S0-CFH-130

Annotated Teacher's Edition

Prentice Hall

LITERATURE

Timeless Voices, Timeless Themes

BRONZE

ISBN 0-13-436017-6

5 6 7 8 9 10   04 03 02 01 00

PRENTICE HALL
Upper Saddle River, New Jersey
Glenview, Illinois
Needham, Massachusetts

Create a fresh enthus
building lifelong c

5 Reasons to choose

1. The finest classic and contemporary literature in a flexible organization
2. Real-life connections that engage and motivate
3. The most comprehensive integrated skills instruction
4. A complete array of customizable resources, including an extensive literature library
5. A wide range of quality technology that enhances and extends literature instruction

Visit us on our companion website at **phlit.phschool.com**

Grade 7 components shown

m for literature while
mmunication skills

Program Components

- ◆ Student Edition
- ◆ Annotated Teacher's Edition
- ◆ Teaching Resources
- ◆ Assessment Success Kit
- ◆ Writing and Language Transparencies
- ◆ Selection Support Workbook
- ◆ Grammar Practice Workbook
- ◆ Literature Library
- ◆ Humanities Pack
- ◆ Interdisciplinary Units
- ◆ Looking at Literature Videotape/Videodisc
- ◆ Listening to Literature Audiocassettes
- ◆ Formal Assessment/Computer Test Bank CD-ROM
- ◆ Literature CD-ROM Library
- ◆ Interactive Student Tutorial CD-ROM
- ◆ Resource Pro® CD-ROM with Literature Database
- ◆ Prentice Hall *Writer's Solution*
  - Writing Lab CD-ROM
  - Language Lab CD-ROM
  - Writers at Work Videotape/Videodisc

The finest classic and contemporary literature in a flexible organization

A perfect blend of classic and contemporary literature is presented in a table of contents that lets you choose a thematic approach, a genre-based approach, or a combination of the two.

Looking at Universal Themes

Finding Yourself

Unit 1

Complete Contents by Genre

Contents ◆ xvii

Complete Contents by Theme

Contents ◆ xxi

Looking at Literary Forms

Nonfiction

Unit 7

Contents ◆ xiii

CONNECTIONS TO TODAY'S WORLD

Many people didn't believe that the Wright brothers would ever get a plane off the ground. If those people could have looked into the future, they would have seen that the Wright brothers' dream led to airplanes, supersonic jets, and even space travel!

John Glenn was the first American to travel around the Earth in space. On February 20, 1962, he orbited (went around) the Earth three times in the spacecraft *Friendship 7*. His return to space at age seventy-seven on board the shuttle *Discovery* makes him the oldest person ever to travel in space. In this on-line interview, he answered questions about his first space journey around the world.

An Astronaut's Answers

John Glenn

The first time you went into space, how did it feel to be all alone except for communication through radio?

In 1962, I looked down from an orbit high above our planet and saw our beautiful Earth and its curved horizon against the vastness of space. I have never forgotten that sight nor the sense of wonder it engendered. Although I was alone in Friendship 7, I did not feel alone in space. I knew that I was supported by my family, my six fellow astronauts, thousands of NASA engineers and employees, and millions of people around the world.

Why did you want to be an astronaut? How did you fly around the Earth three times? Was it hard?

I served as a fighter pilot in World War II and the Korean conflict. After Korea, I graduated from the Naval Test Pilot School and worked as a fighter test pilot. I applied for the astronaut program because I thought it was a logical career step, a challenging opportunity and one in which I could help start a new area of research that would be very valuable to everyone here on Earth. I have always considered myself very fortunate to be selected in the first group of seven astronauts.

An Atlas rocket boosted me into space and I orbited the Earth in my space capsule, the Friendship 7. It certainly was a challenge but one for which I was well prepared. The National Aeronautics and Space Administration (NASA) wanted people who were test pilots and accustomed to working under very unusual

◀ Critical Viewing Why do you think John Glenn needs a special suit and helmet for space travel? [Draw Conclusions]

266 ◆ Proving Yours

Real-life connections that engage and motivate

Literature and Your Life feature helps capture student interest by linking literature to life experiences throughout every selection.

Connections to Today's World feature ties contemporary popular writings-including articles, songs, and television scripts—to the classics.

High Interest Visuals hook students' interest as they begin every selection.

The most comprehensive integrated skills instruction

Writing Process Workshops provide detailed step-by-step writing process instruction in all modes of writing.

- Provides 20 opportunities for extended writing projects
- Linked to the end-of-selection Writing Mini-Lesson through the Writing Skills Focus sections; enables students to build on skills they've already learned

Two **Applying Language Skills** mini-lessons accompany each Writing Process Workshop.

Real-World Reading Skills Workshops help students build skills essential to success in careers and in daily life.

- 20 lessons in each book

Speaking, Listening, and Viewing Workshops provide instruction in real-life communication skills.

Grammar Review provides a review of the grammar skills featured in each unit, following a developmental sequence.

What's Behind the Words: Vocabulary Adventures with Richard Lederer will delight students and increase their vocabulary.

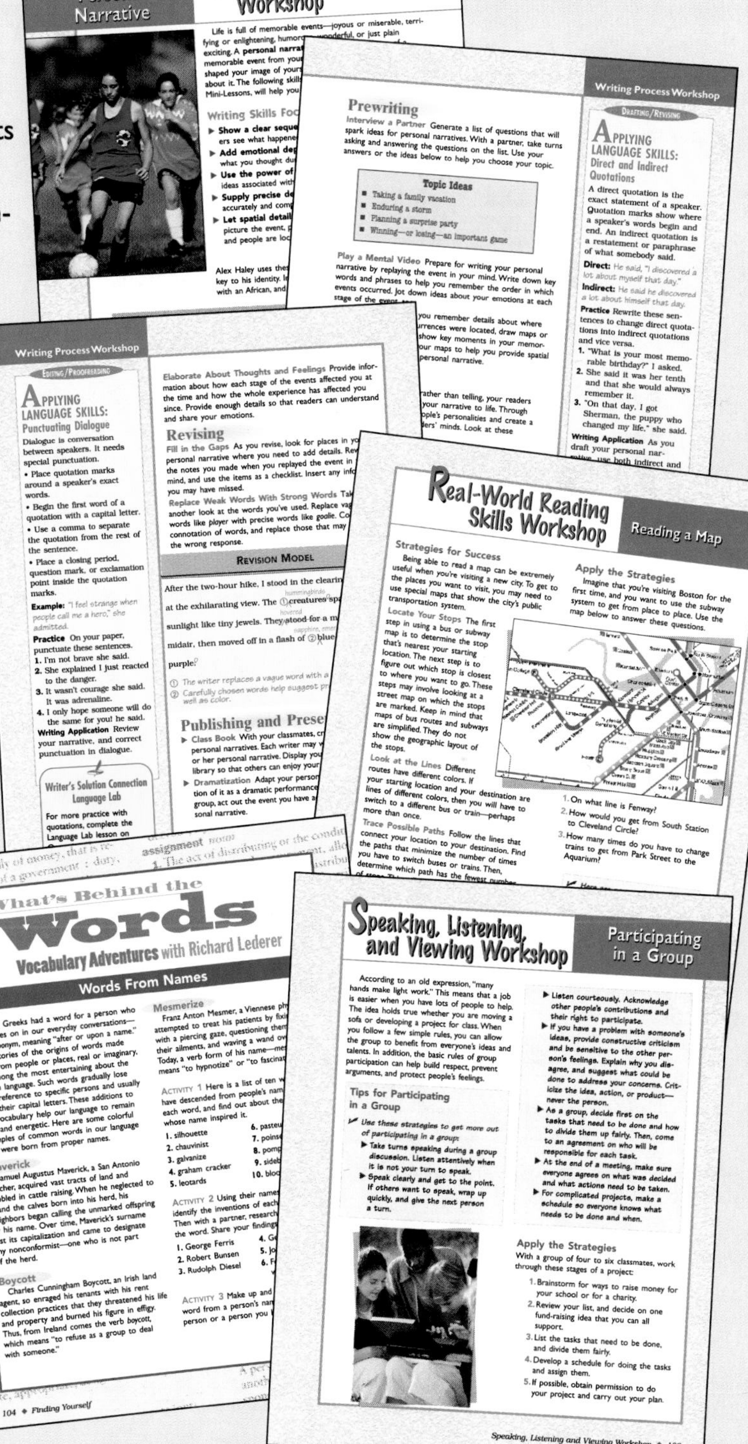

The only literature program to provide complete skills instruction with every selection

Guide for Reading

Meet the Author:
John Steinbeck (1902–1968)

When John Steinbeck received the Nobel Prize for Literature in 1962, it capped a long, successful career in which he established himself as one of our nation's best-loved and most highly regarded writers.

Voice of the Working Class Steinbeck grew up in the Salinas Valley of California, where he became aware of the hard lives of migrant farm workers. After college, he spent five years drifting and writing; he even joined a hobo camp to study the lives of its people. His Pulitzer Prize-winning novel *The Grapes of Wrath* and the novels *Of Mice and Men* and *The Pearl* express sympathy for poor people who are exploited by society.

The Story Behind the Story

Although he had been acclaimed as one of the foremost writers of America's heartland, Steinbeck worried that he had lost touch with the country and its people. He decided to reestablish his ties by driving east to west—from Maine to California—along a northern route. He returned to New York along the southern route, passing through the Mohave Desert, Texas, and the Deep South. Steinbeck published an account of his travels entitled *Travels with Charley,* in 1962. The book's subtitle was "In Search of America."

◆ Literature and Your Life

Connect Your Experience

Think for a moment of trips you've taken—to another country, state, or region. Did the people you meet have attitudes, beliefs, or ways of speaking different from your own? In *Travels with Charley,* John Steinbeck sets out to meet people all across the United States and learns about their different views of life in the process.

Thematic Focus: A Land of Promise

As you follow Steinbeck on his journey, ask yourself what qualities make the United States "a land of promise" for people from all regions of the land.

◆ Background for Understanding

Geography

As Steinbeck travels through the western United States, he finds himself in the Badlands of North Dakota. Located in the western parts of both North and South Dakota, the Badlands are a rugged region of fantastically shaped rock formations separated by valleys. In that barren landscape, there is little vegetation to prevent the erosion of the soft sedimentary rocks. The elevation of the Badlands is between 2,000 and 5,000 feet.

◆ Build Vocabulary

Suffixes: *-ic*

The suffix *-ic* means "like" or "having to do with." The word *diagnostic,* therefore, means "having to do with a diagnosis"—the study of facts.

Word Bank

Which word from the story do you think might mean "the act of inquiring"? Check the Build Vocabulary box on page 356 to see if you chose correctly.

diagnostic
peripatetic
rigorous
maneuver
inquiry
inexplicable
celestial

352 ◆ From Sea to Shining Sea

◆ from Travels with Charley ◆

◆ Literary Focus

Travel Essay

An essay is a short nonfiction work about a particular subject. A **travel essay** focuses on a trip or journey that someone actually made. In it, the writer may include factual information as well as descriptions that reveal how a place looks, sounds, or feels. It is, however, the writer's personal impressions and reflections that make the essay unique.

◆ Reading Strategy

Clarify Details

When you don't completely understand a passage in a travel essay or other piece of writing, take time to stop and **clarify** what is not clear. Sometimes, this may simply involve pausing to think about the meaning of a detail. Other times, it may be necessary to reread a portion of the text or read ahead to piece together the meaning of something. Sometimes, it may even be necessary to go outside the text to find out what something means. Fill out a chart like the one below to clarify details as you read.

Detail to Clarify	Meaning of Detail	Strategy Used: Pause, Read Ahead, Read Back, Use Other Source

Guide for Reading ◆ 353

Before Reading

Engage your students and prepare them to read each selection.

- **An extensive author biography** brings the author to life for students.
- **Build Vocabulary** previews new words and teaches a vocabulary-building strategy.
- **Background for Understanding** provides context related to history, science, culture, and more.
- **Reading Strategy** helps students read more critically and with a higher level of comprehension.
- **Literary Focus** teaches a literary form or element.

During Reading

Two types of support help students through the selections:

- **Reading Strategy** prompts guide students in using the strategy introduced before the selection.

> **◆ Reading Strategy**
> Is this a fact or an impression? How do you know?

- **Literary Focus** prompts help students see how the literary element is illustrated in specific passages.

> **◆ Literary Focus**
> In what specific ways is this passage typical of a descriptive essay?

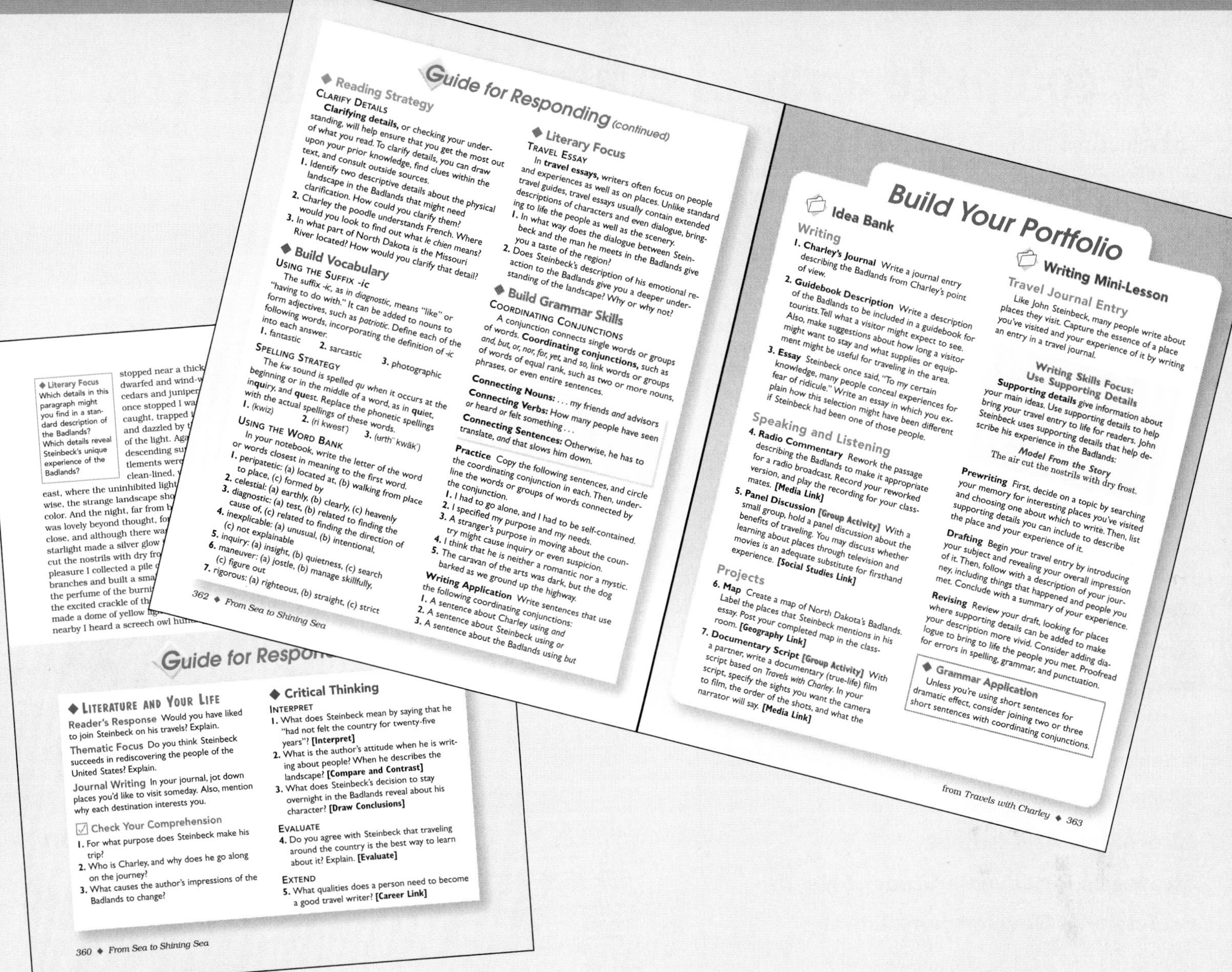

Guide for Responding (continued)

◆ Reading Strategy

CLARIFY DETAILS

Clarifying details, or checking your understanding, will help ensure that you get the most out of what you read. To clarify details, you can draw upon your prior knowledge, find clues within the text, and consult outside sources.

1. Identify two descriptive details about the physical landscape in the Badlands that might need clarification. How could you clarify them?
2. Charley the poodle understands French. Where would you look to find out what *le chien* means?
3. In what part of North Dakota is the Missouri River located? How would you clarify that detail?

◆ Build Vocabulary

USING THE SUFFIX *-ic*

The suffix *-ic*, as in *diagnostic*, means "like" or "having to do with." It can be added to nouns to form adjectives, such as *patriotic*. Define each of the following words, incorporating the definition of *-ic* into each answer.

1. fantastic 2. sarcastic 3. photographic

SPELLING STRATEGY

The *kw* sound is spelled *qu* when it occurs at the beginning or in the middle of a word, as in **quiet**, **inquiry**, and **quest**. Replace the phonetic spellings with the actual spellings of these words.

1. (kwiz) 2. (ri kwest') 3. (ərth' kwāk')

USING THE WORD BANK

In your notebook, write the letter of the word or words closest in meaning to the first word.

1. peripatetic: (a) located at, (b) walking from place to place, (c) formed by
2. celestial: (a) earthly, (b) clearly, (c) heavenly
3. diagnostic: (a) test, (b) related to finding the cause of, (c) related to finding the direction of
4. inexplicable: (a) unusual, (b) intentional, (c) not explainable
5. inquiry: (a) insight, (b) quietness, (c) search
6. maneuver: (a) jostle, (b) manage skillfully, (c) figure out
7. rigorous: (a) righteous, (b) straight, (c) strict

◆ Literary Focus

TRAVEL ESSAY

In **travel essays,** writers often focus on people and experiences as well as on places. Unlike standard travel guides, travel essays usually contain extended descriptions of characters and even dialogue, bringing to life the people as well as the scenery.

1. In what way does the dialogue between Steinbeck and the man he meets in the Badlands give you a taste of the region?
2. Does Steinbeck's description of his emotional reaction to the Badlands give you a deeper understanding of the landscape? Why or why not?

◆ Build Grammar Skills

COORDINATING CONJUNCTIONS

A conjunction connects single words or groups of words. **Coordinating conjunctions,** such as *and, but, or, nor, for, yet,* and *so,* link words or groups of words of equal rank, such as two or more nouns, phrases, or even entire sentences.

Connecting Nouns: . . . my friends *and* advisors

Connecting Verbs: How many people have seen *or* heard or felt something . . .

Connecting Sentences: Otherwise, he has to translate, *and* that slows him down.

Practice Copy the following sentences, and circle the coordinating conjunction in each. Then, underline the words or groups of words connected by the conjunction.

1. I had to go alone, and I had to be self-contained.
2. I specified my purpose and my needs.
3. A stranger's purpose in moving about the country might cause inquiry or even suspicion.
4. I think that he is neither a romantic nor a mystic.
5. The caravan of the arts was dark, but the dog barked as we ground up the highway.

Writing Application Write sentences that use the following coordinating conjunctions:

1. A sentence about Charley using *and*
2. A sentence about Steinbeck using *or*
3. A sentence about the Badlands using *but*

362 ◆ From Sea to Shining Sea

Build Your Portfolio

Idea Bank

Writing

1. **Charley's Journal** Write a journal entry describing the Badlands from Charley's point of view.
2. **Guidebook Description** Write a description of the Badlands to be included in a guidebook for tourists. Tell what a visitor might expect to see. Also, make suggestions about how long a visitor might want to stay and what supplies or equipment might be useful for traveling in the area.
3. **Essay** Steinbeck once said, "To my certain knowledge, many people conceal experiences for fear of ridicule." Write an essay in which you explain how this selection might have been different if Steinbeck had been one of those people.

Speaking and Listening

4. **Radio Commentary** Rework the passage describing the Badlands to make it appropriate for a radio broadcast. Record your reworked version, and play the recording for your classmates. **[Media Link]**
5. **Panel Discussion [Group Activity]** With a small group, hold a panel discussion about the benefits of traveling. You may discuss whether learning about places through television and movies is an adequate substitute for firsthand experience. **[Social Studies Link]**

Projects

6. **Map** Create a map of North Dakota's Badlands. Label the places that Steinbeck mentions in his essay. Post your completed map in the classroom. **[Geography Link]**
7. **Documentary Script [Group Activity]** With a partner, write a documentary (true-life) film script based on *Travels with Charley*. In your script, specify the sights you want the camera to film, the order of the shots, and what the narrator will say. **[Media Link]**

Writing Mini-Lesson

Travel Journal Entry

Like John Steinbeck, many people write about places they visit. Capture the essence of a place you've visited and your experience of it by writing an entry in a travel journal.

Writing Skills Focus: Use Supporting Details

Supporting details give information about your main ideas. Use supporting details to help bring your travel entry to life for readers. John Steinbeck uses supporting details that help describe his experience in the Badlands:

Model From the Story

The air cut the nostrils with dry frost.

Prewriting First, decide on a topic by searching your memory for interesting places you've visited and choosing one about which to write. Then, list supporting details you can include to describe the place and your experience of it.

Drafting Begin your travel entry by introducing your subject and revealing your overall impression of it. Then, follow with a description of your journey, including things that happened and people you met. Conclude with a summary of your experience.

Revising Review your draft, looking for places where supporting details can be added to make your description more vivid. Consider adding dialogue to bring to life the people you met. Proofread for errors in spelling, grammar, and punctuation.

◆ Grammar Application

Unless you're using short sentences for dramatic effect, consider joining two or three short sentences with coordinating conjunctions.

from Travels with Charley ◆ 363

◆ Literary Focus
Which details in this paragraph might you find in a standard description of the Badlands? Which details reveal Steinbeck's unique experience of the Badlands?

Guide for Responding

◆ LITERATURE AND YOUR LIFE

Reader's Response Would you have liked to join Steinbeck on his travels? Explain.

Thematic Focus Do you think Steinbeck succeeds in rediscovering the people of the United States? Explain.

Journal Writing In your journal, jot down places you'd like to visit someday. Also, mention why each destination interests you.

Check Your Comprehension

1. For what purpose does Steinbeck make his trip?
2. Who is Charley, and why does he go along on the journey?
3. What causes the author's impressions of the Badlands to change?

◆ Critical Thinking

INTERPRET

1. What does Steinbeck mean by saying that he "had not felt the country for twenty-five years"? **[Interpret]**
2. What is the author's attitude when he is writing about people? When he describes the landscape? **[Compare and Contrast]**
3. What does Steinbeck's decision to stay overnight in the Badlands reveal about his character? **[Draw Conclusions]**

EVALUATE

4. Do you agree with Steinbeck that traveling around the country is the best way to learn about it? Explain. **[Evaluate]**

EXTEND

5. What qualities does a person need to become a good travel writer? **[Career Link]**

360 ◆ From Sea to Shining Sea

After Reading

Assess students' understanding and **extend** their learning.

☑ **Check Your Comprehension** questions assess students' literal understanding of the selection.

◆ **Critical Thinking** questions assess students' ability to use higher-level thinking skills.

◆ **Reading Strategy** assesses students' mastery of the reading strategy.

◆ **Literary Focus** reinforces students' understanding of the literary element.

◆ **Build Vocabulary** checks students' mastery of both the vocabulary strategy and the words used in the selection. Also includes a Spelling Strategy.

◆ **Build Grammar Skills** provides instruction and practice activities and a writing application.

Build Your Portfolio provides a wealth of activities for students to demonstrate their understanding.

Idea Bank provides:

- Three writing activities keyed to varying performance levels
- Two speaking and listening activities
- Two projects, often linked to cross-curricular topics

Writing Mini-Lesson provides step-by-step writing process instruction.

A complete array of customizable resources.

The Annotated Teacher's Edition provides flexible teaching pathways and cutomized strategies to meet your curricular goals and your students' individual needs. Plus it organizes the program's wealth of materials for reteaching, extension, and assesment.

Teaching Resources

Selection Support: Skills Development

Practice pages for skills taught with each selection:

- ◆ Build Vocabulary
- ◆ Build Spelling Skills
- ◆ Build Grammar Skills
- ◆ Reading Strategy
- ◆ Literary Focus

Beyond Literature

Daily Language Practice

Art Transparencies

Readings From Social Studies

Formal Assessment

- ◆ Selection Tests
- ◆ Unit Tests

Alternative Assessment

Strategies for Diverse Student Needs

Professional Development Library

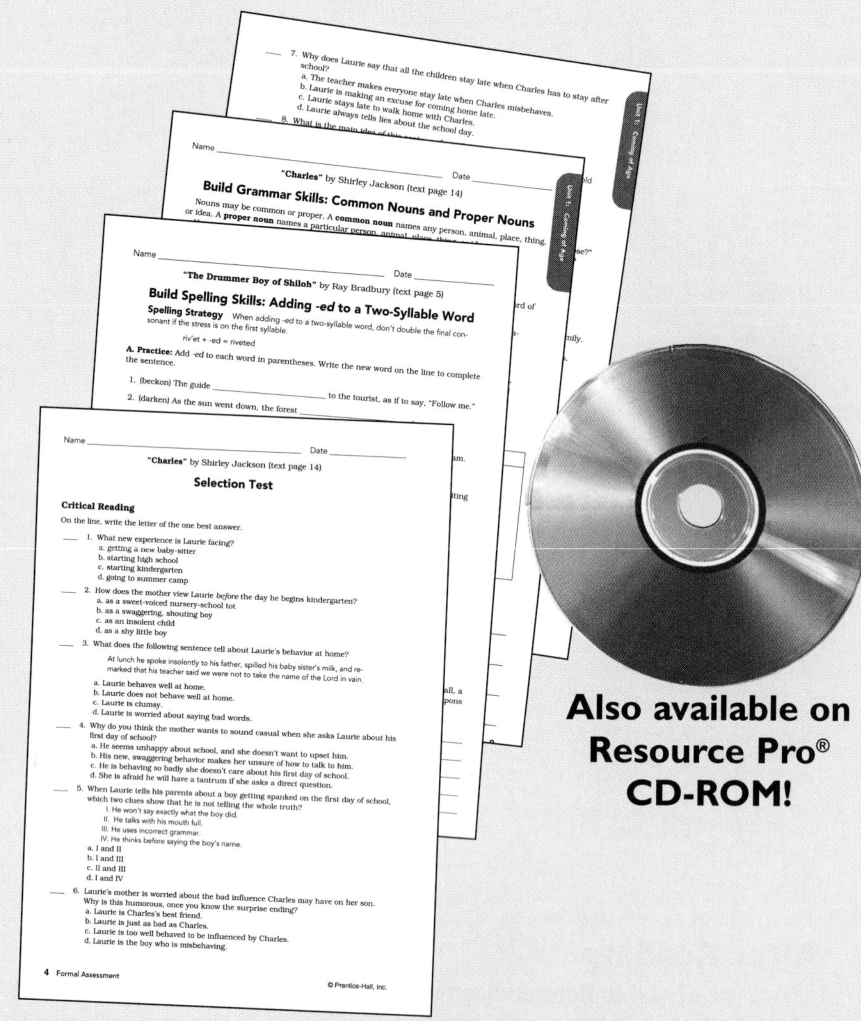

Name ______________________ Date __________

"Charles" by Shirley Jackson (text page 14)

Selection Test

Critical Reading

On the line, write the letter of the one best answer.

___ 1. What new experience is Laurie facing?
a. getting a new baby-sitter
b. starting high school
c. starting kindergarten
d. going to summer camp

___ 2. How does the mother view Laurie *before* the day he begins kindergarten?
a. as a sweet-voiced nursery-school tot
b. as a swaggering, shouting boy
c. as an insolent child
d. as a shy little boy

___ 3. What does the following sentence tell about Laurie's behavior at home?

At lunch he spoke insolently to his father, spilled his baby sister's milk, and remarked that his teacher said we were not to take the name of the Lord in vain.

a. Laurie behaves well at home.
b. Laurie does not behave well at home.
c. Laurie is clumsy.
d. Laurie is worried about saying bad words.

___ 4. Why do you think the mother wants to sound casual when she asks Laurie about his first day of school?
a. He seems unhappy about school, and she doesn't want to upset him.
b. His new, swaggering behavior makes her unsure of how to talk to him.
c. He is behaving so badly she doesn't care about his first day of school.
d. She is afraid he will have a tantrum if she asks a direct question.

___ 5. When Laurie tells his parents about a boy getting spanked on the first day of school, which two clues show that he is not telling the whole truth?
I. He won't say exactly what the boy did.
II. He talks with his mouth full.
III. He uses incorrect grammar.
IV. He thinks before saying the boy's name.
a. I and II
b. I and III
c. II and III
d. I and IV

___ 6. Laurie's mother is worried about the bad influence Charles may have on her son. Why is this humorous, once you know the surprise ending?
a. Laurie is Charles's best friend.
b. Laurie is just as bad as Charles.
c. Laurie is too well behaved to be influenced by Charles.
d. Laurie is the boy who is misbehaving.

4 Formal Assessment © Prentice-Hall, Inc.

Also available on Resource Pro® CD-ROM!

Writing and Language Transparencies

- ◆ Over 100 transparencies for writing and grammar instruction

Assessment Success Kit

- ◆ Supports student performance on standardized tests
- ◆ Includes an Interactive Student Tutorial CD-ROM with standardized test practice

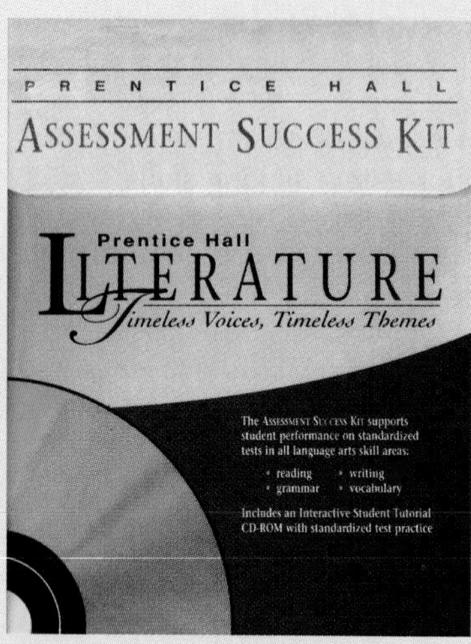

Prentice Hall Literature Library

- The only literature library with mini-anthologies featuring writings from specific regions, cultures, and genre
- More than 40 titles to choose from
- Comprehensive teaching support
- Special hardcovers with a beautiful design for attractiveness and durability
- Uncut editions so students enjoy complete works
- Classic novels by honored writers
- Great drama, including additional Shakespeare offerings

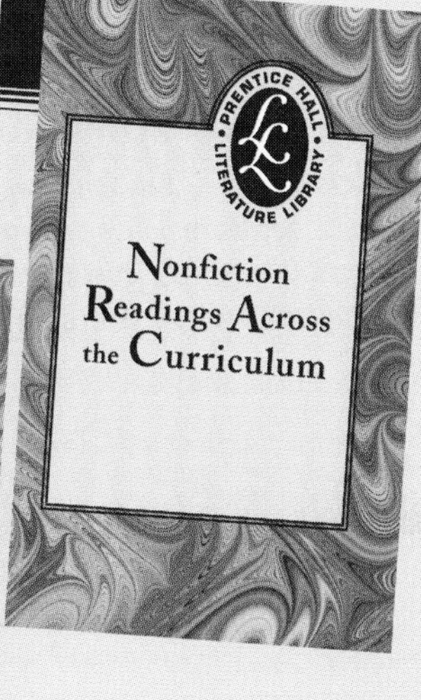

Humanities Pack

- A unique mini-course in the creative arts
- Fine-art transparencies and posters
- Audio CDs
- Performing arts video

PLUS

Interdisciplinary Units

- A complete interdisciplinary exploration for every unit in the literature text

Selection Support Workbook

- Reinforcement for all skills instruction in a consumable format

A wide range of quality technology enhances and extends literature instruction.

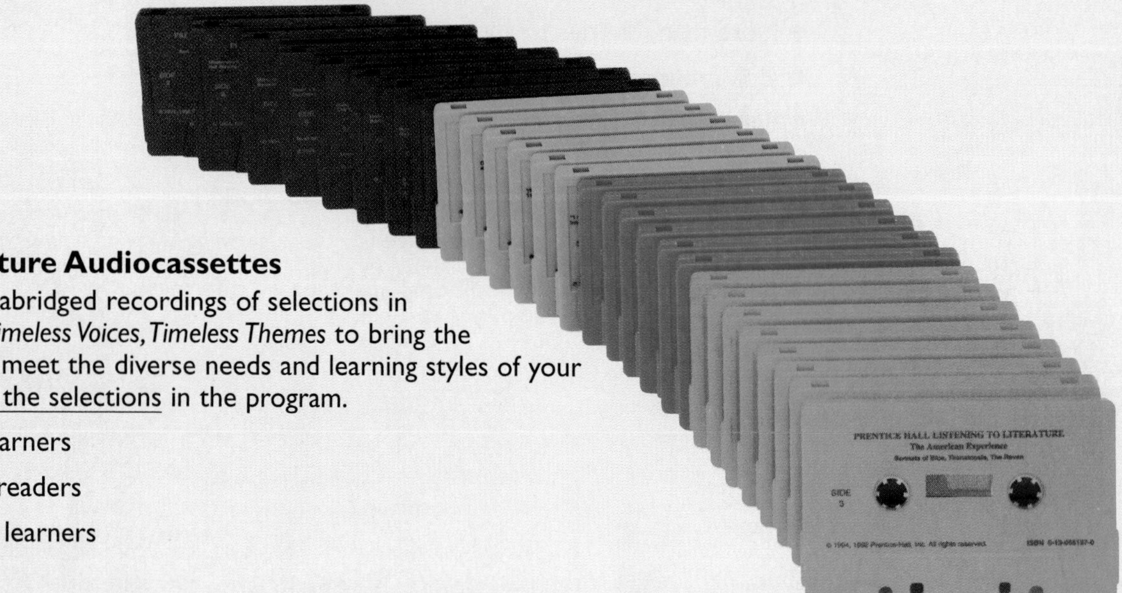

Listening to Literature Audiocassettes

Use these complete, unabridged recordings of selections in *Prentice Hall Literature: Timeless Voices, Timeless Themes* to bring the literature to life and to meet the diverse needs and learning styles of your students. Includes all of the selections in the program.

- Motivate auditory learners
- Help less proficient readers
- Aid English language learners

Looking at Literature Videodiscs and Videotapes

Full-motion video segments provide a wide range of support for the literature—from student response to historical context to connections to today's world.

- Motivate students
- Build background
- Establish relevance
- Encourage class discussion of the literature

Resource Pro and Literature Database CD-ROM

Imagine a complete Teaching Resources, a customizable Lesson Planner, and a wide range of additional literature selections that all fit in one hand! With this CD-ROM, you can customize lesson plans at the touch of a button. You can also review, edit, and print an entire year's worth of blackline masters and other teaching support materials. In addition, more than 100 supplemental literature selections are provided for every grade level.

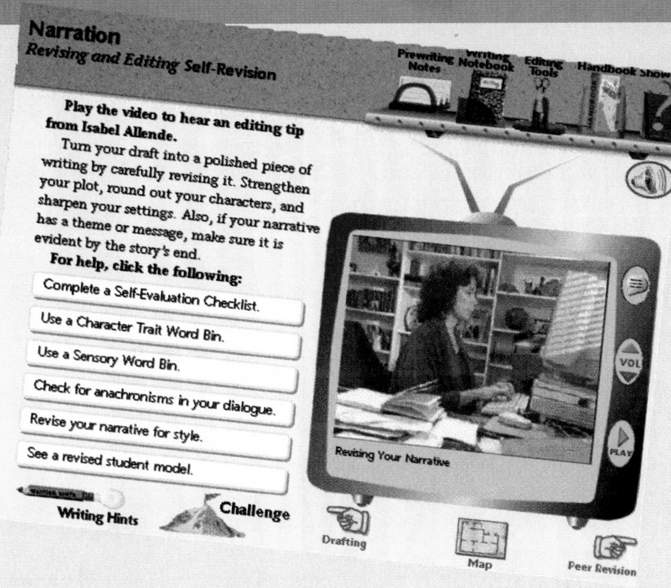
Narration
Revising and Editing Self-Revision
Prewriting Notes
Writing Notebook
Editing Tools
Handbook
Play the video to hear an editing tip from Isabel Allende.
Turn your draft into a polished piece of writing by carefully revising it. Strengthen your plot, round out your characters, and sharpen your settings. Also, if your narrative has a theme or message, make sure it is evident by the story's end.
For help, click the following:
Complete a Self-Evaluation Checklist.
Use a Character Trait Word Bin.
Use a Sensory Word Bin.
Check for anachronisms in your dialogue.
Revise your narrative for style.
See a revised student model.
Writing Hints
Challenge
Revising Your Narrative
VOL
PLAY
Drafting
Map
Peer Revision

Writer's Solution

Writer's Solution, Prentice Hall's award-winning interactive writing instruction program, has been fully integrated into *Prentice Hall Literature: Timeless Voices, Timeless Themes*. Components include:

- ◆ Writing Lab CD-ROM—provides interactive tutorials on the major modes of writing, including Response to Literature
- ◆ Language Lab CD-ROM—provides self-directed instruction and practice in grammar, usage, and mechanics
- ◆ Writers at Work videodisc and videotape—to bring real writers into the classroom
- ◆ Writer's Toolkit networked software—provides tools and activities for all stages of writing

Formal Assessment CD-ROM

All selection tests and unit tests are available on software so you can customize assessment for your students. The software enables you to:

- ◆ Customize tests to ability levels
- ◆ Customize tests by skills objectives
- ◆ Administer tests on-line in the computer lab

Literature CD-ROM Library

Multimedia presentations; hyperlinks to glossaries, indexes, and encyclopedias; and complete, on-line testing are just some of the outstanding features on these interactive CD-ROMs. Titles include the following:

- ◆ How to Read and Understand Poetry
- ◆ How to Read and Understand Drama
- ◆ The Time, Life, and Works of Shakespeare
- ◆ The History of American Literature, Part 1
- ◆ The History of American Literature, Part 2
- ◆ Greek Myths and Legends
- ◆ Science Fiction and Fantasy
- ◆ Myths of Africa, Arabia, Ireland, and Scandinavia
- ◆ Short Story Writing

Interactive Student Tutorial CD-ROM

A tool designed to help students review and prepare for standardized tests.

Internet Home Page

Visit the Prentice Hall Web site at **phschool.com** for features that support *Prentice Hall Literature: Timeless Voices, Timeless Themes:*

- ◆ Visit literary sites through our updated Links.
- ◆ Share ideas through our Faculty Forum electronic bulletin board.
- ◆ Take part in special events, such as electronic dialogues with notable authors.

PH
@school
PRENTICE HALL

www.phlit.phschool.com

Program Planner Unit 1 Finding Yourself

Selection	Reading	Literary Elements/Forms	Vocabulary	Grammar
"The Cat Who Thought She Was a Dog and the Dog Who Thought He Was a Cat," Isaac Bashevis Singer, SE p. 5 Reading Level: Average	• Reading for Success: Literal Comprehension Strategies, SE pp. 4, 9; TR Selection Support, pp. 4, 5 • Use Context Clues, TR Str. for Diverse St. Needs, pp. 1–2 • Model Selection, SE pp. 5–8	• The Moral of a Story, SE pp. 3, 9; TR Selection Support, p. 6	• Prefixes: *pro-*, SE pp. 3, 9; TR Selection Support, p. 1 Word Bank: enthralled, protruded, console, afflicted, vanity, p. 7; anguish, p. 8	• Nouns, SE p. 9; TR Selection Support, p. 3 • WS Language Lab CD-ROM, Using Nouns • WS Gram. Pr. Book, pp. 5–7
"Two Kinds," Amy Tan, SE p. 14 Reading Level: Challenging	• Word Identification, SE pp. 13, 26; TR Selection Support, p. 10 • Apply Word Identification Strategies, TR Str. for Diverse St. Needs, pp. 3–4	• Characters' Motives, SE pp. 13, 26; TR Selection Support, p. 11	• Suffixes: *-ness*, SE pp. 12, 26; TR Selection Support, p. 7 Word Bank: prodigy, p. 15; reproach, mesmerizing, sauciness, p. 16; conspired, debut, p. 21; devastated, fiasco, p. 23	• Common and Proper Nouns, SE p. 26; TR Selection Support, p. 9 • WS Language Lab CD-ROM, Nouns and Different Kinds of Nouns • WS Gram. Pr. Book, p. 7
from **"Song of Myself,"** Walt Whitman; **"I'm Nobody,"** Emily Dickinson; **"Me,"** Walter de la Mare, SE pp. 30, 31, 32 Reading Levels: Average, Easy, Easy	• Read Poetry According to Punctuation, SE pp. 29, 34; TR Selection Support, p. 15 • Read Poetry According to Punctuation, TR Str. for Diverse St. Needs, pp. 5–6	• The Speaker in Poetry, SE pp. 29, 34; TR Selection Support, p. 16	• Related Words: Using Forms of *equal*, SE pp. 28, 34; TR Selection Support, p. 12 Word Bank: assume, loaf, content, equal, banish, bog, p. 30; forlorn, p. 32	• General and Specific Nouns, SE p. 34; TR Selection Support, p. 14 • WS Language Lab CD-ROM, Using Nouns • WS Gram. Pr. Book, Different Kinds of Nouns, p. 7
"My Furthest-Back Person (The Inspiration for *Roots*)," Alex Haley, SE p. 38 Reading Level: Challenging	• Break Down Long Sentences, SE pp. 37, 46; TR Selection Support, p. 20 • Break Down Long Sentences, TR Str. for Diverse St. Needs, pp. 7–8	• Personal Essay, SE pp. 37, 46; TR Selection Support, p. 21	• Prefixes: Using the Prefix *un-*, SE pp. 36, 46; TR Selection Support, p. 17 Word Bank: intrigue, uncanny, p. 39; cherished, queried, eminent, p. 40; destination, p. 45	• Collective Nouns, SE p. 46; TR Selection Support, p. 19 • WS Language Lab CD-ROM, Using Nouns • WS Gram. Pr. Book, Different Kinds of Nouns, p. 6
"The Third Level," Jack Finney, SE p. 50 Reading Level: Average	• Use Context to Unlock Meaning, SE pp. 49, 54; TR Selection Support, p. 25 • Use Context to Determine Meaning, TR Str. for Diverse St. Needs, pp. 9–10	• Time in a Setting, SE pp. 49, 54; TR Selection Support, p. 26	• Suffixes: *-ist*, SE pp. 48, 54; TR Selection Support, p. 22 Word Bank: psychiatrist, arched, p. 50; currency, premium, p. 52	• Concrete and Abstract Nouns, SE p. 54; TR Selection Support, p. 24 • WS Language Lab CD-ROM, Using Nouns • WS Gram. Pr. Book, Nouns, p. 5
"A Day's Wait," Ernest Hemingway, SE p. 72 Reading Level: Average	• Reread, SE pp. 71, 76; TR Selection Support, p. 32 • Reread, TR Str. for Diverse St. Needs, pp. 11–12	• Internal Conflict, SE pp. 71, 76; TR Selection Support, p. 33	• Word Roots: *-vid-*, SE pp. 70, 76: TR Selection Support, p. 29 Word Bank: epidemic, p. 73; evidently, p. 74	• Pronouns, SE p. 76; TR Selection Support, p. 31 • WS Language Lab CD-ROM, Using Pronouns • WS Gram. Pr. Book, Pronouns, pp. 8–10
"The Writer," Richard Wilbur; **"Flint,"** Christina Rossetti; **"Oranges,"** Gary Soto, SE pp. 80, 81, 82 Reading Levels: Average, Easy, Average	• Recognize Signal Words, SE pp. 79, 84; TR Selection Support, p. 37 • Recognize Signal Words, TR Str. for Diverse St. Needs, pp. 13–14	• Sensory Language, SE pp. 79, 84; TR Selection Support, p. 38	• Words From *French*, SE pp. 78, 84; TR Selection Support, p. 34 Word Bank: commotion, clamor, iridescent, p. 80; rouge, tiered, hissing, p. 83	• Pronouns and Antecedents, SE p. 84; TR Selection Support, p. 36 • WS Language Lab CD-ROM, Using Pronouns • WS Gram. Pr. Book, Pronouns, p. 8
"Was Tarzan a Three-Bandage Man?" Bill Cosby, SE p. 88 Reading Level: Average	• Context Clues, SE pp. 87, 90; TR Selection Support, p. 42 • Find Context Clues, TR Str. for Diverse St. Needs, pp. 15–16	• Humorous Anecdote, SE pp. 87, 90; TR Selection Support, p. 43	• Suffixes: *-ly*, SE pp. 86, 90; TR Selection Support, p. 39 Word Bank: incorporate, dejectedly, tourniquets, p. 88	• Personal Pronouns, SE p. 90; TR Selection Support, p. 41 • WS Language Lab CD-ROM, Using Pronouns • WS Gram. Pr. Book, Pronouns, p. 8
"King Arthur: The Marvel of the Sword," Mary MacLeod, SE p. 57 Reading Level: Average			Word Bank: malady, p. 57; remedy, strife,ordained, p. 59; grieved, p. 61	

KEY: SE: Student Edition; ATE: Annotated Teacher's Edition; TR: Teaching Resources; LL: Listening to Literature; WS: Writer's Solution

Writing	Speaking and Listening Viewing and Representing	Projects	Assessment	Technology
• Product Warning, Advertisements, Newspaper Article, SE p. 10 • Mini-Lesson: Fable That Teaches a Lesson [Correct Sequence of Events], SE p. 10 • Fable, TR Alt. Assess., p. 1	• Lecture, Humorous Retelling, SE p. 10 • S/L Mini-Lesson Humorous Retelling, ATE p. 7 • Dual Portrait, TR Alt. Assess., p. 1	• Report on Eastern Europe, Multimedia Report on Mirrors, SE p. 10 • Television News Team, TR Alt. Assess., p. 1	• Selection Test, TR Formal Assessment, pp. 1–3; Assess. Res. Software • Fictional Narative Rubric [for Wr. Mini-Lesson], TR Alt. Assess., p. 82 • TR Alt. Assess., p. 1	• "The Cat Who Thought She Was a Dog and the Dog Who Thought He Was a Cat," LL Audiocassettes • WS Writing Lab CD-ROM, Narration Tutorial
• Job Description, Music Review, Prequel, SE p. 27 • Mini-Lesson: Mother's Diary Entry [Elaborate to Add Emotional Depth], SE p. 27 • Training Manual, TR Alt. Assess., p. 2	• Counseling Conference, Monologue, SE p. 27 • S/L Mini-Lesson Monologue, ATE p. 16 • V/R Mini-Lesson Representing "Two Kinds," ATE p. 24 • Mirror Images, TR Alt. Assess., p. 2	• Television Soundtrack, Report on Chinese Customs, SE p. 27 • Concert, TR Alt. Assess., p. 2	• Selection Test, TR Formal Assessment, pp. 4–6; Assess. Res. Software • Fictional Narative Rubric [for Wr. Mini-Lesson], TR Alt. Assess., p. 82 • TR Alt. Assess., p. 2	• "Two Kinds," LL Audiocassettes • WS Writing Lab CD-ROM, Description Tutorial
• Rules for a Club, Plan for a Celebration, Comparison and Contrast, SE p. 35 • Mini-Lesson: Personal Creed [Using Connotations], SE p. 35 • Role Play, TR Alt. Assess., p. 3	• Telephone Conversation, Three-Way Poetry Contest, SE p. 35 • S/L Mini-Lesson Poetry Reading, ATE p. 32 • Collage, TR Alt. Assess., p. 3	• Multimedia Presentation, Science Fair, SE p. 35 • Music for Poetry, TR Alt. Assess., p. 3	• Selection Test, TR Formal Assessment, pp. 7–9; Assess. Res. Software • Expression Rubric [for Wr. Mini-Lesson], TR Alt. Assess., p. 81 • TR Alt. Assess., p. 3	• "Song of Myself," "I'm Nobody," "Me," LL Audiocassettes • WS Writing Lab CD-ROM, Expression Tutorial
• Captions, Book Jacket, Proposal, SE p. 47 • Mini Lesson: I-Search Paper [Elaborate With Precise Details], SE p. 47 • Map, TR Alt. Assess., p. 4	• Speaker's Introduction, Storytellers' Circle, SE p. 47 • S/L Mini-Lesson Storytellers Circle, ATE p. 42 • V/R Mini-Lesson Film Review, ATE p. 41 • Interview, TR Alt. Assess., p. 4	• Family Chart, Film Review, SE p. 47 • Pantomime, TR Alt. Assess., p. 4	• Selection Test, TR Formal Assessment, pp. 10–12; Assess. Res. Software • Research Report/Paper Rubric [for Wr. Mini-Lesson], TR Alt. Assess., p. 93 • TR Alt. Assess., p. 4	• "My Furthest-Back Person (The Inspiration for *Roots*)," LL Audiocassettes • WS Writing Lab CD-ROM, Reports Tutorial
• Letters, Time-Travel Story, Psychiatrist's Report, SE p. 55 • Mini-Lesson: Description of a Place [Spatial Details], SE p. 55 • Journal Entry, TR Alt. Assess., p. 5	• Oral History, Leisure Time Presentation, SE p. 55 • S/L Mini-Lesson Leisure Time Presentation, ATE p. 52 • Collage, TR Alt. Assess., p. 5	• Poster Series on Train Travel, Survey, SE p. 55 • Role Play, TR Alt. Assess., p. 5	• Selection Test, TR Formal Assessment, pp. 13–15; Assess. Res. Software • Business Letter/Memo Rubric [for Wr. Mini-Lesson], TR Alt. Assess., p. 100 • TR Alt. Assess., p. 5	• "The Third Level," LL Audiocassettes • WS Writing Lab CD-ROM, Description Tutorial
• Inner Monologue, Film Director's Memo, Definition, SE p. 77 • Mini-Lesson: A Day of Anticipation [Elaborate to Make Writing Personal], SE p. 77 • Metric Chart, TR Alt. Assess., p. 6	• Medal Presentation Speech, Panel Discussion, SE p. 77 • S/L Mini-Lesson: Panel Discussion, ATE p. 73 • Anecdote,TR Alt. Assess., p. 6	• Comparison Chart, Advice Pamphlet, SE p. 77 • Illustrations TR Alt. Assess., p. 6	• Selection Test, TR Formal Assessment, pp. 18–20; Assess. Res. Software • Fictional Narrative Rubric [for Wr. Mini-Lesson], TR Alt. Assess., p. 82 • TR Alt. Assess., p. 6	• "A Day's Wait," LL Audiocassettes • WS Writing Lab CD-ROM, Narratives Tutorial
• Description, He Said, She Said, Critique, SE p. 85 • Mini-Lesson: Description [Sensory Language], SE p. 85 • Personal Narrative, TR Alt. Assess., p 7	• Dialogue, Song Lyrics, SE p. 85 • S/L Mini-Lesson: Song Lyrics, ATE p. 81 • Poetry Reading,TR Alt. Assess., p. 7	• Informative Brochure, Illustrated Chart, SE p. 85 • Background Music Description, TR Alt. Assess., p. 7	• Selection Test, TR Formal Assessment, pp. 21–23; Assess. Res. Software • Description Rubric [for Wr. Mini-Lesson], TR Alt. Assess., p. 84 • TR Alt. Assess., p. 7	• "The Writer," "Flint," "Oranges," LL Audiocassettes • WS Writing Lab CD-ROM, Description Tutorial
• Letter of Recommendation, SE p. 91 • Mini-Lesson: Essay [Provide Reasons], SE p. 91 • Book Jacket, TR Alt. Assess., p. 8	• Stand-up Routine, Role Play, SE p. 91 • Storytelling, TR Alt. Assess., p. 8;	• Comic Strip, Scrapbook of Heroes, SE p. 91 • Imitation, TR Alt. Assess., p. 8	• Selection Test, TR Formal Assessment, pp. 24–26; Assess. Res. Software • Persuasion Rubric [for Wr. Mini-Lesson], TR Alt. Assess., p. 92 • TR Alt. Assess., p. 8	• "Was Tarzan a Three-Bandage Man?" LL Audiocassettes • WS Writing Lab CD-ROM, Persuasion Tutorial
• Job Description, Speech, Legend, SE p. 63	• Debate, SE p. 63 • V/R Mini-Lesson: Chess Pieces, ATE p. 60	• Timeline, Coat of Arms, SE p. 63	• Selection Test, TR Formal Assessment, pp. 16–17; Assess. Res. Software	• "King Arthur: The Marvel of the Sword," LL Audiocassettes

Program Planner Unit 2 Common Threads

Selection	Reading	Literary Elements/Forms	Vocabulary	Grammar
from ***In Search of Our Mothers' Gardens,*** Alice Walker, SE p. 111 Reading Level: Challenging	• Reading for Success: Interactive Reading Strategies, SE pp. 110, 117; TR Selection Support, pp. 47–48 • Ask Questions, TR Str. for Diverse St. Needs, pp. 17–18 • Model Selection, SE pp. 111–116	• Tribute, SE pp. 109,117; TR Selection Support, p. 49	• Word Roots: *-nym-,* SE pp. 109, 117; TR Selection Support, p. 44 Word Bank: mutilated, vibrant, anonymous, p. 111; profusely, radiant, illuminates, hindered, p. 115	• Verbs, SE p. 117; TR Selection Support, p. 46 • WS Language Lab CD-ROM, Using Verbs • WS Gram. Pr. Book, Action Verbs, p. 11
"Seventh Grade," Gary Soto; **"Melting Pot,"** Anna Quindlen, SE pp. 122, 128 Reading Levels: Average, Average	• Relate to Your Experiences, SE pp. 121, 132; TR Selection Support, p. 53 • Relate to Your Own Experience, TR Str. for Diverse St. Needs, pp. 19–20	• Tone, SE pp. 121, 132; TR Selection Support, p. 54	• Prefixes: *inter-,* SE pp. 120, 132; TR Selection Support, p. 50 Word Bank: elective, scowl, ferocity, p. 123; conviction, p. 125; sheepishly, p. 127; fluent, bigots, p. 129; interloper, p. 130	• Action Verbs and Linking Verbs, SE p. 132; TR Selection Support, p. 52 • WS Language Lab CD-ROM, Using Verbs • WS Gram. Pr. Book, Linking Verbs, pp. 12–13
"Fable," Ralph Waldo Emerson; **"Thumbprint,"** Eve Merriam; **"If—,"** Rudyard Kipling, SE pp. 136, 137, 138 Reading Levels: Easy, Easy, Average	• Paraphrase, SE pp. 135, 140; TR Selection Support, p. 58 • Paraphrase, TR Str. for Diverse St. Needs, pp. 21–22	• Rhyme, SE pp. 135, 140; TR Selection Support, p. 59	• Prefixes: *uni-,* SE pp. 134, 140; TR Selection Support, p. 55 Word Bank: spry, p. 136; unique, base, p. 137; impostors, virtue, p. 139	• Verb Tenses, SE p. 140; TR Selection Support, p. 57 • WS Language Lab CD-ROM, Using Verbs • WS Gram. Pr. Book, The Six Tenses of Verbs, p. 66
"Rip Van Winkle," Washington Irving, SE p. 144 Reading Level: Challenging	• Break Down Long Sentences, SE pp. 143, 158; TR Selection Support, p. 63 • Break Down Long Sentences, TR Str. for Diverse St. Needs, pp. 23–24	• Historical Setting, SE pp. 143, 158; TR Selection Support, p. 64	• Word Roots: *-cline-,* SE pp. 142, 158; TR Selection Support, p. 60 Word Bank: martial, domestic, p. 145; wistfully, majestic, incomprehensible, p. 149; melancholy, declined, p. 151	• Verb Tenses, SE p. 158; TR Selection Support, p. 62 • WS Language Lab CD-ROM, Verb Tense • WS Gram. Pr. Book, Verb Tenses, p. 66
"Mother to Son," Langston Hughes; **"The Courage That My Mother Had,"** Edna St. Vincent Millay; **"The Village Blacksmith,"** Henry Wadsworth Longfellow; **"The Hummingbird That Lived Through Winter,"** William Saroyan, SE pp. 168, 169, 170, 172 Reading Levels: Average, Average, Average, Average	• Question, SE pp. 167, 176; TR Selection Support, p. 68 • Question, TR Str. for Diverse St. Needs, pp. 25–26	• Symbol, SE pp. 167, 176; TR Selection Support, p. 69	• Prefixes: *trans-,* SE pp. 166, 176; TR Selection Support, p. 65 Word Bank: quarried, brooch, p. 169; brawny, p. 171; pathetic, p. 173; transformation, p. 174	• Principal Parts of Verbs, SE p. 176; TR Selection Support, p. 67 • WS Language Lab CD-ROM, Principal Parts of Verbs • WS Gram. Pr. Book, Verbs, pp. 11–14
from ***The Midwife's Apprentice,*** Karen Cushman, SE p. 181 Reading Level: Average			• TR Selection Support, p. 70 Word Bank: roamed, frail, p. 181; nimble, p. 182; devotion , p. 184	

KEY: SE: Student Edition; ATE: Annotated Teacher's Edition; TR: Teaching Resources; LL: Listening to Literature; WS: Writer's Solution

Writing	Speaking and Listening Viewing and Representing	Projects	Assessment	Technology
• Slogans, Walker Family Story, Literary Analysis, SE p. 118 • Mini-Lesson: Tribute [Vivid Words], SE p. 118 • Interview and Paragraph, TR Alt. Assess., p. 9	• Television Commercial, How-to Speech, SE p. 118 • S/L Mini-Lesson: How-to Speech, ATE p. 114 • V/R Mini-Lesson: Close-up, ATE p. 113 • Oral Performance,TR Alt. Assess., p. 9	• Sharecropping Report, Garden Plan, SE p. 118 • A Letter to the Author, TR Alt. Assess., p. 9	• Selection Test, TR Formal Assessment, pp. 35–37; Assess. Res. Software • Description Rubric [for Wr. Mini-Lesson], TR Alt. Assess., p. 84 • TR Alt. Assess., p. 9	• from *In Search of Our Mothers' Gardens,* LL Audiocassettes • WS Writing Lab CD-ROM, Description Tutorial
• Letter to Mr. Bueller, Personal Narrative, Welcome Pamphlet, SE p. 133 • Mini-Lesson: Guidelines [Develop Each Point], SE p. 133 • Dialogue, TR Alt. Assess., p. 10	• Dramatic Revue, Neighbor-hood Meeting, SE p. 133 • S/L Mini-Lesson: Neighbor-hood Meeting, ATE p. 126 • V/R Mini-Lesson: Today's Melting Pot, ATE p. 130 • Photo Essay, TR Alt. Assess., p. 10	• Food Festival, Community Work, SE p. 133 • Interview and Paragraph, TR Alt. Assess., p. 10	• Selection Test, TR Formal Assessment, pp. 38–40; Assess. Res. Software • How to Process Explanation Rubric [for Wr. Mini-Lesson], TR Alt. Assess., p. 87 • TR Alt. Assess., p. 10	• "Seventh Grade," "Melting Pot," LL Audiocassettes • WS Writing Lab CD-ROM, Exposition Tutorial
• If– Poem, Response, Introduction, SE p. 141 • Mini-Lesson: Persuasive Argument [Grab Readers' Interest], SE p. 141 • Film Review, TR Alt. Assess., p. 11	• Poetry Reading, Class Poll, SE p. 141 • S/L Mini-Lesson: Class Poll, ATE p. 138 • Humorous Dialogue, TR Alt. Assess., p. 11	• Thumbprint Display, Living Biography, SE p. 141 • Music Album, TR Alt. Assess., p. 11	• Selection Test, TR Formal Assessment, pp. 41–43; Assess. Res. Software • Persuasion Rubric [for Wr. Mini-Lesson], TR Alt. Assess., p. 92 • TR Alt. Assess., p. 11	• "Fable," "Thumbprint," "If—," LL Audiocassettes • WS Writing Lab CD-ROM, Persuasion Tutorial
• Memoir, Newspaper Article, Comparison-and-Contrast Essay, SE p. 159 • Mini-Lesson: Description of a Trip Through Time [Engage the Senses], SE p. 159 • Gossip Session, TR Alt. Assess., p. 12	• Talk Show Appearance, Dramatization, SE p. 159 • S/L Mini-Lesson: Talk Show Appearance, ATE p.147 • V/R Mini-Lesson: Creating a Storyboard, ATE p. 155 • Illustration, TR Alt. Assess., p. 12	• Oral Presentation, Geography Update, SE p. 159 • Illustrated Research Report, TR Alt. Assess., p. 12	• Selection Test, TR Formal Assessment, pp. 44–46; Assess. Res. Software • Description Rubric [for Wr. Mini-Lesson], TR Alt. Assess., p. 84 • TR Alt. Assess., p. 12	• "Rip Van Winkle," LL Audiocassettes • WS Writing Lab CD-ROM, Description Tutorial
• Response Poem, Public-Service Announcement, Analysis of a Symbol, SE p. 177 • Mini-Lesson: Pep Talk [Stress Main Idea], SE p. 177 • Report on Animal Symbolism, TR Alt. Assess., p. 13	• Song, An Unexpected Meeting, SE p. 177 • S/L Mini-Lesson: Song, ATE p. 174 • V/R Mini-Lesson: Symbols and Slogans, ATE p. 172 • Human Interest Story, TR Alt. Assess., p. 13	• Survey, Internet Research, SE p. 177 • Scene, TR Alt. Assess., p. 13	• Selection Test, TR Formal Assessment, pp. 47–49; Assess. Res. Software • Problem/ Solution Rubric [for Wr. Mini-Lesson], TR Alt. Assess., p. 88 • TR Alt. Assess., p. 13	• "Mother to Son," "The Courage That My Mother Had," "The Village Blacksmith," "The Hummingbird That Lived Through Winter," LL Audiocassettes • WS Writing Lab CD-ROM, Persuasion Tutorial
• Letter, Advertisement, Time-Travel Log, SE p. 185	• Health Lesson, SE p. 185	• Medieval Festival, SE p. 185	• Selection Test, TR Formal Assessment, pp. 50–51 Assess. Res. Software	• from *The Midwife's Apprentice,* LL Audiocassettes

Program Planner Unit 3 What Matters

Selection	Reading	Literary Elements/Forms	Vocabulary	Grammar
"The Third Wish," Joan Aiken, SE p. 199 Reading Level: Average	• Reading for Success: Interactive Reading Strategies, SE pp. 198, 205; TR Selection Support, pp. 75–76 • Model, SE pp. 199–204 • Clarify, TR Str. for Diverse St. Needs, pp. 27–28	• Modern Fairy Tale, SE pp. 197, 205; TR Selection Support, p. 77	• Suffixes: *-ous,* SE pp. 197–205; TR Selection Support, p. 72 Word Bank: extricate, p. 199; presumptuous, composure, rash, remote, p. 200; malicious, p. 202	• Adjectives, SE p. 205; TR Selection Support, p. 74 • WS Language Lab CD-ROM, Using Modifiers • WS Gram. Pr. Book, Adjectives, pp. 15–19
"A Boy and a Man," James Ramsey Ulman; from ***Into Thin Air,*** Jon Krakauer, SE pp. 210, 218 Reading Levels: Average, Challenging	• Predict, SE pp. 209, 220; TR Selection Support, p. 81 • Predict, TR Str. for Diverse St. Needs, pp. 29–30	• Conflict With Nature, SE pp. 209, 220; TR Selection Support, p. 82	• Prefixes: *mal-*, SE, pp. 208, 220; TR Selection Support, p. 78 Word Bank: prone, taut, pummeled, p. 213; reconnoiter, p. 215; malevolent, denigrate, p. 219	• Placement of Adjectives, SE p. 220; TR Selection Support, p. 80 • WS Language Lab CD-ROM, Using Modifiers • WS Gram. Pr. Book, Adjective Practice, pp. 15–19
"The Iceman," Don Lessem, SE p. 223 Reading Level: Average			• TR Selection Support, p. 83 Word Bank: emblems, delicacies, wielding, p. 224	
"The Charge of the Light Brigade," Alfred, Lord Tennyson; from ***Henry V,*** William Shakespeare; **"Lonely Particular,"** Alice Walker; **"The Enemy,"** Alice Walker, SE pp. 230, 232, 234, 235 Reading Levels: Average, Challenging, Average, Average	• Reading Poetic Contractions, SE pp. 229, 236; TR Selection Support, p. 88 • Reading Poetic Contractions, TR Str. for Diverse St. Needs, pp. 31–32	• Repetition, SE pp. 229, 236; TR Selection Support, p. 89	• Homophones, SE pp. 228, 236; TR Selection Support, p. 85 Word Bank: dismayed, blundered, volleyed, reeled, sundered, p. 231	• Possessive Adjectives, SE p. 236; TR Selection Support, p. 87 • WS Language Lab CD-ROM, Using Modifiers • WS Gram. Pr. Book, Adjectives, pp. 15–19
"The Californian's Tale," Mark Twain; **"Valediction,"** Seamus Heaney, SE pp. 246, 252 Reading Levels: Average, Average	• Summarize, SE pp. 245, 254; TR Selection Support, p. 93 • Summarize, TR Str. for Diverse St. Needs, pp. 33–34	• Local Color, SE pp. 245, 254; TR Selection Support, p. 94	• Suffixes: *-ify,* SE pp. 244, 254; TR Selection Support, p. 90 Word Bank: balmy, predecessors, humiliation, abundant, desolation, p. 247; furtive, gratify, p. 248; apprehensions, p. 250	• Adverbs, SE p. 254; TR Selection Support, p. 92 • WS Language Lab CD-ROM, Using Modifiers • WS Gram. Pr. Book, Adverbs, pp. 20–22
"Stopping by Woods on a Snowy Evening," Robert Frost; **"Four Skinny Trees,"** Sandra Cisneros; **"Miracles,"** Walt Whitman, SE pp. 260, 261, 262 Reading Levels: Average, Average, Average	• Respond to Levels of Meaning, SE pp. 259, 264; TR Selection Support, p. 98 • Respond to Levels of Meaning, TR Str. for Diverse St. Needs, pp. 35–36	• Levels of Meaning, SE pp. 259, 264; TR Selection Support, p. 99	• Related Words: Forms of *ferocious,* SE pp. 258, 264; TR Selection Support, p. 95 Word Bank: downy, ferocious, p. 261; exquisite, distinct, p. 262	• Adverbs Modifying Adjectives and Adverbs, SE p. 264; TR Selection Support, p. 97 • WS Language Lab CD-ROM, Using Modifiers • WS Gram. Pr. Book, Adverbs, pp. 20–22

KEY: SE: Student Edition; ATE: Annotated Teacher's Edition; TR: Teaching Resources; LL: Listening to Literature; WS: Writer's Solution

Writing	Speaking and Listening Viewing and Representing	Projects	Assessment	Technology
• Journal Entry, Obituary, Analysis, SE p. 206 • Mini-Lesson: Modern Fairy Tale [Elaborate on Key Ideas], SE p. 206 • Prose Poem, TR Alt. Assess., p. 14	• Song Lyrics, Radio Drama, SE p. 206 • S/L Mini-Lesson: Song Lyrics, ATE p. 202 • Illustration, TR Alt. Assess., p. 14	• Poster on the Number Three, Multimedia Report, SE p. 206 • Paragraph, TR Alt. Assess., p. 14	• Selection Test, TR Formal Assessment, pp. 60–62; Assess. Res. Software • Fictional Narative Rubric [for Mini-Lesson], TR Alt. Assess., p. 82 • TR Alt. Assess., p. 14	• "The Third Wish," LL Audiocassettes • WS Writing Lab CD-ROM, Narration Tutorial
• Advertisement, Movie Proposal, Autobiographical Incident, SE p. 221 • Mini-Lesson: Persuasive Letter [Order of Importance] SE p. 221 • Magazine Article, TR Alt. Assess., p. 15	• Dialogue, Rescue Interview, SE p. 221 • S/L Mini-Lesson: Dialogue, ATE p. 212 • V/R Mini Lesson: Illustrating a Scene, ATE p. 216 • Science Report, TR Alt. Assess., p. 15	• Glacier Research, How-to Guide, SE p. 221 • Collage, TR Alt. Assess., p. 15	• Selection Test, TR Formal Assessment, pp. 63–65; Assess. Res. Software • Persuasion Rubric [for Mini-Lesson], TR Alt. Assess., p. 92 • TR Alt. Assess., p. 15	• "A Boy and a Man," from *Into Thin Air,* LL Audiocassettes • WS Writing Lab CD-ROM, Persuasion Tutorial
• Journal Entry, TV News Story, Letter, SE p. 227	• Telephone Interview, SE p. 227	• Research, Model Tools SE, p. 227	• Selection Test, TR Formal Assessment, pp. 66–67 Assess. Res. Software	• "The Iceman," LL Audiocassettes
• Letter for Future Generations, Eyewitness Report, Evaluation of a Poet's Message, SE p. 237 • Mini-Lesson: Report [Accuracy], SE p. 237 • Biographical Sketch, TR Alt. Assess., p. 16	• Poetry Reading, Debate, SE p. 237 • S/L Mini-Lesson: Debate, ATE p. 234 • V/R Mini-Lesson; Images of War, ATE p. 231 • Song Festival, TR Alt. Assess., p. 16	• Museum Exhibit, Oral History, SE p. 237 • Internet Oral Report, TR Alt. Assess., p. 16	• Selection Test, TR Formal Assessment, pp. 68–70; Assess. Res. Software • Research Rubric [for Wr. Mini-Lesson], TR Alt. Assess.; p. 93 • TR Alt. Assess., p. 16	• "The Charge of the Light Brigade," from *Henry V,* "Lonely Particular," "The Enemy," LL Audiocassettes • WS Writing Lab CD-ROM, Reports Tutorial
• Journal Entry, Letter Home, Behavior Analysis, SE p. 255 • Mini-Lesson: Character Sketch [Specific Examples], SE p. 255 • Poem, TR Alt. Assess., p. 17	• Public Reading, Dramatization, SE p. 255 • S/L Mini-Lesson; Public Reading, ATE p. 251 • Art History, TR Alt. Assess., p. 17	• Portrait of a Lady, Multimedia Presentation, SE p. 255 • Poem, TR Alt. Assess., p. 17	• Selection Test, TR Formal Assessment, pp. 71–73; Assess. Res. Software • Description Rubric, [for Wr. Mini-Lesson], TR Alt. Assess.; p. 84 • TR Alt. Assess., p. 17	• "The Californian's Tale," "Valediction," LL Audiocassettes • WS Writing Lab CD-ROM, Description Tutorial
• Reminiscence, Travel Brochure, Letter to Author, SE p. 265 • Mini-Lesson: Poem About Your Environment [Precise Words], SE p. 265 • Multimedia Presentation Plan, TR Alt. Assess., p. 18	• Weather Commentary, "Sounds of Home" Tape, SE p. 265 • V/R Mini-Lesson: "Sounds of Home" Tape, ATE p. 262 • Seasons Report, TR Alt. Assess., p. 18	• A Picture of Miracles, Survey and Chart, SE p. 265 • Debate, TR Alt. Assess., p. 18	• Selection Test, TR Formal Assessment, pp. 74–76; Assess. Res. Software • Poetry Rubric [for Wr. Mini-Lesson], TR Alt. Assess., p. 95 • TR Alt. Assess., p. 18	• "Stopping by Woods on a Snowy Evening," "Four Skinny Trees," "Miracles," LL Audiocassettes • WS Writing Lab CD-ROM, Creative Writing Tutorial

Program Planner Unit 4 Resolving Conflicts

Selection	Reading	Literary Elements/Forms	Vocabulary	Grammar
"The Night the Bed Fell," James Thurber, SE p. 279 Reading Level: Challenging	• Reading for Success: Strategies for Constructing Meaning, SE pp. 278, 283; TR Selection Support, pp. 103–104 • Identify Causes and Effects, TR Str. for Diverse St. Needs, pp. 37–38 • Model Selection, SE pp. 279–282	• Humorous Essay, SE pp. 277, 283; TR Selection Support, p. 105	• Prefixes: *ex-,* SE pp. 277, 283; TR Selection Support, p. 100 Word Bank: ominous, allay, p. 279; fortitude, perilous, deluge, pungent, extricate, p. 281; culprit, p. 282	• Prepositions, SE p. 283; TR Selection Support, p. 102 • WS Language Lab CD-ROM, Prepositions and Prepositional Phrases • WS Gram. Pr. Book, Prepositions, pp. 23–24
"All Summer in a Day," Ray Bradbury; **"Primer Lesson,"** Carl Sandburg, SE pp. 288, 294 Reading Levels: Average, Easy	• Envision Setting and Actions, SE pp. 287, 296; TR Selection Support, p. 109 • Envision Setting and Actions, TR Str. for Diverse St. Needs, pp. 39–40	• Setting, SE pp. 287, 296; TR Selection Support, p. 110	• Word Roots: *-vita-,* SE pp. 286, 296; TR Selection Support, p. 106 Word Bank: concussion, p. 289; slackening, vital, surged, p. 291; tumultuously, resilient, savored, p. 293	• Prepositional Phrases, SE p. 296; TR Selection Support, p. 108 • WS Language Lab CD-ROM, Prepositional Phrases • WS Gram. Pr. Book, Prepositional Phrases, pp. 23–24
"The Highwayman," Alfred Noyes; **"The Dying Cowboy,"** Folk Song; **"The Real Story of a Cowboy's Life,"** Geoffrey C. Ward, SE pp. 300, 306, 309 Reading Levels: Average, Easy, Average	• Identify Cause and Effect, SE pp. 299, 312; TR Selection Support, p. 114 • Indentify Cause and Effect, TR Str. for Diverse St. Needs, pp. 41–42	• Suspense, SE pp. 299, 312; TR Selection Support, p. 115	• Compound Nouns, SE pp. 298, 312: TR Selection Support, p. 111 Word Bank: torrent, p. 301; landlord, cascade, tawny, bound, strive, p. 303; brandished, p. 304	• Adjective and Adverb Phrases, SE p. 312; TR Selection Support, p. 113 • WS Language Lab CD-ROM, Prepositional Phrases, Using Modifiers • WS Gram. Pr. Book, Prepositional Phrases That Act as Adjectives and Adverbs, pp. 44–45
"The Little Lizard's Sorrow," from *Vietnam,* Translated by Mai Vo-Dinh, SE p. 315 Reading Level: Average			• TR Selection Support, p. 116 Word Bank: emitting, p. 315; gaunt, pauper, chortle, domestic, p. 316; harassed, p. 318	
"The Dying Detective," Sir Arthur Conan Doyle, dramatized by Michael and Mollie Hardwick, SE p. 328 Reading Level: Challenging	• Draw Conclusions, SE pp. 327, 340; TR Selection Support, p. 121 • Draw Conclusions, TR Str. for Diverse St. Needs, pp. 43–44	• Staging, SE pp. 327, 340; TR Selection Support, p. 122	• Suffixes: *-ology,* SE pp. 326, 340; TR Selection Support, p. 118 Word Bank: agitated, p. 329; pathological, p. 331; implore, methodical, p. 332; irksome, p. 337	• Interjections, SE p. 340; TR Selection Support, p. 120 • WS Language Lab CD-ROM, Punctuation • WS Gram. Pr. Book, End Marks, p. 97
"Justin Lebo," Phillip Hoose; **"The Rider,"** Naomi Shihab Nye; **"Amigo Brothers,"** Piri Thomas; **"The Walk,"** Thomas Hardy, SE pp. 346, 351, 352, 359 Reading Levels: Average, Average, Average, Average	• Make Inferences, SE pp. 345, 360; TR Selection Support, p. 126 • Make Inferences, TR Str. for Diverse St. Needs, pp. 45–46	• Third-Person Point of View, SE pp. 345, 360; TR Selection Support, p. 127	• Prefixes: *re-,* SE pp. 344, 360; TR Selection Support, p. 123 Word Bank: realign, yield, p. 346; coalition, p. 350; devastating, p. 353; superimposed, perpetual, p. 354; dispelled, p. 357; evading, p. 358	• Coordinating Conjunctions, SE p. 360; TR Selection Support, p. 125 • WS Language Lab CD-ROM, Coordinating Conjunctions • WS Gram. Pr. Book, Conjunction Practice, p. 25

KEY: SE: Student Edition; ATE: Annotated Teacher's Edition; TR: Teaching Resources; LL: Listening to Literature; WS: Writer's Solution

Writing	Speaking and Listening Viewing and Representing	Projects	Assessment	Technology
• Invitation, Home Name Proposal, News Report, SE p. 284 • Mini-Lesson: Humorous Essay [Punchy Conclusion], SE p. 284 • Contest Poster, TR Alt. Assess., p. 19	• Skit, Guided Tour, SE p. 284 • S/L Mini-Lesson: Skit, ATE p. 281 • Sound Track,TR Alt. Assess., p. 19	• Sleep Research, Game Collection, SE p. 284 • Magazine Research, TR Alt. Assess., p. 19	• Selection Test, TR Formal Assessment, pp. 85–87; Assess. Res. Software • Narrative Based on Personal Experience Rubric [for Wr. Mini-Lesson], TR Alt. Assess., p. 83 • TR Alt. Assess., p. 19	• "The Night the Bed Fell," LL Audiocassettes • WS Writing Lab CD-ROM, Narration Tutorial
• Diary Entry, Travel Brochure, Teacher's Report, SE p. 297 • Mini-Lesson: Remembrance [Show, Don't Tell], SE p. 297 • Author Report, TR Alt. Assess., p. 20	• Lecture, Dramatization, SE p. 297 • S/L Mini-Lesson: Dramatization, ATE p. 290 • V/R Mini-Lesson: Using Color, ATE, p. 292 • Illustration, TR Alt. Assess., p. 20	• Internet Research, Multimedia Report, SE p. 297 • Science Report, TR Alt. Assess., p. 20	• Selection Test, TR Formal Assessment, pp. 88–90; Assess. Res. Software • Description Rubric [for Wr. Mini-Lesson], TR Alt. Assess., p. 84 • TR Alt. Assess., p. 20	• "All Summer in a Day," "Primer Lesson," LL Audiocassettes • WS Writing Lab CD-ROM, Description Tutorial
• Wanted Poster, Letter of Appeal, Narrative Poem, SE p. 313 • Mini-Lesson: Police Report [Facts and Examples], SE p. 313 • Film Review, TR Alt. Assess., p. 21	• Poetry Reading, Ballad Collection, SE p. 313 • S/L Mini-Lesson: Oral Report, ATE p. 308 • Skit,TR Alt. Assess., p. 21	• Oral Reports on Legendary Figures, Geography Comparison, SE p. 313 • Music Search, TR Alt. Assess., p. 21	• Selection Test, TR Formal Assessment, pp. 91–93; Assess. Res. Software • Research Report Rubric [for Wr. Mini-Lesson], TR Alt. Assess., p. 93 • TR Alt. Assess., p. 21	• "The Highwayman," "The Dying Cowboy," "The Real Story of a Cowboy's Life," LL Audiocassettes • WS Writing Lab CD-ROM, Reports Tutorial
• Rules of the Game, Lecture, Folk Tale, SE p. 319	• Folk Tale Exchange, SE p. 319	• Lizard Presentation, Report on Vietnamese History, SE p. 319	• Selection Test, TR Formal Assessment, pp. 94–95 Assess. Res. Software	• "The Little Lizard's Sorrow" LL Audiocassettes
• Monologue, Scene, Memo to a Drama Coach, SE p. 341 • Mini Lesson: Critical Review [Language to Evaluate], SE p. 341 • Internet Research, TR Alt. Assess., p. 22	• Dramatic Scene, Lawyer's Argument, SE p. 341 • S/L Mini-Lesson: Dramatic Scene, ATE p. 337 • V/R Mini-Lesson: Many Faces of Sherlock Holmes, ATE p. 336 • Film Review,TR Alt. Assess., p. 22	• Multimedia Biography, Crime-Solvers' Club, SE p. 341 • Tropical Disease Report, TR Alt. Assess., p. 22	• Selection Test, TR Formal Assessment, pp. 96–98; Assess. Res. Software • Critical Review Rubric [for Wr. Mini-Lesson], TR Alt. Assess., p. 98 • TR Alt. Assess., p. 22	• "The Dying Detective," LL Audiocassettes • WS Writing Lab CD-ROM, Response to Literature Tutorial
• Journal Entry, Citizenship Award, Comparison-and-Contrast Essay, SE p. 361 • Mini Lesson: Volunteering Handbook [Address Your Audience], SE p. 361 • Music Report, TR Alt. Assess., p. 23	• School Interviews, How-to Fair, SE p. 361 • S/L Mini-Lesson: School Interviews, ATE p. 355 • V/R Mini-Lesson: Flowchart, ATE, p. 348 • Fundraising Survey, TR Alt. Assess., p. 23	• Community Participation, Flow Chart, SE p. 361 • Author Report, TR Alt. Assess., p. 23	• Selection Test, TR Formal Assessment, pp. 99–101; Assess. Res. Software • Research Report/Paper Rubric [for Wr. Mini-Lesson], TR Alt. Assess., p. 93 • TR Alt. Assess., p. 23	• "Justin Lebo," "The Rider," "Amigo Brothers," "The Walk," LL Audiocassettes • WS Writing Lab CD-ROM, Exposition Tutorial

Program Planner Unit 5 Just for Fun

Selection	Reading	Literary Elements/Forms	Vocabulary	Grammar
"Our Finest Hour," Charles Osgood, SE p. 375 Reading Level: Average	• Reading for Success: Strategies for Reading Critically, SE pp. 374, 377; TR Selection Support, pp. 131–132 • Distinguish Fact From Opinion,TR Str. for Diverse St. Needs, pp. 47–48 • Model Selection, SE pp. 375–376	• Humor, SE pp. 373, 377; TR Selection Support, p. 133	• Suffixes: *-ment,* SE pp. 373, 377; TR Selection Support, p. 128 Word Bank: correspondent, p. 375; bewilderment, p. 376	• Subjects and Predicates, SE p. 377; TR Selection Support, p. 130 • WS Gram. Pr. Book, Complete Sentences and Predicates, p. 29
"Cat on the Go," James Herriot, SE p. 382 Reading Level: Average	• Understand Bias, SE pp. 381, 394; TR Selection Support, p. 137 • Understand Bias, TR Str. for Diverse St. Needs, pp. 49–50	• Character Traits, SE pp. 381, 394; TR Selection Support, p. 138	• Prefixes: *in-,* SE pp. 380, 394; TR Selection Support, p. 134 Word Bank: grotesquely, emaciated, p. 383; inevitable, sauntered, p. 385; distraught, despondent, intrigued, p. 387; surreptitiously, p. 392	• Compound Subject and Predicates, SE p. 394, TR Selection Support, p. 136 • WS Language Lab CD-ROM, Agreement With Compound Subjects
"The Luckiest Time of All," Lucille Clifton; **"Father William,"** Lewis Carroll; **"The Microscope,"** Maxine Kumin; **"In Just—,"** E. E. Cummings; **"Sarah Cynthia Sylvia Stout Would Not Take the Garbage Out,"** Shel Silverstein, SE pp. 398, 400, 403, 404, 405 Reading Levels: Average, Average, Average, Average, Easy	• Recognize Author's Purpose, SE pp. 397, 408; TR Selection Support, p. 142 • Recognize Author's Purpose, TR Str. for Diverse St. Needs, pp. 51–52	• Hyperbole, SE pp. 397, 408; TR Selection Support, p. 143	• Words With Multiple Meanings, SE pp. 396, 408; TR Selection Support, p. 139 Word Bank: incessantly, sage, supple, p. 401; withered, p. 405; curdled, rancid, p. 406	• Complete and Incomplete Sentences, SE p. 408, TR Selection Support, p. 141 • WS Language Lab CD-ROM, Sentence Fragments • WS Gram. Pr. Book, The Basic Sentence, p. 28
"Zoo," Edward D. Hoch; **"The Hippopotamus,"** Ogden Nash; **"The Caterpillar,"** Ogden Nash; **"The Blind Men and the Elephant,"** John Godfrey Saxe; **"How the Snake Got Poison,"** Zora Neale Hurston, SE pp. 418, 420, 421, 422, 424 Reading Levels: Average, Easy, Easy, Average, Average	• Evaluate Author's Message, SE pp. 417, 426; TR Selection Support, p. 147 • Evaluate an Author's Message, TR Str. for Diverse St. Needs, pp. 53–54	• Character's Perspective, SE pp. 417, 426; TR Selection Support, p. 148	• Related Words: Forms of *wonder,* SE pp. 416, 426; TR Selection Support, p. 144 Word Bank: interplanetary, wonderment, awe, p. 418; inclined, observation, wondrous, p. 422; immensity, p. 425	• Direct and Indirect Objects, SE p. 426, TR Selection Support, p. 146 • WS Language Lab CD-ROM, Styling Sentences • WS Gram. Pr. Book, Direct and Indirect Objects, pp. 33–37
"A Letter to a Clockmaker," Charles Dickens; **"Stepping Out With My Baby,"** Paul Reiser, SE pp. 430, 431 Reading Levels: Average, Average	• Distinguish Fact From Opinion, SE pp. 429, 434; TR Selection Support, p. 152 • Distinguish Fact From Opinion, TR Str. for Diverse St. Needs, pp. 55–56	• Humorous Commentary, SE pp. 429, 434; TR Selection Support, p. 153	• Prefixes: *auto-,* SE pp. 428, 434; TR Selection Support, p. 149 Word Bank: reluctance, confi-dential, automatically, p. 430	• Subject Complements, SE p. 434, TR Selection Support, p. 151 • WS Language Lab CD-ROM, Styling Sentences • WS Gram. Pr. Book, Subject Complements, pp. 38–39
"Let's Steal the Moon," Blanche Serwer-Bernstein, SE p. 437 Reading Level: Easy			• TR Selection Support, p. 154 Word Bank: patriarch, luminary, p. 437; marauders, p. 438	

KEY: SE: Student Edition; ATE: Annotated Teacher's Edition; TR: Teaching Resources; LL: Listening to Literature; WS: Writer's Solution

Writing	Speaking and Listening Viewing and Representing	Projects	Assessment	Technology
• Statement of Apology, Comparison-and-Contrast Essay, Career Advice, SE p. 378 • Mini-Lesson: Report for a Newscast [The 5 W's], SE p. 378 • Oral Report, TR Alt. Assess., p. 24	• Interpreter's Explanation, Humorous Anecdote, SE p. 378 • S/L Mini-Lesson: Humorous Anecdote, ATE p. 375 • Illustration, TR Alt. Assess., p. 24	• News Show, Report on the News, SE p. 378 • Media Report, TR Alt. Assess., p. 24	• Selection Test, TR Formal Assessment, pp. 110–112; Assess. Res. Software • Research Report/Paper Rubric [for Wr. Mini-Lesson], TR Alt. Assess., p. 93 • TR Alt. Assess., p. 24	• "Our Finest Hour," LL Audiocassettes • WS Writing Lab CD-ROM, Reports Tutorial
• Pet Story, Monologue, Biographical Sketch, SE p. 395 • Mini-Lesson: Directory of Places [Supply Background Information], SE p. 395 • Community Resource Report,TR Alt. Assess., p. 25	• Career Interview, Musical Retelling, SE p. 395 • S/L Mini-Lesson: Career Interview, ATE p. 390 • V/R Mini-Lesson: Comic Strip, ATE p. 387 • TV Film Review,TR Alt. Assess., p. 25	• Training Profile, Pet Care Brochure, SE p. 395 • Book Report,TR Alt. Assess., p. 25	• Selection Test, TR Formal Assessment, pp. 113–115; Assess. Res. Software • Research Report/Paper Rubric [for Wr. Mini-Lesson], TR Alt. Assess., p. 93 • TR Alt. Assess., p. 25	• "Cat on the Go," LL Audiocassettes • WS Writing Lab CD-ROM, Exposition Tutorial
• Postcard From Sarah, Seasonal Description, Literary Review, SE p. 409 • Mini-Lesson: Humorous Poem [Use Imaginative Words], SE p.409 • Oral Performance,TR Alt. Assess., p. 26	• Dramatization, Interview, SE p. 409 • S/L Mini-Lesson: Interview, ATE p. 401 • V/R Mini-Lesson: Visual Representation of a Poem, ATE p. 406 • Cartoon or Comic Strip, TR Alt. Assess., p. 26	• Report on Good-Luck Charms, Microscope Presentation, SE p. 409 • Oral Report, TR Alt. Assess., p. 26	• Selection Test, TR Formal Assessment, pp. 116–118; Assess. Res. Software • Poetry Rubric [for Wr. Mini-Lesson], TR Alt. Assess., p. 95 • TR Alt. Assess., p. 26	• "The Luckiest Time of All," "Father William," "The Microscope," "In Just-," "Sarah Cynthia Sylvia Stout Would Not Take the Garbage Out," LL Audiocassettes • WS Writing Lab CD-ROM, Creative Writing Tutorial
• Advertising Flyer, Humorous Poem, Comparison-and-Contrast Essay, SE p. 427 • Mini-Lesson: Report [Topic Sentences and Supporting Details], SE p. 427 • Oral Performance TR Alt. Assess., p. 27	• Zoo Commercial, Animal Game, SE p. 427 • S/L Mini-Lesson: Animal Game, ATE p. 420 • Illustration TR Alt. Assess., p. 27	• Pet Show, Metamorphosis, SE p. 427 • Report TR Alt. Assess., p. 27	• Selection Test, TR Formal Assessment, pp. 119–121; Assess. Res. Software • Research Report/Paper Rubric [for Wr. Mini-Lesson], TR Alt. Assess., p. 93 • TR Alt. Assess., p. 27	• "Zoo," "The Hippopotamus," "Caterpillar," "The Blind Men and the Elephant," "How the Snake Got Poison," LL Audiocassettes • WS Writing Lab CD-ROM, Exposition Tutorial
• Letter of Response, Personal Narrative, Comparison-and-Contrast Essay, SE p. 435 • Mini-Lesson: Letter of Complaint [Letter Format], SE p. 435 • Poem, TR Alt. Assess., p. 28	• Charles Dickens Presentation, Review, SE p. 435 • S/L Mini-Lesson: Dickens Presentation, ATE p. 431 • V/R Mini-Lesson: Personification in Drawings, ATE p. 432 • Design for a Mobile,TR Alt. Assess., p. 28	• Report on the 1850's, Sitcom Guide, SE p. 435 • Portmanteau Words, TR Alt. Assess., p. 28	• Selection Test, TR Formal Assessment, pp. 122–124; Assess. Res. Software • Business Letter/Memo Rubric [for Wr. Mini-Lesson], TR Alt. Assess., p. 100 • TR Alt. Assess., p. 28	• "A Letter to a Clockmaker," LL Audiocassettes • WS Writing Lab CD-ROM, Expression Tutorial
• Outlining a Process, Extending the Tale, Critical Review, SE p. 439	• Storytelling, SE p. 439	• Map Research, Jewish Emigration, SE p. 439	• Selection Test, TR Formal Assessment, pp. 125–126 Assess. Res. Software	• "Let's Steal the Moon," LL Audiocassettes

Program Planner Unit 6 Short Stories

Selection	Reading	Literary Elements/Forms	Vocabulary	Grammar
"After Twenty Years," O. Henry, SE p. 453 Reading Level: Challenging	• Reading for Success: Strategies for Reading Fiction, SE pp. 452, 459; TR Selection Support, pp. 159–160 • What Happens Next, TR Str. for Diverse St. Needs, pp. 57–58 • Model Selection, SE pp. 453–458	• Suprise Ending, SE pp. 451, 459; TR Selection Support p. 161	• Word Roots: *-spec-*, SE pp. 451, 459; TR Selection Support, p. 156 Word Bank: spectators, intricate, p. 453; destiny, p. 455; dismally, absurdity, simultaneously, p. 457	• Clauses, SE p. 459; TR Selection Support, p. 158 • WS Language Lab CD-ROM, Styling Sentences • WS Gram. Pr. Book, Diagraming Clauses, p. 56
"Rikki-tikki-tavi," Rudyard Kipling, SE p. 464 Reading Level: Challenging	• Predict, SE pp. 463, 476; TR Selection Support, p. 165 • Predict, TR Str. for Diverse St. Needs, pp. 59–60	• Plot, SE pp. 463,476; TR Selection Support, p. 166	• Word Roots: *-viv-*, SE pp. 462, 476; TR Selection Support, p. 162 Word Bank: revived, draggled, p. 465; flinched, p. 467; mourning, consolation, cunningly, p. 473	• Simple and Compound Sentences, SE p. 476; TR Selection Support p. 164 • WS Language Lab CD-ROM, Varying Sentence Length and Structure • WS Gram. Pr. Book, Simple and Compound Sentences, pp. 28–30
"Papa's Parrot," Cynthia Rylant; **"Stolen Day,"** Sherwood Anderson, SE pp. 481, 484 Reading Level: Easy, Average	• Indentify With a Character, SE pp. 479, 488; TR Selection Support, p. 170 • Indentify With a Chracter, TR Str. for Diverse St. Needs, pp. 61–62	• Characterization, SE pp. 479, 488; TR Selection Support, p. 171	• Word Roots: *-flam-*, SE pp. 478, 488; TR Selection Support, p. 167 Word Bank: resumed, p. 482; inflammatory, rheumatism, solemn, p. 484	• Complex Sentences, SE p. 488; TR Selection Support, p. 169 • WS Language Lab CD-ROM, Sentence Errors and Styling Sentences
"Heartache," Anton Chekhov; **"Suzy and Leah,"** Jane Yolen, SE pp. 506, 512 Reading Level: Average, Average	• Make Inferences, SE pp. 505, 520; TR Selection Support, p. 177 • Make Inferences, TR Str. for Diverse St. Needs, pp. 69–70	• Setting, SE pp. 505, 520; TR Selection Support, p. 178	• Suffixes: *-ee,* SE pp. 504, 520; TR Selection Support, p. 174 Word Bank: conspiring, ponderous, indignantly, quavering, p. 509; insignificant, p. 511; refugee, p. 513	• Adverb Clauses, SE p. 520; TR Selection Support, p. 176 • WS Language Lab CD-ROM, Adverbs • WS Gram. Pr. Book, Adverb Clauses, p. 53
"Ribbons," Laurence Yep; **"The Treasure of Lemon Brown,"** Walter Dean Myers, SE pp. 524, 532 Reading Level: Average, Average	• Ask Questions, SE pp. 523, 540; TR Selection Support, p. 182 • Ask Questions, TR Str. for Diverse St. Needs, pp. 65–66	• Theme, SE pp. 523, 540; TR Selection Support, p. 183	• Word Roots: *-sens,* SE pp. 522, 540; TR Selection Support, p. 179 Word Bank: sensitive, meek, coax, laborious, p. 525; exertion, p. 526; impromptu, ajar, tentatively, p. 533	• Adjective Clauses, SE p. 540; TR Selection Support, p. 181 • WS Language Lab CD-ROM, Adjectives • WS Gram. Pr. Book, Adjective Clauses, p. 52

KEY: SE: Student Edition; ATE: Annotated Teacher's Edition; TR: Teaching Resources; LL: Listening to Literature; WS: Writer's Solution

Writing	Speaking and Listening Viewing and Representing	Projects	Assessment	Technology
• Friendship list, Letter From Prison, Police Reports, SE p. 460 • Mini-Lesson, Prequel [Use Dialogue], SE p. 460 • Explanation, TR Alt. Assess., p. 29	• News Bulletin, Tabloid Television, SE p. 460 • S/L Mini-Lesson: Tabloid Television, ATE p. 457 • V/R Mini-Lesson: Illustrating the Story, ATE p. 455 • Performance and Discussion, TR Alt. Assess., p. 29	• Wanted Poster, New York in 1900, SE p. 460 • Research Report, TR Alt. Assess., p. 29	• Selection Test, TR Formal Assessment, pp. 135–137; Assess. Res. Software • Description Rubric [for Mini-Lesson], TR Alt. Assess., p. 84 • TR Alt. Assess., p. 29	• "After Twenty Years," LL Audiocassettes • WS Writing Lab CD-ROM, Creative Writing Tutorial
• Picture Book for First Graders, Letter, Comparison and Contrast Essay, SE p. 477 • Mini-Lesson: Report on Natural Enemies [Details to Describe the Environment], SE p. 477 • News Feature, TR Alt. Assess., p. 30	• Play-by-Play Account, First-Aid Demonstration, SE p. 477 • S/L Mini-Lesson: First Aid Demonstration, ATE p. 473 • Report, TR Alt. Assess., p. 30	• Wildlife Collage, Multimedia Report, SE p. 477 • Round Table Discussion, TR Alt. Assess., p. 30	• Selection Test, TR Formal Assessment, pp. 138–140; Assess. Res. Software • Research Report/Paper Rubric [for Wr. Mini-Lesson] TR Alt. Assess., p. 93 • TR Alt Assess., p. 30	• "Rikki-tikki-tavi," LL Audiocassettes • WS Writing Lab CD-ROM, Reports Tutorial
• Diary Entry, Review, Comparing Literary Works, SE p. 489 • Mini-Lesson: Continuation [Show, Don't Tell], SE p. 489 • Readers Theater, TR Alt. Assess., p. 31	• Television Interview, Dramatic Reading, SE p. 489 • S/L Mini-Lesson: Dramatic Reading, ATE, p. 482 • Interview, TR Alt. Assess., p. 31	• Health Statistics, Report, SE p. 489 • Paragraph, TR Alt Assess., p. 31	• Selection Test, TR Formal Assessment, pp. 141–143; Assess. Res. Software • Fictional Narrative Rubric [for Wr. Mini-Lesson], TR Alt. Assess., p. 82 • TR Alt Assess., p. 31	• "Papa's Parrot," "Stolen Day," LL Audiocassettes • WS Writing Lab CD-ROM, Creative Writing Tutorial
• Sympathy Note, Diary Entries, Analytic Essay, SE p. 521 • Mini-Lesson: Introduction to an Exhibition [Necessary Context/Background], SE p. 521 • Brochure, TR Alt. Assess., p. 32	• Questions and Answers, Talk Radio, SE p. 521 • S/L Mini-Lesson: Questions and Answers, ATE , p. 516 • V/R Mini-Lesson: Comparing and Contrasting Cultures, ATE, p. 509 • Paragraph, TR Alt. Assess., p. 32	• Snow Statistics, Research Report, SE p. 521 • Round Table Discussion, TR Alt. Assess., p. 32	• Selection Test, TR Formal Assessment, pp. 146–148; Assess. Res. Software • Research Report/Paper [for Wr. Mini-Lesson], TR Alt. Assess., p. 93 • TR Alt. Assess., p. 32	• "Heartache," "Suzy and Leah," LL Audiocassettes • WS Writing Lab CD-ROM, Exposition Tutorial
• Treasure Description, Diary, Story Review, SE p. 541 • Mini-Lesson: Character Analysis [Support With Evidence], SE p. 541 • Advertisement, TR Alt. Assess., p. 33	• Monologue, Blues Presentation, SE p. 541 • S/L Mini-Lesson: Monologues ATE, p. 529 • V/R Mini-Lesson: Intergenerational Friendship Quilt, ATE, p. 538 • Newspaper Feature, TR Alt. Assess., p. 33	• Travel Brochure, Report, SE p. 541 • Illustration, TR Alt. Assess., p. 33	• Selection Test, TR Formal Assessment, pp. 149–151; Assess. Res. Software • Definition/Classification Rubric [for Wr. Mini-Lesson], TR Alt. Assess., p. 86 • TR Alt. Assess., p. 33	• "Ribbons," "The Treasure of Lemon Brown," LL Audiocassettes • WS Writing Lab CD-ROM, Response to Literature Tutorial

Program Planner Unit 7 Nonfiction

Selection	Reading	Literary Elements/Forms	Vocabulary	Grammar
"How to Enjoy Poetry," James Dickey, SE p. 557 Reading Level: Average	• Reading for Success: Strategies for Reading Nonfiction, SE pp. 556, 561; TR Selection Support, pp. 187–188 • Recognize the Organization,TR Str. for Diverse St. Needs, pp. 67–68 • Model Selection, SE pp. 557–560	• Expository Essay, SE pp. 555, 561; TR Selection Support, p. 189	• Prefixes: *inter-,* SE pp. 555, 561; TR Selection Support, p. 184 Word Bank: prose, inevitability, p. 559; interacts, vital, p. 560	• The Four Functions of Sentences, SE p. 561; TR Selection Support, p. 186 • WS Language Lab CD-ROM, Styling Sentences • WS Gram. Pr. Book, The Four Functions of Sentences, p. 40
"No Gumption," Russell Baker; **"The Chase"** from ***An American Childhood,*** Annie Dillard, SE pp. 566, 576 Reading Levels: Average, Average	• Understanding the Author's Purpose, SE pp. 565, 582; TR Selection Support, p. 193 • Understand the Author's Purpose, TR Str. for Diverse St. Needs, pp. 69–70	• Autobiography, SE pp. 565, 582; TR Selection Support, p. 194	• Word Roots: *-pel-,* SE pp. 564, 582; TR Selection Support, p. 190 Word Bank: gumption, p. 567; paupers, crucial, p. 569; aptitude, p. 571; translucent, p. 578; compelled, perfunctorily, p. 581	• Participles and Participial Phrases, SE p. 582; TR Selection Support, p. 192 • WS Language Lab CD-ROM, Participles and Participial Phrases • WS Gram. Pr. Book, Participles in Phrases, pp. 47–48
"Winslow Homer: America's Greatest Painter," H. N. Levitt, **"Nolan Ryan, Texas Treasure,"** William W. Lace, SE pp. 586, 590 Reading Levels: Average, Average	• Set a Purpose for Reading, SE pp. 585, 594; TR Selection Support, p. 198 • Set a Purpose for Reading, TR Str. for Diverse St. Needs, pp. 71–72	• Biography, SE pp. 585, 594; TR Selection Support, p. 199	• Prefixes: *sub-,* SE pp. 584, 594: TR Selection Support, p. 195 Word Bank: cantankerous, subtle, brutality, vanquished, p. 587; serenity, subservient, p. 589; hostility, p. 592	• Appositives and Appositive Phrases, SE p. 594; TR Selection Support, p. 197 • WS Language Lab CD-ROM, Styling Sentences • WS Gram. Pr. Book, Appositives, p. 46
"Independence Hall," Charles Kuralt; **"Rattlesnake Hunt,"** Majorie Kinnan Rawlings; from ***Barrio Boy,*** Ernesto Galarza; **"I Am a Native of North America,"** Chief Dan George; **"All Together Now,"** Barbara Jordan, SE pp. 604, 607, 611, 615, 618 Reading Levels: Average, Average, Average, Average, Average	• Identify Main Points, SE pp. 603, 620; TR Selection Support, p. 203 • Identify the Author's Main Points, TR Str. for Diverse St. Needs, pp. 73–74	• Essay, SE pp. 603, 620; TR Selection Support, p. 204	• Word Roots: *-mort-,* SE pp. 602, 620; TR Selection Support, p. 200 Word Bank: anonymous, p. 605; unanimously, p. 606, desolate, p. 607; mortality, p. 609; formidable, p. 613; communal, p. 615; tolerant, p. 619	• Subject and Object Pronouns, SE p. 620; TR Selection Support, p. 202 • WS Language Lab CD-ROM, Pronoun Case • WS Gram. Pr. Book, Pronoun Case, pp. 69–71
"Tenochtitlan: Inside the Aztec Capital," Jacqueline Dineen, SE p. 623 Reading Level: Average			• TR Selection Support, p. 205 Word Bank: outskirts, reeds, p. 627; goblets, p. 628	

KEY: SE: Student Edition; ATE: Annotated Teacher's Edition; TR: Teaching Resources; LL: Listening to Literature; WS: Writer's Solution

Writing	Speaking and Listening Viewing and Representing	Projects	Assessment	Technology
• Reader's Log, Limerick, How-to Essay, SE p. 562 • Mini-Lesson: Essay of Praise [Clearly Express the Main Points], SE p. 562 • Literature Report, TR Alt. Assess., p. 34	• Poetry Listening, Choral Reading, SE p. 562 • S/L Mini-Lesson: Choral Reading, ATE p. 558 • Rhymes, TR Alt. Assess., p. 34	• Anthology of Essays, Poetry Home Page, SE p. 562 • Poster, TR Alt. Assess., p 34	• Selection Test, TR Formal Assessment, pp. 160–162; Assess. Res. Software • Expression Rubric [for Wr. Mini-Lesson], TR Alt. Assess., p. 81 • TR Alt. Assess., p 34	• "How to Enjoy Poetry," LL Audiocassettes • WS Writing Lab CD-ROM, Expression Tutorial
• Personality Profile, Personal Narrative, Extended Definition, SE p. 583 • Mini-Lesson: Comparison-and-Contrast Essay [Clear and Logical Organization], SE p. 583 • Magazine Poster, TR Alt. Assess., p. 35	• Dialogue of Authors, Oral Interpretation, SE p. 583 • S/L Mini-Lesson: Dialogue of Authors, ATE p. 580 • V/R Mini-Lesson: Self-Portraits, ATE p. 571 • Story Theater,TR Alt. Assess., p. 35	• Book Report, Multimedia Presentation, SE p. 583 • Sound Track, TR Alt. Assess., p. 35	• Selection Test, TR Formal Assessment, pp. 163–165; Assess. Res. Software • Comparison/Contrast Rubric [for Wr. Mini-Lesson], TR Alt. Assess., p. 90 • TR Alt. Assess., p. 35	• "The Chase" from *An American Childhood,* LL Audiocassettes • WS Writing Lab CD-ROM, Exposition Tutorial
• Baseball Card, Song of Praise, Proposal for a Documentary, SE p. 595 • Mini-Lesson: Instructional Guide [Thoroughness], SE p. 595 • Poem, TR Alt. Assess., p. 36	• Gallery Talk, Award Presentation, SE p. 595 • S/L Mini-Lesson: Award Presentation, ATE p. 591 • Letter to the Editor, TR Alt. Assess., p. 36	• Book Circle, Biographical Report, SE p. 595 • Paragraph, TR Alt. Assess., p 36	• Selection Test, TR Formal Assessment, pp. 166–168; Assess. Res. Software • How-to/Process Explanation Rubric [for Wr. Mini-Lesson], TR Alt. Assess., p. 87 • TR Alt. Assess., p 36	• "Winslow Homer: America's Greatest Painter," "Nolan Ryan, Texas Treasure," LL Audiocassettes • WS Writing Lab CD-ROM, Exposition Tutorial
• Anecdote, Essay for a Broadcast, Introduction to an Anthology, SE p. 621 • Mini-Lesson: Reflective Essay [Necessary Background], SE p. 621 • Brochure, TR Alt. Assess., p. 37	• Press Conference, Book Talk, SE p. 621 • S/L Mini-Lesson: Press Conference, ATE p. 618 • Illustration Notes,TR Alt. Assess., p. 37	• Essay "Fortune Cookies," Timeline, SE p. 621 • Round Table Discussion, TR Alt. Assess., p. 37	• Selection Test, TR Formal Assessment, pp. 169–171; Assess. Res. Software • Expression Rubric [for Wr. Mini-Lesson], TR Alt. Assess., p. 81 • TR Alt. Assess., p. 37	• "Independence Hall," "Rattlesnake Hunt," from *Barrio Boy,* "I Am a Native of North America," "All Together Now," LL Audiocassettes • WS Writing Lab CD-ROM, Narration Tutorial
• Community Events Poster, Ancient Call-in Show, Campaign Speech, SE p. 629	• Interview, SE p. 629	• Visual Essay, SE p. 629	• Selection Test, TR Formal Assessment. pp. 172–173; Assess. Res. Software	• "Tenochtitlan: Inside the Aztec Capital," LL Audiocassettes

Program Planner Unit 8 Drama

Selection	Reading	Literary Elements/Forms	Vocabulary	Grammar
"A Christmas Carol: Scrooge and Marley, Act I," Charles Dickens, dramatized by Israel Horovitz, SE p. 644 Reading Level: Average	• Reading for Success: Strategies for Reading Drama, SE pp. 643, 661; TR Selection Support, p. 210 • Envision,TR Str. for Diverse St. Needs, pp. 75–76	• Elements of Drama, SE pp. 643, 661; TR Selection Support, p. 211	• Word Roots: *-bene-*, SE pp. 642, 661; TR Selection Support, p. 207 Word Bank: implored, morose, p. 647; destitute, p. 649; misanthrope, void, p. 651; ponderous, benevolence, p. 653	• Subject and Verb Agreement, SE p. 661; TR Selection Support, p. 209
"A Christmas Carol: Scrooge and Marley, Act II," Charles Dickens, dramatized by Israel Horovitz, SE p. 663 Reading Level: Average	• Question, SE pp. 662, 682; TR Selection Support, p. 215 • Question, TR Str. for Diverse St. Needs, pp. 77–78	• Characterization and Theme in Drama, SE pp. 662, 682; TR Selection Support, p. 216	• Word Roots: *-aud-*, SE pp. 662, 682: TR Selection Support, p. 212 Word Bank: astonish, p. 663; compulsion, severe, p. 665; meager, threadbare, p. 667; audible, gnarled, p. 671; dispelled, p. 677	• Verb Agreement With Collective Nouns, SE p. 682; TR Selection Support, p. 214 • WS Language Lab CD-ROM, Subject/Verb Agreement • WS Gram. Pr. Book, Agreement Between Subjects and Verbs, pp. 72–74
from ***Sarafina!* "Bring Back Nelson Mandela"** Hugh Masekela, SE p. 685 Reading Level: Average			• TR Selection Support, p. 217	
"The Monsters Are Due on Maple Street," Rod Serling, SE p. 696 Reading Level: Average	• Predict, SE pp. 695, 712; TR Selection Support, p. 222 • Predict, TR Str. for Diverse St. Needs, pp. 79–80	• Conflict in Drama, SE pp. 695, 712; TR Selection Support, p. 223	• Word Roots: *-sist-,* SE pp. 694, 712; TR Selection Support, p. 219 Word Bank: flustered, sluggishly, p. 699; assent, persistently, defiant, p. 701; metamorphosis, p. 703; scapegoat, p. 706	• Pronoun and Antecedent Agreement, SE p. 712; TR Selection Support, p. 221 • WS Language Lab CD-ROM, Pronouns • WS Gram. Pr. Book, Agreement Between Pronouns and Antecendents, p. 77

KEY: SE: Student Edition; ATE: Annotated Teacher's Edition; TR: Teaching Resources; LL: Listening to Literature; WS: Writer's Solution

Writing	Speaking and Listening Viewing and Representing	Projects	Assessment	Technology
• Invitation, Dramatic Scene, SE p. 661 • Analysis, TR Alt. Assess., p. 38	• V/R Mini-Lesson: Journey to the Past, ATE p. 657 • Illustration, TR Alt. Assess., p. 38	• Set Design, SE p. 661 • Research Report, TR Alt. Assess., p 38	• Selection Test, TR Formal Assessment, pp. 182–184; Assess. Res. Software • TR Alt. Assess., p. 38	• "A Christmas Carol: Scrooge and Marley, Act I," LL Audiocassettes
• Casting Memo, Contrasting Obituaries, Drama Critic's Review, SE p. 683 • Mini-Lesson: Scrooge's Persuasive Speech [Support With Evidence], SE p. 683 • Review, TR Alt. Assess., p. 39	• Dramatic Monologue, SE p. 683 • S/L Mini-Lesson: Dramatic Monologue, ATE p. 670 • V/R Mini-Lesson: Set Model, ATE p. 675 • Dialogue and Performance, TR Alt. Assess., p. 39	• Winter Holidays, Set Model, SE p. 683 • Letter to Marley, TR Alt. Assess., p 39	• Selection Test, TR Formal Assessment, pp. 185–187; Assess. Res. Software • Persuasion Rubric [for Wr. Mini-Lesson], TR Alt. Assess., p. 92 • TR Alt. Assess., p. 39	• "A Christmas Carol: Scrooge and Marley, Act II," LL Audiocassettes • WS Writing Lab CD-ROM, Persuasion Tutorial
• Protest Slogan,Classroom Lecture, Memoir, SE p. 687	• Dramatic Performance, SE p. 687	• Flag, SE p. 687	• Selection Test, TR Formal Assessment, pp.188–189 Assess. Res. Software	• from *Sarafina!* "Bring Back Nelson Mandela," LL Audiocassettes
• Neighborhood Code, Alien's Report, Drama Review, SE p. 713 • Mini Lesson: Final Scene [Script Format], SE p. 713 • Research Report, TR Alt. Assess., p. 40	• Performance, Conflict-Resolution Meeting, SE p. 713 • S/L Mini-Lesson: Performance, ATE p. 698 • V/R Mini-Lesson: Visual Imagery, ATE, p. 707 • Photo Essay, TR Alt. Assess., p. 40	• The Scientific View, Casting Sketches, SE p. 713 • Social Studies Report, TR Alt. Assess., p. 40	• Selection Test, TR Formal Assessment, pp. 190–192; Assess. Res. Software • Drama Rubric [for Wr. Mini-Lesson], TR Alt. Assess., p. 96 • TR Alt. Assess., p. 40	• "The Monsters Are Due on Maple Street," LL Audiocassettes • WS Writing Lab CD-ROM, Creative Writing Tutorial

Program Planner Unit 9 Poetry

Selection	Reading	Literary Elements/Forms	Vocabulary	Grammar
"Lochinvar," Sir Walter Scott, SE p. 727 Reading Level: Average	• Reading for Success: Strategies for Reading Poetry, SE pp. 726, 731; TR Selection Support, pp. 227 • Paraphrase the Lines, TR Str. for Diverse St. Needs, pp. 81–82 • Model Selection, SE pp. 727–730	• Ballad, SE pp. 725, 731; TR Selection Support, p. 228	• Words With Multiple Meanings, SE pp. 725, 731; TR Selection Support, p. 224 Word Bank: dauntless, consented, laggard, bar, tread, fret, p. 729	• Degrees of Comparison, SE p. 731, TR Selection Support, p. 226 • WS Language Lab CD-ROM, Modifiers • WS Gram. Pr. Book, Using the Comparative and Superlative Degrees, p. 80
"The Cremation of Sam McGee," Robert Service, SE p. 736 Reading Level: Average	• Identify the Speaker, SE pp. 735, 742; TR Selection Support, p. 232 • Identify the Speaker, TR Str. for Diverse St. Needs, pp. 83–84	• Narrative Poetry, SE pp. 735, 742; TR Selection Support, p. 233	• Shades of Meaning, SE pp. 734, 742; TR Selection Support, p. 229 Word Bank: cremated, whimper, p. 737; ghastly, stern, loathed, p. 739; grisly, p. 740	• Irregular Comparison of Modifiers, SE p. 742, TR Selection Support, p. 231 • WS Language Lab CD-ROM, Comparatives • WS Gram. Pr. Book, Using the Comparative and Superlative Degrees, p. 80
"Washed in Silver," James Stephens; **"Barter,"** Sara Teasdale; **"Winter,"** Nikki Giovanni; **"Down by the Salley Gardens,"** William Butler Yeats, SE pp. 746, 747, 748, 749 Reading Levels: Easy, Average, Easy, Average	• Use Your Senses, SE pp. 745, 750; TR Selection Support, p. 237 • Use Your Senses, TR Str. for Diverse St. Needs, pp. 85–86	• Lyric Poetry, SE pp. 745, 750; TR Selection Support, p. 238	• Word Roots: *-rad-*, SE pp. 744, 750; TR Selection Support, p. 234 Word Bank: radiance, strife, ecstasy, p. 746; burrow, p. 748	• Correct Use of *good* and *well,* SE p. 750, TR Selection Support, p. 236 • WS Gram. Pr. Book, Glossary of Troublesome Adjectives and Adverbs, p. 81
"Seal," William Jay Smith; **"The Pasture,"** Robert Frost; **"Three Haiku,"** Matsuo Bashō, SE pp. 754, 755, 756 Reading Levels: Average, Average, Easy	• Read According to Punctuation, SE pp. 753, 758; TR Selection Support, p. 242 • Read According to Punctuation, TR Str. for Diverse St. Needs, pp. 87–88	• Form in Poetry, SE pp. 753, 758; TR Selection Support, p. 243	• Synonyms, SE pp. 752, 758; TR Selection Support, p. 239 Word Bank: swerve, utter, p. 754; pasture, totters, p. 755	• Placement of *only,* SE p. 758, TR Selection Support, p. 241
"Tanka" Myoe and Minamoto No Sanetomo, SE p. 761 Reading Level: Easy			• TR Selection Support, p. 244	
"Martin Luther King," Raymond Richard Patterson; **"Annabel Lee,"** Edgar Allan Poe; **"Feelings About Words,"** Mary O'Neill, SE pp. 772, 774, 776 Reading Levels: Easy, Average, Average	• Paraphrase, SE pp. 771, 778; TR Selection Support, p. 249 • Paraphrase, TR Str. for Diverse St. Needs, pp. 89–90	• Rythm and Rhyme, SE pp. 771, 778; TR Selection Support, p. 250	• Word Root: *-found-,* SE pp. 770, 778; TR Selection Support, p. 246 Word Bank: beset, profound, p. 772; coveted, p. 775; squat, saunter, preen, pomp, p. 777	• Pronouns in Comparisons, SE p. 778, TR Selection Support, p. 248 • WS Language Lab CD-ROM, Special Problems With Pronouns 2
"Full Fathom Five," William Shakespeare; **"Onomatopeia,"** Eve Merriam; **"Maestro,"** Pat Mora, SE pp. 782, 783,784 Reading Levels: Average, Easy, Average	• Listen as You Read Poetry, SE pp. 781, 786; TR Selection Support, p. 254 • Listen as You Read Poetry, TR Str. for Diverse St. Needs, pp. 91–92	• Sound Devices, SE pp. 781, 786; TR Selection Support, p. 255	• Words based on *onomatopoeia,* SE pp. 780, 786; TR Selection Support, p. 251 Word Bank: knell, sputters, p. 782; maestro, snare, p. 784	• Commonly Confused Verbs: *lay* and *lie,* SE p. 786, TR Selection Support, p. 253 • WS Language Lab CD-ROM, Using Verbs • WS Gram. Pr. Book, Glossary of Troublesome Verbs, p. 68
"Aunt Leaf," Mary Oliver; **"Fog,"** Carl Sandburg; **"Life,"** Naomi Long Madgett; **"Loo-Wit,"** Wendy Rose, SE pp. 790, 792, 793, 794 Reading Levels: Average, Easy, Easy, Average	• Respond to Poetry, SE pp. 789, 796; TR Selection Support, p. 259 • Respond to Poetry, TR Str. for Diverse St. Needs, pp. 93–94	• Figurative Language, SE pp. 789, 796; TR Selection Support, p. 260	• Prefixes: *dis-,* SE pp. 788, 796; TR Selection Support, p. 256 Word Bank: haunches, p. 792; buttes, crouches, unravel, dislodge, p. 794	• Correct use of *like* and *as,* SE p. 796, TR Selection Support, p. 258

KEY: SE: Student Edition; ATE: Annotated Teacher's Edition; TR: Teaching Resources; LL: Listening to Literature; WS: Writer's Solution

Writing	Speaking and Listening Viewing and Representing	Projects	Assessment	Technology
• Farewell Letter, Editorial, Sequel, SE p. 732 • Mini-Lesson: Updated Ballad [Refrain], SE p. 732 • Country Profile, TR Alt. Assess., p. 41	• Skit, Missing Persons Description, SE p. 732 • S/L Mini-Lesson: Skit, ATE p. 729 • Ballad in Performance, TR Alt. Assess., p. 41	• Search Report, Illustrated Storyboard, SE p. 732 • Illustration, TR Alt. Assess., p. 41	• Selection Test, TR Formal Assessment, pp. 201–203; Assess. Res. Software • Poetry Rubric [for Wr. Mini-Lesson], TR Alt. Assess., p. 95 • TR Alt. Assess., p. 41	• "Lochinvar," LL Audiocassettes • WS Writing Lab CD-ROM, Creative Writing Tutorial
• Tabloid Article, Wildernes Code, Tall Tale, SE p. 743 • Mini-Lesson: Diary Entry [Sensory Details], SE p. 743 • Oral Performance, TR Alt. Assess., p. 42	• Weather Report, Conversation SE p. 743 • S/L Mini-Lesson: Weather Report, ATE p. 738 • V/R Mini-Lesson: Map, ATE p. 739 • Wildlife Report, TR Alt. Assess., p. 42	• Yukon Research, Map, SE p. 743 • Tourist Brochure, TR Alt. Assess., p. 42	• Selection Test, TR Formal Assessment, pp. 204–206; Assess. Res. Software • Expression Rubric [for Wr. Mini-Lesson], TR Alt. Assess., p. 81 • TR Alt. Assess., p. 42	• "The Cremation of Sam McGee," LL Audiocassettes • WS Writing Lab CD-ROM, Expression Tutorial
• Recommendation, Nature Poem, Literary Response, SE p. 751 • Mini-Lesson: Introduction to a Poetry Collection [Elaborate on an Idea], SE p. 751 • Radio Advertisement, TR Alt. Assess., p. 43	• Lyrics Presentation, Dramatic Reading, SE p. 751 • S/L Mini-Lesson: Dramatic Reading, ATE p. 748 • Photo Essay, TR Alt. Assess., p. 43	• Seasonal Preparations, Nature Walk, SE p. 751 • Musical Selection, TR Alt. Assess., p. 43	• Selection Test, TR Formal Assessment, pp. 207–209; Assess. Res. Software • Definition/Classification Rubric [for Wr. Mini-Lesson], TR Alt. Assess., p. 86 • TR Alt. Assess., p. 43	• "Washed in Silver," "Barter," "Winter," "Down by the Salley Gardens," LL Audiocassettes • WS Writing Lab CD-ROM, Exposition Tutorial
• Personal Letter, Advertisement, Concrete Poem, SE p. 759 • Mini-Lesson: Poem Describing an Animal [Four-Line Stanza], SE p. 759 • Author Report, TR Alt. Assess., p. 44	• Poetry Reading, Performance Group, SE p. 759 • S/L Mini-Lesson: Poetry Reading, ATE p. 756 • Musical Haiku, TR Alt. Assess., p. 44	• Aquariam Lecture, Research Project, SE p. 759 • Illustration, TR Alt. Assess., p. 44	• Selection Test, TR Formal Assessment, pp. 210–212; Assess. Res. Software • Poetry Rubric [for Wr. Mini-Lesson], TR Alt. Assess., p. 95 • TR Alt. Assess., p. 44	• "Seal," "The Pasture," "Three Haiku," LL Audiocassettes • WS Writing Lab CD-ROM, Creative Writing Tutorial
• Directions, Tanka, Artistic Goals, SE p. 763	• Group Reading, SE p. 763	• Illustrations, A Poet's Life, SE p. 763	• Selection Test, TR Formal Assessment, pp. 213–214; Assess. Res. Software	• "Tanka," LL Audiocassettes
• Couplet, Liner Notes, Critical Review, SE p. 779 • Mini-Lesson: Remembrance of a Person [Specific Examples], SE p. 779 • Oral Performance, TR Alt. Assess., p. 45	• Oral Interpretation, Poetry Drumbeat, SE p. 779 • S/L Mini-Lesson: Poetry Drumbeat, ATE p. 774 • Respond to a Speech, TR Alt. Assess., p. 45	• Missing Person Investigation, Multimedia Presentation, SE p. 779 • Poster, TR Alt. Assess., p. 45	• Selection Test, TR Formal Assessment, pp. 215–217; Assess. Res. Software • Description Rubric [for Wr. Mini-Lesson], TR Alt. Assess., p. 84 • TR Alt. Assess., p. 45	• "Martin Luther King," "Annabel Lee," "Feelings About Words," LL Audiocassettes • WS Writing Lab CD-ROM, Description Tutorial
• School Cheer, Radio Spot, Poem With Artful Alliteration, SE p. 787 • Mini-Lesson: Analysis of a Poem [Clear and Logical Organization], SE p. 787 • Ad Scrapbook, TR Alt. Assess., p. 46	• Silly, Sensational Storytelling, Poetry Singing, SE p. 787 • S/L Mini-Lesson: Silly, Sensational Storytelling, ATE p. 784 • Song Anthology, TR Alt. Assess., p. 46	• Onomatopoeia Factory, Shakespeare and Exploration, SE p. 787 • Career Report, TR Alt. Assess., p. 46	• Selection Test, TR Formal Assessment, pp. 218–220; Assess. Res. Software • TR Alt. Assess., p. 46	• "Full Fathom Five," Onomatopoeia," "Maestro," LL Audiocassettes • WS Writing Lab CD-ROM, Response to Literature Tutorial
• E-mail Response, Personified Weather Report, Analysis, SE p. 797 • Mini-Lesson: Extended Definition [Topic Statement], SE p. 797 • Interview, TR Alt. Assess., p. 47	• Television Newscast, Simile Slam, SE p. 797 • S/L Mini-Lesson: Television Newscast, ATE p. 792 • Pantomime, TR Alt. Assess., p. 47	• Illustrated Figure of Speech, Dancing With "Aunt Leaf," SE p. 797 • Cliché Watch, TR Alt. Assess., p. 47	• Selection Test, TR Formal Assessment, pp. 221–223; Assess. Res. Software • Definition/Classification Rubric [for Wr. Mini-Lesson], TR Alt. Assess., p. 86 • TR Alt. Assess., p. 47	• "Aunt Leaf," "Fog," "Life," "Loo-Wit," LL Audiocassettes • WS Writing Lab CD-ROM, Exposition Tutorial

Program Planner Unit 10 Myths, Legends, and Folk Tales

Selection	Reading	Literary Elements/Forms	Vocabulary	Grammar
"Popocatepetl and Ixtlaccihuatl," Juliet Piggott, SE p. 811 Reading Level: Average	• Reading for Success: Strategies for Reading Legends, Folk Tales, and Myths, SE pp. 810, 817; TR Selection Support, pp. 264–265 • Predict, TR Str. for Diverse St. Needs, pp. 95–96 • Model Selection, SE pp. 811–816	• Legend, SE pp. 809, 817; TR Selection Support, p. 266	• Prefixes: *be-*, SE pp. 809, 817; TR Selection Support, p. 261 Word Bank: beseiged, decreed, relished, brandishing, p. 813; unanimous, refute, routed, edifice, p. 815	• Commas With Interrupters, SE p. 817; TR Selection Support, p. 263 • WS Language Lab CD-ROM, Commas • WS Gram. Pr. Book, Commas That Set Off Added Elements, p. 100
"The People Could Fly," Virginia Hamilton; **"The Algonquin Cinderella,"** Idries Shah; **"Yeh-Shen: A Cinderella Story From China,"** Ai-Ling Louie; **"His Just Reward,"** Lone Thygesen-Blecher and George Blecher; **"Djuha Borrows a Pot,"** Inea Bushnaq, SE pp. 822, 825, 829, 833, 834 Reading Levels: Average, Average, Average, Easy, Easy	• Recognize Cultural Context, SE pp. 821, 836; TR Selection Support, p. 270 • Recognize Cultural Context,TR Str. for Diverse St. Needs, pp. 97–98	• Folk Tales, SE pp. 821, 836; TR Selection Support, p. 271	• Related Words: *undaunted*, SE pp. 820, 836; TR Selection Support, p. 267 Word Bank: croon, p. 823; shuffle, p.824; sage, undaunted, p. 830	• Commas in a Series, SE p. 836; TR Selection Support, p. 269 • WS Language Lab CD-ROM, Puntuation • WS Gram. Pr. Book,Commas That Separate Basic Elements, p. 98
"All Stories Are Anansi's," Harold Courlander, SE p. 841 Reading Level: Average			• TR Selection Support, p. 272 Word Bank: yearned, p. 841; gourd, p. 843; acknowledge, p. 844	
"Phaëthon, Son of Apollo," Olivia E. Coolidge; **"Demeter and Persephone,"** Anne Terry White; **"Narcissus,"** Jay Macpherson; **"Icarus and Daedalus,"** Josephine Preston Peabody, SE pp. 854, 858, 862, 864 Reading Levels: Average, Average, Average, Average	• Predict, SE pp. 853, 868; TR Selection Support, p. 277 • Predict, TR Str. for Diverse St. Needs, pp. 99–100	• Myth, SE pp. 853, 868; TR Selection Support, p. 278	• Word Roots: *-domin-*, SE pp. 852, 868; TR Selection Support, p. 274 Word Bank: mortal, p. 855; dissuade, p. 856; dominions, p. 859; avenging, deluded, lament, p. 863; vacancy, substained; 866	• Commas After Introductory Phrases, SE p. 868; TR Selection Support, p. 276 • WS Language Lab CD-ROM, Commas • WS Gram. Pr. Book, Commas That Set Off Added Elements, p. 100
"The Lion and the Statue," Aesop; **"The Fox and the Crow,"** Aesop, SE pp. 872, 873 Reading Levels: Easy, Easy	• Recognize Storyteller's Purpose, SE pp. 871, 874; TR Selection Support, p. 282 • Recognize Storyteller's Purpose, TR Str. for Diverse St. Needs, pp. 101–102	• Fable, SE pp. 871, 874; TR Selection Support, p. 283	• Prefixes: *sur-*, SE pp. 870, 874; TR Selection Support, p. 279 Word Bank: glossy, surpass, flatterers, p. 872	• Quotation Marks, SE p. 874; TR Selection Support, p. 281 • WS Language Lab CD-ROM, Quotation Marks • WS Gram. Pr. Book, Quotation Marks, pp. 105–106

KEY: SE: Student Edition; ATE: Annotated Teacher's Edition; TR: Teaching Resources; LL: Listening to Literature; WS: Writer's Solution

Writing	Speaking and Listening Viewing and Representing	Projects	Assessment	Technology
• Diary Entry, New Ending, Essay About Cultural Context, SE p. 818 • Mini-Lesson: Explanation of Natural Wonder [Sequence of Events], SE p. 818 • Film Proposal, TR Alt. Assess., p. 48	• TV News Report, Musical Accompaniment SE p. 818 • S/L Mini-Lesson: TV News Report, ATE p. 815 • Volcano Time Line, TR Alt. Assess., p. 48	• Aztec City, Volcano Model, SE p. 818 • History Report, TR Alt. Assess., p. 48	• Selection Test, TR Formal Assessment, pp. 232–234; Assess. Res. Software • Fictional Narrative Rubric [for Wr. Mini-Lesson], TR Alt. Assess., p. 82 • TR Alt. Assess., p. 48	• "Popocatepetl and Ixtlaccihuatl," LL Audiocassettes • WS Writing Lab CD-ROM, Exposition Tutorial
• Book Jacket, Story Sequel, Reader Review, SE p. 837 • Mini-Lesson: Essay on Cultural Context [Elaborate to Support an Idea], SE p. 837 • Photo Essay, TR Alt. Assess., p. 49	• Retelling, Role Play, SE p. 837 • S/L Mini-Lesson: Retelling, ATE p. 833 • V/R Mini-Lesson: Book Illustrations, ATE p. 830 • Story Theater, TR Alt. Assess., p. 49	• Folk-Tale Festival, Puzzle Challenge, SE p. 837 • Evaluation, TR Alt. Assess., p. 49	• Selection Test, TR Formal Assessment, pp. 235–237; Assess. Res. Software • Research Report/Paper Rubric [for Wr. Mini-Lesson], TR Alt. Assess., p. 93 • TR Alt. Assess., p. 49	• "The People Could Fly," "The Algonquin Cinderella," "Yeh-Shen: A Cinderella Story From China," "His Just Reward," "Djuha Borrows a Pot," LL Audiocassettes • WS Writing Lab CD-ROM, Exposition Tutorial
• Help-Wanted Ad, Argument, Folk Tale, SE p. 845	• Performance, SE p. 845 • S/L Mini-Lesson: Performance, ATE, p. 843	• Storytelling Festival, Spider Profile, SE p. 845	• Selection Test, TR Formal Assessment, pp. 238–239; Assess. Res. Software	• "All Stories Are Anansi's," LL Audiocassettes
• News Article, Autobiography, Myth, SE p. 869 • Mini-Lesson: Modern Myth [Use an Outline], SE p. 869 • Modern-Day Myth, TR Alt. Assess., p. 50	• Oral Reading, Radio Advice Show, SE p. 869 • S/L Mini-Lesson: Radio Advice Show, ATE p. 866 • Debate, TR Alt. Assess., p. 50	• Model, Comparison Chart, SE p. 869 • Myth Summary, TR Alt. Assess., p. 50	• Selection Test, TR Formal Assessment, pp. 240–242; Assess. Res. Software • Fictional Narrative Rubric [for Wr. Mini-Lesson], TR Alt. Assess., p. 82 • TR Alt. Assess., p. 50	• "Phaëthon, Son of Apollo," "Demeter and Persephone," "Narcissus," "Icarus and Daedalus," LL Audiocassettes • WS Writing Lab CD-ROM, Narration Tutorial
• Journal Entry, Fable, Fable Essay, SE p. 875 • Mini-Lesson: Introduction to a Collection of Fables [Use Appropriate Sources], SE p. 875 • Oral Report, TR Alt. Assess., p. 51	• Television Dialogue, Monologue, SE p. 875 • Promotional Copy, TR Alt. Assess., p. 51	• Multicultural Fables, Web Site Review, SE p. 875 • Comic Strip, TR Alt. Assess., p. 51	• Selection Test, TR Formal Assessment, pp. 243–245; Assess. Res. Software • Research Report/Paper Rubric [for Wr. Mini-Lesson], TR Alt. Assess., p. 93 • TR Alt. Assess., p. 51	• "The Lion and the Statue," "The Fox and the Crow," LL Audiocassettes • WS Writing Lab CD-ROM, Reports Tutorial

Skills Workshops

Unit	Writing Process Workshops	Applying Language Skills	Real-World Reading Workshops	Speaking and Listening Workshops
Finding Yourself	Pesonal Narrative, p. 64 Firsthand Biography, p. 98	Direct and Indirect Quotations; Punctuating Dialogue, pp. 65, 66 Varying Sentence Beginnings; Avoid Run-on Sentences, pp. 99, 100	Understanding an Author's Purpose, p. 67 Making Inferences, p. 101	Participating in a Group, p. 103
Common Threads	Descriptive Essay, p. 160 Summary, p. 186	Using Precise Nouns; Spelling Noun Plurals, pp. 161, 162 Using Objective Language; Eliminating Unnecessary Words, pp. 187, 188	Reading a Map, p. 163 Recognizing Key Words, p. 189	Understanding Body Language, p. 191
What Matters	Persuasive Letter, p. 238 How-to Essay, p. 266	Friendly Letter Format; Formal and Informal Language, pp. 239, 240 Using Time Transitions; Avoid Sentence Fragments, pp. 267, 268	Recognizing Bias, p. 241 Following Directions, p. 269	Active Listening, p. 271
Resolving Conflicts	Problem-Solution Essay, p. 320 Persuasive Essay, p. 362	Use the Correct Homophone; Avoid Clichés, pp. 321, 322 Connotations; Frequently Confused Words, pp. 363, 364	Challenging an Article, p. 323 Recognizing Charged Words, p. 365	Handling a Confrontational Situation, p. 367
Just for Fun	Humorous Anecdote, p. 410 Letter of Proposal, p. 440	Specific vs. Vague Words; Spelling Contractions With *Have,* pp. 411, 412 Business-Letter Format; Writing Organization Names Correctly, pp. 441, 442	Interpreting Charts and Graphs, p. 413 Reading Product Labels, p. 443	Giving Feedback, p. 445
Short Stories	Short Story, p. 498 Critical Review, p. 544	Vary Tag Words; Using Correct Verbs, pp. 499, 500 Vary Sentence Beginnings; Writing Titles Correctly, pp. 545, 546	Reading Novels and Other Extended Works, p. 501 Varying Reading Rate for Nonfiction, p. 547	Follow Oral Directions, p. 549
Nonfiction	Biographical Report, p. 596 Report on a Current Event, p. 630	Documenting Sources; Avoiding Double Negatives, pp. 597, 598 Use Synonyms for Variety; Capitalize Proper Nouns, pp. 631, 632	Reading for Specific Information, p. 599 Using Headlines and Text Structure in Newspapers, p. 633	Speaking Persuasively, p. 635
Drama	Response to a Drama, p. 688 Radio Script, p. 714	Unity; Correcting Stringy Sentences, pp. 689, 690 Spoken vs. Written Language; Use Punctuation to Show Emotion, pp. 715, 716	Understanding an Internet Web Page, p. 691 Evaluating Media Messages, p. 717	Evaluating a Presentation, p. 719
Poetry	Song Lyrics, p. 764 Comparison-and-Contrast Essay, p. 798	Figurative Language; Commas After Interjections, pp. 765, 766 Vary Sentence Length; Avoid Double Comparisons, pp. 799, 800	Interpreting Song Lyrics, p. 767 Distinguishing Between Fact and Opinion, p. 801	Conducting a Telephone Interview, p. 803
Myths, Legends, and Folk Tales	Cause-and-Effect Essay, p. 846 Research Report, p. 876	Transitions to Show Cause and Effect; Punctuating Introductory Elements, pp. 847, 848 Sentence Variety; Bibliographic Form, pp. 877, 878	Evaluating an Argument, p. 849 Evaluating Sources of Information, 879	Giving an Oral Presentation, p. 881

Copper
Bronze
Silver
Gold
Platinum
The American Experience
The British Tradition

SERIES AUTHORS

The series authors guided the direction and the philosophy of Prentice Hall Literature: Timeless Voices, Timeless Themes. *Working closely with the development team, they contributed to the pedagogical integrity of the program and to its relevance for today's teachers and students.*

Heidi Hayes Jacobs
Department of Curriculum and Teaching
Teachers College
Columbia University
New York, New York
Heidi Hayes Jacobs has served as an educational consultant to over 1,000 schools nationally and internationally. A frequent contributor to professional journals, she has published two best-selling books through ASCD: Interdisciplinary Curriculum: Design and Implementation *and* Mapping the Big Picture: Integrating Curriculum and Assessment K–12. *She has been on the faculty of Teachers College, Columbia University, since 1981, and her years as a teacher of high-school, middle-school, and elementary-school students in Utah, Massachusetts, and New York provide the fundamental background of her experience.*

Richard Lederer
Author, speaker, columnist, and teacher
San Diego, California
Richard Lederer celebrates the English language as the best-selling author of more than ten books, including Anguished English *and* The Miracle of Language. *He writes a syndicated weekly column, "Looking at Language," and he is the Grammar Grappler for* Writer's Digest. *His work has also appeared in publications such as* The New York Times, Sports Illustrated, National Review, *and* Reader's Digest. *Well-known as a speaker and a presenter, Lederer has entertained and informed a wide variety of audiences, including the National Council of Teachers of English. For many years, he taught English at St. Paul's School in Concord, New Hampshire.*

Sharon Sorensen
Author, speaker, and consultant
Mt. Vernon, Indiana
An educator with more than thirty years of classroom experience, Sharon Sorensen has taught both secondary language arts and language arts methods at the university level. She has also published over eighty articles and has authored or co-authored more than twenty-five books on writing, writing process, and the teaching of writing, including How to Write Short Stories, How to Write Research Papers, *and* Webster's New World Student Writing Handbook. *She and her husband live in a self-created wildlife sanctuary in rural Indiana, where they are active in the National Audubon Society.*

PROGRAM ADVISORS

The program advisors provided ongoing input throughout the development of Prentice Hall Literature: Timeless Voices, Timeless Themes. *Their valuable insights ensure that the perspectives of teachers throughout the country are represented within this literature series.*

Diane Cappillo
Language Arts Department Chair
Barbara Goleman Senior High School
Miami, Florida
Past President of the Dade County Council of Teachers of English.

Anita Clay
English Instructor
Gateway Institute of Technology
St. Louis, Missouri
Former Middle School Team Leader; Former Chair, High School English Department.

Mary Curfman
Teacher of English
Clark County School District
Las Vegas, Nevada

Ellen Eberly
Teacher of Language Arts
Catholic Memorial
West Roxbury, Massachusetts

Nancy M. Fahner
Language Arts Instructor
Ingham Intermediate School District
Mason, Michigan
Recipient of Charlotte, Michigan, Teacher of the Year Award, 1992. Curriculum Coordinator for School-to-Work Program.

Terri Fields
Language Arts and Communication Arts Teacher, Author
Sunnyslope High School
Phoenix, Arizona
Recipient of Arizona Teacher of the Year and U.S. WEST Outstanding Arizona Teacher awards.

Susan J. Goldberg
Teacher of English
Westlake Middle School
Thornwood, New York
President, Westchester Council of English Educators. President-Elect, New York State English Council.

Argelia Arizpe Guadarrama
Secondary Curriculum Coordinator
Phar–San Juan–Alamo Independent School District
San Juan, Texas
Recognized by Texas Education Agency for work on Texas Assessment of Academic Skills.

V. Pauline Hodges, Ph.D.
Teacher and Educational Consultant
Forgan High School
Forgan, Oklahoma
President, National Rural Education Association. Former Language Arts Coordinator, Jefferson County, Colorado.

Jennifer Huntress
Secondary Language Arts Coordinator
Putnam City Schools
Oklahoma City, Oklahoma
National trainer for writing evaluation, curriculum integration, and alternative assessment strategies.

Angelique McMath Jordan
Teacher of English
Dunwoody High School
Dunwoody, Georgia
Teacher of the Year at Dunwoody High School, 1991.

Thomas S. Lindsay
Assistant Superintendent
Mannheim School District 83
Franklin Park, Illinois

Carol McKee
Middle School Language Arts Research Teacher
Fayette County Public Schools
Lexington, Kentucky
Past President, Kentucky Middle School Association.

Nancy L. Monroe
Teacher of English and ACT Preparation
Bolton High School
Alexandria, Louisiana
Past President of the Rapides Council of Teachers of English and the Louisiana Council of Teachers. National Advanced Placement Consultant.

Rosemary A. Naab
Chair, English Department
Archbishop Ryan High School
Archdiocese of Philadelphia
Philadelphia, Pennsylvania
English Curriculum Committee. Awarded Curriculum Quill Award by the Archdiocese of Philadelphia.

Ann Okamura
Teacher of English
Laguna Creek High School
Elk Grove, California
Participant in the College Board Pacesetters Program. Formerly K–12 District Resource Specialist in Writing, Competency Assessment, Foreign Languages, and the Elk Grove Writing Project. Fellow in the San Joaquin Valley Writing Project and the California Literature Project.

Scott Phillips
Teacher of English
Ford Middle School
Allen, Texas
District Curriculum Committee Member.

Jonathan L. Schatz
Teacher of English/Team Leader
Tappan Zee High School
Orangeburg, New York
Creator of a literacy program to assist students with reading in all content areas.

John Scott
Teacher of English
Hampton High School
Hampton, Virginia
Recipient of the Folger Shakespeare Library Renaissance Forum Award. Participant in four National Endowment for the Humanities teacher programs.

Ken Spurlock
Assistant Principal
Boone County High School
Florence, Kentucky
Former Teacher of English at Holmes High School and District Writing Supervisor. Twice elected President of Kentucky Council of Teachers of English.

Joan West
Teacher of English
Oliver Middle School
Broken Arrow, Oklahoma
Runner-up, Middle Grades Teacher of the Year.

Rick Wormeli
Teacher of English
Rachel Carson Middle School
Herndon, Virginia
Disney's Outstanding English Teacher of the Year, 1996.

CONTRIBUTING WRITERS

Elaine Epstein
Former Teacher of English
Lynbrook High School
Lynbrook, New York

Bruce Goldstone
Children's Book Author
New York, New York

W. Frances Holder
Former Teacher of English
Palos Verdes United School District
Palos Verdes, California

Emily Hutchinson
Former Teacher of English
Jordan High School
Los Angeles, California

Howard Kutcher
Teacher of English
Conrad Middle School
Red Clay Consolidated School District
Wilmington, Delaware

Lisa Moore
Former Teacher of English
Wayland High School
Wayland, Massachusetts

Jacqueline M. Regan
Former Teacher of English
Newington High School
Newington, Connecticut

Stacey Sparks
Former Librarian
Cuyahoga County Public Library System
Cuyahoga County, Ohio

MULTICULTURAL REVIEW BOARD

Jocelyn Chadwick-Joshua
Director of American Studies
The Dallas Institute of Humanities and Culture
Dallas, Texas

Clara M. Chu
Assistant Professor, Department of Library and Information Science
University of California at Los Angeles
Los Angeles, California

Nora A. Little Light Bird
Department of Special Education
Montana State University
Billings, Montana

K. Tsianina Lomawaima
Associate Professor, American Indian Studies
University of Arizona
Tucson, Arizona

Larry L. Martin
Chair of History, Geography, and International Studies
Coppin State College
Baltimore, Maryland

Sunita Sunder Mukhi
Program Associate
Cultural Programs Division
Asia Society
New York, New York

Julio Noboa Polanco
Professor, Department of Teaching
The University of Northern Iowa
San Antonio, Texas

Alfredo Sámano
Educational Consultant
Region 4, Education Service Center
Houston, Texas

A. J. Williams-Meyers
Professor, Black Studies Department
SUNY–College at New Paltz
New Paltz, New York

Prentice Hall

LITERATURE

Timeless Voices, Timeless Themes

BRONZE

PRENTICE HALL
Upper Saddle River, New Jersey
Needham, Massachusetts

ISBN 0-13-435294-7

2 3 4 5 6 7 8 9 10   02 01 00 99

PRENTICE HALL

ACKNOWLEDGMENTS

Grateful acknowledgment is made to the following for permission to reprint copyrighted material:

Miriam Altshuler Literary Agency as agent for Walter Dean Myers
"The Treasure of Lemon Brown" by Walter Dean Myers from *Boy's Life Magazine,* March 1983. Copyright © 1983 by Walter Dean Myers. Reprinted by permission of Miriam Altshuler Literary Agency as agent for Walter Dean Myers.

Américas
"Lather and Nothing Else" by Hernando Téllez. Reprinted from *Américas,* a bimonthly magazine published by the General Secretariat of the Organization of American States in English and Spanish. Reprinted by permission of *Américas* magazine.

Arte Publico Press
"Maestro" by Pat Mora is reprinted with permission from the publisher of *Borders* (Houston: Arte Publico Press—University of Houston, 1986).

Susan Bergholz Literary Services, New York
"Four Skinny Trees" from *The House on Mango Street.* Copyright © 1984 by Sandra Cisneros. Published by Vintage Books, a division of Random House Inc., and in hardcover by Alfred A. Knopf, 1994. Reprinted by permission of Susan Bergholz Literary Services, New York. All rights reserved.

Brandt & Brandt Literary Agents, Inc.
"The Third Wish" from *Not What You Expected: A Collection of Short Stories* by Joan Aiken. Copyright © 1974 by Joan Aiken. Reprinted by permission of Brandt & Brandt Literary Agents, Inc.

Broadway Books, a division of Bantam Doubleday Dell Publishing Group
From *Tiger: A Biography of Tiger Woods* by John Strege. Copyright ©1997 by John Strege. Used by permission of Broadway Books, a division of Bantam Doubleday Dell Publishing Group.

Clarion Books/Houghton Mifflin Company
Excerpt from *The Midwife's Apprentice* by Karen Cushman. Copyright © 1995 by Karen Cushman. Reprinted by permission of Clarion Books/Houghton Mifflin Company. All rights reserved.

Don Congdon Associates, Inc.
"The Third Level" by Jack Finney, published in *Collier's,* October 7, 1950. Copyright © 1950 by Crowell Collier, renewed 1977 by Jack Finney. "All Summer In A Day" by Ray Bradbury, published in *The Magazine of Fantasy and Science Fiction,* March 1, 1954. Copyright © 1954, renewed 1982 by Ray Bradbury. Reprinted by permission of Don Congdon Associates, Inc.

Harold Courlander
"All Stories Are Anansi's" from *The Hat-Shaking Dance and Other Ashanti Tales from Ghana* by Harold Courlander with Albert Kofi Prempeh. Copyright © 1957 by Harcourt Brace Jovanovich, Inc.; 1985 by Harold Courlander. Reprinted by permission of the author.

Crown Publishers, Inc.
From *The Iceman* by Don Lessem. Copyright © 1994 by Don Lessem. Reprinted by permission of Crown Publishers, Inc.

Curtis Brown, Ltd.
"Suzy and Leah" by Jane Yolen. Copyright © 1993 by Jane Yolen. First appeared in *American Girl Magazine,* published by The Pleasant Company. Reprinted by permission of Curtis Brown, Ltd.

Delacorte Press, a division of Bantam Doubleday Dell Publishing Group, Inc.
"The Luckiest Time of All" from *The Lucky Stone* by Lucille Clifton. Copyright © 1979 by Lucille Clifton. Used by permission of Delacorte Press, a division of Bantam Doubleday Dell Publishing Group, Inc.

Doubleday, a division of Bantam Doubleday Dell Publishing Group, Inc.
"Two Tankas" from *From the Country of Eight Islands* by Hiroaki Sato and Burton Watson. Copyright © 1981 by Hiroaki Sato and Burton Watson. Used by permission of Doubleday, a division of Bantam Doubleday Dell Publishing Group, Inc. "After Twenty Years" by O. Henry from *The Complete Works of O. Henry.*

Enslow Publishers, Inc.
"Nolan Ryan: Texas Treasure" from *Sports Great Nolan Ryan,* Enslow Publishers, Inc., P.O. Box 699, Springfield, NJ 07081, © 1993 by William W. Lace. Reprinted by permission of the publisher.

(Acknowledgments continue on p. 947.)

Looking at Universal Themes

Unit 1

Finding Yourself

Unit 2 Looking at Universal Themes

Common Threads

Unit 3

Looking at Universal Themes

What Matters

Unit 4

Looking at Universal Themes

Resolving Conflicts

Looking at Universal Themes

Unit 5

Just for Fun

Unit 6

Looking at Literary Forms

Short Stories

Unit 7

Looking at Literary Forms

Nonfiction

Unit 8

Looking at Literary Forms

Drama

Looking at Literary Forms

Unit 9

Poetry

Unit

Looking at Literary Forms

Myths, Legends, and Folk Tales

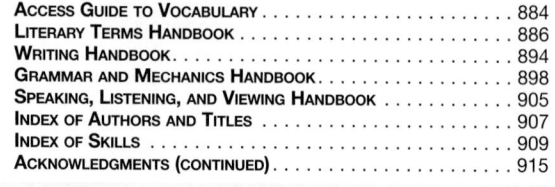

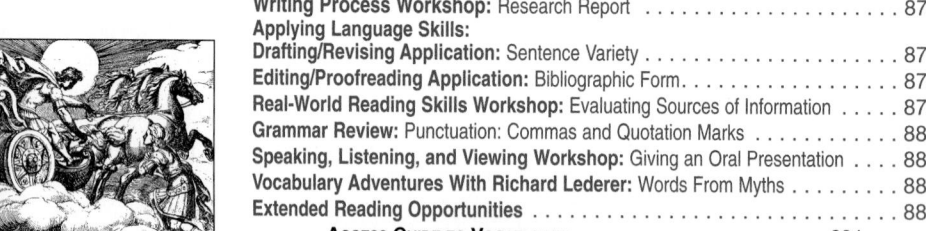

Complete Contents by Genre

Short Story

Drama

Nonfiction

Complete Contents by Genre

NONFICTION (CONTINUED)

POETRY

Complete Contents by Genre

Poetry (continued)

Myths, Legends, and Folk Tales

Complete Contents by Theme

Finding Yourself

Just For Fun

What Matters

Complete Contents by Theme

Resolving Conflicts

Common Threads

The World Around Us

Complete Contents by Theme

The World Around Us (continued)

Setting Goals

Achieving a Balance

Prentice Hall
LITERATURE
Timeless Voices, Timeless Themes

xxiii

Planning Instruction and Assessment

Unit Objectives

1. To read selections in different genres that develop the theme of "Finding Yourself"
2. To apply a variety of reading strategies, particularly literal comprehension strategies, appropriate for reading these selections
3. To recognize literary elements used in these selections
4. To increase vocabulary
5. To learn elements of grammar and usage
6. To write in a variety of modes about situations based on the selections
7. To develop speaking and listening skills, by completing activities
8. To view images critically and create visual representations

Meeting the Objectives Each selection provides instructional material and portfolio opportunities by which students can meet unit objectives. You will find additional practice pages for reading strategies, literary elements, vocabulary, and grammar in the **Selection Support** booklet in the **Teaching Resources** box.

Setting Goals Work with your students at the beginning of the unit to set goals for unit outcomes. Plan what skills and concepts you wish students to acquire. You may match instruction and activities according to students' performance levels or learning modalities.

Portfolios Students may keep portfolios of their completed work or of their work in progress. The Build Your Portfolio page of each selection provides opportunities for students to apply the concepts presented.

Humanities: Art

Untitled, by Steve Dininno

In addition to being an award-winning illustrator, Steve Dininno has published poetry. In this painting, the people are finding their way through the dark. Use these questions for discussion:

1. How are the people in the painting finding their way? *They are using the bicycle's searchlight.*
2. Do you think the people are having fun? Why or why not? *The people are pedaling uphill in the dark, which is difficult and may not be fun; because the people are riding a type of bicycle that is usually used for fun, they might be having fun.*

Untitled, Steve Dininno

Art Transparencies

The **Art Transparencies** booklet in the **Teaching Resources** box offers fine art to make connections to other curriculum areas.

To make connections to the theme of Unit 1, "Finding Yourself," you may wish to use Art Transparency 13, p. 55, *Holding Tilts* by Philomena Williamson. A contemporary artist, Williamson creates paintings that depict the struggle of the transitional period between childhood and adulthood. Use one of the booklet's activities to help students explore the art through discussion of the painting, a writing activity, or by creating their own paintings.

Beyond Literature

Each unit presents Beyond Literature features that lead students into an exploration of careers, communities, and other subject areas. In this unit, students will examine nature's unique creatures, explore genealogy on the Internet, and find out about opportunities for young writers in the workplace. In addition, the **Teaching Resources** box contains a **Beyond Literature** booklet of activities. Using literature as a springboard, these activity pages offer students opportunities to connect literature to other curriculum areas and to the workplace and careers, community, media, and humanities.

UNIT 1

Finding Yourself

One of the most rewarding searches you'll ever conduct is the discovery of the qualities that make you an individual. The literature in this unit will introduce you to people of all generations who have dedicated themselves to this search. You'll meet a girl who struggles to find who she really is and a boy who imitates his heroes as he creates his own style. You'll encounter a man who travels across the world and another who journeys back in time—each in search of himself. As you read about all of these characters, you may discover something about yourself!

Connections

Within this unit, you will find selections and activities that make connections beyond literature. Use these selections to connect students' understanding and appreciation of literature beyond the traditional literature and language arts curriculum.

Encourage students to connect literature to other curriculum areas. You may wish to coordinate with teachers of other disciplines to determine ways to team teach and further extend instruction.

Connections to Today's World

Use these selections to guide students to recognize the relevance of literature to contemporary writings. In this unit, students will read an excerpt from Tiger Woods's biography.

Connecting Literature to Social Studies

Each unit contains a selection that connects literature to social studies. In this unit, students will explore the Middle Ages through a story from the legend of King Arthur.

Assessing Student Progress

The tools that are available to measure the degree to which students meet the unit objectives are listed below.

Informal Assessment

The questions in the Guide for Responding sections are a first level of response to the concepts and skills presented with the selection. As a brief, informal measure of students' grasp of the material, these responses indicate where further instruction and practice are needed. The practice pages in the **Selection Support** booklet provide for this type of instruction and practice.

You will also find literature and reading guides in the **Alternative Assessment** booklet, which students can use for informal assessment of their individual performances.

Formal Assessment

The **Formal Assessment** booklet contains Selection Tests and Unit Tests.

Selection Tests measure comprehension and skills acquisition for each selection or group of selections.

Each Unit Test provides students with 30 multiple-choice questions and 5 essay questions designed to assess students' knowledge of the literature and skills taught in the unit.

Each Alternative Unit Test: Standardized-Test Practice provides 15 multiple-choice questions and 3 essay questions based on two new literature selections not contained in the student book. The questions on the Alternative Unit Test are designed to assess students' ability to compare and contrast selections, applying skills taught in the unit.

Alternative Assessment

For portfolio and alternative assessment, the **Alternative Assessment** booklet contains Scoring Rubrics, Assessment sheets, and Learning Modalities activities.

Scoring Rubrics provide writing modes that can be applied to Writing activities, Writing Mini-Lessons, and Writing Process Workshop lessons.

Assessment sheets for speaking and listening activities provide peer and self-assessment direction.

Learning Modalities activities appeal to different learning styles. Use these as an alternative measurement of students' growth.

Prepare and Engage

OBJECTIVES

1. To read, comprehend, and interpret a short story
2. To relate a short story to personal experience
3. To apply literal comprehension reading strategies
4. To recognize the moral of a story
5. To build vocabulary in context and learn the prefix *pro-*
6. To recognize nouns
7. To write a fable that teaches a lesson by using a correct sequence of events
8. To respond to a short story through writing, speaking and listening, and projects

SKILLS INSTRUCTION

Vocabulary: Prefixes: *pro-*
Spelling: Words With *gu* (gw)
Grammar: Nouns
Reading for Success: Literal Comprehension Strategies
Literary Focus: The Moral of a Story
Writing: Correct Sequence of Events
Speaking and Listening: Humorous Retelling (Teacher Edition)
Critical Viewing: Analyze; Support

PORTFOLIO OPPORTUNITIES

Writing: Product Warning; Advertisements; Newspaper Article
Writing Mini-Lesson: Fable That Teaches a Lesson
Speaking and Listening: Lecture; Humorous Retelling
Projects: Report on Eastern Europe; Multimedia Report on Mirrors

More About the Author
Isaac Bashevis Singer first worked as a proofreader and then as a journalist, following in the writing footsteps of his older brother. When he emigrated from Poland to New York City, Singer wrote for the Jewish Daily Forward, a Yiddish-language newspaper. Singer also wrote most of his fictional works in Yiddish, which were later translated into English. Several of his works have been made into movies, including the story "Yentl." Because Singer was a long-time resident of the Upper West Side in Manhattan, West 86th Street in that neighborhood was renamed for him after his death.

Guide for Reading

Meet the Author:

Isaac Bashevis Singer (1904–1991)

As a boy in Poland, Isaac Bashevis Singer became fascinated with the real-life stories he witnessed in his father's "courtroom." However, his father was neither a lawyer nor a judge. The man was a rabbi, a Jewish religious leader, who settled disputes among the poor Jews of Warsaw, Poland's capital.

The Writer as Judge Later, as a writer, Singer would settle the problems of his own made-up characters. He did this using the language he spoke as a youth and heard in his father's "court": Yiddish. This language, related to German, was spoken by Eastern European Jews and is still used by many Jews.

Far and Not So Far In one way, Singer left his father's world. He came to the United States in 1935 and, over the years, became famous for his novels and stories. Eventually, he won the Nobel Prize for Literature. In another way, though, Singer never really left his father's world. The stories that won him such a wide audience were often based on what he saw and heard as a boy.

The Story Behind the Story

As a religious Jew, Singer's father believed that people should not take pride in their appearance. It is likely that he banned or limited the use of mirrors in his household. You'll see the influence of this attitude in this story.

◆ Literature and Your Life

Connect Your Experience

You'd still be yourself in a world without mirrors. However, some part of you would be missing—something that appears often, is as personal as a fingerprint, but weighs nothing: your reflection in the glass! Without that reflection, you couldn't have an accurate mental picture of yourself.

The characters in this story live happily in a mirrorless world and don't know at first that anything is missing.

Thematic Focus: Finding Yourself

In reading this story, think about whether the image looking out from a mirror is really the same as the self that looks in.

◆ Background for Understanding

Social Studies

The painting on the next page tells you that mirrors have been known for many years. However, the Skibas in this story, peasant farmers from Eastern Europe, regard a mirror as a "luxury."

That's because, as peasants, they have practically no money. They work a small plot of land, producing enough food for their own needs and perhaps a little extra to sell. As a society relies more on technology, peasant farming tends to disappear. However, there are still people in today's world who live much as the Skibas do.

Prentice Hall Literature Program Resources

REINFORCE / RETEACH / EXTEND
Selection Support Pages
Build Vocabulary: Prefixes: *pro-*, p. 1
Build Spelling Skills, p. 2
Build Grammar Skills: Nouns, p. 3
Reading for Success: Literal Comprehension Strategies, pp. 4–5
Literary Focus: The Moral of a Story, p. 6
Strategies for Diverse Student Needs, pp. 1–2
Beyond Literature Cross-Curricular Connection: Psychology, p. 1

Formal Assessment Selection Test, pp. 1–3, Assessment Resources Software
Alternative Assessment, p. 1
Resource Pro CD-ROM
"The Cat Who Thought She Was a Dog and the Dog Who Thought He Was a Cat"—includes all resource material and customizable lesson plan
Listening to Literature Audiocassettes
"The Cat Who Thought She Was a Dog and the Dog Who Thought He Was a Cat"

MODEL SELECTION

The Cat Who Thought She Was a Dog and the Dog Who Thought He Was a Cat

◆ Literary Focus

The Moral of a Story

A short story is like a magical mirror: It shows you your own life reflected in the lives of others. In other words, a story uses the actions of characters to give you a **moral,** a guide for living, that you can apply to your own life.

Sometimes you have to figure out the moral yourself. However, in Singer's tale and in many others, you can find the moral stated, usually toward the end. It may be spoken by the author or by a character.

Peasant shows his wife up in the mirror, undated painting

◆ Build Vocabulary

Prefixes: *pro-*

You'll meet a character in this story whose teeth *protruded.* The prefix *pro-* can mean "forward or before in place or time, or in front of," and the word part *-trude* means "to jut out." Teeth that protrude jut out in front of the lip. On your paper, use a graphic organizer like the one at right to help you think of other *pro-* words.

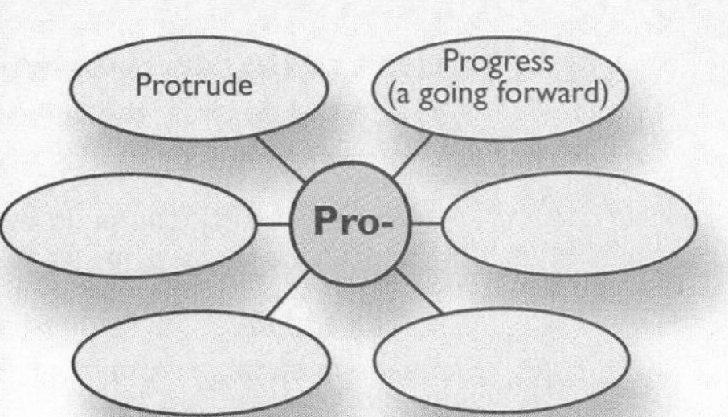

Word Bank

Look over these words from the story. Which word refers to a quality that causes a person to enjoy looking in a mirror? Check the Build Vocabulary box on page 7 to see if you chose correctly.

enthralled
protruded
console
afflicted
vanity
anguish

Write the following phrase on the board: "A world without mirrors." Then have students freewrite about activities that would be difficult to perform if people did not have access to mirrors. Follow with a class discussion in which students share their observations. Then lead students into the story by explaining that the characters in this story live in a mirrorless world. How might the introduction of mirrors change their lives?

◆Build Grammar Skills

Nouns If you wish to introduce the grammar concept for this selection before students read, refer to the instruction on p. 9.

Customize for *Less Proficient Readers*

To help students understand the similarities and differences between the dog and cat in this story, discuss the complex title. As they read, have students list details about the cat and the dog in a character chart, including how the two animals react to the mirror that Jan Skiba buys.

Customize for *More Advanced Students*

Singer invites the reader into his story by asking questions, such as "But must all creatures be exactly alike in their own kind?" Challenge students to answer these questions as they read, and use the questions to predict what will happen in the story.

Humanities: Art

Peasant shows his wife up in the mirror, by Jan Massys

In this picture, Jan Massys (1509–1575) uses exaggerated facial features to emphasize the woman's interest in her reflection. Use these questions for discussion:

1. From the look on his face, what might the man be thinking? *He might be glad that his wife is enjoying the mirror.*
2. Do you think the painting is funny or serious? Explain. *The painting seems funny because the characters look almost like cartoon characters.*

Preparing for Standardized Tests

Reading and Vocabulary This model selection presents four literal comprehension strategies that will help students as they read. These strategies will also help students with reading comprehension items on standardized tests.

Context clues can help students determine the meaning of an unfamiliar word, such as *hut* in the sentence "He lived . . . in a one-room hut with a straw roof." *Lived, one room,* and *straw roof* are clues that *hut* is a humble shelter.

Write this sample test question on the board and have students select the best answer to replace the underlined word :

When Jan Skiba saw the <u>disruption</u> caused by the mirror, he decided his family didn't need it.

(A) pleasure (C) happiness
(B) work (D) disturbance

Point out to students that Skiba would probably want his family to have *pleasure* or *happiness,* so *(A)* and *(C)* are incorrect; and a mirror probably doesn't cause *work,* so *(B)* is not the best answer. Because the sentence indicates that the mirror has a bad effect, *(D)* is the best answer.

Reading for Success

The Reading for Success page in each unit presents a set of problem-solving strategies to help readers understand authors' words and ideas on multiple levels. Good readers develop a bank of strategies from which they can draw as needed.

Unit 1 introduces strategies for literal comprehension. Students must understand a work on its literal level before they apply higher-level critical thinking strategies. Literal comprehension strategies help readers attack text on a surface level—understanding vocabulary, sentence structure, and sometimes complex language.

These strategies for literal comprehension are modeled with "The Cat Who Thought She Was a Dog and the Dog Who Thought He Was a Cat." Each green box shows an example of the thinking process involved in applying one of these strategies. Additional notes provide support for applying these strategies throughout the selection.

How to Use the Reading for Success Page

- Introduce the literal comprehension strategies, presenting each as a problem-solving procedure.
- Before students read the story, have them preview it, looking at the annotations in the green boxes that model the strategies.
- To reinforce these strategies after students have read the story, have them do the Reading for Success, pp. 4–5, in **Selection Support**. These pages give students an opportunity to read a selection and practice literal comprehension strategies by writing their own annotations.

Reading Strategies: Support and Reinforcement

Using Boxed Annotations and Prompts

Throughout the unit, the notes in green, red, and maroon boxes are intended to help students apply reading strategies, understand the literary focus, and make a connection with their lives. You may use boxed material in these ways:

- Have students pause at each box and respond to its prompt before they continue reading.
- Urge students to read through the selection, ignoring the boxes. After they complete the selection, they may go back and review the text, responding to the prompts.

Reading for Success

Literal Comprehension Strategies

Reading is not that different from athletics. Just as you need to be light on your feet to play basketball or baseball, you need to be light on your mental feet when you read. The following strategies will get you on your mental toes and moving toward understanding.

Break down long sentences.

- Don't read a sentence word by word. Look at groups of meaningful words.
- Find the subject, the person, place, or object that the sentence is discussing. Also, find key words that tell you about the subject. The subject and the words that tell you about it don't always appear together:

subject

The *peddlers* who bought groats, chickens, eggs, honey, calves, and whatever was available from the peasants in the village *never came to Jan Skiba's poor hut*.

tells you about the subject

Apply word identification strategies.

- When you come to an unfamiliar word, divide it into syllables and word parts to find familiar elements. When you encounter the word *bedazzled,* break it into its parts:

be + dazzled

You probably know *dazzled,* so you can guess that *bedazzled* means "to be dazzled, or blinded."

Use context to determine meaning.

- Use the context, the surroundings, of an unfamiliar word to find clues to its meaning. Nearby words may provide examples of the unfamiliar word:

From his sack the peddler drew yellow beads, false pearls, tin earrings, rings, brooches, colored kerchiefs, garters, and other such *trinkets*.

If all the items mentioned are examples of *trinkets,* then the word probably means "a small ornament or piece of jewelry."

Reread or read ahead.

- If you're confused by passages, reread them to make sense of words or ideas.
- Read ahead, keeping in mind any questions. You may find the answers later.

As you read the following story by Isaac Bashevis Singer, look at the notes in the boxes. The notes demonstrate how to apply these strategies to a work of literature.

Model a Reading Strategy: Use Context to Determine Meaning

Tell students that when they are reading stories with an unfamiliar setting, they may encounter words they don't recognize. These unfamiliar words may not keep them from understanding the story, but knowing the purpose of the words will help them to appreciate the story more. Show students how to use context clues to grasp the meanings of words such as *gulden* and *groshen* by modeling this kind of thinking:

> In this paragraph, a peddler has come to Jan Skiba's hut. The peddler is showing Jan Skiba and his wife things that they can buy with gulden. The characters are discussing the *price* of a mirror. I see that the price is "a lot of money for poor peasants," so *gulden* must be a form of money. Jan Skiba's wife agrees to *pay* the peddler five groshen a month, so *groshen* must be money, too.

Point out to students that they can check the meanings of these words, or if they are curious about how much a gulden and a groshen are worth, they can research their monetary value in an encyclopedia or a dictionary with a money table.

MODEL

The Cat Who Thought She Was a Dog and the Dog Who Thought He Was a Cat

Isaac Bashevis Singer

"Then Came a Dog and Bit the Cat" from Had Gadya (Tale of a Goat), 1919, E. Lissitzky, The Jewish Museum, New York, New York

1 ▲ **Critical Viewing** Singer includes humorous touches in his story. What details does this artist use to create humor? Explain. **[Analyze]**

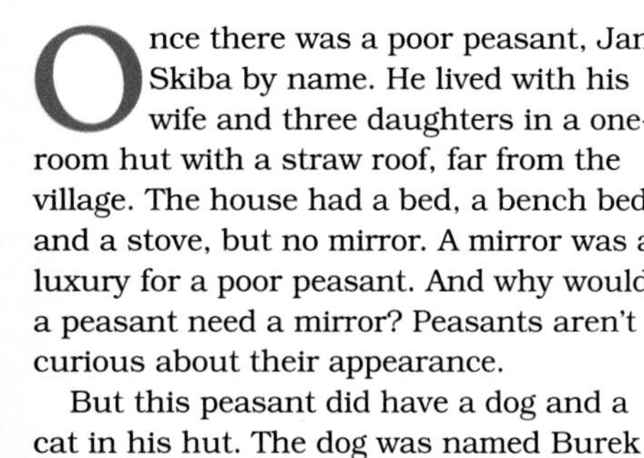

Once there was a poor peasant, Jan Skiba by name. He lived with his wife and three daughters in a one-room hut with a straw roof, far from the village. The house had a bed, a bench bed, and a stove, but no mirror. A mirror was a luxury for a poor peasant. And why would a peasant need a mirror? Peasants aren't curious about their appearance.

But this peasant did have a dog and a cat in his hut. The dog was named Burek and the cat Kot. They had both been born within the same week. As little food as the peasant had for himself and his family, he still wouldn't let his dog and cat go hungry. Since the dog had never seen another dog and the cat had never seen another cat and they saw only each other, the dog thought he was a cat and the cat thought she was a dog. 2 True, they were far from being alike by nature. The dog barked and the cat meowed. The dog chased rabbits and the cat lurked after mice. 3 But must all creatures be exactly like their own kind? The peasant's children weren't exactly alike either. Burek and Kot

> **Break down** this long sentence, and you'll see that its main part is "the dog thought he was a cat and the cat thought she was a dog."

Develop Understanding

One-Minute Insight Jan Skiba lives a simple life with his wife, his daughters, a dog, and a cat in a small hut. When a peddler sells them a mirror, the family members see themselves in a disappointing new light. Even the cat and the dog find the mirror disturbing and turn on each other. Jan returns the mirror, deciding that harmony is more valuable than a reflection. Through this plot sequence, Singer shows readers that it's what is inside a person, not the outward appearance, that counts.

▶Critical Viewing◀

❶ **Analyze** *The cat and dog turn, or whirl, as they fight and their fangs and claws are exaggerated.*

Reading for Success

❷ **Break Down Long Sentences** To break down this sentence, guide students to find the subject of each part and key words that tell about the subjects. *Cat and dog are subjects and saw and thought are key words which point out the animals' mixed-up perceptions of themselves.*

Reading for Success

❸ **Use Context to Determine Meaning** Guide students to use context clues to ascertain the meaning of the word *lurked.* Point out that the cat's lurking is compared to the dog's chasing. Then ask students what they think the cat is doing. *The cat is sneaking up on its prey, lying in wait.*

Humanities: Art

"Then Came a Dog and Bit the Cat" from *Had Gadya (Tale of a Goat),* 1919, by Eleazar Lissitzsky

This painting is an artist's view of part of the Hebrew folk song "Had Gadya," which means "an only kid" (orphaned baby goat). Have students look at the painting and think about how it fits with the title of the story. *Students may say that the picture helps them predict that the cat and dog in the title will fight each other in the story.*

Block Scheduling Strategies

Consider these suggestions to take advantage of extended class time:

- Before students read the story, introduce the Reading for Success strategies, p. 4. Suggest that as they read, students keep a log to monitor their reading strategies. Supplement by having students work as a class to answer the Reading for Success questions on p. 9. Then have students apply the strategies as they annotate Reading for Success practice selection, pp. 3–4, in **Selection Support.**
- Have students read independently, then discuss the Literary Focus, p. 9. Form students into four discussion groups based on whether they strongly agree; agree; disagree; or strongly disagree with Jan Skiba's decision to give back the mirror. Ask each group to summarize their discussion for the rest of the class before they answer the Critical Thinking questions.
- To prepare students for the Writing Mini-Lesson, have them work in the Using Nouns section of the *Writer's Solution Language Lab CD-ROM.*

▶Critical Viewing◀

❶ **Support** *The painting shows a horse, a chicken, farm equipment, and a shed or barn in the background.*

Clarification

❷ Peddlers who go from town to town to barter or sell are no longer common today; most shoppers go to stores to buy what they need. However, similar merchants still exist —some in mall booths, others on urban street corners or at street fairs. Modern-day "peddlers" may offer wares such as souvenirs, snacks, jewelry, or crafts—often the same type of trinkets and doodads that the peddler offers Jan Skiba and his family.

Customize for *English Language Learners*

Students will find words in this story that are uncommon in modern, everyday English. Assist them by replacing words such as *groats* and *gulden* with words that may be more familiar, such as *oats* or *dollar,* in order for them to understand the meaning of the sentences where these words appear.

Customize for *Intrapersonal Learners*

Ask students to put themselves in the position of the peddler and then Jan Skiba or his wife during the exchange of the mirror and the first installment of paying for it. Suggest that students examine each character's individual outlook on the situation: the peddler's concern about the Skibas' ability to pay for the mirror; Jan Skiba's desire for his wife and daughters to have something special; and the wife's desire to have the mirror for her daughters and herself. Encourage students to describe their impressions of the characters' thoughts and attitudes.

La Cour d'un Ferme (The Farmyard), Marc Chagall

❶ ▲ Critical Viewing What details in this painting illustrate that Singer's story is set in a rural area far from a village? **[Support]**

lived on good terms, often ate from the same dish, and tried to mimic each other. When Burek barked, Kot tried to bark along, and when Kot meowed, Burek tried to meow too. Kot occasionally chased rabbits and Burek made an effort to catch a mouse.

❷ The peddlers who bought groats,[1] chickens, eggs, honey, calves, and whatever was available from the peasants in the village never came to Jan Skiba's poor hut. They knew that Jan was so poor he had nothing to sell. But one day a peddler happened to stray there. When he came inside and began to lay out his wares, Jan Skiba's wife and daughters were bedazzled by all the pretty doodads. From his sack the peddler drew yellow beads, false

1. **groats** (grōtz) *n.*: Coarsely cracked grains, especially wheat, buckwheat, oats, or barley.

Humanities: Art

La Cour d'une Ferme (The Farmyard), by Marc Chagall

Marc Chagall (1887–1985) lived much of his life in Paris, yet his art reflects a fondness for his native Russia. He often painted images of country life that were a sharp contrast to the urban lifestyle he lived in his adopted city. In this painting, the house is simple, and the animals roam freely in the farmyard. Use the following questions for discussion:

1. Ask students to compare and contrast the house in this painting to the house in the story. *Both are farmhouses, but the one in the painting seems much larger than the Skibas' hut.*
2. Who is the person in the window? What is he or she doing? *It may be the farmer or his wife, letting fresh air into the room, tossing feed to the animals, or simply looking out the window.*
3. Like the Skibas' cat and dog, the animals in this painting are not penned. What does the animals' freedom suggest about their status? *They are important enough to roam among the people with whom they live; they may be considered members of the family.*

pearls, tin earrings, rings, brooches, colored kerchiefs, garters, and other such trinkets. But what enthralled the women of the house most was a mirror set in a wooden frame. They asked the peddler its price and he said a half gulden, which was a lot of money for poor peasants. After a while, Jan Skiba's wife, Marianna, made a proposition to the peddler. She would pay him five groshen a month for the mirror. The peddler hesitated a moment. The mirror took up too much space in his sack and there was always the danger it might break. He, therefore, decided to go along, took the first payment of five groshen from Marianna, and left the mirror with the family. He visited the region often and he knew the Skibas to be honest people. He would gradually get his money back and a profit besides.

> Use **context clues** to see that *proposition* means "a plan offered for consideration." The next sentence provides the clue; it explains the plan.

The mirror created a commotion in the hut.
3 Until then Marianna and the children had seldom seen themselves. Before they had the mirror, they had only seen their reflections in the barrel of water that stood by the door. Now they could see themselves clearly and they began to find defects in their faces, defects they had never noticed before. Marianna was pretty but she had a tooth missing in front and she felt that this made her ugly. One daughter discovered that her
4 nose was too snub and too broad; a second that her chin was too narrow and too long; a third that her face was sprinkled with freckles. Jan Skiba too caught a glimpse of himself in the mirror and grew displeased by his thick lips and his teeth, which protruded like a buck's. That day, the women of the house became so absorbed in the mirror they didn't cook supper, didn't make up the bed, and neglected all the other household tasks. Marianna had heard of a dentist in the big city who could replace a missing tooth, but such things were expensive. The girls tried to console each other that they were pretty enough and that they would find suitors, but they no longer felt as jolly as before. They had been afflicted with the vanity of city girls. The one with the broad nose kept trying to pinch it together with her fingers to make it narrower; the one with the too-long chin pushed it up with her fist to make it shorter; the one with the freckles wondered if there was a salve[2] in the city that could remove freckles. But where would the money come from for the fare to the city? And what about the money to buy this salve? For the first time the Skiba family deeply felt its poverty and envied the rich.

> **Break down** *reflections* into its parts: *re + flect- ions.*

> **Reread** this paragraph to understand why the family envied the rich.

But the human members of the household were not the only ones affected. The dog and the cat also grew disturbed by the mirror. The hut was low and the mirror had been hung just above a bench. The first time the cat sprang up on the bench and saw her image in the mirror, she became terribly perplexed. She had never before seen such a creature. Kot's whiskers bristled, she began to meow at her reflection and raised a paw to it, but the other creature meowed back and raised her paw too. Soon the dog jumped up on the bench, and when he saw the other dog he became wild with rage and shock. He barked at the other dog and showed him his teeth, but the other barked back and bared his fangs too. So great was the distress of Burek and Kot that for the first time in their lives they turned on each other. Burek took a bite 5
out of Kot's throat and Kot hissed and spat at him and clawed his muzzle. They both started

2. **salve** (sav) *n.*: Lotion or ointment used to soothe or heal.

◆ Build Vocabulary

enthralled (en thrôld′) *v.*: Fascinated; charmed

protruded (prō tro͞od′ id) *v.*: Stuck out; extended

console (kən sōl′) *v.*: Comfort; make less sad

afflicted (ə flik′ tid) *v.*: Received pain or suffering

vanity (van′ ə tē) *n.*: The quality of being very proud of one's appearance

◆ Literature and Your Life

3 If, like the Skibas, you had never seen your reflection, how would you react to the thought that you were about to view yourself? *Students may suggest reactions that include excitement or uneasiness and possibly a mixture of these responses.*

Reading for Success

4 **Reread or Read Ahead** This passage requires readers to understand the meaning of *defect.* Point out that by reading ahead, students will find examples of defects, or "flaws." *Students should find such examples as too many freckles, a snub nose, and a narrow chin.*

◆ Critical Thinking

5 **Interpret** How does the fight between the cat and dog make the situation seem even worse than it did when the human family members were worrying about their appearances? *The situation between the cat and the dog seems worse because they are attacking each other whereas the family members were just upset with themselves.*

Customize for *Less Proficient Readers*

Help students apply word identification strategies to a word that may be difficult for them. Point out that Jan Skiba is *displeased* with his appearance. Model breaking down this word into syllables to find its familiar parts: *dis + pleased.* Tell students the prefix *dis-* usually means "the opposite of." Then encourage them to apply the meaning of the prefix to define *displeased* as "the opposite of being pleased or happy."

Customize for *Interpersonal Learners*

Form small groups of students, and instruct each group to act out a different scene of the story. Students can take on different roles, such as Burek, Kot, Jan, Marianna, and a narrator. After they present their scenes, have students discuss insights into the characters and events that they gained from acting out the story.

Speaking and Listening Mini-Lesson

Humorous Retelling

This lesson supports the Speaking and Listening activity on p. 10.

Introduce Show students that Singer's use of details, description, and questions to the reader makes this a good story to retell. Point out that there is no dialogue until the last page of the story.

Develop Tell students that retelling a story offers an opportunity to heighten the effects of certain parts by exaggerating details, using vocal effects, and incorporating the audience's response as the reteller relates the story. With the class, develop a list of criteria for retelling a story.

Apply Have students tell the story as the peddler. Encourage them to elaborate by adding dialogue for one or more of the characters, transitions, and humorous details. Invite them to retell the story for groups of children from a class of younger students.

Assess Evaluate students' retellings based on the criteria that the class developed, and use the Peer Assessment: Dramatic Performance form, p. 107, in **Alternative Assessment.**

◆Literary Focus

❶ The Moral of a Story Point out that Singer uses the village priest to state the moral of the story. What does he say is the problem with the glass mirror? *A glass mirror only shows the appearance of a person, not who the person really is.*

Reinforce and Extend

Answers

◆Literature and Your Life

Reader's Response Students may say they would need more time to get ready to go to school, or to go out with their friends, because they wouldn't be able to see themselves. Others may say they would pay less attention to their appearance.

Thematic Focus Students may say that the characters forget that they were happy with themselves before they saw their reflections.

☑ Check Your Comprehension

1. The house is a small hut with only one room. The Skibas are poor peasant farmers.
2. They don't fight like most cats and dogs. They get along and they try to copy each other.
3. A peddler comes to the hut and shows the Skibas the mirror. They can't afford it, but then Marianna makes an arrangement to pay a little bit every month.
4. The humans worry about their appearance instead of doing chores. The animals attack their reflections and then attack each other.
5. Skiba gives the mirror back to the peddler.

◆Critical Thinking

1. All the items are jewelry or attractive things that aren't absolutely necessary.
2. The humans hardly recognize who they really are and become aware of flaws in their appearance. The mirror causes the dog and cat to fight with each other as if they didn't know one another.
3. The reactions are funny because they are silly and exaggerated. It's funny that the cat and dog try to fight with their reflections. It's sad when the people start to think less of themselves and the animals turn on each other.

to bleed and the sight of blood aroused them so that they nearly killed or crippled each other. The members of the household barely managed to separate them. Because a dog is stronger than a cat, Burek had to be tied outside, and he howled all day and all night. In their anguish, both the dog and the cat stopped eating.

When Jan Skiba saw the disruption the mirror had created in his household, he decided a mirror wasn't what his family needed. "Why look at yourself," he said, "when you can see and admire the sky, the sun, the moon, the stars, and the earth, with all its forests, meadows, rivers, and plants?" He took the mirror down from the wall and put it away in the woodshed. When the peddler came for his monthly installment, Jan Skiba gave him back the mirror and in its stead, bought kerchiefs and slippers for the women. After the mirror disappeared, Burek and Kot returned to normal. Again Burek thought he was a cat and Kot was sure she was a dog. Despite all the defects the girls had found in themselves, they made good marriages. The village priest heard what had happened at Jan Skiba's house and he said, "A glass mirror shows only the skin of the body. The real image of a person is in his willingness to help himself and his family and, as far as possible, all those he comes in contact with. This kind of mirror reveals the very soul of the person." ❶

◆ Build Vocabulary

anguish (aŋ´ gwish) *n.*: Great suffering; agony

Guide for Responding

◆ Literature and Your Life

Reader's Response List some ways in which your life would be different without mirrors.

Thematic Focus What understanding of themselves do the characters lose when they discover their reflections in the mirror?

Skit [Group Activity] Reenact the commotion that occurs in the hut when Marianna and her daughters first see themselves in the mirror.

☑ Check Your Comprehension

1. Briefly describe the Skibas' house and way of life.
2. What is special about their cat and dog?
3. List the events leading up to the purchase of the mirror by the Skibas.
4. What problems does the mirror create for the human and animal characters?
5. How does Jan Skiba solve these problems?

◆ Critical Thinking

Interpret

1. What is similar about all the goods that the peddler shows Marianna? **[Connect]**
2. In what way does the mirror, a strange new object, cause the humans and the animals to become strangers to themselves? **[Analyze]**
3. Why are the characters' reactions to the mirror both funny and sad? **[Interpret]**
4. Why does the simple fact that Skiba has removed the mirror have such a dramatic effect on the family? **[Draw Conclusions]**

Evaluate

5. Could a dog think it's a cat and a cat think it's a dog? Why or why not? **[Criticize]**

Apply

6. Would it be possible for our society to do without mirrors? Explain. **[Speculate]**

Beyond the Selection

FURTHER READING

Other Works by Isaac Bashevis Singer

The Estate
The Death of Methuselah

Other Works on the Theme of Finding Yourself

The View from Saturday, E. L. Konigsburg
Bridge to Terabithia, Katherine Paterson
Great Expectations, Charles Dickens

INTERNET

We suggest the following sites on the Internet (all Web sites are subject to change).

For more information on Isaac Bashevis Singer and his Nobel Prize:
http://www.nobel.se/laureates/literature-1978.html

For an interview with Singer:
http://www.salonmagazine.com/books/int/1998/04/cov_si_28int.html

We *strongly recommend* that you preview these sites before you send students to them.

Guide for Responding (continued)

◆ Reading for Success

Literal Comprehension Strategies

Review the reading strategies and the notes showing how to understand a writer's words. Then apply them to answer the following.

1. Break down the word *commotion* into its parts and find a familiar word hidden inside it.
2. Break down the sentence on page 7 that begins "So great was the distress . . ." What is the subject? What are the key words that tell you about the subject?
3. Using context clues, find the meaning of *perplexed* on page 7. Explain how you figured out the meaning.

◆ Build Vocabulary

Using the Prefix *pro-*

Explain how each italicized *pro-* word includes the meaning "before, ahead, in front of, or forth":

> Today, factories *produce* mirrors. Then advertisers *promote* them by showing models *promenading* along a street with mirrors. The ad *promises* people that they will look like models. This system is called *progress*.

Spelling Strategy

The *gw* sound following *n*, as in *anguish*, is spelled *gu*. Write the words containing the *gu* spelling of the *gw* sound that fit the following definitions:

1. Human speech: l ___?___
2. A black-and-white bird that lives in the Arctic: p ___?___
3. To become weak; to lose energy: l ___?___

Using the Word Bank

On your paper, write the word or phrase whose meaning is closest to that of the first word.

1. enthralled: (a) fascinated, (b) stalled, (c) enjoyed
2. protruded: (a) intruded, (b) stuck out, (c) protected
3. console: (a) help, (b) comfort, (c) go alone
4. afflicted: (a) troubled, (b) calmed, (c) beat
5. vanity: (a) beauty, (b) large mirror, (c) excessive pride
6. anguish: (a) tears, (b) suffering, (c) anger

◆ Literary Focus

The Moral of a Story

Singer ends his tale with a **moral,** a guide for living, so that the story won't really end with the last printed word. He wants you to keep thinking about this moral and apply it to your own life. In this way, the true ending of the story is you.

To give the full statement of the moral, Singer uses a character who is more educated than the Skibas: the village priest.

1. In your own words, express the moral stated by the priest.
2. Explain how something in your own experience supports or goes against the moral in this story.

◆ Build Grammar Skills

Nouns

Nouns are words that name a person, animal, place, thing, or idea. Without nouns, we couldn't use language to talk about the world. Singer needs and uses every kind of noun in his story:

Person *peasant, daughter*	**Thing** *mirror, trinket*
Animal *cat, rabbit*	**Idea** *soul, rage*
Place *village, city*	

Practice Find the nouns in these sentences and tell what kind of item they name.

1. The peasant had a dog and a cat in his hut.
2. The peddlers never came to the hut.
3. There was a mirror in his sack.
4. All day, the women looked into the mirror.
5. The family felt true distress.

Writing Application Answer the following questions in full sentences. Then, circle the nouns you've used.

1. What kind of home do the Skibas have?
2. Where is their farm located?
3. How does the mirror change life in the house?
4. Which animals use the mirror?
5. What happens to the mirror?

4. Once the mirror is gone, the characters no longer worry about their appearance and flaws.
5. Students should support their responses with examples from their own reading or observations. Some may say it's not possible because dogs are dogs by nature and cats are cats.
6. Students may say that it would be possible to live without mirrors because we only use them to see ourselves. Some may say that without mirrors we would have to rely on other people to tell us what we look like.

Reading for Success

1. *com + motion; motion*
2. The sentence is about the *distress* of Burek and Kot. Key words are *great* and *turned on each other.*
3. The sentences following the word *perplexed* explain that Kot had "never before seen such a creature" and that she tries to swat at her own reflection. She is confused, so *perplexed* must mean "confused."

◆Build Vocabulary

Using the Prefix *pro-*

In *produce, pro-* means "to bring forth"; in *promote* it means "move forward or forth"; in *promenading* it means "walking before or forth"; in *promising* it means "sending your word forth"; in *progress* it means "moving forward or ahead."

Spelling Strategy

1. language; 2. penguin; 3. languish

Using the Word Bank

1. a 3. b 5. c
2. b 4. a 6. b

◆Literary Focus

1. Students may say that the moral is that one's true self is shown in one's actions, not one's appearance.
2. Students should use examples from their experiences. Some may say that they agree with the moral because they have changed their opinions about people after they have gotten to know them.

◆Build Grammar Skills

Practice

1. peasant: person; dog: animal; cat: animal; hut: thing
2. peddlers: persons; hut: thing
3. mirror: thing; sack: thing
4. day: idea; women: persons; mirror: thing
5. family: persons; distress: idea

Writing Application

Possible responses: 1. hut; 2. village; 3. troubles or distress; 4. cat or dog; 5. priest

Writer's Solution

For additional instruction and practice, use the lesson in the *Writer's Solution Language Lab CD-ROM* on Using Nouns and the practice pages on Nouns, pp. 5–7, in the *Writer's Solution Grammar Practice Book.*

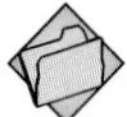

Idea Bank

Following are suggestions for matching the Idea Bank topics with your students' performance levels and learning modalities:

Customize for
Performance Levels
Less Advanced Students: 1, 4, 5
Average Students: 2, 4, 5, 6
More Advanced Students: 3, 6, 7

Customize for
Learning Modalities
Verbal/Linguistic: 1, 2, 3, 4, 5, 6
Visual/Spatial: 7
Bodily/Kinesthetic: 5
Logical/Mathematical: 6, 7
Interpersonal: 6
Intrapersonal: 4

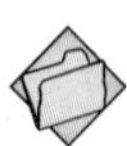

Writing Mini-Lesson

Refer students to the Writing Handbook in the back of the book for instructions on the writing process and for further information on fables.

Writer's Solution

Writing Lab CD-ROM

Have students complete the tutorial on Narration. Follow these steps:

1. Use the Conflict Wheel activity to spark an idea for a fable.
2. Have students draft on the computer.
3. Use the Transitional Word Bin to gather words to connect the events in the fable.
4. Have students work together on the peer-evaluation checklist.

You will need approximately 90 minutes of class time to complete these steps.

Writer's Solution Sourcebook

Have students use Chapter 3, "Narration," pp. 66–101, for additional support. This chapter includes in-depth instruction on developing well-rounded characters, p. 88.

Build Your Portfolio

Idea Bank

Writing

1. **Product Warning** Mirror-makers have taken Singer's story to heart and are attaching a warning to their product. Write a warning they can place in the corner of every mirror.
2. **Advertisements** The Skibas have to sell their quarreling cat and dog. Write two ads for them: one to sell a cat that thinks it's a dog and the other to sell a dog that thinks it's a cat.
3. **Newspaper Article** As a reporter for the local village paper, write an article about the strange events at the Skibas' house. Begin with a lead, a paragraph telling readers *who, what, when, where,* and *how.* **[Career Link]**

Speaking and Listening

4. **Lecture** You're a village teacher who has heard about the Skibas' problems. Using the Skiba household as an example, deliver a lecture to your class on the dangers of vanity. **[Performing Arts Link]**
5. **Humorous Retelling** The peddler in Singer's tale had a funny story to tell his next customers. Retell the story as the peddler might have told it, adding humorous details. **[Performing Arts Link]**

Projects

6. **Report on Eastern Europe** **[Group Activity]** With several classmates, write a report on peasant life in Eastern Europe centuries ago. Divide the work so that one person gathers statistics, another finds out about day-to-day life, and a third weaves the report together. **[Social Studies Link]**
7. **Multimedia Report on Mirrors** Research fantastic facts about the history and uses of mirrors. For example, find out about convex mirrors and funhouse mirrors. Then, including materials like photographs, actual mirrors, diagrams, and video clips, create a presentation for the class. **[Media Link]**

Writing Mini-Lesson

Fable That Teaches a Lesson

Singer's story reads like a fable, a brief tale in which animal characters teach a lesson about life. Write such a fable yourself. Use Singer's cat and dog or other animal characters to teach a lesson, and have a character state the lesson at the end.

Writing Skills Focus: Correct Sequence of Events

Your audience will be confused if they can't follow the **sequence of events.** To hold your audience and teach your lesson, you must tell what happened in the right order. For example, in this passage from his story, Singer uses words that clarify the sequence of events:

Model From the Story

But *one day* a peddler happened to stray there. *When* he came inside . . . *After a while,* Jan Skiba's wife, Marianna, made a proposition to the peddler. . . .

Prewriting Start by choosing the lesson you'll teach at the end of your fable. Then, think of the animal characters you'll use, and jot down the order of events.

Drafting Write the lesson first. Then, tell the events leading up to it, referring to your outline as you draft. Use time words to clarify the sequence of events—words like *after a while, when,* and *then.* Make your fable more than just an outline by having animal characters show silly human weaknesses.

Revising Read your fable to classmates. If they can't follow the events or don't seem amused, add time words to clarify the sequence or exaggerate actions to heighten the humor.

◆ Grammar Application

Be sure you've used a variety of kinds of nouns so that readers can picture the world you're describing.

ASSESSMENT OPTIONS

Formal Assessment, Selection Test, pp. 1–3, and Assessment Resources Software. The selection test is designed so that it can be easily customized to the performance levels of your students.

Alternative Assessment, p. 1, includes options for less advanced students, more advanced students, and verbal/linguistic learners, intrapersonal learners, visual/spatial learners, logical/mathematical learners, and interpersonal learners.

PORTFOLIO ASSESSMENT

Use the following rubrics in the **Alternative Assessment** booklet to assess students' writing:
Product Warning: Technical Description/Explanation, p. 102
Advertisements: Description, p. 84
Newspaper Article: Summary, p. 85
Writing Mini-Lesson: Fictional Narrative, p. 82

PART 1 *Inventing Yourself*

Untitled, Jean-Francois Podevin

Humanities: Art

Untitled, by Jean-François Podevin

Jean-François Podevin was born in France and is famous because of his illustrations for magazines, book jackets, and posters. His work centers on the idea of "spontaneous artistic combustion"—the belief in an artist's original spark of creativity. Podevin begins all his works with a sketch and then elaborates with various media including pen, pencil, camera, paint, and computer. To him, the piece is successful if the finished image still contains the spontaneity of the original sketch.

Help students connect the art to the theme "Finding Yourself" by answering the following questions:

1. *Finding yourself* means "looking past your appearance to the different parts that make you a unique person." How does the image in this picture suggest finding yourself? *Students may note that the man in the picture seems to be put together like a puzzle.*
2. What is the mood of the man in the picture? *Students may say the man seems serious, as if he is examining his reflection.*

One-Minute Planning Guide

The selections in this section focus on the the theme of finding one's identity. "The Cat Who Thought She Was a Dog and the Dog Who Thought He Was a Cat" describes what happens to a family when they see their reflections in a mirror for the first time. "Two Kinds" presents the struggle of a girl who finds that she can be two kinds of a daughter. An excerpt from *Song of Myself,* "I'm Nobody," and "Me" are three poems that consider the question "Who am I?" "My Furthest-Back Person" follows the author as he finds his roots in another country. In "The Third Level," the narrator travels back in time and discovers an era in which he feels he belongs. In "King Arthur: The Marvel of the Sword," Arthur discovers his destiny to become king of all England.

Customize for
Varying Students Needs

When assigning the selections in this section to your students, keep in mind the following factors:

"The Cat Who Thought She Was a Dog and the Dog Who Thought He Was a Cat"
- An accessible short story with a moral that introduces the theme of identity and self-worth

"Two Kinds"
- A story of a girl's attempt to establish her own identity while trying to please her mother
- A longer and more challenging short story (11 pp.)

from *Song of Myself*
- An excerpt from a classic poem
- Students may need help recognizing the theme

"I'm Nobody"
- A short, witty poem
- Helps students understand Emily Dickinson's style

"Me"
- A poem exploring self-worth

"My Furthest-Back Person"
- A personal narrative about tracing family from a relative's stories

"The Third Level"
- An exciting short story about time travel

"King Arthur: The Marvel of the Sword"
- A classic story retold
- An opportunity for connecting literature to social studies

Prepare and Engage

OBJECTIVES

1. To read, comprehend, interpret, and respond to a story
2. To relate a story to students' personal experience
3. To apply word identification strategies
4. To recognize characters' motives
5. To build vocabulary in context and learn the suffix *-ness*
6. To recognize common and proper nouns
7. To write a diary entry using elaboration to add emotional depth
8. To respond to the story through writing, speaking and listening, and projects

SKILLS INSTRUCTION

Vocabulary: Suffixes: *-ness*

Spelling: Adding *-ness* to Words Ending With *y*

Grammar: Common and Proper Nouns

Literary Focus: Characters' Motives

Reading Strategy: Apply Word Identification Strategies

Writing: Elaborate to Add Emotional Depth

Speaking and Listening: Monologue (Teacher Edition)

Viewing and Representing: Representing "Two Kinds" (Teacher Edition)

Critical Viewing: Speculate; Connect; Infer; Evaluate; Compare and Contrast

PORTFOLIO OPPORTUNITIES

Writing: Job Description; Music Review; Prequel

Writing Mini-Lesson: Mother's Diary Entry

Speaking and Listening: Counseling Conference; Monologue

Projects: Television Soundtrack; Report on Chinese Customs

More About the Author

When she isn't writing, **Amy Tan** sings in a rock band with Stephen King and other authors. They raise money for causes, such as promoting literacy and aiding the homeless. Tan enjoys singing lead on such standards as "These Boots Are Made for Walking" and "Leader of the Pack."

Tan admits to being rebellious by nature and this trait has influenced her life as a first-generation Chinese American growing up in California. However, she has reconciled the Chinese and American aspects of her identity.

Guide for Reading

Meet the Author:

Amy Tan (1952–)

Amy Tan has struggled to find herself. The author grew up as the second-youngest child in a Chinese American family from California. As a youngster, Tan was pulled between mainstream American culture and the Chinese traditions that her mother kept alive.

Success, Experiments, Success Tan showed early signs of being a writer. At age eight, she published an essay entitled "What the Library Means to Me" in a local paper. However, she went to a number of different colleges and held a variety of jobs—from carhop to educational counselor—before achieving spectacular success with her first novel.

From Book to Movie That first novel, *The Joy Luck Club*, explores life in a Chinese American community. Nominated for a National Book Award, the novel also inspired a movie of the same title.

Finding Herself, Again Tan reports that she struggled with her fear of failure while writing her second novel, *The Kitchen God's Wife*. However, that book and her third, *The Hundred Secret Senses*, have been widely praised.

The Story Behind the Story

Amy Tan used details from her own life to create characters in "Two Kinds." Like the young woman in the story, Tan resisted her Chinese heritage when she was young.

◆ Literature and Your Life

Connect Your Experience

You stand at the plate ready to hit a homer or at the microphone ready to dazzle the crowd. Most people love to star in their own daydreams of greatness. However, when you star in a dream that someone else has for you, you may feel divided in half, like the woman on the opposite page. This is the problem that a teenager faces in "Two Kinds."

Thematic Focus: Inventing Yourself

The mother of the young woman in "Two Kinds" has high hopes for her daughter. Notice what happens when the daughter tries to fulfill her mother's hopes.

◆ Background for Understanding

History

In 1949, the Communist party seized control of China, following years of civil war. Like the mother in this story, a number of Chinese, who feared the communists, fled to the United States. Many of them had lost everything except their hopes for a better future. They placed these hopes, a heavy but invisible burden, on the shoulders of the children born in the new land.

◆ Build Vocabulary

Suffixes: *-ness*

In "Two Kinds," the narrator describes a girl's "sauciness." *Sauciness* means "the quality of being lively." It combines the adjective *saucy* ("lively") with the suffix *-ness*, meaning "the quality or condition of."

Word Bank

Which of these words from the story do you think are nouns? Check the Vocabulary Boxes to see if you are right.

prodigy
reproach
mesmerizing
sauciness
conspired
debut
devastated
fiasco

Prentice Hall Literature Program Resources

REINFORCE / RETEACH / EXTEND

Selection Support Pages

Build Vocabulary: Suffixes: *-ness*, p. 7
Build Spelling Skills, p. 8
Build Grammar Skills: Common and Proper Nouns, p. 9
Reading Strategy: Apply Word Identification Strategies, p. 10
Literary Focus: Characters' Motives, p. 11

Strategies for Diverse Student Needs, pp. 3–4

Beyond Literature Cross-Curricular Connection: Performing Arts, p. 2

Formal Assessment Selection Test, pp. 4–6, Assessment Resources Software

Alternative Assessment, p. 2

Writing and Language Transparencies Open Mind Organizer, p. 90

Resource Pro CD-ROM "Two Kinds"—includes all resource material and customizable lesson plan

Listening to Literature Audiocassettes "Two Kinds"

Two Kinds

Literary Focus

Characters' Motives

It's no accident that **motive** sounds like *motor*. Motives are the engines of personality—the emotions and goals that drive characters this way or that. Some powerful motives are love, anger, hope, and ambition. Acting together, emotional engines like these can sometimes spin characters around or set them on a collision course.

In "Two Kinds," the narrator explains and hints at the different motives that influence her and her mother. On a sheet of paper, keep track of these motives by filling in a chart like the one below.

Reading Strategy

Word Identification

Sometimes words can look like a secret code. However, by using simple methods of **word identification,** dividing words into syllables and recognizable word parts, you can break the code. The trick is to find something familiar in what at first looks unfamiliar.

In this story, two words that might trip you up are *uneven* and *instructor.* Run your finger over these words, breaking them into syllables and looking for familiar words:

- The first syllable of *uneven* is the prefix *un-*, followed by the word *even.*
- *Instructor* contains the word *instruct.*

Use this strategy to unlock the meaning of other unfamiliar words.

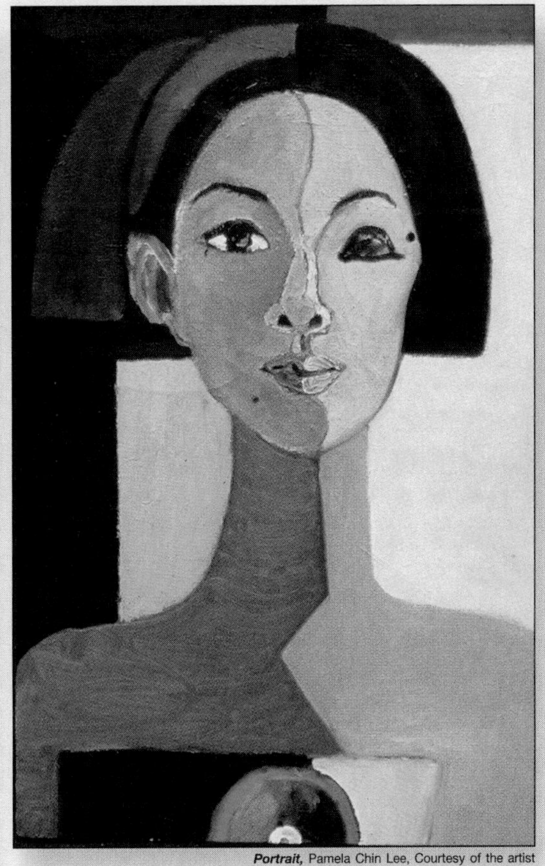

Portrait, Pamela Chin Lee, Courtesy of the artist

	Narrator	Mother
Passage from story:	"I was filled with a sense that I would soon become *perfect.* My mother and father would adore me."	"America was where all my mother's hopes lay. She had come here . . . after losing everything in China. . . ."
Motive:	**Need for *love***	***Hope* for a better future**
Passage from story: **Motive:**		
Passage from story: **Motive:**		

Interest Grabber To help students appreciate what it might be like to be pushed to fulfill the dreams that someone else has for them, engage them in the following activity. Have each student write a brief description of a personal dream on a piece of paper. For example, some students may dream of becoming a professional athlete or a musician. Have students fold up the pieces of paper. Then place all of the pieces in a basket. Pass the basket around the room, and have each student pull out one of the folded pieces of paper. Then have students open the pieces of paper and imagine that what is written on the pieces of paper is a dream that someone has for them. Allow 5 minutes for students to freewrite about how they'd feel about being pushed toward this goal. Then explain that the main character in this story is pushed to reach a goal that someone else has for her.

Build Grammar Skills

Common and Proper Nouns If you wish to introduce the grammar concept taught with this story, refer to the instruction on p. 26 before students read the story.

Customize for
Less Proficient Readers
Because this story is long and complex, students may have greater success if they read it in small sections, stopping to review and summarize what has happened in each section. Students may also benefit from listening to all or some of the story on audiocassette.

Listening to Literature Audiocassettes

Customize for
More Advanced Students
Suggest that students keep a log to note parts of the story when the narrator feels pressured. Explain to students that these notes will show the gradual process that leads to turning points when the character sees herself in different ways.

Preparing for Standardized Tests

Grammar The grammar concept for this story is common and proper nouns. Standardized tests may include questions that test students' understanding of the capitalization of nouns.

Point out to students that common nouns name people, places, things, and ideas. Proper nouns are specific nouns and, therefore, must be capitalized. Write these nouns on the board: *boy, schumann, state, game, school, america, test.* Call on volunteers to capitalize the words that are proper nouns: *Schumann* and *America.* Then give students this sample test question:

Identify the sentence that capitalizes nouns correctly.

(A) Auntie Lindo and uncle Tin were there.
(B) She had talked to Mr. chong.
(C) All I knew was the capital of California.
(D) My Mother thought I could be a Chinese Shirley Temple.

Students should recognize that *(C)* is the only sentence with all of its nouns capitalized correctly.

For additional practice, use **Selection Support,** p. 9, on Common and Proper Nouns.

Humanities: Art

For information about *Portrait,* by Pamela Chin Lee, see p. 23.

Develop Understanding

One-Minute Insight "Two Kinds" addresses a question almost everyone wonders about while growing up: "Who am I?" It also explores the clash of cultures that first-generation children of immigrants can experience. In the story, an immigrant Chinese mother wants her American-born daughter, Jing-mei, to be a famous prodigy. To that end, she pushes the reluctant girl to excel as an actress, a geography ace, then a math whiz, and on and on; finally, the mother provides piano lessons for her daughter to become a performing musician. Initially the mother and daughter share the desire for fame. As failures mount, Jing-mei rebels against her mother's demands. The story climaxes with a terrible argument in which Jing-mei says hurtful things to her mother. Nevertheless, when Jing-mei is grown, she makes peace with her mother and herself, realizing that she's two kinds of daughter—one who follows her own mind and one who is an obedient daughter.

Customize for
English Language Learners
English language learners may have difficulty understanding the descriptions in this story because of the use of unfamiliar phrases. Help students by using gestures and body language to communicate the meanings of descriptive phrases, such as "pursing her lips," "performed listlessly," "entranced by the music," "conduct his frantic silent sonatas," "applauded," " squabbling over crayons and dolls," "dawdled over it," and "beaming and shouting."

Customize for
Visual/Spatial Learners
Invite students to describe what they see in the photograph on this page. Tell them that it represents the story's setting in San Francisco's Chinatown. Encourage them to use this and other visuals accompanying the story to help them appreciate the cultural influence of the setting.

Block Scheduling Strategies

Consider these suggestions to take advantage of extended class time:

- Encourage students to explore the literary focus for this story. Have them read the selection in small groups, stopping occasionally to discuss evidence of the characters' motives. Then have them use what they have discussed to complete the Literary Focus, p. 26.
- Either before or after students read the selection, show a segment from the movie adaptation of *The Joy Luck Club*. Follow with a class discussion in which students compare and contrast viewing the movie with reading Tan's writing. Which is more effective? Why?
- If you have access to technology, have students work on the *Writer's Solution Writing Lab CD-ROM* to complete all or part of the Writing Mini-Lesson. Follow the suggestions on p. 27 to help you structure class time.

Two Kinds

from The Joy Luck Club

Amy Tan

y mother believed you could be anything you wanted to be in America. You could open a restaurant. You could work for the government and get good retirement. You could buy a house with almost no money down. You could become rich. You could become
1 instantly famous.

"Of course you can be prodigy, too," my mother told me when I was nine. "You can be best anything. What does Auntie Lindo know? Her daughter, she is only best tricky."

America was where all my mother's hopes lay. She had come here in 1949 after losing everything in China: her mother and father, her family home, her first husband, and two daughters, twin baby girls. But she never looked back with regret. There were so many ways for things to get better.

We didn't immediately pick the right kind of prodigy. At first my mother thought I could 3
be a Chinese Shirley Temple.[1] We'd watch Shirley's old movies on TV as though they were training films. My mother would poke my arm and say, "*Ni kan*"[2]—You watch. And I would see Shirley tapping her feet, or singing a sailor song, or pursing her lips into a very round O while saying, "Oh my goodness."

"*Ni kan*," said my mother as Shirley's eyes flooded with tears. "You already know how. Don't need talent for crying!"

Soon after my mother got this idea about Shirley Temple, she took me to a beauty training school in the Mission district[3] and put me in the hands of a student who could barely hold the scissors without shaking.

◆ **Build Vocabulary**

prodigy (präd´ ə jē) *n.*: Child of unusually high talent

2 ◄ Critical Viewing San Francisco's Chinatown, seen here, uses both the English and Chinese languages. How might such a mix affect the narrator's sense of herself? **[Speculate]**

1. **Shirley Temple:** American child star of the 1930's, she starred in her first movie at age three and won an Academy Award at age six.
2. ***Ni kan*** (nē kän)
3. **Mission district:** Residential district in San Francisco, California.

◆Literary Focus

❶ **Characters' Motives** In these opening paragraphs, we learn that the mother insists that her daughter can be a prodigy. Why does she want this type of achievement for her daughter? *She is motivated by hope. She faced many hardships in China, but America seems to be the land of opportunity. She hopes her daughter will benefit from what she has not had.*

►Critical Viewing◄

❷ **Speculate** Like the mix of languages in one place, Jing-mei has a mix of both cultures within herself. *Students should recognize that this mix creates internal conflict and conflict between the narrator and her mother.*

◆Literature and Your Life

❸ Point out that Jing-mei's mother has high expectations for her to be a prodigy. What are some of the things parents expect from their children? Why might parents have such expectations? *Students may suggest such things as school grades, musical talent, athletic ability, and social skills. Guide students to recognize that parents often want their children to achieve success that they could not achieve themselves.*

Customize for
Verbal/Linguistic Learners
Amy Tan uses nonstandard English for the mother's dialogue. Point out that this type of "broken" English is not intended to be derogatory, but is using the mother's speech patterns to make the character seem real to readers—it represents the communication of a person whose first language is not English. Help students analyze the nonstandard elements in the mother's speech, adding missing words to complete the thoughts in standard English.

Cross-Curricular Connection: Social Studies

China Fictional stories are often influenced by reality. The mother in "Two Kinds" came to the United States in 1949 in order to escape a war in her native China.

In order to understand why the mother emigrated, have students research more about the conditions in China in the 1940's. They can use your school's media center or the local library for sources such as history books and news magazines from that time. Ask your school librarian to assist, or help students find information such as the following:

- The Japanese invasion of China during World War II weakened the Nationalists led by Chiang Kai-shek, and they endured most of the front-line fighting. Mao Tse-tung and the Communists, however, were able to establish popular reforms in the less troubled areas that they controlled. By the end of the war in 1945, the Communists controlled the North, which had a population of 100 million.
- Although far superior in numbers and supported by the United States, the city-centered Nationalist government was plagued by corruption and a weak economy.
- By the middle of 1948, the Communists equaled the Nationalists in number and in 1949 they crossed the Yangtze River to defeat the Nationalist army, establishing Communism in China.

Have students share their findings. Then discuss how the establishment of a new government might motivate people to leave their homeland.

◆Literature and Your Life

1 Point out that, at times, we picture ourselves as Jing-mei is imagining herself here. Suggest that students consider their own grand aspirations, maybe succeeding as a professional athlete or a recording superstar. Encourage them to use their own attitudes about wanting to be successful or famous to help them identify with Jing-mei.

Comprehension Check ☑

2 Check that students understand who is talking in this passage. Guide them to realize that *it* represents the prodigy that supposedly lives within Jing-mei, as if the prodigy exists separately from the real person. The words suggest an inner voice that warns the daughter to find her calling before it's too late. Discuss how she can avoid responsibility for her actions by imagining a separate being who can help her reach her goals—or let her fail.

◆Reading Strategy

3 **Apply Word Identification Strategies** Students should break the word into syllables and identify the word *sort* and suffix *-ment:* as- + sort + -ment; *recognizing the word* sort, *which means "type, or kind," can lead them to guess that an assortment of magazines is a variety of types of magazines.*

◆Critical Thinking

4 **Infer** Have students think about the tests described in this paragraph. Ask whether they are a good way to measure abilities. *Some students may answer yes—they measure Jing-mei's talent or ability in these areas; others may say no—the tests are too varied and are not connected to her interests.*

Instead of getting big fat curls, I emerged with an uneven mass of crinkly black fuzz. My mother dragged me off to the bathroom and tried to wet down my hair.

"You look like Negro Chinese," she lamented, as if I had done this on purpose.

The instructor of the beauty training school had to lop off these soggy clumps to make my hair even again. "Peter Pan is very popular these days," the instructor assured my mother. I now had hair the length of a boy's, with straight-across bangs that hung at a slant two inches above my eyebrows. I liked the haircut and it made me actually look forward to my future fame.

1 In fact, in the beginning, I was just as excited as my mother, maybe even more so. I pictured this prodigy part of me as many different images, trying each one on for size. I was a dainty ballerina girl standing by the curtains, waiting to hear the right music that would send me floating on my tiptoes. I was like the Christ child lifted out of the straw manger, crying with holy indignity. I was Cinderella stepping from her pumpkin carriage with sparkly cartoon music filling the air.

In all of my imaginings, I was filled with a sense that I would soon become *perfect.* My mother and father would adore me. I would be beyond reproach. I would never feel the need to sulk for anything.

2 But sometimes the prodigy in me became impatient. "If you don't hurry up and get me out of here, I'm disappearing for good," it warned. "And then you'll always be nothing."

Every night after dinner, my mother and I would sit at the Formica kitchen table. She would present new tests, taking her examples from stories of amazing children she had read in *Ripley's Believe It or Not,* or *Good Housekeeping, Reader's Digest,* and a dozen other magazines she kept in a pile in our bathroom. My mother got these magazines from people whose houses she cleaned. And since she cleaned many houses each week, we had a great assortment. She would look through them all, searching for stories about remarkable children.

> **◆ Reading Strategy** What familiar word and common suffix can you find in the word *assortment*? 3

The first night she brought out a story about a three-year-old boy who knew the capitals of all the states and even most of the European countries. A teacher was quoted as saying the little boy could also pronounce the names of the foreign cities correctly.

"What's the capital of Finland?" my mother asked me, looking at the magazine story.

All I knew was the capital of California, because Sacramento was the name of the street we lived on in Chinatown. "Nairobi!"[4] I guessed, saying the most foreign word I could think of. She checked to see if that was possibly one way to pronounce "Helsinki"[5] before showing me the answer.

The tests got harder—multiplying numbers in my head, finding the queen of hearts in a deck of cards, trying to stand on my head without using my hands, predicting the daily temperatures in Los Angeles, New York, and London. 4

One night I had to look at a page from the Bible for three minutes and then report everything I could remember. "Now Jehoshaphat had riches and honor in abundance and . . . that's all I remember, Ma," I said.

And after seeing my mother's disappointed face once again, something inside of me began to die. I hated the tests, the raised hopes and failed expectations. Before going to bed that night, I looked in the mirror above the bathroom sink and when I saw only my face staring back—and that it would always be

◆ Build Vocabulary

reproach (ri prōch´) *n.:* Disgrace; blame

mesmerizing (mez´ mər īz´ iŋ) *adj.:* Hypnotizing

sauciness (sô´ sē nes) *n.:* Liveliness; boldness; spirit

---

4. **Nairobi** (nī rō´ bē): Capital of Kenya, a country in east central Africa.

5. **Helsinki** (hel siŋ´ kē)

Speaking and Listening Mini-Lesson

Monologue

This mini-lesson supports the Speaking and Listening activity in the Idea Bank on p. 27.

Introduce Explain that writers often use inner conversation —"talking to yourself"— to help readers get inside a character's mind. A monologue (*mono-* instead of *dia-*logue, because it is only one person) reveals what the character is thinking and feeling.

Develop Give students these tips for developing a monologue:

- Review the story from the beginning to the point the monologue will take place and make a list of events and conflicts to include in a monologue.
- Write a script of the character's exact words.
- Try out and revise monologues with partners.
- To deliver a monologue, speak clearly and confidently, make eye contact, and use effective gestures and body language.

Apply Allow time for each student to develop and perform a 3-minute monologue for the class. Instruct students, as audience members, to listen carefully and to take notes during the performances.

Assess Evaluate each student's performance in terms of preparation, speaking, composure, eye contact, and body language. Have "audience" members use the Peer Assessment: Dramatic Performance form, p. 107 in **Alternative Assessment,** to evaluate the performances of their classmates.

5 this ordinary face—I began to cry. Such a sad, ugly girl! I made high-pitched noises like a crazed animal, trying to scratch out the face in the mirror.

And then I saw what seemed to be the prodigy side of me—because I had never seen that face before. I looked at my reflection, blinking so I could see more clearly. The girl staring back at me was angry, powerful. This girl and I were the same. I had
6 new thoughts, willful thoughts, or rather thoughts filled with lots of won'ts. I won't let her change me, I promised myself. I won't be what I'm not.

Mandarin Square: Badge with peacock-insignia-3rd civil rank. China, 17th–20th century, Unknown artist, Yale University Art Gallery

▲ **Critical Viewing** Which characters in the story are best suggested by this peacock, a symbol of arrogance and pride? **[Connect]** 8

So now on nights when my mother presented her tests, I performed listlessly, my head propped on one arm. I pretended to be bored. And I was. I got so bored I started counting the bellows of the foghorns out on the bay while my mother drilled me in other areas. The sound was comforting and reminded me of the cow jumping over the moon. And the next day, I played a game with myself, seeing if my mother would give up on me before eight bellows. After a while I usually counted only one, maybe two bellows at most. At last she was beginning to give up hope.

Two or three months had gone by without any mention of my being a prodigy again. And
7 then one day my mother was watching *The Ed Sullivan Show* [6] on TV. The TV was old and the sound kept shorting out. Every time my mother got halfway up from the sofa to adjust the set, the sound would go back on and Ed would be talking. As soon as she sat down, Ed would go silent again. She got up, the TV broke into loud piano music. She sat down. Silence. Up and down, back and forth, quiet and loud. It was like a stiff embraceless dance between her and the TV set. Finally she stood by the set with her hand on the sound dial.

She seemed entranced by the music, a little frenzied piano piece with this <u>mesmerizing</u> quality, sort of quick passages and then teasing lilting ones before it returned to the quick playful parts.

"*Ni kan*," my mother said, calling me over with hurried hand gestures. "Look here."

I could see why my mother was fascinated by the music. It was being pounded out by a little Chinese girl, about nine years old, with a Peter Pan haircut. The girl had the <u>sauciness</u> of a Shirley Temple. She was proudly modest like a proper Chinese child. And she also did this fancy sweep of a curtsy, so that the fluffy skirt of her

> ◆ **Literature and Your Life**
> Have you ever dreamed of being a television star? Explain. 9

6. ***The Ed Sullivan Show:*** Popular variety show, hosted by Ed Sullivan, that ran from 1955 to 1971.

Humanities: Art

Mandarin Square: Badge with peacock-insignia—3rd civil rank, Qing dynasty, Kangxi period (1622–1722)

This strutting peacock is a work of colorful needlecraft, done with gold-wrapped silk threads on satin. This fabric art is an example of Chinese art. Discuss the following questions:

1. How does the medium—hand-stitching with expensive fabric and thread—influence your appreciation of the piece? How do you imagine it being displayed? *The delicate hand work and costly materials make the piece unique and valuable. Since it is a cloth, it might be on a piece of clothing or a banner.*
2. How does the peacock represent attitudes of the mother and daughter in the story? *Students may note that the peacock's pride and arrogance represent the mother's pride and arrogance about wanting to fulfill her daughter's potential. They may also think that the daughter is displaying her own pride and arrogance by standing up to her mother.*

◆Literary Focus

5 Characters' Motives Play the recording of this passage to emphasize the drama of the scene. Ask students what motivates the narrator to attack her reflection. *She feels worthless because she is failing her mother's tests and not meeting expectations; so she feels ugly both on the inside and the outside.*

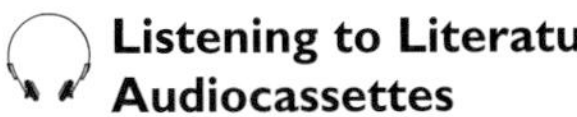

Listening to Literature Audiocassettes

6 Characters' Motives Discuss why this moment marks a turning point for the daughter. Have students describe the change that comes over her. You may wish to use the Open Mind Organizer, p. 90, in **Writing and Language Transparencies** to help students determine the character's motive. *She feels angry and powerful enough to stand up to her mother, who she feels is trying to make her into something she's not.*

Clarification

7 *The Ed Sullivan Show* (1955–1971) was one of early TV's most popular programs. It showcased performers, including Barbra Streisand, Elvis Presley, and the Beatles, as well as a variety of other entertainment: animal acts, rock bands, comedians, jugglers, dancers, ventriloquists, and opera singers.

▶Critical Viewing◀

8 Connect Tell students that *arrogant* means "having or showing too much pride or feelings of being superior." *At this point, the mother is arrogant and the daughter has too much pride to give in to her mother's wishes.*

◆Literature and Your Life

9 Students should elaborate on their dreams or explain why they have never had this particular type of dream. *Some students may describe thoughts of identifying with TV stars; others may perceive TV personalities as removed from their everyday lives.*

Customize for
Bodily/Kinesthetic Learners
Encourage students to reenact the mother's "stiff embraceless dance" with the TV set. Ask them to explain whether the mother's actions are conscious or unconscious. Guide them to recognize that, once again, the mother's desire for her daughter to become a prodigy is revealed.

◆Literary Focus

❶ Characters' Motives Mr. Chong and the mother agree to trade services. Have students work in pairs to evaluate what each gives and gets in this exchange. They may use a chart like the one below:

Trade	Mr. Chong	Mother
Gives	Piano lessons	House cleaning
Receives	House cleaned	Piano lessons for daughter

Which of the two receives a direct benefit from the deal? What does this tell you about the other person's motives? *Mr. Chong directly benefits—he gets his house cleaned. The mother's motives are concern and love for her daughter. Jing-mei actually receives the benefits of her mother's sacrifice.*

◆Critical Thinking

❷ Draw Conclusions Tell students that this is a crucial moment for the daughter. What does Jing-mei do that she hasn't done before? *For the first time Jing-mei shows her mother how angry and hurt she feels.*

▶Critical Viewing◀

❸ Infer Point out to students that both Chinese and American cultures are represented in the photograph of Chinatown on these two pages. *Students may notice old American cars and old styles of Western clothing, including the men's hats.*

Customize for *Interpersonal Learners*

To help understand characters' motives, have pairs of students read the dialogue between the mother and daughter as they argue about the piano lessons. Encourage students to read the dialogue twice, switching roles. Then ask them to explain what makes each character angry.

white dress cascaded slowly to the floor like the petals of a large carnation.

In spite of these warning signs, I wasn't worried. Our family had no piano and we couldn't afford to buy one, let alone reams of sheet music and piano lessons. So I could be generous in my comments when my mother bad-mouthed the little girl on TV.

"Play note right, but doesn't sound good! No singing sound," complained my mother.

"What are you picking on her for?" I said carelessly. "She's pretty good. Maybe she's not the best, but she's trying hard." I knew almost immediately I would be sorry I said that.

"Just like you," she said. "Not the best. Because you not trying." She gave a little huff as she let go of the sound dial and sat down on the sofa.

The little Chinese girl sat down also to play an encore of "Anitra's Dance" by Grieg.[7] I remember the song, because later on I had to learn how to play it.

Three days after watching *The Ed Sullivan Show*, my mother told me what my schedule would be for piano lessons and piano practice. She had talked to Mr. Chong, who lived on the first floor of our apartment building. Mr. Chong

❶ was a retired piano teacher and my mother had traded housecleaning services for weekly lessons and a piano for me to practice on every day, two hours a day, from four until six.

When my mother told me this, I felt as though I had been sent to hell. I whined and then kicked my foot a little when I couldn't stand it anymore.

❷ "Why don't you like me the way I am? I'm *not* a genius! I can't play the piano. And even if I could, I wouldn't go on TV if you paid me a million dollars!" I cried.

---

7. **Grieg** (grēg): Edvard Grieg (1843–1907), Norwegian composer.

❸ ▶ **Critical Viewing** What details in the photograph and the story tell you that the action takes place in an earlier time? **[Infer]**

Humanities: Music

"Anitra's Dance," by Edvard Grieg (composed in 1874–1875)

The works of Norwegian composer Edvard Grieg (1843–1907) reflect the character of his homeland. One of his most famous works is the music he wrote for Henrik Ibsen's dramatic poem, *Peer Gynt,* which is based on Scandinavian folklore. "Anitra's Dance" is a waltz that captures the spirit of the Troll King's daughter. Play a recording of "Anitra's Dance." Invite students' responses to the changes in mood of the piece, and how it musically supports the story.

1. Do you think "Anitra's Dance" is too difficult a piece for a 9-year-old? *Students may answer that although it may be difficult, a 9-year-old could handle the music with enough practice.*
2. What do you think of the mother's criticism of the little girl's performance? *Some students may say that the mother's criticism is too harsh—she shouldn't expect an average child to play like a concert pianist; others may think she could be right and the girl is not playing musically.*

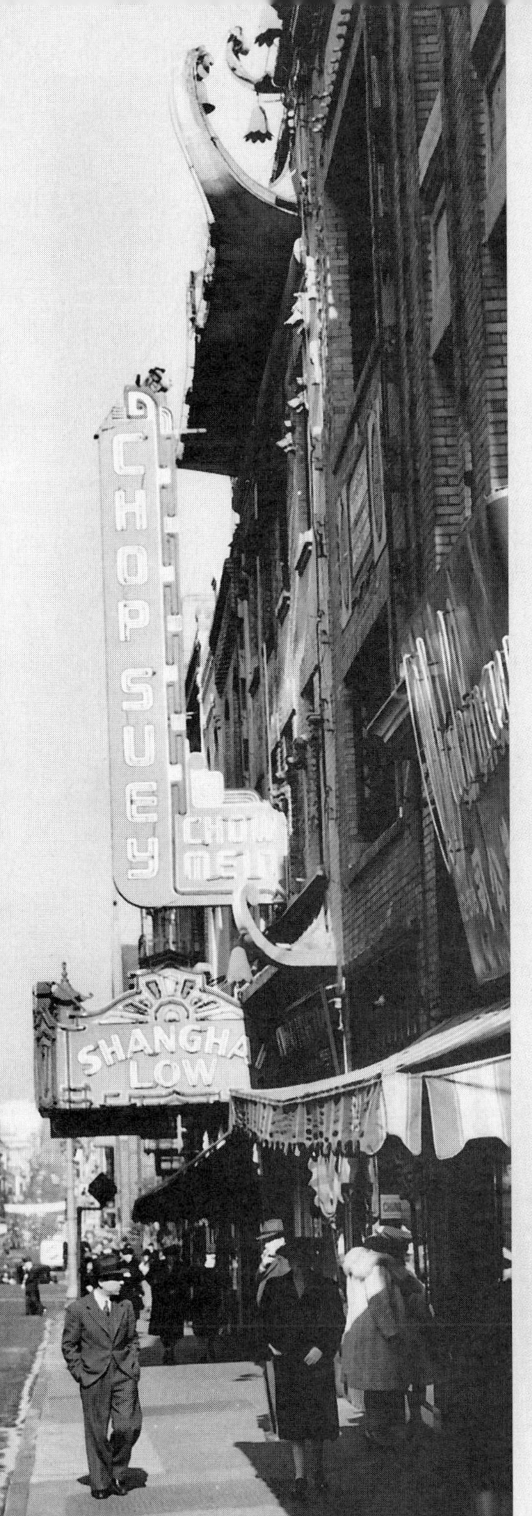

My mother slapped me. "Who ask you be genius?" she shouted. "Only ask you be your best. For you sake. You think I want you be genius? Hnnh! What for! Who ask you!"

"So ungrateful," I heard her mutter in Chinese. "If she had as much talent as she has temper, she would be famous now."

Mr. Chong, whom I secretly nicknamed Old Chong, was very strange, always tapping his fingers to the silent music of an invisible orchestra. He looked ancient in my eyes. He had lost most of the hair on top of his head and he wore thick glasses and had eyes that always looked tired and sleepy. But he must have been younger than I thought, since he lived with his mother and was not yet married.

I met Old Lady Chong once and that was enough. She had this peculiar smell like a baby that had done something in its pants. And her fingers felt like a dead person's, like an old peach I once found in the back of the refrigerator; the skin just slid off the meat when I picked it up.

I soon found out why Old Chong had retired from teaching piano. He was deaf. "Like Beethoven!"[8] he shouted to me. "We're both listening only in our head!" And he would start to conduct his frantic silent sonatas.

Our lessons went like this. He would open the book and point to different things, explaining their purpose: "Key! Treble! Bass! No sharps or flats! So this is C major! Listen now and play after me!" ❹

And then he would play the C scale a few times, a simple chord, and then, as if inspired by an old, unreachable itch, he gradually added more notes and running trills and a pounding bass until the music was really something quite grand.

I would play after him, the simple scale, the simple chord, and then I just played some nonsense that sounded like a cat running up and down on top of garbage cans. ❺

8. **Beethoven** (bā´ tō´ vən): Ludwig van Beethoven (1770–1827), German composer who began to lose his hearing in 1801. By 1817 he was completely deaf. Some of his greatest pieces were written when he was deaf.

Clarification

❹ Explain, or have a student who plays an instrument explain, the musical terms used in this paragraph. Treble notes are high (the right-hand side of a piano keyboard), and bass notes are low (the left-hand keys). Sharps and flats are used in music to change the key of music, which is usually based on an 8-note scale. Sometimes the key is minor, which may make the music sound eerie or sad. Music that is written and played in a major key may sound more "normal" or pleasant to listeners.

Comprehension Check ☑

❺ Point out that at the time of this story, all garbage cans would have been made of metal. Ask students to describe what a cat running up and down on top of garbage cans might sound like. *Students may suggest that the sound would be loud, clanging, unmusical, like metal banging together.*

Customize for *Musical/Rhythmic Learners*

Ask students to think of a time when they may have seen someone tapping their fingers or feet while listening to music through headphones. Then have them use these memories and add their own experience to reproduce Mr. Chong's musical attitude. Ask each student to think of a song or piece of music. Then ask volunteers to tap out the rhythm with their fingers while their classmates observe. Encourage the observers to note the body language of the musical tappers, as they concentrate on "tapping to silent music."

Customize for *Verbal/Linguistic Learners*

Point out the author's descriptive words that draw a vivid picture of Old Lady Chong, as seen through Jing-mei's eyes. Encourage these students to find other examples of descriptive language that appear in the piece. Then invite them to write a descriptive paragraph expressing their impressions about someone they know outside of school, using figurative language.

Cultural Connection

Neighborhoods This story is set in Chinatown, San Francisco. Explain to students that many American cities and towns have neighborhoods in which members of one cultural group tend to live, work, shop, and gather for social events (some places have several different cultural areas). These areas are characterized by businesses that cater to needs and interests of the particular culture, such as restaurants, and shops that sell foods, fabrics, crafts, books, newspapers, or other items from their homelands. Invite students to identify cultural neighborhoods in or near your community. Discuss why cultural neighborhoods exist. Explore the need for familiarity and the desire to keep cultures alive and preserve traditions.

Encourage students to explore their own cultural identification. If they have relatives who can provide information about traditions, foods, and so forth, ask them to gather information and make a presentation to the class. For students whose cultural background is more diverse, suggest that they research a culture that interests them.

▶Critical Viewing◀

❶ **Connect** *Two kinds of Chinese culture appear in the painting. For instance, the girl wears modern clothes and a man in traditional Chinese clothing walks in the background.*

Clarification

❷ In addition to teaching musical notes and rhythms, piano teachers expect students to use the technique required for successfully playing the instrument. Holding the hands properly allows a pianist to use each finger independently of the others in order to avoid hitting an extra key and for each musical note to sound clearly. Chords are two or more notes played simultaneously, so the keys must be struck at exactly the same time to produce the sound that is intended. The fingers must strike the piano keys sharply to produce the sharp sound of a *staccato* note. Scales and arpeggios are series of notes moving up and down the keyboard, and they should be played so that the sounds are produced evenly. To produce accurate sounds, pianists must develop their hand and finger muscles. This requires repetition and practice, like any other physical exertion.

◆Literary Focus

❸ **Characters' Motives** Why is the daughter determined not to try? Do you think she has any desire to play well? *She wants to get back at her mother and prove that her mother's efforts to turn her into a prodigy are not good. Students may recognize Jing-mei's interest in playing the piano, which she chooses to ignore in order to spite her mother.*

Chinese Girl Under Lanterns, Winson Trang

❶ ▲ Critical Viewing How does the contrast between the modern and the traditional in this painting reflect the title of Tan's story? **[Connect]**

Old Chong smiled and applauded and then said, "Very good! But now you must learn to keep time!"

So that's how I discovered that Old Chong's eyes were too slow to keep up with the wrong notes I was playing. He went through the motions in half-time. To help me keep rhythm, he stood behind me, pushing down on my right shoulder for every beat. He balanced pennies on top of my wrists so I would keep them still as I slowly played scales and arpeggios.[9] ❷ He had me curve my hand around an apple and keep that shape when playing chords. He marched stiffly to show me how to make each finger dance up and down, staccato[10] like an obedient little soldier.

He taught me all these things, and that was how I also learned I could be lazy and get away with mistakes, lots of mistakes. If I hit the wrong notes because I hadn't practiced enough, I never corrected myself. I just kept playing in rhythm. And Old Chong kept conducting his own private reverie.

So maybe I never really gave myself a fair chance. I did pick up the basics pretty quickly, and I might have become a good pianist at that young age. ❸ But I was so determined not to try, not to be anybody different that I

9. **arpeggios** (är pej´ ē ōz) *n.*: Notes in a chord played in quick succession instead of at the same time.

10. **staccato** (stə kät´ ō) *adv.*: Played crisply, with distinct breaks between notes.

Cultural Connection

Chinese Culture

Point out to students the Chinese lanterns, decorations, and the Cantonese restaurant in the image on this page. Explain that the Chinese immigrants who have have made their homes in the United States have brought many cultural influences with them.

Chinese lanterns have special meaning in Chinese holidays and festivals, including the Chinese New Year and the Chinese Lantern Festival. Most lanterns are made from a technique called paper cutting, which is an ancient Chinese art form. Paper cutting was one of the crafts that young girls were taught, and, in earlier times, upon which they were judged as prospective brides. In addition to lanterns, paper cuttings adorn windows, lamps, and doors in the home to bring good luck. Paper cuttings are made by elaborate and precise work with either a knife or scissors.

Cantonese cuisine is just one type of Chinese cuisine, but it is by far the most popular in America today. Cantonese cooking is varied and uses expensive ingredients, including fish, seafood, birds, snakes, and even insects. The popular dish *chop suey* is actually not a Chinese dish, but was first improvised by Cantonese restaurants to please visitors to China from abroad. Other popular Cantonese dishes include *sweet and sour pork, chow mein, wontons,* and *fried rice.*

Encourage students to research more about Chinese food and crafts, using the library or community resources. Have students share their findings with the rest of the class.

learned to play only the most ear-splitting preludes, the most discordant hymns.

Over the next year, I practiced like this, dutifully in my own way. And then one day I heard my mother and her friend Lindo Jong both talking in a loud bragging tone of voice so others could hear. It was after church, and I was leaning against the brick wall wearing a dress with stiff white petticoats. Auntie
4 Lindo's daughter, Waverly, who was about my age, was standing farther down the wall about five feet away. We had grown up together and shared all the closeness of two sisters squabbling over crayons and dolls. In other words, for the most part, we hated each other. I thought she was snotty. Waverly Jong had gained a certain amount of fame as "Chinatown's Littlest Chinese Chess Champion."

"She bring home too many trophy," lamented Auntie Lindo that Sunday. "All day she play chess. All day I have no time do nothing but dust off her winnings." She threw a scolding look at Waverly, who pretended not to see her.

> ◆ **Literary Focus**
> 5 What motivates the mother to brag about her daughter?

"You lucky you don't have this problem," said Auntie Lindo with a sigh to my mother.

And my mother squared her shoulders and bragged: "Our problem worser than yours. If we ask Jing-mei wash dish, she hear nothing but music. It's like you can't stop this natural talent."

And right then, I was determined to put a stop to her foolish pride.

A few weeks later, Old Chong and my mother conspired to have me play in a talent show which would be held in the church hall. By then, my parents had saved up enough to buy me a secondhand piano, a black Wurlitzer spinet[11] with a scarred bench. It was the showpiece of our living room.

For the talent show, I was to play a piece called "Pleading Child" from Schumann's[12] *Scenes from Childhood*. It was a simple, moody piece that sounded more difficult than it was. I was supposed to memorize the whole thing, playing the repeat parts twice to make the piece sound longer. But I dawdled over it, playing a few bars and then cheating, looking up to see what notes followed. I never really listened to what I was playing. I daydreamed about being somewhere else, about being someone else.

The part I liked to practice best was the fancy curtsy: right foot out, touch the rose on the carpet with a pointed foot, sweep to the side, left leg bends, look up and smile.

My parents invited all the couples from the Joy Luck Club[13] to witness my debut. Auntie Lindo and Uncle Tin were there. Waverly and her two older brothers had also come. The first two rows were filled with children both younger and older than I was. The littlest ones got to go first. They recited simple nursery rhymes, squawked out tunes on miniature violins, twirled Hula Hoops, pranced in pink ballet tutus, and when they bowed or curtsied, the audience would sigh in unison, "Awww," and then clap enthusiastically.

When my turn came, I was very confident. I remember my childish excitement. It was as if I knew, without a doubt, that the prodigy side of me really did exist. I had no fear whatsoever, no nervousness. I remember thinking to 6
myself, This is it! This is it! I looked out over the audience, at my mother's blank face, my father's yawn, Auntie Lindo's stiff-lipped smile, Waverly's sulky expression. I had on a white dress layered with sheets of lace, and a pink bow in my Peter Pan haircut. As I sat down I

11. **spinet** (spin´ it) *n.*: Small, upright piano.

12. **Schumann** (sho͞o´ män): Robert Alexander Schumann (1810–1856), German composer.

13. **Joy Luck Club:** Four Chinese women who have been meeting for years to socialize, play games, and tell stories from the past.

◆ Build Vocabulary

conspired (kən spīrd´) *v.*: Planned together secretly

debut (dā byo͞o´) *n.*: First performance in public

◆Build Grammar Skills

4 Common and Proper Nouns Tell students that proper nouns name specific people, animals, places, things, or ideas and are always capitalized. Then point out the word *Waverly*. In addition to the context clues of the sentence, students should recognize this word as the name of a person because it is capitalized.

◆Literary Focus

5 Characters' Motives *Students may say that the mother brags because she is competing with Auntie Lindo; to make her daughter seem more accomplished than she really is; in order to defend her from Auntie Lindo's disguised insult.*

◆Build Vocabulary

6 Suffixes: *-ness* Have students look at the word *nervousness*. Point out that the suffix *-ness* means "the state or quality of being." Adding *-ness* to the adjective *nervous* changes the word into a noun, meaning "having the quality of being nervous."

Humanities: Music

Scenes from Childhood, by Robert Schumann

Schumann wrote the 13 short piano pieces of *Scenes from Childhood* because his wife remarked that he seemed like a child sometimes. Instead of reacting negatively, he composed brief musical imitations of child-like actions, such as "All About Strange Lands and People," "Curious Story," "The Knight of the Rocking-Horse," and "Almost too Serious." When *Scenes from Childhood* was published in the 1800's, a critic said that a musical imitation of a child couldn't be taken seriously. Schumann thought this criticism was "stupid." Schumann titled the music after it was composed and stated that the titles for *Scenes from Childhood* were actually performance directions.

There are 30 of these short pieces altogether. When Schumann gave them to his wife—a professional musician—he said that she must forget that she was a virtuoso and simply play them for the impression they make. The piece the daughter is preparing for the talent show, "The Pleading Child," sounds like a pleading or whining child.

1. Why do you think the author chose the "The Pleading Child" for the daughter to play? *She probably wanted the daughter to sound as though she is pleading with her mother not to play the piano.*
2. How is the daughter's preparation for her piano performance a scene from childhood? *She is excited and more interested in how she will curtsy and appear to the audience than how well she will perform.*

◆Reading Strategy

❶ **Apply Word Identification Strategies** *Students should break envisioned into en + vi + sioned. The familiar word is vision, so envisioned must have something to do with seeing people.*

◆Critical Thinking

❷ **Draw Conclusions** Even after things have gone wrong, Jing-mei keeps playing. How have her lessons with Mr. Chong allowed her to keep playing? What is different about her wrong notes now? *She usually ignores how they sound, and Mr. Chong can't hear them. As the audience hears the wrong notes, she notices them, too.*

Clarification

❸ In music, the term *repeat* means what the word itself indicates: portions or all of the music is repeated, sometimes twice.

◆Literary Focus

❹ **Characters' Motives** Why is Old Chong beaming and shouting while everyone else in the room is quiet? *He is happy and showing support for his student. Because he is deaf, he hasn't heard her bad performance.*

◆Critical Thinking

❺ **Infer** Jing-mei is experiencing a mix of feelings. Ask students why they think she is confused by her mother's reaction to her poor performance. *Students should recognize that Jing-mei wants her mother's approval; despite her rebellious attitude, she feels guilty about not pleasing her mother.*

Customize for
English Language Learners

When familiar adjectives describe nouns in an unexpected way, students may have trouble grasping the meaning of the phrase. Show students how to make connections between familiar usage of the words that they know and the usage they are reading. Present the expressions *blank face* and *sour notes*. Students may know *blank* and *sour* in other contexts, such as *blank paper* or *sour milk*. Guide students to connect *blank paper*—paper without marks—and a *blank face*—a face without expression. In the same manner, help them realize that *sour milk* tastes bad, *sour* notes sound bad.

---

❶ **◆ Reading Strategy** Break the word *envisioned* into syllables. What familiar word is hidden inside?

envisioned people jumping to their feet and Ed Sullivan rushing up to introduce me to everyone on TV.

And I started to play. It was so beautiful. I was so caught up in how lovely I looked that at first I didn't worry how I would sound. So it was a surprise to me when I hit the first wrong note and I realized something didn't sound quite ❷ right. And then I hit another and another followed that. A chill started at the top of my head and began to trickle down. Yet I couldn't stop playing, as though my hands were bewitched. I kept thinking my fingers would adjust themselves back, like a train switching to the right track. I played this strange ❸ jumble through two repeats, the sour notes staying with me all the way to the end.

When I stood up, I discovered my legs were shaking. Maybe I had just been nervous and the audience, like Old Chong, had seen me go through the right motions and had not heard anything wrong at all. I swept my right foot out, went down on my knee, looked up and smiled. The room was quiet, except for Old ❹ Chong, who was beaming and shouting, "Bravo! Bravo! Well done!" But then I saw my mother's face, her stricken face. The audience clapped weakly, and as I walked back to my chair, with my whole face quivering as I tried not to cry, I heard a little boy whisper loudly to his mother, "That was awful," and the mother whispered back, "Well, she certainly tried."

And now I realized how many people were in the audience, the whole world it seemed. I was aware of eyes burning into my back. I felt the shame of my mother and father as they sat stiffly throughout the rest of the show.

We could have escaped during intermission. Pride and some strange sense of honor must have anchored my parents to their chairs. And so we watched it all: the eighteen-year-old boy with a fake mustache who did a magic show and juggled flaming hoops while riding a unicycle. The breasted girl with white makeup who sang from *Madama Butterfly* and got honorable mention. And the eleven-year-old boy who won first prize playing a tricky violin song that sounded like a busy bee.

After the show, the Hsus, the Jongs, and the St. Clairs from the Joy Luck Club came up to my mother and father.

"Lots of talented kids," Auntie Lindo said vaguely, smiling broadly.

"That was somethin' else," said my father, and I wondered if he was referring to me in a humorous way, or whether he even remembered what I had done.

Waverly looked at me and shrugged her shoulders. "You aren't a genius like me," she said matter-of-factly. And if I hadn't felt so bad, I would have pulled her braids and punched her stomach.

But my mother's expression was what devastated me: a quiet, blank look that said she had lost everything. I felt the same way, and it seemed as if everybody were now coming up, like gawkers at the scene of an accident, to see what parts were actually missing. When we got on the bus to go home, my father was humming the busy-bee tune and my mother was silent. I kept thinking she wanted ❺ to wait until we got home before shouting at me. But when my father unlocked the door to our apartment, my mother walked in and then went to the back, into the bedroom. No accusations. No blame. And in a way, I felt disappointed. I had been waiting for her to start shouting, so I could shout back and cry and blame her for all my misery.

I assumed my talent-show fiasco meant I never had to play the piano again. But two days later, after school, my mother came out of the kitchen and saw me watching TV.

"Four clock," she reminded me as if it were any other day. I was stunned, as though she were asking me to go through the talent-show torture again. I wedged myself more tightly in front of the TV.

"Turn off TV," she called from the kitchen five minutes later.

Beyond the Classroom

Workplace Skills

Preparedness Ask for a volunteer to explain why the girl performed so poorly during the recital: *She had not practiced enough, so she wasn't prepared when it was time for her to perform.* Tell students that in any workplace setting, being prepared is important to performing duties. Offer this example: "In the local firehouse, the fire truck's gas tank is empty, the firefighters' gear is misplaced, and the fire hoses are leaking. Then the fire bell rings." Invite students to discuss what will happen next. Lead students to see that not being prepared affects job performance and may affect others who depend on that performance. Continue by explaining to students how you prepare for your day of teaching.

Ask students to choose a job or profession and to write a paragraph about what the person holding that position must do to be prepared. Have them also write down some consequences that might follow if the person is not prepared.

I didn't budge. And then I decided. I didn't have to do what my mother said anymore. I wasn't her slave. This wasn't China. I had listened to her before and look what happened. She was the stupid one.

She came out from the kitchen and stood in the arched entryway of the living room. "Four clock," she said once again, louder.

"I'm not going to play anymore," I
6 said nonchalantly. "Why should I? I'm not a genius."

She walked over and stood in front of the TV. I saw her chest was heaving up and down in an angry way.

> 7 ◆ **Literary Focus**
> What word in this paragraph gives you a clue to the mother's motive?

"No!" I said, and I now felt stronger, as if my true self had finally emerged. So this was what had been inside me all along.

"No! I won't!" I screamed.

She yanked me by the arm, pulled me off the floor, snapped off the TV. She was frighteningly strong, half pulling, half carrying me toward the piano as I kicked the throw rugs un-
8 der my feet. She lifted me up and onto the hard bench. I was sobbing by now, looking at her bitterly. Her chest was heaving even more and her mouth was open, smiling crazily as if she were pleased I was crying.

"You want me to be someone that I'm not!" I sobbed. "I'll never be the kind of daughter you want me to be!"

"Only two kinds of daughters," she shouted in Chinese. "Those who are obedient and those who follow their own mind! Only one kind of daughter can live in this house. Obedient daughter!"

"Then I wish I wasn't your daughter. I wish you weren't my mother," I shouted. As I said these things I got scared. It felt like worms and toads and slimy things crawling out of my chest, but it also felt good, as if this awful

Portrait, Pamela Chin Lee, Courtesy of the artist

▲ **Critical Viewing** Do you think this image accurately portrays the "two kinds" of daughters the mother describes? **[Evaluate]** 9

side of me had surfaced, at last.

"Too late change this," said my mother shrilly.

And I could sense her anger rising to its breaking point. I wanted to see it spill over. And that's when I remembered the babies she

◆ Build Vocabulary

devastated (dev´ ə stā tid) *v.*: Destroyed; completely upset

fiasco (fē as´ cō) *n.*: Complete failure

◆Critical Thinking

6 Evaluate Jing-mei says she will not play the piano anymore because she's not a genius. Do you think this is a good reason to quit playing? *No. Students should realize that you don't have to be a "genius" to play the piano. They should also suggest that the real reason may be that she is angry and feeling rebellious about her mother's wishes; she may be afraid of failure, too.*

◆Literary Focus

7 Characters' Motives *Students should identify the word angry as a clue that the mother is motivated by anger at this point.*

◆Critical Thinking

8 Analyze Why does the mother react so strongly to the daughter's show of defiance? Students know enough about the characters to suggest several reasons: *Children were more respectful of their parents in China; the mother has been embarrassed in public by the daughter's refusal to practice; the mother has sacrificed to provide lessons for her daughter; the mother has not scolded her daughter for her poor performance, but now the daughter is screaming at her.*

▶Critical Viewing◀

9 Evaluate *Students should recognize that the two-sided face in the portrait accurately portrays the two-sided nature of the daughter's relationship with her mother.*

Customize for
Interpersonal Learners
Discuss with students how Jing-mei feels about her mother's response to the recital performance and her ongoing expectations of her daughter. Have students role-play the scenes between the mother and daughter to explore each character's motives. Urge students to use gestures and facial expressions to the various responses.

Humanities: Art

Portrait, by Pamela Chin Lee

Pamela Chin Lee was born in Kingston, Jamaica, and earned a Bachelor of Fine Arts degree from the Rhode Island School of Design. Her works include paintings and illustrations.

This painting shows two sides to one person. The colors of the right side of the painting are lighter and brighter. Encourage students to cover one side of the portrait to reveal only one half of the woman at a time, describing the differences they see. Use the following questions for discussion:

1. What message do you think the artist wishes to convey? *Students may suggest that the artist is showing that there are two sides to everyone.*
2. How do the colors of the painting help you see different parts of the person? *Students may suggest that the yellow background and pink and purple of the right side of the person show a happier or lighter side of her personality.*
3. Why do you think this painting might illustrate a story called "Two Kinds"? *The painting shows the two kinds of people or two kinds of personalities within one person that the story may describe.*

▶Critical Viewing◀

❶ **Compare and Contrast** *The girl in the photograph is dressed similarly to the description of how the narrator is dressed for the talent show, but she looks happy to be at the piano, which is very different from the narrator.*

◆Critical Thinking

❷ **Draw Conclusions** What does the mother's reaction reveal about what she is feeling? *The mother is usually outspoken about her disapproval of her daughter's actions. Her silence shows that in this case she has been deeply hurt and disappointed.*

◆Literature and Your Life

❸ We all depend on others' support and hope to help us believe in ourselves. Why do you think the daughter thinks her mother has betrayed her? *Students may suggest the daughter expected her mother to keep pushing her to play the piano or accomplish something.*

◆Literary Focus

❹ **Characters' Motives** *Students should note the word forgiveness as a clue that the mother's motive is to make peace with her daughter.*

Customize for
Interpersonal Learners
Ask students why the girl is scared by the things she says to her mother. Encourage small discussion groups to talk about saying hurtful things to those we love. Students should contrast the immediate feeling of release, of "getting it off one's chest," with later feelings of shame, or regret.

❶ ▲ **Critical Viewing** How does this photograph of the author compare with the story's narrator? **[Compare and Contrast]**

had lost in China, the ones we never talked about. "Then I wish I'd never been born!" I shouted. "I wish I were dead! Like them."

❷ It was as if I had said the magic words. Alakazam!—and her face went blank, her mouth closed, her arms went slack, and she backed out of the room, stunned, as if she were blowing away like a small brown leaf, thin, brittle, lifeless.

It was not the only disappointment my mother felt in me. In the years that followed, I failed her so many times, each time asserting my own will, my right to fall short of expectations. I didn't get straight A's. I didn't become class president. I didn't get into Stanford. I dropped out of college.

For unlike my mother, I did not believe I could be anything I wanted to be. I could only be me.

And for all those years, we never talked about the disaster at the recital or my terrible accusations afterward at the piano bench. All that remained unchecked, like a betrayal that was now unspeakable. So I never found a way to ask her why she had hoped for something so large that failure was inevitable. ❸

And even worse, I never asked her what frightened me the most: Why had she given up hope?

For after our struggle at the piano, she never mentioned my playing again. The lessons stopped. The lid to the piano was closed, shutting out the dust, my misery, and her dreams.

> ◆ **Literary Focus** What is the mother's motive in offering the piano? ❹

So she surprised me. A few years ago, she offered to give me the piano, for my thirtieth birthday. I had not played in all those years. I saw the offer as a sign of forgiveness, a tremendous burden removed.

"Are you sure?" I asked shyly. "I mean, won't you and Dad miss it?"

"No, this your piano," she said firmly. "Always your piano. You only one can play."

"Well, I probably can't play anymore," I said. "It's been years."

"You pick up fast," said my mother, as if she knew this was certain. "You have natural talent. You could been genius if you want to."

"No I couldn't."

"You just not trying," said my mother. And she was neither angry nor sad. She said it as if to announce a fact that could never be disproved. "Take it," she said.

But I didn't at first. It was enough that she had offered it to me. And after that, every time I saw it in my parents' living room, standing in front of the bay windows, it made me feel proud, as if it were a shiny trophy I had won back.

Last week I sent a tuner over to my parents' apartment and had the piano reconditioned, for purely sentimental reasons. My mother had died a few months before and I had been getting things in order for my

Viewing and Representing Mini-Lesson

Representing "Two Kinds"
This mini-lesson will extend students' understanding of the daughter's conflict with her mother and her internal conflict by visually representing "two kinds."

Introduce Remind students that throughout the story, the daughter has felt that she is one person while her mother wants her to be another person. Have them review the story's images for how artists and photographers choose to represent two sides of a person or of a culture such as Chinese American.

Develop Point out that people and cultures may be composed of two sides that coexist in harmony or two sides in conflict like the daughter in this story. Have students choose a medium or method to represent "two kinds." To appeal to different learning modalities, suggest the following:

- a dance duet
- recordings or musical performances
- a collage
- a videotape recording of a person's actions
- a poem

Apply Have students create their representations and present them to the class, followed by a short, oral explanation.

Assess Evaluate students' representations based on how well the concept of "two kinds" has been addressed, and whether students' explanations indicate a deeper understanding of the concept. Encourage students to ask and answer questions after each presentation.

father, a little bit at a time. I put the jewelry in special silk pouches. The sweaters she had knitted in yellow, pink, bright orange—all the colors I hated—I put those in moth-proof boxes. I found some old Chinese silk dresses, the kind with little slits up the sides. I rubbed the old silk against my skin, then wrapped them in tissue and decided to take them home with me.

After I had the piano tuned, I opened the lid and touched the keys. It sounded even richer than I remembered. Really, it was a very good piano. Inside the bench were the same exercise notes with handwritten scales, the same secondhand music books with their covers held together with yellow tape.

I opened up the Schumann book to the dark little piece I had played at the recital. It was on the left-hand side of the page, "Pleading Child." It looked more difficult than I remembered. I played a few bars, surprised at how easily the notes came back to me.

And for the first time, or so it seemed, I noticed the piece on the right-hand side. It was called "Perfectly Contented." I tried to play this one as well. It had a lighter melody but the same flowing rhythm and turned out to be quite easy. "Pleading Child" was shorter but slower; "Perfectly Contented" was longer, but faster. And after I played them both a few times, I realized they were two halves of the same song. 5

Guide for Responding

◆ Literature and Your Life

Reader's Response What advice would you have given the mother and daughter?

Thematic Focus In what ways can parents' hopes and expectations *help* children to create their own identities?

Gift Exchange With several classmates, choose presents for the mother and grown-up daughter to exchange in order to restore harmony.

☑ Check Your Comprehension

1. List the ways in which the mother tries to make her daughter into a prodigy.
2. Describe what happens at the talent show.
3. After the show, what occurs when the mother forces the daughter to practice?
4. How does the mother surprise the daughter years later?
5. What does the daughter finally discover about the piano piece she had played at the recital?

◆ Critical Thinking

Interpret

1. What do the daughter's failures on the nightly tests reveal about her abilities? **[Infer]**
2. Compare and contrast the daughter's use of the word *prodigy* with her mother's. **[Compare and Contrast]**
3. In the argument after the recital, why do the daughter's final words have such a powerful effect on her mother? **[Analyze]**
4. What have the mother and daughter learned from their conflict? **[Draw Conclusions]**

Evaluate

5. Do you agree with the daughter's statement that people can't be anything they want to be? Why or why not? **[Criticize]**

Extend

6. What does this story suggest about differences between some immigrant parents and their American-born children? **[Social Studies Link]**

Beyond the Selection

FURTHER READING

Other Works by Amy Tan

The Kitchen God's Wife
The Hundred Secret Senses
The Moon Lady (children's book)
The Chinese Siamese Cat (children's book)

INTERNET

We suggest the following sites on the Internet (all Web sites are subject to change).

For *The Joy Luck Club* and Amy Tan:
http://www.luminarium.org/contemporary/amytan

For additional information about Asian American culture:
http://www.jadedragon.com

We *strongly recommend* that you preview these sites before you send students to them.

◆ Critical Thinking

5 Infer How do the two pieces of music represent the contrasts in the young girl? *The "pleading child" searches for her true identity and is unhappy and confused. She will become "perfectly contented" in her life only when she accepts the different sides of herself.*

Reinforce and Extend

Answers

◆ Literature and Your Life

Reader's Response Students may advise the mother and daughter to stop arguing and to remember their love for one another.

Thematic Focus Parents can encourage children to discover themselves by allowing them to explore their interests and arranging for them to take special lessons.

☑ Check Your Comprehension

1. She pushes her, tests her, and arranges for piano lessons.
2. At the talent show, Jing-mei plays badly, embarrassing her parents and herself.
3. They argue, and the daughter says mean things to her mother.
4. She surprises her daughter by offering her the piano.
5. She discovers that it goes with another piece, titled "Perfectly Contented."

◆ Critical Thinking

1. She has neither the knowledge nor the interests of the prodigies her mother wants her to imitate.
2. The mother thinks of a *prodigy* as a child who wins fame for a special talent or for exceptional knowledge. The daughter associates the word *prodigy* with something she can't achieve.
3. The daughter uses terrible memories of China to hurt her mother.
4. The mother accepts that the daughter must go her own way, and the daughter learns that she cannot be who her mother wants her to be and can only be herself.
5. Some may say that when people try hard and have realistic expectations, they can be what they want to be. Others may say people are limited by their abilities and outside forces.
6. Parents may have hopes and dreams for their children that the children don't want or can't fulfill.

Answers

◆Reading Strategy

1. You can break *assortment* down and find the familiar word, *sort,* and a familiar suffix, *-ment.*
2. *Crazed* contains most of the word *crazy* and the verb ending *-ed.*
3. This word contains the word *applaud* and the verb ending *-ed.*
4. This word contains the word *embrace* and the ending *-less.*

◆Build Vocabulary

Using the Suffix *-ness*

Mother: stubbornness, hopefulness
Daughter: rebelliousness, sauciness, sadness

Spelling Strategy

1. happiness; 2. messiness; 3. filthiness; 4. silliness

Using the Word Bank

prodigy; debut; mesmerizing; reproach; sauciness; fiasco; conspired; devastated

◆Literary Focus

1. Having lost everything in China, the mother places all her hopes on her daughter and constantly pressures her to achieve fame and success.
2. Her laziness reflects her angry determination not to be what her mother wants.
3. She thinks that by listening to her mother, she was embarrassed at the recital. Now she is angry and feels that her mother and her requests are not worth the trouble.

◆Build Grammar Skills

Practice

1. Common noun: piano
2. Common nouns: name, teacher; proper noun: Mr. Chong
3. Common nouns: recital, piece; proper noun: Schumann
4. Common nouns: mother, daughter, chess; proper noun: Auntie Lindo
5. Common noun: mother; proper noun: China

Writing Application

Possible responses:

1. Change *Old Lady Chong* to *the woman.*
2. Change *Auntie Lindo* and *Uncle Tin* to *My aunt* and *my uncle.*

Guide for Responding *(continued)*

◆ Reading Strategy

Apply Word Identification Strategies

Some words in this story may seem odd until you use **word identification** to break them into syllables and familiar word parts. The word *expectation,* for example, might look too big for anyone's good. Inside it, however, you'll find the two-syllable word *expect* combined with the word ending *-ation.* You can guess that *expectation* means "the action of expecting or waiting for something."

Explain how word identification can help you make sense of these words from the story:

1. assortment
2. crazed
3. applauded
4. embraceless

◆ Build Vocabulary

Using the Suffix *-ness*

Use the suffix *-ness* to change the adjectives describing each character into the qualities that each character possesses:

1. Mother: stubborn; hopeful
2. Daughter: rebellious; saucy; sad

Spelling Strategy

If the final *y* in a word is preceded by a consonant, change the *y* to *i* when adding a suffix like *-ness:* saucy + -ness = sauciness. Write the following words correctly.

1. happy + -ness
2. messy + -ness
3. filthy + -ness
4. silly + -ness

Using the Word Bank

Replace each italicized word or phrase with the word from the Word Bank that has the same meaning.

The *child genius* sat down at the piano for her *first appearance* on stage. Her *hypnotic* performance was beyond *blame,* and her *boldness* won her admirers. The clarinetist sensed that his own efforts were a *failure.* Everything and everyone had *plotted* against him, and he felt *destroyed.*

◆ Literary Focus

Characters' Motives

In this story, the **characters' motives**—the reasons for their actions—power them into a head-on collision. The daughter reveals some of her motives directly. Looking in the mirror, she sees the anger she feels toward her mother. She also reveals her mother's motives, especially when describing what her mother lost in China and hopes for in America.

1. How do Chinese losses and American hopes explain why the mother pressures her daughter?
2. Why is the daughter careless when she practices at the piano?
3. Why does the daughter no longer wish to please her mother after the recital?

◆ Build Grammar Skills

Common and Proper Nouns

This story contains **common nouns,** which name people, places, things, and ideas in general, and **proper nouns,** which refer to specific people, places, things, and ideas. As this sentence indicates, common nouns are not capitalized, but proper nouns are:

Sacramento (proper) was the *name* (common) of the *street* (common) we lived on in *Chinatown* (proper).

Practice On your paper, identify common and proper nouns in these sentences.

1. She said that she couldn't play the piano.
2. The name of her teacher was Mr. Chong.
3. At the recital, she played a piece by Schumann.
4. Her mother competed with Auntie Lindo, whose daughter played chess.
5. Because they weren't living in China, she felt that she didn't have to do what her mother said.

Writing Application Rewrite these sentences, replacing the proper nouns with common nouns.

1. I met Old Lady Chong once in the Mission district and that was enough.
2. Auntie Lindo and Uncle Tin were there.

Writer's Solution

For additional instruction and practice, use the lesson in the *Writer's Solution Language Lab CD-ROM* on Nouns and Different Kinds of Nouns and the practice, pp. 5–6, in the *Writer's Solution Grammar Practice Book.*

Build Your Portfolio

Idea Bank

Writing

1. **Job Description** Briefly describe what the mother believes a prodigy should be able to do. Write your descriptions under these words: *Wanted! A Prodigy Who Can . . .*
2. **Music Review** Using details provided in the story, write a review of the daughter's performance at the recital. Imagine you are writing the review for a local newspaper. **[Career Link]**
3. **Prequel** Write an episode that comes before the events of this story. Briefly describe the mother's experiences in fleeing China. Base your account on details from the story's third paragraph and on your own imagination.

Speaking and Listening

4. **Counseling Conference** **[Group Activity]** Role-play a meeting of the daughter, the mother, and a guidance counselor. Have the mother and daughter express their disagreements, and have the counselor try to resolve them. **[Health Link]**
5. **Monologue** The daughter in the story has a moment alone in the bathroom after failing her mother's tests. Perform the speech that she might give as she looks at her face in the mirror. **[Performing Arts Link]**

Projects

6. **Television Soundtrack** You're producing a teleplay based on "Two Kinds." Choose two musical themes for the soundtrack—one for the daughter and one for the mother. Record your choices, and play them for the class. **[Music Link; Media Link]**
7. **Report on Chinese Customs** Use encyclopedias and books on China to learn what the Chinese believe about raising children. Write a report that will help students understand why the mother in the story insists on obedience. **[Social Studies Link]**

Writing Mini-Lesson

Mother's Diary Entry

You may feel closer to the daughter in this story than to the mother. However, stretch your imagination by looking at events through the mother's eyes. Choose an episode and write a diary entry about it as if you were the mother. Assume that the mother writes English well.

Writing Skills Focus: Elaborate to Add Emotional Depth

In writing diary entries and remembrances, it's important to reveal emotions. **Elaborate** to add emotional depth by stating how you feel about people and events. Also, use words that convey strong feelings, like *frenzied* rather than *hurried.* Notice how Amy Tan uses statements of emotion and emotional words in this passage:

Model From the Story

I began to cry. Such a sad, ugly girl! I made high-pitched noises like a crazed animal, trying to scratch out the face in the mirror.

Prewriting Choose an event that prompted strong feelings in the mother. Then, recall her experiences in China and her goals for her daughter. Keeping these in mind, jot down words that reflect the mother's feelings about the event.

Drafting As the mother, describe what happened. Elaborate on your factual account by stating how you feel about your daughter's behavior and including emotional words from your Prewriting list.

 **Grammar Application**

Use proper nouns that give a Chinese flavor to the diary entry.

Revising Have a classmate read the entry to see whether it is true to the mother's character and expresses strong feelings. If your entry is emotionally boring, replace flat words like *unpleasant* with crackling words like *hateful.*

✓ ASSESSMENT OPTIONS

Formal Assessment, Selection Test, pp. 4–6, and Assessment Resources Software. The selection test is designed so that it can be easily customized to the performance levels of your students.

Alternative Assessment, p. 2, includes options for less advanced students, more advanced students, interpersonal learners, verbal/linguistic learners, visual/spatial learners, intrapersonal learners, bodily/kinesthetic learners, and musical/rhythmic learners.

PORTFOLIO ASSESSMENT

Use the following rubrics in the **Alternative Assessment** booklet to assess student writing:
Job Description: Definition/Classification, p. 86
Music Review: Critical Review, p. 98
Prequel: Description, p. 84
Writing Mini-Lesson: Fictional Narrative, p. 82

Idea Bank

Following are suggestions for matching the Idea Bank topics with your students' performance levels and learning modalities:

Customize for *Performance Levels*

Less Advanced Students: 1, 5
Average Students: 2, 4, 5, 6
More Advanced Students: 3, 4, 5, 6, 7

Customize for *Learning Modalities*

Verbal/Linguistic: 1, 2, 3, 4, 5, 7
Interpersonal: 4
Intrapersonal: 5
Logical/Mathematical: 7
Musical/Rhythmic: 6

Writing Mini-Lesson

Refer students to the Writing Handbook at the back of the book for instruction on the writing process and for further information on expression.

 ***Writer's Solution***

Writers at Work Videodisc

To expose students to another writer who promotes Asian American culture, like Amy Tan, play the segment featuring June Choi. Have students compare and contrast the type of writing Choi does with Tan's writing.

Play frames 43192 to 51872

Writing Lab CD-ROM

Have students complete the tutorial on Description. Follow these steps.

1. Have students use the Sensory Word Bin to find words that elaborate to add emotional depth.
2. Have students draft on computer.
3. Suggest that students use the revision checker to help them spot vague adjectives in their writing.

Allow about 60 minutes to complete these steps.

Writer's Solution Sourcebook

Have students use Chapter 2, "Description," pp. 32–65, for additional support. The chapter includes in-depth instruction on using vivid and precise verbs, p. 59.

Prepare and Engage

OBJECTIVES

1. To read, comprehend, and interpret three poems
2. To relate poems to personal experience
3. To read poetry according to punctuation
4. To understand the speaker in poetry
5. To build vocabulary in context and learn forms of *equal*
6. To identify general and specific nouns
7. To write a personal creed focusing on the connotations of words
8. To respond to the poems through writing, speaking and listening, and projects

SKILLS INSTRUCTION

Vocabulary: Using Forms of *equal*
Spelling: Words With *qu* (kw)
Grammar: General and Specific Nouns
Reading Strategy: Read Poetry According to Punctuation
Literary Focus: The Speaker in Poetry
Writing: Using Connotations
Speaking and Listening: Poetry Reading (Teacher Edition)

PORTFOLIO OPPORTUNITIES

Writing: Rules for a Club; Plan for a Celebration; Comparison and Contrast
Writing Mini-Lesson: Personal Creed
Speaking and Listening: Telephone Conversation; Three-Way Poetry Contest
Projects: Multimedia Presentation; Science Fair

More About the Authors
Walt Whitman worked hard for recognition. He paid to publish his book of poetry, *Leaves of Grass,* and set the type for the first edition. Whitman also wrote anonymous newspaper reviews to draw attention to his poetry.

Emily Dickinson rarely left her home, but she led a full and active life. To the world, her most important activity was writing poetry. After Dickinson's death, her sister found hundreds of poems along with instructions to burn them—luckily, she chose not to.

Walter de la Mare's poetry shows how he could see the world through a child's eyes. At the age of 35, a yearly pension from the British government allowed him the time to devote himself to his writing.

Guide for Reading

Meet the Authors:

Walt Whitman (1819–1892)

There are two Walt Whitmans, related but different. One is a real person, and the other is the self he invented. The real Whitman grew up in Brooklyn, New York, and tried many jobs—from teaching to news reporting. During the Civil War, he traveled to Washington, D.C., to nurse his wounded brother and stayed to help other wounded soldiers.

All this time, the real Whitman was inventing a character based on himself. This character first appears in "Song of Myself." Striding out from the poem's free-flowing lines, the invented Whitman is confident and larger than life. [For more information on Whitman, see page 258.]

Emily Dickinson (1830–1886)

Walt Whitman traveled around, but Emily Dickinson hardly ever ventured outside Amherst, Massachusetts, where she was born. Quietly, however, she was writing the 1,775 poems that would make her famous after her death. In these brief lyrics, she created a poetic self that flashes with humor and intelligence.

Walter de la Mare (1873–1956)

While still a teenager, Walter de la Mare began working on statistics in a London office. Numbers were part of his daily life. By night, however, he escaped into the world of his imagination, writing poems for adults and children. In the poem "Me," de la Mare writes about the mystery of being one of a kind, not a statistic.

◆ Literature and Your Life

Connect Your Experience

Standing alone, like the man in the photograph on the opposite page, you may feel like a small part of a large world. With friends, you may feel just the right size, an important member of the group. When you look at objects under a microscope, you may suddenly feel like a giant. These poets explore what it means to be unique—whether you're feeling large or small.

Thematic Focus: Inventing Yourself

As you read these poems, think about the self that is you. How much of it did you create?

◆ Background for Understanding

Literature

Just as each individual creates a special self, every country creates a unique set of literary works. Walt Whitman and Emily Dickinson both contributed to the special character of American literature. Whitman used free verse, poems without regular rhythms to capture the American spirit. Dickinson gave American poetry the gift of looking inward.

◆ Build Vocabulary

Related Words: Forms of *equal*

In math, *equal* quantities are "the same as each other." Whitman also uses the word *equal* to mean "the same" when he says "with equal cheerfulness I can wait." A related form of this word is *unequal,* meaning "not the same."

Word Bank

Look over these words from the poems. Describe a place where you might *loaf.* Check the Build Vocabulary box on page 30 to see if loafing is something you really can do in the place you described.

assume
loaf
content
equal
banish
bog
forlorn

Prentice Hall Literature Program Resources

REINFORCE / RETEACH / EXTEND

Selection Support Pages
Build Vocabulary: Using Forms of *equal,* p. 12
Build Spelling Skills: Words With *qu* (kw), p. 13
Building Grammar Skills: General and Specific Nouns, p. 14
Reading Strategy: Read Poetry According to Punctuation, p. 15
Literary Focus: The Speaker in Poetry, p. 16

Strategies for Diverse Student Needs, pp. 5–6

Beyond Literature Cultural Connection: Fame, p. 3

Formal Assessment Selection Test, pp. 7–9, Assessment Resources Software

Alternative Assessment, p. 3

Resource Pro CD-ROM
Excerpt from *Song of Myself;* "I'm Nobody"; "Me"

Listening to Literature Audiocassettes
Excerpt from *Song of Myself;* "I'm Nobody"; "Me"

Song of Myself ◆ I'm Nobody ◆ Me

◆ Literary Focus

The Speaker in Poetry

Starting to read a poem is like answering a telephone call. Suddenly you "hear" a voice saying the words of the poem—the voice of the **speaker.** This speaker might be the poet or a character that the poet has created.

In these poems, the poets seem to be speaking as themselves. Listen to the words they stress and the rhythms of their speech, just as you would listen to an unknown voice on the telephone. These clues will help you understand who the speakers are and what they are telling you.

◆ Reading Strategy

Read Poetry According to Punctuation

By **reading according to punctuation,** pausing with commas and stopping with end marks, you'll hear a human voice in a poem. Otherwise, the speaker will sound like a weird computer voice, halting along.

In reading each poem, pause at commas, ellipsis marks (three dots), and dashes. Stop longer at end marks, making questions sound like questions and stressing statements that end with exclamation points. Don't stop at the ends of lines if there is no punctuation. Create a reading copy of each poem with notes like these:

Stress first statement. Full pause.   Read as question. Full pause.

I'm nobody! Who are you?

Preparing for Standardized Tests

Grammar and Analogies Knowledge of general and specific nouns may help students with analogy sections of standardized tests. Write the following analogy on the board and tell students it is read, "oak is to tree as daisy is to what?" *flower*

oak : tree :: daisy : _____

The object of an analogy question is to determine the relationship between the first two items and then apply the same relationship to fill in the missing part. Most standardized tests offer a choice of words to complete an analogy.

song : music :: poem : _____

(A) description (C) literature
(B) words (D) books

Remind students that more than one answer may complete an analogy, but they should select the best answer. In the example above, *(B) words* completes the analogy, but *(C) literature* is the best answer. Use Build Grammar Skills on p. 34 to be sure students can distinguish between general and specific nouns. For additional practice, use **Selection Support,** p. 14.

Stimulate students' interest in the poems' themes of identifying the self by having them write five clues about their own identity on a piece of paper. Clues might include information such as "I sit in the front row," "I have brown hair," or "I like cats," and end with the question, "Who am I?" Ask for their lists of clues, and read each one, allowing the class to speculate about the identity of each student.

◆ Build Grammar Skills

General and Specific Nouns If you wish to introduce the grammar concept for this selection before students read, refer to the instruction on p. 34.

Customize for
Less Proficient Readers

To help less proficient readers understand the poems, define and discuss each vocabulary word before reading. Then have students follow along in their books as you read each poem aloud, modeling how to Read Poetry According to Punctuation. After they hear the poems, help students paraphrase the phrases that have vocabulary words. For example, paraphrase "I lean and loaf at my ease" as "I hang out whenever I want to."

Customize for
More Advanced Students

Invite students to write poems that allow them "to sing their own songs." Encourage them to describe themselves or some aspect of themselves. Challenge them to use vivid and precise words in their descriptions.

Customize for
English Language Learners

Listening to oral interpretations of the poems may help English language learners comprehend the poems and understand the reading strategy of these poems. Play the audiocassette of these poems twice, encouraging students to follow the printed words as they listen the second time. Have them discuss the readers' interpretations of each form of punctuation.

Listening to Literature Audiocassettes

Develop Understanding

Song of Myself allows readers to appreciate how the speaker enjoys life, relaxing and enjoying his or her place in the world. Descriptions offer clues about who the speaker is—someone who is comfortable in his or her own skin.

◆Literary Focus

1 The Speaker in Poetry Point out that the poem's speaker talks directly to the reader. Then ask students what the speaker's message to the reader is. *Students may respond that the speaker tells the reader that they are equals and what is good for the speaker is good for the reader.*

◆Critical Thinking

2 Deduce Whitman's book of poetry, *Leaves of Grass,* refers to people (leaves) as being part of society or a large group (grass). In this poem, what does a single spear of grass represent? *Students should understand Whitman's analogy and identify a spear of grass as one person or a member of society.*

◆Critical Thinking

3 Infer Does the speaker care if the world knows about him or her? *No, the speaker doesn't care, because he or she is content whether the world is aware or not.*

◆Build Vocabulary

4 Forms of *equal* Have students think about the last two lines of the poem and the definition of *equal.* Then ask them to use their understanding of *equal* to paraphrase these lines. *Possible answer: It will give me the same amount of happiness to come into my own now or later.*

Customize for
Visual/Spatial Learners

Students may pick up clues to the meaning of the poem by looking at the picture of the girl on p. 30. Have them study the picture and describe what they see. You may want to guide them by suggesting that they think about whether she looks happy or sad, content or impatient, excited or calm, and so forth.

from
Song of Myself
Walt Whitman

I celebrate myself,
And what I <u>assume</u> you shall assume,
For every atom belonging to me as good belongs to you.

I <u>loaf</u> and invite my soul,
I lean and loaf at my ease . . . . observing a spear of summer grass.

* * *

I exist as I am, that is enough,
If no other in the world be aware I sit <u>content</u>,
And if each and all be aware I sit content.

One world is aware, and by far the largest to me, and that is myself,
And whether I come to my own today or in ten thousand or ten million years,
I can cheerfully take it now, or with <u>equal</u> cheerfulness I can wait.

◆ Build Vocabulary

assume (ə so͞om′) *v.*: Believe to be a fact
loaf (lōf) *v.*: Spend time idly
content (kən tent′) *adj.*: Happy enough
equal (ē′ kwəl) *adj.*: Of the same amount
banish (ban′ ish) *v.*: Send away; exile
bog (bäg) *n.*: Small marsh or swamp

Block Scheduling Strategies

Consider these suggestions to take advantage of extended class time:

- Focus on the reading strategy: First, have students listen to the audiocassette, noting how poetry is read according to punctuation. Next, have students read aloud in pairs, using the Reading Strategy, p. 34. To reinforce understanding, use **Selection Support,** p. 15; the Speaking and Listening Mini-Lesson, p. 32, of the Teacher Edition; and/or have students Stage a Three-Way Poetry Contest, p. 35.
- For project-oriented instruction, have students read independently and then work in pairs to complete the Cross-Curricular Activity: Classifying Plants, p. 33. Or, have them research and complete a Multimedia Presentation, p. 35.
- To help prepare students for the Writing Mini-Lesson, p. 35, have them complete Literary Focus, p. 16, of **Selection Support,** and the Comparison and Contrast activity, p. 35. Then have students write a personal creed, forming small groups to revise, and discuss Writing Focus: Using Connotations.

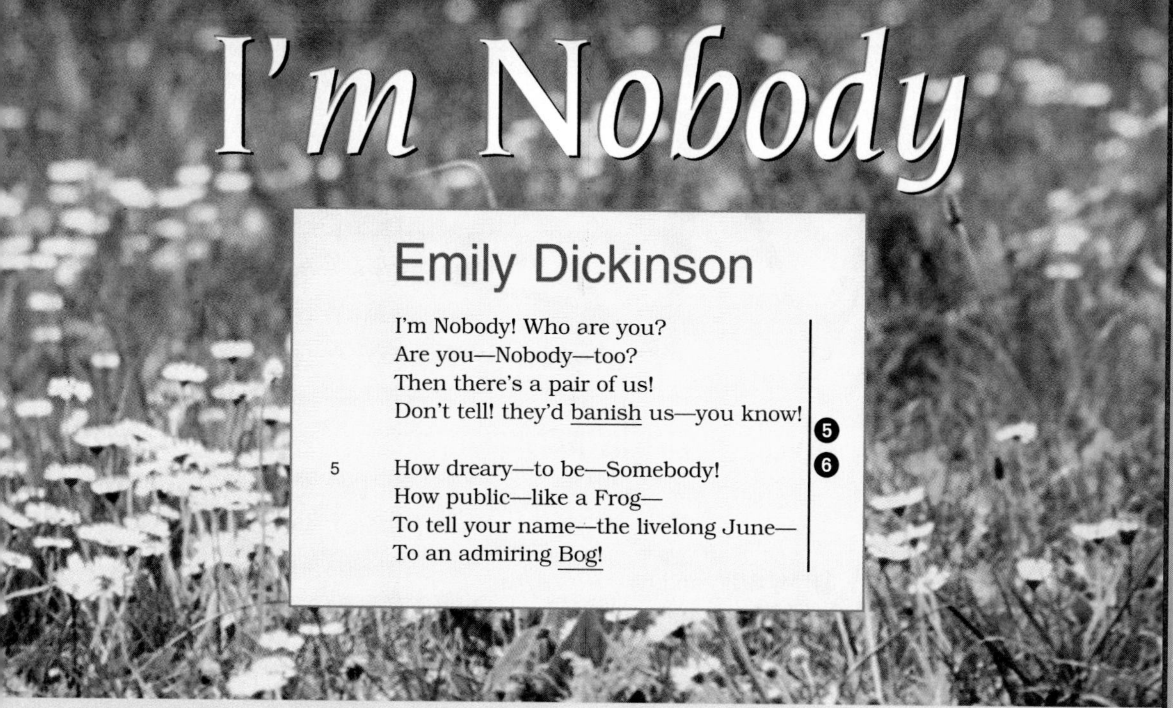

I'm Nobody

Emily Dickinson

I'm Nobody! Who are you?
Are you—Nobody—too?
Then there's a pair of us!
Don't tell! they'd banish us—you know! ❺

How dreary—to be—Somebody! ❻
How public—like a Frog—
To tell your name—the livelong June—
To an admiring Bog!

Guide for Responding

◆ Literature and Your Life

Reader's Response Which of these poets would make a better companion on a hike? At a school basketball game? Explain.

Thematic Focus What is unusual or surprising about the selves that these poets present?

Sketch Make a quick line drawing of Whitman loafing or of a secret meeting between two Nobodies.

☑ Check Your Comprehension

1. Describe three things Whitman does in the first five lines of "Song of Myself."
2. What fact is "enough" for Whitman?
3. What does Dickinson ask and tell the reader in the first stanza of "I'm Nobody"?
4. In "I'm Nobody," how do Somebodies behave like frogs?

◆ Critical Thinking

INTERPRET

1. How can Whitman's loafing be a celebration of himself? **[Infer]**
2. What advice about living is Whitman passing on to readers? **[Draw Conclusions]**
3. Name three traits that Dickinson's Somebodies share, and explain your choices. **[Deduce]**
4. For Dickinson, what two key differences make Nobodies better than Somebodies? Explain. **[Draw Conclusions]**

EVALUATE

5. Do you agree with Dickinson that it's better to be Nobody than Somebody? Explain. **[Criticize]**

COMPARE LITERARY WORKS

6. In what ways do both of these poets create a special bond with the reader? **[Connect]**

One-Minute Insight In "I'm Nobody," Emily Dickinson celebrates privacy and one's right to be different. She then pokes gentle fun at those who need to trumpet their names to the world.

◆ Reading Strategy

❺ Read Poetry According to Punctuation Invite two volunteers to each read a stanza of the poem aloud, pausing at dashes and stressing exclamations. Then ask them how the punctuation affects the reading of the poem. *Students should note the rhythm created by the dashes and the enthusiasm or intensity that the exclamation points indicate.*

◆ Literary Focus

❻ The Speaker in Poetry Point out that Dickinson is playing with the terms *nobody* and *somebody*. In fact, she means the very opposite of what is usually indicated by these terms. What does the speaker's humorous description of *Somebodies* tell you about how she feels? *She thinks that those who try to be important in the eyes of others are wasting their time.*

Reinforce and Extend

Answers

◆ Literature and Your Life

Reader's Response Students may think Whitman would be fun on a hike because he's relaxed and enjoys nature, and Dickinson would be good for a game because she doesn't have to be the center of attention.

Thematic Focus Students may think the fact that Whitman loafs or Dickinson chooses to be a "nobody" is unusual.

☑ Check Your Comprehension

1. He celebrates himself, he loafs, and he observes a spear of grass.
2. The fact that he is himself is enough.
3. She asks if the reader is a Nobody and tells the reader that she is a Nobody.
4. They want to be seen and heard, just like a frog croaking in a swamp.

◆ Critical Thinking

1. Loafing allows time for enjoying one's self and life, in general.
2. He advises readers to be content and cheerful and to like themselves.
3. Possible responses: Somebodies are boring because they talk about themselves; foolish because they don't care who looks up to them as long as someone does; and they are public because they want to feel important.
4. Nobodies don't care about being known to the world, and they don't brag about themselves like dreary Somebodies.
5. Students should support their answers with observations from their own experiences or ideas; for example, some students may disagree because they want to be well known.
6. Both poets directly address the reader as "you." Whitman says the reader is as good as he is. Dickinson invites the reader into a friendly conspiracy.

Develop Understanding

One-Minute Insight Walter de la Mare's poem, "Me," reveals the wonder and uniqueness of each individual. The speaker is saying, "Whatever I am, whether tree, flower, or human being, I will always be 'just me.'"

◆Literary Focus

❶ The Speaker in Poetry Is the speaker a child, teenager, young adult, or old adult? Have students support their answer to this question. *Students may think that the speaker sounds like a child because of the poem's simple comparisons and focus on "me."*

◆Build Grammar Skills

❷ General and Specific Nouns Have students list the living things found in lines 5–12 under the headings "General Noun" or "Specific Noun." *General Noun: tree, flower. Specific Noun: willow, elder, aspen, thorn, cypress, primrose, pink, violet.*

Clarification

❸ All three flowers mentioned are small, delicate plants that flower in late spring and early summer. The primrose is traditionally yellow, but ranges from white to pink, purple, and blue; a pink *(dianthus)* is usually pink or white; and violets are pictured on the student pages.

Customize for
Logical/Mathematical Learners
Have students use a Venn diagram to find the similarities and differences amongst the three poems.

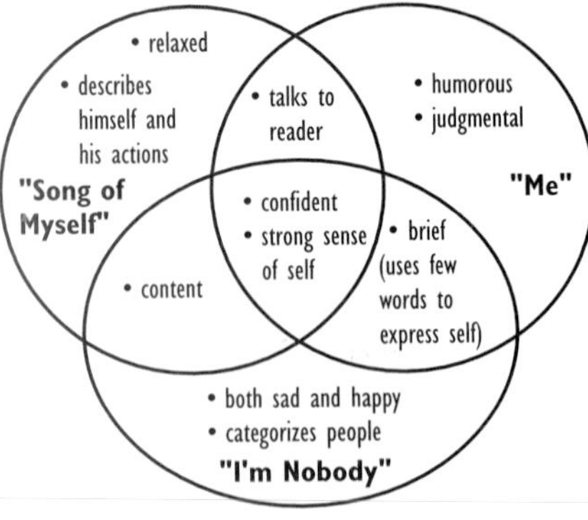

Me

Walter de la Mare

As long as I live
I shall always be
❶ My Self—and no other,
Just me.

Like a tree.

Like a willow or elder,
An aspen, a thorn,
Or a cypress[1] forlorn.
❷

Like a flower,
For its hour
A primrose, a pink,
❸ Or a violet—
Sunned by the sun,
And with dewdrops wet.

Always just me.

1. **cypress** (sī′ prəs) *n.*: Evergreen, cone-bearing tree whose branches or sprigs are used as a symbol of grief or mourning.

◆ Build Vocabulary
forlorn (fôr lôrn′) *adj.*: Alone and miserable

32 ◆ *Finding Yourself*

Speaking and Listening Mini-Lesson

Poetry Reading
This mini-lesson supports the Speaking and Listening activity in the Idea Bank on p. 35.

Introduce Point out that punctuation in poems often indicates where a reader should pause. Also, changing tone of voice helps communicate the thoughts and mood of the poems.

Develop As students develop their readings, urge them to consider these points:
- What are the poem's thoughts and moods?
- How does punctuation indicate the poem should be read?

Apply Have students create a script including pauses and vocal changes. You may want them to work in pairs with one student as reader and one as coach. Invite them to perform their poetry readings for the class as part of the Three-Way Poetry Contest.

Assess Evaluate readings by using these criteria: vocal effects, overall delivery, and attention to punctuation. Or, have students use the Peer Assessment: Oral Interpretation form, p. 106, in **Alternative Assessment.**

Beyond Literature

Science Connection

Nature's One-of-a-Kind Creations
In "Me," de la Mare compares his own uniqueness to that of various trees and flowers. Did you know that for every kind of tree and flower, there may be dozens—or even hundreds—of unique variations? Botanists are scientists who study and classify plants according to their characteristics. For most of us, a rose is a rose, but for botanists, there are actually hundreds of different types of roses—each one unlike every other one.

Cross-Curricular Activity
Classifying Plants Choose a plant, and do research to find out how many variations of it exist. Visit a local nursery or consult Internet and library resources. Then, use your findings to create an illustrated chart that shows your plant and the characteristics botanists use to classify it. Post your chart in the classroom or the school library.

Guide for Responding

◆ Literature and Your Life

Reader's Response Would you like to meet the speaker of this poem? What do you think he or she would be like?

Thematic Focus Does De la Mare give you the feeling that people are able to create their own identities? Why or why not?

Comparison Game With a group of classmates, take turns writing sentences that compare people to trees, flowers, or animals. Each person should complete the statement "I am most like a . . ." and then explain the comparison. Be original in your responses.

☑ Check Your Comprehension

1. What will the poet be as long as he lives?
2. To what trees and flowers does he compare himself?

◆ Critical Thinking

INTERPRET

1. What is similar about the things to which de la Mare compares himself? **[Connect]**
2. How is the message of "Me" both comforting and limiting? **[Draw Conclusions]**

EVALUATE

3. Is "Me" successful in suggesting the mystery of being a "Self"? Explain. **[Criticize]**

EXTEND

4. In what way is a person in society "Just me" and more than "Just me"? **[Social Studies Link]**

Beyond the Selection

FURTHER READING

Other Works by the Authors
Leaves of Grass, Walt Whitman
Final Harvest: Emily Dickinson's Poems, T. H. Johnson (ed.)
The Listeners and Other Poems, Walter de la Mare

Other Works on the Theme of Finding Yourself
I Feel a Little Jumpy Around You, Naomi Shihab Nye and Paul B. Janeczo (eds.)

INTERNET
We suggest the following sites on the Internet (all Web sites are subject to change).
To learn more about Walt Whitman: **http://www.liglobal.com/walt**
For Emily Dickinson: **http://www.planet.nte/pkrisxle/emily/dickinson.html**
For de la Mare: **http://www.columbia.edu/acis/bartleby/mbp/48.html**
We *strongly recommend* that you preview these sites before you send students to them.

Beyond Literature

Encourage students to think of a plant that has variations, such as lettuce (iceberg; bib) or tomato (cherry; plum). Students might start their research with an encyclopedia or reference book on botany. Suggest that they use both pictures and words to depict the variations. Their charts should clearly show the plant, and the variations should be labeled with defining characteristics.

Reinforce and Extend

Answers

◆ Literature and Your Life

Reader's Response Students' responses should be based on an attribute they believe they share with a plant or animal, such as "I am strong like an oak tree."

Thematic Focus Students may suggest that de la Mare says there is nothing you can do to change who you are.

☑ Check Your Comprehension

1. The poet will always be "just me."
2. The poet compares himself to a willow, elder, aspen, thorn, and cypress (trees), and to a primrose, pink, and violet (flowers).

◆ Critical Thinking

1. Most students will see that he compares himself to plants—trees and flowers. Some may see that plants, like people, are living things with special identities.
2. It's comforting to know that you'll always be yourself, but it is also limiting that you may never be anything else.
3. Students may say yes because de la Mare compares himself to things that we don't know what it would be like to be.
4. Possible response: Each individual person is "just me" because each is independent. However, as daughters or sons, students, and friends, people are also part of relationships and groups that are more than "just me."

Answers

◆Reading Strategy

1. The six pauses should be at the five commas and the ending period.
2. The period requires the longest pause because it indicates the end of a sentence.
3. There are six brief pauses and two longer pauses.
4. The first brief pause is after "Self" (line 3).

◆Build Vocabulary

Using Forms of *equal*
equals; unequal; equality

Spelling Strategy
1. questions; 2. quill

Using the Word Bank
1. c 2. e 3. a 4. d
5. b 6. f

◆Literary Focus

1. Many students will see that the long lines and sentences show that the speaker has thought a lot about who he is.
2. Possible response: In the first stanza, the speaker capitalizes "Nobody" and places it in an exclamation. This shows that she is happy or proud to be a Nobody. In the second stanza, the speaker stresses "Frog" and "Bog" by using rhyming words and capitalization. By comparing Somebodies to frogs croaking in a bog, she makes them seem silly and self-important.

◆Build Grammar Skills

Practice
1. general
2. specific
3. specific
4. general
5. general

Writing Application
Possible response: Three examples of balls are a volleyball, a basketball, and a baseball.

Writer's Solution

For additional instruction and practice, use the lesson in the *Writer's Solution Language Lab CD-ROM* on Using Nouns and the practice page on Different Kinds of Nouns, p. 7, in the *Writer's Solution Grammar Practice Book.*

Guide for Responding *(continued)*

◆ Reading Strategy

Read Poetry According to Punctuation

You heard the human voices in these poems by **reading poetry according to punctuation,** pausing briefly at commas and longer at end marks. You didn't make the voices sound stiff by pausing at the ends of lines where there was no punctuation.

1. In the last three lines of "Song of Myself," find six places where you should pause.
2. Which place requires the longest pause? Why?
3. How many brief pauses are there in lines 5–8 of "I'm Nobody"? How many longer pauses?
4. Where is the first brief pause in "Me"?

◆ Build Vocabulary

Using Forms of *equal*

Equal means "the same as," but related forms of the word express this sameness in different ways. Using each word only once, choose the form of *equal* that fits best in each blank.

unequal equals equality

Because poetry is so personal, one poet never exactly __?__ another. Also, poets are __?__ in their achievements. However, these three poets, like all fine writers, display an __?__ of spirit.

Spelling Strategy

The *kw* sound following the e in *equal* is spelled *qu*. Fill in the blanks with a suitable word containing the *qu* spelling of the *kw* sound:

1. Often Dickinson's poems ask __?__ that are hard to answer.
2. Living many years ago, Whitman and Dickinson probably wrote with a __?__ and ink.

Using the Word Bank

On your paper, match each word in the first column with the word that is closest in meaning to it in the second column.

1. assume	**a.** identical
2. loaf	**b.** sad
3. equal	**c.** suppose
4. bog	**d.** swamp
5. forlorn	**e.** relax
6. banish	**f.** remove

◆ Literary Focus

The Speaker in Poetry

The **speaker** is the voice or character who narrates a poem. The speakers of these poems reveal themselves in the words and rhythms they use. De la Mare, for example, repeats the phrase "just me" and uses lines that are very brief. These clues suggest that the speaker feels both special and small.

1. In "Song of Myself," what do the long lines and long sentences indicate about the speaker?
2. In "I'm Nobody," how does the speaker stress words in a humorous way to show that Nobodies are special but Somebodies are not?

◆ Build Grammar Skills

General and Specific Nouns

In using nouns to refer to people, places, or things, imagine that you're operating a movie camera. A **general noun,** like *tree,* is a wide-angle shot that takes in a group of related items. There are many kinds of trees in the group. A **specific noun,** like *oak,* is a close-up shot of a single item. An oak is one type of tree.

Notice how De la Mare follows a wide-angle shot (general noun) with a series of quick close-ups (specific nouns):

Like a tree.

Like a willow or elder,
An aspen, a thorn,
Or a cypress forlorn.

Practice On your paper, indicate whether each italicized noun is general or specific.

1. De la Mare compares human life to that of a *flower.*
2. The poet doesn't mention a *daisy.*
3. For Dickinson, a Somebody is like a *frog.*
4. Whitman writes about many types of *vehicles.*
5. For Whitman, each *person* was special.

Writing Application On your paper, fill in a plural general noun in the first blank and three specific nouns in the following blanks: Three examples of __?__ are a __?__, a __?__, and a __?__.

Build Your Portfolio

Idea Bank

Writing

1. **Rules for a Club** Dickinson's poem "I'm Nobody" reads like an invitation to a club. Write the rules for a Happy-to-Be-Nobody Club. Include entrance requirements and procedures for meetings.
2. **Plan for a Celebration** Your school is honoring Whitman with a Self-Celebration Day. Write the plan for a day on which all students can express and celebrate what makes them special.
3. **Comparison and Contrast** In an essay, compare two of these poems, focusing on their ideas about a person's self. For example, what elements are similar and different about Dickinson's "Nobody" and de la Mare's "just me"?

Speaking and Listening

4. **Telephone Conversation** With a partner, improvise a phone conversation between any two of these poets. Make the poets sound as they do in their poems. **[Performing Arts Link]**
5. **Three-Way Poetry Contest** Stage a competition among these poets as they read from their work. A panel can rate the performances based on the quality of the poems and the drama of the presentation. **[Performing Arts Link]**

Projects

6. **Multimedia Presentation** Dramatize the life of Whitman or Dickinson in a multimedia presentation. Research the poet's life, gathering film clips, slides, photographs, and books. Then, weave these materials into a script and present it to the class. **[Media Link]**
7. **Science Fair** **[Group Activity]** What do scientists think is special about each person? Stage a fair to answer this question. One student can demonstrate fingerprinting, and others can present information on genes and DNA. **[Science Link]**

Writing Mini-Lesson

Personal Creed

Each of these poems is a kind of personal creed, a statement of the poet's deepest beliefs. In prose, write your own personal creed. Think of it as a statement of your beliefs that could appear under your photograph in a school yearbook. It will tell your classmates and teachers about the ideas and loyalties that guide your life.

Writing Skills Focus: Using Connotations

Because your creed will express deep feelings, you must focus on the **connotations** of words—the emotions and ideas they stir up. Even when two words have the same dictionary meaning, they often have different connotations. For example, *to celebrate* sounds grander and more festive than *to honor* in the following:

Model From the Poem

I celebrate myself,
And what I assume you shall assume . . .

Prewriting Write "I believe ______" several times on a sheet of paper and fill in the blanks with words and phrases. Then, substitute words with similar dictionary meanings and different connotations to see which ones you prefer.

Drafting Imagine that you're answering a close friend who has just asked, "What do you believe in?" Refer to your prewriting notes for key words and phrases.

◆ Grammar Application

Where possible, replace general nouns like *relative* with specific nouns that have more feeling, like *father* or *mother*.

Revising Have classmates look over your creed and describe the feelings that key words stir up in them. If a word's connotations aren't right for your purpose, replace the word with a synonym.

Idea Bank

Following are suggestions for matching the Idea Bank topics with your students' performance levels and learning modalities:

Customize for *Performance Levels*

Less Advanced Students: 2, 4, 7
Average Students: 1, 4, 5, 7
More Advanced Students: 3, 5, 6, 7

Customize for *Learning Modalities*

Verbal/Linguistic: 1, 2, 3, 4, 5, 6
Interpersonal: 4, 5, 6, 7
Musical/Rhythmic: 5
Visual/Spatial: 6
Logical/Mathematical: 1, 2, 7
Bodily/Kinesthetic: 7

Writer's Solution

Writing Lab CD-ROM

Have students complete the tutorial on Expression. Follow these steps:

1. Have students use the Cluster Map activity to come up with a topic.
2. Have students draft on computer.
3. Have students use the Descriptive Word Bin to come up with precise and vivid words.

You will need approximately 70 minutes of class time to complete these steps.

Writer's Solution Sourcebook

Have students use Chapter 1, "Expression," pp. 1–29, for additional support. This chapter includes in-depth instruction on considering your audience and purpose.

✓ ASSESSMENT OPTIONS

Formal Assessment, Selection Test, pp. 7–9, and Assessment Resources Software. The selection test is designed so that it can be easily customized to the performance levels of your students.

Alternative Assessment, p. 3, includes options for less advanced students, more advanced students, verbal/linguistic learners, interpersonal learners, visual/spatial learners, and musical/rhythmic learners.

PORTFOLIO ASSESSMENT

Use the following rubrics in the **Alternative Assessment** booklet to assess student writing:
Rules for a Club: How-to/Process Explanation, p. 87
Multimedia Presentation: Multimedia Report, p. 94
Comparison and Contrast: Comparison/Contrast, p. 90
Writing Mini-Lesson: Expression, p. 81

Guide for Reading

OBJECTIVES

1. To read, comprehend, and interpret an essay
2. To relate an essay to personal experience
3. To break down long sentences
4. To analyze a personal essay
5. To build vocabulary in context and learn the prefix *un-*
6. To develop skill in using collective nouns
7. To write an I-Search paper using precise details
8. To respond to an essay through writing, speaking and listening, and projects

SKILLS INSTRUCTION

Vocabulary: Prefixes: *un-*
Spelling: Words With Prefixes
Grammar: Collective Nouns
Reading Strategy: Break Down Long Sentences
Literary Focus: Personal Essay
Writing: Elaborate With Precise Details
Speaking and Listening: Storytellers' Circle (Teacher Edition)
Viewing and Representing: Film Review (Teacher Edition)
Critical Viewing: Analyze; Identify

PORTFOLIO OPPORTUNITIES

Writing: Captions; Book Jacket; Proposal
Writing Mini-Lesson: I-Search Paper
Speaking and Listening: Speaker's Introduction; Storytellers' Circle
Projects: Family Chart; Film Review

More About the Author

Before publishing *Roots* in 1976, **Alex Haley** worked as the Coast Guard's chief journalist and as a magazine writer. He received hundreds of rejection slips over a period of 8 years before he sold his first article. His first major work, *The Autobiography of Malcolm X* (1965), was an authoritative and widely read narrative based on Haley's interviews with the Nation of Islam spokesman.

As Haley explains in this essay, he then became interested in tracing his family's history. Over the next 12 years, he spent $80,000 and traveled half a million miles in researching *Roots*. He completed the book in 1976, the year of the United States' Bicentennial, and dedicated it "as a birthday offering to my country."

Meet the Author:

Alex Haley (1921–1992)

Alex Haley grew up in Tennessee and Alabama. As a teenager, he wanted to see more of the world, so he joined the Coast Guard. It was while aboard ships, lying in his bunk at night, that he started to imagine and write sea adventure stories.

A Writer on His Own
After twenty years with the Coast Guard, Haley retired to begin a full-time career as a writer. He wrote several books, but his best-known work is *Roots: The Saga of an American Family.* "My Furthest-Back Person" explains how he began this book.

A Television Mini-Series Haley's *Roots* tells about the history of his family in Africa and the United States. An immediate bestseller, it led to a television mini-series that was viewed by 130 million people. The book and the mini-series inspired many people to research their own family histories.

The Story Behind the Essay
As a boy in Tennessee, Haley would sit on the porch, listening to his grandmother and great aunts tell stories about the family's "furthest-back person." These stories prompted him to find out more about the mysterious African named "Kin-tay."

◆ Literature and Your Life

Connect Your Experience

Photographs, family stories, and heirlooms such as the quilt on the facing page can help people re-create their family's history. However, most of us can't trace our family's roots for more than a few generations. This was true of Alex Haley, whose distant relatives were brought to the United States as slaves. In this essay, he describes how he struggled to find his missing roots.

Thematic Focus: Inventing Yourself

Sometimes you learn who you are by discovering who your ancestors were. Notice how Haley's research gives him a new sense of himself.

◆ Background for Understanding

Social Studies

Alex Haley began his research at the National Archives in Washington, D.C. This agency was established in 1934 to store government records. There, Haley found population lists with the names of his great-grandparents. In Africa, he found another way to keep records: in the memory of a tribal "historian" who could recite centuries of history!

◆ Build Vocabulary

Prefixes: *un-*

Haley uses the word "*uncanny*." The prefix *un-* means "not or the opposite of." Combined with *canny*, which can mean "comfortable," it creates a word meaning "strange, in a way that is not comfortable."

Word Bank

Which of these words from the essay might be related to the word *question?*

intrigue
uncanny
cherished
queried
eminent
destination

Prentice Hall Literature Program Resources

REINFORCE / RETEACH / EXTEND

Selection Support Pages
Build Vocabulary: Prefixes: *un-*, p. 17
Build Spelling Skills, p. 18
Build Grammar Skills: Collective Nouns, p. 19
Reading Strategy: Break Down Long Sentences, p. 20
Literary Focus: Personal Essay, p. 21

Strategies for Diverse Student Needs, pp. 7–8

Beyond Literature Cross-Curricular Connection: Social Studies, p. 4

Formal Assessment Selection Test, pp. 10–12, Assessment Resources Software

Alternative Assessment, p. 4

Resource Pro CD-ROM
"My Furthest-Back Person"—includes all resource materials and customizable lesson plan

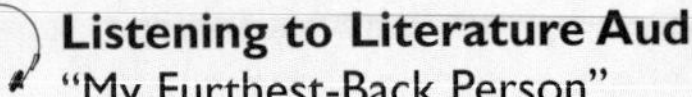

Listening to Literature Audiocassettes
"My Furthest-Back Person"

My Furthest-Back Person (*The Inspiration for* Roots)

***The Purple Quilt* (detail),** 1986: acrylic on canvas, tie-dyed and printed fabric, 91 x 72, Faith Ringgold, Courtesy of Bernice Steinbaum

◆ Literary Focus

Personal Essay

The word *essay,* which means "a brief, nonfiction discussion of a topic," sounds cold and distant. However, imagine sitting on a porch with a writer who talks to you like a friend. That's just what **personal essays** do—they place you close to authors who tell you about their lives.

From the first sentence, Haley's writing reveals the elements of a personal essay. With its conversational style, its use of the pronoun "I," and its focus on Haley's own life, it speaks to you like a porch companion: "One Saturday in 1965 I happened to be walking. . . ."

◆ Reading Strategy

Break Down Long Sentences

When you read, you create meaning from words. To build up meaning, you must sometimes **break down long sentences**—find the subject of the sentence (what it is about) and what the sentence is saying about the subject.

You can break down this sentence by Haley by placing the subject at the beginning:

Haley's Sentence: One Saturday in 1965 I happened to be walking past the National Archives. . . .

Rearranged Sentence: I happened to be walking past the National Archives one Saturday in 1965.

Preparing for Standardized Tests

Vocabulary General vocabulary test questions on standardized tests often evaluate students' knowledge of affixes. Students can develop their ability to apply affixes, such as this selection's vocabulary skill, Using the Prefix *un-*, to derivatives.

Ask students to explain the difference between *happy* and *unhappy*. Point out that they can apply their knowledge of how the prefix *un-* changes the meaning of *happy* to its opposite and determine the meanings of many words that begin with *un-*. Write the following sample question on the board:

Choose the best word or phrase that means the opposite of unspent.
(A) wasted (C) paid
(B) saved (D) used

Knowing the meaning of the prefix *un-* will help students choose the correct answer, *(B) saved.* For practice using the prefix *un-*, use the Build Vocabulary activity, p. 46.

Interest Grabber Play the "telephone game." Begin by whispering a sentence to the first student and having each student whisper what he or she heard, down the line. When the last student has heard the sentence, have him or her write it on the board. Then write the original sentence. Have students reverse the order aloud to try to find where changes occurred in the message. Then explain to the class that adaptations caused by passing along information this way are similar to the adaptations of Alex Haley's family history that he discovers in "My Furthest-Back Person."

◆ Build Grammar Skills

Collective Nouns If you wish to introduce the grammar concept taught with this essay, use the instruction on p. 46 before students read the essay.

Customize for *Less Proficient Readers*

Help students jot down notes about the topic of each section of text. The notes should consist of a phrase or two—just enough to remind students of what they have read. For instance, have them write "Grandma's stories" after reading p. 39.

Customize for *More Advanced Students*

Students may be interested in doing their own genealogical research. Offer them some research tips:

- Interview relatives.
- Look for clues in deeds to family farms, county records, old city telephone directories, and family Bibles that list births and deaths.
- Examine old photos for clues.
- Use the Web. See Beyond Literature: Technology Connection, p. 44.

Humanities: Art

The Purple Quilt, by Faith Ringgold

Faith Ringgold is known for her colorful, soft sculptures and story quilts. Like Alex Haley, her work is influenced by the African American community and her family.

Ask students what impressions they get from looking at this section of Ringgold's quilt art. *Responses may include a family portrait, class picture, a flag, or a range of other impressions.*

Develop Understanding

One-Minute Insight In his essay, Haley tells the story behind *Roots: The Saga of An American Family*. After years of intense research, Haley traces one branch of his family tree back to the Kinte clan in what is today called the Republic of the Gambia. In an emotional moment, he listens as a Gambian *griot* recounts the history of the Kinte clan. The moment climaxes in Haley's realization that Kunta Kinte of the griot's tale is his own ancestor—the very same "Kin-tay" of his grandmother's stories. By discovering the details of his ancestry, Haley has found himself.

Team Teaching Strategy

The historical and geographical aspects of Haley's essay about researching his family history offer a strong connection to social studies. You may want to coordinate with a social studies teacher to plan ways to extend instruction.

Customize for *English Language Learners*

As students read, help them paraphrase and simplify some of the selection's longer sentences. For example, on p. 39, the sentence beginning "The microfilm rolls were delivered, and I turned them . . ." might be paraphrased as, "The microfilm rolls were brought to me. I looked at them with interest. I saw many names."

Customize for *Visual/Spatial Learners*

Have students use a globe or world map to trace Alex Haley's travels throughout North America, Europe, and Africa, as he researches his family's ancestral roots.

Block Scheduling Strategies

Consider these suggestions to take advantage of extended class time:

- Before reading, have students complete the Journal Writing activity in Literature and Your Life, p. 45. Then have them work with partners to read the selection and answer Critical Thinking questions on p. 45.
- Alternatively, have students read the essay independently and then meet in small groups to discuss the impact of a personal essay such as Haley's. Ask them to complete the Literary Focus and Build Grammar Skills on p. 46, and/or complete the accompanying **Selection Support,** p. 19 and p. 21. Encourage them to apply what they have learned about personal essays as you teach the Speaking and Listening Mini-Lesson on p. 42 of the Teacher Edition.
- If you have access to technology, have students use the *Writer's Solution Writing Lab CD-ROM* to prepare for and complete the Writing Mini-Lesson.

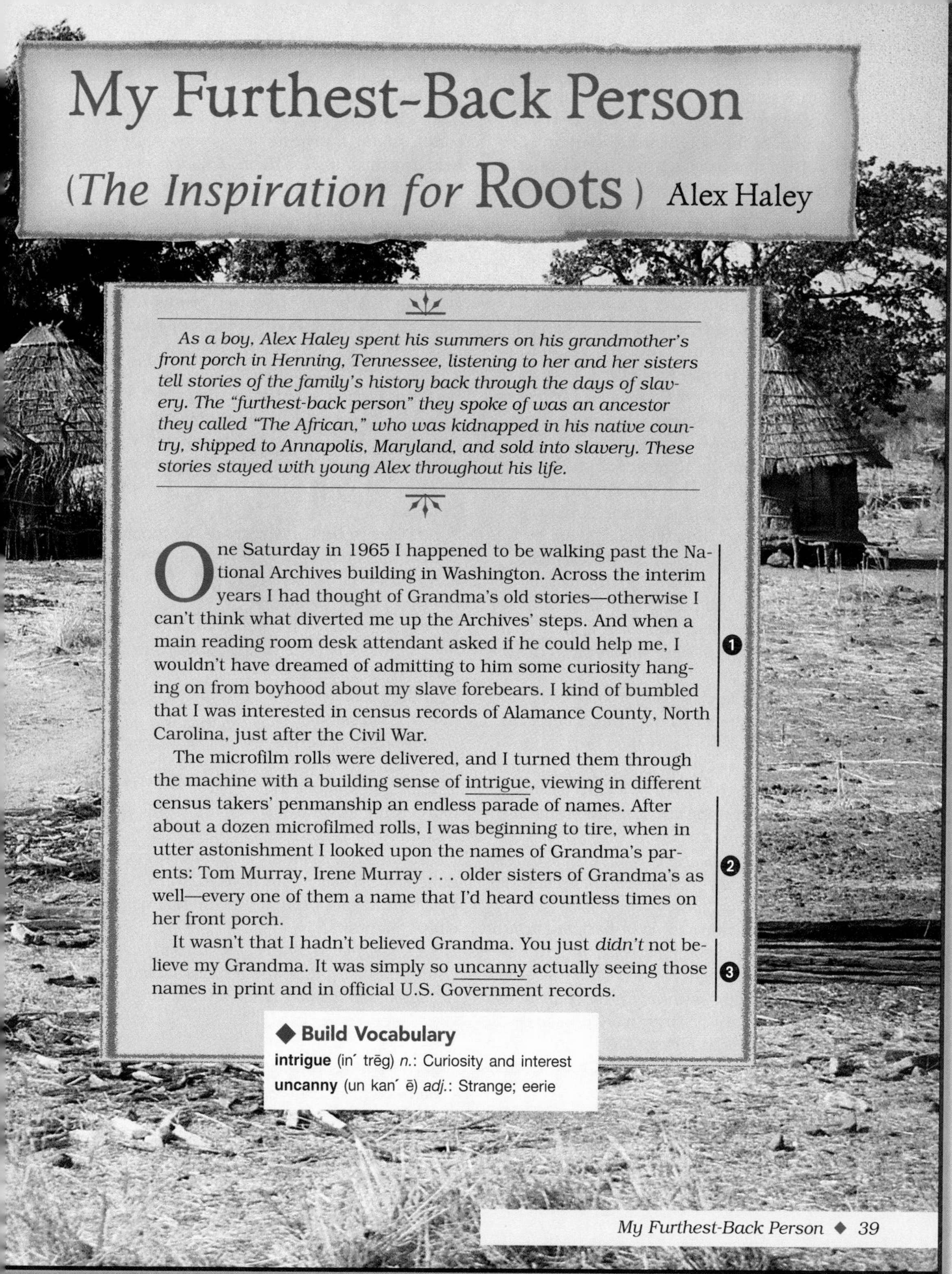

My Furthest-Back Person

(*The Inspiration for* Roots) Alex Haley

As a boy, Alex Haley spent his summers on his grandmother's front porch in Henning, Tennessee, listening to her and her sisters tell stories of the family's history back through the days of slavery. The "furthest-back person" they spoke of was an ancestor they called "The African," who was kidnapped in his native country, shipped to Annapolis, Maryland, and sold into slavery. These stories stayed with young Alex throughout his life.

One Saturday in 1965 I happened to be walking past the National Archives building in Washington. Across the interim years I had thought of Grandma's old stories—otherwise I can't think what diverted me up the Archives' steps. And when a main reading room desk attendant asked if he could help me, I wouldn't have dreamed of admitting to him some curiosity hanging on from boyhood about my slave forebears. I kind of bumbled that I was interested in census records of Alamance County, North Carolina, just after the Civil War. ❶

The microfilm rolls were delivered, and I turned them through the machine with a building sense of intrigue, viewing in different census takers' penmanship an endless parade of names. After about a dozen microfilmed rolls, I was beginning to tire, when in utter astonishment I looked upon the names of Grandma's parents: Tom Murray, Irene Murray . . . older sisters of Grandma's as well—every one of them a name that I'd heard countless times on her front porch. ❷

It wasn't that I hadn't believed Grandma. You just *didn't* not believe my Grandma. It was simply so uncanny actually seeing those names in print and in official U.S. Government records. ❸

◆ Build Vocabulary

intrigue (in´ trēg) *n.*: Curiosity and interest

uncanny (un kan´ ē) *adj.*: Strange; eerie

◆ Literary Focus

❶ **Personal Essay** Ask students to find clues in the first paragraph that tell them this is a personal essay. *Use of the pronoun "I," Haley's conversational style, the way he refers to his grandmother as "Grandma," and the personal feelings he shares are clues.*

◆ Reading Strategy

❷ **Break Down Long Sentences** Read the sentence "After about a dozen . . . on her front porch" aloud to the class. Have them locate the subject and then paraphrase by breaking this long sentence down into shorter sentences and placing "I" at the beginning of each piece. *I looked at microfilm rolls. I got tired. I was surprised to find names of Grandma's relatives.*

◆ Literature and Your Life

❸ Invite students to share their reactions to Haley's comments about his grandmother. *Some students may be amused. Others may make a connection between Haley's feelings about Grandma and their own feelings about a grandparent or other relative.*

Customize for *Visual/Spatial Learners*

Suggest that students use the photograph on these pages to visualize Haley's search for information. Ask them to explain how he might feel when arriving in an African village such as the one pictured here. Encourage students to use this and other visuals accompanying the story to follow Haley's journey.

Humanities: Television Film

The TV mini-series *Roots* (1977), which was based on the book *Roots: The Saga of An American Family*, was a cultural phenomenon in the U.S. It was one of the most popular shows in American TV history. A sequel aired in 1979 as *Roots: The Next Generations*. Another sequel, *Queen* (1993), also appeared as a book and TV mini-series.

Roots spurred much interest in family trees. According to a recent *American Demographics* article, more than 100 million Americans are now looking for their roots and 64 million have written a family history or created a family tree. One resource is the Kinte Foundation, created in 1972 by Haley and his brothers to store records that aid in tracing African American genealogy.

1. Why do you think the TV mini-series *Roots* was so popular when it first aired? *Possible answers: It was different from other TV shows; it was about a family; it told a true personal story.*
2. What might motivate you to begin a new and difficult project such as tracing your roots? *Students should support answers they give, such as a strong interest and seeing someone else involved in a similar project.*

◆ Critical Thinking

❶ **Draw Conclusions** How might others' interest in Haley's search help him find the information he needs? *They might offer suggestions or bring him documents quickly.*

◆ Build Vocabulary

❷ **Using the Prefix *un-*** Tell students that *tongue* may mean "language." Then point out the word *unknown.* Ask students to break the word into its parts, and discuss its meaning in relation to a tongue, or language. *The word* unknown *breaks down into* un- + known. Unknown-tongue *means a language that is "not known."*

◆ Reading Strategy

❸ **Break Down Long Sentences** Ask students to find the subject of this sentence and place it at the beginning. Then find the words that tell you about the subject. Dr. Jan Vansina *was particularly intriguing . . . .*

◆ Literary Focus

❹ **Personal Essay** Elicit responses such as the following: *This detail makes the essay more personal by letting you see the author as a child.*

◆ Build Grammar Skills

❺ **Collective Nouns** Point out the word *family.* Tell students that it is a collective noun because its singular form names a group of people. To help reinforce this concept, you may also want to point out the word *brothers* in the previous paragraph. Help students see that this noun also names a group of people, but it does so because the *-s* forms a plural of the noun *brother.* Therefore, *brothers* is not a collective noun.

During the next several months I was back in Washington whenever possible, in the Archives, the Library of Congress, the Daughters of the American Revolution Library. ❶ (Whenever black attendants understood the idea of my search, documents I requested reached me with miraculous speed.) In one source or another during 1966 I was able to document at least the highlights of the cherished family story. I would have given anything to have told Grandma, but, sadly, in 1949 she had gone. So I went and told the only survivor of those Henning front-porch storytellers: Cousin Georgia Anderson, now in her 80's in Kansas City, Kan. Wrinkled, bent, not well herself, she was so overjoyed, repeating to me the old stories and sounds; they were like Henning echoes: "Yeah, boy, that African say his name was *'Kin-tay'*; he say the banjo was *'ko,'* an' the river *'Kamby Bolong,'* an' he was off choppin' some wood to make his drum when they grabbed 'im!" Cousin Georgia grew so excited we had to stop her, calm her down, "You go 'head, boy! Your grandma an' all of 'em—they up there watching what you do!"

That week I flew to London on a magazine assignment. Since by now I was steeped in the old, in the past, scarcely a tour guide missed me—I was awed at so many historical places and treasures I'd heard of and read of. I came upon the Rosetta stone in the British Museum, marveling anew at how Jean Champollion, the French archaeologist, had miraculously deciphered its ancient demotic and hieroglyphic texts[1] . . .

The thrill of that just kept hanging around in my head. I was on a jet returning to New York when a thought hit me. Those strange, ❷ unknown-tongue sounds, always part of our family's old story . . . they were obviously bits of our original African *"Kin-tay's"* native tongue. What specific tongue? Could I somehow find out?

1. **demotic and hieroglyphic texts** (dē mät´ ik and hī´ ər ō´ glif´ ik) *adj.:* Ancient Egyptian writing, using symbols and pictures to represent words.

Back in New York, I began making visits to the United Nations Headquarters lobby; it wasn't hard to spot Africans. I'd stop any I could, asking if my bits of phonetic sounds held any meaning for them. A couple of dozen Africans quickly looked at me, listened, and took off—understandably dubious about some Tennesseean's accent alleging "African" sounds.

My research assistant, George Sims (we grew up together in Henning), brought me some names of ranking scholars of African linguistics. One was particularly intriguing: a Belgian- and English-educated Dr. Jan Vansina; he had spent his early career living in West African villages, studying and tape-recording countless oral histories that were narrated by certain very old African men; he had written a standard textbook, "The Oral Tradition." ❸

So I flew to the University of Wisconsin to see Dr. Vansina. In his living room I told him every bit of the family story in the fullest detail that I could remember it. Then, intensely, he queried me about the story's relay across the generations, about the gibberish of "*k*" sounds Grandma had fiercely muttered to herself while doing her housework, with my brothers and me giggling beyond her hearing at what we had dubbed "Grandma's noises." ❹

> **◆ Literary Focus**
> In what way does this detail about giggling boys make the essay personal?

Dr. Vansina, his manner very serious, finally said, "These sounds your family has kept sound very probably of the tongue called 'Mandinka.'" ❺

I'd never heard of any "Mandinka." Grandma just told of the African saying "*ko*" for banjo, or "*Kamby Bolong*" for a Virginia river.

◆ Build Vocabulary

cherished (cher´ ishd) *adj.:* Beloved; valued
queried (kwir´ ēd) *v.:* Asked
eminent (em´ ə nənt) *adj.:* Distinguished or outstanding

Cross-Curricular Connection: Social Studies

Transatlantic slave trade began during the early sixteenth century and continued until the 1880's. More than 11 million Africans were transported to lives of servitude in the Americas. Enslaved people mainly came from the area that was called Guinea, extending south more than 3,700 miles from the Senegal River through modern-day Gambia, Ghana, Nigeria, Zaire, and Angola.

Trade routes followed a triangular pattern. Ships from Europe sailed to Africa with manufactured goods such as knives, guns, and cloth, which were bartered to the local rulers for slaves. The second leg of the triangle, known as the middle passage, crossed the Atlantic to the Americas or the Caribbean, where the Africans were sold as slaves. Traders then bought molasses, cotton, and tobacco to take back to Europe.

Today, Republic of the Gambia is a nation of 1.2 million people on the Atlantic Coast near the western tip of Africa. Have students find Gambia on a map and deduce why its location lent itself to slave-trading. *Gambia's location on the Atlantic Ocean in western Africa allowed easy trade routes between Europe, the Americas, and Africa.*

Among Mandinka stringed instruments, Dr. Vansina said, one of the oldest was the "*kora.*"

"*Bolong,*" he said, was clearly Mandinka for "river." Preceded by "*Kamby,*" it very likely meant "Gambia River."

Dr. Vansina telephoned an eminent Africanist colleague, Dr. Philip Curtin. He said that the phonetic "*Kin-tay*" was correctly spelled "*Kinte,*" a very old clan that had originated in Old Mali. The Kinte men traditionally were blacksmiths, and the women were potters and weavers.

6 I knew I must get to the Gambia River.

The first native Gambian I could locate in the U.S. was named Ebou Manga, then a junior attending Hamilton College in upstate Clinton, N.Y. He and I flew to Dakar, Senegal, then took a smaller plane to Yundum Airport, and rode in a van to Gambia's capital, Bathurst. Ebou and his father assembled eight Gambia government officials. I told them Grandma's stories, every detail I could remember, as they listened intently, then reacted. "'*Kamby Bolong*' of course is Gambia River!" I heard. "But more clue is your forefather's saying his name was '*Kinte.*'" Then they told me something I would never ever have fantasized—that in places in the back country lived very old men, commonly called *griots,* who could tell centuries of the histories of certain very old family clans. As for *Kintes,* they pointed out to me on a map some family villages, Kinte-Kundah, and Kinte-Kundah Janneh-Ya, for instance. 7

The Gambian officials said they would try to help me. I returned to New York dazed. It is embarrassing to me now, but despite Grandma's stories, I'd never been concerned much with Africa, and I had the routine images of African people living mostly in exotic jungles. But a compulsion now laid hold of me to learn all I could, and I began devouring books about Africa, especially about the slave trade. Then one Thursday's mail contained a letter from one of the Gambian officials, inviting me to return there.

Monday I was back in Bathurst. It galvanized me when the officials said that a *griot* had been located who told the *Kinte* clan history—his name was Kebba Kanga Fofana. To reach him, I discovered, required a modified safari: renting a launch to get upriver, two land vehicles to carry supplies by a round-about land route, and employing finally 14 people, including three interpreters and four musicians, since a *griot* would not speak the revered clan histories without background music. 9 10

◆ **Reading Strategy** Break down this sentence to explain what "galvanized" Haley, making him pay attention.

8 ▶ **Critical Viewing** This photograph and the one on page 43 are stills from the television mini-series about Haley's experience. What does the posture of the actors reveal about the relationship between their characters? **[Analyze]**

Comprehension Check ☑

6 Why must Haley get to the Gambia River? *The two African scholars have told him that "Kamby Bolong," which was one of the phrases his ancestor said, meant "Gambia River." He thinks if he goes there, he'll find more information.*

Clarification

7 Explain that an African *griot* (grē′ō) is a musician and entertainer whose performance includes tribal histories and genealogies. In a society without a written language, an oral historian serves a most important function—he or she is the source of the group's collective "memory."

▶Critical Viewing◀

8 **Analyze** Suggested response: *The posture of the actors shows one man standing above another man who is in chains. This may indicate that one is in command of the other.*

◆Reading Strategy

9 **Break Down Long Sentences** Possible response: *Hearing that "a griot had been located who told the Kinte clan history" galvanized, or convinced, Haley that he was on the right track and should keep searching.*

Clarification

10 Point out that Africa, the world's second largest continent, contains every kind of land: deserts (including the world's largest—the Sahara), rain forests, swamps, beaches, mountains, and grasslands.

Viewing and Representing Mini-Lesson

Film Review

This mini-lesson supports the Film Review project in the Idea Bank on p.47.

Introduce Tell students that, with a partner, they will present a give-and-take film review after viewing *Roots.* Discuss examples of this type of film review that they may have seen on TV. Point out that film reviewers describe what they see with a critical eye so that their audience can decide whether they may want to see the film.

Develop Give students these tips:

- List the elements you want to criticize, and be sure to review each one.
- Select segments, or clips, of the film that support your opinions.
- Compare segments of the film to corresponding sections of the book *Roots,* to help understand the filmmaker's choices for telling the story.
- Practice with your partner before presenting to your audience.

Apply Have each pair of students make a 3–5-minute multimedia oral presentation to the class, using clips to support their review.

Assess Check that students review and comment on acting, direction, setting, camera work, soundtrack, and story and that presentations are lively, fair, and well supported. Have students use the Peer Assessment: Speaker/Speech form, p.188, in **Alternative Assessment,** to evaluate their own and other reviews.

◆ Literature and Your Life

❶ As Haley nears what may be his ancestors' home, his feelings intensify. Invite students to explain what they think it's like to be a tourist in a strange place. Is it comfortable? Exciting? Why? *Students may suggest feelings of being confused, homesick, or overwhelmed. They may explain that these feelings are a result of differences among people and cultures.*

◆ Critical Thinking

❷ **Connect** In what way do the Gambians' feelings about seeing Haley mirror his feelings about seeing them? *Students may note that Haley has never seen a Gambian—just as the Gambians have never seen an African American.*

Clarification

❸ The official language of the Republic of the Gambia is English, due to several hundred years as a British possession; Gambia achieved independence in 1965. However, more than 40 percent of its people are Mandinka and speak that language.

◆ Critical Thinking

❹ **Compare and Contrast** Ask students to compare and contrast Alex Haley and the griot he meets in the Gambia. *They are alike in that they are both storytellers and interested in family history. They are different because the griot uses music and tells the story aloud, while Haley tells his story through writing.*

Customize for *Musical/Rhythmic Learners*

Suggest that students retell Haley's story as a *griot* might, using music and/or drumming as background. They may want to research *griots* first, or develop their own style based on Haley's description.

The boat Baddibu vibrated upriver, with me acutely tense: Were these Africans maybe viewing me as but another of the pith-helmets?[2] After about two hours, we put in at James Island, for me to see the ruins of the once British-operated James Fort. Here two centuries of slave ships had loaded thousands of cargoes of Gambian tribespeople. The crumbling stones, the deeply oxidized swivel cannon, even some remnant links of chain seemed all but impossible to believe. Then we continued upriver to the left-bank village of Albreda, and there put ashore to continue on foot to Juffure,[3] village of the *griot*. Once more we stopped, for me to see *toubob kolong*, the "white man's well," now almost filled in, in a swampy area with abundant, tall, saw-toothed grass. It was dug two centuries ago to "17 men's height deep" to insure survival drinking water for long-driven, famishing coffles[4] of slaves.

Walking on, I kept wishing that Grandma could hear how her stories had led me to the "*Kamby Bolong*." (Our surviving storyteller Cousin Georgia died in a Kansas City hospital during this same morning, I would learn later.) Finally, Juffure village's playing children, sighting us, flashed an alert. The 70-odd people came rushing from their circular, thatch-roofed, mud-walled huts, with goats bounding up and about, and parrots squawking from up in the palms. I sensed him in advance somehow, the small man amid them, wearing a pillbox cap and an off-white robe—the *griot*. Then the interpreters went to him, as the villagers thronged around me. ❶

And it hit me like a gale wind: every one of them, the whole crowd, was *jet black*. An enormous sense of guilt swept me—a sense of being some kind of hybrid . . . a sense of being impure among the pure. It was an awful sensation.

The old *griot* stepped away from my interpreters and the crowd quickly swarmed around him—all of them buzzing. An interpreter named A.B.C. Salla came to me; he whispered: "Why they stare at you so, they have never seen here a black American." And that hit me: I was symbolizing for them twenty-five millions of us they had never seen. What did they think of me—of us? ❷

Then abruptly the old *griot* was briskly walking toward me. His eyes boring into mine, he spoke in Mandinka, as if instinctively I should understand—and A.B.C. Salla translated: ❸

"Yes . . . we have been told by the forefathers . . . that many of us from this place are in exile . . . in that place called America . . . and in other places."

I suppose I physically wavered, and they thought it was the heat; rustling whispers went through the crowd, and a man brought me a low stool. Now the whispering hushed—the musicians had softly begun playing *kora* and *balafon*, and a canvas sling lawn seat was taken by the *griot*, Kebba Kanga Fofana, aged 73 "rains" (one rainy season each year). He seemed to gather himself into a physical rigidity, and he began speaking the *Kinte* clan's ancestral oral history; it came rolling from his mouth across the next hours . . . 17th- and 18th-century *Kinte* lineage details, predominantly what men took wives; the children they "begot," in the order of their births; those children's mates and children. ❹

Events frequently were dated by some proximate[5] singular physical occurrence. It was as if some ancient scroll were printed indelibly within the *griot's* brain. Each few sentences or so, he would pause for an interpreter's translation to me. I distill here the essence:

The *Kinte* clan began in Old Mali, the men generally blacksmiths ". . . who conquered fire," and the women potters and weavers.

2. **pith-helmets** *jargon:* Tourists or hunters on safari, who traditionally wore this type of fabric-covered hard hat.
3. **Juffure** (jo͞o′ fo͞o rā)
4. **coffles** (kôf′ əlz) *n.*: Groups of animals or slaves chained or tied together in a line.
5. **proximate** (präks′ ə mət) *adj.*: Near in time.

Speaking and Listening Mini-Lesson

Storytellers' Circle

This mini-lesson supports the Speaking and Listening activity on p. 47.

Introduce Discuss the elements of a good story with students: plot, interesting characters, and a vivid setting. Point out that storytelling requires performance skills as well as a good story.

Develop Have students choose a family story or another story that interests them. Ask them to outline the story's plot. To tell the story orally, they should memorize the plot. Here are some storytelling techniques:

- Learn the plot by envisioning it as a series of images in your head, like a movie or a set of slides.
- Make a "comic strip" of the plot.
- Draw a story map of the story's events.
- Tell a partner a one-minute version.

Apply Have students prepare to tell their stories. Encourage them to explore different styles of telling. Will they sit, stand, or move around? Will they use gestures or vary their voice for each character? Videotape students telling their stories.

Assess Play students' tapes of their performances. Evaluate each storyteller on his or her attention to plot, characterization, setting, as well as clarity of speaking, and entertainment quality. Have students use the Peer Assessment: Dramatic Performance form, p. 107, in **Alternative Assessment** to evaluate their own and others' storytelling performances.

5 ▶ Critical Viewing Which paragraph of the essay does this photograph bring to life? **[Identify]**

One large branch of the clan moved to Mauretania from where one son of the clan, Kairaba Kunta Kinte, a Moslem Marabout holy man, entered Gambia. He lived first in the village of Pakali N'Ding; he moved next to Jiffarong village; ". . . and then he came here, into our own village of Juffure."

In Juffure, Kairaba Kunta Kinte took his first wife, ". . . a Mandinka maiden, whose name was Sireng. By her, he begot two sons, whose names were Janneh and Saloum. Then he got a second wife, Yaisa. By her, he begot a son, Omoro."

The three sons became men in Juffure. Janneh and Saloum went off and found a new village, Kinte-Kundah Janneh-Ya. "And then Omoro, the youngest son, when he had 30 rains, took as a wife a maiden, Binta Kebba.

"And by her, he begot four sons—Kunta, Lamin, Suwadu, and Madi . . ."

Sometimes, a "begotten," after his naming, would be accompanied by some later-occurring detail, perhaps as ". . . in time of big water (flood), he slew a water buffalo." Having named those four sons, now the *griot* stated such a detail.

"About the time the king's soldiers came, the eldest of these four sons, Kunta, when he had about 16 rains, went away from his village, to chop wood to make a drum . . . and he was never seen again . . ."

6 ◆ Reading Strategy Who is the subject of the sentence, and what did he do?

Goose-pimples the size of lemons seemed to pop all over me. In my knapsack were my cumulative notebooks, the first of them including how in my boyhood, my Grandma, Cousin Georgia and the others told of the African "*Kin-tay*" who always said he was kidnapped near his village—while chopping wood to make a drum . . . 7

I showed the interpreter, he showed and told the *griot*, who excitedly told the people; they grew very agitated. Abruptly then they formed a human ring, encircling me, dancing and chanting. Perhaps a dozen of the women carrying their infant babies rushed in toward me, thrusting the infants into my arms conveying, I would later learn, "the laying on of hands . . . through this flesh which is us, we are you, and you are us." The men hurried me into their mosque, their Arabic praying later being translated outside: "Thanks be to Allah for returning the long lost from among us." Direct descendants of Kunta Kinte's blood brothers were hastened, some of them from nearby villages, for a family portrait to be taken with me, surrounded by actual ancestral sixth cousins. More symbolic acts filled the remaining day.

When they would let me leave, for some reason I wanted to go away over the African

▶ Critical Viewing◀

5 Identify *The photograph shows the paragraph beginning "I showed the interpreter . . . ," because it describes Haley being surrounded by the joyful villagers as they realize he is related to them by blood.*

◆ Reading Strategy

6 Break Down Long Sentences Students should answer: *Kunta is the subject. He "went away from his village, to chop wood . . . ," but never came back.*

◆ Literary Focus

7 Personal Essay Why do you think Haley included this detail about goose-pimples? *Haley used this detail to show how the griot's story made him feel and how important hearing that story was to him.*

Customize for
English Language Learners

Explain to students that *begot* in the first and third full paragraphs on this page means "to father a baby." Make sure they understand that the *griot* is listing the family's ancestors in order from the most distant to the most recent. It may help to draw a Haley family tree on the board. For example:

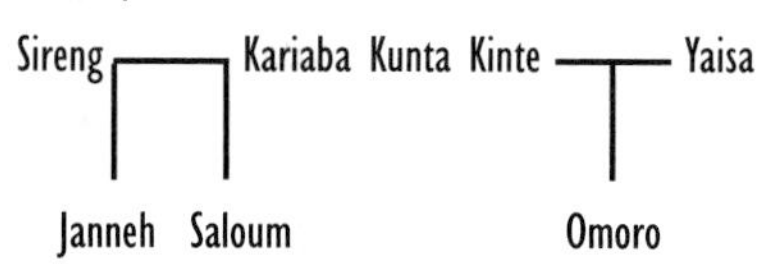

Beyond the Classroom

Career Connection

Journalism Haley worked for many years as a journalist. Although journalists must be good writers, they spend as much—or more—time researching as writing. Researching may include reading books, magazines, or newspapers, or they may search the Internet. Journalists also interview people who are experts in their field or who have experience or knowledge relevant to their topic.

Have students contact a newspaper, magazine, or television or radio station and interview journalists about their jobs. How do they find their topics? What interview questions do they ask? How do they organize their notes before writing? What do they like/dislike about their jobs?

Community Connection

Community Elders A *griot* is an older respected community leader. Have students identify an elder of their family or community. Encourage students to talk to them about family/community history. What stories can these local "griots" tell?

◆ Literary Focus

❶ **Personal Essay** Students may respond: *Haley makes readers feel as if they are his close friends by sharing his deepest emotions with them.*

◆ Critical Thinking

❷ **Interpret** Ask students to explain what Haley means by this statement. *Each person has millions of ancestors, who have all helped to shape that person's past.*

◆ Reading Strategy

❸ **Break Down Long Sentences** Help students identify the subject, verb, and direct object of this sentence. Then guide them to restate it as a simple sentence. *subject*—feverish searching; *verb*—identified; *direct object*—Colonel O'Hare's Forces: *Feverish searching identified Colonel O'Hare's forces that were sent to protect James Fort in 1767.*

◆ Literature and Your Life

❹ Elicit responses such as the following: *People may have a mixture of feelings such as excitement, awe, and pride when they see family names in old records.*

Beyond Literature

Make sure that students' research on the Internet is supervised by you or another adult. You may want to choose one or two Web pages to guide students' research, and suggest that they use information from those pages as a starting point to continue their research, using other sources.

land. Dazed, silent in the bumping Land Rover, I heard the cutting staccato of talking drums. Then when we sighted the next village, its people came thronging to meet us. They were all—little naked ones to wizened elders—waving, beaming; amid a cacophony of crying out; and then my ears identified their words: "*Meester Kinte! Meester Kinte!*"

Let me tell you something: I am a man. But I remember the sob surging up from my feet, flinging up my hands before my face and bawling as I had not done since I was a baby . . . the jet-black Africans were jostling,[6] staring . . . I didn't care, with the feelings surging. If you really knew the odyssey of us millions of black Americans, if you really knew how we came in the seeds of our forefathers, captured, driven, beaten, inspected, bought, branded, chained in foul ships, if you really knew, you needed weeping . . .

> **◆ Literary Focus** ❶
> How do these details of his reaction create a close bond between you and Haley?

❷

Back home, I knew that what I must write, really, was our black saga, where any individual's past is the essence of the millions'. Now flat broke, I went to some editors I knew, describing the Gambian miracle, and my desire to pursue the research; Doubleday contracted to publish, and Reader's Digest to condense the projected book; then I had advances to travel further.

What ship brought Kinte to Grandma's "Naplis" (Annapolis, Md., obviously)? The old *griot's* time reference to "king's soldiers" sent me flying to London. ❸ Feverish searching at last identified, in British Parliament records, "Colonel O'Hare's Forces," dispatched in mid-1767 to protect the then British-held James Fort whose ruins I'd visited. So Kunta Kinte was down in some ship probably sailing later that summer from the Gambia River to Annapolis.

Now I feel it was fated that I had taught myself to write in the U.S. Coast Guard. For the sea dramas I had concentrated on had given me years of experience searching among yellowing old U.S. maritime records. So now in English 18th Century marine records I finally tracked ships reporting themselves in and out to the Commandant of the Gambia River's James Fort. And then early one afternoon I found that a Lord Ligonier under a Captain Thomas Davies had sailed on the Sabbath of July 5, 1767. Her cargo: 3,265 elephants' teeth, 3,700 pounds of beeswax, 800 pounds of cotton, 32 ounces of Gambian gold and 140 slaves; her destination: "Annapolis."

That night I recrossed the Atlantic. In the Library of Congress the Lord Ligonier's arrival was one brief line in "Shipping In The Port Of Annapolis—1748–1775." I located the author, Vaughan W. Brown, in his Baltimore brokerage office. He drove to Historic

6. **jostling** (jäs′ ling) *v.*: Bumping and pushing, as in a crowd.

Beyond Literature

Technology Connection

Genealogy on the Internet If you wanted to find your "furthest-back person," how would you do it? The Internet is a great place to start. A net search of the key word *genealogy* will give you links to organizations and journals that specialize in genealogy, like the National Genealogical Society. Their home pages have lists of resources and tips for how to use them. Or you can do a more specific search based on where your family came from or your family's ethnic group.

Cross-Curricular Activity

Digging Up Your Roots Use the Internet to learn about your family history. Then, create a family tree based on what you discover. Share your results with classmates, describing the steps you took to get the information.

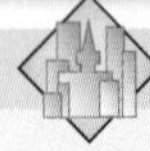

Beyond the Classroom

Workplace Skills

Point out that Alex Haley successfully interviews many people in his search for his family's roots. Then tell students that interviewing skills are essential for a wide variety of jobs.

Discuss with students what makes a good interviewer, such as being prepared, asking questions appropriate to the topic, speaking clearly, and listening carefully.

Invite students to brainstorm for a list of jobs that require interviewing skills. Possibilities include newspaper/television reporter, telephone surveyor, personnel manager, pollster, market researcher, lawyer, nurse, and psychologist. Discuss which kinds of questions elicit the most information from interviewees, establishing that yes-and-no questions are the least productive.

Invite students to choose one of these jobs, and, with a partner, take turns as interviewer/interviewee in conducting an interview based on the type of questions someone with that job would ask.

Annapolis, the city's historical society, and found me further documentation of her arrival on Sept. 29, 1767. (Exactly two centuries later, Sept. 29, 1967, standing, staring seaward from an Annapolis pier, again I knew tears.) More help came in the Maryland Hall of Records. Archivist Phebe Jacobsen found the Lord Ligonier's arriving customs declaration listing, "98 Negroes"—so in her 86-day crossing, 42 Gambians had died, one among the survivors being 16-year-old Kunta Kinte. Then the microfilmed Oct. 1, 1767, Maryland Gazette contained, on page two, an announcement to prospective buyers from the ship's agents, Daniel of St. Thos. Jenifer and John Ridout (the Governor's secretary): "from the River GAMBIA, in AFRICA . . . a cargo of choice, healthy SLAVES . . ."

◆ **Literature and Your Life**
What feelings do you think people have as they research family records in this way? Explain. 4

◆ **Build Vocabulary**
destination (des´ tə nā´ shən) *n.*: The place to which something is being sent

Guide for Responding

◆ Literature and Your Life

Reader's Response What questions would you like to ask Haley about his experience?

Thematic Focus Some people say that our identity is the story we tell about ourselves. How did Haley's research help him tell a better story about himself?

Journal Writing Jot down what you know about your own family's ancestry and what you'd like to learn. List possible sources of information, like family photographs, letters and diaries, and government records.

☑ Check Your Comprehension

1. What does Haley discover "One Saturday in 1965"?
2. Tell how clues from the "family's old story" lead Haley to Gambia as the family's original home.
3. Summarize what Haley learns on his second trip to Gambia.
4. Describe Haley's reaction to villagers calling him *"Meester Kinte!"*
5. What does Haley decide to write?

◆ Critical Thinking

INTERPRET

1. How is Haley's quest, from the very beginning, both a mental puzzle and an emotional thrill? **[Interpret]**
2. What is similar and different about the African sounds in Haley's family stories and the writing on the Rosetta stone? **[Compare and Contrast]**
3. In what way are the tales of the *griot* and the tales of Haley's family like two parts of the same puzzle? **[Connect]**
4. When villagers greeted Haley as *"Meester Kinte,"* what did he find that had been lost for 200 years? **[Draw Conclusions]**

EVALUATE

5. Was it "fated" that Haley would solve the mystery of "the African," or was it just chance? Explain. **[Make a Judgment]**

EXTEND

6. This essay suggests that, in addition to being special, a person needs to feel part of a larger group. Explain why you agree or disagree. **[Social Studies Link]**

Beyond the Selection

FURTHER READING

Other Works by Alex Haley

Roots: The Saga of An American Family

Queen: The Story of An American Family

Other Works on the Theme of Finding Yourself

Beginners' Ancestor Research Kit, Philip Beck

Ancestors: A Beginner's Guide to Family History and Genealogy, by Jim Willard, Terry Willard, and Jane Wilson

INTERNET

We suggest the following sites on the Internet (all Web sites are subject to change).

For more information about Alex Haley:
http://www.historychannel.com/community/roots/transcript4.html

For genealogy information:
http://www.kbyu. org/ancestors/

We *strongly recommend* that you preview these sites before you send students to them.

Reinforce and Extend

Answers

◆ Literature and Your Life

Reader's Response Students' questions should focus on Haley's search and his reactions to that search.

Thematic Focus Students may comment that Haley's research lets him tell a more complete story about himself, filling in details about his family's links to Gambia.

☑ Check Your Comprehension

1. He discovers the names of his great-grandparents in the records of the National Archives.
2. Haley finds someone who identifies the words he knows as part of a language called Mandinka that is spoken in Gambia.
3. He hears a history of the Kinte clan, including Kunta Kinte, who disappeared from his village. Haley realizes Kunta Kinte is probably his African ancestor.
4. Haley becomes very emotional.
5. He decides to write about his family.

◆ Critical Thinking

1. It is a mental puzzle because he must find and put together evidence of his family's history like pieces of a puzzle. It is an emotional thrill because he learns more about his family and himself.
2. They are similar in that both need to be deciphered. They are different because the African sounds are heard and the writing on the Rosetta stone is seen.
3. Haley's relatives told about the family's history back to the first African ancestor brought to America. The *griot* tells the part that happened before in Africa. Together they complete the family history.
4. He found the connection to his African ancestors that had almost been lost.
5. Some students may say it was chance that Haley's search began when he walked past the National Archives. Others may say Haley was always interested in his family's history, just like his grandmother and Cousin Georgia.
6. Students should support their responses with examples of people asserting or denying their group identities.

Answers

◆ **Reading Strategy**

1. Subject: "I"; about the subject: "began making visits to the United Nations Headquarters lobby . . ."
2. Subject: "I"; about the subject: "wanted to go away over the African land."

◆ **Build Vocabulary**

Using the Prefix *Un-*

1. Africa was unmapped (not mapped or charted) for him because he knew so little about it.
2. That Haley broke down in tears when villagers greeted him as "Meester Kinte" shows he was unafraid (not afraid) to show his emotions.

Spelling Strategy

1. uneven; 2. replace;
3. unnecessary; 4. reelect

Using the Word Bank

1. Yes; *cherished* means "held dear."
2. Yes; he was highly respected for his achievements.
3. No; Haley went to Gambia, not Ghana.
4. No; the more he discovered, the more interested he was.
5. Yes; it made him feel a little strange or eerie.
6. Yes; people probably asked him for advice since he had spent years researching his own family history.

◆ **Literary Focus**

1. The phrase "Let me tell you something" makes the reader feel close to Haley because it sounds as if he is speaking to us in conversation.
2. The exact words shouted by the villagers—"Meester Kinte"—make the essay personal by putting the reader in Haley's shoes; we hear what he heard.
3. Haley's confession of emotion—"the sob surging up from my feet . . ."—lets the reader share his deep feelings.

◆ **Build Grammar Skills**

Practice

1. family; 2. crew; 3. flock;
4. people; majority; 5. dozen

Writing Application

Possible responses:

1. The orchestra practiced the symphony.
2. The team is playing well this year.
3. The army went to war.

Guide for Responding *(continued)*

◆ **Reading Strategy**

BREAK DOWN LONG SENTENCES

When you **break down long sentences,** you find the subject and what the sentence tells about it. Now test your skills again. On your paper, underline the subject of each sentence, and circle the words that tell you about the subject.

1. Back in New York, I began making visits to the United Nations Headquarters lobby. . . .
2. When they would let me leave, for some reason I wanted to go away over the African land.

◆ **Build Vocabulary**

USING THE PREFIX *un-*

Use your knowledge of the prefix *un-* ("not" or "the opposite of") to answer these questions.

1. Why was Africa *unmapped* territory for Haley before he began his research?
2. What incident in Gambia proves that Haley was *unafraid* of showing his emotions?

SPELLING STRATEGY

When you add a prefix to a word, you don't change the spelling of the original word:

un- + canny = uncanny

Write the following words correctly.

1. un- + even   **3.** un- + necessary
2. re- + place   **4.** re- + elect

USING THE WORD BANK

Answer each question yes or no. Then explain your responses.

1. If a project is *cherished*, is it valued?
2. Was Alex Haley an *eminent* writer?
3. Was Ghana Haley's *destination* in Africa?
4. Did the *intrigue* of the quest decrease for Haley?
5. Did seeing his great-grandparents' names in census records give Haley an *uncanny* feeling?
6. Is it likely that people *queried* Haley about how to find their own roots?

◆ **Literary Focus**

PERSONAL ESSAY

A **personal essay** is a brief nonfiction account about a memorable event from the writer's life. Haley's essay gives you the feeling of sitting comfortably with him as he tells you about his life. To create that special bond with you, he uses phrases from casual conversation, such as "I wouldn't have dreamed of . . ." and "I kind of bumbled that I was interested. . . ." He also includes precise details, like his cousin's words, that help you experience what he did. Finally, he expresses emotions that you can share with him.

Reread the last six paragraphs of the essay. Find these elements in the passage you've read, and explain how each makes the essay more personal.

1. conversational phrases
2. people's exact words
3. expressions of emotion

◆ **Build Grammar Skills**

COLLECTIVE NOUNS

Haley's essay is about individuals and the groups from which they come. Therefore, it isn't surprising that he uses **collective nouns,** words whose singular form names a group of persons, animals, or objects. *Crowd,* for example, is a collective noun:

The *crowd* surrounded him.

Other examples are *team, jury, herd,* and *audience.*

Practice On your paper, write these sentences. Then underline the collective noun in each.

1. Haley was interested in the history of his family.
2. In Africa, the crew of the boat took him upriver.
3. He saw the flock circling over the boat.
4. He met many people, and the majority were nice.
5. A dozen of the African musical instruments were unknown to him.

Writing Application Write sentences with each of the following collective nouns: *orchestra, team, army.*

Writer's Solution

For additional instruction and practice, use the lesson in the *Writer's Solution Language Lab CD-ROM* on Using Nouns and the practice page on Different Kinds of Nouns, p. 6, in the *Writer's Solution Grammar Practice Book.*

Build Your Portfolio

Idea Bank

Writing

1. Captions Write brief but informative captions for three or four photographs in your family's album. Identify the people in each picture, the occasion on which it was taken, and the date.

2. Book Jacket A jacket, the paper cover of a book, contains interesting information about the book and the author. Write jacket copy for *Roots*, the book that came out of Haley's experiences in "My Furthest-Back Person."

3. Proposal As Haley, write a proposal that will interest a publisher to want to publish your book. Explain what you'll include and what you've done so far. Also, explain why your book will appeal to a wide audience.

Speaking and Listening

4. Speaker's Introduction Suppose that Alex Haley could speak to your class. Briefly introduce him to your classmates, telling them who he is and what he'll discuss. **[Performing Arts Link]**

5. Storytellers' Circle Get together with two or three classmates and tell one another stories about your families. Record your performance, and play the recording for the class. **[Performing Arts Link; Social Studies Link]**

Projects

6. Family Chart Ask your teacher how to chart family births, marriages, and deaths. Then, create a chart for your own family or for one that is famous in history. Interview people, research family records, or study history books to gather facts. **[Social Studies Link; Art Link]**

7. Film Review **[Group Activity]** Rent one or more of the episodes in the television mini-series *Roots*. Then, with a group, review the film for classmates. Each group member can discuss a different element of the film, including the acting, directing, setting, camera work, soundtrack, and story. **[Social Studies Link; Media Link]**

Writing Mini-Lesson

I-Search Paper

Haley's personal essay is in some ways very much like an I-Search paper. This type of paper not only reports on a topic but also describes the adventure involved in the research itself. Write an I-Search paper about a topic that interests you. As Haley does in his essay, include the story of *how* you learned as you report on *what* you learned.

Writing Skills Focus: Elaborate With Precise Details

You can bring writing to life by giving readers **precise details** rather than general statements. Haley uses such details to make you a partner in his discoveries. For example, his remark about the varying penmanship of census takers is a detail that helps you *see* the microfilmed rolls:

Model From the Essay

. . . I turned them through the machine with a building sense of intrigue, viewing in different census takers' penmanship an endless parade of names.

Prewriting Research a topic that interests you by reading books and encyclopedia articles. Also, interview people who know about the subject. Besides taking notes on the facts you learn, record details of your research adventure: people you meet and places to which you travel.

Drafting Using precise details, weave your research adventure into your report on the facts.

Revising Scan your paper for dull, general statements, like "I read the rolls of microfilm and found the names." Spice them up with precise details: "There, *hovering in and out of focus*, were the names for which I was looking."

◆ **Grammar Application**

With a highlighter pen, identify any collective nouns you've used.

Idea Bank

Following are suggestions for matching the Idea Bank topics with your students' performance levels and learning modalities:

Customize for *Performance Levels*

Less Advanced Students: 1, 7
Average Students: 2, 4, 5, 6, 7
More Advanced Students: 3, 5, 6, 7

Customize for *Learning Modalities*

Visual/Spatial: 1
Verbal/Linguistic: 2, 3, 4, 5, 7
Bodily/Kinesthetic: 5
Interpersonal: 4, 5, 7
Logical/Mathematical: 6
Intrapersonal: 5

Writing Mini-Lesson

Refer students to the Writing Handbook in the back of the book for instructions on the writing process and for further information on reports.

Writer's Solution

Writing Lab CD-ROM

Have students complete the tutorial on Reports. Follow these steps:

1. Have students use the Inspirations for Reports to stimulate topic ideas.
2. Suggest students use the Notecard activity to help them group their information.
3. Have students use the unity and coherence revision checker.

Writer's Solution Sourcebook

Have students use Chapter 7, "Reports," pp. 200–233, for additional support. The chapter includes in-depth instruction on organizing information, p. 222.

✓ ASSESSMENT OPTIONS

Formal Assessment, Selection Test, pp. 10–12, and Assessment Resources Software. The selection test is designed so that it can be easily customized to the performance levels of your students.

Alternative Assessment, p. 4, includes options for less advanced students, more advanced students, visual/spatial learners, verbal/linguistic learners, interpersonal learners, and bodily/kinesthetic learners.

PORTFOLIO ASSESSMENT

Use the following rubrics in the **Alternative Assessment** booklet to assess student writing:
Captions: Technical Description/Explanation, p. 102
Book Jacket: Description, p. 84
Proposal: Business Letter/Memo, p. 100
Writing Mini-Lesson: Research Report/Paper, p. 93

Prepare and Engage

OBJECTIVES

1. To read, comprehend, and interpret a story
2. To relate a story to personal experience
3. To use context to unlock meaning
4. To analyze the importance of time in a story setting
5. To build vocabulary in context and learn the suffix *-ist*
6. To develop skill in using concrete and abstract nouns
7. To write a description of a place using spatial details
8. To respond to the story through writing, speaking and listening, and projects

SKILLS INSTRUCTION

Vocabulary: Suffixes: *-ist*
Spelling: Adding Suffixes: *-ist*
Grammar: Concrete and Abstract Nouns
Reading Strategy: Use Context to Unlock Meaning
Literary Focus: Time in a Setting
Writing: Spatial Details
Speaking and Listening: Leisure Time Presentation (Teacher Edition)
Critical Viewing: Support

PORTFOLIO OPPORTUNITIES

Writing: Letters; Time-Travel Story; Psychiatrist's Report
Writing Mini-Lesson: Description of a Place
Speaking and Listening: Oral History; Leisure Time Presentation
Projects: Poster Series on Train Travel; Survey

More About the Author
Jack Finney published *The Third Level,* a collection of short stories, soon after his science-fiction novel *The Body Snatchers* was made into a movie in the 1950's. These short stories secured his reputation as a fantasy writer. Publication of *Time and Again* brought him a devoted following of readers who enjoyed his well-researched and richly detailed descriptions of New York City life in the 1880's. Through stories such as "The Third Level," Finney suggests to readers that extraordinary adventures can be found in ordinary places, including a busy train station in a large city.

Guide for Reading

Meet the Author:
Jack Finney (1911–1995)

When you read the writings of Jack Finney, you have to wonder whether he really did learn the secret of time travel. This fantastic idea is at the heart of many of his works, including "The Third Level" and the novel *Time and Again.* When Finney explores the idea of moving through time, he maps out an escape route for travel from a harsh present to an appealing past.

Finney was born in Milwaukee, Wisconsin. After graduating from college, he went to New York City to seek his fortune. While working in advertising, Finney began a second career writing short stories and novels. His science-fiction novel *The Body Snatchers* brought him wider recognition and eventually inspired two film versions.

The Story Behind the Story

Even though "The Third Level" deals with time travel—a fictional and to-date impossible occurrence—the story's characters and setting are drawn from Finney's own experience. Like the writer, the main character has come from the Midwest to New York City. In the story, he makes a reverse trip.

◆ Literature and Your Life

Connect Your Experience

You've probably gotten a glimpse of life in the late 1800's from movies and television. Based on what you know or what you can assume from the photograph on the facing page, what might you like about life in that time? Compare your thoughts to the reactions of this story's narrator, as he travels back to 1894 and finds that time period strangely appealing.

Thematic Focus: Inventing Yourself

How do the time and place in which you live help to shape you? What might happen if your likes and dislikes didn't fit well with your surroundings?

◆ Background for Understanding

History

"The Third Level" is set in New York City's Grand Central Station. Completed in 1913, Grand Central is one of the world's most famous train stations. The huge main room of the station is connected to railroad platforms, subways, and streets by a series of tunnels. In "The Third Level," a tunnel takes an unexpected turn.

◆ Build Vocabulary

Suffixes: *-ist*

The character in "The Third Level" frequently mentions his *psychiatrist.* The word *psychiatrist* ends with the suffix *-ist,* meaning "someone who is skilled in." *Psychiatry* deals with illnesses of the mind, so a *psychiatrist* is skilled in curing these illnesses.

Word Bank

Which of these words might describe the shape of a doorway? Check the Build Vocabulary boxes to see if you chose correctly.

psychiatrist
arched
currency
premium

Prentice Hall Literature Program Resources

REINFORCE / RETEACH / EXTEND
Selection Support Pages
Build Vocabulary: Suffixes: *-ist,* p. 22
Build Spelling Skills, p. 23
Build Grammar Skills: Concrete and Abstract Nouns, p. 24
Reading Strategy: Use Context to Unlock Meaning, p. 25
Literary Focus: Time in a Setting, p. 26
Strategies for Diverse Student Needs, pp. 9–10

Beyond Literature Cross-Curricular Connection: Science, p. 5
Formal Assessment Selection Test, pp. 13–15, Assessment Resources Software
Alternative Assessment, p. 5
Writing and Language Transparencies Series of Events Chain, p. 66; Sunburst Organizer, p. 94
Resource Pro CD-ROM "The Third Level"
Listening to Literature Audiocassettes "The Third Level"

The Third Level

◆ Literary Focus

Time in a Setting

Setting is the time and place in which a story's events occur. In Finney's story, time plays an especially important role, as the main character walks down a corridor in Grand Central Station and discovers that he has been transported back to 1894. As you read, record the details of 1894 that contrast with the details of the contemporary setting on a chart like the following:

Clues That Show Charley Is in Present	Clues That Show Charley Is in 1894

◆ Reading Strategy

Use Context to Unlock Meaning

In a story like "The Third Level" with an unusual or unfamiliar setting, you'll come across place names, slang, or other words that you don't recognize. When you encounter a name or a word you don't know, use its **context**—the words, phrases, and sentences around it—to figure out its meaning. Look at this example:

> I . . . glanced at the stack of papers at his feet. It was the *World*; and the *World* hasn't been published for years.

At first glance, you might wonder why a stack of papers would be called the *World*. The capitalization and italics indicate the title of a published work. Context clues such as "papers" and "published" provide further information to help you conclude that the *World* was a newspaper.

Place a chair at the front of the classroom. Invite students to join you in imagining that the chair is a vehicle that can go backward or forward in time. Then invite volunteers to sit in the time-travel chair and time travel. Encourage them to explain their decision to go forward or backward and to narrate their "journey." Explain to students that in "The Third Level," a man unexpectedly travels back to a time that is more appealing to him than the time in which he lives.

◆ Build Grammar Skills

Concrete and Abstract Nouns

The grammar concept taught with this story is concrete and abstract nouns. To introduce the concept, write the phrase "a ticket to the past" on the board. Explain that *ticket* is a concrete noun because it is something you can hold in your hand, while *past* is an abstract noun because you can't experience it through any of the five senses. If you wish to explore the concept of concrete nouns before students read the story, refer to the instruction on p. 54.

Customize for
More Advanced Students

Have students research life in the 1950's, the era in which "The Third Level" was written. Then, using the information they find, the details of the story, and their own knowledge of the present, ask them to create a chart that examines the pros and cons of living in each time period.

	1890's	1950's	Present
Pros			
Cons			

Preparing for Standardized Tests

Reading Point out to students that using context to unlock the meanings of words (the reading strategy taught with this selection) can help them with unfamiliar words. On standardized tests, they may be asked to identify the correct definition of a word as it is used in a sentence or paragraph.

To help students prepare for test questions that require them to use context clues, tell them they should think about the words and phrases around the word they are defining.

Have students read the following sentence and choose the answer that best defines the underlined word:

During Charley's time travel, he <u>traversed</u> through the nineteenth century.
(A) jumped (C) traveled
(B) ran (D) drove

Although all of the answers are words that show movement, *(C) traveled* is the only word that makes sense to use to move *through* a century. For practice using context, use **Selection Support,** p. 25, Reading Strategy: Use Context to Unlock Meaning.

Customize for
Less Proficient Readers

Have students track the story's events starting with Charley's decision to take the subway home, which is described in the third paragraph on p. 50. The Series of Events Chain, p. 66, in **Writing and Language Transparencies** may help them record the events that follow and lead to the final outcome of the story.

Develop Understanding

One-Minute Insight Through an uncommon series of events, the author of "The Third Level" describes the common urge to escape a complicated modern world. In this story, "an ordinary guy named Charley" enters New York City's Grand Central Station and, after making his way through an unfamiliar corridor, finds himself on a mysterious third level of the bustling train station. Charley realizes that he has somehow traveled 50 years into the past. Longing for the simple life of the nineteenth century, Charley decides to buy train tickets to a peaceful, quiet town called Galesburg, Illinois. Unable to purchase tickets with modern money, he leaves the third level and returns home. Although his wife and friends doubt the experience he reports, Charley returns to Grand Central Station many times to try to find the third level again. In this story, the author captures the popular desire to find happiness and one's true self by escaping to another place or time.

◆ Literary Focus

❶ Time in a Setting Help students identify details that offer clues to a modern, urban setting, such as hurrying uptown, the apartment, the subway, and the bus.

◆ Critical Thinking

❷ Interpret Have students explain why the author compares Grand Central to a tree. *Students should recognize that the author is suggesting that the tunnels and staircases of Grand Central are like roots.*

Customize for
English Language Learners
English language learners may have difficulty with the story's descriptive phrases and expressions. To understand the action of "*ducking* into an arched doorway," and "*fussing* with a stamp collection," have peer tutors pantomime the action indicated by the verbs. Ask peer tutors to help clarify the meanings of other words, as necessary.

The Third Level

Jack Finney

he presidents of the New York Central and the New York, New Haven and Hartford railroads will swear on a stack of timetables that there are only two. But I say there are three, because I've *been* on the third level at Grand Central Station.[1] Yes, I've taken the obvious step: I talked to a psychiatrist friend of mine, among others. I told him about the third level at Grand Central Station, and he said it was a waking-dream wish fulfillment. He said I was unhappy. That made my wife kind of mad, but he explained that he meant the modern world is full of insecurity, fear, war, worry and all the rest of it, and that I just want to escape. Well, who doesn't? Everybody I know wants to escape, but they don't wander down into any third level at Grand Central Station.

But that's the reason, he said, and my friends all agreed. Everything points to it, they claimed. My stamp collecting, for example; that's a "temporary refuge from reality." Well, maybe, but my grandfather didn't need any refuge from reality; things were pretty nice and peaceful in his day, from all I hear, and he started my collection. It's a nice collection, too, blocks of four of practically every U.S. issue, first-day covers, and so on. President Roosevelt collected stamps, too, you know.

❶ Anyway, here's what happened at Grand Central. One night last summer I worked late at the office. I was in a hurry to get uptown to my apartment so I decided to take the subway from Grand Central because it's faster than the bus.

> **◆ Literary Focus**
> What details of setting does this paragraph provide?

Now, I don't know why this should have happened to me. I'm just an ordinary guy named Charley, thirty-one years old, and I was wearing a tan gabardine[2] suit and a straw hat with a fancy band; I passed a dozen men who looked just like me. And I wasn't trying to escape from anything; I just wanted to get home to Louisa, my wife.

I turned into Grand Central from Vanderbilt Avenue, and went down the steps to the first level, where you take trains like the Twentieth Century. Then I walked down another flight to the second level, where the suburban trains leave from, ducked into an arched doorway heading for the subway—and got lost. That's easy to do. I've been in and out of Grand Central hundreds of times, but I'm always bumping into new doorways and stairs and corridors. Once I got into a tunnel about a mile long and came out in the lobby of the Roosevelt Hotel. Another time I came up in an office building on Forty-sixth Street, three blocks away.

Sometimes I think Grand Central is growing like a tree, pushing out new corridors and staircases like roots. There's probably a long tunnel that nobody knows about feeling its way under the city right now, on its way to Times Square, and maybe another to Central Park. ❷ And maybe—because for so many people through the years Grand Central *has* been an exit, a way of escape—maybe that's how the tunnel I got into . . . But I never told my psychiatrist friend about that idea.

The corridor I was in began angling left and slanting downward and I thought that was wrong, but I kept on walking. All I could hear was the empty sound of my own footsteps and I didn't pass a soul. Then I heard that sort of

1. **Grand Central Station:** Large train station in New York City.

2. **gabardine** (gab′ ər dēn′): Cloth of wool, cotton, rayon, or other material used for suits and dresses.

◆ Build Vocabulary

psychiatrist (sī kī′ ə trist) *noun used as adj.*: Medical doctor specializing in illnesses of the mind

arched (ärcht) *adj.*: Curved

Block Scheduling Strategies

Consider these suggestions to take advantage of extended class time:

- Have students listen to "The Third Level" on the literature audiocassette. Encourage them to note words and phrases that describe the atmosphere of the story's setting. Have them complete the Writing Mini-Lesson. Then invite them to apply what they have learned about details and description to one of the writing activities in the Idea Bank on p. 55.

Listening to Literature Audiocassettes

- As an alternative, use Build Vocabulary and Build Grammar Skills to begin the class time. Then have students read the selection independently. Allow them to meet in groups to discuss Reader's Response and Thematic Focus and answer questions on p. 53.
- After students read the selection, have them answer the Literary Focus questions on p. 54 and use **Selection Support,** p. 26. They can begin working on the Poster Series project in the Idea Bank, p. 55, keeping Time in a Setting in mind.

hollow roar ahead that means open space and people talking. The tunnel turned sharp left; I went down a short flight of stairs and came out on the third level at Grand Central Station. For just a moment I thought I was back on the second level, but I saw the room was smaller, there were fewer ticket windows and train gates, and the information booth in the center was wood and old-looking. And the man in the booth wore a green eyeshade and long black sleeve protectors. The lights were dim and sort of flickering. Then I saw why; they were open-
3 flame gaslights.

There were brass spittoons[3] on the floor, and across the station a glint of light caught my eye; a man was pulling a gold watch from his vest pocket. He snapped open the cover, glanced at his watch, and frowned. He wore a derby hat,[4] a black four-button suit with tiny lapels, and he had a big, black, handle-bar mustache. Then I looked around and saw that everyone in the station was dressed like eighteen-ninety-something; I never saw so many beards, sideburns and fancy mustaches in my life. A woman walked in through the train gate; she wore a dress with leg-of-mutton sleeves[5] and skirts to the top of her high-buttoned shoes. Back of her, out on the tracks, I caught a glimpse of a locomotive, a very small Currier & Ives[6]

> ◆ Reading Strategy Using the beards and mustaches as a clue, what do you think *sideburns* are? 5

3. **spittoons** (spi to͞onz′): Jarlike containers into which people spit. Spitting in public was a more accepted habit in the past.

4. **derby hat:** Stiff felt hat with a round crown and curved brim.

5. **leg-of-mutton sleeves:** Sleeves that puff out toward the shoulder and resemble a leg of mutton (lamb or sheep).

6. **Currier & Ives:** These nineteenth-century American printmakers became famous for their pictures of trains, yachts, horses, and scenes of nature.

4 ▼ **Critical Viewing** List three specific details to prove this photograph was taken in modern New York City. **[Support]**

◆ Literary Focus

3 Time in a Setting Ask students to identify the author's details that clue Charlie and readers to the fact that he has gone back in time. *Students may note the ticket seller's eyeshade and sleeve protectors, gaslights, spittoons, and the man with the gold watch.*

▶Critical Viewing◀

4 Support *Students should list details such as people wearing modern clothes, the lighted schedule board, and electric lights at the ticket counters.*

◆ Reading Strategy

5 Use Context to Unlock Meaning *Most students will recognize that because beards and mustaches are types of facial hair, sideburns are whiskers or facial hair on the side of the face.*

Customize for ***Visual/Spatial Learners***

Encourage students to consider the author's visual description of the corridors of Grand Central growing like tree roots. Have them review the paragraph that begins at the bottom of p. 50 and follow Charley's detour to the third level. Ask them to draw a map of his route, using clues such as "angling left," "slanting downward," "sharp left," and "down a short flight of stairs."

Humanities: Architecture

Grand Central Terminal New York City's railroad station was built by a team of engineers and architects to accommodate railroads in the middle of a busy city. Cornelius Vanderbilt, who once controlled all rail routes into New York, first built a railroad station on the site in 1869. The building that Charley enters in the story, however, was not completed until 1913. The "third level" actually would have been Vanderbilt's original station. The main concourse of today's Grand Central measures 470 feet by 150 feet with windows 60 feet high. The ceiling is decorated with nearly 2,500 stars. Grand Central's tunnels for subway, commuter, and long-distance train tracks extend almost a mile under city streets, and smaller tunnels with side entrances allow people to get to surrounding streets and office buildings.

1. How do you react when you are in a busy, bustling place? *Students may say that busy places are interesting, overwhelming, or fun.*
2. What might the expression "it's like Grand Central Station" mean? *Students should realize that the busy train station is sometimes referred to when people are in busy situations or places.*

▶Critical Viewing◀

❶ **Support** *Students should list details such as the horse-drawn vehicles, cobblestone streets, and old trolleys.*

◆Critical Thinking

❷ **Infer** Ask students what they think Charley means by "summer evenings were twice as long" in 1894. Encourage students to think about their own summer experiences to answer the question. *Students should infer that because people sat on porches and talked, summer evenings seemed longer than those of a modern, fast-paced world in which people have less time to relax.*

Comprehension Check 

❸ Why does Charley hurry out of the third level of Grand Central? *The clerk at the ticket window thought that Charley was trying to buy tickets with counterfeit money.*

Clarification

❹ In 1894, the price of a pound of butter was 26 cents. A half gallon of milk (delivered) was 14 cents. Five pounds of flour cost 12 cents, and five pounds of sugar cost 28 cents.

Comprehension Check 

❺ Why does Charley open the envelope postmarked July 18, 1894? *He is curious about the envelope that has suddenly appeared in his collection.*

Customize for *Intrapersonal Learners*

Invite students to share activities that they pursue on their own, such as Charley's stamp collecting. Encourage them to relate their interest in their individual activities to Charley's personal interest in stamps. Discuss with them why he might have gone back to his stamps to try to take his mind off the third level.

Customize for *Logical/Mathematical Learners*

Challenge students to come up with a way to help Charley and his wife find the third level again. They may suggest mapping the terminal to determine which corridors are false leads, or retracing the steps of his first journey back to 1894.

locomotive with a funnel-shaped stack. And then I knew.

To make sure, I walked over to a newsboy and glanced at the stack of papers at his feet. It was the *World;* and the *World* hasn't been published for years. The lead story said something about President Cleveland. I've found that front page since, in the Public Library files, and it was printed June 11, 1894.

I turned toward the ticket windows knowing that here—on the third level at Grand Central—I could buy tickets that would take Louisa and me anywhere in the United States we wanted to go. In the year 1894. And I wanted two tickets to Galesburg, Illinois.

Have you ever been there? It's a wonderful town still, with big old frame houses, huge lawns and tremendous trees whose branches meet overhead and roof the streets. And in 1894, summer evenings were twice as long, ❷ and people sat out on their lawns, the men smoking cigars and talking quietly, the women waving palm-leaf fans, with the fireflies all around, in a peaceful world. To be back there with the First World War still twenty years off, and World War II over forty years in the future . . . I wanted two tickets for that.

The clerk figured the fare—he glanced at my fancy hatband, but he figured the fare—and I had enough for two coach tickets, one way. But when I counted out the money and looked up, the clerk was staring at me. He nodded at the bills. "That ain't money, mister," he said, "and if you're trying to skin me you won't get very far," and he glanced at the cash drawer beside him. Of course the money in his drawer was old-style bills, half again as big as the money we use nowadays, and different-looking. I turned away and got out fast. There's nothing nice about jail, ❸ even in 1894.

And that was that. I left the same way I came, I suppose. Next day, during lunch hour, I drew three hundred dollars out of the bank, nearly all we had, and bought old-style currency (that *really* worried my psychiatrist friend). You can buy old money at almost any coin dealer's, but you have to pay a premium. My three hundred dollars bought less than two hundred in ❹ old-style bills, but I didn't care; eggs were thirteen cents a dozen in 1894.

But I've never again found the corridor that leads to the third level at Grand Central Station, although I've tried often enough.

Louisa was pretty worried when I told her all this, and didn't want me to look for the third level any more, and after a while I stopped; I went back to my stamps. But now we're *both* looking, every weekend, because now we have proof that the third level is still there. My friend

❶ ▼ Critical Viewing List three specific details to prove this photograph was taken in New York City at an earlier time. **[Support]**

◆ Build Vocabulary

currency (kʉr´ ən sē) *n.:* Money

premium (prē´ mē əm) *n.:* Additional charge

Speaking and Listening Mini-Lesson

Leisure Time Presentation

This mini-lesson supports the Speaking and Listening activity in the Idea Bank on p. 55.

Introduce Have students describe how they spend their free time. Point out that a range of activities and "inactivities" are considered leisure.

Develop Have students list leisure categories, such as sports, games, and music. Place students in groups, based on their choice of category, to research and prepare a presentation. Help them use your school's media center to research late-nineteenth-century leisure activities.

Apply Have students organize their materials and prepare their presentations. Encourage them to consider the format they will use, such as videotaping an outdoor activity or role-playing a scene of activity. They may want to use photographs, props, or drawings.

Assess Include students' contributions during preparations in your evaluation, and have students use the Self-Assessment: Speaking and Listening Progress form, p. 109, in **Alternative Assessment.**

Sam Weiner disappeared! Nobody knew where, but I sort of suspected because Sam's a city boy, and I used to tell him about Galesburg—I went to school there—and he always said he liked the sound of the place. And that's where he is all right. In 1894.

Because one night, fussing with my stamp collection, I found—well, do you know what a first-day cover is? When a new stamp is issued, stamp collectors buy some and use them to mail envelopes to themselves on the very first day of sale; and the postmark proves the date. The envelope is called a first-day cover. They're never opened; you just put blank paper in the envelope.

That night, among my oldest first-day covers, I found one that shouldn't have been there. But there it was. It was there because someone had mailed it to my grandfather at his home in Galesburg; that's what the address on the envelope said. And it had been there since July 18, 1894—the postmark showed that—yet I didn't remember it at all. The stamp was a six-cent, dull brown, with a picture of President Garfield. Naturally, when the envelope came to Granddad in the mail, it went right into his collection and stayed there—till I took it out and opened it. 5

The paper inside wasn't blank. It read:

941 Willard Street
Galesburg, Illinois
July 18, 1894

Charley:

I got to wishing that you were right. Then I got to believing you were right. And, Charley, it's true; I found the third level! I've been here two weeks, and right now, down the street at the Daly's, someone is playing a piano, and they're all out on the front porch singing, "Seeing Nellie home." And I'm invited over for lemonade. Come on back, Charley and Louisa. Keep looking till you find the third level! It's worth it, believe me! 6

The note was signed *Sam*.

At the stamp and coin store I go to, I found out that Sam bought eight hundred dollars' worth of old-style currency. That ought to set him up in a nice little hay, feed and grain business; he always said that's what he really wished he could do, and he certainly can't go back to his old business. Not in Galesburg, Illinois, in 1894. His old business? Why, Sam was my psychiatrist.

Guide for Responding

◆ Literature and Your Life

Reader's Response As it is described, is Galesburg in 1894 a place to which you would like to go? Why or why not?

Thematic Focus What advice would you give Charley and Louisa about reinventing themselves to fit into an 1894 world?

☑ Check Your Comprehension

1. According to Charley's psychiatrist, how can Charley's visit to the third level be explained?
2. What makes Charley think he has traveled to another time?
3. What proof does Charley get that the third level exists?

◆ Critical Thinking

Interpret

1. Contrast life in the modern world and life in Galesburg in 1894. **[Compare and Contrast]**
2. What evidence suggests that Charley feels out of place in modern times? **[Support]**
3. In what two ways does the stamp collection provide a link to life in Galesburg? **[Connect]**
4. How does Sam's attitude toward the third level change during the story? **[Analyze]**

Apply

5. What leads some people to believe that life in previous times was simpler or better than life in the present? Do you agree or disagree with this view? **[Explain]**

◆ Literature and Your Life

6 Ask students what they might do if they received a letter from a friend inviting them to join her or him in another time. *Some students may say they wouldn't want to leave the present. Others may say that they would leave if the other time period seemed more exciting.*

Reinforce and Extend

Writing Mini-Lesson

Answers

◆ Literature and Your Life

Reader's Response Some students may say they'd like to go to Galesburg because it seems friendly and peaceful. Others may say that it seems dull and slow-paced.

Thematic Focus Students may suggest that Charley and Louisa prepare themselves for a slower pace and lack of modern conveniences.

☑ Check Your Comprehension

1. The psychiatrist says Charley's visit is a response to Charley's wish to escape from the problems of the modern world.
2. He sees that his new surroundings look as if they're from the past.
3. Charley receives a letter from Sam, dated July 18, 1894, in which Sam tells of finding the third level.

◆ Critical Thinking

1. Modern life is hectic and "full of insecurity, fear, war, and worry"; life in Galesburg in 1894 is peaceful, relaxing, and nice.
2. Charley's psychiatrist calls him unhappy and says he wants to escape. Charley's friends say he tries to avoid reality.
3. The stamp collection was started by Charley's grandfather in Galesburg, and Charley finds the letter from Sam in his collection.
4. At first Sam doesn't believe it exists, but then he finds it and tells Charley and Louisa to keep looking for it.
5. Some students may say people believe life was simpler in the past because they think there was less to worry about. Others may disagree, saying that there are always things to worry about.

Beyond the Selection

FURTHER READING

Other Works by Jack Finney

About Time: Twelve Stories
Time and Again
From Time to Time

Other Works About Time Travel

Back to Before, Jan Slepian
Charlotte Sometimes, Penelope Farmer
A Connecticut Yankee in King Arthur's Court, Mark Twain
A Wrinkle in Time, Madeleine L'Engle

INTERNET

We suggest the following sites on the Internet (all Web sites are subject to change).

For additional information about Jack Finney:
http://members.aol.com/leahj/finney.htm

For links to information about life in the 1890's:
http://lcweb2.loc.gov/detroit/dethome.html

We *strongly recommend* that you preview these sites before you send students to them.

Answers

◆ Reading Strategy

1. Twentieth Century is the name of a particular train. The word *like* links *trains* to *Twentieth Century*; also, the capital letters suggest a name or title.
2. *Skin* means "to cheat or deceive." "That ain't money" suggests that the clerk believes that Charley is trying to con him with fake money.

◆ Build Vocabulary

Using the Suffix *-ist*

1. someone who creates art
2. someone who works with chemicals
3. someone who writes novels
4. someone who does scientific work
5. someone who works on teeth

Spelling Strategy

1. botanist
2. hairstylist
3. zoologist
4. typist

Using the Word Bank

1. arched
2. currency
3. psychiatrist
4. premium

◆ Literary Focus

1. The room he enters is smaller, with fewer ticket windows and train gates.
2. The old-looking wood information booth, clothing on the men and women, gaslights, spittoons, facial hair on the men, the pocket watch, and an old locomotive are all clues of the past.
3. It brings out his desire to live a more peaceful life.
4. He describes the type of activities that Charley misses and wants to have; he urges Charley and Louisa to keep looking for the third level.

◆ Build Grammar Skills

Practice

1. abstract
2. concrete
3. concrete
4. concrete
5. abstract
6. abstract

Writing Application

Possible responses:

1. idea
2. clothing
3. tickets
4. happiness

Guide for Responding *(continued)*

◆ Reading Strategy

Use Context to Unlock Meaning

Using **context**—the surrounding words, phrases, and sentences—can help you determine the meaning of unfamiliar words, objects, or slang from another time period. There are many types of context clues, including description, example, restatement, and comparison or contrast.

Use context to define the italicized words. Identify the clues you used and explain your answer.

1. ". . . where you take trains like the *Twentieth Century.*"

2. "That ain't money, mister, " he said, "and if you're trying to *skin* me you won't get very far."

◆ Build Vocabulary

Using the Suffix *-ist*

The suffix *-ist* means "someone who is skilled in or practices." Write a definition explaining what each of the following people practices.

1. artist **2.** chemist **3.** novelist **4.** scientist **5.** dentist

Spelling Strategy

Follow these rules when adding *-ist* to words:

If the word ends in a silent e preceded by a consonant, drop the *e:*

manicure + -ist = manicurist

If the word ends in *y,* drop the *y* when the *y* sounds like a long *e:*

psychiatry + -ist = psychiatrist

On your paper, add *-ist* to the following words.

1. botany **2.** hairstyle **3.** zoology **4.** type

Using the Word Bank

On your paper, complete each sentence with a word from the Word Bank.

1. An ___?___ window offers a better view of the cityscape than a narrow, square one.

2. When you visit another country, you have to exchange American dollars for foreign ___?___.

3. A ___?___ may help those experiencing extreme sadness or anger.

4. Tickets for the hottest concert of the year were available only at a ___?___.

◆ Literary Focus

Time in a Setting

Setting is the time and place of a story's action. When a story shifts from the present to the past, as "The Third Level" does, you have to determine when the action is taking place. You also have to consider how that changing time affects the characters. Answer the following questions. You may refer to your chart to help you.

1. What detail first hints that Charley has entered the Grand Central Station of 1894?

2. Identify at least three other details that show that the third level is in the past.

3. How does travel to 1894 change Sam?

4. What does Sam's letter say that suggests life in Galesburg in 1894 is better than life in modern-day New York City?

◆ Build Grammar Skills

Concrete and Abstract Nouns

Concrete nouns refer to physical things that can be seen, heard, tasted, smelled, or touched. **Abstract nouns** refer to ideas, qualities, or feelings that can't be experienced through the five senses. Look at these nouns from the story:

Concrete: apartment, president, ticket

Abstract: insecurity, war, worry

An *apartment* can be touched or seen. *Insecurity* can only be described or experienced.

Practice Identify each of the following as either a concrete or an abstract noun.

1. wish **2.** corridor **3.** mustache **4.** envelope **5.** fear **6.** reality

Writing Application Copy and complete the following sentences on your paper. Use either a concrete or an abstract noun as indicated.

1. Louisa explained her ___?___ about how to reach the third level. (abstract)

2. They dressed in ___?___ from 1894. (concrete)

3. The clerk gave Charley two ___?___ to Galesburg. (concrete)

4. Sam and Charley were filled with ___?___ when they saw each other again. (abstract)

Writer's Solution

For additional instruction and practice, use the lesson in the *Writer's Solution Language Lab CD-ROM* on Using Nouns. You may also use the practice page on nouns, p. 5, in the *Writer's Solution Grammar Practice Book.*

Build Your Portfolio

Idea Bank

Writing

1. Letters Write a letter from Charley asking Sam about Galesburg and the third level. Then, write Sam's response, with details about the 1890's.

2. Time-Travel Story Like Charley, you make a turn down an unfamiliar corridor and step into the past. Write a story to describe your experience.

3. Psychiatrist's Report Imagine you are a psychiatrist who believes the third level is a product of Charley's imagination. Using examples from the story, write a report explaining your opinion.

Speaking and Listening

4. Oral History Interview an older relative or friend about the time period of his or her childhood. Find out about fashion, fun, and issues of concern. Record the oral history, and present it with visuals from the period. **[Social Studies Link]**

5. Leisure Time Presentation [Group Activity] In a group, learn more about leisure activities in the late nineteenth century. Each group member should research a different topic, such as sports, games, and music. Then, describe to the class the activities the people of Galesburg might have enjoyed. **[Performing Arts Link; Social Studies Link]**

Projects

6. Poster Series on Train Travel In 1894, passenger train travel was far more important than it is today. Using the Internet or reference books, research train travel in the late 1800's. Present your findings in several colorful posters. **[Art Link; Social Studies Link]**

7. Survey Write a survey about time travel, providing three or four answer choices for each question. For example, you might ask people whether they believe in the possibility of time travel or what time period they might choose to visit if it were possible. Conduct the survey, and plot the results on a bar graph. **[Math Link]**

Writing Mini-Lesson

Description of a Place

Jack Finney uses vivid description to re-create the atmosphere, or mood, of a time long gone. Like Finney's 1894 Grand Central Station, the locations you visit today will become a later generation's "ancient history." Write a description to help readers of the distant future see the physical details and experience the mood of a place in today's world.

Writing Skills Focus: Spatial Details

Help readers picture the place you are describing by using **spatial details.** Use such words and phrases as *above, behind,* and *in front of* that tell where things are located in space. Notice how Finney organizes his spaces to lead readers through Grand Central Station.

Model From the Story

Then I heard that sort of hollow roar *ahead* that means open space and people talking. The tunnel turned sharp *left*; I went *down* a short flight of stairs and came *out on* the *third level*. . . .

Prewriting If possible, visit the place you've chosen, and take notes on its physical details. Jot down words such as *bustling, tense,* or *dim* to describe the atmosphere.

Drafting Begin with a vivid detail of atmosphere, such as the sounds or movement in the place. Then, use your notes to build a complete picture of the scene.

◆ Grammar Application

Use concrete nouns, such as *scoreboard,* to show a space's physical elements. Use abstract nouns, such as *excitement,* to convey emotions.

Revising Review your description, noting places where additional vivid details could make the atmosphere more realistic.

✓ ASSESSMENT OPTIONS

Formal Assessment, Selection Test, pp. 13–15, and Assessment Resources Software. The selection test is designed so that it can easily be customized to the performance levels of your students.

Alternative Assessment, p. 5, includes options for less advanced students, more advanced students, verbal/linguistic, intrapersonal, visual/spatial, interpersonal, bodily/kinesthetic, logical/mathematical, and musical/rhythmic learners.

PORTFOLIO ASSESSMENT
Use the following rubrics in the **Alternative Assessment** booklet to assess student writing:
Letters: Expression, p. 81
Time-Travel Story: Fictional Narrative, p. 82
Writing Mini-Lesson: Description, p. 84
Psychiatrist's Report: Business Letter/Memo, p. 100

Idea Bank

Following are suggestions for matching the Idea Bank topics with your students' performance levels and learning modalities:

Customize for
Performance Levels
Less Advanced Students: 1, 2, 5
Average Students: 2, 4, 5, 6
More Advanced Students: 3, 5, 6, 7

Customize for
Learning Modalities
Verbal/Linguistic: 1, 2, 3, 4, 5, 7
Logical/Mathematical: 7
Visual/Spatial: 6
Bodily/Kinesthetic: 5
Interpersonal: 4, 5, 7
Intrapersonal: 2

Writing Mini-Lesson

Refer students to the Writing Handbook in the back of the book for instruction on the writing process and for further information on description. Have students use the Sunburst Organizer in **Writing and Language Transparencies,** p. 94, to arrange their prewriting examples.

Writer's Solution

Writing Lab CD-ROM
Have students complete the tutorial on Description. Follow these steps:

1. Have students use the Cluster Diagram to help them narrow their topic.
2. Have students draft on the computer.
3. Encourage students to use the Sensory Word Bin activity to gather vivid descriptive words.
4. Use the revision checker to find and replace weak adjectives in their description.

You will need approximately 90 minutes of class time to complete these steps.

Writer's Solution Sourcebook
Have students use Chapter 2, "Description," pp. 32–65, for additional support. This chapter includes in-depth instruction on gathering sensory details and organizing details in spatial order, p. 53.

Prepare and Engage

OBJECTIVES

1. To read, comprehend, and interpret a story that has a social studies focus
2. To relate a story with a social studies focus to personal experience
3. To connect literature to social studies
4. To respond to Social Studies Guiding Questions
5. To respond to the story through writing, speaking and listening, and projects

SOCIAL STUDIES GUIDING QUESTIONS

Reading about the legend of King Arthur will help students discover answers to these Social Studies Guiding Questions:

- How did the belief system of England during the Middle Ages affect its history, government, and economy?
- What was the pattern of day-to-day life in England during the Middle Ages?

Interest Grabber Display a set of chess pieces. Ask students to describe or suggest what each piece portrays: king, queen, bishop, knight, rook (castle), and pawn (common person). Help them see that these characters (and castles) are elements of medieval times. Then have students brainstorm for a list of games, books, TV shows, movies, and computer games in which some or all of the characters are medieval knights or kings, such as the TV movie *Merlin*; the movie *First Knight*; the musical *Camelot*; the comic strip *Prince Valiant*; and the book *Ivanhoe*. Guide students to identify the qualities and activities of these characters. Then have them look for these traits in the characters of "King Arthur: The Marvel of the Sword."

Map Study

Historical Maps The connection between geography and history is often a key to understanding why events happened. For example, to understand young Arthur's danger, students can use the map on this page to understand that England was being invaded. To help relate the map to history and further understand Merlin's concern for Arthur, have students read Wars and Invasions on this page.

CONNECTING LITERATURE TO SOCIAL STUDIES

MEDIEVAL TIMES

King Arthur: The Marvel of the Sword *by Mary MacLeod*

TEENAGER ELECTED PRESIDENT. You may have wondered if a headline like this could ever appear in a newspaper. Actually, an event like this did happen—in another country and another time. The story is part of English legend.

ATLANTIC OCEAN
IRELAND
ENGLAND
SCANDINAVIA
DENMARK
Baltic Sea
GERMANY
FRANCE (Normandy)
ITALY
Vikings 900's
Vikings 800's
Anglo-Saxons 450–650
Normans 1066
N
0 150 300 mi
0 150 300 km

Invasions of England, A.D. 450–1066

The Making of a Legend Legends are tales that are loosely based on historical facts. These stories may not be entirely true, but they do reflect a group's identity: what it wishes for and values.

Campfires and Castles The legend of King Arthur began to be told more than a thousand years ago. Whispered over open campfires and recited in drafty castles, it reflected the yearning of the English people to be united under a wise and brave ruler. The details changed with every telling, but the legend always expressed this same yearning.

Wars and Invasions This story gathered power during a perilous time in English history. In the middle of the fifth century A.D., tribes of sea-rovers began invading England from Northern Europe. These invaders gradually settled in England, but fresh dangers threatened the English people. The land was divided by warring kingdoms as noblemen struggled for power. Also, new invaders kept coming from across the water: Vikings from Scandinavia and Denmark in the ninth century, and Normans from France in 1066.

A King Who Never Was? Maybe King Arthur really lived during the time of the first invaders. Maybe he won victories against these sea-rovers. These maybes don't add up to historical fact, but people needed to hear about a great king like Arthur as long as times remained perilous. In "The Marvel of the Sword," you'll meet this legendary king when he is a teenager.

Prentice Hall Literature Program Resources

REINFORCE / RETEACH / EXTEND

Selection Support Pages
Build Vocabulary, p. 27
Connect Legend to Social Studies, p. 28

Formal Assessment Selection Test,
pp. 16–17, Assessment Resources Software

Writing and Language Transparencies
Sunburst Organizer, p. 94

Resource Pro CD-ROM
"King Arthur: The Marvel of the Sword"

Listening to Literature Audiocassettes
"King Arthur: The Marvel of the Sword"

Connection to Prentice Hall World Explorer
Medieval Times to Today
Ch. 5, "Europe in the Middle Ages"
Ch. 6, "A New Age in Europe"

King Arthur: The Marvel of the Sword

Mary MacLeod

When Uther[1] Pendragon, King of England, died, the country for a long while stood in great danger, for every lord that was mighty gathered his forces, and many wished to be king. For King Uther's own son, Prince Arthur, who should have succeeded him, was but a child, and Merlin, the mighty magician, had hidden him away.

Now a strange thing had happened at Arthur's birth.

Some time before, Merlin had done Uther a great service, on condition that the King should grant him whatever he wished for. This the King swore a solemn oath to do. Then Merlin made him promise that when his child was born it should be delivered to Merlin to bring up as he chose, for this would be to the child's own great advantage. The King had given his promise so he was obliged to agree. Then Merlin said he knew a very true and faithful man, one of King Uther's lords, by name Sir Ector,[2] who had large possessions in many parts of England and Wales, and that the child should be given to him to bring up.

On the night the baby was born, while it was still unchristened, King Uther commanded two knights and two ladies to take it, wrapped in a cloth of gold, and deliver it to a poor man whom they would find waiting at the postern gate of the Castle. This poor man was Merlin in disguise, although they did not know it. So the child was delivered unto Merlin and he carried him to Sir Ector, and made a holy man christen him, and named him Arthur; and Sir Ector's wife cherished him as her own child.

> **Connecting Literature to Social Studies**
> Which details make this account seem more legendary than historical? Why? ❶

Within two years King Uther fell sick of a great malady, and for three days and three nights he was speechless. All the Barons[3]

1. **Uther** (yo͞o thər)
2. **Ector** (ek´ tôr)

3. **Barons** (bar´ ənz) *n.*: Members of the lowest rank of British nobility.

◆ **Build Vocabulary**

malady (mal´ ə dē) *n.*: Illness; disease

One-Minute Insight This selection from Mary MacLeod's retelling of the legend of King Arthur is the story of how Arthur becomes king of all England. Prior to the death of Arthur's father, King Uther, Merlin the magician delivers the baby Arthur to Sir Ector and his wife to raise. The land is in chaos because there is no ruler, so Merlin devises a test to determine the rightful king—the man who can pull the sword from a stone in the churchyard will be king. Many barons and knights attempt the feat, but they consistently fail. When Arthur is a youth, he succeeds in pulling the sword from the stone. However, he has to pull the sword on four more occasions before he is accepted as rightful heir to the throne. The legend reveals Arthur's strong character traits, and as events transpire, Arthur finds himself as King of England. We learn that it will take a very special person—a true "noble"—to make England a strong, united nation.

Team Teaching Strategy

"King Arthur: The Marvel of the Sword" offers an opportunity to team teach with a social studies teacher, creating a cross-curricular unit on medieval times.

Connecting Literature to Social Studies

❶ **Legend vs. History** Have students list details from their first page of reading. Then help them identify which details seem less likely to be historical facts, suggesting that the story is legendary, not historical. *Merlin was a magician; King Uther gave his son and heir to Merlin; the baby Arthur was wrapped in a cloth of gold.*

Customize for *Less Proficient Readers*

To help students understand the medieval setting of the story, have them preview the art in their books. You may also wish to find examples of illustrations and art from different versions of the story of King Arthur for students to view and relate to the "age" of the legend. Alternatively, show a film adaptation to view elements of medieval legends.

Preparing for Standardized Tests

Social Studies Reading Selections
Standardized tests often include reading selections in which students are called on to think critically about material from various curriculum areas. The test format may require students to evaluate all possible answers in order to identify the one best answer. To offer students practice in thinking critically to answer questions, have them read p. 57. Then, on the board, write the following set of answers to the boxed prompt:

(A) Uther Pendragon was the King of England.
(B) Merlin is a mighty magician.
(C) King Uther and Merlin have an agreement.
(D) Arthur is a baby when King Uther dies.

Guide students to review details and recognize that *(B)* is the best answer to the question. Mention that some tests ask for the one *best* answer, yet provide another answer that may answer the question. They must read carefully to choose the best, or "correct," answer. For additional practice, you may want to provide answers to each of the selection prompts, as *(A)–(D)*, for students to evaluate and determine the correct answer.

▶ Critical Viewing ◀

❶ **Connect** Students should have no trouble identifying the baby, the knights, and one of the ladies. If they are confused about which person is Merlin, tell them to look for the one who is receiving the baby.

Links Across Time

❷ The setting for the legend of King Arthur is England during the Middle Ages (A.D. 500–1500), the period between the end of ancient times and the beginning of modern times. Following the collapse of the Roman empire, the new inhabitants of western Europe were under constant attack from northern invaders. The system known as feudalism that developed during this time provided protection from invaders and structure for medieval society. A king or queen was at the top of the system, followed by nobles, then knights, and finally, peasants. In return for protection and land to own or use, each person (a vassal) owed loyalty, service, and payment to the person (a lord) above him or her.

Customize for *English Language Learners*

Make sure students understand that the author's style uses modern English in a way that reflects the formalities and rhythm of the original story. Have them work with a proficient partner to understand such terms as *look ye all, bid him pray for my soul, whoso pulleth this sword,* and so on. Have them demonstrate their understanding with pantomime, where appropriate.

Customize for *More Advanced Students*

As students read about Arthur becoming king, they can use events and characters as a springboard to research more of the King Arthur legends, including the well-known Round Table. Suggest they start with a list of research questions such as these:

- What were the major events of King Arthur's life?
- When and why did King Arthur begin the Round Table?
- Who were the Knights of the Round Table?

Guide students to use a variety of sources. Have them present their findings, using the format they feel best fits their information, such as an oral or written report, a timeline or chart, or a dramatic interpretation.

MERLIN TAKETH THE CHILD ARTHVR INTO HIS KEEPING

Drawing from an 1894 edition of Sir Thomas Malory's Le Morte d'Arthur, Aubrey Beardsley

❶ ▲ Critical Viewing Identify in the picture these details from the story: "two knights and two ladies," the baby "wrapped in a cloth of gold," and Merlin disguised as a "poor man." **[Connect]**

Block Scheduling Strategies

Consider these suggestions to take advantage of extended class time:

- After using the Interest Grabber to draw students into the selection, play the audiocassette of "King Arthur: The Marvel of the Sword." Ask students to form two groups according to their agreement with the Barons' reluctance or the Commoners' insistence about Arthur's right to the throne. Have them discuss the Thematic Focus on p. 62 and summarize their group's discussion for the entire class, or debate the issue, using the Speaking and Listening activity on p. 63.
- Alternatively, have students use the Sunburst Organizer, p. 94, in **Writing and Language Transparencies** to gather and organize their thoughts and materials for the Viewing and Representing Mini-Lesson on p. 60 of the Teacher's Edition or for writing a legend in the Idea Bank on p. 63.
- Use *World Explorer: Medieval Times to Today*, Chapter 5, "Europe in the Middle Ages" to team teach or to further extend connecting literature to social studies.

were in sorrow, and asked Merlin what was best to be done.

"There is no remedy," said Merlin. "God will have His Will. But look ye all, Barons, come before King Uther tomorrow, and God will make him speak."

So the next day Merlin and all the Barons came before the King, and Merlin said aloud to King Uther:

"Sir, after your days shall your son Arthur be King of this realm and all that belongs to it?"

Then Uther Pendragon turned and said in hearing of them all: "I give my son Arthur God's blessing and mine, and bid him pray
2 for my soul, and righteously and honorably claim the crown, on forfeiture of my blessing."

And with that, King Uther died.

But Arthur was still only a baby, not two years old, and Merlin knew it would be no use yet to proclaim him King. For there were many powerful nobles in England in those days, who were all trying to get the kingdom
3 for themselves, and perhaps they would kill the little Prince. So there was much strife and debate in the land for a long time.

When several years had passed, Merlin went to the Archbishop of Canterbury[4] and counseled him to send for all the lords of the
4 realm,[5] and all the gentlemen of arms, that they should come to London at Christmas, and for this cause—that a miracle would show who should be rightly King of the realm. So all the lords and gentlemen made themselves ready, and came to London, and long before dawn on Christmas Day they were all gathered in the great church of St. Paul's to pray.

When the first service was over, there was seen in the churchyard a large stone, four-square, like marble, and in the midst of it was like an anvil of steel, a foot high. In this was stuck by the point a beautiful sword, with naked blade, and there were letters written in gold about the sword, which said thus:

Whoso pulleth this sword out of this stone and anvil is rightly King of all England. 5

Then the people marveled, and told it to the Archbishop.

"I command," said the Archbishop, "that you keep within the church, and pray unto God still; and that no man touch the sword till the service is over."

So when the prayers in church were over, all the lords went to behold the stone and the sword; and when they read the writing some of them—such as wished to be king—tried to pull the sword out of the anvil. But not one could make it stir. 6

"The man is not here, that shall achieve the sword," said the Archbishop, "but doubt not God will make him known. But let us provide ten knights, men of good fame, to keep guard over the sword."

So it was ordained, and proclamation was made that everyone who wished might try to win the sword. And upon New Year's Day the Barons arranged to have a great tournament, in which all knights who would joust[6] or tourney[7] might take a part. This was ordained to keep together the Lords and Commons, for

4. **Canterbury** (kan′ tər ber′ ē) *n.*: Cathedral and sacred shrine in Canterbury, a town southeast of London. In medieval times, many English people made pilgrimages or journeys to Canterbury.
5. **realm** (relm) *n.*: Kingdom.

6. **joust** (jowst) *v.*: To take part in a combat between two knights on horseback with lances.
7. **tourney** (toor′ nē) *v.*: To compete; to take part in a tournament.

◆ Build Vocabulary

remedy (rem′ ə dē) *n.*: Medicine or treatment that cures illness

strife (strīf) *n.*: Trouble; conflict; struggle

ordained (ôr dān′ əd) *v.*: Ordered; decreed

CONNECTING LITERATURE TO SOCIAL STUDIES

CONNECTING LITERATURE TO SOCIAL STUDIES

3 Draw Conclusions In this passage, we learn that the nobles would fight among themselves to gain control of the kingdom and, perhaps, kill the baby prince to do it. What does this say about the nobles' respect for the role of the king? *The nobles would only respect a king who was personally strong enough to demand their loyalty; they would not follow a weak king.*

Links Across Time

4 Merlin's visit to the Archbishop of Canterbury introduces a new character to the story. Historically, the power of the Archbishop to summon all the lords is a sign of the power of the Roman Catholic Church in the Middle Ages. In addition to performing church services and providing spiritual leadership, the church also made laws and set up courts to enforce those laws, collected taxes, received lands from lords in exchange for services performed by the clergy, and acted as advisors to kings. The church could even prevent war by threatening to excommunicate (remove from church life) any lord who threatened to rebel against the king.

Clarification

5 Have students look at the verb *pulleth* in this sentence. Tell students that the archaic suffix *-eth* is used for verbs (the *knight pulleth* or the *knights pulleth*). Then guide them to rewrite the subject and verb in modern English as "whoever pulls." As they continue reading the story, suggest that students look for other verbs ending in *-eth*, such as *taketh, sticketh, holdeth*. They may want to rewrite the phrases or sentences where they appear in order to clarify meaning.

CONNECTING LITERATURE TO SOCIAL STUDIES

6 Make a Judgment Ask students whether they think the method described in this passage would be a good way to test our nation's leaders today. *Students should see that physical strength is not a basis for leadership; there is no such thing as a test to determine leadership ability; the criteria for judging our modern-day leaders are different from those for judging a legendary king.*

Humanities: Art

Merlin Taketh the Child Arthur Into His Keeping, drawing from an 1894 edition of Sir Thomas Malory's *Le Morte d'Arthur*

This illustration depicts Merlin receiving the baby Arthur into his care. The print is similar to the woodcut block prints used for illustration during medieval times, a relief printing technique, and this illustration displays a typically intricate border pattern.

During the fifteenth century, many books were made in England using wood block printing. A separate block was made for each page, and because cutting letters in wood was difficult, many of the books were mostly pictures with a line of text to explain the illustration on each page (as in this print, although usually not as elaborate).

1. How does this illustration help you to imagine the story's setting? *The knights in armor, the clothing of the ladies and Merlin, the castle walls, and the buildings of the town in the valley below show that the story takes place a long time ago.*
2. How does the artist show that the story involves fantasy? *The border art has fantastic creatures in it.*

Connecting Literature to Social Studies

❶ **Leadership Potential** At this point in the story, Arthur has agreed to retrieve his brother's sword, and when he can't find it, he decides to take the sword in the stone to make sure that Sir Kay has a sword for the joust. *Based on what Arthur does to help his brother, students should see that a good ruler's qualities include being generous, good-natured, loyal, dutiful, resourceful, purposeful, and loving.*

❷ **Make a Judgment** Ask students whether they think Arthur is a hero because he pulled the sword from the stone. Why? *Some students may say no—the mere act of pulling the sword is not heroic and at this point only Arthur knows he has done so. Others may say yes—the miracle of the sword in the stone is that only a hero can pull it from the stone.*

Comprehension Check ☑

❸ Why does Arthur ask Sir Ector why he is King of England? *Arthur's true identity has been a secret to everyone but Sir Ector and Merlin.*

◆ Literature and Your Life

❹ Students may recall situations in which they were asked to assume a responsibility for which they thought they weren't prepared. Invite students to share their thoughts about taking on responsibility and what is required to handle responsibility successfully.

Connecting Literature to Social Studies

❺ **Danger in Medieval England** *As a child, Arthur might not have been able to keep the fact that he would be king a secret and his life would be in danger; if the heir to the throne were killed, the kingdom would be torn by civil war.*

the Archbishop trusted that it would be made known who should win the sword.

On New Year's Day, after church, the Barons rode to the field, some to joust, and some to tourney, and so it happened that Sir Ector, who had large estates near London, came also to the tournament; and with him rode Sir Kay, his son, with young Arthur, his foster brother.

As they rode, Sir Kay found he had lost his sword, for he had left it at his father's lodging, so he begged young Arthur to go and fetch it for him.

"That will I, gladly," said Arthur, and he rode fast away.

But when he came to the house, he found no one at home to give him the sword, for everyone had gone to see the jousting. Then Arthur was angry and said to himself:

> **Connecting Literature to Social Studies** ❶
> What qualities does Arthur display that suggest he will be a good ruler?

"I will ride to the churchyard, and take the sword with me that sticketh in the stone, for my brother, Sir Kay, shall not be without a sword this day."

When he came to the churchyard he alighted,[8] and tied his horse to the stile, and went to the tent. But he found there no knights, who should have been guarding the sword, for they were all away at the joust. ❷ Seizing the sword by the handle he lightly and fiercely pulled it out of the stone, then took his horse and rode his way, till he came to Sir Kay his brother, to whom he delivered the sword.

As soon as Sir Kay saw it, he knew well it was the sword of the Stone, so he rode to his father Sir Ector, and said:

"Sir, lo, here is the Sword of the Stone, wherefore[9] I must be King of this land."

When Sir Ector saw the sword he turned back, and came to the church, and there they all three alighted and went into the church, and he made his son swear truly how he got the sword.

"By my brother Arthur," said Sir Kay, "for he brought it to me."

"How did you get this sword?" said Sir Ector to Arthur.

And the boy told him.

"Now," said Sir Ector, "I understand you must be King of this land."

"Wherefore I?" said Arthur. "And for what cause?" ❸

"Sir," said Ector, "because God will have it so; for never man could draw out this sword but he that shall rightly be King. Now let me see whether you can put the sword there as it was, and pull it out again."

"There is no difficulty," said Arthur, and he put it back into the stone.

Then Sir Ector tried to pull out the sword, and failed; and Sir Kay also pulled with all his might, but it would not move.

"Now you shall try," said Sir Ector to Arthur.

"I will, well," said Arthur, and pulled the sword out easily.

At this Sir Ector and Sir Kay knelt down on the ground. ❹

"Alas," said Arthur, "mine own dear father and brother, why do you kneel to me?"

"Nay, nay, my lord Arthur, it is not so; I was never your father, nor of your blood; but I know well you are of higher blood than I thought you were."

> **Connecting Literature to Social Studies** ❺
> Why was it important to keep Arthur's true identity a secret even from him?

Then Sir Ector told him all, how he had taken him to bring up, and by whose

8. **alighted** (a līt′ əd) *v.*: Dismounted; got down off a horse.

9. **wherefore:** Why.

Viewing and Representing Mini-Lesson

Chess Pieces

In this mini-lesson students will extend their understanding of Arthur and medieval times by representing the characters of the legend.

Introduce Use a traditional chess set to discuss the game of chess and the names and moves of each chess piece. Explain that chess was introduced to England in 1013 and that the game's essence (a battle involving members of different social groups) and game pieces reflect the feudal system of medieval times.

Develop Have students list the characters of the legend, and categorize them in relation to the chess pieces: Merlin; Arthur and Uther—kings; Sir Ector and Sir Kay—knights; the Archbishop of Canterbury—bishop. Help students relate the characters and the chess pieces further by discussing the common people (not lords or knights) who are pawns, and telling them that King Arthur later marries Queen Guenivere.

Apply Divide students into six groups, assigning a different chess piece to each. Have them research England in the Middle Ages to find images and information about the person or place their chess piece represents; then create representations of each piece. Supply mixed media materials, such as clay, magazines, and posterboard, for the task.

Assess Have students present their chess pieces to the class and explain the social role and rank of the pieces or characters, both on the chess board and in medieval society. Evaluate students on their group work, research, and presentations.

◀ Critical Viewing In what ways does this picture explain the respect that Merlin seems to command throughout the story? **[Interpret]** ❻

CONNECTING LITERATURE TO SOCIAL STUDIES

Free Public Library of Philadelphia

command; and how he had received him from Merlin. And when he understood that Ector was not his father, Arthur was deeply grieved.

"Will you be my good, gracious lord, when you are King?" asked the knight.

"If not, I should be to blame," said Arthur, "for you are the man in the world to whom I am the most beholden, and my good lady and mother your wife, who has fostered and kept me as well as her own children. And if ever it be God's will that I be King, as you say, you shall desire of me what I shall do, and I shall not fail you: God forbid I should fail you."

"Sir," said Sir Ector, "I will ask no more of you but that you will make my son, your foster brother Sir Kay, seneschal[10] of all your lands."

"That shall be done," said Arthur, "and by my faith, never man but he shall have that office while he and I live."

Then they went to the Archbishop and told him how the sword was achieved, and by whom.

On Twelfth Day all the Barons came to the stone in the churchyard, so that anyone ❼
who wished might try to win the sword. But not one of them all could take it out, except Arthur. Many of them therefore were very angry, and said it was a
great shame to them and to the country to be ❽
governed by a boy not of high blood, for as yet none of them knew that he was the son of King Uther Pendragon. So they agreed to delay the decision till Candlemas, which is the ❾
second day of February.

But when Candlemas came, and Arthur once more was the only one who could pull

10. **seneschal** (sen´ ə shəl) *n.*: Person in charge of household arrangements.

◆ **Build Vocabulary**

grieved (grēvd) *adj.*: Saddened; overcome by grief

▶ Critical Viewing ◀

❻ **Interpret** *Students may observe that Merlin seems thoughtful and wise, which reassures people and encourages them to admire and respect him.*

◆ LITERATURE AND YOUR LIFE

❼ Arthur's feat must be repeated for the Archbishop and Barons to witness. Invite students to share how they think Arthur might feel about proving something he has already done. *Some students may think Arthur will accept the fact that such an important event must be witnessed in order to be believed; others may feel that Arthur is being slighted by having to prove he is the rightful king.*

CONNECTING LITERATURE TO SOCIAL STUDIES

❽ **Infer** Point out to students that sometimes when an outcome of a situation is not what we want, we require extra proof in order to accept or believe it. Ask students whether the Barons would have asked Arthur to pull the sword again if they had known he was of noble blood. *Students should realize that the Barons would still find a reason to object, because most still wanted to be king themselves.*

Links Across Time

❾ Tournaments for knights were often held on holidays. In medieval times, many of the celebrated holidays in England corresponded to the calendar of the Church of England—for example, Twelfth Day, Candlemas, Easter, and the Feast of Pentecost.

Customize for *Visual/Spatial Learners*

In addition to the map on p. 56, encourage students to use other maps to understand what England was like during the time Arthur was a boy.

Customize for *Less Proficient Readers*

As students reach the climax, let them listen to a portion of the audiocassette, noting how the reader heightens the dramatic effect by adjusting rate, volume, pitch, and tone.

Listening to Literature Audiocassettes

Humanities: Art

Image of Merlin This print shows Merlin in quiet repose in the woods. It is reminiscent of medieval woodcut prints in books of that time period. Illustrators like to use wood block printing because of the dramatic effect given by the sharp contrasts and expressive lines that the technique provides.

1. What is the mood of the print? *Merlin seems thoughtful and quiet.*
2. How does the artist's use of light and dark contribute to the portrayal of Merlin in this story? *The figure of Merlin is light, but he is surrounded by darkness, which may indicate mystery or something dangerous.*
3. Why does the artist use a circle for the shape of the print? *Circles can represent the world or something that is endless. Merlin may be pushing against the way of the world, simply thinking about the world around him or considering the endless dangers that Arthur faces.*
4. Why is Merlin pictured alone in the woods? *Merlin may need to be alone for what he needs to do in order to help Arthur; the woods may be his home.*

Connecting Literature to Social Studies

❶ **Class Conflict** Possible Answer: *The nobles did not want a commoner to rule them and each hoped to become king himself. The common people knew that the man who passed the test was the true king.*

Reinforce and Extend

Answers

◆ **Literature and Your Life**

Reader's Response Students may suggest feelings of excitement, being overwhelmed, astonishment, fright, or doubt. They may also recognize that Arthur probably reacted with a combination of feelings.

Thematic Focus Students may say that one cannot simply declare his or her greatness to others; it must be proven and witnessed in order to be accepted and believed.

☑ **Check Your Comprehension**

1. Uther gives Arthur to Merlin, who puts Arthur in the care of Sir Ector to be raised as his son.
2. Arthur pulls the sword from the stone after he can't find his brother's sword.
3. The Barons are angry that a common boy should rule and insist that Arthur draw the sword again.
4. After repeatedly drawing the sword, the common people demand that Arthur be accepted as their king.

More About the Author

Mary MacLeod (?–1914) was a writer known for retelling classic stories from medieval times to make them accessible to the modern reader. She was an expert at adapting medieval texts so that the meaning and cadences of the original were preserved. The story presented here is from her book *King Arthur and His Knights,* which closely follows Sir Thomas Malory's *Le Morte d'Arthur* (c. 1469), the best-known of many works recounting the Arthurian legend. Another book by Mary MacLeod is *Stories from the Faerie Queen,* which retells *The Faerie Queen,* an epic poem by Edmund Spenser, written between 1590 and 1596.

out the sword, they put it off till Easter; and when Easter came, and Arthur again prevailed in the presence of them all, they put it off till the Feast of Pentecost.

Then by Merlin's advice the Archbishop summoned some of the best knights that were to be—such knights as in his own day King Uther Pendragon had best loved, and trusted most—and these were appointed to attend young Arthur, and never to leave him night or day till the Feast of Pentecost.

❶ When the great day came, all manner of men once more made the attempt, and once more not one of them all could prevail but Arthur. Before all the Lords and Commons there assembled he pulled out the sword, whereupon all the Commons cried out:

> **Connecting Literature to Social Studies**
> What conclusion can you draw from the fact that the common people, rather than the nobles, demand that Arthur be crowned?

"We will have Arthur for our King! We will put him no more in delay, for we all see that it is God's will that he shall be our King, and he who holdeth against it, we will slay him."

And therewith they knelt down all at once, both rich and poor, and besought pardon of Arthur, because they had delayed him so long.

And Arthur forgave them, and took the sword in both his hands, and offered it on the altar where the Archbishop was and so he was made knight by the best man there.

After that, he was crowned at once, and there he swore to his Lords and Commons to be a true King, and to govern with true justice from thenceforth all the days of his life.

Guide for Responding

◆ **Literature and Your Life**

Reader's Response If you were Arthur, how would you feel about suddenly discovering you were king? Why?

Thematic Focus Why does the deed by which Arthur discovers his identity have to be witnessed by others?

☑ **Check Your Comprehension**

1. How does Arthur become part of Sir Ector's family?
2. What surprising event occurs on New Year's Day?
3. Describe the reaction of the Barons to this event.
4. In what way does Arthur finally become king?

◆ **Critical Thinking**

Interpret

1. Why do Sir Ector and then the Barons ask Arthur to pull the sword out again and again? **[Infer]**
2. What message does this tale convey about division and unity in a kingdom? **[Draw Conclusions]**
3. Does Arthur seem like a hero to you? Why or why not? **[Make a Judgment]**
4. Arthur is recognized as king after pulling a magic sword from a stone. In what ways do we choose and test our leaders today? **[Social Studies Link]**

Meet the Author

Mary MacLeod (? –1914) made legendary heroes come alive for children by rewriting Shakespeare's plays and the classic tales of Robin Hood and King Arthur. Like many people who have retold the tales of King Arthur, MacLeod based her stories on those of Sir Thomas Malory, who wrote *Le Morte d'Arthur* (French for "The Death of Arthur"), which was published in 1485. It was Malory who first compiled the tales of King Arthur and his Knights of the Round Table.

Beyond the Selection

FURTHER READING

Other Works by Mary MacLeod

Stories from the Faerie Queene
A Book of Ballad Stories

Other Works About the Legend of King Arthur

A Connecticut Yankee in King Arthur's Court, Mark Twain
The Illustrated Encyclopaedia of Arthurian Legends, Ronan Coghlan
The Sword in the Stone, T. H. White

INTERNET

We suggest the following Internet site (all Web sites are subject to change).

This site includes full text of many works of Arthurian literature, related articles, maps, timelines, and additional resources:
http://www.brittania.com/history/arthur

You will also find related information on the broader topic of medieval England on the Internet.

We *strongly recommend* that you preview these sites before you send your students to them.

CONNECTING LITERATURE TO SOCIAL STUDIES

The King Arthur of legend is a national hero of the English people. He may have been loosely modeled on a real leader, but many details of his story were made up and revised in constant retellings.

Although these retellings varied, certain details stayed the same: The teenage Arthur goes on to establish his court at Camelot. There he assembles the greatest knights of the day, who sit as equals at the famous Round Table. Often, these knights go out on adventures, rescuing ladies in distress and righting wrongs.

To people living during the Middle Ages (1066–1485) and after, Arthur and his knights came to represent the gentlemanly traits that nobles were supposed to have: loyalty, bravery, courtesy, and honor. Even in this story about the young Arthur, you can see evidence of these traits.

1. What is the chief detail that makes this story a legend rather than a historical account? Explain.
2. Identify two gentlemanly traits displayed by young Arthur, and support your choices.
3. Why might this account of young Arthur have comforted people during times of danger?

Idea Bank

Writing

1. **Job Description** As a nobleman of England, write a job description for a king. First, briefly describe the job and its duties. Then, list the physical and mental traits that an applicant for the throne should demonstrate.
2. **Speech** Arthur will have to give a speech to present himself and his policies to his people. Write such a speech for him. Include one or two things he plans to do in order to protect the country.
3. **Legend** Extend the legend of King Arthur by creating another adventure for him. For example, you may want to describe how he passes a different kind of test. Among the characters you can include are the magician Merlin.

Speaking and Listening

4. **Debate** Role-play the debate that the Barons might have had while deciding whether Arthur should be king. Have one side support him and the other argue against him. Present your debate to a small group of classmates.

Projects

5. **Timeline** Create a timeline showing the wars and invasions that troubled English history, which may have helped to foster the legend of King Arthur. Cover the years A.D. 500–1500.
6. **Coat of Arms** Create a coat of arms for Arthur, a special decoration that he can display on his shield. To find out more about coats of arms, research the topic heraldry in an encyclopedia. Then use what you learn—and what you already know about Arthur—to design his coat of arms.

Further Reading, Listening, and Viewing

- Graeme Fife's *Arthur the King* (1991) explains the mysteries of the Arthurian legend.
- T. H. White's *The Once and Future King* (1958) is a humorous retelling of the legend.
- Persia Woolley's *Queen of the Summer Stars* (1990) is about Guinevere, Arthur's queen.
- Alan Jay Lerner and Frederick Loewe's *Camelot* (1960) is a musical based on the legend.

✓ ASSESSMENT OPTIONS

ASSESSMENT OPTIONS

Formal Assessment, Selection Test, pp. 16–17, and Assessment Resources Software. The selection test is designed so that it can be easily customized to the performance levels of your students.

PORTFOLIO ASSESSMENT

Use the following rubrics and assessment form in the **Alternative Assessment** booklet to assess student writing:

Job Description: Description, p. 84
Speech: Self-Assessment: Speech, p. 104
Legend: Fictional Narrative, p. 82

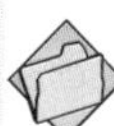

Idea Bank

Following are suggestions for matching the Idea Bank topics with your students' performance levels and learning modalities:

Customize for
Performance Levels

Less Advanced Students: 2, 6
Average Students: 3, 4, 5,
More Advanced Students: 1, 5

Customize for
Learning Modalities

Verbal/Linguistic: 1, 2, 3, 4
Visual/Spatial: 5, 6
Interpersonal: 4

Answers

◆ Critical Thinking

1. Sir Ector needs to witness the act for himself in order to believe Arthur and Kay; the Barons do not want Arthur to rule and hope he will eventually fail to pull the sword out of the stone.
2. It is better to have a united kingdom to avoid war and suffering; the king must be respected by his subjects to be an effective ruler.
3. Students may say Arthur is a hero because of his good qualities and his acceptance by the people as their king; or, he is not a hero because he hasn't done anything except pull a sword from a stone.
4. We elect leaders by voting. Our leaders can be voted out of office if they perform poorly or don't keep their promises. Debates, town meetings, and news coverage are some ways voters can find out about the qualities of their leaders.

CONNECTING LITERATURE TO SOCIAL STUDIES

1. The chief detail is the miracle of the sword in the stone. A sword that can only be drawn by one man regardless of strength is a test that could not happen in real life. This fantasy detail combined with facts about medieval England make the story a legend.
2. Arthur addresses Sir Ector courteously. He shows kindness and loyalty when he volunteers to retrieve Sir Kay's sword. He shows respect when he promises to treat his adoptive family well.
3. They might believe a hero may come forth to save them. The tale may be a source of inspiration never to give up hope.

Prepare and Engage

Establish Writing Guidelines
Before students begin, review the elements of a personal narrative:

- A personal narrative is a true story about a memorable experience or event in the writer's life.
- The writer's thoughts and insights about the event help to re-create the experience.

You may want to distribute the scoring rubric for Narrative Based on Personal Experience, p. 83 in **Alternative Assessment**, to make students aware of the criteria on which they will be evaluated. See the suggestions on p. 66 for how you can customize the rubric to this workshop.

Refer students to the Writing Handbook for instruction on the writing process and further information on narrative writing.

Writer's Solution

Writers at Work Videodisc
To introduce students to narration and to show them how Denise Chavez uses elements of personal narrative, play the videodisc segment on Narration (Ch. 3). Have students discuss how Chavez considers her audience when she writes.

Play frames 22000 to 31088

Writing Lab CD-ROM
If you have access to computers, you may want to have students use the tutorial on Narration to write their personal narratives. Follow these steps:

1. Students can review the interactive model of a personal narrative.
2. Have students use the Sunburst Diagram to generate words to describe the setting of their narrative.
3. Students can draft on computer.
4. Have students review the tips for punctuating dialogue in the Proofreading section.

Writer's Solution Sourcebook
Students can find additional support, including inspirations for ideas and models from literature, in the chapter on Narration, pp. 67–101.

Connect to Literature Unit 7, "Nonfiction," includes an example of a personal narrative: Russell Baker's "No Gumption."

Narrative Writing

Personal Narrative

Writing Process Workshop

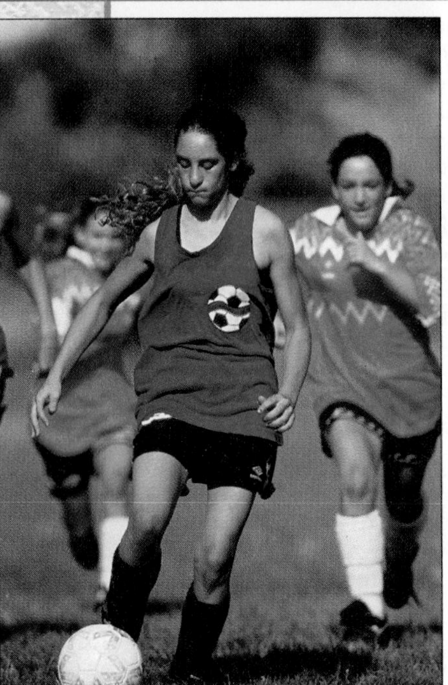

Life is full of memorable events—joyous or miserable, terrifying or enlightening, humorous, wonderful, or just plain exciting. A **personal narrative** is a written account of a memorable event from your own life. Re-create an event that shaped your image of yourself by writing a personal narrative about it. The following skills, introduced in this part's Writing Mini-Lessons, will help you write your personal narrative.

Writing Skills Focus

- **Show a clear sequence of events** to help your readers see what happened first, next, and last. (See p. 10.)
- **Add emotional depth** by providing details that show what you thought during the event. (See p. 27.)
- **Use the power of connotations** by considering the ideas associated with the words you choose. (See p. 35.)
- **Supply precise details** that describe your experience accurately and completely. (See p. 47.)
- **Let spatial details create the setting.** To help readers picture the event, provide information about where objects and people are located. (See p. 55.)

Alex Haley uses these skills to describe how he discovered a key to his identity. In this passage, Haley shares his notebook with an African, and both realize they are distantly related.

Model From Literature

from "My Furthest-Back Person" by Alex Haley

I showed the interpreter, he showed and told the *griot,* who excitedly told the people; they grew very agitated. ① Abruptly then they formed a human ring, encircling me, dancing and chanting. ② Perhaps a dozen of the women carrying their infant babies rushed in toward me, thrusting the infants into my arms conveying, I would later learn, "the laying on of hands . . . through this flesh which is us, we are you, and you are us." ③

① The author makes the sequence of events clear by listing them in the order in which they occurred.

② By describing the circle of dancers, Haley offers spatial information to help readers see the action.

③ Haley's precise details help bring the events to life.

Cultural Connection

Personal Heritage Point out to students that a personal narrative allows a writer to share his or her personal heritage with readers. Often, personal narratives are written to explain an incident that shaped the writer's identity, such as Alex Haley's "My Furthest-Back Person." In his narrative, Haley introduces readers to his African heritage and explains his feelings about discovering an important link to his identity. Reading his personal narrative, readers discover both African and African American cultures. As Haley's narrative reveals, the experience of becoming aware of one's culture and personal heritage is a memorable event.

As students plan their writing, encourage them to think of an event in their lives that has special meaning—an incident that may be unique to their upbringing or cultural background. It may be helpful for you to read aloud excerpts from other personal narratives to show students examples of diversity. You may want to use passages of "Two Kinds," p. 15, from Amy Tan's *The Joy Luck Club,* which is based on her experience of growing up in a Chinese American environment.

Prewriting

Interview a Partner Generate a list of questions that will spark ideas for personal narratives. With a partner, take turns asking and answering the questions on the list. Use your answers or the ideas below to help you choose your topic.

Topic Ideas

- Taking a family vacation
- Enduring a storm
- Planning a surprise party
- Winning—or losing—an important game

Play a Mental Video Prepare for writing your personal narrative by replaying the event in your mind. Write down key words and phrases to help you remember the order in which events occurred. Jot down ideas about your emotions at each stage of the event, too.

Draw a Map To help you remember details about where people, objects, and occurrences were located, draw maps or pictures. On your maps, show key moments in your memorable event. You can use your maps to help you provide spatial details as you draft your personal narrative.

Drafting

Use Dialogue Showing, rather than telling, your readers what people say will bring your narrative to life. Through dialogue, you can reveal people's personalities and create a moving picture in your readers' minds. Look at these examples.

Telling	Showing (Dialogue)
My sister and I argued until Dad, thoroughly fed up, yelled at us.	"Did not." "Did so." "Did not!" "Kids!" Dad yelled, thoroughly fed up with us. "Knock it off!"
The phone woke him at three in the morning.	"Uh . . . hello?" he said, rubbing his eyes and squinting at the alarm. "Who?—what *time* is it? Do you know what time it is?!"

DRAFTING/REVISING

APPLYING LANGUAGE SKILLS: Direct and Indirect Quotations

A direct quotation is the exact statement of a speaker. Quotation marks show where a speaker's words begin and end. An indirect quotation is a restatement or paraphrase of what somebody said.

Direct: *He said, "I discovered a lot about myself that day."*

Indirect: *He said he discovered a lot about himself that day.*

Practice Rewrite these sentences to change direct quotations into indirect quotations and vice versa.

1. "What is your most memorable birthday?" I asked.
2. She said it was her tenth and that she would always remember it.
3. "On that day, I got Sherman, the puppy who changed my life," she said.

Writing Application As you draft your personal narrative, use both indirect and direct quotations.

Writer's Solution Connection Writing Lab

For help choosing a topic, use the Inspirations in the Narration Tutorial.

Applying Language Skills

Direct and Indirect Quotations Have students pay attention to the verbs they use when writing dialogue. Remind students that often when they tell a story they may misuse the word "goes" for "says," as in "Then he goes, 'Stop it!'" rather than "Then he says, 'Stop it!'"

Answers

Suggested responses:

1. I asked her what is her most memorable birthday.
2. She said, "It was my tenth and I'll always remember it."

Writer's Solution

For additional instruction and practice, have students use the *Writer's Solution Language Lab CD-ROM,* Writing Dialogue, in the Composing Unit.

Develop Student Writing

Prewriting

Remind students to think about their audience as they plan their personal narratives. Make sure that they are aware that their audience will not have the personal experience that the writer has with the subject.

Customize for *Less Proficient Writers*

Students who are having difficulty writing dialogue may find it helpful to record their drafts on a tape recorder. When they listen to their recordings, have them follow along with their writing and note whether the dialogue seems realistic.

Customize for *English Language Learners*

Help students identify and add transition words to connect the events of their narratives. Have these students use a graphic organizer such as the Series of Events Chain, p. 66, in **Writing and Language Transparencies** to organize the events of their narrative. Then ask them to number the events chronologically. Show them how they can replace the numbers with transition words, such as *first, then, next,* and *later,* to make their writing flow smoothly and help readers understand the sequence of events.

Drafting

Remind students, as they draft, that dialogue will help show, rather than tell. Students may find group work helpful for testing their dialogue. Writers can assign readers for each speaker of their dialogue. Both readers and listeners in the groups should listen for dialogue that seems confusing or lifeless. As students read and listen to one another's writing, encourage them to brainstorm for ways to make dialogue more revealing and exciting.

Writer's Solution

Writing Lab CD-ROM

Students can develop strategies for writing their drafts by using the five interactive models in the drafting section of the tutorial on Narration. Using the Transitional Word Bin will help them gather words to connect the events in their story. They can drag the words from the bin into the correct place in their drafts.

Revising

You may want to have students work with peer reviewers to revise their personal narratives. Encourage reviewers to provide critical support, advising their peers where they could use more details to elaborate or replace indirect quotations with dialogue.

Writer's Solution

Writing Lab CD-ROM
In the tutorial on Narration, the Peer-Evaluation Checklist and tips for working with a peer editor can guide students through the editing phase.

Publishing

In addition to creating a class book, encourage students to consider sending copies of their personal narratives to friends or relatives.

Reinforce and Extend

Review the Writing Guidelines
After students complete their writing, review the characteristics of a personal narrative.

Applying Language Skills

Punctuating Dialogue Show students that when a quotation is placed at the beginning of a sentence, the period is changed to a comma: "Take a left at the white house," she said.

Answers

1. "I'm not brave," she said.
2. She explained, "I just reacted to danger."
3. "It wasn't courage," she said. "It was adrenaline."

Writer's Solution

For additional practice, complete the Quotation Marks With Direct Quotations lesson in the *Writer's Solution Grammar Practice Book*, pp. 105–106.

EDITING/PROOFREADING

APPLYING LANGUAGE SKILLS: Punctuating Dialogue

Dialogue is conversation between speakers. It needs special punctuation.

- Place quotation marks around a speaker's exact words.
- Begin the first word of a quotation with a capital letter.
- Use a comma to separate the quotation from the rest of the sentence.
- Place a closing period, question mark, or exclamation point inside the quotation marks.

Example: "I feel strange when people call me a hero," she admitted.

Practice On your paper, punctuate these sentences.

1. I'm not brave she said.
2. She explained I just reacted to the danger.
3. It wasn't courage she said. It was adrenaline.
4. I only hope someone will do the same for you! he said.

Writing Application Review your narrative, and correct punctuation in dialogue.

Writer's Solution Connection
Language Lab

For more practice with quotations, complete the Language Lab lesson on Quotation Marks, Colons, and Semicolons.

Elaborate About Thoughts and Feelings Provide information about how each stage of the events affected you at the time and how the whole experience has affected you since. Provide enough details so that readers can understand and share your emotions.

Revising

Fill in the Gaps As you revise, look for places in your personal narrative where you need to add details. Review the notes you made when you replayed the event in your mind, and use the items as a checklist. Insert any information you may have missed.

Replace Weak Words With Strong Words Take another look at the words you've used. Replace vague words like *player* with precise words like *goalie*. Consider the connotation of words, and replace those that may provoke the wrong response.

REVISION MODEL

After the two-hour hike, I stood in the clearing marveling at the exhilarating view. The ① ~~creatures~~ hummingbirds sparkled in the sunlight like tiny jewels. They ~~stood for a moment~~ hovered in midair, and then moved off in a flash of ② ~~blue, green, and purple.~~ sapphire, emerald, and amethyst.

① The writer replaces a vague word with a precise word.
② Carefully chosen words help suggest preciousness as well as color.

Publishing and Presenting

- **Class Book** With your classmates, create a class book of personal narratives. Each writer may wish to illustrate his or her personal narrative. Display your book in the school library so that others can enjoy your writing.
- **Dramatization** Adapt your personal narrative or a section of it as a dramatic performance. Working solo or in a group, act out the event you have adapted from your personal narrative.

ASSESSMENT		4	3	2	1
PORTFOLIO ASSESSMENT Use the rubric on Narrative Based on Personal Experience in the **Alternative Assessment** booklet, p. 83, to assess the students' writing. Add these criteria to customize this rubric to this assignment.	**Punctuating Quotations**	Dialogue is consistently punctuated correctly.	Punctuation of quotations has minor errors.	Punctuation of quotations is inconsistent or incorrect.	Quotations are difficult to read because punctuation is incorrect.
	Elaboration	The narrative uses precise details and dialogue to give the reader a clear idea of the experience.	The narrative uses details and dialogue, but inconsistently.	The narrative uses details but provides no insight or dialogue for the experience.	The narrative uses no dialogue and key parts lack details, making the narrative hard to follow.

Real-World Reading Skills Workshop

Understanding an Author's Purpose

Strategies for Success

You probably read the cartoon pages of the newspaper differently from the way you read the guidelines for behavior at the local pool. While a cartoonist usually works to amuse, the director of a community pool creates a list of rules to establish and maintain order and safety—a completely different purpose. As these examples illustrate, each piece of writing you encounter has a unique purpose. Some common purposes are to entertain, to inform, and to persuade. As a reader, if you can identify a writer's purpose, you can get more out of what you read.

Scan Writing for Clues to Purpose Before you read an essay or article thoroughly, quickly scan the pages for clues to help you identify the author's purpose. The title, language, style, and form the author chooses are important clues to his or her purpose. For example, descriptive essays use more poetic language than police reports do. Make a guess about the author's intention, and adjust your reading to suit that purpose.

Adjust Your Expectations Once you have identified the author's probable purpose, you can prepare yourself mentally. If the author's purpose is to describe or to tell a story, get ready to enjoy the images and events the author creates. If the author's purpose is to inform or explain, prepare yourself to gather useful information from your reading.

✔ *Here are other situations in which it's important to recognize the author's purpose:*

- ▶ Newspaper articles
- ▶ Political campaigns
- ▶ Advertisements

Apply the Strategies

An inventory is usually a detailed list of items that catalogs the stock of a business. However, in "Thanksgiving Inventory," the writer takes stock of a different kind. Read this section to determine the writer's purpose.

from Thanksgiving Inventory

by Roger Rosenblatt, *Time* Magazine

Then I drive home, where I make more entries still. In the mail are new pictures of the children; I share a cup of hot chocolate with the dog; the wind kicks up; the fat pine on the front lawn trembles its skirts in the late afternoon; shadows smudge the hedges; day hookslides into night. I think of high school baseball, then basketball. The orange moon hangs so low it looks as if it is about to fall to earth and bounce.

This inventory is getting out of hand. Last week alone I made more than a thousand new entries, and I never erase the old ones. If this keeps up, I will require a dozen ledgers, and even then my accounts will be woefully incomplete. Every year is the same. I prepare my inventory for Thanksgiving, to say grace, and always come up short.

1. What is unusual about the items in the writer's inventory?
2. What is the writer's attitude toward his inventory?
3. What is the writer's purpose? How do you know?
4. (a) How would the details be different if the writer were trying to persuade you that you have much to be thankful for? (b) Rewrite the article to reflect this purpose.

Introduce the Strategies

Students will be familiar with nonfiction articles from newspapers, magazines, and their social studies texts; they read stories from this literature anthology. Discuss what differentiates writing that is meant to inform from writing that is intended for enjoyment. For example, a story usually entertains readers, whereas a newspaper editorial tries to persuade readers. Encourage students to identify examples of writing that address different purposes. Remind students that as they begin to read, they should ask the question "What is the author trying to achieve?"

Customize for
Visual/Spatial Learners
As students read the excerpt from "Thanksgiving Inventory," have them represent the scenes the writer describes by sketching or clipping magazine pictures. Encourage visual learners to analyze the author's use of descriptive words such as "smudge" or "hookslides" and try to implement these in their visual representations. Ask students to point out phrases in the article that they find difficult to produce as images.

Apply the Strategies

Have students read the excerpt from "Thanksgiving Inventory" once before examining it in detail. Then discuss why the author might be taking the inventory. Guide students to use their answers to this question to determine the author's purpose for writing the article. Make sure they notice that the author states his purpose for the inventory in the last sentence.

Answers

1. The items in the inventory are unusual because they are descriptions of scenes and events rather than objects or materials.
2. Despite his statement that his inventory is "getting out of hand," he seems proud of it and glad that there is so much for which he can be thankful.
3. His purpose is to inform or remind readers that the list of everyday occurrences and items in life for which we can be grateful is endless. After listing many kinds of things he appreciates, the writer explains in the last paragraph that he is preparing for Thanksgiving.
4. (a) If the writer were trying to persuade, he probably would use more direct language in order to convince readers to accept his point of view.
(b) Students should rewrite the article using a persuasive tone that convinces readers to be thankful.

◆Build Grammar Skills

Reviewing Nouns

The selections in Part I include instruction on the following:

- Common and Proper Nouns
- General and Specific Nouns
- Collective Nouns
- Concrete and Abstract Nouns

This instruction is reinforced with the Build Grammar Skills practice pages in **Selection Support,** pp. 3, 9, 14, and 24.

As you review nouns, you may wish to include the following:

- Compound Nouns

Compound nouns are two or more words that function as a single noun; the parts of a compound noun may be written as separate words, one word, or a hyphenated word. Give students some examples of compound words such as *homework* (single word), *great-aunt* (hyphenated word), and *telephone book* (separate words). Then write the following headings on the board and have students list compund nouns that fall into each category.

Single Word	Hyphenated Word	Separate Words

Customize for
Less Proficient Readers

Suggest that students do the following: When identifying collective nouns, ask themselves, "Is the noun singular, but still names a group of people or things?" If yes, then it is a collective noun. When identifying abstract nouns, ask, "Can I touch, hear, taste, smell, or see it?" If no, then it is an abstract noun.

Writer's Solution

For additional practice and support using nouns, use the practice pages on nouns, pp. 5–7, in the *Writer's Solution Grammar Practice Book.*

Nouns — Grammar Review

Nouns are the words that name. They name persons, places, things, and ideas or qualities.

Person	peddler, author, Walt Whitman
Thing	city, mirror, money, Grand Central Station
Idea or quality	loveliness, knowledge, luck, freedom

Nouns fall into these categories:

Common (See p. 26.)	writer, town, river
Proper (See p. 26.)	Jack Finney, Galesburg, Columbia River
Concrete (See p. 54.)	piano, library, finger, San Francisco
Abstract (See p. 54.)	humor, jealousy, anger
Collective (See p. 46.)	family, crowd, herd, team, jury

Practice 1 List the nouns in the sentences that follow. Next to each, identify the noun as common or proper; then label any nouns that are collective or abstract.

1. Amy Tan loses her confidence during a disaster at a recital.
2. The audience claps, but the people see her embarrassment as she walks to her chair.
3. While touring Africa, Alex Haley discovers a connection to his family.
4. The writer realizes the truth behind the stories he loved as a child.
5. Charley's visit to Grand Central Station leads him on a fantastic journey.

Practice 2 Rewrite the following paragraph, filling in each blank with a noun.

We share many ____ in common, but we all have our own special qualities that set us apart. Your unique ____ is affected by many factors. Your ____, your ____, and your ____ all shape the things you think, the ____ you like, even the ____ you wear. While some parts of your "self" stay constant over time, other ____ are always changing. Every new ____ you have adds to your own particular values and beliefs.

Grammar in Writing

✔ *When you write, let nouns work for you. Use specific nouns to help your reader see precisely what you are describing.*

General noun: The peddler in Jan Skiba's village sold many *items.*

Specific nouns: The peddler in Jan Skiba's village sold *beads, false pearls, rings,* and *kerchiefs.*

Use a thesaurus—a reference book containing synonyms—to help you select specific nouns.

Answers

Practice 1

1. Amy Tan (proper); confidence (common, abstract); disaster (common); recital (common)
2. audience (common, collective); people (common, collective); embarrassment (common); chair (common)
3. Africa (proper); Alex Haley (proper); connection (common); family (common, collective)
4. writer (common); truth (common, abstract); stories (common); child (common)
5. Charley's (proper); visit (common); Grand Central Station (proper); journey (common)

Practice 2

Possible responses for each of the nine blanks are:

1. traits; characteristics; feelings; beliefs; things
2. self; personality; character; nature

3–5. beliefs; ideas; upbringing; surroundings; education; feelings; emotions; family; background; culture; language; religion; friends; failures; successes; experiences

6. people; food; places; ideas; things
7. clothes; shoes; hats; things
8. sides; aspects; traits; features
9. experience; encounter; adventure

PART 2 Testing Yourself

Racer, Diana Ong

One-Minute Planning Guide

The selections in this section focus on the theme of "Testing Yourself." "A Day's Wait" tells the story of a young boy mistakenly facing what he thinks is a life-and-death situation. Bill Cosby relates a humorous anecdote about mimicking his childhood heroes in "Was Tarzan a Three-Bandage Man?" Richard Wilbur writes about his daughter's literary determination in "The Writer." "Flint" is a poem that compares the strength of flint to the beauty of precious gems. In "Oranges," Gary Soto describes a young boy's courage in proving his worth to his first crush.

Customize for
Varying Student Needs

When assigning the selections in this section, keep in mind the following factors:

"A Day's Wait"
- A short story by Ernest Hemingway
- Students may need help with the theme

"The Writer"
- A short poem

"Flint"
- A short poem that compares and contrasts strength and beauty

"Oranges"
- A short story by Gary Soto
- Students may relate to the narrator's experiences

"Was Tarzan a Three-Bandage Man?"
- A humorous anecdote by Bill Cosby
- Includes a Connection to Today's World about Tiger Woods

Humanities: Art

Racer, by Diana Ong

Diana Ong (1940–) is a graphic artist living in Jacksonville, Florida. She trained at the National Academy of Arts and the School of Visual Arts in New York City. Ong is a pioneer in the artistic field of using computer graphics programs as a medium for fine art. Use these questions for discussion:

1. How does the artist suggest the movement of the racer? *Students may say that the lines the artist uses in the painting suggest movement, creating the hair flowing back from the runner's face, and the running motion of the runner's legs.*
2. The title of this painting is *Racer.* How does the image of a racer relate to the theme "Testing Yourself"? *Students may say that racers compete not only against other runners but they also have to compete against themselves, to improve their times.*
3. Do you think a photograph of a racer would be a better representation? Why or why not? *Some students may prefer the detailed accuracy of a photograph to the abstract detail of this painting. Their opinions should be supported.*

Prepare and Engage

OBJECTIVES

1. To read, comprehend, and interpret a short story
2. To relate a short story to personal experience
3. To reread as a reading strategy
4. To analyze internal conflict
5. To build vocabulary in context and learn the word root *-vid-*
6. To develop skill in using pronouns
7. To write a narrative using elaboration to make writing personal
8. To respond to the story through writing, speaking and listening, and projects

SKILLS INSTRUCTION

Vocabulary: Word Roots: *-vid-*
Spelling: Changing Adjectives With *-ent* to Nouns With *-ence*
Grammar: Pronouns
Reading Strategy: Reread
Literary Focus: Internal Conflict
Writing: Elaborate to Make Writing Personal
Speaking and Listening: Panel Discussion (Teacher Edition)
Critical Viewing: Speculate; Connect

PORTFOLIO OPPORTUNITIES

Writing: Inner Monologue; Film Director's Memo; Definition
Writing Mini-Lesson: A Day of Anticipation
Speaking and Listening: Medal Presentation Speech; Panel Discussion
Projects: Comparison Chart; Advice Pamphlet

More About the Author
As a boy, **Ernest Hemingway** often fished and hunted with his father, a physician, near his home in Oak Park, Illinois. At age 17, he decided to pursue his love of writing by taking a job as a cub reporter with the *Kansas City Star*. There, he was first exposed to journalistic writing, a style that gets to the point and doesn't waste words. Later, he applied elements of this style to works of fiction like "A Day's Wait."

After World War I, Hemingway lived in Paris and became acquainted with other expatriate writers such as F. Scott Fitzgerald and Gertrude Stein. They encouraged and influenced his interest in writing.

His sympathy for the culture and lifestyles in France and Europe became a part of his writing style.

Guide for Reading

Meet the Author:
Ernest Hemingway (1899–1961)

Ernest Hemingway earned international fame for his gripping tales of war and adventure. Amazingly, most of his writing was based on his own true-life experiences.

Restless for excitement, Hemingway left home as soon as he graduated from high school. Just before his nineteenth birthday, he was wounded in World War I. While hospitalized in Italy, he received a medal for heroism. These experiences became the basis for a number of short stories and the novel *A Farewell to Arms*.

A Life of Adventure Hemingway went on to travel the world, using his experiences as material for his writing. African safaris inspired stories like "The Snows of Kilimanjaro." Involvement with the Spanish Civil War sparked the novel *For Whom the Bell Tolls*. His observations of bullfighting in Spain provided material for *The Sun Also Rises*.

THE STORY BEHIND THE STORY
Hemingway's writing celebrates heroes and explores the nature of courage. In much of his writing, he dramatizes the importance of bravery in the face of death and of life's everyday problems. "A Day's Wait" is not about war or outdoor adventures, but it still deals with the quiet courage needed to face fear.

◆ Literature and Your Life

CONNECT YOUR EXPERIENCE
When you're waiting for a party, time seems to drag. When you're waiting to have a tooth drilled, time races by. As the photograph on the next page suggests, lying in bed when you're sick can be the worst kind of waiting. In addition to the fact that you feel bad and you're bored, you have plenty of time to worry. In "A Day's Wait," a young boy experiences this worst kind of waiting.

THEMATIC FOCUS: Testing Yourself
Major problems in our lives force us to examine who we are. In "A Day's Wait," an illness causes a boy to discover his inner reserve of courage.

◆ Background for Understanding

SCIENCE
In this story, a doctor measures a boy's temperature in degrees Fahrenheit (°F). On this scale, water freezes at 32°F and boils at 212°F. Although Fahrenheit is used in the United States, most of the world measures temperature in degrees Celsius (°C). In that system, water freezes at 0°C and boils at 100°C. A confusion about these scales sets off part of the trouble in "A Day's Wait."

◆ Build Vocabulary

WORD ROOTS: *-vid-*
In this story, you'll encounter the word *evidently*, which contains the root *-vid-*, meaning "to see." *Evidently* means "obviously" or "easily able to be seen."

WORD BANK
Which of these words from the story do you think tells how something is done? Check the Build Vocabulary boxes on pages 73 and 74 to see whether you chose the correct word.

epidemic
evidently

Prentice Hall Literature Program Resources

REINFORCE/RETEACH/EXTEND

Selection Support Pages
Build Vocabulary: Word Roots: *-vid-*, p. 29
Build Spelling Skills, p. 30
Build Grammar Skills: Pronouns, p. 31
Reading Strategy: Reread, p. 32
Literary Focus: Internal Conflict, p. 33

Strategies for Diverse Student Needs, pp. 11–12

Beyond Literature Activity Page Cross-Curricular Connection: Math, p. 6

Formal Assessment Selection Test, pp. 18–20, Assessment Resources Software

Alternative Assessment, p. 6

Writing and Language Transparencies Series-of-Events Chain, p. 66

Resource Pro CD-ROM
"A Day's Wait"—includes all resource materials and customizable lesson plan

Listening to Literature Audiocassette
"A Day's Wait"

A Day's Wait

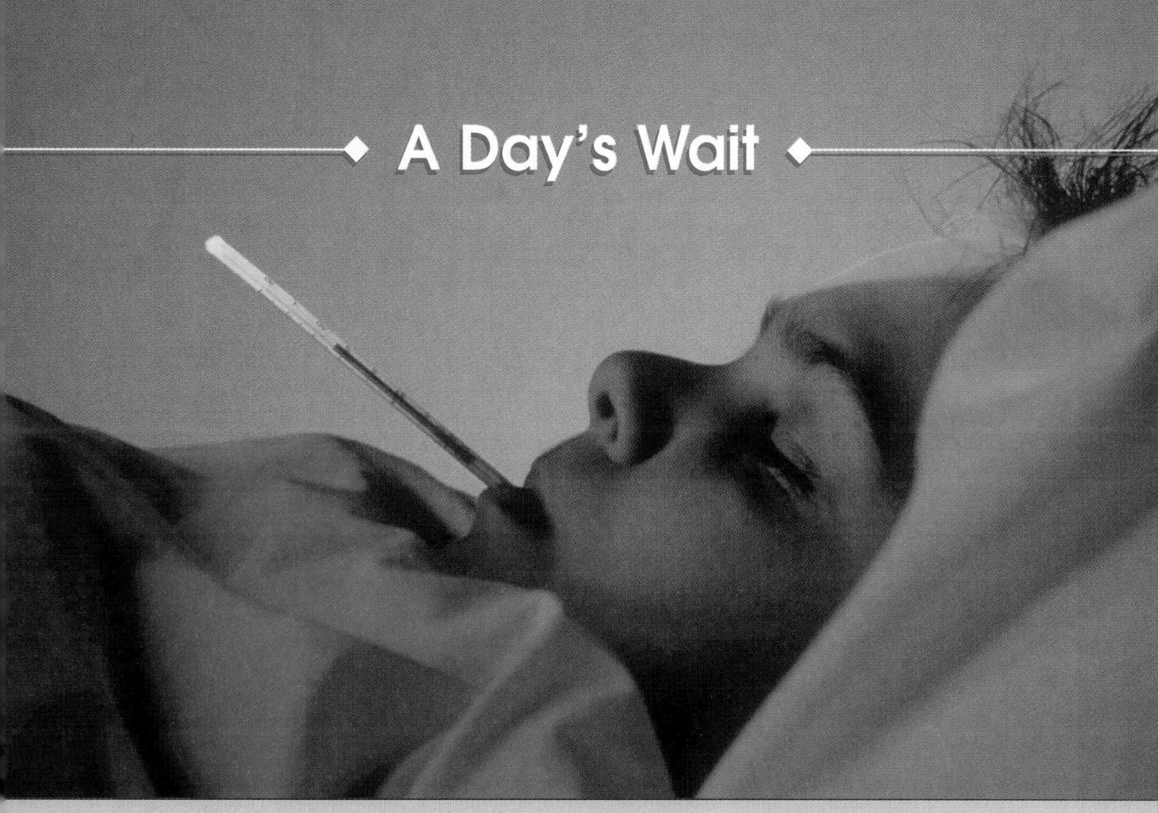

◆ Literary Focus

Internal Conflict

Most fiction centers around a **conflict,** which is a struggle between opposing forces. An **internal conflict** is one that takes place inside a character's mind. The struggle may be to overcome a fear, learn how to manage anger, or decide between two options of equal value. "A Day's Wait" is a story of a boy's internal conflict. Because you do not know the boy's thoughts, you discover his conflict through his actions and words.

◆ Reading Strategy

Reread

Reading can be a many-step process. When you **reread,** you read again for a particular purpose. You might pause to reread a passage that's unclear, or reread an entire story to find answers to unresolved questions. Through this process, you can gain new understanding. For example, you might find clues that explain why the boy in this story is so worried. Use a chart like the one below to record questions that come to mind or details that seem unclear as you read for the first time. Then, reread all or part of the story, focusing on finding answers to your questions.

Reading Questions	Rereading Answers
Why won't the boy stay in bed if he is sick?	

Preparing for Standardized Tests

Vocabulary Using word roots is a helpful skill when students are asked to recognize a an unfamiliar word on standardized tests.

The root *-vid-* means "to see." Knowing this meaning will help students determine the definition of other words that share this word root. Write this sentence on the board: *The boy was watching a video.* Tell students that the root word of video means "to see," which would help them understand the meaning of video if they did not already recognize the word.

Have students consider the following sample test question:

Write the letter of the word that is closest in meaning to the word *evident.*

(A) joyful (C) eventful
(B) dental (D) apparent

Based on the root word *-vid-,* the word *evident* can be defined as "easily seen." Therefore, the best answer is *(D) apparent,* which has nearly the same meaning as *evident.* The other three choices are not close in meaning. For practice in using the word root *-vid-,* use Build Vocabulary in **Selection Support,** p. 29.

Ask students to remember a time when they became sick. Did someone explain the illness and let them know they would be okay, or were they afraid they might be sick forever? Have volunteers role-play a doctor and patient visit where the doctor and patient discuss symptoms, possible treatment and outcomes, as well as the questions and fears of the patient. Have students consider whether or not a sick and feverish person usually feels good enough to think rationally and ask specific questions. Lead students into this selection by explaining that it is about a boy who faces unanswered questions and fears after waking up one morning ill with a fever.

◆ Build Grammar Skills

Pronouns If you wish to introduce the grammar concept for this selection before students read, refer to the instruction on p. 76.

Customize for *Less Proficient Readers*

Suggest that students read the selection with a partner. After they read a page silently, have them take turns summarizing the events on the page. Suggest that students reread the page if one partner has questions about the details of the summary.

Customize for *More Advanced Students*

Suggest that students make notes about the main character as they read. Have them use these notes to formulate unanswered questions and possible answers they may have about the story details and the plot. For example, the boy's mother is not mentioned in the short story. Students could speculate about the reason she is absent. They might wish to expand on the boy's experiences at school in France and explore reasons why he seems unfamiliar with life in the United States. Suggest that students dig deeper into Hemingway's unstated meanings.

Develop Understanding

One-Minute Insight In "A Day's Wait," a young boy is terrified by his sudden illness, but bravely hides his fears. Unaware of the boy's true feelings, his father leaves the house to go for a walk. Returning, the father finally realizes how tormented the boy has been all day. The simple misunderstanding and source of the boy's fears is finally revealed at the end of the story. The boy's quiet resolve demonstrates how some people face distressing situations with courage and concern for others.

◆ Reading Strategy

❶ **Reread** Point out to students that the dialogue in this passage has no words that identify each speaker. Have students reread the passage to identify which lines of dialogue are the narrator's and which are the boy's.

◆ Build Grammar Skills

❷ **Pronouns** Tell students that pronouns take the place of nouns in a sentence and that some nouns name persons. Ask them to explain why the narrator's identity is unknown at this point. *The narrator has only been identified by the pronoun I. The noun that I replaces must be known in order to confirm the narrator's identity.*

Customize for
English Language Learners
Before students begin reading, explain words and phrases from the story that may be difficult to understand, for example: "influenza," "lightheaded," "prescribed," "varnished with ice," "thermometer," and "slack."

A Day's Wait

Ernest Hemingway

He came into the room to shut the windows while we were still in bed and I saw he looked ill. He was shivering, his face was white, and he walked slowly as though it ached to move.

"What's the matter, Schatz?"[1]

"I've got a headache."

❶ "You better go back to bed."

"No. I'm all right."

"You go to bed. I'll see you when I'm dressed."

But when I came downstairs he was dressed, sitting by the fire, looking a very sick and miserable boy of nine years. When I put my hand on his forehead I knew he had a fever.

"You go up to bed," I said, "you're sick."

"I'm all right," he said.

When the doctor came he took the boy's temperature.

"What is it?" I asked him.

"One hundred and two."

Downstairs, the doctor left three different medicines in different colored capsules with instructions for giving them. One was to bring down the fever, another a purgative, the third to overcome an acid condition. The germs of influenza can only exist in an acid condition, he explained. He seemed to know all about influenza and said there was nothing to worry about if the fever did not go above one hundred and four degrees. This was a light epidemic of flu and there was no danger if you avoided pneumonia.

❷ Back in the room I wrote the boy's temperature down and made a note of the time to give the various capsules.

1. **Schatz** (shäts): German term of affection, used here as a loving nickname.

Block Scheduling Strategies

Consider these suggestions for taking advantage of extended class time:

- In order to understand and enjoy reading Hemingway, students must have good comprehension of details included in the story. Because temperature is a very crucial detail, before students read discuss Background for Understanding, p. 70, as a class. After reading, discuss why the background information was so important to understanding the story. Then have students independently complete Guide for Responding questions, p. 75. Invite students to discuss their individual answers in small groups.
- For practice applying the reading strategy of rereading, ask students to fill in the chart shown in Reading Strategy, p. 71, as they reread the story. After rereading, have them discuss Reading Strategy questions on p. 76 in small groups. Then, have students complete the Writing Mini-Lesson, p. 77. Remind them to reread their stories during the Revising stage of the mini-lesson.
- To focus on the main character's internal conflict, have students review Literary Focus, p. 71. Have them discuss and answer the Literary Focus questions, p. 76, in small groups. Students can then use what they have discussed to complete the Inner Monologue writing activity, p. 77.

3 ▲ Critical Viewing In this story, a father and son spend time apart. How might time in a natural setting like this one help the father to stay calm? **[Speculate]**

"Do you want me to read to you?"

"All right. If you want to," said the boy. His face was very white and there were dark areas under his eyes. He lay still in the bed and seemed very detached from what was going on.

I read aloud from Howard Pyle's *Book of Pirates;* but I could see he was not following what I was reading.

4 "How do you feel, Schatz?" I asked him.

"Just the same, so far," he said.

5 I sat at the foot of the bed and read to myself while I waited for it to be time to give another capsule. It would have been natural 5
for him to go to sleep, but when I looked up he was looking at the foot of the bed, looking very strangely.

"Why don't you try to go to sleep? I'll wake you up for the medicine."

"I'd rather stay awake."

After a while he said to me, "You don't have to stay in here with me, Papa, if it bothers you."

"It doesn't bother me."

"No. I mean you don't have to stay if it's going to bother you."

I thought perhaps he was a little lightheaded

◆ Build Vocabulary

epidemic (ep´ ə dem´ ik) *n.*: Outbreak of a contagious disease

▶ Critical Viewing ◀

3 **Speculate** *Students may suggest that the quiet and solitude of the surroundings would give the father an opportunity to settle his thoughts.*

◆ Literary Focus

4 **Internal Conflict** The boy's detachment and the comment "so far" suggest that he is expecting something worse to happen, but he doesn't share this fear with his father. Ask students why he doesn't talk about his internal conflict. *He is scared and imagining bad things, but he doesn't want to show that he is afraid or worry his father.*

Comprehension Check ☑

5 How long does the father sit by the bed reading to himself? *He probably sits by the bed for quite a while because he waits until it is time to give his son his next capsule. He is surprised that the boy is still awake.*

Customize for *Less Proficient Readers*

Be sure that students understand what the word *detached* means. Ask three volunteers to demonstrate detachment by having two students engaged in an activity while the third student stands alone, absorbed in his or her own thoughts.

Customize for *Bodily/Kinesthetic Learners*

Invite interested volunteers to create a silent dramatization of the story. Suggest that they create roles for the father, the boy, and the doctor. Students should use body language and facial gestures that show their understanding of the miscommunication among the characters and the internal struggles of the boy.

Speaking and Listening Mini-Lesson

Panel Discussion

This mini-lesson supports the Speaking and Listening activity in the Idea Bank, p. 77.

Introduce Explain to students that an informational panel discussion about childhood illnesses is an excellent means of making important information available to the public.

Develop Suggest that students list jobs that need to be accomplished in order to have a successful panel discussion. Set up committees as needed.

- Establish a date and time.
- Decide if special guests should be invited to listen to the panel discussion—parents, community members, another class.
- Invite speakers—nurse, doctor, parent, hospital worker. Discuss whether to ask each participant to make a short presentation about the topic in addition to being prepared to answer questions.
- Plan questions to ask the panel and select moderators to be prepared to ask the questions.
- Set up the speakers' table and seating for guests.

Apply Conduct the panel discussion meeting.

Assess Use Self-Assessment: Speaking and Listening Progress form, p. 109 in **Alternative Assessment.**

▶ Critical Viewing◀

❶ **Connect** *The boy in the picture has a thermometer in his mouth, he is wrapped up in his blanket, his eyes are closed, his hair is messy, and he is in bed.*

◆ Critical Thinking

❷ **Infer** What can you infer from the father's decision to go hunting? *The father doesn't think there is any real cause for alarm about the boy's illness.*

◆ Reading Strategy

❸ **Reread** Have students reread the description of the walk in the woods. What do these details reveal? *The details show that the setting of the story is in the country in the wintertime and the man enjoys being outdoors and hunting with his dog.*

Comprehension Check ☑

❹ Ask students why the boy makes the statement "You can't come in. You mustn't get what I have" and what it reveals about his character. *The boy is worried that he might die and someone else will catch the illness that he has. He reveals that he is a brave and caring person.*

◆ Literary Focus

❺ **Internal Conflict** *When the boy says, "I don't worry, but I can't keep from thinking," he indicates that he is worried about something, but doesn't want to admit it. His father's observation that he is "holding tight on to himself about something" supports this idea.*

Customize for *Bodily/Kinesthetic Learners*

Suggest that students tense up their shoulders and back to relate to the boy's feelings during most of the story. Then have them relax to show how he feels at the end. Have them discuss which posture feels better and why.

1 ▶ **Critical Viewing** What details in this picture suggest that the boy in the picture is as sick as the boy in the story? **[Connect]**

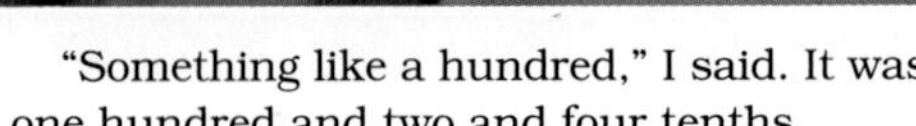

2 and after giving him the prescribed capsules at eleven o'clock I went out for a while. It was a bright, cold day, the ground covered with a sleet that had frozen so that it seemed as if all the bare trees, the bushes, the cut brush and all the grass and the bare ground had been varnished with ice. I took the young Irish setter for a little walk up the road and along a frozen creek, but it was difficult to stand or walk on the glassy surface and the red dog slipped and slithered and I fell twice,
3 hard, once dropping my gun and having it slide away over the ice.

We flushed[2] a covey[3] of quail under a high clay bank with overhanging brush and I killed two as they went out of sight over the top of the bank. Some of the covey lit in trees but most of them scattered into brush piles and it was necessary to jump on the ice-coated mounds of brush several times before they would flush. Coming out while you were poised unsteadily on the icy, springy brush they made difficult shooting, and I killed two, missed five, and started back pleased to have found a covey close to the house and happy there were so many left to find on another day.

At the house they said the boy had refused to let anyone come into the room.

4 "You can't come in," he said. "You mustn't get what I have."

I went up to him and found him in exactly the position I had left him, white-faced, but with the tops of his cheeks flushed by the fever, staring still, as he had stared at the foot of the bed.

I took his temperature.

"What is it?"

"Something like a hundred," I said. It was one hundred and two and four tenths.

"It was a hundred and two," he said.

"Who said so?"

"The doctor."

"Your temperature is all right," I said. "It's nothing to worry about."

"I don't worry," he said, "but I can't keep from thinking."

"Don't think," I said. "Just take it easy."

"I'm taking it easy," he said and looked straight ahead. He was evidently holding tight on to himself about something.

"Take this with water."

"Do you think it will do any good?"

"Of course it will."

I sat down and opened the *Pirate* book and commenced to read, but I could see he was not following, so I stopped.

"About what time do you think I'm going to die?" he asked.

"What?"

"About how long will it be before I die?"

"You aren't going to die. What's the matter with you?"

"Oh, yes, I am. I heard him say a hundred and two."

"People don't die with a fever of one hundred

◆ **Literary Focus** How does Schatz's response hint at an inner conflict? 5

2. **flushed** (flusht) *v.*: Drove from hiding.
3. **covey** (kuv´ ē) *n.*: Small flock of birds.

◆ Build Vocabulary

evidently (ev´ ə dent´ lē) *adv.*: Clearly; obviously

Humanities: Literature

Ernest Hemingway Although Ernest Hemingway's award-winning writing style is sometimes described as simple, it often has many hidden layers. Students can simply read the story "A Day's Wait" and think about a boy who is afraid because he is ill. Or they can think about what is not specifically written and analyze the terror and isolation a child might feel who has been educated in France and is certain he will die—because of his misunderstanding about temperature readings. An adult reading the story might find even deeper layers of meaning.

Students may understand more easily if this writing style is described to them, using Hemingway's own words, as an "iceberg." The written words and plot of the story are only the tip of the iceberg that can be seen above the water. Much of the story is left unwritten so that the reader must feel it and then draw his or her own conclusions.

Reading Hemingway's writing is similar to looking at fine art or listening to classical music. It may take many readings of a variety of his works to truly appreciate the complexity of the literature.

and two. That's a silly way to talk."

"I know they do. At school in France the boys told me you can't live with forty-four degrees. I've got a hundred and two."

> ◆ **Reading Strategy**
> 6 Reread the first two pages of the story to see why Schatz thought he was going to die.

He had been waiting to die all day, ever since nine o'clock in the morning.

"You poor Schatz," I said. "Poor old Schatz. It's like miles and kilometers.[4] You aren't going to die. That's a different thermometer. On that thermometer thirty-seven is normal. On this kind it's ninety-eight."

"Are you sure?"

"Absolutely," I said. "It's like miles and kilometers. You know, like how many kilometers we make when we do seventy miles in the car?"

"Oh," he said.

But his gaze at the foot of the bed relaxed slowly. The hold over himself relaxed too, finally, and the next day it was very slack and he cried very easily at little things that were of no importance.

4. **kilometers** (ki läm′ ə tərz) *n.*: A kilometer is 1,000 meters or about 5/8 of a mile.

Guide for Responding

◆ Literature and Your Life

Reader's Response Do you find the boy's actions courageous, touching, or silly? Explain.

Thematic Focus How does the boy's illness cause him to test his image of himself? What does he discover?

Journal Entry What do people learn from their experiences with anxiety? Write about a time when you worried about something that turned out to be less of a problem than you originally imagined. What lesson did you take away from the experience?

☑ Check Your Comprehension

1. What starts the boy's concern over dying?
2. How does the boy spend his day of illness?
3. What does the boy's father do while the boy is ill?
4. Why does the boy think he will die?
5. How does the father explain the mistake to his son?

◆ Critical Thinking

Interpret

1. What is the meaning of the story's title? **[Interpret]**
2. Describe two ways in which the boy shows courage or concern for others. **[Connect]**
3. Why does the boy cry easily the next day? **[Analyze Cause and Effect]**
4. How do you think the confusion over the boy's illness will change the relationship between the boy and his father? **[Speculate]**
5. What long-term effect might this "day's wait" have on the boy? **[Analyze Cause and Effect; Speculate]**

Apply

6. In his novels, Hemingway often celebrated bravery. How does the boy's behavior in "A Day's Wait" illustrate Hemingway's ideal of courage? **[Draw Conclusions]**

Extend

7. Name two jobs in which the boy's quiet bravery would be valuable. Explain how this quality would be useful in each job. **[Career Link]**

Beyond the Selection

FURTHER READING

Other Works by Ernest Hemingway

The Short Stories

Other Works With the Theme of Testing Yourself

On the Far Side of the Mountain, Jean Craighead George

The Night Journey, Kathryn Lasky

Dogsong, Gary Paulsen

INTERNET

We suggest the following sites on the Internet (all Web sites are subject to change).

For more on Ernest Hemingway: **http://www.ee.mcgill.ca/~nverever/hem/pindex.html**

For links to short stories written by students: **http://www.ipl.org/cgi-bin/youth/youth.out.pl?sub=rzn3000**

We *strongly recommend* that you preview these sites before you send students to them.

◆ Reading Strategy

6 Reread *The boy hears the doctor say that his temperature is 102°, but doesn't hear that there is no problem unless the fever goes above 104°. He thinks something is wrong because his father spends time at his bedside. Having gone to school in France, he misunderstands his fever, believing that it is very high and he will surely die.*

Reinforce and Extend

Answers

◆ Literature and Your Life

Reader's Response Many students will find the boy's behavior courageous because he faced his fears alone. Some will think he was foolish not to have explained his fears sooner.

Thematic Focus The boy's illness causes him to test whether he has the strength to face death alone. He discovers that he can be brave and caring even when he is frightened.

☑ Check Your Comprehension

1. He hears the doctor report his temperature as 102°.
2. He waits to die.
3. He stays with the boy for a while and then goes hunting.
4. His temperature is 102°F., and in France he was told that people can't live with a temperature higher than 44°C.
5. He explains that body temperature can be measured with different units. In one system 37°C. is normal, whereas in the other system 98°F. is normal.

◆ Critical Thinking

1. The boy waits the whole day to die, and a day like that can seem like an eternity.
2. The boy shows courage because he does not cry or complain. He shows concern when he tells his father that he doesn't need to stay and not to come in because he might get sick, too.
3. He isn't preparing to die anymore, so he can let go of his emotions.
4. They learned to communicate better and might be closer as a result.
5. The boy knows how to face death.
6. Despite fear, the boy controls his emotions and considers others.
7. A police officer must handle tense situations with calm courage; a nurse assists and reassures others.

Answers

◆ Reading Strategy

1. The boy keeps his feelings hidden, and because the father knows that the illness is not serious, he doesn't notice his fears.
2. The boy went to school in France, where his schoolmates told him that a body temperature of 44°C. is deadly.
3. Students may suggest they want to know more about the boy's mother, where the boy and his father live, the boy's real name, or why the boy went to school in France.

◆ Build Vocabulary

Using the Word Root *-vid-*

1. video; 2. evidence

Spelling Strategy

1. residence; 2. patience;
3. insistence; 4. difference

Using the Word Bank

1. epidemic; 2. evidently

◆ Literary Focus

1. Although the boy feels terrified, he wants to be brave both for himself and for his father.
2. Some examples of unusual statements are "You don't have to stay if it's going to bother you"; "You can't come in. You mustn't get what I have"; and "Do you think it will do any good?" Some examples of unusual actions are that the boy won't go to sleep; he stares vacantly; and he wants to be alone.

◆ Build Grammar Skills

Practice

1. we; 2. you, it; 3. himself, he;
4. It, him; 5. Who

Writing Application

1. The boy believes he is going to die.
2. The boy wonders how his father could hunt now.
3. His temperature is high; it is 102°F.
4. When readers understand his fears, they can appreciate his behavior.

Guide for Responding *(continued)*

◆ Reading Strategy

Reread

Rereading passages of text will help you answer questions and clear up areas of confusion. You can truly appreciate the behavior of the boy in "A Day's Wait," for example, once you understand what triggers his fear. Rereading may also reveal that an author has omitted certain information for a reason. Reread "A Day's Wait" to answer each of the following questions.

1. Why doesn't the boy's father notice his son's fear?
2. How did the boy become confused about his condition?
3. What information has the author not included that would have improved your understanding of the story?

◆ Build Vocabulary

Using the Word Root *-vid-*

The following words contain the root *-vid-*, meaning "to see." Complete the sentences with one of these words:

video evidence

1. Sports analysts review the ___?___ to get a better look at close plays.
2. His white face and tense expression were ___?___ of the boy's fear.

Spelling Strategy

The *-ent* in *evident* makes the word an adjective, a word that describes a noun. Many words that end in *-ent* have a related noun form that ends in *-ence*, like *evidence*. Write the related noun form of these words:

1. resident **3.** insistent
2. patient **4.** different

Using the Word Bank

On your paper, complete the paragraph with words from the Word Bank.

People in the tiny Italian village were terrified. A terrible ___?___ had caused dozens of people to fall ill. ___?___, a germ had made its way into the water supply.

◆ Literary Focus

Internal Conflict

An **internal conflict** is a struggle within a character's mind. In "A Day's Wait," the boy's statements and actions suggest that he is responding to an inner conflict rather than to the actual situation.

1. What conflicting feelings does the boy have?
2. List two examples of unusual statements or actions that point to the boy's internal conflict.

◆ Build Grammar Skills

Pronouns

A **pronoun** is a word that takes the place of a noun or a group of words acting as a noun. Pronouns offer writers another way to identify people, places, and things. For instance, Hemingway uses the nouns "boy" and "Schatz" to refer to his main character, and he uses the pronouns "he" and "him" in place of these nouns. Here are the most common pronouns:

I	me	my	hers	herself
she	us	mine	its	themselves
he	you	our	their	who
it	them	ours	myself	whose
we	him	your	ourselves	which
they	her	his	himself	

Practice Write the following sentences. Circle the pronouns.

1. As readers, we understand the father's actions.
2. How would you explain it to the boy?
3. The boy finally tells himself he will survive.
4. It makes him feel much better.
5. Who will research Hemingway's life?

Writing Application Copy the following sentences, replacing the italicized words with pronouns.

1. The boy believes *the boy* is going to die.
2. The boy wonders how *the boy's* father could hunt now.
3. His temperature is high; *the temperature* is 102°F.
4. When readers understand his fears, *readers* can appreciate his behavior.

Writer's Solution

For additional practice and support using pronouns, use the practice pages on pronouns, pp. 8–10, in the *Writer's Solution Grammar Practice Book*. You may also use the lesson in the *Writer's Solution Language Lab CD-ROM* on Using Pronouns.

Build Your Portfolio

Idea Bank

Writing

1. **Internal Monologue** Describe the thoughts running through the boy's mind as he waits to die. Write a monologue—the speech or thoughts of a single character—that captures his feelings.
2. **Film Director's Memo** Imagine that you are directing a movie based on this story. Choose a scene, and describe camera shots that will capture the boy's internal conflict. Explain why each shot would be effective. **[Career Link]**
3. **Definition** "A Day's Wait" shows that courage is sometimes tested in the most unexpected ways. Write a definition of courage. Use your own experiences or those of people you know to illustrate your definition.

Speaking and Listening

4. **Medal Presentation Speech** Deliver a speech in which you award the boy a medal for courage. Explain how his behavior in the face of fear has earned him this medal.
5. **Panel Discussion** Organize an information session about children's health. Invite outside speakers or the school nurse to speak about common childhood illnesses. Prepare a list of specific questions. Then, host the visit, welcoming your guests and directing the conversation. **[Health Link]**

Projects

6. **Comparison Chart** Many Americans know that cakes bake at 350°F and that kids wear shorts if the weather hits 70°F. List significant temperatures like these, and calculate their Celsius equivalents. Use the formula $°C = \frac{5}{9} \times (°F - 32)$. Show results in an illustrated chart. **[Math Link]**
7. **Advice Pamphlet [Group Activity]** With classmates, develop a pamphlet to help parents deal with common childhood ailments. One person can research the symptoms children may experience, while others can list tips for keeping children comfortable. **[Health Link]**

Writing Mini-Lesson

A Day of Anticipation

In "A Day's Wait," a boy fearfully anticipates his own death. Imagine how different the story would have been if the boy had been looking forward to a happy occasion. The boy probably would have been anxious for time to pass as quickly as possible, and he might have struggled to contain his excitement. Recall a day you spent anticipating an event or decision. Write a narrative telling the story of that day.

Writing Skills Focus: Elaborate to Make Writing Personal

Draw readers into your personal experience. Provide details to show how the events of that anxious day made you feel. Tell readers, for example, that your heart jumped every time the phone rang, that time seemed to stand still, or that you were surprised at how calm you became as the event drew near.

Prewriting Choose the day about which you will write. Then write an hour-by-hour list of events that occurred during the day. Next to each event, list the emotion it triggered.

Drafting Begin by identifying the anticipated event or by providing a vivid example of your emotions. Then, unfold the day's story, showing the events and your reactions. Conclude your essay by describing what finally happened and the impact the event had on your feelings.

Revising Review your story to identify places where you simply recount events. In these spots, elaborate by adding details that explain how the events made you feel.

◆ Grammar Application

Find the places where your use of nouns is repetitive. Replace some nouns, especially names, with pronouns. Pronouns will make your story flow more smoothly.

ASSESSMENT OPTIONS

Formal Assessment, Selection Test, pp. 18–20, and Assessment Resources Software. The selection test is designed so that it can be easily customized to the performance levels of your students.

Alternative Assessment, p. 6, includes options for less advanced students, more advanced students, interpersonal learners, logical/mathematical learners, verbal/linguistic learners, bodily/kinesthetic learners, and visual/spatial learners.

PORTFOLIO ASSESSMENT

Use the following rubrics in the **Alternative Assessment** booklet to assess student writing:
Inner Monologue: Expression Rubric, p. 81
Film Director's Memo: Technical Description/Explanation Rubric, p. 102
Definition: Definition Rubric, p. 86
Writing Mini-Lesson: Fictional Narrative Rubric, p. 82

Idea Bank

Following are suggestions for matching the Idea Bank topics with your students' performance levels:

Customize for *Performance Levels*
Less Advanced Students: 3, 4, 7
Average Students: 1, 4, 6, 7
More Advanced Students: 2, 5, 7

Customize for *Learning Modalities*
Verbal/Linguistic: 1, 2, 3, 4, 5
Interpersonal: 5, 7
Intrapersonal: 3
Visual/Spatial: 2, 6
Logical/Mathematical: 6

Writing Mini-Lesson

Refer students to the Writing Handbook in the back of the book for instruction on the writing process and for further information on writing narratives. Have students use the Series of Events Chain in **Writing and Language Transparencies,** p. 66, to arrange their prewriting examples.

Writer's Solution

Writers at Work Videodisc
Writing Lab CD-ROM
Have students complete the tutorial on Narratives. Follow these steps:

1. Have students view the interactive model of a personal narrative.
2. Suggest that students use the Plot Outliner activity to map the plot of their narrative.
3. Allow students to draft on computer.
4. When revising, have students use the revision checker to determine when they need to vary the language in their narratives.

Writer's Solution Sourcebook
Have students use Chapter 3, "Narration," pp. 66–101, for additional support. This chapter includes in-depth instruction on developing narrative elements, p. 85.

Prepare and Engage

OBJECTIVES

1. To read, comprehend, and interpret three poems
2. To relate poetry to personal experience
3. To recognize signal words
4. To respond to sensory language
5. To build vocabulary in context and use words from the French language
6. To develop skill in identifying and using pronouns and antecedents
7. To write a description of a fire, using sensory language
8. To respond to the poems through writing, speaking and listening, and projects

SKILLS INSTRUCTION

Vocabulary: Words From French
Spelling: Words With *ie* Before *r*
Grammar: Pronouns and Antecedents
Reading Strategy: Recognize Signal Words
Literary Focus: Sensory Language
Writing: Sensory Language
Speaking and Listening: Dialogue (Teacher Edition)
Critical Viewing: Interpret; Extend

PORTFOLIO OPPORTUNITIES

Writing: Jewelry Description; He Said, She Said; Poetry Critique
Writing Mini-Lesson: Description of a Fire
Speaking and Listening: Dialogue; Song Lyrics
Projects: Informative Brochure; Illustrated Chart

More About the Authors

Richard Wilbur has twice won the Pulitzer Prize for his poetry collections. He is also known for his translations of French plays, and for writing the lyrics for the comic opera *Candide*.

Christina Rossetti often spent time in the country with her grandfather when she was a young girl. Themes of nature and wilderness are recurrent in her poetry.

Gary Soto has said that the girl in the poem "Oranges" was 2 inches taller than he was, and he was surprised when she accepted his invitation to go for a walk. In reality he bought a 10-cent bag of popcorn for his date, but in the poem he changed it to chocolate because he thought chocolate sounded more romantic.

Guide for Reading

Meet the Authors:

Richard Wilbur (1921–)

Although Richard Wilbur is known for his writing, he originally planned to be a cartoonist. He created cartoons for his college magazine and later secretly thought that if he failed at other things, he could always be a comic-strip artist. Instead, he has become an award-winning poet.

By the time he reached 30, Wilbur had published two collections of poetry and established himself as an important young writer. In 1987, Wilbur was appointed poet laureate of the United States.

Christina Rossetti (1830–1894)

Poor health forced Christina Rossetti to live a quiet life, but it did not keep her from writing. When she was twenty, Rossetti published her first poems in a magazine produced by her brother. She went on to write many volumes of prose and poetry, including verses for young people, of which "Flint" is an example.

Gary Soto (1952–)

Gary Soto grew up in an industrial neighborhood in Fresno, California. Although the neighborhood was poor, Soto loved it and was deeply saddened when the old buildings were torn down in the 1960's. He says that much of his writing is a reaction to the loss of this happy childhood place.

In fact, Soto's short-story collection *Baseball in April* and his poetry collection *Living Up the Street* reflect his fondness for youth. [For more information about Soto, see page 120.]

◆ Literature and Your Life

Connect Your Experience

Like the geode pictured on the opposite page, everyone has an outer appearance that often conceals an inner drama. Think how exciting it is when you see the inner core of someone else or when someone sees what matters to you. In these poems, look for strength waiting just below the surface.

Thematic Focus: Testing Yourself

When situations test you, you may find your strength somewhere beyond the public part of your personality. These poems remind you that the same applies to others—sometimes you need to look past appearances to find their true identity, too.

◆ Background for Understanding

Science

Christina Rossetti's poem is about flint—a hard, gray rock. If you strike a piece of flint sharply against steel, sparks will fly, and you can start a fire. Centuries before the invention of matches, flint was an everyday necessity. To start a fire, a person would put a small pile of twigs on pieces of wood. Sparks from the flint and steel would then ignite a fire.

◆ Build Vocabulary

Words From French

English has borrowed many words from French. In "Oranges," Gary Soto refers to *rouge*, a French word meaning "red." In English, *rouge* describes a cosmetic, now known as *blusher*, used to color the cheeks.

Word Bank

Which of these words from the poems sounds like the noise it might describe?

commotion
clamor
iridescent
rouge
tiered
hissing

Prentice Hall Literature Program Resources

REINFORCE / RETEACH / EXTEND

Selection Support Pages
Build Vocabulary: Words From French, p. 34
Build Spelling Skills, p. 35
Build Grammar Skills: Pronouns and Antecedents, p. 36
Reading Strategy: Recognize Signal Words, p. 37
Literary Focus: Sensory Language, p. 38

Strategies for Diverse Student Needs, pp. 13–14

Beyond Literature Cross-Curricular Connection: Science, p. 7

Formal Assessment Selection Test, pp. 21–23

Alternative Assessment, p. 7

Writing and Language Transparencies
Sensory Language Chart, p. 78

Resource Pro CD-ROM
"The Writer"; "Flint"; "Oranges"

Listening to Literature Audiocassettes
"The Writer"; "Flint"; "Oranges"

◆ The Writer ◆ Flint ◆ Oranges ◆

◆ Literary Focus

Sensory Language

Sensory language appeals to your sense of sight, hearing, taste, smell, or touch. Poets use sensory language to make the world of a poem come alive. To appreciate a poem fully, read with your senses as well as your mind. For example, when you read Soto's description of cars "hissing by," call up your memories of this noise. When Soto and Rossetti describe fire, remember how a fire sounds and smells. Use a chart like the one below to record words and phrases appealing to each sense.

◆ Reading Strategy

Recognize Signal Words

Poets use language in creative ways. They may include different ideas, jumping from one thought or image to another. One way to follow the flow of ideas is to pay attention to words such as *first*, *but*, and *then* that **signal** relationships between the elements in a poem. As you read the poetry of Wilbur, Rossetti, and Soto, find signal words to help you make connections among the words and ideas.

	Sight	Sound	Smell	Taste	Touch
"Flint"	Emerald green grass		grass		

Preparing for Standardized Tests

Grammar This selection's grammar skill is identifying pronouns and their antecedents. Tell students that an antecedent is the noun to which a pronoun refers. Grammar portions of standardized tests may require students to correctly apply this skill. Often the antecedent appears before the pronoun, but not always. Show this variance, in order, by writing the following sentences on the board:

My *daughter* writes in *her* room.
In *her* room, my *daughter* writes.

Then give students a sample test question.

Identify the pronoun(s) that refer to Richard Wilbur in this sentence.

Richard Wilbur wrote a poem about himself and his daughter.

(A) himself (C) himself and his
(B) his (D) his and her

The correct answer is *(C)*. Both *himself* and *his* are pronouns that refer to the antecedent *Richard Wilbur*. *(A)* and *(B)* each name only one of the two pronouns, and *(D)* names a pronoun that is not used in the sentence.

To help students understand the sensory details in these poems, introduce items that represent each of the senses. For example, have them smell a rose and come up with a list of words to describe its aroma, pass around a smooth rock and have them describe the way it feels, or scratch your nails on the board and have them describe the sound. Tell students that the words they have used to describe what they sensed are examples of sensory language. Explain that in the poems they are about to read, the poets use sensory language to make the poems come alive.

◆ Build Grammar Skills

Pronouns and Antecedents If you wish to introduce the grammar concept for this selection before students read, refer to the instruction on p. 84.

Customize for *Less Proficient Readers*

You may wish to have students read along as they listen to the recording of each poem. Encourage them to notice how the reader pauses in response to punctuation marks within the poem rather than at the end of each line.

Listening to Literature Audiocassettes

Customize for *More Advanced Students*

Suggest that students compare and contrast the poets' styles as they read the three poems by filling out the following chart:

	"The Writer"	"Flint"	"Oranges"
Rhyme	None	ABCB	None
Structure	3-line stanzas	Quatrains	Free verse
Point of View	First	Third	First

Customize for *English Language Learners*

Poets' visual descriptions often use familiar words in ways that students may have difficulty grasping. Have students point out words they know and then discuss or pantomime the phrases where they appear, such as "drop like a glove," "to catch the world's desire," and "she lifted a chocolate."

Develop Understanding

In "The Writer," the speaker observes his daughter writing and thinks about her inevitable struggle for maturity as she tries to find her place in the world.

◆ Critical Thinking

❶ **Interpret** Point out that Wilbur makes references to a ship *(prow, gunwale, cargo)*. Ask students what the ship may symbolize. *The ship symbolizes the daughter's voyage through life.*

◆ Literary Focus

❷ **Sensory Language** Ask students to point out sensory details in this passage. *Students should point out "light breaks," "tossed with linden," "a commotion of typewriter-keys," and "a chain hauled over a gunwale."*

Clarification

❸ Students may be unfamiliar with the sound of typewriter keys. Describe the metallic noise and help them compare it to the softer sound of a computer keyboard's keys.

◆ Build Grammar Skills

❹ **Pronouns and Antecedents** Tell students that a pronoun replaces a noun, and the antecedent is the noun it replaces. Draw students' attention to the pronoun *it* in line 8, and lead them to identify its antecedent as *cargo*. Explain to them that *some* is a different pronoun referring to the same antecedent.

◆ Critical Thinking

❺ **Connect** Ask students what wish the speaker is referring to in lines 32 and 33. *The speaker wants his daughter to grow up happy.*

▶Critical Viewing◀

❻ **Interpret** Students may say the image might illustrate the lines "It lifted off from a chair-back . . . clearing the sill of the world."

Customize for
Visual/Spatial Learners
Have students create images from the poems on paper. They can draw, paint, or use magazine pictures for their images.

The Writer

Richard Wilbur

In her room at the prow[1] of the house
❶ Where light breaks, and the windows are tossed with linden,[2]
My daughter is writing a story.
❷

I pause in the stairwell, hearing
❸ From her shut door a commotion of typewriter-keys
Like a chain hauled over a gunwale.[3]

Young as she is, the stuff
❹ Of her life is a great cargo, and some of it heavy:
I wish her a lucky passage.

But now it is she who pauses,
As if to reject my thought and its easy figure.
A stillness greatens, in which

The whole house seems to be thinking,
And then she is at it again with a bunched clamor
Of strokes, and again is silent.

I remember the dazed starling[4]
Which was trapped in that very room, two years ago;
How we stole in, lifted a sash

And retreated, not to affright it;
And how for a helpless hour, through the crack of the door,
We watched the sleek, wild, dark

And iridescent creature
Batter against the brilliance, drop like a glove
To the hard floor, or the desk-top,

And wait then, humped and bloody,
For the wits to try it again; and how our spirits
Rose when, suddenly sure,

It lifted off from a chair-back,
Beating a smooth course for the right window
And clearing the sill of the world.

It is always a matter, my darling,
Of life or death, as I had forgotten. I wish
❺ What I wished you before, but harder.

▶ Critical Viewing Which lines from "The Writer" might this image illustrate? Explain. **[Interpret]** ❻

◆ Build Vocabulary

commotion (kə mō′ shən) *n.*: Noisy rushing about

clamor (klam′ ər) *n.*: Loud, sustained noise

iridescent (ir′ i des′ ənt) *adj.*: Shimmering with colors; having shifting rainbow colors, like a soap bubble

1. **prow** (prou) *n.*: Front part of a ship or boat.
2. **linden** (lin′ dən) *n.*: Type of tree.
3. **gunwale** (gun′ əl) *n.*: Upper edge of the sides of a ship or boat.
4. **starling** (stär′ liŋ) *n.*: Bird with black feathers that shine in a greenish or purplish way.

Block Scheduling Strategies

Consider these suggestions to take advantage of extended class time:

- Introduce sensory details as the literary focus for these poems. As students read, have them note examples of sensory language on the Sensory Language Chart from the **Writing and Language Transparencies,** p. 78. Then have them complete the Literary Focus activities and compare answers.
- Discuss the thematic focus of the poems before you have students read. Then have students form groups to answer the Critical Thinking questions on p. 83. When they get to the last question on comparing literary works, have them re-form into groups based on their answer. Then have students stage a class debate on which poem they thought was most successful in following the theme.
- After students read the poems, have students work in groups to complete the Writing Mini-Lesson in the *Writer's Solution Writing Lab CD-ROM*. If time permits, have students read their descriptions to the class.

...nde Famille (The Great Family), Rene Magritte, Private Collection/Lauros-Giraudon, Paris

FLINT

Christina Rossetti

❼ An emerald is as green as grass;
A ruby red as blood;
❽ A sapphire shines as blue as heaven;
A flint lies in the mud.

A diamond is a brilliant stone,
To catch the world's desire;
❾ An opal holds a fiery spark;
❿ But a flint holds fire.

Beyond Literature

Workplace Connection

Opportunities for Young Writers Like many young people, the girl in "The Writer" takes her creativity seriously. Most writers, young or old, dream of publishing their work. But where do you publish when you're twelve or thirteen years old? There are a number of publications and contests for student writers. "Creative Kids," "READ," "Skipping Stones," and *Merlyn's Pen* are among the most well known, but there are many others.

Activity

Go for It! Use the library or the Internet to compile a list of names and addresses of publications and contests that specialize in student writing. Then, choose one and submit your best work. Most publications list submission guidelines in each issue. For contests, contact sponsoring organizations for submission rules.

Speaking and Listening Mini-Lesson

Song Lyrics
This mini-lesson supports the Speaking and Listening activity in the Idea Bank on p. 85.

Introduce Point out to students that a successful interpretation of a poem or any other piece of literature communicates the message of the writing to an audience. Discuss students' experiences with successful interpretations of different types of writing.

Develop Divide the class into groups of 3 and have each group review the poem, "Flint." Ask students to assign tasks within their groups to prepare music for the poem, write additional verses, and prepare to present.

Apply Give students the Peer Assessment: Oral Interpretation form, p. 106, in **Alternative Assessment.** As a class, adapt the form to evaluate a presentation of song lyrics. Then, allow time for students to complete their preparations and rehearse or record their song lyrics.

Assess Have students use their adapted assessment forms to evaluate their classmates' presentation.

Develop Understanding

One-Minute Insight In "Flint," Christina Rossetti compares flint to precious gems, implying that the key to one's identity lies beneath the surface.

◆ Literary Focus

❼ **Sensory Language** Have students cite examples of sensory language in lines 1–4. *Students' response should include "green as grass," "red as blood," and "blue as heaven."*

◆ Critical Thinking

❽ **Compare and Contrast** Ask students to compare and contrast flint and the jewels described in the first verse. *Students may respond that they are all stones, but the jewels are colorful and the flint is muddy.*

◆ Build Vocabulary

❾ **Recognize Signal Words** Have students identify the signal word in line 8, and ask what relationship the word signals. *The signal word is* but. *It signals that flint has something more important than the other stones' beauty.*

◆ Literature and Your Life

❿ Ask students to think of objects that are plain or unattractive but capable of something important, such as a pencil that can write a story or a baseball bat that can hit a home run.

Humanities: Art

La Grande Famille (The Great Family), 1963, by René Magritte

Belgian artist René Magritte (1898–1967) is best known for his surrealistic paintings. His art explores relationships between reality and mystery, often presenting ordinary objects in unexpected ways.

1. What images do the poems on these pages share with the artwork? *There is a bird in both "The Writer" and the painting. "Flint" refers to a heavenly blue color, like the blue sky in the painting.*
2. Look more deeply into the meaning of the poems and the painting. What message do they share? *Students' responses should indicate looking beyond the surface to discover a deeper or hidden truth about someone or something.*

Develop Understanding

One-Minute Insight The speaker in Gary Soto's "Oranges" is a 12-year-old boy taking his first walk with a girl. Trying to impress her, he offers to buy her something, then realizes he cannot afford what she wants. He solves his problem creatively, helping him feel confident and lucky.

▶Critical Viewing◀

❶ **Extend** *Students may suggest an image of a boy and girl in a store because it shows the setting of the story.*

◆ Literary Focus

❷ **Sensory Language** Ask students to point out examples of sensory language in lines 1–8. *Examples of sensory language include "cold," "weighted down with two oranges," "frost cracking," "breath before me."*

◆ Reading Strategy

❸ **Recognize Signal Words** Ask students to discuss how the signal word *then* helps them understand the situation. *Students may say that then helps them understand that he first places the nickel on the counter, before he offers the orange as a replacement for the money he doesn't have.*

Comprehension Check ☑

❹ Ask students what it is that the lady knows. *She knows the boy doesn't have enough money for the candy, and he doesn't want the girl to know.*

◆ Literary Focus

❺ **Sensory Language** Ask students to identify sensory language in lines 44–46, including the sense to which each example appeals. *Students may identify the phrase "cars hissing past," which appeals to hearing; "fog hanging like old coats between the trees," which appeals to sight.*

Customize for
Bodily/Kinesthetic Learners
You may want to have volunteers act out the story behind "Oranges" to show how the poem progresses. You will need a student to be the speaker or narrator, one to be the girl, and one to be the saleslady.

GARY SOTO

Three Fruit, Ashton Hinrichs

❶ ▲ Critical Viewing This painting of oranges seems to suit Gary Soto's poem. What other image might you suggest? Defend your choice. **[Extend]**

The first time I walked
With a girl, I was twelve,
Cold, and weighted down
With two oranges in my jacket. ❷
December. Frost cracking
Beneath my steps, my breath
Before me, then gone,
As I walked toward
Her house, the one whose
Porchlight burned yellow
Night and day, in any weather.
A dog barked at me, until
She came out pulling
At her gloves, face bright
With rouge. I smiled,
Touched her shoulder, and led
Her down the street, across
A used car lot and a line
Of newly planted trees,
Until we were breathing
Before a drug store. We
Entered, the tiny bell
Bringing a saleslady
Down a narrow aisle of goods.
I turned to the candies
Tiered like bleachers,
And asked what she wanted—
Light in her eyes, a smile
Starting at the corners
Of her mouth. I fingered
A nickel in my pocket,
And when she lifted a chocolate ❸
That cost a dime,
I didn't say anything.
I took the nickel from
My pocket, then an orange,
And set them quietly on
The counter. When I looked up,
The lady's eyes met mine, ❹
And held them, knowing
Very well what it was all
About.

Humanities: Art

Three Fruit, by Ashton Hinrichs

Invite volunteers to describe what they see in this colorful, expressive still life. Point out how the diagonal lines in this painting contrast with the round shapes of the fruit. Help students link the artwork to "Oranges" by asking the following questions:

1. How are the oranges in the artwork similar to the oranges in the poem? *The oranges in both are brightly colored and stand out against their backgrounds.*
2. If the speaker in "Oranges" were to paint a painting of his orange, how would it differ from this? *Students may say the speaker would make the background of the painting a dull gray like the gray December in the poem.*
3. Compare and contrast the painting and lines 43–56 of the poem. *The poem's description of the orange in the gray setting offers a similar balance of colors as the painting's fruit against the blue background; the poem offers more sensory descriptions than the painting can visually portray, such as sound of the cars hissing, dampness of fog, and holding the girl's hand.*

Outside,
A few cars hissing past,
Fog hanging like old ❺
Coats between the trees.
I took my girl's hand
In mine for two blocks,
Then released it to let
Her unwrap the chocolate.
I peeled my orange
That was so bright against
The gray of December ❻
That, from some distance,
Someone might have thought
I was making a fire in my hands.

◆ **Build Vocabulary**

rouge (ro͞ozh) *n.*: Reddish cosmetic used to color cheeks

tiered (tird) *adj.*: Stacked in rows

hissing (his′ iŋ) *adj.*: Making a sound like a prolonged *s*

Guide for Responding

◆ Literature and Your Life

Reader's Response Do you think that you are most like the speaker in "The Writer," "Flint," or "Oranges"? Explain.

Thematic Focus Explain how these poems celebrate qualities that are revealed only through careful examination.

☑ Check Your Comprehension

1. Describe the daughter's actions in "The Writer."
2. In "The Writer," how do the speaker and his daughter respond to the starling's situation?
3. What objects are the subject of "Flint"?
4. Where does Rossetti say that flint can be found?
5. Describe the girl in "Oranges" when she first comes out of her house.
6. Why does the speaker in "Oranges" pay for the candy with a nickel and an orange?

◆ Critical Thinking

Interpret

1. According to the speaker of "The Writer," how are his daughter and the starling similar? **[Compare and Contrast]**
2. What does the speaker of "The Writer" conclude about the ways he can affect his daughter's life? **[Synthesize]**
3. What comparision does the speaker of "Flint" see between flint and precious gems? **[Infer]**
4. Explain the saleslady's reaction in "Oranges" when the speaker offers an orange. **[Analyze]**
5. What does the remaining orange come to represent to the speaker in "Oranges"? **[Infer]**

Apply

6. How might "Flint" help people better understand one another? **[Relate]**

Compare Literary Works

7. Which poem do you think is most successful in describing the need to see beyond initial expectations? Explain. **[Evaluate]**

◆ Critical Thinking

❻ **Interpret** Ask students why the author ends the poem by comparing the orange to a fire in his hands. *Some students may say that the orange is like a fire because it contrasts against the gray December sky.*

Reinforce and Extend

Answers

◆ Literature and Your Life

Reader's Response Some students will say they are most like the speaker of "Flint" because they look beyond the surface to determine the worth of a person or an object. Others will say they are most like the speaker in "Oranges" because they share similar experiences.

Thematic Focus They show that what appears to be one thing on the outside can always be looked at in a different way.

☑ Check Your Comprehension

1. She is using a typewriter to write something.
2. They carefully raise a window and then leave the room.
3. Different stones are the subject.
4. Flint can be found in the mud.
5. Her face is bright with rouge and she is putting on gloves.
6. He does not have enough money.

◆ Critical Thinking

1. They are similar in that they are both trying hard for something: the daughter to write and the bird to escape.
2. He can only wish that she finds her way, but he cannot help her.
3. Flint has the same inner value as a gem's outer preciousness.
4. She sees that he doesn't have enough money, so she takes the orange to avoid embarrassing him in front of the girl.
5. The orange may represent how he feels about the girl; it may also stand for the potential of their relationship.
6. It might help people understand that everyone has qualities underneath their external appearance.
7. Some students may say "Flint" is most successful because it provides a clear example of flint lying in the mud like something you might pass over even though it has a valuable quality.

Beyond the Selection

FURTHER READING

Other Works by the Authors

Things of This World, Richard Wilbur

A Choice of Christina Rossetti's Verse, Elizabeth Jennings (ed.)

New and Selected Poems, Gary Soto

Other Works About Inventing Yourself

The Phantom Tollbooth, Norton Juster

Island of the Blue Dolphins, Scott O'Dell

INTERNET

We suggest the following sites on the Internet (all Web sites are subject to change).

For Richard Wilbur: **http://www.theatlantic.com/atlantic/issues/95sep/wilbur.htm**

For Christina Rossetti: **http://www.stg.brown.edu/projects/hypertext/landow/victorian/crossetti/crov.html**

For Gary Soto: **http://www.garysoto.com**

We *strongly recommend* that you preview these sites before you send students to them.

Answers

◆ Reading Strategy

1. Students may suggest the word *but* in line 8, which signals the comparison between all the jewels and flint.
2. "The Writer": Students may list *but* in line 10, which links the image of the speaker pausing with that of the daughter pausing. The word *before* in line 33 connects the speaker's final wish to his opening wish for "a lucky passage."

   "Oranges": Students may list the word *until* in line 12, which links the dog barking and the girl coming out of the house. The word *when* in line 38 links the speaker looking up and the lady's eyes meeting his.

◆ Build Vocabulary

Using Words From French

1. a chest of drawers
2. physical or bodily structure
3. stylish
4. a small shop
5. a meeting place
6. an overused or trite expression

Spelling Strategy

1. pier
2. fierce
3. cashier
4. pierce

Using the Word Bank

Sample responses:

1. The silence of the cave was broken by a snake hissing, followed by the clamor and commotion of hikers scrambling to escape.
2. The three-tiered white cake was topped with a bride and groom.
3. The lake's surface looked iridescent in the moonlight.
4. The bright rouge enhanced the model's cheekbones.

◆ Literary Focus

1. Possible responses: "The Writer"—wild, dark and iridescent; brilliance; humped and bloody. "Flint"—green as grass, red as blood, brilliant, fiery spark. "Oranges"—light in her eyes, fog hanging, the gray of December.
2. Possible responses: "The Writer" —like chain hauled over a gunwale; stillness greatens; bunched clamor. "Oranges"—Frost cracking; tiny bells; cars hissing past.
3. (a) taste; (b) sight; (c) smell; (d) touch; (e) hearing

Guide for Responding *(continued)*

◆ Reading Strategy

Recognize Signal Words

By acting as road signs that direct the flow of ideas, **signal words**—like *then, now, next, after*, and *but*—help you follow a poet's ideas. In "Oranges," for example, the word *as* links two actions happening at the same time: *As* he walked, he heard a dog bark. He hears this sound *until* he sees his date. In "The Writer," the words "I remember" tell you that the speaker is about to describe a memory of a past event.

1. Identify a key signal word in "Flint," and explain the relationship to the ideas it suggests.
2. List two signal words each from "The Writer" and "Oranges." Explain how each word links the ideas around it.

◆ Build Vocabulary

Using Words From French

The word *rouge*, which appears in "Oranges," comes from French. Other French words, now common in English, are listed below. With a partner, discuss each one. Jot down a definition for each word you recognize. Check your definition in an English dictionary.

1. bureau **4.** boutique
2. physique **5.** rendezvous
3. chic **6.** cliché

Spelling Strategy

The rule "Use *i* before *e* except after *c*" also holds true when *i* and *e* appear before *r*. For example, *i* comes before *e* in *tier*. On your paper, complete the following words by filling in the blanks with *i* and *e*.

1. p_ _ r **3.** cash _ _ r
2. f _ _ rce **4.** p _ _ rce

Using the Word Bank

Write sentences according to the directions below. Provide enough context to demonstrate the meaning of the italicized words.

1. Use the words *hissing, clamor*, and *commotion* to describe a scary scene.
2. Use the word *tiered* to describe a wedding cake.
3. Use the word *iridescent* to describe a lake.
4. Use the word *rouge* to describe a model's face.

◆ Literary Focus

Sensory Language

Sensory language refers to words and phrases that appeal to the senses. The sensory language in these poems helps you experience the ideas and images in them. For example, "Flint" includes sensory language that displays the jewels in vivid color. "Oranges" lets you experience the street sounds and the feel of a nickel. The vivid description of the starling in "The Writer" enables you to picture the trapped bird.

1. List three sensory details that help you see specific images in these poems.
2. List three sensory details that help you hear the images in these poems.
3. To which of your senses do the following words appeal? (a) salty, (b) purple, (c) fragrant, (d) silky, (e) squeak

◆ Build Grammar Skills

Pronouns and Antecedents

A **pronoun** takes the place of a noun. The noun that a pronoun replaces is called its **antecedent**. Most antecedents come before the pronouns that take their place. Look at this example:

antecedent pronoun

The first time I walked with a *girl* . . . *She* came out pulling at her gloves.

Practice In the following sentences, pronouns are italicized. Identify the antecedent for each one.

1. My daughter is writing in *her* room.
2. Trapped inside, the bird hit the window again. *It* finally escaped after many tries.
3. Rubies, emeralds, and sapphires are jewels. *They* are brightly colored.
4. The saleslady accepted the offer. *She* traded the candy bar for the orange.
5. As my girl and I left the store, *we* smiled.

Writing Application Using "Oranges" as an inspiration, describe the first time you met someone. In a paragraph, use at least three pronouns and identify the antecedent for each one.

◆ Build Grammar Skills

1. daughter
2. bird
3. jewels
4. saleslady
5. My girl and I

Writing Application

Students' paragraphs should contain at least 3 pronouns with their antecedents correctly identified.

Writer's Solution

For additional instruction and practice, use the lesson in the *Writer's Solution Language Lab CD-ROM* on Using Pronouns. You may also use the practice page on pronouns, p. 8, in the *Writer's Solution Grammar Practice Book.*

Build Your Portfolio

Idea Bank

Writing

1. **Jewelry Description** Write descriptions of jewelry for a humorous catalogue. Besides items containing traditional diamonds and rubies, include some pieces of flint jewelry. The more outrageous your descriptions, the better.
2. **He Said, She Said** Rewrite "Oranges" from the girl's point of view. Describe her feelings as she waits for the boy, walks with him, picks out the candy, and watches him pay for it.
3. **Poetry Critique** In a review for a poetry magazine, write a critique of "The Writer." Tell readers what message you think the poet conveys and whether you think he conveys it effectively.

Speaking and Listening

4. **Dialogue** In "Oranges," the speaker and the saleswoman communicate silently when he hands her the nickel and the orange. With a partner, create a dialogue that expresses their thoughts.
5. **Song Lyrics** **[Group Activity]** With a group, work to make "Flint" into a song. One person can choose or create music for the poem, while another can write additional verses with the same length and rhythm. A third person can direct a rehearsal or recording. **[Music Link]**

Projects

6. **Informative Brochure** By letter or telephone, contact experts such as veterinarians and wildlife rehabilitators to find out how to care for injured wild birds and animals. Ask for tips on avoiding potentially dangerous animals. Turn your findings into a brochure. **[Science Link; Health Link]**
7. **Illustrated Chart** Research the list of precious and semiprecious stones in "Flint." In addition to the scientific characteristics of each one, find out the cultural meaning of each one. For example, emerald is the May birthstone, and diamonds are often set in engagement rings. Present your findings in a colorful chart. **[Science Link]**

Writing Mini-Lesson

Description of a Fire

Two of these poets use the power of fire in their writing. A fire is one of the most captivating things in the world. It can be comforting or terrifying, but it is always powerful. Write a description that captures the energy of a fire.

Writing Skills Focus: Sensory Language

A fire appeals to many senses. Therefore, to make your description complete, include vivid details about how it looks, sounds, feels, and smells. Describe its color, size, and shape. Imagine how it sounds, how it smells, how hot it is, and how the smoke makes you feel.

Prewriting Decide what kind of fire you want to describe. For example, you might choose a bonfire, forest fire, fire in a fireplace, or fire in an outdoor grill. Imagine how that fire would look, smell, feel, and sound. Jot down words to help describe the fire.

Drafting Write your first draft. Organize your details according to the senses to which they appeal. For example, you might begin with how the fire smells and move on to how it looks.

Revising Review your sensory details. Are they varied and precise? Can you replace any of your descriptive words and phrases with more vivid and original alternatives?

◆ Grammar Application

Look at all the pronouns in your description. For each one, be sure the antecedent is obvious. If necessary, replace a pronoun with a noun or clarify the context so that the antecedent is clear.

ASSESSMENT OPTIONS

Formal Assessment, Selection Test, pp. 21–23, and Assessment Resources Software. The selection test is designed so that it can easily be customized to the performance levels of your students.

Alternative Assessment, p. 7, includes options for less advanced students, more advanced students, verbal/linguistic learners, musical/rhythmic learners, and intrapersonal learners.

PORTFOLIO ASSESSMENT

Use the following rubrics in the **Alternative Assessment** booklet to assess student writing:

Jewelry Description: Description, p. 84
He Said, She Said: Fictional Narrative, p. 82
Poetry Critique: Literary Analysis/Interpretation, p. 99
Writing Mini-Lesson: Description, p. 84

Idea Bank

Following are suggestions for matching the Idea Bank topics with your students' performance levels and learning modalities:

Customize for
Performance Levels

Less Advanced Students: 1, 4, 5
Average Students: 2, 5, 6, 7
More Advanced Students: 3, 4, 6, 7

Customize for
Learning Modalities

Verbal/Linguistic: 1, 2, 3, 4, 6
Bodily/Kinesthetic: 4
Interpersonal: 4, 5, 6
Visual/Spatial: 1, 6, 7
Musical/Rhythmic: 5
Intrapersonal: 3, 7

Writing Mini-Lesson

Refer students to the Writing Handbook in the back of the book for instruction on the writing process and for further information on descriptive writing.

Writer's Solution

Writers at Work Videodisc

To further students' understanding of sensory language, have them watch the segment on Will Hobbs and his tip on gathering sensory details.

Play frames 20324 to 21291

Writing Lab CD-ROM

Have students complete their descriptions by using the tutorial on Description. Follow these steps:

1. Have students look at the interactive model of an observation.
2. Suggest that they complete the Sensory Word Bin activity to gather descriptive details.
3. Let students draft on computer.
4. Have students use the interactive checklist when revising.

Allow about 90 minutes to complete these steps.

Writer's Solution Sourcebook

Have students use Chapter 2, "Description," pp. 32–65, for additional support. This chapter includes in-depth instruction on using vivid and precise verbs.

OBJECTIVES

1. To read, comprehend, and interpret a humorous anecdote
2. To relate a humorous anecdote to personal experience
3. To use context clues to help determine meaning of unfamiliar words
4. To analyze a humorous anecdote
5. To build vocabulary in context and learn the suffix *-ly*
6. To develop skill in using personal pronouns
7. To write an essay of opinion, providing reasons
8. To respond to a humorous anecdote through writing, speaking and listening, and projects

SKILLS INSTRUCTION

Vocabulary: Suffixes: *-ly*
Spelling: Words with *qu* for the *k sound*
Grammar: Personal Pronouns
Reading Strategy: Context Clues
Literary Focus: Humorous Anecdote
Writing: Provide Reasons
Critical Viewing: Infer

PORTFOLIO OPPORTUNITIES

Writing: Letter of Recommendation; Definition of a Hero; Humorous Story
Writing Mini-Lesson: Essay of Opinion
Speaking and Listening: Stand-up Routine; Role Play
Projects: Comic Strip; Scrapbook of Heroes

More About the Author
In 1965, **Bill Cosby** became the first African American to play a lead in a TV series. He starred opposite a white actor in the TV show *I Spy*. During that series, Cosby won three of his five Emmy awards for Best Actor. He has also won five Grammy awards for Best Comedy Album. Besides pursuing his acting and stand-up comedy careers, Cosby has earned a doctorate in education and has written several best-selling books including *Fatherhood.*

Guide for Reading

Meet the Author:
Bill Cosby (1937–)

Even as a boy, comedian Bill Cosby showed a talent for comedy. Once described as a student who would rather "clown than study," Cosby later earned a track-and-field college scholarship. He never stopped being funny, however. While in college, he practiced comedy routines in Philadelphia night spots and coffeehouses. Today, live performances and recordings of Cosby's comedy routines are big sellers. You may know him best from his appearances in popular ad campaigns and his television series, including *Cosby* and *Kids Say the Funniest Things.*

This essay is based on Cosby's childhood experiences, but the comedian changed his beliefs as he grew up. As kids, Cosby's friends idolized boxers. Later, the comedian would promote education instead of boxing gloves. Cosby once said, "I think there's a lot to be said for fighting at the blackboard, with a piece of chalk as a weapon."

The Story Behind the Story

Young people hold a special place in Cosby's heart and in his comedy. Family and friends fill his comedy routines. The famous cartoon versions of Fat Albert and Junior are based on Cosby's boyhood friends. Fat Albert and Junior make an appearance in this story, which focuses on familiar childhood challenges.

◆ Literature and Your Life

Connect Your Experience

When you see your favorite sports hero sink a basket at the buzzer, you probably imagine yourself in his or her place. Similarly, you might see yourself in the role of other heroes—actors, rock stars, politicians. In this selection, you'll learn about Bill Cosby's boyhood heroes and discover how he tried to copy them.

Thematic Focus: Testing Yourself

Each time he finds a new hero, the young Bill Cosby tests out a new personality. In the process, he may learn more about himself than he does about his heroes.

◆ Background for Understanding

Sports

In this piece, Bill Cosby expresses admiration for two famous African American sports figures—baseball great Jackie Robinson and boxer Sugar Ray Robinson. In 1947, Jackie Robinson, pictured on the next page, broke baseball's color barrier. Until then, the Major Leagues were closed to nonwhite players. Sugar Ray Robinson's powerful combination punches won him the middleweight championship five times between 1951 and 1960.

◆ Build Vocabulary

Suffixes: *-ly*

Bill Cosby describes his behavior with the word *dejectedly.* The suffix *-ly* usually indicates that a word is an adverb, a word that tells how something is done:

Young Bill sighed *dejectedly*.

Word Bank

Which of these words might refer to something that must be "turned" to work? Check the Build Vocabulary box on page 88 to see whether you are correct.

incorporate
dejectedly
tourniquets

Prentice Hall Literature Program Resources

REINFORCE / RETEACH / EXTEND

Selection Support Pages
Build Vocabulary: Suffixes: *-ly*, p. 39
Build Spelling Skills: p. 40
Build Grammar Skills: Personal Pronouns, p. 41
Reading Strategy: Context Clues, p. 42
Literary Focus: Humorous Anecdote, p. 43

Strategies for Diverse Student Needs, pp. 15–16

Beyond Literature Workplace Skills
Oral Communication, p. 8

Formal Assessment Selection Test, pp. 24–26, Assessment Resources Software

Alternative Assessment, p. 8

Resource Pro CD-ROM "Was Tarzan a Three-Bandage Man?"—includes all resource material and customizable lesson plan.

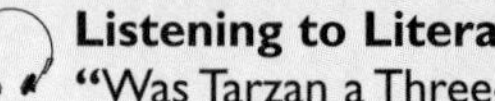

Listening to Literature Audiocassettes
"Was Tarzan a Three-Bandage Man?"

◆ Was Tarzan a Three-Bandage Man? ◆

◆ Literary Focus

Humorous Anecdote

As a comedian, Bill Cosby is known for his **humorous anecdotes,** which are brief, funny stories. Writers use several devices to bring out the humor in anecdotes. One device is exaggeration—stressing ridiculous actions or stretching reality to humorous lengths. Another device is contrast, creating a difference between what is outrageous and what is more usual. For example, Cosby contrasts his silliness with his mother's expectations of normal behavior.

As you read, note examples of exaggeration and contrast in a chart like the one below.

Exaggeration	Contrast
Pigeon-toed walking is painful.	

◆ Reading Strategy

Context Clues

Context, the words and phrases around a word, can help you understand a word you might not know. Context may contain a variety of clues to the meaning of a word—synonyms, detailed descriptions, or examples of the unknown word. Look at this passage from Cosby's writing:

> we *walked* pigeon-toed, a painful form of *locomotion* . . .

By looking at the relationship among the words, you can see that *walking* is an example of a type of *locomotion*. Since you know that *walking* is a form of movement, you might easily guess that *locomotion* means "movement."

Preparing for Standardized Tests

Grammar Standardized test questions may test a student's ability to recognize whether personal pronouns are used properly in a sentence. Being able to correctly identify personal pronouns and whether they are singular or plural may help students answer test questions. Write this sample text question on the board:

Choose the sentence in which the pronoun is used properly:

(A) They is the fastest man in baseball.
(B) Them is the fastest man in baseball.
(C) She is the fastest man in baseball.
(D) He is the fastest man in baseball.

Have a volunteer read each sentence out loud. Guide students to understand that answers (*A*) and (*B*) contain plural pronouns used incorrectly with a singular verb. In (*C*), *she* refers to a woman and the sentence discusses a man. (*D*) is the only sentence in which the pronoun is used correctly. For further practice in using pronouns, have students review Build Grammar Skills on p.90 or use **Selection Support** p. 41.

Interest Grabber Ask students to think about someone they look up to in their own lives and then freewrite for 5 minutes about that person, giving reasons why they admire him or her. For example, students might choose to write about a parent, a friend, a neighbor, a teacher, or a well-known person such as a celebrity or sports figure. Point out the pictures of Jackie Robinson on p. 87 and Sugar Ray Robinson on p. 89. Introduce the selection by explaining that just as many young people today look up to Bill Cosby, he admired sports figures when he was young.

◆ Build Grammar Skills

Personal Pronouns If you wish to introduce the grammar concept for this selection before students read, refer to the instruction on p. 90.

Customize for
Less Proficient Readers
Because much of this selection is dialogue with variant spellings to mark dialect, suggest that students read along in their books as they listen to the audiocassette. Point out that Cosby's spellings of words help make the dialogue come to life.

Listening to Literature Audiocassettes

Customize for
More Advanced Students
Students may be interested in researching one of the personalities mentioned in this selection. Suggest that they use library reference materials or the Internet to begin. Have students look up information on Bill Cosby, Jackie Robinson, Sugar Ray Robinson, Buddy Helm, or Booker T. Washington and write a short report to share with the class.

Customize for
English Language Learners
Students may find it easier to understand the selection if they have help recognizing some of the techniques Cosby uses to create humor. Explaining examples of mock threats, funny body imagery, and exaggeration will help make the humor more accessible. Invite volunteers to locate and explain examples, such as the exaggerated warning his mother gives about his legs falling off if he keeps trying to change their shape.

Develop Understanding

In "Was Tarzan a Three-Bandage Man?" Bill Cosby humorously recalls his youthful adoration of American sports heroes. Despite his mother's questions, comments, and suggestions of others to imitate, Bill and his friends persisted in copying the behavior and attire of boxers, baseball players, and football stars. They never realized that their attempts to be tough and cool actually made them look foolish.

Team Teaching Strategy

The sports themes of this selection provide a strong connection to physical education. You may wish to coordinate with a physical education teacher to plan ways of extending instruction.

◆Literary Focus

❶ **Humorous Anecdote** Cosby illustrates how ridiculous his actions were, by the responses of his mother. When he tries to walk like his hero, his mother demands to know why he is walking so funny. Have students read the mother's dialogue carefully to see why her responses provide humor in the anecdote. Ask students to role-play the first interaction between Bill and his mother.

◆Reading Strategy

❷ *Students may say that the remark suggests that Bill's brain is so small it would fit under a Band-Aid. Exaggerating the small size of Bill's brain is funny because we know that human brains cannot possibly be that tiny.*

Customize for
Bodily/Kinesthetic Learners
The conversation between young Bill and his mother probably was accompanied by body language, including facial expressions. Invite students to act out the scene between these two characters. Encourage students to recall the types of facial expressions that they may have seen Bill Cosby use in a TV show or interview.

Was Tarzan a Three-Bandage Man?

Bill Cosby

In the days before athletes had learned how to incorporate themselves, they were shining heroes to American kids. In fact, they were such heroes to me and my friends that we even imitated their walks. When Jackie Robinson,[1] a pigeon-toed[2] walker, became famous, we walked pigeon-toed, a painful form of locomotion unless you were Robinson or a pigeon.

❶ "Why you walkin' like that?" said my mother one day.

"This is Jackie *Robinson's* walk," I proudly replied.

"There's somethin' wrong with his shoes?"

"He's the fastest man in baseball."

"He'd be faster if he didn't walk like that. His mother should make him walk right."

A few months later, when football season began, I stopped imitating Robinson and began to walk bowlegged[3] like a player named Buddy Helm.

"Why you always tryin' to change the shape of your legs?" said my mother. "You keep doin' that an' they'll fall off—an' I'm not gettin' you new ones."

Although baseball and football stars inspired us, our real heroes were the famous prize fighters, and the way to emulate a fighter was to walk around with a Band-Aid over one eye. People with acne walked around that way too, but we hoped it was clear that we were worshipping good fists and not bad skin.

1. **Jackie Robinson:** First African American to play Major League baseball, Robinson began his career with the Brooklyn Dodgers in 1945.
2. **pigeon-toed** (pij´ ən tōd) *adj.*: Having the feet turned in toward each other.
3. **bowlegged** (bō´ leg ed) *adj.*: Having legs that are curved outward.

The first time my mother saw me being Sugar Ray,[4] not Jackie Robinson, she said, "What's that bandage for?"

"Oh, nuthin'," I replied.

"Now that's a new kinda stupid answer. That bandage gotta be coverin' somethin'—besides your entire brain."

"Well, it's just for show. I wanna look like Sugar Ray Robinson."

> **◆ Reading Strategy**
> How does the suggestion that the bandage covers Bill's entire brain use exaggeration to create humor? ❷

"The fastest man in baseball."

"No, that's a different one."

"You doin' Swiss Family Robinson[5] next?"

"Swiss Family Robinson? They live in the projects?"

"You'd know who they are if you read more books instead of makin' yourself look like an accident. Why can't you try to imitate someone like Booker T. Washington?"[6]

4. **Sugar Ray Robinson:** Boxer who was world welterweight champion from 1945 to 1951, defending his title five times.
5. **Swiss Family Robinson:** Fictional family stranded on a desert island.
6. **Booker T. Washington** (1856–1915): African American educator and author.

> **◆ Build Vocabulary**
>
> **incorporate** (in kôr´ pôr āt) *v.*: Form into a legal business
>
> **dejectedly** (dē jek´ tid lē) *adv.*: Sadly; showing discouragement
>
> **tourniquets** (tʉr´ ni kits) *n.*: Devices used to stop bleeding in an emergency, as a bandage tightly twisted to stop the flow of blood

Block Scheduling Strategies

Consider these suggestions to take advantage of extended class time:

- Focus on the grammar skill, personal pronouns. Before reading the selection, introduce personal pronouns on p. 90. Have students work in pairs to complete the practice exercise and the Writing Application. To reinforce understanding use **Selection Support,** p. 41, or the Using Pronouns section of the *Writer's Solution Language Lab CD-ROM*.
- After students read the selection, review the elements of a humorous anecdote. Have them complete the Literary Focus questions on p. 90. Then, have students work in groups on either the comic strip or one of the speaking and listening options from the Idea Bank, p. 91. Remind them to use what they have learned about humor to complete the activities.
- Have students work in groups to answer the Critical Thinking questions on p. 89. Then, independently complete the Writing Mini-Lesson on p. 91. Have them exchange papers with a partner and use the Peer Conferencing Notes in **Alternative Assessment,** pp. 72–75.

"Who does he play for?"

"Bill, let's put it this way: you take off that bandage right now or I'll have your father move you up to stitches."

The following morning on the street, I dejectedly told the boys, "My mother says I gotta stop wearin' a bandage. She wants my whole head to show."

"What's wrong with that woman?" said Fat Albert. "She won't let you do *nuthin'*."

"It's okay, Cos," said Junior, "'cause one bandage ain't enough anyway. My brother says the really tough guys wear two."

"One over each eye?" I asked him.

"Or one eye and one nose," he said.

"Man, I wouldn't want to mess with no two-bandage man," said Eddie.

3 And perhaps the toughest guys of all wore tourniquets around their necks. We were capable of such attire, for we were never more ridiculous than when we were trying to be tough and cool. Most ridiculous, of course, was that our hero worshipping was backwards: we should have been emulating the men who had *caused* the need for bandages.

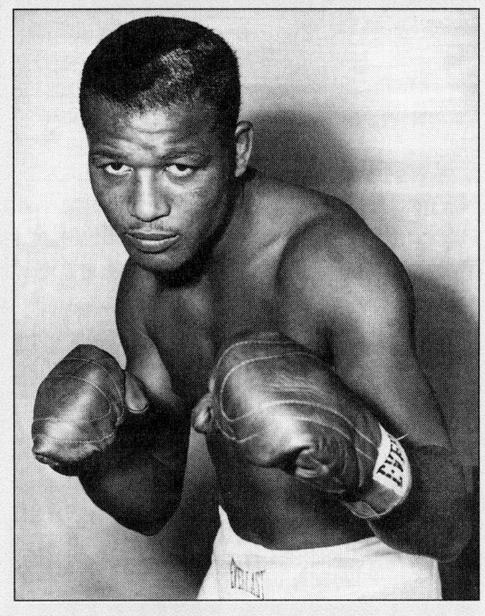

▲ Critical Viewing Why might young boys like Cosby and his friends idolize a man like Sugar Ray Robinson, pictured here? **[Infer]** 4

Guide for Responding

◆ Literature and Your Life

Reader's Response What heroes do you imitate? What qualities in them do you admire?

Thematic Focus The young Cosby believes that imitating heroes will bring out the best of his abilities. In what other ways can people test their strengths?

☑ Check Your Comprehension

1. Name two ways in which Cosby and his friends imitate their heroes.
2. What is a three-bandage man?
3. Whom does Cosby's mother suggest he idolize?

◆ Critical Thinking

Interpret

1. Why does young Bill want to walk like Jackie Robinson and Buddy Helm? **[Infer]**
2. How does Cosby's mother view her son's hero worship in general? **[Interpret]**
3. Who do you think is more understanding of the other's behavior—Cosby or his mother? Why? **[Compare and Contrast]**
4. How does Cosby's attitude toward his choice of boyhood heroes change in time? **[Analyze]**

Apply

5. This story seems to suggest a definition of a role model. What is that definition? **[Generalize]**

Extend

6. What does this story say about how sports figures should live and behave? **[Physical Education Link]**

Beyond the Selection

FURTHER READING

Other Works by Bill Cosby

Fatherhood
Time Flies

Other Humorous Anecdotes

Forever Erma, Erma Bombeck
My Life and Hard Times, James Thurber
Growing Up, Russell Baker

INTERNET

We suggest the following sites on the Internet (all Web sites are subject to change).

For information on Bill Cosby:
http://marketing.cbs.com/primetime/cosby/bios/bcosby.shtml

We *strongly recommend* that you preview this site before you send students to it.

◆ Literary Focus

3 Humorous Anecdote Point out to students that Cosby's use of the term *tourniquet* is another example of his humorous techniques. A device twisted tightly to stop bleeding worn around a neck is certainly not a normal item of clothing and is intended to be a humorous exaggeration.

▶Critical Viewing◀

4 Infer *Cosby and his friends admired Sugar Ray Robinson because he was African American like them, and he looked tough and strong.*

Reinforce and Extend

Answers

◆ Literature and Your Life

Reader's Response Students may name family, friends, or famous people because they admire their strengths and personal qualities.

Thematic Focus People can try to do well in school, learn new skills, or help others to test their abilities.

☑ Check Your Comprehension

1. They imitate their walks and wear bandages like them.
2. A three-bandage man is someone who is so tough he needs three bandages to cover all his wounds.
3. Cosby's mother suggests he idolize Booker T. Washington.

◆ Critical Thinking

1. He wants to be cool like them.
2. She thinks he's being silly about whom he chooses to imitate.
3. Students may say that Cosby's mother is not understanding, because she doesn't want him to imitate his hero. Others may say Cosby is less understanding because he thinks his mom won't let him do anything.
4. At first Cosby is inspired by baseball and football stars, then prize fighters. Finally he realizes he should worship the men who hurt the prize fighters.
5. A role model is someone you look up to and try to copy.
6. Some students may say that they think sports figures have a responsibility to behave well because so many kids look up to them. Others may give reasons and disagree.

Answers

◆Reading Strategy

1. Meaning: imitate. Clue: The verb *emulate* links the prize fighters to the kids walking around with bandages like their heroes.
2. Meaning: clothing or accessory. Clue: The word *attire* refers to a tourniquet worn around the neck, so attire must mean something that is worn.

◆Build Vocabulary

Using the Suffix *-ly*

1. ridiculously; Can you believe how ridiculously she is dressed today?
2. stupidly; Junior gawked stupidly at Bill's latest costume.
3. painfully; Mrs. Cosby walked painfully in her high-heeled shoes.

Spelling Strategy

1. bouquet; 2. racquet; 3. antique

Using the Word Bank

1. A belt can be wrapped around the injured leg to stop the flow of blood.
2. Yes, he or she would probably feel saddened by the funeral.
3. Yes, that action would turn it into an official business.

◆Literary Focus

1. Cosby's mother exaggerates to create the wacky image of young Bill's legs falling off.
2. Cosby uses contrast when his mother compares the size of his bandage to the size of his brain.
3. (a) Cosby conveys a message that his attempts to look cool make him look ridiculous. (b) Humor emphasizes how funny the boys looked.

◆Build Grammar Skills

Personal Pronouns

Practice

1. his (third); their (third)
2. them (third)
3. they (third)
4. we (first)
5. you (second)

Writing Application

Possible responses:

1. Each day *he* wears a bandage. third person singular
2. *He* likes to strut like a winner. third person singular
3. They idolized Jackie Robinson. third person plural

Guide for Responding (continued)

◆ Reading Strategy

Context Clues

When you study the **context** of a word—the words and ideas surrounding it—you can uncover clues to its meaning. Use the context to determine the meaning of each italicized word in the following passages. Then, explain what clue the context provided.

1. "our real heroes were the famous prize fighters, and the way to *emulate* a fighter was to walk around with a Band-Aid over one eye."
2. "the toughest guys of all wore tourniquets around their necks. We were capable of such *attire*. . . ."

◆ Build Vocabulary

Using the Suffix *-ly*

The suffix *-ly,* meaning "in this way," usually indicates that the word is an adverb. Add *-ly* to each word listed here to create an adverb. Then write a sentence using the new word.

1. ridiculous
2. stupid
3. painful

Spelling Strategy

In certain words that come from French, the *k* sound is spelled *qu*, as in *tourniquet.* On your paper, use the definitions provided to fill in the missing letters of the words containing the *qu* spelling of the *k* sound.

1. Bunch of flowers held together: b _ _ _ _ _ t
2. Sports equipment used to hit a tennis ball: r _ c _ _ _ t
3. A very old and valuable piece of furniture: a _ _ _ _ _ e

Using the Word Bank

On your paper, answer these questions. Explain each answer.

1. Which would be a more effective *tourniquet* for a deep cut on the leg—a chair or a belt?
2. Would you describe someone at a funeral as "walking *dejectedly* to the car"?
3. If you wanted to expand your car-washing business, might you *incorporate* it?

◆ Literary Focus

Humorous Anecdote

A **humorous anecdote,** such as Bill Cosby's story, relates a brief, funny, and often true experience to make a point. Techniques of comedy, including exaggeration and contrast, can help writers bring out the humor in otherwise ordinary stories.

1. Identify a scene in which Cosby uses exaggeration.
2. Identify a scene in which Cosby uses contrast.
3. (a) What message do you think Cosby conveys? (b) How does humor add to his message?

◆ Build Grammar Skills

Personal Pronouns

Writers use **personal pronouns** to identify the person speaking (first person), the person spoken to (second person), or the person, place, or thing spoken about (third person). This chart shows the most common personal pronouns:

	SINGULAR	PLURAL
First person	I, me, mine	we, us, our, ours
Second person	you, your, yours	you, your, yours
Third person	he, she, him, her, his, it, its	they, them, their, theirs

Notice that Cosby uses the first-person pronouns *us* and *our* to identify himself and his friends:

> Although . . . football stars inspired *us, our* real heroes were . . . prize fighters.

Practice Write the personal pronouns in each sentence on your paper. Then, identify each as first, second, or third person.

1. Cosby and his friends try to act like their heroes.
2. A boxer is popular with them for a while.
3. They switch favorites every week.
4. We also admire actors and celebrities.
5. Who is inspiring to you?

Writing Application Answer the following questions using personal pronouns. For each, identify the type of personal pronoun you used.

1. What does Junior wear every day?
2. How did Bill like to walk?
3. Whom did Bill and his friends idolize?

Writer's Solution

For additional instruction and practice, use the lesson in the *Writer's Solution Language Lab CD-ROM* on Using Pronouns. You may also use the practice page on pronouns, p. 8, in the *Writer's Solution Grammar Practice Book.*

Build Your Portfolio

Idea Bank

Writing

1. **Letter of Recommendation** Write a letter recommending one of your heroes for a teen role model award. Explain why your hero deserves this award.
2. **Definition of a Hero** Describe the qualities or behaviors you admire most in others. Write a few paragraphs giving your personal definition of a hero.
3. **Humorous Story** Write a funny story about a teenager who trades places for a day with a personal hero. Use exaggeration and contrast to increase the humor of your story.

Speaking and Listening

4. **Stand-up Routine** Jot down a few of the techniques used by your favorite comedians. Then, use your notes to help you develop, rehearse, and stage an original comedy routine or perform an already published one. **[Performing Arts Link]**
5. **Role Play** With a partner, discuss what makes the scenes between Bill and his mother authentic. Then, role-play the scenes for classmates using gestures and body language. **[Performing Arts Link]**

Projects

6. **Comic Strip** Choose an incident from your own life and present it humorously in comic-strip form. Create at least three panels, and include captions or speech balloons to help communicate the action. **[Art Link]**
7. **Scrapbook of Heroes** **[Group Activity]** Working with a group, identify public figures you think might make good role models. Each group member should research at least one person's accomplishments and personal life. Then, organize the group's findings in a scrapbook, with group members contributing photographs and informative captions for their chosen role models. Share your scrapbook with the class.

Writing Mini-Lesson

Essay of Opinion

In his writing, Bill Cosby pokes fun at his boyhood practice of idolizing his sports heroes. He also raises an important question: Are stars worthy of young people's admiration and respect? Write an opinion essay in which you explain whether you think athletes make good role models.

Writing Skills Focus: Provide Reasons

Make your essay effective by **providing concrete and convincing reasons** to support your opinion. Don't simply write: "I think sports figures are good role models." Add impact with a clearly stated reason. For example, when asked why he is imitating Jackie Robinson's walk, Bill Cosby replies: "He's the fastest man in baseball." The reason—Robinson's speed—helps readers understand *why* Cosby wants to imitate Robinson.

Prewriting Make a chart of the pros and cons of holding athletes up as role models. Jot down the names of athletes whose behavior supports each side. Then study your list to decide where you stand.

Drafting Begin your essay by stating your opinion. Follow with two or three supporting reasons. If you can, give a real-life example for each reason. You might put each reason and its example in a separate paragraph. End by forcefully restating your opinion.

◆ Grammar Application

Avoid repeating names of people too often. Create connections by using personal pronouns—such as *he, she, I,* or *they*—after you have named people or groups.

Revising Review your essay to be sure that your argument makes sense. Strengthen weak reasons and replace boring examples with more vivid or convincing situations.

Idea Bank

Following are suggestions for matching the Idea Bank topics with your students' performance levels and learning modalities:

Customize for *Performance Levels*
Less Advanced Students: 1, 5, 6
Average Students: 2, 5, 6, 7
More Advanced Students: 3, 4, 7

Customize for *Learning Modalities*
Verbal/Linguistic: 1, 2, 3
Visual/Spatial: 6, 7
Bodily/Kinesthetic: 4, 5
Logical/Mathematical: 7
Interpersonal: 5, 7
Intrapersonal: 1, 2, 3, 6

Writing Mini-Lesson

Refer students to the Writing Handbook in the back of the book for instructions on the writing process and for further information on persuasive writing.

Writer's Solution

Writing Lab CD-ROM
Have students complete the tutorial on Persuasion. Follow these steps:

1. Look at the interactive model of an essay of opinion.
2. Use the Pros and Cons Chart activity to learn to distinguish opposing positions.
3. Have students draft on computer.
4. Have them use the Self-Evaluation Checklist when revising.

Writer's Solution Sourcebook
Have students use Chapter 6, "Persuasion," pp. 166–199, for additional support. The chapter includes in-depth instruction on writing an essay in support of an opinion, and includes helpful suggestions on how to avoid faulty reasoning, p. 189.

✓ ASSESSMENT OPTIONS

Formal Assessment, Selection Test, pp. 24–26, and Assessment Resources Software. The selection test is designed so that it can be easily customized to the performance levels of your students.

Alternative Assessment, p. 8, includes options for less advanced students, more advanced students, visual/spatial learners, verbal/linguistic learners, intrapersonal learners, and bodily/kinesthetic learners.

PORTFOLIO ASSESSMENT
Use the following rubrics in the **Alternative Assessment** booklet to assess students writing:
Letter of Recommendation: Persuasion, p. 92
Definition of a Hero: Expression, p. 81
Humorous Story: Fictional Narrative, p. 82
Writing Mini-Lesson: Persuasion, p. 92

Connections to Today's World

Tiger Woods is a world-famous athlete, of both Asian and African heritage. His dedication to the sport of golf from a very young age and his well-developed talent and ability have provided inspiration and motivation to many young people. With the help and support of his parents, among others, Tiger constantly challenges himself to focus on being a good person as well as an excellent golfer. This excerpt from his biography is a literature connection to the challenges of life and successful ways of dealing with them.

Team Teaching Strategy

The emphasis on sports training and golf competition in this selection provides an excellent opportunity for connections to the physical education curriculum. You may want to coordinate with a physical education teacher to find ways to extend instruction.

More About the Author

John Strege covered Los Angeles's professional baseball and football teams—the Dodgers, the Angels, and the Raiders, before he started writing about golf. Strege is also a sports columnist and reporter on general assignment for the *Orange County Register.*

More About Tiger Woods

Tiger Woods grew up in Cypress, California. As a child he watched his father, Earl, hit golf balls and tried to imitate his swing. At the age of 2, Tiger appeared on the *Mike Douglas Show,* and putted golf balls with comedian Bob Hope. Playing tournaments as an amateur, Tiger Woods won six consecutive United States Golf Association (USGA) championships and won the U.S. Junior Amateur competition in 1991 at the age of 15.

After two years at Stanford University, Tiger won the NCAA (National Collegiate Athletic Association) Championship in 1996. In 1997, he became the youngest PGA Masters Tournament winner at the age of 21. He also broke racial barriers by becoming the first player of Asian or African heritage to win a major championship. Some have called Tiger Woods the best golfer in the world.

Connections to Today's World

Tiger: A Biography of Tiger Woods

John Strege

Thematic Connection

Testing Yourself

Have you ever wondered what it would be like to be a world-famous athlete? Competitors like golf professional Tiger Woods must perform at their best over and over—even when they don't feel their best. Each time Tiger plays, he puts himself to the test. He has been doing this regularly since he was thirteen years old.

Woods is just one of many athletes who have dedicated themselves to their sport at a young age. Some, like Woods, have achieved national and even world recognition. In 1998, Tara Lipinski became the youngest figure skater to win an Olympic gold medal. She was fifteen years old at the time.

Being the Best in Your Field

Most young athletes never become as well known as Woods and Lipinski, but many do get noticed within their sport. The three Sanderson brothers of Heber City, Utah, all won awards at wrestling's important regional Junior Olympics. At age thirteen, Angela Moscarelli held fifteen national archery records. At age twelve, Kelly Quinn broke new ground as the only female ice hockey player in her league and hoped to be ready for the 2002 women's Olympic ice hockey team. Ten-year-old fly fisherman Jake Howard even received a $5,000 scholarship for winning the Casting Kids national championship.

The Cost of Success

These young athletes take competition very seriously. Most train very hard, sometimes for several hours each day. They all learn, as Tiger Woods does, the importance of commitment—of never quitting.

This section from Tiger Woods's biography focuses on a personal test. As you read, think about the tests you face in your life—preparing for a music performance, winning a key basketball game, earning money for a group or school trip, showing your readiness for a new responsibility at home. Consider how these tests ask of you the same blend of dedication and perspective successful young athletes must develop.

John Strege
(1939–)

As a reporter, John Strege met Tiger Woods when the golfer was making news at the age of fourteen. Through attendance at many golf tournaments, Strege came to know Woods and his family, and the writer and the golfer became friends. This familiarity paid off. Strege's biography of Tiger Woods, released in 1997, was noted for its author's knowledge of the family.

Cultural Connection

Sports in History We can trace the beginnings of sports as we know them today to the ancient Greeks. The ideal Greek male had a healthy body as well as a trained mind. Boys received athletic training in school. The first Olympic games took place in Greece in 776 B.C.

Across cultures and throughout history, many games have been played with clubs and balls. The ancient Roman game of *pangea* appears to be the forerunner to field hockey, and Native American versions of stickball are forerunners to the modern game of lacrosse.

During the Middle Ages, people in Europe enjoyed a game known as *Jeu de Malle,* in which a ball was knocked from one place to another, using the fewest number of hits. The game eventually became known as *kolf* in the Netherlands, *goff* in England and *gowf* in Scotland. Today, we think of the east coast of Scotland as the place where the modern game of golf took root.

Using the Internet and library resources, interested students might research the history of a sport they enjoy and write a report to be collected as a class book on the history of sports.

from

Tiger: A Biography of Tiger Woods

John Strege

He was as thin as a steel shaft and lighter than graphite.[1] He stood five-feet-five and weighed one hundred seven pounds, which, if a fair fight was the objective, would have required he be matched against a 4-iron. In this instance, his opponent was a heavyweight, John Daly, the Arkansas Player of the Year in 1986 and 1987, and already a legend, on a local scale, for his prodigious length.

The site was Texarkana Country Club in Texarkana, Arkansas, on a golf course that, according to a local newspaper, had never before been played by a black. Until then Woods had considered himself only a golfer. Suddenly, he had become a black golfer, which puzzled him. He was thirteen and only vaguely aware of the social impact a talented black player might have on the game.

Tiger was there to play in the Big I, short for the Insurance Youth Golf Classic, a prestigious event on the American Junior Golf Association tour. The Big I created excitement among the juniors: in the final round they were paired with professional golfers. Daly was among the twenty pros recruited to participate with the sixty juniors,

1. **graphite** (graf´ īt´) *n.*: Lightweight material used to make golf clubs.

◆ Build Vocabulary

objective (əb jek´ tiv) *n.*: Goal

prodigious (prō dij´ əs) *adj.*: Amazing

prestigious (pres tij´ əs) *adj.*: Having an impressive reputation

Develop Understanding

One-Minute Insight

Tiger: A Biography of Tiger Woods chronicles the beginnings of Tiger's amazing career in golf. He was introduced to the game at a very early age by his father, Earl. His father has occasionally been criticized by some for putting pressure on Tiger to excel. On the contrary, he once remarked that he didn't care what Tiger became, as long as he was a good citizen. At competitions, Tiger's father was often dismayed to observe parents criticizing their talented children in public. Because of Tiger's success and personal determination, he was recruited by Stanford University. Tiger Woods is a modern-day sports hero who challenges and inspires us all.

Customize for *Less Proficient Readers*

Before students begin reading, discuss the technical vocabulary in this selection with them, referring to the Golf Glossary, p. 94. Encourage them to jot down unfamiliar terms as they read. Later, they can use the Golf Glossary or dictionary to interpret the meanings of these terms. Then, suggest they reread the selection for a clearer understanding.

Customize for *More Advanced Students*

Tiger Woods has had extraordinary success in his career as a golfer. As they read, encourage students to note his personal qualities that contribute to this success. Suggest that they create a chart like the one below.

Conflict	Resolution	Personal Quality That Helps Tiger
Not many people make it as pro golfers.	Tiger continues his education.	He considers the consequences and prepares for them.

Customize for *English Language Learners*

Use pictures from a sports or golf magazine to help students understand golf terms and concepts such as *driver, shot,* and *tee.*

Speaking and Listening Mini-Lesson

Interview

In this lesson, students will use speaking and listening skills to interview a local athlete.

Introduce Have students study the results of high school athletics in the local newspaper.

Develop As a class, list elements of a good interview on the board, including the following:

- Good preparation
- Appropriate questions
- The interviewer speaks clearly and looks directly at the person being interviewed
- The interviewer listens to answers and adjusts questions accordingly

Apply You may want to contact the athletic director at a local high school to locate athletes willing to be interviewed. Instruct students to prepare a list of questions. In pairs, have them conduct an interview to share with the class either on videotape or audiotape.

Assess Have students use the Self-Assessment: Speaking and Listening Progress form, pp. 109–110, in **Alternative Assessment.**

Thematic Connection

❶ Ask students to explain what Tiger's quote tells about what he expects of himself. *Instead of being impressed with Daly, a professional golfer who beat him, Tiger expects to exceed Daly in his golfing abilities.*

Clarification

❷ Explain to students that college recruiters compete to try to enroll outstanding high school athletes to play for their teams. Schools often give athletes scholarships in hopes of building a winning college team that will attract funding and donations. Stanford University in Palo Alto, California, has a strong academic reputation, but still counts on successful athletics programs to provide income.

Customize for *Verbal/Linguistic Learners*

Interested students might wish to read the "Faces in the Crowd" feature of *Sports Illustrated* magazine, highlighting the achievements of young athletes in all sports. Students might submit names of local athletes, supported with evidence, who merit inclusion in an upcoming issue, to the editors of the magazine.

Customize for *Logical/Mathematical Readers*

The par for the Texarkana Country Club where Tiger played Daly is 72. Have students read the paragraph beginning "Tiger remained ahead at the turn . . . ." and try to determine Daly's final score. Refer them to the Golf Glossary, as needed. Ask volunteers to share what they learn with the class.

CONNECTIONS TO TODAY'S WORLD

and he was paired with Woods. Through four holes, Woods was ahead of Daly, who turned to a friend and said loud enough to be heard by those in the gallery, "I can't let this thirteen-year-old beat me."

Tiger remained ahead at the turn, three-under par to Daly's one-under par. But Daly's four birdies on the back nine and three on the last four holes enabled him to defeat Woods. Still, Tiger's score was better than those posted by eight of the twenty professionals, and he finished second in the tournament.

❶ Three years later, Tiger was asked what he recalled about playing with Daly that day. "I don't remember too much, except he wasn't a smart player," he said. "He'd take his driver and go over trees. He's got to throttle back."[2]

Daly, conversely, had been indelibly[3] impressed. "That kid is great," he said. "Everybody was applauding him and nobody applauded me. He's better than I'd heard."

Few people knew of Daly then, but Tiger's legend had already begun to blossom and was steadily expanding. He was still only thirteen when his first college recruiting letter arrived in the mail. Dated March 28, 1989, it read in part: ❷

> Dear Tiger,
> Here at Stanford I'm finding that it is never too early to get word out to you exceptional young men.

It had been sent by Wally Goodwin, the golf coach at Stanford, who a few years before had been tipped off about Woods by Tom Sargent, the professional at Yorba Linda Country Club. Goodwin was reintroduced to the name when he had seen Woods featured in *Sports Illustrated*'s "Faces in the Crowd." He sent off the first of several letters he would mail to Woods in the next five years. Tiger wrote back to him in April:

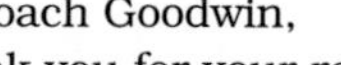

> Dear Coach Goodwin,
> Thank you for your recent letter expressing Stanford's interest in me as a ❸

2. **throttle back:** Ease up.
3. **indelibly** (in del´ ə blē) *adv.*: Lastingly; permanently.

GOLF GLOSSARY

THE COURSE:

tee: Flat area from which the golfer takes the first stroke, or shot, for a given hole

fairway: Path between the tee and the green

green: Area of closely mown grass around the hole

THE CLUBS:

Clubs are numbered from 1 to 9 to indicate the angle of a club. Clubs with a greater number will produce higher and shorter shots.

irons: Clubs with thin, bladelike heads; used for accuracy

woods: Clubs with large, thick heads; used for long shots

driver: Number 1 wood; used off the tee

THE SCORING:

par: Number of strokes assigned to a specific hole or course for comparative purposes

three-under par: Score of three strokes less than par

bogey (bō´ gē): Score of one-over par on a hole

birdie: Score of one-under par on a hole

eagle: Score of two-under par on a hole

ace: Hole in one; when the tee shot goes into the hole

Beyond the Classroom

Career Connection

Careers Related to Sports Many individuals pursue careers in sports, not just as athletic participants, but as coaches, writers, caretakers, programmers, and team owners. For example, someone who designs clothes and likes sports might work at a design company for athletic sportswear. A person who likes being outside and enjoys golf could be a caddy or a golf course groundskeeper. Career opportunities range from direct involvement in a sport, such as horse groom, caddy, or referee; to indirect, such as sports writer, sports psychologist, or manager.

Challenge students to brainstorm for a list of sports-related occupations. Ask students to choose one of the jobs that interests them and learn more about it. Suggest that students use the Internet and library for preliminary research. To gain further information, they may wish to formulate a list of questions and talk to someone who works in the field. Have students report their findings to the class.

future student and golfer. At first it was hard for me to understand why a university like Stanford was interested in a thirteen-year-old seventh grader. But after talking with my father I have come to better understand and appreciate the honor you have given me. I further appreciate Mr. Sargent's interest in my future development by recommending me to you.

I became interested in Stanford's academics **4** while watching the Olympics and Debi Thomas. My goal is to obtain a quality business education. Your guidelines will be most helpful in preparing **3** me for college life. My GPA this year is 3.86 and I plan to keep it there or higher when I enter high school.

I am working on an exercise program to increase my strength. My April USGA handicap is 1 and I plan to play in SCPGA and maybe some AJGA tournaments this summer. My goal is to win the Junior World in July for the fourth time and to become the first player to win each age bracket. Ultimately I would like to be a PGA professional. Next February I plan to go to Thailand and play in the Thai Open as an amateur.

I've heard a lot about your golf course and I would like to play it with my dad some time in the future.

Hope to hear from you soon.

Sincerely,
Tiger Woods 5-5/100
(*his weight and height*)

"There's no way this youngster wrote the letter," a disbelieving Goodwin said. "It was absolutely a perfect letter. I called Tida[4] after that. I said, 'It's hard for me to believe that Tiger wrote that letter himself.' She said, 'Coach, he wrote every word himself.'

"I was having a team meeting in my office. There were three academic All-Americans. One guy was being a smart aleck. I said, 'Listen, buster, I got a letter from a little black kid in Los Angeles that writes a letter better than any of you guys in this room can write. It's got capital letters, punctuation, every sentence has a verb in it. It's perfect.' They said, 'Come on, coach.' So I got the letter, made copies and gave one to each guy. Dead silence."

Later that year, Tiger admitted that he was 90 percent certain that he would attend Stanford, although he had not yet even started the eighth grade. He intended to earn a college degree, as a safeguard against failing to earn a living from golf. It was only a contingency plan[5] as he fully expected to excel at the game and to some day win the Masters and the U.S. Open. He already rated his game an A, primarily because he seldom made mental mistakes. On the golf course, he likened himself to a thirty-year-old in a thirteen-year-old body.

His maturity at such a young age led to countless charges that Earl was a stage father living vicariously[6] through his son's success **5** and applying undue pressure on Tiger to measure up to unrealistic standards. But the Woodses simply presented professional golf as an option to Tiger, never a requirement.

---

4. **Tida:** Tiger's mother.

5. **contingency** (kən tin′ jən sē) **plan:** Plan to cover the possibility of an unexpected event.

6. **vicariously** (vī ker′ ē əs lē) *adv.*: Imagined participation in another's experience.

Thematic Connection

3 Ask students what this letter tells them about Tiger Woods and his attempts to test himself. *He sets clear goals for himself such as getting a business education, maintaining his GPA, and increasing his strength. His interest in Stanford's golf course indicates a desire to learn new skills.*

Clarification

4 Debi Thomas, the only African-American figure skater to win an Olympic medal, was the United States national champion in 1986. In 1988, she won a bronze medal in the Olympics at the age of 21.

◆Critical Thinking

5 Infer Read this sentence aloud to the class, and discuss the footnote for the word *vicariously*. Ask students what "stage father" means. *The word stage suggests a public performance. The clues that Earl is accused of living through his son and pressuring Tiger to fulfill his own standards indicate that a stage father is a parent who pressures his child to become a star, regardless of the child's wishes.*

Customize for
Visual/Spatial Learners

Students may understand the selection better if they have a visual guide. From a book about golf, provide them with an outline of a golf course and review terms used in this article such as "back nine" and "short putt." Interested students might enjoy sketching a golf course or miniature golf course to see how the holes, sand traps, and obstacles are designed and laid out.

Cross-Curricular Connection: Science

Golf and the Environment There are more than 15,000 golf courses in the United States. The land used for these recreation sites covers an area larger than the states of Rhode Island and Delaware combined. Since 1990, more than 350 courses have been built or expanded, raising environmental concerns about land use. Golf courses can require extensive irrigation, chemical fertilizers, and pesticides, but as awareness is increased, this is changing.

Many new golf courses are designed to reclaim wasteland, convert old landfills, and benefit wildlife. Golf architect Michael Hurdzan is a leader of this movement—he holds a doctorate in environmental and turfgrass studies. Cloverdale Golf Club in Washington is an example of an innovative course designed with the future in mind. Its fairways follow the paths of ancient riverbeds and imprints of cattle hooves, and its layout leaves boulders and thickets of brush in place.

Encourage students to find out more about the efforts being made by designers, engineers, and computer specialists to create golf courses that do not endanger the environment.

Comprehension Check ☑

❶ Ask students to describe Earl's reaction to overbearing stage parents in golf. *He is disgusted when he observes a father bitterly scolding his son for a poor performance.*

◆Critical Thinking

❷ **Infer** Ask students whether they believe Earl Woods is a stage father who unnecessarily pushes his son to excel. *Mr. Woods is a warm, caring person. He is genuinely proud of his son and more concerned that Tiger become a good person than a winning golfer.*

◆Critical Thinking

❸ **Analyze** Ask students to explain what the author means when he writes that Tiger has a "psychological advantage." *Since Tiger is under no pressure to constantly please his parents, he can enjoy playing golf and is free to relax and concentrate on mastering the sport.*

Clarification

❹ Jack Nicklaus was by far the best player of his time—the Michael Jordan of golf. During the years 1962–1986, he won 18 major championships and was named Player of the Year five times on the Professional Golfers' Association tour. His legendary achievements are ones to which all other golfers are often compared.

Customize for *Intrapersonal Learners*

The interaction between the players and their parents provides an opportunity to discuss the dynamics of high-pressured situations. Invite students to share what they think it is like to play in an American Junior Golf tournament. Ask what pressures might be put on them to win. Then encourage them to explain how those pressures might affect one's performance and attitude. Talk about how Tiger Woods and his parents avoid some of the tension and problems that many of the other players and their families experience. Conclude by discussing how the more successful attitudes of the Woodses might be applied to other stressful situations in life.

CONNECTIONS TO TODAY'S WORLD

"He isn't living anyone else's expectations," said Jay Brunza, a long-time family friend and Woods's sports psychologist. "He plays the game for the joy and passion within himself. If he said, 'I'm tired of golf. I want to collect stamps,' his parents would say, 'Fine, son,' and walk him down to the post office." ❶

Overbearing stage parents were not in short supply on the American Junior Golf Association tour. The AJGA is comprised of the best junior golfers in the country, male and female, and conducts tournaments throughout the year. At one such event, Earl witnessed a father berating his son for playing poorly, leaving Earl shaking his head in disgust. Similar scenes played out at other tournaments, with children frequently walking away from parents in mid-scolding.

"It's not necessary for Tiger to play professionally," Earl said. "If he wants to be a fireman in Umpity-Ump, Tennessee, that's fine as long as he's an upright citizen. There's no pressure. He doesn't have to provide for Dad's welfare. He doesn't have to buy me a home. I already have a home. He doesn't have to buy me a car. I have four cars. I'm set for life. My goal for Tiger is for him to be an upright, contributing citizen." ❷

When Tiger lost to Dennis Hillman in the semifinal of the U.S. Junior Amateur in 1990, his disappointment was apparent. He stared impassively ahead as he and Earl began driving away from the club. Moments later, Tiger reached over and hugged his father and said, "Pop, I love you."

"That made the whole thing worthwhile for me," Earl said. "I'm very proud that Tiger is a better person than he is a golfer."

His mother and father were atypical of the parents of athletic prodigies in that, though Tiger rarely lost a junior tournament, he received the same postround reception from his parents as he did when he won. So Tiger, unafraid of failing and disappointing his parents, had a psychological advantage over those who shied away from pressure and tended to play not to lose. ❸

After a tournament, he and his dad would discuss the round and identify the problem areas that needed work, but his mother stressed that, "he doesn't have to be Jack Nicklaus." ❹

Viewing and Representing Mini-Lesson

Golf Visual Representation

In this lesson, students will look at visuals of the game of golf and create an interpretation.

Introduce Show students a videotaped golf tournament, or pictures in magazines and books.

Develop Discuss the colors, lines, shapes, texture, and elements of composition seen on the golf course and at the competition. Students should note the sharp angle created by a golfer in mid-swing, the greens, the sky, flags at the holes, sandtraps, hills, the length of the fairway, trees, bright clothing, and the colorful crowd of people watching the game.

Apply Have students create a visual representation of golf. Provide materials and time for students to create. They might choose to use tissue paper, tempera paint, water color, torn paper, or a collage of magazine photos.

Assess Have students display their representations for the class and explain why they chose the elements that they did. Evaluate students' work based on their presentation and explanation to the class.

CONNECTIONS TO TODAY'S WORLD

Once when Tiger was ten, he was on the course and was faced with several options on a particular shot. He chose a peculiar one from Earl's perspective. After the round, Earl asked him why he had hit that shot.

"Because that's what I thought you wanted me to do," Tiger said.

"Tiger," Earl said, "you're not out there playing for me. You're out there playing for yourself. On the golf course you're the boss. You do what you want to do."

From then on he understood that he had to perform only to the standards he had established for himself. There was never
5 parental pressure on Tiger to win; anything was an acceptable outcome as long as an appropriate effort was made to avoid losing.
6 Once, his effort failed to measure up, a mistake compounded by the fact that his father was a witness: At the Orange Bowl Junior Classic in Miami, Tiger was leading when he missed a short putt, which ignited a short fuse. He sulked the rest of the round, losing his lead and eventually the tournament. It was apparent that he had quit on himself, the one mistake Earl would not tolerate, and it exposed Earl's military expertise at upbraiding a subordinate.

Earl's lecture, delivered at decibels with which Tiger was unfamiliar, centered on the theme that golf owes no one anything, least of all success, and that quitting is a flagrant foul, intolerable. Even golf's most prolific winner, Jack Nicklaus, was renowned in part for the manner in which he accepted defeat. Even when he was losing, when he was far removed from contention, he continued to grind, as if a U.S. Open victory hung in the balance with each shot. From Earl's lesson, Tiger learned the importance of behaving similarly if he wanted to achieve the same level of greatness. 6

Thematic Connection

TESTING YOURSELF

Like the other selections in this unit, this section from Tiger Woods's biography highlights the importance of testing your own ideas and pushing yourself to the limits of your abilities.

1. Jot down a few words that describe each of the following characters in the face of a challenge: (a) the daughter in "Two Kinds," (b) Alex Haley in "My Furthest-Back Person," (c) the boy in "A Day's Wait," (d) young Bill Cosby in "Was Tarzan a Three-Bandage Man?"

2. (a) What qualities do the people named in question 1 share? (b) How does Tiger Woods demonstrate these qualities?

3. For centuries, human beings have been challenging themselves—to climb mountains, win races, walk on the moon. Why do you think people are so drawn to tests or challenges? Explain.

◆ Critical Thinking

INTERPRET

1. What does Tiger's letter to Coach Goodwin show about his character? **[Analyze]**

2. How do Earl Woods's responses affect his son? **[Analyze Causes and Effects]**

3. How does Tiger's personal development affect his golf game? Be specific. **[Connect]**

4. What can you conclude from this article about the qualities necessary to become a successful competitive athlete? **[Draw Conclusions]**

APPLY

5. How can you apply the lessons Tiger Woods learned to the tests in your life? **[Relate]**

EXTEND

6. In sports, accomplishments may be easy to see. How is accomplishment measured in fields such as the performing or fine arts? **[Art Link]**

Beyond the Selection

FURTHER READING

Other Works About Tiger Woods

Training a Tiger: A Father's Guide to Raising a Winner in Both Golf and Life, Earl Woods with Pete McDaniel

Other Works on the Theme of Testing Yourself

Into Thin Air, Jon Krakauer

Fever Pitch, Nick Hornby

INTERNET

We suggest the following Internet sites (all Web sites are subject to change).

For more information about golf: **http://www.golfweb.com**

For more information about Tiger Woods: **http://www.tigerwoods.com**

We *strongly recommend* that you preview these sites before you send students to them.

◆ LITERATURE AND YOUR LIFE

5 Ask students to think about someone they may know who is very talented and wishes to advance in a chosen field. What kind of advice do they think Tiger's parents might give to this person's parents? *Tiger's parents would probably advise them to let their child make their own decisions and set their own goals and dreams.*

◆ Critical Thinking

6 Draw Conclusions Ask students what causes Earl Woods to become disappointed with Tiger. *Tiger's father expects him to be a good sport and learn from his mistakes. He is unhappy when Tiger quits on himself and pouts about playing poorly.*

Answers

Thematic Connection

1. Possible responses are:
   (a) stubborn, determined, angry
   (b) determined, resourceful, hopeful
   (c) resigned, brave, determined
   (d) creative, determined, good-humored
2. (a) They are all determined and face challenges.
   (b) Through dedication, perseverance, and a willingness to learn, Tiger Woods shows he is determined to be an excellent golfer and a good person.
3. People enjoy the thrill of testing their limits and of learning about their own strengths and weaknesses in addition to achieving something difficult.

◆ Critical Thinking

1. It demonstrates that he knows who he is and what he can do and that he has a long-range plan for his life.
2. Tiger appreciates his father's love and support; he does not feel pressured; and he learns from his father.
3. Tiger has learned that on the golf course, he is responsible for his own actions and setting his own standards.
4. An athlete needs skill, dedication, perseverance, and confidence.
5. Students may say they learned the importance of doing the best they can to achieve their goals.
6. Accomplishment is sometimes measured by money, celebrity status, peer opinion, or number and prestige of performances.

Prepare and Engage

Establish Writing Guidelines
Before students begin, review the characteristics of a firsthand biography:

- A firsthand biography is a life story about someone with whom the writer has a close personal relationship.
- The writer of a firsthand biography is able to provide insights not found in researched biographies.

You may wish to distribute the scoring rubric for Narrative Based on Personal Experience, p. 83 in **Alternative Assessment,** to inform students of the criteria on which they will be evaluated. See p. 100 for suggestions on customizing the rubric to this workshop.

Refer students to the Writing Handbook in the back of the book for instruction on the writing process and for further information on writing biographies.

Writers at Work Videodisc
Have students view the videodisc to learn how Denise Chavez develops narrative elements.

Writer's Solution

Writing Lab CD-ROM
Have students use the tutorial on Narration to complete all or part of their biographies. Follow these steps:

1. Have students review the Firsthand Biography interactive model.
2. Students can use the Inspirations for Narration examples of firsthand biographies.
3. Have students use the Transition Word Bin to gather words to connect the events in their firsthand biographies as they draft.
4. Students can use the interactive student model in the Proofreading section to help them revise.

Play frames 25977 to 28374

Writer's Solution Sourcebook
For additional support, have students use the chapter on Narration, pp. 67–101.

Connect to Literature *Tiger: A Biography of Tiger Woods* by John Strege, p. 93 of Unit 1, is a firsthand biography that is written from a third-person point of view.

Narrative Writing

Firsthand Biography

Writing Process Workshop

How do people become who they are? One way of exploring this question is to examine the life of someone you know. You can do this by writing a firsthand biography. This is a life story written by someone who has a close relationship with the subject of the biography. Because you are writing about someone you know personally, you can provide insights not found in biographies based on research. Use the following skills, introduced in this section's Writing Mini-Lessons, as you write your firsthand biography.

Writing Skills Focus

- **Elaborate** to make your writing personal by providing details about how you feel about the subject. (See p. 77.)
- **Use sensory language**—details that appeal to the senses—to create vivid images. (See p. 85.)
- **Supply reasons or examples** to support the statements you make about the subject. (See p. 91.)
- **Make sure that your facts are accurate.**
- **Provide necessary context** so readers have enough background to understand your subject.

The writer uses these skills in the following firsthand biography of her grandfather.

Writing Model

I yelp as a spray of icy lake water splashes me and the rough, warm boards of the swimming dock. Above the roar of the motorboat, I hear a triumphant whoop. ① Grandpa has just learned to water-ski.

Grandpa is the most amazing person I know. He can repair a car, play the banjo, and bake the world's best chocolate-chip cookies. ② Curious and full of energy, he is always eager to learn new things. Grandma teases him about either behaving himself or getting more insurance, but she loves him just the way he is. ③ Grandpa is my oldest friend—and maybe my best friend.

① Sensory details in these sentences appeal to the senses of touch and hearing.
② Here, the writer provides reasons why the subject is "amazing."
③ Elaboration helps reveal the writer's affection for the subject.

Beyond the Classroom

Career Connection

Journalism Point out to students that the skills they will use in writing their firsthand biographies are also used by journalists to research and write a profile of a particular person.

To provide both an interesting and accurate portrayal of a subject, the journalist conducts interviews both with the subject and with people who know that person. Journalists may use written, audiotaped, or videotaped notes of their interviews to organize their personal profiles and to make sure their profiles accurately reflect their research. Explain also that personal profiles differ from regular objective reporting because, as with firsthand biographies, the journalist's personal and subjective opinions about the subject are often included in the article.

Suggest that students find personal profiles of well-known people in magazines or newspapers. Have them annotate the article in the same manner used in the Writing Model on this page. Using their annotations, discuss how the professional journalists used narrative writing techniques to write their firsthand biographies.

Prewriting

Take Stock of Your Choices To help you think of potential subjects for your firsthand biography, create a list of people whom you know personally whose achievements or experiences make them interesting. Use your list or the topic ideas below to help you choose your subject.

Topic Ideas

- My most unusual relative
- An everyday hero
- An outstanding achiever

Conduct Interviews Gather details for your firsthand biography by interviewing your subject and the people who know him or her well. Before each interview, make a list of questions that will help you get a good picture of the subject's childhood, achievements, or goals and dreams.

Develop a Timeline Use a timeline similar to this one to organize the information you have gathered about your subject. This will give you a clear idea of when important events took place in your subject's life.

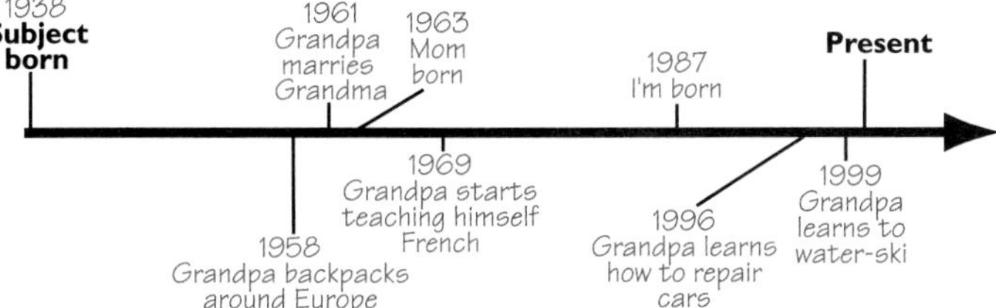

Drafting

Use Your Notes Refer to your interview notes as you draft your firsthand biography. The information in your notes will help you provide necessary background and ensure accuracy when you report facts or quote words from your interviews.

Share Your Feelings Instead of just recounting important dates and events, supply the details and feelings that will add a personal touch to your biography.

Finish With a Flourish Wrap up your firsthand biography by summarizing the most important ideas about your subject. Briefly touch upon the reasons for your opinions about your subject. Finally, explain what conclusions you think people can draw from the subject's life and achievements.

DRAFTING/REVISING

APPLYING LANGUAGE SKILLS: Varying Sentence Beginnings

You can make your writing more lively and interesting by varying your sentence structure. Start some sentences with a subject. Start other sentences with phrases.

Start with a subject:

The man is an inspiration.

He always tries new ideas and activities.

Start with a phrase:

Skilled and patient, the man is an inspiration.

Even at sixty, he always tries new activities.

Practice Rewrite the following sentences so that they start with a phrase.

1. Grandpa patiently explained what he was doing as he fussed with poles, pegs, and ropes.
2. The process suddenly began to make sense.

Writing Application As you draft your firsthand biography, make sure you vary your sentences.

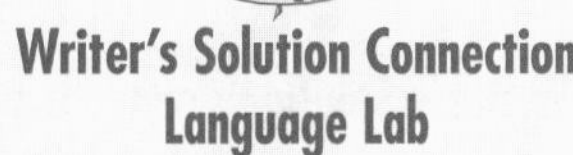

Writer's Solution Connection Language Lab

For instruction in sentence beginnings and types of sentences, see the lesson on Varying Sentence Structure.

Develop Student Writing

Prewriting

Advise students that the subject of their firsthand biography should be someone they know personally. Explain that they should know enough facts about the subject beforehand to be able to tell fact from fiction when conducting and checking their interviews.

Customize for ***Less Proficient Writers***

Suggest that students use a timeline to organize their interview questions in addition to using one to organize their notes. In that way, their notes will flow in chronological order as they ask their questions, simplifying the drafting process.

Customize for ***English Language Learners***

Students can acquire additional vocabulary to create vivid images by using the Sensory Language Chart graphic organizer, p. 78 in **Writing and Language Transparencies.** To generate sensory words to add to the chart, collect magazine pictures of different environments and people engaged in various activities. Help supply students with sensory words appropriate to each scene, such as *warm, sweet, smooth, bright,* or *shout.* Have students refer to the chart as they write their firsthand biographies.

Drafting

Students' firsthand biographies should be personal, as well as factual. Suggest that they think of their audience as an awards committee that is honoring the "Most Interesting Person of the Year." As they draft, students can focus on what they personally think of the subject, the reasons for their opinions, and why the facts of the subject's life will be of interest to others.

Applying Language Skills

Varying Sentence Beginnings Explain to students that when they vary sentence structure by beginning a sentence with a phrase, they must make sure that the reader can tell what the introductory phrase refers to. For example, if they changed the sentence *Sam could not catch Grandpa because he ran too fast* to *Because he ran too fast, Sam could not catch Grandpa,* the reader may think it is Sam who ran too fast. Demonstrate how to move the noun and change the pronoun to make the meaning clear: *Because Grandpa ran too fast, Sam could not catch him.*

Answers

Practice

1. As he fussed with poles, pegs, and ropes, Grandpa patiently explained what he was doing.
2. Suddenly, the process began to make sense.

Writer's Solution

For additional instruction and practice, have students complete the practice page on Participles in Phrases in the *Writer's Solution Grammar Practice Book,* p. 48.

Writer's Solution

Writing Lab CD-ROM

To help students draft these first-person narratives, have them use the video clip on point of view in the Drafting section of the tutorial on Narration to learn the differences between first- and third-person points of view. They may also use the Interactive Model From Literature from "Last Cover" by Paul Annixter to learn how a professional writer uses first-person point of view.

Revising

Have partners use the Peer Conferencing Notes: Writer form, p. 72 in **Alternative Assessment.** They can use these notes to revise their drafts.

Writer's Solution

Writing Lab CD-ROM

Students may use the revision checker and the interactive checklist to evaluate and revise their drafts.

Publishing

Students might use their firsthand biographies to start a family or community history book. Encourage them to add biographies of other family and community members throughout the year and to illustrate the biographies with photos and mementos.

Reinforce and Extend

Review the Writing Guidelines

After students complete their writing, review the criteria for writing a firsthand biography.

Applying Language Skills

Avoid Run-on Sentences Suggest that students identify run-on sentences by determining whether there are two or more sets of complete subjects and complete predicates.

Answers

Practice

Possible answers are:

1. Grandpa loved dinosaurs, so he went to the museum.
2. He knows a lot. He still studies.

For additional practice, have students complete the practice exercises in the Correcting Run-ons lesson in the *Writer's Solution Grammar Practice Book,* p. 59.

EDITING/PROOFREADING

Applying Language Skills: Avoid Run-on Sentences

A **run-on sentence** is two or more complete sentences written as if they were a single sentence. There are two kinds of run-on sentences:

No punctuation: It was 1965 he was on his own in Europe.

Separation by comma: It was 1965, he was on his own in Europe.

To correct a run-on sentence:

- Use a comma and a coordinating conjunction: It was 1965, and he was on his own in Europe.
- Use a semicolon: It was 1965; he was on his own in Europe.
- Use a period and begin a new sentence: It was 1965. He was on his own in Europe.

Practice Correct these run-on sentences.

1. Grandpa loved dinosaurs he went to the museum.
2. He knows a lot he still studies.

Writing Application Correct run-on sentences you see in your firsthand biography.

Writer's Solution Connection
Language Lab

For more help punctuating run-on sentences, see the lessons on Sentence Errors.

Revising

Use a Checklist The following checklist will help you revise your firsthand biography.

- Is my writing interesting and vivid?
  As you revise, look for places where you can add sensory details or elaborate to make the biography more personal.
- Are events listed in the proper sequence?
  Consult the timeline you prepared earlier.
- Is my biography accurate?
  Check your notes to make sure that you haven't made any mistakes.

Revision Model

Grandpa's oldest brother recalls, "He was into everything, even as a baby. He never walked when he could run. ① Some things never change." Grandpa was born in ② ~~1937,~~ 1938 the youngest of three boys. His family lived in a ③ cozy red brick house at what was then the edge of town.

① Changing the order of the sentences puts events in the proper sequence.
② The writer revised this date to ensure accuracy.
③ More sensory details make objects and events easier to picture.

Publishing and Presenting

- **Hall of Fame** With classmates, prepare a bulletin board display that shows photographs or portraits of the subjects of your firsthand biographies. Write captions that let viewers identify each person and preview the essays. Then, arrange your biographies on a shelf beneath the bulletin board so that visitors to your "hall of fame" can learn more about the people featured there.
- **Oral Tribute** Using the information in your firsthand biography, prepare a short speech that explains why you selected the subject and what that person means to you.

✓ ASSESSMENT		4	3	2	1
PORTFOLIO ASSESSMENT Use the rubric on Narrative Based on Personal Experience in the **Alternative Assessment** booklet, p. 83, to assess students' writing. Add these criteria to customize this rubric to this assignment.	**Varying Sentence Beginnings**	The writer has creatively varied sentence beginnings throughout the biography.	The writer has varied sentence beginnings, but some sentences sound redundant.	The writer has varied sentence beginnings, but used the same subject or phrase more than once.	The writer has not varied sentence beginnings. Most sentences sound redundant.
	Avoid Run-on Sentences	There are no run-on sentences in the biography.	There is one or two run-on sentences in the biography.	There are several run-on sentences in the biography.	Most of the sentences in the biography are run-on sentences.

Real-World Reading Skills Workshop

Making Inferences

Strategies for Success

If a writer tried to spell out every single bit of background information about a topic, the resulting writing wouldn't be very interesting and would take too much time and concentration to dig through it! Instead, authors expect you to **make inferences**—to use your own knowledge and imagination to supply information that they don't state directly. When you make inferences in your reading, you're using a skill that you use just about every day in real life, without even realizing it. For example, if you see puddles outside, you infer that it has rained. Or, if you see your friend slam her books down, you can infer she's angry about something.

Look for Clues Read the text carefully. Take note of the information that the author provides, such as time and place and the people's actions, opinions, and reactions. Consider this example: *Spike Johnson walked to the plate slowly, as a hush fell over the crowd.* The detail that he's walking to the plate helps you infer that the author is writing about a baseball game. The facts that Spike is walking slowly and that the crowd is hushed are good clues that it's a crucial moment in the game.

Use Your Experience To make inferences, readers must combine their own knowledge with the information given by the author. In some cases, it may be helpful to think about a similar situation that you have experienced. Consider another example: *Alex wrung his hands and his voice was shaky as he talked to the coach.* Using the details provided (Alex's hand-wringing and his shaky voice) along with your knowledge of what this behavior means, you can infer that Alex is nervous.

Apply the Strategies

Read the article at the bottom of the first column, and make inferences to answer the questions that follow. List the clues in the article that helped you make each inference.

1. What sport is the article about?
2. What part of the game does the writer describe?
3. What is the player about to do?
4. What has the player done to prepare for the game?
5. What does the player always do before his shot?

The Moment of Truth

by Don Pollero

Many lonely practice hours in the gym lead up to the moment when the game clock is down to the last few seconds. A player stands alone on the line, pounding the ball a routine three bounces. Was all that practice enough to make the shot with the game on the line? The crowd holds its breath, waiting for his shot.

Here are other situations in which you can use the strategies for making inferences:

- Watching television
- Looking at a painting
- Listening to music

Introduce the Strategies

Explain to students that an inference is similar to an educated guess. By picking up clues and details and considering what information the author does and does not include, the reader can make an inference as to the author's intended, but perhaps not stated, purpose. Just as you read a person's body language to find signals to his or her mood or meaning, you can read more in a text to see what a character's actions mean.

Customize for
Less Proficient Readers
Suggest that students keep a reading log as they read, jotting down key words and phrases that may be clues to hidden meaning. Tell students to consider what adjectives and adverbs the writer uses in describing people or places. After reading, have students refer to their notes to understand how the author has written.

Apply the Strategies

Remind students that they may want to read the article twice to make sure they have picked up all important details. You may want to have students work in small groups to discuss what clues they have found to make the inferences.

Answers

1. The article is about basketball. Clues include: the game is practiced in the gym, it is played to a clock, the player stands alone, bounces the ball three times, and tries to make a shot.
2. The writer describes the end of the game, when the "clock is down to the last few seconds."
3. The player is about to try to shoot a basket. Clues include: the player stands alone, he pounds the ball three times, and the crowd waits for his shot.
4. The player has practiced many hours in the gym.
5. The player always bounces the ball three times before the shot. The writer uses the word "routine" to describe this.

◆ Build Grammar Skills

The selections in Part 2 include instruction on the following:

- Pronouns
- Pronouns and Antecedents
- Personal Pronouns

This information is reinforced with the Build Grammar Skills practice pages in **Selection Support,** pp. 31, 36, and 41.

As you review pronouns, you may wish to include the following:

- Gender and Number of Pronouns

A personal pronoun must agree with its antecedent in number, person, and gender.

The number of a pronoun indicates whether it is *singular* or *plural.* The person of a pronoun indicates whether the pronoun refers to the *first person* (the one speaking), the *second person* (the one spoken to), or the *third person* (the one spoken about).

Nouns referring to males, such as *father,* are *masculine* in gender. Nouns referring to females, such as *mother,* are *feminine.* Nouns that refer to neither males nor females such as *book* or *truth,* are *neuter.* Only third-person singular pronouns indicate gender.

- Possessive Pronouns

Seven personal pronouns are possessive pronouns or possessive adjectives. They are pronouns because they have antecedents; they are adjectives because they modify nouns and answer the question *Which one?*

Possessive Pronouns

my your his her
its our their

- Interrogative Pronouns

All (five) relative pronouns except *that* can also be interrogative pronouns. An interrogative pronoun begins a question.

Interrogative Pronouns

what which who
whom whose

- Demonstrative Pronouns

Prounouns that direct attention to one or more nouns are called demonstrative pronouns. There are four.

Demonstrative Pronouns

Singular	*Plural*
this, that	these, those

Demonstrative pronouns may appear before or after their antecedents.

- Relative Pronouns

One of the demonstrative pronouns, that, can also be used as a relative pronoun. A relative pronoun begins a subordinate clause and connects it to another idea in the sentence. For more instruction on subordinate clauses, refer to pp. 520, 540, and 548.

Pronouns

Grammar Review

nominal adjective "our"] —pro·nom'i·nally adv.
pro·noun (prō'noun') n. [altered (infl. by NOUN) < pronomen < pro, for + nomen, NOUN] Gram. any relationship or signal words that assume the fu within clauses or phrases while referring to othe the sentence or in other sentences: I, you, them, it, myself, anybody, etc. ... pronouns

A **pronoun** is a word that takes the place of a noun or a group of words acting as a noun (see page 76). Pronouns provide another way to identify the people, places, and things in writing.

The pronoun's **antecedent** is the noun (or group of words acting as a noun) to which the pronoun refers (see page 84).

antecedent pronoun
Even though *flint* is a dull, gray rock, *it* contains fire.

Personal pronouns (see page 90) refer to the person speaking (first person), the person spoken to (second person), or the person or thing spoken about (third person).

	Singular	Plural
First Person	I, me, my, mine	we, us, our, ours
Second Person	you, your, yours	you, your, yours
Third Person	he, him, his, she, her, hers, it, its	they, them, their, theirs

Practice 1 Write the personal pronouns in these sentences. Identify each pronoun as being in the first, second, or third person.

1. Ernest Hemingway's writing shows his belief in courage.
2. When people first read Hemingway, they immediately notice his short sentences.
3. If you could ask him, he might explain it.
4. Which style do you prefer?
5. I guess we all have our own preferences.

Practice 2 Rewrite the paragraph below, replacing repeated nouns with pronouns.

The writing in this section deals with testing yourself—an important part of life. As young people try to figure out what is important, *young people* try many things. Bill Cosby had several sports heroes, yet *Cosby* has become not an athlete but a comedian. Tiger Woods, however, has shown that his own athletic work pays off. Tiger Woods's determination helped *Tiger Woods* compete in golf on a professional level. Woods and Cosby can teach all of us about personal tests. *Woods* and *Cosby* may be heroes to the next generation.

Grammar in Writing

✔ *Pronouns make your writing flow smoothly. However, look out for pronouns that could refer to more than one antecedent.*

Vague: When the boy explained his confusion to his father, he laughed.

(He could refer to the boy or his father.)

Clear: When the boy explained his confusion to his father, his father laughed.

Be sure that the pronouns you use have a definite and clear antecedent.

Writer's Solution

For additional practice and support in using pronouns, use the practice pages on pronouns in the *Writer's Solution Grammar Practice Book,* pp. 8–10.

Answers

Practice 1

1. his (third)
2. they (third); his (third)
3. you (second); him (third); he (third); it (third)
4. you (second)
5. I (first); we (first); our (first)

Practice 2

The writing in this section deals with testing yourself—an important part of life. As young people try to figure out what is important, *they* try many things. Bill Cosby had several sports heroes, yet *he* has become not an athlete, but a comedian. Tiger Woods, however, has shown that his own athletic work pays off. Tiger Woods's determination helped *him* compete in golf on a professional level. Woods and Cosby can teach all of us about personal tests. *They* may be heroes to the next generation.

Speaking, Listening, and Viewing Workshop

Participating in a Group

According to an old expression, "many hands make light work." This means that a job is easier when you have lots of people to help. The idea holds true whether you are moving a sofa or developing a project for class. When you follow a few simple rules, you can allow the group to benefit from everyone's ideas and talents. In addition, the basic rules of group participation can help build respect, prevent arguments, and protect people's feelings.

Tips for Participating in a Group

Use these strategies to get more out of participating in a group:

- Take turns speaking during a group discussion. Listen attentively when it is not your turn to speak.
- Speak clearly and get to the point. If others want to speak, wrap up quickly, and give the next person a turn.
- Listen courteously. Acknowledge other people's contributions and their right to participate.
- If you have a problem with someone's ideas, provide constructive criticism and be sensitive to the other person's feelings. Explain why you disagree, and suggest what could be done to address your concerns. Criticize the idea, action, or product—never the person.
- As a group, decide first on the tasks that need to be done and how to divide them up fairly. Then, come to an agreement on who will be responsible for each task.
- At the end of a meeting, make sure everyone agrees on what was decided and what actions need to be taken.
- For complicated projects, make a schedule so everyone knows what needs to be done and when.

Apply the Strategies

With a group of four to six classmates, work through these stages of a project:

1. Brainstorm for ways to raise money for your school or for a charity.
2. Review your list, and decide on one fund-raising idea that you can all support.
3. List the tasks that need to be done, and divide them fairly.
4. Develop a schedule for doing the tasks and assign them.
5. If possible, obtain permission to do your project and carry out your plan.

Introduce the Strategies

Point out to students that every time they get together with friends and plan a joint activity, they are participating in a group decision. Participating in any group requires that each individual contribute. Invite students to share examples of successful group decisions and activities in which they have participated. Remind them that participation does not mean individually choosing what one wants to do, but choosing what works best for the group.

Apply the Strategies

Remind groups, as they speak and listen to one another, to keep their goal of a fund-raising event in mind.

Assessment

Students should be assessed not only on the success of the group, but on their individual contributions, as well. You may want them to use the Speaking and Listening Progress Self-Assessment form in **Alternative Assessment,** pp. 109–110.

Customize for
Interpersonal Learners

Suggest that interpersonal learners use their interpersonal skills to encourage less willing students to contribute to the group.

Customize for
Logical/Mathematical Learners

Encourage students to help establish the relationship between the goal the group is trying to achieve and the steps needed to make it happen. Encourage them to outline the steps carefully before the group proceeds. Suggest that they contribute to the group by developing schedules.

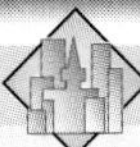

Beyond the Classroom

Workplace Skills

Working as a Team Many jobs require workers to participate in a group, or work as a team. The skills of speaking, listening, and cooperating with others are building blocks for successful teamwork. Have students brainstorm for a list of careers in which group work is essential, such as a construction crew whose workers rely on each other for assistance and safety, doctors and nurses who work together as a surgery team, chefs and staff who prepare and serve food, and assembly line workers who each complete parts of a larger task. Divide the class into groups and have each group focus on one of the careers on the list. Ask them to identify each "team player" and his or her role and responsibilities to the work group and summarize what they think makes a team of workers in that field successful. When groups are finished, have them present their summaries to the class.

◆Build Vocabulary

What's Behind the Words

To research words from names, students will need to locate the meanings and derivations of words using sources such as a dictionary or encyclopedia.

Tell students that most dictionaries add a note in the word entry if the word was named after a person. For example, following the entry *Maverick* is "after Samuel A. Maverick, Texas pioneer who did not brand his cattle." Then students may want to use the Internet or an encyclopedia for further information on the person.

More Vocabulary Adventures

For additional exploration of words from names, you may wish to have students complete this activity:

- Like people's names, place names provide the English language with a great many common words, often the names of products associated with a particular city or area. Identify the sources of the following words:

1. denim	4. cantaloupe
2. jeans	5. frankfurter
3. brussels sprouts	6. hamburger

Answers

1. Nimes, France	4. Cantalupo, Italy
2. Genoa, Italy	5. Frankfurt, Germany
3. Brussels, Belgium	6. Hamburg, Germany

What's Behind the Words

Vocabulary Adventures with Richard Lederer

Words From Names

The Greeks had a word for a person who lives on in our everyday conversations—*eponym*, meaning "after or upon a name." Stories of the origins of words made from people or places, real or imaginary, are among the most entertaining about the English language. Such words gradually lose their reference to specific persons and usually shed their capital letters. These additions to our vocabulary help our language to remain alive and energetic. Here are some colorful examples of common words in our language that were born from proper names.

Maverick

Samuel Augustus Maverick, a San Antonio rancher, acquired vast tracts of land and dabbled in cattle raising. When he neglected to brand the calves born into his herd, his neighbors began calling the unmarked offspring by his name. Over time, Maverick's surname lost its capitalization and came to designate any nonconformist—one who is not part of the herd.

Boycott

Charles Cunningham Boycott, an Irish land agent, so enraged his tenants with his rent collection practices that they threatened his life and property and burned his figure in effigy. Thus, from Ireland comes the verb *boycott*, which means "to refuse as a group to deal with someone."

Mesmerize

Franz Anton Mesmer, a Viennese physician, attempted to treat his patients by fixing them with a piercing gaze, questioning them about their ailments, and waving a wand over them. Today, a verb form of his name—*mesmerize*—means "to hypnotize" or "to fascinate."

Activity 1 Here is a list of ten words that have descended from people's names. Define each word, and find out about the person whose name inspired it.

1. silhouette	**6.** pasteurize
2. chauvinist	**7.** poinsettia
3. galvanize	**8.** pompadour
4. graham cracker	**9.** sideburns
5. leotards	**10.** bloomers

Activity 2 Using their names as clues, identify the inventions of each of these people. Then with a partner, research the story behind the word. Share your findings with the class.

1. George Ferris	**4.** George Pullman
2. Robert Bunsen	**5.** Joseph Guillotin
3. Rudolph Diesel	**6.** Ferdinand Count von Zeppelin

Activity 3 Make up and clearly define a new word from a person's name. It can be a famous person or a person you know.

Answers

Activity 1

1. *silhouette,* the outline or general shape of something. Inspired by Etienne de Silhouette, a French finance minister who practiced making portrait silhouettes by cutting them out of paper.
2. *chauvinist,* an excessive patriot. Inspired by Chauvin, a soldier in Napoleon's army noted for loud-mouthed patriotism.
3. *galvanize,* to stimulate or excite by electric shock. Inspired by Galvani, an Italian physiologist who found that electricity may result from chemical activity.
4. *graham cracker,* a cracker made of unsifted whole wheat flour. Named for Sylvester Graham, a reformer of dietetics.
5. *leotards,* close-fitting one-piece garments worn by dancers and gymnasts. Named after Jules Leotard, a French gymnast.
6. *pasteurize,* to expose (milk, cheese, etc.) to a high temperature to destroy microorganisms and prevent fermentation. Named for Louis Pasteur, French chemist who invented this process.
7. *poinsettia,* a plant native to Mexico and Central America, having variously lobed leaves and brilliant scarlet, pink, or white bracts. Named for Joel R. Poinsett, American diplomat who discovered the plant in Mexico.
8. *pompadour,* a hairstyle where the hair is raised over the forehead in a roll. Inspired by the Marquise de Pompadour.
9. *sideburns,* short whiskers extending from the hairline to below the ears and worn with an unbearded chin. Inspired by Ambrose Everett Burnside, Union general in the U.S. Civil War.
10. *bloomers,* full, loose trousers gathered at the knee, formerly worn by women for athletics. Named for Amelia Jenkins Bloomer, an American reformer who introduced the outfit.

Activity 2

1. ferris wheel	4. pullman car
2. bunsen burner	5. guillotine
3. diesel engine	6. zeppelin (airship)

Activity 3

Sample response: Jordan, a high-tech basketball sneaker inspired by Michael Jordan.

Extended Reading Opportunities

Because finding yourself is a lifelong process, the search is a popular topic for writers and readers alike. Here are suggestions for your further exploration of the subject.

Suggested Titles

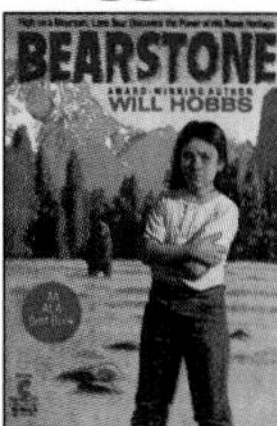

Bearstone
Will Hobbs

Will Hobbs tells the tale of Cloyd, a Native American boy who struggles to build a future for himself. His people, the Utes, once lived among the stark peaks and lush valleys of southwestern Colorado, the region where this modern-day story takes place.

Cloyd's knowledge of his ancestors helps him deal with his problems in the present. His broken family and his bitterness make it hard for him to accept help until he meets an older white man named Walter Landis.

Where the Red Fern Grows
Wilson Rawls

Although still a ten-year-old, Billy is desperate for a hunting dog, and he sets his mind on getting one. From the day he raises enough money and hikes twenty miles to town, he begins his own journey to adulthood. Billy's experiences with his dogs, Old Dan and Little Ann, teach him about fear, responsibility, ingenuity, friendship, strength, and death.

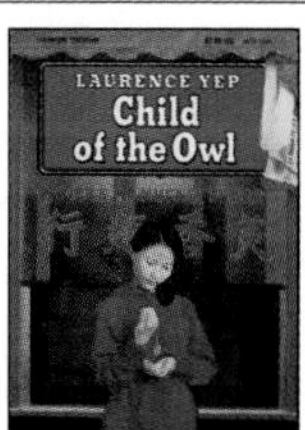

Child of the Owl
Laurence Yep

After her father is hospitalized, twelve-year-old Casey is sent to live with her grandmother in San Francisco's bustling Chinatown. While adjusting to her colorful new home, she begins to discover aspects of her family history and Chinese heritage she never knew before. In this novel, a grandmother's wisdom helps change a tough, independent girl with no real sense of home to a young woman with a new sense of who she is and where she belongs.

Other Possibilities

Missing Pieces	Norma Fox Mazer
Maniac McGee	Jerry Spinelli
My Brother, My Sister, and I	Yoko Kawashima Watkins
Hold Fast to Dreams	Andrea Davis Pinkney

Planning Students' Extended Reading

All of the works listed on this page are good choices for extending the theme "Finding Yourself." Following is some information that may help you choose which to teach.

Customize for *Varying Student Needs*

When assigning the selections in this part to your students, keep in mind the following factors.

- *Bearstone* is a contemporary novel whose theme of Native American heritage can provide an opportunity for class discussion of the importance of people's cultural backgrounds.
- *Where the Red Fern Grows* is a classic contemporary novel for young readers. However, it does have some sensitivity issues listed below.
- *Child of the Owl* is another award-winning novel about growing up Chinese American. It may be of special interest to students whose parents moved here from another country.

Sensitive Issues The subject matter of hunting in *Where the Red Fern Grows* may not be appropriate for some students. You may wish to use caution when assigning this book to readers for whom violence to animals is a personally sensitive issue. However, this book may also provide excellent discussion opportunities about the realities of animal death and the laws of nature.

Literature Study Guides

Literature study guides are available for *Bearstone* and *Child of the Owl.* The guides include section summaries, discussion questions, and activities.

Planning Instruction and Assessment

Unit Objectives

1. To read selections in different genres that develop the theme of "Common Threads"
2. To apply a variety of reading strategies, particularly strategies for interactive reading, appropriate for reading these selections
3. To recognize literary elements used in these selections
4. To increase vocabulary
5. To learn elements of grammar and usage
6. To write in a variety of modes about situations based on the selections
7. To develop speaking and listening skills, by completing activities
8. To view images critically and create visual representations

Meeting the Objectives Each selection provides instructional material and portfolio opportunities by which students can meet unit objectives. You will find additional practice pages for reading strategies, literary elements, vocabulary, and grammar in the **Selection Support** booklet in the **Teaching Resources** box.

Setting Goals Work with your students at the beginning of the unit to set goals for unit outcomes. Plan what skills and concepts you wish students to acquire. You may match instruction and activities according to students' performance levels or learning modalities.

Portfolios Students may keep portfolios of their completed work or of their work in progress. The Build Your Portfolio page of each selection provides opportunities for students to apply the concepts presented.

Humanities: Art

Untitled, by David Ridley

David Ridley's painting shows an endless line of people linked together. Use these questions for discussion:

1. Do the painting's figures look alike or different? Explain. *Some students may perceive them as the same because of their shapes; others may perceive the varied colors as making them look different.*
2. What do you think the artist wants to convey by showing the linked figures? *Students may say that people can join together despite differences.*

Untitled, © David Ridley

Art Transparencies

The **Art Transparencies** booklet in the **Teaching Resources** box offers fine art to help students make connections to other curriculum areas and high-interest topics.

Beyond Literature

Each unit presents Beyond Literature features that lead students into an exploration of other areas. In this unit, students will explore the immigrant experience, and make career and science connections. In addition, the **Teaching Resources** box contains a **Beyond Literature** booklet of activities. Using literature as a springboard, these activity pages offer students many opportunities to connect literature to areas.

UNIT **2**

Common Threads

No matter how different we may be from people around the world, we share experiences that bring us all together. The literature in this unit will show you just how strong those common threads can be. You'll read about athletes who compete for glory. You'll meet a woman inspired by her mother's creative influence. You may see yourself in a boy who does foolish things to make an impression. Read on—the people you meet in this unit may let you discover new connections to your world!

Connections

Within this unit, you will find selections and activities that make connections beyond literature. Use these selections to connect students' understanding and appreciation of literature beyond the traditional literature and language arts curriculum.

Encourage students to connect literature to other curriculum areas. You may wish to coordinate with teachers in other curriculum areas to determine ways to team teach and further extend instruction.

Connections to Today's World

Use these selections to guide students to recognize the relevance of literature to contemporary writings. In this unit, students will read an excerpt from a magazine article about the 1998 U.S. Women's Hockey Team.

Connecting Literature to Social Studies

Each unit contains a selection that connects literature to social studies. In this unit, students will read an excerpt about young people's lives in the Middle Ages.

Assessing Student Progress

The tools that are available to measure the degree to which students meet the unit objectives are listed below.

Informal Assessment

The questions in the Guide for Responding sections are a first level of response to the concepts and skills presented with the selection. As a brief informal measure of students' grasp of the material, these responses indicate where further instruction and practice are needed. The practice pages in the **Selection Support** booklet provide for this type of instruction and practice.

You will also find literature and reading guides in the **Alternative Assessment** booklet, which students can use for informal assessment of their individual performances.

Formal Assessment

The **Formal Assessment** booklet contains Selection Tests and Unit Tests.

Selection Tests measure comprehension and skills acquisition for each selection or group of selections.

Each **Unit Test** provides 30 multiple-choice questions and 5 essay questions designed to assess students' knowledge of the literature and skills taught in the unit.

Each **Alternative Unit Test: Standardized-Test Practice** provides 15 multiple-choice questions and 3 essay questions based on 2 new literature selections not contained in the Student Edition. The questions on the Alternative Unit Test are designed to assess students' ability to compare and contrast selections, applying skills taught in the unit.

Alternative Assessment

For portfolio and alternative assessment, the **Alternative Assessment** booklet contains Scoring Rubrics, Assessment Sheets, and Learning Modalities activities.

Scoring Rubrics provide writing modes that can be applied to Writing Mini-Lessons and to Writing Process Workshop lessons.

Assessment Sheets for speaking and listening activities.

Learning Modalities Activities appeal to different learning styles. Use these as an alternative measurement of students' growth.

Prepare and Engage

OBJECTIVES

1. To read, comprehend, interpret, and respond to a tribute
2. To relate a tribute to personal experience
3. To apply interactive reading strategies
4. To analyze the characteristics of a tribute
5. To build vocabulary in context and learn the root *-nym-*
6. To recognize verbs
7. To write a tribute using vivid words
8. To respond to the tribute through writing, speaking and listening, and projects

SKILLS INSTRUCTION

Vocabulary:
Word Roots: *-nym-*

Spelling:
The Short *i* Sound in *-nym-*

Grammar:
Verbs

Literary Focus:
Tribute

Reading Strategy:
Interactive Reading Strategies

Writing:
Use Vivid Words

Speaking and Listening:
How-to Speech (Teacher Edition)

Viewing and Representing:
Close-up (Teacher Edition)

Critical Viewing:
Support, Analyze

PORTFOLIO OPPORTUNITIES

Writing: Slogans; Walker Family Story; Literary Analysis

Writing Mini-Lesson: Tribute

Speaking and Listening: Television Commercial; How-to Speech

Projects: Sharecropping Report; Garden Plan

More About the Author

Alice Walker won recognition for her talent and intelligence early in her life. Overcoming poverty and partial blindness, she graduated at the top of her high school class and received a scholarship to Spelman College in Atlanta. Her many awards include not only the Pulitzer Prize and the American Book Award for *The Color Purple,* but also the Lillian Smith Award from the National Endowment for the Arts, and the Rosenthal Award from the National Institute of Arts and Letters. Walker's participation in the Civil Rights movement during the 1960's became the subject of two of her novels. Many of Walker's works focus on women and their strengths.

Guide for Reading

Meet the Author:

Alice Walker (1944–)

Since her childhood in rural Georgia, Alice Walker's life has been shaped by the love and power of women. First, there was Walker's mother, who stood at the center of her large family. An African American woman with limited education and income, she shared her artistic spirit and creations with her family and community. Later, there were the many African and African American ancestors Walker discovered. Characters based on these women appear in many of Walker's works.

Becoming a Writer Despite her family's size and limited financial resources, Walker went to college. There, she wrote her first book of poems—about a summer trip to Africa and her work in the civil rights movement. Walker's work blossomed from there, and she became very popular. *The Color Purple,* for example, won the Pulitzer Prize and became a successful movie.

THE STORY BEHIND THE ESSAY

This essay is a tribute to Alice Walker's mother, who, in Walker's words, "made a way out of no way." Walker wrote the essay in 1983 as a way to honor the creative influence that helped her achieve great success with *The Color Purple* and other works. This essay has turned out to be a creative influence, too, inspiring Walker's fictional story *Everyday Use.*

[For more on Alice Walker, see page 228.]

◆ LITERATURE AND YOUR LIFE

CONNECT YOUR EXPERIENCE

Think about a special someone—your older brother, a grandparent, or maybe your fourth grade teacher. Somehow this special person may have changed your life or shaped who you are today. In this essay, Alice Walker shares her memories of the person who had the strongest impact on her life, her mother.

THEMATIC FOCUS: Common Threads

As you read, think about how the talents of one generation reappear in the next generation.

◆ Background for Understanding

HISTORY

Like many African American families in the South just after the Civil War, Alice Walker's ancestors lived the difficult life of sharecroppers—working on plantations for landowners who no longer had slaves to work the fields. In return for land, seed, and tools, these former slaves and poor whites gave the landowners a percentage of their crops at harvest time. Sharecroppers worked long hours and dreamed of buying land of their own eventually. However, many fell into debt and were fortunate if they had enough food for their families.

Prentice Hall Literature Program Resources

REINFORCE / RETEACH / EXTEND

Selection Support Pages
Build Vocabulary: Word Roots: *-nym-*, p. 44
Build Spelling Skills, p. 45
Build Grammar Skills: Verbs, p. 46
Reading Strategy: Interactive Reading Strategies, p. 47
Literary Focus: Tribute, p. 49

Strategies for Diverse Student Needs, pp. 17–18

Beyond Literature Study Skills: Classifying, p. 9

Formal Assessment Selection Test, pp. 35–37, Assessment Resources Software

Alternative Assessment, p. 9

Writing and Language Transparencies
Cluster Organizer, p. 82

Resource Pro CD-ROM
from *In Search of Our Mothers' Gardens*—includes all resource material and customizable lesson plan

Listening to Literature Audiocassettes
from *In Search of Our Mothers' Gardens*

◆ Literary Focus

TRIBUTE

The piece you're about to read is a **tribute,** a literary expression of gratitude or admiration, to honor a special person. A tribute often contains anecdotes, or brief stories, that show the qualities of the honored person and includes an explanation of the subject's importance to the writer. As you read, you get to know both the subject and the writer. Use a graphic organizer like the one below to note what you learn about Walker and her mother.

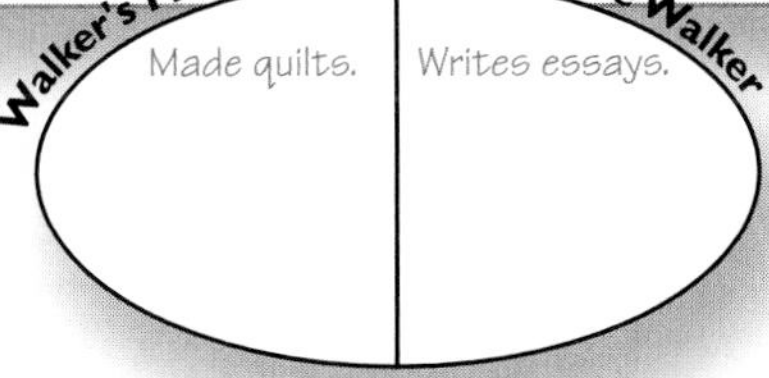

◆ Build Vocabulary

WORD ROOTS: *-nym-*

Alice Walker describes an extraordinary quilt created by an "anonymous Black woman in Alabama." The word *anonymous* contains the root *-nym-*, meaning "name." *Anonymous* means "without name." No one knows who made the quilt.

WORD BANK

Look over these words from the essay. Can you identify which two words have to do with light?

mutilated
vibrant
anonymous
profusely
radiant
illuminates
hindered

101962

Preparing for Standardized Tests

Grammar Ability to correctly identify parts of speech, such as verbs (the grammar concept for this selection), will give students a basis for answering grammar questions and applying editing skills on standardized tests. You may wish to refer to the verb instruction on p. 117 to help prepare students for practice with verbs in a standardized test format.

Write the following sample question and answers on the board:

Her day began before sunup.

Identify the verb in this sentence.

(A) day (C) before
(B) began (D) sunup

Students should recognize that *(B) began* expresses action. Then give students this sample:

Her day is long and busy.

Identify the verb in this sentence.

(A) day (C) is
(B) long (D) busy

Guide students to see that *(C) is* expresses the state of being long and busy. For additional practice with verbs, use **Selection Support**, p. 46.

Interest Grabber Show students an apple and discuss its various qualities. Then invite them to consider how they might show appreciation of an apple's natural beauty. For example, they could paint a picture of it, write a poem about it, bake an apple pie, plant its seeds, or compost its core and stem. Then lead students into the selection by telling them that Alice Walker describes her mother's creative expression of her appreciation of nature through her garden, while Walker expresses herself through her writing.

◆ Build Grammar Skills

Verbs If you wish to introduce the grammar concept for this selection before students read, refer to the instruction on p. 117.

Customize for *Less Proficient Readers*

You may want to show students a book of flowers. Encourage them to identify the names of flowers that Walker uses in the selection and help them pronounce the names. (See the flowers listed on p. 114.)

Customize for *More Advanced Students*

In addition to the section of verse, Walker's poetic writing in this essay lends itself to oral interpretation. Invite students to prepare a reading of the essay, selecting the sections they will read, determining the speaker's (Walker's) tone, and deciding on appropriate vocal inflections and gestures. Have students present their oral interpretations to the class after the other students have read the essay independently. Discuss how oral interpretation enhances Walker's tribute.

Customize for *English Language Learners*

The descriptions of gardening activities may be unfamiliar to students, but, in fact, students may recognize the activities. Pantomime actions such as "dividing clumps of bulbs," "uprooting and replanting roses," and "pruning branches."

Reading for Success

The Reading for Success page in each unit presents a set of problem-solving strategies to help readers understand authors' words and ideas on multiple levels. Good readers develop a bank of strategies from which they can draw as needed.

Unit 2 introduces strategies for interactive reading. It is important for students to interact with what they read in order to find meaning. These strategies for interactive reading give readers an array of approaches for mastering a text: reading purposefully, relating the literature to one's own experience, asking questions, and paraphrasing.

These strategies for interactive reading are modeled with the excerpt from *In Search of Our Mothers' Gardens*. Each green box shows an example of the thinking process involved in applying one of these strategies. Additional notes provide support for applying these strategies throughout the selection.

How to Use the Reading for Success Page

- Introduce the interactive reading strategies, presenting each as a problem-solving procedure.
- Before students read the selection, have them preview it, looking at the annotations in the green boxes that model the strategies.
- To reinforce these strategies after students have read the selection, have them use Reading for Success, p. 47, in **Selection Support.** That page gives students an opportunity to read a selection and practice interactive reading strategies by writing their own annotations.

Reading Strategies: Support and Reinforcement

Using Boxed Annotations and Prompts

Throughout the unit, the notes in green, red, and maroon are intended to help students apply reading strategies, understand the literary focus, and make a connection with their lives. You may use boxed material in these ways:

- Have students pause at each box and respond to its prompt before they continue reading.
- Urge students to read through the selection, ignoring the boxes. After they complete the selection, they may go back and review the text, responding to the prompts.

Reading for Success

Interactive Reading Strategies

Whether you're watching a horror movie, singing in a chorus, or learning about ancient cultures, you have to be involved to get the most from your experience. Reading is no different—you must actively participate to get the most from your reading. By interacting with literature, you'll better understand what you read. These strategies will help you read interactively.

Set a purpose for reading.

- For every piece of writing you encounter, determine your purpose for reading. For example, you may read:
  - To learn about history
  - To study a writer's work
  - To find out more about someone you respect

  You might read Alice Walker's essay to see why she honors a special person.
- Look for details in your reading that help you meet your purpose. For example, look for Walker's ideas about her mother. Find examples of experiences the two women share.

Relate to your own experience.

- People, even in very different settings, often share emotions and ideas. Find ways that your experiences relate to those of the writer or the character.

Ask questions.

- Make the reading an active experience by asking questions like these:
  - Why do the characters behave as they do?
  - What causes events to happen?
  - Why does the writer include certain information?

Look for answers to your questions as you read.

Paraphrase.

- Paraphrasing is simply restating in your own words. When you paraphrase sentences or paragraphs, you make their meaning clear to yourself.

  Walker's Words: For stories, too, were subject to being distracted, to dying without conclusion.

  Paraphrase: Stories could be interrupted or not even finished.

As you read the following essay by Alice Walker, look at the notes in the boxes. The notes show you how to apply these strategies to your reading.

Model a Reading Strategy: Use Paraphrasing to Clarify Meaning

Tell students that when they read certain passages and the meaning is not completely clear to them, they can paraphrase the passage—put it into their own words for better understanding. The verse form of the poem on p. 115 might be challenging to some students. Show them how to restate the poem and make its meaning clearer by modeling a prose paraphrase of the poem:

> In this poem Walker describes African American mothers whose hard lives made them strong, like soldiers. The white scarves they wore were like generals' uniforms. Their lives were like battles to be won. Walker compares their homes with battlefields that have buried mines and booby traps. To overcome these obstacles, women struggled to show their children the goals of education and advancement; they never had the experience themselves.

You may want to point out to students that paraphrasing provides a way to understand Walker's meaning, but it sacrifices the power and beauty of her poetic language.

MODEL

from *In Search of Our Mothers' Gardens*

Alice Walker

1 My mother made all the clothes we wore, even my brothers' overalls. She made all the towels and sheets we used. She spent the summers canning vegetables and fruits. She spent the winter evenings making quilts enough to cover all our beds.

During the "working" day, she labored beside—not behind—my father in the fields. Her day began before sunup, and did not end until late at night. There was never a moment for her to sit down, undisturbed, to unravel her own private thoughts; never a time free from interruption—by work or the noisy inquiries of her many children. And yet, it is to my mother—and all our mothers who were not famous—that I went in search of the secret of what has fed that muzzled[1] and often mutilated, but vibrant, creative spirit that the black woman has inherited, and that pops out in wild and unlikely places to this day.

2 The statement beginning with "And yet" identifies Alice Walker's main idea. You can now **set a purpose** to find supporting ideas throughout the essay.

But when, you will ask, did my overworked mother have time to know or care about feeding the creative spirit?

3 The answer is so simple that many of us have spent years discovering it. We have constantly looked high, when we should have looked high—and low. 3

For example: in the Smithsonian Institution[2] in Washington, D.C., there hangs a quilt unlike any other in the world. In fanciful,[3] inspired, and yet simple and identifiable figures, it portrays the story of the Crucifixion.[4] It is considered rare, beyond price. Though it follows no known pattern of quilt-making, and though it is made of bits and pieces of worthless rags, it is obviously the work of a person of powerful imagination and deep spiritual feeling. Below this quilt I saw a note that says it was made by "an anonymous Black woman in Alabama, a hundred years ago."

If we could locate this "anonymous" black woman from Alabama, she would turn out to be one of our grandmothers—an artist who left her mark in the only materials she could afford, and in the only medium her position in society allowed her to use.

1. **muzzled** (muz´ əld) *adj.*: Prevented from expressing itself.

2. **Smithsonian Institution:** Group of museums with exhibits in the fields of science, art, and history.
3. **fanciful** (fan´ si fəl) *adj.*: Playfully imaginative.
4. **the Crucifixion** (kro͞o´ sə fik´ shən): Jesus Christ's suffering and death on the cross.

◆ Build Vocabulary

mutilated (myo͞ot´ əl āt´ id) *adj.*: Damaged or injured

vibrant (vī´ brənt) *adj.*: Lively and energetic

anonymous (ə nän´ ə məs) *adj.*: With no name known

Develop Understanding

One-Minute Insight Alice Walker begins this tribute to her mother and to "mothers who were not famous" by describing her search for the secret behind the creative spirit of African American women. She discovers this secret in the efforts of women who use any available medium to express themselves. Her own mother, a sharecropper, told stories and created beautiful gardens. The stories provide a foundation for Walker's writing, and the gardens show Walker the value of creative expression. In her writing, Walker follows the threads of creativity that link generations.

◆ Literary Focus

1 Tribute A tribute describes a person's traits. Ask students what they learn about Alice Walker's mother from the opening paragraph. *She worked hard making clothes and linens, canning food, and working in the fields.*

Reading for Success

2 Set a Purpose After students read the first two paragraphs of the selection, have them state a purpose for reading. For instance, noting the difficult life that Walker's mother led, they might want to find out how her "vibrant, creative spirit . . . pops out in wild and unlikely places." Encourage them to set other purposes as they continue reading.

◆ Critical Thinking

3 Analyze Ask students what Walker means when she states that ". . . we should have looked high—and low." *Possible response: She means that the creative spirit can be found in humble (low) places, such as within the woman who used "bits and pieces of worthless rags" to make a beautiful quilt.*

Customize for
Interpersonal Learners
To provide practice in paraphrasing, suggest that partners read the selection together, taking turns paraphrasing difficult paragraphs.

Block Scheduling Strategies

- Before students read the selection, introduce the Reading for Success Strategies, p. 110. Suggest that as they read, students keep a log to monitor their reading strategies. Supplement by having students work as a class to answer the Reading for Success questions on p. 117. Then have students apply the strategies as they annotate the Reading for Success practice selection, p. 47, in **Selection Support**.
- Alternatively, students may begin with Build Vocabulary and Build Grammar Skills and then read the selection independently. Have groups discuss Reader's Response and Thematic Focus and answer questions on p. 116.
- Guide students to discuss Background for Understanding, p. 108, and Literary Focus, p. 109. Then have them listen to the excerpt from *In Search of Our Mothers' Gardens* on audiocassette. As they listen, encourage them to complete their graphic organizers from Literary Focus, p. 109, and note vivid words that the author uses in her tribute.

Listening to Literature Audiocassettes

◆Literature and Your Life

❶ Ask volunteers to describe creative endeavors of their mothers, aunts, or grandmothers. Encourage them to tell if they have ever shared in these activities and, if so, what they learned from the experience.

Reading for Success

❷ **Set a Purpose** Remind students that the author set out to find the "secret of what has fed that muzzled and often mutilated, but vibrant, creative spirit that the black woman has inherited." Ask them what the first paragraph reveals about the results of this search. *Walker explains that the creative activities of mothers and grandmothers often inspire the drive to create in later generations.*

◆Critical Thinking

❸ **Generalize** Explain to students that, like Walker and her mother, everyone has stories to tell about their lives. Ask students why these stories are important. *Possible response: The stories of each person's life reflect a place, a time, and a culture. The sum of these stories tells about our history.*

Reading for Success

❹ **Paraphrase** Help students with the sentence in the second paragraph that begins "Only recently did I fully realize this . . ." by *paraphrasing:* "This is what I realized after listening to my mother's stories for years. I have known the stories, and I have known the manner in which my mother told the stories. I have absorbed the knowledge that her stories must be recorded." Tell students that breaking a sentence into smaller sentences is a way to paraphrase text.

Comprehension Check ☑

❺ In what way does Alice Walker continually pay tribute to her mother's stories? *Students should understand that Walker uses her mother's stories as inspiration and bases much of her writing on those same stories.*

◆Critical Thinking

❻ **Cause and Effect** Ask students why Walker's mother did not always finish her stories. *She had to stop her stories to take care of chores such as preparing dinner and picking cotton.*

> Use this information to achieve your **purpose for reading.** Creativity is not limited to famous wealthy artists.

❶ ❷ And so our mothers and grandmothers have, more often than not anonymously, handed on the creative spark, the seed of the flower they themselves never hoped to see: or like a sealed letter they could not plainly read.

And so it is, certainly, with my own mother. Unlike "Ma" Rainey's songs,[5] which retained their creator's name even while blasting forth from Bessie Smith's mouth,[6] no song or poem will bear my mother's name. Yet so many of the stories that I write, that we all write, are my mother's stories. Only recently did I fully realize this: that through years of listening to
❸ my mother's stories of her life, I have absorbed
❹ not only the stories themselves, but something of the manner in which she spoke, something of the urgency that involves the knowledge that her stories—like her life— must be recorded. It is probably for this reason that so
❺ much of what I have written is about characters whose counterparts in real life are so much older than I am.

But the telling of these stories, which came from my mother's lips as naturally as breathing, was not the only way my mother showed herself as an artist. For stories, too, were sub-
❻ ject to being distracted, to dying without conclusion. Dinners must be started, and cotton must be gathered before the big rains. The artist that was and is my mother showed itself to me only after many years. This is what I finally noticed:

Like Mem, a character in *The Third Life of Grange Copeland,*[7] my mother adorned with

5. **"Ma" Rainey's songs:** Gertrude ("Ma") Rainey, one of America's first blues singers, lived during the early years of this century.
6. **Bessie Smith's mouth:** Bessie Smith was a well-known blues singer (1898?–1937), who knew and learned from "Ma" Rainey.
7. ***The Third Life of Grange Copeland:*** The title of a novel by Alice Walker.

Cross-Curricular Connection: Music

Blues Music The sound of blues has its origins in a blending of African and American traditions. Some elements of blues can be traced to the African call-and-response chant, in which a solo line is answered with a choral response, while the theme of most blues songs reflects the struggles of African American people.

Blues singer Ma Rainey was born in Georgia in 1886. She began performing at age 14, and was probably the first woman to sing the blues with vaudeville, minstrel, and tent shows.

Born in Tennessee in 1894, Bessie Smith began singing in the 1920's with the help of Ma Rainey. After working in tent shows, she went to New York for her first recording session. An instant success, Rainey earned the title "Empress of the Blues" with her robust unrestrained style. Invite students to listen and respond to a recording of one or both singers.

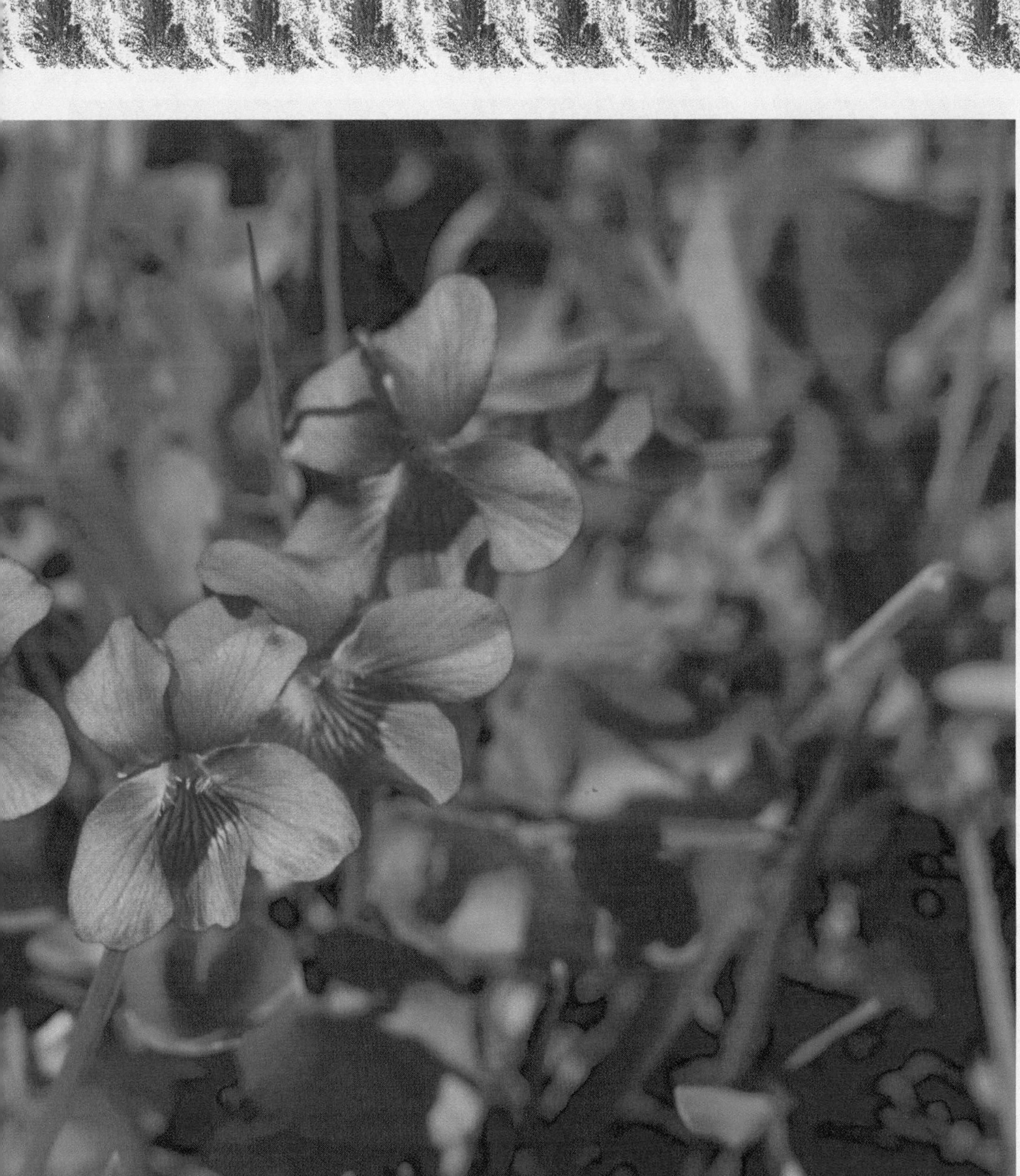

▲ Critical Viewing This essay describes a woman's love of gardening. How can planting and caring for a garden be a creative process? **[Support]** 7

▶Critical Viewing◀

7 Support *The cultivation of plants and flowers is creative because the gardener watches plants grow and decides what they need to thrive and bloom, such as the amount of light, water, or fertilizer. The arrangement of flowers in gardens depends upon an understanding of what colors and shapes will complement one another and also show personal taste.*

Customize for *Less Proficient Readers*

Help students summarize the author's ideas to this point—state the most important points of the writing. Alice Walker set out to find the source of the creative spirit that exists in African American women such as her mother. A quilt she saw showed her that creativity is found in in all kinds of places and that creative people make use of materials on hand. She considers her mother's stories to be a result of this drive to create.

Viewing and Representing Mini-Lesson

Close-up

This mini-lesson will help students extend the idea of creative representation, based on a close-up photograph.

Introduce Have students study the close-up photograph of flowers on these two pages.

Develop Discuss how a close-up view shows details of this flower. Help students focus on specific details of the flowers, such as the colors, the number of petals, and the stripes surrounding the stamen (the center of the flower). Then discuss how tributes, which give detailed information about a person, are like close-up photographs.

Apply Ask students to think of a creative person they admire—someone they know or have learned about through reading or another source. Discuss how they might represent this person in a close-up. For example, they might represent a pianist by showing a hand on a keyboard. Then have them select a medium such as drawing, painting, photography, video, or written words to use in creating a close-up of the person. Help students find the appropriate materials for their close-ups—you may want to encourage them to select a realistic medium for the means you and they have available. Allow time for students to create their close-up representations.

Assess Have students share their work with the class, explaining their choice of subject and medium. Evaluate students' work based on their successsful completion of the assignment and their explanations.

▶Critical Viewing◀

❶ **Analyze** *Different plants require different quantities of water and varying amounts of growing space. A gardener also has to know the seasons that different flowers bloom and how to time the planting of various flowers if he or she wants them to bloom at the same time.*

Reading for Success

❷ **Ask Questions** Point out that a reader who is reading interactively may have asked him-or herself, "How did Walker's mother find the time to create beautiful gardens?" Guide students to find the answer. *She worked before she left home for the fields. When she returned, she worked until dark.*

Reading for Success

❸ **Paraphrase** Invite a volunteer to read the paraphrase aloud. Ask students if they feel it captures the ideas of the writer. *Most students will agree because the paragraph describes the beautiful flowers produced by her gardening skills and their effect on Walker's memories of poverty.*

❶ ▲ **Critical Viewing** Gardens like this one and the one Walker's mother kept include many varieties of plants. How might such a blend make a garden more difficult to maintain? **[Analyze]**

flowers whatever shabby house we were forced to live in. And not just your typical straggly[8] country stand of zinnias, either. She planted ambitious gardens—and still does—with over fifty different varieties of plants that bloom profusely from early March until late November. Before she left home for the fields, she watered her flowers, chopped up the grass, ❷ and laid out new beds. When she returned from the fields she might divide clumps of bulbs, dig a cold pit,[9] uproot and replant roses, or prune branches from her taller bushes or trees—until night came and it was too dark to see.

Whatever she planted grew as if by magic, and her fame as a grower of flowers spread over three counties. Because of her creativity with her flowers, even my memories of poverty are seen through a screen of blooms—sunflowers, petunias, roses, dahlias, forsythia, spirea, delphiniums, verbena . . . and on and on.

> **Paraphrase** this paragraph in this way: "She was a talented gardener whose ability to create beauty softened my experience of our poverty." ❸

And I remember people coming to my mother's yard to be given cuttings from her flowers; I hear again the praise showered on ❹ her because whatever rocky soil she landed on, she turned into a garden. A garden so

8. **straggly** (strag´ lē) *adj.*: Spread out in an irregular way.
9. **cold pit:** Hole in which seedlings are planted at the beginning of the spring.

Speaking and Listening Mini-Lesson

How-to Speech

This mini-lesson supports the Speaking and Listening activity in the Idea Bank on p. 118.

Introduce Invite a volunteer to give instructions to the class on getting to the school cafeteria from your classroom. Ask the rest of the class to evaluate whether the instructions adequately explain how to make the short trip.

Develop Use students' evaluation of the previous instructions to discuss the elements of an effective how-to speech. Elicit from them that the goal of the instructions and steps to take must be clear, steps must in the proper order, and to maintain interest, the explanation must be engaging and show how creativity can improve the end product.

Apply After students have selected a topic for their how-to speech, suggest that they jot down notes or create an outline for their speeches. You may wish to have them work with a partner to try out their speeches. Encourage listeners to ask questions about steps that may be unclear or confusing as to the order of the steps. Encourage students to use visuals such as charts and pictures to help keep their audience interested.

Assess Evaluate students' speeches on clarity, completeness, and delivery, or use the Peer Assessment: Speaker/Speech form, p. 105, in **Alternative Assessment.**

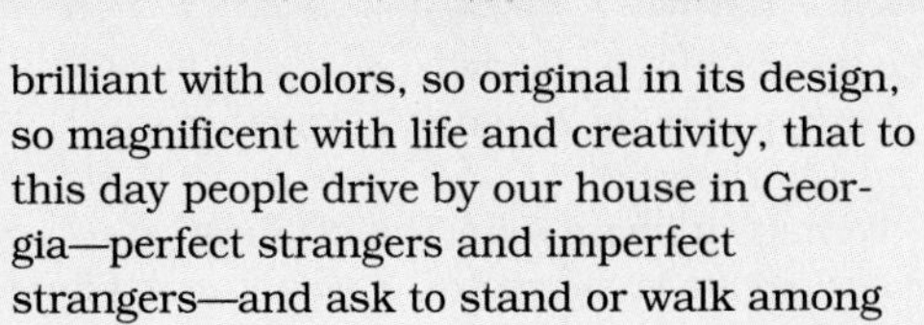

brilliant with colors, so original in its design, so magnificent with life and creativity, that to this day people drive by our house in Geor-
4 gia—perfect strangers and imperfect strangers—and ask to stand or walk among my mother's art.

Relate this passage to your own experience by recalling your own excitement over a colorful sunset or a sleek new skateboard.

5 I notice that it is only when my mother is working in her flowers that she is radiant, almost to the point of being invisible—except as Creator: hand and eye. She is involved in work
6 her soul must have. Ordering the universe in the image of her personal conception of Beauty.

When you **ask** why Walker includes this information, you may see her love and appreciation for her mother.

Her face, as she prepares the Art that is her gift, is a legacy[10] of respect she leaves to me, for all that illuminates and cherishes life. She has handed down respect for the possibilities—and the will to grasp them.

For her, so hindered and intruded upon in so many ways, being an artist has still been a daily part of her life. This ability to hold on, even in very simple ways, is work black women have done for a very long time.

This poem is not enough, but it is something, for the woman who literally covered the holes in our walls with sunflowers:

7 **Ask** what qualities Walker emphasizes in the poem.

They were women then
My mama's generation
Husky of voice—Stout of
Step
With fists as well as
Hands
How they battered down
Doors
And ironed
Starched white
Shirts
How they led
Armies
Headragged[11] Generals
Across mined[12]
Fields
Booby-trapped[13]
Kitchens
To discover books
Desks
A place for us
How they knew what we
Must know
Without knowing a page
Of it
Themselves.

Guided by my heritage of a love of beauty and a respect for strength—in search of my mother's garden, I found my own.

And perhaps in Africa over two hundred years ago, there was just such a mother; perhaps she painted vivid and daring decorations in oranges and yellows and greens on the walls of her hut; perhaps she sang—in a voice

10. **legacy** (leg´ ə sē) *n.*: Something handed down by a parent or an ancestor.

11. **headragged** (hed´ ragd) *adj.*: With head wrapped around by a rag or kerchief.

12. **mined** (mīnd) *adj.*: Filled with buried explosives that are set to go off when stepped on.

13. **booby-trapped** (bo͞o´ bē trapt) *adj.*: With bombs or mines hidden and set to go off when someone touches or lifts an object.

◆ Build Vocabulary

profusely (prō fyo͞os´ lē) *adv.*: Freely or plentifully

radiant (rā´ dē ənt) *adj.*: Filled with light; shining brightly

illuminates (i lo͞o´ mə nāts´) *v.*: Brightens; sheds light on

hindered (hin´ dərd) *adj.*: Held back

◆Literary Focus

4 Tribute Ask students why they think that Walker mentions that many people knew of her mother's gardens. *Possible response: She wanted to emphasize that her mother was recognized by people as an artist. This confirms her feeling that her mother was artistic.*

Reading for Success

5 Relate to Your Own Experience Ask students what in their own experiences is similar to Walker's experience of looking at her mother's gardens. *Students may describe experiences that inspired them.*

◆Critical Thinking

6 Draw Conclusions Have students comment on why this information is important to the main idea of the tribute. *It makes a connection between the gardens and the concepts of creativity and beauty.*

Reading for Success

7 Ask Questions Ask students why they think Walker includes this description of a mother in Africa over 200 years ago. *She wants to reinforce the idea that the creative spirit is passed from generation to generation and that this connects African with African American women.*

Customize for
Musical/Rhythmic Learners
Have students read the poem aloud or read it to them. Point out that some lines in the poem only contain one word. Have students find examples of this technique. Ask them why they think Walker uses this technique. You may also want to have students develop a choral reading of the poem for their classmates.

Cross-Curricular Connection: Social Studies

Sharecroppers Alice Walker's parents were called sharecroppers because they helped farm land that was owned by someone else in order to share the crops. During the 1930's and 1940's, sharecroppers, many of whom were African Americans, farmed much of the land in the South. Sharecroppers were allowed to keep a percentage of the crops to sell. The other portion was given to the landowner, who also provided a house, a plot for growing vegetables, seeds and fertilizer for the crops, and mules and plows. In many cases, the landowner also owned the local grocery store and gave sharecroppers credit to buy their groceries until the crops came in.

Explain to students that even though they earned a small amount of money by selling the crops they raised, sharecroppers benefited little from the arrangement and were a symbol of the poverty in the rural South during this time. Suggest that students research this topic for more information about sharecroppers and why this was so.

Reinforce and Extend

Answers

◆ Literature and Your Life

Reader's Response Students may cite the creative talents of storytelling and gardening that Walker admires. They also may observe Mrs. Walker's sense of responsibility, her efficient use of time, and her obvious love for her family.

Thematic Focus Some students will agree, citing examples such as parent-child acting or writing pairs. Others will disagree, saying that creativity is a highly personal trait.

☑ Check Your Comprehension

1. Walker lived in rural Georgia, in "shabby" homes on or near farmland.
2. She manages household chores, cares for the family, makes clothing, works in the fields, and tells stories.
3. She reveals herself as an artist in the gardens she creates, the stories she tells, and in her sewing.
4. The garden is known throughout her part of Georgia. People come to see her flower choices, planting patterns, and flower cuttings.
5. She has left Walker a love for beauty, an understanding of strength, and the desire to pursue her dreams.

◆ Critical Thinking

1. She means the source of creativity can be found in many places.
2. The quilt maker was a woman who created a work of art with no artistic training and few materials.
3. It provides a contrast to the creative spirit.
4. She might say that her mother is an artist because she loves beauty and also creates it.
5. Walker feels that the creative spirit exists in many women.
6. Students may say that the poem is a fitting tribute to her mother because it shows her own creative spirit, a legacy from her mother.
7. (a) Students may say that beauty in everyday settings is as important as famous artworks in museums. (b) Some may say that all art is important because it expresses the artist's creativity; others may say that trained artists produce more important artworks.

like Roberta Flack's[14]—*sweetly* over the compounds of her village; perhaps she wove the most stunning mats or told the most ingenious[15] stories of all the village storytellers. Perhaps she was herself a poet—though only her daughter's name is signed to the poems that we know.

Perhaps Phillis Wheatley's[16] mother was also an artist.

Perhaps in more than Phillis Wheatley's biological life is her mother's signature made clear.

14. **Roberta Flack's:** Roberta Flack is a contemporary African American singer.
15. **ingenious** (in jēn´ yəs) *adj.*: Clever and inventive.
16. **Phillis Wheatley's:** Phillis Wheatley (1753?–1784) was a poet, considered the first important black writer in America.

Guide for Responding

◆ Literature and Your Life

Reader's Response Which of Walker's mother's personal qualities do you most admire? Why?

Thematic Focus Walker says that our skills and creativity are passed on to us from our parents. Do you agree with her? Why or why not?

Journal Writing Each person finds his or her own ways to express creativity—from experimenting with clothing styles to writing original music. List some ways in which you are creative. What do these creative expressions mean to you?

☑ Check Your Comprehension

1. Briefly describe the home and setting of Alice Walker's childhood.
2. What role does Walker's mother play in the household?
3. In what two ways did Walker's mother reveal herself as an artist?
4. Why do people visit the garden Walker's mother created?
5. What legacies, or gifts, has Walker's mother given her daughter?

◆ Critical Thinking

Interpret

1. What does Walker mean when she writes, "We have constantly looked high, when we should have looked high—and low"? **[Interpret]**
2. How does the anecdote of the quilt hanging in the Smithsonian Institution clarify Walker's point? **[Support]**
3. For Walker, how does the setting emphasize the power of her mother's creative spirit? **[Connect]**
4. If Walker were to summarize what makes her mother an artist, what would she say? **[Synthesize]**
5. Why does Walker call this essay "In Search of *Our* Mothers' Gardens" instead of "In Search of *My* Mother's Garden"? **[Analyze]**

Evaluate

6. Do you think Walker's poem is a fitting tribute to her mother? Explain. **[Criticize]**

Extend

7. (a) What does this story suggest about the importance of practical arts like gardening and quilting compared with fine arts like painting and sculpting? (b) Explain whether you agree with that suggestion. **[Art Link]**

Beyond the Selection

FURTHER READING

Other Works by Alice Walker

"Longing to Die of Old Age" (essay) from *Living by the Wind*

"Everyday Use" (short story) from *In Love and Trouble*

"For My Sister Molly Who in the Fifties" (poem) from *Revolutionary Petunias and Other Poems*

INTERNET

Additional information about Alice Walker can be found on the Internet. We suggest the following site (all Web sites are subject to change).

http://www.luminarium.org/contemporary/alicew/

We *strongly recommend* that you preview this site before you send students to it.

Guide for Responding *(continued)*

◆ Reading Strategy

Interactive Reading Strategies

When you **read interactively,** you increase your participation in the experience of reading. Review the strategies and the notes showing how to interact with the text. Then, apply them to answer the following.

1. List some questions that came to you while reading. Tell whether you found answers as you read.
2. Find and paraphrase the sentence near the end of the essay, beginning "Guided by my heritage . . ."
3. How did your own knowledge or experience help you appreciate Walker's tribute to her mother?

◆ Build Vocabulary

Using the Word Root *-nym-*

The word *anonymous* is built around the word root -*nym*-, meaning "name." On your paper, complete these word equations containing the root -*nym*-. Then, use the examples to help you define each word.

1. homo (the same) + -nym- = ___?___
Example: there/they're/their
2. anto (the opposite) + -nym- = ___?___
Example: here/there
3. pseudo (fake) + -nym- = ___?___
Example: William Sydney Porter/O. Henry

Spelling Strategy

In the -*nym*- root, always spell the short *i* sound with *y*. Add -*nym* to the end of each word part. Write the complete word correctly on your paper.

1. acro + **2.** hetero + **3.** syno +

Using the Word Bank

Identify the word that means the opposite of the first word.

1. radiant: (a) dull, (b) joyful, (c) shining
2. vibrant: (a) alive, (b) weak, (c) eager
3. illuminates: (a) lights, (b) darkens, (c) explains
4. anonymous: (a) unknown, (b) evil, (c) credited
5. profusely: (a) scarcely, (b) frequently, (c) loudly
6. mutilated: (a) damaged, (b) whole, (c) silly
7. hindered: (a) aided, (b) delayed, (c) frustrated

◆ Literary Focus

Tribute

A **tribute** is a literary expression of admiration. In her essay, Alice Walker shows appreciation for her mother's strength and creativity through a vivid and admiring portrait of the woman. Using anecdotes (brief stories) and description, she says "thank you" and "you're wonderful." Through the process of sharing her memories of her mother, Walker also provides readers a glimpse of her own personality.

1. What qualities does Walker admire about her mother?
2. Identify one anecdote Walker uses to describe her mother. How does this story support Walker's tribute?
3. How would you describe Walker's attitude toward her mother?

◆ Build Grammar Skills

Verbs

Verbs are words that express action or state of being. Some verbs show physical action, like *throwing*. Others show mental action, like *thinking*. Verbs like *am*, *is*, *are*, *was*, or *were* show a state of being.

My mother *made* all the clothes we *wore*. . . .
The artist that *was* and *is* my mother . . .

Practice Identify the verbs in these sentences. Then, explain whether each verb expresses a physical action, mental action, or state of being.

1. People drive by our house in Georgia.
2. All my mother's plants grew as if by magic.
3. I admire my mother's courage and strength.
4. Today, my mother might be a professional artist.
5. They handed on the creative spark.

Writing Application Use the following verbs in sentences.

1. create
2. believe
3. express
4. honor
5. remember

◆ Reading Strategy

1. Have volunteers read their questions aloud and explain what answers they did or did not find.
2. "With my mother's help, I found my own love of beauty and respect for strength."
3. Students' answers should indicate a relationship between their experiences and those of the author. For instance, their own mothers, or an aunt or a grandmother, may influence them in some of the ways that Walker's mother influenced her.

◆ Build Vocabulary

Using the Word Root: *-nym-*

1. homonym; "a word spelled and pronounced like another, but having a different meaning"
2. antonym; "a word with the opposite meaning of another word"
3. pseudonym; "a false or assumed name"

Spelling Strategy

1. acronym
2. heteronym
3. synonym

Using the Word Bank

1. a
2. b
3. b
4. c
5. a
6. b
7. a

◆ Literary Focus

1. She admires her mother's talent, energy, devotion, and strength.
2. Possible response: Walker remembers people coming to admire her mother's gardens. This shows how her mother's talents give joy to many people and helps Walker see her mother's art through others' eyes.
3. Walker's attitude is one of admiration, respect, gratitude, and love.

◆ Build Grammar Skills

Practice

1. drive; physical action
2. grew; physical action
3. admire; mental action
4. might be; state of being
5. handed; mental action

Writing Application

Make sure students use the verbs accurately to express physical action or mental action.

Writer's Solution

For additional instruction and practice, use the using verbs lesson in the *Writer's Solution Language Lab CD-ROM.* You may also use Action Verbs, p. 11, in the *Writer's Solution Grammar Practice Book.*

Idea Bank

Following are suggestions for matching the Idea Bank topics with your students' performance levels and learning modalities:

Customize for
Performance Levels
Less Advanced Students: 1, 4, 7
Average Students: 2, 5, 6
More Advanced Students: 3, 4, 5

Customize for
Learning Modalities
Verbal/Linguistic: 1, 2, 3, 4
Interpersonal: 5, 6
Visual/Spatial: 7
Logical/Mathematical: 5, 7
Musical/Rhythmic: 6

Writing Mini-Lesson

Refer students to the Writing Handbook in the back of the book for instructions on the writing process and for further information on expression. Have students use the Cluster Organizer in Writing and Language Transparencies, p. 82, to arrange their prewriting examples.

Writer's Solution

Writing Lab CD-ROM
Have students complete the tutorial on Description. Follow these steps:

1. Have students use the Cluster Diagram to narrow their topics.
2. Let students draft on computer.
3. Have students use the Sensory Word Bin activity to gather descriptive details.
4. When revising, encourage students to use the Word Bin to find and replace vague adjectives.

Writer's Solution Sourcebook
Have students use Chapter 2, "Description," pp. 32–65, for additional support. This chapter includes in-depth instruction on using vivid verbs and using modifiers, pp. 59–61.

Build Your Portfolio

Idea Bank

Writing

1. **Slogans** Use Walker's essay to create five to ten slogans about mothers. You might begin each with the words *A good mother . . .*
2. **Walker Family Story** Write one of the stories Alice Walker's mother might have told. Use details from the essay and aspects of her personality to choose a plot and theme.
3. **Literary Analysis** For Alice Walker and her mother, a garden is more than just a collection of plants. In an essay, use the details in Walker's writing to discuss the symbolic meaning that gardens hold for the Walkers.

Speaking and Listening

4. **Television Commercial** Write and present the introduction you would give if Alice Walker were speaking to students at your school. Use the information in the material on page 108 as well as what you've learned about Walker from her essay. **[Media Link]**
5. **How-to Speech** Like gardening and quilting, many daily chores can bring out a person's creative talents. Choose a skill that requires an artistic flair—such as gift wrapping or food preparation. In a brief how-to speech, explain the activity and show how creativity can improve the products.

Projects

6. **Sharecropping Report** Walker's parents, grandparents, and great-grandparents lived the life of sharecroppers. Find out more about the living and working conditions sharecropping produced. Share your findings in a written report. **[Social Studies Link]**
7. **Garden Plan** **[Group Activity]** Plan a garden using the plants named in Walker's essay or others of your choosing. Use graph paper to sketch your plan. If possible, create the garden at home or in the classroom. **[Science Link]**

Writing Mini-Lesson

Tribute

By the time you've finished reading Alice Walker's tribute, her mother seems like an old friend. You learn about the strong connection between mother and daughter and between artist and teacher. Choose an important person in your life, and write a tribute to that person. Think of it as a way to thank someone for help, guidance, or concern.

Writing Skills Focus: Vivid Words

For a tribute to be effective, your readers must feel as if they know the subject personally. Describe the person with words that add precise detail and help readers "see" the action. Notice how Walker creates an image of the garden.

Model From the Selection

A garden so brilliant with colors, so original in its design, so magnificent with life and creativity, that to this day . . . perfect strangers and imperfect strangers . . . ask to stand or walk among my mother's art.

Prewriting List people who have been important in your life. Choose the person you think you can describe most fully. Jot down vivid details about this person's appearance, traits, special quirks, and—most important—what this person means to you.

Drafting Develop your tribute with anecdotes that capture your subject's qualities and interactions with you. Make the stories believable with vivid descriptions of your subject's behavior.

Revising Review your essay. If your tribute doesn't read as if it honors a real person, replace ordinary verbs, nouns, and adjectives with vivid words that bring the portrait to life.

 **Grammar Application**

Use specific verbs in your tribute. When possible, replace forms of *be* with action verbs.

✓ ASSESSMENT OPTIONS

Formal Assessment, Selection Test, pp. 35–37, and Assessment Resources Software. The selection test is designed so that it can easily be customized to the performance levels of your students.

Alternative Assessment, p. 9, includes options for less advanced students, more advanced students, and interpersonal learners, verbal/linguistic learners, musical/rhythmic learners, and visual/spatial learners.

PORTFOLIO ASSESSMENT
Use the following rubrics in the **Alternative Assessment** booklet to assess student writing:
Slogans: Expression, p. 81
Walker Family Story: Fictional Narrative, p. 82
Literary Analysis: Literary Analysis/Interpretation, p. 99
Writing Mini-Lesson: Description, p. 84

PART 1 *Fitting In*

Friends, Diana Ong

One-Minute Planning Guide

The selections in this section focus on the theme of "Fitting In." An essay from *In Search of Our Mothers' Gardens* explores creative inspiration. "Seventh Grade" is the story of a boy who tries to impress the girl he likes. "Melting Pot" probes the benefits and complications of cultural diversity. "Fable," "Thumbprint," and "If—" examine individuality as it applies to fitting in. In the timeless tale of "Rip Van Winkle," readers discover what it's like to try and fit in after a 20-year sleep.

Customize for *Varying Students' Needs*

When assigning the selections in this section to your students, keep in mind the following factors:

from *In Search of Our Mothers' Gardens*

- Students may need help with abstract concepts

"Seventh Grade"

- Explores issues to which students will relate
- Appealing writing style for middle grade students

"Melting Pot"

- Short essay
- An accessible survey of cultural diversity

"Fable"

- Short poem that demonstrates the uniqueness of individuals

"Thumbprint"

- Examines personal identity

"If—"

- A longer, and more difficult poem

"Rip Van Winkle"

- Classic tale
- A longer short story (14 pp.)
- Complex sentence structure and difficult vocabulary may impede some students' understanding and appreciation

Humanities: Art

Friends, by Diana Ong

Diana Ong (born 1940) trained at the National Academy of Arts and the School of Visual Arts in New York and has gained recognition as a pioneer in computer graphic design as a fine artist. She was one of the first major artists in that arena. Because painting on a computer involves using a pressure-sensitive pad and seeing the reaction happen on screen, Ong says she feels like her ideas travel from her brain to her hand to her computer.

Help students connect the art to the theme of Part 1, "Fitting In," by answering the following questions:

1. Describe the faces of the people in the painting. *Students may say that most of the people look like women; they all have different color hair, different colors on their faces, and they seem to be different ages.*
2. Do the women in the painting seem to "fit in"? *Students may say that because the title of the painting is "Friends," it represents the closeness among them; they also seem to fit together in the painting.*

OBJECTIVES

1. To read, comprehend, and interpret a short story and an essay
2. To relate a short story and an essay to personal experience
3. To strategize to relate experiences to literature
4. To recognize the tone of a literary work
5. To build vocabulary in context and learn the prefix *inter-*
6. To recognize action verbs and linking verbs
7. To write guidelines that develop each point
8. To respond to a short story and an essay through writing, speaking and listening, and projects

SKILLS INSTRUCTION

Vocabulary: Prefixes: *inter-*

Spelling: Words With *c* and *k* for the *k* Sound

Grammar: Action Verbs and Linking Verbs

Reading Strategy: Relate to Your Experiences

Literary Focus: Tone

Writing: Develop Each Point

Speaking and Listening: Neighborhood Meeting (Teacher Edition)

Critical Viewing: Connect

PORTFOLIO OPPORTUNITIES

Writing: Letter to Mr. Bueller; Personal Narrative; Welcome Pamphlet

Writing Mini-Lesson: Guidelines

Speaking and Listening: Dramatic Revue; Neighborhood Meeting

Projects: Food Festival; Community Work

More About the Authors

Gary Soto did not always write stories with the kind of gentle humor found in "Seventh Grade." His early writings paint a grim portrait of the hardships and poverty of working-class Mexican Americans in California. As a teenager, Soto thought about being a priest, a hobo, a paleontologist, and a geographer, but finally decided to become a poet.

Anna Quindlen has always shown interest in the ties that bind people, and tries to understand the tensions that can break those bonds. Besides her essays and novels, Quindlen has also written two books for children.

Guide for Reading

Meet the Authors:

Gary Soto (1952–)

Gary Soto has a lot in common with Victor, a character in "Seventh Grade." Soto grew up in Fresno and once harvested crops in the fields of California.

Finding His Place

Soto began writing while in college. In the fiction and poetry he's written since, he reaches back to the sense of belonging he felt in Fresno. He often writes for young adults—who he knows are also searching for their community, their place. [For more on Soto, see page 78.]

Anna Quindlen (1953–)

Anna Quindlen spent five years reporting for *The New York Times*, covering issues relating to her family and her neighborhood.

As a reporter, Quindlen wrote regular columns and earned a Pulitzer Prize. She left the newspaper to write novels and has published two bestsellers, *One True Thing* and *Black and Blue*.

The Story Behind the Essay

"Melting Pot" originally appeared in "Life in the 30's," a popular column that Quindlen wrote for five years. In the column, she spoke from her perspective as a working mother. She addressed issues of concern to other people in her age group.

◆ Literature and Your Life

Connect Your Experience

You're wearing the perfect outfit, you've found the coolest way to walk, and you're ready to amaze your friends. Then, you freeze in horror when a classmate gives your shoes an odd look. Now you feel like two people—the one you think you present and the one others are seeing. When the main character in "Seventh Grade" feels these pangs, he wonders what he needs to do to belong.

Thematic Focus: Fitting In

What do these selections reveal about the ways people try to fit in to their schools and communities?

◆ Background for Understanding

Social Studies

Since the 1970's, immigrants have been coming to the United States at a faster rate than at any time since the start of the twentieth century. Many of the new arrivals come from Asia, the Pacific Islands, and Latin America. As Quindlen's essay describes, neighborhoods in and around large cities are often most strongly affected by the constant arrival of new citizens.

◆ Build Vocabulary

Prefixes: *inter-*

Anna Quindlen says she fears some people see her as an *interloper*. Understanding that the prefix *inter-* means "among or between" can help you see that *interloper* means "someone who pushes in between others."

Word Bank

Which of these words from the selections do you think might describe an angry expression? Check the Build Vocabulary boxes to see if you were right.

elective
scowl
ferocity
conviction
sheepishly
fluent
bigots
interloper

Prentice Hall Literature Program Resources

REINFORCE / RETEACH / EXTEND

Selection Support Pages

Build Vocabulary: Prefixes: *inter-*, p. 50
Build Spelling Skills, p.51
Build Grammar Skills: Action Verbs and Linking Verbs, p. 52
Reading Strategy: Relate to Your Experiences, p. 53
Literary Focus: Tone, p. 54

Strategies for Diverse Student Needs, pp. 19–20

Beyond Literature Community Connection: Cultural Backgrounds, p. 10

Formal Assessment Selection Test, pp. 38–40, Assessment Resources Software

Alternative Assessment, p. 10

Writing and Language Transparencies Cluster Organizer, p. 82

Resource Pro CD-ROM "Seventh Grade"; "Melting Pot"—includes all resource material and customizable lesson plan

Listening to Literature Audiocassettes "Seventh Grade"; "Melting Pot"

◆ Seventh Grade ◆ Melting Pot ◆

◆ Literary Focus

Tone

The **tone** of a literary work is the writer's attitude toward the subject and characters. The tone can often be described in one word, such as *formal, playful,* or *serious.* Tone is revealed in a writer's choice of words and details and even in the sentence structure. For example, Anna Quindlen says that her children are having dinner with her Ecuadorian neighbors and that her neighbors' choice to teach their son only English seems natural to her. These details show Quindlen's affection toward her neighbors.

◆ Reading Strategy

Relate to Your Experiences

Once you grasp the tone of a literary work, you'll probably find yourself comparing your own attitude toward the subject and characters with the writer's attitudes. Doing so will help draw you into the literature. To become even more involved with your reading, try to **relate** the literature **to your own experiences**—look for common ground between the characters' lives and your own. For example, you may have had an experience similar to a character's or met someone who reminded you of a character. Use a chart like the one below to note such connections.

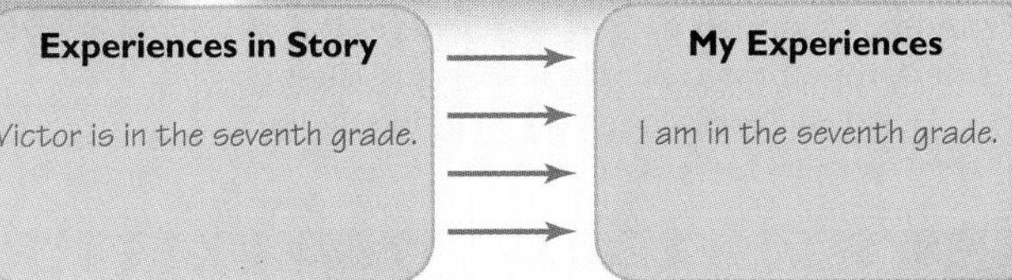

Experiences in Story
Victor is in the seventh grade.
My Experiences
I am in the seventh grade.

Preparing for Standardized Tests

Reading Standardized test questions may require students to evaluate a situation by choosing the most reasonable action. Students who can relate literature to their experiences (the reading strategy for this selection) may be better able to choose the best answer for questions that require inference and interpretation.

Write this sample test item on the board and ask students to select the best answer:

Anna Quindlen's two boys were having dinner with the Ecuadorian family next door. When a dish with unfamiliar ingredients was served, the older boy—

(A) pretended not to be hungry
(B) asked what was in the dish
(C) told a funny joke about tacos
(D) offered to clear the table

Most students have experienced a time when they were served a food they might not have chosen, but, as guests, they didn't want to insult the host. Based on such experience, students should see that *(B)* is the only choice that is neither offensive nor inappropriate.

To help students appreciate the experiences of the main character of this story, invite them to recall their first day of seventh grade. Encourage them to consider their feelings by asking these questions: "Was there someone special you wanted to see?" "Did you exaggerate any of your abilities to impress someone you wanted to know?" "Did you do anything to get attention?" Allow them 5 minutes to freewrite about feelings and thoughts they have when remembering their first day of seventh grade. Then explain that the main character of the first selection they will read wants to impress a girl he likes. What might happen?

◆ Build Grammar Skills

Action Verbs and Linking Verbs

If you wish to introduce the grammar concept for this selection before students read, refer to the instruction on p. 132.

Customize for
Less Proficient Readers

The characters in "Seventh Grade" try different tactics to impress others. Students can use the Cluster Organizer, p. 82, in **Writing and Language Transparencies,** to help follow this pattern of tactics. Have them write the phrase "Impressing Someone" in the central circle, and then list the main characters in the cells around it. As they notice what a character does to impress others, they can fill in the organizer to help relate the story to their own experiences.

Customize for
More Advanced Students

Both of these selections explore the challenge of being accepted by new people; in one case, an individual, in the other, a group. They must adapt to new environments, issues, and demands, while trying to maintain their true selves. Challenge students to work together as a group to compare and contrast the main character's attitude in "Seventh Grade" with the author's attitude in "Melting Pot." Based on what they discover about these attitudes, have them create a list of suggestions for fitting in.

One-Minute Insight

On the first day of seventh grade, Victor and his friend try to hide their insecurities and impress the girls in their class. With his sights on Teresa, Victor signs up for French class to be near her. In that class, Victor takes a risk, impulsively implying that he knows French when he really doesn't. Victor's enthusiasm leads him into an embarrassing situation, but the sensitive teacher helps him save face. Victor learns that teachers can be kind, that girls are approachable, and that taking a risk to fit in can pay off.

◆Literary Focus

1 Tone Based on the first paragraph, ask students to suggest what the writer's attitude is toward the subject of seventh grade. Students should use clues such as the "wobbly card table" and the comparison of France and Fresno to recognize that the writer is not using a formal tone.

Spelling Strategy

2 This selection's spelling strategy guides students to recognize that the letters *c* or *k* are used to spell the *k* sound in words, depending upon the vowel that follows. In *computer card, c* forms the *k* sound in each word because *c* is followed by *o* or *a.*

◆Literature and Your Life

3 Relate to Your Experiences Students may realize that Victor is taking French for a private reason, although he has an explanation other than his interest for Teresa. Invite students to suggest why he might choose to explain it this way. *Students may suggest embarrassment or fear of rejection from Teresa.*

Customize for *English Language Learners*

Because this story uses Spanish and French words, it offers extra challenges to students who don't speak either of these languages and are acquiring English. Point out that the phrases in these languages are printed in italics. Then help students distinguish between words that are actually Spanish or French and Victor's attempts to speak French, which are printed in regular type.

Seventh Grade

Gary Soto

On the first day of school, Victor stood in
1 line half an hour before he came to a wobbly card table. He was handed a packet of pa-
2 pers and a computer card on which he listed his one elective, French. He already spoke Spanish and English, but he thought some day he might travel to France, where it was cool; not like Fresno, where summer days reached 110 degrees in the shade. There were rivers in France and huge churches, and fair-skinned people everywhere, the way there were brown people all around Victor.

Besides, Teresa, a girl he had liked since they were in catechism classes at Saint Theresa's, was taking French, too. With any luck they would be in the same class. Teresa is going to be my girl this year, he promised himself as he left the gym full of students in 3
their new fall clothes. She was cute. And good in math, too, Victor thought as he walked down the hall to his homeroom. He ran into his friend, Michael Torres, by the water fountain that never turned off.

They shook hands, *raza*-style, and jerked their heads at one another in a *saludo de vato.*[1] "How come you're making a face?"

1. ***raza*-style . . . *saludo de vato*** (säl o͞o´ dō dā bä´ tō): Spanish gestures of greeting between friends.

Block Scheduling Strategies

Consider these suggestions to take advantage of extended class time:

- After students read the short story and essay, have them focus on the Social Studies Connection activity on p. 131. Then provide class time for students to begin work on one or both of the Idea Bank projects, p. 133.
- Alternatively, divide the class into three groups. With one group, work on the selections' skills, while the second group reads "Seventh Grade" and the third group reads "Melting Pot" independently. Allow students within each reading group to meet and discuss the questions on pp. 127 and 131. Then have the groups switch instructional activities.
- If you have access to technology, have students work on the *Writer's Solution Writing Lab CD-ROM* to complete all or part of the Writing Mini-Lesson.

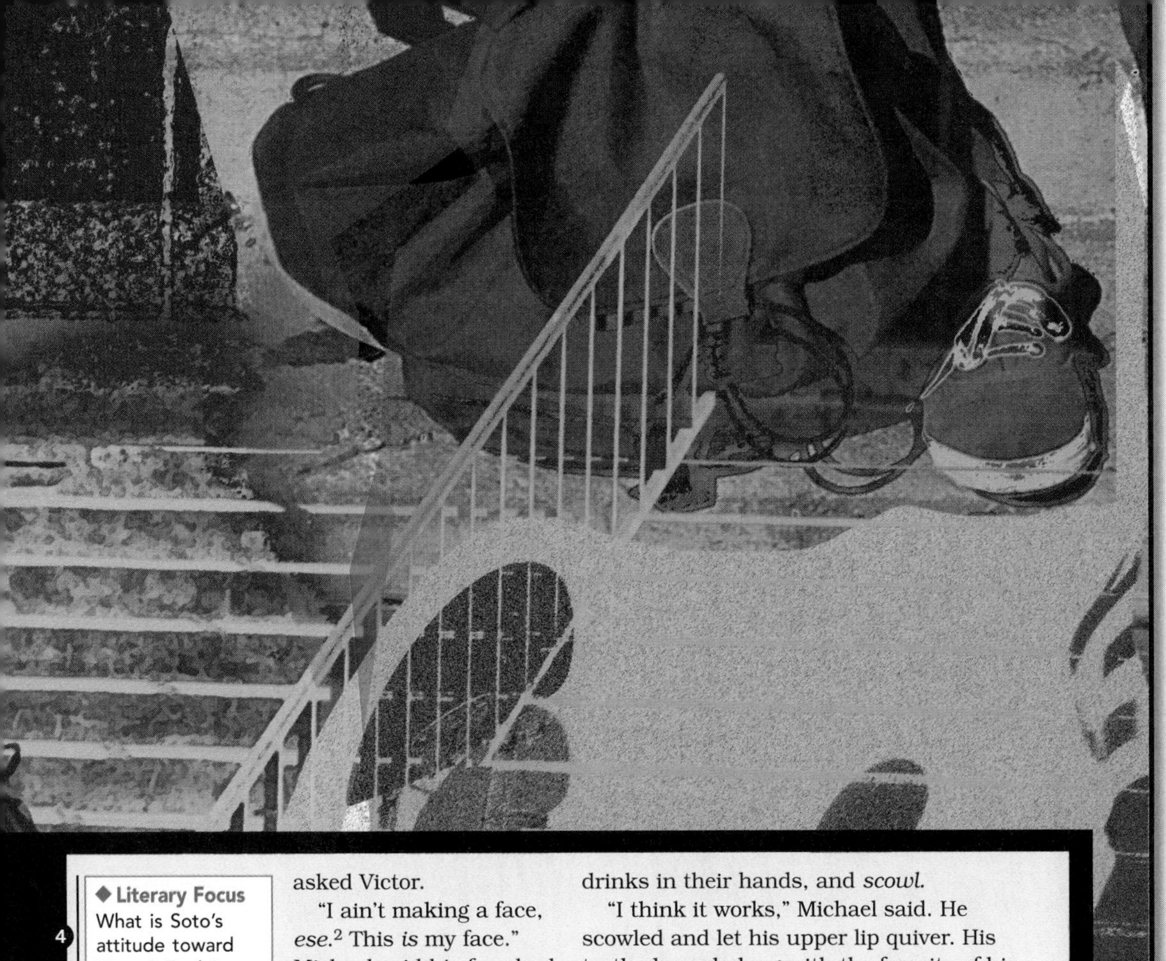

4 **◆ Literary Focus** What is Soto's attitude toward Victor? Explain.

asked Victor.

"I ain't making a face, *ese.*[2] This *is* my face." Michael said his face had changed during the sum-
5 mer. He had read a *GQ* magazine that his older brother had borrowed from the Book Mobile and noticed that the male models all had the same look on their faces. They would stand, one arm around a beautiful woman, and *scowl.* They would sit at a pool, their rippled stomachs dark with shadow, and *scowl.* They would sit at dinner tables, cool drinks in their hands, and *scowl.*

"I think it works," Michael said. He scowled and let his upper lip quiver. His teeth showed along with the ferocity of his soul. "Belinda Reyes walked by a while ago and looked at me," he said.

Victor didn't say anything, though he

2. ***ese*** (es´ ā): Spanish word for "man."

◆ Build Vocabulary

elective (ē lek´ tiv) *n.*: Optional course or subject in a school or college curriculum

scowl (skoul) *v.*: Lower eyebrows and corners of the mouth; look angry or irritated

ferocity (fə räs´ ə tē) *n.*: Fierceness; wild force

◆Literary Focus

4 Tone *Possible responses: Soto seems protective of Victor in his embarrassing situation; the tone shows in the description of Victor with his head down, in the detail about Victor's blushing, and in Victor's frustration at not saying something "clever"; Soto pokes fun at Victor, but very gently.*

◆Reading Strategy

5 Clarification Tell students that *GQ* stands for *Gentleman's Quarterly,* which is the title of a men's fashion magazine. If possible, display a recent issue so students can get a feel for *GQ's* style and tone.

Customize for *Bodily/Kinesthetic Learners*

The body language used by characters in this story can help students better appreciate its tone. Invite students to act out some of the physical gestures Soto describes, such as the *raza*-style handshake, Michael's scowl, Teresa's graceful walk, and Victor's furtive glances at Teresa.

Cultural Connection

Greetings Victor greets his friend Michael with a *raza*-style handshake and a *saludo de vato.* Soto describes these greetings to add authentic details to his story, set in a largely Hispanic neighborhood of Fresno, California. Forms of greeting vary from culture to culture. For example, Japanese people traditionally bow or lower their heads to greet one another with respect; young American athletes may give each other elaborate knuckle-to-knuckle fist and hand greetings to show enthusiasm.

Have students research different forms of greetings among cultures. They may focus on formal or informal greetings, or any related expressions or gestures that are specific to a culture or region. One source of information might be international traveler's guides that alert visitors to key local customs so they can avoid giving offense or being misinterpreted. Students can present their findings orally, act out and describe the greetings, or prepare a multimedia presentation.

Comprehension Check ☑

❶ When Victor first saw Michael he was scowling. Why is he scowling now? *He is still practicing to be like the models in GQ in order to impress girls.*

◆Literature and Your Life

❷ Encourage students to identify with Victor's experiences on the first day of a new school year. How have their own experiences compared or contrasted with Victor's? *Students may express more general concerns, such as acceptable dress and appearance. Most students will remember trying to avoid notice rather than attract it, as Victor does, on the first day of the school year.*

◆Critical Thinking

❸ **Infer** Ask students to describe Victor's attitude toward school. *He seems to enjoy the social aspects of it, but has less interest in the classes he is taking, especially math.*

▶Critical Viewing◀

❹ **Connect** *The bright light shining on the people's faces suggests the feeling in a literal way. Their cheerful expressions convey a "sunny" mood.*

Customize for
Verbal/Linguistic Learners
Soto uses precise verbs, such as *herded* and *lingered,* to paint a vivid picture of school life. Encourage students to look for other precise verbs, such as *propelled* and *trudged.*

thought his friend looked pretty strange. They talked about recent movies, baseball, their parents, and the horrors of picking grapes in order to buy their fall clothes. Picking grapes was like living in Siberia,[3] except hot and more boring.

1 "What classes are you taking?" Michael said, scowling.

"French. How 'bout you?"

"Spanish. I ain't so good at it, even if I'm Mexican."

"I'm not either, but I'm better at it than math, that's for sure."

A tinny, three-beat bell propelled students to their homerooms. The two friends socked each other in the arm and went their ways, Victor thinking, man, that's weird. Michael thinks making a face makes him handsome.

On the way to his homeroom, Victor tried a scowl. He felt foolish, until out of the corner of his eye he saw a girl looking at him. Umm, he thought, maybe it does work. He scowled with greater conviction.

In homeroom, roll was taken, emergency cards were passed out, and they were given a bulletin to take home to their parents. The principal, Mr. Belton, spoke over 2
the crackling loudspeaker, welcoming the students to a new year, new experiences, and new friendships. The students squirmed in their chairs and ignored him. They were anxious to go to first period. Victor sat calmly, thinking of Teresa, who sat two rows away, reading a paperback 3
novel. This would be his lucky year. She was in his homeroom, and would probably be in his English and math classes. And, of course, French.

The bell rang for first period, and the students herded noisily through the door. Only Teresa lingered, talking with the homeroom teacher.

"So you think I should talk to Mrs.

3. **Siberia** (sī bir′ ē ə): Region in northern Asia known for its harsh winters.

▼ **Critical Viewing** Soto describes the students' mood as "sunny" on the first day of school. How does this photograph convey that 4
feeling? **[Connect]**

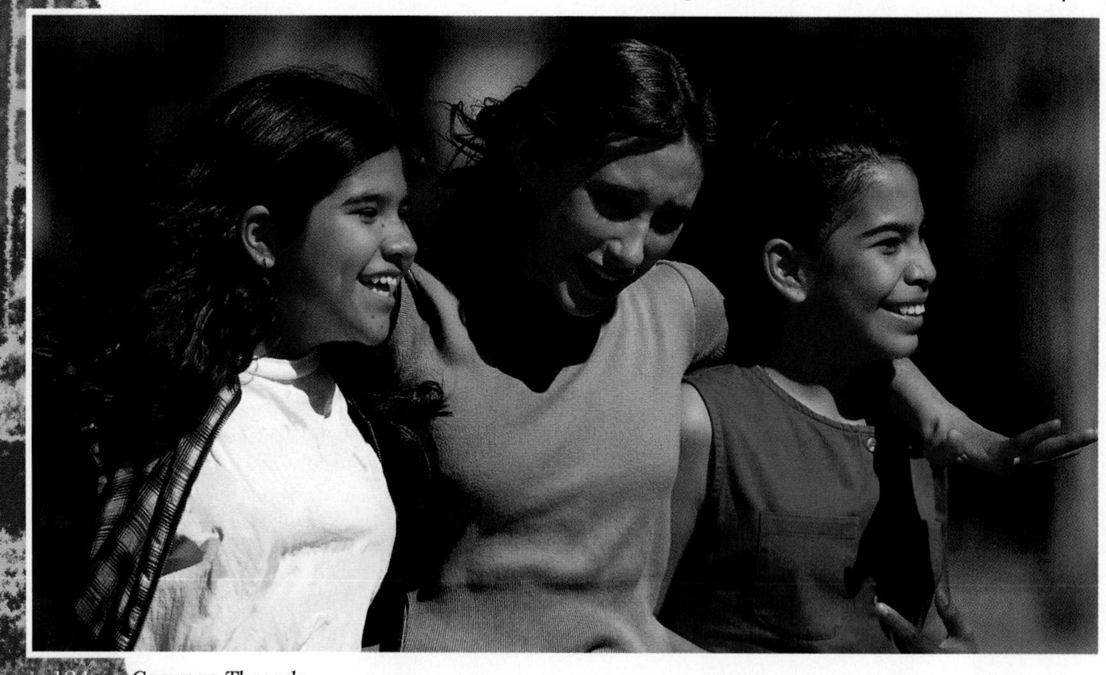

Beyond the Classroom

Career Connection

Translator Victor knows some Spanish and thinks it might be good to learn French. He's right. Point out to students that speaking another language is not only helpful for personal travel, but that there are also job possibilities for those who are fluent in another language, such as being a translator.

There are different kinds of translators—many are used by the government and having a business background is useful for this job; technical translators also need technical writing skills; court translators must be completely fluent in the second language (including slang); and academic translators interpret foreign text, giving them the most creative expression as translators.

Many translators like their jobs because they get to travel. Some jobs require translators to have done some cultural studies, as well as language studies, or spent time in the country of the language they speak.

Because of the need for communication between all peoples and cultures, the need for translation will continue to exist.

Gaines?" she asked the teacher. "She would know about ballet?"

"She would be a good bet," the teacher said. Then added, "Or the gym teacher, Mrs. Garza."

Victor lingered, keeping his head down and staring at his desk. He wanted to leave when she did so he could bump into her and say something clever.

He watched her on the sly. As she turned to leave, he stood up and hurried to the door, where he managed to catch her eye. She smiled and said, "Hi, Victor."

He smiled back and said, "Yeah, that's me." His brown face blushed. Why hadn't he said, "Hi, Teresa," or "How was your summer?" or something nice?

5 As Teresa walked down the hall, Victor walked the other way, looking back, admiring how gracefully she walked, one foot in front of the other. So much for being in the same class, he thought. As he trudged to English, he practiced scowling.

In English they reviewed the parts of speech. Mr. Lucas, a portly man, waddled down the aisle, asking, "What is a noun?"

"A person, place, or thing," said the class in unison.

"Yes, now somebody give me an example of a person—you, Victor Rodriguez."

"Teresa," Victor said automatically. Some of the girls giggled. They knew he had a crush on Teresa. He felt himself blushing again.

"Correct," Mr. Lucas said. "Now provide me with a place."

6 Mr. Lucas called on a freckled kid who answered, "Teresa's house with a kitchen full of big brothers."

After English, Victor had math, his weakest subject. He sat in the back by the window, hoping that he would not be called on. Victor understood most of the problems, but some of the stuff looked like the teacher made it up as he went along. It was confusing, like the inside of a watch.

After math he had a fifteen-minute break, then social studies, and, finally, lunch. He bought a tuna casserole with buttered rolls, some fruit cocktail, and milk. He sat with Michael, who practiced scowling between bites.

Girls walked by and looked at him.

"See what I mean, Vic?" Michael scowled. "They love it."

"Yeah, I guess so."

They ate slowly, Victor scanning the horizon for a glimpse of Teresa. He didn't see her. She must have brought lunch, he thought, and is eating outside. Victor scraped his plate and left Michael, who was busy scowling at a girl two tables away.

The small, triangle-shaped campus bustled with students talking about their new classes. Everyone was in a sunny mood. Victor hurried to the bag lunch area, where he sat down and opened his math book. He moved his lips as if he were reading, but his mind was somewhere else. He raised his eyes slowly and looked around. No Teresa. 7

He lowered his eyes, pretending to study, then looked slowly to the left. No Teresa. He turned a page in the book and stared at some math problems that scared him because he knew he would have to do them eventually. He looked to the right. Still no sign of her. He stretched out lazily in an attempt to disguise his snooping.

Then he saw her. She was sitting with a girlfriend under a plum tree. Victor moved to a table near her and daydreamed about taking her to a movie. When the bell sounded, Teresa looked up, and their eyes met. She smiled sweetly and gathered her books. Her next class was French, same as Victor's. 8 9

They were among the last students to arrive in class, so all the good desks in the back had already been taken. Victor

◆ Build Vocabulary

conviction (kən vik′ shən) *n.:* Belief

◆Critical Thinking

5 Infer Victor obviously admires more than Teresa's graceful walk. Ask students to describe the qualities of Teresa's character. Have them identify the story details on which they base their description. *Possible answers: Teresa is good at math, reads for pleasure, and is interested in ballet; she is intelligent and artistic; she is confident because she approaches her teacher for advice; and she is independent because she doesn't rush out with the other students.*

◆Critical Thinking

6 Infer Point out that the freckled kid's answer, a sentence using a noun that names a place, hints that he knows Teresa's family, and that he recognizes that Victor has a crush on Teresa and is teasing him for it. Ask students what they think his comment means. *Teresa has several older brothers who are protective of her, so Victor better watch out!*

◆Literary Focus

7 Tone Focus on this passage to help students detect Gary Soto's attitudes toward Victor and Michael through the tone of his writing. Guide them to notice the gently humorous description of Michael as "busy scowling at a girl two tables away." Soto offers a sympathetic picture of love-struck Victor, who pretends to study but is thinking about Teresa.

◆Build Grammar Skills

8 Action Verbs and Linking Verbs The grammar skill in this selection asks students to identify action and linking verbs. This passage has examples of each kind. Ask students to identify the three verbs in this passage. Then, help students classify the verbs as action or linking verbs. *In the first sentence,* smiled *and* gathered *are both action verbs; in the next sentence,* was *is a linking verb.*

◆Critical Thinking

9 Speculate Point out Teresa's sweet smile toward Victor. Have students speculate about what this response to Victor may reveal about Teresa. *Students may say that she already seems to like Victor.*

◆Reading Strategy

❶ Relate to Your Experiences Discuss with students why Victor continues to try to bluff his way out by "making noises that sounded French." *Students may suggest that he can't find any way out and is simply being carried where his bluff is taking him.*

◆Critical Thinking

❷ Draw Conclusions Ask why Mr. Bueller doesn't comment on Victor's "French." What does the teacher's action reveal about him? *Mr. Bueller knows that Victor has no idea how to speak French, but he chooses not to humiliate the boy and just moves on to the next part of the lesson. He must be a nice person not to embarrass a student.*

Comprehension Check ☑

❸ What does Victor think the outcome of his failed attempt to speak French will be with Teresa? *Victor probably thinks he has lost his chances with her.*

◆Literary Focus

❹ Tone Guide students to understand that Mr. Bueller is the only well-defined adult in the story. *Students may suggest that he comes across as a real person who was once young and foolish himself. He could have forced the issue of Victor's fake French; instead, he recalled his own youthful actions, thus showing his caring side through the author's voice.* Point out that Mr. Bueller's attitudes may represent the writer's attitude.

◆Reading Strategy

❺ Relate to Your Experiences *Students probably will identify with Victor's feelings of embarrassment.*

was forced to sit near the front, a few desks away from Teresa, while Mr. Bueller wrote French words on the chalkboard. The bell rang, and Mr. Bueller wiped his hands, turned to the class, and said, "*Bonjour*."[4]

"*Bonjour*," braved a few students.

"*Bonjour*," Victor whispered. He wondered if Teresa heard him. Mr. Bueller said that if the students studied hard, at the end of the year they could go to France and be understood by the populace.

One kid raised his hand and asked, "What's 'populace'?"

"The people, the people of France."

Mr. Bueller asked if anyone knew French. Victor raised his hand, wanting to impress Teresa. The teacher beamed and said, "*Trés bien. Parlez-vous français*?"[5]

Victor didn't know what to say. The teacher wet his lips and asked something else in French. The room grew silent. Victor felt all eyes staring at him. He tried to bluff his way out by making noises that sounded French.

"La me vave me con le grandma," he said uncertainly.

Mr. Bueller, wrinkling his face in curiosity, asked him to speak up.

❶ Great rosebushes of red bloomed on Victor's cheeks. A river of nervous sweat ran down his palms. He felt awful. Teresa sat a few desks away, no doubt thinking he was a fool. Without looking at Mr. Bueller, Victor mumbled, "Frenchie oh wewe gee in September."

Mr. Bueller asked Victor to repeat what he had said.

"Frenchie oh wewe gee in September," Victor repeated.

❷ Mr. Bueller understood that the boy didn't know French and turned away. He walked to the blackboard and pointed to the words on the board with his steel-edged ruler. ❷

"*Le bateau*," he sang.

"*Le bateau*," the students repeated.

"*Le bateau est sur l'eau*,"[6] he sang.

"*Le bateau est sur l'eau*."

Victor was too weak from failure to join the class. He stared at the board and wished he had taken Spanish, not French. Better yet, he wished he could start his life over. He had never been so embarrassed. He bit his thumb until he tore off a sliver of skin.

The bell sounded for fifth period, and Victor shot out of the room, avoiding the stares of the other kids, but had to return for his math book. He looked sheepishly at the teacher, who was erasing the board, then widened his eyes in terror at Teresa who stood in front of him. "I didn't know you knew French," she said. "That was good." ❸

Mr. Bueller looked at Victor, and Victor looked back. Oh please, don't say anything, Victor pleaded with his eyes. I'll wash your car, mow your lawn, walk your dog—anything! I'll be your best student and I'll clean your erasers after school.

Mr. Bueller shuffled through the papers on his desk. He smiled and hummed as he sat down to work. He remembered his college years when he dated a girlfriend in borrowed cars. She thought he was rich because each time he picked her up he had a different car. It was fun until he had spent all his money on her and had to write home to his parents because he was broke. ❹

> **◆ Literary Focus**
> How do Mr. Bueller's thoughts and actions create a sympathetic tone?

Victor couldn't stand to look at Teresa. He was sweaty with shame. "Yeah, well, I

4. ***Bonjour*** (bōn zhōōr′): French for "Hello"; "Good day."
5. ***Trés bien. Parlez-vous français?*** (trā byan pär lā′ vōō frän sā′): French for "Very well. Do you speak French?"
6. ***Le bateau est sur l'eau.*** (lə bä tō′ ā sōōr lō): French for "The boat is on the water."

Speaking and Listening Mini-Lesson

Neighborhood Meeting
This lesson supports the Speaking and Listening activity on p. 133.

Introduce In American neighborhoods, meetings sometimes are held to discuss problems affecting the neighborhood. Such meetings may occur regularly or may be called whenever events need action. Participants may include elected and appointed officials, community leaders, journalists, and interested citizens.

Develop Brainstorm with students for a list of problems that neighborhood residents might face. Guide them to think beyond neighbor-to-neighbor grievances for issues that affect a large number of people, such as a traffic light that is needed for safety, funding required to improve a playground, or assistance for elderly residents. Help groups assign roles to play, including the residents presenting the problem, board members, other residents, and perhaps a journalist.

Apply Have groups practice and present their meetings. After their presentations, hold a question-and-answer session during which students, in character, field questions from the class.

Assess Evaluate students' presentations based on their group preparation, speaking, and composure, or use the Peer Assessment: Dramatic Performance form, p. 107, in **Alternative Assessment.**

picked up a few things from movies and books and stuff like that." They left the class together. Teresa asked him if he would help her with her French.

"Sure, anytime," Victor said.

"I won't be bothering you, will I?"

"Oh no, I like being bothered."

"*Bonjour*," Teresa said, leaving him outside her next class. She smiled and pushed wisps of hair from her face.

"Yeah, right, *bonjour*," Victor said. He turned and headed to his class. The rosebushes of shame on his face became bouquets of love. Teresa is a great girl, he thought. And Mr. Bueller is a good guy.

He raced to metal shop. After metal shop there was biology, and after biology a long sprint to the public library, where he checked out three French textbooks.

He was going to like seventh grade.

> **◆ Reading Strategy**
> Recall a time when you pretended to know something you did not in order to impress someone. How did you feel? 5

> **◆ Build Vocabulary**
> **sheepishly** (shēp′ ish lē) *adv.*: In a shy or embarrassed way

Guide for Responding

◆ Literature and Your Life

Reader's Response What would you say to Victor about the way he tries to impress Teresa? What advice would you give him?

Thematic Focus Deciding how to "fit in" may be one of the biggest choices the characters in "Seventh Grade" make. How do Victor and Michael change themselves in an effort to belong?

Journal Writing Although he may be your age, Victor might handle his life very differently from the way you approach yours. In your journal, identify the ways in which you and Victor are alike and different. What would you have done in his place?

☑ Check Your Comprehension

1. At what time of year does the story take place?
2. What are Victor's goals for seventh grade?
3. Why does Michael scowl?
4. What does Victor do to try to impress Teresa?
5. What does Mr. Bueller do to help Victor?

◆ Critical Thinking

INTERPRET

1. Why does Victor pretend to know French? **[Analyze]**
2. How do Michael's scowls really affect the girls? **[Analyze Cause and Effect]**
3. How do the impressions Victor, Michael, and Mr. Bueller create prevent people from seeing their real selves? **[Draw Conclusions]**
4. Using examples from the story to support your answer, describe Teresa. **[Support]**
5. What do you predict will happen when Victor tries to tutor Teresa? **[Speculate]**
6. What lesson can you learn from Victor's experiences? **[Draw Conclusions]**

APPLY

7. Why do you think people try so hard to create a good impression? **[Synthesize]**

EXTEND

8. Though his reason is purely social, Victor does choose to study a third language. Do you think young Americans should speak more than one language? Why or why not? **[Social Studies Link]**

Beyond the Selection

FURTHER READING

Other Works by Gary Soto

The Elements of San Joaquin
Baseball in April and Other Stories
Summer on Wheels

Other Works About Fitting In

"The Monsters Are Due on Maple Street," Rod Serling
Barrio Boy, Ernesto Galarza
The Joy Luck Club, Amy Tan

INTERNET

We suggest the following sites on the Internet (all Web sites are subject to change).

For more about Gary Soto:
http://www.garysoto.com

For more about Gary Soto's poetry:
http://www.poets.org/lit/poet/gsotofst.htm

We *strongly recommend* that you preview these sites before you send students to them.

Reinforce and Extend

Answers

◆ Literature and Your Life

Reader's Response Students may say that the impression may be positive, but it isn't worth it because Teresa will find out later and then think badly of Victor.

Thematic Focus Michael scowls in an attempt to look like a model and Victor pretends to know French to seem worldly and knowledgeable.

☑ Check Your Comprehension

1. It takes place on the first day of school.
2. He hopes that Teresa, a girl in his class, will become his girlfriend.
3. He thinks it will impress girls.
4. He uses his elective to take French and then pretends he can speak French.
5. He doesn't let Teresa know about Victor's ignorance of French.

◆ Critical Thinking

1. He wants to impress Teresa with his knowledge.
2. They probably think, as Victor does, that he looks strange.
3. Because people do not see their real characters, they miss finding out who they are.
4. Because she thinks that Victor can speak French, Teresa may be easily fooled or impressed by how things seem. Her warm smiles toward Victor suggest that she is a nice person and she'd like to get to know him.
5. Teresa will soon discover that Victor can't speak French. When she finds out the truth, she may lose interest in him; or, she may be touched by his efforts to impress her.
6. Possible response: It is impossible to predict other people's reactions.
7. Students may suggest that people may do whatever they think is needed to be accepted, valued, or liked by others.
8. Some students may say that young Americans should learn several languages to be able to communicate with others around the world or Americans of different cultures.

One-Minute Insight The speaker of "Melting Pot" describes her changing urban neighborhood both from the viewpoint of an outsider who only arrived recently, and as an insider who was the daughter of immigrants. She considers the idea of being accepted in a multicultural community: how people regard their neighbors as "us" or "them," and how they may hold broad prejudices against some ethnic groups as a whole but relax the prejudices as they get to know individual members of those groups.

Clarification

❶ In Israel Zangwill's 1908 play about immigration, *The Melting Pot,* America was first called ". . .the great Melting Pot where all the races of Europe are melting and reforming!" Over time, "melting pot" came to include immigrants from every part of the world. In cultural context, *melting pot,* which literally means a pot where something is melted, originally described a welcome breakdown of racial and national prejudices in order to form a homogenous culture.But now, to some, it has come to suggest an unwelcome loss of ethnic identity. After students read the essay, you might ask them which meaning of "melting pot" the title suggests.

◆Literary Focus

❷ **Tone** Guide students to recognize the serious tone of this essay, based on a factual opening.Ask them whether they think the serious tone will apply to the entire essay. *Students should realize that a serious opening indicates a serious tone for the piece; however, there may be examples of a humorous or playful tone, as well.*

Clarification

❸ Tell students that "No Irish Need Apply" was an affront to the many impoverished Irish immigrants who poured into America in the mid-nineteenth century to escape the terrible conditions in Ireland at the time. Americans, who had arrived before the Irish, hated the needy newcomers who threatened to take jobs from those immigrants already established here.

❶

Melting Pot

Anna Quindlen

❷ My children are upstairs in the house next door, having dinner with the Ecuadorian family that lives on the top floor. The father speaks some English, the mother less than that. The two daughters are fluent in both their native and their adopted languages, but the youngest child, a son, a close friend of my two boys, speaks almost no Spanish. His parents thought it would be better that way. This doesn't surprise me; it was the way my mother was raised, American among Italians. I always suspected, hearing my ❸ grandfather talk about the "No Irish Need Apply" signs outside factories, hearing my mother talk about the neighborhood kids, who called her greaseball, that the American fable of the melting pot was a myth. Here in our neighborhood it exists, but like so many other things, it exists only person-to-person.

The letters in the local weekly tabloid[1] suggest that everybody hates everybody else here, and on a macro level they do. The old-timers are

1. **tabloid** (tab′ loid′) *n.*: Small newspaper.

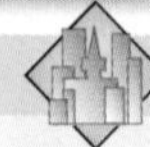

Beyond the Classroom

Career Connection

Community Activist In the melting-pot neighborhood Anna Quindlen describes, residents get together to discuss issues that concern everyone, regardless of their diverse backgrounds. Some communities have regular outlets for such expression, and some have people whose job it is to facilitate cooperation among neighbors.

Invite interested students to learn about the kinds of people whose efforts can influence a community to pull together for the common good. Community activists do things for their neighborhoods. They may be environmentalists, people interested in saving local landmarks, and community organization workers, such as senior citizen center workers, neighborhood safety patrols, urban park rangers, or community garden advisors. Students might interview community leaders, look through local newspapers or newsletters, contact block associations, or talk to long-time residents about ways that the neighborhood has united to face issues together. Students can present their findings as oral or written reports.

angry because they think the new moneyed professionals are taking over their town. The professionals are tired of being blamed for the neighborhood's rising rents, particularly since they are the ones paying them. The old immigrants are suspicious of the new ones. The new ones think the old ones are bigots. Nevertheless, on a micro level most of us get along. We are friendly with the Ecuadorian family, with the Yugoslavs across the street, and with the Italians next door, mainly by virtue of our children's sidewalk friendships. It took awhile. Eight years ago we were the new people on the block, filling dumpsters with old plaster and lath, . . . (sitting) on the stoop with our demolition masks hanging around our necks like goiters.[2] We thought we could feel people staring at us from behind the sheer curtains on their windows. We were right. 4 5

My first apartment in New York was in a gritty warehouse district, the kind of place that makes your parents wince. A lot of old Italians lived around me, which suited me just fine because I was the granddaughter of old Italians. Their own children and grandchildren had moved to Long Island and New Jersey. All they had was me. All I had was them. 6

I remember sitting on a corner with a group of half a dozen elderly men, men who had known one another since they were boys sitting together on this same corner, watching a glazier install a great spread of tiny glass panes to make one wall of a restaurant in the ground floor of an old building across the street. The men laid bets on how long the panes, and the restaurant, would last. Two years later two of the men were dead, one had moved in with his married daughter in the suburbs, and the three remaining sat and watched dolefully as people waited each night for a table in the restaurant. "Twenty-two dollars for a piece of veal!" one of

2. **goiters** (goit′ ərz) *n.*: Swellings in the lower front of the neck caused by an enlarged thyroid gland.

◆ Build Vocabulary

fluent (flo͞o′ ənt) *adj.*: Able to write or speak easily and smoothly

bigots (big′ əts) *n.*: Narrow-minded, prejudiced people

Clarification

4 Explain that *micro level* describes the smallest, most specific link: person-to-person, not large-group-to-large-group.

◆ Literature and Your Life

5 Ask students to relate this account to their own experiences in their schools, neighborhoods, or in the community in general. Even students who live and go to school in a relatively homogenous area may be familiar with variety in family background, family structure, political belief, or social custom.

◆ Literary Focus

6 **Tone** Ask students what this anecdote tells them about the author's attitude toward her subject. *Students may say that the use of "I" creates a personal tone, while the short sentences suggest a casual tone, meant to reach a wide audience.*

Customize for
More Advanced Students
Present the term *gentrification* to students. Challenge them to find its meaning, to explain how it fits the situation Quindlen describes in this passage, and to infer why gentrification is often regarded with scorn and fear by an area's long-time residents. Gentrification is the renewal or upgrading of a run-down urban area. This process stimulates commercial and residential growth, but often displaces poorer people when new residents with more money than previous residents move into the area. These old men scorn gentrification because they fear it will change their neighborhood into a place they no longer feel welcome or comfortable and are not recognized.

Comprehension Check ☑

❶ Ask students to explain why long-time residents feel that "change comes hard." *Students may say that as a neighborhood changes, people who have lived there for a long time are pushed out to make way for newcomers. This process threatens long-time residents and makes them feel abandoned, confused, and resentful.*

▶Critical Viewing◀

❷ **Connect** *Students might suggest that the different doors (which reflect different architectural styles, from Georgian to Victorian and 1920's bungalow) could symbolize the diversity of people in Anna Quindlen's melting pot. The doors all serve the same purpose and are all acceptable in their own ways.*

Beyond Literature

Guide students to be sensitive in their interviews. While an immigrant, recent or established, may appear easy-going about his or her status in the United States, remarks by students could cause pain or annoyance. Encourage students to let their interviewees introduce topics and do most of the talking.

Customize for
Less Proficient Readers
Help students appreciate the humor of Quindlen's description of squid/calamari/sushi. She describes it from three neighborhood points of view. The Italians see squid as *calamari* (its Italian name), the Asians and young professionals who eat out in restaurants see it as *sushi* (a Japanese dish with raw fish and rice), and the do-it-yourself, outdoor types see it as something used to bait hooks to catch fish. Quindlen's tone lets her express a difference in outlook.

---

them would say, apropos of nothing.[3] But when I ate in the restaurant they never blamed me. "You're not one of them," one of the men explained. "You're one of me." It's an argument familiar to members of almost any embattled race or class: I like you, therefore you aren't like the rest of your kind, whom I hate.

❶ Change comes hard in America, but it comes constantly. The butcher whose old shop is now an antiques store sits day after day outside the pizzeria here like a lost child. The old people across the street cluster together and discuss what kind of money they might be offered if the person who bought their building wants to turn it into condominiums. The greengrocer stocks yellow peppers and fresh rosemary for the gourmands, plum tomatoes and broadleaf parsley for the older Italians, mangoes for the Indians. He doesn't carry plantains, he says, because you can buy them in the bodega.[4]

Sometimes the baby slips out with the bath water. I wanted to throw confetti the day that a family of rough types who propped their speakers on their station wagon and played heavy metal music at 3:00 A.M. moved out. I stood and smiled as the seedy bar at the corner was transformed into a slick Mexican restaurant. But I liked some of the people who moved out at the same time the rough types did. And I'm not sure I have that much in common with the singles who have made the restaurant their second home.

Yet somehow now we seem to have reached a nice mix. About a third of the people in the neighborhood think of squid as calamari, about a third think of it as sushi, and about a third think of it as bait. Lots of the single people who have moved in during the last year or two are easygoing and good-tempered about all the kids. The old Italians have become philosophical about the new Hispanics, although they still think more of them should know English. The firebrand community organizer with the storefront on the block, the one who is always talking about people like us as though we stole our houses out of the open purse of a ninety-year-old blind widow, is pleasant to my boys.

Drawn in broad strokes, we live in a pressure cooker: oil and water, us and them. But if you come around at exactly the right time, you'll find members of all these groups gathered around complaining about the condition of the streets, on which everyone can agree. We melt together, then draw apart. I am the granddaughter of immigrants, a young professional—either an interloper or a longtime resident, depending on your concept of time. I am one of them, and one of us.

❷ ▲ **Critical Viewing** In what ways do the doors accompanying this essay illustrate its title? **[Connect]**

3. **apropos** (ap´ rə pō´) **of nothing:** Without connection.
4. **bodega** (bō dā´ gə) *n.*: Small Hispanic grocery store.

◆ Build Vocabulary

interloper (in´ tər lō´ pər) *n.*: Person who intrudes on another's rights or territory

---

Viewing and Representing Mini-Lesson

Today's Melting Pot
In this mini-lesson, students will extend their understanding of the United States as a melting pot by creating other examples that represent this concept.

Introduce Review the origin of the term "melting pot" (see Clarification, p. 128). Discuss what happens when a chef puts separate ingredients into a pot and cooks them. Students may say that the result blends the tastes of each ingredient into a new dish that echoes the individual flavors. Explain that this is one analogy for a multicultural society.

Develop Have students list other ways to represent a multicultural community. They might suggest visuals such as a rainbow, salad bar, patchwork quilt, or a spray of mixed flowers; some may envision musical ideas such as a medley. Invite students to imagine ways in which separate parts maintain their uniqueness as they contribute to a new whole.

Apply Have individuals or pairs work to create a visual, musical, or artistic representation of American multicultural society. Supply assorted materials, such as fabric, paint, posterboard, and so forth.

Assess Have students share their representations with the class and explain how their project captures the essence of multicultural America as they see it, or as they would like it to be. Evaluate students on their group work, the originality and clarity of their presentations, and their ability to describe and support their ideas.

Beyond Literature

Social Studies Connection

The Immigrant Experience Like Anna Quindlen's Ecuadorian neighbors, the hundreds of thousands of people who emigrate to the United States each year face tough choices. Should they learn English and teach their children American ways, or should they keep to the old traditions? How can they create a home in their adopted country without missing the community they left behind? Pulled in opposite directions, immigrants may feel unsure of who they are or where they belong.

Cross-Curricular Activity

Get to Know an Immigrant In your family or community, locate someone who emigrated to the United States. With an adult's help, ask at neighborhood churches or temples, local senior citizen centers, or even ethnic restaurants. Interview an immigrant about his or her experiences. Find out the easiest and most difficult things about settling in a new country. Share your findings with the class.

Guide for Responding

◆ Literature and Your Life

Reader's Response Would you like to live in Anna Quindlen's neighborhood? Why or why not?

Thematic Focus Why do you think Anna Quindlen is accepted by the long-time residents of her neighborhood?

Cultural Catalog With a partner, list the cultures represented in the "Melting Pot" neighborhood. Compare these with the cultures represented in your classroom, school, or neighborhood.

☑ Check Your Comprehension

1. What countries and ethnic groups do the people in Anna Quindlen's neighborhood represent?
2. What role did Quindlen's children play in helping the family fit into the neighborhood?
3. How does Quindlen get along with her neighbors?
4. How do the people in the neighborhood get along "on a micro level"?

◆ Critical Thinking

Interpret

1. What beliefs do most of the neighborhood residents share? **[Connect]**
2. How do these shared beliefs both unite and divide the residents? **[Interpret]**
3. What does Quindlen's choice of neighborhood reveal about what she finds important? **[Analyze]**
4. What advice would Quindlen give on how people of different cultures can get along with one another? **[Draw Conclusions]**

Evaluate

5. Do you think it's possible to be "one of them" and "one of us"? Explain. **[Make a Judgment]**
6. What does this story suggest about the way people live in American city neighborhoods? **[Social Studies Link]**

Compare Literary Works

7. In what ways do "Seventh Grade" and "Melting Pot" remind us to look beyond people's appearances before making any judgments? **[Connect]**

Beyond the Selection

FURTHER READING

Other Works by Anna Quindlen

Living Out Loud

Thinking Out Loud

Other Works About Communities

Amigo Brothers, Piri Thomas

"I Am a Native of North America," Chief Dan George

INTERNET

We suggest the following site on the Internet (all Web sites are subject to change).

For more on Anna Quindlen, including links to audio interviews:

http://www.erols.com/maura/webgrrls/quindlen

We *strongly recommend* that you preview the site before you send students to it.

Reinforce and Extend

Answers

◆ Literature and Your Life

Reader's Response Students may say that they would like living in Quindlen's neighborhood because it seems to be a successful mix of people from different backgrounds.

Thematic Focus The long-time residents accept Quindlen because they simply like her as a person, and may sense some kinship with her based on her background as the daughter of immigrants.

☑ Check Your Comprehension

1. They come from Ecuador, Ireland, Yugoslavia, Italy, India, Mexico, and other unnamed Hispanic cultures.
2. Her children's neighborhood friends brought the families together despite differences in their backgrounds.
3. She gets along well with most of her neighbors on an individual level, but is sometimes caught between opposing groups.
4. They appreciate each other as individuals, despite negative attitudes they may have toward ethnic groups in general.

◆ Critical Thinking

1. Most residents share the belief that change is unavoidable but not necessarily desirable.
2. They unite residents who are already there, whatever their background, against newcomers. They divide them from each other until the next newcomers turn old newcomers into "us."
3. It suggests that she values personal relationships and thinks it is important to know people of many different backgrounds.
4. Quindlen probably would advise people to get to know their neighbors as individuals, not as members of a stereotypical group.
5. Possible answer: It is possible because one can be part of many groups.
6. It suggests that city dwellers live among diverse cultural groups in an ever-changing environment. It also suggests that neighborhoods may change more rapidly in cities.
7. Possible answer: Each person has something unique to offer his or her community.

Answers

◆Reading Strategy

1. Students should clearly identify the story experience and its connection to their own lives, such as the first day of seventh grade and wanting to impress someone.
2. Noting Quindlen's experience of feeling stared at as a newcomer, students may link it to their own experiences as a new student or as an outsider moving into a new neighborhood.

◆Build Vocabulary

Using the Prefix *inter-*

1. international; 2. intersect; 3. interrupt

Spelling Strategy

1. keen; 2. scare; 3. skeleton; 4. score; 5. curvy; 6. kite

Using the Word Bank

1. f 2. h 3. d 4. b 5. a 6. c 7. e 8. g

◆Literary Focus

1. Soto seems to encourage Victor's actions. He creates a teacher who is understanding of Victor's behavior.
2. Soto's tone is sympathetic, friendly, understanding, funny, and supportive.
3. Although some characters or anecdotes are fearful, satisfied, angry, and excited, students may say that the tone of "Melting Pot" is hopeful and sympathetic. Quindlen works to blend the experiences into a lesson about how to fit into a diverse community.

◆Build Grammar Skills

Practice

1. seems: linking
2. are: linking
3. speaks: action
4. smiled: action
5. was: linking

Writing Application

Paragraphs will vary; check that students have circled action verbs and underlined linking verbs.

Guide for Responding *(continued)*

◆ Reading Strategy

Relate to Your Experiences

The people, places, and events in these selections may seem more alive when you **relate** them **to your own experiences.** For example, Victor's classroom antics might remind you of a time you tried to improvise an answer. Find other ways to connect and compare these writers' experiences with your own.

1. Identify two links between your experiences and the actions in "Seventh Grade."

2. Name one experience, situation, or feeling described in "Melting Pot" that you can link to your own life.

◆ Build Vocabulary

Using the Prefix *inter-*

The prefix *inter-* means "among or between." On your paper, complete each sentence with one of the words below. Use each word once.

international interrupt intersect

1. Quindlen's neighborhood has an __?__ feeling.

2. Many cultures __?__ in the neighborhood.

3. Mr. Bueller doesn't want Victor to __?__ during instruction.

Spelling Strategy

English words frequently use *c* for the *k* sound before the vowels *a*, *o*, or *u*, as in *scowl*, and the *k* before e and *i*. On your paper, complete each word correctly with either *c* or *k*.

1. _een **3.** s_eleton **5.** _urvy
2. s_are **4.** s_ore **6.** _ite

Using the Word Bank

On your paper, match each numbered word with its lettered definition.

1. fluent **a.** prejudiced people
2. interloper **b.** angry expression
3. elective **c.** fierceness
4. scowl **d.** optional course
5. bigots **e.** belief
6. ferocity **f.** able to communicate easily
7. conviction **g.** in a shy way
8. sheepishly **h.** intruder

◆ Literary Focus

Tone

A writer's **tone** refers to his or her attitude toward a subject. You can determine a writer's tone through his or her word choice, sentence structure, and descriptive details. For example, when Anna Quindlen says her neighborhood seems "to have reached a nice mix," you get the feeling that she is comfortable and pleased with that evaluation.

1. What details from "Seventh Grade" suggest that Soto likes Victor and enjoys the boy's behavior?

2. Describe the tone of "Seventh Grade." Support your answer.

3. Would you describe the tone of "Melting Pot" as fearful, satisfied, angry, or excited? Explain.

◆ Build Grammar Skills

Action Verbs and Linking Verbs

An **action verb** tells what action is occurring: Victor *spoke* in French. A **linking verb** joins the subject of a sentence with a word or expression that describes or renames the subject: Victor *sounded* silly. Common linking verbs include *seem*, *look*, *appear*, *sound*, *stay*, and forms of *be*. Notice that this sentence uses both action and linking verbs:

action verb action verb
Victor *didn't say* anything, though he *thought* his
linking verb
friend *looked* pretty strange.

Practice On your paper, identify the action and linking verbs in these sentences.

1. Anna's neighborhood seems busy and vibrant.

2. Many residents are hopeful about the peaceful feelings in the community.

3. Victor already speaks Spanish and English.

4. Mr. Bueller smiled at Victor's behavior.

5. Victor was embarrassed.

Writing Application In a paragraph, describe your first day of seventh grade. Then, circle the action verbs and underline the linking verbs you used.

Writer's Solution

For additional instruction and practice, use the Using Verbs section of in the *Writer's Solution Language Lab CD-ROM,* and the practice pages on linking verbs, pp. 12–13 in the *Writer's Solution Grammar Practice Book.*

Build Your Portfolio

Idea Bank

Writing

1. **Letter to Mr. Bueller** Imagine that you are Victor, as a young boy or as an adult. Write a letter of appreciation to Mr. Bueller, explaining what his actions have meant to you.
2. **Personal Narrative** In "Seventh Grade," Soto details Victor's first day of school. Write a brief narrative to describe your first day at school, at camp, or on the job. Capture the newness, excitement, or anxiety you may have felt.
3. **Welcome Pamphlet** Suppose that new tenants have moved into the apartment next to Anna Quindlen's. In a pamphlet, provide a brief description of the people, the stores, the restaurants, and the unique qualities of the neighborhood.

Speaking and Listening

4. **Dramatic Revue** **[Group Activity]** Work with classmates to create a revue expressing the seventh grade experience. You might include brief speeches, music, poems, and skits. One person should act as emcee to introduce each segment of the revue. **[Performing Arts Link]**
5. **Neighborhood Meeting** Role-play a meeting of a neighborhood improvement board. Acting as residents, two students should present a problem they can't solve. Other group members should act as board members and help the neighbors resolve their differences. **[Community Link]**

Projects

6. **Food Festival** Quindlen's grocer stocks a variety of ethnic foods. Sample the ethnic foods available in your community, and share the best with your class. Beyond the exotic flavors, provide information about each food for classmates.
7. **Community Work** Like Victor's job of picking grapes, employment in an area is often related to a local product or industry. Find out about the jobs that are available in your community. Present your findings in a report. **[Social Studies Link]**

Writing Mini-Lesson

Guidelines

Looking back on the events in "Seventh Grade," Victor might see his actions more clearly. He may have been more prepared for seventh grade if someone had given him some helpful tips. In a set of guidelines, give today's seventh graders some advice for getting along with others and being honest about themselves.

Writing Skills Focus: Develop Each Point

When writing guidelines or instructions, it helps to list the main ideas or steps point by point. You can then **develop each point** with specific details. For example, one main idea in your brochure might be developed this way:

Model

Be honest about who you are.

- Don't be afraid to share your strengths and your weaknesses to help others know the real "you."
- Think about how others will react if you lie to them and they find out.

Prewriting Review Victor's actions to list behaviors to encourage and those to avoid. Add ideas from your own experience to the list. Jot down details you might use to develop each listed idea.

Drafting Address your main points in order of importance. Provide examples or specific suggestions to develop each one.

◆ Grammar Application

Use action verbs to tell readers clearly how to behave. Add linking verbs to identify or describe the results of different behaviors.

Revising Your guidelines are intended for students your own age. Be sure you address your readers in a friendly, conversational way. Revise any language that may be too formal or confrontational.

ASSESSMENT OPTIONS

Formal Assessment, Selection Test, pp. 38–40, and Assessment Resources Software. The selection test is designed so that it can be easily customized to the performance levels of your students.

Alternative Assessment, p. 10, includes options for less advanced students, more advanced students, visual/spatial learners, interpersonal learners, verbal/linguistic learners, and bodily/kinesthetic learners.

PORTFOLIO ASSESSMENT

Use the following rubrics in the **Alternative Assessment** booklet to assess student writing:

Letter to Mr. Bueller: Expression, p. 81
Personal Narrative: Narrative Based on Personal Experience, p. 83
Welcome Pamphlet: Description, p. 84
Writing Mini-Lesson: How-to Process Explanation, p. 87

Idea Bank

Following are suggestions for matching the Idea Bank topics with your students' performance levels and learning modalities:

Customize for *Performance Levels*

Less Advanced Students: 2, 4, 6
Average Students: 1, 4, 6, 7
More Advanced Students: 3, 5, 7

Customize for *Learning Modalities*

Verbal/Linguistic: 1, 2, 3, 4, 5, 6, 7
Visual/Spatial: 3, 6
Bodily/Kinesthetic: 4, 5, 6
Logical/Mathematical: 5, 7
Musical/Rhythmic: 4
Interpersonal: 4, 5, 6
Intrapersonal: 1, 2, 3, 7

Writing Mini-Lesson

Refer students to the Writing Handbook in the back of the book for instructions on the writing process and for further information on writing guidelines.

Writer's Solution

Writing Lab CD-ROM

Have students complete the tutorial on Exposition: Giving Information. Follow these steps:

1. Have students use the Chain of Events chart to list main ideas.
2. Let students draft on computer.
3. Encourage students to use Notecard Activities to arrange details by order of importance.
4. Have students use the Proofreading Checklist when revising.

Writer's Solution Sourcebook

Have students use Chapter 4 "Exposition: Giving Information," pp. 102–133, for additional support. This chapter includes in-depth instruction on organizing details, p. 122, and using exact nouns, p. 128.

Prepare and Engage

OBJECTIVES

1. To read, comprehend, and interpret three poems
2. To relate poetry to personal experience
3. To paraphrase to get at the meaning of a poem
4. To recognize types of rhymes
5. To build vocabulary in context and learn the prefix *uni-*
6. To develop skill in using verb tenses
7. To use a strong opening to grab readers' interest in a persuasive essay
8. To respond to poetry through writing, speaking and listening, and projects

SKILLS INSTRUCTION

Vocabulary: Prefixes: *uni-*

Spelling: Using *qu* to make the *k* sound

Grammar: Verb Tenses

Reading Strategy: Paraphrasing

Literary Focus: Rhyme

Writing: Grab Reader's Interest

Speaking and Listening: Class Poll (Teacher Edition)

PORTFOLIO OPPORTUNITIES

Writing: "If—" Poem; Response; Introduction

Writing Mini-Lesson: Persuasive Argument

Speaking and Listening: Poetry Reading; Class Poll

Projects: Thumbprint Display; Living Biography

More About the Authors

Ralph Waldo Emerson was widely sought as a lecturer. It was the nation's young people who were most receptive to the ideas of this often controversial writer and philosopher.

Eve Merriam's attraction to poetry began at an early age. In talking about poetry, she stressed the "joy of the sound of language." She said that she would sometimes spend weeks looking for precisely the right word to use in a poem.

Rudyard Kipling wrote his jungle classics *The Jungle Book* and *Kim* not while living in India or England, but from his home in New England. When he won the Nobel Prize for Literature, he was the first author from England to do so.

Guide for Reading

Meet the Authors:

Ralph Waldo Emerson (1803–1882)

Ralph Waldo Emerson had a lifelong motto. This phrase, "*Trust yourself,*" helped direct many of his decisions and actions. Emerson believed in people's inborn judgment—their ability to evaluate the world and make the right choices. From his Boston boyhood to his years as a minister, Emerson worked hard at understanding his world. In writing about his ideas, he changed the way many people viewed their place in the world.

Eve Merriam (1916–1992)

"Words are fun!" might have been Eve Merriam's motto. Merriam found the world an entertaining place. She especially enjoyed words—for what they mean, how they look on a page, how they sound. Even as a child in Philadelphia, Merriam loved to make up rhymes. [For more on Eve Merriam, see page 780.]

Rudyard Kipling (1865–1936)

"Be brave, and do what needs to be done" would be a suitable motto for Rudyard Kipling. His approach to life may have dated back to growing up in India at a time when it was ruled by the British. In that time and place, a British boy was expected to be brave and to know where he was going. The poem "If—" outlines some of these expectations. "If—" is a tiny part of Kipling's work. His novels, plays, and other writings won him a Nobel Prize for Literature in 1907. [For more on Kipling, see page 462.]

◆ Literature and Your Life

Connect Your Experience

There are moments in our lives when we feel a great sense of accomplishment—imagine passing a tough exam, mastering a rollerblading trick, or getting the lead role in a play. At these times, we celebrate our achievements, our determination, and our own special abilities. The memory of these successes may even help us through difficult times later in life.

Thematic Connection: Fitting In

These poems show how even the successful feeling of being an individual gives people shared experiences and helps them to fit in.

◆ Background for Understanding

Science

Eve Merriam's poem takes a scientific approach to the concept of individuality. Every person—even an identical twin—is different from everyone else. This difference is evident not just in personality or appearance, but in actual scientific ways. For example, no two human beings have the same fingerprint. The pattern of ridges in the skin is different on each person's fingertips. That is why fingerprints can be used to identify people, even when their appearance has changed.

◆ Build Vocabulary

Prefixes: *uni-*

These poets explore individuality. Once you know that the prefix *uni-* means "one," you can see why Eve Merriam uses the word *unique,* meaning "like no other," in her exploration.

Word Bank

Which word from the poems might describe people who aren't who they appear to be?

spry
unique
base
impostors
virtue

Prentice Hall Literature Program Resources

REINFORCE / RETEACH / EXTEND

Selection Support Pages
Build Vocabulary: Prefixes: *uni-,* p. 55
Build Spelling Skills, p. 56
Build Grammar Skills: Verb Tenses, p. 57
Reading Strategy: Paraphrasing, p. 58
Literary Focus: Rhyme, p. 59

Strategies for Diverse Student Needs, pp. 21–22

Beyond Literature Career Connection: Individual Choices, p. 11

Formal Assessment Selection Test, pp. 41–43, Assessment Resources Software

Alternative Assessment, p. 11

Writing and Language Transparencies Open Mind Organizer, p. 90

Art Transparencies Transparency 4, *Personal Appearance*

Resource Pro CD-ROM "Fable"; "Thumbprint"; "If—"

Listening to Literature Audiocassettes "Fable"; "Thumbprint"; "If—"

◆ Fable ◆ Thumbprint ◆ If— ◆

◆ Literary Focus

RHYME

Rhyme is the repetition of sounds at the ends of words. Rhyme that occurs at the end of lines is called **end rhyme. Exact rhyme** refers to words that sound exactly alike except for the beginning consonant, like *disgrace* and *place*. **Half rhymes** are words whose sounds are similar but not identical, like *squirrel* and *quarrel*.

Rhyme is important for several reasons. You begin to listen for it, and the expectation of sounds repeated keeps you interested. A poet may also vary the **rhyme scheme,** or pattern of rhymes, to call your attention to a passage.

◆ Reading Strategy

PARAPHRASE

Poets may use words in unusual ways, or they may play with sentence order. One way to help you get to the meaning of a poem is to **paraphrase** it. When you paraphrase, you restate lines in your own words. Look at this example:

Kipling's Version: If you can trust yourself when all men doubt you, / But make allowance for their doubting too . . .

Paraphrased: If you can be confident when others question you, / while understanding why they doubt you . . .

Use a chart like the one below to paraphrase passages from these poems.

Poet's Words	Paraphrase

Interest Grabber Ask students to write brief self-descriptions on index cards. They should describe only their characters and personalities, not their physical appearances, leaving their names off their cards. When they finish, shuffle all of the cards together and read the descriptions aloud. Invite volunteers to match the descriptions with the students who wrote them. Discuss with students whether the descriptions on the cards portrayed their classmates the way they see them. Lead students into the poems by telling them that we are not always perceived as we think. What gives individuals their identity?

◆ Build Grammar Skills

Verb Tenses If you wish to introduce the grammar concept for this selection before students read, refer to the instruction on p. 140.

Customize for
Less Proficient Readers
The three poems in the selection, which present three different writing styles, are not equally easy to grasp. To help students comprehend the poets' messages, encourage them to take the time to reread all or parts of the poems and to break down poems into small sections.

Customize for
More Advanced Students
Have students identify and compare the different voices and tones of the three poems. Guide them to appreciate that "Fable" is written as a conversation between a mountain and a squirrel, that "Thumbprint" is presented from an exuberant first-person point of view, and that "If—" sounds like a lecture from a wise elder to a child. Challenge students to analyze and explain the strengths of each presentation as they read.

Customize for
English Language Learners
Recast each poem in the selection as if it were a dialogue: between a mountain and a squirrel, between Merriam and a friend, and between Kipling and his son. Allow teams of students acquiring English to stop and ask questions about what the speakers are saying.

Preparing for Standardized Tests

Spelling Standardized tests may assess students' knowledge of spelling rules. Write this sentence on the board: "The ballet dancer stood in a perfect arabesque." Tell students that because the spelling of the word *arabesque* ends with *que,* it is pronounced with a *k* sound at the end. Then point out that the correct spelling of this *k* sound requires adding the letter e to *qu.* You may want to mention that words that end with *que* are borrowed from French. Then give students this sample test item:

The cliqu ate lunch together every day.

Choose the correct spelling of the underlined word.

(A) click (C) clicque
(B) clique (D) No mistake

Students should recognize that *(A) click* is a homonym and sounds the same as *clique,* but doesn't have the correct meaning in this context. Then they should apply the spelling rule, "when using *qu* to make the *k* sound at the end of the word, add an *e,*" and select *(C) clique* as the correct spelling. For additional practice, use **Selection Support,** p. 55.

Develop Understanding

One-Minute Insight "Fable" is a conversation between a mountain and a squirrel. The poet makes the point that all things, no matter how large or small, have their own unique talents that allow them to fit in the world; a tiny squirrel is as unique and valuable as a huge mountain.

◆ Reading Strategy

❶ **Paraphrasing** Define *former* as "first in order of two or more things cited or understood" and *latter* as "the second of two groups or things or the last of several groups or things referred to." Then ask students to paraphrase line 3. *The mountain called the squirrel "Little Prig."*

◆ Literary Focus

❷ **Rhyme** Have a student read the poem aloud. Ask listeners to identify the end rhymes that are exact and those that are half-rhymes. *Half-rhymes: squirrel/quarrel, make/track, put/nut; exact rhyme: Prig/big, weather/together, year/sphere, disgrace/place, I/spry, track/back.*

◆ Literature and Your Life

❸ Ask students whether they think the mountain or the squirrel shows more self-confidence and have them explain their answers. *Students should recognize that the mountain relies on its size for its confidence, whereas the squirrel recognizes its own unique talents.*

Customize for
Less Proficient Readers
Use the Open Mind Organizer, p. 90 in **Writing and Language Transparencies,** to help students identify the points that each character in the poem makes. Students can record the mountain's ideas on one organizer and the squirrel's thoughts on another.

Customize for
Visual/Spatial Learners
Use Art Transparency 4, p. 19, in **Art Transparencies,** to help students explore the concept of individuality as they read the poems. *Personal Appearance*, by Miriam Schapiro, shows individuality using color, texture, and form.

Fable

Ralph Waldo Emerson

❶ The mountain and the squirrel
Had a quarrel;
And the former called the latter 'Little Prig.'
Bun replied,
'You are doubtless very big;
But all sorts of things and weather
Must be taken in together,
❷ To make up a year
❸ And a sphere.
And I think it no disgrace
To occupy my place.
If I'm not so large as you,
You are not so small as I,
And not half so spry.
I'll not deny you make
A very pretty squirrel track;
Talents differ; all is well and wisely put;
If I cannot carry forests on my back,
Neither can you crack a nut.'

◆ Build Vocabulary
spry (sprī) *adj.*: Full of life; active; nimble

Block Scheduling Strategies

Consider these suggestions to take advantage of extended class time:

- Introduce the Reading Strategy, Paraphrase, on p. 140. Then have pairs of students read the poems and take turns paraphrasing lines. Encourage them to discuss the poem's meaning as they read. Then have students independently use what they have gained from paraphrasing to answer the questions on pp. 137 and 139.
- If you have access to technology, have students use the *Writer's Solution Writing Lab CD-ROM* to prepare for and complete the Writing Mini-Lesson. Use the suggestions on p. 141 to structure class time.
- To help students appreciate the importance of rhyme, have them listen to the recording of each poem. Then have them answer the Literary Focus questions on p. 140. Encourage them to use a rhyme scheme as they complete the writing activity, "If—" Poem, in the Idea Bank on p. 141.

Listening to Literature Audiocassettes

Thumbprint

Eve Merriam

On the pad of my thumb
are whorls, whirls, wheels
in a unique design:
mine alone.
What a treasure to own!
My own flesh, my own feelings.
No other, however grand or base,
can ever contain the same.
My signature,
thumbing the pages of my time.
My universe key,
my singularity.
Impress, implant,
I am myself, ❹
of all my atom parts I am the sum.
And out of my blood and my brain
I make my own interior weather,
my own sun and rain.
Imprint my mark upon the world, ❺
whatever I shall become.

◆ **Build Vocabulary**

unique (yōō nēk′) *adj.*: Unlike any other; singular

base (bās) *adj.*: Lowly; inferior

Guide for Responding

◆ Literature and Your Life

Reader's Response Which of these poems comes closest to stating your life motto? Explain.

Thematic Focus Based on the ideas in their poems, which of these poets might be a better team member? Which might be more successful in an individual effort? Explain.

Read Aloud Read these poems aloud. For "Fable," use voice and gesture to capture the personalities of the mountain and the squirrel.

☑ Check Your Comprehension

1. Summarize the conversation in "Fable."
2. What does Eve Merriam describe in "Thumbprint"?
3. What are the "whorls, whirls, wheels" Merriam describes?

◆ Critical Thinking

Interpret

1. Why does the squirrel compare its place in the world to the parts of a year? **[Interpret]**
2. What does Emerson suggest about the value of the individual? **[Draw Conclusions]**
3. Why is the speaker's thumbprint so precious to her? **[Analyze]**
4. How does a thumbprint help Merriam make a point about individuality ? **[Infer]**

Extend

5. How might these poems help family members, classmates, or co-workers understand one another better? **[Social Studies Link]**

Compare Literary Works

6. What message do these poems share? **[Compare and Contrast]**

Develop Understanding

One-Minute Insight In "Thumbprint," Merriam explores the uniqueness of her thumbprint to emphasize and celebrate her individuality.

◆ Literature and Your Life

❹ Discuss with students whether the speaker of this poem might find it easy or difficult to fit in with other people. *Some students may suggest that confidence as an individual may allow the speaker to deal well with others; some students may suggest that the speaker believes in uniqueness too much to fit in with others.*

◆ Build Grammar Skills

❺ **Verb Tenses** Point out that verbs can express action that takes place in the present, in the past, and in the future. Guide them to recognize the action taking place in the present in these lines (*make, imprint*) and in the future (*shall become*).

Customize for *Verbal/Linguistic Learners*

Point out the sound device of alliteration (repetition of initial consonant sounds) that the poet uses in the second line, "whorls, whirls, wheels." Tell students that, like rhyme, poets use alliteration to create musical effects and to draw attention to words and ideas. Have students write sentences about themselves, using alliteration. For instance, "I am tall, tan, and talkative."

Reinforce and Extend

Answers

◆ Literature and Your Life

Reader's Response Some students will choose "Fable" because it recognizes everyone's value and talents. Others will select "Thumbprint" for the way it celebrates individuality.

Thematic Focus Emerson would probably make a better team player because he recognizes everyone's ability to contribute. Merriam might be better suited to individual efforts as she seems more interested in recognizing how each person is unique.

Check Your Comprehension

1. A mountain and a squirrel argue about who is more important.
2. She describes her thumbprint.
3. They are the pattern of her thumbprint.

◆ Critical Thinking

1. Bun sees each individual as a part necessary to complete the whole.
2. He suggests that individuals each have something unique to contribute.
3. It makes her unique.
4. It allows her to make her mark on the world; without it she might be unrecognizable.
5. Students may suggest that they describe the importance and value of each individual but don't deny the existence of others' individuality.
6. They honor others' differences as well as unique contributions.

"If—" is a poem describing conditions that, if fulfilled, allow a child to become a successful adult.

Clarification

❶ In elementary logic, conditional "if-then" statements (if *p*, then *q*) are called implications. They have two parts: the hypothesis and the conclusion. The "if" part of the statement is the hypothesis. For example, "If you live in Denver, then you live in Colorado." If the boy in the poem meets the conditions set forth, then he will become a man.

◆Literature and Your Life

❷ Point out to students that the ideas Kipling expresses in this first stanza reflect choices that everyone faces in daily life. Discuss with them situations when they must decide between doing what they believe is right or doing what others expect. For instance, you may want to present students with a scenario such as completing a homework assignment or going out with a group of friends.

Customize for *Logical/Mathematical Learners*

Challenge students to come up with a reasonable "then" conclusion for each "if" statement in the poem. To get them started, provide an example, such as the following, for the "if" statement in the first two lines: ...then you may be the one to find a solution to the problem that's causing people around you to simply lose their heads and place blame.

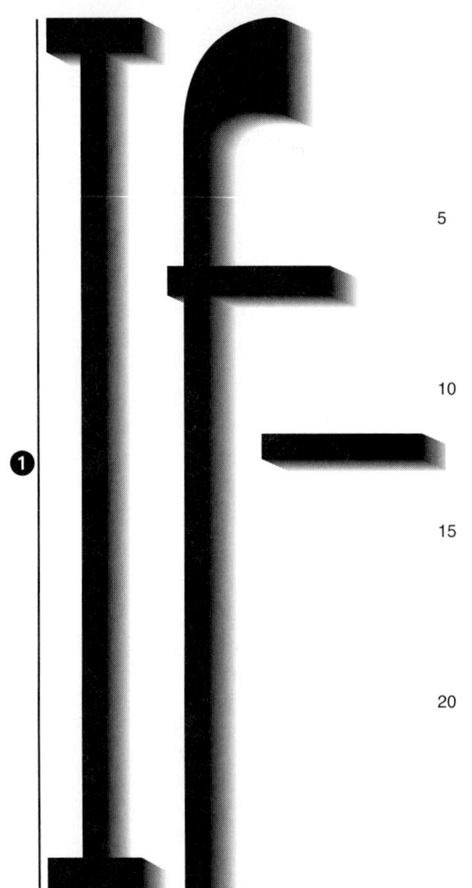

❶

Rudyard Kipling

If you can keep your head when all about you
  Are losing theirs and blaming it on you,
If you can trust yourself when all men doubt you,
  But make allowance for their doubting too;
If you can wait and not be tired by waiting,
  Or being lied about, don't deal in lies,
Or being hated, don't give way to hating,
  And yet don't look too good, nor talk too wise: ❷

If you can dream—and not make dreams your master;
  If you can think—and not make thoughts your aim;
If you can meet with Triumph and Disaster
  And treat those two impostors just the same;
If you can bear to hear the truth you've spoken
  Twisted by knaves to make a trap for fools,
Or watch the things you gave your life to, broken,
  And stoop and build 'em up with worn-out tools:

If you can make one heap of all your winnings
  And risk it on one turn of pitch-and-toss,
And lose, and start again at your beginnings
  And never breathe a word about your loss;
If you can force your heart and nerve and sinew
  To serve your turn long after they are gone,
And so hold on when there is nothing in you
  Except the Will which says to them: "Hold on!" ❸

Speaking and Listening Mini-Lesson

Class Poll
This mini-lesson supports the Speaking and Listening activity on p. 141.

Introduce Discuss with students that Kipling's suggestions for successful living are not rules, but guidelines. Mention that their classmates will probably find some of the guidelines more useful than others.

Develop Point out that the goal of an effective survey is to obtain data and examine what participants believe. Suggest to students that they use survey answer choices such as "strongly agree," "agree," "disagree," "strongly disagree." You may wish to provide samples of survey forms for students to use as examples.

Apply Divide the class into groups and have them assign survey tasks. Guide students to reach group agreement on how the guidelines will be rewritten and presented and the survey answer choices that will be used. Encourage students to predict the results of their surveys prior to conducting them. Invite groups to survey other seventh-grade students, or students from other grade levels.

Assess After students have tabulated their results and shared their findings, discuss their experiences with conducting a survey. Assess students on their group work and presentations. In addition, use the Initial Self-Assessment: Speaking and Listening form, p. 103 in **Alternative Assessment,** for students to assess their own survey experience.

If you can talk with crowds and keep your virtue,
  Or walk with Kings—nor lose the common touch,
If neither foes nor loving friends can hurt you,
  If all men count with you, but none too much;
❹ If you can fill the unforgiving minute
  With sixty seconds' worth of distance run,
Yours is the Earth and everything that's in it,
  And—which is more—you'll be a Man, my son!

◆ Build Vocabulary

impostors (im päs´ tər z) *n.*: People who trick or deceive others by pretending to be what they are not

virtue (vʉr´ cho͞o) *n.*: Moral goodness

Guide for Responding

◆ Literature and Your Life

Reader's Response Which of the conditions described in this poem would you find hardest to fulfill? Which might be easiest to fulfill? Explain.

Thematic Focus According to "If—," what does an individual need to do to fit in with the group?

Journal Writing Choose a line or two from Kipling's poem that reminds you of an experience you've had. In a brief journal entry, explain what happened and what you learned from the experience.

☑ Check Your Comprehension

1. List three situations and behaviors the speaker includes in "If—."
2. What happens if all the conditions are met?

◆ Critical Thinking

Interpret

1. What is similar about many of the conditions Kipling describes? **[Connect]**
2. Why does Kipling advise treating Triumph and Disaster as impostors? **[Interpret]**
3. What qualities does Kipling value in people? **[Draw Conclusions]**

Apply

4. How does the poem celebrate the individual while acknowledging the group? **[Support]**

Extend

5. Which jobs might suit a person who meets the conditions of the poem? **[Career Link]**

Beyond the Selection

FURTHER READING

Other Works by Ralph Waldo Emerson

The Complete Works of Ralph Waldo Emerson

The Letters of Ralph Waldo Emerson

Other Works by Eve Merriam

A Sky Full of Poems

It Doesn't Always Have to Rhyme

Other Works by Rudyard Kipling

The Jungle Book

Kim

INTERNET

We suggest the following sites on the Internet (all Web sites are subject to change).

For more on Ralph Waldo Emerson:
http://www.geocities.com/athens/7687/1emerson.html

For Eve Merriam's unique poem about a city with an impossible-to-rhyme name, visit:
http://www.union.edu/alumni/SchenectadyPoem.html

For information on Rudyard Kipling's Nobel Prize:
http://www.almaz.com/nobel/literature/1907a.html

We *strongly recommend* that you preview these sites before you send students to them.

◆ Reading Strategy

❸ **Paraphrasing** Ask students to restate the poet's words to get at their meaning. *Possible responses: Stick to your own ideas when dealing with a group; or, don't forget who you are when you are with others.*

◆ Literary Focus

❹ **Rhyme** Have students identify the end rhymes in lines 25–33 and tell whether they are exact or half. *Exact rhyme: virtue/you, touch/much, run/son; half-rhyme: minute/in it.*

Reinforce and Extend

Answers

◆ Literature and Your Life

Reader's Response Some students may say it is most difficult not to lie when lied to; others may say that trying again after losing big is something they have difficulty doing.

Thematic Focus A person needs to be true to his or her beliefs.

☑ Check Your Comprehension

1. Possible responses: waiting without getting impatient; not lying when lied to; take winning or losing the same without gloating or acting disappointed; not wasting time.
2. If the conditions are met, the child becomes an adult.

◆ Critical Thinking

1. Many of the conditions contrast behavior within a group with what an individual should do.
2. He believes that changes in fortune don't matter much. They only seem to matter, much like an imposter appears to be someone else.
3. He values common sense, persistence, calmness, honesty, integrity, optimism, fairness, perseverance, and patience.
4. It suggests that individuals can be proud of their talents and uniqueness without bragging.
5. Any kind of job that requires leadership.

Answers

◆Reading Strategy

1. Possible response: If you can try again when you lose and stick with tasks when you are tired.
2. Possible response: Every part of the universe has its value. We should cherish each part for its contribution.
3. Possible response: My thumbprint stands for all the ways I'm different from everyone else and for all the ways I can affect the world.
4. Students may notice a lack of emotion, rhyme, musical quality, or sensory detail in their restatements.

◆Build Vocabulary

Using the prefix *uni-*

1. A union joins many individuals together.
2. To unite individuals means to bring them together.
3. The universe includes all individuals.
4. An individual can be seen as a unit of a larger group.

Spelling Strategy

1. mystique; 2. technique; 3. physique; 4. boutique

Using the Word Bank

1. Yes, because spry means "quick, moves easily, agile."
2. A bride is unique because she is dressed differently than the others and will stand out in the photo.
3. An imposter pretends to be someone else.
4. It is a virtue because it is a quality worth admiring.
5. No, because base means "of lesser value."

◆Literary Focus

1. put/nut
2. alone/own; This rhyme highlights the speaker's ownership of the unique thumbprint.
3. you/too; waiting/hating; lies/wise; aim/same; virtue/you; touch/much; minute/in it; run/son
4. "If—" is the most regular with each stanza except the first, maintaining an abab/cdcd rhyme scheme.

◆Build Grammar Skills

Practice

1. past; 2. present; 3. present; 4. future; 5. past

Guide for Responding *(continued)*

◆ Reading Strategy

PARAPHRASE

The mysteries in these poems become clear as you **paraphrase** them, or restate the lines in your own words.

1. Paraphrase lines 17–24 of "If—."
2. Paraphrase all of "Fable."
3. Paraphrase lines 5–20 of "Thumbprint."
4. How are your paraphrases different from the original lines?

◆ Build Vocabulary

USING THE PREFIX *uni-*

Remember that the prefix *uni-* means "one." On your paper, explain how each word connects individuals and the group.

1. union **2.** unite **3.** universe **4.** unit

SPELLING STRATEGY

The word *unique* demonstrates this spelling rule: When using *qu* to make the *k* sound at the end of a word, add an *e*.

On your paper, write these words, completing them with the correct spelling of the *k* sound that uses *qu*. Then, use each word in a sentence.

1. mysti____
2. techni____
3. physi____
4. bouti____

USING THE WORD BANK

On your paper, answer the following questions. Explain each answer.

1. Would a good dancer be a *spry* person?
2. Who is more likely to be *unique* in a group photo—a soccer player in a team picture or a bride posing with her family?
3. Why would you expect an *impostor* to use a false name?
4. Is truthfulness a *virtue* or a fault?
5. Would you expect a *base* metal to be valuable?

◆ Literary Focus

RHYME

The repetition of sounds in two or more words, called **rhyme,** is a common element of poetry. Rhymed lines usually occur in a pattern called a rhyme scheme. Once you recognize the pattern, you expect rhymes in particular places.

1. A **half rhyme** pairs words that sound similar but not identical. Identify a half rhyme that Emerson uses in "Fable."
2. Identify the first rhyme in "Thumbprint" and the idea it highlights.
3. The rhyming sound used in the first, second, and fourth groups of lines of "If—" is spelled in many different ways. Write the words that contain this rhyming sound.
4. Which of these poems has the most regular rhyme scheme? Explain.

◆ Build Grammar Skills

VERB TENSES

Verbs are words that indicate action. Verbs have **tenses,** different forms that tell at what time something happens—in the present, in the past, or in the future.

Present tense: I *make* my own interior weather. . . .

Past tense: The mountain and the squirrel/*Had* a quarrel;/ And the former *called* the latter "Little Prig."

Future tense: *I'll [will]* not *deny* you make/ A very pretty squirrel track. . . .

Practice Identify the tense of each verb.

1. She *pressed* her thumb firmly on the inkpad.
2. The advice in "If—" *lingers* in my mind.
3. The mountain and the squirrel *compare* their strengths and weaknesses.
4. The mountain *will respect* the squirrel now.
5. Rudyard Kipling *believed* in being brave.

Writing Application Write a paragraph to describe what sets you apart from the crowd. In your writing, use each of the three tenses twice.

Writing Application

Responses will include students' perceptions of their individuality and uniqueness. They should support their views with examples. To use the future tense, students can describe how they plan to assert their individuality in the future.

Writer's Solution

For additional instruction and practice, use the lesson in the *Writer's Solution Language Lab CD-ROM* on Using Verbs, and the practice page on The Six Tenses of Verbs, p. 66 in the *Writer's Solution Grammar Practice Book.*

Build Your Portfolio

Idea Bank

Writing

1. **If— Poem** Write a poem modeled after Kipling's. Begin every other line or every fourth line with the words "If you can . . ." Focus on presenting an approach to life that can benefit readers.
2. **Response** How might the mountain reply to the squirrel's views? Write the mountain's response, in prose or poetry.
3. **Introduction** Poetry collections often have a common theme that draws the poems together. Write a brief introduction to appear at the beginning of a collection that includes these three poems. Explain the thematic focus of the collection, and identify how each poem fits the theme.

Speaking and Listening

4. **Poetry Reading** Choose one of the three poems, and read it aloud for the class. Use the punctuation to guide the way you read, and vary the tone and volume of your voice to emphasize key words and lines.
5. **Class Poll [Group Activity]** Kipling sets guidelines for living successfully. With a group, conduct a survey to discover which of Kipling's rules are most important to your classmates. Divide these tasks: rewrite the poem as a list of guidelines; prepare copies of the survey; tabulate results. Share your findings with the class. **[Math Link]**

Projects

6. **Thumbprint Display** Use a science reference book to compare classmates' thumbprints with typical patterns. Then, create thumbprint artwork by combining different patterns and ink colors. **[Science Link; Art Link]**
7. **Living Biography** Present a look at the life of either Emerson or Kipling. Conduct research to learn more about the times in which the writer lived. Then, put together a presentation, including props, slides, text clips, maps, photographs, and other materials you have found about the writer.

Writing Mini-Lesson

Persuasive Argument

Each of these poems takes a position about the importance of individuality—of standing out in the crowd. Make your own case for individuality. Write a persuasive essay that explains whether you should be allowed to dress as you choose, decorate your own bedroom, or choose your future job.

Writing Skills Focus: Grab Readers' Interest

Before you convince readers of your ideas, you must get their attention. **Grab readers' interest** with a strong opening that appeals to their emotions and introduces your subject. Consider these strategies:

- Use a startling anecdote.
- Offer compelling statistics.
- Ask a bold question.

Prewriting In one column of a two-column chart, list the positive aspects of being able to choose your own style, interests, and future. For example, people who like their jobs may be more productive. In the second column, list the potential negative effects of such freedom of choice. For example, if people are given the right to choose their clothing style, they may dress in ways others don't like.

Drafting As you draft, use both columns of your chart to make your argument. Use your chart to provide evidence that supports your opinion.

Revising Read your essay aloud to a classmate to confirm that your position is clear and convincing. If your opening sounds flat or dull to your partner, strengthen it to make it more inviting.

Grammar Application

Make sure you keep all verbs in the same tense, unless you are referring to events from a different time.

✓ ASSESSMENT OPTIONS

Formal Assessment, Selection Test, pp. 41–43, and Assessment Resources Software. The selection test is designed so that it can be easily customized to the performance levels of your students.

Alternative Assessment, p. 11, includes options for less advanced students, more advanced students, visual/spatial learners, verbal/linguistic learners, bodily/kinesthetic learners, intrapersonal learners, and musical/rhythmic learners.

PORTFOLIO ASSESSMENT

Use the following rubrics in the **Alternative Assessment** booklet to assess student writing:
"If—" Poem: Poetry, p. 95
Response: Expression, p. 81
Introduction: Summary, p. 85
Writing Mini-Lesson: Persuasion, p. 92

Idea Bank

Following are suggestions for matching the Idea Bank topics with your students' performance levels and learning modalities:

Customize for
Performance Levels
Less Advanced Students: 1, 4
Average Students: 2, 4, 5, 6
More Advanced Students: 3, 6, 7

Customize for
Learning Modalities
Verbal/Linguistic: 1, 2, 3, 4, 5, 7
Visual/Spatial: 2, 4, 6, 7
Logical/Mathematical: 1, 3, 4
Interpersonal: 5
Intrapersonal: 3

Writing Mini-Lesson

Refer students to the Writing Handbook in the back of the book for instructions on the writing process and for further information on persuasion.

Writer's Solution

Writers at Work Videodisc

To introduce students to persuasive writing, have students view the segment featuring Joseph Bruchac. Have students discuss how Bruchac discovers ideas to help persuade his readers.

Play frames 4 to 9282

Writing Lab CD-ROM

Have students complete the tutorial on Persuasion. Follow these steps:

1. Have students view model of an essay supporting an opinion.
2. Encourage students to use the Pros and Cons Chart activity to learn to distinguish opposing positions.
3. Let students draft on computer.
4. When revising, use the Peer-Evaluation Checklist.

Writer's Solution Sourcebook

Have students use Chapter 6, "Persuasion," pp. 166–199, for additional instruction. This chapter includes in-depth instruction on writing supporting sentences and using commas, pp. 194–195.

Guide for Reading

OBJECTIVES

1. To read, comprehend, and interpret a story
2. To relate a story to personal experience
3. To break down long sentences
4. To analyze elements used to create a historical setting
5. To build vocabulary in context and learn the word root *-cline-*
6. To distinguish among perfect verb tenses
7. To write a description of a trip to the future using words that engage the senses
8. To respond to the story through writing, speaking and listening, and projects

SKILLS INSTRUCTION

Vocabulary: Word Roots: *-cline-*
Spelling: Adding the Suffix *-able*
Grammar: Verb Tenses
Reading Strategy: Break Down Long Sentences
Literary Focus: Historical Setting
Writing: Engage the Senses
Speaking and Listening: Talk Show Appearance (Teacher Edition)
Viewing and Representing: Storyboard (Teacher Edition)
Critical Viewing: Infer; Analyze; Connect

PORTFOLIO OPPORTUNITIES

Writing: Memoir; Newspaper Article; Comparison-and-Contrast Essay
Writing Mini-Lesson: Description of a Trip Through Time
Speaking and Listening: Talk Show Appearance; Dramatization
Projects: Oral Presentation; Geography Update

Meet the Author:

Washington Irving (1783–1859)

Born in New York City the year the American Revolution ended, Washington Irving was the first American writer to become famous in Europe as well as at home.

The Comic Edge While still in his teens, Irving began writing and publishing humorous essays. His first big success was A *History of New York* (1809). Written under the pen name Diedrich Knickerbocker, this supposedly scholarly work was actually a spoof of history books and a comic look at politics. In 1820, he published a story collection, *The Sketch Book of Geoffrey Crayon, Gent.* (which included "Rip Van Winkle"). It made him the most famous American writer of his day.

An American in Europe Irving wrote all his life, publishing stories, essays, and biographies. An enthusiastic traveler, he also served at various times as a diplomat in Madrid and London.

THE STORY BEHIND THE STORY

While living in England when he was a young man, Irving read old German folk tales in search of subjects he could use for stories of his own. These tales frequently appeared in Irving's later writings, slightly changed and set in an American landscape. One of the German tales that appealed to Irving was the inspiration for "Rip Van Winkle."

◆ LITERATURE AND YOUR LIFE

CONNECT YOUR EXPERIENCE

At some time in your life, you were probably out of school or away from home for a period of several days or weeks. When you returned, you may have discovered that you'd missed out on events that people were now talking about. You may even have noticed changes had taken place. Imagine what it would be like if, like Rip Van Winkle, you returned home after being away for years.

THEMATIC FOCUS: Fitting In

After a long absence, Rip Van Winkle finds he no longer fits in. As you read, notice how common experiences play a part in how comfortable people feel in a group.

◆ Background for Understanding

GEOGRAPHY

The Catskill Mountains, located northwest of New York City, are now a popular resort area. In the eighteenth century, however, the Catskills were still remote, wild, densely wooded, and largely unsettled. As the map indicates, the area was cut through with rocky gorges formed by "kills," or creeks. Villages and farms dotted the Hudson River valley. Much of "Rip Van Winkle" takes place in one of these small villages.

◆ Build Vocabulary

WORD ROOTS: *-cline-*

In "Rip Van Winkle," Irving uses the word *declined*. The word root *-cline-*, meaning "lean" or "bend," is a key to the meaning of *decline*, "to bend downward or away."

WORD BANK

Which word from the story might mean "royal" or "grand"?

martial
domestic
wistfully
majestic
incomprehensible
melancholy
declined

More About the Author
Washington Irving's witty and entertaining stories combine history, biography, and legend. His popular tales, including the adventures of Ichabod Crane ("The Legend of Sleepy Hollow") and Rip Van Winkle, made Irving the leader of American literary life in the early nineteenth century. Irving is one of the few writers of his era whose works continue to be read by later generations. Washington Irving spent the last years of his life at his home in Tarrytown, New York, near Rip Van Winkle's Catskill Mountains.

Prentice Hall Literature Program Resources

REINFORCE / RETEACH / EXTEND

Selection Support Pages
Build Vocabulary: Word Roots: *-cline-*, p. 60
Build Spelling Skills, p. 61
Build Grammar Skills: Verb Tenses, p. 62
Reading Strategy: Break Down Long Sentences, p. 63
Literary Focus: Historical Setting, p. 64
Strategies for Diverse Student Needs, pp. 23–24
Beyond Literature Cross-Curricular Connection: Social Studies, p. 12

Formal Assessment Selection Test, pp. 44–46, Assessment Resources Software
Alternative Assessment, p. 12
Writing and Language Transparencies Series of Events Chain, p. 66; Sensory Language Chart, p. 78
Daily Language Practice, p. 12
Resource Pro CD-ROM "Rip Van Winkle"

Listening to Literature Audiocassettes "Rip Van Winkle"

Rip Van Winkle

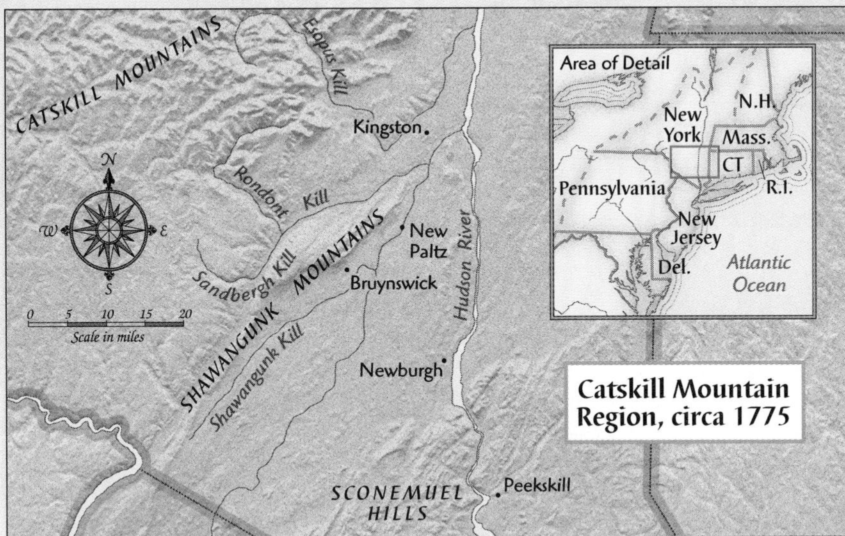

◆ Literary Focus

Historical Setting

A story's **setting** is the time and place in which the action occurs. Stories that are set in a specific period in the past have a **historical setting.** "Rip Van Winkle," for example, is set in a village in the Catskills in the mid-1700's. The region's settlers were Dutch, but revolution was in the air. As the story opens, New York is a British colony. By the end, the American Revolution is over, and George Washington is President. Use a chart like the one below to note historical details of "Rip Van Winkle."

Details of Historic Setting

Before His Sleep	After Sleep
New York is a British colony.	

◆ Reading Strategy

Break Down Long Sentences

Washington Irving wrote at a time when long, complex sentences were a mark of style. **Breaking down long sentences** in this story will help you understand them. First, use punctuation to help you find manageable sections. Then, identify *who* the sentence is about and *what* that person is doing. In this example, key sections are shown in red and details are bracketed off.

". . . If left to himself, / he would have whistled life away/[in perfect contentment]; but his wife kept continually dinning in his ears / [about his idleness, / his carelessness, / and the ruin / he was bringing on his family. . . .]"

Preparing for Standardized Tests

Spelling The spelling portion of standardized tests may require students to select correctly spelled words that have the suffix *-able*. Have students read the following sentence and choose the word that is spelled correctly to complete the sentence.

At first, Rip's story did not seem ________.

(A) believable (C) believvable
(B) believeable (D) believible

In the example above, *(A) believable* is the correct answer. When adding the suffix *-able* to a word that ends in silent e, usually drop the e before adding the suffix. To offer students practice in spelling words with the suffix *-able* correctly, use **Selection Support,** p. 61, Build Spelling Skills.

To prepare students for standardized tests, you may want to share suggestions to help them perform their best:

- Read and listen to each test question carefully.
- Before responding to a question, be sure you know what is being asked so that you can select the best answer.

Invite students to imagine this scenario: "In the morning, on the way to school, you notice that the houses look different—they are painted different colors and there are new cars in front of them. Upon arriving at school, you notice that the building has been renovated and the flag that hangs in front has different colors and symbols on it. The usual crowd of students stands at the door, but you do not recognize anyone. You ask about certain students and teachers you saw and spoke to yesterday and are told they are no longer at the school."

Encourage students to suggest what they might think if they encountered those circumstances. Discuss with them how the similar but different nature of the situation might be confusing. Then introduce the story by telling them that the main character wakes one morning to find the people in his life gone and the environment changed. How might he feel? How will he determine what has happened to bring about these changes?

◆ Build Grammar Skills

Verb Tenses If you wish to explore the concept of perfect verb tenses before students read the story, refer to the instruction on p. 158.

Customize for
Less Proficient Readers
Have students track significant events in the story, beginning with Rip's hike into the Catskills to hunt squirrels. You may wish to have them use the Series of Events Chain, p. 66 in **Writing and Language Transparencies,** to record each important event. Suggest that students subdivide the boxes by drawing horizontal rules to accommodate all the events.

Customize for
More Advanced Students
Before students read the selection, have them research the Dutch settlement of the Hudson River Valley. Suggest that students jot down facts they learn from their research. As students read, they can add specific information from the story to support the facts they recorded.

Develop Understanding

One-Minute Insight One afternoon, in the mountains near his home, Rip Van Winkle encounters a strange man with a thick beard and unusual clothing. The stranger wants Rip to help him carry a keg up the mountain. Rip helps the man, and they soon come upon a group of odd-looking men playing a game of bowling. As Rip watches the men at their game, he drinks from the keg and soon falls into a deep sleep. He awakens and discovers that he has been asleep for 20 years. Rip is bewildered by the changes, but when he is reunited with his daughter, he settles back into life in the village. Through the story of Rip Van Winkle, Washington Irving reminds readers of what is gained and what is lost through the passage of time.

Team Teaching Strategy

The historical setting of Irving's story provides a strong connection to social studies. You may want to coordinate with a social studies teacher to plan ways of extending instruction.

Customize for *English Language Learners*

Help English language learners understand the meanings of unfamiliar expressions as they read the story. For example, for phrases such as "great antiquity," "insuperable aversion," and "domestic adherent," use more familiar words such as *old, dislike,* and *friend.*

◆Critical Viewing

1 Infer Point out to students that *atmosphere* refers to the general mood established by a work of art or literature. *Students may describe the atmosphere as threatening because of the dark woods, the man's anxious expression, and the dog's fearful look. Most students will predict that the story is about something that happens to the man in the woods.*

Rip Van Winkle

Washington Irving

Rip in the Mountains, Albertus Del Orient Brower, Shelburne Museum, Shelburne, Vermont

1 ▲ Critical Viewing Describe the atmosphere of this painting. What can you learn about Rip Van Winkle from the artist's presentation? **[Infer]**

Whoever has made a voyage up the Hudson must remember the Catskill mountains. They are a branch of the great Appalachian family,[1] and are seen away to the west of the river, swelling up to a noble height, and lording it over the surrounding country. Every change of season, every change of weather, indeed every hour of the day, produces some change in the magical hues and shapes of these mountains, and they are regarded by all the good wives, far and near, as perfect barometers. When the weather is fair and settled, they are clothed in blue and purple, and print their bold outlines on the clear evening sky; but sometimes, when the rest of the landscape is cloudless, they will gather a hood of gray vapors about their summits,

1. **Appalachian** (ap´ ə lā´ chən) **family:** Group of mountains extending from southern Quebec in Canada to northern Alabama.

Block Scheduling Strategies

Consider these suggestions to take advantage of extended class time:

- Have students explore the literary focus of "Rip Van Winkle." Arrange students in small groups. Have them read the story independently. Then allow groups to discuss the details and events that create the historical setting. Reinforce students' understanding of historical setting by having them answer the Literary Focus questions on p. 158 on their own, or by using **Selection Support,** p. 63.
- If you have access to technology, have students work on the *Writer's Solution Language Lab CD-ROM* and *Writer's Solution Writing Lab CD-ROM* to prepare for and complete all or part of the Writing Mini-Lesson. Alternatively, have students complete the activity on p. 12 of **Daily Language Practice.**
- Have students work in small groups on the Projects in the Idea Bank on p. 159, or research the geography and history of the Hudson Valley.

which, in the last rays of the setting sun, will glow and light up like a crown of glory.

At the foot of these fairy mountains, the voyager may have seen the light smoke curling up from a village, whose shingle roofs gleam among the trees, just where the blue tints of the upland melt away into the fresh green of the nearer landscape. It is a little village, of great antiquity, having been founded by some of the Dutch colonists, in the early times of the province, just about the beginning of the government of the good Peter Stuyvesant,[2] (may he rest in peace!) and there were some of the houses of the original settlers standing within a few years,[3] built of small yellow bricks brought from Holland, having latticed windows and gable fronts,[4] surmounted with weathercocks.

In that same village, and in one of these very houses (which, to tell the precise truth, was sadly timeworn and weather-beaten), there lived many years since, while the country was yet ❷ a province of Great Britain, a simple good-natured fellow, of the name of Rip Van Winkle.

> **◆ Reading Strategy**
> Break this sentence into parts. How does the punctuation help you understand it?

He was a descendant of the Van Winkles who figured so gallantly in the chivalrous days of Peter Stuyvesant, and accompanied him to the siege of Fort Christina. He inherited, however, but little of the <u>martial</u> character of his ancestors. I have observed that he was a simple good-natured man; he was, moreover, a kind ❸ neighbor, and an obedient henpecked husband. Indeed, to the latter circumstance might be owing that meekness of spirit which gained him such universal popularity; for those men are most apt to be obsequious and conciliating abroad, who are under the discipline of shrews at home. Their tempers, doubtless, are rendered pliant and malleable in the fiery furnace of <u>domestic</u> tribulation which is worth all the sermons in the world for teaching the virtues of patience and long-suffering. ❸ A termagant[5] wife may, therefore, in some respects, be considered a tolerable blessing; and if so, Rip Van Winkle was thrice blessed.

Certain it is, that he was a great favorite among all the good wives of the village, who, as usual with the amiable sex, took his part in all family squabbles; and never failed, whenever they talked those matters over in their evening gossipings, to lay all the blame on Dame Van Winkle. The children of the village, too, would shout with joy whenever he approached. He assisted at their sports, made their playthings, taught them to fly kites and shoot marbles, and told them long stories of ghosts, witches, and Indians. Whenever he went dodging about the village, he was surrounded by a troop of them, hanging on his skirts, clambering on his back and playing a thousand tricks on him with impunity; and not a dog would bark at him throughout the neighborhood.

The great error in Rip's composition was an insuperable aversion to all kinds of profitable labor. It could not be from the want of perseverance; for he would sit on a wet rock, with a rod as long and heavy as a Tartar's lance,[6] and fish all day without a murmur, even though he should not be encouraged by a single nibble. He

2. **Peter Stuyvesant** (stī′ və sənt): The last governor of New Netherland, a Dutch colony, before it was taken over by the English in 1664 and renamed New York.
3. **within a few years:** Until recently; this story was written during the early part of the 19th century.
4. **gable fronts:** Triangular wall shapes where two roof slopes meet.

5. **termagant** (tər′ mə gənt) *adj.*: Scolding.
6. **Tartar's** (tär′ tərz) **lance:** The Tartars were one of the Mongolian tribes that invaded Europe about 700 years ago; these warriors used lances, which are long, heavy spears.

◆ Build Vocabulary

martial (mär′ shəl) *adj.*: Suitable for war

domestic (dō mes′ tik) *adj.*: Of the home and family

◆Reading Strategy

❷ Break Down Long Sentences
Guide students to use the commas and parentheses in the sentence to identify its separate sections. Suggest that students write the sentence on a sheet of paper, using slashes to break it into manageable parts. Then have a student paraphrase the key ideas in the sentence. *A simple, good-natured fellow named Rip Van Winkle lived in a time-worn, weather-beaten house in the village.*

Comprehension Check ☑

❸ Check to see that students understand Irving's point in this passage. *Rip's mild temperament was forged by his domineering wife.* Encourage students to look up the definitions of *henpecked, obsequious, conciliating, pliant,* and *malleable.* Ask students to explain the narrator's statement that "A termagant wife may . . . be considered a tolerable blessing." Have students discuss whether they agree or disagree with the statement. *Irving is saying that having a scolding wife forces a husband to become patient and tolerant.*

Customize for *Interpersonal Learners*

Have students work with partners to begin a character web on which they list the traits of Rip Van Winkle as presented on this page.

kind

good-natured

Rip Van Winkle

Suggest that students write Rip's name in a center circle and then list character traits and examples that illustrate each trait. Students may want to add to the web as they read the story.

Humanities: Art

Rip in the Mountains, by Albertus Del Orient Brower

Albertus Del Orient Brower (1814–1887) is known for his landscape paintings of the Catskill Mountains and scenes of the California Gold Rush. He is one of several well-known artists, including George Cruikshank, N. C. Wyeth, and Maxfield Parrish, who have been inspired by and illustrated Washington Irving's imaginative stories. The paintings on pp. 146 and 151 were also done by Brower. Encourage students to note the similarity of style in all three paintings.

1. In what ways does the painting support the description of the story's historical setting? *Students may note the wooded mountains rising from the river and the figure wearing old clothing and carrying an old gun.*
2. Who is the person in the painting? What is he doing? *Rip Van Winkle and his dog appear to be listening to a sound in the woods.*
3. Suppose the person shown in the painting appeared in your school. Would he stand out or fit in? Why? *Students may say that he would stand out because of his clothes.*

◆Critical Thinking

❶ Speculate Have students suggest reasons why "Rip was ready to attend to anybody's business but his own . . ." *Some students may say that Rip helps others in order to escape his wife's nagging; others may suggest that Rip helps others because they show more appreciation for his efforts than his wife does.*

◆Critical Thinking

❷ Analyze Discuss the practice of rationalizing, or giving plausible but untrue reasons for one's conduct. Ask students to give examples of rationalizing. Have students review Rip's reasoning in this passage. Then ask students to analyze Rip's complaints about his farm to decide if Rip is giving sound reasoning or is rationalizing. *Students should recognize that Rip is rationalizing. His neglect of his farm is the reason that "everything about it went wrong."*

▶Critical Viewing◀

❸ Infer Ask students who the woman in the picture is and have them speculate about what she is doing. Remind students of what they already know about Rip and his wife as they determine which person is Rip. *The woman is probably Rip's wife, and she is no doubt scolding the men for their laziness. Rip is probably the man walking with the dog and making his escape behind her. Both he and the dog resemble the same figures in Brower's other illustration on p. 144.*

Customize for
Visual/Spatial Learners
After they discuss the critical viewing question on this page, you may want to encourage students to describe what else they see in the painting. Point out that the picture helps readers imagine the historical setting described in the story.

would carry a fowling piece[7] on his shoulder for hours together, trudging through woods and swamps, and up hill and down dale, to shoot a few squirrels or wild pigeons. He would never refuse to assist a neighbor even in the roughest toil, and was a foremost man at all country frolics for husking Indian corn, or building stone fences; the women of the village, too, used to employ him to run their errands, and to do such little odd jobs as their less obliging husbands would not do for them. In a word, Rip was ready to attend to anybody's business but his own;
❶ but as to doing family duty, and keeping his farm in order, he found it impossible.

7. **fowling piece:** Type of shotgun for hunting wild fowl or birds.

In fact, he declared it was of no use to work on his farm; it was the most pestilent[8] little
piece of ground in the whole country; everything ❷
about it went wrong, and would go wrong, in spite of him. His fences were continually falling to pieces; his cow would either go astray, or get among the cabbages; weeds were sure to grow quicker in his fields than anywhere else; the rain always made a point of setting in just as he had some outdoor work to do; so that though his estate had dwindled away under his

8. **pestilent** (pes´ təl ənt) *adj.*: Annoying; troublesome.

▼ Critical Viewing Which person in the painting is Rip? How do you know? **[Infer]** ❸

Rip at the Inn, Albertus Del Orient Brower, Shelburne Museum, Shelburne, Vermont

Cross-Curricular Connection: Social Studies

In 1609, English explorer Henry Hudson claimed the area around what is now known as the Hudson River for the Dutch. Several years later, the Dutch West India Company established the colony of New Netherland in the Hudson River Valley. The Dutch had sailed across the Atlantic Ocean to make money in the fur trade. In 1664, the British took control of New Netherland and renamed the area New York.

Have small groups of students use resources in the school's library or media center to find information about one or more of these topics:

- Algonquian-speaking groups who lived in the Hudson River Valley during the time of the Dutch arrival
- Effect on the area of the French defeat of the British in 1763
- Daily life in Dutch towns in New York during the 1700's

Invite students to give brief oral presentations on topic(s) they researched.

management, acre by acre, until there was little more left than a mere patch of Indian corn and potatoes, yet it was the worst conditioned farm in the neighborhood.

His children, too, were as ragged and wild as if they belonged to nobody. His son Rip, an urchin[9] begotten in his own likeness, promised to inherit the habits, with the old clothes of his father. He was generally seen trooping like a colt at his mother's heels, equipped in a pair of his father's cast-off galligaskins,[10] which he had much ado to hold up with one hand, as a fine lady does her train in bad weather.

Rip Van Winkle, however, was one of those happy mortals, of foolish, well-oiled dispositions, who take the world easy, eat white bread or brown, whichever can be got with least thought or trouble, and would rather starve on a penny than work for a pound.[11] If left to himself, he would have whistled life away in perfect contentment; but his wife kept continually dinning in his ears about his idleness, his carelessness, and the ruin he was bringing on his family. Morning, noon, and night, her tongue was incessantly going, and everything he said or did was sure to produce a torrent of household eloquence. Rip had but one way of replying to all lectures of the kind, and that, by frequent use, had grown into a habit. He shrugged his shoulders, shook his head, cast up his eyes, but said nothing. This, however, always provoked a fresh volley from his wife; so that he was fain[12] to draw off his forces, and take to the outside of the house—the only side which, in truth, belongs to a henpecked husband.

4 Rip's sole domestic adherent was his dog Wolf, who was as much henpecked as his master; for Dame Van Winkle regarded them as companions in idleness, and even looked upon Wolf with an evil eye, as the cause of his master's going so often astray. 4 True it is, in all points of spirit befitting an honorable dog, he was as courageous an animal as ever scoured the woods—but what courage can withstand the ever-enduring and all-besetting terrors of a woman's tongue? The moment Wolf entered the house his crest fell, his tail drooped to the ground or curled between his legs, he sneaked about with a gallows air, casting many a sidelong glance at Dame Van Winkle, and at the least flourish of a broomstick or ladle, he would fly to the door with yelping precipitation.[13]

Times grew worse and worse with Rip Van Winkle as years of matrimony rolled on; a tart temper never mellows with age, and a sharp tongue is the only edged tool that grows keener with constant use. For a long while he used to console himself, when driven from home, by frequenting a kind of perpetual club of the sages, philosophers, and other idle personages of the 5
village; which held its sessions on a bench before a small inn, designated by a portrait of His Majesty George the Third. Here they used to sit in the shade through a long, lazy summer's day, talking listlessly over village gossip, or telling endless sleepy stories about nothing. But it would have been worth any statesman's money to have heard the profound discussions that sometimes took place when by chance an old newspaper fell into their hands from some passing traveler. How solemnly they would listen to 6
the contents, as drawled out by Derrick Van Bummel, the schoolmaster, a dapper, learned little man, who was not to be daunted by the most gigantic word in the dictionary; and how sagely they would deliberate upon public events some months after they had taken place.

The opinions of this group were completely controlled by Nicholas Vedder, a patriarch of the village, and landlord of the inn, at the door of which he took his seat from morning till night,

9. **urchin** (ər´ chin) *n.*: Mischievous boy.
10. **galligaskins** (gal´ i gas´ kinz) *n.*: Loosely fitting breeches worn in the 16th and 17th centuries.
11. **pound** *n.*: British unit of money.
12. **fain** (fān) *adj.*: Old-fashioned word meaning "glad."
13. **precipitation** (pri sip´ ə tā´ shən) *n.*: Great speed.

◆Reading Strategy

4 Break Down Long Sentences Have students reread this sentence and break it down into shorter parts. Invite a volunteer to write the sentence on the board, using brackets and/or slashes to break it down, and then tell the meaning of the sentence. *Students may break down the sentence in this way: Rip's sole domestic adherent was his dog Wolf / [who was as much henpecked / as his master; / for Dame Van Winkle regarded them as companions / in idleness, / and even looked upon Wolf / with an evil eye, / as the cause / of his master's going so often astray.] The sentence says that Rip's dog, who was Rip's only friend in the house, was disliked by Dame Van Winkle, who thought the dog lazy and partly to blame for Rip's idleness.*

◆Literature and Your Life

5 Point out that Rip finds relief from his wife's constant nagging by joining his friends at the village inn. Have students suggest reasons why Rip chooses to console himself in this way. Encourage students to identify with Rip's need to escape by recalling their own ways of escaping from pressure from others. *Students may suggest that Rip goes to the inn because he feels accepted for who he is by his friends and finds pleasure in idle talk and passionate discussions.*

◆Critical Thinking

6 Infer What does this passage seem to indicate about the way news reaches Rip's village during the time of the story? *Students should infer that news comes slowly to the village and that old newspapers appear there only by chance from passing travelers.*

Speaking and Listening Mini-Lesson

Talk Show Appearance

This mini-lesson supports the Speaking and Listening activity in the Idea Bank on p. 159.

Introduce Discuss talk shows that students have seen on television. Explain that although these shows appear casual and spontaneous, much preparation goes into producing the shows.

Develop Arrange students in groups. Instruct them to discuss the various roles for the performance. Have students choose their roles and work together to plan the talk show. Direct them to write a script and a set of instructions for the actors and to select any props they may want to use.

Apply Allow time for students to rehearse the talk show. Then have them perform the show for the rest of the class.

Assess Evaluate students' performances in terms of preparation, characterization, and clarity of speaking. Have students use the Peer Assessment: Dramatic Performance form, p. 107, in **Alternative Assessment,** to evaluate the performances of their classmates.

◆ Literature and Your Life

❶ Suggest that students use the painting on p. 146, as well as the information in this passage, to help them understand the effect of Dame Van Winkle's appearance at the inn. *Students may say that they would feel angry and embarrassed if they were in Rip's place.*

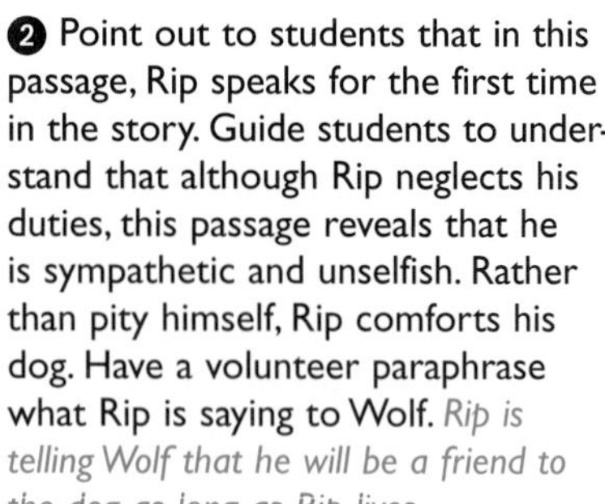

Comprehension Check ☑

❷ Point out to students that in this passage, Rip speaks for the first time in the story. Guide students to understand that although Rip neglects his duties, this passage reveals that he is sympathetic and unselfish. Rather than pity himself, Rip comforts his dog. Have a volunteer paraphrase what Rip is saying to Wolf. *Rip is telling Wolf that he will be a friend to the dog as long as Rip lives.*

◆ Critical Thinking

❸ **Analyze** Have a volunteer read the paragraph aloud. Then ask students to describe the mood that the author conveys in the passage. Have students name words and phrases that help create the mood. *Some students may say that the mood is one of loneliness, citing words and phrases such as* "lonely," "scarcely lighted by the reflected rays of the setting sun," *and* "long blue shadows." *Others may say that the mood is foreboding. They may mention* "deep mountain glen," "heavy sigh," *and* "terrors" *as words and phrases that help set the mood.*

Customize for *Verbal/Linguistic Learners*

Point out the author's vivid description of the landscape in which Rip finds himself at the end of the afternoon. Encourage students to identify other examples of descriptive language in the story. Have volunteers read aloud their favorite descriptive passages from the story.

just moving sufficiently to avoid the sun and keep in the shade of a large tree; so that the neighbors could tell the hour by his movements as accurately as by a sundial. It is true, he was rarely heard to speak, but smoked his pipe incessantly. His adherents, however (for every great man has his adherents), perfectly understood him, and knew how to gather his opinions. When anything that was read or related displeased him, he was observed to smoke his pipe vehemently, and to send forth short, frequent, and angry puffs; but when pleased, he would inhale the smoke slowly and tranquilly, and emit it in light and placid clouds; and sometimes, taking the pipe from his mouth, and letting the fragrant vapor curl about his nose, would gravely nod his head in token of perfect approbation.

From even this stronghold the unlucky Rip was at length routed by his termagant wife, who would suddenly break in upon the
❶ tranquillity of the assemblage and call the members all to naught; nor was that august personage, Nicholas Vedder himself, sacred from the daring tongue of this terrible virago,[14] who charged him outright with encouraging her husband in habits of idleness.

> . . . he saw that it would be dark long before he could reach the village, and he heaved a heavy sigh . . .

Poor Rip was at last reduced almost to despair; and his only alternative, to escape from the labor of the farm and clamor of his wife, was to take gun in hand and stroll away into the woods. Here he would sometimes seat himself at the foot of a tree, and share the contents of his wallet[15] with Wolf, with whom he sympathized
❷ as a fellow-sufferer in persecution. "Poor Wolf," he would say, "thy mistress leads thee a dog's
life of it; but never mind, my lad, whilst I live ❷
thou shalt never want a friend to stand by thee!" Wolf would wag his tail, look wistfully in his master's face, and if dogs can feel pity I verily believe he reciprocated the sentiment with all his heart.

In a long ramble of the kind on a fine autumnal day, Rip had unconsciously scrambled to one of the highest parts of the Catskill mountains. He was after his favorite sport of squirrel shooting, and the still solitudes had echoed and re-echoed with the reports of his gun. Panting and fatigued, he threw himself, late in the afternoon, on a green knoll, covered with mountain herbage, that crowned the brow of a precipice. From an opening between the trees he could overlook all the lower country for many a mile of rich woodland. He saw at a distance the lordly Hudson, far, far below him, moving on its silent but majestic course, with the reflection of a purple cloud, or the sail of a lagging bark,[16] here and there sleeping on its glassy bosom, and at last losing itself in the blue highlands.

On the other side he looked down into a deep mountain glen, wild, lonely, and shagged,[17] the bottom filled with fragments from the
impending[18] cliffs, and scarcely lighted by the ❸
reflected rays of the setting sun. For some time Rip lay musing on this scene; evening was gradually advancing; the mountains began to throw

14. **virago** (vi rā′ gō) *n.*: Quarrelsome woman.
15. **wallet** (wôl′ it) *n.*: Bag for carrying provisions.
16. **bark** (bärk) *n.*: Any boat, especially a small sailing boat.
17. **shagged** (shagd) *adj.*: Shaggy or rough.
18. **impending** (im pend′ iŋ) *adj.*: Overhanging.

Cross-Curricular Connection: Social Studies

The Hudson River rises in the Adirondack Mountains in northeast New York and flows south for 315 miles through the state of New York. It empties into the Atlantic Ocean at New York City. An important commercial waterway, the Hudson is linked by a canal system to the Great Lakes.

The Hudson River was discovered in 1524 by Florentine navigator Giovanni da Verrazano but was explored by Henry Hudson in 1609. For many years before Hudson's arrival, the Algonquins lived in the forests near the river. They called the Hudson "the river that flows two ways," because its tidal waters allowed them to catch both freshwater and saltwater fish.

Have students use a map or a globe to trace the course of the Hudson. Instruct them to list cities and geographical features that appear along the river's course.

3 their long blue shadows over the valleys; he saw that it would be dark long before he could reach the village, and he heaved a heavy sigh when he thought of encountering the terrors of Dame Van Winkle.

As he was about to descend, he heard a voice from a distance hallooing, "Rip Van Winkle! Rip Van Winkle!" He looked round, but could see nothing but a crow winging its solitary flight across the mountain. He thought his fancy[19] must have deceived him, and turned again to descend, when he heard the same cry ring through the still evening air: "Rip Van Winkle!
4 Rip Van Winkle!"—at the same time Wolf bristled up his back, and giving a low growl, skulked to his master's side, looking fearfully down into the glen. Rip now felt a vague apprehension stealing over him; he looked anxiously in the same direction, and perceived a strange figure slowly toiling up the rocks, and bending under the weight of something he carried on his back. He was surprised to see any human being in this lonely and unfrequented place, but sup-
5 posing it to be some one of the neighborhood in need of his assistance, he hastened down to yield it.

On nearer approach he was still more surprised at the singularity of the stranger's appearance. He was a short, square-built old fellow, with thick bushy hair, and a grizzled[20] beard. His dress was of the antique Dutch fashion—a cloth jerkin[21] strapped round the waist—several pairs of breeches, the outer one of ample volume, decorated with rows of buttons down the sides and bunches at the knees. He bore on his shoulder a stout keg, that seemed full of liquor, and made signs for Rip to approach and assist him with the load. Though rather shy and
6 distrustful of this new acquaintance, Rip complied with his usual alacrity; and mutually relieving one another, they clambered up a narrow gully, apparently the dry bed of a mountain 6
torrent. As they ascended, Rip every now and then heard long rolling peals, like distant thunder, that seemed to issue out of a deep ravine, or rather cleft, between lofty rocks, toward which their rugged path conducted. He paused for an instant, but supposing it to be the muttering of one of these transient thundershowers which often take place in mountain heights, he proceeded. Passing through the ravine, they came to a hollow, like a small amphitheater, surrounded by perpendicular precipices, over the brinks of which impending trees shot their branches, so that you only caught glimpses of the azure sky and the bright evening cloud. During the whole time, Rip and his companion had labored on in silence; for though the former marvelled greatly what could be the object of carrying a keg of liquor up this wild mountain, yet there was something strange and incomprehensible about the unknown that inspired awe and checked familiarity.

On entering the amphitheater, new objects of wonder presented themselves. On a level spot in the center was a company of odd-looking per- 7
sonages playing at ninepins. They were dressed in a quaint outlandish fashion; some wore short doublets,[22] others jerkins, with long knives in their belts, and most of them had enormous 8
breeches, of similar style with that of the guide's. Their visages,[23] too, were peculiar; one had a large

> **◆ Literary Focus**
> What details in this paragraph help create the historical setting?

19. **fancy** (fan´ sē) *n.*: Imagination.
20. **grizzled** (griz´ əld) *adj.*: Gray.
21. **jerkin** (jər´ kin) *n.*: Short, closefitting jacket worn in the 16th and 17th centuries.
22. **doublets** (dub´ lits) *n.*: Closefitting jackets.
23. **visages** (viz´ ij iz) *n.*: Faces.

◆ Build Vocabulary

wistfully (wist´ fəl lē) *adv.*: With longing

majestic (mə jes´ tik) *adj.*: Grand; lofty

incomprehensible (in´ käm pri hen´ sə bəl) *adj.*: Not able to be understood

Cultural Connection

Clothing In two events of the story, Rip is perplexed by the clothing worn by people he encounters. The peculiar clothes worn by the men playing ninepins and the unfamiliar fashions worn by villagers he meets after his long sleep surprise and bewilder him. Similarly, when he returns to the village, Rip's clothing and appearance evoke a curious response from those that observe him.

Discuss with students various clothing styles they associate with different periods in American history or with various cultural groups. Link the discussion to the thematic focus, "Fitting In," by talking about the role that fashion plays in defining people's identities and their desire to fit in with others.

Encourage students to look through books and magazines archived at your local library to find examples of clothing styles of the past 50 years. Have students make sketches, or bring to school pictures, of clothing to share with classmates.

◆Critical Thinking

4 **Analyze** Why does Rip become uneasy after he hears his name called in the woods? *Possible answers: He is surprised that another person is in such a remote part of the woods; Wolf's growling and skulking make Rip anxious; Rip does not recognize the figure in the distance.*

◆Critical Thinking

5 **Make a Judgment** In spite of Rip's apprehension, he hurries toward the stranger. What does this reveal about Rip's character? *Students may suggest that Rip is willing to take risks to help another person.*

◆Critical Thinking

6 **Analyze** Point out that *alacrity* means "promptness of response" or "cheerful readiness." Ask students why Rip cheerfully responds to the stranger's signal for help, even though he distrusts the stranger. *Some students may say that Rip is always ready to help others, no matter what the circumstance; others may say that he helps the man because his curiosity is stronger than his distrust.*

Clarification

7 The game of ninepins is a form of bowling, one of the oldest and most popular indoor sports. Archaeological evidence suggests that people have competed in bowling for thousands of years. In ninepins, the bowler rolls the ball at nine wooden pins set in a diamond formation. The game is popular in northern Europe. The Dutch brought their version of the game with them to the Hudson River Valley in the 1600's.

◆Literary Focus

8 **Historical Setting** *The descriptions of the clothing worn by the characters are of historical dress.*

Customize for *English Language Learners*

Have native speakers help English learners with unfamiliar words and phrases by using facial expressions, gestures, and body language to pantomime meanings of words and phrases on this page such as *descend, bristled up his back, skulked, toiling,* and *hastened.* For example, for *skulked,* students might hunch the shoulders and crouch, with a fearful or anxious expression.

◆Critical Thinking

❶ **Connect** What evidence suggests that the odd-looking men are from an earlier time? *The men's general appearance reminds Rip of figures in an old painting he has seen in the village parson's parlor.*

◆Critical Thinking

❷ **Infer** Ask students why they think the men playing ninepins are so silent and melancholy. *Students may perceive that the men "maintained the gravest face" because they are indeed ghosts who have returned from the grave for a special purpose.*

Clarification

❸ Thunder Mountain in the Catskills is thought to be the setting for Rip's encounter. The sound of rolling balls crashing against ninepins is one of many mythical explanations of what causes thunder. Some primitive people thought that thunder was the roar of angry gods. Thunder is really caused by the violent expansion of the air after it has been heated by lightning.

◆Literary Focus

❹ **Historical Setting** Have students describe the change in setting that is set in motion by Rip's actions in this passage. You may want to play the recording of this passage to emphasize its importance as a turning point in the story. *Drinking the stranger's beverage causes Rip to fall into his long sleep.*

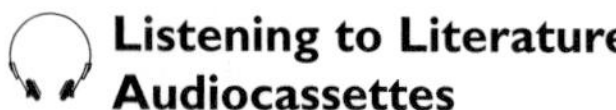

Listening to Literature Audiocassettes

Customize for
Bodily/Kinesthetic Learners
Encourage students to pantomime the passage in which Rip and the stranger approach the men playing ninepins and Rip is signaled to wait on the men. Before students reenact the scene, guide them to use context to determine that *smote* (the past tense of *smite*) means "struck." Rip's knees are knocking together.

beard, broad face, and small piggish eyes; the face of another seemed to consist entirely of nose, and was surmounted by a white sugar-loaf hat,[24] set off with a little red cock's tail. They all had beards, of various shapes and colors. There was one who seemed to be the commander. He was a stout old gentleman, with a weather-beaten countenance,[25] he wore a laced doublet, broad belt and hanger,[26] high-crowned hat and feather, red stockings, and high-heeled shoes, with roses in them. The whole group reminded Rip of the figures in an old Flemish[27] ❶ painting, in the parlor of Dominie Van Shaick, the village parson, and which had been brought over from Holland at the time of the settlement.

What seemed particularly odd to Rip was, that though these folks were evidently amusing ❷ themselves, yet they maintained the gravest face, the most mysterious silence, and were, withal, the most melancholy party of pleasure he had ever witnessed. Nothing interrupted the stillness of the scene but the noise of the balls, ❸ which, whenever they were rolled, echoed along the mountains like rumbling peals of thunder.

As Rip and his companion approached them, they suddenly desisted from their play, and stared at him with such fixed, statuelike gaze, and such strange, lackluster[28] countenances, that his heart turned within him, and his knees smote together. His companion, now emptied the contents of the keg into large flagons,[29] and made signs to him to wait upon the company. He obeyed with fear and trembling; they quaffed[30] the liquor in profound silence, and then returned to their game.

By degrees Rip's awe and apprehension subsided. He even ventured, when no eye was fixed upon him, to taste the beverage, which he found had much of the flavor of excellent Hollands.[31] He was naturally a thirsty soul, and was soon tempted to repeat the draft. One taste provoked another; and he reiterated his visits to the flagon so often that at length his senses were overpowered, his eyes swam in his head, his head gradually declined, and he fell into a deep sleep.

On waking, he found himself on the green knoll whence he had first seen the old man of ❹ the glen. He rubbed his eyes—it was a bright sunny morning. The birds were hopping and twittering among the bushes, and the eagle was wheeling aloft, and breasting the pure mountain breeze. "Surely," thought Rip, "I have not slept here all night." He recalled the occurrences before he fell asleep. The strange man with a keg of liquor—the mountain ravine—the wild retreat among the rocks—the woebegone party at ninepins—the flagon— "Oh! that flagon! that wicked flagon!" thought Rip— "what excuse shall I make to Dame Van Winkle?"

He looked round for his gun, but in place of the clean, well-oiled fowling piece, he found an old firelock lying by him, the barrel incrusted with rust, the lock falling off, and the stock worm-eaten. He now suspected that the grave roysters[32] of the mountain had put a trick upon him, and having dosed him with liquor, had robbed him of his gun. Wolf, too, had disappeared, but he might have strayed away after a squirrel or partridge. He whistled after him and shouted his name, but all in vain; the echoes repeated his whistle and shout, but no dog was to be seen.

He determined to revisit the scene of the last evening's gambol,[33] and if he met with any of

---

24. **sugar-loaf hat:** Hat shaped like a cone.
25. **countenance** (koun´ tə nəns) *n.*: Face.
26. **hanger** (haŋ´ ər) *n.*: Short sword that hangs from the belt.
27. **Flemish** (flem´ ish) *adj.*: Referring to the former country of Flanders in northwest Europe.
28. **lackluster** (lak´ lus´ tər) *adj.*: Lacking brightness; dull.
29. **flagons** (flag´ ənz) *n.*: Containers for liquids with a handle, narrow neck, spout, and sometimes a lid.
30. **quaffed** (kwäft) *v.*: Drank in a thirsty way.
31. **Hollands** *n.*: Drink made in the Netherlands.
32. **roysters** (rois´ tərs) *n.*: People who are having a good time at a party.
33. **gambol** (gam´ bəl) *n.*: Play; frolic.

the party, to demand his dog and gun. As he rose to walk, he found himself stiff in the joints, and wanting in his usual activity. "These mountain beds do not agree with me," thought Rip,
5 "and if this frolic should lay me up with a fit of the rheumatism, I shall have a blessed time with Dame Van Winkle." With some difficulty he got down into the glen: he found the gully up which he and his companion had ascended the preceding evening; but to his astonishment a
6 mountain stream was now foaming down it, leaping from rock to rock, and filling the glen with babbling murmurs. He, however, made shift to scramble up its sides, working his toilsome way through thickets of birch, sassafras, and witch hazel, and sometimes tripped up or 6
entangled by the wild grapevines that twisted their coils or tendrils from tree to tree, and spread a kind of network in his path.

At length he reached to where the ravine had opened through the cliffs to the amphitheater; 8
but no traces of such opening remained. The

◆ Build Vocabulary

melancholy (mel´ ən käl´ ē) *adj.*: Sad; gloomy

declined (dē klīnd´) *v.*: Bent or sank downward

7 ▼ Critical Viewing What has changed about Rip's appearance in this painting? **[Analyze]**

Rip Van Winkle Asleep, Albertus Del Orient Brower, Shelburne Museum, Shelburne, Vermont

Clarification

5 Rheumatism is a term for various conditions characterized by pain or inflammation in joints, muscles, or fibrous tissue of the body.

◆Literature and Your Life

6 Point out that Rip begins to try to make sense of what has happened since his evening with the odd-looking men. His first reaction is to look for logical explanations. Suggest that students consider their own reactions when presented with a mystery or a problem. Do they respond with logic, or do they let their minds think in new ways? Invite volunteers to give examples of both ways of thinking to solve a problem.

▶Critical Viewing◀

7 **Analyze** Have students contrast the images of Rip in the paintings on pp. 144 and 146 with the image in this painting. *Students will notice that Rip's hair has turned white and that he has grown a mustache and beard. They may also note that Rip's face appears older and that his clothes are tattered.*

Comprehension Check ☑

8 Check to be sure that students understand that Rip has retraced his steps from the previous "night." Rip is seeking the place where he first encountered the men playing ninepins. You may want to have students "retrace their steps" by rereading the passage on the previous page that begins "On waking . . ." Students should understand that Rip awakens in a different part of the forest from where he fell asleep.

Humanities: Art

Rip Van Winkle Asleep, by Albertus Del Orient Brower

Along with the paintings on pp. 144 and 146, Brower's artwork virtually illustrates "Rip Van Winkle." Brower obviously was intrigued by the story. Use the following questions for discussion:

1. Compare and contrast the natural setting of this painting with that in the painting on p. 144. *In general, the setting is similar, with nearly the same view of the river. The trees and greenery are similar. Rip's immediate surroundings differ, though. The woods in the painting on p. 144 are darker and denser; the ground is cluttered with more rocks and tree trunks.*
2. What might a caption for this painting say? Students may suggest captions such as these: *"Rip sleeps soundly, unaware that he has become an old man 'overnight.'" "Rip is on the verge of a rude awakening."*
3. What might the artist be saying about the passage of time? *Students may suggest he is saying that time changes humans more dramatically than it changes nature.*

◆Literature and Your Life

❶ Invite students to tell how they might feel if they were in Rip's place at this moment. *Students may say that they would feel bewildered or confused. They may elaborate by saying that they would wonder if they had imagined the encounter with the strange men and were losing their minds.*

▶Critical Viewing◀

❷ **Connect** You may wish to have students read p. 153 before answering this question. *The villagers mock Rip and a dog barks at him; the Catskills are visible in the distance; a large, rickety wooden building with a sign identifying it as the Union Hotel stands in the background, its windows broken and mended; a flag with stars and stripes flies from a pole; the sign at the former inn features a likeness of George Washington; a man in the foreground has handbills in his pockets.*

◆Critical Thinking

❸ **Connect** Ask students to describe how the villagers' first impressions of Rip mirror Rip's feelings at seeing them. *Students may say that Rip is a stranger to them as they are to him. If the villagers' clothes seem unfamiliar to Rip, Rip's clothing must look strange to them.*

rocks presented a high impenetrable wall, over which the torrent came tumbling in a sheet of feathery foam, and fell into a broad deep basin, black from the shadows of the surrounding forest. Here, then, poor Rip was brought to a stand. He again called and whistled after his dog; he was only answered by the cawing of a flock of idle crows, sporting high in air about a dry tree that overhung a sunny precipice; and who, secure in their elevation, seemed to look down and scoff at the poor man's perplexities. What was to be done? The morning was passing away, and Rip felt famished for want of his breakfast. He grieved to give up his dog and gun; he dreaded to meet his wife; but it would not do to starve among the mountains. He shook his head, shouldered the rusty firelock, and with a heart full of trouble and anxiety, turned his steps homeward. ❶

As he approached the village he met a number of people, but none whom he knew, which somewhat surprised him, for he had thought himself acquainted with everyone in the country round. Their dress, too, was of a different fashion from that to which he was accustomed. They all stared at him with equal marks of surprise, ❸

❷ ▼ **Critical Viewing** Which details in this painting relate to details in the story? **[Connect]**

Return of Rip Van Winkle, 1849, John Quidor, National Gallery of Art, Washington, DC

Humanities: Art

Return of Rip Van Winkle, c. 1849, by John Quidor

John Quidor (1801–1881), born in Tappan, New York, is known for his imaginative scenes inspired by literary themes. Washington Irving was a personal friend of Quidor. The romantic style of Quidor's painting was unpopular during his time. As a result, he was forced to support himself by painting signs, banners, and fire engines. Today, Quidor is considered one of America's most original painters and his work is appreciated for its humor and vitality.

This painting depicts a disheveled and confused Rip walking into town. The Dutch-styled buildings in the background are appropriate to old New York. On the right flies an American flag, symbolic of the changes that have taken place during Rip's 20-year sleep.

1. What might Rip be saying in this scene? *Students may say that Rip is trying to explain who he is and what has happened.*
2. What do the faces of the villagers reveal about their feelings toward Rip? *They seem to be amused by the old man.*

3 and whenever they cast their eyes upon him, invariably stroked their chins. The constant recurrence of this gesture induced Rip, invol-
4 untarily, to do the same, when, to his astonishment, he found his beard had grown a foot long!

He had now entered the outskirts of the village. A troop of strange children ran at his heels, hooting after him, and pointing at his gray beard. The dogs, too, not one of which he recognized for an old acquaintance, barked at him as he passed. The very village was altered; it was larger and more populous. There were rows of houses which he had never seen before, and those which had been his familiar haunts had disappeared. Strange names were over the doors—strange faces at the windows—every thing was strange. His mind now misgave him; he began to doubt whether both he and the world around him were not bewitched. Surely this was his native village, which he had left but the day before. There stood the Catskill mountains—there ran the silver Hudson at a dis-
5 tance—there was every hill and dale precisely as it had always been—Rip was sorely perplexed—"That flagon last night," thought he; "has addled[34] my poor head sadly!"

It was with some difficulty that he found the way to his own house, which he approached with silent awe, expecting every moment to hear the shrill voice of Dame Van Winkle. He found the house gone to decay—the roof fallen in, the windows shattered, and the doors off the hinges. A half-starved dog that looked like Wolf was skulking about it. Rip called him by name, but the cur snarled, showed his teeth, and passed on. This was an unkind cut indeed—"My very dog," sighed poor Rip, "has forgotten me!"

He entered the house, which, to tell the truth, Dame Van Winkle had always kept in neat order. It was empty, forlorn, and apparently abandoned. This desolateness overcame all his
6 fears—he called loudly for his wife and children —the lonely chambers rang for a moment with his voice, and then all again was silence.

He now hurried forth, and hastened to his old resort, the village inn—but it too was gone. A large rickety wooden building stood in its place, with great gaping windows, some of them broken and mended with old hats and petticoats, and over the door was painted, "The Union Hotel, by Jonathan Doolittle." Instead of the great tree that used to shelter the quiet little Dutch inn of yore, there now was reared a tall, naked pole, with something on the top that looked like a red nightcap,[35] and from it was fluttering a flag, on which was a singular assemblage of stars and stripes—all this was strange and incomprehensible. He recognized on the sign, however, the ruby face of King George, under which he had smoked so many a peaceful pipe; but even this was singularly metamorphosed.[36] The red coat was changed for one of blue and buff, a sword was held in the hand instead of a scepter, the head was decorated with a cocked hat, and underneath was painted in large characters, GENERAL WASHINGTON. 7

> **◆ Literary Focus**
> What historical changes seem to have taken place since Rip was here last? How do you know?

There was, as usual, a crowd of folk about the door, but none that Rip recollected. The very character of the people seemed changed. There was a busy, bustling, disputatious tone about it, instead of the accustomed drowsy tranquillity. He looked in vain for the sage Nicholas Vedder, with his broad face, double chin, and fair long pipe, uttering clouds of tobacco smoke instead of idle speeches; or Van Bummel, the schoolmaster, doling forth the contents of an ancient newspaper. In places of these, a lean, bilious-looking[37] fellow, with his pockets full

34. **addled** (ad´ əld) *v.*: Muddled and confused.

35. **red nightcap:** Liberty cap, used by colonists to symbolize their freedom from Great Britain.

36. **metamorphosed** (met´ ə môr´ fōzd) *v.*: Changed.

37. **bilious** (bil´ yəs) **-looking** *adj.*: Looking cross or bad-tempered.

◆Build Grammar Skills

4 Verb Tenses Point out the verb *had grown.* Explain that this verb is in the past perfect tense. The past perfect shows a past action that ended before another action began. Challenge students to find two additional examples of the use of the past perfect tense on pages 151 and 152. *The first example is* had opened, *in the sentence that begins "At length he reached . . ."; the second example is* had thought, *in the sentence that begins "As he approached the village . . ."*

◆Critical Thinking

5 Interpret What are the only things that seem not to have changed in Rip's world? *The Catskill Mountains, the Hudson River, and the surrounding hills and dales are unchanged.*

◆Critical Thinking

6 Analyze Why does Rip call for his wife and children? *Rip feels sad and lonely when he realizes that he has apparently lost everything that was familiar to him.*

◆Literary Focus

7 Historical Setting *The Revolutionary War has been fought since Rip was in the village. Signs of this include the name of the hotel, the liberty cap on the flagpole, the United States flag, the face of George Washington on the tavern's swinging sign, and the man with handbills promoting citizens' rights.*

Customize for *English Language Learners*

As students continue to read, help them paraphrase and break down longer sentences. For example, the sentence on this page that begins "Instead of the great tree . . ." might be paraphrased as, "The tree near the inn was gone. In its place was a tall pole. A red cap was on top of the pole. A flag with stars and stripes fluttered from the pole. All these changes were hard to understand."

Cross-Curricular Connection: Social Studies

The American Revolution lasted from 1775 to 1783. As a result of the war, 13 colonies on the Atlantic seaboard of North America won independence from Great Britain and became the United States.

Washington Irving's father was a veteran of the Revolutionary War. He named his youngest son after his commander-in-chief George Washington.

In order for students to understand the changes that took place during Rip's sleep, have them work in small groups to research the events and climate of the American Revolution and the period of time following the war. Suggest that they focus their research on finding answers to questions such as these:

- What factors led to the American Revolution?
- Who were the important leaders in the Revolution? Why were they important?
- What political structure was established in the United States following the American Revolution?

◆Reading Strategy

❶ Break Down Long Sentences Have students use brackets and slashes to break down the sentence that begins "Rip was equally at a loss . . ." Invite a volunteer to write the sentence on the board and show a way to break it down into shorter sections. *One possible way to break down the sentence is "Rip was [equally] at a loss / to comprehend the question; / when a [knowing / self-important / old] gentleman, [in a sharp cocked hat,] made his way / through the crowd, [putting them to the right and left / with his elbows / as he passed,] and planting himself / before Van Winkle, [with one arm akimbo, / the other resting on his cane, / his keen eyes and sharp hat penetrating, / as it were, / into his very soul,] demanded [in an austere tone,] 'what brought him / to the election/with a gun on his shoulder, / and a mob at his heels. / and whether he meant to breed a riot / in the village?'"*

◆Critical Thinking

❷ Analyze Cause and Effect Discuss with students why the townspeople may be suspicious of Rip. Help them analyze why the bystanders call Rip a tory and a spy. *The bystanders think that Rip is on the side of the British, who, until the Revolutionary War, ruled Rip's colony. Rip describes himself as "a loyal subject of the king," because at the time he fell asleep, he and everyone else in the village were British subjects.*

Customize for
Visual/Spatial Learners
Have students relate the images in the painting on p. 152 to the description of Rip's confrontation by the villagers. Ask them to identify the "knowing, self-important old gentleman" in the painting.

of handbills, was speaking vehemently about rights of citizens—elections—members of Congress—liberty—Bunker's Hill—heroes of seventy-six—and other words, which were a perfect Babylonish jargon[38] to the bewildered Van Winkle.

The appearance of Rip, with his long grizzled beard, his rusty fowling piece, his uncouth dress, and an army of women and children at his heels, soon attracted the attention of the tavern politicians. They crowded round him, eyeing him from head to foot with great curiosity. The orator bustled up to him, and, drawing him partly aside, inquired "on which side he voted?" Rip stared in vacant stupidity. Another short but busy little fellow pulled him by the arm, and, rising on tiptoe, inquired in his ear, "whether he was Federal or Democrat?"[39] Rip was equally at a loss to comprehend the question; when a knowing, self-important old gentleman in a sharp cocked hat made his way through the crowd, putting them to the right and left with his elbows as he passed, and
❶ planting himself before Van Winkle, with one arm akimbo,[40] the other resting on his cane, his keen eyes and sharp hat penetrating, as it were, into his very soul, demanded, in an austere tone, "what brought him to the election with a gun on his shoulder, and a mob at his heels, and whether he meant to breed a riot in the village?" "Alas! gentlemen," cried Rip, somewhat dismayed, "I am a poor, quiet man, a native of the place, and a loyal subject of the king, God bless him!"

> "Rip's heart died away at hearing of these sad changes in his home and friends, and finding himself thus alone in the world."

Here a general shout burst from the bystanders— "A tory![41] a tory! a spy! a refugee! hustle him! away with him!" It was with great ❷ difficulty that the self-important man in the cocked hat restored order; and, having assumed a tenfold austerity of brow, demanded again of the unknown culprit, what he came there for, and whom he was seeking. The poor man humbly assured him that he meant no harm, but merely came there in search of some of his neighbors, who used to keep about the tavern.

"Well, who are they? Name them."

Rip bethought himself a moment, and inquired, "Where's Nicholas Vedder?"

There was a silence for a little while, when an old man replied, in a thin, piping voice, "Nicholas Vedder! why, he is dead and gone these eighteen years! There was a wooden tombstone in the churchyard that used to tell all about him, but that's rotten and gone too."

"Where's Brom Dutcher?"

"Oh, he went off to the army in the beginning of the war; some say he was killed at the storming of Stony Point[42]—others say he was drowned in a squall at the foot of Antony's Nose.[43] I don't know—he never came back again."

"Where's Van Bummel, the schoolmaster?"

38. **Babylonish** (bab´ ə lō´ nish) **jargon:** Language he could not understand.
39. **Federal or Democrat:** Two political parties.
40. **akimbo** (ə kim´ bō) *adj.*: Hand on hip, with elbow pointing outward.
41. **tory** (tôr´ ē): Person who supported the British during the American Revolution.
42. **Stony Point:** Town on the Hudson River where a Revolutionary War battle was fought in 1779.
43. **Antony's Nose:** Mountain on the Hudson River.

Beyond the Classroom

Career Connection

Members of Congress Rip learns that his friend Derrick Van Bummel is now in Congress. Explain that in the United States, Congress is the legislative branch of the federal government, composed of the House of Representatives and the Senate. Senators and representatives to Congress are elected to promote and uphold the interests of those they represent.

Have students contact the office of a United States senator or representative by phone, mail, or e-mail to find out about duties and responsibilities of a member of Congress. Ask students to take notes and give presentations to the class on what they learn.

Ask students to think about whether they would like to serve as a member of Congress. Have them write a paragraph in which they express their thoughts about this suggestion, giving reasons for their responses.

"He went off to the wars, too, was a great militia general, and is now in Congress."

Rip's heart died away at hearing of these sad changes in his home and friends, and finding himself thus alone in the world. Every answer puzzled him too, by treating of such enormous lapses of time, and of matters which he could not understand; war—Congress—Stony Point—he had no courage to ask after any more friends, but cried out in despair, "Does nobody here know Rip Van Winkle?"

"Oh, Rip Van Winkle!" exclaimed two or three, "Oh, to be sure! that's Rip Van Winkle yonder, leaning against the tree."

Rip looked, and beheld a precise counterpart of himself, as he went up the mountain: apparently as lazy, and certainly as ragged. The poor fellow was now completely confounded. He doubted his own identity, and whether he was himself or another man. In the midst of his bewilderment, the man in the cocked hat demanded who he was, and what was his name.

3 "Goodness knows," exclaimed he, at his wit's end; "I'm not myself—I'm somebody else—that's me yonder—no—that's somebody else got into my shoes—I was myself last night, but I fell asleep on the mountain, and they've changed my gun, and everything's changed, and I'm changed, and I can't tell what's my name, or who I am!"

The bystanders began now to look at each other, nod, wink significantly, and tap their fingers against their foreheads. There was a whisper, also, about securing the gun, and keeping the old fellow from doing mischief, at the very suggestion of which the self-important man in the cocked hat retired with some precipitation. At this critical moment a fresh, comely[44] woman pressed through the throng to get a peep at the gray-bearded man. She had a chubby child in her arms, which, frightened at his looks, began to cry, "Hush, Rip," cried she, "hush, you little fool; the old man won't hurt you." The name of the child, the air of the mother, the tone of her voice, all awakened a train of recollections in his mind. "What is your name, my good woman?" asked he.

"Judith Gardenier."

"And your father's name?"

"Ah! poor man, Rip Van Winkle was his name, but it's twenty years since he went away from home with his gun and never has been heard of since—his dog came home without him; but whether he shot himself, or was carried away by the Indians, nobody can tell. I was then but a little girl."

Rip had but one question more to ask; but he put it with a faltering voice:

> ◆ **Literature and Your Life**
> Why do you think Rip asks about his wife in a "faltering" voice?

"Where's your mother?" 4

"Oh, she too had died but a short time since; she broke a blood vessel in a fit of passion at a New England peddler."

There was a drop of comfort, at least, in this intelligence.[45] The honest man could contain himself no longer. He caught his daughter and her child in his arms. "I am your father!" cried he— "Young Rip Van Winkle once—old Rip Van Winkle now! Does nobody know poor Rip Van Winkle?"

All stood amazed, until an old woman, tottering out from among the crowd, put her hand to her brow, and peering under it in his face for a moment, exclaimed, "Sure enough! it is Rip Van 5 Winkle—it is himself! Welcome home again, old neighbor. Why where have you been these twenty long years?"

Rip's story was soon told, for the whole twenty long years had been to him but as one night. The neighbors stared when they heard it; some were seen to wink at each other, and put their tongues in their cheeks: and the self-important man in the cocked hat, who, when

44. comely (kum´ lē) *adj.*: Attractive; pretty.

45. intelligence (in tel´ ə jəns) *n.*: News.

◆Critical Thinking

3 Analyze Why does Rip seem confused about who he is? *Students may need to reread the previous two paragraphs to understand that the villagers have identified another person as Rip Van Winkle. Noticing that this person looks very much like he did on the day he went up the mountain, Rip is now thoroughly confused about his own identity.*

◆Literature and Your Life

4 Make sure that students understand that a *faltering* voice is one that wavers, stammers, or is weak. Invite volunteers to read aloud Rip's question about his wife, demonstrating the way Rip might have asked the question. *Rip's voice falters because he fears that his wife may still be alive.*

◆Critical Thinking

5 Draw Conclusions How do you think Rip feels at this point in the story? *Students may conclude that Rip feels happy, relieved, and reassured that he has not lost his identity.*

Customize for
Interpersonal Learners
Invite several students to perform a dramatic reading of the passage that begins "Goodness knows . . ." and ends with Rip's welcome home by the old woman who recognizes him. Have students read the parts of the narrator, Rip, Rip's daughter, and the old woman. Suggest that students read through the passage together once and then present the reading for the class.

Viewing and Representing Mini-Lesson

Creating a Storyboard

Through this mini-lesson, students will demonstrate and reinforce their understanding of key events in the story.

Introduce Explain that a storyboard is a planning tool for a movie, television show, or commercial. It consists of a series of panels or sketches arranged to show important scenes.

Develop Have students create storyboards that show main events in the plot for a movie version of "Rip Van Winkle." Ask students to write a caption below each picture. Reassure students that the drawings do not need to be elaborate. They can use simple shapes to indicate figures in the panels.

Apply Provide students with posterboard and markers to create their storyboards. After students are done, invite volunteers to display their storyboards for the class and explain what each panel represents.

Assess Evaluate students' storyboards based on how well students cover and explain key events in the story.

◆Literature and Your Life

❶ Peter Vanderdonk, the oldest resident of the village, corroborates Rip's story about the strange-looking men. In what ways can a community's older inhabitants influence the community? *They can serve as a community's "memory" because they have witnessed more changes over the years than have younger members of the community. They can also be sources of advice and wisdom to younger members of the community.*

Clarification

❷ Henry Hudson was the first explorer along the Hudson River, which was named after him. The *Half-Moon* is the name of the ship that he sailed from Holland to North America.

Comprehension Check

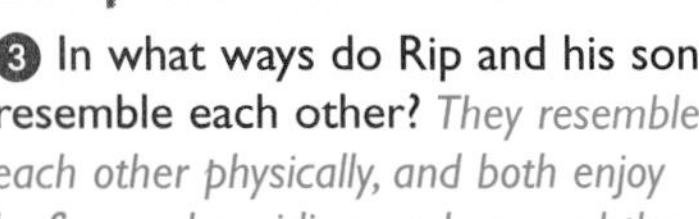

❸ In what ways do Rip and his son resemble each other? *They resemble each other physically, and both enjoy loafing and avoiding work around the house.*

◆Critical Thinking

❹ **Draw Conclusions** Why might Rip prefer the company of younger people? *Students may conclude that in Rip's mind, he is 20 years younger than his former cronies. Although Rip's body aged during the 20 years he was asleep, his mind may not have aged at all.*

◆Literary Focus

❺ **Historical Setting** *The passage indicates that there has been a revolutionary war, that Rip is no longer a subject of the king of England, and that he is a citizen of the United States.*

the alarm was over, had returned to the field, screwed down the corners of his mouth, and shook his head—upon which there was a general shaking of the head throughout the assemblage.

It was determined, however, to take the opinion of old Peter Vanderdonk, who was seen slowly advancing up the road. He was a descendant of the historian of that name, who wrote one of the earliest accounts of the province. Peter was the most ancient inhabitant of the village, and well versed in all the wonderful events and traditions of the neighborhood. He recollected Rip at once, and corroborated his
❶ story in the most satisfactory manner. He assured the company that it was a fact, handed down from his ancestor the historian, that the Catskill mountains had always been haunted by strange beings. That it was affirmed that
❷ the great Henry Hudson, the first discoverer of the river and country,[46] kept a kind of vigil there every twenty years, with his crew of the *Half-Moon;* being permitted in this way to revisit the scenes of his enterprise, and keep a guardian eye upon the river, and the great city called by his name. That his father had once seen them in their old Dutch dresses playing at ninepins in a hollow of the mountain; and that he himself had heard, one summer afternoon, the sound of their balls, like distant peals of thunder.

To make a long story short, the company broke up, and returned to the more important concerns of the election. Rip's daughter took him home to live with her; she had a snug, well-furnished house, and a stout, cheery farmer for a husband, whom Rip recollected for one of the urchins that used to climb upon his back. As to Rip's son and heir, who was the ditto of himself, seen leaning against the tree, he was employed
❸ to work on the farm; but evinced an hereditary disposition to attend to anything else but his business.

Rip now resumed his old walks and habits; he soon found many of his former cronies, though all rather the worse for the wear and
tear of time; and preferred making friends ❹
among the rising generation, with whom he soon grew into great favor.

Having nothing to do at home, and being arrived at that happy age when a man can be idle with impunity, he took his place once more on the bench at the inn door, and was reverenced as one of the patriarchs of the village, and a chronicle of the old times "before the war." It was some time before he could get into the regular track of gossip, or could be made to comprehend the strange events that had taken place during his torpor. How that there had been a revolutionary war—that the country had thrown off the yoke of old England—and that, instead of being a subject of his Majesty George the Third, he was now a free
citizen of the United States. ❺
Rip, in fact, was no politician; the changes of states and empires made but little impression on him; but there was one species of despotism under which he had long groaned, and that was—petticoat government. Happily that was at an end; he had got his neck out of the yoke of matrimony, and could go in and out whenever he pleased, without dreading the tyranny of Dame Van Winkle. Whenever her name was mentioned, however, he shook his head, shrugged his shoulders, and cast up his eyes; which might pass either for an expression of resignation to his fate, or joy at his deliverance.

> ◆ **Literary Focus**
> What clues in this passage show the story's historical setting?

He used to tell his story to every stranger that arrived at Mr. Doolittle's hotel. He was observed, at first, to vary on some points every time he told it, which was, doubtless, owing to his having so recently awaked. It at last settled down precisely to the tale I have related, and not a man, woman, or child in the neighborhood, but

46. **country:** Area around the Catskills.

Cross-Curricular Connection: Social Studies

Henry Hudson Point out to students that Henry Hudson (c. 1565–1611) was an English sea captain. In 1609, he led an expedition to North America for the Netherlands. Hudson explored what are now known as New York Harbor and the Hudson River.

The year after Hudson claimed the Hudson River Valley for the Dutch, he explored northern Canada for the English. When Hudson sailed into an icy bay, the crew feared for their lives and asked Hudson to turn back. When Hudson refused, the crew mutinied, setting their captain adrift in an open boat in Hudson Bay. No trace of Hudson was ever found.

Have students research more about the adventurer and explorer, Henry Hudson. We suggest the following Web site, although it is subject to change:
http://www.georgian.net/rally/hudson

We *strongly recommend* that you preview this site before you send students to it. When students have completed their research, discuss how Hudson became a legend to the old Dutch inhabitants of the Hudson River Valley.

6 knew it by heart. Some always pretended to doubt the reality of it, and insisted that Rip had been out of his head, and that this was one point on which he always remained flighty. The old Dutch inhabitants, however, almost universally gave it full credit. Even to this day they never hear a thunderstorm of a summer afternoon about the Catskills, but they say Henry Hudson and his crew are at their game of ninepins; and it is a common wish of all henpecked husbands in the neighborhood, when life hangs heavy on their hands, that they might have a quieting draft out of Rip Van Winkle's flagon. 6

Guide for Responding

◆ Literature and Your Life

Reader's Response Which part of the story did you find the most entertaining? Explain.

Thematic Focus Rip was well liked before he disappeared for twenty years. How did his absence affect his relationships with other people?

Journal Writing At the end of the story, Rip fits in better with young people than he does with his old friends. Write a journal entry to explore why this may have been so.

☑ Check Your Comprehension

1. Describe the "great error" in Rip's character.
2. Why does Rip go for a walk in the mountains?
3. Summarize what happens between the time Rip sets out and the time he returns to the village.
4. (a) What is Rip's reaction when he reenters the village? (b) How do the villagers react to Rip?
5. According to the story, what really happened to Rip in the mountains?

◆ Critical Thinking

Interpret

1. Why do Rip and his wife have such a stormy marriage? **[Analyze]**
2. A sentence in the story says that a quarrelsome wife may be considered a blessing. What does this mean? **[Interpret]**
3. How do Dame Van Winkle's personality and Rip's personality differ? **[Contrast]**
4. Compare and contrast Rip's life after his long sleep with his earlier life. **[Compare and Contrast]**
5. Reread the last sentence of the story. What might be Irving's purpose in ending the story with this statement? **[Analyze]**

Evaluate

6. How might Rip's life have been different if his wife and he had been more suited to each other? **[Hypothesize]**

Apply

7. Major historic changes take place while Rip is asleep. Imagine that you were to fall into a similar sleep. What changes in the country and in the world do you think you would discover when you awoke? **[Social Studies Link]**

Beyond the Selection

FURTHER READING

Other Works by Washington Irving

"The Legend of Sleepy Hollow"
The Sketch Book
Tales of a Traveller
A Tour on the Prairies

INTERNET

We suggest the following sites on the Internet (all Web sites are subject to change).

For additional information about Washington Irving and the Hudson River Valley setting of "Rip Van Winkle":
http://www.hudsonriver.com/history.htm
http://www.hudsonvalley.org/

We *strongly recommend* that you preview these sites before you send students to them.

◆ Critical Thinking

6 Analyze Ask students whether they think Irving intended his tale to be serious or entertaining. *Students may see the ending, stated almost like a moral, as an indication that the story was written to be thought-provoking, but entertaining.*

Reinforce and Extend

Answers

◆ Literature and Your Life

Reader's Response Some students may say they most enjoyed the account of Rip's return to his village; others may have liked reading about Rip's adventurous night on the mountain.

Thematic Focus Rip preferred younger people to his old friends.

☑ Check Your Comprehension

1. Rip didn't want to work for a living.
2. Rip wants to escape farm duties and his wife's sharp tongue.
3. After a day of hunting, Rip meets a stranger and goes with him to where odd-looking men are playing a game; Rip falls asleep and awakens to notice changes but doesn't realize until returning to his village that he has been asleep for 20 years.
4. Rip is surprised at unfamiliar faces and the changes in his village. The villagers are suspicious of Rip.
5. Rip met up with the ghosts of Henry Hudson and his crew and fell into a deep sleep.

◆ Critical Thinking

1. Rip isn't responsible, and his wife nags him.
2. Having such a wife can teach a husband patience and tolerance.
3. Dame Van Winkle is ill-tempered and impatient; Rip is friendly and easygoing.
4. Rip continues his idle life, hiking in the woods and talking to friends. He can come and go as he pleases without being scolded.
5. Irving may have wanted readers to remember the story.
6. Students may hypothesize that Rip might never have escaped to the woods and met the strange men.
7. Students may cite amazing new inventions, advances such as cures for diseases, or the elimination of wars.

Answers

◆Reading Strategy

Possible responses:

1. "How solemnly they would listen / to the contents, / [as drawled out by Derrick Van Bummel, / the schoolmaster, / a dapper, learned little man, / who was not to be daunted by the most gigantic word in the dictionary]; and how sagely they would deliberate / upon public events some months after they had taken place."

   "As to Rip's son [and heir,] [who was the ditto of himself, / seen leaning against the tree,] he was employed / to work on the farm; / but evinced an hereditary disposition to attend to anything else but his business."
2. The men would listen to Derrick Van Bummel read the paper and then discuss the events even though they were old news. Rip's son was hired to work on the farm, but, like his father, he spent more time helping others than taking care of his own chores.

◆Build Vocabulary

Using the Word Part *-cline-*

1. a chair that leans back
2. a slope or surface that leans
3. turned down

Spelling Strategy

1. comfortable
2. valuable
3. usable
4. winnable
5. doable
6. laughable

Using the Word Bank

1. S
2. S
3. A
4. A
5. A
6. S
7. S

◆Literary Focus

1. The village is described as being a province of Great Britain; the narrator refers to old clothing such as galligaskins and women's dress trains; the inn features a portrait of King George the Third.
2. The building that replaces the village inn features a "Union Hotel" sign; a nearby pole has a liberty cap on top and a flag with stars and stripes; the sign that featured a portrait of King George had been changed to a portrait of George Washington; people are using terms that refer to the American Revolution and its aftermath.

◆Build Grammar Skills

1. past perfect
2. present perfect
3. future perfect
4. past perfect
5. present perfect

Writing Application

Students' paragraphs should demonstrate the use of *have, has,* and *had* added to past participle verb forms.

Writer's Solution

For additional instruction and practice, use the verb tense lesson in the using verb section of *Writer's Solution Language Lab CD-ROM.* You may also use the practice page on verb tenses, p. 66, in the *Writer's Solution Grammar Practice Book.*

Guide for Responding *(continued)*

◆ Reading Strategy

BREAK DOWN LONG SENTENCES

In reading "Rip Van Winkle," you may have had to go back and reread some of the long sentences, **breaking them down** into shorter parts in order to understand them better.

1. Choose two long sentences from the story, and write them out. Use brackets and slashes to show how you broke each one down.
2. Write the meaning of each sentence as you understand it.

◆ Build Vocabulary

USING THE WORD ROOT *-cline-*

The word root *-cline-* means "lean, bend, or turn." Knowing this can help you figure out the meaning of words that contain *-cline-*. On a piece of paper, write a definition for each italicized word.

1. Watching television, he dozed off in his *recliner.*
2. She was forced to push her bike up the *incline.*
3. He *declined* her invitation to the party.

SPELLING STRATEGY

When you add the suffix *-able* to most words, do not change the spelling of the original word:

wash + -able = washable

If the word ends in silent e, drop the *e:*

like + -able = likable

If the word ends in a consonant preceded by a single vowel, you usually double the final consonant:

swim + -able = swimmable

On your paper, write the word that results when *-able* is added to each of the following words.

1. comfort	**3.** use	**5.** do
2. value	**4.** win	**6.** laugh

USING THE WORD BANK

Decide whether the following word pairs are synonyms, which mean the same thing, or antonyms, which mean opposite things. On your paper, write *S* for synonym and *A* for antonym.

1. martial, warlike	**5.** domestic, foreign
2. wistfully, longingly	**6.** majestic, regal
3. melancholy, cheerful	**7.** declined, wilted
4. incomprehensible, understandable	

◆ Literary Focus

HISTORICAL SETTING

Every story has a **setting,** a time and place in which the action occurs. Some stories have a **historical setting** that places them in a specific period from the past. "Rip Van Winkle," for example, is set in New York's Hudson River valley both before and after the American Revolution.

1. When the story opens, what details of the village reflect the story's historical setting?
2. What details indicate that the American Revolution has been fought and won while Rip has slept?

◆ Build Grammar Skills

VERB TENSES

In addition to the simple present, past, and future tenses, verbs have **perfect tenses.** Perfect verb tenses use *have, has,* or *had* added to the past form of the verb, which is usually made by adding *-d* or *-ed* to the main part of the verb.

The **present perfect tense** shows an action that began in the past and continues into the present:

Whoever *has voyaged* up the Hudson must remember the Catskill Mountains.

The **past perfect tense** shows a past action that ended before another began:

Rip *had* unconsciously *scrambled* to one of the highest parts of the Catskill Mountains.

The **future perfect tense** shows a future action that will have ended before another begins. This tense also uses the helping verb *will:*

By the time Rip awakens, his wife *will have died.*

Practice Indicate whether the verb tenses below are present perfect, past perfect, or future perfect.

1. Rip had argued with his wife.
2. She has scolded him all day.
3. The villagers will have forgotten Rip.
4. He had slept for a long time.
5. Have you climbed the Catskills?

Writing Application Write a paragraph in which you use all three perfect verb tenses.

Build Your Portfolio

Idea Bank

Writing

1. **Memoir** Write a passage that Rip might have composed for his memoirs. In it, describe Rip's encounter with the ghosts of Hudson's crew.
2. **Newspaper Article** Imagine that you are a reporter in the square when Rip returns. Write an article about him for the village newspaper.
3. **Comparison-and-Contrast Essay** The action of "Rip Van Winkle" takes place within a few miles, but the story spans twenty years. In an essay, compare and contrast Rip's surroundings before and after his twenty-year sleep.

Speaking and Listening

4. **Talk Show Appearance** **[Group Activity]** Imagine that Rip or his wife were invited to appear on a talk show. With a group, write and perform the show. Divide these roles in your group: host, audience members, and Dame or Rip Van Winkle. Use details from the story to help you create believable characters.
5. **Dramatization** With a group, choose a scene from the story and act it out. Feel free to add dialogue not included in Irving's story to bring the scene to life. **[Performing Arts Link]**

Projects

6. **Oral Presentation** Settings that inspired Washington Irving also captured the imaginations of many painters, most notably, Thomas Cole and Frederick Church, whose work came to be known as the Hudson River School. Find out more about these artists, and prepare a brief presentation about their work. **[Art Link]**
7. **Geography Update** Conduct research to find out how the Catskills have changed since the early 1700's to the present. Investigate changes caused by exploration, settlement, and land use. Create a report using the maps and photographs you have found. **[Social Studies Link]**

Writing Mini-Lesson

Description of a Trip Through Time

Much can happen in twenty years. When Rip wakes up after his long, long nap, he barely recognizes his own village. Not a face looks familiar. People are strangely dressed. Only the mountains are unchanged. Imagine that you wake up tomorrow morning to find that twenty years have passed. What would it be like? Write a short description of your experience.

Writing Skills Focus: Engage the Senses

Description can be most effective when it **engages the senses.** A vague statement like "Everything was different" doesn't let a reader see what you're describing. "The saplings we had planted were now leafy maples" provides a better image. Notice how Irving engages the sense of hearing as he describes an empty house:

Model From the Story

> . . . the lonely chambers *rang* for a moment with his voice, and then all again was *silence*.

Prewriting Spend some time jotting down ideas about what the world might look like in twenty years. In a five-column chart, list words that appeal to each sense: sight, hearing, taste, smell, and touch.

Drafting As you write, form a mental picture of what you are describing. Use your chart to choose words that convey images of your future world.

◆ Grammar Application

Since your description is set in the future, there may be many actions that begin in the past, present, or future and continue. Be sure that you have used perfect tenses correctly.

Revising Check to make sure your description tells a clear story. Then, improve your writing by replacing vague words with more vivid ones.

Idea Bank

Following are suggestions for matching the Idea Bank topics with your students' performance levels and learning modalities:

Customize for
Performance Levels
Less Advanced Students: 1, 4
Average Students: 2, 4, 5, 6
More Advanced Students: 3, 5, 7

Customize for
Learning Modalities
Verbal/Linguistic: 1, 2, 4, 5, 6
Visual/Spatial: 3, 6, 7
Bodily/Kinesthetic: 4, 5
Logical/Mathematical: 7
Interpersonal: 4, 5
Intrapersonal: 1, 7

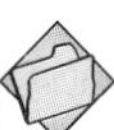

Writing Mini-Lesson

Refer students to the Writing Handbook in the back of the book for instructions on the writing process and for further information on description. Have students use the Sensory Language Chart in **Writing and Language Transparencies**, p. 78, to arrange their prewriting examples.

Writer's Solution

Writing Lab CD-ROM
Have students complete the tutorial on Description. Follow these steps:

1. Have students create a Cluster Diagram to help them narrow their topic.
2. Have students draft on computer.
3. Encourage students to use the Sensory Word Bin Activity to gather descriptive details.
4. When revising, have students use the interactive checklist to evaluate their descriptions.

Writer's Solution Sourcebook
Have students use Chapter 2, "Description," pp. 32–65, for additional support. This chapter includes in-depth instruction on using vivid verbs and using modifiers, pp. 59–61.

ASSESSMENT OPTIONS

Formal Assessment, Selection Test, pp. 44–46, and Assessment Resources Software. The selection test is designed so that it can be easily customized to the performance levels of your students.

Alternative Assessment, p. 12, includes options for less advanced students, more advanced students, visual/spatial learners, verbal/linguistic learners, and bodily/kinesthetic learners.

PORTFOLIO ASSESSMENT
Use the following rubrics in the **Alternative Assessment** booklet to assess student writing:
Memoir: Narrative Based on Personal Experience, p. 83
Newspaper Article: Summary, p. 85
Comparison-and-Contrast Essay: Comparison/Contrast, p. 90
Writing Mini-Lesson: Description, p. 84

Prepare and Engage

Establish Writing Guidelines
Before students begin, review the characteristics of a descriptive essay:

• A descriptive essay brings to life a thing, a place, or an experience that the writer knows about.
• The essay is focused and elaborates with vivid details.

You may want to distribute the scoring rubric for Description, p. 84 in **Alternative Assessment,** to make students aware of the criteria on which they will be evaluated. See p. 162 for suggestions for customizing the rubric to this workshop.

Refer students to the Writing Handbook in the back of the book for instruction on the writing process and for further information on descriptive writing.

Writer's Solution

Writers at Work Videodisc
To review the key elements of description and for Will Hobbs's thoughts on descriptive writing, play the videodisc segment on Description (Ch. 2). Discuss with students what Hobbs says about using the five senses to describe something.

Play frames 11106 to 20321

Writing Lab CD-ROM
Have students work in the tutorial on Description to complete all or part of their personal narratives. Follow these steps:

1. Students can review the interactive models of descriptive writing.
2. Encourage students to use the interactive organizing activity to choose a method for organizing their descriptions.
3. Have students draft on the computer.
4. Suggest that students use the revision checker for vague adjectives.

Writer's Solution Sourcebook
Students can find information on using vivid and precise verbs, in the chapter on Description (pp. 32–65).

Connect to Literature Unit 6, "Nonfiction," includes an example of a descriptive essay: Anais Nin's "Forest Fire."

Descriptive Writing

Descriptive Essay

Writing Process Workshop

Have words ever caused you to think, "Wow, I feel like I'm there!" Good description can transport readers to another place. When you write a long description in which several paragraphs contribute to one mood, you're writing a **descriptive essay.** For this assignment, choose a real place that inspires a definite mood. The following skills, introduced in this section's Writing Mini-Lessons, will help you write your descriptive essay.

Writing Skills Focus

▶ **Use vivid words.** Paint a word picture that's sharp, precise, and in focus. (See page 118.)

▶ **Develop each point** by moving slowly through the topic of your description. (See page 133.)

▶ **Grab your readers' interest.** Make your first detail a strong one. (See page 141.)

▶ **Engage many senses.** Think about all five senses—and don't forget to use your imagination. (See page 159.)

Washington Irving uses these writing skills to make you feel as if you're hiking into Sleepy Hollow.

Model From Literature

from *The Legend of Sleepy Hollow* by Washington Irving

. . . the voyager may have seen the light smoke curling up from a village, ① whose shingle roofs gleam among the trees, just where the blue tints of the upland melt away into the fresh green of the nearer landscape. It is a little village, of great antiquity, having been founded by some of the Dutch colonists, in the early times of the province, just about the beginning of the government of the good Peter Stuyvesant, . . . and there were some of the houses of the original settlers ② standing within a few years, built of small yellow bricks brought from Holland, ③ having latticed windows and gable fronts, surmounted with weathercocks.

① The smoke appeals to two senses: sight and smell.

② The writer zooms in—bringing a wide description of the landscape into a closer focus on the houses.

③ Instead of using a vague word like *stones*, the writer calls them *small yellow bricks from Holland.* Now that's precise!

Cross-Curricular Connection: Science

Observation Point out to students that one type of descriptive writing is an observation, which is fundamental to scientific research. Scientists keep observational journals to record details of their work. Journals such as these can then be of use to other researchers because they help them reproduce the scientific work and use the information to plan new research.

When documenting details of observation, scientists must note how an experiment was planned and carried out, what equipment was used, as well as the end results. The journal writing must be as descriptive and detailed as possible and may even include drawings, diagrams, and charts. Have students research and identify the steps used in scientific experiments. Then have them use journal writing to describe some of their own observations. Suggest that students pick an object and record as many details as possible. Remind them to be specific by developing each point, using vivid words and engaging many senses. Invite students to share their observations with the class by placing them in a central location for their classmates to read during free time.

Prewriting

Use Photographs and Memories To help you choose a topic, remember recent vacations or special days that were filled with excitement. If you have photographs, dig them out. Look through yearbooks or flip through a calendar to jump start your memory. If you still can't find a place or event you'd like to describe, consider these topic ideas:

Topic Ideas

- A corner of your room
- Your favorite camping site
- A movie theater just before the lights go down

Make a Sensory Chart One of the easiest ways to explore all five senses is to make a sensory chart. Can you guess what kind of place this chart describes?

SIGHT	SMELL	SOUND	TASTE	TOUCH
Roller coaster	Sausage frying	Screams	Fried dough	Soft tickets
Babies in strollers	Horse stalls	Rock music	Candy apples	Cold metal railings
Games of chance	Cotton candy	"Tickets, please!"	Lemonade	Drizzle in air

Convey a Mood What feeling do you want to convey about this place? Once you've named it, make a list of details that work together to support that feeling.

Choose Your Order Should you begin at the bottom and move to the top? How about top to bottom—or left to right? Choose a spatial order that makes sense. Don't confuse your audience by wandering around aimlessly or jumping from point to point.

Drafting

Hook Your Readers Make your first detail strong and impressive. Hook your readers' interest from the very first sentence.

Vary Your Sentences Descriptions can get boring if sentences all sound the same. Try using questions, exclamations, and quotations. Mix short sentences with long ones. Don't be afraid to experiment.

DRAFTING/REVISING

APPLYING LANGUAGE SKILLS: Using Precise Nouns

A **general noun,** which names a broad class of people, places, or things, is vague. A **precise noun** is the opposite; it is specific, concrete, and clear. Make your nouns as precise as possible.

General:

The *animal* ran up the *tree* with *something* in his mouth.

Precise:

The *raccoon* ran up the *sycamore* tree with a *trout* in his *teeth*.

Practice On your paper, rewrite these sentences to make the nouns more precise.

1. The place was full of plants.
2. Put your clothes in the room.
3. Let's build something with this stuff.
4. The man held a toy.

Writing Application As you write your descriptive essay, make your nouns precise.

Writer's Solution Connection Language Lab

For more practice with precise nouns, complete the Language Lab lesson on Exact Nouns.

Applying Language Skills

Using Precise Nouns Explain to students that using precise nouns will help bring their descriptions to life. For example, when describing a bench under a *tree,* saying that the bench is under the *weeping willow* helps convey the mood of the place, and also creates a more accurate image of the place.

Answers

Possible responses:

1. The sunroom was full of African violets.
2. Put your sweatpants in your bedroom.
3. Let's build a fort with these cushions.
4. The professor held a Frisbee.

 ***Writer's Solution***

For additional instruction and practice have students use the Using Nouns lesson in the *Writer's Solution Language Lab CD-ROM.*

Develop Student Writing

Prewriting

If students are having trouble coming up with a topic, suggest that they think about a room in their home, a particular spot where they spend time at school, or a place where they meet friends.

Customize for *Less Proficient Writers*

Suggest to students that they choose to write about a place that is convenient for them to visit. This way, they can actually observe and take notes about details while they are there.

Customize for *Visual/Spatial Learners*

Start students on their descriptions by having them sketch their chosen topics. Encourage them to consider how words can help engage all five senses. For instance a colorful drawing of a rose appeals to sight, but the words "the perfume of the deep red rose wafted toward me" engage the senses of sight and smell.

Drafting

Have students use the Sensory Language Chart, p. 78 in **Writing and Language Transparencies,** to gather details that will help them come up with vivid words. As they write, encourage them to refer back to the sensory details they have entered in their charts. Suggest to students that they show rather than tell the reader what they are describing.

 ***Writer's Solution***

Writing Lab CD-ROM

In the section of the tutorial on Description, students can view interactive writing models to see how different writers begin their drafts. In addition, students can use the Transitional Word Bin to choose words that show spatial order.

Revising

You may want to have students work with peer reviewers, looking for wordiness or places where action verbs could be used instead of the verb *to be*.

Writer's Solution

Writing Lab CD-ROM

In the tutorial on Description, have students use the revision checker to help them spot vague adjectives in their writing.

Publishing

In addition to tape recordings or a collection of essays, have students read their essays to the class and then show photos or videotapes of the places they describe.

Reinforce and Extend

Review the Writing Guidelines

After students have completed their papers, review the characteristics of a descriptive essay.

Applying Language Skills

Spelling Noun Plurals Explain to students that for nouns that do not form regular plurals, they will have to rely on reference sources until they learn the proper plural forms.

Answers

1. sharp wits
2. pretty ladies
3. blueberry patches
4. fancy stores

Writer's Solution

For additional practice, complete the Plural and Possessive Nouns lesson in the *Writer's Solution Language Lab CD-ROM.*

Writing Process Workshop

EDITING/PROOFREADING

Applying Language Skills: Spelling Noun Plurals

Singular nouns name one person, place, or thing. **Plural** nouns name more than one person, place, or thing. Usually, to make a singular noun plural, you add *-s* or *-es*. Add *-es* to words that end in *s* (glasses), *ch* (churches), and *x* (mixes). If a noun ends in *y*, change the *y* to an *i* and add *-es* (candies).

A few nouns stay the same whether they are singular or plural: deer, deer. Other plurals don't seem to follow any rules: children; mice; teeth.

Practice Make these singular noun phrases plural. If necessary, use a dictionary for reference.

1. sharp wit
2. pretty lady
3. blueberry patch
4. fancy store

Writing Application As you edit your descriptive essay, check that you have spelled all plural nouns correctly.

Writer's Solution Connection
Writing Lab

For help revising vague adjectives in your description, use the Word Bins in the tutorial for Description in the Writing Lab CD-ROM.

Mark Places to Use Precise Details Avoid pausing in your first draft to fill in the precise details you don't have. Just mark the place where you can go back and insert details, like a player's name or uniform number.

Revising

Whittle Wordiness Good descriptions don't use unnecessary words. They don't repeat. For example, you could whittle "a mouth that looked really dangerous, like it could really hurt you" to "sharp teeth." The more you say with fewer words, the stronger your writing will be.

Use Action Verbs It might be a temptation to write sentences that use the verb *to be*. (Her hat *was* red. His face *is* leathery.) As you revise, circle forms of *to be* and replace them with action verbs.

Revision Model

① ~~The beach was nice.~~ As the waves ~~moved~~ ② crashed onto the beach, they sent up a fine cool spray ③ that tasted salty and smelled vaguely of seaweed. The sand, soft and warm under our feet, was sprinkled with shells and smooth pebbles.

① Deleting a weak first sentence allows the writer to begin with a strong detail.
② The writer uses a more vivid word.
③ These details appeal to the senses of taste and smell.

Publishing and Presenting

Musical Descriptions Make a tape recording of your descriptive essay accompanied by music that reflects the mood of your writing. Play your recording for a friend who has never been to the place you describe.

Book of Places With a group of classmates, create a collection of descriptive essays that are illustrated by photographs or drawings. Display the finished collection in your school library.

✓ ASSESSMENT

PORTFOLIO ASSESSMENT

Use the rubric on Description in the ***Alternative Assessment*** booklet, p. 84, to assess students' writing. Add these criteria to customize this rubric to this assignment.

	4	3	2	1
Vivid Words	The description consistently uses vivid words and paints a sharp, precise word picture.	The description combines vivid words and vague details.	Most of the description is vague.	The description includes too few vivid words to create a word picture.
Precise Nouns	The writer consistently uses precise nouns.	The writer uses a mixture of precise nouns and general nouns.	The writer includes some, but far too few, precise nouns.	The writer uses a few precise nouns, and mostly relies on general nouns.

Real-World Reading Skills Workshop

Reading a Map

Strategies for Success

Being able to read a map can be extremely useful when you're visiting a new city. To get to the places you want to visit, you may need to use special maps that show the city's public transportation system.

Locate Your Stops The first step in using a bus or subway map is to determine the stop that's nearest your starting location. The next step is to figure out which stop is closest to where you want to go. These steps may involve looking at a street map on which the stops are marked. Keep in mind that maps of bus routes and subways are simplified. They do not show the geographic layout of the stops.

Look at the Lines Different routes have different colors. If your starting location and your destination are lines of different colors, then you will have to switch to a different bus or train—perhaps more than once.

Trace Possible Paths Follow the lines that connect your location to your destination. Find the paths that minimize the number of times you have to switch buses or trains. Then, determine which path has the fewest number of stops. This will be your best route.

Note the Direction Look at the ends of the routes to make sure you catch the bus or train that is headed in the correct direction. For example, if you were going from Central to Park Street on Boston's subway, you'd take the train that is traveling toward Braintree, not the one that's heading to Alewife.

Apply the Strategies

Imagine that you're visiting Boston for the first time, and you want to use the subway system to get from place to place. Use the map below to answer these questions.

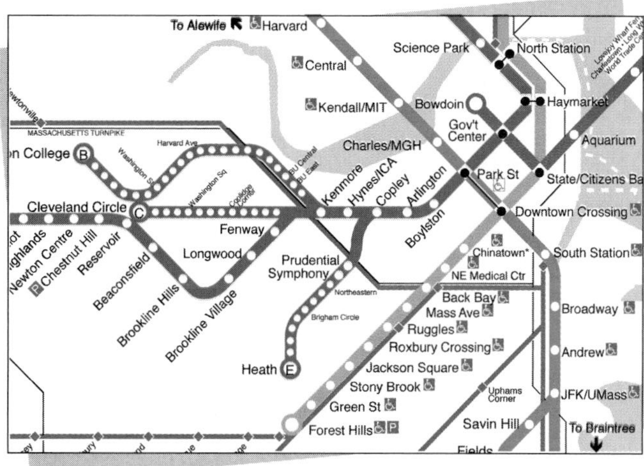

1. On what line is Fenway?
2. How would you get from South Station to Cleveland Circle?
3. How many times do you have to change trains to get from Park Street to the Aquarium?

Here are some other situations in which reading a map can be helpful:

- Helping a driver find the way to a new place
- Providing directions to your home
- Planning a walking tour
- Reading news magazines

Introduce the Strategies

Students will probably be familiar with maps from their social studies textbooks. Point out that subway and bus maps are also drawings that represent areas. Knowing how to read a map is useful when trying to give or follow directions, and when planning routes for driving or using public transportation.

Customize for
More Advanced Learners
Challenge students to create their own maps. Suggest that they map out their routes to school or the path from the gym to their lockers. Encourage them to use color coding and clear markings to help their map readers. Then invite pairs of students to swap maps and follow the routes. After they have tried out the maps, have students make suggestions to their partners for clarifying the maps.

Apply the Strategies

Tell students that sometimes when one looks at a map for the first time it can seem overwhelming. Make map reading manageable by suggesting that they find a reference point—a place where they can orient themselves. For example, many maps of shopping malls and other areas include a spot on the map that indicates "You Are Here" as a reference point. To follow a particular route, most people find it easier to understand if they trace a path with their fingers.

Answers

1. Green Line
2. Take the Red Line for two stops until you get to Park Street; then switch to the Green Line, which ends at Cleveland Circle.
3. Once. If you start on the Green Line at Park Street, change to the Blue Line at Government Center, and go one stop; you'll be at the Aquarium.

◆Build Grammar Skills

Reviewing Verbs and Verb Tenses
The selections in Part I include instruction on the following:
- Verbs
- Action Verbs and Linking Verbs
- Verb Tenses

This instruction is reinforced with the Build Grammar Skills practice pages in **Selection Support,** pp. 46, 51, 56, and 61.

As you review verbs, you may wish to include the following:
- Contractions With Verbs

Verbs often come in contracted form. Verb contractions are common in everyday speech. Guide students to complete the following chart:

Common Contractions With Verbs		
Verbs with *not*	are not do not was not were not	*aren't* *don't* *wasn't* *weren't*
Pronouns with *will*	I will you will she will they will	*I'll* *you'll* *she'll* *they'll*
Pronouns and Nouns with the Verb *be*	I am you are who is Joan is	*I'm* *you're* *who's* *Joan's*
Pronouns with *would*	I would he would we would they would	*I'd* *he'd* *we'd* *they'd*

To help students understand verb tenses, encourage them to review the chart on this page and the chart on p. 66 of the *Writer's Solution Grammar Practice Book* for examples of conjugations of verbs.

Writer's Solution

For additional practice and support using verbs and verb tenses, use practice pp. 11–14 and 66 in the *Writer's Solution Grammar Practice Book.*

Verbs

Grammar Review

verb (vurb) *n.* a word that shows action or a condition of being: some verbs are used to link a subject with words that tell about the subject, or to help other verbs show special features /In "The children ate early" and "Cactuses grow slowly," the words "ate" and "grow" are *verbs.* In "He is asleep," the word "is" is a linking *verb.* In "Where have you gone?", the word "hav...

A **verb** tells what the subject of a sentence does or is. Verbs that tell what the subject *does* are **action verbs**. Verbs that tell what the subject *is* are **linking verbs.** (See page 132.)

Verbs change form to show time. The six tenses of verbs are given in the following chart. Note that some tenses add helping verbs—such as *have, has, had,* and *will*—to the main verb.

Verb Tense	Helping Verb	Verb Ending	Examples
Simple Tenses (See page 140.)			
Present	none	none or -s, -es	I look; he looks
Past	none	-*ed* (for regular verbs)	You looked
Future	will or shall	none	We will look
Perfect Tenses (See page 158.)			
Present Perfect	have or has	-*ed* (for regular verbs)	They have looked; she has looked
Past Perfect	had	-*ed* (for regular verbs)	I had looked
Future Perfect	will have or shall have	-*ed* (for regular verbs)	It will have looked

Practice 1 Copy the numbered sentences on a piece of paper. Underline main verbs twice. Underline helping verbs once. Then, identify the verb tense, and indicate whether the main verb is a linking verb or an action verb.

1. Alice Walker remembers her mother's garden.
2. Victor will be more careful and will not boast anymore.
3. The people in Quindlen's neighborhood have changed.
4. The squirrel collected and ate nuts.
5. Rip Van Winkle had gone hunting in the mountains.

Practice 2 Rewrite the following paragraph, putting the given verb into the tense indicated in parentheses.

When I first (meet, *past*) Caroline, I (think, *past*) we (have, *past*) nothing at all in common. Until that year, she (spend, *past perfect*) all her life in London. In contrast, I (grow, *past*) up on a ranch that (is, *present*) far away from any city. After I (learn, *past perfect*) more about Caroline, however, I (find, *past*) that we (share, *past*) many interests. For example, we (is, *present*) both crazy about horses. After we (finish, *present perfect*) high school, we (hope, *present*) to start a riding school. By that time, we (gain, *future perfect*) a lot of experience from working at my aunt's stable during school vacations.

Grammar in Writing

✓ *When you write, be careful to use verb tenses correctly. Avoid changing tenses when events occur at the same time, but do change tenses when you want to show that events did not occur at the same time.*

Answers

Practice 1

1. main verb: *remembers*—present tense, action verb
2. main verb: *be*—future tense, linking verb; main verb: *boast*—future tense, action verb; helping verb: *will*—future tense, linking verb
3. main verb: *changed*—present perfect tense, action verb; helping verb: *have*—present perfect tense, linking verb
4. main verb: *collected*—past tense, action verb; main verb: *ate*—past tense, action verb
5. main verb: *hunting*—past perfect tense, action verb; helping verbs: had *gone*—past perfect tense, linking verb

Practice 2

When I first *met* Caroline, I *thought* we *had* nothing at all in common. Until that year, she *had spent* all her life in London. In contrast, I *grew* up on a ranch that *is* far away from any city. After I *had learned* more about Caroline, however, I *found* that we *shared* many interests. For example, we *are* both crazy about horses. After we *have finished* high school, we *hope* to start a riding school. By that time, we *will have gained* a lot of experience from working at my aunt's stable during school vacation.

Part 2 *Shared Dreams*

Untitled (Two Girls Talking), Pierre-Auguste Renoir

One-Minute Planning Guide

The selections in this section focus on the theme of shared dreams. A group of three poems and a short story—"Mother to Son," "The Courage That My Mother Had," "The Village Blacksmith," and "The Hummingbird That Lived Through Winter" —explores the use of symbols that represent shared attitudes and approaches to life. "The Midwife's Apprentice" describes the shared dreams of two friends in the Middle Ages.

Customize for ***Varying Student Needs***

When assigning the selections in this section to your students, keep in mind the following factors:

"Mother to Son"

- A poem that gently encourages readers to meet the challenges of life

"The Courage That My Mother Had"

- Accessible, yet challenging use of symbol

"The Village Blacksmith"

- A longer, descriptive poem

"The Hummingbird That Lived Through Winter"

- A very short story
- First-person narrator

"The Midwife's Apprentice"

- Excerpted from a Newbery Medal winner
- An opportunity for connecting literature to social studies

Humanities: Art

Untitled *(Two Girls Talking),* 1878, by Pierre-Auguste Renoir

Pierre-Auguste Renoir (1841–1919) was a French painter and leader of the Impressionist movement. Like most of his peers, Renoir was interested in re-creating the qualities of light and atmosphere on canvas. Many of his paintings focus on the human form, and Renoir is known for his ability to portray subjects through brilliant colors and the harmony of lines. During the last 20 years of his life, Renoir suffered from arthritis, but he continued to paint by strapping brushes to his arm.

Help students connect the art to theme of Part 2, "Shared Dreams," with these questions:

1. What kind of mood does Renoir create by using soft colors and lines? *Students may say he creates a dreamy mood, as the image seems slightly blurred like a memory.*
2. How do the two women in the painting illustrate the theme "Shared Dreams"? *Students may suggest that they look like they're having a deep conversation, maybe about their dreams.*

Prepare and Engage

OBJECTIVES

1. To read, comprehend, and interpret three poems and a short story
2. To relate poems and a short story to personal experience
3. To question while reading
4. To understand literary symbols
5. To build vocabulary in context and learn the prefix *trans-*
6. To learn the principal parts of irregular verbs
7. To write a pep talk
8. To respond to poems and a short story through writing, speaking and listening, and projects

SKILLS INSTRUCTION

Vocabulary: Prefixes: *trans-*
Spelling: Plurals of Words Ending in *ch*
Grammar: Principal Parts of Irregular Verbs
Reading Strategy: Question
Literary Focus: Symbol
Writing: Stress Main Idea
Speaking and Listening: Song (Teacher Edition)
Viewing and Representing: Symbols and Slogans (Teacher Edition)
Critical Viewing: Connect

PORTFOLIO OPPORTUNITIES

Writing: Response Poem; Public-Service Announcement; Analysis of a Symbol
Writing Mini-Lesson: Pep Talk
Speaking and Listening: Song; An Unexpected Meeting
Projects: Survey; Internet Research

More About the Authors

Langston Hughes was born in Missouri, but he also lived in Mexico, West Africa, Paris, Venice, and Genoa before settling in Harlem.

Edna St. Vincent Millay graduated from Vassar College in 1917 and then moved to Greenwich Village New York City to write.

Henry Wadsworth Longfellow attended Bowdoin College where he became friends with Nathaniel Hawthorne. After graduation, he became a professor of modern languages.

William Saroyan won the Pulitzer Prize for his play *The Time of Your Life* but he declined the prize because he believed that business should not support art.

Guide for Reading

Meet the Authors:

Langston Hughes (1902–1967)

Langston Hughes was one of the main figures in the Harlem Renaissance, a creative movement that took place in the 1920's in the New York City community of Harlem. Hughes and other artists and writers used their talents to celebrate their African American heritage.

Edna St. Vincent Millay (1892–1950)

Edna St. Vincent Millay was born and raised in Rockland, Maine. When just nineteen, she wrote the first of many emotional poems. "The Courage That My Mother Had" is a moving example of the intense feelings her poetry expresses.

Henry Wadsworth Longfellow (1807–1882)

Henry Wadsworth Longfellow's poetry was just as popular in his time as the best-loved television programs are today. Longfellow was part of a group that was called the Fireside Poets because their family audiences would read poems, including "The Village Blacksmith," aloud while sitting around their fireplaces.

William Saroyan (1908–1981)

William Saroyan's childhood was a difficult time. He spent part of it in an orphanage and left school at twelve. Saroyan writes often about the Armenian immigrants he knew as a boy.

◆ Literature and Your Life

Connect Your Experience

You look to adults to provide guidance and to set an example. As you grow into adulthood, you'll probably continue to draw upon the wisdom of those who are older or more experienced. In these selections, writers celebrate the inspiring strength and wisdom of mothers, fathers, and neighbors.

Thematic Focus: Shared Dreams

As you read about the values these writers find important, consider whether you share their hopes and goals for life.

◆ Background for Understanding

History

In his poem, Longfellow describes in vivid detail the work of a blacksmith in a small New England village in the 1800's. At the time, blacksmiths played a key role in village life, making and repairing horseshoes and iron tools used in the fireplace. The blacksmith would heat the iron until it was red-hot and then shape it with a heavy hammer. Because horses were the main means of transportation and because people used a fireplace to cook their meals, blacksmiths were in high demand at the time.

◆ Build Vocabulary

Prefixes: *trans-*

The hummingbird in Saroyan's story completes a *transformation*. The prefix *trans-* means "across, over, or beyond." A *transformation* is a change from one form to another.

Word Bank

Which of these words from the selections might describe a strong and muscular person?

quarried
brooch
brawny
pathetic
transformation

Prentice Hall Literature Program Resources

REINFORCE / RETEACH / EXTEND

Selection Support Pages
Vocabulary: Prefixes: *trans-*, p. 65; Spelling, p. 66; Grammar: Principal Parts of Irregular Verbs, p. 67; Reading Strategy: Question, p. 68; Literary Focus: Symbol, p. 69
Strategies for Diverse Student Needs, pp. 25–26
Beyond Literature Study Skills: Make an Outline, p. 13
Formal Assessment Selection Test, pp. 47–49, Assessment Resources Software
Alternative Assessment, p. 13

Writing and Language Transparencies
Main Idea and Supporting Details, p. 70
Daily Language Practice, p. 32
Resource Pro CD-ROM
"Mother to Son"; "The Courage That My Mother Had"; "The Village Blacksmith"; The Hummingbird That Lived Through Winter"

Listening to Literature Audiocassettes
"Mother to Son"; "The Courage That My Mother Had;"; "The Village Blacksmith"; The Hummingbird That Lived Through Winter"

Mother to Son ◆ The Courage That My Mother Had ◆ The Village Blacksmith ◆ The Hummingbird That Lived Through Winter

The Banjo Lesson, © 1894, Mary Cassatt, The Adolf D. and Wilkins C. Williams Fund, Virginia Museum of Fine Arts, Richmond

◆ Literary Focus

Symbol

A **symbol** is an object that conveys an idea beyond itself. For example, a dove with an olive branch is a symbol of peace. A crown is a symbol of a king's authority. Symbols are frequently used to express an idea in a concrete and memorable way. To identify symbols, look for objects that call to mind specific associations or seem to take on extra importance in a literary work. For each selection, record details relating to such objects. Use the organizer below as you read "Mother to Son." On each step, note a detail about the staircase. Create similar organizers for the other selections.

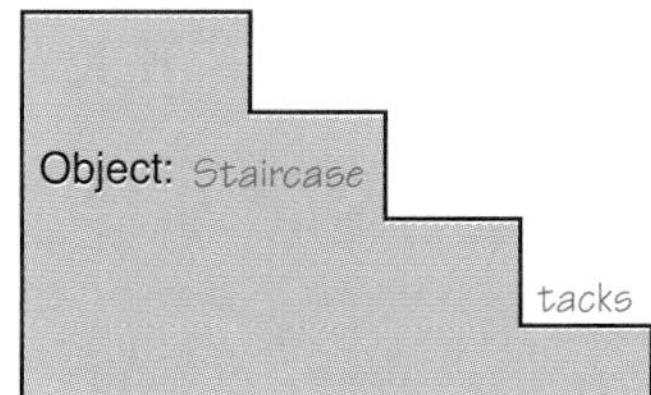

◆ Reading Strategy

Question

One way to get a better understanding of what you read is to create questions based on the text and then see if you can answer them. Begin with the common question words *who, what, where, when, why*, and *how*. For example, when Edna St. Vincent Millay uses the image of New England rock, you might ask what the rock represents to the poet. Search for the answers to your questions as you read, and you'll find an understanding of the selection easy to reach.

Preparing for Standardized Tests

Grammar This selection provides a table of common irregular verbs whose principal parts break the standard rules for forming the past tense and/or past participle. Grammar, usage, and writing sections of standardized tests may ask students to apply the correct form of an irregular verb in a sentence, either in open-ended writing or in multiple-choice items. Present the following sample test item:

The blacksmith go to the church last Sunday.

Which is the best way to write the sentence?

(A) The blacksmith have gone to church last Sunday.
(B) The blacksmith went to church last Sunday.
(C) The blacksmith going to church last Sunday.
(D) Best as it is

The table on page 176 shows the simple past tense of the verb *to go* as *went*. Point out that the time clue "last Sunday" requires past tense, which eliminates *(C)* and *(D)*. *(A)* is a faulty construction, so *(B)* is correct. For additional practice, use Build Grammar Skills in **Selection Support,** p. 67.

Ask students: "What is the best advice you've ever received?" Encourage them to consider why the advice was important, when they heard it, who gave it to them, and so forth. Then have them jot down a few lines about how the advice helped them. Tell students that the works they will read are about the advice or influence of other people.

◆ Build Grammar Skills

Principal Parts of Irregular Verbs If you wish to introduce the grammar skill for this selection before students read, refer to the instruction on p. 176.

Customize for
Less Proficient Readers
Have students listen to the recordings of these poems. Encourage them to pay attention to the rhythms of the poems and any words or phrases that the readers emphasize. Then have them listen again and follow along in their books.

Listening to Literature Audiocassettes

Customize for
More Advanced Students
The poems and story that students will read reveal the respect that a younger person holds for a mother or other adult. Invite students to think of a person that they respect and determine a symbol for that respect. Ask them to describe the symbol and how it conveys the idea.

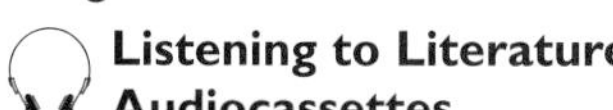

The Banjo Lesson, by Mary Cassatt

Mary Cassatt (1844–1926) studied and worked in France when it was difficult for her to achieve status as a woman artist in America. She is well known for her work that conveys a mother-and-child theme.

1. Do you think these figures are enjoying the banjo lesson? Why? *Students may note concentration and contentment as signs of enjoyment.*
2. What is the relationship between these two people? *Most students will identify the relationship as mother and daughter.*

Develop Understanding

One-Minute Insight In "Mother to Son," the speaker shares her experiences with her son and tells him to expect life not to be easy, yet never to give up.

◆Literary Focus

❶ Symbol The poet uses a stairway as a symbol for the progress of life. What other symbol can you think of to describe the progress of life? *Students may suggest a path, a river, or a road.*

▶Critical Viewing◀

❷ Connect *Students may note that the woman seems to be listening; her tilted head suggests that she may be thinking about something serious; she has a determined look.*

Customize for
English Language Learners
The dialect used in this poem may confuse students. Examples include "I'se" for "I have"; " 'Cause" for "because"; "you finds" for "you find"; and "kinder" for "kind of." Read the dialect aloud to help clue students into the meaning of unfamiliar spellings. Ask volunteers to restate the dialect in standard English.

Humanities: Art

Organdy Collar, 1936, by Edmund Archer

Edmund Archer (1904–1986) was one of the three original curators for the Whitney Museum of American Art, located in New York. Archer is best known for his sensitive portraits, like this one. Discuss these questions:

1. What is the mood of the woman in the painting? *Students may say that she looks serious, thoughtful, or tired.*
2. Do you think this portrait portrays the woman in the poem? *Students may say yes because she seems the right age and has a wise and tired look about her.*

Mother to Son

Langston Hughes

Organdy Collar, 1936, Edmund Archer, Whitney Museum of American Art

Well, son, I'll tell you: ❶
Life for me ain't been no crystal stair.
It's had tacks in it,
And splinters,
And boards torn up,
And places with no carpet on the floor—
Bare.
But all the time
I'se been a-climbin' on,
And reachin' landin's,
And turnin' corners,
And sometimes goin' in the dark
Where there ain't been no light.
So boy, don't you turn back.
Don't you set down on the steps
'Cause you finds it's kinder hard.
Don't you fall now—
For I'se still goin', honey,
I'se still climbin',
And life for me ain't been no crystal stair.

▲ **Critical Viewing** What details of the painting on this page convey the emotion of the poem? **[Connect]** ❷

Block Scheduling Strategies

Consider these suggestions to take advantage of extended class time:

- Introduce the reading strategy before students read. While they read, have them begin a list of questions about the selections. Then have them discuss their questions in groups, suggesting answers based on their reading. Together, they can answer the Reading Strategy questions on p. 176.
- As an alternative, begin class time by introducing the vocabulary and the grammar skill, p. 176. Have students read the selections and work in groups to answer the Guide for Responding questions that appear on pp. 169, 171, and 175. Introduce "The Village Blacksmith" with the **Daily Language Practice** lesson, p. 32.
- Have pairs of students work on the Writing Mini-Lesson on p. 177. If they have access to technology, encourage them to use the tutorial on Persuasion in the *Writer's Solution Writing Lab CD-ROM.*

The Courage That My Mother Had

Edna St. Vincent Millay

The courage that my mother had
Went with her, and is with her still:
Rock from New England quarried;
Now granite in a granite hill.

❹

The golden brooch my mother wore
She left behind for me to wear;
I have no thing I treasure more:
Yet, it is something I could spare.

Oh, if instead she'd left to me
❺ The thing she took into the grave!—
❻ That courage like a rock, which she
Has no more need of, and I have.

◆ Build Vocabulary

quarried (kwôr′ ēd) *adj.*: Carved out of the ground

brooch (brōch) *n.*: Large ornamental pin worn on a blouse or dress

Guide for Responding

◆ Literature and Your Life

Reader's Response Would you like to know the mothers described in these poems? Why or why not?

Thematic Focus How can a parent's courage or endurance help children achieve their dreams?

☑ Check Your Comprehension

1. In "Mother to Son," what advice does the mother give to her son?
2. Where is the speaker's mother in "The Courage That My Mother Had"?
3. For what quality does the speaker of "The Courage That My Mother Had" wish?

◆ Critical Thinking

Interpret

1. (a) In "Mother to Son," what does the mother say about her life? (b) What comparison does she make to develop this point? **[Analyze]**
2. In lines 14–17 of "Mother to Son," what does the mother say about how to live? **[Synthesize]**
3. Explain lines 3–4 in "The Courage That My Mother Had." **[Analyze]**
4. Why does Millay compare her mother to New England granite? **[Interpret]**
5. Why would Millay rather have her mother's character than a brooch made of gold? **[Infer]**
6. Describe the feeling that the speaker expresses in "The Courage That My Mother Had." **[Interpret]**

Evaluate

7. The speaker in Millay's poem implies that courage is a quality you either have or don't have. Can we learn qualities such as courage or perseverance? Explain. **[Criticize]**

Compare Literary Works

8. What qualities do you think the women in "Mother to Son" and "The Courage That My Mother Had" share? **[Connect]**

One-Minute Insight

In "The Courage That My Mother Had," the speaker pays tribute to her late mother and wishes she had her courage.

Clarification

❸ Edna St. Vincent Millay's mother, Cora, divorced when her daughter was only 8 years old. Cora was from a strong New England background and worked as a nurse. The family lived in several New England towns. Cora encouraged Edna to submit her poem "Renascence" to a poetry contest, which earned her a scholarship to Vassar.

◆ Literary Focus

❹ **Symbol** Ask students to identify which is a better symbol for the speaker's mother—the golden brooch or granite—and explain why. *Students should recognize that the brooch does not convey the idea of the mother's courage and strength like the rock does.*

◆ Literature and Your Life

❺ Discuss with students whether the speaker actually has any of her mother's positive qualities. *Students may say that the fact that the speaker appreciates her mother's brooch but recognizes that it is only material may indicate that she shares strong qualities with her mother.*

◆ Reading Strategy

❻ **Question** Encourage students to question why the poet wishes she had her mother's courage. *Students may say the poet may have been looking for courage or strength at the time she wrote the poem, possibly due to a difficult situation in her life.*

Reinforce and Extend

Answers

◆ Literature and Your Life

Reader's Response Students may say they'd like to know the mothers because they seem strong and brave.

Thematic Focus Students may say that if parents show strong qualitites, they may inspire their children to do the same.

☑ Check Your Comprehension

1. She says not to give up, even if life is hard.
2. She is buried in a cemetery.
3. She wishes for courage.

◆ Critical Thinking

1. (a) Her life has not been smooth or easy, but she has kept going. (b) She compares her life to a stairway of splinters, worn carpet, and abrupt turns.
2. One should live by not turning back, giving up, or falling down.
3. The mother was as courageous as a rock, and she is now buried.
4. She uses granite to portray her mother's rock-hard strength and courage.
5. She values courage and character more than wealth and possessions.
6. She expresses admiration and a desire for her mother's courage.
7. Some students will say that a person can learn to be brave by following the examples of others. Others will say that we are or aren't born with these qualities and can't learn them.
8. Both characters show deep commitment to their tasks in life; they seem brave, strong, and determined.

The speaker of "The Village Blacksmith" describes the life of a strong, simple, hardworking blacksmith. In this lifestyle, the speaker finds an inspiring model of a worthy life made up of honest attitudes and a deep love of family and community.

◆Critical Thinking

❶ **Draw Conclusions** Ask students what they know about the blacksmith from this description. *Students should conclude that he is honest and sincere.*

◆Literary Focus

❷ **Symbol** Ask students what the image of the sexton ringing the village bell might symbolize and how it compares to the noises of the blacksmith's shop. *The sexton's ringing of the bells signals the end of the day and is a reminder of everyday life, just as the noise of the blacksmith's shop is a symbol of daily labor and life.*

Clarification

❸ Explain to students that *chaff* is the husks of grains and grasses separated during threshing, the mechanical process of separating grain or seeds from a plant. Chaff scatters in a similar manner as scattering sparks.

Customize for *Musical/Rhythmic Learners*

This poem includes many effective sound devices, such as alliteration, onomatopoeia, and repetition. Help students use the Literary Terms Handbook in the back of the book to review these literary devices and identify examples of them within the poem. Then have them form groups and present an oral interpretation of the poem to the class, with musical or rhythmic accompaniment.

The Village Blacksmith

Henry Wadsworth Longfellow

Under a spreading chestnut tree
The village smithy[1] stands;
The smith, a mighty man is he,
With large and sinewy[2] hands;
And the muscles of his brawny arms
Are strong as iron bands.

His hair is crisp,[3] and black, and long,
His face is like the tan;
His brow is wet with honest sweat,
❶ He earns whate'er he can,
And looks the whole world in the face,
For he owes not any man.

Week in, week out, from morn till night,
You can hear his bellows[4] blow;
❷ You can hear him swing his heavy sledge,[5]
With measured beat and slow,
Like a sexton[6] ringing the village bell,
When the evening sun is low.

And children coming home from school
Look in at the open door;
They love to see the flaming forge,
And hear the bellows roar,
And catch the burning sparks that fly
❸ Like chaff from a threshing floor.

He goes on Sunday to the church,
And sits among his boys;
He hears the parson pray and preach,
He hears his daughter's voice,

---

1. **smithy** (smith´ ē) *n.*: Workshop of a blacksmith.
2. **sinewy** (sin´ yo͞o wē) *adj.*: Tough and strong.
3. **crisp** (krisp) *adj.*: Closely curled and wiry.
4. **bellows** (bel´ ōz) *n.*: Device for quickening the fire by blowing air on it.
5. **sledge** (slej) *n.*: Sledgehammer; a long, heavy hammer, usually held with both hands.
6. **sexton** (seks´ tən) *n.*: Church official in charge of ringing the bells.

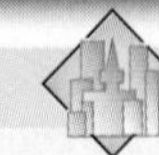

Beyond the Classroom

Workplace Skills

Job Satisfaction Discuss with students what it might be like to have the blacksmith's job. Encourage them to express how they think they would respond to hard physical labor all day long. Point out that it is not always possible to choose an easy job. Lead them to understand that the blacksmith derives satisfaction from his job because he is dedicated and honest about his work. In addition, his family and church are just as important as his job.

Have students brainstorm for a list of qualities that the blacksmith applies to his life and job—qualities that allow him to toil long and hard six days a week. Their list may include dedication, determination, satisfaction in a task well-done, helping others, and balancing work with other activities. Then ask them to choose a job and write a description of how they could apply those qualities to be successful in it. Have them share their descriptions with the class by reading them aloud or posting them on a bulletin board.

Singing in the village choir,
And it makes his heart rejoice.

It sounds to him like her mother's voice,
Singing in Paradise!
He needs must think of her once more,
How in the grave she lies;
And with his hard, rough hand he wipes
A tear out of his eyes.

❹ Toiling—rejoicing—sorrowing,
Onward through life he goes;
Each morning sees some task begin,
Each evening sees it close;
Something attempted, something done,
Has earned a night's repose.

Thanks, thanks to thee, my worthy friend,
For the lesson thou hast taught!
Thus at the flaming forge of life
Our fortunes must be wrought;
Thus on its sounding anvil shaped
Each burning deed and thought. ❺

◆ **Build Vocabulary**

brawny (brôn´ ē) *adj.*: Strong and muscular

Guide for Responding

Beyond Literature

Career Connection

Modern Metalwork The intense manual effort that Longfellow describes has been eased by new technology. Now, machines do most of the work. Instead of a hammer and an anvil, forging presses force red-hot metal into shape by squeezing it into molds called dies. This process creates such common products as tools and engine parts.

Cross-Curricular Activity

Career Profile Today, there are plenty of jobs involving metalwork. Discover what you can about these careers. Research the metalwork at nearby factories, repair shops, or industrial centers. Interview someone who works with metal to find out about educational requirements and job responsibilities. Then, share your findings with the class.

◆ Literature and Your Life

Reader's Response Do you admire the blacksmith? Explain.

Thematic Focus How do the blacksmith's actions reflect the values and beliefs he shares with his community?

☑ Check Your Comprehension

1. Describe the blacksmith's appearance.
2. Why is the blacksmith able to look the whole world in the face?

◆ Critical Thinking

INTERPRET

1. Which details tell you that the blacksmith is an honest, hard-working man? **[Connect]**
2. What does the tear in his eye reveal about him? **[Infer]**
3. Based on this poem, what is Longfellow's philosophy of life? **[Draw Conclusions]**

EXTEND

4. The village blacksmith symbolized the hard work that Americans prized in Longfellow's time. What occupations do you think symbolize the values of the United States today? **[Career Link]**

◆ Critical Thinking

❹ **Relate** Ask students to consider how lines 37–38 summarize the poem to this point. *Toiling refers to what the blacksmith does in stanzas 1–4; he rejoices in stanza 5; he experiences sorrows in stanza 6; line 38 implies that his life is a simple pattern of toiling, rejoicing, and sorrowing.*

◆ Critical Thinking

❺ **Interpret** Ask students to explain the meaning of lines 45–48 in their own words. *Possible reponse: Our lives are determined by the work we put into them and how we respond to life determines who we truly are.*

Beyond Literature

Modern metal workers have different methods and tools than the village blacksmith did, but many modern artisans proudly preserve traditional skills. We suggest the following Internet site (all Web sites are subject to change).

For more on metal working today and blacksmithing in the 21st century:

http://www.anvilfire.com

We *strongly recommend* that you preview the site before you send students to it.

Reinforce and Extend

Answers

◆ Literature and Your Life

Reader's Response Some students may say they admire the blacksmith for his honest approach to work and life.

Thematic Focus Students may say that the blacksmith's attention to his work, day after day at a hot, tiring job, shows the values of dedication and perseverance, and a sense of responsibility.

☑ Check Your Comprehension

1. He is large, broad-shouldered, with big hands and strong, muscular arms. He has long, curly, dark hair and tan skin.
2. The blacksmith can look the whole world in the face because he depends on no one else for his living.

◆ Critical Thinking

1. He is "wet with honest sweat," "he owes not any man," and his arms "are strong as iron bands."
2. The tear reveals that he loved and misses his wife.
3. Some students may say that Longfellow believes the philosophy to life is working hard and honestly, rejoicing in one's family and community, and resting.
4. Students may suggest police officers, firefighters, doctors, and so forth.

In "The Hummingbird That Lived Through Winter," Dikran, a boy's old and nearly blind neighbor, finds a half-dead hummingbird in his garden one cold winter's day. He and the boy work to revive the tiny bird. When it regains its strength and wants to fly, they release it into the cold. When spring comes and the other hummingbirds return, the old man leads the narrator to see that they represent life that continues.

Team Teaching Strategy

The weather conditions in this story and environmental needs of hummingbirds lend themseleves to a science connection. You may want to coordinate with a science teacher to come up with ideas for extending instruction.

Customize for *Visual/Spatial Learners*

The photograph on this page shows a female ruby-throated hummingbird feeding her young. Encourage students to study this picture and note details about the color, size, and setting of the picture. Then have them read the story and create a representation of the hummingbird that appears in the story. Invite volunteers to share their images with the class, explaining the details from the story that guided them in creating their hummingbird representation.

The Hummingbird That Lived Through Winter

William Saroyan

Viewing and Representing Mini-Lesson

Symbols and Slogans

This mini-lesson extends the selection's Literary Focus, which is symbol.

Introduce Almost anything can be an effective symbol. But one must first decide what idea to symbolize. Ask students to think of a dream they have, a goal they aspire to, or a trait they hope to develop; and some way to symbolize it. To establish context for the symbols, have them also consider an accompanying motto or slogan to help convey its meaning. Have students suggest symbols with which they may be familiar, such as the panda as a symbol for the World Wildlife Fund (WWF).

Develop After students select a concept to symbolize, have them plan a format, such as a bookmark, bumper sticker, computer screensaver, stickers or button—anything that can quickly inspire those who see it.

Apply Provide materials, such as art supplies, magazines, and computer or media access. Guide students to pare their representation to its essence—a visual symbol and a slogan. Invite students to preview their symbolic ideas to peers to elicit feedback on ways to make the representation more effective.

Assess Evaluate representations on how effectively students capture ideas visually and with the written slogans. Consider wit, originality, and inspirational value, as well as the effectiveness of the format.

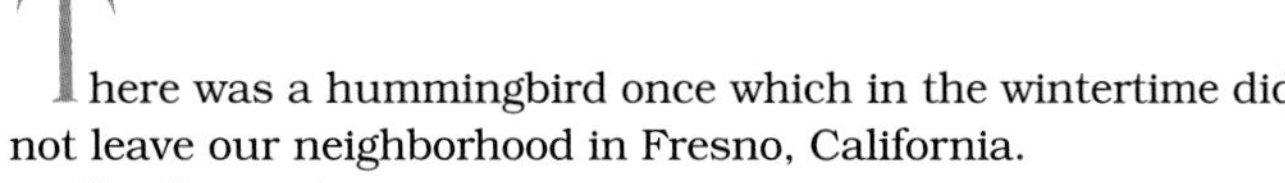

There was a hummingbird once which in the wintertime did not leave our neighborhood in Fresno, California.

I'll tell you about it.

Across the street lived old Dikran,[1] who was almost blind. He was past eighty and his wife was only a few years younger. They had a little house that was as neat inside as it was ordinary outside—except for old Dikran's garden, which was the best thing of its kind in the world. ❶ Plants, bushes, trees—all strong, in sweet black moist earth whose guardian was old Dikran. All things from the sky loved this spot in our poor neighborhood, and old Dikran loved *them*. ❷

One freezing Sunday, in the dead of winter, as I came home from Sunday School I saw old Dikran standing in the middle of the street trying to distinguish what was in his hand. Instead of going into our house to the fire, as I had wanted to do, I stood on the steps of the front porch and watched the old man. He would turn around and look upward at his trees and then back to the palm of his hand. He stood in the street at least two minutes and then at last he came to me. He held his hand out, and in Armenian[2] he said, "What is this in my hand?"

I looked.

"It is a hummingbird," I said half in English and half in Armenian. Hummingbird I said in English because I didn't know its name in Armenian.

"What is that?" old Dikran asked.

"The little bird," I said. "You know. The one that comes in the summer and stands in the air and then shoots away. The one with the wings that beat so fast you can't see them. It's in your hand. It's dying."

"Come with me," the old man said. "I can't see, and the old lady's at church. I can feel its heart beating. Is it in a bad way? Look again, once."

I looked again. It was a sad thing to behold. This wonderful little creature of summertime in the big rough hand of the old peasant. ❸ Here it was in the cold of winter, absolutely helpless and pathetic, not suspended in a shaft of summer light, not the most ❹

1. **Dikran** (dĕk´ rän)
2. **Armenian** (är mē´ nē ən): Language spoken in Armenia, a country in southwestern Asia, bordering Georgia, Turkey, Iran, and Azerbaijan.

◆ Build Vocabulary

pathetic (pə thet´ ik) *adj.*: Arousing pity, sorrow, and sympathy

◄ Critical Viewing What information in the Beyond Literature Connection on page 175 helps you understand this photograph of a hummingbird? Explain. **[Connect]**

◆Critical Thinking

❶ **Draw Conclusions** Discuss with students what the garden reveals about Dikran. *Students may say that the beautiful garden shows that Dikran may be old, but he still is capable of and enjoys tending it well.*

Comprehension Check ☑

❷ What does the author mean by "All things from the sky loved this spot . . ."? *Because of the many flowers and plants in the garden, all types of birds and flying insects are attracted to it.*

◆Reading Strategy

❸ **Question** Review with students the title of this story. Given the title and the details in this passage, ask students what questions come to mind to give them a purpose to continue reading. You may wish to have students use charts to record their questions and note the answers that they find.

Question	The Answer I Found
What will Dikran and the boy do?	

◆Literary Focus

❹ **Symbol** Point out that Saroyan describes the hummingbird as a "creature of summertime." Talk with students about how that description contrasts with the bird's present condition. *Students may say that the bird's condition suggests the opposite of summer, for it has lost its vigor and barely moves, and therefore seems more like the "dead of winter" mentioned earlier.*

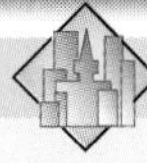

Beyond the Classroom

Career Connection

Working in Nature Students who feel a strong connection with nature may want to follow a path that will lead them to a career working outside. Have students form interest groups based on a branch of nature that interests them, such as animals, plants, minerals, or wetlands. Within each group, have students brainstorm for a list of possible job opportunities, or situations where they have seen adults at work. For instance, students who like working with people outdoors might consider jobs as park rangers, trail guides, or clerks at a garden shop or tree nursery. Animal lovers might consider wildlife research, veterinary medicine, farming, or animal grooming, breeding, or training.

Have students investigate their ideas on the Internet, in the library, or by talking with people who work in nature. They might write letters of inquiry to places like state wildlife agencies or local parks to see if there are any opportunities for interns or volunteers their age.

◆Literary Focus

1 Symbol Ask students what winter or summer might symbolize to a man who loves his garden and the birds that visit it. *Possible answers: The winter represents a time when nature is asleep and the man, himself, takes a rest; summer stands for renewal and energy.*

Thematic Focus

2 Shared Dream Ask students what a person's "will and love" can do for another. *Students may suggest that will and love can spur someone on, give support, and encourage them to keep going even if they lack the will themselves.*

◆Critical Thinking

3 Analyze Dikran knows that the boy cannot recognize the hummingbird. Ask students why he might ask this question. What lesson is he trying to teach the boy? *Students may say he wants to teach the boy that life goes on, even if one individual dies.*

Customize for *English Language Learners*

To help students understand the meanings of phrases such as "shoot upwards," "suspend itself in space," and "spun about," use your hands to imitate the movements of the bird.

alive thing in the world, but the most helpless and heartbreaking.

"It's dying," I said.

The old man lifted his hand to his mouth and blew warm breath on the little thing in his hand which he could not even see.

1 "Stay now," he said in Armenian. "It is not long till summer. Stay, swift and lovely."

We went into the kitchen of his little house, and while he blew warm breath on the bird he told me what to do.

"Put a tablespoonful of honey over the gas fire and pour it into my hand, but be sure it is not too hot."

This was done.

After a moment the hummingbird began to show signs of fresh 2 life. The warmth of the room, the vapor of the warm honey—and, well, the will and love of the old man. Soon the old man could feel the change in his hand, and after a moment or two the hummingbird began to take little dabs of the honey.

"It will live," the old man announced. "Stay and watch."

The transformation was incredible. The old man kept his hand generously open, and I expected the helpless bird to shoot upward out of his hand, suspend itself in space, and scare the life out of me—which is exactly what happened. The new life of the little bird was magnificent. It spun about in the little kitchen, going to the window, coming back to the heat, suspending, circling as if it were summertime and it had never felt better in its whole life.

The old man sat on the plain chair, blind but attentive. He listened carefully and tried to see, but of course he couldn't. He kept asking about the bird, how it seemed to be, whether it showed signs of weakening again, what its spirit was, and whether or not it appeared to be restless; and I kept describing the bird to him.

When the bird was restless and wanted to go, the old man said, "Open the window and let it go."

"Will it live?" I asked.

"It is alive now and wants to go," he said. "Open the window."

I opened the window, the hummingbird stirred about here and there, feeling the cold from the outside, suspended itself in the area of the open window, stirring this way and that, and then it was gone.

"Close the window," the old man said.

We talked a minute or two and then I went home.

The old man claimed the hummingbird lived through that winter, but I never knew for sure. I saw hummingbirds again when

◆ Build Vocabulary

transformation (trans′ fər mā′ shən) *n.*: Change in condition or outward appearance

Speaking and Listening Mini-Lesson

Song

This mini-lesson supports the Speaking and Listening activity in the Idea Bank on p. 177.

Introduce Songs can inspire listeners with catchy, heroic, or sweet melodies, rhythms, and lyrics. Play an inspiring song, such as a patriotic anthem, for the class. Talk about the aspects of the song that lend encouragement.

Develop Have students work in pairs or independently. Present these options: Select an existing poem about courage to set to music; revise "The Courage That My Mother Had" and set it to an original or existing melody; or create original lyrics and melody for a song that gets at the importance of courage. Students who play instruments may arrange to accompany themselves.

Apply Set aside time for students to perform their songs, either live or by playing an audio- or videotaped recording of it. Students might prepare lyric sheets for the audience so they can follow along.

Assess Evaluate students on originality, choice of musical style, presentation, and how well they meet the challenge of the assignment.

summer came, but I couldn't tell one from the other.

One day in the summer I asked the old man.

"Did it live?"

"The little bird?" he said.

"Yes," I said. "That we gave the honey to. You remember. The little bird that was dying in the winter. Did it live?"

3 "Look about you," the old man said. "Do you see the bird?"

"I see humming*birds*," I said.

"Each of them is our bird," the old man said. "Each of them, each of them," he said swiftly and gently.

Beyond Literature

Science Connection

Hummingbirds—Nature's Wonder
Saroyan's narrator is fascinated by the hummingbird, a tiny bird that can suspend itself in midair by beating its wings 50 times each second! Hummingbirds hover over flowers long enough to feed on their nectar before darting away—at speeds of up to 60 miles per hour. Since this motion expends energy, the birds spend nights in deep sleep.

Cross-Curricular Activity
Multimedia Report With classmates, learn more about hummingbirds. Check the Internet, read books, or speak with bird specialists at a local college or zoo. Then, create a multimedia presentation using artwork, models, or videos to accompany an oral report that captures this amazing bird's spirit.

Guide for Responding

◆ Literature and Your Life

Reader's Response Would you have let the hummingbird go again, or would you have tried to keep it inside until spring? Explain.

Thematic Focus How does working together to save the hummingbird change the relationship between the boy and the old man?

☑ Check Your Comprehension

1. Describe "old Dikran's" personality and appearance.
2. What do the narrator and Dikran do to help the hummingbird?
3. What happens to the hummingbird while it is in Dikran's house?
4. How does Dikran respond to the narrator's question about whether the bird lived?

◆ Critical Thinking

Interpret

1. How does Dikran feel about nature and living creatures? **[Infer]**
2. What does the narrator think about the old man's efforts to save the bird? **[Interpret]**
3. Why does Dikran let the bird go? **[Analyze]**
4. Compare and contrast the two characters' ways of looking at the world. **[Compare and Contrast]**

Apply

5. The narrator says the bird "began to show signs of life." What does he mean by this expression? Whom do you know who fits this description? **[Relate]**

Extend

6. From a scientist's view, is it likely that the hummingbird survived the winter? Why or why not? **[Science Link]**

Beyond the Selection

FURTHER READING

Other Works by the Authors

I Wonder as I Wander, Langston Hughes

The Harp-Weaver and Other Poems, Edna St. Vincent Millay

The Courtship of Miles Standish and Other Poems, Henry Wadsworth Longfellow

My Name Is Aram, William Saroyan

INTERNET

We suggest the following sites on the Internet (all Web sites are subject to change).

For more information about Langston Hughes, go to: **http://ie.uwindsor.ca/jazz/hughes.html**

For more on Henry Wadsworth Longfellow, go to: **http://www.auburn.edu/~vestmon/longfellow.html**

For more on William Saroyan, go to: **http://www.pbs.org/newshour/essays/rodriguez_5-26.html**

We *strongly recommend* that you preview the sites.

Beyond Literature

Students can find a vast array of hummingbird resources at this Internet address: **http://www.derived.com/hummers**

Another useful Web site is the Patuxent Bird Identification Center at **http://www.mbr.nbs.gov/id/framlst/framlst.html** which contains identification tips, life-history data, and photos.

We *strongly recommend* that you preview these sites before you send students to them.

Reinforce and Extend

Answers

◆ Literature and Your Life

Reader's Response Some students may say that they would have kept the bird inside to protect it; others may say that they would have released it because it seemed to want to go.

Thematic Focus They share the goal of saving the bird.

☑ Check Your Comprehension

1. He is an older person and almost blind. He is kind, neat, well organized, careful, patient, and wise.
2. They bring it inside, warm it with their breath and hands, feed it honey, and let it regain its strength.
3. It recovers and begins to fly.
4. Dikran points out that each of the birds is their bird.

◆ Critical Thinking

1. Dikran enjoys nature and living things and takes care of them.
2. At first he is skeptical but then he is awed at the bird's change.
3. He believes it is ready to go.
4. Dikran believes in the coexistence of humans and nature. The boy is less sure of himself and believes in the hard reality of what he observes.
5. It means that the bird revives after being so lifeless; it begins to breathe, move, and drink.
6. It's unlikely that the bird survived; most fragile, small birds such as hummingbirds cannot survive the cold of winter.

Answers

◆Reading Strategy

1. Possible answers: She may have died in childbirth, or when their daughter was young, perhaps of a disease common in those times. Answering this question helps to create a fuller portrait of the blacksmith by giving him an emotional side.
2. Students may suggest that she has faced many obstacles and sees her son facing some of the same challenges. She wants to tell him that life can be hard but he should not give up. Answering this question gives the reader insight into what the speaker has gone through and how she feels about her son.
3. He may feel strongly about nature because it is a constant symbol of life and rebirth and he is growing old. Answering this question helps readers appreciate Dikran's desire to help the hummingbird and his answer to the boy at the end of the story.

◆Build Vocabulary

Using the Prefix *trans-*

Sample sentences:

1. translate; The boy can translate Armenian into English.
2. transcontinental; Transcontinental journeys can take days or weeks.
3. translucent; Translucent curtains let in light but give us privacy.

Spelling Strategy

1. watches; 2. churches; 3. ditches; 4. sketches

Using the Word Bank

1. pathetic; 2. brawny; 3. quarried; 4. brooch; 5. transformation

◆Literary Focus

1. (a) The brooch symbolizes the speaker's mother. (b) The speaker says it was left behind for her to wear and she treasures it.
2. (a) The bird symbolizes hope and life. (b) The bird is compared to summer and it is brought back to life by warm air, honey, and love.
3. A blacksmith is an effective symbol for strength and hard work because his job requires these traits.

Guide for Responding *(continued)*

◆ Reading Strategy

Question

When you **question** as you read, you can often unlock the meaning of a work of literature. You can ask why a character says or does something or wonder about a writer's choices of details or plot. For example, if you asked why Millay used the image of a rock, you might have concluded that rocks are strong and enduring. These, in turn, are qualities that Millay links to her mother's courage. Consider these questions, and then explain how answering them adds to your reading.

1. In "The Village Blacksmith," how and when do you think the blacksmith's wife died?
2. In "Mother to Son," why might the speaker want to give this advice to her son?
3. Why does Dikran feel so strongly about nature?

◆ Build Vocabulary

Using the Prefix *trans-*

Words that include the prefix *trans-* involve change or movement. They tell about moving people, ideas, or objects "across, over, through, and beyond." Add *trans-* to these words or word parts to create a word fitting the definition supplied. Then, use each word in a sentence.

1. *-late*: Change from one language into another
2. *-continental*: Extending across a continent
3. *-lucent*: Something that light can shine through

Spelling Strategy

To make the plural of words ending in *ch*, always add -es, as in brooches. On your paper, make these words plural.

1. watch **2.** church **3.** ditch **4.** sketch

Using the Word Bank

On your paper, complete each sentence with the correct word from the Word Bank.

1. She was ___?___ in her grief over the old man's death.
2. After weight-training, his body became ___?___ .
3. The gravestones are ___?___ nearby.
4. Millay remembers her mother's gold ___?___ .
5. The man's efforts caused a ___?___ in the bird.

◆ Literary Focus

Symbol

A **symbol** is an object that conveys an idea or message beyond itself. The writers in this grouping use symbols to suggest important ideas. For example, in "Mother to Son," the "dark" symbolizes confusion and "light" stands for knowledge. Because they give you simple and concrete pictures, these symbols let you get closer to Hughes's ideas about life's struggles.

1. (a) What does the brooch in "The Courage That My Mother Had" represent? (b) How do you know?
2. (a) What does the hummingbird symbolize for Dikran? (b) What details help you decide?
3. In "The Village Blacksmith," why is a blacksmith an effective symbol for the strength to keep going and the value of hard work?

◆ Build Grammar Skills

Principal Parts of Verbs

Every verb (word expressing an action or state of being) has four main forms, called its **principal parts.** These parts are used to form verb tenses, the forms that show time. Regular verbs, such as *climb,* form their past tense and past participles by adding *-ed* or *-d.* Irregular verbs, such as *be,* form their past tense and/or past participles in different ways.

Base (present)	Present Participle	Past	Past Participle
reach	reaching	reached	(have, has, had) reached
earn	earning	earned	(have, has, had) earned
am, be	being	was, were	(have, has, had) been
go	going	went	(have, has, had) gone

Practice On your paper, complete the following chart.

Base (present)	Present Participle	Past	Past Participle
	talking	talked	
	choosing		(have, has, had) chosen
find			(have, has, had) found

Writing Application Write four sentences about one of the selections in this grouping. In each sentence, use a different principal part of the verb *try.*

◆Build Grammar Skills

Writing Application

Possible responses:

1. Try not to give up.
2. She is trying to teach her son.
3. The woman tried to be strong.
4. They have tried to succeed.

Writer's Solution

For additional instruction and practice, use the lesson in the *Writer's Solution Language Lab CD-ROM* on Principal Parts of Verbs, and the practice pages on Verbs, pp. 11–14 in the *Writer's Solution Grammar Practice Book.*

Build Your Portfolio

Idea Bank

Writing

1. Response Poem Write a poem that could be called "Son to Mother." Answer the mother's advice, using speech patterns that a real boy would use. Follow Hughes's example by using a comparison to describe the son's life.

2. Public-Service Announcement A public-service announcement, or PSA, is a message that attempts to educate, advise, or persuade the public to respond to an issue of public concern. Write the text of a PSA intended to encourage respect for adults and the older generation.

3. Analysis of a Symbol Choose a symbol in one of the works you just read. In an essay, explain what the symbol represents. Use evidence from the text to support your interpretation.

Speaking and Listening

4. Song Using "The Courage That My Mother Had" as an inspiration, write a song in which you explain the importance of courage. Add music to your lyrics. **[Music Link]**

5. An Unexpected Meeting Role-play a meeting among the writers whose work is presented here. Have each writer give the others advice about life. Use the poems and story plus what you know about the writers' lives to make them sound realistic. **[Performing Arts Link]**

Projects

6. Survey [Group Activity] Ask adults in your community to identify the one quality in people that they most value. Divide these tasks among a group: collect the data, tabulate results on a chart or graph, and write a brief summary of the conclusions you draw from the information. **[Math Link]**

7. Internet Research Go on-line to learn about one of the authors presented here. Collect facts about the writer's life and work. If possible, share examples of his or her writing with the class.

Writing Mini-Lesson

Pep Talk

Like a coach giving a pep talk before the big game, each of these writers—Longfellow, Hughes, Millay, and Saroyan—offers encouragement about facing life's challenges. Imagine that you have to give a similar pep talk—to a friend with a problem, to your teammates before the debate finals, to a younger brother or sister entering a new school. Choose a situation, and write the pep talk that you might give to encourage extra effort or to inspire bravery.

Writing Skills Focus: Stress Main Idea

Because you give a pep talk when there's a problem to be solved, you want listeners to remember your advice. If you **stress the main idea**—by repeating it, restating it several ways, or putting it in your opening and concluding paragraphs—your message is sure to be received. Notice how Langston Hughes restates the main idea that life isn't easy.

Model From the Poem

Life for me ain't been no crystal stair.
It's had tacks in it,
And splinters,
And boards torn up,

Prewriting Once you've chosen a situation, list the problems your audience might face. For each, explain why your audience is up for the challenge.

Drafting Address each problem individually, but always return to your main point—that no problem is impossible to conquer.

Revising Read your draft to classmates, and ask whether they feel encouraged or inspired by it. If the talk is not working, go back to your draft, and find places to stress your main idea more strongly.

◆ Grammar Application

Make sure you have correctly formed the past and past participle forms of irregular verbs.

✓ ASSESSMENT OPTIONS

Formal Assessment, Selection Test, pp. 47–49, and Assessment Resources Software. The selection test is designed so that it can be easily customized to the performance levels of your students.

Alternative Assessment, p. 13, includes options for less advanced students, more advanced students, verbal/linguistic learners, visual/spatial learners, and bodily/kinesthetic learners.

PORTFOLIO ASSESSMENT

Use the following rubrics in the **Alternative Assessment** booklet to assess student writing:
Public Service Announcement: Persuasion, p. 92
Response Poem: Poetry, p. 95
Analysis of a Symbol: Literary Analysis/Interpretation, p. 99
Writing Mini-Lesson: Problem/Solution, p. 88

Idea Bank

Following are suggestions for matching the Idea Bank topics with your students' performance levels and learning modalities:

Customize for *Performance Levels*
Less Advanced Students: 2, 6, 7
Average Students: 1, 4, 6, 7
More Advanced Students: 3, 5

Customize for *Learning Modalities*
Verbal/Linguistic: 1, 2, 3, 6
Bodily/Kinesthetic: 5, 6
Logical/Mathematical: 3, 6, 7
Musical/Rhythmic: 2, 4
Interpersonal: 1, 4, 6
Intrapersonal: 2, 3, 4, 7

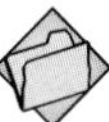

Writing Mini-Lesson

Refer students to the Writing Handbook in the back of the book for instructions on the writing process and for further information on persuasive writing.

You might provide students with the Main Idea and Supporting Details Organizer in **Writing and Language Transparencies,** p. 70, to help them plan their pep talk.

Writer's Solution

Writing Lab CD-ROM
Have students complete the tutorial on Persuasion. Follow these steps:

1. Have students use the Topic Web activity to develop a variety of topics.
2. Allow students to draft on computer.
3. Encourage students to use the Transition Word Bin activity to find transitional words and phrases to use in their draft.
4. Have students use the Self-Evaluation Checklist when revising.

Writer's Solution Sourcebook
Have students use Chapter 6, "Persuasion," pp. 166–199, for additional support. The chapter includes in-depth instruction on avoiding faulty reasoning, p. 189.

Connections to Today's World

In 1998, people around the world were inspired by the team effort exhibited by the U.S. Women's Hockey team in achieving their shared dream—winning the gold medal in the first women's Olympic ice hockey tournament in Nagano, Japan. Their victory and performance were a huge step forward for women's ice hockey and women's sports in America. In the competition, the female athletes on all the teams displayed a will to compete and an intensity to win, proving to the world that women are ready for grittier sports that were formerly the domain of men alone. This piece is excerpted from a longer article Johnette Howard wrote for *Sports Illustrated* magazine in March, 1998.

Thematic Connection

❶ Ask students to explain how Tueting's brother shares and participates in his sister's dream. *He accompanies the team to Japan to watch his sister play and he joins in the victory celebration by tossing the foam-rubber Uncle Sam hat onto the ice for his sister to wear.*

Customize for *English Language Learners*

This selection contains sports terms and expressions, such as *camp, drum major, sealed the victory,* and *nudging in,* as well as terms specific to the sport of hockey. Help students to understand the meaning of these unfamiliar words or phrases by using sketches, or by a video of a hockey game. For example, call on knowledgeable students to identify the leftwinger, the goalie, and an empty net goal, and examples of spectacular saves and high stepping on the ice.

Connections to Today's World

In the following article, sportswriter Johnette Howard tells the story of the dream shared by teammates. Showing the courage and determination that Hughes and Longfellow celebrate, the members of the U.S. Women's Hockey Team worked together to achieve their dream—winning a gold medal at the 1998 Winter Olympics.

Johnette Howard

By the time the clock struck midnight and the pop of champagne corks was heard at the victory party, the game's particulars had begun to fade from conversation. The feelings were what the U.S. women ice hockey players wanted to review: the lumps in their throats, the chills that ran down their spines, the eye-dampening sight of goalie Sarah Tueting high-stepping around the ice like a crazed drum major after the U.S. won the gold medal game 3–1 against archnemesis Canada. Sandra Whyte, Tueting's onetime housemate in Boston, had sealed the victory, nudging in a 40-foot empty-net goal that the sellout crowd in Nagano's Big Hat stadium traced on its excruciatingly slow path to the net with a steadily building roar of *oh-oh-ooOOHH!* "I'm sure all of us will see ourselves celebrating on tape tomorrow and say, 'I did *what*?' said U.S. forward A.J. Mleczko.

"All I could think was, We just won a gold medal—did we not just win a gold
❶ medal?" said Tueting, an apple-cheeked Dartmouth junior-to-be who made 21 saves, many of them spectacular, in the final, and then floated into both the postgame press conference and the victory party wearing a two-foot-tall foam-
rubber Uncle Sam hat that her brother, ❶
Jonathon, had tossed onto the ice. Suddenly those despair-filled months in 1996, when Tueting was ready to quit hockey at age 19 because she'd never been invited to a U.S. national team tryout, seemed long, long ago. "I had gone home that summer, taken the Olympic posters off my bedroom wall and told everyone I was through," Tueting said. "Then August came, and I got a letter inviting me to camp. I made the national team. In the space of two weeks I went from quitting hockey to putting my life on hold to chase this dream. And now look."

In winning the six-team inaugural women's Olympic tournament with a 6–0 record, the U.S. team eclipsed Picabo Street[1] as America's feel-good story of the Winter Games. On Sunday, General Mills announced that it had chosen Tueting and her teammates to adorn its post-Olympics

1. **Picabo** (pēk´ ə bo͞o) **Street:** Member of the U.S. Women's Ski Team who came back from a serious injury to win two gold medals at the 1998 Olympic Winter Games.

More About the Author

Johnette Howard is a sportswriter who has contributed many articles to *Sports Illustrated* on topics as diverse as baseball, boxing, and speed skating.

Cross-Curricular Connection: Physical Education

Women's Sports Women's team sports are on the upswing, as indicated by the introduction of ice hockey as an Olympic sport. Inform students that it wasn't too long ago that very few people knew that women played basketball professionally or that girls could participate in Little League baseball.

Have students find out about and report to the class on the beginnings of some women's team sports or leagues. For example, they can look into the Ladies Professional Baseball League, research the beginnings of college women's basketball, or find out about the history of girls' team sports in your area. Encourage them to survey women of all ages to determine when and if they were permitted to participate in team sports. Alternatively, students can find out about individuals who made a difference in the growth and success of women's team sports, such as Senda Berenson, who introduced women's basketball to Smith College in 1892. Invite students to post their findings on a class bulletin board.

2 ▲ **Critical Viewing** This photograph was taken moments after the medal ceremony at the 1998 Olympic Winter Games. What details show the women saw their victory as a team effort? **[Analyze]**

Wheaties box. Just hours after the gold medal game on Feb. 17, the *Late Show with David Letterman* rushed 10 of the U.S. players to a Nagano TV studio to read a Top Ten List titled "Cool Things About Winning an Olympic Gold Medal."

Sportswriters walked into the final grousing about having to cover it and walked out gushing that it was the best thing they'd ever seen. A felicitous[2] line by *Washington Post* columnist Michael Wilbon, who called Mleczko "the first leftwinger I've ever had a crush on," was typical.

3 That stretching sound you hear is attitudes about women athletes continuing to expand. After the 1996 Atlanta Summer Olympics and now the Nagano Games, it's clear that the U.S.'s female athletic heroes don't have to play what Billie Jean King has jokingly called the "good clothes sports"—figure skating, tennis and golf. Women never lacked the strength or will to compete in the grittier sports, just the opportunity. When they get the chance, they can produce stirring results. 3 As the U.S. men's Olympic goalie, Mike Richter of the New York Rangers, said admiringly after watching the U.S. women play Canada, "You felt so good for them, the way they were just bleeding for each other to win every game." 4

2. **felicitous** (fə lis′ i təs) *adj.*: Appropriate or well-chosen.

1. (a) What was Sarah Tueting's dream in college? (b) Why did she nearly give up on this dream?
2. (a) Why did sportswriters complain about covering the finals? (b) Why did they "walk out gushing"?
3. Drawing on your reading of this article and the other selections in this part, describe what it takes to make shared dreams come true.

Beyond the Selection

FURTHER READING

Other Works About Women's Ice Hockey

She Shoots . . . She Scores: Complete Guide to Girls' and Women's Hockey, Barbara Stewart

Our Goal Is Gold: A Pictorial Profile of the 1998 USA Hockey Team

On the Edge: Women Making Hockey History, Elizabeth Etue and Megan K. Williams

INTERNET

We suggest the following site on the Internet (all Web sites are subject to change).

For more on the women's hockey team at the 1998 Nagano Olympics:

http://cnnsi.com/olympics/events/1998/nagano/

We *strongly recommend* that you preview this site before you send students to it.

▶Critical Viewing◀

2 **Analyze** *The players in the photo show their team spirit by the way they huddle together around the large American flag, proudly displaying medals, flowers, and small flags, all emblems of team effort and shared victory.*

Thematic Connection

3 Ask students to explain how the victory of the United States women's ice hockey team may affect the dreams of other female athletes. *Other female athletes may now expect to achieve their dream of recognition by the sports world because the hockey team achieved this same dream.*

Clarification

4 Mike Richter was the goalie on the underdog 1980 United States men's Olympic ice hockey team that shocked the sports world by winning the gold medal.

Looking at Literature Videodisc/Videotape

To provide background for students, and to motivate them to read "Golden Girls: The 1998 U.S. Women's Hockey Team," play Chapter 2 of the videodisc. This chapter will give students an overview of the history of the modern Olympics. Discuss how the 1998 women's hockey team stayed true to the Olympic spirit.

Chapter 2

Answers

1. (a) She wanted to play hockey for the United States national team. (b) She had never been invited to a team tryout.
2. (a) Sportswriters probably thought that women's ice hockey would be dull, poorly played, and of little interest to anyone but the participants. (b) By the end of the tournament, the writers were convinced that the intensity and desire of the players could generate a great deal of excitement.
3. Students may say that teamwork and perseverance help shared dreams come true.

Prepare and Engage

OBJECTIVES

1. To read, comprehend, and interpret a selection that has a social studies focus
2. To relate a story with a social studies focus to personal experience
3. To connect literature to social studies
4. To respond to Social Studies Guiding Questions
5. To respond to the story through writing, speaking and listening, and projects

SOCIAL STUDIES GUIDING QUESTIONS

Reading about the special relationship between two young people during the Middle Ages will help students discover answers to these Social Studies Guiding Questions:

- How did the belief system of England during the Middle Ages affect its history, government, and economy?
- What was the pattern of day-to-day life in England during the Middle Ages?

Invite a volunteer to describe the details of his or her daily routine to prepare for school, while the rest of the class takes notes on what is needed for each step of the routine. Then have students list the basic needs of day-to-day life, including food, shelter, clothing, recreation, and education. Tell students that this story takes place in a time when most communities were small and isolated. Guide them to see how these features increased the ways people depended on one another for their basic needs.

Map Study

Viewing a Diagram Picturing the physical setting of a time period is useful for understanding a historical story. A diagram is a plan or sketch that shows the parts of something and where they are placed. The diagram on this page helps make sense of the medieval community, including and surrounding a manor house, by depicting the common areas where people lived and worked. To help relate the diagram to the medieval time period and further understand the characters in the story, have students read Peasants and Lords on this page.

CONNECTING LITERATURE TO SOCIAL STUDIES

MEDIEVAL TIMES

The Midwife's Apprentice *by Karen Cushman*

FIRST BATH IN MONTHS! Believe it or not, such an occurrence wouldn't be unusual in the England of six hundred years ago. People bathed very rarely—some doctors even believed dangerous diseases could get through uncovered skin.

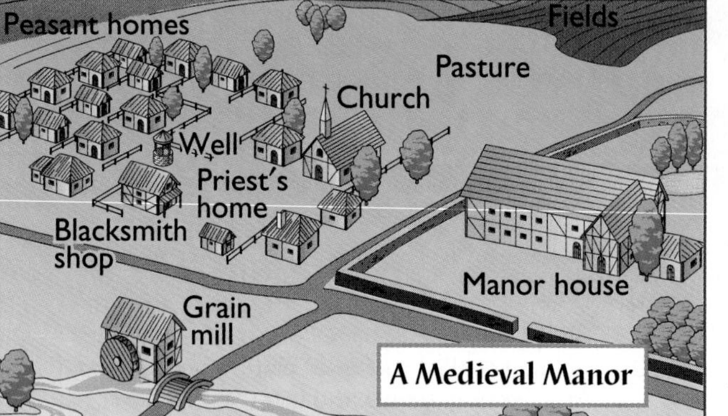

A Medieval Manor

Peasants and Lords In England in the fourteenth century, people spent their days just trying to survive. If they lived in the country, their lives centered around a manor house, like the one pictured here—usually the home of a lord, a member of a class just below the king in importance. The manor functioned as a complete community, inhabited not only by the lord and his family, but also by peasants who worked for the lord in return for protection from roving gangs.

Village Life The peasants led simple lives. The men plowed fields and grew crops. Many raised sheep for wool and milk. Women walked to the village well to get fresh water. They spun yarn and wove cloth from sheep's wool to make clothing. Food was simple—bread made from local grains and vegetables from the garden.

At the Manor Children helped in the fields or at home. Like the boy in this story, some worked in the manor at such chores as roasting meat over a fire with a hand crank. When the lord was home—for he might be away in the king's service—the manor would fill with parties. Though a boy would then work harder, he might enjoy the excitement in the manor's hall.

Shared Dreams Life was hard, and young people grew up very fast. Still, just like you, children of the time yearned for friendship and wondered if others found them attractive. In *The Midwife's Apprentice*, you'll meet two fictional young people whose lives are set during this distant age.

Prentice Hall Literature Program Resources

REINFORCE / RETEACH / EXTEND

Selection Support Pages
Build Vocabulary, p. 70
Connect Historical Fiction to Social Studies, p. 71

Formal Assessment Selection Test, pp. 50–51, Assessment Resources Software

Readings from Social Studies

Writing and Language Transparencies
Sensory Language Chart, p. 78

Resource Pro CD-ROM
"The Midwife's Apprentice"—includes all resource material and customizable lesson plan

Listening to Literature Audiocassettes
"The Midwife's Apprentice"

Connection to Prentice Hall World Explorer
Medieval Times to Today
Ch. 5, "Europe in the Middle Ages"
Ch. 6, "A New Age in Europe"

from The Midwife's Apprentice

Karen Cushman

Alyce, a homeless child, is taken in by a sharp-tongued midwife (a woman who helps others with childbirth). She makes the girl her apprentice. One day, Alyce finds Edward, another homeless child. Although she is not able to care for him herself, Alyce persuades the cook at the local baron's manor to give the boy a job and a place to stay. Alyce promises Edward that she will return for him when she can. Months pass. Alyce has an argument with the midwife and takes a job working at an inn. Now that she has an income of her own and a place to live, Alyce returns to the manor to reclaim Edward.

While they ate their bread-and-bacon supper, while Alyce helped Edward mound up straw in a corner of the kitchen, while she sat by watching for him to go to sleep, all the while Edward talked of life on the manor. He told her of the silken-robed lords and ladies who came for feasts and rode out to hunt and danced like autumn leaves in the candlelit great hall, of the visiting knights who clanked their swords against each other as they practiced in the school yard, of the masons who slapped mortar and bricks together to build a great new tower at the corner of the hall that looked to stretch near all the way to heaven. He described the excitement of buying and selling at the great autumn horse fair, the nervous preparations accompanying the arrival of some velvet-shod bishop or priest, and the thrill of watching the baron's men ride out to confront a huge maddened boar who had roamed too close to the village. And he complained at his lot, doing all the smallest tasks, not being allowed to help with the threshing and ploughing, being teased for being so little and frail and tied to Cook's skirts and fit for nothing but gathering eggs. Finally as his eyes looked near to closing, he said, "Tell me a story, Alyce."

"I don't know any stories."

"For sure you do. Everyone does."

"Well, Jennet told me that one night a visiting mayor fell out of bed, hit his head, and thought he was a cat, so he slept all night on the floor watching the mouseholes."

"That is no story, Alyce. Cook tells me stories. A story should have a hero and brave deeds."

"Well then, once there was a boy who for all he was so small and puny was brave enough to do what he must although he didn't like it and was sometimes teased. Is that a story?"

> **Connecting Literature to Social Studies**
> How is Edward's life at the manor different from that of a peasant boy living in the village? **1**

"Close enough, Alyce." And he closed his eyes.

When the moon shone through the misty clouds and two owls hooted in the manor yard, Edward and Alyce slept, each comforted

◆ Build Vocabulary

roamed (rōmd) *v.*: Wandered

frail (frāl) *adj.*: Delicate or weak

Develop Understanding

One-Minute Insight This excerpt from *The Midwife's Apprentice* captures a brief episode in the lives of two young people during the Middle Ages. Once homeless, they have formed a bond of friendship and now Alyce is visiting Edward at the manor where he lives and works. When the two friends help with the community's sheep washing, Alyce—who lives a struggling existence—discovers beauty in the surroundings and in herself. As students read about the dreams of these characters from long ago, they will discover that people of other times and cultures share the same need for friends, admiration, and fun.

Team Teaching Strategy

"The Midwife's Apprentice" offers team teaching opportunities with a social studies teacher and with a health or science teacher. You may wish to coordinate for a cross-curricular unit on medieval times that includes geography and historical aspects of the time period, including issues of diet and personal hygiene.

Customize for
Less Proficient Readers
Have students use the Sensory Language Chart, p. 78 in **Writing and Language Transparencies,** to list details about the setting. Noting details as they read should help students orient themselves to the story setting and encourage them to focus on the ways that the setting is recognizable despite the historical time period.

CONNECTING LITERATURE TO SOCIAL STUDIES

1 Compare and Contrast Point out to students that village children lived in simple one-room homes and spent their days working in the fields. *Possible responses: Edward sees visiting nobles and knights; he does chores for the cook instead of field work; he sleeps in the manor kitchen instead of living in a small house.*

Preparing for Standardized Tests

Critical Thinking Standardized tests often ask students to read a passage and respond to multiple-choice questions. Remind students that they must think critically and analyze information in order to draw conclusions. Setting details, and characters' actions and words provide information in a fictional passage. Have students practice their critical thinking skills by rereading p. 181 for clues about Edward's goals and dreams. Then write the following question and answer choices on the board:

When he grows up, Edward wants to become a _______

(A) cook (C) mason
(B) knight (D) mayor

Review the information and answer choices with students. Help them rule out *(A)* because of Edward's complaints about chores; *(C)* because it is not well-supported by the text; and *(D)* because it is a minor detail. Based on Edward's description of the knights, *(A)* is the best answer to the question. For more practice, use the Connecting Literature to Social Studies question on p. 182.

▶Critical Viewing◀

1 Infer *Students may infer that medieval peasants raised sheep and cows, lived in small houses, and wore simple clothing.*

Connecting Literature to Social Studies

2 Draw Conclusions *Possible response: Edward eats mostly the same few foods and hasn't tried many other kinds of foods.*

Customize for *English Language Learners*

To help students recognize words and understand the hectic nature of the sheep-washing scene, call on native speakers to demonstrate and pantomime. Write descriptions such as "barking of dogs," "lathering their backs," and "coughing and sputtering" on the board. Have volunteers imitate the sounds and actions. Then help students locate these words in the text.

Customize for *More Advanced Students*

Have students research the aspects of medieval life described by Edward:

- The guild system that apprenticed masons and other craftspeople
- Knights, their armor and battle training
- Hunting and harvest festivals

Invite students to share their findings with the class through role play, posters, or oral reports.

Humanities: Art

Farmyard with woman milking cow, by Simon Bening

Simon Bening (1484–1561) was a Flemish book illustrator. This illustration was one of many created for calendars of the time. Like snapshots, the pictures illustrate events related to a particular month.

How does this illustration help you imagine washing the sheep? *The line of sheep and lack of machinery show that the task is difficult and time-consuming.*

Farmyard with woman milking cow, from the Da Costa Book of Hours, Bruges, c. 1515

1 ▲ **Critical Viewing** What can you infer about medieval life from this painting? **[Infer]**

by knowing the other was safe and warm and sheltered and not too very far away.

The next day being the day the woolly black-faced sheep were washed before shearing, Alyce and Edward ate their breakfast down by the river to watch the great event.

Edward finished his breakfast first. "I'm still hungry, Alyce, and there is nothing about here to eat but grass. Do you know if grass is good for people to eat?"

"Try it."

He did. "It be good for exercising my teeth and making my mouth taste better, but it tastes like . . . grass, I would say."

"Then do not eat it."

"What is the best thing you ever ate, Alyce?"

"Hot soup on a cold day, I think."

"Once long ago a monk gave me a fig. It was a wonderful thing, Alyce, soft and sweet. After that I had nothing to eat for three days but the smell of the fig on my fingers. Are you ever going to finish that bread, Alyce?"

And Alyce gave him her bread, which is what Edward wanted and Alyce intended all along.

> **Connecting Literature to Social Studies**
> What conclusion about his life experience can you draw from Edward's reaction to eating a fig? 2

Part of the river had been dammed to form a washing pool. Men stood in the waist-deep water while the hairy shepherds, looking much like sheep themselves, drove the woolly beasts into the water to have their loose fleeces pulled off and then be scrubbed with the strong yellow soap. The river was noisy with the barking of dogs, the bleating of sheep, the calling and cursing of men, and the furious bawling[1] of those lambs separated from their mothers. Edward soon took on the job of matching mothers and babies. He snatched up the bawling lambs and ran from mother to mother until he made up the right pair, whereupon they would knock him out of the way in their hurry to nuzzle each other.

As the day grew hotter the river looked cooler, and finally Alyce tucked her skirt up into her belt and waded in. The weary men were glad of another pair of hands and soon had Alyce helping. First she held the woolly black faces while they were scrubbed, but one old ewe took offense at Alyce's handling and, standing up with her front feet on Alyce's chest, pushed the girl into the water. Alyce, coughing and sputtering, traded jobs with the man who was lathering their backs. Fleeces clean, the sheep swam to the bank and scrambled out of the water, nimble as goats and hungry as pigs.

By midafternoon they were finished. While Edward and the shepherds drove the sheep to their pens across the field, Alyce stretched and wiped her wet hands on her wet skirt. What a

1. **bawling** (bôl′ iŋ) *n.*: Loud or angry cries.

◆ Build Vocabulary

nimble (nim′ bəl) *adj.*: Moving quickly and lightly

Block Scheduling Strategies

Consider these suggestions to take advantage of extended class time:

- As students read, encourage them to take notes to prepare for the Medieval Festival project in the Idea Bank on p. 185. You may wish to use *World Explorer: Medieval Times to Today,* Chapter 5, "Europe in the Middle Ages," to further extend connecting literature to social studies and help students research for the festival.
- Call on volunteers to read aloud the information on p. 180. Then have students follow along in their books as they listen to the audiocassette of "The Midwife's Apprentice." After the first page of reading, stop the recording, and have students study the diagram on p. 180 to help picture the setting of the manor. Invite students to offer their own observations about the setting and time period and then continue reading the story independently or listening to the recording.

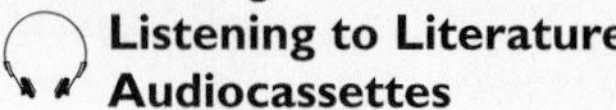

Listening to Literature Audiocassettes

3 wonder, she thought, looking at her hands. How white they were and how soft. The hours of strong soap and sudsy fleece had accomplished what years of cold water never had—her hands were really clean. There was no dirt between her fingers, around her nails, or ground into the lines on her palms. She sat back against a tree, held her hands up before her, and admired them. How clean they were. How white.

Suddenly she sat forward. Was the rest of her then that white and clean under all the dirt? Was her face white and clean? Was Will Russet right—was she even *pretty* under the dirt? There never had been one pretty thing about her, just skinny arms and big feet and dirt, but lately she had been told her hair was black and curly and her eyes big and sad
4 and she was mayhap even pretty.

Alyce looked about. The washing was done and the sheep driven to the barn to dry off for tomorrow's shearing. The river was empty but for great chunks of the greasy yellow soap floating here and there. Alyce found a spot a bit upriver from the befouled[2] washing pool, pulled off her clothes, and waded in. She rubbed her body with the yellow soap and a handful of sandy gravel until she tingled. Squatting down until the water reached her chin, she washed her hair and watched it float about her until she grew chilled.

Alyce stood up in the shallow water and looked at herself. Much cleaner, although a

5 **Connecting Literature to Social Studies**
Why does Alyce look around before she begins to bathe?

6 ▼ **Critical Viewing** Judging from their clothing, which of the women in this painting do you think is of higher social rank? Explain. **[Compare and Contrast; Support]**

Garden in the interior of a palace: a young lady and her servant, from Recueil de miniatures

2. **befouled** (bē fould′) *adj.*: Dirty.

CONNECTING LITERATURE TO SOCIAL STUDIES

Links Across Time

3 Living conditions in medieval Europe were filthy and disease-ridden. One disease, the Black Death, wiped out a third of Europe's population in just 4 years. Most medieval Europeans feared that bathing would lead to chills and death. They avoided baths except in the summer months. It was not unusual for poorer Europeans to have lice.

Clarification

4 Explain to students that the word "mayhap" blends *may* and *hap (happen)*. It can be interpreted as "maybe" or "perhaps."

CONNECTING LITERATURE TO SOCIAL STUDIES

5 Infer *Alyce wants to be sure that no one sees her, and she also may be embarrassed by her newfound desire to be clean.*

►Critical Viewing◄

6 Compare and Contrast; Support *Students should recognize that the woman on the right is of higher rank: she wears a fancy dress with a train and large sleeves that would interfere with work; her hair hangs loose, which also would keep her from performing manual labor. The woman on the left is dressed simply in a uniform-like dress; her hair is covered and she wears an apron.*

Customize for *Visual/Spatial Learners*

Encourage students to note the layers of clothing that the people in the painting wear. This detail may help them understand Alyce's reactions to undressing.

Humanities: Art

Garden in the Interior of a Palace, by an unknown 15th-century French artist

This painting is similar to the illustration, or illumination, on p. 182, and probably was quite small since books of that time were collections of miniature paintings. Illuminations were painted with gold, silver, or other bright colors. The designs were elaborate, especially considering the fact that they were quite small—about the size of a paperback book. The decorative aspects of illuminations were often enhanced by a border, such as the one that appears around Bening's farmyard scene. Use these questions for discussion of the paintings on pp. 182 and 183.

1. Where, in the story's setting, might this scene take place? *Students should conclude from the buildings and gardens that the ladies are at the manor house.*
2. Judging from the pictures on pp. 182 and 183, would you want to live in medieval times? *Some students may think that the colorful depictions are appealing; others may recognize that the lives of people of lower rank might be difficult and not so pleasant.*

Links Across Time

1 Life in the middle ages was extremely difficult compared to how we live today. It was not uncommon for people to be injured and lose an arm or a leg. Medical knowledge was limited, and diseases such as smallpox claimed lives or left scars. Dental hygiene and dentures were virtually nonexistent, so rotted teeth were typical and once they came out were not replaced. Alyce, indeed, is lucky to have good health, even at such a young age.

Reinforce and Extend

Answers

◆ Literature and Your Life

Reader's Response Students may say that they'd like being outdoors, seeing knights, and not going to school; they might dislike the lack of modern conveniences and the dirt.

Thematic Focus Both want to be safe, warm, and near one another. Both want to feel safe and special.

☑ Check Your Comprehension

1. He is a servant boy.
2. She is visiting Edward, the one person that she is close to.
3. They help wash the sheep.
4. She bathes in the river.

Answers

◆ Critical Thinking

1. He wants to share his excitement and include her in his manor life.
2. Besides realizing she is pretty and enjoys being clean, she acknowledges that Edward is very important to her.

More About the Author

Karen Cushman has focused most of her books on the experiences of ordinary young people living in other times. She became captivated by young adult literature with its themes of "coming of age," "the acceptance of responsibility," and "development of compassion" during her own daughter's teenage years. *Catherine, Called Birdy* was chosen as a 1994 Newbery Honor Book, and *The Midwife's Apprentice* won the Newbery Medal in 1995.

bit pink and wrinkled from her long soak. 1 And pretty? Mayhap even that, for she had all her teeth and all her limbs, a face unmarked by pox, and perhaps, now, more of happiness and hope than of sadness in those big eyes that even the midwife had remarked on.

She washed her clothes, pulled them on still wet and drippy, and ran for the kitchen to dry a bit before the fire.

Too soon it was time to bid Edward goodbye. "Be assured I will not be far from here, and I promise to come back for Christmas and Easter and your saint's day. And to see when that front tooth grows in again." Edward grinned. He had enjoyed the day, done a man's job, and been carried home on the shoulders of a giant of a shepherd called Hal. He was satisfied with his place at the manor, the devotion of the cook, and the friendship of Alyce. He suddenly felt not so small.

Alyce gave him a hug and a smack and felt that tickling in her throat and stinging in her eyes that meant she might cry again, now she knew how to do it. She went down the path from the manor, stopping every few steps to turn and wave until finally the path curved and Edward was lost from sight and all she could see was the way ahead.

◆ Build Vocabulary

devotion (di vō´ shən) *n.*: Loyalty or deep affection

Guide for Responding

◆ Literature and Your Life

Reader's Response What would you like and dislike about living in Edward's and Alyce's world? Explain.

Thematic Focus What dreams do Alyce and Edward share?

☑ Check Your Comprehension

1. What is Edward's role at the manor?
2. Why is Alyce at the manor?
3. What chore do Edward and Alyce share?
4. What does Alyce do at the river when the work is done?

◆ Critical Thinking

Interpret

1. Why does Edward tell Alyce so much about his life at the manor? **[Infer]**
2. What does Alyce learn about herself during her time with Edward? **[Interpret]**
3. What do Edward and Alyce want from each other? Explain how their expectations differ. **[Draw Conclusions]**

Apply

4. What does this story suggest about the ways people's dreams remain the same, despite the passage of history? **[Generalize]**

Extend

5. How important are cleanliness and physical appearance in people's lives today? **[Health Link]**

Meet the Author

Karen Cushman (1941–) Writing lets Karen Cushman go anywhere she wants—if only in her imagination. In stories and poems, Cushman has been taking imaginary journeys to distant lands and earlier ages since she was a girl. She didn't realize people could make a living writing until much later—after time spent raising her daughter and working in museums. At the age of fifty, she finally began a novel that took her more than three years to complete.

Travels Through Time Given her interest in museums, it's not surprising that many of Cushman's books are historical. Her first novel, *Catherine, Called Birdy,* is set in medieval times, as is *The Midwife's Apprentice.* Cushman sees young people—no matter what century they live in—facing similar issues as they grow into adulthood.

Beyond the Selection

FURTHER READING

Other Works by Karen Cushman

Catherine, Called Biddy

The Ballad of Lucy Whipple

Other Words About Everyday Life in Medieval Europe

The Early Middle Ages, James A. Corrick

The Trumpeter of Krakow, Eric P. Kelly

The Untold Tale, Eric Christian Haugaard

Life in a Medieval Village, Gwyneth Morgan

INTERNET

We suggest the following Internet sites (all Web sites are subject to change.)

For more information about life in medieval times:

http://tp-junior.advanced.org/4051/credits/htm

http://www.learner.org/exhibits/middleages/feudal.html

http://www.edu:8080/~MA/MA.HTM

We *strongly recommend* that you preview these sites before you send students to them.

Connecting Literature to Social Studies

The world was in many ways a dangerous place in medieval times—governments were unstable, leaders struggled for power, death came quickly from disease. In this uncertain world, people stayed in clearly assigned roles. Lords served the king, on and off the battlefield. For this service, they received lands where they established manors. In exchange for a place to live and protection from outsiders, peasants worked the land of the lords and swore their loyalty to the lords. The Church also played an important role—as a gathering place, a source of guidance, and a strict lawmaker.

For people like Alyce and Edward, the road probably held many problems but few surprises. You can begin to see in this story what they want from life and how these dreams may unfold.

1. What has Edward experienced in his life at the manor that might make him interested in stories with a hero and brave deeds?
2. What details show how Edward's and Alyce's roles compare with those of the manor lords?
3. How might the clear roles and understandable problems of their time help Edward and Alyce as they grow up?

Idea Bank

Writing

1. **Letter** As Alyce, write a letter to Edward about your visit to the manor. Explain what it meant to you and how you feel about returning soon.
2. **Advertisement** Write an ad to attract young workers for the manor. Use the information on page 180 and details from the story to make your ad realistic. **[Media Link]**
3. **Time-Travel Log** Imagine that you've suddenly awakened on the manor. Write a log entry describing what you experience in a day's visit. Include enough detail so others can learn from your travel.

Speaking and Listening

4. **Health Lesson** You're a modern-day health counselor who has studied medieval times. Present some advice that would benefit Edward and Alyce. Focus your remarks on their diet and personal hygiene. **[Health Link]**

Projects

5. **Medieval Festival** **[Group Activity]** Research and stage a fair modeled on the autumn horse fair Edward attends or a typical medieval midsummer village fair. Create booths to sell foods and other products. If possible, wear costumes and play historical music. **[Social Studies Link]**

Further Reading, Listening, and Viewing

- Elizabeth Janet Gray's *Adam of the Road* (1987) tells the story of a young boy on his own during medieval times.
- Stephen Biesty's *Cross-Sections: Castle* (1994) shows the inner workings of a medieval castle and its nearby village.
- Dorothy Van Woerkom's *A Pearl in the Egg: A Tale of the Thirteenth Century* (1980) captures everyday life in medieval England.
- *The Middle Ages* (1993) is a BBC documentary that includes castles, medieval life, and a peasant revolt.
- *The Castle* (1988) is a video version of David Macauley's popular book.

ASSESSMENT OPTIONS

Formal Assessment, Selection Test, pp. 50–51 and Assessment Resources Software. The selection test is designed so that it can be easily customized to the performance levels of your students.

PORTFOLIO ASSESSMENT
Use the following rubrics in the **Alternative Assessment** booklet to assess student writing:
Letter: Expression, p. 81
Advertisement: Persuasion, p. 92
Time-Travel Log: Fictional Narrative, p. 82

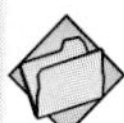

Idea Bank

Following are suggestions for matching the Idea Bank topics with your students' performance levels and learning modalities:

Customize for
Performance Levels
Less Advanced Students: 1, 5
Average Students: 2, 5
More Advanced Students: 3, 4

Customize for
Learning Modalities
Verbal/Linguistic: 1, 2, 3
Interpersonal: 4, 5
Intrapersonal: 1, 3
Bodily/Kinesthetic: 5
Musical/Rhythmic: 5

Answers *(continued)*

◆Critical Thinking

3. They want to give each other the security of a family; Edward has begun to find security at the manor, while Alyce still looks mostly to Edward for companionship.
4. The story suggests that everyone shares the dream to be valued by those around them and enjoy the security and comfort of others.
5. In modern times, people have the resources and time to use for cleanliness and appearance; physical appearance plays a major role in most people's lives today.

Connecting Literature to Social Studies

1. He has seen visiting knights with their swords in the courtyard; he has heard the cook's stories.
2. Possible responses: Edward sleeps on straw on the kitchen floor and is content to be an onlooker to the manor's exciting life; Alyce has rarely paid attention to her appearance and tells a story that shows her unimaginative view of life; the manor lords, however, dress in silken robes, attend festivals and banquets, meet with bishops, prepare for battle, and appear to do little everyday work.
3. The roles of medieval times help Edward and Alyce by removing the question of "What do I want to do when I grow up?" Young people of this time simply worked to survive and did what was expected of them.

Prepare and Engage

Establish Writing Guidelines
Review the key characteristics of a summary:

- A summary provides only the most important details
- A summary should recount events in chronological order and use transitions to clarify the order of events

You may want to distribute the scoring rubric for Summary, p. 85 in **Alternative Assessment,** to make students aware of the criteria on which they will be evaluated. See the suggestions on p. 188 for how you can customize the rubric to this workshop.

Refer students to the Writing Handbook for instruction on the writing process and further information on expository writing.

Writer's Solution

Writers at Work Videodisc
To introduce students to expository writing and author Richard Lederer's ideas about learning from writing, play the videodisc segment on Exposition: Giving Information (Ch. 4). Ask them how Lederer gets his ideas for writing.

Play frames 31956 to 41222

Writing Lab CD-ROM
If your students have access to computers, you may want to have them work in the tutorial on Exposition to complete all or part of their summaries. Follow these steps:

1. Suggest that students use the Chain of Events chart to narrow their topics.
2. Have students draft on computer.
3. Students can use the Timeline activity to arrange events of their summaries in chronological order.
4. When revising, have students use the Revision Checker for unity and coherence.

Writer's Solution Sourcebook
Students can find additional support, including in-depth instruction on using exact nouns and building paragraphs, on pp. 128–129.

Connect to Literature Unit 7, "Nonfiction," includes an example of expository writing: Virginia Shea's "Netiquette: Do's and Don'ts on the Information Highway."

Expository Writing

Summary

Writing Process Workshop

After you've read a long story or essay, you may be asked to write about its overall purpose and its most important points. When you do this, you write a **summary.** A summary doesn't include your opinions or judgments; it sticks to the facts. It answers the question, "What is the writing about?"

For this assignment, choose a piece of prose you have enjoyed—from this unit or elsewhere. Read the piece again before you begin to write your summary.

Writing Skills Focus

- **Stress the main ideas.** Supporting details don't belong in summaries. (See p. 177.)
- **Use key words** from the writing to make the subject of your summary clear.
- **Be brief.** Make each word count. If a word doesn't help make a point, delete it.

Notice how this writer uses these skills to write a summary of "Golden Girls."

Writing Model

"Golden Girls" by Johnette Howard ① describes how the U.S. Women's Hockey Team beat the Canadian team in the 1998 Olympics. ② The writer suggests that this victory shows how women's athletics are changing in the world. The article also shows how the U.S. and Canadian teams have been rivals for a long time. Many of the teammates are quoted. ③ The players describe what it felt like to win and what they plan to do now that the Olympics are over. ④

① Title and author are clear, correct, and right up front.

② This topic sentence could stand alone as a one-sentence summary.

③ Specific names aren't included—just main ideas.

④ *Olympics* is a key word. It's in the first sentence and the last.

Beyond the Classroom

Workplace Skills
Tell students that the ability to write a summary is important for many different types of jobs. For example, a critic has to summarize the work to be critiqued in order to explain its basic elements. A doctor may summarize a patient's condition to an assisting physician or nurse. A construction worker may summarize the progress of a building site for his foreman or the architect. Remind students that a summary contains only the most important information. It should be concise and to the point, without including details.

Tell students that television and radio broadcasters summarize news for their listeners and viewers. Discuss with them what makes a successful broadcaster. You may want to have students listen to a radio broadcast in class and then discuss whether students think the event is summarized effectively.

Prewriting

Choose Your Subject If you're having trouble deciding on the material you want to summarize, choose from the ideas suggested in the topic box.

Topic Ideas

- Story from your literature textbook
- Article from a magazine
- Current movie
- Section of your social studies textbook

Use Key Words Identify the important words you'll use in your summary. For example, in an article about a new law, you'll probably use *law* and *senators* often. Make a list of synonyms, like *legislation* and *politicians,* to help you avoid repetition.

Write an Outline or Plan Since a summary is a type of informative writing, it's good to map things out before you begin to draft. Whether you prefer a formal outline, a list of notes, or a graphic organizer, write a plan that shows, in order, the main ideas you wish to cover.

Title, Author
Who?
What?
Where?
When?
Why?
How?

Drafting

Write a Topic Sentence Whether your summary is a few, brief sentences or runs to many paragraphs, begin by writing a single sentence that expresses what the writing is about. This sentence should include the name of the work and the name of the writer.

Remember That Less Is More Good summaries are clear and precise. Their language is crisp and to the point. Use as few words as possible to cover the main ideas.

DRAFTING/REVISING

Applying Language Skills: Using Objective Language

A summary presents events factually. To avoid giving your opinions about the material, eliminate words that evaluate. Instead, let the facts tell the story. If necessary, quote others' opinions.

Conveying an Opinion: The women's hockey team won in an amazing victory over a sluggish competitor.

Staying Objective: The women's hockey team beat its rival by a 4–2 margin.

Using a Quotation: The coach said, "The women's hockey team win was amazing."

Practice Rewrite these sentences to make them more objective.

1. He did his best work near the end of his tragically short life.
2. Surprisingly, thousands of crazy fans grabbed his books off the shelves.

Writing Application As you revise your summary, replace opinions with facts.

Writer's Solution Connection Writing Lab

For more examples of summaries, refer to the About Exposition screen in the Exposition: Giving Information tutorial.

Develop Student Writing

Prewriting

When deciding on topic ideas for a summary, have students think about whether they will be able to include all the important information. If not, suggest that they narrow their topic. For example, instead of writing a summary of an entire play, they may choose to concentrate on just one of the scenes or acts.

Customize for *Less Proficient Writers*

To help students organize the events in their summaries, have them use the Series of Events Chain in **Writing and Language Transparencies,** p. 66. Start them off by helping them to identify the beginning event in the topic of their summary.

Drafting

Advise students that although they will not include details in their summaries, they must provide significant information. For example, when writing a summary of a story, students should include the title and author of the work, the main characters, and the story's main events.

Writer's Solution

Writing Lab CD-ROM

Students can develop strategies for writing their drafts by using the interactive model of a summary in the drafting section of the tutorial on Exposition: Giving Information.

Applying Language Skills

Using Objective Language Point out to students that different words may provide different connotations, or implied meanings, such as opinions. Encourage them to review their writing for words that may imply something other than facts.

Answers

Suggested responses:

1. He continued to work until the end of his short life.
2. Thousands of fans bought his books.

Writer's Solution

For additional instruction and practice, have students use the lesson from *Writer's Solution Language Lab CD-ROM,* Considering Audience and Purpose, in the Composing section.

Revising

When students work with peer reviewers, remind them to make sure that enough information is included, the relationships between events are clearly shown, and any unnecessary words are eliminated.

 **Writer's Solution**

Writing Lab CD-ROM

In the tutorial on Exposition: Giving Information, have students use the Self-Evaluation Checklist to help them assess their own writing.

Publishing

For other publishing opportunities, you may want to suggest that students submit their summaries to the school newspaper.

Reinforce and Extend

Review the Writing Guidelines

After students complete their writing, review the characteristics of a summary. Discuss with students ways for making their writing brief, based on what they have learned through completing the assignment.

Applying Language Skills

Eliminating Unnecessary Words

Suggest to students that when revising their summaries, they look to eliminate details that don't support the topic and to delete repetitive information.

Answers

1. Her face was colorless.
2. The book is about freedom.

 **Writer's Solution**

For additional practice, complete the Shortening Sentences That Are Too Long lesson in the *Writer's Solution Grammar Practice Book*, p. 119.

EDITING/PROOFREADING

APPLYING LANGUAGE SKILLS: Eliminating Unnecessary Words

In all good writing, less is more. This means that saying something in a few words is more effective than saying it using a lot of words. Prune your writing down to the words that really matter. Be on the lookout for these culprits:

Repetition: The hazy sky was heavy and hazy.

Redundancy: My first reaction was an initial shock.

Filler Phrases: They were, in fact, frightened.

Awkward Wordiness: Arthur pulled the sword out of the stone that it was stuck into.

Practice Rewrite these sentences to eliminate unnecessary words.

1. Her face was white, pale, and colorless.
2. It seems that the book, in fact, is probably about freedom.

Writing Application As you revise your summary, eliminate unnecessary words.

Writer's Solution Connection Writing Lab

For more practice, see the Eliminating Unnecessary Words lesson in the Language Lab CD-ROM.

Revising

Read Your Summary Aloud Often, the ear hears what the eye misses. When you *hear* your writing, you'll catch awkward phrases, left-out words, repetition, and mechanical mistakes that your eyes have skipped right over. Read slowly. Stop after each sentence to think about its smoothness (or lack of smoothness). Mark changes immediately—you may forget them later.

Peer Review Ask someone who hasn't read the writing you're summarizing to read your summary. See if it makes sense to them. Ask them to point out what they didn't understand.

REVISION MODEL

In the article "Origami Tips," Audrey Samuels provides ~~a number of~~ ① helpful hints~~, along with decorative photographs of intricate finished works~~. ② Her first tip is to read carefully through the instructions for a model ~~that you like~~ ①. Her second tip is to make sure your paper is perfectly square. ~~If the paper is not perfectly square, then the white backing of the paper will show where it shouldn't.~~ ③

① These words don't help to make the point.
② This information was cut to keep the summary brief.
③ Supporting details like these do not belong in a summary.

Publishing and Presenting

▶ **Broadcast [Group Activity]** Radio and television broadcasters summarize events, films, news stories, and biographies all the time. With a group, videotape a newscast in which you report your summaries. Assign an anchor, reporters, and a camera operator. Then, write a script that ties all your reports together. Share your video with the class.

ASSESSMENT

PORTFOLIO ASSESSMENT Use the rubric on Summary in the **Alternative Assessment** booklet, p. 85, to assess the students' writing. Add these criteria to customize this rubric to this assignment.

	4	3	2	1
Using Objective Language	The writer consistently uses objective language in the summary.	The writer uses objective language a majority of the time.	The writer uses subjective and objective language indiscriminately.	The writer does not use objective language.
Presentation of Facts	The facts of the summary are presented in full, and in a clear order.	The facts of the summary are generally complete, but not always clear	Some of the facts of the summary are missing, and they are not always clear.	The facts of the summary are incomplete and not presented clearly.

Real-World Reading Skills Workshop

Recognizing Key Words

Strategies for Success

All the words in a piece of writing are important—but some are more important than others. These **key words** act to unlock the meaning of a passage or of an entire piece of writing. Without the key words, the meaning of the entire passage would be lost. Follow these tips for recognizing key words in your reading:

Find the Subject and Verb A sentence cannot be complete without a subject and a verb. The subject is who or what the sentence is about. The verb tells what the subject is or does. For example, in the sentence *My mother planted flowers*, the subject is *mother* and the verb is *planted*. The subject and verb are the key words in most sentences.

Look for Instruction Words If you've ever taken a test, performed a science experiment, followed a recipe, or built a model, you know that the words that give instructions are important to your success. The key words in instructions include verbs that give commands. For example, in the sentence *Stir until the ingredients are well mixed*, the command verb is *stir*.

Almond Cloud

1. Add 1 cup of boiling water to 2 packets of unflavored gelatin and 1/2 cup sugar.
2. Stir until gelatin and sugar are completely dissolved.
3. Add 1 cup of milk and 1 tablespoon of almond extract. Stir.
4. Pour mixture into an 8" square cake pan. Refrigerate until set.
5. Cut in squares and serve.

Look for Signals To make their ideas easier to understand, writers use signal words or phrases. Some signals show the importance of ideas—*most importantly, last but not least*, and *primarily*, to name a few. Other signals explain the relationships among ideas—*because, in contrast, despite*, and *after*, for example. Still others count off the writer's main points—*first, second, third*, and so on. Signal words are crucial, because they help you to identify and follow the writer's main points.

Apply the Strategies

Read the recipe on this page. Then, answer the questions that follow.

1. What are the key verbs in step 1?
2. Identify the key word in step 2 that tells how long the step takes.
3. What are two important actions in step 3?
4. What are the key words in step 4? Explain.

Here are some other situations in which recognizing key words can be helpful:

- *Reading science or social studies textbooks*
- *Using instruction manuals*
- *Completing summer job applications*

Introduce the Strategies

Ask volunteers to share experiences they may have had when they failed to pay attention to key words, such as which direction to turn or how much sugar to add to a recipe. Point out to students that missing key words can cause disasters in some circumstances. Identifying key words enables the reader to pay attention to the most important details of what he or she is reading.

Customize for
Less Proficient Readers
In order to help students recognize key words, tell them that instruction words are usually commands and, therefore, may not have a noun as a subject. For example, in the instruction "Read the paragraph closely," the verb in the sentence is the command "read." The subject in the sentence has disappeared, as is common with commands. The subject is an implied "you" as in "[You] read the paragraph closely."

Customize for
Bodily/Kinesthetic Learners
Encourage students to "go through the motions" as they read. Experiencing the movement indicated by the writing may help them identify key words.

Apply the Strategies

As students read the recipe, have them identify and write down key words. You may want to point out that some steps have more key words than others. Have students explain why each word is important, what instruction it gives, or what essential action it indicates. Then guide them to identify whether the key words are subjects (amounts) or verbs (actions), instruction words (how), or signal words (in what manner).

Answers

Suggested responses:

1. Add
2. Completely
3. Add; stir
4. Pour; 8" square pan; Refrigerate

◆Build Grammar Skills

Reviewing Principal Parts of Verbs

The selections in Part 2 include instruction on the following:

- Principal Parts of Irregular Verbs

This instruction is reinforced with the Build Grammar Skills practice pages in **Selection Support,** p. 67.

As you review the parts of verbs, you may wish to begin with the following:

- Principal Parts of Regular Verbs

A verb shows action or the state of being. Here are four sentences, each using one of the principal parts of the regular verb *climb.*

Present	She climbs the stairway of life.
Present Participle	She is climbing the stairway of life.
Past	She climbed the stairway of life.
Past Participle	She has climbed the stairway of life.

Encourage students to keep a list of irregular verbs that give them trouble in their writing. They can create their own chart for reference.

Writer's Solution

For additional practice using verbs, use the practice page on action verbs, p. 11, and helping verbs, p. 14, in the *Writer's Solution Grammar Practice Book.*

Principal Parts of Verbs

Grammar Review

A **verb** tells what the subject of a sentence does or is. The **principal parts of a verb** are the four forms of a verb from which all other tenses and forms are created. For regular verbs, principal parts are formed in a predictable way. The principal parts of irregular verbs are not formed in the same way, so you must memorize them (see page 176).

Principal Part	Regular Formation	Examples (regular)	Examples (irregular)
Base (present) Form		play; like	am, be; freeze; run
Past Form	adds *-ed* or *-d*	played; liked	was, were; froze; ran
Present Participle	adds *-ing*	playing; liking	being; freezing; running
Past Participle	adds *-ed* or *-d*	played; liked	been; frozen; run

The present and past participles are always used with helping verbs (verbs that work together with the main verb, such as *has, have, be, was, may,* and *will*). The past participle is always used in forming the perfect tenses.

Practice 1 Identify the principal part of each italicized verb, and tell whether the verb is regular or irregular.

1. Alyce *helped* when Edward *was feeding* the sheep.
2. The mother *is comparing* life to stairs.
3. She *wished* for her mother's courage.
4. The blacksmith *shaped* the iron.
5. After it *drank* some sweetened water and *became* warm enough, the hummingbird *flew* away.

Practice 2 Rewrite the following paragraph, replacing each verb in parentheses with the principal part indicated.

For years, the Coyotes had (be, *past participle*) the worst football team in the state. They (be, *past*) so bad that their opponents' scores (look, *past*) like basketball scores. It (get, *past*) so bad that no one (want, *past*) to coach the team. Then, Miss Garcia, the English teacher, (step, *past*) in. She (know, *past*) exactly what the team (need, *past*). She (build, *past*) up the team's morale and (teach, *past*) players to think like a team. She (give, *past*) them a dream to share and believe in. At first, the other teams (laugh, *past*) about the Coyotes having a "girl coach." No one is (laugh, *present participle*) now. This year, the Coyotes (be, *present*) the regional champs.

Grammar in Writing

✓ ***Using the correct principal parts can be tricky, especially when you are dealing with irregular verbs. Keep in mind that irregular verbs do not form past forms or past participles in the usual way.***

Answers

Practice 1

1. help, regular; feed; irregular
2. compare, regular
3. wish, regular
4. shape, regular
5. drink, irregular; become, irregular; fly, irregular

Practice 2

For years, the Coyotes *had been* the worst football team in the state. They *were* so bad that their opponents' scores *looked* like basketball scores. It got so bad that no one *wanted* to coach the team. Then Miss Garcia, the English teacher *stepped* in. She *knew* exactly what the team *needed.* She *built* up the team's morale, *taught* players to think like a team. She *gave* them a dream to share and believe in. At first, the other teams *laughed* about the Coyotes having a "girl coach." No one is *laughing* now. This year, the Coyotes *are* the regional champs.

Speaking, Listening, and Viewing Workshop

Understanding Body Language

Communication involves more than just speaking words. It also involves the unspoken messages that you send in the way you stand, gesture, and look as you speak. In fact, most of the messages your listeners receive come from your body language—even though you and they may not be aware of it.

Don't Slouch Your posture sends a strong message about your attitude. Hunching over when you speak says that you are unsure of what you are saying or that you are trying to hide something. Slouching as you listen says that you are not fully attentive. Sitting or standing straight says that you are confident and interested in the conversation.

Make Eye Contact Maintaining good eye contact sends the message that you are attentive and trustworthy. However, keep in mind that the correct amount of eye contact varies greatly from culture to culture. You may need to adjust your behavior to make the other person comfortable.

Tips for Using Good Body Language

✓ *Follow these suggestions to communicate effectively:*

- Gesture purposefully. Vague or repetitive gestures can distract.
- Smile. A friendly face helps to ensure a friendly conversation. It also affects the tone of your voice. This is why it is important to smile even when talking on the telephone.
- If your listeners seem to be getting annoyed or confused, your body language might be sending the wrong message. You may need to make adjustments.

Apply the Strategies

With a partner, analyze the body language in the photograph on this page. Then, role-play the following situations several times, experimenting with different body language. Note your partner's reactions, and discuss what you've learned.

1. At lunch, you tell a new student about your school, your town, and your interests.
2. You are being interviewed for a job as a baby sitter.

Introduce the Strategies

You may want to use pictures from magazines or videotapes to illustrate different types of body language to students. Have them comment on the way a person is sitting or standing, hand gestures, facial expressions, and movement both noticeable (standing up or sitting down) and subtle (shifting feet).

Apply the Strategies

Remind students to concentrate on all aspects of their body language, including facial gestures, hand and feet movements, posture, and eye contact. As they replay the situations, encourage partners to alternate between roles, trying different body language to convey varying messages.

Customize for
Visual/Spatial Learners
Encourage students to draw or sketch examples of different types of body language, or find examples of drawings in cartoons or comics. Have them show their representations to the class and explain what types of body language are represented by each.

Beyond the Classroom

Workplace Skills

Body Language Explain to students that good use of body language is helpful in all aspects of a job, from job interviews to job performances. Have students brainstorm for a list of job scenarios where body language would take on extra importance. Start them off by suggesting the following:

- Interviewing for a position in a prestigious company
- Explaining a serious illness
- Trying to sell a new soft drink
- A foreman instructing his crew about a job that requires explosives

Then have students form groups and role-play a job scenario that they select, using only body language. You may want to review the various types of body language for them to be aware of, including facial expressions, hand gestures, eye contact, movement of feet, and posture. Allow students to use props. Have each group perform its scenario. As a class, discuss which body language is appropriate and how it can be improved.

◆ Build Vocabulary

What's Behind the Words

Dictionaries usually identify the origin of words, either in the definition itself or in a note after the definition that names the country of origin. Often, however, the name of the country is abbreviated and students may need to look up the abbreviation in the dictionary guide.

Answers

Activity 1

1. aardvark, African
2. anchovy, Spanish
3. bazaar, Middle Eastern
4. canoe, Native American
5. coyote, Mexican
6. flannel, Welsh or British
7. moose, Algonquian
8. oasis, Egyptian
9. polo, Tibetan
10. shingle, British
11. sauna, Finnish
12. tattoo, Tahitian

Activity 2

Possible responses:

macaroni, pasta	Italian
tortilla	Mexican
eggroll	Chinese
crepe	French
pita	Middle East
chutney	Hindi
sauerkraut, strudel	German
pierogi	Polish
borscht	Russian
curry	Indian
paprika	Hungarian

What's Behind the Words

Vocabulary Adventures With Richard Lederer

Words Borrowed From Around The World

Ralph Waldo Emerson praised "English speech, the sea which receives tributaries from every region under heaven." Dorothy Thompson, using a more common metaphor, referred to "that glorious and imperial mongrel, the English language." What each is saying in a different way is that the English vocabulary flows from many sources. On top of the native store of old Anglo-Saxon words, English has been helping itself to foreign words throughout its history. These borrowings from languages all over the world have enriched our vocabulary with beauty, vitality, color, variety, and precision.

Words Are History

If English had been left to develop in isolation, it would have borrowed fewer words. But English not only rubbed elbows with other languages, it collided head-on with several. When things happen to people—conquest, trade, exploration, immigration—things happen to their language as well. The vocabulary is enhanced as the people encounter new customs, inventions, and ideas. Each word adopted into English is a part of our history.

Our musical vocabulary would be almost mute without the words we have adopted from the Italian language—words such as *alto, cello, maestro, opera, solo, tempo,* and *violin.* Our language would be far less seaworthy without adoptions from the seafaring Dutch: *cruise, deck, dock, freight, skipper,* and *yacht.* How would we describe western life without the Spanish contributions *adobe, bronco, canyon,* and *stampede?*

Our Democratic Language

To appreciate how spongelike our English language is, examine the following list:

Arabic	camel
Australian	boomerang
Bengali	bungalow
Danish	skill
German	kindergarten
Hawaiian	ukulele
Hungarian	saber
Maori	kiwi
Portuguese	molasses
Swedish	smorgasbord
Yiddish	kosher

English is the most democratic and hospitable language that has ever existed. As the poet Carl Sandburg once said, "The English language hasn't got where it is by being pure."

ACTIVITY 1: Using your dictionary, identify the origin of each of the following words:

1. aardvark	**5.** coyote	**9.** polo
2. anchovy	**6.** flannel	**10.** shingle
3. bazaar	**7.** moose	**11.** sauna
4. canoe	**8.** oasis	**12.** tattoo

ACTIVITY 2: Identify ten foods that get their names from foreign languages. Identify the language from which each food comes.

Extended Reading Opportunities

The shared interests, heritage, and dreams that bind people together in friendships and communities have been examined in many works of literature. Following are a few that can help you explore common threads.

Suggested Titles

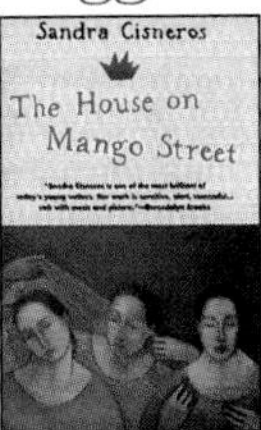

The House on Mango Street
Sandra Cisneros

Esperanza Cordero does not think she fits in, and she longs to move away from her Chicago neighborhood. However, she still learns a lot about life from her Mango Street neighbors. She discovers that there are many different kinds of people in the world and each has something to give.

Each chapter of this book seems like a poem as well as a section of a novel. Whether you think of it as poetry or prose, you will have a hard time putting this book down.

It's Our World, Too!
Phillip Hoose

In this book, you will meet young people who are taking action to make shared dreams come true—taking stands against racism or crime, assisting those in need, working to save the environment, and helping to create a world of peace.

In addition to presenting profiles of people who are making a difference, the book describes young people who have made a difference in American history. It also gives advice that will help readers make a difference in their own communities.

Letters From Rifka
Karen Hesse

This fictional portrait of the immigrant experience is based on the real-life experiences of the author's great-aunt. Twelve-year-old Rifka Nebrot's letters to her cousin Tovah are written in the blank spaces in a book of poetry. In her letters, Rifka describes the fear, disease, hardship, and other problems she and her family endure as they travel to America.

Rifka's problems are not over when she arrives at Ellis Island in New York. Will she be able to convince the officials to admit her to the United States? Read this novel and find out.

Other Possibilities

The Italian American Family Album	Dorothy and Thomas Hoobler, Editors
Freedom Songs	Yvette Moore
The Trumpet of the Swan	E. B. White
Black Star, Bright Dawn	Scott O'Dell

Planning Students' Extended Reading

All of the works listed on this page are good choices for extending the theme of Unit 2 "Common Threads." Following is some information that may help you choose which to teach.

Customize for *Varying Student Needs*

When assigning the selections in this part to your students, keep in mind the following factors.

- *The House on Mango Street* is a best-selling novel that reads as a series of vignettes. Each chapter can be read independently and offers opportunities for discussion about ethnic diversities.
- *It's Our World, Too* is a collection of true stories about young people.
- *Letters from Rifka* is a fictional account based on a true story of a young woman's escape from persecution in her native country. This book offers a good opportunity for a tie-in with social studies.

Sensitive Issues The stories in *The House on Mango Street* address a wide variety of life's issues. You may wish to use caution when assigning this book to readers who have traditional expectations regarding literary subject matter.

Literature Study Guides Literature study guides are available for *The House on Mango Street* and *Letters from Rifka*. The guides include section summaries, discussion questions, and activities.

Planning Instruction and Assessment

Unit Objectives

1. To read selections in different genres that develop the theme of "What Matters"
2. To apply a variety of reading strategies, particularly strategies for interactive reading, appropriate for reading these selections
3. To recognize literary elements used in these selections
4. To increase vocabulary
5. To learn elements of grammar and usage
6. To write in a variety of modes about situations based on the selections
7. To develop speaking and listening skills, by completing activities
8. To view images critically and create visual representations

Meeting the Objectives Each selection provides instructional material and portfolio opportunities by which students can meet unit objectives. You will find additional practice pages for reading strategies, literary elements, vocabulary, and grammar in the **Selection Support** booklet in the **Teaching Resources** box.

Setting Goals Work with your students at the beginning of the unit to set goals for unit outcomes. Plan what skills and concepts you wish students to acquire. You may match instruction and activities according to students' performance levels or learning modalities.

Portfolios Students may keep portfolios of their completed work or of their work in progress. The Build Your Portfolio page of each selection provides opportunities for students to apply the concepts presented.

Humanities: Art

Couple on the Road, by Diana Ong

Diana Ong (1940–) is one of the first artists to translate computer graphic design into fine art.

1. Do you think the couple in the painting are looking down the road or facing the viewer? *They may be looking down the road; or they are facing the viewer.*
2. "What Matters" about the title of the painting *Couple on the Road?* *Students may say that the title represents what the artist is showing—facing life hand-in-hand.*

Couple on the Road, Diana Ong

Art Transparencies

The **Art Transparencies** booklet in the **Teaching Resources** box offers fine art to help students make connections to other curriculum areas and high-interest topics.

Beyond Literature

Each unit presents Beyond Literature features that lead students into an exploration of careers, communities, and other subject areas. In this unit, students will explore the challenge of mountain climbing, and make history and geography connections. In addition, the **Teaching Resources** box contains a **Beyond Literature** booklet of activities. Using literature as a springboard, these activity pages offer students opportunities to connect literature to other curriculum areas and to the workplace and careers, community, media, and humanities.

UNIT 3

What Matters

To navigate a life filled with options and distractions, each of us has to set priorities and answer a tough question: What matters most? The literature in this unit presents a variety of answers to this very personal question. You'll read about a man who weighs his wife's happiness in his choices, and you'll struggle with a boy who balances his parents' wishes against his own. Some writers will help you see nature in a fresh light. Read thoughtfully. In the end, you might see your own priorities from a new angle.

Connections

Within this unit, you will find selections and activities that make connections beyond literature. Use these selections to connect students' understanding and appreciation of literature beyond the traditional literature and language arts curriculum.

Encourage students to connect literature to other curriculum areas. You may wish to coordinate with teachers in other curriculum areas to determine ways to team teach and further extend instruction.

Connections to Today's World

Use these selections to guide students to recognize the relevance of literature to contemporary writings. In this unit, students will read the song lyrics for "On My Own" from *Les Misérables.*

Connecting Literature to Social Studies

Each unit contains a selection that connects literature to social studies. In this unit, students will read about the exciting discovery of the body of a man who lived over 5000 years ago.

Assessing Student Progress

The tools that are available to measure the degree to which students meet the unit objectives are listed below.

Informal Assessment

The questions in the Guide for Responding sections are a first level of response to the concepts and skills presented with the selection. As a brief informal measure of students' grasp of the material, these responses indicate where further instruction and practice are needed. The practice pages in the **Selection Support** booklet provide for this type of instruction and practice.

You will also find literature and reading guides in the **Alternative Assessment** booklet, which students can use for informal assessment of their individual performances.

Formal Assessment

The **Formal Assessment** booklet contains Selection Tests and Unit Tests.

Selection Tests measure comprehension and skills acquisition for each selection or group of selections.

Each Unit Test provides students with 30 multiple-choice questions and 5 essay questions designed to assess students' knowledge of the literature and skills taught in the unit.

Each Alternative Unit Test: Standardized-Test Practice provides 15 multiple-choice questions and 3 essay questions based on two new literature selections not contained in the student book. The questions on the Alternative Unit Test are designed to assess students' ability to compare and contrast selections, applying skills taught in the unit.

Alternative Assessment

For portfolio and alternative assessment, the **Alternative Assessment** booklet contains Scoring Rubrics, Assessment Sheets, and Learning Modalities activities.

Scoring Rubrics provide writing modes that can be applied to Writing Mini-Lessons and to Writing Process Workshop lessons.

Assessment Sheets for speaking and listening activities.

Learning Modalities Activities appeal to different learning styles. Use these as an alternative measurement of students' growth.

Prepare and Engage

OBJECTIVES

1. To read, comprehend, and interpret a short story
2. To relate a short story to personal experience
3. To apply interactive reading strategies
4. To analyze the characteristics of a modern fairy tale
5. To build vocabulary in context and learn the suffix *-ous*
6. To develop skill in recognizing and using adjectives
7. To write a modern fairy tale elaborating on key details
8. To respond to the short story through writing, speaking and listening, and projects

SKILLS INSTRUCTION

Vocabulary: Suffixes: *-ous*
Spelling: Adding *-ous* to Base Words
Grammar: Adjectives
Literary Focus: Modern Fairy Tale
Reading for Success: Interactive Reading Strategies
Writing: Elaborate on Key Ideas
Speaking and Listening: Song Lyrics (Teacher Edition)
Critical Viewing: Relate; Analyze

PORTFOLIO OPPORTUNITIES

Writing: Journal Entry; Obituary; Analysis
Writing Mini-Lesson: Modern Fairy Tale
Speaking and Listening: Song Lyrics; Radio Drama
Projects: Poster; Multimedia Report

More About the Author
As a child, **Joan Aiken** went on walks with her younger brother and told him stories when he grew tired. Then, as he grew older, the two children shared details about fantasy countries they invented. Aiken began writing when her husband died of lung cancer, leaving her to take care of their two children. She was inspired by writers like Edgar Allan Poe and Rudyard Kipling. In her works for children, Aiken has used her own children as critics of her writing to ensure that her stories contain the same sense of right and wrong that children naturally possess.

Guide for Reading

Meet the Author:

Joan Aiken (1924–)

As a child, Joan Aiken loved to take walks in the fields by her house, creating stories to amuse herself. Aiken was strongly influenced by her father, the American poet Conrad Aiken. Her mother contributed to her imagination by reading aloud from the works of Charles Dickens, Jane Austen, and countless other classic English writers.

English Roots
Born and schooled in England, Aiken continues to live both there and in the United States. She has received awards for her writing from both countries, including the Lewis Carroll Shelf Award and the Edgar Allan Poe Award from the Mystery Writers of America.

The Story Behind the Story

Joan Aiken has the special ability to bring new life to traditional literary forms. Her imaginative stories combine pieces of historical fiction, fairy tales, and horror stories and usually deal with fantastic or mysterious events. As you'll see, "The Third Wish" gives a twist to the predictable fairy-tale form. In fact, the story comes from a collection whose title sums up the appeal of Aiken's work—*Not What You Expected.*

◆ Literature and Your Life

Connect Your Experience

Imagine that you could have three wishes granted to you. Do you know what your wishes would be? This is the situation of Mr. Peters in "The Third Wish," a person whose life has always been routine, even humdrum. As you read, think about how Mr. Peters's wishes compare with wishes you might make in a similar situation.

Thematic Focus: What Matters

When Mr. Peters has to decide whose happiness is most important, he must weigh everything that matters to him. You may be surprised at the values he reveals.

◆ Background for Understanding

Literature

"The Third Wish" features the swan, a long-necked waterbird known for its grace. Joan Aiken enhances the physical characteristics of swans by adding magical qualities. She is not the first writer to transform a swan into a mystical creature. Throughout time, swans have appeared in myths and legends. In some legends, swans represent feminine qualities. In others, they lead a wanderer on a mysterious journey. Aiken picks up this mythical pattern as she describes the mysterious journey of her main character in "The Third Wish."

Prentice Hall Literature Program Resources

REINFORCE / RETEACH / EXTEND

Selection Support Pages
Build Vocabulary: Suffixes: *-ous,* p. 72
Build Spelling Skills, p. 73
Build Grammar Skills: Adjectives, p. 74
Reading for Success: Interactive Reading Strategies, pp. 75–76
Literary Focus: Modern Fairy Tale, p. 77

Strategies for Diverse Student Needs, pp. 27–28

Beyond Literature Cross-Curricular Connection: Science, p. 14

Formal Assessment Selection Test, pp. 60–62, Assessment Resources Software

Alternative Assessment, p. 14

Writing and Language Transparencies Series of Events Chain, p. 66; Cluster Organizer, p. 82

Art Transparencies Art 2, *Cascading Leaves*

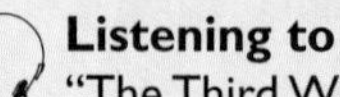
Resource Pro CD-ROM
"The Third Wish"—includes all resource material and customizable lesson plan

Listening to Literature Audiocassettes "The Third Wish"

The Third Wish

Literary Focus

Modern Fairy Tale

The elements of a **modern fairy tale** are the same as those in traditional fairy tales: mysterious and fantastic events, magic and wishes, and animals with unusual abilities. Modern fairy tales also include details and concerns related to contemporary life.

In "The Third Wish," a lonely Englishman stumbles into the realm of fantasy one evening while driving home in his car. As you read the story, record the elements of a modern fairy tale in a chart like the one below.

Build Vocabulary

Suffixes: *-ous*

A character in "The Third Wish" describes Mr. Peters as being "presumptuous." This word is derived from the word *presume.* The suffix *-ous* means "full of" or "characterized by." *Presumptuous* means "characterized by presuming or taking too much for granted"—in other words, being too bold or daring for your own good.

Word Bank

Which of these words from the selection describes a person who is full of bad intent, or malice? Check the Build Vocabulary boxes to see if you are correct.

extricate
presumptuous
composure
rash
remote
malicious

Mysterious and Fantastic Events	Magic and Wishes	Unusual Animals	Details About Contemporary Life
		Talking swan	

Preparing for Standardized Tests

Grammar Tell students that adjectives are words that modify or describe nouns. Some standardized tests may require students to identify adjectives and the nouns that they modify. Read the following sentence: "In his hands were a withered leaf and a white feather." Tell students that *withered* modifies *leaf* and *white* modifies *feather.* Explain that these adjectives answer the question "What kind?" Write the following on the board:

As Mr. Peters entered a straight, empty stretch of road he seemed to hear a faint crying.

Have students pick the adjectives in the sentence and the words they modify:

(A) *straight* modifies *stretch; faint* modifies *crying*
(B) *straight* and *empty* modify *stretch; faint* modifies *hear*
(C) *straight* and *empty* modify *stretch; faint* modifies *crying*
(D) *empty* modifies *stretch; faint* modifies *crying*

The correct answer is (C); both *straight* and *empty* modify the noun *stretch* (in *stretch of road*).

Interest Grabber Remind students that characters in fairy tales are often given three wishes. Ask each student to write three wishes anonymously on a piece of paper, fold the paper, and give it to you. Read some of the responses aloud and lead a discussion about the kinds of things students wished for. Try to point out any potential misinterpretations or problems with the wishes.

Build Grammar Skills

Adjectives If you wish to introduce the grammar concept for this selection before students read, refer to the instruction on p. 205.

Customize for
Less Proficient Readers
Ask students to track the story's events starting with the swan's release as described in the first paragraph on p. 200. Have them use the Series of Events Chain, p. 66, in **Writing and Language Transparencies.**

Customize for
More Advanced Students
Remind students that in fairy tales, animals often turn into humans, and vice versa. In this story, some of the humans have animal counterparts. As students read, instruct them to compare and contrast the qualities of the humans in the story with those of their animal counterparts.

Customize for
Verbal/Linguistic Learners
Ask students to recall other literary works that feature swans. Remind them of Hans Christian Andersen's "The Ugly Duckling" or the Greek myth of Leda and the Swan, which was also the subject of a poem by William Butler Yeats. Encourage students to read one or more of these works and note what the swan seems to symbolize. Have students share their findings with the rest of the class.

Reading for Success

The Reading for Success page in each unit presents a set of problem-solving strategies to help readers understand authors' words and ideas on multiple levels. Good readers develop a bank of strategies from which they can draw as needed.

Unit 3 introduces strategies for interactive reading. These strategies include predicting, clarifying, summarizing, and responding. Using these strategies will help students find meaning in what they read.

The interactive reading strategies are modeled in "The Third Wish." Each green box shows an example of the thinking process involved in applying one of the strategies. Additional notes provide support for applying these strategies throughout the selection.

How to Use the Reading for Success Page

- Introduce the interactive reading strategies, presenting each as a problem-solving procedure.
- Be sure students understand what each strategy involves and under what circumstances to apply it.
- Before students read the selection, have them preview it, looking at the annotations in the green boxes that model the strategies.
- To reinforce these strategies after students have read the selection, have them use Reading for Success, pp. 75–76, in **Selection Support.** These pages give students an opportunity to read a selection and practice interactive reading strategies by writing their own annotations.

Reading Strategies: Support and Reinforcement

Using Boxed Annotations and Prompts

Throughout the unit, the notes in green, red, and maroon are intended to help students apply reading strategies, understand the literary focus, and make a connection with their lives. You may use boxed material in these ways:

- Have students pause at each box and respond to its prompt before they continue reading.
- Urge students to read through the selection, ignoring the boxes. After they complete the selection, they may go back and review the text, responding to the prompts.

Reading for Success

Interactive Reading Strategies

Reading is like many activities in our lives—the more actively we participate, the more we get out of it. When you get truly involved in your reading, or read interactively, you'll better remember what you read. These strategies will help you become an interactive reader:

Predict what will happen.

When you read a story, your mind may race ahead, predicting what a character might do or how a conflict might be resolved. Look for clues or hints in the story to help you predict what is likely to occur. Look at this example:

Title:	"The Third Wish"
Predictions:	This story will be about a person granted three wishes. The last wish will be most important.

As you read, revise your predictions according to events in the story.

Clarify.

Only you know what you don't understand. When you read a passage you find difficult or confusing, take the time to pause to clarify the meaning. Try these strategies:

- ▶ Reread a section slowly to find out what the author is really saying.
- ▶ Ask questions to resolve the confusion.
- ▶ Look up a word in the dictionary, or get information from another source.

Summarize what you have read.

As you read a selection, pause occasionally to review and restate what has happened so far. This will help you to identify the most important ideas.

Respond.

You may understand a work of literature best when it evokes strong feelings. Get to know your own reactions by asking yourself what the selection meant to you. Use these questions to get you started:

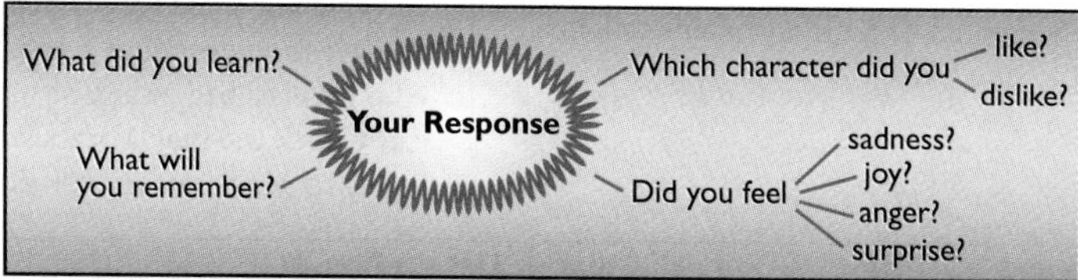

As you read "The Third Wish," look at the notes in the boxes. The notes demonstrate how to apply these strategies to a work of literature.

Model a Reading Strategy: Predict What Will Happen

Students can increase their reading comprehension by making predictions about events that may occur later in the story. To illustrate how to form these hypotheses, model your thinking process:

> After Leita marries Mr. Peters, she seems unhappy with her life as a human being. I can guess that she may become a swan again. I find out that Mr. Peters is worried about Leita and read that he offers to use his second wish to turn her back into a swan. Even though Leita turns him down, I still think she may end up as a swan. I know that Mr. Peters really wants a wife, so I think that if he uses his second wish to turn Leita back to a swan, he may use his third wish for another wife. When I find out how Mr. Peters uses his second wish, I can decide whether I want to change my prediction about the third wish.

Suggest that students record their predictions in their journals. At the end of the story they can see how close they came to the true outcome of the story. This will help them determine whether the reading strategy of predicting what will happen aided their comprehension of the story.

▲ **Critical Viewing** In this story, a swan has magical powers. What details of the photograph make this swan look powerful? **[Relate]** 1

Once there was a man who was driving in his car at dusk on a spring evening through part of the forest of Savernake. His name was Mr. Peters. The primroses were just beginning but the trees were still bare, and it was cold; the birds had stopped singing an hour ago.

As Mr. Peters entered a straight, empty stretch of road he seemed to hear a faint crying, and a struggling and thrashing, as if somebody was in trouble far away in the trees. He left his car and climbed the mossy bank beside the road. Beyond the bank was an open slope of beech trees leading down to thorn bushes through which he saw the gleam of water. He stood a moment waiting to try and discover where the noise was coming from, and presently heard a rustling and some strange cries in a voice which was almost human—and yet there was something too hoarse about it at one time and too clear and sweet at another. Mr. Peters ran down the hill and as he neared the bushes he saw something white among them which was trying to extricate itself; coming closer he found that it was a swan that had become

From these details, you can **predict** that this swan will become important in the story. 2

◆ **Build Vocabulary**

extricate (eks´ tri kāt´) *v.*: To set free

Develop Understanding

In "The Third Wish", Mr. Peters frees a swan he finds entangled in the brush. When the swan changes into the King of the Forest, Mr. Peters demands three wishes for saving him. First, he wishes for a wife, and the next day marries a beautiful woman named Leita. Before long, however, Mr. Peters learns that Leita used to be a swan, and that she misses her earlier life. Seeing his wife so unhappy, Mr. Peters must decide what really matters and how to use his remaining wishes.

▶Critical Viewing◀

1 **Relate** *Possible response: The swan looks powerful because its neck is pushed back, its head is turned downward, as if it is ready to strike, and its feathers are puffed and majestic-looking.*

Reading for Success

2 **Predict** *Students should recognize that the swan's early emergence in the story, the compelling details of its struggle, and the fact that Mr. Peters stops to help it all signify that the swan will become important in the story.*

Customize for *English Language Learners*

This modern fairy tale uses figurative language and terms with which students may be unfamiliar. To help them, pantomime, draw, or explain expressions such as "holding the snaky head well away with the other hand," "assumed great dignity," "outskirts of the forest," "his heart swelled with grief," "communicating in some wordless manner," and "his hands, clasped on his breast."

Block Scheduling Strategies

Consider these suggestions to take advantage of extended class time:

- Before students read the selection, introduce the Reading for Success strategies, p. 198. Suggest that as they read, students keep a log to monitor their reading strategies. Supplement by having students work in groups to answer the Reading for Success questions on p. 205. Then have them complete practice pages in **Selection Support,** pp. 75–76.
- Introduce the literary focus, modern fairy tale, before students read the selection. As they read, have them record elements in a chart like the one on p. 197. Then have them get together in small groups to answer the Literary Focus questions on p. 205.
- To prepare for the Speaking and Listening Mini-Lesson, p. 202, have them work with a partner to brainstorm for favorite song lyrics.
- If you have access to technology, have students use the *Writer's Solution Writing Lab CD-ROM* tutorial on Creative Writing to prepare for and complete the Writing Mini-Lesson.

◆Literary Focus

1 Modern Fairy Tale Ask students to identify the first characteristic of a fairy tale in the story. *The swan changes into a little man in green who has a golden crown and a long beard.*

Art Transparency Display Art Transparency 2, p. 11 in **Art Transparencies,** to suggest to students the setting in the story, which takes place near water, like the scene in this painting. Emphasize two important elements in this story that are depicted in the painting: the water and the leaves. After they have read the first three pages of the story, ask students to explain why the water is important, leading them to see that it was necessary to Leita's life. Ask them also to state the significance of the leaves—three leaves represent the three wishes that Mr. Peters is granted.

Customize for
Bodily/Kinesthetic Learners
Have students pantomime the character of the swan/man as he is described on this page. Encourage them, through their performance, to convey the dignity and vanity of the swan, as well as the unfriendliness and impatience of the "little man."

◆Critical Thinking

2 Analyze Character Ask students to use details from the text to give a brief analysis of the King of the Forest. *Students may respond that the King of the Forest is described as having "fierce glittering eyes" and "looked by no means friendly," and that his conversation with Mr. Peters seems haughty and condescending. The King of the Forest does not seem to respect humans.*

entangled in the thorns growing on the bank of the canal.

The bird struggled all the more frantically as he approached, looking at him with hate in its yellow eyes, and when he took hold of it to free it, it hissed at him, pecked him, and thrashed dangerously with its wings which were powerful enough to break his arm. Nevertheless he managed to release it from the thorns, and carrying it tightly with one arm, holding the snaky head well away with the other hand (for he did not wish his eyes pecked out), he took it to the verge of the canal and dropped it in.

The swan instantly assumed great dignity and sailed out to the middle of the water, where it put itself to rights with much dabbling and preening, smoothing its feathers with little showers of drops. Mr. Peters waited, to make sure that it was all right and had suffered no damage in its struggles. Presently the swan, when it was satisfied with its appearance, floated in to the bank once more, and in a moment, instead of the
1 great white bird, there was a little man all in green with a golden crown and long beard, standing by the water. He had fierce glittering eyes and looked by no means friendly.

"Well, Sir," he said threateningly, "I see you are presumptuous enough to know some of the laws of magic. You think that because you have rescued—by pure good fortune—the King of the Forest from a difficulty, you should have some fabulous reward."

"I expect three wishes, no more and no less," answered Mr. Peters, looking at him steadily and with composure. 2

"Three wishes, he wants, the clever man! Well, I have yet to hear of the human being who made any good use of his three wishes—they mostly end up worse off than they started. Take your three wishes then"—he flung three dead leaves in the air—"don't blame me if you spend the last wish in undoing the work of the other two."

◆ Build Vocabulary

presumptuous (prē zump′ cho͞o əs) *adj.*: Overconfident; arrogant

composure (kəm pō′ zhər) *n.*: Calmness of mind

rash (rash) *adj.*: Thoughtless

remote (ri mōt′) *adj.*: Far away from everything else

Beyond the Classroom

Career Connection

Child Care/Education Some students may be interested in a career—such as teaching preschool or working in a day-care center—in which they will have to entertain young children. Lead students to the idea that reading and telling stories are educational and fun ways to engage young children.

Ask students what techniques effective storytellers use. Discuss techniques such as speaking clearly, using different voices for each character, and using intonation and body language to reflect the mood of the scene. Then ask students what types of voices each character in "The Third Wish" might have.

Have interested students make audio recordings of the story, using the techniques mentioned. If possible, give the audiocassettes to elementary teachers in your area to use in their listening centers. Suggest that—after their students have listened to the selection several times—they make drawings of the story to send to your students.

Mr. Peters caught the leaves and put two of them carefully in his briefcase. When he looked up, the swan was sailing about in the middle of the water again, flicking the drops angrily down its long neck.

Mr. Peters stood for some minutes reflecting on how he should use his reward. He knew very well that the gift of three magic wishes was one which brought trouble more often than not, and he had no intention of being like the forester who first wished by mistake for a sausage, and then in a rage wished it on the end of his wife's nose, and then had to use his last wish in getting it off again. Mr. Peters had most of the things which he wanted and was very content with his life. The only thing that troubled him was that he was a little lonely, and had no companion for his old age. He decided to use his first wish and to keep the other two in case of an emergency. Taking a thorn he pricked his tongue with it, to remind himself not to utter <u>rash</u> wishes aloud. 4 Then holding the third leaf and gazing round him at the dusky undergrowth, the primroses, great beeches and the blue-green water of the canal, he said:

3 You might **respond** with amusement to the story of the forester.

"I wish I had a wife as beautiful as the forest."

A tremendous quacking and splashing broke out on the surface of the water. He thought that it was the swan laughing at him. Taking no notice he made his way through the darkening woods to his car, wrapped himself up in the rug and went to sleep.

When he awoke it was morning and the birds were beginning to call. Coming along the track towards him was the most beautiful creature he had ever seen, with eyes as blue-green as the canal, hair as dusky as the bushes, and skin as white as the feathers of swans. 5

"Are you the wife that I wished for?" asked Mr. Peters.

"Yes, I am," she replied. "My name is Leita." 6

She stepped into the car beside him and they drove off to the church on the outskirts of the forest, where they were married. Then he took her to his house in a <u>remote</u> and lovely valley and showed her all his treasures—the bees in their white hives, the Jersey

Reading for Success

3 **Respond** Ask students to respond to the story of the forester. *Most students will respond with feelings of amusement, but encourage other responses, such as impatience with the forester's foolishness.*

◆Build Grammar Skills

4 **Adjectives** Tell students that adjectives are words that describe or modify nouns or pronouns. Discuss with students the meaning of the vocabulary word *rash.* Point out that it describes the noun *wishes*. Ask students to find adjectives that describe nouns in the next sentence. *Students should identify* third, dusky, great, blue-green, *and* beautiful.

◆Literature and Your Life

5 Ask students to think of a time when they received something they had always wanted. Ask them if receiving it changed their life in the way that they had hoped. *Discuss that sometimes receiving a desired object results in disappointment and also that desired objects sometimes lose their appeal after a short time.*

6 **Clarification** Leita is a name associated with Leda. In classical mythology Zeus, in the form of a swan, comes to Leda. From their union two children are born, Helen and Pollux. The story has been commonly used in art and literature. Correggio has painted *Leda and the Swan* and W. B. Yeats has written the poem "Leda and the Swan."

Humanities: Literature

Fairy Tale Although fairy tales have long been popular among children, it is believed that they were originally meant for adults. Most fairy tales have several versions from different times and countries. For example, there were found to be 345 versions of Cinderella (dating from 1544 to 1892) from countries such as China, Ireland, and North America. In each version, the same basic episodes exist with variations on the specific characters. The fairy godmother, for example, may be a magical animal or a dead mother.

Jacob and Wilhelm Grimm are among the most famous collectors of fairy tales. They wrote down tales from oral narration by peasants in Germany. Among their most famous stories are "Hansel and Gretel," "Rumpelstiltskin," and "Snow White." Hans Christian Andersen was a Danish writer who wrote 168 fairy tales, including such classics as "The Princess and the Pea" and "The Ugly Duckling."

Have students choose a specific fairy tale to investigate. Have them begin their research by locating the origin of the tale, then continue by finding different versions. Finally, have them share their findings with the class.

Students might try this Web site (all Web sites are subject to change).

http://www.darkgoddess.com/fairy

We *strongly recommend* that you preview the site before you send students to it.

Reading for Success

1 Summarize Explain to students that interactive readers pause periodically in their reading to summarize the events of the story thus far.

Reading for Success

2 Respond Have students share their responses about the cause of Leita's unhappiness. *Some students may sympathize with Leita, while others may feel concerned for Mr. Peters, who is troubled by Leita's feelings.*

◆Critical Thinking

3 Infer Ask students why they think Mr. Peters knows that "when a human being marries a bird it always leads to sorrow." *Students may say Mr. Peters knows this fact just as he knows other laws of magic.*

◆Reading Stratgey

4 Clarify Remind students that in fairy tales, characters often repeat the same actions over and over again. Ask why this might be so. *Some students may say that it gives the story a predictable pattern.*

---

1 **Summarize** the events of the story this way: When Mr. Peters rescued a swan who turned out to be the King of the Forest, he was granted three wishes. Mr. Peters used one wish to ask for a wife, and Leita appeared.

cows, the hyacinths, the silver candlesticks, the blue cups and the luster bowl for putting primroses in. She admired everything, but what pleased her most was the river which ran by the foot of his garden.

"Do swans come up there?" she asked.

"Yes, I have often seen swans there on the river," he told her, and she smiled.

Leita made him a good wife. But as time went by Mr. Peters began to feel that she was not happy. She seemed restless, wandered much in the garden, and sometimes when he came back from the fields he would find the house empty and she would return after half an hour or so with no explanation of where she had been. On these occasions she was always especially tender and would put out his slippers to warm and cook his favorite dish—Welsh rarebit[1] with wild strawberries—for supper.

One evening he was returning home along the river path when he saw Leita in front of him, down by the water. A swan had sailed up to the verge and she had her arms round its neck and the swan's head rested against her cheek. She was weeping, and as he came nearer he saw that tears were rolling, too, from the swan's eyes.

2 You might **respond** to Leita's crying by remembering a time when you felt very sad.

"Leita, what is it?" he asked, very troubled.

"This is my sister," she answered. "I can't bear being separated from her."

Now he understood that Leita was really a swan from the forest, and this made him very sad because when a human being marries a bird it always leads to sorrow. 3

"I could use my second wish to give your sister human shape, so that she could be a companion to you," he suggested.

"No, no," she cried, "I couldn't ask that of her."

"Is it so very hard to be a human being?" asked Mr. Peters sadly.

"Very, very hard," she answered.

"Don't you love me at all, Leita?"

"Yes, I do, I do love you," she said, and there were tears in her eyes again. "But I missed the old life in the forest, the cool grass and the mist rising off the river at sunrise and the feel of the water sliding over my feathers as my sister and I drifted along the stream."

"Then shall I use my second wish to turn you back into a swan again?" he asked, and his tongue pricked to remind him of the old King's words,

Clarify that Mr. Peters pricked his tongue when he made his first wish, to remind himself not to make rash wishes. 4

1. **Welsh rarebit:** A dish of melted cheese served on crackers or toast.

◆ Build Vocabulary

malicious (mə lish′ əs) *adj.*: Spiteful; hateful

Speaking and Listening Mini-Lesson

Song Lyrics

This mini-lesson supports the Speaking and Listening activity in the Idea Bank on p. 206.

Introduce Invite students to cite favorite song lyrics while a volunteer writes them on the board. Help students analyze how the lyrics express different emotions.

Develop Have students form groups to discuss what emotions Leita's song should convey. Then have them write a short song. Suggest that students reread the story to gather ideas for lyrics. If students have difficulty creating a melody, they can use a tune with which they are familiar. Encourage students who have musical training to apply their skills to their creation.

Apply Have students present their songs to the class. Some groups may elect to sing their song with no accompaniment, while others may prefer to play an audiocassette recording of music in the background or have a group member accompany them. Suggest that students who are not comfortable singing read the words of their song.

Assess Evaluate students' songs on how well they convey the emotions that Leita felt as a human, or adapt the Peer Assessment: Dramatic Performance, p. 107, in **Alternative Assessment.**

and his heart swelled with grief inside him.

"Who will take care of you?"

"I'd do it myself as I did before I married you," he said, trying to sound cheerful.

She shook her head. "No, I could not be as unkind to you as that. I am partly a swan, but
5 I am also partly a human being now. I will stay with you."

Poor Mr. Peters was very distressed on his wife's account and did his best to make her life happier, taking her for drives in the car, finding beautiful music for her to listen to on
6 the radio, buying clothes for her and even suggesting a trip round the world. But she said no to that; she would prefer to stay in their own house near the river.

He noticed that she spent more and more time baking wonderful cakes—jam puffs, petits fours, eclairs and meringues. One day he saw her take a basketful down to the river and he guessed that she was giving them to her sister.

He built a seat for her by the river, and the two sisters spent hours together there, communicating in some wordless manner. For a time he thought that all would be well, but then he saw how thin and pale she was growing.

One night when he had been late doing the account he came up to bed and found her weeping in her sleep and calling:

> The story events lead you to **predict** what must happen to Leita. 7

"Rhea! Rhea! I can't understand what you say! Oh, wait for me, take me with you!"

Then he knew that it was hopeless and she would never be happy as a human. He stooped down and kissed her goodbye, then took another leaf from his notecase, blew it out of the window, and used up his second wish.

Next moment instead of Leita there was a sleeping swan lying across the bed with its head under its wing. He carried it out of the house and down to the brink of the river, and then he said, "Leita! Leita!" to waken her, and gently put her into the water. She gazed round her in astonishment for a moment, and then came up to him and rested her head lightly against his hand; next instant she was flying away over the trees towards the heart of the forest.

He heard a harsh laugh behind him, and turning round saw the old King looking at him with a <u>malicious</u> expression.

"Well, my friend! You don't seem to have managed so wonderfully with your first two wishes, do you? What will you do with the last? Turn yourself into a swan? Or turn Leita back into a girl?"

"I shall do neither," said Mr. Peters calmly. "Human beings and swans are better in their own shapes."

But for all that he looked sadly over towards the forest where Leita had flown, and walked slowly back to his house.

Next day he saw two swans swimming at the bottom of the garden, and one of them wore the gold chain he had given Leita after their marriage; she came up and rubbed her

◀ **Critical Viewing** What experiences pictured here might Leita miss as a human? **[Analyze]** 8

Comprehension Check ☑

5 Why is Mr. Peters distressed when Leita refuses his offer to turn her back into a swan? *He is distressed to learn that her life as a human is difficult and that she is not happy.*

◆ Critical Thinking

6 Infer Ask students why they think that Leita turns down Mr. Peters's offer to take her around the world. *Leita wants to stay near the river and her sister.*

Reading for Success

7 Predict Ask students to share their predictions about what will happen to Leita, and to explain the story events that led them to their predictions. *Students who predict that Leita will return to her life as a swan should cite the following story events: Leita's weeping, her statement that she wants to remain near the river, her baking treats for and spending time with her sister.*

▶Critical Viewing◀

8 Analyze Possible response: *Leita might miss such experiences as swimming in the lake, enjoying the sound of the reeds rustling, and the company of the other swan.*

Cross-Curricular Connection: Science

Swans Explain to students that swans are a type of waterfowl related to ducks and geese. They are characterized by heavy bodies, short legs, wide webbed feet, and usually white feathers. Swans tend to fly in groups in a "V" pattern. They form lifelong bonds with one mate and both parents share responsibility for guarding the nest and caring for the young.

Share with students that there are eight different species of swans. The most well known are the mute swan, the whistling swan, and the trumpeter swan. The other species are the Bewick's swan, the whooping swan, the blacknecked swan, the Coscoraoba swan, and the black swan, whose plumage is all black.

Have students form groups and research one species of swan. Suggest that students cover such areas as physical characteristics, habitat, and diet. Then encourage students to present their findings in an illustrated report that includes photographs or drawings of their swans.

Reading for Success

Answers

◆ Literature and Your Life

Reader's Response Students may say that they would advise Mr. Peters to wish for things rather than people.

Thematic Focus He learns that the happiness of the person he loves is more important than having his wishes fulfilled.

☑ Check Your Comprehension

1. Mr. Peters rescues a swan who is really the King of the Forest and who can grant magic wishes.
2. Mr. Peters holds the third leaf and wishes for a wife. Then he goes to sleep. In the morning, he sees a woman walking toward him.
3. Mr. Peters wishes that Leita return to her swan form.
4. He spends time with two swans. He talks to them and they protect him.
5. He never makes a third wish.

◆ Critical Thinking

1. Mr. Peters loves his wife enough to sacrifice his own happiness for hers.
2. He is happy that Leita stayed close by as his companion throughout his life, therefore fulfilling his first wish.
3. The story's ending shows that Mr. Peters finds a companion for his old age after all, even though she wasn't a human.
4. Some students may say that he used his wishes wisely because he had no way of knowing how his wish for a wife would turn out. Others may say that he should have taken time to think about what he wanted.
5. Most students will say that his statement that "wishes . . . don't always better you" shows he would not have used his third wish.

head against his hand.

Mr. Peters and his two swans came to be well known in that part of the country; people used to say that he talked to swans and they understood him as well as his neighbors.

Many people were a little frightened of him. There was a story that once when thieves tried to break into his house they were set upon by two huge white birds which carried them off bodily and dropped them into the river.

> Compare the story's ending with your **prediction** to see if you were right.

As Mr. Peters grew old everyone wondered at his contentment. Even when he was bent with rheumatism[2] he would not think of moving to a drier spot, but went slowly about his work, with the two swans always somewhere close at hand.

Sometimes people who knew his story would say to him:

"Mr. Peters, why don't you wish for another wife?"

"Not likely," he would answer serenely. "Two wishes were enough for me, I reckon. I've learned that even if your wishes are granted they don't always better you. I'll stay faithful to Leita."

One autumn night, passers-by along the road heard the mournful sound of two swans singing. All night the song went on, sweet and harsh, sharp and clear. In the morning Mr. Peters was found peacefully dead in his bed with a smile of great happiness on his face. In his hands, which lay clasped on his breast, were a withered leaf and a white feather.

2. **rheumatism** (roo´ me tiz əm) *n.*: Pain and stiffness of the joints and muscles.

Guide for Responding

◆ Literature and Your Life

Reader's Response If you could give advice to Mr. Peters about how to use his third wish, what would you tell him?

Thematic Focus As the story unfolds, what does Mr. Peters learn about the things that matter to him?

☑ Check Your Comprehension

1. How does Mr. Peters get an opportunity to ask for three wishes?
2. How is his first wish granted?
3. What is Mr. Peters's second wish?
4. Describe Mr. Peters's life after his second wish is granted.
5. What is his third wish?

◆ Critical Thinking

Interpret

1. Mr. Peters turns his wife back into a swan. What does this show about him? **[Infer]**
2. Why does Mr. Peters die with a look of happiness on his face? **[Analyze]**
3. Explain the story's ending. **[Draw Conclusions]**

Evaluate

4. Do you think Mr. Peters wisely used the three wishes granted to him? **[Evaluate]**

Apply

5. If Mr. Peters were alive today, do you think he would have used his third wish? Why or why not? **[Speculate]**

Beyond the Selection

FURTHER READING

Other Works by Joan Aiken

Not What You Expected
A Creepy Company: Ten Tales of Terror
A Fit of Shivers: Tales for Late at Night
The Wolves of Willoughby Chase

Other Fairy Tales

Snow White and Rose Red: A Modern Fairy Tale, Regina Doman
The Complete Fairy Tales of the Brothers Grimm, Jack Zipes (trans.)

INTERNET

Additional information about Joan Aiken can be found on the Internet. We suggest the following sites on the Internet (all Web sites are subject to change).

http://ocean.st.usm.edu/~dajones/findaids/aiken.htm

For an interview with Joan Aiken, go to:
http://www.locusmag.com/Issues/1998/05/Aiken.html

We *strongly recommend* that you preview these sites before you send students to them.

Guide for Responding *(continued)*

◆ Reading for Success

Interactive Reading Strategies

Review the reading strategies and the notes showing how to interact with the story. Then apply them to answer the following questions.

1. Summarize the events that lead up to Mr. Peters's three wishes.
2. At what point in this story would you predict what each of the three wishes might be? Why?
3. Do you think Mr. Peters used his second wish wisely? Explain.

◆ Build Vocabulary

Using the Suffix *-ous*

The suffix *-ous,* meaning "full of" or "characterized by," makes a noun an adjective. On a sheet of paper, add *-ous* to the word in parentheses to complete each sentence.

1. She looked __?__ in that silly outfit. (ridicule)
2. The __?__ firefighter rescued the child. (courage)
3. With her diamond barrettes and her dark glasses, the actress looked very __?__. (glamour)

Spelling Strategy

When you add *-ous* to words that end with *ce* pronounced like *s*, change the final *e* to *i* before adding the suffix: *malice* + *-ous* = *malicious.*

Add *-ous* to these nouns to create adjectives. Then, write sentences using each new word.

1. space
2. grace
3. vice

Using the Word Bank

On your paper, match each word in the first column with a word that means the same in the second column.

1. extricate	**a.** far
2. composure	**b.** thoughtless
3. presumptuous	**c.** free
4. rash	**d.** calmness
5. remote	**e.** spiteful
6. malicious	**f.** arrogant

◆ Literary Focus

Modern Fairy Tale

Because it contains both old-fashioned and contemporary elements, "The Third Wish" is a **modern fairy tale.** Aiken uses such classic fairy-tale elements as magic, wishes, and the unexpected behavior of animals. She also incorporates contemporary twists and issues in the setting, characters, and plot of the story.

1. What details of the setting in "The Third Wish" make it a modern fairy tale?
2. (a) In what ways is Mr. Peters like the main character in a traditional fairy tale? (b) How is he different and more contemporary?
3. How does Leita represent a character specific to a modern fairy tale?

◆ Build Grammar Skills

Adjectives

Adjectives are words that modify or describe nouns or pronouns. They tell more about the nouns or pronouns they modify by answering the questions *what kind, which one, how many,* and *how much.* In the following sentence, Aiken uses adjectives to inform the reader about "how many" wishes Mr. Peters expects. She also tells "what kind" of man Mr. Peters is.

"*Three* wishes, he wants, the *clever* man!"

Practice Copy these sentences. Underline each adjective, and draw an arrow to the word it modifies. Then, tell what question it answers.

1. He climbed the mossy bank beside the road.
2. He had fierce glittering eyes and powerful white wings.
3. Leita made him a good wife.
4. He heard a harsh laugh behind him.
5. Next day he saw two swans.

Writing Application On your paper, write a paragraph using the following adjectives.

1. careful
2. vivid
3. happy
4. astonished

◆ Build Grammar Skills

Practice

1. He climbed the mossy bank beside the road. (bank; *what kind?*)
2. He had fierce glittering eyes and powerful, white wings. (eyes, *what kind?*; wings, *what kind?*)
3. Leita made him a good wife. (wife; *what kind?*)
4. He heard a harsh laugh behind him. (laugh; *what kind?*)
5. Next day he saw two swans. (day; *which one?*; swans; *how many?*)

Writer's Solution

For additional instruction and practice, use the lesson in the *Writer's Solution Language Lab CD-ROM* on Using Modifiers. You may also use the pages on Adjectives, pp. 15–19, in the *Writer's Solution Grammar Practice Book.*

Reading for Success

1. Mr. Peters is driving, hears a strange noise, and goes to investigate. He finds a swan tangled in the brush and he sets it free. The swan changes into the King of the Forest, and Mr. Peters demands that he be given three wishes in return for his efforts.
2. Some students may say that they predicted Mr. Peters's first wish when they learned that he was lonely and his second wish when Leita became unhappy. They may have predicted that he would not use his third wish, because his first two wishes turned out badly.
3. Many students will say that Mr. Peters uses his second wish wisely because he is happier seeing Leita happy.

◆ Build Vocabulary

Using the Suffix *-ous*

1. ridiculous
2. courageous
3. glamorous

Spelling Strategy

1. spacious
2. gracious
3. vicious

Using the Word Bank

1. c
2. d
3. f
4. b
5. a
6. e

◆ Literary Focus

1. Students should note the conveniences of modern society such as a car, the radio, and Mr. Peters's offering Leita a trip around the world.
2. (a) He is like a character in a traditional fairy tale because he receives three wishes in return for saving the King of the Forest. (b) He is different because he lives in the modern world and seems to know about the laws of magic.
3. Leita represents a character specific to a modern fairy tale because she changes from human to animal but lives in a world with cars and radios.

Idea Bank

Following are suggestions for matching the Idea Bank topics with your students' performance levels and learning modalities:

Customize for
Performance Levels
Less Advanced Students: 1, 5, 7
Average Students: 2, 4, 5, 6, 7
More Advanced Students: 3, 4, 6

Customize for
Learning Modalities
Verbal/Linguistic: 1, 2, 3, 5
Interpersonal: 4, 5
Visual/Spatial: 6, 7
Bodily/Kinesthetic: 5
Logical/Mathematical: 6
Musical/Rhythmic: 4

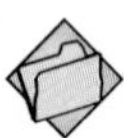

Writing Mini-Lesson

Refer students to the Writing Handbook in the back of the book for instruction on the writing process and for further information on creative writing. Have students use the Cluster Organizer in **Writing and Language Transparencies,** p. 82, to arrange their prewriting examples.

Writer's Solution

Writing Lab CD-ROM

1. Have students view the video clip on how to get started gathering details.
2. Have students draft on computer.
3. Encourage students to use the Concrete Images Word Bin to see lists of sensory images.
4. Suggest that students view interactive writing tips when revising.

Writer's Solution Sourcebook
Have students use Chapter 8, "Creative Writing," pp. 234–263, for additional support. This chapter includes in-depth instruction on formatting dialogue and using concrete language pp. 261–263.

Build Your Portfolio

Idea Bank

Writing

1. **Journal Entry** As the King of the Forest, write a journal entry describing how you were rescued by Mr. Peters.
2. **Obituary** An obituary is a notice of someone's death. Write an obituary for Mr. Peters, including facts about his death. Add colorful details of Mr. Peters's life to make the obituary interesting.
3. **Analysis** "The Third Wish" has a message for readers. In an essay, identify the message and cite story details to support your interpretation. Include your reaction to the idea the story stresses.

Speaking and Listening

4. **Song Lyrics [Group Activity]** If Leita were to sing a song about her experiences as a swan, what would the lyrics of her song say? With one or two classmates, write the music and lyrics of Leita's song and perform it for your class. **[Music Link]**
5. **Radio Drama** Mr. Peters had an extraordinary experience when he saved the King of the Forest. Create a radio script that portrays the rescue, and act it out for your class. Add sound effects to bring the action to life. **[Performing Arts Link]**

Projects

6. **Poster on the Number Three** Like Aiken's story, many fairy tales include three wishes. Common wisdom says that good things happen in threes. The ancient Greeks had three major gods. The Greek philosopher Pythagoras considered three perfect because it represents a beginning, middle, and an end. Compile a poster of mathematical data about the number three: its square root, its factors, and its relationship to geometric shapes. **[Math Link]**
7. **Multimedia Report** Research fairy tales from different cultures. Note their countries of origin, characters, magic elements, and messages. Gather maps, book jackets, illustrations, and videos to create a multimedia report. **[Media Link]**

Writing Mini-Lesson

Modern Fairy Tale

"The Third Wish" takes place in the modern world, but it contains fantasy and magic—elements of traditional fairy tales. Choose a traditional fairy tale with which you're familiar, and write a retelling of it in a modern setting.

Writing Skills Focus: Elaborate on Key Ideas

Let your readers know you've updated your story by **elaborating on key ideas.** For example, if you decide to include an electronic fairy godmother who appears via e-mail, you might provide supporting details such as these:

- The hero spends a lot of time at the computer.
- A computer crash and restart signals the appearance and disappearance of the fairy godmother.
- At the end of the story, the computer seems strangely normal again.

Prewriting List the events in your story. Brainstorm for ways to update the setting, and jot down your best ideas.

Drafting Begin with the traditional opening sentence of a fairy tale: "Once upon a time . . ." As you draft your story, refer to your list of events, and include the details of the setting you've planned.

◆ **Grammar Application**

Look for places in your story where adjectives can provide more information.

Revising Check that the events of your story lead smoothly from one point to the next. If necessary, add more information to make the characters, plot, and setting easier for your readers to understand.

✓ ASSESSMENT OPTIONS

Formal Assessment, Selection Test, pp. 60–62, and Assessment Resources Software. The selection test is designed so that it can easily be customized to the performance levels of your students.

Alternative Assessment, p. 14, includes options for less advanced students, more advanced students, visual/spatial learners, interpersonal learners, verbal/linguistic learners, and musical/rhythmic learners.

PORTFOLIO ASSESSMENT
Use the following rubrics in the **Alternative Assessment** booklet to assess student writing:
Journal Entry: Expression, p. 81
Obituary: Description, p. 84
Analysis: Response to Literature, p. 97
Writing Mini-Lesson: Fictional Narrative, p. 82

Part 1 Risking It All

Untitled, Anatar Dayal

One-Minute Planning Guide

The selections in this part take a look at risks, with the theme of "Risking It All." The boy in "A Boy and a Man" risks his life to save the life of another. In an excerpt from the bestseller *Into Thin Air,* the author describes the risks and fears of climbing Mount Everest. *The Iceman* offers a hypothesis about the risks a man took 5,000 years ago—although the elements claimed his life, they preserved his body for scientists to study. "The Charge of the Light Brigade," a speech from Shakespeare's *Henry V,* and the poems "Lonely Particular" and "The Enemy" survey the risks of war and battles.

Customize for
Varying Student Needs

When assigning the selections in this part, keep in mind these factors:

"A Boy and a Man"
- Excerpt from *Banner in the Sky*
- Suspenseful

from *Into Thin Air*
- Excerpt from a nonfiction bestseller

from *The Iceman*
- Overview of an unusual and exciting archaeological find
- Opportunities for social studies connections

"The Charge of the Light Brigade"
- Famous, challenging poem from *Henry V*
- Short excerpt
- Less proficient readers and English language learners will need help with Shakespearean language

"Lonely Particular" and "The Enemy"
- Short but challenging poems about the impact of war

Humanities: Art

Untitled, by Anatar Dayal

Point out to students that the lines in this image probably mean that this is an engraving rather than a painting. In engraving, a design is drawn or traced onto a plate, and then incised by hand or by the application of acid. The plate is then inked, wiped clean, covered with a sheet of paper, and put through a press. The ink remaining in the incisions stands out on the paper in slight relief.

Help students connect the art to the theme of "Risking It All" by answering the following questions:

1. What do you think the person in the boat is feeling? *Students may say the person is frightened by the size of the wave that looks as if it's going to take over the boat.*
2. Do you think the artist has exaggerated the size of the wave? Why or why not? *Some students may say the artist made the wave extremely big to emphasize the risk that the sailor on the boat is taking.*

Prepare and Engage

OBJECTIVES

1. To read, comprehend, and interpret a story and an essay
2. To relate a story and an essay to personal experience
3. To predict story events
4. To analyze conflict with nature
5. To build vocabulary in context and learn the prefix *mal-*
6. To understand how to place adjectives correctly
7. To write a persuasive letter, organizing details by order of importance
8. To respond to the story through writing, speaking and listening, and projects

SKILLS INSTRUCTION

Vocabulary: Prefixes: *mal-*
Spelling: Words With Double Consonants
Grammar: Placement of Adjectives
Reading Strategy: Predict
Literary Focus: Conflict With Nature
Writing: Order of Importance
Speaking and Listening: Dialogue (Teacher Edition)
Critical Viewing: Speculate; Respond

PORTFOLIO OPPORTUNITIES

Writing: Advertisement; Movie Proposal; Autobiographical Incident
Writing Mini-Lesson: Persuasive Letter
Speaking and Listening: Dialogue; Rescue Interview
Projects: Glacier Research; How-to Guide

More About the Authors
James Ullman has said that people climb mountains for the same reasons they listen to music or look at the stars—these are all experiences of the spirit. He believes that "a man is never more a man than when he is striving for what is beyond his grasp."

With no formal training in writing, **Jon Krakauer** took a risk when he quit his work as a carpenter and fisherman in 1983 to begin writing full time. Since then, he has achieved significant success as an author, being named National Magazine Award Finalist in both 1994 and 1997. His best-selling book *Into Thin Air* describes an ill-fated expedition to the summit of Mt. Everest in 1996.

Guide for Reading

Meet the Authors:

James Ramsey Ullman (1907–1971)

Born in the shadow of the mountain-like skyscrapers of New York City, James Ramsey Ullman developed a love for climbing that made him feel more at home in Tibet than on New York's crowded streets. Although he personally did not climb Mt. Everest, he was a member of the first American expedition to the mountain.

Climbing and Writing Ullman was also a talented writer who worked as a reporter and wrote fiction and plays. He combined his love of climbing and his writing skill in *Banner in the Sky*, which won a Newbery Honor award. Five of Ullman's books became films, including *The White Tower, River of the Sun,* and *Banner in the Sky*.

Jon Krakauer (1954–)

Family outings in Oregon set the stage for Jon Krakauer's interest in mountaineering. By his early twenties, he had attempted several difficult mountain ascents. His first book-length publication, *Eiger Dreams: Ventures Among Men and Mountains,* was a collection of essays about climbing the Eiger, one of the toughest peaks of the Alps. He was well prepared for the challenge of climbing Mt. Everest and writing about it in his best-selling book *Into Thin Air.*

◆ Literature and Your Life

Connect Your Experience

You may have felt your heart race as you experienced the risks and rewards of downhill skiing, extreme skateboarding, or white-water rafting. These selections describe the heart-pounding danger and excitement of mountaineering—a challenge most of us may never have the courage or opportunity to experience firsthand.

Thematic Focus: Risking It All

Characters in these narratives risk it all to reach a goal, help someone in trouble, and overcome their fear.

◆ Background for Understanding

Geography

In "Into Thin Air," Jon Krakauer describes a dangerous hike across a glacier. Glaciers are huge ice chunks that develop where more snow falls than melts. Snow builds in layers until the glacier's crushing weight pushes it across the land. Since the surface of a glacier is rigid and it cannot flow like the compacted layers below, the layers do not move at the same speed. Stress builds until the surface cracks and deep crevasses appear. In addition to these dangerous cracks, those hiking across glaciers face deadly icefalls—avalanches of glacial ice.

◆ Build Vocabulary

Prefixes: *mal-*

The word *malevolent* combines the prefix *mal-*, meaning "bad or evil" and *-volence,* meaning "to wish." *Malevolent* means "wishing harm to others." You can see how these writers might call the mountains *malevolent,* since each could harm the climbers.

Word Bank

Which of these words from the selections do you think are verbs? Why?

prone
taut
pummeled
reconnoiter
malevolent
denigrate

Prentice Hall Literature Program Resources

REINFORCE / RETEACH / EXTEND

Selection Support Pages
Build Vocabulary: Prefixes: *mal-*, p. 78
Build Spelling Skills: p. 79
Build Grammar Skills: Placement of Adjectives, p. 80
Reading Strategy: Predict, p. 81
Literary Focus: Conflict With Nature, p. 82

Strategies for Diverse Student Needs, pp. 29–30

Beyond Literature Study Skills: Planning a Study Routine, p. 15

Formal Assessment Selection Test, pp. 63–65, Assessment Resources Software

Alternative Assessment, p. 15

Writing and Language Transparencies Sunburst Organizer, p. 95

Resource Pro CD-ROM "A Boy and a Man"; from *Into Thin Air*

Listening to Literature Audiocassettes "A Boy and a Man"; from *Into Thin Air*

A Boy and a Man ◆ *from* Into Thin Air

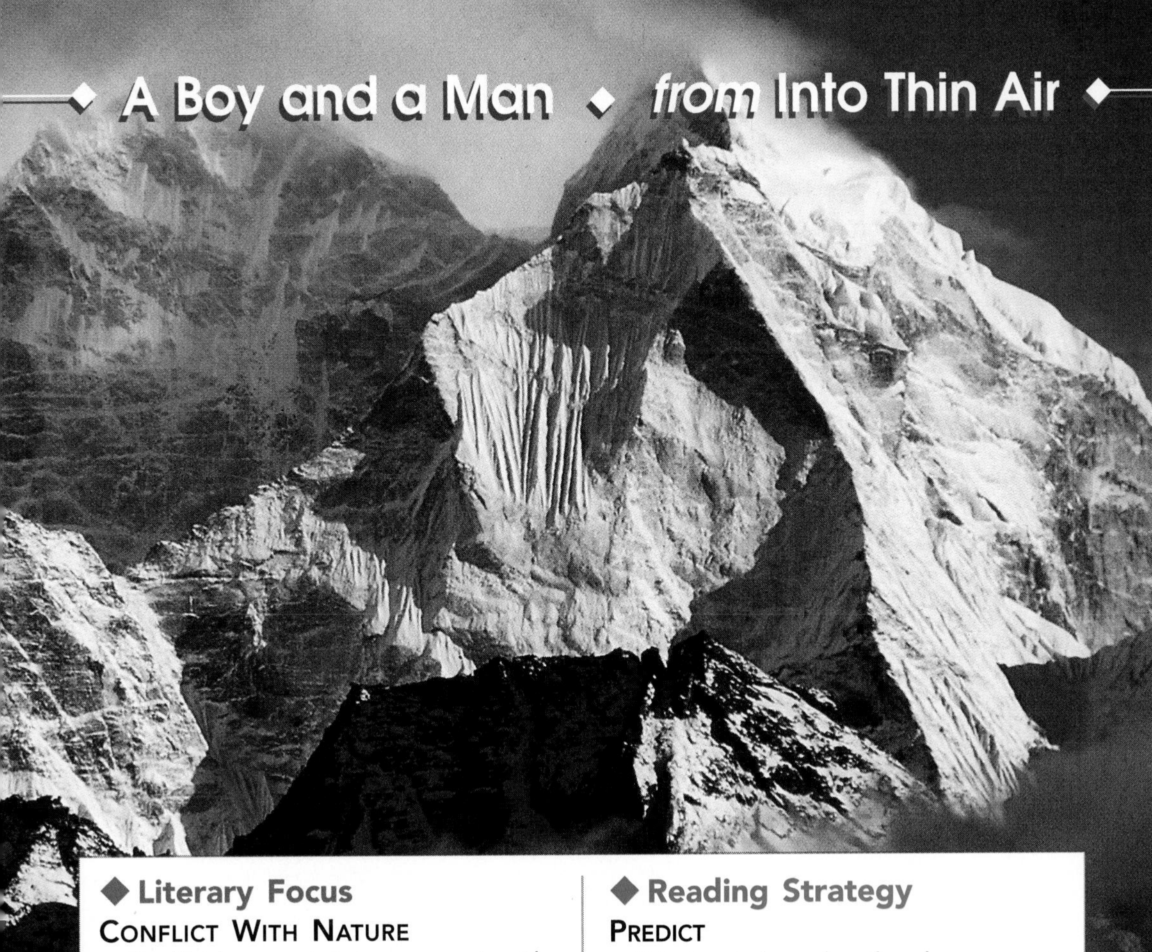

◆ Literary Focus

Conflict With Nature

Conflict is a struggle between opposing sides or forces. Most stories are built around a conflict. Conflicts may occur between characters, with nature, with society, or within an individual. Both these stories feature a conflict with nature in which people are pitted against the elements. In each case, the conflict focuses specifically on a struggle against an icy glacier, resulting in a chilling, life-or-death adventure.

◆ Reading Strategy

Predict

Gripping stories such as these keep you wondering what's going to happen next. Based on information the author provides, you can **predict,** or make an informed guess about, the events to follow. When you come to a place where the action could go in several directions, ask yourself: What details does the author provide about the conflict that suggest what will happen? Then, read to find out whether your prediction is correct. Keep track of your predictions by filling in a chart like the one below.

Detail or Hint	My Prediction	Actual Outcome
Rudi hears the voice in the crevasse.	He will try to rescue the man.	

Interest Grabber To engage student interest, show all or part of the film *Everest* (available from your local video store), which chronicles the adventures of an international crew of climbers assisting in the making of an IMAX movie. After viewing the film, which conveys the beauty and excitement—but also the danger—of climbing, ask students whether they consider mountaineering a valid sport or an unwarranted risky adventure.

◆Build Grammar Skills

Placement of Adjectives If you wish to introduce the grammar concept for this selection before students read, refer to the instruction on p. 220.

Customize for *Less Proficient Readers*

You may want to review the vocabulary words in these selections before students read. If possible, locate an encyclopedia article, magazine article, or book on mountain climbing and refer to any illustrations or pictures that will help clarify the technical vocabulary.

Customize for *More Advanced Students*

Students may enjoy doing preliminary research on mountain climbing before reading these selections. Encourage them to look at the footnoted words in the selections and then find pictures or illustrations of such words as *chimney, crevasse, crampons, serac,* and *stalagmites.* Ask students to share their findings with the class.

Preparing for Standardized Tests

Vocabulary Standardized tests often require students to choose the best definition for a word as it is used in a sentence. Knowing the definition of common prefixes will help students identify correct meanings.

For example, if asked to define the word *unconsciously,* students can begin by identifying the prefix *un-*. Since *un-* means "not," students can determine that *unconscious* means "not conscious" or "without awareness, sensation, or cognition."

Write the following sentence on the board, asking students to identify the best definition of the underlined word. Remind them to identify the prefix and use its meaning to help them find the correct answer.

After spending weeks at a high altitude, the mountain climber was maladjusted to life on the ground.

(A) trying
(B) poorly adapted
(C) expected
(D) well suited

Students can eliminate both *(A)* and *(C)* because they don't make sense in the sentence. In the context of the sentence, *(D)* is inaccurate, so *(B)* is the correct answer. If students know the prefix *mal-* means "not," they should be able to deduce that *maladjusted* means "not adjusted" or "unable to adapt."

One-Minute Insight Rudi is walking on a mountain glacier when he discovers a man trapped in a crevasse. Knowing the man will soon freeze, Rudi creates a makeshift rope and pulls the man to safety. He discovers that the man is Captain Winter, a famous mountaineer. As the two talk, Winter learns that Rudi is the son of an Alpine guide who died trying to climb the Citadel, a treacherous peak that Winter wants to climb. As they continue their conversation about the Citadel, Rudi realizes that because he has risked his life to save this man, he is now treated as an adult by Winter.

Customize for
English Language Learners
Explain to students that in selections such as these, which describe daring adventures, writers use a variety of verbs to illustrate characters' actions. You may want to use pantomime to illustrate the following action words: *wrenched, pummeled, flapping, threaded, flexed,* and *munching.*

Customize for
Interpersonal Learners
After students read the selection, arrange them in pairs and have them role-play the conversation that occurs between Rudi and Captain Winter following the rescue. Then have students change partners and assume the other role. Encourage students to share what they discovered about the characters during the activity.

Customize for
Visual/Spatial Learners
Students may understand the story better if they use the visual clues given by the author to sketch or draw certain elements. As they read, encourage students to create a rendering of the setting, the characters, or the actions. Then ask them to show their representations to the class, including commentary on how the author's description helped them create their images.

A Boy and a Man

from *Banner in the Sky*

James Ramsey Ullman

Block Scheduling Strategies

Consider these suggestions to take advantage of extended class time:

- Encourage students to focus on the reading strategy for the selection. As they read each selection, have them complete charts like the one on p. 209. After they finish reading, have students work in groups to complete the Reading Strategy questions on p. 220.
- Alternatively, have students read each selection independently and then meet in small groups to answer and discuss the Critical Thinking questions. Then encourage students to form small groups and work on the Cross-Curricular Activity in Beyond Literature feature on p. 217, or one of the projects from the Idea Bank on p. 221.
- If students have access to technology, have them work in pairs to complete the Writing Mini-Lesson using the *Writer's Solution Writing Lab CD-ROM* tutorial on Persuasion.

1 The crevasse[1] was about six feet wide at the top and narrowed gradually as it went down. But how deep it was Rudi could not tell. After a few feet the blue walls of ice curved away at a sharp slant, and what was below the curve was hidden from sight.

"Hello!" Rudi called.

"Hello—" A voice answered from the depths.

"How far down are you?"

"I'm not sure. About twenty feet, I'd guess."

"On the bottom?"

"No. I can't even see the bottom. I was lucky and hit a ledge."

The voice spoke in German, but with a strange accent. Whoever was down there, Rudi knew, it was not one of the men of the valley.

"Are you hurt?" he called.

"Nothing broken—no," said the voice. "Just shaken up some. And cold."

"How long have you been there?"

"About three hours."

Rudi looked up and down the crevasse. He was thinking desperately of what he could do.

"Do you have a rope?" asked the voice.

"No."

"How many of you are there?"

"Only me."

There was a silence. When the voice spoke again, it was still quiet and under strict control. "Then you'll have to get help," it said.

Rudi didn't answer. To get down to Kurtal would take at least two hours, and for a party to climb back up would take three. By that time it would be night, and the man would have been in the crevasse for eight hours. He would be frozen to death.

"No," said Rudi, "it would take too long."

"What else is there to do?"

Rudi's eyes moved over the ice-walls: almost vertical, smooth as glass. "Have you an ax?" he asked.

"No. I lost it when I fell. It dropped to the bottom."

"Have you tried to climb?"

"Yes. But I can't get a hold."

There was another silence. Rudi's lips tightened, and when he spoke again his voice was strained. "I'll think of something," he cried. "I'll think of *something*!"

"Don't lose your head," the voice said. "The only way is to go down for help."

"But you'll—"

"Maybe. And maybe not. That's a chance we'll have to take."

The voice was as quiet as ever. And, hearing it, Rudi was suddenly ashamed. Here was he, safe on the glacier's surface, showing fear and despair, while the one below, facing almost certain death, remained calm and controlled. Whoever it was down there it was a real man. A brave man. 2

Rudi drew in a long, slow breath. With his climbing-staff he felt down along the smooth surface of the ice walls.

"Are you still there?" said the voice.

"Yes," he said.

"You had better go."

1. **crevasse** (krə vas′) *n.*: Deep crack, especially in a glacier.

Clarification

❶ This story takes place in the Swiss Alps. Set the scene for the story by bringing in pictures of the Alps from travel guide books, such as Baedeker's *Switzerland*. The view from the Jungfraujoch toward the Wengernalp is particularly impressive.

◆Critical Thinking

❷ **Infer** Ask students to answer the following questions: What impresses Rudi about the man in the crevasse? Why is Rudi "suddenly ashamed"? How does this help him to think of a possible solution? *Rudi is impressed by the man's control. He is ashamed to show fear and despair when the man, who is in extreme danger, remains calm. Inspired by the man, Rudi calms himself, which enables him to think clearly and come up with a solution.*

Customize for *Bodily/Kinesthetic Learners*

Have students imagine they are in Rudi's situation. Then have them pantomime the action of drawing in a long, slow breath. Ask students what they can infer about Rudi based on this description. *He may be concentrating on making a decision or he may feel frustrated by the difficult choice in front of him.*

Cross-Curricular Connection: Science

Mountains Explain to students that mountains are parts of the Earth's surface that rise above the surrounding regions. Because of their high elevation, mountains serve as barriers to atmospheric pressure, creating differing climates on opposite sides. For example, the Himalayas actually block the polar gusts of air from Siberia and Russia, creating warmer winter weather in India.

Mountains are formed by various disturbances within the Earth's crust. There are three types of mountains:

- Fold mountains are created when the Earth's plates collide, pushing the Earth's crust upward.
- Block mountains are land masses that have been raised upward between fault lines.
- Volcanic mountains are created from lava and ash from volcanoes.

Have students use library reference sources or the Internet to find out more about the Alps or the Himalayas. In particular, have them research how these mountains were formed and what influence they have on the weather in surrounding countries.

◆Critical Thinking

❶ **Infer** Ask students why Rudi is lowering the staff into the crevasse. *He might be trying to use it as a rope, or he might be trying to judge distance.*

◆Reading Strategy

❷ **Predict** Ask students to predict what will happen next, based on what they have read so far. *Students might guess that Rudi will take off the rest of his clothes and lengthen the rope.*

◆Literary Focus

❸ **Conflict With Nature** Ask students how the environment adds to Rudi's difficulties rescuing the man. Encourage them to use a cluster diagram to record their ideas. *If he gets too cold, he will not have the strength to lift the man, and he might suffer frostbite or become ill from exposure.*

"Wait—"

❶ Lying flat on the glacier, he leaned over the rim of the crevasse and lowered the staff as far as it would go. Its end came almost to the curve in the walls.

"Can you see it?" he asked.

"See what?" said the man.

Obviously he couldn't. Standing up, Rudi removed his jacket and tied it by one sleeve to the curved end of the staff. Then, holding the other end, he again lay prone and lowered his staff and jacket.

"Can you see it now?" he asked.

"Yes," said the man.

"How far above you is it?"

"About ten feet."

Again the staff came up. Rudi took off his shirt and tied one of its sleeves to the dangling sleeve of the jacket. This time, as he lay down, the ice bit, cold and rough, into his bare chest; but he scarcely noticed it. With his arms extended, all the shirt and half the jacket were out of sight beneath the curve in the crevasse.

"How near are you now?" he called.

❷ "Not far," said the voice.

"Can you reach it?"

"I'm trying."

There was the sound of scraping bootnails; of labored breathing. But no pull on the shirt-sleeve down below.

"I can't make it," said the voice. It was fainter than before.

"Wait," said Rudi.

For the third time he raised the staff. He took off his trousers. He tied a trouser-leg to the loose sleeve of the shirt. Then he pulled, one by one, at all the knots he had made: between staff and jacket, jacket and shirt, shirt and trousers. He pulled until the blood pounded in his head and the knots were as tight as his strength could make them. This done, he stepped back from the crevasse to the point where his toes had rested when he lay flat. ❸ With feet and hands he kicked and scraped the ice until he had made two holes. Then, lying down as before, he dug his toes deep into them. He was naked now, except for his shoes, stockings and underpants. The cold rose from the ice into his blood and bones. He lowered the staff and knotted clothes like a sort of crazy fishing line. ❸

The trousers, the shirt and half of the jacket passed out of sight. He was leaning over as far as he could.

"Can you reach it now?" he called.

"Yes," the voice answered.

"All right. Come on."

"You won't be able to hold me. I'll pull you in."

"No you won't."

He braced himself. The pull came. His toes went taut in their ice-holds and his hands tightened on the staff until the knuckles showed white. Again he could hear a scraping sound below, and he knew that the man was clawing his boots against the ice-wall, trying both to lever himself up and to take as much weight as possible off the improvised lifeline. But the wall obviously offered little help. Almost all his weight was on the lifeline. Suddenly there was a jerk, as one of the knots in the clothing slipped, and the staff was almost wrenched from Rudi's hands. But the knot held. And his hands held. He tried to call down, "All right?" but he had no breath for words. From below, the only sound was the scraping of boots on ice.

How long it went on Rudi could never have said. Perhaps only for a minute or so. But it seemed like hours. And then at last—at last—it happened. A hand came into view around the curve of the crevasse wall; a hand gripping the twisted fabric of his jacket, and then a second hand rising slowly above it. A head appeared. A pair of shoulders. A face was raised for an instant and then lowered. Again one hand moved slowly up past the other.

But Rudi no longer saw it, for now his eyes were shut tight with the strain. His teeth were clamped, the cords of his neck bulged, the muscles of his arm felt as if he were being drawn one by one from the bones that held them. He began to lose his toeholds. He was being dragged forward. Desperately, frantically, he dug in with his feet, pressed his

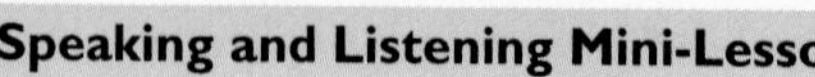

Speaking and Listening Mini-Lesson

Dialogue

This mini-lesson supports the Speaking and Listening activity in the Idea Bank on p. 221.

Introduce Explain that a dialogue is an exchange of ideas between two or more people. It can be written, as in the conversation between Rudi and Captain Winter, or it can be spontaneous, as when students meet in the hallway. Arrange students in groups of three and have them decide which role each will play in the dialogue.

Develop Encourage students to brainstorm what each person will say to the others about mountain climbing. Have them consider each person's age, experience level, and motivation for climbing as they develop their ideas.

Apply Some students may want to write out scripts for their dialogue, while others will prefer to jot down notes that they can refer to as they speak. Remind students to take turns speaking and to respond appropriately to questions. Encourage students to stand in a semicircle facing the class and to speak clearly.

Assess Evaluate students' work based on creativity, clarity of presentation, and how well they understand the characters. Alternatively, have students use the Peer Assessment: Dramatic Performance form, p. 107 in **Alternative Assessment.**

whole body down, as if he could make it part of the glacier. Though all but naked on the ice, he was pouring with sweat. Somehow he stopped the slipping. Somehow he held on.

> **◆ Reading Strategy**
> Predict what will happen to Rudi and the man. Do you have confidence in Rudi's ability to hold on to the staff?

4 But now suddenly the strain was even worse, for the man had reached the lower end of the staff. The slight "give" of the stretched clothing was gone, and in its place, was rigid deadweight on a length of wood. The climber was close now. 5 But heavy. Indescribably heavy. Rudi's hands ached and burned, as if it were a rod of hot lead that they clung to. It was not a mere man he was holding, but a giant; or a block of granite. The pull was unendurable. The pain unendurable. He could hold on no longer. His hands were opening. It was all over.

And then it *was* over. The weight was gone. There was a scraping sound close beneath him; a hand on the rim of ice; a figure pulling itself up onto the lip of the crevasse. The man was beside Rudi, turning to him, staring at him.

6 "Why—you're just a boy!" he said in astonishment.

Rudi was too numb to move or speak. Taking the staff from him, the man pulled up the line of clothes, untied the knots and shook them out.

"Come on now. Quickly!" he said.

Pulling the boy to his feet, he helped him dress. Then he rubbed and pummeled him un-
7 til at last Rudi felt the warmth of returning circulation.

"Better?" the man asked, smiling.

Rudi nodded. And finally he was able to speak again. "And you, sir," he said, "you are all right?"

The man nodded. He was warming himself now: flapping his arms and kicking his feet together. "A few minutes of sun and I'll be as good as new."

Nearby, a black boulder lay embedded in the glacial ice, and, going over to it, they sat down. The sunlight poured over them like a warm bath. Rudi slowly flexed his aching fingers and saw that the man was doing the same. And then the man had raised his eyes and was looking at him.

"It's a miracle how you did it," he said. "A boy of your size. All alone."

"It was nothing." Rudi murmured.

"Nothing?"

"I—I only—"

"Only saved my life." said the man.

For the first time, now, Rudi was really seeing him. He was a man of perhaps thirty, very tall and thin, and his face, too, was thin, with a big hawklike nose and a strong jutting chin. His weather-browned cheeks were clean-shaven, his hair black, his eyes deep-set and gray. And when he spoke, his voice was still almost as quiet as when it had been muffled by the ice-walls of the crevasse. He is—what?—Rudi thought. Not Swiss, he knew. Not French or German. English, perhaps? Yes, English. . . . And then suddenly a deep excitement filled him, for he knew who the man was.

"You are Captain Winter?" he murmured.

"That's right."

"And I—I have saved—I mean—"

Rudi stopped in confusion. and the Englishman grinned. "You've saved," he said, smiling, "one of the worst imbeciles that ever walked on a glacier. An imbecile who was so busy looking 8
up at a mountain that he couldn't even see what was at his feet."

Rudi was wordless—almost stunned. He looked at the man. and then away in embarrassment, and he could scarcely believe what had happened. The name of Captain John Winter was known through the length and breadth of the Alps. He was the foremost

◆ Build Vocabulary

prone (prōn) *adj.:* Lying face downward

taut (tôt) *adj.:* Tightly stretched

pummeled (pum´ əld) *v.:* Beat

◆Reading Strategy

4 Predict Elicit responses such as the following: *Rudi will be able to hold the staff because he seems strong and determined, or Rudi doesn't seem like he will be able to hold on to the staff because the pain is too much.*

◆Literary Focus

5 Conflict With Nature Ask students to name some of the different aspects of Rudi's struggle here. To help them, suggest they consider what might keep Rudi from succeeding in pulling the man up. *The cold, the weight of the man, the slippery ice, and Rudi's pain and fatigue might all keep Rudi from succeeding.*

◆Critical Thinking

6 Speculate Ask students why the man might be surprised that Rudi is "just a boy." *He is surprised because Rudi exhibits strength and bravery that one would expect from an older person.*

Clarification

7 Explain that the man is rubbing and pummeling Rudi in order to boost his circulation. This will help Rudi avoid frostbite, a serious condition that occurs when body tissue becomes extremely cold.

◆Critical Thinking

8 Infer Explain that *imbecile* is a synonym for *fool* or *idiot.* Then ask students why Captain Winter refers to himself as an imbecile in this passage. *Winter refers to himself as an imbecile because his fall into the crevasse made him seem more like a fool than like a famous mountaineer.*

Cross-Curricular Connection: Social Studies

Geography Share with students that the Alps are Europe's most extensive mountain system, stretching from the Mediterranean coast of France through Italy, Switzerland, Germany, Austria, Slovenia, and into Liechtenstein. The chain of mountains is over 600 miles long and covers an area of more than 80,000 square miles. The peaks average 6,000 to 8,000 feet, with some towering above 10,000 feet. Historically, the Alps have created a barrier between Mediterranean cultures and those to the north.

Invite groups of students to compose questions about the climate, topography, vegetation and animal life, and cultural and historical influence of the Alps. Then have them use atlases, encyclopedias, the Internet, and other available reference sources to find answers to their questions. Ask groups to share their questions and answers with the class.

◆Critical Thinking

1 Deduce Point out to students that Rudi and Captain Winter use the past tense when speaking of Rudi's father. Then ask them why they think Rudi's heart swelled and why the two are looking at the mountain. *Rudi is probably thinking of his father with pride and love; the two might have been looking at the mountain because it had something to do with Rudi's father and the way he died.*

Comprehension Check ☑

2 What does Captain Winter mean by this statement? *He means that it is lucky he fell in a way that did not crush the chocolate bar.*

◆Critical Thinking

3 Speculate Ask students why Rudi's heart is pounding and why Captain Winter's desire to climb the Citadel interests him. *He may be reminded of his father's death, or he may be excited to meet someone who is interested in accomplishing what his father set out to do.*

◆Literature and Your Life

4 *Some students may say they have been called "crazy" because they wanted to do things like go bungee jumping or cliff diving. They may have thought twice or they may have done it anyway because of the thrill.*

Customize for
English Language Learners
You may want to help students by discussing and clarifying some of the idiomatic terms and usages on this page (*got his voice back, before my day, heart swelled, eyes fixed,* etc.).

mountaineer of his day, and during the past ten years had made more first ascents of great peaks than any other man alive. Rudi had heard that he had come to Kurtal a few days before. He had hoped that at least he would see him in the hotel or walking by in the street. But actually to meet him—and in this way! To pull him from a crevasse—save him . . . . It was incredible!

Captain Winter was watching him. "And you, son," he asked. "What is your name?"

Somehow the boy got his voice back. "Rudi," he said. "Rudi Matt."

"Matt?" Now it was the man's turn to be impressed. "Not of the family of the great Josef Matt?"

"He was my father," Rudi said.

Captain Winter studied him with his gray eyes. Then he smiled again. "I should have known," he said. "A boy who could do what you've done—"

"Did you know my father, sir?"

"No, unfortunately I didn't. He was before my day. But ever since I was a boy I have heard of him. In twenty years no one has come
1 to the Alps and not heard of the great guide,
Josef Matt."

Rudi's heart swelled. He looked away. His eyes fixed on the vast mountain that rose before them, and then he saw that Captain Winter was watching it too.

Unconsciously the Englishman spoke his thoughts. "Your father was—" He caught himself and stopped.

"Yes," said Rudi softly. "he was killed on the Citadel."

There was a silence. Captain Winter reached into a pocket and brought out an unbroken bar
2 of chocolate. "Lucky I fell on the other side," he
grinned.

He broke the bar in two and handed half to Rudi.

"Oh, no, sir, thank you. I couldn't."

"When I meet a boy your age who can't eat chocolate," said Winter. "I'll be glad to stay in a crevasse for good."

Rudi took it, and they sat munching. The sun was warm on their thawing bodies. Far above, it struck the cliffs and snowfields of the Citadel, so brightly that they had to squint against the glare.

Then there was Winter's quiet voice again. "What do you think, Rudi?"

"Think, sir?"

"Can it be climbed?"

"Climbed? The Citadel?"

"Your father thought so. Alone among all the guides of Switzerland, he thought so." There was another pause. "And I think so too." said Captain Winter.

The boy was peering again at the shining heights. And suddenly his heart was pounding so hard that he was sure the Englishman
must be able to hear it. "Is—is that why you 3
have come here, sir?" he asked. "To try to climb the Citadel?"

"Well, now—" Winter smiled. "It's not so simple, you know. For one thing, there's not a guide in the valley who would go with me."

"I have an uncle, sir. He is—"

"Yes, I know your uncle. Franz Lerner. He is the best in Kurtal, and I've spoken to him. But he would not go. Anything but that, he said. Any other peak, any route, any venture. But not *that*, he said. Not the Citadel."

"He remembers my father—"

"Yes, he remembers your father. They all remember him. And while they love and respect his memory, they all think he was crazy." Winter chuckled softly. "Now they think *I'm* crazy," he added. "And maybe they're right too," he said.

> **◆ Literature and Your Life** 4
> Have you ever had a goal others called "crazy"? Did this make you think twice?

"What will you do. sir?" asked Rudi. "Not try it alone?"

"No, that crazy I'm not." Winter slowly stroked his long jaw. "I'm not certain what I'll do." he went on. "Perhaps I'll go over to the next valley. To Broli. I've been told there is a guide there—a man called Saxo. Do you know him?"

"Yes—Emil Saxo. I have never met him. but I have heard of him. They say he is a very

5 ▲ **Critical Viewing** What details of this photograph might inspire Rudi? Explain. **[Speculate]**

great guide."

"Well, I thought perhaps I'd go and talk with him. After a while. But first I must reconnoiter some more. Make my plans. Pick the route. If there *is* a route."

"Yes, there is! Of course there is!"

6 Rudi had not thought the words. They simply burst out from him. And now again he was embarrassed as the man looked at him curiously.

"So?" said Captain Winter. "That is interesting, Rudi. Tell me why you think so."

"I have studied the Citadel many times, sir."

"Why?"

◆ Build Vocabulary

reconnoiter (rē kə noit´ ər) *v.*: Look around

"Because—because—" He stopped. He couldn't say it. 6

"Because you want to climb it yourself?"

"I am not yet a grown man. sir. I know I cannot expect—"

"I wasn't a grown man either," said the Captain, "when I first saw the Citadel. I was younger than you—only twelve—and my parents had brought me here for a summer holiday. But I can still remember how I felt when I looked up at it, and the promise I made myself that some day I was going to climb it." He paused. His eyes moved slowly upward. "Youth is the time for dreams, boy," he murmured. "The trick is, when you get older, not to forget them." 7

Rudi listened, spellbound. He had never heard anyone speak like that. He had not known a grown man could think and feel like that.

Then Winter asked:

▶Critical Viewing◀

5 Speculate *Rudi might be inspired by the beauty of the sheer ice, by the strength displayed by the strong hold of the climber's legs, and by the grasps of the boots that are holding the climber in position.*

◆Critical Thinking

6 Analyze Character Point out to students that in this passage Rudi is described as *embarrassed* and unable to finish his sentence. What do these things show about Rudi's character? *Rudi seems to be nervous and unsure of himself talking to Captain Winter. Rudi may feel like he is only a boy with no valid opinions when talking to Winter, his idol.*

◆Critical Thinking

7 Interpret Ask students what Captain Winter means here. *Young people think of all the things they can do with their lives and imagine themselves in all sorts of situations. When people get older, their responsibilities often keep them from doing what they would really love to do.*

Humanities: Photography

Cascade de Glaces (Waterfall of Ice), by Jean-Marc Boivin

Jean-Marc Boivin is not only a photographer, but also a leading Alpinist and the first person to hang glide from the top of Mt. Everest. This color photograph of a mountain climber scaling a wall of ice illustrates the danger and difficulty involved in the activity. Have students look carefully at this photograph and the others used in "A Boy and a Man" and the excerpt from *Into Thin Air.* Then use questions such as the following to discuss how the photographs connect to the selections and enhance students' understanding.

1. How do these photographs help you understand the setting of the selections? *Possible response: They provide a feeling of the ruggedness, coldness, beauty, and danger of the settings.*
2. Based on these photographs, what mental and physical characteristics do you think a person needs to climb a mountain? *Possible response: People must be physically strong, conditioned, and flexible. Mentally, they must be focused, brave, and disciplined.*

◆Critical Thinking

❶ Interpret Discuss the phrase *threaded their way* with students. Explain that it implies the people were slowly and carefully making their way between boulders, icy spots, and other obstacles, similar to the way thread is pushed through the eye of a needle. Ask how this usage helps students visualize the scene. *It helps students imagine the people walking on a difficult surface, picking their way, rather than walking quickly and easily down an open pathway.*

◆Critical Thinking

❷ Speculate Ask students to complete Rudi's statements, explaining what it is his mother is afraid of and does not want him to do. *Possible response: She is afraid he might also be killed; she does not want him to be a mountain climber.*

◆Reading Strategy

❸ Predict Ask students to predict the favor they think Rudi will ask of Captain Winter. *Students may say that Rudi wants Winter to include him in his plans to climb the Citadel, or to continue to talk to him about it at a later time.*

◆Critical Thinking

❹ Draw Conclusions Ask students why Rudi will be in trouble if his mother or uncle finds out he has been in the mountains. *Possible response: He has been forbidden to go to the mountains because his mother and uncle don't think it's safe.*

"This east face, Rudi—what do you think of it?"

"Think of it, sir?"

"Could it be climbed?"

Rudi shook his head. "No, it is no good. The long chimney[2] there—you see. It looks all right: it could be done. And to the left, ledges"—he pointed—"they could be done too. But higher up, no. They stop. The chimney stops, and there is only smooth rock."

"What about the northeast ridge?"

"That is not good either."

"It's not so steep."

"No, it is not so steep," said Rudi. "But the rocks are bad. They slope out, with few places for holds."

"And the north face?"

Rudi talked on. About the north face, the west ridge, the southwest ridge. He talked quietly and thoughtfully, but with deep inner excitement, for this was the first time in his life that he had been able to speak to anyone of these things which he had thought and studied for so long. . . . And then suddenly he stopped, for he realized what he was doing. He, Rudi Matt, a boy of sixteen who worked in the kitchen of the Beau Site Hotel, was presuming to give his opinions to one of the greatest climbers in the world.

But Captain Winter had been listening intently. Sometimes he nodded. "Go on," he said now, as Rudi paused.

"But I am only—"

"Go on."

And Rudi went on . . .

"That doesn't leave much," said the captain a little later.

"No, sir," said the boy.

"Only the southeast ridge."

"Yes, sir."

"That was the way your father tried, wasn't it?"

"Yes, sir."

"And you believe it's the only way?"

"Yes, sir."

Captain Winter rubbed his jaw for a moment before speaking again. Then—"That also is very interesting to me, Rudi," he said quietly, "because it is what I believe too."

Later, they threaded their way down the Blue Glacier. For a while they moved in silence. Then Captain Winter asked: ❶

"What do you do, Rudi?"

"Do, sir?"

"Are you an apprentice guide? A porter?"

Rudi swallowed. "No sir."

"What then?"

He could hardly say it. "A—dishwasher."

"A dishwasher?"

"In the Beau Site Hotel. It is my mother, sir. Since my father died, you see, she is afraid—she does not want—" Rudi swallowed again. "I am to go into the hotel business," he murmured. ❷

"Oh."

Again they moved on without speaking. It was now late afternoon, and behind them the stillness was broken by a great roaring, as sun-loosened rock and ice broke off from the heights of the Citadel.

When they reached the path Rudi spoke again, hesitantly. "Will you please do me a favor, sir," he asked. ❸

"Of course," said Winter.

"Before we come to the town we will separate. And you will please not tell anyone that I have been up here today?"

The Englishman looked at him in astonishment. "Not tell anyone? You save my life, boy, and you want me to keep it a secret?"

"It was nothing, sir. Truly. And if you say that I have been in the mountains, my mother and uncle will hear, and I will be in trouble." Rudi's voice took on a note of urgency. "You will not do it, sir? You will promise—please?" ❹

Winter put a hand on his shoulder. "Don't worry," he said. "I won't get you in trouble." Then he smiled and added: "Master Rudi Matt—dishwasher."

They walked down the path. The sun sank. Behind them, the mountain roared.

2. **chimney** (chim′ nē) *n.:* In mountain climbing, a deep, narrow crack in a cliff face.

Viewing and Representing Mini-Lesson

Illustrating a Scene

Introduce Ask students how selections like this one differ from the books they read as small children. Lead them to see that stories such as this one rely on words rather than pictures to present ideas.

Develop Have students imagine the scene described on p. 216: The characters are moving down Blue Glacier while the sun is causing rock and ice to break off and fall from the Citadel behind them. Ask them what colors they see and what lines and shapes help create the images in their mind.

Apply Ask students to create illustrations for the scene. Invite them to use the medium they prefer (paint, charcoal, cut paper, collage, and so on). Encourage students to use color in a way that expresses the warmth of the sun contrasting with the cold ice of the glacier. They may want to depict the characters and the setting in a realistic way, or they might prefer to express the feeling of the scene abstractly. Have each student think of a title for his or her illustration.

Assess As students display their illustrations, discuss the feeling conveyed by each. Ask what effect the illustration would have on a reader's interpretation of the scene. Evaluate students' work based on interpretation of the scene and creativity.

Beyond Literature

Sports Connection

The Challenge of Mountain Climbing Mountain climbing may never be as popular as such sports as baseball or hockey, but that doesn't prevent a small group of professionals, along with thousands of amateurs, from considering it a serious sport. Mountain climbing is guided by a set of rules, just as any sport is. Each climb is rated on its technical difficulty. Climbs requiring the most difficult moves are assigned the highest rating. The first climber making the trip up a mountain usually has the honor of suggesting the appropriate rating for the climb, but the rating can be adjusted if others challenge the first climber's assessment. Rigorous training and conditioning are required for those who want to experience the thrill of climbing to the highest points on Earth.

Cross-Curricular Activity

Comparing Mountains With a group, conduct research to find out the ratings of some of the highest mountains in the world. Make a colorful map or chart to record your findings.

Guide for Responding

◆ Literature and Your Life

Reader's Response Would you like to know Rudi? Explain why or why not.

Thematic Focus Both Rudi and Captain Winter took risks. However, each displayed a unique kind of bravery. What did you admire about each of these characters?

Journal Writing Rudi was not completely sure of his own power to save Captain Winter. In a journal entry, write about a time when your own ability surprised you.

☑ Check Your Comprehension

1. How does Rudi make a lifeline?
2. Why was Captain Winter astonished when he met his rescuer face to face?
3. Why is Rudi "almost stunned" when he learns the identity of the man he has saved?
4. Why had Captain Winter come to Switzerland?
5. How did Rudi's father die?

◆ Critical Thinking

Interpret

1. Captain Winter says, "Youth is the time for dreams." What is Rudi's dream? **[Interpret]**
2. Why has Rudi been unable to fulfill his dream? **[Speculate]**
3. How might giving Captain Winter advice about mountain climbing help Rudi to solve his own problem? **[Generalize]**
4. Climbing the Citadel would pose problems for both Rudi and Captain Winter. State the problems for each. Then, compare and contrast them. **[Compare and Contrast]**
5. Why do you think this story is called "A Boy and a Man"? **[Analyze]**

Evaluate

6. Why do you think that Rudi was willing to risk his life to save Captain Winter? **[Make a Judgment]**

Apply

7. Why do people sometimes keep secret their dreams and plans? **[Generalize]**

Beyond Literature

Help students prepare for their research by giving the names and locations of the following mountains: Mt. McKinley or Denali (Alaska), Mt. Acongua (Argentina), the Matterhorn (Switzerland/Italy), Mt. Kilimanjaro (Africa), Mt. Everest (Nepal/China), and Mt. Jaya (New Guineau). Tell students that a good place to begin their research is in an encyclopedia.

Reinforce and Extend

Answers

◆ Literature and Your Life

Reader's Response Many students will think that Rudi is someone they would like to know because he is brave and responsible, has an interesting life, and could be counted on for help in times of trouble.

Thematic Focus Possible response: Rudi showed physical courage in saving Captain Winter and moral courage in putting aside his own goals in consideration of his family's feelings. Captain Winter showed courage by keeping calm in a life-threatening situation. Also, he showed his bravery by planning to climb the Citadel.

☑ Check Your Comprehension

1. He constructed the lifeline from his clothes, which he tied together.
2. He was surprised because Rudi was a 16-year-old boy.
3. Captain Winter is the most famous mountaineer in the world.
4. Captain Winter came to Switzerland to climb the Citadel.
5. He died climbing the Citadel.

◆ Critical Thinking

1. Rudi's secret dream is to climb the Citadel.
2. Rudi's mother does not want him to climb the mountain.
3. Giving advice on a subject about which he is so knowledgeable could give Rudi the confidence to follow his dream.
4. Rudi would be going against the wishes of his mother. Captain Winter would not be going against anyone's wishes, but would be considered "crazy." Both would face extreme danger.
5. The story is about a growing friendship between a boy, Rudi, and a man, Captain Winter. Although they are different in age, they have much in common.
6. Most students will say that Rudi was a caring person who could not let another person die, even if he had to risk his life.
7. Students may say that people keep their dreams secret because they are afraid others might ridicule them.

Develop Understanding

One-Minute Insight In this excerpt from *Into Thin Air,* Jon Krakauer details his climb through the Icefall, a dangerous passage on the way to the summit of Mt. Everest.

Clarification

❶ Explain that the icefall Krakauer describes is called the Khumbu Icefall, at the first part of the southern route on Mt. Everest. The massive glacier presides over a steep landscape below it, and tons of glacial ice shift and crash every day. More climbers have died on the Icefall than on any other part of Everest.

◆Literary Focus

❷ **Conflict With Nature** Ask students to identify specific elements of nature that conflict with Krakauer's climb. *Students may note the avalanches, the compression of the crevasses, the sun warming the ice and making ladders unsteady.*

▶Critical Viewing◀

❸ **Respond** Elicit a response such as this: *It seems treacherous because the man seems to be hanging on only by the rope and the spikes in his boots.*

◆Literature and Your Life

❹ Have students think of a time when they were so absorbed in a task that they lost track of what was going on around them. *Students may describe practicing for a sports event, studying for an exam, or playing an instrument.*

Clarification

❺ Tell students that "Hall" refers to Rob Hall, the New Zealand climber who led the expedition to which Krakauer belonged. Hall was one of eight climbers who died on that expedition.

Customize for ***Less Proficient Readers***
You may want to read the selection aloud with students to clarify difficult words or phrases. In particular, you may want to define the following words: *orthodox, repertoire, gloaming, crevasses, phantasmal, buttresses, unfettered,* and *off-kilter.*

from Into Thin Air

Jon Krakauer

In April 1996, writer John Krakauer joined an expedition to the top of Mount Everest. Krakauer survived to write a book about his experience, but before the trip was over, eight climbers had lost their lives. Here, Krakauer describes one of the terrifying ordeals of his climb.

If the Icefall required few orthodox climbing techniques, it demanded a whole new repertoire of skills in their stead—for instance, the ability to tiptoe in mountaineering boots and crampons[1] across three wobbly ladders lashed end to end, bridging a heart-stopping chasm. There were many such crossings, and I never got used to them. ❶

At one point I was balanced on an unsteady ladder in the predawn gloaming, stepping tenuously from one bent rung to the next, when the ice supporting the ladder on either end began to quiver as if an earthquake had struck. A moment later came an explosive roar as a large serac[2] somewhere close above came crashing down. I froze, my heart in my throat, but the avalanching ice passed fifty yards to the left, out of sight, without doing any damage. After waiting a few minutes to regain my composure I resumed my herky-jerky passage to the far side of the ladder.

The glacier's continual and often violent state of flux added an element of uncertainty to every ladder crossing. As the glacier moved, crevasses would sometimes compress, buckling ladders like toothpicks; other times a crevasse might expand, leaving a ladder dangling in the air, only tenuously supported, with neither end mounted on solid ice. ❷ Anchors securing the ladders and lines routinely melted out when the afternoon sun warmed the surrounding ice and snow. Despite daily maintenance, there was a very real danger that any given rope might pull loose under body weight.

But if the Icefall was strenuous and terrifying, it had a surprising allure as well. As dawn washed the darkness from the sky, the shattered glacier was revealed to be a three-dimensional landscape of phantasmal beauty. The temperature was six degrees

1. **crampons** (kram´ pənz) *n.*: Iron spikes on shoes to prevent slipping.
2. **serac** (sə rak´) *n.*: High, pointed mass of ice.

◀ Critical Viewing What impression of the climb does this photograph give you? **[Respond]** ❸

Cross-Curricular Connection: Social Studies

The Himalayan Mountains, located along the northern border of the Indian subcontinent, make up the world's highest mountain range. Included among their peaks is Mt. Everest, which—at 29,108 feet above sea level—reaches the highest point on Earth.

Mt. Everest was first climbed successfully on May 29, 1953. Edmund Hillary of New Zealand and Tenzing Norgay, a Sherpa guide from Nepal, were the first people to set foot on the summit. Prior to that time, all expeditions had failed because equipment was not available to help climbers cope with the lack of oxygen and harsh weather conditions. In 1963, the first American expedition successfully climbed the mountain.

The 1996 expedition that Krakauer describes ended in tragedy, with a record number of deaths. Krakauer was on an assignment for *Outside* magazine to write an article on the commercialization of Everest, where novices pay up to $65,000 to be "guided" to the summit.

Have students do research on Krakauer's story and the conflict surrounding it. Then have them share their findings with the class.

Fahrenheit. My crampons crunched reassuringly into the glacier's rind. Following the fixed line, I meandered through a vertical maze of crystalline blue stalagmites.[3] Sheer rock buttresses seamed with ice pressed in from both edges of the glacier, rising like the shoulders of a <u>malevolent</u> god. Absorbed by my surround- 4 ings and the gravity of the labor, I lost myself in the unfettered pleasures of ascent, and for an hour or two actually forgot to be afraid.

Three-quarters of the way to Camp One, 5 Hall remarked at a rest stop that the icefall was in better shape than he'd ever seen it: "The route's a bloody freeway this season." But only slightly higher, at 19,000 feet, the ropes brought us to the base of a gargantuan, perilously balanced serac. As massive as a twelve-story building, it loomed over our heads, leaning 30 degrees past vertical. The route followed a natural catwalk that angled sharply up the overhanging face: we would have to climb up and over the entire off-kilter tower to escape its threatening tonnage.

Safety, I understood, hinged on speed. I huffed toward the relative security of the serac's crest with all the haste I could muster, but since I wasn't acclimatized my fastest pace was no better than a crawl. 6 Every four or five steps I'd have to stop, lean against the rope, and suck desperately at the thin, bitter 7 air, searing my lungs in the process.

I reached the top of the serac without it collapsing and flopped breathless onto its flat summit, my heart pounding like a jackhammer. A little later, around 8:30 A.M., I arrived at the top of the Icefall itself, just beyond the last of the seracs. The safety of Camp One didn't supply much peace of mind, however: I couldn't stop thinking about the ominously tilted slab a short distance below, and the fact that I would have to pass beneath its faltering bulk at least seven more times if I was going to make it to the summit of Everest. Climbers who snidely <u>denigrate</u> this as the Yak Route, I decided, had obviously never been through the Khumbu Icefall.

3. **stalagmites** (stə lag′ mīts′) *n.*: Cone-shaped mineral deposits.

◆ Build Vocabulary

malevolent (mə lev′ ə lənt) *adj.*: Wishing evil or harm to others

denigrate (den′ ə grāt′) *n.*: Discredit; put down; belittle

Guide for Responding

◆ Literature and Your Life

Reader's Response What thoughts might you have had if you were crossing the Icefall?

Thematic Focus Jon Krakauer and his fellow climbers risked their lives to climb Mount Everest. Why do you think Krakauer was willing to risk everything to make it to the top?

☑ Check Your Comprehension

1. Give two reasons why the ladder crossings on the Icefall were dangerous.
2. Why did the Icefall attract Krakauer in spite of its dangers?
3. Why did Krakauer have difficulty climbing the twelve-story serac?

◆ Critical Thinking

Interpret

1. Why do you think Krakauer never got used to crossing the chasms? **[Analyze]**
2. From what you have read, how would you rate Krakauer's skills as a mountaineer? **[Infer]**
3. Despite fear, Krakauer continued across the Icefall. What does this tell you about his character? **[Draw Conclusions]**

Compare Literary Works

4. Compare the environment of "A Boy and a Man" and the environment of the excerpt from *Into Thin Air.* **[Compare and Contrast]**

Clarification

6 Tell students that acclimatization, or the ability to adjust to a new climate, is an essential part of mountaineering above 9,000 feet. In high altitudes, the atmospheric pressures change and there is a shortage of oxygen. A climber who has not acclimatized is subject to high-altitude sickness, which includes headaches, dizziness, nausea, and vomiting.

◆Critical Thinking

7 **Infer** Ask students why the author believes that safety hinges on speed. *Since the serac is leaning over him in an off-kilter way, it is possible it will slip and crash down on him.*

Reinforce and Extend

Answers

◆Literature and Your Life

Reader's Response Students might say they have fearful thoughts; others might enjoy the adventure.

Thematic Focus Students may think he wanted to prove to himself that he could reach the summit.

☑ Check Your Comprehension

1. They could collapse; glacier movement could cause the ladders to compress or stretch; anchors could melt from the ice, causing ropes to pull loose.
2. He found it beautiful. The stalagmites and the color of the ice mesmerized him.
3. Speed was important, but since he was not acclimatized, he had to rest often.

◆Critical Thinking

1. Possible response: There was constant, changing danger at each crossing.
2. Students may say Krakauer is a good mountaineer because he knows the dangers facing him and he succeeded in his climb.
3. Students may say that to feel fear and continue is a mark of courage. Krakauer appears to be a courageous, thoughtful man.
4. Students may say that both environments are dangerous and challenging, but that Mt. Everest and the Icefall seem more so because of the dangers detailed in the text.

Beyond the Selection

FURTHER READING

Other Works by the Authors

Banner in the Sky, James Ramsey Ullman
Into the Wild, Jon Krakauer
Eiger Dreams: Ventures Among Men and Mountains, Jon Krakauer

Other Works About Risking It All

Hatchet, Gary Paulsen
Ultimate Sports: Short Stories by Outstanding Writers for Young Adults, Donald R. Gallo
On the Edge, Martin Dugard

INTERNET

The following Web site offers a virtual high-mountain tour:
http://www.cs.berkeley.edu/~qtluong/gallery/slides-alps/alp-show2.html

For information on Krakauer's climb, go to:
http://outside.starwave.com/magazine/0996/9609/feev.html

Be aware that Web sites may have changed from the time we published this information. We *strongly recommend* that you preview these sites before you send students to them.

Answers

◆Reading Strategy

1. Possible response: (a) I thought Rudi would rescue Captain Winter. (b) Rudi seemed to know what he was doing and he seemed very strong.
2. (a) Some students will predict Rudi will climb the Citadel because (b) he has a great interest in it, he seems to have studied which way to do it, and because Winter wants someone to climb with him.
3. Krakauer survived to write about his experience; he successfully arrives at Camp One—one of the hurdles of the expedition.

◆Build Vocabulary

Using the Prefix *mal-*

1. malfunctioned: did not function correctly
2. malnourished: poorly nourished
3. malformed: badly formed or misshapen

Spelling Strategy

1. recon-noiter
2. begin-ning
3. al-lure
4. in-nocent

Using the Word Bank

1. reconnoiter
2. taut
3. denigrate
4. prone
5. malevolent
6. pummeled

◆Literary Focus

1. Possible response: Captain Winter fell down a crevasse, the cold weather means he may die if not rescued, the ice makes the walls of the crevasse slippery, and the ice makes it hard to get a toehold.
2. The most terrifying environmental threat is the perilously balanced serac that was as high as a twelve-story building.
3. Rudi uses a climbing staff, and he and Winter both wear jackets and boots. Krakauer uses ladders, ropes, and crampons.

◆Build Grammar Skills

1. scraping modifies *sound*
2. lucky modifies *I*
3. afraid modifies *she*
4. terrifying modifies *climb*
5. vertical modifies *maze;* crystalline modifies *stalagmites*

Guide for Responding *(continued)*

◆ Reading Strategy

PREDICT

When you **predict,** you make a guess about the outcome of a story using details the author provides. Making and revising your predictions based on the information in each paragraph keeps you an active participant in the reading process.

1. (a) Did you predict that Rudi in "A Boy and a Man" would successfully rescue Captain Winter? (b) On what facts or beliefs did you base this prediction?
2. (a) Do you predict that Rudi will climb the Citadel? (b) What details in "A Boy and a Man" support your prediction?
3. Krakauer reaches the summit of Mount Everest and safely returns. What details in this passage from *Into Thin Air* help you predict his success?

◆ Build Vocabulary

USING THE PREFIX *mal-*

The prefix *mal-* means "bad" or "badly." On a sheet of paper, write the words formed by adding *mal-* to these words. Then, write a definition for the new word.

1. functioned **2.** nourished **3.** formed

SPELLING STRATEGY

When you break a word with double consonants at the end of a line, divide it between the two consonants: *pum-meled.*

Copy the following words on your paper, dividing them as if you reached the end of a line.

1. reconnoiter **3.** allure
2. beginning **4.** innocent

USING THE WORD BANK

Replace each italicized word or phrase with the word from the Word Bank that means the same.

The lieutenant was in the field to **(1)** *investigate* the area which was to be attacked. His body was **(2)** *tense.* He thought that the situation was potentially dangerous, even though he had heard others **(3)** *belittle* the threat. As he lay in a **(4)** *flat* position on the ground, he saw where the **(5)** *evil* enemy had been **(6)** *beaten up* by cannon fire. Knowing the enemy was retreating, the lieutenant felt reassured.

◆ Literary Focus

CONFLICT WITH NATURE

Conflict is a struggle between two opposing forces. In both fiction and nonfiction, conflict provides interest, suspense, and tension. Both of these narratives feature a **conflict with nature** in which characters face the elements in a fierce struggle for survival. The main characters struggle against high, forbidding mountain environments.

1. Identify three details in "A Boy and a Man" that show that a conflict with nature can be brutal.
2. Describe the most terrifying environmental threat in *Into Thin Air.*
3. What protection do characters in both narratives use against the elements?

◆ Build Grammar Skills

PLACEMENT OF ADJECTIVES

Both Ullman and Krakauer make their writing more descriptive by using **adjectives,** words that modify nouns or pronouns. Adjectives can be placed in several different parts of a sentence. Sometimes, they come directly before the noun they modify. Sometimes, they follow linking verbs such as *am, is, are, was,* and *were* to modify the subject of the sentence.

Before a Noun: Captain Winter brought out an *unbroken* bar of chocolate.

After a Linking Verb: The Icefall was *strenuous.*

Practice Copy these sentences on your paper. Underline each adjective, and draw an arrow to the word it modifies.

1. Again he could hear a scraping sound below.
2. I was lucky and hit a ledge.
3. You can see that she is afraid.
4. The climb was terrifying.
5. I meandered through a vertical maze of crystalline stalagmites.

Writing Application Write a paragraph describing a time when you faced extreme cold, extreme heat, or another serious weather condition. In your paragraph, use three adjectives before nouns and three adjectives following linking verbs.

Writer's Solution

For additional instruction and practice, use the lesson in the *Writer's Solution Language Lab CD-ROM* on Using Modifiers. You may also use the adjective practice page, pp. 15–19, in the *Writer's Solution Grammar Practice Book.*

Build Your Portfolio

Idea Bank

Writing

1. **Advertisement** Imagine Jon Krakauer has started a travel agency for mountaineers. Write an advertisement for his new business.
2. **Movie Proposal** A mountaineering movie based on either of these narratives could be very successful. Choose one of the pieces and write a proposal to a film studio to convince them that the story would make a successful film.
3. **Autobiographical Incident** Even though you may not have climbed Mount Everest yet, you've probably pushed yourself to reach a difficult goal. In an essay, describe the challenge you faced and the steps you took to succeed.

Speaking and Listening

4. **Dialogue [Group Activity]** Pretend that Rudi, Captain Winter, and Jon Krakauer have met at a mountaineering convention. With two classmates, prepare and present the conversation that takes place among the three climbers.
5. **Rescue Interview** "A Boy and a Man" describes a dramatic rescue. Interview your local fire chief to find out how professional rescue teams work where you live. Prepare your questions in advance and share the information you discover with the class. **[Community Link]**

Projects

6. **Glacier Research** "A Boy and a Man" takes place on a glacier, a huge mass of ice. Use library resources to learn more about glaciers. For example, prepare a report explaining how glaciers are formed, how far they travel in a year, or how they affect the Earth's surface. **[Science Link]**
7. **How-to Guide** The characters in these narratives put themselves in danger's path. However, most people are unprepared when nature's fury strikes home. In a brochure, outline the ways people can prepare for such unexpected natural events as hurricanes, floods, or blizzards.

Writing Mini-Lesson

Persuasive Letter

You want Rudi to be part of the group you are organizing to climb the Citadel. However, his family wants him to choose a safer life. Write a letter to Rudi's mother persuading her to let her son join you.

Writing Skills Focus: Order of Importance

When you write to persuade, you want to convince your reader that your position is right. To make your argument most effective, arrange your ideas in **order of importance.** Build from your least important to your most important reason or piece of evidence. This strategy will leave your reader thinking about your strongest point.

Prewriting Review "A Boy and a Man" to gather details that support your opinion. Jot down a list of reasons that prove that Rudi should become part of the team. Next, rank the items on your list from the least important to the most important.

Drafting Your persuasive letter should begin with your opinion—Rudi should be part of your team. Then, write your reasons beginning with the least important and ending with the most important. For each reason you cite, give examples or details to support your idea. Remember you are writing to Rudi's mother, so use reasonable and polite language. Let your argument speak for itself.

Revising Check your letter to be sure that you have used the proper form, heading, and salutation. If you have not concluded with your strongest point, adjust your ending. Don't forget to sign your letter.

◆ Grammar Application

Add specific adjectives to make your arguments more powerful.

ASSESSMENT OPTIONS

Formal Assessment, Selection Test, pp. 63–65, and Assessment Resources Software. The selection test is designed so that it can easily be customized to the performance levels of your students.

Alternative Assessment, p. 15, includes options for less advanced students, more advanced students, visual/spatial learners, verbal/linguistic learners, logical/mathematical learners, and interpersonal learners.

PORTFOLIO ASSESSMENT

Use the following rubrics in the **Alternative Assessment** booklet to assess student writing:
Advertisement: Persuasion, p. 92
Movie Proposal: Persuasion, p. 92
Autobiographical Incident: Narrative Based on Personal Experience, p. 83
Writing Mini-Lesson: Persuasion, p. 92

Idea Bank

Customize for *Performance Levels*

Following are suggestions for matching the Idea Bank topics with your students' performance levels:
Less Advanced Students: 1, 4, 6
Average Students: 2, 4, 5, 6, 7
More Advanced Students: 3, 5, 7

Customize for *Learning Modalities*

Verbal/Linguistic: 1, 2, 4, 5, 6
Interpersonal: 4, 6
Visual/Spatial: 3, 6
Logical/Mathematical: 7
Intrapersonal: 1, 2, 3, 7

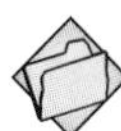

Writing Mini-Lesson

Refer students to the Writing Handbook in the back of the book for instruction on the writing process, and for further information on persuasive writing. Have students use the Sunburst Organizer in **Writing and Language Transparencies,** p. 94, to arrange their prewriting examples.

Writer's Solution

Writing Lab CD-ROM

Have students complete the tutorial on Persuasion. Follow these steps:

1. Have students view the video clip in the Prewriting section to see examples of persuasive evidence.
2. Encourage students to use the Pros and Cons Chart activity to distinguish opposing viewpoints.
3. Allow students to begin drafting on computer.
4. Have students view the Writing Hints on reading drafts twice to help them revise.

Writer's Solution Sourcebook

Have students use Chapter 6, "Persuasion," pp. 166–199. This chapter includes in-depth instruction on writing supporting sentences and using commas, pp. 194–195.

Prepare and Engage

OBJECTIVES

1. To read, comprehend, and interpret a selection that has a social studies focus
2. To relate a selection with a social studies focus to personal experience
3. To connect literature to social studies
4. To respond to Social Studies Guiding Questions
5. To respond to the selection through writing, speaking and listening, and projects

SOCIAL STUDIES GUIDING QUESTIONS

Reading about the reconstructed life of a Copper Age man will help students discover answers to these Social Studies Guiding Questions:

- What methods do people use today to try to understand cultures of the past?
- What was daily life like in the Copper Age?

To hook students into the jigsaw puzzle aspects of archaeological research, do the following: Have each student write on a slip of paper an everyday item he or she uses (a calculator, a baseball cap, a pencil, and so on). Place the slips of paper into a container and pull them out at random. Have the class imagine that archaeologists in the year A.D. 7,000 have discovered that item. Discuss what clues the archaeologists could glean from that item about the clothing, tools, and physical appearance of today's middle school students.

Map Study

Locator Maps The connection between geography and history is often a key to understanding how and why events happened. For example, to understand how Ötzi's body could be preserved in ice for 5,000 years, students can note the mountainous (and therefore possibly cold) region in which his body was discovered. To more fully appreciate the significance of the location, have students read "Preserved in Ice" on this page.

CONNECTING LITERATURE TO SOCIAL STUDIES

PREHISTORIC TIMES

from The Iceman *by Don Lessem*

SCIENCE FICTION In the movie *Jurassic Park,* scientists discover a tiny piece of a dinosaur's body. It had been preserved in amber for millions of years. These Hollywood scientists use it to clone several living dinosaurs. The movie was science fiction—a made-up story based on scientific knowledge of things that could happen.

Scientific Fact In the real world, scientists actually do discover remains of the world as it existed long before history was recorded and passed down from one generation to another. This period is known as the *prehistoric* era.

Tools, Artifacts, and Art If a period precedes written history, how do we know anything about it? We know from the many discoveries scientists have made in various parts of the world. Some scientists dig in places where they believe people once lived. They uncover tools and other artifacts that prehistoric people used in their daily lives. They discover drawings on the walls of caves. Once in a great while, the search uncovers the remains of a human being.

Prehistoric Body Found

N
0 150 mi
0 150 km
area of map
Zürich
Innsbruck
AUSTRIA
SWITZERLAND
Iceman discovered
Milan
ITALY
Adriatic Sea

Preserved in Ice When a creature dies, its body slowly changes into the elements that make up the Earth. This process is called *decomposition.* One way to stop decomposition is to freeze the dead body. Sometimes this freezing happens naturally. If an animal or a person dies in a very cold climate, the dry, icy air will keep the body from decomposing. Suppose this happens in a place where the climate is always very cold. How long do you think the body of a dead person could be preserved? You'll find an answer in "The Iceman."

Prentice Hall Literature Program Resources

REINFORCE / RETEACH / EXTEND

Selection Support Pages
Build Vocabulary, p. 83
Connect Scientific Evidence to Social Studies, p. 84

Formal Assessment Selection Test, pp. 66–67, Assessment Resources Software

Readings From Social Studies

Writing and Language Transparencies
Timeline, p. 74; Main Idea and Supporting Details Organizer, p. 70; Sunburst Organizer, p. 94

Resource Pro CD-ROM
from *The Iceman*—includes all resource material and customizable lesson plan

Listening to Literature Audiocassettes
from *The Iceman*

Connection to Prentice Hall World Explorer
Ancient Times
Ch. 1, "The Beginnings of Human Society"

from THE ICEMAN

by Don Lessem

In 1991, hikers in the mountains of northern Europe found the body of a 5,300-year-old man. It was perfectly preserved by the snow that had covered it for so long. Scientists of many kinds used information gathered from the man, whom they named Ötzi, to create a picture of European life in the Copper Age. ❶

Ötzi and the everyday objects that were found beside him are unique and wonderfully preserved clues to daily life in a time that has long been mysterious. With their help, we can imagine what life might have been like in the Copper Age[1] and how Ötzi lived and died. We can never be certain, but it may have been something like this:

Ötzi may have been a shepherd herding sheep, a trader trading stone and metal for tools, or even a medicine man in search of messages from gods. Whatever the reason, Ötzi had hiked high into the mountains. He was strong and well equipped, perhaps a leader among his people.

1. **Copper Age** (käp′ ər) *n.*: Period lasting from 5,000 B.C. to 3,500 B.C., when copper was the most advanced metal in use.

Preparing for Standardized Tests

Reading for Information Standardized tests often include informational reading selections in which students are called on to accurately identify factual data. Tell students that the key to answering questions of this type is careful reading—both of the passage and of the question. Have students practice by reading this page. Then write this question and these answer choices on the chalkboard:

According to scientists, Ötzi was which of the following?

(A) a trader of stone and metal
(B) a shepherd herding sheep
(C) a medicine man
(D) any of the above

(D) is the only correct answer because it accurately reflects the archaeologists' speculation about Ötzi's life. *(A)*, *(B)*, and *(C)* exclude other possibilities, conclusions that the text does not support. Highlight the words *may have been* in the text to show that scientists were speculating. For further practice, you might ask students to find other such signal words (for example *if*) that indicate speculation about facts.

Develop Understanding

One-Minute Insight

This selection from *The Iceman* reconstructs the life of a man, called Ötzi, who lived over 5,000 years ago in the European Alps. From data gathered and interpreted by scientists and archaeologists, Ötzi's identity comes into focus. He lived during the Copper Age, was perhaps a trader, medicine man, or shepherd, and carried a much-valued ax. His clothing and tools showed the many skills of his people. When faced with danger, he responded resourcefully. Reading about this real individual's experiences will help bring ancient history to life for students.

Team Teaching Strategy

The text from *The Iceman* offers an opportunity to team teach with a science teacher, creating a cross-curricular unit on the ways science facilitates our knowledge of history. Alternatively, you might team teach with a social studies teacher to create a unit on ancient history.

Customize for *Less Proficient Readers*

To help students place the selection in its historical context, show them a timeline of ancient history (such as the one found in World Explorer: *Ancient Times,* p. 25). Have students record the timeline data on a copy of the Timeline Organizer, p. 74, in **Writing and Language Transparencies.** Instruct them to leave space at the top of the timeline for additional dates. After reading the first selection page, help students place Ötzi's experiences on the timeline.

Clarification

❶ Explain that scientists used Ötzi's ax to date him to the Copper Age. The ax blade was made of almost pure copper, which people used after the Stone Age but before they learned to use bronze, another metal, for tool-making. Scientists used a method called carbon-dating to more exactly determine Ötzi's age. Carbon-dating measures how much carbon (an element present in all living things and some objects)has decayed. Because carbon decays at a constant rate, scientists can estimate a specimen's age.

Customize for
More Advanced Students
Organize students in teams to read the full text of Don Lessem's *The Iceman.* Challenge teams to discuss the scientific findings in Lessem's book. Ask them to agree or disagree with the inferences scientists made from the findings. What, if any, other interpretations could they make from the data?

Links Across Time

❶ By around 7,000 years ago, many people lived in small farming settlements. Ancient peoples had discovered that farming could supply many of their food needs year-round, sometimes with leftovers for future years. Food surpluses meant that some people could focus on other efforts, such as skilled tool-making and needlework. The products made by these skilled workers not only improved villagers' lives, but also made trade possible. Increasing skill also led to inventions such as the wheel and axle, in use by some civilizations by around 3500 B.C.

CONNECTING LITERATURE TO SOCIAL STUDIES

❷ **A Packing List** Have students list details from their reading up to this point. Remind them to read carefully to distinguish those objects scientists discovered with Ötzi from those they can only speculate he carried. *Ötzi carried a copper ax, hard flints, and a huge bow. He may also have carried meat or additional flint and copper materials for trading.*

CONNECTING LITERATURE TO SOCIAL STUDIES

❸ **Connect** Invite a student to read this paragraph aloud to note details related to temperature. *Students should recognize that Ötzi's clothing, the stuffing in his shoes, and his fur cap all suggested to scientists that he faced cold temperatures.*

The tattoo lines on his knee, foot, and back may have been religious emblems or a sign of his bravery or status.

Ötzi was a welcome visitor to the villages along his route. If he was a shepherd, he would have brought the villagers meat (since wool was not yet used for clothing). If he was a trader, he would
❶ have brought them flint for tools or copper for weapons.

Ötzi may have admired the villagers' talents. They used wheeled wagons and plows to farm. They sewed linen clothes and shoes expertly. They fed him butter and other delicacies.

The villagers may have been impressed with the hard flints Ötzi had brought—wonderful stones for making daggers and knives—and with his fine ax. But Ötzi would not part with the ax. He had traveled far to the south and traded away many of his belongings to the copper workers for his ax.

❷ **Connecting Literature to Social Studies** What objects did Ötzi have with him on his trip into the mountains?

Ötzi was handy and so found many uses for his ax. He had been wielding it lately to make a new bow to replace the one he'd traded away or broken. It was a huge bow, taller than he was. It took all his strength to pull the bowstring.

Ötzi had been hunting since he was a child. He had learned to feather his arrows at an angle to make them spin in flight and hold their course. After crossing the mountains, Ötzi planned to finish his new bow and arrows. Then he could hunt in the woods for ibex,[2] deer, and boar, and kill threatening bears and wolves. But for now, his mind was on traveling across the treeless high mountains in the thin, cold air.

❸ **Connecting Literature to Social Studies** What clues did scientists use to support their conclusion about the cold temperature Ötzi faced?

In the soft deerskin suit and grass cape made for him by the village tailors, Ötzi was dressed for chill mountain weather. He had stuffed his shoes with mountain grass to protect his feet from the cold. He wore a fur cap on his head.

But the autumn air turned even colder than Ötzi had expected. He huddled in the shelter of a rock hollow. He was too cold and tired to eat the last of the antelope meat and berries he had brought with him.

Ötzi tried to start a fire. He had flint to strike a spark and strips
❹ of felt to help the fire along. But far above the tree line,[3] Ötzi could

2. **ibex** (ī´ beks´) *n.*: European wild goats.
3. **tree line** *n.*: Line above which trees will not grow.

◆ Build Vocabulary

emblems (em´ blәmz) *n.*: Symbols, signs, or badges
delicacies (del´ i ke sēz) *n.*: Foods that are rare and tasty
wielding (wēld´ iŋ) *v.*: Using with skill

▶ **Critical Viewing** John Gurche (left) of the Denver Museum used a copy of the Iceman's skull (right) to reconstruct a head (center). Why do you think he gave his model a ruddy complexion and a beard? **[Infer]**

Block Scheduling Strategies

Consider these suggestions to take advantage of extended class time:

- After discussing "Preserved in Ice" from p. 222, invite students to share their knowledge of the archaeological process. Use the Interest Grabber as a springboard to inform students further about archaeology. Then have students work in teams to generate the presentation outlined in the Viewing and Representing Mini-Lesson on p. 225.
- Invite students to use the Main Idea and Supporting Details organizer, p. 70, in **Writing and Language Transparencies** to organize information for their TV News Story or Research Report in the Idea Bank on p. 227.
- To help students capture the atmosphere of Ötzi's final days, play the audiocassette of *The Iceman.* Pause the recording to ask and discuss the boxed prompts. Then work as a group to complete a simplified Sunburst Organizer, p. 95, in **Writing and Language Transparencies,** with data about Ötzi's character and experiences.

◆Critical Thinking

4 Analyze Ask students whether they would describe Ötzi as a resourceful person. Invite them to use details from the selection to support their answers. *Most students will say that Ötzi is resourceful, citing his efforts to light a fire as well as earlier details about his preparations for cold weather and his trading successes.*

Customize for *English Language Learners*

Make sure students understand that all the events described in the selection are based on inferences drawn by scientists. Point out words such as *if* and *may have been,* explaining that these are signals to readers of the text's inferences.

Customize for *Logical/Mathematical Learners*

Challenge students to outline a likely barter scenario between Ötzi and either the northern villagers or southern copper workers. Remind them to first identify the relative values of the objects and services being bartered. If students wish, invite them to role-play their scenario for the class.

▶Critical Viewing◀

5 Infer *Since the man was outside, he would be exposed to the elements and his skin would be rough, sunburned and/or windburned—ruddy, or reddish colored; his beard may have helped keep him warm and he probably did not have a razor to shave.*

Customize for *Visual/Spatial Learners*

Group students to brainstorm costumes and make-up for a dramatic version of Ötzi's final days. Have them sketch or describe their ideas, listing necessary modern materials.

Viewing and Representing Mini-Lesson

Multimedia Report

This mini-lesson will extend students' understanding of the archaeological research in *The Iceman* by exploring ways that historical information can be interpreted and then communicated to others.

Introduce Explain to students that the model of Ötzi's head shown on this page was created by an artist from the dead man's skeleton and other scientific knowledge. Piecing this data together involves making educated guesses but also makes Ötzi much more accessible to those who study him. With a face, he becomes a real person for scientists and readers.

Develop Have students list details from the text about Ötzi's appearance and experiences. Then urge them to brainstorm for ways to represent these details to an exhibit audience. They might consider recorded journal entries, a repeating live or video-taped role play, tool displays, a route map, or dioramas.

Apply Have students prepare a chosen aspect of the exhibit and present it to the class. If possible, help the class organize all the pieces into a single, traveling exhibit for your school.

Assess Consider students' brainstorming contributions and their groupwork efforts, along with the actual exhibit products. Use the Scoring Rubric for a Multimedia Report form, p. 94, in **Alternative Assessment** to evaluate the final exhibit product.

Connecting Literature to Social Studies

1 Infer/Speculate *Students may speculate that scientists found evidence of his final resting position in Ötzi's skeleton or in the ways his clothing had decayed. Accept any speculation that builds from scientific data to inference.*

Reinforce and Extend

Answers

◆ Literature and Your Life

Reader's Response Students may say they would search for Ötzi because he was a fellow human in need. Others may say they wouldn't go, as Ötzi was a stranger.

Thematic Focus He faced the risks of exhaustion, starvation, exposure to cold, and meeting hostile strangers.

Journal Writing Entries should reflect excitement, curiosity, and the eagerness to move forward.

☑ Check Your Comprehension

1. He was a shepherd herding sheep, a trader trading stone and metal, or a traveling medicine man.
2. He carried many tools; he had tattoo lines that may have indicated status built on strength.
3. He lacked firewood, and perhaps falling snow put out the fire.
4. His body may have been covered by snow.

find no branches to keep a fire going. Perhaps falling snow snuffed out the few sparks he had created.

Ötzi's only hope for survival was to move on through the mountain pass and down into the valley. But he was too weak to move. Maybe he was sick or injured.

Ötzi carefully laid his belongings, including his beautiful ax, against the rocks around him. He lay down to sleep on his left side atop a large stone as the snow fell through the frigid air.

> **Connecting Literature to Social Studies**
> 1 How do scientists know Ötzi rested on his left side?

Days later, when Ötzi did not appear, other shepherds, or friends from the village, may have come looking for him. If they came upon the spot where he lay down, they would have found only a blanket of snow.

In cold isolation, Ötzi had quietly died. Five thousand years later, his snow blanket was finally removed. At last Ötzi was found, along with his treasures. Their value is beyond measure, for they give us our best view yet of the lost world of our Copper Age ancestors.

Guide for Responding

◆ Literature and Your Life

Reader's Response Suppose that you lived in one of the villages that Ötzi visited. Would you have joined the search party that went out to look for him? Why or why not?

Thematic Focus What risks did Ötzi face during his travels?

Journal Writing How would you feel if you were one of the archaeologists or scientists who initially studied Ötzi? Write a journal entry to describe your first day's findings.

☑ Check Your Comprehension

1. What are some possible explanations for Ötzi's traveling so far from home?
2. What evidence is there that Ötzi was probably very strong?
3. Why was Ötzi unable to build a fire to protect himself from the cold?
4. Why did the villagers have trouble finding Ötzi when they went looking for him?

◆ Critical Thinking

Interpret

1. Do you think Ötzi would have felt free to enter a village where he was a stranger? Why or why not? **[Infer]**
2. What could Ötzi have done to avoid dying in the snowstorm? **[Speculate]**

Apply

3. Why do scientists find the details of Ötzi's life useful? **[Assess]**
4. Why was Ötzi more at risk than a traveler along the same route would be today? **[Apply]**

Meet the Author

Don Lessem (1952–) has explained prehistoric times in more than a dozen books. He is best known as a dinosaur expert who edits a newspaper called *Dino Times*. It includes a column he writes using the name of Dino Don.

Lessem was a consultant on the movie *Jurassic Park*, and he is the host of a Microsoft CD-ROM about dinosaurs. *The Iceman* is Lessem's book about the discovery and study of the man who came to be called Ötzi.

More About the Author

Don Lessem's interest in science and history dates from a childhood visit to New York City's Museum of Natural History. Though he notes that his interest fell dormant for the years that he studied Oriental art and wrote humorous books for adults, Lessem rediscovered his passion in 1988 while visiting a paleontology dig in Montana. His experiences on the dig led to a continuing friendship with paleontologist Jack Horner. Fascinated by what he calls "the scavenger hunting that is much of the science," Lessem brings tremendous enthusiasm to all his writings about scientific discoveries and the people and methods behind them.

Beyond the Selection

FURTHER READING

Other Works by Don Lessem

Jack Horner: Living With Dinosaurs
Inside the Amazing Amazon
Dinosaurs to Dodos: Encyclopedia of Extinct Animals

Other Works About Ancient Times and Archaeology

Maroo of the Winter Caves, Ann Turnbull
The Visual Dictionary of Ancient Civilizations, Emily Hill, editor
Dar and the Spear Thrower, Marjorie Cowley
Tombs and Treasures, Catherine Charley

INTERNET

We suggest the following Internet sites (all Web sites are subject to change).

For information about the use of tools in prehistoric life, visit:
http://www.ncl.ac.uk/~nantiq/menu.html

For more on Don Lessem and his work, visit:
http://www.giganotosaurus.com

You might also find related information under the topics *prehistoric civilizations* and *Iceman.*

We *strongly recommend* that you preview these sites before you send your students to them.

Connecting Literature to Social Studies

The Iceman's remains were not discovered by scientists. They were found by two people who were hiking in the mountains on the border between Italy and Austria. The local police used a jackhammer to break up the ice surrounding the body. Other people tried digging it out with axes. All this digging ruined some of the artifacts lying near the body. It took several days before a scientist examined the body and realized it was old, deciding that it was probably more than 1,000 years old. The body was then flown by helicopter to a place where it could be studied. Only after more study did scientists learn that the body was actually 5,000 years old. The local people began calling it Ötzi because it was found near a valley named Ötzal.

1. Why was Ötzi's ax so important to him?
2. Identify three details from the selection that reveal how people probably lived during Ötzi's time.
3. Why are scientists interested in the remains of someone who lived thousands of years ago?

Idea Bank

Writing

1. **Journal Entry** If Ötzi could read and write, he might have kept a journal of his travels. Write the entry he might have made just before going to sleep the night he could not build a fire.
2. **TV News Story** Imagine that a TV camera crew has taped the police and the scientists digging up Ötzi's remains. Write a script to be read by the anchorperson of a news program that will show the tape.
3. **Letter** Write a letter to the editor of a newspaper. Tell why you think the discovery and study of Ötzi's remains are important to the world.

Speaking and Listening

4. **Telephone Interview** Learn more about the fields of science that study prehistory. Find an expert at a local museum or university, and arrange a telephone interview. Prepare questions in advance. Then, share what you learn with classmates. **[Career Link]**

Projects

5. **Research** Use an encyclopedia and other library resources to research the Copper Age and the Bronze Age. Report to the class on how metals were made and used during those two periods.
6. **Model Tools** Find out more about the technology of the Copper and Bronze ages. Use what you discover to make models of several tools used during the Copper and Bronze ages.

Further Reading

- John Napier's *The Origins of Man* (1968) gives information about the earliest humans.
- William Jaspersohn's *How People First Lived* (1985) is about prehistoric communities.
- Isaac Asimov's *How Did We Find Out About Our Human Roots?* (1979) explains some of the methods scientists use to study prehistory.

✓ Assessment Options

Formal Assessment, Selection Test, pp. 66–67, and Assessment Resources Software. The selection test is designed so that it can be easily customized to the performance levels of your students.

PORTFOLIO ASSESSMENT
Use the following rubrics and assessment forms in the **Alternative Assessment** booklet to assess student writing:
Journal Entry: Writing Self-Assessment, p. 78
TV News Story: Technical Description/ Explanation, p. 102
Letter: Response to Literature, p. 97

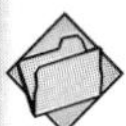

Idea Bank

Following are suggestions for matching the Idea Bank topics with your students' performance levels and learning modalities:

Customize for *Performance Levels*
Less Advanced Students: 1, 6
Average Students: 3, 4, 6
More Advanced Students: 2, 5

Customize for *Learning Modalities*
Verbal/Linguistic: 1, 2, 3, 4
Visual/Spatial: 6
Interpersonal: 4
Bodily/Kinesthetic: 6
Logical/Mathematical: 2, 5

Answers

▸Critical Thinking

1. Possible response: He may have been wary of possible hostility in villagers but would have known that he had desirable trading goods and the means to protect himself.
2. Possible response: He could have returned to the village.
3. They help scientists learn about life in the Copper Age.
4. Ötzi lacked the automobile club, cell phone, motels, or other ways to get help and shelter that a modern traveler would have.

Connecting Literature to Social Studies

1. Ötzi needed his ax for fashioning tools and protecting himself. Also, he'd traded a great deal to get it so he valued it.
2. Possible response: Ötzi's carefully made weapons suggest that people of his time hunted for food and that they regularly faced physical danger. His carefully sewn clothing suggests that people lived a settled enough life to spend time on skilled workmanship. His preparations for the cold suggest that he, at least, traveled regularly.
3. Possible response: Learning how humans lived thousands of years ago helps scientists draw conclusions about the ways the human race has developed since that time.

Prepare and Engage

OBJECTIVES

1. To read, comprehend, and interpret four poems
2. To relate poems to personal experience
3. To read and understand poetic contractions
4. To analyze the use of repetition
5. To build vocabulary in context and learn about homophones
6. To develop skill in using possessive adjectives
7. To write a report focusing on factual accuracy
8. To respond to the poems through writing, speaking and listening, and projects

SKILLS INSTRUCTION

Vocabulary: Homophones
Spelling: Words With *-ed* Endings
Grammar: Possessive Adjectives
Reading Strategy: Poetic Contractions
Literary Focus: Repetition
Writing: Accuracy
Speaking and Listening: Debate (Teacher Edition)
Viewing and Representing: Images of War (Teacher Edition)
Critical Viewing: Analyze; Connect

PORTFOLIO OPPORTUNITIES

Writing: Letter for Future Generations; Eyewitness Report; Evaluation of a Poet's Message
Writing Mini-Lesson: Report
Speaking and Listening: Poetry Reading; Debate
Projects: Museum Exhibit; Oral History

More About the Authors
Alfred, Lord Tennyson In 1850, Queen Victoria appointed Tennyson England's poet laureate, the country's national poet. He had just published *In Memoriam,* an elegy on the death of his college friend Arthur Hallam.

William Shakespeare was not only a playwright, poet, and actor. He was a member of Lord Chamberlain's Men, a successful acting company in London. He and his fellow actors often performed for Queen Elizabeth.

Alice Walker graduated as valedictorian of her high school class. At Spelman College, she took part in civil rights demonstrations before she transferred to Sarah Lawrence College in New York.

Guide for Reading

Meet the Authors:

Alfred, Lord Tennyson (1809–1892)

Alfred, Lord Tennyson was the most popular British poet of his day. Many of his poems focused on nature. Others dealt with significant historical events. In "The Charge of the Light Brigade," a poem based on a newspaper account of a battle between English and Russian troops, he honored the courage of the English cavalry who fought against overwhelming odds.

William Shakespeare (1564–1616)

We are sure that William Shakespeare was born in Stratford-on-Avon, England, but no one knows much about his early life. He became England's greatest poet and foremost playwright. Shakespeare wrote thirty-seven plays. His historical dramas, such as *Henry V,* instilled the English people with pride in their heritage and provided them with a model of patriotism. [For more information on Shakespeare, see page 780.]

Alice Walker (1944–)

Alice Walker was born the eighth and last child in a poor family in Eatonton, Georgia. She developed a love of reading and writing at an early age, and she has gone on to establish herself as one of today's best-known and most-loved writers. In many of her works, she expresses her concerns about social injustice. [For more information on Walker, see page 108.]

◆ Literature and Your Life

Connect Your Experience

You may have heard the battle stories of people who have fought for our country in a war. Yet you probably have a hard time imagining what it is like to be in battle. The pieces you're about to read will bring the experiences of battle to life and give you an appreciation of the sacrifices that soldiers make.

Thematic Focus: Risking It All

As you read, think about the courage it takes for soldiers to risk their lives in battle.

◆ Background for Understanding

History

Fought between 1853 and 1856, the Crimean War pitted Russia against the combined armies of Great Britain, France, and what is now Turkey. It was the first war to be covered by journalists at the front line, and citizens at home learned about it in a graphic way. "The Charge of the Light Brigade" commemorates the Battle of Balaklava, in which a confusion in orders led 600 lightly armed British troops to charge a heavily armed Russian fortification. Three fourths of the British were killed.

◆ Build Vocabulary

Homophones

Homophones, words that sound the same but have different meanings, can cause confusion. For example, *real* means "genuine" or "true," but *reel* can mean to "stagger" or "sway."

Word Bank

Which of these words from the poems might mean "made a foolish mistake"?

dismayed
blundered
volleyed
reeled
sundered

Prentice Hall Literature Program Resources

REINFORCE / RETEACH / EXTEND

Selection Support Pages
Build Vocabulary: Homophones, p. 85
Build Spelling Skills, p. 86
Build Grammar Skills: Possessive Adjectives, p. 87
Reading Strategy: Poetic Contractions, p. 88
Literary Focus: Repetition, p. 89

Strategies for Diverse Student Needs, pp. 31–32

Beyond Literature Career Connection, p. 16

Formal Assessment Selection Test, pp. 68–70, Assessment Resources Software

Alternative Assessment, p. 16

Writing and Language Transparencies
Series of Events Chain, p. 66

Daily Language Practice, p. 38

Resource Pro CD-ROM "The Charge of the Light Brigade"; from *Henry V;* "Lonely Particular"; "The Enemy"

Listening to Literature Audiocassettes "The Charge of the Light Brigade"; from *Henry V,* "Lonely Particular"; "The Enemy"

The Charge of the Light Brigade
from Henry V ◆ Lonely Particular ◆ The Enemy

◆ Literary Focus

Repetition

Repetition is the repeated use of words, phrases, or rhythms. Poets use repetition to add to the music of poetry, to emphasize ideas, and to help establish mood or atmosphere. Look at these famous lines from Tennyson's poem:

Theirs not to make reply,
Theirs not to reason why,
Theirs but to do and die.

Notice how the use of repetition in this example creates rhythm and adds emphasis to the ideas Tennyson is expressing.

◆ Reading Strategy

Reading Poetic Contractions

To achieve a specific rhythm, or pattern of sound, poets often use **poetic contractions.** These words, which appear mostly in poetry, are abbreviated versions of common words. Remember that in a contraction, an apostrophe replaces missing letters. For example, you may see the contraction *ne'er* for "never" or *o'er* for "over." To understand these words, supply the missing letters. Use a chart like the following to clarify the contractions in these poems.

Contraction	Meaning
Sab'ring	sabering
call'd	
remembr'red	
ne'er	
accurs'd	

Interest Grabber To engage students' interest, play a scene from a movie—for example, the 1993 film *Gettysburg*—in which soldiers are about to charge a greater foe. Ask students to try to put themselves in the soldiers' shoes. Challenge them to explain how or why soldiers can overcome their fears and go forth to risk it all upon command. Explain that the selections they will read are about soldiers risking it all.

◆Build Grammar Skills

Possessive Adjectives If you wish to introduce the grammar concept for this selection before students read, refer to the instruction on p. 236.

Customize for
Less Proficient Readers

The archaic language of the first two poems may make comprehension difficult for students. Have students read the poems in pairs or in small groups. Groups can complete the Series of Events Chain in **Writing and Language Transparencies,** p. 66, to help them follow the action in the Tennyson poem.

Customize for
More Advanced Students

Inform students that in the poems they are about to read, the poets express distinctly different views on war and warfare. Guide them to look for these differences as they read, and to compare and contrast the poets' positions. Ask them to consider which poet's view most closely resembles their own.

Humanities: Art

The Interior of the Redan,
by G. Shaw-Lefevre

This photograph from the Crimean War shows the Redan, a Russian fortification from which the British were driven back in 1855. Have students look at the photograph and cite details that strike them. *Students may cite the cannon, the general wrecked atmosphere of the fort, the sea in the background.*

Preparing for Standardized Tests

Vocabulary This selection presents homophones—words that sound alike but have different meanings, such as *hare* and *hair.* Standardized tests may evaluate students' ability to identify sentences that use homophones correctly. Present the following sample question:

In which sentence is the underlined word used correctly?

(A) The general left all his medals to his air.
(B) The army had to altar its plans.
(C) Soldiers ate any fowl they could find in local farmers' barnyards.
(D) The bold general was the idle of many young soldiers.

In *(C),* the word *fowl* is used correctly, as *fowl* means "poultry." *(A)* is wrong: *air* is the mixture of gases that form the Earth's atmosphere. An *heir* is "a person who inherits the property of another." *(B)* is the wrong choice: an *altar* is a religious platform. *Alter* is a verb that means "to change." *(D)* is incorrect: an admired figure is an *idol,* not *idle,* an adjective that means "not working." For further practice, use Build Vocabulary Skills in **Selection Support,** p. 85.

Develop Understanding

One-Minute Insight Tennyson's poem describes an actual event—the valiant but ill-fated charge of the British 27th Lancers at Russian troops during the Crimean War. The poet immortalizes the sacrifice of the men who risked it all in that battle—neither the first nor last time that lives were lost as a result of errors in command.

▶Critical Viewing◀

1 Analyze Possible response: *There are many soldiers on horseback fighting only a few on the ground. There are many dead soldiers on the ground.*

Customize for
English Language Learners
To help students understand the battle-related terminology in this poem, provide photos or explanations of cannon, sabers, shot and shell, volley, battery, mines, ranks, scars, and wounds. Point out that here *cannon* is used as the plural form of the word.

Customize for
Musical/Rhythmic Learners
Students may enjoy listening to the poem read aloud. Encourage students to note the rhyme and rhythm of the poem, the repetition of key words and phrases, and the use of dialogue within the poem. Ask students what music or sounds they would include as elaboration to make the scene of war come alive.

Listening to Literature Audiocassettes

Humanities: Art

Charge of the Light Brigade at the Battle of Balaklava, 1854, Artist Unknown

This painting is a commemorative painting—its purpose is to depict an actual historical event. Note that the artist has rendered the scene realistically to show the horror of the battle and the soldiers' bravery. Ask students to note three realistic details in the painting. *Students might mention the color of the sky, the expressions on the soldiers' faces, the artist's rendering of animals and men, or the soldiers' uniforms.*

The Charge of the Light Brigade

Alfred, Lord Tennyson

Charge of the Light Brigade at the Battle of Balaklava, 1854, Artist Unknown

1 ▲ **Critical Viewing** The Charge of the Light Brigade led to tremendous losses for the British. What in this painting confirms that the battle was unbalanced? **[Analyze]**

Block Scheduling Strategies

Consider these suggestions to take advantage of extended class time:

- Introduce the Reading Strategy, Reading Poetic Contractions, on p. 229. Have students fill out the contraction chart as they read. Then have them get together in groups to compare their charts and complete the Reading Strategy exercise on p. 236. For additional practice, have them use the lesson in **Selection Support,** p. 88.
- Have students consider the theme Risking It All as they read the four poems. Have them get together in groups to answer the Critical Thinking questions on pp. 233 and 235. Then have them complete the Debate on p. 237, using the Speaking and Listening Mini-Lesson, p. 234 (Teacher's Edition).
- To reinforce grammar, mechanics, and usage skills, as well as provide additional background on William Shakespeare, work with small groups on Week 17 of **Daily Language Practice,** p. 38.
- If students have access to technology, encourage them to work in pairs on the Writing Mini-Lesson, using the tutorial on Reports from the *Writer's Solution Writing Lab CD-ROM.*

1

❷ Half a league,[1] half a league,
Half a league onward,
All in the valley of Death
  Rode the six hundred.
"Forward, the Light Brigade!
❸ Charge for the guns!" he said:
Into the valley of Death
  Rode the six hundred.

2

"Forward, the Light Brigade!"
Was there a man dismayed?
Not though the soldier knew
❹ Someone had blundered:
Theirs not to make reply,
❺ Theirs not to reason why,
Theirs but to do and die,
Into the valley of Death
  Rode the six hundred.

3

Cannon to right of them,
Cannon to left of them,
Cannon in front of them
  Volleyed and thundered;
Stormed at with shot and shell,
Boldly they rode and well,
Into the jaws of Death,
Into the mouth of Hell
  Rode the six hundred.

4

Flashed all their sabers bare,
Flashed as they turned in air,
Sab'ring the gunners there,
Charging an army, while
  All the world wondered:
Plunged in the battery[2] smoke
Right through the line they broke:
Cossack[3] and Russian
Reeled from the saber stroke
  Shattered and sundered.
Then they rode back, but not,
  Not the six hundred.

5

Cannon to right of them,
Cannon to left of them, ❻
Cannon behind them
  Volleyed and thundered;
Stormed at with shot and shell,
While horse and hero fell,
They that had fought so well
Came through the jaws of Death,
Back from the mouth of Hell,
All that was left of them,
  Left of six hundred.

6

When can their glory fade?
O the wild charge they made!
  All the world wondered.
Honor the charge they made!
Honor the Light Brigade,
  Noble six hundred!

1. **league** (lēg) *n.*: Three miles.

2. **battery:** Fortification equipped with heavy guns.
3. **Cossack** (käs´ ak´): People of southern Russia famous as horsemen and cavalrymen.

◆ Build Vocabulary

dismayed (dis mād´) *adj.*: Afraid; without confidence
blundered (blun´ dərd) *v.*: Made a foolish mistake
volleyed (väl´ ēd) *v.*: Fired together
reeled (rēld) *v.*: Fell back from a blow
sundered (sun´ dərd) *v.*: Broken apart

◆ Literary Focus

❷ **Repetition** Discuss with students the effects of the repetition in these lines. Help them appreciate that it sets up a rhythm for the poem that recalls the pounding of horses' hooves.

Clarification

❸ The term *light* in Light Brigade refers to the nature of the weaponry the soldiers carried into battle, not the size of the military unit. These cavalry soldiers were lightly armed.

Comprehension Check ☑

❹ Ask students to explain why the soldiers obeyed their commander's orders. Students should understand that soldiers are trained to obey and follow all orders given by officers, without question.

◆ Build Vocabulary

❺ **Homophones** Homophones are words that sound alike but have different spellings and meanings. Point out the homophone *theirs* in this passage. Students should not confuse this possessive pronoun with the contraction *there's*, which often begins sentences.

◆ Literary Focus

❻ **Repetition** Ask students to explain how the repetition of lines from the third stanza shows the progress of the battle. *Students may say that now the cannons are behind the soldiers, that they have come back from the jaws of death, and that fewer than 600 returned.*

Viewing and Representing Mini-Lesson

Images of War

This mini-lesson supports the Museum Exhibit project in the Idea Bank on p. 237.

Introduce Tell students that the experience of war has been chronicled in diary entries; expressed in poetry, prose, and song; painted, sculpted, danced, photographed, and filmed. Challenge them to create a multimedia presentation that characterizes their own view of war.

Develop Provide these tips to groups: Share researching and presenting tasks.
Review media choices together. Decide on the best way to present sounds and images.
Do a trial run of the presentation before sharing it with the class.

Apply Have each group give 5- to 10-minute presentations. Encourage them to explain their choice of materials.

Assess Make sure that students have represented the war in a variety of ways, and that their presentations reflect a team effort. You may want to adapt the Multimedia Report rubric in **Alternative Assessment,** p. 94.

One-Minute Insight On the eve of the battle of Agincourt (1415), in which King Henry V's small British army would face a much larger French force, the king inspires his soldiers to battle. He tells his troops that those who risk their lives to fight with him that day will think better of themselves for having done so and will always look back at the day with pride, having taken their place in history alongside their king.

Clarification

❶ The St. Crispian's Day speech is from Act IV, Scene III, of the play. It takes place in the English camp. Henry delivers the speech right after he and his noblemen have learned that their French foes outnumber their force by a factor of five (according to Shakespeare). Historians believe that the actual difference was less, although still significant.

◆Critical Thinking

❷ **Deduce** Ask students to read these lines and then deduce what "to stand a' tiptoe" means. *Students should deduce that it means to hold one's head high, to be proud.*

◆Critical Thinking

❸ **Paraphrase** Ask a volunteer to paraphrase these lines to make clear Henry's emphasis. *He says that although much gets forgotten, all who fight with him will remember their part in that glorious day, and so will generations that follow.*

Clarification

❹ Crispin and Crispian were two martyrs thought to have come from Rome to preach Christianity in Gaul toward the end of the third century. They preached by day and made shoes by night, until Emperor Maximian ordered their beheading.

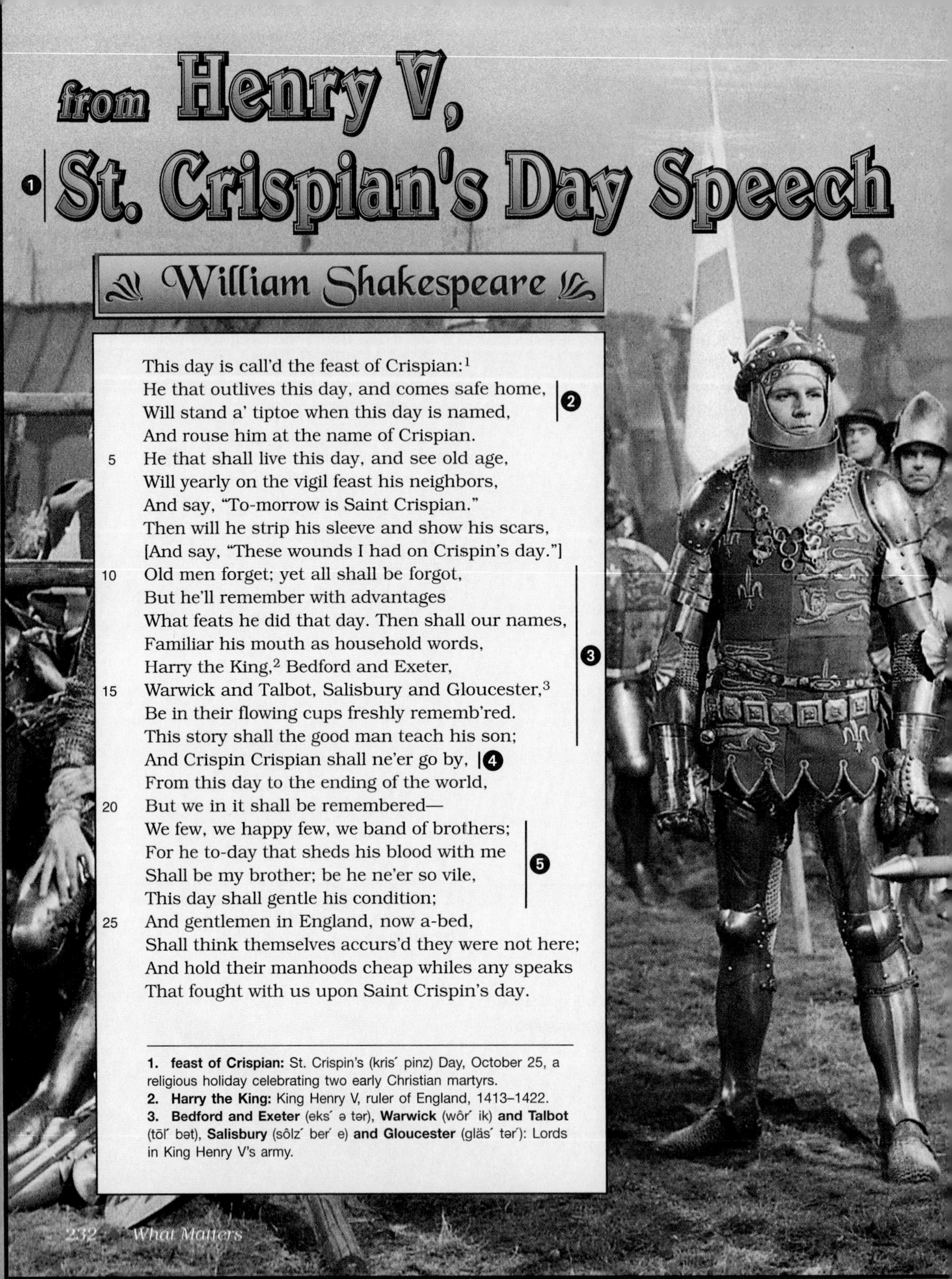

from Henry V, ❶ St. Crispian's Day Speech

William Shakespeare

This day is call'd the feast of Crispian:[1]
He that outlives this day, and comes safe home, ❷
Will stand a' tiptoe when this day is named,
And rouse him at the name of Crispian.
He that shall live this day, and see old age,
Will yearly on the vigil feast his neighbors,
And say, "To-morrow is Saint Crispian."
Then will he strip his sleeve and show his scars,
[And say, "These wounds I had on Crispin's day."]
Old men forget; yet all shall be forgot,
But he'll remember with advantages
What feats he did that day. Then shall our names,
Familiar his mouth as household words, ❸
Harry the King,[2] Bedford and Exeter,
Warwick and Talbot, Salisbury and Gloucester,[3]
Be in their flowing cups freshly rememb'red.
This story shall the good man teach his son;
And Crispin Crispian shall ne'er go by, ❹
From this day to the ending of the world,
But we in it shall be remembered—
We few, we happy few, we band of brothers;
For he to-day that sheds his blood with me
Shall be my brother; be he ne'er so vile, ❺
This day shall gentle his condition;
And gentlemen in England, now a-bed,
Shall think themselves accurs'd they were not here;
And hold their manhoods cheap whiles any speaks
That fought with us upon Saint Crispin's day.

1. **feast of Crispian:** St. Crispin's (kris´ pinz) Day, October 25, a religious holiday celebrating two early Christian martyrs.
2. **Harry the King:** King Henry V, ruler of England, 1413–1422.
3. **Bedford and Exeter** (eks´ ə tər), **Warwick** (wôr´ ik) **and Talbot** (tôl´ bət), **Salisbury** (sôlz´ ber´ e) **and Gloucester** (gläs´ tər): Lords in King Henry V's army.

Humanities: Performing Arts

There are two movie versions of *Henry V,* each British. Interestingly, in each, the director played the title role. Sir Laurence Olivier played Henry V in his 1945 film, and Kenneth Branagh did so in his 1989 work. Olivier earned a special Academy Award for his achievement as actor, director, and producer. For Branagh, the film marked his impressive directorial debut.

Play for students the scene from each film in which Henry delivers his St. Crispian's Day speech. Ask students to notice how each director has chosen to film this pivotal scene and to listen for the music each has selected to accompany the speech. Then have students discuss their responses to the following questions:

1. Which actor's performance is more compelling? Why? *Responses will vary but should be based on which of the two speeches they found more stirring and more convincing as a rallying cry.*
2. Which version of the scene is more effective? Explain. *Students might base their responses upon their opinions of the set design, the music, the camera angles the director uses, or how the scene is framed and lit.*

6 ◀ Critical Viewing Laurence Olivier, pictured in armor here, had the title role in the 1944 film version of *Henry V.* What elements of his body language suggest the royalty and leadership the speech conveys? **[Connect]**

Beyond Literature

History Connection

Who was Henry V? Henry V was one of England's greatest leaders, a soldier-king who conquered a large part of France. His first military campaign in 1415 led England against France and ended in the crushing defeat of the French at the Battle of Agincourt, where a starving English army defeated a well-rested French one several times its size. Shakespeare dramatized this battle in his play *Henry V.* Long marches and several battles finally took their toll on King Henry. He died in 1422 at the height of his power. His nine-month old son, Henry VI, succeeded him to the throne. Not long after, the English lost all the land they had taken from the French.

Cross-Curricular Activity

History at the Movies William Shakespeare's depiction of Henry V did more to immortalize this ambitious king than any history book ever could. Hollywood has taken the playwright's work to the silver screen, producing several versions of Shakespeare's play. Read at least two reviews of a recent making of *Henry V.* What did the reviewers think of it? Share your findings with the class.

Guide for Responding

◆ Literature and Your Life

Reader's Response Would Alfred, Lord Tennyson or William Shakespeare make a better war correspondent for television news? Explain.

Thematic Focus In what ways are the soldiers asked to risk it all in "The Charge of the Light Brigade" and in the St. Crispian's Day speech?

Journal Writing What advice might a member of the Light Brigade give to a soldier who had just heard Henry's St. Crispian's Day speech? In a journal entry, explore this question.

☑ Check Your Comprehension

1. The soldiers in "The Charge of the Light Brigade" realize someone had blundered. Why do they still go into battle?
2. What was the outcome of the battle?
3. Why does Henry V say that the world will always remember St. Crispian's Day?

◆ Critical Thinking

Interpret

1. What is the spirit of the Light Brigade's cavalrymen as they make their charge? **[Infer]**
2. Describe the speaker's feelings about the cavalrymen. **[Speculate]**
3. What reasons might Henry V have had for calling all the soldiers, both noble and common, his brothers? **[Analyze]**
4. What does the St. Crispian's Day speech tell you about the character of Henry V? **[Infer]**

Evaluate

5. Henry V's St. Crispian's Day speech is considered by many to be one of the greatest speeches an actor can perform. Based on your reading, why do you think this is so? **[Assess]**
6. Could a poem like "The Charge of the Light Brigade" be written today about a modern battle? **[Make a Judgment]**

Compare Literary Works

7. How does the representation of courage presented in these two selections differ? **[Contrast]**

Thematic Focus

❺ **Risking it All** What does Henry say are the rewards for risking it all in this battle? *All those who fight by his side will be his brothers, will be proud of what they have done, and will be beloved and remembered for what they did.*

▶Critical Viewing◀

❻ **Connect** *Henry stands proud and straight, in a heavily decorated suit of armor, with his soldiers behind him; the man whom he addresses is bowing.*

Beyond Literature

If students have access to technology, suggest they begin their search for reviews of *Henry V* at The Internet Movie Database, **http://www.us.imdb.com.**

Customize for
Logical/Mathematical Learners

Have students use a Venn diagram to record the similarities and differences between "The Charge of the Light Brigade" and "St. Crispian's Day Speech."

"The Charge of the Light Brigade"
- about the Crimean War
- soldiers were defeated

Both:
- glorify war
- about difficult battles

"St. Crispian's Day Speech"
- about the Battle of Agincourt
- soldiers were victorious

Reinforce and Extend

Answers

◆ Literature and Your Life

Reader's Response Lord Tennyson, because he gives a step-by-step description.

Thematic Focus In both battles soldiers are asked to take up arms against a more powerful foe.

☑ Check Your Comprehension

1. Soldiers are disciplined to follow orders from their officers and not ask questions.
2. The Light Brigade was badly defeated; only a few survived.
3. The world will remember the bravery of the few soldiers who fought as brothers against a much larger enemy.

◆ Critical Thinking

1. They go boldly forth without question.
2. The speaker is proud of their bravery.
3. Possible response: Because Henry is going into battle himself, he calls any man who enters battle alongside him his brother.
4. It suggests that Henry was an inspiring leader who recognized the value of all his soldiers, noble and common alike.
5. Possible response: The speech contains emotion and passion and is convincing.
6. A poem could be written about a modern battle but it would have to be updated for modern battle techniques.
7. Both armies fought against overwhelming odds; the soldiers at Agincourt had an inspiring leader; those at Balaklava fought bravely and desperately despite the mistaken orders of their blundering officers.

A general who now fires on his own men to prod them into battle was once a frightened foot soldier who fled the enemy's guns. His aggressive response to cowardice within his troops overcompensates for his own former weakness.

◆Critical Thinking

❶ **Infer** Have students read the first four lines and then ask students what the poet means by "that other time." *Students should recognize that these lines refer to a time in the General's life before he became a General.*

Clarification

❷ Point out to students that shooting deserters and harshly treating cowardice in battle have been common military practices throughout history. This general is not the first to have ordered officers to fire at men who try to leave the scene of a battle.

◆Critical Thinking

❸ **Interpret** What is hypocritical about the General's behavior? *He, who now shoots his men for what he sees as cowardice, was once guilty of that same response to battle.*

Customize for
Verbal/Linguistic Learners
Guide students to recognize the contrast between *lonely* and *crowding* and between *particular* and *general*. Students can notice that, as a frightened young soldier, the General acted as a lone individual, but as a commanding officer interested only in his "cause," he cannot treat soldiers as individuals.

LONELY PARTICULAR

Alice Walker

When the people knew you
That other time
❶ You were not as now
A crowding General.
Firing into your own
Ranks;
Forcing the tender skin
Of men
❷ Against the guns
The very sun
To mangled perfection
For your cause.

Not General then
But frightened boy.
The cheering fell
Within the quiet
That fed your
❸ Walks
Across the mines.
A mere foot soldier,
Marching the other way:
A lonely Particular.

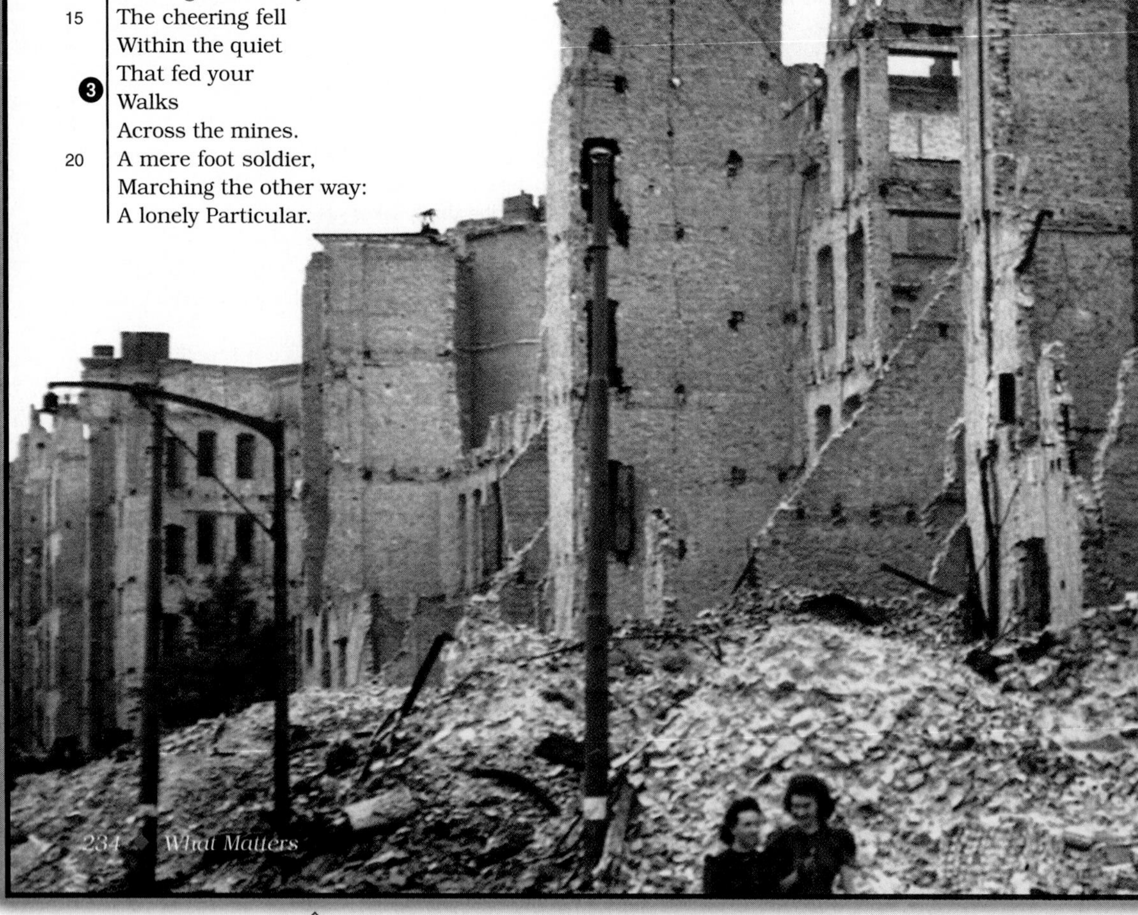

Speaking and Listening Mini-Lesson

Debate
This mini-lesson supports the Speaking and Listening activity in the Idea Bank on p. 237.

Introduce Discuss with students the importance of listening attentively and respectfully to each presenter.

Develop Divide the class into three groups, each responsible for the position of one of the writers. Instruct debaters to be prepared to defend their positions with lines from the selections. Suggest to groups that they have different members responsible for each attribute in question. Assign one or more students the role of moderator.

Apply Hold the debate. Remind students to speak in turn. You may wish to record the debate on audiotape or videotape.

Assess Evaluate the debating teams on their ability to state correctly and clearly their writer's views on courage, loyalty, honor, and war, and on their adherence to all aspects of the debate format. Have students use the Peer Assessment: Speaker/Speech form, p. 105, in **Alternative Assessment** to evaluate their own and others' arguments on behalf of the writers.

THE ENEMY

Alice Walker

in gray, battle-scarred Leningrad[1]
a tiny fist unsnapped to show
crumpled heads
of pink and yellow flowers
snatched hurriedly on the go
in the cold spring shower—

consent or not
countries choose
cold or hot
win or lose
to speak of wars
yellow and red
but there is much
let it be said
for children.

1. **Leningrad** (len´ in grad´) *n.*: Important city in the former Soviet Union, renamed St. Petersburg, in 1991.

Guide for Responding

◆ Literature and Your Life

Reader's Response What would you like to say to the General in "Lonely Particular"? What questions would you ask "The Enemy"?

Thematic Focus A loyal and courageous soldier risks everything fighting the enemy. Do you think Alice Walker believes soldiers should be asked to risk their lives for their country?

☑ Check Your Comprehension

1. Why is the General in "Lonely Particular" firing?
2. How has the General changed since his youth?
3. What is the setting of "The Enemy"?
4. In "The Enemy," who is holding the pink and yellow flowers?

◆ Critical Thinking

Interpret

1. How does the relationship between the words "general" and "particular" help you interpret the meaning of "Lonely Particular"? **[Connect]**
2. What might have caused the General to fire into his own ranks? **[Analyze Cause and Effect]**
3. What do you think Walker thinks about war? Explain. **[Draw Conclusions]**

Evaluate

4. Explain whether the General in "Lonely Particular" is fit to lead soldiers. **[Assess]**

Compare Literary Works

5. Which poem presents a stronger case for Walker's position on war? Explain. **[Distinguish]**

Develop Understanding

This poem presents a view of the far-reaching risks involved in any war. Innocent children, as well as the armed soldiers, are among its victims.

Clarification

❹ Leningrad was the site of one of the worst German-Soviet battles in World War II. The Germans came to Leningrad in September 1941 and the battle didn't end until January 1944. Nearly one million people died.

◆ Critical Thinking

❺ **Analyze** Guide students to see that by reducing war to a series of polar opposites—consent or not, cold as in cold war or hot, win or lose—the poet negates its purpose.

Reinforce and Extend

◆ Literature and Your Life

Reader's Response Students might ask the general how he could treat his men so badly. They might ask "The Enemy" how any war is justified.

Thematic Focus Students may say that Alice Walker believes that no "cause" of war is worth dying for.

☑ Check Your Comprehension

1. To keep his soldiers from fleeing.
2. In his youth he, too, fled in fright.
3. The setting is Leningrad, in Russia.
4. A dead child is holding the flowers.

◆ Critical Thinking

1. They show the contrast between the strong General and the frightened soldier he once was.
2. Possible response: He doesn't want his soldiers to display cowardice as he once did.
3. She is against war. Each poem expresses the cruelty of war.
4. Possible response: He is unfit to lead because he would risk wounding his own soldiers to stop them from being cowards.
5. Some students may say that firing on terrified soldiers to spur them on is the stronger antiwar statement; others may say the death of innocent children is stronger.

Beyond the Selection

FURTHER READING

Other Works by the Authors

Idylls of the King, Alfred, Lord Tennyson
Romeo and Juliet, William Shakespeare
Once: Poems, Alice Walker

Other Works About War

The Red Badge of Courage, Stephen Crane
Collected Poems, Wilfred Owen

INTERNET

We suggest the following sites on the Internet (all Web sites are subject to change).

For a brief biography of Alfred, Lord Tennyson: **http://mirrors.org.sg/victorian/tennyson/tennybio.html**

For information about the Battle of Balaklava: **http://www.pinetreeweb.com/13th-balaklava.htm**

For the complete works of William Shakespeare: **http://the-tech.mit.edu/Shakespeare/works.html**

For Alice Walker information: **http://www.luminarium.org/contemporary/alicew**

We *strongly recommend* that you preview these sites.

Answers

◆Reading Strategy

Evaluate students on the delivery of their readings, as well as on how well they spoke the contracted words.

◆Build Vocabulary

Using Homophones

1. real; 2. reel; 3. vial; 4. vile

Spelling Strategy

1. volleyed; 2. blundered; 3. wondered; 4. regretted

Using the Word Bank

1. (e) frightened
2. (a) bungled
3. (b) barraged; attacked
4. (d) wavered
5. (c) separated

◆Literary Focus

1. It expresses the repeated firing of cannon all around the charging brigade, creating a sense of frantic conflict.
2. (a) Lines 17, 26, 38, 49, and 55; (b) The repetition reinforces the low number of soldiers in the brigade; (c) The changing line shows how the number of soldiers decreases as the battle progresses.

◆Build Grammar Skills

Practice

1. their, sabers; 2. their, glory; 3. our, names; his, mouth; 4. his, blood; my, brother; 5. your, walks

Writing Application

Possible responses:

1. My uncle fought in Vietnam.
2. Our grandfather fought in the Battle of the Bulge.
3. His cousin played Henry V in the local theater.
4. Their regiment lost many men in the battle.

Writer's Solution

For additional instruction and practice, use the lesson in the *Writer's Solution Language Lab CD-ROM* on Using Modifiers, and the practice pages on adjectives, pp. 15–19, in the *Writer's Solution Grammar Practice Book*.

Guide for Responding *(continued)*

◆ Reading Strategy

Reading Poetic Contractions

Henry V's St. Crispian's Day speech includes **poetic contractions** that help maintain the poetic rhythm. Practice reading the speech aloud. Read *accurs'd (accursed)* as two syllables, *rememb'red* as three syllables, *remembered* as four, and *ne'er (never)* as one syllable. When you are ready, read the speech aloud for your class.

◆ Build Vocabulary

Using Homophones

Homophones are words that sound alike but have different spellings and meanings. On a sheet of paper, write the proper word in the following sentences. Use a dictionary to help you.

1. His ring was made of __?__ gold. (real, reel)
2. The cowboy and his horse began to __?__ as they chased the calf. (real, reel)
3. The doctor gave the __?__ of medicine to his patient. (vile, vial)
4. Rotting meat gives off a __?__ smell. (vile, vial)

Spelling Strategy

When you add *-ed* to a verb whose last syllable is stressed, double the final consonant if it is preceded by a vowel:

commit + -ed = committed

Exceptions include words ending in *r, w, x,* and *y*. In those cases, do not double the final letter:

follow + -ed = followed dismay + -ed = dismayed

Write the following words correctly on a sheet of paper:

1. volley + -ed =
2. blunder + -ed =
3. wonder + -ed =
4. regret + -ed =

Using the Word Bank

On your paper, match each word in the first column with the word or words closest in meaning in the second column.

1. dismayed	**a.** bungled
2. blundered	**b.** barraged; attacked
3. volleyed	**c.** separated
4. reeled	**d.** wavered
5. sundered	**e.** frightened

◆ Literary Focus

Repetition

Repetition in poetry is the repeated use of words, phrases, or rhythmic patterns. Poets use repetition to emphasize key ideas. For example, in his poem, Tennyson uses repetition to leave readers with an unforgettable impression of the sights and sounds of actual battle.

1. What is the effect of the repetition in these lines: "Cannon to right of them,/Cannon to left of them,/Cannon in front of them"?
2. In the first stanza, Tennyson repeats the line "Rode the six hundred." (a) Scan the rest of the poem to identify the lines that repeat the words "six hundred." (b) What is the effect of the repetition of these words? (c) What is the effect of the changing of the line as the battle progresses?

◆ Build Grammar Skills

Possessive Adjectives

While all **adjectives** modify nouns or pronouns, some adjectives show ownership by answering the question *whose*. The personal pronouns *my, your, his, her, our, their,* and *its* modify nouns and tell *whose*. These pronouns are therefore sometimes called **possessive adjectives.** Notice that the pronoun *his* functions as an adjective in this line spoken by Henry V:

"Then will he strip *his* sleeve and show *his* scars."

Practice On your paper, identify the possessive adjectives in the following lines from the poems. Then, indicate which noun each modifies.

1. Flashed all their sabers bare, . . .
2. When can their glory fade?
3. Then shall our names,/Familiar his mouth as household words, . . .
4. For he to-day that sheds his blood with me/Shall be my brother; . . .
5. Within the quiet/That fed your/Walks . . .

Writing Application On your paper, write three sentences or a short poem using the following possessive adjectives.

1. my **2.** our **3.** his **4.** their

Build Your Portfolio

Idea Bank

Writing

1. Letter for Future Generations As one of King Henry's soldiers, you are moved by his St. Crispian's Day speech. In a letter for future generations of your family, describe how Henry V's words made you feel that fateful day.

2. Eyewitness Report As one of the British reporters on the front lines of the battle described in "The Charge of the Light Brigade," provide a description for readers back home. Use vivid language that will help readers "see" the event.

3. Evaluation of a Poet's Message These poems present different views of the responsibilities of soldiers and leaders. Choose one of the poems. Analyze the message it conveys about war. Then, in an essay identify the message of the poem, and tell whether you agree or disagree with it.

Speaking and Listening

4. Poetry Reading With a group, present a dramatic reading of each of the poems in this section. Add appropriate music or visuals to enhance your presentation. **[Performing Arts Link]**

5. Debate [Group Activity] With a small group, conduct a debate among the three writers that explores their positions on courage, loyalty, honor, or war. Each group member can take the part of a writer. Present the debate to your class.

Projects

6. Museum Exhibit [Group Activity] Create an exhibit about an important war in history. Decide which conflict your group will study. Use the library and the Internet for research. Create dioramas, three-dimensional maps, and posters to present your information. **[Media Link]**

7. Oral History Conduct an interview with someone who has served in the armed forces. Prepare questions in advance, and take notes or tape record the interview. Present your findings to your class. **[History Link]**

Writing Mini-Lesson

Report

Tennyson uses poetry to describe a battle that occurred during his lifetime. However, you can find more factual information about the Crimean War in encyclopedias and history books. Choose an important historical battle, and write a factual report about the causes of the battle and its outcome.

Writing Skills Focus: Accuracy

While Tennyson's language tugs at reader's emotions, you should strive to inform your audience. To achieve this purpose, concentrate on **accuracy**—provide a true, fair report of the events. Use these tips to guide you:

- Use as many sources as possible. If a detail appears in two sources, you can generally be assured of its accuracy.
- Be careful as you take notes. Copy statistics exactly. Avoid changing the meaning when you put information into your own words.

Prewriting Begin with a source such as an encyclopedia, which will give an overview of the battle. Find two other books to give you further information. As you read, note the countries involved, the dates of the battle, the numbers of soldiers killed, and the reason for the fight.

Drafting Devote each paragraph in your essay to a specific topic. For example, in one paragraph, address the causes of the battle; in another, describe the location and duration of the fighting; and in another, describe the weapons and technology used.

Revising When you revise, check your draft against your notes to be sure you have accurately reported the facts.

◆ Grammar Application

Check your use of possessive adjectives. Do they show ownership or a clear relationship?

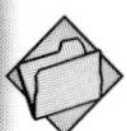

Idea Bank

Following are suggestions for matching the Idea Bank topics with your students' performance levels and learning modalities:

Customize for *Performance Levels*

Less Advanced Students: 1, 7
Average Students: 2, 4, 5, 7
More Advanced Students: 3, 4, 5, 6

Customize for *Learning Modalities*

Verbal/Linguistic: 1, 2, 3, 4, 5, 7
Visual/Spatial: 3, 6
Logical/Mathematical: 5
Musical/Rhythmic: 4
Interpersonal: 4, 5, 6
Intrapersonal: 1, 2, 3

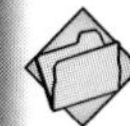

Writing Mini-Lesson

Refer students to the Writing Handbook in the back of the book for instructions on the writing process and for further information on reports.

Writing Lab CD-ROM

Have students complete the tutorial on Reports. Follow these steps:

1. Have students view interactive models of reports.
2. Encourage students to use the Topic Web activity to break their topic into narrower topics.
3. Suggest that students use the notecard template when taking notes.
4. Have students draft on computer.

Writer's Solution Sourcebook

Have students use Chapter 7, "Reports," pp. 201–234, for additional support. The chapter includes in-depth instruction on gathering and organizing information, pp. 219–222.

✓ ASSESSMENT OPTIONS

Formal Assessment, Selection Test, pp. 68–70, and Assessment Resources Software. The selection test is designed so that it can be easily customized to the performance levels of your students.

Alternative Assessment, p. 16, includes options for less advanced students, more advanced students, verbal/linguistic learners, musical/rhythmic learners, interpersonal learners, and logical/mathematical learners.

PORTFOLIO ASSESSMENT

Use the following rubrics in the **Alternative Assessment** booklet to assess student writing:
Letter for Future Generations: Expression, p. 81
Eyewitness Report: Description, p. 84
Evaluation of Poet's Message: Response to Literature, p. 97
Writing Mini-Lesson: Research Report, p. 93

Prepare and Engage

Establish Writing Guidelines
Review the following key characteristics of a persuasive letter:

- A persuasive letter attempts to convince the reader to agree with what the writer is saying.
- A persuasive letter uses compelling evidence for its position.

You may want to distribute the scoring rubric for Persuasion, p. 92 in **Alternative Assessment,** to make students aware of the criteria on which they will be evaluated. See the suggestions on p. 240 for how you can customize the rubric to this workshop.

Refer students to the Writing Handbook in the back of the book for instruction on the writing process and further information on persuasive writing.

Writer's Solution

Writers at Work Videodisc
To introduce students to persuasive writing, and to show them what author Joseph Bruchac says about learning from writing, play the videodisc segment on Exposition: Giving Information (Ch. 6). Have students discuss how Bruchac gets his ideas for writing.

Play frames 31956 to 41222

Writing Lab CD-ROM
If your students have access to computers, you may want to have them work in the tutorial on Persuasion to complete all or part of their letters. Follow these steps:

1. Have students view the Writing Inspirations for Persuasion to choose a writing topic.
2. Encourage students to use the Topic Web activity to narrow their topic.
3. Let students draft on computer.
4. When revising, have students use the Proofreading Checklist.

Writer's Solution Sourcebook
Students can find additional support, including in-depth instruction on writing supporting sentences and using commas in the chapter on Persuasion, pp. 166–200.

Persuasive Writing

Persuasive Letter

Writing Process Workshop

If you've ever tried to convince your parents to let you get a pet or argued with a friend that one musical group is better than another, you've used persuasion. Persuasion is writing or speaking that tries to convince people to agree with a writer's perspective. Write a **persuasive letter** about something that really matters to you. Your letter should try to get someone to see things your way or to take a certain action. The following skills, introduced in this section's Writing Mini-Lessons, will help you write your persuasive letter.

Writing Skills Focus

▶ **Elaborate on key ideas.** To really convince your reader, include facts and details that prove your arguments are sound. (See p. 206.)

▶ **Organize your main points by order of importance.** Begin with your least important point and work up to the most important one, or do just the opposite. (See p. 221.)

▶ **Be accurate.** Double-check the facts you use, and document your sources. (See p. 237.)

In this model, a girl who wants to convince her parents to let her learn a potentially dangerous activity uses these skills in her request.

Model

Dear Mom and Dad,
The YMCA is offering a rock-climbing course, and I really want to sign up. You'll be happy to know that the motto of the program is "Safety First." In fact, there are only three students to every instructor. ① The course brochure says the class is designed for beginners with a "taste for adventure." That sounds just like me!
Classes meet from 10:00 to 12:30 on Saturday mornings beginning the first of next month. . . . ②

① The writer begins with her most important point: the course is safe. Then, she supports this point with details.

② The writer should double-check these facts for accuracy.

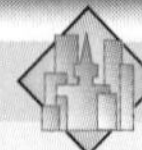

Beyond the Classroom

Workplace Skills

Writing Proposals Tell students that the ability to write persuasively is important in many jobs. Explain that in several careers, people have to write a formal proposal, letter, or memo persuading someone to take a certain course of action. Ask students to suggest reasons why a company might prefer to have a written proposal for a new project, rather than simply having a discussion about it. Elicit responses such as the following: *Companies might prefer written proposals because they are easy to copy and distribute to a large number of people. Also, in a written proposal, the ideas are clearly outlined and easy to follow and remember. A company can refer back to a written proposal to check facts and to make sure that details are accurate.*

Prewriting

Choose Your Topic The topic of your letter should be something that really matters to you. Get your ideas into focus by completing this sentence: "I want to persuade _______ to __________." For example, you might want to persuade a friend to support a worthy cause, or convince an employer to offer you a job. If you'd like, consider these ideas:

Topic Ideas

Young people should/should not

- Get a driver's license at 15
- Wear a uniform to school
- Eat a vegetarian diet

Conduct Research Look for support beyond your own ideas. At the library, check nonfiction books, encyclopedias, magazine articles, CD-ROM references, and the Internet. Double-check your facts by consulting at least two sources.

Prepare Counterarguments To strengthen your letter, be aware of arguments against your position, and decide how to address them. Use a chart like the one below to jot down arguments for both sides.

Rock Climbing

Pros	Cons
Rock climbing builds	It can be dangerous.
strength and stamina.	
Learning rock climbing	A class might be
will build confidence.	expensive.

Drafting

Write a Strong Beginning Even if you save your most powerful argument for the end of your letter, begin in a way that will really grab your readers' attention. Consider using a snappy statistic, an emotional appeal, a question, or a strong statement.

Keep to a Planned Organization Whether you decide to begin with your strongest argument or build up to a grand finale, be sure your arguments follow the pattern you decide.

DRAFTING/REVISING

APPLYING LANGUAGE SKILLS: Friendly Letter Format

Follow these pointers when you write a friendly letter.

- Use correct state abbreviations.
- Use a comma after the greeting.
- Begin the closing with a capital letter and follow it with a comma.

A friendly letter includes these five parts:

Heading	48 Plains Road Harrison, TX 74040
Greeting	Dear Mr. Backman,
Body	I would like to go to the Art Museum on our field trip.
Closing	Your student,
Signature	Sam Scribner

Practice Write these parts of a friendly letter correctly.

1. dover Ohio 44622
2. sincerely yours
3. dear michelle

Writing Application In your friendly letter, follow the proper format.

Writer's Solution Connection Writing Lab

To help you follow the proper format, draft your letter in the Letter Shell in the tutorial on Expression.

Develop Student Writing

Prewriting

Encourage students to take into consideration the person to whom they are addressing the letter. If they are writing a letter to a friend, for example, they may be able to predict the friend's counterarguments. On the other hand, if they are writing a letter to someone they don't know, they should make sure to keep the letter formal and respectful.

Customize for
Less Proficient Writers

Students may get more from their research if they work together. Have students discuss their topics with the class and pair up students who have chosen similar topics. You may want to have one student represent the "pro" side and the other student represent the "con" side. When doing research, encourage students to take notes on points that counter their argument, as well as on points that support their argument.

Writer's Solution

Writing Lab CD-ROM

Students can use an interactive chart in the Prewriting section of the tutorial on Persuasion to explore the difference between facts and opinions. In addition, have them use the Pros and Cons Chart activity to learn to distinguish opposing positions.

Drafting

Tell students that they should clearly identify their letter's purpose in their introduction. In addition, students should decide if they need to introduce themselves to the person to whom they are writing. Give them this example of a letter written to a senator about the speed limit. The first sentence might be: "I am a concerned citizen of New York and I am writing to you because I think the speed limit should be lowered."

Applying Language Skills

Friendly Letter Format Provide students with different example of closings and greetings. Tell them that if they don't have the name of a specific person to address, they can use the general greeting *To Whom It May Concern.* Some variations on closings include *Respectfully yours,* and *Sincerely.*

Answers

1. Dover, OH 44622
2. Sincerely yours,
3. Dear Michelle,

Writer's Solution

For additional instruction and practice have students use the practice pages on Writing Different Kinds of Letters in the *Writer's Solution Grammar Practice Book,* pp. 142–143.

Revising

Remind reviewers that their job is not to argue against the position in the letter but to tell the writer if his or her argument is convincing. Encourage students to suggest additional evidence if they are familiar with the topic.

Writer's Solution

Writing Lab CD-ROM

In the tutorial on Persuasion, have students use a question-and-answer form to create a Peer-Evaluation Checklist.

Publishing

In addition to mailing the letter or making it a speech, students can swap letters with classmates. Have students respond to the letters they have received, using the techniques they have learned.

Applying Language Skills

Formal and Informal Language

You may want to have students read their writing aloud to help them determine how formal or informal their language sounds. Remind students to remain consistent with the type of language they use in their letters.

Answers

Possible responses:

1. View the program at 7 o'clock tonight.
2. This rule is an impediment.
3. Why didn't you write back?

EDITING/PROOFREADING

APPLYING LANGUAGE SKILLS: Formal and Informal Language

The language in your writing should depend on your audience and purpose. When you use **formal language,** you write in full sentences, follow all rules of grammar, and avoid slang. Use formal language for serious letters to people you do not know. **Informal language** sounds like speech—relaxed and casual. Use it with friends and family.

Formal:

Please consider me for the position of lifeguard. I am well qualified and dependable.

Informal:

I'd love to land the lifeguard job.

Practice On your paper, make the formal sentences informal—and vice versa.

1. Check out the show at 7.
2. This rule is such a drag.
3. I hereby protest that you did not return my note.

Writing Application In your persuasive letter, use the language that best suits your audience and purpose.

Writer's Solution Connection
Language Lab

For additional instruction and practice, see the unit on Composing.

Revising

Listen to Your Letter Ask a classmate to read your letter aloud to you. You may hear something that you missed with your eyes. When your classmate has finished reading, ask questions such as these:

- Which of my reasons was strongest? Weakest?
- Did I offer enough evidence to convince you of my argument?
- Can you think of any way a reader could disagree?

Revise according to the feedback you receive.

Check Your Facts Check all the facts, quotations, and statistics you used in your letter. Make sure they are accurate and that they support your position directly and clearly.

REVISION MODEL

Since I know I'll want to pursue rock climbing when I get older, I think taking this class now ① , in the safety of a gymnasium, will help give me the knowledge I'll need. The instructor has ~~two~~ ② five years of climbing experience, including climbs at Glacier National Park and Yosemite.

① *The writer adds more details to convince an anxious reader.*

② *To be completely accurate, the writer corrects a fact.*

Publishing and Presenting

Make It a Speech Deliver your letter as a speech to the class. Use the tone of your voice, gestures, and even visual aids or props as added persuasive details.

Mail It Hand deliver, mail, or send your letter via computer e-mail. Ask for a reply, to see if your persuasion worked.

✓ ASSESSMENT		4	3	2	1
PORTFOLIO ASSESSMENT Use the rubric on Persuasion in the **Alternative Assessment** booklet, p. 92, to assess students' writing. Add these criteria to customize this rubric to this assignment.	**Friendly Letter Format**	The letter includes the five parts of a friendly letter; each part is punctuated correctly.	The letter includes the five parts of a friendly letter; there are a few punctuation errors.	The letter does not include all the parts of a friendly letter; there are punctuation errors.	The assignment is not written in letter form; there are punctuation errors.
	Organization	The letter is logically organized and all counter-arguments are addressed.	The letter is generally easy to follow and most counterarguments are addressed.	The letter is hard to follow at times and the argument is hard to distinguish.	The letter is poorly organized and provides no basis for argument.

Real-World Reading Skills Workshop

Recognizing Bias

Strategies for Success

When a writer's personal opinions come through in a story or news report, he or she is revealing a *bias*. Certain types of writers—reporters, for instance—are supposed to be objective. They are expected to stick to the facts and keep their personal opinions out of their writing. Recognizing bias while you read will help you sort out fact from opinion.

Watch for Loaded Words Loaded words do more than just state the facts. They reveal the writer's personal opinion. For instance, one sports reporter may write about a "losing pitcher," while another describes the same athlete as a "sloppy losing pitcher." The word *sloppy* is a loaded word that shows the writer's bias.

Look Out for Stereotypes Stereotypes label an entire group as being a certain way without looking at the different members of that group. For instance, a writer who reports that "men are reckless drivers" creates a stereotype about male drivers. If the writer had done more research, he or she might have learned that some men—and some women—drive recklessly, but not all. Stereotypes like this one reveal bias.

Be Aware of One-Sided Arguments Bias is also revealed when a writer presents only one side of an argument. For instance, a reporter who reports only the views of one political candidate presents a one-sided argument. The reader does not get the whole story.

Apply the Strategies

Read the newspaper article on this page. Then, answer the questions that follow.

1. Do you see any loaded words in the article? List them.
2. Has the writer created a stereotype? Explain.
3. Did the writer present any one-sided arguments? If so, what might be the other side of that argument?

Skateboard Madness

On Saturday, the warm spring weather brought out crowds of inconsiderate kids with skateboards. Wild skateboarders clogged sidewalks and made walking difficult. The town should allow skateboarding only in parks and playgrounds.

✔ *Here are other places to be on the lookout for bias:*

- A letter written to a newspaper's editorial page
- A candidate's speech about an opponent
- A hometown sports report about a rival team
- An eyewitness account of an automobile accident

Introduce the Strategies

Discuss with students the kinds of writing that are biased, such as editorials, critiques, and advertising. Point out that recognizing bias will allow students to make more informed decisions. Recognizing bias means distinguishing between fact and opinion.

Customize for
Less Proficient Readers
Remind students that when reading critically, they should keep in mind the intention of the author. Does the author want the reader to do something—such as buy an item, vote for a certain person, or believe in an idea? These are cases where the writing can be—and usually is—biased.

Apply the Strategies

Share with students that one way to determine bias is to try to summarize the information given, to strip it down to the bare facts. Once the information is summarized, it is easier to see whether loaded words have been used.

Answers

1. inconsiderate, wild, clogged
2. The writer creates a stereotype by labeling the skateboarders as "wild" and "inconsiderate."
3. The writer says that skateboarding should be allowed only in parks and playgrounds. The other side of this argument is that maybe the parks and playgrounds are too crowded to have room for the skateboarders, or that many kids use their skateboards for transportation as well as recreation.

◆Build Grammar Skills

Reviewing Adjectives

The selections in Part I include instruction on the following:

- Adjectives
- Placement of Adjectives
- Possessive Adjectives

This instruction is reinforced with the Build Grammar Skills practice pages in **Selection Support,** pp. 74, 80, and 87.

As you review adjectives you may wish to discuss the following:

- **Articles (adjectives)** Three adjectives—*a, an,* and *the*—are called articles. *The* is called a *definite article* because it refers to a specific noun. *A* and *an* are called *indefinite articles* because they refer to any one of a class of nouns.
- **Nouns Used as Adjectives** A noun used as an adjective answers the question *What kind?* or *Which one?* about a noun that follows it.
- **Proper Adjectives** A proper adjective is a proper noun used as an adjective, or an adjective formed from a proper noun.

Writer's Solution

For additional practice and support using adjectives, use the practice pages on adjectives, pp. 15–19, in the *Writer's Solution Grammar Practice Book.*

Adjectives

Grammar Review

An **adjective** is a word that modifies or describes a noun or a pronoun. (See page 205.) By answering the questions *what kind, which one, how many, how much,* and *whose,* adjectives make the words they modify more vivid and precise.

Placement of Adjectives An adjective may come before the word it modifies or after a linking verb, modifying the subject. (See page 220.)

Position	Example
Before the Word It Modifies	The *graceful* swan glided by.
After a Linking Verb	The swan was *graceful.*

Possessive Adjectives The personal pronouns *my, your, his, her, its, our,* and *their* modify nouns and tell *whose.* These pronouns are sometimes called **possessive adjectives.** (See page 236.)

His speech was inspiring.

Practice 1 Copy these sentences. Underline each adjective, and draw an arrow to the word it modifies.

1. His wish was for a beautiful and gentle wife.
2. The snow-capped mountains are beautiful but dangerous.
3. Many climbers have lost their lives while attempting to scale the rugged peaks.
4. The brigade was brave but outnumbered.
5. Some of the courageous men who fought with Henry V lived to tell their grandchildren about the fierce battle.

Practice 2 Rewrite the following paragraph, putting adjectives into the blanks.

__?__ people think that the __?__ way to discover what really matters is to engage in activities that push your __?__ and __?__ abilities to the limit. Such activities can be risky, even __?__. However, by paying attention to safety and taking __?__ precautions, you can avoid taking __?__ risks.

Grammar in Writing

✔ *Some adjectives have been overused to the point where they are empty, or meaningless. Empty adjectives—nice, cute, special, awful, and interesting, to name a few—do little to make meanings stronger or clearer. When revising, replace empty adjectives with precise adjectives.*

Answers

Practice 1

1. His modifies *wish;* beautiful and gentle modify *wife*
2. *snow-capped, beautiful, dangerous* modify *mountains*
3. *many* modifies *climbers; their* modifies *lives; rugged* modifies *peaks*
4. *brave* and *outnumbered* modify *brigade*
5. *courageous* modifies *men; their* modifies *grandchildren; fierce* modifies *battle*

Practice 2

Sample response:

Some people think that the best way to discover what really matters is to engage in activities that push your physical and mental abilities to the limit. Such activities can be risky, even dangerous. However, by paying attention to safety and taking appropriate precautions, you can avoid taking foolish risks.

PART 2 *Moments of Insight*

The Voice, 1930, Agnes Pelton, Collection of the Jonson Gallery of the University of New Mexico Art Museum, Albuquerque

One-Minute Planning Guide

The selections in this section explore moments of insight as their theme. With a surprise ending, "The Californian's Tale" follows the narrator's journey to a moment of insight about a strange situation he encounters. Grouped with this short story, the lyrics to "On My Own" from *Les Misérables* offer a lyrical insight and "Valediction" a poetic insight. In "Stopping by Woods on a Snowy Evening," the speaker experiences a gentle moment of insight in nature. The narrator of "Four Skinny Trees" finds a moment of insight related to nature in a city setting. In "Miracles," the speaker finds moments of insight—miracles—in everyday life.

Customize for *Varying Students Needs*

When assigning the selections in this section to your students, keep in mind the following factors:

"The Californian's Tale"
- A short story with a surprise ending
- Mark Twain's classic storytelling style

"On My Own"
- Song lyrics

"Valediction"
- A poem by a Nobel Prize-winning writer

"Stopping by Woods on a Snowy Evening"
- Well-known poem
- Accessible poetic description

"Four Skinny Trees"
- A short prose piece

"Miracles"
- A positive outlook on what the world has to offer

Humanities: Art

The Voice, 1930, by Agnes Pelton

Agnes Pelton (1881–1961) was known as a pioneer in American abstract art. She lived in Greenwich Village in the 1910's where she experimented with progressive art. That led to her exhibition in the 1913 Armory Show, the first major exhibition of modern art in the United States. In 1921, she moved to the Hayground windmill in Water Mill, New York, and began painting portraits of summer visitors. In 1932, she moved to California and began painting abstract images influenced by the desert scenery. She is known for using bright colors and complicated shapes to capture the essence of nature within an abstraction.

Help students connect the art to the theme of Part 2, "Moments of Insight," by answering the following questions:

1. What does the shape in the painting remind you of? *Students may say the shape looks like a flower or a plant.*
2. How can studying the abstract design of this painting cause a moment of insight? *Students may say that because the painting is abstract, it allows the viewer to see in it more than a straight image.*
3. What types of visual images do you think depict moments of insight? *Students may suggest flashes of light or bursts of color.*

Prepare and Engage

OBJECTIVES

1. To read, comprehend, and interpret a short story and a poem
2. To relate a short story and a poem to personal experience
3. To summarize parts of a story and a poem
4. To explore local color in a story
5. To build vocabulary in context and learn the suffix *-ify*
6. To identify adverbs
7. To write a character sketch
8. To respond to a short story and a poem through writing, speaking and listening, and projects

SKILLS INSTRUCTION

Vocabulary: Suffixes: *-ify*

Spelling: Words With a Silent *l*

Grammar: Adverbs

Reading Strategy: Summarize

Literary Focus: Local Color

Writing: Specific Examples

Speaking and Listening: Public Reading (Teacher Edition)

Critical Viewing: Draw Conclusions; Connect

PORTFOLIO OPPORTUNITIES

Writing: Journal Entry; Letter Home; Behavior Analysis

Writing Mini-Lesson: Character Sketch

Speaking and Listening: Public Reading; Dramatization

Projects: Portrait of a Lady; Multimedia Presentation

More About the Authors

Mark Twain first used his pen name in 1863 to sign an amusing travel account. As a boy, Samuel Langhorne Clemens was a name synonymous with trouble, not unlike that of his famous literary character, Tom Sawyer. He was known for such antics as putting snakes in his aunt's sewing basket and dropping a watermelon shell on his brother's head. When he was 11 years old, his father died and Twain went to work in print shops and newspaper offices—always carrying a book along with him.

Seamus Heaney was the oldest of nine children who grew up on a farm in County Derry, Ireland. In addition to poetry, he writes nonfiction. Some of his essays examine poets he admires, such as Gerard Manley Hopkins and Robert Lowell.

Guide for Reading

Meet the Authors:

Mark Twain (1835–1910)

In his youth, Mark Twain worked as a Mississippi riverboat pilot before heading west to prospect for gold. He never struck it rich through gold, but Twain's experiences in the camps gave him the raw material for success in writing. Soon, he was penning humorous reports for a local newspaper. He was on his way to becoming one of America's most popular storytellers.

The Story Behind the Story

Because Twain loved meeting colorful characters and studying the way that people fool even themselves, life in the prospectors' camps provided him with the material to make great stories. You'll see both these elements at work in "The Californian's Tale."

Seamus Heaney (1939–)

Seamus Heaney is one of Ireland's most beloved contemporary poets. Much of his early work focuses on everyday life in the Irish countryside where he was born. His most recent poetry deals with Irish history, culture, and politics.

Nobel Prize Winner

Heaney has won numerous awards and honors, including the 1995 Nobel Prize for Literature.

◆ Literature and Your Life

Connect Your Experience

Open a school yearbook, and you'll see rows of smiling young faces. In truth, you know little of the lives that go with the faces. As you read Twain's tale and Heaney's poem, remember that behind every picture lies a story—but it's not necessarily the story you imagine.

Thematic Focus: Moments of Insight

In "The Californian's Tale," the narrator tries to piece together a strange situation. As you read, you may reach a moment of insight before he does.

◆ Background for Understanding

History

The California Gold Rush of 1849 brought thousands to California, eager to strike it rich. Often, men left wives and family behind to make their fortunes. They lived in terrible conditions. In the first year of the Gold Rush, nearly 10,000 died. There were few women present to nurse the sick, prepare healthy food, and keep a home. No wonder the prospector in this story saw a woman's presence as a treasure worth more than gold!

◆ Build Vocabulary

Suffixes: *-ify*

The narrator of "The Californian's Tale" seeks to *gratify* his host by admiring various objects in his house. *Gratify* means "to please." The suffix *-ify* indicates that *gratify* is a verb.

Word Bank

Which of these words from the selections do you think might mean "those who came before"? What in the word suggests "before"? Check the Build Vocabulary boxes to see if you are correct.

balmy
predecessors
humiliation
abundant
desolation
furtive
gratify
apprehensions

Prentice Hall Literature Program Resources

REINFORCE / RETEACH / EXTEND

Selection Support Pages
Build Vocabulary: Suffixes: *-ify,* p. 90
Build Spelling Skills, p. 91
Build Grammar Skills: Adverbs, p. 92
Literary Focus: Local Color, p. 94
Reading Strategy: Summarize, p. 93

Strategies for Diverse Student Needs, p. 33

Beyond Literature Cultural Connection, p. 17

Formal Assessment Selection Test, pp. 71–73, Assessment Resources Software

Alternative Assessment, p. 17

Writing and Language Transparencies
Sunburst Graphic Organizer, p. 94; Cluster Organizer, p. 82

Resource Pro CD-ROM "The Californian's Tale"; "Valediction"

Listening to Literature Audiocassettes "The Californian's Tale"; "Valediction"

Looking at Literature Videodisc/Videotape "The Californian's Tale"

The Californian's Tale ◆ Valediction

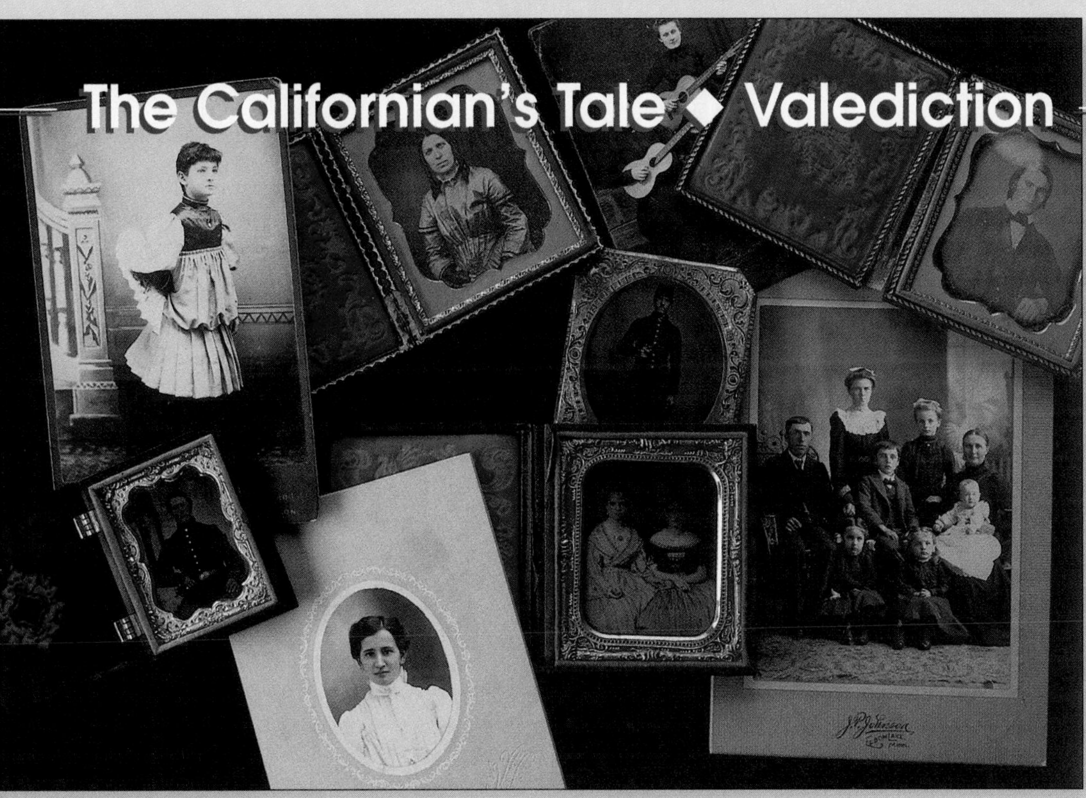

◆ Literary Focus

Local Color

Local color, the use of detail specific to a region, adds authenticity to a story. To help readers see the mining camp of his story, Twain includes descriptions of the people, places, and customs of these makeshift towns. For example, Twain provides these details of the cabins: "dirt floor, never-made beds, tin plates and cups, bacon and beans and black coffee, and nothing of ornament but war pictures . . . tacked to the log walls."

As you read, keep a chart like the one below to note details of local color that bring "The Californian's Tale" to life.

◆ Reading Strategy

Summarize

If you want to describe a story to someone who hasn't read it or a movie to someone who hasn't seen it, you'd probably do so by summarizing. When you **summarize,** you state briefly in your own words the main points and key details of the action. If you summarize as you read by stopping after each paragraph, page, or episode to note key events, you will improve your understanding of the story.

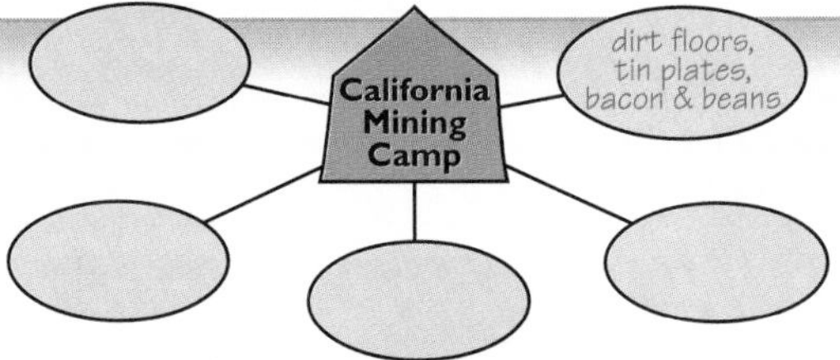

Display a magazine photo of a country-style home and ask students to speculate about the owner of the home. Then add a photograph of a woman and ask students to imagine that she owns the home in the picture. Ask students to use both photos to help describe the woman: who she is, how old she is, what she does for a living, where she lives, what her family is like, and so on. To introduce the selection, tell students that the narrator of the story is a gold prospector who tells the strange story of a man he met in California who lives in a lovely, well-cared-for home in a gold mining town. The narrator is shown a photograph of the man's young wife and slowly learns the truth about her.

◆ Build Grammar Skills

Adverbs If you wish to introduce the grammar concept for this selection before students read, refer to the instruction on p. 254.

Customize for *Less Proficient Readers*

"The Californian's Tale" contains many details that lead up to the surprise ending. To help students better understand the events, suggest that they make a timeline chart as they read.

- **Wednesday**: Narrator visits Henry
- **Thursday**: Tom visits and reads letter
- **Friday**: Joe visits and reads letter
- **Saturday**: Wife expected home; Charley arrives to read letter; Tom and Joe arrive to decorate for a welcome-home party; Henry falls asleep, he's put to bed; Narrator learns truth about Henry's wife

Customize for *More Advanced Students*

Point out to students that "The Californian's Tale" is told from a first-person point of view. Challenge students to speculate about what might happen to the narrator after the story's ending. Suggest that students write another chapter to the story.

Preparing for Standardized Tests

Reading Summarizing, the Reading Strategy taught with this selection, is a skill often tested in critical-reading sections of standardized tests. To help students practice applying their ability to summarize to a standardized test format, present and discuss the following sample question after students have finished reading:

At the end, the narrator finally realizes that

(A) Henry cannot stay up late.
(B) mining can be risky.
(C) mail service is unreliable.
(D) the wife has been dead for years.

Students should determine which choice best completes the summarizing statement in light of all the details of the story. The best answer is *(D)*.

As an extension activity, have groups of students construct their own standardized test questions by pulling paragraphs from the story and preparing a series of multiple-choice answers summarizing the paragraph they've chosen. For more practice, use Reading Strategy: Summarize in **Selection Support,** p. 93.

Develop Understanding

One-Minute Insight The story's narrator is a gold prospector who meets a man named Henry in a nearly deserted gold mining town. The narrator is deeply impressed by the well-cared-for comforts of Henry's cabin, which he attributes to his young wife. Henry invites the narrator to stay with him until Saturday, when his wife will be returning from a family visit. As Saturday approaches, the narrator meets Henry's neighbors, who plan a welcoming party. The narrator discovers, however, that Henry's wife is never coming home and that the neighbors help him maintain a false sense of hope that she will come back. The story conveys the message that it is sometimes less painful to mislead someone than to force them to face the truth.

◆Literary Focus

❶ **Local Color** Have students continue to fill in the chart introduced on p. 245. They should look for details in the opening paragraph of the selection about the nearly deserted areas that which were once booming mine towns filled with people, homes, and businesses.

Clarification

❷ Tuttletown is a town in Tuolumne County, California. Named after Anson A. H. Tuttle, who built the first log cabin there in 1858, the town started as a camp for gold prospectors who found rich claims in nearby Mormon Gulch. Twain stayed nearby during the winter of 1864–1865.

▶Critical Viewing◀

❸ **Draw Conclusions** Based on the people's attire, students may conclude that life in a mining camp is rugged, and that those in the camps faced cold weather.

Customize for
English Language Learners
Twain's use of local color and choice of words may be challenging for students. You may want to read the story aloud, stopping to explain and paraphrase difficult phrases or unusual word choices. For example, the phrase "be to them thenceforth as one dead" might be restated as "from then on, they'll think he's dead."

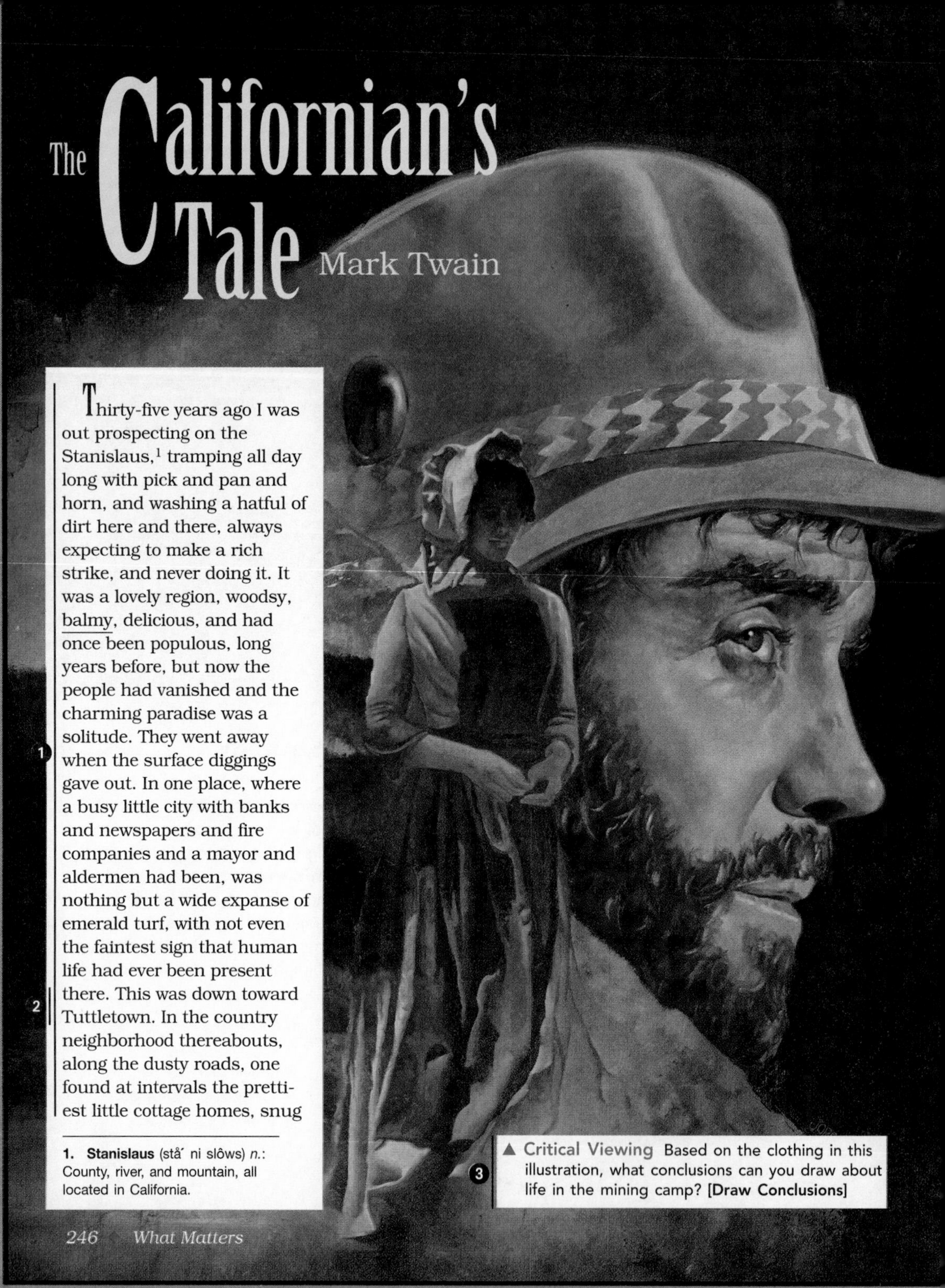

The Californian's Tale

Mark Twain

Thirty-five years ago I was out prospecting on the Stanislaus,[1] tramping all day long with pick and pan and horn, and washing a hatful of dirt here and there, always expecting to make a rich strike, and never doing it. It was a lovely region, woodsy, balmy, delicious, and had once been populous, long years before, but now the people had vanished and the charming paradise was a solitude. They went away
1 when the surface diggings gave out. In one place, where a busy little city with banks and newspapers and fire companies and a mayor and aldermen had been, was nothing but a wide expanse of emerald turf, with not even the faintest sign that human life had ever been present
2 there. This was down toward Tuttletown. In the country neighborhood thereabouts, along the dusty roads, one found at intervals the prettiest little cottage homes, snug

1. **Stanislaus** (stä́ ni slôws) *n.*: County, river, and mountain, all located in California.

3 ▲ Critical Viewing Based on the clothing in this illustration, what conclusions can you draw about life in the mining camp? **[Draw Conclusions]**

Block Scheduling Strategies

Consider these suggestions to take advantage of extended class time:

- To preserve the surprise ending element of the selection, suggest that students read the entire selection without stopping. Before students begin reading, introduce the story using Background for Understanding, p. 244.
- Introduce the Reading Strategy, p. 245, and ask students to fill out the main events/details charts after they read. Then have them form groups and answer the Reading Strategy questions, p. 254.
- Have students answer the Guide for Responding questions, p. 253. Then have them work in groups to complete the Beyond Literature activity, p. 251, or the Multimedia Presentation from the Idea Bank, p. 255.
- Devote class time to the Writing Mini-Lesson, p. 255, focusing on the key steps of the writing process. If students have access to technology, have them work in pairs on the tutorial on Description in the *Writer's Solution Writing Lab CD-ROM* to complete their sketches.

and cozy, and so cobwebbed with vines snowed thick with roses that the doors and windows were wholly hidden from sight—sign that these were deserted homes, forsaken years ago by defeated and disappointed families who could neither sell them nor give them away. Now and then, half an hour apart, one came across solitary log cabins of the earliest mining days, built by the first gold-miners, the predecessors of the cottage-builders. In some few cases these cabins were still occupied; and when this was so, you could depend upon it that the occupant was the very pioneer who had built the cabin;
4 and you could depend on another thing, too—that he was there because he had once had his opportunity to go home to the States rich, and had not done it; had rather lost his wealth, and had then in his humiliation resolved to sever all communication with his home relatives and friends, and be to them thenceforth as one dead. Round about California in that day were scattered a host of these living dead men—pride-smitten poor fellows, grizzled and old at forty, whose secret thoughts were made all of regrets and longings—regrets for their wasted lives, and longings to be out of the struggle and done with it all.

It was a lonesome land! Not a sound in all those peaceful expanses of grass and woods but the drowsy hum of insects; no glimpse of man or beast; nothing to keep up your spirits and make you glad to be alive. And so, at last, in the early part of the afternoon, when I caught sight of a human creature, I felt a most grateful uplift. This person was a man about forty-five years old, and he was standing at the gate of one of those cozy little rose-clad cottages of the sort already referred to. However, this one hadn't a deserted look; it had the look of being lived in and petted and cared for and looked after; and so had its front yard, which was a garden
5 of flowers, abundant, gay, and flourishing. I was invited in, of course, and required to make myself at home—it was the custom of the country.

◆ **Reading Strategy**
Summarize the narrator's main reasons for liking the cottage so much.

It was delightful to be in such a place, after long weeks of daily and nightly familiarity with miners' cabins—with all which this implies of dirt floor, never-made beds, tin plates and cups, bacon and beans and black coffee, and nothing of ornament but war pictures from the Eastern illustrated papers tacked to the log walls. That was all hard, cheerless, materialistic desolation, but here was a nest which had aspects to rest the tired eye and refresh that something in one's nature which, after long fasting, recognizes, when confronted by the belongings of art, howsoever cheap and modest they may be, that it has unconsciously been famishing and now has found nourishment. I could not have believed that a rag carpet could feast me so, and so content me; or that there could be such solace to the soul in wall-paper and framed lithographs,[2] and bright-colored tidies[3] and lamp-mats, and Windsor chairs,[4] and varnished what-nots, with sea-shells and books and china vases on them, and the score of little unclassifiable tricks and touches that a woman's hand distributes about a home, which one sees without knowing he sees them, yet would miss in a moment if they were taken away. The delight that was in my heart showed in my face, and the man saw it and was pleased; saw it so plainly that he answered it as if it had been spoken.

"All her work," he said, caressingly; "she did it all herself—every bit," and he took the room in with a glance which was full of affectionate

---

2. **lithographs** (lith´ ə grafs´) *n.*: Type of print.
3. **tidies** (tid´ ēz) *n.*: Ornamental chair coverings that protect the back, armrests, and headrest.
4. **Windsor chairs** (win´ zər) *n.*: Wooden chairs popular in the 18th century. They had spreading legs, a back of spindles, and usually a saddle seat.

◆ Build Vocabulary

balmy (bäm´ ē) *adj.*: Soothing; mild; pleasant
predecessors (pred´ ə ses´ ərz) *n.*: Those who came before
humiliation (hyo͞o mil´ ē ā´ shən) *n.*: Embarrassment; feeling of hurt pride
abundant (ə bun´ dənt) *adj.*: Plentiful
desolation (des´ ə lā´ shən) *n.*: Loneliness; emptiness; misery

◆Critical Thinking

4 Interpret Ask students to explain what the narrator means by "regrets for their wasted lives, and longings to be out of the struggle and done with it all." Elicit responses such as: *The old miners regret never finding gold and being too proud to return to their families. Now they are older and seem to be waiting to die, to be done with the struggle of life.*

◆Reading Strategy

5 Summarize The narrator is charmed by the cozy, well-cared-for cottage. He is cheered by the flowers and the homey, inviting look of the place after enduring the hardships of a miner's dreary life.

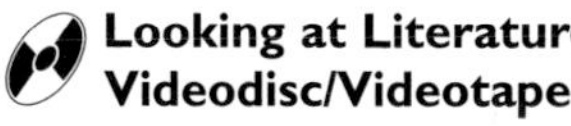

Looking at Literature Videodisc/Videotape

To provide historical background on the California Gold Rush, play Chapter 3 of the videodisc. This segment features historical photos and information on the California forty-niners. Discuss why there were so many towns like the one in Twain's story following the gold rush of the 1840's and 1850's.

Chapter 3

Customize for *Logical/Mathematical Learners*

Students may wish to do research into the value of gold bullion in today's financial market and compare it to the value of gold at the time of the California Gold Rush. To expand the activity, students might study the difference in the cost of living for specific items such as food, clothing, mining supplies, and lodging. Suggest that they compute answers to problems such as: How much gold would a miner have to find each year to pay for supplies? How much gold would a miner have to find to "strike it rich" and go home a wealthy person?

Cross-Curricular Connection: Social Studies

The California gold rush lured thousands to seek fabulous wealth. A California "forty-niner" once said that the gold rush forever changed America. Eager prospectors dropped everything to try to strike it rich. Most prospectors were men in their twenties from the eastern United States, but people came from all over the world to try their luck. Because of the gold rush, California's immigrant population grew to become the largest in America. When all the surface gold had been found, solitary miners lost out at getting rich. Only large-scale mining companies with massive equipment and large numbers of workers had any hope of extracting gold from the hills. Many individual miners gave up and returned to their former lives, or dropped out of sight and lived simply in small cabins in the mountains.

Students may wish to do further research about the California Gold Rush and what happened to the miners and the towns after the gold played out and the rush ended.

◆ Critical Thinking

1 Infer Ask students to attempt to explain why the narrator is so delighted by the room and its furnishings. What does this reveal about the narrator's life? *Students may say the narrator hasn't seen such an inviting and clean room for a long time. The cleanliness and whiteness of the room contrast with the dirty, rugged, and rough conditions found in mining camps. Some students may note that the narrator may be reminded of the home of his childhood.*

◆ Literary Focus

2 Local Color All of the details describing the bedroom develop local color by providing a dramatic contrast to the descriptions of the region in the first several paragraphs.

◆ Build Spelling Skills

3 Silent *l* Draw students' attention to the words *would* and *could.* Guide them to notice that those words, and others like them, such as *chalk* and *should*, have an unpronounced *l*.

Clarification

4 Tell students that a daguerreotype is an early kind of photographic print that was made using a light-sensitive, silver-coated copper plate. The name honors its inventor, the French artist Louis Jacques Mandé Daguerre (1789–1851).

◆ Literature and Your Life

5 Have students share their reaction to the revelation of the age of Henry's wife, the woman in the photograph. Some students may react with surprise, expecting that she would have been older. Others may be aware that women in the past married at much younger ages than they customarily do nowadays.

worship. One of those soft Japanese fabrics with which woman drape with careful negligence the upper part of a picture-frame was out of adjustment. He noticed it, and rearranged it with cautious pains, stepping back several times to gauge the effect before he got it to suit him. Then he gave it a light finishing pat or two with his hand, and said: "She always does that. You can't tell just what it lacks, but it does lack something until you've done that—you can see it yourself after it's done, but that is all you know; you can't find out the law of it. It's like the finishing pats a mother gives the child's hair after she's got it combed and brushed, I reckon. I've seen her fix all these things so much that I can do them all just her way, though I don't know the law of any of them. But she knows the law. She knows the why and the how both; but I don't know the why; I only know the how."

He took me into a bedroom so that I might wash my hands; such a bedroom as I had not seen for years: white counterpane, white pillows,
1 carpeted floor, papered walls, pictures, dressing-table, with mirror and pin-cushion and dainty toilet things; and in the corner
2 a wash-stand, with real china-ware bowl and pitcher,[5] and with soap in a china dish, and on a rack more than a dozen towels—towels too clean and white for one out of practice to use without some vague sense of profanation. So my face spoke again, and he answered with gratified words:

> **◆ Literary Focus**
> What details in this passage develop the local color?

"All her work; she did it all herself—every bit. Nothing here that hasn't felt the touch of her hand. Now you would think—But I mustn't talk so much."

By this time I was wiping my hands and glancing from detail to detail of the room's belongings, as one is apt to do when he is in a new place, where everything he sees is a comfort to his eye and his spirit; and I became conscious, in one of those unaccountable ways, you know, that there was something there somewhere that the man wanted me to discover for myself. I knew it perfectly, and I knew he was trying to help me by furtive indications with his eye, so I tried hard to get on the right track, being eager to gratify him. I failed several times, as I could see out of the corner of my eye without being told; but at last I know I must be looking straight at the thing—knew it from the
pleasure issuing in invisible waves from him. 3
He broke into a happy laugh, and rubbed his hands together, and cried out:

"That's it! You've found it. I knew you would. It's her picture."

I went to the little black-walnut bracket on
the farther wall, and did find there what I had 4
not yet noticed—a daguerreotype-case. It contained the sweetest girlish face, and the most beautiful, as it seemed to me, that I had ever seen. The man drank the admiration from my face, and was fully satisfied.

"Nineteen her last birthday," he said, as he put the picture back; "and that was the day we
were married. When you see her—ah, just wait 5
till you see her!"

"Where is she? When will she be in?"

"Oh, she's away now. She's gone to see her people. They live forty or fifty miles from here. She's been gone two weeks to-day."

"When do you expect her back?"

"This is Wednesday. She'll be back Saturday, in the evening—about nine o'clock, likely."

I felt a sharp sense of disappointment.

"I'm sorry, because I'll be gone by then," I said, regretfully.

"Gone? No—why should you go? Don't go. She'll be so disappointed."

She would be disappointed—that beautiful creature! If she had said the words herself they could hardly have blessed me more. I was feeling a deep, strong longing to see her—a longing so supplicating, so insistent, that it made me afraid. I said to myself: "I will go straight away from this place, for my peace of mind's sake."

"You see, she likes to have people come and

5. **wash-stand, with real china-ware bowl and pitcher:** Items used for washing before sinks and indoor plumbing were available.

◆ Build Vocabulary

furtive (fur′ tiv) *adj.*: Sneaky

gratify (grat′ i fī′) v.: To please

Humanities: Photography

Most people today take photography for granted. Almost anyone can use a simple camera to capture scenic wonders or family events. We expect to see photographs displayed in homes and used as illustrations in the news media. However, photography has existed for fewer than 200 years. Early photography was a laborious and slow process, quite expensive, and thus often available only to the rich. By the time of the Civil War, photography had grown into a medium of journalism, history, art, politics, science, and entertainment.

As an Extension activity, have students examine historical photos. They can browse the Internet, examine art or history books, or scan old family albums for examples to study. Students might compare and contrast old portraits with modern ones, or create family stories based on group shots. Others may analyze old photos for artistic elements such as composition, design, or symbolism. Conclude by creating a photo wall to represent the students' artistic views of a theme, such as loneliness, loss, or surprise.

stop with us—people who know things, and can talk—people like you. She delights in it; for she knows—oh, she knows nearly everything herself, and can talk, oh, like a bird—and the books she reads, why, you would be astonished. Don't go; it's only a little while, you know, and she'll be so disappointed."

I heard the words, but hardly noticed them, I was so deep in my thinkings and strugglings. He left me, but I didn't know. Presently he was back, with the picture-case in his hand, and he held it open before me and said:

"There, now, tell her to her face you could have stayed to see her, and you wouldn't."

That second glimpse broke down my good resolution. I would stay and take the risk. That night we smoked the tranquil pipe, and talked
6 till late about various things, but mainly about her; and certainly I had had no such pleasant and restful time for many a day. The Thursday followed and slipped comfortably away. Toward twilight a big miner from three miles away came—one of the grizzled, stranded pioneers—
and gave us warm salutation, clothed in grave 6
and sober speech. The he said:

"I only just dropped over to ask about the little madam, and when is she coming home. Any news from her?"

"Oh yes, a letter. Would you like to hear it, Tom?"

"Well, I should think I would, if you don't mind, Henry!"

Henry got the letter out of his wallet, and said he would skip some of the private phases, if we were willing; then he went on and read the bulk of it—a loving, sedate, and altogether charming and gracious piece of handiwork, with a postscript full of affectionate regards and messages to Tom, and Joe, and Charley, and other close friends and neighbors.

As the reader finished, he glanced at Tom, and cried out:

"Oho, you're at it again! Take your hands away, and let me see your eyes. You always do that when I read a letter from her. I will write and tell her."

7 ▼ **Critical Viewing** Why would a cabin such as the one pictured here be unusual in the mining camps? **[Connect]**

◆Reading Strategy

6 Summarize Ask students to summarize what happens in this passage. *Students may say that the narrator decides to stay on to meet the wife. He and Henry stay up late talking. On Thursday night, another old miner stops by.*

▶Critical Viewing◀

7 Connect Guide students to realize that a well-tended cabin with flowers would have been unusual to see in a mining camp for a number of reasons. *Students may answer that most miners were so busy prospecting for gold and fabulous wealth that they would not take the time to plant flowers and keep a tidy yard and garden.*

Beyond the Classroom

Career Connection

Home Improvement Henry's wife had worked very hard in "The Californian's Tale" to maintain an attractive and comfortable home. Today, people find careers in home-comfort jobs, such as interior decoration; the design and installation of home lighting, heating, air conditioning, or ventilation systems; cleaning service and maintenance; and landscaping.

Have groups brainstorm for ideas about what makes a home comfortable and inviting, such as adequate space, lighting, ventilation, handicapped ramps, and decoration. Stress to students that each family has different needs and wishes on home improvement decisions.

Then have them think about the jobs required to help residents achieve and maintain a comfortable and attractive home. For example, students may suggest selling, designing, installation, and upkeep. Students can browse through home magazines or talk to interior designers, architects, home furnishings dealers, and others to learn how they assist their customers and what services they offer. Suggest that they look at employment advertisements for possible job openings and needed qualifications, as well as career development resources for information on specific skills and education required for various careers. Encourage students to share their findings with the class.

◆Build Vocabulary

❶ **Suffixes: *-ify*** Point out the word *satisfied.* Explain that, as it is written, this is the past tense of a verb that ends in *-ify*. Challenge students to give the *-ify* form of the verb—*satisfy*.

◆Reading Strategy

❷ **Summarize** Have students summarize the situation at this point in the story, including the narrator's feelings, Henry's mood, and the impact of Charley's arrival. *Possible summary: Henry's uneasy behavior as he waits irritates the narrator, who loses patience and then feels bad for his sharp words. Charley, another old miner, arrives and calms Henry.*

◆ Literary Focus

❸ **Local Color** Students may point to phrases and clauses such as "don't you fret," "as sure as you are born," and "let's get to decorating."

◆Critical Thinking

❹ **Deduce** Ask students to review the narrator's description of the nearly deserted mining town in the first four paragraphs of the story. Given this lonely setting, what guests would be expected to attend a party? *Students may say that the idea of even having a party is odd, since there are few residents—men or women—in the town at all. This may be a good clue that something is not quite "right" about the story.*

Customize for
Musical/Rhythmic Learners

Ask students familiar with stringed instruments to share and explain what kinds of sounds and music a "fiddler" would play and the difference in a fiddle's sound compared with that of a banjo. Students may also enjoy discussing the kinds of music that Henry's friends might have played at the welcome home party. To further extend the activity, students could make a list of the names of songs that the miners might have known and been able to play.

"Oh no, you mustn't, Henry. I am getting old, you know, and any little disappointment makes me want to cry. I thought she'd be here herself, and now you've got only a letter."

"Well, now, what put that in your head? I thought everybody knew she wasn't coming till Saturday."

"Saturday! Why, come to think, I did know it. I wonder what's the matter with me lately? Certainly I knew it. Ain't we all getting ready for her? Well, I must be going now. But I'll be on hand when she comes, old man!"

Late Friday afternoon another gray veteran tramped over from his cabin a mile or so away, and said the boys wanted to have a little gaiety and a good time Saturday night, if Henry thought she wouldn't be too tired after her long journey to be kept up.

"Tired? She tired! Oh, hear the man! Joe, *you* know she'd sit up six weeks to please any one of you!"

When Joe heard that there was a letter, he asked to have it read, and the loving messages in it for him broke the old fellow all up; but he said he was such an old wreck that *that* would happen to him if she only just mentioned his name. "Lord, we miss her so!" he said.

Saturday afternoon I found I was taking out my watch pretty often. Henry noticed it, and said, with a startled look:

"You don't think she ought to be here so soon, do you?"

I felt caught, and a little embarrassed; but I laughed, and said it was a habit of mine when I was in a state of expectancy. But he didn't
❶ seem quite satisfied; and from that time on he began to show uneasiness. Four times he walked me up the road to a point whence we could see a long distance; and there he would stand, shading his eyes with his hand, and looking. Several times he said:

"I'm getting worried, I'm getting right down worried. I know she's not due till about nine o'clock, and yet something seems to be trying to warn me that something's happened. You don't think anything has happened, do you?"

I began to get pretty thoroughly ashamed of
❷ him for his childishness; and at last, when he repeated that imploring question still another time, I lost my patience for the moment, and spoke pretty brutally to him. It seemed to shrivel him up and cow him; and he looked so wounded and so humble after that, that I detested myself for having done the cruel and unnecessary thing. And so I was glad when Charley, another veteran, arrived toward the ❷
edge of the evening, and nestled up to Henry to hear the letter read, and talked over the preparations for the welcome. Charley fetched out one hearty speech after another, and did his best to drive away his friend's bodings and apprehensions.

"Anything *happened* to her? Henry, that's pure nonsense. There isn't anything going to happen to her; just make your mind easy as to that. What did the letter say? Said she was well, didn't it? And said she'd be here by nine o'clock, didn't it? Did you ever know her to fail of her word? Why, you know you never did. Well, then, don't you fret; she'll *be* here, and that's absolutely certain, and as sure as you are born. Come, now, let's get to decorating—not much time left." ❸

> **◆ Literary Focus**
> Which words in the dialogue here help to show local color?

Pretty soon Tom and Joe arrived, and then all hands set about adorning the house with flowers. Toward nine the three miners said that as they had brought their instruments they might as well tune up, for the boys and girls would soon be arriving now, and hungry for a good, old-
fashioned break-down. A fiddle, a banjo, and a ❹
clarinet—these were the instruments. The trio took their places side by side, and began to play some rattling dance-music, and beat time with their big boots.

It was getting very close to nine. Henry was standing in the door with his eyes directed up the road, his body swaying to the torture of his mental distress. He had been made to drink his wife's health and safety several times, and now Tom shouted:

◆ Build Vocabulary

apprehensions (ap′ rē hen′ shənz) *n.*: Fears; anxious feelings

Beyond the Classroom

Community Connection

Social Services Without the help of his loyal friends, Henry's life after the disappearance of his wife could have been much worse. Communities today offer a variety of social services to people who live alone so that they can have more productive and connected lives. For instance, some agencies arrange to deliver meals to house-bound senior citizens. Community centers provide meals and activities for the homeless, after-school programs for children of single parents, or recreation facilities where teenagers and single people can get together in safe environments. Support groups help individuals locate companions, roommates, foster parents, volunteer shoppers, or readers.

Have students investigate the social services available in your area for people who live alone, especially those who cannot get around on their own and who may have no friends or family members nearby to help them.

Some students may wish to find out how to serve as a volunteer or make plans to organize an event, such as a bake sale, to raise money to donate to a support agency.

"All hands stand by! One more drink, and she's here!"

Joe brought the glasses on a waiter, and served the party. I reached for one of the two remaining glasses, but Joe growled, under his breath:

"Drop that! Take the other."

Which I did. Henry was served last. He had hardly swallowed his drink when the clock began to strike. He listened till it finished, his face growing pale and paler; then he said:

"Boys, I am sick with fear. Help me—I want to lie down!"

They helped him to the sofa. He began to nestle and drowse, but presently spoke like one talking in his sleep, and said: "Did I hear horses' feet? Have they come?"

One of the veterans answered, close to his ear: "It was Jimmy Parrish come to say the party got delayed, but they're right up the road a piece, and coming along. Her horse is lame, but she'll be here in half an hour."

"Oh, I'm *so* thankful nothing has happened!"

He was asleep almost before the words were out of his mouth. In a moment those handy men had his clothes off, and had tucked him into his bed in the chamber where I had washed my hands. They closed the door and came back. Then they seemed preparing to leave; but I said: "Please don't go, gentlemen. She won't know me; I am a stranger."

They glanced at each other. Then Joe said:

"She? Poor thing, she's been dead nineteen years!"

"Dead?"

"That or worse. She went to see her folks half a year after she was married, and on her way 5
back, on a Saturday evening, the Indians captured her within five miles of this place, and she's never been heard of since."

"And he lost his mind in consequence?"

"Never has been sane an hour since. But he only gets bad when that time of the year comes round. Then we begin to drop in here, three days before she's due, to encourage him up, and ask if he's heard from her, and Saturday we all come and fix up the house with flowers, and get everything ready for a dance. We've done it every year for nineteen years. The first Saturday there was twenty-seven of us, without 6
counting the girls; there's only three of us now, and the girls are all gone. We drug him to sleep, or he would go wild; then he's all right for another year—thinks she's with him till the last three or four days come round; then he begins to look for her, and gets out his poor old letter, and we come and ask him to read it to us. Lord, she was a darling!"

Beyond Literature

Geography Connection

The Rise of the Gold Rush Towns
"Gold!" The cry rang out across the country. Discovered in 1848 at Sutter's Mill, California, gold—and the chance at immediate wealth—was the reason more than 80,000 people rushed west. Boom towns sprang up overnight, as settlements were founded to support prospecting activities. Dirty and often overcrowded, these towns were composed mostly of men. They were dangerous, lawless places. To create a sense of order, the residents in the towns established small, grassroots democracies. Eventually, the gold would be depleted at each of the sites. With the gold gone, most of the people left, the streets grew bare, and the buildings empty. How do you think it would feel to be the last person living in such a ghost town?

Cross-Curricular Activity
Gold Rush Towns Map Conduct research on the locations of several gold rush towns in the West during the middle of the nineteenth century. Draw a map that shows the locations of these towns. Share your map with the class, and discuss what happened to these towns.

◆Reading Strategy

5 Summarize Ask students to summarize what they have just learned about Henry's marriage, in terms of the amount of time he and his wife had spent together as husband and wife. *Henry has been without his wife far longer than they lived together. She has been gone for nineteen years. They were married only for six months when she went away and never returned.*

◆Literary Focus

6 Surprise Endings Invite students to share their honest reactions to the story's ending. Some may have sensed that there was something "off" about the way Henry spoke about his wife. Some clues Twain gives include Henry's agitation, the narrator's discomfort about meeting the wife, the unusual way the miners show up to ask questions and read the letter, and plans for a party on the night the wife is supposed to return home.

Beyond Literature

Geography Connection

Because photography had been developed by the time of the California Gold Rush, historical photographic images of miners and boom towns exist. Suggest that students locate photographs in books about that period in history. They can also use the Internet. Two helpful sites are California's Gold Rush Country at **http://www.goldrush1849.com** and the Oakland Museum of California's Gold Rush exhibit at **http://www.museumca.org/goldrush.html.** Remember, all Web sites are subject to change. We *strongly recommend* that you preview these sites before you send students to them.

Speaking and Listening Mini-Lesson

Public Reading
This mini-lesson supports the Public Reading activity in the Idea Bank on p. 255.

Introduce Before radio, television, or films, it was a popular entertainment to hear a live performance of a reading or storytelling. As a lecturer and storyteller, Mark Twain was one of the nation's earliest and most popular standup comics.

Develop Humorists like Twain did not just read words in a flat, uninteresting tone of voice. They added dialect and dramatic interpretation to engage and entertain the audience. Discuss how to enliven a public reading:

- Use an appealing tone of voice.
- Make eye contact with the audience members.
- Use gestures.
- Use simple props if appropriate.

Have students select a passage to read aloud and practice before a mirror, or work in pairs to listen to each other practice.

Apply Students can give readings for the entire class or for small groups. You may wish to plan the order of presentations so that the excerpted readings reflect the correct story order.

Assess Evaluate students on how well they use their faces, bodies, and voices to build drama, bring characters or scenes to life, and create overall impressions. Or use the Peer Assessment: Oral Interpretation form, p. 106, in **Alternative Assessment.**

In this poem the speaker yearns for the woman who has left, expressing his inner turmoil and longing in language rich with sea imagery.

Clarification

❶ Have students look up the poem's title in the dictionary. A *valediction* is "something said in parting, or the act of bidding or saying farewell." It may help some students to know this word before they read. Others may be able to determine its meaning after they read the poem.

◆Critical Thinking

❷ **Analyze** Guide students to notice the regular rhyme and rhythm of lines 1–4. Ask them to explain how the mood of the poem changes in lines 5–13 as the rhyme scheme and rhythm of the lines shift. *Students may say that lines 5–13 rock in an unbalanced way, symbolizing the turmoil the speaker feels.*

◆Reading Strategy

❸ **Summarize** Ask students to summarize the final three lines of the poem. *Possible response: The narrator feels that without her presence, he does not know who he is.*

Customize for *Verbal/Linguistic Learners*

Seamus Heaney weaves nautical imagery throughout this poem. Help students appreciate his choice by discussing what deeper meaning "to be at sea" holds (to be lost or bewildered). Help them identify other nautical terms, such as *strand, unmoored, pitched,* and *mutiny*.

❶ Valediction[1]

Seamus Heaney

Lady with the frilled blouse
And simple tartan[2] skirt,
Since you have left the house
Its emptiness has hurt
All thought. In your presence
Time rode easy, anchored
❷ On a smile; but absence
Rocked love's balance, unmoored
The days. They buck and bound
Across the calendar
Pitched from the quiet sound
Of your flowertender
Voice. Need breaks on my strand;
You've gone, I am at sea.
Until you resume command
❸ Self is in mutiny.

1. **valediction** (val′ ə dik′ shən) *n.*: The act of saying farewell.
2. **tartan** (tär′ tən) *n.*: Woolen cloth with plaid pattern, commonly worn in the Scottish Highlands, where each clan has its own plaid.

Guide for Responding

◆ Literature and Your Life

Reader's Response Were you surprised by the ending of "The Californian's Tale," or did you guess what was coming? Explain your response.

Thematic Focus At the end of "The Californian's Tale," the narrator understands the true nature of Henry's situation. How do you think he felt about Henry and the other men once he understood? Explain.

☑ Check Your Comprehension

1. In "The Californian's Tale," what is special about Henry's house?
2. Where does Henry say his wife is?
3. Why do Tom, Joe, and Charley come to Henry's house?
4. What has happened to Henry's wife?
5. Explain the speaker's situation in "Valediction."

◆ Critical Thinking

INTERPRET

1. Why is Henry's cottage so appealing to the narrator in "The Californian's Tale"? **[Analyze]**
2. Henry's wife was just nineteen when she disappeared. What do you think she was like? **[Speculate]**
3. (a) Why do the miners go to such lengths to help Henry? (b) What does their behavior say about their own lives? **[Infer]**
4. What can you infer about the relationship between the speaker and the "Lady with the frilled blouse" in "Valediction"? **[Infer]**

APPLY

5. (a) What does "The Californian's Tale" say about the value of a woman in the home? (b) Explain whether this idea has changed since the time when the story takes place. **[Synthesize]**

COMPARE LITERARY WORKS

6. "The Californian's Tale" and "Valediction" are about men who are at a loss when the women in their lives leave. Compare and contrast the ways in which each man deals with his loss. **[Compare and Contrast]**

Reinforce and Extend

Answers

◆ Literature and Your Life

Reader's Response Students may say that they got hints, so they weren't surprised by the ending.

Thematic Focus The narrator may have felt sorry for Henry and his sadness and glad that the miners were helping him. He admired the friendship the miners gave to Henry.

☑ Check Your Comprehension

1. Henry's house is special because it is so well cared for. In an area where most people have moved away and abandoned their homes because the gold rush days have ended, his house is unusual.
2. Henry explains that his wife has gone to visit her family.
3. The miners come to visit Henry to help him overcome his sadness and to keep him company.
4. She was captured by the Indians and never heard from again.
5. The speaker is at sea because his lady has left.

◆ Critical Thinking

1. The cottage is cozy, homey, and clean. Because he has been living in dirty mining camps, the narrator has not been in such an inviting place for a long time.
2. Possible response: She was young, lively, friendly, and caring.
3. (a) They feel sorry for him, and act as family to him. (b) Their own lives are probably just as lonely and empty as Henry's.
4. The reader can infer a very strong feeling, maybe even love, between the speaker and the "Lady with the frilled blouse."
5. Possible responses: (a) A woman in the home can hold things together, smooth the rough routines of life, and bring comfort to her husband. (b) Today, some women choose not to marry, marry later in life, and work outside the home at their own careers.
6. Possible response: Both men feel lonely. Henry, however, suffers from an inability to accept the reality of his loss. The speaker in "Valediction" is more aware of his pain, and realizes how much the woman's absence changes his life.

Beyond the Selection

FURTHER READING

Other Works by Mark Twain

Life on the Mississippi
The Adventures of Tom Sawyer
Puddn'head Wilson

Other Works by Seamus Heaney

Station Island
Door Into the Dark
Death of a Naturalist

INTERNET

We suggest the following sites on the Internet (all Web sites are subject to change).

For Mark Twain resources:
http://marktwain.miningco.com

For more information about Seamus Heaney:
http://sunsite.unc.edu/dykki/poetry/heaney-cov.html

We *strongly recommend* that you preview the sites before you send students to them.

Answers

◆Reading Strategy

1. The narrator stops by to visit Henry for a short visit and, to the visitor's delight, Henry shows off his lovely home. When the narrator washes up in the bedroom, Henry shows him his beloved wife's picture and invites him to stay until she returns home.
2. The narrator and Henry visit. Henry's miner friends Tom, Joe, and Charley come by and ask about Henry's wife and share his letter. On Saturday, they arrive to decorate for a welcome home party.
3. Saturday evening, Henry becomes more worried and anxious about his wife's late return. His friends play music to entertain him and drug his beverage so that he will eventually fall asleep and not suffer.

◆Build Vocabulary

Using the Suffix *-ify*

1. testify; 2. solidify

Spelling Strategy

1. calm; 2. palms; 3. walked; 4. talking

Using the Word Bank

1. A *furtive* glance is very quick and sneaky.
2. A farmer would be very glad to have an *abundant* or plentiful crop.
3. You might reassure your friend that everything will be okay to calm his or her *apprehensions* and anxiety.
4. The *predecessor* of digital watches are watches with hands to tell time.
5. You would not need mittens on a *balmy,* pleasant night.
6. You might do or say something nice to *gratify* or please your sister.
7. A good way to overcome *humiliation* is to do something that will be praised.
8. You might expect to find *desolation* in a place where people are miserable and lonely.

◆Literary Focus

1. Examples include "nothing of ornament but war pictures...tacked to the log walls"; "never-made beds"; "bacon and beans and black coffee."
2. Examples include "to ask about the little madam"; "they're up the road a piece, and coming along."
3. Possible details include honking taxis, graffiti on the walls, buses, bustling crowds, and tall buildings.

Guide for Responding *(continued)*

◆ Reading Strategy

SUMMARIZE

When you **summarize** as you read, you stop to restate the main events of the action so far. As you do so, it is important to note the key points and important details, but keep your summary short by leaving out any descriptive information.

1. Summarize the events that lead Henry to beg the narrator to stay to meet his wife.
2. Summarize the events that take place between Wednesday and Saturday.
3. Summarize the events of Saturday night.

◆ Build Vocabulary

USING THE SUFFIX *-ify*

The suffix *-ify* indicates that a word is a verb showing action. Use *-ify* to create a verb from the word in italics in each sentence below. Write your answers on a sheet of paper.

1. As a witness, you may be asked to give *testimony* in a trial. Be prepared to __?__.
2. Ice is water in a *solid* state. If you cool water to the freezing point, it will __?__.

SPELLING STRATEGY

In the word *balmy,* the *l* is silent. Fill in the blanks with other common words that include this silent letter.

Though he tried to remain c__?__, Henry was anxious and upset. The p__?__ of his hands were sweaty. He w__?__ to the end of the road and back, t__?__ to himself about his absent wife.

USING THE WORD BANK

Answer these questions. Explain each response.

1. How long might a *furtive* glance take?
2. Would a farmer be happy with an *abundant* crop?
3. How could you calm your friend's *apprehensions?*
4. What was the *predecessor* to digital watches?
5. Would you need mittens on a *balmy* night?
6. What could you do to *gratify* your sister?
7. What is a good way to overcome *humiliation?*
8. Where would you expect to find *desolation?*

◆ Literary Focus

LOCAL COLOR

Mark Twain creates **local color** by providing details specific to the California mining region where his story is set. These details include the look of the landscape, the colorful language of the people who live there, and the style of clothing and furniture.

1. Review the second and third paragraphs of the story to identify three details of local color.
2. Find two examples of unusual language that add to the local color.
3. Name five details of local color you would expect to find if this story were set in a busy city.

◆ Build Grammar Skills

ADVERBS

An **adverb** is a word that modifies or describes a verb, an adjective, or another adverb. Adverbs provide information by answering the questions *how, when, where, how often,* or *to what extent.* Many adverbs end in the suffix *-ly*. Here are examples from "The Californian's Tale":

They went *away. (Where* did they go?)
"All her work," he said *caressingly. (How* did he say it?)
"She *always* does that." *(When* does she do that?)
Certainly I had had no such pleasant time. *(To what extent* had he not had a pleasant time?)

Practice On your paper, identify each adverb and the word it modifies. Tell what question it answers.

1. Doors were wholly hidden from sight.
2. Thursday followed and slipped comfortably away.
3. "Well, I must be going now."
4. He rose hourly to pace the floor.
5. I began to get pretty thoroughly ashamed of him.

Writing Application Write sentences using each of the following adverbs. For each sentence, identify the verb modified.

1. completely
2. unfortunately
3. sadly
4. nearly
5. wisely

◆ Build Grammar Skills

Practice

1. wholly modifies *were hidden* (To what extent?)
2. comfortably (How?) and away (Where?) modify *slipped*
3. now modifies *must be going* (When?)
4. hourly modifies *rose* (How often?)
5. thoroughly modifies *ashamed* (How?) pretty modifies *thoroughly* (How?)

Writing Application

Possible responses:

1. Henry had completely lost his mind.
2. The narrator unfortunately didn't know the whole story.
3. Tom listened sadly to the letter.
4. The miners nearly found gold.
5. Wisely, the miners put Henry to bed.

Writer's Solution

For additional instruction and practice, refer students to the lesson on Using Modifiers in the *Writer's Solution Language Lab CD-ROM* or the practice page on adverbs in the *Writer's Solution Grammar Practice Book,* pp. 20–22.

Build Your Portfolio

Idea Bank

Writing

1. **Journal Entry** Write a journal entry telling about a day in the life of one of Henry's friends, a miner.
2. **Letter Home** Imagine that Henry's wife has spent the last nineteen years living with the Indian tribe that captured her. Write a letter that she might have written to Henry, telling about her life and explaining why she could not return to the mining camp.
3. **Behavior Analysis** The miners in "The Californian's Tale" believe their deception protects Henry. In an essay, defend or criticize their behavior. Refer to "Valediction" if it helps your argument.

Speaking and Listening

4. **Public Reading** Mark Twain was a performer as well as a writer. He toured the country giving public readings from his work. Appearing as Twain, read an excerpt to your class from "The Californian's Tale." **[Performing Arts Link]**
5. **Dramatization [Group Activity]** With a group, dramatize the ending of "The Californian's Tale," beginning with the miners' arrival for the party. Add dialogue to make your scene sound as much like Twain's writing as possible. **[Performing Arts Link]**

Projects

6. **Portrait of a Lady** Draw, paint, or make a collage to convey a portrait of the lady in "Valediction." Place her in a setting suggested by the poet's language. **[Art Link]**
7. **Multimedia Presentation** With a group, create a multimedia presentation about the California Gold Rush. In addition to explaining what you learn from research, use maps, photographs, newspaper reports, music, and diary entries to bring the subject to life. Present your report to the class. **[Social Studies Link; Technology Link]**

Writing Mini-Lesson

Character Sketch

Mark Twain uses actions, dialogue, and descriptive details to paint a word picture of the characters in his story. However, he leaves readers to piece together these elements of his narrator. Write a character sketch of the narrator of "The Californian's Tale," based on details in the text that show what kind of person he is.

Writing Skills Focus: Specific Examples

Bring the character to life by showing **specific examples** of his actions, gestures, and attitudes. Instead of telling that he is a tall man, for example, show him stooping to pass through a doorway. Notice how much Twain conveys about Henry in this description.

Model From the Story

"All her work," he said, caressingly; "she did it all herself—every bit," and he took the room in with a glance which was full of affectionate worship.

Prewriting Review the story, jotting down what you know about the narrator. Where did he come from? Why is he prospecting? How does he walk and talk?

Drafting Show the character in action. Describe how he looked, acted, and talked. End with a statement revealing your impression of him, such as, "He was one of the ___?___est men I'd ever met."

◆ Grammar Application

Look for places where you might add an adverb to explain *where, when,* or *how* action takes place.

Revising Check to see that you include specific examples to show what the character is like. Add more action and dialogue, if necessary, to bring him to life.

Idea Bank

Following are suggestions for matching the Idea Bank topics with your students' performance levels and learning modalities:

Customize for *Performance Levels*

Less Advanced Students: 1, 4, 5, 6
Average Students: 2, 5, 6, 7
More Advanced Students: 3, 7

Customize for *Learning Modalities*

Verbal/Linguistic: 1, 2, 3, 4, 5
Visual/Spatial: 1, 6, 7
Bodily/Kinesthetic: 4, 5, 7
Musical/Rhythmic: 4, 7
Interpersonal: 4, 5, 7
Intrapersonal: 1, 2, 3, 6

Writing Mini-Lesson

Refer students to the Writing Handbook in the back of the book for instructions on the writing process and for further information on description.

Writer's Solution

Writing Lab CD-ROM

Have students complete the tutorial on Description. Follow these steps:

1. Have students create a Cluster Diagram to help them narrow their topic.
2. Allow students to draft on computer.
3. Have students use the Word Bin to replace vague adjectives with more precise words.

Writer's Solution Sourcebook

Have students use Chapter 2, "Description," pp. 32–65, for additional support. The chapter includes in-depth instruction on using modifiers, pp. 60–61.

✓ ASSESSMENT OPTIONS

Formal Assessment, Selection Test, pp. 71–73, and Assessment Resources Software. The selection test is designed so that it can be easily customized to the performance levels of your students.

Alternative Assessment, p. 17, includes options for less advanced students, more advanced students, musical/rhythmic learners, verbal/linguistic learners, visual/spatial learners, and interpersonal learners.

PORTFOLIO ASSESSMENT

Use the following rubrics in the **Alternative Assessment** booklet to assess student writing:
Journal Entry: Fictional Narrative, p. 82
Letter Home: Fictional Narrative, p. 82
Behavior Analysis, Persuasion, p. 92
Writing Mini-Lesson: Description, p. 84

Connections to Today's World

Students may recognize the image on this page as the logo for the musical *Les Misérables*. The illustration shows young Cosette, the waiflike orphan whose life intersects with and influences many events in Victor Hugo's epic novel. The story tells of freedom, love, hate, hope, suffering, determination, idealism, honor, and redemption. In these song lyrics, Eponine, another character of the story, describes loneliness similar to Henry's in "The Californian's Tale."

Enrichment

Victor Hugo (1802–1885) often used a theme of liberty and freedom in his writings that portrayed the sufferings of ordinary people. Because he was an activist at a time of political unrest in France, he lived in exile for almost 20 years. His novel *Les Misérables* is the story of Jean Valjean, an escaped convict, who tries to live a good life in the face of overwhelming odds and great prejudice. The musical based on this novel has achieved enormous success worldwide and has been affectionately dubbed "Les Miz."

Customize for *Musical/Rhythmic Learners*

Obtain a recording of "On My Own" to play for the class. You may wish to have students read the lyrics first and then hear the music, or have them follow along as they listen.

More About the Author

Herbert Kretzmer was born in South Africa but has lived in London since the mid-1950's. For over eighteen years, he was chief drama critic for the London paper *Daily Express*. He spends his time working as a journalist and a songwriter. Song lyrics he has written include those for a BBC television program entitled "That Was the Week That Was," for a West End musical *Our Man Crichton,* and for the play *The Four Musketeers*. He has received both Tony and Grammy awards for his work on the musical *Les Misérables*.

Connections to Today's World

Mark Twain's "The Californian's Tale" and Seamus Heaney's "Valediction" show us that loss and the loneliness it creates can be paralyzing. In fact, such topics have provided rich sources of inspiration through the ages. In 1862, the French writer Victor Hugo wrote *Les Misérables* ("The Miserable Ones"), a gripping novel based on the French riots of 1832. During the 1980's, the book was transformed into a musical play so appealing that it has been translated into at least seven languages. In this song from the musical, the character Eponine sings of her love for the rebel Marius.

from

Les Misérables

On My Own

Alain Bloubil
Herbert Kretzmer
John Caird
Trevor Nunn
Jean-Marc Natel

Humanities: Musical Theatre

Musical theater dates back to the late Middle Ages when musical pieces with accompanying lyrics were interspersed with comedic dialogues. The first known musical is thought to be *Le Jeu de Robin et Marion* by Adam de la Halle in 1283.

In the fifteenth century, Punch and Judy puppet plays were extremely popular but violent musical comedies. It was Mozart's *The Magic Flute* (1791) that became the model for musical theater as we know it today. Musical theater combines the main story elements of a romance, and a mixture of dialogue and song to portray the story.

Some popular musicals of the twentieth century are by Rogers and Hammerstein (*Show Boat, Oklahoma!*) and Andrew Lloyd Webber (*Cats, Phantom of the Opera*). Others include *Annie* by Thomas Meehan, *Hair* by Gerome Ragnit and James Rado, and *Rent* by Jonathan Larson.

Have students, working in groups, select a specific musical to research. Encourage them to find information on the history of the musical, as well as the actual story line. If possible, have them obtain and share pictures, videotape segments, reviews, or recordings of the musical.

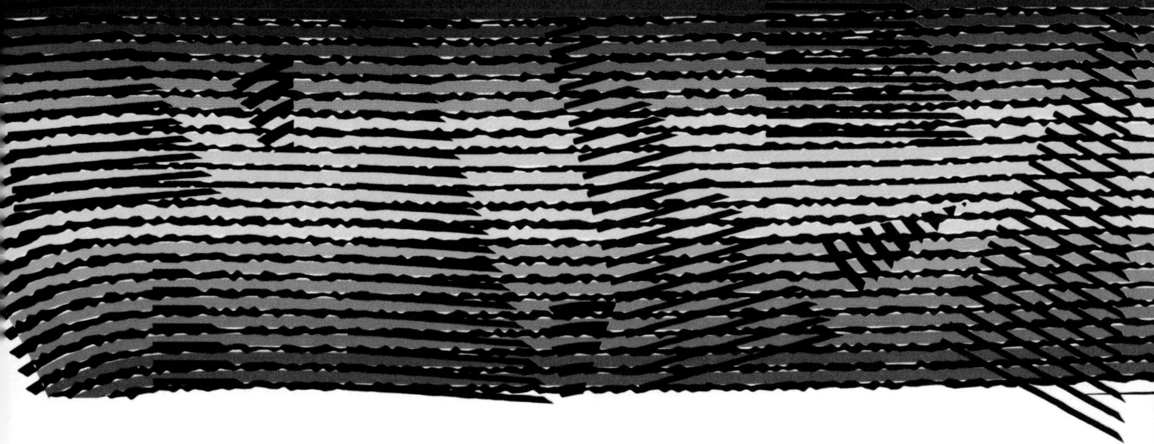

CONNECTIONS TO TODAY'S WORLD

And now I'm all alone again
Nowhere to turn, no one to go to
Without a home, without a friend,
Without a face to say hello to.
And now the night is near
Now I can make believe he's here. ❶

Sometimes I walk alone at night
When everybody else is sleeping
I think of him and then I'm happy
With the company I'm keeping
The city goes to bed
And I can live inside my head.

On my own
Pretending he's beside me
All alone, I walk with him till morning
Without him
I feel his arms around me
And when I lose my way I close my eyes
And he has found me

In the rain the pavement shines like silver
All the lights are misty in the river
In the darkness, the trees are full of starlight
And all I see is him and me for ever and
forever

And I know it's only in my mind
That I'm talking to myself and not to him
And although I know that he is blind
Still I say, there's a way for us

I love him
But when the night is over
He is gone, the river's just a river
Without him the world around me changes
The trees are bare and everywhere
The streets are full of strangers

I love him
But every day I'm learning
All my life I've only been pretending
Without me his world will go on turning ❷
A world that's full of happiness
That I have never known!

I love him
I love him
I love him
But only on my own.

1. What does Eponine do to relieve her loneliness?
2. What lines of the song convey Eponine's "moment of insight"? Explain.
3. Compare and contrast what you know of Eponine in *Les Misérables* and Henry in "The Californian's Tale." In what ways are they similar? In what ways are they different?

◆Reading Strategy

❶ Summarize Ask students to summarize the first two stanzas about Eponine's life. *She is a loner who has no home, and no friends. As she roams the city streets at night, her only companion is her thoughts of her beloved.*

Thematic Focus

❷ Moments of Insight Discuss with students what Eponine is facing in this passage. *She realizes that she has invented her relationship with Marius, that he doesn't notice her, and that no matter how much she wants him to love her, she will never have happiness with him.*

Answers

1. Eponine makes believe that Marius is with her; she thinks of him and then she is happy.
2. Students may cite lines 1–4, 11–14, 24–25, 29–30, or 35–44 as moments of insight.
3. Possible response: Henry and Eponine both mourn loves they cannot have. However, Henry was married, so he and his wife did share their love, if only for a short time. Eponine loves Marius from a distance and has never known his love in return. Henry's loss drives him mad; Eponine's loss is just one more disappointment in her sad life.

Beyond the Selection

FURTHER READING

For More About *Les Misérables*

Les Misérables: History in the Making, Edward Behr
Les Misérables, Abridged Edition, Victor Hugo, Charles Wilbout, James Robinson

For More About Musical Theatre

Making Musicals: An Informal Introduction to the World of Musical Theatre, Tom Jones

INTERNET

We suggest the following site on the Internet (all Web sites are subject to change).

For more information about Herbert Kretzmer and *Les Misérables*:
http://www.lesmis.com

For more information about *Les Misérables* and Victor Hugo:
http://www.rural.escape.ca/wideman/hugo/

We *strongly recommend* that you preview the sites before you send students to them.

Prepare and Engage

OBJECTIVES

1. To read, comprehend, and interpret three poems
2. To relate poems to personal experience
3. To respond to levels of meaning
4. To identify levels of meaning
5. To build vocabulary in context and learn forms of *ferocious*
6. To develop skill in using adverbs to modify adjectives and adverbs
7. To write a poem about your environment using precise words
8. To respond to poetry through writing, speaking and listening, and projects

SKILLS INSTRUCTION

Vocabulary: Related Words: Forms of *ferocious*
Spelling: Using s to Spell a z Sound
Grammar: Adverbs Modifying Adjectives and Adverbs
Reading Strategy: Respond to Levels of Meaning
Literary Focus: Levels of Meaning
Writing: Precise Words
Speaking and Listening: "Sounds of Home" Tape (Teacher Edition)
Critical Viewing: Infer; Connect

PORTFOLIO OPPORTUNITIES

Writing: Reminiscence; Travel Brochure; Letter to the Author

Writing Mini-Lesson: Poem About Your Environment

Speaking and Listening: Weather Commentary; "Sounds of Home" Tape

Projects: A Picture of Miracles; Survey and Chart

More About the Authors

In his poetry, **Robert Frost** illustrates his passion for the details of the world around him. He was an amateur botanist and naturalist with a deep love of nature. This poem first appeared in 1923.

Sandra Cisneros grew up with six brothers. Before becoming a writer, Cisneros taught high school dropouts in the barrios in Chicago.

Walt Whitman attended elementary school in Brooklyn, New York, and spent his summers on Long Island. From 1864 to 1868 he was the editor of the *Brooklyn Daily Eagle,* a popular newspaper at the time. He was fired because of his antislavery views.

Guide for Reading

Meet the Authors:

Robert Frost (1875–1963)

Robert Frost was born in San Francisco but moved to New England when he was only ten. This region would prove to be most inspirational to him. Frost's most popular poetry describes New England country life and landscapes. Of these, "Stopping by Woods on a Snowy Evening" is considered one of his best. Frost won the Pulitzer Prize four times—more than any other poet. [For more information on Frost, see page 752.]

Sandra Cisneros (1954–)

Sandra Cisneros was born and raised in Chicago. Because her parents were born in Mexico, she grew up speaking English and Spanish. She writes both poetry and fiction about subjects she knows best—memories of her childhood and her Mexican heritage. Her feelings about growing up in the city are reflected in "Four Skinny Trees."

Walt Whitman (1819–1892)

Walt Whitman worked at many occupations during his life. He was a printer, carpenter, teacher, and newspaper reporter. Known by many as the father of modern American poetry, Whitman abandoned regular rhythm and rhyme in favor of free verse that followed no set pattern. Because of his unusual style, publishers refused to publish *Leaves of Grass,* his long poem about America. Undiscouraged, Whitman published the first edition himself. [For more information on Whitman, see page 28.]

◆ Literature and Your Life

Connect Your Experience

Whether you live on a farm, in a tree-lined neighborhood, or in a crowded city, where you live probably has a big influence on the way you see the world. In the pieces that follow, Frost, Cisneros, and Whitman describe the settings that surround them and express how these places shape their thoughts and feelings.

Thematic Focus: Moments of Insight

As you read, consider how each unique setting leads a narrator to a moment of insight.

◆ Background for Understanding

Literature

Robert Frost is one of America's best loved poets. Most frequently, Frost sets his work in the stark natural landscape of rural northern New England. This region is known for its natural beauty, harsh winters, and picture-postcard villages. There, isolated from America's bustling cities, Frost's speakers confront difficult and life-changing choices—which road to take, what commitments to honor, how connected each person should be to others.

◆ Build Vocabulary

Related Words: Forms of *ferocious*

Cisneros uses the word *ferocious* to describe trees: "They send ferocious roots beneath the ground." *Ferocious* is an adjective meaning "fierce" or "savage." The noun form *ferocity* refers to the state of being ferocious.

Word Bank

Which of these words from the selections do you think means "as light and fluffy as goose feathers"?

downy
ferocious
exquisite
distinct

Prentice Hall Literature Program Resources

REINFORCE / RETEACH / EXTEND

Selection Support Pages
Build Vocabulary: Related Words: Forms of *ferocious,* p. 95
Build Spelling Skills, p. 96
Build Grammar Skills: Adverbs Modifying Adjectives and Adverbs, p. 97
Reading Strategy: Respond to Levels of Meaning, p. 98
Literary Focus: Levels of Meaning, p. 99

Strategies for Diverse Student Needs, pp. 35–36

Beyond Literature Cross-Curricular Connection: Science, p. 18

Formal Assessment Selection Test, pp. 74–76
Assessment Resources Software

Alternative Assessment, p. 18

Resource Pro CD-RM "Stopping by Woods on a Snowy Evening"; "Four Skinny Trees"; "Miracles"

Listening to Literature Audiocassettes "Stopping by Woods on a Snowy Evening"; "Four Skinny Trees"; "Miracles"

Stopping by Woods on a Snowy Evening
Four Skinny Trees ◆ Miracles

◆ Literary Focus

Levels of Meaning

Many works of literature contain different **levels of meaning.** Beyond the literal meaning —what the words actually say—the work may contain deeper meanings that relate more broadly to life. "Four Skinny Trees," for example, is literally about four trees that grow outside a young woman's home. On a deeper level, it is about how she identifies with these trees. On the deepest level, it is about all young people and their struggle to make a place for themselves. Use a chart like the one below to identify the levels of meaning in these selections.

White Veil, 1909, William L. Metcalf, Museum of Art, Rhode Island School of Design

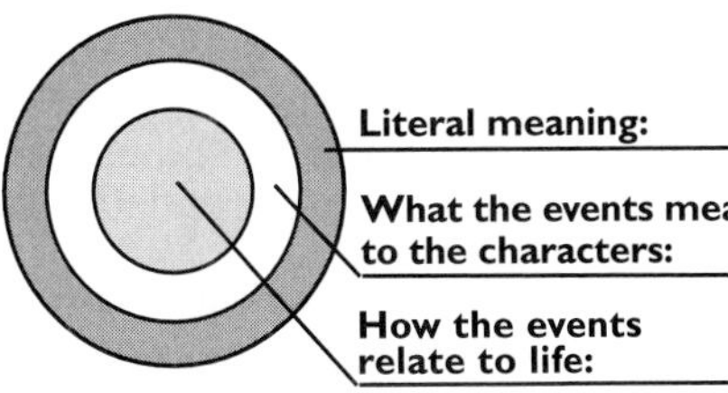

◆ Reading Strategy

Respond to Levels of Meaning

Whenever you read a work of literature, you **respond to each level of meaning** in a personal way. Something the author says—at a literal level or at a deeper level—triggers an emotional response in you. You may relate what the writer says to your own experience. Or you may simply agree or disagree with the message.

As you read these selections, ask yourself how they relate to you personally. What does each writer say that connects to you?

Preparing for Standardized Tests

Reading Critical-reading sections on standardized tests may evaluate students' grasp of levels of meaning—the reading strategy taught with these poems. For instance, an item may ask them to identify a deeper meaning for a literal statement. Use the following sample test question:

The speaker in Walt Whitman's poem "Miracles" says, "Every cubic inch of space is a miracle."

This means that miracles

(A) have a size you can calculate.
(B) are usually spacious.
(C) can be found anywhere.
(D) come in small boxes.

Students who know about levels of meaning will recognize that this is a broad statement about life in general. Although cubic inch is a mathematical measure of volume, the statement is not about the size of miracles *(A)*, nor can miracles be found in boxes *(D)*. The line from the poem uses the word space but doesn't mean that miracles take up space *(B)*. Therefore, the best choice is *(C)*, a deeper restatement of the meaning. For further practice, use Literary Focus: Levels of Meaning in **Selection Support,** p. 99.

Slowly read the following list of words, giving the students time to think carefully about each word and how it relates to the list: soft, feathery, cold, icy, frosty, crunchy, wet, boots, shovel, sled, flakes, winter, and storm. Ask for a show of hands to see how many students were able to determine the topic of the list, which was snow. Have volunteers tell which word gave them the final clue for their correct guess. Ask students to brainstorm additional words they might add to the list. Poets make careful use of vivid words to allow readers to imagine a scene and bring it into clear focus. Explain that the selections explore ideas inspired by the writer's surroundings. Suggest that students pay close attention to the choice of words.

◆ Build Grammar Skills

Adverbs Modifying Adjectives and Adverbs To introduce the grammar concept for this selection before students read, refer to the instruction on p. 264.

Customize for
Less Proficient Readers
It may help students to hear the readings of these selections to grasp how intonation, rhyme, rhythm, and emphasis can help determine meaning or highlight key concepts.

Listening to Literature Audiocassettes

Customize for
More Advanced Students
Each selection benefits from a sound device or structural form that helps advance its meaning. Challenge students to identify the rhyme scheme of the Frost poem, and the instances of repetition in the Cisneros piece and the Whitman poem. Have them think about how each structure supports the writer's message.

Humanities: Art

The White Veil, 1909, by William Metcalf

This painting depicts a country hillside in winter. Have students interpret the title. *Possible answer: the white veil may be the gauzy effect you get looking through snow as it falls.*

Develop Understanding

One-Minute Insight As he is traveling in a horse-drawn sleigh one night, the speaker of "Stopping by Woods on a Snowy Evening" pauses in the woods to watch the snow fall before going on his way. Although he admires the quiet beauty, he is drawn by his obligations to continue on. The poem captures how the the fast pace of life and the obligations that people have can lead them to miss out on opportunities to appreciate the simple beauty of nature.

◆Literary Focus

❶ **Levels of Meaning** After students read the first two stanzas of the poem, have them describe the literal meaning of the lines. Then ask them how the events of the lines relate to life. *Students may say that the speaker and his horse have stopped in the woods to watch the snow falling. This could represent a moment of peace and reflection that one indulges in sometimes.*

Customize for
English Language Learners
Some students may find it easier to understand the poems by trying to form sentences out of the lines. For example, write the first stanza of Frost's poem on the board as a long sentence. Explain that in that line, Frost has inverted the subject. Rework the sentence on the board to begin, "I think I know whose woods these are." Explain to students that techniques like these may help them understand the selections better.

Customize for
Musical/Rhythmic Learners
Read the pieces aloud, or play the audiocassette, so students can appreciate the musical elements of repetition, rhythm, and cadence. Or play a recording of the choral arrangement of the poem from the "Frostiana" song cycle by American composer Randall Thompson.

Encourage students to identify the rhyme scheme of each stanza of Frost's poem as AABA, BBCB, CCDC, DDDD.

Listening to Literature Audiocassettes

Stopping by Woods on a Snowy Evening

Robert Frost

Whose woods these are I think I know.
His house is in the village, though;
He will not see me stopping here
To watch his woods fill up with snow.

❶

My little horse must think it queer
To stop without a farmhouse near
Between the woods and frozen lake
The darkest evening of the year.

He gives his harness bells a shake
To ask if there is some mistake.
The only other sound's the sweep
Of easy wind and downy flake.

The woods are lovely, dark, and deep,
But I have promises to keep,
And miles to go before I sleep,
And miles to go before I sleep.

Block Scheduling Strategies

Consider these suggestions to take advantage of extended class time:

- Introduce the Literary Focus and Reading Strategy on p. 259. Encourage students to read the poems twice, looking for deeper levels of meaning each time they read. Then, form students into groups to complete the Literary Focus and Reading Strategy questions on p. 264.
- Use the Viewing and Representing Mini-Lesson on p. 262 to have students complete the "Sounds of Home" tape in the Idea Bank, p. 265.
- Have students listen to the recordings of poems while they follow along in their books.

Listening to Literature Audiocassettes

- Introduce the grammar concept (adverbs modifying adjectives and adverbs, p. 264). Have them work in pairs to complete the Build Grammar activity. If students have access to computers, allow them to complete the Writing Mini-Lesson using the tutorial on Creative Writing in the *Writer's Solution Writing Lab CD-ROM*.

Four Skinny Trees

Sandra Cisneros

They are the only ones who understand me. I am the only one who understands them. Four skinny trees with skinny necks and pointy elbows
2 like mine. Four who do not belong here but are here. Four raggedy excuses planted by the city. From our room we can hear them, but Nenny just sleeps and doesn't appreciate these things.

Their strength is secret. They send ferocious roots beneath the ground. They grow up and they grow down and grab the earth between their hairy toes and bite the sky with violent teeth and never quit their anger. This is how they keep.

Let one forget his reason for being, they'd all droop like tulips in a glass, each with their arms around the other. Keep, keep, keep, trees say when I sleep. They teach.

When I am too sad and too skinny to keep keeping, when I am a tiny thing against so many bricks, then it is I look at trees. When there is
3 nothing left to look at on this street. Four who grew despite concrete. Four who reach and do not forget to reach. Four whose only reason is to be and be.

◆ Build Vocabulary

downy (doun´ ē) *adj.*: Soft and fluffy

ferocious (fə rō´ shəs) *adj.*: Fierce; savage

◀ Critical Viewing What emotions does a wintry scene like the one pictured here bring out in the speaker of "Stopping by Woods . . ."? **[Infer]**

Guide for Responding

◆ Literature and Your Life

Reader's Response Which selection more closely reflects the setting where you live? Explain.

Thematic Focus How do the physical settings of the selections contribute to each narrator's insights into life?

☑ Check Your Comprehension

1. Describe the setting—both the time and the place—of "Stopping by Woods . . . ."
2. Why has the speaker in "Stopping by Woods . . ." stopped here?
3. Where are the "Four Skinny Trees" described in this selection?
4. What physical characteristics do the trees and the speaker share?

◆ Critical Thinking

Interpret

1. "Stopping by Woods on a Snowy Evening" takes place on "The darkest evening of the year." How does this description affect the meaning of the poem? **[Connect]**
2. What comment about life is Frost making when he writes, "But I have promises to keep, /And miles to go before I sleep"? **[Draw Conclusions]**
3. In "Four Skinny Trees," the speaker says that she can "hear" the trees from her room. What does this reveal about her relationship with the trees? **[Infer]**
4. (a) According to "Four Skinny Trees," what lessons can the trees teach? (b) Who can learn these lessons? **[Generalize]**

Evaluate

5. Do you think the speaker in "Stopping by Woods . . ." honors his promises? Explain. **[Deduce]**

Compare Literary Works

6. Compare and contrast the role of nature in these two selections. **[Compare and Contrast]**

One-Minute Insight

The speaker of "Four Skinny Trees," a young girl living in a city neighborhood, feels isolated and misunderstood. She identifies with the four scrawny trees that grow outside her window in an unlikely, inhospitable environment, and looks to them for strength and inspiration in her own life.

◆ Literary Focus

2 Levels of Meaning Ask students what different levels of meaning they can identify in this passage. *On a literal level, the speaker describes the four skinny trees outside her window. On a deeper level, she expresses her connection with the four skinny trees that she feels are as out of place in the city as she is. On the deepest level, she says that, like the trees, she is unnoticed and unappreciated.*

Thematic Focus

3 Moments of Insight How do the trees give the poet insight into who she is? *Possible response: She feels like the trees—out of place and awkward. By seeing how the trees manage to live and grow despite all odds, she is inspired to keep trying herself.*

Customize for *English Language Learners*

Figurative language, sentence fragments, and unidentified antecedents in "Four Skinny Trees" may challenge students acquiring English. Help them break down the piece to understand its meaning. For instance, identify "They" as the trees by the speaker's room. Rephrase lines like "keep keeping" as "keep on going."

Reinforce and Extend

Answers

◆ Literature and Your Life

Reader's Response Urban students may identify with the Cisneros piece; suburban or rural students may feel more response to the Frost poem.

Thematic Focus Frost uses the peace of the winter night as a moment to reflect on his own life and duties; Cisneros compares herself with trees struggling to grow in an unnatural environment.

☑ Check Your Comprehension

1. It is the evening of a dark winter day deep in the snowy, quiet woods.
2. He wants to watch the snow fall and appreciate the quiet beauty.
3. They grow outside the speaker's window in a city neighborhood.
4. The speaker and the trees are both skinny and ragged.

◆ Critical Thinking

1. Possible response: It suggests bleakness, emptiness, or despair.
2. Life is too complex and busy to allow time for simple pleasures.
3. She feels so close to them that she believes they can communicate with her.
4. (a) Trees can teach persistence, strength, and hope. (b) Anyone who notices how hard the trees work to grow and live in a hostile environment can learn a lesson.
5. His actions in the poem suggest that he does honor his commitments.
6. Trees comfort the speakers in both pieces. In the Frost poem, the woods offer peace and beauty; in the other piece, the trees are models of strength and determination.

In "Miracles," the speaker exuberantly expresses his belief that all life is miraculous, listing examples of miracles that he finds in common events.

◆Critical Thinking

1 Connect Whitman begins this poem with a question. Ask students to react to this opening. Is it effective? Why? *Students may say that the question makes them want to read on to learn the answer; it draws them into a "conversation" with the speaker.*

◆Reading Strategy

2 Infer Have students reread lines 15–16. Then ask them what the speaker means by "the whole referring, yet each distinct . . ." *Possible response: Each example he lists above refers to the whole of life, yet each example is in itself a different and unique part of life.*

◆Literature and Your Life

3 Invite students to add their own examples of miracles to Whitman's list. *Sample responses: icicles on a tree, a rainbow after a storm, flowers blooming, leaves crunching underfoot, looking out the car window, or playing soccer with friends.*

◆Reading Strategy

4 Respond to Levels of Meaning Ask students whether they agree with the last line "What stranger miracles are there?" *Some students may agree with Whitman, while others may say stranger miracles exist and Whitman asked the question to make them think.*

Miracles

Walt Whitman

Why, who makes much of a miracle?
As to me I know of nothing else but miracles,
Whether I walk the streets of Manhattan,
Or dart my sight over the roofs of houses toward the sky,
Or wade with naked feet along the beach just in the edge of the water,
Or stand under trees in the woods,
Or talk by day with any one I love . . .
Or sit at table at dinner with the rest.
Or look at strangers opposite me riding in the car,
Or watch honeybees busy around the hive of a summer forenoon[1]
Or animals feeding in the fields,
Or birds, or the wonderfulness of insects in the air,
Or the wonderfulness of the sundown, or of stars shining so quiet and bright,
Or the exquisite delicate thin curve of the new moon in spring;
These with the rest, one and all, are to me miracles,
The whole referring, yet each distinct and in its place.

To me every hour of the light and dark is a miracle,
Every cubic inch of space is a miracle,
Every square yard of the surface of the earth is spread with the same,
Every foot of the interior swarms[2] with the same.

To me the sea is a continual miracle,
The fishes that swim—the rocks—the motion of the waves—
  the ships with men in them,
What stranger miracles are there?

1. **forenoon** (fôr′ no͞on′) *n.*: Morning.
2. **swarms** (swôrmz) *v.*: Is filled or crowded.

◆ Build Vocabulary

exquisite (eks kwi′ zit) *adj.*: Very beautiful, especially in a delicate way

distinct (di stiŋkt′) *adj.*: Separate and different

Viewing and Representing Mini-Lesson

"Sounds of Home" Tape

This mini-lesson supports and extends the Speaking and Listening activity on p. 265 to include a visual representation.

Introduce The sounds heard in everyday life are different in various locations and areas of the country. Point out to students that a honking horn brings to mind a very different environment than chirping crickets.

Develop Have students brainstorm for ideas of sounds that are typical of the environment in which they live. They may choose to list the sounds found in the school, their home, the streets, or their neighborhoods. Establish groups of students to work together based on their interests.

Apply Have students work with their group to audiotape the sounds they have chosen. As they work together, have the students set goals for their group and decide how they would like to represent their sounds. They may choose to form a collage of art materials that portray the sounds, or assemble photographs that illustrate the sounds. Some students may wish to set their sounds with a musical background, or even to perform a dance or movement as an illustration.

Assess Invite students to play their "Sounds of Home" audiotape for the class and then display or perform their representations of the audiotape. Have class members identify the sounds each group taped and discuss how the group chose to represent the sounds. Evaluate students based on the goals each group set and whether they were able to achieve what they were trying to represent.

La Bonne Aventure (Good Fortune), 1939, René Magritte, Museum Boymans-van Beuningen, Rotterdam

5 ▶ Critical Viewing Identify a line in the poem that relates to this painting. Explain your choice. **[Connect]**

Guide for Responding

◆ Literature and Your Life

Reader's Response Name something in your environment that is a miracle to you.

Thematic Focus How does the speaker's attitude reflect a moment of insight?

Journal Writing The speaker says that every experience is a miracle. In your journal, discuss the way this attitude could change the way you live.

☑ Check Your Comprehension

1. Which people does the speaker consider to be miracles?
2. List five of the physical settings, or places, mentioned in the poem.
3. Name four events that Whitman calls miracles.

◆ Critical Thinking

Interpret

1. "Miracles" begins and ends with a question. What impact does this have on you? **[Connect]**
2. In what way is the sea a "continual miracle"? **[Infer]**
3. How does your definition of "miracle" contrast with the speaker's definition? **[Compare and Contrast]**

Evaluate

4. From what you know about the speaker in "Miracles," do you think he is a contented person? Explain. **[Evaluate]**

Apply

5. Do you think that people today see the world around them as full of miracles? Explain. **[Relate]**

Beyond the Selection

FURTHER READING

Other Works by the Authors

Collected Poems of Robert Frost
The House on Mango Street, Sandra Cisneros
Leaves of Grass, Walt Whitman

Other Works on the Theme of What Matters

The Space Between Our Footsteps, Naomi Shahib Nye (ed.)
Learning to Live in the World, William Stafford et al.
Earth-Shattering Poems, Liz Rosenberg

INTERNET

We suggest the following sites on the Internet (all Web sites are subject to change).

To see a virtual exhibit of Robert Frost materials, including part of the poem in the poet's own handwriting: **http://www.lib.virginia.edu/exhibits/frost/english.html**

For links to many Walt Whitman Web sites: **http://www.oz.net/wlbbooks/wwic/WWICmenu.html**

We *strongly recommend* that you preview these sites before you send students to them.

▶Critical Viewing◀

5 Connect Students may identify line 13 and 14 because of the poetic details about sundown and the curve of the new moon.

Reinforce and Extend

Answers

◆Literature and Your Life

Reader's Response Possible response: my cat, a swamp, a garden, a skyscraper.

Thematic Focus Students may say recognizing miracles makes a person understand what is most important.

☑ Check Your Comprehension

1. Anyone he loves, his companions, and strangers.
2. Possible responses: Manhattan, the beach, the woods, in a train, near a beehive.
3. Possible responses: wading on the beach, standing under trees, talking to people, watching bees.

◆Critical Thinking

1. By asking and ending with direct questions, the poet involves readers in what he is writing.
2. It's never still; its tides constantly move in and out.
3. Students may feel that a miracle is something that cannot be explained; others may agree with the speaker who sees miracles in all aspects of life.
4. Students may say that the speaker is a contented person because he finds so much in the world around him that pleases him and brings deep joy and satisfaction.
5. Students may say that people who are accustomed to special effects and scientific advances may not see the world as full of miracles.

Humanities: Art

La Bonne Aventure (Good Fortune), 1939, by René Magritte

Magritte (1898–1967) is renowned for his surrealistic style. In his paintings, ordinary subjects appear in unusual combinations that often create an air of mystery or absurdity. Discuss what is unusual about the combination of details in the painting. *The moon and stars are in front of the house rather than above it in the sky.*

Answers

◆Literary Focus

1. Possible response: (a) He might have stopped because his horse is tired, he is tired himself and needs a rest, and the woods make him feel a sense of peace. But then he realizes it is not time for him to stop and sleep yet. (b) The events remind him of his responsibilities and obligations. (c) People everywhere need to stop and rest to renew themselves even though they have many duties and responsibilities ahead of them.
2. (a) The speaker in "Miracles" lists many miracles and wonderful occurences in life. (b) This literal list reminds the speaker that he is constantly surrounded by miracles. (c) People everywhere need to recognize and appreciate the miracles that surround them in their everyday life and to be content.

◆Build Vocabulary

Using Forms of *ferocious*

1. ferociously; 2. ferocious; 3. ferocity

Spelling Strategy

1. desert; 2. noise; 3. compose

Using the Word Bank

1. (c) fluffy; 2. (b) fierce; 3. (b) beautiful; 4. (a) separate

◆Reading Strategy

1. Students' answers will vary depending on which selection they identified with.
2. Students might note that they understand a selection better each time they read it because they become more familiar with the ideas it contains.

◆Build Grammar Skills

Practice

1. extremely modifies the adjective *popular*
2. quite modifies the adjective *lonely*
3. carefully modifies the verb *read;* very modifies the adverb *carefully*
4. never modifies the verb *happen*; almost modifies the adverb *never*
5. rather modifies the adverb *eloquently*; eloquently modifies the verb *write*

Guide for Responding *(continued)*

◆ Literary Focus

Levels of Meaning

Each of these selections has several **levels of meaning.** The literal meaning consists simply of the details and events in each work. Another level of meaning can be found in the insights that the characters have as a result of the events in each work. On the deepest level, the events lead readers to a general understanding of all people or of life.

1. (a) What is the literal meaning of "Stopping By Woods on a Snowy Evening"? (b) Of what do the events of the poem remind the speaker? (c) How can his experience apply to the experiences of people everywhere?

2. (a) What is the literal meaning of "Miracles"? (b) What does the poem's list remind the speaker? (c) How can his feelings and ideas apply to people everywhere?

◆ Build Vocabulary

Using Forms of *ferocious*

Ferocious is an adjective meaning "fierce" or "savage." Related forms of the word express the same meaning as different parts of speech. Use these forms of *ferocious* to complete each sentence.

ferocious ferociously ferocity

1. The roots grew ___?___.

2. The ___?___ roots grew under the concrete.

3. Their ___?___ caused the concrete to crack.

Spelling Strategy

The z sound you hear in *exquisite* is spelled with an s. For each clue below, write a word that uses an s spelling for a z sound.

1. A dry, sandy region: d___?___

2. A loud, disturbing sound: n___?___

3. To create a piece of writing or music: c___?___

Using the Word Bank

On your paper, write the word that best defines the first word.

1. downy: (a) below, (b) crusty, (c) fluffy

2. ferocious: (a) fat, (b) fierce, (c) famous

3. exquisite: (a) small, (b) beautiful, (c) extra

4. distinct: (a) separate, (b) loud, (c) similar

◆ Reading Strategy

Respond to Levels of Meaning

Once you've identified all the **levels of meaning** in a work of literature, decide whether you agree with the message the work sends. Your response may be different from that of your classmates because your experiences, memories, and attitudes are different from one another.

1. For one of these selections, write down two or three lines or passages that moved you or meant something to you. Explain your response.

2. You probably found that the more you read a selection and thought about it, the more it meant to you. What might be some reasons for this?

◆ Build Grammar Skills

Adverbs Modifying Adjectives and Adverbs

Often, **adverbs** modify or describe a verb. They can also modify an adjective or another adverb. The following adverbs are commonly used to modify adjectives and other adverbs: *too, so, very, quite, much, more, rather, usually, almost.* Look at these examples:

Modifying Adjectives: When I am *too* sad and *too* skinny to keep keeping . . . *(How* sad and *how* skinny*?)*

Modifying Adverbs: The snow falls *more* silently in the forest. *(How* silently*?)*

Practice Copy the sentences below. Underline each adverb. Then, identify whether the adverb modifies an adjective, another adverb, or a verb.

1. Frost's poems are extremely popular.

2. Cisneros's piece makes one feel quite lonely.

3. I read Whitman's poem very carefully.

4. Miracles almost never happen to me!

5. The three poets write rather eloquently.

Writing Application Copy the sentences below, adding an adverb to each one.

1. The tree grows slowly. *(How slowly?)*

2. Cisneros lived happily in Chicago. *(How happily?)*

3. That night, he was tired. *(How tired?)*

4. He greets strangers warmly. *(How warmly?)*

5. We walked quickly through the snow. *(How quickly?)*

Writing Application

Possible responses:

1. The tree grows more slowly.
2. Cisneros lived quite happily in Chicago.
3. That night, he was extremely tired.
4. We walked very quickly through the snow.

Writer's Solution

For additional instruction and practice, use the lesson in the *Writer's Solution Language Lab CD-ROM* on Using Modifiers, and the practice pages on adverbs, pp. 20–22 in the *Writer's Solution Grammar Practice Book.*

Build Your Portfolio

Idea Bank

Writing

1. Reminiscence Sandra Cisneros describes an important element of the setting in which she grew up. In a description, explain how a place or a scene holds special meaning for you.

2. Travel Brochure Imagine that you have chosen "Stopping by Woods on a Snowy Evening" and the photograph on page 260 to appear in a travel brochure. Write the text you would include to encourage visitors to travel to New England.

3. Letter to the Author In a letter to the writer, respond to one of the works in this grouping. For example, tell Whitman whether you agree with his philosophy, or explain to Frost whether you might have made the same decision he did. Support your ideas with lines from the work.

Speaking and Listening

4. Weather Commentary Many of nature's "miracles" are observable each day. Others, like rainbows and lunar eclipses, are not quite as common. Give a brief presentation to explain one of nature's usual or unusual miracles. **[Science Link]**

5. "Sounds of Home" Tape [Group Activity] The street scene that Cisneros describes would sound much different from Frost's wintry forest. With a group, collect audio material to convey the environment in which you live. Use an audiotape to record the sounds that are "home" to you and your neighbors. **[Social Studies Link]**

Projects

6. A Picture of Miracles Create a collage of images that reflect what you consider to be miracles. Consider the wonders of nature and those of human creation. **[Art Link]**

7. Survey and Chart Ask friends and neighbors to identify the everyday events that they consider miracles. Chart their responses to create a mathematical response to Whitman's poem. **[Mathematics Link]**

Writing Mini-Lesson

Poem About Your Environment

Imagine that, like Frost, you are stopping to watch something on your way home from school or that, like Cisneros, you are looking out of a window from your room at home. Write a poem about where you are and what you see. As part of your description, tell something about yourself.

Writing Skills Focus: Precise Words

Choose **precise words** to convey exactly what you mean. A well-chosen word can clinch a description or bring a feeling into clear focus. Notice, for example, how Frost chooses a single word to describe the lake and a single word to describe the evening. What do these words tell you about winter at the time the poem is set?

Model From the Poem

My little horse must think it queer
To stop without a farmhouse near
Between the woods and *frozen* lake
The *darkest* evening of the year.

Prewriting Decide where you are. Jot down some descriptive words about the setting and what you see. Then, jot down some words that describe how you feel at this time.

Drafting Write a few lines or verses, sketching out your poem with words or phrases from your list. As you draft, be open to a variety of structures your poem might take. Reread what you have written to develop patterns you want to use.

◆ Grammar Application

Look for places where you can use an adverb to clarify an adjective or another adverb to make a description precise.

Revising Change individual words to describe the environment more accurately. Also, change words, phrases, or lines to suit the patterns of rhyme or rhythm you've chosen.

ASSESSMENT OPTIONS

Formal Assessment, Selection Test, pp. 74–76, and Assessment Resources Software. The Selection Test is designed so that it can be easily customized to the performance levels of your students.

Alternative Assessment, p. 18, includes options for less advanced students, more advanced students, visual/spatial learners, musical/rhythmic learners, logical/mathematcial learners, verbal/linguistic learners, and bodily/kinesthetic learners.

PORTFOLIO ASSESSMENT

Use the following rubrics in the **Alternative Assessment** booklet to assess student writing:
Reminiscence: Narrative Based on Personal Experience, p. 83
Magazine Caption: Description, p. 84
Letter to the Author: Respond to Literature, p. 97
Writing Mini-Lesson: Poetry, p. 95

Idea Bank

Following are suggestions for matching the Idea Bank topics with your students' performance levels and learning modalities:

Customize for *Performance Levels*
Less Advanced Students: 2, 4, 7
Average Students: 1, 4, 5, 6, 7
More Advanced Students: 3, 5, 6

Customize for *Learning Modalities*
Verbal/Linguistic: 1, 2, 3, 6
Visual/Spatial: 2, 6, 7
Bodily/Kinesthetic: 4, 5
Logical/Mathematical: 1, 4, 6
Interpersonal: 6, 7
Intrapersonal: 3, 7

Writing Mini-Lesson

Refer students to the Writing Handbook in the back of the book for instructions on the writing process and for further information on creative writing.

Writer's Solution

Writers at Work Videodisc
Have students view the videodisc segment on Creative Writing (Ch. 8), featuring poet Nikki Giovanni, to learn her views on the importance of using precise, exact words. Have students discuss how she chooses her words carefully to help them write their poems.

Play frames 26472 to 27449

Writing Lab CD-ROM
Have students complete the tutorial on Creative Writing, using these steps:

1. Have students view annotated models of similes and metaphors to help them use figurative language.
2. Let students draft on computer.
3. Encourage students to use the Concrete Image Word Bin to see lists of sensory images.
4. When revising, have students use the Interactive Self-Evaluation Checklist for poetry.

Writer's Solution Sourcebook
Have students use Chapter 8, "Creative Writing," pp. 234–263, for additional support. The chapter includes in-depth instruction on using concrete language, pp. 262–263.

Prepare and Engage

Establish Writing Guidelines
Review the following key characteristics of a how-to essay:

- A how-to essay tells the reader how to do something.
- The essay is organized logically and chronologically for easy understanding.

You may want to distribute the scoring rubric for How-to/Process Explanation, p. 87 in **Alternative Assessment,** to make students aware of the criteria on which they will be evaluated. See the suggestions on p. 268 for how you can customize the rubric to this workshop.

Refer students to the Writing Handbook in the back of the book for instruction on the writing process and further information on expository writing.

 ***Writer's Solution***

Writers at Work Videodisc
To introduce students to the key elements of description and to hear Richard Lederer's thoughts on expository writing, play the videodisc segment on Exposition: Giving Information (Ch. 4). Have students discuss how Lederer chooses and organizes information for his first draft.

Play frames 31956 to 41222

Writing Lab CD-ROM
If your students have access to computers, you may want to have them work in the tutorial on Exposition: Giving Information to complete all or part of their how-to essays. Follow these steps:

1. Suggest that students use Inspirations for expository writing to explore possible topics.
2. Have students use the Cluster Diagram activity to help them choose and organize details.
3. Students can also draft on the computer.
4. When revising, have students use the revision checker for unity and coherence.

Writer's Solution Sourcebook
Students can find additional support, including instruction on using exact nouns and building paragraphs, in the chapter on Exposition: Giving Information (pp. 103–133).

Expository Writing

How-to Essay

Writing Process Workshop

How do you ride a unicycle? What are the skills in juggling? Are there rules for decorating a room? **How-to essays** answer questions like these. A how-to essay is a written, step-by-step explanation of a process.

Choose a process that you enjoy—perhaps inspired by a selection from this unit—and write a how-to essay that will help readers perform the process, even if it's something they've never done before. The following skills, covered in the Writing Mini-Lessons, will help you write an effective how-to essay.

Writing Skills Focus

▶ **Give specific examples** to help readers understand each step in the process. (See p. 255.)

▶ **Use precise words** to make your essay clear and easy to follow. (See p. 265.)

▶ **Present the steps in the order in which they occur.** Also, don't forget the important details of each step.

Inspired by descriptions in "The Californian's Tale," this writer is working on a how-to essay about decorating a bedroom. Notice how she uses the skills mentioned above.

Model

When preparing to paper your walls, your first step is to choose a color. ① You can visit hardware stores, paint stores, or even some department stores. ② You have a few decisions to make. Decide whether you want a glossy or a flat finish, a textured or smooth paper, or a large or small pattern. Most stores that sell wallpaper will give you samples to take home. Tape these up in the room you'll be decorating. Then, look at the patterns from various distances. ③

① The word *first* indicates the order in which to perform the steps.

② The writer includes three specific examples of places to research wallpaper.

③ Precise words like *glossy* and *flat* help readers decide how to proceed.

 **Beyond the Classroom**

Career Connection

Technical Writer Tell students that one career in which knowing how to write an effective how-to essay is crucial is that of a technical writer. These writers take subjects and write about them in simpler terms so readers can easily grasp the information. Most technical writers work in a specific industry and must not only be proficient writers, but also know or study the industry itself.

Technical writers may create pamphlets or brochures explaining how to operate a piece of equipment, or how to install a computer program. Industries that use technical writers vary greatly and include such areas as banking and finance, electronics, pharmaceuticals, and manufacturing. Have students write a brief how-to essay on how to work a home appliance. Have them pick an appliance with which they are familiar, such as a VCR, microwave, or dishwasher. Then have them create a step-by-step guide on how to operate that equipment. Encourage volunteers to read their instructions in class. Then discuss whether the writer has included all the necessary steps and details.

Prewriting

Brainstorm With a Partner With a classmate, list activities you know well. Look for activities that readers will find useful or interesting. Together, go over your list, and choose the topics you like best. Consider the skills on this list:

Topic Ideas

- How to wrap a gift
- How to play a sport or game
- How to get ready for school in fifteen minutes flat
- How to sing in harmony

Gather Information Conduct some research before you write. Find books or magazines on your topic, or interview an expert. In your notes, jot down specific information and vocabulary that will help readers follow your essay.

List the Steps Write out the steps in your process in the order in which they occur. Using a Chain-of-Events Organizer like the one below will help you make sure that you haven't left anything out.

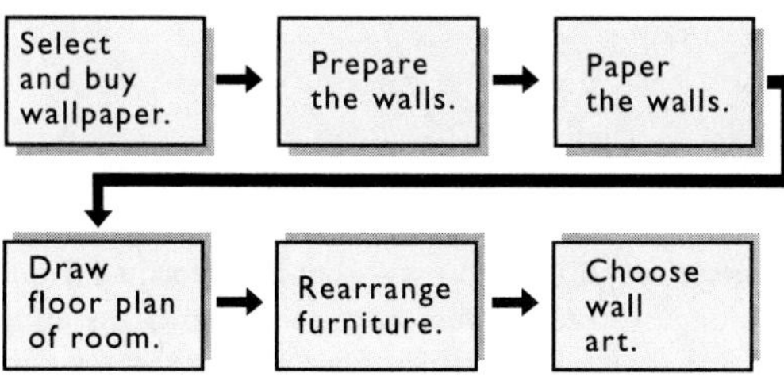

Drafting

Add a Diagram To help readers follow your explanation, create a drawing or diagram. Include any necessary labels or captions, and refer to the diagram in your essay.

Keep Your Essay Organized Imagine that you are writing for someone who has never done what you're describing. Use clear steps that proceed in the correct order. You may want to make each step a separate paragraph. As you draft, use language that is clear and concrete.

DRAFTING/REVISING

Applying Language Skills: Using Time Transitions

Since sequencing is critical to a step-by-step process, use time transitions to clarify the order of events. Time transitions are words that show chronological order or the passage of time. They include words such as *first, during, later, next, after, then,* and *finally* as well as phrases such as *in about an hour* or *when the dough begins to rise*. Time transitions will guide your readers smoothly through the steps of the process you are describing.

Practice On your paper, add time transitions to clarify meaning in this paragraph about in-line skating.

> Put on your skates. Put on your protective gear. Take it slow and easy. Get comfortable stopping. Go a little faster. Practice. You're skating like a pro!

Writing Application As you write your how-to essay, make sure each step is introduced by a clear time transition.

Writer's Solution Connection
Writing Lab

For more examples of time transitions, use the Transition Word Bin in the tutorial on Exposition.

Develop Student Writing

Prewriting

If students are having trouble coming up with a topic, suggest that they flip through popular magazines for ideas. Most magazines have how-to sections or tips for making an activity easier.

Customize for
Visual/Spatial Learners
Students may want to create a diagram as the first step in writing their draft. Then, once they have the diagram filled in and labeled, they may be able to see more clearly the steps they need to address in their writing.

Customize for
English Language Learners
Students may have difficulty coming up with precise terms to use in their how-to essays. Encourage them to use a thesaurus to come up with alternative words that may be more accurate and precise. Or, review their drafts with them, and point out which words are too vague.

Drafting

Tell students to make sure that their essay includes an introduction that identifies the subject. The body of their essay should include the precise details needed to make the instructions clear.

Writer's Solution

Writing Lab CD-ROM
In the section of the tutorial on Exposition: Giving Information, students can view an interactive writing model of a how-to essay. In addition, students can use the Transitional Word Bin to come up with words to indicate the relationships among their ideas.

Applying Language Skills

Using Time Transitions Explain to students that, when using time transitions, they should remember to vary the ones they use. Also, explain that some transitions are separated from the rest of the sentence with a comma, as in the following example: "When the mixture is smooth, pour it into the bowl."

Answers

Suggested response:
First, put on your skates. *Next,* put on your protective gear. *Begin* by taking it slow and easy. *Then,* get comfortable stopping. *Now,* go a little faster. Practice. *Finally,* you're skating like a pro!

Revising

Encourage peer reviewers to suggest alternative words or phrases that will make the essay more clear. Have them comment on whether the essay includes or needs an introduction to identify the subject.

Writer's Solution

Writing Lab CD-ROM

In the tutorial on Exposition: Giving Information, have students use the proofreading checklist for complete sentences, punctuation, subject-verb agreement, spelling, and capitalization.

Publishing

In addition to a demonstration, or a class anthology, have students swap papers and try to complete the instructions in each other's essays. Then have them discuss with each other any problems they encountered.

Reinforce and Extend

Review the Writing Guidelines

After students have completed their papers, review the characteristics of a how-to essay.

Applying Language Skills

Answers

1. A color that you really like is a good choice for painting your walls.
2. Keep stirring until it boils.
3. When you stand in the box, water may be thrown at you.

Writer's Solution

For additional practice, complete the Basic Sentence lesson in the *Writer's Solution Grammar Practice Book,* p. 28.

EDITING/PROOFREADING

APPLYING LANGUAGE SKILLS: Avoid Sentence Fragments

A **sentence fragment** is a group of words that may look like a sentence but isn't. A fragment is missing a subject, a predicate, or both. Therefore, it does not express a complete thought. Be on the lookout for sentence fragments—and correct them.

Fragment:
About six inches into the dirt.

Complete Sentence:
Dig about six inches into the dirt.

Fragment:
After packing for a vacation.

Complete Sentence:
After packing for a vacation, you'll find the rest is easy!

Practice Rewrite these sentence fragments to make them complete sentences.

1. A color that you really like.
2. Stirring until it boils.
3. When you stand in the box.

Writing Application Proofread your essay to make sure all of your sentences are complete.

Writer's Solution Connection
Language Lab

For additional practice, complete the Sentence Fragments lessons in the Problems With Sentences unit.

Revising

Test It Ask someone who is unfamiliar with your topic to read your essay. Ask questions such as these:

- Do you understand the process?
- Which part was most clear? Most confusing?
- Is the order clear and logical?
- Do you think you could perform the process using this essay as a guide?

Be Precise Review your draft, circling all words that feel general, vague, or abstract. For example, notice how this writer improves her draft by replacing general phrases with specific examples and precise words that make the process more clear.

REVISION MODEL

Before you put up the paper, prepare the walls by spackling ① any holes or cracks. Use a ② putty knife ~~flat edged tool~~ to apply the spackle evenly. Then, sand the area ③ with fine-grit paper.

① The writer added more examples to explain when this step is necessary.
② A more precise phrase replaces a vague description.
③ These words clarify the materials required.

Publishing and Presenting

- **Demonstrate** A how-to essay that is performed live is called a demonstration. Demonstrate your process using props to show how to perform the process step by step. For fun, videotape your demonstration.
- **Make a Class Anthology** Work with your classmates to combine your essays into a booklet called "How to Do Almost Everything." Have someone make a table of contents. Someone else can write an introduction. Display the book in your school or local library, where people can make copies of essays that interest them.

✓ ASSESSMENT

PORTFOLIO ASSESSMENT

Use the rubric on How-to/Process Explanation, p. 87 in the **Alternative Assessment** booklet, to assess the students' writing. Add these criteria to customize this rubric to this assignment.

	4	3	2	1
Using Transitions	The writer consistently uses transitions, including time transitions that clarify the order of events.	The writer generally uses transitions effectively, but the order of events is slightly confusing.	The writer uses transitions sparingly, confusing the order of events.	The writer uses few or no transitions, and the order of events is unclear.
Organization	The essay is logically organized, and all vital information is included.	The essay is logically organized, but some details may have been left out.	The essay is not logically organized, and some vital information has been left out.	The essay shows no signs of organization and lacks vital information.

Real-World Reading Skills Workshop

Following Directions

Strategies for Success

When you build a model airplane, take an exam, or cook a frozen pizza, you need to follow written directions. Directions tell you the steps in a process, as well as the order in which to perform them. If you read directions carefully and follow them exactly, your model, exam, or pizza is likely to come out well. If you misread directions or perform steps in the wrong order, you might end up with a mess instead.

Read Everything First Begin by reading the directions slowly and carefully, without actually performing any of the steps. Be sure that you understand the directions and that you have the tools you need to complete the task. Estimate how long the process will take.

Take a Test Run Now that you understand the process, walk through it in your mind, picturing each step in turn. You may wish to hold tools in your hands as you imagine certain steps. Ask yourself questions like these: What problems am I likely to run into? Might I need assistance?

Follow the Process Exactly Start with the first step and follow through to the last, performing each exactly as directed. Work slowly and carefully. If you come to a step that doesn't make sense, read the directions again. If necessary, ask for help.

Apply the Strategies

You can't get your computer started. Its monitor has gone dark. It isn't making any sounds. Read the directions on this page from a computer trouble-shooting manual. Then, answer the questions.

Computer Trouble-shooting Manual

Chapter 1

If your computer doesn't seem to be working, follow these steps:

Step 1 Make sure the computer is plugged in.

Step 2 Make sure the computer's power switch is turned on.

Step 3 Make sure the monitor's power switch is turned on.

Step 4 Make sure the cable connecting the monitor to the computer is securely attached.

Step 5 If your computer still does not work, call the service hotline.

1. Should you call the service hotline right away?
2. How many switches must be checked?
3. Should you check switches or the monitor cable first?
4. Estimate how long it would take you to perform steps 1 through 3.

✔ *Here are other situations in which you need to follow directions carefully:*

- ▶ Programming a VCR
- ▶ Assembling furniture
- ▶ Loading film into a camera

Introduce the Strategies

Discuss with students on what other types of occasions they would have to know how to follow directions. Ask them if they've ever encountered directions that were confusing. Explain that knowing how to follow directions now will help them conquer not only minor tasks but also major academic tasks such as standardized tests and exams.

Customize for
English Language Learners
Explain to students that many times instructions are accompanied by a drawing or diagram. If students have difficulty understanding a specific term, tell them to look for a diagram, a drawing, or even a glossary that will help them identify the term's meaning or location.

Apply the Strategies

Remind students to read the directions through once before actually performing any of the steps.

Answers

1. No
2. Two
3. Switches
4. Possible reponse: It should take only about a minute or two to complete the first three steps, provided you know where all the switches are.

◆Build Grammar Skills

Reviewing Adverbs
The selections in Part 2 include instruction on the following:

- adverbs
- adverbs modifying adjectives and adverbs

This instruction is reinforced with the Build Grammar Skills practice pages in **Selection Support,** pp. 92 and 97.

As you review adverbs you may wish to review the following:

- Adjective or Adverb? Sometimes, the same word can be either an adverb or an adjective, depending upon how it is used in a sentence. Although many adverbs are formed by adding *-ly* to an adjective, a few words ending in *-ly* are adjectives.

Adjective The miners had a yearly celebration of her birthday.

Adverb They celebrated yearly.

Generally, adverbs and adjectives have different forms. If a word ends in *-ly* it is necessary to determine whether it modifies a verb (adverb) or whether it modifies a noun or a pronoun (adjective).

Writer's Solution

For additional practice and support using adverbs, use the practice pages on adverbs, pp. 20–22 in the *Writer's Solution Grammar Practice Book.*

Answers

Practice 1

1. certainly modifies *was* (verb); quite modifies *harmless* (adjective)
2. easily modifies *passed* (verb)
3. restlessly modifies *shook* (verb); *questioningly* modifies *looked* (verb)
4. strongly, defiantly, there modify *grow* (verb); so modifies *very* (adverb); very modifies *many* (adjective)
5. everywhere modifies *are* (verb); around modifies *look* (verb); really modifies *try* (verb)

Practice 2
Possible response:

Suddenly, all the pieces fall into place, and you finally understand what is really happening. You clearly understand why someone is behaving in a certain way, know what factors actually caused something to happen, or come to grips with your own feelings. Although moments of insight are quite common, they always feel extremely significant. They can strike you anytime, anywhere, and for any reason.

Adverbs — Grammar Review

An **adverb** is a word that modifies, or describes, a verb, an adjective, or another adverb. (See pages 254 and 264.) Adverbs answer the questions *how, when, where, how often,* and *to what extent.*

Question Answered	Examples
Adverb Modifying a Verb	
How?	The snow falls *softly* on the ground.
When?	The snow falls *late* in the day.
Where?	The snow falls *everywhere.*
How often?	Snow *usually* falls by January 1.
To what extent?	The snow *barely* dusts the ground.
Adverb Modifying an Adjective	
To what extent?	The snow is *very* deep.
Adverb Modifying Another Adverb	
To what extent?	The snow is falling *quite* quickly.

Practice 1 Copy these sentences. Underline each adverb, and draw an arrow to the word it modifies. Identify whether the modified word is a verb, an adjective, or an adverb.

1. Henry was certainly unstable, but he was quite harmless.
2. He felt that time passed easily in her presence.
3. The horse shook its harness restlessly and looked at its owner questioningly.
4. The skinny trees grow strongly and defiantly there by the wall that is built of so very many bricks.
5. There are miracles everywhere; look around and really try to see the world's beauty.

aventuros < aventure, ADVENTURE] 1 fond of adv... take chances; daring 2 full of danger; risky —adv. —ad·ven'tur·ous·ness n.
ad·verb (ad'vurb') n. [ME adverbe < L adverbi... verbum, a word] any of a class of words used gene... verb, an adjective, another adverb, a phrase, or a cl... ing time, place, manner, degree, cause, etc.: Engli... end in -ly (Ex.: fast, carefully, then)
ad·ver·bial (ad vur'bē əl, əd-) adj. 1 of an adve... nature or function of an adverb 3 used to form... adverbial suffix] —n. Linguis. a word or... grammatical fu...

Practice 2 Write the following paragraph, putting adverbs into the blanks.

___?___, all the pieces fall into place, and you ___?___ understand what is ___?___ happening. You ___?___ understand why someone is behaving in a certain way, know what factors ___?___ caused something to happen, or come to grips with your own feelings. Although moments of insight are ___?___ common, they ___?___ feel ___?___ significant. They can strike you ___?___, ___?___, and for any reason.

Grammar in Writing

✔ ***Remember to use an adverb, not an adjective, to modify a verb.***

Incorrect: He listened intent to the man's story. (Intent is an adjective.)

Correct: He listened intently to the man's story. (Intently is an adverb modifying *listened.*)

Speaking, Listening, and Viewing Workshop

Active Listening

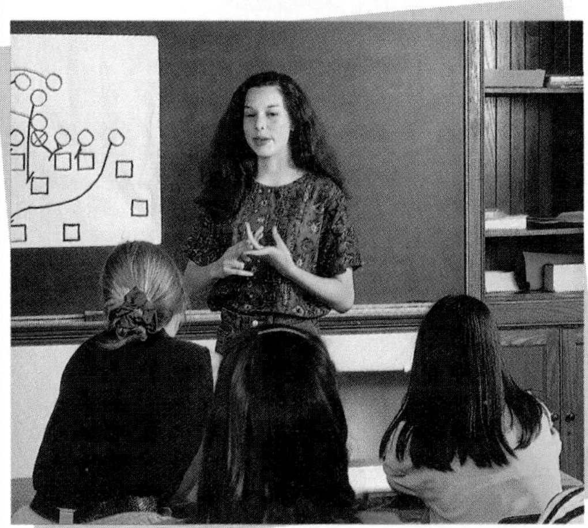

School assemblies, television newscasts, and talk shows are possible opportunities for learning. In fact, you can learn more in class, at home, or while talking with friends if you listen actively. Use these strategies to help you to become an active listener in any listening situation.

Get the Big Picture As you listen, identify the speaker's topic and purpose. Often the speaker will tell you *why* the topic is important to you. Use that information to help you make a connection to the topic.

Add Your Own Knowledge Once you've identified the speaker's focus, consider what you already know about the subject. Make connections between your interests and the topic. These connections will help keep you focused on what you hear.

Notice the Details A good newspaper reporter always looks for the following details: *who? what? when? where? why?* and *how?* Listen carefully for the answers to these questions. They will help you to understand the speaker's main points.

Take Notes Some people actually get more out of listening when they take notes. Organizing the information helps you to see the connections the speaker makes. You may even be less likely to forget important details. However, you don't need to record the speaker's exact words.

Apply the Strategies

These activities will help you become a better active listener:

1. With a partner, arrange to listen to the same newscast. Take notes, and summarize the first three stories in the newscast. The next day, compare your summaries. Which summaries are more complete? Why?
2. Invite a guest to speak to your class. During the visit, answer these questions.
   a. What is the topic?
   b. What do I know about this topic?
   c. What three facts have I learned?
   d. What questions do I have?

Tips for Active Listening

- Imagine that the speaker is talking directly to you.
- As you listen, summarize the main points of the presentation or discussion.
- Ask questions if there is something you do not understand.

Introduce the Strategies

Explain to students that listening is a more active phase of hearing. Tell students that when you have an in-depth conversation with someone, you usually respond to the person's voice through body language, eye contact, and facial expressions as well as by verbal expressions that show that you are listening. Remind students to use these strategies in everyday conversations as well as in more formal settings.

Apply the Strategies

Explain to students that most news broadcasters begin by announcing the subject of their stories. Then they fill in the details. Summaries should contain the basics of the stories—the events that happened and the people involved.

Customize for
Less Proficient Learners
You may suggest that students videotape the broadcasts they will view, or the speaker coming to the classroom. Then, they can go back and view the tape to pick up any information they missed the first time around.

Beyond the Classroom

Workplace Skills
Active Listening Explain to students that active listening skills can be a big part of many jobs. Sales, customer service, and counseling are just a few of the careers that require active listening. In addition, knowing how to listen actively will help workers get the most out of meetings and conferences. Have students get together in groups to pick a career to research. In particular, have them try to find information on the daily life of a worker in that career, including to whom the worker would report. Encourage students to think of situations where active listening is crucial to that job. For example, a writer must bring her drafts to an editor and listen to her comments, or a football player must listen to strategies from his coach. Suggest that students talk to people in their career area about their jobs and the people to whom they need to listen. Then have them share their findings with the rest of the class.

◆Build Vocabulary

What's Behind the Words

Tell students that acronyms differ from other abbreviations in that they are pronounced as a single word and not as a series of separate letters. Acronyms are used by many businesses as well as political units, such as NATO (North Atlantic Treaty Organization). Suggest to students that they use an encyclopedia or dictionary when working on Activity 1.

Answers

Activity 1

1. CARE: Cooperative for American Relief Everywhere, Inc.
2. laser: light amplification by stimulated emission of radiation
3. OPEC: Organization of the Petroleum Exporting Countries
4. scuba: self-contained underwater breathing apparatus
5. sonar: sound navigation and ranging
6. UNICEF: United Nations Children's Fund

What's Behind the Words

Vocabulary Adventures With Richard Lederer

Acronyms

Increasingly in modern life, our American vocabulary is filled with words formed from capital letters. We turn on the TV, for example, and watch shows on channels such as ABC, CBS, ESPN, NBC, and TNT. We use A.M. and P.M. to separate light from darkness and B.C. and A.D. to identify vast stretches of time.

Letters Into Words

Other letter series have become actual words in the English language. In 1941, at the start of World War II, the word *radar* was coined to describe a radio device used to locate an object by means of waves reflected from the object and received by the sending unit. The letters in *radar* form not only an acronym ("*ra*dio *d*etecting *a*nd *r*anging"), but an apt palindrome for the two-way reflection of radio waves. Words such as *snafu* ("*s*ituation *n*ormal, *a*ll *f*ouled *u*p"), AWOL ("*a*bsent *w*ithout *l*eave"), *flak* (from the German "*F*leiger-*A*bwehr-*K*anone"), and WAVES (*W*omen *A*ccepted for *V*olunteer *E*mergency *S*ervice) also came out of World War II.

Words like these are called acronyms, a label coined from two Greek roots: *acros,* "top," and *onyma,* "word or name." Because acronyms are generally fashioned from the capital letters, or tops, of words, the label seems especially appropriate.

Bacronyms

The years since World War II have brought a new refinement to the art of acronyming. This is the reverse acronym—or bacronym—in which the letters are arranged to form a word that already exists and that cleverly underscores some quality of the words that formed it. Thus ZIP codes, for "zone improvement plan," are meant to add zip or to speed our mail services, while VISTA volunteers (Volunteers in Service to America) provide wider horizons (vistas) to needy Americans.

Other activist groups that have coined sprightly acronyms to name themselves include GASP (Group Against Smoking Pollution), ACTION (American Council to Improve Our Neighborhoods), CORE (Congress of Racial Equality), and JOBS (Job Opportunities for Better Skills).

The Future of Acronyms

Acronyms say a lot in a compressed space. They seem especially suited to the rush of modern life, in which people are constantly striving to make things smaller and faster. It is safe to assume that American acronymania will continue to boom for many years.

ACTIVITY 1 Supply the complete phrase that lies behind each acronym.

1. CARE **3.** OPEC **5.** sonar
2. laser **4.** scuba **6.** UNICEF

ACTIVITY 2 Make up your own bacronym, in which the initials stand for actual words. Examples: ACRONYM: American Committee Running on Names Yielding Mischief. STARS: Students Teaching About Responsible Sailing.

Extended Reading Opportunities

Life's challenges often help people identify what matters most to them. In these novels, characters find themselves in situations that force them to decide.

Suggested Titles

Old Yeller
Fred Gipson

This classic tale of a boy and his dog is set on a frontier farm in 1860's Texas. Travis, a fourteen-year-old boy, is forced to assume responsibility for the safety of his family and their farm. He is aided in this task by Old Yeller, a big yellow dog who wanders onto their land one day, beaten and malnourished. Bound by devotion, the two face many challenges to their survival.

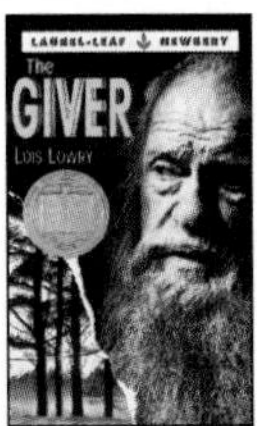

The Giver
Lois Lowry

Jonas lives in a world without war, poverty, or discontent—a world of Sameness where everything is the same day after day. He is appointed the title of Receiver of Memory and takes on the critical role of storing all the memories of his community. As part of his training, he learns that Sameness was once a place where pain and conflict—as well as sunshine and color—were part of everyone's experience. Suddenly, Jonas must decide what is most important in life.

Amos Fortune, Free Man
Elizabeth Yates

Amos Fortune was born the son of an African king, but at 15 years of age, Amos was captured by slave traders. After traveling to Massachusetts, he was sold into slavery. Even though he knows his own royal heritage, Amos works as a slave and, after 45 years, he is finally able to buy his freedom. The story of Amos Fortune may help you see your life—and what matters—in a new way.

Other Possibilities

I, Juan de Pareja	Elizabeth Borton de Treviño
Jazz: My Music My People	Morgan Monceaux
The Well	Mildred Taylor
Waiting for the Rain	Sheila Gordon

Planning Students' Extended Reading

All of the works listed on this page are good choices for extending the theme "What Matters." The following information may help you choose which to teach.

Customize for *Varying Student Needs*

When assigning the selections in this part to your students, keep in mind the following factors.

- *Old Yeller* is a classic novel that also has been adapted into a Disney movie.
- The author of *The Giver* did not intend for the story to symbolize or represent any particular belief system, but some students may perceive it as such.
- The historical events of *Amos Fortune, Free Man* may need to be put in context for some students.

Literature Study Guides

Literature study guides are available for *Old Yeller* and *The Giver*. The guides include section summaries, discussion questions, and activities.

Planning Instruction and Assessment

Unit Objectives

1. To read selections in different genres that develop the theme of "Resolving Conflicts"
2. To apply a variety of reading strategies, particularly strategies for constructing meaning, appropriate for reading these selections
3. To recognize literary elements used in these selections
4. To increase vocabulary
5. To learn elements of grammar and usage
6. To write in a variety of modes about situations based on the selections
7. To develop speaking and listening skills, by completing activities
8. To view images critically and create visual representations

Meeting the Objectives Each selection provides instructional material and portfolio opportunities by which students can meet unit objectives. You will find additional practice pages for reading strategies, literary elements, vocabulary, spelling, and grammar in **Selection Support** in the **Teaching Resources** box.

Setting Goals Work with your students at the beginning of the unit to set goals for unit outcomes. You may match instruction and activities according to students' performance levels or learning modalities.

Portfolios Students may keep portfolios of their completed work or of their work in progress. The Build Your Portfolio page of each selection provides opportunities for students to apply the concepts presented.

Humanities: Art

The Fight Interrupted, by William Mulready

William Mulready (1786–1863), an Irish painter, designed a stamped sheet of paper in 1893. It became known as the Mulready envelope and was important to postage reform.

1. What conflicts do you see in this painting? *The man holds one boy by the ear and scolds another; in the right corner, a boy talks to another who looks as if he's been in a fight.*
2. What might be the story behind the painting? *A teacher breaks up a fight in a schoolyard.*

The Fight Interrupted, William Mulready, Victoria & Albert Museum

Art Transparencies

The **Art Transparencies** booklet in the **Teaching Resources** box offers fine art to help students make connections to other curriculum areas and high-interest topics.

Beyond Literature

Each unit presents Beyond Literature features that lead students into an exploration of careers, communities, and other subject areas. In this unit, students will explore Venus, and make science and community connections. In addition, the **Teaching Resources** box contains a **Beyond Literature** booklet of activities. Using literature as a springboard, these activity pages offer students opportunities to connect literature to other curriculum areas and to the workplace and careers, community, media, and humanities.

UNIT **4**

Resolving Conflicts

Conflicts are a fact of life. The trick to living graciously is to find a way to solve these problems without compromising your beliefs or hurting someone else. The selections in this unit show you a range of problem-solving behaviors. As you read about two boys who must face each other in the boxing ring, a detective who cleverly solves a crime, and a bicycle rider who speeds away from loneliness, decide what techniques you might use to resolve the same problems.

Connections

Within this unit, you will find selections and activities that make connections beyond literature. Use these selections to connect students' understanding and appreciation of literature beyond the traditional literature and language arts curriculum.

Encourage students to connect literature to other curriculum areas. You may wish to coordinate with teachers in other curriculum areas to determine ways to team teach and further extend instruction.

Connections to Today's World

Use these selections to guide students to recognize the relevance of literature to contemporary writings. In this unit, students will connect modern detective work to that of Sir Arthur Conan Doyle's Sherlock Holmes by reading an article about animals' crime-solving techniques.

Connecting Literature to Social Studies

Each unit contains a selection that connects Literature to Social Studies. In this unit, students will read a Vietnamese folk tale.

Assessing Student Progress

The tools that are available to measure the degree to which students meet the unit objectives are listed below.

Informal Assessment

The questions in the Guide for Responding sections are a first level of response to the concepts and skills presented with the selection. As a brief, informal measure of students' grasp of the material, these responses indicate where further instruction and practice are needed. The practice pages in the **Selection Support** booklet provide for this type of instruction and practice.

You will also find literature and reading guides in the **Alternative Assessment** booklet, which students can use for informal assessment of their individual performances.

Formal Assessment

The **Formal Assessment** booklet contains Selection Tests and Unit Tests.

Selection Tests measure comprehension and skills acquisition for each selection or group of selections.

Each Unit Test provides students with 30 multiple-choice questions and 5 essay questions designed to assess students' knowledge of the literature and skills taught in the unit.

Each Alternative Unit Test: Standardized-Test Practice provides 15 multiple-choice questions and 3 essay questions based on two new literature selections not contained in the student book. The questions on the Alternative Unit Test are designed to assess students' ability to compare and contrast selections, applying skills taught in the unit.

Alternative Assessment

For portfolio and alternative assessment, the **Alternative Assessment** booklet contains Scoring Rubrics, Assessment sheets, and Learning Modalities activities.

Scoring Rubrics provide writing modes that can be applied to Writing activities, Writing Mini-Lessons, and Writing Process Workshop lessons.

Assessment sheets for speaking and listening activities provide peer and self-assessment direction.

Learning Modalities activities appeal to different learning styles. Use these as an alternative measurement of students' growth.

Prepare and Engage

OBJECTIVES

1. To read, comprehend, and interpret a humorous essay
2. To relate a humorous essay to personal experience
3. To apply strategies for constructing meaning
4. To understand a humorous essay
5. To build vocabulary in context and learn the prefix *ex-*
6. To recognize prepositions
7. To write a humorous essay that ends with a punchy conclusion
8. To respond to a humorous essay through writing, speaking and listening, and projects

SKILLS INSTRUCTION

Vocabulary: Prefixes: *ex-*
Spelling: Spell the *j* Sound With *g*
Grammar: Prepositions
Reading Strategy: Strategies for Constructing Meaning
Literary Focus: Humorous Essay
Writing: End With a Punchy Conclusion
Speaking and Listening: Skit (Teacher Edition)
Critical Viewing: Analyze; Assess

PORTFOLIO OPPORTUNITIES

Writing: Invitation; Home Name Proposal; News Report
Writing Mini-Lesson: Humorous Essay
Speaking and Listening: Skit; Guided Tour
Projects: Sleep Research; Game Collection

More About the Author
James Grover Thurber has been called one of America's greatest twentieth-century humorists. *The New Yorker* magazine sent him rejection slips for his first twenty submissions before deciding to hire him in 1927. Thurber was a staff writer and managing editor of the literary magazine until 1933. After leaving *The New Yorker*, he remained a major contributor and continued writing books and short stories.

In his writing, Thurber is known for gently poking fun at himself and others. His stories, essays, and cartoons expose basic truths about human nature.

Guide for Reading

Meet the Author:
James Thurber (1894–1961)

According to James Thurber, if you had grown up in his Columbus, Ohio, childhood home, your days would have been filled with absurd and almost unbelievable events. Thurber recounts many of these humorous events in his writings—always with affection for his sometimes silly relatives.

A Permanent Fixture at *The New Yorker* Thurber pursued a long writing career. After working as a newspaper reporter, he found the perfect creative outlet in the literary magazine *The New Yorker.* There, he could write essays that gently poked fun at his family and the rest of the world. Thurber's humor made the magazine extremely popular.

THE STORY BEHIND THE ESSAY

To James Thurber, life's humor came from the contrast between the chaos of a moment and the calm understanding that comes when looking back at it. In writing about his family in "The Night the Bed Fell," Thurber calmly recounts an example of the total confusion he remembers as part of his childhood.

◆ LITERATURE AND YOUR LIFE

CONNECT YOUR EXPERIENCE

The funniest moments can come out of simple misunderstandings. For example, imagine strolling through a store with a friend, joking about something funny, and realizing that the person standing next to you is not your friend. Suddenly, you see that you've been talking to a complete stranger! James Thurber shows you what happens when a simple confusion is compounded by the interpretations of seven people in his family.

THEMATIC FOCUS: Trouble Brewing

In "The Night the Bed Fell," each character has a different—but equally mistaken—view of the events. Each new misunderstanding leads to more confusion and more humor. As you read, think about how communication failures can lead to problems.

◆ Background for Understanding

THE ARTS

Though an early accident left him blind in first one and then both eyes, it did not prevent James Thurber from pursuing a dual career as a writer and cartoonist for *The New Yorker*. Instead, his poor eyesight led him to develop his own readily identifiable style of simple line drawing. Like the cartoon on the opposite page, which illustrated "The Night the Bed Fell," many of his cartoons enhance the humor of the situations he describes.

Prentice Hall Literature Program Resources

REINFORCE / RETEACH / EXTEND
Selection Support Pages
Build Vocabulary: Prefixes: *ex-*, p. 100
Build Spelling Skills, p. 101
Build Grammar Skills: Prepositions, p. 102
Reading for Success: Strategies for Constructing Meaning, pp. 103–104
Literary Focus: Humorous Essay, p. 105
Strategies for Diverse Student Needs, pp. 37–38
Beyond Literature: Workplace Skills: Effective Communication, p. 19

Formal Assessment Selection Test, pp. 85–87, Assessment Resources Software
Alternative Assessment, p. 19
Daily Language Practice, pp. 24–27
Resource Pro CD-ROM
"The Night the Bed Fell"—includes all resource material and customizable lesson plan

Listening to Literature Audiocassettes "The Night the Bed Fell"

MODEL SELECTION

The Night the Bed Fell

"Briggs Suffocating" by James Thurber

◆ Literary Focus

Humorous Essay

Humorous essays are brief works of nonfiction meant to amuse readers. In these essays, writers sometimes create humor by contrasting the reality of a situation with the characters' mistaken views of what is happening. In "The Night the Bed Fell," for example, every member of a household has a different yet equally misguided interpretation of a chaotic series of events. Use an organizer like the one below to record the contrasting views of events.

◆ Build Vocabulary

Prefixes: *ex-*

Thurber uses the word *extricate*, which contains the prefix *ex-*, meaning "out." This prefix contributes to the word's meaning—*extricate* means "to set free or to get out of a tangle."

Word Bank

Which of these words from the essay might refer to a criminal? Check the Build Vocabulary boxes to see if you chose correctly.

ominous
allay
fortitude
perilous
deluge
pungent
extricate
culprit

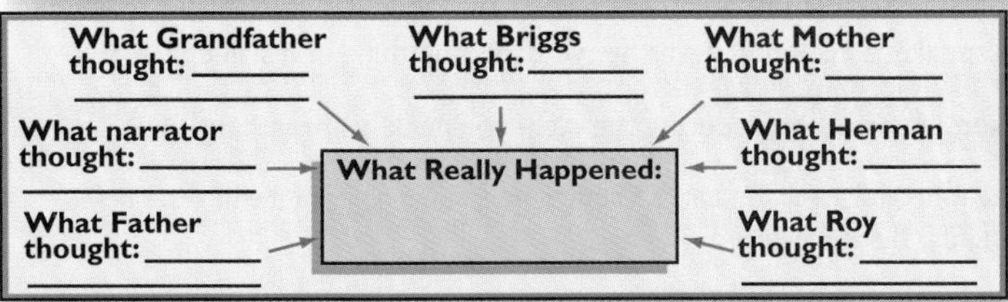

Preparing for Standardized Tests

Vocabulary Being able to select the most suitable antonym for a given word is a skill that will help students answer questions on standardized tests. Ask students to complete the following sample test question:

Write the letter of the word that is opposite in meaning to the word in italics.

Aunt Gracie *suspected* that burglars were always breaking into the house.

(A) doubted (C) complained
(B) expected (D) wished

Students who know that suspected means "believed" or "thought to be true" can look at the choices and select a word that means "did not believe" or "thought to be false." Discuss the choices and lead students to understand that *(A)* is the best answer. Remind students that they must read the directions carefully so that they do not mistakenly choose a synonym. For further practice, use Build Vocabulary in **Selection Support,** p. 100.

Interest Grabber Lead students in a game of "Telephone." Have them get in line, and then ask the first person to whisper a message into the next person's ear, and so on down the line. After the last person has received it, ask him or her to say the message out loud. Compare this message with the original message, and discuss as a group the often humorous ways in which a message can become garbled or misunderstood. Tell students that in this humorous essay, a series of misunderstandings cause some comical events to unfold.

◆ Build Grammar Skills

Prepositions If you wish to introduce the grammar concept for this selection before students read, refer to the instruction on p. 283.

Customize for
Less Proficient Readers
This selection includes difficult words that are not defined in the text. Examples include *passel, dissuading,* and *presently*. Have students look up the meanings, and create an informal glossary to accompany the story.

Customize for
More Advanced Students
Thurber's theatrical sense surfaces in this humorous essay. For example, he clearly sets up the camphor bottle (p. 279) as an important prop that might be used in a play or skit. Ask students to predict what role this prop may play in the action. As they read, have them identify other props that will become a part of the plot. Challenge them to discuss how they might adapt this essay for the stage.

Humanities: Art

Briggs Suffocating, 1933, by James Thurber

This black-and-white cartoon is an original illustration that Thurber drew to accompany this essay. Use these questions for discussion:

1. What can you predict about the story from this cartoon? *Someone will awaken in the night.*
2. What moods does it convey? *surprise, anxiety, fear, confusion*

Reading for Success

The Reading for Success page in each unit presents a set of problem-solving strategies to help readers understand authors' words and ideas on multiple levels. Good readers develop a bank of strategies from which they can draw as needed.

Unit 4 introduces strategies for constructing meaning. These strategies give readers an array of approaches for mastering a text: envisioning, making inferences, drawing conclusions and identifying causes and effects.

The strategies are modeled with the selection *The Night the Bed Fell.* Each green box shows an example of the thinking process involved in applying one of these strategies. Additional notes provide support for applying these strategies throughout the selection.

How to Use the Reading for Success Page

- Introduce the reading strategies about constructing meaning, presenting each as a problem-solving procedure.
- Before students read the selection, have them preview it, looking at the annotations in the green boxes that model the strategies.
- To reinforce these strategies after students have read the selection, have them use Reading for Success, pp. 103–104 in **Selection Support.** These pages give students an opportunity to read a selection and practice constructing meaning by writing their own annotations.

Reading Strategies: Support and Reinforcement

Using Boxed Annotations and Prompts

Throughout the unit, the notes in green, red, and maroon are intended to help students apply reading strategies, understand the literary focus, and make a connection with their lives. You may use boxed material in these ways:

- Have students pause at each box and respond to its prompt before they continue reading.
- Urge students to read through the selection, ignoring the boxes. After they complete the selection, they may go back and review the text, responding to the prompts.

Reading for Success

Strategies for Constructing Meaning

To understand a work of literature fully, you must go beyond a simple scan of the page to put the writer's ideas together in your own mind. What idea does he or she want to communicate? What does the work mean to you? In looking for answers to these questions, you construct the meaning of the work for you. Use these strategies to help you construct meaning:

Envision.

- Use details that the author provides to help you picture in your mind the places, people, and events in a piece of writing. Don't limit yourself to just your sense of sight, however. Use your imagination to experience sounds, tastes, smells, and physical sensations as well. For example, use your sense of hearing to experience this detail from Thurber's essay:

> We later heard *ominous creakings* as he crawled into bed.

Make inferences.

- It's a reader's job to fill in details the author doesn't provide. You can do so by making inferences based on the details that *are* provided, combined with your own knowledge and experience. For example, from the descriptions in the essay, you can infer that Thurber's house and family are large.

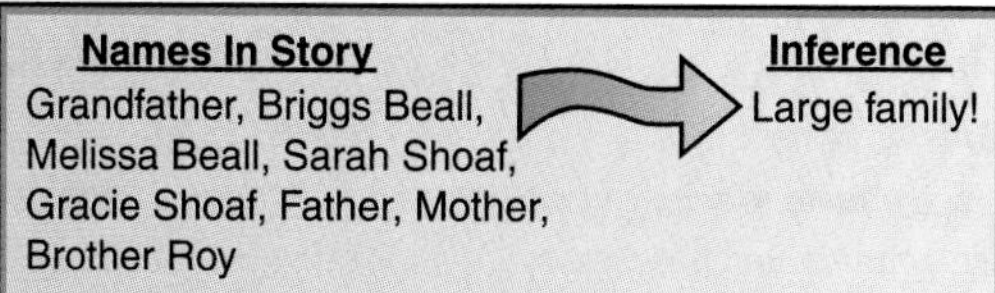

Names In Story
Grandfather, Briggs Beall, Melissa Beall, Sarah Shoaf, Gracie Shoaf, Father, Mother, Brother Roy
Inference
Large family!

Draw conclusions.

- A conclusion is a general statement that you can support with details from the text. A series of inferences can lead you to a conclusion. For example, if a character behaves badly and suffers as a result of his actions, you can conclude that the writer is making a point about how this type of behavior should be avoided.

Identify causes and effects.

- Look carefully at the relationship of events. Identify causes and effects. Notice how the cause—an action, feeling, or situation—brings about a result—the effect. Look at this example:

> *Cause:* The speaker's cousin believes he will stop breathing in his sleep.
>
> *Effect:* He gets up every hour during the night to check his breathing.

As you read the following essay by James Thurber, look at the notes in the boxes. These notes model how to use the strategies.

Model a Reading Strategy: Drawing Conclusions to Clarify Meaning

Tell students that a series of inferences based on details can lead them to draw conclusions as they read. Model the process with the second column of text on p. 279.

As I read, I learn that Briggs believes he will suffocate in his sleep. Because he is worried about this problem, he sets an alarm clock to go off every hour. I infer that Briggs's concerns are exaggerated, and also that waking up every hour will disturb his sleep and the narrator's. Using these inferences, I can draw conclusions about the narrator's cleverness by noting the way that he outsmarts Briggs. The narrator says that he will wake up if somebody quits breathing in the same room with him. As I read on, I learn that the narrator predicts that Briggs will test him, so he stays awake while pretending to be asleep. From these details, I conclude that the narrator is smart, and determined to get a good night's sleep because he sees through his cousin's "crotchets" and finds a way to work around them.

MODEL

The Night the Bed Fell

James Thurber

I suppose that the high-water mark of my
youth in Columbus, Ohio, was the night
the bed fell on my father. It makes a better
1 recitation (unless, as some friends of mine
have said, one has heard it five or six times)
2 than it does a piece of writing, for it is almost
necessary to throw furniture around, shake
doors, and bark like a dog, to lend the proper
atmosphere and verisimilitude[1] to what is admittedly a somewhat incredible tale. Still, it did take place.

It happened, then, that my father had decided to sleep in the attic one night, to be away where he could think. My mother opposed the notion strongly because, she said, the old wooden bed up there was unsafe: it was wobbly and the heavy headboard would crash down on father's head in case the bed fell, and kill him. There was no dissuading him, however, and at a quarter past ten he closed the attic door behind him and went up the narrow twisting stairs. We later heard ominous creakings as he crawled into bed. Grandfather, who usually slept in the attic bed when he was with us, had disappeared some days before. On these occasions he was usually gone six or eight days and returned growling and out of temper, with the news that the Federal Union[2] was run by a passel of blockheads and that the Army of the Potomac[3] didn't have a chance.

> Read this paragraph to **draw a conclusion** about the subject and tone of the essay. It will be about an incredible night in his family's history. The story contains funny, hard-to-believe but true events.

We had visiting us at this time a nervous first cousin of mine named Briggs Beall, who believed that he was likely to cease breathing when he was asleep. It was his feeling that if he were not awakened every hour during the night, he might die of suffocation. He had been accustomed to setting an alarm clock to ring at intervals until morning, but I persuaded him to abandon this. He slept in my room and I told him that I was such a light sleeper that if anybody quit breathing in the same room with me, I would wake instantly. He tested me the first night—which I had suspected he would—by holding his breath after my regular breathing had convinced him I was asleep. I was not asleep, however, and called to him. This seemed to allay his fears a little, but he took the precaution of putting a glass of spirits of camphor[4] on a little table at the head of his bed. In case I didn't arouse him until he was almost gone, he said, he would sniff the camphor, a powerful reviver. Briggs was not the only member of his family who had his crotchets.[5] Old Aunt Melissa Beall (who could whistle like a man, with two fingers in her mouth) suffered under the premonition that she was destined to die on South High Street, because she had been born on South High Street and married on South

1. **verisimilitude** (ver′ ə si mil′ ə to͞od′) *n.*: Appearance of being true or real.

2. **Federal Union:** Northern side during the Civil War. He is under the illusion that the Civil War has not yet ended.
3. **Army of the Potomac:** One of the northern armies during the Civil War.
4. **spirits of camphor:** Liquid with a powerful odor.
5. **crotchets** (kräch′ əts) *n.*: Peculiar or stubborn ideas.

◆ Build Vocabulary

ominous (äm′ ə nəs) *adj.*: Threatening

allay (a lā′) *v.*: Put to rest; calm

Develop Understanding

One-Minute Insight

In this humorous essay, characters' mistaken ideas set off a chain reaction that produces total confusion. As the narrator's bed collapses during the night, each character responds in his or her own bizarre way.

Customize for *English Language Learners*

Help students interpret some of the idiomatic phrases and expressions used in the selection. You can help them by restating the expressions in other terms, or by working through a word-by-word explanation. Examples include "met his Maker" (died), "out of temper" (in a bad mood), or "foggy with sleep" (groggy).

Customize for *Visual/Spatial Learners*

Students are more likely to enjoy this essay if they clearly understand the locations and movements of all the characters. From Thurber's description, have students draw a simple map diagram of the house. Suggest that they locate each person's bedroom. Then, they can indicate key events in captions, and illustrate people's movements with small arrows.

Reading for Success

1 Draw Conclusions Guide students to notice the narrator's aside, given in parentheses. Ask them to explain what this remark suggests about the storyteller and his audience. *The narrator has told the story often, which means that he thinks that it's a good one and he enjoys telling it. Among his audience are friends who have heard him tell and retell the tale.*

Thematic Focus

2 Trouble Brewing This passage alerts readers that trouble is brewing. Challenge students to tell how they know that the trouble will be comical and not serious. *The narrator reminds us that it is a true story, and asks readers to imagine wild goings-on and barking dogs to understand just how chaotic the event is.*

Block Scheduling Strategies

Consider these suggestions to take advantage of extended class time:

- Discuss the Reading for Success strategies on p. 278, and remind students to review the prompt boxes as they read. After reading, have students work in groups to answer the Reading for Success questions on p. 283.
- To help students prepare for the Writing Mini-Lesson (p. 284), have groups work through the tutorial on Narration in the *Writer's Solution Writing Lab CD-ROM,* or do related activities in the *Writer's Solution Sourcebook.*
- Introduce the exercises in **Daily Language Practice,** pp. 24-27 to give students practice with grammar, usage, and mechanics as they learn facts about James Thurber's life.
- Have students complete the Journal Writing activity on p. 282. Invite volunteers to tell their humorous stories to the class.

Reading for Success

❶ **Draw Conclusions** What is the family's general attitude toward one another's quirkiness? Discuss how the introductory character descriptions prepare readers for what comes later. *Family members accept one another as they are, despite their strange behavior. This sets up the expectation that anything is possible in this eccentric family.*

◆Literary Focus

❷ **Humorous Essay** Point out the transition that opens this paragraph: "But I am straying . . ." Discuss why the narrator would intentionally supply details about his eccentric relatives. *Events will seem more humorous if the narrator sets up outlandish expectations in his readers.*

Reading for Success

❸ **Envision** Ask students why it is important for readers to understand the locations of key people. *By accurately picturing the action in their minds, readers will better appreciate the humor of the story.*

▶Critical Viewing◀

❹ **Analyze** *She is scaring away burglars to protect her family.*

High Street. Then there was Aunt Sarah Shoaf, who never went to bed at night without the fear that a burglar was going to get in and blow chloroform[6] under her door through a tube. To avert this calamity—for she was in greater dread of anesthetics than of losing her household goods—she always piled her money, silverware, and other valuables in a neat stack just outside her bedroom, with a note reading: "This is all I have. Please take it and do not use your chloroform, as this is all I have." Aunt Gracie Shoaf also had a burglar phobia, but she met it with more fortitude. She was confident that burglars had been getting into her house every night for forty years. The fact that she never
❶ missed any thing was to her no proof to the contrary. She always claimed that she scared them off before they could take anything, by throwing shoes down the hallway. When she went to bed she piled, where she could get at them handily, all the shoes there were about her house. Five minutes after she had turned off the light, she would sit up in bed and say "Hark!" Her husband, who had learned to ignore the whole situation as long ago as 1903, would either be sound asleep or pretend to be sound asleep. In either case he would not respond to her tugging and pulling, so that presently she would arise, tiptoe to the door, open it slightly and heave a shoe down the hall in one direction, and its mate down the hall in the other direction. Some nights she threw them all, some nights only a couple of pair.

Use details about Aunt Sarah to **picture** her daily before-bed antics.

❷ But I am straying from the remarkable incidents that took place during the night that the bed fell on father. By midnight we were all in bed. The layout of the rooms and the disposition[7] of their occupants is important to an
❸ understanding of what later occurred. In the front room upstairs (just under father's attic bedroom) were my mother and my brother Herman, who sometimes sang in his sleep,

"Aunt Gracie Shoaf Throwing Shoes" by James Thurber

▲ **Critical Viewing** How would Gracie Shoaf defend the actions shown in this drawing? **[Analyze]** ❹

usually "Marching Through Georgia" or "Onward, Christian Soldiers." Briggs Beall and myself were in a room adjoining this one. My ❸
brother Roy was in a room across the hall from ours. Our bull terrier, Rex, slept in the hall.

My bed was an army cot, one of those affairs which are made wide enough to sleep on comfortably only by putting up, flat with the middle section, the two sides which ordinarily hang down like the sideboards of a drop-leaf table. When these sides are up, it is perilous to roll too far toward the edge, for then the cot is likely to tip completely over, bringing the whole bed down on top of one, with a tremendous banging crash. This, in fact, is precisely what happened about two o'clock in the morning. (It was my mother who, in recalling the scene later, first referred to it as "the night the bed fell on your father.")

Always a deep sleeper, slow to arouse (I had lied to Briggs), I was at first unconscious of what

6. **chloroform** (klôr´ ə fôrm´) *n.:* Substance used at one time as an anesthetic, or pain-killer, during operations because it can cause a person to pass out.
7. **disposition** (dis´ pə zish´ ən) *n.:* Arrangement.

Humanities: Art

Illustrations by James Thurber, 1933, 1961

Thurber often illustrated his humorous writing with his own stylized cartoons until his eyesight grew so poor in the late 1940's that he had to give up drawing altogether. The cartoons that accompany this selection were created by Thurber to illustrate this essay. They have been called gesture drawings, simple in the use of line and space, yet complex in their ability to convey humor. Use these questions for discussion:

1. What scenes do the cartoons portray? *Briggs waking up in fear that he might have stopped breathing; Aunt Gracie Shoaf tossing shoes down the hall; Rex attacking Briggs as the would-be culprit*
2. What makes these simple illustrations so effective? *Students may say that knowing that the cartoonist and author are the same person makes the cartoons especially suitable; they may see the quirkiness of the art as an echo of the quirky characters; simple drawings, like simple narratives, allow audiences to fill in details from their own imagination.*

had happened when the iron cot rolled me onto the floor and toppled over on me. It left me still warmly bundled up and unhurt, for the bed rested above me like a canopy. Hence I did not 5 wake up, only reached the edge of consciousness and went back. The racket, however, instantly awakened my mother, in the next room, who came to the immediate conclusion that her worst dread was realized: the big wooden bed upstairs had fallen on father. She therefore screamed, "Let's go to your poor father!" It was this shout, rather than the noise of my cot falling, that awakened Herman, in the same room with her. He thought that mother had become, for no apparent reason, hysterical. "You're all right, Mamma!" he shouted, trying to calm her. They exchanged shout for shout for perhaps ten seconds: "Let's go to your poor father!" and "You're all right!" That woke up Briggs. By this time I was conscious of what was going on, in a vague way, but did not yet realize that I was under my bed instead of on it. Briggs, awakening in the midst of loud shouts of fear and apprehension, came to the quick conclusion that he was suffocating and that we were all trying to "bring him out." With a low moan, he grasped the glass of camphor at the head of his bed and instead of sniffing it poured it over himself. The room reeked of camphor. "Ugf, ahfg," choked Briggs, like a drowning man, for he had almost succeeded in stopping his breath under the deluge of pungent spirits. He leaped out of bed and groped toward the open window, but he came up against one that was closed. With his hand, he beat out the glass, and I could hear it crash and tinkle on the alleyway below. It was at this juncture that I, in trying to get up, had the uncanny sensation of feeling my bed above me! Foggy with sleep, I now suspected, in my turn, that the whole uproar was being made in a frantic endeavor to extricate me from what must be an 8 unheard-of and perilous situation. "Get me out of this!" I bawled. "Get me out!" I think I had the nightmarish belief that I was entombed in a mine. "Gugh," gasped Briggs, floundering in his camphor.

By this time my mother, still shouting, pursued by Herman, still shouting, was trying to open the door to the attic, in order to go up and get my father's body out of the wreckage. The door was stuck, however, and wouldn't yield. Her frantic pulls on it only added to the general banging and confusion. Roy and the

6 **Identify cause and effect**—the noise made by young Thurber falling out of and under his bed awakens his mother. This causes her to think that her husband has fallen out of his bed.

Use Briggs's assumption that everyone is worried about him, along with the earlier details about his anxiety about going to sleep, to **make the inference** that he thinks mostly about his own situation.

◆ Build Vocabulary

fortitude (fôrt´ ə to͞od´) *n.*: Firm courage

perilous (per´ ə ləs) *adj.*: Dangerous

deluge (del´ yo͞oj´) *n.*: Great flood or rush of anything

pungent (pun´ jənt) *adj.*: Sharp-smelling

extricate (eks´ trə kāt´) *v.*: Set free; disentangle

"Briggs and Rex" by James Thurber

7 ▶ Critical Viewing Everyone, including the dog, jumped into action the night the bed fell. How does this make the events even funnier? **[Assess]**

◆Build Spelling Skills

5 The spelling strategy for this selection is spelling the *j* sound with g. Have students find the word in this sentence to which the spelling strategy applies. *edge*

Reading for Success

6 Identify Cause and Effect Have students identify the true cause of Thurber's mother's anxiety. *The actual cause is Thurber's cot collapsing onto the floor, but his mother is confused and thinks that it is his father's bed that has fallen.*

▶Critical Viewing◀

7 Assess *Students may say that the family has fallen into such chaos that even the dog gets into the act.*

Reading for Success

8 Make Inferences Help students make the inference that young Thurber is even more confused upon finally awakening because of the uproar around him.

Speaking and Listening Mini-Lesson

Skit

This mini-lesson supports the Speaking and Listening activity in the Idea Bank on p. 284.

Introduce Tell students that many of Thurber's humorous stories have been adapted for TV, film, and stage. Discuss story elements that lend themselves to drama, such as quirky characters, chaotic action, and the narrator's matter-of-fact tone.

Develop Divide the class into groups. Each group can decide whether to portray the entire story, or to dramatize a certain moment. Discuss jobs that group members might assume, such as casting director, actors, script writer, vocal coach, or stage manager. Students may wish to add sound effects, as the narrator suggests.

Apply Allow time for groups to plan, prepare, rehearse, and perform their skits.

Assess Assess students on their ability to bring the essay to life. You might want to have students use the Peer Assessment: Dramatic Performance form, p. 107, in **Alternative Assessment.**

Reinforce and Extend

Answers

◆ Literature and Your Life

Reader's Response Students may say that they would enjoy visiting, but not living with, the Thurbers. The family is likeable, but such zaniness may not appeal to all students.

Thematic Focus Their expectations lead them to assume that a problem exists when it really doesn't.

☑ Check Your Comprehension

1. Mr. and Mrs. Thurber, James, his brothers Herman and Roy, cousin Briggs Beall, and Rex, the dog
2. Mr. Thurber is in the attic, above Mrs. Thurber's room. James and Briggs are in the bedroom next to Mrs. Thurber's. Roy is in his bedroom across the hall. Rex, the dog, is in the upstairs hall. The rooms are so close together that Mrs. Thurber mistakes which room the crash comes from.
3. He believes that he will suffocate in his sleep unless he is awakened at intervals during the night.
4. Mrs. Thurber awakens and begins shouting. Herman awakens and tries to calm his mother. Briggs awakens, pours camphor on himself, and smashes the window. James wakes up and begins to shout. His mother runs to the attic door and pulls on it. Roy and the dog awaken. Mr. Thurber awakens and cries out. Mrs. Thurber shouts that her husband is dying. Briggs shouts that he's fine. Thurber and Briggs join the others. The dog jumps on Briggs. Mr. Thurber emerges.

◆ Critical Thinking

1. He is setting the scene for the crazy antics that will follow.
2. Many have peculiar ideas and are easily excitable.
3. When people first wake up, their sensory perceptions may be a little off, and it takes them a while to respond appropriately.
4. Some family members expect problems. Others are poor listeners and excitable.
5. The story ends on a happy note.
6. Possible response: Sturdier beds, better communication skills.
7. You may make mistakes if you are half asleep.

dog were now up, the one shouting questions, the other barking.

Father, farthest away and soundest sleeper of all, had by this time been awakened by the battering on the attic door. He decided that the house was on fire. "I'm coming, I'm coming!" he wailed in a slow, sleepy voice—it took him many minutes to regain full consciousness. My mother, still believing he was caught under the bed, detected in his "I'm coming!" the mournful, resigned note of one who is preparing to meet his Maker. "He's dying!" she shouted.

"I'm all right!" Briggs yelled to reassure her. "I'm all right!" He still believed that it was his own closeness to death that was worrying mother. I found at last the light switch in my room, unlocked the door, and Briggs and I joined the others at the attic door. The dog, who never did like Briggs, jumped for him—assuming that he was the culprit in whatever was going on—and Roy had to throw Rex and hold him. We could hear father crawling out of bed upstairs. Roy pulled the attic door open, with a mighty jerk, and father came down the stairs, sleepy and irritable but safe and sound. My mother began to weep when she saw him. Rex began to howl. "What in the name of heaven is going on here?" asked father.

The situation was finally put together like a gigantic jigsaw puzzle. Father caught a cold from prowling around in his bare feet but there were no other bad results. "I'm glad," said mother, who always looked on the bright side of things, "that your grandfather wasn't here."

◆ Build Vocabulary

culprit (kul′ prit) *n.*: Guilty person

Guide for Responding

◆ Literature and Your Life

Reader's Response Do you think you would enjoy living with, or even visiting, a family like James Thurber's? Explain.

Thematic Focus Several characters in the story worry about the night. How do these fears contribute to the problems that develop?

Journal Writing In a journal entry, describe a time when confusion led to comedy in your home or school.

☑ Check Your Comprehension

1. Who is in the house on the night described?
2. Describe the layout of the rooms. Why is their placement important to the plot of the story?
3. What is Briggs's crotchet, or peculiar idea?
4. In chronological, or time, order, list the actions that occur after Thurber's bed collapses.

◆ Critical Thinking

INTERPRET

1. Why does Thurber begin the essay with a description of his relatives? **[Interpret]**
2. In what ways are Thurber's relatives similar? **[Compare and Contrast]**
3. How does the fact that all the characters were asleep when Thurber's bed fell cause them to act especially strangely? **[Analyze]**
4. Why does the collapse of Thurber's bed lead to such confusion and odd behavior among his family? **[Draw Conclusions]**
5. What evidence is there that Thurber felt affection for his family? **[Support]**

APPLY

6. What changes can you suggest to avoid future confusion in the Thurber household? **[Resolve]**

EXTEND

7. What does this story suggest about the importance of being fully awake before joining in the events around you? **[Health Link]**

Beyond the Selection

FURTHER READING

Other Works by James Thurber

My Life and Hard Times
The Years With Ross

Other Humorous Essays About Families

"No Gumption," Russell Baker
"The Night the Ghost Got In," James Thurber
"The Sneaker Crisis," Shirley Jackson

INTERNET

We suggest the following site on the Internet (all Web sites are subject to change).

For more about James Thurber, including a self-portrait:
http://home.earthlink.net/~ritter/thurber/index.html

We *strongly recommend* that you preview the site before you send students to it.

Guide for Responding (continued)

◆ Reading for Success

Strategies for Constructing Meaning

Review the reading strategies and the notes showing how to construct meaning. Then, apply them to answer the questions.

1. List three sensory details that show the night's confusion.

2. What event causes Briggs Beall to awaken?

3. (a) What experiences from your own life might relate to this story? (b) How does such a connection help you understand the essay?

◆ Build Vocabulary

Using the Prefix *ex-*

The common prefix *ex-* means "out." For example, *exclude* means "to leave out," and *expand* means "to spread out." Match each word to its definition.

1. exalt	**a.** to go beyond the limit
2. exceed	**b.** to breathe out
3. exhale	**c.** to raise high

Spelling Strategy

You often spell the *j* sound with a *g*, as in *pungent.* When this sound appears at the end of a word, as in *deluge*, always use *ge*. Use the definitions below to write words containing *j* spelled with *g*.

1. the trick of pulling a rabbit out of a hat: ma___?___

2. a larger-than-life figure: le___?___

3. photograph, painting, or moving picture: im___?___

4. a number indicating the amount of years you've lived: ag___?___

Using the Word Bank

On your paper, write the letter of the word that is most opposite in meaning to the first word.

1. fortitude: (a) strength, (b) weakness, (c) courage

2. ominous: (a) favorable, (b) dull, (c) scary

3. deluge: (a) flood, (b) drought, (c) shower

4. extricate: (a) rescue, (b) revolve, (c) capture

5. culprit: (a) lawyer, (b) offender, (c) victim

6. perilous: (a) risky, (b) exciting, (c) secure

7. allay: (a) partner, (b) irritate, (c) calm

8. pungent: (a) moldy, (b) tangy, (c) bland

◆ Literary Focus

Humorous Essay

A **humorous essay** is a brief work of nonfiction meant to amuse. In "The Night the Bed Fell," Thurber creates the fun by showing both what is really happening and what each character thinks is happening. For example, Thurber's mother believes that her husband lies crushed in the wreckage of his bed, but he is really safely asleep.

1. Contrast what actually happens when the bed falls with what each character thinks happens.

2. Would the essay be as funny if you were as confused about what happened as the characters were? Why or why not?

3. At the beginning of the essay, Thurber writes that he prefers to tell the story orally because he can add physical effects. Do you think such antics would make this funny tale even funnier? Explain.

◆ Build Grammar Skills

Prepositions

A **preposition** is a word that relates a noun or pronoun that follows it to another word in the sentence. Here are some common prepositions: *above, behind, below, near, into, through, outside, inside, beyond, off, on, over, to, up,* and *with*. Some prepositions—such as *ahead of, because of,* and *in addition to*—consist of more than one word. Look at these examples:

On these occasions he returned *out of* temper.
Father had been awakened *by* the noise.
I didn't realize I was *under* my bed not *on* it.

Practice On your paper, write the prepositions in each sentence.

1. The room was underneath the attic bedroom.

2. Mrs. Thurber slept in that room, too.

3. Two were in the room next to Herman's.

4. Roy slept in a room across the hall from them.

5. The dog, Rex, slept in front of Roy's door.

Writing Application Rewrite each practice sentence using a different preposition. Explain how the meaning of the sentence changes.

◆ Build Grammar Skills

Practice

1. underneath; 2. in; 3. in, next to; 4. in, across, from; 5. in; of

Writing Application

Possible responses:

1. The room was above the attic bedroom.
2. Mrs. Thurber slept outside that room, too.
3. Two were beneath the room next to Herman's.
4. Roy slept behind a room near the hall between them.
5. The dog, Rex, slept outside Roy's door.

Writer's Solution

For additional instruction and practice, use the lesson in the *Writer's Solution Language Lab CD-ROM* on prepositions and prepositional phrases, and the practice page on prepositions, pp. 23–24 in the *Writer's Solution Grammar Practice Book.*

Answers

◆ Reading Strategy

1. Possible responses: the noises of Briggs jumping about, the dog barking, people shouting, glass breaking
2. Mrs. Thurber and Herman are shouting at each other.
3. (a) Responses are likely to focus on humorous misunderstandings among family members. (b) It helps students empathize with the affectionate way Thurber tells the story.

◆ Build Vocabulary

Using the Prefix *ex-*

1. c
2. a
3. b

Spelling Strategy

1. magic; 2. legend; 3. image; 4. age

Using the Word Bank

1. b
2. a
3. b
4. c
5. c
6. c
7. b
8. c

◆ Literary Focus

1. Thurber's cot falls, but Mrs. Thurber thinks the attic bed has fallen. When she calls out, Herman thinks she is hysterical and tries to calm her. Briggs hears shouts and thinks he's suffocating. Thurber awakes under the cot and thinks he's in a mine. Mr. Thurber hears noise and thinks that the house is on fire. Mrs. Thurber hears her husband shout and thinks he's dying. Briggs thinks Mrs. Thurber is shouting because he is suffocating, and tries to calm her. Rex thinks that Briggs has caused all the trouble and jumps on him.
2. Students should realize that readers can best appreciate the humor of the events by knowing both the characters' mistaken impressions and the truth.
3. Students may say that sound effects and actions would make the story even funnier if they were performed skillfully.

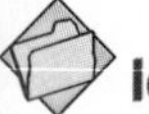

Idea Bank

Following are suggestions for matching the Idea Bank topics with your students' performance levels and learning modalities:

Customize for
Performance Levels

Less Advanced Students: 1, 4, 7
Average Students: 2, 4, 5, 6, 7
More Advanced Students: 3, 4, 5, 6

Customize for
Learning Modalities

Verbal/Linguistic: 1, 2, 3, 5, 6
Visual/Spatial: 4, 5, 7
Bodily/Kinesthetic: 4, 5, 7
Logical/Mathematical: 3, 5, 6, 7
Musical/Rhythmic: 4
Interpersonal: 4, 7
Intrapersonal: 1, 2, 3, 5, 6

Writing Mini-Lesson

Refer students to the Writing Handbook in the back of the book for instructions on the writing process and for further information on narrative writing.

Writer's Solution

Writers at Work Videodisc

Have students view the videodisc segment on Narration (Ch. 3), featuring Denise Chavez, to see how she uses what she knows when she writes. Have students discuss the importance of using dialogue that suits the narrative and that meets the needs of an audience to help them write their humorous essays.

Play frames 31091 to 31478

Writing Lab CD-ROM

Have students complete the tutorial on Narration. Follow these steps:

1. Guide students to develop the narrative elements of character, plot, and setting, and find ways to hold readers' interest.
2. Have students draft on computer.
3. Have students use the interactive student model to guide them through the proofreading phase.

Allow about 60 minutes of class time to complete these steps.

Writer's Solution Sourcebook

Have students use Chapter 3, "Narration," pp. 66–101, for additional support. The chapter includes in-depth instruction on using transitions to show time order, pp. 95–96.

Build Your Portfolio

Idea Bank

Writing

1. **Invitation** The Thurbers are planning a party. Write an invitation describing the amusements in store for guests. If you like, decorate your invitation with Thurberlike cartoons. **[Art Link]**
2. **Home Name Proposal** In some communities, homes are named to reflect the personality or interest of the occupants. Given the goings-on that Thurber reports, suggest a name for his home. Present your idea in a written proposal.
3. **News Report** As a local journalist, write a news report of the events at Thurber's house. Include important facts about who was involved, what happened, when the events occurred, and where the action took place. **[Media Link]**

Speaking and Listening

4. **Skit [Group Activity]** With a few classmates, dramatize the confusion at the Thurber home. In preparation for a performance, one student can write the final script, another can select or create music to fit the mood, and another can direct a rehearsal. **[Performing Arts Link]**
5. **Guided Tour** Draw a plan of the Thurber house as it is described in the essay. Then, present a tour of the evening's events, using a pointer to explain each character's movements. **[Art Link]**

Projects

6. **Sleep Research** Some of the confusion in the essay grows out of the fact that the characters are half asleep. Research the effect of sleep on the senses. Find out how sensory information can be distorted by the sleeping state. Share your findings with the class. **[Science Link]**
7. **Game Collection** Learn about games such as Telephone, in which the fun and humor come from misunderstandings. Consult game books and exchange ideas with classmates. Then, play several games in class, analyzing how the confusion leads to humor.

Writing Mini-Lesson

Humorous Essay

You may think that your life experiences could never be as funny as Thurber's. However, though you may not have an aunt as unusual as Melissa Beall, you've surely had an especially funny experience. Write an essay telling the story of your experience. Use some of Thurber's techniques to get the most humor out of the events.

Writing Skills Focus:
Punchy Conclusion

There's nothing worse than knowing your audience "doesn't get the joke." To avoid this fate, end your story with a **punchy conclusion.** This might be a joke or a summarizing comment that ties all the pieces together. Notice how Thurber ends his essay with a clinching reminder of his family's unusual outlook on life.

Model From the Story

"I'm glad," said mother, who always looked on the bright side of things, "that your grandfather wasn't here."

Prewriting Brainstorm with family or friends to recall favorite amusing stories. Once you've chosen your story, list the main events in sequence. Find the funniest sequence, experimenting with the most effective concluding element.

Drafting Write the conclusion first. Get the punch line—the clincher—down, and then go back to the beginning to narrate the events. Add exaggeration and contrast where it will create humor.

◆ Grammar Application

Make sure your prepositions describe the relationships between words accurately.

Revising Read your essay aloud. Do listeners laugh in the places you expected? If the concluding punch line doesn't tie it all together for them, reorganize events or add more exaggeration and contrast.

✓ ASSESSMENT OPTIONS

Formal Assessment, Selection Test, pp. 85–87, and Assessment Resources Software. The selection test is designed so that it can be easily customized to the performance levels of your students.

Alternative Assessment, p. 19, includes options for less advanced students, more advanced students, verbal/linguistic learners, visual/spatial learners, interpersonal learners, and musical/rhythmic learners.

PORTFOLIO ASSESSMENT

Use the following rubrics in the **Alternative Assessment** booklet to assess student writing:
Invitation: Business Letter/Memo, p. 100
Home Name Proposal: Persuasion, p. 92
News Report: Summary, p. 85
Writing Mini-Lesson: Narrative Based on Personal Experience, p. 83

PART 1 *Trouble Brewing*

View of Toledo, Domenikos Theotokopoulos, The Metropolitan Museum of Art

One-Minute Planning Guide

The selections in this part focus on the theme of "trouble brewing." In "All Summer in a Day," a young girl's classmates punish her for being different. "Primer Lesson" is a short poem that warns against using proud words. "The Highwayman" takes a poetic look at a British outlaw. "The Dying Cowboy" describes a character who has strong feelings about where he wants to be buried, while "The Real Story of a Cowboy's Life" deglamorizes life on the range. In "The Little Lizard's Sorrow" a haggard traveler proves to be a match for a rich, greedy landowner.

Customize for *Varying Students Needs*

When assigning the selections in this section, keep in mind the following factors:

"All Summer in a Day"
- A classic science-fiction story
- Provides an opportunity for science research on Venus

"Primer Lesson"
- A very short poem
- Students may need help with theme

"The Highwayman"
- A long classic poem
- Students may need help with vocabulary

"The Dying Cowboy"
- Some students may know this folk ballad
- Surprise ending

"The Real Story of a Cowboy's Life"
- Interesting, real-life look at cowboys

"The Little Lizard's Sorrow"
- A Vietnamese folk tale
- An opportunity for connecting literature with social studies

Humanities: Art

View of Toledo, c. 1597, by Domenikos Theotokopoulos

Domenikos Theotokopoulos (1541–1614) is more commonly known as El Greco, or "The Greek." Born in Crete, El Greco eventually settled in Spain and became one of that country's most important artists. He is especially well known for his paintings that express the mystery of Catholicism.

El Greco moved to Venice when he was in his twenties and studied under the aging artist Titian. In 1577, he moved to Toledo, Spain, where he spent the rest of his life. He did several works for the church there, which had enormous power in the community. *View of Toledo* is one of El Greco's most famous works and can be seen at the Metropolitan Museum of Art in New York City.

El Greco's paintings are known for their strong contrasts of color and light. He has been called a prophet of modern art. Have students study the painting and then ask the following questions:

1. How does this painting relate to the theme "Trouble Brewing"? *Students may say that the sky looks ominous above the city, as if a storm is about to break.*
2. Look at the colors El Greco uses in this painting. How do they contribute to the mood of the painting? *Students may say that he uses vivid greens for the landscape and an array of blues for the sky, but the city itself is very plain and grey. This makes nature seem more powerful than the man-made buildings.*

Prepare and Engage

OBJECTIVES

1. To read, comprehend, and interpret a story and a poem
2. To relate a story and poem to personal experience
3. To envision setting and actions
4. To analyze setting
5. To build vocabulary in context and learn the word root *-vita-*
6. To recognize prepositional phrases
7. To write a remembrance that brings events to life for the reader
8. To respond to the story and poem through writing, speaking and listening, and projects

SKILLS INSTRUCTION

Vocabulary:
Word Roots: *-vita-*

Spelling:
Words With *tu (choo)*

Grammar:
Prepositional Phrases

Reading Strategy:
Envision Setting and Actions

Literary Focus:
Setting

Writing:
Show, Don't Tell

Speaking and Listening:
Dramatization (Teacher Edition)

Viewing and Representing:
Using Color (Teacher Edition)

Critical Viewing:
Distinguish; Connect; Evaluate

PORTFOLIO OPPORTUNITIES

Writing: Diary Entry; Travel Brochure; Teacher's Report

Writing Mini-Lesson: Remembrance

Speaking and Listening: Lecture; Dramatization

Projects: Internet Research; Multimedia Report

More About the Authors

Ray Bradbury does not drive a car and has never flown. Yet his fantastic imagination allows his readers to enter all kinds of strange worlds. He has won many awards, including the World Fantasy Award for lifetime achievement and the Grand Master Award from the Science Fiction Writers of America. An astronaut has even named a lunar landmark, *Dandelion Crater,* after Bradbury's book, *Dandelion Wine*.

Carl Sandburg won a Pulitzer Prize for his poetry in 1951. In addition to his poetry, he was a noted historian and biographer.

Guide for Reading

Meet the Author:

Ray Bradbury (1920–)

As a boy, Ray Bradbury loved magicians, circuses, and the stories of science-fiction novelist Edgar Rice Burroughs.

Bradbury began his own writing almost by accident. He couldn't afford to buy the sequel to a Burroughs novel, so he invented a sequel. Writing his own story ending proved to be the beginning of an award-winning career as a science-fiction writer.

The Story Behind the Story

In 1950, Bradbury published a story about a group of Earthmen struggling through the rainy world of Venus. This story made him wonder how a child would react to the sun's brief appearances on Venus. To answer this question, he wrote "All Summer in a Day."

Carl Sandburg (1878–1967)

Carl Sandburg is one of America's most beloved poets. When his poetry first appeared, however, it created a stir because it lacked set rhyme and rhythm. In addition, because Sandburg used the language of the common people, some critics thought his poetry was rough and crude. [For more information on Sandburg, see page 788.]

◆ Literature and Your Life

Connect Your Experience

Watching the sun break through the clouds after a storm, you may feel as if you're welcoming back a good friend. Imagine how you'd feel to see the sun if it had been raining for seven years! This is the situation for schoolchildren in Ray Bradbury's story. How do you think they'll act as the rain ends and the sun finally appears?

Thematic Focus: Trouble Brewing

One child in "All Summer in a Day" remembers seeing the sun before. Why might its appearance be different for her? Why is it important for others to respect her feelings?

◆ Background for Understanding

Science

"All Summer in a Day" is set on Venus, the second planet from the sun. Today, we know that Venus has a surface temperature of almost 900°F, more than twice the oven temperature for roasting chicken. In 1950, when Bradbury wrote his story, Venus was a mystery planet. Some scientists believed that its clouds concealed a watery world. That's probably why Bradbury describes Venus as a place of soggy jungles and almost continuous rain.

◆ Build Vocabulary

Word Roots: *-vita-*

A girl in this story is not doing well on Venus, where she lives. Her parents feel that it is *vital* that they take her back to Earth. The word *vital,* which means "necessary for life," contains the root *-vita-,* meaning "life."

Word Bank

Look over these words from the story. Which two words are past tense verbs?

concussion
slackening
vital
surged
tumultuously
resilient
savored

Prentice Hall Literature Program Resources

REINFORCE / RETEACH / EXTEND

Selection Support Pages
Build Vocabulary: Word Roots: *-vita-*, p. 106
Build Spelling Skills, p. 107
Build Grammar Skills: Prepositional Phrases, p. 108
Reading Strategy: Envision Setting and Actions, p. 109
Literary Focus: Setting, p. 110

Strategies for Diverse Student Needs, pp. 39-40

Beyond Literature Activity Page Cross-Curricular Connection: Science, p. 20

Formal Assessment Selection Test, pp. 88–90, Assessment Resources Software

Alternative Assessment, p. 20

Writing and Language Transparencies Sensory Language Chart, p. 78

Resource Pro CD-ROM "All Summer in a Day"

Listening to Literature Audiocassettes "All Summer in a Day"

Looking at Literature Videodisc/Videotape "All Summer in a Day"

◆ Literary Focus

Setting

A story's **setting,** its place and time, is the world in which its characters live. That world can be anywhere and any time—a sunny street in a modern city or another planet whose sky is always torn by lightning. In some stories, the setting is just a background for the events. In others, like this story, the setting drives the characters' actions. The children on Bradbury's rainy Venus, for instance, would give almost anything for a glimpse of the sun.

◆ Reading Strategy

Envision Setting and Actions

You can live in a story's setting just as the characters do. All you need are your senses. Practice using them by imagining that the picture above is a window. As you look through it, watch the dark clouds fly by and listen for the wind that carries them. Apply this same technique to the story. **Envision** the setting and the actions by finding details that help you sense the world that Bradbury creates. Then, as you read, fill out a chart like the one below to capture sensory details.

Situation	Sights, Sounds, Smells, Physical Sensations
At the classroom window	
In the tunnels	
In the sun-filled jungle	
In the closet	

Preparing for Standardized Tests

Grammar Recognizing prepositional phrases (the skill for this selection) is the first step to using them correctly. Point out that a prepositional phrase is a group of words that begins with a preposition and ends with a noun or pronoun:

The poems *by* the <u>children</u> describe the sun.

Grammar and usage portions of standardized tests may require students to identify prepositional phrases in sentences. Write the following sample test item on the board for students:

Identify the prepositional phrase.

Scientists predicted sunshine for Friday.

(A) sunshine for Friday.
(B) scientists predicted sunshine
(C) for Friday
(D) predicted sunshine

Guide students to recognize the preposition *for* in the sentence. Knowing that the prepositional phrase begins with *for*, students should see that *Friday* is the object of the preposition. Therefore, *(C)* is the correct answer.

To help draw students into the story setting, close the shades to darken the room and play a recording of rain for a few minutes. Ask students to describe how the constant sound of rain affects their mood. Encourage them to think about how they would feel if the rain didn't stop for seven years. Would they get used to it? Discuss areas of life that relentless rain would impact, such as limiting outdoor activity, rarely seeing the sun, and feeling damp. Ask students how their mood might change when the rain stops, and then ask how they would feel when it begins to rain again.

◆Build Grammar Skills

Prepositional Phrases The grammar concept taught with this story is prepositional phrases. Write the phrase "all summer in a day" on the board. Underline *in a day* and tell students it is a prepositional phrase. If you wish to explore the concept of prepositional phrases further before students read the story, refer to the instruction on p. 296.

Customize for
More Advanced Students

After discussing the Guide for Reading pages, but before students read the story, have them chart their own story line based on the setting. After reading, have students chart Bradbury's story line and compare and contrast the two charts.

Characters:	
Rising Action (Complications):	
Turning Point:	
Falling Action (Resolutions):	
Ending:	

Customize for
Less Proficient Readers

To help less proficient readers appreciate the visual descriptions and the revealing dialogue of this story, have them listen to the recording of the selection. Or, have students of mixed ability work in pairs and practice reading sections of dialogue and descriptive passages.

Listening to Literature Audiocassettes

Develop Understanding

One-Minute Insight

The setting of this story is the planet Venus. On Ray Bradbury's Venus, it rains constantly, and the sun appears only once every seven years. A group of school children eagerly awaits the moment the sun will appear. Margot, who arrived on the planet more recently, remembers sunshine and is pining away in the rainy climate. She doesn't fit in with the other children, mainly because she knows the warmth and joy of sunlight. As the brief appearance of the sun nears, Margot becomes the group's victim when she is locked in a closet and forgotten. She remains in the closet while her classmates enjoy the sunshine. The sequence of events illustrates the need for tolerance and sensitivity. The story also captures how members of a group can take on a mob mentality and cease to act according to their individual beliefs.

Team Teaching Strategy

Because of its setting, "All Summer in a Day" provides an excellent opportunity for making connections to science. You may want to coordinate with a science teacher to come up with ideas for extending instruction.

Customize for *English Language Learners*

English language learners may be unfamiliar with the figurative language and terms used in this story. Pantomime "the world ground to a standstill" by engaging in movement and slowly coming to a stop; use chart paper to sketch a rooftop and draw a chain of drops for ". . . clear bead necklaces on the roof." Pantomime "if they tagged her and ran," and "clutched her hands to her ears . . ."

Customize for *Interpersonal Learners*

In this story, a group teams against one person, based on their perceptions of her as being different. Invite interpersonal learners to observe the characters' interaction. After they read the story, have students role-play the confrontational scene between the children. Then, encourage them to express what they discovered about the characters.

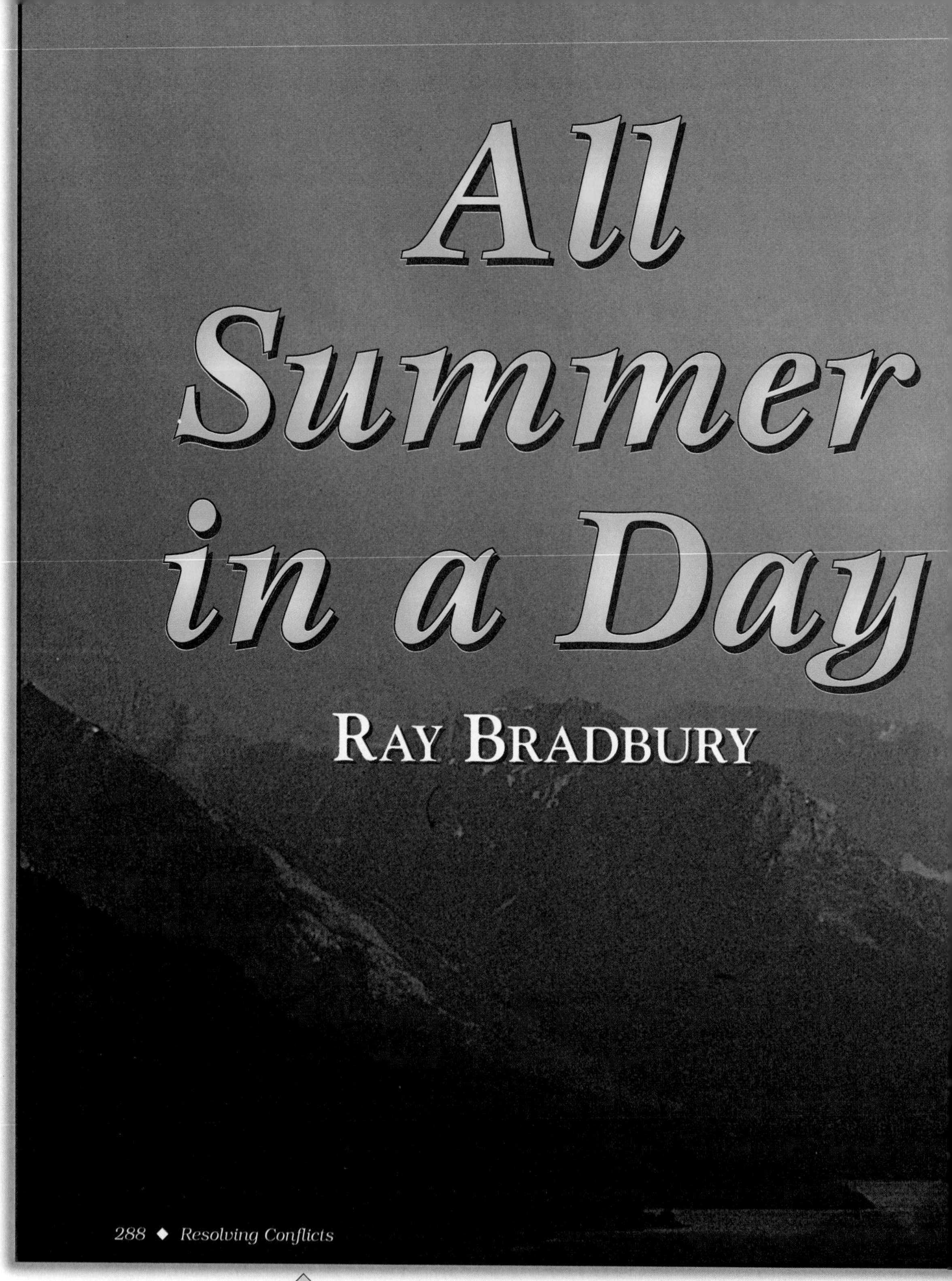

All Summer in a Day

RAY BRADBURY

Block Scheduling Strategies

Consider these suggestions to take advantage of extended class time:

- To structure class time, have students alternate between working independently and with learning buddies. Students might work on their own to read the selection independently, answer questions from Guide for Responding, complete **Selection Support** pages for Grammar (p. 108) and Vocabulary (p. 106), and complete the Writing Mini-Lesson. After the first three instructional activities, allow students to briefly meet with learning buddies to discuss how they would feel if they were one of the characters. Encourage students to use what they discover in buddy conferences as they write a remembrance.
- To help students prepare for the Writing Mini-Lesson, teach the Speaking and Listening Mini-Lesson on p. 290, and/or use the Dramatization activity in the Idea Bank on p. 297.
- Have students work in small groups on the Projects in the Idea Bank on p. 297, or research the planet Venus for the Science Connection in **Beyond Literature** on p. 20.

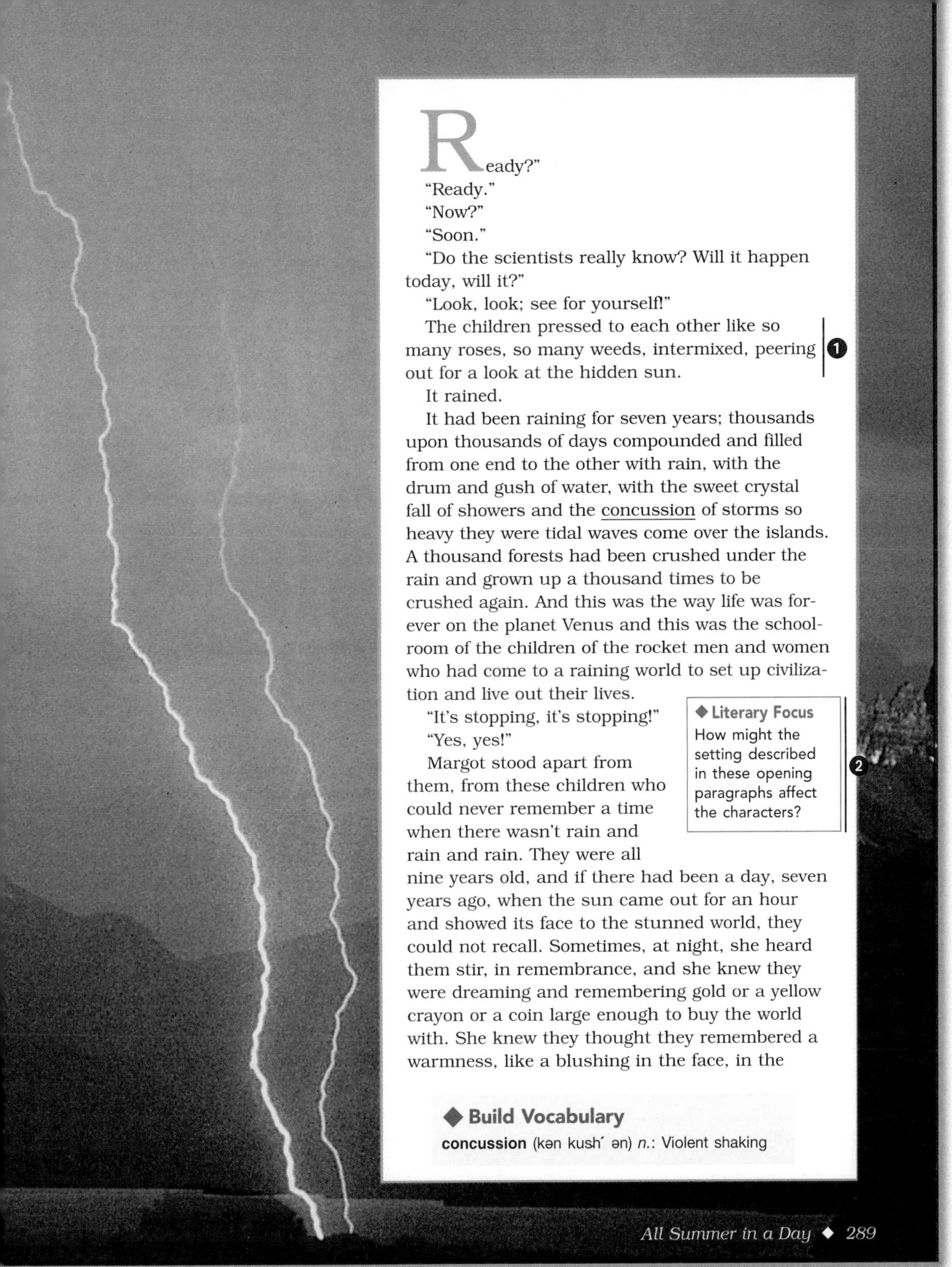

"Ready?"

"Ready."

"Now?"

"Soon."

"Do the scientists really know? Will it happen today, will it?"

"Look, look; see for yourself!"

The children pressed to each other like so many roses, so many weeds, intermixed, peering out for a look at the hidden sun. 1

It rained.

It had been raining for seven years; thousands upon thousands of days compounded and filled from one end to the other with rain, with the drum and gush of water, with the sweet crystal fall of showers and the concussion of storms so heavy they were tidal waves come over the islands. A thousand forests had been crushed under the rain and grown up a thousand times to be crushed again. And this was the way life was forever on the planet Venus and this was the schoolroom of the children of the rocket men and women who had come to a raining world to set up civilization and live out their lives.

"It's stopping, it's stopping!"

"Yes, yes!"

Margot stood apart from them, from these children who could never remember a time when there wasn't rain and rain and rain. They were all nine years old, and if there had been a day, seven years ago, when the sun came out for an hour and showed its face to the stunned world, they could not recall. Sometimes, at night, she heard them stir, in remembrance, and she knew they were dreaming and remembering gold or a yellow crayon or a coin large enough to buy the world with. She knew they thought they remembered a warmness, like a blushing in the face, in the

◆ **Literary Focus**
How might the setting described in these opening paragraphs affect the characters? 2

◆ Build Vocabulary

concussion (kən kush´ ən) *n.*: Violent shaking

◆Reading Strategy

1 Envision Settings and Actions Encourage students to recall a time when they looked out a window to see something different or special. Then, ask students to explain how they picture the children, based on this description. *They are crowded together, looking out the window.*

◆Literary Focus

2 Setting *The setting is a schoolroom on Venus, a world of constantly falling rain. Some students may suggest that those who live in such a setting might become sad and depressed because they never got to see the sun. They would be very excited about the prospect of finally seeing the sun for a few minutes.*

Customize for *Visual/Spatial Learners*

The photograph on these pages can help establish the setting of the story. Have students discuss what the images of lightning and an overcast landscape bring to mind. Encourage them to use this and other visuals accompanying the story to help them picture characters' actions and changes in the setting.

Looking at Literature Videodisc/Videotape

To provide background for students and motivate them to read "All Summer in a Day," play Chapter 4 of the videodisc. This segment provides an overview of meteorology and a meteorologist's job. Discuss how a meteorologist's job on Venus might be different from a meteorologist's job on Earth.

Chapter 4

Cross-Curricular Connection: Science

The atmosphere of Venus, as Ray Bradbury describes it, is pure fiction. Venus is relatively close to Earth and similar in size and mass. These factors led Bradbury and scientists to assume that Venus and Earth shared other features, but until the early 1990's little was actually known about the planet.

Scientists now know that Venus doesn't have a rainy climate. Thick, sulfuric clouds cover the planet's surface with only small traces of water vapor. A surface temperature of about 480° C (887° F) is the result of the greenhouse effect. The atmosphere cannot support plant life.

The spacecraft *Magellan* has been gathering and relaying to Earth a significant amount of data about Venus and its atmosphere. One source of documentation on *Magellan's* findings is "Venus Unveiled," an episode of the PBS TV program, *Nova*. You may want to obtain "Venus Unveiled," or another documentary on Venus, for the class to watch. Go to **http://www.pbs.org/wgbh/nova** for information on obtaining *Nova* videos. However, please be aware that the site may have changed from the time we published this information.

►Critical Viewing◄

❶ Distinguish Students may observe that the forest in the picture looks damp and has lots of vines and undergrowth, as the story's descriptions indicate.

◆Build Grammar Skills

❷ Prepositional Phrases After you have introduced prepositional phrases, ask students to find two prepositional phrases in the sentence that begins, "All day yesterday. . .": (in class; about the sun) and then to identify the prepositions (in; about).

◆Critical Thinking

❸ Infer Why does the boy doubt that Margot wrote the poem? *Possible responses: He thinks the poem is too good for her to have written, or he just wants to pick on her.*

◆Literary Focus

❹ Setting How does the setting of the story affect Margot? *Possible responses: She is faded, or washed out, by the rain; she is withdrawn because she is unhappy that it rains so much.*

Untitled, Rob Wood, Illustration by Wood Ronsaville Harlin, Inc.

❶ ▲ Critical Viewing What aspects of the story's setting do you see in this picture? [Distinguish]

body, in the arms and legs and trembling hands. But then they always awoke to the tatting drum, the endless shaking down of clear bead necklaces upon the roof, the walk, the gardens, the forests, and their dreams were gone.

❷ All day yesterday they had read in class about the sun. About how like a lemon it was, and how hot. And they had written small stories or essays or poems about it:

I think the sun is a flower,
That blooms for just one hour.

That was Margot's poem, read in a quiet voice in the still classroom while the rain was falling outside.

❸ "Aw, you didn't write that!" protested one of the boys.

"I did," said Margot. "I *did*."

"William!" said the teacher.

But that was yesterday. Now the rain was slackening, and the children were crushed in the great thick windows.

"Where's teacher?"

"She'll be back."

"She'd better hurry, we'll miss it!"

They turned on themselves, like a feverish wheel, all fumbling spokes.

Margot stood alone. She was a very frail girl who looked as if she had been lost in the rain for years and the rain had washed out the blue from her eyes and the red from her mouth and the yellow from her hair. She was an old photograph dusted from an album, whitened away, and if she spoke at all her voice would be a ghost. ❹ Now she stood, separate, staring at the rain and the loud wet world beyond the huge glass.

"What're *you* looking at?" said William.

Margot said nothing.

"Speak when you're spoken to." He gave her a shove. But she did not move; rather

Speaking and Listening Mini-Lesson

Dramatization

This mini-lesson supports the Speaking and Listening Activity in the Idea Bank on p. 297.

Introduce Point out that a dramatization is the performance of a story. Hearing and seeing a story performed can bring out certain literary elements of the writing, such as tone and characterization. Divide the class into drama groups. Have each group discuss the effects they wish to create in dramatizing the scene.

Develop Guide each group to consider these points:

- Convey ideas with actions, as well as words.
- Convey emotions that fit the characters.
- Present narrative. Will one or several people read it? Can narrative be replaced with dialogue or newly created action?

Apply Have students prepare their scripts. Some roles will be small, so in addition to performing, students can create costumes, props, backdrops, or sound effects. One student can direct. Invite students to present their dramatizations to the class.

Assess Have students note variations among the group dramatizations. Evaluate students' work based on the effectiveness of their preparation and ability to engage the audience, or use the Peer Assessment form for a dramatic performance, p. 107, in **Alternative Assessment.**

she let herself be moved only by him and nothing else.

They edged away from her, they would not look at her. She felt them go away. And this was because she would play no games with them in the echoing tunnels of the underground city. If they tagged her and ran, she stood blinking after them and did not follow. When the class sang songs about happiness and life and games her lips barely moved. Only when they sang about the sun and the summer did her lips move as she watched the drenched windows.

And then, of course, the biggest crime of all was that she had come here only five years ago from Earth, and she remembered the sun and the way the sun was and the sky was when she was four in Ohio. And they, they had been on Venus all their lives, and they had been only two years old when last the sun came out and had long since forgotten the color and heat of it and the way it really was. But Margot remembered.

"It's like a penny," she said once, eyes closed.

"No, it's not!" the children cried.

5 "It's like a fire," she said, "in the stove."

"You're lying, you don't remember!" cried the children.

But she remembered and stood quietly apart from all of them and watched the patterning windows. And once, a month ago, she had refused to shower in the school shower rooms, had clutched her

6 hands to her ears and over her head, screaming the water mustn't touch her head. So after that, dimly, dimly, she sensed it, she was different and they knew her difference and kept away.

There was talk that her father and mother were taking her back to Earth next year; it seemed vital to her that they do so, though it would mean the loss of thousands of dollars to her family. And so, the children hated her for all these reasons of big and little consequence. They hated her pale snow face, her waiting silence, her thinness, and her possible future.

"Get away!" The boy gave her another push. "What're you waiting for?"

Then, for the first time, she turned and looked at him. And what she was waiting for was in her eyes.

"Well, don't wait around here!" cried the boy savagely. "You won't see nothing!"

Her lips moved.

"Nothing!" he cried. "It was all a joke, wasn't it?" He turned to the other children. "Nothing's happening today. *Is* it?"

They all blinked at him and then, understanding, laughed and shook their heads. "Nothing, nothing!"

"Oh, but," Margot whispered, her eyes helpless. "But this is the day, the scientists 7 predict, they say, they *know*, the sun . . ."

"All a joke!" said the boy, and seized her roughly. "Hey, everyone, let's put her in a closet before teacher comes!"

"No," said Margot, falling back.

They surged about her, caught her up and bore her, protesting, and then pleading, and then crying, back into a tunnel, a room, a closet, where they slammed and locked the door. They stood looking at the door and saw it tremble from her beating and throwing herself against it. They heard her muffled cries. Then, smiling, they turned and went out and back down the tunnel, just as the teacher arrived.

"Ready, children?" She glanced at her watch.

◆ Build Vocabulary

slackening (slak′ ən iŋ) *v.*: Easing; becoming less active

vital (vīt′ əl) *adj.*: Necessary to life; critically important

surged (surjd) *v.*: Moved in a violent swelling motion

Cultural Connection

The conflict in "All Summer in a Day" arises from differences between the characters. Margot is from Earth's "culture," where the sun often shines, while Venusians rarely see the sun. Her descriptions of the sun spoil the other children's excitement. Respect for cultural differences is important, and when one has the benefit of a unique experience, he or she must be sensitive to others' lack of that experience. William can't tolerate Margot's experience of sunshine, and she can't understand why he disrespects her experience.

"Heat of the moment" action is often regretted. Based on the outcome, the children might act differently—given the opportunity.

Initiate a discussion about differences and tolerance. Guide students to identify what tolerance requires, such as sensitivity to other people's feelings, allowances for personal experiences, and respect for differences. Ask students to suggest how Margot and William might have been more sensitive to each other and more tolerant of the cultural differences between life on Earth and on Venus.

◆Literature and Your Life

5 Margot is having difficulty sharing her memory of sunshine so that the other children respect her experience. Invite students to share times when they were able to share an experience so that others understood and respected it. Encourage them to explain what made it possible to share the experience positively with others. *Students may cite experiences such as taking a trip or accomplishing a new skateboard maneuver; they should recognize that positive sharing requires consideration of others' different experiences.*

◆Critical Thinking

6 **Draw Conclusions** Ask students why they think Margot is afraid of the shower water. *Students should see that she is somehow equating the shower with the endless Venusian rains.*

◆Critical Thinking

7 **Infer** Have students consider the behavior of Margot's classmates when they lock her in the closet. Encourage students to recognize that no one stops or even questions what is taking place. Ask them to suggest why people might follow along this way. *Students should recognize the mob mentality that overtakes the group at the instigation of one person; in following his lead and remaining part of the crowd, they temporarily feel no individual responsibility for their actions.*

Customize for *Logical/Mathematical Learners*

Have students compute how many times a Venusian would experience sunshine during an average lifetime of 70 to 80 Earth years. Then, have them use the Internet or call the National Weather Bureau to obtain statistics on the number of sunny days in your local area during the past year (they may need to subtract the number of days it rained from 365). Have students prepare a chart or graph for the class that represents the sunshine opportunities during a lifetime on rainy Venus compared to a year in your community.

▶Critical Viewing◀

❶ **Connect** Suggested response: *The people in the painting are dancing wildly, joyfully, similar to the children's play in the sunshine.*

◆Reading Strategy

❷ **Envision Setting and Actions** *Possible responses: The sun shines brightly and burns; it is colorful; the sun seems to appear larger than it does from Earth.*

◆Literary Focus

❸ **Setting** Ask students to describe changes in the setting when the rain stops. They might continue the sensory detail chart suggested on p. 287 as they read about the period of time that the children are outside in the sunshine. Alternatively, use the Sensory Language Chart in **Writing and Language Transparencies,** p. 78.

Situation	Sights, Sounds, Smells, Physical Sensations
Just outside the tunnel	*bright, quiet, colorful, warm*
In the jungle	*silent, fresh, burning, alive*

Humanities: Art

A New Planet, by K. F. Yuon

The active figures in this painting indicate that an exciting event is taking place. The colors of the sky carry out the tone of excitement, as do the upward bursts of light. The overall visual effect is energized.

1. How does the painting reflect the mood and actions of the children playing in the sunlight? *The children are excited, too; they are energized by the sunshine in the same way the people in the painting are energized by the rays of light.*
2. Based on the story, what title would you choose for this painting? *Possible responses: Sunshine, A Day Without Rain, Dancing in the Sun*

A New Planet, K.F. Yuon, Tretiakov Gallery, Moscow, Russia

❶ ▲ **Critical Viewing** How do the emotions of the people in this painting compare with those of the characters in the story? **[Connect]**

"Yes!" said everyone.

"Are we all here?"

"Yes!"

The rain slackened still more.

They crowded to the huge door.

The rain stopped.

It was as if, in the midst of a film concerning an avalanche, a tornado, a hurricane, a volcanic eruption, something had, first, gone wrong with the sound apparatus, thus muffling and finally cutting off all noise, all of the blasts and repercussions and thunders, and then, second, ripped the film from the projector and inserted in its place a peaceful tropical slide which did not move or tremor. The world ground to a standstill. The silence was so immense and unbelievable that you felt your ears had been stuffed or you had lost your hearing altogether. The children put their hands to their ears. They stood apart. The door slid back and the smell of the silent, waiting world came in to them.

The sun came out.

It was the color of flaming bronze and it was very large. And the sky around it was a blazing blue tile color. And the jungle burned with sunlight as the children, released from their spell, rushed out, yelling, into the springtime.

◆ **Reading Strategy** How do you picture the sun based on this description? ❷

❸

"Now, don't go too far," called the teacher after them. "You've only two hours, you know. You wouldn't want to get caught out!"

But they were running and turning their faces up to the sky and feeling the sun on their cheeks like a warm iron; they

Viewing and Representing Mini-Lesson

Using Color

Introduce Ask students what tone and message they think the colors in K. F. Yuon's painting convey.

Develop Color impressions are quick, yet they last a long time. If we see too many colors at once, they visually overwhelm us—but we may be bored without enough color. Ask students how they would react to seeing purple cheese on a pizza or a blue happy face logo. Invite them to suggest what certain colors bring to mind.

Apply Ask students to create a color image, first by drawing an ordinary item, such as a car, chair, or tree. Then ask them to decide what message they would like to convey with color. Encourage them to use *A New Planet* as a model for using colors; their colors do not have to stay within lines or take on a particular shape. Direct students to title their finished work.

Assess Have students show their work to the class, explaining color choice, and what the message of their artwork is. Evaluate students' work based on their titles and explanations.

were taking off their jackets and letting the sun burn their arms.

3 "Oh, it's better than the sun lamps, isn't it?"

"Much, much better!"

They stopped running and stood in the great jungle that covered Venus, that grew and never stopped growing, tumultuously, even as you watched it. It was a nest of octopi, clustering up great arms of flesh-like weed, wavering, flowering in this brief spring. It was the color of rubber and ash, this jungle, from the many years without sun. It was the color of stones and white cheeses and ink, and it was the color of the moon.

The children lay out, laughing, on the jungle mattress, and heard it sigh and squeak under them, resilient and alive. They ran among the trees, they slipped and fell, they pushed each other, they played hide-and-seek and tag, but most of all they squinted at the sun until tears ran down their faces, they put their hands up to that yellowness and

> **◆ Literature and Your Life**
> Describe a time when your experience of something was much better than what you'd expected.

4 that amazing blueness and they breathed of the fresh, fresh air and listened and listened to the silence which suspended them in a blessed sea of no sound and no motion. They looked at everything and savored everything. Then, wildly, like animals escaped from their caves, they ran and ran in shouting circles. They ran for an hour and did not stop running.

And then—

In the midst of their running one of the girls wailed.

Everyone stopped.

5 The girl, standing in the open, held out her hand.

"Oh, look, look," she said, trembling.

They came slowly to look at her opened palm.

In the center of it, cupped and huge, was a single raindrop. 5

She began to cry, looking at it.

They glanced quietly at the sky.

"Oh, Oh."

A few cold drops fell on their noses and their cheeks and their mouths. The sun faded behind a stir of mist. A wind blew cool around them. They turned and started to walk back toward the underground house, their hands at their sides, their smiles vanishing away.

A boom of thunder startled them and like leaves before a new hurricane, they tumbled upon each other and ran. Lightning struck ten miles away, five miles away, a mile, a half mile. The sky darkened into midnight in a flash.

They stood in the doorway of the underground for a moment until it was raining hard. Then they closed the door and heard the gigantic sound of the rain falling in tons and avalanches, everywhere and forever.

"Will it be seven more years?"

"Yes. Seven."

Then one of them gave a little cry.

"Margot!"

"What?"

"She's still in the closet where we locked her."

"Margot."

They stood as if someone had driven them, like so many stakes, into the floor. They looked at each other and then looked away. They glanced out at the world that 6
was raining now and raining and raining

◆ Build Vocabulary

tumultuously (to͞o mulʹ cho͞o əs lē) *adv.*: Noisily and violently

resilient (ri zilʹ yənt) *adj.*: Springing back into shape

savored (sāʹ vərd) *v.*: Enjoyed

◆Reading Strategy

4 Envision Setting and Actions
How does Bradbury help his readers envision the children's response to the sun? *Bradbury compares their actions to "animals escaped from their caves," and uses words like wildly.*

Comprehension Check ☑

5 Why does the girl begin to cry? *She knows the raindrop means that the heavy rains are returning.*

◆Reading Strategy

6 Envision Setting and Actions
Ask students to explain how Bradbury "shows" the reader that the children feel bad about locking Margot in the closet. *Possible responses: the children stand "as if someone had driven them, like so many stakes, into the floor;" they can't meet each other's glances; their faces are "solemn and pale."*

Customize for
Bodily/Kinesthetic Learners
Turn off the lights and ask the class to sit, without moving a muscle, for three minutes. Then, turn on the lights and allow students to move freely about the classroom for one minute, giving them a 15-second warning before the time is gone. Have them compare and contrast their moods and physical reactions from both segments of the activity. Then, ask them to suggest how they might feel if the motionless part of the activity lasted much longer and they still had only a brief time to move. Finally, ask them how they felt when you told them they had only a few seconds of movement time left.

Beyond the Classroom

Career Connection

Science Fiction Careers Discuss what it takes to create science fiction, for example an interest in and knowledge about science and its effect on culture. Science fiction writers imagine life on another planet or in the future. Ray Bradbury predicted virtual reality and interactive television years before they actually existed.

Guide students to list science-fiction genres, including stories, television shows, movies, computer games, and comic books. Discuss pros and cons of each genre, such as special, visual, sound, and computer-generated effects, and inspiring and relying on the imaginations of readers.

Interested students can find out more about science-fiction careers by writing to the creator of their favorite science-fiction genre. Address a letter to a writer in care of the agent or publisher (your local library is one source for this address) and to a TV or film writer in care of the production company. Alternatively, challenge students to research who developed a computer game and to write to that person in care of the software publisher.

Develop Understanding

One-Minute Insight In "Primer Lesson," Carl Sandburg cautions that you should be careful how you use proud words because once they are spoken, you cannot take them back.

Critical Viewing

1 Evaluate *The intense colors and large size of the sun work well to illustrate the sun in the story; the figure standing alone could be Margot.*

◆Critical Thinking

2 Predict Ask students to predict what Margot will say to the children who locked her in the closet. How will this incident affect her? *Based on Margot's previous responses to the children's teasing, she may say nothing. However, it seems likely that missing the sunshine will make things worse for her and she will be very sad.*

Comprehension Check ☑

3 Does the title of the poem reflect the caution Sandburg gives about using proud words? *Students will probably infer that the title of the poem concerning a simple lesson cautions about the wisdom of choosing words carefully.*

◆Critical Thinking

4 Speculate What is the lesson Margot and the other children might learn from the poem? *Students may say that if Margot hadn't used proud words to describe her memories of the sun, the other students would not have become jealous of her. If the other children hadn't used proud words, Margot wouldn't have missed the sun.*

Beyond Literature

As students research Venus, they can search for data that has been obtained by the spacecraft *Magellan,* or contact NASA:
NASA/Washington, DC 20546
(202) 358-0000
http://www.jpl.nasa.gov/magellan

Sunrise IV, Arthur Dove, Hirshhorn Museum and Sculpture Garden, Smithsonian Institution

(1) ▲ **Critical Viewing** How well does the painting fit the story? **[Evaluate]**

steadily. They could not meet each other's glances. Their faces were solemn and pale. They looked at their hands and feet, their faces down.

"Margot."

One of the girls said, "Well . . .?"

No one moved.

"Go on," whispered the girl.

They walked slowly down the hall in the sound of cold rain. They turned through the doorway to the room in the sound of the storm and thunder, lightning on their faces, blue and terrible. They walked over to the closet door slowly and stood by it.

Behind the closet door was only silence.

(2) They unlocked the door, even more slowly, and let Margot out.

Primer[1] Lesson (3)

Carl Sandburg

Look out how you use proud words.
When you let proud words go, it is
not easy to call them back.
They wear long boots, hard boots; they
walk off proud; they can't hear you
calling—
Look out how you use proud words. (4)

1. **primer** (prim´ ər) *adj.:* From a simple textbook for teaching basic reading and morals.

Humanities: Art

Sunrise IV, 1937, by Arthur Dove

Arthur Dove (1880–1946) was one of the first abstract painters. Abstract paintings do not represent a subject realistically. Instead, they attempt to convey the essences of a subject through color, shape, and form.

Sunrise IV is from a series of sunrise pictures that Dove painted. He has taken a brilliant sunrise and reduced it to a few simple geometric shapes and colors that express the essence of what he saw. In this painting, as in all of his works, Dove expresses his deep love of nature. Have students examine the piece and discuss these questions:

1. How does the painting give you the feeling of a sunrise? *The colorful shapes seem to rise and expand like sunlight. The colors, intense in the center and more subdued in the surrounding bands, convey the brightness of the sun.*
2. How would the children in the story, including Margot, react to this painting? *The children would probably like the painting because it would remind them of the fun they had playing outside in the sunshine. Margot might take comfort from the painting, or it might cause painful memories.*

Beyond Literature

Science Connection

Exploring Venus Venus is the closest planet to Earth and is a near twin in size. However, that's where the similarity ends. The average surface temperature on Venus is 887 degrees Fahrenheit, eight times hotter than any region on Earth. In addition, its atmosphere is dramatically different from that of Earth, consisting mostly of sulfuric acid and sulfur dioxide. Finally, Venus rotates only once every 243 days, in contrast to Earth, which rotates once every 24 hours.

Cross-Curricular Activity

Museum Exhibit With a group of classmates, search the Internet or use library resources to learn more about Venus. Gather maps, charts, photographs, and other materials. Label each of the visuals you gather. Then, assemble the materials you gather into a museum exhibit that you can display in the classroom.

Guide for Responding

◆ Literature and Your Life

Reader's Response What is your reaction to how Margot is treated by the other students? Why?

Thematic Focus The other children's impulsive actions kept Margot from seeing the sun, which mattered very much to her. What would you like to say to the other children?

Journal Writing This story takes place in a world that is almost completely sunless. In a journal entry, jot down some ways in which you would adjust to life on Venus.

☑ Check Your Comprehension

1. Why are all the students excited at the start of the story?
2. Why does Margot know more about the sun than her classmates do?
3. What do the children do to Margot just before the rain stops?
4. What do the children do during the two hours that they are outdoors?
5. What happens to Margot at the very end?
6. In "Primer Lesson," what makes "proud words" dangerous?

◆ Critical Thinking

INTERPRET

1. Why are the children unkind to Margot? **[Infer]**
2. Why do the children reject Margot's descriptions of what the sun is like? **[Infer]**
3. Why do you think that all of the children go along with the prank that is played against Margot? **[Draw Conclusions]**
4. How do you think the children intend for their prank to end? **[Speculate]**
5. How do they feel when they remember what they have done to Margot? **[Analyze]**
6. What lessons does this story teach that can be applied to life in our world? **[Generalize]**
7. What quality of "proud words" does Sandburg stress in saying they wear "hard boots"? **[Interpret]**
8. Read the footnoted definition of *primer*. Why do you think Sandburg called his poem "Primer Lesson"? **[Generalize]**

EXTEND

9. How do you think the other children will treat Margot in the future? **[Predict]**

COMPARE LITERARY WORKS

10. How can you apply the message of "Primer Lesson" to "All Summer in a Day"? **[Connect]**

Beyond the Selection

FURTHER READING

Other Works by Ray Bradbury

The Martian Chronicles
Fahrenheit 451
The Illustrated Man

Other Works About Resolving Conflicts

Maniac Magee, Jerry Spinelli
Child of the Owl, Laurence Yep
Anne of Green Gables, L. M. Montgomery

INTERNET

For more information about Ray Bradbury, visit the following Web site:

http://www.pracapp.com/infomine/A733612060/output2.html

Please be aware, however, that the site may have changed from the time we published this information.

We *strongly recommend* that you preview the site before you send students to it.

Reinforce and Extend

Answers

◆ Literature and Your Life

Reader's Response Students may feel compassion for Margot and her situation.

Thematic Focus Students may wish to tell the children they were mean. Some students might like to ask the children to consider how they would feel if they were in Margot's place.

☑ Check Your Comprehension

1. The children are excited because they hope to see the sun.
2. Margot remembers the sun because she lived on Earth, but the others have always lived on Venus.
3. They lock Margot in a closet.
4. They run and play, look at the sky, and squint at the sun.
5. At the very end, the children let Margot out of the closet.
6. You cannot take them back.

◆ Critical Thinking

1. They dislike Margot because she is different from them. She doesn't join in their games, and she remembers what sunlight is like.
2. The other children resent Margot's memories of the sun.
3. The children go along with the prank because they dislike Margot. They may feel less responsibility because it was William's idea, not theirs.
4. They may have thought the teacher would find Margot in the closet and free her.
5. The children feel bad when they realize that Margot, who longed for the sun more than any of them, didn't get to see it.
6. Possible responses: Treat all people with kindness and respect; treat others as you wish to be treated.
7. Sandburg stresses the fact that proud words may hurt others.
8. Sandburg wanted his poem to teach a simple lesson about choosing words carefully.
9. Some students may believe that the children will treat Margot better. Others may feel that the children will be embarrassed and avoid her even more.
10. If the boy hadn't used proud words, the other children might not have been cruel to Margot.

Answers

◆Reading Strategy

1. Possible details are constant hard rain; the sound of rain like a "tatting drum"; dark, sunless days.
2. Possible details are sun on their cheeks "like a warm iron"; sky is "a blazing blue tile color"; breathing "fresh, fresh air."
3. Details such as "long boots, hard boots" describe proud words.

◆Build Vocabulary

Using the Word Root *-vita-*

1. vitality; 2. vitamins; 3. vital signs

Spelling Strategy

1. saturated; 2. actuality; 3. situation

Using the Word Bank

1. Yes; you cannot live without water.
2. If you savored a meal, you liked it very much.
3. Slackening rain is decreasing.
4. No; a feather falls lightly to the floor, so it doesn't cause any shaking.
5. Yes; a baseball can absorb a hit while retaining its shape.
6. Electricity surging through a computer could cause electrical damage to the circuits.
7. Children playing tumultuously would be very noisy.

◆Literary Focus

1. The most essential details of the setting are that the children are on Venus, where it rains all the time, and that the sun is about to reappear for the first time in seven years.
2. Margot is unhappy on Venus. She is pale and withdrawn. She does not play with the other children and misses Earth and its sunshine.
3. The other children on Venus are able to enjoy life, play games, sing songs, and form friendships even though they, too, long for the appearance of the sun.
4. Students should base their answers on their knowledge of groups of children.

Guide for Responding *(continued)*

◆ Reading Strategy

Envision Setting and Actions

Envisioning details that appeal to your senses in various scenes will help you to participate in the story. You can better understand the struggle between Margot and her classmates by contrasting the rainy period and the few hours of sunlight.

1. List three sensory details that show why living on Venus is difficult.

2. List three sensory details that show how the students enjoy the rare appearance of the sun.

3. What details in "Primer Lesson" help you envision "proud words"?

◆ Build Vocabulary

Using the Word Root *-vita-*

You will recognize the word root *-vita-*, meaning "life," in these words and expressions:

vitamins   vitality   vital signs

On your paper, match the words with their meanings.

1. A feeling of being alive: ___?___

2. Elements in food that are essential for life: ___?___

3. The body's indicators of life: ___?___

Spelling Strategy

In some words, like *tumultuously*, the *choo* sound is spelled *tu*. Write the following sentences, completing the spelling of the *choo* sound.

1. Constant rains sa__rated Bradbury's Venus.

2. In ac__ality, there is no rain on Venus.

3. The fictional si__ation makes a good story.

Using the Word Bank

Answer the following questions. Explain each answer.

1. Is water *vital* to life?

2. Is a meal that you *savored* one that you liked?

3. Is *slackening* rain increasing or decreasing?

4. When a feather lands on the floor, does it produce a *concussion?*

5. Would you describe a baseball as *resilient?*

6. If electricity *surged* through your computer, what effect would it have?

7. If children play *tumultuously*, are they quiet?

◆ Literary Focus

Setting

The **setting** of "All Summer in a Day"—the time and place in which events occur—plays a key role in the characters' actions and the events in the plot.

1. What details of the setting are most essential?

2. How is Margot affected by the story's setting?

3. How are the other children affected by it?

4. Could events similar to those in this story occur in a different setting? Explain.

◆ Build Grammar Skills

Prepositional Phrases

A **preposition** relates a noun or pronoun that appears with it to another word in the sentence. A **prepositional phrase** is a group of words that begins with a preposition and ends with a noun or pronoun. The noun or pronoun following a preposition is called the **object of the preposition.**

Common Prepositions				
about	behind	during	off	to
above	below	except	on	toward
across	beneath	for	onto	under
after	beside	from	outside	until

In this example, the prepositional phrases are in italics. The prepositions are printed in boldface, and the objects of the prepositions are underlined:

The children pressed ***to*** *each other,* ***like*** *so many roses* . . . peering out ***for*** *a look* ***at*** *the hidden sun.*

Practice Copy the following sentences, and underline the prepositional phrases. Identify the preposition and the object of each preposition.

1. It had been raining for seven years.

2. Margot stood apart from these children.

3. They had read in class about the sun.

4. She would play no games with them in the echoing tunnels of the underground city.

5. The sky darkened into midnight in a flash.

Writing Application Add at least two prepositional phrases to each of the following sentences.

1. It rains heavily.

2. One boy spoke.

◆Build Grammar Skills

1. Prep. Phrase: for seven years; Prep.: for; OP: years
2. Prep. Phrase: from these children; Prep.: from; OP: children
3. Prep. Phrases: in class, about the sun; Prep.: in, about; OP: class, sun
4. Prep. Phrases: with them, in the echoing tunnels, of the underground city; Prep.: with, in, of; OP: them, tunnels, city
5. Prep. Phrases: into midnight, in a flash; Prep.: into, in; OP: midnight, flash

Writing Application

Possible responses:

1. It rains heavily in Maryland in the spring.
2. One boy in the room spoke to Sean about weather.

Writer's Solution

For additional instruction and practice, use the lesson in the *Writer's SolutionLanguage Lab CD-ROM* on Prepositional Phrases and the practice pages on prepositional phrases, pp. 23–24, in the *Writer's Solution Grammar Practice Book.*

Build Your Portfolio

Idea Bank

Writing

1. **Diary Entry** Write a diary entry that Margot might have composed on the night following the events in the story.
2. **Travel Brochure** Write a pamphlet for tourists who want to visit Venus. Advertise interesting sights, fun activities, and cultural institutions. Also, say something favorable about the weather.
3. **Teacher's Report** As Margot's teacher, write a report on the incident described in the story. Keep your report as objective as possible. Include statements from the children involved and suggest appropriate discipline.

Speaking and Listening

4. **Lecture** If you were the teacher, what would you say to your class after discovering what they had done to Margot? Reread "Primer Lesson," and then deliver a lecture to the class in response to their treatment of Margot.
5. **Dramatization [Group Activity]** With a group, act out the scene in which Margot is locked in the closet. Feel free to add dialogue not included in Bradbury's story. **[Performing Arts Link]**

Projects

6. **Internet Research** Use the Internet to find out about weather conditions on different planets. Investigate temperature, atmosphere, and the length of a year. Share your findings, and identify the Web sites you used. **[Science Link]**
7. **Multimedia Report** Create a multimedia report on life in a place with a large average rainfall. Gather maps, charts, photographs, and, if possible, video. Put these materials together, along with written text, in a report that you can present to the class. **[Media Link]**

Writing Mini-Lesson

Remembrance

As time passes, our feelings about key events often change. Imagine how the children in Bradbury's story might have felt years later when they looked back on how they had treated Margot. Put yourself in the place of one of the characters, and write a **remembrance**—a piece of writing that describes people, places, and events from the past.

Writing Skills Focus: Show, Don't Tell

As you develop your remembrance, **show** the events instead of **telling** readers about them. Dramatize the situation through dialogue and detailed description. Instead of simply writing, "The other students picked on Margot," Bradbury dramatizes how the students picked on her. Look at the following example:

Model From the Story

"What're *you* looking at?" said William.
Margot said nothing.
"Speak when you're spoken to." He gave her a shove. But she did not move. . . .

Prewriting Choose the character from whose point of view you will write. Then, jot down how that character might feel years after the incident.

Drafting Begin your remembrance by revealing how you feel now about the event. Then, follow with a detailed description of what happened. In your description, focus on dramatizing the events, rather than simply telling what happened. End by revealing what you learned from the experience.

Revising Revise your remembrance by looking for places where you can improve your descriptions. Replace vague words with more vivid ones, or add dialogue or other details.

◆ Grammar Application

Use prepositional phrases to add descriptive or informative details to your remembrance.

✓ ASSESSMENT OPTIONS

Formal Assessment, Selection Test, pp. 88–90, and Assessment Resources Software. The selection test is designed so that it can be easily customized to the performance levels of your students.

Alternative Assessment, p. 20, includes options for less advanced students, more advanced students, visual/spatial learners, interpersonal learners, logical/mathematical learners, and verbal/linguistic learners.

PORTFOLIO ASSESSMENT

Use the following rubrics in the **Alternative Assessment** booklet to assess student writing:
Diary Entry: Narrative Based on Personal Experience Rubric, p. 83
Travel Brochure: Description Rubric, p. 84
Teacher's Report: Summary Rubric, p. 85
Writing Mini-Lesson: Description Rubric, p. 84

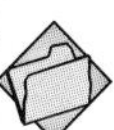

Idea Bank

Following are suggestions for matching the Idea Bank topics with your students' performance levels and learning modalities:

Customize for *Performance Levels*
Less Advanced Students: 1, 4, 6
Average Students: 2, 5, 6
More Advanced Students: 3, 5, 7

Customize for *Learning Modalities*
Visual/Spatial: 2, 5, 7
Verbal/Linguistic: 1, 3, 5, 7
Bodily/Kinesthetic: 5
Interpersonal: 5
Intrapersonal: 1, 6, 7
Logical/Mathematical: 6, 7

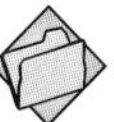

Writing Mini-Lesson

Refer students to the Writing Handbook in the back of the book for further instruction and information.

Writer's Solution

Writers at Work Videodisc
Have students view the videodisc segment on Description (Ch. 7) featuring Will Hobbs to see how he uses descriptive words to show, not tell. Have students discuss his use of description to help them write their remembrances.

Play frames 11106 to 20321

Writing Lab CD-ROM
Have students complete their remembrances by using the tutorial on Description. Follow these steps:

1. Have students use the Sensory Word Bin and the Descriptive Word Bin to find words that show, rather than tell.
2. Have students draft on computer.
3. Have students use the vague adjectives revision checker to help them revise.

Allow about 70 minutes to complete these steps.

Writer's Solution Sourcebook
Have students use Chapter 2, "Description," pp. 32–65, for additional support. This chapter includes in-depth instruction on descriptive writing, pp. 53–58, and a model of a remembrance, p. 38.

Prepare and Engage

OBJECTIVES

1. To read, comprehend, and interpret a narrative poem, a ballad, and an essay
2. To relate a poem, a ballad, and an essay to personal experience
3. To identify cause and effect
4. To appreciate suspense
5. To build vocabulary in context and learn about compound nouns
6. To develop skill in using adjective and adverb phrases
7. To write a police report using facts and examples
8. To respond to a narrative poem, a ballad, and an essay through writing, speaking and listening, and projects

SKILLS INSTRUCTION

Vocabulary: Compound Nouns

Spelling: Hyphenated Compound Adjectives

Grammar: Adjective and Adverb Phrases

Reading Strategy: Identify Cause and Effect

Literary Focus: Suspense

Writing: Use Facts and Examples

Speaking and Listening: Oral Report (Teacher Edition)

Critical Viewing: Connect

PORTFOLIO OPPORTUNITIES

Writing: Wanted Poster; Letter of Appeal; Narrative Poem

Writing Mini-Lesson: Police Report

Speaking and Listening: Poetry Reading; Ballad Collection

Projects: Oral Report; Geography Comparison

More About the Authors

Alfred Noyes was a very popular poet during the early 1900's. His epic poem, *Drake,* based on the exploits of Sir Francis Drake, appeared in serial form in a magazine from 1906 to 1908. Readers waited eagerly for each installment.

Geoffrey C. Ward, formerly the editor of *American Heritage* magazine, is a Franklin D. Roosevelt scholar and the author of several books on this American president. The coauthor of *The Civil War* and *Baseball,* and the principal writer on the TV documentaries upon which those two books are based, Ward is currently writing scripts for several film biographies.

Guide for Reading

Meet the Authors:

Alfred Noyes (1880–1958)

Alfred Noyes, born in Staffordshire, England, was both a poet and a critic. He wrote frequently about the English countryside and legends. Despite his great love for England's history, Noyes moved to New Jersey to teach at Princeton University. This new location did not stop him from writing poems about English history, especially of legendary figures like Robin Hood.

Geoffrey C. Ward (1940–)

From *The Civil War* to *The West* and *Baseball,* historian Geoffrey C. Ward balances legend against fact to bring the American past to life in successful television documentaries. Ward has combined his own writing talent and knowledge of history with Ken Burns's distinctive filmmaking style to co-create these award-winning PBS series.

Folk Ballads

Before printed books were easily available, stories were passed along orally. Told around an evening fire, some stories became songs, called ballads. Today, these ballads carry on the legends of the American West. Many focus on larger-than-life heroes. Some, like "The Dying Cowboy," tell a tragic tale with a twist of humor.

◆ Literature and Your Life

Connect to Your Experience

Who's your favorite athlete, film character, or figure from history? These people—who can perform amazing physical tasks or think fast to get out of a tight spot—seem bigger than the rest of us. They mix independence, strength, and determination. As you read these selections, think about how personalities from history and legend compare with today's giants.

Thematic Focus: Trouble Brewing

As you encounter the larger-than-life personalities in these selections, ask yourself whether they attract difficulty or are just better able to cope with it.

◆ Background for Understanding

History

Like Bess, a main character in "The Highwayman," Englishman Alfred Noyes saw British outlaws as dashing, romantic figures. So when Noyes visited Bagshot, Heath, England—a lonely region once terrorized by these highway thieves—perhaps a local legend caught his imagination and inspired him to write his famous poem.

◆ Build Vocabulary

Compound Nouns

The word *landlord,* which appears in "The Highwayman," is a compound noun combining two words, *land* and *lord.* A landlord is the owner of a business or property.

Word Bank

Which two of these words from the selections might describe a waterfall?

torrent
landlord
cascade
tawny
bound
strive
brandished

Prentice Hall Literature Program Resources

REINFORCE / RETEACH / EXTEND

Selection Support Pages
Build Vocabulary: Compound Nouns, p. 111
Build Spelling Skills, p. 112
Build Grammar Skills: Adjective and Adverb Phrases, p. 113
Reading Strategy: Identify Cause and Effect p. 114
Literary Focus: Suspense, p. 115

Strategies for Diverse Student Needs, pp. 41–42

Beyond Literature Cultural Connection: Cowboy Language and Cuisine, p. 21

Formal Assessment Selection Test, pp. 91–93, Assessment Resources Software

Alternative Assessment, p. 21

Daily Language Practice, pp. 34-35

Resource Pro CD-ROM
"The Highwayman," "The Dying Cowboy," "The Real Story of a Cowboy's Life"—includes all resource material and customizable lesson plan

Listening to Literature Audiocassettes
Includes all selections

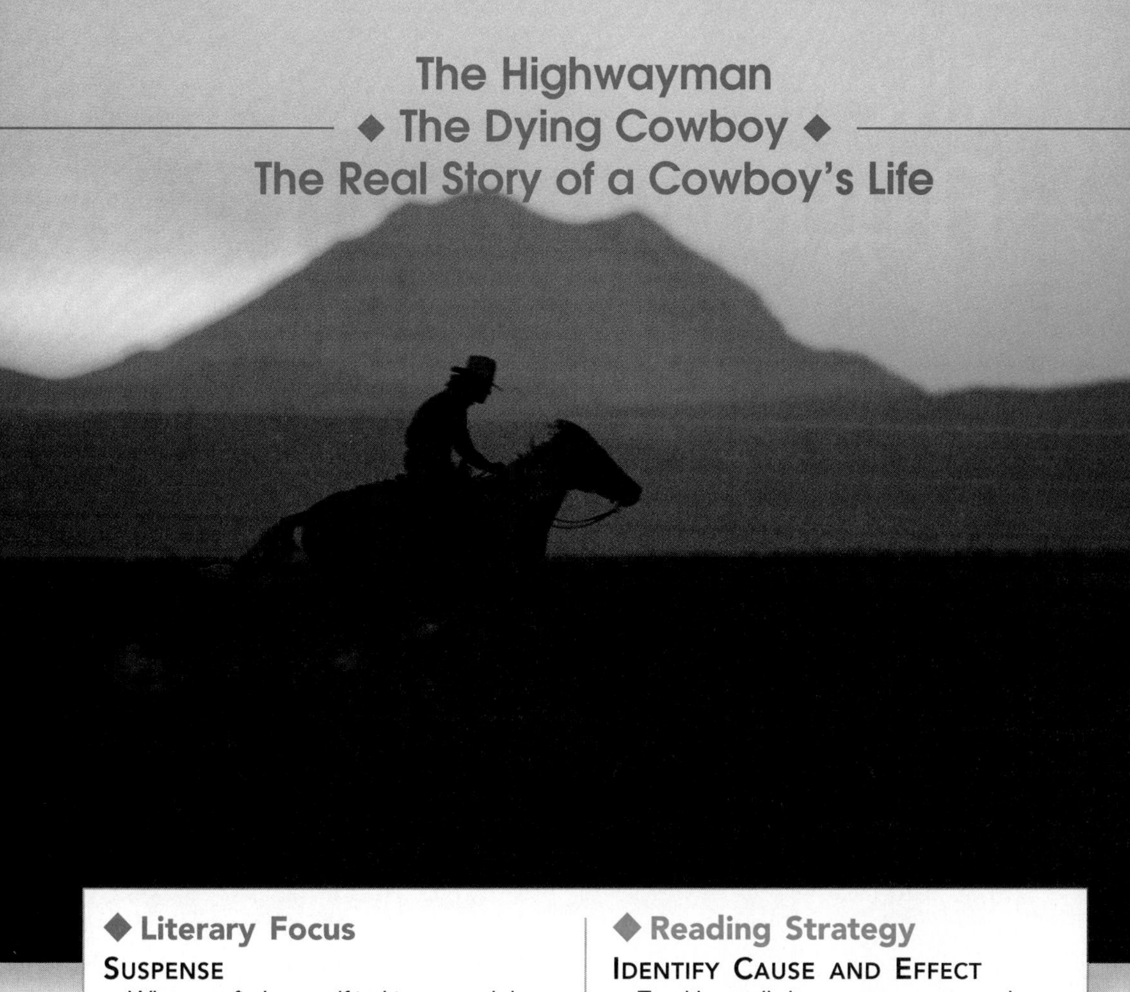

The Highwayman ◆ The Dying Cowboy ◆ The Real Story of a Cowboy's Life

◆ Literary Focus

Suspense

When you find yourself inching toward the edge of your seat in a movie theater, **suspense** is at work. This sense of uncertainty about how events will unfold also plays an important role in works of literature. Suspense makes you want to keep reading. Writers create suspense by presenting life-or-death danger or by building tension before a problem is resolved. In "The Highwayman," a stormy setting and the character's fear help build the poem's suspense.

◆ Reading Strategy

Identify Cause and Effect

Trouble usually has a **cause,** a reason that explains why it occurs. In "The Highwayman," an outlaw goes "after a prize," knowing the dangers he's up against. What he may not anticipate, however, is the **effect,** or result of his decision. Each event becomes a cause for the next event, linking causes and effects and propelling the action forward. Use a chart like the one below to record causes and effects as you read these selections.

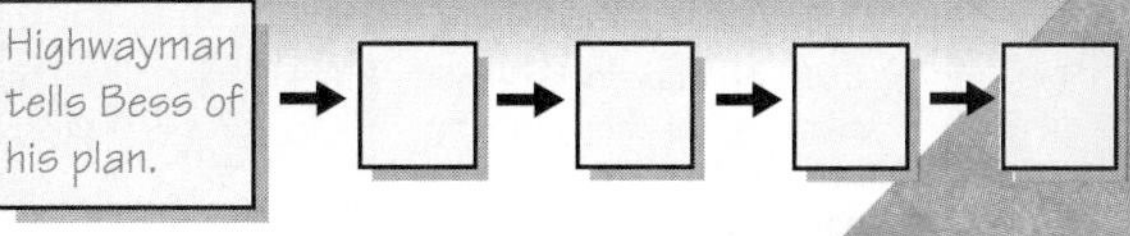
Highwayman tells Bess of his plan.

Interest Grabber

Tell students that actors often say it is more fun to play a villain than a hero. Ask them to speculate as to why this may be so. Next, ask students to explain what, if anything, makes outlaws so interesting, and what qualities make some outlaws more likeable than others. Inform students that in the poem "The Highwayman" they'll read about a notorious bandit who is portrayed as a dashing, romantic figure. Have them predict why he might be so appealing.

◆ Build Grammar Skills

Adjective and Adverb Phrases If you wish to introduce the grammar concept before students read, refer to the instruction on p. 312.

Customize for *Less Proficient Readers*

"The Highwayman" uses some words that may be unfamiliar to students. Help them use context and their dictionaries to determine the meanings of words not defined in the footnotes, such as: *torrent, claret, doeskin, hollows, cobbles, peaked, cascade, redcoat, throbbed,* and *brandished.*

Customize for *More Advanced Students*

Inform students that in the days of horse-drawn carriages, highwaymen were thieves who preyed on their victims on lonely stretches of road. Although these outlaws were feared by travelers, famous highwaymen like Robin Hood, Pancho Villa, and Jesse James are the stuff of legends. Have students, as they read "The Highwayman," try to separate factual from legendary details.

Preparing for Standardized Tests

Grammar The grammar concept for this selection is prepositional phrases used as adjectives and adverbs. Explain to students that prepositional phrases include the preposition and its object, and can function as adjectives modifying nouns or pronouns, or as adverbs modifying verbs or other adverbs or adjectives. Standardized tests may evaluate students' understanding of these adjective and adverb phrases. Present the following sample test question:

Identify the sentence that contains an adverb phrase.

(A) The hill on the horizon is five miles away.
(B) The cowboys in the front are riding point.
(C) The floods in early spring posed hazards.
(D) Often they rode by moonlight.

Students should recognize that in each of the first three choices, the prepositional phrases modify nouns (hill, cowboys, floods) and are therefore adjective phrases. In *(D)*, the correct choice, the prepositional phrase modifies the verb *rode.* For further practice, use Build Grammar Skills in **Selection Support,** p. 113.

Develop Understanding

This narrative poem tells a romantic tale of love, betrayal, honor, and death. A dashing robber loves Bess, an innkeeper's daughter, who loves him in return. He stops at the inn to tell Bess he is off to get a "prize," but will return before morning. Tim, who works at the inn and is jealous of their love, overhears their talk. He informs authorities, an action that sends soldiers to the inn. While awaiting the highwayman's return, the soldiers mistreat Bess and tie her up with a gun aimed at her heart. When the highwayman returns, Bess frees one hand and fires the gun to warn him of the ambush, killing herself in the process. The highwayman rides away, but returns in a fury after hearing of her death. He is killed by the soldiers.

Customize for
English Language Learners
Guide students to rephrase lines with inverted word order into standard form, in order to better understand them. For example, students can restate the beginning of line 13 as "He clattered over the cobbles . . ." Also, point out that the poet uses contractions to make the poem scan. Play the audiocassette to help students appreciate this technique.

Listening to Literature Audiocassettes

Customize for
Verbal/Linguistic Learners
Discuss with students that narrative poems, like "The Highwayman," tell a story. They combine poetic devices (rhythm, rhyme, and repetition) with elements of fiction, such as plot, character, dialogue, and setting, to create tension and to vividly present dramatic events. Guide students, as they read, to focus not only on the tale of love and betrayal, but also on the poetic devices. In particular, guide them to notice how Noyes uses repetition to create a song-like rhythm and focus readers' attention on key details of the story.

The Highwayman

Alfred Noyes

▲ Critical Viewing What elements of the poem's setting does this illustration capture? [Connect]

Block Scheduling Strategies

Consider these suggestions to take advantage of extended class time:

- Have students read independently and then work through the Guide for Responding questions, pp. 305, 308, and 311, in pairs or small groups.
- Allow volunteers to read sections of "The Highwayman" aloud to the class.
- Devote class time to having students work in small groups on the projects in the Idea Bank on p. 313, or to work on the writing activities. Invite students to post their Wanted Posters and Letters of Appeal, and to share their findings about ballads.
- To help students prepare for the Writing Mini-Lesson, refer them to p. 221 of the Reports chapter in *Writer's Solution Sourcebook,* where they will find pointers for conducting interviews.
- Give students practice in grammar, usage, and mechanics by having them complete the exercises in **Daily Language Practice,** p. 34.

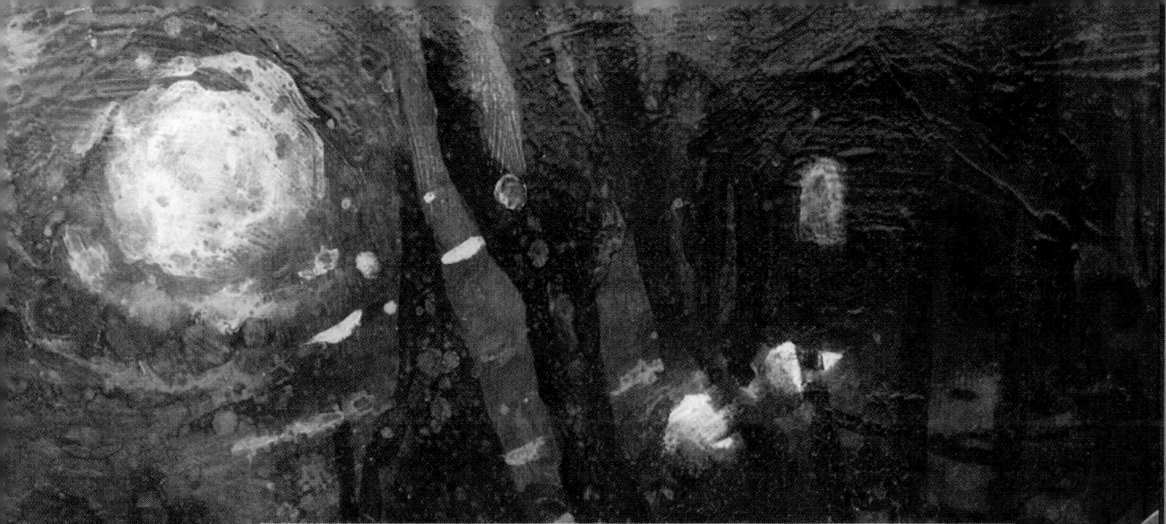

Part One

The wind was a torrent of darkness among the gusty trees. ❶
The moon was a ghostly galleon[1] tossed upon cloudy seas.
The road was a ribbon of moonlight over the purple moor,[2] ❷
And the highwayman came riding—
Riding—riding—
The highwayman came riding, up to the old inn door.

He'd a French cocked-hat on his forehead, a bunch of lace at his chin, ❸
A coat of the claret velvet, and breeches[3] of brown doeskin.
They fitted with never a wrinkle. His boots were up to the thigh. ❹
And he rode with a jeweled twinkle,
His pistol butts a-twinkle,
His rapier hilt[4] a-twinkle, under the jeweled sky.

Over the cobbles he clattered and clashed in the dark innyard.
He tapped with his whip on the shutters, but all was locked and barred.
He whistled a tune to the window, and who should be waiting there ❺

1. **galleon** (gal´ ē ən) *n.*: Large Spanish sailing ship.
2. **moor** (moor) *n.*: Open, rolling land with swamps.
3. **breeches** (brich´ iz) *n.*: Trousers that reach to or just below the knee.
4. **rapier** (rā´ pē ər) **hilt:** Large cup-shaped handle of a rapier, which is a type of sword.

◆ Build Vocabulary
torrent (tôr´ ənt) *n.*: Flood

◆Literary Focus

❶ **Suspense** Have students notice the metaphors in the first three lines. Ask them to tell what kind of mood these help to create. *Students may respond that the mood created is eerie, mysterious, and foreboding.*

Clarification

❷ Explain that the purple color of the moor may refer to heather, a flowering plant that grows on the English and Scottish moors. Heather grows low to the ground and has scalelike leaves and stalks of small, bell-shaped, purplish-pink flowers. Refer to the bottom note on this page for more on moors.

Clarification

❸ Explain to students that a cocked hat is a three-corned one with its brim turned up around the edge. Point out that cocked hats are those they have frequently seen in pictures of Revolutionary War soldiers.

◆Critical Thinking

❹ **Deduce** What does the highwayman's appearance suggest about him? *Students may say that his colorful, elegant clothes make him look romantic and glamorous, and that his gleaming sword handle and pistol make him seem both brave and dangerous. They may also observe that such extravagance suggests he is good at what he does.*

◆Critical Thinking

❺ **Draw Conclusions** What evidence is there that the highwayman and Bess have met like this before? *Students may say that Bess responds to his whistle, a signal.*

Cross-Curricular Connection: Geography

Moors The setting of this narrative poem is the English moors. These are known for their isolation and the sense of foreboding they inspire, and have been used by numerous authors as fictional settings. Have students use a map of Great Britain to locate the moors on the east coast of England, just south of the border with Scotland.

To give students a sense of the feelings of dread and apprehension associated with the moors, encourage them to read "The Hounds of the Baskervilles," by Sir Arthur Conan Doyle. The eerie setting of the moors and the local superstitions associated with them figure prominently in this dark mystery featuring Sherlock Holmes. Students can also view the film (the 1939 version with Basil Rathbone as the wily detective), which is available on videotape.

Clarification

❶ Inform students that a "love knot" was a special way of braiding hair that signified that a young woman was in love.

◆Critical Thinking

❷ **Infer** What can you infer about Tim, based on the poet's description of him? *Students may suggest that he is the opposite of the highwayman: graceless, dirty, grubby, and with messy hair.*

Thematic Focus

❸ **Trouble Brewing** Why do you think Noyes has introduced the character of Tim? What do you think the ostler will do now that he has heard the highwayman's plan? *Students may predict that since Tim loves Bess, he is jealous of the highwayman and will sabotage the planned rendezvous.*

◆Literary Focus

❹ **Suspense** Why do you think the poet emphasizes the word moonlight here? *Students may know that crazy things are often thought to take place in moonlight. Here, moonlight may hint of the possibility of "crazy" or wild behavior to come. You may wish to point out that the terms* lunacy *and* lunatic *have the same derivation as* lunar *and similar terms related to the moon.*

Comprehension Check ☑

Before students read on, you may wish to have them summarize what has happened in the story thus far. Guide students to recall the ominous opening, the secret meeting between the highwayman and Bess, the highwayman's plan to steal gold and then return to her, and the fact that Tim, whose eyes "were hollows of madness," overhears all.

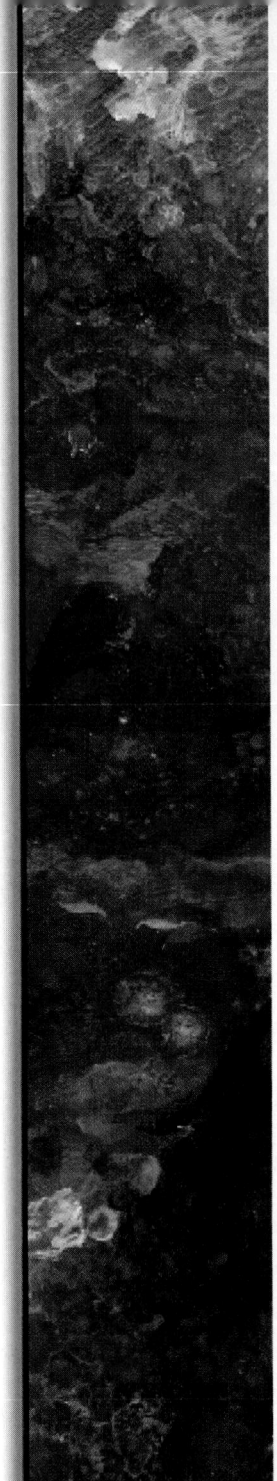

But the landlord's black-eyed daughter,
    Bess, the landlord's daughter,
❶ Plaiting[5] a dark red love knot into her long black hair.

And dark in the dark old innyard a stable wicket[6] creaked
Where Tim the ostler[7] listened. His face was white and peaked.
His eyes were hollows of madness, his hair like moldy hay,
❷ But he loved the landlord's daughter,
    The landlord's red-lipped daughter.
Dumb as a dog he listened, and he heard the robber say—
"One kiss, my bonny[8] sweetheart, I'm after a prize to-night,
❸ But I shall be back with the yellow gold before the morning
    light;
Yet, if they press me sharply, and harry[9] me through the day.
Then look for me by moonlight,
    Watch for me by moonlight,
❹ I'll come to thee by moonlight, though hell should bar the
    way."

He rose upright in the stirrups. He scarce could reach her
    hand,
But she loosened her hair in the casement.[10] His face burnt
    like a brand[11]
As the black cascade of perfume came tumbling over his
    breast;
And he kissed its waves in the moonlight,
    (O, sweet black waves in the moonlight!)
Then he tugged at his rein in the moonlight, and galloped
    away to the west.

Part Two

He did not come in the dawning. He did not come at noon;
And out of the tawny sunset, before the rise of the moon,
When the road was a gypsy's ribbon, looping the purple moor,
A redcoat troop came marching—
    Marching—marching—
King George's men[12] came marching, up to the old inn door.

---

5. **plaiting** (plāt´ iŋ) *adj.*: Braiding.
6. **stable wicket** (stā´ bəl wik´ ət): Small door or gate to a stable.
7. **ostler** (äs´ lər) *n.*: Person who takes care of horses at an inn or a stable.
8. **bonny** (bän´ ē) *adj.*: Scottish for "pretty."
9. **harry** (har´ ē) *v.*: To disturb by constant attacks.
10. **casement** (kās´ mənt) *n.*: Window frame that opens on hinges.
11. **brand** (brand) *n.*: Piece of burning wood.
12. **King George's men:** Soldiers serving King George of England.

Cross-Curricular Connection: Art

Color Different colors evoke certain responses in people. Ask students, for example, what feelings or ideas they associate with the color yellow, or what it means to be "blue." In literature, writers use color to symbolize different emotions. For instance, students can notice how prominently the color red figures in this poem. They can point to Bess's red lips and her red love knot. They may know that claret, the color of the highwayman's velvet coat, is the purplish-red color of red wine. Discuss why the poet made red his color of choice *(It is symbolic of blood, death, and love)*. Ask them to identify other colors used frequently in the poem and why they think the poet chose those colors.

Have students discuss colors and responses that seem to go together. Have them consider such expressions as "green with envy." Have interested students look back at other selections they've read recently to see how the writer used color to convey an idea or feeling symbolically. Did a character always wear a particular color? If so, why? What color was the sky? A building? A coat?

They said no word to the landlord. They drank his ale instead
But they gagged his daughter, and bound her, to the foot of
her narrow bed.
Two of them knelt at her casement, with muskets at their
(5) side!
There was death at every window;
And hell at one dark window;
For Bess could see, through her casement, the road that *he*
would ride.

They had tied her up to attention, with many a sniggering
jest.[13]
They had bound a musket beside her, with the muzzle
beneath her breast!
(6) "Now, keep good watch!" and they kissed her. She heard the
doomed man say—
Look for me by moonlight;
Watch for me by moonlight;
I'll come to thee by moonlight, though hell should bar the
way!

She twisted her hands behind her; but all the knots held
good!
(7) She writhed her hands till her fingers were wet with sweat or
blood!
They stretched and strained in the darkness, and the hours
crawled by like years,
Till, now, on the stroke of midnight,
Cold, on the stroke of midnight,
The tip of one finger touched it! The trigger at least was hers!

(8) The tip of one finger touched it. She strove no more for the
rest.
Up, she stood up to attention, with the muzzle beneath her
breast.
She would not risk their hearing; she would not strive again;
For the road lay bare in the moonlight;
Blank and bare in the moonlight;

13. **sniggering** (snig´ ər iŋ) **jest:** Sly joke.

◆ Build Vocabulary

landlord (land´ lôrd) *n.*: Person who keeps a rooming house, inn, etc.
cascade (kas kād´) *n.*: Waterfall or anything tumbling like water
tawny (tô´ nē) *adj.*: Tan; yellowish brown
bound (bound) *v.*: Tied
strive (strīv) *v.*: Struggle

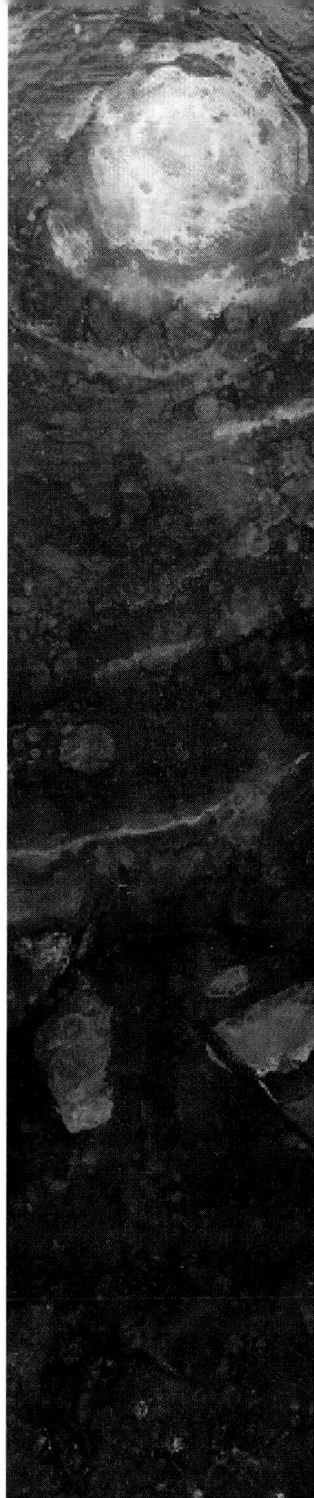

Comprehension Check ☑

(5) Why have the soldiers come to the inn? Why have they tied up Bess? *They have probably been summoned by Tim and are waiting at the inn for the highwayman to return. They tie up Bess to prevent her from warning him of their presence.*

◆ Reading Strategy

(6) **Identify Cause and Effect** Ask students to suggest how the brutal behavior of the soldiers affects their attitude toward the highwayman. *Students may say that compared with the soldiers, with their rude and villainous behavior, the highwayman appears honorable.*

◆ Critical Thinking

(7) **Make a Judgment** What do Bess's actions tell us about her? *Students may say that her painful attempts at freeing herself are heroic and that they show her loyalty to the highwayman.*

◆ Build Grammar Skills

(8) **Adjective and Adverb Phrases** Prepositional phrases that modify nouns and pronouns are adjective phrases. Those that modify verbs, adjectives, and other adverbs are adverb phrases. Point out both the adjective phrase *of one finger* that modifies *tip,* and the adverb phrase *for the rest* that modifies *strove.*

Cultural Connection

Signaling Signals, or nonverbal ways to communicate, differ from culture to culture. When the highwayman whistles, Bess comes to the window; the two had a prearranged signal. For as long as people have been communicating, they have been using one kind of nonverbal signal or another to express ideas. Ask students to identify times when words won't do and signals are necessary. Guide them to recognize that overcoming distance or loud noise, needing to be silent, or needing to communicate when language is a barrier are some reasons why signals are so important.

Challenge students to come up with examples of how people signal one another in different cultures, or at different times throughout history. Guide them to identify traditional ways that people have communicated across great distances (e.g., smoke signals or musical tones) and in closer address (hand gestures, facial expressions, body language, etc.). Invite students to demonstrate their signals.

Clarification

1 Direct students' attention to the repeated words *tlot-tlot,* which indicate horses' hoof beats. Explain that the use of words that imitate sounds is called *onomatopoeia*. Ask students to suggest other examples of sound-imitating words (*buzz, tweet,* etc.) Point out that Noyes probably made up *tlot-tlot* rather than use the more common *clip-clop* because it is less common and more onomatopoetic.

◆Reading Strategy

2 Identify Cause and Effect What are the effects of the musket shot? *The shot warns off the highwayman, but does not tell him that Bess is dead.*

Thematic Focus

3 Trouble Brewing Why does the highwayman return to the inn? *Some students may say that he wants to avenge Bess's death. Others may say that he feels responsible for her death and will sacrifice himself to keep his honor.*

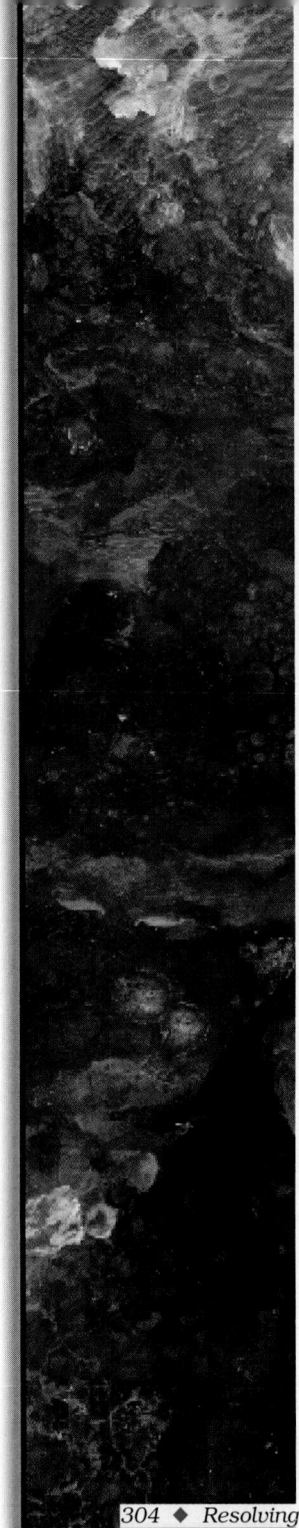

And the blood of her veins, in the moonlight, throbbed to
her love's refrain.

Tlot-tlot; tlot-tlot! Had they heard it? The horsehoofs ringing
clear;
Tlot-tlot, tlot-tlot, in the distance? Were they deaf that they
did not hear?
Down the ribbon of moonlight, over the brow of the hill,
The highwayman came riding—
1 Riding—riding—
The redcoats looked to their priming![14] She stood up, straight
and still.

Tlot-tlot, in the frosty silence! *Tlot-tlot,* in the echoing night!
Nearer he came and nearer. Her face was like a light.
Her eyes grew wide for a moment; she drew one last deep
breath,
Then her finger moved in the moonlight,
Her musket shattered the moonlight,
Shattered her breast in the moonlight and warned him—
2 with her death.

He turned. He spurred to the west; he did not know who stood
Bowed, with her head o'er the musket, drenched with her own
blood!
Not till the dawn he heard it, and his face grew gray to hear
How Bess, the landlord's daughter,
The landlord's black-eyed daughter,
Had watched for her love in the moonlight, and died in the
darkness there.

Back, he spurred like a madman, shouting a curse to the sky,
3 With the white road smoking behind him and his rapier
<u>brandished</u> high.
Blood-red were his spurs in the golden noon; wine-red was his
velvet coat;
When they shot him down on the highway,
Down like a dog on the highway,
And he lay in his blood on the highway, with a bunch of lace
at his throat.

. . . .

14. priming (prī´ miŋ) *n.*: Explosive used to set off the charge in a gun.

◆ Build Vocabulary

brandished (bran´ dishd) *adj.*: Waved in a threatening way

And still of a winter's night, they say, when the wind is in
the trees,
When the moon is a ghostly galleon tossed upon cloudy
seas,
When the road is a ribbon of moonlight over the purple moor,
A highwayman comes riding—
Riding—riding—
A highwayman comes riding, up to the old inn door.

❹

Over the cobbles he clatters and clangs in the dark innyard.
He taps with his whip on the shutters, but all is locked and
barred.
He whistles a tune to the window, and who should be
waiting there
But the landlord's black-eyed daughter,
Bess, the landlord's daughter,
Plaiting a dark red love knot into her long black hair.

Guide for Responding

◆ Literature and Your Life

Reader's Response Who do you think was more brave—Bess or the highwayman? Why?

Thematic Focus What choices do Bess and the highwayman make that lead to trouble?

Poll Ask several classmates to supply three adjectives to describe the highwayman. Identify the adjectives most frequently used. What conclusion can you draw about this larger-than-life figure based on the results?

☑ Check Your Comprehension

1. Describe the two main characters of the poem.
2. Where and when does most of the action take place?
3. Use lines 25–30 to explain the highwayman's plans.
4. Why does Bess think she needs to warn the highwayman?
5. Use lines 75–80 to summarize how she communicates her warning.

◆ Critical Thinking

Interpret

1. What evidence is there to suggest that Bess and the highwayman have met on many moonlit nights? **[Infer]**
2. Find three details that make the highwayman appear a romantic, or dashing, figure. **[Connect]**
3. How does the repetition of the color red add to the poem's romantic quality? **[Support]**
4. What elements of the setting add to the poem's romantic quality? **[Support]**
5. What do the last two stanzas suggest about the love between Bess and her highwayman? **[Draw Conclusions]**

Evaluate

6. Would the poem have been as effective if it had ended at line 90? Explain. **[Evaluate]**

Extend

7. What can you learn from this poem about life in eighteenth-century England? **[Social Studies Link]**

Cross-Curricular Connection: Social Studies

Robin Hood Ask students to discuss what they know of Robin Hood of Sherwood Forest, the legendary thirteenth-century outlaw who reportedly stole from the rich and gave to the poor. Then, have them do research to find out more about the Robin Hood legend, King John, who was king of England at the time (reigned 1199–1216), and Robin's archenemy, the Sheriff of Nottingham. Invite students to share their findings in an oral report.

Interested students might enjoy watching *The Adventures of Robin Hood,* the 1938 film starring Errol Flynn as the swashbuckling bandit, or another, more recent film version. Have them compare the depiction of the character of this outlaw with the portrayal of the highwayman in the poem.

Clarification

❹ Guide students to recognize that the italic print of the last two stanzas sets them apart from the rest of the poem. Then, discuss that these stanzas act as an epilogue, or closing section, and are themselves a separate legend based on the story that just ended. These stanzas imply that the love between Bess and the highwayman was so strong that it continues even after they've died.

Reinforce and Extend

Answers

◆ Literature and Your Life

Reader's Response Have students support their answers.

Thematic Focus Bess's choice to love a robber invites trouble, while the highwayman's choice to visit Bess and then tell her of his planned robbery invites danger.

☑ Check Your Comprehension

1. The highwayman is a stylish and daring outlaw. Bess, the beautiful daughter of an innkeeper, is a brave and faithful young woman.
2. Most of the action takes place at an English inn, during two nights.
3. He plans to steal gold and then return to Bess at the inn.
4. The soldiers have set a trap for him and await his return.
5. She fires the musket, killing herself. He hears the shot and realizes that something is wrong.

◆ Critical Thinking

1. They have a secret signal—a whistle.
2. Students may refer to his fancy dress and weapons, his scorn for danger, his appearances by moonlight, and his love for Bess.
3. Red is often associated with love and death.
4. The moonlight and wind create an eerie, mysterious atmosphere that adds a romantic quality.
5. It is strong enough to continue after their deaths.
6. Possible response: No. The last two stanzas make it clear that the story has become a legend.
7. Possible response: Roads were dangerous; people traveled by horse or carriage and carried gold with them; some men wore elaborate clothing; outlaws could be shot on sight, without trial.

One-Minute Insight

This traditional cowboy ballad tells of one cowhand's dying request not to be buried on the open prairie. He wants to be buried at his home, near his family, but the demands of a cattle drive make his wish an impossible one to accommodate.

Customize for
More Advanced Students
Inform students that although cowboys rode on the "lone prairie," they themselves, contrary to popular western lore, were not loners. They worked and lived in groups and crowded into the same places in the towns they eventually reached. Guide students, as they read this piece and the one that follows, to look for examples of the team effort demanded by cattle drives, and of how each member of those teams was responsible not only for the successful completion of the task, but for the well-being of others on the drive.

Clarification

❶ Explain to students that a "traditional" work has no known author or composer, and has been passed down orally over the years. Tell them that this song and others like it were used by cowboys to pass the time and to settle the herds. Like other traditional cowboy ballads, it is simple and repetitive. Like any work from oral tradition, its exact words may vary from one rendition to the next.

Clarification

❷ Discuss with students that cowboys did not live on the open prairie; they just passed through it on the cattle drives.

Clarification

❸ Inform students that this indented stanza is the refrain of the song. Tell students that a refrain is a verse repeated at intervals within a song or poem. Point out that in this song, the first line of the refrain is the same each time, but that the other lines change.

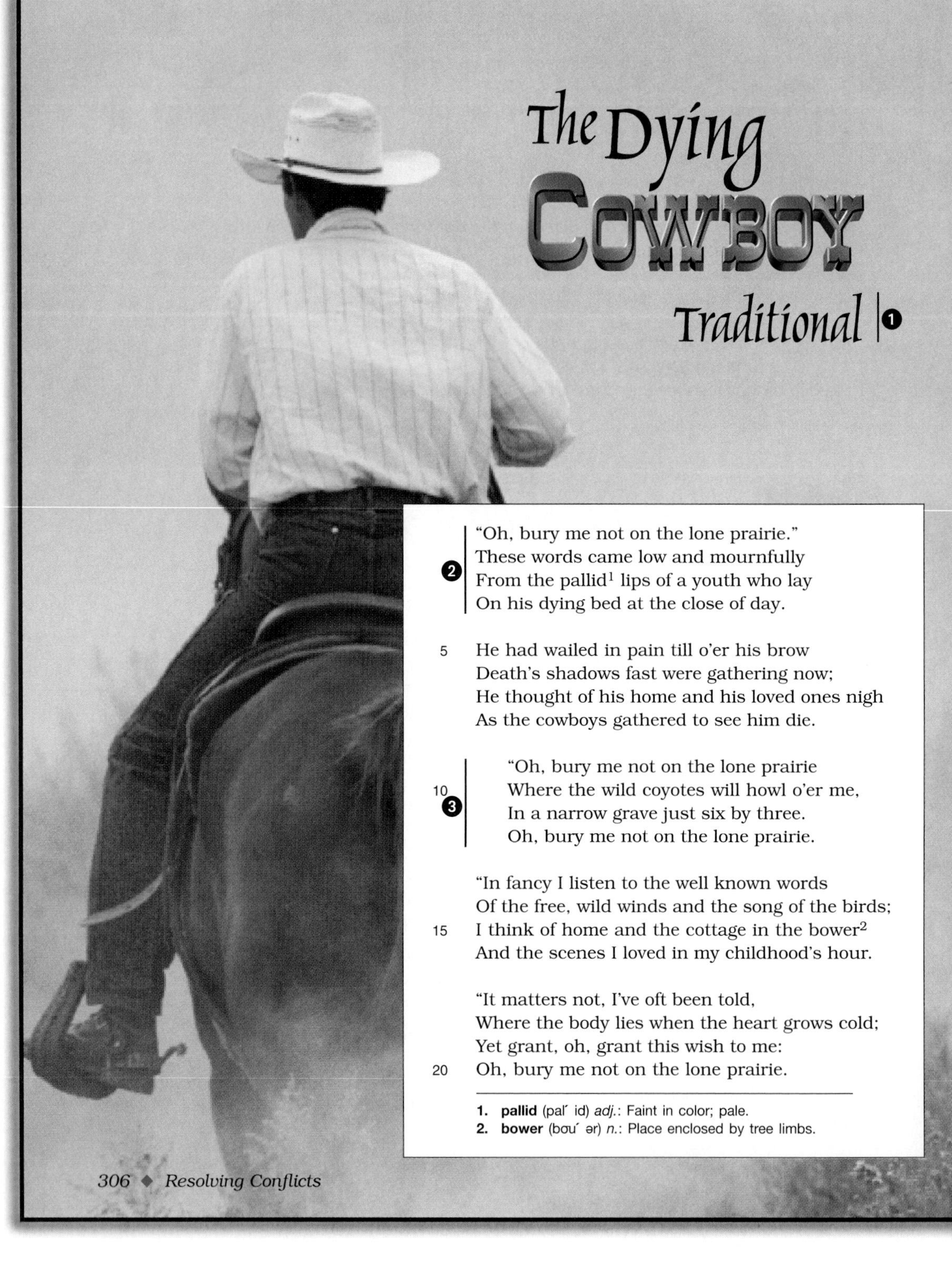

The Dying Cowboy

Traditional ❶

❷ "Oh, bury me not on the lone prairie."
These words came low and mournfully
From the pallid[1] lips of a youth who lay
On his dying bed at the close of day.

He had wailed in pain till o'er his brow
Death's shadows fast were gathering now;
He thought of his home and his loved ones nigh
As the cowboys gathered to see him die.

❸ "Oh, bury me not on the lone prairie
Where the wild coyotes will howl o'er me,
In a narrow grave just six by three.
Oh, bury me not on the lone prairie.

"In fancy I listen to the well known words
Of the free, wild winds and the song of the birds;
I think of home and the cottage in the bower[2]
And the scenes I loved in my childhood's hour.

"It matters not, I've oft been told,
Where the body lies when the heart grows cold;
Yet grant, oh, grant this wish to me:
Oh, bury me not on the lone prairie.

1. **pallid** (pal′ id) *adj.*: Faint in color; pale.
2. **bower** (bou′ ər) *n.*: Place enclosed by tree limbs.

"Oh, then bury me not on the lone prairie,
In a narrow grave six foot by three,
Where the buffalo paws o'er a prairie sea.
Oh, bury me not on the lone prairie.

"I've always wished to be laid when I died
In the little churchyard on the green hillside; 4
By my father's grave there let mine be,
And bury me not on the lone prairie.

"Let my death slumber be where my mother's prayer
And a sister's tear will mingle there,
Where my friends can come and weep o'er me;
Oh, bury me not on the lone prairie.

"Oh, bury me not on the lone prairie
In a narrow grave just six by three,
Where the buzzard waits and the wind blows free;
Then bury me not on the lone prairie.

"There is another whose tears may be shed
For one who lies on a prairie bed;
It pained me then and it pains me now—
She has curled these locks, she has kissed this brow.

"These locks she has curled, shall the rattlesnake kiss?
This brow she has kissed, shall the cold grave press?
For the sake of the loved ones that will weep for me,
Oh, bury me not on the lone prairie.

"Oh, bury me not on the lone prairie
Where the wild coyotes will howl o'er me,
Where the buzzards sail and wind goes free.
Oh, bury me not on the lone prairie.

"Oh, bury me not—" And his voice failed there.
But we took no heed of his dying prayer; 5
In a narrow grave just six by three
We buried him there on the lone prairie.

Where the dewdrops glow and the butterflies rest,
And the flowers bloom o'er the prairie's crest;
Where the wild coyote and winds sport free
On a wet saddle blanket lay a cowboy-ee.

◀ **Critical Viewing** What aspects of a cowboy's life do the photograph and "The Dying Cowboy" suggest? **[Connect]** 

◆Build Vocabulary

4 Compound Nouns Compound nouns are nouns formed by combining two separate words. Discuss the compound nouns in this line *(churchyard; hillside)*. Invite students to suggest other compound nouns they could form *(schoolyard, hilltop, etc.)* by piecing together the smaller words.

◆Reading Strategy

5 Identify Cause and Effect Why do the other cowboys "take no heed" of the dying cowboy's request? *They are in the midst of a cattle drive, many day's travel from the man's home. The demands of their mutual task (made even harder by the impending absence of this dying man) make assigning men to this extra task an impossibility.*

▶Critical Viewing◀

6 Connect *Possible response: They suggest a life in the saddle through a rugged, dusty, lonely landscape.*

Cross-Curricular Connection: Music

Music of the Cowboys Not all cowboys sang just to soothe cattle; some made a career of it. Gene Autry is perhaps the most famous of the many cowboy singers who were popular movie and television stars in the 1940's and 1950's. During these years, westerns were the genre of choice in America. Autry, dubbed "America's Favorite Cowboy," wrote over 200 songs. His signature song is "Back in the Saddle Again," but Autry wrote another one that many students will know: "Rudolph the Red-Nosed Reindeer."

If possible, obtain and play for students the songs of Gene Autry and other cowboy singers, such as the Sons of the Pioneers and Roy Rogers. What common themes or features do the songs share? How are they different from the music students listen to today? How are they similar?

Customize for
Musical/Rhythmic Learners
Invite students to find a version of this song to play for classmates. Alternately, ask students who know the ballad to play or sing it. Or, ask volunteers to write their own tunes and arrangements for the song, and to perform them.

Reinforce and Extend

Answers

◆ Literature and Your Life

Reader's Response Some students will be surprised that the cowboy does not get his wish. Others may have guessed that the wish would be too difficult to fulfill.

Thematic Focus Possible response: It is often difficult to know where life's choices will lead, but people can try to weigh the possible outcomes of each decision.

☑ Check Your Comprehension

1. He doesn't wish to be buried on the lonely prairie; rather, near the home he left behind.
2. He wants to be buried near his childhood home, next to his father's grave, so that his family and girlfriend will mourn him. He finds the prairie desolate.

◆ Critical Thinking

1. The cowboy sees the prairie as lonely and bleak, while his companions can see its positive traits.
2. He loves and misses them.
3. Students may say that the song suggests thinking carefully about choices and where they may lead.
4. Possible responses: (a) It conveys a sense of loneliness and isolation. (b) Details are the description of the windswept prairie and the dying cowboy's repeated longing to be buried near his distant home.

"Oh, bury me not on the lone prairie
Where the wild coyotes will howl o'er me,
Where the rattlesnakes hiss and the crow flies free.
Oh, bury me not on the lone prairie."

Oh, we buried him there on the lone prairie
Where the wild rose blooms and the wind blows free;
Oh, his pale young face nevermore to see—
For we buried him there on the lone prairie.

Yes, we buried him there on the lone prairie.
Where the owl all night hoots mournfully,
And the blizzard beats and the winds blow free
O'er his lowly grave on the lone prairie.

And the cowboys now as they roam the plain—
For they marked the spot where his bones were lain—
Fling a handful of roses o'er his grave,
With a prayer to Him who his soul will save.

"Oh, bury me not on the lone prairie
Where the wolves can howl and growl o'er me;
Fling a handful of roses o'er my grave
With a prayer to Him who my soul will save."

Guide for Responding

◆ Literature and Your Life

Reader's Response Were you surprised by this song's ending? Explain.

Thematic Focus The main speaker in "The Dying Cowboy" regrets some of his life choices. How can people identify decisions that may lead to trouble—before it's too late?

Journal Writing In a journal entry, explain the images that the word *cowboy* sparks in your mind.

☑ Check Your Comprehension

1. Summarize the wishes expressed by "The Dying Cowboy."
2. What three reasons does he provide to support his wishes?

◆ Critical Thinking

Interpret

1. How does the cowboy's view of the prairie differ from his companions' view of it? **[Compare and Contrast]**
2. How does the cowboy feel about his family and friends back home? **[Infer]**
3. What messages about life can you find in this song? **[Draw Conclusions]**

Evaluate

4. (a) What impression of a cowboy's life does the song convey? (b) What details contribute to this impression? **[Assess]**

Speaking and Listening Mini-Lesson

Oral Report
This mini-lesson supports the project in the Idea Bank on p. 313.

Introduce Discuss with students how generations of Americans have been fascinated with the legends of western adventurers, heroes, and villains. Tell students that in this activity they will do collaborative research to discover the truth behind the myths surrounding some of these romantic characters.

Develop Brainstorm with students for a list of legendary western figures, such as Davy Crockett, Kit Carson, Jesse James, Wyatt Earp, Doc Holliday, Wild Bill Hickock, Annie Oakley, and Billy the Kid. Have students form groups, each choosing one of these people to research. Guide them to contrast the legendary figure with the real person. Students can use the Internet or the library; encourage them to consult a variety of sources (such as *The West,* from which "The Real Story of a Cowboy's Life" has been taken).

Apply Have each group present its report. Invite them to include clips from videos (such as Ken Burns's *The West,* or other films or documentaries), play evocative songs, or show pictures and photos to enhance the reports.

Assess Evaluate groups on the quality and breadth of research gathered, and on the clarity of the presentation. Or, use the Peer Assessment: Speaker/Speech form, p. 105, in **Alternative Assessment.**

The Real Story of a Cowboy's Life

GEOFFREY C. WARD

A drive's success depended on discipline and planning. According to Teddy Blue,[1] most Texas herds numbered about 2,000 head with a trail boss and about a dozen men in charge—though herds as large as 15,000 were also driven north with far larger escorts. The most experienced men rode "point" and "swing," at the head and sides of the long herd; the least experienced brought up the rear, riding "drag" and eating dust. At the end of the day, Teddy Blue remembered, they "would go to the water barrel . . . and rinse their mouths and cough and spit up . . . black stuff. But you couldn't get it up out of your lungs." ❶

They had to learn to work as a team, keeping the herd moving during the day, resting peacefully at night. Twelve to fifteen miles a day was a good pace. But such steady progress could be interrupted at any time. ❷ A cowboy had to know how to gauge the temperament of his cattle, how to chase down a stray without alarming the rest of the herd, how to lasso[2] a steer using the horn of his saddle as a tying post. His saddle was his most prized possession; it served as his chair, his workbench, his pillow at night. Being dragged to death was the most common death for a cowboy, and so the most feared occurrence on the trail was the nighttime stampede.[3] As Teddy Blue recalled, a sound, a smell, or simply the sudden movement of a jittery cow could set off a whole herd.

> If . . . the cattle started running—you'd hear that low rumbling noise along the ground and the men on herd wouldn't need to come in and tell you, you'd know—then you'd jump for your horse and get out there in the lead,

1. **Teddy Blue:** Edward C. Abbot; a cowboy who rode in a successful trail drive in the 1880's.
2. **lasso** (las´ ō) *v.*: To throw a long rope with a sliding noose at one end over something, then pulling the noose tight and catching it.
3. **stampede** (stam pēd´) *n.*: Sudden rush of panicked animals.

One-Minute Insight This essay describes a cattle drive from the perspective of a real cowboy who rode in one. It portrays the drive as a multifaceted, difficult experience, full of conflict, danger, and reward but not much glamour.

Customize for *Visual/Spatial Learners*

Students can see what a drive must have looked like by watching Part 2: "The Trail," of Volume I of the television mini-series *Lonesome Dove*. They will be able to see clearly the tasks of point, swing, and drag riders, and to witness the many hazards that threaten the success of a cattle drive.

Clarification

❶ Inform students that the era of the cattle drives lasted only about twenty-five years, from the end of the Civil War to about 1890. It was a period in which 10 million head of cattle were driven north from ranches in Texas along one of several trails, such as the Chisholm, the Shawnee, and the Goodnight-Loving. At first, cattle were taken to mining towns and to military forts, where the government bought beef to feed soldiers and the Native American groups on reservations. Later, most cattle were taken to railheads in towns in Kansas and Nebraska, from where they were shipped east by rail to feed people in the growing cities. Although the rough and dangerous conditions and low pay dissuaded most cowboys from participating in more than one drive, Teddy Blue made several. His first was in 1871 and his last in 1883, when he was only 23 years old.

◆Reading Strategy

❷ Identify Cause and Effect
What might interrupt the steady progress of a trail drive? *Students might point to dust storms, floods, and other weather events; problems with settlers; problems with Native Americans; and other unexpected hardships, such as disease or injury to some of the hands.*

Humanities: Photography

The top photograph was taken in the Oklahoma panhandle in about 1880. The men on the hill overlook a river, where others are bathing. The photographer is unknown. The photo below it, by F. M. Steele, shows men riding herd in the 1880's. Use these questions for discussion:

1. How would you describe the men in the two photos? *Students may say that the men, most of whom are young, are dressed similarly in white shirts, some with vests, most wearing hats. One man in the bottom photo is not on horseback. Students can notice the length of rope each rider has, and that the men, for the most part, appear to have stern looks on their faces.*
2. How do these presentations of trail life differ from those given in the piece? *Students may say that the men appear to be taking it easy, even those in the bottom photo, which shows the cattle for which the men are responsible. The calm scene shown here contrasts with the harsh depiction of cattle drives in the essay, which emphasizes their dangers and difficult conditions.*

Thematic Focus

❶ **Trouble Brewing** In what ways did trail bosses formulate procedures to head off trouble? Why did some bosses set up clear guidelines for behavior and work responsibilities, while others made cowboys sign written agreements and kept the cowboys' guns? *Students may say that since cowboys were armed and there was no law to speak of on the open prairie at that time, these were reasonable measures. Some may note that some of the cowboys might have been soldiers and therefore may not have been averse to using their weapons.*

Customize for *Logical/Mathematical Learners*

Provide a map that includes Texas, Oklahoma, Kansas, and Nebraska to help students see where the drives took place. Point out lower Texas, the rivers mentioned on this page, and the Kansas "cow towns" of Abilene, Chetopa, Coffeyville, Ellsworth, Hays, Wichita, Great Bend, Caldwell, and Dodge City.

Comprehension Check ☑

❷ Have students clarify the meaning of this quotation. *Settlers and cowboys were at odds. The cattle trails crossed lands claimed by farmers, who claimed that the cows did damage to their crops. In turn, the cowboys claimed that they had been using the trails before the settlers came in.*

◆Reading Strategy

❸ **Identify Cause and Effect** *Cattle drives ruined crops and spread disease to domestic livestock.*

◆Build Vocabulary

❹ **Compound Nouns** Point out the current meaning of *deadline,* which is the latest time by which a task must be completed. Then, tell students that the word derives from the time of the notorious Confederate military prison at Andersonville, Georgia. Then, a "deadline" referred to a line beyond which a prisoner could go only at the risk of being shot by a guard. At Andersonville, the deadline was set at seventeen feet from the camp fence.

trying to head them and get them into a mill before they scattered. It was riding at a dead run in the dark, with cut banks and prairie dog holes all around you, not knowing if the next jump would land you in a shallow grave.

1 Most cowboys had guns, but rarely used them on the trail. Some outfits made them keep their weapons in the chuck wagon[4] to eliminate any chance of gunplay. Charles Goodnight[5] was still more emphatic: "Before starting on a trail drive, I made it a rule to draw up an article of agreement, setting forth what each man was to do. The main clause stipulated[6] that if one shot another he was to be tried by the outfit and hanged on the spot, if found guilty. I never had a man shot on the trail."

Regardless of its ultimate destination, every herd had to ford[7] a series of rivers—the Nueces, the Guadalupe, the Brazos, the Wichita, the Red. A big herd of longhorns swimming across a river, Goodnight remembered, "looked like a million floating rocking chairs," and crossing those rivers one after another, a cowboy recalled, was like climbing the rungs of a long ladder reaching north.

"After you crossed the Red River and got out on the open plains," Teddy Blue remembered, "it was sure a pretty sight to see them strung out for almost a mile, the sun shining on their horns." Initially, the land immediately north of the Red River was Indian territory, and some tribes charged tolls for herds crossing their land—payable in money or beef. But Teddy Blue remembered that the homesteaders,[8] now pouring onto the Plains by railroad, were far more nettlesome:

2 There was no love lost between settlers and cowboys on the trail. Those jayhawkers would take up a claim right where the herds watered and charge us for water. They would plant a crop alongside the trail and plow a furrow around it for a fence, and then when the cattle got into their wheat or their garden patch, they would come cussing and waving a shotgun and yelling for damages. And the cattle had been coming through there when they were still raising punkins in Illinois.

3 The settlers' hostility was entirely understandable. The big herds ruined their crops, and they carried with them a disease, spread by ticks and called "Texas fever," that devastated domestic livestock. Kansas and other territories along the route soon established quarantine[9] lines, called "deadlines," at the western fringe of settlement, and insisted that trail drives not cross them. Each year, as settlers continued to move in, those deadlines moved farther west. 4

> **◆ Reading Strategy** Identify two effects the cattle drives had on settlers.

Sometimes, farmers tried to enforce their own, as John Rumans, one of Charles Goodnight's hands, recalled:

Some men met us at the trail near Canyon City, and said we couldn't come in. There were fifteen or twenty of them, and they were not going to let us cross the Arkansas River. We didn't even stop. . . . Old man [Goodnight] had a shotgun loaded with buckshot and led the way, saying: "John, get over on that point with your Winchester and point these cattle in behind me." He slid his shotgun across the saddle in front of him and we did the same with our Winchesters. He rode right across, and as he rode up to them, he said: "I've monkeyed as long as I want to with you," and they fell back to the sides, and went home after we had passed.

4. **chuck wagon** *n.*: Wagon equipped like a kitchen to feed cowboys or other outdoor workers.
5. **Charles Goodnight:** Cowboy who rode successful trail drives in the 1880's.
6. **stipulated** (stip′ yo͞o lāt′ id) *v.*: Stated as a rule.
7. **ford** (fôrd) *v.*: To cross a river at its low point.
8. **homesteaders** *n.*: Settlers who obtained land from the government in exchange for a commitment to farm it for at least five years.
9. **quarantine** (kwôr′ ən tēn) **lines** *n.*: Boundaries created to prevent the spread of disease.

Beyond the Classroom

Workplace Skills

Teamwork The demands of a cattle drive called for all participants to work together as a team. Each man had a role, and jobs were interrelated; if the men on the swing neglected their responsibilities or did their work poorly, it would cause problems for the men riding drag.

Similarly, in many kinds of work today, the success of a project requires team effort. Teams of carpenters build houses, teams of attorneys tackle cases, and teams at advertising agencies develop the ads we see on TV.

Discuss with students the kinds of jobs in which teamwork is a key element. Then, have teams of students focus on three or four of these jobs. Have them share the task of interviewing workers to learn about ways that teamwork plays a part in their daily activities. Students can speak with family members, adult friends, and neighbors to gather information. Some may wish to visit an office or factory to gather firsthand knowledge. After they have their data, groups can share the task of consolidating and then presenting their findings to the class.

There were few diversions on the trail. Most trail bosses banned liquor. Goodnight prohibited gambling, too. Even the songs for which cowboys became famous grew directly out of doing a job, remembered Teddy Blue:

> The singing was supposed to soothe [the cattle] and it did; I don't know why, unless it was that a sound they was used to would keep them from spooking at other noises. I know that if you wasn't singing, any little sound in the night—it might be just a horse shaking himself—could make them leave the country; but if you were singing, they wouldn't notice it.

The two men on guard would circle around with their horses on a walk, if it was a clear night and the cattle was bedded down and quiet, and one man would sing a verse of song, and his partner on the other side of the herd would sing another verse; and you'd go through a whole song that way. . . . "Bury Me Not on the Lone Prairie" was a great song for awhile, but . . . they sung it to death. It was a saying on the range that even the horses nickered it and the coyotes howled it; it got so they'd throw you in the creek if you sang it.

The number of cattle on the move was sometimes staggering: once, Teddy Blue rode to the top of a rise from which he could see seven herds strung out behind him; eight more up ahead; and the dust from an additional thirteen moving parallel to his. "All the cattle in the world," he remembered, "seemed to be coming up from Texas."

At last, the herds neared their destinations. After months in the saddle—often wearing the same clothes every day, eating nothing but biscuits and beef stew at the chuck wagon, drinking only water and coffee, his sole companions his fellow cowboys, his herd, and his horse—the cowboy was about to be paid for his work, and turned loose in town.

Guide for Responding

◆ Literature and Your Life

Reader's Response Which detail in "The Real Story of a Cowboy's Life" surprised you the most? Why?

Thematic Focus What facts in this essay show that a cowboy's life was dangerous?

☑ Check Your Comprehension

1. Use the information in "The Real Story of a Cowboy's Life" to identify four uses of a cowboy's saddle.
2. What was the most common cause of death on the trail?
3. Identify two details that explain how violence was kept to a minimum on the trail.
4. According to "The Real Story of a Cowboy's Life," why were songs like "The Dying Cowboy" sung?

◆ Critical Thinking

Interpret

1. (a) What challenges did the landscape present to cowboys on a drive? (b) What challenges did people present? **[Analyze]**
2. What qualifies Teddy Blue as a reliable source of information about cattle drives? **[Infer]**
3. What evidence suggests Teddy Blue liked cattle driving? **[Support]**

Apply

4. Based on "The Real Story of a Cowboy's Life," what kind of person do you think would succeed as a cowboy? **[Apply]**

Compare Literary Works

5. "The Dying Cowboy" and "The Real Story of a Cowboy's Life" present very different versions of life on the prairie. What is the value of each one? **[Evaluate]**

Beyond the Selection

FURTHER READING

Other Works by Alfred Noyes

The Loom of Years
The Torch Bearers

Other Works by Geoffrey Ward

Before the Trumpet: Young Franklin Roosevelt (1882–1905)
The Civil War (with Ken Burns and Ric Burns)

Other Works About Cowboys

Lonesome Dove, Larry McMurtry
The Virginian, Owen Wister

INTERNET

We suggest the following site on the Internet (all Web sites are subject to change).

For more information about Geoffrey C. Ward:

http://pbs.org/weta/thewest/wpages/

We *strongly recommend* that you preview the site before you send students to it.

Thematic Focus

5 Trouble Brewing What do you think these cow towns were like? Why? *Students may say that the towns were rowdy, dangerous, and dirty. The cowboys who descended on them had money in their pockets, were eager for entertainment and relaxation, and were armed. Students may say that there probably were lots of rough young men, some of whom behaved badly, and an absence of the calming influences of families, community, or law enforcement.*

Reinforce and Extend

Answers

◆ Literature and Your Life

Reader's Response Some students may point to the cowboy's greatest fear: being dragged to death.

Thematic Focus Managing the cows safely, crossing rivers, dealing with the elements, storms and other natural events, and the possibility of attack made trail drives dangerous.

☑ Check Your Comprehension

1. A chair, a workbench, a pillow, and a tying post for a lasso.
2. The most common cause of death was dragging during a stampede.
3. Trail bosses commandeered the guns and set rules for behavior and responsibilities.
4. They were sung to settle the cows.

◆ Critical Thinking

1. (a) It presented dust, storms, and rivers to cross. (b) Native Americans charged tolls and may have been unfriendly, and armed homesteaders were also a threat.
2. Blue's knowledge implies that he participated in several drives.
3. Possible response: He did it more than once.
4. Possible response: Someone who wouldn't mind long hours and discomfort, a challenging and dangerous assignment, and many hours outdoors and away from family and community.
5. Possible response: One shows some of the feelings of the individual cowboy on the lonely prairie; the other provides information on the teamwork needed for a cattle drive.

Answers

◆Reading Strategy

1. Bess's fired shot warns off the approaching highwayman; her death sparks him to return to the inn and the fate that awaits him there.
2. (a) Students might cite his desire to be buried in the same cemetery in which his father is buried, and his worry that his loved ones won't be able to mourn his death. (b) His words have little effect on the other cowboys, who'll bury him on the spot and go on with the business of herding cattle.

◆Build Vocabulary

Using Compound Nouns

landlord, lamplight, highway, heartache, heartland, highland, headache, headquarters, headlight, highlight, headway

Spelling Strategy

1. red-lipped
2. black-haired
3. velvet-coated
4. sharp-eyed

Using the Word Bank

1. S
2. A
3. A
4. A
5. S
6. A
7. S

◆Literary Focus

1. Possible response: The action takes place on a moonlit night; Tim overhears the conversation between the highwayman and Bess; we hear the hooves of the highwayman's horse as he returns to the inn before Bess fires the gun.
2. Possible response: His plea is repeated over and over; his wish builds in force; the reader doesn't know what the other cowboys will do.
3. Repeated lines emphasize details and create tension.
4. Possible response: the details about the dangers of a stampede or about the tension between settlers and cowboys

◆Build Grammar Skills

Practice

1. in the blinding moonlight; shone; adverb
2. of Bess's hair; waves; adjective
3. on the lonely prairie; died; adverb
4. of the buzzards; all; adjective/on the cowboy's grave; landed; adverb
5. at the head; rode; adverb/of the herd; head; adjective

Guide for Responding (continued)

◆ Reading Strategy

IDENTIFY CAUSE AND EFFECT

A **cause** makes something happen. An **effect** is what happens. Noting cause-and-effect relationships will help you get at the meaning of a selection. For example, Tim's betrayal of the outlaw's plans in "The Highwayman" gains importance when you realize that it eventually causes Bess's death.

1. Identify two other causes and their effects in "The Highwayman."

2. (a) What causes can you find for the wishes of the "Dying Cowboy"? (b) What effect do his wishes have on the other cowboys' actions?

◆ Build Vocabulary

COMPOUND NOUNS

The word *moonlight* is a compound noun—one made by combining two smaller words. With a partner, piece together the words below into as many compound nouns as you can.

lord	way	lamp	land	high
light	ache	heart	quarters	head

SPELLING STRATEGY

When you make compound adjectives, use a hyphen to separate an adjective and the *-ed* form of a noun: *black* + *eye* become the adjective *black-eyed.* Use the details below to create compound adjectives that describe Bess or the highwayman.

1. red lips
2. black hair
3. velvet coat
4. sharp eye

USING THE WORD BANK

In your notebook, label each word pair with *A* for *antonyms* (words with opposite meanings) and *S* for *synonyms* (words with similar meanings).

1. torrent, flood
2. cascade, trickle
3. brandished, hid
4. bound, unlocked
5. tawny, tan
6. landlord, tenant
7. strive, try

◆ Literary Focus

SUSPENSE

By creating **suspense,** or story tension, writers draw readers into a literary work and lead them to anxiously anticipate the outcome. Suspense often surrounds dangerous or uncertain situations. For example, the secrecy of the meeting between Bess and the highwayman increases the suspense.

1. Identify three details Noyes uses to increase the suspense in "The Highwayman."
2. How does "The Dying Cowboy" build suspense?
3. How do the repeated lines in both poems increase the suspense?
4. What details in "The Real Story of a Cowboy's Life" might be used to create suspenseful writing?

◆ Build Grammar Skills

ADJECTIVE AND ADVERB PHRASES

A **preposition** relates the noun or pronoun following it to another word in the sentence. A **prepositional phrase** includes a preposition and its object. Prepositional phrases can act as **adjectives** modifying nouns or as **adverbs** modifying verbs.

noun prep. phrase

Adjective: The wind was a *torrent* [of darkness.]

verb prep. phrase

Adverb: They *fitted* [with never a wrinkle.]

Practice Copy the following sentences. Bracket each prepositional phrase, and identify the word it modifies. Then, tell whether it functions as an adjective or an adverb.

1. The moors shone in the blinding moonlight.
2. He kissed the tumbling waves of Bess's hair.
3. The dying cowboy died on the lonely prairie.
4. All of the buzzards landed on the cowboy's grave.
5. Experienced men rode at the head of the herd.

Writing Application Write sentences that include these prepositional phrases, used as shown.

1. of his home far away (as an adverb)
2. on the prairie (as an adverb)
3. from the window (as an adjective)

Writing Application

Possible responses:

1. The dying cowboy thought of his home far away.
2. He rode on the prairie.
3. The view from the window was of open prairie.

Writer's Solution

For additional instruction and practice, use the lesson in the *Writer's Solution Language Lab CD-ROM* on prepositional phrases (Using Modifiers unit), and the practice pages on prepositional phrases that act as adjectives and adverbs, pp. 44–45 in the *Writer's Solution Grammar Practice Book.*

Build Your Portfolio

Idea Bank

Writing

1. **Wanted Poster** Write a wanted poster offering a reward for the highwayman's capture. Include a vivid description of him, and mention his known associates and hangouts.
2. **Letter of Appeal** As a loved one of "The Dying Cowboy," write a letter to his companions asking them to send the cowboy home for his burial. Use reasons and details from the song to make your letter effective.
3. **Narrative Poem** Use the events in "The Dying Cowboy" or "The Real Story of a Cowboy's Life" to write a narrative poem—a poem that tells a story. Study "The Highwayman" for tips on structure and technique.

Speaking and Listening

4. **Poetry Reading** Read "The Highwayman" to classmates. To bring out the meaning of the poem, change the speed and volume of your voice, and let punctuation determine your pauses.
5. **Ballad Collection** In recordings or books of musical history, find examples of western and English ballads to share with the class. Then, discuss the stories told by the songs, and identify any elements of suspense. **[Music Link]**

Projects

6. **Oral Report on Legendary Figures [Group Activity]** In a group, research such legendary western figures as Davy Crockett, Kit Carson, or Jesse James. Watch episodes of Geoffrey C. Ward and Ken Burns's series *The West* or consult the companion book. Identify the information each group member will seek. Then, include all the findings in an oral report. **[Social Studies Link]**
7. **Geography Comparison** Using the settings of "The Highwayman" and "The Real Story of a Cowboy's Life," make a chart comparing and contrasting the natural features described. **[Social Studies Link]**

Writing Mini-Lesson

Police Report

"The Highwayman" and "The Dying Cowboy" describe events from a particular point of view—almost as an eyewitness would. However, what would the same events look like through the eyes of an observer who was not involved? Choose a selection, and write a police report recounting its events. To make your report realistic, use a detective's technique: include information from interviews with participants or eyewitnesses.

Writing Skills Focus: Facts and Examples

To explain the events reported, use **facts and examples** to provide the details. Answer the question "*Who* was *where when?*" by saying, for example, "The landlord's daughter met the suspect early on the night of the robbery." Also, use examples to describe the participants' behavior—"The highwayman avoided arrest by shooting at officers, hiding in a wooded area, and adopting a disguise."

Prewriting After choosing your selection, list its events in chronological order. Highlight the places in the sequence where an eyewitness interview or a specific fact would be useful.

Drafting Build on your timeline, adding details about *who, what, when, where,* and *how* to show the key facts of each event. Use eyewitness reports to show different interpretations of the events.

Grammar Application

Make your report more specific by providing details in adjective and adverb phrases.

Revising Make sure your report objectively details what happened. If necessary, add information to help readers understand the *who, what, when, where,* and *how* of the events.

ASSESSMENT OPTIONS

Formal Assessment, Selection Test, pp. 91–93, and Assessment Resources Software. The selection test is designed so that it can be easily customized to the performance levels of your students.

Alternative Assessment, p. 21, includes options for less advanced students, more advanced students, and interpersonal learners, visual/spatial learners, verbal/linguistic learners, bodily/kinesthetic learners, and musical/rhythmic learners.

PORTFOLIO ASSESSMENT

Use the following rubrics in the **Alternative Assessment** booklet to assess student writing:
Wanted Poster: Description, p. 84
Letter of Appeal: Persuasion, p. 92
Narrative Poem: Poetry, p. 95
Writing Mini-Lesson: Research Report, p. 93

Idea Bank

Following are suggestions for matching the Idea Bank topics with your students' performance levels and learning modalities:

Customize for *Performance Levels*
Less Advanced Students: 1, 5
Average Students: 2, 4, 5, 6, 7
More Advanced Students: 3, 4, 6

Customize for *Learning Modalities*
Verbal/Linguistic: 1, 2, 3, 4, 5, 6, 7
Visual/Spatial: 1, 7
Logical/Mathematical: 1, 2, 7
Musical/Rhythmic: 3, 4, 6
Interpersonal: 2, 5, 6
Intrapersonal: 1, 3

Writing Mini-Lesson

Refer students to the Writing Handbook in the back of the book for instruction on the writing process and for further information on writing reports.

Writer's Solution

Writers at Work Videodisc

Have students view the videodisc segment on Reports (Ch. 7), featuring Ellie Fries, to see what she has to say about researching, organizing, and writing a report. Guide them to watch the segment in which she prepares for conducting interviews by discussing how she takes notes.

Play frames 14345 to 15275

Writing Lab CD-ROM

Have students complete the tutorial on Reports. Follow these steps:

1. Have students use the Narrowing Your Topic section to get ideas for how to narrow their topics.
2. Have students use the Gathering Information section, which includes options for taking notes.
3. Have students draft on computer.
4. Have students use the Revising and Editing section for information on the types of revisions they might make.

Allow about 70 minutes of class time to complete these steps.

Writer's Solution Sourcebook

Have students use Chapter 7, "Reports," pp. 200–233, for additional support. The chapter includes in-depth instruction on conducting interviews, p. 221.

OBJECTIVES

1. To read, comprehend, and interpret a selection that has a social studies focus
2. To relate a selection with a social studies focus to personal experience
3. To connect literature to social studies
4. To respond to Social Studies Guiding Questions
5. To respond to the selection through writing, speaking and listening, and projects

Social Studies Guiding Questions

Reading a folk tale from Vietnam will help students discovers answers to this Social Studies Guiding Question:

- What beliefs and values of Buddhism—the dominant religion of Vietnam—are revealed in this folk tale?

Interest Grabber Place two chairs at the front of the room. Invite students to take turns playing a mock game of chess, checkers, or cards as they sit in these chairs. Both players are to imagine the stakes of the game are something precious to them. Ask students to describe their feelings. Do they want to play a game for such important stakes? How might these conditions affect their playing ability? Is it worth risking something you truly care about to win a game? Urge them to keep these questions in mind as they read "The Little Lizard's Sorrow."

Map Study

Regional Maps Explain to students that geography is often an important key to understanding a folk tale's cultural context. The map on this page, for example, shows that Vietnam is in a region of many different nations. It is also in a location many travelers might pass by land or sea. To help students link this information to the story, read aloud "A Region of Diversity" and "Less Is More" on this page. Then, explain that Buddhism came to Vietnam from China, a nation to its north.

CONNECTING LITERATURE TO SOCIAL STUDIES

SOUTHEAST ASIA

The Little Lizard's Sorrow *Retold by Mai Vo-Dinh*

A Region of Diversity Long ago, Southeast Asia's mountains kept people protected and isolated. People had little contact with those who lived outside their own valley. This created a region with a variety of cultures. Through the centuries, traders, explorers, and travelers passed through Southeast Asia, bringing new ideas and religions to the region. The people of Southeast Asia blended these new ideas with their own traditions to create unique ways of life.

Manners for All Vietnam—a tropical country in Southeast Asia—has a strong culture and lively traditions. From the rural villages (where most live) to big cities like Ho Chi Minh City (the former Saigon), many Vietnamese think about what is good for their families. Many in the country also honor the community's rules—caring for older people, greeting visitors, and working at common problems.

Less Is More Like people in many cultures, the Vietnamese look to their religion for guidance. Most practice Buddhism, a religion that teaches that people can overcome life's problems by giving up possessions—serving the world instead of asking it to serve them. These beliefs are revealed in Vietnamese folklore—the stories passed from generation to generation. In "The Little Lizard's Sorrow," for example, a poor stranger and a rich man explore the importance of worldly possessions.

Prentice Hall Literature Program Resources

REINFORCE / RETEACH / EXTEND

Selection Support Pages
Build Vocabulary, p. 116
Theme, p. 117

Formal Assessment Selection Test, pp. 94–95, Assessment Resources Software

Writing and Language Transparencies
Venn Diagram, p. 86

Resource Pro CD-ROM
"The Little Lizard's Sorrow"—includes all resource material and customizable lesson plan

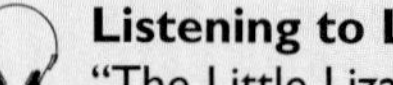

Listening to Literature Audiocassettes
"The Little Lizard's Sorrow"

Connection to Prentice Hall World Explorer Asia and the Pacific
Ch. 4, "South and Southeast Asia: Cultures and History"

The Little Lizard's Sorrow

From Vietnam
Retold by Mai Vo-Dinh

There is in Vietnam a certain species of small lizard only three inches long with webbed feet and a short, round head. They are often seen indoors, running swiftly upside down on the ceiling or along the walls, emitting little snapping cries that sound like "Tssst . . . tssst!" Suppose that you drop an egg on the kitchen floor; the kind of sound you would make then, with the tip of your tongue between your teeth, is like the cry of these harmless, funny little lizards. Sounds of mild sorrow, of genuine shock but somehow humorous regret that seem to say, "Oh, if only I had been . . . If only I had known . . . Oh, what a pity, what a pity . . . Tssst! Tssst!"

There was once a very rich man whose house was immense and filled with treasures. His land was so extensive that, as the Vietnamese say, "Cranes fly over it with outstretched wings," for cranes only do so over very long distances. Wealth breeding vanity, one of the rich man's greatest pleasures was beating other rich men at a game he himself had invented. One player would announce one of his rare possessions, the other would counter the challenge by saying that he, too—if he really did—owned such a treasure. "A stable of fifty buffalos," one man would say. The other would reply, "Yes, I also have fifty of them." It was then his turn to announce, "I sleep in an all-teak[1] bed encrusted with mother-of-pearl."[2] The first player would lose if he slept on cherry planks![3]

> **Connecting Literature to Social Studies**
> 1 Based on this Vietnamese saying, do you think cranes are common birds in Vietnam?

One day, a stranger came to the rich man's house. Judging from his appearance, the gatekeeper did not doubt that the visitor was a madman. He wanted, he said, to play the famous game with the mansion's master. Yet dressed in clothes that looked as if they had been mended hundreds of times, and wearing

1. **teak** (tēk) *adj.*: Yellowish-brown wood used for furniture.
2. **mother-of-pearl** *n.*: Hard, pearly inside of certain seashells.
3. **cherry planks** *n.*: Wood from a cherry tree.

◆ **Build Vocabulary**

emitting (ē mitʹ iŋ) *adj.*: Sending out or uttering

One-Minute Insight

In this traditional Vietnamese folk tale, translator Mai Vo-Dinh retells a story that explains the origins of a sad-looking lizard. As in many other folk tales, a character in this story—a poor stranger—seeks to win a fortune by making himself a bet. He challenges a wealthy man to a game of that man's own invention, each wagering all their possessions. The poor stranger, who owns very little, wins the game through cleverness, and the wealthy man, in regret and sorrow, becomes a sad lizard.

Team Teaching Strategy

"The Little Lizard's Sorrow" can be team taught with a social studies or world cultures teacher, focusing on Vietnam or world folk literature.

Customize for *Less Proficient Readers*

Point out to students that the first paragraph is separated from the story to emphasize its importance. After students read that paragraph, clarify that the folk tale was created to explain the little lizard's sorrowful behavior. Point out that the explanation will be completed at the story's end.

Customize for *English Language Learners*

Make sure students understand how the essential "game of riches" works. Building on the Interest Grabber role-play activity, have two students pantomime the game as it is described in the story, showing that the items mentioned in the story—for example, fifty buffaloes, an all-teak bed encrusted with mother-of-pearl—are considered objects of value in this Vietnamese village.

Connecting Literature to Social Studies

1 **Infer** *Students should make the link that sayings usually arise from the surroundings; therefore, cranes probably are common birds in Vietnam.*

Preparing for Standardized Tests

Make Inferences Standardized tests may ask students to use critical reading strategies to extract information. For example, a test might excerpt a folk tale such as this one and ask students to use text clues and personal experience to make inferences about Vietnam's geography. Model such a question by directing students to the boxed prompt on this page and posting the following answers on the board:

(A) Yes, because sayings in my community are based on familiar parts of the surroundings.
(B) Yes, because cranes are beautiful birds.
(C) No, because the story is about a lizard.
(D) No, because the story says that cranes only fly over the man's land, they never stop there.

As a class, discuss each alternative and guide students to recognize that *(A)* is the correct answer. The facts in *(B)* and *(C)* are accurate but *(B)* doesn't support the *yes* inference and *(C)* makes the incorrect *no* inference. *(D)* misunderstands the saying and thus makes the incorrect *no* inference. For more practice, have students write and answer their own A–D answer alternatives for the other boxed prompts.

Customize for
More Advanced Students
Remind students that in literature, as in life, symbols are objects that stand for ideas beyond their literal existence. For example, a dove is a symbol of peace. As they read "The Little Lizard's Sorrow," ask students to consider the folk tale's symbols. Have them answer the following questions:

- What two symbols can you find in this story? *the lizard; the cup*
- What human feelings are linked to the lizard at the beginning and end of this tale? *regret; self-pity*
- What evidence in the story suggests the coconut-shell cup's importance to the stranger? *The stranger equates it with the rich man's expensive china.*
- What might the cup symbolize? *Objects of true value, not ornaments; useful objects that add something to people's lives.*

Links Across Culture
❶ The visitor, despite his pride, appears to be struggling economically. Many Vietnamese share this struggle, in part because the country has few industries or natural resources. They live in simple wood or bamboo houses, often built on tall stilts to keep dry during heavy seasonal rains, and work long hours harvesting Vietnam's rice crop.

CONNECTING LITERATURE TO SOCIAL STUDIES
❷ **Connect** *The Vietnamese value manners, equally applied to all members of society, rich and poor. Also, it would be important to the rich man to follow the rules of hospitality and of the game itself.*

►Critical Viewing◄
❸ **Support** Possible Response: The folk tale is called "The Little Lizard's Sorrow."

Customize for
Visual/Spatial and Bodily/Kinesthetic Learners
Organize students in groups or pairs across these learning styles. As they listen to you read the text descriptions aloud, challenge them to draw, pantomime, or role-play visually the contrast between the two men.

CONNECTING LITERATURE TO SOCIAL STUDIES

broken straw sandals, the stranger appeared to be anything but a wealthy man. Moreover, his face was gaunt and pale as if he had not ❶ had a good meal in days. But there was such proud, quiet dignity to the stranger that the servant did not dare shut the gates in his face. Instead, he meekly went to inform his master of the unlikely visitor's presence. Intrigued, the man ordered that the pauper be ushered in.

Trying to conceal his curiosity and surprise, the rich man offered his visitor the very best chair and served him hot, perfumed tea.

> **Connecting Literature to Social Studies** ❷ Why do you think a rich Vietnamese man would be especially concerned for his visitor's wishes?

"Well, stranger, is it true that you have deigned[4] to come here to play a game of riches with me?" he began inquiringly.

The visitor was apparently unimpressed by the rich surroundings, giving them only a passing, casual look. Perfectly at ease, sipping his tea from the rare porcelain cup, he answered in a quiet though self-assured voice, "Yes, sir, that is if you, too, so wish."

"Naturally, naturally," the rich man raised his hand in a sweeping motion. "But, may I ask, with your permission, where you reside and what is your honorable occupation?"

The stranger gave a little chortle, visibly amused. "Sir, would you gain any to know about these? I came here simply to play your game; only, I have two conditions, if you are so generous as to allow them."

"By all means! Pray, tell me what they are," the rich man readily inquired.

The visitor sat farther back on the brocaded chair, his voice soft and confidential.

▼ **Critical Viewing** Why is a lizard like the one shown here a good choice for inclusion in a Vietnamese folk tale? **[Support]** ❸

◆ **Build Vocabulary**

gaunt (gônt) *adj.*: Thin and bony

pauper (pô´ pər) *n.*: Extremely poor person

chortle (chor´ təl) *n.*: Amused chuckling or snorting sound

domestic (də mes´ tik) *n.*: Servant for the home

4. **deigned** (dānd) *v.*: Graciously agreed to do something beneath him.

Block Scheduling Strategies
Consider these strategies to take advantage of extended class time:

- Have students read the selection independently. Then, reinforce and extend their understanding by having them work in small groups to complete the Guide for Responding questions, p. 318. Encourage students to take turns reading questions and writing responses.
- Have students use the Venn Diagram, p. 86, in **Writing and Language Transparencies** to prepare for the Folk Tale Exchange activity, p. 319. Present the Speaking and Listening Mini-Lesson on p. 317 of the Teacher's Edition as additional help.
- Use *World Explorer: Asia and the Pacific,* Chapter 4, "South and Southeast Asia: Cultures and History" to clarify the story's setting and cultural context. Then, have students read the story independently before joining groups to answer the Critical Thinking questions, p. 318.

4 "Well, here they are. A game is no fun if the winner does not win anything and the loser does not lose anything. Therefore I would suggest that if I win I would take everything in your possession—your lands, your stables, your servants, your house and everything contained in it. But if you win—" Here the stranger paused, his eyes narrowed ever so slightly, full of humorous malice, "If you win, you would become the owner of everything that belongs to me." The stranger paused again. "And what belongs to me, sir, you will have no idea of. I am one of the most fortunate men alive, sir. . . . And besides that," he added with a knowing look, "I would remain in this house to serve you as a domestic the rest of my life."

For a long moment, the rich man sat back in silence. Another long moment went by, then the rich man spoke: "That's agreed. But, please tell me your other condition."

Eyes dreamy, the stranger looked out of the window. "My second condition, sir, is not so much a condition as a request. I hope you would not mind giving me, a visitor, an edge over you. May I be allowed to ask the first question?"

The rich man thought for a long second, then said, "That is also agreed. Let's begin."

"Do I really understand that you have agreed to both my conditions?" the stranger asked thoughtfully.

Something in the visitor's manner and voice hurt the rich man's pride. He was ready to stake his very life on this game that he himself had created. There was no way out. "Yes," he said. "Yes, indeed I have. Now tell me, please, what do you have that I have not got?" The stranger smiled. Reaching to his feet, he took up his traveling bag, a coarse cotton square tied together by the four ends. Opening it slowly, ceremoniously, he took out an object and handed it to his host without a word. It was an empty half of a coconut shell, old and chipped, the kind poor people use as a container to drink water from. 5

"A coconut-shell cup!" the rich man exclaimed. One could not know whether he was merely amused or completely shattered.

"Yes, sir, a coconut-shell cup. A *chipped* shell cup. I use it to drink from on my wanderings. I am a wanderer," the visitor said quietly.

Holding the shell between his thumb and his forefinger and looking as if he had never seen such an object before, the rich man interrupted, "But, but you don't mean that I do not have a thing like this?"

"No, sir, you have not. How could you?" the stranger replied.

Turning the residence upside down, the man and his servants discovered odds and ends of one thousand and one kinds, but they were unable to produce a drinking cup made from a coconut shell. In the servants' quarters, however, they found a few such utensils, but they were all brand new, not chipped. One could imagine that the servants of such a wealthy man would not deign to drink from a chipped cup. Even a beggar would throw it away. . . .

"You see, sir," the stranger said to the rich man once they were again seated across the tea table, "you see, I am a wanderer, as I have said. I am a free man. This cup here is

Connecting Literature to Social Studies

4 Make a Judgment Ask students whether they think people's attitudes about the importance of winning are influenced by their culture and if so, how. *Students should be able to use the example of America's winner idolatry to recognize that values about the importance of winning vary from culture to culture.*

Connecting Literature to Social Studies

5 Infer Here, we learn that coconut-shell cups are so easy to acquire that even poor people use them regularly. What does this say about Vietnam's vegetation? *Students should recognize that coconut trees must grow commonly in Vietnam for their cups to be available even to a homeless wanderer.*

Customize for
Logical/Mathematical Learners
Ask students how they think the stranger could have predicted that the wealthy man wouldn't have a chipped coconut-shell cup. Point out that though he used logic, he also played the odds. Challenge students to develop a hypothetical math equation to express the likely odds facing the stranger. *Equations should express huge odds against the wealthy man's having such a cup.*

Customize for
Intrapersonal Learners
Have students write a journal entry identifying the stakes they would wager in playing the game from the story. Tell them their wagers may be material objects or ideas such as "freedom." Urge them to relate their feelings about the risks in such a wager to the two men's attitudes in the story. Discuss what each man believes he is risking.

Customize for
Less Proficient Readers
Play the recording for this selection, and help students track the changes in tone and voice as the rich man realizes what has occurred.

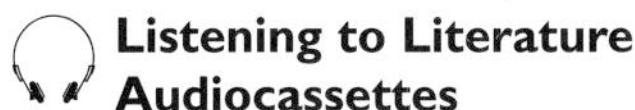
Listening to Literature Audiocassettes

Speaking and Listening Mini-Lesson

Folk Tale Exchange
This mini-lesson supports the Speaking and Listening activity in the Idea Bank on p. 319.

Introduce Have students name countries and cultures of particular interest or familiarity. Point out that some folk tales may appear in the literature of many countries.

Develop Place students in groups, according to the countries or cultures they have named. Help them find folk tale collections in the library (usually in the nonfiction section, organized by country or topic).

Apply Provide the groups with Venn Diagrams, p. 86, in **Writing and Language Transparencies,** on which they can list common themes among pairs of folk tales. Have students base their discussions on the completed Venn Diagrams. Urge each group to choose a representative to exchange findings with other groups.

Assess Use the Speaking and Listening Progress Chart: Teacher Observation, p. 111, in **Alternative Assessment** to track and evaluate individual students' group efforts.

CONNECTING LITERATURE TO SOCIAL STUDIES

1 Interpret *He believed in the Buddhist teaching that his path to peace is through giving up his desire for material things.*

Reinforce and Extend

Answers

◆ LITERATURE AND YOUR LIFE

Reader's Response Possible response: Yes, because people must face the consequences, however unpleasant, of their choices.

Thematic Focus He tries to show the rich man how valuable peace of mind and freedom from material wealth can be. He takes from the rich and gives to the poor. He tries to set an example as someone who is happy with very little.

Check Your Comprehension

1. One person announces a rare possession. The other person counters this, if possible, with a claim to own the same thing. The second person then makes a claim that must be matched by the first. When one person owns something that the other does not, that person wins.
2. The first condition is that the winner gains all the loser's possessions; the second is that he, the stranger, asks the first question.
3. He produces his chipped coconut-shell cup. The rich man does not have anything so broken down and battered.
4. He gives them all away.

More About the Author
Mai Vo-Dinh (1933–), says that the long war in his country affected him in many ways, as it did a generation of his peers. Still, notes Vo-Dinh, "my work cannot . . . be called violent or pessimistic." If anything, Vo-Dinh has tried to show in his work the "faith beyond hope or despair" he sees in his countrymen. For Vo-Dinh, this has meant celebrating Vietnam's rich cultural and literary history in scores of stories, translations, and illustrations.

several years old and my only possession besides these poor clothes I have on. If you do not think me too immodest, I would venture that I treasure it more than you do all of your collections of fine china. But, from this day, I am the owner and lone master of all that belongs to you. . . ."

Having taken possession of the rich man's land, houses, herds and all his other treasures, the stranger began to give them away to the poor and needy people. Then, one day, taking up his old cotton bag, he left the village and no one ever saw him again.

Connecting Literature to Social Studies
Why do you think the stranger gave away all his new possessions and continued his wandering? 1

As for the dispossessed rich man, it is believed that he died of grief and regret and was transformed into this small lizard. Curiously, one sees him scurrying about only indoors. Running up and down the walls, crossing the ceiling, staring at people and furniture, he never stops his "Tssst, Tssst." Vietnamese children, in particular, are very fond of him for he looks so harassed, so funny.

But, oh, such sorrow, such regret, such self-pity.

◆ Build Vocabulary
harassed (hə rast′) *adj.*: Troubled

Guide for Responding

◆ LITERATURE AND YOUR LIFE

Reader's Response Do you feel that the rich man deserved what the stranger did to him? Explain.

Thematic Focus How does the stranger try to solve the universal problem of greed?

Check Your Comprehension

1. Describe the game the rich men play.
2. Identify two game conditions the stranger sets.
3. How does the stranger defeat the rich man?
4. What does the stranger do with the rich man's possessions?

◆ Critical Thinking

INTERPRET

1. Why does the stranger describe himself as one of the most fortunate men alive? **[Interpret]**
2. Why does he treasure his coconut-shell cup more than the rich man treasures his china? **[Connect]**
3. What lesson about living does this folk tale teach? **[Draw Conclusions]**

APPLY

4. J. Brotherton once wrote: "My riches consist not in the extent of my possessions but in the fewness of my wants." Would the stranger agree or disagree with him? Explain. **[Hypothesize]**

EXTEND

5. How does the wager in the folk tale compare with the stakes in a professional sports competition? **[Social Studies Link]**

Meet the Author
Mai Vo-Dinh (1933–)
Because Mai Vo-Dinh was born in Vietnam, his country's struggles for freedom meant that he grew up with war. He has translated works of Vietnamese folk literature, sharing the stories that make a culture special and highlighting the lessons learned from everyday problems.

Mai Vo-Dinh came to live in the United States in 1960, but he has kept strong ties to his homeland through his work as a writer, translator, and book illustrator. With his work, he explores the modern problems people experience. At the same time, he keeps alive Vietnam's long-lasting storytelling traditions.

Beyond the Selection

FURTHER READING

Other Works by Mai Vo-Dinh
Lam Xep (stories)
Doa Sen va Nu Cuoi (The Lotus and The Smile)

Other Works About Vietnam and Reptiles
Sky Legends of Vietnam, Lynett Vuong
My First Pocket Guide : Reptiles & Amphibians, Dr. David Kirshner

INTERNET
We suggest the following Internet sites (all Web sites are subject to change).

For information about Vietnam, visit **http://sunsite.unc.edu/vietnam/unpic.html**

To view the illustrated diary of a Vietnamese girl, visit **http://mcweb.mitsubishi.co.jp/companies/ARTGPRX96/VietNam_E.html**

For data on reptiles, visit **http://www.ukreptiles.com/index4.htm**

We *strongly recommend* that you preview these sites before you send your students to them.

Connecting Literature to Social Studies

Lizards appear in the folk tales of many cultures—each time representing a different idea. Australian aborigines believe the first humans came from lizards. In other cultures, lizards are signs of coming life events, such as death or a new baby. For the Vietnamese, the lizard is known as a sad creature—one who reminds us of the self-pity and regret we feel over our mistakes.

Many Vietnamese practice Buddhism. This religion teaches that people will continue to struggle in life until they give up wanting things. Buddhists believe that even after a body's death, the soul may return in another creature to face problems again and to learn this difficult lesson. That is why the rich man in this folk tale becomes a lizard who scurries around commenting about his sorrow.

1. How does the poor stranger stand for the ideas of Buddhism?
2. Review the information on page 314. Then, identify two details in "The Little Lizard's Sorrow" that reflect the values of Vietnamese communities.

Idea Bank

Writing

1. **Rules of the Game** The "game of riches" teaches a lesson about greed. Write the rules for another game that teaches a lesson you think Americans need to learn.
2. **Lecture** You're the leader of the Vietnamese village in which the rich man lived. Use the story of the "game of riches" to remind your people about the dangers of greed.
3. **Folk Tale** Write a folk tale modeled on "The Little Lizard's Sorrow." Use your tale to address a common problem or value of a culture you know well.

Speaking and Listening

4. **Folk-Tale Exchange** **[Group Activity]** With a group, organize a study of lizard folk tales. First, divide the research by country, and ask each student to find a folk tale featuring a lizard. Then, share the stories within your group. Discuss common themes, and identify how different cultures address them. **[Social Studies Link]**

Projects

5. **Lizard Presentation** Find out all you can about lizards: where they live, what they eat, how they differ from other reptiles. Share what you learn in a presentation. Include illustrations or models. **[Science Link]**
6. **Report on Vietnamese History** Vietnam has been influenced by a number of other countries over the course of history. Learn how China and other nations have influenced Vietnam. Share your findings with the class. **[Social Studies Link]**

Further Reading, Listening, and Viewing

- Heather Forest's collection *Wisdom Tales From Around the World* (1996) shows how other cultures have understood greed.
- *Eyewitness: Reptile* (1991) is a video that includes exciting images of reptiles in their natural environment.
- *The Land I Lost: Adventures of a Boy in Vietnam* (1982), which Mai Vo-Dinh illustrated, is a true first-person account of Quang Nhuong Huynh's childhood in Vietnam.

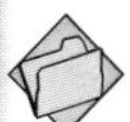

Idea Bank

Following are suggestions for matching the Idea Bank topics with your students' performance levels and learning modalities.

Customize for
Performance Levels
Less Advanced Students: 1, 4
Average Students: 2, 4, 5, 6
More Advanced Students: 3, 5, 6

Customize for
Learning Modalities
Verbal/Linguistic: 1, 2, 3, 4, 6
Visual/Spatial: 5
Interpersonal: 2, 4
Logical/Mathematical: 1
Intrapersonal: 5, 6

◆Critical Thinking

1. He does not need anything more than his clothes and his cup to be happy.
2. It is his only possession and one that he cannot afford to replace. Also, the rich man has so many possessions that they lose their individual value to him.
3. Possible responses: People should value possessions for their real benefits and not accumulate things simply for the sake of vanity; peace of mind and freedom are more valuable than material objects.
4. The stranger would agree; he considers himself lucky because he has few possessions.
5. Possible response: The wagers in professional sports are also governed by rules and played for both financial gain and status. Unlike the story, those betting are not those competing.

Connecting Literature to Social Studies

1. He values his peace of mind over material objects, so much so that he gives away his newly acquired riches. Thus, he stands for the Buddhist idea that peace comes through giving up the desire for possessions.
2. Possible response: The gate keeper's hospitality to the poor stranger because of that man's dignity shows Vietnamese respect for visitors and value of dignity. The careful attention to rules and manners during the game shows the Vietnamese value of order and respect.

✓ Assessment Options

Formal Assessment, Selection Test, pp. 94–95, and Assessment Resources Software. The selection test is designed so that it can be easily customized to the performance levels of your students.

PORTFOLIO ASSESSMENT
Use the following rubrics in the **Alternative Assessment** booklet to assess student writing:
Rules of the Game: Technical Description/Explanation, p. 102
Lecture: Persuasion, p. 92
Folk Tale, Fictional Narrative, p. 82

Prepare and Engage

Establish Writing Guidelines
Review the following key characteristics of a problem-solution essay:

- A problem-solution essay is a type of expository writing, although its primary goal may be to persuade.
- A problem-solution essay presents relevant facts of a problem and a step-by-step proposal for a solution.
- A problem-solution essay must be well organized, and the solution must be supported with facts and/or examples.

You may want to distribute the scoring rubric for Problem-Solution Essay, p. 88 in **Alternative Assessment** to make students aware of the criteria on which they will be evaluated. See the suggestions on p. 322 for how you can customize the rubric to this workshop.

Refer students to the Writing Handbook in the back of the book for instruction on the writing process and further information on exposition.

Writer's Solution

Writers at Work Videodisc
Play the videodisc segment on Exposition: Making Connections (Ch. 5) so students can hear Dimitri Ehrlich's views on exposition.

Play frames 42847 to 52256

Writing Lab CD-ROM
Students can work in the tutorial on Exposition: Making Connections to complete all or part of their problem-solution essays. Follow these steps:

1. Have students view the interactive model of a written solution to a problem.
2. Suggest that students use the Problem Wheels to come up with topic ideas.
3. Allow students to draft on computer.
4. When revising, have students use the Interactive Self-Evaluation Checklist.

Writer's Solution Sourcebook
Students can find in-depth instruction on using prepositions and conjunctions, pp. 161–162, in the chapter on Exposition: Making Connections, pp. 134–165.

Expository Writing

Problem-Solution Essay

Writing Process Workshop

Dangerous intersections, expensive leisure-time activities, polluted beaches—problems are everywhere. However, if you think creatively, solutions are everywhere, too. A **problem-and-solution essay** focuses on a problem and offers one or more possible solutions to it. Choose a problem with which you are familiar, consider a few solutions, and write a problem-and-solution essay. The following skills, introduced in this section's Writing Mini-Lessons, will help you write an effective essay:

Writing Skills Focus

▶ **Show, don't tell.** It isn't enough to tell your readers that something is a problem or that a solution will work. Show specific examples of the problem, and present evidence that demonstrates why your solution will work. (See p. 297.)

▶ **Provide facts and examples** to explain the problem and convince readers that your solutions will work. (See p. 313.)

▶ **End your essay with a strong conclusion.** Tie your ideas together, and finish with a statement that directs your readers to action. (See p. 284.)

Notice how this model demonstrates each of these skills:

Model

When you are new to a school, you may find the first few days awkward and uncomfortable. Since you don't know many people, you may prefer to sit alone at lunch or walk alone to classes and home from school. This may increase your isolation. ①

Fortunately, the problem of being new to a school is easily remedied. First of all, remember that small talk is the rule when speaking with classmates you've just met. Asking people about their interests is often a good tactic. ② People love others who are interested in them! ③

① After the problem is identified, these details help show how it feels.

② The writer offers several suggestions for solving the problem.

③ The last sentence concludes the paragraph by summing up its information in an easy-to-remember statement.

Cross-Curricular Connection: Science

Problems and Solutions Explain to students that some of the basic elements of science deal with problems and solutions. Many scientists are actually inventors who devote themselves to solving a problem, by finding a new way to make or do something. They come up with an idea, and then take steps to experiment and see if their idea works. Most inventors keep precise notes of their work to refer to later. For example, James Watt detailed all the steps that led him to invent a condenser that significantly improved the efficiency of the steam engine.

Encourage students to brainstorm for a list of modern inventions. Start them off by naming the airplane, electron microscope, and television, as inventions of the last century. Then, have students do some research to find out where the idea for the invention came from, how it was created, and by whom. Suggest that students begin their research with an encyclopedia and then move on to a biography or autobiography of the inventor. Have them ask, "What problem was the inventor trying to solve?" Encourage students to share their findings with the class.

Prewriting

Define the Problem With a partner, discuss problems that could inspire good essays. Here are some broad suggestions to get you started:

Topic Ideas

- There's too much ______
- There's not enough ______
- A problem in our school

Browse Through a Newspaper To get ideas or information, look through a current newspaper and jot down subjects that interest you. You also might want to read an advice column, which is a good example of problem-solution writing.

Make a Cluster Diagram Use a cluster diagram to brainstorm for possible solutions, reasons, examples, facts, and other details that you can use when you write.

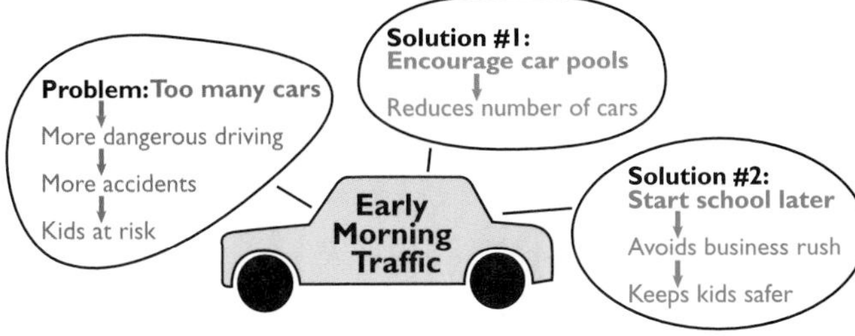

Drafting

Introduce the Problem Begin your essay by making the problem clear. Identify your subject, and grab your readers' attention with a bold statement or a question.

Develop Your Ideas In the body of your essay, build your argument by presenting information. If you are presenting one solution, move through it step by step. If you're suggesting several possible solutions, arrange them in an order that makes logical sense. Treat each one separately and clearly.

Wrap Up Memorably In your conclusion, summarize your main ideas by restating the problem in a sentence or two. Then, list the solutions you propose. State your best solution, and briefly say why it is the best. Finally, leave your readers something to think about, such as:

- A recommendation
- A thought-provoking question
- A prediction

Drafting/Revising

Applying Language Skills: Use the Correct Homophone

Homophones are those tricky words that sound alike but are spelled differently. Proofread carefully for these pesky words. Following are some of the more common homophones. Use a dictionary if you are unsure about the differences in meaning of these pairs and trios.

to, too, two	you're, your
hear, here	sight, site, cite
its, it's	passed, past
buy, by, bye	lead, led
their, there, they're	

Practice Correct the incorrect homophones in the following sentences:

1. I hope to here you've solved you're problem.
2. My essay sited the reports bye they're experts.
3. We just past the new store.

Writing Application As you write your essay, be careful to use the correct homophones.

Writer's Solution Connection Writing Lab

For more on writing the parts of a problem-solution essay, see the annotated student models in the Drafting section of the tutorial on Exposition: Making Connections.

Develop Student Writing

Prewriting

Tell students that the editorial section of the newspaper often has examples of problem-solution essays. Readers or commentators offer solutions to various problems in the local or national community. Another place to look for topic ideas is the letters to the editor sections of magazines.

Customize for *More Advanced Writers*

Suggest that students find an example of a problem-solution essay in a local or national newspaper. Have them identify the problem, and then have them offer a different solution to the problem in the essay. Encourage them to include references to the newspaper story in their essays, pointing out why their solution is better.

Customize for *Less Proficient Writers*

You may want to have students work in pairs on their problem-solution essays. Have students get together and decide on a topic. Then, have them discuss different possible solutions. Encourage them to take notes while they talk. As they draft their essay, they can refer back to their notes.

Drafting

Remind students that good organization is an essential part of a well-written essay. Suggest that they use chronological order to give step-by-step instructions or when re-creating a series of events. You may want students to use the Series of Events Chain in **Writing and Language Transparencies,** p. 66, to help them organize their essays.

Applying Language Skills

Use the Correct Homophone Remind students that spelling checkers on computers cannot determine differences in homophones. If you have used the wrong word, but spelled it correctly, the spelling checker will not find an error. Therefore, suggest that students carefully look for homophones when they revise.

Answers

1. I hope to hear you've solved your problem.
2. My essay cited the reports by their experts.
3. We just passed the new store.

Revising

Suggest that peer reviewers look to make sure enough background information is included about the problem, that the solution is practical and understandable, and that the essay is well organized. In addition, have reviewers read for grammar, mechanics, or spelling errors.

Writer's Solution

Writing Lab CD-ROM

In the tutorial on Exposition: Making Connections, have students use the sentence-length revision checker to help them combine short sentences into longer ones.

Publishing

For other publishing ideas, suggest that students submit their problem-solution essays to the editorial section of the school or local newspaper.

Reinforce and Extend

Review the Writing Guidelines

After students have completed their papers, review the characteristics of a problem-solution essay.

Applying Language Skills

Avoid Clichés

Tell students that clichés are also called *dead metaphors,* meaning they are figures of speech that have lost their figurative sound; they have been so overused that they have lost their imaginative power.

Answers

Possible responses:

1. I feel ravenous.
2. His envy simmered inside his mind, making him feel like a wretched, evil being.
3. Her skin seemed to glow from the inside out.
4. Now, it'll be like sunning yourself on the beach.

EDITING/PROOFREADING

APPLYING LANGUAGE SKILLS: Avoid Clichés

A **cliché** is a phrase that has been repeated too many times. It started out fresh and clever, but it has worn out from overuse. Here are some examples of clichés:

quiet as a mouse

as cool as a cucumber

by the skin of our teeth

avoid it like the plague

Descriptive language needs to be fresh and imaginative. Instead of saying you are "on pins and needles," for example, let your readers see your anxiety in a new light. You could say, "I feel like a sky diver about to jump."

Practice Rewrite these sentences, replacing clichés with clearer, more specific words.

1. I could eat a horse.
2. He was green with envy.
3. Her skin was as white as snow.
4. Now, it'll be smooth sailing.

Writing Application Revise any clichés in your essay. Find your own original ways to express your ideas.

Writer's Solution Connection Language Lab

For more practice with lively comparisons, see the Language Lab lesson on Figurative Language.

Revising

Use Present Tense For word economy and a clean, crisp style, use the present tense for presenting facts.

Use a Peer Reviewer Ask someone else to read your essay. Then, ask them questions such as these:

- Can you identify the problem?
- Is the solution (or solutions) I offer reasonable?
- Do I support each solution with enough facts?
- Is my essay convincing? Why or why not?
- Is my conclusion effective? Why or why not?
- What is the strongest part of my essay? The weakest part?

Use your peer reviewer's response to help you revise your problem-solution essay.

REVISION MODEL

Find out who ~~you're~~ ① your classmates are. Ask them about their hobbies ② , their favorite subjects, and their opinions. Don't forget to ~~share~~ ③ make connections by sharing your own interests and ideas.

① The writer replaced an incorrect homophone.

② The writer provided more examples of conversation topics.

③ This detail strengthens the writer's argument.

Publishing and Presenting

Prepare an Advice Column Turn your essay into a question with an essay-length answer, as if it appeared in an advice column. Combine yours with others and publish them under a collective name, such as *Ask Amanda* or *Dear Donald.*

Be a Talk-Show Guest With a partner, pretend you are a guest on a talk show, and you've been asked to give advice about the problem addressed in your essay. Take turns being the host and the guest, asking and answering questions.

✓ ASSESSMENT		4	3	2	1
PORTFOLIO ASSESSMENT Use the rubric on Problem-Solution Essay in the **Alternative Assessment** booklet, p. 88, to assess the students' writing. Add these criteria to customize this rubric to this assignment.	**Facts and Examples**	The writer uses ample facts and examples to support the solution.	The writer uses facts and examples to support the solution, but some are unclear or misleading.	The writer uses facts and examples, but key elements of the solution are unsupported.	The writer fails to use facts or examples to support the solution.
	Avoiding Clichés	The writer avoids clichés and uses fresh, imaginative descriptive language.	The writer avoids clichés but parts of the essay lack descriptive language.	The writer uses one or two clichés.	The writer uses clichés throughout the essay.

Real-World Reading Skills Workshop

Challenging an Article

Strategies for Success

What would the world be like if people believed everything they read? We would think that certain products could make us more popular, that every scheme could make us rich, and that weight loss without exercise is easy and quick. We tend to trust what we see in print, but not every story is presented truthfully. When you're reading a newspaper article, you should ask questions, check the writer's logic, and consider alternatives.

Be Critical Be ready to question what a writer says. Here are some points on which you can challenge an article:

- **Truth** Reliable journalism is based on research from several sources that can be verified. Unreliable journalism presents stories that may not be truthful. These stories are frequently based on information that is not supported. You should question statements in an article that seem unrealistic or unreasonable.
- **Bias** Good journalism does not take sides or favor a point of view. If a writer has a bias, he or she may not present information objectively.
- **Writer's motive** A *motive* is a purpose for doing something. Consider a writer's reason for writing. Not every writer intends to be totally accurate. A writer's motive may be to entertain, sell copies of the paper, injure someone, or make you agree with him or her.
- **Logical reasoning** Watch out for unsupported statements. Check that the writer's conclusions make sense based on the facts presented in the article.

Apply the Strategies

Read the following newspaper clipping, and answer the questions that follow:

Cabbage Makes You Taller

Muncie, Indiana—James Torres, 14, has grown over three inches since he started eating cabbage just two weeks ago. "Jimmy was short for his age. Now he's taller than many of the students in his class," says the boy's mother. A neighbor confirms the story, saying, "I see Jimmy walking to school every day, and he's definitely taller than he used to be." Do you wish you were taller? A half cup of cabbage three times a day will put you on the right track!

1. Is this story an example of reliable or unreliable journalism? Why?
2. What is one problem with using the neighbor's statement to support the claim about cabbage?
3. Identify at least one other explanation for James Torres's increased height.
4. What questions would you ask about the writer's conclusion that cabbage makes you grow?

Here are some other types of articles in which you should challenge the writer's message:

- Editorials
- Articles about new products or services
- The text of political speeches

Introduce the Strategies

Discuss with students supermarket tabloids, television series about "unexplained mysteries," and other types of writing or media in which the stories and information tend to be unbelievable. Explain that even though we realize that these stories bend the truth, we should apply this kind of questioning to all types of writing and media.

Customize for
Less Proficient Learners
Some students may need help distinguishing fact from opinion. Explain that a fact is something that can be verified as true or false and an opinion is a claim that cannot be verified.

Customize for
More Advanced Learners
Invite students to scan headlines of local tabloids and then write their own stories based on the headlines. For example, if they find a headline *Bat Boy Lives!* they can write a story about the elusive bat boy.

Apply the Strategies

Explain to students that they may want to read an article more than once before deciding on its reliability. Often, as one rereads, the hidden meaning or purpose behind the text becomes more evident.

Answers

1. This is an example of unreliable journalism because none of the sources can be verified.
2. The neighbor's statement that he's taller than he used to be may be true, but it doesn't say he's taller than he was two weeks ago, or that it has anything to do with cabbage.
3. He could be having a growth spurt.
4. Some students may ask for scientific evidence on cabbage and height. Other students may ask why the writer specifies a certain amount of cabbage intake.

◆Build Grammar Skills

Reviewing Prepositions and Prepositional Phrases

The selections in Part 1 include instruction on the following:

- Prepositions
- Prepositional Phrases
- Adjective and Adverb Phrases

This instruction is reinforced with the Build Grammar Skills practice pages in **Selection Support,** pp. 102, 108, and 113.

As you review prepositions and prepositional phrases you may wish to review the following:

- Preposition or Adverb?

Prepositions always have objects. Adverbs do not. You may wish to use the following sentences to help students understand that many words that are considered prepositions can also be adverbs, depending on how they are used.

Prepositions	Adverbs
The school was *near* the forest.	They knew the rain was *near*.
They ran *around* the forest.	No one was *around*.

Customize for
Less Proficient Readers

Remind students that some words are used as prepositions or adverbs. Explain that a preposition begins a prepositional phrase and has an object, such as *underneath the bushes*. Here, *underneath* is the preposition and the object is *bushes*. However, in another sentence, *underneath* can be used as an adverb. For example, *We climbed underneath.*

Writer's Solution

For additional practice and support with phrases, use the practice pages on Prepositions, pp. 23–24 in the *Writer's Solution Grammar Practice Book.*

Prepositions and Prepositional Phrases — Grammar Review

etc., predominate —pre·pon'der·a'tion n.
prep·o·si·tion (prep'ə zish'ən) n. [ME preposicioun < praepositus, pp. of praeponere < prae-, before see PRE- & POSITION): transl. of Gr prothesis, PRO languages, a relation or function word, as English etc., that connects a lexical word, usually a noun syntactic construction, to another element of the verb (Ex.: he went to the store), to a noun (Ex.: music), or to an adj...

A **preposition** is a word that relates a noun or a pronoun to another word in the sentence (see page 283). Here are some examples of prepositions:

Common Prepositions			
about	because of	from	over
above	before	in	past
according to	behind	into	since
across	below	like	through
after	beside	next to	to
against	between	of	toward
ahead of	by	off	under
among	during	on	until
around	except	on top of	up
at	for	out	with

A **prepositional phrase** (see page 296) is a group of words that begins with a preposition and ends with a noun or pronoun, called the object of the preposition.

Preposition	Object of the Preposition
across	the bridge
past	the new supermarket
on top of	the hill

Prepositional phrases can act as adjectives or adverbs (see page 312).

Thurber wrote humorous stories *about his life.*
(adjective)

His stories were illustrated *with funny cartoons.*
(adverb)

Practice 1 Copy these sentences. Underline each prepositional phrase. Identify the word the phrase modifies, and tell whether it acts as an adjective or an adverb.

1. On Venus, the sun appears only once in seven years.
2. Proud words can come between people.
3. Bess waited at her window and looked for her love by moonlight.
4. The cowboys drove the cattle up hills, down valleys, and across the open range.

Practice 2 Write a paragraph about events leading to a conflict, using the prepositional phrases as indicated. Use the phrases in any order.

over the fence *(adverb)*
next to the park *(adjective)*
during the summer *(adverb)*
at a restaurant *(adjective)*

Grammar in Writing

✔ *Do not use the prepositions at or to without an object when the sentence makes sense without the preposition:*

Where are you going ~~to~~?
Where's the party ~~at~~?

✔ *Do not use two prepositions when one will do:*

The poster fell off ~~of~~ the wall.

Answers

Practice 1

1. On Venus, the sun appears only once in seven years. *On Venus* modifies *appears* and acts as an adverb; *in seven years* modifies *once* and acts as an adverb.
2. Proud words can come between people. *Between people* modifies *can come* and acts as an adverb.
3. Bess waited at her window and looked for her love by moonlight. *At her window* modifies *waited* and acts as an adverb; *for her love* modifies *looked* and acts as an adverb; *by moonlight* modifies *looked* and acts as an adverb.
4. The cowboys drove the cattle up hills, down valleys, and across the open range. *Up hills, down valleys,* and *across the open range* modify *drove* and act as adverbs.

Part 2 *Finding Solutions*

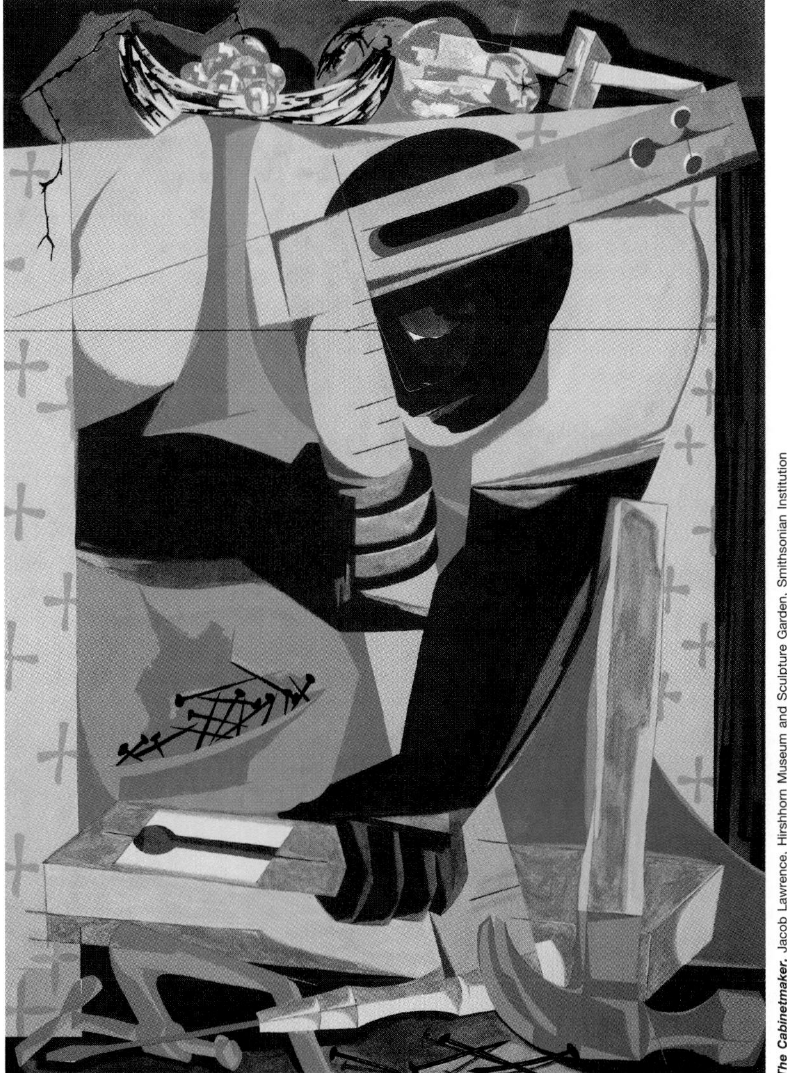

The Cabinetmaker, Jacob Lawrence, Hirshhorn Museum and Sculpture Garden, Smithsonian Institution

One-Minute Planning Guide

The selections in this section focus on the theme of finding solutions. In "The Dying Detective," Sherlock Holmes uses the power of deduction to solve a mystery. "Justin Lebo" is a true story of a boy who turns his own interest in bicycling into a way to help others. "The Rider" is a poem about dealing with loneliness. In "Amigo Brothers," best friends face a serious challenge to their friendship. "The Walk" is a poem about missing someone.

Customize for
Varying Students Needs

When assigning the selections in this section, keep in mind the following factors:

"The Dying Detective"
- A classic mystery
- Introduces students to Sherlock Holmes

"Justin Lebo"
- A true story
- Introduces the idea of charity

"The Rider"
- A brief poem
- Students may need help with the theme

"Amigo Brothers"
- A short story
- An opportunity for research on boxing

"The Walk"
- A classic short poem
- Students may need help with theme

Humanities: Art

The Cabinetmaker, by Jacob Lawrence

Jacob Lawrence (1917–) is widely regarded as one of the most influential African American painters of the twentieth century. His work is characterized by bold colors and lines, and expressive flat forms. Most of his work focuses on the lives, history, and culture of African Americans. He has created numerous narrative series—collections of paintings or images, often strung together with text from his own research.

Lawrence was born in Atlantic City, New Jersey, but moved with his family to Harlem in New York City, in 1926. He studied art at the Harlem Art Workshop and had his first one-man show at the age of twenty-one. His most famous work is *Migration of the Negro*, a collection of sixty paintings showing the flight of southern blacks to the cities of the North after World War II. "The Cabinetmaker" is from a series called *Builders*.

Have students study the painting and then ask the following questions:

1. How do the proportions in the painting contribute to the characterization of the cabinetmaker? *Students may say that the man's enormous shoulders and forearms show him to be strong and hardworking.*
2. How does this painting relate to the theme Finding Solutions? *Students may say that the painting shows a cabinetmaker at work with his tools, trying to find a solution to some type of construction problem.*

OBJECTIVES

1. To read, comprehend, and interpret a play
2. To relate a play to personal experience
3. To draw conclusions
4. To understand staging
5. To build vocabulary in context and learn the suffix *-ology*
6. To develop skill in using interjections
7. To write a critical review using evaluatory language
8. To respond to a play through writing, speaking and listening, and projects

SKILLS INSTRUCTION

Vocabulary: Suffixes: *-ology*

Spelling: Adding *-ing* to Words Ending With Silent e

Grammar: Interjections

Reading Strategy: Draw Conclusions

Literary Focus: Staging

Writing: Language to Evaluate

Speaking and Listening: Dramatic Scene (Teacher Edition)

Viewing and Representing: Many Faces of Sherlock Holmes (Teacher Edition)

Critical Viewing: Hypothesize; Assess; Compare and Contrast; Connect; Interpret

PORTFOLIO OPPORTUNITIES

Writing: Monologue; Scene; Memo

Writing Mini-Lesson: Critical Review

Speaking and Listening: Dramatic Scene; Lawyer's Argument

Projects: Multimedia Biography; Crime-Solvers' Club

More About the Authors

English writer **Michael Hardwick** and his wife, **Mollie Hardwick,** collaborated on this play, but both have written independently. The couple wrote many interpretations of Sherlock Holmes stories, as well as scripts for British-based television series such as *Upstairs, Downstairs.* Many of **Sir Arthur Conan Doyle's** Sherlock Holmes novels and stories have been adapted into movies, television dramas, and plays. His brilliant detective has enduring appeal. In fact, Conan Doyle is credited with sparking the growth of the mystery-detective genre. Devotees, often called "Sherlockians," have formed Holmes-appreciation clubs around the world.

Guide for Reading

Meet the Authors:

Sir Arthur Conan Doyle (1859–1930)

Almost like a combination of his two most famous characters—Sherlock Holmes and Dr. Watson—Sir Arthur Conan Doyle was both a mystery solver *and* a trained medical doctor.

Success as a Writer Doyle was born in Edinburgh, Scotland. When his medical practice struggled, he turned to mystery writing as a way to earn money, achieving immediate success with his Sherlock Holmes stories. In addition to detective stories, Doyle wrote historical and fantasy novels.

Although Holmes was a great success, Doyle often considered killing off the famous detective. Readers protested so wildly to one attempt that Doyle brought Holmes back to life.

Michael Hardwick (1924–1991)
Mollie Hardwick

Fortunately for Michael Hardwick, Doyle wrote many Sherlock Holmes stories. Studying Doyle and writing materials to go with his stories kept Michael Hardwick busy writing for years. Together with his wife, Mollie, he wrote this dramatic version of "The Dying Detective." Michael once said their styles were so similar that even they couldn't tell later who wrote specific passages.

◆ Literature and Your Life

Connect Your Experience

Somewhere in your life there's probably a person whom you know really well. You can finish each other's sentences and predict each other's emotions. What would you do if this person started acting strangely? What if he or she suddenly seemed to dislike you and, although unhappy, insisted on suffering alone? This is the problem Dr. Watson faces in "The Dying Detective."

Thematic Focus: Finding Solutions

In "The Dying Detective," the characters each try to solve different problems. Think about how each man's actions can help the other solve his problem.

◆ Background for Understanding

Mathematics

Detectives solve mysteries with logical deductions—conclusions reached by reasoning from a general statement to a specific one. Look at these two sentences:

Holmes usually speaks clearly and logically.
Today, Holmes is not making sense.

From these statements, you can draw this conclusion:

Something is wrong with Holmes.

As you read, think about how Dr. Watson might use logic to solve the problem of Holmes's strange behavior.

◆ Build Vocabulary

Suffixes: *-ology*

Sherlock Holmes describes a disease as *pathological.* The related word *pathology* is formed from the root *path,* meaning "feeling or suffering," and the suffix *-ology,* meaning "the science or study of disease."

Word Bank

Which of these words do you think might describe a careful and very organized person?

agitated
pathological
implore
methodical
irksome

Prentice Hall Literature Program Resources

REINFORCE / RETEACH / EXTEND

Selection Support Pages
Build Vocabulary: Suffixes: *-ology,* p. 118
Build Spelling Skills, p. 119
Build Grammar Skills: Interjections, p. 120
Reading Strategy: Draw Conclusions, p. 121
Literary Focus: Staging, p. 122

Strategies for Diverse Student Needs, pp. 43–44

Beyond Literature Career Connection: Travel Agent, p. 22

Formal Assessment Selection Test, pp. 96–98
Assessment Resources Software

Alternative Assessment, p. 22

Resource Pro CD-ROM
"The Dying Detective"—includes all resource material and customizable lesson plan

Listening to Literature Audiocassettes
"The Dying Detective"

The Dying Detective

Sherlock Holmes, Frederic Dorr Steele

Reading Strategy

Draw Conclusions

A mystery like "The Dying Detective" is built around the facts the author includes and the information that is held back. When you **draw conclusions,** you use details in the text to make general statements. By identifying the clues Doyle presents, you might unravel the mystery. As you read, be aware of the characters' actions and any unusual remarks. Note the topics that the main characters think are important. With these clues, you may solve a crime before the characters do.

Literary Focus

Staging

The techniques that bring a drama to life—movements, costumes, scenery, lighting, and sound—are called **staging.** Playwrights provide staging directions in brackets that appear in the script. Directors use this information as they plan productions. Readers use the information to visualize the action. The staging directions at the beginning of "The Dying Detective" describe the appearance of Holmes's room. As you read, create a staging chart like the one below for each scene.

	Actors' Movements	Scenery	Lighting and Sound Effects	Costumes
Scene 1:				
Scene 2:				
Scene 3:				

Interest Grabber Write on the board: *Vandals Caught.* Identify examples of the crimes vandals might commit. Then, divide the class into groups in which someone role-plays a suspected vandal. Two others should role-play detectives, and another, a witness. Have groups role-play questioning the suspect, whom you have coached to be evasive and maybe insolent. Afterward, talk about the problems that arise in questioning a suspect, such as deciding whether he or she is telling the truth, and evaluating evidence and alibis. Tell students that they will read about the famed fictional detective, Sherlock Holmes.

Build Grammar Skills

Interjections If you wish to introduce the grammar concept for this selection before students read, refer to the instruction on p. 340.

Customize for
Less Proficient Readers
Mystery writers intentionally plant clues in their stories. Encourage students to read the play all the way through, trying to unravel clues on their own. Then, guide them through a second reading, stopping to discuss issues and questions raised in side notes.

Customize for
More Advanced Students
Of the many traits Sherlock Holmes possesses, an important one in this story is determination. Challenge students, as they read, to look for evidence of determination on the parts of Holmes, Dr. Watson, Mrs. Hudson, and the criminal himself.

Humanities: Art

Sherlock Holmes, by Frederic Dorr Steele

The works of Frederic Dorr Steele have illustrated many Sherlock Holmes stories. Ask these questions:

1. What features in his face suggest that Sherlock Holmes is a brilliant detective? *He seems serious, intently focused, and unruffled.*
2. What signature items does Steele include in this portrait of Holmes? *the double-billed cap, the pipe, and the magnifying glass*

Preparing for Standardized Tests

Grammar This selection provides instruction on interjections that will help students as they read in general, and as they answer certain items on standardized tests. Standardized tests may evaluate students' ability to correctly punctuate a passage that contains an interjection. Provide the following sample test question:

Find the choice that best expresses the sentence in standard written English.

Stop! don't touch that box.

(A) No change
(B) Stop! Don't touch that box.
(C) Stop don't touch that box
(D) Stop, Don't touch that box.

Students who interpret *Stop!* as an interjection will know to set it apart from the rest of the sentence with an exclamation point. This eliminates *(C)* and *(D)*. *(B)* is correct, because the first letter of *Don't* must then be capitalized. For additional practice, use Build Grammar Skills in **Selection Support,** p. 120.

Develop Understanding

One-Minute Insight In the opening scene, Sherlock Holmes, sick in bed, gets a visit from his old friend, Dr. Watson. When Watson tries to fetch a renowned specialist, Holmes insists that he instead summon a man named Culverton Smith. Just before Smith arrives, Holmes orders Watson to hide behind his bed. Smith, believing Holmes to be near death, gloats about a prior murder he has committed by infecting his victim with a rare, deadly disease. He believes he has also infected Holmes. Holmes tricks Smith into turning up a lamp, thus signaling Inspector Morton, who has been waiting outside to arrest Smith. The confession extracted by the wily Holmes, who has faked his illness, is enough to convict Smith.

Customize for
English Language Learners
Use the following strategies to help students determine the meanings of unfamiliar words: Use surrounding words and context clues to find the meaning of *carafe* (pitcher), *adorned* (decorated), *delirium* (daze), *gloat* (brag), and *recumbent* (leaning). Or, think of related words to define *pretense* (false claim), *ensure* (guarantee), and *masterful* (talented).

Customize for
Verbal/Linguistic Learners
Have students form small groups and take turns reading the lines of each character. Suggest that students switch roles at the start of each new scene. One person in each group can read the stage directions. Encourage students to read with suitable character and flair.

Clarification

❶ Sir Arthur Conan Doyle wrote "The Adventure of the Dying Detective," the story upon which this play is based. That story appeared in a collection called *His Last Bow.*

▶Critical Viewing◀

❷ **Hypothesize** *Students may suggest that the audience might wonder how Sherlock Holmes has wound up in such a terrible state. They might assume that the man leaning over the bed is Dr. Watson, and may wonder who the seated man might be.*

The Dying Detective

❶ FROM A STORY BY SIR ARTHUR CONAN DOYLE

Michael and Mollie Hardwick

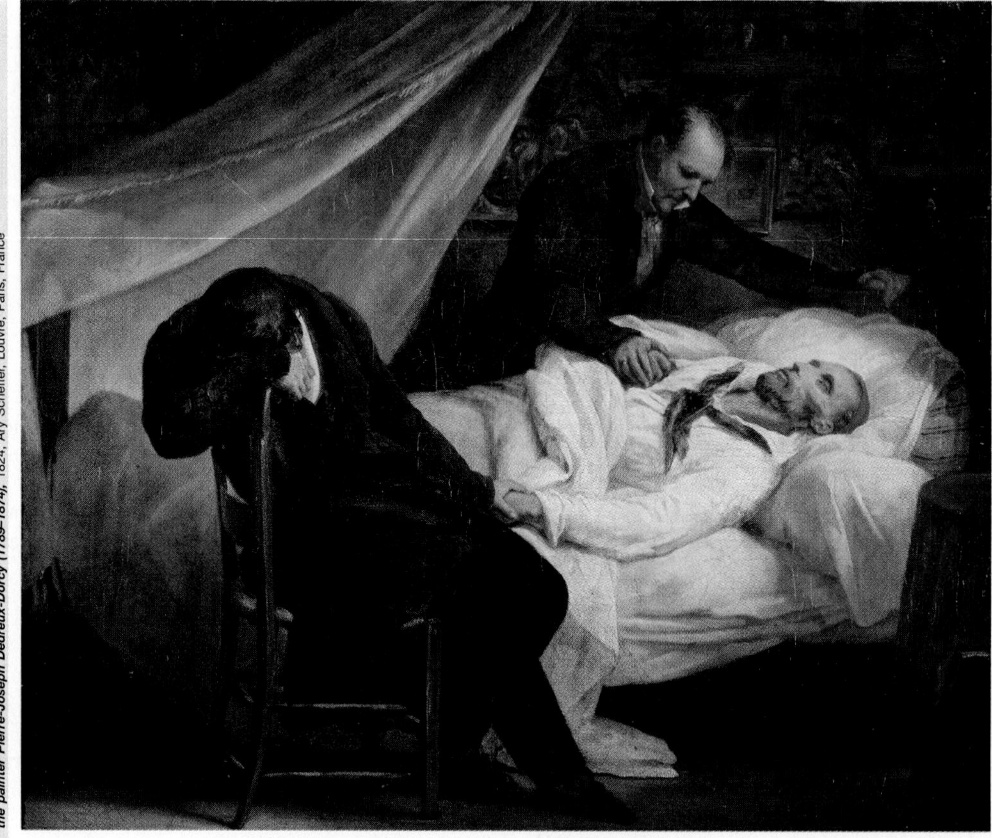

The Death of Theodore Gericault (1791–1824) with his friends Colonel Bro de Comeres and the painter Pierre-Joseph Dedreux-Dorcy (1789–1874), 1824, Ary Scheffer, Louvre, Paris, France

❷ ▲ Critical Viewing If you went to see a production of "The Dying Detective," the curtain might rise on a scene like the one in this painting. How would you expect the audience to respond? **[Hypothesize]**

328 ◆ *Resolving Conflicts*

Humanities: Art

The Death of Theodore Gericault (1791–1824), with his friends Colonel Bro de Comeres and the painter Pierre-Joseph Dedreux-Dorcy (1789–1874), 1824, by Ary Scheffer.

Dutch-born painter Ary Scheffer (1795–1858) received his earliest art lessons from his parents, who were both painters. Scheffer soon moved to Paris, where he studied art professionally. He was only 13 when he had one of his paintings, a scene from Roman history, shown publicly. A leader of the Romantic movement, Scheffer enjoyed widespread popularity for his sentimental scenes based upon literature and history. Use these questions for discussion:

1. What is the mood of the scene? *Students should be able to determine that the mood conveys sadness and grief.*
2. Why do the two men hold Gericault's hands? *Students may assume that the men are trying to comfort Gericault as he approaches death.*

CHARACTERS, IN ORDER OF APPEARANCE

MRS. HUDSON

DR. WATSON

SHERLOCK HOLMES

CULVERTON SMITH: "A great yellow face, coarse-grained and greasy, with heavy double chin, and two sullen, menacing gray eyes which
3 glared at me from under tufted and sandy brows . . ."

INSPECTOR MORTON: Middle-aged, tough, dressed in plain clothes.

Scene 1: Sherlock Holmes's bedroom, *afternoon*

Scene 2: The same, *dusk*

Scene 3: The same, *evening*

Scene 1

[SHERLOCK HOLMES'S *bedroom at 221B Baker Street. The essential features are: a bed with a large wooden head, placed crosswise on the stage, the head a foot or two from one side wall; a small table near the bed-head, on the audience's side, on which stand a carafe of water and a glass, and a tiny metal or ivory box; a window in the back wall, the curtains*
4 *parted; and, under the window, a table or chest of drawers, on which stand a green wine bottle, some wine-glasses, a biscuit-barrel,*[1] *and a lamp. Of course, there may be further lamps and any amount of furnishing and clutter: Holmes's bedroom was adorned with pictures of celebrated criminals and littered with everything from tobacco pipes to revolver cartridges.*]

[*There is daylight outside the window.* SHERLOCK HOLMES *lies in the bed on his back, tucked up to the chin and evidently asleep. He is very pale.* MRS. HUDSON *enters followed by* DR. WATSON, *who is wearing his coat and hat and carrying his small medical bag.* MRS. HUDSON *pauses for a moment.*]

MRS. HUDSON. He's asleep, sir.

[*They approach the bed.* WATSON *comes round to the audience's side and looks down at* HOLMES *for a moment. He shakes his head gravely, then he and* MRS. HUDSON *move away be-* 5
yond the foot of the bed. WATSON *takes off his hat and coat as they talk and she takes them from him.*]

> **◆ Literary Focus**
> What information about the actors and their appearance do these staging directions provide?

WATSON. This is dreadful, Mrs. Hudson. He was perfectly hale and hearty when I went away only three days ago.

MRS. HUDSON. I know, sir. Oh, Dr. Watson, sir, I'm glad that you've come back. If anyone can save Mr. Holmes, I'm sure you can.

WATSON. I shall have to know what is the matter with him first. Mrs. Hudson, please tell me, as quickly as you can, how it all came about.

MRS. HUDSON. Yes, sir. Mr. Holmes has been working lately on some case down near the river—Rotherhithe, I think.

WATSON. Yes, yes. I know.

MRS. HUDSON. Well, you know what he is for
coming in at all hours. I was just taking my 6
lamp to go to my bed on Wednesday night when I heard a faint knocking at the street door. I . . . I found Mr. Holmes there. He could hardly stand. Just muttered to me to help him up to his bed here, and he's barely spoken since.

WATSON. Dear me!

MRS. HUDSON. Won't take food or drink. Just lies there, sleeping or staring in a wild sort of way.

WATSON. But, goodness gracious, Mrs. Hudson,
why did you not send for another doctor in my 7
absence?

MRS. HUDSON. Oh, I told him straightaway I was going to do that, sir. But he got so agitated—almost shouted that he wouldn't allow any

1. **biscuit-barrel** (bis′ kit bar′ əl) *n.*: British term for a container holding cookies or crackers.

◆ Build Vocabulary
agitated (aj′ i tāt′ id) *adj.*: Shaken or upset

◆Literary Focus

❸ Staging Call attention to the cast of characters and the list of scenes. Explain to students that if they were in an audience about to watch the play, they would receive a program with this information to prepare them for the drama. Ask students to speculate about why a cast list is more common in plays than in books. *When you read a book, you can always go back to an earlier page to check something you missed. When you watch a play, you can't go back to review the action; so, it is more important to have knowledge of the characters before the play begins.*

◆Literary Focus

❹ Staging Make certain that students notice the comprehensive list of stage properties listed and described in the stage directions. Tell them that stage properties are called "props" by theatre professionals and audience members as well.

◆Literary Focus

❺ Staging *Dr. Watson has made a first diagnosis and he feels that Holmes's condition is grave enough that he should discuss it with Mrs. Hudson away from Holmes.*

◆Reading Strategy

❻ Draw Conclusions Ask students who they think Mrs. Hudson is. *Students familiar with Sherlock Holmes will know her as Holmes's loyal and discreet housekeeper. Others may need to read on to learn more about her from what she says and how she acts.*

◆Build Grammar Skills

❼ Interjections Interjections are words that express feelings or emotions. Guide students to identify the interjection in this passage, and suggest the emotion or feeling it conveys. *goodness gracious; shows concern*

Block Scheduling Strategies

Consider these suggestions to take advantage of extended class time:

- Use the Interest Grabber (p. 327) to engage students. Or prepare for the selection by discussing the illustrations. Present the Humanities note on p. 330 to acquaint students with the conventions of reading a script.
- Have students read the play on their own, or set up "reader's theatre" groups to read it aloud.
- To help students prepare for the Writing Mini-Lesson, teach the Viewing and Representing Mini-Lesson on p. 336, and/or use the Dramatic Scene activity in the Idea Bank on p. 341.
- If you have access to technology, have students work through some or all of the *Writer's Solution Writing Lab CD-ROM* tutorial on Response to Literature for the Writing Mini-Lesson, p. 341. Others can use class time to work in groups on the Projects in the Idea Bank (p. 341), or to research forensics for the Beyond Literature: Science Connection, p. 339.

◆Reading Strategy

❶ **Draw Conclusions** Guide students to note Watson's reaction when he finds out that Holmes wouldn't let Mrs. Hudson notify him. Is this how a sick person usually acts? What might Holmes's objection be to seeing a doctor? *Many students will wonder why Holmes wouldn't want his friend to tend to him; some will be suspicious of Holmes's handling of his supposed best friend.*

Comprehension Check ☑

❷ Ask students to tell what Holmes threatens to do if Watson tries to come near him. *He'll order Watson out of the house.* Why does he say that Watson should stay back? *He claims that he has a deadly disease that Watson might catch if he comes near.*

◆Reading Strategy

❸ **Draw Conclusions** *Students may conclude that Holmes is frightened or worried, or that he has a hidden motive for keeping Watson at bay.*

◆Reading Strategy

❹ **Draw Conclusions** Ask students to draw conclusions about Dr. Watson's character based on the way he reacts to Holmes. *Students may say that Watson seems unflappable, confident, tolerant, and persistent. He is not flustered by the insulting things Holmes says, and simply does what he believes must be done.*

doctor on the premises. You know how masterful he is, Dr. Watson.

WATSON. Indeed. But you could have telegraphed[2] for me.

[MRS. HUDSON *appears embarrassed.*]

MRS. HUDSON. Well, sir . . .

WATSON. But you didn't. Why, Mrs. Hudson?

MRS. HUDSON. Sir, I don't like to tell you, but . . . well, Mr. Holmes said he wouldn't even have you to see him.

WATSON. What? This is monstrous! I, his oldest friend, and . . .
[HOLMES *groans and stirs slightly.*]

1 Ssh! He's waking. You go along, Mrs. Hudson, and leave this to me. Whether he likes it or not, I shall ensure that everything possible is done.

MRS. HUDSON. Thank you, sir. You'll ring if I can be of help.
[*She exits with* WATSON'S *things.* HOLMES *groans again and flings out an arm restlessly.* WATSON *comes to the audience's side of the bed and sits on it.*]

WATSON. Holmes? It's I—Watson.

HOLMES. [*Sighs*] Ahh! Well, Watson? We . . . we seem to have fallen on evil days.

WATSON. My dear fellow!
[*He moves to reach for* HOLMES'S *pulse.*]

HOLMES. [*Urgently*] No, no! Keep back!

WATSON. Eh?

HOLMES. Mustn't come near.

WATSON. Now, look here, Holmes . . . !

HOLMES. If you come near . . . order you out of the house.

2 **WATSON.** [*Defiantly*] Hah!

HOLMES. For your own sake, Watson. Contracted . . . a disease—from Sumatra.[3] Very little known, except that most deadly. Contagious by touch. So . . . must keep away. 2

WATSON. Utter rubbish. Holmes! Mrs. Hudson tells me she helped you to your bed. There's nothing the matter with her.

HOLMES. Period of . . . incubation.[4] Only dangerous after two or three days. Deadly by now.

WATSON. Good heavens, do you suppose such a consideration weighs with me? Even if I weren't a doctor, d'you think it would stop me doing my duty to an old friend? Now, let's have a good look at you. [*He moves forward again.*]

HOLMES. [*Harshly*] I tell you to keep back!

WATSON. See here, Holmes . . .

HOLMES. If you will stay where you are, I will talk to you. If you will not, you can get out.

> **◆ Reading Strategy** What conclusions can you draw based on Holmes's unusual behavior?

WATSON. Holmes! [*Recovering*] Holmes, you aren't yourself. You're sick and as helpless as a child. Whether you like it or not, I'm going to examine you and treat you.

HOLMES. [*Sneering*] If I'm to be forced to have a doctor, let him at least be someone I've some confidence in.

WATSON. Oh! You . . . After all these years, Holmes, you haven't . . . confidence in me?

HOLMES. In your friendship, Watson—yes. But facts are facts. As a medical man you're a mere general practitioner, of limited experience and mediocre[5] qualifications.

WATSON. Well . . . ! Well, really!

HOLMES. It is painful to say such things, but you leave me no choice.

WATSON. [*Coldly*] Thank you. I'll tell you this, Holmes. Such a remark, coming from you, merely serves to tell me what state your nerves are in. Still, if you insist that you have no

2. **telegraphed** (tel′ ə graf′) *v.:* Sent a message by telegraph, a system that changes codes into electrical impulses and sends them into a distant receiver.
3. **Sumatra** (so͞o mä′ trə): Large island of Indonesia.
4. **incubation** (in′ kyo͞o bā′ shən) *n.:* The phase of a disease between infection and the first appearance of symptoms.
5. **mediocre** (mē′ dē ō′ kər) *adj.:* Neither very good nor very bad.

Humanities: Theatre Arts

In the script for "The Dying Detective," as in most plays, the authors follow accepted standards of formatting and printing so that actors, directors, and readers can follow it. The use of stage direction allows playwrights to explain how they want a set to look or how the director and actors should portray or interpret the characters. By convention, stage directions are presented in italic type, and the lines that a character speaks are presented in regular (or Roman) type. This distinction helps directors or performers identify what to say and what to do. Use these questions for discussion:

1. What conventions can you detect in the way a playwright presents a character's lines? *The character's name appears first in all boldfaced capital letters, followed by a period. Then come the lines themselves, with any pertinent stage directions in brackets.*
2. In what ways do these conventions help readers? How can they be distracting? *They are helpful because readers always know who is speaking and how the author expects that character to act or move, but it can be distracting or confusing when dialogue is interrupted by stage directions.*

4 confidence in me, I will not intrude my services. But what I shall do is to summon Sir Jasper Meek or Penrose Fisher, or any of the other best men in London.

HOLMES. [*Groans*] My . . . dear Watson. You mean well. But do you suppose they—any of them—know of the Tapanuli Fever?

WATSON. The Tap . . . ?

5 **HOLMES.** What do you yourself know of the Black Formosa Corruption?

WATSON. Tapanuli Fever? Black Formosa Corruption? I've never heard of either of 'em.

HOLMES. Nor have your colleagues.[6] There are many problems of disease, many pathological possibilities, peculiar to the East. So I've learned during some of my recent researches. It was in the course of one of them that I contracted this complaint. I assure you, Watson, you can do nothing.

WATSON. Can't I? I happen to know, Holmes, that the greatest living authority on tropical disease, Dr. Ainstree, is in London just now.

HOLMES. [*Beseeching*] Watson!

WATSON. All remonstrance[7] is useless. I am going this instant to fetch him. [*He gets up*]

HOLMES. [*A great cry*] No!

6 **WATSON.** Eh? Holmes . . . my dear fellow . . .

HOLMES. Watson, in the name of our old friendship, do as I ask.

WATSON. But . . .

HOLMES. You have only my own good at heart. Of course, I know that. You . . . you shall have your way. Only . . . give me time to . . . to collect my strength. What is the time now? [WATSON *sits again and consults his watch.*] 6

WATSON. Four o'clock.

HOLMES. Then at six you can go.

WATSON. This is insanity!

HOLMES. Only two hours, Watson. I promise you may go then.

WATSON. Hang it, this is urgent, man!

HOLMES. I will see no one before six. I will not be examined. I shall resist!

WATSON. [*Sighing*] Oh, have it your own way, then. But I insist on staying with you in the meantime. You need an eye keeping on you, Holmes.

HOLMES. Very well, Watson. And now I must sleep. I feel exhausted. [*Drowsily*] I wonder how a battery feels when it pours electricity into a non-conductor?

WATSON. Eh?

HOLMES. [*Yawning*] At six, Watson, we resume our conversation. [*He lies back and closes his eyes.* WATSON *makes as though to move, but thinks better of it. He sits still, watching* HOLMES. *A slow black-out*]

Scene 2

[*The stage lights up again, though more dimly than before, to disclose the same scene. Twilight is apparent through the window.* HOLMES *lies motionless.* WATSON *sits as before, though with his head sagging, half asleep. His chin drops suddenly and he wakes with a jerk. He glances* 7

6. **colleagues** (käl' ēgz) *n.:* Fellow workers.
7. **remonstrance** (ri män' strəns) *n.:* Act of protesting or complaining.

◆ Build Vocabulary

pathological (path' ə läj' i kəl) *adj.*: Due to or related to disease

◄ **Critical Viewing** Why is a magnifying glass like the one pictured here an important tool for Sherlock Holmes? **[Assess]** 8

◆Critical Thinking

❺ Make a Judgment Part of the appeal of the Sherlock Holmes series is a thread of subtle humor that runs through the stories. Conan Doyle himself was a doctor, and could easily have come up with names of real diseases; rather, he chose to make up absurd names. Ask students to give their opinion of this decision, and how, or if, they think it adds humor to the scene. *Students may say that the names sound silly, which adds humor. Some may wonder whether these are real diseases.*

◆Reading Strategy

❻ Draw Conclusions Have students think of other reasons Holmes might have for delaying Watson. Do they suspect that Holmes may have some larger plan in progress? Explain. *Students may say that Holmes stalls Watson to keep him around for some reason, to prevent him from running into someone, or to protect him from some risk or danger.*

◆Literary Focus

❼ Staging Be sure students realize that Scene 2 marks the start of the next section of the play. The main reasons to call for a new scene are to indicate that the set has changed in some way or that a significant period of time has passed. Have students read the stage directions that open Scene 2 to determine why the playwrights call for a new scene. *Students should note that it is now twilight, which would be around 6:00 P.M., when Holmes and Watson will resume their conversation.*

►Critical Viewing◄

❽ Assess Students may say that in a time before high-tech detecting equipment, a magnifying glass could help a good detective find tiny clues, such as hairs, that might otherwise have gone unnoticed.

◆ Critical Thinking

❶ **Interpret** Guide students to notice that, in this passage, Holmes shows a sudden level of vigor that seems to conflict with his grave illness. Discuss whether students think that a dying man would be this alert and emphatic. What does this reveal about Holmes? *Some students may say that people often get one last burst of strength before they die; others may say it makes them suspicious.*

Clarification

❷ Tell students that an asylum is an institution where the sick, especially the mentally ill, receive care. The word was used more commonly in the past than it is today. The point of Holmes's remark is that Watson's actions are driving him insane.

◆ Critical Thinking

❸ **Evaluate** This passage serves two functions. First, it illustrates that Watson is no match for Holmes in terms of cunning. Help students notice that, despite Watson's refusal to "delay another instant," Holmes can easily distract him. Second, the mad delirium adds another touch of humor in what would otherwise be an ominous situation. Ask students to evaluate the effectiveness of this passage in achieving those goals. *Students may appreciate Holmes's ability to derail Watson, and may enjoy the absurd excuse he offers to play for time.*

◆ Literary Focus

❹ **Staging** *Until now, the room has been dim in twilight. When Watson strikes a match to light the lamp, some new light brightens the scene.*

Thematic Focus

❺ **Finding Solutions** Guide students to note that Holmes asks Watson to fetch someone Watson has never heard of, who is not even a medical specialist. Discuss what solutions Holmes may hope to find with Culverton Smith. *Some students may accept Holmes's explanation at face value. Others may suspect that Holmes has a specific reason for inviting Smith to his home.*

---

around, sees the twilight outside, and consults his watch. He yawns, flexes his arms, then proceeds to glance idly about him. His attention is caught by the little box on the bedside table. Stealthily, he reaches over and picks it up.]

HOLMES. [*Very loudly and urgently*] No! No, Watson, no!

❶ **WATSON.** [*Startled*] Eh? What? [HOLMES *starts up onto his elbow.*]

HOLMES. Put it down! Down this instant! Do as I say, Watson!

WATSON. Oh! All right, then. [*Putting the box down.*] Look here, Holmes, I really think . . .

HOLMES. I hate to have my things touched. You know perfectly well I do.

WATSON. Holmes . . . !

HOLMES. You fidget[8] me beyond endurance. You, a doctor—you're enough to drive a patient
❷ into an asylum!

WATSON. Really!

HOLMES. Now, for heaven's sake, sit still, and let me have my rest.

WATSON. Holmes, it is almost six o'clock, and I refuse to delay another instant. [*He gets up determinedly.*]

HOLMES. Really? Watson, have you any change in your pocket?

WATSON. Yes.

HOLMES. Any silver?

WATSON. [*Fishing out his change*] A good deal.

HOLMES. How many half-crowns?

❸ **WATSON.** Er, five.

HOLMES. [*Sighing*] Ah, too few, too few. However, such as they are, you can put them in your watch-pocket—and all the rest of your money in your left trouser-pocket. It will balance you so much better like that.

WATSON. Balance . . . ? Holmes, you're raving! This has gone too far . . . !

8. **fidget** (fij′ it) *v.*: Used here to mean the same as "to irritate."

HOLMES. You will now light that lamp by the window, Watson, but you will be very careful that not for one instant shall it be more than at half flame.

WATSON. Oh, very well. [WATSON *goes to the lamp and strikes a match.*]

HOLMES. I implore you to be careful.

WATSON. [*As though humoring him*] Yes, Holmes. [*He lights the lamp, carefully keeping the flame low. He moves to draw the curtains.*]

◆ **Literary Focus**
How does the stage lighting change during this passage?

HOLMES. No, you need not draw the curtains. [WATSON *leaves them and comes back round the bed.*]

So! Good. You may now go and fetch a specialist.

WATSON. Well, thank heaven for that.

HOLMES. His name is Mr. Culverton Smith, of 13 Lower Burke Street.

WATSON. [*Staring*] Eh?

HOLMES. Well, go on, man. You could hardly wait to fetch someone before.

WATSON. Yes, but . . . Culverton Smith? I've never heard the name!

HOLMES. Possibly not. It may surprise you to know that the one man who knows everything about this disease is not a medical man. He's a planter.

WATSON. A planter!

HOLMES. His plantation is far from medical aid. An outbreak of this disease there caused him to study it intensely. He's a very methodical man, and I asked you not to go before six because I knew you wouldn't find him in his study till then.

WATSON. Holmes, I . . . I never heard such a . . . !

◆ Build Vocabulary

implore (im plôr′) *v.*: Ask or beg earnestly

methodical (mə thäd′ i kəl) *adj.*: Orderly; organized

Cross-Curricular Connection: Social Studies

The original Sherlock Holmes stories were set in and around London in the late nineteenth century. Have students conduct research to find out more about the setting in which the master detective practiced his craft. Some students might locate photographs or paintings of late nineteenth century London and use them to create a display that helps classmates better visualize the setting of the stories. Others might investigate typical architecture, methods of transportation and communication, and clothing and hairstyles of the day to round out the picture. Still others might create a timeline of world events that took place during the period Sherlock Holmes purportedly rid London of its archcriminals.

HOLMES. You will tell him exactly how you have left me. A dying man.

WATSON. No, Holmes!

HOLMES. At any rate, delirious. Yes, not dying, delirious. [*Chuckles*] No, I really can't think why the whole ocean bed isn't one solid mass of oysters.

WATSON. Oysters?

HOLMES. They're so prolific,[9] you know.

WATSON. Great Heavens! Now, Holmes, you just lie quiet, and . . .

HOLMES. Strange how the mind controls the brain. Er, what was I saying, Watson?

WATSON. You were . . .

HOLMES. Ah, I remember. Culverton Smith. My life depends on him, Watson. But you will have to plead with him to come. There is no good feeling between us. He has . . . a grudge. I rely on you to soften him. Beg, Watson. Pray. But get him here by any means.

◆ **Reading Strategy**
What conclusions can you draw based on the change in Holmes's manner?

WATSON. Very well. I'll bring him in a cab, if I have to carry him down to it.

HOLMES. You will do nothing of the sort. You will persuade him to come—and then return before him. [*Deliberately*] Make any excuse so as not to come with him. Don't forget that, Watson. You won't fail me. You never did fail me.

WATSON. That's all very well, Holmes, but . . .

HOLMES. [*Interrupting*] Then, shall the world be overrun by oysters? No doubt there are natural enemies which limit their increase. And yet . . . No, horrible, horrible!

WATSON. [*Grimly*] I'm going, Holmes. Say no more, I'm going!
[*He hurries out.* HOLMES *remains propped up for a moment, staring after* WATSON, *then sinks back into a sleeping posture as the stage blacks out.*]

9. **prolific** (prō lif′ ik) *adj.:* Producing many young.

Scene 3

[*The stage lights up on the same scene.* HOLMES *lies still. It is now quite dark outside. After a moment* WATSON *bustles in, pulling off his coat. He pauses to hand it to* MRS. HUDSON, *who is behind him.*]

WATSON. Thank you, Mrs. Hudson. A gentleman will be calling very shortly. Kindly show him up here immediately.

MRS. HUDSON. Yes, sir.
[*She exits.* WATSON *approaches the bed.*]

HOLMES. [*Drowsily*] Watson?

WATSON. Yes, Holmes. How are you feeling?

HOLMES. Much the same, I fear. Is Culverton Smith coming?

WATSON. Should be here any minute. It took me some minutes to find a cab, and I almost expected him to have got here first.

HOLMES. Well done, my dear Watson.

WATSON. I must say, Holmes, I'm only doing this to humor you. Frankly, I didn't take to your planter friend at all.

HOLMES. Oh? How so?

WATSON. Rudeness itself. He almost showed me the door before I could give him your message. It wasn't until I mentioned the name, Sherlock Holmes . . .

HOLMES. Ah!

WATSON. Quite changed him—but I wouldn't say it was for the better.

HOLMES. Tell me what he said.

7

WATSON. Said you'd had some business dealings together, and that he respected your character and talents. Described you as an amateur of crime, in the way that he regards himself as an amateur of disease.

HOLMES. Quite typical—and surely, quite fair?

WATSON. Quite fair—if he hadn't put such sarcasm into saying it. No, Holmes, you said he bears you some grudge. Mark my words, as soon as he has left this house I insist upon calling a recognized specialist.

◆ **Reading Strategy**

❻ **Draw Conclusions** *Students may say that Holmes implores Watson to say or do whatever it takes to get Culverton Smith to come by, and gives him precise instruction on what to say and do. He does not act like a delirious, dying man.*

◆ **Reading Strategy**

❼ **Draw Conclusions** Have students share the impressions of Culverton Smith that they form from Watson's description of the man. *Students may find Smith, as Watson does, to be rude, and yet surprisingly curious about Holmes.* How does their view of Culverton affect the story's mood of suspense? *Watson implies that Smith doesn't like Holmes, which makes readers more curious about who Smith is and why Holmes has summoned him.*

◆ Critical Thinking

❶ **Speculate** Ask students if they think the fact that Inspector Morton was passing 221B Baker Street just as Watson was returning from Smith's house was a coincidence. If not, why not? *Some students may say that in a busy city like London, it is a possible coincidence. Others may suspect a plan between Holmes and Morton.*

Clarification

❷ Scotland Yard, where London police headquarters rose in 1829, was so named because a medieval palace where Scottish royalty stayed once stood on the spot. London's metropolitan police headquarters have moved twice since 1829 and have been located since 1967 at 10 Broadway, off Victoria Street. Since the first move in 1890, the establishment has been officially named New Scotland Yard.

◆ Literary Focus

❸ **Staging** Encourage students to question Holmes's motives. What explanation does Holmes give to Watson for wanting him to hide behind the bed? Is this a plausible explanation? *Holmes says that Smith will give a more honest medical opinion if no one else is present. Some students may say that this is a humorous touch, while others may think that Watson may be needed later on.*

◆ Literary Focus

❹ **Staging** *On their way up the stairs, Mrs. Hudson must have told Smith that Watson was visiting. Now that she doesn't see him in the room, she feels compelled to give Smith a plausible explanation.*

▶ Critical Viewing ◀

❺ **Compare and Contrast** *Students may find the clothing appropriate to a play set in Victorian London; Watson and Smith would probably be dressed like this.*

HOLMES. My dear Watson, you are the best of messengers. Thank you again.

WATSON. Not at all. Holmes, Holmes—let me help you without any of this nonsense. The whole of Great Britain will condemn me otherwise. Why, my cabmen both inquired anxiously after you; and so did Inspector Morton . . .

❶ **HOLMES.** Morton?

WATSON. Of the Yard. He was passing our door just now as I came in. Seemed extremely concerned.

❷ **HOLMES.** Scotland Yard[10] concerned for me? How very touching! And now, Watson, you may disappear from the scene.

WATSON. Disappear! I shall do no such thing. I wish to be present when this Culverton Smith arrives. I wish to hear every word of this so-called medical expert's opinion.

HOLMES. [*Turning his head*] Yes, of course. Then I think you will just find room behind the head of the bed.

WATSON. What? Hide?

HOLMES. I have reason to suppose that his opinion will be much more frank and valuable if he imagines he is alone with me.
[*We hear the murmur of* MRS. HUDSON'S *and* CULVERTON SMITH'S *voices off-stage.*]

Listen! I hear him coming. Get behind the bed, Watson, and do not budge, whatever happens. *Whatever* happens, you understand?

WATSON. Oh, all right, Holmes. Anything to please you. But I don't like this. Not at all.
[*He goes behind the bed-head and conceals himself.* MRS. HUDSON *enters, looks round the room and then at* HOLMES. SMITH *enters behind her.*]

◆ **Literary Focus** What is the result of this staging direction?

MRS. HUDSON. [*To* SMITH] Oh, Dr. Watson must have let himself out. No doubt he'll be back directly, sir.

SMITH. No matter, my good woman.
[MRS. HUDSON *bristles at this form of address.*]

You may leave me alone with your master.

MRS. HUDSON. As you wish—*sir.*
[*She sweeps out.* SMITH *advances slowly to the bed and stands at the foot, staring at the recumbent* HOLMES.]

SMITH. [*Almost to himself*] So, Holmes. It has come to this, then.
[HOLMES *stirs.* SMITH *chuckles and leans his arms on the bed-foot and his chin on them, continuing to watch* HOLMES.]

10. **Scotland Yard:** The London police, especially the detective bureau.

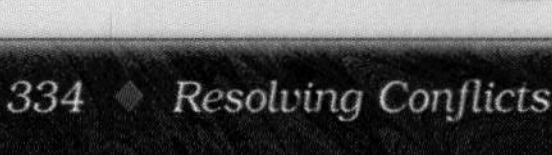

▲ **Critical Viewing** How does the formal clothing of the men compare with the costumes you would expect to see in a production of "The Dying Detective"? **[Compare and Contrast]** ❺

Beyond the Classroom

Career Connection

Investigator In the play, students can find ample evidence that the great Sherlock Holmes is observant, creative, analytical, highly focused, and detail-oriented. Explain to students that there are other types of investigators besides police detectives and private eyes. Invite students who show an interest in investigation, or who demonstrate some of these traits, to research possible career choices involving investigation. Some examples include: insurance investigators, who check that people file accurate claims; environmental investigators, who look for evidence that someone is polluting the air, land, or water; computer investigators, who track down hackers who perpetrate bank or phone fraud; and archaeologists, who use scientific methods and historical facts to investigate the past. Have students share their findings with the class.

HOLMES. [*Weakly*] Watson? Who . . . ? Smith? Smith, is that you?

SMITH. [*Chuckles*]

HOLMES. I . . . I hardly dared hope you would come.

SMITH. I should imagine not. And yet, you see, I'm here. Coals of fire,[11] Holmes—coals of fire!

HOLMES. Noble of you . . .

SMITH. Yes, isn't it?

HOLMES. I appreciate your special knowledge.

SMITH. Then you're the only man in London who does. Do you know what is the matter with you?

HOLMES. The same as young Victor—your cousin.

SMITH. Ah, then you recognize the symptoms. Well, then, it's a bad look-out for you. Victor was a strong, hearty young fellow—but a dead man on the fourth day. As you said at the time, it *was* rather surprising that he should contract an out-of-the-way Asiatic[12] disease in the heart of London—a disease of which I have
6 made such a very special study. [*Chuckles*] And now, you, Holmes. Singular coincidence, eh? Or are you going to start making accusations once again—about cause and effect and so on?

HOLMES. I . . . I knew you caused Victor Savage's death.
[SMITH *comes round the bed.*]

SMITH. [*Snarling*] Did you? Well, proving it is a different matter, Holmes. But what sort of a game is this, then—spreading lying reports about me one moment, then crawling to me for help the next?

HOLMES. [*Gasping*] Give . . . give me water. For . . . pity's sake, Smith. Water!
[SMITH *hesitates momentarily, then goes to the table and pours a glass from the carafe.*]

11. **Coals of fire:** Reference to a biblical passage, Proverbs 25:21–22, about revenging oneself on an enemy.
12. **Asiatic** (ā zhē at′ ik): Related to Asia, largest continent in the Eastern Hemisphere.

SMITH. You're precious near your end, my friend, but I don't want you to go till I've had a word with you.
[*He holds out the glass to* HOLMES, *who struggles up feebly to take it and drinks.*]

HOLMES. [*Gulping water*] Ah! Thank . . . thank you. Please . . . do what you can for me. Only 7
cure me, and I promise to forget.

SMITH. Forget what?

HOLMES. About Victor Savage's death. You as good as admitted just now that you had done it. I swear I will forget it.

SMITH. [*Laughs*] Forget it, remember it—do as you like. I don't see you in any witness-box, Holmes. Quite another shape of box, I assure 8
you. But you must hear first how it came about.

HOLMES. Working amongst Chinese sailors. Down at the docks.

SMITH. Proud of your brains, aren't you? Think yourself smart? Well, you've met a smarter one this time.
[HOLMES *falls back, groaning loudly.*]

Getting painful, is it?
[HOLMES *cries out, writhing in agony.*]

SMITH. That's the way. Takes you as cramp, I fancy?

HOLMES. Cramp! Cramp!

SMITH. Well, you can still hear me. Now, can't you just remember any unusual incident—just about the time your symptoms began?

HOLMES. I . . . can't think. My mind is gone! Help me, Smith!

SMITH. Did nothing come to you through the post, for instance?

HOLMES. Post? Post?

SMITH. Yes. A little box, perhaps?

HOLMES. [*A shuddering groan*]

SMITH. [*Closer; deadly*] Listen! You *shall* hear me! Don't you remember a box—a little ivory 9
box? [*He sees it on the table and holds it up.*] Yes, here it is on your bedside table. It came on

Comprehension Check ☑

❻ What happened to Victor Savage and what links Culverton Smith to that event? *Victor Savage, who was a strong young man, unexpectedly died of a disease on which Smith claims to be an expert.* Does Smith actually confess to the crime? *His words imply a link, but he stops short of admitting his responsibility.*

◆Reading Strategy

❼ **Draw Conclusions** Discuss these questions to help students draw their own conclusions: Why has Holmes summoned a suspected murderer? Why does Smith come to 221B Baker Street if he knows that Holmes suspects him of killing Victor Savage? *Holmes arranges for Smith to come to see him to entrap him and enjoy outsmarting him; Smith comes to gloat because he is confident that Holmes is dying of the same "disease" that killed Victor.*

◆Critical Thinking

❽ **Interpret** What kind of box does Smith allude to here? *He is talking about a coffin.*

Clarification

❾ Ask students whether they recall points in the story when the little box was mentioned, and determine whether they forgot it or expected it to have a role in the story. *It was listed among the props in the stage directions at the beginning of the play; in Scene 2, Watson absently picks it up, and Holmes commands him to put it down.*

Humanities: Literature

Detectives After Sir Arthur Conan Doyle, the best known English author of detective stores is Agatha Christie (1890–1976). In fact, she is the most widely translated author in English. Her answer to Sherlock Holmes was the clever Hercule Poirot, a Belgian detective living in England, whose vanity, if not ability, far exceeds that of Holmes. But Christie's most original creation is the formidable Jane Marple, the first famous woman detective in fiction.

Miss Marple, a remarkably insightful, elderly spinster, lives in the quaint English village of St. Mary Mead and is well aware that criminals can be as deceitful in the country as in the city. Though she is not a professional, her talent for uncovering murderers and solving crimes confounds the local policemen, and she has admirers at Scotland Yard. Her social life consists of the usual leisure activities of a village, such as gardening, teas, and charity events, and she is treated generously by the local gentry, who respect, and occasionally fear, her talent, and are grateful for her discretion.

She appears in over fifteen books, including *The Body in the Library* and *A Pocket Full of Rye*. She has been portrayed on film and television, most memorably by Joan Hickson on the PBS *Mystery* series.

▶Critical Viewing◀

❶ **Connect** *The photo suggests that close examination is an important skill for a detective; in this play, close examination of the small box probably saved Holmes's life.*

Clarification

❷ "Entering the valley of the shadow" is a Biblical reference, or allusion, to Psalm 23, a sacred poem from the Old Testament. That verse includes the words, "Yea, though I walk through the valley of the shadow of death, I will fear no evil . . ." Here, Smith uses that allusion to taunt Holmes about his supposedly imminent death.

◆Reading Strategy

❸ **Draw Conclusions** *When Holmes asks Smith to turn up the light, it's not so that he can see Smith clearly, but to send some kind of signal.*

Wednesday. You opened it—do you remember?

HOLMES. Box? Opened? Yes, yes! There was . . . sharp spring inside. Pricked my finger. Some sort of joke . . .

SMITH. It was no joke, Holmes. You fool! Who asked you to cross my path? If you'd only left me alone I would never have hurt you.

HOLMES. Box! Yes! Pricked finger. Poison!

SMITH. [*Triumphantly*] So you do remember. Good, good! I'm glad indeed. Well, the box leaves this room in my pocket, and there's your last shred of evidence gone. [*He pockets it.*] But you have the truth now, Holmes. You can die knowing that I killed you. You knew too much about what happened to Victor Savage, so you must share his fate. Yes, Holmes, you are very near your end now. I think I shall sit here and watch you die. [*He sits on the bed.*]

HOLMES. [*Almost a whisper*] The . . . shadows . . . falling. Getting . . . so dark. I can't see. Smith! Smith, are you there? The light . . . for charity's sake, turn up the light!

[SMITH *laughs, gets up and goes to the light.*]

SMITH. Entering the valley of the shadow, eh, Holmes? Yes, I'll turn up the light for you. I can watch your face more plainly, then. [*He turns the flame up full.*] There! Now, is there any *further* service I can render you? 2

HOLMES. [*In a clear, strong voice*] A match and my pipe, if you please. 3

[*He sits bolt upright.* SMITH

◆ **Reading Strategy** Notice how eager Holmes is to see Culverton Smith. Draw a conclusion based on this detail.

❶ ▼ **Critical Viewing** What does this photograph suggest about the importance of close examination? What role might such an examination play in this drama? **[Connect]**

Viewing and Representing Mini-Lesson

Many Faces of Sherlock Holmes

In this mini-lesson, students will compare and contrast different portrayals of Sherlock Holmes to assess how different acting styles, mannerisms, or other factors influence the portrayal of this character.

Introduce Tell students that Sherlock Holmes has been depicted on film (and later, on television) more often, and by more actors, than any other fictional character. This fascination with the great detective began during the age of silent films, and continues to this day.

Develop Help students locate various versions of Sherlock Holmes stories on film or videotape: from full-length feature films to television shows, from faithful adaptations of the Conan Doyle stories to comic satires. Have groups select two or three examples to view and then compare, contrast, and evaluate in terms of mood, strengths, weaknesses, messages, or overall effect.

Apply Have groups present their findings, including representative moments from the films they compared. Encourage students to give their reviews of actors, directors, or particular portrayals that they think are most effective.

Assess Evaluate students on their work as a group, and on preparation, analysis, and presentation. Help students field questions about the judgments they make.

spins round to see him.]

SMITH. Eh? What the devil's the meaning of this?

HOLMES. [*Cheerfully*] The best way of successfully acting a part is to *be* it. I give you my 4 word that for three days I have neither tasted food nor drink until you were good enough to pour me out that glass of water. But it's the tobacco I find most irksome.
[*We hear the thud of footsteps running upstairs off-stage.*]

Hello, hello! Do I hear the step of a friend?
5 [INSPECTOR MORTON *hurries in.*]

MORTON. Mr. Holmes?

HOLMES. Inspector Morton, this is your man.

SMITH. What is the meaning of . . . ?

MORTON. Culverton Smith, I arrest you on the charge of the murder of one Victor Savage, and I must warn you that anything you say . . .

SMITH. You've got nothing on me! It's all a trick! A pack of lies!
[*He makes to escape.* MORTON *restrains him.*]

MORTON. Keep still, or you'll get yourself hurt!

SMITH. Get off me!

MORTON. Hold your hands out!
[*They struggle.* MORTON *gets out handcuffs and claps them on* SMITH'S *wrists.*]

That'll do.

HOLMES. By the way, Inspector, you might add the attempted murder of one Sherlock Holmes to that charge. Oh, and you'll find a small box in the pocket of your prisoner's coat. Pray, 6 leave it on the table, here. Handle it gingerly, though. It may play its part at his trial.
[MORTON *retrieves the box and places it on the table.*]

SMITH. Trial! You'll be the one in the dock,[13] Holmes. Inspector, he asked me to come here. He was ill, and I was sorry for him, so I came. Now he'll pretend I've said anything he cares to invent that will corroborate[14] his insane suspicions. Well, you can lie as you like, Holmes. My word's as good as yours.

HOLMES. Good heavens! I'd completely forgotten him!

MORTON. Forgotten who, sir?

HOLMES. Watson, my dear fellow! Do come out!
[WATSON *emerges with cramped groans.*]

I owe you a thousand apologies. To think that I should have overlooked you!

WATSON. It's all right, Holmes. Would have come out before, only you said, whatever happened, I wasn't to budge.

SMITH. What's all this about?

HOLMES. I needn't introduce you to my witness, my friend Dr. Watson. I understand you met somewhat earlier in the evening.

SMITH. You . . . you mean you had all this planned?

HOLMES. Of course. To the last detail. I think I may say it worked very well—with your assistance, of course. 7

SMITH. Mine?

HOLMES. You saved an invalid trouble by giving my signal to Inspector Morton, waiting outside. You turned up the lamp.
[SMITH *and* WATSON *are equally flabbergasted.*]

MORTON. I'd better take him along now, sir. [*To* SMITH] Come on.
[*He bundles* SMITH *roughly toward the door.*]

We'll see you down at the Yard tomorrow, perhaps, Mr. Holmes?

HOLMES. Very well, Inspector. And many thanks.

WATSON. Goodbye, Inspector.
[MORTON *exits with* SMITH.]

[*Chuckles*]

Well, Holmes?

13. **dock** (däk) *n.:* Place where the accused sits or stands in court.
14. **corroborate** (kə räb´ ə rāt´) *v.:* Support; strengthen.

◆ Build Vocabulary

irksome (ʉrk´ səm) *adj.:* Tiresome or annoying

Comprehension Check ☑

❹ Ask students to describe Holmes's admission in their own words. *Holmes was just pretending to be sick; in order to do so convincingly, he didn't eat or drink for three days.*

◆Reading Strategy

❺ **Draw Conclusions** Challenge students to think back to an earlier detail in the play. What had Inspector Morton been waiting for when Watson ran into him in the street outside 221B Baker Street? *He was waiting for a signal from Holmes.* Why had Holmes acted so surprised to hear that Morton was in the neighborhood? *Holmes did not want Watson to suspect that he and Morton had made any arrangements.*

Comprehension Check ☑

❻ How did Smith murder Savage, and how did he try to murder Holmes? *Smith poisoned Savage with the same infection that would have killed Holmes, had the sleuth opened the box and been pricked.*

Thematic Focus

❼ **Finding Solutions** Ask students to summarize Holmes's plan. Have them describe each character's part in the plan to catch Smith. *Holmes pretended to be sick so that Watson would bring Smith, whom Holmes suspected of murder and attempted murder, to 221B Baker Street. Holmes had Inspector Morton wait outside until he saw a prearranged signal—from a lamp—at which point he'd come in and arrest Smith. Mrs. Hudson's concern moved the plan along, as did Watson's eagerness to help his friend.*

Speaking and Listening Mini-Lesson

Dramatic Scene

This mini-lesson supports the Speaking and Listening activity in the Idea Bank, p. 341.

Introduce Discuss with students that the preparation involved in acting out a scene from a play can help them understand the characters and their actions.

Develop Have students form groups and choose a scene to play. Suggest that they jot down important character traits or motives they hope to convey. For example, for Holmes, they might write *crafty* or *sly.* Guide groups to keep costumes and scenery to a minimum, but to be sure that the elements they select are effective.

Apply Have students plan their scenes and practice variations of their roles until they are happy with the results. Then, set aside time for groups to present their scenes, preferably arranged in the order in which they appear in the play.

Assess Evaluate students' dramatic scenes based on preparation; interpretation of characters; effective use of voice, gestures, props, and scenery; and faithfulness to the spirit of the play. Or, use the Peer Assessment: Dramatic Performance form, p. 107, in **Alternative Assessment.**

Thematic Focus

1 Finding Solutions Tell students that dissimulation is the act of hiding something. Discuss the solution Holmes found so that he could involve Watson in his plan to catch Smith without letting Watson's weakness spoil things. *Holmes didn't tell Watson his plan because he knew that Watson wasn't good at keeping secrets. Had Watson known the truth, he'd never have been able to persuade Smith to visit Holmes.*

◆ Literature and Your Life

2 *Possible responses: Some students might enjoy being able to outsmart a foe; others might feel unable to pull off such deceit.*

Comprehension Check ☑

3 What does Holmes really think of Watson's medical talents? *Holmes greatly respects Watson's abilities as a doctor. That's why he made sure to keep Watson away. If he'd gotten close enough to Holmes to examine him, Watson would have known at once that Holmes wasn't sick.*

Thematic Focus

4 Finding Solutions What problem had Culverton Smith hoped to solve by killing Vincent Savage? *Smith saw a chance to become rich. He wanted the money that Savage stood to inherit; with Savage out of the way, the money would go to Smith.*

HOLMES. Well, Watson, there's a bottle of claret over there—it is uncorked—and some biscuits in the barrel. If you'll be so kind, I'm badly in need of both.
[WATSON *goes to fetch them.*]

WATSON. Certainly. You know, Holmes, all this seems a pretty, well, elaborate way to go about catching that fellow. I mean, taking in Mrs. Hudson—*and me*—like that. Scared us half to death.

HOLMES. It was very essential that I should make Mrs. Hudson believe in my condition. She was to convey it to you, and you to him.

WATSON. Well . . .

HOLMES. Pray do not be offended, my good Watson. You must admit that among your many talents, dissimulation scarcely finds a place. If
1 you'd shared my secret, you would never have been able to impress Smith with the urgent necessity of coming to me. It was the vital point of the whole scheme. I knew his vindictive nature, and I was certain he would come to gloat over his handiwork.
[WATSON *returns with the bottle, glasses and barrel.*]

WATSON. But . . . but your appearance, Holmes. Your face! You really do look ghastly.

HOLMES. Three days of absolute fast does not improve one's beauty, Watson. However, as you know, my habits are irregular, and such a feat means less to me than to most men. For the rest, there is nothing that a sponge won't cure. Vaseline to produce the glistening forehead; belladonna[15] for the watering of the eyes; rouge over the cheekbones and crust of beeswax round one's lips. . . .

2 **◆ Literature and Your Life**
Holmes explains his scheme here. How would you feel to have tricked Smith this way?

WATSON. [*Chuckling*] And that babbling about oysters! [*He begins pouring the wine.*]

HOLMES. Yes. I've sometimes thought of writing a monograph on the subject of malingering.[16]

WATSON. But why wouldn't you let me near you? There was no risk of infection.

HOLMES. Whatever I may have said to the contrary in the grip of delirium, do you imagine that I have no respect for your medical talents? Could I imagine that you would be 3
deceived by a dying man with no rise of pulse or temperature? At four yards' distance I *could* deceive you.
[WATSON *reaches for the box.*]

WATSON. This box, then . . .

HOLMES. No, Watson. I wouldn't touch it. You can just see, if you look at it sideways, where the sharp spring emerges as you open it. I dare say it was by some such device that poor young Savage was done to death. He stood 4
between that monster and an inheritance, you know.

WATSON. Then it's true, Holmes! You . . . you might have been killed, too!

HOLMES. As you know, my correspondence is a varied one. I am somewhat on my guard against any packages which reach me. But I saw that by pretending he had succeeded in his design I might be enabled to surprise a confession from him. That pretense I think I may claim to have carried out with the thoroughness of a true artist.

WATSON. [*Warmly*] You certainly did, Holmes. Er, a biscuit? [*He holds out the barrel.*]

HOLMES. On second thought, Watson, no thank you. Let us preserve our appetite. By the time I have shaved and dressed, I fancy it will just be a nice time for something nutritious at our little place in the Strand.[17]
[*They raise their glasses to one another and drink. The curtain falls.*]

15. **belladonna** (bel ə dän′ ə) *n.:* Poisonous European plant.

16. **monograph on . . . malingering:** Study on the subject of pretending to be ill in order to avoid work.

17. **the Strand:** London's main shopping and entertainment district; also, the name of a specific street within this district.

Cross-Curricular Connection: Science

In this play, Sherlock Holmes intentionally deprives himself of food and water for three days as part of an elaborate plan to capture a murderer. Of course, in this work of fiction, Holmes suffers no ill effects from his fast. However, in reality, the human body needs daily food and water for survival and for good health.

Invite interested students to investigate the minimum daily requirements for adults in terms of water and food. Students might interview doctors, nutritionists, biologists, or health care workers. They might do research in the library or on the Internet. Have them try to find out how a real person might act after three days without food and water. What symptoms would the person display? How would the person feel? What bodily systems or functions would be at risk? How long would it take the body to recover? Students can share their findings in the form of a report, or they can hold a class discussion in which they share the information they learned.

Beyond Literature

Science Connection

Catching Criminals With Science
Unlike Sherlock Holmes, who catches Culverton Smith with a clever trick, today's detectives often use scientific evidence. They analyze this evidence with the help of forensic experts, who study the chemical makeup of tiny pieces of material—hair, fabric, or soil, for example—from a crime scene to link it with an accused criminal. They may also evaluate fingerprints, blood, and teeth to help identify crime victims and criminals or to study a victim's body for clues that reveal how a crime was committed.

Cross-Curricular Activity
Can You Make a Match? Two ways in which forensic experts can trace who has been at a crime scene is by matching hair samples and shoe impressions. With a group of classmates, conduct the following experiment. At home or in another classroom, have each group member make an ink print of his or her shoe. Then, work together to match the prints to the shoes that each of you is wearing. Finally, discuss the experience.

Guide for Responding

◆ Literature and Your Life

Reader's Response If you were Watson, how would you feel about Holmes at the end of this play? Why?

Thematic Focus Holmes traps a murderer through deception. Why do you think Holmes chose this method for catching Culverton Smith?

List If Culverton Smith didn't visit, the outcome of the story would have changed drastically. With a partner, make a list of the possible outcomes of Holmes's risky trap.

☑ Check Your Comprehension

1. What kind of disease does Holmes claim to have?
2. What reasons does Sherlock Holmes give for not letting Dr. Watson treat him?
3. How does this deception suit Holmes's plan to bring Culverton Smith to justice?
4. What criminal doings does Holmes trick Smith into revealing?
5. What is the real reason that Holmes asks Culverton Smith to turn up the light?

◆ Critical Thinking

Interpret

1. Why does Sherlock Holmes make wild statements to Watson about batteries, coins, and oysters? **[Infer]**
2. Why doesn't Holmes tell Watson of his plan for proving Smith a murderer? **[Analyze Cause and Effect]**
3. Explain the importance of Watson's hiding place in Holmes's plot against Smith. **[Interpret]**
4. How do Watson's feelings about Holmes change during the play? **[Connect]**
5. What qualities does Holmes value in his friends? Support your answer. **[Draw Conclusions]**

Evaluate

6. (a) In what ways is Watson suited to deceiving Smith? (b) In what ways is Watson suited to being deceived by Holmes? **[Assess]**

Extend

7. Compare and contrast Holmes's methods to those of modern crime fighters, real or fictional. **[Literature Link; Career Link]**

Beyond the Selection

FURTHER READING

Other Works by Sir Arthur Conan Doyle
"A Study in Scarlet"
"The Red-Headed League"
"The Adventure of the Speckled Band"

Other Works with Legendary Detectives
Murder on the Orient Express (with Hercule Poirot), Agatha Christie
Miss Marple: The Complete Short Stories, Agatha Christie
The Long Goodbye (with Phillip Marlowe), Raymond Chandler
Fer-de-Lance (with Nero Wolfe), Rex Stout

INTERNET
We suggest the following sites on the Internet (all Web sites are subject to change).

For more information about Sir Arthur Conan Doyle:
http://members.home.net/sherlock1/sherlocktron.html

For the complete text of the original story:
http://www.citsoft.com/holmes/last_bow/dying.detective.txt

We *strongly recommend* that you preview these sites before you send students to them.

Beyond Literature

Students interested in forensic science can find additional information in the library or on the Internet. This Web site presents easy forensic experiments young people can do:
http//www.eecs.umich.edu/mathscience/funexperiments/agesubject/lessons/newton/mrdrmysr.html

We *strongly recommend* that you preview this site before you send students to it.

Reinforce and Extend

Answers

◆ Literature and Your Life

Reader's Response Possible responses: hurt, deceived, angry, admiring, awestruck.

Thematic Focus Possible response: The play implies that he'd tried several other methods, with no luck.

☑ Check Your Comprehension

1. Holmes claims to have a rare and deadly tropical disease.
2. Holmes says that Watson lacks the talent and experience to treat his condition.
3. Since Watson doesn't know that Holmes is pretending to be sick, he agrees to fetch Smith.
4. He tricks Smith into revealing that he murdered Victor Savage and tried to murder Holmes.
5. The light signals the inspector to come in and arrest Smith.

◆ Critical Thinking

1. He wants Watson to think that he is delirious.
2. He believes Watson is too honest to complete the deception.
3. Watson must be hidden so Smith will think that only the dying Holmes can hear his confession.
4. Watson is first concerned, then hurt, and finally admiring.
5. He values loyalty, trust, and openness.
6. (a) He appears incapable of deceit. (b) He is trusting.
7. Some students may compare Holmes's use of logic and observation with the methods of fictional crime fighters who use superhuman powers, such as X-ray vision or invincible strength, or those of modern police detectives who fight crime with forensic science and technology.

Answers

◆ Reading Strategy

1. (a) He is pale; he needed help to get upstairs; he groans; he seems weak and delirious.(b) He is firm in giving Watson precise orders about Culverton Smith.
2. Possible answers: when Holmes makes Watson hide; when Holmes tells Smith that he knew Smith had caused Savage's death; when Holmes asks for his pipe
3. (a) They are close friends who believe in one another, even when the circumstances are odd.
   (b) Watson does exactly what Holmes asks, even when it seems odd; Holmes protects Watson by withholding information that might put his plan in jeopardy.

◆ Build Vocabulary

Using the Suffix *-ology*

1. the branch of science that studies various forms of life
2. the study of God and religion
3. the study of humans, including our origins, customs, and cultures

Spelling Strategy

1. agitating
2. examining
3. disclosing
4. balancing

Using the Word Bank

1. implore
2. methodical
3. agitated
4. irksome
5. pathological

◆ Literary Focus

1. The set consists of Sherlock Holmes's bedroom, with usual bedroom furnishings and a clutter of his personal effects. The room has a window that faces the street.
2. Holmes is in bed for the entire play; the window is used to signal for the police at just the right moment; the box is the prop that initiates the drama and, at the end, is revealed to be a key piece of evidence.
3. Possible answers: The audience wonders when and if Watson will emerge, or whether he will call attention to himself; they may wonder whether Holmes will need Watson to rescue him.

◆ Build Grammar Skills

Practice

1. Ouch! That box has a sharp spring in it.
2. Oh, no! The spring seems to contain poison.
3. Ah …uh … What do we do now?
4. Look! It never actually pricked your skin.
5. Phew! What a close call!

Writing Application

Possible responses:

1. Wow! You are lucky Smith agreed to come.
2. Good grief! Did you think I'd leave it to chance?
3. Thank heavens! I knew I could count on you.

Writer's Solution

For additional instruction and practice on using exclamation marks with interjections, use the Punctuation unit in the *Writer's Solution Language Lab CD-ROM*. You may also use the practice page on end marks, p. 97 in the *Writer's Solution Grammar Practice Book*.

Guide for Responding *(continued)*

◆ Reading Strategy

Draw Conclusions

As in any other mystery, certain key pieces of information aren't revealed until the end of this play. If you **drew conclusions** by making general statements that the facts of the play could support, you may have solved the mystery before the final scene. For example, Holmes recovers strength every time Watson's actions lead away from the plan. You could use this fact to conclude that the detective is not really dying.

1. (a) List three facts about Holmes's condition that might fool the audience into believing he's ill.
(b) List one detail that hints he is not truly dying.
2. At what exact moment would an audience understand the true situation?
3. (a) What can you conclude about the relationship between Holmes and Watson? (b) What details support this conclusion?

◆ Build Vocabulary

Using the Suffix *-ology*

Knowing that *-ology* means "the study or science of" can help you solve the mystery behind some unfamiliar words. Use the clues provided to define these words. Check a dictionary to adjust your definition.

1. biology (*bio-* means "life")
2. theology (*theo-* means "God")
3. anthropology (*anthropo-* means "human")

Spelling Strategy

When you add the suffix *-ing* to verbs ending in silent e, drop the *e: implore + -ing = imploring.* On your paper, add *-ing* to each of these verbs:

1. agitate **2.** examine **3.** disclose **4.** balance

Using the Word Bank

Identify the word from the Word Bank that has the same meaning as each word or phrase following.

1. beg strongly: ___?___
2. organized: ___?___
3. upset: ___?___
4. annoying: ___?___
5. concerning disease: ___?___

◆ Literary Focus

Staging

In this play, **staging**—the scenery, lighting, sound, special effects, costumes, props, and stage directions—plays a key role in getting you to the edge of your seat. For example, all the action of the play takes place in one room. This increases the suspense because the audience does not know what the characters who leave the room may be saying to each other.

1. Describe the set of "The Dying Detective."
2. How are the bed, window, and box important to the plot?
3. Picture Watson in his hiding place behind the bed. How does this use of staging create suspense?

◆ Build Grammar Skills

Interjections

Because they use dialogue, plays often contain **interjections**—words that express feeling and emotion. Interjections function independently of a sentence. Exclamation points often follow interjections, which are also capitalized if they appear at the beginning of a sentence. Interjections can express a variety of emotions—from surprise to pain to disapproval.

Concern: *Dear me!*
Urgency: *No, no!* Keep back!
Hurt: *Oh!* Don't you have any confidence in me?
Surprise: *Good heavens!* I completely forgot him!

Practice Rewrite these sentences. Underline the interjections, and correct punctuation when necessary.

1. Ouch. That box has a sharp spring in it.
2. Oh no. The spring seems to contain poison.
3. Ah, uh, what do we do now?
4. Look. It never actually pricked your skin.
5. Phew. What a close call.

Writing Application Complete each sentence with an interjection that fits the emotion indicated.

1. (joy) You are lucky Smith agreed to come.
2. (surprise) Did you think I'd leave it to chance?
3. (impatience) I knew I could count on you.

Build Your Portfolio

Idea Bank

Writing

1. **Monologue** Without giving away too much of the action, write a speech that Holmes can deliver to the audience at the beginning of the play. Have him give readers or viewers a few clues about the outcome. **[Performing Arts Link]**
2. **Scene** Write a scene that takes place outside Holmes's bedroom, to give viewers at least a few clues to what is really going on. If necessary, invent new characters. **[Performing Arts Link]**
3. **Memo to a Drama Coach** Recall a short story you have recently enjoyed. Write a memo to the drama club coach describing in detail how you would stage the story. Specify sets and props you'd use. **[Art Link]**

Speaking and Listening

4. **Dramatic Scene [Group Activity]** With a few classmates, perform a scene from the play. In rehearsal, discuss how each role should be played, and practice the lines. Design costumes and scenery. **[Performing Arts Link]**
5. **Lawyer's Argument** Present an opening argument at Culverton Smith's trial. Use facts from the play and your own knowledge from movies or television of suspected criminals' rights. Then, outline the strategy you would use to defend—or prosecute—Smith. **[Career Link]**

Projects

6. **Multimedia Biography** Research Sherlock Holmes to learn more about this popular literary character. Tell his life story to the class, using maps, music, or video clips to enhance your presentation. **[Media Link]**
7. **Crime-Solvers' Club [Group Activity]** With a group, gather facts about popular crime solvers from television, books, and movies. Discuss how they solve crimes—with special gadgets or talents, with strength or mental quickness. Share your observations with the class.

Writing Mini-Lesson

Critical Review

Would you recommend "The Dying Detective" to a friend? That is the question a drama critic answers when reviewing a play. Imagine that you have just seen the play performed. Write a critical review in which you identify what worked about the performance and what didn't. Focus on the plot, dialogue, and staging as they appear in the script.

Writing Skills Focus: Language to Evaluate

In a critical review, you express an opinion. **Language to evaluate**—words that praise or criticize—conveys that opinion. Make these words as specific as possible. For example, *splendid* reflects stronger praise than *good*. Use words that show precisely how you feel.

Mild Dislike: It was *disappointing*.
Strong Dislike: It was *horrible*.
Mild Praise: It was *well written*.
High Praise: It was *brilliant*.

Prewriting Start by making a two-column chart of elements you liked and those you disliked in the written script. Highlight those elements about which you feel most strongly.

Drafting Picture yourself in the emptying theater, just after the show has ended. Describe your reactions to the plot, staging, and acting. You could begin with a feature you loved—or hated. Use evaluating words to make your feelings clear.

◆ **Grammar Application**

Where possible, use interjections like *Wow!* or *No!* to express your reactions to the play. However, avoid using too many of these words.

Revising Reread your review, and identify opinions that are not well supported or don't clearly communicate your feelings. If necessary, add details from the play. Replace general words, like *interesting*, with more precise words, like *suspenseful*.

Idea Bank

Following are suggestions for matching the Idea Bank topics with your students' performance levels and learning modalities:

Customize for *Performance Levels*
Less Advanced Students: 2, 7
Average Students: 3, 4, 7
More Advanced Students: 1, 5, 6

Customize for *Learning Modalities*
Verbal/Linguistic: 1, 2, 3, 4, 5, 6, 7
Visual/Spatial: 2, 4, 6
Bodily/Kinesthetic: 1, 4
Logical/Mathematical: 1, 2, 5
Musical/Rhythmic: 6
Interpersonal: 4, 7
Intrapersonal: 1, 2, 3, 5, 6

Writing Mini-Lesson

Refer students to the Writing Handbook in the back of the book for instructions on the writing process and for further information on writing critical reviews.

Writer's Solution

Writing Lab CD-ROM
Have students complete the tutorial on Response to Literature. Follow these steps:

1. Have students use the About Response to Literature introduction to establish goals.
2. Have students examine the writing model that is a review of a literary work.
3. Have students draft on computer.
4. Have students use the language variety revision checker.

Allow about 60 minutes of class time to complete these steps.

Writer's Solution Sourcebook
Have students use Chapter 9, "Response to Literature," pp. 264–295, for more support. The chapter includes in-depth instruction on varying sentence length and structure, pp. 292–293.

ASSESSMENT OPTIONS

Formal Assessment, Selection Test, pp. 96–98, and Assessment Resources Software. The selection test is designed so that it can be easily customized to the performance levels of your students.

Alternative Assessment, p. 22, includes options for less advanced students, more advanced students, verbal/linguistic learners, logical/mathematical learners, interpersonal learners, and visual/spatial learners.

PORTFOLIO ASSESSMENT
Use the following rubrics in the **Alternative Assessment** booklet to assess student writing:
Monologue: Peer Assessment: Speaker/Speech, p. 105
Scene: Drama, p. 96
Memo to a Drama Coach: Business Letter/Memo, p. 100
Writing Mini-Lesson: Critical Review, p. 98

Connections to Today's World

This article deals with a modern approach to crime detection. Here, the U.S. Department of Agriculture agents use highly skilled dogs to sniff out possible infringements of health and safety rules without having to deceive people or put anyone at risk.

More About the Author
Print journalist **Susan Essoyan** has written many articles for the *Los Angeles Times*, and specializes in stories about Hawaii.

Customize for
Less Proficient Readers
Preview the selection with students and clarify unfamiliar expressions or terms, such as *in concert with, passes muster, seizures, prohibited,* and *contraband.* Then have students read the article aloud, stopping to discuss sentences or ideas that may be unclear. Guide students to draw conclusions about the reasons for the success of the Beagle Brigade.

CONNECTIONS TO TODAY'S WORLD

In Arthur Conan Doyle's time, detectives were called on to solve crimes using logic and deduction. More modern techniques rely on technology to test DNA evidence, provide videotaped surveillance records, scan the contents of packages, and interpret fingerprints. In some fields, like airport security, even animals are getting in on the problem-solving action. This article introduces you to the dogs who work at Honolulu's airport.

NOSING AROUND U.S. BORDERS

Susan Essoyan

The well-dressed tourist took her eyes off the baggage carousel for a moment, smiled and cooed in Japanese, "Hello, little Mr. Woof-Woof. Here you are."

She plopped her bag on the ground for the veteran detective, a beagle called Junior, who trotted forward to get a whiff. When the dog finished and turned away, signaling that the bag had passed inspection, the woman dissolved into laughter.

"They think he's cute," said Junior's handler, Mike Simon, the U.S. Department of Agriculture's (USDA) senior canine officer in Honolulu. Travelers don't object to Junior's search, which is
1 not always the case with traditional inspections. "He's more like a mascot," Simon said.

Despite Junior's engaging personality, the 6-year-old dog has a serious mission: to help protect U.S. agriculture from foreign pests and diseases. He and the 60 other dogs in the USDA's Beagle Brigade cruise international airports across the country in search of forbidden fruit, vegetables, plants and meat.

Many international travelers don't realize that even a single piece of fruit packed in a suitcase has the potential to unleash a pest that could devastate U.S. crops. Working in concert with X-ray and visual searches conducted by the USDA's Animal and Plant Health Inspection Service, the Beagle Brigade helps to prevent prohibited goods from crossing U.S. borders.

The brigade began in 1984 with one dog at Los Angeles International Airport but has proved so effective teams now patrol 20 international airports in the United States. John F. Kennedy International Airport in New York has the largest contingent with 10 dogs, and Bangor, Maine, the smallest with just one working part time. Across the country, the Beagles and their handlers are responsible for about 60,000 seizures of prohibited agricultural products yearly.

Simon, who founded the program, recommended Beagles because they are less intimidating than larger breeds and have a keen sense of smell and a lot of stamina.

"Beagles keep their puppy-like appearance their whole life," Simon said. "The whole inspection process can have an unpleasant image because we take things from people. But when the dog finds something, the people aren't as upset."

The Beagles make their rounds on leashes, sporting green vests marked "Agriculture's Beagle Brigade" and "Protecting American Agriculture." They are 2
efficient detectives, circling baggage

Beyond the Classroom

Career Connection

Dog Trainer The USDA Beagle Brigade succeeds because teams of dedicated dog lovers train beagles for certain tasks they are naturally suited to do. Have groups of students discuss what traits or interests a person should have to successfully train dogs, such as a love of and respect for animals, patience, and an ability to teach. Ask if they envision themselves in such a career. Suggest that interested students learn more about this kind of work by interviewing local people who train dogs: a breeder or a pet store owner, for example. Remind students to inquire about the job's responsibilities, rewards, and drawbacks. As an alternative, students could find out how dogs are trained for other roles, such as guiding, rescuing, acting, or farming. There are many books for young adults on this topic.

CONNECTIONS TO TODAY'S WORLD

3 ▲ **Critical Viewing** Describe the action shown in this photograph. **[Interpret]**

2 carousels while passengers collect their luggage, rather than requiring people to stand in line to be checked one by one.

The dogs put in eight-hour days, with each hour on duty followed by an hour off. When a dog locates a suspect package, it signals its handler by sitting down.

4 "We can't have a dog that attacks its target—not when we're dealing with Gucci bags," Simon said.

With a sense of smell at least 100 times better than a human's, Junior can pick up the scent of an orange lingering in a bag amid an array of smells from laundry to cosmetics. Trained Beagles with a year's experience have a success rate of about 80 percent. After two years on the job, the figure jumps to 90 percent. When they make a find, the dogs are rewarded with a biscuit.

The six Beagles working for the USDA in Honolulu have the most varied assignments. Along with airport duties, they check cruise ships, military bases, cargo holds, and mail depots. Hawaiian inspectors must check items arriving from foreign countries and those headed from Hawaii to the mainland.

The Honolulu dogs are invaluable in inspecting domestic mail heading to the rest of the United States. While an X-ray is considered invasive under the Privacy Act, having a Beagle sniff the air outside parcels passes muster. Since 1990, more than 2,000 federal warrants have been issued to search mail packages in Honolulu based on Beagle Brigade signals, with 95 percent of them turning up prohibited items, Simon said.

All contraband is seized for disposal. People who mail such packages are fined; travelers who fail to declare such items can be fined up to $100.

In 1992, the Hawaiian Department of Agriculture followed the USDA's lead by creating its own Beagle team. The dogs are used to uncover brown tree snakes that try to enter Hawaii from Guam. The reptile has wiped out several bird species on Guam and would wreak havoc on Hawaii's native ecosystem if it made it ashore.

◆ **Build Vocabulary**

intimidating (in tim′ ə dāt′ iŋ) *adj.*: Causing fear

stamina (stam′ ə nə) *n.*: Endurance

1. What does the Beagle Brigade do?
2. Why are beagles especially good for this type of work?
3. How do the dogs help resolve conflicts?

▶Critical Viewing◀

❶ **Interpret** Ask students: Who is Junior and what is his job? *He is a beagle who sniffs baggage to determine whether it contains any items that would endanger the country's ecosystem.*

◆Reading Strategy

❷ **Draw Conclusions** Ask students to explain why so many travelers prefer to have beagles climb all over their luggage than to have a person check their bags. *The Beagle Brigade is faster; people don't have to waste time waiting in lines.*

▶Critical Viewing◀

❸ **Interpret** *A handler watches as a member of the Beagle Brigade searches cargo.*

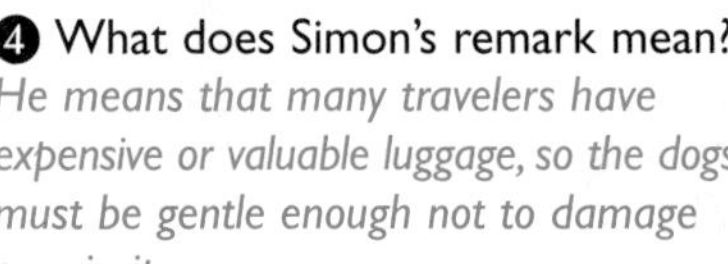

Comprehension Check ☑

❹ What does Simon's remark mean? *He means that many travelers have expensive or valuable luggage, so the dogs must be gentle enough not to damage or ruin it.*

Answers

1. Dogs in the Beagle Brigade sniff baggage at international airports to locate harmful products that the USDA does not allow to enter the country.
2. Beagles have a sharp sense of smell, and they have lots of energy.
3. Beagles are small, puppy-like in appearance, and nonthreatening to most people.

Beyond the Selection

FURTHER READING

Other Articles About Working Dogs

"Susan Butcher," Bill Littlefield

"TV's Top Dogs," Deborah Starr Seibel

INTERNET

We suggest the following site on the Internet (all Web sites are subject to change).

For more information on the USDA Beagle Brigade: **http://www.usda.gov/news/releases/1995/03/0232**

We *strongly recommend* that you preview the site before you send students to it.

Prepare and Engage

OBJECTIVES

1. To read, comprehend, and interpret an essay, a story, and two poems
2. To relate third-person point of view to personal experience
3. To make inferences
4. To recognize third-person point of view
5. To build vocabulary in context and learn the prefix *re-*
6. To recognize and use coordinating conjunctions
7. To write a volunteering handbook
8. To respond to the selections through writing, speaking and listening, and projects

SKILLS INSTRUCTION

Vocabulary:
Prefixes: *re-*

Spelling:
Using a Hyphen With the Prefix *re-*

Grammar:
Coordinating Conjunctions

Reading Strategy:
Make Inferences

Literary Focus:
Third-Person Point of View

Writing:
Address Your Audience

Speaking and Listening:
School Interviews (Teacher Edition)

Viewing and Representing:
Flowchart (Teacher Edition)

Critical Viewing:
Connect; Compare and Contrast; Analyze; Cause and Effect; Hypothesize

PORTFOLIO OPPORTUNITIES

Writing: Journal Entry; Citizenship Award; Comparison-and-Contrast Essay
Writing Mini-Lesson: Volunteering Handbook
Speaking and Listening: School Interviews; How-to Fair
Projects: Community Participation; Flowchart

Guide for Reading

Meet the Authors:

Phillip Hoose

Phillip Hoose was inspired to write about people making a difference in their communities. The energy and compassion he saw led him to write *It's Our World, Too,* a collection of essays about young people working to help others. "Justin Lebo" comes from that book.

Naomi Shihab Nye (1952–)

As a teenager, Naomi Shihab Nye probably felt the loneliness she discusses in her poem. Her family moved from its home in St. Louis, Missouri, to Jerusalem, Israel, when she was fourteen. While Nye now values the chance to learn about her Arab heritage, the move wasn't easy. Nye's poems often focus on such real-life experiences—what she calls "true things."

Piri Thomas (1928–)

Reading Piri Thomas's autobiography, *Down These Mean Streets,* you know that growing up in New York City's Spanish Harlem was a challenge. Like the boys he creates in "Amigo Brothers," Thomas had to overcome the problems of his surroundings. The road was bumpy before Thomas "dreamt positive."

Thomas Hardy (1840–1928)

Thomas Hardy lived during the Victorian Era, a time when writers spun stories of morals, manners, and money. Hardy, considered to be the greatest novelist of his time, was buried in London's Westminster Abbey when he died.

◆ Literature and Your Life

Connect Your Experience

Sometimes your energy overflows. You think of exciting projects and feel sure you can conquer any challenge. What happens, though, when solving one problem creates another? That is what the characters in "Amigo Brothers" and "Justin Lebo" face.

Thematic Focus: Finding Solutions

The characters in these selections confront loneliness, isolation, and boredom—problems that face many of us at one time or another. As you read, notice how they solve the problems that might limit freedom.

◆ Background for Understanding

Sports

"Amigo Brothers" is the story of two teenage boxers with championship dreams. Competing against each other, they both want to represent their club in the annual Golden Gloves tournament. In this tournament—probably the most famous amateur boxing event in the United States—local and regional elimination bouts lead to the final championship matches.

◆ Build Vocabulary

Prefixes: *re-*

Justin Lebo *realigns* the wheels of his bikes. If you know that *aligns* means "puts in line" and that the prefix *re-* means "again," you can easily determine the meaning of this word.

Word Bank

Which of these words from the selections might refer to a group working toward a common goal? What word clue helps you decide?

realign
yield
coalition
devastating
superimposed
perpetual
dispelled
evading

More About the Authors

Phillip Hoose has tried to help solve social problems by working with tenant organizations and the Nature Conservancy.

Naomi Shihab Nye travels widely, using her poetry as a way to promote international understanding. She lives in San Antonio, Texas.

Piri Thomas began writing in 1956. Since then, he has also become involved in volunteer work.

Thomas Hardy left behind a career as an architect to write a number of popular novels and poems.

Prentice Hall Literature Program Resources

REINFORCE / RETEACH / EXTEND

Selection Support Pages
Build Vocabulary: Prefixes: *re-*, p. 123
Build Spelling Skills, p. 124
Build Grammar Skills: Coordinating Conjunctions, p. 125
Reading Strategy: Make Inferences, p. 126
Literary Focus: Third-Person Point of View, p. 127

Strategies for Diverse Student Needs, pp. 45–46

Beyond Literature Cross-Curricular Connection: Physical Education, p. 23

Formal Assessment Selection Test, pp. 99–101, Assessment Resources Software

Alternative Assessment, p. 23

Writing and Language Transparencies
Venn Diagram, p. 86

Resource Pro CD-ROM
"Justin Lebo"; "The Rider"; "Amigo Brothers"; "The Walk"

Listening to Literature Audiocassettes
"Justin Lebo"; "The Rider"; "Amigo Brothers"; "The Walk"

Justin Lebo ◆ The Rider
Amigo Brothers ◆ The Walk

◆ Literary Focus

Third-Person Point of View

Point of view refers to the angle or position from which a writer tells a story. When using a **third-person point of view,** a writer or narrator stands outside the action to describe it. From this position, the narrator gives you information about characters that even they don't know. Narrators in "Amigo Brothers" and "Justin Lebo" tell you about the thoughts, feelings, and actions of many people. As you read, look for details that only the third-person point of view could provide.

◆ Reading Strategy

Make Inferences

When you **make inferences**—guesses based on evidence—you supply information an author omits. Making inferences allows you to get a fuller understanding of the people and situations writers present. For example, since Justin Lebo loves to fix bikes, you can infer that he has mechanical ability. As you read, use an organizer like this one to record key details and to make inferences based on each detail.

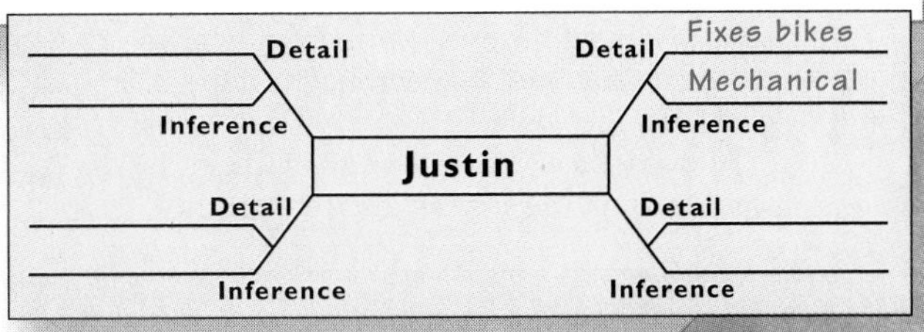

Preparing for Standardized Tests

Make Inferences To answer reading comprehension questions on standardized tests, students are often required to make inferences. Point out that students can use prior knowledge and logical thinking to add to the information in the text.

Write the following question on the board:

Justin and his father poured alcohol on the frame and rubbed until the old paint disappeared.

What can you infer from this sentence?

(A) Justin and his father bought alcohol at the drug store.
(B) Alcohol can be used as a paint remover.
(C) Justin and his father like to work on bicycles.
(D) People can repair bicycles more quickly when they work together.

Point out that while *(A)*, *(C)*, and *(D)* might be true statements, they cannot be inferred from the information provided. Explain that since alcohol was rubbed onto the frame until the paint disappeared, it can be inferred that alcohol works as a paint remover, and *(B)* is the best answer.

Arrange students in groups of four or five. Have each group brainstorm for specific problems in your school or community that young people might be able to work to solve, such as not enough money in the school budget to buy new band uniforms; trash or graffiti cluttering the school grounds; community residents with no place to eat Thanksgiving dinner. Ask students to avoid focusing on large, general problems such as world hunger or political conflicts. Have them select three ideas and write one idea on each slip of paper. Have each group randomly draw a problem from the pile. Encourage groups to think of and list creative actions that could be taken to solve the problem found on their paper. Invite groups to share their problem-and-solution lists for the class. Lead students into the selections by telling them that the characters in each one must find creative ways to solve their problems.

◆Build Grammar Skills

Coordinating Conjunctions If you wish to introduce the grammar concept for this selection before students read, refer to the instruction on p. 360.

Customize for *Less Proficient Readers*

Most students will find these selections interesting and enjoyable to read. They may have difficulty, however, moving smoothly from one selection to another and connecting the poetry to the story and essay. Have students read the selections independently and then stop to discuss with a partner how each selection relates to the theme and to the other selections.

Customize for *More Advanced Students*

Ask students to consider how "Justin Lebo" and "Amigo Brothers" would change if they were written from the first-person point of view. For example, ask them to consider who would narrate "Amigo Brothers" and how the change in narrator might affect the readers' feelings toward the characters. Then have them choose a passage from one of the selections and rewrite it from the first-person point of view.

Develop Understanding

One-Minute Insight Ten-year-old Justin Lebo loves bikes; he loves to work on them and to race them. After buying and restoring a beat-up old bike, Justin realized that riding the bike was not nearly as much fun as the challenge of rebuilding it. Soon, he was rebuilding another. Since he already had two racing bikes, Justin decided to donate the rebuilt bikes to the Kilbarchan Home for Boys. The boys were so thrilled with the bikes that Justin set himself the goal of rebuilding a bike for each of the twenty-one boys by Christmas. At first, he had trouble finding the money to buy the old bikes and parts, but people soon began donating used bikes and money to help him meet his goal. By Christmas, each boy at the home had a reconditioned bike to ride. Justin's creativity and determination and his generous nature helped him find a way to solve a problem.

Team Teaching Strategy

The cost and time spent on Justin's volunteer work and the Viewing and Representing: Flowchart activity on p. 348 offer opportunities to relate the selection to math. You may want to work with a math teacher to coordinate ways of extending instruction.

◆Literary Focus

1 Third-Person Point of View *The narrator refers to the characters by name or by the third-person pronoun* he. *First-person pronouns, such as* I *or* we, *do not appear.*

Customize for *English Language Learners*

To help students understand the selection, provide a drawing or photograph of a BMX-style bicycle with labels attached to identify parts, such as pedals, grips, spokes, brakes, and so forth. As students read, have them refer to the illustration and labels to clarify meaning.

JUSTIN LEBO

Phillip Hoose

Something about the battered old bicycle at the garage sale caught ten-year-old Justin Lebo's eye. What a wreck! It was like looking at a few big bones in the dust and trying to figure out what kind of dinosaur they had once belonged to.

It was a BMX bike with a twenty-inch frame. Its original color was buried beneath five or six coats of gunky paint. Now it showed up as sort of a rusted red. Everything—the grips, the pedals, the brakes, the seat, the spokes—was bent or broken, twisted and rusted. Justin stood back as if he were inspecting a painting for sale at an auction. Then he made his final judgment: perfect.

Justin talked the owner down to $6.50 and asked his mother, Diane, to help him load the bike into the back of their car.

When he got it home, he wheeled the junker into the garage and showed it proudly to his father. "Will you help me fix it up?" he asked. Justin's hobby was bike racing, a passion the two of them shared. Their garage barely had room for the car anymore. It was more like a bike shop. Tires and frames hung from hooks on the ceiling, and bike wrenches dangled from the walls.

At every race, Justin and his father would adjust the brakes and realign the wheels of his two racing bikes. This was a lot of work, since Justin raced flat out, challenging every gear and part to perform to its fullest. He had learned to handle almost every repair his father could and maybe even a few things he couldn't. When Justin got really stuck, he went to see Mel, the owner of the best bike shop in town. Mel let him hang out and watch, and he even grunted a few syllables of advice from between the spokes of a wheel now and then.

> **◆ Literary Focus** 1
> What details in this passage demonstrate that it is told from a third-person point of view?

Now Justin and his father cleared out a work space in the garage and put the old junker up on a rack. They poured alcohol on the frame and rubbed until the old paint began to yield, layer by layer. They replaced the broken pedal, tightened down a new seat, and restored the grips. In about a week, it looked brand new.

◆ Build Vocabulary

realign (rē´ ə līn´) *v.*: Readjust into a straight line or into proper coordination

yield (yēld) *v.*: Give way to pressure or force

Block Scheduling Strategies

Consider these suggestions to take advantage of extended class time.

- Have students work in small groups to read the selections and answer the Critical Thinking questions. Then have groups plan the Community Project activity on p. 350.
- Alternatively, have students read the story independently and then meet in groups to discuss ways people can make a difference in their community. Ask them to complete the Reading Strategy, Literary Skills, and Build Grammar Skills on p. 360, and/or complete the accompanying **Selection Support,** pp. 123–127.
- Have students use information they develop completing the Cross-Curricular Activity, p. 350, and School Interview in the Idea Bank, p. 361, as they write their Volunteering Handbook.
- If you have access to technology, have students use the *Writer's Solution Writing Lab CD-ROM* to prepare for and complete the Writing Mini-Lesson.

Justin wheeled it out of the garage, leapt aboard, and started off around the block. He stood up and mashed down on the pedals, straining for speed. It was a good, steady ride, but not much of a thrill compared to his racers.

Soon he forgot about the bike. But the very next week, he bought another junker at a yard sale and fixed it up, too. After a while it bothered him that he
2 wasn't really using either bike. Then he
realized that what he loved about the old bikes wasn't riding them: it was the challenge of making something new and useful out of something old and broken.

Justin wondered what he should do with them. They were just taking up space in the garage. He remembered that when he was younger, he used to live
3 near a large brick building called the
Kilbarchan Home for Boys. It was a place
for boys whose parents couldn't care for 3
them for one reason or another.

▲ **Critical Viewing** Like the father and son in this photograph, Justin and his father fix bicycles together. How might such a hobby bring two people together? **[Connect]** 4

He found "Kilbarchan" in the phone book and called the director, who said the boys would be thrilled to get two bicycles. The next day when Justin and his mother unloaded the bikes at the home, two boys raced out to greet them. They leapt aboard the bikes and started tooling around the semicircular driveway, doing wheelies and pirouettes, laughing and shouting.

The Lebos watched them for a while, then started to climb into their car to go home. The boys cried after them, "Wait a minute! You forgot your bikes!" Justin

◆Literary Focus

2 Third-Person Narrator Discuss the information the third-person narrator provides about Justin. Ask students what they might not know if Justin were narrating the story himself. *If Justin were the narrator, he might not reveal directly that he was bothered about not using the bikes and that he enjoyed the challenge of making something useful out of something old and broken.*

Clarification

3 Kilbarchan Home for Boys was established in 1831 in Paterson, New Jersey. It is the oldest continuously operating residential facility for children in need in the United States. The home provides professional treatment and a safe, nurturing environment to young men who have severe emotional or behavioral problems. The goal of treatment is to teach the residents attitudes and skills necessary to cope with their difficulties and become self-sufficient.

▶Critical Viewing◀

4 Connect *Possible response: Working together on a project gives two people time to share thoughts and ideas. It also makes clear what the people have in common and allows them to build a relationship based on mutual interests.*

Customize for *Bodily/Kinesthetic Learners*

Have students who are familiar with riding bikes describe for the class the actions involved in tooling around (riding) and doing wheelies (popping the front tire up and riding on the rear tire) and pirouettes (spinning on the rear tire with the front tire off the ground).

Cultural Connection

Bicycles Bicycles have become increasingly popular worldwide, and in many countries, bicycles outnumber automobiles. The demand for safe places to ride has been so great that many communities have established special bicycle lanes along streets and in parks and recreation areas. Bicycles are used for transportation, recreation, and racing by many cyclists. In fact, bicycle racing is one of the most popular sports in the world and has long been an event in the Olympic Games.

Unless you are a beginner, as you pedal down the street on a bicycle, you don't stop to think about what is making the pedals work and keeping you balanced upright. Gyroscopic forces and centrifugal force are two scientific principles that help the bicycle to stay upright.

The five main types of bicycles include

(1) mountain bikes with heavy-duty springs suited to riding over rough ground
(2) road bikes with thin tires meant to be ridden on paved roads
(3) hybrids, which are a cross between mountain and road bikes
(4) juvenile bikes, which include smaller styles of adult bikes, BMX bikes for racing on dirt tracks, and freestyle bikes designed for doing tricks
(5) specialty bikes, including the "bicycle built for two," or tandem bike, and recumbent bikes, which are pedaled from an almost lying-down position

Interested students may wish to find out more about maintenance requirements, safe riding practices, racing, and types of bicycles.

◆Reading Strategy

❶ **Make Inferences** *Justin's thoughts indicate that he is sensitive, and understands that not having enough to go around can cause problems within a group. He is also concerned about the happiness of all the kids at the home. He seems to be a caring and generous person.*

◆Literary Focus

❷ **Third-Person Point of View** Point out the use of the first-person *I* in this paragraph. Discuss that Justin's words are enclosed in quotation marks, indicating that these are his words and not those of the narrator. Ask students what else in the paragraph indicates the third-person point of view. *The narrator knows and reveals Justin's mother's thoughts—that she had rarely seen him more determined—which would not have been indicated had the story been told in first-person.*

Comprehension Check ☑

❸ Ask students why Justin needs to make only nineteen bikes for twenty-one boys. *He has already made two bikes; nineteen more will equal twenty-one.*

◆Reading Strategy

❹ **Make Inferences** Ask students what they can infer about Justin's parents from the information in this paragraph. *Justin's parents are generous and interested in helping others. They want to encourage Justin's desire to help others.*

---

explained that the bikes were for them to keep. "They were so happy," Justin remembers. "It was like they couldn't believe it. It made me feel good to see them happy."

On the way home, Justin was silent. His mother assumed he was lost in a feeling of satisfaction. But he was thinking about what would happen once those bikes got wheeled inside and everyone saw them. How would all those kids decide who got the bikes? Two bikes could cause more trouble than they would solve. Actually, they hadn't been that hard to build. It was fun. Maybe he could do more. . . .

❶ ◆ **Reading Strategy** What kind of person do Justin's thoughts suggest he is?

❷ "Mom," Justin said as they turned onto their street, "I've got an idea. I'm going to make a bike for every boy at Kilbarchan for Christmas." Diane Lebo looked at Justin out of the corner of her eye. She had rarely seen him so determined.

❸ When they got home, Justin called Kilbarchan to find out how many boys lived there. There were twenty-one. It was already June. He had six months to make nineteen bikes. That was almost a bike a week. Justin called the home back to tell them of his plan. "I could tell they didn't think I could do it," Justin remembers. "I knew I could."

Justin knew his best chance was to build bikes almost the way GM or Ford builds cars: in an assembly line. He would start with frames from three-speed, twenty-four-inch BMX bicycles. They were common bikes, and all the parts were interchangeable. If he could find enough decent frames, he could take parts off broken bikes and fasten them onto the good frames. He figured it would take three or four junkers to produce enough parts to make one good bike. That meant sixty to eighty bikes. Where would he get them?

Garage sales seemed to be the only hope. It was June, and there would be garage sales all summer long. But even if he could find that many bikes, how could he ever pay for them? That was hundreds of dollars.

He went to his parents with a proposal. "When Justin was younger, say five or six," says his mother, "he used to give some of his allowance away to help others in need. His father and I would donate a dollar for every dollar Justin donated. So he asked us if it could be like the old days, if we'd match every dollar he put into buying old bikes. We said yes." ❹

Justin and his mother spent most of June and July hunting for cheap bikes at garage sales and thrift shops. They would haul the bikes home, and Justin would start stripping them down in the yard.

But by the beginning of August, he had managed to make only ten bikes. Summer vacation was almost over, and school and homework would soon cut into his time. Garage sales would dry up when it got colder, and Justin was out of money. Still, he was determined to find a way.

At the end of August, Justin got a break. A neighbor wrote a letter to the local newspaper describing Justin's project, and an editor thought it would make a good story. One day a reporter entered the Lebo garage. Stepping gingerly through the tires and frames that covered the floor, she found a boy with cut fingers and dirty nails, banging a seat onto a frame. His clothes were covered with grease. In her admiring article about a boy who was devoting his summer to help kids he didn't even know, she said Justin needed bikes and money, and she printed his home phone number.

Overnight, everything changed. "There must have been a hundred calls," Justin says. "People would call me up and ask me to come over and pick up their old bike. Or I'd be working in the garage, and a station wagon would pull up. The driver

Viewing and Representing Mini-Lesson

Flowchart

This mini-lesson supports the Flowchart project in the Idea Bank on p. 361.

Introduce Provide examples of flowcharts for students to look at. These might include actual computer flowcharts, recipe books with step-by step directions, or "how-to" books that give detailed directions. Point out that flowcharts show, step by step, how a specific process is accomplished. The steps can be described in writing or illustrated. In an actual flowchart, each step is usually connected to the following (and preceding) steps by a line or directional arrow.

Develop Have individuals or groups of students research Henry Ford's assembly-line process. They can locate information in an encyclopedia, in library books about Henry Ford or automobiles, in some history textbooks, or on the Internet. Ask students to make notes about the main steps in the assembly-line process and then to brainstorm for ways to illustrate these steps.

Apply Have students use long strips of butcher paper and colored markers to create their flow charts. Remind them to use directional arrows to show the order in which the steps progress. If students are not comfortable drawing illustrations, they can cut pictures from magazines or newspapers and glue these onto the flowchart to illustrate the steps.

Assess Evaluate students' work based on whether they have prepared a meaningful representation of a flowchart with steps shown in accurate sequence.

Bicycles, Robert Vickrey, 32 1/2" x 46" © Robert Vickrey/Licensed by VAGA, New York, NY

5 ▲ Critical Viewing How does the mood of this photograph compare with the mood at the Kilbarchan Home when Justin brings his bicycles? **[Compare and Contrast]**

would leave a couple of bikes by the curb. It just snowballed."

6 By the start of school, the garage was overflowing with BMX frames. Pyramids of pedals and seats rose in the corners. Soon bike parts filled a toolshed in the backyard and then spilled out into the small yard itself, wearing away the lawn.

More and more writers and television and radio reporters called for interviews. Each time he told his story, Justin asked for bikes and money. "The first few interviews were fun," Justin says, "but it reached a point where I really didn't like doing them. The publicity was necessary, though. I had to keep doing interviews to get the donations I needed."

By the time school opened, he was working on ten bikes at a time. There 7 were so many calls now that he was beginning to refuse offers that weren't the exact bikes he needed.

As checks came pouring in, Justin's money problems disappeared. He set up a bank account and began to make bulk orders of common parts from Mel's bike shop. Mel seemed delighted to see him. Sometimes, if Justin brought a bike by the shop, Mel would help him fix it. When 8 Justin tried to talk him into a lower price for big orders, Mel smiled and gave in. He respected another good businessman. They became friends.

▶Critical Viewing◀

5 Compare and Contrast *Possible response: The mood of the photograph seems sad, because of the subdued lighting, the long shadows, and the boy's body language. The mood at the boys' home was happy and upbeat, with the boys riding around on their new bicycles.*

◆Critical Thinking

6 Deduce Ask students what they can deduce from the details in this paragraph. *So many bikes were dropped off that there was scarcely room at the Lebos' home to hold all their parts.*

◆Critical Thinking

7 Connect Discuss how Justin might be able to work on ten bicycles at one time. Ask students what information from earlier in the selection helps them understand how he can do this. *Justin built the bikes using an assembly-line process, the way automobile manufacturers build cars.*

◆Reading Strategy

8 Make Inferences Ask students what they can infer about business people from this passage and what details they used to make the inference. *Good business people spend their money wisely. Justin tries to negotiate a better price when he places a large order.*

Beyond the Classroom

Community Connection

Small Businesses Discuss with students that communities are made up of people, businesses, and organizations that work together in many ways. Small businesses are an important asset to the business community, and can provide a variety of products and services. Businesses owned or operated by one person are called single proprietorships. The owners may employ a small number of employees to help run the business. These small businesses might include bike shops, like the one owned by Mel in the selection, barber shops, hair salons, restaurants, coffee shops, book stores, hardware stores, flower shops, and so forth. These businesses provide goods or services to the people who live nearby, and the owners are often well acquainted with their customers.

If the owner of a small business runs out of money, gets sick, or dies, the business often closes. To encourage small businesses, the United States government offers assistance through the Small Business Administration (SBA) with affordable loans, training, and information. The SBA offers special programs to women and minority groups to encourage business ownership.

Have students suggest examples of small businesses in your community and tell what goods or service the business provides. Discuss how the community would be different without these small businesses.

In "The Rider," Naomi Shihab Nye describes how activities such as rollerskating or bike riding can help people overcome loneliness.

◆Reading Strategy

❶ Make Inferences Ask students what they can infer about the speaker's feelings by connecting these lines to earlier ones. *She is feeling lonely and hopes that bicycling works as well as rollerskating in outrunning loneliness.*

▶Critical Viewing◀

❷ Analyze *The blurred focus shows the rider pedaling hard and fast, like the speaker. The rider is smiling and appears happy, like the speaker, who has left loneliness behind.*

Beyond Literature

Many community projects are developed and maintained by volunteers. Discuss with students the need for volunteer help to accomplish the goals of a community project. Organized volunteer opportunities are often made known through established service agencies such as the United Way, Habitat for Humanity, or the Red Cross. Encourage students to contact someone from a volunteer organization for ideas on how best to address community problems.

The week before Christmas Justin delivered the last of the twenty-one bikes to Kilbarchan. Once again, the boys poured out of the home and leapt aboard the bikes, tearing around the snow.

And once again, their joy inspired Justin. They reminded him how important bikes were to him. Wheels meant freedom. He thought how much more the freedom to ride must mean to boys like these who had so little freedom in their lives. He decided to keep on building.

"First I made eleven bikes for the children in a foster home my mother told me about. Then I made bikes for all the women in a battered women's shelter. Then I made ten little bikes and tricycles for the kids in a home for children with AIDS. Then I made twenty-three bikes for the Paterson Housing Coalition."

In the four years since he started, Justin Lebo has made between 150 and 200 bikes and given them all away. He has been careful to leave time for his homework, his friends, his coin collection, his new interest in marine biology, and of course his own bikes.

Reporters and interviewers have asked Justin Lebo the same question over and over: "Why do you do it?" The question seems to make him uncomfortable. It's as if they want him to say what a great person he is. Their stories always make him seem like a saint, which he knows he isn't. "Sure it's nice of me to make the bikes," he says, "because I don't have to. But I want to. In part, I do it for myself. I don't think you can ever really do anything to help anybody else if it doesn't make you happy.

"Once I overheard a kid who got one of my bikes say, 'A bike is like a book; it opens up a whole new world.' That's how I feel, too. It made me happy to know that kid felt that way. That's why I do it."

◆ Literature and Your Life

Have you ever done something nice for someone else because it made you feel happy?

◆ Build Vocabulary

coalition (kō´ ə lish´ ən) *n.*: Association or organization formed for a specific purpose

Beyond Literature

Community Connection

Making a Difference Justin Lebo isn't the only young person to help others, finding personal satisfaction through the process. In communities across the nation, people volunteer and improve the lives of others. Some volunteering opportunities can be found through organizations—serving food in a soup kitchen, working with a group to teach adults to read, or joining others to build houses for those who might not otherwise be able to afford them. In contrast, some volunteering opportunities are not organized: People may bring home groceries for their elderly neighbors, or a few adults might get together to help a mother of triplets manage her newborns.

Cross-Curricular Activity

Community Project In discussion with a group, identify some problems in your community. Consider the environment, housing, or the condition of public spaces, for example. Talk with parents and teachers to find out what problems residents may have already identified. After choosing an issue, look for ways that your group can get involved. Make your plans as specific as possible. With your teacher's help, offer your help to an appropriate organization.

Cross-Curricular Connection: Math

Story Problems Remind students that many math problems are word problems or "story problems" that present a mathematical problem in words. In these types of problems, students must determine a mathematical equation that can be used to calculate the answer to the word question. The descriptions of Justin's volunteer activities contain many mathematical ideas and opportunities for computation that can be written as story problems. For example, from information included in the selection, have students read and answer the following story problem:

> Justin paid $6.50 for the first bike he rebuilt. How much money will he need in order to buy 60 to 80 bikes? *He will need $390 for 60 bikes and $520 for 80 bikes, so $390–$520 is the range of money he will need.*

Invite students to write other mathematical word problems based on the story. Collect their word problems, and work to answer them with the class. Possible word problems include:

- If Justin needs to rebuild 19 bicycles before Christmas and has only 6 months to do it, how long does he have to work on each bike?
- What is the total cost of each renovated bicycle that Justin gives to the children's home?

The Rider

Naomi Shihab Nye

A boy told me
if he rollerskated fast enough
his loneliness couldn't catch up to him,

the best reason I ever heard
for trying to be a champion.

What I wonder tonight
1 pedaling hard down King William Street
is if it translates to bicycles.

A victory! To leave your loneliness
panting behind you on some
street corner
while you float free into a cloud
of sudden azaleas,
luminous pink petals that have
never felt loneliness,
no matter how slowly they fell.

2 ▲ **Critical Viewing** What details of this photograph convey the feelings the poem describes? **[Analyze]**

Guide for Responding

◆ Literature and Your Life

Reader's Response What does riding a bicycle mean to you? Explain.

Thematic Focus How do bicycles help Justin Lebo and the speaker of "The Rider" to solve problems?

Journal Writing What skills could you share, as Justin Lebo shares his mechanical abilities? In a journal entry, describe the talents you have that could help others.

☑ Check Your Comprehension

1. What special talent does Justin Lebo have?
2. How does he use his talent to help the boys at Kilbarchan?
3. What obstacles must Justin overcome to accomplish his plan?
4. In the first stanza of "The Rider," against whom or what is the boy racing?
5. What is the speaker of the poem doing?

◆ Critical Thinking

Interpret

1. Find two examples that show Justin Lebo likes a challenge. **[Connect]**
2. In accomplishing his goal, how does Justin give inspiration to others and receive it from them? **[Analyze Cause and Effect]**
3. What does Justin learn from his project? **[Draw Conclusions]**
4. What words in "The Rider" help communicate the idea of freedom? **[Support]**
5. What do the two activities described in "The Rider" have in common? **[Compare]**

Apply

6. What are some ways in which the speaker of "The Rider" could help others? **[Apply]**

Compare Literary Works

7. Do you think Justin Lebo would agree with the ideas presented in "The Rider"? Why or why not? **[Connect]**

Reinforce and Extend

Answers

◆ Literature and Your Life

Reader's Response Accept all supported answers.

Thematic Focus Possible response: Bikes help Justin Lebo to bring freedom to people in need. For the speaker of "The Rider," a bike offers an escape from loneliness.

☑ Check Your Comprehension

1. He is good at riding and fixing bicycles.
2. He repairs and rebuilds old bikes for the boys.
3. He has to find and pay for used bikes and parts. He sets himself a goal to do all the work in a certain amount of time.
4. He is racing against loneliness.
5. The speaker is riding a bicycle.

◆ Critical Thinking

1. Possible response: He bargains an owner down to $6.50 for an old bike. He sets himself a goal to rebuild nineteen bikes before Christmas.
2. He shows his parents and others that he cares, he can solve problems, and he won't give up. He is inspired by the generosity of his parents, Mel, and people in the community, and by the boys' excitement over the bikes.
3. Possible response: He learns that persistence pays off, that problems can be solved creatively, that helping others makes you feel good.
4. "Float free into a cloud of sudden azaleas"
5. Possible response: They are both physical activities that are challenging and may help people work through loneliness.
6. Possible response: He or she could teach other people to ride bikes or use sports to help them feel better.
7. Possible response: Yes. He believes that bike riding offers freedom to people in need, and riding to escape loneliness is an example of such a freedom.

Beyond the Selection

FURTHER READING

Other Works by the Authors

Hoosiers: The Fabulous Basketball of Indiana, Phillip Hoose

Habibi, Naomi Shihab Nye

Never in a Hurry: Essays on People and Places, Naomi Shihab Nye

Other Works on the Theme of Finding Solutions

Zebra and Other Stories, Chaim Potok

How to Make the World a Better Place: 116 Ways You Can Make a Difference, Jeffrey Hollender

INTERNET

We suggest the following sites on the Internet (all Web sites are subject to change).

For more poems by and information about Naomi Shihab Nye:
http://www.wnet.org/archive/lol/nye.html

For information about children making a difference in a community:
http://www.childrensfoundation.org/

We *strongly recommend* that you preview these sites before you send students to them.

One-Minute Insight Antonio and Felix have grown up as good friends in a Puerto Rican neighborhood in New York City. The seventeen-year-olds are both fine boxers with championship dreams. After they learn they will meet as opponents in the ring, tension builds between them. Finally, they agree to go into the ring as strangers. When fight day arrives, they fight evenly for two rounds, but must be pried apart by the final bell. When they rush back toward each other, the crowd believes they will resume fighting. Instead, they embrace and silently agree on a solution to the problems raised by a competition between friends.

Team Teaching Strategy

The emphasis on the sport of boxing and physical fitness in the selection offers opportunities to coordinate instruction with a physical education teacher.

◆Reading Strategy

❶ **Make Inferences** Ask students what they can infer about Felix and Antonio from the detail that they live in a tenement. *Their families probably do not have a lot of money.*

◆Literary Focus

❷ **Third-Person Point of View** *A narrator is telling the story, since the characters are referred to by name or by third-person pronouns. Also, the narrator knows what both Antonio and Felix are thinking.*

Customize for
Bodily/Kinesthetic Learners
Ask a volunteer familiar with boxing to demonstrate techniques such as *feinting, haymaker, bob and weave, overhand right, left hook, right cross, straight left, jab,* and *countered.*

Customize for
Visual/Spatial Learners
The photographs on these pages can help students imagine how Antonio and Felix looked as they practiced or boxed in the championship match. Based on these photographs, discuss with students their impressions of boxers and the sport of boxing.

Amigo Brothers

Piri Thomas

Antonio Cruz and Felix Vargas were both seventeen years old. They were so together in friendship that they felt themselves to be brothers. ❶ They had known each other since childhood, growing up on the lower east side of Manhattan in the same tenement building on Fifth Street between Avenue A and Avenue B.

Antonio was fair, lean, and lanky, while Felix was dark, short, and husky. Antonio's hair was always falling over his eyes, while Felix wore his black hair in a natural Afro style.

Each youngster had a dream of someday becoming lightweight champion of the world. Every chance they had the boys worked out, sometimes at the Boys Club on 10th Street and Avenue A and sometimes at the pro's gym on 14th Street. Early morning sunrises would find them running along the East River Drive, wrapped in sweat shirts, short towels around their necks, and handkerchiefs Apache style around their foreheads.

While some youngsters were into street negatives, Antonio and Felix slept, ate, rapped, and dreamt positive. Between them, they had a collection of *Fight* magazines second to none, plus a scrapbook filled with torn tickets to every boxing match they had ever attended, and some clippings of their own. If asked a question about any given fighter, they would immediately zip out from their memory banks divisions, weights, records of fights, knock-outs, technical knock-outs,[1] and draws or losses.

❷ **◆ Literary Focus** Who is telling this story? How can you tell?

Each had fought many bouts representing their community and had won two gold-plated medals plus a silver and bronze medallion. The difference was in their style. Antonio's lean form and long reach made him the better boxer, while Felix's short and muscular frame made him the better slugger. Whenever they had met in the ring for sparring sessions, it had always been hot and heavy.

Now, after a series of elimination bouts,[2] they had been informed that they were to meet each other in the division finals that were scheduled

1. **technical knock-outs:** Occasions when a fight is stopped because one of the fighters is too hurt to continue, even though he is on his feet.
2. **elimination bouts:** Matches in which only the winners go on to fight in other matches.

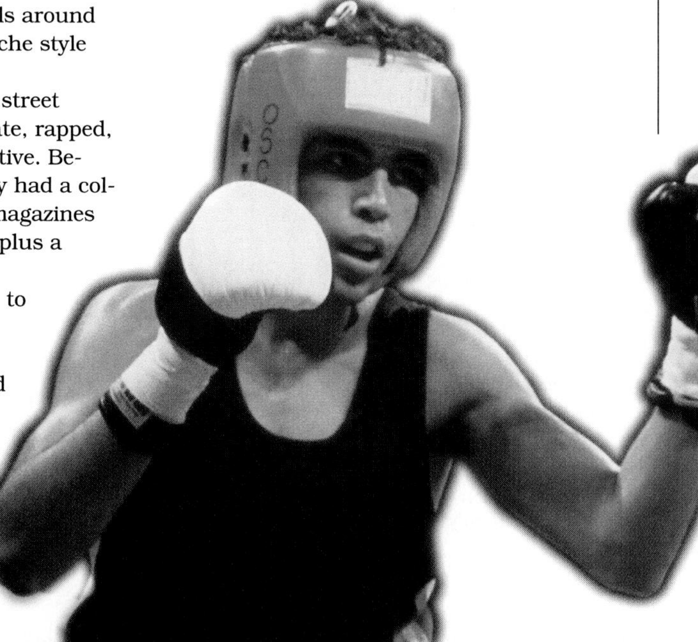

Cross-Curricular Connection: Physical Education

Boxing The sport of boxing dates back to ancient Greece and was an event in the first Olympic games held in 776 B.C. Boxing in eighteenth-century England was a brutal, bare-knuckled sport enjoyed chiefly for wagering. Early guidelines added a veneer of civility by forbidding such actions as hair pulling. The Queensbury rules of 1857 signaled the arrival of the modern sport. These rules, still used today, emphasize skill and mandate the use of gloves.

In modern amateur boxing, competitors fight in twelve different weight divisions. Boxing bouts are no longer than three rounds of three minutes each. The fighters use extra-heavy gloves and protective devices such as headgear. The Golden Gloves Association, founded in 1927, is a major amateur boxing organization.

Invite interested students to research opportunities to learn and practice boxing in your school or community. Encourage them to report back to the class with their findings.

for the seventh of August, two weeks away—the winner to represent the Boys Club in the Golden Gloves Championship Tournament.

The two boys continued to run together along the East River Drive. But even when joking with each other, they both sensed a wall rising between them.

One morning less than a week before their bout, they met as usual for their daily workout. They fooled around with a few jabs at the air, slapped skin, and then took off, running lightly along the dirty East River's edge.

Antonio glanced at Felix who kept his eyes purposely straight ahead, pausing from time to time to do some fancy leg work while throwing one-twos followed by upper cuts to an imaginary jaw. Antonio then beat the air with a barrage of body blows and short devastating lefts with an overhand jaw-breaking right. After a mile or so, Felix puffed and said, "Let's stop a while, bro. I think we both got something to say to each other."

Antonio nodded. It was not natural to be acting as though nothing unusual was happening when two ace-boon buddies were going to be blasting each other within a few short days.

They rested their elbows on the railing separating them from the river. Antonio wiped his face with his short towel. The sunrise was now creating day.

Felix leaned heavily on the river's railing and stared across to the shores of Brooklyn. Finally, he broke the silence.

"Man, I don't know how to come out with it."

Antonio helped. "It's about our fight, right?"

"Yeah, right." Felix's eyes squinted at the rising orange sun.

"I've been thinking about it too, *panín*. In fact, since we found out it was going to be me and you, I've been awake at night, pulling punches on you, trying not to hurt you."

"Same here. It ain't natural not to think about the fight. I mean, we both are *cheverote* fighters and we both want to win. But only one of us can win. There ain't no draws in the eliminations." 4

Felix tapped Antonio gently on the shoulder. "I don't mean to sound like I'm bragging, bro. But I wanna win, fair and square."

◆ **Reading Strategy** What can you infer about Felix and Antonio's relationship from this conversation? 5

Antonio nodded quietly. "Yeah. We both know that in the ring the better man wins. Friend or no friend, brother or no . . ."

Felix finished it for him. "Brother. Tony, let's promise something right here. Okay?"

"If it's fair, *hermano*, I'm for it." Antonio admired the courage of a tugboat pulling a barge five times its welterweight size.

◆ **Build Vocabulary**

devastating (dev´ əs tāt´ iŋ) *adj.*: Destructive; overwhelming

◄ **Critical Viewing** Felix and Antonio box against each other in "Amigo Brothers." What does the protective gear in this photograph suggest about boxing? **[Analyze Cause and Effect]** 6

◆Reading Strategy

3 Make Inferences Ask students how they think the boys are feeling. *Possible response: They are uncomfortable, because each wants to win but doesn't want to defeat a friend in order to do so.*

Comprehension Check ☑

4 Ask students why this fight is so important to both Felix and Antonio. *Both fighters have championship dreams; this match is the division final, and the winner will represent the Boys Club in the Golden Gloves Tournament.*

◆Reading Strategy

5 *Possible response: Felix and Antonio admire and respect each other. They do not want to hurt each other, but neither fighter wants to give up the chance to become a champion.*

►Critical Viewing◄

6 Analyze; Cause and Effect *Possible response: The gear suggests that boxing can be a dangerous sport and that participants must protect themselves from serious injury, particularly to their heads.*

Customize for *Verbal/Linguistic*

Suggest that students research aspects of Puerto Rican culture and history, including the postwar immigration to the mainland United States, "El Barrio" in New York City, the statehood and independence movements, or the Puerto Rican world boxing champions who may have inspired the story characters.

Cultural Connection

Slang is an informal language composed of words or phrases that certain groups of people make up or use in new or unusual ways. These groups of people might live in a certain area, be of a similar age, engage in common activities, or share other interests. Sometimes, slang terms come to be used by the general population. For example, *veg out* (relax and do nothing), *pig out* (eat too much), *vibes* (feelings), *hang loose* (relax), and so forth are examples of more widely used slang expressions.

Technical slang terms are usually labeled *jargon* and are often used in a specific business or industry. Terms such as: *the Net, memory,* and *chips* are examples of computer jargon that those familiar with a computer recognize immediately.

Slang is often considered inappropriate to use in writing or school work. Slang expressions and meanings change rapidly and are sometimes difficult to define accurately. Some people use slang to be modern or popular, others because it is informal and seems friendly.

Invite groups of students to identify examples of slang in this selection, such as *bro, ace-boon buddy, heavy, psyching up, split, fight flick,* and *ghetto grapevine*. Then, ask them to define each term and speculate about how and why the term might have originated. Encourage volunteers to share their ideas with the class.

◆Critical Thinking

❶ **Make a Judgment** Ask students if they think Felix and Antonio will solve their problem by staying apart until the fight and if they will ever be able to act as if nothing had happened. *Most students will agree that staying apart will help them prepare to fight each other. Students might disagree about whether the outcome of the fight will affect the friendship between the fighters. Encourage students to give reasons for their opinions.*

Comprehension Check ☑

❷ Point out the Spanish terms in these sentences, as well as those that appeared earlier. Then, direct students' attention to the box on p. 355 that defines these terms. Have students reread the sentences, inserting the English translation in place of the Spanish terms.

◆Reading Strategy

❸ **Make an Inference** Ask students why the kids don't bother Felix, but instead go about their own business. *They are put off by his obvious boxing ability.*

Customize for *Visual/Spatial Learners*

Invite interested students to create a pictorial map of New York City depicting the places mentioned in the selection, with drawings that indicate what occurs in each location. Students might include a movie theater in the South Bronx, Tompkins Square Park, the East River Drive (which may be indicated as FDR Drive on some maps), the boys' apartment building, and the various gyms. Remind students to include a compass rose to show direction.

"It's fair, Tony. When we get into the ring, it's gotta be like we never met. We gotta be like two heavy strangers that want the same thing and only one can have it. You understand, don'tcha?"

"*Sí*, I know." Tony smiled. "No pulling punches. We go all the way."

"Yeah, that's right. Listen, Tony. Don't you think it's a good idea if we don't see each other until the day of the fight? I'm going to stay with my Aunt Lucy in the Bronx. I can use Gleason's Gym for working out. My manager
❶ says he got some sparring partners with more or less your style."

Tony scratched his nose pensively. "Yeah, it would be better for our heads." He held out his hand, palm upward. "Deal?"

"Deal." Felix lightly slapped open skin.

"Ready for some more running?" Tony asked lamely.

"Naw, bro. Let's cut it here. You go on. I kinda like to get things together in my head."

"You ain't worried, are you?" Tony asked.

"No way, man." Felix laughed out loud. "I got too much smarts for that. I just think it's cooler if we split right here. After the fight, we can get it together again like nothing ever happened."

The amigo brothers were not ashamed to hug each other tightly.

"Guess you're right. Watch yourself, Felix. I hear there's some pretty heavy dudes up in
❷ the Bronx. *Suavecito*, okay?"

"Okay. You watch yourself too, *sabe*?"

Tony jogged away. Felix watched his friend disappear from view, throwing rights and lefts. Both fighters had a lot of psyching up to do before the big fight.

The days in training passed much too slowly. Although they kept out of each other's way, they were aware of each other's progress via the ghetto grapevine.

The evening before the big fight, Tony made his way to the roof of his tenement. In the quiet early dark, he peered over the ledge. Six stories below the lights of the city blinked and the sounds of cars mingled with the curses and the laughter of children in the street. He tried not to think of Felix, feeling he had succeeded in psyching his mind. But only in the ring would he really know. To spare Felix hurt, he would have to knock him out, early and quick.

> **◆ Literature and Your Life**
> How would you prepare for the challenge of the next day?

Up in the South Bronx, Felix decided to take in a movie in an effort to keep Antonio's face away from his fists. The flick was *The Champion* with Kirk Douglas, the third time Felix was seeing it.

The champion was getting hit hard. He was saved only by the sound of the bell.

Felix became the champ and Tony the challenger.

The movie audience was going out of its head. The challenger, confident that he had the championship in the bag, threw a left. The champ countered with a dynamite right.

Felix's right arm felt the shock. Antonio's face, superimposed on the screen, was hit by the awesome blow. Felix saw himself in the ring, blasting Antonio against the ropes. The champ had to be forcibly restrained. The challenger was allowed to crumble slowly to the canvas.

When Felix finally left the theatre, he had figured out how to psyche himself for tomorrow's fight. It was Felix the Champion vs. Antonio the Challenger.

He walked up some dark streets, deserted except for small pockets of wary-looking kids wearing gang colors. Despite the fact that he was Puerto Rican like them, they eyed him as
a stranger to their turf. Felix did a fast shuffle, ❸
bobbing and weaving, while letting loose a torrent of blows that would demolish whatever got in its way. It seemed to impress the brothers, who went about their own business.

Finding no takers, Felix decided to split to his aunt's. Walking the streets had not relaxed him, neither had the fight flick. All it had done was to stir him up. He let himself quietly into his Aunt Lucy's apartment and went straight

◆ Build Vocabulary

superimposed (so͞o´ pər im pōzd´) *adj.*: Put or stacked on top of something else

perpetual (pər pech´ o͞o əl) *adj.*: Constant; unending

Cross-Curricular Connection: Language

Foreign Language Study Felix and Antonio use many Spanish words in their conversations. Ask students if they are familiar with any of the Spanish words in the list on p. 355.

Young children learn their native language easily by listening to and imitating their parents and those around them. Many studies have indicated that children ten and under can learn a foreign language more easily and quickly than older students. For this reason, some schools begin foreign language instruction in the early grades.

Ask students to list and discuss reasons why learning a foreign language at any age is important:

- communication with more people
- understanding of the grammar of a foreign language increases understanding of English grammar
- awareness of other cultures and countries
- travel in a foreign country

Invite students to discuss with family members and friends the languages they have studied and what they feel they gained from their experiences.

to bed, falling into a fitful sleep with sounds of the gong for Round One.

Antonio was passing some heavy time on his rooftop. How would the fight tomorrow affect his relationship with Felix? After all, (4) fighting was like any other profession. Friendship had nothing to do with it. A gnawing doubt crept in. He cut negative thinking real quick by doing some speedy fancy dance steps, bobbing and weaving like mercury.[3] The night air was blurred with perpetual motions of left hooks and right crosses. Felix, his *amigo* brother, was not going to be Felix at all in the ring. Just an opponent with another face. Antonio went to sleep, hearing the opening bell for the first round. Like his friend in the South Bronx, he prayed for victory, via a quick clean knock-out in the first round.

Large posters plastered all over the walls of (5) local shops announced the fight between Antonio Cruz and Felix Vargas as the main bout.

The fight had created great interest in the neighborhood. Antonio and Felix were well liked and respected. Each had his own loyal following. Antonio's fans counted on his boxing skills. On the other side, Felix's admirers trusted in his dynamite-packed fists.

Felix had returned to his apartment early in the morning of August 7th and stayed there, hoping to avoid seeing Antonio. He turned the radio on to *salsa* music sounds and then tried to read while waiting for word from his manager.

The fight was scheduled to take place in Tompkins Square Park. It had been decided that the gymnasium of the Boys Club was not large enough to hold all the people who were sure to attend. In Tompkins Square Park, everyone who wanted could view the fight, whether from ringside or window fire escapes or tenement rooftops.

The morning of the fight Tompkins Square was a beehive of activity with numerous workers setting up the ring, the seats, and the guest speakers' stand. The scheduled bouts began shortly after noon and the park had begun filling up even earlier.

The local junior high school across from Tompkins Square Park served as the dressing room for all the fighters. Each was given a separate classroom with desk tops, covered with mats, serving as resting tables. Antonio thought he caught a glimpse of Felix waving to him from a room at the far end of the corridor. He waved back just in case it had been him.

The fighters changed from their street clothes into fighting gear. Antonio wore white trunks, black socks, and black shoes. Felix wore sky blue trunks, red socks, and white boxing shoes. Each had dressing gowns to match their fighting trunks with their names neatly stitched on the back.

---

3. **mercury** (mur´ kyo͞o rē) *n.*: The element mercury, also known as quicksilver because it is so quick and fluid. This element was named after the Roman god Mercury, who because of his speed and quick thinking served as the messenger of the gods.

Spanish Terms

amigo (ə mē´ gō) *adj.*: Spanish for "friend" (usually a noun)
panín (pä nēn´) *n.*: Spanish for "pal"
cheverote (che bē rō´ te): Spanish for "great"
hermano (ar mä´ no) *n.*: Spanish for "brother"
suavecito (swä ve sē´ tō): Spanish for "take it easy"
sabe (sä bā´) *v.*: Spanish for "understand?"
salsa (säl´ sä) *n.*: Latin American music
señores y señoras (sen yo´ res ē se nyo´ räs): Spanish for "Gentlemen and Ladies"
mucho corazón (mo͞o´ chō cô rä sôn´): Spanish for "much courage"

◆Critical Thinking

4 Connect Ask students what Antonio's thoughts have in common with those of the speaker in "The Rider." *They both have negative thoughts or feelings that they overcome through physical activity.*

Comprehension Check ☑

5 Ask students why the fight between Antonio and Felix would be the main bout. *The two were fighting to see who would represent the Boys Club in the Golden Gloves Championship Tournament.*

Customize for *Logical/Mathematical*

Suggest that students research the number of English-speaking people in the world. Have them prepare a graph that compares the numbers of people who speak English, Spanish, French, or other languages. If possible, have students locate the numbers of countries where residents are bilingual (able to speak and understand two languages), in which case they might wish to use a Venn Diagram (p. 86 in **Writing and Language Transparencies**) to illustrate their numbers.

Speaking and Listening Mini-Lesson

School Interviews

This mini-lesson supports the Speaking and Listening activity in the Idea Bank on p. 361.

Introduce Explain that the purpose of an interview is to gather information. Generally, an interview takes place between two people: the person conducting the interview and the person being interviewed.

Develop Once students decide whom they will interview, ask them to develop a list of questions. The questions asked will vary, depending on the kind of information they wish to obtain, but should be planned carefully in advance.

Apply Remind students to listen carefully during the interview, and to take accurate notes so they will remember exactly what was said. If possible, they may want to use a tape recorder in addition to their note-taking. Following the interview, have students review their notes to make sure they are clear. Encourage them to organize the notes before they make their presentations to the class.

Assess Evaluate students' interviews based on the quality and organization of information gathered and on clarity of presentation. You may want to have students complete the Peer Assessment: Speaker/Speech form, p. 105, in **Alternative Assessment.**

Comprehension Check ☑

❶ Ask students to explain why Felix was relieved. *He was relieved because the fight before his was over quickly. He was anxious to get his own fight under way.*

◆Reading Strategy

❷ **Make Inferences** Ask students how they think the fighters are feeling. Have students point out details that help them make this inference. *Possible response: They are nervous and worried about fighting. Antonio is trying to be cool and turns slowly to look at Felix. The fighters quickly turn away from each other because they are embarrassed and nervous.*

◆Literary Focus

❸ **Third-Person Point of View** *The narrator tells the reader that the announcer is proud to be able to speak both English and Spanish.*

▶Critical Viewing◀

❹ **Hypothesize** *Possible response: It helps the judges and the fans tell who is who and makes it easier for them to focus on a particular competitor.*

The loudspeakers blared into the open windows of the school. There were speeches by dignitaries, community leaders, and great boxers of yesteryear. Some were well prepared, some improvised on the spot. They all carried the same message of great pleasure and honor at being part of such a historic event. This great day was in the tradition of champions emerging from the streets of the lower east side.

Interwoven with the speeches were the sounds of the other boxing events. After the sixth bout, Felix
1 was much relieved when his trainer Charlie said, "Time change. Quick knock-out. This is it. We're on."

Waiting time was over. Felix was escorted from the classroom by a dozen fans in white T-shirts with the word FELIX across their fronts.

Antonio was escorted down a different stairwell and guided through a roped-off path.

As the two climbed into the ring, the crowd exploded with a roar. Antonio and Felix both bowed gracefully and then raised their arms in acknowledgment.

Antonio tried to be cool, but even as the roar was in its first birth, he turned slowly to meet Felix's eyes looking directly into his.
2 Felix nodded his head and Antonio responded. And both as one, just as quickly, turned away to face his own corner.

Bong—bong—bong. The roar turned to stillness.

"Ladies and Gentlemen. *Señores y Señoras.*"

The announcer spoke slowly, pleased at his bilingual efforts.

"Now the moment we have all been waiting for—the main event between two fine young Puerto Rican fighters, products of our lower east side. In this corner, weighing 134 pounds, Felix Vargas. And in this corner, weighing 133 pounds, Antonio Cruz. The winner will represent the Boys Club in the tournament of champions, the Golden Gloves. There will be no draw. May the best man win."

◆ **Literary Focus** How does the narrator help you learn about the announcer? 3

The cheering of the crowd shook the window panes of the old buildings surrounding Tompkins Square Park. At the center of the ring, the referee was giving instructions to the youngsters.

"Keep your punches up. No low blows. No punching on the back of the head. Keep your heads up. Understand. Let's have a clean fight. Now shake hands and come out fighting."

Both youngsters touched gloves and nodded. They turned and danced quickly to their corners. Their head towels and dressing gowns were lifted neatly from their shoulders by their trainers' nimble fingers. Antonio crossed himself. Felix did the same.

BONG! BONG! ROUND ONE. Felix and Antonio turned and faced each other squarely in a fighting pose. Felix wasted no time. He came in fast, head low, half hunched toward his right shoulder, and lashed out with a straight left. He missed a right cross as Antonio slipped the punch and countered with one-two-three lefts that snapped Felix's head back, sending a mild shock coursing through him. If Felix had any small doubt about their friendship affecting their fight, it was being neatly dispelled.

▲ **Critical Viewing** In boxing matches, as in many other sporting events, competitors wear contrasting colors. Why do you think this is true? **[Hypothesize]** 4

Humanities: Photography

Sports Photography The photographs on these pages show Oscar de la Hoya in the blue shirt and A. Khamatov in the red shirt. The photographs were taken by professional photographer David Madison. Television news programming uses video recordings of sports events, but magazines and newspapers publish clear and exciting still photographs. Sports photographers provide pictures of exciting moments in fast-moving sporting events, such as boxing matches, football games, gymnastics competitions, baseball games, and track meets.

Particular skills and a lot of practice are needed to capture meaningful sports images. It takes only a split second to push the button on a camera, but a good sports photographer must anticipate the action and move at precisely the right instant, or the photograph of a winning moment may be lost forever. Sports photographers must also know what kinds of film and camera are required to freeze action and produce a sharp, clear image rather than a blurred, fuzzy one that cannot be published.

Have students view the photographs in this selection as they discuss the following questions:

1. What actions are frozen in time by the photographer? *Possible response: bouncing, steps, jabs, punches*
2. How do these photographs help you understand what is happening in the story? *Possible response: They show examples of the gear and some of the boxing movements that are described in the selection.*

5 Antonio danced, a joy to behold. His left hand was like a piston pumping jabs one right after another with seeming ease. Felix bobbed and weaved and never stopped boring in. He knew that at long range he was at a disadvantage. Antonio had too much reach on him. Only by coming in close could Felix hope to achieve the dreamed-of knockout.

Antonio knew the dynamite that was stored in his *amigo* brother's fist. He ducked a short right and missed a left hook. Felix trapped him against the ropes just long enough to pour some punishing rights and lefts to Antonio's hard midsection. Antonio slipped away from Felix, crashing two lefts to his head, which set Felix's right ear to ringing.

Bong! Both *amigos* froze a punch well on its way, sending up a roar of approval for good sportsmanship.

Felix walked briskly back to his corner. His right ear had not stopped ringing. Antonio gracefully danced his way toward his stool none the worse, except for glowing glove burns, showing angry red against the whiteness of his midribs.

"Watch that right, Tony." His trainer talked into his ear. "Remember Felix always goes to the body. He'll want you to drop your hands for his overhand left or right. Got it?"

Antonio nodded, spraying water out between his teeth. He felt better as his sore midsection was being firmly rubbed.

Felix's corner was also busy.

"You gotta get in there, fella." Felix's trainer poured water over his curly Afro locks. "Get in there or he's gonna chop you up from way back."

Bong! Bong! Round two. Felix was off his stool and rushed Antonio like a bull, sending a hard right to his head. Beads of water exploded from Antonio's long hair.

Antonio, hurt, sent back a blurring barrage of lefts and rights that only meant pain to Felix, who returned with a short left to the head followed by a looping right to the body. Antonio countered with his own flurry, forcing Felix to give ground. But not for long.

Felix bobbed and weaved, bobbed and weaved, occasionally punching his two gloves together.

Antonio waited for the rush that was sure to come. Felix closed in and feinted[4] with his left shoulder and threw his right instead. Lights suddenly exploded inside Felix's head as Antonio slipped the blow and hit him with a piston-like left catching him flush on the point of his chin. 6
Bedlam[5] broke loose as Felix's legs momentarily buckled. He fought off a series of rights and lefts and came back with a strong right that taught Antonio respect.

Antonio danced in carefully. He knew Felix had the habit of playing possum when hurt, to

◆ **Build Vocabulary**

dispelled (dis peld′) *v.*: Driven away; made to disappear

4. **feinted** (fānt′ əd) *v.*: Pretended to make a blow.
5. **Bedlam** (bed′ ləm) *n.*: Condition of noise and confusion.

◆Critical Thinking

5 Compare and Contrast Point out the author's use of the words *piston* and *boring.* Ask them why the author might use words associated with engines and machines to describe the motions of the two fighters. *Antonio's left hand is moving so fast and rhythmically that it is almost like the piston of an engine as it moves up and down. Felix keeps moving closer and closer to his opponent, like a drill.*

Comprehension Check ☑

6 Discuss with students whether this paragraph means that Antonio did not respect Felix before the punch was thrown. Lead them to recognize that previously Antonio had hurt Felix. The right-handed punch is simply a reminder to Antonio that Felix is still dangerous.

Customize for *Verbal/Linguistic Learners*

Have students locate examples in the fight scene of particularly vivid descriptions that appeal to the senses such as: *dynamite…stored in his fist; glowing glove burns, showing angry red against the whiteness of his midribs; Beads of water exploded from Antonio's long hair; Lights suddenly exploded inside Felix's head….* Discuss with students how colorful descriptions like these help them imagine the scenes and enhance their understanding of the selection.

Beyond the Classroom

Career Connection

Sports Careers Discuss with students that in addition to the actual participants, most competitive sports events require the services of many people. A referee or umpire is the person who makes sure the game or match is conducted fairly and by the rules. These are generally part-time jobs. For example, a store clerk or an engineer might work as a referee for a Friday night football game. Often referees volunteer their time to help community organizations, such as youth soccer or baseball leagues.

You may want to focus on the role of boxing referees. Explain that the primary duties of a boxing referee are to ensure a fair fight and to prevent injuries if possible. Certain punches—those to the back of the head, kidney area, or below the belt—are prohibited because of their potential to cause serious injury. A boxing referee can end a fight at any time if he or she believes either fighter is in distress.

Invite students to discuss other careers with a connection to sports: trainers, coaches, physical education teachers, specialists in sports medicine, salespersons of sports clothing and equipment, gymnasium staff, and so forth. Suggest that interested students investigate the training, experience, and education required to pursue a career in the field of sports.

◆Reading Strategy

❶ **Make Inferences** *Possible response: Both fighters wanted badly to win the match and to do it as quickly as possible.*

◆Critical Thinking

❷ **Make Judgments** Ask students who they think is fighting better up to this point, and why. *Some students will think that Felix is fighting better, since he has knocked Antonio down. Others will think that Antonio is fighting better, since he was able to get up and fight back.*

Comprehension Check ☑

❸ Ask students why hurt fighters might act in this way. *They are probably dazed and unable to think clearly, since a smile is neither an expected nor appropriate expression for a fighter in this situation.*

◆Critical Thinking

❹ **Conclude** Ask students what conclusions they can draw about Antonio and Felix's friendship from the story's ending. *The boys are still close friends and care more about each other than about who won the match.*

---

sucker an opponent within reach of the powerful bombs he carried in each fist.

A right to the head slowed Antonio's pretty dancing. He answered with his own left at Felix's right eye that began puffing up within three seconds.

Antonio, a bit too eager, moved in too close and Felix had him entangled into a rip-roaring, punching toe-to-toe slugfest that brought the whole Tompkins Square Park screaming to its feet.

> **◆ Reading Strategy**
> ❶ What do the fierce fighting efforts of Antonio and Felix tell you about their feelings?

Rights to the body. Lefts to the head. Neither fighter was giving an inch. Suddenly a short right caught Antonio squarely on the chin. His long legs turned to jelly and his arms flailed out desperately. Felix, grunting like a bull, threw wild punches from every direction. Antonio, groggy, bobbed and weaved, evading most of the blows. Suddenly his head cleared. His left flashed out hard and straight catching Felix on the bridge of his nose.

❷ Felix lashed back with a haymaker,[6] right off the ghetto streets. At the same instant, his eye caught another left hook from Antonio. Felix swung out trying to clear the pain. Only the frenzied screaming of those along ringside let him know that he had dropped Antonio. Fighting off the growing haze, Antonio struggled to his feet, got up, ducked, and threw a smashing right that dropped Felix flat on his back.

Felix got up as fast as he could in his own corner, groggy but still game. He didn't even hear the count. In a fog, he heard the roaring of the crowd, who seemed to have gone insane. His head cleared to hear the bell sound at the end of the round. He was very glad. His trainer sat him down on the stool.

❸ In his corner, Antonio was doing what all fighters do when they are hurt. They sit and smile at everyone.

The referee signaled the ring doctor to check the fighters out. He did so and then gave his okay. The cold water sponges brought clarity to both *amigo* brothers. They were rubbed until their circulation ran free.

Bong! Round three—the final round. Up to now it had been tic-tac-toe, pretty much even. But everyone knew there could be no draw and this round would decide the winner.

This time, to Felix's surprise, it was Antonio who came out fast, charging across the ring. Felix braced himself but couldn't ward off the barrage of punches. Antonio drove Felix hard against the ropes.

The crowd ate it up. Thus far the two had fought with *mucho corazón*. Felix tapped his gloves and commenced his attack anew. Antonio, throwing boxer's caution to the winds, jumped in to meet him.

Both pounded away. Neither gave an inch and neither fell to the canvas. Felix's left eye was tightly closed. Claret red blood poured from Antonio's nose. They fought toe-to-toe.

The sounds of their blows were loud in contrast to the silence of a crowd gone completely mute. The referee was stunned by their savagery.

Bong! Bong! Bong! The bell sounded over and over again. Felix and Antonio were past hearing. Their blows continued to pound on each other like hailstones.

Finally the referee and the two trainers pried Felix and Antonio apart. Cold water was poured over them to bring them back to their senses.

They looked around and then rushed toward each other. A cry of alarm surged through Tompkins Square Park. Was this a fight to the death instead of a boxing match?

The fear soon gave way to wave upon wave of cheering as the two *amigos* embraced.

No matter what the decision, they knew they would always be champions to each other. ❹

BONG! BONG! BONG! "Ladies and Gentlemen. *Señores* and *Señoras*. The winner and representative to the Golden Gloves Tournament of Champions is . . ."

The announcer turned to point to the winner and found himself alone. Arm in arm the champions had already left the ring.

> **◆ Build Vocabulary**
> **evading** (ē vād′ iŋ) *adj.*: Keeping away from or avoiding

6. **haymaker:** Punch thrown with full force.

Humanities: Film

Sports Movies The night before the important fight, Felix goes to the movies to see Kirk Douglas in *The Champion*. Movies and television programs about sports are quite common. Students may be surprised to learn that in one movie video guide, there are more than 150 movies listed under the subject heading of Boxing.

Suggest that interested groups of students find resources that would help them locate movies with various sports-related themes. Students may wish to conduct their research at the library with video guides, magazines, or newspapers; at the video store with the help of a clerk or store reference materials; or on the Internet. They may be able to obtain the information from a plot synopsis, from reviews, or from marketing and advertising information.

Students may find that looking for a specific sport will help them narrow their search. For an activity, students may wish to view a movie with a sports theme and answer the following kinds of questions about it:

- Is the sports activity most often the main theme, or a small element, of the plot?
- What can be learned from watching the movie about the rules of the sport and the training required for participation?
- Why do you think there are so many movies made about sports?
- How were you able to determine that the sport would be a part of the movie before watching it? Was it the title, the publicity photos, or the movie synopsis that gave you clues?

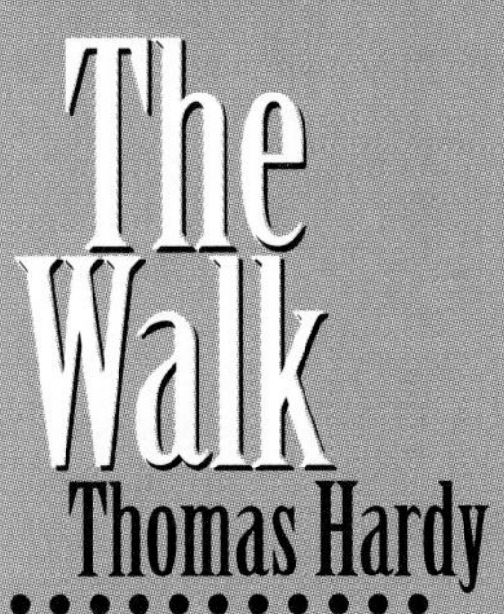

You did not walk with me
Of late to the hilltop tree
By the gated ways,
As in earlier days;
You were weak and lame,
So you never came,
And I went alone, and I did not mind,
Not thinking of you as left behind.

I walked up there today
Just in the former way;
Surveyed[1] around
The familiar ground
By myself again:
What difference, then?
Only that underlying sense
Of the look of a room on returning thence. ❺

1. **surveyed** (sər vād′) *v.*: Looked at in a careful and thorough way.

Guide for Responding

◆ Literature and Your Life

Reader's Response How do you feel when you have to be separated from a friend for a time? Explain.

Thematic Focus Antonio thinks that at the fight, he and Felix should imagine they're strangers. In what other ways might he solve this problem?

Discussion What might have happened had the fight ended differently? With a small group, discuss the connection between "The Walk" and such an ending.

☑ Check Your Comprehension

1. What dream do the boys share?
2. What event creates a wall between them?
3. What agreement do they make while jogging?
4. Describe the way the boys leave the ring at the end of the fight.
5. Why is the speaker of "The Walk" alone?

◆ Critical Thinking

Interpret

1. Why is boxing so important to Antonio and Felix? **[Infer]**
2. Why do the boys decide not to see each other until the fight? **[Interpret]**
3. How does their relationship both help and hurt the boys during the fight? **[Analyze]**
4. What do the boys discover they value as much as or more than winning? **[Draw Conclusions]**
5. Why is the event described in "The Walk" different from the way it used to be? **[Interpret]**
6. How does the speaker of "The Walk" feel about this change? **[Infer]**

Apply

7. What lesson from "Amigo Brothers" could you apply to your own life? Explain. **[Apply]**

Compare Literary Works

8. What advice would the speaker of "The Walk" give to the boys of "Amigo Brothers"? Explain. **[Speculate; Connect]**

Beyond the Selection

FURTHER READING

Other Works by Piri Thomas

Stories From El Barrio
Down These Mean Streets

Other Works by Thomas Hardy

Tess of the D'Urbervilles
Selected Short Stories and Poems (Everyman Paperback Classics)

Other Stories About Friendship and Solving Problems

Baseball in April: And Other Stories, Gary Soto
Athletic Shorts: Six Short Stories, Chris Crutcher

INTERNET

We suggest the following sites on the Internet (all Web sites are subject to change).

For more information about Piri Thomas, visit the following Web site:
http://www. cheverote.com/bio.html

For more information about Thomas Hardy, visit the following Web site:
http://pages.ripco. com:8080/~mws/timeline.html

We *strongly recommend* that you preview these sites before you send students to them.

In "The Walk" Thomas Hardy describes a friendship that endures, even when the friends cannot be together as they once were.

◆ Reading Strategy

❺ **Make Inferences** Ask students why the speaker does not mind that the friend was left behind. *The speaker feels as if the friend is present, since the place visited was filled with memories.*

Reinforce and Extend

Answers

◆ Literature and Your Life

Reader's Response Students should recall a specific situation in which they were separated from a friend and then explain how they felt.

Thematic Focus Accept all reasonable answers.

☑ Check Your Comprehension

1. Both want to be lightweight champion of the world.
2. The friends must fight against each other in the division finals.
3. They agree to fight as if they were strangers and to fight to win.
4. They leave arm in arm as friends before the winner is announced.
5. The speaker's friend is weak and lame and cannot come along.

◆ Critical Thinking

1. Boxing is one way the boys can excel and achieve recognition.
2. To lessen the pressure of the upcoming fight, which was affecting their friendship in a negative way.
3. Possible response: It helps them because they know each other's fighting style. It challenges them because they don't want to physically hurt each other.
4. They value their friendship.
5. One of the friends is no longer able to be there.
6. The speaker accepts it, because the friend is still there in memories.
7. Possible response: Friendship is more important than winning or losing. People should not jeopardize friendships in order to win.
8. Possible response: Enjoy your friendship, and hold on to the memories.

Answers

◆Reading Strategy

1. (a) Justin's relationship with Mel is friendly and seems to be a relationship between equals. (b) Justin is confident and comfortable dealing with adults; he chooses friends with common interests.
2. The speaker is lonely, likes to ride a bicycle, and notices color and beauty in nature.
3. (a) They are proud of their neighborhood and enjoy living there. (b) They want to stay away from street negatives; they want to represent their neighborhood in the boxing championship.
4. They were close friends who used to walk together to the hilltop tree. One is now ill and can no longer make the walk.

◆Build Vocabulary

Using the Prefix *re-*

Possible responses:

1. I need to review the story.
2. I cannot recall the details.
3. I will renew my subscription.
4. Can you recycle this plastic bag?
5. The birds will reappear in the spring.
6. Let's reheat this cold pizza for lunch.

Spelling Strategy

1. repaint; 2. relive; 3. rebuild; 4. renew; 5. react; 6. reenter

Using the Word Bank

1. c; 2. e; 3. f; 4. g; 5 a; 6. h; 7. b; 8. d

◆Literary Focus

1. (a) His mother assumes he is lost in a feeling of satisfaction. (b) He is thinking about how two bikes for twenty-one boys might cause more problems than they would solve.
2. Possible response: If the story of "Amigo Brothers" were told from one boy's view, the story would be more personal to that character. For example, it might minimize the other boy's honesty or athletic talent and maximize the speaker's suffering.

Guide for Responding *(continued)*

◆ Reading Strategy

Make Inferences

When you **make inferences,** you use the information the writers tell you to draw conclusions about details that are left out. This strategy helps you more fully understand the characters in the literature you read.

1. (a) Describe Justin Lebo's relationship with Mel. (b) What inferences about Justin can you make based on this relationship?
2. What can you infer about the speaker of "The Rider"?
3. (a) How do the boys in "Amigo Brothers" feel about their neighborhood? (b) What details help you answer?
4. What do you learn about the relationship between the speaker and the person being addressed in "The Walk"?

◆ Build Vocabulary

Using the Prefix *re-*

The prefix *re-* means "again." Use these words in sentences to demonstrate each word's meaning.

1. review	**3.** renew	**5.** reappear
2. recall	**4.** recycle	**6.** reheat

Spelling Strategy

In most cases, you do not use a hyphen when adding the prefix *re-* to a word: *realign* not *re-align.* On your paper, add *re-* to the following words:

1. paint **2.** live **3.** build **4.** new **5.** act **6.** enter

Using the Word Bank

On your paper, match the word on the left with its definition on the right.

1. realign	**a.** put on top of something
2. yield	**b.** made to disappear
3. coalition	**c.** adjust so the parts work together
4. devastating	**d.** avoiding
5. superimposed	**e.** give way to pressure
6. perpetual	**f.** group formed for a common goal
7. dispelled	**g.** overwhelming; damaging
8. evading	**h.** never stopping

◆ Literary Focus

Third-Person Point of View

When a writer uses the **third-person point of view,** the narrator speaks from outside the events to communicate the thoughts, feelings, and actions of many different characters. Characters are referred to by name or as "he" or "she." This point of view lets writers provide details you'd miss if one of the characters narrated the story. For example, you couldn't know how both boys in "Amigo Brothers" feel if either one of them were telling the story.

1. Justin Lebo is silent as he and his mom drive away from Kilbarchan for the first time. (a) What does his mother think about this silence? (b) What is Justin thinking?
2. In what ways would "Amigo Brothers" be different if Felix or Anthony told the story?

◆ Build Grammar Skills

Coordinating Conjunctions

Coordinating conjunctions —including *and, but, for, nor, or, so,* and *yet*—connect words of a similar kind. They can also connect larger groups of words, such as phrases or even entire sentences. In these examples, the coordinating conjunctions are circled. The words they connect are italicized.

Nouns: Everyone could view the fight, whether from *ringside* (or) *fire escapes* (or) *rooftops.*

Verbs: Mel let him *hang out* (and) *watch.*

Prepositional Phrases: He stored bicycles *in the garage* (and) *on the driveway.*

Practice On your paper, circle the coordinating conjunction in each sentence. Then, underline the words or phrases connected by the conjunction.

1. Which do you prefer, bicycling or roller skating?
2. Odds were against him, but Justin wouldn't quit.
3. The two friends had to fight each other, so they decided to stay apart until the big day.
4. Before and after the fight, they were friends.
5. Justin used old or new parts.

Writing Application Write a paragraph summarizing one of the selections. In it, use and identify three different coordinating conjunctions.

◆Build Grammar Skills

1. bicycling *or* roller skating
2. Odds were against him, *but* Justin wouldn't quit.
3. The two friends had to fight each other, *so* they decided to stay apart until the big day.
4. Before *and* after
5. old *or* new

Writer's Solution

For additional instruction and practice, use the lesson in the *Writer's Solution Language Lab CD-ROM* on coordinating conjunctions. You may also use the conjunction practice page, p. 25, in the *Writer's Solution Grammar Practice Book.*

Build Your Portfolio

Idea Bank

Writing

1. **Journal Entry** Imagine that you're one of the "Amigo Brothers." In a journal entry, describe your thoughts and feelings when you discover that you will fight your best friend.
2. **Citizenship Award** Using Justin Lebo's actions as a model, create the criteria for a student citizenship award. Consider the achievements or personal characteristics a person would need in order to win. **[Social Studies Link]**
3. **Comparison-and-Contrast Essay** Compare and contrast two characters from the selections presented here. For example, you might consider comparing Felix to Justin Lebo. In an essay, identify the character's similarities and differences.

Speaking and Listening

4. **School Interviews** Interview classmates who do something to make a difference or who have displayed a special skill. Learn about their accomplishments, and gather advice for other students. Share your findings with the class.
5. **How-to Fair [Group Activity]** Justin Lebo uses his talents to help his community. The people in "The Rider" help themselves through physical activity. Organize a fair in which students demonstrate their skills. Each presenter should explain how his or her talent could help other members of the community. **[Social Studies Link]**

Projects

6. **Community Participation** The "Amigo Brothers" made use of a Boys Club program. Find out about organizations that offer activities for young people in your area. Describe the programs in a list for the class.
7. **Flowchart** Justin Lebo modeled his small business on the big-business ideas of a very successful man. Research the ideas of Henry Ford, and create a flowchart that outlines his assembly-line process.

Writing Mini-Lesson

Volunteering Handbook

Justin Lebo worked by himself, but your classmates might prefer to join an organization that helps others. To help others choose the group that works best for them, research and write a handbook of volunteer opportunities. Include basic information about each organization.

Writing Skills Focus: Address Your Audience

You are writing for classmates, not Wall Street investors. It is important to **keep your audience in mind** and to choose information that readers can use. Consider these tips:

- Include material to help readers make a wise decision. A group's policies about teen volunteers is more useful than its policies on charitable contributions.
- Use language your audience will understand.
- Avoid overly technical information.

Prewriting Gather organizations from library or other sources and through your guidance counselor. For each organization you find interesting, record the name, address, phone number, volunteer requirements, goals, and projects in process.

Drafting Arrange the entries alphabetically or by topic. List the same information about every entry, in the same order. For each entry, briefly explain the appeal to your audience.

◆ Grammar Application

Combine short, choppy sentences gracefully using coordinating conjunctions.

Revising Read your handbook to make sure that entries contain the necessary facts. Double-check that entries are chosen and written for an audience of young volunteers. If necessary, replace "grown-up" entries like a driving service for older residents with "kid friendly" entries like a park cleanup group.

ASSESSMENT OPTIONS

Formal Assessment, Selection Test, pp. 99–101, and Assessment Resources Software. The selection test is designed so that it can easily be customized to the performance levels of your students.

Alternative Assessment, p. 23, includes options for less-advanced students, more advanced students, musical/rhythmic learners, interpersonal learners, logical/mathematical learners, and verbal/linguistic learners.

PORTFOLIO ASSESSMENT

Use the following rubrics in the **Alternative Assessment** booklet to assess student writing:
Journal Entry: Expression Rubric, p.81
Citizenship Award: Definition/Classification Rubric, p. 86
Comparison-and-Contrast Essay: Comparison/Contrast Rubric, p. 90
Writing Mini-Lesson: Research Report/Paper Rubric, p. 93

Idea Bank

Following are suggestions for matching the Idea Bank topics with your student's performance levels and learning modalities:

Customizing for *Performance Levels*

Less Advanced Students: 1, 4, 6
Average Students: 2, 4, 5, 6, 7
More Advanced Students: 3, 4, 5, 7

Customizing for *Learning Modalities*

Verbal/Linguistic: 1, 2, 3, 4
Interpersonal: 4, 5, 6
Visual/Spatial: 7
Intrapersonal: 1, 2, 3, 7
Bodily/Kinesthetic: 5, 7

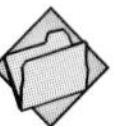

Writing Mini-Lesson

Refer students to the Writing Handbook in the back of the book for instructions on the writing process and for further information on expository writing.

Writer's Solution

Writing Lab CD-ROM

Have students complete the tutorial on Exposition: Giving Information. Follow these steps:

1. Have students use the Topic Web activity to find appropriate subtopics.
2. Suggest that students use the Cluster Diagram activity to choose and organize details.
3. Allow students to draft on computer.
4. Have students use the Proofreading Checklist when revising.

Writer's Solution Sourcebook

Have students use Chapter 4, "Exposition: Giving Information," pp. 102–133, for additional support. This chapter includes in-depth instruction on considering audience and purpose, pp. 120–121.

Prepare and Engage

Establish Writing Guidelines
Review the following key characteristics of a persuasive essay:

- A persuasive essay attempts to get the reader to take action or believe a position on an issue.
- A persuasive essay must include logical information to back up the writer's opinion.

You may want to distribute the scoring rubric for Persuasion, p. 92 in **Alternative Assessment,** to make students aware of the criteria on which they will be evaluated. See the suggestions on p. 364 for how you can customize the rubric to this workshop.

Refer students to the Writing Handbook in the back of the book for instruction on the writing process and further information on persuasion.

Writer's Solution

Writers at Work Videodisc
To introduce students to persuasive writing and to have them see how Joseph Bruchac discovers ideas to persuade his readers, play the videodisc segment on Persuasion (Ch. 6). Have students discuss how Bruchac answers the question *What is persuasive writing?*

Play frames 4 to 9282

Writing Lab CD-ROM
If your students have access to computers, you may want to have them work in the tutorial on Persuasion to complete all or part of their persuasive essays. Follow these steps:

1. Have students view the interactive model of an essay supporting an opinion.
2. Suggest that students use the Topic Wheel activity to spark ideas for topics.
3. Allow students to draft on computer.
4. Have students use the Self-Evaluation Checklist when revising.

Writer's Solution Sourcebook
Students can find additional support, including in-depth instruction on writing supporting sentences, p. 194, in the chapter on Persuasion, pp. 166–199.

Persuasive Writing

Persuasive Essay

Writing Process Workshop

Persuasion is everywhere. Commercials persuade us to buy new products. Billboards persuade us to see new films. Politicians give speeches to persuade voters to elect them to office. In a **persuasive essay,** a writer attempts to persuade an audience to take action or to think a certain way. The following skills, introduced in the Writing Mini-Lessons, will help you write an effective persuasive essay.

Writing Skills Focus

- ▶ **Use language to evaluate**—words that praise or criticize—to convey your opinions precisely. (See p. 341.)
- ▶ **Address your audience.** Make sure your word choices, tone, and style are suitable for the person or people for whom you are writing. (See p. 361.)
- ▶ **Provide facts and examples to support your opinions.**

After reading the essay "Justin Lebo," one writer decided to persuade other young people to do something to make others happy.

Model

Sure, the residents of Montello Manor were born many years before we were, but most of them are lively, funny, and interested in the same things we are. ① They just need someone to be with. ② They love to tell stories, but they need someone who will listen. Many of them have trouble seeing well enough to read, but they love to be read to. They also enjoy walking in the gardens outside and playing cards and board games. You could help them write a letter or tape-record a memory for their family. ③

① Evaluative words like *lively* and *funny* show the writer's positive evaluation of the residents.

② This sentence is an opinion, which the writer supports with examples.

③ The essay's informal tone is appropriate for an audience of teenagers.

Beyond the Classroom

Workplace Skills

Persuasive Writing Tell students that the ability to write a persuasive essay can come into play in many jobs. Different types of commercial writers are hired to write speeches for politicians, to write copy for advertisers, and to write editorials for newspapers or magazines. In addition, people with careers other than as writers may have to write proposals to their managers or supervisors to persuade them to take a course of action.

Have students get together in groups and choose a group career. Then have them think of a situation where persuasive writing might occur. For example, a group might choose sanitation worker as their career. A situation arises because the dump is closing. The persuasive writing might occur when the worker suggests new ways to promote recycling to the community. Suggest that students scan local papers for editorials that may be career related. Then have them share their findings with the class.

Prewriting

Choose a Cause With a partner, discuss actions that you might want to persuade others to take. Consider national and local issues, and choose a topic that's important to you. Then, identify your position. Here are some suggestions to get you started:

Topic Ideas

- Volunteerism
- Endangered species
- Required military service

Make a Plan Organize your ideas by creating an outline, a web, or other type of plan for your essay. Here's an example:

I. Introduction
  A. Montello Manor
  B. Mrs. Campbell
II. The Residents
  A. Need social interaction
  B. Examples of activities
    1. reading
    2. playing games
    3. going for walks
III. The Rewards
  A. Personal satisfaction
  B. Lasting friendships
  C. Experience for future jobs
IV. Conclusion
  A. Statistics about Montello Manor
  B. Quotation by Mrs. Campbell

Drafting

Use Emotion, Reason, or Both As you write your essay, keep in mind the "angle" that will best suit your audience. Here are some different types of appeals you might use:

TYPE OF APPEAL	EXAMPLE
Feelings and Emotions	Imagine being old, lonely, and confined to one place.
Sense of Right and Wrong	Helping others is the right thing to do.
Self-Interest	You can learn a lot from an older person.

DRAFTING/REVISING

APPLYING LANGUAGE SKILLS: Connotations

If you look up a word in a dictionary, you find its denotation. **Denotation** is the exact meaning (or meanings) of a word. However, words also create feelings and associations, called **connotations.** Although some pairs of words mean basically the same thing, some words have positive connotations and others have negative connotations.

Positive	**Negative**
mellow	lazy
joking	mocking
assertive	bossy

Practice From each pair in parentheses, choose the word with the positive connotation.

1. These hats are (cheap, inexpensive).
2. My uncle is (clever, conniving).
3. The music was (calming, boring).
4. My little sister is (active, wild).

Writing Application Pay close attention to the connotations of the words you choose for your persuasive essay.

Writer's Solution Connection Writing Lab

To learn more about distinguishing fact from opinion, see the Prewriting section in the tutorial on Persuasion.

Develop Student Writing

Prewriting

Tell students that they can look at community and national newspapers to get topic ideas. Suggest that they look in the editorial section for examples of persuasive essays.

Customize for
Less Proficient Writers
Some students may benefit from using the Main Idea and Supporting Details Organizer in **Writing and Language Transparencies,** p. 70. Once they have chosen a position on an issue, they can record it in the space marked *Main Idea.* Then they will have to identify three details or facts to support their position. If students cannot come up with supporting details, they may want to change the topic.

Drafting

Remind students that they should include an introduction, body, and conclusion in their essay. The introduction should clearly state the position of the writer. The body develops and supports that position, using facts and details. The conclusion should restate the position clearly and summarize the most important reasons.

Connect to Literature Unit 7, "Nonfiction," includes an example of a persuasive essay: Barbara Jordan's "All Together Now."

Applying Language Skills

Connotations Remind students that one way to come up with alternative words to avoid unwanted connotations is to use a thesaurus, or synonym finder. Many word-processing programs have a thesaurus built in that will suggest replacements for the highlighted word. Tell students to consult a dictionary to find the exact denotation of the suggested synonym.

Answers

1. These hats are *inexpensive.*
2. My uncle is *clever.*
3. The music was *calming.*
4. My little sister is *active.*

Revising

Have students work with peer reviewers to consider whether the issue is appropriate; whether there is enough evidence; and whether the essay is well organized.

 ***Writer's Solution***

Writing Lab CD-ROM

Have students use the Self-Evaluation Checklist, in the tutorial on Persuasion for revision checklist items.

Publishing

Suggest that students create a class anthology of their persuasive essays. Or, have students match essays about the opposing sides of the same issue.

Reinforce and Extend

Review the Writing Guidelines

After students have completed their papers, review the characteristics of a persuasive essay.

Applying Language Skills

Frequently Confused Words

Discuss other examples of commonly confused words, such as *amount,* which refers to a mass or unit; *number,* which refers to individual items being counted; *beside,* which means "close to" and *besides,* which means "in addition to."

Answers

1. May I bring flowers when I visit?
2. Bill accepted my birthday card.
3. Let's keep this secret among the three of us.

 ***Writer's Solution***

For additional support, suggest that students use the practice page on Fifteen Common Usage Problems, p. 83, in the *Writer's Solution Grammar Practice Book.*

EDITING/PROOFREADING

APPLYING LANGUAGE SKILLS: Frequently Confused Words

Some words are frequently confused with other words that sound similar or are related in meaning. Here are some examples:

Accept is a verb that means *to receive* or *to agree to.*
Except is a preposition that means *other than* or *leaving out.*

Among is used with three or more items.
Between is used with only two items.

Can refers to the ability to do something.
May refers to having permission to do something.

Practice Correct the commonly confused words in these sentences.

1. Can I bring flowers when I visit?
2. Bill excepted my birthday card.
3. Let's keep this secret between the three of us.

Writing Application As you write your persuasive essay, be careful to use the correct word.

Writer's Solution Connection
Language Lab

For more help with revision, use the Revision Checkers in the tutorial on Persuasion.

Appeal to Your Audience Use words that your audience will know. If you're writing for teenagers, your language should be informal and fun. If you're writing to a government official, your language should be formal and serious.

Present One Opinion; Many Facts The point you are trying to make is your opinion. It's the only opinion that should appear in your essay. The rest of your essay should contain facts: details, statistics, evidence, or descriptions. Facts will make your case strong and persuade your audience.

Revising

Use a Checklist Use a checklist to help you determine places that need revision. Your checklist might include these questions:

- Are the words I use appropriate for my audience?
- Would I be convinced by this essay?
- Are my opinions supported by facts, statistics, and examples?

REVISION MODEL

It is important that we take measures to ~~conserve the remaining habitats of these endangered species~~ ① protect the places where these nearly extinct birds live. This can help preserve these ~~interesting~~ ② fascinating and unusual birds for future generations.

① The writer simplified this phrase so it was better suited for the intended audience.
② Stronger language of evaluation reveals how the writer feels.

Publishing and Presenting

- **Give a Speech** Like written essays, persuasive speeches are delivered to motivate the audience to take up an action or change their opinions. Deliver your essay as a speech. Use gestures, tone, and volume to make your point dramatic and clear.
- **Spread the Word** Most newspapers will publish well-written persuasive essays if they appeal to the newspaper's audience. Submit your essay to a school, local, or big-city newspaper, and see what happens.

✓ ASSESSMENT

PORTFOLIO ASSESSMENT
Use the rubric on Persuasion in the **Alternative Assessment** booklet, p. 92, to assess the students' writing. Add these criteria to customize this rubric to this assignment.

	4	3	2	1
Main Idea and Supporting Details	The essay includes a clearly stated main idea and several developed supporting details.	The essay includes a clearly stated main idea and supporting details, but the details need development.	The essay includes a main idea and only one supporting detail.	The essay's main idea is unclear and is not supported.
Connotations	The essay uses words with appropriate connotations.	Most of the words in the essay have appropriate connotations.	Some of the words in the essay have misleading connotations.	Many of the words in the essay have inappropriate connotations, making the essay seem conflicting.

Real-World Reading Skills Workshop

Recognizing Charged Words

Strategies for Success

Language can be very powerful. Some words are meant to strike the reader or listener as funny, inspirational, or hurtful. Certain words, chosen for their power, can cause strong reactions. Recognizing when such *charged words* are being used helps you better understand why they are being used.

Be on the Lookout Charged words are often used as attention-getters. This is especially true in advertising. Words or phrases like *big savings, going fast,* and *act now* are used to grab your attention. It's important to be able to tell the difference between words that are just trying to hook your interest and those that give important information.

Distinguish Between Fact and Opinion A fact is a statement that can be proved: *The mayor raised taxes.* However, when a charged word is added, a basic fact becomes an opinion—something that reveals beliefs or attitudes and that cannot be proved. *The mayor sneakily raised taxes.* In this revised sentence, the word *sneakily* shows that the writer has an opinion about the mayor's action.

Don't Be Tricked by Stereotypes Charged words are often used to label an entire group of individuals. In these cases, the charged words create stereotypes and prevent the reader or listener from getting a true picture. Charged words can be hurtful when they are used unfairly to label people.

Apply the Strategies

Read the poster below. Then, answer the questions that follow.

The public pool should be closed at night. Rowdy teenagers cannot be trusted to swim safely. They make too much noise and never follow rules. Join smart people who want to stop nighttime swimming.

1. Identify the charged words used on the poster.
2. Why do you think these charged words are being used?
3. How much of what is on the poster do you think is fact? How much is opinion?
4. Rewrite the poster without using charged words.

Here are some other places where charged words may show up:
- Newspaper editorials
- Political advertisements
- Letters to the editor of a newspaper or magazine

Introduce the Strategies

Provide students with magazines or newspapers. Suggest that students flip through and look for advertisements that use charged words. Then, discuss the different techniques used in an advertisement and ways students can use their critical thinking skills to analyze the ad.

Customize for
More Advanced Learners
Encourage students to find examples of charged words in newspaper editorials or other forms of persuasive writing. Have them write a brief analysis of the piece, highlighting instances of charged words or stereotypes. Have them discuss whether these words or phrases add to or take away from the persuasive element of the piece.

Apply the Strategies

Tell students that when looking for charged words, they should read every sentence carefully. Remind them that when reading persuasive writing, they should look for concrete facts or details to support the position.

Answers

Possible responses:

1. Charged words include *rowdy, never,* and *smart.*
2. The charged words are being used to create a negative image of the group of people the poster is trying to keep out.
3. There are no facts on the poster. Most of the poster is opinions, based on stereotypes about teenagers.
4. The public pool should be closed at night. There are no lifeguards on duty to protect children from serious injury. In addition, residents in nearby homes may be bothered by excess noise. Join us in trying to keep our children safe and our neighborhood quiet.

◆Build Grammar Skills

Reviewing Interjections and Conjunctions
The selections in Part 2 include instruction on the following:

- Interjections
- Coordinating Conjunctions

This instruction is reinforced with the Build Grammar Skills practice pages in **Selection Support,** pp. 120 and 125.

As you review interjections and conjunctions you may wish to review the following:

- Correlative Conjunctions
Correlative conjunctions are matched pairs of conjunctions that connect similar kinds of words or groups of words. Examples of correlative conjunctions include *both...and, either . . . or, neither . . . nor, not only . . . but also,* and *whether . . . or.*
- Subordinating Conjunctions
Subordinating conjunctions connect two complete ideas by making one of the ideas subordinate to or less important than the other. For more instruction and practice on subordinating conjunctions, see pp. 520 and 540.

Customize for
Less Proficient Readers
Remind students that to understand interjections, it helps to think of them as part of a dialogue. When reading sentences with interjections, suggest that students read the sentences aloud, imagining what kind of emotion a character engaging in this dialogue would be trying to convey.

Writer's Solution

For additional practice and support with interjections and conjunctions, use the practice pages on Interjections and Conjunctions, pp. 25–26 in the *Writer's Solution Grammar Practice Book.*

Interjections and Conjunctions

Grammar Review

different forms of a verb
con·junc·tion (kən juŋk′shən) *n.* 1 a joining together; combination [*High winds, in conjunction with rain, made travel difficult.*] 2 a word used to join other words, phrases, or clauses [*"And," "but," "or," and "if" are conjunctions.*]
con·jure (kän′jər) *v.* to practice magic or

An **interjection** is a word or phrase that expresses emotion and has no grammatical relation to the rest of the words in a sentence. (See page 340.) Use an exclamation point after an interjection that expresses strong feeling; use a comma after one that expresses mild emotion.

Emotion	Strength of Emotion	Example
Agreement	Mild	*Yes,* I would like to go with you.
Excitement	Strong	*Wow!* Look at all this stuff.
Alarm	Mild	*Uh, oh,* I think those boxes are falling.
Urgency	Strong	*Hey!* Watch out!
Concern	Strong	*Goodness!* Are you okay?
Relief	Strong	*Whew!* I'm glad we didn't break anything.

A **conjunction** is a word that links two or more words or groups of words. **Coordinating conjunctions**—including *and, but, for, nor, or, so,* and *yet*—connect words of a similar kind. They can also connect phrases, clauses, or entire sentences. (See page 360.)

Practice 1 Copy these sentences. Circle each interjection. Underline each conjunction, and identify the words, phrases, or clauses each connects.

1. Holmes is both clever and a good actor.
2. He pretended to be dying so the murderer would confess.
3. Well, I was amazed and inspired by Justin, but I had to wonder what his friends thought about his bike project.
4. After fighting their boxing match, Felix and Anthony remained good friends.
5. No, I don't think the speaker in "The Walk" will change his habits or visit his friend.

Practice 2 Rewrite each of the following pairs of sentences as a single sentence, following the directions given in parentheses.

1. Ellen loves mysteries. She reads them often. (*Add a coordinating conjunction.*)
2. Holmes wanted to trap a killer. Holmes wanted to avoid hurting Watson. (*Add a coordinating conjunction.*)
3. Are you listening to me? Are you ignoring me? (*Add an interjection and a coordinating conjunction.*)

Grammar in Writing

✔ ***Even when writing dialogue, avoid overusing interjections. Using them too often lessens their dramatic impact and can be annoying.***

Answers
Practice 1

1. Holmes is both clever and a good actor.
2. He pretended to be dying so the murderer would confess.
3. Well, I was amazed and inspired by Justin, but I had to wonder what his friends thought about his bike project. (circle *Well*)
4. After fighting their boxing match, Felix and Anthony remained good friends.
5. No, I don't think the speaker in "The Walk" will change his habits or visit his friend. (circle *No*)

Practice 2
Possible responses:

1. Ellen loves mysteries *so* she reads them often.
2. Holmes wanted to trap a killer *but* he wanted to avoid hurting Watson.
3. *Hey!* Are you listening to me *or* are you ignoring me?

Speaking, Listening, and Viewing Workshop

Handling a Confrontational Situation

Disagreement can be healthy. If everyone always agreed, we'd never have new ideas. When a disagreement turns to confrontation, however, it's time to think carefully about how you listen and speak. Try to take the anger out of the situation.

Listen Actively Sometimes we think we know what someone is going to say. We hear a few words, stop listening, and begin planning what we're going to say next. Break this dangerous habit. Instead, make sure you understand what someone really means before you respond. Ask questions to get him or her to explain. Ask for examples, if that will help.

This is the first step in handling a potential confrontation—trying to avoid it in the first place. People like to be heard. Even when you disagree, if you give the speaker respect in listening, you can have a healthy disagreement, not a confrontation.

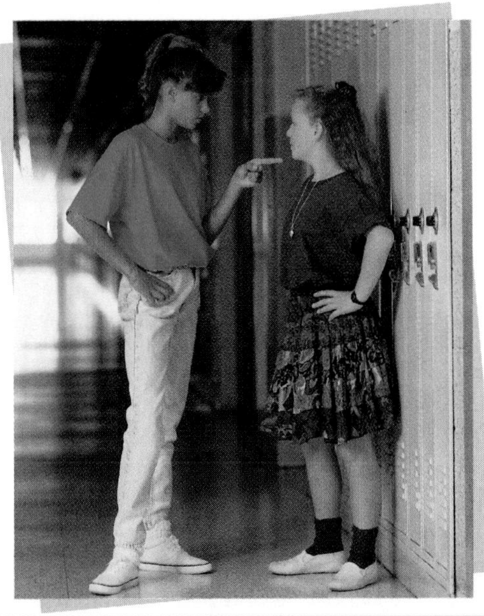

Use "I" When you speak or respond, say things you can be certain of: what *you* think and feel. In other words, don't say, "You're wrong!" but say, "I still don't understand why that's important to you," or even, "I can't agree." Name-calling and blaming just make people emotional. The real point gets lost.

Seek Common Ground Find ways to be on the same side. If a conflict arises out of an athletic competition, for example, remember that both sides love the game. Make sure to tell the other person whenever you agree with something he or she is saying.

Apply the Strategies

As a group, share stories of confrontations you have witnessed—in real life, in books, or in movies. Choose three of those confrontations to evaluate. Discuss the following:

1. What was the disagreement?
2. Why did the disagreement escalate into a confrontation?
3. How was the confrontation resolved?
4. What should or could have been done differently?

Tips for Handling a Confrontational Situation

If you want to keep your cool during a tense situation, use these strategies:

- The best response to an insult can be a shrug. It helps defuse the situation and shows your strength or confidence.
- If you feel yourself getting angry, take a deep breath and be still for a few seconds.
- If all else fails, walk away. You can return to express your feelings when you are calmer.

Introduce the Strategies

Encourage students to think of different situations where they have witnessed or been a part of a confrontation. Explain that a confrontation differs from a disagreement in that *confront* means "to face, especially in hostility or defiance." Confrontations are more hostile than disagreements.

Apply the Strategies

Explain to students that they should try to keep a hold on the anger that they feel when a disagreement begins. If they feel that they are getting angry, encourage them to back down and take a few moments to relax and try to think differently about the situation. Tell students to try to see the issue from the other person's point of view. In addition, to make sure students are not being vocally aggressive, they should imagine how they would react if the words they say to someone else were said to them.

Cross-Curricular Connection: Social Studies

Law Explain to students that when confrontational situations occur that cannot be resolved, we rely on the law to protect and govern us. The law, by definition, means all the rules applied in the courts and enforced by the power of the state. Laws have existed in cultures since the Sumerians invented Hammurabi's Code. While early law concentrated on maintaining civil order, preventing violent crimes, protecting property, and enforcing moral standards, the modern law extends to many areas of human conduct.

Explain to students that there are different types of lawyers to conduct lawsuits for clients or advise them in legal matters. A corporate lawyer works for a corporation and tries to ensure the legality of commercial transactions. The corporate lawyers for two sides work together to try to negotiate the best terms for both parties. Trial lawyers have clients who are undergoing trial for either civil or criminal cases. Their job is to present facts and evidence that persuade the jury to believe their client. An attorney serves as legal counsel to clients in all matters pertaining to the law. Other professions dealing with the law include private investigators, judges, police officers, and paralegals. Suggest that students do some preliminary research on a law-related career that interests them. Or, have them watch a law-related television program or movie and analyze the job the lawyer does in terms of handling confrontations. Encourage students to share their findings with the class.

◆Build Vocabulary

What's Behind the Words Explain that a metaphor is a type of figurative language, which makes writing more imaginative. Used in the right way, metaphors can make writing more powerful, more exciting, and more striking. Most commonly, metaphors are used in descriptive writing.

Customize for
English Language Learners
Some students may not be familiar with baseball terminology. Encourage students with a knowledge of the sport to provide explanations for the phrases used in these paragraphs, such as *go to bat, touch base, way off base, first base, screwball, out in left field, hardball,* and *two strikes*.

Customize for
Bodily/Kinesthetic Learners
Students interested in movement and those knowledgeable in sports can work together to make these metaphors come to life. Review the sports metaphors on this page and ask for volunteers to explain what they mean. Then encourage other students to act out the action, to show it to the rest of the class.

Answers
Activity 1
1. boxing
2. pool or billiards
3. darts
4. tennis
5. golf
6. bullfighting

What's Behind the Words

Vocabulary Adventures With Richard Lederer

The Sports Origins of Common Phrases

A teacher once asked a student, "What's a metaphor?" The student answered, "For cows to eat grass in." Well . . . actually, a metaphor (met-uh-for) is a figure of speech that compares one thing to another, blending ideas in creative ways. Did you know that you speak in metaphors every day?

The metaphors that are common in a culture tell us a lot. With many of the expressions we use every day, we honor the prominent place of sports in our society.

Take Me Out to the Ballgame

In the early days of the twentieth century, a college professor explained, "To understand America, you must first understand baseball." Baseball is not only America's pastime but the most popular athletic metaphor in the American language. Right off the bat, we bat around a few ideas and then go to bat for someone. If we don't touch base with others, we may find ourselves way off base or not able to get to first base.

Please don't think me a screwball who's out in left field with two strikes against me. I'm playing vocabulary hardball here, and I call 'em as I see 'em. And what I see are ballpark figures (of speech) like *in there pitching, bush league operation, major league performance, play the field, a smash hit, safe by a mile, take a rain check, hit and run,* and *pinch-hit for somebody.*

Sportspeak

Here are the origins of some sporty words and expressions that have moved into our general vocabulary:

To hold the line comes from the game of football, while *up for grabs* derives from the jump ball in basketball.

A *kingpin* is the number-one pin in bowling, the one that stands in front of all the others. Hit correctly, it causes all the other pins to fall. That's why we also use the word *kingpin* to refer to the most critical person—the leader or the chief—in a business or project.

No holds barred, meaning "without restriction," originates from wrestling matches, in which no holds were disallowed, producing a wild, unstructured contest.

When we say *this is where I draw the line,* we lay down a definite limit. The phrase started in tennis. When the sport was first introduced in the fourteenth century, there were no exact dimensions for the court, so players drew lines and agreed that the ball couldn't be hit beyond those lines.

ACTIVITY 1 Identify the sport from which each of these phrases comes.

1. saved by the bell
2. behind the eight ball
3. hit the bullseye
4. the ball's in your court
5. below par
6. take the bull by the horns

Extended Reading Opportunities

Trouble—and someone's response to it—can reveal a person's character, culture, and creativity. Explore the imaginative ways that the characters in these novels solve their troubles.

Suggested Titles

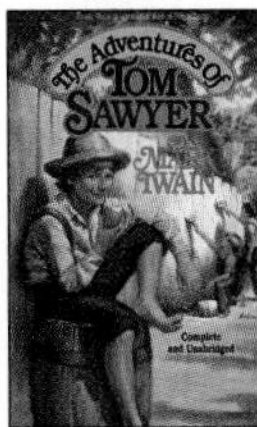

The Adventures of Tom Sawyer
Mark Twain

In this classic tale of a boyhood in nineteenth-century Mississippi, you'll follow Tom Sawyer as he plays pranks and gets caught up in one adventure after another. Tom is full of energy and a natural leader among his friends. His life seems charmed, until he witnesses a murder one night. Knowing his life is in danger, he runs away from home. Yet Tom's luck holds as he plays pirate on a deserted island, attends his own funeral, and even steals the murderer's treasure.

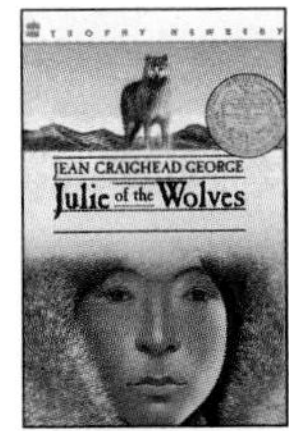

Julie of the Wolves
Jean Craighead George

At the age of thirteen, Julie leaves her home village in Alaska to travel on her own to San Francisco. When she gets lost in the wilderness, she has to rely on wolves—animals she has befriended—to help her survive. In one scene, all the wolves join together to fight a bear. While hiking through the cold landscape, Julie must decide what truly matters to her. This thrilling adventure story of her struggle will have you on the edge of your seat!

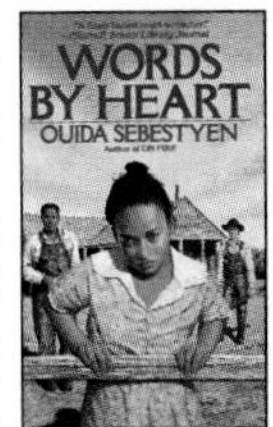

Words by Heart
Ouida Sebestyen

In this moving novel of a twelve-year-old girl's struggle with racism, you'll see how conflict can challenge personal actions and beliefs. Lena wants to win a contest at school, but when she does, someone plunges a butcher knife into the family's kitchen table. Suddenly, Lena wonders if she has overstepped the bounds set for her as the only African American girl in a small town. The knife's implied threat is only the beginning, and Lena must solve the problem of how to confront her enemy—with vengeance or forgiveness.

Other Possibilities

The Kid's Guide to Service Projects	Barbara A. Lewis
What I Had Was Singing: The Story of Marian Anderson	Jeri Ferris
One Proud Summer	Marsha Hewitt and Claire McKay
Profiles in Courage	John F. Kennedy

Planning Students' Extended Reading
All of the works listed on this page are good choices for extending the theme "Resolving Conflicts." The following information may help you choose which to teach.

Customize for
Varying Student Needs
When assigning the selections in this part to your students, keep in mind the following factors:

- *The Adventures of Tom Sawyer* is a classic novel about a young boy's life on the Mississippi River. It introduces students to the humor of Mark Twain. In addition, it can offer an opportunity for cross-curricular study in the areas of early twentieth-century America, Mississippi, and slavery.
- *Julie of the Wolves* is an award-winning novel about an Eskimo girl who learns to appreciate her heritage. However, it does have some sensitive issues, listed below.
- *Words by Heart* is a novel about the struggle of being an outsider in a small town. It has some sensitive issues, listed below.

Sensitive Issues In *Julie of the Wolves,* the main character is involved in an arranged marriage and adult relationship. However, this story may open up opportunities for discussions on cultural differences.

Words by Heart deals with the violent results of racism, including death. However, it may offer opportunities to discuss racism and racial conflict.

Literature Study Guides
Literature study guides are available for *The Adventures of Tom Sawyer, Julie of the Wolves,* and *Words by Heart.* The guides include section summaries, discussion questions, and activities.

Planning Instruction and Assessment

Unit Objectives

1. To read selections in different genres that develop the theme of "Just for Fun"
2. To apply a variety of reading strategies, particularly strategies for reading critically, appropriate for reading these selections
3. To recognize literary elements used in these selections
4. To increase vocabulary
5. To learn elements of grammar and usage
6. To write in a variety of modes about situations based on the selections
7. To develop speaking and listening skills, by completing activities
8. To view images critically and create visual representations

Meeting the Objectives Each selection provides instructional material and portfolio opportunities by which students can meet unit objectives. You will find additional practice pages for reading strategies, literary elements, vocabulary, and grammar in the **Selection Support** booklet in the **Teaching Resources** box.

Setting Goals Work with your students at the beginning of the unit to set goals for unit outcomes. Plan what skills and concepts you wish students to acquire. You may match instruction and activities according to students' performance levels or learning modalities.

Portfolios Students may keep portfolios of their completed work or of their work in progress. The Build Your Portfolio page of each selection provides opportunities for students to apply the concepts presented.

Humanities: Art

Snap the Whip, by Winslow Homer

Winslow Homer (1836–1910), a nineteenth-century American painter, began his career as a magazine illustrator in Boston. His earliest paintings focused on simple country life. Later, his paintings focused on the sea, forest, and mountains.

1. Do the children look like they are having fun as they play Snap the Whip? *Students may say the game seems like fun, although snapping off the end might hurt.*

Snap the Whip, Winslow Homer, Butler Institute of American Art, Youngstown, Ohio

Art Transparencies

The **Art Transparencies** booklet in the **Teaching Resources** box offers fine art to help students make connections to other curriculum areas and high-interest topics.

The art transparency of Winslow Homer's *Snap the Whip,* Art Transparency 12, p. 51, will help students connect to the theme of "Just for Fun." Homer's appreciation of a lively game inspired him to portray some fun. Use one of the booklet's activities to help students explore the art through discussion of the painting, a writing activity, or by playing their own game.

Beyond Literature

Each unit presents Beyond Literature features that lead students into an exploration of careers, communities, and other subject areas. In this unit, students will read and learn about wild and domestic cats, and make technology and media connections. In addition, the **Teaching Resources** box contains a **Beyond Literature** booklet of activities. Using literature as a springboard, these activity pages offer students opportunities to connect literature to other curriculum areas and to the workplace and careers, community, media, and humanities.

UNIT 5

Just for Fun

Words have the power to spark emotion—fear, sadness, surprise—even anger. In this unit, you'll find literature to make you laugh. You'll meet an unusual cat, a stubborn child, and a curious shopkeeper. The behavior of each of these quirky characters produces amusing results. Read on to see how the most common activities can be funny when they are seen through the eyes of a writer with a sense of humor.

Connections

Within this unit, you will find selections and activities that make connections beyond literature. Use these selections to connect students' understanding and appreciation of literature beyond the traditional literature and language arts curriculum.

Encourage students to connect literature to other curriculum areas. You may wish to coordinate with teachers in other curriculum areas to determine ways to team teach and further extend instruction.

Connections to Today's World

Use these selections to guide students to recognize the relevance of literature to contemporary writings. In this unit, students can use the popular cartoon character, Garfield, to connect to one of James Herriot's veterinary patients.

Connecting Literature to Social Studies

Each unit contains a selection that connects Literature to Social Studies. In this unit, students will read a Yiddish folk tale.

Assessing Student Progress

The tools that are available to measure the degree to which students meet the unit objectives are listed below.

Informal Assessment

The questions in the Guide for Responding sections are a first level of response to the concepts and skills presented with the selection. As a brief, informal measure of students' grasp of the material, these responses indicate where further instruction and practice are needed. The practice pages in the **Selection Support** booklet provide for this type of instruction and practice.

You will also find literature and reading guides in the **Alternative Assessment** booklet, which students can use for informal assessment of their individual performances.

Formal Assessment

The **Formal Assessment** booklet contains Selection Tests and Unit Tests.

Selection Tests measure comprehension and skills acquisition for each selection or group of selections.

Each Unit Test provides students with 30 multiple-choice questions and 5 essay questions designed to assess students' knowledge of the literature and skills taught in the unit.

Each Alternative Unit Test: Standardized-Test Practice provides 15 multiple-choice questions and 3 essay questions based on two new literature selections not contained in the student book. The questions on the Alternative Unit Test are designed to assess students' ability to compare and contrast selections, applying skills taught in the unit.

Alternative Assessment

For portfolio and alternative assessment, the **Alternative Assessment** booklet contains Scoring Rubrics, Assessment sheets, and Learning Modalities activities.

Scoring Rubrics provide writing modes that can be applied to Writing activities, Writing Mini-Lessons, and Writing Process Workshop lessons.

Assessment sheets for speaking and listening activities provide peer and self-assessment direction.

Learning Modalities activities appeal to different learning styles. Use these as an alternative measurement of students' growth.

OBJECTIVES

1. To read, comprehend, and interpret an essay
2. To relate an essay to personal experience
3. To apply critical reading strategies
4. To analyze the use of humor
5. To build vocabulary in context and use the suffix *-ment*
6. To distinguish between subjects and predicates
7. To write a news report that answers *What? Who? Where? When?* and *Why?*
8. To respond to the essay through writing, speaking and listening, and projects

SKILLS INSTRUCTION

Vocabulary:
Suffixes: *-ment*

Spelling:
Words With Double *r*

Grammar:
Subjects and Predicates

Reading for Success:
Strategies for Reading Critically

Literary Focus:
Humor

Writing:
The 5 W's

Speaking and Listening:
Humorous Anecdote (Teacher Edition)

PORTFOLIO OPPORTUNITIES

Writing: Statement of Apology; Comparison-and-Contrast Essay; Career Advice

Writing Mini-Lesson: Report for a Newscast

Speaking and Listening: Interpreter's Explanation; Humorous Anecdote

Projects: News Show; Report on the News

More About the Author
Charles Osgood is known as the "poet in residence" at CBS Radio. His writing and broadcasting skills have earned him many awards. In 1990, he was inducted into the National Association of Broadcasters Hall of Fame. A native New Yorker, Osgood lives with his wife and children in New Jersey. In his spare time, he enjoys playing the piano and the five-string banjo.

Guide for Reading

Meet the Author:
Charles Osgood (1933–)

As a reporter, Charles Osgood has covered such serious topics as politics, the economy, and war. However, lighter subjects and everyday experiences interest him most. In addition to the formal news pieces he writes for radio and television, his special broadcasts—called *Newsbreak* and *The Osgood File*—highlight his unique, humorous slant on life. Osgood may be best known for his rhyming commentaries that poke fun at current events. For example, he once wrote in rhyme, "We've all really had it with trouble and woe. And if those things exist, why, we don't want to know."

Man of the Media Born before television came into people's homes, Osgood grew up loving radio. He eventually got a job announcing the Army Band during his years in the service. From professional radio work, Osgood moved into television, becoming the anchor on the *CBS Evening News* in 1972. When Charles Kuralt retired as anchor of the CBS news program *Sunday Morning* in 1994, Osgood's style earned him the job as the new anchor.

The Story Behind the Essay

Osgood usually covers news stories—describing the *who, what, where, when, how,* and *why* of events. In "Our Finest Hour," he turns the reporter's lens on himself to describe a chaotic newscast he once anchored.

◆ Literature and Your Life

Connect Your Experience

At one time or another, you've probably had a carefully planned event turn into a disaster. Just imagine what it would be like to have such an experience on live television in front of millions of viewers. This is the type of situation that Osgood describes in his essay about a newscast that went terribly wrong.

Thematic Focus: Just For Fun

This essay shows you that you can have fun even when a simple plan goes completely wrong.

◆ Background for Understanding

Media

The people who report the news may seem relaxed, but because their work is broadcast live, they are actually under a great deal of pressure. The newsroom buzzes with activity until the broadcast is over. When a story changes, copy is written and rewritten until the moment it is read. Teleprompters roll scripts as the anchors read. Pre-recorded stories are cued, waiting for precisely the right moment before the tapes roll. Earphones allow directors and producers to communicate with the anchors even during the broadcast. Since this all happens live, anchors must handle any mistakes—mispronunciations, incorrect graphics, technical difficulties with live interviews, or even more unexpected disasters—as they occur.

Prentice Hall Literature Program Resources

REINFORCE / RETEACH / EXTEND

Selection Support Pages
Build Vocabulary: Suffixes: *-ment,* p. 128
Build Spelling Skills, p. 129
Build Grammar Skills: Subjects and Predicates, p. 130
Reading for Success: Strategies for Reading Critically, pp. 131–132
Literary Focus: Humor, p. 133

Strategies for Diverse Student Needs, pp. 47–48

Beyond Literature Career Connection: Journalist, p. 24

Formal Assessment Selection Test, p. 110–112, Assessment Resources Software

Alternative Assessment, p. 24

Writing and Language Transparencies
Series of Events Chain, p. 66

Resource Pro CD-ROM
"Our Finest Hour"—includes all resource material and customizable lesson plan

Listening to Literature Audiocassettes
"Our Finest Hour"

◆ Our Finest Hour ◆

◆ Literary Focus

HUMOR

Humor is writing that is meant to evoke laughter. One of the best ways to create humor is to describe real-life bloopers and blunders. In this essay, for example, Charles Osgood recounts a disastrous live newscast in which just about everything goes wrong. While the situation he describes is clearly funny to readers, Osgood takes a subtle approach. He never admits that the events he endured were humorous. Indeed, he probably did not find them humorous until later.

◆ Build Vocabulary

SUFFIXES: *-ment*

Charles Osgood admits his bewilderment in the face of disaster. The word *bewilderment* contains the suffix *-ment*, meaning "the condition of." When combined with *bewilder*, meaning "to confuse or perplex," the suffix *-ment* produces the word *bewilderment*, meaning "the condition of confusion."

WORD BANK

Which of these words from the essay names a person who contributes stories to the news?

correspondent
bewilderment

Preparing for Standardized Tests

Grammar Explain to students that the subject and predicate are the two basic parts of the sentence. The subject names who or what the sentence is about, and the predicate includes the verb or verb phrase that tells what the subject does, what is done to the subject, or what the condition of the subject is. Some portions of standardized tests may have questions about identifying subjects and predicates.

Write the following sample test question on the board:

Nobody in there knew anything about this piece either.

The *simple subject* and *simple predicate* of this sentence are:

(A) there, knew
(B) nobody, either
(C) anything, knew
(D) nobody, knew

Guide students to see that *(D)* is the correct answer. *Nobody* answers the question *who?* and *knew* is the action of the subject.

Spark students' interest in Osgood's essay by having a class discussion in which students share examples of movies and television programs in which humor arises from a series of blunders. If appropriate, you might even encourage groups of students to act out especially humorous scenes from the movies or programs being discussed. Following the discussion, explain that the piece they're about to read focuses on a series of blunders that take place during a live television broadcast. As they read, have them consider whether the blunders would have been amusing to viewers at the time of the broadcast.

◆ Build Grammar Skills

Subjects and Predicates If you wish to introduce the grammar concept before students read, refer to the instruction on p. 377.

Customize for
Less Proficient Readers
Have students work in small groups to track the events described in the essay. Display the Series of Events Chain, p. 66, in **Writing and Language Transparencies.** Point out the labels on the organizer. Then direct students to jot down incidents in the order they are described by the author. Explain that the boxes can be subdivided with horizontal rules if there are more events than boxes.

Customize for
More Advanced Students
Explain to students that the essay they are about to read contains examples of informal English and is written in a conversational style. Have students pick out words and phrases that illustrate this informal style. Then suggest that students rewrite a portion of the essay in a formal style. When they have finished, have them compare the two styles and suggest the strengths/weaknesses of each one. Ask students to decide which style they think works better for this story.

Reading for Success

The Reading for Success page in each unit presents a set of problem-solving strategies to help readers understand authors' words and ideas on multiple levels. Good readers develop a bank of strategies from which they can draw as needed.

Unit 5 introduces strategies for reading critically. These strategies offer students an approach to applying higher-level critical thinking skills. They help readers analyze what they read on a level beyond literal comprehension, through understanding the author's bias, recognizing the author's purpose, evaluating the author's message, and distinguishing fact from opinion.

The strategies for reading critically are modeled with this essay. Each green box shows an example of the thinking process involved in applying one of the strategies.

How to Use the Reading for Success Page

- Introduce the strategies for reading critically, presenting each as a problem-solving procedure.
- Before students read the essay, have them preview it, looking at the annotations in the green boxes that model the strategies.
- To reinforce these strategies after students have read the essay, have them complete Reading for Success, pp. 131–132, in **Selection Support.** These pages give students an opportunity to read a selection and practice strategies for reading critically by writing their own annotations.

Reading Strategies: Support and Reinforcement

Using Boxed Annotations and Prompts

Throughout the unit, the notes in green, red, and maroon boxes are intended to help students apply reading strategies, understand the literary focus, and make a connection with their lives. You may use boxed material in these ways:

- Have students pause at each box and respond to its prompt before they continue reading.
- Urge students to read through the selection, ignoring the boxes. After they complete the selection, they may go back and review the text, responding to the prompts.

Reading for Success

Strategies for Reading Critically

Some people think that being critical is the same as being negative. However, being a critical reader doesn't mean that you necessarily respond negatively to what you read. It means that you take the time to analyze carefully what you read and to consider how effectively an author has put together a piece of writing.

Understand the author's bias.

▶ Recognize that writers often present an issue through their own bias—their unique perspective on a subject. Look for details that might reveal a writer's opinion. Use what you know about the writer's background and knowledge. For example, each of the people shown in the chart below might describe a disastrous newscast differently.

A writer's bias influences the details he or she presents. Keep this in mind as you read—you might be getting only half the story.

Recognize the author's purpose.

▶ Authors generally write to achieve a purpose, such as the following:
• to entertain • to inform • to call to action • to reflect on experiences
Notice the author's choice of words and the details he or she includes. These clues will help you determine an author's purpose.

Evaluate the author's message.

▶ When you evaluate an author's message, you make a judgment about how effectively the writer has proved his or her point. First, identify the writer's message. Then, look to see whether this message has been supported. Also, consider whether the writer is qualified to write on a subject.

Distinguish fact from opinion.

▶ It's important to distinguish facts from opinions.
Fact: A statement that can be proved true by consulting a reliable source.
Opinion: A belief that is based on a writer's attitude or values.
Writers should back up their opinions with facts, not simply cite a series of opinions without any support.

As you read this essay by Charles Osgood, look at the notes along the sides. The notes demonstrate how to apply these strategies to a work of literature.

Model a Reading Strategy: Understand the Author's Bias

Critical readers know that writers often have a personal bias through which their ideas are filtered. In order to demonstrate how to understand Osgood's bias in this essay, model your thinking for students:

Osgood states in his introduction that anchoring is mostly "sitting there" and "telling some stories." He goes on to talk about his experience "in the business." I know that because Osgood has had other jobs in the news broadcasting business. His statement about the "easy" job of being an anchor is biased. Someone who had not been involved in the business may have found anchoring a complicated job. As I continue reading, I learn that Osgood encounters a lot of problems while filling in for Roger Mudd. He says that he tried to give an "obvious cue" to go to commercial, but it took the control room a "while to register." I recognize bias here because Osgood thinks he's given an obvious cue, but apparently, it is not so obvious to the people in that control room.

MODEL

Our Finest Hour

Charles Osgood

Only occasionally do most reporters or correspondents get to "anchor" a news broadcast. Anchoring, you understand, means sitting there in the studio and telling some stories into the camera and introducing the reports and pieces that other reporters do. It looks easy enough. It is easy enough, most of the time . . .

It was back when I was relatively new at CBS News. I'd been in the business a while, but only recently had moved over to CBS News. I was old, but I was new. It was a Saturday night and I was filling in for Roger Mudd[1] on the *CBS Evening News*. Roger was on vacation. The regular executive producer[2] of the broadcast, Paul Greenberg, was on vacation, too. And so was the regular cameraman and the regular editor and the regular director. Somewhere along the line we had one too many substitutes that night.

> Comical repetition of the word *regular* indicates Osgood's **purpose**—to entertain.

I said "Good evening" and introduced the first report and turned to the monitor to watch it. What I saw was myself looking at the monitor. Many seconds passed. Finally there was something on the screen. A reporter was beginning a story. It was not the story I had introduced. Instead, it was a different story by a different reporter. This was supposed to be the second item in the newscast. So I shuffled my script around and made the first piece second and the second piece first. When I came back on camera, I explained what it was we had seen and reintroduced the first piece. Again there was a long, awkward pause. I shuffled my papers. I scribbled on the script. I turned to the monitor. Finally, the floor director, who was filling in for the regular floor director, cued me to go on. So I introduced the next report. It didn't come up either, so I said we'd continue in just a moment. Obvious cue for a commercial, I thought, but it took a while to register in the control room. When a commercial did come up, there was a frantic scramble in the studio to reorganize what was left of the broadcast. But by now everything had come undone.

> It is a **fact** that a commercial was shown. It is an **opinion** that the studio became frantic.

When the commercial was over, I introduced a piece from Washington. What came up was a series of pictures of people who seemed to be dead. One man was slumped over a car wheel. Two or three people were lying in the middle of the street. Another man was propped up against the wall of the building, his eyes staring vacantly into space. Then came the voice of Peter Kalisher. "This was the town where everyone died," he said. I knew nothing whatsoever about this piece. It was not scheduled for the broadcast. Peter Kalisher was in Paris as far as I knew. But there had been nothing on the news wires about everybody in Paris having died. ❶ In the "fishbowl," the glassed-in office where the executive producer sits, there were at least three people yelling into telephones. Nobody in there knew anything about this piece either. The story was

> The **author's bias** as anchor influences the way he describes the "fishbowl."

1. **Roger Mudd:** *CBS News* reporter from 1961 to 1980. He was a backup anchorperson for Walter Cronkite during the time of this story.
2. **executive producer:** Person responsible for the quality of the newscast.

◆ Build Vocabulary

correspondent (kôr′ ə spän′ dənt) *n.*: Person hired by a news organization to provide news from a distant place

Develop Understanding

One-Minute Insight

When reporter Charles Osgood fills in for the regular network anchor on a live television newscast, a comedy of errors ensues. The essay illustrates how one error can lead to confusion that produces other errors and shows how humor can arise from a series of blunders.

◆ Literary Focus

❶ **Humor** How does this description add to the humor of the essay? *The humor lies in the contrast between what is expected and what happens. The reader can imagine television viewers, as well as Charles Osgood, prepared for images relating to a report from Washington. Instead, images of dead people appear on the screen.*

Customize for *English Language Learners*

This essay contains many examples of technical vocabulary related to television production. To help students, provide them with definitions of these terms before they read. Include definitions for *broadcast, editor, director, script, monitor, floor director, studio,* and *control room.*

Block Scheduling

Consider these suggestions to take advantage of extended class time:

- Before students read the essay, introduce the Reading for Success strategies, p. 374. Have them apply the strategies while reading. Then, have students form groups to answer the Reading for Success questions on p. 377. For additional support, use the practice pages in **Selection Support,** pp. 131–132.
- If you have access to technology, have students work on the *Writer's Solution Writing Lab CD-ROM* to prepare for and complete all or part of the Writing Mini-Lesson.

Speaking and Listening Mini-Lesson

Humorous Anecdote

This mini-lesson supports the Speaking and Listening activity in the Idea Bank on p. 378.

Introduce Explain that an anecdote is a brief story about an interesting, amusing, or strange event. Anecdotes are told to entertain or to make a point.

Develop As students write their anecdotes, encourage them to consider these questions:

- In what ways can the introduction prepare the audience for a humorous story?
- How can voice tone and pitch help convey humor?
- In what ways can gestures and facial expressions add humor to the story?

Apply Have students rehearse their anecdotes with partners, giving constructive feedback to each other. Then have students tell their anecdotes to the class.

Assess Evaluate students' anecdotes based on preparation, vocal effects, and overall delivery. Have students use the Peer Assessment: Speaker/Speech form, p. 105, in **Alternative Assessment.**

Reinforce and Extend

Answers

◆ Literature and Your Life

Reader's Response Some students may say they would have told viewers that the broadcast was experiencing "technical difficulties"; others may say that, like the author, they would have muddled through.

Thematic Focus Students may say that Osgood saw the humor in the story and wanted to share it with others.

☑ Check Your Comprehension

1. He was filling in for Roger Mudd, who was on vacation.
2. Charles Osgood, the substitute anchor, introduces one news report after another, none of which is supported by the images on-screen.

◆ Critical Thinking

1. Possible responses: He was able to stay in control because he had extensive experience working in television; he was able to go with the flow of the broadcast despite the problems occurring.
2. Most or all of the people working that night were substitutes, and they didn't have enough experience to know what to do when something went wrong.
3. Possible responses: "grace under pressure," "calm professionalism," or "cool and collected" because he stayed in control even though nothing was going right with the newscast.
4. Possible responses: A reporter gathers information for a story; the ability to listen carefully is an important skill. A newswriter writes the script for a newscast based on reporters' notes; the ability to write clearly and concisely is an important skill. An executive producer coordinates the entire newscast; the ability to stay focused on many things at once is crucial to success.

about some little town in France that was demonstrating the evils of cigarette smoking. Seems the population of the town was the same number as smoking-related deaths in France in a given year. It was a nice story well told, but since nobody in authority at CBS News, New York, had seen it or knew what was coming next, they decided to dump out of it and come back to me. I, of course, was sitting there looking at the piece with bewilderment written all over my face, when suddenly, in the midst of all these French people pretending to be dead, I saw myself, bewilderment and all.

All in all, it was not the finest broadcast CBS News has ever done. But the worst part came when I introduced the "end piece," a feature story that Hughes Rudd had done about raft racing on the Chatahoochie River.[3] Again, when I finished the introduction, I turned to the monitor and, again, nothing happened. Then, through the glass window of the "fishbowl," I heard a loud and plaintive wail. "What is going on?" screamed the fill-in executive producer. I could hear him perfectly clearly, and so could half of America. The microphone on my tie-clip was open. Standing in the control room watching this, with what I'm sure must have been great interest, was a delegation of visiting journalists from the People's Republic of China.[4] They must have had a really great impression of American electronic journalism. The next Monday morning, sitting back at the radio desk where I belonged, I became aware of a presence standing quietly next to my desk. It was Richard Salant, the wise and gentle man who was then president of CBS News. He'd been waiting until I finished typing a sentence before bending over and inquiring softly: "What *was* going on?"

> When you **evaluate the author's message,** you may decide that Osgood's experience as a journalist qualifies him to make this statement.

3. **Chatahoochie River** (cha tə hü′ chē): River running south through Georgia and forming part of the borders of Georgia, Alabama, and Florida.

4. **People's Republic of China:** Official name of China.

◆ Build Vocabulary

bewilderment (bē wil′ dər mənt) *n.*: State of confusion

Guide for Responding

◆ Literature and Your Life

Reader's Response How would you have responded if you were the anchorperson when this situation occurred?

Thematic Focus Charles Osgood chose not only to tell this story to friends, but to publish it—and share it with total strangers. Why would he want to relive this disaster?

☑ Check Your Comprehension

1. Why was Charles Osgood anchoring the news on the night he describes?
2. Summarize the events of the newscast Osgood describes.

◆ Critical Thinking

INTERPRET

1. Charles Osgood stays calm despite the trouble. Give two reasons to explain how he was able to stay in control. **[Hypothesize]**
2. Why did the telecast go so badly? **[Analyze]**

EVALUATE

3. Use two or three words to evaluate Osgood's job performance that night. Explain your answer. **[Make a Judgment]**

EXTEND

4. Besides the anchor, name three other people who help create a newscast. For each, name a skill that is critical to success. **[Career Link]**

Beyond the Selection

FURTHER READING

Other Works by Charles Osgood

Osgood on Speaking: How to Think on Your Feet Without Falling on Your Face

The Osgood Files

INTERNET

We suggest the following sites on the Internet (all Web sites are subject to change).

For more information about Charles Osgood: **http://www.cbsradio.com/osgood/bio.html**

For more information about CBS News: **http://www.cbs.com**

We *strongly recommend* that you preview these sites before you send students to them.

Guide for Responding (continued)

◆ Literary Focus

Humor

In presenting a minute-by-minute account of a situation that kept getting worse, Charles Osgood uses a matter-of-fact style that enhances the **humor,** or comic effect, of his essay. Osgood's choice of words and details help him achieve his purpose of evoking laughter.

1. How does the title "Our Finest Hour" add to the humor of this essay?

2. How does the first paragraph set up readers to be surprised by the story of the telecast?

3. Identify three details that add to the humor of the error-filled telecast.

4. (a) Which detail did you find funniest? Why? (b) How did its placement in the essay affect the humor?

◆ Build Vocabulary

Using the Suffix *–ment*

When the suffix *-ment* is added to many verbs, it forms nouns such as *bewilderment* or *amusement* that name a "state or condition of." Add the suffix *-ment* to the following verbs, and use each new word in a sentence.

1. excite
2. disappoint
3. content
4. bombard

Spelling Strategy

When you write words like *correspondent,* remember that they have the double consonant *r.* Using each clue below, write a word with a double *r.*

1. Talk while someone else talks: int___?___

2. The relationship between pen pals: co___?___

3. Edit a page for errors: co___?___

Using the Word Bank

On your paper, write the word or phrase whose meaning is closest to that of the first word.

1. correspondent: (a) one who finds letters, (b) one who contributes news, (c) one who speaks out of turn

2. bewilderment: (a) state of jumbled confusion, (b) state of inactivity, (c) state of determination

◆ Reading for Success

Strategies for Reading Critically

Review the reading strategies and the notes on how to read a written work critically. Then, apply them to answer the following:

1. (a) Identify two facts presented in "Our Finest Hour." (b) Identify two opinions.

2. What experiences qualify Charles Osgood to write about news anchoring?

3. Provide a detail that reveals the author's bias.

4. (a) What do you think is Charles Osgood's message? (b) Explain whether you believe he is successful at conveying that message to readers.

◆ Build Grammar Skills

Subjects and Predicates

Every complete sentence has two parts. The **subject** is the part that names whom or what the sentence is about. The **simple subject** is the noun or pronoun that answers the question *who* or *what* about the sentence. The **predicate** is the part that tells something about the subject. The **simple predicate** is the verb or verb phrase that tells *what* action the subject performs. In this example, the subject and predicate are each bracketed. The simple subject and simple predicate are circled.

[subject: The floor (director)] [predicate: (cued) me to go on.]

Practice Write the following sentences on your paper. For each, underline the subject once and the predicate twice. Then, circle the simple subject and the simple predicate.

1. We had one too many substitutes that night.

2. I turned to the monitor.

3. Everything had come undone.

4. The microphone on my tie-clip was open.

5. It was not the finest broadcast.

Writing Application Write a five-sentence paragraph about a time when events got out of hand despite your best attempts to stay organized. In each sentence, underline the subject once and the predicate twice. Then, circle the simple subject and the simple predicate.

◆ Build Grammar Skills

1. We had one too many substitutes that night. [circle "We" and "had"]
2. I turned to the monitor. [circle "I" and "turned"]
3. Everything had come undone. [circle "everything" and "had come"]
4. The microphone on my tie-clip was open. [circle "microphone" and "was"]
5. It was not the finest broadcast. [circle "it" and "was"]

Writer's Solution

For additional instruction and practice, use the lesson in the *Writer's Solution Grammar Practice Book* on Complete Sentences and Predicates, p. 29.

Answers

◆ Literary Focus

1. The title states the opposite of what the newscast turned out to be.
2. The information leads readers to think that anchoring the news is fairly easy.
3. Students may mention Osgood's shuffling of papers while waiting for the story to appear on-screen, the unscheduled story from France, Osgood's attempt to cue for a commercial.
4. (a) Possible response: The funniest detail is the account of the staff's reaction to the pictures of "dead" people. It shows that the newscast has gone from wobbly to absurd. (b) The detail is placed at a point where readers might expect things to improve, but they only get worse.

◆ Build Vocabulary

Using the Suffix *-ment*

Possible responses:

1. excitement; Viewers reacted with excitement to the news.
2. disappointment; The newscast was a source of disappointment.
3. contentment; The editor's expression showed contentment.
4. bombardment; The bombardment of letters surprised the station owner.

Spelling Strategy

1. interrupt
2. correspondence
3. correct

Using the Word Bank

1. (b)
2. (a)

Reading for Success

1. Possible responses: (a) Osgood was substituting for Roger Mudd. The microphone on his tie clip was on. (b) The broadcast was not CBS's finest newscast. The visiting journalists were unimpressed with American electronic journalism.
2. He has had experience as an anchor, a reporter, and a broadcaster.
3. He claims that anchoring "is easy enough."
4. (a) Possible response: His message is that we can often look back with humor at an awful moment. (b) He successfully conveys the humor of a disastrous situation.

Idea Bank

Following are suggestions for matching the Idea Bank topics with your students' performance levels and learning modalities:

Customize for
Performance Levels
Less Advanced Students: 1, 5
Average Students: 2, 5, 6
More Advanced Students: 3, 4, 6, 7

Customize for
Learning Modalities
Verbal/Linguistic: 1, 2, 3, 4
Visual/Spatial: 6, 7
Interpersonal: 4, 5, 6, 7
Intrapersonal: 1, 2

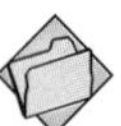

Writing Mini-Lesson

Refer students to the Writing Handbook in the back of the book for instruction on the writing process, and for further information on reports.

Writer's Solution

Writing Lab CD-ROM
Have students complete the tutorial on Reports. Follow these steps:

1. Have students use the Sunburst Diagram activity for possible topic ideas.
2. Suggest that students use the Topic Web activity to narrow their topic.
3. Have students draft on computer.
4. When revising, suggest that students use the Unity and Coherence revision checker.

Writer's Solution Sourcebook
Have students use Chapter 7, "Reports," pp. 200–233, for additional support. This chapter includes in-depth instruction on organizing information, pp. 222–223.

Build Your Portfolio

Idea Bank

Writing

1. **Statement of Apology** Imagine that Charles Osgood read a statement to express the network's apology to viewers. Write that statement, providing an explanation for the mistakes that took place on the evening news.
2. **Comparison-and-Contrast Essay** Think of a moment in your life when you encountered a disaster, despite careful planning. In an essay, compare and contrast your experience with the one Osgood describes.
3. **Career Advice** Using the information that Osgood presents in this essay, write a letter he might present to new reporters. Give the new staff useful tips for success in television news. **[Career Link]**

Speaking and Listening

4. **Interpreter's Explanation** As the guide that the network has hired, provide an explanation for the Chinese guests. Convey a positive idea about American network newscast practices, despite the errors the visitors have just seen. **[Career Link]**
5. **Humorous Anecdote** Relate a funny, real-life experience to the class. Rehearse your speech, paying attention to how the tone and pitch of your voice add humor. **[Performing Arts Link]**

Projects

6. **News Show [Group Activity]** In a group, create a telecast of school news. One student can serve as anchor and others can report the stories. Include visual aids, maps, and interviews to enhance the telecast. **[Media Link]**
7. **Report on the News** Watch television to discover just how many news programs are available. In a presentation, compare and contrast the variety of newscasts you've seen. Include video clips to support your points. **[Media Link]**

Writing Mini-Lesson

Report for a Newscast

Even though news anchors and reporters may appear chatty in front of the camera, they are usually reading copy that has been written in advance. Choose an event that you'd like to see covered on the evening news. Then, write the copy for the report. You can report on a serious current issue, a local event, or a person or place of interest.

Writing Skills Focus: The 5 W's

Like any good reporter, make sure your report answers the critical questions—the **5 W's:**

- *What* happened?
- *Who* was involved?
- *Where* did it happen?
- *When* did it happen?
- *Why* did it happen?

In written news reports, these questions are answered in the opening paragraph. You can provide details, quotations, or eyewitness accounts in later paragraphs.

Prewriting As you gather information, keep a list of facts about the event that answer each of the 5 W's. If you interview any sources, take accurate notes so you can include them in your report.

Drafting Write a first sentence that will grab listeners' attention. Then, answer the 5W's in the first paragraph. As you write the rest of your report, continue to provide information that explains the event to viewers.

Revising Read your news report aloud to a small group of classmates. Do listeners want to know more after hearing your first sentence? If they can't answer the 5 W's about the event you're describing, add or rearrange the details.

◆ Grammar Application
Review your news report to be sure that every sentence has a subject and a predicate.

✓ ASSESSMENT OPTIONS

Formal Assessment, Selection Test, pp. 110–112, and Assessment Resources Software. The selection test is designed so that it can be easily customized to the performance levels of your students.

Alternative Assessment, p. 24, includes options for less advanced students, more advanced students, verbal/linguistic learners, musical/rhythmic learners, interpersonal learners, and visual/spatial learners.

PORTFOLIO ASSESSMENT
Use the following rubrics in the **Alternative Assessment** booklet to assess student writing:
Statement of Apology: Expression, p. 81
Comparison-and-Contrast Essay: Comparison/Contrast, p. 90
Career Advice: Business Letter/Memo, p. 100
Writing Mini-Lesson: Research Report/Paper, p. 93

PART 1 # *Quirky Characters*

Essor, 1981, Andre Rouillard

One-Minute Planning Guide

The selections in this section focus on the theme of quirky characters. In "Cat on the Go," a cat defies death to assert his unique personality. In "The Luckiest Time of All," an old woman shares a well-worn family story in her own distinctive voice. The poems "Father William," "The Microscope," "in Just-," and "Sarah Cynthia Sylvia Stout Would Not Take the Garbage Out," though different in many ways, share a common thread. Each describes a singular—and memorably quirky—character.

Customize for *Varying Student Needs*

When assigning the selections in this section to your students, keep in mind the following factors:

"Cat on the Go"
- Students may need help with some British terminology
- The selection is fairly long; you may want to divide the piece up into sections for struggling readers

"The Luckiest Time of All"
- Students may need help with the dialect in this story

"Father William"
- The strong rhythm of this poem makes it ideal for reading aloud

"The Microscope"
- Provides an opportunity for a connection to science

"in Just-"
- Students may be surprised by Cummings's unusual use of spacing, punctuation, and capitalization

"Sarah Cynthia Sylvia Stout Would Not Take the Garbage Out"
- Amusing, accessible poem with a solid rhyme scheme

Humanities: Art

Essor, 1981, by Andre Rouillard

Tell students that the name of this painting, *Essor*, is the French word for flight. Explain that this painting is an example of surrealism, an artistic movement of the early twentieth century centered around such artists as Andre Breton and Joan Miro. Surrealism, as opposed to traditionalism, emphasizes fantasy.

Have students study the painting and then ask the following questions:

1. What elements of this painting are fantastical or surreal? *Students should be able to identify that the main character in the painting has lost half of his head, there is a bird drinking out of his head, and the top of his head resembles a kite.*
2. How do you think these elements of surrealism or fantasy relate to the theme of quirky characters? *Students should recognize that elements of surrealism, such as the details in the painting, are unnatural, or odd, or quirky.*

Guide for Reading

OBJECTIVES

1. To read, comprehend, and interpret an essay
2. To relate an essay to personal experience
3. To understand bias
4. To identify character traits
5. To build vocabulary in context and learn the prefix *in-*
6. To develop skill in using compound subjects and predicates
7. To write a directory of places that supplies background information
8. To respond to a narrative essay through writing, speaking and listening, and projects

SKILLS INSTRUCTION

Vocabulary:
Using the Prefix *in-*
Spelling:
Silent *gh*
Grammar:
Compound Subjects and Predicates
Reading Strategy:
Understand Bias
Literary Focus:
Character Traits
Writing:
Supply Background Information
Speaking and Listening:
Career Interview (Teacher Edition)
Viewing and Representing:
Comic Strip (Teacher Edition)
Critical Viewing:
Speculate, Support, Connect

PORTFOLIO OPPORTUNITIES

Writing: Pet Story; Monologue; Biographical Sketch
Writing Mini-Lesson: Directory of Places
Speaking and Listening: Career Interview; Musical Retelling
Projects: Training Profile; Pet Care Brochure

More About the Author
James Herriot is the pen name of James Alfred Wight, who grew up in Glasgow, England. After serving in the Royal Air Force during World War II, Herriot answered an ad for a veterinarian who was willing to serve in a remote rural area. Herriot began writing in 1966, when his wife urged him to make good on his threats to record his real-life experiences in a book. Herriot's books, with their sentimental animal tales and gentle philosophies, have sold over 50 million copies worldwide.

Meet the Author:

James Herriot (1916–1995)

At the early age of 24, James Herriot became a trained veterinarian. However, it wasn't until he was in his fifties that he combined his two loves—animals and writing—into the first of his books, *All Creatures Great and Small*. This work served as the basis for a television series.

Dual Dedication Herriot was so dedicated to both of his passions that he never even took a day off at Christmas. At the time he was writing, British veterinarians were not allowed to advertise, so although he was born James Alfred Wight, he adopted the pen name of James Herriot. This allowed him to publish accounts of his experiences.

Herriot continued his veterinary practice into his seventies, splitting his time between treating his animal patients and signing autographs for his many fans.

The Story Behind the Essay

Herriot's books—written directly from his experience—are widely known for their lively descriptions of characters he met, both animal and human. "Cat on the Go," from his book *All Things Wise and Wonderful*, describes an unforgettable cat that he and his wife adopted.

◆ Literature and Your Life

Connect Your Experience

If you've ever had a pet or have interacted with someone else's pet, you know that animals have distinctive personalities. Some pets can even perform tricks or behave in ways that will amaze you. In this story, you'll meet Oscar, a very unusual cat with a surprising habit.

Thematic Focus: Quirky Characters

As you read about this cat's adventures, notice how his strange behavior charms most of the people he meets.

◆ Background for Understanding

Science

James Herriot's veterinary practice gave him endless material for his writing. Veterinarians have a strong scientific education and complete a four-year postgraduate program before becoming licensed. Usually, they specialize in either small animals, such as house pets, or large animals, such as horses and farm animals. Like doctors, veterinarians sometimes have to perform surgery to save an animal's life. Through medical advances, veterinarians now have access to sophisticated equipment and a wide range of medicines. As you'll discover, the medicine and equipment available at the time of the story wasn't so advanced.

◆ Build Vocabulary

Prefixes: *in-*

In this story, an infection seems *inevitable*. *Evitable* means "avoidable." When the prefix *in-* meaning "not" is added, it creates "inevitable," meaning "not avoidable."

Word Bank

Which of these words from the story might you use to describe an action that is completed in a disgusting way?

grotesquely
emaciated
inevitable
sauntered
distraught
despondent
intrigued
surreptitiously

Prentice Hall Literature Program Resources

REINFORCE / RETEACH / EXTEND

Selection Support Pages
Build Vocabulary: Prefixes: *in-*, p. 134
Build Spelling Skills, p. 135
Build Grammar Skills: Compound Subjects and Predicates, p. 136
Reading Strategy: Understand Bias, p. 137
Literary Focus: Character Traits, p. 138

Strategies for Diverse Student Needs, pp. 49–50

Beyond Literature Workplace Skills: Responding in an Emergency, p. 25

Formal Assessment Selection Test, pp. 113–115, Assessment Resources Software

Alternative Assessment, p. 25

Resource Pro CD-ROM
"Cat on the Go"—includes all resource material and customizable lesson plan

Listening to Literature Audiocassettes
"Cat on the Go"

Cat on the Go

Happy Cat, Christian Pierre

Literary Focus

Character Traits

Character traits are the qualities that make a person, or even an animal, an individual. For example, one person may seem calm; another, excitable. One person may be musical; another, athletic. It is these character traits that determine how each person behaves and interacts with others.

Use a chart like the one below to record the traits of each real-life person and animal in Herriot's essay.

Reading Strategy

Understand Bias

Just like the characters in a literary work, every writer has unique personality traits that contribute to that writer's **bias**—the knowledge and interest that a writer brings to a subject. You can see bias through the author's choice of words. For example, Herriot describes the cat's fur as "auburn and copper-gold," not plain brown. From this choice of words, you can tell that he thinks this is a special cat. As you read, look for more evidence of bias. Think about how Herriot's bias affects the way information is presented and the way you respond to it.

Preparing for Standardized Tests

Reading Standardized tests often present analogies to evaluate students' understanding of relationships and concepts. Knowing how to interpret words that include the prefix *in-* can help students complete some analogies. Complete this sample analogy:

energetic is to inactive as ___?___ is to incurable

(A) restored
(B) injured
(C) pampered
(D) adopted

Students who know the meaning of the prefix *in-* will see that the first pair of words are opposites: *energetic* means "full of energy," while *inactive* means "not active." To correctly complete the analogy, the student needs to select a word that means the opposite of *not curable.* The best choice is *(A), restored.* For more practice, use Build Vocabulary in **Selection Support,** p. 134.

Interest Grabber Ask students to imagine that a well-loved pet that belongs to their family or to a friend has gotten lost. Have students design a lost animal poster or newspaper want ad intended to help locate the animal. Remind students that they need to give accurate information about the animal and a good description of the pet. Have students share their descriptions with the class. Discuss how they might feel about the loss. Guide students into the selection by explaining that a very sick stray cat is adopted by a couple and nursed back to health. The couple must face hard choices when the cat's original owners appear to claim their lost pet.

Build Grammar Skills

Compound Subjects and Predicates If you wish to introduce the grammar concept for this selection before students read, refer to the instruction on p. 394.

Customize for
Less Proficient Readers
Parts of this narrative essay, in which the author describes the cat's serious injury and the surgery he performs, may be hard for readers to understand. It may help if you suggest common synonyms for words such as *abdomen* (stomach), *syringe* (needle), or *sutures* (stitches).

Customize for
More Advanced Students
Challenge your more advanced students by having them consider the ways in which Herriot's essay and the experiences it describes would have been different if the author had not been a veterinarian.

Humanities: Art

Happy Cat, by Christian Pierre

Christian Pierre lives, works, and exhibits in Jacksonville, Florida. Her paintings are often featured on book covers or in illustrations and are prized by collectors. Her work is sometimes described as urban folk art. Ask: In what way does this image fit the title of the story? Why? *The cat looks like it is ready to go—ready to blast off into outer space.*

Develop Understanding

In this gently humorous essay, "Cat on the Go," a rural veterinarian saves the life of a badly injured stray cat, adopts it, and grows to love its unusual behavior. Then the cat's original owners find him. The doctor and his wife reluctantly give the cat back to its rightful family. Later, when they pay a surprise visit to the family and the cat, they not only learn a lesson about family pride, but they get to once again appreciate the cat's odd but endearing habits. They learn that at times, doing the right thing can be painful and confusing.

◆Critical Thinking

❶ **Analyze** Have students explain how Herriot captures their interest at the start of the essay. *He opens with an urgent call for help, which makes us want to know what the problem is and how things will turn out.*

▶Critical Viewing◀

❷ **Speculate** Students may say that the cat looks like it is longing for attention.

◆Critical Thinking

❸ **Infer** Challenge students to find details in this scene that reveal that Herriot is a veterinarian. *His house has a consulting room, the girl brings an injured cat to him, both men study the animal's injuries.*

Customize for
English Language Learners
Students acquiring American English may have difficulty when they come upon phrases in British English, such as "don't fancy this" or "have a go." The rustic Yorkshire accents and colloquial speech patterns also make it harder for some students to read. Help them by "translating" these phrases into American English, or by having students read in pairs to talk through expressions they might not understand at first glance. Others may get a better appreciation for the piece from hearing it. You might have students follow along as they listen to the recording of the selection.

Listening to Literature Audiocassettes

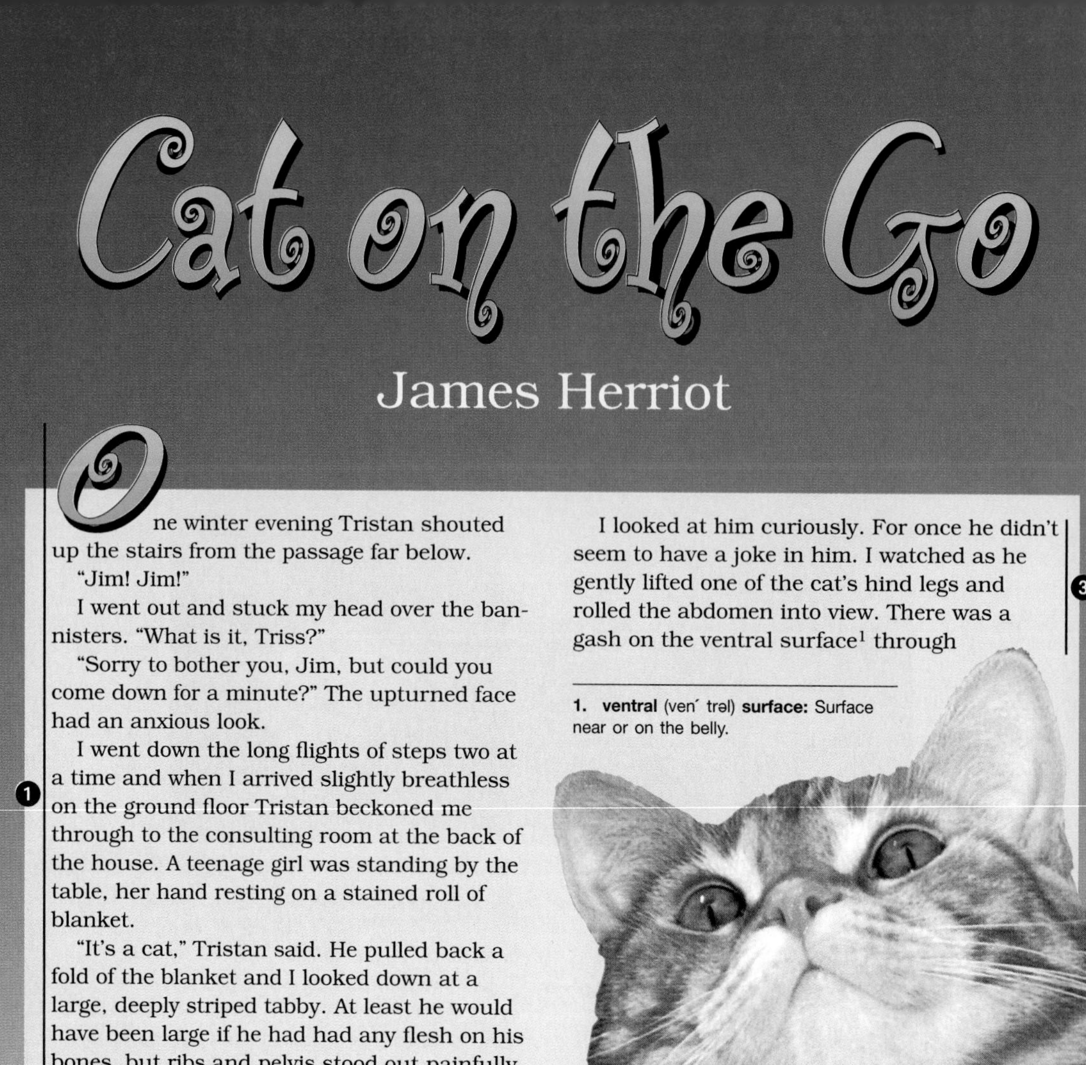

Cat on the Go

James Herriot

One winter evening Tristan shouted up the stairs from the passage far below.

"Jim! Jim!"

I went out and stuck my head over the banisters. "What is it, Triss?"

"Sorry to bother you, Jim, but could you come down for a minute?" The upturned face had an anxious look.

❶ I went down the long flights of steps two at a time and when I arrived slightly breathless on the ground floor Tristan beckoned me through to the consulting room at the back of the house. A teenage girl was standing by the table, her hand resting on a stained roll of blanket.

"It's a cat," Tristan said. He pulled back a fold of the blanket and I looked down at a large, deeply striped tabby. At least he would have been large if he had had any flesh on his bones, but ribs and pelvis stood out painfully through the fur and as I passed my hand over the motionless body I could feel only a thin covering of skin.

Tristan cleared his throat. "There's something else, Jim."

I looked at him curiously. For once he didn't seem to have a joke in him. I watched as he gently lifted one of the cat's hind legs and rolled the abdomen into view. There was a gash on the ventral surface[1] through ❸

1. **ventral** (ven´ trəl) **surface:** Surface near or on the belly.

❷ ▶ Critical Viewing What human emotions does the cat in this photograph seem to convey? Explain your response. **[Speculate]**

Block Scheduling Strategies

Consider these suggestions to take advantage of extended class time:

- After using the Interest Grabber to draw students into the essay, play the audiocassette of "Cat on the Go" as students read along. Follow with a class discussion about how the reading enhances the humor of the story, and their understanding of it.

Listening to Literature Audiocassettes

- As an alternative, have students read the essay independently. Then reinforce and extend the selection skills by having students work together in small groups to discuss and complete the Guide for Responding questions, pp. 393–394. Encourage students to take turns reading questions and writing responses.
- If students have access to technology, have them use the tutorial on Exposition: Giving Information, in the *Writer's Solution Writing Lab CD-ROM,* to prepare for and complete all or part of the Writing Mini-Lesson.

which a coiled cluster of intestines spilled
3 grotesquely onto the cloth. I was still shocked and staring when the girl spoke.

"I saw this cat sittin' in the dark, down Brown's yard. I thought 'e looked skinny, like, and a bit quiet and I bent down to give 'im a
4 pat. Then I saw 'e was badly hurt and I went home for a blanket and brought 'im round to you."

"That was kind of you," I said. "Have you any idea who he belongs to?"

The girl shook her head. "No, he looks like a stray to me."

"He does indeed." I dragged my eyes away from the terrible wound. "You're Marjorie Simpson, aren't you?"

5 "Yes."

"I know your Dad well. He's our postman."

"That's right." She gave a half smile then her lips trembled.

"Well, I reckon I'd better leave 'im with you. You'll be going to put him out of his misery. There's nothing anybody can do about . . . about that?"

I shrugged and shook my head. The girl's eyes filled with tears, she stretched out a hand and touched the emaciated animal then turned and walked quickly to the door.

"Thanks again, Marjorie," I called after the
6 retreating back. "And don't worry—we'll look after him."

In the silence that followed, Tristan and I looked down at the shattered animal. Under the surgery lamp it was all too easy to see. He had almost been disemboweled[2] and the pile of intestines was covered in dirt and mud.

"What d'you think did this?" Tristan said at length. "Has he been run over?"

"Maybe," I replied. "Could be anything. An attack by a big dog or somebody could have kicked him or struck him." All things were possible with cats because some people seemed to regard them as fair game for any cruelty.

Tristan nodded. "Anyway, whatever happened, he must have been on the verge of starvation. He's a skeleton. I bet he's wandered miles from home."

"Ah well," I sighed. "There's only one thing
to do. Those guts are perforated in several 7
places. It's hopeless."

Tristan didn't say anything but he whistled under his breath and drew the tip of his forefinger again and again across the furry cheek. And, unbelievably, from somewhere in the scraggy chest a gentle purring arose.

The young man looked at me, round eyed. "My God, do you hear that?"

"Yes . . . amazing in that condition. He's a good-natured cat."

Tristan, head bowed, continued his stroking. I knew how he felt because, although he preserved a cheerfully hard-boiled attitude to our patients he couldn't kid me about one thing: he had a soft spot for cats. Even now, when we are both around the sixty mark, he often talks to me about the cat he has had for many years. It
is a typical relationship— 8
they tease each other unmercifully—but it is based on real affection.

◆ **Literary Focus**
Both men believe the situation is hopeless, yet they operate anyway. What character traits does this decision reveal?

"It's no good, Triss," I said gently. "It's got to be done." I reached for the syringe but something in me rebelled against plunging a needle into that mutilated body. Instead I pulled a fold of the blanket over the cat's head.

"Pour a little ether onto the cloth," I said. "He'll just sleep away."

Wordlessly, Tristan unscrewed the cap of the ether bottle and poised it above the head. Then from under the shapeless heap of blanket we heard it again: the deep purring which increased in volume till it boomed in our ears like a distant motorcycle.

Tristan was like a man turned to stone, hand gripping the bottle rigidly, eyes staring

2. **disemboweled** (dis′ im bou′ əld) *v.*: Lost its intestines.

◆ **Build Vocabulary**

grotesquely (grō tesk′ le) *adv.*: In a strange or distorted way

emaciated (ē mā′ shē āt′ id) *adj.*: Extremely thin; starving

Clarification

4 The story Herriot tells is set in Yorkshire, a county in northern England. Some of the characters speak in the dialect of that area. One feature of the dialect is the dropping of the letter *h* in words like *he* and *him.* Herriot uses this dialect to give readers local color of the region.

◆ Reading Strategy

5 Understand Bias Herriot's stories are based on his many years of living in a rural area of northern England. There, as in other small towns the world over, people tend to know their neighbors and form close friendships and ties. Ask students what they can tell from this passage about Herriot's relationship to the people in his town. *He seems to know the people in the area quite well, and likes them.*

Comprehension Check ☑

6 What problem does Herriot face? *The cat that Marjorie has brought in is badly injured; Herriot must decide what to do for the suffering animal.*

Build Spelling Skills

7 The spelling strategy for this piece focuses on the silent blend *gh.* Have students find the word in this line that has this blend. *sighed* Because the *gh* is silent, the word is pronounced SIDE, but is spelled as shown.

◆ Literary Focus

8 Character Traits The decision reveals their deep love for animals. Even if the odds are poor, they are dedicated and willing to try almost anything to help a suffering animal.

Beyond the Classroom

Community Connection

Animal Welfare Caring people take their responsibility to animals seriously. Most communities have public agencies or private organizations whose mission is to help animals in need. They may be called animal shelters, animal rescue centers, or pet adoption agencies. Some offer temporary care for stray or injured animals; others serve as clearinghouses to match up families with pets who need homes; still others exist to monitor animal protection laws or to deal with health threats animals may pose to the public. The staff may consist of animal health workers, veterinarians, public relations people, administrators, and environmental scientists.

Have interested students learn more about the agencies or organizations in your area that serve the needs of animals, or deal with human health and safety issues related to animals. Students might begin by listing questions about animals, and then finding out where to go to get those questions answered. For instance:

- Whom do you notify if a deer is hit by a car?
- Whom do you call if you suspect an animal may be rabid?
- Who can help if your pet has a litter of babies you cannot keep?
- Whom do you contact if your pet is lost or stolen?

Students can conclude their investigation by publishing a pamphlet or list of useful contacts in your area.

◆Build Grammar Skills

1 Compound Subjects and Predicates The verbs in a sentence with a compound predicate share the same subject. This sentence is an example: the single subject, *he,* has the compound predicate *looked* and *gulped.* Help students understand that the subject is implicitly repeated.

◆Critical Thinking

2 Infer Students should sense the reluctance both men feel to give up on the injured cat, even though the situation is very grave. What does this show about the men? *They have a deep love for animals and a strong urge to try to help them at any cost.*

◆Critical Thinking

3 Defend Some readers may be disturbed by the graphic details of the surgery. Others may have difficulty comprehending the medical details. But the author consciously chose to include these details. Have students discuss why Herriot chooses to give technical details about the operation, even though it may be unpleasant to some readers. *The technical details support the point that Herriot is indeed a skilled veterinarian with experience healing sick and injured animals. The details increase our respect for Herriot's dedication and our curiosity to know what will happen to the cat.*

◆Reading Strategy

4 Understand Bias The author views the cat as a patient, as physicians see their human patients; he hopes for the best, and is pleased to think that the cat is comfortable. All of this shows a concern and love for cats.

Customize for *Logical/Mathematical Learners*

Students might be interested in researching the number of stray animals that must be cared for each year at your local animal shelter. They could collect data on the number of animals that are adopted and how many must be euthanized because homes cannot be found for them. They can make a graph or chart to illustrate this information.

down at the mound of cloth from which the purring rose in waves of warm friendly sound.

1 At last he looked up at me and gulped. "I don't fancy this much, Jim. Can't we do something?"

"You mean, put that lot back?"

"Yes."

"But the bowels are damaged—they're like a
2 sieve in parts."

"We could stitch them, couldn't we?"

I lifted the blanket and looked again. "Honestly, Triss, I wouldn't know where to start. And the whole thing is filthy."

He didn't say anything, but continued to look at me steadily. And I didn't need much persuading. I had no more desire to pour ether onto that comradely purring than he had.

"Come on, then," I said. "We'll have a go."

With the oxygen bubbling and the cat's head in the anesthetic mask we washed the whole prolapse[3] with warm saline.[4] We did it again and again but it was impossible to remove every fragment of caked dirt. Then we started the painfully
3 slow business of stitching the many holes in the tiny intestines, and here I was glad of Tristan's nimble fingers which seemed better able to manipulate the small round-bodied needles than mine.

Two hours and yards of catgut[5] later, we dusted the patched up peritoneal[6] surface with sulfanilamide[7] and pushed the entire mass back into the abdomen. When I had sutured muscle layers and skin everything looked tidy but I had a nasty feeling of sweeping undesirable things under the carpet. The extensive damage, all that contamination—peritonitis[8] was <u>inevitable</u>.

"He's alive, anyway, Triss," I said as we began to wash the instruments. "We'll put him onto sulfapyridine and keep our fingers crossed." There were still no antibiotics at that time but the new drug was a big advance.

The door opened and Helen came in. "You've been a long time, Jim." She walked over to the table and looked down at the sleeping cat. "What a poor skinny little thing. He's all bones."

"You should have seen him when he came in." Tristan switched off the sterilizer and screwed shut the valve on the anesthetic machine. "He looks a lot better now."

She stroked the little animal for a moment. "Is he badly injured?"

"I'm afraid so, Helen," I said. "We've done our best for him but I honestly don't think he has much chance."

"What a shame. And he's pretty, too. Four white feet and all those unusual colors." With her finger she traced the faint bands of auburn and copper-gold among the gray and black.

Tristan laughed. "Yes, I think that chap has a ginger Tom somewhere in his ancestry."

Helen smiled, too, but absently, and I noticed a broody look about her. She hurried out to the stock room and returned with an empty box. "Yes . . . yes . . ." she said thoughtfully. "I can make a bed in this box for him and he'll sleep in our room, Jim."

"He will?"

"Yes, he must be warm, mustn't he?"

"Of course."

Later, in the darkness of our bed-sitter,[9] I looked from my pillow at a cozy scene. Sam in his basket on one side of the flickering fire and the cat cushioned and blanketed in his box on the other.

As I floated off into sleep it was good to know that my patient was so comfortable, but I wondered if he would be alive in the morning. . . .

> **◆ Reading Strategy** How does this passage reveal the author's bias toward cats? 4

3. **prolapse** (prō´ laps) *n.:* Internal organ—here, the intestines—that has fallen out of place.
4. **saline** (sā´ līn) *n.:* Salt solution.
5. **catgut** (kat´ gut´) *n.:* Tough string or thread used in surgery.
6. **peritoneal** (per´ i tō nē´ əl) *adj.:* Having to do with the membrane that lines the abdomen.
7. **sulfanilamide** (sul´ fə nil´ ə mīd) *n.:* Sulfa drugs were used to treat infections before penicillin and other antibiotics were discovered.
8. **peritonitis** (per´ i tō nīt´ is) *n.:* Inflammation of the abdominal lining.
9. **bed-sitter:** British term for a one-room apartment.

Beyond the Classroom

Career Connection

Working With Animals To become a veterinarian, a person needs a college degree followed by post-graduate work in animal medicine, and an internship at an animal health facility. But there are other ways people who love animals can work with them. Brainstorm with students for a list of possible jobs that involve the care, health, or safety of animals, such as:

- dog walker
- pet sitter
- animal groomer
- animal trainer
- veterinarian's aide
- breeder
- animal shelter worker
- zoo keeper

Discuss what training and personality traits would be necessary for such jobs.

Students might talk to the manager of a pet shop, a zoo keeper, or an animal shelter worker to learn about opportunities that may exist for volunteer or part-time work for young people who enjoy working with animals and would like to help.

I knew he was alive at 7:30 a.m. because my wife was already up and talking to him. I trailed across the room in my pajamas and the cat and I looked at each other. I rubbed him under the chin and he opened his mouth in a rusty miaow. But he didn't try to move.

"Helen," I said. "This little thing is tied together inside with catgut. He'll have to live on fluids for a week and even then he probably won't make it. If he stays up here you'll be spooning milk into him umpteen times a day."

5 "Okay, okay." She had that broody look again.

It wasn't only milk she spooned into him over the next few days. Beef essence, strained broth and a succession of sophisticated baby foods found their way down his throat at regular intervals. One lunch time I found Helen kneeling by the box.

6 "We shall call him Oscar," she said.

"You mean we're keeping him?"

"Yes."

I am fond of cats but we already had a dog in our cramped quarters and I could see difficulties. Still I decided to let it go.

"Why Oscar?"

"I don't know." Helen tipped a few drops of chop gravy onto the little red tongue and watched intently as he swallowed.

One of the things I like about women is their mystery, the unfathomable part of them, and I didn't press the matter further. But I was pleased at the way things were going. I had been giving the sulfapyridine every six hours and taking the temperature night and morning, expecting all the time to encounter the roaring fever, the vomiting and the tense abdomen of peritonitis. But it never happened.

7 It was as though Oscar's animal instinct told him he had to move as little as possible because he lay absolutely still day after day and looked up at us—and purred.

His purr became part of our lives and when he eventually left his bed, sauntered through to our kitchen and began to sample Sam's dinner of meat and biscuit it was a moment of triumph. And I didn't spoil it by wondering if he was ready for solid food; I felt he knew.

From then on it was sheer joy to watch the furry scarecrow fill out and grow strong, and as he ate and ate and the flesh spread over his bones the true beauty of his coat showed in the glossy medley of auburn, black and gold. We had a handsome cat on our hands.

Once Oscar had fully recovered, Tristan was a regular visitor.

He probably felt, and rightly, that he, more than I, had saved Oscar's life in the first place and he used to play with him for long periods. His favorite ploy was to push his leg round the corner of the table and withdraw it repeatedly just as the cat pawed at it.

Oscar was justifiably irritated by this teasing but showed his character by lying in wait for Tristan one night and biting him smartly[10] in the ankle before he could start his tricks. 8

From my own point of view Oscar added many things to our menage.[11] Sam was delighted with him and the two soon became firm friends. Helen adored him and each evening I thought afresh that a nice cat washing his face by the hearth gave extra comfort to a room.

Oscar had been established as one of the family for several weeks when I came in from a late call to find Helen waiting for me with a stricken face.

"What's happened?" I asked.

"It's Oscar—he's gone!"

"Gone? What do you mean?"

"Oh, Jim, I think he's run away."

I stared at her. "He wouldn't do that. He often goes down to the garden at night. Are you sure he isn't there?"

◆ Build Vocabulary

inevitable (in ev´ ə tə bəl) *adj.*: Certain to happen

sauntered (sôn´ tərd) *v.*: Strolled

10. **smartly** (smart´ lē) *adv.*: Sharply.

11. **menage** (mā näzh´) *n.*: Household.

◆Literary Focus

5 Character Traits The word *broody* can mean "ready to hover over or protect offspring," or "inclined to dwell moodily on one's thoughts." Discuss with students how these meanings might apply to the way Helen looks. What is she thinking? *Students may say that she is feeling protective of the cat, as if it were her own; that she is thinking how she might become more involved in the cat's care; or that she is weighing the option of getting more involved with the cat.*

◆Critical Thinking

6 Interpret How is giving the cat a name a hopeful sign that he might recover? *Students may say that giving a name to the cat makes him seem more like a member of the family, and implies a hopeful future.*

◆Reading Strategy

7 Understand Bias Ask students to explain what Herriot's evaluation of Oscar's behavior in this paragraph implies about Herriot's view of cats. *Herriot thinks that cats are intelligent and can sense what is good for them.*

◆Critical Thinking

8 Relate Have students respond to this new snag. Did they expect this problem? Are they worried? Discuss how the author keeps the reader's interest in the essay by introducing a new problem, now that Oscar has recovered physically.

Cross-Curricular Connection: Science

Antibiotics are chemical substances that can prevent or slow the growth of some infections. At the time of Herriot's story, antibiotics were not widely available. In fact, antibiotics did not become commonly used until World War II, when penicillin was shipped to battlefield hospitals to keep wounds from getting infected.

Have interested students research the work of Scottish bacteriologist Alexander Fleming, who accidentally discovered penicillin in 1928. They can then learn how Australian scientist Howard Florey proceeded with penicillin research, and finally, how the Northern Regional Research Laboratory in Peoria, Illinois, made the breakthroughs that enabled that drug's widespread use.

Alternatively, students could learn how penicillin and other antibiotics work, where they come from, how they are introduced into the body, and what happens to people who are allergic to them. Students can present their findings in the form of oral or written reports, displays, or multimedia reports.

◆Literary Focus

❶ **Character Traits** She is emotional, but she tries to control and hide her feelings. She is being realistic about Oscar's history.

◆Literature and Your Life

❷ Ask students to compare Oscar's behavior to the behavior of cats they know. How would they characterize Oscar's behavior, by comparison. Does it seem ordinary? Odd? *Answers will vary, but students should give details to support their answer.*

▶Critical Viewing◀

❸ **Support** Like this cat, Oscar is described as having a coat showing a "glossy medley of auburn, black and gold."

"Absolutely. I've searched right into the yard. I've even had a walk round the town. And remember." Her chin quivered. "He . . . he ran away from somewhere before."

◆ Literary Focus What character traits are revealed by Helen's quivering chin? 1

I looked at my watch. "Ten o'clock. Yes, that is strange. He shouldn't be out at this time."

As I spoke the front door bell jangled. I galloped down the stairs and as I rounded the corner in the passage I could see Mrs. Heslington, the vicar's[12] wife, through the glass. I threw open the door. She was holding Oscar in her arms.

"I believe this is your cat, Mr. Herriot," she said.

"It is indeed, Mrs. Heslington. Where did you find him?"

She smiled. "Well it was rather odd. We were having a meeting of the Mothers' Union at the church house and we noticed the cat sitting there in the room."

"Just sitting . . .?" 2

"Yes, as though he were listening to what we were saying and enjoying it all. It was unusual. When the meeting ended I thought I'd better bring him along to you."

"I'm most grateful, Mrs. Heslington." I snatched Oscar and tucked him under my arm. "My wife is distraught—she thought he was lost."

It was a little mystery. Why should he suddenly take off like that? But since he showed no change in his manner over the ensuing week we put it out of our minds.

12. **vicar** (vik´ ər) *n.*: Parish priest.

◀ **Critical Viewing** What information in the essay suggests Oscar might look like the cat in this photograph? **[Support]** 3

Humanities: Art

Cartoons Oscar exhibits unusual and quirky qualities that could easily be found illustrated in a comic strip or on a Saturday morning cartoon show.

Cartoons are sketches or drawings, or a series of drawings that are meant to entertain, tell a story, communicate a message, or even make an editorial comment. Cartoons are created for many different reasons and done for a variety of media—newspapers, books, magazines, comic books, advertisements, educational materials—and even animated for television and movies. Often cartoons combine a drawing and words to depict the chosen message, but other times, the drawing itself gives the entire message. Animated cartoons have voice accompaniments.

Artists or cartoonists do not always draw the figures they use in cartoons realistically. They often choose a physical feature or personality trait to exaggerate. For example, Oscar might be depicted as having an unusually long nose because he is so nosy and curious, and not because he actually looks that way. Editorial or political cartoons drawn of famous or well-known people often exaggerate a nose, ears, hair, or size to make the drawing recognizable to the viewer.

Students may wish to make a scrapbook collection of cartoons from local newspapers or magazines that they find enjoyable or humorous. The Viewing and Representing Mini-Lesson on p. 387 will give students a further opportunity to design a cartoon.

Then one evening a man brought in a dog for a distemper[13] inoculation and left the front door open. When I went up to our flat I found that Oscar had disappeared again. This time Helen and I scoured the marketplace and side
4 alleys in vain and when we returned at half past nine we were both despondent. It was nearly eleven and we were thinking of bed when the doorbell rang.

It was Oscar again, this time resting on the ample stomach of Jack Newbould. Jack was a gardener at one of the big houses. He hiccuped gently and gave me a huge benevolent smile. "Brought your cat, Mr. Herriot."

"Gosh, thanks, Jack!" I said, scooping up Oscar gratefully. "Where the devil did you find him?"

5 "Well, s'matter o' fact 'e sort of found me."

"What do you mean?"

Jack closed his eyes for a few moments before articulating carefully. "Thish is a big night, tha knows, Mr. Herriot. Darts championship. Lots of t'lads round at t'Dog and Gun—lotsh and lotsh of 'em. Big gatherin'."

"And our cat was there?"

"Aye, he were there, all right. Sitting among t'lads. Shpent t'whole evenin' with us."

"Just sat there, eh?"

"That 'e did." Jack giggled reminiscently. "By gaw 'e enjoyed 'isself. Ah gave 'em a drop out of me own glass and once or twice ah thought 'e was going to have a go at chuckin' a dart. He's some cat." He laughed again.

As I bore Oscar upstairs I was deep in thought. What was going on here? These sudden desertions were upsetting Helen and I felt they could get on my nerves in time.

> ◆ **Literary Focus**
> What can you tell
> 6 about Oscar's
> personality from
> his actions?

I didn't have long to wait till the next one. Three nights later he was missing again. This time Helen and I didn't bother to search—we just waited.

He was back earlier than usual. I heard the door bell at nine o'clock. It was the elderly Miss Simpson peering through the glass. And she wasn't holding Oscar—he was prowling on the mat waiting to come in.

Miss Simpson watched with interest as the cat stalked inside and made for the stairs. "Ah, good, I'm so glad he's come home safely. I knew he was your cat and I've been intrigued by his behavior all evening."

"Where . . . may I ask?"

"Oh, at the Women's Institute. He came in shortly after we started and stayed there till the end."

"Really? What exactly was your program, Miss Simpson?"

"Well, there was a bit of committee stuff, then a short talk with lantern slides by Mr. Walters from the water company and we finished with a cake-making competition."

"Yes . . . yes . . . and what did Oscar do?"

She laughed. "Mixed with the company, apparently enjoyed the slides and showed great interest in the cakes."

"I see. And you didn't bring him home?"

"No, he made his own way here. As you know, I have to pass your house and I merely rang your bell to make sure you knew he had arrived."

"I'm obliged to you, Miss Simpson. We were a little worried."

I mounted the stairs in record time. Helen was sitting with the cat on her knee and she looked up as I burst in.

"I know about Oscar now," I said.

"Know what?"

13. **distemper** (dis tem´ pər) *adj.*: Infectious viral disease of young dogs.

◆ Build Vocabulary

distraught (dis trôt´) *adj.*: Extremely upset

despondent (di spän´ dənt) *adj.*: Lacking hope; depressed

intrigued (in trēg d´) *v.*: Fascinated

◆Build Grammar Skills

❹ Compound Subjects and Predicates Unlike the sentence students examined on p. 384, this sentence has a compound subject. Help students identify the subject. *Helen and I.*

◆Literary Focus

❺ Character Traits Invite students to describe Jack Newbould, based on the character traits they can gather from the details in this passage. *Jack is a fun-loving, sociable guy who plays darts competitively. He has a sense of humor, likes cats, and goes to the Dog and Gun too often.*

◆Literary Focus

❻ Character Traits Oscar enjoys being with groups of people, and he is very curious about their activities.

Viewing and Representing Mini-Lesson

Comic Strip

This mini-lesson supports the Literary Focus for this selection, and echoes the "Garfield" piece in the Connections to Today's World feature, p. 393.

Introduce Have students discuss the ways in which comic strips can convey character traits—the way characters are drawn and how they look; how they move, speak, or act; and how they are shown interacting with others. Propose the idea of creating a comic strip to represent the quirky charm of Oscar/Tiger, based on details from the narrative essay.

Develop Form groups of students in which at least one member enjoys drawing and the others share skills such as having a sense of humor, being a strong reader, or being well organized. Have each group create a two- to four-panel comic strip that captures a scene from "Cat on the Go." It should convey the quirkiness of Oscar/Tiger and the genuine affection the humans feel for him.

Apply Allow time for groups to discuss, plan, sketch, color, create dialogue, and revise the comic strips. Encourage group give-and-take to achieve the best results.

Assess Display the comic strips in the classroom, or duplicate them so that each group can have access to them. Evaluate the strips in terms of originality, accuracy in reflecting the story, and success in capturing character traits.

Thematic Focus

❶ **Quirky Characters** In this passage, Herriot and Helen attribute human traits to Oscar. Be sure students understand the meaning of each description. For instance, a socialite is a prominent person who spends a lot of time at social events. A high stepper likes to prance about, often in rich circumstances. A cat-about-town, like a "man-about-town," is a worldly and socially active creature. How do these human traits highlight Oscar's quirkiness? *Students may say that by giving him human traits, Herriot and Helen show their appreciation for Oscar, and express awe at how much like a human he behaves.*

◆Reading Strategy

❷ **Understand Bias** Note how the author describes Oscar as looking both ways, as a person would before crossing the street. Do cats really look both ways before they cross a street? What does this reveal about Herriot's attitudes toward Oscar? *Again, Herriot gives human traits to this unusual cat, which shows his respect and admiration for Oscar. He believes Oscar is very intelligent.*

◆Critical Thinking

❸ **Connect** Based on the details in this passage, what blow do you expect? *Students may guess that this man and his boys are Oscar's original owners.*

◆Literature and Your Life

❹ Some students will cite the "finders keepers" rule; others may say that Herriot and Helen should return Oscar to his rightful family. Encourage students to realize that doing the right thing isn't always an easy thing to do.

"Why he goes on these nightly outings. He's not running away—he's visiting."

"Visiting?"

"Yes," I said. "Don't you see? He likes getting around, he loves people, especially in
❶ groups, and he's interested in what they do. He's a natural mixer."

Helen looked down at the attractive mound of fur curled on her lap. "Of course . . . that's it . . . he's a socialite!"

"Exactly, a high stepper!"

"A cat-about-town!"

It all afforded us some innocent laughter and Oscar sat up and looked at us with evident pleasure, adding his own throbbing purr to the merriment. But for Helen and me there was a lot of relief behind it; ever since our cat had started his excursions there had been the gnawing fear that we would lose him, and now we felt secure.

From that night our delight in him increased. There was endless joy in watching this facet of his character unfolding. He did the social round meticulously, taking in most of the activities of the town. He became a familiar figure at whist drives,[14] jumble sales,[15] school concerts and scout bazaars. Most of the time he was made welcome, but was twice ejected from meetings of the Rural District Council who did not seem to relish the idea of a cat sitting in on their deliberations.

At first I was apprehensive about his making his way through the streets but I watched him once or twice and saw that he looked both
❷ ways before tripping daintily across. Clearly he had excellent traffic sense and this made me feel that his original injury had not been caused by a car.

Taking it all in all, Helen and I felt that it
❸ was a kind stroke of fortune which had brought Oscar to us. He was a warm and cherished part of our home life. He added to our happiness.

When the blow fell it was totally unexpected. ❸
I was finishing the evening surgery.[16] I looked round the door and saw only a man and two little boys.

"Next, please," I said.

The man stood up. He had no animal with him. He was middle-aged, with the rough weathered face of a farm worker. He twirled a cloth cap nervously in his hands.

"Mr. Herriot?" he said.

"Yes, what can I do for you?"

He swallowed and looked me straight in the eyes. "Ah think you've got ma cat."

"What?"

"Ah lost ma cat a bit since." He cleared his throat. "We used to live at Missdon but ah got a job as plowman to Mr. Horne of Wederly. It was after we moved to Wederly that t'cat went missin'. Ah reckon he was tryin to find 'is way back to his old home."

"Wederly? That's on the other side of Brawton—over thirty miles away."

"Aye, ah knaw, but cats is funny things."

"But what makes you think I've got him?"

He twisted the cap around a bit more. "There's a cousin o' mine lives in Darrowby and ah heard tell from 'im about this cat that goes around to meetin's. I 'ad to come. We've been huntin' everywhere."

"Tell me," I said. "This cat you lost. What did he look like?"

"Gray and black and sort o' gingery. Right bonny[17] 'e was. And 'e was allus goin' out to gatherin's."

A cold hand clutched at my heart. "You'd better come upstairs. Bring the boys with you."

◆ Literature and Your Life
What would you do in Jim and Helen's place? ❹

14. **whist** (hwist) **drives:** Attempts to raise money for charities and other purposes by playing the card game whist.
15. **jumble sales:** British term for sales of contributed articles to raise money for charity.
16. **surgery** (sur′ jər ē) *n.*: British term for "office hours."
17. **bonny** (bän′ ē) *adj.*: Pretty.

Beyond the Classroom

Workplace Skills

Flexibility In "Cat on the Go," Dr. Herriot faces many situations he cannot fully anticipate. When Marjorie Simpson brings him the injured cat, he simply stops what he was doing and cares for it. In the workplace, the ability to be flexible and "go with the flow" is a valuable skill. Someone who is flexible can be counted on to do whatever is needed, when it is needed.

Talk with students about aspects of flexibility, such as an ability to make quick decisions, to "switch gears" smoothly, and to make do with whatever is at hand. Discuss how flexibility can influence students' school or home obligations. For example, a surprise test may spur a flexible student to rethink homework plans to make time to study. A flexible babysitter will abandon plans for an art project if the children show interest in a game or other activity. A flexible person who enjoys sports will have alternate plans in case of bad weather.

To help students understand the trait of flexibility better, have pairs of students select a situation that demands flexibility and role-play it. Or, they might choose to contrast how flexible and inflexible people might react to the same situation. In addition they might list jobs that they believe require significant flexibility, such as teaching or customer service.

Helen was putting some coal on the fire of the bed-sitter.

"Helen," I said. "This is Mr.—er—I'm sorry, I don't know your name."

"Gibbons, Sep Gibbons. They called me Septimus because ah was the seventh in family and it looks like ah'm goin' t'same way 'cause we've got six already. These are our two youngest." The two boys, obvious twins of about eight, looked up at us solemnly.

I wished my heart would stop hammering. "Mr. Gibbons thinks Oscar is his. He lost his cat some time ago."

My wife put down her little shovel. "Oh . . . oh . . . I see." She stood very still for a moment then smiled faintly. "Do sit down. Oscar's in the kitchen, I'll bring him through."

She went out and reappeared with the cat in her arms. She hadn't got through the door before the little boys gave tongue.

"Tiger!" they cried. "Oh, Tiger, Tiger!"

The man's face seemed lit from within. He walked quickly across the
5 floor and ran his big work-roughened hand along the fur.

"Hullo, awd lad," he said, and turned to me with a radiant smile. "It's 'im, Mr. Herriot. It's 'im awright, and don't 'e look well!"

"You call him Tiger, eh?" I said.

"Aye," he replied happily. "It's them gingery stripes. The kids called 'im that. They were brokenhearted when we lost 'im."

As the two little boys rolled on the floor our Oscar rolled with them, pawing playfully, purring with delight.

Sep Gibbons sat down again. "That's the way 'e allus went on wi' the family. They used to play with 'im for hours. By gaw we did miss 'im. He were a right favorite."

I looked at the broken nails on the edge of the cap, at the decent, honest, uncomplicated Yorkshire[18] face so like the many I had grown to like and respect. Farm men like him got thirty shillings a week in those days and it was reflected in the threadbare jacket, the cracked, shiny boots and the obvious hand-me-downs of the boys.

> **◆ Reading Strategy**
> Do you think the
> author respects peo- 6
> ple like Sep Gibbons?
> Explain.

But all three were scrubbed and tidy, the man's face like a red beacon, the children's knees gleaming and their hair carefully slicked across their foreheads. They looked like nice people to me. I didn't know what to say.

Helen said it for me. "Well, Mr. Gibbons." Her tone had an unnatural brightness. "You'd better take him."

The man hesitated. "Now then, are ye sure, Missis Herriot?"

"Yes . . . yes, I'm sure. He was your cat first."

"Aye, but some folks 'ud say finders keepers or summat like that. Ah didn't come 'ere to demand 'im back or owt of t'sort."

"I know you didn't, Mr. Gibbons, but you've had him all those years and you've searched for him so hard. We couldn't possibly keep him from you."

He nodded quickly. "Well, that's right good of ye." He paused for a moment, his face serious, then he stooped and picked Oscar up. "We'll have to be off if we're goin' to catch the eight o'clock bus."

Helen reached forward, cupped the cat's head in her hands and looked at him steadily for a few seconds. Then she patted the boys' heads. "You'll take good care of him, won't you?"

"Aye, missis, thank ye, we will that." The two small faces looked up at her and smiled.

"I'll see you down the stairs, Mr. Gibbons," I said.

On the descent I tickled the furry cheek resting on the man's shoulder and heard for the last time the rich purring. On the front door step we shook hands and they set off down the street. As they rounded the corner of Trengate they stopped and waved, and I waved back at the man, the two children and the cat's head looking back at me over the shoulder.

It was my habit at that time in my life to▼ 7

18. **Yorkshire:** Region of northern England.

◆Literary Focus

5 Character Traits Have students explain the kind of person they think Sep Gibbons is, based on these details. *Students may say that he is a warm, friendly man. Although he is not wealthy, he wants to do whatever he can to make his children happy.*

◆Reading Strategy

6 Understand Bias Students may say that the author respects people like Sep Gibbons because he describes Sep and his boys kindly. He respects the fact that they are well-mannered, affectionate, and attempt to put their best foot forward.

◆Literary Focus

7 Character Traits Why does Herriot walk up the stairs "like an old man"? *He is reluctant to return to life without Oscar, and feels sad about losing him, so he moves slowly, as an old man might. He is afraid that Helen will be unhappy and upset.*

Cultural Connection

Animals that have been kept as pets differ in various regions of the world and during different periods of history.

It is known that ancient Egyptians worshipped the cat as a god as long as three or four thousand years ago. The Egyptian goddess, Bastet, was depicted in statues and pictures with a cat's head and the body of a woman. If an Egyptian house cat died, the family shaved their eyebrows as a sign of mourning. Cat mummies have even been found that were prepared as royally as that of a king.

Cats may have been valued as pets by some earlier civilizations because they were able to help control the rodent population that spread disease and filth.

In Hong Kong, an island in the South China Sea, songbirds have replaced cats and dogs as the most popular pet. In that densely populated city, bird owners, most often older gentlemen, carry their songbirds in cages to the parks so that the birds can sing in new surroundings. Walking their birds gives Hong Kong residents a reason to escape crowded apartments and noisy streets, and to meet old friends under trees festooned with singing birds in cages. Bird walkers may even travel with caged pets by subway.

Invite students to investigate the kinds of animals that are kept as pets in other cultures and have been kept as pets historically. Suggest that students analyze reasons why pets are cared for and enjoyed.

▶Critical Viewing◀

❶ Connect This cat has Oscar's coloring, and is shown in a rural environment, which fits Oscar's background. The picture does not show his interaction with people, but it does show him "on the go."

◆Critical Thinking

Speculate Pause at this point to ask students to suggest what they think may happen in the narrative once Oscar goes back to his original owners. *Some students may say that the story will end with Oscar getting sick and being brought to Herriot for care. Others may guess that Oscar misses Herriot and Helen.*

Customize for
Verbal/Linguistic Learners
Students may enjoy planning and writing another chapter to Oscar's life. They might write a chapter in which he disrupts a meeting, or causes an argument and debate over whether he should be allowed to visit. Alternatively, they may conclude that Oscar attempts to go back to visit Herriot and Helen, gets lost again, and has adventures.

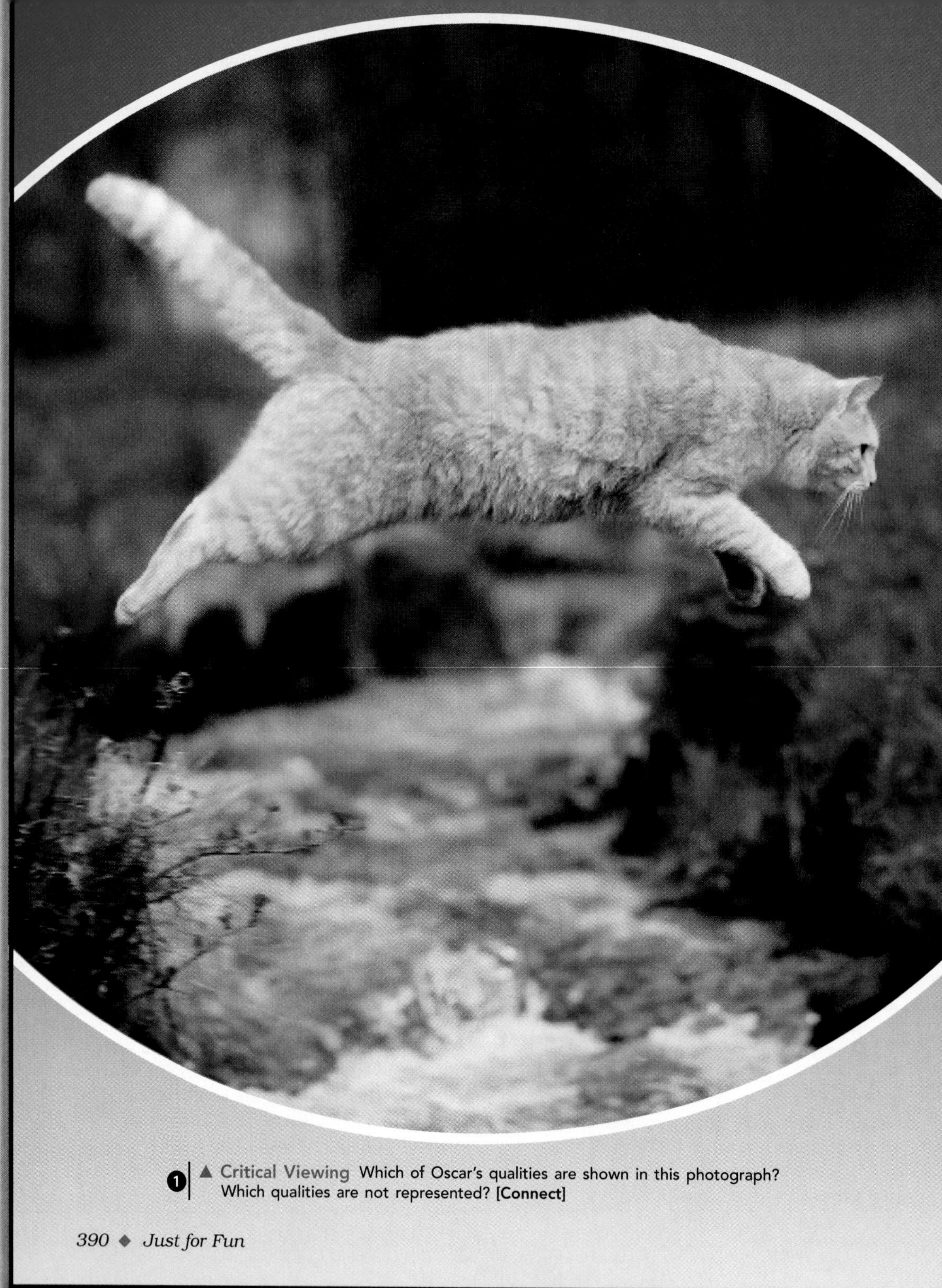

❶ ▲ Critical Viewing Which of Oscar's qualities are shown in this photograph? Which qualities are not represented? **[Connect]**

Speaking and Listening Mini-Lesson

Career Interview

This mini-lesson supports the Speaking and Listening activity in the Idea Bank on p. 395.

Introduce Talk about the benefits of an interview for getting firsthand information. Tell students that when they want to interview a busy person, they need to schedule an appointment or contact another possible interviewee. Talk about how to contact a vet (consult the Yellow Pages of your local telephone directory, or go on the Internet), how to ask for an interview, and how best to prepare so that the time is well spent.

Develop Have students work in pairs or small groups. Have them role-play practice: calling for the appointment, introducing themselves and explaining the task, and asking questions and noting responses. Point out that this task involves planning (preparing for the interview), speaking (asking questions), listening (taking in details), and organizing (sharing facts).

Apply Allow adequate time for students to conduct their interviews—in person, over the phone, or by mail. When they have gathered their data, have them determine how best to share it: in a written report, an oral report, or a graphic display.

Assess Evaluate the interviews by how well students achieve their goal, how effectively their interviews went, and how clearly they impart information to classmates.

mount the stairs two or three at a time but on this occasion I trailed upwards like an old man, slightly breathless, throat tight, eyes prickling.

I cursed myself for a sentimental fool but as I reached our door I found a flash of consolation. Helen had taken it remarkably well. She had nursed that cat and grown deeply attached to him, and I'd have thought an unforeseen calamity like this would have upset her terribly. But no, she had behaved calmly and rationally.

It was up to me to do as well. I adjusted my features into the semblance of a cheerful smile and marched into the room.

2 Helen had pulled a chair close to the table and was slumped face down against the wood. One arm cradled her head while the other was stretched in front of her as her body shook with an utterly abandoned weeping.

I had never seen her like this and I was appalled. I tried to say something comforting but nothing stemmed the flow of racking sobs.

Feeling helpless and inadequate I could only sit close to her and stroke the back of her head. Maybe I could have said something if I hadn't felt just about as bad myself.

You get over these things in time. After all, we told ourselves, it wasn't as though Oscar had died or got lost again—he had gone to a good family who would look after him. In fact he had really gone home.

3 And of course, we still had our much-loved Sam, although he didn't help in the early stages by sniffing disconsolately where Oscar's bed used to lie then collapsing on the rug with a long lugubrious sigh.

There was one other thing, too. I had a little notion forming in my mind, an idea which I would spring on Helen when the time was right. It was about a month after that shattering night and we were coming out of the cinema at Brawton at the end of our half day. I looked at my watch.

"Only eight o'clock," I said. "How about going to see Oscar?"

Helen looked at me in surprise. "You mean—drive on to Wederly?"

"Yes, it's only about five miles."

A smile crept slowly across her face. "That would be lovely. But do you think they would mind?"

"The Gibbons? No, I'm sure they wouldn't. Let's go."

Wederly was a big village and the plowman's cottage was at the far end a few yards beyond the Methodist chapel. I pushed open the garden gate and we walked down the path.

A busy-looking little woman answered my knock. She was drying her hands on a striped towel.

"Mrs. Gibbons?" I said.

"Aye, that's me."

"I'm James Herriot—and this is my wife."

Her eyes widened uncomprehendingly. Clearly the name meant nothing to her.

"We had your cat for a while," I added.

Suddenly she grinned and waved her towel at us. "Oh aye, ah remember now. Sep told me about you. Come in, come in!"

4 The big kitchen-living room was a tableau[19] of life with six children and thirty shillings a week. Battered furniture, rows of much-mended washing on a pulley, black cooking range and a general air of chaos.

Sep got up from his place by the fire, put down his newspaper, took off a pair of steel-rimmed spectacles and shook hands.

He waved Helen to a sagging armchair. "Well, it's right nice to see you. Ah've often spoke of ye to t'missis."

His wife hung up her towel. "Yes, and I'm glad to meet ye both. I'll get some tea in a minnit."

She laughed and dragged a bucket of muddy water into a corner. "I've been washin' football jerseys. Them lads just handed them to me tonight—as if I haven't enough to do."

As she ran the water into the kettle I peeped

19. **tableau** (tab´ lō) *n.*: Dramatic scene or picture.

◆Literary Focus

2 Character Traits Discuss new insights into Helen, based on this passage. How does she really feel about Oscar's return to the Gibbons family? Why did she hide these feelings earlier? *Helen is very upset at losing Oscar, but she did not want to reveal her true feelings to the Gibbons family, who were so glad to have found their lost cat. She didn't want to be selfish.*

Thematic Focus

3 Quirky Characters Although this story has focused mainly on Oscar, Sam is a quirky character, too. Have students tell what seems quirky about Sam. *Herriot describes Sam as having near-human qualities. He seems to search for Oscar, and collapses with a sigh when he cannot find him.*

◆Literary Focus

4 Character Traits In this passage, the narrator describes the Gibbonses at home. What character traits can students discern about the family from the description of their surroundings and about how they greet Herriot and Helen? *Students will note that the big family is boisterous and cordial. They are poor, but they welcome Herriot and Helen graciously and do not seem ashamed of their modest home.*

Cross-Curricular Connection: Science

Cat Communication In the selection, Herriot and Tristan decide not to use ether to put Oscar to sleep when he is so badly wounded because they hear purring coming from the badly injured animal.

Purring is the sound a friendly, contented cat often makes. The sound is generally thought to be caused by the vocal cords vibrating as a cat inhales and exhales air. However, some scientists believe the purring sound is caused by vibrations in the wall of a blood vessel in the chest that occurs when the blood flow increases. Although purring usually means a cat is happy, it has been noticed that some cats purr when they are sick.

In addition to purring, cats use a variety of vocal sounds and behaviors to communicate their feelings without words. Ask students if they have ever heard a cat fight late at night under their windows outside. If so, they will be interested to know that the horrible sound the cats make is called *caterwauling.* A contented cat may lie on its back or chest with its eyes closed in total bliss and if you stroke him, he will rumble with a purr. An angry or frightened cat will crouch down low, lay back its ears, switch its tail back and forth, and growl or wail to express itself quite effectively.

Suggest that interested students observe a cat's behavior and note other forms of communication a cat employs.

Thematic Focus

1 Quirky Characters What is quirky about what Mrs. Gibbons tells Helen and Herriot? *She tells them that Tiger is out, but that he's due home soon, as if the cat can tell time or keep to a regular schedule.*

Beyond Literature

Science Connection Students might begin their research by gathering basic background facts from an encyclopedia article or a book on cats. Armed with information, they can move into the cat research.

surreptitiously around me and I noticed Helen doing the same. But we searched in vain. There was no sign of a cat. Surely he couldn't have run away again? With a growing feeling of dismay I realized that my little scheme could backfire devastatingly.

It wasn't until the tea had been made and poured that I dared to raise the subject.

"How—" I asked diffidently. "How is—er—Tiger?"

1 "Oh, he's grand," the little woman replied briskly. She glanced up at the clock on the mantelpiece. "He should be back any time now, then you'll be able to see 'im."

As she spoke, Sep raised a finger. "Ah think ah can hear 'im now."

He walked over and opened the door and our Oscar strode in with all his old grace and majesty. He took one look at Helen and leaped onto her lap. With a cry of delight she put down her cup and stroked the beautiful fur as the cat arched himself against her hand and the familiar purr echoed round the room.

"He knows me," she murmured. "He knows me."

Sep nodded and smiled. "He does that. You were good to 'im. He'll never forget ye, and we won't either, will we mother?"

"No, we won't, Mrs. Herriot," his wife said as she applied butter to a slice of gingerbread. "That was a kind thing ye did for us and I 'ope you'll come and see us all whenever you're near."

"Well, thank you," I said. "We'd love to—we're often in Brawton."

I went over and tickled Oscar's chin, then I turned again to Mrs. Gibbons. "By the way, it's after nine o'clock. Where has he been till now?"

She poised her butter knife and looked into space.

"Let's see, now," she said. "It's Thursday, isn't it? Ah yes, it's 'is night for the Yoga class."

◆ **Build Vocabulary**

surreptitiously (sʉr′ əp tish′ əs lē) *adv.*: Secretly

Beyond Literature

Science Connection

Cats—Domestic and Wild You may be familiar with the many breeds of cats that are domesticated. These cats are trainable and friendly to humans. However, there are some species of cat that live in the wild, scavenging food for themselves and marking out a space to call their own. While Oscar is treated as a house cat, his roaming demonstrates some behaviors of wild cats.

All felines are solitary creatures who travel a specific range or territory. They spend a large portion of their day covering this range, searching for food and defending their territory from invaders.

Wildcats—like the bobcat and Canada lynx—are generally longer and stronger than house cats. They have shorter tails and tufts of fur on their ears. These cats prowl at night and may be more vicious than a typical house cat.

Cross-Curricular Activity

Categorizing Cats Conduct research to learn the species of cats common in your region. Identify the breeds of cats your friends and neighbors keep as pets, and collect information on as many breeds as possible. Find out about wildcats that may roam free in your state.

Create an illustrated report to share your findings with classmates.

Beyond the Selection

FURTHER READING

Other Works by James Herriot

All Creatures Great and Small

Every Living Thing

Other Works About Cats

One-Eyed Cat, Paula Fox

The Incredible Journey, Sheila Burnford

INTERNET

We suggest the following sites on the Internet (all Web sites are subject to change).

For more information about James Herriot: **http://www.geocities.com/Athens/acropolis/3907/herriot2.html**

For more on Jim Davis and Garfield: **http://www.garfield.com/paws/jimdavis**

We *strongly recommend* that you preview these sites before you send students to them.

Connections to Today's World

From the Herriots' home in England to the homes of many of your friends and neighbors, cats are beloved by people the world over. Those of us who don't own a furry feline may enjoy the witty commentary of Jim Davis's Garfield, a cat who visits our homes in daily newspapers and in collections of Davis's funny cartoons.

Garfield

Jim Davis

DO YOU KNOW WHY I DON'T CHASE BIRDS ? WELL, I'LL TELL YOU
MY UNCLE HUBERT ONCE CAUGHT A 30-POUND CANARY IN CHICAGO
THEY LAST SPOTTED HIM OVER DALLAS, TEXAS
6-23
JIM DAVIS

1. According to the cartoon, what happened to Hubert?
2. Compare the characterization of Garfield with that of Oscar in "Cat on the Go."

Guide for Responding

◆ Literature and Your Life

Reader's Response How have you felt when, like the Herriots, you've had to give up something that meant a lot to you?

Thematic Focus What do the Herriots discover about the cat that makes them laugh?

Journal Writing Is it better that the Herriots had the chance to know Oscar, or would they have been better off not meeting him? In a journal entry, explore your response.

☑ Check Your Comprehension

1. Explain how Doctor Herriot helped the cat.
2. What is Helen Herriot's response to the cat?
3. Where does the cat go each time it wanders off from the Herriots' home?
4. How does the community react to the cat?
5. How is the cat reunited with its owners?
6. Where is the cat when the Herriots go to visit?

◆ Critical Thinking

INTERPRET

1. What effect does the injured cat's purring have on Herriot and Tristan? **[Analyze Cause and Effect]**
2. (a) Identify three places where neighbors spot the cat. (b) What do these places have in common? **[Generalize]**
3. Why do the Herriots give up the cat instead of claiming "finders keepers"? **[Analyze]**
4. After the cat leaves, what details of their life tell you the Herriots had become attached to him? **[Support]**

EVALUATE

5. How does Herriot's enjoyment of the cat increase your interest in the essay? **[Assess]**
6. Do you think that the Herriots did the right thing in returning Oscar to the Gibbons family? Explain your answer. **[Evaluate]**

APPLY

7. Why do you think that many people enjoy having pets? **[Generalize]**

◆ Critical Thinking

1. They are so moved by the good-natured purring of such a badly injured animal that they do what they can to try to save him.
2. (a) At a meeting of the Mothers' Union at the church house; at the darts championship; at the Women's Institute meeting; (b) Each is a gathering of a group of people in a public meeting place.
3. They believe it is their obligation to return the cat to its original owners, who have missed it deeply.
4. They were upset; they made plans to visit the Gibbons family to see the cat.
5. Possible answer: Herriot makes the cat such a likeable character that you can't help but enjoy reading about him.
6. Most students will say that they did the right thing, but others may feel that since Herriot and Helen did so much to save the cat's life, they earned the right to keep him.
7. Possible answers: They like animals; they want to care for a living creature; the pet entertains and soothes them; they like the companionship.

Connections to Today's World

More About the Author

Jim Davis was born in Marion, Indiana, in 1945. Although he grew up with several dozen cats, he has no cats today because his wife is allergic. His "Garfield" comic strip, which first appeared on June 19, 1978, in 41 newspapers, now appears in over 2,500 papers around the world.

Thematic Focus

Quirky Characters Brainstorm with students to list some of the quirky cat characters they know from cartoons, comics, or fiction, such as Garfield, Sylvester, the Cheshire Cat, or Morris. Discuss the quirks that help these famous cats capture the imagination. What distinguishes Garfield from the others?

Answers

1. The canary flew away with him.
2. Like Oscar, Garfield seems to have humanlike traits. Unlike Oscar, Garfield shares his thoughts with his audience in his balloon messages.

Reinforce and Extend

Answers

◆ Literature and Your Life

Reader's Response Encourage students to share their experiences and include details about the event and how they felt.

Thematic Focus They find it amusing that the cat's quirky behaviors seem almost human.

☑ Check Your Comprehension

1. He performed life-saving surgery.
2. She makes the cat comfortable and does everything she can to help it get better.
3. The cat shows up at meetings of various groups of people, where he is interested in watching and listening.
4. The people in the community enjoy Oscar's visits.
5. Sep Gibbons hears a rumor about a cat who enjoys going to meetings. He travels to Herriot's home to see if the cat might be his missing pet.
6. He is visiting a yoga class.

Answers

◆Reading Strategy

1. *Part of our lives* means that the author sees the cat as a member of the family; the verbs *sauntered* and *sample* make the cat seem almost human; *it was a moment of triumph* shows how glad Herriot is that the cat has survived.
2. Sample responses: *He wouldn't do that* [run away] shows that Herriot believes that Oscar thinks he's as much a part of the family as Herriot and Helen do; *He's visiting* shows that Herriot believes that Oscar makes choices as a human might.

◆ Build Vocabulary

Using the Prefix *in-*

1. inconsistent; The weather is inconsistent at this time of year.
2. incapable; Cats are incapable of speech.
3. insincere; I would be insincere if I said that I love cats.

Spelling Strategy

1. thought; 2. fought; 3. drought

Using the Word Bank

1. sauntered; 2. intrigued;
3. distraught or despondent;
4. emaciated; 5. grotesquely;
6. inevitable; 7. surreptitiously;
8. despondent or distraught

◆Literary Focus

1. It shows that Tristan cares for animals and trusts in Dr. Herriot's ability to heal them.
2. It shows that he is a trained and experienced veterinarian and a scientist.
3. He is curious, good-natured, fun-loving, unpredictable, and attractive.

◆Build Grammar Skills

Practice

1. unscrewed, poised (comp. pred.)
2. essence, broth, food (comp. subj.)
3. galloped, rounded (comp. pred.)
4. Helen, I (comp. subj.)
5. would fill, have (comp. pred.)

Writing Application

Possible responses:

1. Herriot and Tristan worked to save the cat.
2. I'd give money to help stray animals or take them in myself.
3. Oscar or Tiger is a good name for a ginger cat.

Guide for Responding *(continued)*

◆ Reading Strategy

Understand Bias

A writer's **bias** is the knowledge, background, interests, and attitude that he or she brings to a piece of writing. You can detect a writer's bias through the details a writer includes. If you remember that bias affects the information the writer presents, you can read a piece of literature objectively.

1. What bias do the italicized words in this statement reveal? "His purr became a *part of our lives* and when he eventually left his bed, *sauntered* . . . to our kitchen and began to *sample* Sam's dinner of meat and biscuit *it was a moment of triumph.*"

2. Find two other examples in the story that show Herriot's bias. Explain each one.

◆ Build Vocabulary

Using the Prefix *in-*

Add the prefix *in-*, meaning "not," to the following words. Then, write sentences using the new words.

1. consistent (following the same pattern)

2. capable (able; skilled)

3. sincere (honest; truthful)

Spelling Strategy

In words like *distraught,* the letters *gh* are silent. Finish the sentences with words that follow this rule.

1. I th___?___ I asked you to feed the cat.

2. Mrs. Herriot f___?___ back tears.

3. The dr___?___ caused a terrible water shortage.

Using the Word Bank

Use the Word Bank to complete these sentences.

1. The cat ___?___ into the room gracefully.

2. The movie's complicated plot ___?___ me.

3. The child became so ___?___ he cried.

4. After a crash diet, he looked ___?___.

5. Intestines spilled ___?___ onto the table.

6. Despite all my excuses, the speeding ticket was ___?___.

7. Stealing glances, she looked at him ___?___.

8. When the cat left, the family became ___?___.

◆ Literary Focus

Character Traits

Character traits are the qualities that make a person or an animal an individual. As the events unfold, Oscar, Tristan, Doctor Herriot, and Helen reveal their special traits in what they do and say.

1. Tristan brings an injured and starving cat to James Herriot. What traits does this behavior reveal?

2. Herriot includes technical details about the operation, even though they might seem unpleasant. What does this say about him?

3. Which character traits make Oscar so well loved by the Herriots?

◆ Build Grammar Skills

Compound Subjects and Predicates

A **compound subject** is two or more subjects that have the same verb. Similarly, a **compound predicate** contains two or more verbs that have the same subject. Both compound subjects and compound predicates are joined by conjunctions, such as *and* or *or*. Look at these examples:

compound subject

Tristan and *I* looked down at the shattered animal.

compound predicate

I *shrugged* and *shook* my head.

Practice Write these sentences on your paper. Underline compound subjects once and compound predicates twice.

1. Tristan unscrewed the cap and poised it above the head.

2. Beef essence, strained broth, and baby food found their way down his throat.

3. I galloped downstairs and rounded the corner.

4. Helen and I felt that it was a kind stroke of fortune that brought Oscar to us.

5. He would either fill out or have trouble surviving.

Writing Application Create sentences using the following items as directed.

1. Herriot and Tristan (compound subject)

2. give or take (compound predicate)

3. Oscar or Tiger (compound subject)

Writer's Solution

For more instruction and practice, use the lesson in the *Writer's Solution Language Lab CD-ROM* on Agreement with Compound Subjects.

Build Your Portfolio

Idea Bank

Writing

1. **Pet Story** Using "Cat on the Go" as a model, write an amusing episode featuring your pet or an animal you know. Include, as Herriot did, realistic dialogue and vivid descriptions.
2. **Monologue** Write a speech from Oscar's point of view. Describe your injury, your feelings about the Herriots, and your evening habits. Explain your feelings about returning to the Gibbonses.
3. **Biographical Sketch** Using the details provided in "Cat on the Go" and the author information on page 380, write a biographical sketch of James Herriot. In your essay, identify the character traits that made him a good doctor.

Speaking and Listening

4. **Career Interview** Interview a veterinarian to find out more about the job Herriot describes. Ask questions to learn what makes the job tough and what makes it rewarding. Share your findings with the class. **[Career Link]**
5. **Musical Retelling [Group Activity]** With a group, set this story to music. Review the piece to determine where the mood changes. For each section, write a summary of the action, and identify music that captures the mood. Combine your summaries with the music, and perform your retelling for the class. **[Music Link]**

Projects

6. **Training Profile** Use the Internet and the library to research the educational requirements needed to get into a school of veterinary medicine. For each school you find, learn what it takes to get a D.V.M. degree. **[Career Link]**
7. **Pet-Care Brochure** Visit an animal shelter or pet store to find out about the responsibilities of pet ownership. In a pamphlet, teach others the daily tasks that need to be done, and offer suggestions for making a pet feel at home. Illustrate your brochure, and share it with classmates.

Writing Mini-Lesson

Directory of Places

Oscar's habit of visiting meetings and groups reveals not only his sociable side but also his resourcefulness. Imagine how much easier his travel would have been if he had used a directory of places to visit. Research your community to find clubs or meetings Oscar might have liked to visit. Then, create a directory of community information.

Writing Skills Focus: Supply Background Information

Your directory will be more useful if it provides more than just names and addresses. **Supply background information on local clubs**—details such as history, goals, major accomplishments, and special programs. These details will make the directory a good resource for any newcomer to your community.

Model

Wederly Art Club: 2-07 High Street. Celebrating its fiftieth year, the Art Club offers classes in a variety of media, including painting, sculpting, and computer animation. Each year, the club creates the floats for the summer parade.

Prewriting Check the library and telephone book to find interesting places in your community. Jot down phone numbers, addresses, and information describing their activities. Decide whether you will organize your directory alphabetically or by category.

Drafting Use your notes to create entries on clubs and activities. Keep directory entries brief.

◆ Grammar Application

Compound subjects or predicates can help you avoid short, choppy sentences.

Revising Confirm the accuracy of your information against your notes. Add illustrations, colors, logos, or bullets to make your directory attractive.

Idea Bank

Following are suggestions for matching the Idea Bank topics with your students' performance levels and learning modalities:

Customize for *Performance Levels*
Less Advanced Students: 1, 4
Average Students: 2, 4, 5, 7
More Advanced Students: 3, 4, 5, 6

Customize for *Learning Modalities*
Verbal/Linguistic: 1, 2, 3, 4, 6, 7
Visual/Spatial: 7
Logical/Mathematical: 4, 6, 7
Musical/Rhythmic: 5
Interpersonal: 4, 5, 7
Intrapersonal: 1, 2, 3, 6

Writing Mini-Lesson

Refer students to the Writing Handbook in the back of the book for instructions on the writing process and for further information on creating a directory.

Writer's Solution

Writing Lab CD-ROM

Have students complete the tutorial on Exposition: Giving Information. Follow these steps:

1. Have students use the Prewriting section of the tutorial to learn how to narrow a topic and gather information.
2. Have students draft on computer.
3. Have students use Proofreading Checklist and the Revision Checker for homonyms.

Allow about 60 minutes of class time to complete these steps.

Writer's Solution Sourcebook

Have students use Chapter 4, "Exposition: Giving Information," pp. 102–133, for additional support. The chapter includes in-depth instruction on building paragraphs to supply adequate information, p. 129.

ASSESSMENT OPTIONS

Formal Assessment, Selection Test, pp. 113–115, and Assessment Resources Software. The selection test is designed so that it can be easily customized to the performance levels of your students.

Alternative Assessment, p. 25, includes options for less advanced students, more advanced students, interpersonal learners, logical/mathematical learners, verbal/lingusitic learners, and visual/spatial learners.

PORTFOLIO ASSESSMENT

Use the following rubrics in the **Alternative Assessment** booklet to assess student writing:
Pet Story: Fictional Narrative, p. 82
Monologue: Expression, p. 81
Biographical Sketch: Description, p. 84
Writing Mini-Lesson: Research Report/Paper, p. 93

Prepare and Engage

OBJECTIVES

1. To read, comprehend, and interpret a short story and four poems
2. To relate a story and poems to personal experience
3. To recognize author's purpose
4. To identify and analyze hyperbole
5. To build vocabulary in context and use words with multiple meanings
6. To distinguish between complete and incomplete sentences
7. To write a humorous poem using imaginative words
8. To respond to the selections through writing, speaking and listening, and projects

SKILLS INSTRUCTION

Vocabulary: Using Words With Multiple Meanings
Spelling: Words With *-cess*
Grammar: Complete and Incomplete Sentences
Reading Strategy: Recognize Author's Purpose
Literary Focus: Hyperbole
Writing: Use Imaginative Words
Speaking and Listening: Dramatization (Teacher Edition)
Viewing and Representing: Visual Representation (Teacher Edition)
Critical Viewing: Analyze; Connect; Assess; Speculate

PORTFOLIO OPPORTUNITIES

Writing: Postcard From Sarah; Seasonal Description; Literary Review
Writing Mini-Lesson: Humorous Poem
Speaking and Listening: Dramatization; Interview
Projects: Report on Good-Luck Charms; Microscope Presentation

More About the Authors

Lucille Clifton's best-known work is *Generations,* a poetic memoir based on five generations of her family.

Lewis Carroll suffered from a stammer, which disappeared when he spoke with children.

Maxine Kumin won a Pulitzer Prize in 1973 for her volume of poetry entitled *Up Country.*

Innovative poet **E. E. Cummings** was also a talented painter and had several one-man shows.

Shel Silverstein served in the Armed Forces in the Korean War, and drew many cartoons for the magazine *Pacific Stars and Stripes.*

Guide for Reading

Meet the Authors:

Lucille Clifton (1936–)

Lucille Clifton has worked hard to overcome discrimination and become a successful writer. Whether in poetry or prose, she often writes about the value of sharing family traditions.

Lewis Carroll (1832–1898)

Lewis Carroll is the pen name of Charles Dodgson, a mathematics professor who was born in England. Under his pen name, Dodgson wrote *Alice's Adventures in Wonderland* and *Through the Looking Glass.* His poems are noted for their clever wordplay, nonsensical meanings, and delightfully zany fantasy worlds.

Maxine Kumin (1925–)

Maxine Kumin writes children's books, as well as volumes of poetry, fiction, and nonfiction. She often plays with the lines in her poems to create a look that reflects the subject of her writing.

E. E. Cummings (1894–1962)

Edward Estlin Cummings's poetry shows his original use of language and uncommon use of punctuation. His style caused much controversy during his lifetime—a controversy that continues today.

Shel Silverstein (1932–1999)

Shel Silverstein is a cartoonist, a composer, a folk singer, and a writer. He is best known to people of all ages for two books of poetry, *Where the Sidewalk Ends* and *A Light in the Attic.* Although his poems are humorous, they contain a message for all.

◆ Literature and Your Life

Connect Your Experience

There are many reasons to look for humor and happiness in daily life. You may joke to relieve the tension of a bad day, or you may smile with joy on the first warm spring morning. Like you, characters in these selections find comedy and satisfaction in life's daily experiences.

Thematic Focus: Quirky Characters

As you encounter the quirky characters in each selection, think about whether they remind you of anyone you know.

◆ Background for Understanding

Literature

Dialect is the form of a language spoken by people in a specific region or group. Dialects differ from the standard language in pronunciation, grammar, and word choice. For example, the varieties of English spoken in Boston, Chicago, or Dallas are quite different from each other. In "The Luckiest Time of All," Clifton uses a dialect from the rural South. Because she uses words like *usta* for "used to" and *nothin* for "nothing," she lets readers enjoy the unique way her narrator tells a story.

◆ Build Vocabulary

Words With Multiple Meanings

Sage is one of many English words that have multiple meanings. In "Father William," the word means "a very wise person." *Sage,* however, is also the name of an herb used in cooking.

Word Bank

Look over these words from the selections. How might *rancid* food smell?

incessantly
sage
supple
withered
curdled
rancid

Prentice Hall Literature Program Resources

REINFORCE / RETEACH / EXTEND

Selection Support Pages
Build Vocabulary: Multiple Meanings, p. 139
Build Spelling Skills, p. 140
Build Grammar Skills: Complete and Incomplete Sentences, p. 141
Reading Strategy: Recognize Author's Purpose, p. 142
Literary Focus: Hyperbole, p. 143

Strategies for Diverse Student Needs, pp. 51–52

Beyond Literature Study Skills: Outlining, p. 26

Formal Assessment Selection Test, pp. 116–118, Assessment Resources Software

Alternative Assessment, p. 26

Writing and Language Transparencies
Sensory Language Chart, p. 78

Resource Pro CD-ROM "The Luckiest Time of All"; "Father William"; "The Microscope"; "in Just-"; "Sarah Cynthia Sylvia Stout . . ."

Listening to Literature Audiocassettes "The Luckiest Time of All"; "Father William"; "The Microscope"; "in Just-"; "Sarah Cynthia Sylvia Stout . . ."

The Luckiest Time of All ◆ Father William
The Microscope ◆ in Just-
[S]arah Cynthia Sylvia Stout Would Not Take the Garbage Out

◆ Literary Focus

HYPERBOLE

"I'm so hungry I could eat a horse!"

"I haven't seen you for ages."

Everyday speech is full of examples of **hyperbole,** or exaggeration for effect. Writers use hyperbole to create humor or to emphasize a point. For example, when a character in "The Luckiest Time of All" describes a dog chasing after her, she says, "He lit out after me and I flew!" As you read, keep a list like the one below to note examples of hyperbole in these selections.

HYPERBOLE — I flew!

◆ Reading Strategy

RECOGNIZE AUTHOR'S PURPOSE

When you are prepared for a strange reflection as you face a fun-house mirror, you can enjoy the view. However, you might be terrified if you were expecting a realistic image. **Recognizing an author's purpose,** or reason, for writing can be equally helpful as you face a piece of literature. This purpose might be to influence you, to educate you, to make you laugh, or to make you think. A purpose shapes the language and details a writer uses. For example, in "Father William," Lewis Carroll creates a ridiculous character in an old man who turns somersaults and offers to sell his son his healing ointment. These details enhance the humor of the poem.

Preparing for Standardized Tests

Vocabulary Standardized test questions may require students to recognize multiple meanings of words. Provide students with opportunities to evaluate the appropriateness of words when their meanings shift. Write these sentences and word choices on the board. Ask students to find the word that fits in both of the sentences.

Anton carefully placed the sack of flour on the ___?___.

He looked at the ___?___ of fish under his microscope.

(A) counter (C) shelf
(B) scales (D) fins

Students should recognize that *(B) scales* is the only word that fits in both sentences. *(A)* and *(C)* both fit in the first sentence but not in the second, and *(D)* fits in the second sentence but not in the first. In the first sentence, *scales* means "an instrument for weighing"; in the second it means "small stiff plates that cover the bodies of fish." For additional practice with multiple-meaning words, use **Selection Support,** p. 139.

Interest Grabber Stimulate students' interest in quirky characters by asking them to think of peculiar characters they know from television, film, or comics. Remind them of such characters as Bill Nye the Science Guy, C3PO from *Star Wars,* and Data from *Star Trek.* Ask students to jot down notes on what makes these characters quirky and whether they like or dislike their oddities. Explain that the selections they are about to read contain more quirky characters.

▸ Build Grammar Skills

Complete and Incomplete Sentences If you wish to introduce the grammar concept for this selection before students read, refer to the instruction on p. 408.

Customize for
Less Proficient Readers
Explain that often a character seems quirky in relation to another "normal" character. Have students fill out a chart like the one below to note the opposing characters in the selections and the details that create the characters.

Selection: Father William	
Character	**Details**
Father William	stands on his head
his son	asks a lot of questions

Customize for
More Advanced Students
Each of the selections students are about to read contains an element of humor. Ask students to determine how humor is created in each selection and to what end humor is used. Is the selection silly to amuse readers? Does the selection use humorous irony to teach a lesson? Have students take notes as they read each selection, trying to pinpoint each writer's development of humor. Then have students compare and contrast the effects of humor in these selections.

One-Minute Insight Elzie tells her great-granddaughter Tee a story of how she and her friend once went to a traveling show. At the show grounds, the two friends are amused by the performance of a dancing dog. People begin throwing pennies on the ground, and the girls join in. In her excitement, Elzie throws her "lucky stone," which accidentally hits the dog's nose. The dog begins to chase Elzie. She is rescued by a young boy named Amos Pickens. The incident causes her to become acquainted with Pickens, who would later become her husband. The story illustrates how events can have unexpected consequences that can change a person's life forever.

◆ Critical Thinking

❶ **Infer** Ask students why people threw pennies. *They were rewarding the dog's owner for the dog's performance.*

◆ Reading Strategy

❷ **Recognize Author's Purpose** What details in this passage provide evidence that the author's purpose is to amuse readers? *The description of the dog chasing Elzie and the people laughing at the "new show" are humorous highlights in the story.*

▶ Critical Viewing ◀

❸ **Analyze** Students should recognize that an activity such as quilting brings family members together to work on a project and to share stories of their lives.

Customize for
English Language Learners
The southern dialect and figures of speech in the story may present challenges for students as they read. Have students try to rephrase sentences in standard English. For example, "Dancin dancin dancin till people started throwin pennies out of they pockets" can be rewritten "Dancing, dancing, dancing, until people started throwing pennies out of their pockets." In addition, clarify meanings of figures of speech by paraphrasing. For example, explain that *grinnin fit to bust* means "wearing a big smile."

The Luckiest Time of All

Lucille Clifton

Mrs. Elzie F. Pickens was rocking slowly on the porch one afternoon when her Great-granddaughter, Tee, brought her a big bunch of dogwood blooms, and that was the beginning of a story.

"Ahhh, now that dogwood reminds me of the day I met your Great-granddaddy, Mr. Pickens, Sweet Tee.

"It was just this time, spring of the year, and me and my best friend Ovella Wilson, who is now gone, was goin to join the Silas Greene. Usta be a kinda show went all through the South, called it the Silas Greene show. Somethin like the circus. Me and Ovella wanted to join that thing and see the world. Nothin wrong at home or nothin, we just wanted to travel and see new things and have high times. Didn't say nothin to nobody but one another. Just up and decided to do it.

"Well, this day we plaited our hair and put a dress and some things in a crokasack[1] and started out to the show. Spring day like this.

"We got there after a good little walk and it was the world, Baby, such music and wonders as we never had seen! They had everything there, or seemed like it.

"Me and Ovella thought we'd walk around for a while and see the show before goin to the office to sign up and join.

"While we was viewin it all we come up on this dancin dog. Cutest one thing in the world next to you, Sweet Tee, dippin and movin and head bowin to that music. Had a little ruffly skirt on itself and up on two back legs twistin and movin to the music. Dancin dancin dancin till people started throwin pennies out of they pockets. ❶

"Me and Ovella was caught up too and laughin so. She took a penny out of her pocket and threw it to the ground where that dog was dancin, and I took two pennies and threw 'em both.

"The music was faster and faster and that dog was turnin and turnin. Ovella reached in her sack and threw out a little pin she had won from never being late at Sunday school. And me, laughin and all excited, reached in my bag and threw out my lucky stone!

"Well, I knew right off what I had done. Soon as it left my hand it seemed like I reached back out for it to take it back. But the stone was gone from my hand and Lord, it hit that dancin dog right on his nose!

"Well, he lit out after me, poor thing. He lit out after me and I flew! Round and round the Silas Greene we run, through every place me and Ovella had walked before, but now that dancin dog was a runnin dog and all the people was laughin at the new show, which was us! ❷

"I felt myself slowin down after a while and I thought I would turn around a little bit to see how much gain that cute little dog was makin on me. When I did I got such a surprise! Right behind me was the dancin dog and right behind him was the finest fast runnin hero in the bottoms of Virginia.

1. **crokasack** (krō′ kər sak) *usually spelled croker sack, n.:* Bag made of burlap or similar material.

▲ **Critical Viewing** Why would an activity like the quilting shown here provide a good opportunity for sharing family stories? **[Analyze]** ❸

Block Scheduling Strategies

Consider these suggestions to take advantage of extended class time:

- Lead a discussion of the Literary Focus, p. 397. Then have students listen to the selections on audiocassette, encouraging them to keep a list of examples of hyperbole, using a graphic organizer like the one shown in Literary Focus. Finally, have them answer the Literary Focus questions on p. 408.

Listening to Literature Audiocassettes

- Once students have finished reading, have a class discussion in which students compare and contrast the selections. Have each student choose his or her favorite. Then divide the class into groups according to students' choices. Follow with a debate about which is the best piece in the grouping and why.
- If students have access to technology, have them work in pairs on the tutorial on Creative Language in the *Writer's Solution Writing Lab CD-ROM* to complete the Writing Mini-Lesson.

"And that was Mr. Pickens when he was still a boy! He had a length of twine in his hand and he was twirlin it around in the air just like the cowboy at the Silas Greene and grinnin fit to bust.

4 "While I was watchin how the sun shined on him and made him look like an angel come to help a poor sinner girl, why, he twirled that twine one extra fancy twirl and looped it right around one hind leg of that dancin dog and brought him low.

"I stopped then and walked slow and shy to where he had picked up that poor dog to see if he was hurt, cradlin him and talkin to him soft and sweet. That showed me how kind and gentle he was, and when we walked back to the dancin dog's place in the show he let the dog loose and helped me to find my stone. I told him how shiny black it was and how it had the letter *A* scratched on one side. We searched and searched and at last he spied it!

5 "Ovella and me lost heart for shows then and we walked on home. And a good little way, the one who was gonna be your Great-granddaddy was walkin on behind. Seein us safe. Us walkin kind of slow. Him seein us safe. Yes." Mrs. Pickens' voice trailed off softly and Tee noticed she had a little smile on her face.

"Grandmama, that stone almost got you bit by a dog that time. It wasn't so lucky that time, was it?"

Tee's Great-grandmother shook her head and laughed out loud.

"That was the luckiest time of all, Tee Baby. It got me acquainted with Mr. Amos Pickens, and if that ain't luck, what could it be! Yes, it was luckier for me than for anybody, I think. Least mostly I think it."

Tee laughed with her Great-grandmother though she didn't exactly know why.

"I hope I have that kind of good stone luck one day," she said. 6

"Maybe you will someday," her Great-grandmother said.

And they rocked a little longer and smiled together.

Guide for Responding

◆ Literature and Your Life

Reader's Response Have you ever met someone "by chance"? What happened?

Thematic Focus Would you describe Great-grandmother as quirky? Explain.

Journal Writing Great-grandmother's story sounds as if it has been told countless times. In a journal entry, tell a story about yourself that you have heard others tell many times.

☑ Check Your Comprehension

1. Who tells the story about the lucky stone and the Silas Greene show?
2. Who is listening to the story?
3. Why does Tee think Great-grandmother's stone was not so lucky at first?
4. What is Great-grandmother's reason for believing that the stone was lucky for her?

◆ Critical Thinking

INTERPRET

1. What details show that Great-grandmother and Ovella were adventurous? **[Support]**
2. Mr. Pickens cradles the dog and speaks softly to it. What can you tell about his character from these actions? **[Infer]**
3. What was Mr. Pickens's real intention in saving Great-grandmother from the dog and in following her home? **[Draw Conclusions]**
4. Would you say that Great-grandmother is happy with her life? Support your opinion with examples. **[Speculate]**

APPLY

5. What does this story suggest about the importance of family stories? **[Apply]**

◆ Critical Thinking

1. They wanted to leave home to join the Silas Greene show and see the world, and they didn't tell anyone else they were leaving.
2. Mr. Pickens is kind and gentle. Even though he wanted to capture the dog, he didn't want to hurt it.
3. Mr. Pickens probably liked Great-grandmother, and he wanted to impress her by rescuing her from the dog and looking out for her on her way home.
4. She seems happy with her life because she has pleasant memories that she recalls with smiles and laughter.
5. Students may say this story suggests that family stories are important because they preserve a family's history. Also, family members can learn important lessons from stories such as these.

Comprehension Check ☑

4 How does Amos capture the dog? *He uses a length of twine to lasso one of the dog's hind legs, which causes the dog to fall.*

◆ Critical Thinking

5 **Infer** Ask students why they think Elzie and Ovella lose interest in joining the Silas Greene show. *Students will probably say that the girls change their minds because the adventure with the dog has filled their appetites for new experiences.*

◆ Literature and Your Life

6 Point out that Tee hopes for good luck such as that her great-grandmother had in the story she tells. Invite students to describe "good stone luck" they have experienced in their lives. *Some students may say they have good-luck charms that they believe have worked, whereas others will say they have not had such experiences.*

Reinforce and Extend

Answers

◆ Literature and Your Life

Reader's Response Students may describe close friendships that developed from chance meetings at school, in their neighborhoods, or during vacations.

Thematic Focus Some students may say that as a young girl Great-grandmother was quirky because she wanted to leave home to join a traveling show. Others may suggest that her way of speaking is quirky.

☑ Check Your Comprehension

1. Great-grandmother tells the story.
2. Tee, the great-granddaughter, listens to the story.
3. The stone hit the dog, which caused the dog to chase Great-grandmother.
4. She was able to meet her future husband because of the stone.

Develop Understanding

One-Minute Insight Father William's son is unsure what to make of his father, who stands on his head, performs back-somersaults, eats an entire goose, and balances an eel on the end of his nose. Again and again, the son questions his father about feats that seem ridiculous or impossible for a man of his age. For each question, the father has a response just as outlandish as his behavior. Through the use of humor, the poem calls attention to the fact that people often have mistaken assumptions about how older people should act.

◆Literary Focus

❶ **Hyperbole** Have students identify an example of hyperbole in this stanza. *Students should recognize that the son's description of the father* incessantly *standing on his head is an exaggeration, because people cannot stand on their heads without stopping.*

◆Reading Strategy

❷ **Recognize Author's Purpose** Have students guess the author's purpose in the poem, based on the first two stanzas. Ask them to give supporting reasons for their responses. *The writer's purpose is to entertain and amuse because the description of the father standing on his head and his explanation for the behavior are humorous.*

▶Critical Viewing◀

❸ **Connect** The drawing illustrates the third stanza, lines 9–12, in which the son describes the father as turning "a back-somersault in at the door."

Customize for
Musical/Rhythmic Learners
Point out the use of rhythm in "Father William." Invite students to read the poem aloud, one student reading the part of the son and the other reading the part of the father. Discuss how the rhythm adds to the humor of the poem. Students may want to read the poem aloud a second time as others tap out the rhythm.

Father William

Lewis Carroll

You Are Old, Father William, 1865, Sir John Tenniel

❶ "You are old, Father William," the young man said,
  "And your hair has become very white;
And yet you incessantly stand on your head—
  Do you think, at your age, it is right?"

❷ "In my youth," Father William replied to his son,
  "I feared it might injure the brain;
But, now that I'm perfectly sure I have none,
  Why, I do it again and again."

▲ **Critical Viewing** Which stanza or group of lines does this drawing illustrate? **[Connect]** ❸

Humanities: Art

You Are Old, Father William, 1865, by Sir John Tenniel

Sir John Tenniel (1820–1914) is the first and best-known illustrator of *Alice in Wonderland.* A political cartoonist as well as a children's book illustrator, Tenniel lost an eye during a fencing bout as a young boy. He always drew from imagination or memory, never from models.

As students view the illustrations on pp. 400 and 401, use the following for discussion:

1. Have students describe the son's expressions in the two drawings. *In the first drawing, the son appears to be shocked at his father's behavior; in the second, he seems puzzled.*
2. Compare and contrast the physical appearance of the father and son in the drawings. *Both are dressed in old-fashioned clothing and both have hats. The son is tall and thin, whereas the father is short and fat.*

"You are old," said the youth, "as I mentioned before.
And have grown most uncommonly[1] fat;
Yet you turned a back-somersault in at the door—
Pray, what is the reason of that?" ❹

"In my youth," said the sage, as he shook his gray locks,
"I kept all my limbs very supple
By the use of this ointment—one shilling[2] the box—
Allow me to sell you a couple?" ❺

"You are old," said the youth, "and your jaws are too weak
For anything tougher than suet;[3]
Yet you finished the goose, with the bones and the beak—
Pray, how did you manage to do it?" ❻

1. **uncommonly** (un käm´ ən lē) *adv.*: Remarkably.
2. **shilling** (shil´ iŋ) *n.*: British coin.
3. **suet** (so͞o´ it) *n.*: Fat used in cooking.

You Are Old Father William II, 1865, Sir John Tenniel

◆ Build Vocabulary

incessantly (in ses´ ənt lē) *adv.*: Without stopping

sage (sāj) *n.*: Very wise man

supple (sup´ əl) *adj.*: Flexible

▲ Critical Viewing How do the illustrations contribute to the humor of the characters? **[Assess]** ❼

Clarification

❹ Point out the word *Pray* at the beginning of line 12. Explain that in contexts such as this, *pray* is used to introduce a question, a plea, or a request.

◆ Build Vocabulary

❺ **Using Words With Multiple Meanings** The vocabulary concept for these selections focuses on words that have more than one meaning. Point out the words *locks* in line 13 and *box* in line 15. Explain that *locks* can refer to hair on the head or fastenings operated by keys. *Box* can refer to a container or can mean "to hit with the hand." Invite students to suggest additional meanings of *locks* and *box.*

◆ Critical Thinking

❻ **Analyze** Ask students why they think the son continues to question his father. *Some students may say that the son wants to influence his father to "act his age." Others may say the son is genuinely curious about his father's abilities.*

▶Critical Viewing◀

❼ **Assess** The illustrations contribute to the humor of the characters because they exaggerate their physical characteristics: Father William is extremely fat and mischievous-looking; his son is lanky, curious, and looks a bit worn out.

Customize for
Visual/Spatial Learners
Suggest that students use the illustrations on pp. 400 and 401 to visualize or create their own illustrations for the first and fourth stanzas of the poem. Ask them to describe what details they would include in their drawings.

Customize for
Interpersonal Learners
Invite pairs of students to read the poem aloud, one student reading the part of the son and the other reading the part of the father. After students read the poem, have them discuss insights into the characters that they gained from reading the poem.

Speaking and Listening Mini-Lesson

Interview

This mini-lesson supports the Speaking and Listening activity in the Idea Bank on p. 409.

Introduce Explain that understanding characters' traits and motives can help readers recognize an author's purpose. Divide the class into pairs and have them choose characters for their interviews.

Develop Encourage students to brainstorm for a list of questions and then develop the list into a logical series. Remind them to review the story for clues to the characters' traits. Have them decide which partner will be the character and which partner will ask questions.

Apply Allow time for students to rehearse and revise their interviews. Suggest that they experiment with body language and voices. When they are ready, have them present their interviews to the class.

Assess Evaluate the interviews in terms of preparation, overall effectiveness, and understanding of the characters, or use the Peer Assessment: Dramatic Performance form, p. 107, in **Alternative Assessment.**

◆ **Critical Thinking**

❶ **Speculate** Point out to students that the father uses the phrase "In my youth" in replying to his son's questions that begin with "You are old." Ask students why the poet repeats these phrases in the poem. *Students may speculate that the poet wants to emphasize the son's feeling that his father acts inappropriately for his age. Students may also guess that the father wants to emphasize that habits formed in one's youth can be helpful in old age.*

◆ **Critical Thinking**

❷ **Draw Conclusions** Why does the father refuse to answer any more questions? *Students may conclude that the father is simply tired of answering his son's questions. Some may say that the father dislikes his son's characterizing him as an old man. By stopping his son's questions, the old man reaffirms his position of power in the house.*

Reinforce and Extend

Answers

◆ **LITERATURE AND YOUR LIFE**

Reader's Response Some students may say that Father William's first reply—that he has no brain—is the most ridiculous because it makes no sense.

Thematic Focus He stands on his head, he somersaults through the door, he eats the bones and beak of the goose.

☑ **Check Your Comprehension**

1. He says he has no brain, so he finds no harm in doing it.
2. He has kept his limbs supple by using an ointment.
3. He strengthened his jaw by arguing legal cases with his wife.
4. The son thinks his father is too old and weak to do what he does.
5. Father William refuses to answer another question and sends his son away.

"In my youth," said his father, "I took to the law,
  And argued each case with my wife;
And the muscular strength, which it gave to my jaw
  Has lasted the rest of my life." ❶

"You are old," said the youth, "one would hardly suppose
  That your eye was as steady as ever;
Yet you balanced an eel on the end of your nose—
  What made you so awfully clever?"

"I have answered three questions, and that is enough,"
  Said his father. "Don't give yourself airs!
Do you think I can listen all day to such stuff?
  Be off, or I'll kick you downstairs!" ❷

Guide for Responding

◆ **LITERATURE AND YOUR LIFE**

Reader's Response Which of Father William's replies do you think is the most ridiculous? Why?

Thematic Focus Identify three things about Father William that make him an unusual man.

Journal Writing Record a question that someone has asked recently about your behavior. Then, create a reply as zany as those of Father William.

☑ **Check Your Comprehension**

1. What reason does Father William give for incessantly standing on his head?
2. What enables him to do back-somersaults?
3. Why is he able to eat an entire goose—bones and all?
4. Why does the son think his father should not be able to do the things that he does?
5. How does the poem end?

◆ **Critical Thinking**

INTERPRET

1. What is it about Father William's physical condition that makes his behavior so absurd? **[Infer]**
2. In general, how does the son regard his father? **[Interpret]**
3. What does the father think about his own behavior? **[Infer]**
4. Do you think the poem presents a typical conversation between this father and son? Explain. **[Speculate]**
5. Why is it comical that Father William refuses to answer any more questions? **[Analyze]**

APPLY

6. How would the poem's humor change if Father William had different physical characteristics? **[Hypothesize]**

COMPARE LITERARY WORKS

7. Compare the relationship between generations in "The Luckiest Time of All" with the one in "Father William." **[Compare and Contrast]**

◆ **Critical Thinking**

1. Father William seems too fat to be able to stand on his head or do back-somersaults.
2. The son thinks his father should act his age. Some students may say that the son admires his father's abilities.
3. The father seems proud of his behavior.
4. Most students will say that although sons often ask their fathers questions, the conversation is not typical, because it is about an absurd situation. The father seems to act more like a child and the son more like a worrisome father.
5. Father William acts as if his son is being ridiculous with "such stuff" as his questions, but actually the father's behavior is absurd.
6. Students may say that the poem wouldn't be as funny if Father William were younger and lean.
7. Tee and her great-grandmother seem comfortable with each other; Tee seems to learn from her older relative. The son in "Father William" worries about his father's behavior and thinks it is abnormal. He doesn't seem to respect his father, and his father doesn't seem to care about his son's opinions.

THE MICROSCOPE

Maxine Kumin

❸ Anton Leeuwenhoek was Dutch.
He sold pincushions, cloth, and such.
The waiting townsfolk fumed and fussed
As Anton's dry goods gathered dust.

He worked, instead of tending store,
At grinding special lenses for
A microscope. Some of the things
He looked at were:
mosquitoes' wings,
the hairs of sheep, the legs of lice,
the skin of people, dogs, and mice;
ox eyes, spiders' spinning gear,
fishes' scales, a little smear
of his own blood,
and best of all,
❹ the unknown, busy, very small
bugs that swim and bump and hop
inside a simple water drop.

Impossible! Most Dutchmen said.
This Anton's crazy in the head.
We ought to ship him off to Spain.
He says he's seen a housefly's brain.
He says the water that we drink
Is full of bugs. He's mad, we think!

They called him *dumkopf,* which means dope.
That's how we got the microscope.

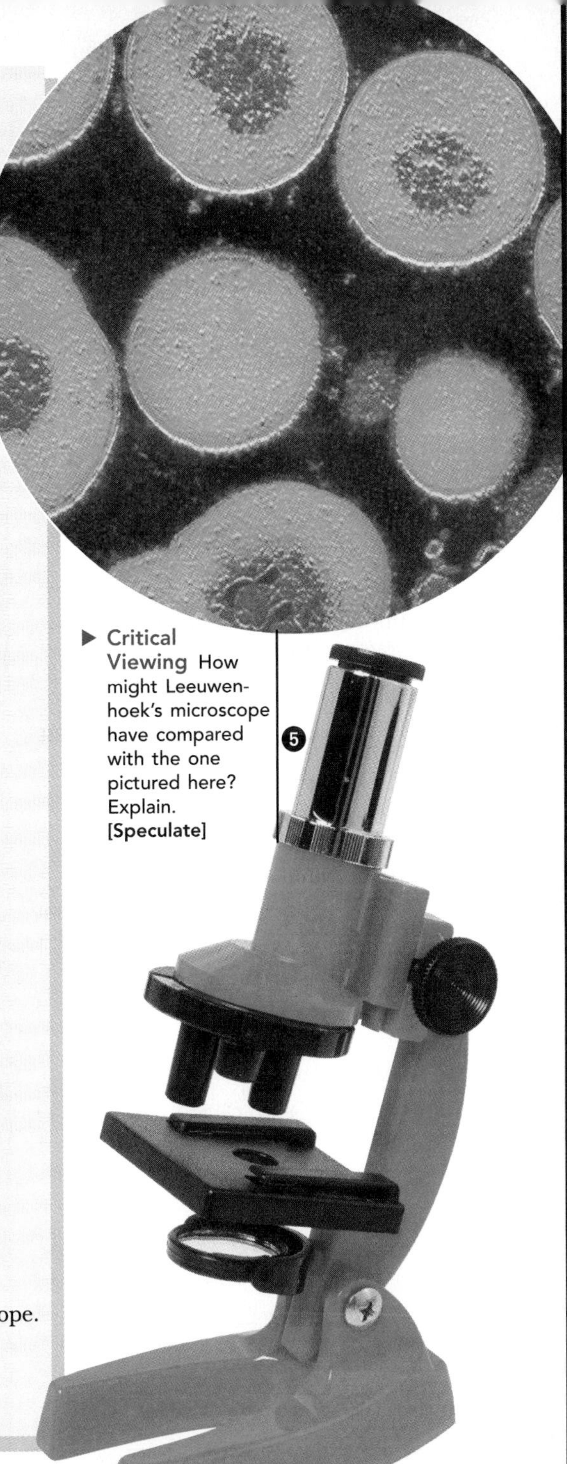

▶ **Critical Viewing** How might Leeuwenhoek's microscope have compared with the one pictured here? Explain. **[Speculate]** ❺

Develop Understanding

One-Minute Insight Anton Leeuwenhoek preferred to study tiny things under a microscope than tend his dry goods store. This infuriated his neighbors, who thought that Anton was crazy for peering through a lens. The poem captures how gifted people are sometimes misperceived by others.

◆Reading Strategy

❸ Recognize Author's Purpose Ask students to suggest ways that the writer of "The Microscope" informs readers about a historical character. *Students may say that the poet informs the reader through facts about Leeuwenhoek: he was Dutch, he owned a dry goods store, he spent much of his time examining objects under a microscope.*

◆Critical Thinking

❹ Infer Ask students why the poet calls Leeuwenhoek's study of "the unknown, busy, very small bugs" in water the "best of all." *Students may say that studying bugs in the water is "best" because at that time it seemed most crazy to think there were bugs in the water.*

▶Critical Viewing◀

❺ Speculate Leeuwenhoek's microscope was probably a lot simpler than the one pictured here. Since he made the first microscope, it probably wasn't so advanced to have a tray to lay the specimen on, three lenses, and an adjusting focus.

Cross-Curricular Connection: Science

Anton Leeuwenhoek Dutch amateur scientist Anton van Leeuwenhoek *(LAY vuhn hook)* (1632–1723) was among the first people to make important observations of microscopic life. As a cloth merchant, Leeuwenhoek first developed the microscope to study the quality of cloth. He began to notice tiny moving objects, which he called *animalcules.* These microorganisms included what are now known as bacteria, protozoa, and rotifers.

Leeuwenhoek studied the blood of humans and other mammals, fish, birds, and tadpoles to learn how nutrients are transported. He was the first person to correctly identify red blood cells.

Have students conduct research to learn more about Leeuwenhoek and the development and use of the microscope. Encourage students to create charts or illustrations that demonstrate how magnified images reach the eye. Alternatively, they can create a diagram of the type of microscope Leeuwenhoek made and compare it to a modern microscope. For more information on Leeuwenhoek, suggest that students go to the following site: **http://www.ucmp.berkeley.edu/history/leeuwenhoek.html**

All Web sites are subject to change, and we *strongly recommend* you preview this site before you send students to it. Encourage students to share their findings and/or projects with the class.

Develop Understanding

In "in Just–," E. E. Cummings celebrates the joys of spring, which include the whistle of the balloonman, mud puddles, and outdoor play with friends. The unusual arrangement of the poem's words and lines adds to the eccentric descriptions of "the balloonman."

◆Reading Strategy

❶ Recognize Author's Purpose Ask students why the poet uses the words *mud-luscious* and *puddle-wonderful* in the poem. *Students may say that Cummings created the words to amuse readers and perhaps to evoke images of children splashing barefoot through spring mud puddles.*

Customize for *Verbal/Linguistic Learners*
Point out words and phrases that appeal to the senses in "in Just–," such as "mud-luscious" and "whistles far and wee." Have students use the Sensory Language Chart, p. 78, in **Writing and Language Transparencies,** to record sensory language in the poem. Encourage them to add words and phrases they might use in a poem about spring.

Reinforce and Extend

Answers

◆Literature and Your Life

Reader's Response Students may suggest memories such as the sights and smells of flowers or playing outdoors with friends.

Thematic Focus Leeuwenhoek seemed quirky because he neglected his business to study things so small no one else could see and no one else believed existed.

☑ Check Your Comprehension

1. Anton Leeuwenhoek is the main character.
2. He owns a dry goods store.
3. He grinds lenses for a microscope and studies various things under the microscope.
4. The poem describes children's reactions to the distant whistle of a balloonman.
5. They are playing games, such as marbles, pirates, hopscotch, and jump-rope.

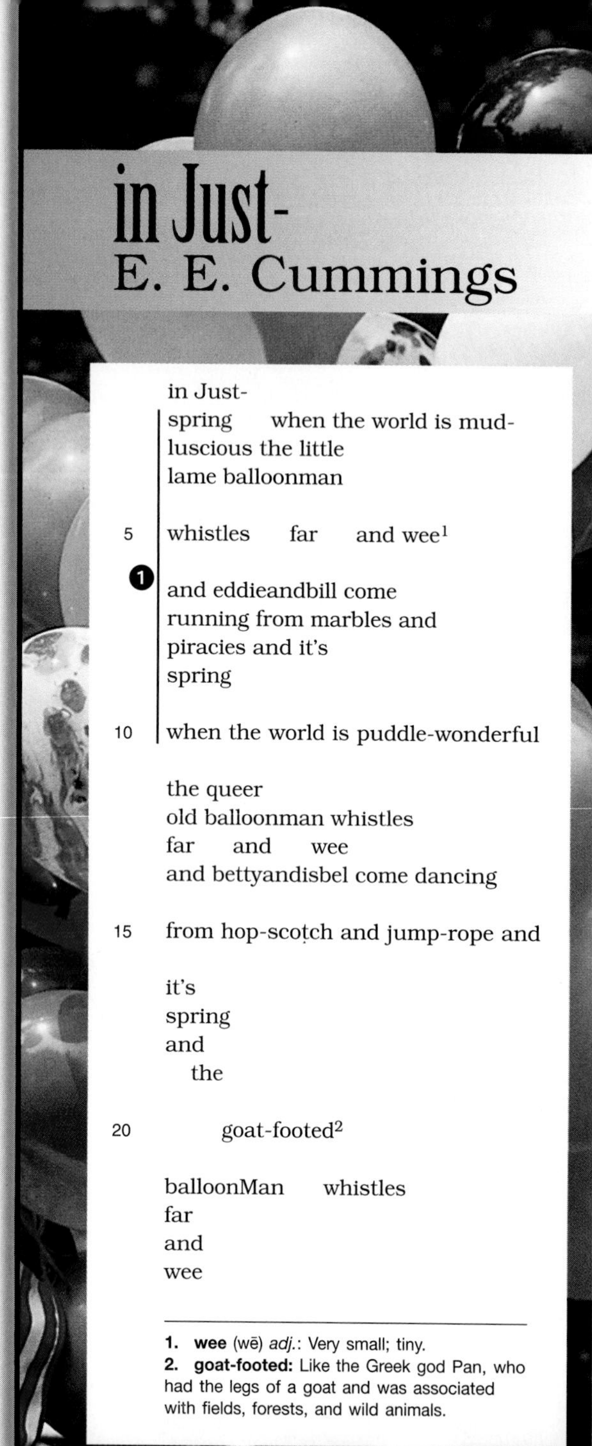

in Just-

E. E. Cummings

in Just-
spring when the world is mud-
luscious the little
lame balloonman

whistles far and wee[1]

❶ and eddieandbill come
running from marbles and
piracies and it's
spring

when the world is puddle-wonderful

the queer
old balloonman whistles
far and wee
and bettyandisbel come dancing

from hop-scotch and jump-rope and

it's
spring
and
the

goat-footed[2]

balloonMan whistles
far
and
wee

1. **wee** (wē) *adj.*: Very small; tiny.
2. **goat-footed:** Like the Greek god Pan, who had the legs of a goat and was associated with fields, forests, and wild animals.

Guide for Responding

◆ Literature and Your Life

Reader's Response What memories of spring does "in Just-" call up for you?

Thematic Focus Use "The Microscope" to explain Anton Leeuwenhoek's quirkiness.

Group Activity With a partner, choose a season and brainstorm for the words you'd use to describe it. To make your list vivid, include words that appeal to all five senses.

☑ Check Your Comprehension

1. Who is the main character in the poem "The Microscope"?
2. What is this person's occupation?
3. What is this person's hobby?
4. What event does the poem "in Just-" describe?
5. What are the children doing when they hear the whistle?

◆ Critical Thinking

Interpret

1. What was unusual about the items Leeuwenhoek studied in "The Microscope"? **[Infer]**
2. Why did the townsfolk think Leeuwenhoek was "crazy in the head"? **[Interpret]**
3. In "in Just-," what is the effect of the poet's writing "eddieandbill" instead of "Eddie and Bill"? **[Analyze]**
4. How does the description of the balloonman change as the poem progresses? **[Interpret]**
5. The Greek god Pan inspired people with his flute playing. What effect does the balloonman's whistling have on the children? **[Analyze]**

Apply

6. What reasons might poets have for playing with the physical arrangements of words, phrases, or lines in poetry? **[Synthesize]**

Extend

7. In what ways did the "dumkopf," Anton Leeuwenhoek, change the world? **[Science Link]**

◆Critical Thinking

1. Students may say that the things Leeuwenhoek studied were unusual because they were small parts of things that few other people had studied before.
2. They thought that Leeuwenhoek was "crazy" because he claimed to see bugs in the water.
3. Running the names together makes the two people seem like they are a unit, two friends who are very close.
4. As the poem progresses, the balloonman's description becomes stranger: from little and lame, to queer and old, to goat-footed.
5. The balloonman's whistle draws children away from their games.
6. Students may say that poets play with physical arrangements of words and phrases to add another visual dimension to the poem, to evoke new images, or to create a different kind of rhythm.
7. Leeuwenhoek's development of the microscope allowed scientists to discover and study microscopic life. Through the use of microscopes, scientists can now study bacteria and viruses and find cures for diseases.

Sarah Cynthia Sylvia Stout Would Not Take the Garbage Out

Shel Silverstein

❷ Sarah Cynthia Sylvia Stout
Would not take the garbage out!
She'd scour[1] the pots and scrape the pans,
Candy[2] the yams and spice the hams,
And though her daddy would scream and shout,
She simply would not take the garbage out.
And so it piled up to the ceilings:
Coffee grounds, potato peelings,
Brown bananas, rotten peas,
Chunks of sour cottage cheese.
It filled the can, it covered the floor,
❸ It cracked the window and blocked the door
With bacon rinds[3] and chicken bones,
Drippy ends of ice cream cones,
Prune pits, peach pits, orange peel,
Gloppy glumps of cold oatmeal,
Pizza crusts and withered greens,
Soggy beans and tangerines,
Crusts of black burned buttered toast,
Gristly bits of beefy roasts . . .
❹ The garbage rolled on down the hall,
It raised the roof, it broke the wall . . .

1. **scour** (skour) *v.*: Clean by rubbing vigorously.
2. **candy** (kan′ dē) *v.*: Coat with sugar.
3. **rinds** (rīndz) *n.*: Tough outer layers or skins.

◀ Critical Viewing
Does the exaggerated style of the cartoon on this page better suit this poem than a realistic photograph might? Explain. **[Make a Judgment]**

◆ Build Vocabulary

withered (with′ ərd) *adj.*: Dried up

Develop Understanding

Sarah Cynthia Sylvia Stout refuses to take out the garbage. Nothing, not even her father's screams and shouts, can persuade her to remove the garbage from the house. Like an expanding monster, the garbage fills the house, bursts through windows and doors, raises the roof, and reaches to the sky. "Sarah Cynthia Sylvia Stout . . ." carries a gentle message about household responsibilities.

◆ Critical Thinking

❷ **Speculate** Ask students why they think Sarah helps out in some ways but refuses to take out the garbage. *Some students may say that Sarah doesn't want to do such a dirty chore.*

Comprehension Check 

❸ As of line 12, what has happened to the garbage so far? *It has piled up to the ceilings, filled the can, covered the floor, cracked the window, and blocked the door.*

◆ Literary Focus

❹ **Hyperbole** Have students describe the effect of the hyperbole in lines 21 and 22. *Students may say that the description of garbage rolling down a hall, raising a roof, and breaking a wall creates a humorous, exaggerated effect.*

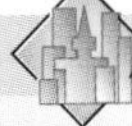

Beyond the Classroom

Community Connection

Garbage Collection and Disposal
Discuss with students ways to dispose of household garbage. Explain that in most communities, nonrecyclable household waste is collected and deposited in landfills. In a sanitary landfill, wastes are compacted often and covered with soil to keep out insects and rats. Other methods of waste disposal include incinerators, biodegradation, ocean disposal, chemical detoxification, and injection. Point out that much of the garbage described in the poem could have been composted, or recycled to be used to enrich soil. Have students conduct research on one of these topics:

- Landfills and their effect on the environment
- Making compost out of household wastes
- Alternative methods of waste disposal

Suggest that students start their research with an encyclopedia or on the Internet. For information on landfills, have students go to:

http://www.enviroweb.org/enviroissues/landfills

For general information on waste disposal, direct students to the U.S. Department of Energy Office of Waste Management at **http://www.em.doe.gov/em30**

All Web sites are subject to change, and we *strongly recommend* you preview these sites before you send students to them.

Invite students to give presentations to the class based on their findings.

◆ Critical Thinking

❶ Analyze Point out to students the poet's use of adjectives such as *green, curdled, moldy, dried up,* and *rancid.* How do these words add to the images in the poem? *Students should realize these adjectives all describe rotting food, which adds to creating an image of smelly, gross-looking food.*

◆ Critical Thinking

❷ Infer What motivates Sarah to agree finally to take the garbage out? *Sarah realizes that she has lost her neighbors and friends because of the spreading garbage. Most students will realize that the fear of loneliness motivates her to agree to take out the garbage.*

Clarification

❸ Explain that the Golden Gate refers to a strait that connects San Francisco Bay with the Pacific Ocean. Have students find New York and the Golden Gate on a United States map.

Customize for *English Language Learners*

Some of the names of garbage items mentioned in the poem may be unfamiliar to students. Encourage students to point out troubling words and ask volunteers to give a definition of the foods in question.

Customize for *Visual/Spatial Learners*

Have students use the images in the poem to create their own illustrations to go along with the story. Encourage them to use the details given by the poet in their representations. Allow students to draw, paint, or make a collage out of magazine pictures.

Greasy napkins, cookie crumbs,
Globs of gooey bubblegum,
Cellophane from green baloney,
Rubbery blubbery macaroni,
Peanut butter, caked and dry,
❶ Curdled milk and crusts of pie,
Moldy melons, dried up mustard,
Eggshells mixed with lemon custard,
Cold french fries and rancid meat,
Yellow lumps of Cream of Wheat.
At last the garbage reached so high
That finally it touched the sky.
And all the neighbors moved away,
And none of her friends would come to play.
❷ And finally Sarah Cynthia Stout said,
"OK, I'll take the garbage out!"
But then, of course, it was too late
The garbage reached across the state,
❸ From New York to the Golden Gate
And there, in the garbage she did hate,
Poor Sarah met an awful fate,
That I cannot right now relate[4]
Because the hour is much too late.
But children, remember Sarah Stout
And always take the garbage out!

4. **relate** (ri lāt´) *v.*: Tell.

◀ **Critical Viewing** The author created the illustrations accompanying the poem. How does this art enhance the humor of the poem? **[Assess]**

◆ Build Vocabulary

curdled (kʉr´ dəld) *adj.*: Thickened; clotted
rancid (ran´ sid) *adj.*: Spoiled and smelling bad

Viewing and Representing Mini-Lesson

Visual Representation of a Poem

In this lesson, students will use the sensory images and details of a poem to help them create a visual representation.

Introduce Have students reread each poem and then pick one that they will represent. Tell them to think not just about the physical details in each poem, but also about the feelings the poems evoke. Explain that even though "Sarah Cynthia Sylvia Stout . . ." offers the most elaborate details, a poem such as "in Just–" may allow students more flexibility in their work.

Develop Point out that writers use vivid descriptions such as those in the poem to help readers picture people, objects, and events. Encourage students to reread their poem and jot down essential details they will include in their representation.

Apply Provide students with a variety of materials with which to create visual representations such as collages, drawings, paintings, or sculptures of the images in the poem. Have students share their representations with the class. Encourage students to explain how they created their representations.

Assess Evaluate students' representations on originality, attention to detail, and overall effectiveness of reflecting the poem.

Beyond Literature

Technology Connection

New Uses for Recycled Materials Sarah Cynthia may not have cared about the garbage she was accumulating, but more and more products are being made from recycled—and recyclable—materials. You probably know that glass and plastic bottles are recycled into new containers. However, you may not have known that some plastic is converted into insulation for maintaining an even temperature in homes and offices. In addition, recycled glass is used in road pavement, and coal ashes are used in cement.

Cross Curricular Activity

Community Research If your community has a recycling program, find out more about it. Call local officials to get information about what happens to recycling materials that are collected. Then, create a flowchart to show the path from curb side to new product. Refer to your chart as you make a presentation to classmates.

Guide for Responding

◆ Literature and Your Life

Reader's Response Do you sympathize more with Sarah or her father? Why?

Thematic Focus If you were asked to describe Sarah with one word, what word would you choose?

Group Activity In a small group, brainstorm for a list of chores that young people are often asked to complete. Then, vote to rank these jobs on a scale from least pleasant to most fun.

☑ Check Your Comprehension

1. Name four chores that Sarah Cynthia Sylvia Stout does at home.
2. What does her father do when Sarah refuses to take out the garbage?
3. What happens to the garbage?
4. What do Sarah's friends and neighbors do as the situation progresses?
5. What finally happens to Sarah?

◆ Critical Thinking

Interpret

1. At what point in the poem does the poet begin to use exaggeration? **[Distinguish]**
2. What is the effect of the continuing exaggeration? **[Analyze]**
3. What reason might the poet have—besides the fact that it is "late"—for not telling readers what happened to Sarah? **[Infer]**
4. What do you think was Sarah's "awful fate"? **[Speculate]**

Apply

5. Find two lines in the poem that do not rhyme. What is the effect of this break in rhyme? **[Synthesize]**

Extend

6. What local rules exist in your area to prevent Sarah's situation from actually happening? **[Community Link]**

Beyond the Selection

FURTHER READING

Other Works by the Authors

The Lucky Stone, Lucille Clifton
Through the Looking-Glass and What Alice Found There, Lewis Carroll
Connecting the Dots: Poems, Maxine Kumin
Is 5, E. E. Cummings
The Giving Tree, Shel Silverstein

INTERNET

We suggest the following sites on the Internet (all Web sites are subject to change).

For more information about authors Lewis Carroll, Lucille Clifton, and Shel Silverstein:
http://www.scils.rutgers.edu/special/kay/author.html

For more on Maxine Kumin:
http://www.poets.org/LIT/poet/mkumifst.htm

For more on E. E. Cummings:
http://www.poets.org/LIT/poet/eecumfst.htm

We *strongly recommend* that you preview these sites before you send students to them.

Beyond Literature

Suggest that students begin their research by calling their local Department of Sanitation. They can also do research on the Internet. Two valuable Web sites include the Global Recycling Network at **http://grn.com:80/grn** and the Database of Recycling Centers at **http://www.1800cleanup.org**

Remember, all Web sites are subject to change, and we *strongly recommend* you preview these sites before you send students to them.

Reinforce and Extend

Answers

◆ Literature and Your Life

Reader's Response Some students may sympathize with Sarah's father, who has to live with the smelly garbage. Other students will think he should just take it out himself.

Thematic Focus Students may mention words such as *quirky, stubborn, lazy, weird.*

☑ Check Your Comprehension

1. She scours the pots, scrapes the pans, candies the yams, and spices the hams.
2. He screams and shouts.
3. It fills the house, touches the sky, and reaches across her state and the whole country.
4. The neighbors moved away, and Sarah's friends no longer come to play.
5. She met an unknown, "awful fate."

◆ Critical Thinking

1. The poet begins to use exaggeration in line 7: "And so it piled up to the ceilings."
2. It adds to the humor of the poem.
3. Possible response: By leaving it to the readers' imagination, the poet makes her "fate" seem more terrible than can be put in words.
4. Students may guess that Sarah was buried by the garbage.
5. Lines 37 and 38 do not rhyme. They stop the reader and signal a change in events.
6. Students may mention local trash pickup and disposal, recycling programs, and regulations against the buildup of trash around houses.

Answers

◆Reading Strategy

1. Possible responses: She uses dialect as spoken by the great-grandmother, and she uses vivid descriptions such as that of the dancing dog.
2. The name is unusually long, and all the names within it begin with the *s* sound. Students may also mention that the rhythm of the name spoken aloud produces a humorous effect.
3. Kumin might not have told about Anton's neglect of his store nor described people's reactions to him, which seem funny now in light of his discovery.

◆ Build Vocabulary

Using Words With Multiple Meanings

1. In the first sentence, *staple* means "the chief part of"; in the second sentence, it refers to a short metal wire that holds papers together.
2. In the first sentence, *pitcher* means "a container for holding liquids"; in the second sentence, it refers to someone who throws a ball.

Spelling Strategy

1. necessary
2. recess
3. access

Using the Word Bank

1. Yes; a faucet that drips without stopping will waste water.
2. No; a baseball bat is smooth, but it isn't flexible.
3. No; thickened or clotted milk is probably not good for drinking.
4. Yes; advice from a wise man is worth listening to.
5. Yes; black bananas are likely to be spoiled and smelly.
6. No; a dried-up salad would not be appetizing.

◆Literary Focus

1. Students may say that eating an entire goose is the most exaggerated behavior, because it's unlikely that someone would eat the bones and beak.
2. Possible response: "He says the water that we drink/Is full of bugs," an exaggeration that sounds as though drinking water is full of normal-sized bugs.
3. Possible response: The garbage "raised the roof," "touched the sky," and "reached across the state." These possibilities are unlikely or impossible.

Guide for Responding *(continued)*

◆ Reading Strategy

Recognize Author's Purpose

All of the pieces in this grouping were written for a similar purpose—to entertain and amuse readers. This purpose is evident in the writers' choice of language, details, and events.

1. Identify two examples in "The Luckiest Time of All" that show that the narrator tells the story to entertain her listener.

2. What do you find humorous about the name Sarah Cynthia Sylvia Stout?

3. Imagine that Kumin's purpose were to provide scholarly information about the microscope. How would her poem "The Microscope" be different?

◆ Build Vocabulary

Using Words With Multiple Meanings

Like *sage,* which can refer to a wise person or an herb, many words in English have multiple meanings. On your paper, explain the different meanings of the italicized words in each set of sentences.

1. Rice is a *staple* in their diet.
One *staple* can't hold that many pages!

2. Fill the *pitcher* with iced tea.
Give the *pitcher* the ball.

Spelling Strategy

The ses sound in *incessantly* is spelled *cess.* On your paper, write a word that contains *cess* to complete each of the following sentences.

1. To avoid disaster, it is n___?___ to take the garbage out.

2. The boys play marbles during r___?___ at school.

3. Without a password, you can't a___?___ the file.

Using the Word Bank

Answer each question, and explain your answer.

1. Will a faucet that *incessantly* drips waste water?

2. Is a baseball bat smooth and *supple?*

3. Is *curdled* milk good for drinking?

4. Would you listen to the advice of a *sage?*

5. Might black bananas be *rancid?*

6. Would a *withered* salad be appetizing?

◆ Literary Focus

Hyperbole

Hyperbole is exaggeration for effect. For example, "Butter doesn't melt in her mouth" and "I'm walking on air" each overstate an idea. Hyperbole is used to create emphasis, humor, or drama. Without hyperbole, the poem about Sarah Stout would not be nearly so funny and dramatic, and "Father William" might simply become a charming character sketch.

1. In your opinion, which of Father William's behaviors is exaggerated the most? Explain.

2. Find an example of hyperbole in "The Microscope." Explain your choice.

3. Find three examples of hyperbole in "Sarah Cynthia Sylvia Stout . . ." Explain each example.

4. Why does hyperbole make people laugh?

◆ Build Grammar Skills

Complete and Incomplete Sentences

A **complete sentence** contains both a subject and a verb. It expresses a complete thought. If a sentence does not meet these requirements, it is **incomplete** and may not be understood. Because people often do not speak in complete sentences, dialogue may include incomplete sentences.

s v
Complete: Elzie rocked gently on the porch.

s
Incomplete: Spring day like this

Practice Copy these examples on your paper. If an item is a complete sentence, underline the subject once and the verb twice. If it is not a sentence, write *incomplete.*

1. Tee brought her great-grandmother a bunch of dogwood blooms.

2. Something like the circus.

3. Between you and me, Father William.

4. When the world is puddle-wonderful.

5. He looked through the lenses of a microscope.

Writing Application Rewrite each incomplete sentence above, adding a subject or a verb to make the sentence complete.

4. Hyperbole creates ridiculous and humorous images in the mind's eye.

◆Build Grammar Skills

1. Tee brought her great-grandmother a bunch of dogwood blooms.
2. Incomplete
3. Incomplete
4. Incomplete
5. He looked through the lense of a microscope.

Writing Application

Possible responses:

2. The Silas Greene show is something like the circus.
3. Between you and me, Father William, your behavior is absurd.
4. Spring is a time when the world is puddle-wonderful.

Writer's Solution

For additional instruction and practice, use the lesson in the *Writer's Solution Language Lab CD-ROM* on Sentence Fragments in the section on Problems With Sentences. You may also use the practice page on The Basic Sentence, p. 28, in the *Writer's Solution Grammar Practice Book.*

Build Your Portfolio

Idea Bank

Writing

1. **Postcard From Sarah** Write a postcard or letter from Sarah Cynthia Sylvia Stout that explains what happened to her.
2. **Seasonal Description** Cummings joined words like *mud* and *luscious* together to make *mud-luscious*. Create combinations of words like these to capture the essence of a season. Then, use these words in an essay about your favorite season.
3. **Literary Review** Write a review of one of the selections you've just read. Summarize the poem or story, state the author's message, and then explain whether you think the author successfully conveyed that message.

Speaking and Listening

4. **Dramatization [Group Activity]** With a group, choose a scene from "The Luckiest Time of All" to bring to life. After a planning meeting, assign these tasks: write the script, plan the costumes and set, and direct the rehearsal. Perform your scene for the class. **[Performing Arts Link]**
5. **Interview** Work with a partner to plan and stage an interview with a character from one of the selections. Develop a series of questions and answers, and present the interview to classmates.

Projects

6. **Report on Good-Luck Charms** Elzie had her lucky stone, baseball players have their rally caps, and many of your classmates have their own good-luck charms. In an illustrated report, explain the variety of modern good-luck objects. Include quotations from friends and family about why they believe these items bring them luck.
7. **Microscope Presentation** Using library resources, learn about Leeuwenhoek's invention. Include photographs, a microscope, and Kumin's poem. If possible, demonstrate use of the microscope as part of your presentation. **[Science Link]**

Writing Mini-Lesson

Humorous Poem

In their work, writers often describe everyday experiences with comic results. Lewis Carroll creates a silly conversation between a father and his son. Shel Silverstein imagines the absurd consequences of a child's decision to avoid her chores. Choose a memorable experience or event from your life, and write a humorous poem about it.

Writing Skills Focus: Use Imaginative Words

In your poem, **use imaginative words** to add humor to the story you tell. Consider these techniques as you experiment:

- Lucille Clifton adds humor by spelling words as Elzie pronounces them. "Usta be a kinda show went all through the South," she says.
- E. E. Cummings creates new words, such as "puddle-wonderful," to describe spring.
- Shel Silverstein chooses words beginning with the same sound to make his poem fun: "Crusts of black burned buttered toast/Gristly bits of beefy roasts . . ."

Prewriting List words and phrases that will bring the experience to life. If you like, choose the key words to use as the start of rhyming lists.

Drafting Set the pattern of rhyme you wish to use. If you plan to write without regular rhyme, consider how to shape your poem on the page. Then, refer to your list as you draft your poem.

Revising Fine-tune words, phrases, and lines to correct rhyme or physical shape. Feel free to create new words if you need them—or create them just for fun.

◆ Grammar Application

If your poem is written in complete sentences, check to be sure that each sentence contains a subject and a verb.

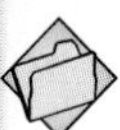

Idea Bank

Following are suggestions for matching the Idea Bank topics with your students' performance levels and learning modalities:

Customize for *Performance Levels*
Less Advanced Students: 1, 4, 6
Average Students: 2, 4, 5, 6
More Advanced Students: 3, 5, 7

Customize for *Learning Modalities*
Verbal/Linguistic: 1, 2, 3
Visual/Spatial: 6, 7
Bodily/Kinesthetic: 4
Interpersonal: 4, 5
Intrapersonal: 1, 2, 3

Writing Mini-Lesson

Refer students to the Writing Handbook in the back of the book for instructions on the writing process and for further information on Creative Writing.

Writer's Solution

Writing Lab CD-ROM

Have students complete the tutorial on Creative Writing. Follow these steps:

1. Have students view the Inspirations for Creative Writing for possible topic ideas.
2. Tell students to view the models of sound devices in poetry.
3. Encourage students to use the Concrete Image Word Bin to help them gather images for their poems.
4. Suggest that students use the Interactive Self-Evaluation Checklist for poetry when revising.

Writer's Solution Sourcebook

Have students use Chapter 8, "Creative Writing," pp. 234–263, for additional support. This chapter includes in-depth instruction on using concrete language, p. 262.

✓ ASSESSMENT OPTIONS

Formal Assessment, Selection Test, pp. 116–118, and Assessment Resources Software. The selection test is designed so that it can easily be customized to the performance levels of your students.

Alternative Assessment, p. 26, includes options for less advanced students, more advanced students, verbal/linguistic learners, bodily/kinesthetic learners, interpersonal learners, visual/spatial learners, and logical/mathematical learners.

PORTFOLIO ASSESSMENT

Use the following rubrics in the **Alternative Assessment** booklet to assess student writing:
Postcard From Sarah: Expression, p. 81
Seasonal Description: Description, p. 84
Literary Review: Critical Review, p. 98
Writing Mini-Lesson: Poetry, p. 95

Prepare and Engage

Establish Writing Guidelines
Review the following key characteristics of a humorous anecdote:

- A humorous anecdote is a brief story about a true, humorous event.
- Humorous anecdotes are often used to entertain an audience by illustrating a point.

You may want to distribute the scoring rubric for Expression, p. 81, in **Alternative Assessment,** to make students aware of the criteria on which they will be evaluated. See the suggestions on p. 412 for how you can customize the rubric to this workshop.

Refer students to the Writing Handbook in the back of the book for instruction on the writing process and further information on expression.

Writer's Solution

Writers at Work Videodisc
To introduce students to expressive writing and to show them how Gary Soto describes his ideas about expression, play the videodisc segment on Expression (Ch. 1.) Have students discuss what Soto says about embellishing topics.

Play frames 320 to 9204

Writing Lab CD-ROM
If your students have access to computers, you may want to have them work in the tutorial on Expression to complete all or part of their humorous anecdotes. Follow these steps:

1. Have students view the interactive model of an anecdote.
2. Suggest that students use the Cluster Map activity to come up with new topic ideas.
3. Allow students to draft on computer.
4. Have students use the Interactive Self-Evaluation Checklist when revising.

Writer's Solution Sourcebook
Students can find additional support, including in-depth instruction on using specific details, in the chapter on Expression, pp. 1–31.

Narrative Writing

Humorous Anecdote

Writing Process Workshop

An old expression says that "laughter is the best medicine." It's true that sometimes when you're feeling down, hearing a funny story can pick you right up again.

Brighten someone's day by writing a **humorous anecdote,** a short, funny story that will make your audience laugh. The following skills, introduced in this section's Writing Mini-Lessons, will help you.

Writing Skills Focus

▶ **Answer the five W's.** Help your audience get the most enjoyment from your humorous anecdote: tell *who* was involved, *what* happened, *when* and *where* the action took place, and *why* the whole thing was so funny. (See p. 378.)

▶ **Supply the background.** Just as every good joke has a "setup," every humorous anecdote needs details and background that build to a funny "punch line." (See p. 395.)

▶ **Use imaginative words** to add to the humor of your story and make it come to life. (See p. 409.)

Notice how Charles Osgood uses these skills in his essay "Our Finest Hour."

Model From Literature

from "Our Finest Hour" by Charles Osgood

When the commercial was over, I introduced a piece from Washington. What came up was a series of pictures of people who seemed to be dead. . . . I knew nothing whatsoever about this piece. It was not scheduled for the broadcast. . . . In the "fishbowl," the glassed-in office where the executive producer sits, ① there were at least three people yelling into telephones. Nobody in there knew anything about this piece either. ②

① *This sentence tells when, who, what, and where.*

② *By giving background that explains what the "fishbowl" is, Osgood helps readers picture this funny scene.*

Beyond the Classroom

Using Humor Tell students that humor can be used in a number of situations to ease tension, introduce a topic, or bring people together. Encourage students to think of situations where they have heard jokes, or laughed at something someone else has said. Remind them of political officials who use humor when giving a speech, or how parents might use humor to address a touchy subject.

Have students keep a journal, noting incidents where humor creeps into their lives. They can note specific incidents that happen to them, things they have heard of through other people, or examples of humor they see on television or in films. After one week, have students review their journals. Encourage volunteers to share their findings with the class, and try to discuss whether the use of humor has been effective in specific situations.

Prewriting

Decide What's Funny A humorous anecdote is short, funny, and often tells about real people. If you have trouble coming up with an idea, try one of the following strategies:

Brainstorming Suggestions

- Skim your journal for funny stories about you and people you know.
- Ask friends and family members to share hilarious stories.
- Flip through photo albums or scrapbooks to stir up amusing memories.
- Read a biography to find a funny episode in the life of a famous person.

Jot Down the Five W's Use a chart like the one below to record the *who, what, where, when,* and *why* of your story. Once you have all these facts on paper, writing your humorous anecdote will be a breeze!

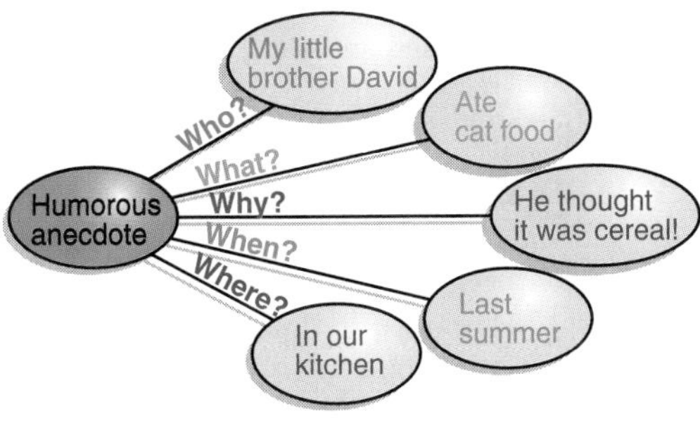

Brainstorm for Wacky Words Before you begin to write, brainstorm for words that will add zing to your anecdote. For example, if a little boy ate cat food by mistake, he might *squinch* up his face in disgust.

Drafting

Use a Humorous Technique There are several ways to make a funny story even funnier. Choose one of the following techniques, and work it into your anecdote as you draft.

- ▶ Add an unexpected twist at the end.
- ▶ Use exaggeration.
- ▶ Contrast a serious tone with a ridiculous situation.
- ▶ Include unusual details of setting and character.

DRAFTING/REVISING

APPLYING LANGUAGE SKILLS: Specific vs. Vague Words

Some words are **vague** and general. They are commonly used and are broad in meaning. Other words are **specific.** They are unusual, crisp, and precise. In most writing, especially in storytelling, it's better to use words that are specific.

Vague:
It tasted bad.

Precise:
It tasted revolting.

Practice Replace the italicized vague words in these sentences with more specific ones.

1. My brother *ate* the *stuff.*
2. He *reacted.*
3. My mother *moved* toward him.
4. It was so *funny,* I had to *laugh.*

Writing Application As you write your humorous anecdote, replace vague words with words that are more specific.

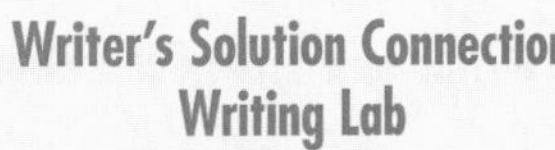

Writer's Solution Connection Writing Lab

To avoid using vague adjectives, use the Revision Checker in the tutorial on Description.

Develop Student Writing

Prewriting

Remind students that often things that are funny to them are not funny to other people. The object of writing a humorous anecdote is to re-create a situation to make it funny for readers, including all necessary details and explanations.

Customize for
Interpersonal Learners
Suggest that students work together on their humorous anecdotes. Have them form pairs and have one student tell a funny story, while the other person writes down what is said. Then the writer must work with the storyteller to gather vivid details and re-create the humor in the event.

Customize for
More Advanced Writers
Suggest that students take their humorous anecdote one step further by turning it into a script for a comedy routine. Have them view a televised comedy routine or listen to a recording of one, noting how the comedian introduces and develops the story. Encourage students to write their scripts and perform the skits for the class.

Drafting

Remind students that they must include their personal reactions and feelings in their humorous anecdotes. Encourage them to jot down notes about how they felt as the event occurred. As they write their drafts, have students refer to their notes to remind them of how they perceived the event.

Applying Language Skills

Specific vs. Vague Words Tell students that one way to come up with specific words is to think of sensory details. When students find vague words in their writing, have them ask themselves, "How is this [bad]?" Ask them to consider which senses the word affects and then be more specific.

Answers

Possible responses:

1. My brother wolfed down the brown soup.
2. He jumped up and down with joy.
3. My mother sidled toward him.
4. It was so hysterical, I had to shriek with laughter.

Writer's Solution

For additional instruction and practice, have students use the lesson on Using Precise Words in the *Writer's Solution Grammar Practice Book,* p. 116.

Revising

Encourage students to use peer reviewers when revising their work. In addition to looking for weak words, have reviewers look for places to add details to increase the humor or simply to suggest where the humor doesn't work.

Writer's Solution

Writing Lab CD-ROM

In the tutorial on Expression, have students use the Revision Checker to help them vary the way they begin their sentences.

Publishing and Presenting

For other publishing ideas, suggest that students include their anecdotes on postcards or in letters to friends or family who remember or were part of the event.

Reinforce and Extend

Review the Writing Guidelines

After students have completed their papers, review the characteristics of a humorous anecdote.

Applying Language Skills

Spelling Contractions With *Have*

Remind students that the reason people often misspell these types of contractions is because when we speak we often pronounce words like *would've* as "would of."

Answers

1. You *would've* been amazed.
2. I *should've* put the cat food away.
3. I *could've* laughed for hours.
4. He *could've* been sick!

EDITING/PROOFREADING

APPLYING LANGUAGE SKILLS: Spelling Contractions With *Have*

Several **contractions** are made from the word *have.* Here are a few:

would've	would have
could've	could have
should've	should have

In writing contractions, be careful not to write *would of* or *could of* when you mean *would've* or *could've.*

Practice On your paper, rewrite these sentences using contractions with *have.* Correct any errors.

1. You would of been amazed.
2. I should of put the cat food away.
3. I could of laughed for hours.
4. He could of been sick!

Writing Application As you write your humorous anecdote, spell all contractions with *have* correctly.

Writer's Solution Connection Language Lab

For more instruction on writing dialogue, see the lesson on Quotation Marks in the Language Lab.

Include Dialogue A good story includes dialogue. Include questions and exclamations. Keep the dialogue short, crisp, and easy to read.

Time Your Punch Line Your anecdote will be funniest if you don't give away your ending too early in the story. Keep your audience guessing. Build suspense. Then, serve up a hilarious punch line.

Revising

Include Necessary Information Your audience won't "get" the joke if you don't give them all the information they need. Have a friend read your anecdote. Then, ask if more background information could make it funnier.

Replace Weak Words Don't settle for boring, everyday words. When you notice them, circle them. Use a dictionary, thesaurus, peer reviewer, or your own imagination to replace them.

REVISION MODEL

① horrified and disgusted. howled with laughter.

He looked ~~surprised and sick.~~ I ~~started to laugh.~~

② As soon as he could talk,

He grabbed a glass, ran to the sink, and screamed,

"Yick! How could Fluffy eat this stuff?!"

① The writer adds interest and flair by replacing dull words with vivid and precise ones.

② The writer provides more detail to tell *when* events happened.

Publishing and Presenting

▶ **Tell It** Plan a Funny Stories Festival for a slow afternoon. Take turns telling your anecdotes aloud, using voice, gesture, and movement to add to the humor. If possible, videotape your performances and share the tape with another class.

▶ **Find a Magazine** Many magazines—for example, *Reader's Digest*—publish humorous anecdotes sent in by their readers. Submit your anecdote for publication. This could be the beginning of a career in comedy writing!

✓ ASSESSMENT

PORTFOLIO ASSESSMENT

Use the rubric on Description in the **Alternative Assessment** booklet, p. 84, to assess students' writing. Add these criteria to customize this rubric to this assignment.

	4	3	2	1
Humorous Technique	The writer successfully uses a humorous technique while also telling about an event.	The writer uses a humorous technique but some of the points in the event are unclear.	The writer attempts to use a humorous technique but fails to tell about key points in the event.	The writer fails to use a humorous technique, and the key points in the event are unclear.
Specific Words	The writer uses specific words consistently throughout the anecdote.	The writer mostly uses specific words; there are a few cases of vague words.	The writer uses more vague words than specific words.	The writer uses very few to no specific words.

Real-World Reading Skills Workshop

Interpreting Charts and Graphs

Strategies for Success

Whether you are researching a report or reading the newspaper, you may find information in charts and graphs. Charts and graphs can help you compare several pieces of related information quickly. Follow these guidelines for interpreting charts and graphs:

Identify the Topic Use the title, captions, and label of the chart or graph to identify its topic. The article in which the chart or graph appears will also provide information. Understanding the purpose of the graph will help you to read it accurately.

Study the Elements Follow these steps to study all the information given in the chart or graph:

- ▶ Identify the type of chart or graph: The most common types are bar graphs, line graphs, and pie charts.
- ▶ Read the key, which tells you what the elements on the graph represent.
- ▶ Note the labels and units of measurement on the graph.
- ▶ Identify the number of items shown on the graph.

Read the Graph To read a pie chart, compare the values represented by the "wedges" to the value of the whole "pie."

To read a bar or line graph:

1. Start at the left side, and locate the first point or bar on the graph.
2. Trace your finger downward to the horizontal axis to see what the point or bar represents.
3. Look across from the point or top of the bar to the vertical axis, and find the unit of measurement.
4. Repeat this process for each point or bar.

Apply the Strategies

Your teacher has asked you to help plan activities for this year's school fair based on the events that were most popular last year. Use the graph to answer the questions that follow.

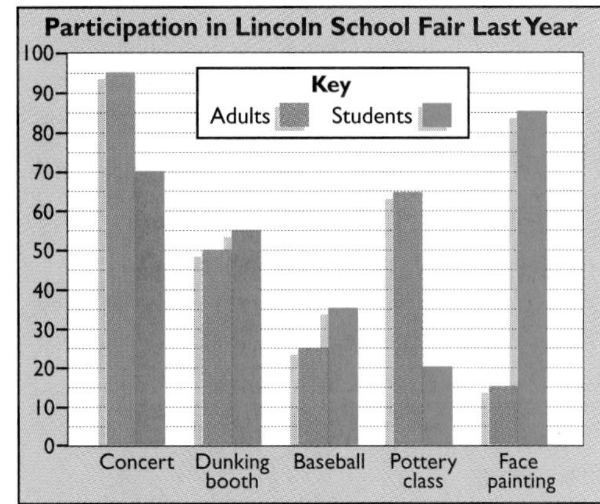

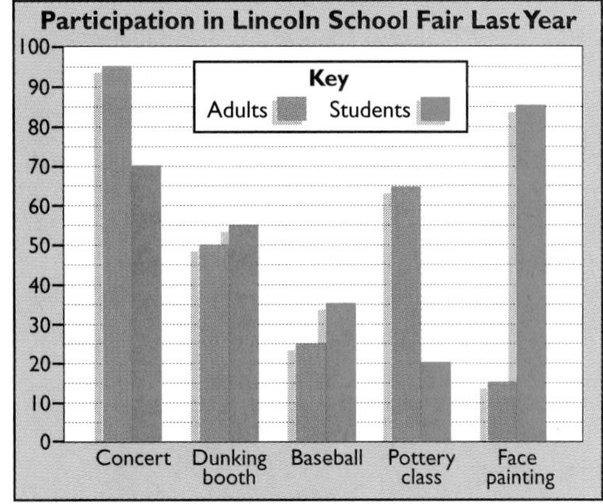

1. Which activity was most popular with adults? With students?
2. Which activity came closest to having the same number of adult and student participants?
3. Which activity had the greatest difference in interest between adults and students?
4. In order to please the most people, which three events would you recommend holding again at this year's fair?

Here are other situations in which you need to interpret charts and graphs:

- ▶ *Comparing sports statistics*
- ▶ *Reading newspapers and magazines*
- ▶ *Doing research*

Introduce the Strategies

Ask students what kinds of graphs and charts they have encountered in everyday life. They should be familiar with different types of graphs and charts from their classes in social studies and science. Have volunteers name different types of graphs or charts they have seen and explain how the information was presented in each.

Customize for
Less Proficient Readers

Students may get a better grasp on graphs and charts by converting the data to written sentences. When they look at the graph or chart, have them first identify the topic of the chart. Then have them complete this sentence: "This [chart/graph] shows the relationship between ____ and ____." As students begin to interpret data at fixed points on the graph or chart, encourage them to create sentences like the one above to better understand the information they are viewing.

Customize for
More Advanced Students

Suggest that students take the information in the graph on p. 413 and make a different type of graph or chart to represent the same information. Have them share their new graphs or charts with the rest of the class. Discuss with students which graph seems the most effective and why.

Apply the Strategies

Explain to students that different types of charts or graphs are used for different purposes. Bar graphs usually compare quantities within categories, line graphs usually show changes over time, and pie charts usually show proportions. As a first step, have students identify what type of graph they are viewing.

Answers

1. The concert was most popular with adults; the face painting was most popular with students.
2. The dunking booth came closest to having the same number of adult and student participants.
3. Face painting had the greatest difference in interest between adults and students.
4. Students should recognize that the three events that were popular for both adults and students were the concert, the dunking booth, and baseball.

◆Build Grammar Skills

Reviewing Subjects and Predicates

The selections in Part I include instruction on the following:

- Subjects and Predicates
- Compound Subjects and Predicates
- Complete and Incomplete Sentences

This instruction is reinforced with the Build Grammar Skills practice pages in **Selection Support,** pp. 130, 136, and 141.

As you review subjects and predicates you may wish to review the following:

- **Complete Subjects and Predicates** A complete subject of a sentence is the subject and any words related to it, such as adjectives. A complete predicate of a sentence is the verb and any words related to it, such as adverbs or adverbial phrases. Compound subjects and compound predicates are joined by conjunctions.

Customize for
Less Proficient Readers

Suggest that students fill out a chart like the one that follows when analyzing sentences for subjects and predicates:

subject	
words related to subject	
predicate	
words related to predicate	
conjunctions	

With this chart, students should be able to determine whether a sentence is complete or incomplete.

Writer's Solution

For additional practice and support with phrases, use the practice pages on The Basic Sentence, p. 28, Complete Sentences and Predicates, p. 29, and Compound Subjects and Verbs, p. 30, in the *Writer's Solution Grammar Practice Book.*

Subjects and Predicates

Grammar Review

SEND

sen·tence (sen′təns) *n.* 1 a group of words that is used to tell, ask, command, or exclaim something, usually having a subject and a predicate: a sentence begins with a capital letter and ends with a period, question mark, or exclamation point

A sentence is a group of words that expresses a complete thought. Every sentence consists of two parts: the **subject** and the **predicate.** The subject states whom or what the sentence is about. The predicate tells what the subject is or does. (See page 377.)

subject | *predicate*

The young Sarah Stout | refused to take out the garbage.

Simple Subject and Simple Predicate Each complete subject and predicate contains a simple subject and simple predicate. The simple subject is the main word in the complete subject, and the simple predicate is the verb or verb phrase in the predicate. (See page 377.)

subject | *predicate*

The young (*Sarah Stout*) | (*refused*) to take out the garbage.

Compound Subjects and Compound Verbs Some sentences may have more than one subject or verb. A **compound subject** is two or more subjects that have the same verb and are linked by a coordinating conjunction such as *and* or *or.* A **compound predicate** is two or more verbs that have the same subject and are linked by a coordinating conjunction such as *and* or *or.* (See page 394.)

Compound Subject: The *producers* and *technicians* were panicking in the control room.

Compound Verb: They *looked* at the monitors and *gasped* at the video.

Every complete sentence has both a subject and a verb. (See page 408.)

Practice 1 Copy the following sentences into your notebook. Underline the complete subject once and the complete predicate twice. Then, circle the simple subject and the simple predicate, and label those that are compound.

1. Sarah scoured the pots and scraped the pans.
2. The garbage reached across the state.
3. You are old, Father William.
4. In my youth, I took to the law and argued each case with my wife.
5. This day, we plaited our hair and put a dress and some things in a crokasack and started out to the show.

Practice 2 In a paragraph, describe someone you would label a "quirky character." In your paragraph, use two sentences with compound subjects and two with compound verbs.

Grammar in Writing

✔ *You can cut down on wordiness and repetition by combining sentences using compound subjects and verbs.*

Repetitive: Father William turned somersaults. Father William stood on his head.

Revised: Father William turned somersaults and stood on his head.

Answers

Practice 1

1. *Sarah* scoured the pots and scraped the pans. (circle simple subject *Sarah,* circle simple predicates *scoured* and *scraped*) compound predicate
2. *The garbage* reached across the state. (circle simple subject *garbage,* circle simple predicate *reached*)
3. *You* are old, *Father William.* (circle simple subject *you,* circle simple predicate *are*)
4. In my youth, *I* took to the law and argued each case with my wife. (circle simple subject *I,* circle simple predicates *took* and *argued*) compound predicate
5. This day, *we* plaited our hair and put a dress and some things in a crokasack and started out to the show. (circle simple subject *we,* circle simple predicates *plaited, put, started*) compound predicate

PART 2 *Mixed Messages*

Central Park, Gustavo Novoa, Wally Findlay Galleries, New York

Humanities: Art

Central Park, by Gustavo Novoa

Gustavo Novoa is a contemporary artist who began his art training at the Ecole des Beaux Arts in Paris, and continued his studies at the Academy of Fine Arts, Santiago, Chile. Most of his paintings include jungle animals or mythical beasts in a richly colored and detailed setting.

Explain to students that Central Park is the most popular park in New York City. The 800-acre park is surrounded by tall apartment buildings and hotels.

1. What details do you find unusual about this painting of Central Park? *Students will probably say that the animals seem out of place for a park in New York City.*
2. How do you think this painting relates to the theme "Mixed Messages"? *Students may say that the contrast between the city in the background and the lush greenery of the park mixes two settings, as well as the type of animals who seem to roam the park freely as people would.*

One-Minute Planning Guide

The selections in this section focus on the theme of mixed messages. "Zoo" turns the concept of a zoo inside out. A pair of poems— "The Hippopotamus" and "The Caterpillar"—look at the eccentricities of two animals. "The Blind Men and the Elephant" focuses on mix-ups that occur from seeing a part, rather than the whole. "How the Snake Got Poison" details the benefits and drawbacks of being a snake. In "A Letter to a Clockmaker," a famous writer humorously describes a broken clock. In "Stepping Out With My Baby," a man has problems communicating with his young son. Finally, "Let's Steal the Moon" tells of one town's attempt to capture the moon for their own purposes.

Customize for *Varying Student Needs*

When assigning the selections in this section to your students, keep in mind the following factors:

"Zoo"
- A short science-fiction story

"The Hippopotamus" and "The Caterpillar"
- Two short rhyming poems

"The Blind Men and the Elephant"
- A rhyming poem
- Students may need help with vocabulary

"How the Snake Got Poison"
- A folk tale
- Students may need help with dialect

"A Letter to a Clockmaker"
- A short letter
- Introduction to Charles Dickens

"Stepping Out With My Baby"
- A humorous essay

"Let's Steal the Moon"
- A short folk tale
- Students may need help analyzing theme

Prepare and Engage

OBJECTIVES

1. To read, comprehend, and interpret stories and poems
2. To relate character's perspective to personal experience
3. To evaluate an author's message
4. To understand a character's perspective
5. To build vocabulary in context and learn forms of the word *wonder*
6. To recognize direct and indirect objects
7. To write a report in which topic sentences are supported by details
8. To respond to stories and poems through writing, speaking and listening, and projects

SKILLS INSTRUCTION

Vocabulary:
Related Words: Forms of *wonder*

Spelling:
Words With the Suffix *-ity*

Grammar:
Direct and Indirect Objects

Reading Strategy:
Evaluate Author's Message

Literary Focus:
Character's Perspective

Writing:
Topic Sentences and Supporting Details

Speaking and Listening:
Animal Game (Teacher Edition)

Critical Viewing:
Summarize; Connect; Speculate

PORTFOLIO OPPORTUNITIES

Writing: Advertising Flyer; Humorous Poem; Comparison-and-Contrast Essay

Writing Mini-Lesson: Report

Speaking and Listening: Zoo Commercial; Animal Game

Projects: Pet Show; Metamorphosis

More About the Authors

Edward D. Hoch says that his strength as a writer stems from his good imagination.

Ogden Nash is considered by many to be the best American writer of light, humorous poems.

There is a final verse—not included in the selection—of **John Godfrey Saxe's** poem. It's entitled "The Moral" and points out that although all of the "disputants . . . rail on . . ." none understands what the others mean or what an elephant is.

Zora Neale Hurston was born in Eatonville, Florida, the first incorporated all-black township, where she experienced no racial prejudice.

Guide for Reading

Meet the Authors:

Edward D. Hoch (1930–)

After Edward Hoch graduated from college, he worked as a researcher and copy writer for an advertising agency. He uses these skills in science-fiction and mystery writing. A sense of humor has come in handy, too, as you'll see in his story "Zoo."

Ogden Nash (1902–1971)

Ogden Nash became famous for his ability to look at life from an unusual angle. Packed with a comical punch, his wise and witty poems continue to delight. Readers of all ages look to his work for fun and insight into life's absurdities.

John Godfrey Saxe (1816–1887)

John Godfrey Saxe lived during a time when writers and readers enjoyed poems that told stories. Saxe added humor to his verse, which has remained popular to this day. "The Blind Men and the Elephant," his most famous verse, is based on a tale from ancient India.

Zora Neale Hurston (1891–1960)

In addition to forging a successful career writing her own stories and essays, Zora Neale Hurston traveled throughout the South collecting African American folk tales. When she wrote the tales on paper, she preserved the exact language in which they had been told. This allowed her to honor the oral tradition and made the tales available to a wider audience.

◆ Literature and Your Life

Connect Your Experience

Science-fiction writers like to invent wild beings who live in the outer reaches of space, but creatures here on Earth are pretty amazing, too. Observe a caterpillar up close or an elephant from afar. These selections may help you see the animal kingdom in a completely new way.

Thematic Focus: Mixed Messages

In their confusion, the characters in these selections expend a lot of misplaced energy. Imagine how their experiences would be different if they understood everything the first time!

◆ Background for Understanding

Science

In this grouping, you'll encounter only a few of the millions of animals who roam the Earth. To help their study of the animal kingdom, scientists have developed a classification system. Animals are classed together based on features they share. For example, the mammal class includes such diverse species as humans, cats, elephants, and dolphins. The 4,500 species of mammals have backbones, warm blood, and well-developed brains.

◆ Build Vocabulary

Related Words: Forms of *wonder*

Wonder and its related words convey a sense of surprise and amazement. *Wonder* can be a noun or a verb. *Wonderment* is also a noun, and *wondrous* and *wonderful* are adjectives.

Word Bank

Which of these words from the selections might mean hugeness?

interplanetary
wonderment
awe
inclined
observation
wondrous
immensity

Prentice Hall Literature Program Resources

REINFORCE / RETEACH / EXTEND

Selection Support Pages
Build Vocabulary: Forms of *wonder,* p. 144
Build Spelling Skills, p. 145
Build Grammar Skills: Direct and Indirect Objects, p. 146
Reading Strategy: Evaluate Author's Message, p. 147
Literary Focus: Character's Perspective, p. 148

Strategies for Diverse Student Needs, pp. 53–54

Beyond Literature Cross-Curricular Connection: Science, p. 27

Formal Assessment Selection Test, pp. 119–121, Assessment Resources Software

Alternative Assessment, p. 27

Writing and Language Transparencies Series of Events Chain, p. 66; Sunburst Organizer, p. 94

Resource Pro CD-ROM Includes all selections

Listening to Literature Audiocassettes Includes all selections

Looking at Literature Videodisc/ Videotape "The Blind Men and the Elephant"

Zoo ◆ The Hippopotamus ◆ The Caterpillar ◆ The Blind Men and the Elephant ◆ How the Snake Got Poison

◆ Reading Strategy

Evaluate Author's Message

A message is the idea that a writer wants to convey. In "Hippopotamus," for example, Nash weighs an animal's perspective against his own to decide that animals and humans each find beauty in their own species. You **evaluate an author's message** by first identifying the message and then judging whether it is true, clearly reasoned, and well supported.

1

◆ Literary Focus

Character's Perspective

You might laugh when people in movies make fools of themselves. Yet if you were in the same situation, you might feel more like crying. The same is true of characters in a story or poem. A **character's perspective,** or the position from which he or she views events, will affect his or her actions, reactions, and attitudes. This perspective can be based on knowledge, ability, and former experiences. As you read, use a chart like the one below to track the ways each character's perspective affects his or her understanding of events.

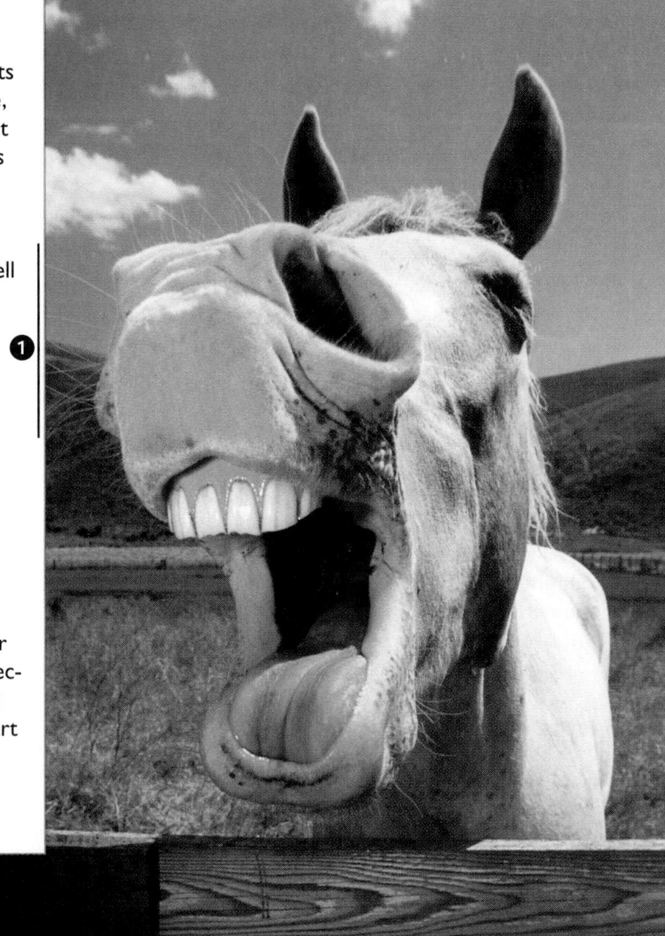

Perspective	Understanding of Events	Actions

Preparing for Standardized Tests

Vocabulary Knowledge of related words will help students as they read in general, and with analogy sections of standardized tests. The object of an analogy question is to determine the relationship between the first two items, and then apply the same relationship to fill in the missing part from among a choice of words. Present the following sample test question:

wonderment : wondrous :: joyfulness : ___

(A) joy (C) joys
(B) joyous (D) enjoyment

Discuss with students why *(B)* is the best choice for completing the analogy. Point out that both *wonderment* and *wondrous* are related forms of *wonder*; that *wonderment* is a noun and *wondrous*, an adjective. Both *joyfulness* and *joyous* are forms of *joy*; and like the two terms of the first pair, *joyfulness* is a noun, and *joyous* is an adjective. For further practice, use Build Vocabulary in **Selection Support,** p. 144.

Ask students if they think it is ever possible to be right and wrong at the same time. Begin a discussion by reading aloud the following:

Jen: We get homework constantly—three times a week.
Tom: We hardly get any homework at all—only three times a week.

Tell students that the pieces they will read focus on how a character's perspective affects the way he or she views events.

◆ Build Grammar Skills

Direct and Indirect Objects If you wish to introduce the grammar concept for this selection before students read, refer to the instruction on p. 426.

◆ Critical Thinking

1 Speculate Refer students to this picture of a mule. Ask them to predict what its appearance here indicates about the selections that follow. *Students may predict that the pieces will be lighthearted and will involve animals.*

Customize for
Less Proficient Readers
Tell students that although many poets, especially modern poets, shun the sing-song style of poetry, here this style is intentional. Guide students to read the Nash and Saxe poems aloud in a sing-song rhythm to appreciate the cleverness of the rhyming. Help them appreciate, for example, the unlikely rhythm and rhyme of "delight the eye" and "hippopotami" in the first Nash poem.

Customize for
More Advanced Students
Discuss with students the universality of certain perceptions and reactions. For example, many organisms are at once fascinated by and fearful of one another. In "Zoo," ask students to look for these and other common emotions the Earth people and Kaan people display.

Develop Understanding

One-Minute Insight In "Zoo," a story about a traveling interplanetary zoo, each creature understands things from his or her own perspective. According to the humans who line up to see them, the horse-spiders from Kaan are an exotic breed displayed in cages. To the horse-spiders, however, it is they who are protected by the bars as they observe the strange and fascinating humans.

Team Teaching Strategy

You may want to coordinate with a science teacher to discuss ideas for extending instruction, particularly as students work on the Speaking and Listening activity about animals, and the Metamorphosis project in the Idea Bank on p. 427.

◆Reading Strategy

1 Evaluate Author's Message Guide students to appreciate how the writer builds suspense quickly and effectively. Ask them what they can infer about this zoo. *The zoo will feature an array of strange and amazing creatures from other planets.*

Thematic Focus

2 Mixed Messages How is Professor Hugo less like a scholar and more like a carnival barker? *His multicolored clothing and master-of-ceremonies approach to zoo-keeping indicate that he is more of a showman than a scientist.*

◆Literary Focus

3 Character's Perspective *The crowd's perspective of viewing them through the bars of cages makes the zoo's creatures appear strange and a bit frightening to the people of Earth.*

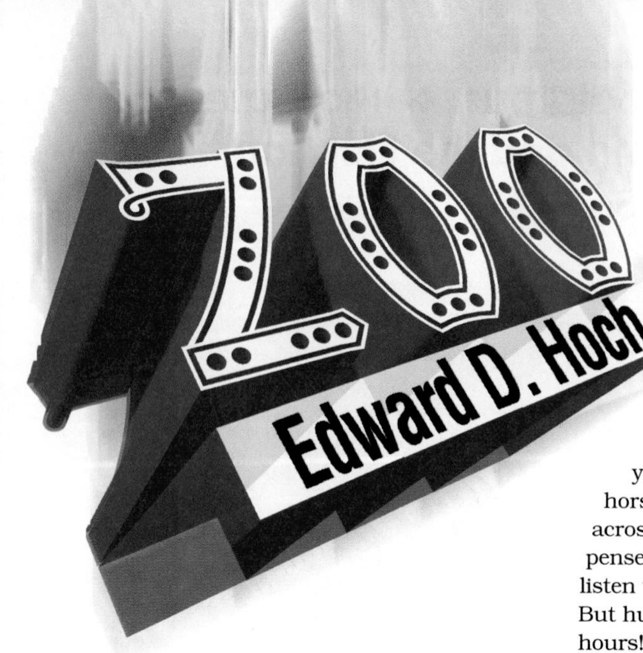

1 The children were always good during the month of August, especially when it began to get near the twenty-third. It was on this day that the great silver spaceship carrying Professor Hugo's Interplanetary Zoo settled down for its annual six-hour visit to the Chicago area.

Before daybreak the crowds would form, long lines of children and adults both, each one clutching his or her dollar and waiting with wonderment to see what race of strange creatures the Professor had brought this year.

In the past they had sometimes been treated to three-legged creatures from Venus, or tall, thin men from Mars, or even snakelike horrors from somewhere more distant. This year, as the great round ship settled slowly to earth in the huge tri-city parking area just outside of Chicago, they watched with awe as the sides slowly slid up to reveal the familiar barred cages. In them were some wild breed of nightmare—small, horse-like animals that moved with quick, jerking motions and constantly chattered in a high-pitched tongue. 1 The citizens of Earth clustered around as Professor Hugo's crew quickly collected the waiting dollars, and soon the good Professor himself made an appearance, wearing his many-colored rainbow cape and top hat. "Peoples of Earth," he called into his microphone.

The crowd's noise died down and he continued. "Peoples of Earth, this year you see a real treat for your single dollar—the little-known horse-spider people of Kaan—brought to you across a million miles of space at great expense. Gather around, see them, study them, listen to them, tell your friends about them. But hurry! My ship can remain here only six hours!" 2

And the crowds slowly filed by, at once horrified and fascinated by these strange creatures that looked like horses but ran up the walls of their cages like spiders. "This is certainly worth a dollar," one man remarked, hurrying away. "I'm going home to get the wife." 3

> **◆ Literary Focus** Why would the crowd's perspective affect the way people view Hugo's Zoo?

All day long it went like that, until ten thousand people had filed by the barred cages set into the side of the spaceship. Then, as the six-hour limit ran out, Professor Hugo once more took the microphone in hand. "We must go now, but we will return next year on this date. And if you enjoyed our zoo this year, telephone your friends in other cities about it. We will land in New York tomorrow, and next week on to London, Paris,

◆ Build Vocabulary

interplanetary (in′ tər plan′ ə ter′ ē) *adj.*: Between planets

wonderment (wun′ dər ment) *n.*: Astonishment

awe (ô) *n.*: Mixed feelings of fear and wonder

Block Scheduling Strategies

Consider these suggestions to take advantage of extended class time:

- After reading "How the Snake Got Poison," have students complete the Journal Writing activity on p. 425. Then have them meet in small groups to read their entries aloud in an "animal gripe session."
- Invite volunteers to read the poems and the folk tale aloud. Alternatively, play the recording.

Listening to Literature Audiocassettes

- Allow students to work on the Speaking and Listening activities in the Idea Bank, p. 427. Provide time for small groups to play the Animal Game or to create a Zoo Commercial.
- To help students prepare for the Writing Mini-Lesson, direct students to *Writer's Solution Sourcebook,* Chapter 4, Exposition: Giving Information. To help them with topic sentences and supporting sentences, refer them to the Building Paragraphs unit of the *Writer's Solution Language Lab CD-ROM.*

Rome, Hong Kong, and Tokyo. Then on to other worlds!"

He waved farewell to them, and as the ship rose from the ground, the Earth peoples agreed that this had been the very best Zoo yet. . . .

Some two months and three planets later, the silver ship of Professor Hugo settled at last onto the familiar jagged rocks of Kaan, and the odd horse-spider creatures filed quickly out of their cages. Professor Hugo was there to say a few parting words, and then they scurried away in a hundred different directions, seeking their homes among the rocks.

In one house, the she-creature was happy to see the return of her mate and offspring. She babbled a greeting in the strange tongue and hurried to embrace them. "It was a long time you were gone. Was it good?"

And the he-creature nodded. "The little one enjoyed it especially. We visited eight worlds and saw many things."

The little one ran up the wall of the cave. "On the place called Earth it was the best. The creatures there wear garments over their skins, and they walk on two legs."

"But isn't it dangerous?" asked the she-creature.

"No," her mate answered. "There are bars to protect us from them. We remain right in the ship. Next time you must come with us. It is well worth the nineteen commocs it costs."

And the little one nodded. "It was the very best Zoo ever. . . ."

◆ **Reading Strategy** Why does she think human beings are dangerous? 

▼ **Critical Viewing** After you've read "Zoo," suggest two captions for this illustration—one from the people's perspective and one from the animals'. **[Summarize]** 5

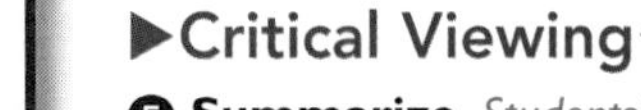

◆Reading Strategy

4 Evaluate Author's Message *Students may say that, like people on Earth, people from other worlds are afraid of the unknown.*

▶Critical Viewing◀

5 Summarize *Students' captions will vary and are likely to reflect perceptions of differences in physical appearance. For example, to the Kaan creatures, the Earthlings are two-legged and open-mouthed, and have eyes that don't protrude from their faces.*

Customize for
English Language Learners

Students may find some of the words in "Zoo" difficult: *breed, chattered, horrified, fascinated, jagged, scurried,* and *garments*. Guide students to read with a partner, using context clues and consulting a dictionary to determine meanings.

Cultural Connection

Zoos Also called zoological gardens or zoological parks, zoos have been around for a long time—it is believed that people began creating them as early as 4500 B.C. Kings and other rulers often had zoos built according to their own designs. In China, in about 1000 B.C., Wen Wang established a 1,500-acre zoological garden, which he named "The Garden of Intelligence." The Greeks also had collections of captive animals, and Alexander the Great collected animals on his military expeditions. During his trek through Mexico, Hernán Cortés came upon a zoo so large that it needed a staff of 300 keepers. A zoo in Vienna, Austria, has been open since 1752. The word *zoo,* however, did not come into use until the late nineteenth century. It was an abbreviation, frequently used for the zoological gardens in London.

Modern zoos try to house animals in natural habitats wherever possible. In rural areas, open-range zoos have been in existence since the early 1930's.

One of the main purposes of zoos is to study animals. To provide for this scientific research, visitors often fund zoos by paying admission fees. Discuss with students what they have observed at zoos they have visited, read about, or seen on TV. Then encourage them to think about the zoo in this story. Invite students to write in their journals about what they think zoos might be like in the future.

Develop Understanding

One-Minute Insight In his poem "The Hippopotamus," Ogden Nash makes the point that hippos may look funny to people, but they look just fine to each other. Nash writes in "The Caterpillar" that this furry, quiet creature is seldom the topic of serious poetry. Both poems feature clever and comical rhymes.

Clarification

❶ Tell students that *hippopotamus* comes from a Greek word that means "river horse." Hippos have large heads, short legs, and four toes on each foot. They are plant-eating, thick-skinned, and nearly hairless mammals that live mostly in or near rivers in sub-Saharan Africa.

◆Critical Thinking

❷ **Connect** Discuss with students the meaning of the expression "Beauty is in the eye of the beholder," and how the poem conveys this message.

▶Critical Viewing◀

❸ **Connect** *Students are likely to point out the hippopotamus's general bulk, its big nostrils, and its apparent, and deceptive, lethargy.*

Customize for *Less Proficient Readers*

Read the poems in advance to identify words that students may find hard to pronounce, such as *hippopotami, Baudelaire,* and *chrysalis.* Help students to correctly pronounce these words to better appreciate the cleverness of the rhymes.

The Hippopotamus

Ogden Nash

Behold the hippopotamus! ❶
We laugh at how he looks to us,
And yet in moments dank and grim
I wonder how we look to him.
Peace, peace, thou hippopotamus! ❷
We really look all right to us,
As you no doubt delight the eye
Of other hippopotami.

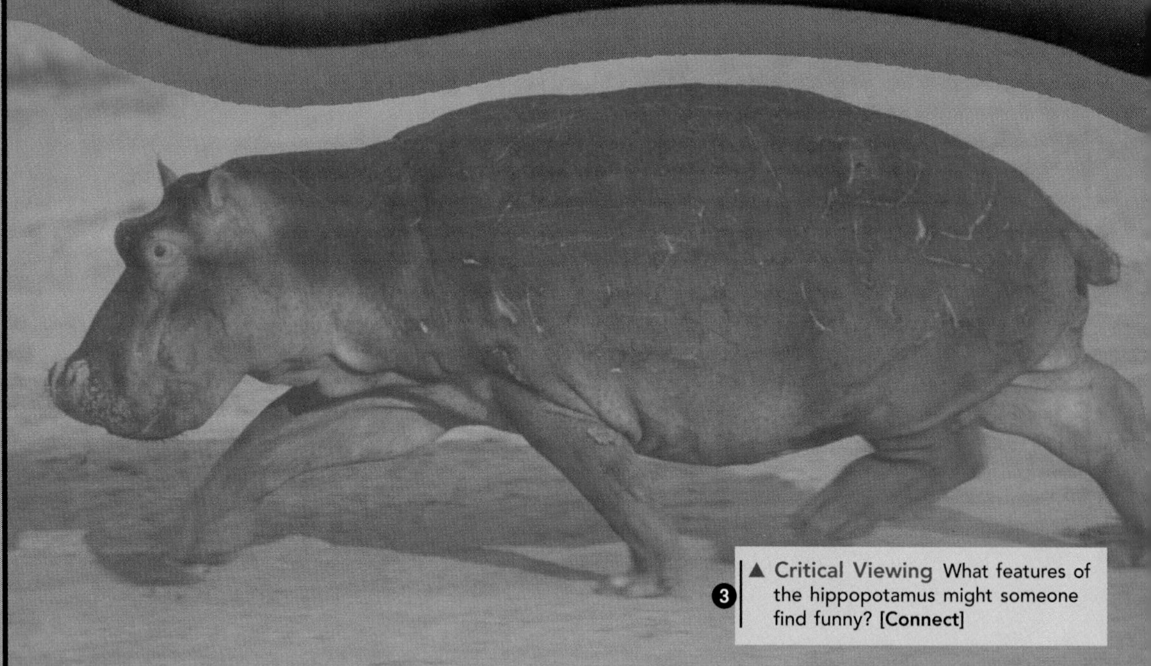

❸ ▲ Critical Viewing What features of the hippopotamus might someone find funny? **[Connect]**

Speaking and Listening Mini-Lesson

Animal Game

This mini-lesson supports the Speaking and Listening activity in the Idea Bank on p. 427.

Introduce Work with students to formulate rules for this game. Help them determine the form in which questions are asked and the manner in which information is shared. Discuss where students can find unusual animal facts. Tell them they should be prepared to identify the source of any fact they use.

Develop Provide time for pairs of students to gather their data and organize their facts in the order in which they plan to present them.

Apply Hold the games. Keep the tone simple and noncompetitive. You may wish to set up a round-robin tournament in which each pair plays every other pair. Or, you might set up brackets for a single-elimination tournament, in which teams compete until there is one winner for the class.

Assess Students should be evaluated on both their research and their guessing. In addition, you may want to use the scoring rubric for Definition/Classification, p. 86, in **Alternative Assessment.**

The Caterpillar

Ogden Nash

I find among the poems of Schiller[1]
No mention of the caterpillar,
Nor can I find one anywhere
In Petrarch[2] or in Baudelaire,[3]
So here I sit in extra session
To give my personal impression.
The caterpillar, as it's called,
Is often hairy, seldom bald;
It looks as if it never shaves;
When as it walks, it walks in waves;
And from the cradle to the chrysalis
It's utterly speechless, songless, whistleless.

1. **Schiller:** Friedrich von Schiller (1759–1805); German dramatist, poet, and historian.
2. **Petrarch:** Francesco Petrarca (1304–1374); Italian poet and scholar.
3. **Baudelaire:** Charles Pierre Baudelaire (1821–1867); French poet.

▲ Critical Viewing Why might a caterpillar, like the one pictured here, be overlooked by the poets that Nash names? **[Speculate]**

Guide for Responding

◆ Literature and Your Life

Reader's Response Were you surprised by the ending of Hoch's story? Explain.

Thematic Focus How do "Zoo," "The Hippopotamus," and "The Caterpillar" each illustrate the concept of mixed messages?

Journal Writing What other animal do you think would make a good subject for a poem by Ogden Nash? In a journal entry, explain your choice.

☑ Check Your Comprehension

1. In "Zoo," what impression do earthlings have of the creatures from Kaan?
2. How do the Kaanians describe humans?
3. What does the speaker of "The Hippopotamus" imagine that the animal thinks?
4. Where has the speaker of "The Caterpillar" looked to find poetry about the animal?

◆ Critical Thinking

Interpret

1. Based on what he tells the earthlings, how do you think Professor Hugo entices the Kaanians to visit Earth? **[Speculate]**
2. What does the way Professor Hugo runs his zoo suggest about him? **[Infer]**
3. (a) In "The Hippopotamus," why does the speaker want to console the animal? (b) What does he say to console him? **[Interpret]**
4. In "The Caterpillar," what qualities of the insect does the speaker celebrate? **[Analyze]**
5. What elements of Nash's poetry tell you the poems are meant to amuse? **[Support]**

Evaluate

6. (a) Do you think Nash likes his subjects? (b) What details in the poems help you decide? **[Assess]**

Extend

7. What facts about the hippopotamus and the caterpillar would you stress in a scientific description? **[Science Link]**

◆ Reading Strategy

❹ Evaluate Author's Message Discuss with students how linking the simple caterpillar with three formidable, serious poets is meant to be ridiculous and funny.

▶ Critical Viewing ◀

❺ Speculate *All three poets were interested in grander, more profound subjects. None of them is known for being humorous.*

Reinforce and Extend

Answers

◆ Literature and Your Life

Reader's Response Most students will find the end of Hoch's story amusing and surprising, but understandable, too.

Thematic Focus Each illustrates the idea that objects and events appear to us through the filter of our own unique points of view. To the Kaan horse-spiders, the Earth people are odd; to the hippo, other hippos are attractive; to one poet, the caterpillar is worthy of a poem.

☑ Check Your Comprehension

1. They are horrified and fascinated by the strangeness of the creatures.
2. They describe them as two-legged creatures that wear clothing.
3. He imagines that it thinks humans are ugly but other hippos are quite attractive.
4. He has looked among the poems of Schiller, Petrarch, and Baudelaire.

◆ Critical Thinking

1. Possible response: He probably tells them that they will see little-known exotic creatures.
2. He understands that people will interpret things from their own perspectives. He intends to profit from this understanding.
3. (a) He thinks the animal needs consolation because humans make fun of its looks. (b) He tells the animal that it looks attractive to others of its kind.
4. He celebrates the way it moves and its soundlessness.
5. Students may point to the cleverness of the rhyming and the choice of topic—animals we find odd or amusing.
6. (a) Answers will vary, but most students are likely to say that he does. (b) He treats the animals with respect.
7. Students' responses will vary, but may include information on the ways the animals move, what they eat, where they live, how long they live, how they reproduce, and how they communicate with one another.

Develop Understanding

One-Minute Insight In "The Blind Men and the Elephant," six men have six different impressions of what an elephant is because they each encounter a different part of the animal. Since each man bases his determination upon a limited examination, each gives a different and misleading description, and none fully understands what an entire elephant is like.

Looking at Literature Videodisc/Videotape

To capture students' interest and motivate them to read, play Chapter 5 of the videodisc. The segment begins with a presentation of "The Blind Men and the Elephant," followed by one student's response to the poem. Ask students to compare and contrast the student's response with their own responses.

Chapter 5

Comprehension Check 

❶ Ask students to paraphrase the first stanza. *Six blind men from Indostan (India) went to see an elephant in order to discover what one is.*

Clarification

❷ Tell students that the apostrophe in *E'en* stands for the missing letter *v.*

Customize for *English Language Learners*

This poem may be challenging for students because of the use of inverse word order—for example, "To learning much inclined"—and archaic vocabulary such as "spake." Encourage students to read in pairs, taking turns reading the stanzas aloud and then discussing important details of each.

Customize for *Less Proficient Readers*

To help students make sense of the ideas and events in the poem, guide them to pause after each stanza and use a Sunburst Organizer, p. 94, or a Series of Events Chain, p. 66, in **Writing and Language Transparencies,** to summarize the information it gives.

The Blind Men and the Elephant

John Godfrey Saxe

It was six men of Indostan
  To learning much inclined,
Who went to see the Elephant
❶ (Though all of them were blind),
That each by observation
  Might satisfy his mind.

The *First* approached the Elephant,
  And happening to fall
Against his broad and sturdy side,
  At once began to bawl:
"God bless me! but the Elephant
  Is very like a wall!"

The *Second,* feeling of the tusk,
  Cried, "Ho! what have we here
So very round and smooth and sharp?
  To me 'tis mighty clear
This wonder of an Elephant
  Is very like a spear!"

The *Third* approached the animal,
  And happening to take
The squirming trunk within his hands,
  Thus boldly up and spake:
"I see," quoth he, "the Elephant
  Is very like a snake!"

The *Fourth* reached out an eager hand,
  And felt about the knee.
"What most this wondrous beast is like
  Is mighty plain," quoth he;
"'Tis clear enough the Elephant
  Is very like a tree!"

The *Fifth,* who chanced to touch the ear,
❷ Said; "E'en the blindest man
Can tell what this resembles most;
  Deny[1] the fact who can,
This marvel of an Elephant
  Is very like a fan!"

1. **deny** (dē nī′) *v.*: Say is untrue; reject.

◆ Build Vocabulary

inclined (in klīnd′) *adj.*: Interested in

observation (äb′ zər vā′ shən) *n.*: The act of noticing details

wondrous (wun′ drəs) *adj.*: Extraordinary

Beyond the Classroom

Workplace Skills

Observation and Perception In this poem, six blind men use their sense of touch to determine what an elephant is. Because they limit their perception of the elephant to one sense, they are unable to get a "complete picture." Discuss with students the importance of observing from more than one perspective. Point out that many job tasks require workers to use multiple senses, such as listening and watching.

Have students work in groups of four or five to brainstorm for a list of job-related tasks that require observation through more than one of the five senses (touch, sight, hearing, smell, and taste). For instance a chef may smell and taste a dish, a salesperson may listen to and watch a client, and a doctor may use touch, sight, and hearing to examine a patient. Encourage students to conduct an informal survey of people they know, as to what types of observation and perception they use in their jobs.

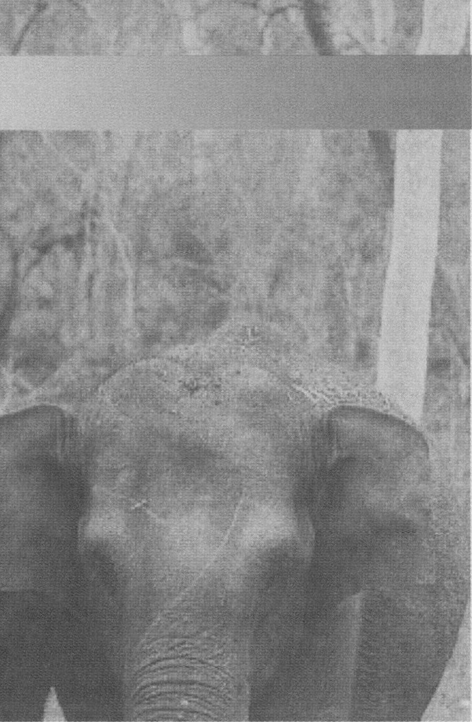

The *Sixth* no sooner had begun
About the beast to grope,
Than, seizing[2] on the swinging tail
That fell within his scope,[3]
"I see," quoth he, "the Elephant
Is very like a rope!"

And so these men of Indostan
Disputed[4] loud and long,
Each in his own opinion
Exceeding[5] stiff and strong,
Though each was partly in the right,
And all were in the wrong! 

---

2. **seizing** (sēz′ iŋ) *v.*: Quickly grabbing.
3. **scope** (skōp) *n.*: Reach or range.
4. **disputed** (di spyo͞ot′ id) *v.*: Argued.
5. **exceeding** (ek sēd′ iŋ) *adv.*: Going beyond.

◀ Critical Viewing The blind men observe six different parts of an elephant. Which of these elements can you see in this photograph? **[Connect]** ❹

Guide for Responding

◆ Literature and Your Life

Reader's Response Explain which description of the elephant was funniest to you.

Thematic Focus Each man receives a different message about the elephant's nature. How might the men arrive at the whole truth?

Journal Writing In a brief journal entry, write about a time when you got only part of a story. Explain the problems this created.

☑ Check Your Comprehension

1. What did the blind men want to find out?
2. How did they observe the elephant without actually seeing it?
3. What did each of the men think the elephant was like? What part did each observe?
4. What did each blind man think of the others' interpretations?

◆ Critical Thinking

Interpret

1. What is the purpose of each of the separate sections, or stanzas, of the poem? **[Analyze]**
2. The men of Indostan are physically blind. In what other ways are they blind? **[Infer]**
3. If the men each observed a part of the elephant accurately, how can each man's conclusion be so wrong? **[Analyze Cause and Effect]**

Apply

4. What advice would you give to these men to help them resolve their conflict? **[Resolve]**

Extend

5. The men of Indostan are not alone in their problematic methods of getting at the truth. Identify a situation in current events that was brought about in the same way. **[Social Studies Link]**

◆ Reading Strategy

❸ Evaluate Author's Message
Have students summarize the poem's message in their own words. *In order to truly understand something, a person must look at the whole of it, and not simply at one of its parts.*

▶Critical Viewing◀

❹ Connect *You can see all six: sides, tusks, trunks, legs, ears, and tail.*

Customize for *Logical/Mathematical Learners*

Guide students to understand the rhyming pattern of the poem: lines 2, 4, and 6 of each stanza rhyme. Point out that each of the stanzas (2–7) describes what one of the blind men examines and ends with a simile beginning "Is very like a. . . ."

Reinforce and Extend

Answers

◆ Literature and Your Life

Reader's Response Students' responses will vary; each description is funny.

Thematic Focus Students may suggest that each man move around the whole elephant, examine all its parts, and then compare their analyses to make a fuller description of the animal.

☑ Check Your Comprehension

1. They wanted to find out what an elephant is like.
2. They used their sense of touch and then compared a characteristic of the elephant to something they already knew.
3. The man who felt its side thought the elephant was like a wall; the one who felt its tusk thought it was like a spear; the one who felt its trunk compared it to a snake; the one who felt its knee thought it was like a tree; the one who touched its ear thought it was like a fan; the one who held its tail thought it was like a rope.
4. Each vigorously disputes the others' interpretations.

◆ Critical Thinking

1. Each gives a different, limited perspective of what an elephant is like.
2. They don't know that they didn't examine the entire elephant; they are unable to accept that other interpretations may be as valid as their own.
3. Each gets only a part of the whole picture; he does not examine all key elements.
4. Students may suggest that to broaden his perspective, each man should examine the other parts of the beast.
5. Examples will vary; have students support their views with facts.

Develop Understanding

One-Minute Insight This folk tale explains how the snake got poison and a rattle. In the tale, the snake goes to God to complain that it lacks protection from its enemies. When God gives the snake poison, the other animals complain. Then God gives the snake a bell (its rattle) to give other creatures fair warning.

Clarification

❶ African American folklore—like the myths, legends, and tales of other cultures—had its origins in the oral traditions of community storytelling. Folk tales are told and retold for instruction and for entertainment. They provide explanations for certain natural phenomena, give insights into the human condition, and offer practical advice. Like Hurston's retelling, folk tales are often humorous. In this story, some of the humor results from dialect, a nonstandard form of English spoken in a particular region. Guide students to recognize the meanings of *de* ("the"), *Ah* ("I"), and *dis* ("this"), among other words that are different from standard words. Students may better grasp the dialect and appreciate the humor in the tale by listening to the recording.

Listening to Literature Audiocassettes

◆Literary Focus

❷ Character's Perspective

Students should realize that at first the snake feels victimized by its lack of protection. Later, the varmints feel victimized by the snake's indiscriminate use of its poison.

How the Snake Got Poison

Zora Neale Hurston

Well, when God made de snake he put him in de bushes to ornament de ground. But things didn't suit de snake so one day he got on de ladder and went up to see God.

"Good mawnin', God."

"How do you do, Snake?"

"Ah[1] ain't so many, God, you put me down here on my belly in de dust and everything trods upon me and kills off my generations. Ah ain't got no kind of protection at all." ❶

God looked off towards immensity and thought about de subject for awhile, then he said, "Ah didn't mean for nothin' to be stompin' you snakes lak dat. You got to have some kind of a protection. Here, take dis poison and put it in yo' mouf and when they tromps on you, protect yo'self."

So de snake took de poison in his mouf and went on back.

So after awhile all de other varmints went up to God.

"Good evenin', God."

"How you makin' it, varmints?"

"God, please do somethin' 'bout dat snake. He' layin' in de bushes there wid poison in his mouf and he's strikin' everything dat shakes de bushes. He's killin' up our generations. Wese skeered to walk de earth." ❷

> **◆ Literary Focus** Notice how both the snake and the varmints see themselves as victims.

So God sent for de snake and tole him:

"Snake, when Ah give you dat poison, Ah didn't mean for you to be hittin' and killin' everything dat shake de bush. I give you dat poison and tole you to protect yo'self when they tromples on you. But you killin' everything dat moves. Ah didn't mean for you to do dat."

De snake say, "Lawd, you know Ah'm down here in de dust. Ah ain't got no claws to fight wid, and Ah ain't got no feets

1. **Ah:** Dialect for "I."

Cultural Connection

Pourquoi Tales Write the word *pourquoi* on the board. Students familiar with French will know that it means "why." Tell students that folk tales that explain origins—like how the snake got poison and a rattle—are sometimes known as *pourquoi tales*. Most cultures have tales that were invented to explain phenomena in nature. Have students think of or research other pourquoi tales and the natural phenomena they attempt to explain. Encourage them to find tales from a variety of cultures. You may wish to refer them to Aesop's fables and to Rudyard Kipling's *Just So Stories,* among other sources. Invite volunteers to retell their favorites to the class. Invite them also to create their own pour quoi tales and either read them aloud or post them in the classroom for others to read.

to git me out de way. All Ah kin see is feets comin' to tromple me. Ah can't tell who my enemy is and who is my friend. You gimme dis protection in my mouf and Ah uses it."

3 God thought it over for a while then he says:

"Well, snake, I don't want yo' generations all stomped out and I don't want you killin' everything else dat moves. Here take dis bell and tie it to yo' tail. When you hear feets comin' you ring yo' bell and if it's yo' friend, he'll be keerful. If it's yo' enemy, it's you and him."

So dat's how de snake got his poison and dat's how come he got rattles.

◆ **Build Vocabulary**

immensity (i menʹ si tē) *n.*: Something extremely large or immeasurably vast

Guide for Responding

◆ Literature and Your Life

Reader's Response In this folk tale, God weighs arguments from two conflicting sides. Would you have made the same decision?

Thematic Focus What mixed message does God give the snake? Explain.

Journal Writing The snake complains about his lot in life. In a journal entry, use another animal's physical traits and write the complaint it might voice if it could.

☑ Check Your Comprehension

1. Why does the snake ask God for protection?
2. (a) Why do the other animals complain to God? (b) How does God respond to their problem?
3. What natural fact does this story explain?

◆ Critical Thinking

INTERPRET

1. The snake's problem could have been solved if God gave him legs or claws. Why couldn't the story end this way? **[Infer]**
2. Reread God's final decision. What seems most important to him? **[Analyze]**

EVALUATE

3. By imitating the exact pronunciation, sentence structure, and language of some African Americans in the South, Zora Neale Hurston used dialect in her writing. How did this choice affect your appreciation of the story? **[Assess]**

EXTEND

4. What does this folk tale illustrate about people and their ways of interacting? **[Social Studies Link]**

Clarification

3 Point out that this sentence is a run-on sentence and that it changes verb tenses. Tell students that Hurston made a conscious choice to write in this way because of the effect it yields: It lends a sense of authenticity to a tale that has its roots in oral tradition.

Answers

◆ Literature and Your Life

Reader's Response Have students support their answers with details from the story.

Thematic Focus God gives the snake poison but no guidelines for how to use it.

☑ Check Your Comprehension

1. It is being stepped on by other creatures.
2. (a) The snake is poisoning them indiscriminately. (b) God gives the snake a rattle to alert the varmints of its presence.
3. It explains the rattlesnake's venom and its warning rattle.

◆ Critical Thinking

1. It had to end the way it does because snakes have poison and rattles, not legs or claws.
2. It seems most important that both snake and varmints live on.
3. Students may say that the dialect helps connect the story with its roots in oral tradition.
4. Possible response: It illustrates that people want the means to protect themselves from their enemies as well as the good sense not to antagonize their friends.

Beyond the Selection

FURTHER READING

Other Works by Edward D. Hoch
Diagnosis Impossible
The Fellowship of the Hand

Other Works by Ogden Nash
Ogden Nash's Zoo
The Tale of Custard the Dragon

Other Works by John Godfrey Saxe
The Library

Other Works by Zora Neale Hurston
Tell My Horse
Dust Tracks on a Road

INTERNET

We suggest the following sites on the Internet (all Web sites are subject to change).

For an interview with Edward D. Hoch:
http://swifty.com/cwc/fp/429609sl.htm

To see selected poems by Ogden Nash:
http://www.westegg.com/nash

For more information about Zora Neale Hurston:
http://www.minorities-jb.com/african/zora.htm

We *strongly recommend* that you preview these sites before you send students to them.

Answers

◆Reading Strategy

1. (a) To truly understand something, a person must look at the whole of it, and not simply at one of its parts. (b) He shows how each blind man has a different interpretation of what an elephant looks like, and that each interpretation is wrong. (c) Students are likely to agree with Saxe's message.
2. Responses will vary. Students who choose "The Hippopotamus" should focus on Nash's idea that beauty is in the eye of the beholder. Those who choose "The Caterpillar" can focus on the idea that the creature is worthy of recognition. Students who pick "How the Snake Got Poison" might focus on the idea that we have what we need to survive as long as we act prudently.

◆Build Vocabulary

Using Forms of *wonder*

1. wonder; 2. wondrously; 3. wondrous

Spelling Strategy

1. density; 2. insanity; 3. scarcity

Using the Word Bank

Possible responses:

1. No; they're afraid of it.
2. Yes; they're totally unique.
3. Yes; an elephant is huge.
4. No; New York and Rome are on the same planet.
5. Example: The night sky is inspirational.
6. Yes; helping those you care about is a natural thing to do.
7. Yes; observation is part of the scientific process.

◆Literary Focus

1. Possible response: You realize that different perspectives are not only possible, but likely; Earthlings would indeed look threatening and odd to those who've never seen them.
2. The different perspectives, each correct but limited, are at odds with one another. Although none of the blind men has a true picture of an elephant, each thinks that he does.

◆Build Grammar Skills

Practice

1. *visit,* direct object
2. *elephant,* indirect object; *shake,* direct object
3. *me,* indirect object; *protection,* direct object
4. *audience,* direct object
5. *children,* indirect object; *tickets,* direct object

Writing Application

Possible responses:

1. I want to write a tale. Direct object: *tale*
2. Send the Kaan people a message from me. Direct object: *message;* indirect object: *people*
3. Tell the snake not to bite. Direct object: *snake*
4. Do you expect them to return to this planet? Direct object: *them*
5. Chase the varmints away. Direct object: *varmints*

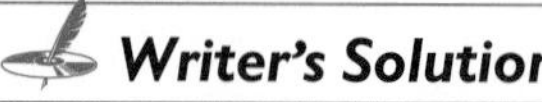

Writer's Solution

For additional instruction and practice, use the lesson in the *Writer's Solution Language Lab CD-ROM* on Styling Sentences, and the practice pages on direct and indirect objects, pp. 33–37 in the *Writer's Solution Grammar Practice Book.*

Guide for Responding *(continued)*

◆ Reading Strategy

EVALUATE AUTHOR'S MESSAGE

You **evaluate an author's message** by first identifying the message, then examining how well it is supported. In "Zoo," Hoch suggests that people often feel superior to others who are different from them. He supports this message by presenting Kaanians, who like a fence to protect them from "dangerous" humans. Your experience will help you decide whether this message rings true.

1. (a) What is the message of "The Blind Men and the Elephant"? (b) How does Saxe support his message? (c) Explain whether you agree or disagree with it.

2. Choose one other selection from this grouping. (a) Identify the message. (b) Identify the reasoning the writer provides to support this message. (c) Explain whether you agree or disagree with it.

◆ Build Vocabulary

USING FORMS OF *wonder*

On your paper, complete the following sentences with the appropriate form of *wonder*. Choose from *wonderment, wonderful, wondrous,* and *wondrously.*

1. The hippopotamus gazed at me with __?__.

2. Snake's poison was __?__ effective.

3. An elephant is a most __?__ creature.

SPELLING STRATEGY

Before you add the suffix *-ity* to nouns ending in e, drop the e: *immense* becomes *immensity*. Add *-ity* to each of the following words, and use each new word in a sentence.

1. dense **2.** insane **3.** scarce

USING THE WORD BANK

Explain your answer to each of these questions.

1. Do varmints view the snake with *wonderment?*

2. Do the people of Earth think the people of Kaan are *wondrous?*

3. Would you be struck by an elephant's *immensity?*

4. Is a flight from New York to Rome *interplanetary?*

5. What inspires a sense of *awe* in you?

6. Would you be *inclined* to help your best friend?

7. Should doctors expect to do a lot of *observation?*

◆ Literary Focus

CHARACTER'S PERSPECTIVE

Each character in these stories views events from a unique **perspective,** or position. For example, in "How the Snake Got Poison," the snake feels victimized without feet. This affects the way he thinks. The other animals—each with its own perspective—are less understanding about his behavior.

1. How does your understanding of the story "Zoo" change when you see things from the perspective of the creatures of Kaan?

2. Six varying perspectives create conflict in "The Blind Men and the Elephant." Explain.

◆ Build Grammar Skills

DIRECT AND INDIRECT OBJECTS

A subject and a verb may require more to complete their meaning. A **direct object** is the noun or pronoun that receives the action of a verb. It answers *whom* or *what* after the verb.

verb D.O.
The creatures wear *garments.* (*Wear what?*)

verb D.O.
Professor Hugo invited *them.* (*Invited whom?*)

A sentence with a direct object can also contain an **indirect object,** which names the person or thing that something is given to or done for. It answers the question *to or for whom* or *to or for what.* Indirect objects appear only before direct objects.

verb I.O. D.O.
Snake told *God* his trouble. (*Told to whom?*)

Practice Identify the direct and indirect objects that appear in the following sentences.

1. We enjoyed our zoo visit this year.

2. The third man gave the elephant a shake.

3. You showed me this protection.

4. The message reached an interplanetary audience.

5. They bought the children tickets to the show.

Writing Application Use the following verbs in sentences with direct and indirect objects. For each, identify the objects you use.

1. write **2.** send **3.** tell **4.** bake **5.** sell

Build Your Portfolio

Idea Bank

Writing

1. **Advertising Flyer** Professor Hugo has recruited a group of humans for an exhibit he'll bring to other planets. Write an advertising flyer telling about these amazing creatures.
2. **Humorous Poem** Using Ogden Nash's verse as a model, write a short poem about an animal. Choose an animal with unusual characteristics or one that is often overlooked.
3. **Comparison-and-Contrast Essay** In "The Blind Men and the Elephant," six men see one object in six different ways. Use the information in the poem to write an essay in which you compare and contrast the accuracy of the conclusions they draw.

Speaking and Listening

4. **Zoo Commercial** Imagine that you are the public relations director for Hugo's Zoo. Create a radio commercial to be aired in several cities. Appeal to a wide audience. **[Career Link]**
5. **Animal Game** Team up with a partner to find out ten unusual facts about an animal. Playing against another team of two, take turns reporting a fact and trying to identify the animal. The first group that guesses an animal correctly wins.

Projects

6. **Pet Show** **[Group Activity]** As these selections remind you, animals come in many shapes and sizes. With several classmates, research the variety of animals that people keep as pets. Interview pet owners, collect photos and videos, and learn more about these animals. Then, present a report to the class. Each group member can describe the unique characteristics of a specific pet. **[Science Link]**
7. **Metamorphosis** Research the care and feeding of caterpillars. Collect specimens and raise them in an indoor exhibit tank or cage. Track their development as they shed their chrysalises and emerge as butterflies or moths. **[Science Link]**

Writing Mini-Lesson

Report

The stories and poems you've just read focus on animals, but they don't provide much factual information. Take a different approach by writing a nonfiction report about an animal that interests you. In your report, focus on the animal's three most outstanding characteristics.

Writing Skills Focus: Topic Sentences and Supporting Details

Keep your writing clear and focused by organizing every paragraph of your report. The **topic sentence** is a general statement that tells the reader what the paragraph is going to be about. **Supporting details** prove the point made in the topic sentence. Look at this outline:

Topic Sentence: Seal pups are hardy animals.

Detail: They swim in ocean water from birth.

Detail: A thick layer of fat protects them.

Detail: At age five weeks, pups are able to catch fish on their own.

Prewriting Use a library, the Internet, or a nearby zoo to research the animal you've chosen. When you've collected enough data, choose the animal's three outstanding characteristics. Make an outline, organizing your report according to these traits.

Drafting In your introduction, provide general facts about the animal. In each of the next three paragraphs, discuss one of the animal's most outstanding characteristics. In your conclusion, summarize and extend by mentioning the animal's value.

Revising Review your notes to make sure your facts are correct. If necessary, add details to support your topic sentences and to make the report more interesting.

◆ Grammar Application

With a highlighter pen, identify any direct or indirect objects you have used.

✓ ASSESSMENT OPTIONS

Formal Assessment, Selection Test, pp. 119–121, and Assessment Resources Software. The selection test is designed so that it can be easily customized to the performance levels of your students.

Alternative Assessment, p. 27, includes options for less advanced students, more advanced students, musical/rhythmic learners, bodily/kinesthetic learners, visual/spatial learners, interpersonal learners, and verbal/linguistic learners.

PORTFOLIO ASSESSMENT

Use the following rubrics in the **Alternative Assessment** booklet to assess student writing:
Advertising Flyer: Description, p. 84
Humorous Poem: Poetry, p. 95
Comparison-and-Contrast Essay: Comparison/Contrast, p. 90
Writing Mini-Lesson: Research Report/Paper, p. 93

Idea Bank

Following are suggestions for matching the Idea Bank topics with your students' performance levels and learning modalities:

Customize for *Performance Levels*

Less Advanced Students: 1, 4, 5, 6
Average Students: 2, 4, 5, 6, 7
More Advanced Students: 3, 7

Customize for *Learning Modalities*

Verbal/Linguistic: 1, 2, 3, 4, 5, 6, 7
Visual/Spatial: 1, 6
Logical/Mathematical: 3, 5, 7
Musical/Rhythmic: 4
Interpersonal: 4, 5, 6
Intrapersonal: 2, 7

Writing Mini-Lesson

Refer students to the Writing Handbook in the back of the book for further instructions on the writing process.

Writer's Solution

Writers at Work Videodisc

Have students view the videodisc segment on expository writing (Ch. 4), featuring Richard Lederer, to see how he organizes his data. Have students discuss his organizing-while-drafting approach.

Play frames 37716 to 38879

Writing Lab CD-ROM

Have students complete the tutorial on Exposition: Giving Information. Follow these steps:

1. Have students use the Narrowing Your Topic section to explore ways to focus their topic.
2. Students can use the Organizing Details section to move through the process of organizing data.
3. Have students use the Drafting section to gain insights into writing the introduction, body, and conclusion.
4. Have students use the Revision Checker for unity and coherence.

Allow about 75 minutes of class time to complete these steps.

Writer's Solution Sourcebook

Have students use Chapter 4, "About Exposition: Giving Information," pp. 103–134, for additional support. The chapter includes in-depth instruction on gathering information, p. 121.

Prepare and Engage

OBJECTIVES

1. To read, comprehend, and interpret a humorous letter and a personal narrative
2. To relate the letter and personal narrative to personal experience
3. To distinguish fact from opinion
4. To analyze humorous commentary
5. To build vocabulary in context and learn the prefix *auto-*
6. To recognize subject complements
7. To write a letter of complaint using standard letter format
8. To respond to the works through writing, speaking and listening, and projects

SKILLS INSTRUCTION

Vocabulary: Prefixes: *auto-*

Spelling Combining *t* with the suffix *-ial*

Grammar: Subject Complements

Reading Strategy: Distinguish Fact From Opinion

Literary Focus: Humorous Commentary

Writing: Formal Letter

Speaking and Listening: Charles Dickens Presentation (Teacher Edition)

Viewing and Representing: Personification in Drawings (Teacher Edition)

Critical Viewing: Hypothesize; Analyze; Infer

PORTFOLIO OPPORTUNITIES

Writing: Letter of Response; Personal Narrative; Comparison-and-Contrast Essay

Writing Mini-Lesson: Letter of Complaint

Speaking and Listening: Charles Dickens Presentation; *Mad About You* Review

Projects: Report on the 1850's; Sitcom Guide

Guide for Reading

Meet the Authors:

Charles Dickens (1812–1870)

With *Oliver Twist, A Christmas Carol,* and *Great Expectations* to his credit, Charles Dickens is one of the world's best-known novelists.

A Childhood of Poverty Born in Portsmouth, England, Dickens began supporting his family at the age of twelve. For the rest of his life, he could not forget what it was like to be poor. As a young man, Dickens became a law apprentice in London, but his main interest was in journalism. He took a job as a political reporter and then began his career as a fiction writer.

In addition to his novels, Dickens wrote many comical sketches and letters. The letter you are about to read shows off the grace and wit of his writing style. [For more about Charles Dickens, see page 642.]

Paul Reiser (1957–)

Of all his accomplishments, Paul Reiser's biggest claim to fame may be the hit television comedy *Mad About You.* The show, produced by and starring Reiser, details the lives of Paul and Jamie Buchman, a young married couple living in New York. Following the birth of Reiser's real-life son, Ezra, a daughter was added to the television family, offering more opportunities for laughs based on Reiser's "honest" comedy.

◆ Literature and Your Life

Connect Your Experience

Such daily chores as doing the laundry, baby sitting, or mowing the lawn might really annoy you. However, as these selections reveal, such routine tasks as fixing a clock and taking an infant on a walk can be a source of humor.

Thematic Focus: Mixed Messages

Notice how these writers discover humor by exploring everyday experiences from unusual angles.

◆ Background for Understanding

Science

Recent research in early childhood development stresses the need to stimulate children at an early age. Scientists now believe that the brain development that occurs within the first years is critical. Every experience helps introduce the brain to new ways of interpreting information. For this reason, parents are encouraged to interact with their new babies as much as they can. Experts suggest playing classical music, reading aloud, hanging mobiles over a baby's crib, and talking to babies as much as possible. In "Stepping Out With My Baby," Paul Reiser tries to follow this advice.

◆ Build Vocabulary

Prefixes: *auto-*

Automatically contains the prefix *auto-* meaning "self." When Reiser reports that he responds *automatically* to an idea, he means that he answers like a self-run machine would—without thinking.

Word Bank

Which of these words from the selections might mean "secret"?

reluctance
confidential
automatically

More About the Authors

Charles Dickens is considered by many to be one of the greatest of all English writers. In his writing he combined a compassion for humble people with exacting skills of observation to create memorable characters like Oliver Twist, David Copperfield, and Tiny Tim.

Paul Reiser has been in several films and has starred in the television sitcom *My Two Dads.* He created *Mad About You* in 1992. Reiser produces and writes for the show as well as playing a leading role.

Prentice Hall Literature Program Resources

REINFORCE / RETEACH / EXTEND

Selection Support Pages
Build Vocabulary: Prefixes: *auto-*, p. 149
Build Spelling Skills, p. 150
Build Grammar Skills: Subject Complements, p. 151
Reading Strategy: Distinguish Fact From Opinion, p. 152
Literary Focus: Humorous Commentary, p. 153

Strategies for Diverse Student Needs, pp. 55–56

Beyond Literature Study Skills: Reading a Flowchart, p. 28

Formal Assessment Selection Test, pp. 122–124, Assessment Resources Software

Alternative Assessment, p. 28

Writing and Language Transparencies Main Idea and Supporting Details Organizer, p. 70

Resource Pro CD-ROM
"A Letter to a Clockmaker"; "Stepping Out With My Baby"—includes all resource material and customizable lesson plan

Listening to Literature Audiocassettes
"A Letter to a Clockmaker"

◆ A Letter to a Clockmaker ◆ Stepping Out With My Baby

◆ Literary Focus

Humorous Commentary

Laughter forms bonds between people. It can sometimes turn strangers into friends or break the tension in uncomfortable situations. Writers use **humorous commentary,** writing that contains amusing personal observations or opinions, to help readers look at life a little less seriously. You are about to see how this technique works in two different forms of writing—a letter and an essay. As you read each selection, notice the topics the writers address, paying attention to the points they make about these topics.

◆ Reading Strategy

Distinguish Fact From Opinion

To show the humor in the subjects they tackle, these writers combine **facts** (statements that can be proved true) and **opinions** (statements that can be supported but not proved). For instance, Reiser starts with a fact: "We arrive at the mailbox." He adds opinion to create comedy: "an exhausting block and a half from home." By **distinguishing fact from opinion,** you form your interpretation of an event rather than just accepting what the author says. Use a chart like the one below to separate facts from opinions.

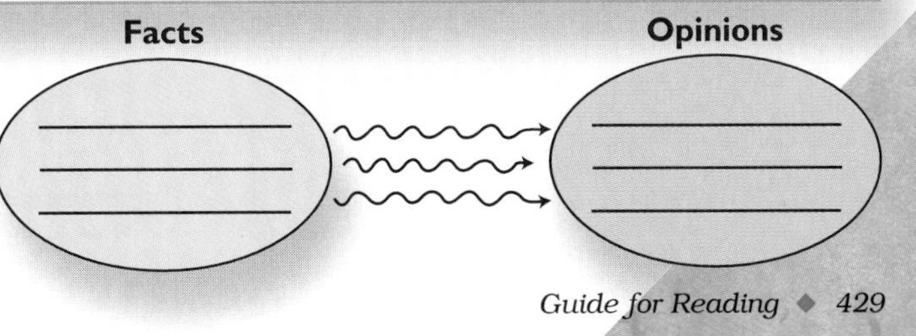

Engage students' interest in these selections by asking them to describe some of the funniest moments they have seen on the television sitcom *Mad About You.* If possible, you may wish to videotape an episode and play the tape for the class. Encourage students to discuss humorous lines spoken by the characters. Point out that they will read a selection by Paul Reiser, the star of *Mad About You,* who sometimes writes the humorous lines they hear on the show. They will also read a funny letter written by Charles Dickens, a well-known English author.

◆ Build Grammar Skills

Subject Complements If you wish to introduce the grammar concept for this selection before students read, refer to the instruction on p. 434.

Customize for
Less Proficient Readers
Both selections contain sentences that are very long. Have students read the selections with a more advanced partner. Suggest that partners work together to break down sentences and paraphrase as they read.

Customize for
More Advanced Students
To give students practice in writing humor of their own, have them choose three or four facts from their fact-and-opinion charts after they read the story. Instruct them to write sentences that combine opinions that humorously elaborate these facts.

Preparing for Standardized Tests

Reading On some standardized tests, students are asked to answer questions that require them to distinguish facts from opinions. To provide practice with this skill, write this passage and question on the board:

> Like many fathers, Paul talks to his infant children to help them learn to speak. On a trip to the mailbox with his infant son, Paul talks to his son about the postal service. He demonstrates depositing the letters in the mailbox. The baby is clearly grateful for all of this guidance. Father and son return home, errand completed.

1. Which sentence states an opinion?
   (A) On a trip to the mailbox with his infant son, Paul talks to his son about the postal service.
   (B) He demonstrates depositing the letter in the mailbox.
   (C) The baby is clearly grateful for all of this guidance.
   (D) Father and son return home, errand completed.

Ask students which sentences could be proved to be true by talking to someone who went along with Paul and the baby. *(A, B,* and *D)* Explain that *(C)* is the correct answer because there is no way to tell if the baby is grateful. It states the writer's opinion.

Develop Understanding

One-Minute Insight In this letter, Dickens uses humor to complain about the service his clock received at the clockmaker's shop. He writes that ever since the clock received a cleaning, it has not worked properly. Personifying the clock, he says that after bringing it home, it struck with "great reluctance." Then it quit striking altogether. Dickens suggests that someone come consult with his clock so the clock can confess what is wrong with it.

◆Literary Focus

1 Humorous Commentary Ask students to identify the topic of the letter. How does Dickens use humor to soften his complaint? *The topic is his clock, which has stopped striking. Dickens makes it sound as if the clock is ill.*

◆Reading Strategy

2 Distinguish Fact From Opinion Ask students to identify the words that help the reader to recognize the second part of this sentence as an opinion. *Students should identify the words* I think.

◆Literary Focus

3 Humorous Commentary Ask students how Dickens gives human qualities to the clock, thus adding humor to the letter. *Dickens makes the clock sound as if it has a mind of its own—it struggles to strike the hour, but finally gives up. When he states that "it may have something on its works that it would be glad to make a clean breast of," he makes it sound as if the clock has something it needs to get off its chest.*

▶Critical Viewing◀

4 Hypothesize *Students may say that Dickens's clock is very large and it has a "face" and "hands." It also makes noise as if it were a member of the household. These "human" features may have given Dickens the idea for his letter.*

A Letter to a Clockmaker

Charles Dickens

My dear Sir:

Since my hall clock was sent to your establishment to be cleaned it has gone (as indeed it always has) perfectly, but has struck with great reluctance, and after enduring internal agonies of a most distressing nature it has now ceased striking altogether. Though a happy release for the clock, this is not a convenience for the household. If you can send down any confidential person with whom the clock can confer, I think it may have something on its works that it would be glad to make a clean breast of.

Faithfully yours,
Charles Dickens.

Higham by Rochester, Kent,
Monday night, Sep. 14, 1863

◀ **Critical Viewing** How might the size and shape of a grandfather clock like the one pictured here prompt Dickens to write "A Letter to a Clockmaker"? **[Hypothesize]** 4

◆ Build Vocabulary

reluctance (ri luk′ təns) *n.*: Unwillingness

confidential (kän′ fə den′ shəl) *adj.*: Entrusted with private or secret matters

automatically (ôt′ ə mat′ ik lē) *adv.*: Without thought; by reflex

Block Scheduling Strategies

Consider these suggestions to take advantage of extended class time:

- Before they begin reading, have students read the Literature and Your Life and Background for Understanding features, p. 428. Have them meet in groups to discuss humorous experiences they have had doing chores at home or caring for younger children.
- Have students use the Main Idea and Supporting Details Organizer, p. 70, in **Writing and Language Transparencies,** to organize their thoughts and materials for the Report on the 1850's in the Idea Bank, p. 435. They can also use the organizer for the prewriting portion of the Writing Mini-Lesson.
- You may want to assign the Beyond Literature Media Connection activity, p. 433, as homework. Then have students compare their conclusions about their findings as an introduction to the *Mad About You* Review in the Idea Bank, p. 435.
- Provide copies of television schedules from newspapers and/or magazines for the Sitcom Guide project in the Idea Bank, p. 435.

Stepping Out With My Baby

Paul Reiser

On his first trip outside the house with his infant son, Paul Reiser describes the stressful experience of being outdoors. Armed with advice from his wife and worried about the opinions of the people who pass him on the street, Reiser endures a barrage of panicked thoughts.

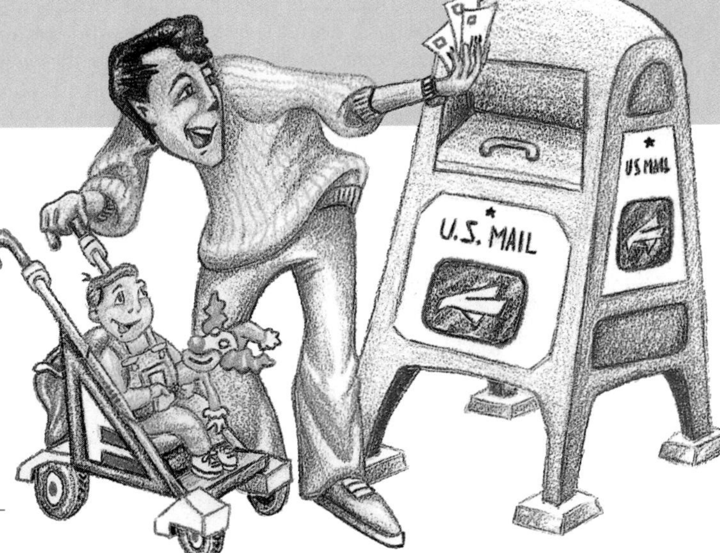

▲ **Critical Viewing** Using the text to help you, describe the action suggested by this illustration. [Analyze] 6

Finally we arrive at the mailbox—an exhausting block and a half from home. Dizzy with the victory of arriving at our destination in more or less one piece, I reach into my pocket, retrieve the now sweaty envelopes, and am about to toss them into the mailbox when I hear a voice. It's my wife's voice, echoing in my head.

"Talk to him."

"Hmm?" I say automatically, totally accepting that my wife might in fact be physically standing next to me, just for a follow-up evaluation on my performance.

"Talk to him. Explain to him what you're doing," the voice in my head suggests.

5 Sometimes I forget that part—talking to my child. Actually *being* with him. When I'm in charge of the kid, I tend to either stare at him like he's television or drift totally into a world of my own, running through my list of things-I-have-to-do-later-when-I'm-not-taking-care-of-the-kid. Or I take the job *so* seriously I become blinded by the severity of the responsibility, and panic. What I seem to miss is the middle ground—the part where you share, teach, learn, play—the part you can actually enjoy. 5

"Right. Talk to him. I'll do that. Thanks," I say to myself, and the voice of the Nice Lady in My Head leaves me alone again.

"So," I say to my buckled-up Beautiful Boy. "This is a mailbox."

And in response, he takes a hearty bite out of his little red corduroy clown's terry-cloth head.

"See? Daddy's going to put these letters into the mailbox. See? . . . What else can I tell you . . . The mailbox is blue."

When in doubt, mention the color. They can't get enough of colors, these kids.

"It's a blue mailbox."

Another ferocious bite-and-tug almost removes the corduroy clown's left ear. Clearly the boy is not that interested—I'll just mail the letters. 7

Develop Understanding

One-Minute Insight Paul Reiser takes his baby with him to mail a letter. When he reaches the mailbox, he imagines his wife's voice telling him to talk to his son. Reiser explains every step of the how-to-mail-a-letter process, from pointing out that the mailbox is big and blue to demonstrating how to open the mouth of the mailbox several times to ensure that the letter goes down. To show his gratitude, his son gives him a "magnificent, otherworldly smile"—as if he hasn't understood a word.

◆Literary Focus

5 Humorous Commentary Ask students to identify the topic of this paragraph and some of Reiser's observations about the topic. *The topic is what Reiser does when he is with his child. He says that sometimes he watches the child as if he were a television, or he panics because he takes his responsibility so seriously.* Point out that these are examples of how a writer can use exaggeration to create humor.

▶Critical Viewing◀

6 Analyze *Students may say that the illustration shows Reiser talking to his son as he identifies the mailbox and its color.*

◆Reading Strategy

7 Distinguish Fact From Opinion Ask students if this sentence is a fact or an opinion. *It is an opinion. Reiser has no way to prove the level of his son's interest in his information about the mailbox.*

Customize for
English Language Learners
Humor can be difficult to understand when it is in an unfamiliar language. Allow volunteers to act out the parts of the narrative that students find difficult. In addition, help students by using gestures and body language to communicate the meanings of phrases such as "drift totally into a world of my own," "violent exchange in my head," and "flick the letters in."

Speaking and Listening Mini-Lesson

Charles Dickens Presentation
This mini-lesson supports the Speaking and Listening activity in the Idea Bank on p. 435.

Introduce Have students find a passage from a short story, novel, or letter written by Charles Dickens. Explain that an oral reading can help a reader interpret literature using his or her own style.

Develop As students begin working, remind them to do the following:

- Become thoroughly familiar with the language of the passage.
- Use body language, tone of voice, pacing, and facial expression to convey the mood of the passage.

Apply Have students practice reading their passages aloud to a partner. Then students can perform their readings for the class. If possible, record their readings on audiocassette.

Assess Have students use the Peer Assessment: Oral Interpretation form, p. 106, in **Alternative Assessment,** to evaluate one another's readings. Be sure students read the checklist before they begin preparing their readings.

◆Literary Focus

❶ **Humorous Commentary** Ask students how Reiser adds humor to the somewhat commonplace topic of talking to a baby. *To describe his own discomfort with making one-sided conversation, Reiser compares the situation to a first date.*

◆Literature and Your Life

❷ Ask students if, like Reiser, they have ever pulled the door of a mailbox open and closed a few times. Ask them why Reiser finds humor in this specific aspect of the letter-mailing chore. Encourage them to name tedious chores, specific aspects of which might be humorous. Students may be surprised to discover that the most annoying aspects of tedious chores are sometimes the most humorous.

◆Build Grammar Skills

❸ **Subject Complements** Write this sentence on the board as follows: "They are wrong." Have students identify its subject as *They.* Point out that *are* is a linking verb and that *wrong* completes the idea about the subject by describing it. Explain that *wrong* is a predicate adjective.

▶Critical Viewing◀

❹ **Infer** *Students may say that both Reiser and the illustration depict the mailbox as being a place where letters are sometimes lost.*

"Explain to him how it works."

"I tried."

"Try again."

"All right, all right. Quit yelling."

Fortunately, no one sees or hears this violent exchange in my head. (See what I mean? They think I'm a guy-with-his-kid, and in fact I'm not only hearing voices but barking back at them.)

"We put the letters in the mailbox, and then the mailman comes and gets them."

❶ Talking to your baby is a lot like being on a first date; you feel like you're either saying too little or too much.

"The postal system was invented by Benjamin Franklin. In Philadelphia. He also invented bifocals."

Probably too much.

"The mailman takes the letters and puts them in a big bag and then he takes them to where they're going. See, this one goes to Aunt Ellen, who sent you that itchy sweater you hate, and this one goes to the Electricity Company so they don't shut off our electricity and force us out of our home." ❶

A little too heavy.

"Forget that. That will never happen."

Then, remembering that Demonstrating is always better than Explaining, I unbuckle him, scoop him up, and illustrate my letter-mailing technique.

"What you want to do is: Pull down the handle, open the mailbox's mouth, and then you *flick* the letters in. You want to get that nice flicking motion in your wrist . . . And then you pull the mouth open-and-closed a few times, to make sure the letters went down. A lot of people will tell you that doesn't do anything. They're wrong. You *must* check. ❸ Otherwise the mailbox will chew up your letter and stick it in a corner where no one can find it for years and years and years." ❷

My son smiles. I pull the handle up and down again. He seems to enjoy the squeaky noise. Who said mailboxes aren't a dynamite activity for youngsters?

As we prepare for our return voyage, I

▲ **Critical Viewing** Why might Reiser characterize the mailbox the way this illustration shows? **[Infer]** ❹

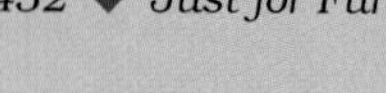

Viewing and Representing Mini-Lesson

Personification in Drawings

In this mini-lesson students will learn about humorous personification in drawings.

Introduce Tell students that, like the writers of these selections, illustrators sometimes give inanimate objects human qualities to add humor to their artworks.

Develop Discuss advertisements that students have seen that use personification for humor—a talking car or laughing box of cereal, for example.

Apply Have students create a humorous drawing of a clock or a mailbox like the one shown on this page by giving the object human qualities. For example, they might depict the clock as if it were ill or the mailbox as if it wanted to chew up people's letters.

Assess Invite students to display their drawings in small groups and explain why they chose certain human qualities to depict. Help students evaluate their drawings by having the other group members point out ways in which the drawings are humorous.

wonder if I've left anything out.

"Now, you may notice, it says here they pick up at eleven A.M., but between you and me it says the same thing on every mailbox, and there's no way that the guy can be at every mailbox in town at the same time, so I say just throw it in whenever you feel like it—it makes no difference. But you know what? You probably won't be mailing things by yourself for a while, so forget that. The main thing for you to remember, I would say, is: The box is blue. It's a big shiny blue box with a squeaky blue mouth."

> **◆ Literary Focus**
> 5 What humorous point does Reiser make in this paragraph?

As I buckle him back in, my son gives me one of those magnificent, otherworldly smiles, and looks at me as if to say, "Dad, I don't know what you're talking about, but you seem like a very nice man."

Beyond Literature

Media Connection

Television's Situation Comedies
Featuring a problem that can be solved in twenty-two minutes, situation comedies have been popular since *I Love Lucy* appeared in 1951. Comedies like *The Brady Bunch* (1967–1974) and *Happy Days* (1974–1984) centered around families and the problems they faced. In the 1990's, well-known stand-up comedians rushed into this arena with their own sitcoms. Popular programs included Paul Reiser's sitcom *Mad About You,* Jerry Seinfeld's self-titled show, and Tim Allen's *Home Improvement.*

Cross-Curricular Activity
Television Review Imagine that you are visiting the United States from another country. As you watch a sitcom from this new angle, take notes on what you learn about American culture. Compare your conclusions with classmates.

Guide for Responding

◆ Literature and Your Life

Reader's Response Explain your reaction to the tone of Dickens's letter to the clockmaker.

Thematic Focus What mixed message does Reiser fear he'll send by talking constantly to his infant son?

Journal Writing Reiser's essay describes the way he felt the first time he took his baby for a walk. In your journal, describe your feelings the first time you did something that would later become completely routine.

☑ Check Your Comprehension

1. According to the letter by Dickens, what is wrong with his clock?
2. What does Dickens want done as a result?
3. What is the errand that Reiser and his son complete?
4. Whose voices does Reiser hear as he completes the walk?
5. What do the voices want him to do?

◆ Critical Thinking

Interpret

1. Why does Dickens write about the clock as if it were a person? **[Analyze]**
2. How do you think the clockmaker responded to Dickens's letter? **[Infer]**
3. Why does the voice in Paul Reiser's head sound like his wife? **[Speculate]**
4. What details in Reiser's story lead you to believe taking care of a baby is hard work? **[Draw Conclusions]**
5. Even though his son can't understand him, Reiser thinks it's important to spend several minutes explaining how a mailbox works. Why? **[Speculate]**

Evaluate

6. Do you think Reiser enjoys being with his son? Explain. **[Assess]**

Compare Literary Works

7. How do these writers reflect the time period in which each lives? **[Distinguish]**

◆ Literary Focus

5 Humorous Commentary
Observe that, once again, Reiser has selected a topic to which most people can connect. *The point that Reiser makes in this paragraph is that most mailboxes list similar times for pickups. Postal workers can only be in one place at one time. Therefore, people shouldn't worry about when they mail their letters.*

Reinforce and Extend

Answers

◆ Literature and Your Life

Reader's Response Most students will find the tone of the letter humorous but formal and will respond to these qualities.

Thematic Focus Reiser is afraid that he might tell his son too much. His son may not understand the information, or he may even be frightened by it.

☑ Check Your Comprehension

1. The clock has quit striking.
2. He would like a person to come to his house and check the clock.
3. They mail some letters.
4. He hears his wife's voice.
5. His wife tells him to talk to his son and to explain what he's doing.

◆ Critical Thinking

1. He does this to add humor to a serious letter.
2. Most students will say that the clockmaker probably replied to his letter by fixing the clock promptly.
3. Reiser seems to depend on his wife to teach him about parenting.
4. Students may observe Reiser's worries about saying the right things and the energy he expends on the smaller tasks of child care.
5. Reiser probably understands that his son learns from what goes on around him.
6. Possible response: Reiser enjoys teaching an uncritical child to do simple things.
7. Possible response: Dickens's letter reflects its time period through its formal tone. Reiser's personal narrative shows a contemporary father actively engaged in raising his child.

Beyond the Selection

FURTHER READING

Other Works by Charles Dickens
A Christmas Carol
Great Expectations
David Copperfield

Other Works by Paul Reiser
Babyhood
Couplehood

INTERNET

Additional information about Paul Reiser and Charles Dickens can be found on the Internet. We suggest the following sites, which are subject to change:
http://www.celebs.net/PaulReiser/prbio.html
http://members.xoom.com/PJMarch/charlesdickens.htm

We *strongly recommend* that you preview these sites before you send students to them.

Answers

◆ Reading Strategy

1. Fact: "... it [the clock] has now ceased striking altogether." This is a fact because it can be proved by watching the clock. Opinion: "Though a happy release for the clock, ..." This is an opinion because it cannot be proved.
2. These are facts because they can be proved: (1) Reiser buckles his son into his stroller; (2) his son smiles at him; (3) his son looks at him. These are opinions because they cannot be proved: (1) his son's smile is magnificent; (2) his son thinks Paul Reiser is a very nice man.

◆ Build Vocabulary

Using the Prefix: *auto-*

1. An autobiography is the story of someone's life, written by himself or herself.
2. Autopilot is a mechanism that allows a plane to fly by itself.
3. An autograph is a person's name, signed by that person.
4. Autonomy is self-government or self-rule.

Spelling Strategy

1. martial; 2. initial; 3. palatial

Using the Word Bank

1. a
2. s
3. a

◆ Literary Focus

1. Dickens says that his clock has experienced "internal agonies of a most distressing nature" and a "happy release" at not having to strike. He says the clock would be glad to "confer" with the clock-maker.
2. Possible responses: Reiser says that being with a baby is like watching television and that his son responds to questions by biting his corduroy clown's head.
3. Neither Dickens's letter nor Reiser's narrative would be as effective because both writers use humor to convey important thoughts and feelings.

◆ Build Grammar Skills

Practice

1. reporter (P. N.)
2. confused (P. A.)
3. popular (P. A.)
4. situation comedy (P. N.)
5. original (P. A.)

Guide for Responding *(continued)*

◆ Reading Strategy

Distinguish Fact From Opinion

To add humor, these writers combine their comical opinions with facts that set up the situations they describe. When you **distinguish fact from opinion,** you ask whether a given statement could be proved to be true. If the answer is yes, the statement is a fact. If the answer is no, the statement is an opinion.

1. Identify one fact and one opinion from Dickens's letter. Explain.

2. Read the last paragraph of Reiser's essay. (a) Identify three facts. (b) Identify two opinions. Explain your answers.

◆ Build Vocabulary

Using the Prefix: *auto-*

The prefix *auto-* means "self." Knowing this prefix can help you determine the meaning of many other English words. Explain how *auto-* affects the meaning of these words:

1. autobiography

2. autopilot

3. autograph (*graph* means writing)

4. autonomy (*nomy* means government or management)

Spelling Strategy

The letter *t* combines with the suffix *-ial* to produce the *shul* sound that you hear in the word *confidential.* The *shul* sound can also be spelled *cial*, but the *tial* spelling is more common. On your paper, complete each sentence with a word that ends with *tial.*

1. Karate and judo are m___?___ arts.

2. Your i___?___ is the first letter of your name.

3. His mansion on the beach is p___?___.

Using the Word Bank

For each of the following pairs of words, write *S* on your paper if the words are synonyms and *A* if they are antonyms.

1. reluctance, eagerness

2. confidential, private

3. automatically, deliberately

◆ Literary Focus

Humorous Commentary

Stand-up comedians often deliver **humorous commentaries,** or amusing observations and opinions, about everyday experiences and events. Humorous commentaries also appear in written form. They are frequently found in newspapers.

1. What amusing comments about his clock does Dickens make in his letter?

2. What amusing observations about babies does Reiser make in his essay?

3. Would either selection be as effective if it were written without humor? Explain.

◆ Build Grammar Skills

Subject Complements

Linking verbs like *be, is,* and *am* show a state of being. They are followed by **subject complements** to complete an idea about a subject. A **predicate noun** renames or identifies the subject; a **predicate adjective** describes the subject. Look at these examples:

Dickens <u>is</u> [L.V.] a world-famous *writer.* [P.N.] (renames subject)

Reiser's new work <u>will be</u> [L.V.] *funny.* [P.A.] (describes subject)

To help you identify complements, note the kind of verb in a sentence. Only linking verbs can have subject complements. Action verbs take direct and indirect objects.

Practice Identify the predicate noun (P.N.) or the predicate adjective (P.A.) in each sentence.

1. Charles Dickens was once a reporter.

2. His family became confused when the clock stopped striking.

3. Reiser's show has been popular for years.

4. It is our favorite situation comedy.

5. Many of the jokes seem original.

Writing Application Write sentences using the following linking verbs. Then, identify the subject complements you use.

1. is **2.** will be **3.** has been **4.** were **5.** are

Writing Application

Possible responses are given:

1. Paul is the baby's father. (*father* P. N.)
2. His wife will be eager for them to return. (*eager* P. A.)
3. Dickens has been a famous writer for years. (*writer* P. N.)
4. Father and son were happy to be together. (*happy* P. A.)
5. Are we nervous about the clock? (*nervous* P. A.)

Writer's Solution

For additional instruction and practice, use the chapter on Styling Sentences in the *Writer's Solution Language Lab CD-ROM,* and Subject Complements, pp. 38–39, in the *Writer's Solution Grammar Practice Book.*

Build Your Portfolio

Idea Bank

Writing

1. Letter of Response If you were the clock-maker who received Dickens's letter, how might you respond? Write a brief note replying to Dickens's request.

2. Personal Narrative Write an essay describing an experience you've had with an infant or toddler who couldn't use language to communicate. In your narrative, explain how the child conveyed his or her needs to you.

3. Comparison-and-Contrast Essay Rewrite Dickens's letter in more modern English. Then, write an essay in which you compare and contrast these two versions.

Speaking and Listening

4. Charles Dickens Presentation Use Internet or library sources to find more samples of Charles Dickens's famous work. Then, choose a brief piece to read aloud to the class. Give an introduction to explain your choice.

5. *Mad About You* Review Watch an episode of Reiser's sitcom *Mad About You*. As you watch, take notes about the comic techniques the show uses. Share your insights with the class. **[Media Link]**

Projects

6. Report on the 1850's [Group Activity] With several classmates, research and report on life in Dickens's time—the 1850's in London. Each person can address a specific question. For example, How did people travel around town? What was the cost of common necessities? What were typical jobs? Share your findings in an illustrated report. **[Social Studies Link]**

7. Sitcom Guide Prepare a list of your favorite sitcoms. For each, write a summary that explains the show's basic premise. Identify the stars and the night and time the show appears. Devise a system to rate each show. **[Media Link]**

Writing Mini-Lesson

Letter of Complaint

If you're like most people, you probably ignore the little frustrations you face every day. What if you could write someone a letter about that finicky locker combination or that bicycle chain that keeps slipping even though it was supposedly fixed? Write a complaint letter about a frustrating or annoying experience that you've had.

Writing Skills Focus: Letter Format

A **formal letter** contains five parts:

1. Heading, including your address and the date, at the top of the page
2. Salutation, or greeting
3. Body
4. Closing
5. Signature

Notice that Dickens chooses the words "My dear Sir" for the salutation and "Faithfully yours" for the closing of his letter to the clockmaker.

Prewriting Choose an annoying incident or experience to describe. Jot down details about it. For example, note what happened, how you felt at the time, and what action you would like taken.

Drafting Write the heading of your letter. Then, choose a salutation. Refer to your notes as you write the body of your letter. Finally, choose a closing phrase and sign your letter.

◆ Grammar Application

Let subject complements work for you. Make them as specific as possible.

Revising Make sure you have explained the situation thoroughly. If necessary, add details to clarify your experience and your request.

Idea Bank

Following are suggestions for matching the Idea Bank topics with your students' performance levels and learning modalities:

Customize for
Performance Levels
Less Advanced Students: 1, 5, 7
Average Students: 2, 4, 6
More Advanced Students: 3, 4, 6

Customize for
Learning Modalities
Verbal/Linguistic: 2, 4
Interpersonal: 5, 6
Visual/Spatial: 5, 7

Writing Mini-Lesson

Refer students to the Writing Handbook in the back of the book for instruction on the writing process, and for further information on writing letters. Have students use the Main Ideas and Supporting Details Organizer in **Writing and Language Transparencies,** p. 70, to arrange their prewriting details.

Writer's Solution

Writing Lab CD-ROM

Have students complete the tutorial on Expression. Follow these steps:

1. Have students complete the Audience Profile activity to help them keep their audience in mind as they write their letters.
2. Have students draft on computer.
3. Suggest that students use the Proofreading Checklist to help them revise their letters.

Writer's Solution Sourcebook
Have students use Chapter 1, "Expression," pp. 1–31, for additional support. The chapter includes in-depth instruction on subject-verb agreement, pp. 25–26, and using pronouns, pp. 27–28.

ASSESSMENT OPTIONS

Formal Assessment, Selection Test, pp. 122–124, and Assessment Resources Software. The selection test is designed so that it can easily be customized to the performance levels of your students.

Alternative Assessment, p. 28, includes options for less advanced students, more advanced students, visual/spatial learners, interpersonal learners, logical/mathematical learners, and verbal/linguistic learners.

PORTFOLIO ASSESSMENT
Use the following rubrics in the **Alternative Assessment** booklet to assess student writing:
Letter of Response: Business Letter/Memo, p. 100
Personal Narrative: Narrative Based on Personal Experience, p. 83
Comparison-and-Contrast Essay: Comparison/Contrast, p. 90
Writing Mini-Lesson: Business Letter/Memo, p. 100

OBJECTIVES

1. To read, comprehend, and interpret a selection that has a social studies focus
2. To relate a selection with a social studies focus to personal experience
3. To connect literature to social studies
4. To respond to Social Studies Guiding Questions
5. To respond to the selection through writing, speaking and listening, and projects

SOCIAL STUDIES GUIDING QUESTIONS

Reading a popular folk tale from the Jewish traditions of Eastern Europe will help students discover answers to these Social Studies Guiding Questions:

- What values and traditions do the people of Eastern Europe have in common?
- What can be learned about a culture by reading its folk tales?

With information from the newspaper or municipal offices, tell students about civic improvements under discussion in your community. Ask students how these changes might be implemented. Have them think of one practical and one foolish method. Urge them to recall both methods as they read this tale about some townspeople who tried to implement a good idea in a silly way.

Humanities: Art

Viewing a Painting Picturing a story's physical setting can help readers understand a folk tale from another culture. Marc Chagall's painting, *Water Carrier by Moonlight,* shows a small Eastern European village like the one in the story. It also reflects Chagall's own past as a Jew born near the Russian-Polish border. To help students make the link between the painting and the story, have them refer back to the painting as they read. When they have finished reading, ask students to compare and contrast their impressions of the village in the painting with those of the town in the folk tale.

CONNECTING LITERATURE TO SOCIAL STUDIES

EASTERN EUROPE

Let's Steal the Moon *by Blanche Serwer-Bernstein*

"DID YOU HEAR THE ONE ABOUT . . . ?"

Even before comedy clubs offered people a chance to laugh at their mistakes, humor was part of most cultures. For enjoyment and education, people passed funny stories from one generation to the next. Such tales can be found in many cultural traditions, including the rich folk heritage of the Jewish people.

Water Carrier by Moonlight, Marc Chagall, © 1989 by The Metropolitan Museum of Art

A History of Wandering The Jews settled in Palestine more than 3,000 years ago. In 63 B.C., their kingdom, Judea, was conquered by the Roman Empire. In A.D. 70, the Romans destroyed the temple in Jerusalem. From that time until the establishment of Israel in 1947, no Jewish state existed.

A Changing Map Many Jews settled in Russia and Eastern Europe—a part of the world where countries and borders were constantly shifting as groups entered, crossed, or settled in the region. For example, in 1795, Russia, Prussia, and Austria moved into Poland, dividing it among themselves. Poland was not independent again until 1918.

Ethnic Conflicts In some Eastern European countries, people of different ethnic groups live together in harmony. For example, in 1993, the Czechs and the Slovaks peacefully agreed to separate Czechoslovakia into two countries. However, in other places, tension between different populations has led to ethnic conflicts. As a result, the map continues to change.

A Town Full of Fools This folk tale comes from Eastern Europe. It was originally told in Yiddish, a language that mixes elements of Hebrew and German. In Jewish folklore, Chelem is a fictional town whose inhabitants are known for their stupidity. The Chelemites, however, consider themselves to be clever, which makes their foolish behavior even funnier.

Prentice Hall Literature Program Resources

REINFORCE / RETEACH / EXTEND

Selection Support Pages
Build Vocabulary, p. 154
Theme, p. 155

Formal Assessment Selection Test, pp. 125–126, Assessment Resources Software

Writing and Language Transparencies
Sunburst Organizer, p. 94

Resource Pro CD-ROM
"Let's Steal the Moon"—includes all resource material and customizable lesson plan

Listening to Literature Audiocassettes
"Let's Steal the Moon"

Connection to Prentice Hall World Explorer
Eastern Hemisphere
Ch. 7, "Europe and Russia: Shaped by History"
Ch. 8, "Cultures of Europe and Russia"
Ch. 10, "Exploring Eastern Europe and Russia"

Let's Steal the Moon

A Yiddish Tale

Blanche Serwer-Bernstein

CONNECTING LITERATURE TO SOCIAL STUDIES

The people of Chelem[1] loved their city and tried to improve it in every way. Whenever they heard of something new and different in another city, they wanted it for themselves. What is good for others is good for us, they reasoned.

Imagine how excited they became when they learned that in some towns the streets were lighted at night. What a brilliant idea! With street lamps there would be no need to stumble in the dark or to come right up to a person and peer closely into his face to recognize him, or guess when you came to a street corner, or lose your way because you made a wrong turn. A wonderful improvement, lamps in the streets! Why hadn't they thought of this before?

> **Connecting Literature to Social Studies**
> 1 How is the city of Chelem governed?

As was the custom, all the citizens of Chelem came together to discuss the appealing new notion of installing lights on their street corners.

As they sat in council, thinking the matter through, a white-bearded patriarch stood up and spoke, "Street lights, my friends, would cost us a great deal of money and where would the money come from? From
2 our fund for the poor? That is forbidden!

"On the other hand, there is a luminary up in the sky that helps us for part of the month and leaves us in the dark for part of the month. There are nights when the moon shines and Chelem has enough light. There are other nights when there is no moon and Chelem is dark. Now, why can't the moon shine for us every night?"

"Why not?" wondered the people of Chelem, looking skyward and shaking their heads thoughtfully.

Then they drew closer to the old man, delighting in his great wisdom as he unfolded his plan. The wise patriarch persuaded the people of Chelem to wait for a night when the moon was large and full, shedding light into every nook and cranny of their dark streets. Then, to put it simply and directly, they would steal the moon and guard her safely until the dark nights of the month, when they would hang her in the skies to light up their streets.

"Steal the moon? Why not?" reasoned the people of Chelem, rubbing their chins in deepest contemplation.

Gimpel, who always had the most advanced ideas, suggested, "While we have it down, why not clean and polish it so that it will be brighter than ever?"

"Polish the moon? Why not?" agreed the people of Chelem, bewildered by the onrush of their own creative ideas.

They had no difficulty at all in capturing the moon. It was a simple matter. They filled a barrel with water and left it open, exposed to the moon's light. Then ten Chelemites stood ready with sackcloth.

The moon, unaware of the plot, moved into the barrel of water. When it was clearly trapped, the Chelemites covered the barrel with the heavy sackcloth and bound it down with thick strong rope. To make certain that everything was as it should be, they put the official seal of Chelem on the barrel and carried it carefully into the Synagogue[2] where it would be safe from all harm. They checked every night to make sure the seal was not broken.

1. **Chelem** (khel´ əm)

2. **Synagogue** (sin´ ə gäg): Place of worship in the Jewish religion.

◆ Build Vocabulary

patriarch (pā´ trē ärk) *n.*: Old, dignified man

luminary (lo͞o´ mə ner´ ē) *n.*: Something that gives off light

Develop Understanding

One-Minute Insight

In this retelling of a traditional Jewish folk tale, the residents of Chelem try to steal the moon to light their city streets. Pleased with their own creativity, the Chelemites amuse readers with their foolish antics.

Team Teaching Strategy

With a social studies teacher, you might develop a cross-curricular unit on Eastern Europe, folk literature, or Jewish history.

Connecting Literature to Social Studies

1 **Make Inferences** *Students should note that the city is governed by a council at which townspeople discuss and agree on plans.*

Links Across Culture

2 The "fund for the poor" refers to the requirement in the Jewish religion that every person give part of his or her income to charity.

Customize for *Less Proficient Readers*

Make sure students understand the humorous tone of the story. Clarify how the moon's light occurs and why that light varies throughout the month. As students read the story aloud, help them to see different aspects of the Chelemites' foolish behavior.

Customize for *English Language Learners*

Urge students to use the roots *pater,* meaning "father," and *lum,* meaning "light," to link Build Vocabulary words to familiar languages. Then pair students with proficient partners to decipher other unfamiliar words.

Customize for *More Advanced Students*

Folk tales offer students an opportunity to learn about other cultures. Offer these topics as starting points:

- Eastern European cultures
- Jewish history
- Foolish folk tales

Invite students to share their knowledge through oral reports, or art projects about a specific culture.

Preparing for Standardized Tests

Stylistic Analysis In responding to the reading passages on standardized tests, students may be asked to critically evaluate and analyze writing style. The test question may require students to consider a writer's word choice, ideas, and mood as they reach an overall conclusion about the passage. To offer students practice in this kind of critical evaluation, have them read the first text column on p. 437. Then, on the board, write the following question and set of answers:

The author's tone or attitude in this folk tale is one of

(A) amusement (C) concern
(B) anger (D) sadness

Guide students to review the language and content of the folk tale to recognize *(A)* as the best answer. Discuss how the words like "imagine" and "wonder" are clues to the story's light tone and help rule out *(B)* and *(D)*. The Chelemites' enthusiasm—shown in "excited" and "brilliant"—helps rules out *(C)*. For additional practice, ask students to repeat the process with other story paragraphs.

Links Across Time

Differing languages and religions have long been two causes of conflict among neighboring towns in this region. For example, even among the many Eastern Europeans tracing their ethnic heritage to the Slavs, at least ten Slavic languages are spoken. Also, in addition to Jews, the region contains Christians and Muslims.

Reinforce and Extend

Answers

◆ Literature and Your Life

Reader's Response Students may say that they did find the Chelemites foolish, but in a likeable way.

Thematic Focus The patriarch tells them it is wrong to take money from the charity fund, but he doesn't seem to feel it is wrong to steal the moon.

☑ Check Your Comprehension

1. They want to use the moon to light their city.
2. They wait until the moon's reflection shows in a bucket. Thinking the bucket now holds the moon, they close the bucket with the town seal and place it in the Synagogue for safety.

◆ Critical Thinking

1. The moon was never in the barrel in the first place. The Chelemites had only captured the moon's reflection.
2. Possible response: The patriarch is a fool because of his silly plan. The description is meant to be funny.
3. Possible reponse: In a group situation, most people want to appear intelligent. They do not want to admit that they don't understand what is being said by others, or be the only one to disagree, for fear of appearing foolish.

More About the Author
Blanche Serwer-Bernstein
(1910–) studied at the Teacher's Institute of Jewish Theological Seminary of America. Her work in child psychology with issues surrounding speech and hearing creates a natural bridge to the study of folklore and oral storytelling. Several of Serwer-Bernstein's books focus on the oral traditions of particular cultures, for example the Jews and Arabs.

Connecting Literature to Social Studies

After two weeks, the nights became very dark and again they began to bump into each other on the streets, bruise their shins, and lose their way because of wrong turns in the darkness.

This was the time! They sent word through the town, and the people gathered to help take the moon out of the barrel and hang it in the sky. They were confident that, with all their minds working on the problem, there would be a way of hoisting it up and securing it there. They knew it was possible, for hadn't they seen the moon up there month after month? Besides, they had collected all the ladders in Chelem and tied them together end to end in preparation for this moment.

Polishing cloths were also gathered in a gigantic heap in front of the Synagogue, where the important event would take place. The women of Chelem vied with each other for positions from which they could help in the polishing.

Then came the moment they had been planning for. They uncovered the barrel carefully, squinting their eyes so that they would not be blinded by the brilliance of the moon's light.

They opened their eyes wide. Their moon was gone! How could that be? They looked at each other in utter confusion.

Who could have released their moon, securely trapped in a water barrel and sealed by the official seal of the city of Chelem? Surely no Chelemite could have done it! Bandits? Marauders from a neighboring town? But the seal remained unbroken! They shook their heads and looked skyward, deeply disturbed by this mysterious happening.

One thing they were sure of. Had they set proper guards over their moon, it would have remained safe and they would have found a way to hang it in the sky. Far from being discouraged, they were confident that they would know how to do it next time.

◆ Build Vocabulary

marauders (mə rôd′ ərs) *n.*: Roaming attackers

Meet the Author

Blanche Serwer-Bernstein (1910–) is a psychologist and a specialist in the education of young children. She said she wrote "Let's Steal the Moon" for two reasons: "The first is that the tales . . . had been 'simmering' in my mind since I had heard them as a child. The second is that folk tales and folklore have a marvelous way of zooming into the fantasy life of a child."

Guide for Responding

◆ Literature and Your Life

Reader's Response Did you like the characters in this story, or did you find their behavior foolish? Explain your response.

Thematic Focus What mixed messages do the Chelemites receive from the wise patriarch?

☑ Check Your Comprehension

1. Why do the Chelemites want to steal the moon?
2. What steps do they take to catch it?

◆ Critical Thinking

INTERPRET

1. What really happened to the moon? **[Apply Prior Knowledge]**
2. The story describes the patriarch as being very wise. Do you think the author really means this? Explain. **[Draw Conclusions]**

EXTEND

3. What does this tale say about the way people sometimes behave in groups? **[Synthesize]**

Block Scheduling Strategies

Consider these suggestions to take advantage of extended class time:

- Post a handful of students' Interest Grabber ideas on the board. Then play the audiocassette of "Let's Steal the Moon."
- Focus a classroom vote and discussion on the Reader's Response, p. 438.
- Have students complete a Sunburst Organizer, p. 94, in **Writing and Language Transparencies,** with character traits typically found in foolish tales. Then organize students in groups for either Extending the Tale or Storytelling from the Idea Bank on p. 439.
- Alternatively, focus on the social studies context of the story. Review the explanatory text from pp. 436 and 439 and answer the questions together. Invite students who conducted the research activities suggested for more advanced students, p. 437, to share their findings. Then use *World Explorer: Eastern Hemisphere,* Chapter 7, "Europe and Russia: Shaped by History," to help students gather information for Map Research and Jewish Emigration in the Idea Bank on p. 439.

CONNECTING LITERATURE TO SOCIAL STUDIES

While the political boundaries and government systems shifted frequently in Eastern Europe, a tradition of folklore could keep a group together by stressing the values the people shared. For this reason, and because some Jews migrated as frequently as the map changed, storytellers traditionally occupied an honorable position in Jewish communities.

In most stories about the people of Chelem, a fool thinks of a ridiculously complex solution to a simple question or problem that any reader could solve. Perhaps this is why tales about fools are so appealing—they make the reader feel superior to the characters.

1. Why would folklore be especially useful to the ethnic groups of Eastern Europe?
2. According to "Let's Steal the Moon," what is the problem in the city of Chelem?
3. How do the people in the town try to solve the problem?
4. Why is the solution foolish?
5. What solution would a truly wise person recommend?

Idea Bank

Writing

1. **Outlining a Process** Imagine that you are one of the townspeople of Chelem. Write a list of steps that have to be followed in order to carry out the plan to steal the moon.
2. **Extending the Tale** Write a sequel to this story to show the townspeople's second attempt to capture the moon. In your story, include dialogue that conveys the characters' silly ideas, their excitement about their new plan, and their reaction to the result.
3. **Critical Review** Blanche Serwer-Bernstein makes a deliberate effort to make this tale humorous. In an essay, cite the specific words, phrases, and details that bring out the humor of the townspeople's decision to steal the moon.

Speaking and Listening

4. **Storytelling** With a group, locate and read more stories about the people of Chelem. Rehearse a reading of two or three tales to find the best ways to bring out the humor of the stories. Add music or illustrations to enhance your presentation.

Projects

5. **Map Research** Use a historical atlas to study the changes in Eastern Europe since 1750. Create several political maps indicating the shifting borders, and include captions explaining the changes. **[Social Studies Link]**
6. **Jewish Emigration** Research the Jewish emigration from Russia and Eastern Europe to the United States between 1880 and 1920. In a chart, indicate the most popular destinations. **[Social Studies Link]**

Further Reading, Listening, and Viewing

- Samuel I. Tenenbaum's *The Wise Men of Chelem* (1965) features more entertaining antics of this community of fools.
- Blanche Luria Serwer's *Let's Steal the Moon* (1970) includes ten more Jewish folk tales.
- Isaac Bashevis Singer's *When Schlemiel Went to Warsaw and Other Stories* (1968) tells more Jewish folk tales.

Beyond the Selection

FURTHER READING

Other Works by Blanche Serwer-Bernstein

Jewish Folktales From Around the World

In the Tradition of Moses and Mohammed: Jewish and Arab Folktales

Other Works About Eastern Europe and Its Folk Traditions

Favorite Folktales From Around the World, Jane Yolen, ed.

Jewish Literature for Children: A Teaching Guide, Cheryl S. Grossman & Suzy Engman

The Silver Crest, Kornei Chukovsky

INTERNET

We suggest the following Internet sites (all Web sites are subject to change).

Search sites about Polish history and culture at:
http://plwww.fuw.edu.pl/index.eng.html

Learn about folk tales through:
http://www.fas.harvard.edu/~folkmyth/fandmwebsites.html

Read Jewish folk tales at:
http://www.tau.ac.il:81/~gila1/folklore/

We *strongly recommend* that you preview these sites before you send your students to them.

Idea Bank

Following are suggestions for matching the Idea Bank topics with your students' performance levels and learning modalities:

Customize for *Performance Levels*

Less Advanced Students: 1, 4
Average Students: 2, 4, 5
More Advanced Students: 3, 5, 6

Customize for *Learning Modalities:*

Verbal/Linguistic: 1, 2, 3, 4, 6
Visual/Spatial: 1, 5, 6
Bodily/Kinesthetic: 4
Logical/Mathematical: 1, 3
Interpersonal: 4

CONNECTING LITERATURE TO SOCIAL STUDIES

1. Possible response: Folklore would help cultures remain intact by providing a way to share values. When politics are unstable, culture becomes a key link among peoples.
2. There isn't enough light at night.
3. They try to take the moon out of the sky in order to store it for future lighting purposes.
4. The moon can neither be taken from the sky nor hung back up artificially.
5. Possible responses: Streetlights, traveling the streets on moonlit nights only

ASSESSMENT OPTIONS

Formal Assessment, Selection Test, pp. 125–126, and Assessment Resources Software. The selection test is designed so that it can be easily customized to the performance levels of your students.

PORTFOLIO ASSESSMENT

Use the following rubrics in the ***Alternative Assessment*** booklet to assess student writing:
Outlining a Process: How-to/Process Explanation, p. 87
Extending the Tale: Fictional Narrative, p. 82
Critical Review: Critical Review, p. 98

Prepare and Engage

Establish Writing Guidelines
Review the following key characteristics of a letter of proposal:

- A letter of proposal attempts to persuade the reader in some way
- It uses business-letter format
- A letter of proposal uses facts and reasons to support the main idea

You may want to distribute the scoring rubric for Persuasion, p. 92, in **Alternative Assessment**. See also the suggestions on p. 442 for customizing the rubric to this workshop.

Refer students to the Writing Handbook in the back of the book for information and instruction.

 ***Writer's Solution***

Writers at Work Videodisc
To show students how Joseph Bruchac defines persuasive writing, play the videodisc segment on Persuasion (Ch. 6.). Have students discuss how Bruchac discovers ideas to persuade his readers.

Play frames 4 to 9282

Writing Lab CD-ROM
If your students have access to technology, you may want to have them work in the tutorial on Persuasion to complete all or part of their letters of proposal. Follow these steps:

1. Have students view interactive models of persuasive writing.
2. Suggest that students use the interactive chart on distinguishing facts from opinions.
3. Have students draft on computer.

Writer's Solution Sourcebook
Students can find additional support in the chapter on Persuasion, pp. 166–199.

Persuasive Writing

Letter of Proposal

Writing Process Workshop

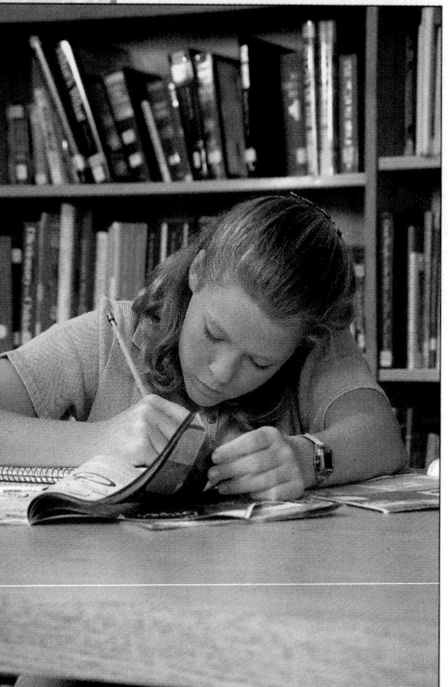

You've got a great idea! Share it with someone who can help you make it happen by writing a **letter of proposal.** In your letter, you'll propose your idea and then offer strong support—reasons, examples, and specific details. The following skills, introduced in this section's Writing Mini-Lessons, will help you draft your letter.

Writing Skills Focus

▶ **Use a topic sentence and supporting details.** Clearly state your main idea. Then, convince your reader with strong supporting details. (See p. 427.)

▶ **Follow letter format.** Stick to the traditional format, which includes a heading, salutation, body, closing, and signature. (See p. 435.)

▶ **Use persuasive words** chosen to convince a specific audience.

After reading Paul Reiser's essay and Ogden Nash's poems, one writer decided to propose a new television show for kids.

Model

Dear Mr. Wilson: ①

I have enjoyed watching your network for many years. Lately, I've been imagining a new show called *Zoo's Alive!* that would both entertain and educate young children. ② Episodes would focus on different unusual animals. Each half-hour show would include four parts: a documentary about the animal's habitat and behavior; a funny cartoon about the animal; a storybook about the animal; and, finally, original poems about the animal written by viewers. For example, the pilot could be about a hippopotamus. ③

① The colon in the greeting follows business-letter format.

② Here's the topic sentence: It's clear and right to the point.

③ Words such as *episode*, *pilot*, and *documentaries* are tailored to the audience: a television network executive.

 **Beyond the Classroom**

Workplace Skills

Making Proposals The ability to formulate well-written proposals is essential in many careers. For example, researchers apply for grants by writing proposal letters. Newspaper and magazine writers send proposal letters about their intended topics to editors. In many cases, writing a letter of proposal is a way for someone to get hired to do a job; that person proposes to do the required work in a certain way, for a certain price, on a certain schedule.

Have students brainstorm for a list of careers in which a worker may be required to write a letter of proposal. Then have them form several groups, each based on one of the careers. Groups should come up with specific scenarios where one "worker" proposes to do something. Encourage groups to divide responsibility so that one or two students draft a proposal letter and the other students form a review board to discuss the proposal. For example, a group of students who choose the career of architect can create a scenario in which a new shopping center needs to be built. Then, students will write a letter of proposal to address how and where the shopping center will be built and the "review board" will decide whether or not the proposal works. Suggest that students share their decisions with the class.

Prewriting

Choose Your Idea First, you have to choose an idea to propose. Then, you can work out some of the details. Here are some suggestions to get the wheels of your mind turning:

Topic Ideas

- School improvement
- Family vacation
- Solving a problem

Brainstorm Ask yourself, "What would have to happen to make my idea a reality?" As you brainstorm, jot down notes. Make a web, a list, or a timeline. Include all kinds of details as you think of them.

Do Some Research Find out more about putting your idea into action. Consider these research routes.

- Ask an expert to discuss your idea with you.
- Check an on-line resource.
- Look up information in the library.
- Find a quotation.

Drafting

Start Strong Grab your reader's attention with a strong beginning sentence. You might try an emotional, personal appeal or a thought-provoking question. Be original. Would you read a letter that began "*Splash!*"? Maybe it's a good way to begin a letter proposing a dunking booth at a school carnival!

Give Reasons and Examples The kind of support you provide depends on your proposal. Here are some suggestions:

Proposal	Support
Fund-raising idea	Statistics about how much money has been raised this way by other organizations
New television show	Details about what the first episode might be like
Change in a law	Examples of times when the old law resulted in injustice, unfairness, or wrongdoing
Family vacation	Photographs, specific costs, maps, and suggested schedules

DRAFTING/REVISING

APPLYING LANGUAGE SKILLS: Business-Letter Format

The standard form for a business letter includes these five parts:

1. **Heading:** Include your address, the recipient's address, and the date.
2. **Greeting:** For a business letter, use the person's name, *Dear Sir, Dear Madam,* or *To Whom It May Concern,* followed by a colon.
3. **Body:** State your business.
4. **Closing:** Capitalize the first letter, and end with a comma.
5. **Signature:** Print or type your full name, and sign your name above it.

Practice What parts of a business letter do these represent? On your paper, capitalize and punctuate them correctly.

1. january 15 1998
2. dear mr. collins
3. sincerely yours

Writing Application As you write your letter of proposal, use correct business-letter format, including correct capitalization and punctuation.

Writer's Solution Connection Writing Lab

For more help with correct letter format, use the Letter Shell in the tutorial on Expression.

Develop Student Writing

Prewriting

Remind students that they must support their proposal with facts and details. To help them gather these details, have them use the Main Idea and Supporting Details Organizer from **Writing and Language Transparencies,** p. 70. Explain that if they cannot come up with enough supporting details, they should consider switching topics.

Customize for
Less Proficient Writers

Students may benefit from working with a partner on their letters of proposal. Encourage partners to choose a topic in which both students are interested. Once they come up with a topic idea, they can each do research and share their results. Have them discuss the evidence they have found: Which evidence is the most convincing and which evidence may be contrary to their position? Partners can work together on drafts and sign their letters with both names.

Customize for
More Advanced Writers

Students may enjoy answering letters of proposal. Have students work in pairs. One student will submit a letter of proposal and the other student will answer the letter. The person answering the letter will have to provide reasons for his or her acceptance or denial of the proposal. He or she should counter each argument the letter details for consideration of the proposal.

Drafting

Remind students that even though their letters should be direct and to the point, they should still contain the basic elements of introduction, body, and conclusion. The introduction and conclusion should state the object of the proposal, and the body of the letter should explain the reasons for the proposal.

Applying Language Skills

Business-Letter Format Tell students that many word processing programs for computers have templates that include all the essential parts of a business letter. Rather than having to set margins for different sections of the letter, the margins have already been set in the template. Suggest that students experiment with templates on word processing programs to which they have access.

Practice

1. Heading: January 15, 1998
2. Greeting: Dear Mr. Collins:
3. Closing: Sincerely yours,

Writer's Solution

For additional instruction and practice, have students use the lesson on Writing Letters in the *Writer's Solution Grammar Practice Book,* pp. 140–143.

Revising

Explain to students that many word processing programs have a built-in thesaurus, which will offer replacement suggestions for a highlighted word. If students have written their drafts with a word processing program, suggest they experiment with this feature.

Writer's Solution

Writing Lab CD-ROM

In the tutorial on Persuasion, have students use the Self-Evaluation Checklist to identify revision checklist items.

Publishing and Presenting

For other publishing ideas, suggest that students stage in-class debates, using the letters of proposals as subject matter. Randomly choose a letter of proposal to read to the class, and have students form "pro" and "con" groups to debate whether they would pass the proposal.

Reinforce and Extend

Review the Writing Guidelines

After students have completed their papers, review the characteristics of a letter of proposal.

Applying Language Skills

Writing Organization Names Correctly Tell students that an easy way to have their proposals turned down is to misspell an organization name. Having a mistake in the address or name of the recipient automatically signals to the recipient that the writer has not been thorough or careful in his or her research.

Answers

1. The United States Postal Service
2. The American Red Cross
3. I.B.M.
4. Wal-Mart Stores, Inc.

EDITING/PROOFREADING

APPLYING LANGUAGE SKILLS: Writing Organization Names Correctly

When writing to an organization, it's important to spell, capitalize, and punctuate correctly. Some businesses, for example, abbreviate parts of their names; others use no abbreviations. Check a telephone book, a business card, or a letterhead for accuracy. Here are a few examples:

Pollero and Sons Flooring
Elliot Office Products, Inc.
Ski & Bike Service Ctr.
American Airlines Inc.
Department of Environmental Protection

Practice Correct the following organization names. Refer to a phone directory for help.

1. the U.S. post office
2. the American red cross inc.
3. International business machines
4. walmart company

Writing Application As you write your letter of proposal, be sure to spell, punctuate, and capitalize all organization names correctly.

Writer's Solution Connection
Language Lab

For more on writing organization names correctly, see the lesson Proper Nouns in the unit on Capitalization.

Write a Strong Conclusion In your conclusion, be polite, positive, creative, and clear. Leave your audience with a strong impression.

Revising

Evaluate Your Word Power Reread your letter to see that you've chosen words and phrases appropriate for your readers. For example, you might mention the "target audience" to a television executive, but you'd talk about "fans" to the manager of a sports team.

Additionally, use a thesaurus to find words that add persuasive punch to your letter. An idea that is "cutting edge" sounds a lot more exciting than a "great" idea.

REVISION MODEL

I think 7:30 P.M. would be ~~a good~~ ① the perfect ~~show time~~ ② time slot for this ~~show~~ program. For most children, it's after dinnertime ③ and before bedtime.

① *Perfect* is a more persuasive word than *good*.
② The writer adds terms that will appeal specifically to the intended audience—a television executive.
③ This detail supports the main point.

Check Your Form Double-check that you have used correct letter form. Be sure that you have included the five parts of a letter, and fix any errors in spelling or punctuation.

Publishing and Presenting

- **Be a Guest at a Business Meeting** Imagine that you've been asked to deliver your proposal orally at a business meeting. In front of the class, spend five minutes making your case.
- **E-mail It** There are many on-line sites from which to share your proposal. Maybe your audience is a government agency, a superintendent's office, a television network, or simply a friend who might be interested in a partnership. Find an e-mail address that makes sense, and send your proposal.

✓ ASSESSMENT

PORTFOLIO ASSESSMENT
Use the rubric on Persuasion in the **Alternative Assessment** booklet, p. 92, to assess students' writing. Add these criteria to customize this rubric to this assignment.

	4	3	2	1
Main Idea and Supporting Details	The proposal includes a clearly stated main idea and several well-developed supporting details.	The proposal includes a clear main idea and several supporting details, some needing more development.	The proposal includes a main idea and only one supporting detail.	The proposal's main idea is unclear and is not supported.
Business-Letter Format	The proposal uses standard business-letter format.	The proposal uses standard business format, but not all puctuation is correct.	The proposal uses letter format, but one or more standard parts of the business format are missing.	The proposal is not in business-letter format.

Real-World Reading Skills Workshop

Reading Product Labels

Strategies for Success

Whether you realize it or not, many of the items you use every day have product labels. The box of cereal you reach for each morning has a label. So does the T-shirt you wear to school and the paint tubes in art class. Knowing how to read a product label helps you to use a product properly and enjoy it with safety.

Read Important Information Labels often carry important information about how a product should and should not be used:

- Food labels list ingredients. This is important information for anyone on a restricted diet. If you are allergic to peanuts, for example, you need to be on the lookout for food products containing peanut oil. Food labels also provide nutritional information. You can find the caloric value of a serving as well as data on sodium and vitamin content.
- Product labels explain how a product should be used. A car wax label, for example, might point out that it works best on a clean, dry surface.
- Medicine labels provide crucial information about proper dosage amounts, as well as information about how often the medicine should be taken.
- Product labels list safety precautions. Is the product you are using flammable, poisonous, or unsafe for small children? Do you need to wear safety goggles or work in a ventilated area? The label lets you know.

Apply the Strategies

Look at the product label below, found in the packaging of a CD-ROM disc. Then, answer the questions that follow.

> No cleaning will be necessary if the compact disc is always held by the edges and is replaced in the case directly after playing. To remove any fingerprints, dust, or dirt, always wipe the compact disc in a straight line, from the center of the disc to the edge. Use a clean, lint-free, dry cloth. Never use any liquid to clean a compact disc.

1. How should a CD-ROM disc be held during cleaning?
2. Does it matter in which direction a CD-ROM disc is wiped?
3. What type of cloth should be used to clean a CD-ROM disc?
4. Should a liquid be used to clean a CD-ROM disc?

Here are situations in which it's important to read the product labels:

- Food labels
- Cleaning instruction labels on clothing
- Safety warnings on cleaning supplies and power tools
- Allergy warnings on medicine labels

Introduce the Strategies

Ask students to volunteer any experiences they have had with reading product labels. Explain that people read labels for different reasons: to understand nutrition information, to find out washing instructions, to see what something is made from.

Customize for
Less Proficient Readers

Students may not recognize technical words used on some labels. Suggest that they use a dictionary to find out what unfamiliar words mean. Explain that many product labels include a phone number for customer inquiries. If consumers need more information about the product, they can call that phone number and speak to a company representative. For example, a carton of organic milk states "Our cows are fed a diet . . . of hay and other healthy things." To find out what those other healthy things are, you can call the dairy and ask.

Customize for
More Advanced Students

Suggest that students write their own product labels for any item they like. Have them share their labels with the rest of the class.

Apply the Strategies

Explain to students that they should read product labels in their entirety to get the most information. Many product labels have warnings that alert consumers to possible hazards, and some contain "fine print" that may include other important information.

Answers

1. The CD-ROM disc should be held by the edges.
2. The disc must be wiped in a straight line, from the center of the disc to the edge.
3. A clean, lint-free, dry cloth should be used.
4. No liquid should be used.

◆Build Grammar Skills

Reviewing Sentence Complements

The selections in Part 2 include instruction on the following:

- Direct and Indirect Objects
- Subject Complements

This instruction is reinforced with the Build Grammar Skills practice pages in **Selection Support,** pp. 146 and 151.

As you review sentence complements you may wish to review the following:

- Distinguishing between prepositions and subordinating conjunctions: Some words can be either prepositions or subordinating conjunctions, such as *until, since,* and *before.* However, subordinating conjunctions connect complete ideas.
- Fragments: Clauses written alone are fragments; therefore they should not be capitalized and punctuated as sentences.

Customize for ***Less Proficient Readers***

Explain to students that sometimes direct objects are found near the beginning of a sentence, especially when the sentence is a question. To help identify the direct object, students may try to rearrange the word order to make the question into a sentence. For example, "What did you do last night?" changes into "You did what last night." Students should recognize *what* as the direct object.

Writer's Solution

For additional practice and support with sentence complements, use the practice pages on Direct Objects, pp. 33–35, Indirect Objects, pp. 36–37, and Subject Complements, pp. 38–39, in the *Writer's Solution Grammar Practice Book.*

Sentence Complements

Grammar Review

com·ple·ment (käm′plə mənt) *n.* 1 the word or words that complete a predicate

A **sentence complement** is a word or a group of words that completes the meaning of a verb. There are four kinds of complements. *Direct objects* and *indirect objects* complete the meaning of an action verb. *Predicate nouns* and *predicate adjectives* are subject complements, which complete the meaning of a linking verb and identify or describe the subject.

Direct Object Receives the action of the verb or shows the result of the action. It answers the questions *whom* or *what.* (See p. 426.)

verb D.O.
I *sent* the clockmaker a *letter.*

Indirect Object Follows an action verb and tells *to whom or what* or *for whom or what* the action of the verb is performed. (See p. 426.)

verb I.O.
I *sent* the *clockmaker* a letter.

Predicate Noun Follows a linking verb and renames the subject. (See p. 434.)

L.V. P.N.
The patient *is* a *clock*

Predicate Adjective Follows a linking verb and describes the subject. (See p. 434.)

L.V. P.A.
My clock *is depressed!*

Practice 1 Copy the following sentences into your notebook. Then, underline the verb in each sentence, and label the complements as indirect object, direct object, predicate noun, or predicate adjective.

1. Ogden Nash writes humorous poetry.

2. Zora Neale Hurston is a famous folklorist.

3. Paul Reiser tells his son a story.

4. Edward Hoch's imagination is creative.

5. All these writers give us their stories.

Practice 2 Write a paragraph describing a funny experience you've had recently. In your paragraph, use two sentences with direct objects, one with an indirect object, one with a predicate noun, and one with a predicate adjective.

Grammar in Writing

✓ ***When writing a sentence with a predicate noun or a predicate adjective, choose the most exact noun or precise adjective to complete your thought.***

Vague Noun: *I Love Lucy* is my favorite show.

Exact Noun: *I Love Lucy* is my favorite comedy.

Vague Adjective: Paul Reiser's essay was good.

Precise Adjective: Paul Reiser's essay was hilarious.

Answers

Practice 1

1. Ogden Nash writes humorous poetry. (*poetry* is the direct object)
2. Zora Neale Hurston is a famous folklorist. (*folklorist* is a predicate noun)
3. Paul Reiser tells his son a story. (*son* is the indirect object; *story* is the direct object)
4. Edward Hoch's imagination is creative. (*creative* is the predicate adjective)
5. All these writers give us their stories. (*us* is the indirect object; *stories* is the direct object)

Speaking, Listening, and Viewing Workshop

Giving Feedback

By providing feedback on your classmates' presentations, reports, or creative writing, you can help them to improve. If you use these guidelines when you respond to someone else's work, your classmates will appreciate your help and be more likely to take your advice.

Balance Criticism With Praise Feedback should include information about what the person did well, as well as how the person could improve. By pointing out only faults, you may hurt someone's feelings. If you offer nothing but praise, the person won't know how to improve his or her work.

Be Constructive Constructive criticism provides helpful recommendations for improvement. For example, saying "You seemed unprepared" is not constructive. Instead, make suggestions for improving preparation, such as "Next time, try practicing your presentation with some classmates ahead of time."

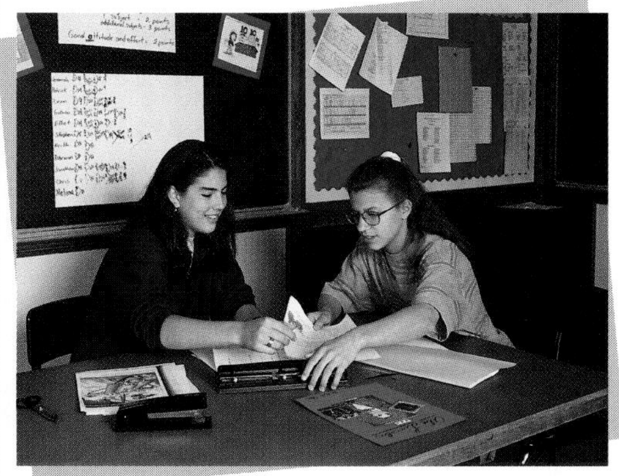

Be Accurate and Specific To be sure that your comments are not influenced by personal feelings, support each criticism with examples from your peer's work. To get beyond a vague comment like "I liked your story," ask yourself why you liked it. For example, you might say, "The way you described the setting made me feel that I was there."

Apply the Strategies

Prepare a brief presentation on a topic of your choice. Then, give your presentation to an audience of two: a reviewer and an observer. Ask the reviewer to give you feedback. When it is your turn to be the reviewer, provide feedback according to these steps:

1. Take careful notes during the presentation.
2. Consider what you will say. Then, deliver constructive feedback.
3. Ask the observer to evaluate the success of the post-presentation meeting.

Tips for Giving Feedback

When giving feedback, follow these strategies:

- *Start with the good points. When you let people know they succeeded in some areas, they will be more likely to accept comments on what they need to do to improve.*
- *Give thoughtful feedback. Avoid blunt comments. Carefully consider what the person did well and where there is room for improvement. Support your feedback with examples.*
- *Don't be emotional. If you speak with too much emotion, the person may feel that you are not being objective and fair.*

Introduce the Strategies

Have students think of different situations in which they have received feedback. Remind them of comments from sports coaches, piano teachers, parents, or friends. Explain that feedback is a general term that includes even negative reactions. Ask students to consider what type of feedback they find the most helpful.

Apply the Strategies

Remind students when they give feedback to use positive body language. Encourage them to make eye contact, to use appropriate hand gestures, and to appear friendly and open. Explain that their goal is to keep the listener's attention and show signs of support.

Assessment
Students should be assessed on the quality of their feedback as well as on how detailed the feedback is. You may also want to use the Speaking and Listening Initial Self-Assessment form in **Alternative Assessment,** p. 103.

Beyond the Classroom

Workplace Skills
Feedback Explain to students that certain careers include the task of giving feedback. Teachers give feedback to their students, counselors to their clients, and coaches to their athletes. Encourage students to interview a teacher or coach they know and ask that person about the role that giving feedback plays in his or her job. Suggest that students ask for specific examples or incidents that reveal how the teacher or coach has learned to be better at giving feedback. Have students write out their questions before the interview and record the interview on videotape or audiotape, if possible. They can then share their findings with the rest of the class.

Community Connection
Counseling Explain to students that most communities offer various types of counseling for different activities. Tell students that often people who need advice on health, business transactions, or legal issues can consult professionals who volunteer their expertise. Oftentimes, this means giving people feedback on their plans or situations. Encourage students to investigate local counseling services and find out what kind of help they provide.

◆ Build Vocabulary

What's Behind the Words

Remind students that collective nouns take a singular verb, as in "The flock of sheep grazes on the hill." Tell students that when consulting a dictionary, they may try looking up the name of the animal or the term for the group. Alternatively, they can look up the name of the animal in an encyclopedia and try to find the name of the group in the article on that animal.

Customize for *English Language Learners*

Students can increase their understanding of everyday words as well as the names of these animal groups by noting other definitions of these terms as they look them up in a dictionary. For example, a group of bees is a "swarm." Another definition of *swarm* (as a verb) is "to move about, along, forth in great numbers, as things or persons."

Answers

Activity 1

1. b
2. a
3. j
4. e
5. c
6. i
7. g
8. f
9. d
10. h

Activity 2

Possible responses: a fluttering of butterflies, a mess of pigs, a slither of worms

Activity 3

1. i
2. j
3. a
4. c
5. d
6. b
7. e
8. f
9. g
10. h

What's Behind the Words

Vocabulary Adventures With Richard Lederer

Names of Animal Groups

You know that a bunch of sheep crowded together is a flock, that a group of antelope loping together is a herd, and that a mass of bees buzzing together is a swarm. However, you may not have ever heard of a labor of moles, a leap of leopards, a flush of mallards, a kindle of kittens, an exaltation of larks, or an ostentation of peacocks.

Labor, leap, flush, kindle, and *exaltation* are only a few examples of collective nouns for animals. Most of these group terms evolved during the Middle Ages, when the complex art of hunting demanded an equally refined vocabulary to name the objects of the chase. Many of these labels reflect the nature of the animals to which they refer.

ACTIVITY 1 Here's your chance to be a groupie. Match the beastly collections in the left-hand column with the animals they describe in the right-hand column. You may consult a good dictionary to help you.

1. bed of	**a.** ants
2. colony of	**b.** clams
3. crash of	**c.** ducks
4. gaggle of	**d.** fish
5. paddling of	**e.** geese
6. parliament of	**f.** lions
7. plague of	**g.** locusts
8. pride of	**h.** monkeys
9. school of	**i.** owls
10. troop of	**j.** rhinoceroses

ACTIVITY 2 For fun, make up your own collective nouns for animals or for people—a prickle of porcupines, an aroma of skunks, a rash of dermatologists, a brace of orthodontists. Work with a partner to create five collective nouns. Then, share your new words with classmates.

ACTIVITY 3 You know that something catlike is *feline* and something doglike is *canine*. But how elegant are you in describing other animals? Match each animal in the left-hand column with its appropriate adjective in the right-hand column. You might need to consult a good dictionary to help you.

1. ape	**a.** apian
2. bear	**b.** aquiline
3. bee	**c.** avian
4. bird	**d.** bovine
5. cow	**e.** elephantine
6. eagle	**f.** equine
7. elephant	**g.** leonine
8. horse	**h.** porcine
9. lion	**i.** simian
10. pig	**j.** ursine

READ MORE ABOUT IT! To add to your store of collective nouns, read James Lipton's *An Exaltation of Larks* (Penguin Books).

Extended Reading Opportunities

To make the most of your leisure reading, consider finding books that celebrate the lighter side of life. The titles below include quirky characters, mixed messages, and lots of laughs!

Suggested Titles

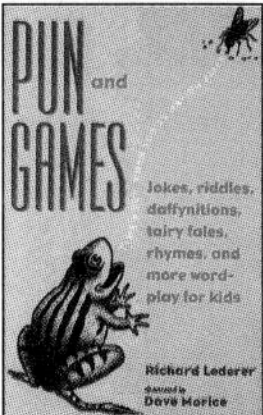

Pun and Games
Richard Lederer
Who would have IOPER8 for a license plate? A surgeon! With this riddle and endless puns, Richard Lederer entertains his reader while poking fun at the English language. Each chapter features a different type of pun. He follows each pun with games, activities, and an invitation for readers to make their own jokes. This book provides a punny way to spend an afternoon. As the frog on the cover croaks, "Time's fun when you're having flies!"

Squashed
Joan Bauer
Ellie Morgan sets a huge goal for herself and her vegetable patch—she wants to grow the largest pumpkin in Iowa! Naming her best-chance pumpkin Max, Ellie works hard, pampers it, and prays that it will grow to 611 pounds. As the narrator, Ellie uses wit and humor to describe the other competitors and the struggles and triumphs of the Rock River Pumpkin Weigh-In.

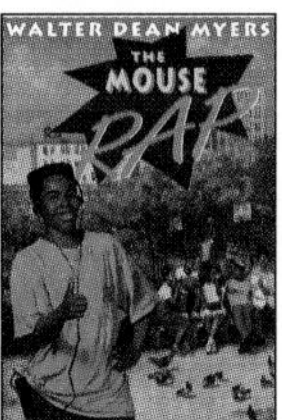

The Mouse Rap
Walter Dean Myers
Fourteen-year-old Mouse (his street name) lives in Harlem. Looking for something to do during the summer, he and his friends get into fights, enter a dance contest, play basketball, and try to find the secret treasure of a 1930's gangster. As if this weren't enough, a girl that Mouse has known for a long time decides she wants them to be a couple, then decides she doesn't, then changes her mind again. In all, the summer turns out to be more eventful than even Mouse had hoped for!

Other Possibilities

The Far Side Gallery	Gary Larson
A Dog's Life	Peter Mayle
Buddy Love Now on Video	Ilene Cooper

Planning Students' Extended Reading

All of the works listed on this page are good choices for extending the theme "Just for Fun." Following is some information that may help you choose which to teach.

Customize for *Varying Student Needs*

When assigning these extended reading selections to your students, keep in mind the following factors:

- *Pun and Games* is a book written especially for students to introduce them to puns, spoonerisms, riddles, and homographs. Each chapter includes a game.
- *Squashed* is a fun, award-winning novel. Because it realistically describes the labor involved with the main character's gardening, this book presents an opportunity for connecting literature to science.
- *The Mouse Rap* is a zany story with characters of all generations. Set in Harlem, this book lends itself to discussions of leisure time, inner cities, and even rap music.

Literature Study Guides

A literature study guide is available for *The Mouse Rap*. The guide includes section summaries, discussion questions, and activities.

Planning Instruction and Assessment

Unit Objectives

1. To read short stories
2. To apply a variety of reading strategies, particularly strategies for reading fiction, appropriate for reading these selections
3. To recognize literary elements used in these selections
4. To increase vocabulary
5. To learn elements of grammar and usage
6. To write in a variety of modes about situations based on the selections
7. To develop speaking and listening skills, by completing activities
8. To view images critically and create visual representations

Meeting the Objectives Each selection provides instructional material and portfolio opportunities by which students can meet unit objectives. You will find additional practice pages for reading strategies, literary elements, vocabulary, and grammar in the **Selection Support** booklet in the **Teaching Resources** box.

Setting Goals Work with your students at the beginning of the unit to set goals for unit outcomes. Plan what skills and concepts you wish students to acquire. You may match instruction and activities according to students' performance levels or learning modalities.

Portfolios Students may keep portfolios of their completed work or of their work in progress. The Build Your Portfolio page of each selection provides opportunities for students to apply the concepts presented.

Humanities: Art

Youth and Old Age, by Norman Rockwell

Norman Rockwell (1894–1978), famous for his magazine covers for *The Saturday Evening Post,* began drawing as a child and studying art at the age of 16. His paintings often tell humorous stories.

1. What do you see happening in this picture? *An old man is telling a story to a boy, perhaps his grandson.*
2. Which of the painting's details show that the man is telling a story? *He leans forward and motions with his arms. The young boy faces him directly and seems intent.*

Youth and Old Age, Norman Rockwell, Photo Courtesy of The Norman Rockwell Museum at Stockbridge, Mass.

Art Transparencies

The **Art Transparencies** booklet in the **Teaching Resources** box offers fine art to help students make connections to other curriculum areas and high-interest topics.

Beyond Literature

Each unit presents Beyond Literature features that lead students into an exploration of careers, communities and other subject areas. In this unit, students will explore snake charming, and make social studies and community connections. In addition, the Teacher's Resource box contains a Beyond Literature booklet of activities. Using literature as a springboard, these activity pages offer students opportunities to connect literature to other curriculum areas and to the workplace and careers, community, media, and humanities.

UNIT 6

Short Stories

Short stories carry you to fictional worlds—both strange and familiar. In the pages of a story, you can meet exceptional people or travel to far-off lands. The possibilities are as endless as the bounds of a writer's imagination, so no two stories are ever alike. There are, however, some elements that all short stories share:

- **Plot** is the sequence of events that hooks you in and keeps you reading.
- **Characters** are the people or animals who take part in the action.
- **Setting** is the time and place of the action.
- **Theme** is the central message expressed in a story.

You will learn about these elements as you read this unit.

Assessing Student Progress

The tools that are available to measure the degree to which students meet the unit objectives are listed below.

Informal Assessment

The questions in the Guide for Responding sections are a first level of response to the concepts and skills presented with the selection. As a brief informal measure of students' grasp of the material, these responses indicate where further instruction and practice are needed. The practice pages in the **Selection Support** booklet provide for this type of instruction and practice.

You will also find literature and reading guides in the **Alternative Assessment** booklet, which students can use for informal assessment of their individual performances.

Formal Assessment

The **Formal Assessment** booklet contains Selection Tests and Unit Tests.

Selection Tests measure comprehension and skills acquisition for each selection or group of selections.

Each Unit Test provides students with 30 multiple-choice questions and 5 essay questions designed to assess students' knowledge of the literature and skills taught in the unit.

Each Alternative Unit Test: Standardized-Test Practice provides 15 multiple-choice questions and 3 essay questions based on two new literature selections not contained in the student book. The questions on the Alternative Unit Test are designed to assess students' ability to compare and contrast selections, applying skills taught in the unit.

Alternative Assessment

For portfolio and alternative assessment, the **Alternative Assessment** booklet contains Scoring Rubrics, Assessment Sheets, and Learning Modalities.

Scoring Rubrics provide writing modes that can be applied to Writing Mini-Lessons and to Writing Process Workshop lessons.

Assessment Sheets provide speaking and listening activities.

Learning Modalities Activities appeal to different learning styles. Use these as an alternative measurement of students' growth.

Connections

Within this unit, you will find selections and activities that make connections beyond literature. Use these selections to connect students' understanding and appreciation of literature beyond the traditional literature and language arts curriculum.

Encourage students to connect literature to other curriculum areas. You may wish to coordinate with teachers in other curriculum areas to determine ways to team teach and further extend instruction.

Connections to Today's World

Use these selections to guide students to recognize the relevance of literature to contemporary writings. In this unit, students will read a press release about the opening of a new exhibit at the Rock and Roll Hall of Fame in Cleveland, Ohio.

Connecting Literature to Social Studies

Each unit contains a selection that connects Literature to Social Studies. In this unit, students will read a short story set in Latin America, written by a Colombian author.

Prepare and Engage

OBJECTIVES

1. To read, comprehend, and interpret a short story
2. To relate a story to personal experience
3. To apply strategies for reading fiction
4. To interpret a surprise ending
5. To build vocabulary in context and learn the word root *-spec-*
6. To identify clauses
7. To write a prequel, using dialogue
8. To respond to a short story through writing, speaking and listening, and projects

SKILLS INSTRUCTION

Vocabulary:
Word Roots: *-spec-*
Spelling:
Words Ending With *-er* or *-or*
Grammar:
Clauses
Reading for Success:
Strategies for Reading Fiction
Literary Focus:
Surprise Ending
Writing:
Use Dialogue
Speaking and Listening:
Tabloid Television (Teacher Edition)
Viewing and Representing:
Illustrating the Story (Teacher Edition)
Critical Viewing:
Connect

PORTFOLIO OPPORTUNITIES

Writing: Friendship List; Letter From Prison; Police Report
Writing Mini-Lesson: Prequel
Speaking and Listening: News Bulletin; Tabloid Television
Projects: Wanted Poster; New York in 1900

More About the Author
O. Henry wrote short stories about life in the Southwest and of adventures in Central America while he was in prison. These stories, which he wrote to earn money to support his daughter, were very popular with magazine readers. When he was released, he took on the alias by which we know William Sydney Porter today. In 1918, the Society of Arts and Sciences secured Porter's place in American literature by establishing the O. Henry Award—given each year to the authors of the best stories published in American magazines.

Guide for Reading

Meet the Author:

O. Henry (1862–1910)

William Sydney Porter, alias O. Henry, is famous for his warm, witty short stories about ordinary people. His tales have crossed the barriers of both language and the media. O. Henry's works have been translated into many languages and have inspired at least two dozen films and television movies—including some in Russian and French.

Traveling Through Texas Porter was born in Greensboro, North Carolina. In 1882, he left home to seek his fortune in Texas. He worked at a ranch, then at a general land office, and later at the First National Bank in Austin. In 1895, Porter joined the *Houston Post* as a reporter and columnist.

Detour Leads to New York After Porter served several months in prison for embezzling bank funds—a crime which he might not have committed—he moved to New York City. He was soon writing stories and publishing his immensely popular books at a rapid rate.

The Story Behind the Story
Like many of his stories, "After Twenty Years" was probably inspired by O. Henry's time in jail—a period during which he learned of the exploits of criminals and gained an understanding of people on both sides of the law.

◆ Literature and Your Life

Connect Your Experience
You've probably had the experience of seeing a friend or family member you hadn't seen in months, even years. During your time apart, your looks may have changed, you may have started dressing in a new way, and you may have developed new interests. Imagine how different someone might look and act if you hadn't seen him or her for twenty years.

Thematic Focus: Trouble Brewing
In this story, two friends go their separate ways, but they promise to meet again in twenty years. Will they recognize each other when they meet again? How will the passage of time affect their friendship?

◆ Background for Understanding

History
The meeting between the two old friends in the story takes place in New York City in the late 1800's or early 1900's. At the time, the city's population had swelled to more than one million people, making it the nation's largest city. Most of the people were packed into what is now downtown Manhattan. People traveled on foot, on horseback, in horse-drawn carriages, or by trolley car. At night, many of the streets were nearly deserted. Policemen, like the one on the next page, patrolled the streets on foot, checking for suspicious activity and deterring criminals with their presence.

Prentice Hall Literature Program Resources

REINFORCE / RETEACH / EXTEND
Selection Support Pages
Build Vocabulary: Word Roots: *-spec-*, p. 156
Build Spelling Skills, p. 157
Build Grammar Skills: Clauses, p. 158
Reading for Success: Strategies for Reading Fiction, pp. 159–160
Literary Focus: Surprise Ending, p. 161
Strategies for Diverse Student Needs, pp. 57–58
Beyond Literature Cross-Curricular Connection: Art, p. 29

Formal Assessment Selection Test, pp. 135–137, Assessment Resources Software
Alternative Assessment, p. 29
Resource Pro CD-ROM
"After Twenty Years"—includes all resource material and customizable lesson plan
Listening to Literature Audiocassettes
"After Twenty Years"

MODEL SELECTION

After Twenty Years

◆ Literary Focus

Surprise Ending

A **surprise ending** is an unexpected twist at the close of a story. Although O. Henry did not invent the surprise ending, he was a master of this technique. While it is not expected, a good surprise ending should make sense to readers and flow logically out of the events preceding it. You'll also find that in stories with surprise endings, the writer often carefully drops hints about it earlier in the story, being careful not to give the surprise away. As you read "After Twenty Years," see whether you can predict the ending.

◆ Build Vocabulary

Word Roots: *-spec-*

Early in the story, O. Henry uses the word *spectators*. The word comes from the root *-spec-*, which means "see." Knowing the meaning of *-spec-* will help you determine that a spectator is a person who watches.

Word Bank

Look over these words from the story. Which words ending in *-y* do you think are adverbs? Which are nouns?

spectators
intricate
destiny
dismally
absurdity
simultaneously

Preparing for Standardized Tests

Reading This model selection presents strategies that will help students as they read fiction and when they encounter reading comprehension sections of standardized tests. Have students read the following passage and then make inferences to complete the sample test item:

> Bob had a pale face, keen eyes, and a small white scar over his right eyebrow. His tie clip was a large diamond, oddly set. For the past twenty years he had hustled around the West, competing with some of the sharpest wits to make his money. His speech was filled with street slang and had a silky tone. Bob is—

(A) a jeweler.
(B) a traveling salesman.
(C) a friendly man.
(D) a shady character.

Help students recognize clues to Bob's character: his showy diamond tie clip, his scar, his use of street slang, his wheeling and dealing lifestyle. Using these clues, they should infer that, *(D)* is the best answer. To practice using strategies for reading fiction, students can write their own annotations, using pp. 159–160 in **Selection Support.**

Interest Grabber Ask students to say whether they think they would recognize someone they know today from a photograph of that person taken many years before. Obtain some twenty-year-old photos of adults with whom all students are familiar, such as yourself or other teachers or celebrities. Present these to groups. Challenge students to identify the person in the photo. Lead them to the story by telling them that it concerns a meeting of two old friends who haven't seen each other in twenty years.

◆ Build Grammar Skills

Clauses If you wish to introduce the grammar concept for this selection before students read, refer to the instruction on p. 459.

◆ Critical Thinking

Analyze Have students examine the photo of the police officer. Ask them to compare his dress, gear, and appearance with that of today's police. *Students may say that the common elements outnumber the differences and that the differences reflect changes in weaponry, protective devices, and clothing styles.*

Customize for
Less Proficient Readers

Tell students that when reading some stories it is not unusual to come across information that seems vague or incomplete. Help them realize that, if they do not fully understand a detail, the writer will clarify matters eventually and make all the pieces fit into place. Encourage students to keep reading and to look for explanations.

Customize for
More Advanced Students

From discussing the Literary Focus on p. 451, students know that this story will contain a surprise ending. Encourage them to be on the lookout for clues that hint at the surprise, and to make guesses as to what it will be. Students can seek clues in characters' actions and words. By identifying with the characters, they may notice an unexpected action or a remark that doesn't quite fit, or is incomplete in a subtle way.

Reading for Success

The Reading for Success page in each unit presents a set of problem-solving strategies to help readers understand authors' words and ideas on multiple levels. Good readers develop a bank of strategies from which they can draw as needed.

Unit 6 introduces strategies for reading fiction. Based on research into techniques good readers use when reading fiction, the strategies outlined on this page will help students become more involved in their reading of stories and novels, and will increase their enjoyment, understanding, and appreciation of fiction.

The strategies are modeled on "After Twenty Years." Each green box shows an example of the thinking process involved in applying one of these strategies. Additional notes provide support for applying these strategies throughout the selection.

How to Use the Reading for Success Page

- Introduce the strategies for reading fiction, presenting each as a problem-solving procedure.
- Before students read the story, have them preview it, looking at the annotations in the green boxes that model the strategies.
- To reinforce these strategies after students have read the story, have them complete pp. 159–160 in **Selection Support**. These pages give students an opportunity to read a selection and practice literal comprehension strategies by writing their own annotations.

Reading Strategies: Support and Reinforcement

Using Boxed Annotations and Prompts

Throughout the unit, the notes in green, red, and maroon boxes are intended to help students apply reading strategies, understand the literary focus, and make a connection with their lives. You may use boxed material in these ways:

- Have students pause at each box and respond to its prompt before they continue reading.
- Urge students to read through the selection, ignoring the boxes. After they complete the selection, they may go back and review the text, responding to the prompts.

Reading for Success

Strategies for Reading Fiction

Fiction is writing that tells about imaginary characters and events. Short stories are brief works of fiction; novels are longer works of fiction. In fiction, the author creates a whole new world for you to explore. Sometimes, this world is strongly based on the real world of today or some time in the past. Other times, this world may be wildly inventive. In order to get the most out of the world the author has created, use the following strategies:

Predict.

As the events of the story unfold, ask yourself what will happen next. Be on the lookout for clues that hint of events to come. To find out whether your predictions are correct, read on.

> **Event:** Policeman walks an isolated beat at night.
> **Predictions:** He will meet someone; he may arrest someone.

Identify with the characters or the situation.

Fiction not only allows you to visit new worlds, but also allows you to experience other lives. By putting yourself in the characters' places or imagining yourself in their situation, you get to live the story with the characters.

Make inferences.

- Writers seldom tell you everything directly. As a result, you need to make inferences, or draw conclusions based on the details the author provides.
- An inference map is a useful way to organize details that the author provides and the inferences you draw from them. A partial inference map for one of the characters in "After Twenty Years" is shown below.

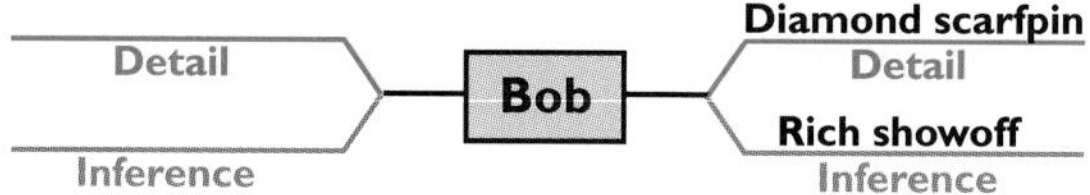

Question.

Stories are more interesting when you ask questions about characters and events. Ask: Why did he or she do that? What does this mean? How does this relate to what's already happened? Is this a hint about events to come? As you read, look for the answers to your questions.

As you read "After Twenty Years," read the side notes, which demonstrate how to apply these strategies to your reading.

Model a Reading Strategy: Ask Questions to Understand Characters and Events

Tell students that as they read stories and become aware that something seems unlikely or doesn't make sense, they can stop and ask questions about events or what the characters say. Asking questions can reveal what the author intends for readers to know. Show students how to ask questions to discover what O. Henry is suggesting in the passage at the top of p. 457 after Bob shows up:

> The first thing that O. Henry tells us about Jimmy Wells is that he is tall. Immediately Bob is "doubtful" that this man is Jimmy. After greeting Jimmy, Bob comments that he doesn't remember Jimmy's being so tall. I ask myself why O. Henry is making so much of Jimmy's height. Then Jimmy says he grew a bit after he was twenty. I know that men don't grow this much after the age of twenty. I wonder whether this man is Jimmy.

Tell students that asking questions not only leads to predictions, but also may help them tap into O. Henry's very special sense of humor.

MODEL

After Twenty Years

O. Henry

The policeman on the beat moved up the avenue impressively. The impressiveness was habitual and not for show, for spectators were few. The time was barely 10 o'clock at night, but chilly gusts of wind with a taste of rain in them had well nigh[1] depeopled the streets.

From the policeman's swagger and careful attention to his duty even when there was no one to admire him, you might **infer** that he is proud of his job.

Trying doors as he went, twirling his club with many intricate and artful movements, turning now and then to cast his watchful eye adown the pacific thoroughfare,[2] the officer, with his stalwart form and slight swagger, made a fine picture of a guardian of the peace. The vicinity was one that kept early hours. Now and then you might see the lights of a cigar store or of an all-night lunch counter; but the majority of the doors belonged to business places that had long since been closed.

When about midway of a certain block the policeman suddenly
1 slowed his walk. In the doorway of a darkened hardware store a man leaned, with an unlighted cigar in his mouth. As the policeman walked up to him the man spoke up quickly.

"It's all right, officer," he said, reassuringly. "I'm just waiting for a friend. It's an appointment made twenty

2 **Predict** what the man is going to tell the policeman.

1. **well nigh** (nī): Very nearly.
2. **pacific thoroughfare:** Calm street.

◆ Build Vocabulary

spectators (spek´ tāt´ ərz) *n.*: People who watch something without taking part; onlookers

intricate (in´ tri kit) *adj.*: Complex; full of complicated detail

Block Scheduling Strategies

Consider these suggestions to take advantage of extended class time:

- Before students begin the story, introduce the Reading for Success strategies on p. 452. Suggest that students keep a log to monitor their use of these reading strategies.
- Have students read independently and then discuss the Literary Focus questions on p. 459 in small groups. Ask them to continue working in their groups on the Reading for Success questions, p. 459. Have them apply the strategies to the Reading for Success practice selection, pp. 159–160, in **Selection Support.**
- To help students complete the Writing Mini-Lesson on p. 460, have groups brainstorm for prequels to stories with which they are familiar, and then share some with the class. After students complete their prequels to this story, invite volunteers to read theirs aloud. Students can critique classmates' efforts with the Reading for Success strategies of identifying with characters, making inferences, and questioning.

Develop Understanding

One-Minute Insight

"After Twenty Years" shows how people change over time—two old friends, one now a shady character wanted by the law, the other, now a police officer, meet as planned after a twenty-year separation. Neither the reader nor the criminal realizes that the uniformed police officer is his old friend. However, the officer recognizes the man, both as his old friend and as one being sought for crimes committed elsewhere. Although he cannot bring himself to make the arrest, the duty-bound cop engages a plain clothes colleague to do so.

Thematic Focus

❶ **Trouble Brewing** What might the police officer think when he sees the man lurking in the darkened doorway? *Possible response: He may think that a man who stays in the shadows, who keeps his cigar unlit, wants to go unnoticed.*

Reading for Success

❷ **Predict** Encourage students to use the story's title along with what they have already read to make their predictions. *Students may say that the story will be about what will happen at a meeting planned twenty years earlier.*

Customize for *English Language Learners*

O. Henry punctuates his writing with precise verbs and modifiers. Help students understand the meanings of these words by providing familiar synonyms and also physical demonstrations. For instance, invite a student who can do so to "twirl" a club, like a baton, with "intricate and artful movements."

Customize for *Visual/Spatial Learners*

Guide students to examine the illustrations that accompany the piece to help them understand where and when the story is set. Ask them to infer what the series of pictures of street lamps indicates about the story. Students may suggest that the lamps will shed light on something, that they will make the truth come to light.

Reading for Success

1 Make Inferences Help students combine the story's information with their own experiences to make other inferences about the man. *Students may say that his "pale" face indicates that he doesn't work outdoors and that his scar may point to a life that has seen some violence.*

Customize for
Interpersonal Learners
Discuss with students that two men made an arrangement to meet twenty years later, no matter what circumstances each found himself in. Ask pairs of students to imagine themselves making that same agreement with a friend. Have each write down a prediction of what he or she and the friend will be up to in twenty years. Then have partners swap descriptions and discuss them.

years ago. Sounds a little funny to you, doesn't it? Well, I'll explain if you'd like to make certain it's all straight. About that long ago there used to be a restaurant where this store stands—'Big Joe' Brady's restaurant."

"Until five years ago," said the policeman. "It was torn down then."

The man in the doorway struck a match and lit his cigar. The light showed a pale, square-jawed face with keen eyes, and a little white scar near his right eyebrow. His scarfpin was a large diamond, oddly set.

> The diamond scarfpin might lead you to **infer** that the man is wealthy and likes to show off. 1

"Twenty years ago tonight," said the man, "I dined here at 'Big Joe' Brady's with Jimmy Wells, my best chum, and the finest chap in the world. He and I were raised here in New York, just like two brothers, together. I was

Humanities: Art

Nighthawks, 1942, by Edward Hopper

Edward Hopper (1882–1967) led a simple and unremarkable life devoted to his art. Best known for his paintings of ordinary urban scenes, houses, and bleak, lonely streets and rooms, he claimed that he did not intend his paintings to show the dark emotions and moods they often do. Rather, he saw them as attempts to capture surroundings, color, and especially the quality of light. Use these questions for discussion:

1. How can you tell that this is a city scene from the past? *Students may refer to the all-night lunch counter, a darkened doorway, and the time as night.*
2. How does the artist create a sense of detachment, or loneliness, in the painting? *Students can point to the mostly solitary figures and their turned-down faces, the dark clothes, and the darkness behind each window.*
3. Is this painting a good illustration for this story? Explain. *Some students may say that the painting captures the story's city setting and somber mood; others may feel that the story's characters should be portrayed.*

Nighthawks, 1942, Edward Hopper, The Art Institute of Chicago

◀ **Critical Viewing** What details in this painting match the setting of the story? **[Connect]** ❷

To **identify** with the man, think about the way you feel about very close friends that you have known for a long time.

eighteen and Jimmy was twenty. The next morning I was to start for the West to make my fortune. You couldn't have dragged Jimmy out of New York; he thought it was the only place on earth. Well, we agreed
❸ that night that we would meet here again exactly twenty years from that date and time, no matter what our conditions might be or from what distance we might have to come. We figured that in twenty years each of us ought to have our destiny worked out and our fortunes made, whatever they were going to be." ❸

◆ **Build Vocabulary**

destiny (des´ tə nē) *n.*: What will necessarily happen to any person or thing; fate

▶Critical Viewing◀

❷ **Connect** *The setting is clearly urban, possibly a street corner in New York City. It is night outside the diner. Across the street from the diner is the recessed doorway of a closed business similar to the one described in the story.*

Reading for Success

❸ **Predict** The man in the doorway tells the police officer about the plan that he and his friend made twenty years before. Ask students to predict whether he will ever meet up with his friend, explaining why or why not. If they think the meeting will occur, ask them if they think it will turn out to be as enjoyable a rendezvous as he seems to think it will be. *Students may predict that the meeting will include some surprises, although they are unlikely to predict its dismal consequences.*

Viewing and Representing Mini-Lesson

Illustrating the Story

Like the Wanted Poster project in the Idea Bank on p. 460, this mini-lesson will extend students' visual sense of the story and its characters.

Introduce Have students imagine that "After Twenty Years" is being made into a TV movie and that they are responsible for the advertising campaign. Tell them that their job is to design a movie poster for bus stops and train platforms, and an illustration for the covers of magazines.

Develop Movie posters and other promotional illustrations are carefully designed to generate interest in the product. Discuss what kinds of visual information usually appear in movie posters and ads, and which ad features students find most effective. Then have students form advertising teams to plan and create their posters and illustrations. If possible, each group should have a student with some drawing ability.

Apply Have group members pool their ideas to create their finished posters and cover illustrations. Each group should share its work as if it were part of an ad presentation for the movie company. Presenters should include rationales for group decisions.

Assess Have the class judge posters and illustrations based on categories they define. Have them choose ones they agree are most effective. Which best capture the essence of the story and its characters? Which make you want to see the movie? Which make you want to avoid it?

Reading for Success

1 Question What has the man been up to in the West? *Students may say that his description of the West as a "big proposition" and his activities "hustling around" lead them to think that he's been speculating, gambling, or involved in some other business activities that may not be on the up and up.*

Reading for Success

2 Identify With the Character The man recalls the exact time of the meeting, even though it took place twenty years ago. Why? Would you? *Students may guess that either the man was a dear friend to Wells or that he has a remarkable memory for certain things, perhaps cards, timetables, or safe combinations. Students will have mixed reactions to whether they would recall this exact detail, but most will indicate that the meeting has carried importance throughout the twenty years.*

Comprehension Check ☑

3 Make sure students understand this passage, which is filled with slang descriptions, some of which may be unfamiliar to them. For example, point out that Bob used all his wits to successfully outsmart other hustlers competing for the same easy money. Living that kind of life required him to think quickly on his feet; he thought of Wells as unequal to such an exciting, fast-paced life full of possibilities and dangers.

Reading for Success

4 Question Ask students to explain why the police officer asked the man if he was going to "call time on him sharp." Ask this question again once students have finished reading the story. *Although many students are unlikely to spot this clue, some may eventually recognize that Wells was trying to find out whether the man would stay there long enough for him to call a plain clothes officer to the meeting place.*

"It sounds pretty interesting," said the policeman. "Rather a long time between meets, though, it seems to me. Haven't you heard from your friend since you left?"

"Well, yes, for a time we corresponded," said the other. "But after a year or two we lost track of each other. You see, the West is a pretty big proposition, and I kept hustling around over it pretty lively. But I know Jimmy will meet me here if he's alive, for he always was the truest, stanchest old chap in the world. He'll never forget. I came a thousand miles to stand in this door to-night, and it's worth it if my old partner turns up." [1]

The waiting man pulled out a handsome watch, the lids of it set with small diamonds.

"Three minutes to ten," he announced. "It was exactly ten o'clock when we parted here at the restaurant door." [2]

"Did pretty well out West, didn't you?" asked the policeman.

"You bet! I hope Jimmy has done half as well. He was a kind of plodder, though, good fellow as he was. I've had to compete with some of the sharpest wits going to get my pile. A man gets in a groove in New York. It takes the West to put a razor-edge on him." [3]

> Up to this point, the man has said only good things about his friend. However, you can **infer** from these statements that the man feels superior to Jimmy.

The policeman twirled his club and took a step or two.

"I'll be on my way. Hope your friend comes around all right. Going to call time on him sharp?" [4]

"I should say not!" said the other. "I'll give him half an hour at least. If Jimmy is alive on earth he'll be here by that time. So long, officer."

"Good-night, sir," said the policeman, passing on along his beat, trying doors as he went.

> The long conversation with the policeman might cause you to ask the **question:** Why is the policeman so interested in the man?

There was now a fine, cold drizzle falling, and the wind had risen from its uncertain puffs into a steady blow. The few foot passengers astir in that quarter hurried dismally and silently along with coat collars turned high and pocketed hands. And in the door of the hardware store the man who had come a thousand miles to fill an appointment, uncertain almost to absurdity, with the friend of his youth, smoked his cigar and waited.

About twenty minutes he waited, and then a tall man in a long overcoat, with collar turned up to his

Beyond the Classroom

Career Connection

Law Enforcement Jimmy has put his efforts into protecting his community as a police officer. There are many different branches of law enforcement, with many kinds of jobs in each—officers who patrol on foot, homicide detectives, the President's Secret Service, FBI agents, and the Attorney General's office. Opportunities abound for those who want to serve their community or country by participating in law enforcement. Of all the jobs in law enforcement, the "cop on the beat" is the most visible.

Have groups of students research and discuss the role of the "beat cop." Encourage them to interview local police officers to find out more about what the job of patrolling the streets involves and what the officers think about their jobs. Students can ask specific questions to learn information such as the size of a beat, the hours of a patrol, how they measure success in their jobs, how officers feel about their communities, and how people respond to them. Have groups share findings. If possible, invite a police officer to address your class.

ears, hurried across from the opposite side of the street. He went directly to the waiting man.

"Is that you, Bob?" he asked, doubtfully.

"Is that you, Jimmy Wells?" cried the man in the door.

"Bless my heart!" exclaimed the new arrival, grasping both the other's hands with his own. "It's Bob, sure as fate. I was certain I'd find you here if you were still in existence. Well, well, well!—twenty years is a long time. The old restaurant's gone, Bob; I wish it had lasted, so we could have had another dinner there. How has the West treated you, old man?"

"Bully;[3] it has given me everything I asked it for. You've changed lots, Jimmy. I never thought you were so tall by two or three inches."

"Oh, I grew a bit after I was twenty."

"Doing well in New York, Jimmy?"

"Moderately. I have a position in one of the city depart-
5 ments. Come on, Bob; we'll go around to a place I know of, and have a good long talk about old times."

The two men started up the street, arm in arm. The man from the West, his egotism enlarged by success, was beginning to outline the history of his career. The other, submerged in his overcoat, listened with interest.

6 At the corner stood a drug store, brilliant with electric lights. When they
7 came into this glare each of them turned simultaneously to gaze upon the other's face.

> **Predict** what the brilliant lights of the drugstore might reveal.

The man from the West stopped suddenly and released his arm.

"You're not Jimmy Wells," he snapped. "Twenty years is a long time, but not long enough to change a man's nose from a Roman to a pug."[4]

> You might **question** why the tall man's statement is important to the action of the story and to the author's message.

"It sometimes changes a good man
8 into a bad one," said the tall man. "You've been under arrest for ten minutes, 'Silky' Bob. Chicago thinks you

3. **Bully:** Very well.

4. **change a man's nose from a Roman to a pug:** A Roman nose has a high, prominent bridge; a pug nose is short, thick, and turned up at the end.

◆ Build Vocabulary

dismally (diz´ məl lē) *adv.*: Gloomily; miserably

absurdity (ab sʉr´ də tē) *n.*: Nonsense; foolishness

simultaneously (sī´ məl tā´ nē əs lē) *adv.*: At the same time

Reading for Success

5 Question Notice that O. Henry does not indicate that the person speaking with Bob is Jimmy Wells. After students read the entire story, you may wish to come back to this point in the text to discuss the clue the author placed here.

Clarification

6 The store is described as being brilliant with electric lights. Point out to students that electric lighting was relatively new technology when O. Henry wrote this story. In fact, it wasn't until the early 1880's that Thomas Edison was able to build a power plant that could light several buildings. In 1882, he provided electric light for 85 buildings in New York City's financial district.

Reading for Success

7 Predict *Students will probably say that the bright lights may reveal something important about one or the other of the men. Some students may be wondering whether perhaps one of the men is not who he appears to be.*

Comprehension Check ☑

8 What is the tall man saying about how time has affected Bob? What does he mean by "Chicago thinks…"? *He is saying that time has turned Bob into a criminal. "Chicago" refers to the police department of that city.*

Speaking and Listening Mini-Lesson

Tabloid Television

This mini-lesson supports the Speaking and Listening activity in the Idea Bank on p. 460.

Introduce Discuss the format, topics, and nature of daytime talk shows. Have students suggest possible interview formats, and guidelines for audience participation that they might use in their own productions.

Develop Select students to act as Jimmy, Bob, and the host. Invite other students to participate as the "studio audience." You may wish to assign a student the role of director, one who will communicate with the interviewer to keep the show and its interview moving. You also might include other characters to be interviewed, such as the plain clothes officer, or other characters from Jimmy's and Bob's past. All participants should know their roles. Peer coaches can help make sure that each participant is fully in character. For example, the actor playing Bob must be cocky, chatty, use slang language effortlessly, and be prepared to name places he's been and tell what he did there.

Apply If possible, videotape the show as students perform. Students may wish to produce and insert commercials for products—perhaps scar-removal cream, plain clothes, or diamond jewelry.

Assess Evaluate students on accuracy of representation and acting and public speaking skills. Assess audience members on the strength of their questions. You can also use the Peer Assessment: Dramatic Performance form, p. 107, in **Alternative Assessment.**

Reading for Success

1 Question Neither man seemed to be who the other one thought he would be.

Reinforce and Extend

Answers

◆ Literature and Your Life

Reader's Response Students may say that he was doing his job or he should have been loyal to his friend.

Thematic Focus People always change over time.

Check Your Comprehension

1. The two men promised to meet twenty years later at the same place from which they parted.
2. Bob believes Jimmy to be a good person, but a bit of a plodder.
3. (a) Bob thinks the West makes a person sharp. (b) He thinks people become complacent in New York.
4. When they step into the light, Bob sees that the other man has a different nose than Jimmy's.
5. He is a plain clothes police officer who has come to arrest Bob.

◆ Critical Thinking

1. Bob is more ambitious and adventurous than Jimmy; Jimmy has stronger ties to his hometown.
2. Both show up for the meeting, a sign that they value friendship. Bob is talkative, boastful, and probably dishonest. Jimmy is more quiet, dedicated to his work, and abides by the law despite personal costs.
3. Jimmy still lives in the city where he grew up; since he patrols a beat, he doesn't seem to want to change his job for a promotion.
4. Students can infer that Bob has moved around quite a bit and gotten some flashy possessions, suggesting he makes a lot of money.
5. It suggests that circumstances can change people in some ways, but not others. Bob may have broken the law, but he is still a loyal friend.
6. Students may say that Jimmy has been more successful since he is a good citizen contributing to society; Bob has succeeded at having an exciting life, although it appears to include illegal activities.
7. (a) O. Henry believes that people change. (b) Students may suggest that people need to recognize and act upon these changes.

may have dropped over our way and wires us she wants to have a chat with you. Going quietly are you? That's sensible. Now, before we go to the station here's a note I was asked to hand to you. You may read it here at the window. It's from Patrolman Wells."

The man from the West unfolded the little piece of paper handed him. His hand was steady when he began to read, but it trembled a little by the time he had finished. The note was rather short.

This surprise ending might prompt you to ask the **question:** What are the clues that would have allowed me to guess that this would happen?

Bob: I was at the appointed place on time. When you struck the match to light your cigar I saw it was the face of the man wanted in Chicago. Somehow I couldn't do it myself, so I went around and got a plain clothes man to do the job. Jimmy. 1

Guide for Responding

◆ Literature and Your Life

Reader's Response Do you think that Patrolman Wells did the right thing? Explain.

Thematic Focus Bob seems to assume that time has not changed him or Jimmy. Why do assumptions like Bob's lead to trouble?

Journal Writing In a journal entry, explain whether you think Jimmy Wells should or should not have arranged for his friend's arrest.

Check Your Comprehension

1. What promise did Bob and Jimmy make to each other twenty years ago?
2. What type of person does Bob believe Jimmy to be?
3. (a) According to Bob, how does the West affect a person? (b) In contrast, how does he say New York affects a person?
4. Why does Bob realize that the man in the long overcoat is not Jimmy?
5. Who is the man in the long overcoat, and why is he pretending to be Jimmy?

◆ Critical Thinking

INTERPRET

1. What can you infer about the personalities of the two men from Bob's decision to go West and Jimmy's decision to remain in New York? **[Infer]**
2. (a) How are Bob and Jimmy similar? (b) How are they different? **[Compare and Contrast]**
3. How much has Jimmy changed over the years? Support your answer with evidence from the story. **[Support]**
4. How has Bob spent his time in the West? **[Infer]**
5. What does this story suggest about the way the passage of time affects people? **[Draw Conclusions]**

EVALUATE

6. Who has been more successful, Bob or Jimmy? Explain your answer. **[Make a Judgment]**

APPLY

7. (a) What do you think is the author's message in this story? (b) How does this message apply to your own life? **[Relate]**

Beyond the Selection

FURTHER READING

Other Works by O. Henry

The Ransom of Red Chief and Other Stories
The Gift of the Magi and Other Stories
Tales of O. Henry

Other Works With Surprise Endings

Back of Beyond: Stories, Sarah Ellis
Mystery Stories, compiled by Helen Cresswell
The Adventures of Sherlock Homes, Sir Arthur Conan Doyle

INTERNET

We suggest the following site on the Internet (all Web sites are subject to change).

For more information about William Sydney Porter's life and work, including photos (one of him as bank teller) and links to other sites:
http://www.utexas.edu/courses/mis311f/history/hist028.htm

We *strongly recommend* that you preview the site before you send students to it.

Guide for Responding (continued)

◆ Reading Strategy

STRATEGIES FOR READING FICTION

Apply the reading strategies and notes showing how to read fiction to answer these questions.

1. What can you tell about Bob's character from the first description of him on page 454?

2. How might the policeman's question—"Going to call time on him sharp?"—on page 456 have helped you predict the story's surprise ending?

◆ Build Vocabulary

USING THE WORD ROOT *-spec-*

The word root *-spec-* means "see" or "look." Define each of the following words, incorporating the definition of *-spec-* into each answer.

1. spectacle
2. prospector
3. respect
4. inspect

SPELLING STRATEGY

Words that describe people who do something or are something often end with the sound ər, which can be spelled *-er* (teacher) or *-or* (professor). Use the *-or* spelling when the word is based on a verb that ends in *-ate*, *-ct*, or *-ess*.

On your paper, write the word that describes a person who performs each of the following actions.

1. decorate	**3.** act	**5.** process
2. direct	**4.** spectate	**6.** collect

USING THE WORD BANK

Answer the following questions. Explain each answer.

1. Can a person avoid his or her *destiny*?

2. Do ordering a book on the Web and receiving the book in the mail happen *simultaneously*?

3. Would you find the *spectators* at a baseball game in the stands or on the field?

4. Is a duck in a three-piece suit an *absurdity*?

5. Would a delighted child regard the perfect birthday gift *dismally*?

6. Which would you describe as *intricate*—a plain sheet of paper or an elaborate piece of lace?

◆ Literary Focus

SURPRISE ENDING

When an author ends a story with an unexpected twist, it is called a **surprise ending.** O. Henry is famous for springing such surprises.

1. Why does the ending come as a surprise?

2. Look back at the story. What clues prepared you for the surprise ending?

3. What does the ending suggest about human relationships and behavior?

◆ Build Grammar Skills

CLAUSES

A **clause** is a group of words with its own subject and verb. The two major types of clauses are independent clauses and subordinate clauses. An independent (main) clause has a subject and verb and can stand by itself as a complete sentence. A subordinate clause has a subject and a verb but is only part of a sentence.

Subordinate Clause — Independent Clause

[When they came into the glare,] (S: they; V: came) [each of them turned to gaze upon the other.] (S: each; V: turned)

Practice Copy the following sentences on your paper. Bracket each clause as in the example above, and identify each as *independent* or *subordinate*. Write *S* above the subject and *V* above the verb.

1. We agreed that night that we would meet again.

2. If Jimmy is alive on earth, he'll be here.

3. When I see him, I'll ask about his life.

4. After he waited twenty minutes, he saw a tall man hurry across the street.

5. When you struck the match, I saw it was the face of the man wanted in Chicago.

Writing Application Using every other line on a piece of paper, write a paragraph about the story. Then, bracket and label the independent and subordinate clauses. For each clause, write *S* above the subject and *V* above the verb.

Answers

▸Reading Strategy

1. His diamond pin and cigar suggest that he has money and likes to show off. The scar suggests that he may be a shady character.
2. Students may realize that the policeman wanted to know what time the meeting would take place so that he could do something for or about the man.

▸Build Vocabulary

Using the Word Root *-spec-*

1. A spectacle is a "strange or remarkable sight."
2. A prospector looks around for things of value, such as gold.
3. If you respect someone, you look at that person with admiration.
3. To inspect a new garment for flaws, you have to look at it carefully.

Spelling Strategy

1. decorator
2. director
3. actor
4. spectator
5. processor
6. collector

Using the Word Bank

1. No; he or she cannot control what will happen.
2. No; the book must be ordered before it can be received.
3. They are in the stands because spectators are onlookers.
4. Yes; the idea of a duck in a suit is nonsensical.
5. No; a delighted child would not regard a gift gloomily.
6. An elaborate piece of lace is intricate because of its detail.

▸Literary Focus

1. Most students will be surprised that the patrolman turned out to be Jimmy Wells and that the man in the overcoat was also a cop.
2. Students may point to Bob's dress and attitude, the police officer's questioning and interest in him, and the appearance of the plain clothes man, who wore his collar up to hide his face.
3. People and relationships change over time, people are not always what they may seem, and people may need to make hard choices between duty and friendship.

◆Build Grammar Skills

Practice

1. Ind: We . . . night; S = We; V = agreed; Sub: that . . . again; S = we; V = would meet
2. Sub: If . . . earth; S = Jimmy; V = is; Ind: he'll . . . here; S = he; V = will be
3. Sub: When . . . him; S = I; V = see; Ind: I'll ask . . . life; S = I; V = ask
4. Sub: After . . . twenty mintues; S = he; V = waited; Ind: he . . . the street; S = he; V = saw
5. Sub: When . . . match; S = you; V = struck; Ind: I saw; S = I; V = saw; Sub: it . . . Chicago; S = it; V = was

Writing Application

Students' paragraphs should have independent and subordinate clauses correctly identified.

For additional instruction and practice, use the lesson in the *Writer's Solution Language Lab CD-ROM* on Styling Sentences, and the practice pages on Diagraming Clauses, p. 56, in the *Writer's Solution Grammar Practice Book*.

Idea Bank

Following are suggestions for matching the Idea Bank topics with your students' performance levels and learning modalities:

Customize for
Performance Levels
Less Advanced Students: 1, 4, 6
Average Students: 2, 3, 4, 6
More Advanced Students: 3, 5, 7

Customize for
Learning Modalities
Verbal/Linguistic: 1, 2, 3, 4, 5, 7
Visual/Spatial: 6, 7
Logical/Mathematical: 3, 5, 6
Interpersonal: 4, 5
Intrapersonal: 1

Writing Mini-Lesson

Refer students to the Writing Handbook in the back of the book for instructions on the writing process and for further information on writing a prequel.

Writer's Solution

Writing Lab CD-ROM
Have students complete the tutorial on Creative Writing. Follow these steps:

1. Have students use the Character Trait Word Bin to establish characters.
2. Suggest that students view interactive writing instruction about character traits to see how dialogue can express a quality.
3. Have students draft on computer.
4. Encourage students to use interactive instruction in verb tense when revising.

Writer's Solution Sourcebook
Have students use Chapter 8, "Creative Writing," pp. 234–263, for additional support. The chapter includes in-depth instruction on using punctuation and formatting dialogue, p. 261.

Build Your Portfolio

Idea Bank

Writing

1. **Friendship List** Make a list of the ten qualities you think are most important in a friend. For each item on your list, write a sentence or two explaining why you included it.
2. **Letter From Prison** Write a letter to Patrolman Wells from "Silky" Bob. In your letter, describe the events of the story from Bob's point of view. Express Bob's feelings about his friend's actions. Is he angry, or does he understand why Jimmy had to turn him in?
3. **Police Report** Imagine that you are Jimmy Wells. Write a report on the arrest of "Silky" Bob. Explain how you discovered the wanted criminal and arranged for him to be brought into police custody. **[Career Link]**

Speaking and Listening

4. **News Bulletin** Write a brief radio news bulletin about the arrest of "Silky" Bob. In the role of a radio announcer, read your bulletin to the class.
5. **Tabloid Television [Group Activity]** With a group, act out an interview of Jimmy and Bob on a daytime talk show after the arrest. Roles for your performance might include Jimmy, Bob, the talk-show host, and members of the studio audience. **[Performing Arts Link]**

Projects

6. **Wanted Poster** Create a wanted poster for "Silky" Bob. Make a drawing that shows what he looks like. Provide information about his real name and aliases, distinguishing characteristics, and crimes. **[Art Link]**
7. **New York in 1900** Create an illustrated report describing life in New York City at the time of "After Twenty Years." Where did people live and work? What did they do for fun? What did the buildings look like? Present your findings to the class. **[Social Studies Link]**

Writing Mini-Lesson

Prequel

In this story, Bob talks fondly of his old friend Jimmy and describes how they were raised together "just like two brothers." The things Bob says, together with the surprise ending, might make you wonder what the friendship was really like, twenty years before. Using what you know about the events and characters, write a prequel, or story before a story, about Bob and Jimmy.

Writing Skills Focus: Use Dialogue

To make your prequel more engaging and realistic, **use dialogue** to show the relationship between Jimmy and Bob. You can also use dialogue to reveal the personalities of the two characters. Notice how O. Henry uses dialogue to hint at Bob's shady activities:

Model From the Story

"You see, the West is a pretty big proposition, and I kept hustling around over it pretty lively."

Prewriting Prepare a two-column chart. In one column, list Bob's characteristics. In the other column, list Jimmy's characteristics.

Drafting Build your prequel around revealing conversations between the two characters. Make sure that what the characters say and how they say it are consistent with their personalities.

Revising Revise your prequel by looking for the passages where you simply describe the characters. Replace these passages with dialogue that shows the characters' personalities and relationships.

◆ Grammar Application

Vary your sentences by using independent and subordinate clauses. You can also show supporting or modifying ideas by attaching them as subordinate clauses to an independent clause.

ASSESSMENT OPTIONS

Formal Assessment, Selection Test, pp. 135–137, and Assessment Resources Software. The selection test is designed so that it can be easily customized to the performance levels of your students.

Alternative Assessment, p. 29, includes options for less advanced students, more advanced students, verbal/linguistic learners, logical/mathematical learners, interpersonal learners, and musical/rhythmic learners.

PORTFOLIO ASSESSMENT
Use the following rubrics in the **Alternative Assessment** booklet to assess student writing:
Friendship List: Expression, p. 81
Letter From Prison: Fictional Narrative, p. 82
Police Report: Problem/Solution, p. 88
Writing Mini-Lesson: Description, p. 84

PART 1 Plot and Character

Illustrated by John Tenniel

One-Minute Planning Guide

The short stories in this section explore the literary elements of plot and character. In "Rikki-tikki-tavi," the plot hinges on a conflict between a clever mongoose and two deadly cobras. "Papa's Parrot" and "Stolen Day" both feature memorable characters who learn important lessons. In "Lather and Nothing Else," a barber faces an agonizing conflict about his own course of action during his country's civil war.

Customize for
Varying Student Needs

When assigning the selections in this section to your students, keep in mind the following factors:

"Rikki-tikki-tavi"

- A longer short story (12 pp.)
- Personification of animals in the story may engage students

"Papa's Parrot"

- Contemporary, accessible story

"Stolen Day"

- Many students will relate to the situation and emotions described by the main character
- Students may need help distinguishing present action from flashback at certain points in the story

"Lather and Nothing Else"

- Short historical fiction piece
- An opportunity for connecting literature to social studies.

Humanities: Art

Illustration From *Through the Looking Glass,* by John Tenniel

John Tenniel (1820–1914) was born in London and is famous for his cartoons in *Punch* magazine as well as his illustrations for Lewis Carroll's classics, *Alice in Wonderland* and *Through the Looking Glass*. He received formal training at the Royal Academy and was knighted in 1893.

Ask students who know the stories of *Alice in Wonderland* or *Through the Looking Glass* to discuss their favorite characters and share the stories' plots with the class. Explain to students that in this scene, Alice meets Tweedledee and Tweedledum. Then discuss these questions:

1. Using this illustration, describe each character. *Students should base their descriptions on the characters' expressions, clothing, and how they are standing in the illustration.*
2. What details of the illustration suggest that the story is fantastical? *Tweedledee and Tweedledum look like overgrown school children. They are exaggeratedly large, have their arms crossed around each other, and seem to look at Alice suspiciously.*

OBJECTIVES

1. To read, comprehend, and interpret a short story
2. To relate a short story to personal experience
3. To apply predicting as a reading strategy
4. To understand the elements of plot
5. To build vocabulary in context and learn the word root *-viv-*
6. To recognize simple and compound sentences
7. To write a factual report on natural enemies, using details to describe the environment
8. To respond to a short story through writing, speaking and listening, and projects

SKILLS INSTRUCTION

Vocabulary: Word Roots: *-viv-*
Spelling: Homophones
Grammar: Simple and Compound Sentences
Reading Strategy: Predict
Literary Focus: Plot
Writing: Details to Describe the Environment
Speaking and Listening: First-Aid Demonstration (Teacher Edition)
Critical Viewing: Assess; Interpret; Analyze; Evaluate; Hypothesize

PORTFOLIO OPPORTUNITIES

Writing: Picture Book for First Graders; Letter; Comparison-and-Contrast Essay

Writing Mini-Lesson: Report on Natural Enemies

Speaking and Listening: Play-by-Play Account; First-Aid Demonstration

Projects: Wildlife Collage; Multimedia Report

More About the Author
Rudyard Kipling's complete works include 35 volumes of stories, novels, essays, sketches, speeches, poetry, and an unfinished autobiography. Critics have debated the merits of his work, but his admirers have included famous poets, such as T. S. Eliot and William Butler Yeats, and scores of everyday readers who have enjoyed his tales, poetry, and enduring children's works.

Guide for Reading

Meet the Author:
Rudyard Kipling (1865–1936)

You may be most familiar with Rudyard Kipling's works through the numerous animated and live-action movies of *The Jungle Book*. Two other works that have become children's classics and have been made into movies are *Kim* and *Captains Courageous*.

An Award-Winning Writer In addition to his famous works for children, Kipling wrote a huge number of other works. His complete works encompass thirty-five volumes of stories, novels, essays, sketches, poetry, speeches, and an unfinished biography. One of his most famous poems, "If—" appears on page 138 in this book.

Kipling's poems and stories made him a celebrity during his lifetime. In 1907, he was awarded the Nobel Prize for Literature. [For more on Kipling, see page 134.]

The Story Behind the Story

Kipling was born in Bombay, India, to English parents. Although he moved to England when he was six, Kipling remained strongly attached to the land of his birth. In 1882, he returned to India to work as a journalist. He was particularly fascinated by the country's wildlife, and he was a keen observer of animal behavior. "Rikki-tikki-tavi," which is set in India and focuses on animal characters, reflects Kipling's love of the Indian landscape and his knowledge of the country's animals.

◆ Literature and Your Life

Connect Your Experience

You have probably seen for yourself that some animals appear to be natural enemies. Birds are the natural enemies of worms, and cats are the natural enemies of birds. In this story, you will meet two natural enemies that you probably have not encountered in everyday life: the mongoose and the cobra.

Thematic Focus: Nature's Wonders

What can we learn from conflicts in nature such as the one between the mongoose and the cobra?

◆ Background for Understanding

Science

The deadly Indian cobra grows to be about six feet long and six inches around. Cobras feed on small animals such as mice and frogs. Just before striking, a cobra raises the front part of its body straight up and spreads the ribs near its head to form a hood.

The mongoose is a brown, furry animal about fifteen inches long from the tip of its pointed nose to the base of its ten-inch tail—about the right size for a cobra's meal. However, a mongoose is fast and fierce. In a battle between a mongoose and a cobra, the cobra usually ends up as the mongoose's meal.

◆ Build Vocabulary

Word Roots: *-viv-*

In this story, a mongoose is revived after it nearly drowns. The word *revived* contains the root *-viv-*, meaning "life," and means "come back to life."

Word Bank

Which of these words from the story might describe action that is done cleverly? Check the Build Vocabulary boxes to see.

revived
draggled
flinched
mourning
consolation
cunningly

Prentice Hall Literature Program Resources

REINFORCE / RETEACH / EXTEND

Selection Support Pages
Build Vocabulary: Word Roots: *-viv-*, p. 162
Build Spelling Skills: p. 163
Build Grammar Skills: Simple and Compound Sentences, p. 164
Reading Strategy: Predict, p. 165
Literary Focus: Plot, p. 166

Strategies for Diverse Student Needs, p. 59
Beyond Literature: Study Skills: Organize Information in a Chart, p. 30

Formal Assessment Selection Test, pp. 138–140, Assessment Resources Software
Alternative Assessment, p. 30
Writing and Language Transparencies Sunburst Organizer, p. 94
Daily Language Practice, p. 14
Resource Pro CD-ROM "Rikki-tikki-tavi"—includes all resource material and customizable lesson plan

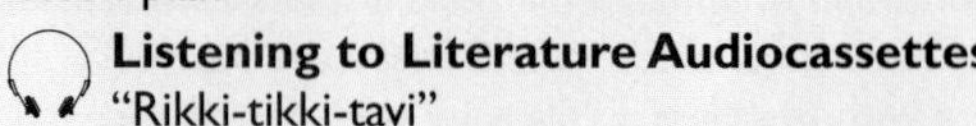

Listening to Literature Audiocassettes "Rikki-tikki-tavi"

Rikki-tikki-tavi

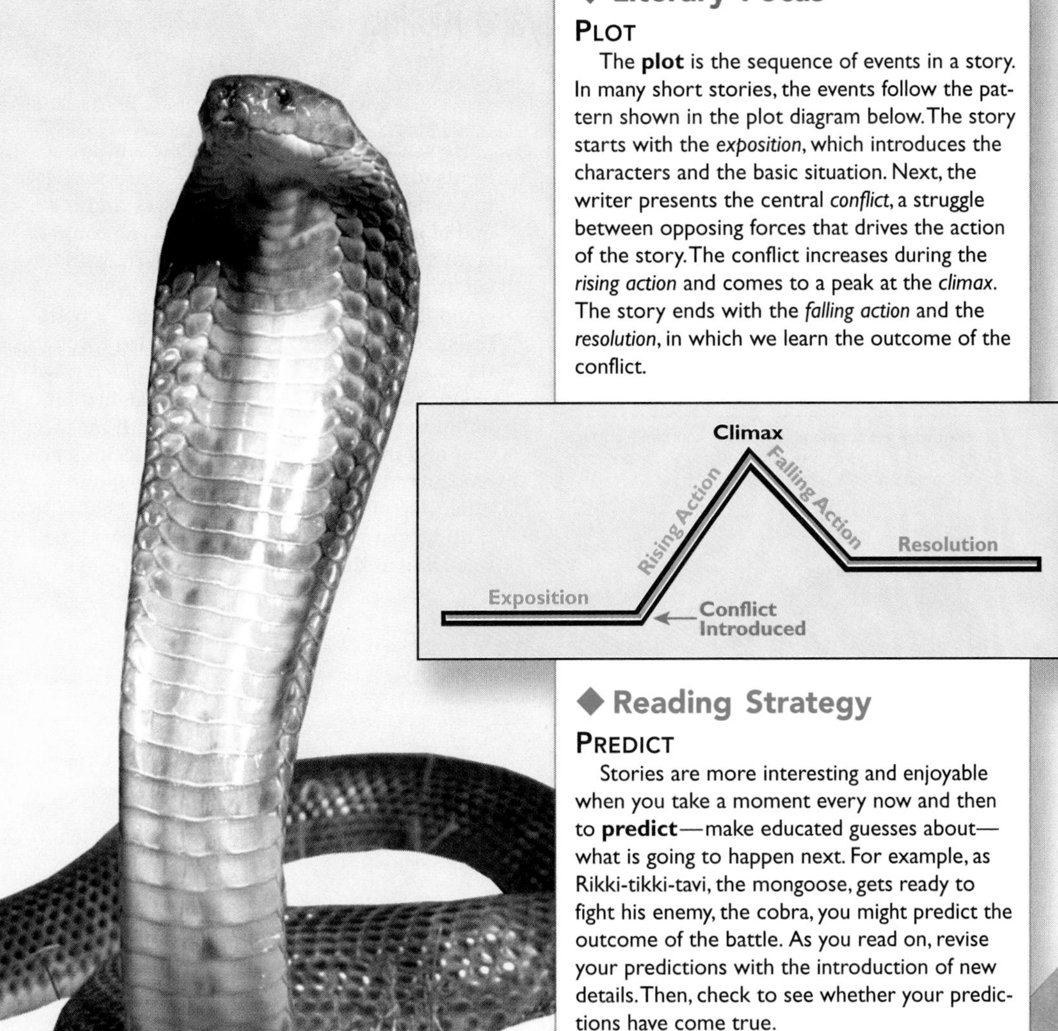

◆ Literary Focus

Plot

The **plot** is the sequence of events in a story. In many short stories, the events follow the pattern shown in the plot diagram below. The story starts with the *exposition*, which introduces the characters and the basic situation. Next, the writer presents the central *conflict*, a struggle between opposing forces that drives the action of the story. The conflict increases during the *rising action* and comes to a peak at the *climax*. The story ends with the *falling action* and the *resolution*, in which we learn the outcome of the conflict.

◆ Reading Strategy

Predict

Stories are more interesting and enjoyable when you take a moment every now and then to **predict**—make educated guesses about—what is going to happen next. For example, as Rikki-tikki-tavi, the mongoose, gets ready to fight his enemy, the cobra, you might predict the outcome of the battle. As you read on, revise your predictions with the introduction of new details. Then, check to see whether your predictions have come true.

Preparing for Standardized Tests

Spelling This selection presents a spelling strategy that can help students with reading in general, as well as with specific mechanics items on standardized tests. Standardized tests may evaluate students' understanding of *homophones*: words that sound alike but have different meanings and spellings. Write the following sample test question on the board and challenge students to answer it:

Identify the sentence in which the correct homophone is used.

(A) In this *tail*, enemies fight to the death.
(B) The water jar *breaks* during the fight.
(C) Nag *rows* up to his full height.
(D) The man *beet* the snake with a stick.

Sentence *(B)* uses the correct homophone; *brakes* stop cars. In *(A)*, the homophone should be *tale*, not *tail*; in *(C)*, it should be *rose*, not *rows*; in *(D)*, it should be *beat*, not *beet*. For additional practice, use Build Spelling Skills in **Selection Support,** p. 163.

Interest Grabber Before students arrive, place a toy cat on one side of a table and a toy dog on the opposite side. When students arrive, ask them to jot down their first reactions to the animals. Then divide the class into small groups to brainstorm for descriptive phrases, adjectives, or idioms that suit these natural enemies. Observe that not even thousands of years of domestication have eliminated their natural enmity. Explore the associations we make between animal behaviors (e.g., aggression, stealth, and curiosity) and human ones. Lead students to the story by telling them that they will read about animal enemies who engage in a "great war" that is made to seem as important as a human conflict.

◆ Build Grammar Skills

Simple and Compound Sentences If you wish to introduce the grammar concept taught with this story, refer to the instruction on p. 476 before students read the story.

Customize for *Less Proficient Readers*

Kipling personifies his animal characters, giving them personality traits similar to those of humans. To help students track the humanlike traits of the nonhuman figures, hand out copies of the Sunburst Organizer (**Writing and Language Transparencies,** p. 94). In the center, have students write: Animal Characters. In each box around it, they can list the key traits of each animal character: Rikki, Nag, Nagaina, Karait, Darzee, and Darzee's wife. This graphic organizer can help them analyze characters and predict how the personified traits of each may influence the plot.

Customize for *More Advanced Students*

Challenge students to identify the key plot elements—exposition, conflict, rising action, climax, falling action, and resolution—as well as devices the author uses to advance the plot, such as flashback, foreshadowing, and repetition. Have students summarize the moral lessons the story tries to teach.

Develop Understanding

One-Minute Insight

Teddy's family, living in India, adopt a young mongoose as a pet. The mongoose, Rikki-tikki-tavi, is the natural enemy of snakes. Two dangerous cobras, Nag and Nagaina, live in the family garden and want to rule over Teddy's house. With the help of Teddy's father and the other animals, Rikki kills Nag and Nagaina and destroys their eggs. Through his triumph he earns the respect and awe of humans and animals alike.

Team Teaching Strategy

You might coordinate with a science teacher to extend instruction. For example, the science teacher could advise students in their research for the Writing Mini-Lesson or provide lessons on natural enemies in the environment of your region.

Clarification

❶ The name Rikki-tikki-tavi sounds like the cry of the mongoose; it is an example of onomatopoeia, the use of words that imitate sounds.

Customize for
English Language Learners
Students acquiring English may not be able to distinguish the names of animals from those of plants in this story. Pair students with native English speakers. Have them make a two-column chart on which to list the names of animals and plants.

Customize for
Bodily/Kinesthetic Learners
Students may better appreciate Rikki's prowess if they compare his motions to the moves of athletes. Students may picture the ready stance of a baseball infielder preparing to move in any direction for a ground ball, or the taut "dance" of a tennis player awaiting a serve. Invite students to act out these and other stances to help classmates visualize Rikki's movements.

Rudyard Kipling

❶ This is the story of the great war that Rikki-tikki-tavi fought single-handed, through the bathrooms of the big bungalow in Segowlee cantonment.[1] Darzee, the tailorbird bird, helped him, and Chuchundra,[2] the muskrat, who never comes out into the middle of the floor, but always creeps round by the wall, gave him advice; but Rikki-tikki did the real fighting.

He was a mongoose, rather like a little cat in his fur and his tail, but quite like a weasel in his head and his habits. His eyes and the end of his restless nose were pink; he could scratch himself anywhere he pleased, with any leg, front or back, that he chose to use; he could fluff up his tail till it looked like a bottle brush, and his war cry as he scuttled through the long grass, was: *"Rikk-tikk-tikki-tikki-tchk!"*

One day, a high summer flood washed him out of the burrow where he lived with his father and mother, and carried him, kicking and clucking, down a roadside ditch. He found a little wisp of grass floating there, and clung to it till he lost his senses. When he revived, he was lying in the hot sun on the middle of a

---

1. **Segowlee cantonment** (sē gou´ lē kan tän´ mənt) *n.*: Living quarters for British troops in Segowlee, India.
2. **Chuchundra** (cho͞o chun´ drə)

Block Scheduling Strategies

Consider these suggestions to take advantage of extended class time:

- Have students read the story on their own, in small groups, or listen to it on audiocassette. Discuss the Thematic Focus on p. 462 to lead into the Writing Mini-Lesson.
- Use the Literary Focus and Reading Strategy on p. 463 to guide pre- and post-reading discussions. Peer groups can answer the Reading Strategy and Literary Focus questions on p. 476.
- Devote class time for students to work in groups on the Projects in the Idea Bank on p. 477, to work independently on their chosen writing activity, or to develop the Writing Mini-Lesson.
- For practice with grammar, usage, and mechanics, have students complete the exercises in **Daily Language Practice,** Week 5, on p. 14.
- If students have access to technology, refer them to the tutorial on Report Writing on the *Writer's Solution Writing Lab CD-ROM* to help them complete the Writing Mini-Lesson.

garden path, very draggled indeed, and a small boy was saying: "Here's a dead mongoose. Let's have a funeral."

"No," said his mother; "let's take him in and dry him. Perhaps he isn't really dead."

They took him into the house, and a big man picked him up between his finger and thumb and said he was not dead but half choked; so they wrapped him in cotton wool, and warmed him, and he opened his eyes and sneezed.

2 "Now," said the big man (he was an Englishman who had just moved into the bungalow); "don't frighten him, and we'll see what he'll do."

It is the hardest thing in the world to frighten a mongoose, because he is eaten up from nose to tail with curiosity. The motto of all the mongoose family is, "Run and find out"; and Rikki-tikki was a true mongoose. He looked at the cotton wool, decided that it was not good to eat, ran all round the table, sat up and put his fur in order, scratched himself, and jumped on the small boy's shoulder.

"Don't be frightened, Teddy," said his father. "That's his way of making friends."

3 "Ouch! He's tickling under my chin," said Teddy.

Rikki-tikki looked down between the boy's collar and neck, snuffed at his ear, and climbed down to the floor, where he sat rubbing his nose.

"Good gracious," said Teddy's mother, "and that's a wild creature! I suppose he's so tame because we've been kind to him."

"All mongooses are like that," said her husband. "If Teddy doesn't pick him up by the tail, or try to put him in a cage, he'll run in and out of the house all day long. Let's give him something to eat."

They gave him a little piece of raw meat. Rikki-tikki liked it immensely, and when it was finished he went out into the veranda and sat in the sunshine and fluffed up his fur to make it dry to the roots. Then he felt better.

"There are more things to find out about in this house," he said to himself, "than all my family could find out in all their lives. I shall certainly stay and find out."

He spent all that day roaming over the house. He nearly drowned himself in the bathtubs, put his nose into the ink on a writing table, and burned it on the end of the big man's cigar, for he climbed up in the big man's lap to see how writing was done. At nightfall he ran into Teddy's nursery to watch how kerosene lamps were lighted, and when Teddy went to bed Rikki-tikki climbed up too; but he was a restless companion, because he had to get up and attend to every noise all through the night, and find out what made it. Teddy's mother and father came in, the last thing, to look at their boy, and Rikki-tikki was awake on the pillow. "I don't like that," said Teddy's mother; "he may bite the child." "He'll do no such thing," said the father. "Teddy's safer with that little beast than if he had a bloodhound to watch him. If a snake came into the nursery now—"

But Teddy's mother wouldn't think of anything so awful.

◆ **Reading Strategy** Teddy's father praises Rikki as a guardian. Based on this detail, what do you predict might happen later in the story? 5

Early in the morning Rikki-tikki came to early breakfast in the veranda riding on Teddy's shoulder, and they gave him banana and some boiled egg; and he sat on all their laps one after the other, because every well-brought-up mongoose always hopes to be a house mongoose some day and have rooms to run about in, and Rikki-tikki's mother (she used to live in the General's house at Segowlee) had carefully told Rikki what to do if ever he came across Englishmen. 6

Then Rikki-tikki went out into the garden to see what was to be seen. It was a large garden,

4 ◄ **Critical Viewing** Does the mongoose shown here appear friendly or hostile? Explain. **[Assess]**

◆ Build Vocabulary

revived (ri vīvd′) *v.*: Came back to consciousness

draggled (drag′ əld) *adj.*: Wet and dirty

Clarification

2 The British ruled India from 1858 to 1947. Many English citizens lived in India during that time. The "big man" and his family are probably in India on government service.

◆Literary Focus

3 Plot Guide students to recognize this passage as part of the exposition, in which readers learn about the main characters. Here, the details about Rikki make readers care about him and show that he is loyal, curious, and charming.

►Critical Viewing◄

4 Assess Some students may perceive the mongoose's "weasel" look as hostile; others may think this mongoose appears friendly since no other animal is challenging it.

◆Reading Strategy

5 Predict *Students may predict that Rikki will save Teddy from a snake.*

◆Build Grammar Skills

6 Simple and Compound Sentences A compound sentence has two or more independent clauses linked by coordinating conjunctions (e.g., *and*, *but*, and *yet*) or semicolons. An independent clause has a subject and a verb and can stand by itself as a complete sentence. This passage is one compound sentence composed of five independent clauses. Challenge students to identify the independent clauses. *"Early in the . . . Teddy's shoulder; they gave him . . . boiled egg; he sat on . . . run about in; Rikki-tikki's mother . . . across Englishmen; She used to . . . at Segowlee."*

Cross-Curricular Connection: Social Studies

British Raj By the early sixteenth century, Dutch, English, French, and Portuguese merchants traded with India. After India's Islamic Mogul Empire fell in 1707, India broke up into separate states with no overall leader. Soon, Britain and France vied to control the fragmented country. In 1756, the English East India Company ousted the French from India and took control of India's foreign trade. With the support of friendly local rulers, Britain began to build a powerful colonial government known as the Raj, from the Indian word for "rule." From 1858 to 1947, the Raj ran India. According to the 1901 census, about 900 British colonial officials ruled nearly 300 million Indians.

Have students research the British Raj. Guide them to explore issues such as the meaning of colonial rule, the goals of colonialism, conflicts between British civil servants and locals, and the rising Indian independence movement. They can research leaders, such as Robert Clive, Warren Hastings, and Mohandas K. Gandhi. Invite students to present their findings as oral or written reports, or multimedia or visual displays.

Clarification

❶ Kipling's names for cobras Nag and Nagaina echo *naja*, the scientific name for the genus of Asian cobras. It comes from the Hindi word for cobra.

◆Critical Thinking

❷ **Infer** Ask students to make inferences about Nag based on the details given in this passage. Draw attention to the "horrid cold sound" Nag makes that startles Rikki.
Students may judge Nag to be an evil character to fear, one associated with death.

▶Critical Viewing◀

❸ **Interpret** *The raised head and spread hood indicate that the cobra is in a state of attack.*

only half cultivated, with bushes as big as summer houses of Marshal Niel roses, lime and orange trees, clumps of bamboos, and thickets of high grass. Rikki-tikki licked his lips. "This is a splendid hunting ground," he said, and his tail grew bottlebrushy at the thought of it, and he scuttled up and down the garden, snuffing here and there till he heard very sorrowful voices in a thornbush.

It was Darzee, the tailorbird, and his wife. They had made a beautiful nest by pulling two big leaves together and stitching them up the edges with fibers, and had filled the hollow with cotton and downy fluff. The nest swayed to and fro, as they sat on the rim and cried.

"What is the matter?" asked Rikki-tikki.

"We are very miserable," said Darzee.

"One of our babies fell out of the nest yesterday and Nag[3] ate him." ❶

"H'm!" said Rikki-tikki, "that is very sad—but I am a stranger here. Who is Nag?"

Darzee and his wife only cowered down in the nest without answering, for from the thick grass at the foot of the bush there came a low hiss—a horrid cold sound that made Rikki-tikki jump back two clear feet. Then inch by inch out of the grass rose up the head and spread hood of Nag, the big black cobra, and he was five feet long from tongue to tail. When he had lifted one third of himself clear of the ground, he stayed balancing to and fro exactly as a dandelion tuft balances in the wind, and he looked at Rikki-tikki with the wicked snake's eyes that never change their expression, whatever the snake may be thinking of. ❷

"Who is Nag?" he said. "*I* am Nag. The great god Brahm[4] put his mark upon all our people when the first cobra spread his hood to keep the sun off Brahm as he slept. Look, and be afraid!"

3. **Nag** (Näg)
4. **Brahm** (bräm): Abbreviation of Brahma, the name of the chief god in the Hindu religion.

▼ Critical Viewing How might a mongoose like Rikki-tikki-tavi know that the cobra pictured here is in a state of attack? **[Interpret]** ❸

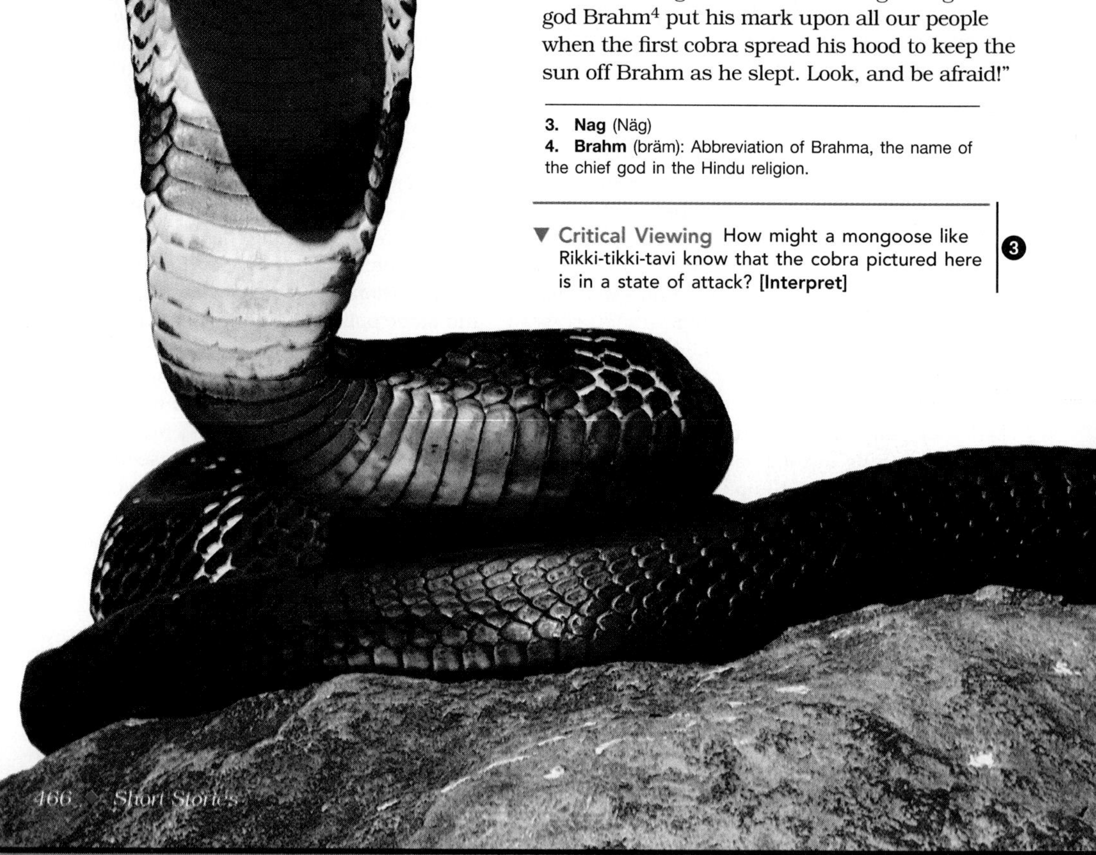

◆ Literary Focus
4 What part of the plot is Rikki's meeting with Nag?

He spread out his hood more than ever, and Rikki-tikki saw the spectacle mark on the back of it that looks exactly like the eye part of a hook-and-eye fastening. He was afraid for the minute; but it is impossible for a mongoose to stay frightened for any length of time, and though Rikki-tikki had never met a live cobra before, his mother had fed him on dead ones, and he knew that all a grown mongoose's business in life was to fight and eat snakes. Nag knew that too, and at the bottom of his cold heart he was afraid.

"Well," said Rikki-tikki, and his tail began to fluff up again, "marks or no marks, do you think it is right for you to eat fledglings out of a nest?"

Nag was thinking to himself, and watching the least little movement in the grass behind Rikki-tikki. He knew that mongooses in the garden meant death sooner or later for him and his family; but he wanted to get Rikki-tikki off his guard. So he dropped his head a little, and put it on one side.

"Let us talk," he said. "You eat eggs. Why should not I eat birds?"

"Behind you! Look behind you!" sang Darzee.

Rikki-tikki knew better than to waste time in staring. He jumped up in the air as high as he could go, and just under him whizzed by the head of Nagaina,[5] Nag's wicked wife. She had crept up behind him as he was talking, to make an end of him; and he heard her savage hiss as the stroke missed. He came down almost across her back, and if he had been an old mongoose he would have known that then was the time to break her back with one bite; but he was afraid of the terrible lashing return stroke of the cobra. He bit, indeed, but did not bite long enough, and he jumped clear of the whisking tail, leaving Nagaina torn and angry.

"Wicked, wicked Darzee!" said Nag, lashing up high as he could reach toward the nest in the thornbush; but Darzee had built it out of reach of snakes; and it only swayed to and fro.

Rikki-tikki felt his eyes growing red and hot (when a mongoose's eyes grow red, he is angry), and he sat back on his tail and hind legs like a little kangaroo, and looked all around him, and chattered with rage. But Nag and Nagaina had disappeared into the grass. When a snake misses its stroke, it never says anything or gives any sign of what it means to do next. Rikki-tikki did not care to follow them, for he did not feel sure that he could manage two snakes at once. So he trotted off to the gravel path near the house, and sat down to think. It was a serious matter for him.

If you read the old books of natural history, you will find they say that when the mongoose fights the snake and happens to get bitten, he runs off and eats some herb that cures him. That is not true. The victory is only a matter of quickness of eye and quickness of foot—snake's blow against mongoose's jump—and as no eye can follow the motion of a snake's head when it strikes, that makes things much more wonderful than any magic herb. Rikki-tikki knew he was a young mongoose, and it made him all the more pleased to think that he had managed to escape a blow from behind. It gave him confidence in himself, and when Teddy came running down the path, Rikki-tikki was ready to be petted.

But just as Teddy was stooping, something flinched a little in the dust, and a tiny voice said: "Be careful. I am death!" It

5. **Nagaina** (nə gī′ nə)

◆ **Build Vocabulary**

flinched (flincht) *v.*: Moved back, as if away from a blow

◆ Literary Focus

4 Plot *Rikki's meeting of Nag introduces the central conflict, which marks the start of the rising action.*

Clarification

5 Before attacking, a cobra flattens its neck by moving its ribs. The neck extends outward like a hood. On the back of the Indian cobra's hood is a mark that looks like a pair of old spectacles, which gave rise to the nickname "spectacled cobra." All cobras have a mark, called an eye, on the back of the open hood, to frighten enemies.

◆ Reading Strategy

6 Predict Ask students to predict why Nag tries to engage Rikki in debate. *Nag wants to distract Rikki to make him vulnerable to attack.*

◆ Critical Thinking

7 Deduce Ask students for evidence from this passage showing that Rikki is young and not yet an expert snake fighter. *He acts from instinct, not experience.*

Cross-Curricular Connection: Science

Poisonous snakes live in many regions of the world. Of nearly 2,700 snake species, about a third are poisonous, but only about 250 species pose a danger to humans.

Invite students to learn about poisonous snakes. Possible topics include poisonous snakes indigenous to your region, how to identify poisonous snakes, how the venom of different snakes works on a victim, or the biology of fangs and venom sacs. Students might make diagrams of fangs and venom sacs, maps of poisonous snake locations, charts on the relative deadliness of venom from different snakes, or diagrams on how to avoid snake bites or how serums can counteract the effect of the poison. You may wish to consult with a science teacher to plan lessons on poisonous snakes.

Clarification

❶ Karait has a name that sounds like krait, a small poisonous snake found in India.

◆Reading Strategy

❷ **Predict** Have students predict why Rikki encounters Karait at this point in the story, and what the outcome may be. *Rikki will probably fight Karait, a small poisonous snake. Their battle may give Rikki practice for the "great war" to come later.*

Spelling

❸ **Homophones** Homophones are words that sound alike but are spelled differently and have different meanings. Challenge students to identify three homophones in this passage, and to give each one's homophonic partner. *so/sew; gait/gate; please/pleas.*

◆Critical Thinking

❹ **Assess** Have students summarize what Rikki has learned to this point in the story. *Rikki has sharpened his fighting skills; he recognizes how important it is for him to stay thin; he has gained confidence.* Then ask students to explain why Rikki seems unimpressed by the fuss the humans make over his feat. *Rikki simply did what mongooses do: fight snakes.*

◆Literary Focus

❺ **Plot** At this point in the story, the author introduces two minor characters: the muskrat Chuchundra and the rat Chua. Ask students to explain how these two advance the plot. *Chuchundra's fears let Rikki boast, which, in turn, makes Chuchundra warn Rikki of danger. Chua, the rat, serves as a spy.*

❶ I was Karait,[6] the dusty brown snakeling that lies for choice on the dusty earth; and his bite ❷ is as dangerous as the cobra's. But he is so small that nobody thinks of him, and so he does the more harm to people.

Rikki-tikki's eyes grew red again, and he danced up to Karait with the peculiar rocking, swaying motion that he had inherited from his family. It looks very funny, but it is so per- ❸ fectly balanced a gait that you can fly off from it at any angle you please; and in dealing with snakes this is an advantage. If Rikki-tikki had only known, he was doing a much more dangerous thing than fighting Nag, for Karait is so small, and can turn so quickly, that unless Rikki bit him close to the back of the head, he would get the return stroke in his eye or lip. But Rikki did not know: his eyes were all red, and he rocked back and forth, looking for a good place to hold. Karait struck out. Rikki jumped sideways and tried to run in, but the wicked little dusty gray head lashed within a fraction of his shoulder, and he had to jump over the body, and the head followed his heels close.

Teddy shouted to the house: "Oh, look here! Our mongoose is killing a snake"; and Rikki-tikki heard a scream from Teddy's mother. His father ran out with a stick, but by the time he came up, Karait had lunged out once too far, and Rikki-tikki had sprung, jumped on the snake's back, dropped his head far between ❹ his fore legs, bitten as high up the back as he could get hold, and rolled away. That bite paralyzed Karait, and Rikki-tikki was just going to eat him up from the tail, after the custom of his family at dinner, when he remembered that a full meal makes a slow mongoose, and if he wanted all his strength and quickness ready, he must keep himself thin.

He went away for a dust bath under the castor-oil bushes, while Teddy's father beat the dead Karait. "What is the use of that?" thought Rikki-tikki. "I have settled it all"; and then Teddy's mother picked him up from the dust and hugged him, crying that he had saved Teddy from death, and Teddy's father said that he was a providence,[7] and Teddy looked on with big scared eyes. Rikki-tikki was rather amused at all the fuss, which, of ❹ course, he did not understand. Teddy's mother might just as well have petted Teddy for playing in the dust. Rikki was thoroughly enjoying himself.

That night, at dinner, walking to and fro among the wineglasses on the table, he could have stuffed himself three times over with nice things; but he remembered Nag and Nagaina, and though it was very pleasant to be patted and petted by Teddy's mother, and to sit on Teddy's shoulder, his eyes would get red from time to time, and he would go off into his long war cry of "*Rikk-tikk-tikki-tikki-tchk!*"

Teddy carried him off to bed, and insisted on Rikki-tikki sleeping under his chin. Rikki-tikki was too well bred to bite or scratch, but as soon as Teddy was asleep he went off for his nightly walk round the house, and in the dark he ran up against Chuchundra the muskrat, creeping round by the wall. Chuchundra is a brokenhearted little beast. He whimpers and cheeps all the night, trying to make up his mind to run into the middle of the room, but he never gets there.

"Don't kill me," said Chuchundra, almost weeping. "Rikki-tikki don't kill me."

"Do you think a snake-killer kills muskrats?" said Rikki-tikki scornfully.

"Those who kill snakes get killed by snakes," said Chuchundra, more sorrowfully ❺ than ever. "And how am I to be sure that Nag won't mistake me for you some dark night?"

"There's not the least danger," said Rikki-tikki; "but Nag is in the garden, and I know you don't go there."

"My cousin Chua, the rat, told me—" said Chuchundra, and then he stopped.

"Told you what?"

"H'sh! Nag is everywhere, Rikki-tikki. You should have talked to Chua in the garden."

"I didn't—so you must tell me. Quick,

6. **Karait** (kə rīt′)

7. **a providence** (präv′ ə dəns): A godsend; a valuable gift.

Chuchundra, or I'll bite you!"

Chuchundra sat down and cried till the tears rolled off his whiskers. "I am a very poor man," he sobbed. "I never had spirit enough to run out into the middle of the room. H'sh! I mustn't tell you anything. Can't you *hear*, Rikki-tikki?"

Rikki-tikki listened. The house was as still as still, but he thought he could just catch the faintest *scratch-scratch* in the world—a noise as faint as that of a wasp walking
6 on a windowpane—the dry scratch of a snake's scales on brickwork.

"That's Nag or Nagaina," he said to himself; "and he is crawling into the bathroom sluice.[8] You're right, Chuchundra; I should have talked to Chua."

He stole off to Teddy's bathroom, but there was nothing there, and then to Teddy's mother's bathroom. At the bottom of the smooth plaster wall there was a brick pulled out to make a sluice for the bath water, and as Rikki-tikki stole in by the masonry curb where the bath is put, he heard Nag and Nagaina whispering together outside in the moonlight.

"When the house is emptied of people," said Nagaina to her husband, "*he* will have to go away, and then the garden will be our own again. Go in quietly, and remember that the big man who killed Karait is the first one to
7 bite. Then come out and tell me, and we will hunt for Rikki-tikki together."

"But are you sure that there is anything to be gained by killing the people?" said Nag.

"Everything. When there were no people in the bungalow, did we have any mongoose in the garden? So long as the bungalow is empty, we are king and queen of the garden; and remember that as soon as our eggs in the melon bed hatch (as they may tomorrow), our children will need room and quiet."

"I had not thought of that," said Nag. "I will 7
go, but there is no need that we should hunt for Rikki-tikki afterward. I will kill the big man and his wife, and the child if I can, and come away quietly. Then the bungalow will be empty, and Rikki-tikki will go."

Rikki-tikki tingled all over with rage and hatred at this, and then Nag's head came through the sluice, and his five feet of cold body followed it. Angry as he was, Rikki-tikki was very frightened as he saw the size of the big cobra. Nag coiled himself up, raised his head, and looked into the bathroom in the dark, and Rikki could see his eyes glitter.

"Now, if I kill him here, Nagaina will know;—and if I fight him on the open floor, the odds are in his favor. What am I to do?" said Rikki-tikki-tavi.

Nag waved to and fro, and then Rikki-tikki-tikki heard him drinking from the biggest water jar that was used to fill the bath. "That is good," said the snake. "Now, when Karait was killed, the big man had a stick. He may have that stick still, but when he comes in to bathe in the morning he will not have a stick. I shall

▲ **Critical Viewing** What role does Darzee, the
tailor-bird, play in the conflict between Rikki-tikki- 8
tavi and Nag? **[Analyze]**

8. **sluice** (slo͞os) Drain.

Comprehension Check 

6 Ask students to explain how Chuchundra's uneasiness helps Rikki. *Chuchundra keeps telling Rikki to hush, which allows him to hear the small sound of a snake crawling into the bathroom sluice.*

◆Literary Focus

7 Plot Discuss with students the plot that Nag and Nagaina have in mind. Guide them to understand that the cobras resent the humans taking over their territory, have reason to fear the "big man," and blame the humans for the presence of the mongoose. Ask students why Nag and Nagaina want Rikki gone. *They want to raise their young with no mongoose to threaten them.*

►Critical Viewing◄

8 Analyze *Darzee is the first character to inform Rikki-tikki-tavi of Nag's threat to the garden inhabitants.*

Cross-Curricular Connection: Social Studies

Cobras, mongooses, and all animals play an important part in Indian lore. Hinduism, the dominant religion of India, is a polytheistic religion, and many of the Hindu gods are either represented as animals or actually are animals. Some of these gods derive from folk religions that have been incorporated into Hindu observance.

These snake deities are often represented as upright stone figures of cobras. In Karnataka state, all families have a snake deity that is thought to be necessary to their welfare. Manasa, a snake goddess worshiped in Assam and Bengal, is believed to fend off snakebites and bring about prosperity. She is sometimes represented in the shape of a woman seated on a snake.

The significance of animals in India is also due in part to the Hindu doctrine of reincarnation. According to this belief, a person's soul never dies. Depending on one's behavior on earth, one may be reborn (or reincarnated) as an animal; the less worthy the soul, the more lowly the animal.

◆Literature and Your Life

❶ Ask students how Rikki's planning of his strategy to fight Nag is related to their own thoughts when they are about to perform a new or difficult action. *Students may say that their minds also race when they are about to do something new or difficult. They may busily plan what to do, worry about what might go wrong, or give themselves pep talks to keep going.*

◆Literary Focus

❷ **Plot** This battle is one climax in the rising action. Have students identify some of the elements in this passage that add tension. *Students may cite the use of short words that move along quickly; vivid words to describe sounds and actions; and repetitive phrases, such as* to and fro, up and down, *and* tighter and tighter. *Frenzied shaking and motion convey a sense of fear, as does Rikki's admission that he thinks he'll die, but hopes to do so without disgracing his family.*

wait here till he comes. Nagaina—do you hear me?—I shall wait here in the cool till daytime."

There was no answer from outside, so Rikki-tikki knew Nagaina had gone away. Nag coiled himself down, coil by coil, round the bulge at the bottom of the waterjar, and Rikki-tikki stayed still as death. After an hour he began to move, muscle by muscle, toward the jar. Nag was asleep, and Rikki-tikki looked at his big back, wondering which would be the best place for a good hold. "If I don't break his back at the first jump," said Rikki, "he can still fight; and if he fights—O Rikki!" He looked at the thickness of the neck below the hood, but that was too much for him; and a bite ❶ near the tail would only make Nag savage.

"It must be the head," he said at last; "the head above the hood; and, when I am once there, I must not let go."

Then he jumped. The head was lying a little clear of the water jar, under the curve of it; and, as his teeth met, Rikki braced his back ❷ against the bulge of the red earthenware to hold down the head. This gave him just one

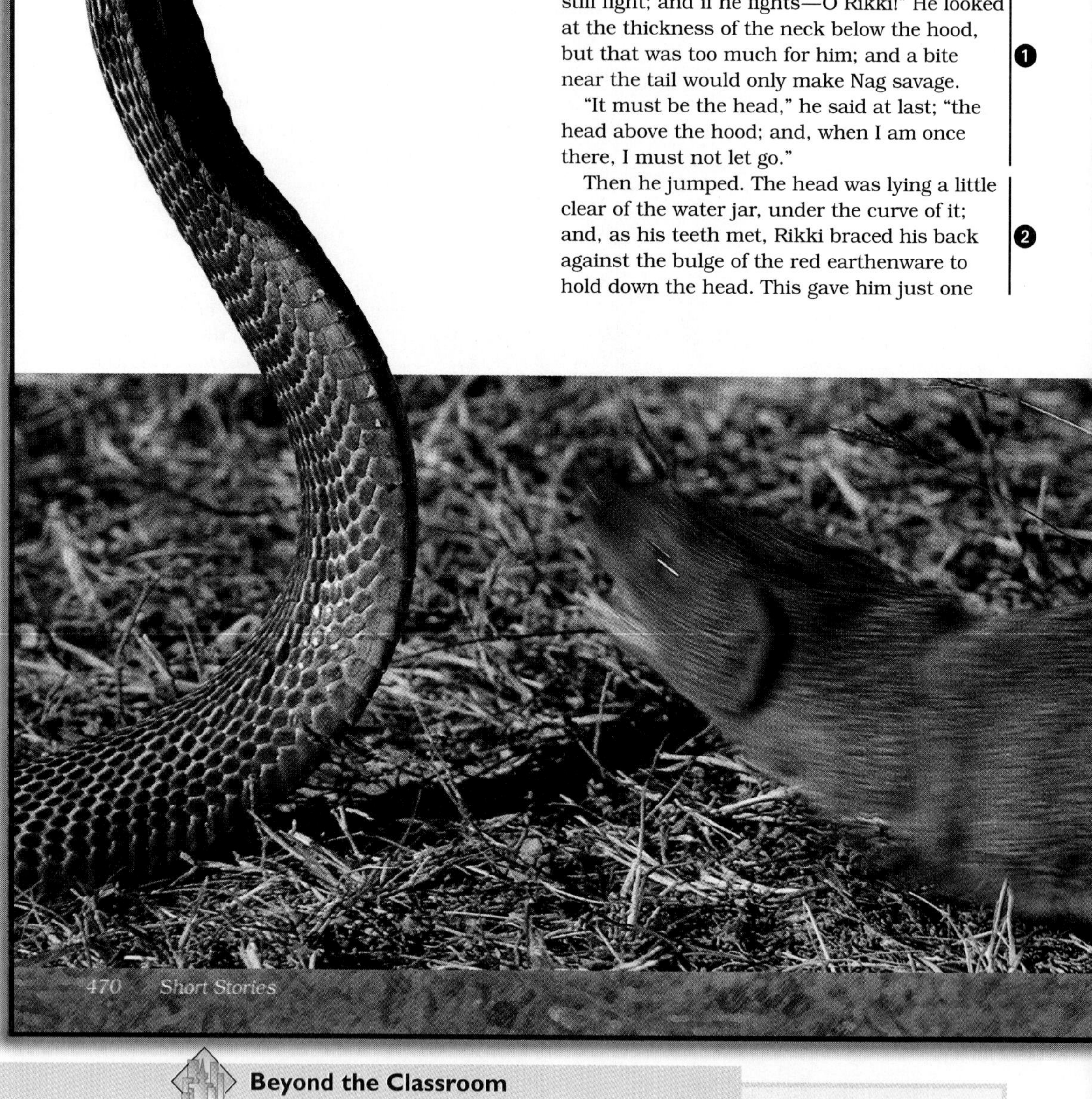

Beyond the Classroom

Community Connection

Coexisting With Wildlife In "Rikki-tikki-tavi," the cobras who live near the bungalow present a serious threat to the humans. In rural areas where wildlife is plentiful, and in urban areas where nature is less evident, people and animals often share a single environment—and problems arise. Many communities have government agencies, businesses, or volunteers who help people and animals coexist safely and with a sense of environmental responsibility. For instance, urban park rangers can make city dwellers aware of the value of local parks as stop-off points on bird migration routes. Exterminators can rid a house of unwanted pests. Wildlife management teams can rescue animals that are injured or trapped. Have students brainstorm for a list of problems that arise when "civilization" overruns natural land. Then have them think of reasonable solutions that help both animals and people. For example, fences can keep wild animals away from domesticated ones; or, planting certain kinds of crops or plants can repel animals without harming them. Students might take an informal trip around the area to see how your community tries to balance human needs with the needs of wildlife.

second's purchase,[9] and he made the most of it. Then he was battered to and fro as a rat is shaken by a dog—to and fro on the floor, up and down, and round in great circles: but his eyes were red, and he held on as the body cart-whipped over the floor, upsetting the tin dipper and the soap dish and the fleshbrush, and banged against the tin side of the bath. As he
2 held he closed his jaws tighter and tighter, for he made sure he would be banged to death, and, for the honor of his family, he preferred to be found with his teeth locked. He was dizzy, aching, and felt shaken to pieces when something went off like a thunderclap just behind him; a hot wind knocked him senseless and red fire singed his fur. The big man had been wakened by the noise, and had fired both barrels of a shotgun into Nag just behind the hood.

9. **purchase** (pur´ chəs): In this case, an advantage.

3 ▼ **Critical Viewing** Basing your answer on the details of this photograph, which animal would you expect to win a match to the death—the cobra or the mongoose? Explain. **[Evaluate]**

Rikki-tikki held on with his eyes shut, for now he was quite sure he was dead; but the head did not move, and the big man picked him up and said: "It's the mongoose again, Alice; the little chap has saved *our* lives now." Then Teddy's mother came in with a very white face, and saw what was left of Nag, and Rikki-tikki dragged himself to Teddy's bedroom and spent half the rest of the night shaking himself tenderly to find out whether he really was broken into forty pieces, as he fancied.

When morning came he was very stiff, but 4
well pleased with his doings. "Now I have Nagaina to settle with, and she will be worse than five Nags, and there's no knowing when the eggs she spoke of will hatch. Goodness! I must go and see Darzee," he said.

Without waiting for breakfast, Rikki-tikki ran to the thornbush where Darzee was singing a song of triumph at the top of his voice. The news of Nag's death was all over the garden, for the sweeper had thrown the body on the rubbish heap.

"Oh, you stupid tuft of feathers!" said Rikki-tikki, angrily. "Is this the time to sing?"

"Nag is dead—is dead—is dead!" sang Darzee. "The valiant Rikki-tikki caught him by the head and held fast. The big man brought the bang-stick and Nag fell in two pieces! He will never eat my babies again."

◆ **Literary Focus** Why is the death of Nag considered part of the rising action of the plot? 5

"All that's true enough; 6
but where's Nagaina?" said Rikki-tikki, looking carefully round him.

"Nagaina came to the bathroom sluice and called for Nag," Darzee went on; "and Nag came out on the end of a stick—the sweeper picked him up on the end of a stick and threw him upon the rubbish heap. Let us sing about the great, the red-eyed Rikki-tikki!" and Darzee filled his throat and sang.

"If I could get up to your nest, I'd roll all your babies out!" said Rikki-tikki "You don't know when to do the right thing at the right time. You're safe enough in your nest there, but it's war for me down here. Stop singing a minute, Darzee."

▶Critical Viewing◀

3 **Evaluate** Some students may think that the cobra's position and flexible body will help it win; others may note the blur of the mongoose in the photo, which means its speed may give it an advantage.

Comprehension Check ☑

4 Ask students why Rikki is so stiff in the morning. *His challenging battle with Nag the night before made his body sore.*

◆Literary Focus

5 **Plot** *Possible response: It is part of the rising action because the danger is not yet over and there are loose ends to tie up. Rikki cannot rest until he deals with Nagaina, who will be furious over her husband's death.*

Comprehension Check ☑

6 Rikki knows that Nag is dead. Why should he worry about Nagaina? *He knows that she'll be angry about Nag's death, and may seek revenge.*

Customize for
Verbal/Linguistic Learners
Have students read the paragraph beginning "Then he jumped" on p. 470 aloud to appreciate the impact of the vivid and precise language the author uses to describe the action.

◆Reading Strategy

❶ **Predict** Ask students to reread this paragraph. Keeping in mind what they already know about life for the garden animals, they can predict what Rikki plans to do. *Students may say that Rikki will destroy the eggs Nagaina laid in the melon bed. He wants Darzee to distract Nagaina.*

◆Critical Thinking

❷ **Support** Ask students to explain why Darzee's wife would risk her life making Nagaina think that she is injured. *Students should understand that Darzee's wife realizes that the eggs will soon become cobras who will threaten the creatures in the garden. She'll risk her safety, and maybe her life, to help Rikki succeed at his plan, by tempting Nagaina to chase her as an easy target.*

Clarification

❸ Most snake eggs have a flexible, leathery, skinlike shell. Snakes hatch by slashing a hole in the shell with a sharp, temporary "egg tooth."

▶Critical Viewing◀

❹ **Hypothesize** *Possible response: the different animals present a variety of personalities and attitudes.*

"For the great, the beautiful Rikki-tikki's sake, I will stop," said Darzee. "What is it, O Killer of the terrible Nag!"

"Where is Nagaina, for the third time?"

"On the rubbish heap by the stables, mourning for Nag. Great is Rikki-tikki with the white teeth."

"Bother my white teeth! Have you ever heard where she keeps her eggs?"

"In the melon bed, on the end nearest the wall, where the sun strikes nearly all day. She had them there weeks ago."

"And you never thought it worthwhile to tell me? The end nearest the wall, you said?"

"Rikki-tikki, you are not going to eat her eggs?"

❶ "Not eat exactly; no. Darzee, if you have a grain of sense you will fly off to the stables and pretend that your wing is broken, and let Nagaina chase you away to this bush! I must get to the melon bed, and if I went there now she'd see me."

Darzee was a featherbrained little fellow who could never hold more than one idea at a time in his head; and just because he knew that Nagaina's children were born in eggs like his own, he didn't think at first that it was fair ❷ to kill them. But his wife was a sensible bird, and she knew that cobra's eggs meant young cobras later on; so she flew off from the nest, and left Darzee to keep the babies warm, and continue his song about the death of Nag. Darzee was very like a man in some ways.

She fluttered in front of Nagaina by the rubbish heap, and cried out, "Oh, my wing is broken! The boy in the house threw a stone at me and broke it." Then she fluttered more desperately than ever.

Nagaina lifted up her head and hissed, "You warned Rikki-tikki when I would have killed him. Indeed and truly, you've chosen a bad place to be lame in." And she moved toward Darzee's wife, slipping along over the dust.

"The boy broke it with a stone!" shrieked Darzee's wife.

"Well! It may be some consolation to you when you're dead to know that I shall settle accounts with the boy. My husband lies on the rubbish heap this morning, but before night the boy in the house will lie very still. What is the use of running away? I am sure to catch you. Little fool, look at me!"

Darzee's wife knew better than to do *that*, for a bird who looks at a snake's eyes gets so frightened that she cannot move. Darzee's wife fluttered on, piping sorrowfully, and never leaving the ground, and Nagaina quickened her pace.

Rikki-tikki heard them going up the path from the stables, and he raced for the end of the melon patch near the wall. There, in the warm litter about the melons, very cunningly hidden, he found twenty-five eggs, about the size of a bantam's eggs,[10] but with whitish skin instead of shell. ❸

10. **bantam's** (ban′ təmz) **eggs**: Small chicken's eggs.

▲ **Critical Viewing** Kipling includes a variety of animals in this story. A mongoose, a cobra, a tailor-bird, a muskrat, and the Coppersmith pictured here. Why might the author choose to include so many animals? **[Hypothesize]** ❹

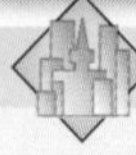

Beyond the Classroom

Workplace Skills

Conflict Resolution In this story, conflict is resolved by battles to the death. This is a real part of nature, but conflicts that arise in the workplace must be solved in other ways. Conflict resolution is an essential workplace skill. Co-workers must resolve problems without resorting to violence. Angry customers and shopkeepers must figure out how to rectify the situation when the customer is dissatisfied with a purchase. Employers and workers need to find reasonable ways to settle conflicts over pay, schedules, or job responsibilities.

Have pairs or small groups brainstorm for conflicts that might arise in a workplace, such as an employee's perpetual lateness to work or a customer's anger when a desired product is out of stock. Then ask students to come up with nonviolent ways to smooth out the conflicts so that each party can save face and reach a satisfactory goal. Have each group role-play their workplace conflict and resolution for the class. Lead a class discussion about the merits of each suggested resolution.

"I was not a day too soon," he said; for he could see the baby cobras curled up inside the skin, and he knew that the minute they were hatched they could each kill a man or a mongoose. He bit off the tops of the eggs as fast as he could, taking care to crush the young cobras, and turned over the litter from time to time to see whether he had missed any. At last there were only three eggs left, and Rikki-tikki began to chuckle to himself, when he heard Darzee's wife screaming:

"Rikki-tikki, I led Nagaina toward the house, and she has gone into the veranda, and—oh, come quickly—she means killing!"

Rikki-tikki smashed two eggs, and tumbled backward down the melon bed with the third egg in his mouth, and scuttled to the veranda as hard as he could put foot to the ground. Teddy and his mother and father were there at early breakfast; but Rikki-tikki saw that they were not eating anything. They sat stone-still, and their faces were white. Nagaina was coiled up on the matting by Teddy's chair, within easy striking distance of Teddy's bare leg, and she was swaying to and fro singing a song of triumph.

"Son of the big man that killed Nag," she hissed, "stay still. I am not ready yet. Wait a little. Keep very still, all you three. If you move I strike, and if you do not move I strike, Oh, foolish people, who killed my Nag!"

Teddy's eyes were fixed on his father, and all his father could do was to whisper, "Sit still, Teddy. You mustn't move. Teddy, keep still."

5 Then Rikki-tikki came up and cried: "Turn round, Nagaina; turn and fight!"

"All in good time," said she, without moving her eyes. "I will settle my account with *you* presently. Look at your friends, Rikki-tikki. They are still and white; they are afraid. They dare not move, and if you come a step nearer I strike."

6 "Look at your eggs," said Rikki-tikki, "in the melon bed near the wall. Go and look, Nagaina."

The big snake turned half round, and saw the egg on the veranda. "Ah-h! Give it to me," she said.

Rikki-tikki put his paws one on each side of the egg, and his eyes were blood-red. "What price for a snake's egg? For a young cobra? For a young king cobra? For the last—the very last of the brood? The ants are eating all the others down by the melon bed." 6

Nagaina spun clear round, forgetting everything for the sake of the one egg; and Rikki-tikki saw Teddy's father shoot out a big hand, catch Teddy by the shoulder, and drag him across the little table with the teacups, safe and out of reach of Nagaina.

"Tricked! Tricked! Tricked! *Rikk-tck-tck!*" chuckled Rikki-tikki. "The boy is safe, and it was I—I—I that caught Nag by the hood last night in the bathroom." Then he began to jump up and down, all four feet together, his head close to the floor. "He threw me to and fro, but he could not shake me off. He was dead before the big man blew him in two. I did it. *Rikki-tikki-tck-tck!* Come then, Nagaina. Come and fight with me. You shall not be a widow long." 7

Nagaina saw that she had lost her chance of killing Teddy, and the egg lay between Rikki-tikki's paws. "Give me the egg, Rikki-tikki. Give me the last of my eggs, and I will go away and never come back," she said, lowering her hood.

"Yes, you will go away, and you will never come back; for you will go to the rubbish heap with Nag. Fight, widow! The big man has gone for his gun! Fight!"

Rikki-tikki was bounding all round Nagaina, keeping just out of reach of her stroke, his little eyes like hot coals. Nagaina gathered herself together, and flung out at him. Rikki-tikki jumped up and backward. Again and again and again she struck, and each time her head came with a whack on the matting of the veranda and she gathered herself together like a watchspring. Then Rikki-tikki danced in a

◆ Build Vocabulary

mourning (môrn´ iŋ) *adj.*: Feeling sorrow for the death of a loved one

consolation (kän´ səl ā´ shən) *n.*: Something that makes you feel better

cunningly (kun´ iŋ lē) *adv.*: Cleverly

◆Reading Strategy

5 Predict Ask students to tell why Rikki challenges Nagaina at this moment, and to predict the outcome of the battle he hopes to undertake. *Rikki hopes that his challenge will distract Nagaina from the humans, thus giving them time to escape. Students may expect Rikki to defeat Nagaina.*

◆Literary Focus

6 Plot Students should recognize that the story is approaching its climax. Ask them to explain why Rikki taunts Nagaina, and to predict what may happen. *Rikki taunts Nagaina to make her so angry that she'll turn away from Teddy and his family to rescue the egg from Rikki and leave to check her other eggs. Students may expect Rikki and Nagaina to fight.*

Comprehension Check ☑

7 Why does Rikki boast about his defeat of Nag? *He tries to lure Nagaina from the humans by saying that he, Rikki, was responsible for Nag's death, not the big man.*

Speaking and Listening Mini-Lesson

First-Aid Demonstration

This mini-lesson supports the Speaking and Listening activity in the Idea Bank on p. 477.

Introduce Provide information about why snakes bite, the harm a bite can cause, and what one should do if bitten. Obtain details from a basic first-aid book, or ask a nurse or science teacher to address the class on this topic.

Develop To grasp the process, students should restate or summarize the steps for giving first-aid for a snake bite. Suggest that they make a flowchart on which they list the steps in order. Urge them to ask questions to ensure that they understand each step enough to explain it to others. Allow adequate time for students to practice. Some may work with a "victim" on whom they can demonstrate the various steps.

Apply Have students present live or videotaped demonstrations to the class. Allow time for a question-and-answer period after the demonstration.

Assess Evaluate for clarity, organization, scientific accuracy, and the presenter's ability to convey information calmly and with authority. Alternatively, use the Peer Assessment: Speaker/Speech form, p. 105, in **Alternative Assessment**.

Comprehension Check ☑

❶ What is Darzee's wife doing, and why? *She wants to distract Nagaina and slow her down so Rikki can catch her.*

◆Reading Strategy

❷ **Predict** Once Nagaina and Rikki disappear down the rat hole, the final action takes place out of sight of the narrator, so readers can only guess what happens. Ask students to predict the outcome of this final struggle. *Most students will predict that Rikki will emerge the winner, despite Darzee's pessimistic view.*

◆Literary Focus

❸ **Plot** Discuss with students the outcome of the final battle. Ask them to explain how the conflict, the "great war," is resolved. *Although the readers get no specific details, Rikki emerges the winner, claiming that Nagaina is dead. The red ants go to check whether this is true.* Ask students to share their responses to the resolution.

Beyond Literature

Cultural Connection

To help students complete the Cross-Curricular Activity, you might guide them to research Buto or Mertseger, snake goddesses in Egyptian mythology. In Japanese mythology, the god Susanoo is associated with snakes. In Indian mythology, Nagas are a fabulous race of snakes who live in a grand underworld kingdom and are noted for trickery and evildoing.

circle to get behind her, and Nagaina spun round to keep her head to his head, so that the rustle of her tail on the matting sounded like dry leaves blown along by the wind.

He had forgotten the egg. It still lay on the veranda, and Nagaina came nearer and nearer to it, till at last, while Rikki-tikki was drawing breath, she caught it in her mouth, turned to the veranda steps, and flew like an arrow down the path, with Rikki-tikki behind her. When the cobra runs for her life, she goes like a whiplash flicked across a horse's neck.

Rikki-tikki knew that he must catch her, or all the trouble would begin again. She headed straight for the long grass by the thornbush, and as he was running Rikki-tikki heard Darzee still singing his foolish little song of
❶ triumph. But Darzee's wife was wiser. She flew off her nest as Nagaina came along, and flapped her wings about Nagaina's head. If Darzee had helped they might have turned her; but Nagaina only lowered her hood and went on. Still, the instant's delay brought
❷ Rikki-tikki up to her, and as she plunged into the rat hole where she and Nag used to live, his little white teeth were clenched on her tail, and he went down with her—and very few mongooses, however wise and old they may be, care to follow a cobra into its hole. It was dark in the hole; and Rikki-tikki never knew when it might open out and give Nagaina room to turn and strike at him. He held on savagely, and struck out his feet to act as brakes on the dark slope of the hot, moist earth.

Then the grass by the mouth of the hole stopped waving, and Darzee said: "It is all over with Rikki-tikki! We must sing his death song. Valiant Rikki-tikki is dead! For Nagaina will surely kill him underground."

So he sang a very mournful song that he made up all on the spur of the minute, and just as he got to the most touching part the
❸ grass quivered again, and Rikki-tikki, covered with dirt, dragged himself out of the hole leg by leg, licking his whiskers. Darzee stopped with a little shout. Rikki-tikki shook some of the dust out of his fur and sneezed. "It is all over," he said. "The widow will never come out again." And the red ants that live between the grass stems heard him, and began to troop down one after another to see if he had spoken the truth. ❸

Rikki-tikki curled himself up in the grass and slept where he was—slept and slept till it was late in the afternoon, for he had done a hard day's work.

"Now," he said, when he awoke, "I will go back to the house. Tell the Coppersmith, Darzee, and he will tell the garden that Nagaina is dead."

The Coppersmith is a bird who makes a noise exactly like the beating of a little hammer on a copper pot; and the reason he is always making it is because he is the town crier to every Indian garden, and tells all the news to everybody who cares to listen. As Rikki-tikki went up the path, he heard his

Beyond Literature

Cultural Connection

Snake Charming Snake charming is one of the oldest forms of entertainment in India. As a snake charmer plays a flutelike instrument, a deadly cobra slithers from a basket onto the ground, raising its head and spreading its hood, as if ready to strike. Instead of attacking, though, the cobra sways back and forth. However, the snake is not dancing. It can barely perceive the music. Instead, it is keeping close watch on the flute, which it regards as a threat. Because snake charmers know exactly how far cobras can move, they sit just out of the cobra's range.

Cross-Curricular Activity
Snakes in Asian Art and Literature
With a group of classmates, learn more about how snakes are depicted in Asian art and literature. Gather photographs, postcards, and copies of folk tales and other literature. Then, arrange your materials to create a classroom display.

Humanities: Music

Indian Classical Music There are two branches of Indian classical music: the Hindustani music of North India and the Carnatic music of South India. Unlike Western music, which features harmony and development of themes, Indian classical music focuses on melodic ideas and rhythm. The music is built around a *drone*, a continual pitch heard throughout a piece; a *raga*, or melodic structure that serves as the basis for improvisation; and a *tala*, or rhythmic structure. Give students a taste of Indian music by playing works performed by the great Indian sitar player Ravi Shankar. Invite students to respond to the feelings the music evokes.

Have interested students learn about Indian melodic instruments, such as the bansuri, bin, santur, sarangi, sarod, shehnai, sitar, and surbahar; as well as the rhythm instruments dholak, pakhawaj, and tabla, and the drone instruments tamboura and swarpeti. Direct students to a useful Internet source at:
http://www.planet.eon.net/~raga/iguide.html
We *strongly recommend* that you preview this site before sending students to it.

> ◆ Literary Focus
> What part of the plot does the Coppersmith's song announce? Explain.

4 "attention" notes like a tiny dinner gong; and then the steady "*Ding-dong-tock!* Nag is dead—*dong*! Nagaina is dead! *Ding-dong-tock!*" That set all the birds in the garden singing, and the frogs croaking; for Nag and Nagaina used to eat frogs as well as little birds.

When Rikki got to the house, Teddy and Teddy's mother and Teddy's father came out and almost cried over him; and that night he ate all that was given him till he could eat no more, and went to bed on Teddy's shoulder, where Teddy's mother saw him when she came to look late at night.

"He saved our lives and Teddy's life," she said to her husband. "Just think, he saved all our lives."

Rikki-tikki woke up with a jump, for all the mongooses are light sleepers.

"Oh, it's you," said he. "What are you bothering for? All the cobras are dead; and if they weren't, I'm here."

Rikki-tikki had a right to be proud of himself; but he did not grow too proud, and he kept that garden as a mongoose should keep it, with tooth and jump and spring and bite, till never a cobra dared show its head inside the walls.

Guide for Responding

◆ Literature and Your Life

Reader's Response Would you enjoy living in India like Teddy and his family? What aspects of living in India do you think you might like? What might you dislike?

Thematic Focus The natural conflict between mongooses and snakes is the basis for Kipling's story. What natural conflicts have you observed that might inspire a good story?

Journal Writing Despite his fear, Rikki faces and beats his enemy. In a journal entry, describe a time when your own fear worked to your benefit.

☑ Check Your Comprehension

1. When does Rikki first meet the cobras?
2. What is Nag and Nagaina's plan to get control of the bungalow?
3. How does Rikki protect Teddy's father from Nag?
4. How does Rikki protect Teddy from Nagaina?
5. What happens to Nagaina at the end?

◆ Critical Thinking

INTERPRET

1. How do the animals in the story resemble humans? **[Support]**
2. What human personality traits might each of the following animals represent? (a) Rikki, (b) Nagaina, (c) Chuchundra, (d) Darzee, (e) Darzee's wife **[Infer]**
3. Compare the personalities of Rikki and the two cobras. **[Compare and Contrast]**
4. (a) How does Nagaina make problems worse for Nag? (b) Does she fight her own battles when she has to? Explain. **[Analyze]**
5. How is "the great war that Rikki-tikki-tavi fought" a battle between good and evil? **[Draw Conclusions]**

EVALUATE

6. Would Rikki's approach to problems in life work better than Darzee's? Explain. **[Assess]**

EXTEND

7. Identify at least three scientific facts Kipling includes in this story. **[Science Link]**

Beyond the Selection

FURTHER READING

Other Works by Rudyard Kipling

Kim

The Jungle Book

Other Works About the Natural World

"The Judgment of the Wind," Harold Courlander and Wolf Leslau

"Rattlesnake Hunt," Marjorie Kinnan Rawlings

INTERNET

We suggest the following sites on the Internet (all Web sites are subject to change).

For more information about Rudyard Kipling: **http://www.bbc.co.uk/education/archive/bookworm/kip.htm**

For facts on cobras: **http://cobras.org**

We *strongly recommend* that you preview these sites before you send students to them.

◆ Literary Focus

4 Plot *It announces the falling action because it occurs after the climactic battle, but before the final resolution.*

Reinforce and Extend

Answers

◆ Literature and Your Life

Reader's Response Students may say that they would enjoy the climate, wildlife, and culture, but that they might dislike having venomous snakes in the area.

Thematic Focus Students may describe conflicts such as cats fighting over territory or conflicts they have seen on television, such as bighorn rams sparring.

☑ Check Your Comprehension

1. Rikki meets the cobras in the garden after hearing Darzee tell of how Nag ate one of his babies.
2. They will kill the humans.
3. Rikki pounces on Nag, then bites him. The fight wakes the father, who gets his gun and shoots Nag.
4. Rikki distracts her by showing her the remaining egg and saying that he has destroyed the rest.
5. Nagaina snatches her egg and races to her rat-hole home, where Rikki kills her.

◆ Critical Thinking

1. They talk and act like humans and have similar relationships. They also show human emotions, such as loyalty, fury, and pride.
2. Possible responses: (a) courage; (b) treachery; (c) cowardice; (d) boastfulness; (e) practicality
3. Rikki is lovable, considerate, and caring of others, whereas the cobras are evil, selfish, and inconsiderate. Both Rikki and the cobras are crafty and intelligent.
4. (a) She stations him in the house where Rikki can attack him. (b) Yes. She does everything she can to save her last egg.
5. It is fought by good Rikki against evil cobras.
6. Rikki is alert and ready to act when necessary; Darzee isn't very smart, and seems incapable of taking decisive action
7. Possible response: Mongooses eat eggs. When its eyes turn red, a mongoose is angry. When a cobra strikes and misses, there is no way to predict what it will do next.

Answers

◆Reading Strategy

1. When Rikki and Nag first meet, each knows he must kill the other. Also, Rikki resists eating as much as he wants because he knows he must remain fit for battle.
2. We know that mongooses like to eat eggs: Rikki eats some his first day in the house. Later Nag remarks that both of them like eggs. Also, the first thing Rikki thinks about after Nag is killed is Nagaina's eggs. He then rushes to Darzee to find out where the eggs are buried.

◆Build Vocabulary

Using the Word Root *-viv-*
1. vivid; 2. vivacious; 3. revival

Spelling Strategy
1. pier; 2. style, flair

Using the Word Bank

1. consolation	4. mourning
2. flinched	5. cunningly
3. draggled	6. revived

◆Literary Focus

1. Rikki nearly drowns in a flood, is rescued by an English family, and decides to live with them. He explores their bungalow and garden, where he meets Darzee and his wife. The two birds are upset because Nag the cobra ate one of their babies.
2. The central conflict is between Rikki and the cobras over who will rule the house and garden.
3. Events include: Nagaina tries to sneak up on Rikki while he talks with Nag; Rikki saves Teddy from Karait and then kills the snake; Rikki talks with Chuchundra and learns the cobras' plan; Rikki kills Nag; Darzee's wife fakes a broken wing to distract Nagaina while Rikki destroys the cobras' eggs; Rikki comes to Teddy's rescue.
4. The climactic scene is Rikki's fight with Nagaina.
5. The conflict is resolved when Rikki kills Nagaina, thus ridding the area of the deadly cobras.

◆Build Grammar Skills

Practice
1. Rikki is curious. He is also brave.
2. Teddy's family might remain in India. They might return to England.
3. The cobras plotted. Then Nag slipped inside.
4. Rikki was not afraid. He didn't hesitate.
5. The mongoose leapt. It bit the snake. It did not bite long enough. The snake broke loose.

Writing Application
Possible response:
Rikki was swept away from home in a flood. He was unconscious. Teddy saw him. Teddy thought the mongoose was dead. Teddy wanted to hold a funeral.

Rikki was swept away from home in a flood; he was unconscious. Teddy saw him and thought he was dead, so Teddy wanted to hold a funeral.

Guide for Responding *(continued)*

◆ Reading Strategy

Predict

To make a **prediction,** you examine clues in the text, and then make an educated guess about what is going to happen next. Review the story to find clues that helped you to predict each of the following:

1. Rikki would eventually fight Nag.
2. The cobra eggs would be destroyed.

◆ Build Vocabulary

Using the Word Root *-viv-*

Use your knowledge of the word root *-viv-*, meaning "life," to complete each sentence with one of the words below. Use each word once.

vivacious revival vivid

1. The toys came in a variety of __?__ colors.
2. She has an outgoing, __?__ personality.
3. During the __?__ of disco music, the fashions of the 1970's made a comeback.

Spelling Strategy

Mourning and *morning* are homophones—they are spelled differently and mean different things, but they have the same pronunciation. On a piece of paper, write the following sentences, correcting the misused homophones.

1. He sat on a peer, fishing.
2. She does everything with stile and flare.

Using the Word Bank

On your paper, write the Word Bank word that best completes each of the following sentences.

1. The contest winner received a trophy, and all the other entrants received __?__ prizes.
2. He __?__ when he saw the dentist's drill.
3. Her hair was __?__ from her fall into the pond.
4. He was gloomy because he was __?__ the death of his pet turtle.
5. The pirate's treasure chest was __?__ concealed in a cave behind a waterfall.
6. The wilted plant __?__ when I watered it.

◆ Literary Focus

Plot

A story's **plot**—the sequence of events—usually begins with the *exposition.* Next, the conflict is introduced and intensifies during the *rising action.* The *climax,* or high point of the story, is followed by the *falling action,* which leads to the *resolution* of the conflict and the tying up of loose ends.

1. What happens during the exposition in "Rikki-tikki-tavi"?
2. What is the conflict in the story?
3. List three events that occur during the rising action of the story.
4. At what point is the climax reached?
5. How is the conflict resolved?

◆ Build Grammar Skills

Simple and Compound Sentences

A **simple sentence** consists of one independent clause (a group of words that has a subject and a verb and can stand by itself as a complete sentence). A **compound sentence** consists of two or more independent clauses. These clauses may be linked by semicolons or by words such as *and, but, or, yet,* and *so.*

Simple Sentence: Rikki fights snakes.
Compound Sentence:

Independent Clause: Rikki was afraid of Nag, but Independent Clause: he fought him anyway.

Practice On your paper, split the following compound sentences into simple sentences.

1. Rikki-tikki is curious; he is also brave.
2. Teddy's family might remain in India, or they might return to England.
3. The cobras plotted, and then Nag slipped inside.
4. Rikki was not afraid, nor did he hesitate.
5. The mongoose leapt; it bit the snake, but it did not bite long enough, for the snake broke loose.

Writing Application Write a paragraph summarizing one of the scenes in "Rikki-tikki-tavi." Use only simple sentences. Then, revise your paragraph, combining some of the simple sentences to form compound sentences.

Writer's Solution

For further instruction and practice, use the lesson in the *Writer's Solution Language Lab CD-ROM* on Varying Sentence Length and Structure, and the practice pages on Simple and Compound Sentences, pp. 28–30, in the *Writer's Solution Grammar Practice Book.*

Build Your Portfolio

Idea Bank

Writing

1. **Picture Book for First Graders** Create a book for first graders about Rikki-tikki-tavi. To make your book easy to read, simplify the story and use short words and sentences. You may either draw the illustrations for your book or describe what they should look like.
2. **Letter** As Teddy, write a letter to your grandmother in England about your pet mongoose. Describe your pet and his adventures. Keep in mind that Teddy did not see all of the events. Feel free to add details that are not in the story.
3. **Comparison-and-Contrast Essay** Write an essay in which you compare and contrast two of the characters from the story.

Speaking and Listening

4. **Play-by-Play Account** Imagine that you are a radio sportscaster. Prepare and perform an exciting play-by-play description to accompany video footage of the big fight between Rikki-tikki-tavi and Nag. **[Performing Arts Link]**
5. **First-Aid Demonstration** Consult the school nurse and other health experts to find out the steps for giving first aid for snake bites. Explain these steps as you demonstrate them for the class. **[Health Link]**

Projects

6. **Wildlife Collage** Use pictures from old magazines, drawings, and other objects to create a collage about wildlife in a specific part of the world, such as southern India or your state. Create a key to explain the images you use. **[Science Link]**
7. **Multimedia Report** **[Group Activity]** With a group, create a multimedia report on life in India. Gather maps, charts, photographs, and, if possible, video. Combine these materials with written text in a report that you can present to the class. **[Social Studies Link; Media Link]**

Writing Mini-Lesson

Report on Natural Enemies

In "Rikki-tikki-tavi," the conflict between natural enemies is described in the form of a fictional story. Another way to describe such a conflict is in the form of a factual report. Choose another pair of natural enemies, and write a report about them.

Writing Skills Focus: Details to Describe the Environment

To help your readers understand the conflict between the enemies described in your report, you need to show how they fit into the natural world. Notice how Kipling provides **details about the environment** to help readers picture Rikki-tikki-tavi's tropical surroundings:

Model From the Story

It was a large garden, only half cultivated, with bushes as big as summer houses of Marshal Niel roses, lime and orange trees, clumps of bamboos, and thickets of high grass.

Prewriting With a partner, brainstorm for a list of natural enemies. Then, conduct research in the library or on the Internet to gather information about one of these pairs of enemies. Collect at least ten facts about the animals.

Drafting As you draft your report, make sure you include plenty of details about what the enemies look like, how they behave, and how they interact. Thoroughly describe the environment in which the enemies are found.

◆ Grammar Application

As you write, be sure to use a mixture of simple and compound sentences in your report.

Revising Revise your report by looking for places where you can improve your descriptions. Replace vague words with more vivid ones and add details.

ASSESSMENT OPTIONS

Formal Assessment, Selection Test, pp. 138–140, and Assessment Resources Software. The selection test is designed so that it can be easily customized to the performance levels of your students.

Alternative Assessment, p. 30, includes options for less advanced students, more advanced students, interpersonal learners, verbal/linguistic learners, visual/spatial learners, and logical/mathematical learners.

PORTFOLIO ASSESSMENT

Use the following rubrics in the **Alternative Assessment** booklet to assess student writing:
Picture Book for First Graders: Summary, p. 85
Letter: Fictional Narrative, p. 82
Comparison-and-Contrast Essay: Comparison/Contrast, p. 90
Writing Mini-Lesson: Research Report/Paper, p. 93

Idea Bank

Following are suggestions for matching the Idea Bank topics with your students' performance levels and learning modalities:

Customize for *Performance Levels*
Less Advanced Students: 1, 6
Average Students: 2, 5, 7
More Advanced Students: 3, 4, 7

Customize for *Learning Modalities*
Verbal/Linguistic: 1, 2, 3, 4
Visual/Spatial: 1, 6, 7
Bodily/Kinesthetic: 4, 5
Logical/Mathematical: 3, 5
Interpersonal: 5
Intrapersonal: 2, 3, 6, 7

Writing Mini-Lesson

Refer students to the Writing Handbook in the back of the book for instructions on the writing process and for further information on writing a report.

Writer's Solution

Writers at Work Videodisc
To introduce students to writing reports, play the segment featuring Ellie Fries. Ask students to note how Fries gathers her information and how she organizes her reports.

Play frames 11077 to 20155

Writing Lab CD-ROM
Have students complete the tutorial on Reports. Follow these steps:
1. Have students review Evaluation Guidelines before they begin their drafts.
2. Suggest that students use the Notecard Activity to help group their information.
3. Let students draft on computer.
4. Have students use the Unity and Coherence revision checker.

Writer's Solution Sourcebook
Have students use Chapter 7, "Reports," pp. 200–233, for additional support. The chapter includes in-depth instruction on avoiding shifts in tense, p. 230.

OBJECTIVES

1. To read, comprehend, and interpret two short stories
2. To relate short stories to personal experience
3. To identify with a character
4. To understand and recognize direct and indirect characterization
5. To build vocabulary in context and learn the word root *-flam-*
6. To develop skill in using complex sentences
7. To write a continuation, focusing on showing, rather than telling, details
8. To respond to short stories through writing, speaking and listening, and projects

SKILLS INSTRUCTION

Vocabulary:
Word Roots: *-flam-*

Spelling:
Words Ending With Silent *n*

Grammar:
Complex Sentences

Reading Strategy:
Identify With a Character

Literary Focus:
Characterization

Writing:
Show, Don't Tell

Speaking and Listening:
Dramatic Reading (Teacher Edition)

Critical Viewing:
Apply Prior Knowledge, Speculate

PORTFOLIO OPPORTUNITIES

Writing: Diary Entry; Review; Comparing Literary Works
Writing Mini-Lesson: Continuation
Speaking and Listening: Television Interview; Dramatic Reading
Projects: Health Statistics; Report

More About the Authors
Cynthia Rylant writes about characters who are isolated in some way from their peers. Her 1993 novel, *Missing May*, won a Newbery Award.

Sherwood Anderson was born and raised in a small town and used his boyhood observations and experiences as material for his short stories. Throughout his writing career he was interested mainly in people who struggled to cope with the changes brought by the emerging modern age.

Guide for Reading

Meet the Authors:

Cynthia Rylant (1954–)

Cynthia Rylant, who grew up in a West Virginia mountain town, was originally planning to be a nurse. However, she fell in love with literature in college, and switched her major to English.

Surrounded by Books Later, while working as a librarian, Rylant discovered children's books and was hooked. Her love of books inspired her to write one of her own. Her first book, *When I Was Young in the Mountains*, was published in 1982. It was soon followed by works of many types—picture books, novels, short stories, poetry, and biographies.

Sherwood Anderson (1876–1941)

As a teenager, Sherwood Anderson was able to attend school only part of the time because he had to work to help support his family. Despite his lack of formal education, Anderson became a successful businessman, the manager of a paint factory.

Change of Scenery In 1912, he shocked those who knew him by moving from Elyria, Ohio, to Chicago, where he devoted himself to writing. His most famous book, *Winesburg, Ohio*, was published in 1921. Anderson and his work had a powerful influence on such writers as Ernest Hemingway and William Faulkner.

◆ Literature and Your Life

Connect Your Experience

At times, you may have made up wild excuses for not doing something you were supposed to do, or maybe you simply avoided doing something and chose not to offer any explanation at all. Both of these stories focus on characters who avoid responsibility and learn important lessons as a consequence of their actions.

Thematic Focus: Personal Codes

These stories illustrate how the mistakes we make can lead to important insights about our actions. As you read, ask yourself how the lessons the characters learn will affect how they act in the future.

◆ Background for Understanding

Science

Medical problems affect events in both these stories. In "Papa's Parrot," a character suffers a heart attack. Heart attacks are caused by a blockage in a blood vessel that supplies blood to the heart muscle. In "Stolen Day," a character says he has "inflammatory rheumatism." The term *rheumatism* is used to describe a number of different diseases, including rheumatoid arthritis. In this disease, the joints swell painfully and gradually break down.

◆ Build Vocabulary

Word Roots: *-flam-*

In "Stolen Day," a boy is convinced he has "inflammatory rheumatism." Once you know that the word root *-flam-* means "flame" or "burn," it's not surprising to learn that a symptom of this disease is that affected joints feel hot.

Word Bank

Which of these words do you think describes someone who is serious?

resumed
inflammatory
rheumatism
solemn

Prentice Hall Literature Program Resources

REINFORCE / RETEACH / EXTEND

Selection Support Pages
Build Vocabulary: Word Roots: *-flam-*, p. 167
Build Spelling Skills, p. 168
Build Grammar Skills: Complex Sentences, p. 169
Reading Strategy: Identify With a Character, p. 170
Literary Focus: Characterization, p. 171

Strategies for Diverse Student Needs, pp. 61–62

Beyond Literature Cultural Connection: Family Guidelines, p. 31

Formal Assessment Selection Test, pp. 141–143, Assessment Resources Software

Alternative Assessment, p. 31

Writing and Language Transparencies, Sunburst Organizer, p. 94

Resource Pro CD-ROM "Papa's Parrot"; "Stolen Day"—includes all resource material and customizable lesson plan

Listening to Literature Audiocassettes "Papa's Parrot"; "Stolen Day"

Papa's Parrot ◆ Stolen Day

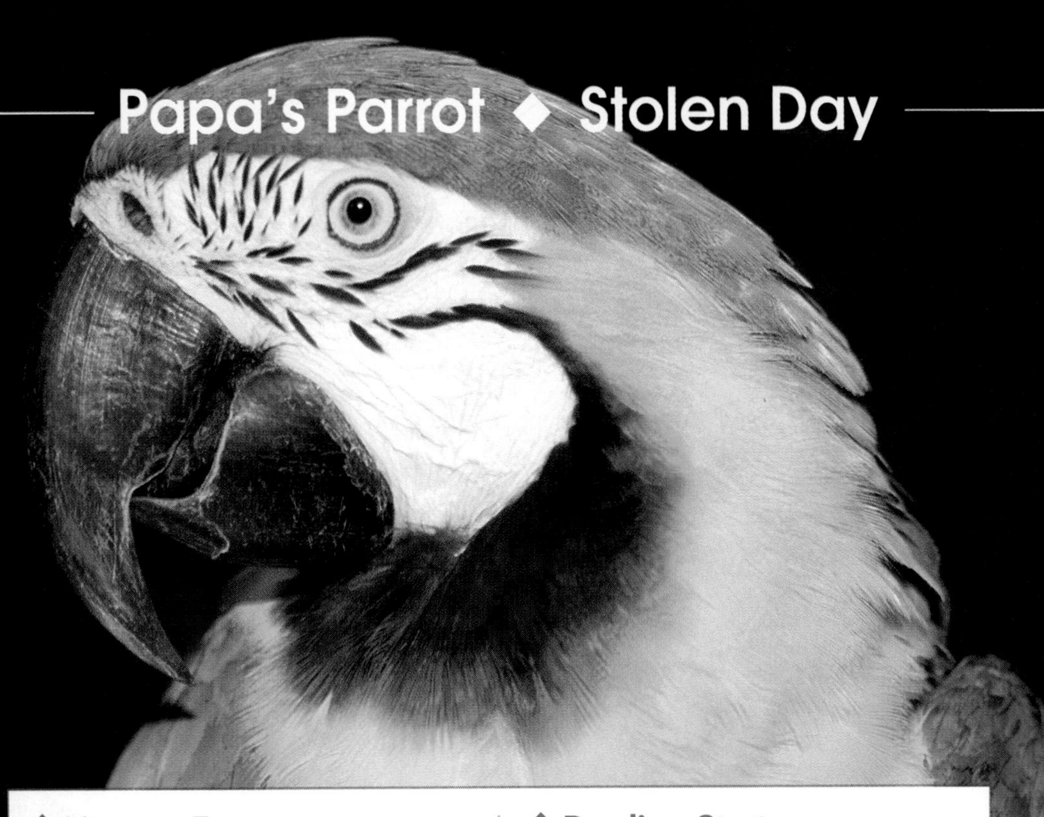

◆ Literary Focus

Characterization

A writer can reveal characters' personalities in two basic ways. When using **direct characterization,** the writer tells you the character's traits: *Rocky was good company.* When using **indirect characterization,** the writer reveals the characters' personalities through the characters' own words, thoughts, and actions and by what other characters say to or about them. In these stories, the authors rely mainly on indirect characterization.

◆ Reading Strategy

Identify With a Character

Stories give you a chance to live another life for a while. To do this, you **identify with a character.** You put yourself in a character's place and think about how you would react to the situations that the character experiences.

As you read each story, fill out a chart like the one below to help you identify with the main character. List each major event, and record the character's reaction to it. Then, note what you might have said or done in the character's place.

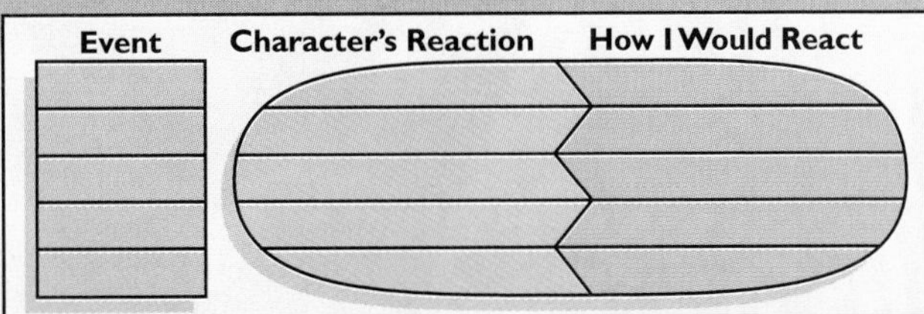

Ask students to recall a time when they or someone they know learned a lesson "the hard way." Discuss the idea that sometimes people can gain important insights from their mistakes. Tell students that in each of the stories they are about to read, a boy learns an important lesson by facing the consequences of his actions.

◆ Build Grammar Skills

Complex Sentences If you wish to introduce the grammar concept for this selection before students read, refer to the instruction on p. 488.

Customize for *Less Proficient Readers*

Students may have difficulty trying to keep track of who is talking in the conversation between Harry and the parrot in the first story. To help them verify who is saying what, have three volunteers read aloud the dialogue and narration on pp. 482–483. One student can read the parrot's lines, another Harry's, and a third the narration.

Customize for *More Advanced Students*

Students reading the first selection will easily identify with Harry. Guide them to read "between the lines" for evidence of what Mr. Tillian's character is like and what is important to him. Encourage them to organize details about Mr. Tillian in a Sunburst Organizer like the one in **Writing and Language Transparencies,** p. 94.

Preparing for Standardized Tests

Grammar The grammar concept for this selection is complex sentences. Standardized tests may include questions that evaluate students' understanding of sentence structure. Explain to students that a sentence is complex only if it has one independent clause and one or more subordinate clauses. Then present the following sample test question:

Identify the sentence that is a complex sentence.

(A) It was Mr. Tillian who bought the parrot.
(B) The boys used to stop by the store to eat candies and sample nuts.
(C) Obeying his mother, the boy went right upstairs and into bed.
(D) The boy went to the pond and caught a large fish.

Students should recognize that *(A)* is the only complex sentence; it has an independent clause and a subordinate clause following the linking word *who.* The other sentences lack subordinate clauses. For further practice, use Build Grammar Skills in **Selection Support,** p. 169.

Develop Understanding

One-Minute Insight Harry Tillian's father owns and operates a nut and candy store, where Harry once spent a good deal of time. As Harry gets older, however, he spends less time at the store. When Mr. Tillian falls ill, Harry learns—with the help of a pet parrot—how much his father misses him, and how he has let his father down.

Clarification

❶ Parrots are tropical or subtropical birds that have curved, hooked bills and often boast crests and brightly colored feathers. Cockatoos, macaws, and parakeets are kinds of parrots. Parrot owners find their birds to be social animals and affectionate companions. Parrots should never be purchased on impulse, however, because they require much care; they are messy and need attention. Also, some of them live as long as 80 years.

◆Critical Thinking

❷ **Speculate** Ask students to guess why the author emphasizes, from the outset, how well Harry and his father get along. *Students might say that their friendship will be tested by events in the story or that the friendship will affect events.*

Customize for
English Language Learners
Play the audiocassette for "Papa's Parrot" and for "Stolen Day" so that, in the first story, students can follow the conversation between Harry and the bird and, in the second story, they can distinguish between what the boy is thinking or imagining and what he is actually saying or doing.

Listening to Literature Audiocassettes

❶ Papa's Parrot

Cynthia Rylant

Block Scheduling Strategies

Consider these suggestions to take advantage of extended class time:

- After students read the stories, have them work in groups to answer the Literary Focus questions, p. 488, to help them distinguish between direct and indirect characterization and to prepare them for the Writing Mini-Lesson, p. 489.
- Have students complete the journal activities following each selection, and have them discuss their entries in small groups.
- Allow class time for students to prepare and present both Speaking and Listening activities, p. 489.
- Have students work in small groups on the Projects in the Idea Bank, p. 489. Suggest that they post their research and graphs in the classroom for classmates to examine.
- If you have access to technology, have students work on the *Writer's Solution Writing Lab CD-ROM* to complete all or part of the Writing Mini-Lesson. Follow the suggestions on p. 489 to help you structure class time.

Though his father was fat and merely owned a candy and nut shop, Harry Tillian liked his papa. Harry stopped
❷ liking candy and nuts when he was around seven, but, in spite of this, he and Mr. Tillian had remained friends and were still friends the year Harry turned twelve.

For years, after school, Harry had always stopped in to see his father at work. Many of Harry's friends stopped there, too, to spend a few cents choosing penny candy from the giant bins or to sample Mr. Tillian's latest batch of roasted peanuts. Mr. Tillian looked forward to
❸ seeing his son and his son's friends every day. He liked the company.

When Harry entered junior high school, though, he didn't come by the candy and nut shop as often. Nor did his friends. They were older and they had more spending money. They went to a burger place. They played video games. They shopped for records. None of them were much interested in candy and nuts anymore.

A new group of children came to Mr. Tillian's shop now. But not Harry Tillian and his friends.

The year Harry turned twelve was also the year Mr. Tillian got a parrot. He went to a pet store one day and bought one for more money than he could really afford. He brought the
❹ parrot to his shop, set its cage near the sign for maple clusters, and named it Rocky.

Harry thought this was the strangest thing his father had ever done, and he told him so, but Mr. Tillian just ignored him.

Rocky was good company for Mr. Tillian. When business was slow, Mr. Tillian would turn on a small color television he had sitting in a corner, and he and Rocky would watch the soap operas. Rocky liked to scream when the romantic music came on, and Mr. Tillian would yell at him to shut up, but they seemed to enjoy themselves.

The more Mr. Tillian grew to like his parrot, and the more he talked to it instead of to people, the more embarrassed Harry became. Harry would stroll past the shop, on his way somewhere else, and he'd take a quick look inside to see what his dad was doing. Mr. Tillian was always talking to the bird. So Harry kept walking.

> ◆ Reading Strategy Put yourself in Harry's place. How would you react to Mr. Tillian talking to his parrot? ❻

At home things were different. Harry and his father joked with each other at the dinner table as they always had—Mr. Tillian teasing Harry about his smelly socks; Harry teasing Mr. Tillian about his blubbery stomach. At home things seemed all right.

But one day, Mr. Tillian became ill. He had been at work, unpacking boxes of caramels, when he had grabbed his chest and fallen over on top of the candy. A customer had found him, and he was taken to the hospital in an ambulance.

Mr. Tillian couldn't leave the hospital. He lay in bed, tubes in his arms, and he worried about his shop. New shipments of candy and nuts would be arriving. Rocky would be hungry. Who would take care of things?

Harry said he would. Harry told his father that he would go to the store every day after
school and unpack boxes. He would sort out ❼
all the candy and nuts. He would even feed Rocky.

So, the next morning, while Mr. Tillian lay in his hospital bed, Harry took the shop key to school with him. After school he left his friends and walked to the empty shop alone. In all the days of his life, Harry had never seen the shop closed after school. Harry didn't even remember what the CLOSED sign looked like. The key stuck in the lock three times, and inside he had to search all the walls for the light switch.

❺ ◀ Critical Viewing What unique ability of parrots is suggested by the combination of the photograph and the title of the story? **[Apply Prior Knowledge]**

◆Literary Focus

❸ **Characterization** Guide students to note the author's use of direct characterization to reveal aspects of Mr. Tillian's personality. Here, the author directly tells how Mr. Tillian feels. Had the author written, "Mr. Tillian smiled broadly when Harry and his friends entered the store," it would have been an example of indirect characterization.

◆Reading Strategy

❹ **Identify With a Character** Ask students to explain why Mr. Tillian buys a parrot and why he ignores his son's disapproval. *Students may say that he is lonely and wants company now that Harry no longer comes by the store. They may say that he ignores Harry's response because he feels abandoned by his son.*

▶Critical Viewing◀

❺ **Apply Prior Knowledge** *Students will probably observe that this parrot appears to be talking, perhaps to Harry's father.*

◆Reading Strategy

❻ **Identify With a Character** *It is likely that most students would respond as Harry does: They would be ashamed and embarrassed by the behavior.*

◆Literary Focus

❼ **Characterization** What do Harry's actions reveal about him? *Possible response: He is responsible; he feels a strong sense of duty.*

Beyond the Classroom

Career Connection

Shopkeeper Small, family-owned businesses, such as the candy and nut store in this story, used to be abundant in America. These were places where the owners were known in the community and where people could socialize. Today, many such businesses have been replaced by chain stores. Is there a future for the enterprising independent shopkeeper?

Discuss this question with students. Then have pairs interview one or more small-store owners in the community to find out about the advantages and disadvantages of owning and operating a small business. They can ask questions to learn about the history of the store and why the present owner chose this way of making a living. Suggest that students tape-record their conversations. Then have whole-class or group discussions in which students compare and contrast what they learned from their interviews. To conclude, invite students to give their views on whether they would like to own and operate a small business one day.

Comprehension Check ☑

❶ Why does the bird say, "Hello Rocky!"? *Parrots mimic what is said to them; Rocky is repeating what he has heard Mr. Tillian say.*

◆Build Grammar Skills

❷ **Complex Sentences** Point out to students that although this sentence is a long one, it is not a complex sentence. It contains several verbs, but it has only one subject (Harry) and therefore is a simple sentence (with a compound predicate). Emphasize that a long sentence is not necessarily a complex one; for it to be complex, it needs to have at least one subordinate clause in addition to its independent clause.

◆Critical Thinking

❸ **Speculate** Ask students to explain why "Chills ran down Harry's back." *Students may say that his uneasy reaction to the constant repetition of "Where's Harry?" shows that the boy feels uncomfortable having the parrot ask where he is when he is right there. Students may also feel that Harry is beginning to understand why the bird is "parroting" this question.*

The shop was as his father had left it. Even the caramels were still spilled on the floor. Harry bent down and picked them up one by one, dropping them back in the boxes. The bird in its cage watched him silently.

Harry opened the new boxes his father hadn't gotten to. Peppermints. Jawbreakers. Toffee creams. Strawberry kisses. Harry traveled from bin to bin, putting the candies where they belonged.

"Hello!"

Harry jumped, spilling a box of jawbreakers.

"Hello, Rocky!"

Harry stared at the parrot. He had forgotten it was there. The bird had been so quiet, and Harry had been thinking only of the candy.

❶ "Hello," Harry said.

"Hello, Rocky!" answered the parrot.

Harry walked slowly over to the cage. The parrot's food cup was empty. Its water was dirty. The bottom of the cage was a mess.

Harry carried the cage into the back room.

"Hello, Rocky!"

"Is that all you can say, you dumb bird?" Harry mumbled. The bird said nothing else.

Harry cleaned the bottom of the cage, refilled the food and water cups, and then put the cage back in its place and resumed sorting the candy. ❷

"Where's Harry?"

Harry looked up.

"Where's Harry?"

Harry stared at the parrot.

"Where's Harry?"

Chills ran down Harry's back. What could the bird mean? It was something from "The Twilight Zone."[1] ❸

"Where's Harry?"

Harry swallowed and said, "I'm here. I'm here, you stupid bird."

1. **"The Twilight Zone":** Science-fiction television series from the 1960's.

◆ Build Vocabulary

resumed (ri zo͞omd′) *v.:* Began again; continued

Speaking and Listening Mini-Lesson

Dramatic Reading

This mini-lesson supports the Speaking and Listening activity in the Idea Bank on p. 489.

Introduce Discuss the elements of good dramatic reading with students. Emphasize the importance of varying the volume and tone of the voice, and the pace of the reading.

Develop Encourage students to practice reading the story and to listen to themselves on audiotape prior to presenting in class. Guide them to listen for how well they convey Harry's feelings. Suggest that each student make a copy of the story and annotate it in the margins to indicate changes to make in their performances—tone of voice, speed and volume of delivery, etc.—related to changes in Harry. Invite students to try a different voice for the parrot.

Apply Record students' performances as they read. Emphasize to the audience the importance of quiet, attentive, and respectful listening.

Assess Evaluate performances based on how well the students capture the changes in and depth of Harry's feelings, and the dramatic elements of the story. Also evaluate how well they project their voices. Alternatively, use the Peer Assessment: Oral Interpretation form, p. 106, or the Peer Assessment: Dramatic Performance form, p. 107, both in **Alternative Assessment.**

"You stupid bird!" said the parrot.

Well, at least he's got one thing straight, thought Harry.

"Miss him! Miss him! Where's Harry? You stupid bird!"

Harry stood with a handful of peppermints.

"What?" he asked.

"Where's Harry?" said the parrot.

"I'm *here*, you stupid bird! I'm here!" Harry yelled. He threw the peppermints at the cage, and the bird screamed and clung to its perch.

> ◆ Literary Focus
> 4 What does Harry's reaction to Rocky reveal about his character?

Harry sobbed, "I'm here." The tears were coming.

Harry leaned over the glass counter.

"Papa." Harry buried his face in his arms.

"Where's Harry?" repeated the bird.

Harry sighed and wiped his face on his sleeve. He watched the parrot. He understood now: someone had been saying, for a long time, "Where's Harry? Miss him."

Harry finished his unpacking and then swept the floor of the shop. He checked the furnace so the bird wouldn't get cold. Then he left to go visit his papa.

Guide for Responding

◆ Literature and Your Life

Reader's Response Should Harry tell his father what he learned from Rocky? Why or why not?

Thematic Focus How might his experience change the way Harry allows himself to interact with others? Explain.

Journal Writing Write about a time when, like Harry, you had an experience that led to a moment of insight. Tell what happened and what the event taught you about yourself.

☑ Check Your Comprehension

1. What does Mr. Tillian do for a living?
2. Why do Harry and his friends visit Harry's father after school?
3. Why do Harry and his friends stop visiting Harry's father?
4. Who is Rocky?
5. Why does Harry have to take care of the shop?
6. What does Rocky say that upsets Harry?

◆ Critical Thinking

Interpret

1. What is Mr. Tillian's motivation, or reason, for buying a parrot? **[Analyze Cause and Effect]**
2. Why is it significant that Mr. Tillian paid "more money than he could really afford" for his parrot? **[Infer]**
3. What can you tell about what motivates Harry from the fact that he walks by his father's shop, looks in, but doesn't stop? **[Interpret]**
4. What motivates Harry to throw peppermints at Rocky? **[Infer]**
5. What does this story suggest about the motivations for people's behavior? **[Draw Conclusions]**

Evaluate

6. In what ways was Harry's behavior irresponsible? Explain. **[Criticize]**

Apply

7. Why might doctors recommend parrots or other pets for older people who are alone? **[Health Link]**

◆ Literary Focus

4 Characterization *Students may say that Harry's reaction to Rocky reveals how much he cares about his father and that he wants to do the right thing. They may suggest that he feels guilty for having stayed away from the store. Others may say that Harry loses his temper easily, or that he doesn't stop to consider the appropriateness or consequences of his actions.*

Reinforce and Extend

Answers

◆ Literature and Your Life

Reader's Response Some students will say that Harry should tell his father and then apologize for the way he has behaved. Others may say that Harry's best course of action would be not to say anything, but to make sure that his future behavior shows how much he really cares about his father.

Thematic Focus Harry realizes that his father thinks about him all the time and misses him, and that he has been neglecting his father by staying away from the store.

☑ Check Your Comprehension

1. He owns a candy and nut shop.
2. They want to buy candy and sample the nuts.
3. They are older, have more spending money, and want to do other things.
4. Rocky is the parrot Mr. Tillian buys to keep him company in the store.
5. His father has had a heart attack and can't leave the hospital.
6. He says, "Where's Harry?" and "Miss him!"

◆ Critical Thinking

1. He is lonely and buys the bird for company.
2. It shows how much he values companionship and misses that of Harry and his friends.
3. Students may infer that Harry cares about his father but is embarrassed by his father's fondness for the parrot. They may suggest that Harry is jealous of the bird, that he senses it to be a substitute for himself.
4. Harry is expressing anger at himself for neglecting his father. Some students may say that his actions reflect a frantic concern for his father's condition.
5. Possible response: People may not be aware of the underlying reasons for their actions or they may behave in an insensitive manner even when their true motivations are basically good.
6. Students may say that Harry did not reach out enough to his father, nor did he make the effort to express his true feelings.
7. Students will suggest that pets provide affection and company. Also, they may observe that older people might welcome the responsibility of pets.

Develop Understanding

One-Minute Insight On the way to school, a boy sees Walter, a classmate who has an illness bad enough to keep him out of school, but not serious enough to keep him from fishing and walking about. Intrigued by Walter's freedom, the boy fakes having the same illness in order to stay home from school and go fishing, too. He lands a big fish and all goes well until his father exposes his trick, and he must face the ridicule of his own family.

◆Critical Thinking

❶ **Hypothesize** Ask students to read the title and to suggest what it might mean. *Students may say that it means taking a day away from an obligation to do what you want, or losing a day to something you don't want to do.*

◆Reading Strategy

❷ **Identify With a Character** Have students describe what the narrator feels toward Walter. *Students may say that he envies Walter's freedom.*

◆Reading Strategy

❸ **Identify With a Character** Here, for the first time, the narrator fools himself into thinking he is ill. Discuss with students that the pain the narrator feels is real, but that he exaggerates it to convince the teacher to send him home. Ask students to explain why his pain goes away. *Once he is out of sight of the teacher and his classmates, he no longer has to exaggerate his discomfort.*

◆Literary Focus

❹ **Characterization** *Since the writer states Earl's traits outright, this description is an example of direct characterization.*

Customize for
Less Proficient Readers
Encourage students to reread passages, as needed, to distinguish between what the boy is saying aloud, what he is thinking and imagining, and what he is actually doing or experiencing.

❶

Stolen Day

Sherwood Anderson

It must be that all children are actors. The whole thing started with a boy on our street named Walter, who had inflammatory rheumatism. That's what they called it. He didn't have to go to school.

❷ Still he could walk about. He could go fishing in the creek or the waterworks pond. There was a place up at the pond where in the spring the water came tumbling over the dam and formed a deep pool. It was a good place. Sometimes you could get some big ones there.

I went down that way on my way to school one spring morning. It was out of my way but I wanted to see if Walter was there.

He was, inflammatory rheumatism and all. There he was, sitting with a fish pole in his hand. He had been able to walk down there all right.

It was then that my own legs began to hurt. My back too. I went on to school but, at the recess time, I began to cry. I did it when the teacher, Sarah Suggett, had come out into the schoolhouse yard.

She came right over to me.

"I ache all over," I said. I did, too.

❸ I kept on crying and it worked all right.

"You'd better go on home," she said.

So I went. I limped painfully away. I kept on limping until I got out of the schoolhouse street.

Then I felt better. I still had inflammatory rheumatism pretty bad but I could get along better.

I must have done some thinking on the way home.

"I'd better not say I have inflammatory rheumatism," I decided. "Maybe if you've got that you swell up."

I thought I'd better go around to where Walter was and ask him about that, so I did—but he wasn't there.

"They must not be biting today," I thought.

I had a feeling that, if I said I had inflammatory rheumatism, Mother or my brothers and my sister Stella might laugh. They did laugh at me pretty often and I didn't like it at all.

"Just the same," I said to myself, "I have got it." I began to hurt and ache again.

I went home and sat on the front steps of our house. I sat there a long time. There wasn't anyone at home but Mother and the two little ones. Ray would have been four or five then and Earl might have been three.

It was Earl who saw me there. I had got tired sitting and was lying on the porch. Earl was always a quiet, solemn little fellow.

He must have said something to Mother for presently she came.

"What's the matter with you? Why aren't you in school?" she asked.

> **◆ Literary Focus**
> Is the narrator's description of Earl an example of direct characterization or indirect characterization? Explain. ❹

I came pretty near telling her right out that I had inflammatory rheumatism but I thought I'd better not. Mother and Father had been speaking of Walter's case at the table just the day before. "It affects the heart," Father had said. That frightened me when I thought of it. "I might die," I thought. "I might just suddenly die right here; my heart might stop beating."

On the day before I had been running a race with my brother Irve. We were up at the

◆ Build Vocabulary

inflammatory (in flam′ ə tôr′ ē) *adj.*: Characterized by pain and swelling

rheumatism (ro͞o′ mə tiz′ əm) *n.*: Painful condition of the joints and muscles

solemn (säl′ əm) *adj.*: Serious; somber

Customize for
English Language Learners
The story contains language specific to fishing. Through illustrations, examples, and descriptions from knowledgeable classmates, help students understand the meanings of these terms. For example, when they read that the boy gets a "bite" on his line and it is a "whopper," point out that the line is the fishing line and the whopper is a typical description of a big fish.

The Pond, 1985, Adele Alsop, Courtesy of Schmidt Bingham Gallery, NYC

5 ▲ **Critical Viewing** Why might Walter or the narrator enjoy spending time at a lake like the one in this painting? **[Speculate]**

fairgrounds after school and there was a half-mile track.

6 "I'll bet you can't run a half-mile," he said. "I bet you I could beat you running clear around the track."

7 And so we did it and I beat him, but afterwards my heart did seem to beat pretty hard. I remembered that lying there on the porch. "It's a wonder, with my inflammatory rheumatism and all, I didn't just drop down dead," I thought. The thought frightened me a lot. I ached worse than ever.

"I ache, Ma," I said. "I just ache."

8 She made me go in the house and upstairs and get into bed.

It wasn't so good. It was spring. I was up there for perhaps an hour, maybe two, and then I felt better.

I got up and went downstairs. "I feel better, Ma," I said.

Mother said she was glad. She was pretty busy that day and hadn't paid much attention to me. She had made me get into bed upstairs and then hadn't even come up to see how I was.

I didn't think much of that when I was up there but when I got downstairs where she was, 8 and when, after I had said I felt better and she only said she was glad and went right on with her work, I began to ache again.

I thought, "I'll bet I die of it. I bet I do."

I went out to the front porch and sat down. I was pretty sore at Mother.

"If she really knew the truth, that I have the inflammatory rheumatism and I may just drop down dead any time, I'll bet she wouldn't care about that either," I thought.

I was getting more and more angry the more thinking I did.

"I know what I'm going to do," I thought; "I'm going to go fishing."

I thought that, feeling the way I did, I might be sitting on the high bank just above the deep pool where the water went over the dam, and suddenly my heart would stop beating.

And then, of course, I'd pitch forward, over the bank into the pool and, if I wasn't dead

▶Critical Viewing◀

5 **Speculate** *Students might suggest that it looks very private and the bank on the far side looks like a perfect place to sit and fish. The scene is also beautiful.*

◆Critical Thinking

6 **Deduce** What does this contest tell you about the real condition of the speaker? How might it explain the pain he would feel in class the next day? *Students can see that he was feeling well enough to win a demanding race. They might suggest that the pain is soreness from the previous day's exertion.*

◆Literary Focus

7 **Characterization** Help students understand that the boy is confused because, despite his physical fitness, he has again fooled himself into thinking that he is ill. Have students be on the lookout for the next time he feels sick and then think about what his motivation might be.

◆Literary Focus

8 **Characterization** Guide students to notice the indirect characterization of the mother. Ask them to explain what her reaction to her son's illness suggests about her and the seriousness of his condition. *Students may say that the mother is wise. She humors him by paying some attention to his complaints, but is aware that they are not serious enough to merit deep concern.*

Humanities: Art

The Pond, 1985, by Adele Alsop

Adele Alsop (born 1948) got her M.F.A. and B.A. from the University of Pennsylvania and also studied at Boston University School of Fine Arts. She lives in Castle Valley, Utah. Known for her landscapes, Alsop has had solo exhibitions since 1973 and has had her paintings in group landscape exhibits since 1972. She has been a visiting lecturer at several colleges. Use these questions for discussion:

1. How is this painting different from many other paintings you have seen? *Possible answer: It almost looks like a color photograph.*
2. Compare and contrast this image with your own mental picture of the place where Walter and the narrator fish. *Possible response: It depicts a more rural scene than one might expect to find within walking distance of the boys' homes.*

◆Literary Focus

❶ Characterization What does this event reveal about the mother's character? *Students can realize now that the mother is truly a caring person. Had she believed that her son was really suffering, she would have shown the concern and care she now demonstrates.*

◆Reading Strategy

❷ Identify With a Character Discuss this humorous contradiction with students and explain that it is an example of the boy's misguided but quite normal call for attention.

◆Literary Focus

❸ Characterization *Students may say that, down deep, he would rather be alive than be a cause for his mother's concern or the object of attention.*

◆Critical Thinking

❹ Draw Conclusions Discuss the following questions: Will the boy now be a hero because of his successful catch? How might his success conflict with his inflammatory rheumatism? Have students review what has happened thus far and predict what will occur now that the boy wants everyone to think he is both a hero and very ill at the same time. *Students may realize that, with his heroics, the boy's ruse is over.*

◆Reading Strategy

❺ Identify With a Character *Students might say they would feel embarrassed, too. They might also be angry with the family for laughing. Some students will recognize that the boy had almost convinced himself that he was sick.*

when I hit the water, I'd drown sure.

They would all come home to supper and they'd miss me.

"But where is he?"

Then Mother would remember that I'd come home from school aching.

She'd go upstairs and I wouldn't be there. One day during the year before, there was a child got drowned in a spring. It was one of the Wyatt children.

Right down at the end of the street there was a spring under a birch tree and there had been a barrel sunk in the ground.

Everyone had always been saying the spring ought to be kept covered, but it wasn't.

So the Wyatt child went down there, played around alone, and fell in and got drowned.

Mother was the one who had found the drowned child. She had gone to get a pail of water and there the child was, drowned and dead.

❶ This had been in the evening when we were all at home, and Mother had come running up the street with the dead, dripping child in her arms. She was making for the Wyatt house as hard as she could run, and she was pale.

She had a terrible look on her face, I remembered then.

"So," I thought, "they'll miss me and there'll be a search made. Very likely there'll be someone who has seen me sitting by the pond fishing, and there'll be a big alarm and all the town will turn out and they'll drag the pond."

❷ I was having a grand time, having died. Maybe, after they found me and had got me out of the deep pool, Mother would grab me up in her arms and run home with me as she had run with the Wyatt child.

> **◆ Literary Focus**
> What do the narrator's thoughts about drowning reveal about his personality? ❸

I got up from the porch and went around the house. I got my fishing pole and lit out for the pool below the dam. Mother was busy—she always was—and didn't see me go. When I got there I thought I'd better not sit too near the edge of the high bank.

By this time I didn't ache hardly at all, but I thought.

"With inflammatory rheumatism you can't tell," I thought.

"It probably comes and goes," I thought.

"Walter has it and he goes fishing," I thought.

I had got my line into the pool and suddenly I got a bite. It was a regular whopper. I knew that. I'd never had a bite like that.

I knew what it was. It was one of Mr. Fenn's big carp.

Mr. Fenn was a man who had a big pond of his own. He sold ice in the summer and the pond was to make the ice. He had bought some big carp and put them into his pond and then, earlier in the spring when there was a freshet, his dam had gone out.

So the carp had got into our creek and one or two big ones had been caught—but none of them by a boy like me.

The carp was pulling and I was pulling and I was afraid he'd break my line, so I just tumbled down the high bank holding onto the line and got right into the pool. We had it out, there in ❹ the pool. We struggled. We wrestled. Then I got a hand under his gills and got him out.

He was a big one all right. He was nearly half

as big as I was myself. I had him on the bank and I kept one hand under his gills and I ran.

I never ran so hard in my life. He was slippery,
4 and now and then he wriggled out of my arms; once I stumbled and fell on him, but I got him home.

So there it was. I was a big hero that day. Mother got a washtub and filled it with water. She put the fish in it and all the neighbors came to look. I got into dry clothes and went down to supper—and then I made a break that spoiled my day.

There we were, all of us, at the table, and suddenly Father asked what had been the matter with me at school. He had met the teacher, Sarah Suggett, on the street and she had told him how I had become ill.

"What was the matter with you?" Father asked, and before I thought what I was saying I let it out.

> ◆ **Reading Strategy** How would you feel at this moment? 5

"I had the inflammatory rheumatism," I said—and a shout went up. It made me sick to hear them, the way they all laughed.

It brought back all the aching again, and like a fool I began to cry.

"Well, I *have* got it—I *have*, I *have*," I cried, and I got up from the table and ran upstairs.

I stayed there until Mother came up. I knew it would be a long time before I heard the last of the inflammatory rheumatism. I was sick all right, but the aching I now had wasn't in my legs or in my back.

Guide for Responding

◆ Literature and Your Life

Reader's Response Do you find the narrator's behavior and ideas realistic? Explain.

Thematic Focus How does his experience affect the way the narrator feels about being honest with himself and others?

Journal Writing The boy knows he has done something wrong, yet he tries to justify his actions. In your journal, consider why people try to convince themselves that they've done the right thing, even when they know they haven't.

☑ Check Your Comprehension

1. What inspires the narrator to think he has "inflammatory rheumatism"?
2. What happens to the narrator in school?
3. What does the narrator do after he gets home?
4. How does his father learn that the narrator left school that day?
5. How does the narrator's family respond when he tells them he has inflammatory rheumatism?

◆ Critical Thinking

INTERPRET

1. Why does the narrator stop limping once he gets away from the schoolhouse street? **[Interpret]**
2. Why is it significant that the boy decides not to tell his family he has inflammatory rheumatism? **[Infer]**
3. (a) What does the narrator mean when he says, "I was having a grand time, having died"? (b) What is his motivation for feeling this way? **[Analyze Causes and Effects]**
4. Do you think that the narrator is fully conscious of his motives? Explain. **[Deduce]**
5. What does this story say about the motivations for people's behavior? **[Draw Conclusions]**

EVALUATE

6. Should the narrator be punished for stealing a day? Why or why not? **[Make a Judgment]**

COMPARE LITERARY WORKS

7. How would you state the theme, or main idea, that lies at the center of "Papa's Parrot" and "Stolen Day"? **[Generalize]**

Beyond the Selection

FURTHER READING

Other Works by Cynthia Rylant

A Couple of Kooks, and Other Stories
Missing May

Other Works by Sherwood Anderson

Winesburg, Ohio
The Triumph of the Egg
Horses and Men

INTERNET

We suggest the following sites on the Internet (all Web sites are subject to change).

For Cynthia Rylant:
http://www.rylant.com

For the Sherwood Anderson page that has a photo of his Clyde, Ohio, home and links to other sites:
http://www.nwohio.com/clydeoh/sherwood.htm

We *strongly recommend* that you preview the sites before you send students to them.

Reinforce and Extend

Answers

◆ Literature and Your Life

Reader's Response Some students may say that the narrator's behavior and ideas are realistic because people can convince themselves of almost anything to justify their behavior. Others may respond that kids who pretend to be sick know that they are faking and fail to feel actual aches and pains.

Thematic Focus The final paragraph suggests that the narrator realizes that he has behaved foolishly and that he'll be teased for it.

☑ Check Your Comprehension

1. He notices that Walter is too sick to go to school but is sometimes well enough to go fishing.
2. He cries during recess, complains of aches all over, and is allowed to go home.
3. He sits on the porch for a while, then goes up to bed. When he is bored with that, he goes fishing.
4. He met the teacher, who told him.
5. They laugh uproariously.

◆ Critical Thinking

1. He no longer needs the excuse of illness to get out of school.
2. He knows deep inside that he is faking it and does not want to get caught imagining a serious disease. He also does not know all the symptoms of the disease.
3. (a) He enjoyed imagining all the attention he would be getting. (b) He feels neglected by his busy mother.
4. Some students will say yes because of the conditions under which he gets his "attacks." Others will think that the narrator lacks self-awareness and believes that he is actually ill.
5. It suggests that people may be unaware of their own motivations.
6. Some students will think he should be punished because playing hooky is not acceptable behavior. Others will argue that the boy truly believed he was ill. Still others might say that his family's response to catching him in the lie is punishment enough.
7. There are unexpected and possibly serious consequences to behaving irresponsibly.

Answers

◆Reading Strategy

1. Students may say that they would try to visit their father more often and to share their feelings more openly.
2. Students may say that they would learn to be more self-aware and understanding of their motivations, and then avoid doing foolish things.
3. Some students may talk about the importance of being honest with themselves and with others. Others may say that it is important to try to understand others' motivations in order to assess what is behind their actions.

◆Build Vocabulary

Using the Word Root *-flam-*

1. Inflame means "to set on fire," "to make or become excited," or "to make or become hot, swollen, and red."
2. Flammable means "easily set on fire."
3. Flamboyant means "having waving curves shaped like flames" or "too showy and ornate."

Spelling Strategy

1. autumn; 2. column; 3. condemn; 4. hymn; 5. solemn

Using the Word Bank

1. solemn; 2. resumed; 3. inflammatory; 4. rheumatism

◆Literary Focus

Possible responses:

1. "Harry told his father that he would go to the store every day after school and unpack boxes." "Chills ran down Harry's back."
2. Indirect: "'If she really knew the truth, that I have the inflammatory rheumatism and I might just drop dead any time, I'll bet she wouldn't care about that either,' I thought." Direct: The boy thought that his mother was ignoring him and not taking him seriously. Indirect: "By this time I didn't ache hardly at all, but I thought. 'With inflammatory rheumatism you can't tell,' I thought. 'It probably comes and goes,' I thought." Direct: By this time the boy felt no aches, but he convinced himself that he still had the disease.
3. Indirect characterization is more effective because it allows readers to draw their own conclusions. It provides details that make it easier to get a full picture of a character.

Guide for Responding *(continued)*

◆ Reading Strategy

Identify With a Character

To fully appreciate a character's experiences, put yourself in his or her place. As the events of the story unfold, **identify with a character** by asking yourself what you would do or how you would feel under the circumstances.

1. If you were in Harry's place, how would you change your behavior in the future?

2. If you were in the narrator's place in "Stolen Day," what would you learn from your feelings at the end of the story?

3. What can you learn from these characters' experiences that might help you in your own life?

◆ Build Vocabulary

Using the Word Root *-flam-*

Knowing that the word root *-flam-* means "burn" or "flame" can help you figure out the meaning of words that contain this root. Define each of the following words, incorporating the meaning of *-flam-*. If necessary, use a dictionary for assistance.

1. inflame **2.** flammable **3.** flamboyant

Spelling Strategy

Almost all words that end with the *m* sound end with *-m* or *-me*. However, a few end with *-mn*. In these words, the letter *n* is silent. There are fewer than a dozen such words. On your paper, complete each of the following words to form a list of the most common *-mn* words.

1. autu_ _ **3.** conde_ _ **5.** sole_ _
2. colu_ _ **4.** hy_ _

Using the Word Bank

On your paper, write the following paragraph, filling in each of the blanks with the appropriate Word Bank word.

The doctor was ____?____ as she examined the sick boy. She had asked him to stop treatment, but he was not improving. Following her instructions, Walter ____?____ taking an anti-____?____ medicine when ____?____ made his joints swollen, feverish, and painful. The medicine reduced his symptons.

◆ Literary Focus

Characterization

In **direct characterization,** the writer tells you about the character's traits. In **indirect characterization,** the writer shows you a character's personality through what he or she says, does, and thinks and by how others interact with the character.

1. Find two examples of indirect characterization of Harry in "Papa's Parrot."

2. Find two examples of indirect characterization of the narrator in "Stolen Day." Rewrite each of the examples you identified as direct characterization.

3. Which is more effective: direct characterization or indirect characterization? Explain.

◆ Build Grammar Skills

Complex Sentences

A **complex sentence** contains one independent clause, which can stand by itself as a complete sentence, and one or more subordinate clauses. A subordinate clause contains a subject and a verb but cannot stand alone. A subordinate clause starts with a word (or words) that links it to the rest of the sentence. Words that introduce subordinate clauses include *after, although, as, as if, because, before, despite, if, so that, that, until, what, when, where, which, while,* and *who.*

Practice Copy the following sentences. Underline the independent clause. Circle the word that introduces the subordinate clause.

1. While Mr. Tillian lay in his hospital bed, Harry took the shop key to school with him.

2. Harry stopped liking candy when he was seven.

3. It was Earl who saw me there.

4. I stayed there until Mother came up.

5. It would be a long time before I heard the last of the inflammatory rheumatism.

Writing Application Copy the following sentences, adding subordinate clauses that provide additional information about *who, where,* or *why.*

1. The boy sat on the riverbank.

2. Mr. Tillian bought a parrot.

◆Build Grammar Skills

Practice

1. Harry took the shop key to school with him; while
2. Harry stopped liking candy; when
3. It was Earl; who
4. I stayed there; until
5. It would be a long time; before

Writing Application

Possible responses:

1. The boy, who was skipping school, sat on the riverbank where the water ran deep and the fish were plentiful.
2. Mr. Tillian bought a parrot, which he hoped would keep him company.

For additional instruction and practice, use the lessons in the *Writer's Solution Language Lab CD-ROM* on Sentence Errors and on Styling Sentences.

Build Your Portfolio

Idea Bank

Writing

1. **Diary Entry** As the narrator of "Stolen Day," compose a diary entry in which you explain your behavior on this day. Discuss the reasons for what you thought and what you did.
2. **Review** Write a review of one of these stories for a student literary magazine. Summarize the events of the story. Then explain why you would or would not recommend the story to your audience. Cite passages from the story for support.
3. **Comparing Literary Works** Write an essay in which you compare and contrast the experiences of the main characters in the two stories.

Speaking and Listening

4. **Television Interview [Group Activity]** Imagine that years after the incidents described in the story, Harry Tillian and his father are asked to appear on a talk show to describe the events in the story. With two other classmates, dramatize this talk-show appearance for the class.
5. **Dramatic Reading** Present a dramatic reading of "Papa's Parrot" to the class. Take some time to practice before your presentation. Vary the tone and volume of your voice to match the main character's feelings about the events described.

Projects

6. **Health Statistics** Through research, gather statistics about rheumatoid arthritis, heart disease, or another health condition. Find out the number of people affected, the age groups they fit into, and cure rates. Then, create a series of graphs to chart your findings. Present your graphs to the class. **[Health Link; Math Link]**
7. **Report [Group Activity]** With a group, create a report on the heart. Divide up topics like these among the members of your group: heart-healthy diets, heart structure, artificial hearts, and heart attacks. **[Science Link]**

Writing Mini-Lesson

Continuation

Both stories end with a conversation just about to take place between a parent and a child. In "Papa's Parrot," Harry is going to visit his father. In "Stolen Day," the narrator's mother is coming upstairs after the narrator has fled to his room. Write a continuation of one of the stories that shows what happens next.

Writing Skills Focus: Show, Don't Tell

As you write your continuation, focus on providing details that get your point across, rather than simply stating what's going on. In other words, **show, don't tell.** Through dialogue and description, lead your readers to the conclusions or insights you want to express.

Prewriting List the emotions you'll want to convey in your continuation. For each, identify actions or dialogue that show this emotion. For example, to convey anger, characters might raise their voices. To show embarrassment, characters might bow their heads or avoid eye contact.

Drafting Sometimes a character's actions say more than his or her actual words. As you relate the conversation, refer to your notes. Then, make sure you include details about the character's gestures and how they speak.

◆ Grammar Application

Use complex sentences to show cause-and-effect relationships, to indicate when actions happened relative to one another, or to provide less important details about people or events.

Revising Revise your continuation by looking for places in the description where you can replace statements about the characters with events that reveal the characters' needs and personalities.

Idea Bank

Following are suggestions for matching the Idea Bank topics with your students' performance levels and learning modalities:

Customize for *Performance Levels*
Less Advanced Students: 1, 2
Average Students: 2, 3, 4, 5
More Advanced Students: 3, 5, 6, 7

Customize for *Learning Modalities*
Verbal/Linguistic: 1, 2, 3, 4, 5, 6, 7
Visual/Spatial: 6
Logical/Mathematical: 3, 6, 7
Musical/Rhythmic: 5
Interpersonal: 2, 4, 7
Intrapersonal: 1, 2

Writing Mini-Lesson

Refer students to the Writing Handbook in the back of the book for instructions on the writing process and for further information on writing dialogue.

Writer's Solution

Writing Lab CD-ROM
Have students complete the tutorial on Creative Writing. Follow these steps:

1. Have students use Word Bin for Emotions to find precise words.
2. Suggest that students view interactive writing instruction about character traits to see how dialogue can express a quality.
3. Have students draft on computer.
4. Encourage students to use interactive instruction in misplaced modifiers when revising.

Writer's Solution Sourcebook
Have students use Chapter 8, "Creative Writing," pp. 234–263, for additional support. The chapter includes in-depth instruction on writing dialogue or a monologue, p. 256.

✓ ASSESSMENT OPTIONS

ASSESSMENT OPTIONS
Formal Assessment, Selection Test, pp. 141–143, and Assessment Resources Software. The selection test is designed so that it can be easily customized to the performance levels of your students.
Alternative Assessment, p. 31, includes options for less advanced students, more advanced students, verbal/linguistic learners, musical/rhythmic learners, interpersonal learners, and logical/mathematical learners.

PORTFOLIO ASSESSMENT
Use the following rubrics in the **Alternative Assessment** booklet to assess student writing:
Diary Entry: Expression, p. 81
Review: Evaluatory Review, p. 91
Comparing Literary Works: Comparison/Contrast, p. 90
Writing Mini-Lesson: Fictional Narrative, p. 82

Prepare and Engage

OBJECTIVES

1. To read, comprehend, and interpret a selection that has a social studies focus
2. To relate a selection with a social studies focus to personal experience
3. To connect literature to social studies
4. To respond to Social Studies Guiding Questions
5. To respond to the selection through writing, speaking and listening, and projects

SOCIAL STUDIES GUIDING QUESTIONS

Reading about the experiences of two men during troubled political times in Colombia will help students discover answers to these Social Studies Guiding Questions:

- What historical events have helped shape Latin America?
- In what ways can a country's civil war affect the everyday lives of its citizens?

To get students thinking about what it's like to lead a double life, pass around U.S. coins for them to examine. If necessary, point out that all the coins show an individual on one side and a symbol of the nation on the other. Then have students flip the coins several times to see how they land. Ask students what it might feel like to be torn between your loyalty to your nation and your loyalty to yourself. Explain that the narrator in "Lather and Nothing Else" faces this situation—complicated by civil war in his nation.

Map Study

Political Maps The connection between geography and social studies is often a key to understanding why events happened. To support students' reading of Two Histories, help them extract details from the map on this page. For example, have students name the countries that border Colombia. Discuss what students know about the political situations in these nations.

CONNECTING LITERATURE TO SOCIAL STUDIES

LATIN AMERICA

Lather and Nothing Else *by Hernando Téllez*

CAN YOU KEEP A SECRET? Imagine that you are living during America's Civil War. You support one side—maybe even spy for its cause—but you live among the other side. Some Americans did face this problem, as did some Colombians during that South American country's years of civil unrest.

BAHAMAS
CUBA
DOMINICAN REPUBLIC
area of map
JAMAICA
HAITI
HONDURAS
PUERTO RICO
Caribbean Sea
NICARAGUA
0 600 mi
0 600 km
COSTA RICA
ATLANTIC OCEAN
PANAMA
VENEZUELA
SURINAME
GUYANA
N
PACIFIC OCEAN
COLOMBIA
0°
Equator
Latin America
ECUADOR
PERU
BRAZIL

Two Histories As in many Latin American nations, the political divisions in Colombia are rooted in the events of the 1500's, when Europeans colonized the land. Native Americans, who had lived in Colombia for thousands of years, lost their land to Spaniards. Spanish landowners became wealthy and helped build big cities like Bogotá, the capital of Colombia.

A Growing Gap Though Colombia became independent from Spain in the early 1800's, the gap between poor peasants of Native American heritage and wealthy, educated city dwellers of European heritage grew wider. Conflict also arose over how to organize the government.

Civil War Breaks Out In the late 1800's, Colombians' anger and frustration finally erupted in civil war. After years of fighting, 100,000 Colombians were dead. Still, the main problems were not solved. During the twentieth century, violence has regularly pierced calm times. One very rocky period from 1948 through the mid-1960's was filled with such fierce fighting that it was known as *La Violencia* (The Violence). In "Lather and Nothing Else," you'll meet a barber who must choose his own role in this violent time.

490 ◆ *Short Stories*

Prentice Hall Literature Program Resources

REINFORCE / RETEACH / EXTEND

Selection Support Pages
Build Vocabulary, p. 172
Theme, p. 173

Formal Assessment Selection Test, pp. 144–145, Assessment Resources Software

Writing and Language Transparencies
Sensory Language Chart, p. 78, Venn Diagram, p. 86; Sunburst Organizer, p. 94; Cause-and-Effect Organizer, p. 62

Resource Pro CD-ROM
"Lather and Nothing Else"—includes all resource material and customizable lesson plan

Listening to Literature Audiocassettes
"Lather and Nothing Else"

Connection to Prentice Hall World Explorer
Latin America
Ch. 1, "Latin America: Physical Geography"
Ch. 2, "Latin America: Shaped by Its History"
Ch. 3, "Cultures of Latin America"
Ch. 6, "Exploring South America"

Lather and Nothing Else

Hernando Téllez

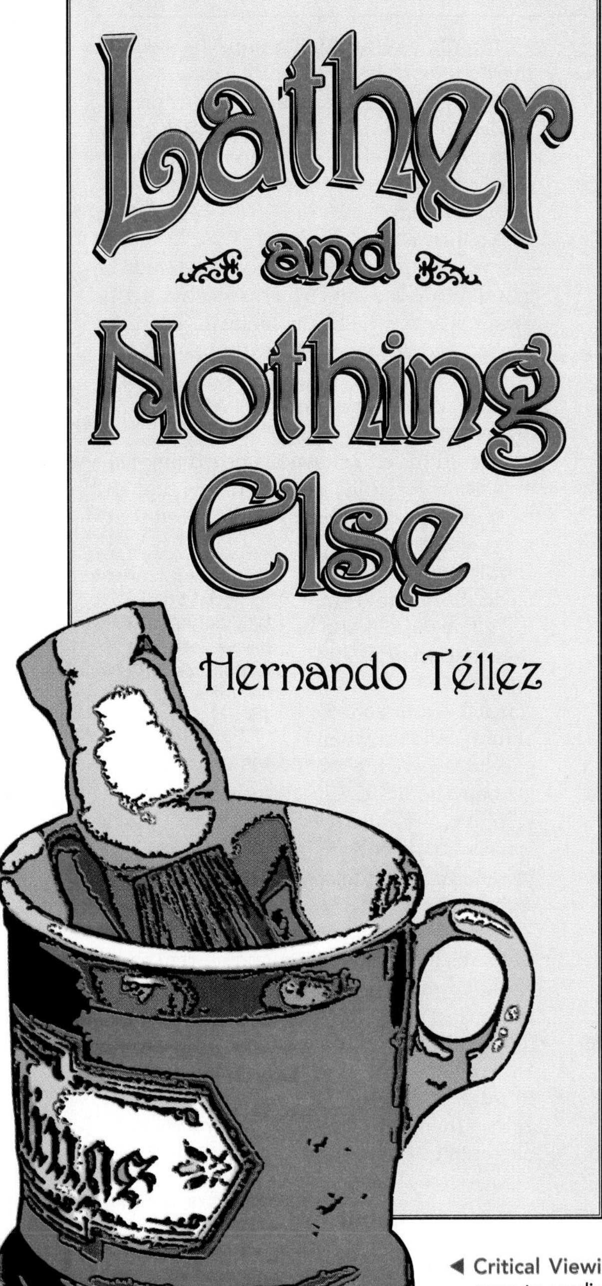

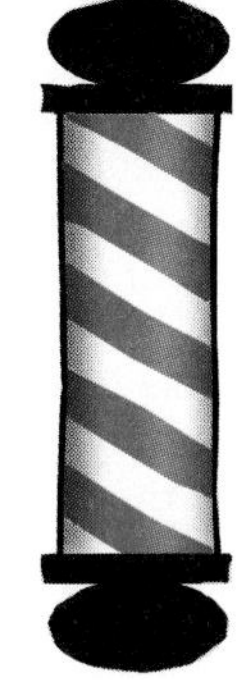

CONNECTING LITERATURE TO SOCIAL STUDIES

He came in without a word. I was stropping[1] my best razor. And when I recognized him, I started to shake. But he did not notice. To cover my nervousness, I went on honing the razor. I tried the edge with the tip of my thumb and took another look at it against the light. ❶

Meanwhile, he was taking off his cartridge-studded belt with the pistol holster suspended from it. He put it on a hook in the wardrobe and hung his cap above it. Then he turned full around toward me and, loosening his tie, remarked, "It's hot as the devil. I want a shave." With that he took his seat.

I estimated he had a four-days' growth of beard, the four days he had been gone on the last foray after our men. His face looked burnt, tanned by the sun.

I started to work carefully on the shaving soap. I scraped some slices from the cake, dropped them into the mug, then

1. **stropping** (sträp´ iŋ) *v.*: Sharpening a blade to a fine edge on a thick band of leather called a strop.

◆ **Build Vocabulary**

foray (fôr´ ā) *n.*: Sudden attack or raid

◀ Critical Viewing Use the title and illustrations on this page to predict the setting of this story. **[Predict]** ❷

One-Minute Insight "Lather and Nothing Else" describes an experience in the life of a small-town barber during Colombia's civil unrest of the late 1940's. A rebel spy, the barber finds himself holding a razor to the chin of Captain Torres of the local military police. As the captain recounts his recent adventures capturing and torturing rebels, the barber agonizes over whether to kill the captain or just give him a great shave. In the end, we learn that the captain has known the barber's true identity all along and perhaps understands his difficult choice.

Team Teaching Strategy

"Lather and Nothing Else" offers an opportunity to team teach with a social studies teacher, creating a cross-curricular unit on Latin American political history.

❶ **Clarification** The barber is using a straight razor, which has a long exposed knifelike blade. Unlike disposable razor blades, more common today, a straight razor is resharpened for repeated use.

Customize for
Less Proficient Readers
Explain that in this story one character shares his inner thoughts and emotions. Remind students of how their own thoughts may jump from topic to topic, and tell them that the barber's thoughts do the same. To help them follow the barber's jumps from external events to internal thoughts, pair students with proficient readers. Play the audiocassette, or have one of the students read the story aloud. Have both partners indicate each time the barber switches from internal to external events.

Listening to Literature Audiocassettes

▶Critical Viewing◀

❷ **Predict** *Because of the shaving mug and barber pole, "lather" must be shaving cream. The story must be set in a barbershop.*

Preparing for Standardized Tests

Critical Reading Standardized tests often include questions that require students to critically analyze elements such as plot, setting, and character. In open-ended test formats, students must develop logically organized and grammatically correct sentences or paragraphs. To offer students practice in thinking critically and developing short answer responses, write the following question on the board:

How might the story's opening be different if it were told from the customer's point of view?

Help students recognize that most of the story's details describe the barber's thoughts and feelings. Students should realize that a different point of view would change the details—and their answers should include examples of some of those details. Model this possible answer:

Told by the customer, the story's opening would focus on his feelings and thoughts as he enters the barber shop. For example, it might describe his physical reactions to the heat and his thick beard or describe his reaction to the barber sharpening a razor.

Connecting Literature to Social Studies

❶ **Speculate** Remind students of the paragraph Civil War Breaks Out on p. 490. Help them identify who is fighting in a civil war (opposing groups of citizens from the same nation). Then direct them to the details on p. 491 about what the customer is wearing. *Students should be able to speculate that the customer is some kind of soldier or policeman. He's probably chasing people fighting for the other side.*

Links Across Time

❷ In 1946, a new political party took over Colombia's government. The Conservatives, as they were called, tried to destroy the opposing party, known as the Liberals. Their methods were very harsh and often violent. In 1948, an important Liberal leader was openly assassinated in Bogotá. Riots followed and began yet another period of increased violence for Colombia.

◆Critical Thinking

❸ **Infer** Ask students if they think the barber is telling the truth here. Did he really enjoy the show? Lead them to infer that the barber is lying. What does this tell readers about him? *He's willing to lie and he's able to do so smoothly enough not to be caught. This suggests that he's probably had some practice at it.*

Connecting Literature to Social Studies

❹ **Analyze** *The barber is a revolutionary for the rebel side. This means that he has a strong interest in how the revolution ends. He's concerned with how his actions can best help the rebel cause.*

Customize for *More Advanced Students*

Students may want to learn more about life in other Latin American nations. Direct them to literature from some of these nations. After they have read a cross-section of Latin American literature, invite students to share their thoughts about the impact of politics on the region's literature.

---

added a little lukewarm water, and stirred with the brush. The lather soon began to rise.

"The fellows in the troop must have just about as much beard as I." I went on stirring up lather.

"But we did very well, you know. We caught the leaders. Some of them we brought back dead; others are still alive. But they'll all be dead soon."

> **Connecting Literature to Social Studies**
> ❶ Given Colombia's political problems, who do you think the customer has been chasing?

"How many did you take?" I asked.

"Fourteen. We had to go pretty far in to find them. But now they're paying for it. And not one will escape; not a single one."

He leaned back in the chair when he saw the brush in my hand, full of lather. I had not yet put the sheet on him. I was certainly flustered. Taking a sheet from the drawer, I tied it around my customer's neck.

He went on talking. He evidently took it for granted that I was on the side of the existing regime.

❷ "The people must have gotten a scare with what happened the other day," he said.

"Yes," I replied, as I finished tying the knot against his nape, which smelt of sweat.

❸ "Good show, wasn't it?"

"Very good," I answered, turning my attention now to the brush. The man closed his eyes wearily and awaited the cool caress of the lather.

I had never had him so close before. The day he ordered the people to file through the schoolyard to look upon the four rebels hanging there, my path had crossed his briefly. But the sight of those mutilated bodies kept me from paying attention to the face of the man who had been directing it all and whom I now had in my hands.

It was not a disagreeable face, certainly. And the beard, which aged him a bit, was not unbecoming. His name was Torres. Captain Torres.

I started to lay on the first coat of lather. He kept his eyes closed.

"I would love to catch a nap," he said, "but there's a lot to be done this evening."

I lifted the brush and asked, with pretended indifference: "A firing party?"

"Something of the sort," he replied, "but slower."

"All of them?"

"No, just a few."

I went on lathering his face. My hands began to tremble again. The man could not be aware of this, which was lucky for me. But I wished he had not come in. Probably many of our men had seen him enter the shop. And with the enemy in my house I felt a certain responsibility.

I would have to shave his beard just like any other, carefully, neatly, just as though he were a good customer, taking heed that not a single pore should emit a drop of blood. Seeing to it that the blade did not slip in the small whorls. Taking care that the skin was left clean, soft, shining, so that when I passed the back of my hand over it not a single hair should be felt. Yes. I was secretly a revolutionary, but at the same time I was a conscientious barber, proud of the way I did my job. And that four-day beard presented a challenge.

> **Connecting Literature to Social Studies**
> Why do you think the barber feels so responsible for how he treats Captain Torres? ❹

I took up the razor, opened the handle wide, releasing the blade, and started to work, downward from one sideburn. The blade responded to perfection. The hair was tough and hard; not very long, but thick. Little by little the skin began to show through. The razor gave out its usual sound as it gathered up layers of soap mixed with bits of hair. I paused to wipe it clean, and

◆ Build Vocabulary

regime (rə zhēm′) *n.*: System or rule of government
nape (nāp) *n.*: Back of the neck
rejuvenated (ri jo͞o′ və nāt′ id) *v.*: Made to feel refreshed; revitalized

Block Scheduling Strategies

Consider these strategies to take advantage of extended class time:

- Use *World Explorer: Latin America,* Chapter 2, "Latin America: Shaped by Its History," to help students understand the story's context. After reading the story, have pairs of students answer the questions on p. 497.
- Have students work in small groups to complete the group activity project, Time Capsule, on p. 497. If possible, provide books and periodicals containing information students will find useful. If you have access to technology, encourage students to use the Internet as a valuable research source.
- Present the Preparing for Standardized Tests lesson on p. 491 after students read the first story page. As students continue reading, urge them to complete a Sunburst Organizer, p. 94, in **Writing and Language Transparencies,** with ideas about Captain Torres's view. Students can use their organizers to prewrite for their Internal Monologue in the Idea Bank on p. 497 and to answer the sample standardized test question about the full selection.

taking up the strop once more went about improving its edge, for I am a painstaking barber.

The man, who had kept his eyes closed, now opened them, put a hand out from under the sheet, felt of the part of his face that was emerging from the lather, and said to me, "Come at six o'clock this evening to the school."

"Will it be like the other day?" I asked, stiff with horror.

"It may be even better," he replied.

"What are you planning to do?"

5 "I'm not sure yet. But we'll have a good time."

Once more he leaned back and shut his eyes. I came closer, the razor on high.

"Are you going to punish all of them?" I timidly ventured.

"Yes, all of them."

The lather was drying on his face. I must hurry. Through the mirror, I took a look at the street. It appeared about as usual; there was the grocery shop with two or three customers. Then I glanced at the clock, two-thirty.

General With Sword, Francisco Vidal. Courtesy of the artist

▲ Critical Viewing What details in this painting suggest both the revolution and the barber shop? [Connect] 6

CONNECTING LITERATURE TO SOCIAL STUDIES

The razor kept descending. Now from the other sideburn downward. It was a blue beard, a thick one. He should let it grow like some poets, or some priests. It would suit him well. Many people would not recognize him. And that would be a good thing for him, I thought, as I went gently over all the throat line. At this point you really had to handle your blade skillfully, because the hair, while scantier, tended to fall into small whorls. It was a curly beard. The pores might open, minutely, in this area and let out a tiny drop of blood. A good barber like myself stakes his reputation on not permitting that to happen to any of his customers.

And this was indeed a special customer. How many of ours had he sent to their death? How many had he mutilated? It was best not to think about it. Torres did not know I was his enemy. Neither he nor the others knew it. It was a secret shared by very few, just because that made it possible for me to inform the revolutionaries about Torres's activities in the town and what he planned to do every time he went on one of his raids to hunt down rebels. So it was going to be very difficult to explain how it was that I had him in my hands and then let him go in peace, alive, cleanshaven.

His beard had now almost entirely disappeared. He looked younger, several years younger than when he had come in. I suppose that always happens to men who enter and leave barbershops. Under the strokes of my razor, Torres was rejuvenated; yes, because I am a good barber, the best in this town, and I say this in all modesty.

◆Critical Thinking

Interpret Why is it a good thing for the captain if people don't recognize him? *He is hated and feared by much of the community, so he will be safer if people don't recognize him. Also, if no one recognizes him, he will be better able to catch the rebel he is chasing.*

Customize for *Visual/Spatial Learners*

As they read or listen to a partner read, have students visualize the details and strong images the writer uses. They can use a Sensory Language Chart, p. 78, in **Writing and Language Transparencies** to record some of these details. Alternatively, students may wish to draw a scene or individual detail.

CONNECTING LITERATURE TO SOCIAL STUDIES

5 **Analyze** In this passage, we learn how costly the revolution has been for the rebels and can guess at the violence of the military regime. Given the dangers, why would an ordinary barber risk his life for the cause? *The barber feels very strongly about bringing change to his country.*

▶Critical Viewing◀

6 **Connect** In the Venn Diagram, p. 86, in **Writing and Language Transparencies,** have students list details from the painting under the headings "The Revolution" and "The Barber Shop." The sword, strips of paper, and blood-red color could all appear in the center section.

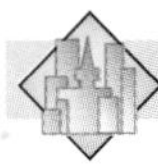

Beyond the Classroom

Workplace Skills

Performance Pride Discuss with students the pride the barber takes in his job skills. Tell students that in any workplace situation, it is important to strive for excellence and take pride in one's work. Tasks should be carefully completed, with attention to detail. As an example, point out that schoolwork, athletic effort, and artistic creations undertaken with pride are usually successful.

Ask students to identify passages from the text that show the barber's pride, for example, the care he takes not to draw any blood. Then have them name a skill in which they take pride and explain how their pride is demonstrated in the results.

Humanities: Art

General With Sword, by Francisco Vidal

Francisco Vidal was born in Barranquilla, Colombia. He trained as a sculptor and painter at the University Atlantico in Colombia and the Art Students League in New York City.

This painting portrays a strong military figure in the foreground against a mostly dark background. The figure appears more like a caricature rather than a real person. Though he is festooned with military decorations, he also seems poised for fighting. His raised sword creates tension and the threat of impending conflict.

Consider these questions for discussion:

1. Does the general in the painting look like anyone you pictured in the story? Explain. *Students are likely to say that the man looks like Captain Torres.*
2. What feelings do you get from the background colors of the painting? *Possible answer: The red causes alarm. It looks like blood, either the captain's or that of the tortured rebels. The black causes sadness because it suggests Colombia's dark times.*

Customize for *Logical/Mathematical Learners*

Tell students to imagine they are undercover military police searching for revolutionaries in the Colombian community. Have them use a "detective's notebook" to record clues about the barber's double life. Invite students to present their clues as "evidence" to the class, who must then vote whether to arrest the barber under suspicion of being a spy.

- nervous reaction to Captain Torres as a customer
- strong curiosity about the captain's chase of the rebels
- morbid horror over the captain's torture sessions

Customize for *English Language Learners*

Point out that this story was originally written in Spanish and then translated into English. Ask students to identify some of the difficulties of translating from one language to another. If possible, provide an original copy of the story for Spanish speakers. Alternatively, pair students with English speakers to translate the English version back to Spanish. Invite Spanish speakers to read portions of the story aloud in Spanish.

Customize for *Bodily/Kinesthetic Learners*

Have students work in pairs to present the story dramatically. Urge them to focus on physical details such as the barber's careful movements in shaving the captain, the contrast between his internal tumult and his external behavior, and the captain's apparent tranquility.

Mexican Market, Ira Moskowitz, Courtesy of the artist

Humanities: Architecture

Mexican Market, by Ira Moskowitz

This painting depicts an open-air market in a town square, in a town much like the one where the story takes place. Squares such as the one in the painting exist in small towns and large cities all around the world. Some have grown naturally at the places where important roads cross. Others, such as the piazzas of the Italian Renaissance, the squares of Washington, D.C., or Brazil's capital of Brasília, were carefully sited by city planners.

No matter their origin, public squares become centers of town life. Farmers and craftspeople from the countryside bring their goods to sell in the town square markets. Important buildings such as churches or courthouses are often built around public squares.

Ask the following question for discussion: How might the ways people use a public square make it hard to keep a secret in a small town? *Students may say that meeting neighbors face to face for business or worship would make it harder to deceive them.*

A little more lather here under the chin, on the Adam's apple, right near the great vein. How hot it is! Torres must be sweating just as I am. But he is not afraid. He is a tranquil man, who is not even giving thought to what he will do to his prisoners this evening. I, on the other hand, polishing his skin with this razor but avoiding the drawing of blood, careful with every stroke—I cannot keep my thoughts in order. ❶

> **Connecting Literature to Social Studies**
> What do you think may be the special challenges of fighting for change in your own country? ❷

Confound the hour he entered my shop! I am a revolutionary but not a murderer. And it would be so easy to kill him. He deserves it. Or does he? No! No one deserves the sacrifice others make in becoming assassins. What is to be gained by it? Nothing. Others and still others keep coming, and the first kill the second, and then these kill the next, and so on until everything becomes a sea of blood. I could cut his throat, so, swish, swish! He would not even have time to moan, and with his eyes shut he would not even see the shine of the razor or the gleam in my eye.

But I'm shaking like a regular murderer. From his throat a stream of blood would flow on the sheet, over the chair, down on my hands, onto the floor. I would have to close the door. But the blood would go flowing, along the floor, warm, indelible, not to be stanched, until it reached the street like a small scarlet river.

I'm sure that with a good strong blow, a deep cut, he would feel no pain. He would not suffer at all. And what would I do then with the body? Where would I hide it? I would have to flee, leave all this behind, take shelter far away, very far away. But they would follow until they caught up with me. "The murderer of Captain Torres. He slit his throat while he was shaving him. What a cowardly thing to do." And others would say, "The avenger of our people. A name to ❸

◆ Build Vocabulary

stanched (stônchd) *v.*: Stopped or slowed down

avenger (ə venj´ ər) *n.*: One who gets even for a wrong or injury

◄ Critical Viewing How does this market scene represent what could be taking place outside the barber's shop? **[Analyze]** ❹

◆Critical Thinking

❶ **Compare and Contrast** How does the author contrast the two characters in this paragraph? What do these contrasts tell you about the state of mind of each man? *The barber is sweating, while the captain is not. This shows that the barber is in a state of turmoil, while the captain seems calm and unaware.*

Connecting Literature to Social Studies

❷ **Generalize** Encourage students to think about the barber's thoughts and conflicting emotions. *Students may say that civil war forces people to fight against members of their community. Also, the tension and fighting may happen in people's own community.*

Links Across Cultures

❸ Harsh dictatorships and revolution have loomed large in Latin America's history. In recent years, however, dictators have fallen in Latin America, as well as in parts of Eastern Europe, Russia, and Africa. This is due in part to the downfall of Communism.

Help the class list countries presently or recently ruled by dictators. Discuss characteristics—political, economical, historical—that these countries share.

►Critical Viewing◄

❹ **Analyze** *The scene shows everyday life in a place such as the one where the story takes place—life goes on normally outside the barbershop.*

Customize for
Less Proficient Readers
Clarify for students that the barber is only imagining the results of killing the captain. Have them use a Cause-and-Effect Organizer, p. 62, in **Writing and Language Transparencies,** to map the barber's thoughts. IF he kills the captain, THEN what will happen? IF he doesn't kill the captain, THEN what will happen?

Speaking and Listening Mini-Lesson

Speech

This mini-lesson supports the Speaking and Listening activity in the Idea Bank on p. 497.

Introduce Point out that speeches often seek to persuade listeners to share the speaker's views. Tell students that it is most effective to choose a position about which they feel strongly.

Develop As students develop their speeches, encourage them to use personal anecdotes or specific facts and details to make their arguments more effective.

Apply Have students write their speeches, marking places where they will pause or emphasize an idea. Urge them to practice with a partner on smooth delivery and appropriate body language. Invite students to deliver their speeches as part of the Gallery of Leaders.

Assess Evaluate speeches with these criteria: logical organization, clear argument, convincing details, oral delivery. If you wish, have student pairs complete the Peer Assessment: Speaker/Speech form, p. 105, in **Alternative Assessment.**

◆ **LITERATURE AND YOUR LIFE**

❶ The barber has faced a very difficult decision. Students may recall tough choices they have faced. Invite them to share their ideas about how to responsibly weigh different options and reach decisions.

Reinforce and Extend

Answers

◆ **LITERATURE AND YOUR LIFE**

Reader's Response Possible response: Given how carefully the barber considers his decision, he probably will not kill the captain. It would be harder to murder the captain after thinking about it so much.

Thematic Focus The barber's personal code dictates that murder is wrong, even when it is in support of a worthy cause.

Check Your Comprehension

1. The barber is immediately nervous.
2. Torres has been tracking down rebels in the countryside.
3. The barber informs the rebels of the regime's plans and activities.

More About the Author

Through his political work and his writing, **Hernando Téllez** was introduced to people and places around the world. He represented his nation as consul to the city of Marseille, a job that perhaps led to his translations of French drama. In addition, this story, which appeared in the author's collection *Ashes for the Wind and Other Tales* (1950), has been very popular and has been translated into several languages.

CONNECTING LITERATURE TO SOCIAL STUDIES

remember"—my name here. "He was the town barber. No one knew he was fighting for our cause."

And so, which will it be? Murderer or hero? My fate hangs on the edge of this razor blade. I can turn my wrist slightly, put a bit more pressure on the blade, let it sink in. The skin will yield like silk, like rubber, like the strop. There is nothing more tender than a man's skin, and the blood is always
❶ there, ready to burst forth. A razor like this cannot fail. It is the best one I have.

But I don't want to be a murderer. No, sir. You came in to be shaved. And I do my work honorably. I don't want to stain my hands with blood. Just with lather, and nothing else. You are an executioner; I am only a barber. Each one to his job. That's it. Each one to his job.

The chin was now clean, polished, soft. The man got up and looked at himself in the glass. He ran his hand over the skin and felt its freshness, its newness.

"Thanks," he said. He walked to the wardrobe for his belt, his pistol, and his cap. I must have been very pale, and I felt my shirt soaked with sweat. Torres finished adjusting his belt buckle, straightened his gun in its holster, and, smoothing his hair mechanically, put on his cap. From his trousers pocket he took some coins to pay for the shave. And he started toward the door. On the threshold he stopped for a moment, and turning toward me he said,

"They told me you would kill me. I came to find out if it was true. But it's not easy to kill. I know what I'm talking about."

Guide for Responding

◆ **LITERATURE AND YOUR LIFE**

Reader's Response Did you think the barber would kill Captain Torres? Why or why not?

Thematic Focus Each of us has a set of rules by which we live. How does the barber's personal code dictate his behavior?

☑ **Check Your Comprehension**

1. How does the barber feel when Captain Torres enters the shop?
2. What has Captain Torres been doing for the past four days?
3. What role does the barber have in the civil war?

◆ Critical Thinking

INTERPRET

1. Why does the barber consider what would "be a good thing" for his enemy? **[Infer]**
2. Why does the barber decide not to kill Captain Torres? **[Interpret]**
3. What message does this story suggest about the effects of civil war on people and their community? **[Draw Conclusions]**

EVALUATE

4. Do you think the barber made the right choice? Why or why not? **[Criticize]**

EXTEND

5. The barber decides that though he is a revolutionary, he is not a murderer. How do you think war might change people's views of their roles—or jobs—in society? Explain. **[Social Studies Link]**

Meet the Author

Hernando Téllez (1908–1966)

Growing up surrounded by Colombia's political unrest shaped Hernando Téllez's life. He became a politician himself and worked as a senator on resolving his country's problems. Téllez also served as a delegate to UNESCO, an organization that uses education and the arts to help people everywhere learn to get along better.

Politics led Téllez toward another main focus of his life—writing. He wrote about politics often, in nonfiction essays and in fictional stories such as "Lather and Nothing Else."

Beyond the Selection

FURTHER READING

Other Works by Hernando Téllez

Ashes for the Wind and Other Tales

Other Works About Latin America and Revolution

El Güero: A True Adventure Story, Elizabeth Borton DeTreviño

José de San Martin: Latin America's Quiet Hero, Jose B. Fernandez

Enchantment of the World: Colombia, Marion Morrison

INTERNET

We suggest the following Internet sites (all Web sites are subject to change).

These sites offer general information on Colombia, with links to specific topics:

http://www.univalle.edu.co/~servinfo/colombia.sp.html

http://www.ddg.com/LIS/aurelia/colombi.htm

http://www.uniandes.edu.co/Colombia/IndiceColombia.html (this site is in Spanish)

We *strongly recommend* that you preview these sites before you send students to them.

Connecting Literature to Social Studies

Colombia is not the only Latin American country to face revolution and civil war. Many of her neighboring countries share a history of conflict between different groups in society.

Though Latin American countries gained independence from Europe one by one in the 1800's, many were then ruled by dictators. Elections have occurred infrequently in most Latin American nations, and citizens have had little say in how their country is run. In addition, governments have sometimes jailed those who speak out for change.

In this century, revolution has broken out in many Latin American nations; for example, Peru, Chile, and Argentina. Like the barber and the captain in this story, these civil wars have set neighbor against neighbor, businessperson against customer.

1. In what ways are the story's setting and characters typical of the political situation in Latin America?
2. How might this story help readers understand the personal and political stakes of revolution and civil war?

Idea Bank

Writing

1. **Letter** As the barber, write a letter to your fellow revolutionaries. Explain why you did not kill your common enemy even though you had the perfect opportunity.
2. **Internal Monologue** Describe the thoughts running through Captain Torres's mind as the barber worked. Consider the captain's view of the political situation and his reasons for behaving as he does.
3. **Story Sequel** What do you think will happen to the barber now? Incorporating what you know about the characters and Latin American history, write a sequel to the story.

Speaking and Listening

4. **Speech** Learn more about the political ideas on both sides of Colombia's civil unrest. Then, deliver a speech asking people to support one side's position. **[Social Studies Link]**

Projects

5. **Gallery of Leaders** Find out about the leader of a Latin American nation—either living today or earlier in the twentieth century. Create a museum exhibit about this person's political and personal life. As a class, assemble all the exhibits into one presentation. **[Social Studies Link]**
6. **Time Capsule [Group Activity]** Within a group, divide the task of researching Colombia's current political and social situation through the Internet, media, and library sources. Identify problems the nation faces. Consider whether the issues raised in the story have been resolved. Then, work together to create a time capsule telling future Colombians about what their nation was like in your lifetime. Where has the country been and where is it headed? **[Social Studies Link]**

Further Reading, Listening, and Viewing

- Marion Morrison's *Enchantment of the World: Colombia* (1990) offers text and pictures about Colombia's past and present.
- Naomi Shihab Nye edited *This Same Sky* (1992), which includes poems by many Latin Americans.
- Lori M. Carlson and Cynthia L. Ventura edited *Where Angels Glide at Dawn: New Stories from Latin America* (1990). This collection includes works by recent Latin American writers.

✓ ASSESSMENT OPTIONS

Formal Assessment, Selection Test, pp. 144–145, and Assessment Resources Software. The selection test is designed so that it can be easily customized to the performance levels of your students.

PORTFOLIO ASSESSMENT
Use the following rubrics and assessment forms in the **Alternative Assessment** booklet to assess student writing:
Letter: Expression, p. 81
Internal Monologue: Writing Self-Assessment, p. 78
Story Sequel: Fictional Narrative, p. 82

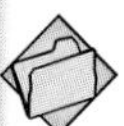

Idea Bank

Following are suggestions for matching the Idea Bank topics with your students' performance levels and learning modalities:

Customize for *Performance Levels*
Less Advanced Students: 1, 6
Average Students: 2, 4, 6
More Advanced Students: 3, 4, 5

Customize for *Learning Modalities*
Verbal/Linguistic: 1, 2, 3, 4
Bodily/Kinesthetic: 4, 5
Visual/Spatial: 5, 6
Interpersonal: 5, 6
Intrapersonal: 2
Logical/Mathematical: 1, 4

***Answers** (continued)*

◆Critical Thinking

1. As he holds the man's life in his hands, he begins to see the captain as a man, to understand the captain's position in the community.
2. The barber does not want to become a murderer, and the honor of his profession is at stake.
3. The story suggests that civil war divides communities, brings violence into peaceful settings, and causes people who would otherwise never think of it to consider murder.
4. Yes, because more killing would not resolve the political situation and would ruin the barber's life. No, because in a revolution you may have to sacrifice lives, even your own, to further the cause.
5. It might force people to consider taking a role they'd never before imagined. For example, the barber has already become a spy and now considers becoming a murderer.

Connecting Literature to Social Studies

1. Students should recognize that the military leadership, civil unrest, violence, and executions outside a legal system are typical of the sociopolitical situation in Latin America.
2. Possible response: By offering readers a very personal look at two realistic people affected by civil war, the story shows what ordinary people stand to lose.

Prepare and Engage

Establish Writing Guidelines
Review the following key characteristics of a short story:

- It is a brief, fictional narrative.
- Most short stories include a main character who faces a conflict.
- Short stories are told by a narrator, who may or may not be a character in the story.

Distribute the scoring rubric for a Fictional Narrative, p. 82, in **Alternative Assessment,** to make students aware of the criteria on which they will be evaluated. See the suggestions on p. 500 for customizing the rubric to this workshop.

Refer students to the Writing Handbook in the back of the book for instruction on the writing process and further information on creative writing.

Writer's Solution

Writers at Work Videodisc
To introduce students to creative writing, and to show them what author Nikki Giovanni says about expressing her ideas in writing, play the videodisc segment on Creative Writing (Ch. 8). Have students discuss Giovanni's writing techniques.

Play frames 22015 to 30765

Writing Lab CD-ROM
If your students have access to computers, you may want to have them work in the tutorial on Creative Writing. Follow these steps:

1. Have students view the Inspirations for Creative Writing to explore possible topics.
2. Suggest that students refer to the Character Trait Word Bin when drafting.
3. Allow students to draft on computer.
4. When students are revising, have them use the interactive instruction on misplaced modifiers.

Writer's Solution Sourcebook
Students can find additional support, including in-depth instruction on punctuating and formatting dialogue, in the chapter on Creative Writing, pp. 234–263.

Narration

Short Story

Writing Process Workshop

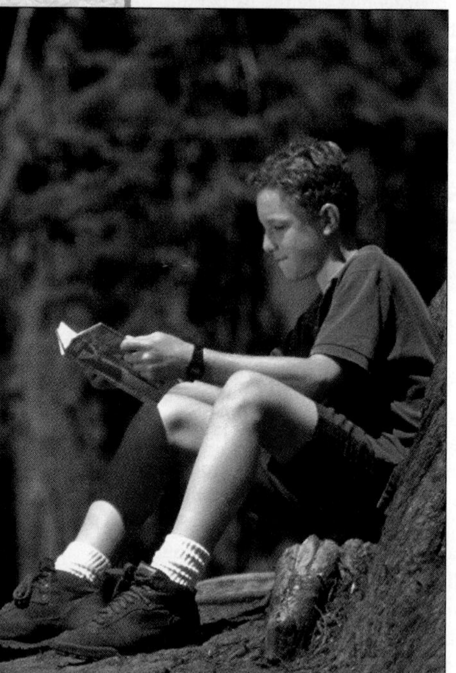

This unit contains short stories written by the masters. Try your hand at writing a **short story** of your own. Your story should be fiction, not fact. You can base it on something that you know—a family, a conflict, or a person—but let your imagination mix with reality to create an original story that no one else could write.

To keep your story short, include only a few events and keep the number of characters down to five or fewer. The following skills, covered in the Writing Mini-Lessons in this part, will help you write your short story.

Writing Skills Focus

▶ To make your story more interesting and engaging, **use dialogue** to help you reveal the personalities of your characters and to move the plot along. (See p. 460.)

▶ **Include descriptive details** to make your setting vivid and real to your readers. (See p. 477.)

▶ **Show, don't tell** what your characters are like, how they behave, and what happens. (See p. 489.)

Cynthia Rylant uses all these skills in this scene from "Papa's Parrot."

Model From Literature

from "Papa's Parrot" by Cynthia Rylant

Harry opened the new boxes his father hadn't gotten to. Peppermints. Jawbreakers. Toffee creams. Strawberry kisses. ① Harry traveled from bin to bin, putting the candies where they belonged.

"Hello!"

Harry jumped, spilling a box of jawbreakers. ②

"Hello, Rocky!" ③

① *Rylant doesn't simply tell us that there are many different kinds of candy. She shows us.*

② *Descriptive details make the story come to life.*

③ *Dialogue also adds life and realism to the story.*

Beyond the Classroom

Career Connection
Tell students that knowing how to write a good story is the basis for many jobs in creative fields. Although many fiction writers work independently creating their own short story collections or novels, there are also writers who are employed by other businesses. For example, many talented story writers write screenplays for television or film. Some writers may come up with the original idea for a film, while others may work developing stories that are already in progress. Often, several writers will collaborate on one project to get it to completion.

Have students do some research on what it takes to develop a film or television show. Suggest that they find out how Hollywood and the movie-making industry have changed over the years. Or they may research a writer who has made a living by writing movies for film, such as Raymond Chandler, Stephen King, or Ray Bradbury. Encourage students to share their findings with the class.

Prewriting

Choose an Idea Perhaps you already have an idea for a story. For example, you might want to add fictional details to tell the story of an actual event. You could write a comic tale like the kind you like to read. If you don't already have the spark for your story, consider one of the ideas listed here.

Topic Ideas

- Surviving a storm
- Taming an animal
- Solving a mystery
- Losing—or making—a friend

Devise a Story Plan Think about your story before you start to write. Use the questions below to generate the information you'll need. Make your answers as detailed as possible.

- Who will be in your story? (character)
- What will happen? (plot)
- When and where will it happen? (setting)
- What is the main character's problem? (conflict)
- What will be the turning point? (climax)

Drafting

Start Strong Experiment with the first sentence of your story. Make it a hook that catches your readers' attention. Here are a few suggestions and examples. Which of them would hook you?

Dialogue:	"Richard, I have something to tell you." Once these words were out, Stacey began to feel better.
An Intriguing Description:	The river rushed past Mia's bare feet, chilling her bones.
A Sound or Noise:	The helicopter's whir stopped our conversation.
A Memory:	When I was three, I gave my teddy bear a haircut.
A Question:	Have you ever insulted someone without realizing it?

Choose a Voice Some stories are told using the first-person voice. ("I answered the phone.") If you choose this voice, decide which character will tell the story. Other stories are told using the third-person voice. ("He answered the phone.") Once you make this choice, stick with it.

DRAFTING/REVISING

APPLYING LANGUAGE SKILLS: Vary Tag Words

Dialogue is a key part of many short stories. While *said* is straightforward and accurate, avoid attaching the same tag words to identify speakers. Choose words that communicate emotion. Notice how each of these examples conveys a different meaning.

Weak Tag Word:

"Stop that," he said.

Stronger Tag Words:

"Stop that," he whined.

"Stop that," he laughed.

"Stop that," he hissed angrily.

Practice Wake up these sentences by replacing the dull tag words with more vivid ones.

1. She said, "Would you go to the store?"
2. "I can't wait for that!" he said.
3. "Please be careful," she said.

Writing Application In your short story, use *said* sparingly. When you can, use other words to convey the emotion of the dialogue.

Writer's Solution Connection Writing Lab

For more on developing characters, use the Character Trait Word Bin in the Prewriting section of the Narration tutorial.

Develop Student Writing

Prewriting

When considering topic ideas for a short story, remind students to write about something with which they are familiar. Even though the story should be made up, they may want to model the setting, characters, or events on places, people, or happenings they know.

If students keep journals, suggest that they flip through them for story ideas.

Customize for *Less Proficient Writers*

Students who have a hard time coming up with story ideas may benefit by working with a partner. First, have them work individually to create charts like the one that follows. Then, with their partners, have them swap ideas about settings, plots, conflicts, and characters, and decide on a final set of elements for a story.

setting	
plot	
conflict	
character	

Customize for *Visual/Spatial Learners*

Remind students that a picture can describe an event. Encourage them to begin their story ideas with a drawing of a setting or character. Then have them add to the drawing, until they have incorporated all the elements of a story. Have them refer to the picture as they write their drafts.

Drafting

Remind students that the events in the story must follow one another in a sequence that won't lose the reader. Suggest that students use the Series of Events Chain in **Writing and Language Transparencies,** p. 66, to help them plot their stories.

Applying Language Skills

Vary Tag Words Tell students that varying tag words not only helps avoid repetition, but also helps describe a character's emotions. Suggest that students review a short story they have read, to gather ideas for different tag words.

Answers

Suggested responses:

1. She begged, "Would you go to the store?"
2. "I can't wait for that!" he exclaimed.
3. "Please be careful," she hissed.

Writer's Solution

For additional instruction and practice, have students use the *Writer's Solution Language Lab CD-ROM* Writing Dialogue lesson in the Composing unit.

Revising

Tell students that they may want to read their stories into a tape recorder. Have them take notes as they listen, looking for weak spots, awkward phrases, and incorrect grammar, as well as well-written sections.

Writer's Solution

Writing Lab CD-ROM

In the tutorial on Creative Writing, have students use the interactive instruction on misplaced modifiers and then correct any mistakes in their own stories.

Publishing

Suggest that students collect their stories in a class anthology. Encourage them to illustrate their stories with pictures, collages, etc.

Reinforce and Extend

Review the Writing Guidelines

After students have completed their papers, review the characteristics of a short story.

Applying Language Skills

Using Correct Verbs

Students may recognize incorrectly used verbs by reading their drafts aloud. Have them flag verbs that sound awkward, and then refer to the verb chart to check their usage.

Answers

1. I saw him in the doorway.
2. The eagle had flown out of the nest.
3. The ice cream has frozen!

Writer's Solution

For additional practice, complete the Verbs lessons in the *Writer's Solution Grammar Practice Book*, pp. 11–14.

EDITING/PROOFREADING

APPLYING LANGUAGE SKILLS: Using Correct Verbs

Regular verbs show action in the past by adding *-ed*. There are many verbs, however, whose past tense and past participles are irregular. You probably know them from using them, but be careful when you proofread. Irregular verbs are frequent sources of errors.

Verb	Past	Past Participle
be	was	(has) been
do	did	(has) done
drive	drove	(has) driven
fly	flew	(has) flown
have	had	(has) had
see	saw	(has) seen
take	took	(has) taken
write	wrote	(has) written

Practice Correct the verb form errors.

1. I seen him in the doorway.
2. The eagle had flew out of the nest.
3. The ice cream has froze!

Writing Application As you revise your story, be careful to use the correct forms of irregular verbs.

Writer's Solution Connection
Language Lab

For more help with irregular verbs, see the Principal Parts of Verbs lesson in the Language Lab CD-ROM.

Show Personality Include rich and lively dialogue in your story. Think about exactly what each character would say—and how to convey emotion through word choice.

▶ "Be careful!" Johanna screamed at her brother.
▶ "Wanna cookie?" Alice mumbled, slurping her milk.

Revising

Cut Down on Modifiers Mark Twain, a great storyteller, once said that writers use adjectives when they can't find the right noun. Look critically at the adjectives and adverbs you use. Can you eliminate them by choosing better nouns and verbs?

Read Aloud The best test of a story's zing is to read it aloud. Your ears will catch awkward sentences that your eyes might miss. Ask a friend or family member to listen, too. Ask your listener questions such as these:

▶ Did you understand the story? If not, what didn't you understand?
▶ Which character did you like? Why?
▶ Was the dialogue clear and believable?
▶ What did you picture as the setting?

REVISION MODEL

① raced

Megan ~~went quickly~~ to the small house on the shore.

② Hey, Nana! shouted

"~~Good afternoon, Grandmother~~," she ~~said~~. "We are here."

① The writer replaced a weak phrase with a stronger verb.
② Revision makes the dialogue more realistic.

Publishing and Presenting

▶ **Submit Your Work** Many magazines publish fiction and accept manuscripts from amateur writers. Find one that appeals to you, and submit your story.

▶ **Stage a Storytelling Festival** With your classmates, hold a Storyteller's Festival. Take turns reading aloud or retelling your stories. Gestures and sound effects will make your storytelling more dramatic and entertaining.

ASSESSMENT

PORTFOLIO ASSESSMENT

Use the rubric on Fictional Narrative in the **Alternative Assessment** booklet, p. 82, to assess the students' writing. Add these criteria to customize this rubric to this assignment.

	4	3	2	1
Dialogue	The dialogue adds to the descriptions of the characters and is punctuated correctly.	The dialogue adds to the descriptions of the characters but is not always punctuated correctly.	The dialogue does not always correspond with the characters and is not always punctuated correctly.	There is little dialogue, and the dialogue used is not appropriate or punctuated correctly.
Using Correct Verbs	All of the verbs in the story are used correctly.	Most of the verbs in the story are used correctly	Few of the verbs in the story are used correctly.	None of the verbs in the story is used correctly.

Real-World Reading Skills Workshop

Reading Novels and Other Extended Works

Strategies for Success

So you want to read a novel, but its 350-page length intimidates you. Or perhaps you need to read a play for a school assignment, but you're not sure you'll be able to finish it in the time allotted. Don't worry. There are strategies you can use to make reading longer works easier.

Plan Your Reading If you need to read a full-length novel, play, or nonfiction book for class, plan ahead. First, find out how long the book is and when you must finish reading it. Then, set aside enough blocks of time to read it all by the due date. Your teacher may assign the reading by chapters or sections. Plan your time in the same way. Try not to let too much time go by between readings. That way, the plot, characters, and other information will stay fresh in your mind.

Scan for Structure Before you start, get an overview of the work. If it's a book, look at the table of contents. If it's a play, check out the list of characters. Flip through the pages to get a feel for the book's organization. This may give you clues to what the book is about. It will also help you plan your reading time.

Read and Check Understanding As you read novels, enjoy the descriptions and dialogue, but don't worry about memorizing passages. Pay attention to the changes that occur. For example, ask yourself how much time passes between chapters, where the events take place, and how a character grows or changes through events.

Keep a Reading Log To stay on top of the plot twists and turns of a longer work, it may be helpful to keep a reading log. After each reading session, summarize the main events, jot down your predictions for the coming chapters, and note any questions you have. Use the log as a refresher before you begin to read again.

Lurking Beyond the Tide

Apply the Strategies

Before answering the questions that follow, skim the table of contents for the novel *Lurking Beyond the Tide*.

1. What do you think this novel might be about?
2. In what kind of environment do you think the action might be set? Give details to support your response.
3. To read this book in three weeks, about how many pages should you read each week? Explain.

Here are some other instances in which you might use your skills at reading novels and other extended works:

- ▶ Reading biographies
- ▶ Reading novellas
- ▶ Reading travel books

Introduce the Strategies

Discuss with students any problems they have encountered while reading novels. Explain that reading a novel takes a lot more patience and time than reading shorter works, but the benefits of being drawn into a longer work are rewarding. You may want to compare a novel to a film, and suggest that students contrast films with their shorter counterparts, television shows.

Customize for
Interpersonal Learners
Some students may get more from reading a novel, if they have a reading partner. Encourage students to form pairs and choose a novel that they both want to read. As they read, encourage them to take notes and stage discussions about the novel.

Apply the Strategies

Tell students that in a novel's table of contents, they can see how long each chapter is by looking at the page numbers. Knowing the chapter length will help in planning a timeline for reading.

Answers
Possible responses:

1. The novel might be about an adventure at sea.
2. The novel is probably set at sea because the chapters include such words as "ocean," "sharks," "tugs," and "boats."
3. You would want to read about 75–80 pages a week. Because the epilogue starts on p. 220, we can assume the book probably has between 225 and 240 pages. If you divide this over 3 weeks, you will get 75–80 pages a week.

◆Build Grammar Skills

Reviewing Sentence Structure
The selections in Part I include instruction on the following:

- Clauses
- Simple and Compound Sentences
- Complex Sentences

 ***Writer's Solution***

For additional practice and support with sentence structure, use the practice pages on Basic Sentence Parts and Patterns, pp. 28–41, in the *Writer's Solution Grammar Practice Book.*

Customize for
Less Proficient Readers
Suggest that students fill out a chart like the one below when analyzing sentence structure:

nouns	
verbs	
subject	
conjunctions	

Then have them identify which words or phrases the conjunctions join.

Answers
Practice 1

1. Bob and Jimmy, who were best friends as kids, agreed to meet again in exactly twenty years. *complex*
2. Rikki is a mongoose that lives with a family in India. *complex*
3. The brave little mongoose killed the deadly cobra. *simple*
4. Mr. Tillian will get out of the hospital soon, but he will rest at home for a few weeks. *compound*
5. Although the boy was sent home from school because he said that he was sick, he did not stay in bed. *complex*

Sentence Structure

Grammar Review

A **sentence** is a group of words that expresses a complete thought. Each sentence contains one or more **clauses,** groups of words with their own subjects and verbs (see page 459). The two major types of clauses are independent clauses and subordinate clauses. An independent (main) clause can stand by itself as a complete sentence. A subordinate clause is only part of a sentence. Sentences can be classified according to the number and types of clauses they contain.

SEND
sen·tence (sen′təns) *n.* **1** a group of words that is used to tell, ask, command, or exclaim something, usually having a subject and a predicate: a sentence begins with a capital letter and ends with a period, question mark, or exclamation point

Sentence Type	Types of Clause(s) in the Sentence
Simple (See p. 476.)	One main clause only
Compound (See p. 476.)	Two or more main clauses
Complex (See p. 488.)	One main clause plus one or more subordinate clauses

Practice 1 Copy these sentences on a piece of paper. Underline main clauses once. Underline subordinate clauses twice. Then, identify each sentence as *simple, compound,* or *complex.*

1. Bob and Jimmy, who were best friends as kids, agreed to meet again in exactly twenty years.

2. Rikki is a mongoose that lives with a family in India.

3. The brave little mongoose killed the deadly cobra.

4. Mr. Tillian will get out of the hospital soon, but he will rest at home for a few weeks.

5. Although the boy was sent home from school because he said that he was sick, he did not stay in bed.

Practice 2
Rewrite the following sentence pairs, combining the ideas to form the types of sentences indicated.

1. (a) This unit features short stories.
(b) Short stories are brief works of fiction. (*complex*)

2. (a) Some stories are closely based on real people and events.
(b) Others are wildly fanciful. (*compound*)

3. (a) Elements of a short story include the plot.
(b) Elements of a short story include the characters. (*simple*)

Grammar in Writing

✔ *Using the same type of sentence over and over again is boring. When you write, use a mixture of different types of sentences. This will help make your writing more lively and interesting.*

✔ *Be careful not to write a subordinate clause as if it were a sentence on its own. Subordinate clauses must always be attached to an independent clause.*

Practice 2

1. This unit features short stories, which are brief works of fiction.
2. Some stories are closely based on real people and events, and others are wildly fanciful.
3. Elements of a short story include the plot and the characters.

PART 2 *Setting and Theme*

Looking Along Broadway Towards Grace Church (detail), 1981, Red Grooms, Courtesy Marlborough Gallery

One-Minute Planning Guide

The selections in this section focus on the setting and theme of "Short Stories." The cold and snowy setting of "Heartache" enhances its theme of loneliness. In "Suzy and Leah," the heartbreak of a war refugee is juxtaposed against the tranquil setting of upstate New York. In "Ribbons," the contrast of life in San Francisco's Chinatown against life in China sets the stage for the differences and ultimate understanding that exist between generations. A stormy night and an abandoned tenement in "The Treasure of Lemon Brown" reflect the characters' outlooks on life.

Customize for
Varying Student Needs

When assigning the selections in this section to your students, keep in mind the following factors:

"Heartache"

- Accessible Anton Chekhov short story
- Uses strong-setting details

"Suzy and Leah"

- Written as diary entries and letters
- Contains vivid characterization

"Ribbons"

- Students can identify with the main character's frustrations and struggles
- Presents a family's intergenerational relationships

"The Treasure of Lemon Brown"

- Presents an intergenerational relationship that evolves out of necessity and develops because of the characters' needs

"Rhythm and Blues, Let the Good Times Roll"

- Connection to media
- Press release format

Humanities: Art

Looking Along Broadway Towards Grace Church (detail), 1981, by Red Grooms

Red Grooms was born in Nashville, Tennessee, in 1937 but moved to New York to attend the New School for Social Research. As an artist, he was involved in the Pop Art movement, collaborating with Claes Oldenburg. In 1959, he staged a multimedia performance in New York entitled *The House That Burns* and was accepted into the Venice Bienalle in 1966. Use the following questions for discussion:

1. What details in the painting clue the viewer into the fact that it is set in New York City? *Students may recognize the tall buildings, the narrow streets, the yellow cabs, the bus with the South Ferry stop illuminated, and the Canal Street sign.*
2. Does the setting appeal to you or do you find it uninviting? Why? *Some students may think the setting is too busy and crowded, while others may think the business is exciting.*
3. How do the artist's color choices contribute to the effect of the painting? *Students may note that the bright colors make the scene seem busy and hectic.*

OBJECTIVES

1. To read, comprehend, and interpret two short stories
2. To relate short stories to personal experience
3. To make inferences
4. To analyze setting
5. To build vocabulary in context and learn the suffix *-ee*
6. To recognize adverb clauses
7. To write an introduction for an exhibition that includes necessary context or historical background
8. To respond to the works through writing, speaking and listening, and projects

SKILLS INSTRUCTION

Vocabulary: Suffixes: *-ee*
Spelling: Adding the Suffix *-ee*
Grammar: Adverb Clauses
Reading Strategy: Make Inferences
Literary Focus: Setting
Writing: Necessary Context/ Background
Speaking and Listening: Questions and Answers (Teacher Edition)
Viewing and Representing: Comparing and Contrasting Cultures (Teacher Edition)
Critical Viewing: Analyze; Support; Compare and Contrast; Respond; Infer; Connect

PORTFOLIO OPPORTUNITIES

Writing: Sympathy Note; Diary Entries; Analytic Essay
Writing Mini-Lesson: Introduction to an Exhibition
Speaking and Listening: Questions and Answers; Talk Radio
Projects: Snow Statistics; Research Report

More About the Authors
In his stories and plays, **Anton Chekhov** is known for skillfully portraying the inner world of troubled characters in common situations.

As a child, **Jane Yolen** was surrounded by writers. Her father was a journalist, her mother wrote short stories, and many family friends were writers. Although Yolen did not have family members in Europe during World War II, she is interested in the Holocaust because of her Jewish heritage.

Guide for Reading

Meet the Authors:

Anton Chekhov (1860–1904)

While still a teen, Anton Chekhov began writing articles and humorous sketches to help support his family. Even though he graduated from medical school and became a successful doctor, writing remained Chekhov's primary career throughout his life.

A Russian Treasure Chekhov is widely considered to be the greatest Russian playwright and short-story writer. His greatest masterpieces are four plays written during the last decade of his life: *The Seagull*, *Uncle Vanya*, *Three Sisters*, and *The Cherry Orchard*.

Jane Yolen (1939–)

Jane Yolen's storytelling career began in first grade, when she wrote a class musical about vegetables. Since then, Yolen has written more than a hundred books. She has produced novels, short stories, poems, plays, and essays.

THE STORY BEHIND THE STORY
Although Yolen is known mainly for her fantasy stories, she found inspiration in her Jewish heritage to write "Suzy and Leah," the story of a Holocaust survivor. Yolen wrote about the Holocaust so that her own children could understand and remember.

◆ Literature and Your Life

CONNECT YOUR EXPERIENCE
When you have a problem, you probably reach out to people close to you for comfort or guidance. Neither of the main characters in these stories has the benefit of such support. In "Heartache," a carriage driver needs to share his sorrow, but he cannot get anyone to listen to him. In "Suzy and Leah," a young girl is afraid to reach out to others and ask for help.

THEMATIC FOCUS: Finding Solutions
As you read these stories, you may find yourself wondering how people can make themselves heard.

◆ Background for Understanding

HISTORY
"Suzy and Leah" is based on true events. Before and during World War II, the Nazi government of Germany persecuted Jews. At first, Jews were forced to identify themselves with yellow stars. Eventually, many Jews were forced to leave their homes. Many were herded into concentration camps, where they were starved, overworked, and killed. Six million Jews died in the Holocaust. Some Jews, however, survived. One group gathered the few belongings they still had and came to a refugee camp in Oswego, New York. The fictional character Leah lives in this camp.

◆ Build Vocabulary

SUFFIXES: *-ee*
Leah is a *refugee*. The word *refugee* is formed by adding the suffix *-ee*, meaning "one who," to the word *refuge*. Thus, a refugee is a person who seeks or has taken refuge.

WORD BANK
Which of these words means "not important"? Check the Build Vocabulary boxes to see if you've chosen correctly.

conspiring
ponderous
indignantly
quavering
insignificant
refugee

Prentice Hall Literature Program Resources

REINFORCE / RETEACH / EXTEND

Selection Support Pages
Build Vocabulary: Suffixes *-ee*, p. 174
Build Spelling Skills, p. 175
Build Grammar Skills: Adverb Clauses, p. 176
Reading Strategy: Make Inferences, p. 177
Literary Focus: Setting, p. 178
Strategies for Diverse Student Needs, pp. 63–64
Beyond Literature Workplace Skills: Communication, p. 32

Formal Assessment Selection Test, pp. 146–148, Assessment Resources Software
Alternative Assessment, p. 32
Resource Pro CD-ROM "Heartache"; "Suzy and Leah"—includes all resource material and customizable lesson plan

Listening to Literature Audiocassettes "Heartache"; "Suzy and Leah"

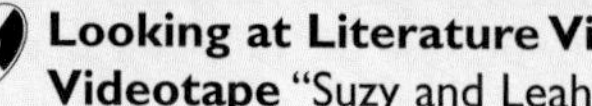

Looking at Literature Videodisc/ Videotape "Suzy and Leah"

Heartache ◆ Suzy and Leah

◆ Literary Focus

Setting

The **setting** of a story is the time and place of the action. The importance of the setting varies. In some stories, the setting is little more than a background. In others, such as "Heartache," the setting highlights the action. In still others, such as "Suzy and Leah," the setting shapes the action.

◆ Reading Strategy

Make Inferences

Short-story writers don't tell you everything there is to know about the characters, setting, and events. Instead, they leave it to you to fill in missing information by **making inferences,** or drawing conclusions, based on the material that is provided. For example, the first paragraph of "Heartache" describes a character and his horse waiting motionless in the snow. From this detail, you might infer that the character is deep in thought or depressed. As you read the stories, jot down key details and record your inferences in a table like the one below.

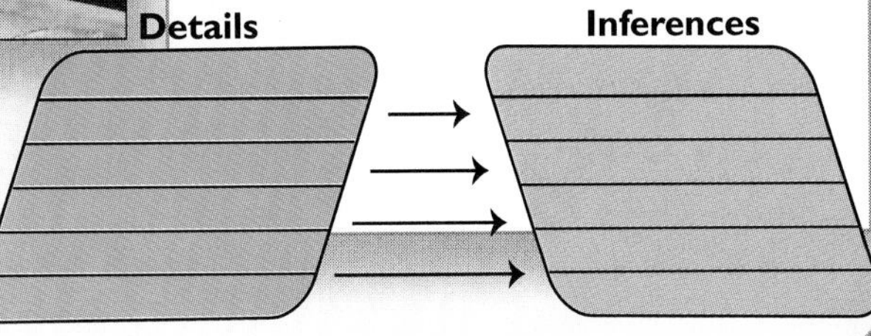

Preparing for Standardized Tests

Reading Standardized tests often ask students to answer questions that require them to make inferences. Read the following passage aloud, then ask students to choose the best answer to the question.

> Leah entered the school wearing a blue dress she had been given at the refugee camp. She lowered her head as she walked past students who were eagerly greeting one another. Waiting to register, she felt a warm blush come over her cheeks.

Leah feels—

(A) impatient (C) sad
(B) uncomfortable (D) angry

Help students identify details and combine them with their own experiences to infer which is the best answer. None of the details indicates that Leah is *(A) impatient* or *(D) angry.* Drawing on their own experiences, students will probably identify *(B)* and *(C)* as possible answers. Although it is possible she feels *sad, (C)* is too specific for the details provided, so *(B)* is the *best* answer to the question.

Divide students into groups of four or five. Instruct one person from each group to wait in the hall while you talk to the rest of the class. Tell students that when the others return from the hallway, they are to be ignored—their group members should not respond to anything these students do or say. After three to five minutes, stop the exercise and encourage the students who were ignored to share their feelings with the class. Help students recognize the frustration and sense of helplessness students may have experienced when they were not "heard." Explain that characters in the stories they will read are unable to communicate with anyone who will actually hear what they have to say.

◆ Build Grammar Skills

Adverb Clauses If you wish to introduce the grammar concept for this selection before students read, refer to the instruction on p. 520.

Customize for *Less Proficient Readers*

Work closely with students to help them apply the reading strategy of making inferences. Guide them in creating a chart, such as the one shown on p. 505, for each story. It may be helpful to read certain passages aloud, pointing out details for them to add to the chart. In addition, review and discuss the Reading Strategy prompts with them.

Customize for *More Advanced Students*

Point out that Chekhov and Yolen use specific details to show the desperate loneliness of characters who have suffered a tragedy. As they read, have students note such details on a chart.

	Heartache	Suzy and Leah
Character:	*Iona*	*Leah*
Setting:	*Russia*	*refugee camp*
Tragedy:	*his son died*	*lost her family*
Details:	*has no family left; has no one to talk to*	*survived the Holocaust; is frightened has no family; doesn't speak English*

Develop Understanding

The dreary setting of "Heartache" reflects the inner turmoil of the main character, Iona Potapov. Iona is hardly aware of the falling snow and darkening sky as he drives customers around his Russian town in a carriage. Even though his customers ridicule him and treat him disrespectfully, Iona attempts to converse with them about a tragic event in his life: the recent death of his son. The customers—first an officer and later three rowdy young men—ignore his attempts to share his tragic story. He returns to the stable, where his misery and dejection continue. The story ends as Iona begins telling the painful story of his loss to his horse.

Customize for *English Language Learners*

English language learners may have difficulty understanding the unfamiliar phrases used for descriptions in these stories. Help students by using gestures and body language to communicate the meanings of phrases from "Heartache," such as "bumped by the nag's muzzle," "on pins and needles," "tugs the reins and clucks," "in measured tones"; and from "Suzy and "Leah," such as "It was so creepy," "pinafore," "prickly as a porcupine," "turn on us," and "screaming my head off."

Customize for *Visual/Spatial Learners*

The photograph on these pages helps establish the setting of "Heartache." Have students use all the visuals accompanying the selections to help them understand the settings of the stories and the characters' reactions to those settings.

Heartache

Block Scheduling Strategies

Consider these suggestions to take advantage of extended class time:

- Before students begin reading, have them read and discuss the Literature and Your Life feature, p. 504. Suggest that they write in their journals about the importance of being able to share feelings and experiences with others.
- After students read the introduction to Literary Focus on p. 505, have small groups create a Setting Chart for each selection with these headings: *Where, When,* and *Details*. Tell them to stop occasionally to add information to their charts as they read. Then direct them to use the information on their charts to discuss the answers to the Literary Focus questions, p. 520.
- Students who work on the Diary Entries activity in the Idea Bank, p. 521, may want to first complete the Speaking and Listening Activity, Questions and Answers to help them hear Leah's and Suzy's tone and style.

Anton Chekhov

Evening twilight. Large wet flakes of snow circle lazily around the just lighted streetlamps and lie on roofs, horses' backs, caps, and shoulders in a thin, soft layer. Cabby Iona Potapov is all white as a ghost. As hunched over as a living body can be hunched, he sits on the box and does not stir. If a whole snowdrift were to fall on him, even then, it seems, he would not find it necessary to shake the snow off himself. . . . His nag, too, is white and motionless. In her motionlessness, angularity of shape, and stick-like straightness, even up close she looks like a penny gingerbread horse. In all probability she is sunk in thought. One who has been torn away from the plow, from the customary grey scenes, and been cast here, into this whirlpool of monstrous light, unceasing din, and rushing people, cannot help thinking. . . . ❶

It has been a long time since Iona and his horse have moved from their place. They left the stable before supper, and still there is no fare. But now evening darkness is descending on the city. The pale light of the streetlamps is surrendering its place to vivid color, and the bustle in the street is becoming noisier. ❷

◆ **Literary Focus** How does the setting of the story reflect Iona's emotional state?

"Cabby, to the Vyborg District!" hears Iona, "Cabby!"

Iona starts, and through eyelashes pasted over with snow he sees an officer in a cloak with a hood.

"To the Vyborg District!" repeats the officer. "What's the matter, are you asleep? To the Vyborg District!"

As a sign of assent Iona tugs the reins, causing the layers of snow to pour off the horse's back and his own shoulders. . . . The officer gets in. The cabby clucks to the horse, stretches his neck out swan-like, raises up, and more from habit than

◀ **Critical Viewing** What details in the first three paragraphs of this story are shown in the photograph? **[Analyze]** ❸

◆ Literary Focus

❶ **Setting** What do you learn about the setting from the first two sentences? *The first sentence tells the time of day that the story occurs—twilight. The second sentence tells the reader that snow is falling gently.*

◆ Literary Focus

❷ **Setting** *Students may say that details such as the cold weather, the large, wet flakes of snow, the descending darkness, and the pale light of the lamplights create a gloomy image in the mind of the reader, which reflects Iona's despondence.*

▶Critical Viewing◀

❸ **Analyze** Have students discuss the somber mood that the details of the photograph create. *Possible responses: "snow," "horse," "caps," "unceasing din," "rushing people," "bustle in the street."*

Customize for
Bodily/Kinesthetic Learners

The author's descriptions of Iona's posture reflects the character's inner thoughts and mood. In the first paragraph he is despondent; in the last paragraph, he attempts to look alert. Invite students to demonstrate the contrast of how he looks, as described in these paragraphs. Then ask them to identify specific words and phrases for each of these looks. *Students may identify "hunched," "does not stir," and "motionless." In the last paragraph, students may identify "tugs the reins," "stretches his neck out swan-like," and "raises up."*

Cultural Connection

Russia—Yesterday and Today The photograph on this page shows nineteenth-century Russia. Tell students that at this time Russia was the center of the Russian empire, a monarchy that was overthrown by the Bolsheviks (communists) in 1917. From 1922 to 1991, Russia was the most powerful state in the USSR (Union of Soviet Socialist Republics) and was under communist rule.

In 1991, a dramatic change took place in Russia. The communist government collapsed, and limited democracy was introduced to the country for the first time. Today, Russia continues to struggle through difficult transitions: from state-owned businesses to privately owned ones, from a planned economy to a market-oriented one, from repression to freedom. During this transition, Russians have faced drastic price increases, a steep rise in unemployment, and a severe shortage of medical supplies.

Encourage interested students to use the Internet or the library to find current information about Russian life.

◆ Reading Strategy

1 **Make Inferences** Ask students what they infer about Iona from this paragraph. What details support this inference? *Students may say that Iona seems confused and dazed, as if he is troubled about something. He drives carelessly, fidgets, rolls his eyes, and seems not to know where he is.*

◆ Literature and Your Life

2 Discuss with students that Iona's passenger uses body language to show that he doesn't want to hear about Iona's problems. Ask students if they have ever experienced a situation in which someone obviously did not want to listen to them. How did they react to this response? How did they handle the situation? *Encourage students to talk about the importance of being a polite and active listener. Also discuss that they will have more success in getting another person to listen to them if they wait until the person is not in the middle of doing something else, or if they warn the person ahead of time that they want to talk.*

Clarification

3 In Russian currency, one ruble equals one hundred kopeks. By today's standards, a ruble is worth about six American cents.

Customize for *English Language Learners*

Some of the language on this page may be difficult for students to interpret. Explain the definitions of words such as *irresolutely* (indecisively), *gnome* (small humanlike creature), and *capriciousness* (whim or impulse). Act out phrases such as "cracking voice" and "sock in the neck." You might illustrate "gangly ones" on the board.

need, waves his whip. The nag stretches her neck too, crooks her stick-like legs, and moves irresolutely from her place . . .

"Where are you heading, you gnome!" almost immediately Iona hears shouts from the dark mass of people moving back and forth. "Where are you going? Keep to the r-r-right!"

"You don't know how to drive! Keep to the right!" says the officer angrily.

The driver of a carriage curses him; a passer-by who was crossing the road and has his shoulder bumped by the nag's muzzle looks at him fiercely and shakes the snow
1 from his sleeve. Iona fidgets on the box, as if on pins and needles, shoves his elbows out to the side and rolls his eyes like a madman, as if he does not understand where he is and why he is here.

"What scoundrels they all are!" jokes the officer. "They are all trying to bump into you or fall under the horse. They're conspiring."

Iona looks around at the passenger and moves his lips . . . Apparently he wants to say something, but nothing comes from his throat except a wheeze.

"What?" asks the officer.

Iona twists his mouth with a smile, strains his throat and wheezes:

"My son, sir . . . er, he died this week."

"Hm! What did he die of?"

Iona turns his whole body around toward the passenger and says:

"Well who knows? From a fever, probably . . . He lay in the hospital three days and died . . . God's will."

"Turn off, you scoundrel!" rings out in the dark. "Where yah crawled out of, you old dog? Use your eyes!"

"Get going, get going . . ." says the passenger. "At this rate we won't get there before tomorrow. Use the whip!"

The cabby again stretches out his neck, raises up, and waves the whip with ponderous
2 grace. Then he looks back at the passenger, but he has closed his eyes and apparently is not disposed to listen. When he has let him out in the Vyborg District, Iona stops by a tavern, hunches over on the box, and again he does not stir . . . The wet snow again paints him and his nag white. One hour passes, another . . .

Cursing each other and stomping their boots loudly on the sidewalk, three young men walk by: two of them are tall and thin, the third is short and hunchbacked.

"Driver, to Policemen's Bridge!" shouts the
hunchback in a cracking voice. "Three of us . . . 3
a twenty-kopek piece!"

Iona tugs the reins and clucks. A twenty-kopek piece is not a proper fare, but he's not interested in the price . . . A ruble or a five-kopek piece, it's all the same to him, as long as he has passengers . . . Bumping into each other and swearing, the young men walk up to the sleigh and all three immediately try to sit down. They begin to solve the question of which two are to sit and which one to stand. After lengthy abuse, capriciousness, and rebukes, they reach the conclusion that since the hunchback is the smallest, he ought to stand.

"Well, drive on," cracks the hunchback, taking his place and breathing down Iona's neck. "Shove off! And, brother, your cap! A worse one couldn't be found in all of Petersburg . . ."

"He, he . . . He, he . . ." laughs Iona. "Whatever you say . . ."

"Well, you 'whatever you say,' drive on! You gonna drive like this the whole way? Yes? And how about a sock in the neck? . . ."

"My head is bursting . . ." says one of the gangly ones. "Yesterday at the Dukmasovs' Vaska and I drank four bottles of cognac between the two of us."

"I don't see why he lies!" the other gangly one says angrily. "He lies like a pig!"

"Really, God punish me . . ."

"That's about as true as that louse's coughs."

"He, he!" snickers Iona. "Jolly fellows!"

"Faugh," says the hunchback indignantly. "Are you going to get going or not, you old rat? Is this the way to drive?"

Behind his back Iona can feel the twisting body and quavering voice of the hunchback.

Humanities: Drama

Chekhov and the Method Most students have seen theater performances in some form. Point out that theater has been a part of civilization for thousands of years and that styles of acting, like styles of painting and literature, have changed over time. People flocked to Shakespeare's plays in the sixteenth century to see actors perform his dramas in a highly dramatic and exciting style. The plays of the nineteenth century often involved huge spectacles, impressive sets, and large casts similar to some of today's Broadway musical productions. However, in the late nineteenth century, plays often emphasized more intimate, psychological drama.

The actors who originally performed Anton Chekhov's plays developed a highly personal, intense mode of acting, which has come to be known as "method acting." Today, actors are still influenced by this style. The goal of method acting is to discover, through the actor's examination of his or her own experiences and emotions, the stage character's inner experience and to communicate that experience to an audience. Explain to students that they may see method actors in films as well as plays. Discuss how actors can show the inner world of Iona through tone of voice, body language, and expression.

▶Critical Viewing◀

4 Support *Students may point out the horses and carriages, the old-fashioned clothing, and the store signs with Russian words.*

◆ Critical Thinking

5 Draw Conclusions Point out that the reader has already learned that Iona is despondent, that his son recently died, and that his first passenger wouldn't talk to him about his loss. Ask students what conclusions they can draw about Iona when they combine these details with those in this sentence. *Students may say that Iona is so lonely that any kind of conversation makes him feel better.*

4 ▲ **Critical Viewing** Find evidence in this photograph to support the fact that it was taken in Russia during the time the story takes place. **[Support]**

5 He hears the abuse directed at him, he sees the men, and little by little the feeling of loneliness begins to lift from his heart. The hunchback goes on abusing him until he is choked by a six-story-high oath and breaks off coughing. The gangly ones begin to talk about a certain Nadezhda Petrovna. Iona looks around at them. Waiting for a short pause, he looks around again and mutters:

"And this week my . . . er . . . son died!"

"We'll all die . . ." sighs the hunchback, wiping his lips after the coughing. "Well, drive on, drive on! Gentlemen, I absolutely cannot go any further like this! When will he get us there?"

◆ Build Vocabulary

conspiring (kən spīr′ iŋ) *v.*: Planning in secret to do something bad

ponderous (pän′ dər əs) *adj.*: Large; heavy

indignantly (in dig′ nənt lē) *adv.*: Angrily

quavering (kwā′ vər iŋ) *adj.*: Shaking; trembling

Viewing and Representing Mini-Lesson

Comparing and Contrasting Cultures

In this mini-lesson, students will extend their understanding of information that historic photographs provide about cultures.

Introduce Point out to students that comparing photographs of cities in different countries taken during the same time period is one way of learning about the cultures the cities represent.

Develop Divide the class into small groups, and ask each group to look in books or on the Internet to find a photograph of a city scene in the United States during the nineteenth century. Then ask them to compare and contrast the photographs they find with the photographs of Russian city life that accompany this story.

Apply When the groups have discussed the similarities and differences of the photos, provide poster board or large sheets of paper on which they can create Venn diagrams. Have each group compare and contrast the photos of the American city with the photos of Russia, using a Venn diagram.

Assess Ask each group to display its Venn diagram for the class, and explain the similarities and differences of the photos. Evaluate students' work on the accuracy of details they have observed from the photos, the appropriate placement of the details on the Venn diagram, and their explanations to the class.

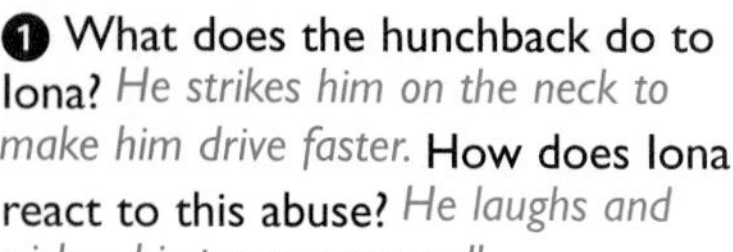

Comprehension Check

❶ What does the hunchback do to Iona? *He strikes him on the neck to make him drive faster.* How does Iona react to this abuse? *He laughs and wishes his passengers well.*

◆ Reading Strategy

❷ **Make Inferences** Discuss with students why they think Iona does not feel the blow on his neck. *Students may say that Iona is so depressed that he feels numb.*

◆ Critical Thinking

❸ **Interpret** Ask students why they think the author states Iona's feelings as a question he asks of himself. Have them explain whether they feel this is an effective technique. *Students may say that by having Iona ask himself a question, the author effectively states the theme of his story.*

◆ Build Grammar Skills

❹ **Adverb Clauses** Point out that although it contains a subject and verb, the following phrase, or clause, cannot stand alone as a sentence: *as if she has understood his thought*. Explain that this is an adverb clause, a clause that modifies a verb, adjective, or other adverb. Ask students what this clause modifies. *Help students conclude that it modifies "begins to run."*

◆ Literary Focus

❺ **Setting** Ask students what these sentences tell about the stable. *Iona is in a place where many people, perhaps other drivers, have gathered for the night. It is dirty, smelly, crowded, and stuffy.*

"You encourage him a little—in the neck!"

"Hear that you old rat? Why I'll whack your neck! . . . If we're going to stand on ceremony with your kind, we might as well go on foot . . . You hear, Snake Gorynych? Or do you spit on your words?"

1 And Iona hears more than feels the thud of a blow on the neck.

"He, he . . ." he laughs. "Jolly fellows . . . God grant you health!"

"Driver, are you married?" asks a tall one.

"Me? He, he . . . Jo-ol-ly fellows! Now I got one wife—the damp earth . . . Ho, ho, ho . . . The grave, that is! . . . My son's died now, and I'm alive . . . Queer thing, death knocked at the wrong door . . . Instead of coming to me, it went to my son . . ."

> **◆ Reading Strategy**
> 2 What can you tell about Iona's character from the way he reacts to the hunchback hitting him on the neck?

And Iona turns around to tell how his son died, but the hunchback sighs lightly and announces that, thank God, they've finally arrived. Receiving his twenty-kopek piece, Iona looks after the carousers disappearing in a dark entrance for a long time. Again he is alone, and again there is silence for him . . . The heartache which had eased for a while, appears again and rends the breast with even greater force.

3 Iona's eyes run anxiously and tormentedly over the crowd surging along both sides of the street: from these thousands of people, can't even one be found who would hear him out? But the crowds run along, not noticing him or his heartache . . . Vast, boundless heartache. If Iona's breast burst and the heartache poured out, it seems it would flood the entire world—but nevertheless people do not see it. It managed to fit into such an insignificant shell that you would not see it in the daylight with a torch . . .

Iona sees a doorkeeper with a sack and decides to talk to him.

"What time would it be now, friend?" he asks.

"After nine . . . Why you stopping here? Move along!"

Iona drives a few steps away, hunches up and surrenders to the heartache . . . He considers it useless to turn to people. But five minutes do not pass before he straightens up, shakes his head as if he felt a sharp pain, and yanks the reins . . . He can't bear it.

"To the stable," he thinks, "to the stable."

And as if she has understood his thought, 4 the nag begins to run at a trot. An hour and a half later Iona is already sitting by a big dirty stove. On the stove, floor, and benches people 5 are snoring. The air is stuffy and full of smells . . . Iona looks at the sleepers, scratches himself and regrets returning home so early . . .

"And I didn't make enough for oats," he thinks. "That's the reason for the heartache. A man who knows his stuff . . . who's full himself and whose horse is full, is always at ease."

In one of the corners a young driver gets up, croaks sleepily, and heads for the waterbucket.

"You want a drink?" asks Iona.

"Obviously!"

"So . . . Your health . . . And, friend, my son died. Did you hear? This week in the hospital . . . A story!"

Iona looks for what effect his words have produced, but sees nothing. The young man has covered his head and is already sleeping. The old man sighs and scratches himself . . . He wants to talk, just as the young man wanted to drink. It will soon be a week since his son died, and he still hasn't talked to anyone about it properly . . . He should speak with good sense, in measured tones . . . He must tell how his son got sick, how he suffered, what he said before death, how he died . . . He should describe the funeral and the trip to the hospital for the deceased's clothes. A daughter, Anisya, remained in the country . . . He should talk about her too . . . Does he have any dearth of things he can talk about now? The listener should moan, sigh, lament . . . And it's even better to talk to women. Even though they are fools, they wail after two words.

"Go see after the horse," thinks Iona. "You'll always manage some sleep . . . You'll probably get enough sleep."

Cross-Curricular Connection: Social Studies

Class-consciousness Explain to students that Iona may be spending the night in the stable with other drivers because he lives in a small village that is far away from the city. During the nineteenth century in Russia, many people who lived in small communities had to travel to the larger cities to find work. As an example, have students look again at the photograph on pp. 506 and 507, which shows peasant women in search of a living in Moscow. Call students' attention to the sacks for carrying belongings.

Discuss with students how Iona's status as a poor person who probably lives in a rural community relates to the treatment he receives from his customers—they may feel that he is uneducated and less informed about subjects than they are because they live in the city. Since they ride in cabs, they also have more money than Iona. Class-consciousness was strong in nineteenth-century Russia. Many Russians like Iona had been slaves, or serfs, until a few decades before this story takes place.

He gets dressed and goes into the stable where his horse is standing. He thinks about oats, hay, about the weather . . . About his son, when he is alone, he cannot think . . . It is possible to talk to someone about him, but by himself it is unbearably painful to think about him and draw his picture.

6 "Chewing?" Iona asks his horse, seeing her shining eyes. "Well, chew, chew . . . If we didn't get enough for oats, we'll eat hay . . . Yes . . . I've already got too old to go out . . . My son should drive, not me . . . He was a real driver . . . If only he were alive . . ."

Iona is silent for a while and continues: "So, my girl . . . Kozma Ionych is gone . . . He left this life . . . Went and died for nothing . . . Now, let's say, you have a little colt, and you are the natural mother of this little colt . . . And suddenly, let's say, this little colt left this life . . . Wouldn't you be sorry?"

The nag chews, listens, and breathes on the hands of her master . . .

Iona is carried away and tells her everything . . .

◆ **Build Vocabulary**

insignificant (inˊ sig nifˊ i kənt) *adj.*: Small; unimposing

Guide for Responding

◆ Literature and Your Life

Reader's Response Would you stop to hear Iona Potapov's story? Explain.

Thematic Focus What should Iona do to deal with his heartache more productively?

Journal Writing When a friend needs someone to talk to, are you a good listener? In a brief journal entry, write about the qualities you think a good listener needs. Then, evaluate your strengths and weaknesses with these skills.

☑ Check Your Comprehension

1. Identify the time of day and season of the year in which this story is set.
2. What is Iona's occupation?
3. How do Iona's passengers treat him?
4. What happened to Iona's son?
5. Who listens to Iona's story in the end?

◆ Critical Thinking

INTERPRET

1. In the first paragraph, Chekhov writes that Iona seems as if he wouldn't bother to shake the snow off himself even if a whole snowdrift were to fall on him. What does this tell you about Iona's state of mind? **[Interpret]**
2. After the officer gets in the cab, why does Iona drive so poorly? **[Infer]**
3. Why do Iona's passengers treat him badly? **[Analyze]**
4. In what ways are Iona and his horse similar? **[Support]**
5. What message about people does "Heartache" convey? **[Draw Conclusions]**

EVALUATE

6. How effective do you find the ending of the story? Explain. **[Make a Judgment]**

APPLY

7. What can individuals and society do to help people who are in situations similar to Iona's? **[Speculate]**

Beyond the Selection

FURTHER READING

Other Works by Anton Chekhov

The Brute and Other Farces
The Kiss and Other Stories
Lady with a Lapdog and Other Stories

Other Short Story Collections

Leaving Home, Hazel Rochman (ed.)
The Call and Other Stories, Robert Westall

INTERNET

We suggest the following sites on the Internet (all Web sites are subject to change).

For summaries of several Chekhov stories, go to: **http://endeavor.med.nyu.edu/lit-med/lit-med-db/webdocs/webauthors/chekhov68-au-.html**

For a Chekhov biography and historical background, visit: **http://www.danworld.com/info/chekhov/bio.shtml**

For several Chekhov stories on-line, go to: **http://eldred.ne.mediaone.net/ac/chekhov.html**

We *strongly recommend* that you preview these sites before you send students to them.

◆ Literature and Your Life

6 Ask students why Iona imagines that his horse is listening to him. Then ask what qualities a good listener must have. *Students may say that a good listener asks questions, makes eye contact, withholds advice unless it is requested, and responds sympathetically.*

Reinforce and Extend

Answers

◆ Literature and Your Life

Reader's Response Many students may not be interested because the story is likely to be long and emotionally painful; others may say that they would listen to Iona because it would make him feel better.

Thematic Focus Students may suggest that he talk to a member of his family or a friend near his home rather than to people who do not know him.

☑ Check Your Comprehension

1. The story takes place at twilight in the winter.
2. Iona is a cab driver.
3. They treat him disrespectfully.
4. He died the week before of a fever.
5. Iona tells his story to his horse.

◆ Critical Thinking

1. He is depressed, so he doesn't care about the snow.
2. He is so preoccupied by his sad thoughts that he can't pay attention.
3. They think he is insignificant, or of a lower status; he is a safe target because he needs the money they pay him.
4. Both are patient and do their jobs with little thought or enthusiasm.
5. The story conveys how important it is for people to be able to share feelings and talk about their problems to others. It also conveys the idea that people may not be willing listeners.
6. Most students will say that the end of the story is effective because it emphasizes how desperately Iona needs to talk about his terrible loss.
7. Discuss the importance of taking time to listen to friends and of learning about services provided by professionals, such as school counselors and social workers.

Develop Understanding

One-Minute Insight This short story, told through the diary entries of two girls, demonstrates how the setting can shape a character's behavior. Leah, a Jewish war refugee from Europe, lives in a camp in upstate New York in 1944. She reveals in diary entries—addressed to her mother who died in the war—how reluctant she is to trust Suzy or the other people who bring food and clothing to the refugee camp. In turn, Suzy reveals in her diary her annoyance at Leah, who keeps her distance at school, never smiles, and refuses Suzy's gestures of friendship. After Suzy reads Leah's letters and learns about the Holocaust from her mother, she begins to understand Leah. She lets Leah read her diary and gives Leah a prized dress. With the possibility of a new friendship, Leah feels that America may be a safe place after all.

◆ Literary Focus

❶ **Setting** Make sure students understand that the "place" that Suzy refers to is the refugee camp where Leah lives. Ask students what these sentences tell about this place. What effect might such a setting have on a person living there? *It is a line of rickety buildings surrounded by high fencing with barbed wire on top. Suzy says it is "just like in the army." Such a setting may cause a person to feel like a prisoner.*

◆ Critical Thinking

❷ **Generalize** Ask students why they think that the author ended the first two letters with these words. *She may have wanted to emphasize that neither girl knew anything about the world in which the other lived.*

◆ Reading Strategy

❸ **Make Inferences** *Students may say that Suzy doesn't seem to understand where the refugees came from or why they act as they do.*

Customize for *Interpersonal Learners*
Have partners read "Suzy and Leah" aloud. Each student can read the letters of one character. Then have partners meet with another pair to discuss the stories.

Suzy and Leah

Jane Yolen

August 5, 1944

Dear Diary,

❶ Today I walked past *that* place, the one that was in the newspaper, the one all the kids have been talking about. Gosh, is it ugly! A line of rickety wooden buildings just like in the army. And a fence lots higher than my head. With barbed wire[1] on top. How can anyone—even a refugee—live there?

I took two candy bars along, just like everyone said I should. When I held them up, all those kids just swarmed over to the fence, grabbing. Like in a zoo. Except for this one girl, with two dark braids and bangs nearly covering her eyes. She was just standing to one side, staring at me. It was so creepy. After a minute I looked away. When I looked back, she was gone. I mean gone. Disappeared as if she'd never been.

Suzy

August 5, 1944

My dear Mutti,[2]

I have but a single piece of paper to write on. And a broken pencil. But I will write small so I can tell all. I address it to you, *Mutti,* though you are gone from me forever. I write in English, to learn better, because I want to make myself be understood.

Today another girl came. With more sweets. A girl with yellow hair and a false smile. Yonni and Zipporah and Ruth, my friends, all grabbed for the sweets. Like wild animals. Like . . . like prisoners. But we are not wild animals. And we are no longer prisoners. Even though we are still penned in.

I stared at the yellow-haired girl until she was forced to look down. Then I walked away. When I turned to look back, she was gone. Disappeared. As if she had never been. ❷

Leah

September 2, 1944

Dear Diary,

I brought the refugee kids oranges today. Can you believe it—they didn't know you're supposed to peel oranges first. One boy tried to eat one like an apple. He made an awful face, but then he ate it anyway. I showed them how to peel oranges with the second one. After I stopped laughing.

Mom says they are going to be coming to school. Of course they'll have to be cleaned up first. Ugh. My hand still feels itchy from where one little boy grabbed it in his. I wonder if he had bugs.

Suzy

> **◆ Reading Strategy**
> What can you infer about Suzy's understanding of the refugees from her thoughts and feelings? ❸

September 2, 1944

My dear Mutti,

Today we got cereal in a box. At first I did not know what it was. Before the war we ate such lovely porridge with milk straight from our cows. And eggs fresh from the hen's nest,

1. **barbed wire:** Twisted wire with sharp points all along it, used for fences and barriers.
2. **Mutti** (moo͝ ´ tē): German equivalent of Mommy.

Cross-Curricular Connection: Social Studies

Safe Haven "Suzy and Leah" is based on historical fact. In 1944, by order of President Roosevelt, 982 refugees from eighteen countries overrun by the Nazis were brought to a camp called Safe Haven in Oswego, New York. Most were Jewish. In Oswego, they were interned in a camp enclosed with barbed wire. Their internment was intended to be temporary—the refugees had signed documents saying they would return to their countries after the war, and Roosevelt planned to return them when it was safe to do so. In 1946, President Truman signed a proclamation that allowed the refugees to stay in the United States and they were permitted to leave the camp; they spread to about seventy communities, getting jobs and attending colleges and universities.

Their story is told in *Haven: The Unknown Story of 1000 World War II Refugees,* by Ruth Gruber a journalist, who was instrumental in bringing these refugees to the United States.

For more information go to:
http://www.syracuse.com/features/safehaven

We *strongly recommend* that you preview this site before sending students to it.

though you know how I hated that nasty old chicken. How often she pecked me! In the German camp, it was potato soup—with onions when we were lucky, without either onion or
4 potato when we were not. And after, when I was running from the Nazis, it was stale brown bread, if we could find any. But cereal in a box—*that* is something.

I will not take a sweet from that yellow-haired girl, though. She
5 laughed at Yonni. I will not take another orange fruit.

Leah

September 5, 1944

Dear Diary,

So how are those refugee kids going to learn? Our teachers teach in English. This is America, after all.

I wouldn't want to be one of them. Imagine going to school and not being able to speak English or understand anything that's going on. I can't imagine anything worse.

Suzy

September 5, 1944

My dear Mutti,

6 The adults of the Americans say we are safe now. And so we must go to their school. But I say no place is safe for us. Did not the Germans say that we were safe in their camps? And there you and baby Natan were killed.

And how could we learn in this American school anyway? I have a little English. But Ruth and Zipporah and the others, though they speak Yiddish[3] and Russian and German, they have no English at all. None beyond *thank you* and *please* and *more sweets.* And then there is little Avi. How could he go to this school? He will speak nothing at all. He stopped speaking, they say, when he was hidden away in a cupboard by his grandmother who was taken by the Nazis after she swore there was no child in the house. And he was almost three days in that cupboard without food, without water, without words to comfort him. Is English a safer language than German?

There is barbed wire still between us and the world.

Leah

3. **Yiddish** (yid′ ish) *n:* Language spoken by eastern European Jews and their descendants. It is written with Hebrew letters and contains words from Hebrew, Russian, Polish, and English.

▲ Critical Viewing How is the expression on this girl's face different from the way Leah's
7 expression is described? When might Leah have been more like the girl in the photograph? **[Compare and Contrast]**

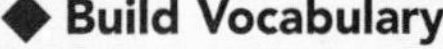

◆ Build Vocabulary

refugee (ref′ yo͞o jē) *n.:* Person who flees home or country to seek shelter from war or cruelty

Clarification

4 Remind students that the Jews who were forced into concentration camps by the Nazis in Germany were starved and forced to suffer unspeakable indignities.

◆ Reading Strategy

5 Make Inferences Ask students what inferences they can make about Leah's character based on her reaction to Suzy's behavior. *Students may say that Leah is protective of Yonni, suspicious, and unwilling to trust people.*

◆ Critical Thinking

6 Compare Ask students to compare Suzy's statement, "I can't imagine anything worse" than not being able to speak English or understand what's going on to Leah's concerns about going to the American school. *Guide students to recognize that Suzy's attitude seems silly and superficial compared to Leah's concerns, which stem from the loss of her mother and brother and the other horrible experiences she has had.*

▶Critical Viewing◀

7 Compare and Contrast *Students may say that the girl in the photograph is smiling and seems relaxed, as Leah probably was before the war changed her life.*

Looking at Literature Videodisc/Videotape

To provide historical background and motivate students to read "Suzy and Leah," play Chapter 6 of the videodisc. In these interviews, Holocaust survivors and the children of Holocaust survivors describe their experiences. Discuss why it is important for their story to be told.

Chapter 6

Cultural Connection

Yiddish Although it is spoken by 540 million people around the world, Yiddish is not a national language anywhere. One of the Germanic languages, Yiddish originated (c.1100) in southwestern Germany as an adaptation by Jews of Middle High German dialects. Hebrew words were later added, especially religious words. Later, when most European Jews moved eastward, words and grammar of various Slavic languages, such as Russian and Polish, were adapted. The Yiddish vocabulary also borrowed from Romance languages and English. The language is written in Hebrew characters.

Yiddish was a predominant language of people who escaped World War II and settled in the United States. As second-, third-, and fourth-generation descendants of these immigrants adopted American customs, the use of Yiddish declined in this country. Yiddish words, however, have found their way into the colloquial language of Americans—for instance, *schlep,* meaning "to travel or to carry something laboriously." To help preserve the language, some American schools and colleges teach Yiddish.

▶Critical Viewing◀

❶ **Respond** *Students will most likely say that it is unusual and disturbing to see terrified women and young children with their arms raised at gunpoint, and by contrast, the relaxed attitude of the Nazi officers holding guns.*

Clarification

❷ Explain that in this sentence Suzy refers to the uniforms worn by the inmates of concentration camps. The uniforms had bold, vertical black and white stripes.

◆ Build Grammar Skills

❸ **Adverb Clauses** Explain that an adverb clause functions as an adverb and has a subject and a verb, but cannot stand alone as a sentence. Guide students to identify the adverb clause in this sentence as "if she had only asked." Point out that *if*, the word that the adverb clause begins with, is a subordinating conjunction. Explain that the adverb clause tells how Suzy would have been more comfortable with her mother's actions. Then ask students to identify the verb phrase that it modifies. *Students should identify "wouldn't have minded."*

◆ Literary Focus

❹ **Setting** Discuss with students that in this sentence the author mentions the farm where Leah lived before the war. Ask them why the author may have included this detail. *She may have wanted to contrast the secure, comfortable existence that Leah had before with the terror she feels now.*

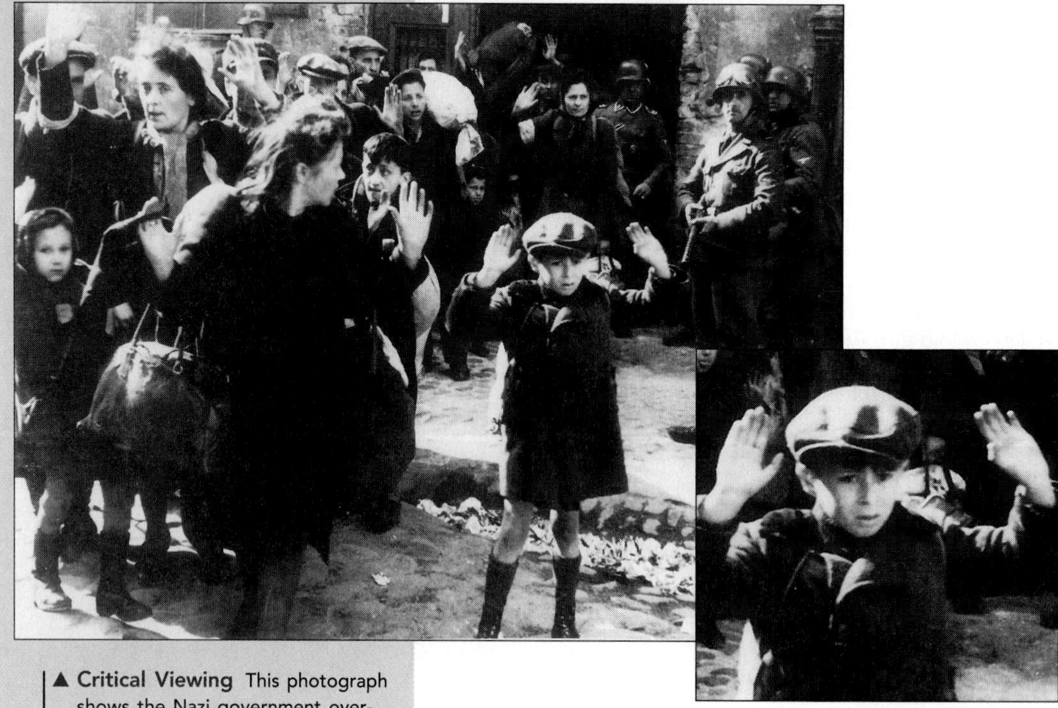

❶ ▲ **Critical Viewing** This photograph shows the Nazi government overseeing Jews leaving their homes. What do you find most surprising about the picture? **[Respond]**

September 14, 1944

Dear Diary,

❷ At least the refugee kids are wearing better clothes now. And they all have shoes. Some of them still had those stripy pajamas on when they arrived in America.

The girls all wore dresses to their first day at school, though. They even had hair bows, gifts from the teachers. Of course I recognized my old blue pinafore. The girl with the dark braids had it on, and Mom hadn't even told me ❸ she was giving it away. I wouldn't have minded so much if she had only asked. It doesn't fit me anymore, anyway.

The girl in my old pinafore was the only one without a name tag, so all day long no one knew her name.

Suzy

September 14, 1944

My dear Mutti,

I put on the blue dress for our first day. It fit me well. ❹ The color reminded me of your eyes and the blue skies over our farm before the smoke from the burning darkened it. Zipporah braided my hair, but I had no mirror until we got to the school and they showed us the toilets. They call it a bathroom, but there is no bath in it at all, which is strange. I have never been in a school with boys before.

Cross-Curricular Connection: Social Studies

The Warsaw Ghetto Focus students' attention on the photographs on this page. Explain that during World War II, Warsaw, the capital of Poland, was the location of the Warsaw Ghetto, where more than 400,000 Jews were confined by Nazi occupation forces. Because of the ghetto's crowded conditions and general deprivation, many Jews died from starvation and disease.

April 19, 1943, marked the beginning of the Warsaw Ghetto Uprising, when more than 2,000 Nazi soldiers, along with members of the Lithuanian militia and Polish police, attacked the ghetto. To counter the surprisingly forceful resistance of the poorly armed Jews, the Nazis set the ghetto on fire block by block and then flooded and smoke-bombed the sewers, which the Jews attempted to use for escape.

Discuss with students the impact of this information. Ask them whether knowing the facts behind the photograph changes their impressions of it.

They have placed us all in low grades. Because of our English. I do not care. This way I do not have to see the girl with the yellow hair who smiles so falsely at me.

5 But they made us wear tags with our names printed on them. That made me afraid. What next? Yellow stars?[4] I tore mine off and threw it behind a bush before we went in.

Leah

September 16, 1944

Dear Diary,

Mr. Forest has assigned each of us to a refugee to help them with their English. He gave me the girl with the dark braids, the one without the name tag, the one in my pinafore. Gee, she's as prickly as a porcupine. I asked if I could have a different kid. He said I was the best English student and she already spoke the best English. He wants her to learn as fast as possible so she can help the others. As if she would, Miss Porcupine.

Her name is Leah. I wish she would wear another dress.

Suzy

September 16, 1944

My dear Mutti,

Now I have a real notebook and a pen. I am writing to you at school now. I cannot take the notebook back to the shelter. Someone there will surely borrow it. I will instead keep it here. In the little cupboard each one of us has been given.

I wish I had another dress. I wish I had a different student helping me and not the yellow-haired girl.

Leah

September 20, 1944

Dear Diary,

6 Can't she ever smile, that Leah? I've brought her candy bars and apples from home. I tried to give her a handkerchief with a yellow flower on it. She wouldn't take any of them. 6

> **◆ Literature and Your Life**
> How would you feel if you had to help someone who didn't act grateful? Would you be understanding or irritated? 7

Her whole name is Leah Shoshana Hershkowitz. At least, that's the way she writes it. When she says it, it sounds all different, low and growly. I laughed when I tried to say it, but she wouldn't laugh with me. What a grouch.

And yesterday, when I took her English paper to correct it, she shrank back against her chair as if I was going to hit her or something. Honestly!

Mom says I should invite her home for dinner soon. We'll have to get her a special pass for that. But I don't know if I want her to come. It's not like she's any fun at all. I wish Mr. Forest would let me trade.

Suzy

September 20, 1944

My dear Mutti,

The girl with the yellow hair is called Suzy Ann McCarthy. It is a silly name. It means nothing. I asked her who she was named for, and she said, "For a book my mom liked." A book! I am named after my great-grandmother on my mother's side, who was an important woman in our village. I am proud to carry on her name.

This Suzy brings many sweets. But I must call them candies now. And a handkerchief. She expects me to be grateful. But how can I be grateful? She treats me like a pet, a pet she does not really like or trust. She wants to feed me like an animal behind bars.

If I write all this down, I will not hold so much anger. I have much anger. And terror besides. *Terror.* It is a new word for me, but an old feeling. One day soon this Suzy and her people will stop being nice to us. They will remember we are not just refugees but Jews, and they will turn on us. Just as the Germans did. Of this I am sure. 8

Leah

4. **yellow stars:** Jews were forced to wear fabric stars during the Holocaust to distinguish them from others.

◆ Reading Strategy

5 Make Inferences Ask students why being asked to wear a name tag frightens Leah. *Leah had at one time been forced to wear a yellow star that identified her as a Jew, and therefore as a person designated for persecution; throwing away the name tag, even though she feels frightened, indicates she is beginning to feel more secure.*

◆ Critical Thinking

6 Analyze and Predict Have students compare these sentences with the last sentence of the previous letter. Tell students that in fiction, authors create a conflict, or a problem to be solved. Ask them what problem these two sentences reveal. How will the problem be solved? *The problem is the lack of understanding between Leah and Suzy and the resentment that results. Students may predict that, after learning more about each other's backgrounds, the girls will better understand each other and grow closer.*

◆ Literature and Your Life

7 Although students will probably agree that Suzy has cause to feel frustrated or irritated by Leah's seemingly ungrateful attitude, many may wonder why she isn't more patient with Leah's behavior. You may want to use this as an opportunity to discuss the importance of trying to see a situation from another person's point of view.

Comprehension Check ☑

8 Why is terror an "old feeling" for Leah? *Students should understand that Leah has suffered years of horror and that she has had little time to feel safe and free from terror.*

Cultural Connection

Naming Traditions Leah's and Suzy's names produce a misunderstanding between the girls. Naming traditions vary from culture to culture. For example, according to Jewish traditions, a child is named for a family member who has died. This is why Leah was named for her great-grandmother.

Although Suzy's mother named her after a character in a book, some families of European descent, especially in earlier times, also named children after their ancestors. They often followed this order:

1st son	=	father's father
2nd son	=	mother's father
3rd son	=	father
4th son	=	father's oldest brother
1st daughter	=	mother's mother
2nd daughter	=	father's mother
3rd daughter	=	mother
4th daughter	=	mother's oldest sister

Invite students to share the naming traditions with which they are familiar. For instance, they might explain how they got their names or how their parents got theirs.

◆ **Reading Strategy**

❶ **Make Inferences** Guide students to notice that this diary entry differs from Suzy's previous ones. Point out, for example, that she pays Leah a compliment and she shows concern for Leah. Ask students what they infer from this entry. *Students may say that Suzy's attitude toward Leah is finally changing.*

◆ **Reading Strategy**

❷ **Make Inferences** *Students may say that Leah feels responsible for and protective of Avi, as if he were her brother. Point out that this feeling of being responsible for someone else may cause her to worry about Avi when she is not around him and add to her "permanent frown lines."*

▶**Critical Viewing**◀

❸ **Support** *Leah and the other refugees eat their meals at the shelter.*

September 30, 1944

Dear Diary,

Leah's English is very good now. But she still never smiles. Especially she never smiles at me. It's like she has a permanent frown and permanent frown lines between her eyes. It makes her look much older than anyone in our class. Like a little old lady.

I wonder if she eats enough. She won't take the candy bars. And she saves the school lunch in her napkin, hiding it away in her pocket. She thinks no one sees her do it, but I do. Does she eat it later? I'm sure they get dinner at the shelter. Mom says they do. Mom also says we have to eat everything on our plates. Sometimes when we're having dinner I think of Leah Shoshana Hershkowitz. ❶

Suzy

September 30, 1944

My dear Mutti,

Avi loves the food I bring home from school. What does he know? It is not even kosher.[5] Sometimes they serve ham. But I do not tell Avi. He needs all the food he can get. He is a growing boy.

◆ **Reading Strategy** What can you infer about Leah from the way she treats Avi? ❷

I, too, am growing fast. Soon I will not fit into the blue dress. I have no other.

Leah

❸ ▼ **Critical Viewing** Part of this story is set in a refugee camp, like the one shown here. What details in the photograph are confirmed in Suzy's letters? **[Support]**

October 9, 1944

Dear Diary,

They skipped Leah up to our grade, her English has gotten so good. Except for some words, like victory, which she pronounces "wick-toe-ree." I try not to laugh, but sometimes I just can't help it!

Leah knows a lot about the world and nothing about America. She thinks New York is right next to Chicago, for goodness sakes! She can't dance at all. She doesn't know the words to any of the top songs. And she's so stuck up, she only talks in class to answer questions. The other refugees aren't like that at all. Why is it only my refugee who's so mean?

Suzy

5. **kosher** (kō′ shər) *adj.*: Fit to eat according to the Jewish laws of diet.

Speaking and Listening Mini-Lesson

Questions and Answers

This mini-lesson supports the Speaking and Listening activity in the Idea Bank on p. 521.

Introduce Point out to students that Suzy and Leah seem to have many unanswered questions about each other's behaviors and attitudes. Discuss how their situation would be different if they verbally communicated the thoughts and feelings revealed in their diaries.

Develop Have students choose partners and select characters to portray. Ask them first to work alone to write about what it would be like to be the character they selected. Then have them write three or four questions they would like to ask the other character.

Apply Have partners ask each other their questions in front of the class or in small groups. Suggest that they use the answers to the questions they listed as a springboard for further questions and answers. When all partners have asked and answered their questions, have them discuss what the questions and answers revealed about each of the characters.

Assess Evaluate students' work on how well they listen to one another's questions and their understanding of their characters as revealed by their answers. If students are keeping a log of their speaking and listening opportunities, have them add this exercise to the Self-Assessment: Speaking and Listening Progress form, p. 109, in **Alternative Assessment.**

October 9, 1944

My dear Mutti,

I think of you all the time. I went to Suzy's house because Mr. Forest said they had gone to a great deal of trouble to get a pass for me. I did not want to go so much, my stomach hurt the whole time I was there.

Suzy's *Mutti* was nice, all pink and gold. She wore a dress with pink roses all over it and it reminded me of your dress, the blue one with the asters. You were wearing it when we were put on the train. And the last time I saw you at the camp with Natan. Oh, *Mutti.* I had to steel my heart against Suzy's mother. If I love her, I will forget you. And that I must never do.

4 I brought back food from her house, though, for Avi. I could not eat it myself. You would like the way Avi grows bigger and stronger. And he talks now, but only to me. He says, "More, Leah, please." And he says "light" for the sun. Sometimes when I am really lonely I call him Natan, but only at night after he has fallen asleep.

Leah

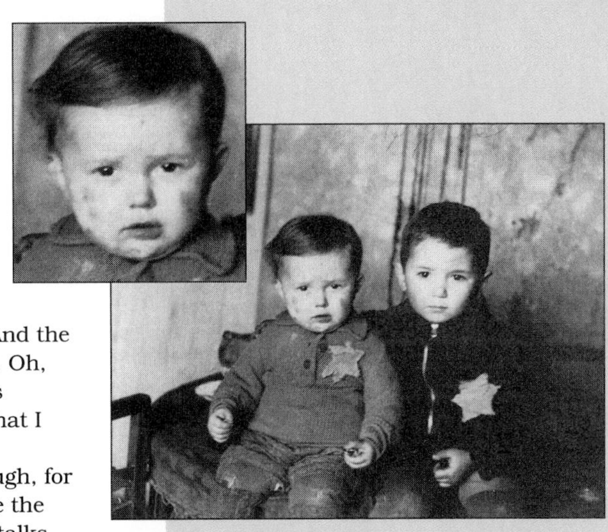

▲ **Critical Viewing** What can you infer about the children in this photograph? Cite details that led you to this inference. **[Infer]** 5

October 10, 1944

Dear Diary,

Leah was not in school today. When I asked her friend Zipporah, she shrugged. "She is ill in her stomach," she said. "What did she eat at your house?"

I didn't answer "Nothing," though that would have been true. She hid it all in a handkerchief Mom gave her. Mom said, "She eats like a bird. How does she stay alive?"

Suzy

October 11, 1944

Dear Diary,

They've asked me to gather Leah's things from school and bring them to the hospital. She had to have her appendix out and nearly died. She almost didn't tell them she was sick until too late. Why did she do that? I would have been screaming my head off with the pain.

Mom says we have to visit, that I'm Leah's American best friend. Hah! We're going to bring several of my old dresses, but not my green one with the white trim. I don't want her to have it. Even if it doesn't fit me anymore.

Suzy

◆ Reading Strategy

4 Make Inferences Ask students why they think that Leah eats so little, hides food, and takes food to Avi. *Students may infer that she eats so little because she wants to save her food for Avi, or that she is too upset to be hungry. They may also say that, because she was not given enough to eat in the concentration camp, she cannot be sure that they will continue to be fed in the United States and wants to save her food.*

▶Critical Viewing◀

5 Infer *Students may say that the boys do not seem happy and that one of them seems ready to cry. To support these ideas, they may point out details about both boys' expressions and the fact that they are leaning on each other.*

Customize for
Less Proficient Readers

Help students understand what Leah means when she says, "I had to steel my heart against Suzy's mother." Explain that Leah felt that she had to fight her impulse to feel affection toward Suzy's mother by making her heart strong, like steel, so she would not forget her own mother. Ask students if they think it was necessary for Leah to do this.

▶Critical Viewing◀

❶ **Connect** *Students may say that the girl on the right looks like Leah because she appears worried, and she seems to be focused on her own thoughts, unlike the other girl who shows interest in what is happening below her.*

◆ Critical Thinking

❷ **Analyze** Discuss with students how Suzy begins this entry by confessing she did something that wasn't right. However, this act resulted in her finally understanding Leah's background. Ask students why this diary entry represents a turning point in the story. *Students should recognize that for the first time Suzy is aware of Leah's history and shows some understanding toward her.*

◆ Literary Focus

❸ **Setting** *The historical context of the story's action is the Holocaust. Leah has lost family members and has been the target of extreme cruelty and hatred. She has also witnessed the violence of war firsthand. These experiences have formed the basis of her personality. This explains why she is unable to trust people, why she hoards food, and why she wants to protect Avi.*

◆ Reading Strategy

❹ **Make Inferences** Ask students why they think Avi is able to speak when Leah becomes ill. *Students may say that Avi's concern for Leah's health helps him overcome the fears that have prevented him from speaking.*

---

❶ ▼ **Critical Viewing** The girls pictured here are looking out of a ship's porthole as they prepare to go to America. Which girl has an expression you'd expect to see on Leah's face? Explain. **[Connect]**

October 12, 1944

Dear Diary,

I did a terrible thing. I read Leah's diary. I'd kill anyone who did that to me!

At first it made no sense. Who were *Mutti* and Natan, and why were they killed? What were the yellow stars? What does kosher mean? And the way she talked about *me* made me furious. Who did she think she was, little Miss Porcupine? All I did was bring candy and fruit and try to make those poor refugee kids feel at home.

Then, when I asked Mom some questions, carefully, so she wouldn't guess I had read Leah's diary, she explained. She said the Nazis killed people, mothers and children as well as men. In places called concentration camps. And that all the Jews—people who weren't Christians like us—had to wear yellow stars on their clothes so they could be spotted blocks and blocks away. It was so awful I could hardly believe it, but Mom said it was true. ❷

How was I supposed to know all that? How can Leah stand any of us? How could she live with all that pain? ❸

Suzy

> ◆ **Literary Focus** Setting includes the historical context of the story's action. How has this shaped Leah's thoughts and behavior?

October 12, 1944

My dear Mutti,

Suzy and her mother came to see me in the hospital. They brought me my notebook so now I can write again.

I was so frightened about being sick. I did not tell anyone for a long time, even though it hurt so much. In the German camp, if you were sick and could not do your work, they did not let you live.

But in the middle of the night, I had so much fever, a doctor was sent for. Little Avi found me. He ran to one of the guards. He spoke out loud for the first time. He said, "Please, for Leah. Do not let her go into the dark." ❹

The doctor tells me I nearly died, but they saved me. They have given me much medicines and soon I will eat the food and they will be sure it is kosher, too. And I am alive. This I can hardly believe. *Alive!*

Cross-Curricular Connection: Social Studies

Always to Remember The National Socialist German Workers' Party (the Nazis) took power in Germany in 1933 when Adolf Hitler became the head of the German government. The Nazis proclaimed the Germans to be the "master race" and blamed specific groups of people for the country's earlier economic problems, as well as Germany's defeat in World War I. Europe's Jews bore the brunt of this blame, suffering most and dying in the largest numbers.

Jewish families, such as Leah's, were terrorized, taken from their homes, forced into labor, or sent to concentration camps—where millions were gassed or died of starvation and disease—in Germany and surrounding European countries. The "Final Solution" was a plan to "exterminate" all of the Jews and others that the Nazis determined to be undesirable in Europe. Germans who did not believe in the Nazis' actions were powerless to stop what was happening. The Allies went to war in 1941, but were unable to stop Hitler and the Nazis until 1945.

Then Suzy came with her *Mutti*, saying, "I am sorry. I am so sorry. I did not know. I did not understand." Suzy did a bad thing. She read my notebook. But it helped her understand. And then, instead of making an apology, she did a strange thing. She took a red book with a lock out of her pocket and gave it to me. "Read this," she said. "And when you are out of the hospital, I have a green dress with white trim I want you to have. It will be just perfect with your eyes."

I do not know what this trim may be. But I like the idea of a green dress. And I have a new word now, as well. It is this: *diary*.

A new word. A new land. And—it is just possible—a new friend.

Leah

Beyond Literature

Social Studies Connection

The U.S. Holocaust Museum Created to keep the memory of the Holocaust alive, the U. S. Holocaust Museum was built in Washington, D.C. One exhibit, "Daniel's Story," is for younger visitors. Through photos and film, children see events through the eyes of a Jewish boy growing up in Nazi Germany. Like Leah, Daniel is fictional, but his story is based on the stories of real people.

Cross Curricular Activity

On-Line Visit Use the Internet to access the U.S. Holocaust Memorial Museum Home Page. Learn more about the Holocaust, and share your findings with the class.

Guide for Responding

◆ Literature and Your Life

Reader's Response How do you think you would have reacted if you had tried to help Leah and she had rejected you?

Thematic Focus Do you think it was wise of Suzy to admit that she had read Leah's diary and to let Leah read her diary? Explain.

Group Discussion This story is about a way in which two people from different worlds learn to understand each other. With classmates, discuss ways in which kids your age can bridge the gaps between different cultures.

☑ Check Your Comprehension

1. What happened to Leah's mother and brother?
2. How are Suzy and Leah forced to get to know each other?
3. Why doesn't Leah eat the food she is given?
4. Why is Leah afraid to go to the hospital?
5. How does Suzy find out that she has misjudged Leah?

◆ Critical Thinking

INTERPRET

1. (a)What do Suzy's reactions to Leah tell you about Suzy? (b)What do Leah's reactions to Suzy tell you about Leah? **[Analyze]**
2. What does Leah mean when she says, "There is barbed wire still between us and the world"? **[Interpret]**
3. How do Suzy's motivations for offering candy to Leah at the story's beginning differ from her motivations for offering her diary to Leah at the end of the story? **[Distinguish]**
4. What has each girl learned from her experience with the other? **[Draw Conclusions]**

EVALUATE

5. Suzy reads Leah's diary and then calls her action "a terrible thing." However, this action leads Suzy to understand Leah better. Would you forgive Suzy? Explain. **[Assess]**

EXTEND

6. How has this story affected your understanding of the Holocaust? **[Social Studies Link]**

Beyond the Selection

FURTHER READING

Other Works by Jane Yolen

Dragon's Blood
The Wild Hunt
The Sea Man

Other Works About the Holocaust

The Diary of a Young Girl, Anne Frank
Number the Stars, Lois Lowry
Bearing Witness: Stories of the Holocaust, Hazel Rochman (ed.)

INTERNET

We suggest the following sites on the Internet (all Web sites are subject to change).

For information on Jane Yolen:
http://www.ipl.org/youth/AskAuthor/Yolen.html

For comments from Jane Yolen:
http://pages.prodigy.com/childrens_writers/janeyole.htm

We *strongly recommend* that you preview these sites before you send students to them.

Beyond Literature

To start students on their research, have them go to the Web site for the United States Holocaust Memorial Museum at **http://www.ushmm.org/index.html.** Tell students that this museum is located in Washington, D.C., but many states have their own Holocaust museums. To find a Holocaust museum near them, suggest that students do their own Internet search, using the key words "Holocaust Museum" and the name of their state.

Reinforce and Extend

Answers

◆ Literature and Your Life

Reader's Response Many students will sympathize with Suzy's frustration; others may say they would try to see the other's point of view.

Thematic Focus Some students will say that Suzy made a wise choice; others will think that it is important to respect the privacy of others.

☑ Check Your Comprehension

1. They were killed in a concentration camp.
2. Suzy is assigned to help Leah with her English at school.
3. Leah saves the food for Avi.
4. In concentration camps sick people were killed.
5. Suzy reads Leah's journal and learns about the Holocaust.

◆ Critical Thinking

1. (a) Suzy has led a privileged life and cannot understand hardship. (b) Leah feels that Suzy treats her like a pet, showing that Leah wants to maintain her pride.
2. Living in the refugee camp still separates Jews from other people.
3. At first, she is doing what she has been told to do. Later, she is motivated by understanding.
4. Suzy has learned that people have different perspectives. Leah has learned that people want to help her and the other refugees.
5. Most students will say that they would forgive Suzy because her actions resulted in a greater understanding between the two girls.
6. Students may say that this story put the Holocaust on a personal level. Students' knowledge about the Holocaust will vary.

Answers

◆ **Reading Strategy**

1. Possible response: Iona is so isolated by his grief that he takes even abusive behavior as some kind of recognition.
2. Possible response: Even though the girls have little understanding of what the other's world is like at the beginning of the story, they are kindred spirits destined for friendship.

◆ **Build Vocabulary**

Using the Suffix -ee

1. employee
2. retiree
3. inductee

Spelling Strategy

1. devotee; 2. awardee; 3. trustee; 4. absentee; 5. examinee

Using the Word Bank

1. b
2. a
3. b
4. a
5. b
6. c

◆ **Literary Focus**

1. "Heartbreak" is set at dusk in a big city in nineteenth-century Russia during the winter.
2. The dreary setting reflects the emotions of the main character, Iona, who has lost his son.
3. "Suzy and Leah" is set in Oswego, New York, near the end of World War II. Suzy lives in the town, and Leah lives in a refugee camp.
4. The setting is essential because the story examines how one's view of the world can be determined by one's experiences. The theme of the story reflects the importance of trying to understand another person's background as a means of understanding the person.

Guide for Responding *(continued)*

◆ Reading Strategy

Make Inferences

To fully understand a story's characters and grasp its message, you have to **make inferences** about the underlying significance of details the author provides. For example, you can make inferences about a character's personality based on details about his or her appearance and actions.

1. What can you infer from Iona's reaction to his three rude passengers: "He hears the abuse directed at him . . . and little by little the feeling of loneliness begins to lift from his heart."

2. Suzy and Leah's first observations of each other end with nearly identical words: "When I looked back, she was gone. . . . Disappeared as if she'd never been." What can you infer from this?

◆ Build Vocabulary

Using the Suffix *-ee*

The suffix -ee indicates a person who is or receives something. Copy the following sentences on your paper. Add -ee to a word from the first sentence to create the word that completes the second sentence.

1. Is he employed there? Yes, he's an __?__ .

2. Is she retired? Yes, she's a __?__.

3. Was he inducted in the army? Yes, he's an __?__.

Spelling Strategy

When you add -ee to a word that ends in the letter e, drop the final e before adding the suffix: *escape + e = escapee*. If the word ends in a consonant, simply add -ee: *appoint + -ee = appointee*.

On your paper, add -ee to the following words.

1. devote **2.** award **3.** trust **4.** absent **5.** examine

Using the Word Bank

On your paper, write the letter of the word closest in meaning to the first word.

1. refugee: (a) soldier, (b) escapee, (c) teacher

2. conspiring: (a) plotting, (b) finding, (c) hiding

3. quavering: (a) steady, (b) shaky, (c) heavy

4. insignificant: (a) unimportant, (b) huge, (c) costly

5. ponderous: (a) simple, (b) heavy, (c) sweet

6. indignantly: (a) quietly, (b) sharply, (c) furiously

◆ Literary Focus

Setting

The **setting** is the time and place in which a story unfolds. The setting may help to set the mood of a story and may even shape the characters and events.

1. Describe the setting of "Heartache."

2. Why is the setting of "Heartache" significant?

3. Describe the setting of "Suzy and Leah."

4. Why is the setting of "Suzy and Leah" essential to the story?

◆ Build Grammar Skills

Adverb Clauses

An **adverb clause** is a subordinate clause (a group of words that has a subject and verb but cannot stand alone as a sentence) that functions as an adverb. The entire clause modifies a verb, adjective, or other adverb. Like one-word adverbs, adverb clauses answer the questions *when, where, how, why,* and *to what extent.* Adverb clauses begin with subordinating conjunctions. Common subordinating conjunctions are *after, as, although, because, if, since, when, unless,* and *until.*

When I held them up, all those kids just swarmed over to the fence, grabbing. (Tells when)

Practice Copy the following sentences. Underline each adverb clause, and draw an arrow to the word it modifies. Then, tell what question the adverb clause answers.

1. I write in English because I want to be understood.

2. I stared at the yellow-haired girl until she was forced to look down.

3. He stopped speaking when he was hidden away in a cupboard.

4. If I write all this down, I will not hold so much anger.

5. I had no mirror until we got to the school.

Writing Application Write each of the following sentences on your paper, adding to each an adverb clause that answers the question.

1. The snow fell on Iona. *(To what extent?)*

2. Only his horse listened to him. *(How?)*

◆ **Build Grammar Skills**

Practice

1. I write in English because I want to be understood. (Tells why)
2. I stared at the yellow-haired girl until she was forced to look down. (Tells how)
3. He stopped speaking when he was hidden away in a cupboard. . . . (Tells when)
4. If I write all this down, I will not hold so much anger. (Tells why)
5. I had no mirror until we got to the school. (Tells when)

Writing Application

Possible responses are given:

1. The snow fell on Iona until he looked like a white statue.
2. Only his horse listened to him as if it understood.

Writer's Solution

For additional instruction and practice, use the lesson in the *Writer's Solution Language Lab CD-ROM* on adverbs. You may also use the practice page on Adverb Clauses, p. 53, in the *Writer's Solution Grammar Practice Book.*

Build Your Portfolio

 Idea Bank

Writing

1. Sympathy Note Imagine that you are a friend of Iona Potapov's son, Kozma. Write a note to comfort Iona. In your note, show that you understand how Iona must be feeling.

2. Diary Entries Write a new pair of diary entries for Suzy and Leah describing events after Leah leaves the hospital. Try to write with each girl's style and tone.

3. Analytic Essay Yolen chose to tell her story through letters. In an essay, evaluate the success of that decision. What are the benefits and disadvantages of telling a story this way?

Speaking and Listening

4. Questions and Answers With a classmate, stage a question-and-answer session between Suzy and Leah in which they ask each other honest questions about their behavior. Base both your questions and answers on information from the story.

5. Talk Radio [Group Activity] Imagine that the characters from "Heartache" called in to a radio talk show to share their opinions about the events in the story and their views on life. Role-play the conversations. Possible roles include: one or two talk-show hosts, Iona, the passengers, and Iona's horse. **[Media Link; Performing Arts Link]**

Projects

6. Snow Statistics To get a better understanding of the setting in "Heartache," use library resources to find the amount of snowfall in the Russian cities of Moscow and St. Petersburg. Construct a bar graph to compare snowfall in those cities with that in your hometown. **[Science Link; Math Link]**

7. Research Report Use Internet, library, and community resources to collect information on the Holocaust. Share what you learn with the class. **[Social Studies Link]**

Writing Mini-Lesson

Introduction to an Exhibition

Imagine that you are helping your local historical museum prepare an exhibit relating to the setting of either "Heartache" or "Suzy and Leah." Write an introductory brochure to help visitors understand what they will see in the exhibits.

Writing Skills Focus: Necessary Context/Background

Your job is to provide the **necessary context or historical background** in your introduction so that museum visitors can understand the photographs and artifacts in your exhibition. Otherwise, visitors will misunderstand or fail to appreciate what they are seeing—just as Suzy misjudged Leah because she did not know much about Leah's background.

Prewriting Select the topic for your exhibition: City Life in Nineteenth-Century Russia or The Holocaust. Then, make a list of questions the introduction to the exhibition should answer. To answer these questions, you may need to do library or Internet research. Record key pieces of information on separate note cards. Remember to include information about your source (author, title, publication information, and page) on each note card.

Drafting Organize your most important findings in logical paragraphs. Begin with the most important facts first. End by explaining how the exhibit relates to this historical background.

◆ Grammar Application

Use adverb clauses to clarify the descriptions in your introduction to an exhibition.

Revising Reread your introduction to make sure that you have provided the background needed to understand the exhibit. Make sure you present accurate information in a logical order. Check that the facts and language are interesting.

 Idea Bank

Following are suggestions for matching the Idea Bank topics with your students' performance levels and learning modalities:

Customize for *Performance Levels*
Less Advanced Students: 1, 4, 7
Average Students: 2, 4, 6, 7
More Advanced Students: 3, 5, 7

Customize for *Learning Modalities*
Verbal/Linguistic: 4, 5, 7
Interpersonal: 4, 5
Logical/Mathematical: 6

 Writing Mini-Lesson

Refer students to the Writing Handbook in the back of the book for instruction on the writing process and for further information on expository writing

 ***Writer's Solution***

Writers at Work Videodisc
To introduce students to expository writing, show them the videodisc segments featuring Richard Lederer. Encourage them to discuss how expository writing leads to learning.

Play frames 31956 to 41222

Writing Lab CD-ROM
Have students complete the tutorial on Exposition: Giving Information. Follow these steps:

1. Have students use the checklist in the Prewriting section to evaluate whether they need to narrow their topics.
2. Suggest that students use the Notecard Activities to see how to arrange details.
3. Have students draft on computer.
4. When revising, have students use the Proofreading Checklist.

Writer's Solution Sourcebook
Have students use Chapter 4, "Exposition: Giving Information," pp. 102–133, for additional support. The chapter includes in-depth instruction on using exact nouns and building paragraphs, pp. 128–129.

ASSESSMENT OPTIONS

Formal Assessment, Selection Test, pp. 146–148, and Assessment Resources Software. The selection test is designed so that it can easily be customized to the performance levels of your students.

Alternative Assessment, p. 32, includes options for less advanced students, more advanced students, and verbal/linguistic learners, intrapersonal learners, visual/spatial learners, logical/mathematical learners, and interpersonal learners.

PORTFOLIO ASSESSMENT
Use the following rubrics in the **Alternative Assessment** booklet to assess student writing:
Sympathy Note: Expression, p. 81
Diary Entries: Fictional Narrative, p. 82
Character Analysis: Critical Review, p. 98
Writing Mini-Lesson: Research Report/Paper, p. 93

Prepare and Engage

OBJECTIVES

1. To read, comprehend, and interpret two stories
2. To relate stories to personal experience
3. To ask questions while reading
4. To recognize the theme of a story
5. To build vocabulary in context and learn the root *-sens-*
6. To identify and use adjective clauses
7. To write a character analysis using supporting evidence
8. To respond to the stories through writing, speaking and listening, and projects

SKILLS INSTRUCTION

Vocabulary: Word Roots: *-sens-*
Spelling: Adding the Suffix *-ious*
Grammar: Adjective Clauses
Reading Strategy: Ask Questions
Literary Focus: Theme
Writing: Character Analysis
Speaking and Listening: Monologue (Teacher Edition)
Viewing and Representing: Intergenerational Friendship Quilt (Teacher Edition)
Critical Viewing: Defend; Connect; Draw Conclusions; Compare and Contrast; Analyze;

PORTFOLIO OPPORTUNITIES

Writing: Treasure Description; Diary; Story Review
Writing Mini-Lesson: Character Analysis
Speaking and Listening: Monologue; Blues Presentation
Projects: Travel Brochure; Report

More About the Authors
Laurence Yep's characters often deal with the issues of being Chinese American. "Ribbons" explores his Chinese heritage through his respect for his own grandmother who was born in China—respect for her individuality and his own desire to become his own person, just as she did.

Walter Dean Myers has gained wide acclaim for his storytelling as well as his ability to depict believable, well-defined characters—many of whom are young African Americans growing up in urban communities.

Guide for Reading

Meet the Authors:

Laurence Yep (1948–)

Laurence Yep was born in San Francisco and grew up in an apartment above his family's grocery store. When a high-school teacher encouraged Yep to send out his stories for publication, he decided to become a professional writer. He is the author of more than a dozen books, including the Newbery Honor Book *Dragonwings*.

The Story Behind the Story

Yep learned about his Chinese heritage from his maternal grandmother. Her influence is seen in "Ribbons" and other works featuring a wise, beloved, strong-willed grandmother.

Walter Dean Myers (1937–)

Born in West Virginia, Myers grew up in the New York City community of Harlem. Although he dreamed of being a professional writer, this seemed impossible because of his poverty and lack of formal education. In 1969, however, his first book won a writing contest and was published. Since then, Myers has published dozens of books and won numerous awards.

◆ Literature and Your Life

Connect Your Experience

Think about a time when you learned something from an older member of your family or community. In these stories, characters discover that by drawing upon an older person's experiences, they gain ideas, information, and skills that can shape their future.

Thematic Focus: Community Ties

These stories may prompt you to wonder: What can people my age learn from older people in my community? What can my generation teach older generations?

◆ Background for Understanding

Music

In "The Treasure of Lemon Brown," a teenager meets a man who was once a famous blues musician. Blues, which have strongly influenced other forms of music, such as jazz and rock, are part of the African American musical heritage. Blues lyrics typically deal with loneliness, sorrow, and life's troubles. As you will discover in the story, Lemon Brown's life has certainly given him the right to sing the blues.

◆ Build Vocabulary

Word Roots: *-sens-*

In "Ribbons," a mother warns her daughter that her grandmother is sensitive about her feet. The word *sensitive* contains the word root *-sens-*, meaning "feel." Knowing this, you can correctly conclude that *sensitive* has something to do with feelings. In "Ribbons," the grandmother is quick to feel offended or angry when anyone mentions her feet.

Word Bank

Which words from the stories are adjectives? Check the Build Vocabulary boxes to see if you are right.

sensitive
meek
coax
laborious
exertion
impromptu
ajar
tentatively

Prentice Hall Literature Program Resources

REINFORCE / RETEACH / EXTEND

Selection Support Pages
Build Vocabulary: Word Roots: *-sens-*, p. 179
Build Spelling Skills: Adding the Suffix *-ious*, p. 180
Build Grammar Skills: Adjective Clauses, p. 181
Reading Strategy: Ask Questions, p. 182
Literary Focus: Theme, p. 183
Strategies for Diverse Student Needs, pp. 65–66
Beyond Literature Media Connection: Documentary, p. 33
Formal Assessment Selection Test, pp. 149–151, Assessment Resources Software
Alternative Assessment, p. 33
Writing and Language Transparencies
Sensory Language Chart, p. 78; Venn Diagram, p. 86; Open Mind Organizer, p. 90
Resource Pro CD-ROM
"Ribbons"; "The Treasure of Lemon Brown"—includes all resource material and customizable lesson plan
Listening to Literature Audiocassettes
"Ribbons"; "The Treasure of Lemon Brown"

Ribbons ◆ The Treasure of Lemon Brown

Four Piece Orchestra, 1944, Ben Shahn, 17 1/2 by 23 1/2 inches © Estate of Ben Shahn/Licensed by VAGA, New York, NY

◆ Literary Focus

Theme

A story's **theme** is its central message or insight into life. Occasionally, the theme is stated directly. More often, however, the theme is implied. The writer provides clues to the theme in the words and experiences of the characters, in the events and setting of the story, and in significant objects that represent ideas or people. For example, if a person in a story comes to accept and love an heirloom, the theme might be an insight into the relationships between generations.

◆ Reading Strategy

Ask Questions

By **asking questions** as you read, you will be better able to understand a story and figure out its theme. For example, you might ask questions like the following:

- Why is the author telling me this?
- Why did the character do or say that?
- How does this event fit into what has happened so far?

As you read these stories, jot down questions in a chart like the one below. Fill in answers as you find them or figure them out for yourself.

Question	Answer
Why is Grandmother sensitive about her feet?	

Preparing for Standardized Tests

Reading Tell students that learning how to answer questions in their minds will help them perform well on standardized tests. The reading strategy that is taught with these selections will help students learn to ask and answer questions as they read.

On a standardized test, students will be given a list of questions to answer—they will not be called upon to generate their own questions. However, they can apply the skill of reading to answer questions in the following way. Advise students that when they take a standardized test, they should preview the questions that accompany a passage, then read with the purpose of answering those questions. For further practice, use **Selection Support,** p. 182, Reading Strategy: Ask Questions.

Create a class "treasure box." Invite students to write on a piece of paper something that they treasure. Have students place their "treasures" in a box, then read them aloud to the class. Discuss the different things that people treasure. Aside from material objects, some students may mention less tangible things like friendship or a special memory. Explain that characters in "Ribbons" and "The Treasure of Lemon Brown" must decide what they treasure in life—and that their choices might be surprising.

◆ Build Grammar Skills

Adjective Clauses If you wish to introduce the grammar concept before students read, refer to the instruction on p. 540.

Customize for
Less Proficient Readers
Help students create Venn diagrams to record the similarities and differences between the narrators and the older characters in these stories. The Venn diagram for "Ribbons" might look like the one shown. Discuss the characters' similarities and differences with students.

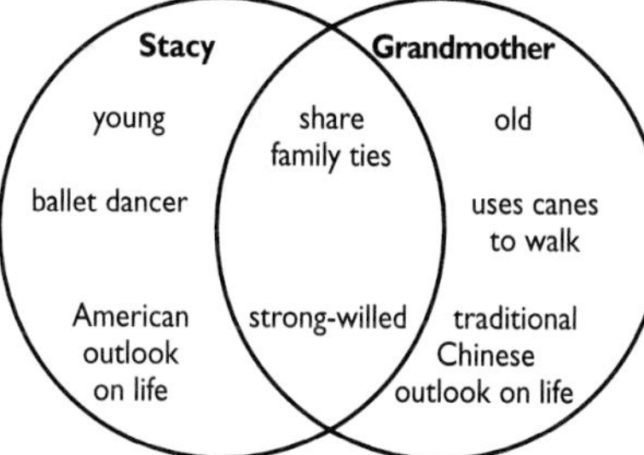

Customize for
More Advanced Students
Have students document character development as they read the stories. Ask them to choose one of the main characters, then write words, phrases, and images that represent the character when first introduced. After students finish reading, have them record new impressions, then compare and contrast the character at the beginning and end of the story.

Humanities: Art

For information about **Four Piece Orchestra,** by Ben Shahn, see p. 534.

Develop Understanding

One-Minute Insight Stacy's life is completely transformed when her grandmother comes from Hong Kong to live with her family in San Francisco. Within minutes of her grandmother's arrival, Stacy feels slighted and ignored by the older woman. Stacy's resentment reaches its peak when one day Grandmother reacts angrily to the sight of Stacy's ballet toe-shoe ribbons. With the help of her mother, Stacy comes to understand her grandmother's fear of the ribbons. Stacy then uses this insight to repair the misunderstanding with her grandmother. Laurence Yep's story illustrates how two people of different cultures and generations can reach past their differences to find a loving bond.

Team Teaching Strategy

The historical and cultural aspects of Yep's story provide a strong connection to social studies. You may want to coordinate with a social studies teacher to plan ways of extending instruction.

▶Critical Viewing◀

1 Defend *Students should notice that the ballet shoes are tied with the ribbons mentioned in the title.*

Customize for
English Language Learners
English language learners may encounter unfamiliar words and phrases in addition to those defined within the story. Have students proficient in English work with English language learners to pantomime words and phrases such as "poked out like six-shooters," "bear hug," and "solemnly."

Ribbons

Laurence Yep

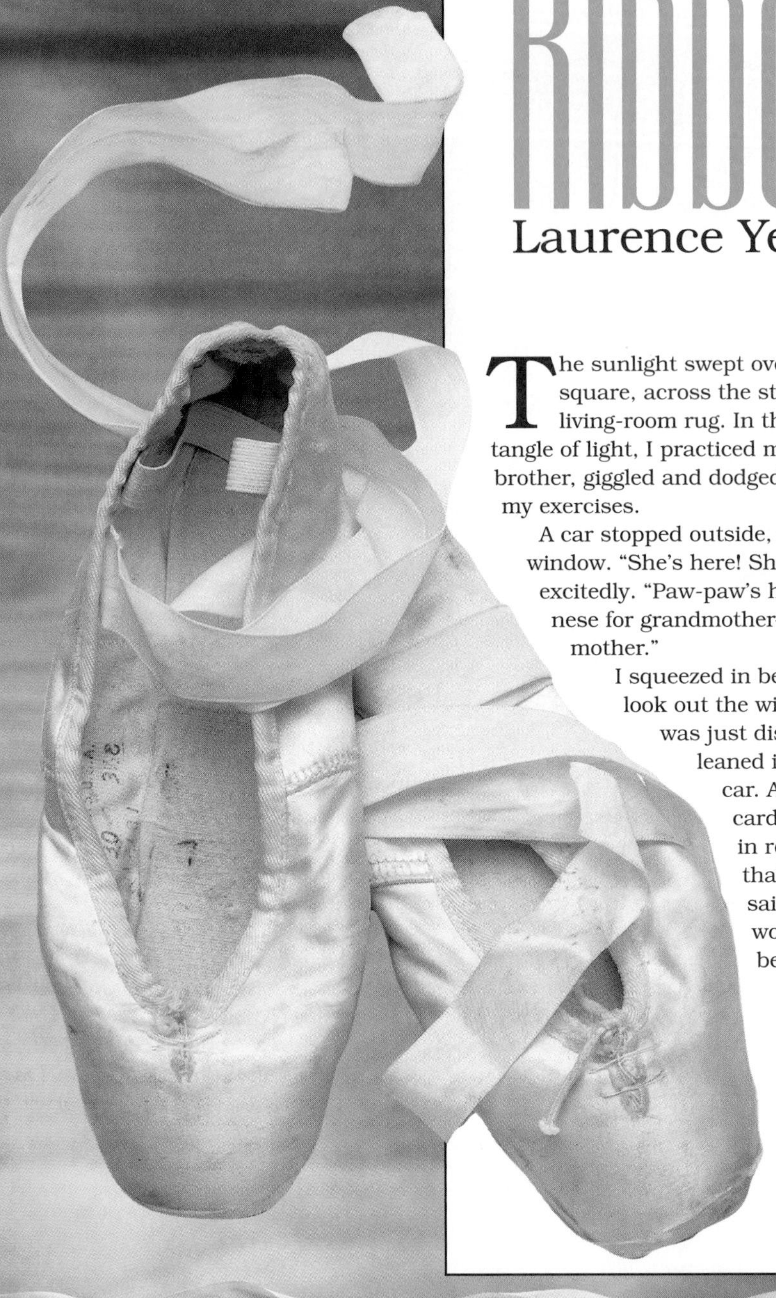

The sunlight swept over the broad grassy square, across the street, and onto our living-room rug. In that bright, warm rectangle of light, I practiced my ballet. Ian, my little brother, giggled and dodged around me while I did my exercises.

A car stopped outside, and Ian rushed to the window. "She's here! She's here!" he shouted excitedly. "Paw-paw's here!" *Paw-paw* is Chinese for grandmother—for "mother's mother."

I squeezed in beside Ian so I could look out the window, too. Dad's head was just disappearing as he leaned into the trunk of the car. A pile of luggage and cardboard boxes wrapped in rope sat by the curb. "Is that all Grandmother's?" I said. I didn't see how it would fit into my old bedroom.

◀ Critical Viewing Why are ballet shoes an appropriate visual accompaniment to this story? **[Defend]** 1

Block Scheduling Strategies

Consider these suggestions to take advantage of extended class time:

- Have students explore the authors' themes in "Ribbons" and "The Treasure of Lemon Brown." After introducing the literary focus, allow students to read the stories in small groups, discussing the thoughts, feelings, and behaviors of the main characters and what these suggest about the stories' themes. Then have students answer the Literary Focus questions on p. 540.
- Use *World Explorer: Asia and the Pacific,* Chapter 2, "East Asia: Cultures and History," to team teach or to further extend the connection in "Ribbons" between literature and social studies.
- If you have access to technology, have students work on the *Writer's Solution Language Lab CD-ROM* and *Writer's Solution Writing Lab CD-ROM* to prepare for and complete all or part of the Writing Mini-Lesson.

Mom laughed behind me. "We're lucky she 2 had to leave her furniture behind in Hong Kong." Mom had been trying to get her mother to come to San Francisco for years. Grandmother had finally agreed, but only because the British were going to return the city to the Chinese Communists in 1997. Because Grandmother's airfare and legal expenses had been so high, there wasn't room in the family budget for Madame Oblomov's ballet school. I'd had to stop my daily lessons.

The rear car door opened, and a pair of carved black canes poked out like six-shooters. "Wait, Paw-paw," Dad said, and slammed the trunk shut. He looked sweaty and harassed.

Grandmother, however, was already using her canes to get to her feet. "I'm not helpless," she insisted to Dad.

Ian was relieved. "She speaks English," he said.

"She worked for a British family for years," Mom explained.

Turning, Ian ran toward the stairs. "I've got the door," he cried. Mom and I caught up with him at the front door and made him wait on the porch. "You don't want to knock her over," I said. For weeks, Mom had been rehearsing us for just this moment. Ian was supposed to wait, but in his excitement he began bowing to Grandmother as she struggled up the outside staircase.

Grandmother was a small woman in a padded silk jacket and black slacks. Her hair was pulled back into a bun behind her head. On her small feet she wore a pair of quilted cotton slippers shaped like boots, with furred tops that hid her ankles.

"What's wrong with her feet?" I whispered to Mom.

"They've always been that way. And don't mention it," she said. "She's <u>sensitive</u> about 3 them."

I was instantly curious. "But what happened to them?"

"Wise grandchildren wouldn't ask," Mom warned.

4 Mom bowed formally as Grandmother reached the porch. "I'm so glad you're here," she said.

Grandmother gazed past us to the stairway leading up to our second-floor apartment. "Why 4 do you have to have so many steps?" she said.

Mom sounded as <u>meek</u> as a child. "I'm sorry, Mother," she said.

Dad tried to change the subject. "That's Stacy, and this little monster is Ian."

"*Joe sun, Paw-paw,*" I said. "Good morning, Grandmother." It was afternoon, but that was the only Chinese I knew, and I had been practicing it.

Mother had coached us on a proper Chinese greeting for the last two months, but I thought Grandmother also deserved an American-style bear hug. However, when I tried to put my arms around her and kiss her, she stiffened in surprise. "Nice children don't drool on people," she snapped at me.

To Ian, anything worth doing was worth repeating, so he bowed again. "*Joe sun, Paw-paw.*"

Grandmother brightened in an instant. "He has your eyes," she said to Mom.

Mom bent and hefted Ian into her arms. "Let me show you our apartment. You'll be in Stacy's room."

Grandmother didn't even thank me. Instead, she stumped up the stairs after Mom, trying to <u>coax</u> a smile from Ian, who was staring at her over Mom's shoulder.

> ◆ **Reading Strategy**
> Ask yourself whether Grandmother's treatment of Stacy will affect Stacy's attitude toward her. 5

Grandmother's climb was long, slow, <u>laborious</u>. *Thump, thump, thump.* Her canes struck the boards as she slowly mounted the

◆ Build Vocabulary

sensitive (sen′ sə tiv′) *adj.*: Easily hurt or irritated; touchy

meek (mēk) *adj.*: Timid; humble; not showing anger

coax (kōks) *v.*: Use gentle persuasion

laborious (la bôr′ ē əs) *adj.*: Taking much work or effort; difficult

Cultural Connection

Social Courtesies People from various cultures have different ways of showing respect toward one another. In "Ribbons," Stacy's mother shows respect by bowing formally to her mother, whereas Stacy, having grown up in America, tries to hug and kiss her grandmother. In some cultures it is customary to shake hands upon meeting. In others, people hug as a way of greeting each other. In the United States, eye contact is encouraged, but in some cultures it is seen as a sign of rudeness.

Encourage groups of students to research the variety of social customs among cultures. Suggest that for part of their research they interview family members, friends, or neighbors whose cultural groups differ from their own. Alternatively, they could interview people they know who have traveled to other countries.

Have student groups share their findings in a presentation and demonstration to the class. Discuss with students why knowing about differences in social rules among cultures is important. Respecting these differences encourages understanding and good will among people of different cultures.

Clarification

2 Hong Kong is an island port on the south coast of China that was a British possession from the early 1840's. As part of a 1984 agreement between Great Britain and China, Hong Kong reverted to Chinese rule in 1997. Uncertain of their future, thousands of Hong Kong residents emigrated to Australia, Canada, and the United States prior to 1997.

◆ Reading Strategy

3 Ask Questions The author seems to be using Stacy's curiosity to indicate an important idea in the story. Help students formulate questions to ask at this point. You may wish to have them add their questions to the charts that they began on p. 523. *Students may ask questions such as "Why is the author describing Grandmother's feet?" or "Why did Mom answer Stacy's question that way?"*

◆ Critical Thinking

4 Infer Introduce the Chinese custom of respect and courtesy for elders. Then ask students whether they think Stacy understands her mother's attitude toward her grandmother. *Students should recognize that the mother's formal greeting and apology are ways of showing respect. Stacy seems to have some difficulty understanding the Chinese custom in this situation.*

◆ Reading Strategy

5 Ask Questions *Students will probably say that Grandmother's rejection of Stacy's affection, her ingratitude for the use of Stacy's room, and her attention to Ian will make Stacy feel resentful.*

Customize for
Bodily/Kinesthetic Learners
Have students assume the roles of family members for Grandmother's arrival. Then ask them to describe the actions of each character. For example, Grandmother walks slowly with canes, Stacy dances in the street, and Dad carries heavy bags and boxes. Guide students to recognize how the family members' actions reveal their individual attitudes.

◆Critical Thinking

1 Interpret Ask students what Stacy's actions and thoughts in this passage reveal. *Stacy's response to Grandmother's boxes shows her vivid imagination; it also shows that Stacy frequently uses dance as a way of expressing herself.*

◆Literature and Your Life

2 Grandmother's arrival in Stacy's home has caused the family to make several important changes. Emphasize that these changes suggest that the family respects and honors older family members. Have students consider times when they have had to make changes because of a new situation at home or in school. Encourage students to use their own attitudes to help them identify with Stacy.

◆Literary Focus

3 Theme Discuss with students how they might react to Stacy's mother's explanation as to why Grandmother spoils Ian. Guide students to understand that, although in American culture boys and girls are usually treated equally, this is not the case in some cultures. Then ask students to connect this incident to the story's theme. *Students should recognize that it reveals to Stacy that she has much to learn about Grandmother's attitudes, behaviors, and feelings, many of which are culturally influenced.*

Customize for *Logical/Mathematical Learners*

According to Stacy's mother, Grandmother "walked across China to Hong Kong." Have students locate China and Hong Kong on a map and use an atlas to estimate how many miles Grandmother may have walked if she began her journey in a city such as Beijing, Shanghai, or Kunming. Students may also determine what conditions she may have faced—for instance, whether she would have walked through mountainous country, and what the temperature may have been.

steps. It sounded like the slow, steady beat of a mechanical heart.

Mom had told us her mother's story often enough. When Mom's father died, Grandmother had strapped my mother to her back and walked across China to Hong Kong to escape the Communists who had taken over her country. I had always thought her trek was heroic, but it seemed even braver when I realized how wobbly she was on her feet.

I was going to follow Grandmother, but Dad waved me down to the sidewalk. "I need you to watch your grandmother's things until I finish bringing them up," he said. He took a suitcase in either hand and set off, catching up with Grandmother at the foot of the first staircase.

1 While I waited for him to come back, I inspected Grandmother's pile of belongings. The boxes, webbed with tight cords, were covered with words in Chinese and English. I could almost smell their exotic scent, and in my imagination I pictured sunlit waters lapping at picturesque docks. Hong Kong was probably as exotic to me as America was to Grandmother. Almost without thinking, I began to dance.

Dad came back out, his face red from exertion. "I wish I had half your energy," he said. Crouching, he used the cords to lift a box in each hand.

I pirouetted,[1] and the world spun round and round. "Madame Oblomov said I should still practice every day." I had waited for this day not only for Grandmother's sake but for my own. 2 "Now that Grandmother's here, can I begin my ballet lessons again?" I asked.

Dad turned toward the house. "We'll see, hon."

Disappointment made me protest. "But you said I had to give up the lessons so we could bring her from Hong Kong," I said. "Well, she's here."

Dad hesitated and then set the boxes down. "Try to understand, hon. We've got to set your grandmother up in her own apartment. That's going to take even more money. Don't you want your room back?"

Poor Dad. He looked tired and worried. I should have shut up, but I loved ballet almost as much as I loved him. "Madame put me in the fifth division even though I'm only eleven. If I'm absent much longer, she might make me start over again with the beginners."

"It'll be soon. I promise." He looked guilty as he picked up the boxes and struggled toward the stairs.

Dad had taken away the one hope that had kept me going during my exile[2] from Madame. Suddenly I felt lost, and the following weeks only made me more confused. Mom started laying down all sorts of new rules. First, we couldn't run around or make noise because Grandmother had to rest. Then we couldn't watch our favorite TV shows because Grandmother couldn't understand them. Instead, we had to watch Westerns on one of the cable stations because it was easier for her to figure out who was the good guy and who was the bad one.

Worst of all, Ian got all of her attention—and her candy and anything else she could bribe him with. It finally got to me on a warm Sunday afternoon a month after she had arrived. I'd just returned home from a long walk in the park with some friends. I was looking forward to something cool and sweet, when I found her giving Ian an ice cream bar I'd bought for myself. "But that was *my* ice cream bar," I complained as he gulped it down.

"Big sisters need to share with little brothers," Grandmother said, and she patted him on the head to encourage him to go on eating.

3 When I complained to Mom about how Grandmother was spoiling Ian, she only sighed. "He's a boy, Stacy. Back in China, boys are everything."

◆ Literary Focus How might this incident relate to the theme of the story?

1. **pirouetted** (pir´ o͞o et´ əd) *v.*: Whirled around on the point of the toe.

2. **exile** (eg´ zīl´) *n.*: Forced absence.

◆ Build Vocabulary

exertion (eg zʉr´ shən) *n.*: Physical work

526 ◆ *Short Stories*

Humanities: Dance

Ballet Stacy wants to share with Grandmother her love of ballet—a beautiful dance form in which dancers seem to float in the air, defying gravity. Ballet is an expressive form of theater that combines dance and music. A ballet may tell a story, or portray a mood or idea.

Ballet movements that look effortless require years of rigorous training and great physical strength and agility. Many professional dancers begin serious training around 8 years of age, and by the age of 12, may take classes every day. Professional dancers continue to take daily classes to maintain their disciplined technique and athletic physical conditioning.

Two kinds of shoes are worn by ballet dancers: soft ballet slippers and hard-toed pointe shoes. Beginners wear slippers with soft soles made of leather or canvas. Male dancers continue with soft-sole slippers, but women must learn to dance gracefully in pointe shoes. To dance in pointe shoes, dancers must have strong, well-developed muscles in their feet and legs. Pointe shoes have long ribbons that are wrapped and tied around the ankles and lower legs.

Three Studies of a Dancer in Fourth Position, ©1879/80, Edgar Degas, Art Institute of Chicago

4 ▲ **Critical Viewing** Which character would be most interested in this painting? Find a sentence on this page to support your answer. **[Connect]**

It wasn't until I saw Grandmother and Ian together the next day that I thought I really understood why she treated him so much better. She was sitting on a kitchen chair with her head bent over next to his. She had taught Ian enough Chinese so that they could hold short, simple conversations. With their faces so close, I could see how much alike they were.

Ian and I both have the same brown eyes,
5 but his hair is black, while mine is brown, like
6 Dad's. In fact, everything about Ian looks more Chinese. Except for the shape of my eyes, I look as Caucasian as Dad. And yet people sometimes stare at me as if I were a freak. I've always told myself that it's because they're ig- 5
norant and never learned manners, but it was 6
really hard to have my own grandmother make me feel that way.

Even so, I kept telling myself: Grandmother is a hero. She saved my mother. She'll like me just as much as she likes Ian once she gets to know me. And, I thought in a flash, the best way to know a person is to know what she 7
loves. For me, that was the ballet.

Ever since Grandmother had arrived, I'd been practicing my ballet privately in the room I now shared with Ian. Now I got out the special

▶Critical Viewing◀

4 Connect *Stacy would be most interested in the painting. Students may cite one or more of these sentences: "And, I thought in a flash, the best way to know a person is to know what she loves. For me, that was the ballet." or "Ever since Grandmother had arrived, I'd been practicing my ballet privately in the room I now shared with Ian."*

◆Reading Strategy

5 Ask Questions Have students suggest questions they might ask themselves as they read this passage. *"Why does Stacy feel that Ian 'looks more Chinese'?" "Is Stacy right in thinking that Grandmother prefers Ian because he looks more Chinese?" or "Why might Stacy feel that people stare at her as if she were 'a freak'?"*

Clarification

6 Heredity is the passing of traits from parents to their children by means of genes. The color of Ian's and Stacy's eyes and hair and the shape of their faces and eyes are examples of physical traits or characteristics that they inherited from their parents.

◆Literature and Your Life

7 Ask students if they agree or disagree with this statement. Encourage them to give reasons for their point of view. *Some students will agree that knowing a person's interests reveals much about that person. Others may say that this type of knowledge doesn't necessarily tell you about a person's character or enable you to predict a person's behavior.*

Humanities: Art

Three Studies of a Dancer in Fourth Position, by Edgar Degas

French painter and sculptor Edgar Degas (1834–1917) was fascinated by ballet. More than half of his statues and paintings reflect this theme, most often in scenes of dancers rehearsing and relaxing. As Degas began a painting, he sketched models in motion so that he could capture the informality and naturalness of the ballet movements and positions. Point out that the words *fourth position,* used in the title, refer to one of the five basic foot positions in ballet. Use these questions for discussion:

1. How would you describe the expressions on the faces shown in the artwork? *Students may say that the faces seem relaxed, as if the dancer is casually practicing, warming up, or waiting for instruction.*
2. In what ways does the artwork suit the story? *The drawing shows a dancer practicing her art, which Stacy does frequently throughout the story.*

◆Critical Thinking

1 Interpret What does the description of the satin ribbons reveal about Stacy's attitude toward ballet? *Her description of the ribbons fluttering around her wrists "as if in a welcoming caress" shows that her toe shoes are prized possessions and very important symbols of success. Stacy takes great pride in being the youngest student wearing toe shoes at Madame Oblomov's school.*

◆Critical Thinking

2 Deduce Why do you think Grandmother is gazing out the window as if she is seeing "a Martian desert"? *Most students will deduce that Grandmother is unhappy and misses her life in Hong Kong. She may be feeling homesick, uncomfortable, or overwhelmed in her new home.*

◆Reading Strategy

3 Ask Questions *Possible responses: Grandmother is startled to see the ribbons in Stacy's hand; students may speculate that Grandmother hates the ribbons because they remind her of something terrible that happened.*

▶Critical Viewing◀

4 Draw Conclusions *Based on Grandmother's angry reaction to the ribbons, her apparent connection of Stacy's callused feet with the ribbons, and the deformed feet shown on the woman in the painting, students may conclude that Grandmother's problems with her own feet are associated with ribbons such as these in some way. Some students may be familiar with the practice of binding feet.*

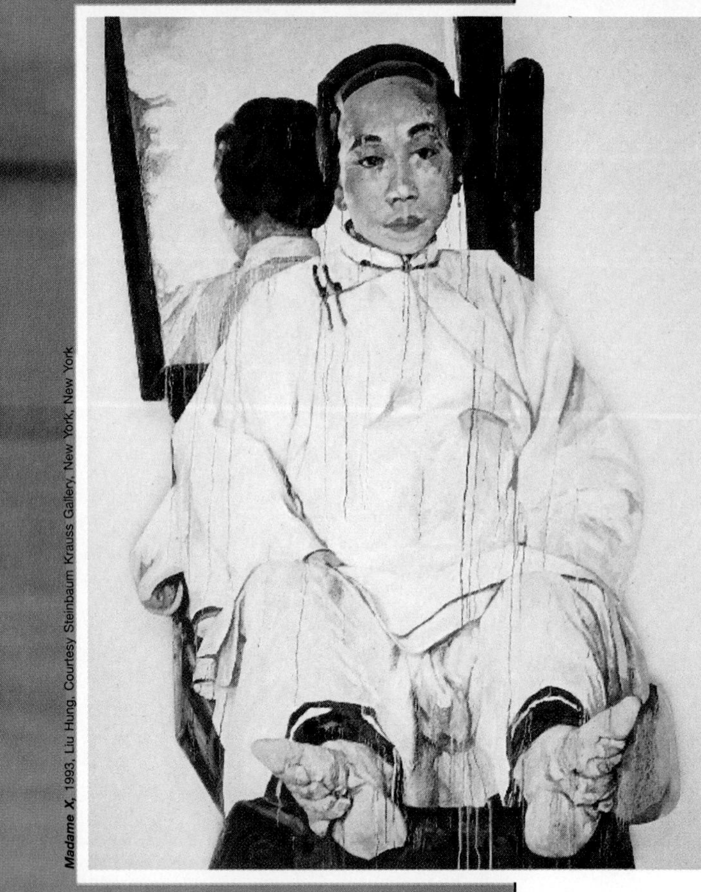

Madame X, 1993, Liu Hung, Courtesy Steinbaum Krauss Gallery, New York, New York

box that held my satin toe shoes. I had been so proud when Madame said I was ready to use them. I was the youngest girl on pointe[3] at Madame's school. As I lifted them out, the satin ribbons fluttered down around my wrists as if in a welcoming caress. 1 I slipped one of the shoes onto my foot, but when I tried to tie the ribbons around my ankles, the ribbons came off in my hands.

I could have asked Mom to help me reattach them, but then I remembered that at one time Grandmother had supported her family by being a seamstress.

Grandmother was sitting in the big recliner in the living room. She stared uneasily out the window as 2 if she were gazing not upon the broad, green lawn of the square but upon a Martian desert.

"Paw-paw," I said, "can you help me?"

Grandmother gave a start when she turned around and saw the ribbons dangling from my hand. Then she looked down at my bare feet, which were callused from three years of daily lessons. When she looked back at the satin ribbons, it was with a hate and disgust that 3 I had never seen before.

"Give those to me." She held out her hand.

I clutched the ribbons tightly against my stomach. "Why?"

"They'll ruin your feet." She lunged toward me and tried to

◆ Reading Strategy Grandmother's reaction might prompt you to ask the question: Why does she hate the ribbons so much?

4 ▲ Critical Viewing Review Grandmother's actions as described on this page and the next one. Then, analyze this painting to draw a conclusion about Grandmother's experiences with ribbons. **[Draw Conclusions]**

3. **on pointe** (pwant) *n.*: Dancing on the tip of the toe.

Humanities: Art

Madame X, by Liu Hung

The artworks of Chinese American artist Liu Hung have been influenced by Chinese poems and writings, as well as by historical writings and photographs. Use these questions for discussion:

1. What do you notice first about this painting? *Some students may say that they notice the woman's feet because of their unusual shape. Others may say they notice the expression on the woman's face.*
2. How is the woman in the painting like Stacy's grandmother? How is she different? *The woman seems dignified but sad like Yep's description of Grandmother. Both women have something wrong with their feet, but, unlike Grandmother, the woman in the painting seems unashamed of her feet.*
3. This painting measures approximately 7 feet by 6 feet. Why do you think the artist made this portrait so large? *Perhaps the artist wanted to make sure the image of the woman and her deformed feet stays in the viewer's mind.*

snatch them away.

Angry and bewildered, I retreated a few steps and showed her the shoe. "No, they're for dancing!"

All Grandmother could see, though, was the ribbons. She managed to totter to her feet without the canes and almost fell forward on her face. Somehow, she regained her balance. Arms reaching out, she stumbled clumsily after me. "Lies!" she said.

"It's the truth!" I backed up so fast that I bumped into Mom as she came running from the kitchen.

Mom immediately assumed it was my fault. "Stop yelling at your grandmother!" she said.

By this point, I was in tears. "She's taken
5 everything else. Now she wants my toe-shoe ribbons."

Grandmother panted as she leaned on Mom. "How could you do that to your own daughter?"

"It's not like you think," Mom tried to explain.

However, Grandmother was too upset to listen. "Take them away!"

Mom helped Grandmother back to her easy chair. "You don't understand," Mom said.

All Grandmother did was stare at the ribbons as she sat back down in the chair. "Take them away. Burn them. Bury them."

Mom sighed. "Yes, Mother."

As Mom came over to me, I stared at her in amazement. "Aren't you going to stand up for me?"

But she acted as if she wanted to break any ties between us. "Can't you see how worked up Paw-paw is?" she whispered. "She won't listen to reason. Give her some time. Let her cool off." She worked the ribbons away from my stunned fingers. Then she also took the shoe.

For the rest of the day, Grandmother just turned away every time Mom and I tried to raise the subject. It was as if she didn't want to even think about satin ribbons.

That evening, after the dozenth attempt, I finally said to Mom, "She's so weird. What's so bad about satin ribbons?"

"She associates them with something awful that happened to her," Mom said.

That puzzled me even more. "What was that?"

She shook her head. "I'm sorry. She made me promise never to talk about it to anyone."

The next morning, I decided that if Grandmother was going to be mean to me, then I would be mean to her. I began to ignore her. 6
When she entered a room I was in, I would deliberately turn around and leave.

For the rest of the day, things got more and more tense. Then I happened to go into the bathroom early that evening. The door wasn't locked, so I thought it was unoccupied, but Grandmother was sitting fully clothed on the edge of the bathtub. Her slacks were rolled up to her knees and she had her feet soaking in a pan of water.

"Don't you know how to knock?" she snapped, and dropped a towel over her feet.

However, she wasn't quick enough, because I saw her bare feet for the first time. Her feet were like taffy that someone had stretched out and twisted. Each foot bent downward in a way 7
that feet were not meant to, and her toes stuck out at odd angles, more like lumps than toes. I didn't think she had all ten of them, either.

"What happened to your feet?" I whispered in shock.

Looking ashamed, Grandmother flapped a hand in the air for me to go. "None of your business. Now get out."

She must have said something to Mom, though, because that night Mom came in and sat on my bed. Ian was outside playing with Grandmother. "Your grandmother's very upset, Stacy," Mom said.

"I didn't mean to look," I said. "It was horrible." Even when I closed my eyes, I could see her mangled feet.

I opened my eyes when I felt Mom's hand on my shoulder. "She was so ashamed of them that she didn't like even me to see them," she said.

"What happened to them?" I wondered.

Mom's forehead furrowed as if she wasn't sure how to explain things. "There was a time back in China when people thought women's feet had to be shaped a certain way to look beautiful. When a girl was about five, her mother would gradually bend her toes under

◆Critical Thinking

5 Interpret Ask students if Stacy's claim that Grandmother has taken everything from her is accurate. Encourage them to give reasons for their opinions. *Some students may agree that Stacy has reasons to be resentful; others may think that Stacy is exaggerating and overreacting and that she should try harder to understand her grandmother.*

◆Literature and Your Life

6 Encourage students to draw on their own experience in conflict with others to discuss pros and cons of Stacy's approach. Have them suggest better ways of resolving conflict. *Students may say that this approach gives short-term satisfaction but does nothing permanent to resolve a conflict. Better solutions include apologizing, listening to the other person's side of the story, having a "cooling-off period" before talking to the person, or having someone mediate the conflict.*

◆Build Grammar Skills

7 Adjective Clauses Explain that an adjective clause functions as an adjective and has a subject and a verb but cannot stand alone as a sentence. Adjective clauses are introduced by *who, whom, whose, which, that, where, when,* or *why.* Have students find an adjective clause in this passage and identify the word it describes. *Possible responses: "that someone had stretched out and twisted" modifies taffy; "that feet were not meant to" modifies way.*

Customize for
English Language Learners
Play the recording of the events described on this page. Use pantomime and facial expressions to illustrate the meanings of unfamiliar words such as *totter, stumbled, panted, ashamed,* and *furrowed.*

Listening to Literature Audiocassettes

Speaking and Listening Mini-Lesson

Monologue This mini-lesson supports the Speaking and Listening activity in the Idea Bank on p. 541.

Introduce Explain that a monologue is a speech made by one character that reveals his or her thoughts and feelings. A monologue does not contain dialogue between two people.

Develop Have students review the story, making notes to develop into a 3- to 5-minute speech from Stacy's point of view. Remind students that they will need to speak clearly and use appropriate body language and gestures in their monologues.

Apply Allow time for students to prepare, rehearse, and revise their monologues with partners. Then have each student perform the monologue for the class. Instruct students in the audience to take notes during the performance.

Assess Evaluate students' performances in terms of preparation, clarity of speaking, composure, and body language. Have students use the Peer Assessment: Dramatic Performance form, p. 107, in **Alternative Assessment,** to evaluate the performances of their classmates.

◆Critical Thinking

❶ Compare and Contrast Have students compare what the ribbons symbolize for Grandmother to what they symbolize for Stacy. *To Grandmother, the ribbons symbolize her old life in China and the painful practice of foot binding; to Stacy, they symbolize her love of ballet.*

◆Literary Focus

❷ Theme Discuss with students what they think the theme of the story is, based on their reading so far. Have them connect this passage with the theme. *Most students will recognize that the theme concerns the importance of patience and understanding in overcoming cultural and generational differences. In this passage, Stacy realizes that her conclusions about Grandmother were wrong. She now understands that Grandmother was trying to protect her and that Grandmother does not understand how important ballet is to her.*

Clarification

❸ Point out that "The Little Mermaid," as originally written by Hans Christian Andersen, ends differently from the animated version of the story. In Andersen's original story, the mermaid dies because she cannot survive outside her natural environment.

◆Critical Thinking

❹ Analyze Cause and Effect Have students explain why Stacy stops reading from "The Little Mermaid" and why Grandmother asks Stacy to continue reading. *Students may say that Stacy is being sensitive to her grandmother's feelings. They may suggest that Grandmother ask Stacy to continue reading because she is trying to reach out to Stacy or because she identifies with the mermaid and wants to hear how the story ends.*

the sole of her foot."

"Ugh." Just thinking about it made my own feet ache. "Her own mother did that to her?"

Mom smiled apologetically. "Her mother and father thought it would make their little girl attractive so she could marry a rich man. They were still doing it in some of the back areas of China long after it was outlawed in the rest of the country."

I shook my head. "There's nothing lovely about those feet."

"I know. But they were usually bound up in silk ribbons." Mom brushed some of the hair from my eyes. "Because they were a symbol of the old days, Paw-paw undid the ribbons as soon as we were free in Hong Kong—even though they kept back the pain."

I was even more puzzled now. "How did the ribbons do that?"

Mom began to brush my hair with quick, light strokes. "The ribbons kept the blood from circulating freely and bringing more feeling to
1 her feet. Once the ribbons were gone, her feet ached. They probably still do."

I rubbed my own foot in sympathy. "But she doesn't complain."

"That's how tough she is," Mom said.

> **◆ Literary Focus**
> How might Stacy's insight relate to the theme of the story?

Finally the truth dawned on me. "And she mistook
2 my toe-shoe ribbons for her old ones."

Mom lowered the brush and nodded solemnly. "And she didn't want you to go through the same pain she had."

I guess Grandmother loved me in her own way. When she came into the bedroom with Ian later that evening, I didn't leave. However, she tried to ignore me—as if I had become tainted by her secret.

When Ian demanded a story, I sighed. "All right. But only one."

Naturally, Ian chose the fattest story he could, which was my old collection of fairy tales by Hans Christian Andersen. Years of
3 reading had cracked the spine so that the book fell open automatically in his hands to the story that had been my favorite when I was small. It was the original story of "The Little Mermaid"—not the cartoon. The picture illustrating 3
the tale showed the mermaid posed like a ballerina in the middle of the throne room.

"This one," Ian said, and pointed to the picture of the Little Mermaid.

When Grandmother and Ian sat down on my bed, I began to read. However, when I got to the part where the Little Mermaid could walk on land, I stopped.

Ian was impatient. "Come on, read," he ordered, patting the page. 4

"After that," I went on, "each step hurt her as if she were walking on a knife." I couldn't help looking up at Grandmother.

This time she was the one to pat the page. "Go on. Tell me more about the mermaid."

So I went on reading to the very end, where the Little Mermaid changes into sea foam. "That's a dumb ending," Ian said. "Who wants to be pollution?"

"Sea foam isn't pollution. It's just bubbles," I explained. "The important thing was that she wanted to walk even though it hurt."

"I would rather have gone on swimming," Ian insisted.

"But maybe she wanted to see new places and people by going on the land," Grandmother said softly. "If she had kept her tail, the land people would have thought she was odd. They might even have made fun of her."

When she glanced at her own feet, I thought she might be talking about herself—so I seized my chance. "My satin ribbons aren't like your old silk ones. I use them to tie my toe shoes on when I dance." Setting the book down, I got out my other shoe. "Look."

Grandmother fingered the dangling ribbons and then pointed at my bare feet. "But you already have calluses there."

I began to dance before Grandmother could stop me. After a minute, I struck a pose on half-toe. "See? I can move fine."

She took my hand and patted it clumsily. I think it was the first time she had showed me any sign of affection. "When I saw those ribbons, I didn't want you feeling pain like I do."

I covered her hands with mine. "I just wanted to show you what I love best—dancing."

Cultural Connection

Changing Appearance Point out that when Stacy's mother explains the practice of foot binding, Stacy reacts with disgust. Throughout history, people have engaged in various practices, including altering the body, to conform to culturally accepted standards of appearance. In certain African cultures, groups stretch their earlobes or gradually elongate their necks by wearing stacks of metal rings; pierced ears have long been considered attractive in many cultures; tattoos have often been deemed an improvement to appearance; some people think that straightened or curled hair may be more attractive.

Students may be interested in researching other practices that people have used to alter their appearances. Lead a discussion about practices that people today might undergo for the sake of cultural standards of beauty or for peer acceptance. Ask students to consider which of these practices might be viewed as dangerous, cruel, or barbaric in the future.

"And I love my children," she said. I could hear the ache in her voice. "And my grandchildren. I don't want anything bad to happen to you."

Suddenly I felt as if there were an invisible ribbon binding us, tougher than silk and satin, stronger even than steel; and it joined her to Mom and Mom to me.

I wanted to hug her so badly that I just did. Though she was stiff at first, she gradually softened in my arms.

"'Let me have my ribbons and my shoes," I said in a low voice. "Let me dance."

"Yes, yes," she whispered fiercely.

5 I felt something on my cheek and realized she was crying, and then I began crying, too.

"So much to learn," she said, and began hugging me back. "So much to learn."

Community Connection

Bridging the Generation Gap Just like Stacy and her grandmother can learn from each other, communities are finding good reasons to bring their oldest and youngest citizens together. In some cities, adopt-a-senior programs allow people your age to build friendships with senior citizens. Students learn about history from those who've actually witnessed it, and the seniors get a chance to enjoy the steady companionship of a new friend.

Cross-Curricular Activity

Volunteer Opportunities Find out about volunteer opportunities to work and interact with senior citizens in your community. You might talk to people in nursing homes and community centers and to senior citizens you know, to learn more about intergenerational programs.

Guide for Responding

◆ Literature and Your Life

Reader's Response What do you think is the hardest part of Stacy's experiences with her grandmother? Why?

Thematic Focus In this story, conflict is created because Stacy and her grandmother come from unique communities and cultures. How are such conflicts resolved?

Journal Writing Stacy may soon enjoy having her grandmother living with her family. In your journal, list the benefits of her situation.

☑ Check Your Comprehension

1. What sacrifices does Stacy make as a result of Grandmother's visit?
2. What changes occur in Stacy's house as a result of Grandmother's visit?
3. How does Stacy learn the secret about Grandmother's feet?
4. Why does Grandmother react so violently to Stacy's ribbons?

◆ Critical Thinking

Interpret

1. What are Stacy's reasons for feeling a little resentful of her grandmother? **[Analyze Cause and Effect]**
2. Why doesn't Grandmother do anything to make Stacy feel better? **[Speculate]**
3. How do her mother's explanations of Chinese culture affect Stacy's attitude toward her grandmother? **[Connect]**
4. How do Stacy and her grandmother eventually come to appreciate each other? **[Deduce]**

Apply

5. What can you learn from this story about getting along with people from different generations? **[Generalize]**

Extend

6. How might an understanding of cultural differences—like those between Stacy and her grandmother—be helpful in the workplace? **[Career Link]**

◆Critical Thinking

5 Speculate Do you think Stacy will be able to resume her ballet lessons? If so, when? In the meantime, what can Stacy do about her desire to dance? *Most students will recognize that Stacy's parents will probably let her resume the lessons after Grandmother is settled in an apartment and as soon as they can afford to pay for the lessons again. In the meantime, although it may be difficult, Stacy can continue to practice what she has already learned from her lessons.*

Beyond Literature

You may want to appoint a committee of students to locate names, addresses, and phone numbers of local senior citizens service organizations that could provide information about volunteer opportunities. Suggest that students consult the yellow pages of the phone book as a starting point, using the guide words "senior citizens." Have students post the information on a classroom bulletin board.

Reinforce and Extend

Answers

◆Literature and Your Life

Reader's Response Students may say that the grandmother's favoritism toward Ian bothers Stacy the most. Being rejected or ignored is also difficult for Stacy.

Thematic Focus The conflicts are resolved when Stacy and her grandmother learn more about each other.

☑ Check Your Comprehension

1. Stacy gives up her room and her daily ballet lessons.
2. Stacy and Ian must be quiet around the house; they cannot watch their favorite television programs; Grandmother spoils Ian.
3. Stacy accidentally sees Grandmother's feet when the grandmother is soaking them; Stacy's mother explains why the feet are deformed.
4. She mistakes the ribbons for those used to bind feet.

◆Critical Thinking

1. Stacy has had to give up her room, her ballet lessons, and even her favorite television programs. Also, Grandmother favors Ian and misunderstands Stacy.
2. Grandmother might not comfort Stacy because in China girls' needs were less important than those of boys. Also, Grandmother seems uncomfortable with displays of affection such as hugging.
3. Stacy begins to understand her grandmother's suffering. She loses her resentment once she understands that her grandmother loves her.
4. They begin to better understand each other's point of view. Stacy's mother explains Grandmother's behavior, and Stacy is able to explain her love of dancing to her grandmother.
5. Students may say the story teaches that getting along involves understanding the other person's experiences, thoughts, and feelings and finding common ground.
6. Possible response: Understanding cultural differences helps people work well together and learn from one another.

In "The Treasure of Lemon Brown," Greg is angry at his father, who won't allow him to play basketball because of poor grades. Instead of going home to study, Greg wanders into an abandoned tenement building to brood. He is frightened when he realizes that he is not alone. From the darkness appears a homeless man, Lemon Brown, who shares his memories of being a blues singer. After chasing away neighborhood thugs who want to steal the "treasure" he has spoken of, Lemon Brown shows his treasure to Greg. Greg begins to understand the legacies, or treasures, that fathers can pass on to their sons.

Team Teaching Strategy

The music history of the blues is an important element in the plot of this story and provides an opportunity to connect literature to music. You may wish to coordinate with a music teacher to find ways to extend instruction.

◆Critical Thinking

1 Interpret What point is Greg's father trying to make? *Greg's father is suggesting that Greg is doing poorly in math because he isn't studying hard enough. Greg is wasting the opportunity to learn, which his father didn't have when he was Greg's age.*

The Treasure of Lemon Brown

Walter Dean Myers

The dark sky, filled with angry, swirling clouds, reflected Greg Ridley's mood as he sat on the stoop of his building. His father's voice came to him again, first reading the letter the principal had sent to the house, then lecturing endlessly about his poor efforts in math.

1 "I had to leave school when I was thirteen," his father had said, "that's a year younger than you are now. If I'd had half the chances that you have, I'd . . ."

Greg had sat in the small, pale green kitchen listening, knowing the lecture would end with his father saying he couldn't play ball with the Scorpions. He had asked his father the week before, and his father had said it depended on his next report card. It wasn't often the Scorpions took on new players, especially fourteen-year-olds, and this was a chance of a lifetime for Greg. He hadn't been allowed to play high school ball, which he had really wanted to do, but playing for the Community Center team was the next best thing. Report cards were due in a week, and Greg had been hoping for the best. But the principal had ended the suspense early when she sent that letter saying Greg would probably fail math if he didn't spend more time studying.

"And you want to play *basketball*?" His father's brows knitted over deep brown eyes. "That must be some kind of a joke. Now you just get into your room and hit those books."

That had been two nights before. His father's words, like the distant thunder that

Morning at the Jackson Ave. Ferry, Gilbert Fletcher, Courtesy of the artist

Cultural Connection

City Neighborhoods At the beginning of the story, Greg is sitting on the *stoop* of his building. Some students may be unfamiliar with terms used to describe a city setting.

Residential neighborhoods in a large city are usually crowded with people and bustling with activity. Because space is limited, dwellings are often close, or even attached, to one another. Children play in the neighborhood parks and school playgrounds rather than a yard or play area around their home. The front porch, or stoop, is a place to sit and visit with neighbors or watch the world hurry by.

The buildings in city neighborhoods may include low-cost housing, abandoned tenement buildings (previously used for residences), row houses, railroad flats (narrow buildings, which are sometimes only 10–12 feet wide), and high-rise buildings.

Students may be interested in researching city neighborhoods and buildings. They may find out more about neighborhoods with prewar buildings, luxury buildings, gentrified neighborhoods, and so forth.

now echoed through the streets of Harlem, still rumbled softly in his ears.

It was beginning to cool. Gusts of wind made bits of paper dance between the parked cars. There was a flash of nearby lightning, and soon large drops of rain splashed onto his jeans. He stood to go upstairs, thought of the lecture that probably awaited him if he did anything except shut himself in his room with his math book, and started walking down the street instead. Down the block there was an old tenement[1] that had been abandoned for some months. Some of the guys had held an impromptu checker tournament there the week before, and Greg had noticed that the door, once boarded over, had been slightly ajar.

Pulling his collar up as high as he could, he checked for traffic and made a dash across the street. He reached the house just as another flash of lightning changed the night to day for an instant, then returned the graffiti-scarred building to the grim shadows. He vaulted over the outer stairs and pushed tentatively on the door. It was open, and he let himself in.

The inside of the building was dark except for the dim light that filtered through the dirty windows from the streetlamps. There was a room a few feet from the door, and from where he stood at the entrance, Greg could see a squarish patch of light on the floor. He entered the room, frowning at the musty smell. It was a large room that might have been someone's parlor at one time. Squinting, Greg could see an old table on its side against one wall, what looked like a pile of rags or a torn mattress in the corner, and a couch, with one side broken, in front of the window.

He went to the couch. The side that wasn't broken was comfortable enough, though a little creaky. From the spot he could see the blinking neon sign over the bodega[2] on the corner.

◆ **Reading Strategy** What questions might this description prompt you to ask?

▼ **Critical Viewing** How do the colors of this painting compare with the mood and description in the story? **[Compare and Contrast]**

1. **tenement** (ten´ əh mənt) *n.*: Old, run-down apartment house.
2. **bodega** (bō dā´ gə) *n.*: Small grocery store serving a Latino neighborhood.

◆ **Build Vocabulary**

impromptu (im prämp´ to͞o) *adj.*: Unscheduled; unplanned

ajar (ə jär´) *adj.*: Open

tentatively (ten´ tə tiv lē) *adv.*: Hesitantly; with uncertainty

◆Critical Thinking

2 Analyze Ask students why they think Greg chooses to walk away from his house instead of going inside. *Some students may suggest that he has chosen to give up on improving his math grade; others may say that Greg is rebelling against his father by not studying.*

▶Critical Viewing◀

3 Compare and Contrast Point out to students that color often invites a reaction. Ask students to think about the color red and the reactions they may have to that color: Red may make them think of anger or excitement. Suggest that students examine the colors used in the painting to answer the question. *The dark colors in the painting help create a dark and lonely mood like the mood created by the description of the tenement building.*

◆Build Grammar Skills

4 Adjective Clauses An adjective clause functions as an adjective, modifying a noun or a pronoun. Have students find one or more adjective clauses in this passage and have them identify the word each clause modifies. *Students should identify one or both of these: "that filtered through the dirty windows from the streetlamps" modifies* light; *"that might have been someone's parlor at one time" modifies* room.

◆Reading Strategy

5 Ask Questions *Possible responses: "Why is Greg looking around the tenement building rather than going home to study?" "Why would Greg go to such a gloomy place when he is already feeling bad?" "Is the building a dangerous place for Greg to be?" or "Does anybody live in this building?"*

Customize for
Visual/Spatial Learners
Encourage students to picture in their minds the inside of the tenement building as described by the story's narrator. Then ask students to draw a diagram that shows the location of the room that Greg enters, using clues provided by the author.

Humanities: Art

Morning at the Jackson Ave. Ferry, by Gilbert Fletcher

Like the room that Greg enters in the tenement building, the room shown in this painting is filled with shadows and patches of light that are filtered through the smudged windows and the doorway onto the wall and floor. Use these questions for discussion:

1. Why do you think the artist chose to paint this scene? *Students may suggest that the artist wanted to show contrasts between dark and light and between loneliness and the companionship symbolized by the telephone shown on the wall.*
2. Describe a place you may have been that reminds you of the one in the painting. *Students may mention an empty train or bus station or an abandoned house.*
3. Why do you think this painting was chosen to illustrate "The Treasure of Lemon Brown"? *The mood of the painting matches that of the first part of the story. The painting shows a place where someone might want to go to be alone.*

◆Critical Thinking

1 Predict Ask students what they think might happen next in the story. *Students will probably guess that someone else is in the room with Greg and that he will discover who the person is.*

▶Critical Viewing◀

2 Connect *As students read further, they will find that music is an important part of Lemon Brown's treasure. He made his living as a blues singer and harmonica player. Brown's battered harmonica and newspaper clippings about his music career are the treasures he gave his son before the son went off to war.*

Customize for
Intrapersonal Learners
Have students analyze the author's description of the room where Lemon Brown seems to be living. You may wish to have them use the Sensory Language Chart, p. 78, in **Writing and Language Transparencies,** to record the sensory impressions that they get from the author's details.

Customize for
Interpersonal Learners
To help students understand how Greg and Lemon Brown begin to learn about each other, have pairs of students choose roles and read aloud the dialogue between the two characters. After reading aloud, encourage students to discuss the insights they gained.

He sat awhile, watching the sign blink first green then red, allowing his mind to drift to the Scorpions, then to his father. His father had been a postal worker for all Greg's life, and was proud of it, often telling Greg how hard he had worked to pass the test. Greg had heard the story too many times to be interested now.

For a moment Greg thought he heard something that sounded like a scraping against the wall. He listened carefully, but it was gone.

Outside the wind had picked up, sending the rain against the window with a force that shook the glass in its frame. A car passed, its
1 tires hissing over the wet street and its red taillights glowing in the darkness.

Greg thought he heard the noise again. His stomach tightened as he held himself still and listened intently. There weren't any more scraping noises, but he was sure he had heard something in the darkness—something breathing!

He tried to figure out just where the breathing was coming from; he knew it was in the room with him. Slowly he stood, tensing. As he turned, a flash of lightning lit up the room, frightening him with its sudden brilliance. He saw nothing, just the overturned table, the pile of rags and an old newspaper on the floor. Could he have been imagining the sounds? He continued listening, but heard nothing and thought that it might have just been rats. Still, he thought, as soon as the rain let up he would leave. He went to the window and was about to look when he heard a voice behind him.

"Don't try nothin' 'cause I got a razor here sharp enough to cut a week into nine days!"

Greg, except for an involuntary tremor[3] in his knees, stood stock still. The voice was high and brittle, like dry twigs being broken, surely not one he had ever heard before. There was a shuffling sound as the person who had been

2 ▼ Critical Viewing What role does music play in this story? **[Connect]**

3. **involuntary** (in väl´ ən ter´ ē) **tremor** (trem´ ər) *n.*: Automatic trembling or shaking.

Four Piece Orchestra, 1944, Ben Shahn, 17 1/2 by 23 1/2 inches © Estate of Ben Shahn/Licensed by VAGA, New York, NY

Humanities: Art

Four Piece Orchestra, by Ben Shahn

Through his realistic paintings, American artist Ben Shahn (1898–1969) sought to influence people's thinking and emotions by drawing attention to social and political events. Help students make connections between the scene shown in the painting and Lemon Brown's treasure. Ask questions such as these:

1. What does this painting show? *It shows three men playing music in an outdoor setting.*
2. Why is the title of the painting "Four Piece Orchestra" if there are only three musicians? *The man playing harmonica is also playing the guitar.*
3. What message do you think the artist wants to convey with his painting? *Students may say that he wants to suggest the diversity of instruments that can be used to create music and he is showing that people of different interests or backgrounds can find common ground through music. Students may point out that the cello player is wearing a suit and tie and the harmonica player is dressed in work clothes—music appeals to all kinds of people.*

speaking moved a step closer. Greg turned, holding his breath, his eyes straining to see in the dark room.

The upper part of the figure before him was still in darkness. The lower half was in the dim rectangle of light that fell unevenly from the window. There were two feet, in cracked, dirty shoes from which rose legs that were wrapped in rags.

"Who are you?" Greg hardly recognized his own voice.

"I'm Lemon Brown," came the answer. "Who're you?"

"Greg Ridley."

"What you doing here?" The figure shuffled forward again, and Greg took a small step backward.

"It's raining," Greg said.

"I can see that," the figure said.

The person who called himself Lemon Brown peered forward, and Greg could see him clearly. He was an old man. His black, heavily wrinkled face was surrounded by a halo of crinkly white hair and whiskers that seemed to separate his head from the layers of dirty coats piled on his smallish frame. His pants were bagged
3 to the knee, where they were met with rags that went down to the old shoes. The rags were held on with strings, and there was a rope around his middle. Greg relaxed. He had seen the man before, picking through the trash on the corner and pulling clothes out of a Salvation Army box. There was no sign of the razor that could "cut a week into nine days."

"What are you doing here?" Greg asked.

"This is where I'm staying," Lemon Brown said. "What you here for?"

"Told you it was raining out," Greg said,
4 leaning against the back of the couch until he felt it give slightly.

"Ain't you got no home?"

"I got a home," Greg answered.

"You ain't one of them bad boys looking for my treasure, is you?" Lemon Brown cocked his head to one side and squinted one eye. "Because I told you I got me a razor."

> **Greg turned, holding his breath, his eyes straining to see in the dark room.**

"I'm not looking for your treasure," Greg answered, smiling. "*If* you have one."

"What you mean, *if* I have one," Lemon
Brown said. "Every man got a treasure. You 5
don't know that, you must be a fool!"

"Sure," Greg said as he sat on the sofa and put one leg over the back. "What do you have, gold coins?"

"Don't worry none about what I got," Lemon Brown said. "You know who I am?"

"You told me your name was orange or lemon or something like that."

"Lemon Brown," the old man said, pulling back his shoulders as he did so, "they used to call me Sweet Lemon Brown."

"Sweet Lemon?" Greg asked.

"Yessir. Sweet Lemon Brown. They used to say I sung the blues so
sweet that if I sang at a 6
funeral, the dead would commence to rocking with the beat. Used to travel all over Mississippi and as far
as Monroe, Louisiana, and 7
east on over to Macon, Georgia. You mean you ain't never heard of Sweet Lemon Brown?"

> **◆ Literature and Your Life**
> Think about the times you have met strange people. In a similar situation, do you think your attitude would be similar to Greg's?

"Afraid not," Greg said. "What . . . what happened to you?"

"Hard times, boy. Hard times always after a poor man. One day I got tired, sat down to rest a spell and felt a tap on my shoulder. Hard times caught up with me."

"Sorry about that."

"What you doing here? How come you didn't go on home when the rain come? Rain don't bother you young folks none."

"Just didn't." Greg looked away.

"I used to have a knotty-headed boy just like you." Lemon Brown had half walked, half shuffled back to the corner and sat down against the wall. "Had them big eyes like you got, I used to call them moon eyes. Look into

◆Critical Thinking

3 Infer What can you tell about Lemon Brown, based on this description? *Students will probably infer that Brown is poor and/or homeless.*

◆Critical Thinking

4 Analyze Why do you think Greg fails to explain more about why he came to the tenement? *Students may suggest that Greg is reluctant to tell a stranger about his anger at his father, or he may be embarrassed by his behavior.*

Comprehension Check ☑

5 Ask students what Lemon Brown means about his treasure. Guide them to recognize that abstract qualities or conditions, such as friendships and memories, can also be considered treasures. *Lemon Brown is saying that everyone has a treasure of some form, whether it is an object or an idea.*

Clarification

6 Blues performers, like the story's character, Sweet Lemon Brown, often traveled from place to place. They played their music, but never stayed in one place very long. As the musicians traveled the south and Texas, they followed the Mississippi River from the Delta, to Memphis, up to St. Louis, and to Chicago, looking for jobs, either as musicians or as factory workers.

◆Literature and Your Life

7 Encourage students to give reasons for their response to the question. *Most students will probably say that, like Greg, they would be cautious because strangers are not always trustworthy, and they would not know how much of his story to believe.*

Humanities: Music

Blues Music The style of Lemon Brown's music—the blues—is based on its improvised musical sound. The "blue" sound comes from playing minor scales or, in some cases, flatting the fifth note of a major scale. These musical effects are enhanced by "bending" notes, which is basically a matter of sliding and shifting the sound of the note as it is played or sung. When lyrics are used with blues songs, they often tell of hard times.

The history of blues is difficult to trace. It has its origins in the spirituals and work songs of African Americans on the plantations of the South. As instruments like acoustic guitars and harmonicas were added to the developing style of the blues, the sad and plaintive sound began to be heard in places where people gathered to listen to music and socialize. Rarely, if ever, did blues musicians play from printed music. Instead, they interpreted songs in their own unique ways, sharing their own memories and treasures with their voices and instruments.

As the blues spread in America, it began to change and influence many other types of music such as jazz and rock and roll.

Students may want to research a blues topic such as the Delta Blues, electronic vs. acoustic blues, prominent blues performers, modern bands who have been influenced by the blues, or blues music today. Encourage students to listen to recordings of the blues as part of their research.

Comprehension Check ☑

1 What reason does Lemon Brown give for not singing the blues anymore? *Lemon Brown said it was foolish to sing about hard times when you have it good.*

◆Critical Thinking

2 **Interpret** When Lemon Brown and Greg hide, what does Lemon Brown's behavior indicate? *Even though he is old and feeble, when Lemon Brown senses danger, he leads Greg to a hiding place and holds his hand as if to reassure Greg that he will protect him from the thugs.*

◆Reading Strategy

3 **Ask Questions** Based on what students know so far, have students speculate about what Greg and Lemon Brown will do and then formulate questions to guide their reading. *Students' questions may reflect their guesses that Greg and Lemon Brown will find another hiding place or might confront the thugs. Students can find answers to their questions by reading ahead.*

Customize for
English Language Learners
Help English language learners understand the meanings of words, phrases, and expressions that may be unfamiliar. Pantomime "half walked, half shuffled," "thugs," "beckoned frantically," and "watch my back."

them moon eyes and see anything you want."

"How come you gave up singing the blues?" Greg asked.

1 "Didn't give it up," Lemon Brown said. "You don't give up the blues; they give you up. After a while you do good for yourself, and it ain't nothing but foolishness singing about how hard you got it. Ain't that right?"

"I guess so."

"What's that noise?" Lemon Brown asked, suddenly sitting upright.

Greg listened, and he heard a noise outside. He looked at Lemon Brown and saw the old man pointing toward the window.

Greg went to the window and saw three men, neighborhood thugs, on the stoop. One was carrying a length of pipe. Greg looked back toward Lemon Brown, who moved quietly across the room to the window. The old man looked out, then beckoned frantically for Greg to follow him. For a moment Greg couldn't move. Then he found himself following Lemon Brown into the hallway and up darkened stairs. Greg fol-
2 lowed as closely as he could. They reached the top of the stairs, and Greg felt Lemon Brown's hand first lying on his shoulder, then probing down his arm until he finally took Greg's hand into his own as they crouched in the darkness.

"They's bad men," Lemon Brown whispered. His breath was warm against Greg's skin.

"Hey! Rag man!" A voice called. "We know you in here. What you got up under them rags? You got any money?"

Silence.

"We don't want to have to come in and hurt you, old man, but we don't mind if we have to."

Lemon Brown squeezed Greg's hand in his own hard, gnarled fist.

There was a banging downstairs and a light as the men entered. They banged around noisily, calling for the rag man.

"We heard you talking about your treasure." The voice was slurred. "We just want to see it, that's all."

"You sure he's here?" One voice seemed to come from the room with the sofa.

"Yeah, he stays here every night."

"There's another room over there; I'm going to take a look. You got that flashlight?"

"Yeah, here, take the pipe too."

Greg opened his mouth to quiet the sound of his breath as he sucked it in uneasily. A beam of light hit the wall a few feet opposite him, then went out.

"Ain't nobody in that room," a voice said. "You think he gone or something?"

"I don't know," came the answer. "All I know is that I heard him talking about some kind of treasure. You know they found that shopping bag lady with that money in her bags."

"Yeah. You think he's upstairs?"

"HEY, OLD MAN, ARE YOU UP THERE?"

Silence.

"Watch my back, I'm going up."

There was a footstep on the stairs, and the beam from the flashlight danced crazily along the peeling wallpaper. Greg held his breath. There was another step and a loud crashing noise as the man banged the pipe against the wooden banister.[4] Greg could feel his temples throb as the man slowly neared them. Greg thought about the pipe, wondering what he would do when the man reached them—what he *could* do.

> **◆ Reading Strategy**
> This tense situation might prompt you to ask what Greg and Lemon Brown will do. How would you expect to find out the answer to this question? 3

Then Lemon Brown released his hand and moved toward the top of the stairs. Greg looked around and saw stairs going up to the next floor. He tried waving to Lemon Brown, hoping the old man would see him in the dim light and follow him to the next floor. Maybe, Greg thought, the man wouldn't follow them up there. Suddenly, though, Lemon Brown stood at the top of the stairs, both arms raised high above his head.

"There he is!" A voice cried from below.

"Throw down your money, old man, so I won't have to bash your head in!"

Lemon Brown didn't move. Greg felt himself near panic. The steps came closer, and still Lemon Brown didn't move. He was an eerie

4. **banister** (ban′ is tər) *n.*: Railing along a staircase.

Beyond the Classroom

Community Connection

Oral History Discuss with students how older adults can provide unique knowledge and information based on their varied life experiences. Explain that an oral history is based on an interview or conversation with an older adult intended to gather information about specific memories and treasures in the adult's past. Information is shared orally, which is why it is called an oral history. Have students brainstorm for a list of topics, such as jobs, holiday celebrations, school experiences, events in history, fashions, or hobbies. As students narrow their topics and plan their questions, suggest interview techniques:

- Take careful notes (students can use a tape recorder if their interview subjects agree).
- Allow interview subjects to tell the stories they like to tell.
- Begin with a period of informal conversation or help with cooking or household chores, asking questions while working together.
- Be prepared to ad lib questions to help interview subjects provide more details.

Have students work in pairs, and encourage them to make appointments for their interviews. Students can write their observations in a report that can be shared with the class.

Disequilibrium, 1987, Catherine Redmond, Courtesy of the artist

4 ▲ Critical Viewing How does a dismal setting like the one in the story and the one in this painting add to the tension of "The Treasure of Lemon Brown"? **[Analyze]**

sight, a bundle of rags standing at the top of the stairs, his shadow on the wall looming over him. Maybe, the thought came to Greg, the scene could be even eerier.

5 Greg wet his lips, put his hands to his mouth and tried to make a sound. Nothing came out. He swallowed hard, wet his lips once more and howled as evenly as he could.

6 *"What's that?"*

7 As Greg howled, the light moved away from Lemon Brown, but not before Greg saw him hurl his body down the stairs at the men who had come to take his treasure. There was a crashing noise, and then footsteps. A rush of warm air came in as the downstairs door opened, then there was only an ominous silence.

Greg stood on the landing. He listened, and after a while there was another sound on the staircase.

"Mr. Brown?" he called.

"Yeah, it's me," came the answer. "I got their flashlight."

Greg exhaled in relief as Lemon Brown made his way slowly back up the stairs. 7

"You OK?"

"Few bumps and bruises," Lemon Brown said.

"I think I'd better be going," Greg said, his breath returning to normal. "You'd better leave, too, before they come back."

"They may hang around outside for a while," Lemon Brown said, "but they ain't getting their nerve up to come in here again. Not with crazy old rag men and howling spooks. Best you stay a while till the coast is clear. I'm heading out west tomorrow, out to east St. Louis."

"They were talking about treasures," Greg said. "You *really* have a treasure?"

"What I tell you? Didn't I tell you every man got a treasure?" Lemon Brown said. "You want to see mine?"

"If you want to show it to me," Greg shrugged.

▶Critical Viewing◀

4 Analyze *Students may say that the dismal setting shown in the painting and the one described in the story carry a sense of gloom or dread, which adds to the tension. Students may say that gloomy pictures make them think that bad things are likely to happen.*

◆Literature and Your Life

5 Have students name physical signs that show fear. Explain that Greg is experiencing the "fight-or-flight response," which often occurs in times of stress. Part of this response is a faster heartbeat and decreased production of saliva. Ask students to think about their own experiences with being startled or afraid. How are they are similar to or different from Greg's? *Greg's response includes the momentary inability to move, rapid breathing, a feeling of panic, throbbing temples, heightened awareness, and dry mouth. In describing their own experiences of the fight-or-flight response, some students may cite a heightened sense of hearing, sight, and smell; increased heartbeat; and a dry mouth.*

◆Critical Thinking

6 Evaluate Ask students whether they think Greg's decision to howl was a good one. *Some students may say that it was effective because it startled the thugs and put them off their guard so that Lemon Brown could overtake them; others may say that the howling was foolish because it could have further angered the thugs.*

◆Critical Thinking

7 Draw Conclusions Ask students what they can conclude about Lemon Brown's physical condition from this passage? *Students may say that Lemon Brown is in better physical shape than they realized, because he hurled his body down the stairs and still was able to walk. Some students may speculate that Brown is hurt but doesn't want to admit it to Greg because he feels protective of him and doesn't want to worry him.*

Humanities: Art

Disequilibrium, by Catherine Redmond

Focus students' attention on the title of the artwork. Explain that *equilibrium* refers to a state of balance. Have students use what they know about the meanings of prefixes to determine that *disequilibrium* means "a loss of balance." Use these questions for discussion:

1. Why do you think the artist titled her painting *Disequilibrium?* *The scene shown in the painting seems out of balance.*
2. What similarities do you see between the scene in the painting and the setting of the story? *Students may observe that the scene in the painting and the setting of the story are both cities. The dark building in the right half of the painting resembles the description of the tenement in the story. Both the painting and the story feature precipitation: The painting shows snow falling, whereas the story takes place during a rainstorm.*

Comprehension Check ☑

❶ Why did Lemon Brown's son stay with his mother's sister? *After Lemon Brown's wife died, he was unable to care for his son because he was traveling around the South making a living as a blues musician.*

Clarification

❷ Explain that *mouth fiddle* is another term for the harmonica, which is also known as a *mouth organ, mouth harp,* and *harp.*

◆ Literary Focus

❸ **Theme** Guide students' responses by focusing their attention on what the clippings and the harmonica symbolize. You may want to point out that the "treasure" had very little cash value—the thieves would have been disappointed. *Students should recognize that Lemon Brown's treasure represents his proudest achievement, which he passed on to his son as an example and which his son treasured as well.*

◆ Critical Thinking

❹ **Draw Conclusions** How has Greg's attitude changed as a result of meeting Lemon Brown? *Possible responses: Greg is no longer in an angry mood; he has begun to understand that his father has a treasure to give him.*

Customize for
Interpersonal Learners

Have students work with partners to create a Venn diagram in which they compare and contrast the characters of Stacy and Greg. You may wish to use the Venn Diagram, p. 86, in **Writing and Language Transparencies.**

"Let's look out the window first, see what them scoundrels be doing," Lemon Brown said.

They followed the oval beam of the flashlight into one of the rooms and looked out the window. They saw the men who had tried to take the treasure sitting on the curb near the corner. One of them had his pants leg up, looking at his knee.

"You sure you're not hurt?" Greg asked Lemon Brown.

"Nothing that ain't been hurt before," Lemon Brown said. "When you get as old as me all you say when something hurts is, 'Howdy, Mr. Pain, sees you back again.' Then when Mr. Pain see he can't worry you none, he go on mess with somebody else."

> "'Course by then I wasn't as much as I used to be, not without somebody to make it worth the while. You know what I mean?"

Greg smiled.

"Here, you hold this." Lemon Brown gave Greg the flashlight.

He sat on the floor near Greg and carefully untied the strings that held the rags on his right leg. When he took the rags away, Greg saw a piece of plastic. The old man carefully took off the plastic and unfolded it. He revealed some yellowed newspaper clippings and a battered harmonica.

"There it be," he said, nodding his head. "There it be."

Greg looked at the old man, saw the distant look in his eye, then turned to the clippings. They told of Sweet Lemon Brown, a blues singer and harmonica player who was appearing at different theaters in the South. One of the clippings said he had been the hit of the show, although not the headliner. All of the clippings were reviews of shows Lemon Brown had been in more than 50 years ago. Greg looked at the harmonica. It was dented badly on one side, with the reed holes on one end nearly closed.

"I used to travel around and make money for to feed my wife and Jesse—that's my boy's
❶ name. Used to feed them good, too. Then his mama died, and he stayed with his mama's sister. He growed up to be a man, and when the war come he saw fit to go off and fight in it. I didn't have nothing to give him except these things that told him who I was, and
what he come from. If you know your pappy ❶
did something, you know you can do something too.

"Anyway, he went off to war, and I went off still playing and singing. 'Course by then I wasn't as much as I used to be, not without somebody to make it worth the while. You know what I mean?"

"Yeah," Greg nodded, not quite really knowing.

"I traveled around, and one time I come home, and there was this letter saying Jesse got killed in the war. Broke my heart, it truly did.

"They sent back what he
had with him over there, and what it was is ❷
this old mouth fiddle and these clippings. Him carrying it around with him like that told me it meant something to him. That was my treasure, and when I give it to him he treated it just like that, a treasure. Ain't that something?"

> ◆ **Literary Focus** ❸
> What might the details about Lemon Brown's treasure tell you about the theme of the story?

"Yeah, I guess so," Greg said.

"You *guess* so?" Lemon Brown's voice rose an octave as he started to put his treasure back into the plastic. "Well, you got to guess 'cause you sure don't know nothing. Don't know enough to get home when it's raining."

"I guess . . . I mean, you're right."

"You OK for a youngster," the old man said as he tied the strings around his leg, "better than those scalawags[5] what come here looking for my treasure. That's for sure."

"You really think that treasure of yours was worth fighting for?" Greg asked. "Against a pipe?"

"What else a man got 'cepting what he can

5. **scalawags** (skal′ ə wagz′) *n.*: People who cause trouble; scoundrels.

Viewing and Representing Mini-Lesson

Intergenerational Friendship Quilt

In this mini-lesson, students will extend their understanding of treasures by visiting with older adults and representing "treasures" for a bulletin board display.

Introduce Tell students that a friendship quilt is made up of quilt squares sewn by different people. Have students measure and determine the size of each "square" for the bulletin board friendship quilt they will create.

Develop Have students work in pairs and think of an older adult they know who would have memories or treasures they might wish to share—a family member, friend, neighbor, or teacher. Students should be prepared to prompt memories by suggesting that the adult share with them a photograph album, a cedar chest of clothing or memorabilia, military uniforms or medals, tools, or books.

Apply Have students visit or talk to the older adult. Then allow time for them to create their "quilt blocks," capturing the essence of the memory treasures that were shared. Encourage students to consider various kinds of paper, fabric, and other materials for their quilt blocks.

Assess Have students describe their quilt block representations as they add them to the bulletin board "friendship quilt." Evaluate students on their ability to work in pairs and whether their quilt blocks and descriptions seem to represent their experiences with older adults.

pass on to his son, or his daughter, if she be his oldest?" Lemon Brown said. "For a big-headed boy you sure do ask the foolishest questions."

Lemon Brown got up after patting his rags in place and looked out the window again.

"Looks like they're gone. You get on out of here and get yourself home. I'll be watching from the window so you'll be all right."

Lemon Brown went down the stairs behind Greg. When they reached the front door the old man looked out first, saw the street was clear and told Greg to scoot on home.

"You sure you'll be OK?" Greg asked.

"Now didn't I tell you I was going to east St. Louis in the morning?" Lemon Brown asked. "Don't that sound OK to you?"

"Sure it does," Greg said. "Sure it does. And you take care of that treasure of yours."

"That I'll do," Lemon said, the wrinkles about his eyes suggesting a smile. "That I'll do."

The night had warmed and the rain had stopped, leaving puddles at the curbs. Greg didn't even want to think how late it was. He thought ahead of what his father would say and wondered if he should tell him about Lemon Brown. He thought about it until he reached his stoop, and decided against it. Lemon Brown would be OK, Greg thought, with his memories and his treasure.

Greg pushed the button over the bell marked Ridley, thought of the lecture he knew 4
his father would give him, and smiled.

Guide for Responding

◆ Literature and Your Life

Reader's Response Do you agree with Greg's decision not to tell his father about Lemon Brown?

Thematic Focus Using Lemon Brown's life experience as a guide, what do you think this story says about the value of family and community ties?

☑ Check Your Comprehension

1. List five facts you learn about Greg at the beginning of the story.
2. Why is Greg upset and angry at the beginning of the story?
3. How does Greg meet Lemon Brown?
4. Why do three men break into the building where Brown is?
5. What is the "treasure" of Lemon Brown?
6. What happened to Brown's son?
7. What is Brown planning to do next?

◆ Critical Thinking

INTERPRET

1. Why doesn't Greg go home when it starts to rain? **[Analyze]**
2. Why does Greg go into the old tenement building? **[Infer]**
3. How does Greg's opinion of Lemon Brown change over the course of the story? **[Compare and Contrast]**
4. What does Brown teach Greg? **[Interpret]**
5. Why do you think Greg smiles at the end of the story? **[Analyze Cause and Effect]**

APPLY

6. If you were to talk to someone younger about what's important in life, what treasures would you share? **[Synthesize]**

COMPARE LITERARY WORKS

7. How are the relationships between Greg and Brown and Stacy and her grandmother similar? How are they different? **[Compare and Contrast]**

Beyond the Selection

FURTHER READING

Other Works by Laurence Yep

Mountain Light
The Serpent's Children
Thief of Hearts

Other Works by Walter Dean Myers

Malcolm X: By Any Means Necessary
Shadow of the Red Moon
Somewhere in the Darkness

INTERNET

We suggest the following sites on the Internet (all Web sites are subject to change).

For more information about Laurence Yep:
http://www.scils.rutgers.edu/special/kay/yep.html

For more information about Walter Dean Myers:
http://www.scils.rutgers.edu/special/kay/myers.html

We *strongly recommend* that you preview these sites before you send students to them.

Reinforce and Extend

Answers

◆ Literature and Your Life

Reader's Response Some students may agree because the decision protects Lemon Brown's privacy and saves Greg from getting into further trouble. Others may note that the thieves are likely to come back and Lemon Brown isn't safe.

Thematic Focus Students may suggest that people of different generations can learn from one another.

☑ Check Your Comprehension

1. Possible responses: Greg is doing poorly in math; he is 14; he is a good basketball player; he wants to play basketball for a team; Greg's father has high expectations for him.
2. His father has told him that he cannot play basketball.
3. He enters an abandoned tenement building where Lemon Brown is staying.
4. They are looking for money or valuables.
5. The treasure is a battered harmonica and old newspaper clippings.
6. He was killed in a war.
7. He is going to St. Louis.

◆ Critical Thinking

1. He wants to avoid his father; he is rebelling against doing what he is told to do.
2. Students may suggest that Greg is seeking shelter from the storm while he broods about his fate or that he wants to do something forbidden and a little dangerous.
3. Greg's opinion changes from fearful to curious to respectful.
4. A person's achievements are a treasure that can be passed on to others. A treasure doesn't have to be worth a lot of money.
5. Greg now sees that his father's hopes for him are a kind of treasure.
6. Students may mention treasures such as honoring family members and friends, acting responsibly, doing one's best, and being kind to others.
7. Both relationships involve older and younger people; in both cases, the two people gain an understanding of each other. Stacy and her grandmother are relatives, whereas Greg and Brown are not.

Answers

◆Reading Strategy

1. The grandmother is sensitive because her feet are deformed from having been bound when she was a young girl. Stacy's mother explains in the text.
2. The grandmother mistakes Stacy's toe-shoe ribbons for the type of ribbons used to bind feet. This is explained in the text.
3. The description explains why Greg avoids going home and sets the stage for the lesson Greg learns about what parents and children can give each other. The answer must be pieced together.

◆Build Vocabulary

Using the Word Root *-sens-*

1. related to perceiving things through the senses
2. lacking feeling
3. an attitude or judgment based on feeling
4. a guard posted to perceive danger

Spelling Strategy

1. glorious
2. laborious
3. furious
4. victorious
5. spacious

Using the Word Bank

1. d
2. e
3. b
4. g
5. h
6. c
7. a
8. f

◆Literary Focus

Possible responses:

1. Through love and understanding, family members can overcome cultural and age differences. Stacy and her grandmother begin to form a bond when they understand each other's point of view.
2. What you become in life can be a treasure to give your children or your parents. Brown's statement that begins "If you know your pappy did something . . ." explains why Brown gave his son the "treasure" and why it pleased him that the treasure was greatly valued by his son.

Guide for Responding *(continued)*

◆ Reading Strategy

Ask Questions

Asking questions as you read a story can help you figure out the author's message. Below are some questions that you might have asked while reading these stories. Answer each question. For each, explain whether the answer was stated directly in the text or whether you had to piece together evidence to get the answer.

1. Why is the grandmother in "Ribbons" sensitive about her feet?
2. How does this explain her conflict with her granddaughter?
3. Why does "The Treasure of Lemon Brown" start with a description of the conflict between Greg and his father?

◆ Build Vocabulary

Using the Word Root *-sens-*

The word root *-sens-* means "feel" or "perceive." On your paper, define each of the following words, using the meaning of *-sens-* in each definition.

1. sensory **2.** insensitive **3.** sentiment **4.** sentry

Spelling Strategy

Adding the suffix *-ious* changes a noun into an adjective. If the noun ends in the letters *y* or *e*, drop the *y* or *e* before adding *-ious*. For each of the following nouns, write the correct *-ious* adjective.

1. glory **2.** labor **3.** fury **4.** victory **5.** space

Using the Word Bank

On your paper, match each of the following words with its definition.

1. tentatively	**a.** timid
2. coax	**b.** slightly open
3. ajar	**c.** touchy
4. laborious	**d.** with uncertainty
5. impromptu	**e.** persuade gently
6. sensitive	**f.** physical work
7. meek	**g.** difficult
8. exertion	**h.** unplanned

◆ Literary Focus

Theme

A **theme** is a central message or insight into life revealed by a literary work. In both stories, the themes are conveyed indirectly through what the characters say and do.

1. Reread the last scene in "Ribbons," which reveals the theme of the story. In your own words, state the theme of "Ribbons." Support your answer.
2. Considering what Lemon Brown tells Greg about his "treasure," what would you say is the theme of "The Treasure of Lemon Brown"? Explain how you arrived at your answer.

◆ Build Grammar Skills

Adjective Clauses

An **adjective clause** is a subordinate clause (group of words that has a subject and a verb but cannot stand on its own as a sentence) that functions as an adjective. Just like single-word adjectives, it modifies a noun or pronoun. Adjective clauses usually begin with a relative pronoun (*who, whom, whose, which,* and *that),* which relates the clause to the word it modifies. Adjective clauses may also begin with the subordinating conjunctions *where, when,* and *why*. Look at this example:

There was an old tenement *that had been abandoned for some months.*

Practice Identify each adjective clause and the word it modifies.

1. He thought of the lecture that awaited him.
2. The inside of the building was dark except for the dim light that filtered through the dirty windows.
3. The person who had been speaking moved a step closer.
4. The person who called himself Lemon Brown peered forward.
5. "I didn't have nothing to give him except these things that told him who I was."

Writing Application Write a paragraph summarizing one of the stories. Use and identify at least three adjective clauses.

◆Build Grammar Skills

1. *that awaited him*; modifies *lecture*
2. *that filtered through the dirty windows;* modifies *light*
3. *who had been speaking*; modifies *person*
4. *who called himself Lemon Brown*; modifies *person*
5. *that told him who I was*; modifies *things*

Writing Application

The adjective clauses in students' paragraphs should modify nouns or pronouns and should begin with relative pronouns or subordinating conjunctions.

Writer's Solution

For additional instruction and practice, use the lesson in the *Writer's Solution Language Lab CD-ROM* on adjectives. You may also use the practice page on Adjective Clauses, p. 52, in the *Writer's Solution Grammar Practice Book.*

Build Your Portfolio

Idea Bank

Writing

1. **Treasure Description** Lemon Brown asserts that every person has a treasure. What is your treasure? In a few paragraphs, describe your treasure, and explain why it is meaningful to you.
2. **Diary** As Stacy or Greg, write a diary entry that describes what you have discovered about yourself and others as a result of the experiences described in the stories.
3. **Story Review** In an essay to appear in a student magazine, write a review of one of the stories. After a brief summary of the action, share your opinion of the story and its message with readers.

Speaking and Listening

4. **Monologue** Assume the role of Stacy, and deliver a speech in which you reflect on the events in "Ribbons." **[Performing Arts Link]**
5. **Blues Presentation** Lemon Brown had been a blues musician. Find out more about this type of music. Listen to recordings of songs and performers. Then, share what you have learned in an oral report. Illustrate your points by playing short excerpts of blues music. **[Music Link]**

Projects

6. **Travel Brochure** Imagine that you own your own travel agency. Design a brochure to promote a tour to Hong Kong—the city where Grandmother lived. Use the Internet and other resources to obtain current tourist, airline, and hotel information. **[Social Studies Link; Career Link; Technology Link]**
7. **Report [Group Activity]** Stacy's grandmother's feet were bound because it was a custom of the culture in which she lived. With a group, find out more about unusual customs in different cultures. Each group member may select a particular culture on which to focus, based on his or her cultural heritage or interests. Present your findings to the class. **[Social Studies Link]**

Writing Mini-Lesson

Character Analysis

Choose one of the main characters from the stories, and write a character analysis of him or her. In your analysis, explore the character's strengths and weaknesses.

Writing Skills Focus: Support With Evidence

After you make a statement about a strong or weak trait in your character, **support** your statement **with evidence** from the story. For example, if you say that one of Greg's father's strengths is determination to succeed, you might use the following passage as evidence:

Model From the Story

His father had been a postal worker for all Greg's life, and was proud of it, often telling Greg how hard he had worked to pass the test.

Prewriting After selecting the character you will analyze, review the story, and gather details about the character. Organize your ideas and information in a chart like the one below.

Strengths	Evidence	Weaknesses	Evidence

Drafting Begin the character analysis with a statement that gives an overall assessment of the character. First, discuss the character's strengths; then, his or her weaknesses. To end, sum up your main points, and draw a conclusion about the character.

Revising Revise your draft by looking for places where you can add details from the story to support your statements.

◆ Grammar Application

As you revise, add adjective clauses as needed to provide more information about your character and his or her behavior.

ASSESSMENT OPTIONS

Formal Assessment, Selection Test, pp. 149–151, and Assessment Resources Software. The selection test is designed so that it can be easily customized to the performance levels of your students.

Alternative Assessment, p. 33, includes options for less advanced students, more advanced students, visual/spatial learners, interpersonal learners, and verbal/linguistic learners.

PORTFOLIO ASSESSMENT

Use the following rubrics in the **Alternative Assessment** booklet to assess student writing:
Treasure Description: Description, p. 84
Diary: Fictional Narrative, p. 82
Story Review: Response to Literature, p. 97
Writing Mini-Lesson: Definition/Classification, p. 86

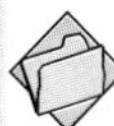

Idea Bank

Following are suggestions for matching the Idea Bank topics with your students' performance levels and learning modalities:

Customize for *Performance Levels*
Less Advanced Students: 1, 4
Average Students: 2, 4, 5, 6
More Advanced Students: 3, 5, 6, 7

Customize for *Learning Modalities*
Verbal/Linguistic: 1, 2, 3, 4, 5
Visual/Spatial: 6
Musical/Rhythmic: 5
Interpersonal: 4, 5, 7
Intrapersonal: 1, 2, 6

Writing Mini-Lesson

Refer students to the Writing Handbook in the back of the book for instructions on the writing process and for further information on responding to literature. Have students use the Open Mind Organizer in **Writing and Language Transparencies,** p. 90, to arrange their prewriting examples.

Writer's Solution

Writing Lab CD-ROM

Have students complete the tutorial on Response to Literature. Follow these steps:

1. Have students use the Topic Web activity to help them divide their topics.
2. Suggest that students use the Character Personality Profile to gather details about the characters.
3. Have students draft on computer.
4. Encourage students to use the Proofreading Checklist when revising their writing.

Writer's Solution Sourcebook

Have students use Chapter 9, "Response to Literature," pp. 264–295, for additional support. This chapter includes in-depth instruction on varying sentence length and structure, pp. 292–293.

Connections to Today's World

As its name suggests, the Rock and Roll Hall of Fame and Museum houses musical treasures. It provides an important link between present and past generations of musicians. In addition, the museum's exhibits highlight the social forces that have shaped the music of the past century. Students may want to visit the museum Web site at the following address: **http://www.rockhall.com/**

We *strongly recommend* that you preview this site before sending students to it. Have students share what they learned from visiting the site.

Clarification

❶ Point out that this is a press release. This information was released to various news media at the time that a new exhibit, "Let the Good Times Roll: A Tribute to Rhythm & Blues," was opened at the Rock and Roll Hall of Fame and Museum. Although the museum is located in Cleveland, Ohio, this press release was sent to newspapers, magazines, and TV and radio stations across the country.

Comprehension Check ☑

❷ Guide students to review and understand the role of R&B music in the development of twentieth-century popular music. Ask: What does R&B stand for? What types of music developed from R&B? *R&B stands for rhythm and blues. Soul, funk, disco, and rap all developed from R&B.*

Thematic Connection

Relate this press release to "Ribbons" and "The Treasure of Lemon Brown" by discussing differences in types of music listened to by older and younger generations of people. Discuss ways that music can forge a link between generations.

Customize for *Musical/Rhythmic Learners*

Encourage students to describe the kind of music they like best and tell why. You may want to suggest that they bring in examples to share with the class. Have students speculate about the types of music that they think Stacy, Greg, Grandmother, and Lemon Brown might listen to.

Connections to Today's World

Blues music—the sort played by Lemon Brown on his treasured harmonica—inspired other forms of American music, including rhythm-and-blues and rock-and-roll. At the Rock and Roll Hall of Fame and Museum, located in Cleveland, Ohio, exhibits celebrate American popular music and show the influence of one generation of musicians upon the next. This press release announces one such exhibit.

❶

Rhythm and Blues, Let the Good Times Roll

Rock and Roll Hall of Fame

The roots of rhythm and blues are complex and deeply woven into the fabric of American history and culture. Like blues, jazz, and country, R&B was, in part, shaped by events far removed from the music. A look at America in the 1940's and '50's reveals how R&B not only was impacted by the many things going on in this country during these two important post-war decades, but also how R&B reflected them in song and sound.

❷ Rhythm & blues evolved into a generic term describing all forms of black popular music: down home blues, big city jump bands, vocal groups, jazz, urban shouters and torchy night club singers. It was rhythm & blues that provided one of the foundations for rock and roll in the early 1950's and, while rock and roll became the mainstream of popular music, rhythm & blues continued its development into an easily recognizable music form.

From R&B came soul, funk, disco and rap—all important African American music forms that still resonate with energy and excitement today.

The Rock and Roll Hall of Fame and Museum honors the men and women who have made unique contributions to the evolution of rock and roll in our new exhibit, "Let the Good Times Roll: A Tribute to Rhythm & Blues."

Facts About The Rock And Roll Hall Of Fame And Museum

The Museum:

The Rock and Roll Hall of Fame and Museum is a 150,000 square-foot facility that serves as the permanent home of the Rock and Roll Hall of Fame. It provides dynamic interactive exhibits, intimate performance spaces, displays from the museum's permanent collection. Exhibits change periodically and showcase specific rock'n'roll eras, styles, milestones and the many facets of the music's evolution. It also houses research facilities and features public programming dedicated to the exploration of the music's enduring impact on global culture. It is the world's first museum dedicated to the living heritage of rock and roll music.

Beyond the Classroom

Career Connection

Public Relations The field of public relations, referred to as PR, connects organizations to the public by various means of communication. PR positions may include publicist, press agent, lobbyist, and various jobs in advertising.

The press release on these pages is an example of a communication tool that PR specialists use to publicize an event. Publicists "release," or distribute, information about events to news media, so that the media can then communicate the details to their readers, listeners, and viewers. After the press release is distributed, a publicist follows up with a contact by telephone, in person, or by mail. More detailed information may be given and interviews may be scheduled. Public relations specialists answer the journalistic questions *who, what, when, where,* and *why.*

Discuss with students the traits that a person who is interested in PR work should have or develop: an enjoyment of interacting with people, an outgoing personality, good writing and verbal skills, and a willingness to keep trying despite negative responses.

CONNECTIONS TO TODAY'S WORLD

◀ Critical Viewing This photograph of Chuck Berry is on the cover of an exhibit brochure. What does it suggest about Berry's importance in rhythm-and-blues music? [Infer] 3

Special Features:

- Exhibits on the roots of rock-and-roll include Gospel, Country, Folk, Blues, and Rhythm-and-Blues, featuring the Museum's collections.
- Working studio from which visiting radio stations can conduct live broadcasts
- 200-seat indoor theater
- Outdoor area for concerts
- Dramatic new multimedia gallery for the Rock and Roll Hall of Fame

Exhibits:

The Museum's exhibits are designed to give the visitor a unique, interactive experience. The Museum's collection is brought to life through a combination of high-tech wizardry and innovative film and video. The Museum offers a comprehensive retrospective on the music's origins, its development, its legends, and its immense impact on global culture.

The exhibitions will take the visitor on a fast-paced journey through the history of rock and roll. They will bring the visitor into the experience, showcasing rock and roll and its impact on society. Major music scenes, specific artists and the music's impact on the way we live will be examined.

◆ **Build Vocabulary**

retrospective (re´ trə spek´ tiv) *n.*: Look on the past

1. What types of music have their origin in rhythm-and-blues?
2. What do the exhibits in the museum show?
3. What can you learn from this article and the stories about the importance of learning from older generations?

▶Critical Viewing◀

3 Infer *Because this photo is on the cover of a brochure about rhythm and blues, it implies that Chuck Berry was a major force in this type of music.*

Customize for
Visual/Spatial Learners
Suggest that students research the wide variety of museums and the diversity of exhibits available to explore in different areas across the country. Students may wish to research in the library or on the Internet, or use travel resources to formulate a list of museums that are geographically unique, and then make a map of their locations. For example, students might map the location of a shell museum located on the ocean or a desert museum in the Southwest that would not be found in any other location in the country.

Customize for
Verbal/Linguistic Learners
Have students use the press release format to write a press release about an upcoming school activity. Alternatively, students may wish to write a press release about a local museum and the exhibits it offers.

Customize for
Interpersonal Learners
Ask students to imagine that a representative of the Rock and Roll Hall of Fame and Museum will be visiting the class soon. Have students compose a list of questions they would like to ask the representative about the museum. Students may wish to role-play the interview with another student and give answers based on the information contained in "Rhythm and Blues, Let the Good Times Roll."

Answers

1. Rock-and-roll, soul, funk, disco, and rap have their origins in rhythm and blues.
2. The exhibits show the origins and development of rock and roll. They showcase its legends and feature information about the worldwide impact on culture of rock-and-roll music.
3. Students may say that the stories and article both show that much can be learned by taking the time to understand ideas and events of the past.

Beyond the Selection

FURTHER READING

Other Works About Blues

The Blues Is a Feeling: Voices and Visions of African American Blues Musicians, James Fraher

The Roots of the Blues: An African Search, Samuel Barclay Charters

Other Works About Museums

Destination Culture: Tourism, Museums and Heritage, Barbara Kirshenblatt-Gimblett

Museum Time Machine: Putting Cultures on Display, Robert Lumley

INTERNET

We suggest the following sites on the Internet (all Web sites are subject to change).

For information about blues:
http://thebluehighway.com/history.html

For information about rock-and-roll:
http://home.earthlink.net/~dpeneny/

To search for information about museums displaying a particular topic, use a keyword such as *museum,* a word that describes the specific topic, or a geographical locator.

We *strongly recommend* that you preview these sites before you send students to them.

Prepare and Engage

Establish Writing Guidelines
Review the following key characteristics of a critical review:

- A critical review is an evaluation of a subject.
- A critical review includes information on the subject being critiqued.
- The writer backs up his or her opinions with specific details.

You may want to distribute the scoring rubric for Critical Review, p. 98, in **Alternative Assessment** to make students aware of the criteria on which they will be evaluated. See the suggestions on p. 546 for customizing the rubric to this workshop.

Refer students to the Writing Handbook in the back of the book for further information.

Writer's Solution

Writers at Work Videodisc
To introduce students to expository writing, and to show them what author Dimitri Ehrlich says about writing a review, play the videodisc segment on Exposition: Making Connections (Ch. 5). Discuss with students Ehrlich's goals in writing a review.

Play frames 42847 to 52256

Writing Lab CD-ROM
If your students have access to computers, you may want to have them work in the tutorial on Exposition: Making Connections to complete all or part of their critical reviews. Follow these steps:

1. Have students use the Cluster Diagram to divide their topic into subtopics.
2. Suggest that students view the video clip on organization.
3. Have students draft on computer.
4. Have students work with a peer adviser when revising, and use the Peer-editing Worksheet.

Writer's Solution Sourcebook
Students can find additional support, including in-depth instruction on writing topic sentences, in the chapter on Exposition: Making Connections, pp. 134–165.

You may wish to refer students to p. 142 for an example of a review of the movie *An American Tale*.

Exposition

Critical Review

Writing Process Workshop

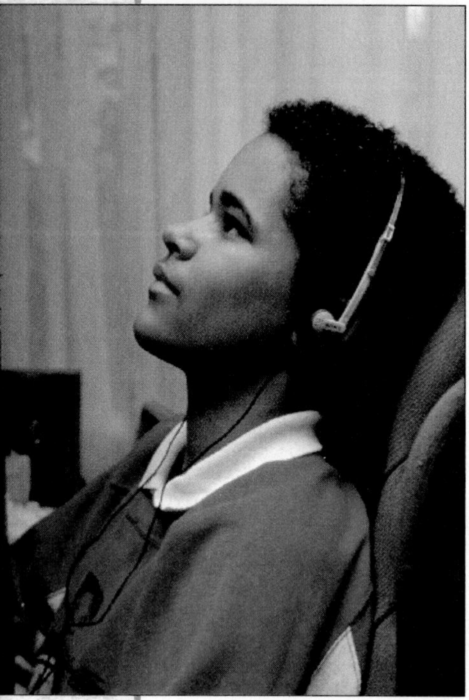

"Did you read the review?" Lots of reviews appear in writing these days: reviews of books, movies, television shows, restaurants, plays, CDs, video games, concerts—you name it. **Critical reviews** describe their subjects in detail and give opinions about their quality. If a reviewer likes something, he or she will rave and sales may sky-rocket. On the other hand, a poor review can discourage others from buying, visiting, reading, or viewing. Now, it's your turn to play critic. The following skills, introduced in Writing Mini-Lessons in this part, will help you write an effective critical review.

Writing Skills Focus

▶ **Give the necessary context.** Provide the background information that your readers will need to understand your review and what you are reviewing. (See p. 521.)

▶ **Support with evidence.** Give specific reasons or examples to back up your opinion. (See p. 541.)

▶ **Elaborate** to convey your reactions to your subject.

Notice how this writer uses all the skills in a review of a blues album.

Model

Bubba Bailey's Blues, a new CD by Ben Bailey (Ragan Records, 1997), is a great introduction to the blues because it includes blues ① of all kinds. For example, "Bubba's Romp" is a playful tune picked on a solo steel-stringed guitar with lyrics that will make you laugh. In contrast, "My Mama's Piano" is a slow, sad song with a beautiful piano riff in the middle that will bring tears to your eye. ② Later, "A Penny for Your Thoughts" rocks wildly in loud, hard rhythms. ③

① This provides necessary information—identifying the CD, the date of its release, and the reviewer's opinion.

② Notice how the writer elaborates by showing how the music evokes playfulness or tears.

③ The writer offers specific examples of songs to support her opinion about the album.

Beyond the Classroom

Career Connection

Critic Explain that a critic's job requires that he or she be experienced with the general topic area under review, such as recordings and music, film, or computer technology. A film critic probably has taken courses in film appreciation and history; a book critic may have studied literature, writing, or journalism; and a food critic will probably have training or background in cooking, food sciences, or health and nutrition. In addition, all critics need good writing skills.

Group students according to fields for which they would like to be critics. Then ask them to find examples of critical reviews in this field. Point out that critics often write regular review columns, so students can look for examples of critics' work in local newspapers and magazines. Suggest that, as they research critical reviews, students gather more than one example. Have groups review the information they have gathered and prepare a brief summary of that information to share with the rest of the class.

Prewriting

Choose a Subject Choose a subject that you know a lot about. It will be easier to describe, and you'll probably find that you have a strong opinion worth supporting. Here are a few suggestions:

Topic Ideas

- Compact disk
- Film you've seen recently
- Play or concert
- Book you've read
- Restaurant you've visited
- Work of art or an exhibit

Include Opinions and Facts State your opinion early in your review. Use facts to support your opinion: statistics, examples, specific details, quotations, even an anecdote. Each piece of evidence makes your case stronger.

Pack In Words That Describe In your review, show, don't tell. For example, don't simply tell your readers that a meal was good. Provide details so that readers see it, taste it, and smell it. If a movie's monster was scary, let your reader feel the ground shake when he passes by.

Drafting

Show Your Reasoning Work carefully on your opinion. Don't settle for simply, "It was good" or "I didn't like it." Elaborate with specific explanations. Once you've written your review, everything in it should support that opinion. Here are some examples:

> Amber's new CD is her best yet because she goes beyond rap.
>
> *Hatchet* was the most suspenseful, exciting, and realistic novel I've ever read.
>
> *Dr. Doolittle* was so funny I never stopped laughing.
>
> The service at Eddie's Diner was great, but the hamburgers were overcooked.

Keep to a Set Length Some reviews are lengthy essays; others are single paragraphs. The length of your review depends on your purpose, audience, and the subject you are reviewing.

DRAFTING/REVISING

Applying Language Skills: Vary Sentence Beginnings

To keep your writing from falling into a dull and predictable pattern, vary the ways you start your sentences. Consider shaking up your writing with these sentence starters:

Phrase:
In his restaurant, Maurice prepares omelets with salsa.

Clause:
Although the flavor is strong, it is not too spicy.

Single-Word Modifier:
Luckily, people love his recipe.

Practice Add phrases, clauses, or single-word modifiers to vary the beginnings of these sentences.

1. He serves side dishes of rice and beans.
2. The burritos are served on hand-painted plates.
3. Prices are reasonable, too.

Writing Application As you draft your critical review, vary your sentence beginnings to avoid a predictable pattern.

Writer's Solution Connection
Writing Lab

To help you gather details for your review, use the Cluster Diagram activity in the Exposition: Giving Information tutorial.

Develop Student Writing

Prewriting

When choosing topics to review, suggest that students pick a topic with which they are not only familiar, but also have had recent experience—a new CD they have been listening to or a movie they have seen recently, for instance. You may want to point out that most reviews address new events or products, and are published before or at the same time a play or movie opens, for example, or a CD or computer game becomes available to buy in stores.

Customize for
Less Proficient Writers
To help students organize the critical points in their review, have them use the Main Idea and Supporting Details Organizer, p. 70, in **Writing and Language Transparencies.** Explain that they should identify the Main Idea as the topic they are reviewing, and use the Supporting Details column to list points they will make in the review, using examples and details about the topic.

Customize for
Interpersonal Learners
Suggest that students work together on their critical reviews. Students can pair up and choose the same topic to review. Have one student write a positive review and one student write a negative review. They can work together to form a preliminary list of pros and cons and begin their drafts using this list.

Drafting

Tell students that one way to organize their reviews is by listing the most important points first and concluding with less important details. They also might want to group their evidence and elaboration by what they liked and disliked. Encourage students to try out different methods of organization.

Applying Language Skills

Vary Sentence Beginnings Encourage students to review their drafts and count how many sentences begin with phrases, clauses, or single-word modifiers, and how many begin with subjects. They can use this information to decide where they should vary their sentence patterns.

Students might read their drafts aloud to check for repetitive sentence beginnings—sometimes it is easier to hear repetition that the eyes have skipped over on paper.

Answers
Suggested responses:

1. With every entree, he serves side dishes of rice and beans.
2. Beautifully prepared, the burritos are served on hand-painted plates.
3. Surprisingly, prices are reasonable, too.

Writer's Solution

For additional instruction and practice, have students use the *Writer's Solution Language Lab CD-ROM* Varying Sentence Structure lesson in the Sentence Style unit or the practice page Using Different Sentence Openers in the *Writer's Solution Grammar Practice Book,* p. 120.

Revising

When revising, remind students to check for the following:

- The opinion is clearly stated in the introduction.
- All relevant factual information is included.
- The supporting details are organized effectively.
- The opinion is restated in the conclusion.

Writer's Solution

Writing Lab CD-ROM

In the tutorial on Exposition: Making Connections, have students use the Sentence-length Revision Checker to vary sentence length and combine short sentences into longer ones.

Publishing

For other publishing ideas, suggest that students send their reviews to local newspapers or submit them to the school newspaper. They might include photographs of the places or items reviewed, if possible.

Applying Language Skills

Writing Titles Correctly

Explain to students that if they punctuate their titles incorrectly, readers may think the review is about a book instead of a short story or a song instead of a CD.

Answers

1. "Ribbons"
2. *The Grapes of Wrath*
3. "America, the Beautiful"

Writer's Solution

For additional practice, complete the Capital for Titles of Things in the *Writer's Solution Grammar Practice Book,* p. 89.

EDITING/PROOFREADING

APPLYING LANGUAGE SKILLS: Writing Titles Correctly

If you refer to a novel, short story, song, or other work, be sure to punctuate the title correctly. Follow these rules:

- Capitalize the first word and all other important words.
- Place quotation marks around titles of short works.
- Underline or italicize the titles of long works.

Look at these examples:

Novel:
A Separate Peace

Short Story:
"The Treasure of Lemon Brown"

Album:
Rites of Passage

Song:
"Closer to Fine"

Practice Rewrite these titles correctly:

1. ribbons (short story)
2. the grapes of wrath (novel)
3. america the beautiful (song)

Writing Application In your critical review, be sure to refer to titles correctly.

Writer's Solution Connection
Writing Lab

For more information on writing titles, see the instruction on punctuation in the Revising and Editing section of the Response to Literature tutorial.

Include the Facts Depending on your subject, you'll want to include certain necessary background information. Here are some questions your review should address:

Restaurant:	Address? Cost? Menu? Atmosphere? Accessibility? Comfort?
Book:	Author? Publisher? Date? Length? Ease of Reading?
Music:	Artist? Producer? Recording Company? Date? Specific Songs?
Film:	Title? Director? Date? Studio? Actors?

Revising

Check Sentence Variety Vary the lengths of your sentences. Combine short sentences into longer ones—or break up longer sentences into shorter ones for emphasis. Inserting a question, a quotation, or an exclamation can jazz up your review.

Don't Repeat Be careful not to repeat words unnecessarily. Also, be on the lookout for redundancy, the unnecessary repetition of an idea.

REVISION MODEL

Elaine's Schooner ① , located at 307 Anchorage Way, provides seafood fare served in a friendly, warm setting. ~~As you~~ ② Time your reservation so you can order the savory Clams Casino or the hearty chowder and take in a beautiful sunset overlooking the bay.

① The writer provides the restaurant's address.
② This advice tells diners the best time to visit.

Publishing and Presenting

Bulletin Board of Reviews Use a bulletin board in a common area of your school to display written reviews. Create an eye-catching title and design for your display.

Review Broadcast Often, critics read their reviews on television and radio programs. Choose an appropriate piece of music to introduce and end your review. Then, work with a partner to record both of your reviews with the accompanying music. Share the recordings with your class.

✓ ASSESSMENT		4	3	2	1
PORTFOLIO ASSESSMENT Use the rubric for Critical Review, p. 98, in **Alternative Assessment** to assess the students' writing. Add these criteria to customize the rubric to this assignment.	**Opinions and Support**	The review contains clear opinions about the topic and supports each opinion with details.	The review contains clear opinions about the topic, but not all opinions are supported.	The review contains opinions, which are not always clearly expressed and some are not supported.	The review contains opinions that are unclear and no supported with details.
	Varying Sentence Beginnings	There is a wide variety of sentence beginnings.	Most of the sentence beginnings are varied; there is some repetition.	Few of the sentence beginnings are varied, and repetition is apparent.	There is no variation among sentence beginnings.

Real-World Reading Skills Workshop

Varying Reading Rate for Nonfiction

Strategies for Success

Consider the variety of ways you approach the nonfiction you encounter every day. You may read your science textbook one way, the box scores another, and a humorous narrative still another. Beyond your changing attitude and interest level about the content of these items, you actually change the speed with which you absorb each one's meaning based on your purpose for reading. To get the most from the nonfiction that you take the time to read, it's important to adjust your reading rate.

Get Your Mind in Gear As your mind rides across the page, make sure it has all the gears it needs to meet your goals. These are some of the ways you might approach nonfiction:

- ▶ **Reading for mastery** Slow reading to memorize facts, understand ideas, and test what is said against your own experience
- ▶ **Attentive reading** Somewhat quicker reading to take in the main ideas and the facts that support them
- ▶ **Skimming** Quick reading to capture the main ideas without focusing on details
- ▶ **Scanning** Quick reading to find specific information by looking for key words in the headings and the text

Learn How to Shift Some kinds of reading require you to be able to shift rapidly from one gear to another. Keep your purpose in mind, and allow yourself to scan at some times and read more attentively at others.

Apply the Strategies

1. You have just picked up Dr. Robert D. Ballard's *The Discovery of the* Titanic. You want to identify the chapter in which Ballard finds the *Titanic*. In looking at the table of contents, what reading rate would you use to do this? Explain.
2. On this page, you'll find an excerpt from Ballard's book. What reading rate would you use to discover the main idea of this passage from the book? Explain your choice.
3. State the main idea of this passage in your own words.

Titanic Found!

Suddenly, out of the gloom, the Boat Deck of the ship came into view. We were on the port side looking at what appeared to be a stack opening—but the funnel was gone, the same forward funnel that had fallen into the water a few minutes before the ship sank, nearly hitting collapsible B, to which a handful of survivors—including Second Officer Lightoller, Colonel Gracie, and Marconi Operator Bride—had been clinging for dear life. Miraculously, its wash had pushed them clear of the hull just in time.

Then I saw it, just off to the starboard side of the bridge—the unmistakable image of a boat davit; and suddenly it hit me square in the stomach. Empty davits: not enough lifeboats.

Before we knew it, Argo had safely passed out over the starboard bow railing and back into the featureless murk. All at once, the bottled-up excitement in the crowded van exploded. People were whooping, hugging, and dancing around . . .

✔ *These types of nonfiction often call for varied reading rates:*

- ▶ Newspaper articles
- ▶ Essays in magazines
- ▶ Written directions

Introduce the Strategies

Discuss with students how they read textbooks for their different school subjects. Ask them what kind of reading strategies they use to get the most out of their assigned reading. Do they take notes? Do they reread? Encourage volunteers to explain their methods and what advantages they provide.

After students have read about the different reading rates on this page, write the following headings on the board and ask students to suggest different types of nonfiction that they might read at each rate.

Reading for Mastery	Attentive Reading	Skimming	Scanning
text-books	newspaper or magazine	movie review	movie listings
	articles, resource materials for a report		

Customize for
Less Proficient Readers
Encourage students to practice different reading rates for nonfiction. They might skim a passage first, and then reread the passage aloud, pausing to note important facts or ideas.

Apply the Strategies

Have students review the strategies for success before they attempt to apply them. Encourage them to consider which of the strategies they have used before and for what types of nonfiction. Remind them that a combination of these strategies may be helpful when approaching a difficult reading assignment.

Answers

Possible responses:

1. You would scan the table of contents to pick up any words in the chapter titles to clue you in to the finding of the *Titanic*.
2. You would read attentively to get to the main idea but not necessarily master all the facts.
3. Ballard is describing finding the *Titanic*, using a robot named Argo passing from the port side to the starboard side of the boat.

◆Build Grammar Skills

Adjective and Adverb Clauses
The selections in Part 2 include instruction on the following:

- Adverb Clauses
- Adjective Clauses

This instruction is reinforced with the Build Grammar Skills practice pages in **Selection Support,** pp. 176 and 181.

As you review adjective and adverb clauses, you may also wish to review the grammar skills from Unit 6, Part 1:

- Clauses

A clause is a group of words with its own subject and verb. An independent (main) clause has a subject and verb and can stand by itself as a complete sentence. A subordinate clause has a subject and a verb but is only part of a sentence.

- Simple and Compound Sentences

A simple sentence consists of one independent clause, and a compound sentence consists of two or more independent clauses.

- Complex Sentences

A complex sentence contains one independent clause and one or more subordinate clauses.

Customize for
Less Proficient Readers
Help students begin to identify clauses in the sentences by having them look for introductory words. Then have them ask, "What question does this clause answer?" They can refer to the chart on this page to see which relationships are expressed by adverb clauses and which are expressed by adjective clauses.

Writer's Solution

For additional practice and support with adjective and adverb clauses, use the practice pages on adjective and adverb clauses, pp. 52–53, in the *Writer's Solution Grammar Practice Book.*

Adverb and Adjective Clauses

Grammar Review

Two types of subordinate clauses are **adverb clauses** and **adjective clauses.** Adverb clauses are used as adverbs, modifying a verb, an adjective, or an adverb (see page 520). Adjective clauses are used as adjectives to modify a noun or pronoun in another clause (see page 540).

There are a number of different words that introduce adverb and adjective clauses, linking them to the rest of the sentence.

Introductory Words for Adverb Clauses

Relationship Expressed	Subordinating Conjunctions
Time (*when?*)	after, as, as soon as, before, until, when, whenever, while
Place (*where?*)	where, wherever
Reason (*why?*)	because, in order that, since, so that
Condition (*under what circumstances?*)	although, even if, even though, if, provided that, though, unless
Manner (*how?*)	as, as if, as though, than

Introductory Words for Adjective Clauses

Relative Pronouns	that, which, who, whoever, whom, whose
Relative Adverbs	where, when

Practice 1 On your paper, write the subordinate clauses in the sentences that follow. Identify each as an adverb or adjective clause. Then, underline the word that introduces each clause. Beside each clause, write the word or phrase it modifies.

1. Although Iona, who is a cab driver, wants to talk about his son, none of his passengers will listen.
2. Leah distrusts everyone because she cannot forget the concentration camp where her mother and brother died.
3. When the Communists took over China, Stacy's grandmother fled to Hong Kong, which was under British rule.
4. Lemon Brown still carries the harmonica that he played when he was a famous blues musician.

Practice 2 Rewrite each set of sentences as one sentence. Use the word given in parentheses to make one sentence an adverb or adjective clause.

1. Elements of short stories include setting and theme. Short stories are a type of fiction. (*which*)
2. The setting is very important. It drives the action. (*when*)
3. To determine the theme, you must look for the clues. The clues are found throughout the story. (*that*)

Grammar in Writing

✔ *If a clause starts with a word that introduces an adverb or adjective clause, it cannot stand by itself as a complete sentence. Adverb and adjective clauses must be linked to main clauses.*

Answers

Practice 1

1. Although Iona wants to talk about his son (adverb clause) modifies *will listen;* who is a cab driver (adjective clause) modifies *Iona*
2. because she cannot forget the concentration camp (adverb clause) modifies *distrusts;* where her mother and brother died (adjective clause) modifies *camp*
3. When the Communists took over China (adverb clause) modifies *fled;* which was under British rule (adjective clause) modifies *Hong Kong*
4. that he played (adjective clause) modifies *harmonica;* when he was a famous blues musician (adverb clause) modifies *played*

Practice 2

1. Elements of short stories, which are a type of fiction, include setting and theme.
2. The setting is very important when it drives the action.
3. To determine the theme, you must look for the clues that are found throughout the story.

Speaking, Listening, and Viewing Workshop

Follow Oral Directions

Every day, your teachers, parents, and friends pass along important information. In some situations, you are specifically told that they are giving you directions; in other cases, you just know that they'll expect you to know how to do something very soon. Whether your sister is telling you to be home for dinner at six o'clock or your friend is asking to borrow your math or your history notes, careful listening is the key. If you follow directions, you'll avoid any confusion or trouble down the road.

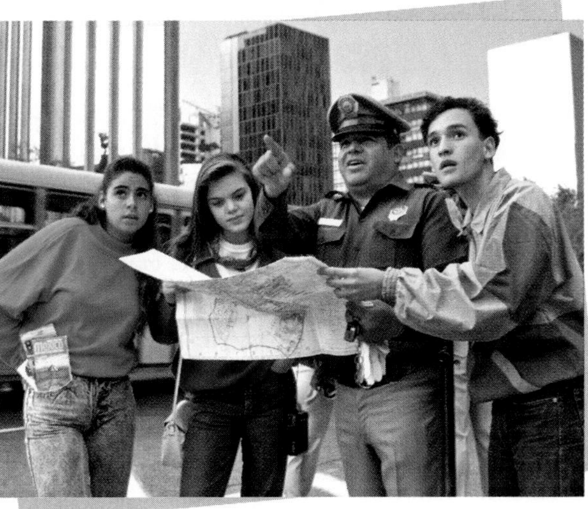

Pay Attention to Key Words

Every sentence spoken to you contains key words that get to the heart of the message. If your teacher tells you, "Be sure to bring two pencils and a blue notebook to class tomorrow," the words *two, pencils,* and *blue notebook* should jump out at you. Different commands or instructions will contain key words. By listening closely, you'll be able to pick them out.

Apply the Strategies

With a group of three, follow the directions in each example below.

1. As one of you gives instructions on how to check out a book from the library, the other two should take notes identifying the key steps. Compare the listeners' notes against each other and then against the speaker's.
2. One group member should create a combination of shapes on a piece of paper. Then, to help the other two create the same design, the first person should give directions. Next, compare the designs on all three pages.

Tips for Following Oral Directions

For help in following oral directions, use these hints:

- Pay attention to every word spoken.
- Look directly at the person speaking to you.
- Repeat the instructions to yourself out loud to make sure you understand them.
- If you have questions, ask.

Introduce the Strategies

Remind students that directions are often given in chronological order, so it is important to listen for the first step of the directions. While listening to directions, if students feel they may have missed a step, encourage them to ask questions, or ask the speaker to stop and repeat the steps. Point out that they may want to wait until the speaker is finished and not interrupt; and it is possible that the speaker will summarize the directions and the missed information will be repeated.

Customize for
Less Proficient Learners
Remind students that other types of key words include transition words, such as *first, next, then,* and *finally.* Listening for these transitions should help the listener form a clear idea of the order of the directions.

Apply the Strategies

Tell students that they should switch places with the others in their groups so everyone has the chance to be the person giving directions. Encourage them to repeat Practice 2, using different shape combinations to make the exercise easier or harder depending on students' success.

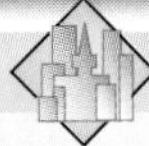

Beyond the Classroom

Workplace Skills

Following Directions Following directions is an essential skill in nearly every job. Even the president of a company must listen to the advice and directions of his or her managers and board of directors.

Discuss job situations where workers must follow directions. Then, encourage students to note situations where directions are given as they participate in team sports, observe family situations, and watch TV programs. Ask them to pay attention to whether the directions are followed correctly and if they aren't, what results.

Form groups of four or five students and have them practice giving and listening to directions. Group members can take turns as listeners, direction givers, and observers: Two group members give and listen to directions while the others observe.

You may want to offer direction scenarios such as searching for a site on the Internet, filling out a catalog order form, or programming a VCR to record a TV program.

◆Build Vocabulary

What's Behind the Words

Discuss with students that some clipped words are so commonplace that we don't even think about their full versions. For instance, people rarely refer to the midday meal as *luncheon*. Encourage students to share examples of clipped words that they typically use.

Point out that some clipped words vary from region to region. If you have students from other parts of the country or other countries, encourage them to volunteer any regional clipped words that they know.

To help students with Activity 1, suggest that they consult a dictionary to find the origin of a clipped word. The longer version of the word is usually included in the entry. For example, the entry for *fridge* reads "a refrigerator."

Answers

Activity 1

1. advertisement
2. delicatessen
3. memorandum
4. telephone
5. automobile
6. fanatic
7. opinion-editorial
8. teenager
9. omnibus
10. gasoline
11. pantaloons
12. zoological garden

Activity 2

Possible responses:
Al for Albert, Tom for Thomas, Jenny for Jennifer, Bob for Robert.

Activity 3

1. *Fab* from fabulous
2. *Coke* from Coca-Cola
3. *Fedex* from Federal Express
4. *Jell-O* from gelatin
5. *Jif* from jiffy
6. *Lux* from luxury
7. *Spray 'n Vac* from spray and vacuum
8. *Tums* from tummy

Activity 4

Possible responses:
(cara)*van*, *prof*(essor), *cord*(uroy)s, (roller)*blading*, (Inter)*net*

What's Behind the Words

Vocabulary Adventures With Richard Lederer

Clipped Words

During a typical day in your life as a student, you may attend classes and take exams in *math, lit,* or *phys ed*. You may hang out in the *gym, lab,* or *libe*, and, if you have a typical American appetite, your menu at lunch may consist of a *burger* or *frank*.

In each italicized example, people have substituted a part of the word for the whole word by clipping off the back part—*math*(ematics), *lab*(oratory), *lunch*(eon)—or the front part (ham)*burger*. Very occasionally, only the middle part of the word is retained, as in *flu* (influenza) and *fridge* (refrigerator).

Compact words

There are scores of words that are clipped in our language. Their popularity arises because people want to communicate as concisely and quickly as possible. They will take advantage of the opportunity to speak or write only part of a word to make themselves understood, especially when the word is one that people use frequently.

The name is the game

You can see this theory at work in the formations of nicknames. When we come to know people well, we usually address them using a familiar clipping of their first name. Most often we lop off the back part, as in *Al, Ben, Doug, Nick, Pam, Rich, Sam,* and *Sue*. We may clip the front of the name, as in *Beth, Becca, Gene,* and *Tina*. Or we may clip away both the front and the back, as in *Liz, Trish,* and *Zeke* (Ezekiel).

It's an ad, ad world

Advertisers often bestow upon their products a clipped name in order to suggest, in a snappy and space-saving way, some outstanding quality of their particular concoction—*Fab, Coke, Fedex, Jell-O, Jif, Lux, Spray 'n Vac,* and *Tums*.

The clip art

It's safe to predict that clipping will remain a productive process for forming new words—an emblem of our impulse as a modern society to scrunch the most meaning into the smallest space.

ACTIVITY 1 From which longer words do the following common clippings derive?

1. ad	**7.** op-ed
2. deli	**8.** teen
3. memo	**9.** bus
4. phone	**10.** gas
5. auto	**11.** pants
6. fan	**12.** zoo

ACTIVITY 2 Make a list of clipped first names of students in your class.

ACTIVITY 3 Identify the longer words from which the brand names mentioned above are coined. How many more examples can you find in your local supermarket?

ACTIVITY 4 In a group, brainstrom for a list of other clipped words you know.

Short stories allow you to take a brief journey to another time or place or to take a quick step in another person's shoes. These collections of stories offer you endless chances for such armchair travel.

Suggested Titles

The Red Pony
John Steinbeck

Written by the Nobel Prize-winning American author John Steinbeck, *The Red Pony* is a book of four related stories that trace the growing pains of a young boy named Jody. In the best-known story, "The Gift," Jody's father gives him a red pony. Jody trains and cares for the pony he loves. However, he discovers there are some tragedies from which he cannot protect the animal. Combined, the four stories show Jody's growth and maturity as he learns to respect life and the land and the people he knows.

Fifty Short Science Fiction Tales
Isaac Asimov and Groff Conklin, Editors

Isaac Asimov—the man who helped make science fiction what it is today—brings together fifty tales of wonder and delight. He presents tales that inspire us with their original views of the future or faraway places. He includes stories that amaze us with their unique technological advances and all the problems these advances bring. Contributing authors to this collection include such favorites as Jack Finney, Isaac Asimov, Robert Heinlein, Arthur Clarke, and Antony Boucher.

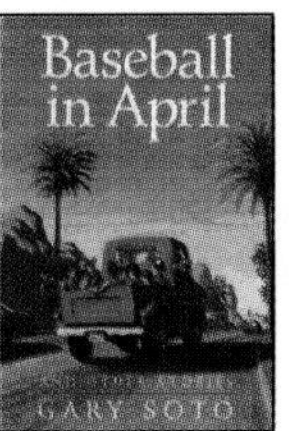

Baseball in April and Other Stories
Gary Soto

In a collection of eleven short stories, Gary Soto focuses on the everyday lives of Hispanic young people growing up in Fresno, California. Through such ordinary events as Little League tryouts, a first date, and a performance in the school talent show, each story shows readers the hopes, desires, and troubles that go along with being a teenager.

Other Possibilities

American Eyes: New Asian American Short Stories for Young Adults	Lori M. Carlson, Editor
Connections: Short Stories	Donald Gallo
8 Plus 1	Robert Cormier

Planning Students' Extended Reading
All of the works listed on this page are good choices for reading short stories. Following is some information that may help you choose which to teach.

Customize for
Varying Student Needs
When assigning these extended reading selections to your students, keep in mind the following factors:

- *The Red Pony* is a classic collection of four short stories by John Steinbeck. There are some sensitive issues listed below.
- *Fifty Short Science Fiction Tales* is a collection of short stories, a few of which are only a page long. These stories allow students to explore surroundings much different from their own. Some of these stories provide an opportunity for discussing the pros and cons of technology in our world.
- *Baseball in April and Other Stories* is a collection of 11 vignettes by acclaimed young adult author Gary Soto. Set in a Mexican American neighborhood in California, these stories offer an opportunity to talk about cultural diversity.

Sensitive Issues The first story in *The Red Pony* includes the death of an animal and the killing of a bird. You may wish to use caution when recommending this book to readers for whom violence to animals is a personally sensitive issue. However, this book may provide excellent discussion opportunities about the realities of animal death and the laws of nature.

Literature Study Guides
A literature study guide is available for *The Red Pony*. This guide includes section summaries, discussion questions, and activities.

Planning Instruction and Assessment

Unit Objectives

1. To read nonfiction selections
2. To apply a variety of reading strategies, particularly strategies for reading nonfiction, appropriate for reading these selections
3. To recognize literary elements used in these selections
4. To increase vocabulary
5. To learn elements of grammar and usage
6. To write in a variety of modes about situations based on the selections
7. To develop speaking and listening skills, by completing activities
8. To view images critically and create visual representations

Meeting the Objectives Each selection provides instructional material and portfolio opportunities by which students can meet unit objectives. You will find additional practice pages for reading strategies, literary elements, vocabulary, and grammar in the **Selection Support** booklet in the **Teaching Resources** box.

Setting Goals Work with your students at the beginning of the unit to set goals for unit outcomes. Plan what skills and concepts you wish students to acquire. You may match instruction and activities according to students' performance levels or learning modalities.

Portfolios Students may keep portfolios of their completed work or of their work in progress. The Build Your Portfolio page of each selection provides opportunities for students to apply the concepts presented.

Humanities: Art

The Mellow Pad, 1945–1951, by Stuart Davis

Stuart Davis (1894–1964) worked as a magazine illustrator, a cartoonist, and a World War I cartographer. His paintings reflect the energy of modern urban life. Many of his paintings resemble collages, such as *The Mellow Pad,* one of his best-known works.

1. What words or letters do you see in the painting? *The words* mellow pad *and* the, *the letters* s *and* x, *and other letter-shapes.*
2. What about this painting reminds you of America? *Students may say the colors or shapes represent the different kinds of people in America.*

The Mellow Pad, 1945–51, Stuart Davis, The Brooklyn Museum, © Estate of Stuart Davis/Licensed by VAGA, New York, NY

Art Transparencies

The **Art Transparencies** booklet in the **Teaching Resources** box offers fine art to help students make connections to other curriculum areas and high-interest topics.

To connect to the art on this page, and to the nonfiction selections that address American life in Unit 7, use Art Transparency 10, p. 43, *Buffalo Road III—Choice* by Peter Jemison. Like Davis's painting, this mixed media work combines American images. Use one of the booklet's activities to help students explore the art through discussion, a writing activity, or oral interpretation.

Beyond Literature

Each unit presents Beyond Literature features that lead students into an exploration of careers, communities and other subject areas. In this unit, students will explore careers in journalism, and make sports and community connections. In addition, the **Teaching Resources** box contains a **Beyond Literature** booklet of activities. Using literature as a springboard, these activity pages offer students opportunities to connect literature to other curriculum areas and to the workplace and careers, community, media, and humanities.

UNIT 7

Nonfiction

Many people who love reading believe that the most interesting literature being written today is nonfiction. The subjects of nonfiction writing are real people, and the events are actual happenings. There are many specific types of nonfiction. Following are the types you'll encounter in this unit:

- A **biography** is the life story of someone written by another person.
- An **autobiography** is a writer's own life story.
- An **expository essay** provides information about a single subject.
- A **narrative essay** tells the story of an actual event.
- A **personal essay** is an informal account of a person's experiences.
- A **reflective essay** reveals a writer's thoughts about an idea or experience.
- A **persuasive essay** presents an argument and attempts to convince readers of this position.

Connections

Within this unit, you will find selections and activities that make connections beyond literature. Use these selections to connect students' understanding and appreciation of literature beyond the traditional literature and language arts curriculum.

Encourage students to connect literature to other curriculum areas. You may wish to coordinate with teachers in other curriculum areas to determine ways to team teach and further extend instruction.

Connections to Today's World

Use these selections to guide students to recognize the relevance of literature to contemporary writings. In this unit, students will read an essay that provides strategies for using the Internet, "Let the Reader Beware: Tips for Verifying Information on the Internet."

Connecting Literature to Social Studies

Each unit contains a selection that connects Literature to Social Studies. In this unit, students will read about an ancient city, looking at maps, drawings, and photographs in the visual essay, "Tenochtitlan: Inside the Aztec Capital."

Assessing Student Progress

The tools that are available to measure the degree to which students meet the unit objectives are listed below.

Informal Assessment

The questions in the Guide for Responding sections are a first level of response to the concepts and skills presented with the selection. As a brief, informal measure of students' grasp of the material, these responses indicate where further instruction and practice are needed. The practice pages in the **Selection Support** booklet provide for this type of instruction and practice.

You will also find literature and reading guides in the **Alternative Assessment** booklet, which students can use for informal assessment of their individual performances.

Formal Assessment

The **Formal Assessment** booklet contains Selection Tests and Unit Tests.

Selection Tests measure comprehension and skills acquisition for each selection or group of selections.

Each Unit Test provides students with 30 multiple-choice questions and 5 essay questions designed to assess students' knowledge of the literature and skills taught in the unit.

Each Alternative Unit Test: Standardized-Test Practice provides 15 multiple-choice questions and 3 essay questions based on two new literature selections not contained in the student book. The questions on the Alternative Unit Test are designed to assess students' ability to compare and contrast selections, applying skills taught in the unit.

Alternative Assessment

For portfolio and alternative assessment, the **Alternative Assessment** booklet contains Scoring Rubrics, Assessment sheets, and Learning Modalities activities.

Scoring Rubrics provide writing modes that can be applied to Writing activities, Writing Mini-Lessons, and Writing Process Workshop lessons.

Assessment sheets for speaking and listening activities provide peer and self-assessment direction.

Learning Modalities activities appeal to different learning styles. Use these as an alternative measurement of students' growth.

OBJECTIVES

1. To read, comprehend, and interpret an expository essay
2. To relate an expository essay to personal experience
3. To apply strategies for reading nonfiction
4. To recognize the characteristics of an expository essay
5. To build vocabulary in context and learn the prefix *inter-*
6. To recognize the four functions of sentences
7. To write an essay of praise in which all main points are clearly expressed
8. To respond to an expository essay through writing, speaking and listening, and projects

SKILLS INSTRUCTION

Vocabulary: Prefixes: *inter-*
Spelling: Changing Adjectives Using *-able* to Noun Forms Using *-ility*
Grammar: The Four Functions of Sentences
Reading for Success: Strategies for Reading Nonfiction
Literary Focus: Expository Essay
Writing: Clearly Express Main Points
Speaking and Listening: Choral Reading (Teacher Edition)
Critical Viewing: Compare and Contrast; Assess

PORTFOLIO OPPORTUNITIES

Writing: Reader's Log; Limerick; How-to Essay
Writing Mini-Lesson: Essay of Praise
Speaking and Listening: Poetry Listening; Choral Reading
Projects: Anthology of Essays; Poetry Home Page

Guide for Reading

Meet the Author:

James Dickey (1923–1997)

The poet who speaks to you in this essay about the joys of poetry and real experience lived a life packed with adventure.

A Life of Action Born in Atlanta, Georgia, Dickey was a football player and motorcycle enthusiast as a young man. During World War II, he served as a radar operator. Then, for a period in the 1950's, he worked for advertising agencies in Atlanta and New York.

Dickey's literary life was active, too. In prize-winning volumes of poetry, like *Buckdancer's Choice*, he spoke of animals, hunting, and his wartime experiences. He also wrote many prose works.

The Poet as Movie Star Dickey's most famous prose work is the novel *Deliverance*, which was also made into a movie. At the end of the movie, a Southern sheriff comes to interview some crime victims. The actor who plays that big but soft-spoken sheriff is the poet himself!

THE STORY BEHIND THE STORY

Just as Dickey urges you to take a chance with poetry, he himself took a chance by plunging into it at age 24. He hadn't yet mastered poetic techniques, but he was full of enthusiasm.

◆ LITERATURE AND YOUR LIFE

CONNECT YOUR EXPERIENCE

The picture on the next page, *The Starry Night*, is familiar and strange at the same time. The artist has taken a sight familiar to you—the sky at night—and given it the strangeness of his own powerful way of seeing.

This essay explains that poets also show you common things with a strange new shine on them. As Dickey says, you can even see the sun with new eyes, through "the special spell that poetry brings to the *fact* of the sun."

THEMATIC FOCUS: Lessons Learned

How does Dickey surprise you into a better understanding of poetry?

◆ Background for Understanding

LITERATURE

As James Dickey says, poetry has been around a long time. It began not with the printed page but with the memory, the breath, and the spoken word. Thousands of years ago, before writing was invented, poets composed and recited long story-poems. They used rhythms, rhymes, and other devices to remember and compose these works. In this essay, Dickey offers advice to modern readers approaching one of the oldest literary forms.

More About the Author
James Dickey began writing poetry while working as an advertising executive for the Coca-Cola Company. Dickey often explored the theme of survival in his poems—perhaps as a result of his experiences as an athlete in school and as a pilot during World War II. As a naturalist, Dickey also wrote frequently about nature. During his lifetime, Dickey wrote over twenty books including books of poetry, novels, and criticism.

Prentice Hall Literature Program Resources

REINFORCE / RETEACH / EXTEND

Selection Support Pages
Build Vocabulary: Prefixes: *inter-*, p. 184
Build Spelling Skills, p. 185
Build Grammar Skills: Four Functions of Sentences, p. 186
Reading for Success: Strategies for Reading Nonfiction, pp. 187–188
Literary Focus: Expository Essay, p. 189
Strategies for Diverse Student Needs, pp. 67–68
Beyond Literature, Cross-Curricular Connection: Music, p. 34
Formal Assessment Selection Test, pp. 160–162, Assessment Resources Software
Alternative Assessment, p. 34
Writing and Language Transparencies KWL, p. 58; Main Idea and Supporting Details, p. 70

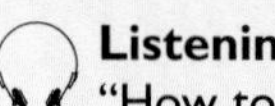

Resource Pro CD-ROM
"How to Enjoy Poetry"—includes all resource material and customizable lesson plan

Listening to Literature Audiocassettes "How to Enjoy Poetry"

MODEL SELECTION

How to Enjoy Poetry

The Starry Night, 1889, Vincent van Gogh, Oil on canvas, 29 x 36 1/4", Collection, The Museum of Modern Art, New York

◆ Literary Focus

Expository Essay

An essay is a short piece of nonfiction in which a writer presents a personal view of a topic. There are many types of essays. One of these is the **expository essay,** in which a writer explains or gives information about a subject. The title of this expository essay, "How to Enjoy Poetry," may remind you of magazine articles that explain a process. However, unlike many how-to articles, this one does not give you rules or steps to follow.

◆ Build Vocabulary

Prefixes: *inter-*

The prefix *inter-*, meaning "between" or "among," suits our computer age. Just think of the *Inter*net, a system of connections "among" computers. In his essay, Dickey uses the word *interacts,* meaning "to affect and be affected by each other."

Gather other *inter-* words with a chart like the one below.

Word Bank

Which of these words from the essay has the same root as the word *vitamin?*

prose
inevitability
interacts
vital

Preparing for Standardized Tests

Reading and Vocabulary Reading
Understanding the author's purpose will help students analyze why a selection was written. Write these passages and questions on the board:

1. Amy Lawrence Lowell was born in 1874. She was a poet and literary biographer who wrote a volume on John Keats.

The purpose of this passage is to—

(A) inform (C) tell a story
(B) state an opinion (D) send a warning

2. There's nothing like reading poetry to help a person relax. The next time you feel the world closing in, grab a book of poetry and read, read, read.

The purpose of this passage is to—

(A) educate (C) entertain
(B) persuade (D) organize ideas

Passage 1 states facts and gives information, so *(A)* is the correct answer. Passage 2 attempts to convince the reader, so *(B)* is the best answer. For additional practice with strategies for reading nonfiction, use **Selection Support,** pp. 187–188.

Interest Grabber Bring several leaves and rocks to class, and have students pass them around, feel them, smell them, and study their features carefully. Ask students to write in their journals for five minutes describing these simple natural items in detail. Explain that in this essay James Dickey asks, "What is more fascinating than a rock, if you really feel it and *look* at it, or more interesting than a leaf?" To lead students into the essay about understanding poetry, explain that Dickey believes that an appreciation of poetry begins simply—as simply as focusing on these objects from nature.

◆ Build Grammar Skills

The Four Functions of Sentences If you wish to introduce the grammar concept for this selection before students read, refer to the instruction on p. 561.

Customize for
Less Proficient Readers
Have students read aloud and discuss each of the main headings in the selection. Then ask them to write the headings on a sheet of paper. After they read the selection, have them write a short summary of each section. To facilitate a better understanding, guide a discussion of students' summaries.

Customize for
More Advanced Students
Suggest that students find examples of Dickey's poetry on the Internet or in the library. Have them select a poem to read to a small group of students. Have students list elements of Dickey's poetry that correspond to his advice about enjoying poetry.

Customize for
English Language Learners
Have students listen to the recording of "How to Enjoy Poetry." Then with partners who are proficient in English, have students discuss the main points of the essay.

Listening to Literature Audiocassettes

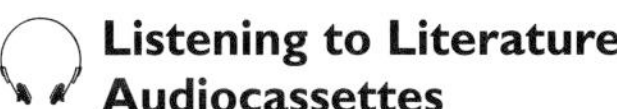

Humanities: Art

For information about *The Starry Night,* by Vincent van Gogh, see p. 559.

Reading for Success

The Reading for Success page in each unit helps readers understand authors' words and ideas on multiple levels. Good readers develop a bank of strategies from which they can draw as needed.

Unit 7 introduces strategies for reading nonfiction. Many students who do quite well at reading fiction find themselves at a loss in social studies or science classes because reading nonfiction sometimes requires a different approach from that used to read fiction.

Strategies for reading nonfiction help students set a purpose for reading, then identify the author's main points and purpose for writing. These strategies are modeled with "How to Enjoy Poetry." Each green box shows an example of the thinking process involved in applying one of these strategies. Additional notes provide support for applying the strategies throughout the selection.

How to Use the Reading for Success Page

- Introduce the strategies for reading nonfiction, presenting each as a problem-solving procedure.
- Before students read the essay, have them preview it, looking at the annotations in the green boxes that model the strategies.
- To reinforce these strategies after students have read the story, have them do the Reading for Success, pp. 187–188, in **Selection Support.** These pages help students practice literal comprehension strategies by writing their own annotations.

Reading Strategies: Support and Reinforcement

Using Boxed Annotations and Prompts

Throughout the unit, the notes in green, red, and maroon boxes are intended to help students apply reading strategies, understand the literary focus, and make a connection with their lives. You may use boxed material in these ways:

- Have students pause at each box and respond to its prompt before they continue reading.
- Urge students to read through the selection, ignoring the boxes. After they complete the selection, they may go back and review the text, responding to the prompts.

Reading for Success

Strategies for Reading Nonfiction

You're bombarded with facts and ideas from every direction. When you scan a cereal box, read a textbook, or cruise the Internet, you make decisions about what, who, and how much to believe. These strategies will help you read the nonfiction you encounter every day.

Set a purpose for reading.

A nonfiction work can cover a lot of territory. To give yourself a reason to read, use your own questions to guide you. Include the questions—and the answers—in a KWL chart, like this one:

K	W	L
What do I *know* about the subject?	What do I *want* to know about it?	What have I *learned* about it?
(Fill this in before you read.)	(Fill this in before and as you read.)	(Fill this in after you have read.)

Identify the author's main points.

Usually, an author wants to convey one or two main ideas. The rest of the information supports those ideas. Look for the main points at the beginning or end of the work. Other clues to the main ideas are signal words like *summary*, *conclusion*, and *meaning*.

Recognize the organization.

If you recognize how the work is organized, you'll be able to read it more easily. Here are some general ways in which authors organize nonfiction:

Chronological Order: Earliest event → latest event

Order of Importance: Most important item → least important item

Spatial Order: left → right ***or*** top → bottom

Understand the author's purpose.

You can better approach a nonfiction work if you understand why it was written. To identify the author's purpose, look for clues like these:

Clue	Purpose
Silly or exaggerated situations	to amuse
Advice to believe or do something	to persuade
Facts or explanations	to inform

As you read the following essay by James Dickey, look at the notes in the boxes. The notes demonstrate how to apply these strategies to a work of literature.

Model a Reading Strategy: Identify the Author's Main Points

Tell students that when they read nonfiction, it is important to identify the author's main points, and decide whether the author supports these ideas with details. Help students identify main points and look for supporting material by modeling this kind of thinking:

> In the last section of Dickey's essay, he says, "you will begin to see things by means of words, and words by means of things." I think this statement says a lot about reading poetry and I know that the author placed it near the end of his essay, so I think it may be one of his main points. When I look back through the essay, I find information that supports this idea. For instance, in the "Where to Start" section Dickey states, "Think and feel," and then suggests questions to help understand Mark Van Doren's poem. He also says that rhyme helps you believe and keep an idea. Then I look back at the end of the essay again and see that the rest of the information in the section also supports the idea.

MODEL

How to Enjoy POETRY

James Dickey

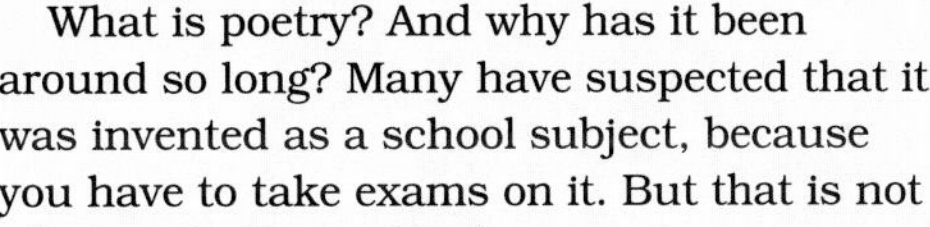

What is poetry? And why has it been around so long? Many have suspected that it was invented as a school subject, because you have to take exams on it. But that is not what poetry is or why it is still around. That's not what it feels like, either. When you really feel it, a new part of you happens, or an old part is renewed, with surprise and delight at being what it is. ❷

> **Set a purpose** for reading. Jot down what you want to learn about poetry and how this information might help you enjoy it more.

Where Poetry Is Coming From

From the beginning, people have known that words and things, words and actions, words and feelings, go together, and that they can go together in thousands of different ways, according to who is using them. Some ways go shallow, and some go deep.

Your Connection With Other Imaginations

The first thing to understand about poetry is that it comes to you from outside you, in books or in words, but that for it to live, something from within you must come to it and meet it and complete it. Your response with your own mind and body and memory and emotions gives the poem its ability to work its magic; if you give to it, it will give to you, and give plenty.

When you read, don't let the poet write down to you; read up to him. Reach for him from your gut out, and the heart and muscles will come into it, too.

Simultaneous Contrasts: Sun and Moon, 1913, Robert Delaunay, Collection, The Museum of Modern Art

▲ Critical Viewing How does this painting—subtitled *Sun and Moon*—compare with *The Starry Night* on page 555? [Compare and Contrast] ❶

Develop Understanding

One-Minute Insight In "How to Enjoy Poetry," James Dickey explains that poets select words to describe things, actions, or feelings that we can all recognize. In turn, readers interact with these words by comparing them with their own experiences. Thus readers draw from their own experiences to enjoy a poem that expresses another person's point of view. Dickey felt that the more a person can experience the beauty and rhythm of poetic language, the more that person will create new connections and ultimately understand new meanings.

▶Critical Viewing◀

❶ **Compare and Contrast** *Both paintings show natural objects in the sky; both artists used dark blue and green with orange and yellow. While* The Starry Night *is more realistic, both artists have created a very personal view of something we all see and know.*

◆ Literary Focus

❷ **Expository Essay** Point out that the main idea of an expository essay is often stated in the first paragraph. Ask students to identify the sentence that states the main idea in this paragraph. *"When you really feel it, a new part of you happens, or an old part is renewed, with surprise and delight at being what it is."*

Humanities: Art

Simultaneous Contrasts: Sun and Moon, 1913, by Robert Delaunay

Explain that this style of painting, called Orphism, is based on Cubism, an artistic style in which the artist attempts to show different views of the same object all at once. In this painting, the viewer must interact with the artwork by deciding which shapes represent the sun and moon.

1. How would you interpret this painting? *Possible response: By placing the moon and sun in a circle, the artist shows that natural objects are interconnected and continuous—unending like a circle.*
2. How is the painting like a poem? *It is like a poem because it shows one person's interpretation of familiar things.*

Block Scheduling Strategies

Consider these suggestions to take advantage of extended class time:

- Review the Background for Understanding, p. 554, then ask students why they think some people don't enjoy reading poetry. Explain that this selection was written for those people, as well as for people who enjoy poetry. After reading, have students form groups to discuss the Critical Thinking questions, p. 560.
- Before students read the selection, introduce the Reading for Success strategies, p. 556. Distribute the KWL Organizer from **Writing and Language Transparencies,** p. 58, for students to use before, during, and after reading. Suggest that small groups review their completed charts. Then have students apply all the reading strategies as they annotate the Reading for Success practice selection, pp. 187–188, in **Selection Support.**
- Have Verbal/Linguistic Learners, Visual/Spatial Learners, and Interpersonal Learners work together to create graphics and text for the How-to Essay and/or the Poetry Home Page in the Idea Bank, p. 562.

Reading for Success

❶ Set a Purpose for Reading After students have read this section, ask them if any of the questions from their KWL Organizers have been answered. Has the information in these sections made them think of new questions to add to the chart?

Reading for Success

❷ Understanding Author's Purpose Ask students what this sentence shows about the author's purpose for writing. *The sentence tells the reader to open up to the moment in order to understand the world. The author's purpose is to persuade the reader to enjoy every moment and to discover the mystery of existence in a simple object.*

◆ Literature and Your Life

❸ After students have read these lines, ask them to name objects that have caused them to reflect on the beauty of the world. Have they been awed by the beauty of any objects listed in the poem? *Encourage students to elaborate by giving details of the objects they find beautiful.*

Customize for *Visual/Spatial Learners* Have students reread the next to last paragraph on this page. Discuss Dickey's suggestion that the reader personalize the images that a poet paints with words. Encourage students to draw their own personal versions of the horse, corn, brambles, or river.

Which Sun? Whose Stars?

These boldface headings are clues to the **organization.** Each section gives different tips for enjoying poetry.

The sun is new every day, the ancient philosopher Heraclitus[1] said. The sun of poetry is new every day, too, because it is seen in different ways by different people who have lived under it, lived with it, responded to it. Their lives are different from yours, but by means of the special spell that poetry brings to the *fact* of the sun—everybody's sun; yours, too—you can come into possession of many suns: as many as men and women have ever been able to imagine. Poetry makes possible the deepest ❶ kind of personal possession of the world.

The most beautiful constellation in the winter sky is Orion,[2] which ancient poets thought looked like a hunter, up there, moving across heaven with his dog Sirius.[3] What is this hunter made out of stars hunting for? What does he mean? Who owns him, if anybody? The poet Aldous Huxley[4] felt that he did, and so, in Aldous Huxley's universe of personal emotion, he did.

Up from among the emblems of the
wind into its heart of power,
The Huntsman climbs, and all his
living stars
Are bright, and all are mine.

Where to Start

The beginning of your true encounter with poetry should be simple. It should bypass all classrooms, all textbooks, courses, examinations, and libraries and go straight to the things that make your own existence exist: to your body and nerves and blood and muscles. Find your own way—a secret way that just maybe you don't know yet—to open yourself as wide as you can and as deep as you can to the moment, the *now* of your own existence and the endless mystery of it, and perhaps at the same time to one other thing that is not you, but is out there: a handful of gravel is a good place to start. So is an ice cube—what more mysterious and beautiful *interior* of something has there ever been? ❷

Dickey continues to say that poetry is not just a classroom subject. One of his **main points** seems to be that readers should find their "own way" to poetry.

As for me, I like the sun, the source of all living things, and on certain days very good-feeling, too. "Start with the sun," D. H. Lawrence[5] said, "and everything will slowly, slowly happen." Good advice. And a lot *will* happen.

What is more fascinating than a rock, if you really feel it and *look* at it, or more interesting than a leaf?

Horses, I mean; butterflies, whales;
Mosses, and stars; and gravelly
Rivers, and fruit. ❸

Oceans, I mean; black valleys; corn;
Brambles, and cliffs; rock, dirt, dust,
ice . . .

Go back and read this list—it is quite a list, Mark Van Doren's[6] list!—item by item. Slowly. Let each of these things call up an image out of your own life.

Think and feel. What moss do you see? Which horse? What field of corn? What brambles are *your* brambles? Which river is most yours?

The Poem's Way of Going

Part of the spell of poetry is in the rhythm of language, used by poets who understand how powerful a factor rhythm can be, how compelling and unforgettable. Almost anything put into rhythm and rhyme is more memorable than the same thing said in prose. Why this is, no one knows completely,

1. **Heraclitus** (her′ ə klī′ təs): Greek philosopher who lived about 500 B.C.
2. **Orion** (ō rī′ ən)
3. **Sirius** (sir′ ē əs)
4. **Aldous Huxley:** English poet, essayist, and novelist (1894–1963).
5. **D. H. Lawrence:** English poet and novelist (1885–1930).
6. **Mark Van Doren:** American poet, teacher, and critic (1894–1972).

Speaking and Listening Mini-Lesson

Choral Reading

This mini-lesson supports the Speaking and Listening activity in the Idea Bank on p. 562.

Introduce Explain that in a choral reading, a group reads together, the way a chorus sings together. During the reading, individuals, small groups, or the entire chorus take turns reading the words. This varied grouping of voices gives rich texture to the reading and adds interest to the words.

Develop Divide students into groups, and then have them follow these steps:

- Select a poem that lends itself to a variety of expression.
- Use punctuation marks as cues for pacing and pauses.
- Use tone of voice, volume, and pacing to express the poem's mood.
- Enunciate every word clearly.
- Decide which individual voices, or groups of voices, should perform specific lines.
- Practice the reading.

Apply Have students perform their choral readings. Students may want to record their readings on audiotape.

Assess Evaluate students' readings on diction and how well they express the poem's mood. You may also want to have students assess their listening skills using the Listening: Self-Assessment form, p. 108, in **Alternative Assessment.**

The Starry Night, 1889, Vincent van Gogh, Oil on canvas, 29 x 36 1/4", Collection, The Museum of Modern Art, New York

4 ▲ Critical Viewing Dickey says that a poet in some ways "owns" what he or she describes. In Dickey's sense of the word, does Vincent Van Gogh "own" the night sky he painted here? **[Assess]**

though the answer is surely rooted far down in the biology by means of which we exist; in the circulation of the blood that goes forth from the heart and comes back, and in the repetition of breathing. Croesus[7] was a rich Greek king, back in the sixth century before Christ, but this tombstone was not his:

5 *No Croesus lies in the grave you see;*
I was a poor laborer, and this suits me.

That is plain-spoken and definitive. You believe it, and the rhyme helps you believe it and keep it.

Some Things You'll Find Out

Writing poetry is a lot like a contest with yourself, and if you like sports and games and competitions of all kinds, you might like to try writing some. Why not? 6

The possibilities of rhyme are great. Some of the best fun is in making up your own limericks. There's no reason you can't invent limericks about anything that comes to your mind. No reason. Try it.

The problem is to find three words that rhyme and fit into a meaning. "There was a young man from . . ." *Where* was he from? What situation was he in? How can these things fit into the limerick form—a form everybody knows—so that the rhymes "pay off," and give that sense of completion and inevitability

7. **Croesus** (krē´ səs)

◆ **Build Vocabulary**

prose (prōz) *n.:* Nonpoetic language

inevitability (in ev´ ə tə bil´ i tē) *n.:* Certainty

Humanities: Art

The Starry Night, 1889, by Vincent van Gogh

Although his work was not well known during his lifetime, Vincent van Gogh is now the most widely recognized Postimpressionist painter. With its strong colors and bold brush strokes, *The Starry Night* is characteristic of his recognizable painting style.

Vincent van Gogh spent the last two years of his life in southern France. In spite of his struggles with mental illness and dejection over his lack of commercial success, he produced some of his most important artworks, including *The Starry Night,* during those years.

Use the following questions for discussion:

1. Why do you think van Gogh chose to paint this scene? *Possible response: He wanted to capture the beauty of the night sky by showing his personal impression of it.*
2. How is the painting like the poetry that James Dickey describes? *Possible response: In the same way that poets use words, van Gogh used colors, lines, and shapes to create an idea that reaches out to the viewer. Van Gogh exaggerated the night sky to call attention to his feelings.*

▶Critical Viewing◀

4 **Assess** Discuss the unique view of the sky depicted in the image. *Students may say that the artist owns the sky in the artwork because it is his personal view of it, one that no one else can imagine. The bold brushstrokes and colors express his sense of ownership.*

Reading for Success

5 **Identify the Author's Main Points** Have a volunteer read this poem aloud. Point out that the poem helps to support one of Dickey's main ideas. Ask students what idea it is. *He includes this poem to show how rhythm and rhyme make an idea more memorable.*

◆Build Grammar Skills

6 **The Four Functions of Sentences** Lead students to note the question mark at the end of this sentence. Explain that one function of a sentence is to ask a question. Ask students what purpose they think this question serves. *Students may say that Dickey wants readers to ask this question of themselves. The purpose of the question is to persuade the reader to try writing poetry.*

Customize for
English Language Learners
Students may need extra help with the phrase "rooted far down in the biology by means of which we exist." Breathe slowly and deeply, inviting students to imitate you. Then pat your chest to imitate the rhythm of a heartbeat. Explain that Dickey feels that the importance of rhythm in poetry is based on the rhythms of the human body.

Customize for
Musical/Rhythmic Learners
Tell students that the painting *The Starry Night* moved singer Don McLean to write a song about van Gogh called "Vincent." If possible, locate a recording so that the students can hear the song. Students may want to discuss McLean's poetic song lyrics and use of language; lyrics to the song can be found at the following Internet site: **http://www.rpi.edu/~holtd/Mclean/Songsf/vincent.htm**

We *strongly recommend* that you preview this site before you send students to it. (All Web sites are subject to change.)

◆Critical Thinking

1 Analyze Ask students what they think Dickey means when he says that poetry will deepen one's life. *Poets cause readers to consider objects, feelings, and ideas from another person's point of view. As a result, the reader makes new connections which lead to greater understanding.*

Reinforce and Extend

Answers

◆Literature and Your Life

Reader's Response Some students may say that they know they like a poem when they find themselves reading it over and over; others may say that they like poems that make them think.

Thematic Focus Reading poetry is an interactive process in which the reader must call on his or her own knowledge and experiences while also opening up to the poet's ideas.

☑ Check Your Comprehension

1. Poetry comes from outside you.
2. Each poet who writes about the sun sees it in a different way.
3. They make the words of a poem memorable.
4. He compares it to "sports and games and competitions of all kinds."
5. It causes a person to make new connections and to have new ideas.

◆Critical Thinking

1. Readers must apply their own experience and knowledge to poetry.
2. Reading poetry gives the reader "ownership" of the object described in a poem, such as the sun or a rock, because each poem provides a different view of something familiar.
3. It is like a heartbeat or the rhythm of breathing.
4. Dickey tells how to let poetry affect one's feelings rather than how to analyze its language.
5. Responses should include objects that students find beautiful or remarkable in some way.
6. Most students will point out that Dickey mentions natural objects such as the sun, a leaf, and a rock in his essay.

that is so deliciously memorable that nothing else is like it?

How It Goes With You

1 The more your encounter with poetry deepens, the more your experience of your own life will deepen, and you will begin to see things by means of words, and words by means of things.

You will come to understand the world as it interacts with words, as it can be re-created by words, by rhythms and by images.

You'll understand that this condition is one charged with vital possibilities. You will pick up meaning more quickly—and you will *create* meaning, too, for yourself and for others.

Connections between things will exist for you in ways that they never did before. They will shine with unexpectedness, wide-openness, and you will go toward them, on your own path. "Then . . ." as Dante[8] says, ". . . Then will your feet be filled with good desire." You will know this is happening the first time you say, of something you never would have noticed before, "Well, would you look at *that*! Who'd 'a thunk it?" (Pause, full of new light)

"*I* thunk it!"

Dickey explains how poetry can enrich your world. His **purpose** is to get you to read poetry with an open mind, to take a chance with it.

8. **Dante** (dän′ tā): Italian poet (1265–1321).

◆ Build Vocabulary

interacts (in′ tər akts′) *v.*: Affects and is affected by

vital (vīt′ əl) *adj.*: Essential to life; living

Guide for Responding

◆ Literature and Your Life

Reader's Response How do you know when you like a poem? What reasons do you generally give?

Thematic Focus What is the main lesson that Dickey teaches about enjoying poetry?

Poetry Gift Exchange Give someone the gift of a poem. Read the poem aloud to your partner, and explain why you like it.

☑ Check Your Comprehension

1. What is the "first thing" Dickey wants you "to understand about poetry"?
2. Why is the "sun of poetry . . . new every day"?
3. Why are rhythm and rhyme important to poetry?
4. To what kinds of activities does Dickey compare the writing of poetry?
5. According to Dickey, how can poetry enrich a person's life?

◆ Critical Thinking

Interpret

1. What does Dickey mean when he says that poetry only lives if "something from within you" meets and completes it? **[Interpret]**
2. How does poetry help you to take "personal possession of the world"? **[Interpret]**
3. In what way could the rhythm of poetry be related to human biology? **[Infer]**
4. How does Dickey's approach to enjoying poetry differ from the way that poetry is sometimes taught? **[Draw Conclusions]**

Apply

5. Dickey says you can enjoy poetry more by focusing on yourself and also on "one other thing that is not you." Which "other thing" would you choose? Why? **[Apply]**

Extend

6. Do you think that a poem could include images and ideas from the sciences? Why or why not? **[Science Link]**

Beyond the Selection

FURTHER READING

Other Works by James Dickey

The Whole Motion: Collected Poems: 1942–1995

James Dickey: The Selected Poems, 1998

Other How-to Works

How to Write a Poem, Margaret Ryan

Creative Nonfiction: How to Live It and Write It, Lee Gutkind

INTERNET

Additional information about James Dickey can be found on the Internet. We suggest the following site (all Web sites are subject to change): **http://www.pbs.org/newshour/bb/remember/1997/dickey_1-20.html**

We *strongly recommend* that you preview this site before you send students to it.

Guide for Responding (continued)

◆ Reading for Success

STRATEGIES FOR READING NONFICTION

Review the strategies for reading nonfiction and the notes showing how to apply them. Then, use what you've learned to answer these questions.

1. What purpose did you have for reading this essay?
2. What are three main points that Dickey makes in this essay?
3. Choose a phrase that best expresses the organization of this essay, and explain your choice: chronological order, order of importance, spatial order, or an informal collection of tips and suggestions.
4. In your own words, express Dickey's purpose for writing this essay.

◆ Build Vocabulary

USING PREFIXES: *inter-*

Knowing that *inter-* means "between" or "among," match each *inter-* word in the first column with its definition in the second column.

1. interview	**a.** concerning relations among nations
2. interact	**b.** a meeting between people
3. international	**c.** to make a firm joining between things
4. interlock	**d.** to affect and be affected by something

SPELLING STRATEGY

When you change certain adjectives ending in *-able* to their noun forms ending in *-ility*, you drop the *-le* ending:

inevitable + -ility = inevitability

On your paper, add *-ility to* correctly spell the noun forms of these adjectives:

1. probable **2.** irritable **3.** durable **4.** reliable

USING THE WORD BANK

Explain whether each item is true or false.

1. Usually *prose* contains many rhymes.
2. A reader who *interacts* with a poem will get more out of it.
3. For Dickey, poetry doesn't offer *vital* possibilities.
4. Rhymes that work give a poem a sense of *inevitability.*

◆ Literary Focus

EXPOSITORY ESSAY

An **expository essay** is one that explains a subject, but Dickey's essay is expository in a special way. Instead of outlining steps you can follow to enjoy poetry, he gives you a feel for what poetry is and what it can do for you. Most importantly, Dickey includes his own feelings in his explanation. When he says that poetry has to do with "the endless mystery" of your life, you know how much he values poetry.

1. Identify three facts in the opening paragraphs that explain poetry to readers.
2. Does Dickey consider poetry a subject to be studied or a way to respond to life? Explain.
3. Identify three suggestions that Dickey offers for increasing your enjoyment of poetry.
4. (a) Find a passage in which Dickey expresses his own feelings about poetry. (b) Explain how it adds to his explanation.

◆ Build Grammar Skills

THE FOUR FUNCTIONS OF SENTENCES

You can classify sentences into four categories based on their function.

- **Declarative** (making statements): The possibilities of rhyme are great.
- **Interrogative** (asking questions): Who owns him, if anybody?
- **Imperative** (giving commands): Don't let the poet write down to you; read up to him.
- **Exclamatory** (calling out or emphasizing): "*I* thunk it!"

Practice On your paper, identify which function each sentence performs.

1. What does he mean?
2. Some ways go shallow, and some go deep.
3. Try it.
4. I really enjoyed that poem!
5. New connections between things will exist for you.

Writing Application On your paper, write sentences that serve each of the four functions. Include the words *enjoy poetry* in each sentence.

Reading for Success

1. Most students will say that their purpose was to learn how to enjoy poetry.
2. You must respond to poetry with your own body and mind. Rhythm and rhyme make poetry memorable. Poetry can enrich your life.
3. Some students will say it is written in order of importance. Dickey begins and ends with his most important ideas, how to respond to poetry and why it is meaningful. In the middle sections of the essay, he discusses how to begin encountering poetry and why writing poetry is fun. Other students may say that it is more like an informal collection of tips because all the ideas are equally important.
4. He wants to persuade people to enjoy, read, and write poetry.

◆Build Vocabulary

Using the Prefix *inter-*

1. b
2. d
3. a
4. c

Spelling Strategy

1. probability
2. irritability
3. durability
4. reliability

Using the Word Bank

1. F
2. T
3. F
4. T

◆Literary Focus

1. Possible response: Words can be used to describe actions, things, and feelings. Poetry comes from outside you. Poetry makes it possible to possess the world.
2. It is a way to respond to life because it helps you make new connections and find new meanings.
3. Possible response: "Read up to the poet." Find an object that is beautiful and respond to it. Write a limerick.
4 Possible response: (a) "When you really feel it, a new part of you happens, or an old part is renewed, with surprise and delight at being what it is." (b) This adds to Dickey's explanation because it describes his surprise and delight in reading poetry.

◆Build Grammar Skills

Practice

1. interrogative
2. declarative
3. imperative
4. exclamatory
5. declarative

Writing Application

Possible responses:

1. Enjoy poetry by reading more of it.
2. I enjoy poetry most when I'm alone.
3. Did James Dickey enjoy poetry when he was young?
4. I really enjoy poetry!

Writer's Solution

For additional instruction and practice, use the lesson on Styling Sentences in the *Writer's Solution Language Lab CD-ROM*. You may also use The Four Functions of Sentences, p. 40 in the *Writer's Solution Grammar Practice Book*.

Idea Bank

Following are suggestions for matching the Idea Bank topics with your students' performance levels and learning modalities:

Customize for *Performance Levels*
Less Advanced Students: 1, 4
Average Students: 2, 4, 5, 7
More Advanced Students: 3, 5, 6, 7

Customize for *Learning Modalities*
Verbal/Linguistic: 1, 2, 3, 4, 5, 6
Interpersonal: 5, 7
Visual/Spatial: 7
Logical/Mathematical: 3
Intrapersonal: 4
Musical/Rhythmic: 4, 5

Writing Mini-Lesson

Refer students to the Writing Handbook in the back of the book for instructions on the writing process and for further information on essays. Have students use the Main Idea and Supporting Details Organizer in **Writing and Language Transparencies,** p. 70, to arrange their prewriting examples.

Writer's Solution

Writing Lab CD-ROM
Have students complete the tutorial on Expression. Follow these steps:

1. Have students record details about the benefits of their chosen activity in a Sunburst Diagram.
2. Allow students to draft on computer.
3. Encourage students to use the interactive model to see how vague language can be made more precise.

Writer's Solution Sourcebook
Have students use chapter 1, "Expression," pp. 1–31, for additional support.

Build Your Portfolio

Idea Bank

Writing

1. **Reader's Log** List the nonfiction you've read during a week. Include newspaper and magazine articles, information on packages, books, and CD liner notes.
2. **Limerick** Write a limerick—a five-line poem with three beats in the rhyming first, second, and fifth lines and two beats in the rhyming third and fourth lines. Here's an example: "A puppy whose hair was so flowing/There really was no means of knowing/Which end was his head,/Once stopped me and said,/"Please, sir, am I coming or going?"
3. **How-to Essay** Write a step-by-step explanation of a process. It can involve anything you do, such as cooking a meal, playing a musical instrument, or assembling a model airplane.

Speaking and Listening

4. **Poetry Listening** Play recordings of poets reading from their work. Hand out copies of the poems so students can follow along. Then, discuss how readers vary their speed and emphasis to convey a message. **[Performing Arts Link]**
5. **Choral Reading [Group Activity]** Choose a poem for choral reading, like "The Cremation of Sam McGee." Give a reading of the poem, with different people or groups of people reading different parts of it. **[Performing Arts Link]**

Projects

6. **Anthology of Essays** Find several essays in which a person deeply involved in a field explains it to beginners. Collect the essays in an anthology, and write a brief introduction explaining what the essays have in common.
7. **Poetry Home Page** Using Dickey's essay, design an Internet Home Page for poetry. Include ideas from the essay and quotations from poems, to encourage people to read more poetry. Also, indicate the kind of graphics that would go on the page. **[Media Link]**

Writing Mini-Lesson

Essay of Praise

Think of a sport, hobby, or subject that you love as much as James Dickey loves poetry. Then, write an essay in praise of this pursuit. Imagine that you're writing for classmates who don't necessarily share your interest or knowledge. Tell them why this activity is so rewarding and what they can do to appreciate it.

Writing Skills Focus: Clearly Express the Main Points

Get your message across by clearly expressing two or three **main points** about your interest. At the beginning of his essay, Dickey alerts readers to a main point by using the phrase "The first thing to understand . . ."

Model From the Essay

The first thing to understand about poetry is that it comes to you from outside you, in books or in words, but that for it to live, something from within you must come to it and meet it and complete it.

Prewriting After choosing the activity you'll write about, jot down three main points to convey. Also, brainstorm to gather experiences you've had that support your main points.

Drafting Imagine that you're talking to a friend about your chosen activity. Tell your friend why this pursuit is so rewarding and what he or she can do to learn more about it. Hook your friend by describing what this activity *feels* like. Add explanations later.

◆ Grammar Application

In your draft, highlight examples of the different sentence functions.

Revising Scan your Prewriting notes, making sure you've included the main points you wanted to convey. Check that you've supported these points with descriptions of your own experience and feelings.

✓ ASSESSMENT OPTIONS

Formal Assessment, Selection Test, pp. 160–162, and Assessment Resources Software. The selection test is designed so that it can easily be customized to the performance levels of your students.

Alternative Assessment, p. 34, includes options for less advanced students, more advanced students, and verbal/linguistic learners, musical/rhythmic learners, interpersonal learners, and visual/spatial learners.

PORTFOLIO ASSESSMENT
Use the following rubrics in the **Alternative Assessment** booklet to assess student writing:
Reader's Log: Technical Description/Explanation, p. 102
Limerick: Poetry, p. 95
How-to Essay: How-to/Process Explanation, p. 87
Writing Mini-Lesson: Expression, p. 81

Part 1 *Biography and Autobiography*

Self-Portrait, 1967, Andy Warhol, The Andy Warhol Foundation, Inc.

One-Minute Planning Guide

This section of the Nonfiction unit introduces examples of biography and autobiography. In "No Gumption," Russell Baker humorously recounts his entry into the business world. "The Chase" is an excerpt from Annie Dillard's autobiography about an exciting moment in a Pittsburgh winter. The biographical pieces, "Winslow Homer, America's Greatest Painter" and "Nolan Ryan, Texas Treasure" introduce two 20th-century Americans who each earned a place at the top of his field.

Customize for *Varying Students Needs*

"No Gumption"
- A short, autobiographical essay
- Set in the Depression

"The Chase"
- An excerpt from Annie Dillard's autobiography *An American Childhood*
- A personal reflection on excitement, adventure, and heroism

"Winslow Homer: America's Greatest Painter"
- A short biographical essay
- Provides an opportunity for connecting literature with art history

"Nolan Ryan, Texas Treasure"
- An easy-to-read biography of a well-known sports figure

Humanities: Art

Self-Portrait, 1967, by Andy Warhol

Andy Warhol (1928–1987) is probably the most famous artist of the 20th century. He spearheaded the avant-garde pop art movement with his silkscreened images of celebrities and consumer goods. In addition to being a painter, Warhol was also a printmaker, a photographer, a filmmaker, the producer of the rock band The Velvet Underground, the publisher of the magazine *Interview*, and the author of several books.

In much of his art—including his images of celebrities such as Marilyn Monroe and Elizabeth Taylor—Warhol explored the ideas of glamour and youth. This painting, one of a series of self-portraits, was made by enlarging a Polaroid image and then silkscreening it onto a canvas.

Have students study the painting and then ask:

1. What differences do you see in the four images that make up *Self-Portrait?* *Each image has slightly different color variations.*
2. What effect does the repetition of these images have on you? *Students may say they come to see the image as not just a face but a mixture of shape, color, and shadow.*

Prepare and Engage

OBJECTIVES

1. To read, comprehend, and interpret two autobiographical essays
2. To relate autobiographical essays to personal experience
3. To understand the author's purpose
4. To identify autobiographical writing
5. To build vocabulary in context and learn the word root *-pel-*
6. To use participles and participial phrases
7. To write a comparison-and-contrast essay, using a logical organization
8. To respond to autobiography through writing, speaking and listening, and projects

SKILLS INSTRUCTION

Vocabulary: Word Roots: *-pel-*
Spelling: Adding Suffixes
Grammar: Participial Phrases
Reading Strategy: Understand the Author's Purpose
Literary Focus: Autobiography
Writing: Organization
Speaking and Listening: Dialogue (Teacher Edition)
Viewing and Representing: Portraits (Teacher Edition)
Critical Viewing: Infer; Compare and Contrast

PORTFOLIO OPPORTUNITIES

Writing: Personality Profile; Personal Narrative; Extended Definition
Writing Mini-Lesson: Comparison-and-Contrast Essay
Speaking and Listening: Dialogue of Authors; Oral Interpretation
Projects: Book Report; Multimedia Presentation

More About the Authors
Russell Baker gained journalistic experience reporting for the *Baltimore Sun* and *The New York Times.* The second volume of his autobiography, *The Good Times,* covers this period of his life. His more recent pursuits include hosting the popular PBS series *Masterpiece Theater.*
Annie Dillard resolved to experience life more fully, following a near-fatal bout with pneumonia in 1971. She moved to Tinker Creek and kept a journal detailing her observations of nature. Over the four seasons she spent near Tinker Creek, Dillard filled more than 20 volumes, often writing for 16 hours a day.

Guide for Reading

Meet the Authors:

Russell Baker (1925–)

Nonfiction is about facts, but no one says that it can't be funny. As a newspaper columnist and author, Russell Baker has found humor in news stories and in his own life story.

Facing Economic Trouble You'll see how Baker's humor emerges even as he writes about problems he faced early in life. As a result of the country's failing economy, his family moved often in search of better opportunities.

Eventually, Baker went on to a successful career in journalism. He won a Pulitzer Prize for his "Observer" column in the *The New York Times* and another for his autobiography *Growing Up,* from which this essay comes.

Annie Dillard (1945–)

As a child, Annie Dillard loved reading, drawing, and observing the natural world. While attending college in Virginia, she lived near a creek in a valley of the Blue Ridge Mountains. In 1974, she published *Pilgrim at Tinker Creek,* which describes her exploration of that environment. The book won the Pulitzer Prize for Nonfiction.

This essay comes from *An American Childhood,* Dillard's autobiographical account of growing up in Pittsburgh, Pennsylvania.

◆ Literature and Your Life

Connect Your Experience

Imagine trying to paint someone you see only in mirrors—yourself! That's what artist Norman Rockwell did when he created the painting on the next page. Perhaps your self-portrait would include humorous touches, like Rockwell's. These selections by Russell Baker and Annie Dillard are self-portraits that use words instead of paint. Like the brush strokes of a humorous painting, some of their words will tickle your funny bone.

Thematic Focus: Moments of Insight

As you read, ask yourself what these authors discover about themselves or about life.

◆ Background for Understanding

Social Studies

"No Gumption" is set during the Depression, a period of economic troubles that began in 1929 when the value of stocks fell rapidly. By 1933, one out of every three workers in the United States was unemployed! That's why Baker's mother considers a good job so important. It wasn't until the early 1940's that the economy recovered completely.

◆ Build Vocabulary

Word Roots: *-pel-*

Since the root *-pel-* means "to drive," it gives a push to words in which it appears. Dillard writes, for example, "we compelled him to follow our route." *Compelled* means "forced." It combines *com-* ("together") and *-pelled* ("drove").

Word Bank

Which of these words from the essays appears in the titles of certain kinds of tests?

gumption
paupers
crucial
aptitude
translucent
compelled
perfunctorily

Prentice Hall Literature Program Resources

REINFORCE / RETEACH / EXTEND
Selection Support Pages
Build Vocabulary: Word Roots: *-pel-*, p. 190
Build Spelling Skills, p. 191
Build Grammar Skills: Participial Phrases, p. 192
Reading Strategy: Author's Purpose, p. 193
Literary Focus: Autobiography, p. 194
Strategies for Diverse Student Needs, p. 69
Beyond Literature Media Connection: Documentary Films, p. 35
Formal Assessment Selection Test, pp. 163–165, Assessment Resources Software
Alternative Assessment, p. 35
Writing and Language Transparencies Venn Diagram, p. 86
Daily Language Practice, p. 30
Resource Pro CD-ROM "No Gumption"; "The Chase"
Listening to Literature Audiocassettes "The Chase" from *An American Childhood*

Looking at Literature Videodisc/Videotape "No Gumption"

◆ No Gumption ◆
The Chase *from* An American Childhood

The Deadline, Norman Rockwell, Photo Courtesy of The Norman Rockwell Museum at Stockbridge

◆Literary Focus

Autobiography

Every day you tell people stories from your own life history. In an **autobiography**—the story of a person's life written by that person—a writer does the same thing in a more formal way. An autobiography includes the key events of a person's life and reveals his or her struggles, values, and ideas.

In reading these two autobiographical essays, enjoy the stories that the authors tell you, but also look deeper. Ask yourself who or what the author struggles against and what the author wants from life.

◆Reading Strategy

Understand the Author's Purpose

An **author's purpose** is his or her reason for writing. Writers of autobiography could have many different reasons for telling their life story. Their purposes might include explaining themselves and their values, teaching lessons in life, entertaining, boasting, or a combination of these.

As you read the essays, use a chart like the one below to figure out the writer's purpose or purposes:

Passage	Possible Purpose
The flaw in my character . . . was lack of "gumption."	To explain himself. To entertain by making fun of himself.

Interest Grabber Read aloud the following: "I began working in journalism when I was eight years old." Tell students that this sentence begins Russell Baker's autobiographical essay. Annie Dillard begins with the statement, "Some boys taught me to play football." Challenge students to think of experiences from their own lives that have had an important effect on them. Then ask them to compose an opening sentence for an autobiographical essay that will capture readers' interest. Invite volunteers to read their sentences aloud.

◆Build Grammar Skills

Participles and Participial Phrases If you wish to introduce the grammar concept for this selection before students read, refer to the instruction on p. 582.

Customize for
Less Proficient Readers
To help them recognize the humor in these selections, arrange students in groups and have them take turns reading aloud. Encourage them to identify humorous lines or passages and discuss what makes them funny.

Customize for
More Advanced Students
Have students review the details Dillard provides about the man who gives chase. Challenge students to write a character sketch describing the man: what he looks like, what job he has, whether or not he has children of his own, his age, and so on. Encourage students to be imaginative in their descriptions.

Humanities: Art

The Deadline, by Norman Rockwell

New York-born Norman Rockwell (1894–1978) was a popular illustrator, best known for his *Saturday Evening Post* cover illustrations. Tell students that this is a self-portrait. Ask what Rockwell's problem is? How can you tell? *He must come up with ideas for a cover illustration by a certain time and seems to be having trouble. Clues include the "Due Date" flag, the way he is scratching his head, the shuffled papers, and the title* The Deadline.

Preparing for Standardized Tests

Grammar The ability to identify and correctly use participles and participial phrases will help students perform well on the grammar portion of a standardized test. After reviewing participles and participial phrases (see Build Grammar Skills, p. 582), write the following on the board:

Identify the sentence that contains a participle and tell the word it modifies.

(A) Annie ran through the falling snow.
(B) Annie saw the snow falling.
(C) Annie ran fast through the city.
(D) Annie described the incident in an essay.

Remind students that a participle is a verb that acts as an adjective to modify a noun or pronoun. Therefore, students should realize that *(A)* is the correct answer: *falling* is used as a participle to modify *snow*. Guide students to see that while *(B)* and *(D)* both contain verbs, they are not used as participles. *(C)* contains the adjective *fast*, which is not a verb form, and therefore not a participle. For more practice with participles and participial phrases, use Build Grammar Skills in **Selection Support,** p. 192.

Develop Understanding

One-Minute Insight Russell Baker's mother is worried that her eight-year-old son shows no gumption, or incentive, so she arranges for him to work for *The Saturday Evening Post.* She hopes that selling magazines will make him more competitive and give him some ambition in life. Baker is not an enthusiastic or successful salesperson—especially in contrast with his spunky younger sister, Doris, who loves selling papers. When Baker brings home a composition that his teacher has praised, his mother suggests that maybe he could be a writer. Baker embraces the idea because he imagines that writers do not need gumption.

Customize for
English Language Learners
Arrange students of varying English proficiency levels in small groups. Working with one group at a time, read aloud the selection, stopping from time to time for students to discuss what is happening. As you read, have students note words or phrases that help them understand something about the young boy in the selection. Invite volunteers to share their ideas with the group.

◆Literary Focus

❶ **Autobiography** Ask students what clues in the opening sentence let them know that this selection is an autobiography. *Since this unit includes only nonfiction, the author's use of the pronoun I signals that he is writing about himself, and thus it is an autobiography.*

◆Critical Thinking

❷ **Interpret** After reading the first paragraph ask students what they think Mrs. Baker expects of her son. *Students will probably realize that Baker's mother wants him to be a success in life and expects him to work hard with that goal in mind.*

NO GUMPTION

Russell Baker

Block Scheduling Strategies

Consider these suggestions to take advantage of extended class time.

- After students read Connections to Today's World, p. 574, have them do an Internet search, gathering and evaluating information about a periodical such as *The Saturday Evening Post* or *The New York Times.* Alternatively, have students conduct Internet research on the Great Depression and then incorporate their findings in the Multimedia Presentation in the Idea Bank, p. 583.
- To give students practice in grammar, usage, and mechanics, have them work in small groups to complete the exercises in Week 13 of **Daily Language Practice,** p. 30.
- Students can work in discussion groups to respond to the Critical Thinking questions on pp. 573 and 581.
- Have students work in small groups, using the *Writer's Solution Writing Lab CD-ROM* to complete the Writing Mini-Lesson on p. 583.

❶ I began working in journalism when I was eight years old. It was my mother's idea. She wanted me to "make something" of myself and, after a level-headed appraisal[1] of my strengths, decided I had better start young if I was to
❷ have any chance of keeping up with the competition.

The flaw in my character which she had already spotted was lack of "gumption." My idea of a perfect afternoon was lying in front of the radio rereading my favorite Big Little Book,[2] *Dick Tracy Meets Stooge Viller*. My mother despised inactivity. Seeing me having a good time in repose, she was powerless to hide her disgust. "You've got no more gumption than a bump on a log," she said. "Get out in the kitchen and help Doris do those dirty dishes."

My sister Doris, though two years younger than I, had enough gumption for a dozen people. She positively enjoyed washing dishes, making beds, and cleaning the house. When she was only seven she could carry a piece of short-weighted cheese back to the A&P, threaten the manager with legal action, and come back triumphantly with the full quarter-pound we'd paid for and a few ounces extra thrown in for forgiveness. Doris could have made something of herself if she hadn't been a girl. Because of this defect, however, the best
she could hope for was a career as a nurse or ❸
schoolteacher, the only work that capable females were considered up to in those days.

This must have saddened my mother, this twist of fate that had allocated all the gumption to the ❹ daughter and left her with a son who was content with Dick Tracy and Stooge Viller. If disappointed, though, she wasted no energy on self-pity. She would make me make something of myself whether I wanted to or not. "The Lord helps those who help themselves," she said. That was the way her mind worked.

> ◆ **Reading Strategy** Which portions of this paragraph indicate that Baker is showing himself as less than perfect in order to entertain the reader?

She was realistic about the difficulty. Having sized up the material the Lord had given her to mold, she didn't overestimate what she

1. **appraisal** (ə prā′ zəl) *n.*: Judgment of something's or someone's quality.
2. **Big Little Book:** A small, inexpensive illustrated book that often portrayed the adventures of comic-strip heroes like Dick Tracy.

◆ **Build Vocabulary**

gumption (gump′ shən) *n.*: Courage; enterprise

◀ Critical Viewing These magazine covers are from the 1930's, when Russell Baker was a boy. What can you infer about his childhood based on these illustrations? **[Infer]** ❺

◆Critical Thinking

❸ **Draw Conclusions** Point out that, even though Baker is using humor when he refers to his sister's gender as a "defect," his reference to limited opportunities for women is historically correct. Ask students what they can tell about people's roles in society during Baker's youth from this passage. *Women did not have equal opportunity in the workplace. Women were not expected to work outside the home and those who did had few choices for careers.*

◆Reading Strategy

❹ **Understand the Author's Purpose** *Baker gently pokes fun at himself for having no gumption. He compares himself unfavorably with his younger sister in this respect and indicates that he was content with Dick Tracy and Stooge Viller.*

▶Critical Viewing◀

❺ **Infer** *Possible response: The boys are dressed differently from children today, but their activities are familiar and they are obviously having fun. Students should recognize that, even though details of his environment were different, Baker would have felt and acted much like modern eight-year-olds.*

Humanities: Periodicals

The Saturday Evening Post Claimed by its publishers to have descended from Ben Franklin's *Pennsylvania Gazette, The Saturday Evening Post* contained only sixteen unillustrated pages and had a circulation of just 2,000 when it was purchased by Cyrus Curtis in 1897. Curtis recognized its potential, however, and with the help of editor George Horace Lorimer turned *The Saturday Evening Post* into "America's magazine."

Over the years, the magazine shifted its focus from business to general interest—including fiction, humor, and articles on a variety of topics. Lively cover illustrations were created by noteworthy illustrators, including N. C. Wyeth, J. C. Leyendecker, and, of course, Norman Rockwell. The covers came to symbolize the ideal of everyday life in America.

Have students locate a collection of *The Saturday Evening Post* cover illustrations, either in books about Norman Rockwell or by visiting Internet sites devoted to the subject. Have them select an interesting cover, and write a short essay explaining what the illustration reveals about American life at that time.

◆Critical Thinking

❶ **Connect** Ask students to recall what Baker said about his sister's opportunities. Ask them to consider why people asked only boys if they wanted to become President. *At the time, no one even considered the possibility that girls would ever aspire to such a position.*

Clarification

❷ Discuss with students what an interrogation is. Ask them if they think Baker is actually being interrogated. Why do they think he describes the event as such? *Students should recognize that this example of exaggeration is used for comic effect, keeping up the lighthearted tone of the piece.*

▶Critical Viewing◀

❸ **Compare and Contrast** *Possible response: Baker describes himself as rather lazy and unmotivated, creating an image of someone who might look unkempt. In the picture, he appears neat, scrubbed, and pleasant. He describes himself as being less energetic than his sister, a comparison that some students might feel is reflected in the eyes and expressions of the children in the photograph.*

◆Literary Focus

❹ **Autobiography** *Possible response: He is interested in things that other people don't value. He does not aspire to the kinds of jobs that many boys would want.*

◆Critical Thinking

❺ **Infer** Ask students why Baker's mother tells a "white lie" here. *Students may say that his mother's sole intent is for him to get the job.*

---

could do with it. She didn't insist that I grow up to be President of the United States.

❶ Fifty years ago parents still asked boys if they wanted to grow up to be President, and asked it not jokingly but seriously. Many parents who were hardly more than paupers still believed their sons could do it. Abraham Lincoln had done it. We were only sixty-five years from Lincoln. Many a grandfather who walked among us could remember Lincoln's time. Men of grandfatherly age were the worst for asking if you wanted to grow up to be President. A surprising number of little boys said yes and meant it.

❷ I was asked many times myself. No, I would say, I didn't want to grow up to be President. My mother was present during one of these interrogations.[3] An elderly uncle, having posed the usual question and exposed my lack of interest in the Presidency, asked, "Well, what *do* you want to be when you grow up?"

I loved to pick through trash piles and collect empty bottles, tin cans with pretty labels, and discarded magazines. The most desirable job on earth sprang instantly to mind. "I want to be a garbage man," I said.

My uncle smiled, but my mother had seen the first distressing evidence of a bump budding on a log.

❸ ▲ **Critical Viewing** Baker's description of himself probably creates an image of a boy in your mind. How does your image compare with this photograph of Russell and his sister? **[Compare and Contrast]**

❹ **◆ Literary Focus** What do these details reveal about Russell's character?

3. **interrogations** (in ter´ ə gā´ shənz) *n.*: Situations where a person is formally questioned.

"Have a little gumption, Russell," she said. Her calling me Russell was a signal of unhappiness. When she approved of me I was always "Buddy."

When I turned eight years old she decided that the job of starting me on the road toward making something of myself could no longer be safely delayed. "Buddy," she said one day, "I want you to come home right after school this afternoon. Somebody's coming and I want you to meet him."

When I burst in that afternoon she was in conference in the parlor with an executive of the Curtis Publishing Company. She introduced me. He bent low from the waist and shook my hand. Was it true as my mother had told him, he asked, that I longed for the opportunity to conquer the world of business? ❺ My mother replied that I was blessed with a rare determination to make something of myself.

"That's right," I whispered.

"But have you got the grit, the character, the never-say-quit spirit it takes to succeed in business?"

My mother said I certainly did.

"That's right," I said.

He eyed me silently for a long pause, as though weighing whether I could be trusted to keep his confidence, then spoke man-to-man. Before taking a crucial step, he said, he wanted to advise me that working for the Curtis Publishing Company placed enormous responsibility on a young man. It was one of the great companies of America. Perhaps the

Cross-Curricular Connection: Math

Survey Have groups of students design a classroom survey on career goals. Groups should discuss and agree upon the kinds of questions to ask and how best to word the questions to obtain useful data. Possible topics for survey questions include career goals each student has and why, and goals that parents and care givers have for students.

After the survey is completed, have students analyze the results. They can learn many things from the data: the kinds of jobs most students are interested in, careers favored by most parents, the similarity (or difference) in attitudes toward work held by parents and children, and whether girls and boys have the same career goals.

Students should then organize and display their findings using tables, graphs, or charts. They may choose to display their results on a bulletin board or an overhead projector, or in a written report shared with the class.

greatest publishing house in the world. I had heard, no doubt, of the *Saturday Evening Post*?

Heard of it? My mother said that everyone in our house had heard of the *Saturday Post* and that I, in fact, read it with religious devotion.

Then doubtless, he said, we were also familiar with those two monthly pillars of the magazine world, the *Ladies Home Journal* and the *Country Gentleman.*

Indeed we were familiar with them, said my mother.

Representing the *Saturday Evening Post* was one of the weightiest honors that could be bestowed in the
6 world of business, he said. He was personally proud of being a part of that great corporation.

My mother said he had every right to be.

Again he studied me as though debating whether I was worthy of a knighthood. Finally: "Are you trustworthy?"

My mother said I was the soul of honesty.

"That's right," I said.

The caller smiled for the first time. He told me
8 I was a lucky young man. He admired my spunk. Too many young men thought life was all play. Those young men would not go far in this world. Only a young man willing to work and save and keep his face washed and his hair neatly combed could hope to come out on top in a world such as ours. Did I truly and sincerely believe that I was such a young man?

"He certainly does," said my mother. 8

"That's right," I said.

He said he had been so impressed by what he had seen of me that he was going to make me a representative of the Curtis Publishing Company. On the following Tuesday, he said, thirty freshly printed copies of the *Saturday Evening Post* would be delivered at our door. I would place these magazines, still damp with the ink of the presses, in a handsome canvas bag, sling it over my shoulder, and set forth through the streets to bring the best in journalism, fiction, and cartoons to the American public.

He had brought the canvas bag with him. He presented it with reverence fit for a chasuble.[4] He showed me how to drape the sling over my left shoulder and
across the chest so that 9
the pouch lay easily accessible[5] to my right hand, allowing the best in journalism, fiction, and cartoons to be swiftly extracted and sold to a citizenry whose happiness and security depended upon us soldiers of the free press.

The following Tuesday I raced home from school, put the canvas bag over my shoulder, dumped the magazines in, and, tilting to the left to balance their weight on my right hip, embarked on the highway of journalism.

We lived in Belleville, New Jersey, a commuter town at the northern fringe of Newark. It

7 ▲ **Critical Viewing** What details tell you that this is an old photograph? **[Analyze]**

◆ Build Vocabulary

paupers (pô´ pərz) *n.*: People who are very poor

crucial (kro͞o´ shəl) *adj.*: Of great importance

4. **chasuble:** (chaz´ ə bəl) *n.*: Sleeveless outer garment worn by priests.

5. **accessible** (ak ses´ ə bəl) *adj.*: Easy to get.

◆Critical Thinking

6 Speculate Ask students why they think the man makes such impressive claims about working for the magazine. *Possible response: He is exaggerating to make himself and the job he is offering seem more important to the boy. Maybe he is trying to impress and scare him a bit so he will do a good job of selling magazines.*

▶Critical Viewing◀

7 Analyze *Possible response: The hairstyle and clothing are from an earlier time. The posed and stiff nature of the black-and-white photograph makes it look old.*

Comprehension Check ☑

8 Baker repeatedly says, "That's right," whenever his mother sings his praises. Ask students to explain what motivates *Baker* to give this response. *His motivation is that he enjoys hearing his mother praise him and that he also enjoys "putting one over" on his interrogator.*

◆Reading Strategy

9 Understand the Author's Purpose Guide students to recognize the tone of exaggerated importance in this passage. Ask them why Baker would present information in this way and what he really thinks about his impending responsibility. *The author is writing in a way that entertains the reader. His way of describing the job contrasts with the comparative unimportance of the task itself.*

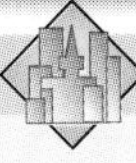

Beyond the Classroom

Career Connection

Sales Jobs Have students discuss career opportunities in sales. Have them brainstorm for the advantages and drawbacks of working in a sales job. Then ask them to talk about the personality traits, skills, and qualities a successful salesperson might need. Suggest to students that people with aptitudes for sales work can achieve financial success.

Guide students to name types of companies that hire salespeople (retail stores, service suppliers, manufacturing companies, etc.). Lead students to see that any company with a product or a service to offer will need salespeople to present those goods or services to the public. Point out to students that fast food employees and waiters and waitresses "sell" their product when they recommend a food or suggest a dessert. Many jobs have an element of sales to them.

Students interested in sales as a career can form a group to investigate more about this field. Encourage them to talk with adults who work in sales to learn about the training and preparation required for sales careers, and report back to the class.

Looking at Literature Videodisc/Videotape

To provide historical background on the Great Depression, play Chapter 7 of the videodisc. This segment features information and historical footage on causes and immediate results of the Stock Market Crash of 1929. Discuss how the economic collapse impacted Baker's family.

Chapter 7

◆ Literary Focus

❶ **Autobiography** *Possible response: Not only does Baker's mother want him to build character, but the family can also use the extra money he might earn from his job.*

◆ Literary Focus

❷ **Autobiography** Ask students why Baker might have included this information in the selection. *This background information gives the reader insight into the personalities of Baker and, more particularly, his mother. It helps readers understand why she is so eager for him to make something of himself.*

Clarification

❸ Explain that, although $30 a week does not sound like very much money today, during the Depression it represented a substantial income.

Customize for *Logical/Mathematical Learners*

Students might enjoy "comparison shopping." Baker's magazines sold for a nickel. Suggest that students check the price of a magazine being sold today to see how the price compares. Ask students to find out what a nickel can buy today. They can also locate various items that are the equivalent cost of a popular magazine being sold today. Have students work in groups to compile their findings into a chart or diagram.

> **◆ Literary Focus**
> In what way does this background help you better understand the situation of Baker's family?

❶ was 1932, the bleakest year of the Depression. My father had died two years before, leaving us with a few pieces of Sears, Roebuck furniture and not much else, and my mother had taken Doris and me to live with one of her ❷ younger brothers. This was my Uncle Allen. Uncle Allen had made something of himself by 1932. As salesman for a soft-drink bottler in Newark, he had an income of $30 a week; wore ❸ pearl-gray spats,[6] detachable collars, and a three-piece suit; was happily married; and took in threadbare relatives.

With my load of magazines I headed toward Belleville Avenue. That's where the people were. There were two filling stations at the intersection with Union Avenue, as well as an A&P, a fruit stand, a bakery, a barber shop, Zuccarelli's drugstore, and a diner shaped like a railroad car. For several hours I made myself highly visible, shifting position now and then from corner to corner, from shop window to shop window, to make sure everyone could see the heavy black lettering on the canvas bag that said *The Saturday Evening Post.* When the angle of the light indicated it was suppertime, I walked back to the house.

"How many did you sell, Buddy?" my mother asked.

"None."

"Where did you go?"

"The corner of Belleville and Union Avenues."

"What did you do?"

"Stood on the corner waiting for somebody to buy a *Saturday Evening Post.*"

"You just stood there?"

"Didn't sell a single one."

"For God's sake, Russell!"

Uncle Allen intervened. "I've been thinking about it for some time," he said, "and I've about decided to take the *Post* regularly. Put me down as a regular customer." I handed him a magazine and he paid me a nickel. It was the first nickel I earned.

Afterwards my mother instructed me in salesmanship. I would have to ring doorbells, address adults with charming self-confidence, and break down resistance with a sales talk pointing out that no one, no matter how poor, could afford to be without the *Saturday Evening Post* in the home.

I told my mother I'd changed my mind about wanting to succeed in the magazine business.

"If you think I'm going to raise a good-for-nothing," she replied, "you've got another think coming." She told me to hit the streets with the canvas bag and start ringing doorbells the instant school was out next day. When I objected that I didn't feel any aptitude for salesmanship, she asked how I'd like to lend her my leather belt so she could whack some sense into me. I bowed to superior will and entered journalism with a heavy heart.

My mother and I had fought this battle almost as long as I could remember. It probably started even before memory began, when I was a country child in northern Virginia and my mother, dissatisfied with my father's plain workman's life, determined that I would not grow up like him and his people, with calluses on their hands, overalls on their backs, and fourth-grade educations in their heads. She had fancier ideas of life's possibilities. Introducing me to the *Saturday Evening Post*, she was trying to wean me as early as possible from my father's world where men left with lunch pails at sunup, worked with their hands until the grime ate into the pores, and died with a few sticks of mail-order furniture as their legacy. In my mother's vision of the better life there were desks and white collars, well-pressed suits, evenings of reading and lively talk, and perhaps—if a man were very, very lucky and hit the jackpot, really made something important of himself—perhaps there might be a fantastic salary of $5,000 a year to support a big house and a Buick with a rumble seat[7] and a vacation in Atlantic City.

6. **spats** (spats) *n.:* Pieces of cloth or leather that cover the upper part of the shoe or ankle.

7. **rumble seat:** In early automobiles, an open seat in the rear of the car that could be folded shut.

Cross-Curricular Connection: Social Studies

The Great Depression Many people blame the Great Depression on the stock market crash of 1929. Other factors contributed as well: an overproduction of goods, overexpansion of credit, reckless speculation in the stock market, and a restriction of trade in foreign markets. As the Depression worsened, up to 16 million people were unemployed, industrial stocks lost up to 80 percent of their value, and 44 percent of U.S. banks failed, taking with them over $2 billion in deposits. Hundreds of thousands of people found themselves unemployed and living on charity. Government programs such as the Civilian Conservation Corps, the Farm Credit Administration, the Works Progress Administration, and the Public Works Administration helped millions of people find jobs. However, the economy did not completely recover until it was stimulated by military expenditures for World War II.

Ask groups of students to discuss how Baker's autobiographical essay might differ if he had grown up during times of plenty. Invite groups to share their ideas with the class.

And so I set forth with my sack of magazines. I was afraid of the dogs that snarled behind the doors of potential buyers. I was timid about ringing the doorbells of strangers, relieved when no one came to the door, and scared when someone did. Despite my mother's instructions, I could not deliver an engaging sales pitch. When a door opened I simply asked, "Want to buy a *Saturday Evening Post*?" In Belleville few persons did. It was a town of 30,000 people, and most weeks I rang a fair majority of its doorbells. But I rarely sold my thirty copies.

4 Some weeks I canvassed the entire town for six days and still had four or five unsold magazines on Monday evening; then I dreaded the coming of Tuesday morning, when a batch of thirty fresh *Saturday Evening Posts* was due at the front door.

"Better get out there and sell the rest of those magazines tonight," my mother would say.

I usually posted myself then at a busy intersection where a traffic light controlled commuter flow from Newark. When the light turned red I stood on the curb and shouted my sales pitch at the motorists.

"Want to buy a *Saturday Evening Post*?"

One rainy night when car windows were sealed against me I came back soaked and with not a single sale to report. My mother beckoned to Doris.

"Go back down there with Buddy and show him how to sell these magazines," she said.

Brimming with zest, Doris, who was then seven years old, returned with me to the corner. She took a magazine from the bag, and when the light turned red she strode to the nearest car and banged her small fist against the closed window. The driver, probably startled at what he took to be a midget assaulting his car, lowered the window to stare, and Doris thrust a *Saturday Evening Post* at him.

> ◆ **Reading Strategy** How does the contrast between Baker and his sister help Baker to explain what he was like? 6

"You need this magazine," she piped, "and it only costs a nickel."

Her salesmanship was irresistible. Before the light changed half a dozen times she disposed of the entire batch. I didn't feel humiliated. To the contrary. I was so happy I decided to give her a treat. Leading her to the vegetable store on Belleville Avenue, I bought three apples, which cost a nickel, and gave her one.

"You shouldn't waste money," she said.

"Eat your apple." I bit into mine.

"You shouldn't eat before supper," she said. "It'll spoil your appetite."

Back at the house that evening, she dutifully reported me for wasting a nickel. Instead of a scolding, I was rewarded with a pat on the back for having the good sense to buy fruit instead of candy. My mother reached into her bottomless supply of maxims[8] and told Doris, "An apple a day keeps the doctor away."

5 ▲ **Critical Viewing** How are the boys in this illustration from the 1930's different from you? How are they the same? [Compare and Contrast]

◆ **Build Vocabulary**

aptitude (ap´ tə to͞od´) *n.*: Talent; ability

8. **maxims** (mak´ simz) *n.*: Wise sayings.

◆ Literature and Your Life

4 Ask students if they have ever had the experience of working hard to complete a job or chore and just as soon as it was done, there was another job waiting. How did this experience make them feel? Invite volunteers to share examples of these experiences. Then ask students why Baker dreaded Tuesday morning. *Just when he was feeling relieved at completing a task he hated, he realized he had to start all over again. He never seemed to get ahead.*

▶Critical Viewing◀

5 Compare and Contrast *Possible response: They are different in that they are younger and they are dressed differently from people today. They are similar in that they enjoy being with friends and playing games.*

◆ Reading Strategy

6 Understand the Author's Purpose *Possible response: By describing his sister's forceful and outgoing behavior, Baker shows himself to be completely unlike her and unable to act in that way. He is more passive and shy. She actually enjoys greeting customers and selling papers, while he hates it.*

Customize for
Bodily/Kinesthetic Learners
Invite groups of three students to role-play Baker and his sister selling newspapers to a client. Have students take turns assuming each role. Following the activity, ask students which role felt more comfortable to them. Encourage them to explain their answers.

Viewing and Representing Mini-Lesson

Self-Portraits

Introduce Have students review the self-portrait of Norman Rockwell on p. 565. Explain that a portrait is an image of a person created by another artist, while a self-portrait is an image of a person created by himself or herself.

Develop Encourage students to imagine young Russell Baker's facial expression when he undertook a job he did not like. Then consider how he looked when he thought about becoming a writer. Point out that a person's feelings can be revealed by the position of the mouth, the look of the eyes, the angles of the eyebrows, and so forth.

Apply Have students fold a sheet of drawing paper in half. On one side of the paper, have them draw a portrait of themselves when they feel discouraged or unhappy. On the other side of the paper have them draw a portrait that portrays their appearance when they are happy and satisfied. Encourage students to add details that will help the viewer understand their feelings, and, if possible, what caused them.

Assess Invite students to display their self-portraits, explaining how they used facial features and details to express certain emotions. Evaluate their work based on their explanations.

▶Critical Viewing◀

❶ **Connect** *Possible response: Although both of these girls are probably older than Doris, the girl in the blue dress seems most like Doris. She looks like a serious, no-nonsense person who will not put up with any foolishness.*

◆Literature and Your Life

❷ *This discovery solves Baker's conflict with having to prove he has gumption by doing a job he hates—selling magazines. Now he can aspire to doing something he actually enjoys doing.*

◆Critical Thinking

❸ **Speculate** Ask students if they think Baker really believes that writing would not be classified as work and that writers do not have to have gumption. Have them explain their answers. *Possible response: He does not really believe these things. As a writer, he knows that writing can be hard work and that it takes gumption to tackle and finish writing assignments. He says these things for the humorous effect.*

Customize for *English Language Learners*

Arrange students of varying ability levels into groups to discuss the maxims used by Baker's mother. Encourage students to explain what each maxim means and then think of other ways to express the maxims. Ask students to repeat any other maxims they may have heard. In addition, students might enjoy creating a maxim of their own.

By the time I was ten I had learned all my mother's maxims by heart. Asking to stay up past normal bedtime, I knew that a refusal would be explained with, "Early to bed and early to rise, makes a man healthy, wealthy, and wise." If I whimpered about having to get up early in the morning, I could depend on her to say, "The early bird gets the worm."

The one I most despised was, "If at first you don't succeed, try, try again." This was the battle cry with which she constantly sent me back into the hopeless struggle whenever I moaned that I had rung every doorbell in town and knew there wasn't a single potential buyer left in Belleville that week. After listening to my explanation, she handed me the canvas bag and said, "If at first you don't succeed . . ."

Three years in that job, which I would gladly have quit after the first day except for her insistence, produced at least one valuable result. My mother finally concluded that I would never make something of myself by pursuing a life in business and started considering careers that demanded less competitive zeal.

One evening when I was eleven I brought home a short "composition" on my summer vacation which the teacher had graded with an A. Reading it with her own schoolteacher's eye, my mother agreed that it was top-drawer seventh grade prose and complimented me. Nothing more was said about it immediately, but a new idea had taken life in her mind. Halfway through supper she suddenly interrupted the conversation.

"Buddy," she said, "maybe you could be a writer."

◆ Literature and Your Life Why does this discovery help solve a conflict Baker has experienced? ❷

I clasped the idea to my heart. I had never met a writer, had shown no previous urge to write, and hadn't a notion how to become a writer, but I loved stories and thought that making up stories must surely be almost as much fun as reading them. Best of all, though, and what really gladdened my heart, was the ease of the writer's life. Writers did not have to trudge through the town peddling from canvas bags, defending themselves against angry dogs, ❸ being rejected by surly strangers. Writers did not have to ring doorbells. So far as I could make out, what writers did couldn't even be classified as work.

I was enchanted. Writers didn't have to have any gumption at all. I did not dare tell anybody for fear of being laughed at in the schoolyard, but secretly I decided that what I'd like to be when I grew up was a writer.

❶ ▲ Critical Viewing Which character in this illustration seems the most like Doris? Explain. **[Connect]**

Cross-Curricular Connection: Social Studies

Communication Technology In the years since Russell Baker sold magazines, the field of journalism and communication has changed a great deal.

Journalism communicates ideas to the public by giving information, entertaining, or expressing editorial opinions. Throughout the years, various media have been used for journalistic communication.

Early American colonists relied on town criers and handwritten notices until 1704, when the *Boston News-Letter* was first published. Other newspapers and magazines soon followed. Radio journalism was added in 1920. Television reporting developed quickly after World War II. Communications satellites were put into use in 1980, and the television industry changed forever. The methods and styles of reporting news have changed rapidly as technology has advanced. With the addition of computer modems and the Internet, journalism has become almost an instant reporting medium.

Suggest that students think about the signing of the Declaration of Independence, imagining that today's communication technology was available at that time. Then open the discussion to include modern examples of communication technology, and have students consider how advances in the field have affected our lives. Ask students to predict what changes they see in their future.

Invite students to write a response to communication technology in their own lives.

Beyond Literature

Career Connection

Careers in Journalism Russell Baker didn't enjoy selling newspapers, but he found writing rewarding. He eventually made newspapers into a career. Journalists inform people about what is happening in the world and help to shape what the public thinks about these events.

Journalists work in one of five main branches of media: newspapers, news services, magazines, radio, and television. Jobs available include columnists, copy editors, editorial writers, feature writers, news editors, photojournalists, reporters, and newscasters. Many of these jobs require at least a college degree in liberal arts or journalism, along with experience on a college paper or radio.

Cross-Curricular Activity
Job Research Research a particular job field of journalism. Find out what the requirements and responsibilities of this job are. If you can, interview a local journalist to get a more accurate idea of the work journalists do. Share your findings with the class through a written or oral report.

Guide for Responding

◆ Literature and Your Life

Reader's Response Do you agree with Baker's mother that he has no "gumption"? Why or why not?

Thematic Focus In what ways does Baker's mother lead him to a discovery of his true talents?

Role Play With a partner, act out a situation in which Baker tries to sell the *Saturday Evening Post* to an adult in Belleville.

☑ Check Your Comprehension

1. Describe how Baker's mother gets him started in "journalism."
2. Explain what success Baker has as a magazine salesman.
3. How does his sister's performance as a salesperson contrast with his?
4. What does his mother conclude after he has worked at the job for three years?
5. What inspires his mother's new plan for his career?

◆ Critical Thinking

Interpret

1. What qualities prevent Baker from being a good salesperson? **[Analyze]**
2. Give two examples that show Baker's sense of humor about his poor salesmanship. **[Support]**
3. Compare Baker's aims in life as a child with the goals his mother sets for him. **[Compare and Contrast]**
4. How much of the idea for Baker's new career plan comes from him, and how much comes from his mother? **[Draw Conclusions]**

Apply

5. What interests of yours could lead to a career? **[Apply]**

Extend

6. What does "No Gumption" reveal about the different expectations people had for boys and for girls in the 1930's? **[Social Studies Link]**

Reinforce and Extend

Answers

◆ Literature and Your Life

Reader's Response Some students will agree that Baker's lack of success in sales proves that he has no gumption. Others will recognize that it takes gumption to stick with a job you do not like.

Thematic Focus By causing him to do something he does not like, Baker's mother helps him recognize the pleasure of doing a job he likes and is suited for.

☑ Check Your Comprehension

1. She encourages a magazine sales manager to hire him.
2. Baker does not have much success, although he tries hard.
3. Baker's sister is a natural salesperson.
4. She concludes that he will never be a successful salesman.
5. Baker receives praise on a school writing composition. His mother reads it and recognizes his talent.

◆ Critical Thinking

1. He enjoys solitary activities more than interacting with others. He is not outgoing and does not behave in an energetic way.
2. Possible responses: He stands on the street corner and waits quietly for someone to ask him about buying a magazine. He rings doorbells and is relieved when no one is home.
3. Baker doesn't think much about his goals in life. His mother wants him to make something of himself.
4. The idea of becoming a writer is mostly his mother's, though Baker decides he likes the idea.
5. Answers will vary according to students' interests.
6. Boys were expected to have big goals for their lives. Girls were not expected to earn a living or aspire to being president.

Beyond the Selection

Other Works Written or Edited by Russell Baker
Russell Baker's Book of American Humor
Inventing the Truth: The Art and Craft of Memoir
Poor Russell's Almanac

Other Autobiographies by Professional Writers
A Girl From Yamhill: A Memoir, Beverly Cleary
The Abracadabra Kid: A Writer's Life, Sid Fleischman
Boy; Tales of Childhood, Roald Dahl

INTERNET
To locate recent *New York Times* articles by Russell Baker, visit the following Web site:
http://www.nytimes.com

Please be aware, however, that the site may have changed from the time we published this information.

We *strongly recommend* that you preview the site before you send students to it.

Connections to Today's World

Tell students that articles from magazines like *The Saturday Evening Post* can be found and read on the Internet. Ask students why people continue to buy newspapers and magazines when they can search for and locate the same material electronically. *Possible responses: Some people do not own or feel comfortable using computers. Others enjoy reading in a comfortable chair or out of doors instead of reading hunched over a computer screen. Some magazines and newspapers are not available on the Internet.*

More About the Author
Reid Goldsborough is the author of the book *Straight Talk About the Information Superhighway.* He is also a contributor to *PC World, MSNBC Interactive, Internet World, Yahoo Internet Life,* and other print and Internet magazines. Copies of his articles can be viewed by visiting his Web site:
http://members.home.net/reidgold/

Please be aware that this Web site may have changed from the time we published this information. We *strongly recommend* that you preview this site before you send students to it.

Customize for
Less Proficient Readers

Explain that Goldsborough uses jargon, or language unique to a particular field. Point out and discuss examples of computer and Internet jargon, such as *Web site* (a page you reach by typing in a certain address), *links* (highlighted words that, when clicked on with a mouse, automatically forward you to another related page), and so forth. Encourage students to note and, as necessary, question other examples of computer and Internet jargon as they read.

Connections to Today's World

In the 1930's, Russell Baker sold copies of *The Saturday Evening Post* on street corners. Since then, a technology explosion has dramatically changed the way people get information. In addition to all-news radio and 24-hour cable news channels, millions of people worldwide have logged onto the Internet. An electronic information network introduced to the American public in the 1990's, the Internet makes vast amounts of information readily available. This essay provides strategies for making the most of this new technology.

Let the Reader Beware

Reid Goldsborough

Tips for Verifying Information on the Internet

The fact is, the Internet is chock full of rumors, gossip, hoaxes, exaggerations, falsehoods, ruses, and scams. Although the Net can reveal useful, factual information that you'd be hard pressed to find elsewhere, it can also appear to be a gigantic electronic tabloid.[1]

Can you ever trust the Internet? Sure you can. You just need to apply critical thinking in evaluating the information and advice you come across. Here's a six-step approach to doing this.

1. Don't judge a Web site by its appearance.

Sure, if a Web site looks professional rather than slopped together, chances are greater that the information within it will be accurate and reliable.

But looks can and do deceive. A flashy site can merely be a marketing front for quack health remedies or an illegal pyramid scheme.

2. Try to find out who's behind the information.

If you're looking at a Web site, check if the author or creator is identified. See if there are links to a page listing professional credentials[2] or affiliations.[3] Be very skeptical if no authorship information is provided.

If you're looking at a message in a Usenet newsgroup or Internet mailing list, see if the author has included a signature—a short, often biographical, description that's automatically appended to the end of messages. Many people include their credentials in their signature or point to their home page, where they provide biographical information.

1. **tabloid** (tab´ lɔid´) *n.*: Newspaper with many pictures and often sensationalized stories.

2. **credentials** (kri den´ shəlz) *n.*: Information that indicates position or authority.
3. **affiliations** (ə fil´ ē ā´ shənz) *n.*: Organizational membership.

Beyond the Classroom

Career Connection

Computer Jobs The ever-changing and expanding field of computers offers many exciting job and career opportunities in:

- research and design
- computer engineering
- programming
- software development and testing
- sales, service, and repairs
- data processing
- Internet specialization
- teaching

Groups of interested students may wish to locate adults presently working in the computer field and interview them about their job experiences, how the industry has changed over the years, and what computer training they received. Others may wish to find out how computers are used in the everyday workplace and how employees are trained. Have students report their findings back to the class.

3. Try to determine the reason the information was posted.

Among those who create Web sites are publishing companies, professional and trade organizations, government agencies, non-profit organizations, for-profit companies, educational institutions, individual researchers, political and advocacy groups, and hobbyists.

Each has its own agenda—sometimes explicit, sometimes hidden. Unearth the agenda and keep it in mind when evaluating the information presented.

Similarly, look behind and between the words posted in Usenet and mailing list discussions. Is the author trying to promote his or her own ends, or be helpful? You can often do both, but not always.

4. Look for the date the information was created or modified.

Unless you're doing historical research, current information is usually more valid and useful than older material.

If the Web site doesn't provide a "last updated" message or otherwise date its content, check out some of its links. If more than a couple are no longer working, the information at the site may no longer be up to date either.

5. Try to verify the same information elsewhere.

This is particularly important if the information is at odds with your previous understanding or if you intend to use it for critical purposes such as an important health, family, or business decision.

Ideally, you should confirm the information with at least two other sources. Librarians and information scientists call this the "principle of triangulation of data." Spending a bit of time validating the material, through the Internet or at a local library, can be well worth the investment.

6. Try to find out how others feel about the reliability and professionalism of the Web site you're looking at.

There are a number of review guides that offer evaluations of other sites. Here are three excellent, relatively new review guides that you may not have heard of:

Argus Clearinghouse
http://www.clearinghouse.net/

Mining Company
http://miningco.com/

Readers Digest's LookSmart
http://www.looksmart.com/

With any information you come across on the Net, the watchword is "Caveat lector"—Let the reader beware.

If you'd like to delve further into the issue of information credibility on the Internet, there are Web sites out there that let you do just that. Here are four good ones.

Evaluating Internet Information
http://www-medlib.med.utah.edu/navigator/discovery/eval.html

Evaluating Quality on the Net
http://www.tiac.net/users/hope/findqual.html

Thinking Critically About World Wide Web Resources
http://www.library.ucla.edu/libraries/college/instruct/critical.htm

Internet Source Validation Project
http://www.stemnet.nf.ca/Curriculum/Validate/validate.html

1. Why does the writer warn people to read information on the Internet critically?
2. Which tip do you think is most useful? Explain.

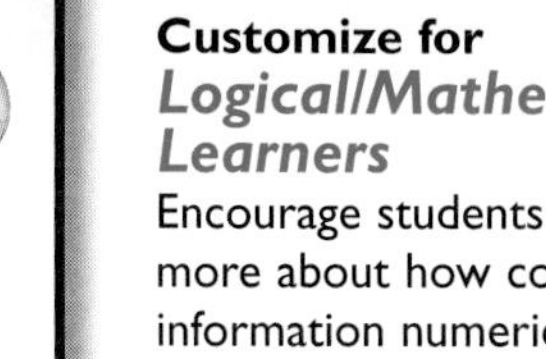

Customize for ***Logical/Mathematical Learners***
Encourage students to find out more about how computers process information numerically using binary numbers. Have them research how a modem, computer, and the Internet can be mathematically connected by means of a telephone line.

Customize for ***Visual/Spatial Learners***
Suggest to students that they design a chart that visually explains how computers, modems, and the Internet are connected for instant access by means of telephone lines. They may wish to work with students who are investigating how computers numerically process information to design a bulletin board that explains the Internet process.

Customize for ***Musical/Rhythmic Learners***
Suggest that interested students search the Internet to find examples of computer-generated or computer-assisted music performances. They may be able to locate information about how computer-generated music and sound are produced and formed. Have them compare and contrast computer-produced music with recordings or music performed live.

Reading Strategy Connection

Ask students to compare and contrast Reid Goldsborough's purpose for writing this article with Russell Baker's purpose for writing "No Gumption." *Russell Baker's purpose is mainly to entertain, but he also informs the reader about his life and the innate differences between people. Reid Goldsborough's purpose is mainly to inform.*

Answers

1. The author warns that the Internet, as well as being quite useful, is also full of useless and misleading information. Users must apply critical thinking in order to find verifiable information.
2. Answers will vary, but students should provide reasons that support their answers.

Develop Understanding

One-Minute Insight Seven-year-old Annie Dillard enjoys playing football with the boys in her neighborhood because it requires her to play wholeheartedly and with concentration and courage. One snowy day, Dillard and the boys are mischievously throwing snowballs at passing cars. A man driving one of the targeted cars stops and jumps out to confront the children. They all run off in different directions, but the man chases after Dillard and her friend Mikey. The two children run down alleys, through backyards, and over fences in hopes of losing the man, but he refuses to give up the chase. Finally the man grabs them. After he catches his breath, he lectures the equally breathless and exhausted children. Dillard is exhilarated, because she has met someone who really challenges her to do her best in the chase.

Customize for
English Language Learners
After students have read the selection, invite volunteers to pantomime the actions and emotions described to make them more understandable.

Customize for
Interpersonal Learners
Arrange students in small groups and have them read the selection aloud. Encourage them to discuss young Dillard's feelings and motivations as they read the selection. Have them use examples from their own lives, as applicable, to explain their ideas about the children's behavior.

Humanities: Photography

Photographs of snowy street scenes are used to illustrate the selection. They help establish the setting by showing how a residential city street might look following a snowfall. Have students look at the photographs as they answer the following questions:

1. How would you feel if you were playing outdoors in one of these places? *Possible responses: Cold; excited about the snowfall.*
2. Would running through the snow be easy or hard? Why? *It would be hard, because you would sink down into the snow and it would keep you from moving quickly and easily. Also, you might slip and fall down.*
3. Which photograph looks more like a well-traveled residential street? Why do you think so? *The photograph on pp. 576–577 looks more like a well-traveled street, since the snow is mostly cleared off the street, showing that it has been plowed and that cars have been driving on it. The street shown in the photograph on pp. 578–579 does not appear to have had much traffic disturbing the snow and the car is still buried.*

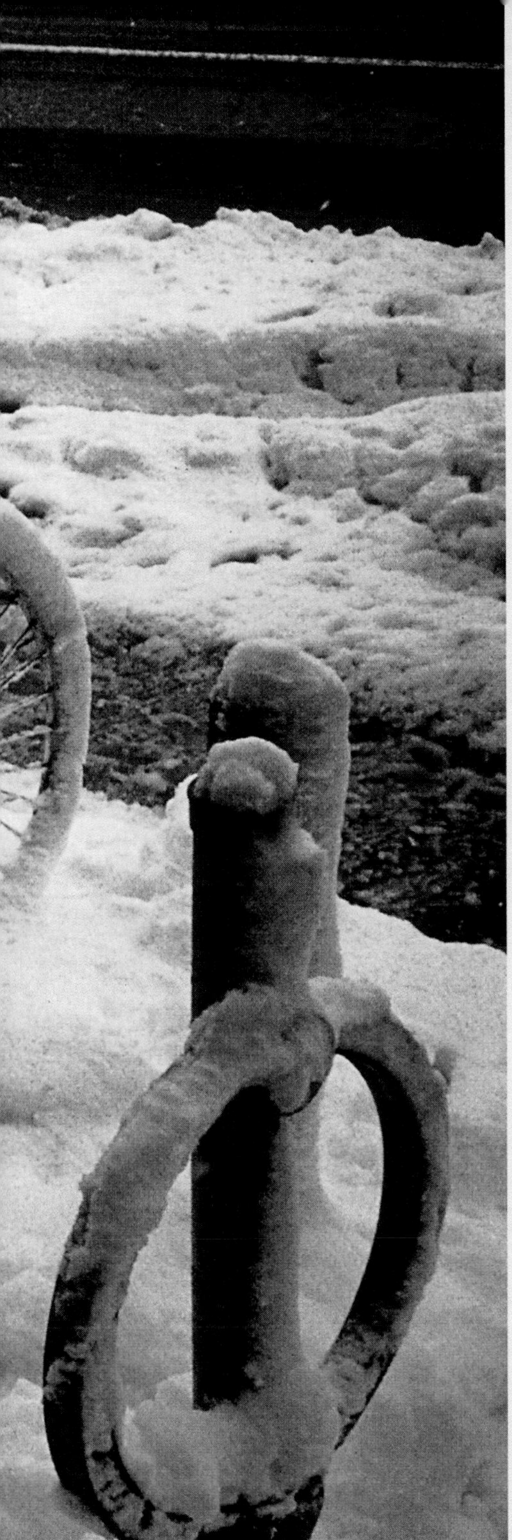

The Chase
from An American Childhood
Annie Dillard

Some boys taught me to play football. This was fine sport. You thought up a new strategy for every play and whispered it to the others. You went out for a pass, fooling everyone. Best, you got to throw yourself mightily at someone's running legs. Either you brought him down or you hit the ground flat out on your chin, with your arms empty before you. It was all or nothing. If you hesitated in fear, you would miss and get hurt: you would take a hard fall while the kid got away, or you would get kicked in the face while the kid got away. But if you flung yourself wholeheartedly at the back of his knees—if you gathered and joined body and soul and pointed them diving fearlessly—then you likely wouldn't get hurt, and you'd stop the ball. Your fate, and your team's score, depended on your concentration and courage. Nothing girls did could compare with it. ❶ ❷ ❸

> ◆ **Reading Strategy** What lesson in life might Dillard be trying to teach in this passage?

Boys welcomed me at baseball, too, for I had, through enthusiastic practice, what was weirdly known as a boy's arm. In winter, in the snow, there was neither baseball nor football, so the boys and I threw snowballs at passing cars. I got in trouble throwing snowballs, and have seldom been happier since. ❹

◀ **Critical Viewing** In what two ways is this photograph of a snow-covered bicycle a good choice for this selection? **[Support]** ❺

◆Literary Focus

❶ **Autobiography** Ask students what word in the first sentence reveals that this selection is an autobiography. *Because the selection is nonfiction, the author's use of the pronoun* me *indicates that she is writing about herself, and it is an autobiography.*

◆Critical Thinking

❷ **Infer** Discuss what students can tell about Annie Dillard from these details. *Possible response: She is not afraid to play hard, and she likes to do her best. She enjoys a challenge.*

◆Reading Strategy

❸ **Understand the Author's Purpose** *Possible response: You succeed in life when you don't hold anything back but give your all. Doing something halfway can only lead to disappointment.*

◆Critical Thinking

❹ **Speculate** Ask students why getting in trouble might have made Dillard so happy. Have them jot down their answers and then check them against what they learn as they read.

▶Critical Viewing◀

❺ **Support** *Possible responses: The photograph illustrates the wintry setting of the story. It also shows that a young girl might live nearby, since the style of the frame is that of a girl's bike.*

On one weekday morning after Christmas, six inches of new snow had just fallen. We were standing up to our boot tops in snow on a front yard on trafficked Reynolds Street, waiting for cars. The cars traveled Reynolds ❶ Street slowly and evenly; they were targets all but wrapped in red ribbons, cream puffs. We couldn't miss.

I was seven; the boys were eight, nine, and ten. The oldest two Fahey boys were there—Mikey and Peter—polite blond boys who lived near me on Lloyd Street, and who already had four brothers and sisters. My parents approved Mikey and Peter Fahey. Chickie McBride was there, a tough kid, and Billy Paul and ❷ Mackie Kean too, from across Reynolds, where the boys grew up dark and furious, grew up skinny, knowing, and skilled. We had all drifted from our houses that morning looking for action, and had found it here on Reynolds Street.

It was cloudy but cold. The cars' tires laid behind them on the snowy street a complex trail of beige chunks like crenellated castle walls.[1] I had stepped on some earlier; they squeaked. We could have wished for ❸ more traffic. When a car came, we all popped it one. In the intervals between cars we reverted to the natural solitude of children.

I started making an iceball—a perfect iceball, from perfectly white snow, perfectly spherical, and squeezed perfectly translucent so no snow remained all the way through. (The Fahey boys and I considered it unfair ❹ actually to throw an iceball at somebody, but it had been known to happen.)

I had just embarked on the iceball project when we heard tire chains come clanking from afar. A black Buick was moving toward us down the street. We all spread out, banged together some regular snowballs, took aim, and, when the Buick drew nigh, fired.

A soft snowball hit the driver's windshield right before the driver's face. It made a smashed star with a

1. **chunks like crenellated** (kren´ əl āt´ əd) **castle walls:** The snow was in rows of square clumps like the notches along the top of castle walls.

◆ Build Vocabulary

translucent (trans lo͞o´ sənt) *adj.*: Able to transmit light but no detail of that light

❺ ▶ Critical Viewing Compare the amount of snow in this photograph with the amount of snow Dillard describes. **[Compare and Contrast]**

Clarification

❶ Explain that Dillard is describing the passing cars as if they were gifts (wrapped in red ribbons) or treats (cream puffs). Ask why she would use this kind of comparison. *The cars passed by so slowly that they were easy targets to hit with snowballs; she thought it was great fun to hit cars with snowballs, and the way she describes the cars indicates her pleasure.*

◆Critical Thinking

❷ **Speculate** Ask students if they think Dillard's parents approved of Chickie, Billy, and Mackie. Have them give reasons for their answers. *Possible response: The parents did not approve of them. Dillard named the boys her parents did approve of. Then she described these three in a way that made them seem like boys her parents might not want her to play with. They may have thought the boys were a bad influence and caused her to get into trouble.*

Comprehension Check 

❸ Ask students what the term "popped it one" means in this context. *It means they hit a car with a snowball.*

◆Critical Thinking

❹ **Infer** Ask students why the children would think it unfair to throw an iceball at someone. *Unlike a snowball, an iceball is hard. It could seriously injure a person or damage a car hit with it.*

Beyond the Classroom

Community Connection

Being a Good Neighbor Point out to students that the children in the selection were acting in a way that could cause harm to their neighbors or their neighbors' property. Then discuss actions and attitudes that make people good neighbors. Write examples on the board as they are suggested. For example:

- Respect others' property.
- Treat people as you would like to be treated.
- Offer help when it is needed.

Arrange students in groups to devise a plan for convincing Annie and her friends not to throw snowballs at cars. Have groups list possible consequences of this behavior to share with the children. Then have them suggest alternative activities that the children might participate in. For example, students might suggest that the children shovel a neighbor's snow-covered walk, or run simple errands for neighbors who are housebound. Invite volunteer groups to share their ideas with the class.

The Chase from An American Childhood ◆ 579

▶Critical Viewing◀

5 Compare and Contrast Elicit responses such as the following: *Dillard says that six inches of snow had just fallen. In the picture, it appears that the snow has just fallen. However, the depth appears to be much more than six inches, based on the amount of snow on top of the car.*

Customize for *Logical/Mathematical Learners*

Challenge students to estimate the depth of the snowfall shown in the photograph. For example, they might determine the height of an average car window and then compare the depth of the snow to the height of the window to arrive at an estimate. Invite students to share their answers and to tell how they arrived at their estimates. To further extend the activity, students might wish to estimate how much precipitation occurred with the snowfall amount.

Cross-Curricular Connection: Physical Education

Winter Sports Point out to the students that Annie Dillard and her friends keep busy playing football when the weather is nice. When it snows, however, the children get bored, and throw snowballs at passing cars.

Have students brainstorm for outdoor sports or activities that can be played in the winter and often require snow or ice for participation. *Possible answers: ice skating, ice hockey, sledding, snow skiing, cross-country skiing, snowboarding, tobogganing, ice fishing. In addition to sports, students might suggest making ice sculptures, snow statues, or buildings.*

Suggest that students select a winter sport or activity that they think might be fun for Dillard and her friends and find out more about where and how it can be played, what equipment is needed, and how much it costs to participate.

Then have volunteers role-play the argument the man who chased them might have given for choosing a winter sport or activity instead of snowballing cars.

◆Critical Thinking

❶ Infer Ask students how they think Dillard expected an adult to behave in a situation like this one. *Possible response: She expected the adult would shout at them from the car window or chase them only a short distance and then give up.*

◆Critical Thinking

❷ Connect Have students recall Dillard's earlier reference to playing football. Then ask why she is comparing the game to the snow chase. *Dillard thinks that a person's fate in a football game depends on courage and concentration. She thinks the same thing is true of this chase, and she is surprised that the man seems as courageous and concentrated as she is.*

◆Literary Focus

❸ Autobiography Elicit responses such as these: *Dillard is motivated and thrilled by a challenge. This chase is especially exhilarating because the man is a worthy opponent.*

◆Build Grammar Skills

❹ Participles and Participial Phrases Ask students to identify the participles in this sentence and to tell what they modify. Staggering, half-blinded, *and* coughing *all are participles modifying* We.

Customize for
Visual/Spatial Learners

Have students draw a simple map of a neighborhood like the one described, and show the route they imagine the children took in trying to escape from the man. Students may wish to create a map legend that will signify obstacles such as fences, garbage cans, and stairs.

hump in the middle.

Often, of course, we hit our target, but this time, the only time in all of life, the car pulled
1 over and stopped. Its wide black door opened;
a man got out of it, running. He didn't even close the car door.

He ran after us, and we ran away from him, up the snowy Reynolds sidewalk. At the corner, I looked back; incredibly, he was still after us. He was in city clothes: a suit and tie, street shoes. Any normal adult would have quit, having sprung us into flight and made his point. This man was gaining on us. He was a thin man, all action. All of a sudden, we were running for our lives.

Wordless, we split up. We were on our turf; we could lose ourselves in the neighborhood backyards, everyone for himself. I paused and considered. Everyone had vanished except Mikey Fahey, who was just rounding the corner of a yellow brick house. Poor Mikey, I trailed him. The driver of the Buick sensibly picked the two of us to follow. The man apparently had all day.

He chased Mikey and me around the yellow house and up a backyard path we knew by heart: under a low tree, up a bank, through a hedge, down some snowy steps, and across the grocery store's delivery driveway. We smashed through a gap in another hedge, entered a scruffy backyard and ran around its back porch and tight between houses to Edgerton Avenue; we ran across Edgerton to an alley and up our own sliding woodpile to the Halls' front yard; he kept coming. We ran up Lloyd Street and wound through mazy backyards toward the steep hilltop at Willard and Lang.

He chased us silently, block after block. He chased us silently over picket fences, through thorny hedges, between houses, around garbage cans, and across streets. Every time I glanced back, choking for breath, I expected
2 he would have quit. He must have been as
breathless as we were. His jacket strained over his body. It was an immense discovery, pounding into my hot head with every sliding, joyous step, that this ordinary adult evidently knew what I thought only children who trained at football knew: that you have to fling
yourself at what you're doing, you have to 2
point yourself, forget yourself, aim, dive.

Mikey and I had nowhere to go, in our own neighborhood or out of it, but away from this man who was chasing us. He impelled us forward; we compelled him to follow our route. The air was cold; every breath tore my throat. We kept running, block after block; we kept improvising, backyard after backyard, running a frantic course and choosing it simultaneously, failing always to find small places or hard places to slow him down, and discovering always, exhilarated, dismayed, that only bare speed could save us—for he would never give up, this man—and we were losing speed.

> **◆ Literary Focus** What does Dillard's exhilaration reveal about her? 3

He chased us through the backyard labyrinths[2] of ten blocks before he caught us by our jackets. He caught us and we all stopped.

We three stood staggering, half blinded,
coughing, in an obscure hilltop backyard: a 4
man in his twenties, a boy, a girl. He had released our jackets, our pursuer, our captor, our hero: he knew we weren't going anywhere. We all played by the rules. Mikey and I unzipped our jackets. I pulled off my sopping mittens. Our tracks multiplied in the backyard's new snow. We had been breaking new snow all morning. We didn't look at each other. I was cherishing my excitement. The man's lower pants legs were wet; his cuffs were full of snow, and there was a prow of snow[3] beneath them on his shoes and socks. Some trees bordered the little flat backyard, some messy winter trees. There was no one around: a clearing in a grove, and we the only players.

It was a long time before he could speak. I had some difficulty at first recalling why we were there. My lips felt swollen; I couldn't see out of the sides of my eyes; I kept coughing.

"You stupid kids," he began perfunctorily.

2. backyard labyrinths (lab´ ə rinths): Areas behind and between the houses were like a kind of maze.
3. prow of snow: V-shaped, like the front of a ship.

Speaking and Listening Mini-Lesson

Dialogue of Authors
This lesson supports the Speaking and Listening activity on p. 583.

Introduce Explain that while these autobiographical essays describe events that actually happened to the authors, a dialogue between the two authors will be fiction. Arrange students in pairs and have them review the essays for ideas.

Develop Guide pairs to consider these questions as they develop their dialogue:

- Where do the authors meet?
- What is the occasion of the meeting?
- What do the two have in common?
- In what ways are they different?
- What will they talk about?

Apply Allow time for pairs to brainstorm and plan their dialogues. Some pairs may want to write out the dialogues, word for word, while others may prefer to prepare note cards to use as they talk. Invite pairs to present their dialogues for the class.

Assess Evaluate each pair's presentation on overall interest, and on accuracy of details included. You might also have students use the Peer Assessment, Dramatic Performance form, p. 107, in **Alternative Assessment.**

We listened perfunctorily indeed, if we listened at all, for the chewing out was redundant, a mere formality, and beside the point. The point was that he had chased us passionately without giving up, and so he had caught us. Now he came down to earth. I wanted the glory to last forever.

But how could the glory have lasted forever? We could have run through every backyard in North America until we got to Panama. But when he trapped us at the lip of the Panama Canal, what precisely could he have done to prolong the drama of the chase and cap its glory? I brooded about this for the next few years. He could only have fried Mikey Fahey and me in boiling oil, say, or dismembered us piecemeal, or staked us to anthills. None of which I really wanted, and none of which any adult was likely to do, even in the spirit of fun. He could only chew us out there in the Panamanian jungle, after months or years of exalting pursuit. He could only begin, "You stupid kids," and continue in his ordinary Pittsburgh accent with his normal righteous anger and the usual common sense.

If in that snowy backyard the driver of the black Buick had cut off our heads, Mikey's and mine, I would have died happy, for nothing has required so much of me since as being chased all over Pittsburgh in the middle of winter—running terrified, exhausted—by this sainted, skinny, furious red-headed man who wished to have a word with us. I don't know how he found his way back to his car. 5

◆ Build Vocabulary

compelled (kəm peld′) *v.*: Forced

perfunctorily (pər fuŋk′ tə rə lē) *adv.*: Without enthusiasm; routinely

Guide for Responding

◆ Literature and Your Life

Reader's Response Would you want the young Annie Dillard as a friend? Why or why not?

Thematic Focus What "immense discovery" does Dillard make as she runs breathlessly through backyards?

Journal Writing Dillard calls the man who chases her "our hero." In a journal entry, write about a time you felt this way about an adult.

☑ Check Your Comprehension

1. What does Dillard like about playing football with the boys?
2. What are Dillard and some of her friends doing "On one weekday morning after Christmas"?
3. Briefly describe how the man chases them.
4. What does the man do when he catches Dillard and her friend?

◆ Critical Thinking

Interpret

1. What connection does Dillard make between playing football and being chased for throwing a snowball? **[Connect]**
2. Why does Dillard call the man who chased her "our hero"? **[Interpret]**
3. What causes the "hero" to come "down to earth"? **[Analyze Cause and Effect]**
4. Does this episode from Dillard's early life have a larger meaning, or is it just an entertaining story? Explain. **[Draw Conclusions]**

Extend

5. The author says that nothing girls did could compare with playing football. Is there still as much of a difference between girls' and boys' activities? Explain. **[Social Studies Link]**

Compare Literary Works

6. Do you think the young Annie Dillard would have liked the young Russell Baker? Why or why not? **[Connect]**

Beyond the Selection

Other Works by Annie Dillard

The Living: A Novel
The Writing Life
Teaching a Stone to Talk: Expeditions and Encounters
Mornings Like This: Found Poems

Other Works About Moments of Insight

But I'll Be Back, Cynthia Rylant
The Pigman, Paul Zindel
Farewell to Manzanar, Jeanne W. Houston, James D. Houston

INTERNET

For more information about Annie Dillard, visit the following Web site:
http://www.wardy.org/dillard/html

Please be aware, however, that the site may have changed from the time we published this information. We *strongly recommend* that you preview the site before you send students to it.

◆ Critical Thinking

5 Draw Conclusions Ask students what they can conclude about Annie Dillard from the ending of this autobiographical essay. *Dillard learned something about herself and about the kind of person she wants to be from the experience of the chase. It is an experience that she will never forget.*

Reinforce and Extend

Answers

◆ Literature and Your Life

Reader's Response Many students will say they would like to have her as a friend because she would be fun to be with—enthusiastic and positive.

Thematic Focus She learns that adults can be courageous and committed—something she believed only children could be.

Check Your Comprehension

1. The game requires courage and concentration.
2. They are throwing snowballs at passing cars.
3. He jumps out of his car, relentlessly chases, and finally catches them.
4. He grabs them by their jackets and lectures them.

◆ Critical Thinking

1. Both require that the participants fling themselves at what they are doing, forgetting themselves and concentrating on the moment.
2. She admires the way he commits himself wholeheartedly to the chase, in a way she thinks only children will.
3. He finally catches the children.
4. It has the larger meaning that the experience and memory of doing something can be as rewarding as the outcome or result.
5. Answers will vary. Students should recognize that there are more opportunities for girls to participate in a variety of sports today.
6. Possible response: Yes, because all the friends she mentions are boys. However, the two might not have been close friends, since Dillard enjoyed the thrill of competition, while Baker liked to read and listen to the radio. Dillard might have liked Baker's sister, Doris, better.

Answers

◆ Reading Strategy

1. He might be trying to show that even successful people experience some failures in their lives. He may also be reminding the reader that different people have different talents.
2. She learns that acting with courage and concentration is its own reward.
3. It was meaningful in her life and she hopes it might be meaningful to others.

◆ Build Vocabulary

Using the Word Root *-pel-*

1. push away
2. push forward
3. push out

Spelling Strategy

1. impelled; 2. admitting; 3. referred

Using the Word Bank

1. b
2. c
3. a
4. b
5. c
6. b
7. a

◆ Literary Focus

1. By presenting his faults, Baker shows that he is an ordinary person with shortcomings—the kind of person readers can understand and with whom they might identify.
2. Student responses will vary but should illustrate Dillard's enthusiastic involvement in the details of everyday experiences.

◆ Build Grammar Skills

1. closed, window
2. running, legs
3. Dazed, we
4. sliding, woodpile
5. exalting, pursuit

Writing Application

Possible responses:

1. He dreaded the wrapped magazines.
2. Angered about the cheese, she went back.

Guide for Responding *(continued)*

◆ Reading Strategy

Understand the Author's Purpose

These authors write about their own lives, but their **purposes,** their reasons for writing, all relate to you. The writers want to share details of their lives to teach you, charm you, convince you, or impress you. Dillard, for example, begins "The Chase" by teaching you about herself and what she valued most in life: "concentration and courage."

1. What might Baker be trying to teach by showing his failures as well as his successes?
2. What does Dillard herself seem to learn about "concentration and courage" from the chase?
3. Why do you think she wants to share this lesson?

◆ Build Vocabulary

Using the Word Root *-pel-*

The root *-pel-* in the word *compelled* means "to push" or "to drive." Explain the meaning of each of these words:

1. *repel* (*re-* means "back" or "away")
2. *propel* (*pro-* means "forward" or "toward")
3. *expel* (*ex-* means "out")

Spelling Strategy

Compel ends in a single consonant coming after a single vowel. It also has the accent on the final syllable. In this case, you usually double the final consonant when adding a suffix starting with a vowel: *compelled.* On your paper, correctly spell the following combinations:

1. impel + -ed **2.** admit + -ing **3.** refer + -ed

Using the Word Bank

Choose the word or phrase that is most nearly opposite in meaning to each first word:

1. gumption: (a) spunk, (b) laziness, (c) loveliness
2. paupers: (a) clerks, (b) puppets, (c) billionaires
3. crucial: (a) unimportant, (b) essential, (c) facial
4. aptitude: (a) test, (b) inability, (c) capacity
5. translucent: (a) admitting light, (b) filled with light, (c) not admitting light
6. compelled: (a) jailed, (b) ignored, (c) dreamed
7. perfunctorily: (a) excitedly, (b) deliberately, (c) jokingly

◆ Literary Focus

Autobiography

These essays come from **autobiographies,** narratives in which the authors tell their life stories. Interestingly, these authors portray themselves in opposite ways. Baker shows himself as a charming loser, a no-gumption kid who stumbles into success at the end. Dillard reveals herself as a girl *with* gumption who dives fearlessly into everything she does.

1. Explain how Baker's humorous confession of his faults makes him more appealing to readers.
2. Show how the chase Dillard describes reveals her passionate approach to life.

◆ Build Grammar Skills

Participles and Participial Phrases

A **participle** is a verb form that acts as an adjective, modifying a noun or a pronoun. **Present participles** end in *-ing*, and **past participles** usually end in *-ed* but may have an irregular ending such as *-t* or *-en.* A **participial phrase** consists of a participle and its modifiers. Look at these examples:

present participle → noun
I could not deliver an *engaging* sales pitch.

past participle → noun
The snowball made a *smashed* star on the window.

participial phrase → pronoun
Brimming with zest, she returned with me.

Practice Identify the participles and participial phrases in these sentences. Indicate the nouns or pronouns that they modify.

1. Doris raised her fist against the closed window.
2. She threw herself mightily at his running legs.
3. Dazed by exhaustion, we froze in our tracks.
4. They ran up the sliding woodpile.
5. After an exalting pursuit, he finally caught them.

Writing Application Combine each pair of sentences by using a participle or participial phrase.

Example: He received a grade. It was passing.
He received a *passing* grade.

1. He dreaded the magazines. They were wrapped.
2. She went back. She was angry about the cheese.

Writer's Solution

For additional instruction and practice, use the lesson in the *Writer's Solution Language Lab CD-ROM* on participles and participial phrases. You may also refer to Participles in Phrases, pp. 47–48, in the *Writer's Solution Grammar Practice Book.*

Build Your Portfolio

Idea Bank

Writing

1. **Personality Profile** Review one of these autobiographical accounts. Then, use it to write a profile of the author, summarizing his or her qualities in a paragraph.
2. **Personal Narrative** Like Baker and Dillard, write about a brief episode from your life. Use language that appeals to the senses so that readers can share your experience. Also, tell readers why the events were important to you.
3. **Extended Definition** Write an extended definition of the word *gumption* as it is used in "No Gumption." Summarize what the word means, and draw on both essays and your own experience to give examples of this quality.

Speaking and Listening

4. **Dialogue of Authors** With a partner, act out a scene in which the young Russell Baker meets the young Annie Dillard. Review their autobiographical accounts for clues about how they would relate to each other. **[Performing Arts Link]**
5. **Oral Interpretation** You can hear the rhythm of the chase in Dillard's description of it. Capture that rhythm as you read her narrative aloud, starting from the moment that the man gets out of his car. **[Performing Arts Link]**

Projects

6. **Book Report** Read Russell Baker's *Growing Up* or Annie Dillard's *An American Childhood*, and report on it to the class. Explain how well the book reveals the author's struggles, values, and ideas about life.
7. **Multimedia Presentation [Group Activity]** Join with classmates to give a presentation on the Depression, the time in which Baker spent his childhood. Use film clips, recordings, photographs, news stories, and speeches to explain that time of economic hardship. **[Social Studies Link; Media Link]**

Writing Mini-Lesson

Comparison-and-Contrast Essay

These autobiographies offer portraits of two young people. Although they grew up twenty years apart, you can introduce them in the pages of your own essay. Write a comparison-and-contrast essay of the young Russell Baker and the young Annie Dillard. Choose three or four points to show how Baker and Dillard are similar or different.

Writing Skills Focus: Clear and Logical Organization

Give your essay a **clear and logical organization** so that readers can understand your ideas. Include an introduction and a conclusion. Also, devote a paragraph to each point of comparison or contrast. Within the paragraph, you can discuss how Baker and Dillard are similar or different with regard to that point.

Model Paragraph Outline:

Paragraph Comparing Their "Gumption"
- Baker lacks it—give examples
- Dillard has it—give examples

Prewriting Focus on three or four points, and jot down similarities or differences for each. Points of comparison or contrast might include gumption, favorite activities, and interaction with adults.

Drafting Referring to your notes, write a paragraph for each point of comparison or contrast. Write the introduction and conclusion after you have written the body of your essay.

◆ Grammar Application

Use participles and participial phrases to combine short sentences.

Revising Be sure that your essay has an introduction that explains your purpose and a conclusion that summarizes your findings. The body of your essay should contain separate paragraphs for each point on which you compare or contrast the authors.

✓ ASSESSMENT OPTIONS

Formal Assessment, Selection Test, pp. 163–165, and Assessment Resources Software. The selection test is designed so that it can easily be customized to the performance levels of your students.

Alternative Assessment, p. 35, includes options for less advanced students, more advanced students, visual/spatial learners, verbal/linguistic learners, musical/rhythmic learners, and bodily/kinesthetic learners.

PORTFOLIO ASSESSMENT

Use the following rubrics in the **Alternative Assessment** booklet to assess student writing:
Personality Profile: Description, p. 84
Personal Narrative: Narrative Based on Personal Experience Rubric, p. 83
Extended Definition: Definition/Classification Rubric, p. 86
Writing Mini-Lesson: Comparison/Contrast Rubric, p. 90

Idea Bank

Following are suggestions for matching the Idea Bank topics with your students' performance levels and learning modalities:

Customize for *Performance Levels*
Less Advanced Students: 1, 4, 7
Average Students: 2, 4, 5, 6, 7
More Advanced Students: 3, 4, 5, 6, 7

Customize for *Learning Modalities*
Verbal/Linguistic: 1, 2, 3, 4, 5, 6
Interpersonal: 4, 7
Visual/Spatial: 7
Musical/Rhythmic: 5
Intrapersonal: 1, 2, 3, 6
Bodily/Kinesthetic: 4, 7

Writing Mini-Lesson

Refer students to the Writing Handbook in the back of the book for instruction on the writing process and for further information on essays. Have students use the Venn Diagram in **Writing and Language Transparencies,** p. 86, to arrange their prewriting examples.

Writer's Solution

Writing Lab CD-ROM
Have students complete the tutorial on Exposition: Making Connections. Follow these steps:

1. Have students record similarities and differences between Dillard and Baker in a Venn diagram.
2. Instruct students to view the video clip about organization.
3. Have students review the annotated student model of a comparison-and-contrast essay.
4. Have students use the sentence-length revision checker.

Writer's Solution Sourcebook
Have students use Chapter 5, "Exposition: Making Connections," pp. 134–165, for additional support. The chapter includes in-depth instruction on using prepositions and conjunctions and writing topic sentences.

Guide for Reading

OBJECTIVES

1. To read, comprehend, and interpret two biographies
2. To relate biographies to personal experience
3. To set a purpose for reading
4. To understand biographies
5. To build vocabulary in context and learn the prefix *sub-*
6. To develop skill in using appositives and appositive phrases
7. To write an instructional guide focusing on thoroughness
8. To respond to biographies through writing, speaking and listening, and projects

SKILLS INSTRUCTION

Vocabulary: Prefixes: *sub-*

Spelling: Add Suffixes to Words Ending in e

Grammar: Appositives and Appositive Phrases

Reading Strategy: Set a Purpose for Reading

Literary Focus: Biography

Writing: Thoroughness

Speaking and Listening: Award Presentation (Teacher Edition)

Critical Viewing: Infer; Assess; Analyze; Draw Conclusions

PORTFOLIO OPPORTUNITIES

Writing: Baseball Card; Song of Praise; Proposal for a Documentary

Writing Mini-Lesson: Instructional Guide

Speaking and Listening: Gallery Talk; Award Presentation

Projects: Book Circle; Biographical Report

Meet the Authors:

H. N. Levitt (1920–)

H. N. Levitt was born and raised in New York City. During World War II, he was a naval officer. After the war, he pursued a career as a playwright and a college professor of drama.

THE STORY BEHIND THE ESSAY

Levitt has always loved the visual arts as well as drama. He learned how to paint at a well-known art school, and he has written often about painters. In this essay, he describes the life and career of the nineteenth-century American artist Winslow Homer.

William W. Lace (1942–)

A native of Fort Worth, Texas, William W. Lace worked for newspapers before joining the University of Texas at Arlington as sports information director. Later, he became the director of college relations for a junior college in Fort Worth.

Lace and his wife, Laura, a public school librarian, live in Arlington, Texas, with their two children. His wife and her book-hungry students inspired Lace to write about Nolan Ryan for young people.

◆ Literature and Your Life

CONNECT YOUR EXPERIENCE

What do you see in the painting on the opposite page? Do you see the work of a contemporary artist or the achievements of all-time strikeout king Nolan Ryan? If you combine these answers, you might see the artist's power—through broad strokes and bright colors—to shape the way you see the athlete. As you read these biographies, think about the way the writers shape your understanding of their subjects.

THEMATIC FOCUS: Wishes, Hopes, Dreams

What do these essays tell you about the goals and ambitions of their subjects?

◆ Background for Understanding

MATHEMATICS

Numbers don't tell the whole story of a life. However, you can suggest people's achievements with statistics, a numerical measure of what they've accomplished. Nolan Ryan's statistics include 5,714 strikeouts, the major league record. The artist Winslow Homer used his arm more gently but just as effectively. He created about 1,000 paintings.

◆ Build Vocabulary

PREFIXES: *sub-*

Levitt's essay explains that many nineteenth-century American painters depicted African Americans in "subservient poses." *Subservient*, meaning "inferior," combines the prefix *sub-*, meaning "under" or "below," with a word part meaning "to serve."

WORD BANK

Which three words from the essays have the same suffix, indicating that they are nouns?

cantankerous
subtle
brutality
vanquished
serenity
subservient
hostility

More About the Authors

H. N. Levitt is a true example of what people call a *Renaissance man*, one who is accomplished in different areas of life. For Levitt, those areas are military life, education, theater, painting, and art criticism.

William W. Lace has written other books, about sports and history, for young adults.

Prentice Hall Literature Program Resources

REINFORCE / RETEACH / EXTEND

Selection Support Pages
Build Vocabulary: Prefixes: *sub-*, p. 195
Build Spelling Skills, p. 196
Build Grammar Skills: Appositives and Appositive Phrases, p. 197
Reading Strategy: Set a Purpose for Reading, p. 198
Literary Focus: Biography, p. 199

Strategies for Diverse Student Needs, pp. 71–72

Beyond Literature Study Skills: Understanding Statistics, p. 36

Formal Assessment Selection Test, pp. 166–168, Assessment Resources Software

Alternative Assessment, p. 36

Art Transparencies, Transparency 12, p. 51

Resource Pro CD-ROM
"Winslow Homer: America's Greatest Painter"; "Nolan Ryan, Texas Treasure"—includes all resource material and customizable lesson plan

Listening to Literature Audiocassettes
"Winslow Homer: America's Greatest Painter"; "Nolan Ryan, Texas Treasure"

Winslow Homer: America's Greatest Painter
◆ Nolan Ryan, Texas Treasure ◆

Nolan Ryan, LeRoy Neiman

◆ Literary Focus

Biography

A **biography** is the story of someone's life told by someone else. Usually, authors write about a famous subject—someone known and of interest to many people. Biographers not only tell you the facts of their subject's lives, they also explain what these facts mean.

◆ Reading Strategy

Set a Purpose for Reading

Setting a purpose, or goal, for reading will help you get the most out of a biography or any other piece of writing. Often, you can phrase your purpose in terms of a question. The titles of these two biographical essays suggest purpose-setting questions to guide your reading. You might ask about Homer, "What makes him America's greatest painter?" You might ask about Ryan, "Why is he a Texas treasure?" Use a KWL chart like the one below to record your answers:

K	W	L
What do I know about Homer?	**What do I want to know about Homer?**	**What have I learned about Homer?**
(Fill this in before you read.)	**Purpose-setting question:** Why is he America's greatest painter?	(Fill this in by answering your question as you read.)

Write the words "Painting" and "Baseball" on the chalkboard. Have students brainstorm for a list of the all-time greats under each category, and write their suggestions on the board. Solicit ideas about what it takes to be a leader in each of these fields, then inform students that they will read biographies about a renowned painter and a champion baseball player.

◆ Build Grammar Skills

Appositives and Appositive Phrases If you wish to introduce the grammar concept for this selection before students read, refer to the instruction on p. 594.

Customize for
Less Proficient Readers
Have students read the selections in small sections, pausing periodically to review and summarize what they have learned so far about the subject of each biography.

Customize for
More Advanced Students
Discuss with students the need to distinguish between fact and opinion when they read biographies. Have students make a two-column table and, as they read, write facts in one column and opinions in the other. When they discuss their choices, students may be surprised to find that there is some disagreement on what are facts and what are opinions.

Fact	Opinion
He took five art lessons	. . . then he went on to become a self-taught genius.

Humanities: Art

Nolan Ryan, by LeRoy Neiman

LeRoy Neiman, best known for his brightly colored, energetic works portraying athletes, was the official artist for five Olympics. As you view the painting on this page, ask: What evidence is there that this painting of Ryan is not from the pitcher's years as a Texas Ranger? *Students who are baseball fans may point to the Houston Astros uniform and the Astrodome locale; others may note the pitcher's youthful appearance.*

Preparing for Standardized Tests

Spelling Standardized tests may include questions that evaluate students' knowledge of spelling strategies for words ending in suffixes. Remind students that when a suffix beginning with a vowel is added to a word ending in e, they should drop that final e. Give the following sample test question:

Identify the sentence in which the underlined word is not spelled correctly.

(A) Most of his contemporaries had left baseball, but Nolan Ryan didn't even think of retiring.
(B) Homer painted scenes of people struggleing against the forces of nature.
(C) Like his paintings, Homer's life was a creative work.
(D) No mistake

Students should recognize that the underlined word in (*B*) is spelled incorrectly. They should also be able to identify the correct spelling as *struggling*. For further practice, use Build Spelling Skills in **Selection Support,** p. 196.

Develop Understanding

One-Minute Insight This essay gives a brief chronological overview of the life of painter Winslow Homer, with an assessment of his character and his art. It portrays the great artist as an independent thinker and a man who struggled and succeeded in his quest to find inner peace.

Team Teaching Strategy

You may want to coordinate with an art teacher, who can present an art appreciation lesson that focuses on the works of Winslow Homer.

Customize for
Visual/Spatial Learners
Guide students to pay particular attention to what Levitt writes about Homer's paintings, because it is especially challenging to capture in words the style and effect of a work of visual art. Encourage students to compare their views about the paintings with the author's views. You may want to show Art Transparency 12, which also appears in the student edition on p. 370, as an additional example of Homer's work.

◆Reading Strategy

❶ Set a Purpose for Reading
Homer is America's greatest painter, according to the author, not only because his work was highly regarded during his lifetime but also because it is featured in America's major museums and collections today.

▶Critical Viewing◀

❷ Infer *Students may observe that soldiers in both armies honored one another and treated one another with respect. They may say that they learn something about the uniforms soldiers wore, and that military behavior was formal.*

Winslow Homer: America's Greatest Painter

H. N. Levitt

Prisoners from the Front, 1866, Winslow Homer, The Metropolitan Museum of Art

▲ **Critical Viewing** What can you learn about the Civil War from this painting by Homer? **[Infer]** 

❶ His oil paintings and watercolors are in all major American museums and collections today. But even when Winslow Homer was alive, they called him America's greatest painter.

That wasn't all they said about him. They also called him crusty, bad-tempered, cantankerous, grouchy, sour as a crab, and surly as a bear. He was all those things, and more.

His brother's wife—and Winslow's only female friend—thought Homer the most courteous gentleman she ever knew. She said he knew what he wanted in life, and he went about getting it without any fuss or feathers.

When it came to painting, he took five lessons, decided that was enough, then went on to become a self-taught genius.

Homer was born into a middle-class family on Feb. 24, 1836. The family lived near the harbor in Boston, so Homer's earliest memories were of ships, sailors, fishermen and the sea.

When he was six, the family moved to Cambridge, directly across the street from Harvard College. Sometimes Winslow's dad would suggest that the boy consider attending Harvard someday. But it was no use. All young Winslow wanted to do was fish and draw.

Humanities: Art

Prisoners From the Front, 1866, by Winslow Homer

The makers of the 1993 film *Gettysburg* were familiar with Winslow Homer's paintings of Civil War scenes. The scene depicted in this painting, for example, was re-created in the movie. In that scene, the Federal lieutenant spoke with the Confederate soldier wearing the floppy hat about what each was fighting for. At that point in the war, neither was altogether sure about the reasons. Use these questions for discussion:

1. Who are these prisoners and what does the painting tell about them? *Students may say that they are captured Confederate soldiers, that they dress differently from one another, range in age from old to young, and that they appear to express different emotions—defiance and resignation, for instance.*
2. What impression do you get of the Federal officer who addresses them? *Students may say that he is formal in appearance and wants to hear what his prisoners have to say.*

After a while, the family realized there was something special about Winslow, because that's all he would do—fish and draw, day in and day out, all year long.

But even if Homer had wanted to go to college, there would have been no money for it. When Homer was 13, his dad sold all and left to make his fortune in the California gold rush. He came back a few years later empty-handed.

But the family remained close. And once they realized how important art was to Homer, they encouraged it. In fact, his brothers se-
3 cretly bought up his paintings at early exhibitions so he wouldn't get discouraged if no one else bought them. Those two brothers remained his best friends all his life.

When the Civil War broke out in 1861, Homer was a young artist already on his way to fame. As a freelance illustrator for *Harper's Weekly*, America's most important news magazine, he was considered one of the country's finest wood-block engravers.

In those days, an artist would cut illustrations into a wood block, which was then inked in black and printed on sheets of paper. Techniques like subtle shadowing and distant perspective were hard to achieve, but Homer's illustrations were unusually lively and strong.

Harper's Weekly offered Homer a good job, and he could have remained a weekly illustrator all his life. But he wanted to work for no one but himself, so he turned the offer down.

Homer left New York to paint the war. He
4 joined Gen. George McClellan's Army of the Potomac[1] as a freelance artist-correspondent. He painted scenes at the siege of Yorktown[2] and did many drawings of Abraham Lincoln, the tall, gaunt, serious president who was desperately trying to keep the Union together.

In a few short years, Homer's Civil War paintings brought him fame at home and abroad. He painted war as no other artist ever had. He emphasized not brutality but rather scenes of loneliness, camp life, endless waiting, and even horseplay on the battlefield.

> ◆ **Literary Focus** 5
> What do you learn about Homer from the way in which he depicted the Civil War?

Homer was a Yankee,[3] but he showed equal concern for soldiers from both the North and South. His paintings did not glorify war; they seemed to cry out for it to end.

His *Prisoners from the Front* made a reputation overnight. This one painting, done in
6 Homer's honest, realistic style, showed the common humanity that linked North and South, victor and vanquished, Americans all. Homer's war paintings give us the best record we have of how the Civil War soldier actually looked and acted.

After the war, railroads and new industries changed America from a rural to an industrial society almost overnight. But Homer paid no attention. He went back to painting the things he liked: country scenes, farmers, beautiful women in fashionable clothes, and kids at play.

He never painted kids with the gushy sentimentalism of other American painters. And he didn't look down on young people. His paintings showed what was then a typical American upbeat attitude marked by humor and innocence. The public loved it.

And then something strange happened. Homer stopped painting. For three years, his brushes sat idle. He left his studio for Europe, but avoided the art world in Paris. Instead, he went to Tynemouth, England, a small fishing port on the North Sea.

It was there, at Tynemouth, that Winslow Homer witnessed the fierce, day-to-day struggle of men and women against the sea. Their

1. **Gen. George McClellan's Army of the Potomac:** McClellan served for a time as the general in chief of the Union Army during the Civil War. The Union Army in the East was known as the Army of the Potomac.
2. **Yorktown:** Yorktown, Virginia, which Gen. McClellan occupied on May 4, 1862.
3. **Yankee:** Native or inhabitant of a northern state.

◆ Build Vocabulary

cantankerous (kan taŋ´ kər əs) *adj.*: Quarrelsome; argumentative

subtle (sut´ əl) *adj.*: Delicately skillful or clever

brutality (bro͞o tal´ ə tē) *n.*: Violence; harshness

vanquished (vaŋ´ kwisht) *n.*: The person defeated (usually a verb)

◆Literary Focus

3 Biography What about Homer's family has an impact on his career as an artist? *His family was supportive of his plans right from the start.*

◆Critical Thinking

4 Assess What does this incident tell you about Homer's character? *He was headstrong, self-motivated, independent, and confident.*

◆Literary Focus

5 Biography *Students may respond that Homer saw beyond the obvious events and issues and was interested in the human side of the war.*

◆Critical Thinking

6 Interpret Ask students to tell whether they agree with Levitt's interpretation of this painting. Have students support their views with details from the painting.

Block Scheduling Strategies

Consider these suggestions to take advantage of extended class time:

- Review the Reading Strategy before students read. Have students, as they read, fill in a chart like the one on p. 585. After reading, have students compare their answers to the Reading Strategy questions on p. 594.
- Introduce the Literary Focus. Have students compare responses to the Literary Focus questions on p. 594.
- Devote class time to having students work in small groups on the Projects in the Idea Bank on p. 595, or to research and discuss statistics for the Sports Connection in Beyond Literature on p. 593. Provide time for students to view one another's baseball cards, examine and comment on the documentary proposals, or listen to performances of the original songs.
- If students have access to technology, have them work in pairs using the tutorial on Exposition: Giving Information, in the *Writer's Solution Writing Lab CD-ROM*, to complete the Writing Mini-Lesson on p. 595.

◆Literary Focus

❶ **Biography** Ask students to try to explain why Homer believed that "nice finishing touches were no longer important." *Students might suggest that once he captured the essence of a subject, Homer felt that he'd accomplished what he set out to do, and he spent no time on less important details. Or they might say that the need to go on to the next painting caused him to stop short of finishing touches on a current work.*

◆Build Vocabulary

❷ **Spelling** Point out that when a suffix begins with a vowel, such as in *-ing*, the final e in the base word should be dropped, as in *using* and *sparkling*.

▶Critical Viewing◀

❸ **Assess** *Some students might say that the power of the sea is conveyed more strongly by churning waves, threatening sharks, and an approaching storm; others may find the man's predicament more strongly conveyed: He seems exhausted from his ordeal, has no sail, mast, nor oars, and has ragged pants, suggesting that he's been at sea for a long time.*

◆Literature and Your Life

❹ *Some students may recall a time when they made a snap decision to change, while others—due to their youth—may find it difficult to relate their own experience to Homer's.*

The Gulf Stream, 1899, Winslow Homer, The Metropolitan Museum of Art

▲ **Critical Viewing** What is conveyed more strongly to you in this painting—the man's predicament or the power of the sea? Explain. **[Assess]** ❸

hard, bitter, dangerous lives made him think critically about his own life and work.

After that, women, children and country life appeared less often in his paintings. What replaced them was the harsh existence of men of the sea. These heroic people became, in his mind, the best examples of mankind. That's apparent in his famous painting *The Life Line.* To Homer, the sea had lost its serenity and had become a powerful force of nature.

❶ Homer began painting larger pictures too, and his style became more bold and powerful. Some complained that his paintings now looked unfinished. But he didn't care. Nice finishing touches were no longer important.

Besides the sea and its people, Homer started painting scenes of the American wilderness. He did big, masculine pictures of hunting and fishing, canoeing the rapids, sitting around the campfire and trekking over rugged trails.

He painted large oils, but he also painted many watercolors. By the time he had hit his stride, he had become America's first great watercolor painter. It was he who developed ❷ the technique of using the white, unpainted paper as sparkling highlight. ❷

Then, at 48, when he was selling just about everything he painted, he did another about-face.

He surprised his family, friends and fellow artists by turning his back on the city and the world of art. He packed up and left to spend the rest of his life—27 years—as a hermit on a rocky cliff overlooking the sea in Prouts Neck, Maine.

> **◆ Literature and Your Life**
> Have you ever made a snap decision to change—like the one described here? ❹

In typical, cantankerous, Yankee fashion, when asked how he could leave New York, the scene of his success, he said, "I left New York to escape jury duty."

In a more serious mood, he told his brother that his new, lonely life was the only setting in which he could do his work in peace, free from visitors and publicity seekers.

Humanities: Art

The Gulf Stream, 1899, by Winslow Homer

This famous painting shows Homer's fascination with the struggle between human beings and the forces of nature. Ask these questions:

1. Why did Homer include the detail of the schooner in the background? *It adds to the drama of the scene by suggesting that there is a possibility, however remote, that the man in the boat may be saved.*
2. Compare this painting with that of the Civil War soldiers on p. 586. Which one do you like better? Why? *Encourage students to express their emotional responses and to point out details of the paintings that evoke those responses.*
3. Write a description of how you would feel if you were the man on the boat or one of the captured soldiers in the Union camp. *Students might say that if they were one of the soldiers, they would feel either despair or relief at being taken out of action; if they were the man in the boat, they might feel terror at the prospect of the approaching storm and the eventuality of being tossed to the circling sharks, or hope that the ship will rescue them.*

Winslow Homer finally came to love his life. It was at Prouts Neck that he finished one of his great masterpieces, *The Gulf Stream*, in 1899.

This painting showed a black man marooned in a broken-masted boat circled by sharks in the Gulf Stream.[4] It was an immediate sensation, but only one of a long series of oils and watercolors that Homer painted of American blacks. This was at a time when blacks were usually depicted as minstrel singers and servants, or in other subservient poses.

In his last years, Homer made another big change. Instead of painting scenes of men struggling against the sea and wilderness, he started painting the sea and wilderness alone.

Like a stubborn tree growing out of a rock, he stood on his lonely cliff and painted the sea, forever untamed and uncontrolled by man. ❺

In 1910, just before he died, he wrote in a letter, "All is lovely outside my house and inside my house and myself." Winslow Homer was a simple, modest, unsentimental man—the kind of American we Americans like.

4. **Gulf Stream:** Warm ocean current flowing from the Gulf of Mexico along the east coast of the United States.

◆ Build Vocabulary

serenity (sə ren´ ə tē) *n.*: Calmness

subservient (səb sʉr´ vē ənt) *adj.*: Inferior

Guide for Responding

◆ Literature and Your Life

Reader's Response Would you like to have known Winslow Homer? Why or why not?

Thematic Focus What do you think Homer wanted to achieve with his art when he reached old age?

Journal Writing Study one of the paintings that accompany this essay. In a journal entry, describe your response to the work.

☑ Check Your Comprehension

1. What caused Homer's family to realize there was "something special" about him?
2. In what ways did Homer's Civil War pictures differ from those of other artists?
3. How did Homer's work change after he lived in England?
4. Why did Homer leave New York to live in Maine?
5. What change occurred in his painting during his "last years"?

◆ Critical Thinking

Interpret

1. In what ways did Homer gain strength from his family? **[Infer]**
2. In your own words, summarize the direction that Homer's art took from the time he returned from the Civil War until his death. **[Analyze]**
3. What do you think might have caused Homer to stop painting for three years? **[Hypothesize]**
4. How does the essay show that Homer "knew what he wanted in life"? **[Support]**

Evaluate

5. Levitt suggests that simplicity, modesty, and lack of sentimentality are values that most Americans share. Explain why you agree or disagree. **[Make a Judgment]**

Extend

6. How would you describe the mood of Homer's painting *The Gulf Stream?* Support your answer with details from the picture. **[Art Link]**

Cross-Curricular Connection: Social Studies

Civil War Images Winslow Homer was not the only artist to cover the Civil War. Because the photographic process at that time was too slow to capture battle action, newspapers and magazines like *Leslie's Weekly, Harper's Weekly,* and *The New York Illustrated News* sent artists to draw what the battles actually looked like. Edwin Forbes, Henry Walke, William and Alfred Waud, and Theodore R. Davis were among the illustrators who, like Homer, got close enough to the action to make quick pen-and-ink sketches of it. These images provide a visual record of the war.

Photographs, too, were important. They illustrated for Americans the Civil War personalities and landscapes, and the horrors of the aftermath of battles. Pioneer photographers like Mathew Brady, Alexander Gardner, and Timothy O'Sullivan made contributions. Have students look through books of Civil War photos and illustrations to appreciate the work of these artists and photographers. Have them explain which pictures move them the most. One source for a variety of images is *The American Heritage Picture History of the Civil War,* by Bruce Catton. Many others are available.

◆ Literary Focus

❺ Biography Why does the author compare Homer to "a stubborn tree growing out of a rock"? *Students may say that he uses this comparison to express the idea that Homer was an individualist whose decisive behavior grew out of his great inner strength and determination.*

Reinforce and Extend

Answers

◆ Literature and Your Life

Reader's Response Possible response: Students would enjoy meeting someone who was so talented and pursued his dreams without compromise.

Thematic Focus Students may suggest that he narrowed his artistic focus solely to landscape or that he was painting a vision of his own peaceful solitude

☑ Check Your Comprehension

1. All he wanted to do was to paint and fish.
2. He didn't paint battle scenes; he tried to accurately depict the soldiers' lives together in the camps.
3. He began to depict the harsh life of people battling the sea.
4. He wanted to work in peace, free from visitors.
5. He began to paint sea wilderness scenes without human figures.

◆ Critical Thinking

1. His family was supportive of and interested in his artistic abilities and unconventional decisions.
2. He became less interested in painting people interacting with one another. At first he painted scenes of the struggle between people and nature. Later he painted nature scenes with no people.
3. Students may suggest that he needed to decide what he wanted to paint.
4. Students may say that he made some unexpected choices in his life, but that each led to his development as an artist.
5. Many responses are likely to reflect teenagers' needs to be liked and accepted by their peers.
6. Possible response: The painting is dramatic; the man's fate is in the balance as he faces death from the elements on one hand and rescue by sailors on the other.

Develop Understanding

One-Minute Insight In this essay, William W. Lace explains why, in his opinion, the pitcher Nolan Ryan is a "Texas Treasure." Lace points not only to Ryan's many successes and accomplishments on the playing field, but to his work ethic and approach to life off the baseball diamond.

Customize for
English Language Learners
Some common words have a very specific meaning for the game of baseball. Help students, as needed, with the many baseball terms and expressions used in the selection, such as *starts, no-hitter, pitch inside, mound, assists, crowd the plate,* and *wild pitches.* Encourage students who are familiar with baseball terminology to help classmates understand any unfamiliar language.

◆Build Grammar Skills

❶ **Appositives and Appositive Phrases** Direct students' attention to the title of this essay and to the appositive phrase it includes. Guide them to understand that "Texas Treasure" is an appositive phrase because it includes a noun and its modifier and explains who Nolan Ryan is.

◆Reading Strategy

❷ **Set a Purpose for Reading** Students may know that pitching a no-hitter is a big achievement and that a pitcher with seven no-hitters to his credit is someone with special talents.

❶ Nolan Ryan, TEXAS TREASURE

William W. Lace

A generation has passed since Nolan Ryan threw his first major league pitch. His fellow players are sometimes just as eager as fans to get his autograph. Texas third baseman Steve Buchele, a southern California native, said, "There wasn't anything more exciting than coming to the games and watching Nolan pitch."

How has Ryan lasted so long? He claims that it's a combination of physical condition and mental attitude.

Ryan has always taken good care of his body. Even after the biggest of games, like his seventh no-hitter, he was up early, working out. "We're working against the clock," he told a reporter. "I can't do this forever. I haven't got much time."

❷ **◆ Reading Strategy** What clues in this passage help answer the purpose-setting question "Why is Ryan a treasure?"

He learned a balanced, healthy diet from his mother, who took pride in putting wholesome meals on the Ryan family table. Even as a young player he was careful about what he ate. He's even more careful now, avoiding meats like bacon or sausage, cream soups, and any other food high in fat. He doesn't eat fried foods and doesn't often eat large meals. When he snacks, he usually chooses fruit.

Ryan's physical conditioning has kept him going long after most players his age have retired. He stays fit during the winter, and during the season, maintains a workout schedule

of weightlifting, throwing, and running that almost never changes. The times are very different from his early days in baseball, when all
3 a pitcher did between starts was throw enough each day to stay loose.

Mental fitness probably has been just as important. Even after 26 major-league seasons, baseball is still fun and challenging to Ryan. Yet, even though it's his living, baseball isn't his whole life. He spends as much time at home with his family as he can. He is keenly interested in cattle raising and operates three ranches in addition to his property near Alvin. He has many other business interests and spends much time on charity work.

The talented pitcher has not allowed fame and fortune to change his personality, as many star athletes have. Ryan remains what he always was—a modest, uncomplicated, man from a middle-class, family-centered background.

"I still represent small-town Texas, and that's fine with me," he once said. "I'm still like the people who lived where I grew up. I've kept my roots. I'm proud of that."

If you didn't know differently, you'd think Ryan was the man next door, working hard to put food on the table and tires on the car. "If you saw him in a shopping mall or talked

▼ **Critical Viewing** Ryan is carried off the field after throwing his record-breaking seventh no-hitter. What details in this photograph tell you this is a historic moment? **[Analyze]** 4

Clarification

3 Up until Ryan's "early days in baseball," the great majority of major league players were not paid the huge salaries most get today. Therefore, it was not uncommon for players to hold winter jobs in order to earn enough money to support their families. Today, players are expected to spend the off-season staying in shape and working on skills. Major league baseball is no longer a seasonal occupation.

▶Critical Viewing◀

4 Analyze *Students may say that the fact that Ryan is being carried off the field by teammates indicates how special the moment is. Guide them to appreciate how much baseball, with all its emphasis on individual records, remains very much a team game. Students can notice Ryan's teammates raising their fists to share the moment of success.*

Speaking and Listening Mini-Lesson

Award Presentation

This mini-lesson supports the Speaking and Listening activity in the Idea Bank on p. 595.

Introduce Have students talk about the kinds of things people might say at an awards presentation. Divide the class into four groups, two each for Homer and Ryan. Have each group select one student to be its emcee and another to be the honoree. Tell students that the honoree should speak, as either man actually might have, in response to the award he is being given.

Develop Provide time for groups to gather and discuss what their emcee will say. Urge students to supplement what they've learned from the selections with facts they learn from library and Internet research and other sources. Have groups divide the tasks of researching, writing and editing the emcee's speech and the honoree's acceptance speech, as well as creating the award they will give him.

Apply Hold the awards presentations, allowing each group's representatives to present and accept.

Assess Evaluate groups' performances on the accuracy and persuasiveness of their award-presentation speeches and on how well the acceptance speeches exemplify the honoree's personality.

▶Critical Viewing◀

1 Draw Conclusions *Students may say that Ryan's face shows that pitching demands great concentration as well as balance and physical exertion.*

Clarification

2 Point out to students that "inside" pitches are the easiest for many batters to hit hard (inside being the side of home plate the batter is on). Only pitchers who can throw the ball hard enough or accurately enough dare to throw inside. One of the benefits that this pitching strategy brings is that it keeps the batter from "crowding the plate," that is, standing near the plate. This makes it harder for the batter to hit pitches thrown on the outside part of the plate.

Clarification

3 Nolan Ryan had a long career even before he played for Texas. First, he pitched for the New York Mets, who drafted him 295th in the 1965 draft. After beginning his career with the Mets, he then played for eight years with the California Angels and for nine years with the Houston Astros. Ryan retired from baseball in 1993, after having pitched for the Rangers for five years. In 1996, the Texas Rangers retired his number, 34.

◆Literary Focus

4 Biography *Although he played for other teams, this passage addresses only Ryan's accomplishments as a Texas Ranger.*

Customize for *Logical/Mathematical Learners*

Students can apply simple proportional reasoning to appreciate the extent of Ryan's benefit to Texas attendance: Sellouts increased five-fold. Instead of an average of one sellout per year, now there were five. Logical thinkers might add that Ryan's presence may not have been the only reason for the increase in attendance: Perhaps the team was improved in other ways, or perhaps it was in the midst of a pennant race during those three seasons.

to him in the grocery store, you'd think he was just another middle-aged guy," said a member of the Rangers' organization.

He's a nice guy off the field, but not necessarily on it. Baseball is still much more than just a game to Ryan. His drive to excel, to win, to help his team is still strong. But Nolan is able to confine this drive to the playing field.

"When I'm out on the mound I don't consider myself a very nice person," he wrote. "I almost hate the players I'm pitching against. I get to feeling a lot of hostility. Normally, I'm a very quiet and reserved person with a peaceful outlook on things. But when I'm pitching I'm anything but that."

1 ▲ **Critical Viewing** What does Ryan's facial expression tell you about the act of pitching? **[Draw Conclusions]**

Ryan wants to be known and remembered as a "gamer," a player who goes all out in every game. He's not afraid to pitch inside to a batter who tries to gain an advantage by standing closer to home plate. He'll make a batter have to duck or leap backward to teach him not to "crowd" the plate. 2

With so many accomplishments so late in his career, Ryan is more famous as a Texas Ranger than he ever was as a Met, Angel, or Astro. There are crowds of fans and autograph seekers wherever the Rangers go. And Ryan's importance to the Rangers goes far beyond his pitching record. He's the player people come to see. 3 4

> ◆ **Literary Focus** How does this passage keep the focus on one particular stage of Ryan's career?

In its first 17 seasons, the Texas franchise[1] had 17 sellout crowds. In three seasons with Nolan Ryan, the team had 15, mostly on nights Ryan pitched. Souvenir program sellers know they can make three times their usual amount when he's on the mound. People hope the programs will turn out to be mementos from another no-hitter.

Ryan is possibly the best-known person in the state of Texas. Watch television, listen to radio, read a newspaper, drive down a freeway, and you'll see or hear Ryan in ads for everything from airlines to blue jeans. He earns an estimated $1 million to $2 million a year from such endorsements.

Ryan holds almost 50 major league records from the important (strikeouts, no-hitters) to the obscure (most assists by a pitcher in a five-game National League Championship Series).

1. **franchise** (fran´ chiz´) *n.*: Team.

◆ Build Vocabulary

hostility (has til´ ə tē) *n.*: Anger; unfriendliness

Beyond the Classroom

Career Connection

Sports Careers Whereas careers as professional athletes are realistic goals for only the very few, careers related to professional sports abound. Discuss with students the many jobs that exist, such as trainer, physical therapist, publicist, agent, coach, scout, sportswriter, referee or umpire, camera operator, statistician, groundskeeper, sports equipment manufacturer or salesperson, and all the positions in sports management. List on the board these and other jobs students suggest.

Invite students to choose one job to investigate further, to find out what the position entails and what skills or credentials an applicant needs in order to qualify. One way students can proceed is to contact professional teams directly, usually through their public relations divisions. Another is to speak with someone they know who actually has such a job. Once students have gathered their information, they can pool their findings to compile a class brochure of sports-related job descriptions, qualifications, and opportunities.

Some, like the ones for most walks and wild pitches in a career, he'd rather not have.

Numbers, however, can't begin to explain the excitement Ryan brings to every game. You know you'll see history made with every strikeout. You may be in on something truly spectacular, like a no-hitter. And Ryan's accomplishments are even more enjoyable because of the kind of person he is as well as the kind of pitcher.

In a country full of sports stars, he somehow stands out. Jim Murray of the *Los Angeles Times* wrote that even though we may have seen Mantle, Mays, Aaron, Rose, and all the rest, "I have a feeling when they talk of the second half of the 20th century in baseball, the most frequently heard question by our generation will be, 'Did you ever see Nolan Ryan pitch?'"

Beyond Literature

Sports Connection

Baseball—A Game of Records Major League baseball players treasure records—but not enough to let them stand forever. In 1974, Hank Aaron broke Babe Ruth's home run record, which had stood for 39 years. In 1995, Cal Ripken, Jr., played in his 2,131st consecutive game, breaking Lou Gehrig's 56-year-old record in the process.

Cross-Curricular Activity

Record-Breakers Chart With a group, research baseball's long-standing records—when they were set and when they were broken. Consider most home runs in a season, most stolen bases, and highest batting average. Record your findings in a chart.

Guide for Responding

◆ Literature and Your Life

Reader's Response Do you admire Nolan Ryan? Why or why not?

Thematic Focus How would you define Ryan's goals on the field and off the field?

Public Service Commercial As Nolan Ryan, do a television commercial encouraging kids to stay fit.

1. What has Ryan done to take care of his body?
2. In what ways does Ryan "still represent small-town Texas"?
3. How does Ryan on the mound differ from Ryan off the mound?
4. What evidence is there that "Ryan is more famous as a Texas Ranger than he ever was as a Met"?
5. In what way does Ryan bring "excitement . . . to every game"?

◆ Critical Thinking

Interpret

1. How are Ryan's off-the-field decisions and activities just as important to his career as what he does on the field? **[Connect]**
2. What do you think enables Ryan to let go of his anger and competitive drive when he steps off the field? **[Infer]**
3. Describe the special qualities that make Ryan different from other sports stars. **[Draw Conclusions]**

Evaluate

4. Do you think a player has to have anger to be a winner? Explain. **[Make a Judgment]**

Apply

5. Would you like to be thought of as a "gamer" in the things you do? Explain. **[Relate]**

Compare Literary Works

6. Do you think Winslow Homer would have enjoyed painting Nolan Ryan? Explain. **[Connect]**

Beyond the Selection

FURTHER READING

Other Works by William W. Lace

Top 10 Football Quarterbacks

The Houston Rockets (Great Sports Teams series)

The Alamo (World History series)

Other Works About Notable Americans

"Martin Luther King," Raymond Richard Patterson

Tin Lizzie, John Dos Passos

Autobiography, Benjamin Franklin

My Bondage and My Freedom, Frederick Douglass

INTERNET

We suggest the following sites on the Internet (all Web sites are subject to change).

To see a photo of Winslow Homer as well as many of his paintings:

http://www.seanet.com/users/lacas/homer.html

For information on the career of Nolan Ryan:

http://www.ghgcorp.com/mingster

We *strongly recommend* that you preview the sites before you send students to them.

Beyond Literature

Students interested in baseball statistics may know that this field has exploded in recent years—there are now more books, more analysis, and better statistical measures of skills and achievements than ever before. Students might enjoy browsing *The Bill James Historical Baseball Abstract* for a new and thoughtful look at the old game of baseball, decade by decade.

Reinforce and Extend

Answers

◆ Literature and Your Life

Reader's Response Students may say that they admire his love of the game and his ability to stay in good condition for so long.

Thematic Focus Students may say that Ryan was focused on doing whatever it took to be successful, to be the best that he could be.

☑ Check Your Comprehension

1. He eats healthy foods and exercises.
2. He remains what he's always been—modest, uncomplicated.
3. On the mound, he's fiercer. Off the field he's a nice person.
4. Ryan achieved many records late in his career and as a result of his long career.
5. With each game, there's the possibility of another no-hitter or of his breaking another record.

◆ Critical Thinking

1. Students may say he needs the calm of his off-the-field life to balance the intensity of competing.
2. Self-knowledge has made him able to keep his personal life and his profession separate.
3. He's modest and unassuming off the field. Students who are sports fans may say that he stayed injury-free and pitched well for a long time.
4. Some students may say that anger keeps a player on edge, which benefits his game. Others may say that anger clouds good judgment.
5. Many students will say that they would like to be known as someone who meets responsibility and always gives his or her best.
6. Some students might say that the challenges Ryan faced would not have been serious enough struggles to interest Homer.

Answers

◆Reading Strategy

1. They supported his desire and efforts to be a painter. His brothers purchased his paintings to keep his career afloat.
2. He ate a healthy diet, kept physically fit, and kept mentally fit by keeping separate his family life and professional life.

◆Build Vocabulary

Using the Prefix *sub-*

subnormal, below normal; *submerging*, placing under water; *subconscious*, less than fully conscious; *substandard*, below standard

Spelling Strategy

1. placement
2. voicing
3. spacious
4. surviving

Using the Word Bank

1. d
2. f
3. a
4. b
5. e
6. g
7. c

◆Literary Focus

1. Possible response: He stopped taking painting lessons after five of them; he turned down steady illustrating work from *Harper's Weekly*; he stopped painting for three years, and when he began again his skills were better than ever.
2. Ordinary off the field: raises cattle; keeps his small-town roots; buys groceries; extraordinary on the field: pitches for 26 years; holds records for strikeouts; has pitched seven no-hitters

◆Build Grammar Skills

Practice

1. Winslow's only female friend; explains wife
2. the scene of his success; explains New York
3. *The Gulf Stream*; explains one of his great masterpieces
4. one for the records; explains no-hitter
5. a southern California native; explains Steve Buchele

Guide for Responding *(continued)*

◆ Reading Strategy

Set a Purpose for Reading

When you **set a purpose** for reading by deciding what you want to learn, you help yourself to get the information you want. If your purpose was to discover why Homer was America's greatest painter, you learned several facts to support this idea. For instance, Homer's paintings of the Civil War showed the "humanity" of soldiers on both sides.

Name two facts that each of these purpose-setting questions would have uncovered.

1. In what ways did Homer's family influence him?
2. Why was Ryan able to have such a long career?

◆ Build Vocabulary

Using the Prefix *sub-*

Use the meaning of the prefix *sub-* ("under" or "below") to define the italicized words in this paragraph:

His performance was *subnormal* tonight. Now, he's *submerging* his arm in ice water. Even if he's not aware of them, questions must be going through the levels of his *subconscious* mind. Can he rise above his *substandard* performance?

Spelling Strategy

When adding suffixes to words ending with e, you usually keep the e when the suffix begins with a consonant but drop the e when the suffix begins with a vowel:

subtle + -ty = subtlety   hostile + -ity = hostility
noise + -less = noiseless   like + -able = likable

On your paper, spell these combinations:

1. place + -ment =   **3.** space + -ious =
2. voice + -ing =   **4.** survive + -ing =

Using the Word Bank

On your paper, match each word in the first column with its definition in the second column

1. subtle	**a.** person defeated
2. brutality	**b.** calmness
3. vanquished	**c.** feeling of unfriendliness
4. serenity	**d.** delicately skillful
5. cantankerous	**e.** argumentative
6. subservient	**f.** violence
7. hostility	**g.** inferior

◆ Literary Focus

Biography

A **biography** is an author's account of the facts and meaning of another person's life. The biographical essay on Ryan, for example, tells you about the facts of his career with the Texas Rangers. It weaves these facts together to present a general idea of the man: He is an ordinary guy with extraordinary skills.

1. Find three examples in Homer's biography that show him as a talented but stubborn loner.
2. Name three facts in Ryan's biography that depict him as ordinary off the field and extraordinary on it.

◆ Build Grammar Skills

Appositives and Appositive Phrases

An **appositive** is a noun placed near another noun or pronoun to explain it. An **appositive phrase** is an appositive and the words that modify it. Appositives and appositive phrases are often set off from the sentence by commas or dashes. Look at these examples:

Appositive: Ryan, *the pitcher*, reached the mound.
Appositive Phrase: Homer loved to paint scenes of the ocean, *the most untamed part of nature.*

Practice On your paper, identify the appositive phrase in each of these sentences. Then, indicate what it explains.

1. His brother's wife, Winslow's only female friend, called Homer a courteous gentleman.
2. Homer left New York, the scene of his success.
3. He finished one of his great masterpieces, *The Gulf Stream*, in 1899.
4. Ryan's seventh no-hitter—one for the records—brought the team a victory over Toronto.
5. Texas third baseman Steve Buchele, a southern California native, was Ryan's teammate.

Writing Application Rewrite these sentences, inserting an appositive or an appositive phrase.

1. Winslow Homer painted in watercolors and oils.
2. During the Civil War, Homer did many drawings of Abraham Lincoln.
3. Ryan is an inspiration to many young athletes.

Writing Application

Possible responses:

1. Winslow Homer, America's greatest painter, painted in watercolors and oils.
2. During the Civil War, the war that ended slavery in the United States, Homer did many drawings of Abraham Lincoln.
3. Ryan, one of the greatest pitchers of his era, is an inspiration to many young athletes.

Writer's Solution

For additional instruction and practice, use the lesson in the *Writer's Solution Language Lab CD-ROM* on styling sentences, and the practice pages on Appositives in Phrases, p. 46 in the *Writer's Solution Grammar Practice Book.*

Build Your Portfolio

Idea Bank

Writing

1. **Baseball Card** Using the following information and the essay on Ryan, design and write the text for a baseball card that summarizes his career: lifetime wins—324; lifetime losses—292; strikeouts—5,714; walks—2,795. **[Art Link]**
2. **Song of Praise** Write a song honoring the achievements of a person you admire. Describe some of those achievements in the song. Also, create a catchy phrase about this person that you can repeat in your lyrics.
3. **Proposal for a Documentary** Write to a television station proposing a documentary film on Homer, Ryan, or a person of your choice. Convince the station's director that the person is worth the attention and that his or her life could inspire a dramatic film. **[Media Link; Career Link]**

Speaking and Listening

4. **Gallery Talk** Imagine that you're giving a talk about the Homer paintings on pages 586 and 588. Explain to museum visitors what is worth noticing about the subjects and about Homer's portrayal of them. **[Art Link; Career Link]**
5. **Award Presentation** As the emcee at a formal dinner, present Winslow Homer or Nolan Ryan with a lifetime achievement award. In your speech, explain why the prize is well deserved.

Projects

6. **Book Circle [Group Activity]** Form a group to read and discuss a biography of a well-known person. Each student should read the book with a different purpose, in order to bring a fresh point of view to the discussion. Then, a group member can sum up the discussion for the class.
7. **Biographical Report** Research the life of someone who interests you. Collect facts and photographs about your subject's career and achievements. Share your report with the class.

Writing Mini-Lesson

Instructional Guide

Nolan Ryan probably knows all the tricks of the trade when it comes to pitching. However, you know the secrets for success in the activities that you do. Publish those secrets in a manual, giving a step-by-step explanation of how to perform a task or a feat that you have mastered.

Writing Skills Focus: Thoroughness

Readers who aren't as familiar with the task as you are may stumble if you leave out some of the steps. That's why **thoroughness,** a complete presentation of details, is essential in a how-to essay. H. N. Levitt shows thoroughness in his biographical essay by explaining wood-block engraving.

Model From the Essay

In those days, an artist would cut illustrations into a wood block, which was then inked in black and printed on sheets of paper.

Prewriting Choose an activity that you understand completely, and jot down all the steps that go into it. Also, jot down positive phrases you can use to encourage readers.

Drafting Remember that you're writing for beginners. Make the activity seem worthwhile, and describe the steps that you might take for granted because of your experience.

Revising Have a classmate who isn't familiar with the activity read your essay. Whenever a passage confuses your classmate, add further explanations or insert steps you may have left out.

◆ Grammar Application

Use appositive phrases to clarify your explanations. Here's an example:

Attach the kite frame, *the two crossed sticks,* to the paper.

ASSESSMENT OPTIONS

Formal Assessment, Selection Test, pp. 166–168, and Assessment Resources Software. The selection test is designed so that it can be easily customized to the performance levels of your students.

Alternative Assessment, p. 36, includes options for less advanced students, more advanced students, verbal/linguistic learners, and visual/spatial learners.

PORTFOLIO ASSESSMENT

Use the following rubrics in the **Alternative Assessment** booklet to assess student writing:

Baseball Card: Summary, p. 85
Song of Praise: Expression, p. 81
Proposal for a Documentary: Persuasion, p. 92
Writing Mini-Lesson: How-to/Process Explanation, p. 87

Idea Bank

Following are suggestions for matching the Idea Bank topics with your students' performance levels and learning modalities:

Customize for
Performance Levels

Less Advanced Students: 1, 5, 7
Average Students: 2, 5, 6, 7
More Advanced Students: 3, 4, 6, 7

Customize for
Learning Modalities

Verbal/Linguistic: 1, 2, 3, 4, 5, 6, 7
Visual/Spatial: 3, 4, 5
Logical/Mathematical: 1, 3, 7
Musical/Rhythmic: 2
Interpersonal: 3, 4, 5, 6
Intrapersonal: 2

Writing Mini-Lesson

Refer students to the Writing Handbook in the back of the book for instructions on the writing process and for further information on expository writing.

Writer's Solution

Writing Lab CD-ROM

Have students complete the tutorial on Exposition. Follow these steps:

1. Have students use the Audience Profile option to gear writing to an intended audience: beginners.
2. Students can use the Organizing Details section to help them arrange data for their guides.
3. Have students draft on computer.
4. Refer students to the Publishing and Presenting section for ideas on ways to create a how-to book.

Allow about 75 minutes of class time to complete these steps.

Writer's Solution Sourcebook

Have students use Chapter 4, "Exposition: Giving Information," pp. 103–134, for additional support. The chapter includes in-depth instruction on considering audience, p. 120.

Prepare and Engage

Establish Writing Guidelines
Review the following key characteristics of a biographical report:

- A biographical report is a summary of a person's life and achievements.
- Biographical reports include the main events of the person's life, including dates and other details.
- A biographical report uses factual information about the time and place the person lived to clearly illustrate the person's life.

You may want to distrubute the scoring rubric for a Research Report/Paper, p. 93 in **Alternative Assessment,** to make students aware of the criteria on which they will be evaluated. See the suggestions on p. 598 for how you can customize the rubric to this workshop.

Refer students to the Writing Handbook in the back of the book for more instruction and information.

Writer's Solution

Writers at Work Videodisc
To introduce students to reports and to show them how Ellie Fries answers the question "What is a report?" play the videodisc segment on Reports (Ch. 7). Have students discuss how Fries gathers information.

Play frames 11077 to 20155

Writing Lab CD-ROM
If your students have access to computers, you may want to have them work in the tutorial on Reports to complete all or part of their biographical reports. Follow these steps:

1. Have students view the Inspirations for Reports to explore possible topics.
2. Suggest that students fill out a KWL chart to see what information they already know and what information they will need to research.
3. Allow students to draft on computer.
4. When revising, have students use the Unity and Coherence Revision Checker.

Writer's Solution Sourcebook
Students can find additional support, including in-depth instruction on organizing information, in the chapter on Reports, pp. 200–233.

Report Writing

Biographical Report

Writing Process Workshop

Certain people intrigue us. Maybe for you, it's sports heroes, political leaders, great explorers, or famous artists. One way to learn more about a person you admire is to research and write a **biographical report.** This kind of writing gives information about a person's life and achievements. Though this report will convey mostly facts, it should also include your own ideas about what makes the person noteworthy. These skills, covered in the Writing Mini-Lessons in this part, will help:

Writing Skills Focus

▶ **Clarify your main points.** Decide what is most interesting or important about your subject, and then focus on those ideas. (See p. 562.)

▶ **Use a clear and logical organization** to help readers follow the story of your subject's life. Chronological order—from first event to last event—may be best. (See p. 583.)

▶ **Tell the story thoroughly.** Be sure you've covered the most important elements of your subject's life. Don't leave out key events. (See p. 595.)

"Winslow Homer: America's Greatest Painter" inspired this writer to study another American great. She uses the skills above in the introduction to a report on Georgia O'Keeffe.

Model

Everyone has a different idea about who is America's greatest painter. In my opinion, it's a woman who began a new style and gave women artists a new role model. ① That woman was Georgia O'Keeffe (1887–1986). ② O'Keeffe painted hundreds of masterpieces in her very long life. ③

① This sentence expresses the two main ideas of this report: O'Keeffe began a new style, and she served as a role model.

② All facts—including dates—are 100 percent accurate.

③ This sentence suggests that this report will trace her very long life, from beginning to end, in clear, chronological order.

Cross-Curricular Connection: History

Biographies Tell students that biographies are especially important when studying history. Biographies have existed in all societies, as commemmorations of the conquests of ancient rulers, as hero legends passed down through oral histories, or as portraits of religious figures who demonstrate a way to live. Through understanding the life and actions of historical figures, we are able to see a clearer picture of the time in which they lived.

Have students form groups and brainstorm for a list of time periods or cultures they would like to know more about. Once they have a general idea, have them do some preliminary research to find a historical figure representative of that time. For example, if they wanted to know more about apartheid and South Africa, they might research Nelson Mandela. Then have students go to the library or start research on the Internet to come up with a list of biographies for their chosen person. Encourage them to share their bibliographies with the class.

Prewriting

Identify Your Subject The first step, of course, is to choose a person to study. You'll want to choose someone whom you admire and want to write about. It's also important that there is ample information available. Here are some general ideas:

Topic Ideas

- World leader
- Sports star
- Writer or artist
- Great entertainer

Research Use more than one source to find your information: library reference books, on-line sources, biographies, video documentaries. Keep track of exactly what sources you use. Include facts that answer questions such as these:

- When and where was he/she born?
- When did he/she get interested in his/her life work?
- How did he/she begin his/her career?
- What were the highlights of his/her life?
- For what is he/she most known or remembered?

Make a Timeline With any writing that is organized chronologically, it's helpful to make a timeline to organize details. Begin with your subject's birth, and move through the years.

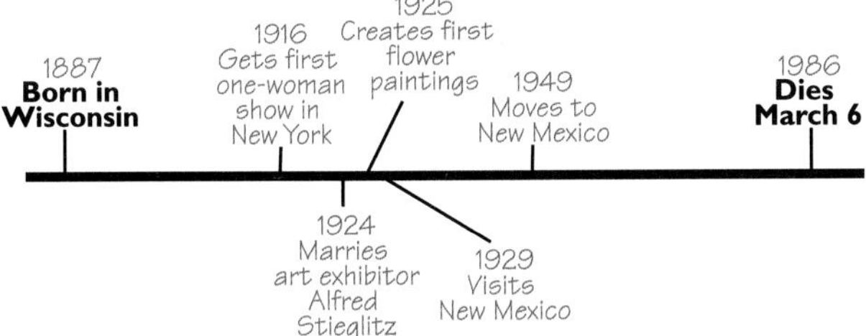

Include a Portrait Sometimes, a picture can say a thousand words. If possible, include a copy of a photograph or portrait of your subject.

Drafting

Write Your Main Idea Before you begin to draft, pause and think: What quality or idea is most important about this person? Write a sentence that expresses your original idea. Use this sentence in your report.

DRAFTING/REVISING

APPLYING LANGUAGE SKILLS: Documenting Sources

At the end of your report, include a **bibliography**—a list of all the sources you've used. Bibliographies are arranged alphabetically. Look at the format and the information included in these examples:

Encyclopedia: "O'Keeffe, Georgia," *Encyclopedia Britannica*, Vol. 25, 1990, pp. 49–74.

Book: Moore, Lisa. *Artists of Courage: Georgia O'Keeffe*. New York: Acme Publishing, 1997.

Article: Brown, Sherrill. "Flowers and Bones: The Art of Georgia O'Keeffe." *Painters and Gardeners Monthly*, November 1992, pp. 90–98.

Practice Make corrections in this bibliography entry for a book. There are four mistakes.

Smith, Thale, American Painters. Boston, Brown Publishing, Inc.

Writing Application When writing your biographical report, be sure to document your sources accurately and completely.

Writer's Solution Connection Writing Lab

For more about documenting sources, see the Drafting section of the Reports tutorial.

Develop Student Writing

Prewriting

Remind students to take detailed notes when researching. To help them organize their notes chronologically, suggest that they use a timeline. Instruct students to enter the key events of their subject's life on the line, moving from birth onward.

Customize for
Less Proficient Writers
When students begin their research, you may want to model a sample timeline for them. Make sure you show them how to organize their details chronologically. Point out that big gaps along the timeline suggest places where more research might be needed.

Drafting

To help students organize their information for writing, suggest they use the Main Idea and Supporting Details Organizer from **Writing and Language Transparencies,** p. 70. Explain that details can include quotes from sources about their subject.

Applying Language Skills

Documenting Sources Tell students that sources must be documented completely so that other people reading the report can find the sources the writer has used. If any of the information is formatted incorrectly, the sources will be much harder to locate.

Answers

Smith, Thale. *American Painters.* Boston: Brown Publishing, Inc.

Mistake # 4: no date

Writer's Solution

For additional instruction and practice have students use the lesson on Looking at Reports in the *Writer's Solution Grammar Practice Book,* p. 133.

Revising

Remind students that their reports should explain any unfamiliar terms, names, or places. Therefore, peer reviewers should note places where there is missing or incomplete information. Also, suggest that reviewers comment on sentence variety, noting places where writers should vary sentence beginnings.

Writer's Solution

Writing Lab CD-ROM

In the tutorial on Reports, have students use the Peer Review checklist for guidance during the editing stage.

Publishing

If your school has a Web page, suggest that students publish their biographies there.

Reinforce and Extend

Review the Writing Guidelines

After students have completed their papers, review the characteristics of a biographical report.

Applying Language Skills

Avoiding Double Negatives

Point out to students that the most common way to make a statement negative is with a single negative word, such as *no, not, none, nothing, never, nobody,* or *nowhere,* or with the contraction *-n't* added to a helping verb.

Answers

1. O'Keeffe never suggests anything original.
2. She didn't make excuses for her art.
3. She has no competition.

Writer's Solution

For additional practice, complete the Avoiding Double Negatives lesson in the *Writer's Solution Language Lab CD-ROM.*

EDITING/PROOFREADING

APPLYING LANGUAGE SKILLS: Avoiding Double Negatives

Negative words, such as *never* or *not,* are used in sentences to deny something. Some writers mistakenly use **double negatives**—two negative words—when one alone is needed. Notice how this example can be corrected in two ways.

Double Negative:

She didn't learn from no one.

Corrected Sentence:

She didn't learn from anyone.

She learned from no one.

Practice Correct the double negatives in these sentences.

1. O'Keeffe never suggests nothing original.
2. She didn't make no excuses for her art.
3. She hasn't got no competition.

Writing Application As you edit your biographical report, correct any double negatives you have included.

Writer's Solution Connection
Language Lab

For more practice, see the Avoiding Double Negatives lesson on the Language Lab CD-ROM.

Choose Active Verbs As you draft your report, choose your verbs carefully. Don't settle for too many *be* verbs. Avoid common, bland verbs like *make, have, do, go,* or *say.* Picture your verbs moving your reader along through the person's life.

Include Time Transitions Words and phrases such as the ones listed here will help your reader keep track of the passage of time, an important factor in biographical writing.

Time Transitions			
after two years	during	formerly	second
as soon as	earlier	in the end	since
at first	eventually	later	soon
at the same time	finally	meanwhile	then
before	first	next	while

Revising

Check Facts and Document Sources As you revise, be your own best editor. Go back to your notes or the books, magazines, or on-line sites you used. Check all your facts. Confirm dates and names. As you fact-check, prepare your bibliography. Be careful and complete.

Create a Catchier Title Take a second look at your title. Many biography titles include the subject's name and a phrase that suggests the main idea. It's a good chance for some word play, but don't go overboard.

Use a Peer Reviewer Ask a classmate to read your report. Together, discuss the following:

- Does the title fit?
- Does the writing flow smoothly?
- Where should information be added? Deleted?
- What was the essay's strongest part? Weakest?

Publishing and Presenting

Anthology of Biographies Combine your report with those of others in a class anthology. Include portraits, if possible. Choose a title, and prepare a table of contents. Make your anthology available to students in other classes.

Ballad Ballads are songs that tell stories—often tales of legendary or famous people. Take the information from your report, and add a sense of humor, rhyme, and rhythm. Write a refrain, or set of lines to be repeated. You might even set your ballad to music. Then, share your poetic biography with classmates.

✓ ASSESSMENT		4	3	2	1
PORTFOLIO ASSESSMENT Use the rubric on Research Report/ Paper in the **Alternative Assessment** booklet, p. 93, to assess the students' writing. Add these criteria to customize the rubric to this assignment.	**Clarity of Main Points**	The report contains several interesting main points, expressed clearly, in a logical order.	The report contains several interesting main points, expressed clearly, but not in a logical order.	The report contains several interesting main points, but they are not expressed clearly or in a logical order.	The report has few to no interesting main points, which are poorly organized and poorly expressed.
	Documenting Sources	All of the sources are clearly noted in a bibliography in the correct format.	All of the sources are noted in the bibliography, but some are in the wrong format.	Most of the sources noted in the bibliography are in the wrong format.	Few sources are noted in the bibliography, and all are in the wrong format.

Real-World Reading Skills Workshop

Reading for Specific Information

Strategies for Success

Wouldn't it be great to have a *User's Guide to Your Life*—a book that gave you all the answers? It would tell you how to make the baseball team, how to do better in math, or how to tell jokes. In reality, the answers to your questions are scattered in hundreds of manuals, books, and encyclopedias. You can find these answers by reading for specific information.

Practice the Moves Learn the moves that will get you through the maze of a reference book. For example, use the sections of a book that may seem as dull as a telephone directory: the table of contents (in the front) and the index (at the back). The table of contents outlines the book's organization. The index is an alphabetized list of the book's subjects. Use them both to get fast facts.

Let Your Fingers Do the Walking Most reference books are not meant to be read cover to cover. By moving your finger and scanning down the table of contents or the index, you'll find the page numbers to direct you to the specific information you need.

Find Key Words When you turn to the page you need, look again for the key word you need, especially in the headings or captions or boldfaced in the text.

Apply the Strategies

Use the table of contents and the index on this page to answer these questions about information in an arts and literature almanac:

1. Which chapter will probably have information on prime-time television? On which page does that chapter begin?
2. Which chapter will probably have information on Andy Warhol and other popular painters? On which page does that chapter begin?
3. On what pages will you find information on the movie *E.T.*?
4. On what pages will you find information about the Academy Awards?

✔ *You may also read for specific information in:*

- ▶ Atlases
- ▶ Textbooks
- ▶ Works of nonfiction
- ▶ Encyclopedias

Almanac of the Arts and Literature of Our Time

Contents

Index

Introduce the Strategies

Discuss with students different types of specific information they may need to look for, such as telephone numbers, word definitions, or information for a report. Ask them where they might find each kind of information. *A phone book, a dictionary, an encyclopedia, or other reference source.* Lead them to recognize that specific information is available from a wide variety of sources.

Customize for
Less Proficient Readers
Have students work in pairs and use one or more reference sources. Encourage them to take turns asking questions about information that is available in the table of contents and index.

Customize for
More Advanced Readers
Invite students to visit your school library or media center and identify the reference section. Ask them to find at least three sources of information that are unfamiliar to them, and identify what types of information they offer. Have them share what they find with the class by creating a chart that can be displayed on a bulletin board or in a place where other students can access the information.

Apply the Strategies

Encourage students to determine how they can identify sources for the specific information they need. For instance, the reference section of a library may offer sources for certain types of information, the card catalogue can be a source for works of nonfiction on particular subjects, or a librarian or media specialist might suggest sources.

Answers

1. Chapter 6; p. 367
2. Chapter 2; p. 75
3. pp. 13 and 25
4. pp. 42, 54, and 76

◆Build Grammar Skills

Reviewing Phrases
The selections in Part I include instruction on the following:

- The Four Functions of Sentences
- Participles and Participial Phrases
- Appositives and Appositive Phrases

This instruction is reinforced with the Build Grammar Skills practice pages in **Selection Support,** pp. 186, 192, and 197.

As you review phrases you may wish to review prepositional phrases with students. In addition, point out that phrases written alone are fragments.

Customize for
Less Proficient Readers
Suggest that students fill out a chart like the one below when analyzing sentences for phrases:

subject	
verb	
nouns	
pronouns	
participle	
appositive phrase	

Then have them try to identify how the participle or the appositive phrase functions in the sentence. Have students ask: What does this phrase modify or identify?

Writer's Solution

For additional practice and support with phrases, use the practice pages on phrases, pp. 44–51 in the *Writer's Solution Grammar Practice Book.*

Phrases — Grammar Review

A **phrase** is a group of words that functions in a sentence as a single part of speech. Phrases do not contain subjects or verbs.

An appositive is a noun or a pronoun placed next to another noun or pronoun to identify or explain it. An **appositive phrase** contains an appositive and its modifiers. (See page 594.)

Russell Baker, *an award-winning journalist* [appositive phrase], sold magazines as a boy.

A **participial phrase** functions as an adjective. (See page 582.) A participle is a verb form that acts as an adjective. Present participles end in *-ing,* and past participles usually end in *-ed,* but they may have an irregular ending such as *-t* or *-en.* A participial phrase contains a participle and its modifiers.

Blazing past batters, [participial phrase] the ball can't be hit.

Amazed by its speed, [participial phrase] hitters stand motionless.

phrase (frāz) *n.* **1** a group of words that is not a complete sentence, but that gives a single idea, usually as a separate part of a sentence ["Drinking fresh milk," "with meals," and "to be healthy" are phrases.]

Practice 1 Identify the appositive phrases and participial phrases in the sentences below. Identify which word each participial phrase modifies, and tell what word each appositive phrase identifies.

1. Biographies, the written stories of people's lives, can teach readers.
2. Engrossed in someone else's struggles, you might understand yourself better.
3. Disappointed by events, Winslow Homer made several changes in his life.
4. Even he, a world-famous painter, had to re-evaluate his work.
5. Reading about his courage, we may feel more inclined to make changes.

Practice 2 Write original sentences using the following phrases, as indicated.

1. the captain of the ship (appositive phrase)
2. a beautiful song (appositive phrase)
3. a mistake with serious consequences (appositive phrase)
4. laughing uncontrollably (participial phrase)
5. wondering about tomorrow (participial phrase)
6. pleased with the news (participial phrase)

Grammar in Writing

✔ *Phrases can help you pack meaning into a sentence. Notice how two sentences can become a single, more informative, one:*

Short Sentences:
Annie Dillard threw snowballs.
She experienced an exciting adventure.

Combined With a Participial Phrase:
While throwing snowballs, Annie Dillard experienced an exciting adventure.

Look for places in your writing to add sophistication with phrases.

Answers
Practice 1

1. the written stories of people's lives—appositive phrase identifies *biographies*
2. Engrossed in someone else's struggles—participial phrase modifies *you*
3. Disappointed by events—participial phrase modifies *Winslow Homer*
4. a world-famous painter—appositive phrase identifies *he*
5. Reading about his courage—participial phrase modifies *we*

Practice 2
Possible responses:

1. Ahab, the captain of the ship, searched for the great white whale.
2. *The Star-Spangled Banner,* a beautiful song, was sung at the beginning of the baseball game.
3. His tardiness, a mistake with serious consequences, prevented him from completing the test.
4. Laughing uncontrollably, he took his seat.
5. Wondering about tomorrow, you can fantasize many things.
6. Pleased with the news, she rushed home to tell her parents.

Part 2 *Types of Essays*

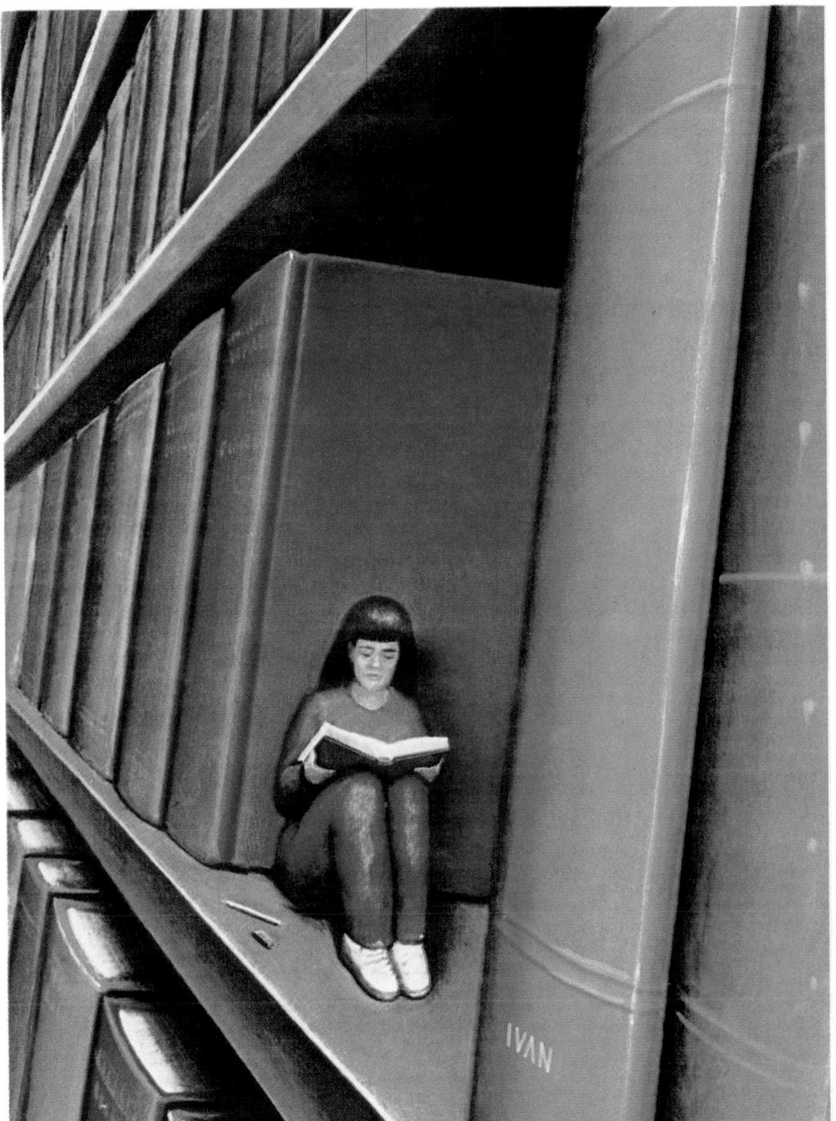

Untitled, Ivan Lee Sanford

One-Minute Planning Guide

The selections in this section are examples of different types of essays. "Independence Hall" is a narrative essay about the Declaration of Independence. In "Rattlesnake Hunt," a descriptive essay, readers join the narrator on an expedition to catch snakes. An essay from *Barrio Boy* is a personal account of a Mexican-born child's experience at his first American school. "I Am a Native of North America" is a reflective essay on the fading culture of Native Americans. "All Together Now" is a persuasive essay about the solution to racial conflicts. In the visual essay "Tenochtitlan: Inside the Aztec Capital," we learn about the history of an ancient Aztec city.

Customize for *Varying Students Needs*

"Independence Hall"
- A short narrative essay
- An opportunity for connecting to social studies

"Rattlesnake Hunt"
- A descriptive essay written in the first person
- An opportunity for connecting to science

from *Barrio Boy*
- A personal essay
- An opportunity for discussing experiences of English language learners

"I Am a Native of North America"
- A reflective essay
- An opportunity to discuss Native American culture

"All Together Now"
- A persuasive essay about race relations

"Tenochtitlan: Inside the Aztec Capital"
- A visual essay
- An opportunity to connect literature with social studies

Humanities: Art

Untitled, by Ivan Lee Sanford

In this picture, the artist uses bright colors and bold lines to create a fantastical image of a miniature child reading a book while sitting on a library shelf. Ask students to examine this picture and then ask the following questions:

1. Do you think the girl in the picture is abnormally small, or that the books in the picture are abnormally large? *Some students will say they think the girl is small because the setting of the books seems normal; other students will say the books seem abnormally large.*
2. The artist has put his name on one of the books in the picture. Ask students to find his name, and then ask them why they think he put his name there. *Students should find the artist's name "Ivan" on the binding of the red book in the lower right hand corner of the image. They may say that he put his name there to sign his painting, relating it to the way that authors put their names on their books.*

Prepare and Engage

OBJECTIVES

1. To read, comprehend, and interpret essays
2. To relate essays to personal experience
3. To identify the main points in an essay
4. To understand the features of essays
5. To build vocabulary in context and learn the word root *-mort-*
6. To develop skill in using subject and object pronouns
7. To write a reflective essay, providing necessary background
8. To respond to essays through writing, speaking and listening, and projects

SKILLS INSTRUCTION

Vocabulary:
Word Roots: *-mort-*

Spelling:
Spell the *it* Sound With *ate*

Grammar:
Subject and Object Pronouns

Reading Strategy:
Identify Main Points

Literary Focus:
Essay

Writing:
Provide Necessary Background

Speaking and Listening:
Press Conference (Teacher Edition)

Critical Viewing:
Infer; Analyze; Evaluate; Compare and Contrast Synthesize

PORTFOLIO OPPORTUNITIES

Writing: Anecdote; Essay; Introduction
Writing Mini-Lesson: Reflective Essay
Speaking and Listening: Press Conference; Book Talk
Projects: Essay "Fortune Cookies"; Timeline

More About the Authors

Charles Kuralt died on July 4, 1997, exactly 221 years after the events he explored in his essay.

Marjorie Kinnan Rawlings is a North Florida literary legend. Her beloved home, Cross Creek, is a national historical site.

Ernesto Galarza was nominated for a Nobel Peace Prize for his work on behalf of Latino rights.

The son of a tribal chief, **Chief Dan George** was named "Tes-wah-no" but his English name was Dan Slaholt, later changed to Dan George.

In 1994, **Barbara Jordon** earned the Presidential Medal of Freedom, our nation's highest civilian award.

Guide for Reading

Meet the Authors:

Charles Kuralt (1934–1997)

Charles Kuralt was the youngest correspondent ever to work at CBS News. Though he anchored with the network, he is probably best remembered for a series he did called *On the Road.* For 13 years, he crossed the country, filing stories that would reveal the flavor of the nation. "Independence Hall" is one of those reports.

Marjorie Kinnan Rawlings (1896–1953)

After starting out as a journalist, Rawlings moved to rural Florida. Later, she would use this region as the setting of her novel *The Yearling.* "Rattlesnake Hunt" introduces you to a scary inhabitant of this area.

Ernesto Galarza (1905–1984)

As a child, Ernesto Galarza moved from Mexico to California. His family struggled to make ends meet, but Galarza eventually became a teacher and writer. In *Barrio Boy*, he tells about his childhood.

Chief Dan George (1899–1981)

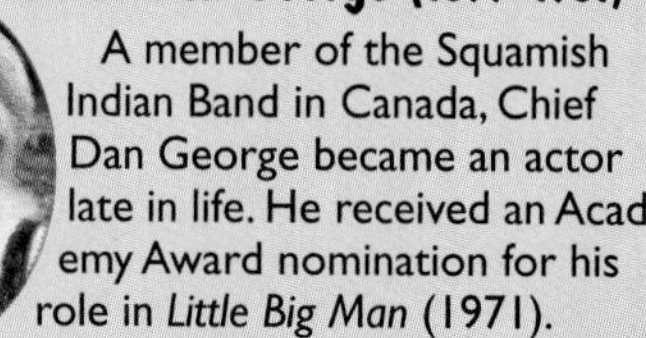

A member of the Squamish Indian Band in Canada, Chief Dan George became an actor late in life. He received an Academy Award nomination for his role in *Little Big Man* (1971).

Barbara Jordan (1936–1996)

Barbara Jordan was the first black Texan elected to Congress. She served three terms and gave a major speech at the 1976 Democratic National Convention.

◆ Literature and Your Life

Connect Your Experience

Everywhere you look, words leap out at you: STOP, GO, BUY, TURN LEFT, PAY HERE. Nobody speaks these words. They're just written on signs, advertisements, and machines.

An essay is the opposite of these impersonal messages. It contains the words of an individual who speaks to you quietly, directly, and personally.

Thematic Focus: Wishes, Hopes, Dreams

How do the essays express each author's viewpoint or goals?

◆ Background for Understanding

Literature

In 1580, the Frenchman Montaigne (män tān´) first used the word *essai* to describe a brief prose work. This French word means "try," and Montaigne's essays were "tries" at understanding. The form caught on, finding its way into the earliest magazines. Today, not only can you read essays in magazines and newspapers, you can "see" them on television.

◆ Build Vocabulary

Word Roots: *-mort-*

The word root *-mort-*, meaning "death," is usually associated with life-and-death matters. In "Rattlesnake Hunt," Rawlings refers to a snake's "mortality," meaning "the fact that it must die": *mortal* ("having to die") + *-ity* ("the fact of").

Word Bank

Which word from these essays replaces the author's name when the author of a piece is unknown? Check the Build Vocabulary boxes to see if you chose correctly.

anonymous
unanimously
desolate
mortality
formidable
communal
tolerant

Prentice Hall Literature Program Resources

REINFORCE / RETEACH / EXTEND

Selection Support Pages
Build Vocabulary: Word Roots: *-mort-*, p. 200
Build Spelling Skills, p. 201
Build Grammar Skills: Subject and Object Pronouns, p. 202
Literary Focus: Essay, p. 204
Reading Strategy: Identify Main Points, p. 203
Strategies for Diverse Student Needs, pp. 79–80
Beyond Literature Media Connection: Advertising, p. 37

Formal Assessment Selection Test, pp. 169–171, Assessment Resources Software
Alternative Assessment, p. 37
Writing and Language Transparencies
Main Idea and Supporting Details, p.70
Daily Language Practice, p. 28
Art Transparency 5
Resource Pro CD-ROM
Includes all selections

Listening to Literature Audiocassettes
Includes all selections

Independence Hall ◆ Rattlesnake Hunt from Barrio Boy ◆ I Am a Native of North America All Together Now

◆ Literary Focus

Essay

An **essay** is a brief prose work in which an author expresses his or her view of a subject. These are the most common types of essays:

- A **narrative essay** is a true story that may focus on a character other than the writer.
- A **descriptive essay** uses vivid sensory details to describe people or places.
- A **personal essay** is an informal account of an episode from a person's own life.
- A **reflective essay** presents a writer's thoughts about ideas or experiences.
- A **persuasive essay** is a series of arguments presented to convince readers to believe or act in a certain way.

In reading, notice the qualities that help you categorize the essays in this group.

Owh! In San Pao, 1951, Stuart Davis, Collection of Whitney Museum of American Art

◆ Reading Strategy

Identify Main Points

Many essays have several **main points,** important ideas that the author wants to convey. The rest of the essay contains ideas, examples, stories, or statistics that support these points. By finding and keeping in mind the main points, you'll be sure to get the message that the author wanted to send.

Most of these authors state their main points directly or give you a clue to them at the beginning or the end of the essay. Use a chart like the one below to identify the main points:

Passage	Hint in Passage	Main Point
John Adams . . . said, ". . . The bridge is cut away."	Cutting a bridge means you can't go back.	There was no turning back once the Declaration of Independence was signed.

Prepare a mock want ad for students that reads: "Essays Needed for New Weekly Paper." Ask them to imagine writing a weekly column about any topic of interest to them. What topics would they explore? Invite students to tell their choices. Display sample syndicated columns as diverse as Dave Barry's humorous essays, Tom and Ray Magliozzi's "Car Talk" column, political satire, or a sports writer's opinion piece from a local paper. Lead students to the selection by saying that they will read five essays in which authors share their views on different issues.

◆ Build Grammar Skills

Subject and Object Pronouns If you wish to introduce the grammar concept before students read, refer to the instruction on p. 620.

Customize for *Less Proficient Readers*

To help students better understand how an author provides details to support main ideas, distribute copies of the Main Idea and Supporting Details Organizer, p. 70 in **Writing and Language Transparencies**. Encourage students to fill out organizers for one or more selections.

Customize for *More Advanced Students*

Challenge students to identify within any one essay some of the traits of other types of essays. Explain that there are features of essays that overlap, and that any essay may contain elements of more than one type. For example, students might conclude that Rawlings's descriptive essay also has elements of narrative, personal, and reflective essays.

Humanities: Art

Owh! In San Pao, 1951, by Stuart Davis

American painter and illustrator Stuart Davis (1894–1964) used an abstract style to capture everyday scenes and objects. Ask: In what ways does this work fit a group of essays?

Possible answer: An essay is a brief piece of writing that expresses a personal view of a topic; this work uses short words and small images to offer an artist's view of modern life.

Preparing for Standardized Tests

Reading This selection presents a strategy to help students in their general reading, and to answer reading comprehension items on standardized tests.

Standardized tests may evaluate students' ability to identify the main points of an essay. Present the following sample test question after students have read "All Together Now" by Barbara Jordan:

Jordan suggests that a realistic way to defeat racism is for parents to encourage their children to–

(A) learn about the civil rights laws that have been passed.
(B) plan to attend another March on Washington.
(C) spend time with people of different racial and ethnic backgrounds.
(D) learn about the situation in Bosnia.

Although *(A)*, *(B)*, and *(D)* reflect ideas mentioned in the essay, the detail that best supports Jordan's thesis is *(C)*. For further practice, use Reading Strategy: Identify the Author's Main Points, in **Selection Support**, p. 203.

Develop Understanding

One-Minute Insight In this narrative essay, a journalist shares information he learned at Independence Hall in Philadelphia. There, in July 1776, members of the Continental Congress created the Declaration of Independence, which led to our nation's birth. The writer presents the details as if memories lingering in the room spoke to him to reveal the dramatic story.

Customize for
English Language Learners
Help students through this essay by restating quotations or archaic expressions in simpler or more modern words. For example, on p. 604, John Dickinson says, "The time is not yet ripe for proclaiming independence." You might help students rephrase this as, "It's too soon to declare our freedom."

▶Critical Viewing◀

❶ **Infer** *Everyone faces the men at the table as they wait to sign; some men stand at attention, as if they know that this is an important moment; the golden light streaming in from the upper right might suggest a bright future.*

Clarification

❷ Tell students that the "wealth of the Empire" refers to all the financial, commercial, and political resources the British Empire had from its far-flung colonies around the world. The American colonies were just one group of British colonies at the time.

◆Literary Focus

❸ **Essay** *It opens with a character giving one side of an argument. It includes descriptive details, such as characterization, that sound like the start of a story.*

Clarification

❹ The Second Continental Congress consisted of representatives from each of the 13 American colonies. The men traveled to Philadelphia to debate how the colonies should deal with their deteriorating relationship with Great Britain.

Independence Hall

Charles Kuralt

The Declaration of Independence, John Trumbull, Yale University Art Gallery

❶ ▲ Critical Viewing What details of this painting convey the importance of the moment that the Declaration of Independence was signed? **[Infer]**

"I say let us wait." John Dickinson of Pennsylvania stood in this hall, July 1st, 1776, and begged the Continental Congress to be reasonable. "The time is not yet ripe for proclaiming independence. Instead of help from foreign powers, it will bring us disaster. I say we ought to hold back any declaration and remain the masters of our fate and our fame. All of Great Britain is armed against us. The ❷ wealth of the Empire is poured into her treasury. We shall weep at our folly."

John Dickinson was not a timid or frightened man. He was a great old Quaker patriot, and he had a good argument. At the moment he spoke, British grenadiers[1] were sweeping down from Canada, British guns were bombarding Charleston, and just ninety miles away an incredible British armada was entering New York harbor—five hundred ships carrying thirty-two thousand troops, the best army in the world. That army could march to Philadelphia and take this building and arrest this Congress any afternoon it chose to do so. So John ❹

◆ **Literary Focus** How can you tell that this essay tells a story? ❸

1. **grenadiers** (gren′ ə dirz′) *n.*: Soldiers in a special unit of the British Army attached to the royal household.

Humanities: Art

The Declaration of Independence, 1786, by John Trumbull

American painter John Trumbull (1756–1843) became interested in art as a child by observing his sister's needlework. Years later, as a student at Harvard, Trumbull met painter John Copley, who inspired him all the more.

This painting, only 30 inches wide, shows 48 figures, grouped naturally and convincingly. Seated at the table is John Hancock; standing before him, from right to left, are Benjamin Franklin, Thomas Jefferson, Robert R. Livingston, Roger Sherman, and John Adams. Use these questions for discussion:

1. How do the flags on the wall and the varied placement of heads add action to what seems like a still scene? *Possible answers: Heads at different levels and angles suggest attention, anticipation, and curiosity; the flags seem to fly over the signers as if to mark a major event.*
2. How might a photo of this event have differed from this artistic view? *Possible answer: A photo might seem less formal or more candid.*

Dickinson pleaded, "Let us not brave the storm in a paper boat."

The delegates paid him respectful attention. John Adams and his cousin, Sam, hot for independence, impatient with the delay, sat listening. Thomas Jefferson sat back in the corner. He had already written the Declaration of Independence. It spoke his thoughts. Beside him, old Benjamin Franklin, also silent, his mind made up.

But every mind was not made up. Pennsylvania and South Carolina were opposed to independence; Delaware divided; New York undecided. All through the spring and into the summer they had sat here and wrangled, their tempers growing hot with the season. Young Edward Rutledge of South Carolina had said of John Adams and the New Englanders, "They will bring us ruin. I dread their low cunning and those leveling principles which men without character and without fortune possess." And John Adams had said of Rutledge, "Rutledge is a perfect bobolink, a swallow, a sparrow, a peacock, excessively vain, excessively weak."

Now, Rutledge and Adams and the rest listened to John Dickinson speaking gravely from the heart: "Declaring our independence at a time like this is like burning down our house before we have another."

5 It was John Adams who rose to his feet. He was not John Dickinson's equal as a speaker, and everything he had to say he had said before. He never said it better than on that July afternoon: "We've been duped and bubbled by the phantom of peace. What is the real choice before us? If we postpone the declaration, do we mean to submit? Do we consent to yield and become a conquered people? No, we do not! We shall fight! We shall fight with whatever means we have—with rusty muskets and broken flints, with bows and arrows, if need be. Then why put off the declaration? For myself, I
6 can only say this: I have crossed the Rubicon.[2] All that I have, all that I am, all that I hope for in this life, I stake on our cause. For me, the die is cast. Sink or swim, live or die, to survive or perish with my country—that is my unalterable resolution!"

That night, John Dickinson went home, put on his militia uniform, and rode away to join his regiment. He could not vote for independence, but he could fight the British. That night, Edward Rutledge changed his mind. South Carolina would not stand in the way of unanimity. That night, Caesar Rodney, a man dying of cancer, rode through the night on horseback in a storm to Philadelphia to cast the deciding vote for Delaware. And so, when Secretary Charles Thomson called the roll on July 2nd, of the twelve colonies voting, all twelve voted for Independence. It was done. What remained was the declaring it.

The next morning, July 3rd, an anonymous note was found on President Hancock's table. It said, "You have gone too far. Take care. A plot is framed for your destruction, and all of you shall be destroyed." It suddenly occurred to them that there might be a lighted powder keg under the floor; there was an uproar. There were volunteers to search the cellar. Then crusty old Joseph Hewes of North Carolina stood up to say, "Mr. President, I am against wasting any time searching cellars. I would as soon be blown to pieces as proclaim to the world that I was frightened by a note."

> **◆ Reading Strategy**
> How does this passage suggest that the delegates may have been uncertain about the outcome of events? 7

8 Without searching any cellars, the Continental Congress proceeded to a consideration of the Declaration of Independence. They're immortal words now, but of course they weren't when Charles Thomson read them for the first time: "When in the Course of human events . . ." And for two days Jefferson sat back in the corner and fumed as they all toyed with his masterpiece. "Did we really have to call the King a tyrant quite so often?" They changed some of the "tyrants" back to "King." "Did we have to bid the British people our everlasting adieu?" They

2. **Rubicon** (ro͞o′ bə kän) *n.:* A limiting line that when crossed commits a person to an unchangeable decision.

◆ Build Vocabulary

anonymous (ə nän′ ə məs) *adj.:* Unsigned; written by a person whose name is unknown

◆Reading Strategy

5 Identify Main Points Ask students, after they read this passage, to summarize how the author feels toward John Adams. *Kuralt knows that Adams was not as good a speaker as Dickinson, but on that day he spoke with remarkable eloquence and power.*

Clarification

6 Clarify the meaning of "crossing the Rubicon" by telling students that the Rubicon was a small river in northern Italy that separated the Roman republic from Cisalpine Gaul. When Julius Caesar lead his army across the Rubicon in 49 B.C., the Roman Senate viewed this move as an act of war. So crossing the Rubicon means knowingly taking a step that will have enormous consequences.

◆Reading Strategy

7 Identify Main Points *Possible answer: The delegates were in "uncharted waters." They faced opposition from their own ranks, from loyalist colonists, and from Great Britain itself. They had no idea how their great experiment in freedom might turn out.*

◆Critical Thinking

8 Assess Have students access the character of Joseph Hewes, based on his comments in this passage. What do his remarks reveal about his commitment to independence? *Hewes is ready to move forward, is not easily threatened, and would rather be remembered for his desire for freedom than for being scared off by what may be an empty threat.*

Block Scheduling Strategies

Consider these suggestions to take advantage of extended class time:

- Using the Interest Grabber (p. 603) as a springboard, have students draft essays on topics of personal interest. Allow volunteers to work together to combine the essays into an editorial section of a "weeky paper." Alternatively, encourage students to submit their essays to the school newspaper.
- Have students complete the Speaking and Listening Mini-Lesson on p. 618. If possible, provide background by showing videotaped footage from a televised press conference. Provide time for students to conduct research on the writers so they can better formulate their questions and answers.
- If you have access to technology, have students work on the *Writer's Solution Writing Lab CD-ROM* to complete all or part of the Writing Mini-Lesson on p. 621.

Clarification

❶ Thomas Jefferson demanded independence and made statements calling for freedom for slaves, as he says in this passage. Yet he himself owned slaves. This apparent contradiction still puzzles historians.

◆ Critical Thinking

❷ **Evaluate** Challenge students to consider the impact of the final document and how the delegates worked to reach a compromise they could live with. *Students may say that the Declaration had to say enough to inspire confidence in the delegates' bold new plan, be powerful enough to force the issue of liberty, yet be softened enough to earn widespread support.*

Customize for *Verbal/Linguistic Learners*

Guide students to think about how much measuring the delegates gave to each word of the Declaration of Independence. Pose these questions:

- Why was it so important to craft the document so carefully?
- Should the particular words someone uses matter? Explain.
- Have there been times in your life when the exact words you chose mattered? Explain.

Reinforce and Extend

Answers

◆ Literature and Your Life

Reader's Response Students should support their views with details from the essay.

Thematic Focus It shows that a national goal is hard to reach. Agreement is not easy to come by and demands serious debate and compromise; it takes courage to chart a new course.

☑ Check Your Comprehension

1. The British were already bombing Charleston, sending armies south from Canada, and sailing a giant armada into the New York harbor.
2. He said that it was time to fight, that nothing would be gained by hesitating.
3. It passed unanimously.
4. They changed "tyrant" to "king" in several places; they removed the "everlasting adieu" to the British people; they took out Jefferson's denunciation of slavery.

❶ struck that out. And Jefferson's mightiest passage, his denunciation[3] of slavery, that was struck out, too, at the insistence of Georgia and South Carolina. Jefferson wrote elsewhere, "Nothing is more certainly written in the book of fate than that these people are to be free."

❷ But finally, all the cuts and changes were done, and what remained was a document still noble enough to inspire the tired delegates and bold enough to hang them all. It was read through one more time to the end: ". . . And for the support of this Declaration, with a firm reliance on the Protection of Divine Providence, we mutually pledge to each other our Lives, our Fortunes and our sacred Honor." There was one final vote, and President Hancock announced the result with the use of a new phrase: "The Declaration of the United States of America is unanimously agreed to." There was no cheering, no fireworks; not yet. The delegates simply walked out into the night of the Fourth of July thinking their own thoughts, some of them no doubt remembering what John Dickinson had said: "This is like burning down our house before we have another." Others hearing Tom Paine: "The birthday of a new world is at hand. We have it in our power to begin the world all over again."

John Adams walked to his boardinghouse to write a letter to a friend. "Well," he said, "the river is passed. The bridge is cut away."

3. **denunciation** (dē nun′ sē ā′ shən) *n.*: Strong criticism.

◆ Build Vocabulary

unanimously (yo͞o nan′ ə məs lē) *adv.*: Overwhelmingly; without disagreement

Guide for Responding

◆ Literature and Your Life

Reader's Response Which of the men named in the essay do you admire most? Why?

Thematic Focus What does this essay indicate about the difficulty of stating and realizing a national dream or goal?

Speech Read aloud the speech that John Adams gave in response to John Dickinson's warnings. (See page 605.) Express not only the ideas but the feelings behind them.

☑ Check Your Comprehension

1. What immediate threats from the British prompted John Dickinson to warn against declaring independence?
2. What did John Adams say in answer to John Dickinson?
3. Give the results of the final vote on the issue of independence.
4. Identify three changes that the Continental Congress made in Jefferson's draft of the Declaration of Independence.

◆ Critical Thinking

Interpret

1. Give two examples from the essay of divisions between northern colonies and southern colonies. **[Analyze]**
2. What do you think persuaded the delegates to vote unanimously for independence? **[Speculate]**
3. Explain how Adams's letter summarizes the situation of the colonies after independence was declared: "the river is passed. The bridge is cut away." **[Interpret]**

Evaluate

4. Do you agree with Joseph Hewes that there was no point in searching the cellar for a bomb? Why or why not? **[Make a Judgment]**

Extend

5. In what ways does Kuralt show that living through a historic event is not as easy as looking back on it? **[Social Studies Link]**

◆ Critical Thinking

1. Edward Rutledge of South Carolina and John Adams of Massachusetts denounced each other. Georgia and South Carolina insisted that slavery be allowed to continue.
2. It would make a stronger statement if all the colonies stood united in the cause.
3. His message is that it's impossible to turn back. In his view, the delegates have cut off ties with Great Britain and will have to survive alone.
4. The note reminded the delegates that they lacked full support. Students may say that these men were serious and level-headed and not likely to panic.
5. As events fade into the past, only the highlights remain. This essay reminds us that before they became heroes, the delegates had struggled to do something unprecedented in a difficult and dangerous situation.

Rattlesnake Hunt

Marjorie Kinnan Rawlings

Ross Allen, a young Florida herpetologist,[1] invited me to join him on a hunt in the upper Everglades[2]—for rattlesnakes. Ross and I drove to Arcadia in his coupé[3] on a warm January day.

I said, "How will you bring back the rattlesnakes?"

"In the back of my car."

My courage was not adequate to inquire whether they were thrown in loose and might be expected to appear between our feet. Actually, a large portable box of heavy close-meshed wire made a safe cage. Ross wanted me to write an article about his work and on our way to the
❸ unhappy hunting grounds I took notes on a mass of data that he had accumulated in years of herpetological research. The scientific and dispassionate detachment of the material and the man made a desirable approach to rattlesnake territory. As I had discovered with the insects and varmints,[4] it is difficult to be afraid of anything about which enough is known, and Ross' facts were fresh from the laboratory.

The hunting ground was Big Prairie, south of Arcadia and west of the northern tip of Lake Okeechobee. Big Prairie is a <u>desolate</u> cattle country, half marsh, half pasture, with islands of palm trees and cypress and oaks. At that time of year the cattlemen and Indians were burning the country, on the theory that the young fresh wire grass that springs up from the roots after a fire is the best cattle forage. Ross planned to hunt his rattlers in the forefront of the fires. They lived in winter, he said, in gopher holes, coming out in the midday warmth to forage, and would move ahead of the flames and be easily taken. We joined forces with a big man named Will, his snake-hunting companion of the territory, and set out in early morning, after a long rough drive over deep-rutted roads into the open wilds.

> ◆ **Literary Focus** ❹ ❺
> Which words and phrases give you a picture of the plant life in this region?

I hope never in my life to be so frightened as I was in those first few hours. I kept on Ross' footsteps, I moved when he moved, sometimes jolting into him when I thought he might leave me behind. He does not use the forked stick of conventional snake hunting, but a steel prong, shaped like an L, at the end of a long stout stick. He hunted casually, calling my attention ❻
to the varying vegetation, to hawks overhead, to a pair of the rare whooping cranes that flapped over us. In mid-morning he stopped short, dropped his stick, and brought up a five-foot rattlesnake draped limply over the steel L. It seemed to me that I should drop in my tracks.

"They're not active at this season," he said

---

1. **herpetologist** (hur′ pə täl′ ə jist) *n.*: Someone who studies reptiles and amphibians.
2. **Everglades:** Large region of swampland in southern Florida, about 100 miles long and 50–75 miles wide.
3. **coupé** (ko͞o pā′) *n.*: Small two-door automobile.
4. **varmints** (vär′ mənts) *n.*: Animals regarded as troublesome.

◆ **Build Vocabulary**

desolate (des′ ə lit) *adj.*: Lonely; solitary

Develop Understanding

In this descriptive essay, the author shares her experiences rattlesnake hunting near the Florida Everglades with an experienced herpetologist. She was at first uneasy around snakes, but as she learned more about them, she grew able to conquer her fears.

Customize for
More Advanced Students

Suggest to students that writers who tell about overcoming their own fears often include a turning point in their narratives—a moment or an event that helps them gain a new perspective on what once frightened them. Have students as they read, look for the turning point in this essay.

◆Reading Strategy

❸ **Identify Main Points** Ask students to determine the author's attitude toward this hunt. *She is afraid and unenthusiastic, but she tries to take an intellectual view to get through it.*

Clarification

❹ The "Indians" Ross refers to are probably the Seminoles. This group of Native Americans fled from areas north of Florida into the Everglades to escape pursuing American soldiers. Although some Seminoles went with the other four "Civilized Tribes" to reservations in Oklahoma, a group remained in Florida to fight to preserve their way of life.

◆Literary Focus

❺ **Essay** *Examples include the description of the country as half marsh and half pasture with wire grass and islands of palm trees and cypress and oaks.*

◆Build Grammar Skills

❻ **Subject and Object Pronouns** Students must know whether to use the subjective or objective cases of pronouns, depending on how they are used in the sentences in which they appear. Help students to identify all the pronouns in this passage and then to determine whether they function as subjects or objects. I *and* he *are subject pronouns;* him, me, *and* us *are object pronouns.*

Cross-Curricular Connection: Science

There are over 2,500 species of snakes in the world; all are carnivorous. Yet of the approximately 400 varieties of venomous snakes, only a few are lethal to humans. Invite interested students to conduct research to learn more about poisonous snakes: where they live, how they hunt, how their poisons kill, and what, if any, antidotes exist to their venom. Students might focus on particular types of venomous snakes, such as rattlesnakes, cobras, and mambas. Students can present their findings in oral reports, written reports, or multimedia presentations to the class. If there is a university or zoo in your area, you might invite a herpetologist to address the class to answer students' questions about poisonous snakes and to tell them about any poisonous snakes that may be indigenous to your area.

◆Literature and Your Life

❶ Encourage students to discuss situations in which they faced their fears, or in which they learned that their preconceived notions about something weren't really accurate.

◆Literary Focus

❷ **Essay** Here, as Rawlings describes her first experience holding a snake, readers may detect the slow change in her attitude. Discuss descriptions that convey change in this passage. *First, she agrees to hold the snake; she realizes that it lies "trustingly" in her hands, it lives and breathes like other creatures, and it is mortal.*

◆Critical Thinking

❸ **Compare and Contrast** Have students compare and contrast the narrator's attitude toward snakes on the first and second mornings of the hunt. *On the first morning, she was reluctant, anxious, and scared; now she feels more bold, brave, and willing to get on with it.*

quietly. "A snake takes on the temperature of its surroundings. They can't stand too much heat for that reason, and when the weather is cool, as now, they're sluggish."

The sun was bright overhead, the sky a translucent blue, and it seemed to me that it was warm enough for any snake to do as it willed. The sweat poured down my back. Ross dropped the rattler in a crocus sack and Will carried it. By noon, he had caught four. I felt faint and ill. We stopped by a pond and went swimming. The region was flat, the horizon limitless, and as I came out of the cool blue water I expected to find myself surrounded by a ring of rattlers. There were only Ross and Will, opening the lunch basket. I could not eat. Will went back and drove his truck closer, for Ross expected the hunting to be better in the afternoon. The hunting was much better. When we went back to the truck to deposit two more rattlers in the wire cage, there was a rattlesnake lying under the truck.

Ross said, "Whenever I leave my car or truck with snakes already in it, other rattlers always appear. I don't know whether this is because they scent or sense the presence of other snakes, or whether in this arid[5] area they come to the car for shade in the heat of the day."

The problem was scientific, but I had no interest.

That night Ross and Will and I camped out in the vast spaces of the Everglades prairies. We got water from an abandoned well and cooked supper under buttonwood bushes by a flowing stream. The camp fire blazed cheerfully under the stars and a new moon lifted in the sky. Will told tall tales of the cattlemen and the Indians and we were at peace.

Ross said, "We couldn't have a better night for catching water snakes."

After the rattlers, water snakes seemed innocuous[6] enough. We worked along the edge of the stream and here Ross did not use his L-shaped steel. He reached under rocks and along the edge of the water and brought out harmless reptiles with his hands. I had said nothing to him of my fears, but he understood them. He brought a small dark snake from under a willow root.

> **◆ Literature and Your Life**
> How would you feel at a moment like this?

"Wouldn't you like to hold it?" he asked. "People think snakes are cold and clammy, but they aren't. Take it in your hands. You'll see that it is warm." ❶

Again, because I was ashamed, I took the snake in my hands. It was not cold, it was not clammy, and it lay trustingly in my hands, a thing that lived and breathed and had mortality like the rest of us. I felt an upsurgence of spirit. ❷

The next day was magnificent. The air was crystal, the sky was aquamarine, and the far horizon of palms and oaks lay against the sky. I felt a new boldness and followed Ross bravely. ❸ He was making the rounds of the gopher holes. The rattlers came out in the mid-morning warmth and were never far away. He could tell by their trails whether one had come out or was still in the hole. Sometimes the two men dug the snake out. At times it was down so long and winding a tunnel that the digging was hopeless. Then they blocked the entrance and went on to other holes. In an hour or so they made the original rounds, unblocking the holes. The rattler in every case came out hurriedly, as though anything were preferable to being shut in. All the time Ross talked to me, telling me the scientific facts he had discovered about the habits of the rattlers.

"They pay no attention to a man standing perfectly still," he said, and proved it by letting Will unblock a hole while he stood at the entrance as the snake came out. It was exciting to watch the snake crawl slowly beside and past the man's legs. When it was at a safe distance he walked within its range of vision, which he had proved to be no higher than a man's knee, and the snake whirled and drew back in an attitude[7] of fighting defense. The rattler strikes only for paralyzing and killing

5. **arid** (ar´ id) *adj.*: Dry and barren.
6. **innocuous** (in näk´ yo͞o əs) *adj.*: Harmless.
7. **attitude:** (at´ ə to͞od´) *n.*: A position or posture of the body.

its food, and for defense.

"It is a slow and heavy snake," Ross said. "It lies in wait on a small game trail and strikes the rat or rabbit passing by. It waits a few minutes, then follows along the trail, coming to the small animal, now dead or dying. It noses it from all sides, making sure that it is its own kill, and that it is dead and ready for swallowing."

A rattler will lie quietly without revealing itself if a man passes by and it thinks it is not seen. It slips away without fighting if given the chance. Only Ross' sharp eyes sometimes picked out the gray and yellow diamond pattern, camouflaged among the grasses. In the cool of the morning, chilled by the January air, the snakes showed no fight. They could be looped up limply over the steel L and dropped in a sack or up into the wire cage on the back of Will's truck. As the sun mounted in the sky and warmed the moist Everglades earth, the snakes were warmed too, and Ross warned that it was time to go more cautiously. Yet
4 having learned that it was we who were the aggressors; that immobility meant complete safety; that the snakes, for all their lightning flash in striking, were inaccurate in their aim, with limited vision; having watched again and again the liquid grace of movement, the beauty of pattern, suddenly I understood that I was drinking in freely the magnificent sweep of the horizon, with no fear of what might be at the moment under my feet. I went off hunting by myself, and though I found no snakes, I should have known what to do. 4

The sun was dropping low in the west. Masses of white cloud hung above the flat marshy plain and seemed to be tangled in the tops of distant palms and cypresses. The sky turned orange, then saffron. I walked leisurely back toward the truck. In the distance I could see Ross and Will making their way in too. The season was more advanced than at the Creek, two hundred miles to the north, and I noticed that spring flowers were blooming among the lumpy hummocks. I leaned over to pick a white violet. There was a rattlesnake under the violet. 5

If this had happened the week before, if it had happened the day before, I think I should have lain down and died on top of the rattlesnake, with no need of being struck and poisoned. The snake did not coil, but lifted its head and whirred its rattles lightly. I

◆ Build Vocabulary

mortality (môr tal′ ə tē) *n.*: The condition of being mortal; having to die eventually

◀ Critical Viewing Why was the author afraid of rattlesnakes, like the one pictured here? **[Analyze]** 6

◆Reading Strategy

4 Identify Main Points Have students restate what the narrator now understands about rattlesnakes that changes her attitude. *Now she understands that the snakes do not hunt humans. It's the other way around; snakes want only to survive.*

Clarification

5 "The Creek" refers to Cross Creek, the author's beloved backwoods farm in Florida. In 1928, she found a rambling old farm house near a remote, run-down orange grove about 20 miles south of Gainesville, between Lochioosa and Orange Lakes. Today her house and grounds are preserved as the Marjorie Kinnan Rawlings State Historical Site. For more information, students can call (904) 466-3672.

▶Critical Viewing◀

6 Analyze *She believed that the snakes would bite her and their venom would kill her.*

Cultural Connection

Despite the apprehension or negative attitudes of individuals, not all cultures fear snakes. One example is the Hopi people of New Mexico. In their religious ceremony known as the Snake Dance, costumed dancers move in pairs. One carries a rattlesnake in his mouth, while a helper occupies the snake's venomous fangs with a feather wisp. When the snakes have been carried across an open area atop a mesa, runners seize the snakes and rush down the mesa to the desert below, where they release the snakes as messengers to the spirits of Earth. Remarkably, few dancers are ever bitten during this dramatic ritual.

Invite interested students to research the attitude toward snakes in other cultures as expressed in religion, folklore, art, and literature. Allow time for students to share their findings with the class.

Thematic Focus

Wishes, Hopes, Dreams Have students consider the ways in which Ross's hopes have been realized. *He has collected enough snakes for his research; he has taught another person to appreciate snakes, and has enjoyed seeing her progress.*

◆Reading Strategy

1 Identify Main Points *It expresses the excitement of overcoming a fear, and the satisfaction a person feels to have done so.*

Reinforce and Extend

Answers

◆Literature and Your Life

Reader's Response Answers will vary, depending on students' sense of adventure, attitude toward snakes, and open-mindedness.

Thematic Focus She comes to realize that fear itself is a greater danger than the imagined or exaggerated dangers of a creature of nature.

☑ Check Your Comprehension

1. She is invited by Ross Allen, a Florida herpetologist, to write an article about his work.
2. Facts include: rattlers live in gopher holes in winter and come out only when they feel warmth; they are sluggish in cool weather; they aren't cold and clammy, but warm; they ignore people who stand perfectly still; a rattler strikes only to paralyze and kill its food, and for defense.
3. She doesn't panic when she finds a rattlesnake under the violet she picks; she tries her best to pick up the snake with the L tool.

◆Critical Thinking

1. She realizes that some of her views about snakes are incorrect, so maybe she should be open-minded to other aspects about snakes.
2. She has new confidence from surviving the first day without incident and from learning so much about snakes from Ross.
3. She has conquered a fear.
4. The essay shows that knowledge helps someone face an unknown situation and face fears.

stepped back slowly and put the violet in a buttonhole. I reached forward and laid the steel L across the snake's neck, just back of the blunt head. I called to Ross:

"I've got one."

He strolled toward me.

"Well, pick it up," he said.

I released it and slipped the L under the middle of the thick body.

"Go put it in the box."

He went ahead of me and lifted the top of the wire cage. I made the truck with the rattler, but when I reached up the six feet to drop it in the cage, it slipped off the stick and dropped on Ross' feet. It made no effort to strike.

"Pick it up again," he said. "If you'll pin it down lightly and reach just back of its head with your hand, as you've seen me do, you can drop it in more easily."

I pinned it and leaned over.

"I'm awfully sorry," I said, "but you're pushing me a little too fast."

He grinned. I lifted it on the stick and again as I had it at head height, it slipped off, down Ross' boots and on top of his feet. He stood as still as a stump. I dropped the snake on his feet for the third time. It seemed to me that the most patient of rattlers might in time resent being hauled up and down, and for all the man's quiet certainty that in standing motionless there was no danger, would strike at whatever was nearest, and that would be Ross.

I said, "I'm just not man enough to keep this up any longer," and he laughed and reached down with his smooth quickness and lifted the snake back of the head and dropped it in the cage. It slid in among its mates and settled in a corner. The hunt was over and we drove back over the uneven trail to Will's village and left him and went on to Arcadia and home. Our catch for the two days was thirty-two rattlers.

I said to Ross, "I believe that tomorrow I could have picked up that snake."

Back at the Creek, I felt a new lightness. I had done battle with a great fear, and the victory was mine.

◆ Reading Strategy
Explain how this passage comes close to stating one of the essay's main points. 1

Guide for Responding

◆ Literature and Your Life

Reader's Response Would you like to go on a rattlesnake hunt? Why or why not?

Thematic Focus In what ways does the rattlesnake hunt change how Rawlings thinks about nature and about herself?

☑ Check Your Comprehension

1. Why does Rawlings go on the hunt?
2. Identify three facts Rawlings learns about rattlers.
3. Note two ways in which Rawlings shows that she has partly overcome her fears.

◆ Critical Thinking

Interpret

1. Why do Rawlings's feelings about snakes change when she holds one? **[Infer]**
2. What might contribute to Rawlings's feeling of "boldness" on the second day? **[Speculate]**
3. Describe the "victory" that Rawlings has won by the end of the hunt. **[Draw Conclusions]**

Apply

4. In what way does this essay support the idea that knowledge drives away fear? **[Defend]**

Cross-Curricular Connection: Ecology

The Florida Everglades is a vast swampy marsh area, one of the world's largest wetland ecosystems. It covers about 5,000 square miles of land, but averages less than a foot in depth. Along with the rattlers living there, the Everglades is the natural habitat of alligators, manatees, giant turtles, fish, deer, the endangered Florida panther, and hundreds of types of birds and insects.

Today, with the growth of cities, highways, agriculture, and the enormous need to supply south Florida with water, the natural balance of the Everglades is at great risk. Help students explore the ecological issues that this unique area faces; recent attempts environmentalists have made to protect and preserve the area; the roles federal, state, and local governments have played to protect it; and its likely future.

from

Barrio Boy

Ernesto Galarza

2 ▶ Critical Viewing Does this photograph effectively convey the emotions that Ernesto might have felt as he enrolled in a new school? Explain. **[Evaluate]**

My mother and I walked south on Fifth Street one morning to the corner of Q Street and turned right. Half of the block was occupied by the Lincoln School. It was a three-story wooden building, with two wings that gave it the shape of a double-T connected by a central hall. It was a new building, 3 painted yellow, with a shingled roof that was not like the red tile of the school in Mazatlán. I noticed other differences, none of them very reassuring.

We walked up the wide staircase hand in hand and through the door, which closed by itself. A mechanical contraption screwed to the top shut it behind us quietly.

4 Up to this point the adventure of enrolling me in the school had been carefully rehearsed. Mrs. Dodson had told us how to find it and we had circled it several times on our walks. Friends in the *barrio*[1] explained that the director was called a principal, and that it was a lady and not a man. They assured us that there was always a person at the school who could speak Spanish.

Exactly as we had been told, there was a sign on the door in both Spanish and English: "Principal." We crossed the hall and entered the office of Miss Nettie Hopley.

Miss Hopley was at a roll-top desk to one side, sitting in a swivel chair that moved on wheels. There was a sofa against the opposite wall, flanked by two windows and a door that opened on a small balcony. Chairs were set around a table and framed pictures hung on the walls of a man with long white hair and 5

1. **barrio** (bär´ ē ō) *n.*: Part of a town or city where most of the people are Hispanic.

Cross-Curricular Connection: Social Studies

Immigration Whereas newcomers from Europe once entered the United States through Ellis Island in the New York harbor, most people from Asia and the Pacific Rim came through Angel Island in San Francisco Bay. Today, most immigrants from Central and South American countries enter California through San Diego and Los Angeles. California schools, like those in any state with a significant immigrant population, have a special mission to help newcomers adjust to their new lives. Have students research the opportunities, outreach programs, and support systems currently available to immigrants in your area. If your area has few immigrant families, then students can learn about ways in which California, New York, Florida, and Texas, which have the greatest immigrant populations, serve the needs of their culturally diverse residents.

Develop Understanding

One-Minute Insight

Young Ernesto from Mexico has just arrived in the United States and at Lincoln School. On his first day, a formidable but friendly principal and her young interpreter greet Ernesto and his mother. His kind, supportive teacher continues the process of welcoming him to his new country and new language. Ernesto and the other immigrant children form a bond as they learn English and adapt to their new lives. The school staff guides them to take pride in their diverse backgrounds.

▶Critical Viewing◀

2 **Evaluate** *Students may say that the boy seems hesitant, perhaps a bit fearful, but curious to fit in to his new environment.*

Clarification

3 Inform students that Mazatlán is a seaport in western Mexico, known for exporting metal ores, tobacco, hides, and shrimp. Tell them that most Americans know it as a beach resort. If any students have been to Mazatlán, invite them to describe it.

◆Reading Strategy

4 **Identify Main Points** Ask students to explain why Ernesto and his mother have rehearsed the interview with the principal. *Students may say that Ernesto and his mother were nervous, or wanted to make a good impression.*

◆Critical Thinking

5 **Deduce** Ernesto and his mother notice the pictures of two men on the office wall. Ask students to deduce from the descriptions who these men are. *Students may say the sad-faced bearded man is Abraham Lincoln, for whom the school is named. They may guess that the other is George Washington, the first U.S. President.*

◆Literary Focus

❶ **Essay** *Students may say that by sharing personal feelings, Galarza makes the essay seem like a story he might share at a family gathering. It brings readers closer to him.*

◆Critical Viewing

❷ **Compare and Contrast** *Like Miss Ryan, this young teacher is working with a group of young children. They seem to be from different ethnic backgrounds. They are discussing a picture whose caption says, "This is the first day I came to school."*

◆Reading Strategy

❸ **Identify the Author's Main Points** Guide students to identify details in this paragraph that show that the narrator is a child. *Students may cite Ernesto's amazement at Miss Hopley's height, exaggerated by the fact that he is so small. He compares her at first to a giant and then wants her protectiveness, as a child might.*

Art Transparency Display Art Transparency 5, a pastel drawing by Mexican American artist Tony Ortega. Have students imagine that Ernesto is one of the young boys seated on the curb, and have them share their ideas about what he and the other people in the picture might be looking at.

◀ Critical Viewing How does the classroom in this photograph compare with Miss Ryan's classroom? **[Compare and Contrast]** ❷

another with a sad face and a black beard.

The principal half turned in the swivel chair to look at us over the pinch glasses crossed on the ridge of her nose. To do this she had to duck her head slightly as if she were about to step through a low doorway.

What Miss Hopley said to us we did not know but we saw in her eyes a warm welcome and when she took off her glasses and straightened up she smiled wholeheartedly, like Mrs. Dodson. We were, of course, saying nothing, only catching the friendliness of her voice and the sparkle in her eyes while she said words we did not understand. She signaled us to the table. Almost tiptoeing across the office, I maneuvered myself to keep my mother between me and the gringo lady. In a matter of seconds I had to decide whether she was a possible friend or a menace.[2] We sat down.

❶ **◆ Literary Focus** In what way does Galarza's honesty about his feelings make the essay seem more personal?

Then Miss Hopley did a formidable thing. She stood up. Had she been standing when we entered she would have seemed tall. But rising from her chair she soared. And what she carried up and up with her was a buxom superstructure,[3] firm shoulders, a straight sharp nose, full cheeks slightly molded by a curved line along the nostrils, thin lips that moved like steel springs, and a high forehead topped by hair gathered in a bun. Miss Hopley was not a giant in body but when she mobilized[4] it to a standing position she seemed a match for giants. I decided I liked her. ❸

She strode to a door in the far corner of the office, opened it and called a name. A boy of about ten years appeared in the doorway. He sat down at one end of the table. He was brown like us, a plump kid with shiny black hair combed straight back, neat, cool, and faintly obnoxious.

Miss Hopley joined us with a large book and some papers in her hand. She, too, sat down and the questions and answers began by way of our interpreter.[5] My name was Ernesto. My mother's name was Henriqueta. My birth

2. **menace** (men´ is) *n.*: Danger; threat.

3. **buxom superstructure:** Full figure.
4. **mobilized** (mō´ bə līzd´) *v.*: Put into motion.
5. **interpreter** (in tur´ prə tər) *n.*: Someone who translates from one language into another.

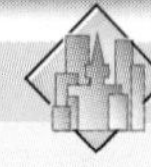

Beyond the Classroom

Career Connection

Careers in Education Ernesto warms to his new principal and teacher, both of whom make him feel welcome and successful. Discuss with students the qualities that make a good teacher or principal. Students may say that good teachers and principals are dedicated to learning more about their academic fields and are caring and supportive, good listeners, observant, and creative problem solvers. Have students identify the qualities of good teaching and good administration that are revealed in this selection. Discuss the personal attributes students think might lead to a career in education. Help interested students learn more about the process of becoming a teacher, teacher's aide, tutor, guidance counselor, or school administrator.

certificate was in San Blas. Here was my last report card from the Escuela Municipal Numero 3 para Varones of Mazatlán,[6] and so forth. Miss Hopley put things down in the book and my mother signed a card.

As long as the questions continued, Doña[7] Henriqueta could stay and I was secure. Now that they were over, Miss Hopley saw her to the door, dismissed our interpreter and without further ado took me by the hand and strode down the hall to Miss Ryan's first grade.

Miss Ryan took me to a seat at the front of the room, into which I shrank—the better to survey her. She was, to skinny, somewhat runty me, of a withering height when she patrolled the class. And when I least expected it, there she was, crouching by my desk, her blond radiant face level with mine, her voice patiently maneuvering me over the awful idiocies of the English language.

During the next few weeks Miss Ryan overcame my fears of tall, energetic teachers as she bent over my desk to help me with a word in the pre-primer. Step by step, she loosened me and my classmates from the safe anchorage of the desks for recitations at the blackboard and consultations at her desk. Frequently she burst into happy announcements to the whole class. "Ito can read a sentence," and small
4 Japanese Ito, squint-eyed and shy, slowly read aloud while the class listened in wonder: "Come, Skipper, come. Come and run." The Korean, Portuguese, Italian, and Polish first graders had similar moments of glory, no less shining than mine the day I conquered "butterfly," which I had been persistently pronouncing in standard Spanish as boo-ter-flee. "Children," Miss Ryan called for attention. "Ernesto has learned how to pronounce *butterfly*!" And I proved it with a perfect imitation of Miss Ryan. From that celebrated success, I was soon able to match Ito's progress as a sentence reader with "Come, butterfly, come fly with me."

Like Ito and several other first graders who did not know English, I received private
lessons from Miss Ryan in the closet, a narrow 5
hall off the classroom with a door at each end. Next to one of these doors Miss Ryan placed a large chair for herself and a small one for me. Keeping an eye on the class through the open door she read with me about sheep in the meadow and a frightened chicken going to see the king, coaching me out of my phonetic ruts in words like *pasture, bow-wow-wow, hay,* and *pretty,* which to my Mexican ear and eye had so many unnecessary sounds and letters. She made me watch her lips and then close my
eyes as she repeated words I found hard to 6
read. When we came to know each other better, I tried interrupting to tell Miss Ryan how we said it in Spanish. It didn't work. She only said "oh" and went on with *pasture, bow-wow-wow,* and *pretty.* It was as if in that closet we were both discovering together the secrets of the English language and grieving[8] together over the tragedies of Bo-Peep. The main reason I was graduated with honors from the first grade was that I had fallen in love with Miss Ryan. Her radiant, no-nonsense character made us either afraid not to love her or love her so we would not be afraid, I am not sure which. It was not only that we sensed she was with it, but also that she was with us.

Like the first grade, the rest of the Lincoln School was a sampling of the lower part of town where many races made their home. My pals in the second grade were Kazushi, whose parents spoke only Japanese; Matti, a skinny Italian boy; and Manuel, a fat Portuguese who would never get into a fight but wrestled you to the ground and just sat on you. Our assortment of nationalities included Koreans, Yugoslavs, Poles, Irish, and home-grown Americans.

At Lincoln, making us into Americans did not mean scrubbing away what made us

6. **Escuela Municipal Numero 3 para Varones of Mazatlán** (es kwā lə mo͞o nē sē päl no͞o´ me rô trās pärä vä rō´ nas mä sät län´): Municipal School Number 3 for Boys of Mazatlán.

7. **Doña** (dô´ nyä): Spanish title of respect meaning "lady" or "madam."

8. **grieving** (grēv´ iŋ) *v.*: Feeling sorrow for a loss.

◆ Build Vocabulary

formidable (fôr´ mi də bəl) *adj.*: Impressive

◆Reading Strategy

4 Identify Main Points Point out that Galarza does not directly state how he feels about Miss Ryan. Rather, he shares anecdotes about things she says and does, so readers can get to know her as well as he has. What opinion of Miss Ryan does Galarza help readers to form? *She is an enthusiastic, encouraging, and kind teacher who makes her students feel good about themselves and their achievements, no matter how small.*

Spelling

5 The spelling strategy examines how the *it* sound at the end of a multisyllable adjective is often spelled with *-ate.* Point out the word in this sentence that fits this pattern: *private.* Encourage students to look for words in this essay, and other essays in this grouping, in which the *it* sound is spelled with *-ate.*

Clarification

6 Encourage students whose first language is not English to explain some of the difficulties encountered by English language learners. Discuss, for example, the fact that in Spanish there is no *w.* Explain that mispronunciations can occur among people who swith languages because different languages have different sounds for certain letters, use different symbols to represent sounds, or may use a totally different alphabet.

Cross-Curricular Connection: Math

Statistics on Diversity Across the United States, many areas have populations that reflect a wide ethnic diversity. Have students conduct a survey to determine the range of languages, nationalities, or places of origin represented in your class, school, or community. Have students work in pairs or small groups to devise and distribute an easy-to-use questionaire. Have them tally and analyze the results mathematically, then present their findings to the class in the form of an annoted chart or graph. You might suggest that students consult with their math teacher for advice on how best to structure the questionaire, tally results, choose a suitable graph, and report findings with accuracy and clarity. To conclude, students might compare the results of their own sample with national or state statistics.

◆Reading Strategy

❶ Identify the Author's Main Points Challenge students to summerize the main point of this paragraph. *Becoming a proud American does not mean losing or denying the special qualities of one's own culture.* What message or lesson does the author try to convey to those who work with immigrants? *He wants people to realize how important it is for immigrants to value their own heritage as they adjust to a new life in America.*

Comprehension Check ☑

In what ways did teachers and administrators at Lincoln School try to make the transition to life in the United States easier for newcomers like Ernesto and his classmates? *School policy permitted children to speak their native tounges on the playground and gave opportunities for them to share their heritage, family accomplishments, art, and cultural values.*

Beyond Literature

In response to the great influx of immigrants from all over the world, educators have been taking direct approaches to the language needs of students from diverse background. You might invite teachers to address the class about some of the techniques they develop to help students whose first language is not English.

Reinforce and Extend

Answers

◆LITERATURE AND YOUR LIFE

Reader's Response Encourage students to share their experiences.

Thematic Focus The school provided a kind, supportive teacher, an understanding, tolerant environment, and an attitude of acceptance of people from many backgrounds.

☑ Check Your Comprehension

1. He goes to enroll in first grade.
2. She is strict, but warm; her height makes Ernesto feel protected.
3. He is suspicious of tall, energetic teachers who loom over students.
4. She gives him support, help, and encouragement, and applauds his succsses.

originally foreign. The teachers called us as our parents did, or as close as they could pronounce our names in Spanish or Japanese. No one was ever scolded or punished for speaking in his native tongue on the playground. Matti told the class about his mother's down quilt, which she had made in Italy with the fine feathers of a thousand geese. Encarnación acted out how boys learned to fish in the Philippines. I astounded the third grade with ❶ the story of my travels on a stagecoach, which nobody else in the class had seen except in the museum at Sutter's Fort. After a visit to the Crocker Art Gallery and its collection of heroic paintings of the golden age of California, someone showed a silk scroll with a Chinese painting. Miss Hopley herself had a way of expressing wonder over these matters before a class, her eyes wide open until they popped slightly. It was easy for me to feel that becoming a proud American, as she said we should, did not mean feeling ashamed of being a Mexican.

Beyond Literature

Community Connection

One School, Many Languages With the steady flow of immigrants so common to communities in the United States, the country's schools welcome students who speak a variety of languages. For example, classrooms across the nation include students with such diverse native languages as Vietnamese, Russian, Polish, and Spanish.

Cross-Curricular Activity
School Research Find out what languages are represented by the students in your school. In addition, learn what special services the school offers students whose first language is not English.

Guide for Responding

◆ LITERATURE AND YOUR LIFE

Reader's Response Have you ever felt the way Ernesto felt in his new school? Explain.

Thematic Focus In what way did the Lincoln School help Galarza realize his dream of "becoming a proud American"?

Journal Writing In your journal, write about the ways you might make a new student feel comfortable at school.

☑ Check Your Comprehension

1. What is the purpose of Galarza's first visit to the Lincoln School?
2. Why does Galarza decide he likes Miss Hopley?
3. Why is Galarza afraid of Miss Ryan at first?
4. In what ways does Miss Ryan help him overcome his fears of her and of the new class?

◆ Critical Thinking

INTERPRET

1. Why did Galarza feel he had to decide immediately whether Miss Hopley "was a possible friend or a menace"? **[Infer]**
2. What does Galarza mean when he says Miss Ryan "was with it" and "with us"? **[Interpret]**
3. In what ways were the seeds of Galarza's success planted in the first grade? **[Speculate]**

APPLY

4. Using this essay, explain the qualities a person needs to help someone feel at home in a new situation. **[Generalize]**

COMPARE LITERARY WORKS

5. In what ways are "Rattlesnake Hunt" and "Barrio Boy" both about overcoming fears? **[Connect]**

◆Critical Thinking

1. He did not understand English, so he didn't know what she was saying to him.
2. He means that she understands the difficulties the children are having, and stands by them and lends her support to everyone.
3. In the first grade, Ernesto learned tolerance, acceptance, trust, and the value of hard work. He also began to build the academic skills that would carry him through his later life.
4. Possible answers include warmth, concern, empathy, friendliness, patience, and persistence.
5. The narrator in each essay tells how he or she faced an unknown and frightening situation. By trusting another person and taking steps foward, each overcame fear.

I Am a Native of North America

Chief Dan George

In the course of my lifetime I have lived in two distinct[1] cultures. I was born into a culture that lived in communal houses. My grandfather's house was eighty feet long. It was called a smoke house, and it stood down by the beach along the inlet.[2] All my grandfather's sons and their families lived in this large dwelling. Their sleeping apartments were separated by blankets made of bull rush reeds, but one open fire in the middle served the cooking needs of all. In houses like these, throughout the tribe, people learned to live with one another; learned to serve one another; learned to respect the rights of one another. And children shared the thoughts of the adult world and found themselves surrounded by aunts and uncles and cousins who loved them and did not threaten them. My father was born in such a house and learned from infancy how to love people and be at home with them.

And beyond this acceptance of one another there was a deep respect for everything in nature that surrounded them. My father loved the earth and all its creatures. The earth was his second mother. The earth and everything it contained was a gift from See-see-am[3] . . . and the way to thank this great spirit was to use his gifts with respect.

I remember, as a little boy, fishing with him up Indian River and I can still see him as the sun rose above the mountain top in the early morning . . . I can see him standing by the water's edge with his arms raised above his head while he softly moaned . . . "Thank you, thank you." It left a deep impression on my young mind.

And I shall never forget his disappointment when once he caught me gaffing for fish[4] "just for the fun of it." "My Son," he said, "the Great Spirit gave you those fish to be your brothers, to feed you when you are hungry. You must respect them. You must not kill them just for the fun of it."

This then was the culture I was born into and for some years the only one I really knew or tasted. This is why I find it hard to accept many of the things I see around me. 2

◆ Literary Focus
Which sentence in this paragraph indicates that the author is reflecting on his experience, trying to understand it? Explain.

I see people living in smoke houses hundreds of times bigger than the one I knew. But the people in one apartment do not even know the people in the next and care less about them. 3

It is also difficult for me to understand the deep hate that exists among people. It is hard to understand a culture that justifies the killing of millions in past wars, and is at this very moment preparing bombs to kill even greater numbers. It is hard for me to understand a culture that spends more on wars and

1. **distinct** (di stinkt′) *adj.*: Separate and different.
2. **inlet** (in′ let) *n.*: Narrow strip of water jutting into a body of land from a river, a lake, or an ocean.
3. **See-see-am:** The name of the Great Spirit, or "The Chief Above," in the Salishan language of Chief George's people.
4. **gaffing for fish:** Using a barbed spear to catch river fish.

◆ Build Vocabulary

communal (kə myo͞o′ nəl) *adj.*: Shared by all

Develop Understanding

One-Minute Insight In this essay, Chief Dan George recalls the traditional ways of life of his people. He questions certain contemporary values and choices, and sadly anticipates the eventual vanishing of his culture. He pleads for love and tolerance as the only hope for a peaceful future.

Customize for *English Language Learners*
Students may be unfamiliar with the Native American traditions described in this essay. Clarify them as much as possible, and answer any questions. Help students recognize the narrator's regret that he and his "white brothers" have not always shared or appreciated the best of each other's cultures.

◆ Literary Focus

2 Essay *He says that his culture was the only one he really knew for part of his life, which is one reason why it may be hard for him to accept some things he sees around him. Although he knows that other cultures have much to offer, he acknowledges the bias of his own upbringing.*

◆ Reading Strategy

3 Identify Main Points Ask students to interpret what the narrator is saying here. How does he weave a symbol of his tradition into a modern observation? How does this observation make readers feel? *He uses the term "smoke house" to describe an apartment building. However, unlike a traditional Native American smoke house, which was a large communal residence where many families lived under one roof, a modern apartment building separates people. Students may feel the poignancy of his observation.*

Beyond the Classroom

Community Connection

Local Environmentalism At the time of this essay, the environmental movement was new, and mainstream attitudes toward preserving and protecting the environment were largely underdeveloped. Since then, attitudes, information, and approaches have changed; today, some degree of environmentalism is a routine way of life for many Americans.

Have students brainstorm for ways that they themselves contribute to protecting or preserving the environment at home, in school, in the community, or elsewere in the area. For instance, does your area sponsor recycling programs? Do air or clean water laws affect the common practices of businesses and farms? Are any local areas targeted for environmental cleanup or restoration? Students can search the Internet; contact local, state, or federal environmental agencies; or speak to knowledgeable area residents about what is being done in your region and what still remains to be done.

▶Critical Viewing◀

1 Synthesize *Some students may say that Chief Dan George would criticize the collage, which shows modern imagery over the form of a buffalo. This may reflect his concern that modern ways are forcing native traditions into the background, soon to be lost forever.*

◆Critical Thinking

2 Compare and Contrast Tell students that Chief Dan George wrote this essay in 1974, a time when the environmental movement was growing in prominence and civil rights issues were in the forefront of political thought. Ask students if Chief Dan George's concerns still hold true today. *Students may say that some issues are still of concern, such as environmental concerns and problems of tolerance among people of different backgrounds; others may say that conditions have improved, although there is still far to go.*

◆Literary Focus

3 Essay Ask students what technique Chief Dan George uses to persuade his audience that love is essential to life. *He gives examples from his own life and experience to support how love has benefited him, hoping readers will share his view.*

Buffalo, 1992, Jaune Smith, Courtesy Steinbaum Krauss Gallery, NYC

1 ▶ **Critical Viewing** Based on the ideas he expresses, do you think Chief Dan George would applaud or criticize this collage? Explain. **[Synthesize]**

weapons to kill, than it does on education and welfare to help and develop.

It is hard for me to understand a culture that not only hates and fights its brothers but even attacks nature and abuses her. I see my white brother going about blotting out nature from his cities. I see him strip the hills bare, leaving ugly wounds on the face of mountains. I see him tearing things from the bosom of mother earth as though she were a monster, who refused to share her treasures with him. I see him throw poison in the waters, indifferent to the life he kills there; and he chokes the air
2 with deadly fumes.

My white brother does many things well for he is more clever than my people but I wonder if he knows how to love well. I wonder if he has ever really learned to love at all. Perhaps he only loves the things that are his own but never learned to love the things that are outside and beyond him. And this is, of course, not love at all, for man must love all creation or he will love none of it. Man must love fully or he will become the lowest of the animals. It is the power to love that makes him the greatest of them all . . . for he alone of all animals is capable of love. 2

Love is something you and I must have. We must have it because our spirit feeds upon it. We must have it because without it we become weak and faint. Without love our self-esteem weakens. Without it our courage fails. Without love we can no longer look out confidently at the world. Instead we turn inwardly and begin to feed upon our own personalities and little by little we destroy ourselves.

You and I need the strength and joy that comes from knowing that we are loved. With it we are creative. With it we march tirelessly. With it, and with it alone, we are able to sacrifice for others.

There have been times when we all wanted so desperately to feel a reassuring hand upon us . . . there have been lonely times when we so wanted a strong arm around us . . . I cannot tell you how deeply I miss my wife's presence when I return from a trip. Her love was 3
my greatest joy, my strength, my greatest blessing.

I am afraid my culture has little to offer yours. But my culture did prize friendship and companionship. It did not look on privacy as a thing to be clung to, for privacy builds up walls and walls promote distrust. My culture lived in big family communities, and from infancy people learned to live with others.

My culture did not prize the hoarding of private possessions; in fact, to hoard was a shameful thing to do among my people. The Indian looked on all things in nature as

Humanities: Art

Buffalo, 1992, by Jaune Quick-to-See Smith

Painter Jaune Quick-to-See Smith (born 1940), who has Slish, French, Cree, and Shoshone ancestors, was raised on the Flathead reservation in Montana. One of Smith's artistic goals is to address the religious beliefs of her ancestors in the context of current Native American issues and problems. Her style combines abstract and representational imagery. *Buffalo* is an oil, collage, and mixed media work. Use these questions for discussion:

1. Smith says that her art, her tribal ties, and her life experiences are intertwined. How does *Buffalo* express this? *Possible answer: The buffalo, a symbol of Native American peoples, is the central figure of the work. Over and around it are other images, such as an American flag, ads, newspaper clippings, and bold strokes that represent the activity of modern life.*
2. What does Smith suggest about the future of the buffalo? *Possible answer: Modern ways smother or overtake the buffalo.*

belonging to him and he expected to share them with others and to take only what he needed.

Everyone likes to give as well as receive. No one wishes only to receive all the time. We have taken much from your culture . . . I wish you had taken something from our culture . . . for there were some beautiful and good things in it.

4 Soon it will be too late to know my culture, for integration[5] is upon us and soon we will have no values but yours. Already many of our young people have forgotten the old ways. And many have been shamed of their Indian ways by scorn[6] and ridicule. My culture is like a wounded deer that has crawled away into the forest to bleed and die alone.

> ◆ **Reading Strategy** What point does Chief Dan George state directly in this paragraph? Summarize it in your own words.

4 5 The only thing that can truly help us is genuine love. You must truly love us, be patient with us and share with us. And we must love you—with a genuine love that forgives and forgets . . . a love that forgives the terrible sufferings your culture brought ours when it swept over us like a wave crashing along a beach . . . with a love that forgets and lifts up its head and sees in your eyes an answering love of trust and acceptance.

This is brotherhood . . . anything less is not worthy of the name.

I have spoken.

5. **integration** (in tə grā′ shən) *n.*: The mingling of different ethnic or racial groups.
6. **scorn** (skôrn) *n.*: Complete lack of respect.

Guide for Responding

◆ Literature and Your Life

Reader's Response Do you agree that "the power to love" is the most important human quality? Why or why not?

Thematic Focus How would the world change if the dream that Chief Dan George expresses came true?

☑ Check Your Comprehension

1. Name three things that people learned from growing up in communal houses.
2. What three things puzzle Chief Dan George about his "white brother"?
3. According to Chief Dan George, what important values could modern society learn from Chief Dan George's culture?
4. Describe the "brotherhood" that Chief Dan George talks about at the end of the essay.
5. According to the author, what makes humans the "greatest of all" creatures?

◆ Critical Thinking

Interpret

1. Sum up the differences between the "two distinct cultures" in which Chief Dan George lived. **[Compare and Contrast]**
2. When Chief Dan George says, "My white brother . . . is more clever than my people," what does he mean by *clever*? **[Interpret]**
3. What values does Chief Dan George think are lacking in modern society? **[Analyze]**

Evaluate

4. Why do you think Chief Dan George wrote about his culture only in the past tense? **[Assess]**

Extend

5. Where might you look to find out if the Squamish people and culture are still alive today? **[Social Studies Link]**

◆ Literary Focus

4 Essay Discuss the tone of this passage and the implications the narrator makes about the behaviors and attitudes of his people and his "white brothers." *Students may describe the tone as wistful or sad; the narrator pleads for the preservation of his beloved culture.*

◆ Reading Strategy

5 Identify Main Points *Possible response: Only the power of love and mutual respect can lead two such different cultures to find true brotherhood, acceptance, pride, and peace.*

Reinforce and Extend

Answers

◆ Literature and Your Life

Reader's Response Accept all responses that are supported.

Thematic Focus Students may say that the world would become a place of harmony between humans and nature, and that different cultures would appreciate and respect each other and share their best traits.

☑ Check your Comprehension

1. They learned to live together, to serve one another, and to respect the rights of others.
2. He can't understand why people hate one another, why they mistreat nature and earth, and how they can show so little love for one another.
3. Modern society could learn to prize friendship and companionship.
4. By brotherhood, he means love, patience, trust, acceptance, peace, and forgiveness among all people.
5. We are made great by our ability to love.

◆ Critical Thinking

1. Possible response: His traditional culture had strong communal ties and deep respect for the land, while the modern culture is more selfish, violent, and materialistic.
2. He means that his "white brothers" have been more successful in spreading their values and ways of life than his culture has been.
3. He feels there is a lack of brotherhood, respect for the earth, and love.
4. He feels that his culture is fading away. Young people have forgotton the "old ways" or are ashamed of those ways.
5. Students might conduct research through the Internet, or check current resource books or periodicals.

Develop Understanding

One-Minute Insight Barbara Jordan, in addressing the Democratic National Convention in 1992, shares her views on the state of race relations in America. She offers suggestions for ways to bring about the American dream of tolerance and equality by starting small: Parents should help their children learn the lessons of human relationships at home, in school, and in all areas of life.

◆Reading Strategy

1 Identify Main Points Discuss with students the difference between the power of legislation and the power of individual attitudes and acts to bring about social change–what Jordan calls "soul force." Guide students to appreciate that, regardless of what laws say or how vigorously they may be enforced, people must develop attitudes that promote social change.

Clarification

2 Tell students that this march is the gathering at which Dr. Martin Luther King, Jr., delivered his famous "I Have a Dream" speech.

◆Critical Thinking

3 Connect Discuss with students the ways in which the narrator's views in this passage parallel the views that Chief Dan George expressed in his essay "I Am a Native of North America." Both narrators know how crucial it is for people of all races and backgrounds to learn to live together in harmony; both believe that one key to this is caring communities.

ALL TOGETHER NOW

BARBARA JORDAN

When I look at race relations today I can see that some positive changes have come about. But much remains to be done, and the answer does not lie in more legislation. We *have* the legislation we need; we have the laws. Frankly, I don't believe that the task of bringing us all together can be accomplished by government. What we need now is soul force—the efforts of people working on a small scale to build a truly tolerant, harmonious society. And parents can do a great deal to create that tolerant society. **1**

We all know that race relations in America have had a very rocky history. Think about the 1960s when Dr. Martin Luther King, Jr., was in his heyday and there were marches and protests against segregation[1] and discrimination. The movement culminated in 1963 with the March on Washington. **2**

Following that event, race relations reached an all-time peak. President Lyndon B. Johnson pushed through the Civil Rights Act of 1964, which remains the fundamental piece of civil rights legislation in this century. The Voting Rights Act of 1965 ensured that everyone in our country could vote. At last, black people and white people seemed ready to live together in peace.

But that is not what happened. By the 1990's the good feelings had diminished. Today the nation seems to be suffering from compassion fatigue, and issues such as race relations and civil rights have never regained momentum.

Those issues, however, remain crucial. As our society becomes more diverse, people of all races and backgrounds will have to learn to live together. If we don't think this is important, all we have to do is look at the situation in Bosnia[2] today. **3**

How do we create a harmonious society out of so many kinds of people? The key is tolerance—the one value that is indispensable in creating community.

1. **segregation** (seg´ rə gā´ shən) *n.*: The practice of forcing racial groups to live apart from each other.

2. **Bosnia** (bäz´ nē ə) *n.*: Country, located on the Balkan Peninsula in Europe, that was the site of a bloody civil war between Muslims and Christians during the 1990's.

Speaking and Listening Mini-Lesson

Press Conference
This mini-lesson supports the Speaking and Listening activity in the Idea Bank on p. 621.

Introduce Discuss with students what a press conferences is, who typically speaks, who attends, and how the information shared at a press conference gets spread. Students may have seen presidential press conferences on TV, or press conferences following natural disasters or events of national concern.

Develop Divide the class into groups of up to eight students. Within each group, one person should assume the role of an essay writer, and the others act as reporters who question the essayist. The "writer" may choose an assistant, or "publicist," who can help field questions. "Reporters" should prepare their questions in advance. Appoint a moderator.

Apply Stage the press conference for the rest of the class or for other groups. Invite audience members to ask additional questions or to call for clarification regarding answers that seem vague.

Assess Evaluate each group member on his or her contribution to the press conference, the clarity of questions and responses, and the general success of the event. You might conclude by having participants evaluate their own performance using the Self-Assessment: Speaking and Listening rubric, p. 103 of **Alternative Assessment.**

If we are concerned about community, if it is important to us that people not feel excluded, then we have to do something. Each of us can decide to have one friend of a different race or background in our mix of friends. If we do this, we'll be working together to push things forward.

One thing is clear to me: We, as human beings, must be willing to accept people who are different from ourselves. I must be willing to
4 accept people who don't look as I do and don't talk as I do. It is crucial that I am open to their feelings, their inner reality.

What can parents do? We can put our faith in young people as a positive force. I have yet to find a racist baby. Babies come into the world as blank as slates and, with their beautiful innocence, see others not as different but as enjoyable companions. Children learn ideas and attitudes from the adults who nurture them. I absolutely believe that children do not adopt prejudices unless they absorb them from their parents or teachers.

The best way to get this country faithful to the American dream of tolerance and equality is to start small. Parents can actively encourage their children to be in the company of people who are of other racial and ethnic backgrounds. If a child thinks, "Well, that person's color is not the same as mine, but she must be okay because she likes to play with the same things I like to play with," that child will grow up with a broader view of humanity.

I'm an incurable optimist. For the rest of the time that I have left on this planet I want to bring people together. You might think of this as a labor of love. Now, I know that love means different things to different people. But what *I* mean is this: I care about you because you are a fellow human being and I find it okay in my mind, in my heart, to simply say to you, I love you. And maybe that would encourage you to love me in return.

It is possible for all of us to work on this—at home, in our schools, at our jobs. It is possible to work on human relationships in every area of our lives.

◆ Build Vocabulary

tolerant (täl′ ər ənt) *adj.*: Free from bigotry or prejudice

Guide for Responding

◆ Literature and Your Life

Reader's Response Does this essay inspire you to change your thinking? Explain.

Thematic Focus How does the word *tolerance* express Jordan's American dream?

Check Your Comprehension

1. How does Jordan summarize the history of race relations from the 1960's to the 1990's?
2. What "one value" is necessary to create "a harmonious society"?
3. According to Jordan, what can parents do to foster a sense of community?

◆ Critical Thinking

INTERPRET

1. In your own words, describe what Jordan means by "compassion fatigue." **[Interpret]**
2. How does the phrase "start small" express two ideas for promoting tolerance? **[Analyze]**

EVALUATE

3. Do you think that Jordan's ideas could work to promote tolerance? Explain. **[Evaluate]**

APPLY

4. In what ways can you apply Jordan's ideas in your life? **[Community Link]**

Beyond the Selection

FURTHER READING

Other Works by Charles Kuralt
North Carolina Is My Home

Other Works by Marjorie Kinnan Rawlings:
The Yearling

Other Works by Ernesto Galarza:
Colleccion Mini Libros

Other Works by Chief Dan George:
My Heart Soars

Other Works by Barbara Jordan:
Legal Immigration: Setting Priorities

INTERNET

We suggest the following sites on the Internet (all Web sites are subject to change).

For an audio excerpt read by Charles Kuralt:
http//:www.simonsays.com/titles/067179745X

For more about Marjorie Kinnan Rawlings:
http//:www.starbanner.com/history/rawlings525.html

For general information on Barbara Jordan:
http//:www.rice.edu/armadillo/Texas/jordan.html

We *strongly reccommend* that you preview these sites before you send students to them.

◆ Reading Strategy

4 Identify the Author's Main Points Ask: What is the impact of the narrator using herself as a model here? *By stating, "I must be willing. . ." or "It is crucial that I am open. . .", Jordan shows that she's not just preaching to others, but intends to put her beliefs into action in her own life. By setting an example, she can inspire others to act in a similar way.*

Reinforce and Extend

Answers

◆ Literature and Your Life

Reader's Response Accept all responses that students support with examples from their own lives.

Thematic Focus Jordan believes that everyone deserves and should demonstrate tolerance so all can enjoy the American dream.

Check your Comprehension

1. She cites marches, protests, demonstrations, civil rights legislation, and growing good feelings, followed by an eventual apathy or retreat from the passion of those times.
2. Tolerance, which is necessary to create an inclusive community.
3. They can work to instill an attitude of tolerance and acceptance in their children.

◆ Critical Thinking

1. People tire of working so hard to bring about peaceful race relations, so they turn away from the issue.
2. It suggests that tolerance must be taught at home, and that major social changes must take place step by step.
3. Students may say that Jordan's ideas could work if all people viewed humankind and life as positively as she does. Also, parents must accept the responsibility for instilling tolerance in thier children.
4. Students may say that they can begin by working for tolerance in their own families, classrooms, communities, or neighborhoods, or in any other small groups to which they belong.

◆Literary Focus

1. Possible responses; the narrator describes the snake cage, the job she'll do for Ross, and the hunting ground and wildlife she sees.
2. It is written in the first person and shares anecdotes about real people, places, and events.
3. He discusses his traditional upbringing and how many of the values and beliefs he grew up with are at odds with modern ways.
4. She wants to persuade her audience to instill tolerance and acceptance at home.

◆Build Vocabulary

Using the Word Root *-mort-*

1. *-mort-* means death, so mortician means "one who works with death." The mortician prepared the body for the funeral.
2. *-al* means suitable for, so mortal means "suitable for or capable of dying." All humans are mortal.
3. *-im* means not, so immortal means "will not die." Our immortal hope is for true peace on earth.

Spelling Strategy

1. moderate; 2. intricate; 3. chocolate

Using the Word Bank

1. No, everyone who voted for it signed his name to it.
2. They vote unanimously when they all vote the same way.
3. Probably not, since a desolate place has a few inhabitants or visitors.
4. Yes, all living creatures will one day die.
5. No, he is small and uncertain, not immpressive and powerful.
6. Yes, in a communal house many things are shared by all.
7. Yes, lack of predjudice and bigotry may prevent conflicts.

◆Reading Strategy

1. Possible answers: *Barrio Boy:* A person can be proud to be American, and still feel pride in his culture; "I Am a Native . . .": Traditional and modern cultures can share much with one another if they can love one another and form bonds of trust; "All Together Now": We must all work to improve human relationships to achieve the American dream of tolerance and equality for all.
2. He suggests that fair-minded people can find ways to compromise and take risks for a greater good.

Guide for Responding (continued)

◆ Literary Focus

Essay

An **essay** is a brief prose work expressing an author's view of a subject. You often know what type it is right away. For example, the first paragraph of the narrative essay "Independence Hall" reveals that the writer will tell a true story.

1. Find three details to confirm that "Rattlesnake Hunt" is a descriptive essay.
2. What elements of the essay from *Barrio Boy* show that it is a personal essay?
3. What ideas or experiences does the writer reflect on in "I Am a Native of North America"?
4. In "All Together Now," what does the writer want to persuade her audience to do?

◆ Build Vocabulary

Using the Word Root *-mort-*

Explain how the word root *-mort-*, meaning "death," helps you understand the meaning of these words. Then, use each word in a sentence.

mortician *n.*: funeral director
mortal *n.*: a being that will eventually die
immortal *adj.*: deathless; living forever

Spelling Strategy

When spelling the *it* sound at the end of multisyllable adjectives, you often use the letters *ate*: *desolate, temperate*. Write the words containing the *ate* spelling that fit the following definitions:

1. average, comfortable: mod___?___
2. complex, involved: intri___?___
3. popular flavor: choc___?___

Using the Word Bank

On your paper, explain your answer to each question.

1. Was the Declaration of Independence *anonymous?*
2. When do delegates vote *unanimously*?
3. Will rattlers be disturbed in a *desolate* place?
4. Do we share *mortality* with all creatures?
5. Does Galarza seem *formidable* to Miss Ryan?
6. Do *communal* houses have things to be shared?
7. Can a *tolerant* attitude help resolve conflicts?

◆ Reading Strategy

Identify Main Points

You can't fully understand these essays until you identify their **main points,** their most important ideas. Often, these ideas appear at the beginning or end of an essay. For example, "Rattlesnake Hunt" states a main point at the end, concluding that by facing fears, you can free yourself of them.

1. Find a stated or suggested main point in *Barrio Boy,* "I Am a Native of North America," and "All Together Now." Express each in your own words.
2. What point does Kuralt hint at in "Independence Hall" by telling about the disagreements among the delegates as well as their unanimous vote?

◆ Build Grammar Skills

Subject and Object Pronouns

Some pronouns change forms depending on their use in a sentence.

Subjective Case	Use in Sentence
I, we	*Subject of a verb*
you	*Subject complement*
he, she, it, they	
Objective Case	**Use in Sentence**
me, us	*Direct object*
you	*Indirect object*
him, her, it, them	*Object of a preposition*

Practice On your paper, identify the case of each italicized pronoun.

1. *We* mutually pledge to each other our lives.
2. It was *they* who went hunting for rattlesnakes.
3. *He* could see *her* rise above *him.*
4. Jordan gave *us* her ideas on the subject.
5. George says, "It is hard for *me* to understand."
6. The classroom was a good one for *them.*
7. *She* had a way of making *us* feel welcome.

Writing Application On your paper, write sentences using personal pronoun forms according to the directions given.

1. Use two subject pronouns.
2. Use one subject and one object pronoun.
3. Use two object pronouns.

◆Build Grammar Skills

Practice

1. subjective; 2. subjective; 3. subjective, objective, objective; 4. objective; 5. objective; 6. objective; 7. subjective, objective

Writing Application

Sample responses:

1. He and I heard all the speakers.
2. They addressed us from the steps of the Lincoln Memorial.
3. Jordan's advice is for them and us as well.

Writer's Solution

For additional instruction and practice, use the Pronoun Case lesson in the *Writer's Solution Language Lab CD-ROM* unit on Using Pronouns, and the practice pages on pronoun case, pp. 69–71 in the *Writer's Solution Grammar Practice Book.*

Build Your Portfolio

Idea Bank

Writing

1. **Anecdote** Write an anecdote—a brief story—based on one of these essays. For example, you might tell what happened to Rawlings on another rattlesnake hunt or what Galarza did on his first day in the second grade.
2. **Essay for a Broadcast** Use one of these essays as the basis for a televised response. Write a narrative or a persuasive essay for a reporter to read on the air. Remember that short sentences with catchy phrases work better on television.
3. **Introduction to an Anthology** Imagine that the essays in this section will be collected in a book. Write an introduction to this anthology. Define what an essay is, and tell about the types of essays that readers will find in the book.

Speaking and Listening

4. **Press Conference [Group Activity]** With a group, stage a press conference in which one of these writers answers reporters' questions about his or her essay. **[Performing Arts Link]**
5. **Book Talk** Give a talk to your class on a recently published book of essays. Gather facts by reading all or part of the book, the information from the inside cover, and reviews of the book in newspapers. **[Performing Arts Link]**

Projects

6. **Essay "Fortune Cookies"** Choose your favorite essay, and write its main points on small strips of paper. Wrap each strip in a package together with a cookie. Then, exchange these essay "fortune cookies" with classmates.
7. **Timeline** Present the history of the essay in the form of an illustrated timeline. Include birth, death, and publication dates for such essayists as Montaigne, Francis Bacon, and Charles Lamb. Also, include information on well-known media "essayists," like Edward R. Murrow and Charles Kuralt. **[Art Link; Media Link]**

Writing Mini-Lesson

Reflective Essay

In "I Am a Native of North America," Chief Dan George reflects on what is important in life. You can write a reflective essay also—by thinking your own thoughts on paper. Start by choosing a subject that has caused you to wonder. It can be anything from the clothing styles of athletes to a concept you've learned in school. Remember that you don't have to know all the answers. It's enough to think about interesting questions.

Writing Skills Focus: Necessary Background

You'll want to take readers along on your reflective journey. That's why you must give them the **necessary background,** the facts they need to follow your thoughts. For example, Chief Dan George gives you background on his childhood so you can understand his comparison of cultures.

Prewriting Flip through the pages of your journal for an idea. Then, choose a subject that has already made you thoughtful. Don't worry if it isn't a life-and-death matter. Big thoughts can grow from little subjects. Freewrite for five to ten minutes, creating a cluster diagram to record your ideas.

Drafting Refer to your diagram as you write. Remember to include information that readers must know in order to understand your thoughts. As you conclude, leave something for the reader to continue thinking about.

Revising Have several classmates read your essay. If they can't follow your thinking, insert more explanations and background material.

◆ Grammar Application

Be sure that you have correctly used subject and object pronouns.

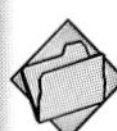

Idea Bank

Following are suggestions for matching the Idea Bank topics with your students' performance levels and learning modalities:

Customize for *Performance Levels*
Less Advanced Students: 1, 6
Average Students: 2, 4, 7
More Advanced Students: 3, 4, 5, 7

Customize for *Learning Modalities*
Verbal/Linguistic: 1, 2, 3, 4, 5, 6, 7
Visual/Spatial: 7
Bodily/Kinesthetic: 4, 5
Logical/Mathematical: 6, 7
Interpersonal: 4, 6
Intrapersonal: 1, 2, 3, 5, 7

Writing Mini-Lesson

Refer students to the Writing Handbook in the back of the book for instructions on the writing process and for further information of reflective essays.

Writer's Solution

Writing Lab CD-ROM
Have students complete the tutorial on Narration. Follow these steps:

1. Have students examine types of narrative writing to get ideas that pertain to their reflective essays.
2. Have students draft on computer.
3. Have students use Character Trait or Transition Word Bins to revise.

Allow 60 minutes of class time to complete these steps.

Writer's Solution Sourcebook
Have students use Chapter 3, "Narration," pp. 66–101, for more support. The chapter includes in-depth instruction on using transitions to show time order, pp. 95–96.

✓ ASSESSMENT OPTIONS

Formal Assessment, Selection Test, pp. 169–171, and Assessment Resources Software. The selection test is designed to that it can be easily customized to the performance levels of your students.

Alternative Assessment, p. 37, includes options for less advanced students, more advanced studens, verbal/linguistic learners, logical/mathematical learners, visual/spatial learners, interpersonal learners, and bodily/kinesthetic learners.

PORTFOLIO ASSESSMENT
Use the following rubrics in the **Alternative Assessment** booklet to assess student writing;
Ancedote: Fictional Narrative, p. 82
Essay for a Broadcast: Persuasion, p. 92
Introduction to an Anthology: Definition/Classification, p. 86
Writing Mini-Lesson: Expression, p. 81

Prepare and Engage

OBJECTIVES

1. To read, comprehend, and interpret a selection that has a social studies focus
2. To relate a selection with a social studies focus to personal experience
3. To connect literature to social studies
4. To respond to Social Studies Guiding Questions
5. To respond to the selection through writing, speaking and listening, and projects

SOCIAL STUDIES GUIDING QUESTIONS

Reading about an early Aztec city will help students answer these questions:

- How did the Aztecs' knowledge of engineering help them solve issues of transportation, food, shelter, and defense?
- How did geography and climate affect the lives of the Aztecs?

Help students arrange the classroom into "islands" of grouped desks. Invite them to brainstorm and role-play ways to solve basic problems such as distributing materials among the "islands." Explain that this selection describes a city built on islands and tells how *its* planners solved basic problems.

Map Study

Historical Maps To grasp the geographic challenges facing planners (and conquerers) of Tenochtitlan, students can use this map made by invader Hernando Cortés.

Humanities: Art

Map of Tenochtitlan, 1524, by Hernando Cortés (1485–1547)

This map was made by the man who led the expedition that conquered Tenochtitlan for the Spaniards. The words on the map are in Latin, the language used on sixteenth-century maps. Ask students why the center of Tenochtitlan might be difficult for enemies to attack. *Defenders could probably cut the bridges to keep enemies out.*

Connecting Literature to Social Studies

GEOGRAPHY

Tenochtitlan: Inside the Aztec Capital *by Jacqueline Dineen*

PLANNING A CITY To create a city, what problems would you face? You'd need food, shelter, and ways to earn a living for thousands of people. Geography—the region's land, climate, and vegetation—would guide your plans.

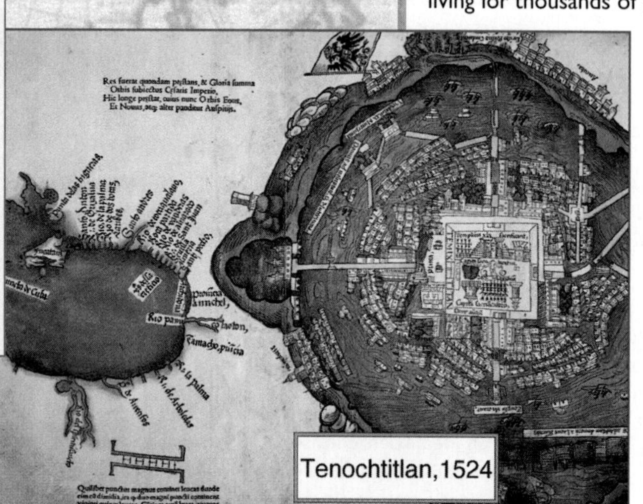

Map of Tenochtitlan, 1524, Hernando Cortes, The Newberry Library, Chicago

A High Valley Mexico is a plateau guarded by two long mountain chains. Some of these mountains are taller than 18,000 feet! A few are volcanic. Even the plateau sits on very high ground—often, more than 4,000 feet above sea level! Along the plateau, there were once many lakes—including Lake Texcoco, where the Aztecs, a native people who controlled the region until the arrival of the Spaniards, built their capital city of Tenochtitlan (te nōch tēt län′) in the 1300's. Set on islands in the lake, Tenochtitlan was safe from invaders, had a mild climate, and offered fertile soil for crops.

The Lake of the Moon Mexico City, which today sits on the drained remains of Lake Texcoco, owes its name to Aztec words meaning "city in the center of the lake of the moon." The city enjoys a fairly dry climate with rainy summers. Limited rain in the winter means farmers must either irrigate or plant crops suited to dry climates.

Window to Another Place The piece you're about to read is a visual essay—a nonfiction piece that blends text and images—that will tell you how the Aztecs built the ancient city of Tenochtitlan on the site where Mexico City stands today. How did the geography of the region shape the way the Aztecs built their city?

Prentice Hall Literature Program Resources

REINFORCE / RETEACH / EXTEND

Selection Support Pages
Build Vocabulary, p. 205
Theme, p. 206

Formal Assessment Selection Test, pp. 172–173, Assessment Resources Software

Resource Pro CD-ROM
"Tenochtitlan: Inside the Aztec Capital"—includes all resource material and customizable lesson plan

Listening to Literature Audiocassettes
"Tenochtitlan: Inside the Aztec Capital"

Connection to Prentice Hall World Explorer
Western Hemisphere
Ch. 12, "Latin America: Shaped by Its History"
Medieval Times to Today
Ch. 3, "The Ancient Americas"

TENOCHTITLAN: Inside the Aztec Capital

Jacqueline Dineen

The Lake City of Tenochtitlan[1]

The city of Tenochtitlan began on an island in the middle of a swampy lake. There the Aztecs built their first temple to Huitzilopochtli.[2] The place was given the name Tenochtitlan, which means "The Place of the Fruit of the Prickly Pear Cactus." Later on the name was given to the city that grew up around the temple. The Aztecs rebuilt their temples on the same site every 52 years, so
1 the first temple eventually became the great Temple Mayor[3] that stood at the center of the city.

The city started as a collection of huts. It began to grow after 1385, while Acamapichtli[4] was king. The Aztecs were excellent engineers. They built three causeways over the swamp to link the city with the mainland. These were raised roads made of stone supported on wooden pillars. Parts of the causeways were bridges. These bridges could be removed to leave gaps and this prevented enemies from getting to the city. Fresh water was brought from the mainland to the city along stone aqueducts.[5]

2 **Connecting Literature to Social Studies** Why might fresh water be so important to a growing city?

The Lake City of Tenochtitlan.

Each grouping of houses in Tenochtitlan was planned so that the houses could be reached through the many waterways. These canals crisscrossed the city, and some are still in and around Mexico City today.

3 ▲ **Critical Viewing** How does this city map compare with modern maps? **[Compare and Contrast]**

1. **Tenochtitlan** (te nōch tēt län′) *n.*: Ancient Aztec capital located in what is now Mexico City.
2. **Huitzilopochtli** (wēt sē pōch′ tlē)
3. **Mayor** (mä yōr′)
4. **Acamapichtli** (ä kä mä pēch′ tlē)
5. **aqueducts** (ak′ wə dukts′) *n.*: Large pipes made for bringing water from a distant source.

Develop Understanding

One-Minute Insight

This visual essay describes the construction of the Aztec capital, Tenochtitlan, and the ways its leaders handled problems accompanying its growth. Founded on an island in a Valley of Mexico lake, the city grew during the late fourteenth century. We learn that the Aztec wealthy and poor lived very differently but that all benefited in some ways from Aztec ingenuity.

Team Teaching Strategy

"Tenochtitlan" presents a rich opportunity to team teach with a social studies or visual arts teacher through a unit on Aztec history or picture essays.

Links Across Time

1 The Aztecs had a sophisticated calendar that measured time in two ways. One method completed its cycle in 365 days (as does our solar calendar) and the other method took only 260 days. When the two methods coincided every 52 years, the Aztecs extinguished and relit all the sacred fires and rebuilt their temples.

Connecting Literature to Social Studies

2 **Infer** *Students should recognize the many uses of fresh water in a growing city, for example, for drinking, bathing, and cooking.*

▶Critical Viewing◀

3 **Compare and Contrast** *Both show the location of structures, bodies of water, and transportation routes. Modern maps usually label these key features and many include a scale.*

Customize for *Less Proficient Readers*

To help students understand the essay, urge them to preview the many captioned illustrations before reading. Have students also note the subheads, which divide the essay into small, manageable sections.

Preparing for Standardized Tests

Visual Images Standardized tests often include visual images—maps, charts, and graphs—from which students must make inferences. Questions may refer to visual facts or to critical conclusions students are expected to draw. To help students practice critically analyzing visuals, have them study the map on p. 623. Then, write the following on the board:

Which statement most accurately describes the map:

(A) It has a key, like a modern map.

(B) It has the labels of a modern map but lacks a key.

(C) Unlike a modern map, it shows important waterways.

(D) It shows important waterways but lacks a modern map's key and labels.

Guide students to recognize that *(D)* is the best answer. Discuss each alternative to help students understand how its information fails to match the map's data. For additional practice, offer students multiple-choice alternatives for other Critical Viewing images.

▶Critical Viewing◀

❶ **Infer** *Students should infer that the cactus provided materials not available in another source. Also, the Aztecs were very resourceful people and would not allow any waste.*

Links Across Time

❷ Arriving in Mexico was an important moment for a man who'd admired explorers since childhood. Cortés was just seven years old when Columbus arrived in the Americas. He was inspired by the older explorer's tales of discovery.

For his expedition to Mexico, Cortés arrived with 508 soldiers, one hundred sailors, and sixteen horses. To keep unhappy sailors from leaving and as an expression of his own confidence in the mission, Cortés burned all his ships after arrival.

Customize for *English Language Learners*

Explain that the selection contains many words from the Aztec language, as well as Spanish names and technical terms used to describe Aztec engineering. Review the numbered glossary items for both meaning and pronunciation.

Customize for *More Advanced Students*

Have students research Aztec culture. In addition, you may have them compare and contrast early civilizations of Middle America by reading pp. 304–312 in the Prentice Hall *World Explorer: Western Hemisphere*. Using data that they gather, challenge students to create a codex about an aspect of Aztec life. Students may work in pairs or use computer graphics programs.

Maguey cactus plants, like these in front of a rebuilt Aztec temple, had many uses. Parts of the plants were used to make medicines. The thorns were used as sewing needles, and fibers of the maguey were spun together and woven into coarse cloth. Pulque, a popular drink, comes from this plant. The maguey even had its own goddess—Mayahuel!

❶ ▲ Critical Viewing Why do you think the Aztecs found so many uses for the cactus plants, like those in this photograph? **[Infer]**

Inside the City The Spaniards' first view of Tenochtitlan was described by one of Cortés's[6] soldiers, Bernal Diaz: "And when we saw all those towns and level causeway leading into Mexico, we were astounded. These great towns and buildings rising from the water, all made of stone, seemed like an enchanted vision." ❷

By that time Tenochtitlan was the largest city in Mexico. About 200,000 people lived there. The houses were one story high and had flat roofs. In the center of the city was a large square. The twin temple stood on one side, and the king's palace on another. Officials' houses made of white stone also lined the square. There were few roads. People traveled in canoes along canals.

Floating Gardens Tenochtitlan was built in a huge valley, the Valley of Mexico, which was surrounded by mountains. Rivers flowed from the mountains into Lake Texcoco, where Tenochtitlan

6. **Hernando Cortés** (er nän´ dō kōr tes´): Spanish adventurer (1485–1547) who conquered what is now central and southern Mexico.

Block Scheduling Strategies

Consider these suggestions to take advantage of extended class time:

- Engage students with the Interest Grabber, posting some suggested solutions on the chalkboard. Then, complete Map Study and have students scan and discuss the selection images, captions, and Critical Viewing prompts. After students read the selection, complete Preparing for Standardized Tests, p. 623.
- Alternatively, focus on literary analysis, beginning with the background material on p. 622 and continuing with discussion of the Connecting Literature to Social Studies prompts and follow-up questions, p. 629. Invite student pairs to respond to the Guide for Responding questions, p. 628. Have pairs brainstorm for ideas and information-gathering strategies for Idea Bank activities, p. 629.
- Use *World Explorer: Western Hemisphere,* Chapter 12, "Latin America: Shaped by Its History," and *World Explorer: Medieval Times to Today,* Chapter 3, "The Ancient Americas," to teach or to further extend the connection between literature and social studies.

stood. The lake was linked to four other shallow, swampy lakes. The land around the lakes was dry because there was very little rain.

> **Connecting Literature to Social Studies**
> 3 What problems might a dry climate cause?

The Aztecs dug ditches and piled up the earth to make islands in the shallow parts of the lake. These chinampas, or swamp gardens, could be farmed. The ditches carried water into larger canals that were used for irrigation[7] and as waterways to the city.

Texcoco and the lake to the south contained fresh water, but the northern lakes contained salt water, which was no good for irrigation. The Aztecs built an embankment[8] 10 miles long to keep out the salt water and also to protect the city from flooding.

---

7. **irrigation** (ir′ ə gā′ shən) *n.*: Act of supplying water by means of ditches, canals, or sprinklers.
8. **embankment** (em bank′ mənt) *n.*: Bank of earth to keep water back.

▼ **Critical Viewing** What does seeing a codex like this one add to your understanding of Aztec culture? **[Connect]** 4

This Aztec codex (the first manuscript presented in modern book form) shows the life of a corn plant over four years. Corn was so precious to the Aztecs that special gods and goddesses were in charge of it. Tlaloc, the God of Rain; Xipe Totec, the God of Planting; and Spring, and the Storm Goddess, are all featured with the corn in this codex.

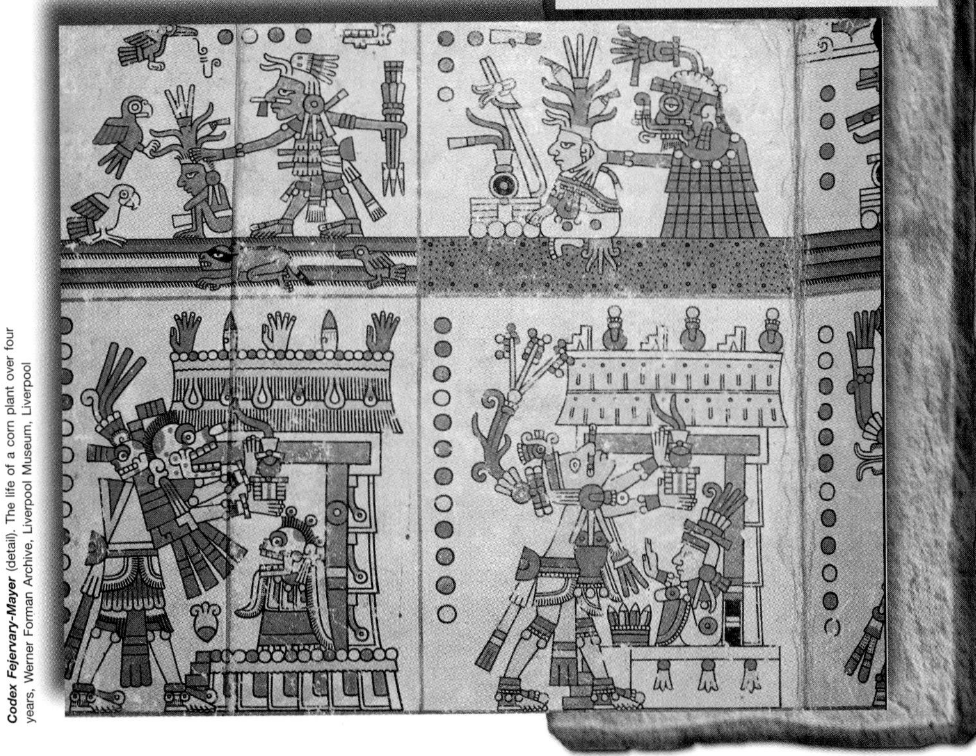

Codex Fejervary-Mayer (detail). The life of a corn plant over four years, Werner Forman Archive, Liverpool Museum, Liverpool

Connecting Literature to Social Studies

3 *In a dry climate, many crops will not grow, and people may not have enough food. Also, animals and people need water to survive.*

▶Critical Viewing◀

4 **Connect** *Students should note that the codex tells them about the importance of corn in Aztec life. It also suggests that the Aztecs were visual communicators interested in color.*

Customize for *Visual/Spatial Learners*

To help students fully understand the Aztecs' incredible engineering feats, challenge them to build a model city. Provide 2–4 inch deep baking tin, dirt or modeling clay, and other supplies for creating buildings and landscape. Have students use the maps on pp. 622–623 as well as the text to create an island city. Urge them to include as many historically accurate features as possible, for example, removable bridges.

Customize for *Logical/Mathematical Learners*

To better imagine the Aztecs' achievements, ask students to sketch the construction projects described. For example, students might create building plans based on descriptions in the essay.

Humanities: Art

Codex Fejervary-Mayer (detail)

Explain that the word *manuscript* comes from the Latin words for "by hand" and "to write," and now refers to writing in its draft forms (even if typed). This manuscript, like other Aztec codices, didn't use letters or script to tell its story. It used symbols called *pictographs* and *ideograms*. These symbols didn't represent the exact object they depicted. Instead, they represented the idea suggested by the object. Thus, a *cow* symbolizes an idea familiar to the educated Aztec.

In this codex, for example, which is read right to left from the top, the corn plant is symbolized by the rain god's wife. As the corn's condition changes with the climate, the rain god's wife appears differently.

1. What do you think the symbols in the codex might have represented to the Aztecs? *Accept all reasonable responses. For example, the birds and underground creatures might symbolize natural enemies to the corn.*
2. How is this manuscript different from modern manuscripts? *Today's manuscripts are written, or more often typed, using words rather than pictures.*
3. Today, how do we use symbols, such as a stop sign, to communicate with people who speak different languages? *Students should note the value of internationally recognized symbols.*

▶Critical Viewing◀

❶ **Analyze** Urge students to read Inside an Aztec Home before answering this question. Comparison with ordinary Aztec homes will help them analyze the image more effectively. *The size of the building, number of rooms, gold detail, and stairs leading ceremoniously to the emperor's throne-like room all suggest his importance.*

Connecting Literature to Social Studies

❷ **Make a Judgment** Point out that the majority of people in Tenochtitlan were farmers and craftspeople. The society was highly stratified; in other words, people didn't move from one class to another. Ask students to describe the advantages and disadvantages of organizing a society in this way. *Students may say that stratified societies are quite stable but also lack flexibility. Thus, if the warrior class were destroyed in battle, no one would be trained to take its place.*

Connecting Literature to Social Studies

❸ **Infer** Ask students what role they think trading had in Aztec society. *Students should be able to infer that trading was an important job in Aztec society, as a lot of food came from outside the city.*

Links Across Time

❹ Chocolate is a food with New World origins. The Aztecs made a bitter drink called *xocoatl* out of the cocoa bean, which Montezuma served to Cortés after he arrived in Tenochtitlan. Cortés brought cocoa back to Spain, and the Spanish soon developed a sweet beverage flavored with cinnamon and vanilla. It became fashionable throughout Europe in the 1600's.

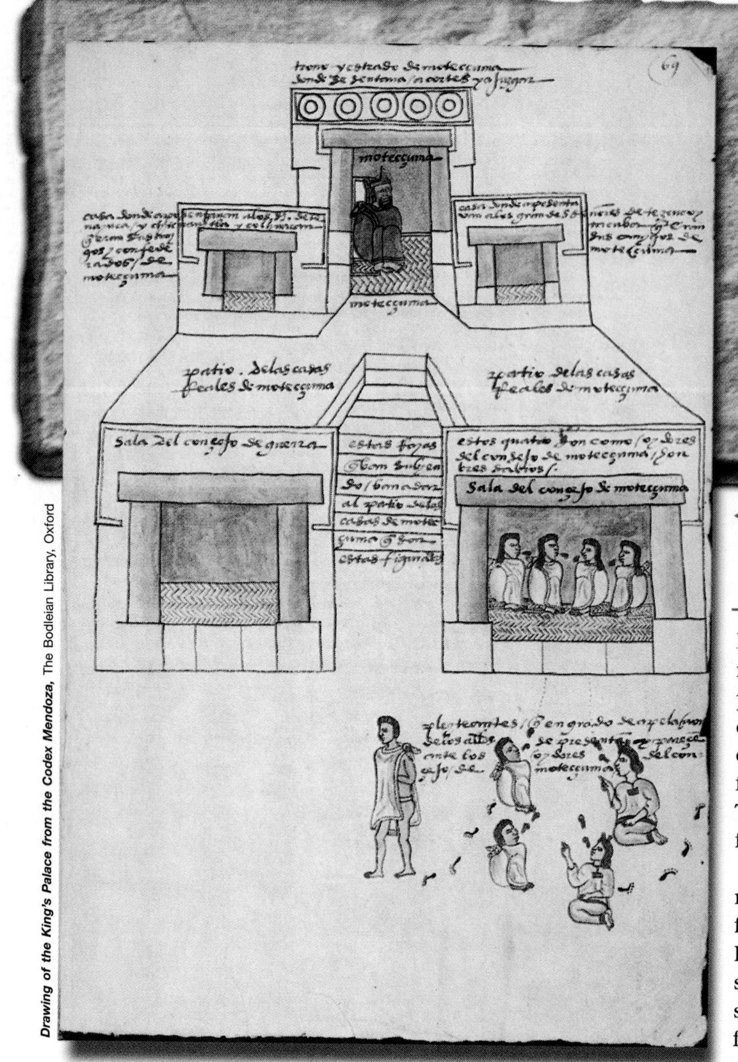

Drawing of the King's Palace from the Codex Mendoza, The Bodleian Library, Oxford

This drawing from the Codex Mendoza shows what the Aztec emperor Montezuma's palace looked like. Practically a small town, it had a main palace and smaller surrounding palaces, council offices, courts of law, and storerooms.

◀ **Critical Viewing** What details in the drawing suggest the emperor's importance? **[Analyze]** ❶

Feeding the People Archaeologists think that when Tenochtitlan was at its greatest, about one million people lived in the Valley of Mexico. That included Tenochtitlan and the 50 or 60 city-states on the mainland surrounding the lakes. Food for all these people had to come from farming.

❷ Historians are not sure how many people in Tenochtitlan were farmers, but they think it may have been between one third and one half of the population. The rest were the nobility, craftspeople, and others. ❸ Each chinampa was only big enough to grow food for one family. Most people in Tenochtitlan depended on food from outside the city.

As the city grew, more and more land was drained for farming and for building. Farmers had no tools except simple hoes and digging sticks, but the loose soil was fertile and easy to turn. The main crop was corn, but farmers also grew tomatoes, beans, chili peppers, and prickly pears. They grew maguey cactus for its fibers and to make a drink called pulque. Cacao trees were grown in the hottest areas. The seeds were used for trading and to make a chocolate drink. ❹

Inside an Aztec Home There were big differences between a rich Aztec home and a poor one. The nobles' houses were like palaces. They were one story high and built

Humanities: Architecture

Drawing of the King's Palace From the Codex Mendoza

When designers want to communicate their ideas to builders, they create a series of drawings. Some drawings are done from an overhead view—these are called "plans." The drawing shown here, called an "elevation," was made facing the building. Notes are added throughout to explain the way rooms will be used, or to indicate the length and width of spaces. Color shows how the building will be decorated.

The emperor's palace was built on two levels, with the emperor's rooms above. Outside (not shown in this drawing) were courtyards and gardens. Each day, officials from around the city visited the palace to learn the king's wishes.

1. What effect do you think this building had on Aztec commoners and on the city officials who visited the emperor? *Visitors were probably awed by the building's splendor and size.*
2. Why might it be difficult to build a structure of this size on land reclaimed from a swamp? *Students should infer that it would be hard to build a large, heavy palace on soft soil.*

around a courtyard. Each of the four sides contained four or five large rooms. The courtyards were planted with flower and vegetable gardens. Some houses on the island in the center of the city were built of adobe—bricks made from mud and dried in the sun. Adobe is still used for building in Mexico today. These grand houses and palaces were whitewashed
5 so that they shone in the sun. The Spanish soldier Bernal Diaz described buildings that looked like "gleaming white towers and castles: a marvelous sight."

There is very little evidence about the buildings in Tenochtitlan and hardly any about the poor people's houses. What we do know has been pieced together from scattered historical records such as documents that record the sale of building sites on the chinampa gardens. All of the poorer people's homes were built on the chinampas on the outskirts of the city. Because the chinampas would not take the weight of stone, houses had to be built of lighter materials such as wattle-and-daub. This was made by weaving reeds together and then plastering them with mud. We know that the outskirts of the city were divided into groups of houses inside walled areas, or compounds. A whole family lived in each compound. The

Connecting Literature to Social Studies
Why wouldn't chinampas support stone houses and buildings? 7

CONNECTING LITERATURE TO SOCIAL STUDIES

◆ Build Vocabulary

outskirts (out′ skurtz′) *n.*: Part of a district far from the center of a city

reeds (rēdz) *n.*: Tall, slender grasses that grow in marshy land

6 ▶ Critical Viewing What can you learn about Aztec technology and skills by examining these stone structures? **[Infer]**

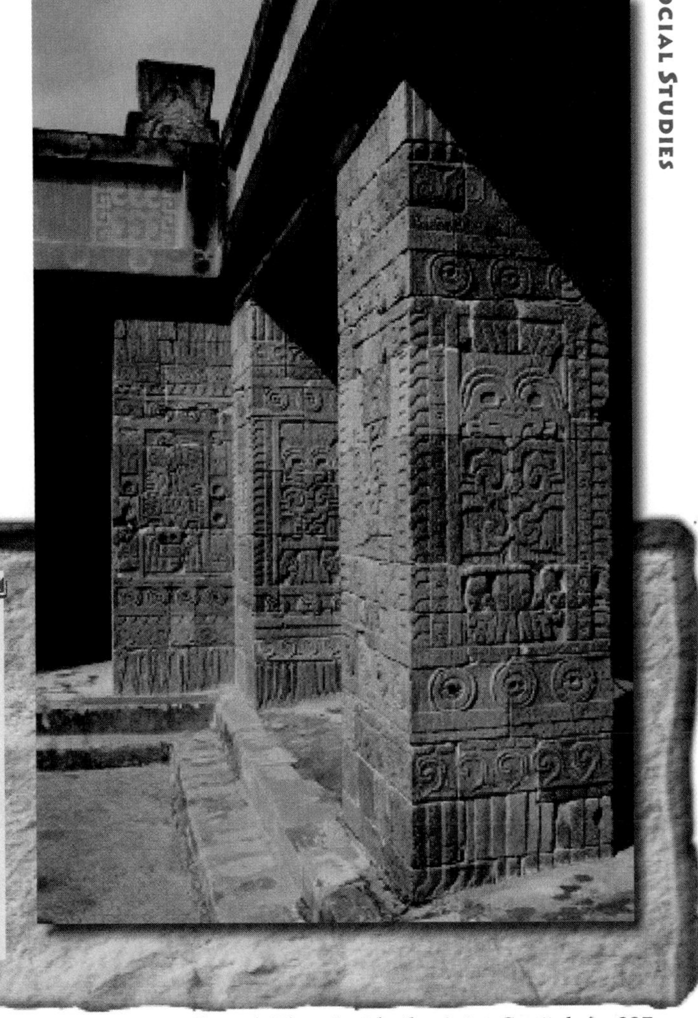

This priest's house is located at Teotihuacan, an Aztec ruin site outside Mexico City. It is probably similar to the homes of Aztec nobles. A doorway opened onto a central courtyard, and the outside walls are decorated with carvings. The houses had flat roofs that were often decorated with flower gardens.

CONNECTING LITERATURE TO SOCIAL STUDIES

5 Tell students that "whitewashed" refers to a white painting gloss, not to a cleaning process. Point out that Tenochtitlan was hot and sunny much of the year. Ask why the Aztecs might have painted their buildings white. *White reflects rather than retains heat. It would help keep the dwellings cool and comfortable.* Then, point out these early architectural choices have made sense for more recent occupants of this region (and the American Southwest nearby) and can still be seen in area buildings.

Links Across Time

The Aztecs were as amazed by the Spanish soldiers as the soldiers were amazed by the Aztecs. One scout reported back to Montezuma:

"We must tell you that we saw a house in the water, out of which came white men, with white hands and faces, and very long, bushy beards, and clothes of every color; white, yellow, red, green, blue, and purple, and on their heads they wore round hats."

▶Critical Viewing◀

6 **Infer** *Students should note that Aztec technology was sophisticated enough to mine, cut, and transport uniform blocks of stone. Craft skills were also advanced, as shown in the intricate carvings*

CONNECTING LITERATURE TO SOCIAL STUDIES

7 **Connect** Refer students back to descriptions of the chinampas and how these "islands" were made. *The chinampas were made of mud and vegetation from the lake bottom and were therefore too soft and unstable to support the weight of a stone building.*

Viewing and Representing Mini-Lesson

Visual Essay

This mini-lesson supports the Visual Essay project in the Idea Bank on p. 629.

Introduce Use this essay to clarify the components with students. Highlight the running text, the drawings, photographs, and extended captions. Explain that blending visuals, text, and captions expands readers' understanding—much like a museum exhibit would.

Develop Have students create charts headed: Text; Pictures; Captions. As they research their essays, students can fill in their charts. Urge students to plan out their essays in storyboard form.

Apply Have students present their visual essays to the class, reading the text aloud and indicating each visual component. Suggest using internal prompts to invite audience participation.

Assess Have students complete the Peer Assessment: Speaker/Speech form, p. 105 in **Alternative Assessment,** as you evaluate presenters for the quality of their research, creativity of design, and effective interaction of text and visual components.

Connecting Literature to Social Studies

1 Draw Conclusions *Students should conclude that religion was important to the Aztecs. For example, they built their temple before their houses, had gods to watch over all the key aspects of life, and placed shrines in their homes.*

Reinforce and Extend

Answers

◆ Literature and Your Life

Reader's Response Possible response: Yes, because there were many challenges to conquer. No, because the Aztecs lacked modern conveniences we now take for granted.

Thematic Focus Possible response: Builders could have created buildings with openings to let in light and reduce smoke, or stabilized the chinampas so that many Aztecs could have sturdier homes.

☑ Check Your Comprehension

1. The city is in the middle of a swampy lake on natural and human-made islands.
2. Wealthy Aztecs lived in elaborate houses centered on a courtyard, mostly in the center of the city. Poor Aztecs lived mostly on outerlying chinampas, in homes built of wattle and daub, or mud-covered reed thatch.
3. Defense was solved by removable causeways. Transportation within the city was solved with canals. Keeping salt water out of the lake was solved with a huge embankment. Food shortages were solved with outside trading and chinampas, reclaimed from the lake.

More About the Author

Jacqueline Dineen uses a skillful mix of description, maps, photographs, and art to give the reader a sense of what it took to create the city of Tenochtitlan. Similar efforts can be seen in the many science and social studies books Dineen has written for schools and children's libraries.

Connecting Literature to Social Studies

family consisted of a couple, their married children, and their grandchildren. Every married couple in the family had a separate house of one or two rooms. All the houses opened onto an outdoor patio that belonged to the whole family.

Outside the house, the families often kept turkeys in pens. The turkeys provided eggs and meat. There was also a beehive for honey. Most families had a bathhouse in the garden.

Furniture and Decoration Aztec houses were very plain inside. Everyone slept on mats of reeds that were spread on the dirt floor at night. Families had cooking pots and utensils made of clay. There were goblets for pulque and other drinks, graters for grinding chilis, and storage pots of various designs. Reed baskets were also used for storage. Households had grinding stones for grinding corn into flour. There was also a household shrine with statues of the gods.

1 **Connecting Literature to Social Studies**
What do you learn about the role religion played in Aztec culture? Explain.

The houses had no windows or chimneys, so they must have been dark and smoky from the cooking fire. There were no doors, just an open doorway. Even the palaces had open doorways with cloths hanging over them.

◆ Build Vocabulary

goblets (gäb′ lits) *n.*: Bowl-shaped drinking containers without handles

Guide for Responding

◆ Literature and Your Life

Reader's Response Would you have enjoyed living in Tenochtitlan? Why or why not?

Thematic Focus Given the resources available to them, how could the leaders of Tenochtitlan have improved community life?

☑ Check Your Comprehension

1. Describe Tenochtitlan's location.
2. Where did both wealthy and poor Aztec people live?
3. Identify three problems faced by the Aztecs, and explain how they solved them.

◆ Critical Thinking

Interpret

1. What do the removable bridges suggest about the relationship between the Aztecs and neighboring peoples? **[Infer]**
2. For what main reason might the Aztecs have created codexes? **[Infer]**
3. Did the city of Tenochtitlan meet the basic needs of its people? Why or why not? **[Draw Conclusions]**

Extend

4. Archaeologists studying Tenochtitlan use artifacts to piece together the puzzle of the past. What skills do you think such a job requires? **[Career Link]**

Meet the Author

Jacqueline Dineen

Jacqueline Dineen probably wishes she could travel back in time to see Tenochtitlan and other ancient civilizations. Bringing these worlds to life for children has been a longtime interest of hers. Dineen pursued that interest during her years as an editor for a London educational publisher and in more than fifty books for children. Sometimes she has focused on specific cultures, as with *The Aztecs* (from which this essay comes) and *The Romans*. In such books as *The Early Inventions* and *Art and Technology Through the Ages*, she's highlighted common human problems and explored how ancient peoples solved them.

Beyond the Selection

FURTHER READING

Other Works by Jacqueline Dineen

Lands of the Bible (Mysterious Places)
Lift the Lid on Mummies: Unravel the Mysteries of Egyptian Tombs and Make Your Own Mummy
People Who Changed the World

Other Works About the Aztecs

Popocatepetl and Ixtlaccihuatl, Juliet Piggott
Growing Up in Aztec Times, Marion Wood
What Do We Know About the Aztecs? Joanna Defrates
The Aztecs, Tim Wood

INTERNET

We suggest the following Internet sites (all Web sites are subject to change).

For information about both historical Tenochtitlan and modern Mexico City, visit these sites:
http://www.adventure.com/ encyclopedia/ general/cthtenoc.html
http://msstate.edu/Archices/History/Latin_ America/Mexico/photos

We *strongly recommend* that you preview these sites before you send your students to them.

CONNECTING LITERATURE TO SOCIAL STUDIES

You might wonder how and why the highly advanced city of Tenochtitlan disappeared. In 1519, Hernando Cortés, the Spanish conquistador, arrived in the beautiful Aztec capital. Because the superstitious emperor Montezuma believed Cortés was a god, the Aztecs did not use geographic defenses but instead welcomed Cortés.

Cortés kidnapped Montezuma and took over his government. In 1521, the Spaniards seized Tenochtitlan and quickly destroyed it. On its main island, they built their city around a square. The Aztecs had to live on the outer islands.

The Spaniards, like the Aztecs before them and the Mexicans after them, had to manage the water around their city. They had to bring in fresh water and irrigate crops. To stop flooding, they filled in Lake Texcoco. Modern Mexico City now sits on this soft lake bottom. As a result, it is sinking—more than 20 feet since 1900! In this essay about the geographic challenges facing the Aztecs, you can see the seeds of these later difficulties.

1. What were some geographic advantages and disadvantages of Tenochtitlan?
2. Explain how geography might have helped the Aztecs succeed in creating their empire.
3. Who has or has had a harder task in maintaining a city: ancient Aztecs or modern Mexicans? Explain.

Idea Bank

Writing

1. **Community Events Poster** Create a poster announcing community happenings in Tenochtitlan. Include as many details about daily life as possible, and illustrate your poster to fit the ancient city's appearance. **[Art Link]**
2. **Ancient Call-in Show** With a partner, write a dialogue for a call-in radio show in which people ask advice about solving life's problems in Tenochtitlan. **[Media Link]**
3. **Campaign Speech** Imagine that you want to be Tenochtitlan's next emperor. Write a speech outlining the main issues that you see facing the city and how you would address these issues. **[Social Studies Link]**

Speaking and Listening

4. **Interview** Call the planning office in your city. Talk to officials there about the jobs of city planners and builders. Find out about the skills these occupations require. Then, determine whether the Aztecs used such skills in making their city. **[Career Link]**

Projects

5. **Visual Essay** Choose a culture that thrived between the years 500 and 1789, and create a visual essay about it. In addition to the running text, include drawings, photographs, and captions. Make your visual essay available for class viewing. **[Social Studies Link]**

Further Reading, Listening, and Viewing

- Elizabeth Baquedano, *Eyewitness: Aztec, Inca, and Maya* (1993) is a book-length picture essay about ancient Latin American cultures.
- John Bierhorst, *Mythology of Mexico and Central America* (1990) shares legends and folk tales of the Aztecs and other ancient peoples.

ASSESSMENT OPTIONS

Formal Assessment, Selection Test, pp. 172–173, and Assessment Resources Software. The selection test is designed so that it can be easily customized to the performance levels of your students.

PORTFOLIO ASSESSMENT
Use the following rubrics and assessment form in the **Alternative Assessment** booklet to assess student writing:
Community Events Poster: Description, p. 84
Ancient Call-in Show: Peer Assessment: Speaker/Speech, p. 105
Campaign Speech: Problem-Solution, p. 88

Idea Bank

Following are suggestions for matching the Idea Bank topics with your students' performance levels and learning modalities:

Customize for *Performance Levels*
Less Advanced Students: 1, 4
Average Students: 2, 4, 5
More Advanced Students: 3, 4, 5

Customize for *Learning Modalities*
Verbal/Linguistic: 1, 2, 3, 4
Visual/Spatial: 1, 5
Interpersonal: 2, 4
Logical/Mathematical: 3

Answers *(continued)*

◆Critical Thinking

1. The Aztecs must have had wars, or at least times of tension, with their neighbors, to justify these defenses.
2. The Aztecs probably created codices to record their history. Codices were also used for religious purposes and for record keeping.
3. Yes, it did. People had food, water, shelter, ways to earn a living, and safety.
4. Archaeologists must be able to analyze information in many forms and make inferences about Aztec life from these minimal clues.

CONNECTING LITERATURE TO SOCIAL STUDIES

1. Advantages include safety from invasion, mild climate, and fertile soil. Disadvantages include lack of rain and the need for irrigation, shortage of farmland and therefore food, the need to bring in fresh water, unstable ground.
2. The location's safety from invasion enabled them to establish themselves more fully. Also, mild climate and fertile soil allowed the culture to flourish and expand.
3. Possible response: The Aztecs faced the more difficult task, as they lacked technology and scientific advances such as sewer systems, heavy earth-moving equipment, and glass for windows. Modern city planners, however, struggle with heavy buildings on unstable soil and crowding.

Prepare and Engage

Establish Writing Guidelines
Review the following key characteristics of a report on a current event:

- A report on a current event summarizes an occurrence in the news.
- It provides factual information on key details of the event.

You may want to distribute the scoring rubric for a Research Report/ Paper, p. 93 in **Alternative Assessment,** to make students aware of the criteria on which they will be evaluated. See the suggestions on p. 632 for how you can customize the rubric to this workshop.

Refer students to the Writing Handbook in the back of the book for instruction on the writing process and further information on reports.

Writer's Solution

Writers at Work Videodisc
To introduce students to reports and to show them how Ellie Fries answers the question "What is a report?" play the videodisc segment on Reports (Ch. 7). Have students discuss how Fries gathers up-to-date information.

Play frames 11077 to 20155

Writing Lab CD-ROM
If your students have access to computers, you may want to have them work in the tutorial on Reports to complete all or part of their reports on current events. Follow these steps:

1. Have students use the Topic Web Activity to narrow their topics.
2. Suggest that students view the skimming tips to learn how to find desired information.
3. Allow students to draft on computer.
4. When revising, have students use the Transition Word Bin activity to select words to connect their ideas.

Writer's Solution Sourcebook
Students can find additional support, including in-depth instruction on organizing information, in the chapter on Reports, pp. 200–233.

Report Writing

Report on a Current Event

Writing Process Workshop

What's happening in the world? A **report on a current event** is a short piece of informative writing that answers the question by summarizing a recent news item. In this workshop, you'll research something in the news that catches your eye. Then, you'll write a report to explain the event to others. The following skills will help you write your report.

Writing Skills Focus

▶ **Provide necessary background** to help readers understand the events you describe in your report. (See p. 621.)

▶ **Follow your interests** as you search for a current event. Choose something that catches your eye—something you would like to learn more about.

▶ **Use the Five W's** to identify the information you'll want to include: *who, what, where, when,* and *why.*

One writer was hooked by a headline that read: **It's Dry, Dry, Dry.** Here's the beginning of her report on wildfires in Florida:

MODEL

This summer has been Florida's worst fire season in over 50 years. ① From Jacksonville to Orlando, new fires have ignited and continued to burn. ② More than 200,000 acres have burned, and many buildings and crops have been destroyed. "The number of fires and the size of them are unbelievable," said one fire lieutenant. The fires are a result of drought plus lightning from storms that dump little or no rain. ③

① This sentence provides background by placing the severity of the fire in context.

② The writer provides information to tell *what* and *where.*

③ This sentence tells why the fires are starting.

Beyond the Classroom

Career Connection

Journalism Tell students that journalism involves the reporting, editing, and managing of newspapers and magazines, and also includes news reporting on radio and television. In addition to reporting on current events, many newspapers include columns and editorials that feature much broader topics.

With the advent of radio and television journalism, reporters can actually provide live reporting while an event is occurring. This "live" reporting is especially important in presidential debates, presidential addresses, and court cases.

Have students form groups and scan a local newspaper for a report on a current event. Encourage them to write a brief summary of the event. Then, have students view or listen to a radio or television report covering the same event. Have them take notes and consider the difference in the quality and type of information given. Ask them to identify which report gave more information and whether any visuals made the story easier to understand. Have students discuss their findings with the rest of the class.

Prewriting

Shop Around Find an event that interests you. Browse through newspapers, listen to the radio, watch television news, or talk to friends about what's happening. Consider these categories to help you pinpoint a current event you'd like to research.

Topic Ideas

- Local or national government
- Business
- Extreme weather conditions
- Conflict
- Trends in fashion or music

Get the Facts Find information about the event you've chosen. Read slowly and carefully. Take notes. Look for answers to questions that begin with the five W's.

Find Another Source Base your report on more than one source. Here are some avenues for information:

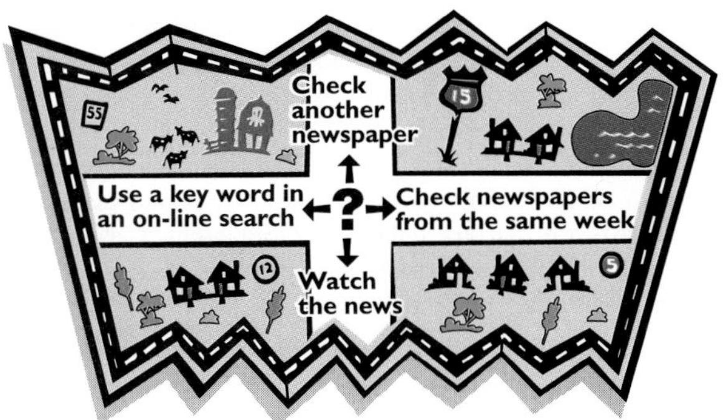

Jot Down Key Words Make a list of three to five important ideas about your current event. You'll want to use them as key words in your report.

Drafting

Report All the Facts As you draft, think about the five W's. Make sure you include information that answers each question: *Who? What? Where? When?* and *Why?*

DRAFTING/REVISING

Applying Language Skills: Use Synonyms for Variety

You'll want to thread certain ideas through your report, but you don't want to repeat the words over and over. For variety, use **synonyms,** words that are similar in meaning. A dictionary or thesaurus might help. Here are some examples:

Instead of repeating . . .	Try . . .
mayor	leader; official
mountain	peak; summit
solution	cure; answer

Practice Replace the italicized words in these sentences with synonyms that make sense.

1. Lightning bolts *start* many fires in dry *places.*
2. The Bulls *beat* the Jazz because of their *better speed.*
3. *Shopping* on the Internet is *common today.*

Writing Application When writing your report on a current event, use synonyms to avoid repetition.

Writer's Solution Connection
Writing Lab

For more instruction on considering your audience, see the Reports tutorial on the Writing Lab CD-ROM.

Develop Student Writing

Prewriting

For more topic ideas, have students consider events occurring at school or in the neighborhood. Tell students to choose a topic broad enough that there is adequate information about it, but not so broad that it can't be easily summarized. Suggest that when they find an article on a topic, they read it to themselves, then try to write down the article's main point in one sentence.

Customize for
Less Proficient Writers

When students have chosen their topic, have them fill out a KWL Organizer, p. 58 in **Writing and Language Transparencies,** to help them focus on what information they already know and what they will have to research. As they find facts and sources, have them go back to their chart and change or add information.

Customize for
More Advanced Writers

Challenge students to report on a current event that has caused a debate in the local or national community. Encourage students to research both sides of the issue and to remain objective in their reporting. They may want to focus on the issue itself and mention the opposing sides, or they may want to focus on the debate, and its resulting problems.

Applying Language Skills

Use Synonyms for Variety If students are working on a computer, remind them that most word processing programs have a built-in thesaurus tool. Students can highlight a word, and the thesaurus will provide a definition and synonyms.

Answers

1. Lightning bolts *begin* many fires in dry areas.
2. The Bulls *whipped* the Jazz because of their *faster pace.*
3. *Buying things* on the Internet is *nothing new.*

Drafting
Tell students to include all necessary background information in their drafts. They may find it helpful to keep the five W's in mind, and answer these questions as they write.

Revising
Peer reviewers should look for a clearly stated main idea, varied sentence beginnings, and visible sources for any quoted material.

Writer's Solution

Writing Lab CD-ROM
Have students use the Peer Review checklist in the tutorial on Reports.

Publishing
Suggest that students compile their reports into a class newspaper. Include a name for the newspaper, a table of contents, and appropriate illustrations or photos.

Reinforce and Extend

Review the Writing Guidelines
After students have completed their papers, review the characteristics of a report on a current event.

Applying Language Skills
Answers
1. President Clinton visited China in June 1998.
2. He debated with Jiang Zemin in the Great Hall of the People.
3. People in Washington and Beijing watched on television.

Writer's Solution

For additional support, complete the practice page on Different Kinds of Nouns in the *Writer's Solution Grammar Practice Book,* p. 6.

EDITING/PROOFREADING

APPLYING LANGUAGE SKILLS: Capitalize Proper Nouns
A **proper noun** is the exact name of a person, place, or thing. Often, proper nouns are one of a kind—and proper nouns are *always* capitalized. Flip through a newspaper, noticing the proper nouns.

People:
Charles Kuralt, Nolan Ryan, Barbara Jordan

Places:
New York City, North America, Tenochtitlan, Independence Hall

Things:
Internet, Statue of Liberty, Godzilla, January

Practice Capitalize the proper nouns in these sentences.
1. President clinton visited china in june 1998.
2. He debated with jiang zemin in the great hall of the people.
3. People in washington and beijing watched on television.

Writing Application As you edit your report, be sure all proper nouns are capitalized.

Writer's Solution Connection Language Lab
For more practice with capitalization, see the Proper Nouns lesson on the Language Lab CD-ROM.

Remember Your Audience Imagine that your audience is your class: teenagers like you. To help you inform them, consider the answers to these questions:
- Would a map help clarify the location of the event?
- Are there key words that need defining?
- Are there key people who must be identified?

Revising
Read Aloud Now that you've written the facts, here's your chance to make your writing smooth and precise. Reading your report aloud will help you hear a word or phrase you've used too often. Be alert to the sound of sentences, and revise those that seem awkward or clunky.

Combine Short Sentences Work to edit short, choppy sentences. Combine them whenever the points they make are closely related. Look at this example:

Short and Choppy:	Smooth and Combined
The mayor announced a new airport. It will be built north of town. It will cost $20 million. The project will take four years.	The mayor announced a four-year project to build a $20 million airport north of town.

Check Facts Confirm the spelling of names and places, especially those that are unfamiliar. Double-check dates, statistics, and any direct quotations you use. Make sure your report is 100 percent accurate.

Use a Peer Reviewer Ask someone to read your report. Use these questions to help get the most out of your reader.
- ▶ Have I included enough information?
- ▶ Can you picture what I'm writing about?
- ▶ Are my sentences clear?
- ▶ Do you see errors in spelling, grammar, or mechanics?

Publishing and Presenting
Newscast Use a video camera to record your report as if you were a television reporter. Watch the news for some tips. Then, rehearse to look and sound like a news anchor.

Current Events Board Find a bulletin board somewhere in your school and label it "In the News." Divide it into four parts: Local, State, National, World. Display your reports, using big, bold headlines for each one. Include copies of photographs if possible. Be sure to keep the board up to date.

✓ ASSESSMENT

PORTFOLIO ASSESSMENT		4	3	2	1
Use the rubric on Research Report/Paper in the **Alternative Assessment** booklet, p. 93, to assess the students' writing. Add these criteria to customize this rubric to this assignment.	**Presentation of Facts**	The report presents all the facts necessary for understanding the event in a clear and orderly fashion.	The report presents all of the facts necessary for understanding the event, but not all are presented clearly.	The report presents most of the facts necessary for understanding the event and in a mostly clear fashion.	The report is missing key facts necessary for understanding the event. The facts are not presented in a clear order.
	Proper Nouns	All of the proper nouns are capitalized correctly.	Most of the proper nouns are capitalized correctly.	Some of the proper nouns are capitalized correctly.	None of the proper nouns is capitalized correctly.

Real-World Reading Skills Workshop

Using Headlines and Text Structure in Newspapers

Strategies for Success

Daily newspapers are an excellent source of information on a wide range of topics. They provide up-to-date articles or subjects as varied as politics, business, sports, human interest, leisure time, and travel. Most newspapers are arranged so that readers can easily find the information they need. Here are some suggestions about how to read a newspaper:

Read Headlines Headlines are written in bold type and announce the major point of the news story that follows. Headlines often use short, attention-getting sentences to catch the reader's eye. Scan these to determine whether an article relates to you.

The Daily News

Mayor Cancels Parade

Monday, May 1. Mayor Daniels announced today that this year's Memorial Day parade would be canceled because of the traffic jams that were caused by last year's parade.

Protests Voiced Parade organizers protested the mayor's decision and hoped to find another site for the event.

Forest Fires Continue to Burn

Monday, May 1. Forest fires raged through several acres of land on the north side of the city. Firefighters from towns and cities all over the county have been called in to help put out the blaze.

Dry Weather Blamed Fire Chief Dave Monore blamed the recent spell of dry weather for creating conditions that led to the fires. Forecasters have predicted a period of rain by the weekend that should help the problem.

Index

World News.......A
Sports...............B
Business...........C
Local News........D
Entertainment...E

Notice Subheads Newspaper articles can be quite long, so they are usually divided into sections. Subheads, or mini-headlines, before each section of a long article let the reader know what information will be covered in the section that follows.

Find the Section You Want Most newspapers are divided into several different sections. A table of contents, or index, may list the sections by name. For instance, there is often a sports section, an arts and entertainment section, and a business section. Don't feel overwhelmed by all the categories—read only what you want or need to know.

Apply the Strategies

Read the front page of the newspaper at left. Then, answer the questions that follow.

1. What headlines do you see?
2. Identify the subheads in each story.
3. Why did the mayor cancel the parade?
4. What caused the forest fires?
5. In which section of the paper could you find baseball scores?
6. How many different sections does this newspaper have?

Here are other situations in which using headlines and text structure can be helpful:

- *Reading a magazine*
- *Reading an article on the Internet*
- *Reading an encyclopedia or atlas*
- *Reading a textbook*

Introduce the Strategies

Ask students if they or members of their family read a daily newspaper. If so, which section do they read first? Encourage students to discuss what parts of the newspaper they read, what sections those parts are found in, and why they read those parts. Explain that often the Sunday edition of a paper has many more sections than a weekday edition. Also, explain that some newspapers have special sections for different days of the week. For example, a science section may come out every Monday, or a food section every Thursday.

Customize for
More Advanced Readers

Explain that many newspapers now have on-line counterparts. Ask students to choose a local or national newspaper that has an on-line version. Have them view the on-line newspaper and make notes as to how it is organized and categorized. Does it have a search mechanism?

Have students compare and contrast the organization of the print version and the on-line version. Have them note if the on-line version has any added features, or is missing sections that the print version has. Encourage students to share their findings with the rest of the class.

Apply the Strategies

Before students answer the questions, ask them how this page differs from an actual newspaper page. Explain that this page has shortened versions of stories, and no photographs, as most newspapers do.

Answers

1. Mayor Cancels Parade; Forest Fires Continue to Burn
2. Protests Voiced; Dry Weather Blamed
3. The parade was canceled because of the traffic jams it caused last year.
4. The forest fire was caused by the recent spell of dry weather.
5. Section B, Sports
6. This newspaper has five sections.

◆Build Grammar Skills

Correct Use of Pronouns
Part 2 of this unit includes instruction on the following:

- Subject and object pronouns

This instruction is reinforced with the Build Grammar Skills practice page in **Selection Support,** p. 202.

As you review the correct use of pronouns, you may wish to include the following:

- Correct pronouns in compound constructions

Remind students to put first-person pronouns last in compuound constructions:

Lee and *I* both made the team.

- Correct pronouns in incomplete constructions

In an incomplete construction, some words are understood rather than stated. Such clauses generally make a comparison and begin with *than* or *as*:

Evelyn is as strong as *he* [is].

In these cases, use the form of the pronoun you would use if the clause were completed.

- Use of *who* and *whom*

Deciding whether to use *who* or *whom* is less confusing when the specific uses of the words are understood: *Who* is subjective and *whom* is objective.

Customize for
Less Proficient Learners
Remind students that personal pronouns refer to the person speaking (subjective case), the person spoken to (objective case), or the person, place, or thing spoken about (objective case).

Writer's Solution

For additional practice and support with phrases, use the practice pages on pronouns, pp. 8–10 in the *Writer's Solution Grammar Practice Book.* If students have access to technology, they can use the Using Pronouns lesson in the *Writer's Solution Language Lab CD-ROM.*

Correct Use of Pronouns

Grammar Review

Pronouns are words that replace nouns. Some pronouns change form depending on their use in a sentence. (See page 620.) Case is the form of the pronoun that shows its use in a sentence.

Subjective Case	Use in Sentence	Example
I, we you	Subject of a Verb	*She* caught a snake.
he, she, it, they	Predicate Pronoun	It was *she.*

Objective Case	Use in Sentence	Example
me, us	Direct Object	Miss Ryan invited *us.*
you him, her, it, them	Indirect Object	She taught *them* tolerance.
	Object of a Preposition	She was happy with *him.*

Practice 1 Identify the case of the italicized pronouns in these sentences.

1. Nonfiction can teach *us* about the world and our interaction with *it.*
2. *I* read two articles on the Internet.
3. *They* could offer *us* more help.
4. After reading *them, she* will write two essays about the Internet.
5. *You* will find *them* useful.
6. *We* should learn from each other.
7. Let *us* take our experiences and share *them.*
8. *It* will make some events seem easier.
9. Let *me* tell you my opinion.
10. When *you* hit trouble, *you*'ll see what *I* mean.

Practice 2 Complete each sentence with the correct pronoun.

1. Charles Kuralt gave (we, us) a vision of the past.
2. (He, him) brought a historic event to life.
3. Between you and (me, I), I liked that essay about the founders best.
4. It was (they, them) who granted (we, us) freedom.
5. (We, us) should be more aware of how (they, them) affected history.
6. Without (they, them), the nation might be different for (we, us).
7. If you ask my classmates and (I, me), I'd guess that (we, us) might not want to take the same risks that they did.

Grammar in Writing

✔ *Mistakes usually occur when a pronoun is part of a compound subject or object. To test whether the form of a pronoun is correct, use the pronoun by itself after the verb or preposition.*

Incorrect: The essay inspired Sam and I.
Test: The essay inspired I.
Correct: The essay inspired Sam and me.

Answers

Practice 1

1. us - objective; it - objective
2. I - subjective
3. They - subjective; us - objective
4. them - objective; she - subjective
5. You - subjective; them - objective
6. We - subjective
7. us - objective; them - objective
8. It - subjective
9. me - objective
10. you - subjective; you - subjective; I - subjective

Practice 2

1. Charles Kuralt gave *us* a vision of the past.
2. *He* brought a historic event to life.
3. Between you and *me,* I liked that essay about the founders best.
4. It was *they* who granted *us* freedom.
5. *We* should be more aware of how *they* affected history.
6. Without *them,* the nation might be different for *us.*
7. If you ask my classmates and *me,* I'd guess that *we* might not want to take the same risks that they did.

Speaking, Listening, and Viewing Workshop

Speaking Persuasively

Candidates for public office use persuasion to convince voters to elect them. Trial lawyers use persuasion to sway juries toward specific verdicts. While you may not be delivering a closing argument anytime soon, you use persuasive tactics every day. Mastering these skills will help you convey your opinions to others—and it should help you change people's minds in the process.

Speak Clearly and Confidently One of the best ways to get someone to believe in your ideas is to believe in them yourself. If you speak clearly and confidently, listeners are more likely to agree with what you say. Use body language and tone of voice to convey your enthusiasm.

Consider Your Audience Persuading your parents to let you see a movie may be a tougher sell than convincing your friend to go with you. Choose the reasons that will sway the person you're addressing.

Organize Your Thoughts Thinking before speaking is always a good rule, especially if you are trying to persuade someone. Keep your goal in mind, and decide the best way to win another person over. Then, present your points in a clear, logical way.

Apply the Strategies

Get together with a small group to role-play the following situations. After two group members act out a scene, the others can give feedback about what worked and what didn't. Share your findings with the class.

1. You argue with a friend over whether you should see a movie or go bicycle riding.
2. You try to persuade a parent to allow you to get an after-school job.
3. You want a salesperson to give you a refund.

Tips for Speaking Persuasively

✔ *To persuade another person to agree with your opinions, follow these suggestions:*

- Use an upbeat tone of voice.
- Listen to objections, and address them in your argument.
- Control your emotions. Don't get angry or shout. Be persuasive, but remain in control.
- Let the facts speak for themselves.

Introduce the Strategies

Encourage students to think of examples of persuasive speaking. Remind them of politicians campaigning on radio or television, telephone fund-raisers requesting support for a cause, a football coach giving a pep talk to the team. Explain that the common thread among these speakers is their intention to make the listener act in a certain way or believe in something. Have students think of situations where they have used persuasive speaking.

Customize for
Bodily/Kinesthetic Leaners
Have students work in pairs to practice using body language to enhance their persuasive speaking. Give them a basic persuasive issue, such as convincing a friend to go to a basketball game. Tell them to try to persuade their partner using only one spoken sentence, "Come with me," and experiment with different types of body language that will support this request. After students have tried this activity several times, encourage them to create a list of persuasive body language and share it with their classmates.

Apply the Strategies

Encourage all students to participate in the role-play as well as the feedback on the role-play. If possible, videotape students' performances; then, have the class comment on them as a group. Have students regroup and do the role-plays with different partners. Then, have them compare the videotaped performances and decide which role-play successfully used the strategies taught.

Speaking and Listening Mini-Lesson

Workplace Skills: Mini-Lesson
Speaking Persuasively Tell students that speaking persuasively is an essential workplace skill. Aside from being useful in professions such as sales and politics, persuasive speaking can also help a person interview for a job or suggest a new procedure for completing a task.

Ask students to brainstorm for a list of work-related situations that involve persuasive speaking: for example, a vacuum cleaner salesperson trying to persuade homemakers or businesses to buy a particular brand of vacuum. Have students get into groups and create scenes to role-play, using the strategies they learned in the lesson.

◆Build Vocabulary

What's Behind the Words

Explain to students that an idiom is an expression particular to a certain language that means something different from the literal meaning of each word. Give them some other examples of common idioms, such as "Keep it down" or to "drop someone a line."

Customize for *English Language Learners*

Some of the more technical language may have to be explained to students to help them understand the meaning of the idiom in question. For example, you might want to explain that "the doldrums" refers to a belt of calm and light winds near the equator, which cause a state of inactivity when sailing. For more help, encourage students to consult a dictionary.

Answers

Activity 1

1. A *budding movie star* is a star who is just developing, as in a bud, an immature plant.
2. *To crop up* means to come about unexpectedly, as in a *crop* is the yield of a harvest.
3. *A farm team* serves as player development, where the best players are "harvested" and brought to the major leagues.
4. *A grass-roots campaign* is a campaign led by common, ordinary people, such as the grass roots, which covers most of the rural areas of the country.
5. *A needle in a haystack* presents the picture of something incredibly small in a stack of hay, which is incredibly big and complex. This expression usually means something difficult to find.
6. *To weed out* means to get rid of something unwanted as in a *weed,* which is a troublesome wild plant that can injure planted crops.

Activity 2

1. *Bitter end* refers to the end of a difficult or unpleasant experience; in nautical terms, *a bitter end* refers to the end of the anchor chain.
2. *The doldrums* refers to a state of inactivity or stagnation as in *the doldrums,* a belt of calm winds that do not allow for movement when sailing.
3. *Hard and fast* means not to be violated (as in a rule); in sailing it means to maneuver to the extreme limit.
4. *A landmark* means a prominent feature, part, or event, as a *landmark* is a prominent object on land that serves as a guide.
5. *Take the wind out of her sails* means to bring someone back to reality just as *take the wind out of her sails* means to bring the boat back from full speed.
6. *The tide is turning* means that the course of events is reversing, as in the tide changing from low to high.

Activity 3

Possible responses: stuffy, chilly, cool, icy, frigid, gloomy, warm

What's Behind the Words

Vocabulary Adventures With Richard Lederer

Idioms From Land, Sea, and Sky

If someone says a concept comes from out of left field, you understand the idea is wacky, but you might not expect it to have anything to do with baseball. Like *out of left field*, many of the expressions we use in everyday speech are idioms—they have meanings different from what they actually say. Many English idioms come from farming, shipping, and the weather.

Down-to-Earth Words

The floor of the house we all share on this planet is the soil. Because the vast majority of Americans now live in cities, we have to some extent lost contact with that soil. Our down-to-earth English words and phrases, however, constantly remind us of our dependence on the earth that supports us:

- Like well-farmed land, the fertile mind of a cultured person is carefully tended and yields a bountiful harvest. We describe such people as *cultivated*.
- Late spring frosts or pests of the insect or human variety can kill a young tree or flower before it has a chance to develop. When we stop a problem in its early stages, we say that we *nip it in the bud*.

Our Seaworthy Language

Four fifths of our planet consists of water, and most of that is ocean. The salt of the sea is indeed on our tongues in phrases like these: I don't wish to *make waves, rock the boat, go overboard, lower the boom* on you, or make you feel *at sea*. I'd rather you *stay on an even keel* and have *smooth sailing*.

- The phrase that old sailors used to describe a ship in shallow water that touches land from time to time was *touch* and *go*. Today, the expression describes any dangerous situation.
- On the high seas, when the weather gets rough, travelers go below deck to ride out the storm and avoid becoming seasick. Thus, they retreat to a location *under the weather*, which gradually has come to mean "feeling ill."

Weather or Not

Now, explore how our language breathes in the air that sustains us all: I don't want to create a *tempest in a teapot* and cause *gales of laughter* in you. Nor do I wish to make a *lightning-quick* decision and *steal your thunder*. But I'm not just *shooting the breeze* either. I'm hoping that your awareness of the weather patterns that stream across our language will put you on *cloud nine*.

ACTIVITY 1 Explain the earthy metaphors embedded in the following expressions: (1) *a budding movie star,* (2) *to crop up,* (3) *a farm team,* (4) *a grass-roots campaign,* (5) *a needle in a haystack,* (6) *to weed out.*

ACTIVITY 2 Explain the sea and sailing metaphors in the following words and expressions: (1) *bitter end,* (2) *the doldrums,* (3) *hard and fast,* (4) *a landmark,* (5) *take the wind out of her sails,* (6) *the tide is turning.*

ACTIVITY 3 Certain people strike us as *cold*, while others radiate a *sunny* disposition. List additional moods and personalities that reflect the weather.

Extended Reading Opportunities

From biographies to history to personal narratives, nonfiction has something to satisfy every interest. Take a look at these suggestions:

Suggested Titles

Eleanor Roosevelt, A Life of Discovery
Russell Freedman

In a biography of one of the most influential twentieth-century Americans, the author traces the life of Eleanor Roosevelt, the former First Lady. Readers follow this strong woman from her childhood, through the troubled period of World War II, to her role in the founding of the United Nations. Throughout his telling, Freedman remains faithful to the spirit of Roosevelt's life.

Twenty-Five Great Moments
Geoffrey C. Ward and Ken Burns With S. A. Kramer

Don Larsen pitches a perfect game in the 1956 World Series. Roberto Clemente pounds his 3,000th hit in 1972. Ken Griffey, Sr., and Ken Griffey, Jr., set a record when they hit back-to-back homers in 1990. Exciting moments like these are described in detail in a companion book to the PBS *Baseball* series. Written expressly for young people, Ward and Burns's book brings the history of baseball to life.

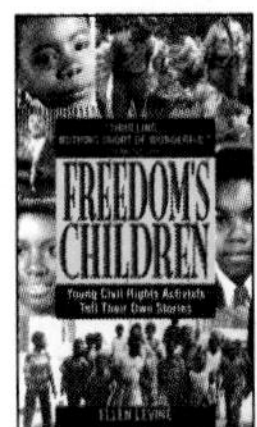

Freedom's Children: Young Civil Rights Activists Tell Their Own Stories
Ellen Levine

From the 1955 Montgomery bus boycott to the 1965 march from Selma to Montgomery, civil rights activity in the South challenged the beliefs, determination, and courage of African Americans. In a book that chronicles these turbulent times, Ellen Levine provides the firsthand accounts of young adults fighting to make a difference.

Other Possibilities

A Summer Life	Gary Soto
Close Encounters: Exploring the Universe With the Hubble Telescope	Elaine Scott
Zlata's Diary: A Child's Life in Sarajevo	Zlata Filipovic

Planning Students' Extended Reading

All of the works listed on this page are good examples of biography and autobiography. Following is some information that may help you choose which to teach.

Customize for *Varying Student Needs*

When assigning the selections in this part to your students, keep in mind the following factors:

- *Eleanor Roosevelt, A Life of Discovery* is a well-written biography of the former First Lady. This biography includes several photographs and presents a good opportunity for team teaching with a social studies unit on Franklin Delano Roosevelt and World War II.
- *Twenty-Five Great Moments* details exciting and memorable events in baseball history, both on and off the field.
- *Freedom's Children: Young Civil Rights Activists Tell Their Own Stories* features first-person accounts of young people who fought for civil rights in the United States between 1955 and 1965. This book provides a solid connection to social studies.

Planning Instruction and Assessment

Unit Objectives

1. To read dramatic works
2. To apply a variety of reading strategies, particularly strategies for reading drama, appropriate for reading dramatizations
3. To recognize literary elements used in these selections
4. To increase vocabulary
5. To learn elements of grammar and usage
6. To write in a variety of modes about situations based on the selections
7. To develop speaking and listening skills, by completing activities
8. To view images critically and create visual representations

Meeting the Objectives Each selection provides instructional material and portfolio opportunities by which students can meet unit objectives. You will find additional practice pages for reading strategies, literary elements, vocabulary, and grammar in the **Selection Support** booklet in the **Teaching Resources** box.

Setting Goals Work with your students at the beginning of the unit to set goals for unit outcomes. Plan what skills and concepts you wish students to acquire. You may match instruction and activities according to students' performance levels or learning modalities.

Portfolios Students may keep portfolios of their completed work or of their work in progress. The Build Your Portfolio page of each selection provides opportunities for students to apply the concepts presented.

Humanities: Art

Performers, by Freshman Brown

Freshman Brown (1941–) sees his art as combining reality and nonreality, the somber and the humorous. Many of his works are inspired by local and national news stories.

1. What is happening in this painting? Why might the figures be wearing masks? *Possible reponses: it looks like a costume party or a performance of some sort; they might be playing characters, or just pretending.*
2. What does the title of the painting tell you? *Students should realize that the title,* Performers, *indicates that a performance is taking place, or about to take place.*

Performers, Freshman Brown

Art Transparencies

The **Art Transparencies** booklet in the **Teaching Resources** box offers fine art to help students make connections to other curriculum areas and high-interest topics.

To make connections to the dramatic elements in Unit 8, you may wish to use Art Transparency 4, p. 19, *Personal Experience* by Miriam Schapiro. Schapiro's mixed media piece is a spirited, lighthearted depiction of a performer. Use one of the booklet's activities to help students explore the art through discussion of the collage painting, a writing activity, or a performance.

Beyond Literature

Each unit presents Beyond Literature features that lead students into an exploration of careers, communities and other subject areas. In this unit, students will explore the relationship between famous names and everyday language, and make language and media connections. In addition, the Teacher's Resource box contains a Beyond Literature booklet of activities. Using literature as a springboard, these activity pages offer students opportunities to connect literature to other curriculum areas and to the workplace and careers, community, media, and humanities.

UNIT 8

Drama

When you read drama—literature meant to be performed—you give your imagination a workout. Use the plays presented in this unit to hear and see the scenes acted before you. As you read, notice the elements that make drama a unique form of writing:

- **Dialogue** is a conversation among characters.
- **Stage directions** are the playwright's notes to actors, directors, and readers. They reveal information about sets, movements, and emotion.
- **Characterization** is the playwright's technique of creating believable characters. The writer can't speak directly to an audience, so dialogue, costume, and gestures show you who each person really is.
- **Theme** is the central message the dramatist shares with the audience.

Connections

Within this unit, you will find selections and activities that make connections beyond literature. Use these selections to connect students' understanding and appreciation of literature beyond the traditional literature and language arts curriculum.

Encourage students to connect literature to other curriculum areas. You may wish to coordinate with teachers in other curriculum areas to determine ways to team teach and further extend instruction.

Connections to Today's World

Use these selections to guide students to recognize the relevance of literature to contemporary writings. In this unit, Gary Larson's "Farside" cartoon offers students a humorous connection to Rod Serling's teleplay from the TV series "The Twilight Zone."

Connecting Literature to Social Studies

Each unit contains a selection that connects Literature to Social Studies. In this unit, students the dramatic lyrics to "Bring Back Nelson Mandela," from the musical, *Sarafina!* provides a connection to drama.

Assessing Student Progress

The tools that are available to measure the degree to which students meet the unit objectives are listed below.

Informal Assessment

The questions in the Guide for Responding sections are a first level of response to the concepts and skills presented with the selection. As a brief, informal measure of students' grasp of the material, these responses indicate where further instruction and practice are needed. The practice pages in the **Selection Support** booklet provide for this type of instruction and practice.

You will also find literature and reading guides in the **Alternative Assessment** booklet, which students can use for informal assessment of their individual performances.

Formal Assessment

The **Formal Assessment** booklet contains Selection Tests and Unit Tests.

Selection Tests measure comprehension and skills acquisition for each selection or group of selections.

Each Unit Test provides students with 30 multiple-choice questions and 5 essay questions designed to assess students' knowledge of the literature and skills taught in the unit.

Each Alternative Unit Test: Standardized-Test Practice provides 15 multiple-choice questions and 3 essay questions based on two new literature selections not contained in the student book. The questions on the Alternative Unit Test are designed to assess students' ability to compare and contrast selections, applying skills taught in the unit.

Alternative Assessment

For portfolio and alternative assessment, the **Alternative Assessment** booklet contains Scoring Rubrics, Assessment sheets, and Learning Modalities activities.

Scoring Rubrics provide writing modes that can be applied to Writing activities, Writing Mini-Lessons, and Writing Process Workshop lessons.

Assessment sheets for speaking and listening activities provide peer and self-assessment direction.

Learning Modalities activities appeal to different learning styles. Use these as an alternative measurement of students' growth.

Reading for Success

The Reading for Success page in each unit presents a set of problem-solving strategies to help readers understand authors' words and ideas on multiple levels. Good readers develop a bank of strategies from which they can draw as needed.

Unit 8 introduces strategies for reading drama. Drama is intended to be experienced as a performance, so reading a drama is fundamentally different from reading other literary forms. Students can benefit from strategies that will help them understand the combination of dialogue and action that make up a drama.

Strategies for reading drama can be applied to "A Christmas Carol" and "The Monsters Are Due on Maple Street." As students read, guide them to apply the strategies of envisioning the action and setting, predicting, questioning, and summarizing the drama. Notes provide support for applying these strategies throughout the selection.

How to Use the Reading for Success Page

- Introduce the strategies for reading drama, presenting each as a problem-solving procedure. Be sure students understand what each strategy involves and under what circumstances to apply it.
- Before students read the plays, have them preview them, looking at the annotations in the green boxes that model the strategies.
- To reinforce these reading strategies after students have read the plays, have them do pp. 210, 215, and 222 in **Selection Support**.

Reading Strategies: Support and Reinforcement

Using Boxed Annotations and Prompts

Throughout the unit, the notes in green, red, and maroon boxes are intended to help students apply reading strategies, understand the literary focus, and make a connection with their lives. You may use boxed material in these ways:

- Have students pause at each box and respond to its prompt before they continue reading.
- Urge students to read through the selection, ignoring the boxes. After they complete the selection, they may go back and review the text, responding to the prompts.

Reading for Success

Strategies for Reading Drama

Although drama shares many elements with stories, essays, and poetry, it is fundamentally different from these forms because it is designed to be performed for an audience. The story is told mostly through what the actors say (dialogue) and what they do (action). Stage directions in the script indicate when and how the actors should move and how they should deliver their lines. Most of the time, stage directions also include descriptions of sets, costumes, props, and sound and lighting effects. In screenplays (dramas written for film or television), the script may also include camera directions. When you read drama, keep in mind that it was written to be performed.

The following strategies will help you interact with the text of drama:

Envision the action and setting.

Reading a drama without envisioning the action and setting is like trying to watch your favorite television program with the picture turned off. To understand and appreciate drama, read the stage directions and use the details to turn on a mental picture.

- How do the actors move? What tone of voice do they use? What goes on between the characters?
- When and where do the events of the drama take place? What do the characters' surroundings look like?

Predict.

As you read, make predictions, or educated guesses, about what you think will happen. Look for hints in the dialogue and action that seem to suggest a certain outcome. As you read on, you will see if your predictions are correct.

Question.

Ask questions about what you read. Some questions that might come to mind as you read a drama may include:

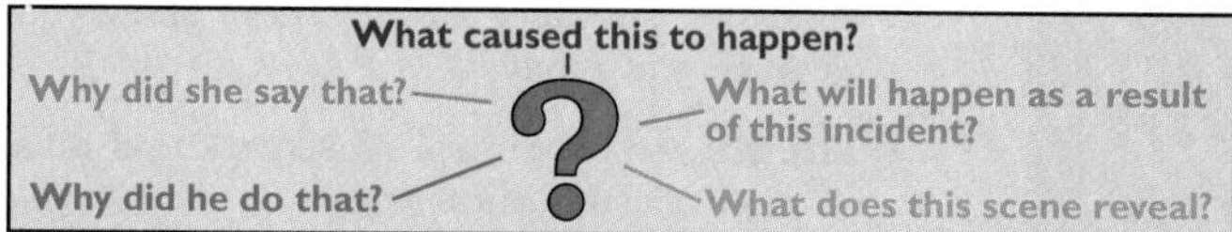
What caused this to happen?
Why did she say that?
What will happen as a result of this incident?
Why did he do that?
What does this scene reveal?

Summarize.

Dramas are often broken into acts or scenes. These natural breaks give you an opportunity to review the action and sum up what has happened.

When you read the selections in this unit, use these general strategies, as well as those specifically suggested with each drama. They will help you gain a better understanding and appreciation for the dramas.

Model a Reading Strategy: Envision the Action and Setting; Predict

Tell students that as they read drama, envisioning the action and setting will help them understand the story that is being told. The mental pictures they form can help them predict what will happen. Show students how to use strategies for reading drama by modeling this kind of thinking:

> As I read the descriptions of the time and place of the play, I begin to form a mental picture of where the action will take place. I know that the play is set in London at Christmastime, so it must be cold, and maybe it is snowy, as well. I'm not sure what the offices and other locations of the play look like, but I can watch for details when these places become the setting of the scenes that take place.
>
> As I read the stage directions for the first scene of the play, I think about ghostly music, the lighting, and the strange description of Jacob Marley. I predict that the play is more of a fantasy than a reality.

As they read, students might note their impressions of the play's scenes in their journals.

PART 1 *Classic Voices*

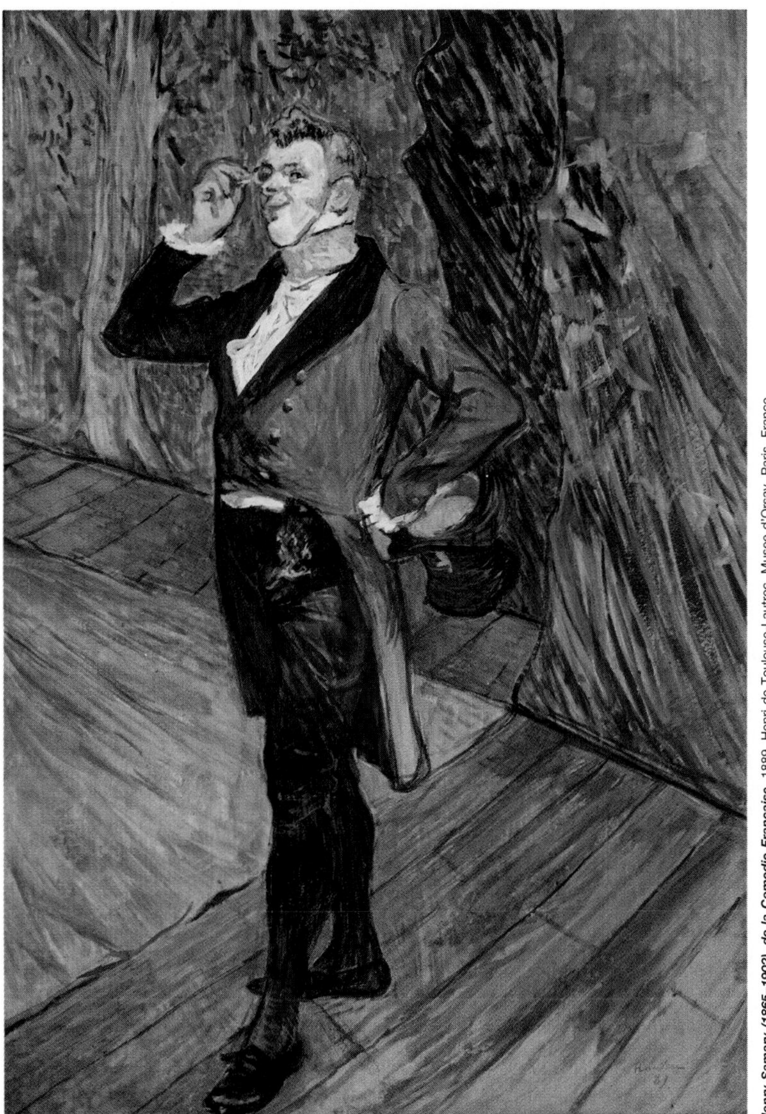

Henry Samary (1865–1902), de la Comedie Francaise, 1889, Henri de Toulouse-Lautrec, Musee d'Orsay, Paris, France

One-Minute Planning Guide

Charles Dickens's classic story *A Christmas Carol*, dramatized by Israel Horovitz and entitled *A Christmas Carol: Scrooge and Marley,* makes up this section of the Drama unit. Most students will be familiar with this timeless story, which has been adapted in many forms, including a Disney movie. Also included as a Connecting Literature to Social Studies feature is a section of the musical *Sarafina!* by Hugh Masekela.

Customize for
Varying Students Needs

When assigning the selections in this section, keep in mind the following factors:

"A Christmas Carol: Scrooge and Marley"

- A long, two-act drama (36 pp.) for which you will want to allow a week to two weeks of class time
- Provides an excellent opportunity to develop speaking and listening skills by having groups of students take turns acting out scenes.

from *Sarafina!*

- Short excerpt from Hugh Masekela's musical
- Provides an excellent opportunity for teaching students about musical dramas, and giving them background on Apartheid and the history of South Africa

Humanities: Art

Henry Samary (1865–1902), de la Comedie Francaise, 1889, by Henri de Toulouse-Lautrec

Henri de Toulouse-Lautrec (1864–1901) was a French painter and lithographer, famous for his paintings of the eccentric performers and people of the cabaret nightlife centered in the Montmartre section of Paris. Toulouse-Lautrec began painting as a child but did not devote himself fully to his art until he was thrown from a horse and left physically challenged. His legs never fully developed, and as an adult he stood at four feet tall. In 1882, he moved to Paris where he became friends with Vincent van Gogh. Bored with professional models, Toulouse-Lautrec began painting circus performers, dancers, and singers. Much of his work is characterized by a "snapshot" view of his subject; rather than paint a whole scene, he seemed to catch a glimpse of his subject in action.

Have students study the painting and then ask the following questions:

1. La Comedie Francaise is the oldest French state theater. Look at the title of this painting. Who do you think Henry Samary was? *Students should be able to deduce that Samary was an actor who was part of the company that performed at La Comedie Francaise.*
2. Look at the details of the man's surroundings. Where do you think the man in this painting is? *Students should notice the wood floor, which looks as if it may be a stage on which the man is standing.*

Prepare and Engage

OBJECTIVES

1. To read, comprehend, and interpret a play
2. To relate elements of drama to personal experience
3. To envision the action in a play
4. To learn about the elements of drama
5. To build vocabulary in context and learn the word root *-bene-*
6. To develop a mastery of subject and verb agreement
7. To respond to the play through writing and projects

SKILLS INSTRUCTION

Vocabulary:
Word Roots: *-bene-*

Spelling:
Words That End With *-stitute*

Grammar:
Subject and Verb Agreement

Reading Strategy:
Envision

Literary Focus:
Elements of Drama

Viewing and Representing:
Journey to the Past (Teacher Edition)

Critical Viewing:
Interpret; Infer; Speculate; Extend

PORTFOLIO OPPORTUNITIES

Writing: Invitation; Dramatic Scene
Project: Set Design

More About the Author
Recalling his childhood, **Charles Dickens** described himself as a lonely boy, as is the young Ebenezer Scrooge in *A Christmas Carol*. From an early age, Charles loved reading and was drawn to the theater. The young Charles performed at local inns, singing songs and reciting short stories by heart.

In 1836, with the publication of the first installment of *The Pickwick Papers,* Dickens married Catherine Hogarth, whose father was editor of the *Evening Chronicle*. The couple had ten children in fifteen years, but the marriage ended in a separation, scandalous for the time, in 1858.

In 1847 Dickens formed his own amateur theater company, which performed in public more than 60 times. He furthered his love for the stage by giving numerous public readings that were well received by critics. Dickens worked furiously until he suffered a stroke that led to his death in 1870. He was halfway through his last novel, *The Mystery of Edwin Drood.*

Guide for Reading

Meet the Author:
Charles Dickens (1812–1870)

The works of Charles Dickens were immensely popular during his lifetime and have remained so. His novels have been made into films, television movies, and even Broadway musicals!

A Difficult Childhood
Dickens spent most of his life in London. When Dickens was twelve, his father was sent to jail for not paying his debts. For several months, the burden of supporting the family fell on young Charles. He had to quit school and work in a factory for ten hours a day, six days a week.

When he was fifteen, Dickens went to work as a law clerk. Later, he became a reporter. In 1833, he began writing humorous pieces for newspapers and magazines under the pen name Boz.

The Turning Point The year 1836 was an eventful one for Dickens. His first book, *Sketches by Boz,* was published in February. Soon after, the first installment of his first novel, *The Pickwick Papers,* was published. Within a few months, *Pickwick,* which was published in twenty monthly installments, was all the rage, and Dickens had become England's most popular author.

The Story Behind the Story
Dickens loved Christmas and longed to see the Christmas spirit of kindness persist throughout the year. This was a driving force behind *A Christmas Carol* and is reflected in many of his other works. [For more on Dickens, see page 428.]

◆ Literature and Your Life

Connect Your Experience
You probably know people who are inconsiderate, self-centered, even cruel. Imagine that there were some way to teach these people a lesson that would lead them to change their behavior. In this play, a greedy, mean-spirited character is taught a lesson he'll never forget.

Thematic Focus: Personal Codes
As you read, take note of how this drama illustrates the importance of being fair and considerate.

◆ Background for Understanding

History
Like most of Dickens's works, *A Christmas Carol* is set in England during the 1800's. This period was characterized by rapid industrial growth and a booming economy. The wealthy lived in great luxury. For the poor and the working class, however, life was hard. Factory workers put in long hours and endured brutal working conditions for low wages. Dickens had great sympathy for the poor and working classes, and you'll find this sympathy reflected in *A Christmas Carol.*

◆ Build Vocabulary

Word Roots: *-bene-*
Scrooge, the main character in *A Christmas Carol,* is not known for his *benevolence.* This word is formed from the word roots *-bene-*, meaning "good," and *-volen-*, meaning "to wish." Thus, you might guess that *benevolence* means "wishing or wanting to do good," or "kindliness."

Word Bank
Which of the Word Bank words do you think means "living in poverty"? Check the Build Vocabulary boxes to find out.

implored
morose
destitute
misanthrope
void
ponderous
benevolence

Prentice Hall Literature Program Resources

REINFORCE / RETEACH / EXTEND

Selection Support Pages
Build Vocabulary: Word Roots: *-bene-*, p. 207
Build Spelling Skills, p. 208
Build Grammar Skills: Subject and Verb Agreement, p. 209
Reading Strategy: Envision, p. 210
Literary Focus: Elements of Drama, p. 211

Strategies for Diverse Student Needs, pp. 75–76

Beyond Literature Study Skills: Research, p. 38

Formal Assessment Selection Test, pp. 182–184, Assessment Resources Software

Alternative Assessment, p. 38

Writing and Language Transparencies Venn Diagram, p. 86

Resource Pro CD-ROM
A Christmas Carol

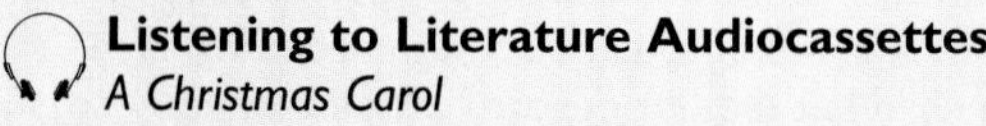

Listening to Literature Audiocassettes
A Christmas Carol

Looking at Literature Videodisc/Videotape *A Christmas Carol*

◆ A Christmas Carol, Act I ◆

◆ Literary Focus

Elements of Drama

As in a movie or television program, the characters in a play are developed entirely through *dialogue* (what the characters say) and actions. Dialogue is one of the two main **elements of drama.** The other main element of drama is *stage directions*. Stage directions, which are printed in italics and enclosed in square brackets, describe what the characters, costumes, and sets look like. They also give instructions about special effects and how the actors should move and speak.

◆ Reading Strategy

Envision

Reading a drama is quite different from seeing a performance on stage. However, you can use the details the playwright provides, along with your imagination, to **envision,** or picture in your mind, what a performance might be like. To help you do so, pay close attention to the stage directions. Look for details that describe how the characters and the setting look. You might use a chart like the one below to help you keep track of these details in each scene.

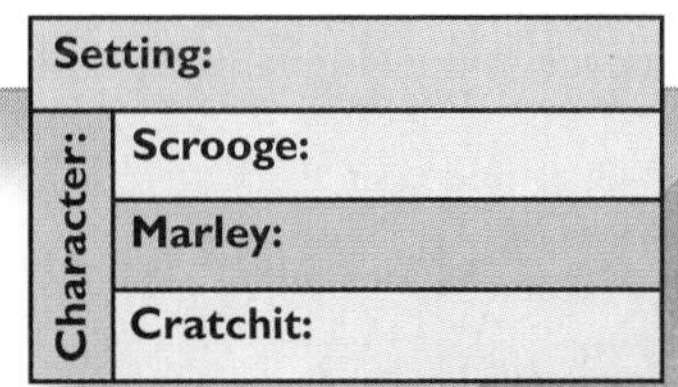

Setting:	
Character:	Scrooge:
	Marley:
	Cratchit:

Preparing for Standardized Tests

Grammar The grammar skill for this selection is subject and verb agreement. Remind students that a verb must agree with its subject in both person and number. Explain that students may be called on to apply this skill to items on a standardized test.

Write the sample test sentence on the board. Instruct students to identify which of the underlined words or phrases contains an error.

<u>In his famous story, *A Christmas Carol*,</u> <u>Charles Dickens teach an important lesson</u> about the need <u>to be compassionate and generous.</u>

(A) In his famous story, *A Christmas Carol,*
(B) Charles Dickens teach an important lesson
(C) to be compassionate and generous
(D) correct as is

Have students identify the subject and verb in each phrase. Then guide them to see that *(B)* is the correct response. The subject, *Charles Dickens,* is a singular noun that does not agree in number with the verb, *teach*, which is plural. For additional practice with subject-verb agreement, use **Selection Support,** p. 209.

Explain to students that in Act I of *A Christmas Carol,* a man revisits four key episodes from his past and learns something important from each event. Have students divide a sheet of paper into four panels. Then ask them to imagine that they are being escorted on a journey to four key scenes from their pasts. Instruct students to make a sketch of each scene or summarize it in words. Have them add a sentence for each panel, in which they tell what lesson can be learned from the scene. Have them compare the lessons that they learned with those learned by Scrooge in this play.

◆ Build Grammar Skills

Subject and Verb Agreement If you wish to introduce the grammar concept for this selection before students read, refer to the instruction on p. 661.

Customize for
Less Proficient Readers

Point out the complete list of characters on p. 644. Explain that the list includes the character of Ebenezer Scrooge at various times of his life. Have students keep their own lists of the play's major characters. Suggest that as students read, they write the names of new characters, adding brief descriptions and additional information, such as character traits, to help them keep track of the characters.

Customize for
More Advanced Students

As students read, have them take notes on contrasts presented in Act I of the play. Their notes may include atmospheric contrasts, such as light and shadows, or character-trait contrasts, such as greed and generosity. Remind them to include contrasts described in the stage directions and dialogue, as well as in the narration by the character of Jacob Marley. Then have students use their notes to create contrast charts of their own design.

Develop Understanding

One-Minute Insight In Act I of *A Christmas Carol,* we meet the stingy and mean-spirited Ebenezer Scrooge. It is the afternoon of Christmas Eve. While people around him cheerfully celebrate the season, Scrooge proclaims the holiday a "humbug." That night, Ebenezer is visited by the ghost of his business partner, Jacob Marley, who warns of the coming of three spirits, whose visits can save Scrooge from a terrible fate. As Marley predicts, the first of the spirits arrives to escort Scrooge on a journey to his past. Scrooge's hard heart begins to soften as he sees himself as a lonely young boy and then as a young man at a turning point in his life. At the end of Act I, Ebenezer Scrooge has returned to his bed, where he will soon be visited by the second spirit.

◆Critical Thinking

1 Infer Direct students' attention to the list of characters. Ask students what they can infer about the time periods covered in the play from the list of characters. *The various Scrooge characters, from "Little Boy Scrooge" to "A Corpse, very like Scrooge," indicate that the play covers several decades in Scrooge's life.*

Customize for
English Language Learners
As students read the play, they may encounter unfamiliar words and expressions, as well as challenging long sentences. To help language learners overcome these challenges, read the play aloud as a class, with students taking turns playing the various parts. Pause often to paraphrase and discuss various passages. For example, paraphrase "Ebenezer Scrooge, not yet dead, which is to say still alive" as "Ebenezer Scrooge, whose life is so dreary, he might as well be dead."

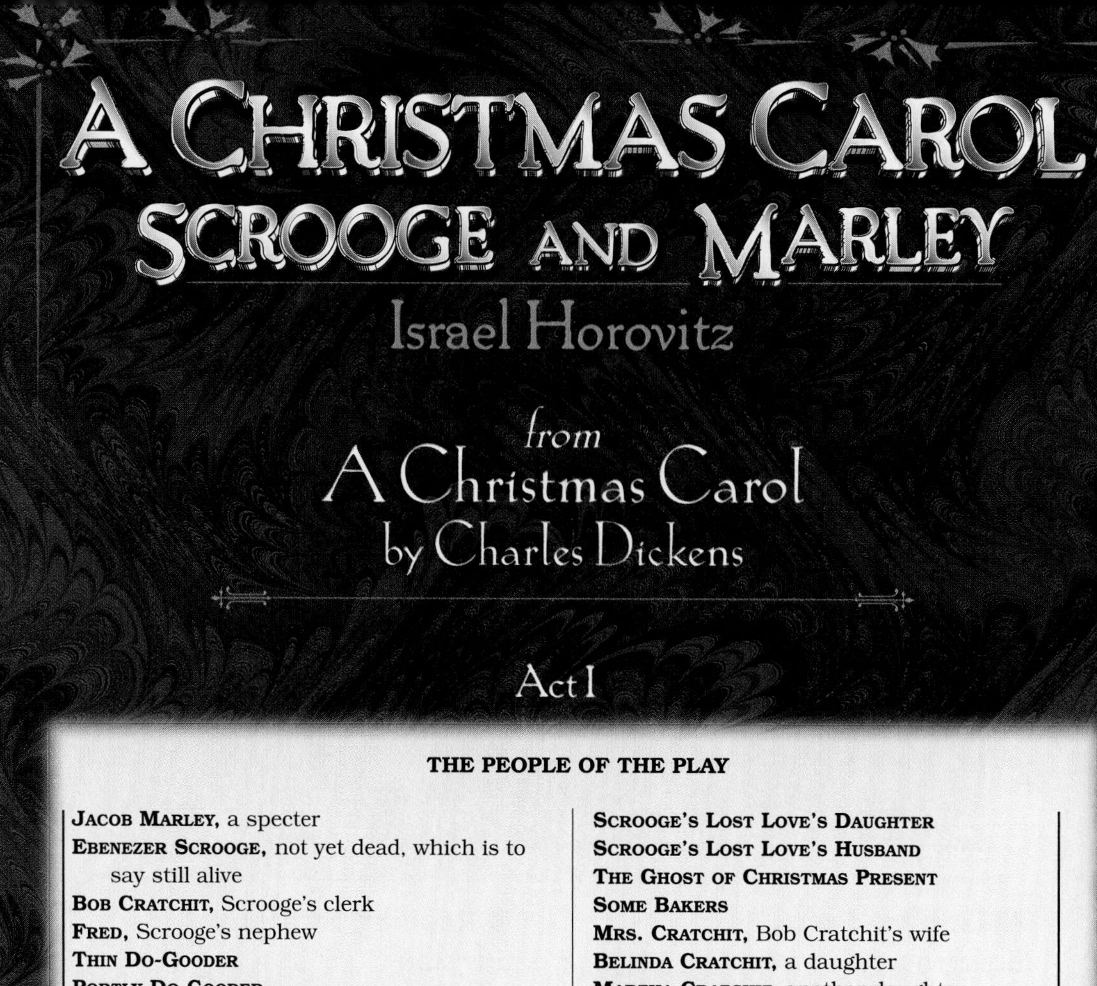

A Christmas Carol: Scrooge and Marley

Israel Horovitz

from
A Christmas Carol
by Charles Dickens

Act I

THE PEOPLE OF THE PLAY

Jacob Marley, a specter
Ebenezer Scrooge, not yet dead, which is to say still alive
Bob Cratchit, Scrooge's clerk
Fred, Scrooge's nephew
Thin Do-Gooder
Portly Do-Gooder
Specters (Various), carrying money-boxes
The Ghost of Christmas Past
Four Jocund Travelers
A Band of Singers
1 **A Band of Dancers**
Little Boy Scrooge
Young Man Scrooge
Fan, Scrooge's little sister
The Schoolmaster
Schoolmates
Fezziwig, a fine and fair employer
Dick, young Scrooge's co-worker
Young Scrooge
A Fiddler
More Dancers
Scrooge's Lost Love
Scrooge's Lost Love's Daughter
Scrooge's Lost Love's Husband
The Ghost of Christmas Present
Some Bakers
Mrs. Cratchit, Bob Cratchit's wife
Belinda Cratchit, a daughter
Martha Cratchit, another daughter
Peter Cratchit, a son
Tiny Tim Cratchit, another son
Scrooge's Niece, Fred's wife
The Ghost of Christmas Future, a mute Phantom 1
Three Men of Business
Drunks, Scoundrels, Women of the Streets
A Charwoman
Mrs. Dilber
Joe, an old second-hand goods dealer
A Corpse, very like Scrooge
An Indebted Family
Adam, a young boy
A Poulterer
A Gentlewoman
Some More Men of Business

Block Scheduling Strategies

Consider these suggestions to take advantage of extended class time:

- Review the Reading Strategy with students before they read Act I. Then instruct students to fill in the chart on p. 643 as they read. Have groups of students compare and discuss their charts and use the information in them to answer the Reading Strategy questions on p. 661.
- Introduce the grammar concept, subject and verb agreement, before students read Act I. After students read this portion of the play, have them work in groups to complete the Build Grammar Skills practice and writing application on p. 661. For additional practice, have students use **Selection Support,** p. 209.
- After students read Act I independently, have them form groups to discuss responses to Reader's Response and Thematic Focus. Then hold a class discussion in which students answer the Critical Thinking questions. Finally, encourage students to reflect on their answers, and then begin work on one of the Idea Bank suggestions on p. 661.

THE PLACE OF THE PLAY
Various locations in and around the City of London, including Scrooge's Chambers and Offices; the Cratchit Home; Fred's Home; Scrooge's School; Fezziwig's Offices; Old Joe's Hide-a-Way.

THE TIME OF THE PLAY
The entire action of the play takes place on Christmas Eve, Christmas Day, and the morning after Christmas, 1843.

Scene 1

2 [*Ghostly music in auditorium. A single spotlight on* JACOB MARLEY, D.C. *He is ancient; awful, dead-eyed. He speaks straight out to auditorium.*]

MARLEY. [*Cackle-voiced*] My name is Jacob Marley and I am dead. [*He laughs.*] Oh, no, there's no doubt that I am dead. The register of my burial was signed by the clergyman, the clerk, the undertaker . . . and by my chief mourner . . . Ebenezer Scrooge . . . [*Pause; remembers*] I am dead as a doornail.

[*A spotlight fades up, Stage Right, on* SCROOGE, *in his counting-house,*[1] *counting. Lettering on the window behind* SCROOGE *reads:* "SCROOGE AND MARLEY, LTD." *The spotlight is tight on* SCROOGE*'s head and shoulders. We shall not yet see into the offices and setting. Ghostly music continues, under.* MARLEY *looks across at* SCROOGE*; pitifully. After a moment's pause*]

I present him to you: Ebenezer Scrooge . . . England's most tightfisted hand at the grindstone, Scrooge! a squeezing, wrenching, grasping, scraping, clutching, covetous, old sinner! secret, and self-contained, and solitary as an oyster. The cold within him freezes his old features, nips his pointed nose, shrivels his cheek, stiffens his gait; makes his eyes red, his thin lips blue; and speaks out shrewdly in his grating voice. Look at him. Look at him . . .

▲ **Critical Viewing** Marley is the first character to appear on stage. What mood would the lighting shown above create for an audience? **[Interpret]** 3

[SCROOGE *counts and mumbles.*]

SCROOGE. They owe me money and I will collect. I will have them jailed, if I have to. They owe me money and I will collect what is due me.

[MARLEY *moves towards* SCROOGE*; two steps. The spotlight stays with him.*]

MARLEY. [*Disgusted*] He and I were partners for I don't know how many years. Scrooge was my sole executor, my sole administrator, my sole assign, my sole residuary legatee,[2] my sole friend and my sole mourner. But Scrooge was

1. **counting house:** Office for keeping financial records and writing business letters.

2. **my sole executor** (ig zek´ yə tər), **my sole administrator, my sole assign** (ə sin´), **my sole residuary legatee** (ri zij´ ōō wer´ ē leg´ ə tē´): Legal terms giving one person responsibility to carry out the wishes of another who has died.

Clarification

❷ Explain that D.C. stands for "downstage center," which refers to the center of the front of the stage, the area closest to the audience. Point out that letters such as these in stage directions tell directors where to position the actors. The letters U.R., for example, mean "upstage right," or the right corner of the rear of the stage. The directions *left* and *right* are oriented from the point of view of the actors and are therefore the opposite of the audience's viewpoint. Draw a diagram like the one shown. Then have students point out where Marley will stand according to the stage directions in this passage.

THE STAGE

Wings (offstage) — Wings (offstage)

Upstage Right	Upstage Center	Upstage Left
Right	Center	Left
Downstage Right	Downstage Center	Downstage Left

Curtain
Apron
Audience

▶Critical Viewing◀

❸ **Interpret** Point out to students that Marley is being lighted from below and the light is red. *Students may say that the lighting probably indicates that Marley's ghost is suffering. It creates a ghostly, foreboding mood.*

Looking at Literature Videodisc/Videotape

To provide motivation for students to read *A Christmas Carol: Scrooge and Marley*, play Chapter 8 of the videodisc. This segment provides an overview of celebrations from a variety of cultures. Have students discuss what the celebrations have in common.

Chapter 8

Humanities: Performing Arts

Playwright **Israel Horovitz** was born in Wakefield, Massachusetts. As a boy, he hated to read books by Charles Dickens but later changed his mind. *A Christmas Carol: Scrooge and Marley* was first performed in Baltimore, in 1978. Horovitz says that his favorite character in the play is Scrooge, who reminds him of his father. Like Dickens, Horovitz is known for his keen ear for dialogue, his social conscience, and the humor in his writing.

Use these questions for discussion:

1. Why do you think the playwright titled his adaptation *A Christmas Carol: Scrooge and Marley?* *Students may speculate that he used this title to distinguish it from the novel, and because Scrooge is the main character and Marley the narrator in the play.*
2. What aspects of Dickens's story might motivate a playwright to adapt it for the theatre? *Students may feel that the characters are colorful, the appearances of a ghost and the spirits make for visually exciting scenes, and Scrooge's transformation might seem all the more touching when viewed onstage.*

◆Literary Focus

❶ **Elements of Drama** Possible responses: Scrooge was not friends with his business partner Marley, and treated his death as another business transaction. Scrooge is cheap and unfeeling, and it appears that most people know him and avoid him.

◆Critical Thinking

❷ **Evaluate** Explain to students that Marley's speaking directly to the audience is known as an *aside*. Through asides, characters in a play reveal directly to the audience their thoughts or other characters' thoughts. A character usually delivers an aside to the audience in confidence, pretending that the other characters cannot hear. Ask students to evaluate the effectiveness of asides such as this. *Possible response: Asides like this one involve the audience in the drama and allow the playwright to give information without having to include extra dialogue.*

◆Literary Focus

❸ **Elements of Drama** Explain that N.B. is an abbreviation of *nota bene*, a Latin term meaning "note well" that is used to call attention to something important. Ask students what a flash-pot might be and why the playwright suggests that Marley's appearances and exits sometimes be accompanied by the explosions of one. *Students may say that a flash-pot is a device that creates a burst of fire and smoke that creates a magical effect. The playwright probably wants to use the effect to get the audience's attention and emphasize Marley's importance in the play.*

◆Reading Strategy

❹ **Envision** Details in the stage directions such as *dismal tank of a cubicle* help the reader picture a cold, half-dark, dreary office.

◆ Literary Focus What key background information is provided in this dialogue? (1)

not so cut up by the sad event of my death, but that he was an excellent man of business on the very day of my funeral, and solemnized[3] it with an undoubted bargain. [*Pauses again in disgust*] He never painted out my name from the window. There it stands, on the window and above the warehouse door: Scrooge and Marley. Sometimes people new to our business call him Scrooge and sometimes they call him Marley. He answers to both names. It's all the same to him. And it's cheaper than painting in a new sign, isn't it? [*Pauses; moves closer to* SCROOGE] Nobody has ever stopped him in the street to say, with gladsome looks, "My dear Scrooge, how are you? When will you come to see me?" No beggars implored him to bestow a trifle, no children ever ask him what it is o'clock, no man or woman now, or ever in his life, not once, inquire the way to such and such a place. [MARLEY *stands next to* SCROOGE *now. They share, so it seems, a spotlight.*] But what does Scrooge care of any of this? It is the very thing he likes! To edge his way along the crowded paths of life, warning all human sympathy to keep its distance.

[*A ghostly bell rings in the distance.* MARLEY *moves away from* SCROOGE, *now, heading* D. *again. As he does, he "takes" the light:* SCROOGE *has disappeared into the black void beyond.* MARLEY *walks* D.C., *talking directly to the audience. Pauses*]

(2) The bell tolls and I must take my leave. You must stay a while with Scrooge and watch him play out his scroogey life. It is now the story: the once-upon-a-time. Scrooge is busy in his counting-house. Where else? Christmas eve and Scrooge is busy in his counting-house. It is cold, bleak, biting weather outside: foggy withal: and, if you listen closely, you can hear the people in the court go wheezing up and down, beating their hands upon their breasts, and stamping their feet upon the pavement stones to warm them . . .

[*The clocks outside strike three.*]

Only three! and quite dark outside already: it has not been light all day this day.

[*This ghostly bell rings in the distance again.* MARLEY *looks about him. Music in.* MARLEY *flies away.*]

[N.B. *Marley's comings and goings should, from time to time, induce the explosion of the odd flash-pot.* I.H.] (3)

Scene 2

[*Christmas music in, sung by a live chorus, full. At conclusion of song, sound fades under and into the distance. Lights up in set: offices of Scrooge and Marley, Ltd.* SCROOGE *sits at his desk, at work. Near him is a tiny fire. His door is open and in his line of vision, we see* SCROOGE'S *clerk,* BOB CRATCHIT, *who sits in a dismal tank of a cubicle, copying letters. Near* CRATCHIT *is a fire so tiny as to barely cast a light: perhaps it is one pitifully glowing coal?* CRATCHIT *rubs his hands together, puts on a white comforter[4] and tries to heat his hands around his candle.* SCROOGE'S NEPHEW *enters, unseen.*]

◆ Reading Strategy How do the stage directions help you envision Scrooge's office? (4)

SCROOGE. What are you doing, Cratchit? Acting cold, are you? Next, you'll be asking to replenish your coal from my coal-box, won't you? Well, save your breath, Cratchit! Unless you're prepared to find employ elsewhere!

NEPHEW. [*Cheerfully; surprising* SCROOGE] A merry Christmas to you, Uncle! God save you!

SCROOGE. Bah! Humbug![5]

NEPHEW. Christmas a "humbug," Uncle? I'm sure you don't mean that.

SCROOGE. I do! Merry Christmas? What right do you have to be merry? What reason have you to be merry? You're poor enough!

NEPHEW. Come, then. What right have you

3. **solemnized** (säl′ əm nīzd′) *v.*: Honored or remembered. Marley is being ironic.

4. **comforter** (kum′ fər tər) *n.*: Long, woolen scarf.
5. **Humbug** (hum′ bug′) *interj.*: Nonsense!

to be dismal? What reason have you to be morose? You're rich enough.

SCROOGE. Bah! Humbug!

NEPHEW. Don't be cross, Uncle.

SCROOGE. What else can I be? Eh? When I live
in a world of fools such as this? Merry Christmas? What's Christmastime to you but a time
of paying bills without any money; a time for
5 finding yourself a year older, but not an hour
richer. If I could work my will, every idiot who
goes about with "Merry Christmas" on his lips,
should be boiled with his own pudding, and
buried with a stake of holly through his heart.
He should!

NEPHEW. Uncle!

SCROOGE. Nephew! You keep Christmas in your own way and let me keep it in mine.

NEPHEW. Keep it! But you don't keep it, Uncle.

SCROOGE. Let me leave it alone, then. Much good it has ever done you!

NEPHEW. There are many things from which I have derived good, by which I have not profited, I daresay. Christmas among the rest. But I am
sure that I always thought of Christmas time,
when it has come round—as a good time: the
only time I know of, when men and women
seem to open their shut-up hearts freely, and
to think of people below them as if they really
were fellow-passengers to the grave, and not 7
another race of creatures bound on other
journeys. And therefore, Uncle, though it has
never put a scrap of gold or silver in my
pocket, I believe that it *has* done me good, and
that it *will* do me good; and I say, God bless it!

[*The* CLERK *in the tank applauds, looks at the furious* SCROOGE *and pokes out his tiny fire, as if in exchange for the moment of impropriety.* SCROOGE *yells at him.*]

▲ **Critical Viewing** Bob Cratchit heats his hands
over a small flame in his office. What does this 6
action communicate to the audience about the
setting? **[Infer]**

◆ Build Vocabulary

implored (im plôrd′) *v.*: Asked or begged earnestly

morose (mə rōs′) *adj.*: Gloomy; ill-tempered

◆Critical Thinking

5 Defend Have students imagine that they are taking part in a debate in which they must defend Scrooge's point of view. Ask students what they might say in support of Scrooge's view of Christmas. *Possible responses: Christmas is often a time of artificial cheerfulness; to pretend to be happy when you are poor is hypocritical. People might well be angry that others have more than they have.*

▶Critical Viewing◀

6 Infer This action shows the audience that Cratchit's cubicle is so cold, thanks to Scrooge's stinginess, that Cratchit is forced to warm his hands over the candle's flame.

◆Critical Thinking

7 Evaluate Have students paraphrase the nephew's argument in favor of Christmas and evaluate its effectiveness. *Scrooge's nephew is saying that Christmas is a time to profit mainly in spiritual and emotional ways rather than in material ways. It is a time to be kinder to others and to erase boundaries that separate people. Students may say that the nephew argues powerfully and eloquently in favor of Christmas, although the argument is lost on his coldhearted uncle.*

Cross-Curricular Connection: Science

Lighting and Heating At the time that Charles Dickens wrote *A Christmas Carol,* either natural gas or gas produced from coal or wood was used for lighting by those who could afford it, and coal was the fuel most often used for heating in cities. The use of candles was still quite common during this period, although kerosene and oil lamps provided brighter lighting.

Gas lighting was available for streetlights by the end of the 18th century, and it was used to illuminate entire streets by 1812 in London and 1817 in Baltimore. Gas lights in homes were a privilege of the wealthy until the late 19th century, when even tenement buildings had gas ducts for lighting and heating.

Electric lighting, provided by arc lamps with carbon electrodes, was in limited use in London and Paris throughout the 19th century, but the electrodes smoked and burned out quickly. It wasn't until the invention of the filament lamp by Thomas Edison in 1879 that electrical lighting on a large scale became possible.

Have students compare 19th-century methods of lighting and heating homes and offices with today's methods. Suggest that students conduct research to find out more about the use of gas for lighting and coal as a source of energy. Some students may want to compare the use of coal in Charles Dickens's time to its uses in modern times. Others may want to investigate the effects of the introduction of electrical energy on people in England and around the world.

Comprehension Check ☑

❶ Have students use a dictionary to explore the meanings of *resolute* and *homage*. Then ask students to paraphrase what Scrooge's nephew is saying in this passage. *The nephew is saying that he is sorry to see Scrooge being so stubborn but that he refuses to let Scrooge's attitude upset him.*

◆Critical Thinking

❷ **Infer** What can you infer about the nephew's character based on this passage? In what ways is the nephew's character similar to that of Bob Cratchit? *Students may say that the nephew is a man of honor and discipline. Even when he is bullied and insulted by his uncle, he stays calm and charitable. Both the nephew and Cratchit seem kind and generous. Both tolerate Scrooge's mistreatment without anger.*

◆Literary Focus

❸ **Elements of Drama** What is humorous about this line of dialogue? *The humor is in the difference between what the portly man expects or hopes for and what the audience knows. Unaware that he is facing one of the most uncharitable of people, the portly man tries to flatter Scrooge in order to influence him to give money to charity.*

◆Literature and Your Life

❹ The portly man is trying to appeal to Scrooge's sympathies for the poor. He tells Scrooge that thousands are lacking "common necessities," while many more do not have "common comforts." Discuss with students the difference between a common necessity and a common comfort. Have students suggest examples of each. Write these on the board. *Students may say that food, shelter, and clothing are necessities and that a CD player, television, and eating in restaurants are comforts.*

SCROOGE. [*To the* CLERK] Let me hear another sound from you and you'll keep your Christmas by losing your situation. [*To the* NEPHEW] You're quite a powerful speaker, sir. I wonder you don't go into Parliament.[6]

NEPHEW. Don't be angry, Uncle. Come! Dine with us tomorrow.

SCROOGE. I'd rather see myself dead than see myself with your family!

NEPHEW. But, why? Why?

SCROOGE. Why did you get married?

NEPHEW. Because I fell in love.

SCROOGE. That, sir, is the only thing that you have said to me in your entire lifetime which is even more ridiculous than "Merry Christmas"! [*Turns from* NEPHEW] Good afternoon.

NEPHEW. Nay, Uncle, you never came to see me before I married either. Why give it as a reason for not coming now?

SCROOGE. Good afternoon, Nephew!

NEPHEW. I want nothing from you; I ask nothing of you; why cannot we be friends?

SCROOGE. Good afternoon!

① **NEPHEW.** I am sorry with all my heart, to find you so resolute. But I have made the trial in homage to Christmas, and I'll keep my Christmas humor to the last. So A Merry Christmas, Uncle!

SCROOGE. Good afternoon!

NEPHEW. And A Happy New Year!

SCROOGE. Good afternoon!

② **NEPHEW.** [*He stands facing* SCROOGE.] Uncle, you are the most . . . [*Pauses*] No, I shan't. My Christmas humor is intact . . . [*Pause*] God bless you, Uncle . . . [NEPHEW *turns and starts for the door; he stops at* CRATCHIT'S *cage.*] Merry Christmas, Bob Cratchit . . .

CRATCHIT. Merry Christmas to you sir, and a very, very happy New Year . . .

SCROOGE. [*Calling across to them*] Oh, fine, a perfection, just fine . . . to see the perfect pair of you: husbands, with wives and children to support . . . my clerk there earning fifteen shillings a week . . . and the perfect pair of you, talking about a Merry Christmas! [*Pauses*] I'll retire to Bedlam![7]

NEPHEW. [*To* CRATCHIT] He's impossible!

CRATCHIT. Oh, mind him not, sir. He's getting on in years, and he's alone. He's noticed your visit. I'll wager your visit has warmed him.

NEPHEW. Him? Uncle Ebenezer Scrooge? *Warmed?* You are a better Christian than I am, sir.

CRATCHIT. [*Opening the door for* NEPHEW; *two* DO-GOODERS *will enter, as* NEPHEW *exits*] Good day to you, sir, and God bless.

NEPHEW. God bless . . . [*One man who enters is portly, the other is thin. Both are pleasant.*]

CRATCHIT. Can I help you, gentlemen?

THIN MAN. [*Carrying papers and books; looks around* CRATCHIT *to* SCROOGE] Scrooge and Marley's, I believe. Have I the pleasure of addressing Mr. Scrooge, or Mr. Marley?

SCROOGE. Mr. Marley has been dead these seven years. He died seven years ago this very night.

PORTLY MAN. We have no doubt his liberality[8] is well represented by his surviving partner . . . [*Offers his calling card*]

SCROOGE. [*Handing back the card; unlooked at*] . . . Good afternoon.

THIN MAN. This will take but a moment, sir . . .

PORTLY MAN. At this festive season of the year, Mr. Scrooge, it is more than usually desirable that we should make some slight provision for the poor and destitute, who suffer greatly at the present time. Many thousands are in want of common necessities; hundreds of thousands are in want of common comforts, sir.

SCROOGE. Are there no prisons?

PORTLY MAN. Plenty of prisons. 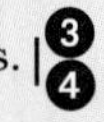

6. **Parliament** (pär′ lə mənt): National legislative body of Great Britain, in some ways like the American Congress.

7. **Bedlam** (bed′ ləm): Hospital in London for the mentally ill.

8. **liberality** (lib′ ər al′ i tē): Generosity.

SCROOGE. And aren't the Union workhouses still in operation?

THIN MAN. They are. Still. I wish that I could say that they are not.

SCROOGE. The Treadmill[9] and the Poor Law[10] are in full vigor, then?

THIN MAN. Both very busy, sir.

SCROOGE. Ohhh, I see. I was afraid, from what you said at first, that something had occurred to stop them from their useful course. [*Pauses*] I'm glad to hear it.

PORTLY MAN. Under the impression that they scarcely furnish Christian cheer of mind or body to the multitude, a few of us are endeavoring to raise a fund to buy the Poor some
5 meat and drink, and means of warmth. We choose this time, because it is a time, of all others, when Want is keenly felt, and Abundance rejoices. [*Pen in hand; as well as notepad*] What shall I put you down for, sir?

SCROOGE. Nothing!

PORTLY MAN. You wish to be left anonymous?

SCROOGE. I wish to be left alone! [*Pauses; turns away; turns back to them*] Since you ask me
6 what I wish, gentlemen, that is my answer. I help to support the establishments that I have mentioned: they cost enough: and those who are badly off must go there.

THIN MAN. Many can't go there; and many would rather die.

SCROOGE. If they would rather die, they had better do it, and decrease the surplus population. Besides—excuse me—I don't know that.

THIN MAN. But you might know it!

SCROOGE. It's not my business. It's enough for a man to understand his own business, and not to interfere with other people's. Mine occupies me constantly. Good afternoon, gentlemen! [SCROOGE *turns his back on the gentlemen and returns to his desk.*]

PORTLY MAN. But, sir, Mr. Scrooge . . . think of the poor.

SCROOGE. [*Turns suddenly to them. Pauses*] Take your leave of my offices, sirs, while I am still smiling.

> ◆ **Reading Strategy**
> How would you expect these visitors
> to react to Scrooge's 7
> comments? What expressions might they show?

[*The* THIN MAN *looks at the* PORTLY MAN. *They are undone. They shrug. They move to the door.* CRATCHIT *hops up to open it for them.*]

THIN MAN. Good day, sir . . . [*To* CRATCHIT] A merry Christmas to you, sir . . .

CRATCHIT. Yes. A Merry Christmas to both of you . . .

PORTLY MAN. Merry Christmas . . .

[CRATCHIT *silently squeezes something into the hand of the* THIN MAN.]

THIN MAN. What's this?

CRATCHIT. Shhhh . . . 8

[CRATCHIT *opens the door; wind and snow whistle into the room.*]

THIN MAN. Thank you, sir, thank you.

[CRATCHIT *closes the door and returns to his workplace.* SCROOGE *is at his own counting table. He talks to* CRATCHIT *without looking up.*]

SCROOGE. It's less of a time of year for being merry, and more a time of year for being loony . . . if you ask me.

CRATCHIT. Well, I don't know, sir . . .

[*The clock's bell strikes six o'clock.*]

Well, there it is, eh, six?

SCROOGE. Saved by six bells, are you?

---

9. **the Treadmill** (tred′ mil′): Kind of mill wheel turned by the weight of persons treading steps arranged around it; this device was used to punish prisoners in jails.

10. **the Poor Law:** The original 17th-century Poor Laws called for overseers of the poor in each parish to provide relief for the needy. The New Poor Law of 1834 made the workhouses in which the poor sometimes lived and worked extremely harsh and unattractive. They became a symbol of the misery of the poor.

◆ **Build Vocabulary**

destitute (des′ tə to͞ot′) *adj. used as n.*: People living in complete poverty

Comprehension Check ☑

❺ What reason does the portly man give for choosing this time of year to seek money for the poor? *The Christmas season is a time of year when the poor might feel especially disadvantaged because others are celebrating their blessings.*

◆Critical Thinking

❻ **Interpret** Ask students to describe how Scrooge supports the poor. *He pays taxes that support the debtors' prisons and workhouses.*

◆Reading Strategy

❼ **Envision** Invite students to use facial expressions to show how the men might react to Scrooge's lack of compassion. *Students may say that the men might show bewildered, surprised, or shocked expressions.*

◆Critical Thinking

❽ **Infer** What does Cratchit squeeze into the hand of the thin man? How do you know? Have students tell what this action reveals about Cratchit's character. *He gives the man money for the poor. This is apparent because Cratchit doesn't want Scrooge to see the donation, and the man thanks him twice. This shows that Cratchit is generous and feels a responsibility toward others, even though he cannot afford to give money to the poor.*

Customize for
Verbal/Linguistic Learners
Assign to five students the roles of Scrooge, Cratchit, the nephew, and the two men seeking money for charity. Have the students conduct a dramatic reading of the dialogue on pp. 648–649. Suggest that students use facial expressions and voice tone to enhance the dialogue.

Cross-Curricular Connection: Social Studies

Debtors' Prison When Charles Dickens was twelve, his father's debts had become so severe that the father was taken to the Marshalsea, a debtors' prison in London. The rest of the family, except for Charles, joined John Dickens in the prison. Six months later, the family was able to leave the prison when Charles's father received an inheritance and was able to pay off his debts. This episode made a profound impression on the young Dickens. It gave him insight into the degradation of poverty, and incentive to pursue his literary career with energy.

Have students conduct research to find out more about debtors' prisons such as the Marshalsea. Suggest that they make notes about daily life in the prisons. Other students may want to learn more about the Poor Law and workhouses in Victorian England. Invite students to give oral presentations on the information they learn from their research.

▶Critical Viewing◀

❶ **Speculate** Students may say that the actor playing Cratchit seems frightened and that he might speak in a small, timid voice to convey his fear of Scrooge. The actor playing Scrooge seems very angry and is likely to use a loud, sharp tone of voice to convey his displeasure with Cratchit.

Comprehension Check 

❷ What agreement does Cratchit make with Scrooge in order to have Christmas Day off? *He agrees to come to work earlier than usual on the day after Christmas.*

◆Literary Focus

❸ **Elements of Drama** The dialogue shows how insensitive Scrooge is to Cratchit's desire to celebrate the holiday with his family. The rest of the dialogue between Scrooge and Cratchit shows how intolerant Scrooge is, even when people try to wish him well.

◆Critical Thinking

❹ **Analyze Causes and Effects** Ask students why Scrooge whacks at the image of the boy at his window. *The boy is singing a Christmas carol, which angers Scrooge, since he believes that Christmas is a "humbug."*

Customize for
Bodily/Kinesthetic Learners
Have students reread the description of Scrooge's walk to his rooms from his offices. Then invite volunteers to pantomime the action. Have one student play the role of Scrooge and six or more students play the roles of passersby, including the boys that Scrooge snaps at.

❶ ▲ **Critical Viewing** What emotion does each actor express in this photograph? Describe the tone of voice that the actors might use to convey this emotion. **[Speculate]**

CRATCHIT. I must be going home . . . [*He snuffs out his candle and puts on his hat.*] I hope you have a . . . very very lovely day tomorrow, sir . . .

SCROOGE. Hmmm. Oh, you'll be wanting the whole day tomorrow, I suppose?

CRATCHIT. If quite convenient, sir.

SCROOGE. It's not convenient, and it's not fair. If I was to stop half-a-crown for it, you'd think yourself ill-used, I'll be bound?

[CRATCHIT *smiles faintly.*]

CRATCHIT. I don't know, sir . . .

SCROOGE. And yet, you don't think me ill-used when I pay a day's wages for no work . . .

CRATCHIT. It's only but once a year . . .

SCROOGE. A poor excuse for picking a man's pocket every 25th of December! But I suppose you must have the whole day. Be here all the earlier the next morning! ❷

CRATCHIT. Oh, I will, sir. I will. I promise you. And, sir . . .

SCROOGE. Don't say it, Cratchit.

CRATCHIT. But let me wish you a . . .

SCROOGE. Don't say it, Cratchit. I warn you . . .

CRATCHIT. Sir!

SCROOGE. Cratchit!

[CRATCHIT *opens the door.*]

CRATCHIT. All right, then, sir . . . well . . . [*Suddenly*] Merry Christmas, Mr. Scrooge!

> **◆ Literary Focus** How does this dialogue help reveal Scrooge's personality? ❸

[*And he runs out the door, shutting same behind him.* SCROOGE *moves to his desk; gathering his coat, hat, etc. A* BOY *appears at his window. . . .*]

BOY. [*Singing*] "Away in a manger . . ."

[SCROOGE *seizes his ruler and whacks at the image of the* BOY *outside. The* BOY *leaves.*] ❹

SCROOGE. Bah! Humbug! Christmas! Bah! Humbug! [*He shuts out the light.*]

A note on the crossover, following Scene 2:

[SCROOGE *will walk alone to his rooms from his offices. As he makes a long slow cross of the stage, the scenery should change. Christmas music will be heard, various people will cross by* SCROOGE, *often smiling happily.*

There will be occasional pleasant greetings tossed at him.

SCROOGE, *in contrast to all, will grump and mumble. He will snap at passing boys, as might a horrid old hound.*

In short, SCROOGE'S *sounds and movements will define him in contrast from all other people who cross the stage: he is the* misanthrope, *the malcontent, the miser. He is* SCROOGE.

This statement of SCROOGE'S *character, by contrast to all other characters, should seem comical to the audience.*

Humanities: Performing Arts

Props Direct students' attention to the photograph on this page. Point out that props, or properties, are an important part of a stage production. They provide additional information for an audience and help establish the theme, period, and mood of a play. Every item on the stage, except for the scenery, is either a *set prop* or a *hand prop*. Furniture and pictures are examples of set props. A sheet of paper or food items are examples of hand props. Items such as eyeglasses or pipes are sometimes called *personal props*.

1. Have students describe the props visible in the photograph. *The photograph shows a desk, a burning candle, a pot that appears to be an inkwell, a metal money box, two ledger sheets, a quill pen, and eyeglasses on both men.*
2. How do these props add to the understanding of the play? *They show that the scene takes place in an office in which ledgers are kept. The candle and the quill pen indicate that the time period of the play is many years ago. The buildup of wax around the candle shows that the workday is near an end.*

During SCROOGE'S *crossover to his rooms, snow should begin to fall. All passers-by will hold their faces to the sky, smiling, allowing snow to shower them lightly.* SCROOGE, *by contrast, will bat at the flakes with his walking-*
5 *stick, as might an insomniac swat at a sleep-stopping, middle-of-the-night swarm of mosquitoes. He will comment on the blackness of the night, and, finally, reach his rooms and his encounter with the magical specter:*[11] MARLEY, *his eternal mate.*]

Scene 3

SCROOGE. No light at all . . . no moon . . . *that* is what is at the center of a Christmas Eve: dead black: void . . .

[SCROOGE *puts his key in the door's keyhole. He has reached his rooms now. The door knocker changes and is now* MARLEY'S *face. A musical sound; quickly: ghostly.* MARLEY'S *image is not at all angry, but looks at* SCROOGE *as did the old* MARLEY *look at* SCROOGE. *The hair is curiously*
6 *stirred; eyes wide open, dead: absent of focus.* SCROOGE *stares wordlessly here. The face, before his very eyes, does deliquesce.*[12] *It is a knocker again.* SCROOGE *opens the door and checks the back of same, probably for* MARLEY'S *pigtail. Seeing nothing but screws and nuts,* SCROOGE *refuses the memory.*]

Pooh, pooh!

[*The sound of the door closing resounds throughout the house as thunder. Every room echoes the sound.* SCROOGE *fastens the door and walks across the hall to the stairs, trimming his candle as he goes; and then he goes slowly up the staircase. He checks each room: sitting*
7 *room, bedrooms, slumber-room. He looks under the sofa, under the table: nobody there. He fixes his evening gruel on the hob,*[13] *changes his jacket.* SCROOGE *sits near the tiny low-flamed fire, sipping his gruel. There are various pictures on the walls: all of them now show likenesses of* MARLEY. SCROOGE *blinks his eyes.*]

Bah! Humbug!

[SCROOGE *walks in a circle about the room. The pictures change back into their natural images. He sits down at the table in front of the fire. A bell hangs overhead. It begins to ring, of its own accord. Slowly, surely, begins the ringing of every bell in the house. They continue ringing for nearly half a minute.* SCROOGE *is stunned by the phenomenon. The bells cease their ringing all at once. Deep below* SCROOGE, *in the basement of the house, there is the sound of clanking, of some enormous chain being dragged across the floors; and now up the stairs. We hear doors flying open.*]

Bah still! Humbug still! This is not happening! 8
I won't believe it!

[MARLEY'S GHOST *enters the room. He is horrible to look at: pigtail, vest, suit as usual, but he drags an enormous chain now, to which is fastened cash-boxes, keys, padlocks, ledgers, deeds, and heavy purses fashioned of steel. He is transparent.* MARLEY *stands opposite the stricken* SCROOGE.]

How now! What do you want of me?

MARLEY. Much!

SCROOGE. Who are you?

MARLEY. Ask me who I *was*.

SCROOGE. Who *were* you then?

MARLEY. In life, I was your business partner: Jacob Marley.

SCROOGE. I see . . . can you sit down?

MARLEY. I can.

SCROOGE. Do it then.

MARLEY. I shall. [MARLEY *sits opposite* SCROOGE, *in the chair across the table, at the front of the fireplace.*] You don't believe in me.

SCROOGE. I don't.

MARLEY. Why do you doubt your senses?

11. **specter** (spek´ tər) *n.*: Ghost.
12. **deliquesce** (del´ ə kwes´) *v.*: Melt away.
13. **gruel** (gro͞o´ əl) **on the hob** (häb): Thin broth warming on a ledge at the back or side of the fireplace.

◆ Build Vocabulary

misanthrope (mis´ ən thrōp´) *n.*: Person who hates or distrusts everyone

void (void) *n.*: Total emptiness

◆Critical Thinking

5 Analyze Scrooge seems to lack a sense of humor. Why, then, do his actions sometimes seem comical? *Students may say that because Scrooge is so thoroughly mean, especially in contrast to those around him, it is easy to laugh at him, particularly when he does such things as batting at harmless flakes of snow.*

◆Reading Strategy

6 Envision What details in these stage directions help the reader picture Marley's face? *"The hair is curiously stirred; eyes wide open, dead: absent of focus . . . The face . . . does deliquesce."*

◆Critical Thinking

7 Infer What new information can the reader learn about Ebenezer Scrooge from this description? *Not only is Scrooge hard on others, he's hard on himself. Scrooge is so miserly that he denies himself proper meals and instead eats a meager dinner such as gruel. Also, he sacrifices comfort to keep his fire low in order to save money on fuel.*

◆Critical Thinking

8 Speculate Why does Scrooge refuse to believe what is happening? *Students may say that Scrooge doesn't believe what is happening because he is stubborn. Others may say that Scrooge believes only what makes sense to him.*

Beyond the Classroom

Career Connection

Employee Benefits In the play, Ebenezer Scrooge grudgingly allows Bob Cratchit to take Christmas Day off with pay. Explain to students that in the United States, common benefits for full-time employees include paid vacations and holidays. Many employers offer two or more weeks of paid vacation per year, in addition to local, state, and federal holidays. Paid vacation time is usually earned after an employee has worked at a business for a minimum number of months or years. In the United States, Christmas day is a legal holiday.

Have students find out more about employee benefits. Suggest that they interview family members, friends, or neighbors who are employed at jobs that offer paid vacations and holidays. Have them ask whether they receive any other paid holidays in addition to legally mandated ones. Students may want to organize their information in a chart. Invite students to give oral presentations of their findings.

Comprehension Check ☑

❶ Scroogethinks that his mind is playing tricks on him. What reason does he give for not believing in Marley's ghost? *He says that the visions he is having are the result of stomach problems from undigested or undercooked foods that have affected his senses.*

◆Literary Focus

❷ **Elements of Drama** Have students paraphrase the playwright's instructions in these stage directions. *Marley's ghost begins to scream, which causes bats to fly and cats to screech. He removes his head from his shoulders and continues to scream. All the pictures in the room show Marley's face as he is screaming. Scrooge falls to his knees in terror.*

◆Critical Thinking

❸ **Analyze** Ask students why Marley puts on the frightening display described in these stage directions. *Possible responses: Marley has grown impatient with Scrooge's denial that his ghost exists. Marley wants to frighten Scrooge into believing in him.*

◆Reading Strategy

❹ **Envision** As students answer the question, encourage them to give specific details that support their responses. *The stage directions help the reader picture Marley's horrifying appearance and actions by giving vivid details such as "Bats fly, cats screech, lightning flashes." The description of Marley's screaming face appearing on all the pictures in the room is chilling and helps the reader envision the special effects.*

▶Critical Viewing◀

❺ **Analyze** Some students may suggest loud, clashing music to accompany the clanging of Marley's chain and the objects attached to it. Others may suggest low, eerie music to enhance the ghostly mood.

Humanities: Performing Arts

Set Design Explain that set designers find ways to help the audience understand a play. They use props and other visual elements to provide a suitable background for the action and to enhance the theme, mood, and setting of a play.

Have students look closely at the set shown in the photograph on this page. Point out the wooden platform that supports Scrooge and Marley and the staircase in the background. Explain that set designers sometimes use a minimum of scenery and props to suggest the mood or spirit of a production.

Have students discuss how the stage set shown in the picture adds to the audience's understanding of Scrooge's encounter with Marley. *The starkness of the set adds to the frightening, bleak atmosphere of the scene and focuses attention on the two main characters.*

SCROOGE. Because every little thing affects them. A slight disorder of the stomach makes them cheat. You may be an undigested bit of
1 beef, a blot of mustard, a crumb of cheese, a fragment of an underdone potato. There's more of gravy than of grave about you, whatever you are!

[*There is a silence between them.* SCROOGE *is made nervous by it. He picks up a toothpick.*]

Humbug! I tell you: humbug!

[MARLEY *opens his mouth and screams a ghosty, fearful scream. The scream echoes about each room of the house. Bats fly, cats screech, lightning flashes.* SCROOGE *stands and walks backwards against the wall.* MARLEY *stands and screams again. This time, he takes his head and lifts it from his shoulders. His head continues to scream.* MARLEY'S *face again appears on every picture in the room: all screaming.* SCROOGE, *on his knees before* MARLEY.]

2
3
4 **◆ Reading Strategy** How do the stage directions help you picture the frightening appearance and actions of Marley's ghost?

Mercy! Dreadful apparition,[14] mercy! Why, O! why do you trouble me so?

MARLEY. Man of the worldly mind, do you believe in me, or not?

SCROOGE. I do. I must. But why do spirits such as you walk the earth? And why do they come to me?

MARLEY. It is required of every man that the spirit within him should walk abroad among his fellow-men, and travel far and wide; and if that spirit goes not forth in life, it is condemned to do so after death. [MARLEY *screams again; a tragic scream; from his ghosty bones.*] I wear the chain I forged in life. I made it link by link, and yard by yard. Is its pattern strange to *you?* Or would you know, you, Scrooge, the weight and length of the strong coil you bear yourself? It was full as heavy and long as this, seven Christmas Eves ago. You have labored on it, since. It is a ponderous chain.

[*Terrified that a chain will appear about his body,* SCROOGE *spins and waves the unwanted* 6
chain away. None, of course, appears. Sees MARLEY *watching him dance about the room.* MARLEY *watches* SCROOGE*; silently.*]

SCROOGE. Jacob. Old Jacob Marley, tell me more. Speak comfort to me, Jacob . . .

MARLEY. I have none to give. Comfort comes from other regions, Ebenezer Scrooge, and is conveyed by other ministers, to other kinds of men. A very little more, is all that is permitted
to me. I cannot rest, I cannot stay, I cannot 7
linger anywhere . . . [*He moans again.*] my spirit never walked beyond our counting-house —mark me!—in life my spirit never roved beyond the narrow limits of our money-changing hole; and weary journeys lie before me!

SCROOGE. But you were always a good man of business, Jacob.

MARLEY. [*Screams word "business"; a flashpot explodes with him.*] *BUSINESS!!!* Mankind was my business. The common welfare was my business; charity, mercy, forbearance, benevolence, were, all, my business. [SCROOGE *is quaking.*] Hear me, Ebenezer Scrooge! My time is nearly gone.

SCROOGE. I will, but don't be hard upon me. 8
And don't be flowery, Jacob! Pray!

MARLEY. How is it that I appear before you in a shape that you can see, I may not tell. I have sat invisible beside you many and many a day. That is no light part of my penance. I am here tonight to warn you that you have yet a chance and hope of escaping my fate. A chance and hope of my procuring, Ebenezer.

14. **apparition** (ap′ ə rish′ ən) *n.:* Ghost.

5 ◀ **Critical Viewing** What music might a director choose to enhance the mood of this scene? Explain. **[Extend]**

◆ Build Vocabulary

ponderous (pän′ dər əs) *adj.:* Very heavy; bulky

benevolence (bə nev′ ə ləns) *n.:* Kindliness

◆Critical Thinking

6 Interpret Why does Marley's ghost carry a chain? What does he mean when he refers to the chain that Scrooge has forged? *Marley's spirit is bound by a chain that was invisible in life but real in death. The chain represents Marley's sins, his obsession with making money, his mistreatment of others, and his lack of compassion. By similar actions, Scrooge has also forged a chain that became obvious to Marley when he died seven years ago.*

Comprehension Check ☑

7 Why is Marley not permitted to rest? *Marley's spirit is condemned to "walk abroad among his fellow-men" because in life he was self-centered and greedy, spending all of his time working at his business rather than helping others.*

◆Critical Thinking

8 Analyze Cause and Effect Point out to students that Scrooge seems not to understand what Marley is trying to tell him. He thinks that Marley is using flowery, or overly fancy, language. Have students tell why Marley is becoming angry with Scrooge. *Marley is trying to tell Scrooge that Scrooge's selfishness will lead to the same fate as Marley's, but Scrooge refuses to understand Marley's point.*

Beyond the Classroom

Community Connection

Caring for Others Marley tells Scrooge that the important business in life is the "common welfare," or caring for others. Point out to students that an important part of growing up is realizing that you cannot think only of yourself. All of us have responsibilities toward family members, friends, neighbors, and others in the community. These responsibilities include caring about people's needs and feelings.

Have students brainstorm a list of gestures that would constitute acts of "charity, mercy, forbearance," and "benevolence" and then write a brief essay about people they know or have read about who have helped the community or another person. You may want to provide students with copies of newspapers or magazines that feature people whose "business" is the common welfare. They might be medical practitioners, service-oriented people, individual philanthropists, or employees of charitable or philanthropic organizations. Ask students to describe the effects these people have had on their communities. Invite volunteers to read their essays aloud.

◆Reading Strategy

❶ Envision How do these stage directions help you picture the scene as Marley leaves Scrooge? *They offer vivid descriptions of Marley's fellow specters as they fly by wrapped in the same kinds of chains and money boxes as Marley wears, and of Marley's actions as he leaves Scrooge's room.*

◆Critical Thinking

❷ Interpret Why do you think this scene includes specters that carry money boxes and chains? *Students may say that the specters are meant to show that, like Marley and Scrooge, many other people tend to be selfish and greedy.*

◆Critical Thinking

❸ Analyze What is unusual about Scrooge's plea? *Up to this point in the story, Scrooge has wanted to be left alone. This is the first time that Scrooge admits that he is frightened and begs not to be left alone.*

◆Literary Focus

❹ Elements of Drama Have students paraphrase the information conveyed through the dialogue in this passage. *Marley is telling the audience that he will continue to be visible to them as the narrator but not to Scrooge, who he believes has already begun to change for the better. Marley then draws attention to Scrooge, who lies in bed waiting for what will happen next.*

Clarification

❺ Point out that the speech Scrooge gives is known in the theater as a *soliloquy*. A soliloquy is a speech in which a character talks to himself or the audience and reveals what he or she is thinking. It is longer than an aside.

SCROOGE. You were always a good friend to me. Thank'ee!

MARLEY. You will be haunted by Three Spirits.

SCROOGE. Would that be the chance and hope you mentioned, Jacob?

MARLEY. It is.

SCROOGE. I think I'd rather not.

MARLEY. Without their visits, you cannot hope to shun the path I tread. Expect the first one tomorrow, when the bell tolls one.

SCROOGE. Couldn't I take 'em all at once, and get it over, Jacob?

MARLEY. Expect the second on the next night at the same hour. The third upon the next night when the last stroke of twelve has ceased to vibrate. Look to see me no more. Others may, but you may not. And look that, for your own sake, you remember what has passed between us!

[MARLEY *places his head back upon his shoulders. He approaches the window and beckons to* SCROOGE *to watch. Outside the window, specters*
1 *fly by, carrying money-boxes and chains. They*
2 *make a confused sound of lamentation.* MARLEY,
after listening a moment, joins into their mournful dirge. He leans to the window and floats out into the bleak, dark night. He is gone.]

3 **SCROOGE.** [*Rushing to the window*] Jacob! No, Jacob! Don't leave me! I'm frightened!

[*He sees that* MARLEY *has gone. He looks outside. He pulls the shutter closed, so that the scene is blocked from his view. All sound stops. After a pause, he re-opens the shutter and all is quiet, as it should be on Christmas Eve. Carolers carol out of doors, in the distance.* SCROOGE *closes the shutter and walks down the stairs. He examines the door by which* MARLEY *first entered.*]

No one here at all! Did I imagine all that? Humbug! [*He looks about the room.*] I did imagine it. It only happened in my foulest dream-mind, didn't it? An undigested bit of . . .

[*Thunder and lightning in the room; suddenly*]

Sorry! Sorry!

[*There is silence again. The lights fade out.*]

Scene 4

[*Christmas music, choral, "Hark the Herald Angels Sing," sung by an onstage choir of children, spotlighted,* D.C. *Above,* SCROOGE *in his bed, dead to the world, asleep, in his darkened room. It should appear that the choir is singing somewhere outside of the house, of course, and a use of scrim*[15] *is thus suggested. When the singing is ended, the choir should fade out of view and* MARLEY *should fade into view, in their place.*]

MARLEY. [*Directly to audience*] From this point forth . . . I shall be quite visible to you, but invisible to him. [*Smiles*] He will feel my presence, nevertheless, for, unless my senses fail me completely, we are—you and I—witness to
the changing of a miser: that one, my partner 4
in life, in business, and in eternity: that one: Scrooge. [*Moves to staircase, below* SCROOGE] See him now. He endeavors to pierce the darkness with his ferret eyes.[16] [*To audience*] See him, now. He listens for the hour.

[*The bells toll.* SCROOGE *is awakened and quakes as the hour approaches one o'clock, but the bells stop their sound at the hour of twelve.*]

SCROOGE. [*Astonished*] Midnight! Why this isn't possible. It was past two when I went to bed. An icicle must have gotten into the clock's works! I couldn't have slept through the whole day and far into another night. It isn't possible that anything has happened to the sun, and this is twelve at noon! [*He runs to window;*
unshutters same; it is night.] Night, still. Quiet, 5
normal for the season, cold. It is certainly not noon. I cannot in any way afford to lose my days. Securities come due, promissory notes,[17] interest on investments: these are things that happen in the daylight! [*He returns to his bed.*] Was this a dream?

---

15. **scrim** (skrim) *n.*: Light, semitransparent curtain.
16. **ferret eyes:** A ferret is a small, weasellike animal used for hunting rabbits; this expression means to look persistently, the way a ferret hunts.
17. **promissory** (präm′ i sôr′ ē) **notes:** Written promises to pay someone a certain sum of money.

[MARLEY *appears in his room. He speaks to the audience.*]

MARLEY. You see? He does not, with faith, believe in me fully, even still! Whatever will it take to turn the faith of a miser from money to men?

SCROOGE. Another quarter and it'll be one and Marley's ghosty friends will come. [*Pauses; listens*] Where's the chime for one? [*Ding, dong*] A quarter *past* [*Repeats*] Half-past! [*Repeats*] A quarter to it! But where's the heavy bell of the hour one? This is a game in which I lose my senses! Perhaps, if I allowed myself another short doze . . .

MARLEY . . . Doze, Ebenezer, doze.

[*A heavy bell thuds its one ring; dull and definitely one o'clock. There is a flash of light.* SCROOGE *sits up, in a sudden. A hand draws back the curtains by his bed. He sees it.*]

SCROOGE. A hand! Who owns it! Hello!

6 [*Ghosty music again, but of a new nature to the play. A strange figure stands before* SCROOGE*—like a child, yet at the same time like an old man: white hair, but unwrinkled skin, long, muscular arms, but delicate legs and feet. Wears white tunic; lustrous belt cinches waist. Branch of fresh green holly in its hand, but has its dress trimmed with fresh summer flowers. Clear jets of light spring from the crown of its head. Holds cap in hand. The Spirit is called* PAST.]

Are you the Spirit, sir, whose coming was foretold to me?

PAST. I am.

MARLEY. Does he take this to be a vision of his green grocer?

SCROOGE. Who, and what are you?

PAST. I am the Ghost of Christmas Past.

SCROOGE. Long past?

PAST. Your past.

SCROOGE. May I ask, please, sir, what business you have here with me?

PAST. Your welfare.

SCROOGE. Not to sound ungrateful, sir, and really, please do understand that I am plenty obliged for your concern, but, really, kind spirit, it would have done all the better for my welfare to have been left alone altogether, to have slept peacefully through this night.

PAST. Your reclamation, then. Take heed!

SCROOGE. My what?

PAST. [*Motioning to* SCROOGE *and taking his arm*] Rise! Fly with me! [*He leads* SCROOGE *to the window.*]

7 **SCROOGE.** [*Panicked*] Fly, but I am a mortal and cannot fly!

PAST. [*Pointing to his heart*] Bear but a touch of my hand *here* and you shall be upheld in more than this!

[SCROOGE *touches the* SPIRIT'S *heart and the lights dissolve into sparkly flickers. Lovely crystals of music are heard. The scene dissolves into another. Christmas music again*]

Scene 5

[SCROOGE *and the* GHOST OF CHRISTMAS PAST *walk together across an open stage. In the background, we see a field that is open; covered by a soft, downy snow: a country road.*]

SCROOGE. Good Heaven! I was bred in this place. I was a boy here!

[SCROOGE *freezes, staring at the field beyond.* MARLEY'S *ghost appears beside him; takes* SCROOGE'S *face in his hands, and turns his face to the audience.*]

8 **MARLEY.** You see this Scrooge: stricken by feeling. Conscious of a thousand odors floating in the air, each one connected with a thousand thoughts, and hopes, and joys, and care long, long forgotten. [*Pause*] This one—this Scrooge—before your very eyes, returns to life, among the living. [*To audience, sternly*] You'd best pay your most careful attention. I would suggest rapt.[18]

[*There is a small flash and puff of smoke and* MARLEY *is gone again.*]

18. **rapt** (rapt) *adj.*: Giving complete attention; totally carried away by something.

◆Critical Thinking

6 Speculate Why does the figure standing before Scrooge appear to be both young and old? *Students may say that perhaps the figure represents the lifetime of a person–past, present, and future–in one spirit. Students who are familiar with* A Christmas Carol *may say that the Spirit looks this way because he foreshadows the old man Scrooge's upcoming return to his youth.*

7 Compare and Contrast Have students describe how the tone of Scrooge's dialogue has changed since the appearance of the Ghost of Christmas Past. Ask them how Scrooge might have reacted had this Spirit appeared the day before in Scrooge's office. *Scrooge sounds polite and humble toward the Spirit. The day before, Scrooge might have yelled angrily at the Spirit and ordered him to leave.*

Comprehension Check ☑

8 Why does the playwright have Marley speak to the audience at this point? What is Marley saying to the audience in this aside? *Students should recognize that Marley is interpreting Scrooge's reaction for the audience, probably because Scrooge is too emotionally overcome to describe his own feelings. Marley is saying that Scrooge's senses are coming alive again because of the sights and smells of his boyhood.*

Customize for *Musical/Rhythmic Learners*

Point out to students that the stage directions on these pages include sound effects and music. Review the types of music and sounds described in the stage directions. Discuss ways in which the music is appropriate for each purpose. If students have access to musical instruments and devices for creating sound effects, invite them to produce examples of the types of music and sounds called for in the stage directions.

◆Literature and Your Life

❶ Have students describe how they feel about Scrooge at this point in the play. *Some students may say that they feel sympathy for Scrooge because he is filled with emotion. Others may say that they sense that he may be changing for the better but that they want to see if the change is real.*

◆Critical Thinking

❷ **Interpret** Have students describe the tone of this passage and paraphrase its meaning. *The Ghost of Christmas Past is using a mocking or sarcastic tone to remind Scrooge of his "Bah, humbug!" attitude toward Christmas cheer.*

◆Literary Focus

❸ **Elements of Drama** What do these stage directions and the dialogue reveal about Scrooge as a young boy? *Scrooge was a lonely boy, whose friends neglected him.*

◆Critical Thinking

❹ **Infer** Why is Scrooge thinking about the boy who appeared at his office the night before? *When Scrooge remembers how lonely he was as a boy, he is reminded of the boy who appeared at his window and how he cruelly chased the boy away by whacking at his image with a ruler.*

◆Critical Thinking

❺ **Speculate** Have students speculate about Scrooge's family life, based on this passage. *Students may guess that Scrooge's father was ill-tempered, since Fan reports that "Father is so much kinder." They may suggest that Scrooge was sent away to boarding school against his will by his father. They may also speculate that Scrooge's mother has died, since Fan doesn't mention her.*

PAST. Your lip is trembling, Mr. Scrooge. And what is that upon your cheek?

SCROOGE. Upon my cheek? Nothing . . . a blemish on the skin from the eating of overmuch grease . . . nothing . . . [*Suddenly*] Kind Spirit of Christmas Past, lead me where you will, but *quickly!* To be stagnant in this place is, for me, *unbearable!*

PAST. You recollect the way?

1 **SCROOGE.** Remember it! I would know it blindfolded! My bridge, my church, my winding river! [*Staggers about, trying to see it all at once. He weeps again.*]

PAST. These are but shadows of things that have been. They have no consciousness of us.

[*Four jocund travelers enter, singing a Christmas song in four-part harmony—"God Rest Ye Merry Gentlemen."*]

SCROOGE. Listen! I know these men! I know them! I remember the beauty of their song!

2 **PAST.** But, why do you remember it so happily? It is Merry Christmas that they say to one another! What is Merry Christmas to you, Mr. Scrooge? Out upon Merry Christmas, right? What good has Merry Christmas ever done you, Mr. Scrooge? . . .

SCROOGE. [*After a long pause*] None. No good. None . . . [*He bows his head.*]

PAST. Look, you, sir, a school ahead. The schoolroom is not quite deserted. A solitary child, neglected by his friends, is left there still.

[SCROOGE *falls to the ground; sobbing as he sees, and we see, a small boy, the young* SCROOGE, *sitting and weeping, bravely, alone at his desk: alone in a vast space, a void.*]

SCROOGE. I cannot look on him!

3 **PAST.** You must, Mr. Scrooge, you must.

SCROOGE. It's me. [*Pauses; weeps*] Poor boy. He lived inside his head . . . alone . . . [*Pauses; weeps*] poor boy. [*Pauses; stops his weeping*] I wish . . . [*Dries his eyes on his cuff*] ah! it's too late!

PAST. What is the matter?

SCROOGE. There was a boy singing a Christmas Carol outside my door last night. I should like to have given him something: that's all. 4

PAST. [*Smiles; waves his hand to* SCROOGE] Come. Let us see another Christmas.

[*Lights out on little boy. A flash of light. A puff of smoke. Lights up on older boy*]

SCROOGE. Look! Me, again! Older now! [*Realizes*] Oh, yes . . . still alone.

[*The boy—a slightly older* SCROOGE *—sits alone in a chair, reading. The door to the room opens and a young girl enters. She is much, much younger than this slightly older* SCROOGE. *She is, say, six, and he is, say, twelve. Elder* SCROOGE *and the* GHOST OF CHRISTMAS PAST *stand watching the scene, unseen.*]

FAN. Dear, dear brother, I have come to bring you home.

BOY. Home, little Fan?

FAN. Yes! Home, for good and all! Father is so much kinder than he ever used to be, and home's like heaven! He spoke so gently to me one dear night when I was going to bed that I was not afraid to ask him once more if you might come home; and he said "yes" . . . you should; and sent me in a coach to bring you. 5 And you're to be a man and are never to come back here, but first, we're to be together all the Christmas long, and have the merriest time in the world.

BOY. You are quite a woman, little Fan!

[*Laughing; she drags at* BOY, *causing him to stumble to the door with her. Suddenly we hear a mean and terrible voice in the hallway, Off. It is the* SCHOOLMASTER.]

SCHOOLMASTER. Bring down Master Scrooge's travel box at once! He is to travel!

FAN. Who is that, Ebenezer?

BOY. O! Quiet, Fan. It is the Schoolmaster, himself!

[*The door bursts open and into the room bursts with it the* SCHOOLMASTER.]

6 ▲ **Critical Viewing** Without knowing about the action of the scene, what can you infer about the relationship of the characters? **[Infer]**

SCHOOLMASTER. Master Scrooge?

BOY. Oh, Schoolmaster. I'd like you to meet my little sister, Fan, sir . . .

[*Two boys struggle on with* SCROOGE'S *trunk.*]

FAN. Pleased, sir . . . [*She curtsies.*]

SCHOOLMASTER. You are to travel, Master Scrooge.

SCROOGE. Yes, sir. I know sir . . .

[*All start to exit, but* FAN *grabs the coattail of the mean old* SCHOOLMASTER.]

BOY. Fan!

SCHOOLMASTER. What's this?

7 **FAN.** Pardon, sir, but I believe that you've forgotten to say your goodbye to my brother, Ebenezer, who stands still now awaiting it . . . [*She smiles, curtsies, lowers her eyes.*] pardon, sir.

SCHOOLMASTER. [*Amazed*] I . . . uh . . . harumph . . . uhh . . . well, then . . . [*Outstretches hand*] Goodbye, Scrooge. 7

BOY. Uh, well, goodbye, Schoolmaster . . .

[*Lights fade out on all but* BOY *looking at* FAN*; and* SCROOGE *and* PAST *looking at them.*]

SCROOGE. Oh, my dear, dear little sister, Fan . . . how I loved her.

PAST. Always a delicate creature, whom a breath might have withered, but she had a large heart . . .

SCROOGE. So she had.

PAST. She died a woman, and had, as I think, children.

SCROOGE. One child. 8

PAST. True. Your nephew.

SCROOGE. Yes.

PAST. Fine, then. We move on, Mr. Scrooge. That warehouse, there? Do you know it?

SCROOGE. Know it? Wasn't I apprenticed[19] there?

PAST. We'll have a look.

[*They enter the warehouse. The lights crossfade with them, coming up on an old man in Welsh wig:* FEZZIWIG.]

SCROOGE. Why, it's old Fezziwig! Bless his heart; it's Fezziwig, alive again!

> **◆ Literature and Your Life**
> What scene from your life might you enjoy seeing again? 9

[FEZZIWIG *sits behind a large, high desk, counting. He lays down his pen; looks at the clock: seven bells sound.*]

Quittin' time . . .

FEZZIWIG. Quittin' time . . . [*He takes off his waistcoat and laughs; calls off*] Yo ho, Ebenezer! Dick!

19. **apprenticed** (ə prenˊ tist) *v.*: Receiving financial support and instruction in a trade in return for work.

▶Critical Viewing◀

6 **Infer** Students may guess that the man who is standing holds power over the man seated at the desk in the foreground. The role of the man seated to the right of the standing man is less clear; he could be an uninvolved observer or associated in some way with the standing man.

◆Critical Thinking

7 **Infer** What can you tell about Fan from the dialogue and stage directions in this passage? *Fan seems to be a courageous advocate for her brother. She also seems aware of the power of using charm to get her way.*

◆Literary Focus

8 **Elements of Drama** Have students describe the information the audience learns from the dialogue in this passage. *The audience learns that the nephew whose dinner invitation Scrooge refused is the son of Scrooge's beloved sister, Fan.*

◆Literature and Your Life

9 Students may mention scenes such as a visit to an exciting place, the scene of a special celebration, an event in which they excelled, such as a sports event or a performance, or an academic achievement.

Viewing and Representing Mini-Lesson

Journey to the Past

Through this mini-lesson, students will extend their understanding of Scrooge's transformation as he revisits his past.

Introduce Have students recall television shows or movies in which a character is changed after being transported to the past. To give an example, ask if anyone has seen the film version of H. G. Wells's *The Time Machine.* Discuss special effects used to show the character's journey and ways in which the character changes.

Develop Have students brainstorm for ways to visually represent such a journey to the past and its effects. Suggest that students think of ways to combine words and pictures, or pictures alone, to convey the emotions a person might experience as he or she revisits a younger self.

Apply Provide students with materials such as drawing paper and recycled magazines with which to create visual representations such as drawings, cartoon panels, or collages. Have students present their representations to the class.

Assess Evaluate students' representations on how well they reflect the concept of an emotional and transforming journey to the past.

Comprehension Check ☑

1 Have students tell where this scene takes place. *It takes place in a warehouse, where Scrooge was an apprentice as a young man.*

◆Reading Strategy

2 **Envision** The dialogue alone doesn't convey the merriment of the evening. The stage directions provide more information about Fezziwig and his family and show Scrooge enjoying himself on a Christmas Eve in his past.

Clarification

3 Point out that the Ghost of Christmas Past is using sarcasm again. He means the opposite of what he is saying here.

◆Critical Thinking

4 **Compare and Contrast** Have students compare and contrast Fezziwig's skills as an employer to those of Scrooge. Students may want to use the Venn diagram, from **Writing and Language Transparencies,** p. 86, as they list similarities and differences between the two men. Encourage students to list specific examples to support their statements of comparison. *Both men are business owners. Fezziwig is kind and generous to his employees, as shown by the Christmas Eve party he gives. Scrooge is mean and uncharitable to Bob Cratchit, as shown by his reluctance to give his employee Christmas Day off.*

Comprehension Check ☑

5 What has Scrooge realized as a result of revisiting Fezziwig's warehouse? *Scrooge sees that Fezziwig's kindness toward his employees made all the difference in their attitudes toward the work. Scrooge enjoyed working for Fezziwig, because Fezziwig treated him with dignity and respect. Scrooge realizes that his meanness to Cratchit has probably made Cratchit's job a miserable one.*

[DICK WILKINS *and* EBENEZER SCROOGE *—a young man version—enter the room.* DICK *and* EBENEZER *are* FEZZIWIG'S *apprentices.*]

SCROOGE. Dick Wilkins, to be sure! My fellow-'prentice! Bless my soul, yes. There he is. He was very much attached to me, was Dick. Poor Dick! Dear, dear!

FEZZIWIG. Yo ho, my boys. No more work tonight. Christmas Eve, Dick. Christmas, Ebenezer!

[*They stand at attention in front of* FEZZIWIG; *laughing*]

Hilli-ho! Clear away, and let's have lots of room here! Hilli-ho, Dick! Chirrup, Ebenezer!

1 [*The young men clear the room, sweep the floor, straighten the pictures, trim the lamps, etc. The space is clear now. A fiddler enters, fiddling.*]

Hi-ho, Matthew! Fiddle away . . . where are my daughters?

[*The* FIDDLER *plays. Three young daughters of* FEZZIWIG *enter followed by six young male suitors. They are dancing to the music. All employees come in: workers, clerks, housemaids, cousins, the baker, etc. All dance. Full number wanted here. Throughout the dance, food is brought into the feast. It is "eaten" in dance, by the dancers.* EBENEZER *dances with all three of the daughters, as does* DICK. *They compete for the daughters, happily, in the dance.* FEZZIWIG *dances with his daughters.* FEZZIWIG *dances with* DICK *and* EBENEZER. *The music changes:* MRS. FEZZIWIG *enters. She lovingly scolds her husband. They dance. She dances with* EBENEZER, *lifting him and throwing him about. She is enormously fat. When the dance is ended, they all dance off, floating away, as does the music.* SCROOGE *and the* GHOST OF CHRISTMAS PAST *stand alone now. The music is gone.*]

2 **◆ Reading Strategy** Why are these stage directions necessary for you to envision what is happening in the play?

3 **PAST.** It was a small matter, that Fezziwig made those silly folks so full of gratitude.

SCROOGE. Small!

PAST. Shhh!

[*Lights up on* DICK *and* EBENEZER]

DICK. We are blessed, Ebenezer, truly, to have such a master as Mr. Fezziwig!

YOUNG SCROOGE. He is the best, best, the very and absolute best! If ever I own a firm of my own, I shall treat my apprentices with the same dignity and the same grace. We have learned a wonderful lesson from the master, Dick!

DICK. Ah, that's a fact, Ebenezer. That's a fact!

PAST. Was it not a small matter, really? He spent but a few pounds[20] of his mortal money on your small party. Three or four pounds, perhaps. Is that so much that he deserves such praise as you and Dick so lavish now?

SCROOGE. It isn't that! It isn't that, Spirit. Fezziwig had the power to make us happy or unhappy; to make our service light or burdensome; a pleasure or a toil. The happiness he gave is quite as great as if it cost him a fortune. 4

PAST. What is the matter?

SCROOGE. Nothing particular.

PAST. Something, I think.

SCROOGE. No, no. I should like to be able to say a word or two to my clerk just now! That's all! 5

[EBENEZER *enters the room and shuts down all the lamps. He stretches and yawns. The* GHOST OF CHRISTMAS PAST *turns to* SCROOGE; *all of a sudden.*]

PAST. My time grows short! Quick!

[*In a flash of light,* EBENEZER *is gone, and in his place stands an* OLDER SCROOGE, *this one a man in the prime of his life. Beside him stands a young woman in a mourning dress. She is crying. She speaks to the man, with hostility.*]

WOMAN. It matters little . . . to you, very little. Another idol has displaced me.

MAN. What idol has displaced you?

20. **pounds** (poundz) *n.*: Common type of money used in Great Britain.

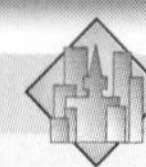

Beyond the Classroom

Career Connection

Office Personnel Remind students that both Scrooge and Fezziwig manage employees who perform clerical tasks. Point out that there are many office jobs that require clerical and managerial skills.

Office workers The specific responsibilities of office workers depend on the services provided by a company. Most clerical jobs require organizational skills. Office clerks are usually expected to use word-processing programs, file, answer telephone calls, open mail, and keep records.

Managers Office managers are required to oversee the work in an office. They may be required to interview job candidates, train and supervise new personnel, monitor the work of people in their department, maintain records, and ensure an adequate inventory of office supplies.

Have students interview clerical workers or managers to find out about specific responsibilities and duties of these jobs. Invite students to share their findings. As a class, review classified advertisements for office workers and managers.

WOMAN. A golden one.

MAN. This is an even-handed dealing of the world. There is nothing on which it is so hard
6 as poverty; and there is nothing it professes to condemn with such severity as the pursuit of wealth!

WOMAN. You fear the world too much. Have I not seen your nobler aspirations fall off one by one, until the master-passion, Gain, engrosses you? Have I not?

SCROOGE. No!

MAN. What then? Even if I have grown so much wiser, what then? Have I changed towards you?

WOMAN. No . . .

MAN. Am I?

WOMAN. Our contract is an old one. It was made when we were both poor and content to
7 be so. You *are* changed. When it was made, you were another man.

MAN. I was not another man: I was a boy.

WOMAN. Your own feeling tells you that you were not what you are. I am. That which promised happiness when we were one in heart is fraught with misery now that we are two . . .

SCROOGE. No!

WOMAN. How often and how keenly I have thought of this, I will not say. It is enough that I *have* thought of it, and can release you . . .

SCROOGE. [*Quietly*] Don't release me, madame . . .

MAN. Have I ever sought release?

WOMAN. In words. No. Never.

MAN. In what then?

WOMAN. In a changed nature; in an altered spirit. In everything that made my love of any worth or value in your sight. If this has never been between us, tell me, would you seek me out and try to win me now? Ah, no!

SCROOGE. Ah, yes!

MAN. You think not?

WOMAN. I would gladly think otherwise if I could, heaven knows! But if you were free today, tomorrow, yesterday, can even I believe that you would choose a dowerless girl[21] —you who in your very confidence with her weigh
everything by Gain; or, choosing her, do I not 8
know that your repentance and regret would surely follow? I do; and I release you. With a full heart, for the love of him you once were.

SCROOGE. Please, I . . . I . . .

MAN. Please, I . . . I . . .

WOMAN. Please. You may—the memory of what is past half makes me hope you will—have pain in this. A very, very brief time, and you will dismiss the memory of it, as an unprofitable dream, from which it happened well that you awoke. May you be happy in the life that you have chosen for yourself . . .

SCROOGE. No!

WOMAN. Yourself . . . alone . . .

SCROOGE. No!

WOMAN. Goodbye, Ebenezer . . .

SCROOGE. Don't let her go!

MAN. Goodbye.

SCROOGE. No!

[*She exits.* SCROOGE *goes to younger man: himself.*]

You fool! Mindless loon! You fool!

MAN. [*To exited woman*] Fool. Mindless loon. Fool . . .

SCROOGE. Don't say that! Spirit, remove me from this place.

PAST. I have told you these were shadows of the things that have been. They are what they are. Do not blame me, Mr. Scrooge.

SCROOGE. Remove me! I cannot bear it!

[*The faces of all who appeared in this scene are now projected for a moment around the stage: enormous, flimsy, silent.*]

---

21. **a dowerless** (dou´ ər les) **girl:** A girl without a dowery, the property or wealth a woman brought to her husband at marriage.

◆Critical Thinking

6 Interpret What complaint is Scrooge making in this passage? Do you think his complaint is fair? *Help students see that Scrooge is saying that the world is harsh for those who are poor, yet it punishes those who try to get rich. Some students may say that this is an unfair characterization. Others may say that life is difficult when you are poor, but that it can also be difficult for the rich, who are often the subjects of envy and criticism.*

Clarification

7 Explain that the contract the woman refers to is an agreement between herself and Scrooge that they would someday marry each other.

◆Critical Thinking

8 Draw Conclusions What reason does Scrooge's fiancée give for leaving him? *She realizes that Scrooge is more interested in the pursuit of money than in the pursuit of their life together.*

Customize for *Verbal/Linguistic Learners*

Have three students assume the roles of Scrooge as a younger man, Scrooge as an old man, and Scrooge's fiancée. Instruct the students to give a dramatic reading of the scene in which the woman breaks her engagement to Scrooge. Remind students to use voice tone to convey emotions as they read the dialogue. Allow time for students to rehearse the reading before presenting it to the class.

Reinforce and Extend

Answers

◆ Literature and Your Life

Reader's Response Some students may mention Scrooge's mistreatment of Cratchit as the meanest thing he does. Others may cite the refusal of his nephew's invitation or his lack of sympathy toward the poor.

Thematic Focus Students may say that Scrooge's lack of compassion and refusal to share his wealth are the most unacceptable, because others suffer as a result this conduct.

☑ Check Your Comprehension

1. In life, he was Scrooge's business partner. He appears in the play as a ghost.
2. He acts as the narrator.
3. Scrooge is demanding and cruel to Cratchit.
4. He comes to invite Scrooge for Christmas dinner.
5. They seek money for the poor.
6. He sees himself as a young boy, lonely and weeping in a schoolroom; as an older boy whose sister has come for him at a boarding school; as a young man celebrating Christmas Eve with his employer; and as an older Scrooge whose fiancée is leaving him.
7. He feels sadness and pity for the lonely boy he was; he feels love for his sister; he admires Fezziwig; and he feels remorse at having lost his fiancée. All the episodes cause him regret for past or present actions.

Leave me! Take me back! Haunt me no longer!

[*There is a sudden flash of light: a flare. The* GHOST OF CHRISTMAS PAST *is gone.* SCROOGE *is, for the moment, alone onstage. His bed is turned down, across the stage. A small candle burns now in* SCROOGE'S *hand. There is a child's cap in his other hand. He slowly crosses the stage to his bed, to sleep.* MARLEY *appears behind* SCROOGE, *who continues his long, elderly cross to bed.* MARLEY *speaks directly to the audience.*]

MARLEY. Scrooge must sleep now. He must surrender to the irresistible drowsiness caused by the recognition of what was. [*Pauses*] The cap he carries is from ten lives past: his boyhood cap . . . donned atop a hopeful hairy head . . . askew, perhaps, or at a rakish angle. Doffed now in honor of regret.[22] Perhaps even too heavy to carry in his present state of weak remorse . . .

[SCROOGE *drops the cap. He lies atop his bed. He sleeps. To audience*]

He sleeps. For him, there's even more trouble ahead. [*Smiles*] For you? The play house tells me there's hot cider, as should be your anticipation for the specter Christmas Present and Future, for I promise you both. [*Smiles again*] So, I pray you hurry back to your seats refreshed and ready for a miser—to turn his coat of gray into a blazen Christmas holly-red.

[*A flash of lightning. A clap of thunder. Bats fly. Ghosty music.* MARLEY *is gone.*]

22. **donned . . . regret:** To *don* and *doff* a hat means to put it on and take it off; *askew* means "crooked," and *at a rakish angle* means "having a dashing or jaunty look."

Guide for Responding

◆ Literature and Your Life

Reader's Response What do you think is the meanest thing Scrooge does in Act I? Explain your answer.

Thematic Focus What aspects of Scrooge's personal code of conduct do you find the most unacceptable? Why?

☑ Check Your Comprehension

1. Who is Marley?
2. What is Marley's purpose in the play?
3. How does Scrooge treat his clerk, Bob Cratchit?
4. For what purpose does Scrooge's nephew come to see Scrooge?
5. Why do the portly man and the thin man visit Scrooge?
6. Which scenes from his past does Scrooge revisit?
7. How does Scrooge react to each one of the episodes from his past?

◆ Critical Thinking

Interpret

1. Why does the Ghost of Christmas Past show Scrooge "shadows of things that have been"? **[Infer]**
2. How do the episodes at the school explain Scrooge's dislike of people? **[Connect]**
3. What does the scene with the young woman reveal about how Scrooge changed as he got older? **[Interpret]**
4. What hints are there that Scrooge may still change for the better? **[Analyze]**
5. Compare and contrast the young Scrooge and the old Scrooge. **[Compare and Contrast]**

Evaluate

6. Assess Scrooge's personality. In what areas does he need improvement? In what areas is he strong? **[Criticize]**

Apply

7. Do you think people like Scrooge are ever really happy? Why or why not? **[Generalize]**

◆ Critical Thinking

1. The ghost wants to remind Scrooge of the pain of his childhood loneliness and of the joys of kindness and love, which Scrooge gave up to make money.
2. They show that Scrooge was lonely and "neglected by his friends," which probably made him bitter.
3. It shows that Scrooge lost his faith in friendship and love and turned exclusively toward the pursuit of wealth.
4. Scrooge begins to show regret for mistreating others such as the boy singing Christmas carols, Cratchit, and his lost love.
5. They are alike in that both are alone. They are different in that the young Scrooge weeps over his loneliness, whereas the old Scrooge has hardened his heart.
6. Possible response: He needs to be kinder to others, but he is hardworking and disciplined.
7. Students may say that people like Scrooge are never truly happy because they lose sight of the purposes of money, such as providing enjoyment to oneself and others, and concentrate only on acquiring it.

Guide for Responding (continued)

◆ Literary Focus

Elements of Drama

Dialogue and stage directions are two of the main **elements of drama.**

1. How does the dialogue in Scene 2 reveal the personalities of Scrooge, his nephew, and Cratchit?

2. Explain what stage directions in Scene 4 would be particularly important to the lighting crew and the costume designer.

◆ Reading Strategy

Envision

The stage directions in a play can help you **envision,** or picture, what is happening.

1. How do the stage directions help you envision the party at Fezziwig's?

2. Why are the stage directions necessary for you to envision Scrooge's reaction to his younger self alone in the schoolroom?

◆ Build Grammar Skills

Subject and Verb Agreement

A **verb** must **agree** with its **subject** in number (singular or plural) and person.

A singular subject must take a singular form of a verb, and a plural subject must use a plural form of the verb. Verbs in the present tense change form to agree with singular or plural subjects.

Practice Copy the following sentences. Underline the subject once and the verb twice. Then, identify the number of the subject.

Example: They owe me money. (plural)

1. He answers to both names.
2. I wish to be left alone!
3. The ghosts terrify Scrooge.
4. A heavy bell thuds its one ring.
5. Scrooge and the Ghost of Christmas Past walk together across an open stage.

Writing Application Choose the correct verb to complete each sentence.

1. The party at Fezziwig's (is, are) fun.
2. Scrooge's relatives (feel, feels) sorry for him.
3. The scenes (frighten, frightens) him.

◆ Build Vocabulary

Using the Word Root *-bene-*

Knowing that the word root *-bene-* means "good" can help you figure out the meaning of words that contain it. On a piece of paper, write a definition for each italicized word.

1. Exercising is *beneficial* to your health.
2. We *benefited* from her wise advice.

Spelling Strategy

Words that end with the letters *-stitute*, such as *destitute*, originally come from a Latin word that means "place" or "stand." The word ending is always spelled *-stitute*. On your paper, write the word that results from adding *-stitute* to each of the following.

1. con____?____ **2.** in____?____
3. sub____?____ **4.** recon____?____

Using the Word Bank

Write the following paragraph on your paper, filling in each blank with the appropriate word from the Word Bank.

The ____?____ beggar ____?____ the sad but wealthy-looking man to show some ____?____. "Don't be a ____?____! Helping others will make your troubles feel less ____?____. You won't feel so ____?____ if you let compassion fill the ____?____ in your heart."

Idea Bank

Writing

1. Invitation In the role of Scrooge's nephew, write a letter to Scrooge to persuade him to join you and your wife for Christmas dinner.

2. Dramatic Scene Write a scene that shows Bob Cratchit's job interview with Scrooge. Use dialogue to reveal Scrooge's stinginess.

Project

3. Set Design Choose a scene from Act 1. Using the descriptions in the stage directions as a starting point, sketch the sets, costumes, and props for the scene. Provide labels and notes on your drawings to help explain your ideas. **[Art Link]**

✓ Assessment Options

Formal Assessment, Selection test, pp. 182–184, and Assessment Resources Software. The selection test is designed so that it can be customized easily to the performance levels of your students.

Alternative Assessment, p. 38, includes options for less advanced students, more advanced students, verbal/linguistic learners, logical/mathematical learners, visual/spatial learners, and interpersonal learners

PORTFOLIO ASSESSMENT

Use the following rubrics in the **Alternative Assessment** booklet:
Invitation: Expression, p. 81
Dramatic Scene: Drama, p. 96

Idea Bank

Following are suggestions for matching the Idea Bank topics with your students' performance levels and learning modalities:

Customize for
Performance Levels
Less Advanced Students: 1
Average Students: 2, 3
More Advanced Students: 2, 3

Customize for
Learning Modalities
Verbal/Linguistic: 1, 2, 3
Visual/Spatial: 3
Intrapersonal: 1, 2

Answers

◆ Literary Focus

1. The dialogue highlights the contrast between the crabby selfishness of Scrooge and the kindness of the nephew and Cratchit.
2. The appearance of the Ghost of Christmas Past and Scrooge's exit with the spirit are striking moments, so the stage directions are especially important.

◆ Reading Strategy

1. Details about the setting, the people, and the people's actions help the reader envision the party.
2. The stage directions help convey what is not said in the dialogue.

◆ Build Grammar Skills

Practice

1. He answers to both names. (singular)
2. I wish to be left alone! (singular)
3. The ghosts terrify Scrooge. (plural)
4. A heavy bell thuds its one ring. (singular)
5. Scrooge and the Ghost of Christmas Past walk together across an open stage. (plural)

Writing Application

1. is; 2. feel; 3. frightens

◆ Build Vocabulary

Using the Word Root *-bene-*

1. good for you or helpful
2. received good

Spelling Strategy

1. constitute 3. substitute
2. institute 4. reconstitute

Using the Word Bank

destitute, implored, benevolence, misanthrope, ponderous, morose, void

Prepare and Engage

OBJECTIVES

1. To read, comprehend, and interpret a play
2. To relate characterization and theme in a drama to personal experience
3. To ask questions during reading
4. To explore characterization and theme in drama
5. To build vocabulary in context and learn the word root *-aud-*
6. To develop skill in using verb agreement with collective nouns
7. To write a persuasive speech using supporting evidence
8. To respond to the play through writing, speaking and listening, and projects

SKILLS INSTRUCTION

Vocabulary: Using the Word Root *-aud-*
Spelling: Words That Begin With *gn-*
Grammar: Verb Agreement With Collective Nouns
Reading Strategy: Question
Literary Focus: Characterization and Theme in Drama
Writing: Support With Evidence
Speaking and Listening: Dramatic Monologue (Teacher Edition)
Viewing and Representing Set Model (Teacher Edition)
Critical Viewing: Analyze; Interpret; Analyze; Compare and Contrast; Analyze Cause and Effect

PORTFOLIO OPPORTUNITIES

Writing: Casting Memo; Contrasting Obituaries; Drama Critic's Review
Writing Mini-Lesson: Scrooge's Persuasive Speech
Speaking and Listening: Dramatic Monologue; Modernization
Projects: Winter Holidays; Set Model

Guide for Reading, Act II

◆ Review and Anticipate

In Act I, you met grumpy, miserly Ebenezer Scrooge. Although the people around him are cheerful and charitable in anticipation of Christmas, Scrooge is as bad-tempered and selfish as ever. However, Scrooge is forced to reexamine his attitude and behavior by the ghost of his old partner, Marley, and by the Ghost of Christmas Past.

From Marley's warning, you know that two more spirits will visit Scrooge. What do you think the Ghosts of Christmas Present and Future will show him? How will Scrooge react? Do you think he will take the Ghosts' lessons to heart? With a partner, jot down your predictions about the outcome of the play.

◆ Literary Focus

CHARACTERIZATION AND THEME IN DRAMA

Characterization is the means through which a writer reveals a character's personality. In drama, characters are revealed mainly through what they say, through what others say about them, and through their actions. A character's physical appearance and gestures may also offer insights into what he or she is like as a person.

The **theme** of a play is its central idea or insight into life. One way to arrive at the theme of a play is to notice how the main character changes. If you can explain why the main character changes for the better—or for the worse—you are probably very close to understanding the theme.

◆ Reading Strategy

QUESTION

You will be able to better understand what is going on in a play—or any work of literature —if you ask **questions** as you read. Some questions you might ask include these:

- Why did he do that?
- What did she mean by that comment?
- How might this incident be significant?

As you read Act II, jot down your questions in a chart like the one on this page. Record the answers to your questions as you encounter them in your reading.

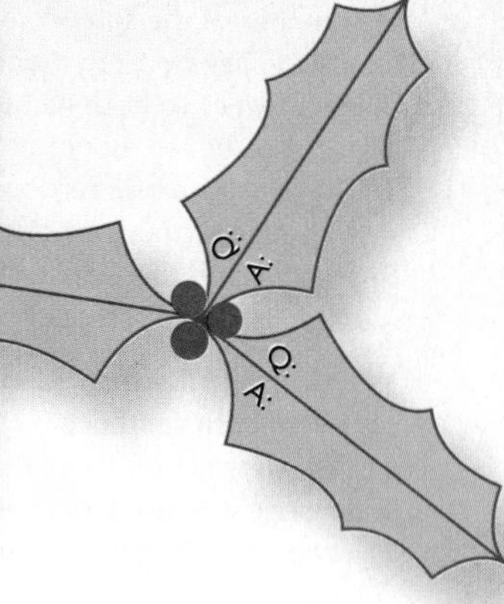

◆ Build Vocabulary

WORD ROOTS: *-aud-*

In Scene 4, Scrooge pleads, "Make me *audible*! I want to talk with my nephew and my niece!" Using the word's context and the knowledge that the word root *-aud-* means "hear," you can determine that *audible* means "able to be heard."

WORD BANK

Look over these words from Act II. Which one might describe the knees in your oldest, most worn-out pair of jeans?

astonish
compulsion
severe
meager
threadbare
audible
gnarled
dispelled

Interest Grabber Have students freewrite about an event in their life that they would like to change. The event should be something for which they are responsible and perhaps regret—by reflecting on mistakes, we can try not to repeat them in the future. Explain that in Act II of the play, Scrooge will see how his actions have affected and will affect the people around him.

Prentice Hall Literature Program Resources

REINFORCE / RETEACH / EXTEND

Selection Support Pages
Build Vocabulary: Word Roots: *-aud-*, p. 212
Build Spelling Skills, p. 213
Build Grammar Skills: Verb Agreement With Collective Nouns, p. 214
Reading Strategy: Question, p. 215
Literary Focus: Characterization and Theme in Drama, p. 216

Strategies for Diverse Student Needs, pp. 77–78

Beyond Literature Cultural Connection: Holiday Observance, p. 39

Formal Assessment Selection Test, pp. 185–187, Assessment Resources Software

Alternative Assessment, p. 39

Writing and Language Transparencies Open Mind Organizer, p. 90; Main Idea and Supporting Details Organizer, p. 70

Resource Pro CD-ROM *A Christmas Carol*

Listening to Literature Audiocassettes *A Christmas Carol*

A CHRISTMAS CAROL: SCROOGE AND MARLEY

Act II

Scene 1

[Lights. Choral music is sung. Curtain. SCROOGE, *in bed, sleeping, in spotlight. We cannot yet see the interior of his room.* MARLEY, *opposite, in spotlight equal to* SCROOGE'S. MARLEY *laughs. He tosses his hand in the air and a flame shoots from it, magically, into the air. There is a thunder clap, and then another; a lightning flash, and then another. Ghostly music plays under. Colors change.* MARLEY'S *spotlight has gone out and now reappears, with* MARLEY *in it, standing next to the bed and the sleeping* SCROOGE. MARLEY *addresses the audience directly.]*

MARLEY. Hear this snoring Scrooge! Sleeping to escape the nightmare that is his waking day. What shall I bring to him now? I'm afraid nothing would astonish old Scrooge now. Not after what he's seen. Not a baby boy, not a rhinoceros, nor anything in between would astonish Ebenezer Scrooge just now. I can think of nothing . . . *[Suddenly]* that's it! Nothing! *[He speaks confidentially.]* I'll have the clock strike one and, when he awakes expecting my second messenger, there will be no one . . . nothing. Then I'll have the bell strike twelve. And then one again . . . and then nothing. Nothing . . . *[Laughs]* nothing will . . . astonish him. I think it will work.

[The bell tolls one. SCROOGE *leaps awake.]*

SCROOGE. One! One! This is it: time! *[Looks about the room]* Nothing!

[The bell tolls midnight.]

Midnight! How can this be? I'm sleeping backwards.

[One again]

Good heavens! One again! I'm sleeping back and forth! *[A pause.* SCROOGE *looks about.]* Nothing! Absolutely nothing!

[Suddenly, thunder and lightning. MARLEY *laughs and disappears. The room shakes and glows. There is suddenly springlike music.* SCROOGE *makes a run for the door.]*

MARLEY. Scrooge!

SCROOGE. What?

MARLEY. Stay you put!

SCROOGE. Just checking to see if anyone is in here.

[Lights and thunder again: more music. MARLEY *is of a sudden gone. In his place sits the* GHOST OF CHRISTMAS PRESENT*—to be called in the stage directions of the play,* PRESENT*—center of room. Heaped up on the floor, to form a kind of throne, are turkeys, geese, game, poultry, brawn, great*

◆ **Reading Strategy**
What questions might the appearance of the Ghost of Christmas Present prompt you to ask about Christmas celebrations in Dickens's time? 1

◆ **Build Vocabulary**

astonish (ə stän′ ish) *v.*: Amaze

Develop Understanding

One-Minute Insight In Act II, the Ghost of Christmas Present escorts Scrooge to the home of his clerk, Bob Cratchit. Unseen, Scrooge meets Cratchit's family, which includes the frail Tiny Tim, who seems doomed to an early death. Scrooge also visits the home of his jovial nephew. Next, the Ghost of Christmas Future escorts Scrooge to several gloomy scenes, including a visit to his own grave. The horrible visions that Scrooge sees show him how careless and thoughtless a man he is and how he will end up—alone, friendless, and ravaged. From Scrooge's experiences in the play, readers learn about the importance of being kind, generous, and compassionate.

◆Build Grammar Skills

Verb Agreement With Collective Nouns If you wish to introduce the grammar concept for this selection before students read, refer to the instruction on p. 682.

◆Reading Strategy

1 Question Students may suggest questions such as these: Were foods such as those described in the stage directions common for Christmas feasts? Were such feasts available only to the rich?

Customize for *Less Proficient Readers*
Have students read Act II one scene at a time, stopping to review and summarize what has happened in each scene. Students may also benefit from listening to all or some of the play on audiocassette.

Listening to Literature Audiocassettes

Customize for *More Advanced Students*
As students read the play, have them explore Scrooge's reactions to the visions that the Spirits show him. Students can fill in the Open Mind Organizer, p. 90, in **Writing and Language Transparencies** with words, phrases, images, and symbols that represent Scrooge's thoughts and feelings at key points in Act II.

Preparing for Standardized Tests

Vocabulary The Build Vocabulary section focuses on the word root *-aud-*, which means "hear." Students can use their knowledge of such word roots to improve their performances on vocabulary sections of standardized tests.

Write the following sample sentences on the board. Ask students to choose the sentence that uses the word *audiologist* most precisely.

(A) The audiologist is specially trained to make plum puddings.
(B) The audiologist tested Tiny Tim's hearing.
(C) You can tell an audiologist from his green robe.
(D) It takes an audiologist to read his lines that well!

Guide students to see that (*B*) is the correct response because the word root *-aud-* refers to hearing, and this is the only answer that mentions hearing. Answers (*A*) and (*C*) are grammatically correct but inaccurate statements about an audiologist, who is a hearing expert. In sentence (*D*), the audiologist is doing something that another kind of expert might do just as well.

▶Critical Viewing◀

❶ **Analyze** The stage directions identify the torch shaped like a horn of plenty, the green robe, and the rusted scabbard.

◆Critical Thinking

❷ **Interpret** Who are the "brothers" that the Ghost of Christmas Present refers to, and why has Scrooge not "walked forth" with the younger brothers? *The Ghost is referring to the Ghosts of Christmas Present that have come before him. Each Christmas, there is a new Ghost of Christmas Present; there have been over eighteen hundred—for the year is in the 1800's—one Christmas per year. Scrooge has not "walked forth," meaning he has not celebrated Christmas.*

◆Literary Focus

❸ **Characterization and Theme in Drama** Point out that Scrooge's first statement shows that he is becoming more sympathetic. Have students analyze the other statements in this passage and tell what they reveal about Scrooge's character. *Possible answers: Scrooge is more willing to learn from the Spirits now. He feels he has learned an important lesson from the Ghost of Christmas Past and now seeks to learn more.*

Customize for
English Language Learners
Sentences such as "Tonight, if you have aught to teach me, let me profit by it" may present a challenge for some students. Have two or more volunteers paraphrase selected dialogue between characters, such as the one between Scrooge and the Ghost of Christmas Present. Encourage students to use pantomime and facial expressions to clarify the meanings of passages.

❶ ▲ **Critical Viewing** Which details of this costume are identified in the stage directions? **[Analyze]**

joints of meat, suckling pigs, long wreaths of sausages, mince-pies, plum puddings, barrels of oysters, red hot chestnuts, cherry-cheeked apples, juicy oranges, luscious pears, immense twelfth cakes, and seething bowls of punch, that make the chamber dim with their delicious steam. Upon this throne sits PRESENT, *glorious to see. He bears a torch, shaped as a Horn of Plenty.*[1] SCROOGE *hops out of the door, and then peeks back again into his bedroom.* PRESENT *calls to* SCROOGE.]

PRESENT. Ebenezer Scrooge. Come in, come in! Come in and know me better!

SCROOGE. Hello. How should I call you?

PRESENT. I am the Ghost of Christmas Present. Look upon me.

[PRESENT *is wearing a simple green robe. The walls around the room are now covered in greenery, as well. The room seems to be a perfect grove now: leaves of holly, mistletoe and ivy reflect the stage lights. Suddenly, there is a mighty roar of flame in the fireplace and now the hearth burns with a lavish, warming fire. There is an ancient scabbard girdling the* GHOST'S *middle, but without sword. The sheath is gone to rust.*]

You have never seen the like of me before?

SCROOGE. Never.

PRESENT. You have never walked forth with younger members of my family; my elder brothers born on Christmases past. ❷

SCROOGE. I don't think I have. I'm afraid I've not. Have you had many brothers, Spirit?

PRESENT. More than eighteen hundred.

SCROOGE. A tremendous family to provide for! [PRESENT *stands*] Spirit, conduct me where you will. I went forth last night on compulsion, and learnt a lesson which is working now. Tonight, if you have aught to teach me, let me profit by it. ❸

PRESENT. Touch my robe.

[SCROOGE *walks cautiously to* PRESENT *and touches his robe. When he does, lightning flashes, thunder claps, music plays. Blackout*]

1. **Horn of Plenty:** A horn overflowing with fruits, flowers, and grain, standing for wealth and abundance.

Block Scheduling Strategies

Consider these suggestions to take advantage of extended class time:

- Have groups of students take turns dramatizing different portions of the play. Follow the performances with a class discussion of the differences between reading and viewing a play.
- Divide students into groups to answer the Critical Thinking and Literary Focus questions. Assign different questions to each group. Then get back together as a class and have each group share the answers it has come up with.
- Allow class time for student presentations of the Writing Mini-Lesson (Persuasive Speech) and/or the Speaking and Listening activities in the Idea Bank (Dramatic Monologue and Modernization).
- Show all or part of one of the film adaptions of Dickens's novel. Follow with a critical discussion in which students compare and contrast the movie with the play they've just read. Which did they like better? Why?

Scene 2

4 [PROLOGUE: MARLEY *stands spotlit,* L. *He speaks directly to the audience.*]

MARLEY. My ghostly friend now leads my living partner through the city's streets.

[*Lights up on* SCROOGE *and* PRESENT]

5 See them there and hear the music people make when the weather is severe, as it is now.

[*Winter music. Choral group behind scrim, sings. When the song is done and the stage is re-set, the lights will fade up on a row of shops, behind the singers. The choral group will hum the song they have just completed now and mill about the streets,*[2] *carrying their dinners to the bakers' shops and restaurants. They will, perhaps, sing about being poor at Christmastime, whatever.*]

PRESENT. These revelers, Mr. Scrooge, carry their own dinners to their jobs, where they will work to bake the meals the rich men and women of this city will eat as their Christmas dinners. Generous people these . . . to care for the others, so . . .

[PRESENT *walks among the choral group and a sparkling incense*[3] *falls from his torch on to their baskets, as he pulls the covers off of the baskets. Some of the choral group become angry with each other.*]

MAN #1. Hey, you, watch where you're going.

MAN #2. Watch it yourself, mate!

[PRESENT *sprinkles them directly, they change.*]

MAN #1. I pray go in ahead of me. It's Christ-
6 mas. You be first!

MAN #2. No, no, I must insist that YOU be first!

MAN #1. All right, I shall be, and gratefully so.

MAN #2. The pleasure is equally mine, for being able to watch you pass, smiling.

2. **mill about the streets:** Walk around aimlessly.
3. **incense** (in′ sens) *n.*: Any of various substances that produce a pleasant odor when burned.

MAN #1. I would find it a shame to quarrel on Christmas Day . . .

MAN #2. As would I.

MAN #1. Merry Christmas then, friend!

MAN #2. And a Merry Christmas straight back to you!

◆ Literature and Your Life 7
Why are some people nicer to each other on holidays?

[*Church bells toll. The choral group enter the buildings: the shops and restaurants; they exit the stage, shutting their doors closed behind them. All sound stops.* SCROOGE *and* PRESENT *are alone again.*]

SCROOGE. What is it you sprinkle from your torch?

PRESENT. Kindness.

SCROOGE. Do you sprinkle your kindness on any particular people or on all people?

PRESENT. To any person kindly given. And to the very poor most of all.

SCROOGE. Why to the very poor most?

PRESENT. Because the very poor need it most. Touch my heart . . . here, Mr. Scrooge. We have another journey.

[SCROOGE *touches the* GHOST'S *heart and music plays, lights change color, lightning flashes, thunder claps. A choral group appears on the street, singing Christmas carols.*]

Scene 3

[MARLEY *stands spotlit in front of a scrim on which is painted the exterior of* CRATCHIT'S *four-roomed house. There is a flash and a clap and* MARLEY *is gone. The lights shift color again, the scrim flies away, and we are in the interior of the* CRATCHIT *family home.* SCROOGE *is there, with the* SPIRIT (PRESENT), *watching* MRS. CRATCHIT

◆ Build Vocabulary

compulsion (kəm pul′ shən) *n.*: A driving, irresistible force

severe (sə vir′) *adj.*: Harsh

◆Build Vocabulary

4 Using the Word Root *-aud-* The vocabulary skill for Act II explores the word root *-aud-*, which means "hear." Point out the word *audience* in the second line of the stage directions on this page. Ask students how the meaning of *-aud-* applies to *audience*. Students may say that an audience is a group of people who are listeners as well as spectators.

Comprehension Check ☑

5 What does Marley want the audience to notice? *He wants them to note that in spite of the harsh weather, people in the streets are in good spirits.*

◆Critical Thinking

6 Interpret Have students explain what happens in this passage. As an extension, ask students how a person on the street might have brought about the same change in the two men. *The Ghost of Christmas Present sprinkles incense on two men who are having angry words with each other. They begin to behave kindly toward each other. A person on the street might have stopped the two and gently reminded them that it's Christmas Day and not a time to quarrel.*

◆Literature and Your Life

7 Students may say that people are nicer to each other on holidays, because holidays are a time for rejoicing and being with loved ones. Holidays are a break from the normal routines of life, and this break can lift one's spirits and make people more relaxed.

Humanities: Music

Christmas Carols The word *carol* is from the French and originally referred to a ring dance accompanied by singing. By the sixteenth century, *carol* had come to mean a Christmas song of joy. Popular Christmas carols throughout the world include "Silent Night," by Franz Gruber, "O Little Town of Bethlehem," by Phillips Brooks, and "God Rest Ye Merry, Gentlemen," based on a London melody popular in English towns during the eighteenth century.

Use these questions for discussion:

1. Why has the playwright included Christmas carolers throughout the play? *Some students may say that they remind Scrooge and the audience of the triumph of joy and kindness over gloom and selfishness. Others may say that they add to the festive atmosphere surrounding the theme of Christmas.*
2. Why do you think Charles Dickens titled his story *A Christmas Carol?* *Students may say that Dickens might have considered his story to be a kind of Christmas carol because it celebrates the joy of Christmas.*

◆Critical Thinking

❶ Speculate Point out that while Scrooge has learned much from the visions shown to him by the Spirits, he has lessons yet to learn. Ask students which statement in this passage reflects the "old Scrooge." Have them speculate about what Scrooge will learn from his visit to the Cratchit home. *The statement "What foolishness!" shows that Scrooge still unfairly places responsibility on others for their misfortune. Students may say that Scrooge will probably learn that the Cratchit family has a lot less money but a lot more joy than Scrooge has.*

◆Literary Focus

❷ Characterization and Theme in Drama Ask students what this passage reveals about how the members of the Cratchit family feel about one another. Encourage them to give specific examples to support their answers. *Students may say that the members of the Cratchit family obviously love and enjoy one another. They may cite examples such as the mother's concern for Martha when she returns from work, Belinda's plot to have Martha hide from their father, and Bob Cratchit's and Martha's hearty greeting of each other.*

Clarification

❸ Explain that a comforter is a long narrow neck scarf that is usually knitted. Bob Cratchit is described as wearing "a threadbare and fringeless comforter," as a way of pointing out that the family is not well off financially.

Customize for *Interpersonal Learners*

Have a group of students conduct a dramatic reading of the dialogue on these pages. Encourage students to use expressive voices in their roles as Scrooge, the Ghost of Christmas, and all of the Crachits, including the baby, Peter.

set the table, with the help of BELINDA CRATCHIT *and* PETER CRATCHIT, *a baby, pokes a fork into the mashed potatoes on his highchair's tray. He also chews on his shirt collar.*]

SCROOGE. What is this place, Spirit?

PRESENT. This is the home of your employee, Mr. Scrooge. Don't you know it?

SCROOGE. Do you mean Cratchit, Spirit? Do you mean this is Cratchit's home?

PRESENT. None other.

1 **SCROOGE.** These children are his?

PRESENT. There are more to come presently.

SCROOGE. On his meager earnings! What foolishness!

PRESENT. Foolishness, is it?

SCROOGE. Wouldn't you say so? Fifteen shillings[4] a week's what he gets!

PRESENT. I would say that he gets the pleasure of his family, fifteen times a week times the number of hours a day! Wait, Mr. Scrooge. Wait, listen and watch. You might actually learn something . . .

MRS. CRATCHIT. What has ever got your precious father then? And your brother, Tiny Tim? And Martha warn't as late last Christmas by half an hour!

[MARTHA *opens the door, speaking to her mother as she does.*]

MARTHA. Here's Martha, now, Mother! [*She*
2 *laughs. The* CRATCHIT CHILDREN *squeal with*
3 *delight.*]

BELINDA. It's Martha, Mother! Here's Martha!

PETER. Marthmama, Marthmama! Hullo!

BELINDA. Hurrah! Martha! Martha! There's such an enormous goose for us, Martha!

MRS. CRATCHIT. Why, bless your heart alive, my dear, how late you are!

MARTHA. We'd a great deal of work to finish up last night, and had to clear away this morning, Mother.

MRS. CRATCHIT. Well, never mind so long as you are come. Sit ye down before the fire, my dear, and have a warm, Lord bless ye!

BELINDA. No, no! There's Father coming. Hide, Martha, hide!

[MARTHA *giggles and hides herself.*]

MARTHA. Where? Here?

PETER. *Hide, hide!*

BELINDA. Not there! *THERE!*

[MARTHA *is hidden.* BOB CRATCHIT *enters, carrying* TINY TIM *atop his shoulder. He wears a threadbare and fringeless comforter hanging down in front of him.* TINY TIM *carries small crutches and*
his small legs are bound in an iron frame 2
brace.] 3

BOB and **TINY TIM.** Merry Christmas.

BOB. Merry Christmas my love, Merry Christmas Peter, Merry Christmas Belinda. Why, where is Martha?

MRS CRATCHIT. Not coming.

BOB. Not coming: Not coming upon Christmas Day?

MARTHA. [*Pokes head out*] Ohhh, poor Father. Don't be disappointed.

BOB. What's this?

MARTHA. 'Tis I!

BOB. Martha! [*They embrace.*]

TINY TIM. Martha! Martha!

MARTHA. Tiny Tim!

[TINY TIM *is placed in* MARTHA'S *arms.* BELINDA *and* PETER *rush him offstage.*]

BELINDA. Come, brother! You must come hear
the pudding singing in the copper. 4
TINY TIM. The pudding? What flavor have we? 5

PETER. Plum! Plum!

TINY TIM. Oh, Mother! I love plum!

4. **fifteen shillings:** A small amount of money for a week's work.

Cultural Connection

Christmas Goose and Plum Pudding
Goose has been a part of Christmas feasts since the Middle Ages, particularly among the English. Of the Cratchits' Christmas goose, Dickens says in his novel, "There never was such a goose . . . Its tenderness and flavor, size and cheapness, were the themes of universal admiration."

The earliest recorded version of English plum pudding was eaten during the reign of Queen Anne, in the early 1700's. It was made of thickened mutton broth, brown bread, raisins, and spices. Today's plum pudding is a dark, firm, rounded dessert, made with bread crumbs, suet, eggs, spices, chopped nuts, and dried and candied fruits—but not plums. During Dickens's time, a proper Christmas pudding took three days to make. Everyone in the household helped prepare the ingredients and stir the pudding. The mixture was then tied tightly in a cloth or pressed into a bowl and lowered into a kettle of boiling water to steam for at least six hours.

[*The children exit the stage, giggling.*]

MRS CRATCHIT. And how did little Tim behave?

BOB. As good as gold, and even better. Somehow he gets thoughtful sitting by himself so much, and thinks the strangest things you ever heard. He told me, coming home, that he hoped people saw him in the church, because he was a cripple, and it might be pleasant to them to remember upon Christmas Day, who made lame beggars walk and blind men see.
4 [*Pauses*] He has the oddest ideas sometimes,
5 but he seems all the while to be growing stronger and more hearty . . . one would never know. [*Hears* TIM'S *crutch on floor outside door*]

PETER. The goose has arrived to be eaten!

BELINDA. Oh, mama, mama, it's beautiful.

MARTHA. It's a perfect goose, Mother!

TINY TIM. To this Christmas goose, Mother and Father I say . . . [*Yells*] *Hurrah! Hurrah!*

OTHER CHILDREN. [*Copying* TIM] *Hurrah! Hurrah!*

[*The family sits round the table.* BOB *and* MRS. CRATCHIT *serve the trimmings, quickly. All sit; all bow heads; all pray.*]

BOB. Thank you, dear Lord, for your many gifts . . . our dear children; our wonderful meal; our love for one another; and the warmth of our small fire—[*Looks up at all*] A merry Christmas to us, my dear. God bless us!

ALL. [*Except* TIM] Merry Christmas! God bless us!

TINY TIM. [*In a short silence*] God bless us every one.

[*All freeze. Spotlight on* PRESENT *and* SCROOGE]

SCROOGE. Spirit, tell me if Tiny Tim will live.

PRESENT. I see a vacant seat . . . in the poor chimney corner, and a crutch without an owner, carefully preserved. If these shadows remain unaltered by the future, the child will die.

> **◆ Literary Focus**
> How does Scrooge's concern for Tiny Tim reflect a change in Scrooge's character? 6

SCROOGE. No, no, kind Spirit! Say he will be spared!

PRESENT. If these shadows remain unaltered by the future, none other of my race will find him here. What then? If he be like to die, he 7 had better do it, and decrease the surplus population.

[SCROOGE *bows his head. We hear* BOB'S *voice speak* SCROOGE'S *name.*]

BOB. Mr. Scrooge . . .

SCROOGE. Huh? What's that? Who calls?

BOB. [*His glass raised in a toast*] I'll give you Mr. Scrooge, the Founder of the Feast!

SCROOGE. Me, Bob? You toast *me*?

PRESENT. Save your breath, Mr. Scrooge. You can't be seen or heard.

MRS. CRATCHIT. The Founder of the Feast, indeed! I wish I had him here, that miser Scrooge. I'd give him a piece of my mind to feast upon, and I hope he'd have a good appetite for it!

BOB. My dear! Christmas Day!

MRS. CRATCHIT. It should be Christmas Day, I am sure, on which one drinks the health of such an odious, stingy, unfeeling man as Mr. Scrooge . . .

SCROOGE. Oh, Spirit, must I? . . .

MRS. CRATCHIT. You know he is, Robert! Nobody knows it better than you do, poor fellow!

BOB. This is Christmas Day, and I should like to drink to the health of the man who employs me and allows me to earn my living and our support and that man is Ebenezer Scrooge . . .

MRS. CRATCHIT. I'll drink to his health for your sake and the day's, but not for his sake . . . a

◆ Build Vocabulary

meager (mē´ gər) *adj.*: Of poor quality; small in amount

threadbare (*th*red´ ber) *adj.*: Worn; shabby

◆Critical Thinking

4 Interpret What does the playwright reveal about Tiny Tim through this dialogue? *Tiny Tim seems well behaved and thoughtful, thinks of others, has a strong faith, and is physically challenged, perhaps as a result of a disease.*

◆Reading Strategy

5 Question What questions might you ask about Tiny Tim as you read Bob Cratchit's dialogue? *Students may suggest questions such as these: Why does Tim sit by himself so much? Why is Tim physically challenged? What is it about Tim's condition that "one would never know"?*

◆Literary Focus

6 Characterization and Theme in Drama Before students answer the question, briefly review with them Scrooge's attitude toward those less fortunate than he, as revealed in Act I of the play. *Scrooge seems genuinely concerned about Tiny Tim's fate. Before the visits by the two Spirits, Scrooge did not care about the suffering of others.*

◆Critical Thinking

7 Connect Have students recall the earlier scene in the play in which they read the phrase "decrease the surplus population." *In Act I, when the two men come to Scrooge's office seeking money for the poor, one of them says that some of those who are destitute would rather die than go to debtors' prison. Scrooge cruelly replies that their deaths would lower the excess population.*

Customize for
Less Proficient Readers
Help students navigate the interactive scene in which Scrooge talks to the Cratchits and to the Ghost of Christmas Present, while Mr. and Mrs. Cratchit talk to each other. You may want to have four students read the scene aloud to see how the dialogue of the characters is interwoven.

◆Critical Thinking

❶ **Infer** Why is Scrooge sure that no one else is toasting him on Christmas Day? *Scrooge now sees how mean and stingy he has been, especially toward Bob Cratchit. He is sure that no one else would drink a toast to the health of such an "unfeeling man."*

▶Critical Viewing◀

❷ **Interpret** Some students may say that placing Tiny Tim on the table highlights his importance in the play as the character who most captures Scrooge's heart. Also, the director may have put Tim on the table because he sings the lead vocal in the family song.

Clarification

❸ The lute is a fretted instrument with a lightweight, pear-shaped body. It is played by plucking the strings with the fingers. Between 1400 and 1700, the lute was perhaps the most popular musical instrument in Europe. Noted English composer John Dowland (c.1563–1626) wrote mostly for the lute.

Customize for *Intrapersonal Learners*

Ask students to put themselves in Scrooge's place at this point in the play. Have them imagine that, as Scrooge, they are keeping a journal of their thoughts and feelings as the Spirits show them visions of Christmases past and present. Instruct students to jot down journal entries that record their reactions to the visions. Encourage them to include questions about what the third Spirit will show them.

Merry Christmas and a Happy New Year to you, Mr. Scrooge, wherever you may be this day!

SCROOGE. Just here, kind madam . . . out of sight, out of sight . . .

BOB. Thank you, my dear. Thank you.

1 **SCROOGE.** Thank *you*, Bob . . . and Mrs. Cratchit, too. No one else is toasting me, . . . not now . . . not ever. Of that I am sure . . .

BOB. Children . . .

ALL. Merry Christmas to Mr. Scrooge.

BOB. I'll pay you sixpence, Tim, for my favorite song.

TINY TIM. Oh, Father, I'd so love to sing it, but not for pay. This Christmas goose—this feast—you and Mother, my brother and sisters close with me: that's my pay—

▲ Critical Viewing Why might a director stage the scene this way, with Tiny Tim standing on the table? **[Interpret]** 2

BOB. Martha, will you play the notes on the lute,[5] for Tiny Tim's song. 3

BELINDA. May I sing, too, Father?

BOB. We'll all sing.

[They sing a song about a tiny child lost in the snow—probably from Wordsworth's poem. TIM *sings the lead vocal; all chime in for the*

5. **lute** (lo͞ot) *n.*: Stringed instrument like a guitar.

Humanities: Literature

The poem referred to is actually a series of poems by William Wordsworth about a three-year-old child who becomes lost in the snow. In "Lucy Gray, or Solitude," a child carries a lantern to town to light her mother's way home through the snow. The child becomes lost, and the parents follow her footsteps until they suddenly disappear in a snowy bank. In "Strange Fits of Passion Have I Known," the moon seems to follow Lucy until suddenly it drops symbolically. In "She Dwelt Among the Untrodden Ways," Lucy is dead. Her brief life is recalled in "Three Years She Grew in Sun and Shower." Read these poems with students, or quote "A Slumber Did My Spirit Seal":

> A slumber did my spirit seal,
> I had no human fears:
> She seemed a thing that could not feel
> The touch of earthly years.

Ask students why such poetry might have meant a lot to the Cratchits. *Students may say that because the Cratchits know that Tiny Tim is very ill, the poems about death give them comfort.*

chorus. Their song fades under, as THE GHOST OF CHRISTMAS PRESENT *speaks.*]

PRESENT. Mark my words, Ebenezer Scrooge. I do not present the Cratchits to you because they are a handsome, or brilliant family. They are not handsome. They are not brilliant. They are not well-dressed, or tasteful to the times. Their shoes are not even waterproofed by virtue of money or cleverness spent. So when the pavement is wet, so are the insides of their shoes and the tops of their toes. These are the Cratchits, Mr. Scrooge. They are not highly special. They are happy, grateful, pleased with one another, contented with the time and how it passes. They don't sing very well, do they? But, nonetheless, they do sing . . . *[Pauses]* think of that, Scrooge. Fifteen shillings a week and they do sing . . . hear their song until its end.

SCROOGE. I am listening.

[*The chorus sings full volume now, until . . . the song ends here.*]

Spirit, it must be time for us to take our leave. I feel in my heart that it is . . . that I must think on that which I have seen here . . .

PRESENT. Touch my robe again . . .

[SCROOGE *touches* PRESENT'S *robe. The lights fade out on the* CRATCHITS, *who sit, frozen, at the table.* SCROOGE *and* PRESENT *in a spotlight now. Thunder, lightning, smoke. They are gone.*]

Scene 4

4 [MARLEY *appears* D.L. *in single spotlight. A storm brews. Thunder and lightning.* SCROOGE *and* PRESENT *"fly" past,* U. *The storm continues, furiously, and, now and again,* SCROOGE *and* PRESENT *will zip past in their travels.* MARLEY *will speak straight out to the audience.*]

MARLEY. The Ghost of Christmas Present, my co-worker in this attempt to turn a miser, flies about now with that very miser, Scrooge, from street to street, and he points out partygoers on their way to Christmas parties. If one were to judge from the numbers of people on their way to friendly gatherings, one might think that no one was left at home to give anyone welcome . . . but that's not the case, is it? Every home is expecting company and . . . [*He laughs.*] Scrooge is amazed.

[SCROOGE *and* PRESENT *zip past again. The lights fade up around them. We are in the* NEPHEW'S *home, in the living room.* PRESENT *and* SCROOGE *stand watching the* NEPHEW: FRED *and his wife, fixing the fire.*]

SCROOGE. What is this place? We've moved from the mines!

PRESENT. You do not recognize them?

SCROOGE. It is my nephew! . . . and the one he married . . .

[MARLEY *waves his hand and there is a lightning flash. He disappears.*]

FRED. It strikes me as sooooo funny, to think of what he said . . . that Christmas was a humbug, as I live! He believed it!

WIFE. More shame for him, Fred!

FRED. Well, he's a comical old fellow, that's the 5
truth.

WIFE. I have no patience with him.

FRED. Oh, I have! I am sorry for him; I couldn't be angry with him if I tried. Who suffers by his ill whims? Himself, always . . .

SCROOGE. It's me they talk of, isn't it, Spirit?

FRED. Here, wife, consider this. Uncle Scrooge takes it into his head to dislike us, and he won't come and dine with us. What's the consequence?

WIFE. Oh . . . you're sweet to say what I think you're about to say, too, Fred . . .

FRED. What's the consequence? He don't lose much of a dinner by it, I can tell you that!

WIFE. Ooooooo, Fred! Indeed, I think he loses a very good dinner . . . ask my sisters, or your bachelor friend, Topper . . . ask any of them. They'll tell you what old Scrooge, your uncle, missed: a dandy meal!

◆Reading Strategy

4 Question Ask students what question they might ask as they read the stage directions for the beginning of Scene 4. Then have them suggest answers to the question. *Students may suggest a question such as this: Why does the playwright include a storm at this point in the play? They may speculate that the storm occurs to heighten the suspense of the scene and to foreshadow coming events.*

◆Critical Thinking

5 Compare and Contrast Have students compare Fred's attitude toward Scrooge with that of his wife. *Students may say that Fred seems more sympathetic toward Scrooge than his wife is.*

Customize for *Visual/Spatial Students*

Review with students the meanings of stage directions such as *D.C., U.R., D.L.,* and *U.* (*downstage center, upstage right, downstage left,* and *upstage*). Have students review the stage directions at the beginning of Scene 4. Then ask a volunteer to draw a diagram on the board that shows the positions of the characters according to these directions.

Beyond the Classroom

Career Connection

Theater Design and Technical Assistants

In the professional theater, a number of persons assist scene designers and technical directors. Their duties include searching for furniture and props, making working drawings, and creating and manipulating scenery. Technical assistants build, assemble, and paint scenery for a production. Property crews make sure that the scenery is kept in good condition. Stage crews are charged with efficient movement and accurate placement of scenery and props during performances and upkeep of materials during the run of a show. These assistants often go unnoticed by the public, but they are key members of a production team because they make possible the smooth execution of directors' and designers' plans.

Have students contact a local theater company or use library resources to learn more about the work of theater assistants and technicians. Encourage students to share their findings.

◆Critical Thinking

❶ **Connect** Remind students that in Act I, the playwright reveals that when Scrooge was a younger man, he lost two people he loved. Have students recall these people and tell how this passage relates to those losses. *Scrooge lost his sister Fan, who died, and his fiancée, who left him because of his greed. Students may say that seeing the happiness between Fred and his wife reminds Scrooge of the happiness he gave up to pursue money. Also, because Fred is reminded of his mother when he looks at Scrooge, Scrooge is reminded of his sister.*

◆Reading Strategy

❷ **Question** Students may mention questions such as these: As Scrooge watches Fred and his wife, does he realize the happiness he missed by not marrying? What might Scrooge say to his nephew if he could become audible?

◆Literature and Your Life

❸ Have students imagine that Scrooge has come to them for advice on what to say to Fred and his wife. What advice would they give him? *Some students may suggest that Scrooge apologize to his nephew for his earlier rudeness and ask to be part of their lives. Others may suggest that Scrooge thank them for the example of loving kindness that they have shown him.*

Comprehension Check ☑

❹ Why will the Ghost of Christmas Present soon end his "life"? *This Spirit's life lasts only as long as Christmas Day.*

◆Critical Thinking

❺ **Connect** Ask students to recall where they read these words earlier in the play. *In speaking to the men who come to his office asking for money for the poor, Scrooge suggests that if the poor can go to workhouses and prisons, they do not need charity.*

FRED. Well, that's something of a relief, wife. Glad to hear it! [*He hugs his wife. They laugh. They kiss.*] The truth is, he misses much yet. I mean to give him the same chance every year, whether he likes it or not, for I pity him. Nay, he is my only uncle and I feel for the old miser . . . but, I tell you, wife: I see my dear and perfect mother's face on his own wizened cheeks and brow: brother and sister they were, and I cannot erase that from each view of him I take . . . ❶

WIFE. I understand what you say, Fred, and I am with you in your yearly asking. But he never will accept, you know. He never will.

FRED. Well, true, wife. Uncle may rail at Christmas till he dies. I think I shook him some with my visit yesterday . . . [*Laughing*] I refused to grow angry . . . no matter how nasty he became . . . [*Whoops*] It was HE who grew angry, wife! [*They both laugh now.*]

SCROOGE. What he says is true, Spirit . . .

FRED and **WIFE.** Bah, humbug!

FRED. [*Embracing his wife*] There is much laughter in our marriage, wife. It pleases me. You please me . . .

WIFE. And you please me, Fred. You are a good man . . . [*They embrace.*] Come now. We must have a look at the meal . . . our guests will soon arrive . . . my sisters, Topper . . .

❷ ◆ **Reading Strategy** What questions might you ask about the episode with Fred and his wife?

FRED. A toast first . . . [*He hands her a glass.*] A toast to Uncle Scrooge . . . [*Fills their glasses*]

WIFE. A toast to him?

FRED. Uncle Scrooge has given us plenty of merriment, I am sure, and it would be ungrateful not to drink to his health. And I say . . . *Uncle Scrooge!*

WIFE. [*Laughing*] You're a proper loon,[6] Fred . . . and I'm a proper wife to you . . . [*She raises her glass.*] *Uncle Scrooge!* [*They drink. They embrace. They kiss.*]

SCROOGE. Spirit, please, make me visible! Make me audible! I want to talk with my nephew and my niece! ❸

[*Calls out to them. The lights that light the room and* FRED *and wife fade out.* SCROOGE *and* PRESENT *are alone, spotlit.*]

PRESENT. These shadows are gone to you now, Mr. Scrooge. You may return to them later tonight in your dreams. [*Pauses*] My time grows short, Ebenezer Scrooge. Look you on me! Do you see how I've aged? ❹

SCROOGE. Your hair has gone gray! Your skin, wrinkled! Are spirits' lives so short?

PRESENT. My stay upon this globe is very brief. It ends tonight.

SCROOGE. Tonight?

PRESENT. At midnight. The time is drawing near!

[*Clock strikes 11:45.*]

Hear those chimes? In a quarter hour, my life will have been spent! Look, Scrooge, man. Look you here.

[*Two gnarled baby dolls are taken from* PRESENT'S *skirts.*]

SCROOGE. Who are they?

PRESENT. They are Man's children, and they cling to me, appealing from their fathers. The boy is Ignorance; the girl is Want. Beware them both, and all of their degree, but most of all beware this boy, for I see that written on his brow which is doom, unless the writing be erased. [*He stretches out his arm. His voice is now amplified: loudly and oddly.*]

SCROOGE. Have they no refuge or resource?

PRESENT. Are there no prisons? Are there no workhouses? [*Twelve chimes*] Are there no prisons? Are there no workhouses? ❺

[*A* PHANTOM, *hooded, appears in dim light,* D., *opposite.*]

Are there no prisons? Are there no workhouses?

6. **a proper loon:** A silly person.

Speaking and Listening Mini-Lesson

Dramatic Monologue
This mini-lesson supports the Speaking and Listening activity in the Idea Bank on p. 683.

Introduce Explain that in a dramatic monologue, an actor reveals the thoughts and feelings of the character she or he is portraying.

Develop Have students review one of Scrooge's experiences with a Christmas Ghost, making notes on information to include in the monologue. Explain that when performing a monologue, students should speak clearly, make eye contact, and use effective gestures.

Apply Allow time for each student to write, rehearse, and revise a three-minute monologue. Have students perform their monologues. Instruct students, as audience members, to take notes during each performance.

Assess Evaluate each student's performance in terms of preparation, speaking composure, eye contact, and body language. Have "audience" members use the Peer Assessment: Dramatic Performance form, p. 107, in **Alternative Assessment,** to evaluate their classmates' performances.

[PRESENT *begins to deliquesce.* SCROOGE *calls after him.*]

SCROOGE. Spirit, I'm frightened! Don't leave me! Spirit!

PRESENT. Prisons? Workhouses? Prisons? Workhouses . . .

[*He is gone.* SCROOGE *is alone now with the* PHANTOM, *who is, of course, the* GHOST OF CHRISTMAS FUTURE. THE PHANTOM *is shrouded in black. Only its outstretched hand is visible from under his ghostly garment.*]

SCROOGE. Who are you, Phantom? Oh, yes, I think I know you! You are, are you not, the Spirit of Christmas Yet to Come? [*No reply*] And you are about to show me the shadows of the things that have not yet happened, but will happen in time before us. Is that not so, Spirit?

[*The* PHANTOM *allows* SCROOGE *a look at his face. No other reply wanted here. A nervous giggle here.*]

Oh, Ghost of the Future, I fear you more than any Specter I have seen! But, as I know that your purpose is to do me good and as I hope to live to be another man from what I was, I am prepared to bear you company.

6 **◆ Literary Focus** What do Scrooge's words to the Ghost of Christmas Future tell you about the play's theme?

[FUTURE *does not reply, but for a stiff arm, hand and finger set, pointing forward.*]

Lead on, then, lead on. The night is waning fast, and it is precious time to me. Lead on, Spirit!

[FUTURE *moves away from* SCROOGE *in the same rhythm and motion employed at its arrival.* SCROOGE *falls into the same pattern, a considerable space apart from the* SPIRIT. *In the space between them,* MARLEY *appears. He looks to* FUTURE *and then to* SCROOGE. *He claps his hands. Thunder and lightning. Three* BUSINESSMEN *appear, spotlighted singularly: One is* D.L.; *one is* D.R.; *one is* U.C. *Thus, six points of the stage should now be spotted in light.* MARLEY *will watch this scene from his position,* C. SCROOGE *and* FUTURE *are* R. *and* L. *of* C.]

FIRST BUSINESSMAN. Oh, no, I don't know much about it either way, I only know he's dead.

SECOND BUSINESSMAN. When did he die?

FIRST BUSINESSMAN. Last night, I believe.

SECOND BUSINESSMAN. Why, what was the matter with him? I thought he'd never die, really . . .

FIRST BUSINESSMAN. [*Yawning*] Goodness knows, goodness knows . . .

THIRD BUSINESSMAN. What has he done with his money? 7

SECOND BUSINESSMAN. I haven't heard. Have you?

FIRST BUSINESSMAN. Left it to his Company, perhaps. Money to money; you know the expression . . .

THIRD BUSINESSMAN. He hasn't left it to me. That's all I know . . .

FIRST BUSINESSMAN. [*Laughing*] Nor to me . . . [*Looks at* SECOND BUSINESSMAN] You, then? You got his money???

SECOND BUSINESSMAN. [*Laughing*] Me, me, his money? Nooooo! [*They all laugh.*]

THIRD BUSINESSMAN. It's likely to be a cheap funeral, for upon my life, I don't know of a living soul who'd care to venture to it. Suppose we make up a party and volunteer?

SECOND BUSINESSMAN. I don't mind going if a lunch is provided, but I must be fed, if I make one.

FIRST BUSINESSMAN. Well, I am the most disinterested among you, for I never wear black gloves, and I never eat lunch. But I'll offer to go, if anybody else will. When I come to think of it, I'm not all sure that I wasn't his most

◆ Build Vocabulary

audible (ô´ də bəl) *adj.*: Loud enough to be heard

gnarled (närld) *adj.*: Knotty and twisted

◆Literary Focus

6 Characterization and Theme in Drama Scrooge tells the Ghost of Christmas Future that in spite of his fear, he is ready to learn from the Ghost because he wants to change his nature. His desire to change from being selfish and mean to being caring and generous is a key to the play's theme, which is that true happiness can be found in love and kindness toward others.

◆Critical Thinking

7 Infer Whom are the men talking about and why are they laughing? *They are talking about Scrooge. Since the men all knew Scrooge to be stingy with money, they are making jokes about Scrooge's leaving his money to others.*

Customize for
Visual/Spatial Learners
Have students make sketches of the stage in which they show the positions of all the actors as described in the stage directions at the bottom of the first column of dialogue on this page. Instruct students to identify the character shown in each position.

Customize for
English Language Learners
Help students understand words on these pages that may be unfamiliar to them. When possible, use pictures, pantomime, and facial expressions to explain meanings of words. For example, for *wizened,* show a picture of a face that is heavily wrinkled; for *rail,* show an angry expression or pantomime scolding; and for *waning,* dim the lights or otherwise show something diminishing or decreasing in size.

Humanities: Literature

A Christmas Carol, by Charles Dickens

Charles Dickens had included Christmas vignettes in his *Sketches by Boz* and *The Pickwick Papers,* but *A Christmas Carol* was his first full-scale treatment of the holiday that he loved as a young boy. Dickens conceived and wrote the story in a few weeks, partly out of financial necessity but also to focus attention on the plight of the poor in England. Dickens said that while writing the book, he laughed and cried as with no other story he had written.

In a review of *A Christmas Carol,* English author William Makepeace Thackeray called it "a national benefit, and to every man and woman who reads it a personal kindness." Scottish author Robert Louis Stevenson wrote of *A Christmas Carol* and another of Dickens's Christmas stories, "Oh, what a jolly thing it is for a man to have written books like these and just filled people's hearts with joy."

Have students discuss reasons for the story's continued popularity, even though it was written more than a century ago.

◆Reading Strategy

❶ **Question** Students may say that they can look for clues in the dialogue and behavior of characters to learn who has died. For example, when Marley laughs at Scrooge's questions, students may guess that Scrooge himself is the dead man.

◆Critical Thinking

❷ **Infer** Refer students to the list of characters on p. 644. Have them locate and identify Joe in the list. Ask students to guess why the women and man have come to Joe's shop. Have them give reasons for their responses. *Students may infer that the women and man have come to sell items that belonged to a dead man, because the third Spirit seems to be showing Scrooge a future in which someone—perhaps Scrooge himself—has died.*

◆Literary Focus

❸ **Characterization and Theme in Drama** Ask students if the attitude of this woman is more like the "old" Scrooge or the "new" Scrooge. Have students give details from the passage to support their answers. *Most students will recognize that her attitude is like that of the "old" Scrooge, because she greedily stole from the dead man, claims that she would have gathered more if she could have, and is eager to know the worth of what she took.*

Customize for *Verbal/Linguistic Learners*

Have volunteers read aloud the dialogue on this page, beginning with the appearance of the First Woman. Discuss with students which of the characters is the most aggressive, or pushy, of the four.

particular friend; for we used to stop and speak whenever we met. Well, then . . . bye, bye!

SECOND BUSINESSMAN. Bye, bye . . .

THIRD BUSINESSMAN. Bye, bye . . .

[They glide offstage in three separate directions. Their lights follow them.]

SCROOGE. Spirit, why did you show me this? Why do you show me businessmen from my streets as they take the death of Jacob Marley. That is a thing past. You are *future!*

[JACOB MARLEY *laughs a long, deep laugh. There is a thunder clap and lightning flash, and he is gone.* SCROOGE *faces* FUTURE, *alone on stage now.* FUTURE *wordlessly stretches out his arm-hand-and-finger-set, pointing into the distance,* U. *There, above them. Scoundrels "fly" by, half-dressed and slovenly. When this scene has passed, a woman enters the playing area. She is almost at once followed by a second woman; and then a man in faded black; and then, suddenly, an old man, who smokes a pipe. The old man scares the other three. They laugh, anxious.*]

1 **◆ Reading Strategy** How would you find out the answer to the question "Who has died"?

FIRST WOMAN. Look here, old Joe, here's a chance! If we haven't all three met here without meaning it!

OLD JOE. You couldn't have met in a better place. Come into the parlor. You were made free of it long ago, you know; and the other
2 two an't strangers [*He stands; shuts a door. Shrieking*] We're all suitable to our calling. We're well matched. Come into the parlor. Come into the parlor . . .

[*They follow him* D. SCROOGE *and* FUTURE *are now in their midst, watching; silent. A truck comes in on which is set a small wall with fireplace and a screen of rags, etc. All props for the scene.*]

Let me just rake this fire over a bit . . .

[*He does. He trims his lamp with the stem of his pipe. The* FIRST WOMAN *throws a large bundle on to the floor. She sits beside it crosslegged, defiantly.*]

FIRST WOMAN. What odds then? What odds, Mrs. Dilber? Every person has a right to take care of themselves. HE always did!

MRS. DILBER. That's true indeed! No man more so!

FIRST WOMAN. Why, then, don't stand staring as if you was afraid, woman! Who's the wiser? We're not going to pick holes in each other's coats, I suppose?

MRS. DILBER. No, indeed! We should hope not!

FIRST WOMAN. Very well, then! That's enough. Who's the worse for the loss of a few things like these? Not a dead man, I suppose?

MRS. DILBER. *[Laughing]* No, indeed!

FIRST WOMAN. If he wanted to keep 'em after he was dead, the wicked old screw, why wasn't he natural in his lifetime? If he had been, he'd
have had somebody to look after him when he 3
was struck with Death, instead of lying gasping out his last there, alone by himself.

MRS. DILBER. It's the truest word that was ever spoke. It's a judgment on him.

FIRST WOMAN. I wish it were a heavier one, and it should have been, you may depend on it, if I could have laid my hands on anything else. Open that bundle, old Joe, and let me know the value of it. Speak out plain. I'm not afraid to be the first, nor afraid for them to see it. We knew pretty well that we were helping ourselves, before we met here, I believe. It's no sin. Open the bundle, Joe.

FIRST MAN. No, no, my dear! I won't think of letting you being the first to show what you've . . . earned . . . earned from this. I throw in mine. [*He takes a bundle from his shoulder, turns it upside down, and empties its contents out on to the floor.*] It's not very extensive, see . . . seals . . . a pencil case . . . sleeve buttons . . .

MRS. DILBER. Nice sleeve buttons, though . . .

FIRST MAN. Not bad, not bad . . . a brooch there . . .

Cross-Curricular Connection: Social Studies

Dickens's London Charles Dickens was drawn to the noisy, bustling streets of nineteenth-century London, which inspired many of his stories. By 1812, when Dickens was born, London was already the largest city in Europe. The author often took long walks throughout the city, after a day of writing, to gather fresh impressions that later found their way into his novels.

Have students use your school's media center or the local library to learn more about life in nineteenth-century London.

Suggest that students focus their research on questions such as these:

- How did the population of London change during Dickens's lifetime?
- What was life like for London's poor?
- How did the railways change London during Dickens's time?

Invite students to share their findings with the class.

OLD JOE: Not really valuable, I'm afraid . . .

FIRST MAN. How much, old Joe?

OLD JOE: [*Writing on the wall with chalk*] A pitiful lot, really. Ten and six and not a sixpence more!

FIRST MAN. You're not serious!

OLD JOE. That's your account and I wouldn't give another sixpence if I was to be boiled for not doing it. Who's next?

MRS. DILBER. Me! [*Dumps out contents of her bundle*] Sheets, towels, silver spoons, silver sugar-tongs . . . some boots . . .

4 **OLD JOE.** [*Writing on wall*] I always give too much to the ladies. It's a weakness of mine and that's the way I ruin myself. Here's your total comin' up . . . two pounds-ten . . . if you asked me for another penny, and made it an open question, I'd repent of being so liberal and knock off half-a-crown.

FIRST WOMAN. And now do MY bundle, Joe.

OLD JOE. [*Kneeling to open knots on her bundle*] So many knots, madam . . . [*He drags out large curtains; dark*] What do you call this? Bed curtains!

FIRST WOMAN. [*Laughing*] Ah, yes, bed curtains!

OLD JOE. You don't mean to say you took 'em down, rings and all, with him lying there?

FIRST WOMAN. Yes, I did, why not?

OLD JOE. You were born to make your fortune and you'll certainly do it.

FIRST WOMAN. I certainly shan't hold my hand, when I can get anything in it by reaching it out, for the sake of such a man as he was, I promise you, Joe.
5 Don't drop that lamp oil on those blankets, now!

OLD JOE. His blankets?

FIRST WOMAN. Whose else's do you think? He isn't likely to catch cold without 'em, I daresay.

OLD JOE. I hope that he didn't die of anything catching? Eh?

FIRST WOMAN. Don't you be afraid of that. I ain't so fond of his company that I'd loiter about him for such things if he did. Ah! You may look through that shirt till your eyes ache, but you won't find a hole in it, nor a threadbare place. It's the best he had, and a fine one, too. They'd have wasted it, if it hadn't been for me.

OLD JOE. What do you mean 'They'd have wasted it?'

FIRST WOMAN. Putting it on him to be buried in, to be sure. Somebody was fool enough to do it, but I took it off again . . . [*She laughs, as do they all, nervously.*] If calico[7] ain't good enough for such a purpose, it isn't good enough then for anything. It's quite as becoming to the body. He can't look uglier than he 6
did in that one!

SCROOGE. [*A low-pitched moan emits from his mouth; from the bones.*] *OOOOOOOoo oooOOOOOoooooOOOOOOOOoooooOOOOOOoo oooOO!*

OLD JOE. One pound six for the lot. [*He produces a small flannel bag filled with money. He divvies it out. He continues to pass around the money as he speaks. All are laughing.*] That's the end of it, you see! He frightened every one away from him while he was alive, to profit us when he was dead! Hah ha ha!

ALL. HAHAHAHAhahahahahahah!

SCROOGE. *OOOoooOOOoooOOOoooOOOooo OOoooOOoooOOOooo!* [*He screams at them.*] Obscene demons! Why not market the corpse itself, as sell its trimming??? [*Suddenly*] Oh, Spirit, I see it, I see it! This unhappy man—this stripped-bare corpse . . . could very well be my own. My life holds parallel! My life ends that way now! 7

[SCROOGE *backs into something in the dark behind his spotlight.* SCROOGE *looks at* FUTURE, *who points to the corpse.* SCROOGE *pulls back the blanket. The corpse is, of course,* SCROOGE, *who screams. He falls aside the bed; weeping.*]

Spirit, this is a fearful place. In leaving it, I shall not leave its lesson, trust me. Let us go!

[FUTURE *points to the corpse.*]

7. **calico** (kal′ ə kō) *n.*: Coarse and cheap cloth.

Clarification

4 Explain that *sixpence* and *crowns* were coins of British currency until the pound sterling was decimalized in 1971. Until then, the pound consisted of 240 *pence,* or pennies, and sixpence was a coin equal to six pennies; a shilling was worth twelve pence; and a crown was worth five shillings, or sixty pence. Until the 1970's, the pound was valued at around five U.S. dollars. Have students conduct research to find the worth of a pound in today's U.S. dollars.

◆Reading Strategy

5 **Question** As students continue to read about the thieves, have them suggest questions they may have about the thieves. Encourage students to speculate about answers to the questions. *Students may suggest questions such as these: How did the thieves know Scrooge? How did they get into his room? How did they know that Scrooge died? They may say that the thieves once worked for Scrooge or knew people who worked for him. Perhaps someone they knew let them in Scrooge's room, having heard about Scrooge's death through gossip on the streets near his home or office.*

Comprehension Check ☑

6 What does the woman admit to in this passage? What was the reason for her actions? *She removed the expensive shirt that the dead man was to be buried in and replaced it with one made of cheap cloth, so that she could sell the expensive shirt.*

◆Critical Thinking

7 **Evaluate** Ask students if they think that Scrooge has seen enough visions and learned enough lessons at this point in the play. Have them tell why or why not. *Some students may say that the final shock of seeing his corpse is lesson enough for Scrooge. Others may say that Scrooge must learn a final lesson when he finds out the fate of Tiny Tim.*

Humanities: Television Film

Television Adaptations Films based on Charles Dickens's *A Christmas Carol* have been shown since 1913. Among the more notable film adaptations are the version starring Alistair Sim (1951) and a musical version titled "Scrooge," starring Albert Finney and Alec Guinness (1970).

On television "Mickey's Christmas Carol," featuring the Disney characters, has appeared since the early 1980's. George C. Scott starred in a television special that first aired in 1984 and is still shown on television today.

Have students meet in small groups to discuss film or television adaptations of *A Christmas Carol* that they have seen. Then have students imagine that they have been chosen to produce and direct a modern version of the story. Ask them to list the actors they would choose to play the major characters. Encourage them to think about where and how they might film the scenes and direct the action. Discuss what kinds of special effects would enhance their filmed, visual portrayal of this story.

◆Critical Thinking

❶ **Speculate** Why did the playwright have Tiny Tim speak without placing him on stage? What effect does this produce? *Students may say that the playwright is using Tim's voice to introduce the next scene. They may also speculate that by doing this the director emphasizes that Tiny Tim has died.*

▶Critical Viewing◀

❷ **Analyze** Students may say that the director placed the actors on the stage floor to emphasize their humble social status. The characters are positioned in a way that shows how close the family is and how they have drawn together since Tiny Tim's death. The actors' somber faces show their heavy mood.

◆Critical Thinking

❸ **Infer** What clue in this passage tells you that Tiny Tim has died? *Mrs. Cratchit speaks of Tim in the past tense: "... he was very light to carry and his father loved him so."*

Customize for *Verbal/Linguistic Learners*

Have students imagine that they are directing the scene on this page for the theater or for a film. Ask them what directions they might give to the actors so that they convey the mood of the scene.

Spirit, let me see some tenderness connected with a death, or that dark chamber, which we just left now, Spirit, will be forever present to me.

[FUTURE *spreads his robes again. Thunder and lightning. Lights up,* U., *in the* CRATCHIT *home setting.* MRS. CRATCHIT *and her daughters, sewing*]

1 **TINY TIM'S VOICE.** [*Off*] And He took a child and set him in the midst of them.

SCROOGE. [Looking about the room; to FUTURE] Huh? Who spoke? Who said that?

MRS. CRATCHIT. [*Puts down her sewing*] The color hurts my eyes. [*Rubs her eyes*] That's better. My eyes grow weak sewing by candlelight. I shouldn't want to show your father weak eyes when he comes home . . . not for the world! It must be near his time . . .

PETER. [*In corner, reading. Looks up from book*] Past it, rather. But I think he's been walking a bit slower than usual these last few evenings, Mother.

MRS. CRATCHIT. I have known him walk with . . .

▲ **Critical Viewing** Why might a director choose to place the actors playing the Cratchits this way? What does their position reveal about their family? **[Analyze]** 2

[*Pauses*] I have know him walk with Tiny Tim upon his shoulder and very fast indeed.

PETER. So have I, Mother! Often!

DAUGHTER. So have I. 3

MRS. CRATCHIT. But he was very light to carry and his father loved him so, that it was not trouble—no trouble.

[BOB, *at door*]

And there is your father at the door.

[BOB CRATCHIT *enters. He wears a comforter. He is cold, forlorn.*]

PETER. Father!

BOB. Hello, wife, children . . .

[*The daughter weeps; turns away from* CRATCHIT.]

Humanities: Theatre Arts

The Guthrie Theater Point out to students that the photographs throughout the play are from a production of *A Christmas Carol* at the Guthrie Theater, in Minneapolis, Minnesota. English director and producer Sir Tyrone Guthrie (1900–1971) founded the theater as one of the first nonprofit regional repertory companies in the United States. The theater opened in 1963 and has become well known for imaginative staging and technical innovation. When available, the theater is also used for book lectures and music concerts.

Encourage interested students to find out more about Sir Tyrone Guthrie and the Guthrie Theater. Have them give an oral presentation based on their findings.

Children! How good to see you all! And you, wife. And look at this sewing! I've no doubt, with all your industry, we'll have a quilt to set down upon our knees in church on Sunday!

MRS. CRATCHIT. You made the arrangements today, then, Robert, for the . . . service . . . to be on Sunday.

BOB. The funeral. Oh, well, yes, yes, I did. I wish you could have gone. It would have done you good to see how green a place it is. But you'll see it often. I promised him that I would walk there on Sunday, after the service. *[Suddenly]* My little, little child! My little child!

> ◆ **Literary Focus**
> 4 How might the differences in the reactions to the two deaths tie in to the theme of the play?

ALL CHILDREN. *[Hugging him]* Oh, Father . . .

BOB. *[He stands]* Forgive me. I saw Mr. Scrooge's nephew, who you know I'd just met once before, and he was so wonderful to me, wife . . . he is the most pleasant-spoken gentleman I've ever met . . . he said "I am heartily sorry for it and heartily sorry for your good wife. If I can be of service to you in any way, here's where I live." And he gave me this card.

PETER. Let me see it!

5 **BOB.** And he looked me straight in the eye, wife, and said, meaningfully, "I pray you'll come to me, Mr. Cratchit, if you need some help. I pray you do." Now it wasn't for the sake of anything that he might be able to do for us, so much as for his kind way. It seemed as if he had known our Tiny Tim and felt with us.

MRS. CRATCHIT. I'm sure that he's a good soul.

BOB. You would be surer of it, my dear, if you saw and spoke to him. I shouldn't be at all surprised, if he got Peter a situation.

MRS. CRATCHIT. Only hear that, Peter!

MARTHA. And then, Peter will be keeping company with someone and setting up for himself!

6 **PETER.** Get along with you!

BOB. It's just as likely as not, one of these days, though there's plenty of time for that, my dear. But however and whenever we part from one another, I am sure we shall none of us forget poor Tiny Tim—shall we?—or this first parting that was among us? 6

ALL CHILDREN. Never, Father, never!

BOB. And when we recollect how patient and mild he was, we shall not quarrel easily among ourselves, and forget poor Tiny Tim in doing it.

ALL CHILDREN. No, Father, never!

LITTLE BOB. I am very happy, I am, I am, I am very happy.

[BOB *kisses his little son, as does* MRS. CRATCHIT, *as do the other children. The family is set now in one sculptural embrace. The lighting fades to a gentle pool of light, tight on them.*]

SCROOGE. Specter, something informs me that our parting moment is at hand. I know it, but I know not how I know it.

[FUTURE *points to the other side of the stage. Lights out on Cratchits.* FUTURE *moves slowing, gliding.* SCROOGE *follows.* FUTURE *points opposite.* FUTURE *leads* SCROOGE *to a wall and a tombstone. He points to the stone.*]

Am *I* that man those ghoulish parasites[8] so gloated over? *[Pauses]* Before I draw nearer to that stone to which you point, answer me one question. Are these the shadows of things that will be, or the shadows of things that MAY be, only? 7

[FUTURE *points to the gravestone.* MARLEY *appears in light well* U. *He points to grave as well. Gravestone turns front and grows to ten feet high. Words upon it:* EBENEZER SCROOGE: *Much smoke billows now from the grave. Choral music here.* SCROOGE *stands looking up at gravestone.* FUTURE *does not at all reply in mortals' words, but points once more to the gravestone. The stone undulates and glows. Music plays, beckoning* SCROOGE. SCROOGE *reeling in terror*]

Oh, no. Spirit! Oh, no, no!

---

8. **ghoulish parasites** (g͞ool' ish par' ə sits): Man and women who stole and divided Scrooge's goods after he died.

◆Literary Focus

4 Characterization and Theme in Drama Lead a discussion in which students compare and contrast the reactions to Scrooge's death with the reactions to Tiny Tim's death. Write students' responses on the chalkboard in a two-column format such as that shown below. Encourage brief responses. Then have students define what quality or qualities in Scrooge and Tiny Tim make the difference in people's reactions.

Scrooge's Death	Tim's Death
unconcern	sadness
ridicule	praise
greed	grief
harsh judgment	fond remembrance

◆Critical Thinking

5 Infer What favor does Bob Cratchit think that Scrooge's nephew might do for Peter? *Students should infer that the nephew might help Peter get a job.*

Comprehension Check ☑

6 What is Bob Cratchit asking of his family in this passage? *He is asking them to honor the memory of Tiny Tim's kind nature by not engaging in arguments over small matters.*

◆Critical Thinking

7 Interpret Why is it important for Scrooge to know if the visions are shadows of things that *will* happen or that *might* happen? *Scrooge's hopes are based on the possibility that he can change his future by changing his behavior. Scrooge wants the lessons he has learned to count for something in his life and the lives of others.*

Viewing and Representing Mini-Lesson

Set Model

This mini-lesson supports the Set Model project in the Idea Bank on p. 683.

Introduce Use the photographs in the play to review with students how scenery and props help establish when and where the action occurs, give information about the characters, and establish mood and atmosphere. Ask students to choose a scene from the play for which to model a set.

Develop Have students make notes and sketches for their set models. Provide them with a variety of materials such as construction paper, wood craft sticks, wood scraps, cloth scraps, cardboard tubes, and recycled aluminum foil.

Apply Have students create their set models for their chosen scenes. Then ask them to display their models for the class and give a brief oral explanation of the models.

Assess Evaluate students' set models on how well they reflect the setting, characterization, mood, and atmosphere of the scene.

◆Literary Focus

❶ Characterization and Theme in Drama The passage shows that Scrooge has completely changed from a greedy, coldhearted miser to a person who is willing to dedicate himself to kindness and charity toward others.

◆Literature and Your Life

❷ Point out to students that Scrooge is being given a second chance in life by the Ghost of Christmas Future. Invite students to discuss times when they or someone they know has been given a second chance to improve a situation or make amends. Have them describe feelings associated with being given a second chance.

◆Critical Thinking

❸ Apply Ask students if they think most people would change their behavior if they were allowed to see their future. Why or why not? *Students may say that whether they would change depends on the future they see. Some students may suggest that those who see a vision of a future such as the one Scrooge saw would change in order to improve the future. Others may say that some people's behavior is so firmly rooted that they would not change, even if shown a bleak future.*

[FUTURE'S *finger still pointing*]

Spirit! Hear me! I am not the man I was. I will not be the man I would have been but for this intercourse. Why show me this, if I am past all hope?

[FUTURE *considers* SCROOGE'S *logic. His hand wavers.*]

Oh, Good Spirit, I see by your wavering hand that your good nature intercedes for me and pities me. Assure me that I yet may change these shadows that you have shown me by an altered life!

[FUTURE'S *hand trembles; pointing has stopped.*]

I will honor Christmas in my heart and try to keep it all the year. I will live in the Past, the Present, and the Future. The Spirits of all Three shall strive within me. I will not shut out the lessons that they teach. Oh, ① tell me that I may sponge away the writing that is upon this stone!

> **◆ Literary Focus**
> How does this passage reveal the theme of the play?

[SCROOGE *makes a desperate stab at grabbing* FUTURE'S *hand. He holds firm for a moment, but* FUTURE, *stronger than* SCROOGE, *pulls away.* SCROOGE *is on his knees, praying.*]

Spirit, dear Spirit, I am praying before you. Give me a sign that all is possible. Give me a sign that all hope for me is not lost. Oh, Spirit, kind Spirit, I beseech thee: give me a sign . . .

[FUTURE *deliquesces, slowly, gently. The* PHANTOM'S *hood and robe drop gracefully to the ground in a small heap. Music in. There is nothing in them. They are mortal cloth. The Spirit is elsewhere.* SCROOGE *has his sign.* SCROOGE *is alone. Tableau. The lights fade to black.*]

Scene 5

[*The end of it.* MARLEY, *spotlighted, opposite* SCROOGE, *in his bed, spotlighted.* MARLEY *speaks to audience, directly.*]

MARLEY. [*He smiles at* SCROOGE:] The firm of Scrooge and Marley is doubly blessed; two misers turned; one, alas, in Death, too late; but the other miser turned in Time's penultimate nick.[9] Look you on my friend, Ebenezer Scrooge . . .

SCROOGE. [*Scrambling out of bed; reeling in delight*] I will live in the Past, in the Present, and in the Future! The Spirits of all Three shall strive within me!

MARLEY. [*He points and moves closer to* SCROOGE'S *bed.*] Yes, Ebenezer, the bedpost is your own. Believe it! Yes, Ebenezer, the room is your own. Believe it!

SCROOGE. Oh, Jacob Marley! Wherever you are, Jacob, know ye that I praise you for this! I praise you . . . and heaven . . . and Christmastime! [*Kneels facing away from* MARLEY] I say it to ye on my knees, old Jacob, on my knees! [*He touches his bed curtains.*] Not torn down. ② My bed curtains are not at all torn down! ③ Rings and all, here they are! They are here: I am here: the shadows of things that would have been, may now be dispelled. They will be, Jacob! I know they will be! [*He chooses clothing for the day. He tries different pieces of clothing and settles, perhaps on a dress suit, plus a cape of the bed clothing: something of color.*] I am light as a feather, I am happy as an angel, I am as merry as a schoolboy. [*Yells out window and then out to audience*] Merry Christmas to everybody! Merry Christmas to everybody! A Happy New Year to all the world! Hallo here! Whoop! Whoop! Hallo! Hallo! I don't know what day of the month it is! I don't care! I don't know anything! I'm quite a baby! I don't care! I don't care a fig! I'd much rather be a baby than be an old wreck like me or Marley! (Sorry, Jacob, wherever ye be!) Hallo! Hallo there!

[*Church bells chime in Christmas Day. A small boy, named* ADAM, *is seen now* D.R., *as a light fades up on him.*]

Hey, you boy! What's today? What day of the year is it?

---

9. **in Time's penultimate nick:** Just at the last moment.

ADAM. Today, sir? Why, it's Christmas Day!

SCROOGE. It's Christmas Day, is it? Whoop! Well, I haven't missed it after all, have I? The Spirits did all they did in one night. They can do anything they like, right? Of course they can! Of course they can!

ADAM. Excuse me, sir?

SCROOGE. Huh? Oh, yes, of course, what's your name, lad?

[SCROOGE *and* ADAM *will play their scene from their own spotlights.*]

ADAM. Adam, sir.

SCROOGE. Adam! What a fine, strong name! Do you know the poulterer's[10] in the next street but one, at the corner?

10. **poulterer's** (pōl′ tər ərz) *n.*: British word for a store that sells chickens, turkeys, and geese.

▲ Critical Viewing How does Scrooge's costume reveal the change in his character? **[Compare and Contrast]** 4

ADAM. I certainly should hope I know him, sir!

SCROOGE. A remarkable boy! An intelligent boy! Do you know whether the poulterer's have sold the prize turkey that was hanging up there? I don't mean the little prize turkey, Adam. I mean the big one! 5

ADAM. What, do you mean the one they've got that's as big as me?

SCROOGE. I mean, the turkey the size of Adam: that's the bird!

ADAM. It's hanging there now, sir.

◆ **Build Vocabulary**

dispelled (dis peld′) *v.*: Scattered and driven away; made to vanish

▶Critical Viewing◀

4 Compare and Contrast Students may say that Scrooge's costume in this photograph is livelier and more colorful than his previous drab costumes, and that this reflects his vibrant new attitude toward life.

◆Critical Thinking

5 Analyze Why does Scrooge call Adam "remarkable" and "intelligent"? *Students may perceive that Scrooge is seeing everything and everyone with "new" eyes and is rediscovering his fellow humans. They may also realize that Scrooge is giddy at having been given a second chance; in his excitement, he may be overstating his feelings.*

Customize for
English Language Learners
Have students identify phrases and passages that may be unfamiliar. Help clarify the meanings of these phrases and passages by paraphrasing them. For example, you may want to paraphrase "I certainly should hope I know him, sir!" as "Of course I know him!"

Customize for
Bodily/Kinesthetic Learners
Have volunteers use body language as they read aloud the dialogue between Scrooge and Adam to demonstrate the characters' intentions and reactions to each other. Encourage students to explain what might be going through each character's mind as the two communicate.

Cultural Connection

Christmas Christmas celebrates the birth of Jesus of Nazareth. Because the exact date of Jesus's birth is not known, the holiday has been celebrated on various dates in December and January throughout the centuries. It is believed that Pope Julius I set the date of Christmas at December 25 in the fourth century, though the Armenian Church celebrates it on January 6.

Christmas traditions reflect the influence of other holiday celebrations taking place during the winter months. For example, the ancient Romans celebrated the Saturnalia, a Winter Solstice observance, on December 17 by exchanging gifts. Germanic and Celtic Yule festivals, also centered on the Winter Solstice, contributed festive foods, decorating with trees, holly, and mistletoe, and good fellowship.

Have students conduct additional research to learn more about topics such as the origin of Santa Claus and Christmas Eve customs in various countries. Invite students to share their findings with the class.

◆ Literature and Your Life

❶ Some students may describe an event from their lives in which they did someone a favor and eventually when they needed help, someone else was there to do a favor for them. Or they may share an experience of giving a gift to someone, when they were just as excited to give the gift as the person was to receive it.

Comprehension Check ☑

❷ What, in addition to money, probably inspired Adam to rush back to Scrooge's house with the poultryman? *Adam was probably inspired by Scrooge's friendliness and flattery of him.*

◆ Critical Thinking

❸ **Speculate** Ask students why Scrooge doesn't want the Cratchits to know who sent the turkey. *Scrooge is acting out of a purely selfless motive: he wants the Cratchits to have a feast for Christmas but wants nothing in return. Also, some students may say that Scrooge does not want the family to feel indebted to him.*

◆ Critical Thinking

❹ **Hypothesize** Have students imagine that the woman on the street is someone who knew the "old" Scrooge. How might she react to this greeting? *Students may say that she might be surprised and perhaps distrustful of his sudden friendliness.*

SCROOGE. It is? Go and buy it! No, no, I am absolutely in earnest. Go and buy it and tell 'em to bring it here, so that I may give them the directions to where I want it delivered, as a gift. Come back here with the man, Adam, and I'll give you a shilling. Come back here with him in less than five minutes, and I'll give you half-a-crown!

ADAM. Oh, my sir! Don't let my brother in on this.

[ADAM *runs offstage.* MARLEY *smiles.*]

MARLEY. An act of kindness is like the first green grape of summer: one leads to another and another and another. It would take a queer man indeed to not follow an act of
1 kindness with an act of kindness. One simply whets the tongue for more . . . the taste of kindness is too too sweet. Gifts—goods—are lifeless. But the gift of goodness one feels in the giving is full of life. It . . . is . . . a . . . wonder.

> **◆ Literature and Your Life**
> Give an example from your experience to support Marley's statements.

[*Pauses; moves closer to* SCROOGE, *who is totally occupied with his dressing and arranging of his room and his day. He is making lists, etc.* MARLEY *reaches out to* SCROOGE:]

ADAM. [*Calling, off*] I'm here! I'm here!

[ADAM *runs on with a man, who carries an enormous turkey.*]

2 Here I am, sir. Three minutes flat! A world record! I've got the poultryman and he's got the poultry! [*He pants, out of breath.*] I have earned my prize, sir, if I live . . .

[*He holds his heart, playacting.* SCROOGE *goes to him and embraces him.*]

SCROOGE. You are truly a champion, Adam . . .

MAN. Here's the bird you ordered, sir . . .

SCROOGE. *Oh, my, MY!!!* look at the size of that turkey, will you! He never could have stood upon his legs, that bird! He would have snapped them off in a minute, like sticks of sealingwax! Why you'll never be able to carry that bird to Camden-Town. I'll give you money for a cab . . .

MAN. Camden-Town's where it's goin', sir?

SCROOGE. Oh, I didn't tell you? Yes, I've written the precise address down just here on this . . . [*Hands paper to him*] Bob Cratchit's house. Now he's not to know who sends him this. Do 3
you understand me? Not a word . . . [*Handing out money and chuckling*]

MAN. I understand, sir, not a word.

SCROOGE. Good. There you go then . . . this is for the turkey . . . [*Chuckle*] and this is for the taxi. [*Chuckle*] . . . and this is for your world-record run, Adam . . .

ADAM. But I don't have change for that, sir.

SCROOGE. Then keep it, my lad. It's Christmas!

ADAM. [*He kisses* SCROOGE'S *cheek, quickly.*] Thank you, sir. Merry, Merry Christmas! [*He runs off.*]

MAN. And you've given me a bit overmuch here, too, sir . . .

SCROOGE. Of course I have, sir. It's Christmas!

MAN. Oh, well, thanking you, sir. I'll have this bird to Mr. Cratchit and his family in no time, sir. Don't you worry none about that. Merry Christmas to you, sir, and a very happy New Year, too . . .

[*The man exits.* SCROOGE *walks in a large circle about the stage, which is now gently lit. A chorus sings Christmas music far in the distance. Bells chime as well, far in the distance. A gentlewoman enters and passes.* SCROOGE *is on the streets now.*]

SCROOGE. Merry Christmas, madam . . . 4

WOMAN. Merry Christmas, sir . . .

[*The portly businessman from the first act enters.*]

SCROOGE. Merry Christmas, sir.

PORTLY MAN. Merry Christmas, sir.

Cross-Curricular Connection: Social Studies

Boxing Day The British and Canadian custom known as Boxing Day is derived from a tradition of the English church. On the day after Christmas, church alms boxes are opened so that the money can be distributed to the poor. Through the years, the tradition grew to include public servants and employees, who took small earthenware boxes around to collect tips and year-end bonuses. The boxes had a slit in the top to admit coins. At the end of the day, the boxes were broken and the money collected.

The custom of giving gifts of money to public servants and employees has continued, but nowadays it takes place before Christmas rather than after, and boxes are no longer used. The name *Boxing Day* has been retained and is still observed as a legal bank holiday in England, Canada, Australia, and other nations once part of the British Commonwealth.

Have two volunteers conduct a debate in which one, acting as the "old" Scrooge, argues against Boxing Day and the other, acting as the "new" Scrooge, argues in favor of the tradition.

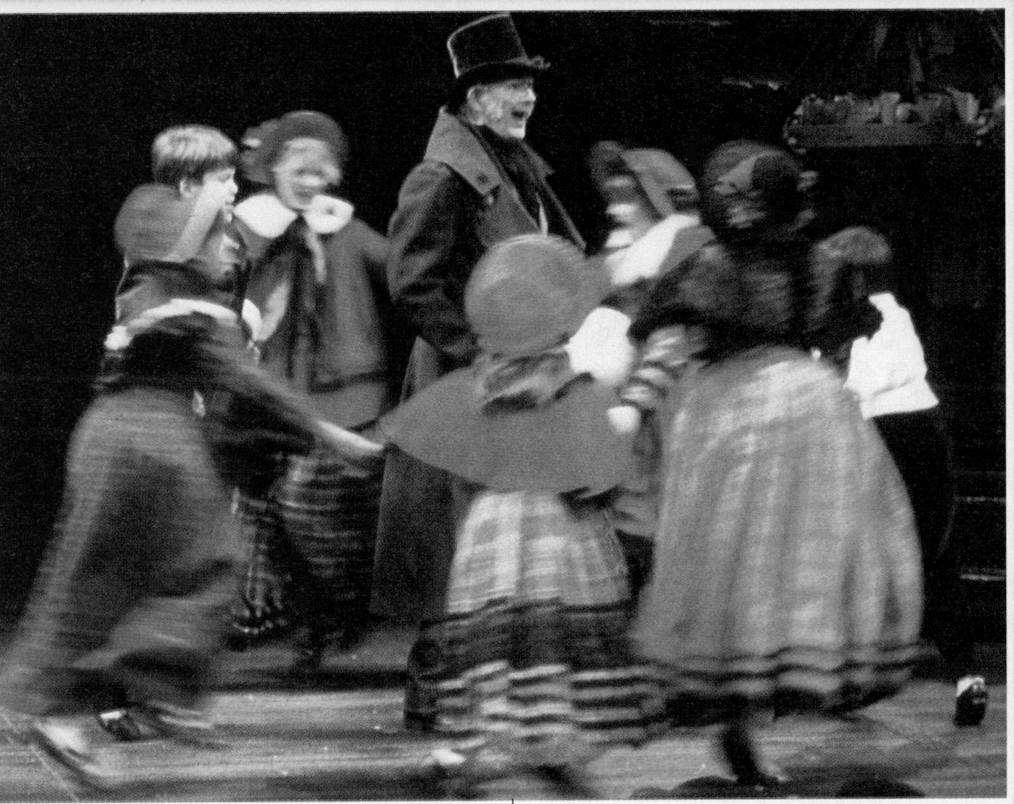

▲ Critical Viewing How do the color and movement in this photo convey Scrooge's new attitude? **[Analyze Cause and Effect]** 7

SCROOGE. Oh, you! My dear sir! How do you do? I do hope that you succeeded yesterday! It was very kind of you. A Merry Christmas.

PORTLY MAN. Mr. Scrooge?

SCROOGE. Yes, Scrooge is my name though I'm afraid you may not find it very pleasant. Allow me to ask your pardon. And will you have the
5 goodness to—[*He whispers into the man's ear.*]

6 **PORTLY MAN.** Lord bless me! My dear Mr. Scrooge, are you *serious!?!*

SCROOGE. If you please. Not a farthing[11] less. A great many back payments are included in it, I assure you. Will you do me that favor?

PORTLY MAN. My dear sir, I don't know what to say to such munifi—

SCROOGE. [*Cutting him off*] Don't say anything, please. Come and see me. Will you?

PORTLY MAN. I will! I will! Oh I will, Mr. Scrooge! It will be my pleasure!

SCROOGE. Thank'ee, I am much obliged to you. I thank you fifty times. Bless you!

[*Portly man passes offstage, perhaps by moving backwards.* SCROOGE *now comes to the room of his* NEPHEW *and* NIECE. *He stops at the door,
begins to knock on it, loses his courage, tries* 8
again, loses his courage again, tries again, fails again, and then backs off and runs at the door, causing a tremendous bump against it. The

11. **farthing** (fär thiŋ) *n.*: Small British coin.

◆Critical Thinking

5 Analyzing Cause and Effect Ask students why Scrooge has decided to give an exceptionally large amount of money to the charity. What does Scrooge mean by "back payments"? *He wants to make up for not having given to the poor in past years.*

Clarification

6 Scrooge interrupts the man before he can finish his statement. The word he begins at the end of the line is *munificence,* which means "great generosity."

▶Critical Viewing◀

7 Analyze Cause and Effect Students may feel that the colorful costumes and lively movement reflect Scrooge's shift from a dull, plodding life to one bursting with vitality.

◆Critical Thinking

8 Interpret Why does it take Scrooge so long to gather the courage to knock on his nephew's door? *Scrooge is probably ashamed of his unkind behavior toward his nephew the day before. Also, having been shown the scene with his nephew and wife by the Ghost of Christmas Present, Scrooge may be afraid that they won't want him to join them for dinner.*

Beyond the Classroom

Career Connection

Costume Design As students view the photograph on this page, point out that the professional production of a play such as *A Christmas Carol* requires artistic decisions by costume designers as well as other specialists.

Costume designers help communicate the mood, period, and meaning of a play. If the play is set in a specific region, country, or historical period, costume designers must conduct research to learn about authentic designs and materials. They then put artistic skills to use by sketching preliminary designs. Costume designers who work on large and expensive theatrical productions must also develop management skills in order to oversee budgets and supervise other professionals.

Have interested students gather further information about this career. Some students might list industries and organizations—for example the movie industry, the television industry, theater and dance companies—that employ costume designers. Other might request information on studies in costume design at colleges and universities.

◆Literature and Your Life

❶ Point out that Scrooge's nephew and niece seem surprised but delighted to see the uncle. Ask students how they might have greeted Scrooge if he were their uncle.

◆Critical Thinking

❷ **Speculate** Have students speculate about what Scrooge might say to his nephew and niece to explain the change in his behavior. *Some students may say that the nephew and niece's welcoming attitude indicates that they need no explanation. Others may say that Scrooge might tell them about the visits of the three Spirits. Others may say that Scrooge might simply apologize for his bad behavior.*

Comprehension Check ☑

❸ Point out that Bob Cratchit does not yet know about Scrooge's change of heart. For Cratchit, this exchange seems entirely normal. Ask students what Cratchit might expect Scrooge to say or do about Cratchit's tardiness. *Students may suggest that Cratchit expects that Scrooge will make him stay late or will deduct money from his salary.*

◆Critical Thinking

❹ **Relate** Have students imagine that it is said of them that they know how to "keep Christmas well." Ask them to describe what they might do to earn this judgment. Encourage them to give specific examples. *Students may name examples of kindness and charity such as giving part of their allowance to the needy, spending time with someone who is lonely, or doing volunteer work.*

Customize for *Interpersonal Learners*

Have students in small groups discuss how Scrooge might live the rest of his life. Pose questions for discussion such as these: Does Scrooge change his business in any way? How does the relationship between Scrooge and his nephew develop? In what specific ways does Scrooge help the Cratchit family? How does Scrooge spend the remaining Christmases of his life?

NEPHEW *and* NIECE *are startled.* SCROOGE, *poking head into room*]

Fred!

NEPHEW. Why, bless my soul! Who's that?

NEPHEW and **NIECE.** [*Together*] How now? Who goes?

SCROOGE. It's I. Your Uncle Scrooge.

NIECE. Dear heart alive!

SCROOGE. I have come to dinner. May I come in, Fred?

1 **NEPHEW.** *May you come in???!!!* With such
2 pleasure for me you may, Uncle!!! What a treat!

NIECE. What a treat, Uncle Scrooge! Come in, come in!

[*They embrace a shocked and delighted* SCROOGE: FRED *calls into the other room.*]

NEPHEW. Come in here, everybody, and meet my Uncle Scrooge! He's come for our Christmas party!

[*Music in. Lighting here indicates that day has gone to night and gone to day again. It is early, early morning.* SCROOGE *walks alone from the party, exhausted, to his offices, opposite side of the stage. He opens his offices. The offices are as they were at the start of the play.* SCROOGE *seats himself with his door wide open so that he can see into the tank, as he awaits* CRATCHIT, *who enters, head down, full of guilt.* CRATCHIT *starts writing almost before he sits.*]

SCROOGE. What do you mean by coming in here at this time of day, a full eighteen minutes late, Mr. Cratchit? Hallo, sir? Do you hear me?

BOB. I am very sorry, sir. I *am* behind my time.

3 **SCROOGE.** You are? Yes, I certainly think you are. Step this way, sir, if you please . . .

BOB. It's only but once a year, sir . . . it shall not be repeated. I was making rather merry yesterday and into the night . . .

SCROOGE. Now, I'll tell you what, Cratchit. I am not going to stand this sort of thing any longer. And therefore . . .

[*He stands and pokes his finger into* BOB'S *chest.*] 3

I am . . . about . . . to . . . raise . . . your salary.

BOB. Oh, no, sir, I . . . [*Realizes*] what did you say, sir?

SCROOGE. A Merry Christmas, Bob . . . [*He claps* BOB'S *back.*] A merrier Christmas, Bob, my good fellow! than I have given you for many a year. I'll raise your salary and endeavor to assist your struggling family and we will discuss your affairs this very afternoon over a bowl of smoking bishop.[12] Bob! Make up the fires and buy another coal scuttle before you dot another i, Bob. It's too cold in this place! We need warmth and cheer, Bob Cratchit! Do you hear me? DO . . . YOU . . . HEAR . . . ME?

[BOB CRATCHIT *stands, smiles at* SCROOGE: BOB CRATCHIT *faints. Blackout. As the main lights black out, a spotlight appears on* SCROOGE: C. *Another on* MARLEY: *He talks directly to the audience.*]

MARLEY. Scrooge was better than his word. He did it all and infinitely more; and to Tiny Tim, who did NOT die, he was a second father. He became as good a friend, as good a master, as good a man, as the good old city knew, or any other good old city, town, or borough in the good old world. And it was always said of him
that he knew how to keep Christmas well, if 4
any man alive possessed the knowledge. [*Pauses*] May that be truly said of us, and all of us. And so, as Tiny Tim observed . . .

TINY TIM. [*Atop* SCROOGE'S *shoulder*] God Bless Us, Every One . . .

[*Lights up on chorus, singing final Christmas Song.* SCROOGE *and* MARLEY *and all spirits and other characters of the play join in. When the song is over, the lights fade to black.*]

---

12. **smoking bishop:** Hot sweet orange-flavored drink.

Beyond the Selection

FURTHER READING

Other Works by Charles Dickens

David Copperfield
Great Expectations
Oliver Twist

Other Works About Christmas

A Different Kind of Christmas, Alex Haley
Fig Pudding, Ralph Fletcher
Thames Doesn't Rhyme With James, Paula Danziger

INTERNET

We suggest the following sites on the Internet (all Web sites are subject to change).

For more information about Charles Dickens: **http://www.bibliomania.com/Fiction/dickens/DickensIntro.html** or, go to: **http://lang.nagoya-u.ac.jp/~matsuoka/Dickens.html**

We *strongly recommend* that you preview these sites before you send students to them.

Beyond Literature

Language Connection

Don't Be a Scrooge Ebenezer Scrooge is such a memorable character that his name has become part of the English language. The term *scrooge* means "a miser who doesn't like people." In other words, a *scrooge* is a person who has the attitude and personality that Ebenezer Scrooge had before Marley's ghost and the ghosts of Christmas Past, Present, and Future showed him the error of his ways.

Cross-Curricular Activity

Famous Names *Scrooge* is not the only name from literature and history to become an everyday expression. For example, a romantic man might be called a *romeo,* after the character in Shakespeare's *Romeo and Juliet.* With a group of classmates, use library and Internet resources to learn more about names that have become part of the language. Share your findings with the class.

Guide for Responding

◆ Literature and Your Life

Reader's Response Do you believe in Scrooge's change of heart? Explain.

Thematic Focus How is Dickens's personal code reflected in Scrooge's transformation?

Journal Writing Do you think that knowing what you'll be like in twenty years would change the way you act now? In a journal entry, explore your response.

☑ Check Your Comprehension

1. Where does Scrooge go with the Ghost of Christmas Present?
2. What fate does the Ghost of Christmas Present foretell for Tiny Tim?
3. What are the dolls that the Ghost of Christmas Present carries?
4. What five scenes does the Ghost of Christmas Future show Scrooge?
5. List five good deeds Scrooge performs at the end of the drama.

◆ Critical Thinking

Interpret

1. How does hearing his own cruel words about "surplus population" and "workhouses" echoed by the Ghost of Christmas Present affect Scrooge? **[Infer]**
2. What does this reaction suggest about Scrooge? **[Assess]**
3. What does Scrooge's desire to talk with his nephew and his niece reveal? **[Interpret]**
4. How does Marley's speech in which he compares acts of kindness to grapes summarize what has happened to Scrooge? **[Connect]**

Evaluate

5. How well does Scrooge live up to the promise he makes at the beginning of Scene 5? **[Make a Judgment]**

Apply

6. How does the Ghost of Christmas Present's explanation about why he gives more kindness to the poor tie to Dickens's experiences and concerns? **[Social Studies Link]**

Beyond Literature

Make sure that students' research on the Internet is supervised by you or another adult. You may want to choose one or two Web pages based on the search word *eponyms* to guide students' research, and suggest that they use information from those pages as a starting point. Explain to students that words such as Reaganomics or Calvinism are words expressing ideas started by certain people, such as Calvin or Reagan. Suggest that students begin their library search with references such as the *Dictionary of Eponyms or Webster's Word Histories.*

Reinforce and Extend

Answers

◆ Literature and Your Life

Reader's Response Students may say that they believe in Scrooge's change of heart because of his pledge to the Ghost of Christmas Future and his acts of kindness on Christmas Day.

Thematic Focus Dickens shows his belief in kindness and charity toward one another through Scrooge's change from miser to benefactor.

☑ Check Your Comprehension

1. He goes to the Cratchit home and to his nephew's home.
2. He says that Tiny Tim will die.
3. The dolls are symbols of Ignorance and Want.
4. He shows Scrooge scenes of businessmen discussing a death, thieves selling the possessions of a dead man, a corpse, the Cratchit home, and Scrooge's gravestone.
5. Scrooge has a turkey sent to the Cratchits, generously tips the delivery boy and the poultryman, pledges money to charity, joins his nephew for Christmas dinner, and gives Bob Cratchit a raise.

◆ Critical Thinking

1. Scrooge probably feels remorse at his cruel remarks.
2. It suggests that he understands the effects of his past behavior and is motivated to change.
3. It shows that Scrooge regrets mistreating his nephew and wants to make amends.
4. Scrooge discovers pleasure in giving to others and thus wants to continue.
5. According to Marley, Scrooge does even more than he promises.
6. Having experienced being poor as a child, Dickens understood the needs of the poor for kindness and compassion.

Answers

◆Reading Strategy

1. He wants Scrooge to see the sacrifices the poor make for the comfort of the rich, in order to show Scrooge why the poor deserve extra kindness. The answer is gained through reading ahead.
2. She has to work late, possibly at the home of someone wealthy. The answer is inferred from her dialogue.
3. They discuss Scrooge's death. Their remarks describe Scrooge without mentioning his name.
4. He will die without help from someone like Scrooge. This is stated directly by the Ghost of Christmas Present.
5. He will send it to the Cratchits. The answer can be found in reading ahead.

◆Build Vocabulary

Using the Word Root *-aud-*

Possible responses:

1. We heard the speech in the school auditorium.
2. Sam failed to hear the director's instructions during his audition.
3. The sound quality of the audiovisual program was excellent.
4. Ms. Hie heard the results of her company's audit.

Spelling Strategy

1. gnome
2. gnat
3. gnaw
4. gnash
5. gnu
6. gnarled

Using the Word Bank

1. threadbare
2. gnarled
3. audible
4. meager
5. compulsion
6. astonish
7. dispelled
8. severe

Guide for Responding *(continued)*

◆ Reading Strategy

QUESTION

Asking questions as you read a drama will help you understand what's going on. Below are some questions you might have asked while reading this play. Provide an answer for each question, explaining how you arrived at your answer.

1. Why does the Ghost of Christmas Present show Scrooge the people carrying their Christmas dinners to work?
2. Why is it possible that Martha Cratchit will not be able to spend Christmas with her family?
3. Whose death do the businessmen discuss?
4. What will happen to Tiny Tim?
5. What will Scrooge do with the turkey?

◆ Build Vocabulary

USING THE WORD ROOT *-aud-*

The word root *-aud-* means "hear." For each of the following words, write a sentence that contains both the word and the meaning of *-aud-*. If a word is unfamiliar, use the dictionary to check its meaning.

1. auditorium **2.** audition **3.** audiovisual **4.** audit

SPELLING STRATEGY

Gnarled is one of a handful of words that start with the letters *gn*. In these words, the letter *g* is silent; the words start with the sound of the letter *n*. Add *gn* to each of the following groups of letters to form a list of the most common *gn* words.

1. __ome **2.** __at **3.** __aw
4. __ash **5.** __u **6.** __arled

USING THE WORD BANK

Identify the Word Bank word that would be best suited for a description of each of the following items.

1. frayed, worn-out clothing
2. ancient, twisted tree
3. loud stereo in the next room
4. amount of food on a dieter's plate
5. unstoppable desire to do something
6. getting an *A* on an exam you thought you failed
7. police sent away a curious crowd
8. a strong allergic reaction

◆ Literary Focus

CHARACTERIZATION AND THEME IN DRAMA

Theme is the central idea or insight about life revealed in a work of literature. Because the **character** of Scrooge is of central importance to the play, understanding how and why he changes will help you understand the theme.

1. Describe three incidents in Act II where Scrooge's reactions show him in the process of changing for the better.
2. For each of these three incidents, what causes Scrooge to change?
3. How is Scrooge's change a key to the play's theme?
4. In your own words, state the theme of the play.

◆ Build Grammar Skills

VERB AGREEMENT WITH COLLECTIVE NOUNS

A **collective noun** names a group. Collective nouns may be either singular or plural. Use a plural verb form with a collective noun when you are referring to the individual parts or members of a group acting separately:

Plural Verb: The group enter the building.

Use a singular verb form when you refer to the group acting together as one unit:

Singular Verb: A group appears on the street.
The family sits at the table.

Practice On your paper, write Correct if the subject and the verb agree. Write the correct form of the verb if the subject and verb do not agree.

1. The army marches in the parade.
2. The club argues about the date of the next meeting.
3. At the thunderclap, the herd scatter in all directions.
4. The band plays a cheerful tune.
5. The group wants different things.

Writing Application For each collective noun, write a sentence that uses it in the form given in parentheses. Make sure that the verb in your sentence agrees with the subject.

1. team (plural) **3.** jury (plural) **5.** crowd (plural)
2. class (singular) **4.** audience (singular)

◆Literary Focus

1. Students may mention Scrooge's concern for Tiny Tim, his desire to be heard by his nephew and niece, and his pledge to the Ghost of Christmas Future.
2. Scrooge sees that Tiny Tim might die; he learns what his nephew and niece think of him; and he sees his name on the gravestone.
3. Scrooge's change shows that it's never too late to make changes for the better in one's life.
4. Students may say the theme is that our happiness and that of others depends on being kind to one another.

◆Build Grammar Skills

Practice

1. Correct
2. argue
3. Correct
4. Correct
5. want

Writing Application

Possible responses:

1. The team disagree about the game plan.
2. Mr. Reed's class hosts an art show.
3. The jury seat themselves.
4. The audience cheers and applauds.
5. The crowd moves past the various exhibits.

Writer's Solution

For additional instruction and practice, use the lessons in the unit on Subject-Verb Agreement in *Writer's Solution Language Lab CD-ROM*, and the practice pages on Agreement Between Subjects and Verbs, pp. 72–74, in the *Writer's Solution Grammar Practice Book*.

Build Your Portfolio

Idea Bank

Writing

1. **Casting Memo** Imagine that you're the casting director for a major new film version of *A Christmas Carol*. List the movie stars you want to play each speaking role. Briefly explain why each actor would be good for the part.
2. **Contrasting Obituaries** Imagine that Scrooge has just died. You have to write the obituary, the article about someone who has recently died. First, imagine that he was never visited by the ghosts and never changed his ways, so you must write about the old Scrooge. Then, write another obituary for the changed Scrooge.
3. **Drama Critic's Review** Write a review of *A Christmas Carol*. Your review should give your readers a clear idea of what the play is about and whether you liked the play and why. End your review by explaining why you do or do not recommend the play. **[Career Link]**

Speaking and Listening

4. **Dramatic Monologue** In the role of Scrooge, tell the story of your experiences with one of the Christmas ghosts.
5. **Modernization [Group Activity]** Set Scrooge's experiences in modern times. With a group, update the setting, language, and characters in a scene from the play. Rehearse, and then perform your scene for the class. **[Performing Arts Link]**

Projects

6. **Winter Holidays [Group Activity]** Prepare a group report on the celebration of winter holidays around the world. Each member of the group might focus on a different holiday: Hanuka, Kwanzaa, or Christmas in various countries. Share your findings with the class. **[Social Studies Link]**
7. **Set Model** Based on the stage directions and your imagination, build a model of the set for a scene in *A Christmas Carol*. Show the scenery and major props, such as furniture. **[Art Link]**

Writing Mini-Lesson

Scrooge's Persuasive Speech

With the help of Marley and the Ghosts of Christmas Past, Present, and Future, Scrooge learned an important lesson about how a person should conduct his or her life. Imagine that he now wants to persuade other people to change their ways. In the role of Scrooge, write a persuasive speech directed at people who have antisocial attitudes.

Writing Skills Focus: Support With Evidence

As you write your speech, **support** your points **with evidence.** Don't simply say, "Don't let business get in the way of your personal relationships." Show your audience the personal costs of letting business and greed run their lives. For example, Scrooge might describe how he lost the woman he loved and how much he now regrets his foolishness.

Prewriting Create an outline in which you list the three to five main points you want to make, leaving space between each point for notes. Then, fill in your outline with evidence to support your points.

Drafting Start your speech with an attention-grabbing story or image. This will help you capture the interest of your audience. Then, use your outline to help you draft the body of your speech. End your speech with a review of your main points. Refer back to the speech's opening, and call on your audience to reform their ways.

Revising Revise your speech by looking for places where you can add evidence or replace weak evidence with stronger evidence. Make sure your ideas are well organized and expressed clearly.

◆ Grammar Application

As you revise, correct places where collective nouns and their verbs do not agree.

Idea Bank

Following are suggestions for matching the Idea Bank topics with your students' performance levels and learning modalities:

Customize for
Performance Levels
Less Advanced Students: 1, 4
Average Students: 3, 4, 5, 7
More Advanced Students: 2, 5, 6, 7

Customize for
Learning Modalities
Verbal/Linguistic: 1, 2, 3, 4, 5
Visual/Spatial: 7
Bodily/Kinesthetic: 4
Intrapersonal: 1, 2, 3, 7
Interpersonal: 5, 6

Writing Mini-Lesson

Refer students to the Writing Handbook in the back of the book for instructions on the writing process and for further information on persuasion. Have students use the Main Idea and Supporting Details Organizer in **Writing and Language Transparencies,** p. 70, to arrange their prewriting examples.

Writer's Solution

Writing Lab CD-ROM
Have students complete the tutorial on Persuasion. Follow these steps:

1. Have students view the interactive model of an essay supporting an opinion.
2. Suggest that students view the Writing Hints on organization.
3. Allow students to draft on computer.
4. When revising, have students use the sentence-opener revising checker activity.

Writer's Solution Sourcebook
Have students use Ch. 6, "Persuasion," pp. 166–199, for additional support. This chapter includes in-depth instruction on avoiding faulty reasoning, p. 189.

✓ ASSESSMENT OPTIONS

Formal Assessment, Selection Test, pp. 185–187, and Assessment Resources Software. The selection test is designed so that it can be easily customized to the performance levels of your students.

Alternative Assessment, p. 39, includes options for less advanced students, more advanced students, verbal/linguistic learners, visual/spatial learners, bodily/kinesthetic learners, and intrapersonal learners.

PORTFOLIO ASSESSMENT
Use the following rubrics in the **Alternative Assessment** booklet to assess student writing:
Casting Memo: Expression, p. 81
Contrasting Obituaries: Expression, p. 81
Drama Critic's Review: Critical Review, p. 98
Writing Mini-Lesson: Persuasion, p. 92

Prepare and Engage

OBJECTIVES

1. To read, comprehend, and interpret a selection that has a social studies focus
2. To relate a selection with a social studies focus to personal experience
3. To connect literature to social studies
4. To respond to Social Studies Guiding Questions
5. To respond to the selection through writing, speaking and listening, and projects

SOCIAL STUDIES GUIDING QUESTIONS

Reading about the freedom struggles of South Africa's youth will help students discover answer to these Social Studies Guiding Questions:

- What factors have shaped South Africa's culture?
- Who is Nelson Mandela and what is his place in the history of South Africa?

Interest Grabber Offer some examples of school or community rules. Then pair students to brainstorm for ways to change a rule they do not like. Remind them to choose orderly and respectful methods but to consider many avenues. For example, they might explore the political process through school government, use art or music to change public opinion, stage a protest to raise students' awareness, or write letters to the teacher. Explain that *Sarafina* uses drama and song to share one young South African woman's plea to change the rules.

Map Study

Political Maps The geography of South Africa can shed some light on its difficult history for students. For example, to understand the isolation black South Africans faced, students can use the map on this page to note the spread-out and remote locations of the homelands. To help relate the map to political events in South Africa and further understand apartheid's discrimination against black South Africans, have students read the background text on this page.

CONNECTING LITERATURE TO SOCIAL STUDIES

AFRICA

from Sarafina! "Bring Back Nelson Mandela"

by Hugh Masekela

South Africa

Tropic of Capricorn
BOTSWANA
NAMIBIA
Pretoria
Johannesburg
SWAZILAND
LESOTHO
SOUTH AFRICA
25°S
30°S
20°E
25°E
0 100 200 mi
0 100 200 km

South Africa: Homelands
KEY

- Bophuthatswana (Tswana)
- KwaNdebele (Matabele)
- Lebowa (North Sotho)
- Venda (Venda)
- Gazankulu (Shangaan)
- KaNgwane (Swazi)
- KwaZulu (Zulu)
- Qwaqwa (South Sotho)
- Ciskei (Xhosa)
- Transkei (Xhosa)

AFRICA AND COLONIAL RULE Africa has a long, rich history of self-government. From the 1600's through the early 1900's, however, most of Africa came under European colonial rule. In the 1650's, the Dutch established a colony in what is now South Africa. Centuries later, the Dutch settlers, who became known as the Boers, struggled for and eventually lost control of the region to the British.

A Segregated Society South Africa became an independent nation in 1910. Although slavery was illegal in the new nation, white South Africans held power and privilege. The whites controlled most of the nation's lands. Blacks were pushed into crowded "homelands" with poor farmland and few services.

Apartheid Takes Hold In 1948, the government created "apartheid"—a set of laws that created total separation of the races. There were four racial groups, but blacks had the fewest rights. Every aspect of their lives—where they lived, worked, and went to school, for example—was restricted.

The Children Revolt During the 1960's, black South Africans worked against apartheid, often at the risk of their lives. Their organizations were outlawed, and protesters—black and white men, women, and children—were jailed, beaten, and even killed for their beliefs. One of these protesters was Nelson Mandela, who was jailed for more than 27 years before being granted his freedom and later becoming South Africa's first black president. In this song from the 1980's musical *Sarafina!*, black South African students sing about Mandela's hoped-for freedom.

Prentice Hall Literature Program Resources

REINFORCE / RETEACH / EXTEND

Selection Support Pages
Build Vocabulary, p. 217
Theme, p. 218

Formal Assessment Selection Test, pp. 188–189, Assessment Resources Software

Writing and Language Transparencies
Main Idea and Supporting Details Organizer, p. 70

Resource Pro CD-ROM
from *Sarafina!* "Bring Back Nelson Mandela"—includes all resource material and customizable lesson plan

Connection to Prentice Hall World Explorer
Africa
Ch. 7, "Exploring Central and Southern Africa"

CONNECTING LITERATURE TO SOCIAL STUDIES

from *Sarafina!*

"Bring Back Nelson Mandela"

Hugh Masekela

Sarafina is a high-school student growing up in the black township of Soweto, South Africa. Despite facing poverty, segregation, violence, and brutal oppression, Sarafina continues to believe in a future of freedom and equality for all South Africans. Her joy and passionate commitment to a better future make her a favorite among her classmates. The musical Sarafina! *ends with Sarafina and her friends singing a song in which they share their dream of Nelson Mandela's release from prison.*

▲ Critical Viewing How do the costumes and gestures of these performers express pride? **[Interpret]**

STUDENTS. [*Singing*] Bring back Nelson Mandela
Bring him back home to Soweto
I want to see him walking down the streets
Of South Africa tomorrow
Bring back Nelson Mandela
Bring him back home to Soweto
I want to see him walking hand in hand
With Winnie Mandela

Develop Understanding

One-Minute Insight This final song from the Broadway musical *Sarafina!* is a joyful and proud call for the release of antiapartheid leader Nelson Mandela from prison. The main characters—students—act out the day of Mandela's release and their star, Sarafina, poses as Mandela to thank the students. The song reveals the hopeful pride of Sarafina and her schoolmates, and celebrates their dedication.

Team Teaching Strategy

With a music, social studies, or drama teacher, you might create cross-curricular units on protest music, apartheid, or drama.

►Critical Viewing◄

1 Interpret *The African fabrics and patterns in the costumes suggest pride in African culture; gestures such as raised and outspread arms express pride in the song's words.*

Customize for *Less Proficient Readers*

To clarify the political context of the musical and song, show photographs from age-appropriate books about the antiapartheid struggle.

Customize for *English Language Learners*

If possible, obtain a recording of the music from *Sarafina!* to play for the class. To help students read the irregularly punctuated song lyrics, have them read along with the recording. As they hear pauses, they can rewrite the song on paper with the punctuation suggested by the audio reading.

Humanities: Musical Theater

Sarafina!, by Hugh Masekela and Mbongeni Ngema

Many of the actors in *Sarafina!* had never been on stage before. They joined the cast because they believed in the play's message. Ask students what they think the experience of performing on stage for the first time might be like. *Responses may range from exciting to terrifying and include actual student experiences.*

Preparing for Standardized Tests

Reading Standardized tests may require students to read and understand materials in many genres. Students who are familiar with the conventions of drama (the genre exemplified by this selection) may be better able to respond to questions about structure and stage directions in a reading passage.

Write this sample test item on the board and ask students to select the best answer:

In this play, who portrays Nelson Mandela?

(A) the real Nelson Mandela
(B) the actress who plays Sarafina
(C) an actor who portrays Mandela
(D) a rotating cast of students

Guide students through the stage directions, pointing out the italicized words [*As Mandela*] within Sarafina's lines. Based on this information, help students conclude that *(B)* is the correct answer.

Customize for
More Advanced Students

This selection can foster students' interest in South Africa's apartheid struggle and its more recent efforts to unite after apartheid. After researching these turbulent times, invite students to complete one of the following activities:

- design a postage stamp honoring the end of apartheid
- create a one-actor show about the life of Nelson Mandela or F. W. de Klerk
- write a report about the role other nations played in ending apartheid

Reinforce and Extend

Answers

◆ Literature and Your Life

Reader's Response Students may mention current leaders or those from history. Feelings might include the hope arising from a clear message and the belief in real change.

Thematic Focus His imprisonment would be likely to anger and sadden the community, while his release would inspire and focus the community.

☑ Check Your Comprehension

1. They ask for Nelson Mandela's return to Soweto.
2. They are gathered to celebrate Mandela's return.
3. She plays herself, a young student activist, and also Nelson Mandela.

More About the Authors

The lives of **Hugh Masekela** and **Mbongeni Ngema** converged one late night in New York City. Ngema's work with South African theater had earned him acclaim both inside and outside of the country (for example, he later received a Best Director Tony Award nomination for *Asinamali!*). While bringing a show to New York City in 1984, he happened upon his countryman Masekela performing at a New York city jazz club. As they shared creative ideas, the promise of *Sarafina!* was born.

SARAFINA. [*Speaking*] There will be millions
of people—millions—from all over the world
in a big open field in Soweto.
The whole place will be vibrating.
Women will be ululating.[1]
Dust will be rising to the sky.
The air will be filled with the sounds of laughter.
People will be rubbing shoulders with one voice one vote one color.
Everybody will be shouting—

STUDENTS. Mandela, Mandela, Mandela!

SARAFINA. [*As Mandela*] My people, today I am free. [*As herself*] And the people will say—

STUDENTS. [*Shouting with joy*] Viva[2] Mandela, Viva!

SARAFINA. [*As Mandela*] We were released from prison because you never forgot us. You constantly demanded our release and carried on the struggle. We are here today not to revenge or to destroy but to build the future . . . where all of us, black and white, can come together and forget the past and work to liberate our land. We should remember that it is only when South Africa is free that all of Africa can be free! [*As herself*] And the people will go wild!

1. **ululating** (yo͞ol′ yo͞o lāt′ iŋ) *v.*: Howling; hooting.
2. **Viva** (vē′ vä) *interj.*: Shout of acclaim that literally means "Live long!"

Guide for Responding

◆ Literature and Your Life

Reader's Response What leaders do you admire? What feelings have they inspired in you?

Thematic Focus How would the imprisonment and release of a leader like Nelson Mandela affect the community he represents?

☑ Check Your Comprehension

1. What do the students ask for in the song's opening lines?
2. Why are millions of people gathered in Soweto?
3. What two roles does Sarafina play?

◆ Critical Thinking

Interpret

1. According to Sarafina's portrayal of Nelson Mandela, why has he been freed? **[Analyze Cause and Effect]**
2. What hopes for South Africa's future does the song convey? **[Infer]**

Apply

3. Based on Mandela's vision for South Africa, do you think he is a leader worth admiring? Why or why not? **[Make a Judgment]**

Extend

4. South Africa is just one place where strong leaders have worked for political change. What are some countries in which major political change is at work or has recently occurred? **[Social Studies Link]**

Meet the Author
Hugh Masekela
Mbongeni Ngema

Lyricist Hugh Masekela and playwright/producer Mbongeni Ngema are two black South African artists committed to political change. When they began to develop *Sarafina!* in 1984, they wanted a musical evoking the rhythms of the music popular in South Africa's black townships. The musical would tell the story of South African children struggling for justice.

As Ngema worked to raise money for the show, he collaborated with Masekela, a jazz musician, to write music and lyrics. With a cast of excited young actors, *Sarafina!* opened in 1987, first in South Africa and then in New York. In its Broadway run, the play was nominated for five Tony awards.

Block Scheduling Strategies

Consider these ideas to take advantage of extended class time:

- After engaging students with the Interest Grabber, invite a social studies teacher to discuss and expand on the background material, p. 684, and perhaps present *World Explorer: Africa,* Chapter 7, "Exploring Central and Southern Africa."
- Have students meet in small groups to discuss the Thematic Focus on p. 686. Tell them to use the discussion as a prewriting activity for the Classroom Lecture or Memoir activity, p. 687.
- Alternatively, have student groups use the Main Idea and Supporting Details Organizer, p. 70 in **Writing and Language Transparencies,** to begin summarizing information for the Dramatic Performance activity on p. 687.
- Use the materials listed under Further Reading, Listening, and Viewing and Beyond the Selection, Teacher's Edition, p. 687, to extend the Connecting Literature to Social Studies questions, p. 687.

Connecting Literature to Social Studies

Even in jail, Nelson Mandela helped lead black South African freedom efforts. Slowly, those efforts succeeded. People around the world pressured the South African government to change.

In 1989, South Africans elected President F. W. de Klerk. He knew that his country's future depended on ending apartheid. He began by releasing Nelson Mandela and other political prisoners.

Once he was freed, Mandela's role in the changing government grew. When elections were held in 1994, with blacks voting for the first time, he was chosen as President. During the 1990's, Mandela worked to unite all South Africans behind his vision: a country where citizens who are safe, educated, and healthy share equal partnership in the economy and government.

1. How does this song capture a moment in South African history?
2. Identify two details in the song that suggest Nelson Mandela's vision for South Africa.
3. How might this song and the musical *Sarafina!* have given black South Africans hope for peace and change?

Idea Bank

Writing

1. **Protest Slogan** As Sarafina, write a slogan calling for Mandela's release and an end to apartheid laws. Make your slogan memorable and punchy—like a song you can't forget.
2. **Classroom Lecture** Once free, Nelson Mandela spoke to South Africans everywhere. Write the speech he might give at a black township school like the one Sarafina attends. What would he say to young black South Africans to show them a place in their country's future?
3. **Memoir** As Nelson Mandela, write several entries for a memoir of your life. Include stories about your time in prison and your efforts for South Africa since you were freed. Add details—from research or your imagination—about how your public role has affected you personally.

Speaking and Listening

4. **Dramatic Performance** Listen to a recorded version of "Bring Back Nelson Mandela." Then, work in a group to stage the song. Include a short summary of the historical background, and share the song with other classes. **[Performing Arts Link]**

Project

5. **Flag** Under apartheid, the South African flag combined colors and symbols from the nation's British and Dutch history. In the 1990's, the country replaced this flag. Conduct research to learn about the new South African flag. Draw the flag on posterboard, and point out significant features to your classmates.

Further Reading, Listening, and Viewing

- *Sarafina!* (1992) is a film version of Mbongeni Ngema's play.
- Peter Gabriel's song "Biko" on the album *Peter Gabriel* (1980) tells the story of murdered protester Steven Biko.
- The documentary film *Voices of Sarafina* (1988) introduces the cast of *Sarafina!*
- Paula Bryant Pratt's book *The End of Apartheid in South Africa* (1995) details this time of great change in South Africa.
- *Long Walk to Freedom* (1995) is Nelson Mandela's own story.

Beyond the Selection

FURTHER READING

Other Works by Mbongeni Ngema

Woza Albert! (with Percy Mtwa & Barney Simon)

Asinamali!

Other Works About South Africa and Apartheid

Nelson Mandela: The Fight Against Apartheid, Steven Otfinoski

Journey to Jo'burg: A South African Story, Beverly Naidoo

INTERNET

We suggest the following Internet sites (all Web sites are subject to change).

For an overview of current events in Africa, visit:
http://www.pbs.org/newshour/bb/africa/africa.html

Study a comparison of Capetown life for black and white South Africans at:
http://www.worldnet-international.com/after.htm

We *strongly recommend* that you preview these sites before you send your students to them.

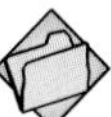

Idea Bank

Following are suggestions for matching the Idea Bank topics with your students' performance levels and learning modalities.

Customize for *Performance Levels*

Less Advanced Students: 1, 5
Average Students: 2, 4, 5
More Advanced Students: 3, 4, 5

Customize for *Learning Modalities*

Verbal/Linguistic: 1, 2, 3, 4
Visual/Spatial: 5; Interpersonal: 4
Intrapersonal: 3, 5;
Bodily/Kinesthetic: 4
Musical/Rhythmic: 1, 4

Answers *(continued)*

◆Critical Thinking

1. He has been freed because of the efforts of black activists.
2. Possible responses: The hopes for a South African future that includes those of all races, for forgiveness and focus on the future, for a free South Africa.
3. Possible response: Yes. He honors his supporters' efforts and seeks positive change rather than revenge.
4. Students may mention Russia, China, or nations of the Middle East.

Connecting Literature to Social Studies

1. It portrays voices of the freedom struggle and longing for change.
2. Mandela calls to build a future, not avenge the past, and he hopes for a black and white partnership.
3. Possible response: They helped South Africans imagine Mandela's freedom and celebrate their pride and hope. They also brought to the world South Africa's plea for help.

ASSESSMENT OPTIONS

Formal Assessment, Selection Test, pp. 188–189, and Assessment Resources Software. The selection test is designed so that it can be easily customized to the performance levels of your students.

PORTFOLIO ASSESSMENT

Use the following rubrics in the **Alternative Assessment** booklet to assess student writing:
Protest Slogan: Persuasion, p. 92
Classroom Lecture: Problem-Solution, p. 88
Memoir: Expression, p. 81

Prepare and Engage

Establish Writing Guidelines
Review the following key characteristics of a response to a drama:

- A response to a drama includes a brief summary of the performance.
- A response to a drama expresses the opinion of the writer.
- The writer's opinion of the drama must be backed up by details from the performance.

You may want to distribute the scoring rubric for Response to Literature, p. 97 in **Alternative Assessment,** to make students aware of the criteria on which they will be evaluated. See the suggestions on p. 690 for how you can customize the rubric to this workshop.

Refer students to the Writing Handbook in the back of the book for instruction on the writing process and further information on Response to Literature.

Writer's Solution

Writers at Work Videodisc
To introduce students to responding to literature and to show them how Naomi Long Midgett describes her feelings about responding to literature, play the videodisc segment on Responding to Literature (Ch. 9.)

Play frames 32401 to 41741

Writing Lab CD-ROM
If your students have access to computers, you may want to have them work in the tutorial on Response to Literature to complete all or part of their responses to a drama. Follow these steps:

1. Have students view the interactive model of responses to a drama.
2. Suggest that students use the Topic Web to divide their topics.
3. Allow students to draft on computer.
4. Have students use the interactive self-evaluation checklist when revising.

Writer's Solution Sourcebook
Students can find additional support, including in-depth instruction on varying sentence length and structure, pp. 292–293, in the chapter on Response to Literature, pp. 264–295.

Response to Literature

Response to a Drama

Writing Process Workshop

Watching a live performance of a play can be a magical experience. A good drama can take you to another time and place. If your imagination is in good shape, reading a play can transport you to a theater in which you see the actors and staging and hear the dialogue and sound effects. In a **response to a drama,** you include your thoughts, feelings, and reactions to a production you've seen or a script you've read. These skills will help you plan, draft, and revise an effective response to a drama:

Writing Skills Focus

▶ **Include a brief summary** to provide the necessary background that readers will need.

▶ **State your opinion clearly** to alert readers to the main point of your essay.

▶ **Support your ideas with evidence** that answers *why* and *how.* (See p. 683.)

Notice how this response to a staged version of *A Christmas Carol* uses these skills:

Model

The play about a miser who changes his stingy ways ① is doubly powerful because it's both funny and scary. ② At one moment, I was laughing at Scrooge and his penny-pinching ways. He looked silly in his red plaid nightshirt, pointed nightcap, and bunny slippers. ③ A few minutes later, I was biting my nails when the darkness set in, mist and smoke blew onto the stage, and, drenched in an eerie blue light, the ghost of Jacob Marley entered, rattling his chains.

① The writer quickly summarizes the outcome of the play.

② This essay will explain why the production created two responses.

③ The writer offers specific evidence to explain why she thought Scrooge was funny.

Cultural Connection

Drama From Around the World Tell students that drama exists in cultures all around the world, but it can take many different forms. Drama from Bali, Thailand, Cambodia, and Indonesia involves rich and elaborate dance movements. Sanskrit drama, performed in India, is highly symbolic—its meaning is conveyed through the use of color, gestures, and spoken words that use varying tones and pitches. Chinese drama, or *ching hsi,* is based on a rigorous tradition of elaborately costumed and made-up actors.

The most famous type of Japanese drama is *No,* which is an elaborate dance form that creates a fantastic atmosphere. The actors move very slowly and manipulate fans, which may represent swords, snow, and so forth. Some other forms of Japanese drama include doll theater and *Kabuki.*

Encourage students to research forms of drama from around the world, comparing their dramatic elements. They may want to create a comparison-and-contrast chart. Have a class presentation in which students can present their findings.

Prewriting

Take a Seat The first step, of course, is to choose a play—if not to attend, then to view or to read. Choose one that interests you and that is written for people your age.

Ideas for Finding a Drama

- Read a play from your library's drama section
- Watch a videotape of a live theatrical performance
- Attend a live performance in your school or community
- See a made-for-television movie

Study the Pros Look in a newspaper or magazine for reviews of plays. Notice what the reviews include, how they begin and end, and whether they are favorable or unfavorable.

List Your Likes and Dislikes With any play, there will be things you like and things you don't like. Make two lists with categories such as these:

WHAT I LIKED	WHAT I DISLIKED
Characters A, B	Character D
Plot Events	Lighting
Staging	
Music	

Compare Notes The best way to discover your own responses is to discuss the play with someone else who has read it or seen it performed. Did you both notice the same things? Did you have similar reactions? As you talk, note the points you might use in your written response.

Drafting

Develop a Main Idea As you begin, pause and think: What was my general response to this play? Write an answer in a single sentence. It should appear early in your response.

Use Rich, Descriptive Details Write about the details that impressed you the most. Include information about sights, sounds, voices, colors, scenes, and actions. You may want to refer to the sets, lighting, and special effects that brought the play to life. Let your reader see, hear, and feel what you did.

Credit the Title, Author, and Performers Be sure to include the full and accurate title (underlined or in italics) and the author's full name. If you see a play performed, keep the program so that you can include the names of actors, directors, and crew.

DRAFTING/REVISING

APPLYING LANGUAGE SKILLS: Unity

Unity means *oneness.* A paragraph has unity when each sentence relates to its topic sentence. An essay has unity when each paragraph supports one idea.

Not Unified:

I liked the set design. The costumes were good, too. During intermission, they served candy canes and Christmas cookies.

Unified:

I liked the set design. Scrooge's house was a simple black table stage left. The cemetery, a single gravestone, was also on the left. In contrast, stage right was full of furniture and life. It was an office, a home, and a ballroom.

Practice Revise this paragraph to make it unified. Add and delete details as necessary.

1. Maria Delfano sang beautifully. Her duets with Scott Gleason were funny and I could hear every word. I also enjoyed her solo, "Baseball Boogie."

Writing Application As you write, use topic sentences to keep your writing unified.

Writer's Solution Connection
Language Lab

For more practice, refer to the Unity in Paragraphs lesson in the Language Lab.

Develop Student Writing

Prewriting

Suggest to students that they take notes while viewing the play that will become the subject of their essay. If they are going to view a live performance, remind them to take a program, if offered. Programs include a list of characters, the names of the actors and actresses, the names of the director and crew, and sometimes a brief summary of the play.

Customize for
More Advanced Learners

Suggest that these students compare a performance of a drama with the written text. Before they view the performance, have students read the play and note what details they think need to be expressed on stage. After students view the performance, have them evaluate the work done by the actors, the director, and the set designer. Have them identify whether the stage performance was true to the written text and what elements of the performance were the strongest. In addition, have students comment on areas where they thought the performance was weak or needed more elaboration.

Drafting

Remind students that when writing their responses, they will want to include details from the performance to provide support for their opinions. If one of their statements is "The costumes were great," students should provide details about the costumes to explain why they think they were great. Suggest that students use the Main Idea and Supporting Details Organizer, p. 70 in **Writing and Language Transparencies,** to organize their thoughts.

Writer's Solution

Writing Lab CD-ROM

In the drafting section of the tutorial on Response to Literature, students can refer to a list of writing hints to help them begin their drafts. In addition, they can view annotated professional and student models to discover ways to write an effective introduction, body, and conclusion.

Applying Language Skills

Unity Tell students that a concept related to unity is **coherence,** which means that each idea logically develops from the previous idea. In a coherent essay, the ideas are organized in a logical manner, transitions are used to show the relationships among ideas, and key words or phrases may be repeated to show connections between sentences or paragraphs.

Answers

Possible responses:

Maria Delfano sang beautifully. I enjoyed both her solo "Baseball Boogie" and her duet with Scott Gleason. Not only did she sing strongly, but she also was able to express the humor of the songs.

Writer's Solution

For additional support, have students use the practice page on Recognizing Paragraphs With Unified Ideas in the *Writer's Solution Grammar Practice Book,* p. 123. If students have access to technology, suggest they use the Unity in Paragraphs lesson in the Building Paragraphs unit in the *Writer's Solution Language Lab CD-ROM.*

Revising

Remind students that they are not reviewing their peers' work to decide whether they agree or disagree, but rather to help them see where more information may be needed or where ideas are unclear. In addition, reviewers can mark for errors in punctuation, spelling, and usage.

Writer's Solution

Writing Lab CD-ROM

In the tutorial on Response to Literature, have students use the peer editor checklist as they review other student's work.

Publishing

For other publishing ideas, suggest that students publish their responses in the school newspaper.

Reinforce and Extend

Review the Writing Guidelines

After students have completed their papers, review the characteristics of a response to a drama.

Applying Language Skills

Correcting Stringy Sentences

Answers

Possible response:

The play shows us life in a small town. It makes us laugh and then it makes us cry.

Writer's Solution

For additional support, use the practice page on Shortening Sentences That Are Too Long, p. 119, in the *Writer's Solution Grammar Practice Book.*

EDITING/PROOFREADING

APPLYING LANGUAGE SKILLS: Correcting Stringy Sentences

Stringy sentences contain many ideas connected by words like *and, so, or,* and *then.*

Stringy Sentence:

Jones has huge teeth and he looks like Dracula so he's really scary and he frightens audiences.

To revise stringy sentences, decide which ideas are closely related and which are not. Break separate ideas into distinct sentences.

Revised Sentences:

Jones has huge teeth, and he looks like Dracula. He's really scary, and he frightens audiences.

Practice Revise this stringy sentence to make it more readable.

The play shows us life in a small town and it makes us laugh and then it makes us cry.

Writing Application As you revise your response to a drama, replace stringy sentences by breaking them into shorter sentences.

Writer's Solution Connection Writing Lab

For advice on keeping a response journal, see the videoclip in the Prewriting section of the Response to Literature tutorial.

Revising

Look at Word Choices As you go through your draft, circle phrases that seem pale, weak, or bland. Go back later, and replace them with some that are more colorful, strong, and delicious to the senses.

REVISION MODEL

① Elmwood Playhouse's recent production of

Lost in Yonkers is a triumph. Set in one room, the play tracks a family's life in the 1940's. Arthur Chill gives a rousing performance as Louie, ② perfectly capturing the New York accent and gestures of a small-time con man.

① The writer provides more context for the review.

② These details support the critic's opinion.

Pair Up! Work with another writer to take turns reading and reacting to each other's work. Use questions such as these to guide you:

- How well has the writer shown how he or she feels about the drama?
- Is there enough evidence to support this feeling?
- Which missing details should be included?
- Do you want to see or read this play? Why or why not?

After a discussion of your work, use your peer reviewer's ideas and reactions to help guide your revision.

Publishing and Presenting

Play Day Set aside a certain time to share your responses orally and to discuss plays that you've seen or read in common. After you've discussed your responses, take a survey to see what kinds of plays your class likes best: dramas, comedies, musicals, science fiction, fantasies, or mysteries.

Write to the Artist Artists usually enjoy getting responses to their work. Send a copy of your response to an actor, director, or playwright. You can send letters to theaters or publishers, and they will forward them. If you get a response, share it with classmates.

ASSESSMENT

PORTFOLIO ASSESSMENT

Use the rubric on Response to Literature in the **Alternative Assessment** booklet, p. 97, to assess the students' writing. Add these criteria to customize this rubric to this assignment.

	4	3	2	1
Stating an Opinion Clearly	An opinion is clearly stated and strongly supported.	An opinion is clearly stated and fairly well supported.	An opinion is implied, but it is not supported.	No opinion is stated or implied.
Unity/ Coherence	Each paragraph supports one idea; all sentences relate to the topic sentence.	Each paragraph supports one idea; most sentences relate to the topic sentence.	Some paragraphs lack topic sentences; sentences do not relate to each other.	There are no topic sentences; ideas are unclear and lack unity.

Real-World Reading Skills Workshop

Understanding an Internet Web Page

The Internet is an excellent source of information on many different topics. For instance, whole sections of the Internet are devoted to subjects such as sports, fashion, music, or cooking. Understanding how an Internet Web page works will help you find the information you want.

Find the Home Pages Every Internet site has a Home Page. The Home Page is like the cover and the table of contents of a magazine or newspaper. Here, important information about the site can be found. For example, you might find a *menu* and instructions about moving through the site.

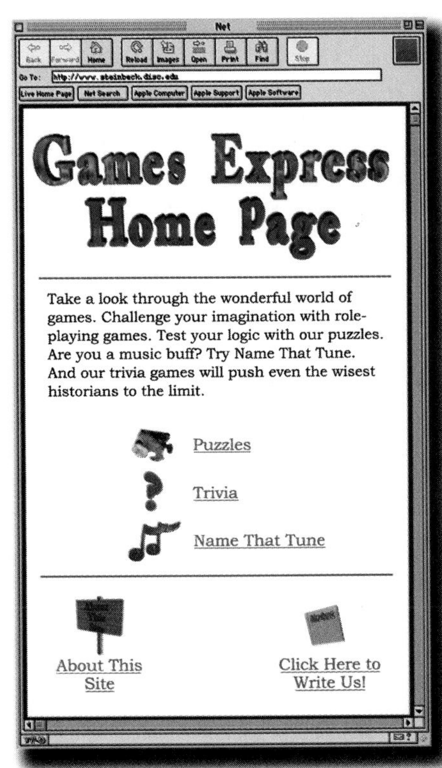

Use the Links A great feature of the Internet is the way everything is connected to everything else. You may have heard of people *surfing the* 'Net. They hop from one page to another by using *links*. Anything can be a link: a word, a sentence, a picture. Links are usually underlined, boxed, or set in a different color from other text on the page.

Click on *About This Site* An Internet Web page is often called a *Web site*. Many Web site Home Pages have a section called *About This Site*. By clicking on *About This Site*, you will find specific information that describes the material on the site and customized directions for finding the information you want.

Apply the Strategies

Look at the Web page pictured here. Then, answer the questions that follow.

1. What type of material is found on this Web page?
2. Is this page the first page of the Web site? How do you know?
3. Identify the links on this Web page.
4. How could you learn more about this Web page and the way it was made?

Here are other situations in which understanding Internet Web pages can be helpful:

- *Conducting research for a school project*
- *Learning more about hobbies and interests*
- *Comparing products and services*

Introduce the Strategies

Many students will be familiar with the World Wide Web and Home Pages. Explain that anyone with access to the right technology can put up a Web page; this includes individuals, companies, and organizations. Web sites are categorized with various search engines as they are created, to make them accessible to viewers.

Apply the Strategies

Explain to students that some of the more complicated or artistic Web sites have links that may seem hidden. Tell students if they come upon a Web site that at first appears to be only an image, they might try moving the mouse around the image until the cursor changes, usually turning into a hand with a pointed finger. Another way to tell if they've found a link is to look at the status bar that usually appears on the bottom of the screen. When a Web page is loading, this status bar shows the progress and signifies completion by the message "Document: Done." When the cursor passes over an embedded link, this status bar will show the address of the linked Web page. To get to the next level, students simply click the mouse button.

Answers

1. This Web page has information about different kinds of games.
2. It is the first page because it is entitled "Games Express Home Page."
3. The links on this page are: Puzzles, Trivia, Name That Tune, About This Site, and Click Here to Write Us.
4. You could go to About This Site, or you could write to the creators of the page, via e-mail, and ask them questions.

◆Build Grammar Skills

Reviewing Subject and Verb Agreement

The selections in Part I include instruction on the following:

- Subject and Verb Agreement
- Verb Agreement With Collective Nouns

This instruction is reinforced with the Build Grammar Skills practice pages in **Selection Support,** pp. 209 and 214.

As you review subject and verb agreement, you may wish to review the following:

- Agreement With Compound Subjects

In making verbs agree, it is important to determine the number of the subject. There are some situations in which the subject (or its number) may be hard to determine.

Two or more singular subjects joined by *or* or *nor* take a singular verb. However, if one of the subjects joined by *or* or *nor* is plural, the verb agrees with the subject that is closest to it in the sentence.
The number of a subject does not change when a prepostional phrase follows it.
Indefinite pronouns *(anybody, anyone, each, either, everybody, everyone, neither, nobody, no one, one, somebody, someone)*, take a singular verb.
Some indefinite pronouns are plural *(both, few, many, several)*, and therefore take a plural verb.
Some indefinite pronouns may be either singular or plural *(all, most, some)*. In these situations, the number is determined by the prepositional phrase that follows it.

Writer's Solution

For additional practice and support with subject and verb agreement, use the practice pages on Agreement Between Subjects and Verbs, pp. 72–74, and Special Problems with Subject-Verb Agreement, pp. 75–76, in the *Writer's Solution Grammar Practice Book.* If students have access to technology, have them use the lessons in the Subject-Verb Agreement unit in the *Writer's Solution Language Lab CD-ROM.*

Subject and Verb Agreement

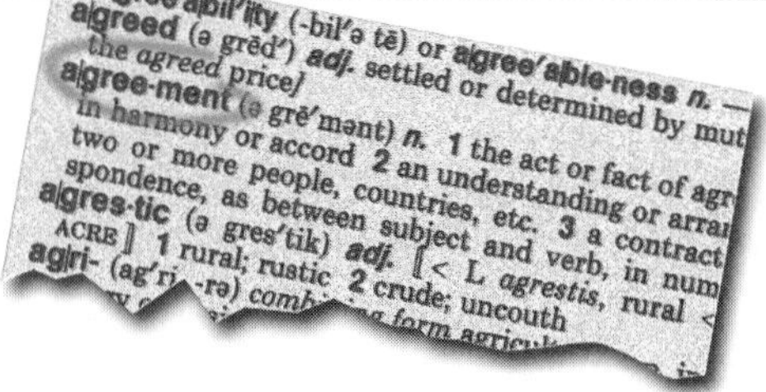

Subject and verb agreement has one main rule: *A verb must agree with its subject in number.* A singular subject must take a singular form of a verb, and a plural subject must use a plural form of the verb. (See p. 661.) Verbs in the present tense change form to agree with singular or plural subjects.

Singular	Plural
It *is*	They *are*
John *thinks*	They *think*

A **collective noun** names a group: *flock, team, club.* Collective nouns may be either singular or plural, depending on their use in a sentence. When a collective noun is a subject, use a singular verb form when you refer to the group acting together as one unit. Use a plural verb form to agree with a collective noun when you are referring to the individual parts or members of a group acting separately. (See page 682.)

A group acting as one takes a singular verb:	The band *plays* carols in December.
Group members acting separately take a plural verb:	The band *go* their separate ways after the concert.

Practice 1 For each of the following sentences, choose the correct verb of the two shown in parentheses, and write it on your paper.

1. Scrooge usually (ignore, ignores) holidays.
2. Ghosts (show, shows) him sad moments.
3. His family (make, makes) him wonder about what matters most.
4. The crowds outside (sing, sings) carols to celebrate the season.
5. Today, our class (read, reads) the play.
6. The audience (disagree, disagrees) over the meaning of the final scene.
7. Most of us (believe, believes) people can really change.

Practice 2 Write a paragraph describing a holiday you've recently celebrated. Use one collective noun with a singular verb and one collective noun with a plural verb. Identify the subject and verb in each sentence. Be sure that the subjects and verbs agree.

Grammar in Writing

✔ *When referring to the individual parts or members of a group acting separately, you may prefer to rewrite the sentences to make your meaning perfectly clear.*

Using a collective noun: The crowd stream out of five exits.

Revised: The people in the crowd stream out of five exits.

Answers

Practice 1

1. Scrooge usually *ignores* holidays.
2. Ghosts *show* him sad moments.
3. His family *makes* him wonder about what matters most.
4. The crowds outside *sing* carols to celebrate the season.
5. Today, our class *reads* the play.
6. The audience *disagree* over the meaning of the final scene.
7. Most of us *believe* people can really change.

PART 2 *Another Dimension*

Tukoer-Ter-Ur, 1989, Victor de Vasarely, © Artists Rights Society (ARS), NY, Private Collection

One-Minute Planning Guide

Part 2 of the Drama unit includes a screenplay of Rod Serling's "The Monsters Are Due on Maple Street," which introduces students to conflict in drama and to the sci-fi television series *The Twilight Zone*.

Customize for
Varying Students Needs
When assigning the selections in this section, keep in mind the following factors:

"The Monsters Are Due on Maple Street"
- A long, two-act play (14 pages)
- Provides an opportunity for researching television

Humanities: Art

Tukoer-Ter-Ur, 1989, by Victor de Vasarely

Victor de Vasarely (1908–1997) was a Hungarian-born French artist, famous for his colorful geometric compositions. Vasarely was a major influence on what is known today as op art, or optical art, a type of abstract art that seeks to create illusions of movement and space through the distortion of lines and color.

Vasarely worked as a graphic designer in Paris for fifteen years, where he also studied science, optics, and color. In the 1940's, he began painting abstract works made up of contrasting shapes and colors. Vasarely became known for his ability to make the canvas appear to bulge out into a three-dimensional form. His later work is marked by varying geometric figures that compose visually confusing patterns.

Have students study the painting and then ask the following questions:

1. Describe what you see. *Some students may describe a box that we are looking into. Other students may say that the small square in the center of the painting seems to pop out at us.*
2. Do you think this painting is a good illustration for the theme "Another Dimension"? *Some students will say that they think this is a good example of the "Another Dimension" theme because the painting convinces our eyes that we are seeing three dimensions when we are only looking at a two-dimensional, flat picture. The way the artist has painted leads us to "another dimension."*

Prepare and Engage

OBJECTIVES

1. To read, comprehend, and interpret a screenplay
2. To relate a conflict in drama to personal experience
3. To make predictions
4. To analyze conflict in drama
5. To build vocabulary in context and learn the word root *-sist-*
6. To recognize pronoun and antecedent agreement
7. To write a final scene using script format
8. To respond to a screenplay through writing, speaking and listening, and projects

SKILLS INSTRUCTION

Vocabulary: Word Roots: *-sist-*
Spelling: *f* Sound Spelled With *ph*
Grammar: Pronoun and Antecedent Agreement
Reading Strategy: Predict
Literary Focus: Conflict in Drama
Writing: Script Format
Speaking and Listening: Performance (Teacher Edition)
Viewing and Representing: Visual Imagery (Teacher Edition)
Critical Viewing: Analyze; Compare and Contrast; Hypothesize; Connect

PORTFOLIO OPPORTUNITIES

Writing: Neighborhood Code; Aliens' Report; Drama Review
Writing Mini-Lesson: Final Scene
Speaking and Listening: Performance; Conflict-Resolution Meeting
Projects: Scientific View; Casting Sketches

More About the Author
Rod Serling began creating *The Twilight Zone* after becoming frustrated with changes to the content of his work. In one production, for example, his sponsors removed an important feature from the New York City skyline simply because the building was named after a competing brand. Creating a series set in worlds that do not really exist gave Serling the artistic control he sought.

Meet the Author:
Rod Serling (1924–1975)

Rod Serling once said that he didn't have much imagination. This is an odd statement from a man who wrote more than 100 television scripts, many of which were highly imaginative science-fiction fantasies.

Beginnings as a Writer Although he worked on his school's newspaper as a teenager, Serling didn't become serious about writing until college, after serving as a paratrooper in World War II. Driven by a love for radio drama, Serling earned second place in a national script contest. Soon after, he landed his first staff job as a radio writer.

Quick Success Serling branched out into writing for a new medium—television—and rocketed to fame. Just five years after he won the contest, everyone wanted to watch—and perform—Serling's work. To speed up production, he began recording his stories on tape instead of typing them.

THE STORY BEHIND THE STORY

In the 1950's and 1960's, television censors banned any script that appeared to question American society. In order to examine society and human nature in his work, Serling disguised social criticism with a science-fiction mask. For example, "The Monsters Are Due on Maple Street" addresses the Cold War mentality. However, by substituting an alien threat for a communist one, Serling avoided censorship.

◆ LITERATURE AND YOUR LIFE

CONNECT YOUR EXPERIENCE

Rumors can spread quickly and become increasingly distorted with each retelling. Sometimes, as in this screenplay, wild rumors have terrible effects.

THEMATIC FOCUS: Community Ties

As the rumors in Serling's drama spread, community ties are stretched to the breaking point. How might your community react in such a situation?

◆ Background for Understanding

HISTORY

This screenplay was written during the Cold War, a period of intense rivalry between the United States and the Soviet Union that lasted from the mid-1940's through the 1980's. Because the Soviet Union had a communist government, the two countries had conflicting political, economic, and social views. Both countries feared that the other was seeking to change its rival's way of life. This suspicion resulted in a massive nuclear arms race and an atmosphere of fear in which people's allegiances were sometimes questioned. As you read Serling's screenplay, think about what sort of statement the author seems to be making about Cold War attitudes.

◆ Build Vocabulary

WORD ROOTS: *-sist-*

In Serling's screenplay, you'll encounter the word *persistently*. The root *-sist-* means "stand." *Persistently* means "standing firmly, especially in the face of an obstacle."

WORD BANK

Which of these words might describe the actions of someone who moves very slowly?

flustered
sluggishly
assent
persistently
defiant
metamorphosis
scapegoat

Prentice Hall Literature Program Resources

REINFORCE / RETEACH / EXTEND

Selection Support Pages
Build Vocabulary: Word Roots: *-sist-*, p. 219
Build Spelling Skills, p. 220
Build Grammar Skills: Pronoun and Antecedent Agreement, p. 221
Reading Strategy: Predict, p. 222
Literary Focus: Conflict in Drama, p. 223

Strategies for Diverse Student Needs, pp. 79–80

Beyond Literature Community Connection: Neighborly Conduct, p. 40

Formal Assessment Selection Test, pp. 190–192, Assessment Resources Software

Alternative Assessment, p. 40

Writing and Language Transparencies Series of Events Chain, p. 66; Timeline p. 74

Resource Pro CD-ROM
"The Monsters Are Due on Maple Street"—includes all resource material and customizable lesson plan

Listening to Literature Audiocassettes
"The Monsters Are Due on Maple Street"

◆ The Monsters Are Due on Maple Street ◆

◆ Literary Focus

Conflict in Drama

Conflict is a struggle between opposing forces that drives the action in a literary work. The conflict can occur within a character or between a character and an outside force, such as another character. Because playwrights can't reveal a character's thoughts the same way a short-story writer would, a conflict that occurs within a character must be presented through what the character says or through what other characters say about him or her. In addition, because dramas tend to be longer works, there may be more than one conflict. As you read, note the conflicts that occur at different levels—between individuals, between groups and individuals, and between groups.

◆ Reading Strategy

Predict

One of the qualities that makes this screenplay successful is Serling's ability to build suspense, a feeling of intense curiosity about the outcome of events. To get the most out of this screenplay or any other piece of suspenseful literature, pause every now and then to **predict,** or make an educated guess, about where the story is headed. Base your predictions on clues that the author provides. You may want to note the clues and your predictions in a chart like the one below, revising as you encounter new information.

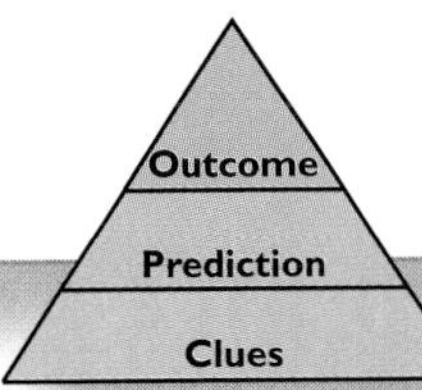

Preparing for Standardized Tests

Grammar Standardized tests usually assess students' understanding of grammar. Understanding pronoun-antecedent agreement will help them with grammar sections of such tests. Remind students that pronouns and antecedents must agree in person, number, and gender. Then, write this sample question on the board:

Choose the best way to write the following sentence:

When the crowd turned on Tommy, ____?____ mother stepped in.

(A) When the crowd turned on Tommy, its mother stepped in.
(B) When the crowd turned on Tommy, their mother stepped in.
(C) When the crowd turned on Tommy, his mother stepped in.
(D) When the crowd turned on Tommy, the mother stepped in.

Guide students to identify "Tommy" as the antecedent of the pronoun. Help them conclude that *(C)* is the correct answer because *his* matches the antecedent in gender, person, and number.

Interest Grabber Stimulate students' interest by telling them that you just heard a rumor about a plan to extend the school day. As students respond to this, do not try to calm their fears. Instead, allow them to protest for a few minutes, asking questions if necessary to maintain their excitement. Then tell them that you made up the rumor. Explain that their emotional response to your statement is similar to that of characters in the selection, who react to rumors when their everyday lives are interrupted by a bright flash of light.

◆ Build Grammar Skills

Pronoun and Antecedent Agreement If you wish to introduce the grammar concept for this selection before students read, refer to the instruction on p. 712.

Customize for *Less Proficient Readers*

Students may not be familiar with the print conventions used in screenplays. Remind students that the play *A Christmas Carol* included stage directions for actors. Pointing out examples, explain that this screenplay includes instructions in bracketed italics for the camera operator, the lighting director, and the sound engineer, as well as for the actors.

Customize for *More Advanced Students*

Suggest that students write a television report to be broadcast the morning following the strange occurrences on Maple Street. Have them follow the journalistic procedures of answering the questions: who, what, when, where, and why. They might wish to interview some of the characters in the screenplay and ask for eyewitness reports. Alternatively, they may wish to interview car repairmen, electricians, or scientists, who may be able to explain the unusual occurrences to the public. Interested students can perform their "broadcasts" for the class.

Develop Understanding

This screenplay explores the effects of prejudice and suspicion. After a bright unknown object flashes across the sky, the astonished neighbors on Maple Street discover that the electricity in their homes is gone, their cars won't start, and they cannot make telephone calls. As the neighbors gather, Tommy, a 14-year-old boy, describes stories he's read about such flying objects and strange occurrences. He tells his neighbors that in these stories, a family is always "sent ahead"—a family that only appears to be human. As neighbors begin to accuse one another of being aliens, the small crowd transforms itself into a mob. Suddenly, they hear footsteps approaching in the darkness. With a single shot, Charlie kills his neighbor Pete Van Horn, who had gone to the next street for help—causing more hysteria and violence.

Meanwhile, the camera cuts to a shot of the side of a metal space craft. Two "figures" discuss how their job is made easy. After all, the most dangerous enemy the neighbors of Maple Street have is themselves.

Customize for
English Language Learners
As students read, point out techniques the author uses to make the dialogue sound realistic. Pronunciation and grammar usage may not be precise. For example, in the sentence, "Nothin' but candles," the *-ing* sound is modified to sound more like actual speech. When Charlie says, "One of 'em'll tip their hand," the author combines the words *them* and *will.* In the sentence, "Tommy, please son . . . honey, don't talk that way—," both the ellipsis and the hyphen indicate pauses. Students can listen for these and similar effects on the audiocassette.

Listening to Literature Audiocassettes

Customize for
Bodily/Kinesthetic Learners
To help students visualize the actions of the play, have them act out one or more scenes for the class. Have them work together to cast the characters, block out their movements and practice the readings.

The Monsters Are Due on Maple Street

Rod Serling

Block Scheduling Strategies

Consider these suggestions to take advantage of extended class time:

- Discuss with students the Background for Understanding, p. 694. Focus especially upon the fear and mistrust that were a part of the era. (See the Cross-Curricular Connection, p. 709.)
- Play the audiocassette of all or part of the screenplay. Look for Customizing notes that make suggestions for how students may receive further benefit from listening to parts of the drama.

Listening to Literature Audiocassettes

- Have groups of students work on the Performance activity in the Idea Bank, p. 713. You might suggest that students complete the Casting Sketches from the Idea Bank to refer to as they plan their movements.
- To review the events in the drama, have partners complete the Series of Events Chain in **Writing and Language Transparencies,** p. 66. Then have them analyze the various conflicts by making a list such as the one shown:

Neighbors ⟶ Aliens
Charlie ⟶ Steve

CHARACTERS

NARRATOR
FIGURE ONE
FIGURE TWO

RESIDENTS OF MAPLE STREET

STEVE BRAND
CHARLIE'S WIFE
MRS. GOODMAN
MRS. BRAND ❶
TOMMY
WOMAN
DON MARTIN
SALLY, Tommy's Mother
MAN ONE
MAN TWO
PETE VAN HORN
CHARLIE
LES GOODMAN

ACT I

[Fade in on a shot of the night sky. The various nebulae and planet bodies stand out in sharp, sparkling relief, and the camera begins a slow pan across the Heavens.]

NARRATOR'S VOICE. There is a fifth dimension beyond that which is known to man. It is a dimension as vast as space, and as timeless as infinity. It is the middle ground between light and shadow—between science and superstition. And it lies between the pit of man's fears and the summit of his knowledge. This is the dimension of imagination. It is an area which we call The Twilight Zone. ❷

[The camera has begun to pan down until it passes the horizon and is on a sign which reads "Maple Street." Pan down until we are shooting down at an angle toward the street below. It's a tree-lined, quiet residential American street, very typical of the small town. The houses have front porches on which people sit and swing on gliders, conversing across from house to house. STEVE BRAND *polishes his car parked in front of his house. His neighbor,* DON MARTIN, *leans against the fender watching him. A Good Humor man rides a bicycle and is just in the process of stopping to sell some ice cream* ❸

◆Reading Strategy

❶ **Predict** Ask students to make predictions about the story based on just the cast list and the title. *Because the title has the word Monsters in it, students may predict that the story will be about two monsters—Figure One and Figure Two—and a group of people.*

Clarification

❷ This narrator's speech is the one that Rod Serling used to introduce each episode of *The Twilight Zone.* The words of the speech, exactly the same throughout a given television season, varied somewhat from one season to the next. Discuss with students how and why his words create an eerie mood.

◆Critical Thinking

❸ **Analyze** Invite a volunteer to read these script notes. In addition to containing stage directions, point out that these notes also give directions for the camera operators. Ask students how they aid the reader as well. *The directions allow readers to picture in their minds what they would see on the screen if they were watching instead of just reading.*

Customize for
Verbal/Linguistic Learners
Invite a strong oral reader to read the narrator's introduction aloud. Discuss how the repetition of words like *between* add rhythm to the speech, and add to its effectiveness.

Customize for
Musical/Rhythmic Learners
The opening of *The Twilight Zone* has a distinctive melody that was always played. Students might enjoy selecting new background music to play with a reading of the narrator's eerie introduction speech.

Humanities: Film

Screenplays Writing screenplays is an important part of creating movies and television series and films—beginning with the idea for a story. Ideas for the story line may come from a book, legend, story, or someone's imagination. The idea may be complex and detailed, or a simple concept that needs to be developed. The idea may be for an ongoing television series with the same characters and similar plots each week or a one-time movie with all new characters and a unique story line. Rod Serling's *Twilight Zone* was a weekly series of television programs, but the plot and characters were different each week. The similarity among episodes was in the style and content of the program and in the narration at the beginning of the program.

Often, screenwriters write screenplays, then send out the script for movie makers to read, and possibly purchase for use. If they cannot sell the script, they do not earn any money for the work. The job of a screenwriter may be finished when the script is purchased. At other times, the writer continues to revise the screenplay as the movie or television program is filmed.

Ask students to think of qualifications that would be necessary in order to write a good screenplay. *Possible answers: a screenwriter must have a good imagination, pay attention to details, have good writing and listening skills, and be creative and flexible.*

◆Critical Thinking

❶ Speculate Discuss Rod Serling's vision of a typical small town in the United States in the 1950's. Ask students to speculate about why he chose this kind of place as the setting of the story. *Students' perceptions of what constitutes a typical small town will vary. They may speculate that Serling wanted to create a scene in which ordinary people are going about their day-to-day activities.*

◆Reading Strategy

❷ Predict *Some students may say that the roar and flash are from an easily explained source, such as a bomb, lightning, a meteor, or an explosion of some sort. Others may guess that they are from an alien spaceship and that there will be contact with visitors from space.*

◆Literary Focus

❸ Conflict in Drama Discuss with students the technique used here in which various unidentified voices grumble about the aftermath of the flash of light. Remind students that conflict in drama occurs between two opposing forces. What conflict may be developing in this scene? *Students may say that a conflict may be developing between the disgruntled neighbors and the source of the problems they discover.*

to a couple of kids. Two women gossip on the front lawn. Another man waters his lawn.]

❶ **NARRATOR'S VOICE.** Maple Street, U.S.A., late summer. A tree-lined little world of front porch gliders, hop scotch, the laughter of children, and the bell of an ice cream vendor.

[*There is a pause and the camera moves over to a shot of the Good Humor man and two small boys who are standing alongside, just buying ice cream.*]

NARRATOR'S VOICE. At the sound of the roar and the flash of light it will be precisely 6:43 P.M. on Maple Street.

[*At this moment one of the little boys,* TOMMY, *looks up to listen to a sound of a tremendous screeching roar from overhead. A flash of light plays on both their faces and then it moves down the street past lawns and porches and rooftops and then disappears.*

Various people leave their porches and stop what they're doing to stare up at the sky. STEVE BRAND, *the man who's been polishing his car, now stands there transfixed, staring upwards. He looks at* DON MARTIN, *his neighbor from across the street.*]

> ❷ **◆ Reading Strategy**
> What do you think the flash is? Predict what effect this event will have on the community.

STEVE. What was that? A meteor?

DON. [*Nods*] That's what it looked like. I didn't hear any crash though, did you?

STEVE. [*Shakes his head*] Nope. I didn't hear anything except a roar.

MRS. BRAND. [*From her porch*] Steve? What was that?

STEVE. [*Raising his voice and looking toward porch*] Guess it was a meteor, honey. Came awful close, didn't it?

MRS. BRAND. Too close for my money! Much too close.

[*The camera pans across the various porches to people who stand there watching and talking in low tones.*]

NARRATOR'S VOICE. Maple Street. Six-forty-four P.M. on a late September evening. [*A pause*] Maple Street in the last calm and reflective moment . . . before the monsters came!

[*The camera slowly pans across the porches again. We see a man screwing a light bulb on a front porch, then getting down off the stool to flick the switch and finding that nothing happens.*

Another man is working on an electric power mower. He plugs in the plug, flicks on the switch of the power mower, off and on, with nothing happening.

Through the window of a front porch, we see a woman pushing her finger back and forth on the dial hook. Her voice is indistinct and distant, but intelligible and repetitive.]

WOMAN. Operator, operator, something's wrong on the phone, operator!

[MRS. BRAND *comes out on the porch and calls to* STEVE.]

MRS. BRAND. [*Calling*] Steve, the power's off. I had the soup on the stove and the stove just stopped working.

WOMAN. Same thing over here. I can't get anybody on the phone either. The phone seems to be dead.

[*We look down on the street as we hear the voices creep up from below, small, mildly disturbed voices highlighting these kinds of phrases:*]

VOICES.

Electricity's off.

Phone won't work.

Can't get a thing on the radio. ❸

My power mower won't move, won't work at all.

Radio's gone dead!

[PETE VAN HORN, *a tall, thin man, is seen standing in front of his house.*]

Speaking and Listening Mini-Lesson

Performance

This mini-lesson supports the Speaking and Listening Activity in the Idea Bank on p. 713.

Introduce The camera directions in a screenplay serve to frame and enhance the most important parts of a scene. Before students begin working, review terms such as *pan*, *fade*, and *long shot*.

Develop Have groups select a scene from the screenplay. Encourage them to work together to add directions for the camera in places where none is given. Suggest that they follow these steps:

- Plan out (block) movements of the characters, view them through the video camera, and make modifications as needed.
- Rehearse the scene before using the video camera to tape.
- Use movements, facial expressions, and tone of voice to convey characters' emotions.
- Speak clearly.

Apply Have students show their videos to the class. Guide a short discussion about the effectiveness of students' video techniques after each video. If videotaped performance is not possible, have students give a live performance of the selected scene.

Assess Evaluate students' performances on the effectiveness of their presentation, or have students complete the Peer Assessment: Dramatic Performance form, p. 107, in **Alternative Assessment.**

VAN HORN. I'll cut through the back yard . . . See if the power's still on on Floral Street. I'll be right back!

[*He walks past the side of his house and disappears into the back yard.*

The camera pans down slowly until we're looking at ten or eleven people standing around the street and overflowing to the curb and sidewalk. In the background is STEVE BRAND'S *car.*]

STEVE. Doesn't make sense. Why should the power go off all of a sudden, and the phone line?

DON. Maybe some sort of an electrical storm or something.

CHARLIE. That don't seem likely. Sky's just as blue as anything. Not a cloud. No lightning. No thunder. No nothing. How could it be a storm?

WOMAN. I can't get a thing on the radio. Not even the portable.

[*The people again murmur softly in wonderment and question.*]

CHARLIE. Well, why don't you go downtown and check with the police, though they'll probably think we're crazy or something. A little power failure and right away we get all flustered and everything.

Woman on telephone as seen through window, William Low, Courtesy of the artist.

STEVE. It isn't just the power failure, Charlie. If it was, we'd still be able to get a broadcast on the portable.

[*There's a murmur of reaction to this.* STEVE *looks from face to face and then over to his car.*]

4 **STEVE.** I'll run downtown. We'll get this all straightened out.

5 [*He walks over to the car, gets in it, turns the key. Looking through the open car door, we see the crowd watching him from the other side.* STEVE *starts the engine. It turns over sluggishly and then just stops dead. He tries it again and this time he can't get it to turn over. Then, very slowly and reflectively, he turns the key back to "off" and slowly gets out of the car.*

The people stare at STEVE. *He stands for a moment by the car, then walks toward the group.*]

▲ **Critical Viewing** What impression does this illustration convey about life on Maple Street? **[Analyze]** 6

◆ Build Vocabulary

flustered (flus′ terd) *adj.*: Nervous; confused

sluggishly (slug′ ish lē) *adv.*: As if lacking energy

◆Critical Thinking

4 Analyze Ask students which character begins to emerge as a leader of the group in this scene. What characteristics of this person make them think so? *Steve appears to be a man who is willing to take action by going downtown to straighten things out and find out what is happening.*

◆Critical Thinking

5 Connect Ask students what the fact that Steve's car won't start may have to do with the preceding events. *Several types of devices have failed (lights, radios, power lawn mower, telephones, and now Steve's car). This adds to the mystery and builds tension because the devices are powered by different sources.*

▶Critical Viewing◀

6 Analyze *The image shows a starry night sky behind a house that appears to be secure and comfortable. The contrast of the dark sky and the lighted house gives the viewer the feeling that something ominous may be lurking in the distance.*

Cross-Curricular Connection: Science

Is There Other Life in the Universe? Discuss with students that many scientists believe that there may be life in the universe beyond our solar system.

First, contrast scientific attempts to make contact with extraterrestrial intelligence with the suspicious "sightings" of spaceships or UFO's. Then tell students about NASA's Origins Program. The goal of this program is to develop new technologies for the exploration of the universe. The technologies will include a succession of telescopes placed in space and connected to observatories on the ground. Students can learn more about this program on NASA's Internet site.

Invite interested students to conduct research on the efforts astronomers are making to search for life forms in the universe, and to communicate with those life forms if they find them. They can find out, for example, how radio signals are used.

◆Literary Focus

❶ Conflict in Drama Ask students to describe how the idea of an alien presence is introduced. *Tommy plants the idea of aliens by referring to "them" and pointing toward the sky. Conflicts in the drama that may occur as a result of an alien presence include: war, alien takeover, panic, and fear among the community members.*

◆Reading Strategy

❷ Predict Ask students if they believe that aliens have caused the disturbance on Maple Street or if it had some other cause. *Some students, particularly those who are fans of science fiction, will embrace the idea of aliens immediately. Others may hold out for a more conventional solution.*

◆Critical Thinking

❸ Infer Ask students to explain why they think that some adults are listening to what Tommy says about aliens, while others want Tommy to "stop that kind of talk." *Students may say that some adults are so confused and mystified that they'll listen to any explanation, while others are reluctant to listen to the boy because his ideas are too frightening.*

Customize for *Visual/Spatial Learners*

Ask students to imagine what Steve looks like. Invite volunteers to suggest actors they might cast in the role of Steve. *Students may say that Steve is a man who takes charge. He is levelheaded, calm, and a good listener. They may envision him looking like an actor whom they see as a responsible person. They may select a favorite actor they would like to see play the role, just because he is a personal favorite.*

STEVE. I don't understand it. It was working fine before . . .

DON. Out of gas?

STEVE. [*Shakes his head*] I just had it filled up.

WOMAN. What's it mean?

CHARLIE. It's just as if . . . as if everything had stopped. [*Then he turns toward* STEVE.] We'd better walk downtown. [*Another murmur of assent at this.*]

STEVE. The two of us can go, Charlie. [*He turns to look back at the car.*] It couldn't be the meteor. A meteor couldn't do *this*.

[*He and* CHARLIE *exchange a look, then they start to walk away from the group.*

We see TOMMY, *a serious-faced fourteen-year-old in spectacles who stands a few feet away from the group. He is halfway between them and the two men, who start to walk down the sidewalk.*]

TOMMY. Mr. Brand . . . you better not!

STEVE. Why not?

TOMMY. They don't want you to.

[STEVE *and* CHARLIE *exchange a grin, and* STEVE *looks back toward the boy.*]

STEVE. Who doesn't want us to?

> **◆ Literary Focus** ❶ What opposing force is introduced here? What kinds of conflicts might result?

TOMMY. [*Jerks his head in the general direction of the distant horizon*] Them!

STEVE. Them?

CHARLIE. Who are them?

TOMMY. [*Very intently*] Whoever was in that thing that came by overhead.

❷ [STEVE *knits his brows for a moment, cocking his head questioningly. His voice is intense.*]

STEVE. What?

TOMMY. Whoever was in that thing that came over. I don't think they want us to leave here. ❷

[STEVE *leaves* CHARLIE *and walks over to the boy. He kneels down in front of him. He forces his voice to remain gentle. He reaches out and holds the boy.*]

STEVE. What do you mean? What are you talking about?

TOMMY. They don't want us to leave. That's why they shut everything off.

STEVE. What makes you say that? Whatever gave you that idea?

WOMAN. [*From the crowd*] Now isn't that the craziest thing you ever heard?

TOMMY. [*Persistently but a little intimidated by the crowd*] It's always that way, in every story I ever read about a ship landing from outer space. ❸

WOMAN. [*To the boy's mother,* SALLY, *who stands on the fringe of the crowd*] From outer space, yet! Sally, you better get that boy of yours up to bed. He's been reading too many comic books or seeing too many movies or something.

SALLY. Tommy, come over here and stop that kind of talk.

STEVE. Go ahead, Tommy. We'll be right back. And you'll see. That wasn't any ship or anything like it. That was just a . . . a meteor or something. Likely as not—[*He turns to the group, now trying to weight his words with an optimism he obviously doesn't feel but is desperately trying to instill in himself as well as the others.*] No doubt it did have something to do with all this power failure and the rest of it. Meteors can do some crazy things. Like sunspots.

DON. [*Picking up the cue*] Sure. That's the kind of thing—like sunspots. They raise Cain[1] with radio reception all over the world. And this thing being so close—why, there's no telling the sort of stuff it can do. [*He wets his lips,*

1. **raise Cain with:** Badly disturb.

Cross-Curricular Connection: Science

Sunspots and Radio Reception Don suggests that the problems on Maple Street are caused by sunspots.

Sunspots occur when the gases on part of the sun's photosphere, or outer layer, become temporarily cooler than the gases around them. Sunspots take only a few days to develop and usually appear in groups. They grow larger, then vanish within a couple of weeks. Sunspots can vary widely in size; a small sunspot may be about 1,000 miles wide, while a large sunspot can be as large as 100,000 miles wide. Every eleven years, the number of sunspots increases dramatically.

Don also claims that sunspots disturb radio reception all over the world. This idea is based on his knowledge that the sun emits radio waves, and large increases in radio emission from small regions of the sun usually occur near sunspots.

Have interested students research scientific discoveries about sunspots and radio emissions. Challenge them to create posters illustrating their findings, and share these with the class.

smiles nervously.] Go ahead, Charlie. You and Steve go into town and see if that isn't what's causing it all.

[STEVE *and* CHARLIE *again walk away from the group down the sidewalk. The people watch silently.*

TOMMY *stares at them, biting his lips, and finally calling out again.*]

TOMMY. *Mr. Brand!*

[*The two men stop again.* TOMMY *takes a step toward them.*]

TOMMY. Mr. Brand . . . please don't leave here.

[STEVE *and* CHARLIE *stop once again and turn toward the boy. There's a murmur in the crowd, a murmur of irritation and concern as if the boy were bringing up fears that shouldn't be brought up; words which carried with them a strange*
4 *kind of validity that came without logic but*
nonetheless registered and had meaning and effect. Again we hear a murmur of reaction from the crowd.

TOMMY *is partly frightened and partly* <u>*defiant*</u> *as well.*]

TOMMY. You might not even be able to get to town. It was that way in the story. Nobody could leave. Nobody except—

STEVE. Except who?

TOMMY. Except the people they'd sent down
5 ahead of them. They looked just like humans.
And it wasn't until the ship landed that—

[*The boy suddenly stops again, conscious of the parents staring at them and of the sudden hush of the crowd.*]

SALLY. [*In a whisper, sensing the antagonism of the crowd*] Tommy, please son . . . honey, don't talk that way—

MAN ONE. That kid shouldn't talk that way . . . and we shouldn't stand here listening to him. Why this is the craziest thing I ever heard of. The kid tells us a comic book plot and here we stand listening—

[STEVE *walks toward the camera, stops by the boy.*]

STEVE. Go ahead, Tommy. What kind of story was this? What about the people that they sent out ahead?

TOMMY. That was the way they prepared things for the landing. They sent four people. A mother and a father and two kids who looked just like humans . . . but they weren't.

[*There's another silence as* STEVE *looks toward the crowd and then toward* TOMMY. *He wears a tight grin.*]

STEVE. Well, I guess what we'd better do then
is to run a check on the neighborhood and see 6
which ones of us are really human.

[*There's laughter at this, but it's a laughter that comes from a desperate attempt to lighten the atmosphere. It's a release kind of laugh. The people look at one another in the middle of their laughter.*]

CHARLIE. There must be somethin' better to do than stand around makin' bum jokes about it.

[*Rubs his jaw nervously*] I wonder if Floral Street's got the same deal we got. [*He looks past the houses.*] Where is Pete Van Horn anyway? Didn't he get back yet?

[*Suddenly there's the sound of a car's engine starting to turn over.*

We look across the street toward the driveway of LES GOODMAN'S *house. He's at the wheel trying to start the car.*]

SALLY. Can you get it started, Les? [*He gets out of the car, shaking his head.*]

GOODMAN. No dice.

◆ Build Vocabulary

assent (ə sent′) *n.*: Agreement

persistently (pər sist′ ənt lē) *adv.*: Firmly and steadily

defiant (dē fī′ ənt) *adj.*: Boldly resisting

◆Reading Strategy

4 Predict Based on the description in these stage directions, ask students to predict what type of actions might occur. *Students will probably agree that the tone of this description is ominous and the resulting actions may be disastrous in some way.*

◆Literary Focus

5 Conflict in Drama Ask students to describe the conflict that is set in motion with Tommy's assertion that aliens might look just like humans. *Students may grasp that tension builds dramatically as people realize for the first time that since aliens can look like humans, there might be aliens among them.*

◆Literature and Your Life

6 Ask students why they think that Steve is attempting to joke with Tommy, especially at this moment when tension is building. *Steve is using humor in the hope that laughter will help his neighbors calm down and be less fearful. Encourage students to discuss experiences they have had when humor helped break the tension felt by a group of people.*

Customize Instruction

Less Proficient Readers

Ask students what differences they notice between the language the characters use and the language the author uses in the stage directions. *Students may say that the characters, who are ordinary people, speak plainly, while the language used in the stage directions is more descriptive and complex.*

Cultural Connection

***The Twilight Zone* and Popular Culture**

During the 1950's and 1960's, some people planned their weekly schedules so that they would not miss even one captivating episode of *The Twilight Zone*. Today, *The Twilight Zone* is part of American pop culture. Entertainers today still imitate its opening narration, and some advertisements include its instantly recognizable theme song. Some of the actors who played in episodes of the show, Robert Redford, Burt Reynolds, and Dennis Hopper later became well-known Hollywood stars.

Featuring aliens, monsters, goblins, robots, and settings on other planets, Rod Serling's stories usually dealt with difficult political and moral issues. A moralist, Serling ended many episodes by having characters pay a penalty for wrongdoing and by giving viewers a philosophical issue to ponder.

Guide a discussion of contemporary television shows. First, have students agree on a list of criteria for quality programming. Then have them name shows that meet these criteria. Do students feel that any of the shows on their list have the same enduring qualities as *The Twilight Zone?*

▶Critical Viewing◀

❶ Compare and Contrast *Students may say that although the bright colors of the houses contrast with the eerie and threatening mood of this scene, they do match the mood at the beginning of the screenplay.*

◆Critical Thinking

❷ Analyze Ask students why they think the crowd suddenly becomes "illogically, wildly, frightened." *The neighbors, who were already frightened, may feel that one more strange event indicates that there really is an immediate and unexplained danger.*

◆Literary Focus

❸ Conflict in Drama *Students should note that the developing conflict is between the mob and Les Goodman. Point out that people in a mob situation do not think rationally as individuals. They tend to ignore reason and feed one another's fears and suspicions.*

Customize for
Less Proficient Readers
As students reach this important point in the drama, let them listen to a portion of the audiocassette, noting how the actors heighten the dramatic effect by adjusting their rate, volume, pitch, and tone.

Listening to Literature Audiocassettes

Overview of family walking dog on the street, William Low, Courtesy of the artist

❶ ▲ **Critical Viewing** How do the colors in this illustration contrast with the mood of the drama? Explain. **[Compare and Contrast]**

[He walks toward the group. He stops suddenly as behind him, inexplicably and with a noise that inserts itself into the silence, the car engine starts up all by itself. GOODMAN *whirls around to stare toward it.*

The car idles roughly, smoke coming from the exhaust, the frame shaking gently.

GOODMAN'S *eyes go wide, and he runs over to his car.*

The people stare toward the car.]

MAN ONE. He got the car started somehow. He got his car started!

❷ *[The camera pans along the faces of the people as they stare, somehow caught up by this revelation and somehow, illogically, wildly, frightened.]*

WOMEN. How come his car just up and started like that?

SALLY. All by itself. He wasn't anywheres near it. It started all by itself.

*[*DON *approaches the group, stops a few feet away to look toward* GOODMAN'S *car and then back toward the group.]*

DON. And he never did come out to look at that thing that flew overhead. He wasn't even interested. *[He turns to the faces in the group, his face taut and serious.]* Why? Why didn't he come out with the rest of us to look?

CHARLIE. He always was an oddball. Him and his whole family. Real oddball.

DON. What do you say we ask him?

[The group suddenly starts toward the house. In this brief fraction of a moment they take the first step toward performing a <u>*metamorphosis*</u> *that changes people from a group into a mob. They begin to head purposefully across the street toward the house at the end.* STEVE *stands in front of them. For a moment their fear almost*

◆ Literary Focus What forces are in conflict now? How has the nature of the conflict changed? ❸

Beyond the Classroom

Workplace Skills

Many business owners and employers feel that having employees from diverse backgrounds enhances productivity, while also helping society as a whole. As a result, an important goal of many businesses is to create diversity in the workplace.

Discuss the fact that "The Monsters Are Due on Maple Street," is about fearful people who reject diversity in their neighborhood. The characters become suspicious when they discover one another's differences. For example, Les Goodman's interest in the stars and Steve Brand's interest in ham radios become suspicious activities. Elicit from students that the resulting prejudices have disastrous effects.

Have students form small groups. Instruct them to create a statement telling how they would like to embrace diversity in the classroom. Have them include a list of several behaviors that will help them understand and enjoy one another's differences. Tell them to place a check mark next to the behaviors that they could use effectively in a business environment. Display the lists in the classroom.

turns their walk into a wild stampede, but STEVE'S *voice, loud, incisive, and commanding, makes them stop.*]

STEVE. Wait a minute . . . wait a minute! Let's not be a mob!

[*The people stop as a group, seem to pause for a moment, and then much more quietly and slowly start to walk across the street.* GOODMAN *stands alone facing the people.*]

GOODMAN. I just don't understand it. I tried to start it and it wouldn't start. You saw me. All of you saw me.

[*And now, just as suddenly as the engine started, it stops and there's a long silence that is gradually intruded upon by the frightened murmuring of the people.*]

GOODMAN. I don't understand. I swear . . . I don't understand. What's happening?

DON. Maybe you better tell us. Nothing's working on this street. Nothing. No lights, no power, no radio. [*And then meaningfully*] Nothing except one car—yours!

4 [*The people pick this up and now their murmuring becomes a loud chant filling the air with accusations and demands for action. Two of the men pass* DON *and head toward* GOODMAN, *who backs away, backing into his car and now at bay.*]

GOODMAN. Wait a minute now. You keep your distance—all of you. So I've got a car that starts by itself—well, that's a freak thing, I admit it. But does that make me some kind of a criminal or something? I don't know why the car works—it just does!

[*This stops the crowd momentarily and now* GOODMAN, *still backing away, goes toward his front porch. He goes up the steps and then stops to stand facing the mob.*

We see a long shot of STEVE *as he comes through the crowd.*]

STEVE. [*Quietly*] We're all on a monster kick, Les. Seems that the general impression holds that maybe one family isn't what we think they are. Monsters from outer space or something. Different than us. Fifth columnists[2] from the vast beyond. [*He chuckles.*] You know anybody that might fit that description around here on Maple Street?

GOODMAN. What is this, a gag or something? This a practical joke or something?

[*We see a close-up of the porch light as it suddenly goes out. There's a murmur from the group.*]

GOODMAN. Now I suppose that's supposed to incriminate me! The light goes on and off. That really does it, doesn't it? [*He looks around the faces of the people.*] I just don't understand this—[*He wets his lips, looking from face to face.*] Look, you all know me. We've lived here five years. Right in this house. We're no different from any of the rest of you! We're no different at all. Really . . . this whole thing is just . . . just weird—

WOMAN. Well, if that's the case, Les Goodman, explain why—[*She stops suddenly, clamping her mouth shut.*]

GOODMAN. [*Softly*] Explain what?

STEVE. [*Interjecting*] Look, let's forget this— 5

CHARLIE. [*Overlapping him*] Go ahead, let her talk. What about it? Explain what?

WOMAN. [*A little reluctantly*] Well . . . sometimes I go to bed late at night. A couple of times . . . a couple of times I'd come out on the porch and I'd see Mr. Goodman here in the wee hours of the morning standing out in front of his house . . . looking up at the sky. [*She looks around*

---

2. **Fifth columnists:** People who help an invading enemy from within their own country.

◆ Build Vocabulary

metamorphosis (met´ ə môr´ fə sis) *n.*: Change of form

◆Critical Thinking

4 Infer Ask students why they think that the neighbors have turned on Goodman simply because his car started by itself. *Students should infer that the neighbors suspect Goodman of being one of "them"—one of the aliens.*

◆Critical Thinking

5 Connect Ask students how Steve's words instructing the people to "forget this" are similar to his earlier attempt at making a joke. *Again, Steve is trying to calm the crowd, this time by attempting to change the subject.*

Cross-Curricular Connection: Social Studies

Fifth Columnists The Spanish Civil War, 1936–1939, was a conflict in which conservative forces, led by Francisco Franco, overthrew the second Spanish republic. The war resulted in a huge death toll. It also marked the beginning of a long era of right-wing dictatorship that ended in 1975 with Franco's death.

After his experiences in and around besieged Madrid during this time, noted author Ernest Hemingway wrote his only full-length play, *The Fifth Column*. Hemingway coined the phrase *fifth columnists* to describe secret subversives working against a country from within that country. The phrase soon became a permanent fixture in the English language.

Ask students if they can think of a historical event, slang word, or activity that has become so well-known that it is often used in the English language. Suggest that students look up Watergate, freestaters, or similar words to see if they can locate the history of the term or expression to help them get started thinking of words we use in the same way as *fifth columnists*.

◆Reading Strategy

❶ **Predict** *Students may predict that Goodman is going to be blamed for the events on Maple Street and that the neighbors may soon become violent.*

◆Critical Thinking

❷ **Analyze** Point out that the drama is divided into two acts. Tell students that a change in acts indicates a pause to mark a change of scene or time, to show a change in perspective, or to create dramatic effect. Ask students why they think Serling started Act II at this point. *Discuss that Serling may have started Act II at this point as a way to highlight this dramatic moment in the story.*

Clarification

❸ Help students see the double message in Charlie's statement about the dark ages. Although Charlie is simply referring to a time when candles were the main source of light, Serling also intended a different meaning. His use of "the dark ages" is a reference to a time when much less was known about many things and suspicion competed with reason as people faced unexpected ideas or unexplainable events. During the Dark Ages, blame was often placed on things or people who were different or misunderstood.

Customize for *English Language Learners*

Help students understand the word *sentry-like* by inviting several students to stand like soldiers in the front of the classroom. To illustrate the word *timorously* have one student read Sally's lines in an anxious and timid voice.

the circle of faces.] That's right, looking up at the sky as if . . . as if he were waiting for something. [*A pause*] As if he were looking for something.

[*There's a murmur of reaction from the crowd again.*

We cut suddenly to a group shot. As GOODMAN *starts toward them, they back away frightened.*]

GOODMAN. You know really . . . this is for laughs. You know what I'm guilty of? [*He laughs.*] I'm guilty of insomnia. Now what's the penalty for insomnia? [*At this point the laugh, the humor, leaves his voice.*] Did you hear what I said? I said it was insomnia. [*A pause as he looks around, then shouts.*] I said it was insomnia! You fools. You scared, frightened rabbits, you. You're sick people, do you know that? You're sick people—all of you! And you don't even know what you're starting because let me tell you . . . let me tell you—this thing you're starting—that should frighten you. As God is my witness . . . you're letting something begin here that's a nightmare!

❶ **◆ Reading Strategy** How do you think the crowd will treat Les Goodman?

❷ ACT II

[*We see a medium shot of the* GOODMAN *entry hall at night. On the side table rests an unlit candle.* MRS. GOODMAN *walks into the scene, a glass of milk in hand. She sets the milk down on the table, lights the candle with a match from a box on the table, picks up the glass of milk, and starts out of scene*

MRS. GOODMAN *comes through her porch door, glass of milk in hand. The entry hall, with table and lit candle, can be seen behind her.*

Outside, the camera slowly pans down the sidewalk, taking in little knots of people who stand around talking in low voices. At the end of each conversation they look toward LES GOODMAN'S *house. From the various houses we can see candlelight but no electricity, and there's an all-pervading quiet that blankets the whole area, disturbed only by the almost whispered voices of the people as they stand around. The camera pans over to one group where* CHARLIE *stands. He stares across at* GOODMAN'S *house.*

We see a long shot of the house. Two men stand across the street in almost sentry-like poses. Then we see a medium shot of a group of people.]

SALLY. [*A little timorously*] It just doesn't seem right, though, keeping watch on them. Why . . . he was right when he said he was one of our neighbors. Why, I've known Ethel Goodman ever since they moved in. We've been good friends—

CHARLIE. That don't prove a thing. Any guy who'd spend his time lookin' up at the sky early in the morning—well, there's something wrong with that kind of person. There's something that ain't legitimate. Maybe under normal circumstances we could let it go by, but these aren't normal circumstances. Why, look at this street! Nothin' but candles. Why, it's like goin' back into the dark ages or somethin'! ❸

[STEVE *walks down the steps of his porch, walks down the street over to* LES GOODMAN'S *house, and then stops at the foot of the steps.* GOODMAN *stands there, his wife behind him, very frightened.*]

GOODMAN. Just stay right where you are, Steve. We don't want any trouble, but this time if anybody sets foot on my porch, that's what they're going to get—trouble!

STEVE. Look, Les—

GOODMAN. I've already explained to you people. I don't sleep very well at night sometimes. I get up and I take a walk and I look up at the sky. I look at the stars!

MRS. GOODMAN. That's exactly what he does. Why this whole thing, it's . . . it's some kind of madness or something.

STEVE. [*Nods grimly*] That's exactly what it is—some kind of madness.

Beyond the Classroom

Career Connection

Astronomy Many misconceptions about alien life forms guide the actions of the people on Maple Street. Clearly, none of the neighbors is an astronomer.

Gather a group of students who are interested in solar systems, galaxies, and the universe. Have them investigate careers in physics and astronomy. They can, for example, contact NASA for information, and explore jobs in the fields of space exploration, satellite technology, and radio and telescope technology, to name just a few.

Have students share with one another the requirements needed to pursue each type of career. Remind students that in addition to needing a solid educational background in science and mathematics, workers in space technology must be creative problem solvers and be able to work with others as a team.

Streetlight, 1930, Constance Coleman Richardson, Indianapolis Museum of Art

4 ▲ Critical Viewing Why does night's darkness, shown in this illustration, make people more fearful? **[Hypothesize]**

CHARLIE'S VOICE. [*Shrill, from across the street*] You best watch who you're seen with, Steve! Until we get this all straightened out, you ain't exactly above suspicion yourself.

STEVE. [*Whirling around toward him*] Or you, Charlie. Or any of us, it seems. From age eight on up!

WOMAN. What I'd like to know is—what are we gonna do? Just stand around here all night?

CHARLIE. There's nothin' else we can do! [*He turns back looking toward* STEVE *and* GOODMAN *again.*] One of 'em'll tip their hand. They got to.

STEVE. [*Raising his voice*] There's something you can do, Charlie. You could go home and keep your mouth shut. You could quit strutting around like a self-appointed hanging judge and just climb into bed and forget it.

CHARLIE. You sound real anxious to have that happen, Steve. I think we better keep our eye on you too!

DON. [*As if he were taking the bit in his teeth, takes a hesitant step to the front*] I think everything might as well come out now. [*He turns toward* STEVE.] Your wife's done plenty of talking, Steve, about how odd you are! 5

CHARLIE. [*Picking this up, his eyes widening*] Go ahead, tell us what she's said.

▶Critical Viewing◀

4 Hypothesize *Students may point out that when one cannot see in the dark, other senses become heightened. For example, a common noise may seem strange, and the feel of a gentle breeze may be more noticeable. These heightened sensations add to people's natural fear of darkness. Discuss that Serling may have created a nighttime setting for Act II to draw on these fears.*

◆Reading Strategy

5 Predict Ask students what they think might happen next. *Students will most likely predict that the crowd is about to turn on Steve.*

Customize for *Bodily/Kinesthetic Learners*

To help students better understand the depth of the characters' mistrust of one another, invite four students to act out the lines on this page, paying particular attention to stage directions like "Whirling around" and "takes a hesitant step." Discuss how the actors' body language helps portray the characters' sense of increasing fear and suspicion.

Humanities: Art

Streetlight, 1930, by Constance Coleman Richardson

Constance Coleman Richardson was born in 1905 in Indianapolis and studied at the Pennsylvania Academy of Fine Arts. She painted many images of the Great Lakes and Far West regions of the United States. Like *Streetlight,* many of her paintings reflect her interest in light and space. This image shows Indianapolis on a summer night.

Have students identify the figures of the mother and child. Ask them how the scene reminds them of Maple Street. Then ask them what details in the painting add an eerie mood to the painting that supports the mood of the drama. *Students may point out the dark setting and the eerie glow. Discuss that in the image the darkness seems to overshadow any human elements.*

◆Literary Focus

❶ **Conflict in Drama** Steve is expressing his anger with his neighbors. Ask students to describe the tone of his speech. What type of conflict does it reveal? *Students should recognize that Steve, who is becoming frustrated as well as angry, is being sarcastic and doesn't really mean what he says. The conflict is now between individuals like Steve and Goodman and also between individuals and the mob.*

◆Critical Thinking

❷ **Compare and Contrast** Discuss with students that people respond differently to the same situations. Ask students to compare the way Steve responds to the mob's accusations with the way his wife does. *Students may notice that while Steve is outraged and angry with the neighbors, his wife attempts to pacify them.*

◆Literature and Your Life

❸ *Students may say that frightened people try to find scapegoats when they feel that things are out of control. Finding a person to blame gives them a false sense of security. In addition, when accusations are flying, finding a scapegoat means they can point the finger away from themselves and they won't find themselves being blamed.*

◆Reading Strategy

❹ **Predict** Discuss with students the role that Tommy has played in the drama thus far. Ask students if they feel his prediction that a monster is coming is correct. *Tommy planted the idea that the problems in the neighborhood were caused by aliens, and he caused the neighbors to suspect one another when he told them that "they" always send a family ahead. Students may be divided on their predictions.*

[*We see a long shot of* STEVE *as he walks toward them from across the street.*]

❶ **STEVE.** Go ahead, what's my wife said? Let's get it all out. Let's pick out every idiosyncrasy of every single man, woman, and child on the street. And then we might as well set up some kind of kangaroo court.[3] How about a firing squad at dawn, Charlie, so we can get rid of all the suspects? Narrow them down. Make it easier for you.

DON. There's no need gettin' so upset, Steve. It's just that . . . well . . . Myra's talked about how there's been plenty of nights you spent hours down in your basement workin' on some kind of radio or something. Well, none of us have ever seen that radio—

[*By this time* STEVE *has reached the group. He stands there defiantly close to them.*]

CHARLIE. Go ahead, Steve. What kind of "radio set" you workin' on? I never seen it. Neither has anyone else. Who you talk to on that radio set? And who talks to you?

STEVE. I'm surprised at you, Charlie. How come you're so dense all of a sudden? [*A pause*] Who do I talk to? I talk to monsters from outer space. I talk to three-headed green men who fly over here in what look like meteors.

[STEVE'S *wife steps down from the porch, bites her lip, calls out.*]

❷ **MRS. BRAND.** Steve! Steve, please. [*Then looking around, frightened, she walks toward the group.*] It's just a ham radio set, that's all. I bought him a book on it myself. It's just a ham radio set. A lot of people have them. I can show it to you. It's right down in the basement.

STEVE. [*Whirls around toward her*] Show them nothing! If they want to look inside our house—let them get a search warrant.

CHARLIE. Look, buddy, you can't afford to—

STEVE. [*Interrupting*] Charlie, don't tell me what I can afford! And stop telling me who's dangerous and who isn't and who's safe and who's a menace. [*He turns to the group and shouts.*] And you're with him, too—all of you! You're standing here all set to crucify—all set to find a scapegoat—all desperate to point some kind of a finger at a neighbor! Well now look, friends, the only thing that's gonna happen is that we'll eat each other up alive—

> **◆ Literature and Your Life**
> Why do people often need to blame a scapegoat for unexplainable events? ❸

[*He stops abruptly as* CHARLIE *suddenly grabs his arm.*]

CHARLIE. [*In a hushed voice*] That's not the only thing that can happen to us.

[*Cut to a long shot looking down the street. A figure has suddenly materialized in the gloom and in the silence we can hear the clickety-clack of slow, measured footsteps on concrete as the figure walks slowly toward them. One of the women lets out a stifled cry. The young mother grabs her boy as do a couple of others.*]

TOMMY. [*Shouting, frightened*] It's the monster! It's the monster! ❹

[*Another woman lets out a wail and the people fall back in a group, staring toward the darkness and the approaching figure.*

We see a medium group shot of the people as they stand in the shadows watching. DON MARTIN *joins them, carrying a shotgun. He holds it up.*]

DON. We may need this.

STEVE. A shotgun? [*He pulls it out of* DON'S *hand.*] Good Lord—will anybody think a thought around here? Will you people wise up? What good would a shotgun do against—

◆ Build Vocabulary

scapegoat (skāp´ gōt´) *n.*: Person or group blamed for the mistakes or crimes of others

3. **kangaroo court:** Unofficial court that does not follow normal rules.

Cross-Curricular Connection: Science

Science Fiction Science fiction, a literary genre based on the effects of science and technology on society, includes stories of fantasy that involve altered time, space, and reality. The writings of two of the earliest science-fiction writers, Jules Verne and H. G. Wells, predicted many future technological advances that have since come true. For example, the characters in Vernes's *Twenty Thousand Leagues Under the Sea* (1870), traveled in a powered submarine; Verne later wrote about weightlessness and space travel. Wells, the author of *The War of the Worlds* (1898), also predicted the advent of space travel and atomic power.

When Rod Serling was young, he might have enjoyed reading popular science-fiction magazines like *Amazing Stories* (1926) and *Astounding Science Fiction* (1937). To create these pulp magazines, a group of writers penned exciting tales in which protagonists battled aliens from other galaxies while wearing metal space suits that looked like diving suits. Talented illustrators styled covers that featured flamboyant "space-opera art." As a result, the genre of science fiction had an audience of its own by the 1930's.

Ask students to brainstorm for changes they predict will come about in the genre of science fiction with the computer age. What new genres might develop, such as interactive stories that are written by several people in different locations?

[*Now* CHARLIE *pulls the gun from* STEVE'S *hand.*]

CHARLIE. No more talk, Steve. You're going to talk us into a grave! You'd let whatever's out there walk right over us, wouldn't yuh? Well, some of us won't!

[*He swings the gun around to point it toward the sidewalk.*

The dark figure continues to walk toward them.

5 *The group stands there, fearful, apprehensive, mothers clutching children, men standing in front of wives.* CHARLIE *slowly raises the gun. As the figure gets closer and closer he suddenly pulls the trigger. The sound of it explodes in the stillness. There is a long angle shot looking down at the figure, who suddenly lets out a small cry, stumbles forward onto his knees and then falls forward on his face.* DON, CHARLIE, *and* STEVE *race forward over to him.* STEVE *is there first and turns the man over. Now the crowd gathers around them.*]

STEVE. [*Slowly looks up*] It's Pete Van Horn.

DON. [*In a hushed voice*] Pete Van Horn! He was just gonna go over to the next block to see if the power was on—

WOMAN. You killed him, Charlie. You shot him dead!

CHARLIE. [*Looks around at the circle of faces, his eyes frightened, his face contorted*] But . . . but I didn't know who he was. I certainly didn't know who he was. He comes walkin' out of the darkness—how am I supposed to know who he was? [*He grabs* STEVE.] Steve—you know why I shot! How was I supposed to know he wasn't a monster or something? [*He grabs* DON *now.*] We're all scared of the same thing. I was just tryin' to . . . tryin' to protect my home, that's all! Look, all of you, that's all I was tryin' to do. [*He looks down wildly at the body.*] I didn't know it was somebody we knew! I didn't know—

6 **◆ Reading Strategy**
Do you think the blackout will be resolved? How?

[*There's a sudden hush and then an intake of breath. We see a medium shot of the living room window of* CHARLIE'S *house. The window is not lit, but suddenly the house lights come on behind it.*]

WOMAN. [*In a very hushed voice*] Charlie . . . Charlie . . . the lights just went on in your house. Why did the lights just go on?

DON. What about it, Charlie? How come you're the only one with lights now?

GOODMAN. That's what I'd like to know.

[*A pause as they all stare toward* CHARLIE.]

GOODMAN. You were so quick to kill, Charlie, and you were so quick to tell us who we had to be careful of. Well, maybe you had to kill. Maybe Peter there was trying to tell us something. Maybe he'd found out something and came back to tell us who there was amongst us we should watch out for— 7

[CHARLIE *backs away from the group, his eyes wide with fright.*]

CHARLIE. No . . . no . . . it's nothing of the sort! I don't know why the lights are on. I swear I don't. Somebody's pulling a gag or something.

[*He bumps against* STEVE, *who grabs him and whirls him around.*]

STEVE. *A gag?* A gag? Charlie, there's a dead man on the sidewalk and you killed him! Does this thing look like a gag to you?

[CHARLIE *breaks away and screams as he runs toward his house.*]

CHARLIE. No! No! Please!

[*A man breaks away from the crowd to chase* CHARLIE.

We see a long angle shot looking down as the man tackles CHARLIE *and lands on top of him. The other people start to run toward them.* CHARLIE *is up on his feet, breaks away from the other man's grasp, lands a couple of desperate punches that push the man aside. Then he forces his way, fighting, through the crowd to once again break free, jumps up on his front*

◆Literary Focus

5 Conflict in Drama Remind students that the climax is the high point of suspense in a story or drama. Point out that Pete Van Horn's murder is the climax of this screen drama. Ask students how the climax relates to the various conflicts they have been following. *Students should note that the climax is the result of the conflicts.*

◆Reading Strategy

6 Predict *Some students may say that the blackout has not been resolved, especially given the developing chaos. They will view Charlie's lights coming on as one in a series of unexplained events. Others may feel that things will return to normal.*

◆Critical Thinking

7 Connect Ask students to recall Goodman's reactions when the crowd's anger and accusations were directed toward him. Ask them to describe how he has changed now that events have changed. *Students will recall that Goodman was initially outraged by the mob's behavior. He identified that behavior as dangerous. They may say that by this point in the plot, he has become one more member of that same mob, and that he is as eager as any of them to point the finger away from himself.*

Viewing and Representing Mini-Lesson

Visual Imagery

In this mini-lesson, students will use imagery created by the screenwriter's words to produce a visual representation.

Introduce Have students read aloud the description of the opening scene on Maple Street, pp. 697–698, and the last scene on Maple Street, pp. 709–710.

Develop Discuss with students that screen-writers use words to communicate ideas that they visualize. Have students discuss how Rod Serling used words to create two very different moods.

Apply Provide magazines, painting and/or drawing tools, and glue. Have students create a collage, painting, drawing, sketch, or a combination of these to show mood changes in the drama. Instruct them to fold a large sheet of drawing paper in half. The left side of the paper can show the beginning of the drama and the right side can show the ending.

Assess Have students present their artworks to the class and explain their choice of media. Ask them to identify the mood and main idea of each side of their creations. Evaluate students on their preparation and presentation.

◆Critical Thinking

1 Analyze Ask students whether they think Charlie really knows who the monster is, as he claims. Ask them to explain why Charlie swears that he does. *Students may say that Charlie is desperate to direct the mob's attention away from himself, and will say almost anything convincingly and vigorously to do so.*

◆Reading Strategy

2 Predict *Students will probably say that more violence will follow and the cause of the problems on Maple Street at the beginning of the story will soon be revealed. Some may predict the arrival of the police or aliens.*

Customize for *Less Proficient Readers*

To help students better understand how the neighbors' fear, suspicion, and accusations lead to the turmoil on Maple Street, you may want to play the audiocassette of the scenes on these pages.

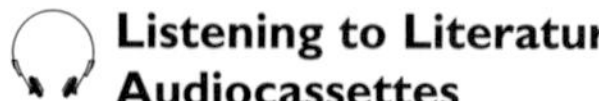
Listening to Literature Audiocassettes

porch. A rock thrown from the group smashes a window alongside of him, the broken glass flying past him. A couple of pieces cut him. He stands there perspiring, rumpled, blood running down from a cut on the cheek. His wife breaks away from the group to throw herself into his arms. He buries his face against her. We can see the crowd converging on the porch now.]

VOICES.

It must have been him.
He's the one.
We got to get Charlie.

[*Another rock lands on the porch. Now* CHARLIE *pushes his wife behind him, facing the group.*]

1 **CHARLIE.** Look, look I swear to you . . . it isn't me . . . but I do know who it is . . . I swear to you, I do know who it is. I know who the monster is here. I know who it is that doesn't belong. I swear to you I know.

GOODMAN. [*Shouting*] What are you waiting for?

WOMAN. [*Shouting*] Come on, Charlie, come on.

MAN ONE. [*Shouting*] Who is it, Charlie, tell us!

DON. [*Pushing his way to the front of the crowd*] All right, Charlie, let's hear it!

[CHARLIE'S *eyes dart around wildly.*]

CHARLIE. It's . . . it's . . .

MAN TWO. [*Screaming*] Go ahead, Charlie, tell us.

CHARLIE. It's . . . it's the kid. It's Tommy. He's the one!

[*There's a gasp from the crowd as we cut to a shot of* SALLY *holding her son* TOMMY. *The boy at first doesn't understand and then, realizing the eyes are all on him, buries his face against his mother.*]

SALLY. [*Backs away*] That's crazy! That's crazy! He's a little boy.

WOMAN. But he knew! He was the only one who knew! He told us all about it. Well, how did he know? How *could* he have known?

[*The various people take this up and repeat the question aloud.*]

VOICES.

How could he know?
Who told him?
Make the kid answer.

DON. It was Charlie who killed old man Van Horn.

WOMAN. But it was the kid here who knew what was going to happen all the time. He was the one who knew!

[*We see a close-up of* STEVE.]

STEVE. Are you all gone crazy? [*Pause as he looks about*] Stop.

[*A fist crashes at* STEVE'S *face, staggering him back out of the frame of the picture.*

There are several close camera shots suggesting the coming of violence. A hand fires a rifle. A fist clenches. A hand grabs the hammer from VAN HORN'S *body, etc. Meanwhile, we hear the following lines.*]

> **◆ Reading Strategy**
> What do you think will happen next on Maple Street? 2

DON. Charlie has to be the one—Where's my rifle—

WOMAN. Les Goodman's the one. His car started! Let's wreck it.

MRS. GOODMAN. What about Steve's radio—He's the one that called them—

MRS. GOODMAN. Smash the radio. Get me a hammer. Get me something.

STEVE. Stop—Stop—

CHARLIE. Where's that kid—Let's get him.

MAN ONE. Get Steve—Get Charlie—They're working together.

[*The crowd starts to converge around the mother, who grabs the child and starts to run with him. The crowd starts to follow, at first*

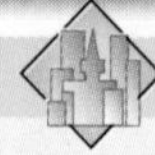

Beyond the Classroom

Career Connection

Jobs in Television "The Monsters Are Due on Maple Street" first aired in 1960, when TV was in its infancy. Nevertheless, its stage directions should give students an idea of the intricacies involved in producing a TV show. Have students reread the stage directions on pp. 708–709 and estimate how many people worked to produce the scene. Discuss the concept that a TV production is the result of the combined talents of many people.

Ask students to name some of the jobs involved in producing a TV show and list these on the board. Students may name: the screenwriter, director, producer, sound engineer, lighting director, camera operator, set designer, actors, makeup artists, grips, costume designers, or stagehands.

Ask students to choose a job from the list that interests them. Group students according to their choices. Have students work together to research the job they selected. They should find out what kind of money the job pays, what kind of training is required, what kinds of qualifications are needed. Students can use the Internet, career guides, videos, biographies, or interviews.

3 ▲ Critical Viewing How does this manipulated photograph help to communicate the ideas of the play? **[Connect]**

walking fast, and then running after him.

We see a full shot of the street as suddenly CHARLIE'S *lights go off and the lights in another house go on. They stay on for a moment, then from across the street other lights go on and then off again.*]

MAN ONE. [*Shouting*] It isn't the kid . . . it's Bob Weaver's house.

WOMAN. It isn't Bob Weaver's house. It's Don Martin's place.

CHARLIE. I tell you it's the kid.

DON. It's Charlie. He's the one.

4 [*We move into a series of close-ups of various people as they shout, accuse, scream, interspersing these shots with shots of houses as the lights go on and off, and then slowly in the middle of this nightmarish morass of sight and sound the camera starts to pull away, until once again we've reached the opening shot looking at the Maple Street sign from high above.* 4

5 *The camera continues to move away until we dissolve to a shot looking toward the metal side of a space craft, which sits shrouded in darkness. An open door throws out a beam of light from the illuminated interior. Two figures silhouetted against the bright lights appear. We get only a vague feeling of form, but nothing more explicit than that.*]

FIGURE ONE. Understand the procedure now? Just stop a few of their machines and radios and telephones and lawn mowers . . . throw them into darkness for a few hours, and then you just sit back and watch the pattern.

FIGURE TWO. And this pattern is always the same?

FIGURE ONE. With few variations. They pick the most dangerous enemy they can find . . . and it's themselves. And all we need do is sit back . . . and watch.

▶Critical Viewing◀

3 Connect *The stream of light at the top of the image brings to mind the flash of light at the beginning of the drama. The lone car on the dark road at night reinforces the fear of the unknown that grips the neighbors of Maple Street.*

◆Critical Thinking

4 Compare and Contrast Have students reread the description of the opening camera shot of Maple Street. Ask them to compare the way the viewer first sees Maple Street and the way it appears now. *Students may note that Serling gives instructions for the same camera angles, but now these cameras show that pandemonium has broken loose on the street. Maple Street, once calm and happy, is now in chaos.*

◆Reading Strategy

5 Predict Ask students to predict what the figures may be. *Students will most likely predict that the figures are aliens. Discuss whether they are surprised at this turn of events.*

Cross-Curricular Connection: Social Studies

McCarthyism During the 1950's Senator Joseph McCarthy abused his powerful position as chairman of the Senate Permanent Subcommittee on Investigations by falsely accusing many scholars, political figures, journalists, and entertainers of being communists.

Citizens became frightened and mistrusted their friends and neighbors. Accusations ruined the careers and reputations of many people, although no accusations were ever proved. McCarthy was finally censured in 1954, six years before the production of "The Monsters Are Due on Maple Street."

To help students understand the theme of the selection, have students reread the Narrator's last speech, p. 710, and discuss how Serling may have written it as a response to McCarthyism. Remind students of Serling's avoidance of censorship in "The Story Behind the Story" on p. 694.

Ask students how turmoil such as that created by McCarthy could have been prevented. Small groups of students can apply their ideas by re-creating a scene of the play in which the neighbors listen to reason. Have each group present their scene to the class.

◆Critical Thinking

1 Draw Conclusions Ask students what Figure One might mean when it says, "Their world is full of Maple Streets." *Students may say that the Figure means that, when they become frightened, many people become suspicious of one another and try to find scapegoats. It might not happen only on Maple Street.*

◆Literary Focus

2 Conflict in Drama Ask students why the narrator refers to thoughts, attitudes, and prejudices as weapons. *Discuss with students that when people's attitudes are prejudicial and suspicious, their actions are not based on facts and reason. These types of thoughts are like weapons because they lead to violence and harm.*

Connections to Today's World

About The Far Side

The Far Side, which was popular for fourteen years from 1980 to 1994, is a series of cartoons that pokes fun at everything from boneless chicken to aliens. Created by Gary Larson, the panel appeared worldwide in more than 1,900 daily and Sunday newspapers and was translated into 17 languages. Today, it is syndicated in 40 countries. Larson has also published 22 books of cartoons.

Answers

1. The cartoon conveys an impression of aliens who are like humans in some ways.
2. Emily will tell Gladys that there is a huge monster in her yard.
3. Aliens are a common subject for humor because extraterrestrial life is a subject about which little is known.

More About the Artist

Gary Larson was born on August 14, 1950, in Tacoma, Washington. Although he loved to draw, he never formally studied art except in required classes and never planned to become a cartoonist. His first love was science. Students might enjoy looking through books of Larson's work at the library to find other cartoon panels with the theme of science.

FIGURE TWO. Then I take it this place . . . this Maple Street . . . is not unique.

1 FIGURE ONE. [*Shaking his head*] By no means. Their world is full of Maple Streets. And we'll go from one to the other and let them destroy themselves. One to the other . . . one to the other . . . one to the other—

[*Now the camera pans up for a shot of the starry sky and over this we hear the* NARRATOR'S *voice.*]

NARRATOR'S VOICE. The tools of conquest do not necessarily come with bombs and explosions and fallout. There are weapons that are simply thoughts, attitudes, prejudices—to be found only in the minds of men. For the record, prejudices can kill and suspicion can destroy and a thoughtless frightened search for a scapegoat has a fallout all its own for the children . . . and the children yet unborn. [*A pause*] And the pity of it is . . . that these things cannot be confined to . . . The Twilight Zone! 2

CONNECTIONS TO TODAY'S WORLD

The possibility of aliens visiting Earth has sparked the imaginations of writers and artists to develop many scenarios. Rod Serling spun tales of fear and conspiracy. In contrast, cartoonist Gary Larson imagined a funnier interaction between humans and creatures from outer space.

The Far Side
by Gary Larson

"Hello, Emily. This is Gladys Murphy up the street. Fine, thanks . . . Say, could you go to your window and describe what's in my front yard?"

"Wonderful! Just wonderful! . . . So much for instilling them with a sense of awe."

1. What impression of aliens does the cartoon to the left convey?
2. Using the cartoon above, what would you expect Emily to tell Gladys?
3. Why do you think Larson chooses aliens as a subject for his comedy?

Beyond Literature

Media Connection

The Twilight Zone "You unlock this door with the key of imagination. Beyond it is another dimension, a dimension of sound, a dimension of sight, a dimension of mind." So began Rod Serling's narration of *The Twilight Zone,* one of the most popular TV shows of all time. The series, whose 156 episodes aired for the first time between 1959 and 1965, combined fantasy and science fiction to examine serious themes such as prejudice, identity, and the effects of technology on society. The premise was so popular that a second series was produced from 1985 to 1987.

Cross-Curricular Activity

TV Review Locate and watch an episode of *The Twilight Zone*. In a review, summarize the plot of the show, and tell readers what the episode suggests about human behavior. Finally, express your opinion about the success of the episode you saw. Share your review with the class.

Guide for Responding

◆ Literature and Your Life

Reader's Response If you were a resident of Maple Street, how would you have responded to the strange events?

Thematic Focus Why does the community turn into an angry and suspicious mob?

Skit In a group, role-play the scene in which the crowd begins to suspect there is an alien among them. Discuss how each of you feels as the scene progresses.

☑ Check Your Comprehension

1. What are the first signs that something strange is happening on Maple Street?
2. How does Tommy explain the strange happenings?
3. How do the other neighborhood residents react to these events?
4. Why does Charlie shoot Pete Van Horn?
5. What happens after the shooting?
6. What is the real cause of the strange occurrences on Maple Street?

◆ Critical Thinking

INTERPRET

1. How does the appearance of the aliens at the end affect your view of the preceding action? **[Analyze]**
2. What qualities in Les Goodman and Steve Brand cause people to become suspicious of them? **[Interpret]**
3. What do the crowd's accusations suggest about how clearly they are thinking? **[Infer]**
4. How does fear contribute to the conflict on Maple Street? **[Analyze Cause and Effect]**
5. How do the events of the play prove the narrator's statement: "The tools of conquest do not necessarily come with bombs and explosions and fallout"? **[Connect]**
6. Who are the real monsters in this play? **[Draw Conclusions]**

APPLY

7. What warning should readers take away from this play? **[Generalize]**

EXTEND

8. Why do you think people's behaviors change when they're in a group? **[Social Studies Link]**

Beyond the Selection

FURTHER READING

Other Works by Rod Serling

The Twilight Zone Complete Stories, Rod Serling

The Zero Hour: The Original Radio Broadcasts: "Program One: The Desperate Witness," Rod Serling (2 audiocassettes)

Other Works About *The Twilight Zone*

In the Zone: The Twilight World of Rod Serling, by Peter Wolfe

INTERNET

We suggest the following sites on the Internet (all Web sites are subject to change).

For more information about Rod Serling: **http://www.scifi.com/twizone/twilite3.html**

For other *The Twilight Zone* sites: **http://www.cgstv.com/twilight.htm**

We *strongly recommend* that you preview these sites before you send students to them.

Beyond Literature

Remind students that when they summarize the plot of the show, they should include the most important events. Students may want to complete the Series of Events Chain in **Writing and Language Transparencies,** p. 66, before they begin writing their review.

Reinforce and Extend

Answers

◆ Literature and Your Life

Reader's Response Some students may say that they would respond with reason. Others might imagine responding fearfully.

Thematic Focus They turn into a mob because they are afraid.

☑ Check Your Comprehension

1. The stove suddenly stops working at the Brand house. Other neighbors discover power failures, dead radios, inoperative lawn mowers and cars that won't start.
2. He thinks aliens have invaded Earth.
3. They panic and then become suspicious of one another.
4. He cannot see well enough to recognize Pete and thinks that a monster is approaching.
5. Hysteria takes over Maple Street.
6. They were caused by the Figures.

◆ Critical Thinking

1. Students may say that the appearance of the aliens makes the preceding action seem even more senseless because it was not only caused by the aliens but predicted as well.
2. They are both different in some way from the crowd.
3. Their thinking is becoming unclear; they jump to conclusions and become suspicious.
4. Fear is the driving force of the conflict.
5. The people's prejudices and attitudes lead to violence.
6. The humans are the real monsters.
7. Avoid prejudice, suspicion, and hatred because they can lead to tragic consequences.
8. Possible response: People may be pressured to conform to the group and may not feel personally responsible for the group's actions.

Answers

◆Reading Strategy

1. Students may say that they expected Steve Brand to become the voice of reason because he listens to Tommy and tries to keep the others calm.
2. Students may note that their own personal experiences suggest that the fears generated by a crowd are often not confirmed. Therefore, they may have predicted that the fears of the neighbors were false.
3. Science-fiction fans may say that they considered aliens a real possibility. Many others will say they were surprised by the ending.

◆Build Vocabulary

Using the Word Root: *-sist-*

1. resist
2. assist; consist

Spelling Strategy

1. headphone
2. biography
3. alphabet

Using the Word Bank

1. a; 2. c; 3. c; 4. a; 5. b; 6. a; 7. c

◆Literary Focus

1. Serling's drama shows conflict between individuals when neighbor turns against neighbor. Men who were friends become suspicious and accuse each other of being alien and strange.
2. Individual neighbors like Mr. Goodman come into conflict with the mob or society when they are perceived as being different by the others in the group.
3. Conflicts also occur within individuals as they try to overcome their own fears.
4. The central conflict is between people and their fears, suspicions, and attitudes.

◆Build Grammar Skills

Practice

1. The aliens had planned their game carefully.
2. Each woman did what she could.
3. Pete showed his fear.
4. Charlie became angry, while Steve tried to solve the puzzle with his mind.
5. The shooting shocked the crowd. It was unexpected.

Guide for Responding *(continued)*

◆ Reading Strategy

Predict

The outcome of this play is not easy to **predict,** or figure out in advance. Still, if you watched for the clues Serling offered, you may have had some idea where the story was headed.

1. Based on Steve Brand's responses to Tommy and the others, what role did you expect him to play in the story? Why?
2. When the crowd begins suspecting Les Goodman and the others, did you think that the crowd's fears would be confirmed? Explain how your own experiences helped you predict.
3. How did you think the play would end? Did you at any point think there might actually be aliens? Why or why not?

◆ Build Vocabulary

Using the Word Root *-sist-*

The word root *-sist-* means "stand." Complete these sentences with *-sist-* words from this list:

consist resist assist

1. He begged them to __?__ acting like a mob.
2. His wife tried to __?__ him, pointing out that the rumors did not __?__ of any real facts.

Spelling Strategy

The *f* sound is sometimes spelled *ph*, as in *metamorphosis*. On your paper, use the definitions provided to complete the words containing the *ph* spelling of the *f* sound.

1. Equipment used to listen to music: he__?__
2. A person's life story: bi__?__
3. Letters in ordered sequence: al__?__

Using the Word Bank

Choose the word most opposite in meaning to the first word.

1. defiant: (a) agreeable, (b) angry, (c) curious
2. persistently: (a) quickly, (b) sadly, (c) occasionally
3. metamorphosis: (a) bloom, (b) choice, (c) stability
4. scapegoat: (a) hero, (b) victim, (c) director
5. flustered: (a) shy, (b) confident, (c) sleepy
6. sluggishly: (a) energetically, (b) newly, (c) dimly
7. assent: (a) confusion, (b) approval, (c) denial

◆ Literary Focus

Conflict in Drama

Conflict is a struggle between opposing forces in a work of literature. In "The Monsters Are Due on Maple Street," several different kinds of conflicts move the play toward its surprising conclusion.

1. How does Serling's play show conflict between individuals?
2. How does the play show conflict between individuals and society?
3. What other conflict occurs in the play?
4. What is the central conflict of the play?

◆ Build Grammar Skills

Pronoun and Antecedent Agreement

A **pronoun** takes the place of a noun. An **antecedent** is the noun for which a pronoun stands. Pronouns should agree with their antecedents in number and gender. *Number* indicates whether a pronoun is singular (referring to one) or plural (referring to more than one). *Gender* indicates whether a pronoun refers to a male or a female. In this example, the plural pronoun *their* agrees with its plural antecedent, *neighbors:*

The *neighbors* have lost *their* ability to think.

Here, the singular pronoun *his* agrees with its singular antecedent *Tommy.*

Tommy gave *his* opinion.

Practice On your paper, complete each sentence with a pronoun that matches the antecedent.

1. The aliens had planned __?__ game carefully.
2. Each woman did what __?__ could.
3. Pete showed __?__ fear.
4. Charlie became angry, while Steve tried to solve the puzzle with __?__ mind.
5. The shooting shocked the crowd. __?__ was unexpected.

Writing Application On your paper, write a sentence with a pronoun that refers to each antecedent. Underline the pronoun.

1. Tommy **2.** Everyone **3.** Each wife **4.** Les

Writing Application

Possible responses:

1. Tommy explained *his* ideas.
2. Everyone in the neighborhood thought that *he* or *she* was in danger.
3. Each wife defended *her* husband.
4. Les explained that *he* has trouble sleeping.

Writer's Solution

For additional instruction and practice, use the lesson in the *Writer's Solution Language Lab CD-ROM* on pronouns. You may also use the Agreement Between Pronouns and Antecedents page, p. 77, in the *Writer's Solution Grammar Practice Book.*

Build Your Portfolio

Idea Bank

Writing

1. **Neighborhood Code** Write a set of rules outlining the way neighbors should treat one another. Use the actions of the Maple Street residents as examples. **[Social Studies Link]**
2. **Aliens' Report** Write a report on the events that Figure One and Figure Two give to their leader on returning. Include recommendations for further action.
3. **Drama Review** In a review for a television guide, write a critique of "The Monsters Are Due on Maple Street." Tell readers whether they should tune in for this episode, and explain why. **[Media Link]**

Speaking and Listening

4. **Performance** **[Group Activity]** With a group, perform a scene from "The Monsters . . ." If possible, use a video camera to film the scene as the camera directions suggest—or try your own camera angles! If a camera is not available, stage the scene for a live audience. **[Performing Arts Link]**
5. **Conflict-Resolution Meeting** **[Group Activity]** Learn about conflict-resolution techniques from school counselors or peer mediators. Then, discuss with a group how these techniques could be used to resolve the conflicts on Maple Street. Summarize your findings for the class.

Projects

6. **The Scientific View** What are some possible scientific explanations for the ways Maple Street machines fail? Talk with electricians or car mechanics. Share their ideas with the class, and discuss which make the most sense. **[Science Link]**
7. **Casting Sketches** To help the actors who will perform the television play, create a series of sketches of different scenes. Think about how people look and move when they are afraid. Capture the movement of the crowd and its growing sense of panic. **[Art Link]**

Writing Mini-Lesson

Final Scene

The end of "The Monsters Are Due . . ." may leave you wondering what happens next. Imagine that you are the television writer hired to create a sequel to the episode. Write the opening scene for a sequel that begins the next morning. Include realistic dialogue and descriptions of camera shots.

Writing Skills Focus: Script Format

Make sure that actors and other crew members can understand the scene you have in mind. Using **script format,** which identifies who is speaking and includes camera angles and stage directions, will help.

Model From the Play

ACT I

[*Fade in on a shot of the night sky. The various nebulae and planet bodies stand out in sharp, sparkling relief, and the camera begins a slow pan across the Heavens.*]

NARRATOR'S VOICE. There is a fifth dimension beyond that which is known to man.

Prewriting Write a list of events that will occur in the scene. Put them in time sequence. Next to each event, briefly describe how the characters are likely to respond. Identify setting elements that should be described in the stage or camera directions.

Drafting Begin by setting the morning scene. Then, show how events have moved forward since the previous night.

Revising Review your scene to make sure characters' actions are consistent with their behavior earlier in the play. Then, look at your script formatting to check that you have identified each character speaking and that the camera angles and stage directions are clear.

◆ Grammar Application

As you draft and revise, make sure your pronouns and antecedents agree.

Idea Bank

Following are suggestions for matching the Idea Bank topics with your students' performance levels and learning modalities:

Customize for *Performance Levels*

Less Advanced Students: 1, 4
Average Students: 2, 4, 5
More Advanced Students: 3, 5, 6

Customize for *Learning Modalities*

Verbal/Linguistic: 1, 2, 3, 4, 5
Interpersonal: 4, 5
Visual/Spatial: 7
Logical/Mathematical: 6
Intrapersonal: 2, 3
Musical/Rhythmic: 4

Writing Mini-Lesson

Refer students to the Writing Handbook in the back of the book for instructions on the writing process and for further information on drama. Have students use the Timeline in **Writing and Language Transparencies,** p. 74, to arrange their prewriting examples.

Writer's Solution

Writing Lab CD-ROM

Have students complete their scenes by using the tutorial on Creative Writing. Follow these steps:

1. Have students use the Concrete Image Word Bin to help them envision and describe the scene's setting.
2. Encourage students to refer to the annotated model of stage directions.
3. Have students use the Interactive Writing Tips as they revise their work.

Writer's Solution Sourcebook

Have students use Chapter 8, Creative Writing, pp. 234–263, for additonal support. This chapter includes in-depth instruction on punctuating and formatting dialogue for a play (p. 261).

✓ ASSESSMENT OPTIONS

Formal Assessment, Selection Test, pp. 190–192, and Assessment Resources Software. The selection test is designed so that it can easily be customized to the performance levels of your students.

Alternative Assessment, p. 40, includes options for less advanced students, more advanced students, verbal/linguistic learners, intrapersonal learners, visual/spatial learners, logical/mathematical learners, and interpersonal learners.

PORTFOLIO ASSESSMENT

Use the following rubrics in the **Alternative Assessment** booklet to assess student writing:
Neighborhood Code: How-to/Process Explanation, p. 87
Aliens' Report: Technical Description/Explanation, p. 102
Drama Review: Critical Review, p. 98
Writing Mini-Lesson: Drama, p. 96

Prepare and Engage

Establish Writing Guidelines
Review the following key characteristics of a radio script:

- A radio script is written in script format, with capitalization to identify the speakers and bracketed text to describe sound effects
- A radio script uses dialogue and sound effects to create an audibly stimulating story

You may want to distribute the scoring rubric for Drama, p. 96 in **Alternative Assessment,** to make students aware of the criteria on which they will be evaluated. See the suggestions on p. 716 for how you can customize the rubric.

Refer students to the Writing Handbook in the back of the book for additional instruction and information on creative writing.

Writer's Solution

Writers at Work Videodisc
To show students how Nikki Giovanni gets her ideas for creative writing, play the videodisc segment on Creative Writing (Ch. 8). Have students discuss Giovanni's writing techniques.

Play frames 22015 to 30765

Writing Lab CD-ROM
If your students have access to computers, you might have them work in the tutorial on Creative Writing to complete all or part of their scripts. Follow these steps:

1. Have students view the Group Project suggestions for writing a fifteen-minute radio script.
2. Suggest that students use the Concrete Image Word Bin to choose sensory images.
3. Encourage students to use the interactive writing instruction about character traits to see examples of expressive dialogue.
4. Have students draft on computer.

Writer's Solution Sourcebook
Students can find additional support, including in-depth instruction on punctuating and formatting dialogue, p. 261, in the chapter on Creative Writing, pp. 234–263.

Creative Writing

Radio Script

Writing Process Workshop

When you go to see a drama, the gestures of the actors, the costumes, and the set help you to understand the events of the play. When you hear a radio play, you have to rely on sounds—those of the actors' voices and of any special effects that convey action. A **radio script** includes the dialogue that characters say and sound-effect advice that will help listeners imagine the action they will never see. Put your imaginations in gear as you write a radio script. The following skills will help you write a script alive with action:

Writing Skills Focus

▶ **Use the proper script format** so readers and actors can understand the directions you provide. (See p. 713.)

▶ **Let your dialogue work for you.** What the characters say—and how they say it—is at the heart of a radio script. Choose each character's dialogue wisely and well.

▶ **Include sounds and noises** of all kinds to bring your script to life.

The following passage from a radio script uses these skills to tell the story of a town that gets hit by a tornado.

Model

SAM. ① Look in the sky just past the horizon! Is that a funnel cloud? [*Sound of wind in the distance.*] ②

LUTHER. Quick! Get inside! Get everyone inside! [*As wind gets stronger and louder, sounds of running feet and slamming doors.*]

SAM. [*Nervously*] Luther! Where are you going? Get back here! [*Now completely panicked and breathless.*] Stay inside, you've got to save yourself! ③

① Script format uses capitalization to identify speakers.

② This precise sound description offers helpful direction.

③ Dialogue develops the conflict of the scene.

Humanities: Drama

Radio Plays Tell students that before TV, many families were entertained by listening to the radio.

In the 1930's, radio series became popular. Sound effects, narration, and various voices drew listeners into dramas and comedies. *The Shadow* was about a crime fighter and started a 25-year run that, at times, had audiences of more than 15 million listeners. Another popular radio show was the *Columbia Workshop,* established in 1936, broadcasting plays by such famous writers as W. H. Auden and Edna St. Vincent Millay.

The first soap operas were broadcast on the radio in the daytime.

Today, radio drama is not as popular due to television and films. However, National Public Radio (NPR) still broadcasts dramas from some of the best-known American writers.

Have students research radio drama. Suggest that they pick one program and write a brief summary of when the program aired, who created it, and what it was about. Then have students share their findings with the rest of the class.

Prewriting

Plan the Plot Think about what will happen in the radio script you write. Choose a conflict that will be dramatic. Here are a few suggestions:

Script Ideas
- Group of friends hikes up a mountain
- Child gets lost at a carnival
- Misunderstanding turns into a comedy

Tune In Many public radio stations still offer radio plays to their audiences. Call a local station to ask when a play is being broadcast, or get a recording from a local library. As you listen, notice how the characters are developed, how the story grows from the dialogue, and how sound effects are used.

Build Suspense Start out in a normal, comfortable way. Let your audience learn about the characters and the setting. Then, introduce the problem, and let the tension grow. Remember that good plots build to a dramatic moment of action or insight. Look at this example:

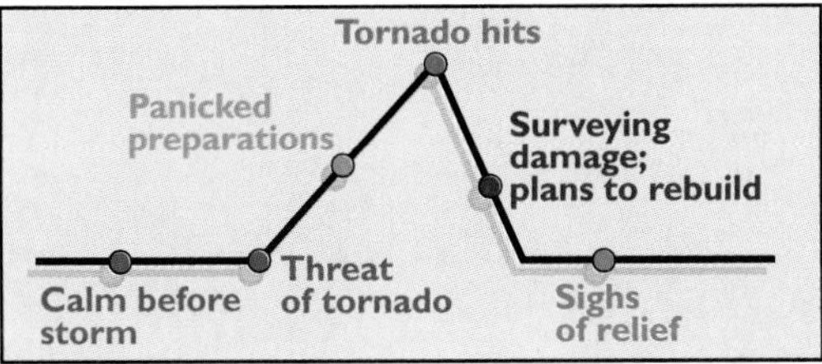

Drafting

Use Realistic Spoken Language To make your dialogue sound like real speech, take note of the way people actually talk. Go to a busy place and listen—on a bus, in the cafeteria, in a school hallway. As you draft, use what you've learned.

Include Stage Directions In brackets in your script, include information about sound effects and how characters should deliver each line.

Find Ways to Add Sound Decide which sounds will enhance the action. A creaky cabinet, a heavy knock on a door, or the ring of a telephone can bring the scenes to life.

DRAFTING/REVISING

APPLYING LANGUAGE SKILLS: Spoken vs. Written Language

Spoken language is loose and free-flowing. We often speak in fragments and use slang. We slur words together and cut things short. In contrast, **written language** is more formal and structured. Look at these examples:

Spoken:
The time? Um, I dunno.

Written:
What time is it? I don't know.

Spoken:
Gotta run. I'm gonna be late.

Written:
I've got to run. I'm going to be late.

Practice Rewrite these spoken sentences into correct written language.

1. When ya comin' home?
2. Any tickets left? We gotta have three.
3. The play was like totally awesome!
4. Wanna go again?

Writing Application When writing a radio script, use spoken language to make dialogue seem real.

Writer's Solution Connection Writing Lab

For more topic ideas, see the Inspirations in the Creative Writing tutorial.

Answers
1. When are you coming home?
2. Do you have any tickets left? We need three.
3. The play was fabulous.
4. Do you want to go again?

Writer's Solution

For additional instruction and practice, have students use the *Writer's Solution Language Lab CD-ROM* Writing Dialogue lesson in the Composing unit.

Develop Student Writing

Prewriting

If possible, bring in an audiocassette tape of a radio drama and play part of it for the class. Suggest that students take notes on the number of characters, the voices the characters use, and sound effects. Then start a class discussion on effective techniques in radio drama.

Customize for *Interpersonal Learners*

Suggest that students work in groups to complete their radio scripts. Students can work together to brainstorm for an outline of a story idea. Then suggest that they each take separate tasks for completing the script. One or two students can be responsible for ensuring that the drama is in proper script format. Other students can be in charge of writing the sound-effect descriptions. When the script is finished, have students perform the drama to look for possible places for improvement.

Drafting

Explain to students that when drafting dialogue for a radio script it may be helpful to speak the dialogue out loud. This way, students may be able to identify which words need to be emphasized and whether the dialogue sounds real or forced. Remind students that different characters may have different ways of speaking and use different types of language.

 ***Writer's Solution***

Writing Lab CD-ROM

Have students view the interactive writing instruction about character traits. They can choose a character trait and see an example of dialogue that expresses that quality.

Applying Language Skills

Spoken vs. Written Language

Explain to students that the difference between spoken and written language is similar to the difference between formal and informal English. Formal English uses traditional standards of correctness and a wide vocabulary, while informal English is conversational in tone, and the sentences are often shorter than those of formal English.

Revising

Encourage students to describe each character in their scripts to a peer reviewer. As the peer reviews the script, have them note where the writer succeeded in developing characters' personalities through dialogue and action, and where characters need more development.

Publishing

For other publishing ideas, suggest that students perform their radio scripts for the rest of the class.

Reinforce and Extend

Review the Writing Guidelines
After students have completed their papers, review the characteristics of a radio script.

Applying Language Skills

Use Punctuation to Show Emotion Explain to students that when actors read scripts, they look to the punctuation to tell them how to perform.

Answers

1. Give me your hand! I'll save you.
2. How can we get out?
3. Um . . . what are you doing?

EDITING/PROOFREADING

APPLYING LANGUAGE SKILLS: Use Punctuation to Show Emotion

In a radio script, you need to describe the emotion the actors should convey. Consider the power of these punctuation marks:

Exclamation points show strong emotion.

Run for your life!

Question marks show direct questions.

Where are you going?

Ellipses create pauses that can show uncertainty or breathlessness.

I can't . . . keep up! . . . Wait . . . for . . me!

Practice Add punctuation to make these sentences more powerful.

1. Give me your hand. I'll save you.
2. How can we get out.
3. Um, what are you doing.

Writing Application Let the punctuation direct the emotions in your radio script.

Writer's Solution Connection
Language Lab

For more practice with end marks, see the Language Lab unit on Punctuation.

Revising

Read Aloud It's essential to hear a script read aloud during the revision process. Ask two or three friends to help you read. They can tell you which lines seemed uncomfortable, awkward, or unbelievable. After the reading, ask the actors to discuss your draft, telling what they liked and did not like.

Add More Sometimes, it's important to add words while you are revising, especially if a character's reasons for action seem unclear. If a line has someone wondering "Why?", add more dialogue to answer the question.

REVISION MODEL

MICHAEL. Turn up the television—I want to hear the score. [*Sound of static* ^(① and changing channels).] Great! They won! We're going to the playoffs!

PATTI. We'd better get tickets to that soccer match. It'll ^(② definitely) sell out soon.

① Stage directions add more information about sound effects.

② This word makes the dialogue more realistic.

Publishing and Presenting

Tape It Radio scripts are meant to be heard! Share your work with an audience by capturing it on tape. Follow these suggestions to record your production successfully:

- Use the stage directions to direct actors and sound effects technicians.
- Rehearse each scene in your script. Plan how actors will deliver the lines, and make sure you are happy with the results on the tape. Run through the action a few times before your final recording.
- Don't take the technology for granted. Be sure the recorder is working, that the sound is clear, and that effects don't overpower voices.
- When you're finished, play the recording for your class—or send it in to a local radio station.

✓ ASSESSMENT		4	3	2	1
PORTFOLIO ASSESSMENT Use the rubric on Drama in the **Alternative Assessment** booklet, p. 96, to assess the students' writing. Add these criteria to customize this rubric to this assignment.	**Script Format**	The script is in the proper format; dialogue and sound directions are clearly indicated.	The script is in the proper format; most dialogue and sound effects are clearly indicated.	Most of the script is formatted; there is some confusion about dialogue and sound effects.	The script is not formatted; dialogue and sound effects are unclear or missing.
	Dialogue	The dialogue is punctuated effectively and helps develop the characters.	Most dialogue is punctuated effectively; it often helps develop the characters.	Some of the dialogue needs more effective punctuation and more development.	Dialogue is not punctuated effectively and does not help build the characters.

Real-World Reading Skills Workshop

Evaluating Media Messages

Strategies for Success

Television, magazines, and the Internet give us lots of information. Messages from these media can entertain us and help us make decisions. Since they can also influence us in subtle ways, it is important to read media messages with a critical eye. Use these skills to help you critically evaluate media messages:

Identify the Writer Try to find out who wrote the message. That will help you figure out the point of view being expressed. It can also reveal a message's intent, even if it isn't stated outright. For example, the makers of Toasty Crispy O's want you to buy their cereal, even if they don't come out and say it directly.

Separate Fact From Opinion Facts are statements that can be checked. If an article says the stock market crashed in 1929, you can look it up and find out whether that's true: It's a fact. If the article says the market crashed because brokers weren't doing their jobs, you can't check that: It's an opinion. Pay attention to the statements you read. Ask yourself: *Is that a fact?*

Ask Questions When you read a media message, ask yourself what information is missing. Is there another point of view? Do you need to know more about the subject? Presenting only one side of the story can change its impact. Ask questions, and get the full story.

Stop Bill 4135A

In June, California voters wisely agreed to give more money to schools to buy delicious dairy products for school cafeterias. That new law made sense. After all, $40 million a year is not a lot to spend when you're buying the healthiest food product around.

Now, Senator Smalley proposes a bill to endanger the health of young people by cutting spending for dairy products. On June 17, the California Senate will vote on Bill 4135A, which would cut dairy spending for public schools to $32 million per year. He says the money can be put to better use. I say you should call your senator and tell him or her to vote against this unhealthy bill.

C.K. Skoda
President, California Dairy League

Apply the Strategies

Read the accompanying paid advertisement. Then, answer the questions that follow.

1. Who wrote the message? How might that person's position and motivation affect the content of the text?
2. List three facts and three opinions that appear in the text.
3. What information is missing from the article? How would the inclusion of this information change the character of the text?

Here are other situations in which you can apply strategies for evaluating media messages:

- Listening to political speeches
- Watching infomercials
- Reading letters to the editor
- Surfing Web sites

Introduce the Strategies

Explain to students that an Internet address, or URL, usually includes the following http://www.[server name] .[type of server]. Explain that the server name is just a name chosen to identify the computer or network hosting the site. The type of server is identified by one of four three-letter abbreviations: *com* (for commercial), *edu* (for educational), *gov* (for governmental), and *org* (for organization). Explain to students that most information from a *gov* or an *org* site should be factually correct, because it is sponsored by the government or a nonprofit organization, and can be verified as a matter of public record. Any commercial (*com*) site is privately funded. Educational sites offer a variety of information. Remind students that many college and university students have Home Pages with *edu* addresses, because they are part of that educational institution.

Apply the Strategies

Remind students to look for biased words as they read. Most factual statements are written in simple, concrete language without descriptive adjectives or adverbs. Facts tell what happened and why, but because they can be verified, they don't need to be explained with descriptive or persuasive language.

Answers

1. The President of the California Dairy League is probably interested in having schools continue to spend money on dairy products.
2. Facts: California voters agreed to give more money to schools for dairy products; Senator Smalley proposes to cut spending on dairy products; the proposed cut is from $40 million to $32 million; the Senate will vote on Bill 4135A on June 17; Senator Smalley says the money can be put to better use.
   Opinions: The new law made sense; $40 million is not a lot to spend on dairy products; dairy products are the healthiest food product; cutting spending on dairy products will endanger the health of young people;
3. Missing information includes what the extra money will be spent on and how much dairy products for schools actually cost. The inclusion of this information would present another side to the issue—explaining what is lost by cutting the spending and what that money would go toward.

◆Build Grammar Skills

Reviewing Pronoun and Antecedent Agreement
The selection in Part 2 includes instruction on the following:

- Pronouns and Antecedent Agreement

This instruction is reinforced with the Build Grammar Skills practice pages in **Selection Support,** p. 221.

As you review usage problems, you may wish to review the following:

- Agreement Between Personal Pronouns and Indefinite Pronouns

Tell students that a singular personal pronoun should be used when its antecedent is a singular indefinite pronoun.

Each of the students read his or her book.

The antecedent in the above sentence is *Each,* which is a singular noun and therefore takes a singular pronoun. When the gender of the antecedent is unclear, it is permissible to use *his or her.*

Writer's Solution

For additional practice and support, use the practice page on Agreement Between Pronouns and Antecedents, p. 77 in the *Writer's Solution Grammar Practice Book.*

Answers

Practice 1

1. Two women noticed that *their* phones weren't working.
2. Pete went to the next block. *He* wanted to see what was happening there.
3. The car wouldn't start. *Its* engine wouldn't turn over.
4. Tommy yelled out a warning, "Mr. Brand . . . *you* better not!"
5. Tommy warned *his* neighbors about aliens. He told *them* what he had heard.

Practice 2

1. Wendy Wasserstein's audience loved *her* plays.
2. The play showed a young man acting in a way that was strange for *him.*
3. Since my friends and I were worried about invasions, the play struck a chord with *us.*

Pronoun and Antecedent Agreement

a·gree (ə grē′) *v.* **1** to be healthful or proper: followed by *with* [This climate *agrees* with me.] **6** *Grammar* to have the same number, person, case, or gender [A verb should *agree* with its subject in number.] **a·greed′, a·gree′ing**

A **pronoun** takes the place of a noun. An **antecedent** is the noun for which a pronoun stands. A pronoun must agree with its antecedent in both person and number. (See page 712.) Singular pronouns refer to singular antecedents. Plural pronouns agree with plural antecedents. Look at this example:

Rod Serling achieved *his* fame with *The Twilight Zone* series.

The pronoun *his* is third person, singular, and masculine. It agrees with its antecedent, Rod Serling, which is also third person, singular, and masculine.

	Singular	Plural
First Person	*I* brought *my* lunch.	*We* brought *our* lunches.
Third Person	*He* brought *his* lunch. *She* brought *her* lunch.	*They* brought *their* lunches.

Practice 1 On your paper, write each of the following sentences, filling in the blanks with the correct pronoun.

1. Two women noticed that __?__ phones weren't working.
2. Pete went to the next block. __?__ wanted to see what was happening there.
3. The car wouldn't start. __?__ engine wouldn't turn over.
4. Tommy yelled out a warning, "Mr. Brand . . . __?__ better not!"
5. Tommy warned __?__ neighbors about aliens. He told __?__ what he had heard.

Practice 2 Revise each sentence according to the directions that follow. Correct pronouns to agree with their new antecedents.

1. Rod Serling's audience loved his plays. (Change *Rod Serling* to *Wendy Wasserstein.*)
2. The play showed average people acting in a way that was strange for them. (Change *average people* to *a young man.*)
3. Since citizens were worried about invasions, the play struck a chord with them. (Change *citizens* to *my friends and I.*)

Grammar in Writing

✔ *A common error in agreement occurs when a writer uses* you *to refer to a noun.*

Incorrect: The *neighbors* are trying to place blame, a mistake *you* shouldn't make when *you're* frightened.

Revised: The *neighbors* are trying to place blame, a mistake *they* shouldn't make when *they're* frightened.

Whenever you use *you* in your writing, make sure it refers only to the person you are addressing—your reader. It should never be used to refer to the person about whom you are writing.

Speaking, Listening, and Viewing Workshop

Evaluating a Presentation

When you watch an infomercial, attend a school assembly, or participate in a walking tour, you experience a presentation on a variety of levels. First, listen for the information presented. Once you've done that, however, take time to judge the quality of the presentation. Use these strategies to help you evaluate a presentation:

Summarize the Message To help you assess whether a presentation was successful, take a moment to sum up what you learned. The simplicity—or difficulty—of this task may reveal the angle of your evaluation. If you can't state briefly what you learned, the presentation may not have been effective.

Be Thorough Many elements combine in a good presentation. Use the following questions to assess a presentation:

- ▶ Was the organization of the presentation clear and logical?
- ▶ Did the presentation contain accurate, interesting information?
- ▶ Did the presenter speak in a way that everyone in the audience could hear?

Evaluate the Bells and Whistles Many presentations have glitzy features such as music, slides, and lots of positive—but empty—talk. After a presentation, consider whether these features actually enhanced the performance. Be critical as you answer questions like these:

- ▶ Did the music fit the message?
- ▶ Did visuals enhance your understanding?
- ▶ Did a humorous anecdote serve a purpose?

Apply the Strategies

With a group, watch a news report, an infomercial, or a live presentation. Then, answer these questions:

1. What was the main idea of the presentation?
2. Identify at least three elements of the presentation that were effective.
3. Identify at least one element of the presentation that could have been improved.
4. In a paragraph, explain whether you would recommend that a friend watch this presentation. Provide evidence to support your evaluation.

Tips for Evaluating a Presentation

✔ *When evaluating a presentation, follow these strategies:*

- ▶ *Note the reaction of other members of the audience.*
- ▶ *Don't get caught up in an emotional reaction. Be sure that your assessment can be supported by evidence.*

Introduce the Strategies

Ask students to share experiences of presentations they have seen and enjoyed. Encourage students to discuss what elements of the presentation they found most intriguing. Ask them if they were more captivated by the subject matter or the way in which the material was presented.

Customize for
Less Proficient Learners
To help students figure out what they have learned from a presentation, have them fill out a KWL Organizer from **Writing and Language Transparencies,** p. 58. Before they view the presentation, have students fill out the columns "What I Know" and "What I Want to Know." After the presentation, have them fill out the "What I Learned" column.

Apply the Strategies

Remind students when viewing presentations to take into consideration who is giving the presentation and why. Encourage them to ask: Is this presentation designed to make me do something or act in a certain way?

◆Build Vocabulary

What's Behind the Words

Remind students that numerical prefixes are added to roots to make new words. For example, *uni-*, meaning "one"; *bi-*, meaning "two"; and *tri-*, meaning "three" can all be added to the word root *cycle*, which comes from the Greek *kyklos*, meaning wheel. Now, you have three new words: unicycle, a bike with one wheel; bicycle, a bike with two wheels; and tricycle, a bike with three wheels.

Customize for *English Language Learners*

Encourage students to share with the class the words for 1 to 10 from other languages. Or, supply the words yourself. In French, *un, deux, trois, quatre, cinq, six, sept, huit, neuf, dix*. In Spanish, *uno, dos, tres, cuatro, cinco, seis, siete, ocho, nueve, diez*. Write these words on the board so students can see how their roots are all similar to the Latin or Greek.

Answers

Activity 1

Possible answers: unicycle, a vehicle with one wheel; unitard, a one-piece leotard; unicorn, a mythical horse with one horn; uniform, a suit worn by all members of a given rank or team; unify, to form into a single unit; union, the act of uniting; unique, existing as the only one or as the sole example; unit, any of a number of things that are equivalent or identical; monochrome, a painting or drawing in different shades of one color; monocle, an eyeglass for one eye; monogamy, marriage with only one person at a time; monolith, a single block of stone of considerable size; monopoly, exclusive control of a commodity or service; monorail, a railroad made up of one rail

Activity 2

E pluribus unum = Out of one, many

What's Behind the Words

Vocabulary Adventures With Richard Lederer

Numerical Prefixes

Let's play a numbers game. Can you name the numbers embedded in each of the following words? What numbers can you find in hexagon, September, octopus, nonagenarian, and decathlon?

Doing a Number on Words

The numbers in the words above are *6, 7, 8, 9,* and *10*. Each of the words contains a Greek or Latin prefix that stands for the numbers six through ten. A hexagon (Latin, *hexa*) is a six-sided figure. September (Latin, *sept*) was once the seventh month of the year. Before the Romans changed their calendar, March was the first month, so September, October, November, and December were suitable names. An octopus (Latin, *octo*) has eight legs. A nonagenarian (Latin, *non, nov*) has reached at least ninety years of age, and a decathlon (Greek, *deka*) consists of exactly ten athletic events.

Counting Off With Prefixes

To discover other numbers hiding in our words, try counting from one to five with prefixes from the classical languages:

Number	Latin	Greek
one	uni	mono
two	duo	di
three	tri	tri
four	quadr	tetra
five	quint	penta

One, Two, Three . . .

The universe is made from two Latin word parts that mean "one world." *Twilight* is literally "the time of two lights," the fading sunset and the emerging light of the moon and stars.

Have you ever wondered if the *tri-* in *trivial* is the same as the *tri-* in *triple*? In fact, *trivial* does derive from the Latin *tri* (three) and *via* (way) and literally means "like something found at a place where three roads meet." In ancient times, shoppers returning from the market often stopped at intersections where three roads converged to exchange idle gossip. Hence, the modern meaning of *trivial:* "common; insignificant."

The Latin *quadr* is in *quarantine,* originally a period of forty days during which ships suspected of carrying disease were banned from port. The *Pentagon* in Washington, D.C., is a famous five-sided building.

Activity 1 *One* is a unique number. It stands for the smallest number—one of any kind—and for the largest number—everything rolled into one unified whole, or union—like the United States or the universe. List as many words as you can that begin with *uni* and *mono,* and tell what they mean.

Activity 2 The motto of our nation is *E pluribus unum*. Use a dictionary to translate those Latin words into English.

Activity 3 Find the meanings of ten words that begin with the numerical prefixes you have learned in this lesson.

Activity 3

Possible responses:

1. monotheism, belief that there is only one God
2. dialogue, a conversation between at least two people
3. triptych, a set of three panels side by side, bearing pictures or carvings
4. quadrille, a square dance for four couples, consisting of five parts or movements, each complete in itself
5. quintessence, the pure and concentrated essence of something
6. hexapod, having six feet
7. septennial, occurring every seven years
8. octant, the eighth part of a circle
9. nonagon, a polygon having nine angles and nine sides
10. decimal, a fraction with an unwritten denominator of 10

Extended Reading Opportunities

Reading a play allows you to enjoy a play at any time, in any place. Consider reading these plays as you extend your exploration of drama.

Suggested Titles

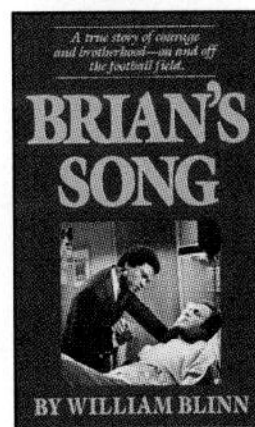

Brian's Song
William Blinn
In a screenplay based on the biography of Brian Piccolo, dramatist William Blinn shares the comic and tragic moments in the life of an athlete dying young. Along with Piccolo, Gale Sayers joined the Chicago Bears in 1965. The two men competed with each other, roomed with each other, and helped each other through injury. The play takes a tragic turn when Piccolo is diagnosed with cancer.

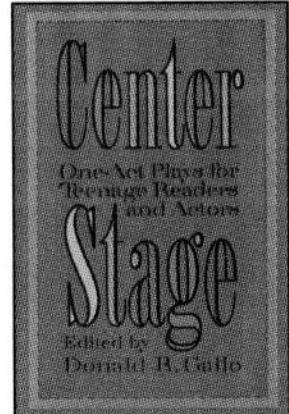

Center Stage: One-Act Plays for Teenage Readers and Actors
Donald R. Gallo, Editor
From an aerobics class for college freshmen to the schoolyard of a city school, this collection of high-interest short plays features young people in a variety of settings. One play, "The War of the Words," pits the "Grunts" against the "Notes" and calls for the audience to vote on the outcome. Chosen especially for young adults, the selections in *Center Stage* feature something for every interest.

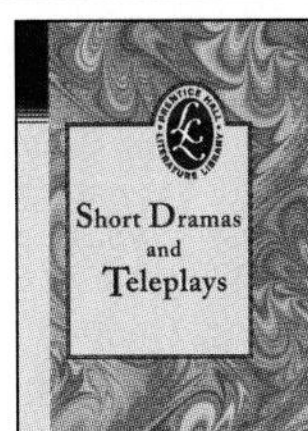

Short Dramas and Teleplays
This anthology of dramas includes classics, one-act plays, and television scripts for readers of all ability levels. In addition to such favorites as *Robin Hood, Oliver Twist,* and *Frankenstein,* you'll find dramatic versions of *The Bishop's Candlesticks, The Red Badge of Courage,* and *I Remember Mama.*

Other Possibilities

¡Aplauso! Hispanic Children's Theater	Joe Rosenberg, Editor
Modern Monologues for Young People	John Murray
Our Town	Thornton Wilder

Planning Students' Extended Reading
All of the works listed on this page are good choices for students' exploration of the genre of drama. The following information will help you choose what to teach:

Customize for
Varying Student Needs
When assigning the selections in this part to your students, keep in mind the following factors:

- *Brian's Song* is a classic story that offers students an opportunity to discuss the meaning of brotherhood. The television movie based on the play has won five Emmy awards.
- *Center Stage: One-Act Plays for Teenage Readers and Actors* is a collection of one-act plays especially selected for young adult readers.
- *Short Dramas and Teleplays,* an offering in the Prentice Hall Literature Library, offers a chance for students to encounter a range of different types of drama. The pieces vary in level of difficulty.

Planning Instruction and Assessment

Unit Objectives

1. To develop skills in reading poetry
2. To apply a variety of reading strategies, particularly strategies for reading poetry
3. To recognize literary elements used in these selections
4. To increase vocabulary
5. To learn elements of grammar and usage
6. To write in a variety of modes about situations based on the selections
7. To develop speaking and listening skills, by completing proposed activities
8. To view images critically and create visual representations

Meeting the Objectives Each selection provides instructional material and portfolio opportunities by which students can meet unit objectives. You will find additional practice pages for reading strategies, literary elements, vocabulary, and grammar in the **Selection Support** booklet in the **Teaching Resources** box.

Setting Goals Work with your students at the beginning of the unit to set goals for unit outcomes. Plan what skills and concepts you wish students to acquire. You may match instruction and activities according to students' performance levels or learning modalities.

Portfolios Students may keep portfolios of their completed work or of their work in progress. The Build Your Portfolio page of each selection provides opportunities for students to apply the concepts presented.

Humanities: Art

Effect of the Sun on the Water, 1905, Andre Derain

Andre Derain (1880–1954) painted in the style of fauvism, which shows the artists's deep, violent brushwork and wild use of colors.

1. Do you think the painting's title fits the art? *Students may say yes, because of the sun's reflection; they may want to see a realistic picture.*
2. How might you relate this painting style to poetry? *Help students relate the painting's figurative expression of the sun on water to the figurative language of poetry.*

Effect of the Sun on the Water, 1905, Andre Derain, © Artists Rights Society (ARS), NY/Giraudon

Art Transparencies

The **Art Transparencies** booklet in the **Teaching Resources** box offers fine art to help students make connections to other curriculum areas and high-interest topics.

Beyond Literature

Each unit presents Beyond Literature features that lead students into an exploration of careers, communities and other subject areas. In this unit, students will explore the Klondike Gold Rush, and make history and science connections. In addition, the **Teaching Resources** box contains a **Beyond Literature** booklet of activities. Using literature as a springboard, these activity pages offer students opportunities to connect literature to other curriculum areas and to the workplace and careers, community, media, and humanities.

UNIT 9

Poetry

Whether telling a story, capturing a single moment, or describing nature in a whole new way, poetry is the most musical of all literary forms. These terms will help you discuss the variety of poetry you'll encounter in this unit:

- **Narrative poetry** tells a story.
- **Lyric poetry** expresses thoughts and feelings.
- **Form** describes the structure of a poem. Some poems are written in regular groups of lines called *stanzas.* Others, like *haiku,* follow strict syllable and line counts.
- **Rhythm, rhyme, and sound devices,** such as *alliteration* and *onomatopoeia,* give poetry its musical quality.
- **Figurative language**—such as *simile, metaphor,* and *personification*—allows the poet to draw vibrant and creative comparisons.

Connections

Within this unit, you will find selections and activities that make connections beyond literature. Use these selections to connect students' understanding and appreciation of literature beyond the traditional literature and language arts curriculum.

Encourage students to connect literature to other curriculum areas. You may wish to coordinate with teachers in other curriculum areas to determine ways to team teach and further extend instruction.

Connections to Today's World

Use these selections to guide students to recognize the relevance of literature to contemporary writings. In this unit, the lyrics of the song, "Abraham, Martin, and John" connect a lyricist's personal response to the assassinations of Martin Luther King and other great leaders of the 1960's.

Connecting Literature to Social Studies

Each unit contains a selection that connects Literature to Social Studies. In this unit, two Japanese tanka connect the Japanese culture to this simple form of poetry.

Assessing Student Progress

The tools that are available to measure the degree to which students meet the unit objectives are listed below.

Informal Assessment

The questions in the Guide for Responding sections are a first level of response to the concepts and skills presented with the selection. As a brief, informal measure of students' grasp of the material, these responses indicate where further instruction and practice are needed. The practice pages in the **Selection Support** booklet provide for this type of instruction and practice.

You will also find literature and reading guides in the **Alternative Assessment** booklet, which students can use for informal assessment of their individual performances.

Formal Assessment

The **Formal Assessment** booklet contains Selection Tests and Unit Tests.

Selection Tests measure comprehension and skills acquisition for each selection or group of selections.

Each Unit Test provides students with 30 multiple-choice questions and 5 essay questions designed to assess students' knowledge of the literature and skills taught in the unit.

Each Alternative Unit Test: Standardized-Test Practice provides 15 multiple-choice questions and 3 essay questions based on two new literature selections not contained in the student book. The questions on the Alternative Unit Test are designed to assess students' ability to compare and contrast selections, applying skills taught in the unit.

Alternative Assessment

For portfolio and alternative assessment, the **Alternative Assessment** booklet contains Scoring Rubrics, Assessment sheets, and Learning Modalities activities.

Scoring Rubrics provide writing modes that can be applied to Writing activities, Writing Mini-Lessons, and Writing Process Workshop lessons.

Assessment sheets for speaking and listening activities provide peer and self-assessment direction.

Learning Modalities activities appeal to different learning styles. Use these as an alternative measurement of students' growth.

Prepare and Engage

OBJECTIVES

1. To read, comprehend, and interpret a ballad
2. To relate a ballad to personal experience
3. To apply strategies for reading poetry
4. To analyze the characteristics of a ballad
5. To build vocabulary in context and learn words with multiple meanings
6. To recognize degrees of comparison
7. To write an updated ballad with a refrain
8. To respond to the ballad through writing, speaking and listening, and projects

SKILLS INSTRUCTION

Vocabulary: Words With Multiple Meanings

Spelling Words With *ea* for Short and Long e Sound

Grammar: Degrees of Comparison

Reading for Success: Strategies for Reading Poetry

Literary Focus: Ballad

Writing: Refrain

Speaking and Listening: Skit (Teacher Edition)

Critical Viewing: Analyze

PORTFOLIO OPPORTUNITIES

Writing: Farewell Letter; Editorial; Sequel

Writing Mini-Lesson: Ballad

Speaking and Listening: Skit; Missing Persons Description

Projects: Search Report; Illustrated Storyboard

More About the Author
Sir Walter Scott spent much of his childhood on his grandfather's farm in Scotland convalescing from a serious illness, possibly polio. During this time, he spent hours exploring the lush Scottish countryside. He also became an avid reader and developed a love for all forms of literature, especially Scottish ballads and legends. One of his first major works is a three-volume collection of Scottish ballads.

Guide for Reading

Meet the Author:

Sir Walter Scott (1771–1832)

When Sir Walter Scott died, people in his native Scotland and in England mourned as if a king had died.

A Varied Life Born into an old and wealthy Scottish family, Scott grew to love his country's history while listening to elderly relatives' stories and accounts. After working briefly—and without much interest—for his lawyer father, Scott explored many different interests. He traveled widely, collected antiques, translated German poetry, and worked as a journalist.

Inventing a New Form of Fiction As "Lochinvar" and his other works show, Scott was a talented poet. In 1813, he was offered the prestigious position of Poet Laureate of England, but he declined the honor; poetry no longer interested him. Instead, he began writing novels based on people and events in Scottish and English history. In the process, he created such classics as *Ivanhoe* and a type of fiction that has remained popular ever since—the historical novel.

THE STORY BEHIND THE STORY

"Lochinvar," like many of Scott's works, reflects his love for the Scottish border ballads, or storytelling songs. His keen ear for the way people spoke and his knowledge of history enabled him to make the past come alive with romance, heroism, and adventure.

◆ LITERATURE AND YOUR LIFE

CONNECT YOUR EXPERIENCE

You've probably seen many movies in which a dashing hero defeats all enemies and walks away with his or her love interest. The poem "Lochinvar" tells such a story, set in the distant past when people fought with swords and the world seemed to be filled with hidden dangers.

THEMATIC FOCUS: Personal Codes

Heroes often live by their own codes of honor. As you read, think about how you would describe Lochinvar's personal code.

◆ Background for Understanding

LITERATURE

In this poem, a knight in shining armor comes to declare his love to a beautiful maiden. Knights were members of the nobility, or upper class, in Europe's Medieval period, which lasted from about 400 to 1400. Their primary duty was to defend the estates of wealthy lords, who provided them with lands in return for their service. In addition, knights were sometimes called upon to travel to distant lands to fight for the king. As a result of their travels, knights were viewed as great adventurers. Because they helped people feel safe in dangerous times, they were also viewed as gallant and romantic heroes.

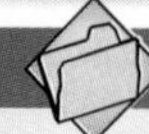

Prentice Hall Literature Program Resources

REINFORCE / RETEACH / EXTEND

Selection Support Pages
Build Vocabulary: Words With Multiple Meanings, p. 224
Build Spelling Skills, p. 225
Build Grammar Skills: Degrees of Comparison, p. 226
Reading for Success: Reading Poetry, p. 227
Literary Focus: Ballad, p. 228

Strategies for Diverse Student Needs, pp. 81–82

Beyond Literature Career Connection: Casting Director, p. 41

Formal Assessment Selection Test, pp. 201–203, Assessment Resources Software

Alternative Assessment, p. 41

Writing and Language Transparencies Cluster Organizer, p. 82; Series of Events Chain, p. 66

Resource Pro CD-ROM
"Lochinvar"—includes all resource material and customizable lesson plan

Listening to Literature Audiocassettes
"Lochinvar"

MODEL SELECTION

◆ Lochinvar ◆

A procession of knights and their squires on their way to do battle, ms. illumination c. 1450

◆ Literary Focus

Ballad

A **ballad** is a song or songlike poem that tells a story, often dealing with adventure or romance. Ballads usually have rhyming lines with a strong, musical rhythm. They are divided into stanzas, or groups, of four or six lines. Ballads usually have a refrain, which is a repeated line or set of lines. In many ballads, including "Lochinvar," the refrain changes a little each time it appears.

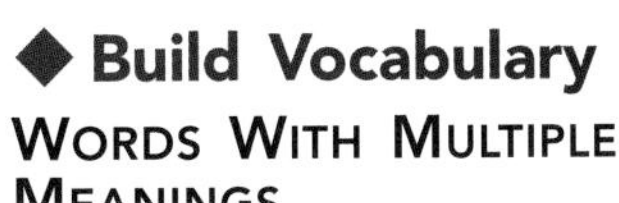

◆ Build Vocabulary

Words With Multiple Meanings

In "Lochinvar," Scott uses the word *bar* as a verb, meaning "to prevent access." The word *bar* has many other meanings, including "a piece of wood or metal used as a barrier." As you read this poem, watch for other words with multiple meanings. Note each word and what you think it means in a chart like the one below.

Word Bank

Which of these words do you think means "to worry"? Check the Build Vocabulary box to see if you chose correctly.

dauntless
consented
laggard
bar
tread
fret

Multiple Meaning Word	What You Think It Means in Poem
brake	
suit	
lead	
bank	

Interest Grabber Write these phrases on the board: *young woman, young man, daring deeds, rebellious acts, anxious parents.* Ask students to name films, novels, or television shows containing these elements. Elicit that the elements are included in many tales of adventure because people of many ages and backgrounds can relate to them. Tell students that this poem, which was written in the early 1800's, contains these elements.

◆ Build Grammar Skills

Degrees of Comparison If you wish to introduce the grammar concept for this selection before students read, refer to the instruction on page 731.

Customize for
Less Proficient Readers
Have students listen to the audiocassette of the poem before reading it on their own. To help them better understand the character of Lochinvar, have them write a few words describing how these characters react to him: the king, the queen, Ellen, Ellen's cousins, the bridegroom.

Listening to Literature Audiocassettes

Customize for
More Advanced Students
Discuss the idea that rhythm contributes to the musical quality of a poem and helps to emphasize ideas. Invite students to prepare a reading of the poem, determining its rhythm and deciding on appropriate vocal inflections. Have students give their readings to the class after everyone has read the poem independently. Discuss how their interpretations enhance the ballad.

Customize for
English Language Learners
Students may be confused by the inverted word order of lines like "where ford there was none." Explain that poets sometimes reverse word order to add to the poem's rhythm or to complete a rhyme scheme. Have volunteers read such lines using standard word order, for example, "where there was no ford."

Preparing for Standardized Tests

Vocabulary Many standardized tests require students to identify the correct definition of a multiple-meaning word (the vocabulary skill with the selection). Write the following sample test question on the board:

Find the word that fits in both of the sentences.

She put a single golden_______ on the chain.
A _______ of sweat appeared on his forehead.

(A) coin (C) bead
(B) drop (D) band

Invite a volunteer to try each word in the first sentence. When students identify *(C)* as the most likely response, ask them to apply the word *bead* to the second sentence. Point out to them that the word that is the correct answer must make sense in both sentences.

Tell students that when they take a standardized test that requires them to mark their answers on a separate answer sheet, they should be sure that the circles, or answer spaces, are filled in neatly and completely and that answer numbers match the item numbers on the test itself.

Reading for Success

The Reading for Success page in each unit presents a set of problem-solving strategies to help students understand authors' words and ideas on multiple levels. Good readers develop a bank of strategies from which they can draw as needed.

Unit 9 introduces strategies for reading poetry. Reading poetry often requires effort beyond that used for reading prose. Not only do poems differ structurally from prose, but they also often condense meaning into a tightly knit cluster of words.

These strategies for reading poetry are modeled with "Lochinvar." Each green box shows an example of the thinking process involved in applying one of these strategies. Additional notes provide support for applying these strategies throughout the selection.

How to Use the Reading for Success Page

- Introduce the strategies for reading poetry, presenting each as a problem-solving procedure.
- Before students read a poem, have them preview it, looking at the annotations in the green boxes that model the strategies.
- To reinforce these strategies after students have the read the poem, have them do the Reading for Success, p. 227, in **Selection Support.** This page gives students an opportunity to read a selection and practice strategies for reading poetry by writing their own annotations.

Reading Strategies: Support and Reinforcement

Using Boxed Annotations and Prompts

Throughout the unit, the notes in green, red, and maroon boxes are intended to help students apply reading strategies, understand the literary focus, and make a connection with their lives. You may use boxed materials in these ways:

- Have students pause at each box and respond to its prompt before they continue reading.
- Urge students to read through the selection, ignoring the boxes. After they complete the selection, they may go back and review the text, responding to the prompts.

Reading for Success

Strategies for Reading Poetry

Sometimes reading poetry is like watching a whodunit movie. It can take a while until you really grasp the story line. You have to listen carefully to what is said (and notice who says it), survey the surroundings to find clues, and keep restating what you know as you put the pieces together. These strategies will help you make poetry less of a mystery:

Identify the speaker.

The speaker is the imaginary voice assumed by the poet. Sometimes, the speaker is the poet. Other times, the speaker is a character created by the poet. Whenever you read a poem, look for clues that will help you make inferences about the speaker's personality, experiences, and attitudes.

Read lines according to punctuation.

- Pause at commas, dashes, semicolons, and ellipsis marks (three or four dots). Stop longer at end marks. Don't stop at the end of a line unless the punctuation indicates that you should.

slight pause full pause

He rode all unarmed, and he rode all alone.

- When sentences end in question marks, read them as questions. When they end with exclamation points, read them with emphasis.

Use your senses.

- Use your senses—sight, hearing, smell, taste, and physical sensation—to understand and experience the poem's world fully.
- Envision the setting and action by painting a mental picture from the poem's words.

Paraphrase the lines.

If you're unsure of the poem's meaning, you may want to restate a line or passage in your own words to help you understand it.

Scott's Version:	So faithful in love, and so dauntless in war, There never was knight like the young Lochinvar.
Paraphrased:	Lochinvar was a great knight. He was a brave soldier and remained true to the woman he left behind while at war.

As you read "Lochinvar," look at the notes in the boxes. They will help you apply the reading strategies to the poem.

Model a Reading Strategy: Use Your Senses to Understand and Experience the Poem's World

Tell students that, when they are reading a narrative poem that takes place in an unfamiliar setting among characters they have just learned about, they can use sensory details to paint a mental picture based on the poem's words. Show students how to use their senses to imagine the scene in which Lochivar joins the wedding celebration:

After Lochinvar remarks that he can find prettier girls than Ellen in Scotland who'd be glad to marry him, Ellen kisses the cup of wine she hands to him. The kiss is intended for Lochinvar. If she makes such a suggestive gesture, it's clear she doesn't take his words seriously. After he drinks the wine, Ellen blushes, looks at him with a sigh, smiles, and sheds a tear.

I know from these details that Ellen is in love with Lochinvar. Scott describes the feel of her hand as "soft," which suggests her youth and beauty and contrasts with Lochinvar's determination and strength.

Lochinvar

Sir Walter Scott

MODEL

A knight and a lady on horseback. Breviary with calendar, May. Flemish School (end 15th)

▲ Critical Viewing What details in this painting tell you it is set in the Medieval period? [Analyze] ❶

Block Scheduling Strategies

Consider these suggestions to take advantage of extended class time:

- Before students read the selection, introduce the Reading for Success strategies, p. 726. After they have read the selection, have students work as a class to answer the Reading for Success questions on p. 731. Then have students apply the strategies as they annotate the Reading for Success practice selection, p. 227, in **Selection Support.**
- Alternatively, students may begin class time with Build Vocabulary and Build Grammar Skills, p. 731, and then read the selection independently. Have them meet in groups to discuss Reader's Response and Thematic Focus and to answer questions on p. 730.
- Guide students in a discussion of Background for Understanding, p. 724, and Literary Focus, p. 725. Then have them listen to "Lochinvar" on audiocassette. As they listen, encourage them to think about the poetic techniques that help to create the musical rhythm of the ballad and to listen for the repeated phrase, *young Lochinvar.*

Listening to Literature Audiocassettes

Develop Understanding

One-Minute Insight Lochinvar arrives at Netherby to find that the wedding of his beloved Ellen to another man has just begun. When the king, Ellen's father, nervously asks Lochinvar the reason for his presence, Lochinvar replies that he has come to dance one dance and drink one drink to celebrate the occasion. Then he takes a cup of wine from Ellen and drinks it. As the guests stand in awe, Lochinvar leads Ellen in a graceful dance. Moving with her toward the open door, he swings Ellen onto his waiting horse with him, and the happy couple races away, vainly pursued by Ellen's kinsmen.

▶Critical Viewing◀

❶ **Analyze** *Students may identify the clothing and the elaborate bridle and harness on the horse as belonging to the Medieval period.*

Customize for *Interpersonal Learners*

To provide practice in paraphrasing, suggest that partners read the selection together, taking turns paraphrasing difficult lines.

Customize for *Visual/Spatial Learners*

Provide practice in reading lines according to punctuation by photocopying all or part of the poem. Suggest that students use markers of different colors to mark commas, periods, question marks, exclamation marks, and quotation marks. Then have them read the poem aloud in small groups, using their marks to guide their reading.

Humanities: Art

A knight and a lady on horseback, Flemish School

Use this question to help students relate the art to the poem.

1. How did the artist use light, especially in the clothing? What might this indicate about the man and woman? *Students may say that the artist used light colors to make it appear that the clothing contains fine gold threads, a sign of wealth. Explain that Lochinvar is a knight, or a member of the upper class.*

◆Literary Focus

❶ **Ballad** After students read the first stanza, ask them to describe their impressions of Lochinvar. *Students may say that Lochinvar is a brave knight who carries only a sword while riding a fine horse. They may also mention that because he is "faithful in love," he probably has a sweetheart.*

Clarification

❷ Explain that a "brake" is a clump of bushes or trees. This stanza emphasizes that Lochinvar is riding swiftly to reach his destination.

Reading for Success

Identify the Speaker Ask students to identify the speaker of the story. *Students may say that because the speaker tells about the actions of Lochinvar and others, the narrator is outside the action. The narrator also uses the pronouns* he *and* his, *indicating the third-person omniscient point of view.*

◆Literary Focus

❸ **Ballad** Remark that lines or parts of lines in ballads are often repeated. Have students compare these lines to the last lines in the first verse. How do they help to contrast Lochinvar, the poem's protagonist, with the bridegroom, his rival? *Line 5 portrays Lochinvar as "So faithful in love, and so dauntless in war," while line 12 portrays the bridegroom as "a laggard in love, and a dastard in war." Explain that before ballads were written down, such repetition of ideas helped early storytellers remember the lines.*

O, young Lochinvar is come out of the West,
Through all the wide Border his steed[1] was the best,
❶ And save his good broadsword[2] he weapons had none;
He rode all unarmed, and he rode all alone.
So faithful in love, and so dauntless in war,
There never was knight like the young Lochinvar.

❷ He stayed not for brake, and he stopped not for stone,
He swam the Eske river[3] where ford there was none;
But, ere he alighted at Netherby[4] gate,
The bride had consented, the gallant came late:
❸ For a laggard in love, and a dastard in war,
Was to wed the fair Ellen of brave Lochinvar.

So boldly he entered the Netherby hall,
Among bridesmen and kinsmen, and brothers and all;
Then spoke the bride's father, his hand on his sword
(For the poor craven[5] bridegroom said never a word),
"O come ye in peace here, or come ye in war,
❹ Or to dance at our bridal, young Lord Lochinvar?"

"I long wooed your daughter, my suit you denied;—
Love swells like the Solway, but ebbs like its tide—
And now I am come, with this lost love of mine,

You can **paraphrase** lines 9–14 as: Before Lochinvar reached Netherby manor, his love, Ellen, had agreed to marry someone else. This other man was slow-moving in love and a cowardly soldier.

Read lines 17–18 **according to the punctuation,** pausing briefly after "here," "war," and "bridal," but not after "in." Noting the final end mark, read the entire sentence as a question.

1. **steed** (stēd) *n.*: Horse.
2. **broadsword** *n.*: Sword with a wide double-edged blade used for slashing rather than thrusting.
3. **Eske river** (esk) *n.*: River near border between England and Scotland.
4. **Netherby** *n.*: Name of the manor where the poem is set.
5. **craven** (krā´ vən) *adj.*: Very cowardly.

Cross-Curricular Connection: Social Studies

Geography of Scotland Scotland is a mountainous country located at the northern end of the island of Great Britain. The Atlantic Ocean borders its western and northern shores, and the North Sea divides its eastern coastline from the European mainland. Many Scottish ballads and legends are associated with the sea. This is not surprising, given that no place in the country is more than 112 km (70 miles) from the coast.

Show students a map of Scotland. Have them note the small islands and inlets along the coastline. Direct students' attention to line 2, "Through all the wide Border his steed was the best." Challenge them to locate the Border region between England and Scotland. Then tell students that a firth is a long, narrow inlet from the sea. Challenge them to find the Solway Firth, which separates the southern boundary of Scotland from England. Ask students what Lochinvar means when he says, "Love swells like the Solway, but ebbs like its tide." *Students may say that Lochinvar means that at one time his love for Ellen grew, but now he is trying to trick her father into believing that he loves her less.*

To lead but one measure, drink one cup of wine.
There are maidens in Scotland more lovely by far,
That would gladly be bride to the young Lochinvar."
The bride kissed the goblet;[6] the knight took it up,
He quaffed off the wine, and he threw down the cup,
She looked down to blush, and she looked up to sigh,
With a smile on her lips and a tear in her eye.
He took her soft hand, ere her mother could <u>bar</u>—
❺ "Now <u>tread</u> we a measure!" said young Lochinvar.

❻ So stately his form, and so lovely her face,
That never a hall such a galliard[7] did grace;
While her mother did <u>fret</u>, and her father did fume,
And the bridegroom stood dangling his bonnet and plume;[8]
And the bridesmaidens whispered, "'Twere better by far
To have matched our fair cousin with young Lochinvar."

One touch to her hand, and one word in her ear,
When they reached the hall door, and the charger stood near;
So light to the croupe the fair lady he swung,
So light to the saddle before her he sprung!
"She is won! we are gone, over bank, bush, and scaur;[9]
They'll have fleet steeds that follow," quoth young Lochinvar.

Bag with scenes of "Minne" (Love) French, c. 1340, Museum fur Kunst und Gewerb, Hamburg, Germany

❼ ▲ Critical Viewing What lines from "Lochinvar" would make the best caption for this tapestry? Explain. **[Connect]**

Use your senses to see the blush on Ellen's cheek and to hear her soft sigh. Picture her smiling lips and a slow-moving tear on her cheek.

◆ Build Vocabulary

dauntless (dônt´ lis) *adj.*: Fearless

consented (kən sent´ id) *v.*: Agreed

laggard (lag´ ərd) *n.*: One who is slow to move, follow, or respond

bar (bär) *v.*: To stop or prevent

tread (tred) *v.*: Walk; dance; step

fret (fret) *v.*: Worry

6. **goblet** (gäb´ lit) *n.*: Drinking cup.
7. **galliard** (gal´ yərd) *n.*: Lively French dance.
8. **plume** (plo͞om) *n.*: Decoration made of a large feather or feathers.
9. **scaur** (skär) *n.*: Steep, rocky hill.

◆ Literary Focus

❹ **Ballad** Review with students the repeated line or lines of refrains and point out that sometimes a refrain changes a little each time it appears. Ask students how the last two lines at the end of each stanza are similar. *The next-to-last line of each stanza ends with a word that rhymes with the word war; the last word in each stanza is* Lochinvar.

◆ Critical Thinking

❺ **Speculate** Make certain that students understand that Lochinvar has ridden his horse a great distance to come to Ellen's wedding. Now, he has taken her in his arms to dance. What might happen next? *Students may guess that he plans to interfere with the wedding in some way.*

◆ Build Vocabulary

❻ **Words With Multiple Meanings** Suggest to students that the word *form* has more than one meaning. Guide students to use context clues to figure out that in this line it means "figure." Challenge students to think of other definitions of the word. *Possible responses: Form can refer to the shape or structure of an object; a document to be completed; or manners set by custom.*

▶Critical Viewing◀

❼ **Connect** *Possible answers: Line 31—"So stately his form, and so lovely her face, . . ." or line 37—"One touch to her hand, and one word in her ear, . . ."*

Customize for
Bodily/Kinesthetic Learners
Have several students act out the parts of Lochinvar, Ellen, the king, the queen, Ellen's cousins, and the bridegroom as described in the sixth stanza. When they have finished, ask them to describe the emotions and personalities they wanted to portray.

Customize for
Less Proficient Readers
Students may have trouble understanding the action in the fourth and fifth stanzas. Help students use context clues to figure out that to "lead a measure" means to guide a partner in a dance; to "quaff" means to drink; and to "tread a measure" means to dance.

Speaking and Listening Mini-Lesson

Skit

This mini-lesson supports the Speaking and Listening activity in the Idea Bank on p. 732.

Introduce Challenge students to present a performance that captures the excitement and romance of this story about medieval times.

Develop Have students form groups and assign the parts of narrator, Lochinvar, Ellen, the king, the queen, the bridegroom, Ellen's cousins, family members, and wedding guests. As students rehearse, remind them to use facial expressions and gestures to capture characters' emotions. Some groups may choose to use simple props.

Apply Have groups perform their skits for the class. You may want to videotape the skits.

Assess Evaluate students' skits by the overall performance and how well the skits demonstrate students' understanding of the poem. Or, have students use the Peer Assessment: Dramatic Performance form, p. 107, in **Alternative Assessment.**

Reading for Success

1 Use Your Senses Ask students how they envision this final scene. *Students may say that they visualize a chaotic scene in which people and horses run in all directions, while the determined couple vanishes in the distance.*

◆ Literature and Your Life

Ask students to name movies or television shows with endings similar to the ending of the ballad. What do students learn from this comparison? *Students may say that this similarity shows that people in medieval times were, in many ways, the same as people today.*

Reinforce and Extend

Answers

◆ Literature and Your Life

Reader's Response Students may say that they hoped the couple would get away because Lochivar seems more worthy than the bridegroom. Ellen obviously thinks so, too.

Thematic Focus Because Lochinvar is "dauntless in war," he is true to his king and nation. He also has a sense of honor because he is "faithful in love" and saves Ellen from an unhappy marriage.

☑ Check Your Comprehension

1. He had been at war.
2. The event is the the wedding of his love, Ellen, to another man.
3. They have been in love for some time, but Ellen's father has not given his consent to their marriage.
4. They run away and are never seen again.

◆ Critical Thinking

1. She loves him.
2. The females are entranced by him; the males do not trust him.
3. Possible response: It shows that he values love above all else.
4. Some students may feel that his actions are justified because he is in love. Others may say that he should have tried to convince Ellen's family of his integrity.
5. Lochinvar is a brave warrior who takes Ellen away to be with him forever.

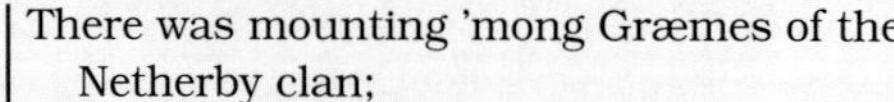

There was mounting 'mong Græmes of the
 Netherby clan;
Forsters, Fenwicks, and Musgraves,[10] they
 rode and they ran;
1 There was racing, and chasing, on Can-
 nobie Lee,
But the lost bride of Netherby ne'er did
 they see.
So daring in love, and so dauntless in war,
Have ye e'er heard of gallant like young
 Lochinvar?

Use the details in this stanza to infer that the **speaker** is impressed by Lochinvar's actions.

10. **Græmes . . . Forsters, Fenwicks, and Musgraves**: Family names.

Guide for Responding

◆ Literature and Your Life

Reader's Response Did you hope that Lochinvar and Ellen would get away? Explain why you did or did not.

Thematic Focus What do the events in the poem tell you about Lochinvar's personal code?

Journal Writing In your journal, explain whether you think Lochinvar is a hero or a scoundrel.

☑ Check Your Comprehension

1. Where had Lochinvar been before arriving at Netherby hall?
2. What event is taking place as he arrives?
3. Describe Lochinvar's previous relationship with Ellen.
4. What do Lochinvar and Ellen do at the end of the poem?

◆ Critical Thinking

Interpret

1. Why do you think Ellen went with Lochinvar, even though she'd agreed to marry another? **[Interpret]**
2. How do the female characters and male characters differ in their response to Lochinvar? **[Compare and Contrast]**
3. What does Lochinvar's behavior at the wedding reveal about his values? **[Infer]**

Evaluate

4. Do you think Lochinvar's actions were justified? Why or why not? **[Evaluate]**

Apply

5. In literature, knightly behavior is characterized by bravery and a romantic attitude toward women. How does this poem illustrate such characteristics? **[Relate]**

Beyond the Selection

FURTHER READING

Other Works by Sir Walter Scott

The Lady of the Lake, a long narrative poem
Minstrelsy of the Scottish Border, a three-volume collection of ballads from the Scottish oral tradition
Ivanhoe
The Heart of Midlothian
Rob Roy
The Bride of Lammermoor

INTERNET

Additional information about Sir Walter Scott can be found on the Internet. We suggest the following site on the Internet (all Web sites are subject to change).
http://lynn.efr.hw.ac.uk:80/EDC/edinburghers/walter-scott.html

We *strongly recommend* that you preview this site before you send students to it.

Guide for Responding (continued)

◆ Reading for Success

Strategies for Reading Poetry

Review the reading strategies and the notes showing how to read poetry. Then, apply these strategies to answer the following:

1. Indicate where the pauses and stops should occur in reading the poem's sixth stanza.
2. List three sensory details that suggest Lochinvar's heroic qualities.
3. Paraphrase the poem's fifth stanza.

◆ Build Vocabulary

Using Words With Multiple Meanings

The word *bar,* which appears in "Lochinvar," has more than one meaning. Several other words with multiple meanings are listed below. With a partner, brainstorm for several definitions for each word. Check your ideas in a dictionary. Then, write a sentence for one definition of the word.

1. brake **3.** lead
2. suit **4.** bank

Spelling Strategy

The short and long e sounds can be spelled with the letters *ea,* as in *tread* (rhymes with *bed*) or *bead* (rhymes with *feed*). Choose an *ea* word below to complete each sentence. Then, write the complete word on your paper.

s_ _t l_ _d h_ _d r_ _d

1. Yesterday, I ___?___ Walter Scott's poem "Lochinvar."
2. Now I can picture Lochinvar in my ___?___.
3. I can see Ellen in her ___?___ upon Lochinvar's horse.
4. Did Lochinvar ___?___ Ellen toward a good choice?

Using the Word Bank

On your paper, complete the paragraph with Word Bank words.

No one dared to ___?___ the way of the ___?___ knight. After all, Ellen had ___?___ to go with him. Her mother did ___?___ some. This worry led her to ___?___ anxiously back and forth across the floor. At least, she knew, he was no ___?___.

◆ Literary Focus

Ballad

A **ballad,** like Scott's poem about Lochinvar, relates a romantic and adventurous story. Structural features, such as a refrain, a strong rhythm, and rhyming lines, give ballads a musical quality.

1. Describe the pattern of rhyming lines in the poem "Lochinvar."
2. Identify the poem's refrain, and explain how it changes each time it is repeated.
3. Do you think that this poem lends itself to being set to music? Explain.

◆ Build Grammar Skills

Degrees of Comparison

Most adjectives and adverbs have three **degrees of comparison:** the positive, the comparative, and the superlative. The positive degree is used when no comparison is being made: *brave.* The comparative is used when two things are being compared: Lochniver was *braver* than the bridegroom. The superlative is used when three or more things are being compared: Lochniver was the *bravest* of all the men there.

To create the comparative form of short (one- or two-syllable) adjectives and adverbs, add *-er* to the positive form. To create the superlative form, add *-est.* For most adjectives and adverbs with two or more syllables, use *more* or *most* with the positive form.

Positive	Comparative	Superlative
young	younger	youngest
late	later	latest
lovely	lovelier	loveliest
boldly	more boldly	most boldly

Practice Write the comparative and superlative forms of these adjectives and adverbs.

1. wide **2.** stately **3.** daring **4.** gladly **5.** light

Writing Application Use the following line as the starting point for a brief summary of the poem. Include all five modifiers listed in parentheses, and use all three forms of comparison.

The Scottish knight Lochinvar rode his horse . . .
(brave, challenging, beautiful, quick, early)

Reading for Success

1. Pauses should occur at each comma and semicolon, with a full stop at the final period.
2. Students may list details such as these: "So boldly he entered the Netherby hall"; "So stately his form"; and "So light to the saddle before her he sprung!"
3. Lochinvar assures the wedding party he no longer loves Ellen and can easily find another love. He has come only to toast the bride and dance with her once. Ellen kisses a cup of wine and hands it to him. He drinks it and throws down the cup. She blushes and smiles. Then, before Ellen's mother can stop them, he takes her hand and asks her to dance.

◆ Build Vocabulary

Words With Multiple Meanings

1. I used my brake to stop my bike.
2. Thomas wore his new gray suit.
3. He played the lead role in the play.
4. I put my earnings in a bank.

Spelling Strategy

1. read
2. head
3. seat
4. lead

Using the Word Bank

bar; dauntless; consented; fret; tread; laggard

◆ Literary Focus

1. The rhyme scheme is AA,BB,CC. Each stanza repeats the first stanza's CC rhyme.
2. The last two lines of each stanza, all of which have the same rhyme, make up the refrain. Each refrain ends with "Lochinvar" but tells something different about him.
3. Students may say that the poem could easily be set to music because the same rhythm is repeated in each stanza. Some may observe that this repetition might pose problems for a composer.

◆ Build Grammar Skills

Practice

wider, widest
statelier, stateliest
more daring, most daring
more gladly, most gladly
lighter, lightest

Writing Application

Sample response: The Scottish knight Lochinvar rode his horse to Netherby hall where Ellen, the most beautiful woman he knew, was about to marry another man, less noble and brave. Her father, who had prevented Lochinvar's marriage to Ellen earlier, asked Lochinvar why he had come. Lochinvar's explanation was quick; he wanted to honor Ellen's wedding to another man. He then accomplished the challenging task of guiding the willing Ellen to his horse for a quick getaway.

Writer's Solution

For additional instruction and practice, use the lesson in the *Writer's Solution Language Lab CD-ROM* on modifiers, or Using the Comparative and Superlative Degrees, p. 80, in the *Writer's Solution Grammar Practice Book.*

Idea Bank

Following are suggestions for matching the Idea Bank topics with your students' performance levels and learning modalities:

Customize for
Performance Levels
Less Advanced Students: 1, 4, 5
Average Students: 2, 5, 6
More Advanced Students: 3, 6, 7

Customize for
Learning Modalities
Verbal/Linguistic: 1, 2, 3, 4, 5
Interpersonal: 4
Visual/Spatial: 5, 7
Logical/Mathematical: 2, 5, 6
Musical/Rhythmic: 3

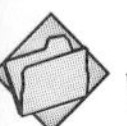

Writing Mini-Lesson

Refer students to the Writing Handbook in the back of the book for instructions on the writing process for further information on poetry. Have students use the Cluster Organizer p. 82, and/or the Series of Events Chain, p. 66 in **Writing and Language Transparencies,** to arrange their prewriting examples.

Writer's Solution

Writing Lab CD-ROM
Have students complete the tutorial on Creative Writing. Follow these steps:

1. Have students review the tips for using similes and metaphors.
2. Encourage students to use the Character Trait Word Bin to help them vividly describe the subjects of their ballads.
3. Have students view the video tip on revising poetry.

Writing Lab CD-ROM
Have students use Chapter 8, "Creative Writing," pp. 234–263, for additional support. This chapter includes in-depth instruction on using concrete language, p. 262.

Build Your Portfolio

Idea Bank

Writing

1. **Farewell Letter** As Ellen, write a letter to your family, explaining why you left with Lochinvar.
2. **Editorial** Write a column for the Netherby newspaper that supports or criticizes the actions taken by Lochinvar and Ellen. Explain your views, using specific examples from the poem.
3. **Sequel** In ballad form, continue the story of Lochinvar in a few more stanzas. Tell readers what happens to Lochinvar and Ellen. How do they escape their pursuers? Where do they go?

Speaking and Listening

4. **Skit [Group Activity]** With a group of classmates, perform the events of the poem. Use gestures and facial expressions to capture the emotions of the story. **[Performing Arts Link]**
5. **Missing Persons Description** As a representative of Ellen's family, create descriptions of Lochinvar and Ellen to help people in other towns search for them. Present these descriptions as they would be used for radio or television announcements. **[Media Link]**

Projects

6. **Search Report** Using library and community resources, such as the local police department, find out what methods are used to locate people who have disappeared. Explain how technology is used in such searches, and identify some organizations focused on locating people. Present your findings in a pamphlet format. **[Social Studies Link]**
7. **Illustrated Storyboard** Using the Background for Understanding on page 724 and further research about knights, create historically accurate illustrations to accompany the poem. Mount these in sequential storyboard form, with lines from the poem included as captions. **[Art Link]**

Writing Mini-Lesson

Updated Ballad

The ballad "Lochinvar" tells the story of a gallant hero from long ago. Like most ballads, the story is one of adventure and romance. Think about someone today—either real or imagined—who could be the hero of a modern-day ballad. Then, tell his or her story in ballad format, using "Lochinvar" as a model.

Writing Skills Focus: Refrain

Ballads have a songlike rhythm. To anchor that rhythm in readers' (or listeners') minds, use a **refrain,** or repeated line or lines. Refrains, which often appear at the end of a stanza, bring readers or listeners back to the main character or idea. For example, notice how Walter Scott ends every stanza with his hero's name, Lochinvar, almost always preceded by "young."

Prewriting Choose a real or imaginary hero for your ballad and list some of his or her personal and physical features. Then, plot the central event you will recount in your ballad. What adventure will occur? How will romance arise?

Drafting Begin by introducing your hero and setting the scene. Then, follow your hero step by step through his or her adventure. As you write, experiment with text that might work as a refrain.

◆ Grammar Application

To paint a vivid picture of your hero and his or her adventures, use comparative and superlative forms of modifiers.

Revising Revise your ballad by adding descriptive details to enhance the sense of romance and adventure. Also, read your refrain aloud. If it seems flat or unmusical, rearrange words or replace it with more rhythmic text.

✓ ASSESSMENT OPTIONS

Formal Assessment, Selection Test, pp. 201–203, and Assessment Resources Software. The selection test is designed so that it can easily be customized to the performance levels of your students.

Alternative Assessment, p. 41, includes options for less advanced students, more advanced students, verbal/linguistic learners, interpersonal learners, musical/rhythmic learners, and visual/spatial learners.

PORTFOLIO ASSESSMENT
Use the following rubrics in the **Alternative Assessment** booklet to assess student writing:
Letter to Family: Expression, p. 81
Editorial: Persuasion, p. 92
Sequel: Poetry, p. 95
Writing Mini-Lesson: Poetry, p. 95

Part 1 *Structure of Poetry*

Le Bassin aux Nympheas—harmonie verte (green harmony), Claude Monet

One-Minute Planning Guide

The selections in this section introduce students to different structures in poetry. "The Cremation of Sam McGee" is a long narrative poem about a journey in the Arctic. The grouping of poems including "Washed in Silver," "Barter," "Winter," and "Down by the Salley Gardens" focuses on lyric poetry. "Seal" is an example of a concrete poem. "The Pasture" is a poem that was originally published as an introduction to an entire volume of poetry. "Three Haiku" and "Tanka" represent forms of Japanese poetry.

Customize for *Varying Student Needs*

When assigning the selections in this section, keep in mind the following factors:

"The Cremation of Sam McGee"
- A long narrative poem
- Opportunity for a geography/history connection

"Washed in Silver," "Barter," "Winter," "Down by the Salley Gardens"
- Reading the poems aloud will help students hear the musical quality of the language

"Seal"
- Humorous concrete poem

"The Pasture"
- Short, two-stanza poem

"Three Haiku"
- Short lines and simple language make these poems accessible

"Tanka"
- Introduces students to tanka
- An opportunity for connecting literature with social studies

Humanities: Art

Le bassin aux Nympheas—harmonie verte (green harmony), by Claude Monet

Claude Monet (1840–1926) was born in Paris and spent his early childhood creating caricatures of his teachers. In 1859, Monet began studying art in Paris and showed in the first Impressionist show in 1874. Impressionism, in general, is a style known for a lack of earth tones, quick brushstrokes, subtle divisions of color, and vibrant chromatic contrasts. This style of painting re-creates outdoor observations by capturing aspects of time of day, light, and weather.

Discuss the following question:

What do you notice about the structures in the painting and how the artist created them? *Students should notice the bridge over the water, the three small waterfalls in the stream, the trees in the background. They may notice that all these structures, except for the possibility of the bridge, are created by altering the brushstrokes and subtly changing the colors. There are no bold outlines of the forms; rather, the forms are rendered through subtle contrasts, suggested rather than stated.*

Prepare and Engage

OBJECTIVES

1. To read, comprehend, and interpret a narrative poem
2. To relate a narrative poem to personal experience
3. To identify the speaker
4. To analyze narrative poetry
5. To build vocabulary in context and distinguish shades of meaning
6. To recognize irregular comparison of modifiers
7. To write a diary entry using sensory details
8. To respond to a narrative poem through writing, speaking and listening, and projects

SKILLS INSTRUCTION

Vocabulary: Shades of Meaning
Spelling: W Sound Spelled With *wh*
Grammar: Irregular Comparison of Modifiers
Reading Strategy: Identify the Speaker
Literary Focus: Narrative Poetry
Writing: Sensory Details
Speaking and Listening: Weather Report (Teacher Edition)
Viewing and Representing Map (Teacher Edition)

PORTFOLIO OPPORTUNITIES

Writing: Tabloid Article; Wilderness Code; Tall Tale
Writing Mini-Lesson: Diary Entry
Speaking and Listening: Weather Report; Conversation
Projects: Yukon Research; Map

More About the Author
During his lifetime, **Robert Service** held an assortment of unusual jobs—from ambulance driver to cook. No doubt, many people he met in these positions later became characters in his poems and novels. Some of his characters also appeared in films based on Service's works. Service himself appeared in one of these films. In 1942, he made an appearance in *The Spoilers,* playing a small part next to one of Hollywood's biggest stars, Marlene Dietrich.

Guide for Reading

Meet the Author

Robert Service (1874–1959)

Robert Service established himself as a poet by introducing readers to the exciting life of Canada's northern wilderness. He could paint a vivid picture of this life because he'd spent many years there himself.

From Banking to Poetry Service came to Canada at age twenty to work for a bank. Sent by the bank to the Yukon Territory, Canada's northernmost territory, Service came face to face with the rough world of trappers and gold prospectors. Soon, he was writing poems about these lively characters.

It didn't take Service long to leave banking for a full-time life of writing. He traveled the Yukon and other Arctic areas for eight years, recording his adventures. Later, Service worked as a newspaper correspondent during both world wars. Though he returned to Canada only briefly during World War II, Service wrote his most popular story poems and novels during this stay.

The Story Behind the Story

Written during Service's brief stay in Canada during World War II, "The Cremation of Sam McGee" is probably the author's best-known poem. As you read, you'll see how the poem reflects Service's firsthand experience with the bitter cold of the Yukon Territory.

◆ Literature and Your Life

Connect Your Experience

When you're too cold or too hot, it can be hard to think about anything but how to get warmer (or cooler)! Imagine what it would be like to spend time out in the wilderness in one of the coldest places in the world. Read this poem and you'll find out.

Thematic Focus: Personal Codes

When people are placed in life-threatening situations, such as being pitted against extreme cold, they may make desperate promises or requests. As you read, consider the importance of fulfilling such a request.

◆ Background for Understanding

Geography

In this poem, two men prospect for gold in Canada's far northwestern Yukon Territory. As you can see from the map on the next page, Yukon's geography is a challenge. Located just east of Alaska, the Yukon stretches to well north of the Arctic Circle. The land is made of high plateaus and even higher mountains. In winter, the temperature reaches -60°F, and much of the ground is permanently frozen. Still, miners have long struggled to get at the territory's mineral wealth.

◆ Build Vocabulary

Shades of Meaning

Loathed is defined as "disliked intensely," "hated," and "abhorred." Each of these definitions gets at the meaning, but none can convey exactly the intensity of the word itself. An awareness of words' shades of meaning can help you appreciate the word choices poets make.

Word Bank

Which two of these words from the poem might you use to describe a horrible sight?

cremated
whimper
ghastly
stern
loathed
grisly

Prentice Hall Literature Program Resources

REINFORCE / RETEACH / EXTEND

Selection Support Pages
Build Vocabulary: Shades of Meaning, p. 229
Build Spelling Skills, p. 230
Build Grammar Skills: Irregular Comparison of Modifiers, p. 231
Reading Strategy: Identify Speaker, p. 232
Literary Focus: Narrative Poetry, p. 233
Strategies for Diverse Student Needs, p. 83
Beyond Literature Cross-Curricular Connection: Geography p. 42

Formal Assessment Selection Test, pp. 204–206, Assessment Resources Software
Alternative Assessment p. 42
Writing and Language Transparencies KWL Organizer, p. 58; Series of Events Chain, p. 66; Sensory Language Chart, p. 78; Venn Diagram, p. 86
Resource Pro CD-ROM
"The Cremation of Sam McGee"—includes all resource material and customizable lesson plan
Listening to Literature Audiocassettes
"The Cremation of Sam McGee"

The Cremation of Sam McGee

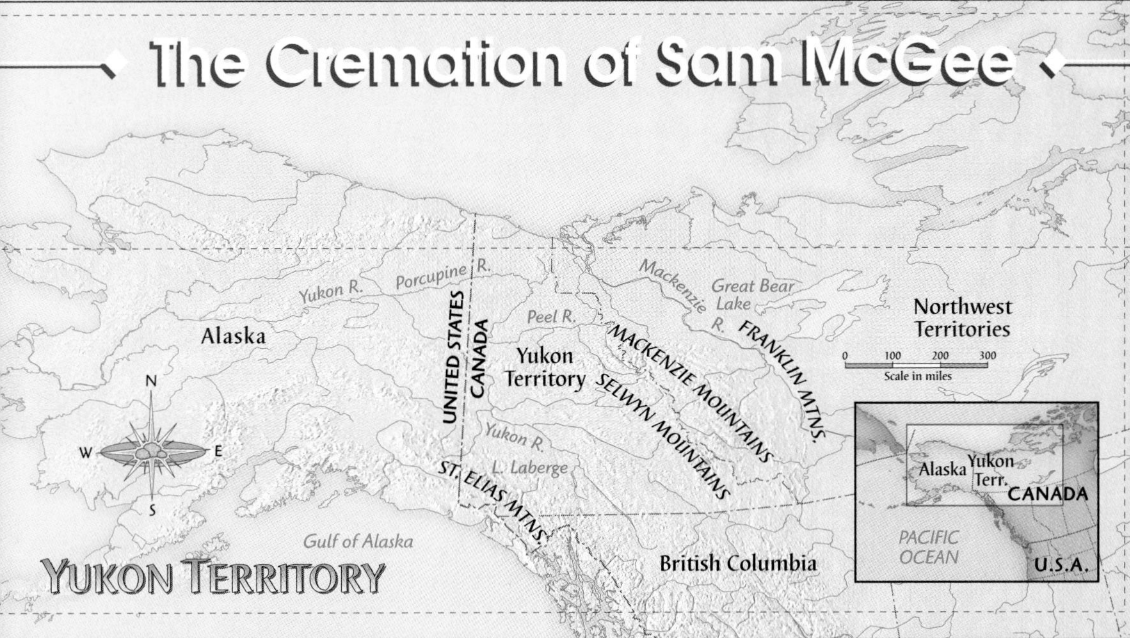

◆ Literary Focus

Narrative Poetry

Narrative poetry is poetry that tells a story. Like a short story, a narrative poem has a plot, characters, and a setting. However, narrative poems generally make much more use of sound than short stories do. Often, rhythm and repetition are used to create a musical effect and to draw your attention to the most important details in the poem.

◆ Reading Strategy

Identify the Speaker

In a narrative poem, the **speaker** is the voice that relates the story. Because the speaker's perspective affects how the story is told, identifying the speaker is one of the keys to unlocking a narrative poem's meaning. As you read "The Cremation of Sam McGee," look for details that reveal the speaker's personality, and take note of his perspective of events. You might use a chart like the one below.

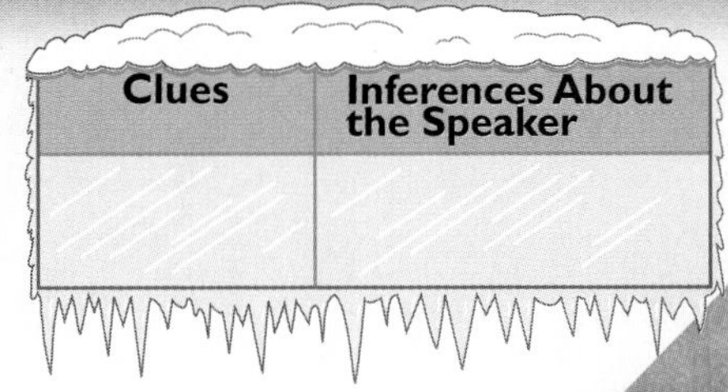

Read aloud this quotation: "The only society I like is that which is rough and tough—and the tougher the better. That's where you get down to bedrock and meet human people." Explain to students that the man who said this also wrote the selection they are about to read. Ask students what they think the quote means and if they agree with it. Then have them tell what it reveals about the poet's personality.

◆ Build Grammar Skills

If you wish to introduce the grammar concept for this selection before students read, refer to the instruction on p. 742.

Customize for *Less Proficient Readers*

To help students better understand the poem's story, briefly summarize its events by drawing and discussing a chart such as the one shown. Have students create a similar chart and add details to it as they read.

Setting	Yukon Territory	**Details**
Characters	Cap, Sam McGee	**Details**
Plot	Two men follow the Dawson trail on a dog sleigh. Sam asks Cap to cremate his body if he dies on the trip.	**Details**

Customize for *More Advanced Students*

Have students note examples of exaggeration as they read the narrative poem. When they finish reading, have small groups discuss their examples. Instruct students to discuss why they think that Service uses this technique in the poem and if, in their opinion, it is effective.

Preparing for Standardized Tests

Grammar Standardized tests may require students to show that they know how to use modifiers correctly. The following test item asks students to demonstrate their understanding of the correct use of a superlative form of a modifier.

Choose the best way to write this sentence.

The stars were shining most brightly than I'd ever seen.

(A) The stars were shining much brightly than I'd ever seen.
(B) The stars were shining more brightly than I'd ever seen.
(C) The stars were shining more brighter than I'd ever seen.
(D) No change

Point out to students that *much/more/most* is an irregular modifier; they simply must know each form of the word and when it should be used. In this sample item, *than* indicates that the modifier should be the comparative form. *(C)* uses the comparative form, but also forms a comparative of bright, which is incorrect. *(B)* is the correct answer, because it uses the comparative form correctly.

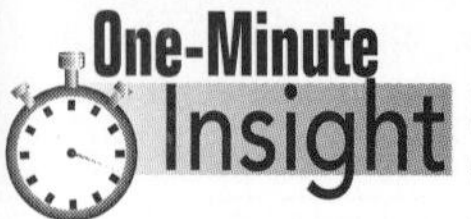

Develop Understanding

One-Minute Insight Like a tall tale, this narrative poem tells a story using exaggeration, humor, and fantasy. On Christmas Day, two prospectors, Sam and Cap, travel across the Yukon on a sleigh pulled by huskies. Unable to bear the bitter cold, Sam tells Cap that he may soon die and requests that Cap cremate his remains. Cap promises to do this.

Cap feels that keeping this promise is a duty, so when the time comes, he lashes Sam's body to his sleigh. Then he pushes on for several more days, looking for fuel. Finally, he fashions a crematorium from an abandoned ship on a frozen lake. After Sam's body burns for awhile, Cap looks into the burning furnace, only to discover that Sam is alive and well—and warm at last.

Customize for
English Language Learners
Students may have difficulty understanding some of the jargon used by the poet. Use gestures, drawings, and the photographs in the book to help students understand words and phrases like "parka," "lashed to the sleigh," "grub," "chum," "spent," and "in a trice."

Customize for
Musical/Rhythmic Learners
To help students hear and enjoy the musical rhythm of the narrative poem, have them listen to the audiocassette. Then guide a discussion about how the rhyme and rhythm enhance the humor at the end of the poem.

Listening to Literature Audiocassettes

The Cremation of Sam McGee

Robert Service

736 *Poetry*

Block Scheduling Strategies

Consider these suggestions to take advantage of extended class time:

- Before they begin to read the poem, discuss with students Background for Understanding, p. 734. Then have them study the map on p. 735. Tell students that, although the events in the story are fictional, many details about the Yukon Territory are accurate. Ask students what they know about the climate and terrain of the Yukon and what they hope to learn from reading the poem. You may want to have small groups of students complete a KWL Organizer, p. 58 in **Writing and Language Transparencies.**
- Play the audiocassette of the poem. Have students complete the chart shown on p. 735 as they listen. Then have students work in small groups to write a short paragraph using details from the poem to describe the speaker's personal code.

Listening to Literature Audiocassettes

- Ask students how they would respond to the Apply question, p. 741. Direct them to form small groups that have members from both sides of the argument. Then have them debate the issue, providing support for their ideas. At the end of the session, invite students who changed their opinions to explain how they were persuaded.

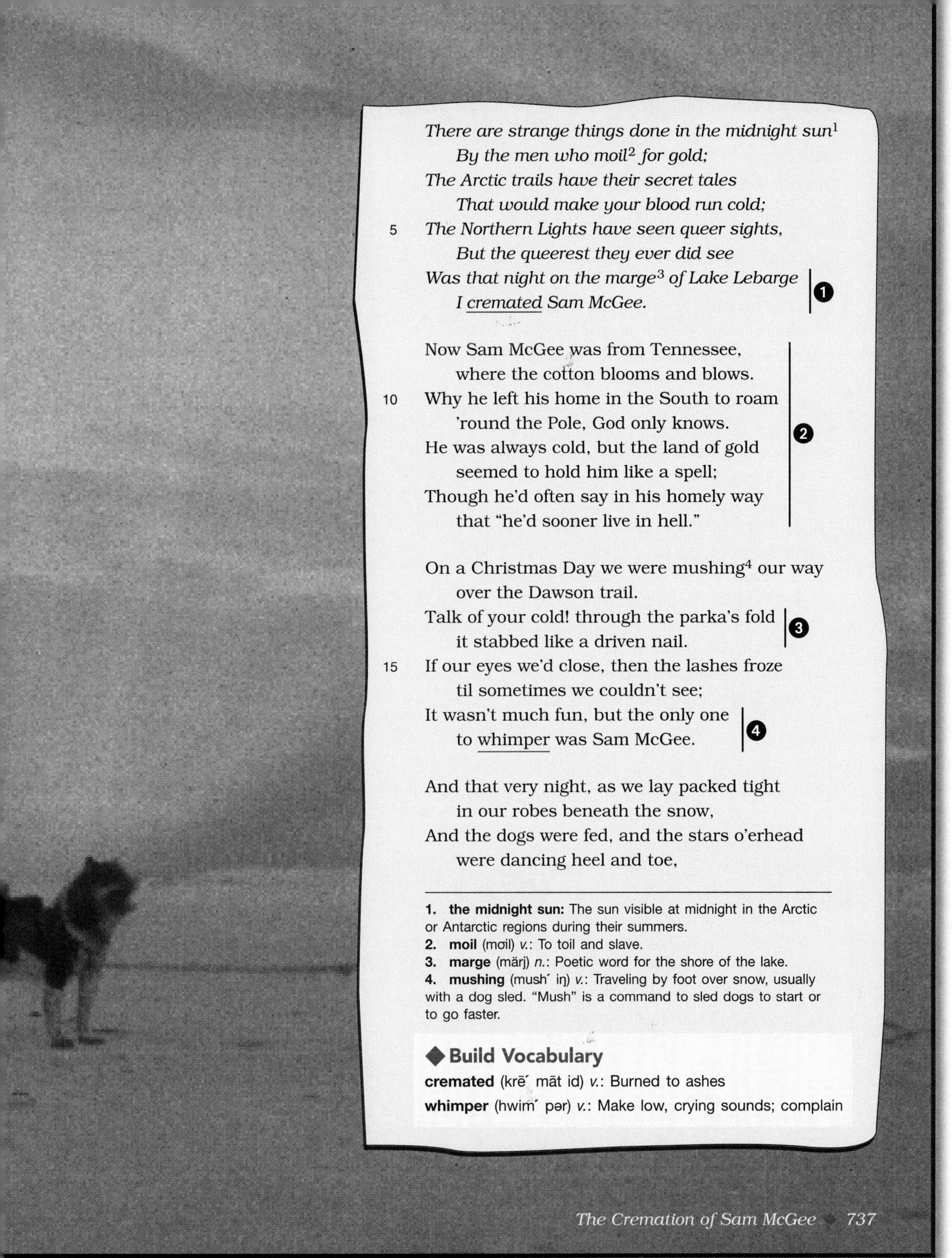

There are strange things done in the midnight sun[1]
By the men who moil[2] *for gold;*
The Arctic trails have their secret tales
That would make your blood run cold;
The Northern Lights have seen queer sights,
But the queerest they ever did see
Was that night on the marge[3] *of Lake Lebarge*
I cremated Sam McGee. ❶

Now Sam McGee was from Tennessee,
where the cotton blooms and blows.
Why he left his home in the South to roam
'round the Pole, God only knows.
He was always cold, but the land of gold
seemed to hold him like a spell;
Though he'd often say in his homely way
that "he'd sooner live in hell." ❷

On a Christmas Day we were mushing[4] our way
over the Dawson trail.
Talk of your cold! through the parka's fold
it stabbed like a driven nail. ❸
If our eyes we'd close, then the lashes froze
til sometimes we couldn't see;
It wasn't much fun, but the only one
to whimper was Sam McGee. ❹

And that very night, as we lay packed tight
in our robes beneath the snow,
And the dogs were fed, and the stars o'erhead
were dancing heel and toe,

---

1. **the midnight sun:** The sun visible at midnight in the Arctic or Antarctic regions during their summers.
2. **moil** (moil) *v.*: To toil and slave.
3. **marge** (märj) *n.*: Poetic word for the shore of the lake.
4. **mushing** (mush´ iŋ) *v.*: Traveling by foot over snow, usually with a dog sled. "Mush" is a command to sled dogs to start or to go faster.

◆ Build Vocabulary

cremated (krē´ māt id) *v.*: Burned to ashes

whimper (hwim´ pər) *v.*: Make low, crying sounds; complain

◆ Reading Strategy

❶ **Identify the Speaker** Lead students to note that the speaker refers to himself as *I* in these lines. Ask students what they learn about the speaker in this stanza. *Students may say that they learn from this stanza that the speaker cremates Sam McGee on the shores of Lake Lebarge.*

◆ Literary Focus

❷ **Narrative Poem** Remind students that, like a story, a narrative poem has characters, a setting, and a plot. Discuss details of setting in this stanza such as "the Pole," "he was always cold," and "land of gold." Then, ask students what they learn about the character of Sam McGee. *He is a prospector who comes from Tennessee; he hates living in the cold.*

◆ Literature and Your Life

❸ Help students recognize that in line 14, the poet compares the sting of the cold to a nail driven through the prospectors' parkas. Ask students if they have ever experienced such cold. *Many students may remember times that they felt cold wind through a heavy coat. Remind students that the winter temperature in the Yukon ranges from -18° to -29° C (0° to -20° F).*

◆ Critical Thinking

❹ **Compare and Contrast** Ask students how the two characters are alike and different. *The speaker is able to withstand the cold; Sam complains about it. Some students may infer from these lines that Sam is weaker than the speaker.*

Customize for
Less Proficient Readers and Musical/Rhythmic Learners

Discuss that the overall rhyme scheme (AA,BB) is enhanced by a pair of rhyming words in each line, for example "McGee" and "Tennessee" (line 9) and "home" and "roam" (line 10). To help them hear this rhythm as they continue reading the poem, invite students to practice reading several lines aloud.

Cross-Curricular Connection: Science

Northern Lights The northern lights, or aurora borealis, are caused when charged particles from the sun hit the atmosphere and are pushed toward the poles by Earth's magnetic fields. They appear in the sky as floating streamers of red, pink, and green. Because the northern lights extend thousands of kilometers from east to west but are only about one kilometer thick from north to south, they produce a curtainlike appearance. The bottom edge of this curtain sometimes has huge crimson folds or is pleated, or both. The Northern Lights are most commonly seen late at night in an area that includes southern Hudson Bay, the southern tip of Greenland, Iceland, the northern tip of the Scandinavian peninsula, the Arctic coast of Siberia, and central Alaska. They occasionally develop further south. In the southern hemisphere, the phenomenon is called aurora australis.

You may want to have interested students find photographs of the northern lights in the school library or on the Internet to share with the class. Discuss how the lights enhance the eerie setting at the beginning of the poem.

◆Critical Thinking

❶ **Analyze** Ask students what Sam fears more than dying. What does this show about Sam? *He fears being buried in an "icy grave." This shows how much he hates the cold.*

◆Literary Focus

❷ **Narrative Poetry** Remind students that an important part of a plot is a problem that must be solved. How might Cap's promise to cremate Sam's remains create a problem? *Students may say that now Cap will have to find a place to carry out Sam's wishes. Be sure that students understand that Cap must first find fuel in the barren landscape.*

◆Critical Thinking

❸ **Interpret** Ask students how Cap feels about hauling Sam's corpse on his sleigh. Why doesn't he simply bury Sam in the ice and snow? *Although carrying Sam's corpse repels Cap, he feels that it is his duty to fulfill his promise to cremate Sam.*

◆Reading Strategy

Identify Speaker Ask students what they have learned about the speaker from the stanzas on this page. What do students think the speaker means when he says that "the trail has its own stern code." *Students may say that the speaker is a man who keeps his word. The stern code of the trail probably involves being able to depend on others to survive the harsh climate.*

He turned to me, and "Cap," says he,
  "I'll cash in[5] this trip, I guess;
And if I do, I'm asking that you
  won't refuse my last request."

Well, he seemed so low that I couldn't say no;
  then he says with a sort of moan:
"It's the cursed cold, and it's got right hold
  till I'm chilled clean through to the bone.
❶ Yet 'tain't being dead—it's my awful dread
  of the icy grave that pains;
So I want you to swear that, foul or fair,
  you'll cremate my last remains."

❷ A pal's last need is a thing to heed,
  so I swore I would not fail;
And we started on at the streak of dawn;
  but God! he looked ghastly pale.
He crouched on the sleigh, and he raved all day
  of his home in Tennessee;
And before nightfall a corpse was all
  that was left of Sam McGee.

There wasn't a breath in that land of death,
  and I hurried, horror-driven,
With a corpse half hid that I couldn't get rid,
  because of a promise given;
It was lashed to the sleigh, and it seemed to say:
  "You may tax your brawn[6] and brains,
❸ But you promised true, and it's up to you
  to cremate those last remains."

Now a promise made is a debt unpaid,
  and the trail has its own stern code.
In the days to come, though my lips were dumb,
  in my heart how I cursed that load.

5. **cash in:** Slang expression meaning "die."
6. **brawn:** (brôn) *n.*: Physical strength.

Speaking and Listening Mini-Lesson

Weather Report

This mini-lesson supports the Speaking and Listening activity in the Idea Bank on p. 743.

Introduce Have students recall weather reports they have seen on television. Discuss the graphics and maps meteorologists use to help explain why certain weather patterns occur.

Develop Have students conduct research using almanacs, encyclopedias, and other reference sources. Then ask how these details from the poem might influence their reports: The poem begins on Christmas Day; the men could see the stars at night; the final scene occurs near a frozen lake.

Apply Have students write a weather report that includes a map and graphics. Ask them to practice their presentation with a partner. Then have them present their report to a small group.

Assess Evaluate students on how well they present and explain facts about the weather. You might also distribute the Peer Assessment: Speaker/Speech form, p. 105 in **Alternative Assessment.**

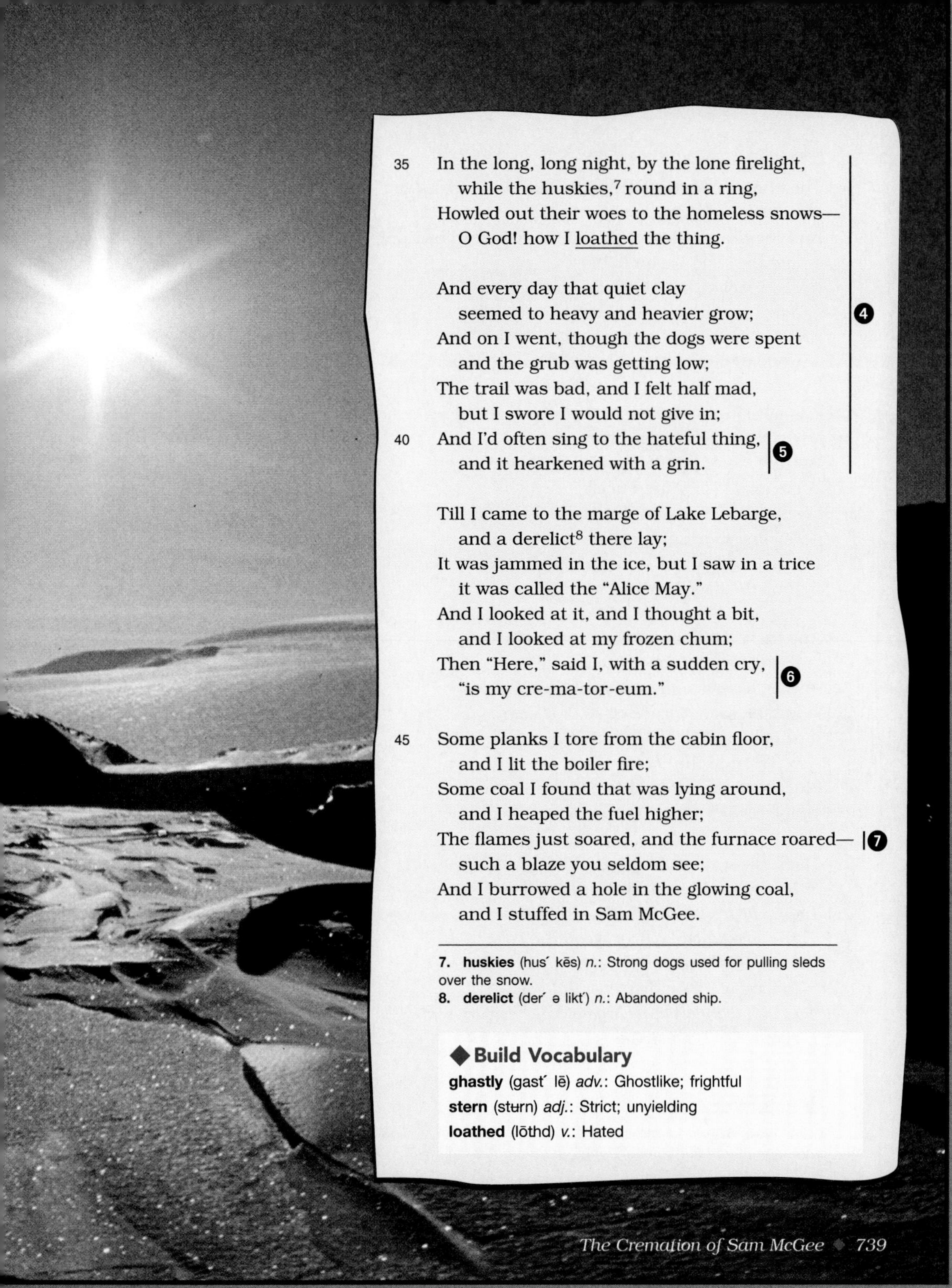

In the long, long night, by the lone firelight,
while the huskies,[7] round in a ring,
Howled out their woes to the homeless snows—
O God! how I loathed the thing.

And every day that quiet clay
seemed to heavy and heavier grow; 4
And on I went, though the dogs were spent
and the grub was getting low;
The trail was bad, and I felt half mad,
but I swore I would not give in;
And I'd often sing to the hateful thing, 5
and it hearkened with a grin.

Till I came to the marge of Lake Lebarge,
and a derelict[8] there lay;
It was jammed in the ice, but I saw in a trice
it was called the "Alice May."
And I looked at it, and I thought a bit,
and I looked at my frozen chum;
Then "Here," said I, with a sudden cry, 6
"is my cre-ma-tor-eum."

Some planks I tore from the cabin floor,
and I lit the boiler fire;
Some coal I found that was lying around,
and I heaped the fuel higher;
The flames just soared, and the furnace roared— 7
such a blaze you seldom see;
And I burrowed a hole in the glowing coal,
and I stuffed in Sam McGee.

7. **huskies** (hus′ kēs) *n.*: Strong dogs used for pulling sleds over the snow.
8. **derelict** (der′ ə likt′) *n.*: Abandoned ship.

◆ Build Vocabulary

ghastly (gast′ lē) *adv.*: Ghostlike; frightful
stern (sturn) *adj.*: Strict; unyielding
loathed (lōthd) *v.*: Hated

◆ Literary Focus

4 Narrative Poetry To help students better understand the character of Cap, elicit that he is growing more discouraged as each day passes. Ask students what may be causing him to feel "half mad." *Students may point out that Cap has been alone with Sam's body for many days, his food is running out, his dogs howl at night, and he is crossing a bleak land with very little variation in scenery.*

◆ Reading Strategy

5 Identify the Speaker Discuss that Cap sings to Sam and imagines that Sam hearkens, or listens, to him while wearing a grin. What do these details indicate about the speaker? *The details show that Cap is losing his grip on reality.*

◆ Critical Thinking

6 Interpret Ask students how this line is different from those that preceded it. What does it indicate about the poem? *This line indicates a change in mood from grim to humorous. It shows that the poem is not as serious as readers may have previously believed.*

◆ Build Vocabulary Skills

7 Shades of Meaning Discuss that the poet could have used words such as *grew* or *climbed* rather than *soared* and *crackled* instead of *roared* to describe the flames of the fire. Why do students think he chose these words? *Students may say that the words paint a picture of a huge, blazing fire in the mind of the reader.*

Customize for
English Language Learners
Help students identify the words used by the poet to refer to Sam's frozen body. *Cap calls Sam's body "that load," "that quiet clay," "the hateful thing," and "my frozen chum."*

Viewing and Representing Mini-Lesson

Map

This mini-lesson supports the Map project in the Idea Bank on p. 743

Introduce Tell students that they will create a map showing the journey in the poem. They will include notes showing where events take place, as well as a key with symbols.

Develop Have students order the events of the poem, using the Series of Events Chain in **Writing and Language Transparencies,** p. 66. Students can use maps of the Yukon Territory or the map on p. 735 for reference.

Apply Ask students to imagine that the journey in the poem begins outside Dawson and ends at Lake Lebarge. Then have them create a map (they can trace one of the maps they are using for reference) showing a route between these points. Suggest that they use symbols to indicate geographical features along the way. Have students display and discuss their maps in small groups.

Assess Evaluate students' maps based on whether they have drawn a map route with notes that accurately shows the principal events of the poem.

◆Critical Thinking

❶ **Interpret** Ask students why they think the poet has Cap say, "I didn't like to hear him sizzle so." *Students may say that the poet included this line to add humor to the poem.*

◆Literary Focus

❷ **Narrative Poem** Ask students how Cap's problem is resolved at the end of the narrative poem. *Cap finally finds fuel for his crematorium when he burns the planks of an abandoned ship. When he looks into the furnace, he discovers that Sam, who is alive, has finally gotten warm.*

◆Literary Focus

❸ **Narrative Poem** Elicit that this stanza is the same as the first stanza. Ask students how this poetic technique is similar to one they discussed while reading "Lochinvar." *Students should recognize this repeated stanza as a refrain.*

Beyond Literature

Some students may want to use the Venn Diagram in **Writing and Language Transparencies,** p. 86, to organize their thoughts before creating their charts. You may also want to suggest that students visit the following site on the Internet to view images of miners during Alaska's gold rush (all Web sites are subject to change).

http://www.educ.state.ak.us/lam/library/hist/goldrush/trail.html

We *strongly recommend* that you preview this site before you send students to it.

❶ Then I made a hike, for I didn't like
  to hear him sizzle so;
And the heavens scowled, and the huskies howled,
  and the wind began to blow.
It was icy cold, but the hot sweat rolled
  down my cheeks, and I don't know why;
And the greasy smoke in an inky cloak
  went streaking down the sky.

I do not know how long in the snow
  I wrestled with grisly fear;
But the stars came out and they danced about
  ere again I ventured near;
I was sick with dread, but I bravely said:
  "I'll just take a peep inside.
I guess he's cooked, and it's time I looked"; . . .
  then the door I opened wide.

❷ And there sat Sam, looking cool and calm,
  in the heart of the furnace roar;
And he wore a smile you could see a mile,
  and he said: "Please close that door.
It's fine in here, but I greatly fear
  you'll let in the cold and storm—
Since I left Plumtree, down in Tennessee,
  it's the first time I've been warm."

❸ *There are strange things done in the midnight sun*
  By the men who moil for gold;
The Arctic trails have their secret tales
  That would make your blood run cold;
The Northern Lights have seen queer sights,
  But the queerest they ever did see
Was that night on the marge of Lake Lebarge
  I cremated Sam McGee.

◆Build Vocabulary

grisly (griz´ lē) *adj.*: Horrible

Cross-Curricular Connection: Social Studies

Primary Source Documents Historians often use information from original documents such as letters, diary entries, ledgers, and official records to accurately describe a certain period in history. Tell students that the following (partial) list is from a letter written in 1897 by Dan Shure to his sister and brother. Shure was gathering materials for himself and a partner to take on a prospecting trip to the Yukon. Discuss with students what the list reveals about the life of a Yukon prospector.

Our latest improved rifles, with plenty of ammunition
Six pairs snow glasses
2 Axes - 3 shovels - 3 picks
3 gold pans and one rocker Also Some quicksilver
1 Frying pan - 1 Baking Pan
1 coffee pot - 6 granite cups
2 large spoons - knives & forks & spoons
4 granite plates - 1 Brace & set of bits
200 ft. $\frac{5}{8}$" rope - Oakum
Batchelors buttons - needles & thread
Leather soles, already cut out
Rubber patches - rubber cement
Our large magnet, also magnifying glass
A quantity of Lime juice to keep off scurvy
Oiled canvas sheet to lay under blanket
Sheet iron stove - Reflector for baking
2 heavy pocket knives - Candle wicks
250 lbs. Bacon Smoked extra heavy - Matches
500 Wheat Flour - Cayenne Pepper
100 Rice - 20 lbs. Coffee - 30 lbs. Tea

History Connection

The Gold Rush Is On! Just like Sam McGee and his buddy, thousands of real people went searching for Yukon gold during the Klondike Gold Rush. Beginning in 1896, when three explorers found gold in a tributary of the Klondike River, the rush took off at breakneck speed. The town of Dawson sprang up to house and serve nearly 25,000 miners. However, the Klondike Gold Rush didn't last long. Few individual prospectors could get at the gold, especially in the Yukon's frozen climate. Big mining groups quickly took over, and the population shrank.

Cross-Curricular Activity

Mining the Past Use encyclopedias, library reference books, and sites on the World Wide Web to find out about mining in the Yukon—in the past and in the present. Focus on how Klondike prospectors searched for gold. Identify the kind of equipment that was used, and find out how the land was manipulated to make mining possible. Then, study the way Yukon mining works today. Create a comparison-and-contrast chart showing the relationship between mining then and now.

Guide for Responding

◆ LITERATURE AND YOUR LIFE

Reader's Response What was your reaction to the ending of the poem? Why?

Thematic Focus Do you admire the narrator for keeping his promise? Why or why not?

One-Liner Ask your classmates what they think their first words would be if they discovered a revived Sam in the furnace.

☑ Check Your Comprehension

1. What problem does Sam McGee have with his surroundings?
2. Why doesn't he go home?
3. What does Sam ask the narrator to promise?
4. How is the narrator supposed to keep his promise?
5. Describe what the narrator finds when he opens the furnace door.

◆ Critical Thinking

INTERPRET

1. What do Sam's fears reveal about his personality? **[Infer]**
2. Why is the speaker so determined to keep his promise? **[Interpret]**
3. What conflicting emotions drive the speaker as he works to fulfill his promise? **[Analyze]**
4. How do you think each character feels at the end of the poem? **[Draw Conclusions]**

APPLY

5. Do you agree with the narrator that "a promise made is a debt unpaid"? Why or why not? **[Make a Judgment]**

EXTEND

6. Speculate about the ways in which modern prospectors might use special equipment and clothing to make their Yukon journeys safer and more comfortable. **[Science Link]**

Reinforce and Extend

Answers

◆ LITERATURE AND YOUR LIFE

Reader's Response Most students will express surprise and delight at the poem's humorous ending. Some students may see the dark humor in this poem as being similar to jokes they have heard.

Thematic Focus Most students will probably admire the narrator for keeping a promise under difficult circumstances.

☑ Check Your Comprehension

1. He hates the cold temperature of the Yukon.
2. He wants to find gold.
3. He asks that the narrator cremate his body when he dies.
4. The narrator must find fuel and a sheltered place for a fire.
5. He finds Sam alive, well, and warm.

◆ Critical Thinking

1. Possible response: He has little confidence in his ability to withstand discomfort.
2. He believes that promises are like "debts unpaid."
3. He feels obligated to Sam but resents the extra load.
4. Sam may feel triumphant because he is finally warm. Cap may feel angry at Sam for taking advantage of his sense of honor.
5. Most students will agree that a promise is a commitment that should be kept.
6. Clothing like down jackets and gloves, warm boots, and synthetic fibers such as polar fleece and capilene would help keep prospectors warm. They might use equipment like portable stoves and body heaters, sleeping bags, and tents.

Beyond the Selection

FURTHER READING

Other Works by Robert W. Service

Best Tales of the Yukon
The Best of Robert Service
Collected Poems of Robert Service

INTERNET

We suggest the following site on the Internet for more information about Robert W. Service (all Web sites are subject to change).

http://www.top.monad.net/~artude/service.html#biography

We *strongly recommend* that you preview this site before you send students to it.

◆Reading Strategy

1. The speaker is named Cap.
2. Possible response: He is an honest man who has strong integrity and takes his promises seriously.
3. Possible response: The story might focus on different details like the cold if it were told from Sam's point of view.

◆Build Vocabulary

Using Shades of Meaning

1. *Frigid* expresses a more intense feeling than *cold*.
2. *Frantic* expresses a feeling of being out of control. *Worried* is less intense.
3. *Grow* describes a slow process. *Expand* describes a more active process.

Spelling Strategy

1. where
2. wear
3. while
4. wily

Using the Word Bank

1. f
2. a
3. e
4. c
5. b
6. d

◆Literary Focus

1. The narrator must find a way to cremate the body of Sam McGee.
2. The poem is set in the Yukon Territory, a region of extreme cold. The setting is central to the story because Sam cannot withstand the extreme temperature.
3. The repetitive rhyme of the poem sometimes creates a bleak mood. ("Talk of your cold! through the parka's fold it stabbed like a driven nail.") At other times, the almost singsong quality suggests an upbeat mood. ("And the dogs were fed, and the stars o'erhead were dancing heel and toe. . . .")

◆Build Grammar Skills

Practice

1. worst
2. less
3. More
4. best
5. better

Guide for Responding *(continued)*

◆ Reading Strategy

Identify the Speaker

The **speaker** is the voice through which a poem is told. Because the speaker's perspective affects how the characters, details, and events are presented, identifying the speaker and drawing conclusions about his personality can help you unlock a poem's meaning.

1. Who is the speaker of "The Cremation of Sam McGee"?

2. How would you describe the speaker's personality and values?

3. How might this poem be different if it were told from another point of view?

◆ Build Vocabulary

Using Shades of Meaning

Both *loathed* and *disliked* describe a degree of hatred, but each of these words suggests a different intensity, or shade of meaning. *Loathed* is much stronger than *disliked*. Identify the different shades of meaning in the following word pairs.

1. cold, frigid **2.** worried, frantic **3.** grow, expand

Spelling Strategy

The *hw* sound in *whimper* and many other words is spelled *wh*. Add either *w* or *wh* to correctly complete each word:

1. __?__ere: word to indicate place

2. __?__ear: to have on the body, as a shirt or jacket

3. __?__ile: as something happens

4. __?__ily: clever

Using the Word Bank

On your paper, write the letter of the best definition for each word.

1. ghastly	**a.** hated
2. loathed	**b.** strict
3. grisly	**c.** burned into ashes
4. cremated	**d.** make low crying sounds
5. stern	**e.** horrible
6. whimper	**f.** frightful; like a ghost

◆ Literary Focus

Narrative Poetry

A **narrative poem** tells a story with characters, a setting, and a plot. For example, "The Cremation of Sam McGee" features two characters—the speaker and Sam McGee—who struggle against the elements of Canada's Yukon Territory.

1. What central conflict drives the poem's plot?

2. Describe the poem's setting and how it affects the story.

3. How do the poem's rhythms create different moods? Give two examples.

◆ Build Grammar Skills

Irregular Comparison of Modifiers

The narrator of "Sam McGee" comments that the trail was bad. If he wanted to compare this trail with another, he could describe one as worse.

A few **modifiers,** such as *good* and *bad,* are **irregular**—their comparative and superlative forms are not constructed in the same way as most other modifiers. Look at these common examples:

Positive	Comparative	Superlative
bad	worse	worst
good	better	best
well	better	best
little	less	least
much	more	most

Practice On your paper, write the correct form of the modifier in parentheses.

1. This was the __?__ trip ever. (*bad*)

2. There was __?__ food than on the last trip. (*little*)

3. __?__ snow fell than last year. (*much*)

4. The __?__ moment of the trip was when she finally reached the warm cabin. (*good*)

5. She slept __?__ there than she had in weeks. (*well*)

Writing Application Write a paragraph describing your reactions to "The Cremation of Sam McGee." Use the comparative or superlative forms of at least four irregular modifiers.

Writing Application

Sample paragraph:

I really like the poem "The Cremation of Sam McGee." My least favorite part was when Sam died because I hate cold weather even more than he does. The best part was the surprise ending. I felt better to learn that Sam was alive after all.

Writer's Solution

For additional instruction and practice, use the lesson in the *Writer's Solution Language Lab CD-ROM* on Comparatives. You may also use the page on Using the Comparative and Superlative Degrees, p. 80, in the *Writer's Solution Grammar Practice Book.*

Build Your Portfolio

Idea Bank

Writing

1. **Tabloid Article** Write an article about the mysterious and unbelievable events described in the poem for the kind of "newspaper" you see at supermarket checkout counters. Exaggerate the details of the narrative as much as you can.
2. **Wilderness Code** Keeping a promise might be especially important in a frontier environment like the Yukon. In a short essay, describe a code of conduct to outline the rules of behavior in this harsh wilderness environment.
3. **Tall Tale** A tall tale is characterized by a larger-than-life hero, humor, references to local places and landmarks, and characters who are common people. Tall tales are invented to entertain, rather than to teach a lesson. Explain how this poem fits into the American tall-tale tradition. Discuss how elements of this poem do or do not fit the different characteristics.

Speaking and Listening

4. **Weather Report** Develop and deliver a report for the Klondike Weather Channel. Using information from the poem, tell prospectors about the conditions they will face. **[Science Link]**
5. **Conversation** Consider what happened after the narrator made his strange discovery. With a partner, role-play a conversation between the narrator and Sam McGee.

Projects

6. **Yukon Research** **[Group Activity]** In a group, divide the task of researching the cultures, geography, and industries of the Yukon. Work together to combine your findings into a single report, including maps and illustrations. **[Geography Link]**
7. **Map** Create an illustrated map of the journey described in the poem. Add notes showing where specific events took place. Include a key explaining the symbols you've used. **[Art Link; Social Studies Link]**

Writing Mini-Lesson

Diary Entry

Imagine the narrator's surprise when he discovers Sam McGee sitting happily in the fire. What other emotions do you suppose he'd feel? Assuming the role of the narrator, write a diary entry about the events described in the poem and what happened afterward.

Writing Skills Focus: Sensory Details

The narrator's journey through the snow wasn't easy. To help readers experience the journey and its surprising conclusion, use vivid **sensory details**—details that capture sights, sounds, smells, tastes, and physical sensations. For example, you might describe the sound of the fire *crackling* or the *biting* cold of the arctic air.

Prewriting Decide how you, as the narrator, feel. Are you relieved that your friend is defrosted? Are you annoyed with Sam for all the trouble he caused? Are you disturbed, or do you take the weird events in stride?

Drafting Begin with a description of how you felt when you found Sam. Use sensory details to paint a picture of that moment. Then, expand the details to support your main emotion with memories from the trip or plans for future action. For example, if your main emotion is anger, you might outline how you will teach Sam a lesson about his behavior.

◆ **Grammar Application**

As you describe your feelings, make sure you use irregular modifiers correctly.

Revising Read your diary entry aloud. Check that your sensory details create a clear picture of your experiences. Confirm that each detail supports your central emotions. If necessary, replace weak sensory details with more commanding words.

ASSESSMENT OPTIONS

Formal Assessment, Selection Test, pp. 204–206, and Assessment Resources Software. The selection test is designed so that it can easily be customized to the performance levels of your students.

Alternative Assessment, p. 42, includes options for less advanced students, more advanced students, verbal/linguistic learners, musical/rhythmic learners, logical/mathematical learners, interpersonal learners, and visual/spatial learners.

PORTFOLIO ASSESSMENT

Use the following rubrics in the **Alternative Assessment** booklet to assess student writing:
Tabloid Article: Description, p. 84
Wilderness Code: Definition/Classification, p. 86
Tall Tale: Comparison/Contrast, p. 90
Writing Mini-Lesson: Expression, p. 81

Idea Bank

Following are suggestions for matching the Idea Bank topics with your students' performance levels and learning modalities:

Customize for *Performance Levels*
Less Advanced Students: 1, 4
Average Students: 2, 4, 5, 6
More Advanced Students: 3, 6, 7

Customize for *Learning Modalities*
Verbal/Linguistic: 1, 2, 3, 4, 5
Interpersonal: 5, 6
Visual/Spatial: 7
Logical/Mathematical: 4, 6
Intrapersonal: 2

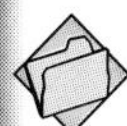

Writing Mini-Lesson

Refer students to the Writing Handbook in the back of the book for instructions on the writing process for further information on personal narratives. Have students use the Sensory Language Chart in **Writing and Language Transparencies,** p. 78, to arrange their prewriting examples.

Writer's Solution

Writing Lab CD-ROM
Have students complete their diary entries by using the tutorial on Expression. Follow these steps:

1. Have students view the video clip from *Star Trek* that gives examples of vivid details used to express personal thoughts.
2. Tell students to use the interactive Notecards activity to organize their details.
3. Encourage students to refer to the Proofreading Checklist during the revision stage.

Writer's Solution Sourcebook
Have students use Chapter 1, "Expression," pp. 1–31, for additional support. This chapter includes in-depth instruction on subject-verb agreement (pp. 25–26) and pronoun use (pp. 27–28).

Prepare and Engage

OBJECTIVES

1. To read, comprehend, and interpret four poems
2. To relate lyric poetry to personal experience
3. To use the senses while reading poetry
4. To analyze lyric poetry
5. To build vocabulary in context and use the word root *-rad-*
6. To recognize the correct use of *good* and *well*
7. To write an introduction to a poetry collection
8. To respond to the poems through writing, speaking and listening, and projects

SKILLS INSTRUCTION

Vocabulary: Word Roots: *-rad-*
Spelling: Using *-sy* to End Words With the *see* Sound
Grammar: Correct Use of *Good* and *Well*
Reading Strategy: Use Your Senses
Literary Focus: Lyric Poetry
Writing: Elaborate on an Idea
Speaking and Listening: Dramatic Reading (Teacher Edition)
Critical Viewing: Compare and Contrast; Relate; Connect

PORTFOLIO OPPORTUNITIES

Writing: Recommendation; Nature Poem; Literary Response
Writing Mini-Lesson: Introduction to a Poetry Collection
Speaking and Listening: Lyrics Presentation; Dramatic Reading
Projects: Seasonal Preparation; Nature Walk

More About the Authors

James Stephens wrote *Crock of Gold* in 1912. Filled with poetic imagery, this novel was adapted as a musical, *Finnian's Rainbow,* in 1947.

Sara Teasdale is known for the power and intensity of her lyrics. Her later poetry encourages women to find fulfillment in their own achievements.

Nikki Giovanni is a poet, essayist, lecturer, and teacher of English at Virginia Polytechnical Institute.

William Butler Yeats served as a senator of the Irish Free State from 1916–1922. He received the Nobel Prize for poetry in 1923.

Guide for Reading

Meet the Authors:

James Stephens (1880–1950)

Growing up in a poor neighborhood in Dublin, James Stephens read everything he could get his hands on. He came to love Ireland's powerful legends and fairy tales. Later, he began to write poetry and novels. "Washed in Silver" captures the magical quality of Irish legends.

Sara Teasdale (1884–1933)

Although her life was short and unhappy, Sara Teasdale left behind a body of poetry charged with emotional intensity. Born in St. Louis, Missouri, Teasdale led a sheltered childhood of carefully chosen schools and travel. She began to write while still young and was quickly successful, winning a Pulitzer Prize in 1918.

Nikki Giovanni (1943–)

Nikki Giovanni's poems share the major events in her life—working for civil rights, celebrating the birth of her son, and experiencing the joys of African American family life. In "Winter," she writes about a universal subject: the changing of the seasons.

William Butler Yeats (1865–1939)

Irish poet William Butler Yeats is regarded as one of the finest poets the world has ever known. His poems offer evidence of his keen powers of observation, a talent sharpened by his study of painting.

◆ Literature and Your Life

CONNECT YOUR EXPERIENCE

Waterfalls cascading downward, mountains rising to the heavens, flowers blooming in a city park—scenes from nature have the power to stir our emotions and imaginations. As these poems reveal, nature can also help people discover themselves.

THEMATIC FOCUS: Nature's Wonders

As you read, take note of what each poet discovers by exploring nature's wonders. How do these discoveries compare with one you've made?

◆ Background for Understanding

SCIENCE

Nikki Giovanni describes the ways people and animals prepare for winter. If you live in a wintry environment, you can turn up the heat and eat hearty foods, but animals don't have this luxury. Some animals—like bears, frogs, and hedgehogs—go into hibernation to survive the cold. Their bodies slip into a state of inactivity. Such life functions as heartbeat, breathing rate, and growth slow until they are almost stopped. In this sleeplike state, hibernating animals burn energy very slowly. That way, the food they have stored as fat can last until the spring.

◆ Build Vocabulary

WORD ROOTS: *-rad-*

James Stephens describes the *radiance* of the moon's light. The root of this word is *-rad-*, which means "spoke or branch." This root offers an important clue to the meaning of *radiance*: "quality of sending out rays of light."

WORD BANK

Which of these words from the poems would you use to describe a place where a groundhog lives?

radiance
strife
ecstasy
burrow

Prentice Hall Literature Program Resources

REINFORCE / RETEACH / EXTEND

Selection Support Pages
Build Vocabulary: Word Roots *-rad-*, p. 234
Build Spelling Skills, p. 235
Build Grammar Skills: Correct Use of *Good* and *Well,* p. 236
Reading Strategy: Use Your Senses, p. 237
Literary Focus: Lyric Poetry, p. 238

Strategies for Diverse Student Needs, pp. 85–86

Beyond Literature Cultural Connection: The Barter System, p. 43

Formal Assessment Selection Test, pp. 207–209, Assessment Resources Software

Alternative Assessment, p. 43

Writing and Language Transparencies Main Idea and Supporting Details Organizer, p. 70

Resource Pro CD-ROM
Includes all selections

Listening to Literature Audiocassettes
Includes all selections

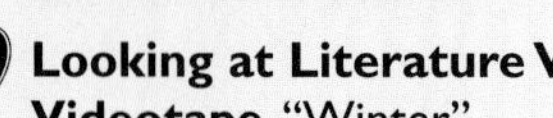

Looking at Literature Videodisc/ Videotape "Winter"

Washed in Silver ◆ Barter ◆ Winter ◆ Down by the Salley Gardens ◆

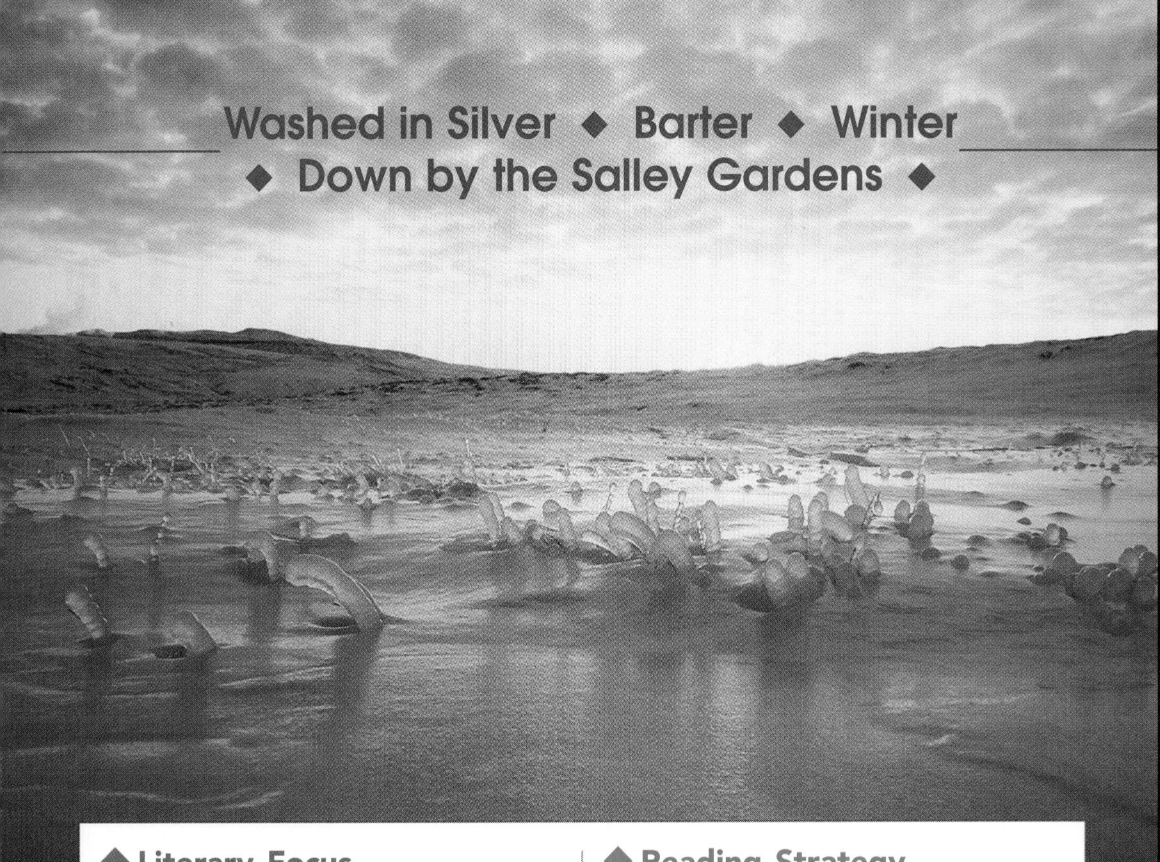

◆ Literary Focus

Lyric Poetry

Nature is a common subject of **lyric poetry,** verse that expresses a poet's personal thoughts and feelings. Once sung to the music of a stringed instrument called a lyre (which gives lyric poetry its name), lyric poetry sweeps you into the poet's world with vivid, musical language. For example, when Sara Teasdale commands "spend all you have for loveliness," you feel the strength of her longing for beauty. These memorable words and phrases echo in your mind like song lyrics (named for the same historical instrument), and the poet's emotions take hold in your mind.

◆ Reading Strategy

Use Your Senses

Most lyric poetry is filled with vivid images, or word pictures. To experience the imagery, **use your senses**—close your eyes and try to see, hear, touch, taste, and smell what the poet describes. For example, you might feel the cool mud around a burrowing frog or hear the lilt of a young woman's voice. Give this process a trial run by studying the photograph above. As you look at it, feel the frigid air around you and see the silvery reflections of sunlight on the icy water. As you read, use a chart like the one below to record the sensations you experience through the poetry.

	Sight	Hearing	Touch	Taste	Smell
Washed in Silver					

Interest Grabber Show students a photograph of a beautiful scene in nature. As students look at the image, have them imagine that they are outdoors enjoying the pictured scene. Ask students what senses they would use to appreciate the sight. Use students' responses to guide them to the conclusion that being in nature increases one's awareness of sights, sounds, smells, tastes, and textures. Tell students that they will need to use their senses to appreciate the four poems they will read.

◆ Build Grammar Skills

Correct Use of *Good* and *Well*
If you wish to introduce the grammar concept for these selections before students read, refer to the instruction on p. 750.

Customize for
Less Proficient Readers
To help students hear the musical quality of these lyric poems, have them listen to the audiocassette of the poems prior to reading. Direct them to listen for words that appeal to the senses.

Listening to Literature Audiocassettes

Customize for
More Advanced Students
Explain that although these poems are based on the poets' experiences in nature, each one has a different focus. Ask students to consider what may have inspired each poet to write his or her poem. Have them meet in small groups to discuss their ideas.

Preparing for Standardized Tests

Grammar Standardized tests may require students to apply editing skills to show their understanding of correct usage. This sample test item uses a test-taking approach that requires students to demonstrate their understanding of the correct use of *good* and *well.*

Choose the best way to write this sentence:

Roger read good when he presented "Winter."

(A) Roger read better when he presented "Winter."
(B) Roger read well when he presented "Winter."
(C) Roger's presentation of "Winter" was well.
(D) No change

Students should apply their knowledge of the correct use of *good* and *well* to recognize that *(A)* changes the meaning of the sentence by using *better*. In addition, choosing just any answer with an adverb may not answer this test item correctly—*(C)* changes the word being modified to *presentation,* requiring an adjective rather than an adverb. In this sample test item, *well* modifies the verb *read*, so *(B)* is the correct answer.

Tell students that when they are taking tests, if they know the material and read the questions carefully, the first answer they select is probably the best choice that they can make.

Develop Understanding

"Washed in Silver" describes a moonlit evening. The speaker describes how the moon shines on the hills and sea creating a sense of awe.

◆Literary Focus

❶ **Lyric Poetry** Discuss that the musical quality of lyric poetry depends on the way the words sound when spoken aloud. Invite a volunteer to read the first verse aloud. Discuss that the poet repeats the *s* sound to help express his feelings about a moonlit evening. Have students identify examples of this alliteration. What other examples of alliteration do they find in the poem? *Students should recognize that the* s *sound occurs at the beginning of "silver," the ending of "hills," and the beginning of "sea." Other examples of alliteration include "silver radiance spills," and "March magnificently."*

◆Reading Strategy

❷ **Use Your Senses** Ask students what "silver tissue" might look and feel like. *Possible response: Tissue feels crisp and looks somewhat transparent. Silver tissue might sparkle as it reflects the light of the moon.*

◆Literature and Your Life

Discuss that moonlight has inspired poets for centuries. Ask students to describe how a beautiful moonlit night makes them feel. Have them contrast this feeling with the feeling they experience on a night with no moon. *Students may agree that moonlight sometimes creates feelings of magnificence. Dark nights, however, may make them feel fearful.*

▶Critical Viewing◀

❸ **Compare and Contrast** Explain that the photograph shows snow-covered trees beside the Dal River in Sweden. *The photograph shows light reflected from a body of water; however there is no moon or hills.*

Washed in Silver

James Stephens

❶ Gleaming in silver are the hills!
Blazing in silver is the sea!

And a silvery <u>radiance</u> spills
Where the moon drives royally!

❷ Clad in silver tissue, I
March magnificently by!

◀ **Critical Viewing** Which details in the poem are represented in the photograph? Which are not? **[Compare and Contrast]** ❸

◆ Build Vocabulary

radiance (rā′ dē əns) *n.*: Quality of shining brightly

strife (strīf) *n.*: Fighting; conflict

ecstasy (ek′ stə sē) *n.*: Overpowering joy

Block Scheduling Strategies

Consider these suggestions to take advantage of extended class time:

- Review the Literary Focus before students read the poems. After they read, have them work in small groups to answer and discuss the Literary Focus questions on p. 750.
- Next, suggest that students reread each poem, while filling in the chart on p. 745. Instruct groups of students to compare and discuss their charts and to answer the Reading Strategy questions on p. 750. For additional practice, use **Selection Support,** p. 237.
- Consider combining the Nature Walk and the Nature Poem activities from the Idea Bank, p. 751. If possible, allow students who participate in the Nature Walk to write their poems while outdoors.
- Have students work in small groups, using the *Writer's Solution Writing Lab CD-ROM* to complete the Writing Mini-Lesson on p. 751.

Barter

Sara Teasdale

❹ Life has loveliness to sell,
All beautiful and splendid things,
Blue waves whitened on a cliff,
Soaring fire that sways and sings,
And children's faces looking up
Holding wonder like a cup.

Life has loveliness to sell,
❺ Music like a curve of gold,
Scent of pine trees in the rain,
Eyes that love you, arms that hold,
And for your spirit's still delight,
Holy thoughts that star the night.

Spend all you have for loveliness,
Buy it and never count the cost;
For one white singing hour of peace
Count many a year of strife well lost, ❻
And for a breath of ecstasy
Give all you have been, or could be.

Guide for Responding

◆ Literature and Your Life

Reader's Response Which poem do you like better—"Washed in Silver" or "Barter"? Why?

Thematic Focus Both poems celebrate the beauty in nature. "Washed in Silver" focuses on one aspect of nature's beauty, while "Barter" mentions several. Based on the details in the poems and the speaker's attitude, explain what you think nature means to each of the poets.

☑ Check Your Comprehension

1. What natural scene does Stephens describe in "Washed in Silver"?
2. What does the speaker in "Barter" say life has to offer people?
3. Name three examples of natural beauty that are mentioned in "Barter."

◆ Critical Thinking

INTERPRET

1. In "Washed in Silver," what does the speaker mean by saying he is "Clad in silver tissue"? **[Interpret]**
2. Explain what the poem's title, "Washed in Silver," means. **[Draw Conclusions]**
3. There is no money in a barter system. Instead, goods and services are used as currency. What are the units of exchange in "Barter"? **[Interpret]**
4. What advice does the speaker give to readers in "Barter?" **[Infer]**

EVALUATE

5. Do you think that the speaker gives good advice in "Barter"? Explain. **[Assess]**

COMPARE LITERARY WORKS

6. Do you think the speaker in "Washed in Silver" would agree with the advice in "Barter"? Explain. **[Literature Link]**

◆ Reading Strategy

❹ **Use Your Senses** Ask students to what senses the images in these lines appeal. What words and phrases does the poet use to achieve this? *The poet uses these words and phrases to appeal to the senses of sight and sound: "Blue waves," "whitened," "Soaring fire," "sways and sings."*

◆ Critical Thinking

❺ **Interpret** Discuss the fact that lyric poetry often contains similes and metaphors in which unlike objects are compared. Ask students to identify the objects that are compared in line 8. *The poet compares music to a curve of gold.* Ask students what type of music they feel the poet is referring to with this comparison. *Accept all reasonable responses.*

◆ Literary Focus

❻ **Lyric Poetry** Invite students to share their interpretations of the poet's personal thoughts and feelings as expressed in this verse. *Students may say that the poet encourages the reader to seek happiness or "one white singing hour of peace," even if its achievement involves pain or strife.*

Customize for
English Language Learners
To help students hear the vivid, musical language of lyric poetry, have them read along as they listen to the recording of the two poems on these pages. Then have them reread the poems silently to themselves.

Listening to Literature Audiocassettes

Reinforce and Extend

Answers

◆ Literature and Your Life

Reader's Response Students may say that they enjoy the imagery and the sound of the words in "Washed in Silver." Others may say that they agree with the advice in "Barter."

Thematic Focus Possible response:
To Stephens, nature is in the wonder of the scenery, as in the passing seasons.
To Teasdale, the beauty of nature can also be seen in human relationships.

☑ Check Your Comprehension

1. He describes a moonlit night.
2. She says life offers loveliness.
3. Students may mention waves, children's faces, and the scent of pine trees.

◆ Critical Thinking

1. The speaker is lit by moonlight.
2. The title indicates that the landscape is bathed in moonlight.
3. They are life's loveliness and life's pain, or strife.
4. The speaker advises readers that peace and happiness are worth the pain it takes to achieve them.
5. Some students may say that the poem encourages them to seek goals without fearing possible risks. Others may say that there is always both beauty and pain.
6. Possible response: Yes, the speaker values nature's beauty and would probably trade a great deal for it.

Develop Understanding

This poem describes activities that help animals and people prepare for winter.

◆Reading Strategy

1 Use Your Senses Ask students how they can use their senses to better understand this verse. *Readers might imagine the smell of the dirt and of clothes hanging outside. They might also imagine the feel of the crisp air.*

◆Critical Thinking

2 Analyze Ask students why they think that the speaker places book collecting in the same verse with bears that store fat and chipmunks that gather nuts. *Students may say that reading provides nourishment for the poet's soul, just as fat and nuts provide nourishment for the animals' bodies.*

▶Critical Viewing◀

3 Relate *In winter, it is difficult to travel outdoors to gather food and other necessities of life.*

Looking at Literature Videodisc/Videotape

Play Chapter 9 of the videodisc, in which Nikki Giovanni stresses the importance of observing the world around her. Ask students to discuss how "Winter" reflects her interest in observation.

Chapter 9

Winter

Nikki Giovanni

(1)
Frogs burrow the mud
snails bury themselves
and I air my quilts
preparing for the cold

Dogs grow more hair
mothers make oatmeal
and little boys and girls
take Father John's Medicine[1]

Bears store fat
chipmunks gather nuts
(2) and I collect books
For the coming winter

1. **Father John's Medicine:** An old-fashioned cough syrup.

◆ Build Vocabulary

burrow (bur´ ō) *v.*: To dig a hole or tunnel, especially for shelter

Cross Country, 1989, Karl J. Kuerner III, David David Gallery

(3) ▶ Critical Viewing Why is winter, as pictured here, a time that demands the preparations the poem describes? **[Relate]**

Speaking and Listening Mini-Lesson

Dramatic Reading

This mini-lesson supports the Speaking and Listening activity in the Idea Bank on p. 751.

Introduce Explain that a dramatic reading helps bring a poem to life. Tell students that to prepare for the reading, they must decide where to take a breath, where to increase or decrease volume, and where to pause or stop. They might also decide whether to use vocal effects such as whispering or raising their voices.

Develop Have students select a poem. Then discuss the following questions with them before they rehearse their dramatic reading:

- What mood should I strive for?
- What vocal effects might create this mood?
- Which punctuation marks in my poem indicate a pause? Which indicate a stop?

Apply Ask students to rehearse their readings with a partner, then perform them for the class.

Assess Have students evaluate each dramatic reading on how readers create a certain mood and how they use their voices to enhance the poem. Or, you may also want to have students use the Peer Assessment form for Oral Interpretation, p. 106, in **Alternative Assessment.**

Down by the Salley[1] Gardens

William Butler Yeats

Down by the salley gardens my love and I did meet;
She passed the salley gardens with little snow-white feet.
She bid me take love easy, as the leaves grow on the tree;
But I, being young and foolish, with her would not agree.

In a field by the river my love and I did stand,
And on my leaning shoulder she laid her snow-white hand.
She bid me take life easy, as the grass grows on the weirs;[2]
❹ But I was young and foolish, and now am full of tears.

1. **salley** (sal′ ē) *n.*: Type of willow tree.
2. **weirs** (wirz) *n.*: Low dams in a river.

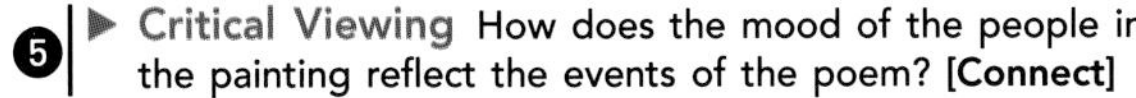

❺ ▶ Critical Viewing How does the mood of the people in the painting reflect the events of the poem? **[Connect]**

Les Adieux (The Good-bye), James L. Tissot, City of Bristol Museum and Art Gallery, England

Guide for Responding

◆ Literature and Your Life

Reader's Response What do you think of the speaker of "Down by the Salley Gardens"? Why?

Thematic Focus What pictures of nature's processes do "Winter" and "Down by the Salley Gardens" create?

Journal Writing In a brief journal entry, describe your impressions of winter.

☑ Check Your Comprehension

1. In "Winter," why are all the characters making preparations?
2. What two things does the speaker do to prepare for this coming season?
3. In Yeats's poem, where do the speaker and his love go?
4. What does the speaker's love ask him to do?
5. How does the speaker respond to her request?
6. What is the result of the speaker's actions?

◆ Critical Thinking

Interpret

1. In "Winter," how do the speaker's actions suggest the coming of winter? **[Connect]**
2. In what ways does this poem suggest that people and animals are alike? **[Compare and Contrast]**
3. In "Down by the Salley Gardens," how does the speaker's love use nature to support her request? **[Connect]**
4. Explain how the speaker and his love differ. **[Compare and Contrast]**
5. What do you think has happened to the love between the two people in "Down by the Salley Gardens"? **[Speculate]**

Evaluate

6. Is it wiser to "take life easy"? Explain. **[Criticize]**

Apply

7. How might an acceptance of natural cycles help people improve their lives? **[Relate]**

Develop Understanding

One-Minute Insight In "Down by the Salley Gardens," the speaker's sweetheart advises him to "take love easy." Because he doesn't heed her advice, he later finds himself alone.

◆ Literary Focus

❹ **Lyric Poetry** Ask students what emotions the speaker expresses in line 8. *feelings of despair and regret that he did not heed his love's advice*

▶ Critical Viewing ◀

❺ **Connect** *Some students may note that the woman is behind a fence and has her head down as if she may be uncertain of her feelings.*

Reinforce and Extend

Answers

◆ Literature and Your Life

Reader's Response Some students may say that he caused his own troubles. Others may feel sorry for him.

Thematic Focus The poems suggest that nature's work comes easily.

☑ Check Your Comprehension

1. They are preparing for winter.
2. She airs quilts and collects books.
3. They go to the salley gardens and to a field by a river.
4. To take love and life easy.
5. He does not heed her advice.
6. He is now "full of tears."

◆ Critical Thinking

1. The speaker is gathering quilts and books to use indoors.
2. They both prepare for winter.
3. She compares taking love and life easy to leaves and grass growing.
4. The speaker wants to live his life vigorously. His love wants him to take a cautious approach to life.
5. Possible response: The woman ended the relationship.
6. Some students may say being relaxed about life results in less pain. Others may say that without pain, there is less growth.
7. Possible response: When people accept the natural rhythms of their bodies, they are more likely to rest when they need to and work when they need to.

Beyond the Selection

FURTHER READING

Other Works by the Authors

Traditional Irish Fairy Tales, James Stephens

The Collected Poems of Sara Teasdale, Sara Teasdale

Ego-Tripping and Other Poems for Young People, Nikki Giovanni

The Collected Poems of W. B. Yeats, W. B. Yeats

INTERNET

We suggest the following sites on the Internet (all Web sites are subject to change).

For more on Sara Teasdale:
http://www.st-louis.mo.us/st-louis/walkofame/inductees/teasdale.html

For Nikki Giovanni, try:
http://pilot.msu.edu/user/jacks302/nikki.htm

For W. B. Yeats:
http://www.golden-dawn.org/bioyeats.html

We *strongly recommend* that you preview these sites before you send students to them.

◆ Literary Focus

1. Possible response: Stephens communicates a feeling of bliss; Teasdale communicates a feeling of appreciation; Giovanni communicates a feeling of being a part of nature; Yeats communicates opposite feelings of joy and despair.
2. Possible response: In "Washed in Silver," Stephens repeats the "s" sound. This adds a musical quality to the poem and emphasizes the word *silver.* In "Barter," Teasdale repeats the line, "Life has loveliness to sell," to support the main idea of the poem. In "Winter," Giovanni repeats the pattern of a noun followed by an active verb to emphasize the activity of winter preparations. In "Down by the Salley Gardens," Yeats repeats much of the first verse in the second to contrast his feelings of joy and pain.
3. Any of the poems would be appropriate. Be certain that students provide support for their opinions.

◆ Reading Strategy

1. Possible responses: "Washed in Silver": "gleaming hills" (sight); "silver tissue" (touch). "Barter": "soaring fire" (touch, hearing); "music like a curve of gold" (hearing, sight, touch). "Winter": "snails bury themselves" (touch; sight); "mothers making oatmeal" (smell, taste). ". . . Gardens": "field by the river" (sight, sound, smell); "she laid her snow-white hand" (touch; sight).
2. "Washed in Silver": sight; "Barter": sight/hearing; "Winter": sight/touch; ". . . Gardens": sight

◆ Build Vocabulary

Word Root *-rad-*

1. *radius* a line segment that joins the center of a circle with any point on its circumference
2. *radiology* branch of medicine that deals with the use of ionizing radiation for diagnosis
3. *radiator* A heating device consisting of connected pipes, typically inside an upright metal structure, used to radiate heat into the surrounding space

Spelling Strategy

1. fantasy
2. courtesy
3. jealousy
4. curtsy

Using the Word Bank

1. c
2. a
3. b
4. a

Guide for Responding *(continued)*

◆ Literary Focus

LYRIC POETRY

Lyric poetry expresses a poet's thoughts and emotions about a topic in lively and musical language.

1. What feelings does each poet communicate?
2. Find an example of repetition in each poem. Explain its effect in the poem.
3. Choose one of the poems, and explain why you think it would be effective if set to music.

◆ Reading Strategy

USE YOUR SENSES

Each of these poets uses vivid images, or word pictures, to capture the wonders of nature and to connect nature to the poet's own experiences. By **using your senses** to see, hear, smell, touch, and taste what the poets are describing, you can fully experience the poems.

1. Identify two details from each poem that appeal to your senses. Name the sense you used for each detail.
2. For each poem, tell which sense you used most in reading.

◆ Build Vocabulary

USING THE WORD ROOT *-rad-*

The root *-rad-*, meaning "spoke or branch," usually indicates that the word in which it is found relates to something spreading out from a center. With this meaning in mind, define the words below.

1. radius **2.** radiology **3.** radiator

SPELLING STRATEGY

When the *see* sound appears at the end of a word, it may be spelled *sy*, as in *ecstasy.* On your paper, correctly spell each of the following words.

1. fanta_ _ **2.** courte_ _ **3.** jealou_ _ **4.** curt_ _

USING THE WORD BANK

Identify the best synonym for each word.

1. radiance: (a) darkness, (b) silliness, (c) glow
2. ecstasy: (a) bliss, (b) misery, (c) boredom
3. strife: (a) agreement, (b) conflict, (c) goal
4. burrow: (a) tunnel, (b) emerge, (c) hurdle

◆ Build Grammar Skills

CORRECT USE OF ***good*** AND ***well***

Good is an adjective (a word that describes a noun or pronoun). ***Well*** can be an adjective, but it is usually an adverb (a word that describes a verb, an adjective, or another adverb). In the following line, the adverb *well* modifies the adjective *lost*:

Count many a year of strife *well lost.*

A common mistake is to use *good* rather than *well* after an action verb. Look at this example:

Incorrect: Teasdale wrote *good* even as a girl.
Correct: Teasdale wrote *well* even as a girl.

Practice On your paper, complete each sentence correctly with either *good* or *well.*

1. The scent of pine trees smelled __?__.
2. The moon lit the hills __?__ last night.
3. Winter is described __?__ in the poem.
4. I think a change of season is __?__ for us all.
5. If you prepare __?__, you can survive the season.

Writing Application Write four sentences: two using *good* correctly and two using *well* correctly.

Beyond Literature

History Connection

The Barter System Teasdale's poem "Barter" refers to an economy in which people use goods and services as currency. For example, you might trade a cow for fruit, cloth, or other goods. You might trade several cows to pay for a carpenter's work. Throughout history, and even today, people in some cultures use barter to meet their needs.

Cross-Curricular Activity

A Barter Community With a group, plan a barter system for a community. What skills or products could the people in the group offer? Which skills would be problematic? Summarize the pros and cons of bartering.

750 ◆ Poetry

◆ Build Grammar Skills

Practice

1. good
2. well
3. well
4. good
5. well

Writing Application

Sample sentences:

1. This is a very good book.
2. The apple tastes good.
3. He can skate well.
4. She did not feel well when she left.

Writer's Solution

For additional instruction, use the Glossary of Troublesome Adjectives and Adverbs, p.81, in the *Writer's Solution Grammar Practice Book.*

Build Your Portfolio

Idea Bank

Writing

1. Recommendation If you were to recommend one of these poems, which one would it be? Choose one of the poems. Then, write a note to a friend recommending that he or she read it. Be sure to explain why you are recommending it.

2. Nature Poem Write a nature poem of your own. Use vivid imagery to capture one or more scenes from nature that stand out in your memory. You might also include personal reflections about the scene or scenes you describe.

3. Literary Response Choose one of the poems that you think presents a meaningful message. In an essay, explain how the poem conveys this message, and tell why the message is important to you. Cite details from the poem for support.

Speaking and Listening

4. Lyrics Presentation Find some song lyrics you find especially meaningful. Read them aloud to your classmates. Explain what the lyrics convey to you, and identify language that is vivid and memorable. **[Music Link]**

5. Dramatic Reading Read one of these poems aloud to the class. Use the punctuation to guide where you pause, and use your voice to add emphasis to the most important lines and images. **[Performing Arts Link]**

Projects

6. Seasonal Preparations [Group Activity] With a group, discuss the economic preparations individuals and businesses in your community make for each season. Each of you can generate a list for one season. Review each other's ideas before creating a single list. **[Social Studies Link]**

7. Nature Walk Nature can be viewed and enjoyed even in cities. Plan a nature walk in your area. Create a map showing your route, and identify sites of particular interest. **[Science Link]**

Writing Mini-Lesson

Introduction to a Poetry Collection

While some people enjoy reading the collected works of a specific writer, others prefer to read poems organized by theme. For example, a book of sports poems or an anthology of poems about facing challenges would appeal to many readers. Write an introduction to a collection that includes the four poems presented here. In your introduction, explain how each poem relates to a theme.

Writing Skills Focus: Elaborate on an Idea

To show readers the connection among the poems in your collection, **elaborate on the ideas** you present. Use these tips to develop your points:

- Gather details that support the idea you'll present.
- Provide vivid examples that make your explanation clear.
- Be sure every general statement is supported by a fact.

Prewriting As you review the poems in this group, consider the ideas that tie them together. Decide on the theme of your collection. Then, jot down details that support this theme.

Drafting Begin with a general statement about the poems and the theme you've chosen. Focus each body paragraph on an individual poem, using your notes to develop the theme of your collection.

◆ Grammar Application

When you describe the poems, make sure to use *good* and *well* correctly.

Revising Remember, your introduction should encourage people to read the collection. As you revise, look for places where you can make each poem's connection to the theme more clear.

ASSESSMENT OPTIONS

Formal Assessment, Selection Test, pp. 207–209, and Assessment Resources Software. The selection test is designed so that it can easily be customized to the performance levels of your students.

Alternative Assessment, p. 43, includes options for less advanced students, more advanced students, verbal/linguistic learners, logical/mathematical learners, intrapersonal learners, visual/spatial learners, and musical/rhythmic learners.

PORTFOLIO ASSESSMENT

Use the following rubrics in the **Alternative Assessment** booklet to assess student writing:
Recommendation: Persuasion, p. 92
Nature Poem: Poetry, p. 95
Literary Response: Response to Literature, p. 97
Writing Mini-Lesson: Definition/Classification, p. 86

Beyond Literature

To help students get started on the activity, discuss with them how they could use their skills to barter with one another. For example, a student who is good in math might offer tutoring to a friend who can repair skateboards.

Idea Bank

Following are suggestions for matching the Idea Bank topics with your students' performance levels and learning modalities:

Customize for *Performance Levels*
Less Advanced Students: 1, 4
Average Students: 2, 4, 5, 6
More Advanced Students: 3, 6, 7

Customize for *Learning Modalities*
Verbal/Linguistic: 1, 2, 3, 4, 5
Interpersonal: 1, 5, 6
Visual/Spatial: 7
Logical/Mathematical: 6
Intrapersonal: 7

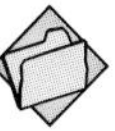

Writing Mini-Lesson

Refer students to the Writing Handbook in the back of the book for instructions on the writing process. Have students use the Main Idea and Supporting Details Organizer in **Writing and Language Transparencies,** p. 70, to arrange their prewriting examples.

Writer's Solution

Writing Lab CD-ROM
Have students use the tutorial on Exposition: Giving Information to complete their introductions. Follow these steps:

1. Have them view the interactive model to hear a writer's insights about purpose.
2. As they draft on computer, direct students to use the Transition Word Bin.
3. Have students use the Self-Evaluation Checklist to help them critically evaluate their writing.

Writer's Solution Sourcebook
Have students use Chapter 4, Exposition: "Giving Information," pp. 102–133, for additional support. This chapter includes in-depth instruction on organizing details (p. 122).

Prepare and Engage

OBJECTIVES

1. To read, comprehend, and interpret two poems and three haiku
2. To relate forms in poems to personal experience
3. To read poetry according to punctuation
4. To recognize different forms of poetry
5. To build vocabulary in context and identify synonyms
6. To understand the placement of the adverb *only* in a sentence
7. To write a poem describing an animal, using four-line stanzas
8. To respond to the poems through writing, speaking and listening, and projects

SKILLS INSTRUCTION

Vocabulary: Synonyms
Spelling: Words With *-ture*
Grammar: Placement of *only*
Reading Strategy: Read According to Punctuation
Literary Focus: Form in Poetry
Writing: Four-Line Stanzas
Speaking and Listening: Poetry Reading (Teacher Edition)
Critical Viewing: Compare and Contrast; Assess

PORTFOLIO OPPORTUNITIES

Writing: Personal Letter; Advertisement; Concrete Poem
Writing Mini-Lesson: Poem Describing an Animal
Speaking and Listening: Poetry Reading; Performance
Projects: Aquarium Lecture, Research Project

More About the Authors

William Jay Smith grew up in Louisiana but lived in Jefferson Barracks, an army post south of St. Louis, Missouri, where his father played clarinet in the Army band. Smith has published over fifty books of poetry, translations, memoirs, and children's verse.

Robert Frost spent two years studying at Yale before he became discouraged and started a new life as a chicken farmer. He did not publish his first volume of poetry until he was forty.

Matsuo Bashō was the son of a samurai. He began writing verse as a youth. He was nicknamed "Bashō" ("banana tree") because he lived in a hut with a banana tree outside.

Guide for Reading

Meet the Authors:

William Jay Smith (1918–)

William Smith was born in Winnfield, Louisiana. He has led a busy life—teaching college students, writing poetry and essays, translating Russian and French poetry, and even serving in the Vermont State Legislature for three years. His most successful writing has been his poetry for young people. When you read "Seal," you will see why. Lively and amusing, it shows that poetry can be pure and simple fun.

Robert Frost (1875–1963)

Born in San Francisco, Robert Frost spent most of his life in New England. At different times, he worked as a farmer and as a part-time teacher. He was not well known as a writer until his first book of poetry, *A Boy's Will* (1913), appeared in Great Britain. Then, almost overnight, he became famous for his poems about New England people and landscapes. Frost had a long and distinguished career as a poet, winning the Pulitzer Prize four times—more than any other poet. [For more information on Robert Frost, see page 258.]

Matsuo Bashō (1644–1694)

Matsuo Bashō was born near Kyoto, Japan. In his three-line poems, he presents a scene in which a momentary feature stands out against an unchanging background. He evokes a whole landscape or an entire season by describing just a few details.

◆ Literature and Your Life

Connect Your Experience

Although we don't always notice, amazing and beautiful events in nature happen all around us—common events, like the appearance of a colorful butterfly or a beautiful sunset, or rare occurrences, like a sun shower or the sighting of a bald eagle. Each of these poems celebrates some aspect of nature. Reading them may help you appreciate natural occurrences you encounter in your life.

Thematic Focus: Nature's Wonders

How do these poets' feelings about and observations of nature compare with your own?

◆ Background for Understanding

Literature

The Japanese consider poetry to be the highest form of literature. As you'll discover when you read the three haiku by Matsuo Bashō—perhaps the most famous of all Japanese poets—Japanese verse is characterized by its brevity and simplicity. In addition, most traditional Japanese poetry presents vivid images of nature that spark associations in the reader's mind. As you read Bashō's haiku, note the thoughts and emotions that each image sparks in your mind.

◆ Build Vocabulary

Synonyms

One way to study a word is to memorize its definition. To become comfortable with a new word, you can also learn its synonyms, the words that mean the same thing. In "The Pasture," a calf *totters* when its mother licks it. Some synonyms of *totter* are *quake, shake,* and *tremble.*

Word Bank

Which of these words do you think might mean "to turn aside from a straight line"?

swerve
utter
pasture
totters

Prentice Hall Literature Program Resources

REINFORCE / RETEACH / EXTEND

Selection Support Pages
Build Vocabulary: Synonyms, p. 239
Build Spelling Skills, p. 240
Build Grammar: Placement of *Only,* p. 241
Reading Strategy: Read According to Punctuation, p. 242
Literary Focus: Form in Poetry, p. 243

Strategies for Diverse Student Needs, pp. 87–88

Beyond Literature Career Connection: Marine Animal Trainer, p. 44

Formal Assessment Selection Test, pp. 210–212, Assessment Resources Software

Alternative Assessment, p. 44

Writing and Language Transparencies
Sensory Language Chart, p. 78; Venn Diagram, p. 86

Resource Pro CD-ROM
"Seal"; "The Pasture"; "Three Haiku"—includes all resource material and customizable lesson plan

Listening to Literature Audiocassettes
"Seal"; "The Pasture"; "Three Haiku"

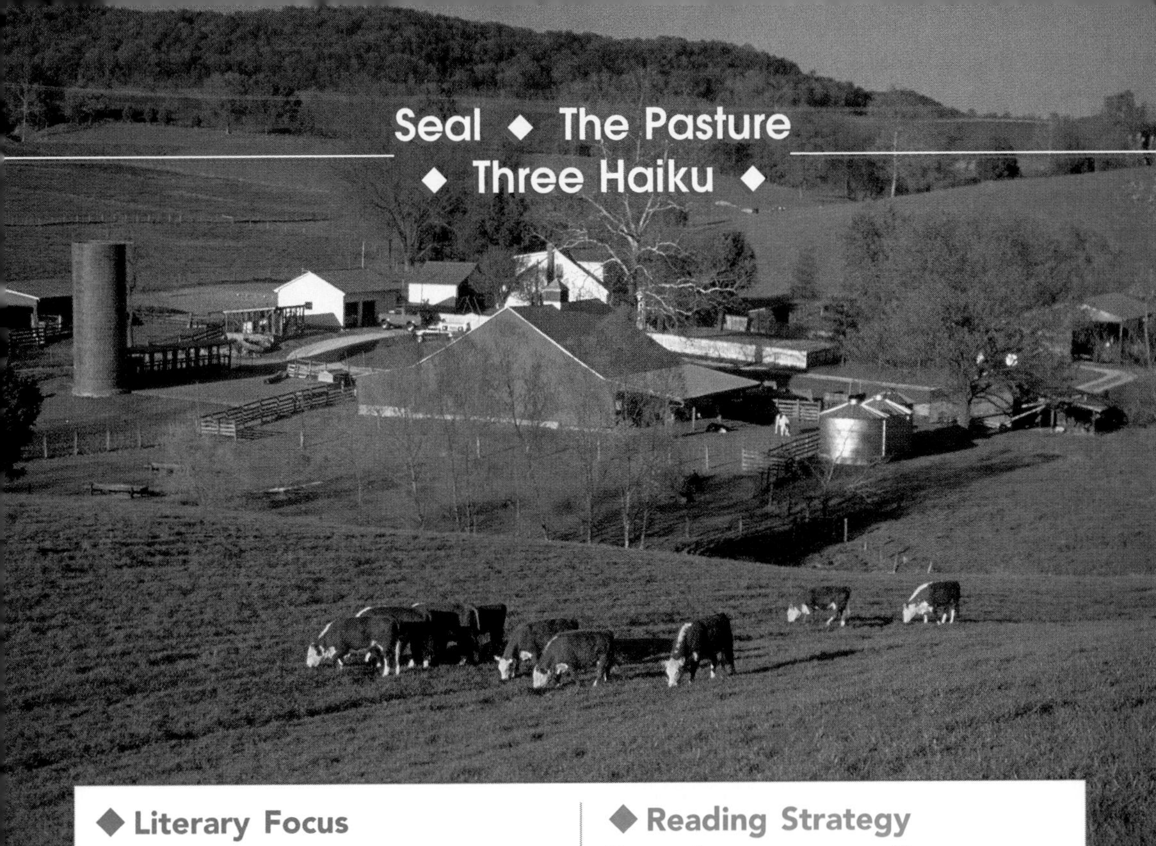

◆ Literary Focus

Form in Poetry

Poetry can take many different forms. Most traditional English poems are divided into stanzas. A **stanza** is a group of lines that might be thought of as corresponding to a paragraph in prose. A **concrete poem** is one with a shape that suggests its subject. The poet arranges the letters and lines to create an image on the page. **Haiku** is a traditional form of Japanese poetry. Haiku always have three lines and seventeen syllables. There are five syllables in the first and third lines, and seven syllables in the second line.

◆ Reading Strategy

Read According to Punctuation

Poets use punctuation the same way prose writers do: to show where thoughts begin and end and how they relate. The structure of poetry, however, can take many forms. Very often the structure of a poem doesn't correspond to the punctuation. You can get around this by **reading according to the punctuation.** Let the punctuation, rather than the line structure, be your guide. If a line ends without a punctuation mark, keep reading until you get to one. Ignore the capital letter at the beginning of a line if it is not also the beginning of a sentence.

I'm going out to fetch the little calf ← No Stop
That's standing by the mother. It's so young ← No Stop
(. ← STOP Full Stop)

Preparing for Standardized Tests

Vocabulary: Synonyms Tell students that their ability to identify *synonyms*, words that have the same meaning, may be tested on standardized tests. Suggest that when students look up a definition for an unknown word, they note any synonyms given with the entry, which will make the word easier to remember.

Ask students to provide a synonym for the word *swerve*. Tell them that the dictionary definition for *swerve* is *to turn aside abruptly in movement.* Therefore, possible synonyms include *turn, veer,* and *curve.*

Write the following sample test question on the board:

Select the best synonym for *fragrant.*

(A) odor (C) stinky
(B) aroma (D) aromatic

Explain to students that the answer is *(D) aromatic* because it comes closest in meaning to fragrant. *(A) odor* and *(B) aroma* are incorrect because they are nouns, not adjectives. *(C) stinky* is incorrect because it has a negative connotation.

Interest Grabber Explain to students that the two poems they are about to read are both based on a poet's inspiration from nature or animals. Ask students to identify the setting in which they live and describe its most outstanding natural characteristics in just a few words. Then ask them to think of a place they have visited that has struck them as particularly beautiful or stunning. Ask them to provide adjectives that describe this place.

◆ Build Grammar Skills

Placement of *Only* If you wish to explore the grammar concept before students read, refer them to the instruction on p. 758.

Customize for
Less Proficient Readers
Students may benefit from hearing the poems read aloud before they read. Have them listen to the audiocassettes as they follow along in their books. Encourage students to note where the speaker seems to take a breath. Explain that the speaker reads according to the punctuation of the poem.

 **Listening to Literature Audiocassettes**

Customize for
More Advanced Students
Suggest to students that they explore the form of these poems. Have them fill out a chart like this one:

	Subject	Form
Seal		
The Pasture		
Three Haiku		

After reading the poems, have students consider whether any of them would work well in another form. Have them make suggestions about ways of changing the form of the poem, while keeping the same subject and theme. Encourage them to discuss their thoughts with the rest of the class.

In the concrete poem "Seal," the poet uses a seal's shape to describe the animal as he dives and swims through the water.

◆ Literary Focus

❶ Form in Poetry Ask students to identify what form of poetry this poem is. *Students should recognize that this poem is a concrete poem.*

◆ Build Vocabulary

❷ Using Synonyms Explain to students that in the first line, the poet uses the word "dives" to describe the poem's action. Have students scan the rest of the poem to find a synonym for the word "dives." *Students should recognize* plunges *as the synonym (line 15).*

◆ Reading Strategy

❸ Read According to Punctuation Point out to students that the poet uses several exclamation marks in this poem. Ask students how they would read the lines ending with these marks. *Students should say that they would read the lines emphatically, to express the wonder the poet finds in the seal's movements.*

Customize for *English Language Learners*

Students may need help distinguishing among the different verbs used in this poem. Suggest that students consult a dictionary, or ask volunteers to explain or pantomime the different action verbs such as *darts, swerves, flip, flicker,* and *zoom.* Ask volunteers to demonstrate a *whoop* and a *bark.*

Customize for *Verbal/Linguistic Learners*

"Seal" has a pronounced rhyme scheme. Encourage students to identify the rhyme scheme as ABCB. Then have students identify how this rhyme scheme influences the poem. Suggest that students rewrite the poem, changing the end words to alter the rhyme.

❶

See how he dives ❷
From the rocks with a zoom!
See how he darts
Through his watery room
Past crabs and eels
And green seaweed,
Past fluffs of sandy
Minnow feed![1]
See how he swims
With a swerve and a twist,
A flip of the flipper,
A flick of the wrist!
Quicksilver-quick,
Softer than spray,
Down he plunges ❸
And sweeps away;
Before you can think,
Before you can utter
Words like "Dill pickle"
Or "Apple butter,"
Back up he swims
Past Sting Ray and Shark,
Out with a zoom,
A whoop, a bark;
Before you can say
Whatever you wish,
He plops at your side
With a mouthful of fish!

1. **feed** (fēd) *n.*: Tiny particles that minnows feed on.

◆ Build Vocabulary

swerve (swʉrv) *n.*: Curving motion

utter (ut´ ər) *v.*: Speak

Block Scheduling Strategies

Consider these suggestions to take advantage of extended class time:

- Before reading the poems, introduce the reading strategy, Read According to Punctuation. To help students understand the application of this strategy, have them listen to the recording while reading along in their books. Have students form groups to answer the Reading Strategy questions on p. 758 and to complete the additional practice page in **Selection Support,** p. 242.

Listening to Literature Audiocassettes

- If students have access to technology, encourage them to use the *Writer's Solution Writing Lab CD-ROM* tutorial on Creative Writing to complete their poems describing an animal.
- Alternatively, suggest that students read the poems and then get together in groups to answer the Critical Thinking questions on pp. 755 and 757. Have students fill out the Venn Diagram in **Writing and Language Transparencies,** p. 86, to compare the poems. Then have students regroup and work on the one of the options from the Idea Bank, p. 759.

The Pasture

Robert Frost

I'm going out to clean the pasture spring:
I'll only stop to rake the leaves away
(And wait to watch the water clear, I may):
I shan't be gone long.—You come too. |❺

I'm going out to fetch the little calf
That's standing by the mother. It's so young
It totters when she licks it with her tongue. |❻
I shan't be gone long.—You come too.

④ ▲ **Critical Viewing** How might life in a rural setting—as shown in this photograph and suggested in "The Pasture"—be different from life in a city? Explain. **[Compare and Contrast]**

◆ Build Vocabulary

pasture (pas´ chər) *adj., usually n.*: In a field used by animals to graze

totters (tät´ ərz) *v.*: Rocks or shakes as if about to fall; is unsteady

Guide for Responding

◆ Literature and Your Life

Reader's Response As you read "The Pasture," did you want to accept the invitation? Why or why not?

Thematic Focus How do you think William Jay Smith feels about the seal in his poem? Support your answer with details from the poem.

Journal Writing Think of some aspect of nature that you enjoy—a particular season, a plant or animal, a time of day, a kind of weather—and describe it. In your journal entry, tell why you like the subject you've chosen.

☑ Check Your Comprehension

1. Sum up the action in "Seal."
2. What motivates the seal to dive from the rocks?
3. What two chores is the speaker in "The Pasture" going to do?

◆ Critical Thinking

Interpret

1. How would you describe the mood of "Seal"? Find at least three words or images that help create this mood. **[Infer]**
2. Although the speaker in "The Pasture" is going out to perform chores, he makes them sound attractive and inviting. What images contribute to this feeling? **[Support]**
3. (a) Who might the "you" be that the speaker of "The Pasture" is addressing? (b) Who do you think is being addressed as "you" in "Seal"? Support your answers. **[Interpret]**

Apply

4. Suppose "Seal" became "Shark." In what ways would this change the poem? **[Modify]**

Compare Literary Works

5. What do the speakers in "The Pasture" and "Seal" have in common? Support your answer with details from the poems. **[Literature Link]**

One-Minute Insight In "The Pasture," the speaker describes spring cleaning on a farm. Instead of avoiding his duties, the speaker looks forward to the signs of a new season.

▶Critical Viewing◀

❹ **Compare and Contrast** *Some students may say that life in this rural setting involves work on the land, walks in the open air, and plenty of nature. Life in the city involves traffic, big buildings, and city blocks.*

◆Reading Strategy

❺ **Read According to Punctuation** Explain that the hyphen in line 4 (and also line 8) indicates a pause. Ask students why they think the poet would want a pause there. *He is showing a change in the speaker's thoughts. With the first part "I shan't be gone long," the speaker is informing someone, then he pauses and thinks, "You come too," as if it has just occurred to him to invite this person to join him.*

◆ Build Vocabulary

❻ **Synonyms** Ask students to find a synonym for the word "totter." *Possible responses:* wobble, stagger, flounder. Explain that the poet might have chosen *totter* to create a rhythm with the other *t* sounds in the line.

Reinforce and Extend

Answers

◆Literature and Your Life

Reader's Response Some students will say yes, wanting to see the new signs of spring and the new calf.

Thematic Focus Smith likes the seal and finds it amusing. Details include his exclamations, playful language, and shape of the poem.

☑ Check Your Comprehension

1. A seal dives from the rocks, swims through the water, and jumps back onto land.
2. The seal wants to get some fish to eat from the water.
3. The speaker is going to clean the pasture spring and to fetch the calf.

◆Critical Thinking

1. The mood is lively and lighthearted. Possible words and images include *flip, flick, quicksilver-quick, dill pickle, apple butter,* and *whoop.*
2. Students may say that the images of the clear water, and the calf's being licked by its mother make the chores seem attractive.
3. (a) The "you" may be someone the speaker lives with because he says he's going out. It's probably someone the speaker has a close relationship with because he wants this person's company. (b) Students may say the "you" is someone who is watching the seal along with the speaker.
4. The poem may change from being lively to being more sinister and perhaps even violent; the outline form of the poem would change as well to something more pointed or knifelike.
5. Both speakers enjoy the natural world and animals; both want to draw readers into their experiences.

These haiku express different images and feelings: a view of a mountain path, mist on a mountain, the smell of flower blossoms. In addition to describing these images, the haiku evoke feelings of surprise and wonder.

◆Critical Thinking

1 Infer Ask students what time of day it is in this poem. *Students should realize that the sun's rising suddenly indicates that it is morning.*

◆Reading Strategy

2 Read According to Punctuation Ask students how having a question mark in the first line brings meaning to the poem. *Because the first line is a question, readers may interpret the poem as the speaker asking a question and then trying to answer it.*

Customize for
Visual/Spatial Learners
Explain that the object of haiku is to present a feeling experienced by the poet. Have students create visual representations of the images in one or all of these haiku. Suggest that they experiment with different mediums to make their representations.

Humanities: Art

Ravens in Moonlight, 1882, by Gengyo

Japanese art is characterized by images of simple, still beauty as well as ornamental grandeur. Have students look at the images, then ask: Do you think this print is more representative of still beauty or ornamental grandeur? *Most students will say this print is representative of still beauty, because the lines, shape, and colors are very simple, yet powerful.*

Three Haiku

Matsuo Bashō

Translated by Daniel C. Buchanan

On sweet plum blossoms
The sun rises suddenly.
Look, a mountain path! 1

Has spring come indeed? 2
On that nameless mountain lie
Thin layers of mist.

Ravens in Moonlight, 1882, Gengyo

Speaking and Listening Mini-Lesson

Poetry Reading

This mini-lesson supports the Speaking and Listening activity in the Idea Bank on p. 759.

Introduce Explain to students that in a poetry reading, volunteers read several poems, usually related by author or theme. This poetry reading will focus on poems by Robert Frost. Suggest that students go to the library or look on the Internet for possible poems to use.

Develop Have students consider the following points when developing their readings:

- Pick poems that are short enough to hold the listener's attention.
- Remember to read according to punctuation.
- Use body language to convey the meanings of the poems.
- Decide whether to provide introductions to the entire reading or introductions to each poem.

Apply Have students get together in groups, and assign different readers for each poem. Encourage them to rehearse the poems in front of a reviewer who will critique their style and use of body language. Suggest that students organize the reading by theme, subject, or date written.

Assess After each reading, have classmates discuss what they liked about the way the poem was read. Evaluate students' work based on the organization of the presentation, students' ability to engage the audience, and how they read the poem according to punctuation.

◀ Critical Viewing ▶ Which haiku is best illustrated by the art on these pages? Explain. [Assess] 4

Temple bells die out. 3
The fragrant blossoms remain.
A perfect evening!

Ravens in Moonlight, 1882, Gengyo

Guide for Responding

◆ Literature and Your Life

Reader's Response Of the three haiku, which do you like best? Why?

Thematic Focus How would you describe Bashō's attitude toward nature?

Group Discussion In a small group, recall moments when you suddenly noticed a change in nature—a change in weather, in cloud formations, or something more dramatic. Did your feelings change in response to nature's change?

☑ Check Your Comprehension

1. What does the speaker notice in the first haiku?
2. What does the speaker observe in the second haiku?
3. What does the speaker reveal about his feelings in the third haiku?

◆ Critical Thinking

INTERPRET

1. Why is the speaker surprised in the first haiku? **[Infer]**
2. In the second haiku, why is he uncertain whether spring has come? **[Interpret]**
3. In the third haiku, why do you think he feels it is a perfect evening? **[Interpret]**

EVALUATE

4. Reread the biography of Bashō on page 752. Then, decide which of these three haiku best illustrates what is said there about his poetry. Explain your choice. **[Assess]**

COMPARE LITERARY WORKS

5. Of the three poets you have read—William Jay Smith, Robert Frost, and Matsuo Bashō—which poet do you think comes closest to expressing your own view of nature? Explain. **[Relate]**

Beyond the Selection 

FURTHER READING

Other Works by the Authors

Laughing Time: Collected Nonsense, William Jay Smith
You Come Too, Robert Frost
On Love and Barley: Haiku of Bashō, Lucien Stryle (ed.)

Other Poetry about Nature

Wooroloo, Frieda Hughes
If You're Not From the Prairie, David Bouchard
Art and Wonder, Kate Farrell (ed.)

INTERNET

We suggest the following sites on the Internet (all Web sites are subject to change).

For information on William Jay Smith:
http://www.theatlantic.com/issues/98sep/poetry.htm

For more on Robert Frost:
http://www.library.utoronto.ca/www/utel/rp/authors/frost.html

For more on haiku and Matsuo Basho:
http://www.big.or.jp/~loupe/links/ehisto/ebasho.html

We *strongly recommend* that you preview these sites before you send students to them.

◆ Critical Thinking

3 Infer From the first line of the poem, what details clue the reader in to the time of day? *Students should recognize that "Temple bells die out" symbolizes a closing, as at the end of day.*

▶Critical Viewing◀

4 Assess *Some students may say the third haiku, because it describes evening and the image looks like evening. Other students will say the first haiku because the colors evoke a sense of light coming up, or sunrise.*

Reinforce and Extend

Answers

◆ Literature and Your Life

Reader's Response Encourage students to support their answers.

Thematic Focus He seems to feel a kinship with nature.

☑ Check Your Comprehension

1. He sees sunlight on blossoms and notices a mountain path.
2. He observes mist on the mountains.
3. He feels contented with the "perfect evening."

◆ Critical Thinking

1. He is surprised because he notices the mountain path only with the rising of the sun.
2. He is uncertain because there is mist on the mountain, which may signify the remains of winter or the wetness of spring.
3. Some students will say the evening is perfect because there is a silence in the air and a lingering aroma from the flowers, which contribute to an intensely serene and enjoyable night.
4. Some students will say that the third poem best illustrates Bashō's work because the dying of the bells represents the change, but the aroma of the flowers is unchanged.
5. Answers will vary. Some students may say that Bashō's view comes closest to their own because it exemplifies a simple, uninterrupted observation, which is how they like to interact with nature.

Answers

◆Reading Strategy

1. (a) It makes more sense the second way. (b) In the second stanza, both the first and second lines end in the middle of a sentence. If you pause at the end of the lines, it doesn't make sense.
2. Some students will say reading according to punctuation adds to the excitement the narrator feels. Other students will say that the short, rhythmic lines already correspond to the punctuation.

◆ Build Vocabulary

Using Synonyms

1. c 2. c 3. a

Spelling Strategy

1. dentures
2. legislature
3. mature

Using the Word Bank

1. a 2. c 3. a 4. b

◆Literary Focus

1. The shape of "The Seal" is like an "S," which can be seen to resemble both the shape of the seal's body, and the movement of his dive into the water.
2. The repetition in the first line of each stanza creates a rhythm, and the repetition in the last line breaks the rhythm.
3. Suggested responses: (1) surprise; (2) uncertainty; (3) contentment

◆Build Grammar Skills

Practice

1. (a) He will watch, but only the snow falling. (b) Of all the people who may be there, he is the sole person who wants to watch the snow fall.
2. (a) Bashō wrote nothing but haiku. (b) No one but Bashō wrote haiku.
3. (a) The seal will sit nowhere but at your side. (b) There is only one seal.
4. (a) The only thing he does is flick his wrist. (b) He has only one wrist to flick.
5. (a) He makes nothing but a zoom when he dives. (b) The only way he gets off the rocks is by diving.

Writing Application

1. I have written only one poem.
2. I can read only one poem at a time.

Guide for Responding *(continued)*

◆ Reading Strategy

Read According to Punctuation

You will better understand poetry you read if you **read it according to punctuation.** This means letting the punctuation, rather than the line division, be your guide to where phrases and sentences begin and end.

1. Read the second stanza of "The Pasture" aloud. Pause at the end of each line. Then, read it aloud according to the punctuation. (a) Which way makes more sense? (b) Why?

2. Does reading "Seal" according to the punctuation change your understanding of it? Explain.

◆ Build Vocabulary

Using Synonyms

Like *totter, shake,* and *tremble,* synonyms are words that are close in meaning. You can often substitute a word's synonym in a sentence. Choose the synonym for each italicized word.

1. She was very *tense* during her solo.
(a) proud, (b) afraid, (c) stiff

2. He bought an *enormous* house.
(a) old, (b) stylish, (c) huge

3. I can't *comprehend* your meaning.
(a) understand, (b) appreciate, (c) discuss

Spelling Strategy

The *cher* sound at the end of a word is often spelled *ture.* After each definition, write a word that fits the definition and contains the *ture* spelling of the *cher* sound.

1. false teeth: de___?___

2. government body that makes laws: legis___?___

3. fully grown or developed: m___?___

Using the Word Bank

Choose the best synonym for each of the following words. Write the letter of your answer on your paper.

1. swerve: (a) turn, (b) flip, (c) shoot

2. utter: (a) shout, (b) murmur, (c) speak

3. pasture: (a) field, (b) lot, (c) yard

4. totters: (a) falls, (b) sways, (c) grows

◆ Literary Focus

Form in Poetry

Many poems follow a specified **form,** or structure. The poems you've just read are examples of three different poetic forms. "Seal" is a *concrete poem* in which the shape suggests its subject. "The Pasture" is divided into groups of lines called *stanzas. Haiku* is a traditional three-line Japanese poem.

1. Explain how the shape of "Seal" relates to its meaning.

2. Both stanzas of "The Pasture" begin with the same words and end with the same line. What is the effect of this repetition?

3. For each haiku by Bashō, choose one word that sums up the emotion expressed in the poem.

◆ Build Grammar Skills

Placement of *only*

The position of the adverb ***only*** can affect the entire meaning of a sentence. Place *only* before the word or phrase it modifies. For example, in "The Pasture," Frost says:

I'll *only* stop to rake the leaves away

Notice how different the meaning would be if he had written:

I'll stop to rake *only* the leaves away

Practice Explain how the placement of *only* changes meaning in each of these sentence pairs.

1. (a) He wished *only* to watch the snow fall.
(b) *Only* he wished to watch the snow fall.

2. (a) Matsuo Bashō wrote *only* haiku.
(b) *Only* Matsuo Bashō wrote haiku.

3. (a) The seal plops *only* at your side.
(b) The *only* seal plops at your side.

4. (a) He *only* flicks his wrist.
(b) He flicks his *only* wrist.

5. (a) He dives from the rocks with *only* a zoom.
(b) He *only* dives from the rocks with a zoom.

Writing Application In your notebook, revise each sentence. Delete the italicized words, but keep the meaning by inserting *only* in the appropriate place.

1. I have written one poem *and no others.*

2. I can read *no more than* one poem at a time.

Build Your Portfolio

Idea Bank

Writing

1. **Personal Letter** Write a letter responding to the invitation in "The Pasture." Explain why you will or will not accept.
2. **Advertisement** Imagine that you are opening a coffeehouse at which great poets, past and present, will read their poetry. You have miraculously signed Robert Frost, William Jay Smith, and Matsuo Bashō to read for the opening night. Create a full-page print advertisement for the grand opening. **[Media Link]**
3. **Concrete Poem** Choose your favorite physical activity, and write a concrete poem about it. First, decide on a shape that resembles or suggests something about your subject. Display your finished poem in the classroom.

Speaking and Listening

4. **Poetry Reading** **[Group Activity]** Work with a group of classmates to read aloud selected poems by Robert Frost. Choose poems you like from a collection of Frost's works. Then, rehearse your readings alone and with the group. Finally, hold a reading for the class.
5. **Performance** **[Group Activity]** Work with a group of classmates to turn "Seal" into a performance piece. Combine a solo or group recitation of the poem with percussion accompaniment and dance movements. **[Performing Arts Link]**

Projects

6. **Aquarium Lecture** Imagine that you are an aquarium guide. Create a short lecture about seals based on "Seal" and library research. Then, deliver your lecture to classmates. **[Science Link]**
7. **Research Project** Use library resources to find out more about Japan during the time of Matsuo Bashō. Topics for research can include Japanese government, society, and culture during this period. Present your findings in the form of an oral or a written report. **[Social Studies Link]**

Writing Mini-Lesson

Poem Describing an Animal

In "Seal," William Jay Smith conveys his appreciation for a lively and lovable sea creature. Write a poem that both describes your favorite animal and conveys your feeling about it. Organize your poem into four-line stanzas.

As you write your stanzas, consider using repetition, as Frost does, to reinforce your main ideas. Try to make the lines about the same length. Choose a different idea for each stanza so that each one adds something new to the poem.

Writing Skills Focus: Four-Line Stanza

Stanzas are like paragraphs in prose or verses in a song. Each stanza can develop an idea, express a feeling, or tell another part of the story. The **four-line stanza** is a traditional poetic form that lends itself to rhythm, rhyme, and repetition.

Model From "The Pasture"

I'm going out to clean the pasture spring:
I'll only stop to rake the leaves away
(And wait to watch the water clear, I may):
I shan't be gone long.—You come too.

Prewriting Make a list of sensory details that describe the animal you chose. Also, jot down your feelings about the animal. Decide whether or not you want your poem to rhyme.

Drafting As you organize your lines into groups of four, experiment by using repetition and/or rhythm. Write at least two four-line stanzas.

◆ Grammar Application

If you use the adverb *only* in your poem, place it before the word or phrase it modifies.

Revising Read the poem aloud. Make sure that each stanza adds something new. Improve descriptions by adding or replacing sensory details. Finally, ask a peer to listen to your poem and suggest ways to improve it.

ASSESSMENT OPTIONS

Formal Assessment, Selection Test, pp. 210–212, and Assessment Resources Software. The selection test is designed so that it can be easily customized to the performance levels of your students.

Alternative Assessment, p. 44, includes options for less advanced students, more advanced students, visual/spatial learners, verbal/linguistic learners, musical/rhythmic learners, and interpersonal learners.

PORTFOLIO ASSESSMENT

Use the following rubrics in the **Alternative Assessment** booklet to assess student writing:
Personal Letter: Expression, p. 81
Advertisement: Persuasion, p. 92
Concrete Poem: Poetry, p. 95
Writing Mini-Lesson: Poetry, p. 95

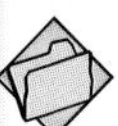

Idea Bank

Following are suggestions for matching the Idea Bank topics with your students' performance levels and learning modalities:

Customize for *Performance Levels*
Less Advanced Students: 1, 5, 6
Average Students: 2, 4, 6, 7
More Advanced Students: 3, 4, 7

Customize for *Learning Modalities*
Verbal/Linguistic: 1, 2, 3, 4, 5, 7
Musical/Rhythmic: 4, 6
Interpersonal: 1, 6
Bodily/Kinesthetic: 6
Logical/Mathematical: 7

Writing Mini-Lesson

Refer students to the Writing Handbook in the back of the book for instruction on the writing process and further information on Creative Writing. Have students use the Sensory Language Chart in **Writing and Language Transparencies,** p. 78, to arrange their prewriting list.

Writing Mini-Lesson

Writers at Work Videodisc

Have students view the videodisc segment on Gary Soto to see how he finds ideas for his poetry.

Play frames 320 to 9204

Writing Lab CD-ROM

Have students complete the tutorial on Creative Writing. Follow these steps:

1. Have students use the Sunburst Diagram activity to explore topic ideas.
2. Suggest that students use the Sensory Image Word Bin to come up with sensory images.
3. Allow students to draft on computer.
4. Encourage students, when revising, to use the Proofreading Checklist for poetry.

Writer's Solution Sourcebook

Have students use Chapter 8, "Creative Writing," pp. 234–263, for additional support. This chapter includes in-depth instruction on using sound devices in poetry, p. 255.

Prepare and Engage

OBJECTIVES

1. To read, comprehend, and interpret a selection that has a social studies focus
2. To relate a selection with a social studies focus to personal experience
3. To connect literature to social studies
4. To respond to Social Studies Guiding Questions
5. To respond to the selection through writing, speaking and listening, and projects

SOCIAL STUDIES GUIDING QUESTIONS

Reading two Japanese tanka will help students discover answers to these Social Studies Guiding Questions:

- What was the importance of poetry in traditional Japanese culture?
- How does the poetic form of tanka exemplify important aspects of Japanese culture, such as beauty, simplicity, and control?

Interest Grabber Place a few familiar natural objects on a classroom table, for example, a vegetable, some leaves, and a rock. Invite students to write on the board descriptive phrases of no more than two words about each object. Poll the class to choose the phrases that best capture the essence of each object. Then explain that the Japanese have a tradition of poetry describing nature's essence with very few words.

Map Study

Regional Maps The connection between geography and history can help students understand how cultures develop. For example, they will more easily understand how Japanese poets created a wholly unique poetic structure—the tanka—when they use the map on this page to note the country's physical isolation. Reading "Islands Apart" on this page can also help students expand their grasp of Japan's historical isolation and link that separation to the poetry.

Connecting Literature to Social Studies

JAPAN

Tanka *by Myoe and Minamoto No Sanetomo*

ISLANDS APART Throughout most of history, few outsiders visited the islands of Japan (located in the Pacific Ocean off the east coast of Asia). As an island nation, its physical separation helped the country create a powerful and unique cultural personality. Although Japan's culture was influenced by others—for example, Japan adopted the Chinese system of writing in the fifth century and Buddhism arrived in the country from China and Korea in the sixth century—Japan's geography gave it some control over which influences it would accept or reject. In fact, Japan closed itself to the world for more than two hundred years, from the 1630's to the 1850's.

Perfect Simplicity Beauty, simplicity, and control are important aspects of Japanese culture, particularly in the arts. A flower arrangement might consist of a single perfect blossom and an interesting twig; a painting might consist of a few brushstrokes that suggest the form of distant mountains. The Japanese passion for elegant simplicity is particularly pronounced in poetry. In tanka, which the Japanese developed about the year 800, poets use just 31 syllables (in the original Japanese, not necessarily in translation!) in five lines to create an image that captures a single moment or aspect of nature.

Shoguns, Priests, and Farmers In traditional Japanese culture, poetry was part of the people's everyday lives—from Buddhist priests to ordinary peasants to warrior leaders. During Japan's medieval times, beginning in the twelfth century, soldier-leaders known as shoguns fought each other to rule the land. They also wrote beautiful poetry, much of it in the tanka form. Here, you can read two tanka, one written by a priest, the other by a shogun from this period.

Prentice Hall Literature Program Resources

REINFORCE / RETEACH / EXTEND

Selection Support Pages
Build Vocabulary, p. 244
Theme, p. 245

Formal Assessment Selection Test, pp. 213–214, Assessment Resources Software

Resource Pro CD-ROM
"Tanka"—includes all resource material and customizable lesson plan

Listening to Literature Audiocassettes
"Tanka"

Connection to Prentice Hall World Explorer
Medieval Times to Today
Ch. 4, "Civilizations of Asia"

TANKA

Ninth Month, Tang-Tai and Ting Kuan-p'eng

Night deepening,
and in this mountain temple
where winds are chill,
over my robe I wear
a layer of autumn mist

—Myoe

◀ **Critical Viewing** What geographic features mentioned in the poem are visible in this traditional Japanese art? **[Connect]** ❶

Develop Understanding

One-Minute Insight Each of these tanka captures a brief aspect of nature. The first, by Myoe, describes night falling in the mountains, perhaps experienced by a monk at a temple. The second poem, by Minamoto No Sanetomo, paints a word picture of a colorful sunset. Both poems evoke a mood of respectful admiration for nature.

Team Teaching Strategy

"Tanka" present an ideal opportunity to team teach with a social studies teacher, creating a cross-curricular unit on medieval Japan.

▶Critical Viewing◀

❶ *Mountains, which are mentioned in the poem, are visible in the art.*

Links Across Culture

Like medieval Europe, society in medieval Japan was structured around a feudal system. Estate owners, called daimyo, hired warriors, called samurai, to protect them. People often lived on self-contained estate, isolated by Japan's rugged mountainous geography. Point out the fine art on this page as example of such a mountain estate. Discuss how the speaker's experience of nature might be impacted by living in such a setting.

Customize for *Less Proficient Readers*

Explain to students that tanka is necessarily abbreviated in its language. Model how to analyze a tanka for its implied meanings—noting the connotative impact of words, hearing the sound rhythms, mentally completing sentences.

Customize for *English Language Learners*

Make sure that students understand the rhythms and tone in each poem. Point out that each tanka could be written out as a single sentence. Read aloud, or play the audiocassette, to help students hear the location of pauses and inflections.

Listening to Literature Audiocassettes

Preparing for Standardized Tests

Interpretive Reading Knowledge of how to read and interpret figurative language will help students perform on standardized tests. Write the following question-and-answer alternatives on the board:

In Minamoto No Sanetomo's tanka, *fabrics* refers to

(A) pieces of cloth wrapped around a man
(B) areas of color in the sky
(C) trees shining in the moonlight
(D) layers of fog and mist

To correctly answer this question, students must read and understand the figurative image described in the poem. Explain that figurative language is not meant to be read literally, but rather helps suggest an image or idea. Help students recognize that the poem describes a sunset, and then guide them to rule out all answers except *(B)*. Use Build Vocabulary, p. 244 in **Selection Support,** to help students expand their vocabulary.

Customize for
More Advanced Students
Provide students with some of the books listed on p. 763. Ask them to read a selection of tanka and haiku and then complete one of these following assignments:

- illustrate a poem
- orally interpret a poem
- find or create a written or oral Japanese version of a poem

CONNECTING LITERATURE TO SOCIAL STUDIES

1 Infer Ask students how this poem shows respect for nature. *The poem conveys admiration for nature's ability to make something special from an everyday occurrence.*

Reinforce and Extend

Answers

◆ Literature and Your Life

Reader's Response Students should be able to support their answer with examples from the poems.

Thematic Focus Both poems use vivid sensory language, capturing natural moments of fog and the sunset.

☑ Check Your Comprehension

1. Myoe's poem takes place in the evening, as dark is settling in; Minamoto's poem is at dusk.
2. He describes fog rolling in on a cool evening.
3. They are the colors of the sunset.
4. Sunset.

Answers

◆ Critical Thinking

1. Myoe: "deepening" suggests natural change; "I wear" suggests the change caused by nature. Minamoto: "swirled," "spreading the sky," and "sinks" suggest movement on a grand scale.
2. Myoe: solitude; Minamoto: awe.

More About the Authors
The poets **Myoe** (1173–1232) and **Minamoto No Sanetomo** (1192–1219) were just two of the many accomplished poets of medieval Japan. With the nation's cultural passion for poetry, almost everyone was writing it, and many were doing so with great talent.

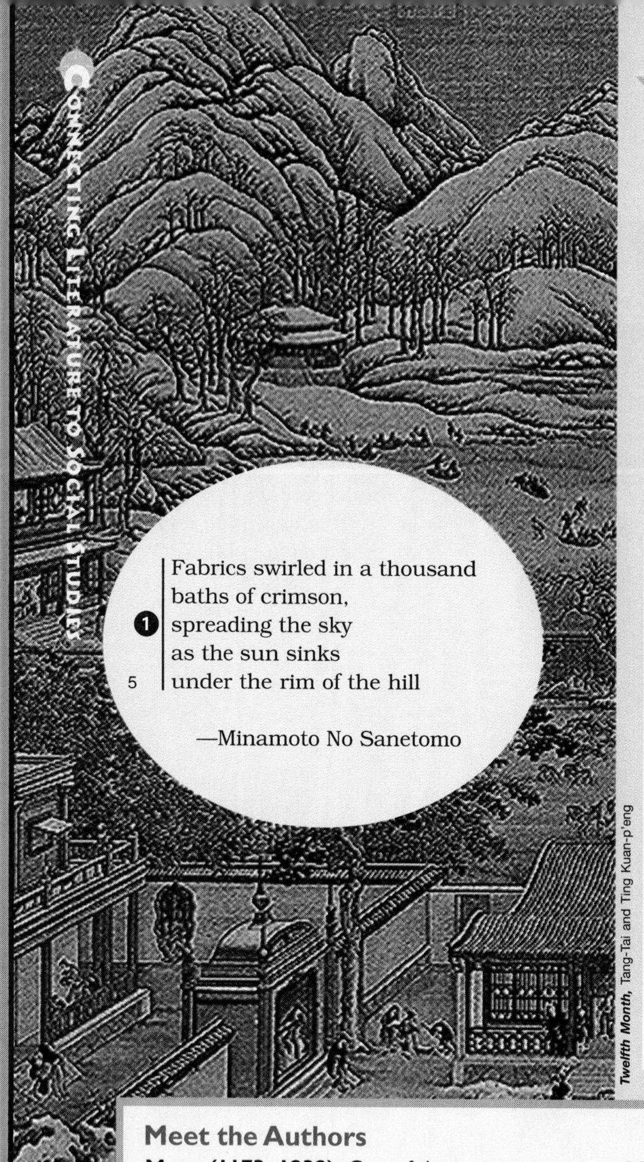

CONNECTING LITERATURE TO SOCIAL STUDIES

Fabrics swirled in a thousand
baths of crimson,
1 spreading the sky
as the sun sinks
under the rim of the hill

—Minamoto No Sanetomo

Twelfth Month, Tang-Tai and Ting Kuan-p'eng

Guide for Responding

◆ Literature and Your Life

Reader's Response Which tanka creates the stronger picture in your mind? Explain.

Thematic Focus How does each poem capture the wonder of nature?

☑ Check Your Comprehension

1. At what time of day does each tanka take place?
2. What natural feature does Myoe describe?
3. Explain the swirling "fabrics" in Minamoto No Sanetomo's tanka.
4. What natural event does Minamoto No Sanetomo describe?

◆ Critical Thinking

INTERPRET

1. How does each poet's language show movement and change? Give two examples. **[Analyze]**
2. What mood does each poem suggest? Explain. **[Draw Conclusions]**

COMPARE LITERARY WORKS

3. How is the point of view different in the two tanka? **[Compare and Contrast]**

EXTEND

4. Why might tanka be especially appreciated by people interested in protecting the environment? **[Science Link; Career Link]**

Meet the Authors

Myoe (1173–1232) One of the main ways that China changed Japanese culture was through the teachings of Buddhist monks. These priests came to Japan and built great monasteries in which to pray and study. Many were skilled artists, architects, and poets. One such monk was the poet Myoe. He was much admired as a man of great faith. In this poem, he seems to connect to nature in a moment of thoughtful solitude.

Minamoto No Sanetomo (1192–1219) Minamoto No Sanetomo was an important figure in his town. He studied with well-known court poet Fujiwara No Teika, and his poems often appeared in collections. As a shogun, he was a military general and also ruler of a region. Though his military role didn't stop him from writing poetry, it resulted in his death in a famous political murder.

Block Scheduling Strategies

Consider these suggestions to take advantage of extended class time:

- After playing the audiocassette "Tanka" to establish the poems' mood, have students meet in groups to work through the following activities in sequence: Map Study, p. 760; Guide for Responding questions, p. 762; and Connecting Literature to Social Studies, p. 763.
- Work with an art teacher to springboard a unit on art in medieval Japan, using *World Explorer: Medieval Times to Today,* Chapter 4, "Civilizations of Asia" and other materials.
- Create an opportunity for students to share their activities and projects from the Idea Bank on p. 763. Help them find productive research sources, and then guide students to choose appropriate organizers from **Writing and Language Transparencies** to structure their material.
- Present the Preparing for Standardized Tests lesson, p. 761 in the Teacher's Edition, and have students complete **Selection Support,** pp. 244–245, on Vocabulary and Theme.

Connecting Literature to Social Studies

Through all Japan's historical changes, nature has remained a central focus of the nation's poetry—and of daily life. Respect for nature, which is important in a place where only a tiny bit of land can be farmed, has helped Japan become and remain a strong nation. You can see that respectful attitude even in these poems from long ago.

1. How do you think Japan's isolation contributed to the development of the tanka form?
2. In what ways do you think these poems show a respect for nature?
3. How does Japanese history help you explain that a lifelong soldier—who solves problems by fighting—and a priest—who solves problems by praying—would share a view of nature?

Idea Bank

Writing

1. **Directions** Imagine that you are meeting a friend at either of the places described in these tanka. Write a set of directions to help your friend find the meeting place. Remember that he or she must travel to Japan first.
2. **Tanka** Write a tanka about a natural scene. You should have five syllables in the first and third lines and seven syllables in the second, fourth, and fifth lines. The lines should not rhyme.
3. **Artistic Goals** Many countries have poet laureates who represent the nation and help set goals for all artists to work toward. As Japan's poet laureate, write a set of guidelines describing goals for Japanese tanka poets.

Speaking and Listening

4. **Group Reading** **[Group Activity]** In many periods of Japanese history, poetry was performed at the court. With a few classmates, review a collection of Japanese poetry to explore the poetry of different time periods. Then, vote on a small sampling to perform for the class.

Projects

5. **Illustrations** If a picture speaks a thousand words, surely you can capture 31 syllables with one picture. Using these or other tanka, create illustrations showing the poet's image. Set your picture in thirteenth-century Japan. **[Art Link]**
6. **A Poet's Life** Both soldiers and priests were poets in medieval Japan. Find out about the life of a Japanese shogun or a Buddhist monk. How did they dress? Where did they live? What were their values and goals in life? Present your findings in an oral report. **[Social Studies Link]**

Further Reading, Listening, and Viewing

- *The Essential Haiku: Versions of Bashō, Buson, and Issa* (1995), edited by Robert Hass, contains a wealth of Japanese poetry.
- Lensey Namioka's *Den of the White Fox* (1997) is an adventure story set in feudal Japan.
- In Myra Cohn Livingston's *Cricket Never Does: A Collection of Haiku and Tanka* (1997), the poet uses Japanese forms to address modern subjects.

Beyond the Selection

FURTHER READING

Other Works by the Poets

Selected poems in *From the Country of Eight Islands,* Hiroaki Sato and Burton Watson (eds.)

Other Works About Japan and Its Poetry

The Japanese, Clare Doran
Samurai of Japan, Michael Gibson
A Samurai Castle, Fiona Macdonald
The Boy and the Samurai, Erik Christian Haugaard

INTERNET

We suggest the following Internet sites (all Web sites are subject to change).

To learn about music from medieval Japan, visit:
http://www.medieval.org/music/world/japan.html

To access the many topics offered by the Institute for Medieval Japanese Studies, visit:
http://columbia.edu/cu/ealac/imjs/

We *strongly recommend* that you preview these sites before you send your students to them.

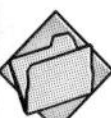

Idea Bank

Following are suggestions for matching the Idea Bank topics with your students' performance levels and learning modalities.

Customize for *Performance Levels*

Less Advanced Students: 1, 4, 5
Average Students: 2, 4, 5, 6
More Advanced Students: 3, 4, 5, 6

Customize for *Learning Modalities*

Verbal/Linguistic: 1, 2, 3, 4, 6
Visual/Spatial: 1, 2, 5
Musical/Rhythmical: 2
Logical/Mathematical: 1
Intrapersonal: 2, 3, 6

Answers *(continued)*

◆Critical Thinking

3. Myoe's is written in the first person, while Minamoto's omits a speaker.
4. It honors and celebrates nature's many beauties. Environmentalists would enjoy this recognition of nature's gifts.

Connecting Literature to Social Studies

1. If Japan had interacted more with other countries, this unique form might have spread, changed, or vanished.
2. They welcome nature as a friend and see its beauty as worth observing.
3. Japan's physical isolation and limited farmland have caused people to respect their surroundings. Both men share the culture's view of nature as an outlet for feelings and artistic ideas.

ASSESSMENT OPTIONS

Formal Assessment, Selection Test, pp. 213–214, and Assessment Resources Software. The selection test is designed so that it can be easily customized to the performance levels of your students.

PORTFOLIO ASSESSMENT

Use the following rubrics and assessment form in the **Alternative Assessment** booklet to assess student writing:
Directions: How-to/Process Explanation, p. 87
Tanka: Poetry, p. 95
Artistic Goal: Writing Self-Assessment, p. 78–79

Prepare and Engage

Establish Writing Guidelines
Review the following key characteristics of song lyrics:

- Song lyrics express a wide variety of moods and emotions.
- Song lyrics are the words to a song
- Song lyrics may contain elements of poetry, such as rhyme and repetition.

You may want to distribute the scoring rubric for Poetry, p. 95 in **Alternative Assessment,** to make students aware of the criteria on which they will be evaluated. See the suggestions on p. 766 for how you can customize the rubric to this workshop.

Refer students to the Writing Handbook in the back of the book for instruction on the writing process and further information on creative writing.

Writer's Solution

Writers at Work Videodisc
To introduce students to expressive writing and to show them how Nikki Giovanni expresses her ideas about creative writing, play the videodisc segment on Creative Writing (Ch. 8.) Have students discuss what Giovanni says about getting her ideas.

Play frames 22015 to 30765

Writing Lab CD-ROM
If your students have access to computers, you may want to have them work in the tutorial on Creative Writing to complete all or part of their song lyrics. Follow these steps:

1. Have students view the interactive model of song lyrics.
2. Suggest that students use Idea Wheel to spark topic ideas.
3. Have students view models of different sound devices used in poetry.
4. Allow students to draft on computer.

Writer's Solution Sourcebook
Students can find additional support, including in-depth instruction on choosing the right form for song lyrics, p. 253, in the chapter on Creative Writing, pp. 253–263.

Connect to Literature Unit 3, "What Matters," includes an example of song lyrics, "On My Own," from the musical, *Les Misérables.*

Creative Writing

Song Lyrics

Writing Process Workshop

A song can convey a powerful message. In a few short lines, it can make you jump for joy or cry with compassion. It can also open your mind to a new way of thinking.

Write your own **song lyrics** that convey a strong emotion or present an interesting idea. Keep in mind that songs are like poetry set to music—they use rhythm, rhyme, repetition, and imagery. For help and inspiration, listen to a few of your favorite songs. The following skills, introduced in this section's Writing Mini-Lessons, will also help you write your lyrics.

Writing Skills Focus

▶ **Write in four-line stanzas.** This poetic form is used in many songs because it lends itself to rhythm, rhyme, and repetition. (See p. 759.)

▶ **Include a refrain—**a repeated line or group of lines that emphasizes a main idea in your song. (See p. 732.)

▶ **Use sensory details** to convey sights, sounds, smells, tastes, and feelings powerfully. (See p. 743.)

▶ **Elaborate on your ideas** by using vivid examples. If you call someone wonderful in your song, explain how and why this is so. (See p. 751.)

Notice how the song "The Dying Cowboy" demonstrates these skills.

Model From Literature

"Oh, bury me not on the lone prairie ①
Where the wild coyotes will howl o'er me,
In a narrow grave just six by three.
Oh, bury me not on the lone prairie. ②

"In fancy I listen to the well-known words
Of the free, wild winds and the song of the birds; ③
I think of home and the cottage in the bower
And the scenes I loved in my childhood's hour. ④

① This refrain is repeated throughout the song.

② Each four-line stanza has a strong rhythm.

③ Sensory details help you feel the wind and hear the birds.

④ In each stanza, the speaker elaborates on his idea: He doesn't want to be buried on the prairie.

Humanities: Music

Musical Theater Share with students that one of the most popular forms of theater today is musical theater, where an entire play is dramatized with interspersions of music accompanied by lyrics. The actors in these plays must also be accomplished singers and, sometimes, dancers.

Encourage students to research popular American musicals from the twentieth century. Before they begin their research, discuss with them whether they know of any songs that originated from musicals, such as "Memory," from *Cats,* "Send in the Clowns," from *A Little Night Music,* "One" from *A Chorus Line,* or "My Favorite Things" from *The Sound of Music.*

If possible, have students bring in recordings from musicals. Encourage students to use information from the recording's liner notes, and from reading the lyrics, to volunteer information on the background of the musical's story. Then, ask students to play their favorite songs and explain what makes the lyrics work and why.

Prewriting

Choose a Topic Many of the best songs are simple but heartfelt. Choose a person, feeling, idea, or message about which you feel strongly. Here are some ideas to get you started:

Topic Ideas

- A unique person
- A special place
- A real-life experience
- A moment in history

Decide on Your Main Idea You might want your song to make a point about social injustice or to present someone as a hero. Identify your main message, and refer to it as you draft. The verses of your song should elaborate on the main idea.

Brainstorm for Sensory Details In a chart like the one below, brainstorm for words and phrases that appeal to the five senses. After recording all the details, you can choose the ones that create the strongest impression.

Summer				
Sights	**Sounds**	**Smells**	**Tastes**	**Feelings**
Kids playing Ferris wheel	Ice-cream truck Crickets	Chlorine Hot dogs	Sweet corn Salty sweat	Excitement Laziness

Drafting

Draft a Refrain A refrain is a repeated line or verse that emphasizes a song's main idea, usually in a catchy way. As you write, find one or more phrases that would make a good refrain.

Use Sound Devices Listen to your favorite songs and you'll hear rhythm, rhyme, and repetition. As a songwriter, work some or all of these sound devices into your own song. If you get stuck looking for words that rhyme, consult a rhyming dictionary. Another effective sound device is alliteration. This is the repetition of a beginning consonant sound, as in "one long, last lingering look."

DRAFTING/REVISING

APPLYING LANGUAGE SKILLS: Figurative Language

Poets and songwriters often use **figurative language,** which includes similes, metaphors, and personification. In a simile, *like* or *as* is used to make a comparison. In a metaphor, one thing is spoken of as if it were something else. In personification, a nonhuman subject is given human characteristics.

Simile:
Her smile was like a watermelon slice.

Metaphor:
Your smile is my sunshine.

Personification:
A smile raced across her face.

Practice On your paper, write a sentence for each item.

1. a cat's purr (simile)
2. anger (metaphor)
3. laughter (personification)

Writing Application When writing your song lyrics, use figurative language to create vivid images.

Writer's Solution Connection
Language Lab

For more help, see the Figurative Language lesson in the unit on Choosing Words.

Develop Student Writing

Prewriting

To help students find an approach to writing song lyrics, suggest that they get together in groups and listen to some popular songs. Have students review the lyrics and determine what messages the songs convey, what poetic devices they use, and how they make the listeners feel. Encourage students to listen to different types of songs.

Customize for
More Advanced Writers

Suggest that students take their song lyrics one step further by turning them into a selection from a musical. Encourage students to outline the story of the entire musical and then identify where this specific song appears in the sequence of events. Have students identify the main characters of the musical and whose song they are writing the lyrics for. Suggest that they write lyrics as a conversation between two of the characters in the musical.

Customize for
Musical/Rhythmic Learners

Suggest that students create a piece of music to go with the lyrics they are going to write. They can use an original piece of music that they have written or one that they know. Encourage these students to review other students' lyrics and suggest pieces of music that they could accompany.

Drafting

Tell students that the most effective songs are the ones that revolve around one topic or idea. Students may find it helpful to write the refrain first and then elaborate from there. The refrain can work like the main idea in an essay. Suggest that students use the Main Idea and Supporting Details Organizer, p. 70, in **Writing and Language Transparencies.** The supporting details can be worked into the stanzas around the refrain.

Applying Language Skills

Figurative Language
Answers

Possible responses:

1. A cat's purr is like an engine running.
2. Her anger was a demon raging inside her.
3. His laughter captured the girl.

Writer's Solution

For additional instruction and practice, have students use the lesson on Figurative Language in the Choosing Words Unit in the *Writer's Solution Language Lab CD-ROM.*

Revising

Students might work with peer reviewers when revising their song lyrics. Tell reviewers to use the checklist on p. 766. Remind them to offer creative solutions to problems. Also encourage them to mark the drafts for any errors in mechanics.

Writer's Solution

Writing Lab CD-ROM

In the tutorial on Creative Writing, have students use interactive instruction on misplaced modifiers.

Publishing

Point out that many popular songs are written by teams. Suggest that students pair up with music students to create an original piece of music to accompany the lyrics.

Reinforce and Extend

Review the Writing Guidelines

After students have completed their papers, review the characteristics of song lyrics.

Applying Language Skills

Commas After Interjections

Remind students that a comma is read as a pause. Therefore, when reading a sentence with an interjection in the beginning, one pauses after the interjection and before the main idea of the sentence.

Answers

1. Well, I'll never forget that day.
2. Oh, I've never seen such a beautiful face.
3. Boy, it was something to see.

Writer's Solution

For additional practice and instruction, use the practice page on Interjections, p. 26, in the *Writer's Solution Grammar Practice Book.*

EDITING/PROOFREADING

Applying Language Skills: Commas After Interjections

An **interjection** is a word or group of words that expresses emotion and functions independently of a sentence.

Although interjections sometimes convey strong emotion and require an exclamation point, interjections in songs are more frequently mild. Punctuate these mild interjections with commas.

Mild Interjection:

Oh, bury me not on the lone prairie.

Practice Rewrite these sentences, punctuating them correctly.

1. Well I'll never forget that day.
2. Oh I've never seen such a beautiful face.
3. Boy it was something to see.

Writing Application Interjections sometimes occur in the refrains of songs. If you use interjections, follow each one with a comma.

Writer's Solution Connection
Writing Lab

Refer to the Revising section of the tutorial on Creative Writing to hear tips from poet Nikki Giovanni.

Revising

Hear the Rhythm Read or sing your lyrics aloud. Is there a clear beat that you can tap to? Switch lines and words around, or add or delete words to create the most musical sounds.

Use a Checklist As you revise your lyrics, ask yourself the following questions:

- **What is the main idea of my song?** Do I elaborate on my main idea in each verse?
- **Have I organized my lyrics into four-line stanzas?** Does each one emphasize my main idea and convey a strong impression?
- **Have I included a refrain?** Is it catchy and effective?
- **Have I effectively used sound devices?** Does my song have a strong, obvious rhythm?
- **Does my song include sensory details?** Can my audience see, hear, smell, taste, and feel my message?

Your answers to questions like these can guide your revision.

Publishing and Presenting

Class Concert Stage a concert in which students recite or sing their lyrics for the class. Those students who play musical instruments may wish to accompany the singers. Students who have chosen the tunes of popular songs may be able to find instrumental tapes in a music store, which they can play for accompaniment.

Lyrics Contest Invite the music teacher in your school to judge a song lyrics contest. Write your lyrics on a piece of paper without your name. Ask the judge to read each and present several awards, such as Best Rhymes, Best Rhythm, Funniest Song, Most Moving Ballad, and Best Blues Song.

Class Anthology Collect your classmates' song lyrics in an anthology. Organize songs according to subject or theme. Add illustrations to accompany your work. Make a table of contents, design a cover, and make your anthology available to other students.

ASSESSMENT		4	3	2	1
PORTFOLIO ASSESSMENT Use the rubric on Poetry in the **Alternative Assessment** booklet, p. 95, to assess the students' writing. Add these criteria to customize this rubric to this assignment.	**Establishes a Main Idea**	The writer establishes a main idea and elaborates on it throughout the lyrics of the song.	The writer establishes a main idea, but elaborates on it only in some of the lyrics of the song.	The writer establishes several ideas, but none of them is strong.	The writer does not establish a main idea.
	Uses Sensory Details	The writer consistently uses sensory details in ways that appeal to the senses	The writer includes sensory details that occasionally appeal to the senses.	The writer includes some sensory details, but they do not effectively appeal to the senses.	The writer includes sensory details, but they do not relate to the topic or appeal to the senses.

Real-World Reading Skills Workshop

Interpreting Song Lyrics

Strategies for Success

When you listen to popular music on the radio or enjoy the music of your favorite CD, you probably respond to both the melody and the message. Like words in poetry, the words of a song—called lyrics—communicate feelings and ideas. You may get more out of your listening if you interpret and respond to the songwriter's words. Use these strategies to help you interpret song lyrics:

Determine the Purpose Like lines of poetry, song lyrics may tell a story, celebrate a moment, express an emotion, or comment on some aspect of life. As you listen, use the images and details to help you identify the purpose of the lyrics. The images that you "see" in your mind's eye are a clue to the songwriter's purpose.

Identify the Mood Reading the lyrics of a song without hearing the music can lead you to draw one conclusion about a song. However, hearing the music might change your first impression. The music that accompanies the lyrics is a good clue to the mood of the song. For example, a slow, sad melody usually accompanies lyrics that express mourning, regret, or loneliness. A fast, bouncy, or upbeat tune often indicates a song's positive message.

Consider the Speaker Identifying the speaker of a poem or the narrator in a short story can help you understand a piece of literature. Applying this strategy can help you get at the meaning of a song. Use the details in the lyrics to draw conclusions about the speaker of a song. Identify the speaker's perspective, notice his or her attitude about the subject, and collect any other facts that the lyrics suggest about the speaker. Then, try to identify with the experiences the speaker describes.

Apply the Strategies

Read the song lyrics below. If possible, listen to a recording of the song. Interpret the song lyrics by answering these questions:

1. What is the mood that the song conveys?
2. Who or what is Shenandoah?
3. Who is the narrator of the song?
4. What is the narrator's message?
5. Have you ever felt the way the narrator feels about a place you know? Explain.

Shenandoah
American Traditional

O Shenandoah, I long to hear you,
Away, you rollin' river.
O Shenandoah, I long to hear you,
Away, we're bound away
'Cross the wide Missouri.

I long to see your fertile valley,
Away, you rollin' river.
I long to see your fertile valley,
Away, we're bound away
'Cross the wide Missouri.

Here are some situations in which interpreting song lyrics can be helpful:

- Watching a musical or opera
- Listening to an advertising jingle
- Listening to an album or a movie soundtrack

Introduce the Strategies

Ask students to make a list of their favorite songs. Then, have them consider whether they appreciate the music or the lyrics more, or the combination of the two. Have them consider what about the lyrics catches their attention. Ask them what purpose the lyrics serve in the songs: Do they tell a story? Evoke an image? Remind the listener of a feeling? Encourage volunteers to bring in lyrics from their favorite CDs and share them with the rest of the class. Explain to students that sometimes, by reading the lyrics of a song separately from listening to the song, they can gain a greater appreciation for the song as a whole.

Apply the Strategies

Remind students to look for interjections in writing that clue the reader into the mood of the speaker. In addition, students should figure out whom the speaker is addressing. You may want to give students some background to this song. Tell them that *Shenandoah* refers to a river flowing from northern Virginia to the Potomac River in West Virginia. The Missouri refers to the Missouri River flowing from Southwest Montana into the Mississippi River, north of St. Louis, Missouri.

Answers

1. The mood of the song is one of longing, regret, and mourning.
2. The Shenandoah is a river and also the river valley in Virginia.
3. The narrator of the song is someone who has moved from the area of the Shenandoah to the area of the Missouri.
4. The narrator's message is that even though he has to go, he misses and thinks fondly of his home.
5. Possible responses: Some students who have moved in their lives may feel similar feelings. Other students may always have stayed in the same place, but they may have strong feelings for that place.

◆Build Grammar Skills

Reviewing Correct Use of Modifiers

The selections in Part I include instruction on the following:

- Degrees of Comparison
- Irregular Comparison of Modifiers
- Correct Use of *Good* and *Well*
- Placement of *Only*

This instruction is reinforced with the Build Grammar Skills practice pages in **Selection Support,** pp. 226, 231, 236, and 241.

As you review modifiers you may wish to review the following:

- Double Comparisons

A double comparison is formed when both *-er* and *more* or both *-est* and *most* are used to compare. A comparison should be formed using only one of these methods.

Comparison	Double Comparison
I write better song lyrics than poetry.	I write more better song lyrics than poetry.
I enjoy song lyrics more than poetry.	I enjoy song lyrics more better than poetry.

Writer's Solution

For additional practice and support with modifiers, use the practice pages on Regular Adjectives and Adverbs, p. 78, Irregular Adjectives and Adverbs p. 79, Using the Comparative and Superlative Degrees, p. 80, and Glossary of Troublesome Adjectives and Adverbs, p. 81, in the *Writer's Solution Grammar Practice Book.*

Correct Use of Modifiers

Grammar Review

modi·fy (mäd'ə fī') *vt.* **-fied', -fy'ing** ⟦ME *modifien* < MFr < L *modificare*, to limit, regulate < *modus*, measure (see MODE) + *facere*, to make: see DO¹⟧ **1** *Gram.* to limit the meaning of; qualify ["old" *modifies* "man" in "old man"] **2** *Linguis.* to change the form of a morpheme to indicate grammatical relations or derivation —*vi.* to be modified —*SYN.* CHANGE —**mod'i·fi'able** *adj.*

Most adjectives and adverbs have three degrees of comparison: the *positive* (used when no comparison is being made), the *comparative* (used when two things are being compared), and the *superlative* (used when three or more things are being compared). (See page 731.)

Comparision of Modifiers To create the comparative form of one- and some two-syllable modifiers, add *-er* to the positive form. To create the superlative form, add *-est.* Some modifiers with two syllables and all those with more than two use *more* or *most* with the positive form.

Positive	Comparative	Superlative
fast	faster	fastest
tall	taller	tallest
popular	more popular	most popular
happily	more happily	most happily

A few adjectives and adverbs are irregular. Their comparative and superlative degrees must be memorized. (See page 742.)

Positive	Comparative	Superlative
bad	worse	worst
many	more	most
good	better	best

Commonly Confused Modifiers *Good* and *well* are especially troublesome modifiers. (See page 750.) *Good* is an adjective. It follows a linking verb. *Well* can be either an adjective or an adverb. Use the adverb *well* after action verbs.

> The seal felt *good* after eating.
> The squirrels have prepared *well.*

Placement of *Only* The position of the adverb *only* can affect the entire meaning of a sentence. Place *only* before the word or phrase it modifies:

> I *only* hope the snow will fall.
> I hope *only* the snow will fall.

Practice 1 Write the following sentences, supplying the correct form of the modifier in parentheses.

1. The speaker endured the weather (bravely) than Sam McGee.
2. The winter is (cold) than the fall.
3. The seals in aquariums may have the (easy) winter situation of all!
4. The calf is the (affectionate) of all the animals.

Practice 2 Correct the errors in these sentences. Write *correct* on your paper if a sentence contains no errors.

1. You speak good, but you write better.
2. Considering the obstacles, we did pretty well.
3. He is good in tough situations.
4. You only may participate in the competition.

Grammar in Writing

✔ *Take care to avoid double comparisions. Do not use both -er and more when forming the comparative degree or both -est and most to form the superlative.*

Incorrect: This winter was more colder than I expected.

Correct: This winter was colder than I expected.

Answers

Practice 1

1. The speaker endured the weather *more bravely* than Sam McGee.
2. The winter is *colder* than the fall.
3. The seals in aquariums may have the *easiest* winter situation of all!
4. The calf is the *most affectionate* of all the animals.

Practice 2

1. You speak well, but you write better.
2. Considering the obstacles, we did pretty well. (correct)
3. He is good in tough situations. (correct)
4. Only you may participate in the competition.

Part 2 *Elements of Poetry*

Double Bass, Triple Head, Gil Mayers, Private Collection

Humanities: Art

Double Bass, Triple Head, by Gil Mayers

This image shows a double bass, also called the contrabass, the largest of the instruments in the violin family and the lowest in range. It produces sounds an octave lower than the written note and is played standing up.

Have students look at the painting above and answer the following questions:

1. Why do you think the artist has included three heads in this painting? *Possible response: The three heads may represent three different people playing the instrument and the variety of music each can play. The different positions of the heads may represent different approaches to the instrument and the different type of music that each produces.*
2. How do you think music relates to poetry? *Possible response: Music relates to poetry in that it can take on a variety of forms and sounds. Just as different poets use different devices to create their poetry, so musicians use different instruments to create their music.*

One-Minute Planning Guide

The selections in this section introduce students to different elements of poetry. "Martin Luther King," "Annabel Lee," and "Feelings About Words" introduce students to rhyme and rhythm. "Full Fathom Five" illustrates alliteration. "Onomatopoeia" is a poetic example of onomatopoeia and "Maestro" uses alliteration and foreign words for sound effects. "Aunt Leaf," "Fog," "Life," and "Loo-Wit" are all examples of poems using figurative language.

Customize for
Varying Students Needs

When assigning the selections in this section, keep in mind the following factors:

"Martin Luther King"
- Short poem of rhyming couplets
- Opportunity to study Martin Luther King, Jr.

"Annabel Lee"
- Introduces students to Edgar Allan Poe's writing
- A good example of rhythm in poetry

"Feelings About Words"
- A poem displaying sensory power of language

"Full Fathom Five"
- From Shakespeare's *The Tempest*
- Students may need help with language

"Onomatopoeia"
- Contains examples of onomatopoeia

"Maestro"
- Contains Spanish words

"Aunt Leaf"
- Figurative language shows the power of imagination

"Fog"
- Very short poem revolving around a single, powerful image
- Extended metaphor
- Opportunity for making connections to science

"Life"
- Short poem using a metaphor

"Loo-Wit"
- Provides an example of personification

Prepare and Engage

OBJECTIVES

1. To read, comprehend, and interpret poems
2. To relate poems to personal experience
3. To paraphrase
4. To determine rhythm and rhyme
5. To build vocabulary in context and learn the word root *-found-*
6. To develop skill in using pronouns in comparisons
7. To write a remembrance of a person
8. To respond to poems through writing, speaking and listening, and projects

SKILLS INSTRUCTION

Vocabulary: Word Roots: *-found-*

Spelling: *kw* Sound Spelled With *qu*

Grammar: Pronouns in Comparisons

Reading Strategy: Paraphrase

Literary Focus: Rhythm and Rhyme

Writing: Use Specific Examples

Speaking and Listening: Poetry Drumbeat (Teacher Edition)

Critical Viewing: Connect; Analyze

PORTFOLIO OPPORTUNITIES

Writing: Couplet; Liner Notes; Critical Review

Writing Mini-Lesson: Remembrance of a Person

Speaking and Listening: Oral Interpretation; Poetry Drumbeat

Projects: Missing Person Investigation; Multimedia Presentation

More About the Authors

Raymond Richard Patterson has taught at the high school and college levels for over thirty years. His poems have appeared in anthologies as well as in his own collections. The themes of grief and rage are evident in his writing.

Edgar Allan Poe earned a meager living from writing, but is one of the best-known American authors. He was fascinated with dark themes, but also embraced reason and logic. "The Murders in the Rue Morgue" is considered the first modern detective story and has become the model for all detective fiction.

Mary O'Neill began writing to entertain her family in a small town near Cleveland, Ohio. She kept her interest in writing even as she made a career in advertising.

Guide for Reading

Meet the Authors:

Raymond Richard Patterson (1929–)

Raymond Patterson's poetry appears in numerous anthologies, as well as in individual collections such as *Elemental Blues*. Patterson's passion for sharing his knowledge of African American history is shown in his newspaper column, "From Our Past," and poems like "Martin Luther King."

Edgar Allan Poe (1809–1849)

Edgar Allan Poe's life is a story of great literary achievement, some literary fame, and much personal loss. His parents were impoverished traveling actors. When Poe was three, his mother died, and Poe went to live with the Allans of Richmond, Virginia.

Although his writing won recognition, it did not bring financial success. Two years after the death of his beloved wife, Virginia, Poe died poor and alone.

The Story Behind the Poem

Poe's biographer Kenneth Silverman believes that the heroine of "Annabel Lee" "represents all of the women he loved and lost." Poe finished the poem about a year after his wife's death and published it in a New York newspaper. He always had a special feeling for the poem. His mother-in-law said, "oh! how he cried!" as he read it aloud to her.

Mary O'Neill (1908–1990)

Mary O'Neill published many stories and poems for young people. Her sense of the magic of words is clear in "Feelings About Words."

◆ Literature and Your Life

Connect Your Experience

Your sense of who you are depends on memory. You'd be incomplete if you couldn't remember those who have loved you or recall those who have contributed to this country.

One role of poetry is to keep memory alive. For example, Poe's fictional "Annabel Lee" is a tribute to a woman or women he had loved. In "Martin Luther King," Patterson honors a national hero.

Thematic Focus: People in Their Variety

As you read, notice the different types of people you meet in these poems.

◆ Background for Understanding

History

Martin Luther King, Jr. (1929–1968), honored in Raymond Richard Patterson's poem, was a great civil rights leader. Using nonviolent methods, he helped end legal discrimination against African Americans in the South and elsewhere in the United States. In 1968, he was shot and killed by an assassin in Memphis, Tennessee.

◆ Build Vocabulary

Word Root: *-found-*

When you use words with the root *-found-*, meaning "bottom," you're probably talking about something deep. Patterson, for example, calls Martin Luther King Jr.'s passion "profound," meaning "deeply felt": *pro-* means "forward to" and *-found* means "the bottom."

Word Bank

Which of these words from the poems looks as if it's closely related to the verb *prune,* meaning "to trim"?

beset
profound
coveted
squat
saunter
preen
pomp

Prentice Hall Literature Program Resources

REINFORCE / RETEACH / EXTEND

Selection Support Pages
Build Vocabulary: Word Root: *-found-,* p. 246
Build Spelling Skills, p. 247
Build Grammar Skills: Pronouns in Comparisons, p. 248
Reading Strategy: Paraphrase, p. 249
Literary Focus: Rhythm and Rhyme, p. 250

Strategies for Diverse Student Needs, pp. 89–90

Beyond Literature Cross-Curricular Connection: Art, p. 45

Formal Assessment Selection Test, pp. 215–217, Assessment Resources Software

Alternative Assessment, p. 45

Daily Language Practice, p. 36

Resource Pro CD-ROM
"Martin Luther King," "Annabel Lee," "Feelings About Words"—includes all resource material and customizable lesson plan

Listening to Literature Audiocassettes
"Martin Luther King," "Annabel Lee," "Feelings About Words"

Martin Luther King ◆ Annabel Lee ◆ Feelings About Words ◆

◆ Literary Focus

Rhythm and Rhyme

Like a song, a poem has patterns of beats and sounds that make it memorable. **Rhythm** is a poem's pattern of stressed (´) and unstressed (˘) syllables. Notice the drumbeat rhythm here:

Hĕ cáme ŭpón ăn áge
Bĕsét bў gríef, bў ráge—

Rhyme is the repetition of a sound at the ends of nearby words—*age/rage*, for example. The pattern of rhyming words at the ends of lines creates the poem's rhyme scheme.

◆ Reading Strategy

Paraphrase

To help you understand the meaning of a poem, you may want to **paraphrase,** or restate, some or all of it. A paraphrase can't replace the music of a poem. However, it can give you a better grip on what a poem is about. The chart below shows how a reader might paraphrase the first stanza, or group of lines, in "Martin Luther King."

Stanza	Paraphrase
1. He came upon an age Beset by grief, by rage—	King was born in a troubled time.
2.	
3.	
4.	

Preparing for Standardized Tests

Reading This selection presents the strategy of paraphrasing, which will help students as they read in general, and as they answer some reading comprehension items on standardized tests. Standardized tests may evaluate students' understanding of a work by asking them to choose the statement that best paraphrases a given passage. Present the following sample test question:

Which statement best paraphrases these lines from the poem "Annabel Lee?"

"For the moon never beams without bringing me dreams / Of the beautiful Annabel Lee"

The speaker of the poem—

(A) has taken up astronomy
(B) remembers his beloved each night
(C) smiles when he imagines Annabel Lee
(D) wishes he could die, too

Students who know how to paraphrase will try to find the statement that gives the same idea in other words. The best answer is *(B).* For further practice, use Reading Strategy: Paraphrase in **Selection Support,** p. 249.

Interest Grabber Tell students that people who use words to persuade you to buy or do things often rely on the feelings and associations that the words convey. Write the words for four or five generic products on the board, such as sunglasses, shampoo, hand lotion, a beverage, and a boot. Divide the class into groups of "advertising executives," whose job it is to come up with names or slogans for new products. Encourage groups to think of words that will evoke the emotions or attitudes they think fit the product. After groups have shared their efforts, guide them to the poems in the grouping by explaining that poets work hard to select the right words to create the images, feelings, or sounds they wish to convey.

◆ Build Grammar Skills

Pronouns in Comparisons If you wish to introduce the grammar concept for this selection before students read, refer to the instruction on p. 778.

Customize for
Less Proficient Readers
Less proficient readers may be better able to appreciate the poems in this grouping if they can hear them read aloud. They can listen to peer readers, or they can listen to the recording of the poems. Have students listen several times to focus on the deeper levels of meaning and on the other skills featured in this selection.

 **Listening to Literature Audiocassettes**

Customize for
More Advanced Students
Repetition in poetry is the use of a word or group of words more than once in a poem. Like rhyme, which is a kind of repetition, this technique can create various effects. For example, it can create a sense of serenity or a feeling of excitement or anticipation, or it can emphasize key words or ideas. Challenge students to look for the uses of repetition in these poems and to speculate about the purposes for it and the effects it has. Have students work together to discuss what they determine about repetition.

Develop Understanding

In just ten lines, the poet captures the essence of Martin Luther King's life and his contribution to America.

Customize for
English Language Learners
Students may find pronouns whose antecedents are not clear. Point out that in this poem, *He, Him,* and *His* refer to Martin Luther King; in "Abraham, Martin and John," *he* refers to a different man in each stanza.

◆Reading Strategy

❶ **Paraphrase** Have students read the poem several times. Then challenge them to paraphrase it, answering these questions: What did King love? (He loved people and righteousness.) What could he not turn aside from? (He couldn't turn from the grief and rage his people felt.) What was his passion? (He wanted love and understanding for all.) Why wouldn't he turn around? (He felt strongly about the cause.) From what does death set him free? (It frees him from all earthly cares and woes.)

◆Critical Thinking

❷ **Apply** Martin Luther King died because he believed in a cause. Ask students whether dying for a cause automatically makes someone a hero. *Students may say that to die for one's beliefs is to make the ultimate sacrifice; not everyone who dies for a cause is a hero, if the cause is unjust.*

▶ Critical Viewing◀

❸ **Connect** *King seems intense, focused, and passionate.*

Martin Luther King

Raymond Richard Patterson

He came upon an age
<u>Beset</u> by grief, by rage—

His love so deep, so wide,
He could not turn aside.

His passion, so <u>profound</u>, ❶
He would not turn around.

He taught this suffering Earth
The measure of Man's worth. ❷

He showed what Man can be
Before death sets him free.

◆ Build Vocabulary
beset (bē set′) *adj.*: Covered; set thickly with
profound (prō found′) *adj.*: Deeply or intensely felt

▶ **Critical Viewing** The photograph on page 773 shows Martin Luther King, Jr., the subject of Patterson's poem. How might the poet describe the leader's expression? **[Connect]** ❸

Guide for Responding

◆ Literature and Your Life

Reader's Response Do you think this poem captures the spirit of Martin Luther King, Jr.? Why or why not?

Thematic Focus What clues to Martin Luther King Jr.'s personality can you find in this poem?

Journal Writing What political heroes inspire you? In a journal entry, explain what this leader has accomplished or what he or she represents to you. **[Social Studies Link]**

☑ Check Your Comprehension

1. Describe the "age" into which King was born.
2. What are two personal qualities that King brought to this "age"?
3. What did King teach "this suffering Earth"?

◆ Critical Thinking

Interpret

1. What does the poet mean by King's "passion, so profound"? **[Interpret]**
2. In your own words, explain the phrases in lines 8–9 that describe King's achievement. **[Draw Conclusions]**

Evaluate

3. Would this poem be suitable for an epitaph, an inscription on King's grave? Explain. **[Make a Judgment]**

Extend

4. If King were alive today, what are the causes for which he might be fighting? **[Hypothesize]**
5. Where might you go to find out more about Martin Luther King Jr.'s life? **[Social Studies Link]**

Reinforce and Extend

Answers

◆Literature and Your Life

Reader's Response Students may say that it captures the essence of the man, but not the details of his struggle.

Thematic Focus Students may cite a deep love and passion for his beliefs, a desire to teach, and the will to prove how worthy people can be, given a chance.

☑ Check Your Comprehension

1. It was an age of turmoil and trouble.
2. He brought love and passion.
3. He taught the importance of each person's worth, and how much a person can accomplish.

◆Critical Thinking

1. It means his belief propelled him to seek equality and justice.
2. These lines mean that King's life is an example of the great and heroic deeds one can accomplish.
3. Students' answers will vary, but should show an awareness that an epitaph must be brief and memorable.
4. Possible answer: civil rights for all persons, regardless of race, religion, gender, or economic status.
5. Possible answers: Information about Martin Luther King might be found in a history textook, a biography, the encyclopedia, or on the Internet.

CONNECTIONS TO TODAY'S WORLD

Martin Luther King Jr.'s life inspired millions. His death caused shock and sadness and moved poets, songwriters, and the public alike. In this song, Richard Holler honors King and three other important Americans who were assassinated.

Abraham, Martin and John

Richard Holler

Has anybody here seen my old friend
  Abraham,[1]
Can you tell me where he's gone?
He freed a lotta people,
but it seems the good die young,
But I just looked around and he's
  gone.

Has anybody here seen my old friend
  John,[2]
Can you tell me where he's gone?
He freed a lotta people,
but it seems the good die young,
But I just looked around and he's
  gone.

Has anybody here seen my old friend
  Martin,[3]
Can you tell me where he's gone?
He freed a lotta people,
but it seems the good die young,
But I just looked around and he's
  gone.

Didn't you love the things they stood
  for?
Didn't they try to find some good for
  you and me?
And we'll be free.
Someday soon,
It's gonna be one day.

Has anybody here seen my old friend
  Bobby?[4]
Can you tell me where he's gone?
I thought I saw him walkin' up over
  the hill,
with Abraham, Martin and John.

1. **Abraham:** Abraham Lincoln (1809–65), the 16th President of the United States, freed the slaves during the Civil War.
2. **John:** John F. Kennedy (1917–63) was the 35th President of the United States.
3. **Martin:** Martin Luther King, Jr. (1929–68), was a famous civil rights leader in the 1960's.
4. **Bobby:** Robert Kennedy (1925–68), a brother of John F. Kennedy, was a political leader and presidential candidate involved in the civil rights movement.

1. What two things do Abraham, Martin, John, and Bobby have in common?
2. What conclusion does the songwriter draw based on their deaths?

Connections to Today's World

"Abraham, Martin and John" was written in 1968, a year of deep turmoil in America. The war in Vietnam was raging, and the bloody Tet offensive began in January of that year. In April, Martin Luther King was assassinated in Memphis. In June, Robert Kennedy, brother of the late President, and former Attorney General of the United States, was killed while campaigning for the presidency. This song, written and composed by Richard Holler and performed by the singer Dion, reached the No. 4 position on the Billboard pop music charts in that year. The poignant lyrics of this song compare four lost American leaders, all of whom worked to bring about freedom, but whose careers and lives were cut short by assassins.

Thematic Focus

4 People in Their Variety In the lyrics of this song, four major American leaders are remembered for their courage in helping minority groups to achieve their rights. Have students volunteer names of current political leaders in today's society, on a national, state, or local level, whose acts demonstrate leadership, courage, and commitment. As you discuss the outstanding men and women, encourage students to consider such qualities as integrity, compassion, and foresight. In what ways do a hero's qualities go beyond culture, gender, or race?

Customize for *Musical/Rhythmic Learners*

Obtain a recording of the original version of "Abraham, Martin, and John" to play for students. Have them listen for the patterns of repetition in the lyrics, and discuss how the melody and pacing of the song enhance its meaning.

Answers

1. All "freed a lotta people" and died young.
2. The good die young.

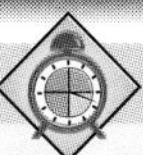

Block Scheduling Strategies

Consider these suggestions to take advantage of extended class time:

- To help students appreciate and understand the poems in this grouping, spend time discussing the Literary Focus and Reading Strategy features on p. 771. Then have students work in pairs to complete **Selection Support** p. 249 and p. 250.
- Divide the class into three groups. Have each group focus on the poems, one at a time. They should read it, discuss it, and answer the Guide for Responding Questions after they finish reading each poem.
- Play a recording of the Connection to Today's World song, "Abraham, Martin and John." Play the recording again, as students read the lyrics in their books on p. 773.
- Devote class time to having students work in small groups on the Projects in the Idea Bank on p. 779.

Develop Understanding

One-Minute Insight In "Annabel Lee," a lyrical, mystical poem, Poe explores the unknown realm of death. The narrator mourns his lost love, Annabel Lee, who was taken from him at a young age, but whom he will never forget.

Clarification

❶ Poe was deeply in love with his young wife, Virginia Clemm, who died of tuberculosis in 1847. Many critics believe that "Annabel Lee" is Poe's response to his wife's tragic death. Other critics have said that the poem is universal, that it speaks to anyone who has ever lost a true love.

Thematic Focus

❷ **People in Their Variety** Point out that in line 2, the narrator describes Annabel Lee as a maiden ". . . whom you may know." Ask students why the poet reaches out to his audience in this way. *Students may say that describing Annabel Lee as someone we may know makes her seem like a real person, not just an imaginary or idealized love.*

◆Critical Thinking

❸ **Interpret** Is the "kingdom by the sea" a real place? *Students may interpret it as an imaginary place that is ever-changing like the motion of the sea; it may stand for an ideal place where the narrator and his love were happy.*

◆Literary Focus

❹ **Rhythm and Rhyme** Point out that rhyme is a form of repetition and that many of the rhymes of this poem are repeated. Ask students to explain the effect of these rhymes. *Students may say that repetition makes it clear that the narrator will never forget Annabel Lee; the steady repetition suggests heartbeats or lapping waves.*

Customize for
English Language Learners
Help students with some of the old-fashioned language of this poem, such as maiden (young woman), wingèd seraphs (angels with wings), and kinsmen (relatives). Have them refer to the footnotes to paraphrase lines that include these words.

❶ *Annabel Lee*

Edgar Allan Poe

It was many and many a year ago,
    In a kingdom by the sea.
❷ That a maiden there lived whom you may know
    By the name of Annabel Lee;—
And this maiden she lived with no other thought
    Than to love and be loved by me.

She was a child and *I* was a child,
    In this kingdom by the sea.
But we loved with a love that was more than love—
    I and my Annabel Lee—
With a love that the wingèd seraphs[1] of Heaven
    Coveted her and me.

❸ And this was the reason that, long ago,
    In this kingdom by the sea,
A wind blew out of a cloud by night
    Chilling my Annabel Lee;
So that her highborn kinsmen[2] came
    And bore her away from me,
To shut her up in a sepulcher[3]
    In this kingdom by the sea.

❹ The angels, not half so happy in Heaven,
    Went envying her and me:—
Yes! that was the reason (as all men know,
    In this kingdom by the sea)
That the wind came out of a cloud, chilling
    And killing my Annabel Lee.

But our love it was stronger by far than the love
    Of those who were older than we—
    Of many far wiser than we—
And neither the angels in Heaven above
    Nor the demons down under the sea,
Can ever dissever[4] my soul from the soul
    Of the beautiful Annabel Lee:—

1. **seraphs** (ser´ əfs) *n.*: Angels.
2. **highborn kinsmen:** Relatives of noble birth.
3. **sepulcher** (sep´ əl kər) *n.*: Vault for burial; grave; tomb.
4. **dissever** (di sev´ ər) *v.*: Separate.

Speaking and Listening Mini-Lesson

Poetry Drumbeat
This mini-lesson supports the Speaking and Listening activity in the Idea Bank on p. 779.

Introduce Talk with students about the concept of stressed and unstressed syllables in poetry and in music. Have them recite a simple poem, such as "Mary Had a Little Lamb," in an exaggerated way to highlight the pattern of stressed and unstressed syllables.

Develop Provide objects that students can use as drums: drums, tambourines, empty containers, rhythm sticks, and so on. Or, suggest that students use a pencil or a ruler to tap on a desk or book. Have student partners work together to determine the drumbeat pattern for whichever poem they choose.

Apply Have groups take turns presenting their poetry drumbeats. Have the audience members of the class compare and contrast the presentations of groups that use the same poem.

Assess Evaluate students on how accurately they capture the rhythmic pattern of the poem, and on how clearly they present stressed and unstressed beats.

For the moon never beams without bringing
me dreams
Of the beautiful Annabel Lee; ❺
And the stars never rise but I see the bright eyes
Of the beautiful Annabel Lee;
And so, all the nighttide,[5] I lie down by the side
Of my darling, my darling, my life and my bride,
In her sepulcher there by the sea—
In her tomb by the side of the sea.

5. **nighttide** (nīt′ tīd′) *n.*: An old-fashioned way of saying nighttime.

◆ Build Vocabulary

coveted (kuv′ it id) *v.*: Wanted greatly

Guide for Responding

◆ Literature and Your Life

Reader's Response Do you think this poem would make a good song? Why or why not?

Thematic Focus Do people today still experience the type of love that the speaker describes in this poem? Explain.

Retelling Review what happens in the poem, and retell the events to classmates as if you were presenting a fairy tale. **[Performing Arts Link]**

☑ Check Your Comprehension

1. At what stage in life did the speaker in the poem fall in love?
2. What caused the death of Annabel Lee?
3. What did Annabel Lee's kinsmen do when she died?
4. Why will nothing be able to separate the speaker's soul from the soul of Annabel Lee?
5. What does the speaker do "all the nighttide"?

◆ Critical Thinking

INTERPRET

1. In your own words, describe the love between the speaker and Annabel Lee. **[Interpret]**
2. In what way does Poe make the events of the story seem distant, like those in a fairy tale? **[Analyze]**
3. How does the last stanza make the sense of sadness in the poem seem immediate and never-ending? **[Support]**

EVALUATE

4. Is the story in this poem realistic? Why or why not? **[Criticize]**

APPLY

5. The poet Countee Cullen once wrote, "Never love with all your heart,/It only ends in aching." Would the speaker in "Annabel Lee" agree? Why or why not? **[Apply]**

COMPARE LITERARY WORKS

6. "Martin Luther King" and "Annabel Lee" are similar in honoring someone who has died. In what ways do they differ? **[Compare and Contrast]**

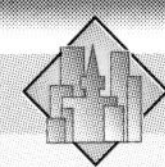

Beyond the Classroom

Community Connection

Memorials Many communities honor local or national heroes, or pay homage to significant places or events that took place in the area. Have students investigate the kinds of memorials that exist in your area. Encourage them to consider such commemorations as parks, schools, streets, or public buildings named for heroes, structures such as monuments or memorial lights dedicated to the dead, or any other special ways that lost lives are remembered with respect and dignity. Students might consult city or county historical societies, or browse through tourist information guides or Internet sites for your area.

Discuss with students the appropriate manner in which to visit a memorial site. If possible, schedule a visit to one of the memorials in your community. You may wish to have students research the developmental process that took place for one or more famous memorials, such as the Vietnam Veterans Memorial in Washington, D.C.

To conclude, students might suggest a recent hero or figure to memorialize, or design a monument to honor that person's achievements in life.

◆ Literary Focus

❺ Rhythm and Rhyme Ask students to explain why they think the poet repeats the name "Annabel Lee" so many times. *Students may say that the repetition of the name is soothing.*

Reinforce and Extend

Answers

◆ Literature and Your Life

Reader's Response Students may say that the repetition is musical and the sad tale is moving.

Thematic Focus Students should support their responses with examples and observations.

☑ Check Your Comprehension

1. He fell in love as a child.
2. A cold wind chilled her. The speaker believes that the wind was sent by angels, jealous of their love.
3. They took her away from the speaker and placed her body in a tomb in a kingdom by the sea.
4. Nothing will separate their souls because their love was stronger than the love of wiser people.
5. He lies "down by the side" of Annabel Lee, possibly in dreams.

◆ Critical Thinking

1. The speaker and Annabel Lee were soulmates. They shared a love so strong that it seemed to last beyond this world.
2. He uses phrases like "many and many a year ago" and "kingdom by the sea" to make his story seem like a fairy tale; the use of angels and a lack of realistic description add to the fairy-tale atmosphere.
3. The poet uses present tense rather than the past. Also, he describes his grief as a feeling that goes on, with no remedy in sight.
4. Some students may feel that the poem is unrealistic because life goes on and most people learn to cope; others may say the story is a realistic view of deep loss.
5. Students may say that the speaker would disagree because he loved with all his heart.
6. "Martin Luther King" honors a real person's achievements; "Annabel Lee" is a fictional person. Both subjects' lives were cut short, but unlike Lee's life, King's had a sense of completion.

Develop Understanding

One-Minute Insight

In this exuberant poem, the speaker expresses some of her own feelings about a wide variety of words, and the power they have to convey emotions, associations, and ideas.

▶ Critical Viewing ◀

❶ **Analyze** *Students may suggest words such as chaos, splash, movement, bright, or swirl.*

◆ Literary Focus

❷ **Rhythm and Rhyme** Point out to students that all of the lines in this poem are short. Discuss why the poet might have chosen to use such short lines. *Students may say that by keeping the lines short, the poet makes the words themselves stand out, and the connections among words in any particular group are clear.*

Customize for
Visual/Spatial Learners
Have students explore the concept of this poem by challenging them to create visual images for words that convey particular ideas. Suggest that they form words in a visual way to convey the word's meaning. For instance, they might write the word *cold* so that it looks as if there were icicles hanging from each letter, or they might write the word *twin* in overlapping pairs of letters.

Dominant Curve, Vasily Kandinsky, Solomon R. Guggenheim Museum, New York, New York

FEELINGS ABOUT WORDS

Mary O'Neill

Some words clink
As ice in drink.
Some move with grace
A dance, a lace.
Some sound thin:
Wail, scream and pin.
Some words are squat:
A mug, a pot,
And some are plump,
Fat, round and dump.
Some words are light:
Drift, lift and bright.
A few are small:
A, is and all.

❷

❶ ▲ Critical Viewing The poet says that every word has a personality. What words would you choose to describe this painting? **[Analyze]**

Humanities: Art

Dominant Curve, April 1936, by Vasily Kandinsky

Russian-born painter Vasily Kandinsky (1866–1944) was an innovator in art. He is thought to be the first artist to paint pictures with no recognizable subject. In addition to painting, he was also a theorist and a teacher who explored the principles of nonrepresentational or "pure" abstraction in art. He believed that painting should be as abstract as music. Use these questions for discussion:

1. What shapes do you see in this work? *Students may cite curves, circles, steps, wedges, rectangles, and squiggles.*
2. In what way does this painting illustrate the poem? *Students may say that the poet plays with the feelings that words convey, and the artist plays with the feelings that colors and shapes convey.*
3. Why do you think Kandinsky called this painting "Dominant Curve"? *Students may note the many curves, including one wide curve that moves vertically through the center of the scene.*

And some are thick,
Glue, paste and brick.
Some words are sad:
❷ "I never had . . ."
And others gay:
Joy, spin and play.
Some words are sick:
Stab, scratch and nick.
Some words are hot:
Fire, flame and shot.
Some words are sharp,
Sword, point and carp.
And some alert:
Glint, glance and flirt.
Some words are lazy:
Saunter, hazy.
❸ And some words preen:
Pride, pomp and queen.
Some words are quick,
A jerk, a flick.
Some words are slow:
Lag, stop and grow,
While others poke
As ox with yoke.
Some words can fly—
There's wind, there's high:
❹ And some words cry:
"Goodbye . . .
Goodbye . . ."

◆ Build Vocabulary

squat (skwät) *adj.*: Short and heavy

saunter (sôn´ tər) *v.*: Walk about idly; stroll

preen (prēn) *v.*: Dress up; show pride in one's appearance

pomp (pämp) *n.*: Impressive show or display

Guide for Responding

◆ Literature and Your Life

Reader's Response Name three of your favorite words, and explain the feelings you have about them.

Thematic Focus O'Neill describes the "personalities" of different words. Do you agree that words can be categorized this way? Explain.

Word Search [Group Activity] With a group, brainstorm for two more examples for each of these kinds of words: "squat," "plump," "light," and "sharp."

☑ Check Your Comprehension

1. List five of the types or categories of words that O'Neill describes.
2. Give one example she uses for each of the five types you have chosen.

◆ Critical Thinking

Interpret

1. Why is *flick* a good example of a word that is quick? **[Support]**
2. Name two ways in which *goodbye* is a word that cries. **[Analyze]**
3. Why does O'Neill call the poem "Feelings About Words"? **[Draw Conclusions]**

Evaluate

4. Do you disagree with any of O'Neill's choices to illustrate certain types of words? Explain. **[Criticize]**

Apply

5. Can two words with the same dictionary definition call up different feelings? Explain. **[Synthesize]**
6. Look at the painting by Wassily Kandinski on page 776. In what way is a poet's love of words similar to an artist's love of color and form? **[Art Link]**

Thematic Focus

❸ **People in Their Variety** In this poem, Mary O'Neill expresses some of her feelings about words. Ask students whether their own feelings about the words in the poem are the same as the poet's. Answers will vary, but students should give reasons to support their responses.

◆ Critical Thinking

❹ **Modify** Discuss the ending of the poem, and how it trails off as if someone is calling out a farewell. Challenge students to think of ways to rewrite the ending to make it more upbeat, or to make it sadder.

Reinforce and Extend

Answers

◆ Literature and Your Life

Reader's Response Encourage students to be specific about why the words they chose are their favorites.

Thematic Focus Most students will see that a word's connotation is, in a way, its unique "personality."

☑ Check Your Comprehension

1. Categories include words that clink, move with grace, sound thin, or are squat, plump, light, small, thick, sad, gay, sick, hot, sharp, alert, lazy, quick, slow
2. Students should choose an example from those available for each of the five categories that they chose.

◆ Critical Thinking

1. It is a one-syllable word with a short *i* sound, giving it a "quick" sound like the movement it describes.
2. *Goodbye* might cry, as in calling a farewell, or in causing tears, as people weep when they part.
3. The poem points out the feelings that she and others associate with certain words.
4. Be sure that students explain their own feelings for choices of words with which they disagree.
5. Students may find it possible. For instance, *scrub* and *wash* both mean to cleanse, but *scrub* connotes a thorough, vigorous cleansing.
6. Students may say that the artist explores color and form in a playful way, much as the poet explores words and their meanings playfully.

Beyond the Selection

FURTHER READING

Other Works by Raymond Richard Patterson
Elemental Blues

Other Works by Edgar Allan Poe
The Black Cat and Other Stories
Complete Poems

Other Works by Mary O'Neill
Words, Words, Words

Other Works About Martin Luther King, Jr.
The Life and Death of Martin Luther King, Jr., by James Haskins

INTERNET

We suggest the following sites on the Internet (all Web sites are subject to change).

For more information about Poe and his life:
http://www.student.virginia.edu/~ravens/poe.html

For links to Martin Luther King, Jr.:
http://pathfinder.com/Life/mlk/mlk.html

We *strongly recommend* that you preview these sites before you send students to them.

Answers

◆Reading Strategy

1. Possible response: King was born in a troubled time. His strong love for others would not let him ignore problems he saw. His deep commitment to others would not let him avoid helping them. In a time of suffering, he showed a person's value, and what can be achieved before death.
2. Possible response: Every night, when the moon and stars come out, I dream of Annabel Lee's bright eyes. In this way, I lie beside the woman I love—who is still my life and my bride—as she lies in her tomb by the sea.
3. Possible response: Some words, like ice in drink, suggest a clinking sound. Some move gracefully, like dance and lace. Some, like wail, scream, and pin, have a thin sound.
4. Possible response: The paraphrase of the O'Neill poem leaves out the quick, two-beat lines and rhymes like clink-drink.

◆Build Vocabulary

Using the Word Root *-found-*
1. b 2. c 3. a

Spelling Strategy
1. correct; 2. acquire; 3. correct; 4. quarrel

Using the Word Bank
1. b 2. a 3. c 4. b 5. a 6. b 7. a

◆Literary Focus

1. 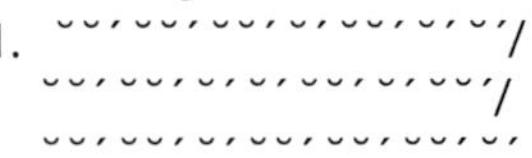

2. The rhyme scheme is: aa bb cc dd ee ff gg hh ii jj hh dd kk ll mm nn hh oo pp qqqq

◆Build Grammar Skills

Practice
1. they (were) 4. she (achieved)
2. she (was) 5. they (were)
3. he (was)

Writing Application
Possible responses:
1. He is sadder than I.
2. They were wiser than we.
3. King was as angry as they.

Guide for Responding *(continued)*

◆ Reading Strategy

Paraphrase

By **paraphrasing** a poem, you can clarify its meaning.

1. Paraphrase each stanza of "Martin Luther King."
2. Paraphrase lines 34–41 of "Annabel Lee."
3. Paraphrase lines 1–6 of "Feelings About Words."
4. Compare one of your paraphrases to the original poem, and find a rhyme or a rhythm that you had to leave out.

◆ Build Vocabulary

Using the Word Root *-found-*

Use your knowledge of the word root *-found-* ("bottom") to match each numbered word with its definition:

1. profound	**a.** one who begins something from the bottom up
2. foundation	**b.** deeply or intensely felt
3. founder	**c.** a structure's support at the bottom

Spelling Strategy

When you spell the *kw* sound in a word, you use the letters *qu,* not a combination with the letter *w:*

squat quality squirm

On your paper, identify and correct the misspelled words.

1. quantity **2.** akwire **3.** quench **4.** kwarrel

Using the Word Bank

On your paper, choose the lettered word or phrase that is closest in meaning to the numbered word.

1. beset: (a) placed in, (b) surrounded by, (c) set again
2. profound: (a) strongly felt, (b) hardly felt, (c) quietly felt
3. coveted: (a) chilled, (b) refused, (c) envied
4. squat: (a) high and mighty, (b) short and heavy, (c) short and sweet
5. saunter: (a) stroll, (b) loaf, (c) hurry
6. preen: (a) take off, (b) dress up, (c) cut with
7. pomp: (a) big display, (b) small ritual, (c) full feast

◆ Literary Focus

Rhythm and Rhyme

Poems create patterns with **rhythm,** an arrangement of stressed and unstressed syllables, and **rhyme,** the repetition of a sound at the ends of words:

- Mark rhythms with (˘) for an unstressed syllable and (´) for a stressed syllable. Example: The word *aside* would be marked ăsíde.
- Rhymes that fall at the ends of lines create a rhyme scheme, which you can analyze by using letters for each rhyme, starting with *a.* For example, the rhyme scheme for "Martin Luther King" is *aa bb cc dd ee.*

1. Mark the rhythm of the first stanza of "Annabel Lee." You'll need the pattern ˘ ˘ ´ as well as ˘ ´.
2. Indicate the rhyme scheme of "Feelings About Words."

◆ Build Grammar Skills

Pronouns in Comparisons

When **pronouns** appear in **comparisons** using *than* or *as,* sometimes words are suggested rather than stated. If you mentally supply the missing words, you can easily select the correct pronoun form to use. When you supply the missing word *were* in the following example, it is clear why Poe used the subject pronoun *we.*

> But our love it was stronger by far than the love/Of those who were older than we [*were*]

Practice On your paper, fill in the unstated word(s), and then choose the correct pronoun.

1. Angels weren't as happy as (them, they) __?__.
2. The highborn kinsmen weren't as noble as (her, she) __?__.
3. No one was sadder than (he, him) __?__.
4. King achieved more than (her, she) __?__.
5. Which leaders were more active than (they, them) __?__?

Writing Application Write three comparisons using *than* or *as,* pronouns, and a word that's only suggested.

Writer's Solution

For additional instruction and practice, use the Special Problems With Pronouns 2 lesson in the *Writer's Solution Language Lab CD-ROM.*

Build Your Portfolio

Idea Bank

Writing

1. Couplet Write two rhyming lines that can be included in "Feelings About Words." Follow this pattern: Some words are ______: / _______, _______, and _______.

2. Liner Notes A singing group has just recorded "Annabel Lee." Write a paraphrase of the poem for the liner notes that will accompany the CD. Your paraphrase will help listeners understand the story told in the poem. **[Career Link]**

3. Critical Review Organizers of a King Day celebration are considering whether to include a reading of Patterson's poem. Review the poem to help them. Decide whether its rhythm, rhymes, mood, and message make it suitable.

Speaking and Listening

4. Oral Interpretation Read one of these poems aloud for the class, stopping at the ends of lines only where there is punctuation. Convey the poet's mood, whether sad or funny. **[Performing Arts Link]**

5. Poetry Drumbeat Drum out the beat of one of these poems as you read it aloud. Give a weak beat to unstressed syllables and a strong one to stressed syllables. Have classmates follow the text silently as they listen. **[Music Link]**

Projects

6. Missing Person Investigation [Group Activity] If possible, find the real identity of Poe's Annabel Lee. Check Web sites on Poe and biographies like Kenneth Silverman's *Mournful and Never-Ending Remembrance*. Present the findings of your investigation to the class.

7. Multimedia Presentation Give a presentation on the life of Martin Luther King, Jr. In addition to an oral report, include news clips, recordings of speeches, photographs, and readings of poems like Patterson's. **[Social Studies Link]**

Writing Mini-Lesson

Remembrance of a Person

Two of these poems, "Annabel Lee" and "Martin Luther King," are types of remembrance. Write a prose remembrance of someone who has been important in your life. Describe this person, your relationship with him or her, and some of the experiences you had together. Above all, show why this person has meant a great deal to you.

Writing Skills Focus: Specific Examples

Use **specific examples,** precise descriptions and detailed stories, to bring your subject to life and show his or her importance to you. For example, don't just say that someone was kind to you. Back up your statement with a story illustrating this person's kindness.

Prewriting Use an outline form like this one to gather information for your remembrance:

I. Description of Person	**II.** Our Relationship
A. Her clothes	**A.** Her kindness
1. Example #1	**1.** Example #1
2. Example #2	**2.** Example #2
B. Her ___?___	**B.** Her ___?___

Drafting Refer to your outline as you write. However, don't hesitate to add examples and descriptions that occur to you while you are drafting.

◆ Grammar Application

To be sure you've used the correct form of the pronoun in *than* or *as* comparisons, mentally fill in the missing words.

Revising Ask a classmate to read your remembrance and describe your subject as specifically as possible. If your reader's description is too general, consider adding more specific examples to your remembrance.

Idea Bank

Following are suggestions for matching the Idea Bank topics with your students' performance levels and learning modalities:

Customize for *Performance Levels*

Less Advanced Students: 1, 4
Average Students: 3, 4, 6
More Advanced Students: 2, 5, 7

Customize for *Learning Modalities*

Verbal/Linguistic: 1, 2, 3, 4
Visual/Spatial: 7
Bodily/Kinesthetic: 4, 5
Logical/Mathematical: 3, 5, 6
Musical/Rhythmic: 4, 5
Interpersonal: 4, 5, 6, 7
Intrapersonal: 1, 2, 3

Writing Mini-Lesson

Refer students to the Writing Handbook in the back of the book for instructions on the writing process and for further information on a remembrance of a person.

Writing Lab CD-ROM

Have students complete the tutorial on Description. Follow these steps:

1. Discuss the types of descriptive writing, their features, and the model of a remembrance.
2. Have students use a Topic Web to narrow their topic.
3. Have students draft on computer.
4. Suggest that students use the Word Bin revision checker to replace vague adjectives with more precise words.

Allow about 70 minutes of class time to complete these steps.

Writer's Solution Sourcebook

Have students use Chapter 2, "Description," pp. 32–65, for additional support. The chapter includes in-depth instruction on organizing details, pp. 53–54.

✓ ASSESSMENT OPTIONS

Formal Assessment, Selection Test, pp. 215–217, and Assessment Resources Software. The selection test is designed so that it can be easily customized to the performance levels of your students.

Alternative Assessment, p. 45, includes options for less advanced students, more advanced students, musical/rhythmic learners, bodily/kinesthetic learners, verbal/linguistic learners, visual/spatial learners, and interpersonal learners.

PORTFOLIO ASSESSMENT

Use the following rubrics in the **Alternative Assessment** booklet to assess student writing:
Couplet: Poetry, p. 95
Liner Notes: Summary, p. 85
Critical Review: Critical Review, p. 98
Writing Mini-Lesson: Description, p. 84

Prepare and Engage

OBJECTIVES

1. To read, comprehend, and interpret poetry
2. To relate poetry to personal experience
3. To listen as you read poetry
4. To appreciate sound devices
5. To build vocabulary in context and learn words based on onomatopoeia
6. To develop skill in using the words *lay* and *lie*
7. To write an analysis of a poem
8. To respond to poetry through writing, speaking and listening, and projects

SKILLS INSTRUCTION

Vocabulary: Words Based on Onomatopoeia

Spelling: Words Beginning With *kn*

Grammar: *lay* and *lie*

Reading Strategy: Listen as You Read Poetry

Literary Focus: Sound Devices

Writing: Clear and Logical Organization

Speaking and Listening: Silly, Sensational Storytelling (Teacher Edition)

Critical Viewing: Synthesize; Compare and Contrast

PORTFOLIO OPPORTUNITIES

Writing: School Cheer; Radio Spot; Poem with Artful Alliteration

Writing Mini-Lesson: Analysis of a Poem

Speaking and Listening: Silly, Sensational Storytelling; Poetry Singing

Projects: Onomatopoeia Factory; Shakespeare and Exploration

More About the Authors

William Shakespeare helped shape the English language by introducing new words and phrases, such as *catch cold, fair play, lousy, laugh it off,* and *foregone conclusion.* He also wrote lines that are memorable to millions of people all over the world.

Eve Merriam wrote dozens of books for children and dozens more for adults. Many of her works tackle social issues such as racial justice. Merriam once said that poets write poems because they must.

Pat Mora believes that geographic location and heritage deeply influence one's life. Her poetry emphasizes the harmony between Mexico and the U. S., with the desert as a common bond between the two cultures.

Guide for Reading

Meet the Author:

William Shakespeare (1564–1616)

Many people regard William Shakespeare as the greatest writer in the English language. In all, Shakespeare wrote 37 plays, many of which are still performed. These include *Romeo and Juliet* and *Hamlet.* He also wrote sonnets and other lyric poems. The song "Full Fathom Five" appears in his play *The Tempest,* which may have been his last work. [For more on Shakespeare, see page 228.]

The Story Behind the Poem

The Tempest was inspired by European exploration in the Americas. The sense of wonder in the play and in "Full Fathom Five" reflects the wonder that Shakespeare felt about this "new world." In fact, the shipwreck referred to in "Full Fathom Five" was based on the wreck of an English ship in Bermuda in 1609.

Eve Merriam (1916–1992)

Eve Merriam's fascination with words began at an early age: "I remember being enthralled by the sound of words." This love, which led her to write poetry, fiction, nonfiction, and drama, is reflected in the poem "Onomatopoeia."

Pat Mora (1942–)

Pat Mora grew up in El Paso, Texas, on the United States/Mexico border. She has written many award-winning stories and poems about her experiences as a Mexican American.

◆ Literature and Your Life

Connect Your Experience

There's something that can quickly change your mood. It doesn't cost any money. You can't hold it in your hands, but it travels in the air and can make different people move to the same rhythm. It's called music.

If you take time to hear it, the music in these poems can make you laugh or feel a sense of wonder.

Thematic Focus: People in Their Variety

How do the people and things in these poems reveal their personalities through the sounds they make?

◆ Background for Understanding

Literature

In Shakespeare's *The Tempest,* a spirit named Ariel sings "Full Fathom Five" to the young prince Ferdinand. The prince and his father, King Alonso, were traveling in a ship that was wrecked on a magical island. Now Ferdinand, wandering the island, hears Ariel sing that his father has drowned. However, Alonso is really alive and will appear at the end of the play.

◆ Build Vocabulary

Words Based on *onomatopoeia*

Onomatopoeia refers to the creation of words to imitate sounds. As you might expect, you'll find examples of this kind of word in the poem "Onomatopoeia": "The rusty spigot/sputters . . . " The dictionary shows that *sputters* was invented long ago to imitate the sound of something that "spits out in small particles."

Word Bank

Which of these words from the poems might describe someone who has *mastered* the art of music?

knell
sputters
maestro
snare

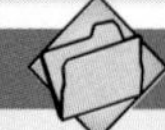

Prentice Hall Literature Program Resources

REINFORCE / RETEACH / EXTEND

Selection Support Pages
Build Vocabulary: Words Based on Onomatopoeia, p. 251
Build Spelling Skills, p. 252
Build Grammar Skills: Commonly Confused Verbs: *lay* and *lie*, p. 253
Reading Strategy: Listen as You Read Poetry, p. 254
Literary Focus: Sound Devices, p. 255

Strategies for Diverse Student Needs, pp. 91–92

Beyond Literature Cross-Curricular Connection: Science, p. 46

Formal Assessment Selection Test, pp. 218–220, Assessment Resources Software

Alternative Assessment, p. 46

Resource Pro CD-ROM
"Full Fathom Five"; "Onomatopoeia"; "Maestro"

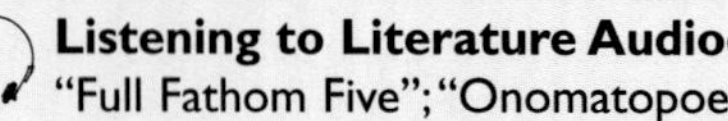

Listening to Literature Audiocassettes
"Full Fathom Five"; "Onomatopoeia"; "Maestro"

◆ Literary Focus

Sound Devices

Poets use **sound devices,** ways of making a work more musical, to appeal to your ear. One device is **onomatopoeia,** the use of words whose sound suggests their meaning, like *sputter.* Another device is **alliteration,** the repetition of sounds at the beginning of words or in stressed syllables: "Full *f*athom *f*ive thy *f*ather lies."

Before you read, tune your ear to these devices by completing this chart:

Onomatopoeia	With Alliteration Added
Sputter	Sprinkly Sputter
Hiss	
Buzz	
Plop	

◆ Reading Strategy

Listen As You Read Poetry

You'll get more out of poetry if you **listen as you read,** hearing a poem's sounds and rhythms. Many poets speak their poems aloud as they write them. Their ear, not their eye, tells them whether a word or line is working.

If possible, read each of these poems softly to yourself, or at least "hear" it in your mind. Listen for the music of the vowel sounds and the sharper music of consonants, like the *t, p,* and *g* sounds in "rusty spigot." Also, hear the chimes of rhymes, like "knell" and "bell."

Preparing for Standardized Tests

Grammar Standardized tests may require students to distinguish between *lay,* meaning "to set or put something down" and *lie,* meaning "to recline." Students also may be tested on the different forms of these verbs. Give students this sample test question:

Identify the sentence that uses the italicized word correctly.

(A) The pianist will *lie* her music next to her on the bench.
(B) Her mother was *laying* down on the sofa, listening to the music on the radio.
(C) Many different forms of coral *lie* on the sea floor, just off shore.
(D) *Lying* his tool kit on the counter, the plumber took a look at the sink.

Point out to students that *lay* always takes a direct object. Then review the forms of *lay* and *lie.* Guide students to recognize that (*C*) is the only sentence in which the correct verb and its form are used. For (*A*) and (*D*), forms of *lay* are needed; For (*B*), *lying* is the correct verb form. For further practice, use Build Grammar Skills in **Selection Support,** p. 253.

Interest Grabber Write a tongue twister such as "She sells sea shells by the sea shore" on the board. Ask volunteers to attempt to say it quickly and without error. Discuss why sentences like this one are pleasing to hear, but hard to say aloud, because of the similarity of sounds. Then lead students to the poems by discussing sound devices such as *alliteration, assonance* (repetition of vowel sounds), and *consonance* (repetition of consonant sounds) that poets use to give rhythm and unity to their poems.

◆ Build Grammar Skills

Commonly Confused Verbs: *lay* and *lie* If you wish to introduce the grammar concept for this selection before students read, refer to the instruction on p. 786.

Customize for
Less Proficient Readers
To help students tune their ears to the poets' use of sound devices, have them create a two-column chart, like the one shown. Ask them to list examples of these sound devices in the appropriate column.

Onomatopoeia	Alliteration

Customize for
More Advanced Students
Challenge students to find what these three poems have in common and how they differ. For instance, students might note that all three poems contain examples of onomatopoeia; that they differ in length and in shape; and that one tells part of a story, another expresses a personal recollection or remembrance, while a third simply is a description.

Customize for
English Language Learners
Because of the sound devices in these poems, students may benefit from hearing them aloud. Play the recording, or call on native-speaking student volunteers to prepare oral interpretations of the poems.

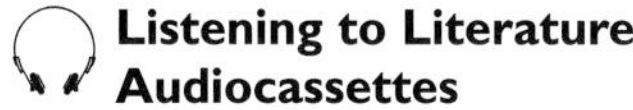

Listening to Literature Audiocassettes

Develop Understanding

One-Minute Insight In this excerpt, a song, from *The Tempest,* we learn that the young prince's father has drowned and has undergone a change on the sea floor. He has become part of the coral life there.

◆Build Grammar Skills

❶ Commonly Confused Verbs: *lay* and *lie* Discuss the distinction between these two verbs. Then point out the father *lies,* or "reclines," at the bottom of the sea, and that *lays,* which means "sets down," and requires a direct object, would be incorrect in this sentence.

Clarification

❷ Coral is a form of marine life having a stonelike skeleton that may be internal or external. Stony coral is the most common and familiar type of coral. Its skeleton is made up almost entirely of calcium carbonate.

◆Critical Thinking

❸ Interpret Discuss with students that a *sea change* is a marked change of some kind, a major transformation. Tell them that when the expression first appeared in 1610, it meant "a change brought about by the sea." Ask them what the sea change of this poem is. *Ferdinand's father has become part of the coral life at the bottom of the sea.*

Customize for
English Language Learners
Students may be unfamiliar with the archaic language that appears in the first poem. Have students find words such as *thy, doth,* and *hark* in the dictionary. Then help them restate the lines where these words appear, using familiar terms to replace the unfamiliar words.

Customize for
Musical/Rhythmic Learners
Invite interested students to set these poems to melody or to give each a rhythmic reading. They might accompany their readings with background music or with sound effects.

Full Fathom Five

WILLIAM SHAKESPEARE

❶ Full fathom[1] five thy father lies,
❷ Of his bones are coral made,
Those are pearls that were his eyes.
Nothing of him that doth fade
But doth suffer a sea change
❸ Into something rich and strange.
Sea nymphs hourly ring his knell.
Ding-dong.
"Hark! Now I hear them—ding-dong, bell."

1. **fathom** (fath´ əm) *n.*: Length of six feet used to measure water depth.

◆ Build Vocabulary

knell (nel) *n.*: Funeral bell

sputters (sput´ ərz) *v.*: Makes hissing or spitting sounds

Block Scheduling Strategies

Consider these suggestions to take advantage of extended class time:

- Focus on the Literary Focus: Sound Devices, p. 781, prior to having students read the selection.
- Have students read the poems, both silently and aloud. Guide them to look for how the poets use onomatopoeia and alliteration to make their poems more lively, musical, and colorful. Have them keep in mind how the sound devices emphasize the mood or meaning of each poem.
- Devote class time to having students prepare and present activities and projects from the Idea Bank, p. 787. Before students begin, discuss which of these activities and projects they would like to develop for their portfolios.
- To help students prepare for the Writing Mini-Lesson, refer them to Literary Focus, p. 255, of **Selection Support,** as well as to Chapter 9, "Response to Literature," in the *Writer's Solution Sourcebook.* You may want to distribute the scoring rubric for Response to Literature, p. 97 in **Alternative Assessment.**

ONOMATOPOEIA

Eve Merriam

4 The rusty spigot
sputters,
utters
a splutter,
spatters a smattering of drops,
gashes wider;
5 slash,
splatters,
6 scatters,
spurts,
finally stops sputtering
and plash!
gushes rushes splashes
clear water dashes.

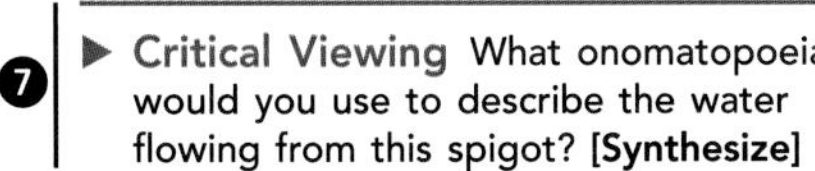

7 ▶ Critical Viewing What onomatopoeia would you use to describe the water flowing from this spigot? **[Synthesize]**

Guide for Responding

◆ Literature and Your Life

Reader's Response Which of these poems was more unusual to you? Why?

Thematic Focus Contrast the "personalities" of the spigot in "Onomatopoeia" and the father in "Full Fathom Five."

Partner Poetry Reading Now that you've listened to these poems yourself, read them aloud to a partner.

☑ Check Your Comprehension

1. What is happening to the father in "Full Fathom Five"?
2. On what object does "Onomatopoeia" focus?
3. In your own words, describe the action in "Onomatopoeia."

◆ Critical Thinking

1. What does Shakespeare mean when he says the father is changing "Into something rich and strange"? **[Interpret]**
2. Which words in "Onomatopoeia" sound most like water? Explain. **[Analyze]**

Evaluate

3. Do the brief lines in "Onomatopoeia" help contribute to the effect of the poem? Explain. **[Criticize]**

Apply

4. In addition to a "rusty spigot," what other thing would be a good subject for a poem entitled "Onomatopoeia"? Why? **[Hypothesize]**

One-Minute Insight "Onomatopoeia" describes the sounds and look of water flowing from a rusty faucet.

◆ Critical Thinking

4 **Hypothesize** Why does the poet choose the word *rusty* to describe the spigot in line 1? *Students may say that she has chosen it for the short* u *sound of the vowel to create assonance (similarity in vowel sounds) and for the consonance, or repetition, of the consonant sound created by the* s *and the* t.

◆ Reading Strategy

5 **Listen as You Read Poetry** Have students read this poem both to themselves and aloud to others so that they may better appreciate its alliteration and onomatopoeia.

◆ Literary Focus

6 **Sound Devices** Guide students to notice the s sound at the end of many lines in this poem. Ask them to describe the effect this sound creates. *Students may point to the hissing sound that identifies flowing water, and the transition from the end of one line to the beginning of the next that mimics the steady flow of the water from the faucet.*

▶ Critical Viewing ◀

7 **Synthesize** *Students' onomatopoetic ideas will vary; invite volunteers to read their descriptions aloud.*

Reinforce and Extend

Answers

◆ Literature and Your Life

Reader's Response Students may find "Onomatopoeia" more unusual because of the short lines and the abundance of sound devices used.

Thematic Focus Students may suggest that the father is now in a permanent and somewhat elegant state, while the spigot creates a changing water flow that varies from a smattering to a gushing.

☑ Check Your Comprehension

1. He is lying under water. His bones have turned into coral and his eyes into pearls.
2. It focuses on a rusty spigot, or faucet.
3. Possible response: At first, the spigot can only spit out a few drops. Gradually, the stream increases until it is flowing freely.

◆ Critical Thinking

1. Possible response: The father appears to be changing from something human into something more like a statue.
2. Students may suggest words such as *splutters, smattering, plash,* or *gush*. They should explain their choices.
3. Students may say that the brief lines recreate the appearance of a long, thin flow of water.
4. Possible response: a creaking door, because words could imitate its sounds and the rhythm of its swing.

Develop Understanding

One-Minute Insight In "Maestro," when a musician bows to the audience after a performance, he hears not the clapping, but only his mother's singing. He recalls the rich musical experiences of his childhood home, in which his mother sang, his father strummed the guitar, and he played the violin.

◆Literary Focus

❶ **Sound Devices** Help students identify the words *clap* and *strummed* as examples of onomatopoeia.

Thematic Focus

❷ **People in Their Variety** Despite the clapping, the musician hears only his mother's voice. Is she in the audience? *Students may say that he hears her voice only in his head, that probably she is not in the audience.*

Comprehension Check ☑

❸ How did the maestro learn music as a child? *He learned by mimicking what his parents played and sang, and by playing with them in a trio.*

◆Critical Thinking

❹ **Analyze** What feelings does the poem evoke, as the maestro thinks back upon his childhood? *Students may say that the poem evokes feelings of home, love, pleasure, and support.*

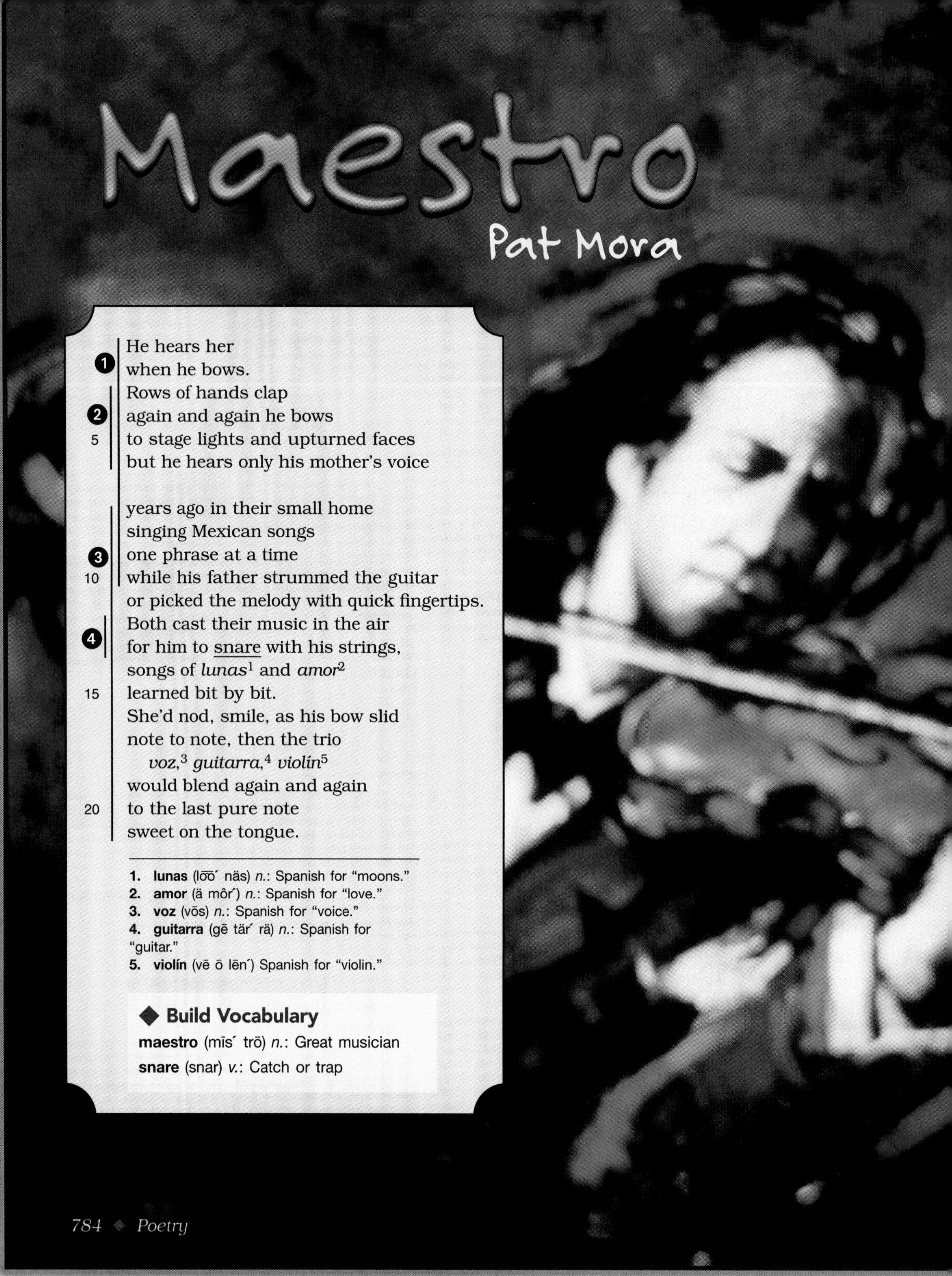

Maestro

Pat Mora

❶ He hears her
when he bows.
❷ Rows of hands clap
again and again he bows
to stage lights and upturned faces
but he hears only his mother's voice

❸ years ago in their small home
singing Mexican songs
one phrase at a time
while his father strummed the guitar
or picked the melody with quick fingertips.
❹ Both cast their music in the air
for him to snare with his strings,
songs of *lunas*[1] and *amor*[2]
learned bit by bit.
She'd nod, smile, as his bow slid
note to note, then the trio
voz,[3] *guitarra,*[4] *violín*[5]
would blend again and again
to the last pure note
sweet on the tongue.

1. **lunas** (lo͞o´ näs) *n.*: Spanish for "moons."
2. **amor** (ä môr´) *n.*: Spanish for "love."
3. **voz** (vōs) *n.*: Spanish for "voice."
4. **guitarra** (gē tär´ rä) *n.*: Spanish for "guitar."
5. **violín** (vē ō lēn´) Spanish for "violin."

◆ Build Vocabulary

maestro (mīs´ trō) *n.*: Great musician

snare (snar) *v.*: Catch or trap

Speaking and Listening Mini-Lesson

Silly, Sensational Storytelling

This mini-lesson supports the Speaking and Listening activity in the Idea Bank on page 787.

Introduce Discuss with students the nature of a cumulative story activity, in which each teller continues a story already begun. Emphasize the need for all participants to listen carefully to what others before them have said.

Develop You may wish to call on a few volunteers and demonstrate the process. As needed, review the meaning of alliteration. Then have students form groups. Each group should choose an order of speaking. Invite students to practice a little to fully understand how the activity works.

Apply Have groups begin their silly, sensational storytelling. If time allows, do the activity one group at a time, so that others can listen to and enjoy all the stories.

Assess Check that all students participate, that each listens to the story that he or she needs to continue, and that students use alliteration in their sentences.

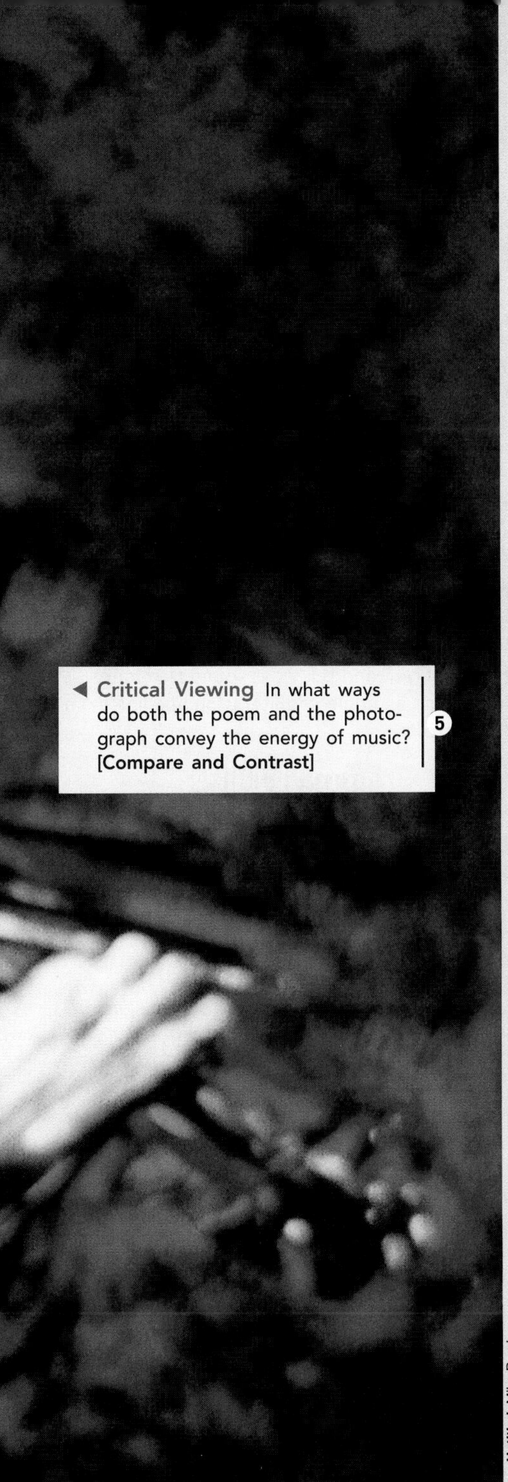

◀ Critical Viewing In what ways do both the poem and the photograph convey the energy of music? **[Compare and Contrast]** 5

Untitled, Mike Reed

Guide for Responding

◆ Literature and Your Life

Reader's Response Would you like to know the family described in "Maestro"? Why or why not?

Thematic Focus How is the musical trio in the poem an example of three different "voices" working together as one?

Group Activity With several classmates, discuss the music you like to hear. Explain your taste in music, and listen to others as they explain theirs.

☑ Check Your Comprehension

1. What is the profession of the person named in the title?
2. What does he recall when he hears the audience's applause?
3. What is his ethnic background?
4. What did each family member contribute to the musical trio?

◆ Critical Thinking

1. Why does the performer hear "only his mother's voice" when he bows? **[Infer]**
2. Which words in the poem convey the feelings in the family without mentioning these feelings directly? **[Analyze]**
3. In what way does this poem use the past to explain the present? **[Draw Conclusions]**

Evaluate

4. Is Mora's use of Spanish words effective? Explain. **[Criticize]**

Apply

5. What does this poem suggest about the importance of the parents' influence on a child? **[Generalize]**

◆Critical Viewing

5 Compare and Contrast

Students may say that both show the intensity and emotional content of the performance and of what life's experiences bring to it.

Reinforce and Extend

Answers

◆Literature And Your Life

Reader's Response Students are likely to say that they would like to know a family that seems so loving and supportive.

Thematic Focus The three different instruments—the voice, the guitar, and the violin—combine to produce one single, harmonious sound.

☑ Check Your Comprehension

1. He is a musician, probably a violinist.
2. He recalls his mother's singing voice and his father playing the guitar.
3. His ethnic background is Mexican.
4. His mother sang, his father played the guitar, and he played the violin.

◆Critical Thinking

1. Possible response: It was her singing that contributed to his love of music.
2. The poem suggests their love for one another by recalling how sweetly they harmonized when they played together.
3. The son's success in the present is attributed to his family's support, teachings, and love of music.
4. Students may suggest that the Spanish words emphasize the reference to Mexican songs that influenced the performer's feelings toward music.
5. The poem suggests that the love, musical sharing, and example that parents provided were a positive influence on the performer when he was a child, indicating that this type of influence is universal.

Beyond the Selection

FURTHER READING

Other Works by the Authors

There Is No Rhyme for Silver, Eve Merriam

Poems From the Planet Earth, Pat Mora

INTERNET

We suggest the following site on the Internet (all Web sites are subject to change).

To find out more about the story of *The Tempest* and when and by whom "Full Fathom Five" is sung:

http://daphne.palomar.edu/Shakespeare/lambtales/Lttemp.htm

We *strongly recommend* that you preview this site before you send students to it.

Answers

◆Reading Strategy

1. Students may hear repeated *r, s, t,* and *sp* sounds.
2. They may hear it in *fathom, of, nothing, doth,* and *something.*
3. Repeated words include *again and again; bit by bit;* and *note to note.*

◆Build Vocabulary

Using Words Based on Onomatopoeia

1. already answered in the book
2. Possible response: steak cooking in a frying pan
3. Possible response: gas escaping from a nozzle
4. Possible response: an arrow moving toward its target
5. Possible response: a passing car on the highway

Spelling Strategy

1. knock; 2. knife; 3. knob

Using the Word Bank

1. Yes; a great musician, or maestro, is needed for that task.
2. No; a knell is a solemn, slowly rung funeral bell.
3. Yes; if it sputters, something is wrong with the water flow.
4. Yes; mice eat cheese and could be trapped, or snared, in their attempt to get it.

◆Literary Focus

1. Possible response: The lines with just one or two words imitate the way a "rusty spigot" coughs up drops of water. The explosive-sounding *sp* and *t* sounds also imitate the coughing of a faucet. The repeated *sh* sound in the last three lines imitates a gushing faucet.
2. The word *ding-dong* imitates the sound of a bell ringing.
3. Possible responses: He hears her; he hears only his; bit by bit; smile as his bow slid; note to note; again and again.

◆Build Grammar Skills

Practice

1. Lay
2. lie
3. laid
4. lain
5. laid

Guide for Responding *(continued)*

◆ Reading Strategy

Listen As You Read Poetry

By **listening as you read these poems,** you heard the rich patterns of sounds in them. Now tune your ears and test your listening skills by answering these questions:

1. Read aloud lines 1–6 of "Onomatopoeia." Which consonant sounds leap out at you? Explain.
2. Reread "Full Fathom Five," listening for the short *o* sound (as in "doth"). In which words do you hear it?
3. "Maestro" creates music with repeated words. Listen for them as you read the poem aloud. Then, write them down.

◆ Build Vocabulary

Using Words Based on *onomatopoeia*

A word based on onomatopoeia sounds like what it describes. For each of these words, fill in a type of sound that it imitates (the first has been done for you).

1. sputter water being coughed from a faucet
2. sizzle ____________
3. hiss ____________
4. zing ____________
5. whiz ____________

Spelling Strategy

In some words, you spell an initial *n* sound *kn: knell.* Other words with this silent *k* before an *n* include *knowledge, knight,* and *knuckle.*

On your paper, write the words with initial *kn* that fit these definitions:

1. A blow, as on a door: __?__
2. A tool for cutting food: __?__
3. A handle on a door: __?__

Using the Word Bank

On your paper, answer each question with *yes* or *no.* Then, explain your answer.

1. Could a *maestro* supervise an orchestra?
2. Does a *knell* usually sound joyful?
3. Would you call a plumber to fix a faucet that *sputters?*
4. Could you use cheese to *snare* a mouse?

◆ Literary Focus

Sound Devices

These poets use a number of **sound devices,** ways to make their poems more musical. One of these is **onomatopoeia,** the use of words that sound like what they mean. You'll find this device not only in "Onomatopoeia" but also in "Maestro." There the word *strummed* imitates the sound of long strokes across the strings of a guitar.

Another sound device is **alliteration,** the repetition of sounds at the beginning of words or in stressed syllables.

1. In addition to the word *sputters* in "Onomatopoeia," how does the whole poem imitate a "rusty spigot"?
2. Find the example of onomatopoeia in "Full Fathom Five," and tell what sound it imitates.
3. Identify an example of alliteration in a line from "Maestro."

◆ Build Grammar Skills

Commonly Confused Verbs: *lay* and *lie*

Lay is a verb meaning "to set or put something down." Its principal parts are *lay, laying, laid, laid. Lay* always takes a direct object. In contrast, *lie* is a verb meaning "to recline." Its principal parts are *lie, lying, lay, lain. Lie* never takes a direct object. Shakespeare uses the present tense of *lie:* "Full fathom five thy father *lies* . . ."

Practice On your paper, choose the correct verb for each sentence.

1. (Lay, Lie) that copy of *The Tempest* on the table.
2. You can (lie, lay) on the couch and listen to the maestro.
3. As he worked on the spigot, he (laid, lay) his wrench down.
4. "I have (lay, lain) underwater for hours," said King Alonso.
5. The maestro has (lain, laid) down his baton for the night.

Writing Application Write a paragraph inspired by one of these poems. Use at least two forms of *lie* and two of *lay.*

Writing Application

Possible response: I can't *lie* down and sleep because of the noisy spigot. For many nights, I have *lain* listening to its sputter. But here is the plumber now. She *lays* down her tools and shakes my hand. While she works, I'll look for the check I wrote for her. I *laid* it aside yesterday.

Writer's Solution

For additional instruction and practice, use the lesson in the *Writer's Solution Language Lab CD-ROM* on Using Verbs, and the Glossary of Troublesome Verbs, p. 68, in the *Writer's Solution Grammar Practice Book.*

Build Your Portfolio

Idea Bank

Writing

1. **School Cheer** Write a cheer to encourage one of your school's athletic teams. Include examples of onomatopoeia and alliteration to give your cheer zing and zest.
2. **Radio Spot** Write a brief radio ad for a product of your choice. Use both onomatopoeia and alliteration to grab listeners' attention. **[Media Link; Career Link]**
3. **Poem With Artful Alliteration** Just as Merriam wrote a poem entitled "Onomatopoeia," write a poem called "Alliteration." In your poem, include examples of alliteration, such as *s*kittish *s*kateboard, *n*oisy *n*eighbors, and *w*ondrous *w*inter.

Speaking and Listening

4. **Silly, Sensational Storytelling** With a circle of classmates, tell a silly, sensational story about someone or something in one of the poems. Each teller should add a sentence with alliteration before passing the story to the next teller in the circle. **[Performing Arts Link]**
5. **Poetry Singing** Listen to a recording of an actor singing "Full Fathom Five" in Act I, Scene ii of *The Tempest*. Then, imitating the actor, sing the poem for the class. **[Performing Arts Link]**

Projects

6. **Onomatopoeia Factory** **[Group Activity]** With classmates, set up a "factory" to create sound words. Add to our stock of sound words (like *hiss*) by assembling words to imitate such sounds as heavy scraping and hearty laughing.
7. **Shakespeare and Exploration** Summarize *The Tempest* for your class. Then, explain how Shakespeare used details from exploration in the Americas in the play. Use the preface to an edition of the play to research this subject. **[Social Studies Link]**

Writing Mini-Lesson

Analysis of a Poem

You analyze when you break something down to see how it works—whether it's a car's engine or a friend's behavior. Now choose one of these poems to analyze. Discuss two of its different elements, like sound devices and characters. Show how these work in the poem and how they work together to create a single feeling or idea.

Writing Skills Focus: Clear and Logical Organization

Your analysis will be easier to read and to write if you use **clear and logical organization:**

- **Introduction**—a paragraph to identify the poem you'll analyze and the elements you'll discuss
- **Body**—two paragraphs to discuss the elements of the poem
- **Conclusion**—a paragraph to explain how the elements of the poem work together

Prewriting Figure out two elements of the poem you can discuss. Among the elements you could discuss are sound devices, rhyme, appearance, images, or characters. Review the poem, and jot down ideas about these elements.

Drafting You don't have to write the sections in the order that they'll appear. Start with the body if you want to get into your discussion right away. You can write the introduction later.

Grammar Application

Be sure that you haven't confused *lie* and *lay*.

Revising Check that your analysis contains an introduction, body, and conclusion. Also, be sure that the conclusion shows how the elements work together. In discussing "Maestro," for example, indicate how the music of the sound devices helps you better understand the musical people in the poem.

ASSESSMENT OPTIONS

Formal Assessment, Selection Test, pp. 218–220, and Assessment Resources Software. The selection test is designed so that it can be easily customized to the performance levels of your students.

Alternative Assessment, p. 46, includes options for less advanced students, more advanced students, visual/spatial learners, interpersonal learners, verbal/linguistic learners, musical /rhythmic learners, and logical/mathematical learners.

PORTFOLIO ASSESSMENT

Use the following rubrics in the **Alternative Assessment** booklet to assess student writing:
School Cheer: Cause-Effect, p. 89
Radio Spot: Persuasion, p. 92
Poem With Artful Alliteration: Poetry, p. 95
Analysis of a Poem: Response to Literature, p. 97

Idea Bank

Following are suggestions for matching the Idea Bank topics with your students' performance levels and learning modalities:

Customize for *Performance Levels*
Less Advanced Students: 1, 4
Average Students: 2, 4, 5
More Advanced Students: 3, 5, 6, 7

Customize for *Learning Modalities*
Verbal/Linguistic: 1, 2, 3, 4, 5, 6, 7
Bodily/Kinesthetic: 5
Logical/Mathematical: 1, 2, 7
Musical/Rhythmic: 1, 2, 3, 4, 5
Interpersonal: 1, 4, 6, 7
Intrapersonal: 2, 3

Writing Mini-Lesson

Refer students to the Writing Handbook in the back of the book for instructions on the writing process and for further information on analyzing poetry.

Writer's Solution

Writers at Work Videodisc
Have students view the videodisc segment on the prewriting phase of writing a response to literature (Ch. 9), featuring Naomi Long Madgett, to see how she focuses her topic.

Play frames 34879 to 35368

Writing Lab CD-ROM
Have students complete the tutorial on Response to Literature. Follow these steps:

1. Have students review the purposes for responding to literature and determine their purpose.
2. Have students learn about strategies for gathering details (freewriting, using a Sunburst Diagram).
3. Have students draft on computer.
4. Have students use a revision checker for varied language and to hear tips from professional writers.

Allow about 70 minutes of class time to complete these steps.

Writer's Solution Sourcebook
Have students use Chapter 9, "Response to Literature," pp. 265–295, for additional support. The chapter includes in-depth instruction on drafting, p. 285.

Prepare and Engage

OBJECTIVES

1. To read, comprehend, and interpret four poems
2. To relate poems to personal experience
3. To respond to poetry
4. To recognize figurative language
5. To build vocabulary in context and learn the prefix *dis-*
6. To use *like* and *as* correctly
7. To write an extended definition
8. To respond to the poems through writing, speaking and listening, and projects

SKILLS INSTRUCTION

Vocabulary: Using the Prefix *dis-*

Spelling: Adding Suffixes to Words Ending With Consonant-Vowel-Consonant

Grammar: Use of *Like* and *As*

Reading Strategy: Respond to Poetry

Literary Focus: Figurative Language

Writing: Topic Statement

Speaking and Listening: Television Newscast (Teacher Edition)

Critical Viewing: Connect; Assess

PORTFOLIO OPPORTUNITIES

Writing: E-mail Response; Personified Weather Report; Analysis

Writing Mini-Lesson: Extended Definition

Speaking and Listening: Television Newscast; Simile Slam

Projects: Illustrated Figure of Speech; Dancing With "Aunt Leaf"

More About the Authors

Mary Oliver is on the faculty of Bennington College and taught at Sweet Briar College and Duke University.

Carl Sandburg played his guitar and sang American folk songs as an interlude to poetry readings. He also wrote a major biography of Abraham Lincoln.

Naomi Long Madgett, in addition to writing poetry, publishes collections of poetry in Detroit, Michigan.

Wendy Rose believes that everyone has the ability to write, draw, or sing, and that people need only self-confidence to tap into that ability and share it with the world.

Guide for Reading

Meet the Authors:

Mary Oliver (1935–)

As a poet, Mary Oliver is known for her fresh perceptions of nature. She received the Pulitzer Prize in Poetry for her book *American Primitive*.

Carl Sandburg (1878–1967)

The son of Swedish immigrants, Carl Sandburg was born in Illinois. Although he won the Pulitzer Prize in both poetry and history, he was not a typical scholar. By the time his first book appeared, he had been a farm worker, a stagehand, a railroad worker, a soldier, and a cook, among other things.

THE STORY BEHIND THE POEM

Sandburg was working as a reporter when he wrote "Fog." He jotted down the poem one day while waiting to interview a Chicago judge for his paper.

Naomi Long Madgett (1923–)

Naomi Long Madgett once said, "I would rather be a good poet than anything else." This ambition has led her to write seven collections of poetry.

Wendy Rose (1948–)

Wendy Rose was born in California, to a Hopi father and a Scots-Irish-Miwok mother. Besides being a poet, she is a painter and a scientist who studies customs and beliefs. "Loo-Wit" is based on legends of the Cowlitz people of Washington State.

◆ LITERATURE AND YOUR LIFE

CONNECT YOUR EXPERIENCE

You've heard people refer to nature as a person: Mother Nature. Although she has her quiet moments, Mother Nature can also get angry. The picture on the facing page shows that you don't want to be there when she blows her top! These poems are like home movies of Mother Nature. They show both her quiet and her angry moods.

THEMATIC FOCUS: Nature's Wonders

How do these poems help you see nature with fresh eyes?

◆ Background for Understanding

SCIENCE

"Loo-Wit" describes the May 18, 1980, eruption of the Mount St. Helens volcano in Washington State. A volcano is an opening in the Earth's crust through which rocks, dust, and ash, or hot liquid rock, can shoot out. The Mount St. Helens eruption killed about 60 people and destroyed about 10,000,000 trees. Hundreds of miles away, volcanic ash "like gray talcum powder" rained down on cities.

◆ Build Vocabulary

PREFIXES: *dis-*

You may have heard the phrase, "don't dis me!" The prefix *dis-*, meaning "away, apart, not, or the opposite," disses every word it can. In "Loo-Wit," it changes *lodge* ("to stay in a resting place") to *dislodge* ("to go away from a resting place").

WORD BANK

Which of these words from the poems describes what a runner does just before starting the 100-yard dash?

haunches
buttes
crouches
unravel
dislodge

Prentice Hall Literature Program Resources

REINFORCE / RETEACH / EXTEND

Selection Support Pages
Build Vocabulary: Prefixes: *dis-*, p. 256
Build Spelling Skills, p. 257
Build Grammar Skills: Correct Use of *like* and *as*, p. 258
Reading Strategy: Respond to Poetry, p. 259
Literary Focus: Figurative Language, p. 260

Strategies for Diverse Student Needs, pp. 93–94

Beyond Literature, Media Connection: Animated Film, p. 47

Formal Assessment Selection Test, pp. 221–223, Assessment Resources Software

Alternative Assessment, p. 47

Writing and Language Transparencies
Cluster Organizer, p. 82; Venn Diagram, p. 86

Resource Pro CD-ROM
"Aunt Leaf"; "Fog"; "Life"; "Loo-Wit"—includes all resource material and customizable lesson plan

Listening to Literature Audiocassettes
"Aunt Leaf"; "Fog"; "Life"; "Loo-Wit"

Aunt Leaf ◆ Fog ◆ Life ◆ Loo-Wit

◆ Reading Strategy

Respond to Poetry

A poem is an open invitation for you to think and feel. **Respond** to its invitation by bringing your understanding to its words, your heartbeat to its rhythms, and your senses to its descriptions. Agree or disagree with its statements, and tap out the beat of its stressed syllables. Enrich its descriptions with your own memories and experiences.

These questions, and those you make up yourself, will help you respond to the poems:

- "Aunt Leaf"—What natural creature would I most like to be?
- "Fog"—When have I seen fog? Did it move or stand still?
- "Life"—To what would I compare life?
- "Loo-Wit"—Is it fun to think of a volcano as a person? Why or why not?

◆ Literary Focus

Figurative Language

You can expect to see figurative language in poetry. **Figurative language** is language that is not meant to be interpreted literally. The following chart lists and describes the major types of figurative language. As you read the poems, look for examples of these types of figurative language.

Type	Description	Example
Simile	Comparison using *like* or *as* to note a similarity in two apparently unlike items	"We'd travel cheerful as birds."
Metaphor	Direct comparison that describes one item as if it were another	"Life is but a toy."
Extended Metaphor	Metaphor that continues past a phrase or sentence	The poem "Fog" develops an extended metaphor.
Personification	Language that gives human traits to something nonhuman	"Loo-Wit" describes a volcano as a woman.

Preparing for Standardized Tests

Punctuation and Capitalization The way that a poem appears on the printed page offers clues to the poet's meaning. Punctuation and capitalization guide readers to experience, understand, and interpret poetry. Recognition of correct punctuation and capitalization usage is often evaluated with standardized tests. Write the following sample test item on the board:

Choose the sentence in which punctuation and capitalization are used correctly.

(A) The fog in San Francisco blanked out the view of the pacific from the window.

(B) The Mount st. Helens eruption could be seen and felt many miles away

(C) Aspen trees, which grow in the mountains of colorado have brilliant gold leaves in the fall.

(D) Cold spring water bubbled down from the rocks and flowed into the clear Blanco River.

Help students to identify the errors in *(A)* (Pacific), *(B)* (St. Helens, away.), and *(C)* (Colorado,). Lead them to see that *(D)* is the only sentence that is correctly punctuated and capitalized.

Write the following on the board: "The tree was like a/an ___?___." Ask volunteers to complete the sentence and then explain why they chose their comparisons. Point out how the type of tree, its location, and the season might affect the comparison made. Tell students that the poems they are about to read include comparisons that can help them think about the natural world in new ways.

◆Build Grammar Skills

Correct Use of *Like* and *As* If you wish to introduce the grammar concept for this selection before students read, refer to the instruction on p. 796.

Customize for *Less Proficient Readers*

To help students locate and understand the figurative language in the poems, have them complete a chart like the one below as they read.

Object or idea described.	To what is it compared?	What do I imagine?
Fog	A cat	A large, soft, gray kitten creeping across the landscape

Customize for *More Advanced Students*

Encourage students to compare the ways in which each writer uses figurative language. They might find it helpful to create a Venn diagram to organize their ideas. Then have students write a short compare-and-contrast essay explaining their ideas.

Customize for *English Language Learners*

Read the poems aloud, or have students listen to the poems on recording. Then, use pantomime and illustration to help students understand the figurative language. For instance, pantomime similes and metaphors such as moving "on little cat feet" and traveling "cheerful as birds"; and illustrate "snakes green as ribbons" and "clearing the twigs from her throat."

Listening to Literature Audiocassettes

Develop Understanding

One-Minute Insight In "Aunt Leaf," the speaker tells about an imaginary friend, described as a great-great-aunt. With this aunt, the speaker takes fanciful journeys during which the two are changed into a variety of wildlife creatures. In the end, the speaker must return to her unimaginative, but kind and solid, family.

◆Reading Strategy

❶ **Respond to Poetry** Ask students what sense the poet appeals to in the opening lines of the poem. Have them give examples to support the answer. *The poet appeals to the sense of sight by describing Aunt Leaf as* dark as hickory *and by using visually descriptive names,* Shining-Leaf, Drifting-Cloud, *or* The-Beauty-of-the Night.

◆Literary Focus

❷ **Figurative Language** Have students locate the example of figurative language in this line. Then ask them to identify it as a simile, a metaphor, an extended metaphor, or personification, and to name the two things being compared. Discuss the image created by this comparison. *The simile* she'd rise up, like an old log in a pool, *compares the aunt with a log. The image is one of a wet, dark log rising slowly and breaking through the surface of the water.*

Customize for
Less Proficient Students
Read the poem aloud with students, helping them to identify the subject, verb, and other important elements in each sentence. Illustrate how students can use punctuation to help them know when to pause and when to continue reading. Encourage students to discuss sentences or phrases they have difficulty understanding.

Aunt Leaf

Mary Oliver

❶ Needing one, I invented her—
the great-great-aunt dark as hickory
called Shining-Leaf, or Drifting-Cloud
or The-Beauty-of-the-Night.

Dear aunt, I'd call into the leaves,
❷ and she'd rise up, like an old log in a pool,
and whisper in a language only the two of us knew
the word that meant *follow*,

and we'd travel
cheerful as birds
out of the dusty town and into the trees
where she would change us both into something quicker—
two foxes with black feet,
two snakes green as ribbons,
two shimmering fish—
and all day we'd travel.

Block Scheduling Strategies

Consider these suggestions to take advantage of extended class time.

- Have students work in small groups to read the poems aloud. Ask them to list examples of figures of speech they find in each poem. Then have groups discuss and compare their lists. For additional practice, use **Selection Support,** p. 260.
- Have students use the Venn Diagram, p. 86, in **Writing and Language Transparencies,** to organize their ideas for writing the Analysis in the Idea Bank, p. 797.
- If you have access to technology, have students use the *Writer's Solution Writing Lab CD-ROM* to prepare for and complete the Writing Mini-Lesson, p. 797.
- Have students listen to the recording of the poems. First, review the reading strategy with students. Encourage them to listen for rhythm patterns and figurative language. Then have groups of students work together to answer the Literary Focus questions on p. 796.

Listening to Literature Audiocassettes

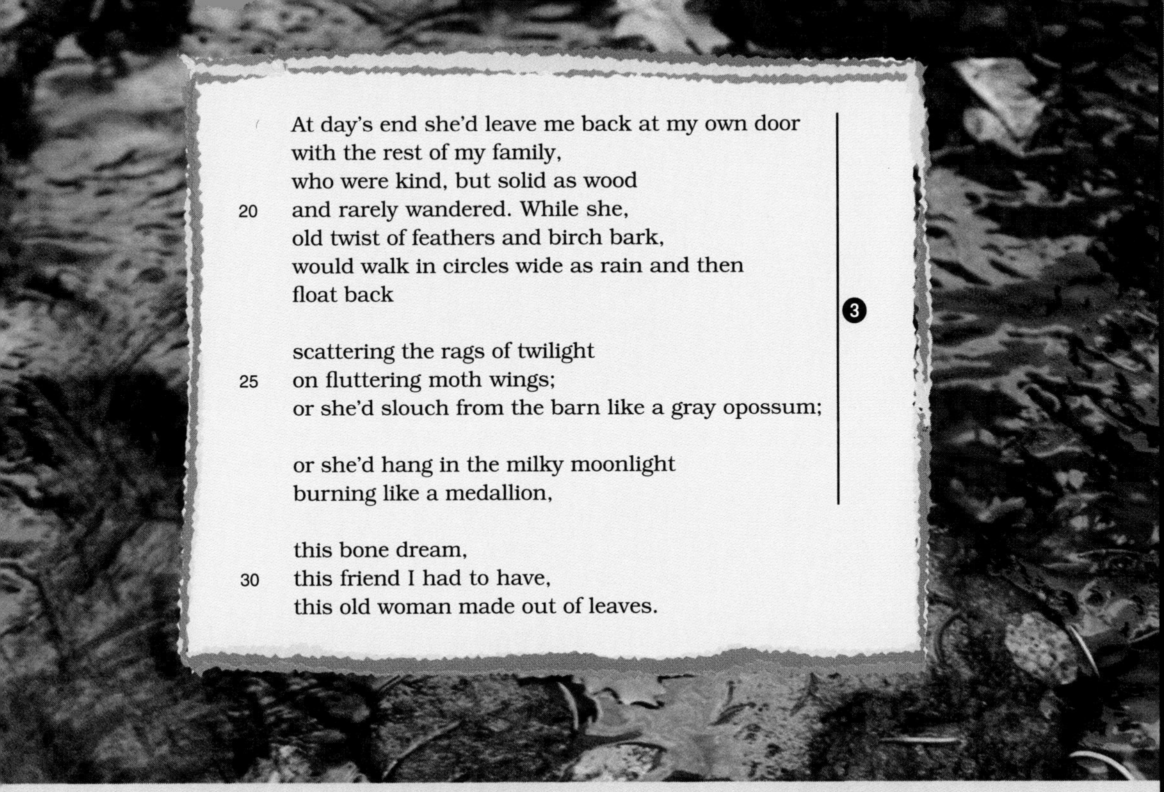

At day's end she'd leave me back at my own door
with the rest of my family,
who were kind, but solid as wood
and rarely wandered. While she,
old twist of feathers and birch bark,
would walk in circles wide as rain and then
float back

scattering the rags of twilight
on fluttering moth wings;
or she'd slouch from the barn like a gray opossum;

or she'd hang in the milky moonlight
burning like a medallion,

this bone dream,
this friend I had to have,
this old woman made out of leaves.

❸

Guide for Responding

◆ Literature and Your Life

Reader's Response Have you ever "traveled" the way the poem's speaker does? Explain.

Thematic Focus Find a word or phrase in the poem that conveys the wonder of nature, and explain your choice.

Journal Writing In your journal, describe an imaginary friend who would suit your personality.

☑ Check Your Comprehension

1. What names did the speaker give her invented great-great-aunt?
2. How did the speaker call to her "aunt," and how did the "aunt" respond?
3. Describe the adventures the speaker had with her "aunt."

◆ Critical Thinking

Interpret

1. In your own words, describe the "aunt" that the speaker invented. **[Interpret]**
2. Contrast the "travel" that the speaker did with ordinary travel. **[Compare and Contrast]**
3. In what way is the speaker different from her family? **[Infer]**
4. Why do you think the speaker "had to have" a friend like this? **[Draw Conclusions]**

Evaluate

5. Is *shimmering* (line 15) a good word to describe a fish? Explain. **[Criticize]**

Apply

6. What does this poem suggest about the power of the imagination? **[Generalize]**

◆ Literary Focus

❸ **Figurative Language** Lead students to locate and identify (by type) four examples of figurative language in these lines and discuss the image created by each comparison. Family as solid as wood, *simile, creates image of sturdy but unmoving people;* she, old twist of feathers and birch bark, *metaphor, creates image of someone light, less sturdy than wood;* she'd slouch . . . like a gray opossum, *simile, creates image of someone moving slowly, close to the ground;* she'd hang . . . burning like a medallion, *simile, creates image of a shining metal disk.*

Reinforce and Extend

Answers

◆ Literature and Your Life

Reader's Response Students may suggest daydreams they've had about being outdoors.

Thematic Focus Possible response: The names used for the great-great-aunt suggest the wonder of nature.

☑ Check Your Comprehension

1. She called her Shining-Leaf, Drifting-Cloud, and The-Beauty-of-the-Night.
2. She'd call "Dear aunt" "into the leaves," and the aunt would whisper a "word that meant *follow.*"
3. Possible response: They'd travel like birds into the trees, then change into foxes, snakes, or fish.

◆ Critical Thinking

1. Possible response: This aunt was like a fairy godmother, who could change herself and the speaker into different creatures.
2. The speaker seems to travel in her mind, rather than traveling on foot or other ordinary ways.
3. She is adventurous and wanders regularly in her imagination, while her family is stolid, if benign.
4. Possible response: She needed to get closer to nature and needed a companion who could help her develop her imagination.
5. Possible response: *Shimmering* is a good word to describe the play of light on a fish's scales.
6. Possible response: The poem suggests that imagination is powerful and can change the way we see and live in the world. It can help us participate more in the world.

Cross-Curricular Connection: Science

Leaves Leaves come in various shapes and sizes, but they all serve a similar purpose—to provide food for plants. Each leaf is like a tiny food factory, gathering water and carbon dioxide from the environment and then using the sun's energy to combine them into glucose and then into starch. This process is called *photosynthesis,* from Greek words meaning "to put together with sunlight." As carbon dioxide and water combine in the leaf, oxygen is released back into the environment.

As well as being essential for providing plant food and maintaining a balanced atmosphere, leaves are used as food (lettuce and cabbage); as flavoring (mint and bay); for beverages (tea and coffee); and as dyes (indigo and henna). Some large leaves are even used to form the roofs and walls of shelters.

Have interested students find answers to questions such as these:

- Why do leaves change color in autumn?
- How does a simple leaf differ from a compound leaf?
- What are the purposes of special leaves, such as pea-plant tendrils or cactus spines?

One-Minute Insight In "Fog," Carl Sandburg describes fog as a cat slowly walking, then sitting, then walking again across the landscape.

Naomi Long Madgett, in "Life," explains that life is like a ticking watch, first entertaining an infant and then being allowed to wind down by a tired old man.

◆Critical Thinking

❶ **Infer** Point out to students that this poem consists of a single image. Ask them what the poet might want the reader to discover by focusing on fog in this way. *Possible response: The poet wants the reader to experience fog as one of nature's wonders instead of as a troublesome weather condition.*

◆Literary Focus

❷ **Figurative Language** Ask students to identify and explain the figurative language Sandburg uses in "Fog." *Sandburg uses an extended metaphor to compare fog to a cat.*

Customize for
Musical/Rhythmic Learners
Have students read "Life" aloud to the rhythm of a ticking clock. If possible, allow the tick-tock rhythm to slow as they get to the end of the poem. Ask students how reading the poem in this way helps them understand its meaning.

❶

FOG

Carl Sandburg

The fog comes
on little cat feet.

❷

It sits looking
over harbor and city
on silent haunches
and then moves on.

◆ **Build Vocabulary**

haunches (hônch´ iz) *n.*: An animal's legs

Beyond Literature

Science Connection

Fog vs. Smog Both fog and smog can cloud your vision, but they are very different in nature. Fog is a mass of microscopic water droplets that hug the ground as a low-flying cloud. Smog, whose name was created by combining the words *smoke* and *fog,* is a form of air pollution. Despite the origins of its name, smog has no relationship to real fog other than being similar in appearance. Smog results from large amounts of pollutants in the air. These pollutants come from the exhausts from automobiles, factory smokestacks, and chimneys. Smog is dangerous and even deadly to people, animals, and plants.

Cross-Curricular Activity

Group Report [Group Activity] With a group, prepare a report on smog. Divide up topics like these: causes of smog; smog prevention; air quality in major cities such as London, Los Angeles, Tokyo, and Beijing; effects of smog on human health. Share your findings with the class in an illustrated report.

Speaking and Listening Mini-Lesson

Television Newscast

This mini-lesson supports the Speaking and Listening activity in the Idea Bank on p. 797.

Introduce Discuss with students the kinds of information that are included in a televised new story. Lead them to see that, like print news stories, an effective and informative television news story answers the questions *Who? What? When? Where?* and *Why?*

Develop After students reread the Background on p. 788, refer them to reference sources, such as an almanac or encyclopedia, or to sites you have preselected on the Internet to gather facts about the Mt. St. Helens eruption. As they research, have students look for answers to the five questions, *Who? What? When? Where?* and *Why?* Suggest that students create note cards to help organize their newscasts.

Apply Give students an opportunity to prepare and rehearse their broadcast news stories. Point out that television reporters may refer to notes or a teleprompter, but, for the most part, they look at the camera in order to make eye contact with the viewing audience. They don't read their stories, and they speak slowly and clearly so that each word can be understood. Have students present their newscasts to the class.

Assess Lead a class discussion about the variations among the newscasts. Evaluate students' work on the quality of preparation and clarity of presentation. Students may evaluate each newscast using the Speaker/Speech form, p. 105, in **Alternative Assessment.**

▶ Critical Viewing In what ways is life like a pocket-watch? [Connect] ❸

Life

Naomi Long Madgett

Life is but a toy that swings on a bright gold chain
Ticking for a little while
To amuse a fascinated infant, ❹
Until the keeper, a very old man,
Becomes tired of the game
And lets the watch run down.

Guide for Responding

◆ Literature and Your Life

Reader's Response Do you agree with the statement in "Life" that "Life is but a toy"? Why or why not?

Thematic Focus Would you call fog one of nature's wonders? Explain.

Pantomime Using gestures, expressions, and movements but not words, express the action in one of these poems.

☑ Check Your Comprehension

1. Describe the setting of "Fog."
2. Identify three things the fog does.
3. In your own words, describe what happens in "Life."

◆ Critical Thinking

INTERPRET

1. What overall impression of fog does the poet create in "Fog"? **[Draw Conclusions]**
2. In your own words, explain what the poem "Life" suggests about life. **[Draw Conclusions]**

EVALUATE

3. Is a ticking watch a good image for life? Why or why not? **[Make a Judgment]**

APPLY

4. What is it about fog that makes it a good subject for a poem? **[Speculate]**

COMPARE LITERARY WORKS

5. What is similar or different about the overall feeling that each of these poems creates? **[Compare and Contrast]**

Beyond the Classroom

Career Connection

Meteorology Natural and human-made weather conditions, including fog, smog, and even the effects of volcanic eruptions, are studied, predicted, and reported by meteorologists. Government agencies, private industry, and television and radio stations use meteorologists. TV's "personality" weather reporters may or may not be meteorologists.

Meteorologists collect data using a variety of instruments; barometers measure air pressure, thermometers measure temperature, hygrometers measure humidity, and anemometers measure wind speed. Weather satellites orbit the earth and send back pictures of weather disturbances and cloud movements. Data is combined and analyzed to determine what the weather will be like at a given place and time.

Have interested students contact a meteorologist in your area to gather information about the field. Students might want to learn about the educational background required, day-to-day responsibilities, and the things the meteorologist likes most and least about his or her job.

▶Critical Viewing◀

❸ **Connect** *Possible response: Each shows in its own way the passing of time.*

◆Literary Focus

❹ **Figurative Language** Ask students to identify and discuss the figurative language used in "Life." *"Life" is a metaphor comparing life to a ticking watch that eventually runs down.*

Reinforce and Extend

Answers

◆Literature and Your Life

Reader's Response Some students may agree with the statement, while others may think that life has more meaning.

Thematic Focus Answers will vary, but students should support their answers with reasons.

☑ Check Your Comprehension

1. The setting of "Fog" is a city with a harbor.
2. The fog comes, looks, and leaves.
3. Possible response: Life is like a watch. It amuses an infant, but an old man grows tired of it and is relieved when it stops.

◆Critical Thinking

1. Possible response: The fog seems delicate and quiet, like a cat.
2. Possible response: It seems to say that life is fascinating when you're very young but you lose interest as you grow older.
3. Answers will vary, but students should be specific in discussing why the image is or is not a good one.
4. Possible response: Fog seems to come and go mysteriously and makes the world into a mysterious place.
5. Possible response: The emotion in "Fog" seems to be an enjoyment of the fog's mystery and quiet. "Life," in contrast, seems to express a discouragement about the way that you lose interest in life as you grow older.

One-Minute Insight

The eruption of Mount St. Helens is personified as an old woman waking up in "Loo-Witt." The eruption itself is described as being started by a "boot scrape" that wakes the old woman. The natural wonder of the volcano's eruption is described as singing.

◆Literary Focus

❶ Figurative Language Ask students who the old woman is and what details they used to make the determination. *She is the volcano. Clues include* spits her black tobacco *(or smoke) and* bumpy bed *(or rocky base).*

Clarification

❷ Have students review the poem and photo to help them figure out the warning of a volcanic eruption.

◆Reading Strategy

❸ Respond to Poetry Ask students what the tone of the last part of the poem is. *Most students will recognize that the tone is free and happy.*

Customize for *Less Proficient Readers*

Suggest that students stop and ask questions about personification details they do not understand. For example, if they do not understand the image in lines 22–26, they could ask what kinds of things get plowed. This will help them understand what Loo-Wit's "skin" is.

Customize for *Visual/Spatial Learners*

Have pictures of volcanoes and volcanic eruptions on hand for students to refer to as they read. The pictures will help students connect personified details with visual images.

Loo-Wit[1]

Wendy Rose

The way they do
this old woman
no longer cares
what others think
but spits her black tobacco
any which way
stretching full length
from her bumpy bed.
Finally up
she sprinkles ashes
on the snow,
cold buttes
promise nothing
but the walk
of winter.
Centuries of cedar
have bound her
to earth,
huckleberry ropes
lay prickly
on her neck.
Around her
machinery growls,
snarls and plows
great patches
of her skin.
She crouches
in the north,
her trembling
the source
of dawn.
Light appears
with the shudder
of her slopes,
the movement
of her arm.
Blackberries unravel,
stones dislodge;
it's not as if
they weren't
warned.

She was sleeping
but she heard the boot
scrape,
the creaking floor,
felt the pull of the blanket
from her thin
shoulder.
With one free hand
she finds her weapons
and raises them high;
clearing the twigs from her
throat
she sings, she
sings,
shaking the sky
like a blanket about her
Loo-wit sings and sings and
sings!

1. **Loo-Wit:** The name given by the Cowlitz People to Mount St. Helens, an active volcano in Washington State. It means "lady of fire."

◆ Build Vocabulary

buttes (byo͞ots) *n.*: Steep hills standing in flat land

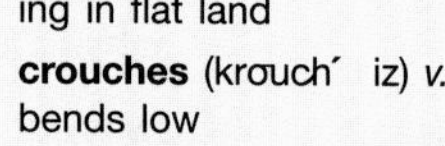

crouches (krouch´ iz) *v.*: Stoops or bends low

unravel (un rav´ əl) *v.*: Become untangled or separated

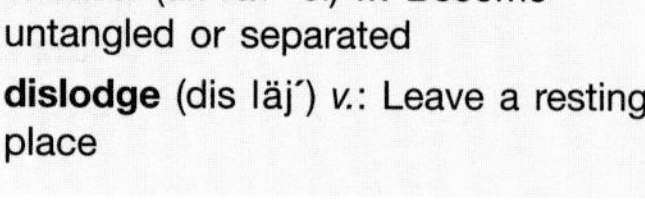

dislodge (dis läj´) *v.*: Leave a resting place

Cross-Curricular Connection: Science

Volcanoes A vent in the earth through which molten rock, or magma, and gas erupt is called a volcano. There are many different kinds of volcanoes and eruptions. These are categorized by the quality and amount of lava, ash, and gas, and the manner in which they flow from the vent. For example, volcanoes of Hawaii and Iceland, which erupt quietly with rivers of fluid lava, are called shield volcanoes. Most of the world's tallest volcanoes are composite volcanoes, which display a cycle of quiet eruptions followed by explosive ones, in which gases, rocks, and thick lava are projected with great force from the vent.

The majority of the Earth's volcanoes were formed millions of years ago in regions called volcanic belts. The Pacific Ocean is surrounded by the largest of these belts, known as the "Ring of Fire." Other volcanoes occur under the surface of oceans, forming underwater mountain ranges. The Hawaiian Islands are the upper portions of mountains formed in this way.

Volcanic activity can have disastrous effects, but there are some economic benefits, as well. Resources such as pumice, sulfur, zinc, copper, and lead have been mined from undersea volcanic deposits. Also, in areas such as Iceland, California, and New Zealand, volcanic energy has been harnessed to create clean and inexpensive geothermal power. Invite students to research other ways in which people, past and present, have suffered from, lived with, and benefited from the power of volcanoes.

▲ Critical Viewing Which lines of the poem best capture the action of this photograph? Explain. [Assess]

Guide for Responding

◆ Literature and Your Life

Reader's Response When have you thought of nature—or something in it—as having a personality? Explain.

Thematic Focus Find a word or phrase in "Loo-Wit" that surprised you into seeing a volcano in a new way. Then, explain your choice.

Volcano's Monologue As Loo-Wit, give a speech expressing what you're feeling and what you intend to do. Combine your speech with appropriate gestures.

☑ Check Your Comprehension

1. To what kind of person does the poet compare Loo-Wit?
2. How does Loo-Wit show that she doesn't care what others think of her?
3. What has bound Loo-Wit to the earth?
4. Describe what Loo-Wit does in lines 46–53.

◆ Critical Thinking

Interpret

1. Who are "they" in line 40? **[Infer]**
2. What picture of humans and their activities does the poem convey? **[Analyze]**
3. What overall impression of Loo-Wit do you get from the poem? Explain. **[Draw Conclusions]**

Apply

4. Why do you think people speak of volcanoes and other natural forces as if they were people? **[Speculate]**

Extend

5. Contrast this poem with a scientific description of a volcano. **[Science Link]**

Compare Literary Works

6. Compare and contrast the portrayal of nature in "Aunt Leaf" and "Loo-Wit." **[Compare and Contrast]**

▶Critical Viewing◀

❹ **Assess** *Most students will agree that lines 50–51 and 54–59 best capture the action of the photograph, since they describe the eruption event.*

Reinforce and Extend

Answers

◆Literature and Your Life

Reader's Response Students may suggest that storms such as hurricanes have personalities.

Thematic Focus Possible response: The phrase "spits her black tobacco" is a vivid way of describing the black smoke and ash that erupt from the volcano.

☑ Check Your Comprehension

1. She compares Loo-Wit to an old woman.
2. She shows she doesn't care by spitting smoke indiscriminately.
3. She has been bound to the earth by old trees and berry bushes.
4. A disturbance below wakes her up; she feels the restraint of the vegetation; and she removes it with an eruption.

◆Critical Thinking

1. "They" refers either to the bushes and rocks or to the people operating the machines.
2. Possible response: Humans have "irritated her skin" with mining, cutting trees, and cultivation.
3. Possible response: She is an old woman who awakens to sing and proclaim her strength.
4. Possible response: People see their own emotions in the forces of nature as a way of understanding natural forces. Also, it is more comforting to feel that nature is angry at us than to think of nature as completely indifferent and nonhuman.
5. A scientific paper would not describe the volcano as a person. It would analyze the quantity and contents of the erupting material and the causes of the eruption.
6. Possible response: In "Aunt Leaf," nature has a human face and can be a friend and a teacher. In "Loo-Wit," nature has a human face but is powerful and dangerous.

Beyond the Selection

FURTHER READING

Other Works by the Authors

New and Selected Poems, Mary Oliver
Rainbows Are Made, Carl Sandburg, Lee Bennett Hopkins, Fritz Eichenberg (illustrators)
Remembrance of Spring: Collected Early Poems (Lotus Poetry), Naomi Long Madgett
Bone Dance: New and Selected Poems, 1965–1993 (Sun Tracks, Vol. 27), Wendy Rose

INTERNET

We suggest the following sites on the Internet (all Web sites are subject to change).

For more poems by and information about Mary Oliver:
http://www.poems.com/westwoli.htm

For more poems by and information about Carl Sandburg:
http://alexia.lis.uiuc.edu/~roberts/sandburg/home.htm

For more poems by and information about Wendy Rose:
http://www.nativeauthors.com/search/bio/biorose.html

We *strongly recommend* that you preview these sites before you send students to them.

Answers

◆Reading Strategy

1. Answers will vary, but students should refer to specific passages and should explain in detail the thoughts they had.
2. Answers will vary. Students should explain their emotional response and indicate the passage or passages to which they responded.
3. Possible responses: "Aunt Leaf" appeals to sight ("dark as hickory"), hearing ("whisper"), and touch ("solid as wood"). "Loo-Wit" appeals to sight ("spits her black tobacco"), hearing ("machinery growls"), and touch ("huckleberry ropes/lay prickly/on her neck").

◆Build Vocabulary

Using the Prefix: *-dis*

For numbers 2 and 3, students may choose either the verb or noun form.

1. dislodge—move away from a resting place
2. disrespect—(noun) a lack of respect; (verb) to have or show a lack of respect
3. dishonor—(verb) bring disgrace to something or someone; (noun) shame, disgrace
4. dissimilar—not alike

Spelling Strategy

1. benefiting
2. traveled
3. unraveled
4. shoveler

Using the Word Bank

crouches, buttes, haunches, unravel, dislodge

◆Literary Focus

1. Possible response: "She'd rise up like an old log," "she'd slouch from the barn like a gray opossum;" These similes indicate that Aunt Leaf is imagined, because the actions are not ones that humans would normally be described as doing.
2. The similes give clear and descriptive visual images of the young speaker's view of life.
3. Life is described as a gold pocket watch.
4. In "Fog," the metaphor begins in the first sentence, where fog is described as coming in on little cat feet. The remaining sentence continues the metaphor, with the subject *It* referring to fog. In "Life," the metaphor begins in the first line, with life described as a toy, and continues throughout the poem, which is only one sentence long.
5. (a) "Loo-Wit" shows the use of personification by describing a volcano as an old woman.
   (b) Possible responses: "this old woman no longer cares what others think," "she sprinkles ashes on the snow," "huckleberry ropes lay prickly on her neck," "She crouches in the north."

◆Build Grammar Skills

1. as if
2. Like
3. as if
4. as
5. as though

Guide for Responding (continued)

◆ Reading Strategy

Respond to Poetry

You **responded** to these poems by thinking about the ideas they stated, feeling the emotions they called up, and using your senses to experience the scenes they described. Now, recall and develop some of your responses to the poems.

1. Which of these poems stated or suggested an idea that made you think more deeply? Explain.
2. To which poem did you have the strongest emotional response? Why?
3. Which poem appealed to three of your senses? Explain.

◆ Build Vocabulary

Using the Prefix *dis-*

Here's your chance to be *dis*respectful and get away with it. Add the prefix *dis-* ("away, apart, not, or the opposite") to these words, and explain the meaning of the word that results.

1. dis- + lodge =
2. dis- + respect =
3. dis- + honor =
4. dis- + similar =

Spelling Strategy

If the last syllable of a word ending with a consonant-vowel-consonant is not stressed, you usually don't double the final consonant when adding an ending:

un rav´ el + -ing = unraveling
ben´ e fit + -ed = benefited

On your paper, correctly spell these combinations.

1. benefit + -ing =
2. travel + -ed =
3. unravel + -ed =
4. shovel + -er =

Using the Word Bank

On your paper, fill in each blank with an appropriate word from the Word Bank. Do not use any word more than once.

I am a proud thunderstorm. I'm not a storm that __?__ behind the __?__, squatting on my __?__. I approach boldly, wanting to __?__ everything you've tied together. Even boulders will __?__ when they hear my thunder-footsteps.

◆ Literary Focus

Figurative Language

Figurative language is not to be taken literally. Types of figurative language include simile, metaphor, and personification.

1. Identify two similes in "Aunt Leaf." Do they indicate that the aunt is a real person or imagined? Explain.
2. How do the similes in "Aunt Leaf" help you see the world as a child would see it?
3. What object is a metaphor for life in "Life"?
4. For either "Fog" or "Life," show how the metaphor continues from the beginning of the poem to the end.
5. (a) How does the poem "Loo-Wit" show the use of personification? (b) Find three details which develop this personification.

◆ Build Grammar Skills

Correct Use of *like* and *as*

As (including *as if* and *as though*) introduces a clause, or group of words that contains a subject and its verb:

They ate their lunch *as* they (s) sat (v) on the grass.

Like introduces a noun or pronoun:

The lemonade tasted *like* sunshine (noun).

Do not use *like* to introduce a clause:

The sandwiches, however, seemed *as if* [not *like*] they needed more mustard. (clause)

Practice On your paper, choose the word or words that correctly complete each sentence.

1. It looks (like, as if) the girl is imaginative.
2. (As, Like) a child, a poet sees things in fresh ways.
3. The baby is acting (like, as if) he needs a nap.
4. He cooks lasagna (like, as) they do in Italy.
5. The volcano erupts (like, as though) it were spitting.

Writing Application Write a short description of a natural object or event. In your description, include sentences that demonstrate the correct use of both *like* and *as*.

Build Your Portfolio

Idea Bank

Writing

1. E-mail Response Write an e-mail note to one of these poets, explaining what you liked or disliked about his or her poem. Be sure to mention the use of figurative language.

2. Personified Weather Report Write a television weather report. However, change the usual approach by describing storms and other weather systems as if they were human. **[Media Link]**

3. Analysis "Life" compares life to a watch. In other metaphors, life is a bowl of cherries, a fleeting melody, a race to the finish, or a climb up a mountain. Choose three of these, and analyze the attitude toward life expressed by each of them.

Speaking and Listening

4. Television Newscast Read the Background for Understanding on page 788 and magazine articles to find out more about the Mount St. Helens eruption. Then, deliver a telecast on the volcano, using figurative language in your report. **[Media Link]**

5. Simile Slam Enter a figurative language contest by choosing your favorite simile from "Aunt Leaf" or another poem you know. Read it to the class, and explain why the simile works so well. Ask the class to select a winner, based on the best reading and the most convincing explanation. **[Performing Arts Link]**

Projects

6. Illustrated Figure of Speech Draw a picture that will help other students understand the concept of a simile, metaphor, or personification. For example, show a volcano that is also an "old woman." **[Art Link]**

7. Dancing With "Aunt Leaf" **[Group Activity]** With several classmates, create and perform a dance showing the adventures of the girl in "Aunt Leaf." **[Performing Arts Link]**

Writing Mini-Lesson

Extended Definition

The poem "Life" is not only a metaphor but also a kind of extended definition. Using prose, write your own extended definition of a great idea, like justice or love. Start with an explanation of the concept. Then, support your explanation with facts, stories, and examples from your reading, viewing, and personal experience.

Writing Skills Focus: Topic Statement

Begin with a **topic statement** that summarizes your main idea or ideas. The first sentence in this model is a topic statement:

Model

Justice means that people get what they truly deserve, not what a government is willing to give them. Too often, justice is confused with the existing court system. . . .

Prewriting Use an organizer like the one below to gather support for your definition (write your topic statement in the center):

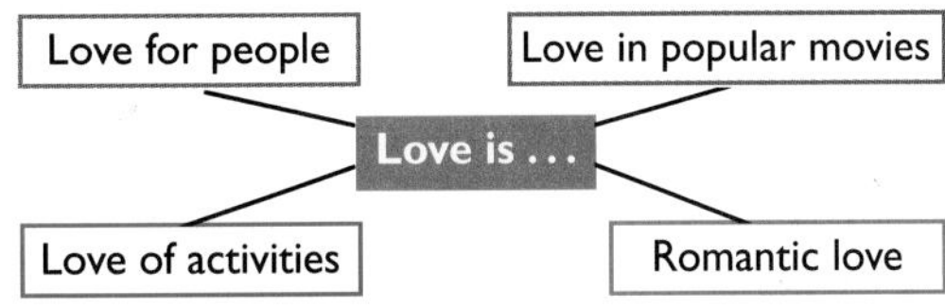

Drafting Write your topic statement. Then, develop your main ideas further in your explanation. Support your ideas with stories and examples from the organizer.

Revising Be sure that your topic statement accurately expresses your main idea, that the explanation develops it, and that your examples support it.

◆ Grammar Application

Check to see that you haven't mistakenly used *like* as a conjunction.

✓ ASSESSMENT OPTIONS

Formal Assessment, Selection Test, pp. 221–223, and Assessment Resources Software. The selection test is designed so that it can easily be customized to the performance levels of your students.

Alternative Assessment, p. 47, includes options for less advanced students, more advanced students, interpersonal learners, verbal/linguistic learners, and bodily/kinesthetic learners.

PORTFOLIO ASSESSMENT

Use the following rubrics in the **Alternative Assessment** booklet to assess student writing:
E-mail Response: Expression Rubric, p. 81
Personified Weather Report: Technical Description/Explanation Rubric, p. 102
Analysis: Literary Analysis/Interpretation, p. 99
Writing Mini-Lesson: Definition/Classification Rubric, p. 86

Idea Bank

Following are suggestions for matching the Idea Bank topics with your student's performance levels and learning modalities:

Customizing for *Performance Levels*

Less Advanced Students: 1, 6, 7
Average Students: 2, 4, 5, 6, 7
More Advanced Students: 3, 4, 5, 6, 7

Customize for *Learning Modalities*

Verbal/Linguistic: 1, 2, 3, 4, 5
Interpersonal: 4, 5
Visual/Spatial: 6
Intrapersonal: 1, 7
Bodily/Kinesthetic: 7
Musical/Rhythmic: 7
Logical/Rational: 3

Writing Mini-Lesson

Refer students to the Writing Handbook in the back of the book for instruction on the writing process and further information on definition/classification. Have students use the Cluster Organizer in **Writing and Language Transparencies,** p. 82, to arrange their prewriting examples.

Writer's Solution

Writing Lab CD-ROM

Have students complete the tutorial on Exposition: Giving Information. Follow these steps:

1. Have students use the Topic Web activity to help them narrow their topics.
2. To help students consider their audience and purpose for writing, have them use the Audience Profile activity
3. Have students draft on the computer.
4. Students can use the guided self-revision activity for their definition.

Writer's Solution Sourcebook

Have students use Chapter 4, "Exposition: Giving Information," 102–133, for additional support. This chapter includes in-depth instruction on expository writing and an excerpt that is an example of the type of expository writing in which the writer provides a definition, pp. 110–112.

Prepare and Engage

Establish Writing Guidelines
Review the following characteristics of a comparison-and-contrast essay:

- Comparison-and-contrast essays point out similarities and differences between two subjects.
- A comparison-and-contrast essay demonstrates the writer's knowledge of the subject as well as his or her ability to analyze.

You may want to distribute the scoring rubric for Comparison/Contrast, p. 90 in **Alternative Assessment,** to make students aware of the criteria on which they will be evaluated. See the suggestions on p. 800 for customizing the rubric to this workshop.

Refer students to the Writing Handbook in the back of the book for instruction on the writing process and further information on expository writing.

Writer's Solution

Writers at Work Videodisc
To introduce students to expressive writing and to show them how Dmitri Ehrlich describes ideas about expository writing, play the videodisc segment on Exposition: Making Connections (Ch. 5.)

Play frames 42847 to 52256

Writing Lab CD-ROM
If your students have access to computers, you may want to have them work in the tutorial on Exposition: Making Connections to complete all or part of their comparison-and-contrast essays. Follow these steps:

1. Have students view the interactive model of a comparison-and-contrast essay.
2. Suggest that students use the Venn Diagram to organize similarities and differences.
3. Allow students to draft on computer.
4. Have students use the Transition Word Bin to find appropriate transitional words and phrases.

Writer's Solution Sourcebook
Students can find additional support, including in-depth instruction on organizing and gathering details for a comparison-and-contrast essay, pp. 151–152 in the chapter on Exposition: Making Connections, pp. 134–165.

Expository Writing

Comparison-and-Contrast Essay

Writing Process Workshop

It's often helpful to think carefully about two things—two poems, two works of art, two people, or two events. Somehow, when you compare and contrast them, both things come into better focus. In a **comparison-and-contrast essay,** you write about how two things are alike and how they are different. These writing skills, covered in the Writing Mini-Lessons in this part, will help you write an effective comparison-and-contrast essay:

Writing Skills Focus

▶ **Specific examples** will make your essay interesting and meaningful. (See p. 779.)

▶ **A clear and logical organization** will help readers follow your argument. Make your case point by point or subject by subject. (See p. 787.)

▶ **Strong topic statements** will guide your writing—and your readers. (See p. 797.)

After reading "Fog," one student decided to look for other poems by Carl Sandburg. He chose to compare and contrast "Fog" with another short poem of Sandburg's: "Grass."

Model

I enjoyed reading both "Fog" and "Grass" by Carl Sandburg. Although they didn't rhyme, they were easy to read. They are similar in their language and style but very different in their meanings. ①

Both poems look short and simple. ② "Fog" has only eight lines. "Grass" has eleven. The words in "Fog" are very simple. The poem almost looks like a children's poem. The words and concepts in "Grass" are a little more advanced, especially the place names, but most of the words and sentences in the poem are short and simple. ③

① This is the topic statement.

② The writer uses a point-by-point organization. This paragraph focuses on the language and length of each poem.

③ By referring to the place names in "Grass," the writer uses a specific example to prove a point.

Beyond the Classroom

Workplace Skills

Compare and Contrast One way to make a well-informed decision is to compare and contrast. When businesses want to advertise a product, they ask an advertising agency to provide them with two or more ideas. By comparing and contrasting these ideas, a decision about which campaign will work best can be made. Decision factors may include the audience to be reached, the cost involved, and the intended formats.

The first step in making an informed choice between two alternatives is to determine a list of criteria. Each alternative can be judged according to these criteria. Then, a general conclusion is made by comparing the results for each alternative in each category. Often the alternatives will measure well in different categories, so the decision will have to be based on individual needs.

Have students study *Consumer Reports,* a magazine that rates products, and select an article with a graphic organizer rating various brands of products. Help students analyze the chart, and then ask them to write an essay comparing and contrasting the results of the two top brands.

Prewriting

Make a Choice You'll need to choose two items that are worth comparing and contrasting. Your subjects should be both alike and different. They must be alike enough to warrant a comparison, but they must also be different enough to make contrasts interesting. Here are a few suggestions:

Topic Ideas

- Two poems or stories by the same poet or writer
- Two ways to do something
- Two famous people who have something important in common
- Two shows or films about the same subject

Use a Venn Diagram In a Venn diagram, each circle represents an item being compared and contrasted. In the overlapping part of the circles, write the similarities. In the two nonoverlapping parts, write the differences. This Venn diagram compares and contrasts two types of bicycles:

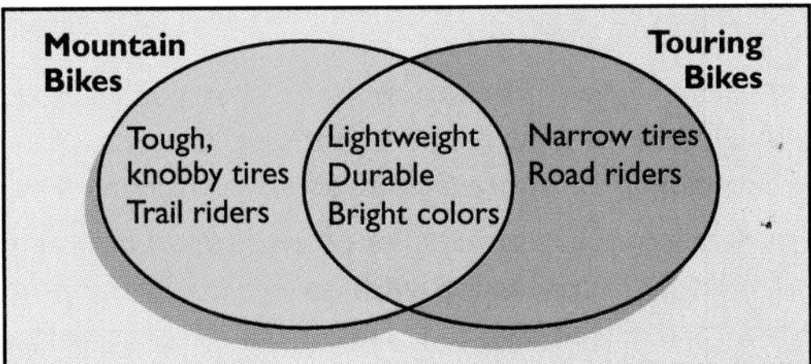

Get Organized There are two general ways to organize a comparison-and-contrast essay. Look at these outlines, showing subject-by-subject and point-by-point organization. Choose the organization that best suits your topic.

Subject by Subject

I. Introduction
II. Mountain Bikes
    Frames; Tires
III. Touring Bikes
    Frames; Tires
IV. Conclusion
    Uses of both bikes

Point by Point

I. Introduction
II. Frames
    Mountain Bikes
    Touring Bikes
III. Tires
    Mountain Bikes
    Touring Bikes
IV. Conclusion
    Uses of both bikes

DRAFTING/REVISING

APPLYING LANGUAGE SKILLS: Vary Sentence Length

When comparing two items, it is easy to use a predictable pattern of sentences. Take care to avoid writing sentences that repeat the same format.

Short Sentences:

The French Open is played on clay courts.

Wimbledon is played on grass.

Try these suggestions to vary sentences:

Combine Sentences:

The French Open is played on clay, but Wimbledon is played on grass.

Use a Subordinate Clause:

While both tournaments are grand slam events, the French Open is played on clay and Wimbledon is played on grass.

Practice Vary the length of the sentences in this paragraph:

The U.S. Open is played in September. The French Open is played in June. Wimbledon is played in July.

Writing Application As you draft, vary the length of sentences in your essay.

Writer's Solution Connection
Writing Lab

To gather details, use the Venn diagram in the Prewriting section of the Exposition tutorial.

Writer's Solution

For additional instruction and practice, have students use the practice page on Improving Sentences, p. 118, in the *Writer's Solution Grammar Practice Book.*

Develop Student Writing

Prewriting

When choosing a topic for a comparison-and-contrast essay, students may want to make a preliminary outline of points they will address, or use a Venn diagram. If there are not enough similarities or differences to discuss, they will want to consider other topic ideas. Tell students that they will want to make sure that they can gather precise details about the similarities and differences of the items they are comparing and contrasting.

Customize for
Less Advanced Learners

Students may have difficulty dividing their topic into points by which to compare and contrast. Suggest that students use the Cluster Organizer from **Writing and Language Transparencies,** p. 82. They can write the main topic idea in the central subject and brainstorm for elements about the subject from which to form the basis for comparison and contrasting.

Customize for
More Advanced Writers

Suggest that students take a different approach to their comparison-and-contrast essays by writing about one thing or person that appears different in different situations. For example, they could compare and contrast an actor and his or her real-life character, or the qualities of water in different states (gas, liquid, solid). Alternatively, suggest that students compare and contrast one thing they know and one thing they want to know more about. For example, if students want to know more about Germany, they can contrast the United States with Germany.

Applying Language Skills

Vary Sentence Length Explain to students that essays with sentences of varying length are more enjoyable to read. One way to achieve variety is to combine short sentences into longer ones.

Answers

Possible response:
The U.S. Open is played in September, while the French Open and Wimbledon are played in the summer. The French Open is played in June, and Wimbledon in July.

Drafting

Remind students that the introduction presents the two items to be compared and contrasted. The body of the essay elaborates on these ideas. Students may want to make all their comparisons before contrasting, or they may want to focus on specific areas first, addressing both similarities and differences.

Revising

With students working in pairs, have writers state the main idea and identify the main issues that their essays will address. Then, the reviewer should note whether the writer fulfills the ideas.

Writer's Solution

Writing Lab CD-ROM

In the tutorial on Exposition: Making Connections, have students use the Sentence-Length Revision Checker to help them evaluate sentence length.

Publishing

Students might create a collection of comparison-and-contrast essays.

Reinforce and Extend

Review the Writing Guidelines

After students have completed their papers, review the characteristics of a comparison-and-contrast essay.

Applying Language Skills

Avoid Double Comparisons

Double comparisons are sometimes used when the writer is trying to overstate his or her position.

Answers

1. Rhinos run faster than hippos.
2. Who is most handsome—a rhino, a giraffe, or a hippo?
3. Rhinos' defenses are better.
4. Hippos are friendlier than rhinos.

EDITING/PROOFREADING

APPLYING LANGUAGE SKILLS: Avoid Double Comparisons

A double comparision occurs when *-er* and *more* or *-est* and *most* are used with the same modifier.

Incorrect:

Mountain bikes are *more better* than touring bikes.

Correct:

Mountain bikes are *better* than touring bikes.

Practice Rewrite each sentence to avoid a double comparison.

1. Rhinos run more faster than hippos.
2. Who is most handsomest—a rhino, a giraffe, or a hippo?
3. Rhinos' defenses are more better.
4. Hippos are more friendlier than rhinos.

Writing Application When writing your comparison-and-contrast essay, use the correct comparative forms of all adjectives and adverbs.

Writer's Solution Connection
Language Lab

For more practice in avoiding double comparisons, complete the Language Lab lesson on Forms of Comparison.

Drafting

Follow a Format Follow the general format for all expository writing—grab your readers' attention in an introduction, present your ideas and details in the body of the essay, and write a conclusion that wraps things up.

Write a Topic Sentence Your topic sentence should be about both subjects. It should address both similarities and differences in general terms.

Add Concrete, Specific Details Do the best job you can. Don't settle for vague, general words. Make your case with specific details like the ones in the chart below.

Don't settle for . . .	When you could write . . .
Living in the city is loud.	In the city, horns honk, sirens wail, and busses belch.
Soccer is challenging.	Would you like to run like a wild horse for a solid hour?
"Fog" means more than you think.	The meaning of this short poem sneaks up on you like a cat.

Revising

Refine Your Topic Sentence Now that you've drafted your essay, look back at your topic statement. Can you make it more interesting or more suited to your essay as a whole?

Punch Up Your Openings and Endings Look at your introduction and conclusion with an eye to bringing more energy into these paragraphs. Grab your readers' interest with the first line. Leave your readers with something to remember. Consider one of these techniques:

- Provide an interesting or surprising fact.
- Supply an informative or entertaining quotation.
- Give a recommendation.
- Ask a thought-provoking question.

Publishing and Presenting

Formal Presentation Imagine that you've been asked to speak to a group of people. Prepare visual aids, and turn your essay into a formal presentation complete with a question-and-answer period. Make your presentation last about ten minutes.

Submit to a Magazine Submit a copy of your essay to a magazine that specializes in the subject you've chosen. Near the magazine's table of contents, you can find publishing information, including an address. Send your work in!

ASSESSMENT

PORTFOLIO ASSESSMENT

Use the rubric on Comparison/Contrast in the **Alternative Assessment** booklet, p. 90, to assess the students' writing. Add these criteria to customize this rubric to this assignment.

	4	3	2	1
Clear Comparisons	The writer consistently makes clear comparisons.	The writer mostly makes clear comparisons.	The writer makes only some clear comparisons.	The writer makes unclear comparisons.
Varying Sentence Length	The writer varies sentence length throughout the essay, making it easier to read.	The writer varies sentence length through most of the essay.	The writer varies sentence length for some of the essay, but some of the essay clearly needs more variation.	The writer does not vary sentence length.

Real-World Reading Skills Workshop

Distinguishing Between Fact and Opinion

Strategies for Success

In your reading, it's important to be able to tell the difference between a fact and an opinion. A fact is something that can be seen or proved. An opinion reveals what the writer believes or thinks about something.

What's a Fact? A story that deals only in facts gives information that can be proved and is not open to debate. In the sentence *The President went to France,* it's very easy to tell fact from opinion. Either the President went to France or he did not. The sentence is stating a fact.

What's an Opinion? Certain words clearly signal that a writer is stating an opinion. For example, in the sentence *I don't think the President should go to France,* the word **think** should jump out at you. Anytime a writer tells you what he or she thinks, you are reading an opinion. Other words that indicate opinions include *believe, should, seems*, and *probably*.

While some words are clues to the opinions that follow, every opinion is not written with such a clear signal. For example, in the sentence *The President was mistaken in planning a trip at this time,* the writer is stating an opinion. As you read, look for sentences that make statements or convey attitudes that can't be proved.

Sort Out the Two Opinions cannot be proved, even if they are stated strongly. Only facts can be proved. Most writing is a combination of fact and opinion. If you read carefully and look for opinion words, you can sort out the two.

Apply the Strategies

Read the accompanying article. Then, follow the directions below:

Rain Causes Trouble in Center of City

Heavy rains flooded the downtown area last night, damaging 12 stores and 26 residences. A 50-person work crew tried to stop the flooding but was probably too tired to build a protective wall. Forecasters predicted the rain, but it seems that the mayor did not pay attention to them. Yesterday was the fifth rainy day in a row. The rain is supposed to end tomorrow.

1. Identify all the statements of fact.
2. Identify all the statements of opinion.
3. List any words that signal an opinion is being given.
4. Rewrite the article using only facts.

✔ *Here are some other situations in which it's important to distinguish between fact and opinion:*

- Political campaigns
- Sales messages
- Celebrity endorsements
- Rumors
- Newspaper editorials
- News commentaries

Introduce the Strategies

Tell students that advertisers often present opinions as fact in order to persuade readers to believe that their product is the best. When advertisers pay spokespeople to comment on the greatness of a product, they are relying on the consumer to value that spokesperson's opinion. Remind students that facts are statements whose reliability can be checked, usually in an encyclopedia or other reference book.

Apply the Strategies

Remind students to read the article carefully, looking for words that clue them into the writer's statement of an opinion. Explain that news reporting is supposed to be objective, giving facts and not opinions. One way to determine whether a newscast has reported facts is to check with other stations reporting on the same subject. If they are reporting the same statistics and data, chances are the facts have been verified.

Answers

1. Heavy rains flooded the downtown area last night, damaging 12 stores and 26 residences. Forecasters predicted the rain. A 50-person work crew tried to stop the flooding. Yesterday was the fifth rainy day in a row.
2. A work crew was too tired to build a protective wall. It seems the mayor did not pay attention to them. The rain is supposed to end tomorrow.
3. probably, seems, supposed to
4. Suggested response: Heavy rains flooded the downtown area last night, damaging 12 stores and 26 residences. A 50-person work crew tried to stop the floodings but could not build a protective wall. Forecasters predicted the rain, but the mayor did not issue a warning to residents. Yesterday was the fifth rainy day in a row. Forecasters predict the rain will end tomorrow.

◆Build Grammar Skills

Reviewing Usage Problems
The selections in Part 2 include instruction on the following:

- Pronouns in Comparisons
- Commonly Confused Verbs: *lie* and *lay*
- Correct Use of *like* and *as*

This instruction is reinforced with the Build Grammar Skills practice pages in **Selection Support,** pp. 248, 253, and 258.

As you review usage problems you may wish to review the following:

- Double Negatives

A double negative is the use of two negative words in a sentence when only one is needed.

Correcting Double Negatives	
Double Negatives	**Corrections**
We never heard no thunder.	We never heard any thunder. We heard no thunder.
I can't see nothing.	I can see nothing. I can't see anything.
She hasn't seen no one.	She has seen no one. She hasn't seen anyone.

Writer's Solution

For additional practice and support with common usage problems, use the practice page on Fifteen Common Usage Problems, p. 83, in the *Writer's Solution Grammar Practice Book.*

Answers

Practice 1

1. No one was prouder than they.
2. He spent more time practicing than she.
3. Sandburg developed better images than I.
4. Not many other poets could write as creatively as he.
5. No one appreciates him more than we.

Practice 2

1. Martin Luther King, Jr. inspired us as no one else has.
2. Aunt Leaf was like a miracle to the child who invented her.
3. Lay the book on the desk.
4. The volcano lay on the village outskirts.
5. Sandburg describes fog as if it were a little cat.

Usage Problems — Grammar Review

To communicate clearly and effectively it's important to speak and write English according to standard usage. Pay attention to the following common usage problems.

Pronouns in Comparisons When pronouns appear in comparisons using *than* or *as*, sometimes words are suggested rather than stated. To choose the correct form of the pronoun, mentally supply the missing words. In this example, the subject pronoun *she* is correct, not *her*. (See page 778.)

> I liked "Onomatopoeia" better than she [did].

Commonly Confused Verbs: *lie* and *lay* The verbs *lay* and *lie* are commonly confused. (See page 786.) *Lay* (*lay, laying, laid, laid*) usually means "to put or place something down." This verb is always followed by a direct object.

> D. O.
> He *lays* his guitar on the table.

In contrast, *lie* (*lie, lying, lay, lain*) usually means "to rest in a reclining position." It is never followed by a direct object.

> After hours of rehearsal, he likes to *lie* down for a nap.

Confusion occurs because the past of *lie* is the same as the present of *lay*.

Correct Use of *like* and *as* The words *like* and *as* are commonly confused. (See page 796.) *Like* is a preposition. It should be followed by its object.

> In Eve Merriam's poem, rushing water sounds *like* a carnival.

As (or *as if* or *as though*) introduces a subordinate clause, or a group of words containing a subject and a verb.

> She describes water *as if* [not like] she has heard it speak to her.

Practice 1 On your paper, choose the correct pronoun to complete each sentence. Explain your answers.

1. No one was prouder than (they, them).
2. He spent more time practicing than (she, her).
3. Sandburg developed better images than (I, me).
4. Not many other poets could write as creatively as (he, him).
5. No one appreciates him more than (we, us).

Practice 2 For each of the following sentences, choose the correct word from the choices in parentheses.

1. Martin Luther King, Jr., inspired us (like, as) no one else has.
2. Aunt Leaf was (like, as) a miracle to the child who invented her.
3. (Lay, Lie) the book on the desk.
4. The volcano (lay, lie) on the village outskirts.
5. Sandburg describes fog (like, as if) it were a little cat.

Grammar in Writing

✓ *If you are unsure about a troublesome verb or commonly confused word, don't hesitate to consult a dictionary or a grammar and usage handbook. Taking a moment to check can save you error or embarrassment.*

Speaking, Listening, and Viewing Workshop

Conducting a Telephone Interview

Imagine what life would be like without the telephone—one of our most commonly used and necessary communications tools. Telephone interviews are a quick way to get information. Whether you are talking to someone across town or on the other side of the world, however, good telephone interviewing strategies should always apply.

Get Information Quickly Using the telephone is often the best way to get information quickly. Whether you are calling a friend or a stranger, begin by saying who you are and why you are calling. *"Hello, Mrs. Adams, this is Katie Green. I'm calling from the Cedar School News, and I'd like to interview you about the history book you wrote."* If the person to whom you are speaking knows why you are calling, he or she can get you the information you need more quickly.

Make It Clear Telephone connections are not always clear, and the person to whom you are speaking might be located in a noisy room. It's important to speak loudly and clearly. Don't shout, but don't mumble or talk to someone else while conducting your interview. Also, turn down the television or radio while you are talking.

Tips for Telephone Interviews

- Write down the questions you want to ask before beginning your interview.
- Try to call at a time that's convenient for the person you're interviewing.
- Ask follow-up questions to clarify answers you don't understand.

Apply the Strategies

To practice your telephone interviewing skills, complete the following exercises:

1. Decide how you would begin a telephone call to the following:
   a. a travel agent to find out about the most popular destinations of the year
   b. a music store owner to learn more about a popular new band
2. Have a friend play along as you role-play these telephone conversations:
   a. You are new in town and need to find out information about the local schools.
   b. You are calling a store to find out about available jobs and how you would apply for them.

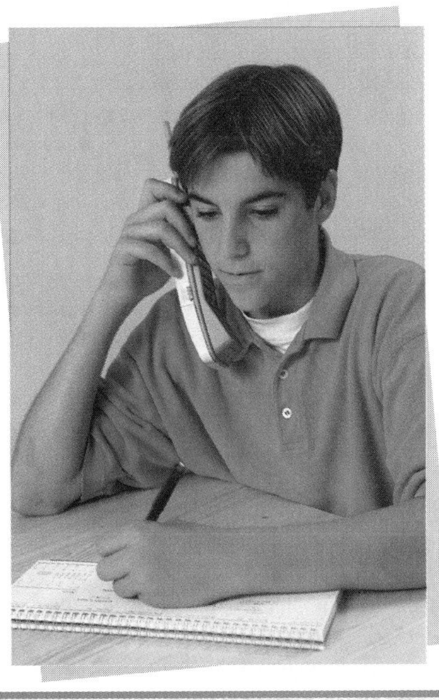

Introduce the Strategies

Tell students that an interview means a conversation between two people, where one person asks questions and the other supplies the answers. Some interviews are formal, such as interviewing for a job, or they can be informal, such as calling a business to ask for directions.

Customize for
Bodily/Kinesthetic Learners
Ask volunteers to mimic a telephone interview in front of the class. Suggest that students do two examples: one of an attentive interviewer and the other of an inattentive interviewer. Have students point out that even though the person on the other end of the line cannot see the person talking, he or she can tell a lot about a person's attitude. When interviewing, remind students to emphasize key words and phrases.

Apply the Strategies

Remind students that they want to make their questions clear, brief, and to the point.

Beyond the Classroom

Workplace Skills

Telephone Interviews Tell students that using the telephone is part of many people's jobs. People who work in production offices of advertisers or movie producers must call different businesses to schedule photo shoots or talent interviews, and to order supplies. Many administrative assistants make travel or catering arrangements for their employers. Before they make these calls, they must know the name and department of the person with whom they want to speak, exactly what they want this person to do, and the name and phone number of any other parties involved.

Gather students in groups. If possible, supply a copy of the local yellow pages. Give students this scenario: You are in charge of putting together a reception for your boss. You must place a reservation at a hotel or restaurant that can hold a banquet, you must find out what types of banquet menus are available and their cost, you must order flowers for the tables, and you will have to have invitations and place holders printed up for the occasion. Tell students that 100 people are expected to attend. Have students locate phone numbers of places to call to fulfill their duties. Then, have them write down next to the phone numbers a list of all the relevant information they need and appropriate questions to find this information. Have each group share their list with the rest of the class.

◆Build Vocabulary

What's Behind the Words

Encourage students to identify musical words and phrases within the first few paragraphs. Ask for volunteers to explain the meaning behind these phrases; *resonate, fiddling around, horning in, fit as a fiddle, play it by ear, strike a responsive chord.* Students may want to refer to a dictionary or an encyclopedia on music to determine these meanings. If they have difficulty, explain that *resonate* means "resound," or "echo with sound"; *fiddling around* means "trifling," or "wasting time"; *fit as a fiddle* means "in perfect health," or "very fit"; *play it by ear* means "improvise"; and *strike a responsive chord* means "produce a response."

Customize for
Musical/Rhythmic Learners

Encourage students to provide the class with a background to musical terminology. If possible, suggest that students bring their instruments to class to demonstrate what it means to "strike a chord" or "play by ear." Suggest that students offer other musical phrases they have heard from music teachers or others.

Answers

Activity 1

1. phonograph = a sound-reproducing machine, using cylinders or disks; commonly, a record player
2. phonics = a method of teaching reading, pronunciation, and spelling based upon the study of speech sounds and their ordinary spelling
3. phonetic = of or pertaining to speech sounds, their production, or their transcription in written symbols
4. cacophony = harsh, discordant sound

Activity 2

Possible responses:

1. concert = from the Italian *concertare,* to decide together; from the Latin *concertus,* to mingle together
2. conductor = from the Latin *con,* with + *duc,* to lead, + *or,* a person that does something
3. orchestra = from the Greek *orcheisthai,* to dance or the space on which the chorus danced
4. prelude = from the Latin *pre,* before + *lude,* to play
5. alto = From the Italian, or Latin *alt(us),* high
6. bass = from the Latin *bassus,* deep or low
7. crescendo = from the Latin *crescere,* to grow
8. percussion = from the Latin *percussus,* struck hard
9. solo = from the Latin *solus,* alone
10. soprano = from the Italian *sopra,* what is above, high
11. tenor = from the Latin *tenere,* to hold
12. tone = from the Greek, *tonos,* strain

What's Behind the Words

Vocabulary Adventures With Richard Lederer

Music Vocabulary

Writers have called music the food of love, the charm that soothes the savage breast, and the universal language. With a golden tongue, it speaks silvery sounds that are music to our ears.

Facing the Music in English

Have you ever considered how many musical words and phrases resonate in our English language? Please don't think that I'm fiddling around and horning in on your life. But I'm feeling fit as a fiddle, and I don't want to play second fiddle, play it by ear, or give you a second-string performance. So hop on the bandwagon as I pull out all the stops and hope to strike a responsive chord in you.

A second-string performance refers to the backup strings that a violinist keeps should a string in the instrument break. When we pull out all the stops, we are acting like the organist who pulls out all the stops, or knobs, in the instrument to bring all the pipes to play.

Music to Our Ears

Almost all the names of musical terms and instruments derive from Greek, Latin, or Italian. The word *music* itself reaches back to the Muses, the nine Greek goddesses of the arts and sciences.

A capella is taken directly from the Italian and means "in chapel style." It refers to choral music that is unaccompanied.

Most music is composed. *Composer* comes from the Latin *componere—com,* "together," and *ponere* "to put." Hence, to *compose* is "to put together."

Harmony reverberates from the Greek *harmonikos,* "an agreement of sounds." The word has been broadened to mean any happy accord, as in "harmony between management and labor."

Songs usually have *lyrics. Lyric* refers directly to the lyre, a stringed, harplike instrument played by the ancient Greeks.

Perhaps the finest flowering of music is the *opera,* a grand drama that is mostly sung. The Italian *opera* is a plural form of the Latin singular *opus* (literally, "a work").

The Latin *rhythmus,* "movement in time," gives us the word *rhythm. Rhythm* contains no *a, e, i, o,* or *u* and only one *y,* yet it is a two-syllable word.

Activity 1 A *symphony* is a harmony of sound, from the Greek *sym,* "together," and *phone,* "sound." When a symphony is being played, the orchestra "sounds together." The root *phone* gives us many other words, including *telephone,* from the Greek *tele,* meaning "far," and *phone,* "sound." A telephone does indeed transmit sound from far away. Define these other words that contain the root *phone:*

1. phonograph **3.** phonetic
2. phonics **4.** cacophony

Activity 2 Investigate the origins of these other common terms in music:

1. concert **5.** alto **9.** solo
2. conductor **6.** bass **10.** soprano
3. orchestra **7.** crescendo **11.** tenor
4. prelude **8.** percussion **12.** tone

Extended Reading Opportunities

The musical rhythms and rhymes of poetry can make a pasture more friendly, a neighborhood more alive, and the search for self more entertaining. Unlock the excitement of poetry with your own review of these titles.

Suggested Titles

You Come Too
Robert Frost

Robert Frost is one of the most celebrated poets in American history and a four-time winner of the Pulitzer Prize. This is a collection of some of his most memorable poems, including "The Road Not Taken," "Acquainted With the Night," and "Stopping by Woods on a Snowy Evening." These poems show Frost's admiration for the New England countryside around him and his overall love of nature and life.

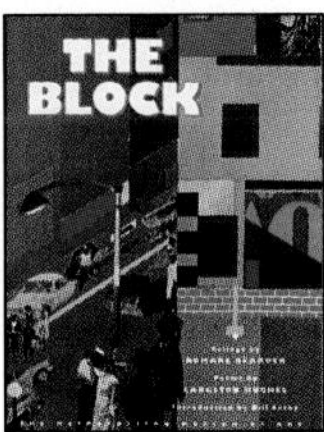

The Block: Poems
Langston Hughes

The setting a poet chooses as a backdrop for his or her work can often have a profound impact on the poetry that emerges. Langston Hughes chose the vibrant neighborhood of New York City's Harlem to celebrate the heritage, traditions, and determination of African Americans. Combining Hughes's insightful poetry with the dazzling work of artist Romare Bearden, this collection honors the urban neighborhood that was an inspiration to both men.

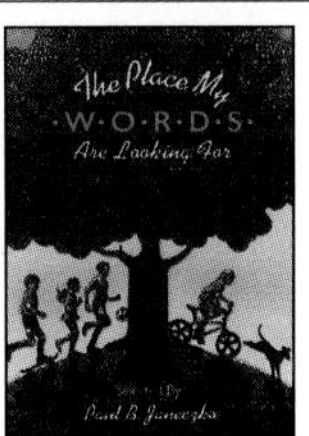

The Place My Words Are Looking For
Paul B. Janeczko

More than thirty poets share their work and their thoughts in this collection. The works of Maxine Kumin, Civ Cedering, Paul Zimmer, Jim Daniels, Gary Soto, and Lillian Morrison are accompanied by brief commentaries by the writers to provide insight into the poets, their motivation, and the stories behind the poems.

Other Possibilities

At the Crack of the Bat: Baseball Poems	Lillian Morrison
Been to Yesterdays	Lee Bennet Hopkins
Falling Up: Poems and Drawings	Shel Silverstein
The Beauty of the Beast: Poems from the Animal Kingdom	Jack Prelutsky, Editor

Planning Students' Extended Reading

All of the works listed on this page are good choices for students' exploration of the genre of poetry. The following information will help you choose what to teach:

Customize for
Varying Student Needs

When assigning the selections in this part to your students, keep in mind the following factors:

- *You Come Too* is a sampler of Robert Frost poems, especially selected for the young adult reader. The collection is illustrated by Thomas W. Nason.
- *The Block: Poems* comprises thirteen poems of Hughes designed to accompany Romare Bearden's 1971 collage of a city block, which now hangs in the Metropolitan Museum of Art. This is a good choice for students interested in multimedia presentations. It includes an introduction by Bill Cosby.
- *The Place My Words Are Looking For* is a collection of poems by thirty-nine contemporary U.S. poets.

Planning Instruction and Assessment

Unit Objectives

1. To develop skills in reading myths, legends, and folk tales
2. To apply a variety of reading strategies, particularly strategies for reading legends, folk tales, and myths, appropriate for reading these selections
3. To recognize literary elements used in these selections
4. To increase vocabulary
5. To learn elements of grammar and usage
6. To write in a variety of modes about situations based on the selections
7. To develop speaking and listening skills, by completing proposed activities
8. To view images critically and create visual representations

Meeting the Objectives Each selection provides instructional material and portfolio opportunities by which students can meet unit objectives. You will find additional practice pages for reading strategies, literary elements, vocabulary, and grammar in the **Selection Support** booklet in the **Teaching Resources** box.

Setting Goals Work with your students at the beginning of the unit to set goals for unit outcomes. Plan what skills and concepts you wish students to acquire. You may match instruction and activities according to students' performance levels or learning modalities.

Portfolios Students may keep portfolios of their completed work or of their work in progress. The Build Your Portfolio page of each selection provides opportunities for students to apply the concepts presented.

Humanities: Art

Sleeping Beauty, by John Dixon Batten

John Dixon Batten (1860–1932) was an English painter known for his interest in fairy tales.

1. Do you think this painting represents a scene from the fairy tale, *Sleeping Beauty*? *Yes. In the fairy tale, a girl pricks her finger and falls asleep for 100 years.*
2. Do you want more information about any of the painting's details? *Possible responses: the black cat and the trapdoor.*

Sleeping Beauty, John Dixon Batten, Christie's Images, London

Art Transparencies

The **Art Transparencies** booklet in the **Teaching Resources** box offers fine art to help students make connections to other curriculum areas and high-interest topics.

To set the stage for Unit 10's myths, legends, and folk tales, use Transparency 11, p. 47, *Koshare Clown Storyteller.* Emily Fragua Tsosie's clay sculpture shows an adult telling a story to two children. Use one of the booklet's activities to help students explore the art through discussion of Pueblo storytellers, writing activities, or by taking on the role of storytellers themselves.

Beyond Literature

Each unit presents Beyond Literature features that lead students into an exploration of careers, communities, and other subject areas. In this unit, students will explore folk tales from around the world, and make science and art connections. In addition, the **Teaching Resources** box contains a **Beyond Literature** booklet of activities. Using literature as a springboard, these activity pages offer students opportunities to connect literature to other curriculum areas and to the workplace and careers, community, media, and humanities.

UNIT 10

Myths, Legends, and Folk Tales

Gods and goddesses, talking animals, strange and wondrous events—these are some of the elements of myths, legends, and folk tales. Although writers retell these stories in print, most of the tales originated long before reading and writing began. They have survived by being handed down from generation to generation. Taken together, these forms make up what is known as the oral tradition of literature:

- **Myths** are anonymous stories involving gods and goddesses. They stress cultural ideals or explain natural occurrences.
- **Legends** are stories that are believed to be based on real-life events and feature larger-than-life people.
- **Folk tales** are stories about ordinary people. Like myths, these stories reveal the traditions and values of a culture.
- **Fables** are stories that feature animals that speak and act like humans. Fables teach morals, or lessons about how to live.

Connections

Within this unit, you will find selections and activities that make connections beyond literature. Use these selections to connect students' understanding and appreciation of literature beyond the traditional literature and language arts curriculum.

Encourage students to connect literature to other curriculum areas. You may wish to coordinate with teachers in other curriculum areas to determine ways to team teach and further extend instruction.

Connections to Today's World

Use these selections to guide students to recognize the relevance of literature to contemporary writings. In this unit, James Thurber's modern folk tale, "The Princess and the Tin Box" helps students connect the genre of myths, folk tales, and legends to contemporary literature.

Connecting Literature to Social Studies

Each unit contains a selection that connects Literature to Social Studies. In this unit, students will read an African folk tale, "All Stories are Anansi's."

Assessing Student Progress

The tools that are available to measure the degree to which students meet the unit objectives are listed below.

Informal Assessment

The questions in the Guide for Responding sections are a first level of response to the concepts and skills presented with the selection. As a brief, informal measure of students' grasp of the material, these responses indicate where further instruction and practice are needed. The practice pages in the **Selection Support** booklet provide for this type of instruction and practice.

You will also find literature and reading guides in the **Alternative Assessment** booklet, which students can use for informal assessment of their individual performances.

Formal Assessment

The **Formal Assessment** booklet contains Selection Tests and Unit Tests.

Selection Tests measure comprehension and skills acquisition for each selection or group of selections.

Each Unit Test provides students with 30 multiple-choice questions and 5 essay questions designed to assess students' knowledge of the literature and skills taught in the unit.

Each Alternative Unit Test: Standardized-Test Practice provides 15 multiple-choice questions and 3 essay questions based on two new literature selections not contained in the student book. The questions on the Alternative Unit Test are designed to assess students' ability to compare and contrast selections, applying skills taught in the unit.

Alternative Assessment

For portfolio and alternative assessment, the **Alternative Assessment** booklet contains Scoring Rubrics, Assessment sheets, and Learning Modalities activities.

Scoring Rubrics provide writing modes that can be applied to Writing activities, Writing Mini-Lessons, and Writing Process Workshop lessons.

Assessment sheets for speaking and listening activities provide peer and self-assessment direction.

Learning Modalities activities appeal to different learning styles. Use these as an alternative measurement of students' growth.

Guide for Reading

OBJECTIVES

1. To read, comprehend, and interpret a legend
2. To relate a legend to personal experience
3. To apply strategies for reading legends, folk tales, and myths
4. To recognize a legend
5. To build vocabulary in context and learn the prefix *be-*
6. To use commas with interrupters
7. To write an explanation of a natural wonder following a sequence of events
8. To respond to a legend through writing, speaking and listening, and projects

SKILLS INSTRUCTION

Vocabulary: Prefixes: *be-*

Spelling: Using *i* Before *e* Except After *c*

Grammar: Commas With Interrupters

Reading for Success: Strategies for Reading Legends, Folk Tales, and Myths

Literary Focus: Legend

Writing: Sequence of Events

Speaking and Listening: TV News Report (Teacher Edition)

Critical Viewing: Connect

PORTFOLIO OPPORTUNITIES

Writing: Diary Entry; New Ending; Essay About Cultural Context

Writing Mini-Lesson: Explanation of a Natural Wonder

Speaking and Listening: TV News Report; Musical Accompaniment

Projects: Aztec City; Volcano Model

More About the Author
Juliet Piggott has also written about wartime nurses in *Queen Alexandra's Royal Army Nursing Corps (Famous Regiments)*, along with her books of Mexican and Japanese folklore and legends. Perhaps Piggott decided to retell this legend because Ixtla, like the author's Shakespearean namesake Juliet, was also tricked into choosing death over life without her true love.

Meet the Author:
Juliet Piggott (1924–1996)

Sometimes it's hard to know how an author became interested in a particular topic. It's easy to imagine, however, that Juliet Piggott found her love for learning about different people and cultures while living in Japan. Her grandfather was a legal advisor to Japan's Prince Ito—a position that probably gave Piggott an up-close view of Japanese culture. Piggott's father was later the head of an organization called the Japan Society. Piggott's interest in Japan inspired her to produce several books on Japanese history and folklore.

The Story Behind the Story

Piggott's interest in folklore was not limited to Japan. The tale you are about to read, which is retold by Piggott, is a Mexican legend that appeared first in her book *Mexican Folk Tales*. Again, her own life experiences may have influenced her interest in Aztec military battles. She knew a great deal about war from her own World War II service in England in the Women's Royal Naval Service and through her marriage to a military historian.

◆ Literature and Your Life

Connect Your Experience

Even in today's technologically advanced society, natural events occur that are beyond our comprehension. We can't accurately predict when a volcano will erupt or explain what determines the exact time that an earthquake will strike. Just imagine how hard it was to understand and predict nature in ancient times. In their efforts to understand and explain events, people came up with fantastic stories like the one you're about to read.

Thematic Focus: Wishes, Hopes, Dreams

This fantastic tale deals with the struggles of a young couple to overcome obstacles that prevent them from fulfilling their dream of being together. What do you expect will be the outcome of their struggles? Why?

◆ Background for Understanding

Culture

This legend comes to us from the Aztec Indians, who controlled a great empire in Mexico about 500 years ago. They were great builders and engineers who constructed cities larger than European cities of that time. Their capital city of Tenochtitlan (te nôch′ tē tlän′), built on a lake, contained an incredible system of canals for transportation and floating gardens for crops. The Spanish conquered the Aztec empire in 1521, but the influence of Aztec culture has continued in Mexico's art, language, and food.

Prentice Hall Literature Program Resources

REINFORCE / RETEACH / EXTEND

Selection Support Pages
Build Vocabulary: Prefixes: *be-*, p. 261
Build Spelling Skills, p. 262
Build Grammar Skills: Commas With Interrupters, p. 263
Reading for Success: Strategies for Reading Legends, Folk Tales, and Myths, pp. 264–265
Literary Focus: Legend, p. 266

Strategies for Diverse Student Needs, pp. 95–96

Beyond Literature Cross-Curricular Connection: Science, p. 48

Formal Assessment Selection Test, pp. 232–234, Assessment Resources Software

Alternative Assessment, p. 48

Resource Pro CD-ROM
"Popocatepetl and Ixtlaccihuatl"—includes all resource material and customizable lesson plan

Listening to Literature Audiocassettes
"Popocatepetl and Ixtlaccihuatl"

Popocatepetl and Ixtlaccihuatl

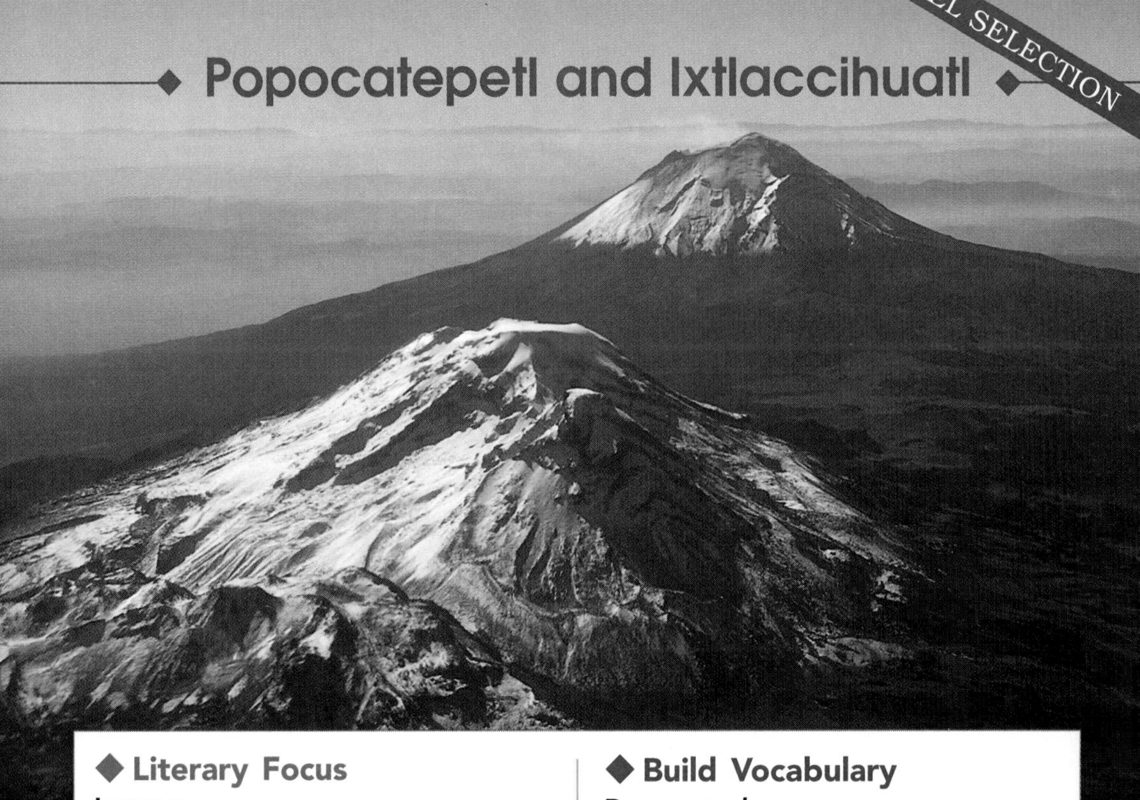

Literary Focus

Legend

"Popocatepetl and Ixtlaccihuatl" is a **legend,** a traditional story about the past believed to be based on real events or people. Legends are part of the oral tradition—they were passed down by word of mouth from generation to generation. The details in a legend become increasingly exaggerated over time. As a result, legends often contain fantastic details and involve larger-than-life characters performing amazing feats.

Legends reveal the values and attitudes of the cultures from which they come. For example, this legend reflects the Aztec belief in loyalty and bravery.

Build Vocabulary

Prefixes: *be-*

In reading this legend, you'll come across the word *besieged*. Its opening prefix *be-*, meaning "make" or "be," is a clue to its meaning, "be under siege." To help get you thinking about other *be-* words, work with a partner to complete a word web like the one below.

Word Bank

Which of these words from the legend do you think is a noun?

besieged
decreed
relished
brandishing
unanimous
refute
routed
edifice

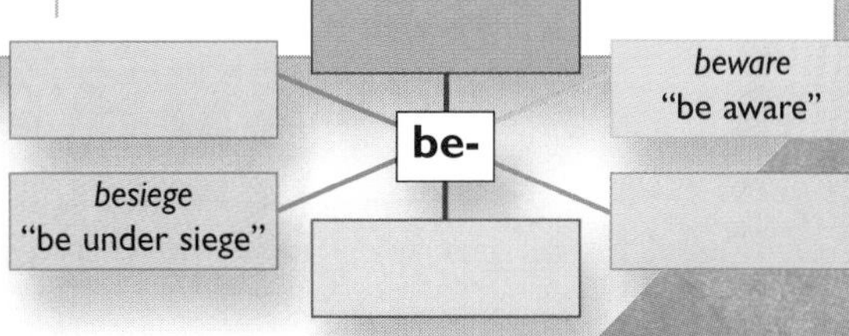

Interest Grabber Write the following headline on the board: *Earthquakes Are Caused by Giant Armadillos Tunneling Underground.* Have students list reasons why such a news story would or would not be believable. Point out that long before there were scientific explanations for natural phenomena, people created explanations based on details from their personal experience. Lead students into the selection by explaining that the legend they are about to read offers an explanation for how two volcanoes in Mexico were formed.

Build Grammar Skills

Commas With Interrupters If you wish to introduce the grammar concept for this selection before students read, refer to the instruction on p. 817.

Customize for
Less Proficient Readers
This legend includes unfamiliar Aztec names that are difficult to read and pronounce, as well as a number of long and complex sentences. To help students grasp the meaning of the story, have them listen to the legend on audiocassette as they follow along in the textbook.

Listening to Literature Audiocassettes

Customize for
More Advanced Students
Invite students to analyze the legend genre by completing a chart like the following as they read:

Realistic Details	Imaginary Details
two volcanoes	smoke in the memory of the princess
Aztec village	pyramid changes to volcano
Powerful Emperor	Popo stood there forever
Tribesmen enemies	
Warrior protectors	

When students have completed the chart, have them use what they have written in the Realistic Details column as the basis for a short paper describing the Aztec culture as described in the legend.

Preparing for Standardized Tests

Grammar Standardized tests may ask students to identify sentences that are correctly punctuated, such as the correct use of commas with interrupters. Explain that interrupters are not essential to the meaning of a sentence, but they help relate ideas to one another. Write these sample sentences on the board, and ask students to select the sentence with correct punctuation.

(A) Volcanoes for the most part, do not cause problems for those who live nearby.
(B) Volcanoes become a problem to say the least when they erupt.
(C) Flows of molten lava have, in some cases, covered entire villages.
(D) It is important, to be aware, of what is happening with a volcano.

Discuss the punctuation errors: *(A)* is missing a comma after *volcanoes, (B)* needs commas to set off *to say the least*, and *(D)* is incorrectly punctuated with commas around *to be aware*. Point out that *(C)* is written correctly, with the interrupter *in some cases* set off with commas. For further practice, have students complete the grammar exercise on p. 817.

Reading for Success

The Reading for Success page in each unit presents a set of problem-solving strategies to help readers understand authors' words and ideas on multiple levels. Good readers develop a bank of strategies from which they can draw as needed.

Unit 10 introduces strategies for reading legends, folk tales, and myths. Students can use these strategies to help find meaning in their reading. To help understand legends, folk tales, and myths, readers can identify the cultural context, reread or read ahead, predict, or recognize the storyteller's purpose.

These strategies are modeled with an excerpt from *Popocatepetl and Ixtlaccihuatl.* Each green box shows an example of the thinking process involved in applying one of these strategies. Additional notes provide support for applying these strategies throughout the selection.

How to Use the Reading for Success Page

- Introduce the reading strategies, presenting each as a problem-solving procedure.
- Before students read the selection, have them preview it, looking at the annotations in the green boxes that model the strategies.
- To reinforce the strategies after students have read the excerpt, have them use Reading for Success, pp. 264–265, in **Selection Support.** These pages give students an opportunity to read a selection and practice the strategies by writing their own annotations.

Reading Strategies: Support and Reinforcement

Using Boxed Annotations and Prompts

Throughout the unit, the notes in green, red, and maroon are intended to help students apply reading strategies, understand the literary focus, and make a connection with their lives. You may use boxed material in these ways:

- Have students pause at each box and respond to its prompt before they continue reading.
- Urge students to read through the selection, ignoring the boxes. After they complete the selection, they may go back and review the text, responding to the prompts.

Reading for Success

Strategies for Reading Legends, Folk Tales, and Myths

Reading legends, folk tales, and myths is a bit like writing a newspaper article about the history of a culture. You must ask: *Who* was important? *What* did they do? *Why* did it matter? *Where* and *when* did the events happen? *What* may happen next? The following strategies can help you find the meaning in a legend, folk tale, or myth:

Identify the cultural context.

- Read the accompanying notes, such as the Background for Understanding on Aztec culture for this legend, to better understand the culture from which the work originated.
- Look for details that suggest how the ancient Aztecs lived and what they found important. You may want to record cultural clues in a chart:

Clue	What This Suggests About the Culture
Ixtla is her father's heir.	The Aztecs believed that a woman could rule.

Reread or read ahead.

- Skim the story for the names of places and characters. Make a list with brief descriptions or notes to help you remember unfamiliar names.
- If you don't understand a certain passage, reread it to look for connections among the words and sentences. It might also help to read ahead, because a word or idea may be clarified further on.

Predict.

Look for clues to help you predict, or make educated guesses about, how the events will unfold. While you read, revise your predictions as you encounter new information.

Recognize the storyteller's purpose.

- Remember that legends, myths, and folk tales are traditional stories that people used to communicate shared beliefs and to explain their world.
- Identify the original storyteller's audience. Knowing that a legend was told by community elders to youngsters around the fire, for example, will help you determine that its purpose was to teach cultural values.

As you read the following Aztec legend, look at the notes in the boxes. These notes demonstrate how to apply reading strategies to a legend.

Model a Reading Strategy: Strategies for Reading Legends, Folk Tales, and Myths

Tell students that when they read a legend, folk tale, or myth that has unfamiliar names of characters or places, it may help to read ahead to understand who the characters are and where events are happening in order to better understand the legend. Model the strategy of reading ahead for students:

> As I begin to read, I see *Tenochtitlan, Ixtlaccihuatl, and Popocatepetl.* These words are unfamiliar to me, so I write them down. Skimming the next pages, I see *Popocatepetl and Ixtlaccihuatl* in the city's description. I am surprised to find that they are also the names of two of the characters. I reread the first page, and I discover the volcanoes also have those names. I jot down these details, and as I read, I use my notes to remember who these characters are and how *Ixtlaccihuatl,* and *Popocatepetl* became the names of volcanoes.

Students also might reread the first few paragraphs to find out how *Ixtlaccihuatl* and *Popocatepetl* relate to the city *Tenochtitlan.*

MODEL

Popocatepetl and Ixtlaccihuatl

Mexican Legend

Juliet Piggott

Before the Spaniards came to Mexico and marched on the Aztec capital of Tenochtitlan[1] there were two volcanoes to the southeast of that city. The Spaniards destroyed much of Tenochtitlan and built another city in its place and called it Mexico City. It is known by that name still, and the pass through which the Spaniards came to the ancient Tenochtitlan is still there, as are the volcanoes on each side of that pass. Their names have not been changed. The one to the north is Ixtlaccihuatl[2] and the one on the south of the pass is Popocatepetl.[3] Both are snowcapped and beautiful, Popocatepetl being the taller of the two. That name means Smoking Mountain. In Aztec days it gushed forth smoke and, on occasion, it does so still. It erupted too

Recognize that the original Aztec storytellers' purpose is to explain something about the two volcanoes. ❶

1. **Tenochtitlan** (te nôch′ tē tlän′): The Spanish Conquered the Aztec capital in 1521.
2. **Ixtlaccihuatl** (ēs′ tä sē′ wät′ əl)
3. **Popocatepetl** (pô pô kä tē′ pet′ əl)

The Volcanos, 1905, Jose Maria Velasco, Courtesy of CDS Gallery, New York

▲ **Critical Viewing** Use the details in the legend to identify each volcano in this painting. **[Connect]** ❷

Develop Understanding

One-Minute Insight "Popocatepetl and Ixtlaccihuatl" is a legend that explains the origin of two volcanoes near present-day Mexico City. A powerful emperor in the Aztec capital of Tenochtitlan has only one child, the beautiful princess Ixtla. Although she loves a brave warrior named Popo, the emperor has forbidden them to marry.

Eventually, the aging emperor offers his daughter's hand in marriage to the warrior who will defeat his enemies. After a lengthy war, the emperor's men prevail, and most soldiers agree that Popo has fought hard and is responsible for the victory, but jealous soldiers hurry back to the city and report that Popo has been killed—news that causes Ixtla to fall ill and die. Popo returns and responds by killing the guilty soldiers and refusing to become Emperor. He then builds two stone pyramids outside the city. He buries Ixtla near the peak of one and then takes his place atop the taller of the two, holding a lighted torch and watching over Ixtla's body for the rest of his days. The two volcanoes stand as reminders of the two lovers who dreamed of always being together.

Reading for Success

❶ **Recognize Storyteller's Purpose** Ask students what the Aztec storytellers might have wanted to explain in the legends about the two volcanoes. *They wanted to explain why the mountains sometimes had smoke or fire coming from their summits.*

▶Critical Viewing◀

❷ **Connect** *The two snowcapped volcano peaks separated by a pass are Ixtlaccihuatl and Popocatepetl. The one on the right, the taller of the two, is Popocatepetl.*

Humanities: Art

The Volcanoes, 1905, by José María Velasco

José María Velasco (1840–1912), a well-known artist from the Mexican school of landscape painting that flourished during the second half of the nineteenth century, included details to show pride in his country's beauty, history, archaeological sites, and monuments, as well as hope for the future.

Landscape artists often try to communicate the many moods of nature through their paintings. Although the word *volcano* suggests violent activity, Velasco's landscape captures a peaceful side of dormant volcanoes.

1. What mood does this landscape convey? How do the colors help communicate this mood? *The picture is calm and serene; the yellows, golds, and browns in the foreground and the pale blues of the mountains help create this mood.*
2. How does the mood of the painting compare with your knowledge about volcanoes? *Possible reponse: People don't often think of volcanoes as being calm and serene. They imagine dangerous activity, such as smoke pouring forth; bright red molten lava spewing from the volcano; and homes being covered with lava and ash.*

Clarification

❶ Corn originated in the Americas and was a staple of the Aztec diet. The Aztecs had a corn god named *Centéotl,* and a goddess, *Chicomecóatl,* who was usually depicted with ears of corn in her hands. After Columbus brought corn back to Europe, it became popular around the world.

Reading for Success

❷ **Read Ahead** Encourage students to read ahead to help them decide if the Emperor is as wise as he is powerful or if they agree with those who doubted his wisdom.

Reading for Success

❸ **Identify the Cultural Context** Ask students what this passage reveals about the Aztec culture. *When judging their leaders, the people placed more value on wisdom than on physical strength, fighting ability, or even wealth.*

◆Critical Thinking

❹ **Infer** Ask students what they can tell about Ixtla's relationship with her father from her actions. *She respects her father's position and cannot imagine defying his wishes.*

Reading for Success

❺ **Predict** Discuss with students what might happen next. Ask them what clues lead them to think so. *Because the Emperor's enemies realize he is no longer ruling, they might decide it is an excellent time to invade and take over Tenochtitlan.*

in Aztec days and has done so again since the Spaniards came. Ixtlaccihuatl means The White Woman, for its peak was, and still is, white.

1 Perhaps Ixtlaccihuatl and Popocatepetl were there in the highest part of the Valley of Mexico in the days when the earth was very young, in the days when the new people were just learning to eat and grow corn. The Aztecs claimed the volcanoes as their own, for they possessed a legend about them and their creation, and they believed that legend to be true.

There was once an Aztec Emperor in Tenochtitlan. He was very powerful. Some thought he was wise as well, whilst others doubted his wisdom. He was both a ruler and a warrior and he kept at bay those tribes living in and beyond the mountains surrounding the Valley of Mexico, with its huge lake called Texcoco[4] in which Tenochtitlan was built. His power was absolute and the splendor in which he lived was very great.

2 Read ahead to see if the emperor makes wise decisions.

It is not known for how many years the Emperor ruled in Tenochtitlan, but it is known that he lived to a great age. However, it was not until he was in his middle years that his wife gave him an heir, a girl. The Emperor and Empress loved the princess very much and she was their only child. She was a dutiful daughter and learned all she could from her father about the art of ruling, for she knew that when he died she would reign in his stead in Tenochtitlan.

Her name was Ixtlaccihuatl. Her parents and her friends called her Ixtla. She had a pleasant disposition and, as a result, she had many friends. The great palace where she lived with the Emperor and Empress rang with their laughter when they came to the parties her parents gave for her. As well as being a delightful companion Ixtla was also very pretty, even beautiful.

Her childhood was happy and she was content enough when she became a young woman. But by then she was fully aware of the great responsibilities which would be hers when her father died and she became serious and studious and did not enjoy parties as much as she had done when younger.

3 Another reason for her being so serious was that she was in love. This in itself was a joyous thing, but the Emperor forbade her to marry. He wanted her to reign and rule alone when he died, for he trusted no one, not even his wife, to rule as he did except his much loved only child, Ixtla. This was why there were some who doubted the wisdom of the Emperor for, by not allowing his heiress to marry, he showed a selfishness and shortsightedness towards his daughter and his empire which many considered was not truly wise. An emperor, they felt, who was not truly wise could not also be truly great. Or even truly powerful.

The man with whom Ixtla was in love was also in love with her. Had they been allowed to marry their state could have been doubly joyous. His name was Popocatepetl and Ixtla and his friends all called him Popo. He was a warrior in the service of the Emperor, tall and strong, with a capacity for gentleness, and very brave. He and Ixtla loved each other very much and while they were content and even happy when they were together, true joy was not theirs because the Emperor continued to insist that Ixtla should not be married when the time came for her to take on her father's responsibilities.

4 This unfortunate but moderately happy relationship between Ixtla and Popo continued for several years, the couple pleading with the Emperor at regular intervals and the Emperor remaining constantly adamant. Popo loved Ixtla no less for her father's stubbornness and she loved him no less while she studied, as her father demanded she should do, the art of ruling in preparation for her reign.

5 When the Emperor became very old he also became ill. In his feebleness he channeled all his failing energies towards instructing Ixtla in statecraft, for he was no longer able to exercise that craft himself. So it was that his enemies, the tribes who lived in the mountains and beyond, realized that the great Emperor in Tenochtitlan was great no longer, for he was only teaching his daughter to rule and not ruling himself.

4. **Texcoco** (tā skō´ kō)

Block Scheduling Strategies

Consider these suggestions to take advantage of extended class time:

- Introduce the Reading for Success strategies on p. 810 before students read the selection. Then read the story as a class, reviewing the Reading for Success annotations in the side notes. Have students work with a partner to complete the Reading for Success practices pages in **Selection Support,** pp. 264–265.
- Alternate class time between working independently and with learning buddies. Have students read the selection and answer comprehension and critical thinking questions independently. Following each of these activities, allow students to briefly meet with learning buddies to discuss Readers' Response and Thematic Focus, p. 816. They can then use their answers to the Readers' Response as they work together to find a Musical Accompaniment for the Speaking and Listening activity in the Idea Bank, p. 818.
- After students decide on a natural wonder to write about, have them complete the Writing Mini-Lesson on p. 818 by using the *Writer's Solution Writing Lab CD-ROM.*

The tribesmen came nearer and nearer to Tenochtitlan until the city was besieged. At last the Emperor realized himself that he was great no longer, that his power was nearly gone and that his domain was in dire peril.

Warrior though he long had been, he was now too old and too ill to lead his fighting men into battle. At last he understood that, unless his enemies were frustrated in their efforts to enter and lay waste to Tenochtitlan, not only would he no longer be Emperor but his daughter would never be Empress.

Instead of appointing one of his warriors to lead the rest into battle on his behalf, he offered a bribe to all of them. Perhaps it was that his wisdom, if wisdom he had, had forsaken him, or perhaps he acted from fear. Or perhaps he simply changed his mind. But the bribe he offered to whichever warrior succeeded in lifting the siege of Tenochtitlan and defeating the enemies in and around the Valley of Mexico was both the hand of his daughter and the equal right to reign and rule, with her, in Tenochtitlan. Furthermore, he decreed that directly he learned that his enemies had been defeated he would instantly cease to be Emperor himself. Ixtla would not have to wait until her father died to become Empress and, if her father should die of his illness or old age before his enemies were vanquished, he further decreed that he who overcame the surrounding enemies should marry the princess whether he, the Emperor, lived or not.

6 Based on your personal experiences and other stories you've read, you might **predict** that the Emperor's bribe may not have the outcome he intends.

Ixtla was fearful when she heard of her father's bribe to his warriors, for the only one whom she had any wish to marry was Popo and she wanted to marry him, and only him, very much indeed.

The warriors, however, were glad when they heard of the decree: there was not one of them who would not have been glad to have the princess as his wife and they all relished the chance of becoming Emperor.

From these details, you can **identify** an important element of the tale's **cultural context:** The Aztecs were a warrior society.

And so the warriors went to war at their ruler's behest, and each fought trebly[5] hard for each was fighting not only for the safety of Tenochtitlan and the surrounding valley, but for the delightful bride and for the right to be the Emperor himself. 7

Even though the warriors fought with great skill and even though each one exhibited a courage he did not know he possessed, the war was a long one. The Emperor's enemies were firmly entrenched around Lake Texcoco and Tenochtitlan by the time the warriors were sent to war, and as battle followed battle the final outcome was uncertain.

The warriors took a variety of weapons with them; wooden clubs edged with sharp blades of obsidian,[6] obsidian machetes,[7] javelins which they hurled at their enemies from troughed throwing boards, bows and arrows, slings and spears set with obsidian fragments, and lances, too. Many of them carried shields woven from wicker[8] and covered in tough hide and most wore armor made of thick quilted cotton soaked in brine. 8

The war was long and fierce. Most of the warriors fought together and in unison, but some fought alone. As time went on natural leaders emerged and, of these, undoubtedly Popo was the best. Finally it was he, brandishing his club and shield, who led the great charge of running warriors across the valley, with their enemies

At this point, you might be able to **predict** the story's outcome. 9

5. **trebly** (tre´ blē) *adv.*: Three times as much; triply.
6. **obsidian** (əb sid´ ē ən) *n.*: Hard, usually dark-colored or black, volcanic glass.
7. **machetes** (mə shet´ ēs) *n.*: Large, heavy-bladed knives.
8. **wicker** (wik´ ər) *n.*: Thin, flexible twig.

◆ Build Vocabulary

besieged (bi sējd´) *adj.*: Surrounded

decreed (di krēd´) *v.*: Officially ordered

relished (rel´ isht) *v.*: Especially enjoyed

brandishing (bran´ dish iŋ) *adj.*: Waving in a menacing way

◆Reading Strategy

6 Predict Have students discuss what they think about the act of bribing. Ask them what they predict may happen as a result of the bribe. *Students may predict a sad outcome from the Emperor's lack of respect for his warriors.*

◆Critical Thinking

7 Assess Ask students to assess the wisdom of the Emperor's offer. Will it achieve the outcome he hopes for? *The offer seems to have inspired the warriors in a way that the Emperor had hoped; they are fighting trebly hard because of the promised prize.*

Reading for Success

8 Identify the Cultural Context Have students notice the specific details about the weapons described here. Ask them what they can tell about the Aztecs from these descriptions. *They were prepared for war, since they possessed so many weapons. Obsidian, wood, cotton, and dried grasses were natural resources that the Aztecs used in making their weapons and shields.*

Reading for Success

9 Predict Ask students to predict how they think the story might end. *Some students will think that Popo will win Ixtla's hand in marriage as a result of his bravery in battle. Others will expect that something bad might keep this from happening.*

Customize for
Visual/Spatial Learners
Suggest that interested students may wish to locate illustrations of the weapons used in battle by the Aztecs: wooden clubs, machetes, javelins, throwing boards, slings, bows and arrows, spears set with obsidian fragments, and lances.

Cultural Connection

Tenochtitlan According to Aztec legend, their god Quetzalcoatl told the people to build their capital city in the place where they would see an eagle holding a snake in its claw while perched atop a cactus growing out of a rock. Hundreds of years passed before a group of people saw just such an eagle. Unfortunately, the rock from which the cactus grew was in the middle of a lake. Believing that they had received a signal from Quetzalcoatl, the Aztecs began the long and difficult process of filling the lake to create a building site for their city.

The original city of Tenochtitlan had a small number of reed huts. In 1519, when the Spaniards arrived, about 150,000 people lived in a 4.5-square-mile city laid out in a grid pattern and surrounded by lush gardens. A ten-mile-long dike protected the city from the lake and controlled flooding.

Many of the Aztec buildings were destroyed as the Spanish colonials arriving after Cortez invaded built what was to become Mexico City. In recent years, archaeological excavations have revealed remnants of the earlier city beneath the foundations of newer buildings.

◆Critical Thinking

1 Assess Remind students that legends often include characters who perform larger-than-life feats. Ask them if they think the battle scene described is realistic or if Popo was made to be a larger-than-life character. *It seems that the battle could have happened this way; there has been nothing in the legend so far that seems supernatural or larger than life.*

Reading for Success

2 Recognizing the Storyteller's Purpose Ask students what lesson or value the storyteller might have wanted the listener to learn from this passage. *Acting out of jealousy to try to hurt others is foolish and cruel, and can cause tragic results.*

Think Critically

3 Analyze Have students discuss how one lie can lead to another. Ask them why one of the men says Popo's body has fallen into Lake Texcoco. *The emperor demands that Popo's body be brought forward for burial. The men must explain why they cannot produce a body, since he is still alive.*

◆Critical Thinking

4 Speculate Why is it possible that Ixtla might not want to hear her father speak about who her husband will be? *Ixtla has just lost the only man she loves. She would not want to hear about other potential husbands.*

fleeing before them to the safety of the coastal plains and jungles beyond the mountains.

1 The warriors acclaimed Popo as the man most responsible for the victory and, weary though they all were, they set off for Tenochtitlan to report to the Emperor and for Popo to claim Ixtla as his wife at last.

2 But a few of those warriors were jealous of Popo. Since they knew none of them could rightly claim the victory for himself (the decision among the Emperor's fighting men that Popo was responsible for the victory had been unanimous), they wanted to spoil for him and for Ixtla the delights which the Emperor had promised.

These few men slipped away from the rest at night and made their way to Tenochtitlan ahead of all the others. They reached the capital two days later, having traveled without sleep all the way, and quickly let it be known that, although the Emperor's warriors had been successful against his enemies, the warrior Popo had been killed in battle.

It was a foolish and cruel lie which those warriors told their Emperor, and they told it for no reason other than that they were jealous of Popo.

3 When the Emperor heard this he demanded that Popo's body be brought to him so that he might arrange a fitting burial. He knew the man his daughter had loved would have died courageously. The jealous warriors looked at one another and said nothing. Then one of them told the Emperor that Popo had been killed on the edge of Lake Texcoco and that his body had fallen into the water and no man had been able to retrieve it. The Emperor was saddened to hear this.

After a little while he demanded to be told which of his warriors had been responsible for the victory but none of the fighting men before him dared claim the successful outcome of the war for himself, for each knew the others would refute him. So they were silent. This puzzled the Emperor and he decided to wait for the main body of his warriors to return and not to press the few who had brought the news of the victory and of Popo's death.

4 Then the Emperor sent for his wife and his daughter and told them their enemies had been overcome. The Empress was thoroughly excited and relieved at the news. Ixtla was only apprehensive. The Emperor, seeing her anxious face, told her quickly that Popo was dead. He went on to say that the warrior's body had been lost in the waters of Lake Texcoco, and again it was as though his wisdom had left him, for he spoke at some length of his not being able to tell Ixtla who her husband would be and who would become

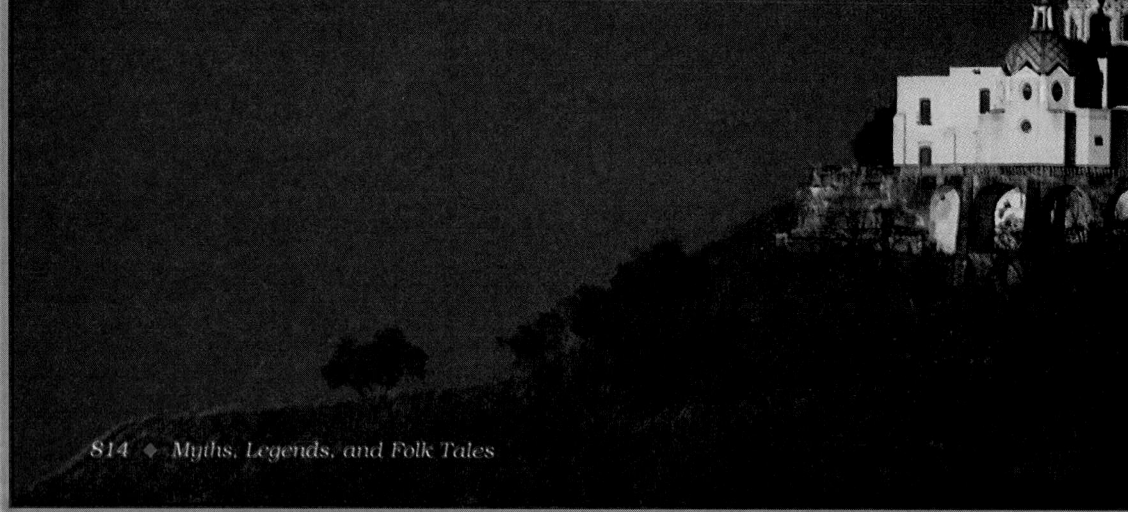

Cross-Curricular Connection: Science

Volcanoes The temperature deep under the surface of the Earth is very hot; temperatures are close to 1200° C, which is hot enough to melt rock. As rock melts and becomes magma, it produces gas, which in turn expands and needs more space. This expanding gas begins to put tremendous pressure on the rock above it, causing the Earth to rise and expand, creating mountains. When the magma finally finds a crack, or weak area, if the pressure is great enough, it bursts forth, or erupts into a volcano spewing rock, dirt, ash, and lava.

Encourage students to think about the terrifying impression a volcano might have on ancient peoples who did not understand what could cause a mountain to produce fire and smoke. Have them consider what it would be like not to understand the science of volcanoes and to be near an erupting volcano.

- What would you see?
- What sounds would you hear?
- How would the vibrations of the Earth make you feel?
- What might you think was happening?

Emperor when the main body of warriors returned to Tenochtitlan.

4 But Ixtla heard nothing of what he told her, only that her beloved Popo was dead. She went to her room and lay down. Her mother followed
5 her and saw at once she was very ill. Witch doctors were sent for, but they could not help the princess, and neither could
6 her parents. Her illness had no name, unless it was the illness of a broken heart. Princess Ixtlaccihuatl did not wish to live if Popocatepetl was dead, and so she died herself.

> **Rereading** the descriptions of Ixtla's feelings for Popo will help you understand her actions.

The day after her death Popo returned to Tenochtitlan with all the other surviving warriors. They went straight to the palace and, with much cheering, told the Emperor that his enemies had been <u>routed</u> and that Popo was the undoubted victor of the conflict.

The Emperor praised his warriors and pronounced Popo to be the new Emperor in his place. When the young man asked first to see Ixtla, begging that they should be married at
7 once before being jointly proclaimed Emperor and Empress, the Emperor had to tell Popo of Ixtla's death, and how it had happened.

Popo spoke not a word.

He gestured the assembled warriors to follow him and together they sought out the few jealous men who had given the false news of his death to the Emperor. With the army of warriors watching, Popo killed each one of them in single combat with his obsidian studded club. No one tried to stop him.

That task accomplished Popo returned to the palace and, still without speaking and still wearing his stiff cotton armor, went to Ixtla's room. He gently lifted her body and carried it out of the palace and out of the city, and no one tried to stop him doing that either. All the warriors followed him in silence.

When he had walked some miles he gestured to them again and they built a huge pile 8
of stones in the shape of a pyramid. They all worked together and they worked fast while Popo stood and watched, holding the body of the princess in his arms. By sunset the mighty
<u>edifice</u> was finished. Popo climbed it alone, carrying Ixtla's corpse with him. There, at the very top, under a heap of stones, he buried the 9

◆ Build Vocabulary

unanimous (yo͞o nan′ ə məs) *adj.*: Based on complete agreement

refute (ri fyo͞ot′) *v.*: Prove someone wrong

routed (rout′ əd) *v.*: Completely defeated

edifice (ed′ ə fis) *n.*: Large structure

Clarification

5 Tell students that people in some cultures rely on witch doctors, or shamans, to help heal sick and injured people. Although witch doctors often have knowledge of the use of herbs and medicinal potions, they rely primarily on spirits or supernatural powers and religious trances to bring about healing.

Reading for Success

6 Rereading Ask students what details they found by rereading to explain Ixtla's actions. *Ixtla loved Popo very much; they had been in love for several years; Popo was the only man she wanted to marry. Because she believed Popo was dead, Ixtla herself no longer wanted to live.*

◆Critical Thinking

7 Infer Ask students why Popo did not speak after he learned of Ixtla's death. *He was so shocked and heart-broken that no words could express what he was feeling.*

◆Literary Focus

8 Legend Remind students that this legend explains the origin of the two volcanoes near Mexico City. How are the stone pyramids related to the volcanoes? *Students might predict that the pyramids Popo builds will become the volcanoes, since their shapes are similar.*

◆Literature and Your Life

9 Suggest that students think of a time when they cared very much about something or someone and things did not turn out well. Have them think about how that made them feel and what they did to try to feel better. Ask for volunteers to share advice they might wish to give Popo to help him deal with his loss.

Speaking and Listening Mini-Lesson

TV News Report

This mini-lesson supports the Speaking and Listening activity in the Idea Bank on p. 818.

Introduce Discuss war correspondents' TV reports that students have seen. Explain that modern technology has made such reports possible. Ask students to imagine that such technology was available to the early Aztecs.

Develop Have students use library reference sources and the Internet to research the Aztecs and Tenochtitlan, focusing on military history and on maps of the city and surrounding area. Encourage students to use what they learn to help them picture the battle scene described in the legend. Ask them to think of details to describe this event for a television audience. Suggest that they organize their ideas on note cards.

Apply Help students find or create visuals such as maps or diagrams to use as they report. Have students present their reports to the class.

Assess Evaluate students' work based on preparation and presentation, or have classmates use the Peer Assessment Speaker/Speech form, p. 105, in **Alternative Assessment.**

◆Literary Focus

❶ **Legend** Ask students what element of a legend is revealed at the end of the story. *The story switches from realistic to imaginary detail.*

Reinforce and Extend

Answers

◆Literature and Your Life

Reader's Response Students may say that they would have also been heartbroken about their loss and angry at the men who lied.

Thematic Focus Most students will recognize that the dream of love shared by Ixtla and Popo was realistic, but circumstances kept them from realizing their dream.

☑ Check Your Comprehension

1. Ixtla's father won't let them marry.
2. The Emperor is thinking only of his own needs, disregarding the needs and wishes of his daughter.
3. Selfishness weakens his position as a ruler and makes the city vulnerable to attack by outsiders.
4. Jealous warriors tell the Emperor a lie—that Popo has been killed, and Ixtla dies of a broken heart.
5. Popo does not want to rule without his beloved Ixtla.

◆Critical Thinking

1. Both Popo and Ixtla were serious, gentle people who wanted the best for Tenochtitlan.
2. The Emperor showed wisdom, such as motivating the warriors by offering his daughter for their efforts; overall, his actions were unwise and caused suffering.
3. The Emperor's selfishness led to the battle; the warriors' jealousy led to Ixtla's death; the love between Ixtla and Popo led to the creation of the two volcanoes.
4. Ixtla's tragic death resulted in the creation of two volcanoes that symbolize the strength and timelessness of true love.
5. The Aztecs honored wisdom, honesty, physical bravery, and loyalty.
6. The power of love continues even after the death of a loved one.
7. Counselors, social workers, psychologists, or clergy might have helped the family and Popo resolve their conflict more happily.

young woman he had loved so well and for so long, and who had died for the love of him.

That night Popo slept alone at the top of the pyramid by Ixtla's grave. In the morning he came down and spoke for the first time since the Emperor had told him the princess was dead. He told the warriors to build another pyramid, a little to the southeast of the one which held Ixtla's body and to build it higher than the other.

He told them too to tell the Emperor on his behalf that he, Popocatepetl, would never reign and rule in Tenochtitlan. He would keep watch over the grave of the Princess Ixtlaccihuatl for the rest of his life.

The messages to the Emperor were the last words Popo ever spoke. Well before the evening the second mighty pile of stones was built. Popo climbed it and stood at the top, taking a torch of resinous pine wood with him.

And when he reached the top he lit the torch and the warriors below saw the white smoke rise against the blue sky, and they watched as the sun began to set and the smoke turned pink and then a deep red, the color of blood.

So Popocatepetl stood there, holding the torch in memory of Ixtlaccihuatl, for the rest of his days.

The snows came and, as the years went by, the pyramids of stone became high white-capped mountains. Even now the one called Popocatepetl emits smoke in memory of the princess whose body lies in the mountain which bears her name. ❶

> This reference to the volcanoes confirms the **storyteller's purpose:** to explain the origins of the volcanoes.

Guide for Responding

◆ Literature and Your Life

Reader's Response If you were either Ixtla or Popo, how would you have responded to the news of the other's death?

Thematic Focus Do you think the dream of love that Ixtla and Popo shared was a realistic one? Explain.

Journal Writing In your journal, share your reactions to the events in the story.

☑ Check Your Comprehension

1. Why are Ixtla and Popo unable to marry?
2. How do the Emperor's actions show his selfishness?
3. What effect does the Emperor's selfishness have on the safety of his kingdom?
4. What leads to Ixtla's death at the end of the war?
5. Why does Popo refuse to become emperor and rule in Tenochtitlan?

◆ Critical Thinking

Interpret

1. What qualities make the two lovers well suited to each other? **[Analyze]**
2. Is the Emperor a wise man? Why or why not? **[Make a Judgment]**
3. In what ways are events caused by the characters' selfishness, jealousy, and love? **[Connect]**
4. How does this story turn tragedy into something positive? **[Interpret]**
5. Based on this legend, what traits do you think the Aztecs admired? **[Draw Conclusions]**

Apply

6. What do you think this legend indicates about the power of love? **[Generalize]**

Extend

7. What kinds of professionals do you think could have helped Ixtla, her father, and Popo resolve their conflict more happily? **[Career Link; Health Link]**

Beyond the Selection

FURTHER READING

Other Works by Juliet Piggott

Japanese Mythology
Mexican Folk Tales

Other Books About Wishes, Hopes, and Dreams

The Beduin's Gazelle, Frances Temple
The Midwife's Apprentice, Karen Cushman, Trina Schart Hyman (illustrator)
The Dreams of Mairhe Mehan, Jennifer Armstrong

INTERNET

We suggest the following sites on the Internet (all sites are subject to change).

For more information about the Aztecs:
http://www.indians.org/welker/aztec.htm

For more information about volcanoes and the eruption status of Popocatepetl at the present time:
http://www.atlsci.com/features/May97_Popocatepetl.html or **http://www,volcanoes.com**

We *strongly recommend* that you preview the sites before you send students to them.

Guide for Responding *(continued)*

◆ Reading for Success

Strategies for Reading Myths, Legends, and Folk Tales

Review the reading strategies and the notes showing how to read myths, legends, and folk tales. Then, apply them to answer the following:

1. (a) At what point were you able to predict the story's outcome? (b) On what did you base your predictions?

2. What does this legend reveal about how the Aztec government worked and how the Aztecs made war?

3. What do you think the original storyteller's main purposes were in creating this legend?

◆ Build Vocabulary

Using the Prefix *be-*

Words that start with the prefix *be-* are usually verbs (action words). They tell you something has been "made" to happen. With this information in mind, work with a partner (and a dictionary, if necessary) to define each of these words:

1. becalm **3.** bewitch
2. befriend **4.** belittle

Spelling Strategy

Use *i* before e except after *c* in words containing the long e sound: *besiege*. Complete the spelling of these words.

1. bel_ _ve **3.** th_ _f
2. f_ _ld **4.** p_ _ce

Using the Word Bank

Write the letter of the definition that best matches each word.

1. besieged	**a.** all in agreement
2. decreed	**b.** prove wrong
3. relished	**c.** large building
4. brandishing	**d.** surrounded by armies
5. unanimous	**e.** waving in a menacing way
6. refute	**f.** especially enjoyed
7. routed	**g.** completely defeated
8. edifice	**h.** officially ordered

◆ Literary Focus

Legend

Legends are tales handed down orally from generation to generation that are believed to have some basis in fact. Like other types of folk literature, legends reveal the values and the beliefs of the culture from which they originate.

1. Which events in this legend might have been based on historical events?

2. Which events are highly imaginative and probably not based on historical events?

3. What inferences can you make about Aztec values and beliefs based on this legend?

◆ Build Grammar Skills

Commas With Interrupters

Writers use **commas** to set off **interrupters**—words or phrases that help relate ideas to one another but that are not essential to the meaning—from the rest of the sentence.

> She was kind and, as a result, she had many friends.

Practice Rewrite the following sentences with correctly placed commas.

1. In Aztec days the volcano gushed forth smoke and on occasion it does so still.

2. Ixtlaccihuatl means The White Woman, for its peak was and still is white.

3. An emperor they felt who was not truly wise could not also be truly great.

4. As time went on natural leaders emerged and of these undoubtedly Popo was the best.

5. He told them too to tell the Emperor on his behalf that he Popocatepetl would never reign and rule in Tenochtitlan.

Writing Application For each of the following interrupters, write a sentence that contains it. Use commas to correctly set off the interrupting text.

1. therefore **2.** on the other hand **3.** some felt

Answers

Reading for Success

1. (a) Many students will say they were able to predict the outcome when Popo had the warriors build a pyramid of rocks. (b) A pyramid would look similar to a volcano so it is a clue to the creation of the volcanoes.
2. The Aztec government was led by an Emperor who had complete power. They made war by sending out an army of warriors with weapons that required hand-to-hand combat.
3. The storyteller's main purpose was to teach values such as wisdom, honesty, and bravery, and to provide an explanation for two volcanoes that were probably very frightening.

◆Build Vocabulary

Using the Prefix *be-*

1. make calm
2. make a friend of
3. influence, as if by witchcraft
4. make to seem small

Spelling Strategy

1. believe
2. field
3. thief
4. piece

Using the Word Bank

1. d
2. h
3. f
4. e
5. a
6. b
7. g
8. c

◆Literary Focus

1. The battle, the report of the jealous warriors, and Ixtla's death might have been based on actual historical events.
2. Popo's building a pyramid and sitting there for the remainder of his life is probably not based on historical events.
3. You can infer that Aztecs placed a value on wisdom, honesty, and bravery. They also believed that there were humanlike explanations for natural phenomena.

◆Build Grammar Skills

1. In Aztec days the volcano gushed forth smoke and, on occasion, it does so still.
2. Ixtlaccihuatl means The White Woman, for its peak was, and still is, white.
3. An emperor, they felt, who was not truly wise could not also be truly great.
4. As time went on natural leaders emerged and, of these, undoubtedly Popo was the best.
5. He told them, too, to tell the Emperor on his behalf that he, Popocatepetl, would never reign and rule in Tenochtitlan.

Writing Application

Make sure students use commas to set off the interrupters in the sentences they write.

Writer's Solution

For additional instruction and practice, use the lesson in the *Writer's Solution Grammar Practice Book*. on Commas That Set Off Added Elements, p. 100. If students have access to technology, they can use the lesson on Commas in the Punctuation unit in the *Writer's Solution Language Lab CD-ROM*.

Idea Bank

Following are suggestions for matching the Idea Bank topics with your students' performance levels and learning modalities:

Customize for
Performance Levels
Less Advanced Students: 1, 5, 7
Average Students: 2, 4, 5, 6, 7
More Advanced Students: 3, 4, 5, 6, 7

Customize for
Learning Modalities
Verbal/Linguistic: 1, 2, 3, 4
Interpersonal: 4, 5
Visual/Spatial: 6, 7
Musical/Rhythmic: 5
Intrapersonal: 1, 2, 3, 6, 7
Logical/Mathematical: 6

Writing Mini-Lesson

Refer students to the Writing Handbook in the back of the book for instruction on the writing process, and for further information on exposition.

Writer's Solution

Writing Lab CD-ROM
Have students complete the tutorial on Exposition: Giving Information. Follow these steps:

1. Have students view the interactive model of an explanation of a process.
2. Suggest that students use the Chain of Events chart to narrow their topics.
3. Have students draft on computer.
4. When revising, suggest that students use the revision checker for unity and coherence.

Writer's Solution Sourcebook
Have students use Chapter 4, "Exposition: Giving Information," pp. 102–133, for additional support. This chapter includes in-depth instruction on building paragraphs, p. 129.

Build Your Portfolio

Idea Bank

Writing

1. **Diary Entry** Imagine that you are either Ixtla, Popo, or a jealous soldier. Choose a critical point in the story. Then, write a journal entry describing the situation and your feelings about it.
2. **New Ending** Like many stories of doomed love, this legend turns on a communication failure. Rewrite the story's ending as if a messenger from Popo had brought Ixtla news of his safety. How might the story end now? Give another explanation of the creation of the two volcanoes.
3. **Essay About Cultural Context** Write a brief essay explaining what this legend reveals about Aztec citizens' values and beliefs, their form of government, and the region in which they lived. Support your points with passages from the legend.

Speaking and Listening

4. **TV News Report** Imagine that you're a war correspondent reporting for a TV station in Tenochtitlan. Using maps and diagrams, describe to your viewers how the war between the Aztec army and its enemies is going. **[Social Studies Link]**
5. **Musical Accompaniment** Choose a piece of music that captures the feelings of Popo and Ixtla upon the discovery of each other's death. Play the piece for the class, and explain why you chose it. **[Music Link]**

Projects

6. **Aztec City** Conduct research to find out what the Aztec city of Tenochtitlan looked like. Then, draw a map of such a city, showing the arrangement of the buildings. **[Art Link]**
7. **Volcano Model** The volcanoes in this tale really exist, about 30 miles from Mexico City. Find out more about volcanoes. Then, build a model of one using the medium of your choice. Ask your science teacher to help find a way to make your volcano "erupt" safely. **[Science Link]**

Writing Mini-Lesson

Explanation of a Natural Wonder

The Aztecs didn't have the scientific knowledge we have today, so they invented stories to explain things that frightened them or made them wonder. Often, these stories explained the origins of objects in nature, such as volcanoes. Now it's your turn to create a tale about how something came to be. Consider writing about a local landmark or a natural feature.

Writing Skills Focus: Sequence of Events

Readers won't understand exactly *how* your natural feature was created unless they can follow the **sequence of events** in your explanation. To help them keep track of this sequence, tell your story in time order. Use signal words like *before* and *still* to help clarify the sequence.

Model From the Story

There was *once* an Aztec Emperor in Tenochtitlan. . . . However, it was not until he was *in his middle years* that his wife gave him an heir, a girl.

Prewriting On separate note cards, list events you can imagine leading up to the creation of your natural feature. Then, arrange your note cards in chronological order.

Drafting If you like, begin your story by introducing the feature you are explaining. Then, referring to your note cards, write your first draft in time order. Clarify the events with time-order words like *in the early days* or *after many seasons*.

◆ Grammar Application

Be sure you've used commas correctly to set apart interrupting material.

Revising Read your story aloud to a classmate. If he or she can't follow the sequence of events, reorganize and add details to make it clearer.

✓ ASSESSMENT OPTIONS

Formal Assessment, Selection Test, pp. 232–234, and Assessment Resources Software. The selection test is designed so that it can easily be customized to the performance levels of your students.

Alternative Assessment, p. 48, includes options for less advanced students, more advanced students, visual/spatial learners, verbal/linguistic learners, and logical/mathematical learners.

PORTFOLIO ASSESSMENT
Use the following rubrics in the **Alternative Assessment** booklet to assess student writing:
Diary Entry: Expression Rubric, p. 81
New Ending: Fictional Narrative Rubric, p. 82
Essay About Cultural Context: Literary Analysis/Interpretation Rubric, p. 99
Writing Mini-Lesson: Fictional Narrative Rubric, p. 82

PART 1

Folk Tales and Legends From Around the World

Illustration from "Russkie Volshebnuie Skazki" by Kochergin, Victoria & Albert Museum, London

One-Minute Planning Guide

The selections in this section are examples of folk tales and legends from around the world. "The People Could Fly" is a classic African American folk tale. "The Algonquin Cinderella" and "Yeh-Shen: A Cinderella Story" are two versions of the popular Cinderella fairy tale. "His Just Reward" and "Djuha Borrows a Pot," are examples of trickster tales. As a Connection to Today's World, James Thurber's modern fairy tale, "The Princess and the Tin Box," follows an updated traditional folk-tale format. Finally, "All Stories Are Anansi's" is an introduction to an Ashanti trickster.

Customize for *Varying Student Needs*

When assigning the selections in this section, keep in mind the following factors:

"The People Could Fly"
- African American folk tale
- Students may need help with dialect

"The Algonquin Cinderella"
- Native American folk tale
- Includes a Beyond Literature feature on Cinderella stories from around the world

"Yeh-Shen: A Cinderella Story From China"
- Chinese folk tale

"His Just Reward"
- Swedish folk tale
- Introduces the "trickster"

"Djuha Borrows a Pot"
- Syrian folk tale
- A "trickster" tale

"The Princess and the Tin Box"
- Classic story by James Thurber
- An opportunity for students to connect folk tales to today's world

"All Stories Are Anansi's"
- West African folk tale
- An opportunity for connecting social studies to literature

Humanities: Art

Illustration from "Russkie Volshebnuie Skazki" by Nikolai M. Kochergin

Nikolai M. Kochergin was a twentieth century Russian poster artist. Russian posters first came into importance after the Russian Revolution in 1917. The posters tried to reach a mass public into boosting revolutionary enthusiasm for a new society. Kochergin also did illustrations, like the one above, for folk tales.

Have students study this illustration and then ask the following questions:

1. What details of the illustration clue the viewer that the setting is Russia? *Students may be able to note that the architecture and the clothing of the people in the background look Russian.*
2. What details of the illustration make the viewer think of legends or folk tales? *Students should see that the man on the horse flying through the sky seems like an image out of a legend; that is, it's supernatural. Also, the size of the man on the horse is larger than life.*

Prepare and Engage

OBJECTIVES

1. To read, comprehend, and interpret five folk tales
2. To relate folk tales to personal experience
3. To recognize cultural context
4. To appreciate folk tales
5. To build vocabulary in context and learn forms of *undaunted*
6. To use commas in a series
7. To write an essay on cultural context, elaborating to support an idea
8. To respond to folk tales through writing, speaking and listening, and projects

SKILLS INSTRUCTION

Vocabulary: Related Words: *undaunted*

Spelling: The Sound *aw* Spelled *au*

Grammar: Commas in a Series

Reading Strategy: Recognize Cultural Context

Literary Focus: Folk Tales

Writing: Elaborate to Support an Idea

Speaking and Listening: Retelling (Teacher Edition)

Viewing and Representing: Book Illustrations (Teacher Edition)

Critical Viewing: Interpret; Connect; Relate; Compare and Contrast

PORTFOLIO OPPORTUNITIES

Writing: Book Jacket; Story Sequel, Reader Review

Writing Mini-Lesson: Essay on Cultural Context

Speaking and Listening: Retelling; Role Play

Projects: Folk-Tale Festival; Puzzle Challenge

More About the Authors

Virginia Hamilton's writing is influenced by her parent's storytelling skills and has won many awards.

Idries Shah was born in North India. As he traveled, he often collected proverbs and folk sayings.

Ai-Ling Louie grew up in New York. The story of Yeh-Shen led her to an ancient Chinese manuscript.

Lone Thygesen-Blecher and George Blecher found many creatures of imagination in the Swedish stories they translated.

Inea Bushnaq recorded over 130 folk tales from the Arab worlds as she prepared *Arab Folktales*.

Guide for Reading

Meet the Authors:

Virginia Hamilton (1936–)

In her many award-winning novels for young readers, Virginia Hamilton uses elements of history, myth, folklore, legend, and dream to bring to life her African American heritage.

Idries Shah (1924–1996)

Idries Shah published more than 30 books in his lifetime, winning six first prizes from the UNESCO International Book Year competition in 1972.

Ai-Ling Louie

When Ai-Ling Louie was a child, her grandmother told her the story "Yeh-Shen," the Chinese version of "Cinderella." Louie later learned that the tale was first written down by Tuan Cheng-shi during the Tang dynasty (A.D. 618–906) and had probably been handed down orally for centuries before that.

Lone Thygesen-Blecher and George Blecher

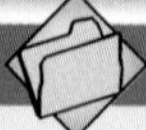

In 1982, Lone Thygesen-Blecher and George Blecher won an award for their translation of the Swedish novel *The Battle Horse*. They have also written *Swedish Folktales*, a collection of tales passed down through the generations.

Inea Bushnaq

Growing up in Jerusalem, Inea Bushnaq was frightened and charmed by the folk tales of her Arabic culture's oral tradition. As an adult, she returned to her homeland to record variations of those tales she heard as a child.

◆ Literature and Your Life

Connect Your Experience

In a difficult situation, you can sometimes look within yourself and find reserves of strength you didn't know you had. Such is the case for many of the characters you're about to meet.

Thematic Focus: Lessons Learned

In these stories, some characters learn lessons, while others teach them. As you read, identify the lesson in each story.

◆ Background for Understanding

History

One way that enslaved Africans kept their hopes alive despite the tremendous hardships they faced was to tell freedom tales—folk tales about the fight for freedom. These tales served an important function: They helped people to believe that they would eventually find freedom from slavery and injustice. As you'll notice in the freedom tale "The People Could Fly," these stories are full of references to the storytellers' native Africa.

◆ Build Vocabulary

Related Words: *undaunted*

The word *daunted* means "afraid or frightened of." Add the prefix *un-*, which means "not," and you'll get the related word *undaunted,* meaning "not afraid or frightened of." You'll encounter the word *undaunted* in "Yeh-Shen: A Cinderella Story From China."

Word Bank

Which word from the selections means "walk with dragging feet"? Check the Build Vocabulary boxes to see if you chose correctly.

croon
shuffle
sage
undaunted

Prentice Hall Literature Program Resources

REINFORCE / RETEACH / EXTEND

Selection Support Pages
Build Vocabulary: Related Words: *undaunted,* p. 267
Build Spelling Skills, p. 268
Build Grammar Skills: Commas in a Series, p. 269
Reading Strategy: Recognize Cultural Context, p. 270
Literary Focus: Folk Tales, p. 271

Strategies for Diverse Student Needs, pp. 97–98

Beyond Literature Community Connection: Volunteerism, p. 49

Formal Assessment Selection Test, pp. 235–237, Assessment Resources Software

Alternative Assessment, p. 49

Resource Pro CD-ROM
"The People Could Fly"; "The Algonquin Cinderella"; "Yeh-Shen: A Cinderella Story From China"; "His Just Reward"; "Djuha Borrows a Pot"

 **Listening to Literature Audiocassettes**

 **Looking at Literature Videodisc/Videotape** "The People Could Fly"

The People Could Fly ◆ The Algonquin Cinderella ◆ Yeh-Shen: A Cinderella Story From China ◆ His Just Reward ◆ Djuha Borrows a Pot

◆ Literary Focus

Folk Tales

Many cultures have **folk tales** that communicate important values and ideas. A folk tale is a story that was composed orally and then passed from person to person by word of mouth. Most folk tales are anonymous: No one knows who first composed them. When modern writers retell a folk tale, they try to capture the feeling and spirit of the tale as it has been told for hundreds of years.

The Ride for Liberty - the Fugitive Slaves, Eastman Johnson

◆ Reading Strategy

Recognize Cultural Context

One way to appreciate a folk tale is to recognize its **cultural context**—details about the time and place of the story and information about the customs and beliefs of its characters. The following selections were first told in many different places and times—from China in the seventh century to the United States during the time of slavery. Keep track of the cultural context of each folk tale by using a chart like the one shown. It will provide a window of understanding into what you read.

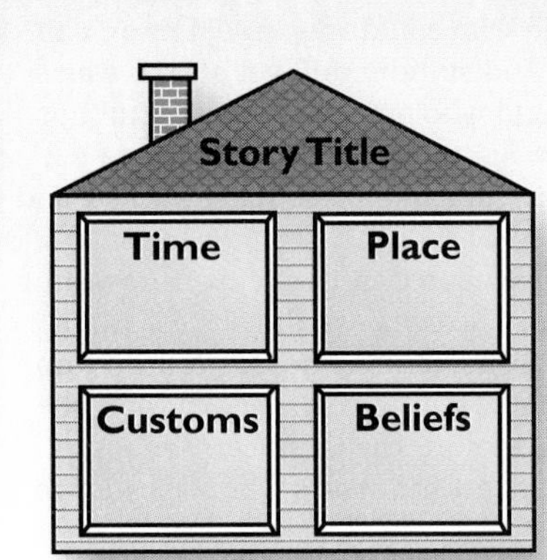

Preparing for Standardized Tests

Grammar Students who can correctly use commas in a series will be able to identify mistakes and select the best answers for standardized test questions that require editing skills. Tell them that commas are used to separate items that are listed together. Use commas when three or more things are listed.

Write this sample test question on the board and ask students to select the best answer:

Which of the following choices is correct?

(A) The king noticed that the woman was tattered, beautiful, and sweet.

(B) The king noticed that the woman was, tattered, beautiful, and sweet.

(C) The king noticed that the woman was beautiful and sweet.

(D) All choices are correct as written.

Help students see that *(B)* includes a comma after the verb; *(C)* does not list three or more items; therefore, *(D)* cannot be the correct answer. Help them realize that by process of elimination, they can determine that *(A)* is the correct answer. However, they should then verify the correct use of commas in that sentence.

Interest Grabber Ask students to think of a memorable celebration in their lives. Then have volunteers orally share their memories with the class as a storyteller might—adding colorful and amusing details to enliven their tales. Lead students into the folk tales they will read by explaining that just as students brings their own memories and even exaggerations to the story of a celebration, folk tales take on the flavor and background of the storyteller who tells the tale. Although folk tales may have been based on a real incident, they are shaped and molded as they are told and retold.

◆ Build Grammar Skills

Commas in a Series If you wish to introduce the grammar concept for this selection before students read, refer to the instruction on p. 836.

Customize for *Less Proficient Readers*

Students may have difficulty reading and understanding written dialect. Letters may be dropped and occasionally sentences have no subject. Tell students that the author chooses to write in this manner in order to make the story sound like spoken language. It may be helpful to play the recording.

Listening to Literature Audiocassettes

Customize for *More Advanced Students*

Have interested students select one of the folk tales and rewrite it as a newspaper article. For example, they might wish to include interviews with characters. Discuss the factual writing style and format of a journalistic article that answers the questions: who? what? when? where? why? and how?

The Ride for Liberty—The Fugitive Slaves, by Eastman Johnson

This image illustrates the idea of freedom tales—folk tales told to help slaves plan for freedom.

What clues does the artist offer about the theme of freedom? *The riders looking behind them as though they are being chased or followed.*

Develop Understanding

In "The People Could Fly," the story is told that long ago in Africa people knew how to fly. When they were captured and sent away in slave ships, it was too crowded and the people who knew how to fly lost their wings. As the enslaved African Americans labored in the fields, they had to work very hard and were often mistreated. An old man, Toby, helps the people to fly away from their misery by whispering magic words that help them remember how to fly. He finally flies himself, leaving those who cannot fly to tell the tale to others.

Team Teaching Strategy

The cultural and historical aspects of these folk tales provide a strong connection to social studies. You may wish to coordinate with a social studies teacher to plan ways of extending instruction.

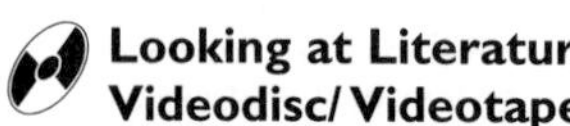

To provide background and insight into the author of "The People Could Fly," play Chapter 10 of the videodisc. Virginia Hamilton discusses the narrative elements that make her stories exciting. Discuss how a strong narrative gives life to a story like "The People Could Fly."

Chapter 10

◆Reading Strategy

❶ Recognize Cultural Context
Information that identifies the cultural background of characters helps readers understand the elements of the story. Ask students to find details that describe the culture. *Possible answers: long ago in Africa, the people knew magic, people could fly, and many people were captured for slavery.*

Customize for
English Language Learners
English Language learners may find it easier to understand these selections by reading and discussing the stories with partners. They might discuss the morals of the stories and lessons learned, unfamiliar vocabulary, and Guide for Responding questions.

The People Could Fly

African American Folk Tale

Virginia Hamilton

They say the people could fly. Say that long ago in Africa, some of the people knew magic. And they would walk up on the air like climbin up on a gate. And they flew like blackbirds over the fields. Black, shiny wings flappin against the blue up there. ❶

Then, many of the people were captured for Slavery. The ones that could fly shed their wings. They couldn't take their wings across the water on the slave ships. Too crowded, don't you know.

The folks were full of misery, then. Got sick with the up and down of the sea. So they forgot about flyin when they could no longer breathe the sweet scent of Africa.

Say the people who could fly kept their power, although they shed their wings. They kept their secret magic in the land of slavery. They looked the same as the other people from Africa who had been coming over, who had dark skin. Say you couldn't tell anymore one who could fly from one who couldn't.

One such who could was an old man, call him Toby. And standin tall, yet afraid, was a young woman who once had wings. Call her Sarah. Now Sarah carried a babe tied to her back. She trembled to be so hard worked and scorned.

The slaves labored in the fields from sunup to sundown. The owner of the slaves callin himself their Master. Say he was a hard lump of clay. A hard, glinty[1] coal. A hard rock pile, wouldn't be moved. His Overseer[2] on horseback pointed out the slaves who were slowin down. So the one called Driver[3] cracked his whip over the slow ones to make them move faster. That whip was a slice-open cut of pain. So they did move faster. Had to.

Sarah hoed and chopped the row as the babe on her back slept.

Say the child grew hungry. That babe started up bawling too loud. Sarah couldn't stop to feed it. Couldn't stop to soothe and quiet it down. She let it cry. She didn't want to. She had no heart to croon to it.

"Keep that thing quiet," called the Overseer. He pointed his finger at the babe. The woman scrunched low. The Driver cracked his whip across the babe anyhow. The babe hollered like any hurt child, and the woman fell to the earth.

The old man that was there, Toby, came and helped her to her feet.

"I must go soon," she told him.

"Soon," he said.

Sarah couldn't stand up straight any longer. She was too weak. The sun burned her face. The babe cried and cried, "Pity me, oh, pity me," say it sounded like. Sarah was so sad and starvin, she sat down in the row.

"Get up, you black cow," called the Overseer. He pointed his hand, and the Driver's whip snarled around Sarah's legs. Her sack dress tore into rags. Her legs bled onto the earth. She couldn't get up.

Toby was there where there was no one to help her and the babe.

"Now, before it's too late," panted Sarah. "Now, Father!"

"Yes, Daughter, the time is come," Toby answered. "Go, as you know how to go!"

1. **glinty** (glint´ ē) *adj.*: Shiny; reflecting light.
2. **Overseer** (ō´ vər sir´) *n.*: Someone who watches over and directs the work of others.
3. **Driver** *n.*: Someone who forced (drove) the slaves to work harder.

Block Scheduling Strategies

Consider these suggestions to take advantage of extended class time:

- In small groups, have students discuss the behaviors of the main characters and what these suggest about the folk tales' themes. Then have students answer the Literary Focus questions on p. 836. For additional practice, they can use **Selection Support,** p. 271, and complete the chart suggested in the Literary Focus note on p. 826 of the Teacher Edition.
- After students have finished reading each selection, have them independently answer the Critical Thinking questions on pp. 824, 828, 832, and 835.
- As a class, students may wish to plan a Folk-Tale Festival from the Idea Bank on p. 837 to share with parents or a younger grade level class.
- After introducing the Literary Focus of folk tales, have students read one or more of the stories. Students may benefit from listening to the recording of the folk tales.

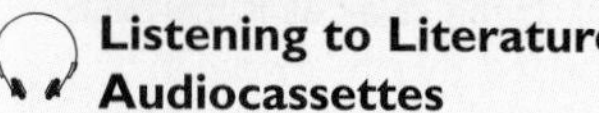

From THE PEOPLE COULD FLY by Virginia Hamilton, illustrated by Leo and Diane Dillon

2 ▲ **Critical Viewing** How does the folk tale explain the unique way the people in this illustration fly? **[Interpret]**

He raised his arms, holding them out to her. "*Kum . . . yali, kum buba tambe,*" and more magic words, said so quickly, they sounded like whispers and sighs.

The young woman lifted one foot on the air. Then the other. She flew clumsily at first, with the child now held tightly in her arms. Then she felt the magic, the African mystery. Say she rose just as free as a bird. As light as a feather.

3 The Overseer rode after her, hollerin. Sarah flew over the fences. She flew over the woods. Tall trees could not snag her. Nor could the Overseer. She flew like an eagle now, until she was gone from sight. No one dared speak about it. Couldn't believe it. But it was, because they that was there saw that it was.

Say the next day was dead hot in the fields. A young man slave fell from the heat. The Driver come and whipped him. Toby come over and spoke words to the fallen one. The words of ancient Africa once heard are never remembered completely. The young man forgot them as soon as he heard them. They went way inside him. He got up and rolled over on the air. He rode it awhile. And he flew away.

Another and another fell from the heat. Toby was there. He cried out to the fallen and reached his arms out to them. "*Kum kunka yali, kum . . . tambe*!" Whispers and sighs. And they too rose on the air. They rode the hot breezes. The ones flyin were black and shinin sticks, wheelin above the head of the Overseer. 4 They crossed the rows, the fields, the fences, the streams, and were away.

"Seize the old man!" cried the Overseer. "I heard him say the magic *words*. Seize him!"

The one callin himself Master come runnin. The Driver got his whip ready to curl around old Toby and tie him up. The slaveowner took his hip gun from its place. He meant to kill old, black Toby. 5

But Toby just laughed. Say he threw back his head and said, "Hee, hee! Don't you know who I am? Don't you know some of us in this field?" He said it to their faces. "We are ones who fly!"

And he sighed the ancient words that were a dark promise. He said them all around to

◆ Build Vocabulary

croon (kro͞on) *v.*: Sing or hum quietly, soothingly

▸Critical Viewing◂

2 Interpret *The people in the folk tale knew how to fly in Africa before they came to America. Toby whispers magic African words that help them remember how to fly.*

◆Literary Focus

3 Folk Tales were often passed down from generation to generation and repeated orally. Suggest that students find details that illustrate how Hamilton writes in the style of a story told aloud. *Students will probably note that the author uses a very informal style of writing that makes it sound as though the story is being told orally. For example, they may note missing sentence subjects and dropped verb endings.*

◆Critical Thinking

4 Speculate Have students think about the reasons why the people want to fly. *The workers are miserable working in the hot son and are being abused by the Overseer; they want to escape from their pain.*

◆Critical Thinking

5 Connect Suggest that students examine the character of Toby to determine why he is able to remember how to fly. Ask them to list Toby's characteristics that make it possible for him to help. *Toby is unafraid of the Overseer and the Master because he remembers the magic and still knows how to fly. He keeps the secret of the magic words hidden until they are needed.*

Humanities: Art

The People Could Fly, by Leo and Diane Dillon

Leo and Diane Dillon have been producing book illustrations as partners since they married in 1957. They have won many awards for their illustrations including the Caldecott Medal two years in a row in 1976 and 1977 for *Why Mosquitoes Buzz in People's Ears* and *Ashanti to Zulu.*

They work as a team when producing their illustrations, passing the artwork back and forth, with each artist adding details until the illustration is completed. A finished illustration is an unusual blend of both artists' talents and imagination, and cannot be attributed to just one or the other.

Suggest that students study the details of the illustration, which is used as the cover illustration of Virginia Hamilton's book, *The People Could Fly.* Use these questions for discussion:

1. What details indicate that the people are actually flying? *Students will note that the background of the illustration is clouds and sky.*
2. What can be learned from the clothing? *Their clothing is ragged and worn as if they are very poor and mistreated.*

Reinforce and Extend

Answers

◆ Literature and Your Life

Reader's Response Students may think that Toby is the most important character in the story because he helps the others gain their freedom.

Thematic Focus Students may think that the Master learned how wrong it was to abuse his workers because they ran away. Others may feel that he did not learn a lesson because he tried to kill Toby.

☑ Check Your Comprehension

1. They lost their wings when they were captured as slaves; the ships were too crowded to carry the wings.
2. The Overseer is mistreating her and her baby; he is striking both of them.
3. Toby tells her the magic words that restore her ability to fly.
4. The slaves who could not fly and stayed behind told the story to their children, and it was passed along from generation to generation.

◆ Critical Thinking

1. Possible answers: the insults of the Overseer, his whipping of Sarah and her child, his constant urging the slaves to work faster; his refusal to allow Sarah to feed and comfort her child.
2. The African words stand for the free life the slaves hope to return to.
3. Flying is a metaphor for being free and living a free life in one's own culture.
4. Students might suggest that the tale would provide hope for freedom and escape from injustice.
5. Students may think that freedom tales were still told because living conditions often improved very little for African Americans after the abolition of slavery.

the others in the field under the whip,

"*. . . buba yali . . . buba tambe. . . .*"

There was a great outcryin. The bent backs straightened up. Old and young who were called slaves and could fly joined hands. Say like they would ring-sing.[4] But they didn't shuffle in a circle. They didn't sing. They rose on the air. They flew in a flock that was black against the heavenly blue. Black crows or black shadows. It didn't matter, they went so high. Way above the plantation, way over the slavery land. Say they flew away to *Free-dom.*

And the old man, old Toby, flew behind them, takin care of them. He wasn't cryin. He wasn't laughin. He was the seer.[5] His gaze fell on the plantation where the slaves who could not fly waited.

"*Take us with you!*" Their looks spoke it but they were afraid to shout it. Toby couldn't take them with him. Hadn't the time to teach them to fly. They must wait for a chance to run.

"Goodie-bye!" The old man called Toby spoke to them, poor souls! And he was flyin gone.

So they say. The Overseer told it. The one called Master said it was a lie, a trick of the light. The Driver kept his mouth shut.

The slaves who could not fly told about the people who could fly to their children. When they were free. When they sat close before the fire in the free land, they told it. They did so love firelight and *Free-dom,* and tellin.

They say that the children of the ones who could not fly told their children. And now, me, I have told it to you.

4. **ring-sing:** Joining hands in a circle to sing and dance.
5. **seer** (sē´ ər) *n.:* One who has supposed power to see the future; prophet.

◆ Build Vocabulary

shuffle (shuf´ əl) *v.:* Walk with dragging feet

Guide for Responding

◆ Literature and Your Life

Reader's Response Who do you think is the most important character in the story? Why?

Thematic Focus Do you think that the Master learned anything in this story? Why or why not?

Group Activity Read the story aloud, switching readers at each paragraph. Is the story more effective when read aloud?

☑ Check Your Comprehension

1. How did the people lose their wings?
2. Why does Sarah tell Toby that she must leave soon?
3. How does Toby help Sarah?
4. Who kept alive the story of the people who could fly?

◆ Critical Thinking

Interpret

1. Describe three details that help you understand the harsh living conditions of the enslaved Africans. **[Support]**
2. Why do you think the author includes African words in the story? **[Interpret]**
3. What do you think "flying" really refers to? **[Draw Conclusion]**

Apply

4. How do you think it would feel to hear this tale if you were an enslaved African? **[Relate]**

Extend

5. Do you think that African American freedom tales were still told after the abolition of slavery in 1865? Why? **[History Link]**

Beyond the Selection

FURTHER READING

Other Works by Virginia Hamilton

The House of Dies Drear
The Planet of Junior Brown
Plain City

Other Works Illustrated by Leo and Diane Dillon

Ashanti to Zulu: African Traditions, Leo Dillon
Why Mosquitoes Buzz in People's Ears: a West African Tale, Verna Aardema

INTERNET

We suggest the following sites on the Internet (all Web sites are subject to change).

For more information about Virginia Hamilton:
http://virginiahamilton.com

For more information about Leo and Diane Dillon's illustrations:
http://www.best.com/~libros/dillon/bio.html

We *strongly recommend* that you preview these sites before you send students to them.

The Algonquin Cinderella

Native American Folk Tale

Retold by Idries Shah

❶ There was once a large village of the MicMac Indians of the Eastern Algonquins,[1] built beside a lake. At the far end of the settlement stood a lodge, and in it lived a being who was always invisible. He had a sister who looked after him, and everyone knew that any girl who could see him might marry him. For
❷ that reason there were very few girls who did not try, but it was very long before anyone succeeded.

This is the way in which the test of sight was carried out: at evening-time, when the Invisible One was due to be returning home, his sister would walk with any girl who might come down to the lakeshore. She, of course, could see her brother, since he was always visible to her. As soon as she saw him, she would say to the girls:

"Do you see my brother?"

"Yes," they would generally reply—though some of them did say "No."

To those who said that they could indeed see him, the sister would say:

"Of what is his shoulder strap made?" Some people say that she would enquire:

"What is his moose-runner's haul?" or "With what does he draw his sled?"

And they would answer:

"A strip of rawhide" or "a green flexible branch," or something of that kind.

Then she, knowing that they had not told the truth, would say:

"Very well, let us return to the wigwam!"[2]

When they had gone in, she would tell them not to sit in a certain place, because it belonged to the Invisible One. Then, after they had helped to cook the supper, they would wait with great curiosity, to see him eat. They could be sure that he was a real person, for when he took off his moccasins they became visible, and his sister hung them up. But beyond this they saw nothing of him, not even when they stayed in the place all night, as many of them did.

1. **Algonquins** (al gäŋ′ kwinz) *n.*: Native Americans living near the Ottawa River in Canada.

2. **wigwam** (wig′ wäm′) *n.*: Indian dwelling made by a dome-shaped framework of poles covered by rush mats or sheets of bark.

Develop Understanding

In "The Algonquin Cinderella," Oochigeaskw and her two sisters live with their father in a village built of lodge homes. A mysterious invisible man lives with his sister in one of the lodges. All the women of the village, including the girl's older sisters, attempt to earn the right to marry him. They must be able to "see" and describe him, but since they cannot actually see him, they guess incorrectly. It isn't until Oochigeaskw, the burn-scarred young girl, goes to the lodge that his belongings are correctly described as a rainbow and the Milky Way. She is correct because she truly can see him and thinks he is wonderful. The man's sister bathes her hair and scars and she becomes a beautiful young woman once again and marries the invisible man.

◆Reading Strategy

❶ **Recognize Cultural Context** Ask students to find details that give the cultural setting of this folk tale. *It takes place in a village of the MicMac Indians of the Eastern Algonquins; the villagers live in lodge dwellings.*

◆Critical Thinking

❷ **Speculate** Have students suggest reasons why the women cannot see the Invisible One. *Students might guess that the women are not kind or worthy enough. They are not truthful about not actually being able to see him, even though they cannot.*

Cross-Curricular Connection: Social Studies

Algonquin Indians "The Algonquin Cinderella" is set in a village of lodge homes built of bent birch saplings covered with birch bark. In addition to their lodges, the Algonquin Indians depended on birch trees in their daily life. They built canoes of birch bark that were light weight and easy to maneuver. Women used birch bark to create cooking pots, needle cases, and decorative designs of animals and people. Men recorded songs and sacred stories on birch bark scrolls.

Many of the Algonquian-speaking tribes lived in Canada in the Ottawa River region of what is now Quebec and Ontario. One of these groups is the MicMac people mentioned in the folk tale. *Algonquian* refers to the language spoken and *Algonquin,* sometimes spelled *Algonkin,* to one of the tribes.

Because they lived too far north to depend entirely on agriculture for food, the Algonquin lived and worked in bands of hunter-gatherers. Their excellent hunting and trapping skills attracted the attention of French fur traders in the early 1600's, and trade was established.

◆Literary Focus

❶ **Folk Tales** The values and lessons taught in folk tales provide many opportunities for students to explore the literary focus of Folk Tales and the theme of "Lessons Learned." As they read, it may help students to understand the lessons and similarities of the stories if they chart some of their observations about the behavior of the characters. This chart can be completed as each folk tale is read.

	Character's Behavior	Lesson Learned
The People Could Fly	*evil Overseer, magic words, hardworking Africans*	*evil doesn't pay, goodness survives*
The Algonquin Cinderella	*wicked sisters, invisible man, hardworking girl*	*wickedness loses, goodness wins*
Yeh-Shen: A Cinderella Story from China	*wicked stepmother, magic fish bones, hardworking girl*	*goodness wins*
His Just Reward	*wicked snake, sly fox, kind man*	*goodness wins*
Djuha Borrows a Pot	*greedy neighbor, clever Djuha*	*greediness does't pay*

▶Critical Viewing◀

❷ **Connect** *Students will probably note that the women decorate their clothing with shells to make it more beautiful. When they go to visit the Invisible One, they wear their finest clothes.*

◆Critical Thinking

❸ **Infer** Ask students to try to understand why the women try to fool the sister and make guesses about the Invisible One's belongings. *The women want to marry him and are pretending to see him.*

▲ **Critical Viewing** This woven fabric demonstrates Algonquin attention to beauty—even in functional items. What details in the folk tale confirm this concern? **[Connect]** ❷

❶ Now there lived in the village an old man who was a widower, and his three daughters. The youngest girl was very small, weak and often ill: and yet her sisters, especially the elder, treated her cruelly. The second daughter was kinder, and sometimes took her side: but the wicked sister would burn her hands and feet with hot cinders, and she was covered with scars from this treatment. She was so marked that people called her *Oochigeaskw*,[3] the Rough-Faced-Girl.

When her father came home and asked why she had such burns, the bad sister would at once say that it was her own fault, for she had disobeyed orders and gone near the fire and fallen into it.

These two elder sisters decided one day to try their luck at seeing the Invisible One. So they dressed themselves in their finest clothes, and tried to look their prettiest. They found the Invisible One's sister and took the usual walk by the water:

When he came, and when they were asked if they could see him, they answered, "Of course." And when asked about the shoulder strap or sled cord, they answered, "A piece of rawhide." ❸

But of course they were lying like the others, and they got nothing for their pains.

The next afternoon, when the father returned home, he brought with him many of the pretty little shells from which wampum[4] was made, and they set to work to string them.

3. **Oochigeaskw** (ō shē´ gā shkə)

4. **wampum** (wäm´ pəm) *n.*: Small beads made of shells used as money by Native Americans.

Humanities: Art

Weaving Household objects that Indians made were created to be beautiful, as well as useful. The woven fabric illustration represents an example of this quest for beauty in daily life. Discuss with students that many kinds of fabric are machine-woven today. If students are unfamiliar with the process of weaving, give a simple demonstration, using construction paper strips of two different colors. Show them how the the weaving is created by laying one set of the strips over and under the other set of strips.

Almost any flexible material can be woven into a number of useful objects, such as fishing nets, baskets, hats, belts, fabric, and blankets. Yucca fibers, thin strips of wood, straw, wheat stalks, reeds, and thread can be used in the weaving process. Suggest that students study baskets and chairs with woven seats to study weaving patterns. Beautiful designs are created by the woven pattern of the materials.

Weaving cloth is a process by which fabric is made by passing various colored threads spun from silk, cotton, wool, or synthetically produced fibers over and under each other. Cloth weaving is often done on looms, where warp or vertical threads are attached to a frame and complex and beautiful patterns woven by passing various colored threads over and under the warp threads in various patterns. Another method is called finger-weaving, used for smaller woven projects such as straps and belts, in which the warp threads are tied together at one end and not attached to a fixed loom.

That day, poor little Oochigeaskw, who had always gone barefoot, got a pair of her father's moccasins, old ones, and put them into water to soften them so that she could wear them. Then she begged her sisters for a few wampum shells. The elder called her a 'little pest,' but the younger one gave her some. Now, with no other clothes than her usual rags, the poor little thing went into the woods and got herself some sheets of birch bark, from which she
❹ made a dress, and put marks on it for decoration, in the style of long ago. She made a petticoat and a loose gown, a cap, leggings and a handkerchief. She put on her father's large old moccasins, which were far too big for her, and went forth to try her luck. She would try, she thought, to discover whether she could see the Invisible One.

She did not begin very well. As she set off, her sisters shouted and hooted, hissed and yelled, and tried
❺ to make her stay. And the loafers around the village, seeing the strange little creature, called out "Shame!"

The poor little girl in her strange clothes, with her face all scarred, was an awful sight, but she was kindly received by the sister of the Invisible One. And this was, of
❻ course, because this noble lady understood far more about things than simply the mere outside which all the rest of the world knows. As the brown of the evening sky turned to black, the lady took her down to the lake.

"Do you see him?" the Invisible One's sister asked.

"I do, indeed—and he is wonderful!" said Oochigeaskw.

The sister asked:

"And what is his sled-string?"

The little girl said:

"It is the Rainbow."

"And, my sister, what is his bow-string?"

"It is The Spirit's Road—the Milky Way."

"So you *have* seen him," said his sister. She took the girl home with her and bathed her. As she did so, all the scars disappeared from her

▼ **Critical Viewing** In what ways do the rainbow and the Milky Way help readers imagine the size and power of the Invisible One? **[Relate]** ❼

◆Critical Thinking

❹ **Interpret** Challenge students to give reasons why Oochigeaskw tries to find clothes to wear and make them more beautiful. *Students will probably realize that she is ashamed of how she looks and wants to make herself as pretty as possible.*

◆Literature and Your Life

❺ **Connect Your Experience** Encourage students to think of a time when they did not feel confident; for example, a time when they were not dressed like everyone else. Ask them to remember how it felt and what they did in order to feel better. Challenge students to think about what advice they might give to Oochigeaskw. *Students may relate various confidence-building measures they have tried to use from their own experiences.*

Comprehension Check ☑

❻ Ask students to explain why the sister of the Invisible One was kind to Oochigeaskw. *Most students will explain that the noble woman could see past her scars and ragged clothes and recognize her gentle good nature.*

►Critical Viewing◄

❼ **Relate** *Being able to control something as wonderful as the Milky Way and a rainbow, made the Invisible One seem to be a very important and powerful person.*

Customize for *English Language Learners*

Students may recognize the elements of the plot in the Cinderella stories and be able to share a folk tale from their own background with the class.

Cross-Curricular Connection: Science

Rainbows and Milky Way
In "The Algonquin Cinderella," Oochigeaskw identifies the Invisible One's sled-string as a rainbow and his bow-string as the Milky Way. Ask students to consider why the storyteller used such terms to describe common everyday objects. Guide students to notice that both are related to the sky and nature, and that both are beautiful and inspirational. Ancient people and Native Americans greatly respected nature and told many stories with nature as an important element.

Rainbows are an awe-inspiring sight, especially when they occur after a ferocious thunderstorm. Scientifically, a rainbow is a large curved band of colors, which is caused by light passing through raindrops, like a prism. Rainbows are seen only in the early morning or late afternoon because the light from the sun, the eyes, and the center of the arc of the rainbow must form a straight line. That straight line is not possible at midday.

The Milky Way is another truly beautiful sight to see—a band of diamondlike stars stretching clear across the night sky. Our Sun, the planets, and Earth are part of a galaxy of stars called the Milky Way. Our solar system is only a very small portion of the galaxy. The Milky Way contains billions of stars, dust, and gases fanning out in a spiral 100,000 light years in diameter.

Encourage interested students to research other sights such as the Northern Lights or solar and lunar eclipses. Then have them write a short tale that incorporates the sight as one of its elements.

Beyond Literature

Students may be surprised to learn how many folk tales around the world contain elements of the plot of Cinderella. In addition to library resources, you may wish to help them explore resources on the Internet. They may find a chart helpful when comparing "Cinderella" names, countries of origin, and differences in the plots that they discover in their research.

Reinforce and Extend

Answers

◆ Literature and Your Life

Reader's Response Possible response: the image of Oochigeaskw dressed in rags, with burns on her body, becoming a finely dressed, beautiful young woman, because it creates such a contrast.

Thematic Focus Pretending to know something is not helpful.

☑ Check Your Comprehension

1. She must be able to see the invisible man.
2. She got her name because she had ugly scars from being burned with hot cinders. The name means Rough-Faced-Girl.
3. They pretend to be able to see him even when they cannot.
4. She is actually able to see the Invisible One; the sister bathes her; the scars disappear; her hair grows back; she marries the Invisible One.

◆ Critical Thinking

1. She questions prospective wives about whether or not they can actually see him.
2. They are embarrassed to admit that they cannot see him; they want to marry him.
3. She succeeds because she has a true spirit; she has had a difficult life and is rewarded for her patience.
4. Students may feel that the elder sister, who was responsible for Oochigeaskw's scars and burns, should be punished, but the second sister, who was kinder, should not be.
5. The crucial test is different. Oochigeaskw must be able to truly see an invisible man, while Cinderella must attend a ball and wear a glass slipper to meet her prince.

body. Her hair grew again, as it was combed, long, like a blackbird's wing. Her eyes were now like stars: in all the world there was no other such beauty. Then, from her treasures, the lady gave her a wedding garment, and adorned her.

Then she told Oochigeaskw to take the *wife's* seat in the wigwam: the one next to where the Invisible One sat, beside the entrance. And when he came in, terrible and beautiful, he smiled and said:

"So we are found out!"

"Yes," said his sister. And so Oochigeaskw became his wife.

Beyond Literature

Culture Connection

Cinderella Around the World The story of a poor hard-working girl suffering under an evil stepmother is known and loved around the world. There are more than nine hundred versions of this classic tale—the oldest has been traced back more than a thousand years to China. The story most Americans are familiar with was written in the 1600's by Charles Perrault, a French writer, and it is the only one with a fairy godmother and a warning to be home by midnight. Yet for all the differences between the stories, the poor girl always manages to escape her stepmother, marry the prince, and live happily ever after.

Cross-Curricular Activity
Comparing Stories Read the Cinderella stories in this book. Then, using library resources, locate one or two others. In a report to classmates, share the stories, describe the similarities and differences among them, and explain why you think the Cinderella model is so popular.

Guide for Responding

◆ Literature and Your Life

Reader's Response What image from the story had the greatest impact on you? Why?

Thematic Focus What lesson does this tale teach its audience?

Group Activity Work with a group to plan and create a comic-book version of "The Algonquin Cinderella."

☑ Check Your Comprehension

1. What task must a girl accomplish in order to marry the mysterious brother?
2. How did Oochigeaskw get her name?
3. What happens when Oochigeaskw's sisters visit the Invisible One?
4. What happens when Oochigeaskw visits the mysterious brother and sister?

◆ Critical Thinking

Interpret

1. How does the Invisible One's sister protect him? **[Interpret]**
2. Why do people in the story pretend to be able to see the Invisible One? **[Infer]**
3. Why do you think Oochigeaskw succeeds where others failed? **[Speculate]**

Evaluate

4. Do you think that the stepsisters should be punished for their behavior? Explain your answer. **[Make a Judgment]**

Extend

5. What do you think is the most important difference between Oochigeaskw's story and the European tale known as "Cinderella"? **[Literature Link]**

Beyond the Selection

FURTHER READING

Other Works About Native Americans

Algonquin Indians, Rita D'Apice, Beatrice Siegel, Patricia Quiri

The Encyclopedia of Native America, Trudy Griffin-Pierce

Indian Handcrafts, C. Keith Wilbur

Other Native American Folk Tales

Native American Story, told by Joseph Bruchac

Echoes of the Elders, The Stories and Paintings of Chief Lelooska, edited by Christine Normandin

INTERNET

We suggest the following sites on the Internet (all Web sites are subject to change).

For more information about Algonquin Indians: **http://dickshovel.netgate.net/alg.html**

For more information about Native American Art: **http://www.nativeweb.org/NativeTech/**

We *strongly recommend* that you preview these sites before you send students to them.

Yeh-Shen: A Cinderella Story From China

Chinese Folk Tale

Retold by Ai-Ling Louie

In the dim past, even before the Ch'in and the Han dynasties, there lived a cave chief of southern China by the name of Wu. As was the custom in those days, Chief Wu had taken
1 two wives. Each wife in her turn had presented Wu with a baby daughter. But one of the wives sickened and died, and not too many days after that Chief Wu took to his bed and died too.

2 Yeh-Shen, the little orphan, grew to girlhood in her stepmother's home. She was a bright child and lovely too, with skin as smooth as ivory and dark pools for eyes. Her stepmother was jealous of all this beauty and goodness, for her own daughter was not pretty at all. So in her displeasure, she gave poor Yeh-Shen the heaviest and most unpleasant chores.

The only friend that Yeh-Shen had to her name was a fish she had caught and raised. It was a beautiful fish with golden eyes, and every day it would come out of the water and rest its head on the bank of the pond, waiting for Yeh-Shen to feed it. Stepmother gave Yeh-Shen little enough food for herself, but the orphan child always found something to share with her fish, which grew to enormous size. 3

> **◆ Reading Strategy**
> In China, many people catch and raise fish as pets. How does this context help you understand Yeh-Shen's situation?

Somehow the stepmother heard of this. She was terribly angry to discover that Yeh-Shen had kept a secret from her. She hurried down to the pond, but she was unable to see the fish, for Yeh-Shen's pet wisely hid itself. The stepmother, however, was a crafty woman, and she soon thought of a plan. She walked home and called out, "Yeh-Shen, go and collect some firewood. But wait! The neighbors might see you. Leave your filthy coat here!" The minute the girl was out of sight, her stepmother slipped on the

Develop Understanding

One-Minute Insight In "Yeh-Shen: A Cinderella Story From China," orphaned Yeh-Shen is mistreated by her stepmother who is jealous of her great beauty. Her only friend is a beautiful fish that she feeds from her meager food supply. The wicked stepmother tricks the girl and kills the fish. The heartbroken girl saves the bones and finds that they have magical powers. With the help of the magic fish bones, Yeh-Shen attends the Festival in a beautiful gown with shoes made of gold. She loses a golden slipper, however, as she flees from her stepmother. The king tries to locate the owner of the golden slipper. When he does, they are soon married. The king banishes the unkind stepmother and stepsister to their cave where they are later killed by falling stones.

Spelling Strategy

1 This selection's spelling strategy guides students to recognize that the *aw* sound can be spelled with *au*. Have students locate the word *daughter* and note that this spelling strategy is used.

◆Critical Thinking

2 **Evaluate** Ask students to evaluate why the stepmother mistreats Yeh-Shen. *Students may say that she mistreats her because she is jealous; Yeh-Shen is beautiful and good, while her own daughter is not.*

◆Reading Strategy

3 **Recognize Cultural Context** *Students may answer that Yeh-Shen's only real friend is her pet fish. Knowing that raising pet fish is a common custom in China helps to identify the setting of the story and its cultural context.*

Humanities: Music

Folk Tales Set to Music

Like artists who paint or draw pictures of characters and scenes from folk tales, musicians also use folk tales as inspiration and the basis of compositions.

Sergei Prokofiev (1891–1953) was a well-known Soviet composer. He composed a ballet arrangement of the Cinderella story, "Cinderella Suites." In addition, he composed a symphonic fairy tale entitled "Peter and the Wolf," which is known and loved by children around the world. It is often their first introduction to classical music. With the help of spoken narration, not only does it tell an exciting story, it introduces the instruments of the orchestra. The sounds of different instruments represent the characters of the story. For example, Peter is played by the string section, the cat is the clarinet, the bird is a flute and the wolf is three French horns. When Peter defies his grandfather's warnings and goes hunting, he must team up with a wily cat, a brave bird and a duck to outsmart the hungry wolf and rescue everyone. The lessons taught in the tale are of the advantages of teamwork and heeding the warnings of adults.

Encourage interested students to locate and listen to the recording of "Cinderella Suites" or "Peter and the Wolf." Ask them to share their impressions of these musical tales with their classmates. Alternatively, students may wish to find recordings of other musical folk tales or information about composers, such as Prokofiev, who have told stories with their music.

Comprehension Check ☑

❶ Who is the old man that Yeh-Shen calls uncle? Is he really her uncle? *He is not a relative; he has been sent by her magical fish to give her a message.*

◆Critical Thinking

❷ **Infer** Have students guess why it is so important for Yeh-Shen to go to the Festival. *Students should note that young women go to the Festival dressed in their finest clothes in hopes of finding a husband to marry. If she cannot go, she will never escape from her miserable life with her stepmother.*

Customize for
Musical/Rhythmic Learners
Folk tales and folk songs are similar because they often tell a story with a cultural setting. Suggest that a group of interested students locate a folk song or a ballad that tells a complete story, and compare it to a folk tale. If possible, they may wish to perform the song as a group or locate a recording to share their findings with the class.

◆Reading Strategy

❸ **Recognize Cultural Context** Challenge students to find details that explain how the Festival helps set the cultural context of the folk tale. *Students may point out that a festival in their own community would probably not be a place where girls would go dressed in their finery to look for a husband.*

Customize for
Verbal/Linguistic Learners
Interested students might enjoy using the story details of Yeh-Shen and rewriting them as a poem.

coat herself and went down again to the pond. This time the big fish saw Yeh-Shen's familiar jacket and heaved itself onto the bank, expecting to be fed. But the stepmother, having hidden a dagger in her sleeve, stabbed the fish, wrapped it in her garments, and took it home to cook for dinner.

When Yeh-Shen came to the pond that evening, she found her pet had disappeared. Overcome with grief, the girl collapsed on the ground and dropped her tears into the still waters of the pond.

"Ah, poor child!" a voice said.

Yeh-Shen sat up to find a very old man looking down at her. He wore the coarsest of clothes, and his hair flowed down over his shoulders.

❶ "Kind uncle,[1] who may you be?" Yeh-Shen asked.

"That is not important, my child. All you must know is that I have been sent to tell you of the wondrous powers of your fish."

"My fish, but sir . . ." The girl's eyes filled with tears, and she could not go on.

The old man sighed and said, "Yes, my child, your fish is no longer alive, and I must tell you that your stepmother is once more the cause of your sorrow." Yeh-Shen gasped in horror, but the old man went on. "Let us not dwell on things that are past," he said, "for I have come bringing you a gift. Now you must listen carefully to this: The bones of your fish are filled with a powerful spirit. Whenever you are in serious need, you must kneel before them and let them know your heart's desire. But do not waste their gifts."

Yeh-Shen wanted to ask the old sage many more questions, but he rose to the sky before she could utter another word. With heavy heart, Yeh-Shen made her way to the dung heap to gather the remains of her friend.

> "Kind uncle, who may you be?" Yeh-Shen asked. "That is not important, my child. All you must know is that I have been sent to tell you of the wondrous powers of your fish."

Time went by, and Yeh-Shen, who was often left alone, took comfort in speaking to the bones of her fish. When she was hungry, which happened quite often, Yeh-Shen asked the bones for food. In this way, Yeh-Shen managed to live from day to day, but she lived in dread that her stepmother would discover her secret and take even that away from her.

So the time passed and spring came. Festival time was approaching: It was the busiest time of the year. Such cooking and cleaning and sewing there was to be done! Yeh-Shen had hardly a moment's rest. At the spring festival young men and young women from the village hoped to meet and to choose whom they would marry. How Yeh-Shen longed to go! But her stepmother had other plans. ❷ She hoped to find a husband for her own daughter and did not want any man to see the beauteous Yeh-Shen first. When finally the holiday arrived, the stepmother and her daughter dressed themselves in their finery and filled their baskets with sweetmeats. "You must remain at home now, and watch to see that no ❸ one steals fruit from our trees," her stepmother told Yeh-Shen, and then she departed for the banquet with her own daughter.

As soon as she was alone, Yeh-Shen went to speak to the bones of her fish. "Oh, dear friend," she said, kneeling before the precious bones, "I long to go to the festival, but I cannot show myself in these rags. Is there somewhere I could borrow clothes fit to wear to the feast?" At once she found herself dressed in a gown of

1. **uncle:** In this case, *uncle* is a term of respect given to an older man and not a blood relation.

◆ Build Vocabulary

sage (sāj) *n.*: Very wise man

undaunted (ən dônt′ id) *adj.*: Not stopping because of fear or failure

Viewing and Representing Mini-Lesson

Book Illustrations

This mini-lesson supports the Book Jacket Writing project in the Idea Bank, p. 837.

Introduce Discuss book jackets with students; what makes them appealing? Color? Images? The design of the title letters? Explain that they will create their own book jackets for a folk tale.

Develop Have students work in groups of three or four to select a folk tale. They may choose to illustrate the setting or cultural context of the tale, portray a character or an element of the plot, or represent the moral of the story. Suggest that they list important details of the story that may be helpful in their portrayal. Groups can assign one student to create the illustration, one to write the blurb, and one to create a title. They may wish to work together for all aspects of the book jacket design. Review the Humanities note on p. 823, so that students can think about the kind of teamwork that Leo and Diane Dillon use for their illustrations. Point out that the illustration does not need to be a drawing or painting. It might be a cartoon, a collage, or a symbolic representation of the folk tale.

Apply Provide a selection of art materials for the students to use as they work on their book jackets. When students have completed their book jackets, create a class display.

Assess Assess students' work on how well their book jackets represent the details of the folk story.

> ◆ Literary Focus
> What role do the fish bones play in this folk tale?

4 azure blue, with a cloak of kingfisher feathers draped around her shoulders. Best of all, on her tiny feet were the most beautiful slippers she had ever seen. They were woven of golden threads, in a pattern like the scales of a fish, and the glistening soles were made of solid gold. There was magic in the shoes, for they should have been quite heavy, yet when Yeh-Shen walked, her feet felt as light as air.

> It wasn't until the blackest part of night, while the moon hid behind a cloud, that Yeh-Shen dared to show her face at the pavilion, and even then she tiptoed timidly across the wide floor.

5 "Be sure you do not lose your golden shoes," said the spirit of the bones. Yeh-Shen promised to be careful. Delighted with her transformation, she bid a fond farewell to the bones of her fish as she slipped off to join in the merrymaking.

That day Yeh-Shen turned many a head as she appeared at the feast. All around her people whispered, "Look at that beautiful girl! Who can she be?"

But above this, Stepsister was heard to say, "Mother, does she not resemble our Yeh-Shen?"

Upon hearing this, Yeh-Shen jumped up and ran off before her stepsister could look closely at her. She raced down the mountainside, and in doing so, she lost one of her golden slippers. No sooner had the shoe fallen from her foot than all her fine clothes turned back to rags. Only one thing remained—a tiny golden shoe. Yeh-Shen hurried to the bones of her fish and returned the slipper, promising to find its mate. But now the bones were silent. Sadly Yeh-Shen realized that she had lost her only friend. She hid the little shoe in her bedstraw, and went outside to cry. Leaning against a fruit tree, she sobbed and sobbed until she fell asleep.

The stepmother left the gathering to check on Yeh-Shen, but when she returned home she found the girl sound asleep, with her arms wrapped around a fruit tree. So thinking no more of her, the stepmother rejoined the party. Meantime, a villager had found the shoe. Recognizing its worth, he sold it to a merchant, who presented it in turn to the king of the island kingdom of T'o Han.

The king was more than happy to accept the slipper as a gift. He was entranced by the tiny thing, which was shaped of the most precious of metals, yet which made no sound when touched to stone. The more he marveled at its beauty, the more determined he became to find the woman to whom the shoe belonged. A search was begun among the ladies of his own kingdom, but all who tried on the sandal found it impossibly small. Undaunted, the king ordered the search widened to include the cave women from the countryside where the slipper had been found. Since he realized it would take many years for every woman to come to his island and test her foot in the slipper, the king thought of a way to get the right woman to come forward. He ordered the sandal placed in a pavilion by the side of the road near where it had been found, and his herald announced that the shoe was to be returned to its original owner. Then from a nearby hiding place, the king and his men settled down to watch and wait for a woman with tiny feet to come and claim her slipper. 6

All that day the pavilion was crowded with cave women who had come to test a foot in the shoe. Yeh-Shen's stepmother and stepsister were among them, but not Yeh-Shen—they had told her to stay home. By day's end, although many women had eagerly tried to put on the slipper, it still had not been worn. Wearily, the king continued his vigil into the night.

It wasn't until the blackest part of night, while the moon hid behind a cloud, that Yeh-Shen dared to show her face at the pavilion, and even then she tiptoed timidly across the wide floor. Sinking down to her knees, the girl 7

◆Literary Focus

4 Folk Tales Point out to students that folk tales often have a fantasy quality to them. Characters may use magical words, or the characters may be magical. *Students will probably note that the fish bones are the equivalent of the fairy godmother in the Cinderella story they probably heard as a child. The fish bones can grant wishes and cause magical things to happen.*

◆Critical Thinking

5 Speculate Why do the fish bones warn Yeh-Shen not to lose the golden slippers, and what do students think will happen if she does? *Students may be able to predict that Yeh-Shen will indeed lose the slipper and the magic bones will lose their power, which is why she was warned to be careful.*

Customize for *Visual/Spatial Learners*

Suggest that interested students might wish to draw a poster announcing the king's search for the owner of the golden slipper. Have students reread the information about the king's offer and include those details on the poster.

◆Build Vocabulary

6 To better understand the meaning of the word and its related words, ask students to paraphrase the sentence that uses the word *undaunted.*

Comprehension Check ☑

7 Why did Yeh-Shen wait until it was dark to go to the pavilion to try on the shoe? *Her stepmother had told her not to come, but she had to go because she knew it was her lost slipper, so she waited until after dark.*

Cultural Connection

Chinese Fashion With the help of the magic fish bones, Yeh-Shen's ragged clothes are transformed into a beautiful blue gown, a cloak of kingfisher feathers, and tiny golden slippers when she attends the Festival. Students may be interested to learn more about Chinese fashion. Common, everyday work clothes consisted of loose trousers for both men and women, cloth slippers and cotton socks, and dark blue cotton tops that buttoned down the center. Very small, dainty feet were prized by women, and men wore their hair in a queue, or pigtail. On special occasions, silk garments and embroidered slippers were worn by those who could afford them. The clothing worn reflected the wealth of the family. If servants were available to do the work, elaborate silk garments were worn daily. Discuss with students why Yeh-Shen wore ragged clothing every day. Lead them to realize that her stepmother assigned her many hard jobs to do each day; she had to work very hard and wouldn't have been able to wear expensive silken gowns even if she owned them.

Reinforce and Extend

Answers

◆ Literature and Your Life

Reader's Response Students will probably wish to meet Yeh-Shen because she is the main character and very beautiful.

Thematic Focus Young children would probably learn that being wicked isn't the best way to earn a reward; being good and working hard is better.

☑ Check Your Comprehension

1. Yeh-Shen was treated badly after her mother died because her stepmother was jealous of her beauty, as her own daughter was not at all pretty.
2. Her stepmother kills and eats it, but the bones have magic powers.
3. She is the only woman whose foot is small enough to fit inside the golden slipper.
4. They are not allowed into the castle; eventually they are crushed to death in their cave home.

◆ Critical Thinking

1. Kind; patient; beautiful; pretty; pitiable
2. He is fascinated by the golden slipper and wants to find the woman whose foot will fit inside.
3. Most students will agree that Yeh-Shen is beautiful because she is patient, kind, and good. They may also point out that she is physically beautiful.
4. She will treat them kindly and respectfully.
5. They are both stories about unloved youngest daughters who find good men to marry. They are both patient and kind, with their true beauty hidden from view—Oochigeaskw's by scars and Yeh-Shen's by tattered clothing.

in rags examined the tiny shoe. Only when she was sure that this was the missing mate to her own golden slipper did she dare pick it up. At last she could return both little shoes to the fish bones. Surely then her beloved spirit would speak to her again.

Now the king's first thought, on seeing Yeh-Shen take the precious slipper, was to throw the girl into prison as a thief. But when she turned to leave, he caught a glimpse of her face. At once the king was struck by the sweet harmony of her features, which seemed so out of keeping with the rags she wore. It was then that he took a closer look and noticed that she walked upon the tiniest feet he had ever seen.

With a wave of his hand, the king signaled that this tattered creature was to be allowed to depart with the golden slipper. Quietly, the king's men slipped off and followed her home.

All this time, Yeh-Shen was unaware of the excitement she had caused. She had made her way home and was about to hide both sandals in her bedding when there was a pounding at the door. Yeh-Shen went to see who it was—and found a king at her doorstep. She was very frightened at first, but the king spoke to her in a kind voice and asked her to try the golden slippers on her feet. The maiden did as she was told, and as she stood in her golden shoes, her rags were transformed once more into the feathered cloak and beautiful azure gown.

Her loveliness made her seem a heavenly being, and the king suddenly knew in his heart that he had found his true love.

Not long after this, Yeh-Shen was married to the king. But fate was not so gentle with her stepmother and stepsister. Since they had been unkind to his beloved, the king would not permit Yeh-Shen to bring them to his palace. They remained in their cave home, where one day, it is said, they were crushed to death in a shower of flying stones.

Guide for Responding

◆ Literature and Your Life

Reader's Response Which character in the story would you most like to meet? Why?

Thematic Focus If you told this tale to a group of young children, what lesson do you think they would learn?

☑ Check Your Comprehension

1. Why was Yeh-Shen treated so badly in her own home?
2. What happens to the fish that Yeh-Shen loves?
3. How does the king find Yeh-Shen?
4. How does fate treat the stepmother and stepsister?

◆ Critical Thinking

Interpret

1. What three words would you use to describe Yeh-Shen? **[Interpret]**
2. Why does the king want to meet Yeh-Shen? **[Infer]**
3. Why do you think Yeh-Shen is described as beautiful? **[Draw Conclusions]**

Apply

4. How do you think Yeh-Shen will treat her own children? **[Speculate]**

Compare Literary Works

5. What basic story elements do both "The Algonquin Cinderella" and "Yeh-Shen" share? **[Compare and Contrast]**

Beyond the Selection

FURTHER READING

Other Cinderella Folk Tales

Tam's Slipper: A Vietnamese Legend, Darrel Lum
A Hmong Cinderella, Jewell Reinhart Coburn
Korean Cinderella: Book 4, Korean Folk Stories for Children, Edward B. Adams
Lily and the Wooden Bowl–From Japan, Alan Schroeder, Yoriko Ito

Other Works About China

D Is for Doufu, An Alphabet Book of Chinese Culture, Maywan Shen Krach
The Spirit of the Chinese Character, Barbara Aria

INTERNET

We suggest the following sites on the Internet (all Web sites are subject to change).

For more information about Cinderella folk tales:
http://www.shens.com or
http://www.acs.ucalgary.ca/~dkbrown/cinderella.html

For more information about Chinese culture:
http://hanwei.com/culture/oldindex.html

We *strongly recommend* that you preview these sites before you send students to them.

HIS JUST REWARD

SWEDISH FOLK TALE

LONE THYGESEN-BLECHER AND GEORGE BLECHER

A man went out into the forest one day looking for a runaway horse. At one point he had to climb across a cleft in the mountain, and that was when he found that a large snake had got its rear end caught in the crevice. 1

The snake said to the man, "If you help free me, I'll see that you get your just reward!"

The man took his staff and pried the rocks apart so that the snake could get out.

"Thanks," said the snake. "Now come over here and I'll give you your just reward."

The man asked what his just reward might be.

"Death," said the snake.

The man said that he wasn't sure that he wanted that, and he suggested that they ask the first creature who came along what one's just reward ought to be.

A bear came along, and the man asked the bear what one's just reward ought to be.

"Death," said the bear.

"You see?" said the snake. "Death *is* one's just reward! So now I'm going to take you."

"But then the man replied, "Let's just walk a little farther and ask someone else."

After a while they met a wolf. And the man asked him what one's just reward ought to be.

"Death," answered the wolf. "That's everybody's just reward."

"There it is," said the snake. "Now you're mine!"

"Just a minute," said the man. "Let us say that the third creature we meet is the final judge, whoever it turns out to be."

In a little while they met a fox. The man asked the fox what one's just reward ought to be, and the fox answered just like the others.

"Death," he said.

"So now I'll bite you to death," said the snake.

When the fox heard that, he said, "Now wait just a moment. We must consider this case more carefully. First of all, what really happened?"

"Well," said the man, " the snake got its tail caught in a crevice."

Then the fox said, "Why don't we go back there to see exactly how it was."

Well, they went back, and the fox asked the man to pry open the rocks again with his staff, and then the snake should put his rear end right in between, just the way it'd been before. Then the man should let the rocks slip back a little. 2

"Was it tighter than this before?" asked the fox.

"Yes," said the snake.

"Let go a little more," said the fox to the man. "Was it tighter than this?"

"Yes."

"Then let go completely. Now, are you in good and tight?"

"It's worse than it was before!" said the snake.

"Well then, you might as well stay there. That way the two of you are even."

So the snake had to stay, and the man avoided getting his just reward. 3

Develop Understanding

One-Minute Insight In "His Just Reward," a man finds a snake caught in a crevice. He works hard to free the snake, and the snake offers to give him his just reward—death. The man suggests they ask another creature for his opinion. The bear and the wolf agree, but the fox offers to investigate the situation further. He has the snake demonstrate exactly how he was caught in the crevice, so the man pries the rocks open and the snake crawls back inside. The fox and the man leave the snake caught in the crevice, and the man does not get his just reward—but the snake does.

◆Critical Thinking

1 Analyze Ask students to determine what kind of man it is who helps the snake escape from the crevice in the mountain. *Students will probably analyze the events and decide that the man is a good-natured man who is willing to help a fellow creature.*

◆Critical Thinking

2 Draw Conclusions Ask students why the author of the folk tale chose to have a fox be the clever animal in this story. *Students will probably think of the phrase "sly as a fox" and conclude that foxes are often thought of as wily and tricky.*

◆LITERATURE AND YOUR LIFE

3 Connect Your Experience Ask students to think about a time when they helped someone else. If the person did not show appreciation, ask them to think about how it made them feel, and why. Suggest that the class list ways of showing appreciation that will show true thankfulness.

Speaking and Listening Mini-Lesson

Retelling

This mini-lesson supports the Speaking and Listening activity in the Idea Bank on p. 837.

Introduce Folk tales are an entertaining and easy way for students to learn the art of storytelling.

Develop Suggest that students select one of the folk tales in the grouping that they would like to retell, and have them consider the following suggestions:

- Do not try to memorize all the details; instead, try to see the story and retell it.
- Use gestures to help tell the story.
- Be sure to have a good beginning and ending.
- Practice telling the story in front of a mirror or with a partner.

Apply Tell the story to the class or a small group.

Assess Have students use the Peer Assessment: Oral Interpretation form, p. 106, in **Alternative Assessment,** to evaluate the performances of their classmates.

Develop Understanding

One-Minute Insight In "Djuha Borrows a Pot," Djuha needs a cooking pot large enough to cook a stewed lamb for dinner, so he borrows a large caldron from his neighbor. When he promptly returns the pot, the neighbor finds a small cooking pot inside. He is happy to keep it after Djuha explains that the large pot gave birth. A few weeks later, Djuha asks to borrow the pot again, but does not return it. When his neighbor complains, he explains that the pot died.

◆ Reading Strategy

❶ **Recognize Cultural Context** Ask students to find details that establish clues as to the cultural context of the selection. *Students may note that the title indicates that the folk tale is Syrian; the name Djuha; the detail that he was cooking lamb; he asks a blessing from Allah.*

◆ Literature and Your Life

❷ Ask students to think of a time they may have had occasion to borrow something from a friend or neighbor. Have them recall the experience and decide if they think it is appropriate to be a trickster as Djuha was when he borrowed the cooking pot. Have students suggest another way Djuha might have behaved. *Students may point out that Djuha should have returned the pot and not tricked his greedy neighbor.*

Djuha Borrows a Pot

Syrian Folk Tale Inea Bushnaq

Bronze cauldron from Daghestan decorated with equestrian figure and two eagles, © The Board of Trustees of the Victoria and Albert Museum, London

One day Djuha[1] wanted to entertain his friends with a dinner of lamb stewed whole with rice stuffing, but he did not have a cooking pot large enough. So he went to his neighbor and borrowed a huge, heavy caldron of fine copper.

❶ Promptly next morning, Djuha returned the borrowed pot. "What is this?" cried the neighbor, pulling a small brass pot from inside the caldron. "Oh yes," said Djuha, "congratulations and blessings upon your house! While your caldron was with me it gave birth to that tiny pot." The neighbor laughed delightedly. "May Allah[2] send blessings your way too," he told Djuha, and carried the two cooking pots into his house.

❷ A few weeks later Djuha knocked on his

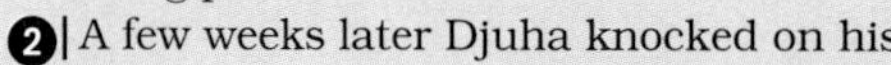

1. **Djuha** (jo͞o′ ə)
2. **Allah** (al′ ə): Name for God in the Muslim religion.

Humanities: Art

Bronze Daghestan Cauldron; Preparing Medicine From Honey, 1224

Large cauldrons or pots made from metals or clay have historically been important cooking utensils. Stews and meals were often cooked in large pots over open fires. Guide students to notice that the cauldron illustrated has feet. Discuss with students what use the feet may have had; point out that the feet kept the pot from sitting directly on the fire and possibly burning the food cooking inside.

Draw students' attention to the decorations on the pot. Ask why the pot might have been decorated, and discuss that people have always tried to make their homes beautiful. By obtaining a pot with handsome decorations, the person who originally owned the pot was no doubt attempting to beautify her or his surroundings.

The Arabic illustration on p. 835 shows a large cooking pot being stirred. The title suggests that a medicine potion is being made from honey. Call students' attention to the writing on the illustration. Ask if they can suggest what it may say. *Students may say that it is a recipe for the medicine, information about the picture, or perhaps information in a medicine textbook.*

neighbor's door again to ask for the loan of the caldron. And the neighbor hurried to fetch it for him. The next day came and went, but Djuha did not return the pot. Several days passed and the neighbor did not hear from Djuha. At last he went to Djuha's house to ask for his property.
2 "Have you not heard, brother?" said Djuha looking very grave. "The very evening I borrowed it from you, your unfortunate caldron—God grant you a long life—died!" "What do you mean, 'died'?" shouted the neighbor. "Can a copper cooking pot die?" "If it can give birth," said Djuha, "it can surely die."

3 ▶ Critical Viewing This Arabic illustration originally accompanied an ancient pharmacology text. In what ways does the artist's style differ from "Western" illustrations you have seen? [Compare and Contrast]

Preparing Medicine from Honey, 1224, The Metropolitan Museum of Art 4

Guide for Responding

◆ Literature and Your Life

Reader's Response How do you feel about letting people borrow your possessions?

Thematic Focus What lesson does the man learn in "His Just Reward"?

☑ Check Your Comprehension

1. In "His Just Reward," how does the man help the snake?
2. How does the snake plan to reward the man for his help?
3. In "Djuha Borrows a Pot," what happens when Djuha returns the pot for the first time?
4. What happens the second time he borrows the same pot?

◆ Critical Thinking

INTERPRET

1. Which character gets "his just reward" in the story with that title? **[Interpret]**
2. In "Djuha Borrows a Pot," why is the neighbor willing to lend Djuha the pot a second time? **[Infer]**
3. On what human frailty does Djuha count to play his trick? **[Analyze]**

COMPARE LITERARY WORKS

4. Does the neighbor who lends Djuha a pot get his "just reward"? Explain. **[Make a Judgment]**

APPLY

5. Why do you think that many cultures tell tales about tricksters like Djuha who use their cunning and wits to get ahead? **[Hypothesize]**

Beyond the Selection

FURTHER READING

Other Works by Lone Thygesen-Blecher and George Blecher

Swedish Folktales and Legends, Lone Thygesen-Blecher and George Blecher

Other Works by Swedish Writers

Pippi Longstocking, Astrid Lindgren

Wonderful Adventures of Nils, Selma Lagerlöf

Other Works by Inea Bushnaq

Arab Folktales, Inea Bushnaq

INTERNET

We suggest the following sites on the Internet (all Web sites are subject to change).

For more information about Swedish folk tales: **http://www.seanet.com/~eldrbarry/rabb/folk/magpie.html**

For more information about Syrian culture: **http://www.syria-online.com/culture/index.html**

To see Farsi writing samples: **http://www.geocities.com/CollegePark/Library/3658**

We *strongly recommend* that you preview these sites before you send students to them.

▶Critical Viewing◀

3 **Compare and Contrast** Point out the writing on the illustration. *Students will probably note that the writing on the illustration and utensils used in the illustration do not look very much like what a Western artist might use. They may also note the title and explain that they don't believe Western pharmacists cook medicines in a pot.*

Clarification

4 The language used on the Arabic illustration is Farsi, sometimes referred to as Persian. Farsi has character shapes that look very different from English letters and numbers. Farsi characters are written from right to left.

Reinforce and Extend

Answers

◆ Literature and Your Life

Reader's Response Some students will say that they are usually willing to share; others will be more reluctant because their belongings may be damaged or lost.

Thematic Focus He learned that being mean and wicked was not wise behavior.

☑ Check Your Comprehension

1. He releases him from a crack in the mountain where he has become trapped.
2. The snake plans to kill the man.
3. He returns the pot with a second smaller pot in addition, saying that the larger pot gave birth to the second.
4. He does not return the pot at all, claiming it has died.

◆ Critical Thinking

1. The snake gets his just reward.
2. He hopes that Djuha will return with a third pot.
3. He counts on the neighbor's being greedy.
4. Students may feel that he was justly punished because he was greedy in the first place.
5. Folk tales about wily tricksters are popular because the qualities of intelligence and cleverness demonstrate that one does not always need strength or power to overcome obstacles.

Answers

◆Literary Focus

1. Trying to see the Invisible One is repeated.
2. Finding the woman whose foot will fit into the tiny golden slipper is the repeated event.
3. When Djuha repeats his action and borrows the pot for a second time, the unexpected result creates humor.

◆Build Vocabulary

Using Forms of *undaunted-*

1. The girl who was usually not afraid of anything felt a little scared when she saw the king.
2. Protecting yourself is something that anybody would be a little afraid to try.

Spelling Strategy

1. The stepmother opened the secret vault.
2. The snake was mauled by a hungry bear.
3. The neighbor eagerly hauled out the pot.

Using the Word Bank

1. undaunted
2. croon
3. shuffle
4. sage

◆Reading Strategy

1. The story shows that despite unjust living conditions, some slaves were able to maintain their faith in freedom and justice.
2. They value people who can see deeply and truly into mysteries that are not apparent to others.
3. The deaths of these two characters reflect the Chinese belief in justice and punishment.

◆Build Grammar Skills

1. Yeh-Shen lived with her father, stepmother, and two stepsisters.
2. The stepmother was jealous of Yeh-Shen's beauty, kindness, and grace.
3. The fish bones granted Yeh-Shen's wishes, desires, and dreams.
4. Yeh-Shen wore a blue gown, a feather cloak, and golden slippers.
5. The stepmother and stepsister were punished for their jealousy, unkindness, and cruelty.

Guide for Responding *(continued)*

◆ Literary Focus

FOLK TALES

Many cultures communicate their values and traditions through **folk tales,** stories passed through the generations by word of mouth. One characteristic of many folk tales is the use of repetition: words, phrases, or events that occur more than once. Repetition makes key events easy to remember. As folk tales were passed from generation to generation, these key repeated events were likely to stay the same, while other details might change with each telling.

1. What event is repeated in "The Algonquin Cinderella"?
2. What similar event is repeated in "Yeh-Shen"?
3. How does repetition contribute to the humor of "Djuha Borrows a Pot"?

◆ Build Vocabulary

USING FORMS OF *undaunted*

The word *undaunted,* which means "not frightened or afraid of," is related to several other words. Paraphrase each of the following sentences in your own words. Use a dictionary to check the meanings of words related to *undaunted.*

1. Even the *dauntless* girl felt nervous as she looked at the king.
2. Defending your life is a *daunting* task.

SPELLING STRATEGY

The sound *aw* can be spelled *au*, as in the words *undaunted* and *cause*. Rewrite each sentence below, correcting the spelling of words with the *aw* sound.

1. The stepmother opened the secret vawlt.
2. The snake was mawled by a hungry bear.
3. The neighbor eagerly hawled out the pot.

USING THE WORD BANK

On your paper, write the word from the Word Bank that best completes each sentence.

1. The flying woman was ___?___ by the shouting man on the ground.
2. She began to ___?___ a happy tune.
3. I saw the old men ___?___ slowly away.
4. The ___?___ gives wise advice to young visitors.

◆ Reading Strategy

RECOGNIZE CULTURAL CONTEXT

When you understand the **cultural context** of folk tales—the time and culture from which they come—you will not only understand the tales better, but you will also learn a lot about the people who created them.

1. What does "The People Could Fly" tell you about the spiritual lives of enslaved people in the United States?
2. The brother in "The Algonquin Cinderella" is invisible. What does this tell you about the values of the Algonquin people?
3. What do you learn about Chinese values from the fate of the stepmother and stepsister in "Yeh-Shen"?

◆ Build Grammar Skills

COMMAS IN A SERIES

Use **commas** to separate items that are listed together. Place a comma before the word *and* when three or more things are listed:

> The youngest girl was very small, weak, and often ill.

Practice On your paper, rewrite the sentences, adding commas to separate items listed in a series.

1. Yeh-Shen lived with her father stepmother and two stepsisters.
2. The stepmother was jealous of Yeh-Shen's beauty kindness and grace.
3. The fish bones granted Yeh-Shen's wishes desires and dreams.
4. Yeh-Shen wore a blue gown a feather cloak and golden slippers.
5. The stepmother and stepsister were punished for their jealousy unkindness and cruelty.

Writing Application Write a sentence that contains each of the following groups of words as a series. Separate the words with commas.

1. shirt, pants, belt, shoes
2. brave, powerful, noble
3. swimming, running, climbing

Writing Application

Answers will vary.

Sample responses:

1. He wished for a new shirt, clean pants, a strong belt, and sturdy shoes.
2. The hero was brave, powerful, and noble.
3. He enjoys swimming in lakes, running in races, and climbing the cliffs.

Writer's Solution

For additional instruction and practice, use the lesson in the *Writer's Solution Language Lab CD-ROM* on punctuation. You may also use the practice page, Commas That Separate Basic Elements, p.98, in the *Writer's Solution Grammar Practice Book.*

Build Your Portfolio

Idea Bank

Writing

1. **Book Jacket** Create a book jacket for a collection of folk tales that includes the stories you have just read. Choose a title, create an illustration, and write a couple of paragraphs about the collection that will make others want to read it.
2. **Story Sequel** Write a continuation of one of the stories. You might choose to introduce new characters, settings, and events as you create your sequel.
3. **Reader Review** Choose one of these stories, and write a short review for others who might want to read it. Include a brief summary that will interest someone in reading the tale.

Speaking and Listening

4. **Retelling** In your own words, retell one of these stories. Review the story to remember the most important events, but add details of your own. Remember that part of the oral tradition involves adding your own personality to your retelling. **[Performing Arts Link]**
5. **Role Play** With a partner, role-play a discussion between Yeh-Shen, the Chinese Cinderella, and Oochigeaskw, the Algon-quin Cinderella. Discuss similarities and differences between the two girls' lives and their experiences.

Projects

6. **Folk-Tale Festival** **[Group Activity]** Hold a class storytelling festival. Each student or team can prepare a story to share with the group. Choose stories from several cultures, and consider using props and music to enhance your presentations. **[Performing Arts Link; Social Studies Link]**
7. **Puzzle Challenge** Djuha and the fox trick others with their cleverness. Stump your classmates with number puzzles. Research brain teasers in puzzle books, and choose the best ones. Then, challenge your classmates to solve them. **[Math Link]**

Writing Mini-Lesson

Essay on Cultural Context

Writing an essay can help you organize your thoughts and share them with others. Think about the cultural context of one of these folk tales. Write an essay explaining how the cultural context influences the story and what the story tells you about the culture it is from. Your essay can include your own reactions to the tale as well.

Writing Skills Focus: Elaborate to Support an Idea

In an essay, it is important to **support your ideas.** After you make a statement, follow it with an example or illustration that shows *why* your statement is true. This will make your writing stronger and more effective. If you have trouble finding details that support a statement, your statement may be too general or it may not be accurate. Try restating your idea. Then, elaborate to support it.

Prewriting Choose a folk tale to study. Then, use a chart or table to jot down ideas about its cultural context. Use reference sources to find out more about the culture.

Drafting Begin each paragraph by clearly stating a main idea. For example, you might say that "The Algonquin Cinderella" reveals values that are important to the Algonquin people. In the body of the paragraph, support this statement with specific details from the story and your research.

◆ Grammar Application

If your draft contains three or more words in a series, separate them with commas.

Revising As you revise, look for ideas that can be further supported with examples. Go back to the folk tale to look for details you might use as support for the ideas in your essay.

Idea Bank

Following are suggestions for matching the Idea Bank topics with your students' performance levels and learning modalities:

Customize for *Performance Levels*

Less Advanced Students: 1, 4, 5, 6
Average Students: 3, 4, 5, 6
More Advanced Students: 2, 3, 5, 7

Customize for *Learning Modalities*

Verbal/Linguistic: 1, 2, 3, 4, 6
Visual/Spatial: 1, 7
Musical/Rhythmic: 4, 6
Interpersonal: 5, 6, 7
Intrapersonal: 1, 2, 3, 4, 7

Writing Mini-Lesson

Refer students to the Writing Handbook in the back of the book for instructions on the writing process and for further information on expository writing.

Writer's Solution

Writing Lab CD-ROM

Have students complete the tutorial on Exposition: Giving Information. Follow these steps:

1. Have students use the Cluster Diagram activity to help them choose and organize details.
2. Suggest that students use the Notecard Activity to gather details.
3. Have students draft on computer.
4. Encourage students to use the Transition Word Bin to find words that will lead their readers from one idea to the next.

Writer's Solution Sourcebook

Have students use Chapter 4, "Exposition: Giving Information," pp. 102–133. This chapter includes in-depth information on using exact nouns, p. 128.

✓ ASSESSMENT OPTIONS

Formal Assessment, Selection Test, pp. 235–237, and Assessment Resources Software. The selection test is designed so that it can be easily customized to the performance levels of your students.

Alternative Assessment, p. 49, includes options for less advanced students, more advanced students, interpersonal learners, visual/spatial learners, verbal/linguistic learners, musical/rhythmic learners, and bodily/kinesthetic learners.

PORTFOLIO ASSESSMENT

Use the following rubrics in the **Alternative Assessment** booklet to assess student writing:
Book Jacket: Summary, p. 85
Story Sequel: Fictional Narrative, p. 82
Reader Review: Evaluation/Review, p. 91
Writing Mini-Lesson: Research Report/Paper, p. 93

Connections to Today's World

Although folk tales are a form of entertainment, they often portray a moral theme, or teach a lesson. Folk tales are filled with characters who are opposites: greedy/unselfish; ugly/beautiful; undaunted/fearful; or lazy/hardworking. Usually, goodness prevails over wickedness, evil, and greed, but not always. In "The Princess and the Tin Box," James Thurber tells the story of a spoiled princess who chooses her husband based on who brings her the largest and most expensive gift. Not only does the folk tale teach a lesson about greed, Thurber writes the moral in a very contemporary and American style.

More About the Author

James Thurber (1894–1961) is a well-known American writer and cartoonist. Although much of his work is known from his time at *The New Yorker* magazine, later in his lifetime he turned to writing fables and fantasy. He wrote *Fables for Our Time* in 1940 and *Further Fables for Our Time* in 1956. The morals of his fables are filled with wisdom and a humorous bite. During the 1950's era of McCarthyism and the fear of Communism in America, many of his writings contained political messages as well.

▶Critical Viewing◀

1 Support *Students may note that the young woman is wearing a very elaborate hairstyle and an expensive dress. They may notice that she is not wearing jewelry, but may realize that wearing jewelry might not have been an acceptable style for young women of that time period. They may think she has a haughty, or superior, expression on her face that makes her seem like the spoiled princess of the story.*

CONNECTIONS TO TODAY'S WORLD

The folk-tale form is nearly universal—most cultures tell stories to pass on traditions, beliefs, and values. In "The Princess and the Tin Box," American humorist James Thurber (1894–1961) updates the traditional folk-tale format by using a marriage contest similar to the one in "Popocatepetl and Ixtlaccihuatl." The results are surprising; however, the story still serves to reveal something about the values of the society in which Thurber wrote.

The Princess and the Tin Box

✦ James Thurber

Portrait of a Young Woman, c. 1470, Piero del Pollaiuolo, The Metropolitan Museum of Art

▲ **Critical Viewing** What details of this portrait reveal that the woman pictured has lived a life like the princess in the story? **[Support]** 1

Once upon a time, in a far country, there lived a king whose daughter was the prettiest princess in the world. Her eyes were like the cornflower, her hair was sweeter than the hyacinth, and her throat made the swan look dusty.

From the time she was a year old, the princess had been showered with presents. Her nursery looked like Cartier's[1] window. Her toys were all made of gold or platinum or diamonds or emeralds. She was not permitted to have wooden blocks or china dolls or rubber dogs or linen books, because such materials were considered cheap for the daughter of a king.

When she was seven, she was allowed to attend the wedding of her brother and throw real pearls at the bride instead of rice. Only the nightingale, with his lyre[2] of gold, was permitted to sing for the princess. The common blackbird, with his boxwood flute, was kept out of the palace grounds. She walked in silver-and-samite slippers to a sapphire-and-topaz bathroom and slept in an ivory bed inlaid with rubies.

On the day the princess was eighteen,

1. **Cartier's:** Well-known upscale jewelry store.

2. **lyre** (līr) *n.*: Harp.

Humanities: Art

Portrait of a Young Woman, c. 1470, by Piero del Pollaiuolo

Italian artist Piero del Pollaiuolo (1443–1496) came from a family of noted Florentine artists during the Renaissance period. His father, Jacopo, was a goldsmith. His brother Antonio was the head of one of Florence's most prestigious and busy art workshops, working in gold, as a painter, sculptor, and engraver, and creating other decorative works. Piero made three of the paintings known as the Seven Virtues displayed in the Uffizi Gallery in Florence, and probably collaborated with Antonio on three more. Their workshop was patronized by the well-known Medici family.

Direct students attention to *Portrait of a Young Woman*. Ask them to speculate about the identity of the young woman. *Students may think she is royalty because the portrait is used to illustrate a story about a princess. Others may believe that she lived in a wealthy family that could afford to pay to have an expensive portrait of her painted to display in their home.*

the king sent a royal ambassador to the courts of five neighboring kingdoms to announce that he would give his daughter's hand in marriage to the prince who brought her the gift she liked most.

The first prince to arrive at the palace rode a swift white stallion and laid at the feet of the princess an enormous apple made of solid gold which he had taken from a dragon who had guarded it for a thousand years. It was placed on a long ebony table set up to hold the gifts of the princess's suitors. The second prince, who came on a gray charger, brought her a nightingale made of a thousand diamonds, and it was placed beside the golden apple. The third prince, riding on a black horse, carried a great jewel box made of platinum and sapphires, and it was placed next to the diamond nightingale. The fourth prince, astride a fiery yellow horse, gave the princess a gigantic heart made of rubies and pierced by an emerald arrow. It was placed next to the platinum-and-sapphire jewel box.

Now the fifth prince was the strongest and handsomest of all the five suitors, but he was the son of a poor king whose realm had been overrun by mice and locusts and wizards and mining engineers so that there was nothing much of value left in it. He came plodding up to the palace of the princess on a plow horse and he brought her a small tin box filled with mica and feldspar and hornblende[3] which he had picked up on the way.

The other princes roared with disdainful laughter when they saw the tawdry gift the fifth prince had brought to the princess. But she examined it with great interest and squealed with delight, for all her life she had been glutted with precious stones and priceless metals, but she had never seen tin before or mica or feldspar or hornblende. The tin box was placed next to the ruby heart pierced with an emerald arrow.

"Now," the king said to his daughter, "you must select the gift you like best and marry the prince that brought it."

❷ The princess smiled and walked up to the table and picked up the present she liked the most. It was the platinum-and-sapphire jewel box, the gift of the third prince.

"The way I figure it," she said, "is this. It is a very large and expensive box, and when I am married, I will meet many admirers who will give me the precious gems with which to fill it to the top. Therefore, it is the most valuable of all the gifts my suitors have brought me and I like it the best."

❸ The princess married the third prince that very day in the midst of great merriment and high revelry. More than a hundred thousand pearls were thrown at her and she loved it.

❹ *Moral: All those who thought the princess was going to select the tin box filled with worthless stones instead of one of the other gifts will kindly stay after class and write one hundred times on the blackboard, "I would rather have a hunk of aluminum silicate than a diamond necklace."*

3. **mica** (mī´ kəh), **feldspar** (feld´ spär´), **hornblende** (hôrn´ blend´) *n.*: Common minerals found in rocks.

◆ Build Vocabulary

disdainful (dis dān´ fəl) *adj.*: Showing arrogance or scorn for someone considered beneath oneself

tawdry (tô´ drē) *adj.*: Cheap and showy; gaudy

glutted (glut´ əd) *v.*: Given more than is needed or wanted

revelry (rev´ əl rē) *n.*: Celebration; noisy merrymaking

1. (a) What choice does the princess make? (b) How does she defend her decision?
2. What details in the moral reveal that the story is meant to amuse?
3. What conclusions can you draw from this story about the values of the society in which Thurber wrote?

CONNECTIONS TO TODAY'S WORLD

Beyond the Selection

FURTHER READING

Other Works by James Thurber

Fables for Our Time

Further Fables for Our Time

Other Works About Princesses

The Barefoot Book of Princesses, Caitlin Matthews

Other Folk Tales From Around the World

Wisdom Tales From Around the World, Heather Forest

INTERNET

We suggest the following sites on the Internet (all Web sites are subject to change).

For more information about James Thurber:
http://www.erols.com/aboyer/thurbertxt.html

For more information about folk tales from around the world:
http://www.acs.ucalgary.ca/~dkbrown/storfolk.html or
http://home.earthlink.net/~bourgoin/folklore.html

We *strongly recommend* that you preview these sites before you send students to them.

◆Critical Thinking

❷ **Draw Conclusions** Based on the gifts the princes bring the princess, have students select the prince they believe would become the wisest king. Ask students if they were surprised at the decision the princess made. *Most students will probably say that the fifth prince who came from a poor kingdom and could not afford jewels but used imagination in his gift would be the best king. Some students will be surprised that the princess was greedy; others will not be.*

Clarification

❸ At weddings, to wish the newly married couple good luck and happiness, guests often throw handfuls of rice at the couple as they depart. In some primitive cultures, eating rice together was actually the way people got married. Point out to students that throwing pearls at the newlyweds was an extravagant and expensive good luck wish, and one of Thurber's humorous details.

Thematic Connection

❹ **Lessons Learned** Suggest that students study the contemporary manner in which James Thurber wrote the moral at the end of the story. Challenge students to work in small groups to write a similar modern-day moral for each of the folk tales they have read. Students might find it helpful to use a chart like the one suggested in the Literary Focus note on p. 826 of the Teacher Edition.

Answers

1. (a) The princess chooses the prince she will marry by choosing the large and expensive gift that he brought. (b) She defended her decision as the best choice because she said many admirers would fill the box with expensive gifts of jewels and it would be even more valuable.
2. The author pokes fun at a classroom punishment of writing on the blackboard.
3. Thurber was writing a moral for a society that he must have considered greedy and selfish.

Prepare and Engage

OBJECTIVES

1. To read, comprehend, and interpret a folk tale that has a social studies focus
2. To relate a folk tale with a social studies focus to personal experience
3. To connect literature to social studies
4. To respond to the Social Studies Guiding Question
5. To respond to the folk tale through writing, speaking and listening, and projects

SOCIAL STUDIES GUIDING QUESTION

Reading the African folk tale will help students discover answers to this Social Studies Guiding Question:

- What factors have shaped Africa's culture?

Have students recall stories in which a character uses her or his brains to outwit a strong and powerful opponent. Invite students to summarize the stories. Then have students imagine that they have been offered a large reward to capture a nest of hornets, a python, and a leopard. They must use their wits and can use only items found in the woods to capture the animals, preferably alive. Have volunteers describe how they would accomplish the task.

Map Study

Political Maps The connection between geography and history is often a key to understanding the folklore of a cultural group. To help students make connections between the Ashanti folk tale and its historical and cultural context, have students read A Powerful Empire and The Empire Falls on this page. Then have them use the map to locate the areas described in the information.

CONNECTING LITERATURE TO SOCIAL STUDIES

AFRICA

All Stories Are Anansi's *Retold by Harold Courlander*

BRAINS BEAT MUSCLES The person with the greatest physical strength doesn't always win. Sometimes a quick-thinking, clever mind can overpower a mighty opponent. Throughout history, people have enjoyed seeing the underdog come out on top. Maybe this is why the clever trickster is so popular in folk tales from Africa and other cultures. A trickster is a character who relies on brains to outwit those who are bigger and stronger. The Ashanti (ə shän′ tē) of western Africa have passed down trickster tales through the generations.

Western Africa
N
SENEGAL
GAMBIA
GUINEA-BISSAU
GUINEA
SIERRA LEONE
LIBERIA
CÔTE D'IVOIRE (IVORY COAST)
BURKINA FASO
GHANA
TOGO
BENIN
NIGERIA
CAMEROON
EQUATORIAL GUINEA
SAO TOME AND PRINCIPE
GABON
0 500 mi
0 500 km
area of map

A Powerful Empire The Ashanti ruled a large empire in western Africa during the 1700's and 1800's. At its height, the Ashanti empire included parts of three modern-day countries—much of Ghana, eastern Ivory Coast, and western Togo.

The Empire Falls During the late nineteenth century, the Ashanti and the British fought each other for control of trade in western Africa. In 1901, the British defeated the Ashanti and made their lands a British colony.

Today, the Ashanti region makes up a large part of Ghana, an independent country. The Ashanti play a major role in Ghana's economic and political development. Most Ashanti work in farming, mining, or forestry. The Ashanti have also earned a reputation as skillful weavers of colorful *kente* cloth. Over the years, the Ashanti have also woven many wonderful stories.

A Sneaky Spider In Ashanti folklore, the slyest trickster is Kwaku Anansi (kwä′ ko͞o ə nän′ sē), the spider. He's so clever, he even tries to trick the most important god—Nyame, the supreme Sky God. As you read about Kwaku Anansi, notice the ways in which he appeals to the fears and vanities of his victims in order to fool them.

Prentice Hall Literature Program Resources

REINFORCE / RETEACH / EXTEND

Selection Support Pages
Build Vocabulary, p. 272
Connect Folk Tale to Social Studies, p. 273

Formal Assessment Selection Test,
pp. 238–239, Assessment Resources Software

Readings From Social Studies

Writing and Language Transparencies
Series of Events Chain, p. 66

Resource Pro CD-ROM
"All Stories Are Anansi's"—includes all resource material and customizable lesson plan

Listening to Literature Audiocassettes
"All Stories Are Anansi's"

Connection to Prentice Hall World Explorer
Africa
Ch. 3, Sec. 2, "The Cultures of West Africa"
Ch. 5, "Exploring West Africa"

All Stories Are Anansi's

African Folk Tale

Harold Courlander

In the beginning, all tales and stories belonged to Nyame,[1] the Sky God. But Kwaku
❶ Anansi,[2] the spider, yearned to be the owner of all the stories known in the world, and he went to Nyame and offered to buy them.

The Sky God said: "I am willing to sell the stories, but the price is high. Many people have come to me offering to buy, but the price was too high for them. Rich and powerful families have not been able to pay. Do you think you can do it?"

❷ Anansi replied to the Sky God: "I can do it. What is the price?"

"My price is three things," the Sky God said. "I must first have Mmoboro,[3] the hornets. I must then have Onini,[4] the great python. I must then have Osebo,[5] the leopard. For these things I will sell you the right to

1. **Nyame** (nē ä´ mē)
2. **Kwaku Anansi** (kwä´ ko͞o ə nän´ sē)
3. **Mmoboro** (mō bō´ rō)
4. **Onini** (ō nē´ nē)
5. **Osebo** (ō sā´ bō)

◆ Build Vocabulary

yearned (yʉrnd) *v.*: Wanted very much

▼ Critical Viewing This nineteenth-century pendant from the Ivory Coast shows a snake catching a frog. What role does the snake play in this folk tale? **[Analyze]** ❸

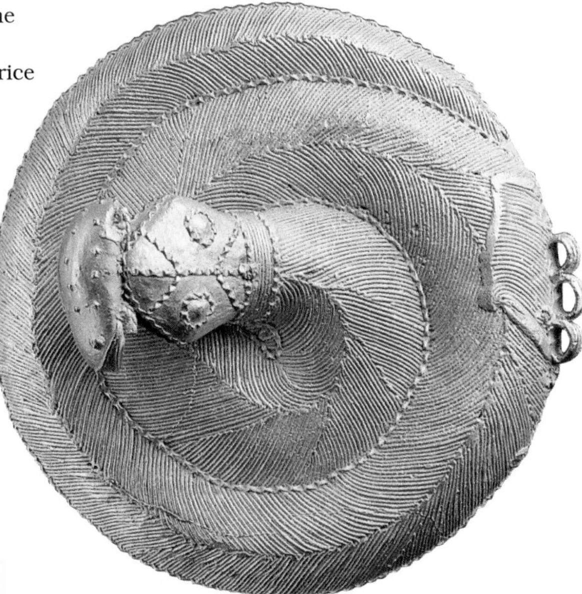

Pendant in the form of a snake catching a frog, Brooklyn Museum

Develop Understanding

One-Minute Insight

In this folk tale, Anansi, trickster figure and hero of many West African tales, seeks to own "all the stories known in the world." Anansi, the spider, goes to the Sky God, to whom the stories belong. The Sky God agrees to sell Anansi the stories if Anansi will bring him the hornets, the great python, and the leopard. The tale describes how Anansi uses his brain to outwit these animals in order to capture them. The tale also provides insight into beliefs and traditions of the Ashanti people, and reveals the great value they place on their folklore.

Team Teaching Strategy

"All Stories Are Anansi's" offers an opportunity to team teach with a social studies teacher, creating a cross-curricular unit on Africa.

Links Across Cultures

❶ In the language of the Ashanti people, *Anansi* means "spider." The word *nan* means "to spin." Ashanti folk tales are known as *Ananisem,* which means "story" and which may or may not be about spiders.

◆Critical Thinking

❷ **Speculate** Why do you think Nyame set such a high price for the stories? *Students may say that the stories are valuable to Nyame, and he is unwilling to give them up easily.*

▶Critical Viewing◀

❸ **Analyze** *Part of the price Anansi must pay for the rights to all the tales and stories is "the great python." Anansi's capture of the snake shows the price of vanity.*

Customize for
Less Proficient Readers
Have students use the Series of Events Chain, p. 66 in **Writing and Language Transparencies,** to keep track of events in the folk tale. Ask students to name the incident that sets the action of the story into motion. Have them write this incident at the top of the organizer. Then have students write the events that follow in the boxes below the beginning event.

Preparing for Standardized Tests

Recognizing Causes and Effects
Comprehension items on standardized tests often focus on cause and effect in a passage. Remind students that cause is the reason that something happens and effect is the result, or what happens. Have students practice recognizing causes and effects by reading the information in the first column of p. 842. Then write this question and these answer choices on the board: Which of these best states the reason that the hornets flew into the gourd?

(A) Nyame asked for the hornets first.
(B) Anansi threw water over the hornets.
(C) The hornets wanted to escape from the rain.
(D) The hornets were foolish.

Review the information from the selection with students. Help them analyze the answer choices to recognize that (C) is the best answer because it states the reason that the hornets flew into the gourd. Lead students to see that the other answers are causes or effects of other events, but only (C) states the direct cause of the hornets' flying into the gourd.

Comprehension Check ☑

❶ How does Anansi persuade the hornets to fly into the gourd? *Anansi pours water on himself and on the hornets to convince the hornets that it is raining; then he suggests that they fly into the gourd to escape the rain.*

CONNECTING LITERATURE TO SOCIAL STUDIES

❷ **Draw Conclusions** Suggest that students review the selection before answering the question. Encourage them to offer details to support their conclusions. *Students may respond that Ghana seems to have a large variety of plants and animals. As examples of animals, students may mention the spider, hornets, python, and leopard. As examples of plants, they may mention gourds, calabashes, grass, vines, bamboo, and tall trees.*

▶Critical Viewing◀

❸ **Connect** *The leopard is accustomed to prowling the forest at night, which leads him to fall into the trap. Some students may say that Anansi also uses the leopard's trust to persuade the leopard to tie the rope to his tail.*

Customize for *More Advanced Students*

As students read the folk tale, have them list traits of Anansi as revealed in the story. Then have students use their lists as a springboard for learning more about Anansi by reading West African stories that feature the trickster, such as those from *The Cow-Tail Switch and Other West African Stories,* by Harold Courlander and George Herzog. Ask them to document whether Anansi retains the same spider form and traits in the stories. Have students present their findings to the class.

tell all stories."

Anansi said: "I will bring them."

He went home and made his plans. He first cut a gourd from a vine and made a small hole in it. He took a large calabash[6] and filled it with water. He went to the tree where the hornets lived. He poured some of the water over himself, so that he was dripping. He threw some water over the hornets, so that they too were dripping. Then he put the calabash on his head, as though to protect himself from a storm, and called out to
❶ the hornets: "Are you foolish people? Why do you stay in the rain that is falling?"

The hornets answered: "Where shall we go?"

"Go here, in this dry gourd," Anansi told them.

The hornets thanked him and flew into the gourd through the small hole. When the last of them had entered, Anansi plugged the hole with a ball of grass, saying: "Oh, yes, but you are really foolish people!"

He took the gourd full of hornets to Nyame, the Sky God. The Sky God accepted them. He said: "There are two more things."

Anansi returned to the forest and cut a long bamboo pole and some strong vines. Then he walked toward the house of Onini, the python, talking to himself. He said: "My wife is stupid. I say he is longer and stronger. My wife says he is shorter and weaker. I give him more respect. She gives him less respect. Is she right or am I right? I am right, he is longer. I am right, he is stronger."

Connecting Literature to Social Studies What can you conclude about the animal and plant life in Ghana from the characters in this folk tale? ❷

When Onini, the python, heard Anansi talking to himself, he said: "Why are you arguing this way with yourself?"

The spider replied: "Ah, I have had a dispute with my wife. She says you are shorter and weaker than this bamboo pole. I say you are longer and stronger."

Onini said: "It's useless and silly to argue when you can find out the truth. Bring the pole and we will measure."

So Anansi laid the pole on the ground, and

▼ **Critical Viewing** What characteristic of the leopard does Anansi use in his trick? **[Connect]** ❸

6. **calabash** (kal′ ə bash′) *n.*: Large fruit that is dried and made into a bowl or cup.

Block Scheduling Strategies

Consider these suggestions to take advantage of extended class time:

- Use the Series of Events Chain, p. 66, in **Writing and Language Transparencies,** to help students as they complete the Speaking and Listening activity in the Idea Bank, p. 845.
- Use *World Explorer: Africa,* Ch. 3, Section 2, "The Cultures of West Africa," and Ch. 5, "Exploring West Africa" to team teach or to further extend connecting literature to social studies.
- Have students listen to the recording of "All Stories Are Anansi's" in segments: (1) from the beginning of the tale to Anansi's pledge to bring the animals to Nyame; (2) through Anansi's offering of the hornets to Nyame; (3) through Anansi's offering of the snake to Nyame; (4) through Anansi's offering of the leopard to Nyame. After each segment, have students write predictions. Collect the predictions and use them to spark a discussion before moving to the next segment. Repeat with each segment.

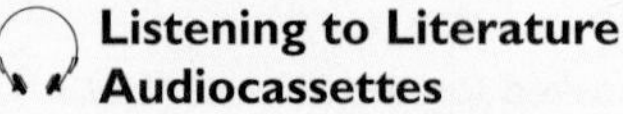

Listening to Literature Audiocassettes

the python came and stretched himself out beside it.

"You seem a little short," Anansi said.

The python stretched further.

"A little more," Anansi said.

"I can stretch no more," Onini said.

"When you stretch at one end, you get shorter at the other end," Anansi said. "Let me tie you at the front so you don't slip."

He tied Onini's head to the pole. Then he went to the other end and tied the tail to the
4 pole. He wrapped the vine all around Onini,
until the python couldn't move.

"Onini," Anansi said, "it turns out that my wife was right and I was wrong. You are shorter than the pole and weaker. My opinion wasn't as good as my wife's. But you were even more foolish than I, and you are now my prisoner."

Anansi carried the python to Nyame, the Sky God, who said: "There is one thing more."

Osebo, the leopard, was next. Anansi went into the forest and dug a deep pit where the leopard was accustomed to walk. He covered it with small branches and leaves and put dust on it, so that it was impossible to tell where the pit was. Anansi went away and hid. When Osebo came prowling in the black of night, he stepped into the trap Anansi had prepared and fell to the bottom. Anansi heard the sound of the leopard falling, and he said: "Ah, Osebo, you are half-foolish!"

When morning came, Anansi went to the pit and saw the leopard there.

"Osebo," he asked, "what are you doing in this hole?"

"I have fallen into a trap," Osebo said. "Help me out."

"I would gladly help you," Anansi said. "But I'm sure that if I bring you out, I will have no thanks for it. You will get hungry,
and later on you will be wanting to eat me 5
and my children."

"I swear it won't happen!" Osebo said.

"Very well. Since you swear it, I will take you out," Anansi said.

He bent a tall green tree toward the ground, so that its top was over the pit, and

▼ **Critical Viewing** Anansi, the spider, is the clever one in this folk tale. What traits of a spider lend themselves to this characterization? **[Defend]** 6

◆ Build Vocabulary

gourd (gôrd) *n.*: Fruit of a certain kind of plant; the dried, hollowed shell of this fruit is used as a drinking cup or dipper

Links Among Cultures

4 In American, African, and West Indian folklore, tricksters take advantage of larger and stronger animal through cunning or magic. Animal tricksters such as Brer Rabbit, Anansi, Turtle, Hare, and Lizard play a variety of roles in folklore literature. Sometimes, these stories pit two tricksters against each other. These timeless tales, passed from generation to generation, were originally brought to the southern United States and the Caribbean West Indies by the first African Americans. Some of the tales eventually returned to Africa.

◆ Literature and Your Life

5 Have students recall what they know about big cats such as leopards. Ask them if they would believe Osebo if they were in Anansi's place. *Students may say that Osebo's word cannot be trusted because he would probably eat Anansi's family if he were hungry enough.*

▶Critical Viewing◀

6 **Defend** *Students may say that spiders are hardworking, as shown by the intricate webs they spin. Students may also mention that spiders are cunning, as shown by the ways in which they catch prey in webs or lure prey into tunnels they build.*

Customize for
Verbal/Linguistic Learners

Point out that for hundreds of years, the oral tradition has kept folk tales such as this one alive while allowing for each storyteller to emphasize different parts of the story. Invite students to use their own words to summarize the story so far. Have the class compare the various retellings.

Speaking and Listening Mini-Lesson

Performance

This mini-lesson supports the Speaking and Listening activity in the Idea Bank on p. 845.

Introduce Point out that performing a folk tale can bring the story's characters to life. Arrange students in groups of five or more, and have the groups choose roles for the presentation.

Develop As students plan and prepare, remind them to use movement and facial expressions to help convey characters' thoughts and actions. Suggest that students research costumes and scenery that reflect the West African setting.

Apply Have groups coordinate all the elements of their performance. Encourage them to rehearse and make changes based on group members' suggestions. Then have groups perform for the class.

Assess Evaluate students' performances in terms of preparation, interpretation of the story, characterization, and appropriate use of sets, props, and costumes. Have students use the Peer Assessment: Dramatic Performance form, p. 107 in **Alternative Assessment,** to evaluate their classmates' performances.

CONNECTING LITERATURE TO SOCIAL STUDIES

1 Generalize *Based on the high price that Nyame set for the right to the stories, most students will say that the Ashanti greatly value their folk tales.*

Reinforce and Extend

Answers

◆ LITERATURE AND YOUR LIFE

Reader's Response Students may say that the capture of the hornets was most impressive, because it required the most ingenuity. Others may say the capture of the snake or the leopard was most impressive because each posed greater danger.

Thematic Focus Students may say that Anansi acts purely out of self-interest and will say anything to get his way. Students are likely to say that they disagree with such a self-serving code of conduct.

☑ Check Your Comprehension

1. He wants to own all the stories and tales.
2. Nyame wants the Mmoboro, the hornets; Onini, the great python; and Osebo, the leopard.
3. Anansi lures the hornets into a gourd by convincing them that it's raining; he plays on the python's vanity by persuading him to lie next to a bamboo pole and then ties the snake to the pole; he traps the leopard in a pit and then kills the leopard after he pretends to rescue him.
4. Nyame gives Anansi the stories.

More About the Author

Harold Courlander's retellings of folklore from Asia, West Africa, and the Caribbean are popular because he keeps the traditional tone of the stories. Regarding folk tales, Courlander has said, "Folk tales . . . have no special meaning for me unless they convey human values, philosophical outlook, cultural heritage. . . ." Courlander's father was a primitive painter, which sparked Courlander's interest in the art and stories of other cultures.

CONNECTING LITERATURE TO SOCIAL STUDIES

he tied it that way. Then he tied a rope to the top of the tree and dropped the other end of it into the pit.

"Tie this to your tail," he said.

Osebo tied the rope to his tail.

"Is it well tied?" Anansi asked.

"Yes, it is well tied," the leopard said.

"In that case," Anansi said, "you are not merely half-foolish, you are all-foolish."

And he took his knife and cut the other rope, the one that held the tree bowed to the ground. The tree straightened up with a snap, pulling Osebo out of the hole. He hung in the air head downward, twisting and turning. And while he hung this way, Anansi killed him with his weapons.

Then he took the body of the leopard and carried it to Nyame, the Sky God, saying: "Here is the third thing. Now I have paid the price."

Nyame said to him: "Kwaku Anansi, great warriors and chiefs have tried, but they have been unable to do it. You have done it. Therefore, I will give you the stories. From this day onward, all stories belong to you. Whenever a man tells a story, he must acknowledge that it is Anansi's tale."

In this way Anansi, the spider, became the owner of all stories that are told. To Anansi all these tales belong.

1 **Connecting Literature to Social Studies** Based on this folk tale, do you think the Ashanti feel that their stories hold great value? Why or why not?

◆ Build Vocabulary

acknowledge (ak näl′ ij) *v.*: Recognize and admit

Guide for Responding

◆ LITERATURE AND YOUR LIFE

Reader's Response Which of Anansi's accomplishments impressed you the most? Why?

Thematic Focus How would you describe Anansi's personal code of behavior? Do you agree or disagree with this code? Explain.

☑ Check Your Comprehension

1. What does Anansi want from Nyame?
2. What does Nyame want to fill this request?
3. How does Anansi capture the hornets, the python, and the leopard?
4. What does Nyame do in the end?

◆ Critical Thinking

INTERPRET

1. What can you infer about the hornets, the python, and the leopard from the fact that they listen to Anansi? **[Infer]**
2. What is Anansi's attitude toward the other animals? **[Interpret]**
3. Why is Anansi able to do what warriors and chiefs have failed to do? **[Draw Conclusions]**

APPLY

4. What lessons does this folk tale teach? Explain. **[Generalize]**

EXTEND

5. Cultures have focused on many different animals in the trickster role. What animal from your natural surroundings would make a good trickster? Why? **[Science Link]**

Meet the Author

Harold Courlander (1908–)

Harold Courlander has studied and written about African, West Indian, Native American, and African American cultures. He has written books on literature and music, novels, and several collections of folk tales from around the world. Courlander is interested in folk tales, he says, because "they convey human values, philosophical outlook, and cultural heritage."

Beyond the Selection

FURTHER READING

Other Works by Harold Courlander

The African

The Cow-Tail Switch and Other West African Stories

The Tiger's Whisker and Other Tales and Legends From Asia and the Pacific

Other Works About Folk Tales

African Folktales and Afro-American Folktales, Roger D. Abrahams

A Ring of Tricksters: Animal Tales From America, the West Indies, and Africa, Virginia Hamilton

Thirty-Three Multicultural Tales to Tell, Pleasant DeSpain

INTERNET

We suggest the following site on the Internet (all Web sites are subject to change).

For more information about West Africa: **http://www.africaonline.com/AfricaOnline/coverkids.html**

We *strongly recommend* that you preview the site before you send students to it.

Connecting Literature to Social Studies

As an Ashanti folk tale, "All Stories Are Anansi's" reveals information about the Ashanti's physical environment, their beliefs, and their traditions. For example, the characters in the story are animals common in western Africa—hornets, pythons, and leopards. In addition, the story's main conflict demonstrates the Ashanti's religious beliefs. The Ashanti people believe that a supreme god, Nyame, created the universe. Nyame has many descendants, who are the gods of villages or geographic regions and features. In this story, Anansi, the trickster, meets with Nyame in order to buy all the stories known. Through cleverness and deceit, Anansi gets his wish.

1. What animal characteristics do you think the Ashanti and other cultures looked for when choosing an animal as their trickster?
2. Note two examples of how Anansi displays trickster traits.
3. Why do you think tricksters like Djuha and Anansi have been such popular characters in folklore?

Idea Bank

Writing

1. **Help-Wanted Ad** Write a help-wanted ad for a trickster. Include a description of qualities the trickster should have.
2. **Argument** Imagine that Anansi now wants to take over Nyame's job. Write the argument he might make to Nyame to explain why the Sky God should allow him to run the universe.
3. **Folk Tale** Write your own folk tale about a trickster like Anansi. Give your character a goal and at least three characters to deceive.

Speaking and Listening

4. **Performance [Group Activity]** With a group of classmates, prepare a performance of "All Stories Are Anansi's." Decide who will play each role. Then, create costumes and sets to fit the western African location. Videotape your play, or perform it live.

Projects

5. **Storytelling Festival** With a group, collect folk tales from different cultures. Look for stories that share similar story lines or characters. For example, you might collect Cinderella stories or trickster tales from around the world. In a presentation, explain the similarities and differences among the stories. Then, retell selected stories to the class. Add music to bring the stories to life.
6. **Spider Profile** Using Internet and library sources, find out about the spiders that live in the western African tropical forests. Describe what they look like, how they behave, and what they eat. Include your own drawing of one such spider or of the fictional Anansi in your report. **[Science Link; Art Link]**

Further Reading, Listening, and Viewing

- Jane Yolen's *Favorite Folktales From Around the World* (1986) is a collection of popular versions of this and other folk tales.
- *Come With Me to Africa* (1993) by Gregory Scott Kreikemeier takes you along on Kreikemeier's African travels while a student.
- *Ghana* (1987) by Martin Hintz offers an overview in pictures and text.

✓ ASSESSMENT OPTIONS

Formal Assessment, Selection Test, pp. 238–239, and Assessment Resources Software. The selection test is designed so that it can be easily customized to the performance levels of your students.

PORTFOLIO ASSESSMENT
Use the following rubrics in the **Alternative Assessment** booklet to assess student writing:
Help-Wanted Ad: Definition/Classification, p. 86
Argument: Persuasion, p. 92
Folk Tale: Fictional Narrative, p. 82

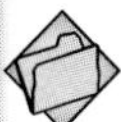

Idea Bank

Following are suggestions for matching the Idea Bank topics with your students' performance levels and learning modalities:

Customize for *Performance Levels*
Less Advanced Students: 1, 4
Average Students: 2, 4, 5, 6
More Advanced Students: 3, 4, 5, 6

Customize for *Learning Modalities*
Verbal/Linguistic: 1, 2, 3, 4, 5, 6
Visual/Spatial: 4, 6
Logical/Mathematical: 2
Bodily/Kinesthetic: 4
Intrapersonal: 1, 2, 3, 6
Interpersonal: 4, 5

◆Critical Thinking

1. Students may infer that all three animals trusted Anansi, perhaps because of past experience with the spider.
2. He thinks they are foolish and easily misled.
3. Anansi uses his wit and cunning instead of physical powers to find clever ways to capture the animals.
4. Students may say that the tale teaches that using your brain can sometimes get you farther than using physical strength.
5. As students think of responses, remind them that tricksters are usually smaller and weaker than most other animals. Students should give plausible reasons to support their responses.

Connecting Literature to Social Studies

1. Students may say that cultures looked for unlikely animals, such as those smaller and weaker, to add a note of surprise or irony to the stories.
2. Examples may include the boldness with which Anansi approaches Nyame for the stories and the cleverness with which Anansi captures the hornets, python, and leopard.
3. Students may say that they are popular because people enjoy seeing a resourceful hero use cleverness to get what it needs from larger, more powerful creatures.

Prepare and Engage

Establish Writing Guidelines
Review the following key characteristics of a cause-and-effect essay:

- A cause-and-effect essay explains the reason for an occurrence.
- A cause-and-effect essay includes supporting facts and details.

You may want to distribute the scoring rubric for Cause-and-Effect Essay, p. 89 in **Alternative Assessment,** to make students aware of the criteria on which they will be evaluated. See the suggestions on p. 848 for how you can customize the rubric to this workshop.

Refer students to the Writing Handbook in the back of the book for instruction on the writing process and further information on expository writing.

 ***Writer's Solution***

Writers at Work Videodisc
To introduce students to expository writing and to show them how Dmitri Ehrlich describes her ideas about expository writing, play the videodisc segment on Exposition: Making Connections (Ch. 5).

Play frames 42847 to 52256

Writing Lab CD-ROM
If your students have access to computers, you may want to have them work in the tutorial on Exposition: Making Connections to complete all or part of their cause-and-effect essays. Follow these steps:

1. Have students use the checklist for defining purpose to help students define their purpose in writing.
2. Suggest that students use the Chain of Events activity to arrange details.
3. Allow students to draft on the computer.
4. Have students use the Transition Word Bin to select transitional words or phrases.

Writer's Solution Sourcebook
Students can find additional support, including in-depth instruction on using prepositions and conjunctions, pp. 161–162, in the chapter on Exposition: Making Connections, pp. 134–165.

Expository Writing

Cause-and-Effect Essay

Writing Process Workshop

In "Popocatepetl and Ixtlaccihuatl," a cause—a young couple's enduring love—leads to an effect—the emergence of a pair of volcanic mountains. Legends and myths often tell *why* a particular event or situation occurred. Another type of writing that answers the question, "Why?" is a **cause-and-effect essay.** Write your own cause-and-effect essay on a topic that interests you. The following skills, introduced in this section's Writing Mini-Lessons, will help you:

Writing Skills Focus

▶ **Clearly explain the sequence of events.** Often, one cause leads to an effect, which in turn leads to its own effect. Make this chain of causes and effects clear in your essay. (See p. 818.)

▶ **Elaborate to support your ideas.** Use specific details and facts that show the connections between events. Be sure to offer reasons for the results you describe. (See p. 837.)

Notice how the writer uses these skills in "Popocatepetl and Ixtlaccihuatl."

Model From Literature

from "Popocatepetl and Ixtlaccihuatl" by Juliet Piggott

The snows came and, as the years went by, the pyramids of stone became high white-capped mountains. ① Even now the one called Popocatepetl emits smoke in memory of the princess whose body lies in the mountain which bears her name. ②

① This sentence shows a clear sequence of events—over time, the pyramids became mountains.

② Details here support the main idea—that Popocatepetl emits smoke in memory of Ixtlaccihuatl.

Cross-Curricular Connection: Science

Action/Reaction Explain to students that one facet of science is the study of how one thing causes a reaction in something else. Chemical reactions are examples of cause and effect. Another area of scientific study of cause and effect is seeking to find the cause of disastrous events. For example, finding the cause for the sinking of the Titanic may be useful knowledge so that safer, more efficient, ships can be built. Scientists also probed into the fiery crash of the Hindenburg, the largest airship ever built, which burst into flames on May 6, 1937. In cases such as these, scientists face the challenge of finding the cause of these tragedies.

Have students brainstorm for a list of disasters that have occurred. Then suggest that they research scientists' findings about the causes of these disasters. Students might begin their research with TV or newspaper reports or on the Internet. Ask them to outline the causes and effects of the disasters; for instance, effects might include safety regulations or changes to aircraft designs. Encourage students to compare and contrast what they discover about cause and effect.

Prewriting

Start With a Question What causes the common cold? Why is the ocean salty? Why did the Union army win the Civil War? Beginning with a good question will give you a strong start.

Topic Ideas

- What causes a disease?
- Why did a historical event happen?
- Why does a rule or law exist?
- Why is a species endangered?
- What causes a certain kind of pollution?

Gather Details Write a list of questions about your topic. Then, conduct research to find the answers. Use the library, on-line resources, or interview an expert on the subject.

Use a Cluster Diagram To clarify the relationships between details, create a cluster diagram. The diagram might consist of a central effect surrounded by several causes, or—as shown below—a central cause surrounded by several effects.

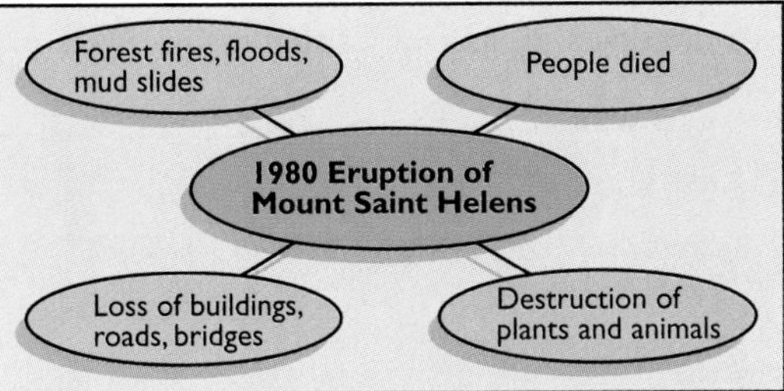

Organize Your Details To show how each cause leads to an effect, organize your details into a flowchart or timeline. Another idea is to write each detail on a separate note card and arrange the cards in the proper order.

Drafting

Write a Strong Introduction Your introduction is the first thing your audience will read, so be sure to grab their attention. You should also explain the importance of your topic and touch on the main points you'll make in your essay.

Write Notes to Yourself Use asterisks (*) to mark places in your draft where you need more information, want to find a better word, or notice a gap in your logic. Write yourself a note in the margin or—if you're working on a computer—in brackets. Later, you can search for the asterisks.

DRAFTING/REVISING

Applying Language Skills: Transitions to Show Cause and Effect

Transitions are like bridges. They connect ideas and sentences. Some transitions show time, and others show location. The ones below show cause and effect.

as a result	meanwhile
as soon as	next
consequently	then
further	therefore
furthermore	when

Practice On your paper, connect the pairs of sentences below with the transitions from the list above.

1. Sam poured birdseed along the path. We provided a bird buffet.
2. I play with the chess club once a week. I've made a lot of new friends.
3. I studied hard. I passed the test.

Writing Application When writing your cause-and-effect essay, use transitions to show the relationships between your sentences.

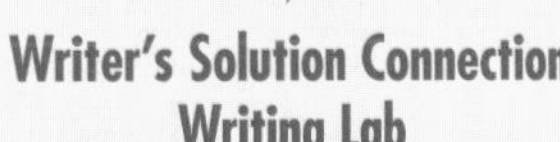

Writer's Solution Connection Writing Lab

For additional help, use the Transition Word Bin in the tutorial on Exposition.

Develop Student Writing

Prewriting

Suggest that students flip through magazines or newspapers to come up with topic ideas. Remind students that they want to pick a topic that is not too large or complex, requiring lengthy explanation. Encourage students to create an outline of steps that answer the question "Why?"

Customize for
More Advanced Writers
Suggest that these students combine the concepts of myths and legends with the framework for a cause-and-effect essay. Have them choose a topic that is mythical, such as, "Why the Sky Turned Green." As they write their essays, have them use factual details to support their fictional topic.

Customize for
Logical/Mathematical Learners
These students may benefit from creating a flowchart to show the steps involved in their topic. Encourage students to begin their charts with the cause and then fill in the steps that lead to the result, with arrows delineating the routes of the action.

Drafting

Remind students that their introductions should clearly state the purpose of their cause-and-effect essays. They may want to introduce their topic in the form of a question, such as "What causes traffic jams on Lincoln Avenue?" The body of their essay should develop the reasons for this effect. The conclusion should summarize the points included in the body and answer the question concisely.

Writer's Solution

Writing Lab CD-ROM
In the drafting section of the tutorial on Exposition: Making Connections, students view annotated student models to hear writer's comments on different types of effective introductions.

For additional support, have students use the practice page on Recognizing Smooth Connections Within Paragraphs in the *Writer's Solution Grammar Practice Book,* p. 126.

Applying Language Skills

Transitions to Show Cause and Effect Explain to students that transitions establish relationships between ideas. In addition to using transitions to show cause and effect, students can use transitions to show the order of events, by words such as *during, after, first, second, next,* and *finally.*

Answers

Possible responses:

1. Sam poured birdseed along the path. Then, we provided a bird buffet.
2. I play with the chess club once a week. As a result, I've made a lot of new friends.
3. I studied hard. Consequently, I passed the test.

Revising

Peer editors can use the checklist on p. 848 when reviewing drafts. Remind them to point out problems and suggest solutions.

 ***Writer's Solution***

Writing Lab CD-ROM
In the tutorial on Exposition: Making Connections, have students use the peer-editing worksheet to help edit.

Publishing

Students might collect their cause-and-effect essays in a class anthology. Have them provide a list of sources so others can research the topic.

Reinforce and Extend

Review the Writing Guidelines
After students have completed their papers, review the characteristics of a cause-and-effect essay.

Applying Language Skills

Punctuating Introductory Elements Commas after introductory elements separate nonessential information from the main subject and verb of the sentence. Often, the introductory words or phrases can be placed elsewhere in the sentence.

Answers

1. In 1492, Columbus "discovered" America.
2. Of course, there were people here already.
3. In his log, Columbus wrote that the people were friendly.

Students can use the practice page on Commas That Set Off Added Elements, p. 100 in the *Writer's Solution Grammar Practice Book.*

EDITING/PROOFREADING

APPLYING LANGUAGE SKILLS: Punctuating Introductory Elements

Some introductory elements are not critical to a sentence. Use a comma to separate the introductory material if the main clause can stand alone.

Prepositional Phrase:
At first light, Columbus landed on San Salvador.

Participle Phrase:
Claiming the land for Spain, he planted a flag.

Transitional Word:
Finally, a European had sailed to the Western Hemisphere.

Subordinate Clause:
When he returned, Columbus was a hero.

Practice Correct the errors in these sentences—if necessary.

1. In 1492 Columbus "discovered" America.
2. Of course there were people here already.
3. In his log Columbus wrote that the people were friendly.

Writing Application When revising, use commas after introductory elements.

Writer's Solution Connection
Writing Lab

If you work with a peer reviewer, refer to the Peer Editing Worksheet in the tutorial on Exposition.

Revising

Use a Checklist As you revise your work, ask yourself the following questions:

- What is the main idea of my essay? How can I make it clearer?
- Have I clearly shown the sequence of causes and effects in my essay? Can I add or change details or transition words to make causes and effects clearer?
- Is there any unnecessary information I should drop from my essay?
- Are there any errors in spelling, grammar, or punctuation?

Answer these questions thoughtfully and thoroughly. Then, use your responses to guide your revision.

REVISION MODEL

When the volcano became active, it made the earth shake, set off avalanches, and sparked an intense series of noises. ~~It~~ ① The first eruption spread a thick layer of volcanic ash over a wide area ② , destroying plant and animal life.

① The writer elaborates to add clarity.
② The writer adds an effect.

Publishing and Presenting

Informative Poster Write the question your essay answers at the top of a big posterboard. Then, use visuals and captions to answer the question based on the information in your essay. Display your poster somewhere in your school.

Talk Show Imagine that your topic is the subject for a talk show. Work with a partner, taking turns being the talk-show host and the guest expert. Answer questions about your topic. Then, ask questions about your partner's topic. Videotape your show if you can.

✓ ASSESSMENT

PORTFOLIO ASSESSMENT
Use the rubric on Cause-and-Effect Essay in the **Alternative Assessment** booklet, p. 89, to assess the students' writing. Add these criteria to customize this rubric to this assignment.

	4	3	2	1
Punctuating Introductory Elements	All introductory elements are punctuated correctly.	Most introductory elements are punctuated correctly.	Some introductory elements are punctuated correctly.	None of the introductory elements is punctuated correctly.
Transitions	The essay includes transitions to link ideas and sentences and to show relationships of cause and effect.	The essay includes transitions that show cause and effect, but some ideas and sentences need to be linked.	The essay has transitions that show some cause and effect, but some sentences and ideas need to be linked.	The essay fails to include transitions to show cause and effect or to link ideas and sentences.

Real-World Reading Skills Workshop

Evaluating an Argument

Strategies for Success

An argument is more than just a quarrel between people. For example, a written argument in a book or a magazine is a formal presentation of an opinion. When a lawyer makes closing statements in a court case, he or she is presenting an argument. Here are some strategies for evaluating the strength of an argument:

Evaluate the Balance Between Logic and Emotion Both logic and emotion play important roles in argument because they are important in how people think. Logical arguments use reasoning to outline an argument clearly. Logical arguments may include pros and cons that need to be considered. An emotional argument offers the writer's feelings on a topic. Although emotional points have merit, an argument that uses only emotional points is usually weak. As you consider the strength of a writer's opinion, look to see that the argument—whether logical or emotional—is supported by reason.

Look for Backup A strong argument will back up its claims with supporting information. This might be in the form of facts, statistics, illustrations, or quotes. For example, the argument that "everybody wants curbside recycling" would be weak unless it offered support. Quotes from residents, poll results, or studies conducted by outside researchers would provide support for the argument.

Apply the Strategies

Read the following persuasive argument. Then, answer the questions that follow.

> **Michael Jordan is the best basketball player in the history of the game. In 1998, his team, the Chicago Bulls, beat the Utah Jazz in a six-game championship series. It was the second time in ten years that the team won three championships in a row!**
>
> **They couldn't have done it without Jordan. His playing was breathtaking, even after 13 years in the league. In the last game of the series, he scored 45 of the Bulls' 87 points and was named the most valuable player of the championship series. That must have been an easy decision.**
>
> **There have been many other great players in the history of the game, but none have had the combination of skills, power, know-how, and drive of Michael Jordan.**

1. What point does the argument make?
2. What does it offer for support?
3. (a) What details appeal to emotion? (b) What details appeal to logic?
4. (a) Overall, do you think the writer presents a strong argument? (b) How could it be stronger?

✔ *Here are other situations in which you'll need to evaluate a written argument:*

- ▶ Information about an election issue
- ▶ Critique of a book or a movie
- ▶ Newspaper editorial

Introduce the Strategies

From TV dramas or films, students may be familiar with closing arguments in a court case. Encourage students to share with the class scenes of arguments they have witnessed. Ask students to identify the two sides of the case and how the lawyer or lawyers appealed to the judge or jury.

Customize for
Less Proficient Readers
To help students evaluate an argument, suggest that they fill out the Main Ideas and Supporting Details Organizer from **Writing and Language Transparencies,** p. 70. In the box for main idea, students should identify the argument. Then, in the supporting details box, they can add the points the argument addresses.

Apply the Strategies

Answers

1. The point of the argument is that Michael Jordan is the best basketball player in the history of the game.
2. Michael scored 45 of the Bulls' 87 points in the last game of the championship series. He was named the most valuable player.
3. (a) Details that appeal to emotion include that his "playing was breathtaking, even after 13 years in the league," that it was an easy decision to name most valuable player, and that Jordan has a "combination of skills, power, know-how, and drive." (b) Details that appeal to logic include that his team won three championships in a row twice in ten years, that he scored 45 of 87 points in the last game, and that he was named most valuable player.
4. (a) Most students will say that the writer presents some details toward a strong argument, but that more specific details could be included. (b) The argument could be stronger if more details or statistics about Jordan's performance throughout his career were included.

◆Build Grammar Skills

Reviewing Punctuation: Commas
The selections in Part I include instruction on the following:

- Commas With Interrupters
- Commas in a Series

This instruction is reinforced with the Build Grammar Skills practice pages in **Selection Support,** pp. 263 and 269.

As you review subject and verb agreement, you may wish to review the following:

- Commas With Compound Sentences

In a compound sentence with two independent clauses, separate the clauses with a comma before the conjunction—*and, but, or, nor, for, so,* or *yet.*

and	At the far end of the settlement stood a lodge, **and** in it lived a being who was always invisible.
but	His sister could see him, **but** the other girls only pretended to know he was there.
or	The older sisters ignored the younger one, **or** they burnt the poor girl's hands and feet.
nor	Oochigeaskw was not pretty, **nor** did she have fine clothes.
for	The bad sister would say it was her own fault, **for** she had gone near the fire and fallen into it.
so	They wanted to see the Invisible One, **so** they they took the usual walk by the water.
yet	The youngest girl was often ill, **yet** her sisters treated her cruelly.

Writer's Solution

For additional practice and support with subject and verb agreement, use the practice pages on Commas That Separate Basic Elements, pp. 98–99, Commas That Set Off Added Elements, pp. 100–101, and Special Uses of the Comma, p. 102, *Writer's Solution Grammar Practice Book.*

Punctuation: Commas

Grammar Review

While an end mark signals a full stop, a **comma** signals a brief pause.

Commas With Interrupters Commas are used to set off interrupters. These are words and phrases that interrupt the flow of a sentence to add information that is not essential to the meaning of the sentence. Commas separate these words from the rest of the sentence. (See page 817.)

Kinds of Interrupters:	
Names of People Being Addressed	I warn you, *Ixtla,* rethink your plan.
Common Expressions	You'll regret your choice, *I believe.*

Commas With a Series Use commas to separate three or more words, phrases, or clauses in a series. (See page 836.)

Series of Words: The Cinderella tale is told in *Europe, North America,* and *Africa.*

Series of Phrases: It is told to *teach a lesson, pass on values,* and *entertain children.*

Series of Clauses: It's interesting to compare *how the stories differ, how they are the same,* and *what each story says about the culture that tells it.*

Practice 1 Write the following sentences, adding commas to set off interrupters.

1. Yeh-Shen of course was blessed with joy.
2. Many women in the Algonquin Cinderella story on the other hand did not find happiness.
3. These stories many believe are worth comparing.
4. Both of them it seems contain evil characters and good ones.
5. Please tell us Mr. Thurber why the princess chose as she did.

press
comm 1 commander 2 commentary 3 commerc 5 committee 6 commonwealth 7 communication
comma (käm'ə) *n.* [L < Gr *komma,* clause in a sent is cut off < *koptein,* to cut off < IE base *(s)kep CAPON, SHAFT] 1 a mark of punctuation (,) used to separation of sentence elements, as in setting off parenthetical elements, items in a series, etc. 2 a s
comma bacillus the bacillus (*Vibrio chol*...

Practice 2 On your paper, write the following sentences, adding commas to separate items listed in a series.

1. Popocatepetl and Ixtlaccihuatl loved each other were committed to each other and died for their beliefs.
2. Ixtla asked begged and pleaded with her father to reconsider his decision.
3. The emperor announced that warriors would compete for Ixtla's hand the leadership of the kingdom and the chance at power.
4. Some warriors were jealous short-sighted and mean-spirited.
5. When Popo learned what truly happened, he wondered who could be so cruel why Ixtla lost faith and what he should do with his life.

Grammar in Writing

Commas in a series can be critical to a correct reading. Notice that the following instructions are unclear when commas are omitted:

Confusing: Review A B and C.
Could mean: Review AB and review C.
or
Review A, review B, and review C.
Clear: Review A, B, and C.

In your writing, use commas to separate items in a series.

Answers

Practice 1

1. Yeh-Shen, of course, was blessed with joy.
2. Many women in the Algonquin Cinderella story, on the other hand, did not find happiness.
3. These stories, many believe, are worth comparing.
4. Both of them, it seems, contain evil characters and good ones.
5. Please tell us, Mr. Thurber, why the princess chose as she did.

Practice 2

1. Popocatepetl and Ixtlaccihuatl loved each other, were committed to each other, and died for their beliefs.
2. Ixtla asked, begged, and pleaded with her father to reconsider his decision.
3. The Emperor announced that warriors would compete for Ixtla's hand, the leadership of the kingdom, and the chance at power.
4. Some warriors were jealous, short-sighted, and mean-spirited.
5. When Popo learned what truly happened, he wondered who could be so cruel, why Ixtla lost faith, and what he should do with his life.

PART 2 Myths and Fables From Ancient Greece

All the evils flying forth into the world on the opening of Pandora's box, colored engraving, 19th-century

One-Minute Planning Guide

This section explores myths and fables from ancient Greece. In "Phaëthon, Son of Apollo," a young man's pride brings about his downfall. "Demeter and Persephone" explains the changing of the seasons. "Narcissus" examines the danger of self-love. "Icarus and Daedulus" is the story of a man and his son who try to fly. Two fables from Aesop, "The Lion and the Statue" and "The Fox and the Crow," provide classic morals.

Customize for *Varying Student Needs*

When assigning the selections in this section, keep in mind the following factors:

"Phaëthon, Son of Apollo"
- Greek myth about pride
- You may want to review footnotes for pronunciation

"Demeter and Persephone"
- Greek myth about the seasons
- Provides an opportunity for a Beyond Literature science connection

"Narcissus"
- A short, classic Greek myth

"Icarus and Daedulus"
- Greek myth about the lure of flying

"The Lion and the Statue"
- Very short fable about how we choose to represent things

"The Fox and the Crow"
- Very short fable about flattery

Humanities: Art

All the evils flying forth into the world on the opening of Pandora's box, 19th century

This engraving illustrates a classic Greek myth. In it, Pandora is the first woman, created out of clay by Hephaestus. Pandora is given beauty by the goddess Aphrodite, arts by the goddess Athena, and cunning by the god Hermes. She is also given a dowry, a box which she is ordered not to open. After marrying Epimetheus, Prometheus' brother, Pandora finds that she cannot resist the temptation to open her magic box. When she does so, she lets out all the evils of the world. The only spirit she manages to keep in the box is Hope.

1. What is Pandora trying to do? *Possible response: She is trying to close the top of the box, to keep the spirits from escaping.*
2. Hope is the only spirit Pandora manages to keep in the box. Do you think this is a good thing? *Some students may say yes because hope gives people the courage to keep fighting when they are plagued with bad luck; other students may say no, because hope can lead to false promises.*

Prepare and Engage

OBJECTIVES

1. To read, comprehend, and interpret four classic Greek myths
2. To relate myths to personal experience
3. To predict
4. To understand and analyze myths
5. To build vocabulary in context and use the word root *-domin-*
6. To develop skill in using commas after introductory phrases
7. To write a modern myth using an outline
8. To respond to the myths through writing, speaking and listening, and projects

SKILLS INSTRUCTION

Vocabulary: Word Roots: *-domin-*

Spelling: Using *su* for Words With the *sw* Sound

Grammar: Commas After Introductory Phrases

Reading Strategy: Predict

Literary Focus: Myth

Writing: Use an Outline

Speaking and Listening: Radio Advice Show (Teacher Edition)

Critical Viewing: Infer; Analyze; Interpret; Predict

PORTFOLIO OPPORTUNITIES

Writing: News Article; Autobiography; Myth

Writing Mini-Lesson: Modern Myth

Speaking and Listening: Oral Reading; Radio Advice Show

Projects: Model; Comparison Chart

More About the Authors

Olivia E. Coolidge was the daughter of a historian and teacher. She herself taught English and Latin. From 1945–1961, Coolidge served as a trustee of Mills College in New York.

Anne Terry White was born in Russia. She attended Brown and Stanford universities and began writing stories to expose her own children to good writing.

Jay Macpherson was part of a group of Canadian poets who wrote following World War II. The group also includes Leonard Cohen, John Newlove, and Daryl Hine.

Josephine Preston Peabody enjoyed writing in a variety of genres. Her stories are filled with thrilling plots, bold characters, and unusual settings.

Guide for Reading

Meet the Authors:

Olivia E. Coolidge (1908–)

Although she is best known for writing biographies, Olivia Coolidge has also written a number of books on myths from ancient Greece, Rome, and Egypt.

Anne Terry White (1896–1980)

Anne Terry White was an authority on ancient Greece. She shares this knowledge in retelling the myth of "Demeter and Persephone." White also explored science, biography, and other topics in her many books for children and young adults.

Jay Macpherson (1931–)

Jay Macpherson is best known for her poetry, which celebrates the power of imagination. Because her poems feature many symbols from myths and legends, it's no surprise that Macpherson has also written a retelling of the Greek myth "Narcissus." Although born in England, Jay Macpherson has lived most of her life in Canada.

Josephine Preston Peabody (1874–1922)

Josephine Preston Peabody was a quick starter. She began writing at thirteen and published her first book—*Old Greek Folk Stories*—when she was twenty-three. "Icarus and Daedalus" is from this collection. Peabody went on to write many poems and plays.

◆ Literature and Your Life

Connect Your Experience

You may know stories—either true or made up—about people who have suffered the consequences of thinking too highly of themselves. As you'll learn from these myths, the ancient Greeks believed that a person was almost sure to be punished for being overly proud or arrogant.

Thematic Focus: Lessons Learned

Sometimes knowledge comes at a price. In these myths, the characters learn their lessons the hard way. As you read, think about easier ways they could have learned the same lessons.

◆ Background for Understanding

Literature

Each of these myths comes from ancient Greece, where people believed in a complex collection of gods and goddesses. The supreme god was Zeus. Zeus ruled with his wife, Hera, from atop Mount Olympus. Beneath Zeus in rank were many lesser gods and goddesses, each linked to ideas or qualities in nature. For example, the goddess Demeter protected the harvest. The god Apollo was linked to poetry, music, and the sun.

◆ Build Vocabulary

Word Roots: *-domin-*

In "Demeter and Persephone," you'll encounter the word *dominions*. Based on the root *-domin-*, meaning "master," *dominions* means "regions over which someone rules."

Word Bank

Which of these words from the myths do you think is the opposite of *persuade*? Check the Build Vocabulary boxes to see if you're correct.

mortal
dissuade
dominions
avenging
deluded
lament
vacancy
sustained

Prentice Hall Literature Program Resources

REINFORCE / RETEACH / EXTEND

Selection Support Pages
Build Vocabulary: Word Roots: *-domin-*, p. 274
Build Spelling Skills, p. 275
Build Grammar Skills: Commas After Introductory Phrases, p. 276
Reading Strategy: Predict, p. 277
Literary Focus: Myth, p. 278

Strategies for Diverse Student Needs, p. 99

Beyond Literature Cultural Connection: Gods and Goddesses of Greek Mythology, p. 50

Formal Assessment Selection Test, pp. 240–242, Assessment Resources Software

Alternative Assessment, p. 50

Writing and Language Transparencies Cluster Organizer, p. 82

Daily Language Practice, p. 60

Resource Pro CD-ROM Includes all selections—includes all resource material and customizable lesson plan

Listening to Literature Audiocassettes Includes all selections

Phaëthon, Son of Apollo ◆ Demeter and Persephone ◆ Narcissus ◆ Icarus and Daedalus

Le Char D'Apollon (Apollo's Chariot) (detail), Odilon Redon, Musee D'Orsay, Paris/Giraudon, Paris

◆ Literary Focus

Myth

Since time began, people have tried to understand the world around them—from how it began to the origins of fire. To help them do so, ancient peoples created **myths,** stories about gods and heroes that explain natural occurrences and express beliefs about right and wrong. Built on an imaginative understanding of nature, myths make sense to us because they explain the world in human terms. In these myths, for example, you will learn how the Greeks explained the sun's daily travel across the sky, the season of winter, and the risks of human pride.

◆ Reading Strategy

Predict

In some myths, characters get into trouble because they happen to be in the wrong place at the wrong time. Most of the time, however, a character's troubles are the result of his or her own actions. As you read, look for clues about what is going to happen and **predict,** or make educated guesses about, where events will lead. Then, read on to see if your predictions were correct. Use a chart like the one below to record clues and your predictions based on these clues.

Clue	Prediction

Preparing for Standardized Tests

Vocabulary Standardized test questions may require students to use their knowledge of word roots in order to understand unfamiliar vocabulary. Write this sentence on the board:

"The problem of how to make wings dominated Daedalus' thoughts."

Remind students that the root *-domin-* means "master." Discuss how knowing this meaning may help them define *dominated* as "controlled" in the sentence. Then write the following sample test question on the board:

Pluto's domination of the underworld gives him power over lesser gods.

In the sentence above, *domination* means—

(A) boredom
(B) enthusiasm
(C) dissatisfaction
(D) control

Help students assess the answer choices. Guide them to see that the only choice relating to the meaning of the root word *-domin-* is *(D)*. The sentence means that Pluto controls, or has mastery over, lesser gods in the underworld.

Interest Grabber Ask students to name occurrences in nature that might cause someone to question why and how. For example, leaves turning colors in the fall, rainbows, or earthquakes. Have students imagine that they lived long ago, before scientists could explain these occurrences scientifically. Tell students to select a natural occurrence, and, in five minutes, write a creative explanation for it. Call on volunteers to share their writing with the class. Introduce the selections by saying that these myths were created thousands of years ago to help people explain natural occurrences.

◆ Build Grammar Skills

Commas After Introductory Phrases If you wish to introduce the grammar concept before students read, refer to the instruction on p. 868.

Customize for *Less Proficient Readers*

Tell students that Greek gods are like humans in some ways—they express emotion and have families—but they also have powers humans lack. As they read, have students keep a list of the gods, their special traits, and how they are like humans.

Customize for *More Advanced Students*

Greek and Roman myths are often studied and compared because many of the characters have the same role but different names:

Greek	Roman
Zeus	Jupiter
Apollo	Apollo
Hermes	Mercury
Demeter	Ceres
Aphrodite	Venus

Students might enjoy doing further research comparing mythological characters in different cultures.

Humanities: Art

Apollo's Chariot, by Odilon Redon (1840–1916)

Ask students what clues to the myth are found in the painting. *The man on the cloud indicates that this myth will have something to do with gods or immortals.*

Develop Understanding

One-Minute Insight "Phaëthon, Son of Apollo" describes the downfall of a mortal who aspires to be a god. Phaëthon, son of the god Apollo and the mortal woman Clymene, often boasts of his divine father, who each day drives the sun's golden chariot across the sky. When another boy expresses doubt about Phaëthon's heritage, Phaëthon visits his father and pleads for help. Apollo promises to give Phaëthon anything he wants. When Phaëthon asks to guide the sun's chariot across the sky, Apollo tries to discourage him; however, Phaëthon proudly insists. The boy is no match for this difficult task, and the chariot veers out of control and swerves too close to Earth. The heat of the sun scorches the earth until Zeus finally hurls a thunderbolt at Phaëthon, sending him crashing to the ground.

Team Teaching Strategy

The cultural, geographical, and historical aspects of these myths offer a strong connection to social studies. You may want to coordinate with a social studies teacher to plan ways to extend instruction.

◆Literary Focus

1 Myths Explain that in many myths, mortals who aspire to be gods are punished in some way. Ask students to find clues in these sentences that indicate that Phaëthon may be in this group. *The sentences point out that Phaëthon is boastful, a negative trait, and that sons of gods and mortal women who become gods must do good deeds to acquire their lofty status.*

Customize for
English Language Learners
Help students understand the family relationships in the myth by drawing a family tree such as the one shown.

Apollo (god) —— Clymene (Mortal)
Phaeton (mortal)

PHAËTHON, SON OF APOLLO

Olivia E. Coolidge

The Chariot of Phaëthon racing through the skies, Copper engraving, 1606

Block Scheduling Strategies

Consider these suggestions to take advantage of extended class time:

- Review the Literary Focus before students read the myths. After they read, discuss as a group their answers to the Literary Focus questions, p. 868.
- Have students work in groups to correct the sentences in **Daily Language Practice,** p.60, which focus on the myth of Icarus and Daedalus
- Have students work in small groups, using the *Writer's Solution Writing Lab CD-ROM* to complete the Writing Mini-Lesson on p. 869.
- Suggest that students listen to the recording of each myth, while filling in the chart on p. 853. Instruct groups of students to compare and discuss their charts and to answer the Reading Strategy questions on p. 868. For additional practice, use **Selection Support,** p. 277.

Listening to Literature Audiocassettes

Though Apollo always honored the memory of Daphne she was not his only love. Another was a mortal, Clymene,[1] by whom he had a son named Phaëthon.[2] Phaëthon grew up with his mother, who, since she was mortal, could not dwell in the halls of Olympus[3] or in the palace of the sun. She lived not far from the East in the land of Ethiopia, and as her son grew up, she would point to the place where Eos,[4] goddess of the dawn, lighted up the sky and tell him that there his father dwelt. Phaëthon loved to boast of his divine father as he saw the golden chariot riding high through the air. He would re-
1 mind his comrades of other sons of gods and mortal women who, by virtue of their great deeds, had themselves become gods at last. He must always be first in everything, and in most things this was easy, since he was in truth stronger, swifter, and more daring than the others. Even if he were not victorious, Phaëthon always
2 claimed to be first in honor. He could never bear to be beaten, even if he must risk his life in some rash way to win.

Most of the princes of Ethiopia willingly paid Phaëthon honor, since they admired him greatly for his fire and beauty. There was one boy, however, Epaphos,[5] who was rumored to be a child of Zeus himself. Since this was not certainly proved, Phaëthon chose to disbelieve it and to demand from Epaphos the deference that he obtained from all others. Epaphos was proud too, and one day he lost his temper with Phaëthon and turned on him, saying, "You are a fool to believe all that your mother tells you. You are all swelled up with false ideas about your father."

Crimson with rage, the lad rushed home to his mother and demanded that she prove to him the truth of the story that she had often told. "Give me some proof," he implored her, "with which I can answer this insult of Epaphos. It is a matter of life and death to me, for if I cannot, I shall die of shame."

"I swear to you," replied his mother solemnly, "by the bright orb of the sun itself that you are his son. If I swear falsely, may I never look on the sun again, but die before the next time he mounts the heavens. More than this I cannot do, but you, my child, can go to the eastern palace of
Phoebus[6] Apollo—it lies not far away—and 4
there speak with the god himself."

The son of Clymene leaped up with joy at his mother's words. The palace of Apollo was indeed not far. It stood just below the eastern horizon, its tall pillars glistening with bronze and gold. Above these it was white with gleaming ivory, and the great doors were flashing silver, embossed with pictures of earth, sky, and sea, and the gods that dwelt therein. Up the steep hill
and the bright steps climbed Phaëthon, 5
passing unafraid through the silver doors, and stood in the presence of the sun. Here at last he was forced to turn away his face, for Phoebus sat in state on his golden throne. It gleamed with emeralds and precious stones, while on the head of the god was a brilliant diamond crown upon which no eye could look undazzled.

Phaëthon hid his face, but the god had recognized his son, and he spoke kindly,

1. **Clymene** (klim´ ə nē)
2. **Phaëthon** (fā´ ə tän)
3. **Olympus** (ō lim´ pəs): Mountain in northern Greece that was known as the home of the gods.
4. **Eos** (ē´ äs)
5. **Epaphos** (ep´ ə fəs)

6. **Phoebus** (fē´ bəs): Means "bright one" in Greek.

3 ◀ Critical Viewing Basing your answer on the details in this illustration, what can you infer about the settings, characters, and events of this myth? **[Infer]**

◆ Build Vocabulary

mortal (môr´ təl) *n.*: Being who must eventually die

◆Reading Strategy

2 Predict Ask students if they have ever known anyone with this characteristic. What do they predict might be in store for Phaëthon? *Students may say that such people often use poor judgment and end up hurting themselves or others.*

▶Critical Viewing◀

3 Infer *Possible response: The illustration indicates that the setting is in the sky among the clouds, the horses appear to be very powerful, the story is probably filled with action.*

◆Critical Thinking

4 Draw Conclusions Ask students why they think that Clymene decides to send her son to see Apollo. *Students may say that she knows Phaëthon well and realizes that he will not be satisfied with her answer but must speak with Apollo personally.*

◆Reading Strategy

5 Literary Focus Review the description of the palace and of Apollo with students. Ask them why they think that the author creates such a lavish setting. *Guide students to conclude that by describing a palace of gold and silver atop a hill, a throne encrusted with jewels, and a crown that no eye can look upon, the author reinforces the reader's view of Apollo as a powerful and wise god.*

Customize for *Visual/Spatial Learners*

Read aloud the description of the palace, throne, and crown. Emphasize these words and phrases: *above, up, passing through, on the head.* Point out that such words and phrases help readers envision the physical arrangement of objects. Some students may want to make a sketch showing the details of the paragraph.

Humanities: Art

The Chariot of Phaëthon Racing Through the Skies

Gather images of Apollo and his son and share them with the class. Explain that Apollo is one of the most important Greek gods, and is associated with beauty, medicine, law, the fine arts, courage, and wisdom. Two Greek maxims, "Know Thyself" and "Nothing in Excess" were inscribed on the walls of his temple at Delphi.

Suggest that students note how mortals are portrayed differently than the gods in the illustrations. Have students point out similarities in the various depictions of Apollo. Many may notice, for example, that he is often shown wearing a laurel wreath. Tell students that one myth describes Apollo's love for Daphne, who fled from him and was turned into a laurel tree. Apollo promised that the tree would always be green, and he wore a laurel wreath from that time on. Later, laurel wreaths were awarded as prizes in athletic and musical competitions. Challenge students to find other myths concerning Apollo to explain symbols they see in the images.

Clarification

❶ An epithet is a word or phrase that is often closely associated with a name to describe someone, such as: Richard *the Lionhearted,* or Michael *Air* Jordan. The term *Phoebus* is used as an epithet with Apollo in this myth.

◆Critical Thinking

❷ **Infer** Ask students what this description of Apollo tells them about him. *He is warm and loving. He is happy that his son has come to visit.*

◆Literary Focus

❸ *They believe that each day Apollo drives the sun in a golden chariot across the sky.*

◆Reading Strategy

❹ **Predict** Invite students to predict what will happen next. *Most students will predict that Phaëthon will have some sort of trouble during his journey across the sky.*

◆Critical Thinking

❺ **Analyze Cause and Effect** What causes the horses to lose control as they soar into the heavens? *The chariot is lighter with only Phaëthon; in addition, Phaëthon is too frightened and dizzy to guide it properly.*

Customize for
Verbal/Linguistic Learners

In 1757, an elegant, light-weight carriage with an open design and ability to negotiate narrow turns was introduced. It was called a *phaeton.* The carriage had a reputation for being dangerous, which only enhanced its appeal for reckless drivers. Ask students why they think the carriage was named after a mythological character. *The carriage with a reputation for being dangerous was appropriately named for a reckless mythological character.*

asking him why he had come. Then Phaëthon plucked up courage and said, "I come to ask you if you are indeed my father. If you are so, I beg you to give me ❶ some proof of it so that all may recognize me as Phoebus' son."

The god smiled, being well pleased with his son's beauty and daring. He took off his crown so that Phaëthon could look at him, and coming down from his throne, he ❷ put his arms around the boy, and said, "You are indeed my son and Clymene's, and worthy to be called so. Ask of me whatever thing you wish to prove your origin to men, and you shall have it."

Phaëthon swayed for a moment and was dizzy with excitement at the touch of the god. His heart leaped; the blood rushed into his face. Now he felt that he was truly divine, unlike other men, and he did not wish to be counted with men any more. He looked up for a moment at his radiant father. "Let me drive the chariot of the sun across the heavens for one day," he said.

❸ **◆ Literary Focus** How do the Greeks explain the sun's daily travel across the sky?

Apollo frowned and shook his head. "I cannot break my promise, but I will dissuade you if I can," he answered. "How can you drive my chariot, whose horses need a strong hand on the reins? The climb is too steep for you. The immense height will make you dizzy. The swift streams of air in the upper heaven will sweep you off your course. Even the immortal gods could not drive my chariot. How then can you? Be wise and make some other choice."

The pride of Phaëthon was stubborn, for he thought the god was merely trying to frighten him. Besides, if he could guide the sun's chariot, would he not have proved his right to be divine rather than mortal? For that he would risk his life. Indeed, once he had seen Apollo's splendor, he did not wish to go back and live among men. Therefore, he insisted on his right until Apollo had to give way.

When the father saw that nothing else would satisfy the boy, he bade the Hours bring forth his chariot and yoke the horses. The chariot was of gold and had two gold-rimmed wheels with spokes of silver. In it there was room for one man to stand and hold the reins. Around the front and sides of it ran a rail, but the back was open. At the end of a long pole there were yokes for the four horses. The pole was of gold and shone with precious jewels: the golden topaz, the bright diamond, the green emerald, and the flashing ruby. While the Hours were yoking the swift, pawing horses, rosy-fingered Dawn hastened to the gates of heaven to draw them open. Meanwhile Apollo anointed his son's face with a magic ointment, that he might be able to bear the heat of the fire-breathing horses and the golden chariot. At last Phaëthon mounted the chariot and grasped the reins, the barriers were let down, and the horses shot up into the air. ❹

At first the fiery horses sped forward up the accustomed trail, but behind them the chariot was too light without the weight of the immortal god. It bounded from side to side and was dashed up and down. Phaëthon was too frightened and too dizzy to pull the reins, nor would he have known anyway whether he was on the usual path. As soon as the horses felt that there was ❺ no hand controlling them, they soared up, up with fiery speed into the heavens till the earth grew pale and cold beneath them. Phaëthon shut his eyes, trembling at the dizzy, precipitous height. Then the horses dropped down, more swiftly than a falling stone, flinging themselves madly from side to side in panic because they

◆ Build Vocabulary

dissuade (di swād′) *v.*: Advise someone against an action

Cross-Curricular Connection: Social Studies

Ancient Greece Ancient Greeks left many legacies to our modern world: the Olympic Games, democracy, trial by jury, and epic poetry. The stories of Greek mythology have provided the basis for sculptures, paintings, music, drama, and literature.

Ancient Greeks believed that the world was a flat disk with Greece in its center. The disk was divided from west to east by a body of water, the Sea, now called the Mediterranean Sea. Around its circumference ran the River Ocean.

To explain their world, the early Greeks created stories about giants, monsters, and enchantresses who lived in the western part of the Sea, and gods who lived around the edge of the Earth. They believed that the Sun, the Dawn, and the Moon rose out of the Sea in the east and drove through the sky to provide light.

Some Greeks believed that the exact center of the Earth was Mount Olympus, Greece's highest mountain peak. Others felt that the center was Delphi. At Delphi, Apollo established the most renowned center for prophecy in the ancient world, the shrine of the Delphic Oracle.

were masterless. Phaëthon dropped the reins entirely and clung with all his might to the chariot rail. Meanwhile as they came near the earth, it dried up and cracked apart. Meadows were reduced to white ashes, cornfields smoked and shriveled, cities perished in flame. Far and wide on the wooded mountains the forests were ablaze, and even the snowclad Alps were bare and dry. Rivers steamed and dried to dust. The great North African plain was scorched until it became the desert that it is today. Even the sea shrank back to pools and caves, until dried fishes were left baking upon the white-hot sands. At
6 last the great earth mother called upon Zeus to save her from utter destruction, and Zeus hurled a mighty thunderbolt at the unhappy Phaëthon, who was still crouched in the chariot, clinging desperately to the rail. 6
The dart cast him out, and he fell flaming in a long trail through the air. The chariot broke in pieces at the mighty blow, and the maddened horses rushed snorting back to the stable of their master, Apollo.

Unhappy Clymene and her daughters wandered over the whole earth seeking the body of the boy they loved so well. When they found him, they took him and buried him. Over his grave they wept and could not be comforted. At last the gods in pity for their grief changed them into poplar trees, which weep with tears of amber in memory of Phaëthon.

Guide for Responding

◆ Literature and Your Life

Reader's Response Have you ever regretted that you didn't take someone's advice? Explain.

Thematic Focus Why do you think Phaëthon rejects Apollo's advice and has to learn his lesson from personal experience?

Journal Writing Phaëthon insists on driving his father's chariot. In a journal entry, explain what you might have wished for in a similar situation.

☑ Check Your Comprehension

1. Why does Phaëthon go to Apollo's palace?
2. Why does Apollo urge Phaëthon to choose a different wish?
3. What is Phaëthon's secret reason for his request?
4. What is the result of this request?
5. What natural features are explained in this myth?

◆ Critical Thinking

Interpret

1. What does Phaëthon's need to "always be first in everything" reveal about his character? **[Infer]**
2. Describe two ways that Phaëthon displays his pride. **[Connect]**
3. How might this story have been different if Phaëthon had resembled his father less? **[Speculate]**
4. What lessons does this myth teach? **[Draw Conclusions]**

Apply

5. Besides refusing to grant Phaëthon's request, how might Apollo have avoided his son's tragic end? **[Modify]**

Extend

6. How do modern scientists explain the sun's movement across the sky? **[Science Link]**

Beyond the Selection

FURTHER READING

Works About Ancient Greece

Ancient Greek Art, Susie Hodge
Greek Gazette, Paul Dowswell

Works About Greek Mythology

Greek Gods and Goddesses, Emma Chichester Clark
Adventures of the Greek Heroes, Mollie McLean, Anne Wilseman
Gods, Men and Monsters From the Greek Myths, Michael Gibson, Giovanni Caselli

INTERNET

We suggest the following sites on the Internet (all Web sites are subject to change.)

For more about ancient Greece:
http://members.aol.com/Donnclass/Greeklife.html

For more about Greek, Roman, and Celtic myths and art:
http://www.loggia.com/myth/myth.html

We *strongly recommend* that you preview these sites before you send students to them.

◆Literary Focus

6 Myth Point out that Zeus must choose between saving the Earth and rescuing Phaëthon. Ask students what lesson can be learned from this myth. *Students may have learned that it is dangerous to be arrogant and to rush impulsively into a risky situation.*

Reinforce and Extend

Answers

◆Literature and Your Life

Reader's Response Students may recall times they have failed to take the advice of a friend, teacher, or parent and been sorry.

Thematic Focus He rejects the advice because he is arrogant, stubborn, and takes unnecessary risks.

☑ Check Your Comprehension

1. He seeks proof that he is Apollo's son.
2. Apollo knows that Phaëthon's choice is dangerous.
3. He wants to become a god.
4. The chariot goes too close to Earth and Zeus must save Earth.
5. It explains the rising and setting of the sun.

◆Critical Thinking

1. It shows that he is arrogant and driven to take risks to prove himself.
2. He insists on proving Epaphos wrong, and on driving the chariot in spite of Apollo's advice.
3. People might have treated him differently and he would have had less to brag about.
4. The story teaches the dangers of false pride.
5. He might have tried to help his son without making a promise.
6. As Earth rotates on its axis, it exposes its surface to the sun.

Develop Understanding

One-Minute Insight "Demeter and Persephone" explains the Earth's seasons. When Pluto, king of the underworld, appears on Earth, Eros causes him to fall in love with Persephone. Pluto kidnaps Persephone and carries her away. When she is unable to find her daughter, Demeter, goddess of the harvest, becomes angry and makes the Earth infertile. Because humankind is threatened with starvation, Zeus asks for Persephone's release—upon the condition that she has not tasted food in the underworld. Pluto reluctantly agrees. Unfortunately, Persephone has tasted four pomegranate seeds, so she must return to Pluto for four months of every year while her mother grieves. These months are known as winter. During the months she is home, the soil is fertile and productive.

▶Critical Viewing◀

1 Analyze *Demeter, the goddess of the harvest is wearing wheat stalks in her hair.*

◆Literary Focus

2 Myth Ask students what natural event these sentences might describe. *They describe a volcano or earthquake.*

Demeter and Persephone

Anne Terry White

Demeter Mourning for Persephone, 1906, Evelyn de Morgan, The De Morgan Foundation, London

1 ▲ **Critical Viewing** What symbols in this painting convey Demeter's role as goddess of the harvest? **[Analyze]**

Humanities: Art

Demeter Mourning for Persephone, by Evelyn de Morgan (1855–1919)

After studying at the Slade School of Fine Art in London, Evelyn de Morgan visited Italy, where her artist uncle lived. There, she became an admirer of Boticelli, whose influence can be seen in her use of soft, frescolike colors. Like *Demeter Mourning for Persephone,* many of de Morgan's paintings show only one or two figures, which are placed on the landscape rather than being incorporated into it. De Morgan is perhaps best known for her artworks showing events from classical mythology. Ask students which event in the story the painting depicts. What clues support their ideas? *In the painting Demeter is shown on her knees with her shoulders and head lowered. This depiction shows her grieving after she has discovered that her daughter is missing, and before she avenges the loss.*

Deep under Mt. Aetna, the gods had
buried alive a number of fearful, fire-
breathing giants. The monsters heaved
and struggled to get free. And so mightily
2 did they shake the earth that Pluto, the
king of the underworld, was alarmed.

"They may tear the rocks asunder and leave the realm of the dead open to the light of day," he thought. And mounting his golden chariot, he went up to see what damage had been done.

Now the goddess of love and beauty, fair
Aphrodite,[1] was sitting on a mountainside
3 playing with her son, Eros.[2] She saw Pluto
as he drove around with his coal-black
horses and she said:

"My son, there is one who defies your power and mine. Quick! Take up your darts! Send an arrow into the breast of that dark monarch. Let him, too, feel the pangs of love. Why should he alone escape them?"

At his mother's words, Eros leaped lightly to his feet. He chose from his quiver[3] his sharpest and truest arrow, fitted it to his bow, drew the string, and shot straight into Pluto's heart.

The grim King had seen fair maids
enough in the gloomy underworld over
which he ruled. But never had his heart
been touched. Now an unaccustomed
warmth stole through his veins. His stern
eyes softened. Before him was a blossom-
ing valley, and along its edge a charming
girl was gathering flowers. She was Persephone,[4] daughter of Demeter,[5] goddess of
4 the harvest. She had strayed from her
companions, and now that her basket
overflowed with blossoms, she was filling
her apron with lilies and violets. The god
looked at Persephone and loved her at once. With one sweep of his arm he caught her up and drove swiftly away.

"Mother!" she screamed, while the flowers fell from her apron and strewed the ground. "Mother!"

And she called on her companions by name. But already they were out of sight, so fast did Pluto urge the horses on. In a few moments they were at the River Cyane.[6] Persephone struggled, her loosened girdle[7] fell to the ground, but the god held her tight. He struck the bank with his trident.[8] The earth opened, and darkness swallowed them all—horses, chariot, Pluto, and weeping Persephone.

From end to end of the earth Demeter sought her daughter. But none could tell her where Persephone was. At last, worn out and despairing, the goddess returned to Sicily. She stood by the River Cyane, where Pluto had cleft[9] the earth and gone down into his own dominions.

Now a river nymph[10] had seen him carry
off his prize. She wanted to tell Demeter
where her daughter was, but fear of Pluto
kept her dumb. Yet she had picked up the 5
girdle Persephone had dropped, and this
the nymph wafted[11] on the waves to the
feet of Demeter.

The goddess knew then that her daughter was gone indeed, but she did not suspect Pluto of carrying her off. She laid the blame on the innocent land.

1. **Aphrodite** (af′ rə dīt′ ē)
2. **Eros** (er′ äs): In Greek mythology, the god of love. identified by the Romans with Cupid.
3. **quiver** (kwiv′ ər) *n.*: Case for arrows.
4. **Persephone** (pər sef′ ə nē)
5. **Demeter** (di mēt′ ər)
6. **River Cyane** (sī′ an): A river in Sicily, an island just south of Italy.
7. **girdle** (gər′ dəl) *n.*: Belt or sash for the waist.
8. **trident** (trīd′ ənt) *n.*: Spear with three points.
9. **cleft** (kleft) *v.*: Split or opened.
10. **river nymph** (nimf): Goddess living in a river.
11. **wafted** (wäft′ əd) *v.*: Carried.

◆ Build Vocabulary

dominions (də min′ yənz) *n.*: Regions over which someone rules

◆Reading Strategy

3 Predict Explain to students that Eros, the god of love, shoots gold-tipped arrows that cause people to fall in love. Ask students to predict what will happen in the story. *Students should predict that Pluto will fall in love.*

◆Critical Thinking

4 Analyze Ask students how the author wanted the reader to feel about Persephone when she wrote this description. *This description of a young woman surrounded by the freshness of newly picked flowers and separated from her companions portrays an image of someone who is both beautiful and vulnerable.*

Clarification

5 In mythology, nymphs are minor gods who appear as beautiful maidens. Nymphs live, and sometimes personify, parts of nature such as rivers, trees, and mountains. The nymph may be frightened to speak to Demeter because she is only a minor god.

Customize for *English Language Learners*

Students may be unfamiliar with some words and phrases in this selection. By using gestures and drawings, review unfamiliar words before they read: "tear asunder," "dark monarch," "stole through his veins," "strewed the ground," "kept her dumb," "sweet pulp," "fare you well."

Cross-Curricular Connection: Social Studies

Greece has long been a popular travel destination because remainders of its ancient civilization can be found everywhere—ruins, broken columns, ancient walls, amphitheaters, and sacred grounds.

The country of Greece consists of a peninsula and approximately 1400 islands, only 169 of which are inhabited. The islands of Greece are very rocky and mountainous. Even so, almost one fourth of the people earn their living in agriculture.

The climate is generally very hot and dry during the summers and mild and wet during winters, but it varies from place to place in the islands. Most precipitation that falls during the year occurs in the wintertime.

The Greeks have a reputation for hospitality and friendliness and a great capacity for enjoying life. Many traditions celebrated in Greece take the form of festivals with dancing, feasting, and singing. Religion is important, with the majority of the population belonging to the Greek Orthodox Church.

◆Literary Focus

1 Myths *In this myth, Demeter's grief causes her to take revenge on the earth. The droughts and floods that she creates result in plagues, hunger, and diseases, which is how ancient Greeks explained these disasters.*

◆Reading Strategy

2 Predict Ask students what they think might happen next, since Zeus knows where Persephone is. *Students may predict that Zeus will intervene in some way and bring Persephone back.*

◆Critical Thinking

3 Connect Ask students how Zeus' actions in this myth are similar to his actions in "Phaëthon, Son of Apollo." *Students may say that in "Phaëthon, Son of Apollo," Zeus saves Earth from the burning sun. In this myth, Zeus again saves Earth—this time from droughts and floods.*

Clarification

4 In many advertisements, the Greek god Hermes, who has wings on his hat and feet, serves as a symbol of a speedy messenger. Advertisers sometimes choose this god to sell products because Hermes is known for his speed and ingenuity.

Customize for *Less Proficient Readers*

Direct attention to Zeus' speech, "Descend to the underworld, my son. . . ." Guide students to use context clues to understand the meanings of the words, *descend* and *bid*.

"Ungrateful soil!" she said. "I made you fertile. I clothed you in grass and nourishing grain, and this is how you reward me. No more shall you enjoy my favors!"

That year was the most cruel mankind had ever known. Nothing prospered, nothing grew. The cattle died, the seed would not come up, men and oxen toiled in vain.
1 There was too much sun. There was too much rain. Thistles[12] and weeds were the only things that grew.
2 It seemed that all mankind would die of hunger.

> **◆ Literary Focus**
> How did the ancient Greeks explain natural disasters, such as drought and disease?

"This cannot go on," said mighty Zeus. "I see that I must intervene." And one by one he sent the gods and goddesses to plead with Demeter.

But she had the same answer for all: "Not till I see my daughter shall the earth bear fruit again."

Zeus, of course, knew well where Persephone was. He did not like to take from his brother the one joyful thing in his life, but he saw that he must if the race of man was to be preserved. So he called Hermes[13] to him and said:

3 "Descend to the underworld, my son. Bid Pluto release his bride. Provided she has not tasted food in the realm of the dead, she may return to her mother forever."

4 Down sped Hermes on his winged feet, and there in the dim palace of the king, he found Persephone by Pluto's side. She was pale and joyless. Not all the glittering treasures of the underworld could bring a smile to her lips.

"You have no flowers here," she would say to her husband when he pressed gems upon her. "Jewels have no fragrance. I do not want them."

When she saw Hermes and heard his message, her heart leaped within her. Her cheeks grew rosy and her eyes sparkled, for she knew that Pluto would not dare to disobey his brother's command. She sprang up, ready to go at once. Only one thing troubled her—that she could not leave the underworld forever. For she had accepted a pomegranate[14] from Pluto and sucked the sweet pulp from four of the seeds.

With a heavy heart Pluto made ready his golden car.[15] He helped Persephone in while Hermes took up the reins.

"Dear wife," said the King, and his voice trembled as he spoke, "think kindly of me, I pray you. For indeed I love you truly. It will be lonely here these eight months you are away. And if you think mine is a gloomy palace to return to, at least remember that your husband is great among the immortals. So fare you well—and get your fill of flowers!"

Straight to the temple of Demeter at Eleusis, Hermes drove the black horses. The goddess heard the chariot wheels and, as a deer bounds over the hills, she ran out swiftly to meet her daughter. Persephone flew to her mother's arms. And the sad tale of each turned into joy in the telling.

So it is to this day. One third of the year Persephone spends in the gloomy abode of Pluto—one month for each seed that she tasted. Then Nature dies, the leaves fall,
the earth stops bringing forth. In spring 5
Persephone returns, and with her come the flowers, followed by summer's fruitfulness and the rich harvest of fall.

---

12. **thistles** (this´ əlz) *n.*: Stubborn, weedy plants with sharp leaves and usually purplish flowers.
13. **Hermes** (hʉr´ mēz): A god who served as a messenger.
14. **pomegranate** (päm´ gran´ it) *n.*: Round fruit with a red leathery rind and many seeds.
15. **car** (kär) *n.*: Chariot.

Cultural Connection

Word Origins Greek mythology has influenced many words and names in the English language. Ask students to consider the Greek god *Apollo*, a powerful god who drove a chariot across the sky, and the NASA space missions named for him. *Jupiter, Mars,* and *Pluto* are planets in our solar system, named for mythological characters. *Venus* is the name of the Evening Star seen in the Northern Hemisphere.

Discuss some of the following word origins. A large undertaking is said to be *herculean*. An area of vulnerability is an *Achilles'* heel. The word *panic* comes from the shepherd god *Pan*. The *Midas* touch refers to the ability to make money. Something huge is said to be *titanic*, from the *Titans*.

Suggest that students look up the definitions of other words from mythology: *echo, nemesis,* and *narcissism*, for example. Interested students can work together to create an illustrated word origins dictionary, which includes words from Greek mythology.

Beyond Literature

Science Connection

The Reasons for the Seasons
The ancient Greeks explained the changing seasons with the story of "Demeter and Persephone." Today, scientists explain these changes differently. The Earth completes one revolution around the sun during the course of a year. As the Earth travels, its tilt causes different parts of its surface to receive more of the sun's light. This tilt pushes part of the Earth toward the sun and the rest away from the sun. In regions getting more sunlight, it is summer. In areas tilting away from the sun's rays, it is winter. At the equator, where the tilting has little effect and the sun's rays remain constant, there is no winter.

Cross-Curricular Activity
Chart the Movements Learn more about how the relationship of the Earth and sun affect the seasons. For example, research the seasonal changes that occur at the North and South poles. Determine what causes autumn and spring. Then, find out what other factors affect seasonal changes. For example, why are places like Iceland, which should be very cold in winter, still mild? Create a poster or a three-dimensional model to demonstrate your findings.

Guide for Responding

◆ Literature and Your Life

Reader's Response For whom do you feel sorrier—Persephone or Pluto? Explain.

Thematic Focus In what way can myths help readers learn truths about life?

Map Search Locate Greece on a world map. What do you think winter is like in this part of the world?

☑ Check Your Comprehension

1. What motivates Pluto to take Persephone to his kingdom?
2. What does Demeter do when she discovers her daughter is lost?
3. How is the situation resolved?
4. How does nature change as Persephone moves between the earth and the underworld?

◆ Critical Thinking

Interpret

1. Why is Persephone unhappy in the underworld? **[Interpret]**
2. What does Pluto's nickname, "the grim King," suggest about his emotional outlook on the world? **[Analyze]**
3. How does Demeter feel when she cannot find her daughter? **[Infer]**
4. How might their experiences in this myth change each of the three main characters? **[Analyze Cause and Effect; Speculate]**

Apply

5. How do the powerful emotions of the three main characters account for the changing of the seasons? **[Synthesize]**

Compare Literary Works

6. How might the myths about Phaëthon and Demeter and Persephone work together to explain changes in nature for the Greeks? **[Connect]**

◆Critical Thinking

Analyze Ask students why they think that Zeus makes it a condition that Persephone may not return to her mother if she has eaten food in the underworld. *Zeus wants to be fair to his brother; he knows that he truly loves Persephone.*

◆Literary Focus

5 Myth Ask students how the explanation of the seasons may have reassured the Ancient Greeks and helped them to understand their world, even though the information is not based on scientific knowledge. *The myth of Persephone reassured them that spring can indeed be depended on to return each year.*

Beyond Literature

Science Connection

To allow more time for the hands-on part of this activity, you may want to have encyclopedias, science books, and books about the solar system available in the classroom rather than requiring students to locate their own references.

Reinforce and Extend

Answers

◆Literature and Your Life

Reader's Response Some may point out that Persephone is an innocent victim, or that Pluto loses the only person he has ever loved.

Thematic Focus Readers can often identify with the lessons learned by characters in myths.

☑ Check Your Comprehension

1. He falls in love with her when he is struck by Eros' arrow.
2. She blames the land for her daughter's disappearance and makes it infertile.
3. Zeus intervenes.
4. When Persephone goes home, spring, summer, and fall occur. When she returns to Pluto, it is winter.

◆Critical Thinking

1. There are no flowers and she misses her mother.
2. He views the world with suspicion and anger.
3. She feels sad, then becomes angry.
4. Persephone might become more grateful for what she has; Pluto might become more loving; Demeter might become less vengeful.
5. When Persephone returns to the underworld, Demeter grieves and vegetation dies. When Persephone returns to earth, her mother's joy brings life back to the fields.
6. "Phaëthon, Son of Apollo" explains night and day. "Demeter and Persephone" explains the seasons.

Develop Understanding

One-Minute Insight The main character in "Narcissus" suffers when he fails to learn important lessons about love. When Narcissus spurns a woman's love, she curses him and hopes that he will love in vain. Her wish is granted by the avenging goddess, Nemesis: Narcissus falls in love with his own reflection in a pool, and cannot return the love of the nymph Echo, who can only repeat the words of love he speaks to his reflection. Narcissus becomes ill with longing and finally dies. When Echo brings other nymphs to weep over his body, they find a single flower in his place. Eventually, Echo pines away as well, until nothing is left but her voice.

◆Literary Focus

❶ **Myth** Ask students to identify the weakness of the main character as revealed in this paragraph. *Although Narcissus is loved by all, his pride lets him love no one in return.*

◆Reading Strategy

❷ **Predict** *Students should recognize that because this is a myth, Narcissus' flaw will have to be punished in some way.*

▶Critical Viewing◀

❸ **Interpret** *This painting conveys Narcissus' vanity because he is gazing at his own reflection, completely absorbed in himself and how beautiful he is.*

Customize for
Visual/Spatial Learners
Students may be interested in seeing a picture of a narcissus flower to help them visualize the ending of the myth.

NARCISSUS

Jay Macpherson

Narcissus at the Spring, Caravaggio, Scala

▲ **Critical Viewing** What personality traits does this painting of Narcissus convey? Explain. **[Interpret]** ❸

❶ As beautiful as Adonis[1] was the ill-fated Narcissus,[2] who from his childhood was loved by all who saw him but whose pride would let him love no one in return. At last one of those who had hopelessly courted him turned and cursed him, exclaiming: "May he suffer as we have suffered! May he too love in vain!" The avenging goddess Nemesis[3] heard and approved this prayer.

There was nearby a clear pool, with shining silvery waters. No shepherd had ever come there, nor beast nor bird nor falling branch marred its surface: the grass grew fresh and green around it, and the sheltering woods kept it always cool from the midday sun.

Here once came Narcissus, heated and tired from the chase, and lay down by the pool to drink. As he bent over the water, his eyes met the eyes of another young man, gazing up at him from the depth of the pool. Deluded by his reflection, Narcissus fell in love with the beauty that was his own. Without thought of food or rest he lay beside the pool addressing cries and pleas to the image, whose lips moved as he spoke but whose reply he could never catch. Echo came by, the most constant of his disdained lovers. She was a nymph who had once angered Hera, the wife of Zeus, by talking too much, and in consequence was deprived of the use of her tongue for ordinary conversation: all she could do was repeat the last words of others. Seeing

❷ **◆ Reading Strategy** What do you predict will happen to Narcissus because of his vanity and pride?

1. **Adonis** (ə dän′ is): Handsome young man loved by Aphrodite, the goddess of love.
2. **Narcissus** (när sis′ əs)
3. **Nemesis** (nem′ ə sis)

Humanities: Art

Narcissus at the Spring, by Caravaggio (1573–1610)

Caravaggio is best known for his stunning use of the chiaroscuro technique, which strongly contrasts light and dark. His work influenced other important painters such as Rembrandt.

Caravaggio depicts Narcissus against a very dark background with light shining on him, almost like a spotlight. Narcissus stares intently at his reflection in a pool of water—obviously engrossed. His strong arms, which support him on either side, add symmetry to the painting. Use the following questions for discussion:

1. How does Caravaggio use light and shadow to convey his ideas? *He shows Narcissus in light, while his reflection is in darkness. Students may say that this difference emphasizes that the object of Narcissus' affection is lifeless.*
2. Why do you think that Caravaggio left Echo out of his depiction of the story? *Including her image would have taken away from the main story, which is that of Narcissus.*

Narcissus lying there, she pleaded with him in his own words. "I will die unless you pity me," cried Narcissus to his beloved. "Pity me," cried Echo as vainly to hers. Narcissus never raised his eyes to her at all, though she remained day after day beside him on the bank, pleading as well as she was able. At last she pined away, withering and wasting with unrequited[4] love, till nothing was left of her but her voice, which the traveler still hears calling unexpectedly in woods and waste places.

As for the cruel Narcissus, he fared no better. The face that looked back at him from the water became pale, thin and haggard,[5] till at last poor Echo caught and repeated his last "Farewell!" But when she came with the other nymphs to lament over his body, it was nowhere to be found. Instead, over the pool bent a new flower, white with a yellow center, which they called by his name. From this flower the Furies, the avengers of guilt, twist garlands to bind their hateful brows.

4. **unrequited** (un ri kwīt´ əd) *adj.*: Unreturned.
5. **haggard** (hag´ ərd) *adj.*: Looking worn from grief or illness.

◆ Build Vocabulary

avenging (ə venj´ iŋ) *adj.*: Taking revenge for an injury or wrong

deluded (di lo͞od´ əd) *adj.*: Fooled; misled

lament (lə ment´) *v.*: Express deep sorrow for; mourn

Guide for Responding

◆ Literature and Your Life

Reader's Response Do you think Narcissus receives a fitting punishment? Why or why not?

Thematic Focus In this myth, Narcissus pays a huge price to learn his lesson. How else might Narcissus have been taught to love others?

Journal Writing Write about a time when you were proud of your skills or personal qualities. How did your pride affect the situation?

✓ Check Your Comprehension

1. What does Narcissus do that causes him to be cursed?
2. How does Narcissus finally fall in love?
3. In what way has Echo's voice been changed and why?
4. How are Echo and Narcissus changed at the end of the myth?

◆ Critical Thinking

INTERPRET

1. Why is it appropriate that Narcissus becomes a flower? **[Interpret; Support]**
2. Explain how the myth's effect would be different if Narcissus simply died, without undergoing a magical change. **[Speculate]**
3. What does this myth suggest about the risks of human pride? **[Draw Conclusions]**
4. What two facts of nature are explained by this myth? **[Connect]**

APPLY

5. Do you think there is a little bit of Narcissus in each of us? Explain. **[Relate; Generalize]**

COMPARE LITERARY WORKS

6. Which of these myths—"Phaëthon, Son of Apollo," "Demeter and Persephone," or "Narcissus"—offers the most appealing explanation of a natural occurrence? **[Evaluate]**

Beyond the Selection

FURTHER READING

Works About Greek Culture

The Greek News, Anton Powell
The Greeks (Look Into the Past), Susan Williams

Works About Mythology From Around the World

Greek and Roman Mythology A to Z: A Young Reader's Companion, Kathleen N. Daly
Demons and Dragons: Myths of China, Japan and India, Stewart Roos
African Myths and Legends, Kathleen Arnott
Chinese Myths and Fantasies, Cyril Burch

INTERNET

We suggest the following sites on the Internet (all Web sites are subject to change.)

For more on Greek Culture:
http://www.culture.gr/welcome.html

For more on Mythology around the world:
http://webhome.idirect.com/~donlong/
or
http://pibweb.it.nwu.edu/~pib/myth.htm

We *strongly recommend* that you preview these sites before you send students to them.

◆ Literature and Your Life

Suggest that students think about whether people who are self-centered like Narcissus harm their relationships with other people. Ask students what advice they might give such a person. *They may suggest being a good listener, or learning to put oneself in another's position.*

Reinforce and Extend

Answers

◆ Literature and Your Life

Reader's Response Some students may say that his punishment is warranted; others may say he probably has good qualities.

Thematic Focus He could have been taught to be aware of others' feelings and to feel compassion for them.

✓ Check Your Comprehension

1. He doesn't return a woman's love.
2. He sees his reflection in a pool.
3. Echo's voice can only repeat others' words as a punishment.
4. Echo pines away until only her voice is left, and Narcissus becomes a flower.

◆ Critical Thinking

1. Like Narcissus, flowers are beautiful but don't last long.
2. If Narcissus simply died, the myth would not teach a lesson.
3. Human pride can alienate people from others, which is harmful.
4. It explains echoes and the flower called the narcissus.
5. Students may point out that as very young children, we are selfish and only want to fulfill our own desires. This tendency can reappear at various times throughout life.
6. Possible answer: "Narcissus" offers the most appealing explanation because it gives a reason for the transient but extraordinary beauty of flowers.

Develop Understanding

One-Minute Insight

In the myth of "Icarus and Daedalus," a boy's impulsive nature brings about harsh consequences. Daedalus, once the master architect for King Minos, finds himself imprisoned on an island along with his son, Icarus. In order to escape, Daedalus puts his inventive mind to work and creates wings from feathers, thread, and wax. As he attaches the wings to Icarus' back, he warns his son not to fly too close to the sun. However, Icarus, preoccupied with the wonder of flight, barely hears his father's warning. Predictably, he soars too close to the sun, melts his wings, and crashes into the sea.

❶ **Clarification** In ancient times, rulers ordered the construction of labyrinths to baffle their enemies. Similar to mazes, these structures were composed of an intricate series of passageways and chambers, with branched paths that led nowhere, or one long circuitous path that led to a central point.

Customize for
Verbal/Linguistic Learners
Remind students that myths helped ancient people explain their beliefs about right and wrong. As students read, have them consider how the myth supports, or does not support, their own principles of fairness. After reading, have interested students write a paper discussing their findings.

Daedalus and Icarus, French colored engraving, 1660

Humanities: Art

Daedalus and Icarus, French colored engraving, 1660

Before the age of technology, bookmakers often used prints called engravings to illustrate their books. To create an engraving, the artist uses a sharp tool to cut a design into a plate made of wood or metal. Next, the plate is inked and wiped clean so that ink remains only in the cut lines. The plate is placed on a press with dampened paper on top of it. When the plate and paper are passed through a press, the image is transferred to the paper. Many prints can be made from a single plate.

This engraving shows Icarus falling into the sea while Daedalus watches. Use the following questions for discussion:

1. How does the artist emphasize the sun? *The sun is the brightest point in the image; a pattern of lines radiating from this bright shape depicts the rays that burn the wings of Icarus.*
2. How does the image capture the tragedy of this myth? *It shows a boy tumbling to his death as his father, who feels responsible, watches.*

ICARUS and DAEDALUS

Josephine Preston Peabody

Among all those mortals who grew so wise that they learned the secrets of the gods, none was more cunning[1] than Daedalus.[2]

He once built, for King Minos of Crete,[3] a wonderful Labyrinth[4] of winding ways so cunningly tangled up and twisted around that, once inside, you could never find your way out again without a magic clue. ❶ But the king's favor veered[5] with the wind, and one day he had his master architect imprisoned in a tower. Daedalus managed to escape from his cell; ❷ but it seemed impossible to leave the island, since every ship that came or went was well guarded by order of the king.

At length, watching the sea-gulls in the air—the only creatures that were sure of liberty—he thought of a plan for himself and his young son Icarus,[6] who was captive with him. ❸

1. **cunning** (kun′ iŋ) *adj.*: Skillful; clever.
2. **Daedalus** (ded′ əl əs)
3. **King Minos** (mī′ nəs) **of Crete**: King Minos was a son of the god Zeus. Crete is a Greek island in the eastern Mediterranean Sea, southeast of Greece.
4. **Labyrinth** (lab′ ə rinth′) *n.*: Maze.
5. **veered** (vird) *v.*: Changed directions.
6. **Icarus** (ik′ ə rəs)

◀ Critical Viewing Use the title of this myth, your knowledge of Greek mythology, and this illustration to predict what will happen to the two mortals in the story. **[Predict]** ❹

◆Critical Thinking

❷ Analyze Causes and Effects Ask students why Daedalus cannot leave the island. *He is imprisoned on the island because he has lost favor with the king.*

◆Critical Thinking

❸ Infer Ask students why they think Daedalus associates sea gulls with liberty. *The birds are independent and can fly freely.*

▶Critical Viewing◀

❹ Predict *Students now know that the story is about a father and son who are held captive on an island. Because the illustration shows a man flying steadily while a boy dives toward the water, students may predict that the man and boy try to fly off the island, and the boy drowns.*

Cross-Curricular Connection: Social Studies

The Palace of Minos and the Minotaur In Greek mythology, King Minos asked Daedalus to construct a prison from which no one could escape. In response, Daedalus designed the labyrinth in Knossos, on the island of Crete. Each year, King Minos punished the people of Athens, who were responsible for the death of his son, by requiring them to send seven young men and seven young women to be eaten by the Minotaur, a dreadful monster that was half man and half bull. The Minotaur was finally killed by the Athenian hero Theseus.

Remind students that although myths are fictional, they are based on aspects of reality. The story may have been based on a real palace located in Knossos, called the Palace of Minos. The sprawling structure with winding corridors was excavated from 1900–1905 by Sir Arthur Evans. It is one of the finest surviving examples of Minoan architecture and has been extensively restored. Students who are interested in architecture may want to find pictures of the restored palace, or other Greek buildings and ruins, to share with the class.

◆Critical Thinking

❶ **Compare and Contrast** Ask students what comparison is made in this sentence. *When Daedalus tries to fly, he moves his arms through the air like a swimmer moving his arms through the water.*

◆Literary Focus

❷ **Myths** Challenge students to think of a character from a previous selection who behaved in a similar manner. What happened to this character? *Like Icarus, Phaëthon paid no attention to his father's warnings. He drove the chariot of the sun too close to Earth and was killed.*

◆Reading Strategy

❸ **Predict** Discuss with students how Icarus reacts to flying. *He is so joyful that he forgets his father's warnings. Students will probably predict that he will fly too close to the sun or too close to Earth.*

◆Literature and Your Life

Point out that in these myths, youthful characters, Phaëthon, Narcissus, and Icarus, make mistakes that cost them their lives. Ask students if they feel that these stories may have been told by adults in ancient Greece to warn their children of life's dangers. If so, how is their message similar to one that might be conveyed by today's adults? *Students might point out that the myths may have helped young Greeks to think twice about making impulsive and dangerous decisions, a message that is as relevant today as it was in ancient times. Challenge students to give examples.*

Little by little, he gathered a store of feathers great and small. He fastened these together with thread, molded them in with wax, and so fashioned two great wings like those of a bird. When they were done, Daedalus fitted them to his own
❶ shoulders, and after one or two efforts, he found that by waving his arms he could winnow[7] the air and cleave it, as a swimmer does the sea. He held himself aloft, wavered this way and that with the wind, and at last, like a great fledgling,[8] he learned to fly.

Without delay, he fell to work on a pair of wings for the boy Icarus, and taught him carefully how to use them, bidding him beware of rash adventures among the stars. "Remember," said the father, "never to fly very low or very high, for the fogs about the earth would weigh you down, but the blaze of the sun will surely melt your feathers apart if you go too near."

For Icarus, these cautions went in at one ear and out by the other. Who could remember to be careful when he was to fly
❷ for the first time? Are birds careful? Not they! And not an idea remained in the boy's head but the one joy of escape.

The day came, and the fair wind that was to set them free. The father bird put on his wings, and, while the light urged them to be gone, he waited to see that all was well with Icarus, for the two could not fly hand in hand. Up they rose, the boy after his father. The hateful ground of Crete sank beneath them; and the country folk, who caught a glimpse of them when they were high above the treetops, took it for a vision of the gods—Apollo, perhaps, with Cupid after him.

At first there was a terror in the joy. The wide vacancy of the air dazed them—a glance downward made their brains reel.

7. **winnow** (win′ ō) *v.*: Beat as with wings.
8. **fledgling** (flej′ liŋ) *n.*: Young bird.

But when a great wind filled their wings, and Icarus felt himself sustained, like a halcyon bird[9] in the hollow of a wave, like a child uplifted by his mother, he forgot everything in the world but joy. He forgot Crete and the other islands that he had passed over: he saw but vaguely that wingèd thing in the distance before him that was his father Daedalus. He longed for one draft of flight to quench the thirst of his captivity: he stretched out his arms to the sky and made towards the highest heavens.

> **◆ Reading Strategy**
> Predict what will happen as the result of Icarus' failure to follow his father's instructions. ❸

Alas for him! Warmer and warmer grew the air. Those arms, that had seemed to uphold him, relaxed. His wings wavered, drooped. He fluttered his young hands vainly—he was falling—and in that terror he remembered. The heat of the sun had melted the wax from his wings; the feathers were falling, one by one, like snowflakes; and there was none to help.

He fell like a leaf tossed down the wind, down, down, with one cry that overtook Daedalus far away. When he returned, and sought high and low for his poor boy, he saw nothing but the birdlike feathers afloat on the water, and he knew that Icarus was drowned.

The nearest island he named Icaria, in memory of the child; but he, in heavy grief, went to the temple of Apollo in Sicily, and there hung up his wings as an offering. Never again did he attempt to fly.

9. **halcyon** (hal′ sē ən) **bird** *n.*: Legendary bird, identified with the kingfisher, which could calm the sea by resting on it.

◆ Build Vocabulary

vacancy (vā′ kən sē) *n.*: Emptiness
sustained (sə stānd′) *adj.*: Supported

Speaking and Listening Mini-Lesson

Radio Advice Show

This mini-lesson supports the Speaking and Listening Activity in the Idea Bank on page 869.

Introduce Discuss with students problems faced by the characters in these myths that are similar to those faced by modern people.

Develop Have groups of students select a myth and list each character's traits. Have them examine the list to determine:

- what each characters wants
- how the character goes about getting it
- if another method would be more successful
- advice from which the character could benefit

Apply Ask each group to list questions that the characters might ask a talk show host, and possible responses. Have them select someone to be the talk show host, while the others "phone in" questions.

Assess Evaluate students' presentations on how well they capture the characters' conflicts. Do their questions show an awareness of the story's meaning? Do their answers show an understanding of the Greek's beliefs about right and wrong?

Beyond Literature

Art Connection

Leonardo da Vinci's Flying Machines Daedalus wasn't the only man to ever attempt flight. People have wanted to fly since the beginning of time. In the 1440's, Italian artist and inventor Leonardo da Vinci worked long and hard to design a human flying machine. He sketched wings that could attach to a person, who would then generate power by flapping his or her arms. In time, Da Vinci gave up on human-powered flight and began to design other flying machines, such as the flying screw, a predecessor of today's helicopter.

Cross-Curricular Connection
Sketch Your Way to the Sky Forget about airplanes and rockets—invent your own flying machine. As you plan your machine, consider the story of Icarus and Daedalus. Think about how the weight of fog affects Icarus' flight and what happens when air can penetrate his wings. Explore different ways to power your machine. Then, sketch your ideas and build your machine from clay, balsa wood, or another medium. Display your finished model, along with those of classmates, in a school hallway.

Guide for Responding

◆ Literature and Your Life

Reader's Response In the same situation, would you have done what Icarus did? Why or why not?

Thematic Focus Do you think that Daedalus was punished by the gods for taking too much pride in his own cleverness? Explain.

Sketch Make a sketch of Icarus—either in his moment of joyful flight or as he realizes his mistake.

☑ Check Your Comprehension

1. Where is Daedalus when the story begins?
2. How does Daedalus plan to escape?
3. Who is Icarus?
4. Summarize the warning Daedalus gives to Icarus.
5. What happens to Icarus at the end of the myth?

◆ Critical Thinking

Interpret

1. In what ways does Daedalus display his "cunning"? **[Analyze]**
2. What does Daedalus reveal about himself in his words to his son? **[Infer]**
3. Icarus flies too close to the sun. What do his actions reveal about his character? **[Infer]**
4. Compare and contrast the reactions of Icarus and Daedalus to the experience of flying. **[Compare and Contrast]**
5. What lesson does this myth teach? **[Draw Conclusions]**

Apply

6. What does the myth suggest about the way people change as they age? **[Generalize]**

Extend

7. To what modern-day professions would Icarus and Daedalus be well suited? Explain. **[Career Link]**

Beyond Literature

Encourage students to look at pictures of a variety of flying machines, such as helicopters, airplanes, and spacecraft, as well as flying animals—dragonflies, wasps, birds, and flying squirrels—before sketching ideas.

Reinforce and Extend

Answers

◆ Literature and Your Life

Reader's Response Students may say that flying would be such fun that they would forget their parent's advice. Others may say that flying might be so frightening that they would be very careful.

Thematic Focus Greek mythology suggests that the gods punish humans for daring too much or for reaching too high.

☑ Check Your Comprehension

1. He is in a tower prison on an island.
2. He builds wings to escape by flying away.
3. Icarus is his son.
4. Don't fly too high near the sun or too low near the water.
5. He flies too close to the sun, loses his wings, and falls into the ocean.

◆ Critical Thinking

1. He designs the Labyrinth and wings.
2. He reveals his life experience, his cautious nature, and his love for his son.
3. He is impulsive. To him, having fun is more important than being careful.
4. Daedalus is cautious; Icarus is adventurous.
5. The myth teaches the importance of caution.
6. It suggests that people learn to be more careful as they grow older.
7. Icarus' adventurous spirit would make him a good astronaut, pilot, or inventor; Daedalus' vision would make him a good engineer or scientist.

Beyond the Selection

FURTHER READING

Other Works by the Authors

The Golden Days of Greece, by Olivia E. Coolidge
The False Treaty, by Anne Terry White
Poems Told Twice: Containing the Boatman and Other Poems, by Jay Macpherson

Other Works About Inventions

100 Inventions That Shaped World History, Bill Yenne
World in the Time of Leonardo DaVinci, Fiona MacDonald
DaVinci: The Painter Who Spoke With Birds, Yves Pinguilly

INTERNET

We suggest the following site on the Internet (all Web sites are subject to change).

To learn more about Greek mythology:
http://www.pantheon.org/mythical/

We *strongly recommend* that you preview this site before you send students to it.

Answers

◆Reading Strategy

1. Zeus needs a solution to preserve the race of humankind, which indicates the need for a compromise.
2. Phaëthon is boastful and competitive, while Narcissus' pride will not allow him to love people. Both characters will learn a lesson.
3. Daedalus warns the boy against rash adventures. This indicates that he knows Icarus may behave recklessly.

◆Build Vocabulary

Word Root *-domin-*

dominant—most masterful
domain—a territory ruled by a master
dominates—is the master

Spelling Strategy

1. suede
2. persuade
3. suite

Using the Word Bank

1. The gods tried to *dissuade* the *mortals* in their *dominions* from *avenging* the gods' actions.
2. Narcissus was left in this condition to *lament* the sad results of his *deluded* self-love.
3. The *vacancy* created by Phaëthon's disappearance forced Clymene into a state of *sustained* grief.

◆Literary Focus

1. "Phaëthon, Son of Apollo": the rising and setting of the sun; the lack of forests in the Alps; the deserts of North Africa
   "Demeter and Persephone": seasonal changes, especially the lack of vegetation in the winter and its return in the spring
   "Narcissus": echoes; the flower, the narcissus
2. Possible response: In "Narcissus," it is Hera's anger that leads to the creation of echoes; in "Phaëthon, Son of Apollo," Apollo's love for his son leads him to make a promise that causes a lack of trees in the Alps and creates the deserts of North Africa.
3. These myths suggest that gods respect human limitations; that gods and humans have an interactive relationship; that people can learn from gods and gods perhaps can learn from people.

Guide for Responding *(continued)*

◆ Reading Strategy

PREDICT

By putting together the clues in a story or myth, you can **predict,** or make educated guesses about, what will happen next.

1. What clues in "Demeter and Persephone" helped you predict the ending of the myth?
2. How did the personality traits of both Phaëthon and Narcissus provide clues about their fates?
3. How does Daedalus' warning to Icarus provide a clue about Icarus' fate?

◆ Build Vocabulary

USING THE WORD ROOT *-domin-*

Complete the paragraph with the listed words containing the root *-domin-*. Explain how the meaning, "master," occurs in each.

dominates domain dominant

Zeus is the __?__ Greek god. He rules a __?__ of lesser gods and goddesses. Each of them __?__ a part of nature or human life.

SPELLING STRATEGY

In some words, like *dissuade*, the *sw* sound is spelled *su*. On your paper, complete the spelling of each word. Use the definitions as a guide.

1. soft and fuzzy type of leather: s _ _ de
2. to convince: pers _ _ de
3. two or more connected rooms: s _ _ te

USING THE WORD BANK

Write sentences according to the directions below. Use context to clearly demonstrate the meaning of the italicized words.

1. Use the words *mortal*, *dominions*, *dissuade*, and *avenging* to describe the relationship between the Greek gods and people.
2. Use the words *deluded* and *lament* to describe Narcissus.
3. Use the words *vacancy* and *sustained* to describe Clymene's reaction to Phaëthon's disappearance.

◆ Literary Focus

MYTH

People of many cultures have created **myths,** stories about gods or heroes, to explain natural occurrences or to express beliefs. Often in myths the explanation of natural occurrences has its roots in the actions of the gods and goddesses involved. The story "Demeter and Persephone," for example, explains why the Earth is unproductive in winter but blooms again in spring.

1. List the natural occurrences and objects that each of these myths explain.
2. Give an example from "Narcissus" and from "Phaëthon, Son of Apollo" of how a god or goddess's emotions resulted in a natural occurrence.
3. What beliefs about the relationship between humans and gods are expressed in these myths?

◆ Build Grammar Skills

COMMAS AFTER INTRODUCTORY PHRASES

Use a comma after **introductory phrases** in sentences. The phrases may be adjectives, adverbs, prepositional phrases, participial phrases, or appositive phrases. Notice the commas Josephine Preston Peabody uses after introductory phrases:

> *Little by little,* he gathered a store of feathers. . . .
> *Without delay,* he fell to work. . . .

Practice On your paper, rewrite each sentence, placing a comma after the introductory phrase.

1. Deep under Mt. Aetna the gods had buried alive a number of fearful, fire-breathing giants.
2. At his mother's words Eros leaped lightly to his feet.
3. Deluded by his reflection Narcissus fell in love with the beauty that was his own.
4. Crimson with rage the lad rushed home.
5. As for the cruel Narcissus he fared no better.

Writing Application On your paper, write sentences containing these introductory phrases.

1. Before you know it
2. After a while
3. Actually

◆Build Grammar Skills

Practice

1. Deep under Mt. Aetna, the gods had buried alive a number of fearful, fire-breathing giants.
2. At his mother's words, Eros leaped lightly to his feet.
3. Deluded by his reflection, Narcissus fell in love with the beauty that was his own.
4. Crimson with rage, the lad rushed home.
5. As for the cruel Narcissus, he fared no better.

Writing Application

Sample sentences:

1. Before you know it, I'll finish this myth.
2. After a while, Zeus decided to intervene.
3. Actually, Zeus has more power than Pluto.

Writer's Solution

Use the practice page, Commas That Set Off Added Elements, p. 100, in the *Writer's Solution Grammar Practice Book.* If students have access to technology, they can use the lesson on Commas in the Punctuation Unit in the *Writer's Solution Language Lab CD-ROM.*

Build Your Portfolio

Idea Bank

Writing

1. News Article Write a news article relating the events that occur in one of the myths. Make sure your article answers the reporter's basic questions: *who, what, when, where,* and *why.* **[Career Link]**

2. Autobiography Imagine that Icarus survived his fall and has lived for years in hiding. As the elderly Icarus, tell the story about your famous flight from your point of view.

3. Myth Compare and contrast two Greek myths that teach a lesson about human behavior. Use at least one myth from this grouping. Compare the lessons learned in the myths, and explain how the myths reflect the values and beliefs of ancient Greece.

Speaking and Listening

4. Oral Reading **[Group Activity]** With a small group, give a dramatic reading of a portion of one of the myths. After assigning roles, practice reading aloud the passages you've chosen. Present your group's interpretation of the myth to the class. **[Performing Arts Link]**

5. Radio Advice Show Using examples from these myths, create a radio advice show outlining acceptable human behavior in ancient Greece. Have a partner "phone in" advice requests or questions. **[Social Studies Link]**

Projects

6. Model Create a model or drawing of either Pluto's underworld or Phaëthon's chariot ride. Use any medium you wish. Let your imagination fill in details that are not supplied in the retellings of the myths. **[Art Link]**

7. Comparison Chart Choose one of the natural occurrences explained in these myths. Then, research the scientific explanation. Create a chart using both text and pictures to compare and contrast the two explanations. **[Science Link]**

Writing Mini-Lesson

Modern Myth

The ancient Greeks created myths to explain natural occurrences. Choose a dramatic natural occurrence, such as a destructive earthquake, or a small occurrence, such as the appearance of dew on the grass. Write a modern myth about the gods or heroes—and their actions—behind this occurrence.

Writing Skills Focus: Use an Outline

Creating an **outline** can help you organize details and events in your myth. In your outline, each Roman numeral might cover a paragraph. Look at this outline of the first paragraph of "Phaëthon, Son of Apollo."

I. Phaëthon
- A. Son of Apollo and Clymene
  - 1. Father a god
  - 2. Mother a mortal
- B. Boastful of divine father
  - 1. Believes mortals can become gods

Prewriting Choose a natural occurrence, flipping through nature magazines for ideas if you like. Then, brainstorm for some ways a god could create this occurrence. For example, an earthquake might be caused by a god stamping his foot. Outline your myth using the model shown above.

Drafting Begin by identifying the natural occurrence or vividly describing human reactions to it. Then, follow your outline to write the myth in greater detail. Be sure to link a god's or hero's action to the resulting occurrence.

Revising Read your myth aloud, listening for unclear links between characters' actions and the plot. Add details or cause-and-effect words such as *because, when,* or *next* to cement these links.

Grammar Application

Make sure the introductory phrases in your myth are set off with commas.

Idea Bank

Following are suggestions for matching the Idea Bank topics with your students' performance levels and learning modalities:

Customize for *Performance Levels*
Less Advanced Students: 1, 4
Average Students: 2, 4, 5, 6
More Advanced Students: 3, 6, 7

Customize for *Learning Modalities*
Verbal/Linguistic: 1, 2, 3, 4, 5
Interpersonal: 4
Visual/Spatial: 6, 7
Logical/Mathematical: 1, 7
Intrapersonal: 6, 7

Writing Mini-Lesson

Refer students to the Writing Handbook in the back of the book for instructions on the writing process and for further information on narrative writing.

Writer's Solution

Writing Lab CD-ROM
Have students complete the tutorial on Narration. Follow these steps:

1. Have students use the Plot Outliner activity to show the course of action in their myth.
2. Suggest that students use the Transitional Word Bins to gather words to connect the events in the myth.
3. Allow students to draft on computer.
4. When revising, suggest that students use the Proofreading Checklist.

Writer's Solution Sourcebook
Have students use Chapter 3, "Narration," pp. 66–101, for additional support. This chapter includes in-depth instruction on using transitions to show time order, pp. 95–96.

✓ ASSESSMENT OPTIONS

Formal Assessment, Selection Test, pp. 240–242, and Assessment Resources Software. The selection test is designed so that it can easily be customized to the performance levels of your students.

Alternative Assessment, p. 50, includes options for less advanced students, more advanced students, verbal/linguistic learners, bodily/kinesthetic learners, interpersonal learners, and musical/rhythmic learners.

PORTFOLIO ASSESSMENT
Use the following rubrics in the **Alternative Assessment** booklet to assess student writing:
News Article: Summary, p. 85
Autobiography: Expression, p. 81
Myth: Comparison/Contrast, p. 90
Writing Mini-Lesson: Fictional Narrative, p. 82

Prepare and Engage

OBJECTIVES

1. To read, comprehend, and interpret two fables
2. To relate fables to personal experience
3. To recognize storyteller's purpose
4. To analyze a fable
5. To build vocabulary in context and learn the prefix *sur-*
6. To use quotation marks to punctuate dialogue correctly
7. To write an introduction to a collection of fables using appropriate sources
8. To respond to the fables through writing, speaking and listening, and projects

SKILLS INSTRUCTION

Vocabulary:
Prefixes: *sur-*

Spelling:
Use the Ending *er* to Describe People

Grammar:
Quotation Marks

Reading Strategy:
Recognize Storyteller's Purpose

Literary Focus:
Fable

Writing:
Use Appropriate Sources

Critical Viewing:
Speculate

PORTFOLIO OPPORTUNITIES

Writing: Journal Entry; Fable; Fable Essay

Writing Mini-Lesson: Introduction to a Collection of Fables

Speaking and Listening: Television Dialogue; Monologue

Projects: Multicultural Fables; Web Site Review

More About the Author
Because **Aesop's** fables are short, enjoyable, and easy to recall, they have been used in schools for centuries and have been adapted and retold by countless writers. One well-known English version is that by Samuel Croxall, originally published in 1722, which includes an "application," or moral, at the end of each fable. Another, by Joseph Jacobs (1894) is known for its faithfulness to early Greek and Latin translations of the ancient texts and for a spare treatment of the tales. The Jacobs versions appear in this selection.

Guide for Reading

Meet the Author:

Aesop (about 620–560 B.C.)

Aesop's fables have been enjoyed for centuries. However, we know very little about the origin of these famous stories—including who actually wrote them.

A Man of Mystery There are different theories about Aesop's identity. Some believe he was a slave who lived on the Greek island of Samos during the sixth century. Others believe that he was a spokesman who defended criminals in court. Still others believe that he was either an advisor or a riddle solver for one of the Greek kings. The most widely held theory, however, is that Aesop wasn't an actual individual at all. Rather, because certain stories in ancient Greece were told over and over, people invented an imaginary author for them.

What We Do Know About Aesop's Fables About 200 years after Aesop's supposed death, a fellow Greek created the first written version of the tales. In the centuries that have followed, the fables have remained very popular and have been enjoyed by people all over the world.

◆ Literature and Your Life

Connect Your Experience

Some stories grab our attention—and our hearts—because they tell about an idea or experience we can all understand. This is true of Aesop's fables, including the ones you're about to read. It is the unusual quality of these stories and their messages that has made them popular for centuries.

Thematic Focus: Community Ties

Stories such as these fables provide a vehicle for communities to share common values and beliefs. As you read, think about how the morals the fables convey apply to your own community.

◆ Background for Understanding

Social Studies

Aesop's fables bring us a small piece of ancient Greek life. From this faraway civilization, we have inherited not only suggestions about manners and conduct, but also a framework for democracy. In Athens during the 400's B.C., men had the right to vote, to serve in an assembly, and to serve on a jury. Every year, citizens participated in the random election of a council of 500 men who debated policy and set law. Although the election of United States leaders is not random, Congress takes many of its practices from the success of Athenian government.

◆ Build Vocabulary

Prefixes: *sur-*

In "The Fox and the Crow," you'll encounter the word *surpass*. Given that the prefix *sur-* means "above" or "over," it makes sense that *surpass* means "be superior to" or "be above all others."

Word Bank

Which of these words from the fables might describe the shiny feathers of a crow?

glossy
surpass
flatterers

Prentice Hall Literature Program Resources

REINFORCE / RETEACH / EXTEND

Selection Support Pages
Build Vocabulary: Prefixes: *sur-*, p. 279
Build Spelling Skills, p. 280
Build Grammar Skills: Quotation Marks, p. 281
Reading Strategy: Recognize Storyteller's Purpose, p. 282
Literary Focus: Fable, p. 283

Strategies for Diverse Student Needs, pp. 101–102

Beyond Literature Cultural Connection: Morals in Fables, p. 51

Formal Assessment Selection Test, pp. 243–245, Assessment Resources Software

Alternative Assessment, p. 51

Writing and Language Transparencies, Cluster Organizer, p. 82

Resource Pro CD-ROM
"The Lion and the Statue"; "The Fox and the Crow"

Listening to Literature Audiocassettes
"The Lion and the Statue"; "The Fox and the Crow"

The Lion and the Statue ◆ The Fox and the Crow

◆ Literary Focus

FABLE

A **fable** is a brief story that teaches a lesson. In Aesop's fables and in many others, the lesson or **moral** is clearly stated as a wise saying at the end of the story.

Fables are short and simple, with relatively undeveloped characters, situations, and conflicts. Fable characters are often animals that act like human beings and illustrate human failings and weaknesses. As you read, look for connections between these animals' attitudes and behaviors and the beliefs and actions of people you know. Keep a chart like the one below to record your reactions.

Behavior in Fable	Reminds Me of . . .

◆ Reading Strategy

RECOGNIZE STORYTELLER'S PURPOSE

When you **recognize a storyteller's purpose,** you can determine how best to read a story. Fables are written for two specific purposes: to teach a lesson and to entertain. As you read, notice how these fables include only those details that achieve one of these purposes. For example, be aware of how characters and situations are sketched briefly enough to set up the problem, relate the outcome, and report the moral.

Preparing for Standardized Tests

Grammar Standardized tests may require students to be able to identify a sentence that is punctuated correctly. Remind students that a speaker's exact words must be set off by quotation marks. Write the following sample test item on the board:

Choose the sentence that is correctly punctuated:

(A) "I'm tired, said the hare," sitting down for a rest.
(B) I'll never catch up with the hare!" exclaimed the turtle.
(C) "Even if I rest," I'll win the race, said the hare.
(D) "Slow and steady wins the race," said the turtle.

Help students identify the errors in *(A), (B),* and *(C)*. In *(A),* the quotation marks should follow *tired* instead of *hare.* Sentence *(B)* needs a quotation mark before *I'll. (C)* needs to have the quotation mark after *rest* moved to follow the word *race. (D)* is correct as written. For additional practice using quotation marks, use **Selection Support,** p. 281.

Interest Grabber Display a picture of some well-known cartoon animals such as Bugs Bunny and the Roadrunner. Discuss with students cartoons, books, and movies that portray animals with human characteristics. Have students list animals and a word that describes each one. For example, they might list *sly fox* or *curious cat.* When students finish, tell them that they will read two fables in which animal characters not only assume human traits but teach lessons about human behavior.

◆ Build Grammar Skills

Quotation Marks If you wish to introduce the grammar concept for this selection before students read, refer to the instruction on p. 874.

Customize for
Less Proficient Readers
Fables are often told orally by storytellers. To help less proficient readers grasp the tone of the dialogue in these fables, have them listen to the recording as they follow along in their books.

Listening to Literature Audiocassettes

Customize for
More Advanced Students
Encourage students to locate and read fables originating in various cultures, for example from Africa or Asia. Then have students meet in groups to retell some of the fables and discuss similarities and differences among them.

Humanities: Art

Aesop, 1492, Venetian woodcut

The portrait of Aesop on p. 870 is a woodcut created by an unknown artist in Venice, Italy, during the Renaissance. Use the following question for discussion:

1. No one knows for sure if Aesop really lived, and if he did, he lived 2,000 years before the woodcut was created. How did the artist make Aesop look? *The artist made Aesop look serious and thoughtful to represent wisdom and learning.*

Develop Understanding

One-Minute Insight In "The Lion and the Statue," a man shows a lion a public statue of Hercules overcoming a lion to prove his point that men are stronger than lions. The lion responds that since it was a man who created the statue, the message was what the man chose it to be and didn't prove anything.

"The Fox and the Crow" is the story of a crow who has a piece of cheese and a greedy fox who wants the same piece of cheese for himself. The fox flatters the crow by complimenting her eyes, her feathers, and her lovely voice. When the crow vainly opens her mouth to caw, her piece of cheese falls to the ground and is eaten by the fox. He advises the crow not to trust flatterers in the future.

Customize for
English Language Learners
Ask English language learners to share with the class the words in their native language for lion, man, statue, fox, crow, and birds. Then, help these students find the English words for these things in the fables. Before reading, you might also wish to review and discuss the footnotes.

▶Critical Viewing◀

❶ **Speculate** *The lion in the statue is shown as weak in comparison to the man. The lion would probably find the statue offensive, since it shows little respect for lions.*

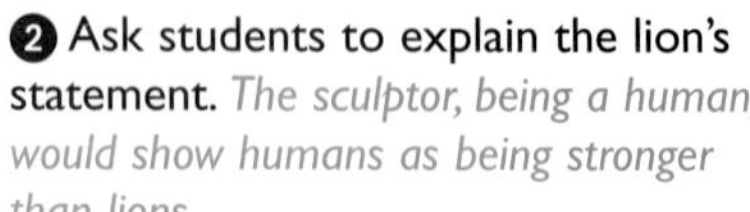

❷ Ask students to explain the lion's statement. *The sculptor, being a human, would show humans as being stronger than lions.*

◆Reading Strategy

❸ **Recognize Storyteller's Purpose** Ask students what the moral of the fable helps them learn about the storyteller's purpose. *The general statement based on events in the story indicates that one purpose of the fable is to teach a lesson.*

The Lion and the Statue

Aesop

❶ ▲ **Critical Viewing** Why would the Lion be bothered by his species' portrayal in the statue shown here? **[Speculate]**

A Man and a Lion were discussing the relative[1] strength of men and lions in general. The Man contended[2] that he and his fellows were stronger than lions by reason of their greater intelligence. "Come now with me," he cried, "and I will soon prove that I am right." So he took him into the public gardens and showed him a statue of Hercules[3] overcoming the Lion and tearing his mouth in two.

"That is all very well," said the Lion, "but proves nothing, for it was a man who made the statue." ❷

We can easily represent things as we wish them to be. ❸

1. **relative** (rel´ ə tiv) *adj.*: Related to another; comparative.
2. **contended** (kən tend´ id) *v.*: Argued.
3. **Hercules** (hʉr´ kyo͞o lēz´): Hero of Ancient Greek mythology known for his strength.

◆ Build Vocabulary

glossy (glôs´ ē) *adj.*: Smooth and shiny
surpass (sər pas´) *v.*: Be superior to
flatterers (flat´ ər ərz) *n.*: Those who praise a person insincerely in order to gain something for themselves

Block Scheduling Strategies

Consider these suggestions to take advantage of extended class time.

- Before reading, have students share any fables that they already know. Lead students to discover elements that the fables share. Then, introduce the Literary Focus. For additional practice, use **Selection Support,** p. 283.
- After reading, allow time for students to role-play the situations in the fables. Then, lead a discussion in which students identify real-life situations to which the lessons in the fables might apply.
- If you have access to technology, have students use the *Writer's Solution Writing Lab CD-ROM* to prepare for and complete the Writing Mini-Lesson, p. 875.
- Have students listen to the audiocassette recording of the fables. Have students meet in groups to discuss and list the features of these fables that make them well suited for telling aloud. Allow time for groups to compare and discuss their lists.

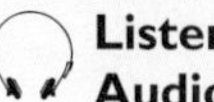

Listening to Literature Audiocassettes

The Fox and the Crow

Aesop

4 A Fox once saw a Crow fly off with a piece of cheese in its beak and settle on a branch of a tree. "That's for me, as I am a Fox," said Master Reynard,[1] and he walked up to the foot of the tree.

"Good day, Mistress Crow," he cried. "How well you are looking today: how glossy your feathers; how bright your eye. I feel sure your voice must surpass that of other birds, just as your figure does; let me hear but one song from you that I may greet you as the Queen of Birds."

The Crow lifted up her head and began to caw her best, but the moment she opened her mouth the piece of cheese fell to the ground, only to be snapped up by Master Fox. "That will do," said he. "That was all I wanted. In exchange for your cheese I will give you a piece of advice for the future—

Do not trust flatterers." 

1. **Master Reynard** (ren´ ərd): The fox in the medieval beast epic *Reynard the Fox*; therefore, a proper name for the fox in other stories.

Guide for Responding

◆ Literature and Your Life

Reader's Response What is your reaction to the moral of each fable? Explain.

Thematic Focus Explain how fables like these might help a community express its values, teach its members how to behave, and create a sense of community identity.

Journal Writing In your journal, write about a time—real or imagined—when someone told you a fable in order to help you understand something.

☑ Check Your Comprehension

1. Summarize the discussion in "The Lion and the Statue."
2. How does the Crow in "The Fox and the Crow" lose the cheese?

◆ Critical Thinking

Interpret

1. What might the statue in "The Lion and the Statue" look like if it were created by a lion? **[Deduce]**
2. In "The Fox and the Crow," how does the Fox's attitude change when he gets the piece of cheese? **[Infer]**
3. What human character traits do the characters in these fables represent? **[Draw Conclusions]**
4. How do the actions of the characters support each fable's moral? **[Connect]**

Evaluate

5. Why might a fable with animal characters teach a lesson better than a tale with human characters? **[Make a Judgment]**

Compare Literary Works

6. How well does each fable teach its lesson? Consider whether or not you find the characters memorable and the lesson important. **[Make a Judgment]**

Beyond the Selection

FURTHER READING

Other Works by Aesop

Aesop's Fables, Illustrated by Jacob Lawrence

Other Works on the Theme of Community Ties

Nothing but the Truth: A Documentary Novel, Avi

Dragons, Gods & Spirits From Chinese Mythology (World Mythology Series), Tao Tao Liu Sanders

Gods and Heroes From Viking Mythology (World Mythology Series), Brian Branston

INTERNET

We suggest the following site on the Internet (all Web sites are subject to change).

For more fables and information about Aesop: **http://www.pacificnet.net/~johnr/aesop**

We *strongly recommend* that you preview the site before you send students to it.

◆ Literary Focus

4 Fable Have students identify elements of a fable that can be found in the opening paragraph. *The main characters are animals. The fox appears to have the human failing of being greedy.*

◆ Reading Strategy

5 Recognizing Storyteller's Purpose Ask students to discuss whether they agree with the lesson taught in this fable. *Most students will agree that someone who is a flatterer might not be completely honest in other ways.*

Reinforce and Extend

Answers

◆ Literature and Your Life

Reader's Response Both fables have common sense morals that seem true and easy to understand.

Thematic Focus The simple morals taught with fables can express the shared values and expectations of a community. Retelling the fables reinforces these shared ideas.

☑ Check Your Comprehension

1. The man tries to convince the lion that men are stronger than lions because of their intelligence. The Lion responds that the statue proves nothing since it was created by a man.
2. The Crow opens her mouth to show off, and the cheese drops out.

◆ Critical Thinking

1. It would probably show the lion overcoming Hercules.
2. He stops flattering the Crow and becomes disdainful of the Crow's vanity.
3. The Lion represents balanced judgment; the Man, pride; the Fox, greed and trickery; the Crow, vanity.
4. The Man's choice of a statue made by a person shows he has skewed facts to fit his ideas. The Fox's stealing of the cheese shows that the Crow should not have trusted his flattering words.
5. Readers may respond to animal characters less defensively than they would to human characters.
6. If students believe one or the other teaches the lesson better and is more memorable, they should give reasons for their choice.

Answers

◆Literary Focus

1. "We can easily represent things as we wish them to be."
   "Do not trust flatterers."
2. It is easy to twist the facts if you want to.
   People who flatter may not be truthful.
3. Students should support their responses with specific reasons.

◆Build Vocabulary

Using the Prefix: *sur-*

1. survey
2. surprise
3. surrenders

Spelling Strategy

1. voter
2. hairdresser
3. photographer
4. believer
5. writer
6. singer
7. painter
8. fighter

Using the Word Bank

1. A car travels much faster than a bicycle.
2. A fan club would contain people likely to flatter you.
3. Polishing wood often makes it glossy.

◆Reading Strategy

1. The animal characters help to make the fables entertaining.
2. The moral supports the purpose of education, since it briefly summarizes the lesson of the story.
3. They probably would not be as entertaining and would give more facts and details.

◆Build Grammar Skills

1. "What other fables have you read?" he asked.
2. "I've read some modern fables by James Thurber," she said. "They were very funny."
3. "I like the fables by La Fontaine," he said.
4. "My favorite," he said, "is the one about not counting your chickens before they're hatched."
5. "I like that one, too," she said. "I also like the one about belling the cat."

Guide for Responding *(continued)*

◆ Literary Focus

FABLE

A **fable** is a brief tale that teaches a lesson called a **moral.** Often, as in the fables you've just read, fables include animal characters that possess human traits.

1. What is the moral of each Aesop fable presented here?
2. Restate the moral of each fable in your own words.
3. Explain why you agree or disagree with each moral.

◆ Build Vocabulary

USING THE PREFIX *sur-*

The prefix *sur-* means "above" or "over." In each sentence, replace the italicized words with a *sur-* word from this list:

surrenders surprise survey

1. From the Acropolis, you can *look over* Athens.
2. Aesop's stories sometimes *take over with an unexpected reaction for* you at the end.
3. The Crow *gives over* the cheese to the Fox.

SPELLING STRATEGY

Use the ending *-er* to describe people who participate in a specific activity: *flatterer.* For each clue below, provide a word ending in *-er.*

1. One who votes
2. One who hairdresses
3. One who takes photographs
4. One who believes
5. One who writes
6. One who sings
7. One who paints
8. One who fights

USING THE WORD BANK

On your paper, write a sentence that answers each question.

1. Would a car *surpass* a bicycle in speed?
2. If you wanted *flatterers*, might you seek a fan club?
3. Would polishing a table make it *glossy?*

◆ Reading Strategy

RECOGNIZE A STORYTELLER'S PURPOSE

Recognizing a storyteller's purpose can help you get the most from these fables. Intended to teach a lesson and to entertain, these fables keep the tension light and the stories short.

1. What part of each fable best supports the storyteller's purpose of entertainment? Explain.
2. What part best supports the purpose of education? Explain.
3. In what ways would the fables be different if they were meant to persuade?

◆ Build Grammar Skills

QUOTATION MARKS

Quotation marks are punctuation marks that set off someone else's exact words. Writers use quotation marks to set off dialogue, or conversations between characters. When the dialogue appears inside a sentence, commas are used to separate the quotation. Notice how Aesop uses quotation marks to indicate that the Crow is speaking:

Quotation marks enclose the Fox's words.

"Good day, Mistress Crow," he cried.

A comma separates the Fox's words from the rest of the sentence.

Practice Rewrite each sentence with correctly placed quotation marks and commas.

1. What other fables have you read? he asked.
2. I've read some modern fables by James Thurber she said. They were very funny.
3. I like the fables by La Fontaine he said.
4. My favorite, he said, is the one about not counting your chickens before they're hatched.
5. I like that one, too, she said. I also like the one about belling the cat.

Writing Application Continue the conversation between the characters from one of the fables. Make sure you use quotation marks correctly.

Writer's Solution

For additional instruction and practice, use the quotation marks lesson in the Punctuation unit of the *Writer's Solution Language Lab CD-ROM* and the practice pages on quotation marks, pp. 105–106, in the *Writer's Solution Grammar Practice Book.*

Build Your Portfolio

Idea Bank

Writing

1. **Journal Entry** In the role of a character from one of the fables, explain what you learned from the events in the story.
2. **Fable** Choose a saying that teaches a lesson about life, and write a fable to illustrate it. Examples of possible sayings include: "Look before you leap" and "He who hesitates is lost."
3. **Fable Essay** Write an essay explaining whether or not you think that fables are useful for teaching children about proper attitudes and behaviors. Support your ideas with specific examples from actual fables.

Speaking and Listening

4. **Television Dialogue [Group Activity]** What if two characters from one of these fables decided to air their differences on a televised talk show? With two classmates, write a dialogue that lets each character explain his or her side. Remember to include a talk-show host. Decide which roles each of you will take. Then, perform your dialogue for the class. **[Performing Arts Link]**
5. **Monologue** Write and perform a monologue—a speech by one character—as either the Crow or the Lion. Talk about the lesson you learned, how you learned it, and how you can apply that lesson to your life in the future. **[Performing Arts Link]**

Projects

6. **Multicultural Fables [Group Activity]** Work with a group to collect fables from different countries. Conduct research to gather the fables. Develop a table of contents. Then, illustrate each fable. **[Social Studies Link]**
7. **Web Site Review** Go on-line to find a Web site of fables. Study its organization and content. Then, in a presentation to the class, evaluate the site. Explain what worked well and how you might improve the collection. **[Technology Link]**

Writing Mini-Lesson

Introduction to a Collection of Fables

In addition to Aesop, fables have been written by many other storytellers from around the world and through the ages. Choose a group of fables—by a certain storyteller or from a specific time period or part of the world. Write an introduction to a collection of these fables.

Writing Skills Focus: Use Appropriate Sources

Your introduction should define the fable form and provide historical background. Find accurate information quickly by **using appropriate sources.** Try some of these:

- Encyclopedias
- Literary reference books such as *Benet's Reader's Encyclopedia*
- Introductions to published fable collections

Prewriting Use note cards to record information from your source materials. Jot down the source for each fact or quotation you include in your notes.

Drafting Begin by explaining what a fable is. Then, share some historical or cultural information about the fables in your collection. Finally, tell readers why they might find these stories from other times and places easy to understand.

◆ Grammar Application

Make sure that you have correctly placed quotation marks when quoting a source's exact words.

Revising Reread your draft for organization and content. Do your ideas flow smoothly? Will your introduction help readers understand the collection? If necessary, return to your sources for additional information. Also, confirm that you have correctly credited any sources used.

✓ ASSESSMENT OPTIONS

Formal Assessment, Selection Test, pp. 243–245, and Assessment Resources Software. The selection test is designed so that it can easily be customized to the performance levels of your students.

Alternative Assessment, p. 51, includes options for less advanced students, more advanced students, verbal/linguistic learners, bodily/kinesthetic learners, visual/spatial learners, and interpersonal learners.

PORTFOLIO ASSESSMENT

Use the following rubrics in the **Alternative Assessment** booklet to assess student writing:
Journal Entry: Expression Rubric, p. 81
Fable: Fictional Narrative Rubric, p. 82
Fable Essay: Persuasion Rubric, p. 92
Writing Mini-Lesson: Research Report/Paper Rubric, p. 93

Idea Bank

Following are suggestions for matching the Idea Bank topics with your students' performance levels and learning modalities:

Customize for *Performance Levels*

Less Advanced Students: 1, 4, 6
Average Students: 2, 4, 6, 7
More Advanced Students: 3, 5, 6, 7

Customize for *Learning Modalities*

Verbal/Linguistic: 1, 2, 3, 4, 5, 6, 7
Interpersonal: 4, 6
Visual/Spatial: 6
Intrapersonal: 1, 2, 3, 5
Bodily/Kinesthetic: 4
Logical/Rational: 7

Writing Mini-Lesson

Refer students to the Writing Handbook in the back of the book for instructions on the writing process and for further information on reports.

Writer's Solution

Writers at Work Videodisc

To introduce students to report writing, play Ch. 7 "Reports." Ask students to discuss how Ellie Fries gathers the most accurate, up-to-date information.

Play frames 11077 to 20155

Writing Lab CD-ROM

Have students complete the tutorial on Reports. Follow these steps:

1. Have students use the interactive KWL chart to prepare for research.
2. Suggest that students view the skimming tips to learn how to quickly find desired information.
3. Allow students to draft on computer.
4. When revising, suggest that students use the Unity and Coherence revision checker.

Writer's Solution Sourcebook

Have students use Chapter 7, "Reports," pp. 200–233. This chapter includes in-depth instruction on citing sources, p. 231.

Prepare and Engage

Establish Writing Guidelines

Review the following key characteristics of a research report:

- A research report provides factual information on a topic.
- A research report uses information gathered from a variety of sources.
- A research report includes a bibliography citing sources used by the writer, and may include footnotes or parenthetical citations.

You may want to distribute the scoring rubric for Research Report/Paper, p. 93 in **Alternative Assessment,** to make students aware of the criteria on which they will be evaluated. See the suggestions on p. 878 for how you can customize the rubric to this workshop.

Refer students to the Writing Handbook in the back of the book for instruction on the writing process and for further information on reports.

Writer's Solution

Writers at Work Videodisc

To introduce students to reports and to show them how Ellie Fries answers the question *What Is a report?*, play the videodisc segment on Reports (Ch. 7).

Play frames 11077 to 20155

Writing Lab CD-ROM

If your students have access to computers, you may want to have them work in the tutorial on Reports to complete all or part of their research reports. Follow these steps:

1. Have students view the interactive model of a library research report.
2. Suggest that students use the Sunburst Diagram activity to come up with topic ideas.
3. Encourage students to use the Outliner Tool to arrange main ideas and details.
4. Have students draft on computer.

Writer's Solution Sourcebook

Students can find additional support, including in-depth instruction on developing an organization plan, p. 223, in the chapter on Reports, pp. 200–232.

Report Writing

Research Report

Writing Process Workshop

One way to learn about a topic—and to share what you've learned—is to write a **research report.** In this workshop, you'll choose and narrow a topic, develop an outline, and conduct research. You'll put it all together into a finished piece of writing, complete with documentation of your sources. The following skills will help you write your report:

Writing Skills Focus

▶ **Narrow your topic** by dividing your subject into subtopics and choosing one on which to focus your report.

▶ **Use an outline** to help you organize your ideas before you begin to write. (See p. 869.)

▶ **Use appropriate sources** that supply accurate information on your topic. Cite these sources in your report. (See p. 875.)

▶ **Use a clear organization.** State your topic in a strong introduction. Offer information about your topic in the body of your report. Summarize your main points in your conclusion.

After reading the myths in this section, one student decided to research growing up in ancient Greece.

Model

Like middle-school students today, students in ancient Greece studied a wide variety of subjects and were taught by several different teachers. ① A *grammatistes* taught reading, writing, and arithmetic. A *kitharistes* taught poetry and music. A *paidotribes* ② taught sports.[1]

① In this body paragraph, the writer focuses on one aspect of the topic—education.

② The writer will cite the source of this information in a footnote at the bottom of the page.

Beyond the Classroom

Workplace Skills

Writing Reports Explain to students that writing reports is an essential skill in many careers. In addition to nonfiction writers, other workers who write reports include scientists, historians, lawyers, teachers, doctors, and office workers. Remind students that the main object of a research report is to provide the reader with accurate information.

As a class, have students brainstorm for a list of careers and the main function of those careers. Then have students consider what information workers in those careers may need to research. For example, a chef's main function is to develop and create recipes for a restaurant. The chef may need to research information on new fat substitutes and their side effects.

Once the class has discovered a few areas where information may be needed, have students break into smaller groups and begin research. Suggest that each group find three different sources of information, including Web sites or articles in encyclopedias, newspapers, books, or magazines. Have students create a bibliography of their sources, using correct bibliographic form.

Prewriting

Narrow Your Topic Some topics are so broad, you could write *several* research reports about them. For example, "Greece" is too big a topic to cover in a brief report. To narrow your topic, keep dividing it into subtopics. Then, choose the one that interests you most. If the subtopic you've chosen can stand alone as a topic, you're ready to begin.

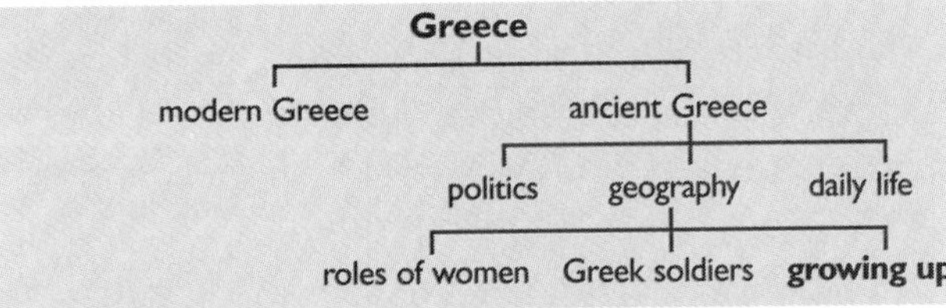

Gather Information In the library, look for information in reference books, nonfiction books, magazines, and on-line services. Consult up-to-date sources to get the most accurate information. Also, try to find the same facts in at least two different sources.

Use Note Cards Record facts and details on note cards, which should also include information about your sources. You'll need this source information when you draft your footnotes and bibliography.

Make an Outline Organize your notes into an outline. The more detailed your outline, the easier your job will be when you begin to draft. Look at this writer's working outline:

Topic: Growing Up in Ancient Greece

I. Education
  A. Education for boys
    1. School: subjects and teachers
    2. Military training
    3. Observational walks
  B. Education for girls
    1. Domestic training

Drafting

Write a Thesis Statement Begin with a thesis statement—a sentence that expresses the main idea of your report. Your thesis statement might be a quotation, fact, description, or question that grabs your readers' attention and makes them want to read more.

DRAFTING/REVISING

Applying Language Skills: Sentence Variety

Your report will be more interesting to read if you vary the length and structure of your sentences. Use both long and short sentences, and include simple, compound, and complex sentences. Notice the variety in this paragraph:

Both boys and girls wore sandals. They also wore chitons, or tunics. The Doric chiton wrapped around the body, while the Ionic chiton fastened across the shoulders.

Practice Revise this paragraph by varying the sentences:

Children played board games. There were games similar to checkers, chess, and dice. Knucklebones was played with animal bones. Knucklebones was popular with girls. Children had other toys, too. They played with yo-yos, hoops, spinning tops, dolls, and balls.

Writing Application Combine shorter sentences with conjunctions and appropriate punctuation to create longer, more complex sentences.

Writer's Solution Connection
Language Lab

For more practice, see the lesson on Varying Sentence Structure in the unit on Styling Sentences.

Develop Student Writing

Prewriting

Explain to students that when taking notes, they should include one piece of information per note card. This way, each note card is precise and can be easily organized. If there are two different facts on one note card, the information cannot be moved around and organized. Suggest that students label their note cards with a general subtopic word or phrase. Then, when ready to outline, students can organize note cards by subtopic.

Customize for
Less Proficient Writers

To help students organize their information into an outline, suggest that they fill out the Main Idea and Supporting Details Organizer, p. 70, in **Writing and Language Transparencies.** Students may want to fill out several copies of the chart. The first copy can list the main topic, with the subtopics as supporting details. Then, students may want to create other organizers for each subtopic—listing the subtopic as main idea, and then filling out the supporting details.

Writer's Solution

Writing Lab CD-ROM

Suggest that students use the Topic Web activity in the Prewriting section to break a broad topic into narrow topics. For additional support on note-taking, suggest that students use the practice pages on Developing Your Note-Taking Skills, pp. 160–161, in the *Writer's Solution Grammar Practice Book.*

For additional instruction and practice, have students use the *Writer's Solution Language Lab CD-ROM* Varying Sentence Structure lesson in the Sentence Style unit.

Applying Language Skills

Sentence Variety

Explain to students that another way to vary their sentences is to vary sentence beginnings. The most common way to begin sentences is with a subject followed by a verb. Suggest to students that they work with their sentences to open with a participial phrase, transition, adverb, or adverb clause.

Answers

Possible response:

Children played board games, similar to checkers, chess, and dice. Knucklebones, played with animal bones, was popular with girls. The children had other toys, too, such as yo-yos, hoops, spinning tops, dolls, and balls.

Drafting

Remind students that when drafting, they should not just copy notes from their note cards. They will need to add transitions to have the sentences flow smoothly. Encourage students to write a strong, interesting introduction that clearly states the thesis.

Writer's Solution

Writing Lab CD-ROM

Suggest that students view the guidelines and models for citing sources using parentheses or footnotes.

Revising

When using a peer reviewer, have them answer the following questions:

1. Is the main idea clearly stated in the introduction?
2. Does the report contain interesting information?
3. Are parts of the report difficult to understand? Does more information need to be included?
4. Are some areas of the report given too much space and other areas not enough?

Publishing

For other publishing ideas, suggest that students provide their reports with a table of contents and visuals. Then create a class table of contents for a cumulative list of subjects.

Reinforce and Extend

Review the Writing Guidelines

After students have completed their papers, review the characteristics of a research report.

Applying Language Skills

Bibliographic Form Explain that a bibliography lists all sources: both the works cited in footnotes or parentheses and the works that have been read but not specifically cited.

Writing Process Workshop

EDITING/PROOFREADING

Applying Language Skills: Bibliographic Form

In your bibliography, you will present information about each source you used:

Article:

Baxter, Zoe. "Fun and Games in Ancient Greece." *National Geographic Explorer*, December 1, 1999: 35.

Encyclopedia Entry:

"Greece (Ancient)." *The World Book Encyclopedia*. 2000 ed.

Book:

Ganeri, Anita. *Ancient Greeks*. New York: Shooting Star Press, 1994.

Interview:

Professor Dina Costalas, interviewed April 20, 2000.

CD-ROM:

"World Wonders: The Acropolis." *Planet Earth*. Macmillan Digital: 1998.

Writing Application As you research your topic, keep a list of the sources you consult. Use proper bibliographic form to create a bibliography of the sources you used. Alphabetize your entries, and then attach your bibliography to the end of your report.

Writer's Solution Connection
Writing Lab

For additional information on citing sources, consult the tutorial on Reports.

Cite Sources Whenever you use another person's exact words or when you use another person's idea, even if you rephrase it in your own words, you must credit your source. There are two ways to do this. You can cite a source in parentheses in the body of your report, or you can cite the source in a footnote at the bottom of the page. Failure to cite a source is called plagiarism—presenting someone else's ideas as your own. Plagiarism is a serious offense.

Parenthetical Citation:	"Life was very different for boys and girls in ancient Greece." (Smith, p. 98)
Footnote:	"Life was very different for boys and girls in ancient Greece."[1]
(bottom of page)	**1.** Smith, p. 98.

Write the Body Develop and support your thesis in the body of your report. Each body paragraph can focus on one aspect of your thesis. Refer to your outline as you draft.

Write the Conclusion Wrap up your report in a conclusion that summarizes your main idea and reemphasizes your thesis.

Revising

Use a Peer Reviewer Ask a classmate who doesn't know much about your subject to read your draft. Take a few minutes to discuss the answers to these questions:

- Is the thesis presented in an interesting way?
- Do the body paragraphs support the thesis statement?
- Is the information clearly presented? Is there enough information?
- Have all sources been accurately cited?

Publishing and Presenting

Class Magazine Combine your report with others into a magazine called *Everything You Always Wanted to Know*. Have volunteers write an introduction, prepare a table of contents, and create illustrations.

Presentation for a Younger Class Before a class of younger students, explain what a research report is and present your report as an example. Show students some of your sources. Encourage them to ask questions after you've finished your presentation.

✓ ASSESSMENT

PORTFOLIO ASSESSMENT		4	3	2	1
Use the rubric on Research Report in the **Alternative Assessment** booklet, p. 93, to assess the students' writing. Add these criteria to customize this rubric to this assignment.	**Organization**	The report includes an introduction, body, and conclusion. Each paragraph has a clearly stated main idea.	The report includes an introduction, body, and conclusion. Most paragraphs have a clearly stated main idea.	The report includes an introduction, body, and conclusion. Many paragraphs lack a clearly stated main idea.	The report lacks a clear organization. There is no distinction of main ideas, an introduction, or a conclusion.
	Citation of Sources	All sources are thoroughly documented in correct bibliographic form.	Most sources are thoroughly documented in correct bibliographic form.	Some sources are thoroughly documented in correct bibliographic form.	There are no sources cited.

Real-World Reading Skills Workshop

Evaluating Sources of Information

Strategies for Success

Research is often the most time-consuming part of preparing a report. In your quest for information, you may look at encyclopedias, books, magazines, and newspapers. Not all sources of information, however, are equally valuable. Follow these guidelines for evaluating your sources:

Investigate the Source Suppose you find a source of information for your report, but it turns out to be a comic book. The information may not be trustworthy. Consider the reputation of a publication before accepting it as a source. For example, not all newspapers are equally reliable. A tabloid—a paper with many pictures and short, sensational stories—is generally less reliable than a large city newspaper.

Consider the Author Before deciding to use a source, investigate its author. Is he or she an expert on the subject? Look in the book for the author's biography. The book jacket may provide more information on the author. Review the author's experience and qualifications to determine whether he or she is knowledgeable enough to write on the subject.

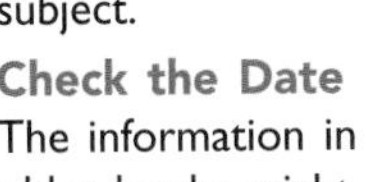

Check the Date The information in older books might not be accurate. For example, if you look for information on Russia in a book from 1990, you might read that Russia is part of the Soviet Union. The book would not say that the Soviet Union was dissolved in 1991.

Apply the Strategies

You are writing a report about the intelligence of dolphins. Look at these sources as you answer the questions that follow:

The World Book Encyclopedia, Volume D, copyright 1998

Dolphins: Geniuses of the Sea, by John Gerald, copyright 1960 by Forest Publishing

"New Research on Dolphin Communication," *The New York Times*, May 5, 1998

"Man Says Dolphin Spoke to Him," *Weekly Examiner*, May 5, 1998

The Lives of Dolphins, by Susan Mendez, copyright 1998 by Prentice Hall

1. Which source would you prefer to use—the encyclopedia or *The New York Times* article? Why?
2. Which of the newspapers would you use? Why?
3. Which of the books would you prefer to use? Why?

Here are other situations in which it is helpful to evaluate sources of information:

- ▶ Listening to television news interviews
- ▶ Reading an advertisement
- ▶ Reading newspaper editorials

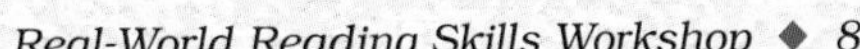

Introduce the Strategies

Remind students that when they are searching for sources, they don't necessarily want to use all the sources they can find. If several sources seem to include the same kind of information, students will want to choose the best source. This might be the source that has the most recent publication date, the source written by the best-known author, or the source with the most accompanying visuals. Tell students that they may also want to include a variety of different sources in their report. Rather than using only books as sources, students might refer to Internet sites and magazine articles for more recently published information.

Apply the Strategies

Remind students that one way to find additional sources is to look at the bibliography of one of the sources. For example, a student who finds a magazine article written by an expert might check the sources the expert cites in the article. In this case, the sources have already been evaluated by an expert.

Answers

1. Students should say *The New York Times* article is preferable because it is more specific, on dolphin communication, rather than just an article on dolphins.
2. Students should use *The New York Times*, because the article is more specific to the information desired. The article in the *Weekly Examiner* sounds as if it may be a tabloid. "Man Says Dolphin Spoke to Him" sounds like the story of one man's experiences, not a scientific study.
3. Students should choose *The Lives of Dolphins* because it has the most recent publication date. The other book was written almost forty years earlier, and may include out-of-date information.

◆Build Grammar Skills

Reviewing Commas and Quotation Marks

The selections in Part 2 include instruction on the following:

- Commas After Introductory Phrases
- Quotation Marks

This instruction is reinforced with the Build Grammar Skills practice pages in **Selection Support,** pp. 276 and 281.

As you review commas and quotation marks, you may wish to go over the following:

- Direct Quotations With Introductory, Concluding, and Interrupting Expressions

Explain to students that expressions such as *she asked, he explained,* or *they said* usually signal accompanying quotations. These expressions can introduce, conclude, or interrupt the quoted material, as in the following examples:

- She asked, "Do you take sugar?"
- "I can't help it," he explained, "I've snored ever since I was a child."
- "The movie was terrible," they said.

Writer's Solution

For additional practice and support, use the practice pages on Commas That Set Off Added Elements, pp. 100–101, and Quotation Marks With Direct Quotations, pp. 105–106, in the *Writer's Solution Grammar Practice Book.* If students have access to technology, suggest they use the Commas and Quotation Marks lessons in the Punctuation unit in the *Writer's Solution Language Lab CD-ROM.*

Answers

Practice 1

1. For years, Narcissus spent his days loving only himself.
2. In their anger, the gods took vengeance on him.
3. "Remember," said Daedalus, "never to fly very low or very high."
4. Mourning his son, Daedalus never attempted to fly again.
5. "You have no flowers here," Demeter told Pluto.
6. "This cannot go on," said mighty Zeus.
7. "Oh, how can I survive without my daughter?" Demeter cried.
8. Happy once again, Demeter welcomed Persephone with springtime and warmth.

Practice 2

Possible responses:

1. Under the setting sun, Demeter began to cry.
2. Gazing at his reflection, Narcissus was mesmerized.
3. For many days and many nights, she wandered the Earth.
4. Dazed by the power of the horses, Phaethon let go of the reins.
5. After six paralyzing minutes, he gave up his grasp and fell toward the Earth.
6. Grabbing the reins, Apollo tried to regain control of the horses.

Punctuation: Commas and Quotation Marks

Grammar Review

to use punctuation marks —**punc'tu·a'tor** *n.*
punc·tu·a·tion (puŋk'cho͞o ā'shən) *n.* ⟦ML *punctua*
the act of punctuating; specif., the act or practice o
ized marks in writing and printing to separate sent
elements or to make the meaning clearer **2** a syste
marks **3** such a mark or marks —**punc'tu·a'tive** *n.*
punctuation mark any of the marks used in punctu
or comma

A **comma** separates introductory phrases from the rest of a sentence. (See page 868.)

Introductory Phrases:	*Inside the shining palace,* Phaëthon saw his father. *Impressed by the splendor,* Phaëthon wanted more.

Quotation marks enclose a person's exact words. A comma separates a direct quotation from the rest of the sentence. (See page 874.)

"You really ought to reconsider," his mother warned.

Phaëthon said, "You can't stop me!"

"You'll see," she said, "you could get hurt."

Practice 1 Rewrite the following sentences, adding commas and quotation marks where needed.

1. For years Narcissus spent his days loving only himself.
2. In their anger the gods took vengeance on him.
3. Remember said Daedalus never to fly very low or very high.
4. Mourning his son Daedalus never attempted to fly again.
5. You have no flowers here Demeter told Pluto.
6. This cannot go on said mighty Zeus.
7. Oh how can I survive without my daughter Demeter cried.
8. Happy once again Demeter welcomed Persephone with springtime and warmth.

Practice 2 Write sentences containing the following introductory words and phrases:

1. Under the setting sun
2. Gazing at his reflection
3. For many days and nights
4. Dazed by the power of the horses
5. After six paralyzing minutes
6. Grabbing the reins

Grammar in Writing

✔ *When writing dialogue, begin a new paragraph with each change of speaker. Look at this example:*

"Come now with me," cried the man, "and I will prove that I am right.

"Where are we going?" asked the Lion.

"I want you to look at this statue," the man said.

"That is all very well," said the Lion, "but proves nothing."

Speaking, Listening, and Viewing Workshop

Giving an Oral Presentation

From time to time, you may be called upon to give an oral presentation. Being able to speak confidently in front of a group of people is an important skill to learn. With practice and attention to the following guidelines, you'll be able to give skillful and interesting oral presentations.

Know Your Material Before giving any type of oral presentation, take some time to review the material you will be presenting. You might spend time rehearsing—by practicing the actual words you'll use in your presentation, you may become more comfortable with the material. This will give you more confidence and make you less likely to lose your place or get confused.

Speak Up Without shouting, use a strong, clear voice that can be heard in the back of the room. Speak slowly enough for listeners to understand what you're saying.

Don't Just Stand There A speaker who appears bored and stiff won't give a successful oral presentation. Use gestures and body language to make your points. To prevent yourself from standing absolutely still, consider incorporating pictures, maps, charts, or graphs. Then, refer to these props as you speak. If you are lively and interested, your listeners will be, too.

Make Eye Contact During your presentation, make eye contact with your audience. Even if you use notes, be sure to glance up at your listeners from time to time.

Apply the Strategies

Take turns giving oral presentations to your classmates about the following topics:

1. News event about which you feel strongly
2. Report on a place you have visited
3. Your favorite relative or friend

Ask your classmates for feedback on your presentation.

Tips for Giving an Oral Presentation

✔ *To give an effective oral presentation to a small or large group, follow these strategies:*

- Know your material.
- Speak loudly and clearly enough for everybody to hear.
- Maintain good eye contact.
- Use body language where appropriate. Be lively, but remain in control.

Introduce the Strategies

Explain to students that many people are nervous about speaking publicly, but that the easiest way to overcome that fear is to practice. Giving a good oral presentation means being able to engage the listener, as well as having extensive knowledge of the subject.

Customize for
Less Proficient Readers
Remind students that in an effective presentation, information is presented in a logical manner. Speakers should introduce their topic, then present the details which support their main idea, and finally conclude by restating the topic. Suggest that students organize their information by using the Main Idea and Supporting Details Organizer, p. 70, in **Writing and Language Transparencies.** They may want to refer to the organizer when they give their presentation.

Apply the Strategies

Remind students that when they give an oral presentation, one of their main goals is to keep the listeners engaged. When speaking on a specific topic, students should remember to explain why this topic is important. Suggest that they use vivid words when describing a place, or include a humorous anecdote when describing a favorite friend or relative. Tell students to give their listeners a reason to care about what they are saying.

Cross-Curricular Connection: Social Studies

Many students may have given oral presentations in social studies or other classes. Explain that oral presentations provide a way for a speaker to share information with a large group of people. Oral presentations often lead into discussions that delve deeper into the subject matter at hand.

Ask students to share with the class topics that they are currently studying in social studies. Encourage them to get together in groups to organize a brief presentation on a social studies subject on which they may have already done some preliminary research. Suggest that students make a brief outline of their topic and try to include drawings, maps, or other visuals to enhance their presentations.

Then, as a class, create a list of the social studies topics to be presented. Encourage students to decide upon an order in which the topics should be addressed. If possible, set aside one class period for students to give their presentations. Have them use the speaking, listening, and viewing skills taught in this lesson. Explain to students that by preparing and giving an oral presentation, students are becoming more familiar with and more knowledgeable about the subject matter, as well as more confident public speakers.

◆Build Vocabulary

What's Behind the Words

Encourage students to consult a dictionary to find the formal definition of the words *herculean, atlas, titanic,* and *tantalize*. Explain that in the dictionary entry, the etymology, or word origin, should note the mythological reference.

Answers

Activity 1

1. flora and fauna: the plants and animals of a particular region or period. Flora is the Roman goddess of spring and flowering plants. Fauna is thought to be the wife or daughter of Faunus, the god of wild nature and fertility, identified with the Greek god Pan.
2. hermetic: made airtight by fusion or sealing. Hermes is the Greek herald and messenger of the gods. He is also the god of roads, trade, and good fortune. He is the patron of tricksters and thieves because he stole a herd of cows from Apollo minutes after he was born. Hermes escorts the souls of the dead to Hades, the underworld.
3. mentor: a wise and trusted counselor. In the *Odyssey,* Mentor was a loyal adviser of Odysseus, and tutor and caretaker of Odysseus' son Telemachus.
4. phobia: an obsessive or irrational fear or anxiety. Phobos is a Greek god of fear, son of Ares and Aphrodite.
5. fury: unrestrained or violent anger, rage, passion, or the like. The Furies are three sisters—daughters of Gaea—who are the goddesses of vengeance. They were created from a drop of blood falling onto the Earth, and they reside in the Under-world where they torment evildoers and sinners.
6. martial: inclined or disposed to war. Mars, the Roman god of war, is the son of Jupiter and Juno, also known as father of Romulus and Remus, founders of Rome. As god of war, he preceded armies into battle, leading them to victory.
7. nemesis: an agent or act of retribution or punishment. Nemesis is the goddess of divine retribution or vengeance. Her father is Darkness, her mother is Night. She pursues those who transgress against the natural order of things with an unrelenting vengeance.

What's Behind the Words

Vocabulary Adventures With Richard Lederer

Words From Myths

Of all the literary sources that feed into our English language, ancient mythology is one of the richest. Today, we constantly speak, hear, write, and read the names of ancient gods and goddesses, heroes and heroines—even if we don't always know it.

Words to Honor Heroes

Because many myths assign supernatural causes to natural occurrences, myths often tell about gods. The ancient gods and heroes of Greek and Roman mythology are not dead at all. Rather, they reside in our English language.

One of the greatest heroes of Greek literature was Hercules, who needed all his power to complete twelve amazingly difficult labors. Today, we use the word *herculean* to describe a mighty effort or a very challenging task.

During his journeys, Hercules met a giant named Atlas, who was condemned to support the heavens on his shoulders. Today, a book of maps is called an *atlas* because the title pages of such collections traditionally show the figure of Atlas with the world on his back.

According to Greek mythology, the Titans were the first children of Mother Earth. They were giants. Once Zeus was born to rule over Olympus, the Titans became his direct enemies. As a result, they posed a threat to all the gods and goddesses of Olympus, and the two groups were frequently at war. Today, we use the word *titanic* to describe anything that is powerful or huge.

A Tantalizing Story

Tantalus, King of Lydia, was such a vile villain that the gods banished him to Hades. In that underworld, he is condemned to stand in a sparkling pool of water with boughs of luscious fruit overhead. When he stoops to drink, the water drains away through the bottom of the pool, and when he reaches to eat, the branches of fruit sway just out of his grasp. Ever since, when something presents itself temptingly to our view but we can't have it, we say it *tantalizes* us.

ACTIVITY 1 A Greek herald in Homer's *Iliad* was a human public-address system, for his voice could be heard all over camp. Today, the adjective *stentorian* means "loud-voiced; bellowing." Locate the sources of the following words that come down to us from mythology. Be sure you know what the word means today, as well as the story of the person from which it comes.

1. flora and fauna
2. hermetic
3. mentor
4. phobia
5. fury
6. martial
7. nemesis

ACTIVITY 2 Go on a scouting expedition to find some of the other myths hiding in everyday English. With a group, complete one of the following scavenger hunts:

1. See what mythology you can find lurking behind the names of our planets or the names of flowers.
2. Take a trip to your local supermarket, and identify the mythological inspiration for many brand names.

Activity 2

Possible responses;

1. planets: Mercury is the Roman god of trade and profit, merchants, and travelers; Mars is the god of war; Venus is the goddess of beauty; Earth is also known as Gaia, the oldest of the goddesses; Saturn is the god of agriculture; Jupiter is the god of light and sky, and the protector of state and laws; Neptune is the god of the sea; Pluto is the god of the Underworld.
2. One example is Ajax, a Greek hero in the Trojan War, who rescued the body of Achilles.

Extended Reading Opportunities

By describing the creation of the world, the adventures of ancient gods and heroes, or the traditions of a culture, folk tales, myths, and legends share timeless stories. Continue your study of folklore with any of these titles.

Suggested Titles

In the Beginning: Creation Stories from Around the World

Virginia Hamilton

Where did we come from, and how did the world begin? These questions have puzzled every culture that ever existed. This illustrated collection of twenty-five creation myths shows some of the answers people once believed and presents a few stories some still hold to be true. Each tale reflects the diverse people who created them and the awe of the universe they shared.

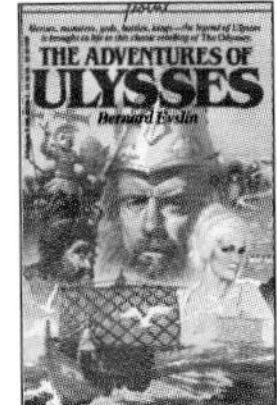

The Adventures of Ulysses

Bernard Evslin

A hero of the brutal Trojan War, Ulysses wants nothing more than to return to his wife and son. But the anger of the gods descends upon him, and he is forced off his course, hopelessly lost. A classic tale of the wandering hero, this story shows how Ulysses must struggle against the elements and battle monsters to return to those he loves.

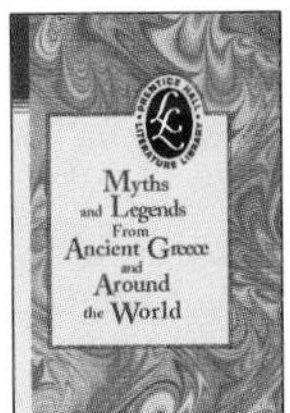

Myths and Legends From Ancient Greece and Around the World

To extend your enjoyment of the genre, this collection provides a wide sampling of ancient folklore. Among the classical myths presented here are the story of Zeus and the creation of mankind; a retelling of Jason and the Golden Fleece; and a narrative about the wanderings of Aeneas. The collection also includes Norse myths describing the death of Balder and a variety of stories from the mythology of world cultures.

Other Possibilities

Ride With the Sun	Harold Courlander
African Folktales: Traditional Stories of the Black World	Roger D. Abrahams, Editor
The Dancing Fox: Arctic Folktales	John Bierhorst, Editor
Greek Myths	Robert Graves

Planning Students' Extended Reading

All of the works listed on this page are good choices for students' exploration of the genre of myths and folk tales. Following is some information that will help you choose what to teach:

Customize for *Varying Student Needs*

When assigning the selections in this part to your students keep in mind the following factors:

- *In the Beginning: Creation Stories from Around the World* includes 25 myths based on the theme of origin from different parts of the world. Includes 42 color illustrations
- *The Adventures of Ulysses* is Homer's classic story the *Odyssey* adapted for young readers.
- *Myths and Legends From Ancient Greece and Around the World* is an offering in the Prentice Hall Literature Library. This anthology offers a chance for students to encounter a range of different types of myth. The pieces vary in level of difficulty.

Literature Study Guides

Literature study guides are available for *The Adventures of Ulysses* and *Myths and Legends From Ancient Greece and Around the World*. The guides include section summaries, discussion questions, and activities.

Access Guide to Vocabulary

KEY TO PRONUNCIATION SYMBOLS USED

Symbol	Key Words	Symbol	Key Words	Symbol	Key Words
a	**a**sp, f**a**t, p**a**rrot	u	**u**p, c**u**t, c**o**lor	m	**m**et, ca**m**el, tri**m**
ā	**a**pe, d**a**te, pl**ay**	ʉr	**ur**n, f**ur**, det**er**	n	**n**ot, fla**nn**el, to**n**
ä	**a**h, c**a**r, f**a**ther	ə	**a** in ago	p	**p**ut, a**pp**le, ta**p**
e	**e**lf, t**e**n, b**e**rry		**e** in agent	r	**r**ed, po**r**t, dea**r**
ē	**e**ven, m**ee**t, mon**ey**		**i** in sanity	s	**s**ell, ca**s**tle, pa**ss**
i	**i**s, h**i**t, m**i**rror		**o** in comply	t	**t**op, ca**tt**le, ha**t**
ī	**i**ce, b**i**te, h**igh**		**u** in focus	v	**v**at, ho**v**el, ha**v**e
ō	**o**pen, t**o**ne, g**o**	ər	p**er**haps, murd**er**	w	**w**ill, al**w**ays, s**w**ear
ô	**a**ll, h**o**rn, l**aw**	b	**b**ed, fa**b**le, du**b**	y	**y**et, on**i**on, **y**ard
o͞o	**oo**ze, t**oo**l, cr**ew**	d	**d**ip, bea**d**le, ha**d**	z	**z**ebra, da**zz**le, ha**z**e
o͝o	l**oo**k, p**u**ll, m**oo**r	f	**f**all, a**f**ter, o**ff**	ch	**ch**in, cat**ch**er, ar**ch**
yo͞o	**u**se, c**u**te, f**ew**	g	**g**et, ha**gg**le, do**g**	sh	**sh**e, cu**sh**ion, da**sh**
yoo	**u**nited, c**u**re, glob**u**le	h	**h**e, **h**ead, **h**otel	th	**th**in, no**th**ing, tru**th**
oi	**oi**l, p**oi**nt, t**oy**	j	**j**oy, a**g**ile, ba**dg**e	*th*	**th**en, fa**th**er, la**th**e
ou	**ou**t, cr**ow**d, pl**ow**	k	**k**ill, ta**ck**le, ba**k**e	zh	a**z**ure, lei**s**ure
		l	**l**et, ye**ll**ow, ba**ll**	ŋ	ri**ng**, a**ng**er, dri**nk**

Literary Terms Handbook

ALLITERATION *Alliteration* is the repetition of initial consonant sounds. Writers use alliteration to draw attention to certain words or ideas, to imitate sounds, and to create musical effects. Shel Silverstein uses alliteration for humorous effect in the title of his poem "Sarah Cynthia Sylvia Stout," on page 405.

ALLUSION An *allusion* is a reference to a well-known person, place, event, literary work, or work of art. Understanding what a writer is saying often depends on recognizing allusions. E. E. Cummings's "goat-footed balloonMan" in the poem "in Just-," on page 404, is an allusion to Greek myths about the god Pan. Pan was a goat-footed god associated with spring.

ANECDOTE An *anecdote* is a brief story about an interesting, amusing, or strange event. Writers tell anecdotes to entertain or to make a point. For example, in "Cat on the Go," on page 382, James Herriot tells several anecdotes about the character named Oscar. Herriot tells these anecdotes to amuse the reader and to reveal Oscar's unusual personality.
See *Narration.*

ANTAGONIST An *antagonist* is a character or force in conflict with a main character, or protagonist. In "Rikki-tikki-tavi," on page 464, there are two antagonists, the cobras Nag and Nagaina. The protagonist is the mongoose, Rikki.
See *Conflict* and *Protagonist.*

ATMOSPHERE See *Mood.*

AUTOBIOGRAPHY An *autobiography* is a form of nonfiction in which a person tells his or her own life story. An autobiography may tell about the person's whole life or only a part of it. This text contains several excerpts from autobiographies, including the selections from Ernesto Galarza's *Barrio Boy,* on page 611.
See *Biography* and *Nonfiction.*

BALLAD A *ballad* is a songlike poem that tells a story, often one dealing with adventure and romance. Most ballads are written in four- to six-line stanzas and have regular rhythms and rhyme schemes. A ballad often features a refrain—a regularly repeated line or group of lines.

Originally, ballads were not written down. They were composed orally and then sung. As these early *folk ballads* passed from singer to singer, they often changed dramatically.

Many writers of the modern era have used the ballad form to create *literary ballads*—written imitations of folk ballads. The influence of the ballad tradition can be seen in Alfred Noyes's "The Highwayman," on page 300.
See *Oral Tradition* and *Refrain.*

BIOGRAPHY A *biography* is a form of nonfiction in which a writer tells the life story of another person. Biographies have been written about many famous historical and contemporary people, but they can also be written about ordinary people. An example of a biography of a famous historical person in the text is "Winslow Homer: America's Greatest Painter," on page 586. Because biographies deal with real people and real events, they are classified as nonfiction.
See *Autobiography* and *Nonfiction.*

BLANK VERSE *Blank verse* is poetry written in unrhymed iambic pentameter lines. The following lines from Robert Frost's "Birches" are written in blank verse:

> When I see birches bend to left and right
> Across the lines of straighter darker trees,
> I like to think some boy's been swinging them.

See *Meter.*

CHARACTER A *character* is a person or animal who takes part in the action of a literary work. The main character is the most important character in a story, poem, or play. A minor character is one who takes part in the action, but who is not the focus of attention.

Characters are sometimes classified as flat or round. A *flat character* is one-sided and often stereotypical. A *round character,* on the other hand, is fully developed and exhibits many traits—often both faults and virtues. Teddy's mother, in Rudyard Kipling's story "Rikki-tikki-tavi," on page 464, is an example of a flat character. In Washington Irving's "Rip Van Winkle," on page 144, the title character is round, or fully developed.

Characters can also be classified as dynamic or static. A *dynamic character* is one who changes or grows during the course of the work. A *static character* is one who does not change. Rip Van Winkle is a dynamic character, while Rip's overbearing wife is a static character.
See *Characterization, Hero/Heroine,* and *Motivation.*

CHARACTERIZATION *Characterization* is the act of creating and developing a character. Writers use two major methods of characterization—*direct* and *indirect*.

When describing a character *directly*, a writer states the character's traits, or characteristics. In "Rip Van Winkle," on page 145, Washington Irving describes Rip directly:

> He inherited, however, but little of the martial character of his ancestors. I have observed that he was a simple good-natured man; he was, moreover, a kind neighbor, and an obedient henpecked husband.

When describing a character *indirectly*, a writer depends on the reader to draw conclusions about the character's traits. Sometimes, the writer describes the character's appearance, actions, or speech. At other times, the writer tells what other participants in the story say and think about the character. The reader then draws his or her own conclusions.
See *Character* and *Motivation*.

CLIMAX See *Conflict* and *Plot*.

CONCRETE POEM A *concrete poem* is one with a shape that suggests its subject. The poet arranges the letters, punctuation, and lines to create an image, or picture, on the page. William Jay Smith's "Seal," on page 754, is a concrete poem. Its swirling shape suggests the form of a seal's body and the way the seal moves.

CONFLICT A *conflict* is a struggle between opposing forces. Conflict is one of the most important elements of stories, novels, and plays because it causes the action.

There are two kinds of conflict: external and internal. An *external conflict* is one in which a character struggles against some outside force. For example, in "A Boy and a Man," on page 210, the character Rudi struggles against nature to save the life of a man who has fallen into a crevasse.

An *internal conflict* is one that takes place within the mind of a character. The character struggles to make a decision, take an action, or overcome a feeling. For example, in "A Day's Wait," on page 72, the boy struggles with his feelings of fear and despair because he believes he is dying.
See *Plot*.

DESCRIPTION A *description* is a portrait, in words, of a person, place, or object. Descriptive writing uses images that appeal to the five senses—sight, hearing, touch, taste, and smell.
See *Image*.

DEVELOPMENT See *Plot*.

DIALECT *Dialect* is the form of a language spoken by people in a particular region or group. The English language is divided into many dialects. British English differs from American English. The English spoken in Boston differs from that spoken in Charleston, Chicago, Houston, or San Francisco. This variety adds richness to the language. Dialects differ in pronunciation, grammar, and word choice.

Writers use dialects to make their characters seem realistic. In "The Luckiest Time of All," on page 398, the narrator uses a dialect from the rural southern United States.

DIALOGUE A *dialogue* is a conversation between characters. In poems, novels, and short stories, dialogue is usually set off by quotation marks to indicate a speaker's exact words. In a play, dialogue follows the names of the characters, and no quotation marks are used.
See *Drama*.

DRAMA A *drama* is a story written to be performed by actors. Although a drama is meant to be performed, one can also read the script, or written version, and imagine the action. The script of a drama is made up of dialogue and stage directions. The *dialogue* is the words spoken by the actors. The *stage directions*, usually printed in italics, tell how the actors should look, move, and speak. They also describe the setting, sound effects, and lighting.

Dramas are often divided into parts called *acts*. The acts are often divided into smaller parts called *scenes*.

DYNAMIC CHARACTER See *Character*.

ESSAY An *essay* is a short nonfiction work about a particular subject. Most essays have a single major focus and a clear introduction, body, and conclusion.

There are many types of essays. A *narrative essay* tells a story about a real-life experience. An *expository essay* relates information or provides explanations. A *persuasive essay*, like "I Am a Native of North America," on page 615, presents and supports an opinion. Most essays contain passages that describe people, places, or objects. However, there are very few purely descriptive essays.
See *Description*, *Exposition*, *Narration*, and *Persuasion*.

EXPOSITION *Exposition* is writing or speech that explains a process or presents information. This Literary Terms Handbook is an example of exposition. So are the introductions to the selections in this text. In the plot of a story or drama, the *exposition*, or introduction, introduces the characters, setting, and basic situation.
See *Plot*.

EXTENDED METAPHOR In an *extended metaphor*, as in a regular metaphor, a subject is described as though it were something else. However, extended metaphor differs from regular metaphor in that several comparisons are made. Carl Sandburg uses extended metaphor in his poem "Fog," on page 792. The poem points out a number of similarities between fog and a cat. See *Metaphor.*

FABLE A *fable* is a brief story or poem, usually with animal characters, that teaches a lesson, or moral. The moral is usually stated at the end of the fable.

The fable is an ancient literary form found in many cultures. The fables written by Aesop, a Greek slave who lived in the sixth century B.C., are still popular with children today. Other famous writers of fables include La Fontaine, the seventeenth-century French poet, and James Thurber, the twentieth-century American humorist. See the fables by Aesop on pages 872–873.
See *Moral.*

FANTASY A *fantasy* is highly imaginative writing that contains elements not found in real life. Examples of fantasy include stories that involve supernatural elements, stories that resemble fairy tales, stories that deal with imaginary places and creatures, and science-fiction stories. In Jack Finney's "The Third Level," on page 50, traveling through time is a fantastic element.
See *Science Fiction.*

FICTION *Fiction* is prose writing that tells about imaginary characters and events. Short stories and novels are works of fiction. Some writers base their fiction on actual events and people, adding invented characters, dialogue, settings, and plots. Other writers of fiction rely on imagination alone to provide their materials.
See *Narration, Nonfiction,* and *Prose.*

FIGURATIVE LANGUAGE *Figurative language* is writing or speech that is not meant to be taken literally. The many types of figurative language are known as *figures of speech.* Common figures of speech include hyperbole, metaphor, personification, and simile. Writers use figurative language to state ideas in vivid and imaginative ways. Carl Sandburg uses figurative language to creatively describe the fog in his poem "Fog," on page 792.
See *Metaphor, Personification, Simile,* and *Symbol.*

FLASHBACK A *flashback* is a section of a literary work that interrupts the sequence of events to relate an event from an earlier time.

FLAT CHARACTER See *Character.*

FOLK TALE A *folk tale* is a story composed orally and then passed from person to person by word of mouth. Folk tales originated among people who could neither read nor write. These people entertained one another by telling stories aloud, often about heroes, adventure, magic, or romance. Eventually, modern scholars like Wilhelm and Jakob Grimm began collecting these stories and writing them down. In this way, folk tales have survived into the present day. In the United States, scholars have also collected folk tales. These tales deal with such legendary heroes as Pecos Bill, Paul Bunyan, Mike Fink, and Davy Crockett.
See *Fable, Legend, Myth,* and *Oral Tradition.*

FOOT See *Meter.*

FORESHADOWING *Foreshadowing* is the use, in a literary work, of clues that suggest events that have yet to occur. Writers use foreshadowing to build their readers' expectations and to create suspense. For example, at the beginning of *The Monsters Are Due on Maple Street,* on page 698, the narrator makes the following statement:

> **NARRATOR'S VOICE.** Maple Street. Six-forty-four P.M. on a late September evening. [*A pause*] Maple Street in the last calm and reflective moment . . . before the monsters came!

The narrator's comment foreshadows, or predicts, what will happen later in the play. It leads the reader or audience to expect the arrival of monsters. Later, the reader or audience is surprised to find out who the monsters really are.

FREE VERSE *Free verse* is poetry not written in a regular rhythmical pattern, or meter. In a free verse poem, the poet is free to write lines of any length or with any number of stresses, or beats. Free verse is therefore less constraining than *metrical verse,* in which every line must have a certain length and a certain number of stresses. Walt Whitman's "Miracles," on page 262, is written in free verse.
See *Meter.*

GENRE A *genre* is a division or type of literature. Literature is commonly divided into three major genres: poetry, prose, and drama. Each major genre is in turn divided into lesser genres, as follows:

1. *Poetry:* lyric poetry, concrete poetry, dramatic poetry, narrative poetry, epic poetry
2. *Prose:* fiction (novels and short stories) and nonfiction (biography, autobiography, letters, essays, and reports)
3. *Drama:* serious drama and tragedy, comic drama, melodrama, and farce

See *Drama, Poetry,* and *Prose.*

HAIKU The *haiku* is a three-line Japanese verse form. The first and third lines of a haiku each have five syllables. The second line has seven syllables. A writer of haiku uses images to create a single vivid picture. See examples of haiku on page 756.

HERO/HEROINE A *hero* or *heroine* is a character whose actions are inspiring or noble. Often, heroes and heroines struggle mightily to overcome foes or to escape difficulties. This is true, for example, of Demeter in "Demeter and Persephone," on page 858. The most obvious examples of heroes and heroines are the larger-than-life characters in myths and legends. However, characters who are more ordinary than Demeter can also act heroically. For example, in Alfred Noyes's poem on page 300, the landlord's daughter, Bess, sacrifices her own life to save that of the highwayman. This is a heroic deed, and Bess is therefore a heroine.

HUBRIS *Hubris* is excessive pride. In "Phaëthon, Son of Apollo," on page 854, the central character is guilty of hubris.

IAMB See *Meter.*

IMAGE An *image* is a word or phrase that appeals to one or more of the five senses. Writers use images to describe how their subjects look, sound, feel, taste, and smell. In "Aunt Leaf" on page 791, Mary Oliver uses the image of a medallion to describe her companion.

IRONY *Irony* is the general name given to literary techniques that involve surprising, interesting, or amusing contradictions. In *verbal irony,* words are used to suggest the opposite of their usual meanings. In *dramatic irony,* there is a contradiction between what a character thinks and what the reader or audience knows to be true. In *irony of situation,* an event occurs that directly contradicts the expectations of the characters, the reader, or the audience.

LEGEND A *legend* is a widely told story about the past, one that may or may not have a foundation in fact. Every culture has its own legends—its familiar, traditional stories. An example of a legend is "Popocatepetl and Ixtlaccihuatl," on page 811. This legend comes from the Aztec Indians of Mexico.
See *Oral Tradition.*

LYRIC POEM A *lyric poem* is a highly musical verse that expresses the observations and feelings of a single speaker. Examples of lyric poems in the text include "Washed in Silver," on page 746, and "Winter," on page 748.

MAIN CHARACTER See *Character.*

METAPHOR A *metaphor* is a figure of speech in which something is described as though it were something else. A metaphor, like a simile, works by pointing out a similarity between two unlike things. In her poem "Life," on page 793, Naomi Long Madgett describes life with metaphors, comparing it to a watch, a toy, and a game. See *Extended Metaphor* and *Simile.*

METER The *meter* of a poem is its rhythmical pattern. This pattern is determined by the number of stresses, or beats, in each line. To describe the meter of a poem, you must *scan* its lines. *Scanning* involves marking the stressed and unstressed syllables, as follows:

The lífe | Ĭ léad | Ĭ wánt | tŏ bé

As you can see, each stress is marked with a slanted line (´) and each unstressed syllable with a horseshoe symbol (˘). The stressed and unstressed syllables are then divided by vertical lines (|) into groups called feet. The following types of feet are common in English poetry:

1. *Iamb:* a foot with one unstressed syllable followed by one stressed syllable, as in the word "bĕgín"
2. *Trochee:* a foot with one stressed syllable followed by one unstressed syllable, as in the word "péoplĕ"
3. *Anapest:* a foot with two unstressed syllables followed by one stressed syllable, as in the phrase "ŏn thĕ séa"
4. *Dactyl:* a foot with one stressed syllable followed by two unstressed syllables, as in the word "háppĭnĕss"
5. *Spondee:* a foot with two stressed syllables, as in the word "dówntówn"

Depending on the type of foot that is most common in them, lines of poetry are described as *iambic, trochaic, anapestic,* or *dactylic.*

Lines are also described in terms of the number of feet that occur in them, as follows:

1. *Monometer:* verse written in one-foot lines:

   Thŭs Í
   Păss bý
   Ănd díe

   —Robert Herrick, "Upon His Departure"

2. *Dimeter:* verse written in two-foot lines:

   Thĕre wás | ă wómăn
   Whŏ lívd | ŏn ă híll.
   Ĭf shé's | nŏt góne,
   Shĕ líves | thĕre stíll.

   —Anonymous

3. *Trimeter:* verse written in three-foot lines:

   Where dips | the rock | y highland

Of Sleuth | Wood in | the lake,
There lies | a leaf | y island
Where flap | ping her | ons wake
The drows | y wat | er rats;
—W. B. Yeats, "The Stolen Child"

4. *Tetrameter:* verse written in four-foot lines:
When wear | y with | the long | day's care,
And earth | ly change | from pain | to pain,
And lost, | and read | y to | despair,
Thy kind | voice calls | me back | again
—Emily Brontë, "To Imagination"

5. *Pentameter:* verse written in five-foot lines:
Amidst | these scenes, | O Pil | grim, seek'st |
thou Rome?
Vain is | thy search |—the pomp | of Rome | is fled
—Francisco de Quevedo, "Rome in Her Ruins"

A complete description of the meter of a line tells the kinds of feet each line contains, as well as how many feet of each kind. Thus, the lines from Quevedo's poem would be described as *iambic pentameter* with one variation, a trochee, in the second line. Blank verse is poetry written in unrhymed iambic pentameter. Poetry that does not have a regular meter is called free verse.
See *Blank Verse* and *Free Verse.*

MINOR CHARACTER See *Character.*

MOOD *Mood,* or *atmosphere,* is the feeling created in the reader by a literary work or passage. Writers use many devices to create mood, including images, dialogue, setting, and plot. Often, a writer creates a mood at the beginning of a work and then sustains this mood throughout. Sometimes, however, the mood of the work changes dramatically. For example, the mood of most of "A Boy and a Man," on page 210, is tense and suspenseful. This mood changes after the man is rescued from the crevasse.

MORAL A *moral* is a lesson taught by a literary work. A fable usually ends with a moral that is directly stated. For example, Aesop's fable "The Fox and the Crow," on page 873, ends with the moral "Do not trust *flatterers.*" A poem, novel, short story, or essay often suggests a moral that is not directly stated. The moral must be drawn by the reader, based on other elements in the work.
See *Fable.*

MOTIVATION A *motivation* is a reason that explains or partially explains a character's thoughts, feelings, actions, or speech. Writers try to make their characters' motivations, or motives, as clear and believable as possible.

Characters are often motivated by needs, such as food and shelter. They are also motivated by feelings, such as fear, love, and pride. In "Suzy and Leah," on page 512, dislike for Leah motivates Suzy to keep her dresses, even though they are too small to fit her well.

MYTH A *myth* is a fictional tale that explains the actions of gods or heroes or the origins of elements of nature. Myths are part of the oral tradition. They are composed orally and then passed from generation to generation by word of mouth. Every ancient culture has its own mythology, or collection of myths. The stories on pages 854–866 are retellings, in writing, of myths from ancient Greece. These Greek myths are known collectively as *classical mythology.*
See *Oral Tradition.*

NARRATION *Narration* is writing that tells a story. Fictional works, such as novels and short stories, are examples of narration. So are poems that tell stories, such as "The Cremation of Sam McGee," on page 736. Narration can also be found in many kinds of nonfiction, including autobiographies, biographies, and newspaper reports. A story told in fiction, nonfiction, poetry, or even in drama is called a narrative.
See *Narrative Poem* and *Narrator.*

NARRATIVE POEM A *narrative poem* is a story told in verse. Narrative poems often have all the elements of short stories, including characters, conflict, and plot. An example of a narrative poem is "The Highwayman," on page 300.

NARRATOR A *narrator* is a speaker or character who tells a story. A *third-person narrator* is one who stands outside the action and speaks about it. A *first-person narrator* is one who tells a story and participates in its action.

In some dramas, like *The Monsters Are Due on Maple Street,* on page 696, there is a separate character called "The Narrator," who introduces, comments on, and concludes the play.
See *Point of View.*

NONFICTION *Nonfiction* is prose writing that presents and explains ideas or that tells about real people, places, objects, or events. Autobiographies, biographies, essays, reports, letters, memos, and newspaper articles are all types of nonfiction.
See *Fiction.*

NOVEL A *novel* is a long work of fiction. Novels contain all the elements of short stories, including characters, plot, conflict, and setting. However, novels are much longer

than short stories. The writer of novels, or the novelist, can therefore develop these elements more fully than a writer of short stories can. In addition to its main plot, a novel may contain one or more subplots, or independent, related stories. A novel may also have several themes.
See *Fiction.*

ONOMATOPOEIA *Onomatopoeia* is the use of words that imitate sounds. *Crash, buzz, screech, hiss, neigh, jingle,* and *cluck* are examples of onomatopoeia.

In her poem "Onomatopoeia," on page 783, Eve Merriam uses words like *sputters, spatters, spurts,* and *plash* to re-create the sounds of water splashing from a faucet.

ORAL TRADITION *Oral tradition* is the passing of songs, stories, and poems from generation to generation by word of mouth. Folk songs, folk tales, legends, and myths all come from the oral tradition. No one knows who first created these stories and poems. The authors are *anonymous.*
See *Folk Tale, Legend,* and *Myth.*

PERSONIFICATION *Personification* is a type of figurative language in which a nonhuman subject is given human characteristics. In "Feelings About Words," on page 776, Mary O'Neill personifies words, describing some as "lazy" and some as full of "pride" and "pomp."

PERSUASION *Persuasion* is writing or speech that attempts to convince the reader or listener to adopt a particular opinion or course of action. Newspaper editorials, letters to the editor, advertisements, and campaign speeches use persuasion.

PLOT *Plot* is the sequence of events in a literary work. In most novels, dramas, short stories, and narrative poems, the plot involves both characters and a central conflict. The plot usually begins with an *exposition* that introduces the setting, the characters, and the basic situation. This is followed by the introduction of the central conflict. The conflict then increases during the *rising action* until it reaches a high point of interest or suspense, the *climax.* The climax is followed by the *falling action,* or end, of the central conflict. Any events that occur during the falling action make up the *resolution,* or *denouement.*

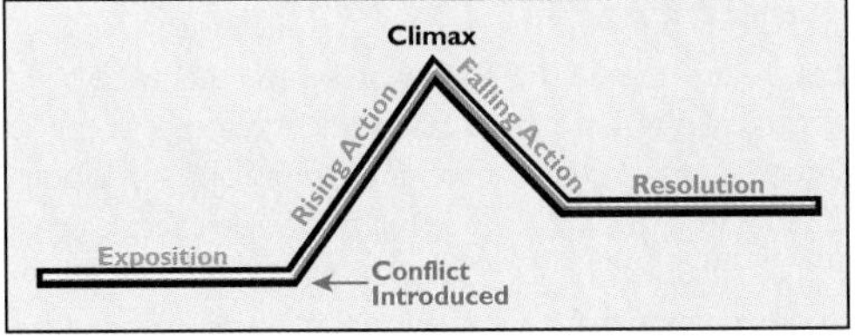

Some plots do not have all these parts. Some stories begin with the inciting incident and end with the resolution. In some, the inciting incident has occurred before the opening of the story.
See *Conflict.*

POETRY *Poetry* is one of the three major types of literature, the others being prose and drama. Defining poetry more precisely isn't easy, for there is no single, unique characteristic that all poems share. Poems are often divided into lines and stanzas and often employ regular rhythmical patterns, or meters. However, some poems are written out just like prose, and some are written in free verse. Most poems make use of highly concise, musical, and emotionally charged language. Many also make use of imagery, figurative language, and special devices of sound such as rhyme.

Major types of poetry include *lyric poetry, narrative poetry,* and *concrete poetry.* Other forms of poetry include *dramatic poetry,* in which characters speak in their own voices, and *epic poetry,* in which the poet tells a long, involved tale about gods or heroes.
See *Concrete Poem, Genre, Lyric Poem,* and *Narrative Poem.*

POINT OF VIEW *Point of view* is the perspective, or vantage point, from which a story is told. Three commonly used points of view are first person, omniscient third person, and limited third person.

In stories told from the *first-person point of view,* the narrator is a character in the story and refers to himself or herself with the pronoun "I." In "Ribbons," on page 524, the character Stacy serves as a first-person narrator.

The two kinds of *third-person point of view,* limited and omniscient, are called "third person" because the narrator uses third-person pronouns such as "he" and "she" to refer to the characters. There is no "I" telling the story.

In stories told from the *omniscient third-person point of view,* the narrator knows and tells about what each character feels and thinks. "Rikki-tikki-tavi," on page 464, is written from the omniscient third-person point of view.

In stories told from the *limited third-person point of view,* the narrator relates the inner thoughts and feelings of only one character, and everything is viewed from this character's perspective. "A Boy and a Man," on page 210, is written from the limited third-person point of view.
See *Narrator.*

PROSE *Prose* is the ordinary form of written language. Most writing that is not poetry, drama, or song is considered prose. Prose is one of the major genres of literature and occurs in two forms: fiction and nonfiction. See *Fiction, Genre,* and *Nonfiction.*

PROTAGONIST The *protagonist* is the main character in a literary work. In "Rikki-tikki-tavi," on page 464, the protagonist, or main character, is Rikki, the mongoose. See *Antagonist* and *Character.*

REFRAIN A *refrain* is a regularly repeated line or group of lines in a poem or song. In "The Dying Cowboy," on page 306, these lines separate the song's verses and stress the song's main idea:

"Oh, bury me not on the lone prairie
Where the wild coyotes will howl o'er me,
In a narrow grave just six by three.
Oh, bury me not on the lone prairie."

In some cases, the refrain varies slightly each time it appears.

REPETITION *Repetition* is the use, more than once, of any element of language—a sound, word, phrase, clause, or sentence. Repetition is used in both prose and poetry. In prose, a situation or character may be repeated with some variations. A subplot, for example, may repeat, with variations, the circumstances presented in the main plot.

Poets make use of many varieties of repetition. *Rhyme, alliteration,* and *rhythm* are all repetitions of sounds or sound patterns. A *refrain* is a repeated line. See *Alliteration, Meter, Plot, Rhyme,* and *Rhyme Scheme.*

RESOLUTION See *Plot.*

RHYME *Rhyme* is the repetition of sounds at the ends of words. Poets use rhyme to lend a songlike quality to their verses and to emphasize certain words and ideas. Many traditional poems contain *end rhymes,* or rhyming words at the ends of lines. See, for example, the end rhymes in Robert Frost's "The Pasture," on page 755. Another common device is the use of *internal rhymes,* or rhyming words within lines. Notice, for example, the internal rhymes in the following passage from Edgar Allan Poe's "Annabel Lee," on page 775:

For the moon never beams without
  bringing me dreams
Of the beautiful Annabel Lee;

See *Rhyme Scheme.*

RHYME SCHEME A *rhyme scheme* is a regular pattern of rhyming words in a poem. To indicate the rhyme scheme of a poem, use lowercase letters. Each rhyme is assigned a different letter, as follows:

Under a spreading chestnut tree *a*
The village smithy stands; *b*
The smith, a mighty man is he, *a*
With large and sinewy hands; *b*
And the muscles of his brawny arms *c*
Are strong as iron bands. *b*

—Henry Wadsworth Longfellow, "The Village Blacksmith"

The rhyme scheme of these lines is thus *ababcb.*

RHYTHM *Rhythm* is the pattern of beats, or stresses, in spoken or written language. See *Meter.*

ROUND CHARACTER See *Character.*

SCIENCE FICTION *Science fiction* is writing that tells about imaginary events that involve science or technology. Many science-fiction stories are set in the future. "All Summer in a Day," on page 288, is a science-fiction story. In this story, Ray Bradbury describes events that take place in the future on the planet Venus.

SENSORY LANGUAGE *Sensory language* is writing or speech that appeals to one or more of the five senses. See *Image.*

SETTING The *setting* of a literary work is the time and place of the action. The time includes not only the historical period—the past, present, or future—but also the year, the season, the time of day, and even the weather. The place may be a specific country, state, region, community, neighborhood, building, institution, or home. Details such as dialects, clothing, customs, and modes of transportation are often used to establish setting.

In most stories the setting serves as a backdrop—a context in which the characters interact. In some stories, the setting is crucial to the plot. For example, the weather on the planet Venus is central to the plot of Ray Bradbury's story "All Summer in a Day," on page 288. Setting can also help to create a mood, or feeling. In "The Third Level," on page 52, the writer's description of a summer evening in a small Illinois town creates a mood of peace and innocence. See *Mood.*

SHORT STORY A *short story* is a brief work of fiction. Like a novel, a short story presents a sequence of events, or plot. The plot usually deals with a central conflict faced by a main character, or protagonist. Like a lyric poem, a short story is concise and creates a single effect, or dominant impression, on its reader. The events in a short story usually communicate a message about life or human nature. This message, or central idea, is the story's theme. See *Conflict, Plot,* and *Theme.*

SIMILE A *simile* is a figure of speech that uses *like* or *as* to make a direct comparison between two unlike ideas. Everyday speech often contains similes, such as "pale as a ghost," "good as gold," and "clever as a fox."

Writers use similes to describe people, places, and things vividly. Poets, especially, create similes to point out new and interesting ways of viewing the world.

SPEAKER The *speaker* is the imaginary voice assumed by the writer of a poem. The speaker is the character who tells the poem. This character, or voice, often is not identified by name. The speaker's voice in Robert Frost's poem "Stopping by Woods on a Snowy Evening," on page 260, carries a sense of quiet sadness, but also mystery.
See *Narrator.*

STAGE DIRECTIONS *Stage directions* are notes included in a drama to describe how the work is to be performed or staged. Stage directions are usually printed in italics and enclosed within parentheses or brackets. Some stage directions describe the movements, costumes, emotional states, and ways of speaking of the characters. This example of stage directions can be found in "The Dying Detective," on page 329.

> **MRS. HUDSON.** He's asleep, sir.
> [*They approach the bed.* WATSON *comes round to the audience's side and looks down at* HOLMES *for a moment. He shakes his head gravely, then he and* MRS. HUDSON *move away beyond the foot of the bed.*]

See *Drama.*

STANZA A *stanza* is a formal division of lines in a poem, considered as a unit. Many poems are divided into stanzas that are separated by spaces. Stanzas often function just like paragraphs in prose. Each stanza states and develops a single main idea.

Stanzas are commonly named according to the number of lines found in them, as follows:

1. *Couplet:* two-line stanza
2. *Tercet:* three-line stanza
3. *Quatrain:* four-line stanza
4. *Cinquain:* five-line stanza
5. *Sestet:* six-line stanza
6. *Heptastich:* seven-line stanza
7. *Octave:* eight-line stanza

Robert Frost's "Stopping by Woods on a Snowy Evening," on page 260, is written in quatrains:

> Whose woods these are I think I know.
> His house is in the village, though;
> He will not see me stopping here
> To watch his woods fill up with snow.

Division into stanzas is common in traditional poetry and is often accompanied by rhyme. Notice, for example, that in the stanzas from the Frost poem, the first, second, and fourth lines rhyme. However, some rhyming poems are not divided into stanzas, and some poems divided into stanzas do not contain rhyme.

STATIC CHARACTER See *Character.*

SURPRISE ENDING A *surprise ending* is a conclusion that is unexpected. Sometimes, a surprise ending follows a false resolution. The reader thinks that the conflict has already been resolved but then is confronted with a new twist that changes the outcome of the plot. Often, a surprise ending is *foreshadowed,* or subtly hinted at, in the course of the work.
See *Foreshadowing* and *Plot.*

SUSPENSE *Suspense* is a feeling of anxious uncertainty about the outcome of events in a literary work. Writers create suspense by raising questions in the minds of their readers. For example, in "A Day's Wait," on page 72, Ernest Hemingway raises questions about whether the boy will recover from his illness.

SYMBOL A *symbol* is anything that stands for or represents something else. Symbols are common in everyday life. A dove with an olive branch in its beak is a symbol of peace. A blindfolded woman holding a balanced scale is a symbol of justice.

THEME A *theme* is a central message, concern, or purpose in a literary work. A theme can usually be expressed as a generalization, or general statement, about people or about life. The theme of a work is not a summary of its plot. The theme is the central idea that the writer communicates.

A theme may be stated directly by the writer, although this is unusual. Instead, most themes are not directly stated but are implied. When the theme is implied, the reader must figure out what the theme is by looking carefully at what the work reveals about people or about life.

WRITING HANDBOOK

THE WRITING PROCESS

The writing process can be roughly divided into a series of stages: prewriting, drafting, revising, editing, proofreading, and publishing. It is important to remember that the writing process is one that moves backward as well as forward. Even while you are moving forward in the creation of your composition, you may still return to a previous stage—to rethink or rewrite.

Following are stages of the writing process, with key points to address during each stage.

Prewriting

In this stage, you plan out the work to be done. You prepare to write by exploring ideas, gathering information, and working out an organization plan. Following are the key steps to take at this stage:

Step 1: Analyze the writing situation. Before writing, analyze the writing assignment. To do this, ask yourself the following questions about each element:

- ***Topic (the subject you will be writing about):*** What exactly are you going to write about? Can you state your subject in a sentence? Is your subject too broad or too narrow?
- ***Purpose (what you want your writing to accomplish):*** Do you want your writing to explain? To describe? To persuade? To tell a story? To entertain? What do you want your audience to learn or to understand?
- ***Audience (the people who will read or listen to your writing):*** Who is your audience? What might they already know about your subject? What basic facts will you have to provide for them?

Step 2: Gather ideas and information. After thinking about the writing situation, you may find that you need more information. If so, you must decide how to gather this information. On the other hand, you may find that you already have too much information—that your topic is too broad. If this is the case, then you must decide how to narrow your topic.

There are many ways to gather information and to narrow a topic. Consider these strategies:

- ***Brainstorm.*** Discuss the topic with a group of people. Try to generate as many ideas as possible. Not all of your brainstormed ideas will be useful or suitable. You'll need to evaluate them later.
- ***Consult other people about your topic.*** Speaking with others may suggest an idea or an approach you did not see at first.
- ***Make a list of questions about your topic.*** Begin your questions with words like *who, what, where, when, why,* and *how.* Then, find the answers to your questions.

Step 3: Organize your notes. Once you have gathered enough information, you will have to organize it. Sort your ideas and notes; decide which points are most important. You can make an outline to show the order of ideas, or you can use some other organizing plan that works for you.

There are many ways to organize and develop your material. Careful organization will make your writing easy to read and understand. The following are common methods of organizing information:

- ***Time Order or Chronological Order*** Events are organized in order of occurrence (from earliest to latest, for example).
- ***Spatial Order*** Details are organized by position in space (from left to right, for example).
- ***Degree Order*** This order is organization by size, amount, or intensity (from coldest to warmest, for example).
- ***Priority Order*** This is organization by importance, value, usefulness, or familiarity (from worst to best, for example).

Drafting

Drafting follows prewriting and is the second stage in the writing process. Working from your prewriting notes and your outline or plan, you develop and present your ideas in sentences and paragraphs. The following are important points to remember about drafting:

- Do not try to make your rough draft perfect. Concentrate on getting your ideas on paper. Once this is done, you can make improvements in the revision and proofreading stages.
- Keep your audience and purpose in mind as you write. This will help you determine what you say and how you say it.
- Don't be afraid to set aside earlier ideas if later

ones work better. Some of the best ideas are those that were not planned at the beginning.

Most papers, regardless of the topic, are developed with an introduction, a body, and a conclusion. Here are tips for developing these parts of a paper:

Introduction In the introduction to a paper, you want to engage your readers' attention and let them know the purpose of your paper. You might use the following strategies in your introduction:

- State your main idea.
- Use an anecdote.
- Startle your readers.
- Take a stand.
- Quote someone.

Body of the paper In the body of your paper, you present your information and make your points. Your *organization* is an important factor in leading readers through your ideas. Your elaboration on your main ideas is also important. *Elaboration* is the development of ideas to make your written work precise and complete. You can use the following kinds of details to elaborate your main ideas:

- Facts and statistics
- Sensory details
- Explanation and definition
- Anecdotes
- Examples
- Quotations

Conclusion The ending of your paper is the final impression you leave with your readers. Your conclusion should give readers the sense that you have pulled everything together. Following are some effective ways to end your paper:

- Summarize and restate.
- State an opinion.
- Tell an anecdote.
- Ask a question.
- Call for action.

Revising

Once you have a draft, you can look at it critically or have others review it. This is the time to make changes on many levels. Revising is the process of reworking what you have written to make it as good as it can be. You may change some details so that your ideas flow smoothly and are clearly supported. You may discover that some details don't work, and you'll need to discard them. Try these strategies:

- Read your work aloud. This is an excellent way to catch any ideas or details that have been left out and to notice errors in logic.
- Ask someone else to read your work. Choose someone who can point out how to improve it.

How do you know what to look for and what to change? Here is a checklist of major writing issues. If the answer to any of these questions is no, then that is an area that needs revision.

1. Does the writing achieve my purpose?
2. Does the paper have a single focus, with all details and information contributing to that focus?
3. Is the arrangement of information clear and logical?
4. Have I elaborated enough to give my audience adequate information?

Editing

When you edit, you look more closely at the language you have used so that the way you express your ideas is most effective.

- Replace dull language with vivid, precise words.
- Cut or change unnecessary repetition.
- Check passive voice; active voice is more effective.
- Replace wordy expressions with shorter, more precise ones.

Proofreading

After you finish your final draft, the last step is to proofread the draft to make it ready for a reader. You may do this on your own or with the help of a partner.

It's useful to have handy both a dictionary and a usage handbook to help you check for correctness. Here are the tasks in proofreading:

- Correct errors in grammar and usage.
- Correct errors in punctuation and capitalization.
- Correct errors in spelling.

Publishing and Presenting

These are some of the many ways in which you can share your work:

- Share your writing in a small group by reading it aloud or by passing it around for others to read.
- Read your work aloud to the class.
- Display your work on a classroom bulletin board.
- Submit your writing to the school literary magazine, or start a literary magazine for your school or for your class.
- Submit your writing to your school or community newspaper.
- Enter your writing in literary contests for student writers.
- Submit your writing to a magazine that publishes work by young people.

The Modes of Writing

Expression

Expression is writing that captures your thoughts, feelings, or experiences. Some expressive writing is private, written only for you to read. Some is written to be shared with an audience—friends, family, or other interested readers. Expressive writing is another way to communicate how you think and feel. You can share your experiences and emotions and reflect on memorable moments in your life. Through expressive writing, you can capture on paper what is most meaningful to you. Expressive writing takes many forms. Here are a few of them:

Personal Letter Writing a personal letter is a good way to share your thoughts and experiences with a friend or family member. In a personal letter, you can express feelings or thoughts you have difficulty talking about directly to the person.

Personal Journal A journal is a book with blank pages in which you record your personal feelings, thoughts, or observations over a period of time. As you write in your journal, you will have a record of the day-to-day happenings or most important events of your own life. Most personal journals are kept private because they are very personal, although some journals have been published to be read by the public.

Personal Memoir In a memoir, you write about significant events from your past and include your thoughts and feelings about those experiences. A memoir may be brief and focus on a single event or it may describe a larger part of your life.

Description

Description is writing that creates a vivid picture for readers, draws readers into a scene, and makes readers feel as if they are meeting a character or experiencing an event firsthand. A description may stand on its own or be part of a longer work, such as a short story.

When you write a description, bring it to life with sensory details, which tell you how your subject looks, smells, sounds, tastes, or feels. You'll want to choose your details carefully, so that you create a single main impression of your subject. These are a few types of descriptions:

Observation In an observation, you describe an event that you have witnessed firsthand, often over an extended period of time. You may focus on an aspect of daily life or on a scientific phenomenon, such as a storm or an eclipse.

Remembrance of People and Places When you write a remembrance, you use vivid descriptive details to bring to life memorable people, places, or events from your past. You include details that convey your feelings about your subject.

Narration

Whenever writers tell any type of story, they are using narration. Most narratives share certain elements—characters, a setting, a sequence of events (or plot, in fiction), and, often, a theme. You might be asked to write one of these types of narration:

Firsthand Biography In a firsthand biography, you tell about the life of a person whom you know personally. You can use your close relationship with the person to help you include personal insights not found in biographies based solely on research.

Short Story Short stories are short fictional narratives in which a main character faces a conflict that is resolved by the end of the story. In planning a short story, focus on developing plot, setting, and characters.

Autobiographical Incident An autobiographical incident tells a true story about a specific event in the writer's life. Because you are the writer and the central figure in an autobiographical incident, this type of writing reveals more about you than about other people.

Exposition: Giving Information

Exposition to give information is writing that informs or explains. In writing expositions that give information, the information you include is factual and the opinions you express should be based on factual information. Here are some types of exposition you may be asked to write:

Summary To write a summary or synopsis of a story, write as few words as possible to give the reader basic information about the plot, characters, and setting without going into detail. To write a summary of an event, present the details as factually as possible and avoid giving personal opinions about what happened.

Classification When writing classification, you put groups of items into categories and define the groups, using facts and examples. For example, you might group animals into categories, such as mammals and reptiles, and define them according to their characteristics.

How-to Composition In a how-to essay, you provide detailed, step-by-step directions that explain a process.

Exposition: Making Connections

Exposition can **make connections** for readers by comparing and contrasting two subjects, by examining a problem and its solution, or by connecting information to an opinion about something. Here are some types of exposition that make connections:

Comparison-and-Contrast Essay A comparison-and-contrast essay points out the similarities and differences between two subjects. For example, when you compare and contrast two objects, you point out the similarities and differences in their physical qualities—how they look and what they're made of—and their functions—how they're used and how they work.

Written Solution to a Problem Writers use exposition to present or explain a problem and to provide a solution. In a written solution to a problem, you identify a specific problem and then suggest one or more solutions supported with facts and examples.

Persuasion

Persuasion is writing or speaking that attempts to convince people to agree with a position or take a desired action. When used effectively, persuasive writing has the power to change people's lives. As a reader and a writer, you will find yourself engaged in many forms of persuasion. Here are a few of them:

Advice Column An advice column provides readers with suggestions for solving problems or improving their lives. When writing an advice column, include facts and other information to support your advice.

Advertisement The purpose of an advertisement is to persuade people to buy something, accept an idea, vote for someone, or support a cause. When you write an advertisement, include imaginative, lively writing that will catch your readers' or viewers' attention. Present your information in an appealing way to make your product or service seem desirable.

Essay Supporting an Opinion In writing an essay to support an opinion, you build an argument and support your opinions with a variety of evidence: facts, statistics, examples, and statements from experts.

Reports

A **report** is writing based on research. People write reports to present information and ideas, to share findings and research, and to explain subjects they have studied. Here are some types of reports:

Biographical Sketch When you write a biographical sketch, include facts about a person's character and achievements. Include the dates and details of the main events in the person's life, presenting the information in chronological order beginning with childhood.

Lab/Experiment Report In a lab/experiment report, you define or explain the purpose of your experiment, describe the materials used, and outline the procedures followed. You also describe your observations and state the conclusions you reached.

Library Research Report When you write a library research report, put together information from books and other library sources. Include details from the research to support a main idea. Also, include footnotes, or credits, to cite your sources.

Creative

Creative Writing blends imagination, ideas, and emotions, and allows you to present your own view of the world. Poems, songs, and dramas are examples of creative writing. The literature in this anthology may inspire you to create your own works, such as these:

Song Lyrics In writing lyrics, or words, for a song, you use many elements of poetry—rhyme, rhythm, repetition, and imagery. Song lyrics convey emotions and make the reader think.

Poem Writing a poem is a way to express thoughts and feelings about a subject. Poems present ideas and stir emotions in readers. In writing poems, use figurative language and sensory images to create strong impact or rhyme; use rhythm and repetition to create a musical quality.

Monologue A monologue is a dramatic speech by a single character. In writing a monologue, choose a subject, and write the details from your subject's point of view.

Response to Literature

In a **response to literature,** you express your thoughts and feelings about a work and often, in so doing, gain a better understanding of the work. Response to literature can take many forms—oral or written, formal or informal. Here are two typical forms:

Reader's Response Journal Entry Your reader's response journal is a record of your feelings about works you've read. Use it to remind yourself of works that you liked or disliked or to provide a source of writing ideas.

Letter to an Author People sometimes respond to a work of literature by writing a letter to the author. You can praise the work, ask questions, or offer constructive criticism.

Grammar and Mechanics Handbook

Nouns A **noun** is the name of a person, place, thing, or idea. A **common noun** names any one of a class of people, places, or things. A **proper noun** names a specific person, place, or thing.

Common Nouns	Proper Nouns
writer	Russell Baker
city	Los Angeles

Pronouns A **pronoun** is a word that stands for a noun or for a word that takes the place of a noun.

A **personal pronoun** refers to (1) the person speaking, (2) the person spoken to, or (3) the person, place, or thing spoken about.

	Singular	Plural
First Person	I, me, my, mine	we, us, our, ours
Second Person	you, your, yours	you, your, yours
Third Person	he, him, his, she, her, hers, it, its	they, them, their, theirs

She is involved in work her soul must have.

—*from* "In Search of Our Mothers' Gardens," Walker, p. 115

They would sit at dinner tables, cool drinks in their hands, and *scowl*.

—"Seventh Grade," Soto, p. 123

A **demonstrative pronoun** directs attention to a specific person, place, or thing.

this lamp *these* rugs

An **interrogative pronoun** is used to begin a question.

What is the title of the story?

Who is the author of "Mother to Son"?

An **indefinite pronoun** refers to a person, place, or thing, often without specifying which one.

Many of the players were tired.

Everyone brought something.

Verbs A **verb** is a word that shows an action, a condition, or the fact that something exists.

An **action verb** indicates the action of someone or something.

Bears store fat
Chipmunks gather nuts. . . .

—"Winter," Giovanni, p. 748

A **linking verb** connects the subject of a sentence with a noun or a pronoun that renames or describes the subject.

She was a very frail girl. . . .

—"All Summer in a Day," Bradbury, p. 290

A **helping verb** can be added to another verb to make a single verb phrase.

They had read in class about the sun.

—"All Summer in a Day," Bradbury, p. 290

Adjectives An **adjective** describes a noun or a pronoun, or gives a noun or a pronoun a more specific meaning. Adjectives answer these questions:

What kind?	*red* rose, *small* bowl
Which one?	*this* spoon, *those* pots
How many?	*four* hours, *many* tomatoes
How much?	*no* rain, *little* money

The **articles** *the, a,* and *an* are adjectives. *An* is used before a word beginning with a vowel sound.

A noun may sometimes be used as an adjective.

family home *science* fiction

Adverbs An **adverb** modifies a verb, an adjective, or another adverb. Adverbs answer the questions *where, when, in what way,* or *to what extent.*

He ran *outside.* (modifies verb *ran*)

She *never* wrote us. (modifies verb *wrote*)

Close the window *quickly.* (modifies verb *close*)

We were *very* sad. (modifies adjective *sad*)

They left *too* suddenly. (modifies adverb *suddenly*)

Prepositions A **preposition** relates a noun or a pronoun following it to another word in the sentence.

across the road *near* the corner
except me *during* the show

Conjunctions A **conjunction** connects other words or groups of words.

A **coordinating conjunction** connects similar kinds or groups of words.

lions *and* tigers small *but* strong

Correlative conjunctions are used in pairs to connect similar words or groups of words.

both Zachary *and* Justin   *neither* they *nor* I

Interjections An **interjection** is a word that expresses feeling or emotion and functions independently of a sentence.

"Ssh! He's waking."

—"The Dying Detective," Hardwick and Hardwick, p. 330

"Now, look here, Holmes!"

—"The Dying Detective," Hardwick and Hardwick, p. 330

Sentences A **sentence** is a group of words with two main parts: a complete subject and a complete predicate. Together, these parts express a complete thought.

A **fragment** is a group of words that does not express a complete thought.

Into the room quietly.

Strolled until night came.

Subject-Verb Agreement To make a **subject** and a **verb agree**, make sure that both are singular or both are plural. Two or more singular subjects joined by *or* or *nor* must have a singular verb. When singular and plural subjects are joined by *or* or *nor,* the verb must agree with the closest subject.

He is at the door.
They drive home every day.
Jeff or *Sam is* absent.
Both *pets are* hungry.
Either the *chairs* or the *table is* on sale.
Neither the *tree* nor the *shrubs were* in bloom.

Phrases A **phrase** is a group of words without a subject and a verb that functions in a sentence as one part of speech.

A **prepositional phrase** is a group of words that includes a preposition and a noun or a pronoun that is the object of the preposition.

near the town   with them
inside our house   beneath the floor

An **adjective phrase** is a prepositional phrase that modifies a noun or a pronoun by telling *what kind, which one,* or *how many.*

Friends *in the barrio* explained that the director was called a principal . . .

—from *Barrio Boy,* Galarza, p. 611

An **adverb phrase** is a prepositional phrase that modifies a verb, an adjective, or an adverb by pointing out *where, when, in what way,* or *to what extent.*

I had not yet put the sheet *on him.*

—"Lather and Nothing Else," Téllez, p. 492

An **appositive phrase** is a noun or a pronoun with modifiers, placed next to a noun or a pronoun to add information and details.

As a freelance illustrator for *Harper's Weekly, America's most important news magazine,* he was considered one of the country's finest woodblock engravers.

—"Winslow Homer: America's Greatest Painter," Levitt, p. 587

A **participial phrase** is a participle modified by an adjective or an adverb phrase or accompanied by a complement. The entire phrase acts as an adjective.

Finding no takers, Felix decided to split to his aunt's.

—"Amigo Brothers," Thomas, p. 354

An **infinitive phrase** is an infinitive with modifiers, complements, or a subject, all acting together as a single part of speech.

He came into the room *to shut the windows* while we were still in bed and I saw he looked ill.

—"A Day's Wait," Hemingway, p. 72

Clause A **clause** is a group of words with its own subject and verb.

An **independent clause** can stand by itself as a complete sentence.

A **subordinate clause** has a subject and a verb, but it cannot stand by itself as a complete sentence; it can only be part of a sentence.

An **adjective clause** is a subordinate clause that modifies a noun or a pronoun by telling *what kind, which one,* or *how many.*

He was a descendant of the Van Winkles *who figured so gallantly in the chivalrous days of Peter Stuyvesant . . .*

—"Rip Van Winkle," Irving, p. 145

An **adverb clause** modifies a verb, an adjective, or an adverb by telling *where, when, in what way, to what extent, under what condition,* or *why.*

"*When I look at race relations today,* I can see that some positive changes have come about."

—"All Together Now," Jordan, p. 618

Summary of Capitalization and Punctuation

Capitalization

Capitalize the first word of a sentence.

At the corner stood a drugstore, brilliant with electric lights.

—"After Twenty Years," O. Henry, p. 457

Capitalize all proper nouns and adjectives.

Amy Tan   Amazon River   Thanksgiving Day
Florida   October   Italian

Capitalize a person's title when it is followed by the person's name or when it is used in direct address.

Doctor   Chief Wu   Dame Van Winkle

Capitalize titles showing family relationships when they refer to a specific person, unless they are preceded by a possessive noun or pronoun.

Aunt Sarah Shoaf   Teddy's mother

Capitalize the first word and all other key words in the titles of books, periodicals, poems, stories, plays, paintings, and other works of art.

from *Into Thin Air*

"All Summer in a Day"   "Valediction"

Capitalize the first word and all nouns in letter salutations and the first word in letter closings.

Dear Mr. Herriot,   Yours truly,

Punctuation

End Marks Use a **period** to end a declarative sentence, an imperative sentence, and most abbreviations.

We read the haiku.

Review the tanka before you recite it.

Use a **question mark** to end a direct question or an incomplete question in which the rest of the question is understood.

Has spring come indeed?

—"Haiku," Bashō, p. 756

"Go ahead, let her talk. What about it?"

—*The Monsters Are Due on Maple Street*, Serling, p. 703

Use an **exclamation mark** after a statement showing strong emotion, an urgent imperative sentence, or an interjection expressing strong emotion.

"It's Oscar—he's gone!"

—"Cat on the Go," Herriot, p. 385

"Get me out of this!"

—"The Night the Bed Fell," Thurber, p. 281

"Bah! Humbug!"

—"A Christmas Carol: Scrooge and Marley," Horovitz, p. 650

Commas Use a **comma** before the coordinating conjunction to separate two independent clauses in a compound sentence.

They were among the last students to arrive in class, so all the good desks in the back had already been taken.

—"Seventh Grade," Soto, p. 125

Use commas to separate three or more words, phrases, or clauses in a series.

There were two filling stations at the intersection with Union Avenue, as well as an A&P, a fruit stand, a bakery, a barber shop, Zuccarelli's drugstore, and a diner shaped like a railroad car.

—"No Gumption," Baker, p. 570

Use commas to separate adjectives of equal rank. Do not use commas to separate adjectives that must stay in a specific order.

He did big, masculine pictures of hunting and fishing. . . .

—"Winslow Homer: America's Greatest Painter," Levitt, p. 588

Use a comma after an introductory word, phrase, or clause.

Naturally, Ian chose the fattest story he could . . .

—"Ribbons," Yep, p. 530

In his corner, Antonio was doing what all fighters do when they are hurt.

—"Amigo Brothers," Thomas, p. 358

Outside the wind had picked up, sending the rain against the window with a force that shook the glass in its frame.

—"The Treasure of Lemon Brown," Myers, p. 534

Use commas to set off parenthetical and nonessential expressions.

We were, of course, saying nothing. . . .

—from *Barrio Boy*, Galarza, p. 612

Use commas with places and dates made up of two or more parts.

Ray Bradbury was born in Waukegan, Illinois.

On July 20, 1969, American astronauts first set foot on the moon.

Use commas after items in addresses, after the salutation in a personal letter, after the closing in all letters, and in numbers of more than three digits.

Linden Lane, Durham, N.C. My dear Sam,

Sincerely yours, 1,372,597

Use a comma to set off a direct quotation.

"Very good," I answered, turning my attention now to the brush.

—"Lather and Nothing Else," Téllez, p. 492

Semicolons Use a **semicolon** to join independent clauses that are not already joined by a conjunction.

The motto of all the mongoose family is, "Run out and find out"; and Rikki-tikki was a true mongoose.

—"Rikki-tikki-tavi," Kipling, p. 465

Use a semicolon to join independent clauses or items in a series that already contain commas.

Your response with your own mind and body and memory and emotions gives the poem its ability to work its magic; if you give to it, it will give to you, and give plenty.

—"How to Enjoy Poetry," Dickey, p. 557

Colons Use a **colon** before a list of items following an independent clause.

The following words are examples of onomatopoeia: *buzz, hiss, jingle,* and *cluck.*

Use a colon in numbers giving the time, in salutations in business letters, and in labels used to signal important ideas.

4:30 A.M. Dear Ms. Mazzilli:

Danger: Landslide Area Ahead

Quotation Marks A **direct quotation** represents a person's exact speech or thoughts and is enclosed in quotation marks.

In 1910, just before he died, he wrote in a letter, "All is lovely outside my house and inside my house and myself."

—"Winslow Homer: America's Greatest Painter," Levitt, p. 589

An **indirect quotation** reports only the general meaning of what a person said or thought and does not require quotation marks.

Mom says I should invite her home for dinner soon.

—"Suzy and Leah," Yolen, p. 515

Always place a comma or a period inside the final quotation mark of a direct quotation.

"It's no good, Triss," I said gently. "It's got to be done."

—"Cat on the Go," Herriot, p. 383

Place a question mark or exclamation mark inside the final quotation mark if the end mark is part of the quotation; if it is not part of the quotation, place it outside the final quotation mark.

As Rikki-tikki went up the path, he heard his "attention" notes like a tiny dinner gong; and then the steady "*Ding-dong-tock!* Nag is dead—*dong!* Nagaina is dead! *Ding-dong-tock!*"

—"Rikki-tikki-tavi," Kipling, pp. 474–475

Does that poem by Robert Frost start with the line, "I'm going out to clean the pasture spring"?

—"The Pasture," Frost, p. 755

Underline or italicize the titles of long written works, movies, television and radio series, lengthy works of music, paintings, and sculptures.

<u>A Christmas Carol</u> *Star Trek*

<u>The Mona Lisa</u>

Use quotation marks around the titles of short written works, episodes in a series, songs, and titles of works mentioned as parts of collections.

"Winter" "Cat on the Go"

"Let's Steal the Moon" "Annabel Lee"

Hyphens Use a **hyphen** with certain numbers, after certain prefixes, with two or more words used as one word, and with a compound modifier that comes before a noun.

fifty-four self-employed

daughter-in-law happy-go-lucky friend

Apostrophes Add an **apostrophe** and -*s* to show the possessive case of most singular nouns.

Aesop's fables　　the author's story

Dickens's novels

Add an apostrophe to show the possessive case of plural nouns ending in -*s* and -*es*.

the bats' squeaks　　the Brookses' home

Add an apostrophe and -*s* to show the possessive case of plural nouns that do not end in -*s* or -*es*.

the women's hats　　the mice's whiskers

Use an apostrophe in a contraction to indicate the position of the missing letter or letters.

"I'd better not say I have inflammatory rheumatism," I decided.

—"Stolen Day," Anderson, p. 484

Glossary of Common Usage

accept, except

Accept is a verb that means "to receive" or "to agree to." *Except* is a preposition that means "other than" or "leaving out." Do not confuse these two words.

The Amigo brothers *accepted* the challenge and prepared for the match.

All the children *except* Margot played.

affect, effect

Affect is normally a verb meaning "to influence" or "to bring about a change in." *Effect* is usually a noun, meaning "result."

The death of his son deeply *affects* Iona.

In James Thurber's essay, the collapse of the bed has many humorous *effects*.

among, between

Among is usually used with three or more items. *Between* is generally used with only two items.

"Zoo" was *among* the stories I liked best.

There was a special relationship *between* Felix and Antonio in "Amigo Brothers."

amount, number

Amount refers to a mass or a unit, whereas *number* refers to individual items that can be counted. Therefore, *amount* generally appears with singular nouns, and *number* appears with plural nouns.

To climb Mt. Everest, Jon Krakauer needed a huge *amount* of determination.

In "The Night the Bed Fell," the family members draw a *number* of mistaken conclusions.

bad, badly

Use the predicate adjective *bad* after linking verbs such as *feel, look,* and *seem.* Use *badly* whenever an adverb is required.

At the beginning of "Amigo Brothers," Felix and Antonio feel *bad* about the upcoming fight.

When Charley finds he's stepped back in time to 1894, he is *badly* confused at first.

because of, due to

Use *due to* if it can logically replace the phrase *caused by.* In introductory phrases, however, *because of* is better usage than *due to.*

Washington Irving's popularity was largely *due to* his use of setting to re-create early America.

Because of the parrot's ability to mimic, Harry learns what his father had said.

beside, besides

Do not confuse these two prepositions, which have different meanings. *Beside* means "at the side of" or "close to." *Besides* means "in addition to."

In Hemingway's "A Day's Wait," the father sits *beside* his son to comfort him.

No one *besides* me had read Twain's "The Californian's Tale."

can, may

The verb *can* generally refers to the ability to do something. The verb *may* generally refers to permission to do something.

Anansi *may* tell all stories if he *can* deliver the hornets, the python, and the leopard to Nyame.

compare, contrast

The verb *compare* can involve both similarities and differences. The verb *contrast* always involves differences. Use *to* or *with* after *compare.* Use *with* after *contrast.*

Stan *compared* Nikki Giovanni's "Winter" *with* Carl Sandburg's "Fog."

Marianna and her daughters' opinions of themselves after they look in the mirror *contrast with* their feelings before seeing the mirror.

different from, different than

Different from is generally preferred over *different than.*

Similes are *different from* metaphors because similes use the words *like* or *as* to make comparisons.

farther, further
Use *farther* when you refer to distance. Use *further* when you mean "to a greater degree or extent" or "additional."

The speaker in Robert Frost's poem is tempted to ride *farther* into the snowy woods.

Reference to age *further* irritates Father William.

fewer, less
Use *fewer* for things that can be counted. Use *less* for amounts or quantities that cannot be counted.

Which animals have *fewer* fangs: sharks or rattlesnakes?

Rikki-tikki-tavi is *less* fearful of the cobra than are the other animals.

good, well
Use the predicate adjective *good* after linking verbs such as *feel, look, smell, taste,* and *seem.* Use *well* whenever you need an adverb.

The speaker in "Oranges" feels *good* about his meeting with the girl.

Rudyard Kipling describes Indian animals *well.*

hopefully
You should not loosely attach this adverb to a sentence, as in *"Hopefully,* the rain will stop by noon." Rewrite the sentence so *hopefully* modifies a specific verb. Other possible ways of revising such sentences include using the adjective *hopeful* or a phrase like "everyone *hopes* that."

James Dickey writes *hopefully* about everyone's ability to enjoy poetry.

At the end of "The Third Level," Charley seems *hopeful* that he will find the third level again.

its, it's
Do not confuse the possessive pronoun *its* with the contraction *it's,* standing for "it is" or "it has."

If a rattler thinks *it's* not seen, it will lie quietly without revealing *its* location.

lay, lie
Do not confuse these verbs. *Lay* is a transitive verb meaning "to set or put something down." Its principal parts are *lay, laying, laid, laid. Lie* is an intransitive verb meaning "to recline." Its principal parts are *lie, lying, lay, lain.*

The seal *lays* its flipper on a rock.

Sam McGee *lies* down in his sleigh.

leave, let
Leave means "to go away" or "to allow to remain." *Let* means "to permit."

After the fox had eaten the cheese, he *left* the crow sitting forlorn and hungry in the tree.

The aliens *let* the people destroy themselves.

like, as
Like is a preposition that usually means "similar to" or "in the same way as." *Like* should always be followed by an object. Do not use *like* before a subject and a verb. Use *as* or *that* instead.

A story *like* "A Boy and a Man" by James Ramsey Ullman uses suspense to hold the reader's interest.

The journey of Icarus does not end *as* he expected.

loose, lose
Loose can be either an adjective (meaning "unattached") or a verb (meaning "to untie"). *Lose* is always a verb (meaning "to fail to keep, have, or win").

There is often only a *loose* connection between the speaker of a poem and the poem's author; sometimes there is no link whatever between the two.

When no one recognizes him, Rip Van Winkle feels that he is *losing* his mind.

many, much
Use *many* to refer to a specific quantity. Use *much* for an indefinite amount or for an abstract concept.

Winslow Homer painted *many* Civil War scenes.

Seamus Heaney has won *much* praise for his poetry about Ireland.

of, have
Do not use *of* in place of *have* after auxiliary verbs like *would, could, should, may, might,* or *must.*

Russell Baker writes that his lack of gumption *must have* saddened his mother.

raise, rise
Raise is a transitive verb that usually takes a direct object. *Rise* is intransitive and never takes a direct object.

All the miners' visits *raise* the speaker's expectations about meeting the lady in "The Californian's Tale."

Rip rubs his eyes, *rises* from the ground, and looks around for his gun.

set, sit
Do not confuse these verbs. *Set* is a transitive verb meaning "to put (something) in a certain place." Its principal parts are *set, setting, set, set. Sit* is an intransitive verb meaning "to be seated." Its principal parts are *sit, sitting, sat, sat.*

The speaker *sets* the planks in the furnace.

Nicholas Vedder would *sit* all day in the doorway to his inn.

than, then
The conjunction *than* is used to connect the two parts of a comparison. Do not confuse *than* with the adverb *then,* which usually refers to time.

Rena liked "Aunt Leaf" more *than* "Life."

Mark Twain worked on a riverboat and *then* moved to California to search for gold.

that, which, who
Use the relative pronoun *that* to refer to things or people. Use *which* only for things and *who* only for people.

The season *that* E. E. Cummings describes is spring.

Lyric poems, *which* express personal emotions, are often brief.

One writer *who* has vividly described the experiences of African Americans is Alice Walker.

their, there, they're
Do not confuse the spelling of these three words. *Their* is a possessive adjective and always modifies a noun. *There* is usually used either at the beginning of a sentence or as an adverb. *They're* is a contraction for "they are."

Teddy and his parents are very happy about *their* new pet.

For most people, *there* are few creatures more terrifying than sharks.

Ron and Nan are in the class production of *The Monsters Are Due on Maple Street,* and *they're* rehearsing in the auditorium right now.

to, too, two
Do not confuse the spelling of these words. *To* is a preposition that begins a prepositional phrase or an infinitive. *Too,* with two *o's,* is an adverb and modifies adjectives and other adverbs. *Two* is a number.

The barber pays close attention *to* the Captain's skin as he gives him a shave.

Josh thought that his paper on Greek myths was *too* short, so he added another paragraph.

Two poems that Thelma especially liked were Edgar Allan Poe's "Annabel Lee" and Nikki Giovanni's "Winter."

unique
Because *unique* means "one of a kind," you should not use it carelessly to mean "interesting" or "unusual." Avoid such illogical expressions as *most unique, very unique,* and *extremely unique.*

Mark Twain's experiences in California gave him a *unique* insight into the gold-mining camps.

when, where, why
Do not use *when, where,* or *why* directly after a linking verb such as *is.* Reword the sentence.

Faulty: Suspense is *when* an author increases the reader's tension.

Revised: An author uses suspense to increase the reader's tension.

Faulty: Mexico is *where* the legend "Popocatepetl and Ixtlaccihuatl" is told.

Revised: The legend "Popocatepetl and Ixtlaccihuatl" is told in Mexico.

who, whom
In formal writing, remember to use *who* only as a subject in clauses and sentences and *whom* only as an object.

Amy Tan, *who* writes about the two worlds of her life, grew up in San Francisco's Chinatown.

Langston Hughes, *whom* we discussed yesterday, was a leader in an important cultural movement during the 1920's called the Harlem Renaissance.

Speaking, Listening, and Viewing Handbook

Communication is the way in which people convey their ideas and interact with one another. The literature in this book is written, which is one form of communication, but much of your personal communication is probably oral or visual. Oral communication involves both speaking and listening. Visual communication involves both conveying messages through physical expression or pictorial representations and interpreting images. Developing strong communication skills can benefit your school life and your life outside of school.

Many of the assignments accompanying the literature in this textbook involve speaking, listening, viewing, and representing. This handbook identifies some of the terminology related to the oral and visual communication you experience every day and the assignments you may do in conjunction with the literature in this book.

Communication

You use many different kinds of communication every day. When you communicate with your friends, your teachers, or your parents, or when you interact with a cashier in a store, you are communicating orally. In addition to ordinary conversation, oral communication includes class discussions, speeches, interviews, presentations, and debates. When you communicate face to face, you usually use more than your voice to get your message across. If you communicate by telephone, however, you must rely solely on your verbal skills. At times, you may use more visual communication than any other kind. For example, when you paint a picture, participate in a dance recital, or prepare a multimedia presentation, you use strategies of visual communication.

The following terms will give you a better understanding of the many elements that are part of oral and visual communication:

BODY LANGUAGE refers to the use of facial expressions, eye contact, gestures, posture, and movement to communicate a feeling or an idea.

CONNOTATION is the set of associations a word calls to mind. The connotations of the words you choose influence the message you send. For example, most people respond more favorably to being described as "slim" rather than as "skinny." The connotation of *slim* is more appealing than that of *skinny.*

EYE CONTACT is direct visual contact with another person's eyes.

FEEDBACK is the set of verbal and nonverbal reactions that indicate to a speaker that a message has been received and understood.

GESTURES are the movements made with arms, hands, face, and fingers to communicate.

LISTENING is understanding and interpreting sound in a meaningful way. You listen differently for different purposes.

Listening for key information: For example, when a teacher gives an assignment, or when someone gives you directions to a place, you listen for key information.

Listening for main points: In a classroom exchange of ideas or information, or while watching a television documentary, you listen for main points.

Listening critically: When you evaluate a performance, song, or a persuasive or political speech, you listen critically, questioning and judging the speaker's message.

MEDIUM is the material or technique used to present a visual image. Common media include paint, clay, and film.

NONVERBAL COMMUNICATION is communication without the use of words. People communicate nonverbally through gestures, facial expressions, posture, and body movements. Sign language is an entire language based on nonverbal communication.

VIEWING is observing, understanding, analyzing, and evaluating information presented through visual means. You might use the following questions to help you interpret what you view:

- What subject is presented?
- What is communicated about the subject?
- Which parts are factual? Which are opinion?
- What mood, attitude, or opinion is conveyed?
- What is your emotional response?

VOCAL DELIVERY is the way in which you present a message. Your vocal delivery involves all of the following elements:

Volume: the loudness or quietness of your voice
Pitch: the high or low quality of your voice
Rate: the speed at which you speak; also called pace
Stress: the amount of emphasis placed on different syllables in a word or on different words in a sentence

All of these elements individually, and the way in which they are combined, contribute to the meaning of a spoken message.

Speaking, Listening, and Viewing Situations

Here are some of the many types of situations in which you apply speaking, listening, and viewing skills:

AUDIENCE Your audience in any situation refers to the person or people to whom you direct your message. An audience can be a group of people sitting in a classroom or auditorium observing a performance or just one person to whom you address a question or a comment. When preparing for any speaking situation, it's useful to analyze your audience, learning what you can about their background, interests, and attitudes so that you can tailor your message to them.

CHARTS AND GRAPHS are visual representations of statistical information. For example, a pie chart might indicate how the average dollar is spent by government, and a bar graph might compare populations in cities over time.

DEBATE A debate is a formal public-speaking situation in which participants prepare and present arguments on opposing sides of a question, stated as a **proposition.**

The two sides in a debate are the *affirmative* (pro) and the *negative* (con). The affirmative side argues in favor of the proposition, while the negative side argues against it. The affirmative side begins the debate, since it is seeking a change in belief or policy. The opposing sides take turns presenting their arguments, and each side has an opportunity for *rebuttal,* in which they may challenge or question the other side's argument.

DOCUMENTARIES are nonfiction films that analyze news events or other focused subjects. You can watch a documentary for the information on its subject.

GROUP DISCUSSION results when three or more people meet to solve a common problem, arrive at a decision, or answer a question of mutual interest. Group discussion is one of the most widely used forms of interpersonal communication in modern society.

INTERVIEW An interview is a form of interaction in which one person, the interviewer, asks questions of another person, the interviewee. Interviews may take place for many purposes: to obtain information, to discover a person's suitability for a job or a college, or to inform the public of a notable person's opinions.

MAPS are visual representations of the Earth's surface. Maps may show political boundaries or physical features. They can also provide information on a variety of other topics. A map's title and its key identify the content of the map.

ORAL INTERPRETATION is the reading or speaking of a work of literature aloud for an audience. Oral interpretation involves giving expression to the ideas, meaning, or even the structure of a work of literature. The speaker interprets the work through his or her vocal delivery. **Storytelling,** in which a speaker reads or tells a story expressively, is a form of oral interpretation.

PANEL DISCUSSION is a group discussion on a topic of interest common to all members of a panel and to a listening audience. A panel is usually composed of four to six experts on a particular topic who are brought together to share information and opinions.

PANTOMIME is a form of nonverbal communication in which an idea or a story is communicated completely through the use of gesture, body language, and facial expressions, without any words at all.

POLITICAL CARTOONS are drawings that comment on important political or social issues. Often, these cartoons use humor to convey a message about their subject. Viewers use their own knowledge of events to evaluate the cartoonist's opinion.

READERS THEATRE is a dramatic reading of a work of literature in which participants take parts from a story or play and read them aloud in expressive voices. Unlike a play, however, sets and costumes are not part of the performance, and the participants remain seated as they deliver their lines.

ROLE PLAY To role-play is to take the role of a person or character and, as that character, act out a given situation, speaking, acting, and responding in the manner of the character.

SPEECH A speech is a talk or address given to an audience. A speech may be **impromptu**—delivered on the spur of the moment with no preparation—or formally prepared and delivered for a specific purpose or occasion.

- *Purposes:* The most common purposes of speeches are to persuade (for example, political speeches), to entertain, to explain, and to inform.
- *Occasions:* Different occasions call for different types of speeches. Speeches given on these occasions could be persuasive, entertaining, or informative, as appropriate. The following are common occasions for speeches:

Introduction: Introducing a speaker at a meeting
Presentation: Giving an award or acknowledging the contributions of someone
Acceptance: Accepting an award or tribute
Keynote: Giving an inspirational address at a large meeting or convention
Commencement: Honoring the graduates of a school

Test Preparation Handbook

Contents

Correlations to Standardized Tests

The reading comprehension skills reviewed in this workshop correspond to the following standardized test sections:

SAT 9	Reading Comprehension
SAT	Critical Reading
ACT	Reading
TerraNova	Reading

Answers

1. The word *prolix* is followed by its definition, "fond of using twenty words where two would do," or wordy. This means that *B*, *wordy*, is the correct answer.
2. The word *veracity* is explained by the fact that the aunt told the truth. Thus *A*, truthfulness, is the correct answer.

Test Preparation Workshop 1

Reading Comprehension — Using Context Clues

Strategies for Success

The reading sections of standardized tests ask you to read a passage and answer questions about word meanings. Some questions require you to figure out the meanings of words by using context clues. Use the following strategies to help you answer this type of test question:

Look for Synonyms and Antonyms Context clues are the words or phrases around an unfamiliar word that give you clues to that word's meaning. Sometimes a passage contains a synonym (word with the same meaning) or an antonym (word with the opposite meaning) for the unfamiliar word. Look at these examples:

> Helen didn't always mean to be **facetious**; still, almost everything she said was humorous. She charmed the audience, who had come in looking **dour** but went away with cheerful smiles on their faces.

1 In this passage, the word **facetious** means—
A funny **C** flattering
B upsetting **D** sad

2 The word **dour** in this passage means—
A relieved **C** gloomy
B expectant **D** happy

For Question 1: From the context, it is clear that *facetious* and *humorous* are synonyms. The correct answer is another synonym, *funny.*

For Question 2: The context suggests that *dour* is the opposite of *cheerful,* so **C** is correct.

Look for Definitions, Explanations, Descriptions, or Examples When you are asked to define an unfamiliar word, reread the passage to see if the word is explained or defined or if a description or examples in the passage can help you figure out the meaning. Look at these examples.

> We went to a **retrospective** of the work of a local artist and saw samples of her lifetime work. She had expressed herself in several **media,** including oils, charcoal, pastels, and watercolor.

1 In this passage, **retrospective** means—
A biographical movie **C** critical lecture
B representative exhibition **D** art store

2 The word **media** in this passage means—
A names **C** materials
B shows **D** decades

For Question 1: The words "samples of her lifetime work" explain what a retrospective is. **B** is correct.

For Question 2: Oils, charcoal, pastels, and watercolor are examples of materials used in art. **C** is correct.

Apply the Strategies

Answer these test questions based on the passage.

> After her car accident, we visited my aunt in the hospital. She is a bit **prolix,** fond of using twenty words where two would do. Still, her **veracity** is admirable. She admitted with charming honesty that the accident had been her fault entirely.

1 In this passage, the word **prolix** means—
A angry **C** distant
B wordy **D** cheerful

2 The word **veracity** in this passage means—
A truthfulness **C** dishonesty
B strength **D** conversation

Additional Test-Taking Tip

Process of Elimination

Tell students that many vocabulary items on standardized tests are multiple-choice. This format allows students to use a process of elimination for determining the meaning of vocabulary items with which they are not familiar. For example, students are probably not familiar with the meaning of the word *veracity*. However, by using context clues and a process of elimination, students can arrive at the correct answer.

Dishonesty is probably not the best answer because dishonesty is not an admirable quality. *Strength* can be considered an admirable quality, but it is probably not the best answer because strength would not be a reason for her to admit that the accident was her fault. Similarly, *conversation* would not cause her to take the blame for the accident. By eliminating the other choices, students can arrive at the correct answer, *truthfulness*.

Test Preparation Workshop 2

Reading Comprehension — Arranging Details in Sequential Order

Strategies for Success

The reading sections of standardized tests require you to read a passage and answer multiple-choice questions about the sequence of details. Use the following strategies to help you answer test questions about sequence:

Read Carefully A passage is not always written in chronological, or time, order. Some passages may start with the most recent event and then go back to tell the story leading up to that event. Other passages may start in the middle of a story and then use a flashback to give background information. You must read carefully to determine sequence. Look at the following example:

> In 1986, the Statue of Liberty got new steel supports, a new torch, and a thorough cleaning. Other than those details, she was in good shape for a hundred-year-old woman. Her story began in 1865 when a group of Frenchmen decided to give the United States a monument to freedom. Sculptor Frederic-Auguste Bartholdi designed and built the monument. Bartholdi sought help from engineer Gustave Eiffel, who years later designed Paris's Eiffel Tower. When Bartholdi finished the Statue of Liberty, it was taken apart, and shipped to New York City. It arrived in 1885 and was dedicated in 1886.

Which event described in the passage happened most recently?

A The Statue of Liberty was dedicated.
B Some Frenchmen decided to build a monument to freedom.
C The Statue of Liberty was taken apart.
D The Statue of Liberty was cleaned.

A happened in 1886, **B** in 1865, **C** in 1885, and **D** in 1986. **D** is correct.

Look for Word Clues When you are asked a question about the sequence of events, look for words that signal the order of events, such as *first, next, lately,* and *last,* to help you determine the sequence. Look at the following question based on the passage above.

Gustave Eiffel advised the sculptor Bartholdi—

A while Eiffel was designing the Eiffel Tower
B before Eiffel designed the Eiffel Tower
C after Eiffel designed the Eiffel Tower
D after 1885

The words "years later designed Paris's Eiffel Tower" tell you that **B** is correct.

Apply the Strategies

Answer the questions based on this passage.

> Justin couldn't believe how much work it was just to get his baby brother ready for an outing in the park. After changing Scott's diaper, he'd put sunscreen on him and found a cap to keep the sun out of his eyes. As they were about to leave, Justin realized he should probably take an extra diaper. Then he thought Scott might get hungry, so he packed a snack. Finally, Justin remembered that Dad always took a few toys in case Scott got bored. By the time Justin had squeezed everything into his backpack, Scott needed another diaper change!

1 Before Justin put sunscreen on Scott, he—

A changed his diaper
B packed some toys
C gave Scott a snack
D found his baseball cap

2 The last thing Justin remembered to pack was—

A a cap **B** toys **C** diaper **D** sunscreen

Correlations to Standardized Tests

The reading comprehension skill reviewed in this workshop correspond to the following standardized test sections:

SAT 9 Reading Comprehension
ACT Reading

Answers

1. (A) changed his diaper
2. (B) toys

Additional Test-Taking Tip

Rephrase the Questions

Point out that test questions can sometimes seem confusing because they discuss the passage in different terms. For example, question 1, contains the word clue *before*. However, the sentence in the passage that contains the correct information begins with the word *after*. Rephrasing the question "Before Justin put sunscreen on Scott, he—" as "Justin put sunscreen on Scott after he—" is one way to correctly locate and verify the answer in the passage.

Remind students that there are many ways to ask questions about passages that describe events in sequential or chronological order. Remind students that rephrasing the question may help them find the correct answer if they are initially confused. In addition, it is a good way to check their work to make sure they have chosen the correct answer.

Correlations to Standardized Tests

The reading comprehension skills reviewed in this workshop correspond to the following standardized test sections:

SAT 9	Reading Comprehension
ACT	Reading
ITBS	Reading Comprehension
TerraNova	Reading

Answers

1. (A) Octopuses would rather flee than fight.
2. (B) Octopuses exhibit intelligence.

Test Preparation Workshop 3

Reading Comprehension

Identify Main Idea

Strategies for Success

The reading sections of standardized tests require you to read a passage and answer multiple-choice questions about main ideas. Use the following strategies to help you answer such questions:

Identify the Stated Main Idea The main idea, the most important point of a passage, is often stated in a topic sentence that summarizes the details in the passage. The topic sentence may be located anywhere in the passage. In some tests, identifying the main idea means finding a restatement of the topic sentence. Read the following:

Mrs. Gomez always does nice things for the young people of the neighborhood. For your birthday, she might present you with a home-baked goodie or a bouquet from her garden. She welcomes youngsters to cool off under her lawn sprinklers. Visitors are encouraged to pick flowers in her garden.

What is the main idea of this passage?

A Mrs. Gomez gives the neighborhood children birthday presents.
B Mrs. Gomez is always doing nice things for the young people of the neighborhood.
C Mrs. Gomez wants you to enjoy her garden.
D Mrs. Gomez welcomes children to cool off under her lawn sprinklers.

A and **D** are details. **C** does not take in all the details in the passage. **B** is correct.

Identify the Implied Main Idea If a main idea is not stated, it is implied or suggested. To identify an implied main idea, look for the answer choice that best summarizes the details in the passage. Look at this example:

One summer Nilda noticed that the weeds were taking over Mrs. Gomez's garden. The day before the woman's eighty-fifth birthday, Nilda had an inspiration. She called eight young people to weed Mrs. Gomez's garden. After three hours, the garden was weed-free and nine happy people were drinking lemonade and eating cake on the porch.

What is the main idea of this passage?

A People over eighty need help gardening.
B Mrs. Gomez's garden needed weeding.
C Several young people pitched in to weed Mrs. Gomez's garden for her birthday.
D Mrs. Gomez loved to celebrate birthdays.

A and **D** do not summarize the information in the passage. **B** is a detail. **C** is correct.

Apply the Strategies

Read this passage and then answer the questions that follow.

Even though they are predators, octopuses would rather flee than fight. Sometimes they avoid enemies by changing their skin patterns to blend in with their surroundings. If this doesn't work, an alarmed octopus can retreat at remarkable speeds.

Just how smart are octopuses? In experiments, some have learned to solve simple puzzles and problems. One scientist has seen an octopus dismantle a dead crab in order to get the food back to its den.

1 What is the main idea of the first paragraph?
A Octopuses would rather flee than fight.
B Octopuses can blend in with their surroundings.
C Octopuses are rapid swimmers.
D Octopuses are predators.

2 What is the main idea of the second paragraph?
A Octopuses can learn to solve puzzles.
B Octopuses exhibit intelligence.
C Octopuses eat crabs.
D An octopus can dismantle a crab.

Additional Test-Taking Tip

Examining Paragraph Structure

Many standardized tests require students to identify the stated or implied main idea of a paragraph. However, most of the time the instructions will not tell them if the main idea is stated or implied. Point out that they should be careful not to assume that an answer is correct just because it is a direct quote from the passage.

Have students look at the example paragraphs above. In the first example, the main idea is stated in the first sentence. Even though choices *B* and *D* are also stated in the passage, they do not offer the best summary of the paragraph's main idea. In the second example, choice *A* is a stereotype that is not expressed in the paragraph. Choice *B* is a detail, and choice *D* is not a summary of the main idea. Although none of the choices are directly stated in the paragraph, item *C* is the best summary of the main idea.

Test Preparation Workshop 4

Reading Comprehension — Author's Point of View and Purpose

Strategies for Success

The reading sections of standardized tests require you to read a passage and answer multiple-choice questions about the author's point of view and purpose. Use these strategies to help you answer such questions:

Recognize the Author's Purpose An author may write primarily to inform, persuade, or entertain readers. To identify an author's purpose, look at the language he or she uses. Facts and details can be presented plainly, or in a way that attempts to convince readers of something. Likewise, if an author aims to entertain, the language may be dramatic or humorous.

Recognize Authors' Points of View Authors' points of view are the way they think and feel about their subjects. Authors may state their point of view directly or imply it through the language they use. If a test question asks you to identify an author's point of view, look for the ways he or she expresses feelings.

Use the following editorial to practice recognizing an author's purpose and point of view.

> Though some may not know it, our class will soon vote on whether formal wear will be required at the annual dance. Many have said that they want to continue the tradition of formal attire. Others say that formal wear is uncomfortable, and too expensive for most students. Though the outcome of the vote means a great deal to all of us, the most important thing is for everyone to cast their votes.

1 In writing this, the author's purpose was to—
A inform readers about the upcoming vote and its importance
B offer an entertaining view of school politics
C encourage a vote for formal clothing
D persuade others to dress up for the dance

Since the letter is neither primarily entertaining nor persuasive, **B**, **C**, and **D** are incorrect. **A** is correct.

2 What is the author's point of view?
A The author wants the tradition of formal wear to continue.
B The author dislikes formal dress.
C The author likes dressing formally.
D The author thinks it is important to be informed and to vote.

The author appears neutral about the outcome of the vote, so **A** and **B** are wrong. There is no evidence supporting **C**. **D** is correct.

Apply the Strategies

Answer the questions based on this passage.

> Bill wrote his parents from camp:
>
> I love this place. There is so much to do and I get to choose my activities. I've tried pottery and working in stained glass. The food is plain but plentiful, and desserts are great. I can't wait to see you on Visitors' Day.
>
> His sister Lillian wrote:
>
> I'm not really enjoying camp. My cabin mates are mean. The activities are OK, but we do the same thing everyday. One good thing is the food. Please write back and say I can come home with you after Visitors' Day.

1 The purpose of Lillian's letter is to—
A inform her parents about camp activities
B complain about the food
C persuade her parents to let her come home
D express her feelings about her cabin mates

2 Lillian and Bill differ in their views of—
A camp activities
B camp food
C seeing their parents
D their cabin mates

Correlations to Standardized Tests

The reading comprehension skills reviewed in this workshop correspond to the following standardized test sections:

ACT	Reading
SAT	Critical Reading
ITBS	Reading Comprehension
TerraNova	Reading

Answers

1. (C) persuade her parents to let her come home
2. (A) camp activities

Additional Test-Taking Tip

Avoid Distractors

Students sometimes have trouble identifying an author's point of view or purpose because incorrect answers often seem like reasonable responses to the text. Point out that it is easier to answer these types of questions correctly after reading the entire passage because the general tone and style of the passage is more important than specific facts or details. Remind students to read carefully and to eliminate answers that do not answer the question.

For example, in question 1 above, the key words *camp activities* in choice *A* might distract students who have not read carefully. However, students can eliminate this choice because the letter does not contain specific information about camp activities. Similarly, *D* describes something that the letter does, but it is not the writer's primary purpose. Students can eliminate *B* quickly because it contradicts the text. Eliminating incorrect answers will allow students to increase their chances of answering correctly, even if they are unsure of the right response.

Correlations to Standardized Tests

The reading comprehension skills reviewed in this workshop correspond to the following standardized test sections:

ACT Reading
SAT 9 Reading Comprehension

Answers

1. (B) soccer has increased in popularity in the United States
2. (B) people of all ages play soccer

Test Preparation Workshop 5

Reading Comprehension — Making Generalizations

Strategies for Success

The reading sections of standardized tests require you to read a passage and answer multiple-choice questions about generalizations. Use the following strategies to help you answer such questions:

Consider the Evidence A generalization is a broad statement that sums up or describes an array of facts and details. A generalization should always be based on facts and details that can be checked for accuracy. Read this example, then answer the question that follows.

> Clara Barton was much younger than her four brothers and sisters. Because she had few playmates, she was very shy as a child. When she was nine, her parents sent her to boarding school, hoping she would overcome her shyness. The opposite happened. After some students laughed at her lisp, she refused to stay at the school. Remarkably, Clara Barton became a teacher herself. When she was refused promotion to the job of principal, she left teaching. She later worked at the U.S. Patent Office, nursed soldiers during the Civil War, and founded the American Red Cross.

The author provides evidence to show that—

A Clara Barton saved many lives
B Clara Barton overcame childhood shyness to achieve many things
C Clara Barton could not stick with one job
D everyone admired Clara Barton

There is no evidence to support **A**, **C**, or **D**. Evidence does show that Barton was shy and accomplished many things. **B** is correct.

Avoid Overgeneralizations An overgeneralization is a statement that is too broad to be supported by the relevant facts. Words like *all, every,* and *always* may signal overgeneralizations. Review the passage above and answer the following question.

Information in the passage shows that—

A Clara Barton was always successful
B Clara Barton had wonderful relationships with all her family
C all people with lisps are shy
D as a child, Clara Barton was mainly with adults

Evidence contradicts **A**. No evidence supports **B**. **C** is an overgeneralization. **D** is correct.

Apply the Strategies

Use the strategies you have learned to answer the questions based on this passage.

> My granddad says that when he was growing up, most people in the United States had never seen a soccer game. Now most towns have leagues for all ages of boys and girls. I read that more young people in the United States play soccer than Little League baseball. Our town even has a soccer league for adults. Granddad watches us play and wonders what sport our children will be playing that we haven't even heard of yet.

1 The author provides evidence to show that—

A his family likes soccer more than baseball
B soccer has increased in popularity in the United States
C baseball is more popular than soccer
D baseball and soccer are the most popular sports in the United States

2 Information in the passage indicates that—

A people in different age groups play soccer
B people of all ages play soccer
C new sports are constantly being developed
D most older people dislike soccer

Additional Test-Taking Tip

Choosing the Right Information

Tell students that sometimes a standardized test will leave out information that most students would know to be true and then refer to the information that is left out in one of the answers. To avoid mistakes, students should reread passages carefully after they have read all the answer choices.

Have students look at the first example above. This passage is about Clara Barton, the woman who founded the American Red Cross. Students probably know from their earlier studies that Clara Barton did indeed save many lives, as stated in choice A. However, this passage refers to Barton's struggle to find a place where she could "fit in." Although the passage comments on her Civil War nursing and her founding of the Red Cross, it leaves out mention of her saving lives.

Test Preparation Workshop 6

Reading Comprehension — Predicting Probable Actions and Outcomes

Strategies for Success

The reading sections of standardized tests require you to read a passage and answer questions about probable outcomes and actions. Use the following strategies to help you answer such questions:

Analyze the Facts Look at the details, facts, and information in the passage. Notice how characters behave and what circumstances surround the actions or dialogue of the passage.

Make Logical Assumptions Remember that writers must make their stories unfold according to some believable logic or pattern. For instance, if you know about one character's personality, you can predict how he or she will behave in future scenes. Look at this example:

Todd slid into a seat just as the newspaper's representative began to talk. "I have just a few suggestions for you new deliverers. First, look at the map that we have attached to your route list, which is alphabetical by customer's last name. Then plan the most efficient route. Finally, rewrite the list in the order you will deliver the papers."

Todd had just begun to follow these directions when Kristina passed his seat. "Are you actually doing that? That's a waste of time. I can figure out my route in my head." Kristina's list, like Todd's, had at least thirty customers on ten different streets. He doubted that anyone could figure out the best route at a glance. But he also knew better than to argue with Kristina. "Come on, my mom will give you a lift," she said. Gratefully Todd accepted.

1 After he gets home, Todd will most likely—
A deliver his papers
B throw away the map he received
C finish rewriting his route list
D call Kristina to thank her for the ride

Evidence suggests that Todd thinks rewriting the list is a good idea, so **C** is correct.

2 The first time Kristina delivers her papers, she will probably—
A not take the most efficient route
B run into Todd
C ask Todd for help
D ask her mother to drive her around

There is no evidence to support **B**, **C**, or **D**. Based on the evidence that Kristina seems determined not to rewrite her list and Todd says her route is long and complicated, **A** is correct.

Apply the Strategies

Answer the questions based on this passage.

Marcie slammed her locker shut and hurried down the hall. She wanted to walk home with Chaney to discuss their weekend plans. Then she remembered that Ms. Weaver was offering extra help in German that afternoon. Marcie hadn't done well on the quiz that day. Ahead she spied Chaney. "Wait up!" she yelled. Chaney turned. "Oh, hi," she smiled. "I wish we could walk home together, Marcie, but I have to go to Ms. Weaver for some extra help. Today's quiz was murder."

1 Marcie will probably—
A walk home alone
B never understand German verbs
C not see Chaney on the weekend
D suggest they both go for extra help

2 If she gets extra help from Ms. Weaver, Marcie will probably—
A miss walking home with Chaney
B do poorly on her next quiz
C understand German verbs better
D neglect her other subjects

Correlations to Standardized Tests

The reading comprehension skills reviewed in this workshop correspond to the following standardized test sections:

ACT Reading
SAT 9 Reading Comprehension

Answers

1. (D) suggest they both go for extra help
2. (C) understand her German verbs better

Additional Test-Taking Tip

Organizing Information

Many standardized tests ask students to read passages and draw inferences, such as conclusions or generalizations, based on the text. Students may find it helpful, when making these deductions, to make a list of the facts that apply to the deduction they are required to make.

For example, in the first example on the student page, the following facts are provided:

1. Todd began to follow the newspaperman's suggestions.
2. Kristina said that she could figure it out in her head.
3. Todd doubted that anyone could figure it out at a glance.
4. Todd stopped writing to accept a ride home.

By looking at the facts as a sequential list, it is easy to see that the next logical items in the sequence would include Todd arriving home and then finishing his list.

Correlations to Standardized Tests

The reading comprehension skills reviewed in this workshop correspond to the following standardized test sections:

SAT 9 Reading Comprehension
ACT Reading
SAT Critical Reading

Answers

1. (C) No student at my school should ever have a boring afternoon.
2. (B) The math team challenges mathematicians.

Test Preparation Workshop 7

Reading Comprehension — Fact and Opinion

Strategies for Success

The reading sections of standardized tests require you to read a passage and answer multiple-choice questions about facts and opinions. Use the following strategies to help you answer such questions:

Recognize Facts A fact can be proven to be true by consulting a reliable source, such as a book or an unbiased expert. When you are asked to identify a fact, ask yourself, "Is it possible to find out whether or not this is true?" Look at this example:

There are many things to see and do in Washington D.C. You can visit the Washington Monument, the Capitol, and the White House. You could spend weeks exploring the many museums that are part of the Smithsonian Institution. The best is the National Museum of American History, where you can see George Washington's false teeth. Some of the city's spots, such as the Vietnam War Memorial, are thought-provoking. For a blend of fun and education, everyone should see Washington, D.C., at least once.

Which of these is a FACT in the passage?

A Washington, D.C., is a fascinating city.
B At the National Museum of American History, you can see George Washington's false teeth.
C The Vietnam War Memorial is thought-provoking and fun.
D Everyone should see Washington, D.C., once.

A, **C**, and **D** cannot be shown to be true. They are the speaker's opinions. **B** is correct.

Recognize Opinions Opinions are statements of belief expressing a writer's attitudes or feelings. A writer may use facts to support opinions, but opinions themselves cannot be proven. When you are asked to identify an opinion, look for a statement that cannot be checked against any objective source. Look at this question based on the passage above:

Which is an OPINION expressed in the passage?

A Washington, D.C., has many attractions.
B Everyone should see Washington, D.C., once.
C The Vietnam War Memorial is in Washington, D.C.
D The Smithsonian Institution includes many museums.

A, **C**, and **D** can be proven to be true by research. **B** is the writer's opinion.

Apply the Strategies

Read the following passage and answer the questions.

No student at my school should ever have a boring afternoon. There are after-school activities for every interest. Athletes can run track or play basketball. The Math Team challenges mathematicians to put their skills to work. There are clubs for readers, history buffs, and cooks. The chess club is best. I've improved my game tremendously since joining. With all these activities, maybe we need a Free-Time Club, for those who just want to relax!

1 Which of these statements is an OPINION?

A There is a club for readers.
B Athletes can run track.
C No student at my school should ever have a boring afternoon.
D I have improved my chess game since joining the Chess Club.

2 Which is a FACT expressed in the passage?

A The best activity is the Chess Club.
B The Math Team challenges mathematicians.
C Maybe we need a Free-Time Club.
D After-school activities cover every interest.

Additional Test-Taking Tip

Ask the Right Questions

Remind students that asking questions about the answer choices can help them determine which are facts and which are opinions. To make the distinction, students should ask "Can this be proven?" Point out that the proof for a particular fact is not always included in the selection. For example, in Question 2, the passage does not reveal how the math club challenges interested students. However, this statement is not an opinion, because it is possible to prove it. For choice *D*, though, the word "every" is a signal that this is not a fact. Even if the passage does not list all the activities that are offered, students should realize that it is impossible to cover every interest students may have. Remind students to use the test of provability to distinguish fact from opinion in the answer choices. In addition, asking questions about the choices is a good way for students to check their work.

Test Preparation Workshop 8

Writing Skills — Sentence Construction

Strategies for Success

The writing sections of standardized tests require you to read a passage and answer multiple-choice questions about sentence construction. Use the following strategies to help you answer such questions:

Recognize Incomplete Sentences and Run-on Sentences Sentences should express complete, unified thoughts. Incomplete sentences lack either a subject or a predicate. Run-on sentences include two or more sentences without proper punctuation between them. You can correct an incomplete sentence by adding to it or by combining it with a sentence or another incomplete sentence. Run-on sentences can be corrected by adding the proper punctuation.

Combine Sentences Sometimes two short sentences that are closely related sound better if they are combined to make a single sentence. Look at the following sample test item:

(1) <u>In 1984, two men were cutting peat They were cutting it from a bog in Lindow Moss, England</u>. Suddenly, they saw a human foot sticking up out of the peat. (2) <u>The men called the police they needed an archaeologist instead</u>. Lindow Man had been dead for about 2,300 years.

Choose the best way to write each underlined section. If it needs no change, choose **D**.

1 **A** In 1984, two men cutting peat from a bog in Lindow Moss, England.
B In 1984, two men were cutting peat they were cutting it from a bog in Lindow Moss, England.
C In 1984, two men were cutting peat from a bog in Lindow Moss, England.
D Correct as is

A is incomplete. **B** is a run-on sentence. **C** is correct because it properly combines two short related sentences.

2 **A** The men called the police, but they needed an archaeologist instead.
B The men called the police, and they needed an archaeologist instead.
C The men called. The police they need an archaeologist instead.
D Correct as is

B corrects the run-on sentence, but the conjunction *and* doesn't work. **C** is punctuated incorrectly. **A** is correct because it properly punctuates a run-on sentence.

Apply the Strategies

Choose the best way to write each underlined section. If it needs no change, choose **D**.

(1) <u>When you eat breakfast cereal. You are actually getting muscle power. From the sun.</u> (2) <u>Plants absorb the sun's energy. They use it to produce glucose</u>. Glucose is changed to starch, which gives humans energy when eaten.

1 **A** When you eat breakfast cereal, you are actually getting muscle power. From the sun.
B When you eat breakfast. Cereal you are actually getting muscle power from the sun.
C When you eat breakfast cereal, you are actually getting muscle power from the sun.
D Correct as is

2 **A** Plants absorb the sun's energy and use it to produce glucose.
B Plants absorb the sun's energy. Using it to produce glucose.
C Plants absorbing the sun's energy. They using it to produce energy.
D Correct as is

Correlations to Standardized Tests

The writing skills reviewed in this workshop correspond to the following standardized test sections:

ACT	English
SAT 9	Language
ITBS	Usage and Expression
TerraNova	Language Arts

Answers

1. (C) When you eat breakfast cereal, you are actually getting muscle power from the sun.
2. (D) Correct as is

Additional Test-Taking Tip

Narrow the Choices

Standardized tests often offer choices that contain answers that are partly correct. Students may find it helpful to mark out answers that they know are at least partly incorrect before attempting to select an answer that is entirely correct. Have students look at the first question in Apply the Strategies above for an example. Students can quickly look at choice *A* and see that "From the sun." is a sentence fragment, so choice *A* should be marked out. In choice *B*, "When you eat breakfast." is a sentence fragment, so answer *B* should also be marked out. Choice *D* says the item is correct as is. Students can quickly see that the underlined item contains the same sentence fragment that eliminated choice A, so answer *D* cannot be correct. Therefore *C* is the only correct answer. For confirmation, students may examine this response and find that the clause "When you eat breakfast cereal," is a subordinate clause modifying *you*. It is proper to separate this clause from the rest of the sentence by using a comma.

Correlations to Standardized Tests

The writing skill reviewed in this workshop corresponds to the following standardized test sections:

SAT 9	Language
ACT	English Usage
ITBS	Usage and Expression

Answers

1. (D) disappointing
2. (B) happily
3. (C) she
4. (A) ever sees
5. (C) comes
6. (A) her
7. (C) had blown

Apply the Strategies

1. (B) is
2. (C) knows
3. (A) their
4. (C) awkward
5. (A) eat

Test Preparation Workshop 9

Writing Skills — Appropriate Usage

Strategies for Success

The writing sections of standardized tests require you to read a passage and answer multiple-choice questions about appropriate usage. Use the following strategies to help you answer such questions:

Use the Correct Form of a Word Some test questions will ask you to choose the correct part of speech, the appropriate form of an adjective or adverb, the correct case of a pronoun, or the correct way to express a negative. Look at these examples:

1 After a _____ performance at the trials, Mark did very well at the meet.
A disappoint **C** disappointment
B disappointed **D** disappointing

An adjective is needed. **B** and **D** are adjectives, but *disappointed* cannot modify *performance*. **D** is correct.

2 The child played _____ in the sandbox.
A happier **C** more happy
B happily **D** happiest

An adverb is needed to modify the verb *played*. **B** is correct.

3 Emily and _____ gave a report about Egypt.
A her **B** him **C** she **D** herself

The correct answer must be in the same case as *Emily*. The answer is **C**.

4 No one _____ that sign.
A ever sees **C** doesn't ever see
B hardly never sees **D** never sees

B, **C**, and **D** form double negatives. **A** is correct.

Use Correct Agreement A verb must agree with its subject in number. A pronoun must agree with its antecedent (the word it stands for). Look at these examples:

5 The brown dog _____ to visit every day.
A come **C** comes
B have come **D** were coming

The verb must agree with the singular subject *dog*. **C** is correct.

6 Luanne lost _____ wallet at the game.
A her **B** its **C** their **D** him

The antecedent, Luanne, is third person singular feminine, so **A** is correct.

Use Correct Verb Tense and Form Some test questions will require you to choose the correct tense of a verb or the correct form of an irregular verb. Look at this example:

7 By the time we got home, the wind _____ down several trees.
A had blew **C** had blown
B blown **D** blowed

The verb describes past action that happened before another past action, so the past perfect tense is needed. **C** is correct.

Apply the Strategies

Choose the words that belong in each space.

About one person in ten __(1)__ left-handed. Nobody __(2)__ for sure why people prefer one hand over the other. Lefties have __(3)__ difficulties in a right-handed world. They may be __(4)__ with objects like scissors and cameras designed for righties.

1 **A** were **B** is **C** are **D** have been

2 **A** don't never know **C** knows
B hardly knows **D** won't never know

3 **A** their **B** them **C** there **D** they

4 **A** awkwardly **C** awkward
B awkwarder **D** most awkwardly

Additional Test-Taking Tip

Define What's Needed

Remind students that an important first step in answering test questions about proper usage is to define what kind of word is required to fit into the blank. Is it an adverb, adjective, verb, or noun? Once students decide what type of word might fit, they can further refine their understanding of what the question calls for. Tell students to ask themselves what characteristics the word in question must have. For example, if they have determined that the correct word is a verb, they should ask themselves what tense the verb must be. By asking themselves a few simple questions like these, students can usually rule out most of the possible choices, leaving the correct answer as the only remaining choice.

Test Preparation Workshop 10

Writing Skills — Spelling, Capitalization, Punctuation

Strategies for Success

The writing sections of standardized tests often require you to read a passage and answer multiple-choice questions about spelling, capitalization, and punctuation. Use the following strategies to help you answer such questions:

Recognize Spelling Errors Check the spelling of the words in the passage you are being tested on. Pay special attention to homophones (to, too, two), double vowels (squeak, not squeek), suffixes (-ness, not –nes), and words containing –ie- or –ei-.

Recognize Capitalization Errors Make sure that the first word in a sentence or a quotation is capitalized, that proper nouns are capitalized, and that no words are capitalized unnecessarily. All the words in a compound proper noun should be capitalized (Middletown City Council).

Recognize Punctuation Errors Check end punctuation, make sure that all necessary commas and no unnecessary commas are there, and notice if both pairs of quotation marks are present. Look at this example:

Read the passage and decide which type of error, if any, appears in each underlined section.

(1) What's it like two hundred miles above Earth (2) Astronaut and Senator John glenn says, (3) "Space is completely black, even when the son is shining." Glenn was the first American to orbit Earth in 1962. (4) Thirty-six years later he went back into space on the space shuttle.

1 **A** Spelling error **B** Capitalization error **C** Punctuation error **D** No error

2 **A** Spelling error **B** Capitalization error **C** Punctuation error **D** No error

3 **A** Spelling error **B** Capitalization error **C** Punctuation error **D** No error

4 **A** Spelling error **B** Capitalization error **C** Punctuation error **D** No error

For question 1: The sentence has no end punctuation, so **C** is correct.

For question 2: *Glenn* is a proper noun and should be capitalized, so **B** is correct.

For question 3: *Son* is a homophone for *sun,* so **A** is correct.

For question 4: There are no errors, so **D** is correct.

Apply the Strategies

Read the passage and decide which type of error, if any, appears in each underlined section.

(1) If you are looking for extreme weather, here's a gide for where to go. (2) In Death Valley California, the temperature has been known to reach 134 degrees Fahrenheit. (3) To cool off, try Prospect Creek Camp, Alaska, where it can go down to eighty degrees below zero. (4) For high winds, climb Mount Washington, new Hampshire, where winds have reached 231 miles per hour.

1 **A** Spelling error **B** Capitalization error **C** Punctuation error **D** No error

2 **A** Spelling error **B** Capitalization error **C** Punctuation error **D** No error

3 **A** Spelling error **B** Capitalization error **C** Punctuation error **D** No error

4 **A** Spelling error **B** Capitalization error **C** Punctuation error **D** No error

Correlations to Standardized Tests

The writing skills reviewed in this workshop correspond to the following standardized test sections:

ACT English
SAT 9 Language
ITBS Spelling; Capitalization

Answers

1. (A) Spelling error
2. (C) Punctuation error
3. (D) No error
4. (B) Capitalization error

Additional Test-Taking Tip

Eliminate Incorrect Answer Choices

One useful strategy for many multiple-choice tests is eliminating incorrect answers. After you eliminate all answers that you know to be wrong, you can work through the remaining choices to see which is most likely correct. If you eliminate three answers, be sure to verify that the fourth answer is correct (if possible). For example, consider question 1 in Apply the Strategies. Note that, in this case, choice *D* cannot be eliminated as a wrong answer until you work through the other choices. Since the first word of the sentence is capitalized and there are no proper nouns requiring capitalization in the rest of the underlined portion, choice *B* can be eliminated. The sentence has an ending punctuation mark, the comma is placed correctly, and there are no missing punctuation marks, so you can also eliminate choice *C*. This means that the correct answer must be either *A* or *D*. If you read the sentence carefully, you will find that the word *guide* is misspelled. Thus, the correct answer is *A*.

Test Preparation Workshop 11

Research Skills

Using Information Resources

Strategies for Success

Some tests require you to review a packet of information resources, and to respond to questions about how you would use these resources to gather information and plan a report on a given subject. Use these strategies:

Review the Packet of Information Skim through the packet to see what types of material are included, such as articles from encyclopedias and computer information.

Scan the Questions Look through the questions to see which types of information are required to answer the questions. Focus on each question separately. The questions are not necessarily related to each other. Locate the best example or piece of information in the packet to answer each question.

Use Correct Sentence Form Write responses to the short-answer questions in complete sentences and include key words. Look at these examples:.

Directions: Suppose that you are writing a report on the life and times of Thomas Alva Edison (1847–1931). Edison is one of the world's most important inventors.
This packet includes several information resources about Thomas Alva Edison:

- an excerpt from an encyclopedia article, "Inventions of the Nineteenth Century"
- a biographical dictionary entry
- *Thomas Alva Edison*, a biography of the inventor: a short excerpt, table of contents, and a list of key dates in Edison's life and career
- Computer screen: on-line index of library books about Thomas Edison

Excerpt from Encyclopedia Article: "Inventions of the Nineteenth Century"

A flood of inventions swept the United States in the late 1800's. By the 1890's Americans were patenting 21,000 new inventions a year. These inventions helped industry to grow and become more efficient. New devices also made daily life easier in many American homes.

Advanced Communication Some remarkable new devices filled the need for faster communication. The telegraph speeded communication within the United States. It still took weeks, however, for news from Europe to arrive by boat. In 1866, Cyrus Field ran an underwater telegraph cable across the Atlantic Ocean, bringing the United States and Europe closer together.

Thomas Edison In an age of invention, Thomas Edison was right at home. In 1876, he opened a research laboratory in Menlo Park, New Jersey. There, Edison boasted that he and his 15 co-workers set out to create "minor" inventions every 10 days and "a big thing every 6 months or so."

Biographical Dictionary

Edison, Thomas Alva A poor student, Thomas Edison grew up to invent the light bulb, the phonograph, and dozens of other devices. Edison once went without sleep for three days working on his phonograph. At last, he heard his own voice reciting "Mary Had a Little Lamb." Edison said, "Genius is one percent inspiration and ninety-nine percent perspiration."

Table of Contents from *Thomas Alva Edison*

Test Preparation Workshop 11

Research Skills

Using Information Resources (cont.)

Short Excerpt from *Thomas Alva Edison*

The key to Edison's success was his approach. He turned inventing into a system. Teams of experts refined Edison's ideas and turned them into practical inventions. Menlo Park became an "invention factory." The results were amazing. Edison became knows as the "Wizard of Menlo Park" for inventing the light bulb, the phonograph, and hundreds of other devices.

Lists of Key Dates from *Thomas Alva Edison*

1847: Born in Milan, Ohio
1852: Moved to Port Huron, Michigan
1869: Was paid $40,000 for improvements to the stock ticker. Opened his first workshop in Newark, New Jersey
1874: Improved the typewriter
1877: Invented the phonograph
1879: Perfected the electric light
1887: Moved to West Orange, New Jersey. Worked on such inventions as the motion picture, a storage battery, a cement mixer, the Dictaphone, and a duplicating machine.
1931: Died at 84 in West Orange, New Jersey

Computer Screen

Library Online Catalog
Subject Search: Thomas Alva Edison

Line	Titles	Subjects
1	2	Edison, Thomas: Early Life
2	4	Edison, Thomas: Bibliography
3	1	Edison, Thomas: Biography

Sample Questions and Explanations

1 Which information given in the encyclopedia article would be LEAST useful for your report?
A the number of patents in the 1890's
B the date Edison opened his laboratory
C Cyrus Field's contributions to communication
D the description of Edison's workshop

The correct answer is **C.** Cyrus Field's contributions are not important to a report on Edison.

2 In which chapter of *Thomas Alva Edison* would you find information about Edison's schooling? ("Early Years" would provide the information.)

3 Which of these sources would you use to find books written about Thomas Alva Edison?
A the encyclopedia article
B the biographical dictionary article
C computer screen
D the biography *Thomas Alva Edison*

The correct answer is **C.** The other sources do not reference other books about Edison.

Apply the Strategies

4 Suppose you are going to write an outline of your report on the life of Thomas Alva Edison. What three main topics would you include?

5 State the main idea of your report.

6 In which source would you find detailed information about Edison's marriage?
A the encyclopedia article
B the biographical dictionary entry
C the main body of the biography
D the list of key dates from the biography

Answers

4. Two possible topic lists are: Edison's Early Years; Edison's Most Famous Inventions; Edison's Later Years; Edison's Childhood; Nineteenth Century Inventions; Edison's Inventions.
5. Students' answers should relate to Edison's importance as an inventor.
6. (C) The most detailed information would appear in the main body of the biography.

Correlations to Standardized Tests

The writing skill reviewed in this workshop corresponds to the following standardized test sections:

SAT 9	Language
ACT	English Usage
ITBS	Usage and Expression
TerraNova	Language Arts

Answers

1. (A) Secretary of State Seward bought Alaska from Russia. The deal was mocked as "Seward's Folly."
2. (A) Delete sentence 3

Test Preparation Workshop 12

Writing Skills Proofreading

Strategies for Success

The writing sections of some standardized tests assess your ability to edit, proofread, and use other writing processes. You are required to look for mistakes in passages and then to choose the best way to correct them.

Check for Incorrect Verb Tense and Errors in Subject-Verb Agreement Check to see that the correct verb tense is used and make the verb agree in number with its subject. If the parts of the subject name more than one thing, use a plural verb. If the parts of the subject refer to the same thing, use a singular verb.

Correct Run-on Sentences Use an end mark and a capital letter to separate main clauses. Use a semicolon between clauses.

Correct Sentence Fragments Add a subject or verb to make a sentence fragment a complete sentence.

Use Supporting Details Effectively Avoid the use of details that interrupt the flow of the passage, and that do not support the main idea.

Sample Passage and Questions:

Directions: A student wrote a paper about Alaska. There are mistakes that need correcting.

(1) Susan Butcher win the Iditarod dog-sled race several times. (2) A large strip of mountains cross Alaska. (3) Despite its challenges, the race attracts more and more racers every year. (4) In the years ahead, racers may come from such far-off countries as Sweden Norway and Denmark.

1 Select the best way to write sentence 1.

A Susan Butcher won the Iditarod dog-sled race several times.

B Susan Butcher will win the Iditarod dog-sled race several times.

C Susan Butcher would have won the Iditarod dog-sled race several times.

D Best as it is

The correct answer is **A.** *Won* is the past tense of the irregular verb *win.*

2 Select the best way to write sentence 2.

A A large strip of mountains crosses Alaska.

B A large strip of mountains do cross Alaska.

C A mountainous strip crosses Alaska.

D Best as it is.

The correct answer is **A.** A large strip of mountains crosses Alaska. The subject is singular and requires a singular verb.

Apply the Strategies

(1) Secretary of State Seward bought Alaska from Russia the deal was mocked as "Seward's Folly." (2) Seward's $7.2 million purchase proved to be a bargain; gold deposits were discovered there three decades later. (3) My uncle told me about a trip he took to Alaska when he was only 12 years old. (4) Prospectors first struck gold in 1889.

1 Which is the best way to write the underlined section in sentence one?

A Secretary of State Seward bought Alaska from Russia. The deal was mocked as "Seward's Folly."

B Secretary of State Seward bought Alaska from Russia, and the deal was mocked.

C Secretary of State Seward bought Alaska. The deal was "Seward's Folly."

D Best as it is

2 Which is the correct way to fix the flow of the passage?

A Delete sentence 3

B Move sentence 4 to the beginning.

C Switch sentences 1 and 2

D Move sentence 1 to the end.

Test Preparation Workshop 13

Writing Skills — Responding to Writing Prompts

Strategies for Success

The writing sections of many standardized tests require you to write an essay based on a writing prompt. Your essay usually is evaluated as a whole, on a 1–6 point scale from *outstanding* to *deficient,* and assessed for focus, content, organization, grammar, usage, and mechanics. Use the following strategies to help you with a writing assessment:

Read the writing prompt The writing prompt consists of two parts. The first part explains the topic you are asked to write about, or the writing situation. The second part provides specific instructions on how to respond to the prompt.

Look for Key Words As you examine the writing prompt, look for key words such as *define, explain, classify,* and *contrast.* These words indicate the purpose of your essay. It is essential that you keep these key words in mind as you develop your essay.

Budget Your Time When writing for a test, you need to be aware of how much time you have. Allow one quarter of your time for gathering ideas, half your time for writing your first draft, and one quarter of your time for revising.

Collect Your Ideas Before you begin writing, jot down key ideas and details that you plan to include. Then, review your ideas and decide on the best organization.

Draft Carefully Because you'll have less time to revise than you might in other writing situations, take care in the words and sentences you use as you draft your essay. Begin with an introduction that presents your main point. Follow with body paragraphs, each focusing on a single subtopic. Then, end with a conclusion restating your point.

Use Transitions As you draft, use transitional words to indicate the connections between ideas. The following words show comparison-and-contrast relationships: *however; nevertheless; yet; likewise; in like manner; on the contrary; similarly; instead;* and *nonetheless.*

Proofread Make sure your descriptions are clear. Check that there are no errors in spelling, grammar, usage, or mechanics.

Key Strategies:

- Focus on the topic and do not include unnecessary information.
- Present the material in an organized manner.
- Provide supporting ideas.
- Write with sentence variety.
- Proofread your work.

Apply the Strategies

Practice the preceding strategies by writing an essay in response to the following prompt.

Sample Writing Prompt

> Everyone looks forward to weekends and a break from the weekday routine. Think about one thing that you like to do on weekends and why. It could be a community activity, an opportunity to be by yourself to play video games or watch television, or it could be sharing time with family members and friends.

Now explain in an essay why this event or activity is important to you. Support your ideas with examples and details.

Using the Test Practice Bank

These tests provide practice test items in reading comprehension and writing skills. For each Test Preparation Workshop that appears in the book, you will find here a page of extra test items that focus on the same skill. In addition, several tests provide practice in a combination of skills, along with writing prompts.

You may choose to have your students use this practice bank from time to time in conjunction with the Test Preparation Workshops; alternatively, you may want students to spend a block of time working on the entire practice bank during a standardized test preparation period.

Correlations to Standardized Tests

The reading comprehension practice items on this page correspond to the following standardized test sections:

ACT	Reading
SAT 9	Reading Vocabulary
SAT	Critical Reading
TerraNova	Reading

Answers

1 (D) After saying that the mother wants Jing-mei to be a *prodigy,* the passage gives examples of what this meant, such as being a math whiz.

2 (J) The context clue "she pushes the girl" suggests that to *excel* is to "outdo others."

3 (A) The words "rebels against" provide a context clue suggesting that *injunctions* means "commands."

4 (H) The words "finally" and "terrible" suggest that the difficulties between mother and daughter reached a peak with their *row,* or quarrel.

5 (B) Because Jing-mei's comments come at the peak of the confrontation between mother and daughter, the context suggests that *malicious* means "hurtful."

6 (J) The words "only later" suggest that the bad feelings between mother and daughter persisted before changing, and that *reconcile* means "make peace."

Test Practice Bank

Reading Comprehension

Using Context Clues

Read the passage, and then answer the questions that follow. Mark the letter of your answer on a bubble sheet if your teacher provides one; otherwise, number from 1 to 6 on a separate sheet of paper, and write the letter of the correct answer next to each number.

"Two Kinds" by Amy Tan addresses a question everyone wonders while growing up: "Who am I?" In the story, an immigrant mother wants her American-born daughter, Jing-mei, to be a famous prodigy. She pushes the girl to excel as an actress, a math whiz, and a musician. As her failures mount, Jing-mei rebels against her mother's injunctions. Finally, they have a terrible row in which Jing-mei makes malicious comments to her mother. Only later, when Jing-mei is grown, is she able to reconcile with her mother.

1 In this passage, the word *prodigy* means—
A faithful servant
B observant witness
C silent partner
D talented child

2 The word *excel* in this passage means—
A assist others
B imitate others
C inspire others
D outdo others

3 In this passage, the word *injunctions* means—
A commands
B emotions
C memories
D treaties

4 The word *row* in this passage means—
A apology
B fable
C quarrel
D sermon

5 In this passage, the word *malicious* means—
A eager
B hurtful
C ordinary
D pleasant

6 The word *reconcile* in this passage means—
A break promises
B find fault
C have struggles
D make peace

Reading Comprehension

Arranging Details in Sequential Order

Read each passage, and then answer the questions that follow. Mark the letter of your answer on a bubble sheet if your teacher provides one; otherwise, number from 1 to 4 on a separate sheet of paper, and write the letter of the correct answer next to each number.

Born in New York City in 1783, Washington Irving was the first American writer to become famous in Europe as well as at home. While still in his teens, he began writing humorous essays. His first successful book was *A History of New York* (1809).

As a young man living in England, Irving read German folk tales in search of subjects he could use for stories of his own. These tales frequently appeared in Irving's later writings, but set in an American landscape. One of these tales inspired the story "Rip Van Winkle," which appeared in *The Sketch Book of Geoffrey Crayon, Gent.*

1 Which of the following events happened first?

A Washington Irving wrote the story "Rip Van Winkle."
B Washington Irving wrote a series of amusing essays.
C Washington Irving authored the book *A History of New York.*
D Washington Irving became a famous writer abroad.

2 When did Washington Irving study German folk tales as research for his writing?

A as a teenager in New York City
B after writing "Rip Van Winkle"
C before visiting England
D before he published *The Sketch Book of Geoffrey Crayon, Gent.*

One afternoon, Rip Van Winkle encounters a strange man with a thick beard and strange clothing in the mountains near his home. The stranger wants Rip to help him carry a keg up the mountain. Rip helps the man, and they soon come upon a group of odd-looking men who are bowling. As Rip watches the game, he sips from the keg and falls into a deep sleep. When he awakens, he discovers that he has slept for 20 years. The changes bewilder him, but after reuniting with his daughter, he settles back into village life.

3 What happens while Rip watches the men bowl?

A Rip is bewildered by the changes he sees.
B Rip helps the bearded man carry a keg.
C Rip drinks from the keg.
D Rip awakes from his sleep.

4 Which event in the passage happened last?

A Rip is shocked by how the village has changed.
B Rip rejoins his daughter.
C Rip returns to the village after a 20-year absence.
D Rip becomes accustomed to the village once more.

Correlations to Standardized Tests

The reading comprehension practice items on this page correspond to the following standardized test sections:

ACT Reading
SAT 9 Reading Comprehension

Answers

1 (B) The humorous or amusing essays mentioned in the passage are those Irving began to write while in his teens, before the events in the other answer choices.
2 (J) The passage states that "Rip Van Winkle" was based on a German folk tale Irving had studied and that "Rip Van Winkle" appeared in *The Sketch Book of Geoffrey Crayon, Gent.* Therefore, Irving must have studied German tales before publishing *The Sketch Book.*
3 (C) The passage states that he sipped from the keg while he watched the game.
4 (J) The text says that Rip settles back into village life, or becomes accustomed to it again, after reuniting with his daughter. These are the final events in the passage.

Correlations to Standardized Tests

The reading comprehension practice items on this page correspond to the following standardized test sections:

ACT Reading
SAT 9 Reading Comprehension
ITBS Reading Comprehension
TerraNova Reading

Answers

1 (B) The first sentence of the passage tells the reader that fairy tales with similar themes come from cultures around the world. In different terms, fairy tales often take slightly differing forms.
2 (G) The final sentence states clearly that Krakauer's earlier experiences with mountaineering and writing about the subject prepared him well to climb Mt. Everest and write about the experience.
3 (C) The details of the passage imply the main idea, that farming could supply enough food to allow the development of other arts and trade.

Reading Comprehension

Identifying Main Idea

Read each passage, and then answer the questions that follow. Mark the letter of your answer on a bubble sheet if your teacher provides one; otherwise, number from 1 to 3 on a separate sheet of paper, and write the letter of the correct answer next to each number.

It is surprising to learn how many different cultures have produced fairy tales with similar themes. For example, there are at least 345 versions of *Cinderella,* from places as diverse as China and Ireland. In each version, the same basic events occur, but the characters vary. In one version, the fairy godmother role is taken by a magical animal.

1 What is the main idea of this passage?
A The Cinderella story is told throughout the world.
B Fairy tales often take slightly differing forms.
C All versions of *Cinderella* have essentially the same plot.
D Fairy tales told in Ireland are similar to those told in China.

Family outings in Oregon set the stage for Jon Krakauer's interest in mountaineering. By the time Krakauer was in his early twenties, he had made several difficult climbs. His first book-length publication was a collection of essays about climbing the Eiger, a peak in the Alps. This prepared him for climbing Mount Everest and writing about his adventure in his book *Into Thin Air.*

2 What is the stated main idea of this passage?
A Jon Krakauer has made difficult climbs, including Mount Everest.
B Jon Krakauer's background qualified him to write about and climb Mount Everest.
C Jon Krakauer has enjoyed climbing mountains since his childhood.
D Jon Krakauer has written much about mountains.

About 7,000 years ago, most people lived in small farming settlements. Ancient peoples had discovered that farming could supply much of their food year-round. Having enough food meant that they could pursue other tasks, such as toolmaking and needlework. Their products improved villagers' lives, and also made trade possible.

3 What is the implied main idea of this passage?
A Farming allowed ancient peoples to grow and store extra food.
B Ancient peoples traded tools and needlework.
C Farming gave ancient peoples the free time to make and trade goods.
D Most ancient peoples lived in small agricultural villages.

Reading Comprehension

Understanding Author's Point of View and Purpose

Read the passage, and then answer the questions that follow. Mark the letter of your answer on a bubble sheet if your teacher provides one; otherwise, number from 1 to 6 on a separate sheet of paper, and write the letter of the correct answer next to each number.

> Besides Sir Arthur Conan Doyle (the creator of Sherlock Holmes), the best British author of detective stories is Agatha Christie. Her answer to Sherlock Holmes is Hercule Poirot, a Belgian detective living in England, whose vanity, if not ability, far exceeds that of Holmes. Christie's most original creation, however, is Jane Marple.
>
> Miss Marple, an elderly and remarkably shrewd woman, lives in the quaint English village of St. Mary Mead. She is well aware that criminals are as common in the country as they are in the city. Although Miss Marple is not a professional, her talent for solving crimes astounds the local police, and she wins admiration at Scotland Yard.

1 The author's main purpose is to—
A describe Agatha Christie's fictional detective Miss Marple
B contrast Arthur Conan Doyle's characters with Agatha Christie's
C describe Hercule Poirot
D show that Miss Marple is the greatest of all detectives

2 How does the author view Arthur Conan Doyle's work?
A The author thinks that Doyle's detective is less vain than Christie's detectives.
B The author likes Doyle's stories more than Christie's.
C The author thinks that Doyle copied Christie's characters.
D The author thinks that Doyle's detective is less shrewd than Christie's detectives.

3 What does the author feel toward Agatha Christie?
A admiration
B jealousy
C compassion
D suspicion

4 The reason the author includes the first sentence is to—
A introduce the reader to Agatha Christie
B indicate a preference for Arthur Conan Doyle
C inform the reader of Agatha Christie's nationality
D describe the type of novels Agatha Christie wrote

5 What does the author feel toward Miss Marple?
A annoyance
B devotion
C fascination
D sympathy

6 How does the author feel toward the character of Hercule Poirot as compared to Sherlock Holmes?
A Poirot is smarter than Sherlock Holmes.
B Poirot is less professional than Holmes.
C Poirot displays less talent than Holmes.
D Poirot is more modest than Holmes.

Correlations to Standardized Tests

The reading comprehension practice items on this page correspond to the following standardized test sections:

ACT	Reading
SAT	Critical Reading
ITBS	Reading Comprehension
TerraNova	Reading

Answers

1 (A) Most of the passage focuses on Agatha Christie's writings and especially on one character, Miss Marple.

2 (G) The author opens the passage by implying that Arthur Conan Doyle was the greatest of all British authors of detective stories, including Agatha Christie.

3 (A) The author clearly admires Agatha Christie, as seen in the opening sentence.

4 (F) By mentioning Arthur Conan Doyle and his character Sherlock Holmes in the first sentence and placing Agatha Christie in Doyle's company, the author introduces the reader to Christie and her work.

5 (C) The author is clearly fascinated by Miss Marple, but not devoted. Nor does the author express feelings of sympathy for the character.

6 (H) When the author says of Poirot that his "vanity, if not ability," exceed Holmes's, the reader knows that the author feels that Poirot's abilities do not exceed Holmes's.

Correlations to Standardized Tests

The reading comprehension practice items on this page correspond to the following standardized test sections:

ACT Reading
SAT 9 Reading Comprehension
SAT Critical Reading
ITBS Reading Comprehension

Answers

1 (C) The description of the setting is most consistent with a medieval country house, especially with mention of "life on the manor" and details such as the straw piled in the corner of the kitchen.
2 (H) It is clear from Edward's complaints and from the words Alyce chooses that Edward's central problem is the teasing he faces and dislikes.
3 (B) The relationship between Edward and Alyce is close, suggesting the affections family members might have for one another.
4 (G) The story that Alyce tells Edward, about a small but brave boy, reflects Edward's actual life and his aspirations.
5 (D) Alyce's words to Edward seem maternal, or motherly, in their protectiveness and support.
6 (H) Alyce's story clearly reflects and restates Edward's actual life, especially in the prominence of the teasing.

Reading Comprehension

Describing Plot, Setting, Character, and Mood

Read the passage, and then answer the questions that follow. Mark the letter of your answer on a bubble sheet if your teacher provides one; otherwise, number from 1 to 6 on a separate sheet of paper, and write the letter of the correct answer next to each number.

While they ate their bread-and-bacon supper, while Alyce helped Edward mound up straw in a corner of the kitchen, while she sat by watching for him to go to sleep, all the while Edward talked of life on the manor. . . . And he complained at his lot, doing all the smallest tasks, . . . being teased for being so little and frail and tied to Cook's skirts and fit for nothing but gathering eggs. Finally as his eyes looked near to closing, he said, "Tell me a story, Alyce."

". . . [O]nce there was a boy who for all he was so small and puny was brave enough to do what he must although he didn't like it and was sometimes teased. Is that a story?"

"Close enough, Alyce." And he closed his eyes.

—*The Midwife's Apprentice* by Karen Cushman

1 What is the most likely setting of this passage?
A a suburban home in the 1950s
B an army hospital in World War II
C a country house in medieval times
D an abandoned hotel in the Old West

2 What is the central problem Edward faces?
A He has to gather straw.
B He wants to stay awake.
C He does not like being teased.
D He does not like Alyce's story.

3 Which of these words best describes the mood of the passage?
A bright
B familial
C jubilant
D suspenseful

4 In this passage, Edward's character is primarily revealed by—
A his words and thoughts
B Alyce's story
C his surroundings
D Alyce's thoughts

5 Based on the passage, which of these words best describes Alyce?
A brilliant
B irritable
C jolly
D motherly

6 How does Alyce's story relate to Edward?
A It recalls how Edward used to behave.
B It explains why Edward is often teased.
C It restates Edward's own story.
D It describes a boy worse off than Edward.

Reading Comprehension

Making Generalizations

Read each passage, and then answer the questions that follow. Mark the letter of your answer on a bubble sheet if your teacher provides one; otherwise, number from 1 to 4 on a separate sheet of paper, and write the letter of the correct answer next to each number.

It is believed that people began creating zoos as early as 4500 B.C. Rulers sometimes designed zoos themselves. In China, in about 1000 B.C., Wen Wang established a 1,500-acre zoological garden, which he named "The Garden of Intelligence." The Greeks also had collections of captive animals, and Alexander the Great collected animals on his expeditions. In Mexico during the 1500's, Hernán Cortés came upon a zoo so large it needed a staff of 300. One zoo in Vienna, Austria, has been open since 1752.

1 Based on the passage, which of these is an accurate generalization about the history of zoos?
A The first zoos were primarily in America.
B Early zoos were sometimes quite elaborate.
C Most zoos were designed by political leaders.
D Most zoos were founded hundreds of years ago.

2 Which of these is an accurate generalization about "The Garden of Intelligence"?
A It contained more animals than European zoos.
B It required more keepers than zoos in Mexico.
C It was the oldest zoo in China.
D It was a large zoo for its time.

Anton van Leeuwenhoek (1632–1723) was among the first people to observe microscopic life. Leeuwenhoek, a cloth merchant, first developed the microscope to examine the quality of cloth. Later, he began to use his microscope to observe drops of water, where he was amazed to find tiny moving organisms. These microorganisms included bacteria, protozoa, and rotifers.

3 Based on the passage, which of these is an accurate generalization about the organisms Leeuwenhoek observed with his microscope?
A They were larger than cloth fibers.
B They consisted mainly of bacteria.
C They could not be seen by unaided human eyes.
D They could easily survive without water.

4 Which of these is an accurate generalization about the career of Anton van Leeuwenhoek?
A He was interested in science as well as business.
B He had an extremely limited knowledge of science.
C He is best known for his work as a cloth merchant.
D He was the first person to observe microorganisms.

Correlations to Standardized Tests

The reading comprehension practice items on this page correspond to the following standardized test sections:

ACT Reading
SAT 9 Reading Comprehension

Answers

1 (B) The passage supports the generalization that early zoos were sometimes elaborate, as seen in details like those concerning Wen Wang's 1,500-acre zoological garden in ancient China.
2 (J) The details of the passage support the generalization that "The Garden of Intelligence" was a large zoo for its time, since it is clearly exceptional as an early zoo, and its great size is emphasized.
3 (C) The details of the passage support the generalization that the organisms Leeuwenhoek saw with his microscope could not be seen without aid, especially the detail concerning Leeuwenhoek's astonishment that such organisms existed at all.
4 (F) Details in the passage concerning his experience as a cloth merchant and scientist support the generalization that Leeuwenhoek was interested in both science and business.

Correlations to Standardized Tests

The reading comprehension practice items on this page correspond to the following standardized test sections:

ACT Reading

SAT 9 Reading Comprehension

Answers

1 (C) The passage ends with the mother suggesting that they take the mongoose home, and the boy's interest in the animal suggests that he will take it home.

2 (J) The boy's interest in the animal and his sympathy for it, expressed by his willingness to provide a funeral for it, tells the reader that the boy will attempt to help the mongoose, as his mother suggests.

3 (B) The passage makes clear that Iona drives a horse-drawn cab and that he is being called by the officer, who needs to be driven somewhere. Iona will probably pick up the officer in his cab.

4 (F) By identifying the man as an officer and having him shout assertively to Iona, Chekhov suggests a man of authority, used to having his way. The officer would probably repeat his order in a louder voice if Iona did not respond at first.

Reading Comprehension

Predicting Probable Actions and Outcomes

Read each passage, and then answer the questions that follow. Mark the letter of your answer on a bubble sheet if your teacher provides one; otherwise, number from 1 to 4 on a separate sheet of paper, and write the letter of the correct answer next to each number.

[Rikki-tikki-tavi] was a mongoose, rather like a little cat in his fur and his tail, but quite like a weasel in his head and his habits. . . .

One day, a high summer flood washed him out of the burrow where he lived with his father and mother, and carried him, kicking and clucking, down a roadside ditch. He found a little wisp of grass floating there, and clung to it till he lost his senses. When he revived, he was lying in the hot sun on the middle of a garden path, very draggled indeed, and a small boy was saying: "Here's a dead mongoose. Let's have a funeral."

"No," said his mother, "let's take him in and dry him. Perhaps he isn't really dead."

—"Rikki-tikki-tavi" by Rudyard Kipling

1 What will probably happen to the mongoose next?
A He will follow the boy home.
B He will be buried near the path.
C He will be taken to the boy's house.
D He will return to his parents' burrow.

2 How will the boy probably react to his mother's suggestion?
A He will refuse to believe her.
B He will try to change her mind.
C He will want to sell the mongoose.
D He will attempt to help the mongoose.

It has been a long time since Iona and his horse have moved from their place. They left the stable before supper, and still there is no fare. But now evening darkness is descending on the city. The pale light of the streetlamps is surrendering its place to vivid color, and the bustle in the street is becoming noisier.

"Cabby, to the Vyborg District!" hears Iona, "Cabby!"

Iona starts, and through eyelashes pasted over with snow he sees an officer in a cloak with a hood.

—"Heartache" by Anton Chekhov

3 What will Iona probably do next?
A He will move his cab away from the officer.
B He will pick up the officer in his cab.
C He will return his horse to the stable.
D He will leave his cab to eat supper.

4 How will the officer probably react if Iona does not respond?
A He will repeat his order in a louder voice.
B He will quietly walk to his destination.
C He will apologize for making a scene.
D He will offer to take Iona to supper.

Reading Comprehension

Distinguishing Fact and Opinion

Read each passage, and then answer the questions that follow. Mark the letter of your answer on a bubble sheet if your teacher provides one; otherwise, number from 1 to 4 on a separate sheet of paper, and write the letter of the correct answer next to each number.

Winslow Homer was not the only artist to cover the Civil War. Because photography at that time was too slow to capture battle action, newspapers and magazines sent artists to draw the battles. Henry Walke was one illustrator who, like Homer, got close enough to the action to make pen-and-ink sketches of it. These images provide a wrenching record of the war.

Photographs, too, were important. They illustrated the Civil War personalities and landscapes as well as the unthinkable aftermath of battle. Pioneer photographers like Mathew Brady and Alexander Gardner made significant contributions to coverage of the war.

1 Which of these is a FACT from the passage?
- **A** Photographs were unimportant in documenting the war.
- **B** Winslow Homer was not the only artist to cover the war.
- **C** Henry Walke's illustrations are a wrenching record of the war.
- **D** Photographs illustrated the aftermath of battles.

2 Which of these is an OPINION expressed in the passage?
- **A** Henry Walke made pen-and-ink sketches of the war.
- **B** Magazines sent artists to draw what the battles looked like.
- **C** Photography was too slow to capture battle action.
- **D** Alexander Gardner made significant contributions to the coverage of the war.

The Florida Everglades is a vast marsh area. It may be the world's most precious wetlands. It covers about 5,000 square miles, but the water averages less than a foot in depth. One of the most fascinating animals there is the rattlesnake. The Everglades is also home to alligators, panthers, and many types of birds.

Today, with the need to supply south Florida's water, the natural balance of the Everglades is at risk. Steps should be taken to protect this treasure.

3 Which of these is a FACT from the passage?
- **A** The Everglades' most fascinating animal is the rattlesnake.
- **B** People should protect the irreplaceable Everglades.
- **C** South Florida uses too much of the Everglades' water.
- **D** The Everglades is home to many types of birds.

4 Which of these is an OPINION expressed in the passage?
- **A** The Everglades is panther habitat.
- **B** The Everglades is one of the most precious wetlands.
- **C** The Everglades is covered by less than a foot of water.
- **D** The Everglades covers about 5,000 square miles of land.

Correlations to Standardized Tests

The reading comprehension practice items on this page correspond to the following standardized test sections:

ACT	Reading
SAT	Critical Reading
SAT 9	Reading Comprehension

Answers

1 (B) The passage states that Homer was not the only artist to cover the war, and offers the example of Henry Walke as another artist who did so. This statement of fact does not depend on anyone's opinion or judgment, and can be verified in independent sources.

2 (J) Opinions are statements that depend on an individual's perspective or judgment and is not subject to independent verification. Whether Alexander Gardner's contributions to war coverage were *significant* is a matter of opinion.

3 (D) That the Everglades is home to many kinds of birds is a fact that can be verified through research in independent sources.

4 (G) It is a matter of opinion whether the Everglades is one of the *most precious* wetlands. It is a matter of individual judgment, not an objectively verifiable statement.

Correlations to Standardized Tests

The reading comprehension practice items on this page correspond to the following standardized test sections:

ACT Reading
SAT 9 Reading Comprehension
TerraNova Reading

Answers

1 (A) It can be inferred from the use of the word *mortal* in the passage that Phaëthon's father, Apollo, is a god. It is not stated plainly.
2 (J) Because the content of the passage concerns immortals, such as Apollo, and the halls of Olympus, the reader sees that this passage is taken from a myth.
3 (B) Phaëthon reminds his friends that, by virtue of great deeds, sons of gods and mortals have become immortal. Readers can infer that this is what Phaëthon hopes will happen.
4 (H) Because readers are told that since Clymene, Phaëthon's mother, could not dwell in the halls of Olympus, readers can infer that mortals cannot enter Olympus.
5 (D) Because Apollo lives where the goddess of dawn lives, and drives a golden chariot across the sky, the golden chariot can be seen to represent the sun.
6 (G) The last sentence says that Phaëthon would risk even his life in a rash attempt to achieve immortality. Knowing how much Phaëthon wants this honor, the reader can infer that Phaëthon may come to harm striving to be godlike.

Reading Comprehension

Drawing Inferences and Conclusions

Read the passage, and then answer the questions that follow. Mark the letter of your answer on a bubble sheet if your teacher provides one; otherwise, number from 1 to 6 on a separate sheet of paper, and write the letter of the correct answer next to each number.

Though Apollo always honored the memory of Daphne she was not his only love. Another was a mortal, Clymene, by whom he had a son named Phaëthon. Phaëthon grew up with his mother, who, since she was mortal, could not dwell in the halls of Olympus or in the palace of the sun. She lived not far from the East in the land of Ethiopia, and as her son grew up, she would point to the place where Eos, goddess of the dawn, lighted up the sky and tell him that there his father dwelt. Phaëthon loved to boast of his divine father as he saw the golden chariot riding high through the air. He would remind his comrades of other sons of gods and mortal women who, by virtue of their great deeds, had become gods at last. . . . He could never bear to be beaten, even if he had to risk his life in some rash way to win.

—"Phaëthon, Son of Apollo" by Olivia E. Coolidge

1 Which of these statements is a sound inference about Phaëthon?
A His father is a god.
B He was once mortal.
C He owns a golden chariot.
D His mother is named Daphne.

2 From what type of literature was this passage taken?
A a ballad
B a biography
C a drama
D a myth

3 What does Phaëthon hope will happen if he is first in everything?
A He will earn his mother's respect.
B He will be transformed into a god.
C He will win a mortal woman's love.
D He will be allowed to visit Ethiopia.

4 Which of these statements is a logical inference about the halls of Olympus?
A Phaëthon was born there.
B Clymene once lived there.
C Only gods may enter there.
D They were built by Apollo.

5 What does Apollo's golden chariot represent?
A the air
B the East
C the land
D the sun

6 What is implied by the last sentence of the passage?
A Phaëthon may take great risks because of his success.
B Phaëthon may come to harm as he strives to be godlike.
C Phaëthon may become arrogant if he behaves dangerously.
D Phaëthon may become discouraged if he behaves recklessly.

Reading Comprehension

Identifying Cause and Effect

Read the passage, and then answer the questions that follow. Mark the letter of your answer on a bubble sheet if your teacher provides one; otherwise, number from 1 to 5 on a separate sheet of paper, and write the letter of the correct answer next to each number.

The highwayman whistled a tune to the window, and Bess, the landlord's daughter, appeared to greet him. Someone else had heard the whistle, too, though: a door squeaked as Tim, the stableman, came close to listen. Tim loved Bess too, and he overheard the robber's promise to return to her by morning. Tim slipped away and set off toward town.

Waiting for the highwayman's return, Bess heard a noise, but not the familiar gait of her sweetheart's horse. Suddenly, there were soldiers at her window. In a moment they were tying her up, and setting a musket aimed at her heart. As the soldiers hid, Tim watched with satisfaction.

Bess struggled with the knots around her wrists and managed to free one hand. Suddenly, she heard the horse's hooves in the distance. What to do? They would surely catch him! Drawing one last breath, she moved her free hand to the trigger of the musket. The silence at the inn was shattered by the gun's roar.

Hearing the sound, the highwayman turned away and headed west. He would come back for Bess another day. He knew she would understand, but he did not know who was slumped on the floor of the inn, her head bowed over a musket.

—adapted from the poem "The Highwayman" by Alfred Noyes

1 What effect did the highwayman's whistle have?
A to signal his sweetheart
B to keep himself awake
C to signal his arrival to Tim
D to alert the soldiers

2 What causes the noise in the yard of the inn when the highwayman and Bess are at the window?
A Bess firing a musket
B Soldiers sneaking into the yard
C Tim entering the yard to listen
D The highwayman whistling

3 Why do the soldiers come to the inn?
A to find a place to stay
B to alert the landlord
C to catch the highwayman
D to protect Bess

4 What causes Tim to leave the yard?
A He has no more work to do.
B He is afraid of the highwayman.
C He is angry at Bess.
D He wants to tell the soldiers about the highwayman's return.

5 Why does Bess fire the musket?
A to frighten the soldiers
B to warn the highwayman
C to show her anger with Tim
D to help catch the highwayman

Correlations to Standardized Tests

The reading comprehension practice items on this page correspond to the following standardized test section:

SAT 9 Reading Comprehension
ACT Reading

Answers

1 (A) The effect of the highwayman's whistle is to signal Bess to come to the window.
2 (H) While Bess and the highwayman are at the window, a door squeaks as Tim comes close to listen. This is the cause of the noise.
3 (C) In the passage, the reader sees that the soldiers tie up Bess and then hide, waiting for the return of the highwayman. They come to the inn in order to catch him.
4 (J) Because the soldiers arrive at the inn just after Tim has sneaked away with knowledge of the highwayman's return, the reader can see that what causes him to leave the inn is his desire to help the soldiers capture the highwayman.
5 (A) Bess fires the musket in hopes that it will cause the highwayman to turn away and avoid the inn. It is a warning.

Correlations to Standardized Tests

The reading comprehension practice items on these two pages correspond to the following standardized test sections:

ACT	Reading
SAT	Critical Reading
ITBS	Reading Comprehension
TerraNova	Reading

Answers

1 (D) It is clear from the details provided that the word *prestigious* means "renowned." One such detail is the inclusion of Arkansas Player of the Year, John Daly, in the match, a player who is described as "legendary."

2 (F) From the text it is clear that Daly's comments about Woods stand *in contrast* to Woods's comments about Daly.

3 (B) That Tiger Woods competed against a *legend* in the match is a matter of opinion, or individual feeling and judgment. There is no independent way to verify if Daly is or ever was a legend.

4 (F) The opening paragraph details the contrast between the slight Tiger Woods and the brawnier John Daly, a "heavyweight."

5 (D) The passage ends with Daly's comments about Woods, in which he makes clear his great respect for the young player's ability. It is probable that in the future Daly will be less confident of beating such a fine player.

Combined Reading and Literary Skills

Read the passage, and then answer the questions that follow. Mark your answers to questions 1 to 9 on a bubble sheet if your teacher provides one; otherwise, number from 1 to 9 on a separate sheet of paper, and write the letter of the correct answer next to each number. Answer number 10 on a separate sheet of paper.

He was as thin as a steel shaft and lighter than graphite.[1] He stood five-feet-five and weighed one hundred seven pounds, which, if a fair fight was the objective, would have required he be matched against a 4-iron. In this instance, his opponent was a heavyweight, John Daly, the Arkansas Player of the Year in 1986 and 1987, and already a legend, on a local scale, for his prodigious length.

The site was Texarkana Country Club in Texarkana, Arkansas. . . .Tiger was there to play in the Big I, short for the Insurance Youth Gold Classic, a prestigious event on the American Junior Gold Association tour. The Big I created excitement among the juniors: in the final round they were paired with professional golfers. Daly was among the twenty pros recruited to participate with the sixty juniors, and he was paired with Woods. Through four holes, Woods was ahead of Daly, who turned to a friend and said loud enough to be heard by those in the gallery, "I can't let this thirteen-year-old beat me."

Tiger remained ahead at the turn, three-under par to Daly's one-under par. But Daly's four birdies on the back nine and three on the last four holes enabled him to defeat Woods. Still, Tiger's score was better than those posted by eight of the twenty professionals, and he finished second in the tournament.

Three years later, Tiger was asked what he recalled about playing with Daly that day. "I don't remember too much, except he wasn't a smart player," he said. "He'd take his driver and go over trees. He's got to throttle back."[2]

Daly, conversely, had been indelibly[3] impressed. "That kid is great," he said. "Everybody was applauding him and nobody applauded me. He's better than I'd heard."

—"Tiger: A Biography of Tiger Woods" by John Strege

1. **graphite:** Lightweight material used to make golf clubs.
2. **throttle back:** Ease up.
3. **indelibly:** Lastingly; permanently.

1 The word *prestigious* in this passage means—
A casual
B questionable
C unexpected
D renowned

2 In this passage, the word *conversely* means—
A in contrast
B in confusion
C lacking control
D without confidence

3 Which of these is an OPINION expressed in this passage?
A Tiger finished second in the tournament.
B Tiger competed against a legend in the Big I.
C Tiger led Daly after four holes.
D Daly had three birdies on the last four holes.

4 What is the main idea of the first paragraph?
A Tiger had to compete against a stronger golfer.
B Although Tiger was thin, he was a powerful golfer.
C Tiger and John Daly were evenly matched opponents.
D John Daly was famous for hitting balls a great distance.

5 What will likely be John Daly's reaction if he plays against Tiger in the future?
A Daly will insist on going first.
B Daly will take Tiger less seriously as a player.
C Daly will ask to compete as a junior.
D Daly will be less confident of winning.

6 You can conclude from the passage that Tiger Woods—
A played well but lacked confidence
B had great skill but rarely practiced
C demonstrated leadership despite being young
D showed great talent for such a young golfer

7 The author's main purpose is to—
A entertain readers with an amusing story about golf
B convince readers to begin playing golf at a young age
C explain why Tiger Woods was not able to beat John Daly
D describe an event from early in Tiger Woods's golfing career

8 What happened during the first four holes of the final round of the Big I?
A Daly scored three birdies.
B Tiger scored better than Daly.
C Tiger recalled golfing with Daly.
D Daly became Player of the Year.

9 Which of these BEST describes the main events of the passage?
A Tiger played against John Daly at the Texarkana Country Club. The crowd applauded Tiger rather than Daly.
B John Daly was much stronger than Tiger. Tiger criticized Daly's playing, but Daly was impressed by Tiger's talent.
C John Daly was determined not to be beaten by Tiger. Daly hit several birdies, which allowed him to defeat Tiger.
D Tiger was paired with John Daly in a golf tournament. Daly beat Tiger, but Tiger showed great promise.

10 Why was Tiger Woods's performance in the Big I so impressive? Support your answer with evidence from the text.

Answers *(continued)*

6 (J) It is clear from the passage that Woods was both a young player at the time of the tournament, and also a player of great composure and talent.

7 (D) The author's purpose can be determined from the details present in the passage and the focus the author brings to the subject. Here, the details concern an event from early in the career of Tiger Woods.

8 (G) The passage states clearly that after the first four holes, Tiger Woods was ahead of John Daly.

9 (D) The three basic statements in this answer cover the main events of the passage accurately.

10 *Possible response:*
Tiger Woods's performance was impressive for several reasons, the first being the high level of the golf he played. In addition, the text makes clear that Tiger was young at the time, only thirteen, and physically small. He played opposite an older, stronger, rather intimidating player, and nearly won. Woods's performance was impressive in part because of his maturity and composure.

Rubric for Evaluating Responses to Writing Prompts				
0	1	2	3	4
Off topic Blank paper Foreign language Illegible, incoherent Not enough content to score	Incorrect purpose, mode, or audience Brief, vague Unelaborated Rambling	Lack of language control Poor organization Correct purpose, mode, audience Some elaboration Some details	Gaps in organization Limited language control Correct purpose, mode, audience Moderately well elaborated Clear, effective language	Organized (perhaps with brief digressions) Correct purpose, mode, audience Effective elaboration Consistent organization Sense of completeness, fluency

Correlations to Standardized Tests

The writing skills items on this page correspond to the following standardized test sections:

ACT	English Usage
SAT 9	Language
ITBS	Usage and Expression
TerraNova	Language Arts

Answers

1 (B) Deleting the period, replacing the comma with a period, and capitalizing the following letter creates two correct sentences.
2 (F) Deleting the period in this section makes the incomplete sentence that follows part of a single correct sentence.
3 (D) The section is correct as it is.

Writing Skills

Sentence Construction

Read the passage. Some sections are underlined. The underlined sections may be one of the following: incomplete sentences, run-on sentences, correctly written sentences that should be combined, correctly written sentences that do not need to be rewritten. Choose the best way to write each underlined section. Mark the letter of your answer on a bubble sheet if your teacher provides one; otherwise, number from 1 to 3 on a separate sheet of paper, and write the letter of the correct answer next to each number.

(1) Good nonfiction is created by men and women. Who use words well what they write has clarity, liveliness, interest, and style. When you read nonfiction, look for these qualities. (2) A persuasive essay is one type of nonfiction. In which a writer tries to convince you to accept a certain idea, or to act a certain way. (3) Writers often state their opinion at the start of the essay and then present a variety of arguments to back up the idea.

1 **A** Good nonfiction is created by men and women: who use words well what they write has clarity, liveliness, interest, and style.
B Good nonfiction is created by men and women who use words well. What they write has clarity, liveliness, interest, and style.
C Good nonfiction is created by men and women who use words well, what they write has clarity, liveliness, interest, and style.
D Correct as is

2 **A** A persuasive essay is one type of nonfiction in which a writer tries to convince you to accept a certain idea or to act a certain way.
B A persuasive essay is one type of nonfiction; in which a writer tries to convince you to accept a certain idea, or to act a certain way.
C A persuasive essay is one type of nonfiction, in which a writer tries to convince you to accept a certain idea. Or to act a certain way.
D Correct as is

3 **A** Writers often state their opinion at the start of the essay; and then they present a variety of arguments, to back up the idea.
B Writers often state their opinion, at the start of the essay and, then, present a variety of arguments to back up the idea.
C Writers, often state their opinion at the start of the essay, and then, present a variety of arguments to back up the idea.
D Correct as is

Writing Skills

Appropriate Usage

Read the passage, and choose the word or group of words that best fits each space. Mark the letter of your answer on a bubble sheet if your teacher provides one; otherwise, number from 1 to 6 on a separate sheet of paper, and write the letter of the correct answer next to each number.

> The poet Oliver Herford (1863–1935) was born in England but __(1)__ most of his life in the United States. There are many stories about Herford's sense of humor and carefree nature. Once, passing a schoolhouse at night, he imagined the typical school day that lay ahead for the teacher and pupils. He entered the school and covered the chalkboard with drawings of animals. The next day, the teachers and pupils __(2)__ both surprised and amused to see the animals cavorting on the board. Another time, after some of his poems were repeatedly rejected by the editor of a magazine, Herford sent __(3)__ back to the editor along with the following note: "Sir: Your office boy __(4)__ continually rejecting these masterpieces. Kindly see that they receive the attention of the editor." The editor __(5)__ by accepting several of the poems. These incidents __(6)__ two of Herford's most beloved qualities: his sense of humor and his fondness for animals as subjects.

1 **A** live
B lived
C will live
D living

2 **A** is
B are
C will be
D were

3 **A** them
B those
C this
D they

4 **A** has been
B will have been
C having been
D are being

5 **A** responds
B will respond
C responded
D should respond

6 **A** have revealed
B will reveal
C revealing
D reveal

Correlations to Standardized Tests

The writing skills practice items on this page correspond to the following standardized test sections:

ACT English Usage
SAT 9 Language
ITBS Usage and Expression

Answers

1 (B) The sentence calls for a verb in the past tense, and among the options only *lived* meets this qualification.

2 (J) The sentence calls for the past tense, plural form of the verb *to be: were.*

3 (A) The pronoun used must match its antecedent, *some of his poems,* in number (plural) and case (objective): *them.*

4 (F) The sentence calls for a form of the verb *to be* that carries the sense of a past action that continues uncompleted, and matches the subject: *has been.*

5 (C) The sentence calls for a form of the verb *to respond* in the past tense: *responded.*

6 (J) The sentence works best with a verb in the present tense that matches the plural form of the subject: *reveal.*

Correlations to Standardized Tests

The writing skills items on this page correspond to the following standardized test sections:

ACT English Usage

SAT 9 Language

ITBS Spelling; Capitalization

Answers

1 (A) The underlined section is correct except for the use of *their,* which should be spelled *there*. This pair of homophones is a frequent cause of confusion for students.

2 (F) In a common mistake, the two words "a lot" are combined: "alot."

3 (C) A comma rather than a period, following the word diet, forms a run-on sentence. The word *diet* should end the first sentence.

4 (H) This section includes an unnecessary colon. No punctuation is needed in this section.

5 (B) This section includes an unnecessary capital letter. Point out to students that the term *medical profession* is not a proper noun.

6 (J) There are no errors in this section.

Writing

Spelling, Capitalization, and Punctuation

Read the passage, and decide which type of error, if any, appears in each underlined section. Mark the letter of your answer on a bubble sheet if your teacher provides one; otherwise, number from 1 to 6 on a separate sheet of paper, and write the letter of the correct answer next to each number.

Their are more people (1) living to be 100 than ever before. (2) Alot of the reason for this is diet, (3) people are simply getting better nutrition throughout their lives. Another reason is: that health (4) care is improving all the time, as the Medical profession (5) is getting better at prevention and early diagnosis of disease. Many doctors (6) now believe that most people will be able to reach the century mark within the next generation.

1 **A** Spelling error
B Capitalization error
C Punctuation error
D No error

2 **A** Spelling error
B Capitalization error
C Punctuation error
D No error

3 **A** Spelling error
B Capitalization error
C Punctuation error
D No error

4 **A** Spelling error
B Capitalization error
C Punctuation error
D No error

5 **A** Spelling error
B Capitalization error
C Punctuation error
D No error

6 **A** Spelling error
B Capitalization error
C Punctuation error
D No error

Writing Tasks

The following activity is designed to assess your writing ability. The prompts will ask you to explain something. You may think of your audience as being any reader other than yourself.

In "Tiger Woods," the author shows the golfer as an exceptionally promising thirteen-year-old player. Living up to such promise is never easy, though.

Write an essay exploring the good and bad aspects of placing such high expectations on young people who excel in their field.

When Tiger Woods played his match against John Daly, he didn't think of the older player as "smart." Was Woods being arrogant, or just confident of his own golf judgement?

Write an essay that defines arrogance and shows the difference between arrogance and confidence. Use Tiger Woods's behavior as an example, but feel free to draw on other examples as well.

A tight, hard-fought match like the one between Tiger Woods and John Daly can remain in the minds of viewers for years.

Write an essay about the attraction of sports for so many viewers. Why do athletic events draw such large crowds? Why do fans get so involved in the actions of their favorite players or teams? Use examples from your own experience.

Rubric for Evaluating Responses to Writing Prompts

0	1	2	3	4
Off topic Blank paper Foreign language Illegible, incoherent Not enough content to score	Incorrect purpose, mode, or audience Brief, vague Unelaborated Rambling	Lack of language control Poor organization Correct purpose, mode, audience Some elaboration Some details	Gaps in organization Limited language control Correct purpose, mode, audience Moderately well elaborated Clear, effective language	Organized (perhaps with brief digressions) Correct purpose, mode, audience Effective elaboration Consistent organization Sense of completeness, fluency

Scoring Rubric

Use this scoring rubric to assess the composition you write in response to the prompts on the previous page. The scale runs from **0** (the poorest) to **4** (the best).

0	1	2	3	4
Blank paper	Vague or brief	Correct purpose, audience, and mode	Correct purpose, audience, and mode	Correct purpose, audience, and mode
In a foreign language	Poorly organized	Organization has lapses	Fair organization	Full, appropriate elaboration
Unreadable because of incoherence or illegibility	Wrong purpose, audience, or mode	Some elaboration and detail	Moderate elaboration and detail	Logical, effective organization
On wrong topic	Loses focus; rambles	Language control is limited	Clear, effective language	Fluent, clear, effective language
Content too scant to score	Lacks elaboration, detail, language control			

Index of Authors and Titles

Page numbers in *italics* refer to biographical information.

Index of Skills

LITERARY TERMS

READING STRATEGIES

GRAMMAR, USAGE, MECHANICS

VOCABULARY

CRITICAL THINKING AND VIEWING

WRITING

Writing Opportunities

Writing Skills

SPEAKING, LISTENING, AND VIEWING

LIFE AND WORK SKILLS

PROJECTS

STAFF CREDITS

The people who made up the *Prentice Hall Literature: Timeless Voices, Timeless Themes* team—representing design services, editorial, editorial services, managing editor, manufacturing and inventory planning, market research, marketing services, on-line services/multimedia development, permissions, product marketing, production services, and publishing processes—are listed below. Bold type denotes core team members.

Laura Bird, Betsy Bostwick, Pam Cardiff, **Megan Chill,** Rhett Conklin, Carlos Crespo, Gabriella Della Corte, Ed de Leon, Donna C. DiCuffa, **Amy E. Fleming, Holly Gordon, Rebecca Z. Graziano, William J. Hanna, Rick Hickox,** Jim Jeglikowski, John Kingston, **Perrin Moriarty,** James O'Neill, **Jim O'Shea, Maureen Raymond,** Rob Richman, Doris Robinson, Gerry Schrenck, Ann Shea, Melissa Shustyk, Annette Simmons, **Rita M. Sullivan, Elizabeth Torjussen**

ADDITIONAL CREDITS

Ernie Albanese, Robert H. Aleman, Diane Alimena, Michele Angelucci, Rosalyn Arcilla, Penny Baker, Anthony Barone, Rui Camarinha, Tara Campbell, Amy Capetta, Lorena Cerisano, Kam Cheng, Elizabeth Crawford, Mark Cryan, Paul Delsignore, Robert Dobaczewski, Irene Ehrmann, Kathryn Foot, Joe Galka, Catalina Gavilanes, Elaine Goldman, Joe Graci, Stacey Hosid, Leanne Korszoloski, Jan Kraus, Gregory Lynch, Mary Luthi, Vickie Menanteaux, John McClure, Frances Medico, Omni-Photo Communications, Inc., Photosearch, Inc., Linda Punskovsky, David Rosenthal, Laura Ross, Rose Sievers, Gillian Speeth/Picture This, Cindi Talocci, Mark Taylor, Lashonda Williams, Jeff Zoda

ACKNOWLEDGMENTS (continued)

Susan Essoyan From "Nosing Around U.S. Borders" by Susan Essoyan. First appeared in *Dog Fancy* magazine, June 1997. Used by permission of the author.

Farrar, Straus & Giroux, Inc. "The Cat Who Thought She Was a Dog and the Dog Who Thought He Was a Cat" from *Naftali the Storyteller and His Horse, Sus* by Isaac Bashevis Singer. Pictures by Margot Zemach. Copyright © 1973, 1976 by Isaac Bashevis Singer. Pictures copyright © 1976 by Margot Zemach. "Seal" from *Laughing Time: Collected Nonsense* by William Jay Smith. Copyright © 1990 by William Jay Smith. Reprinted by permission of Farrar, Straus & Giroux, Inc.

Farrar, Straus & Giroux, Inc., and Faber and Faber Limited "Valediction" by Seamus Heaney. Published by Farrar, Straus & Giroux in the U.S. in *Poems 1965–1975* by Seamus Heaney, copyright © 1966, 1980 by Seamus Heaney. Published by Faber and Faber Ltd. in the U.K. in *Death of a Naturalist* by Seamus Heaney. Reprinted by permission.

M.W. Farrell, executrix for the Estate of Juliet Piggott Wood "Popocatepetl and Ixtlaccihuatl" from *Mexican Folk Tales* by Juliet Piggott. Copyright © 1973 by Juliet Piggott. Reprinted by permission.

Golden Books Family Entertainment "The Bride of Pluto" (retitled "Demeter and Persephone") from *Golden Treasury of Myths and Legends* by Anne Terry White. Copyright © 1959 Western Publishing Company, Inc. All rights reserved. Reprinted by permission.

Reid Goldsborough "Let the reader beware" by Reid Goldsborough (reidgold@ netaxs.com) syndicated columnist, which appeared in *Reading Today,* August/September 1997. Used by permission of the author.

Hal Leonard Corporation "On My Own," music by Claude-Michel Schonberg, lyrics by Alain Boublil, Herbert Kretzmer, John Caird, Trevor Nunn and Jean-Marc Natel. Music and lyrics copyright © 1980 by Editions Musicales Alain Boublil. English lyrics copyright © 1986 by Alain Boublil Music Ltd. (ASCAP). Mechanical and publication rights for the U.S.A. administered by Alain Boublil Music Ltd. (ASCAP) c/o Stephen Tenenbaum & Co., Inc., 1775 Broadway, Suite 708, New York, NY 10019, Tel. (212) 246-7204, Fax (212) 246-7217. International Copyright Secured. All Rights Reserved. This music is copyrighted. Photocopying is illegal. All Performance Rights Restricted.

Harcourt Brace & Company "The Writer" from *The Mind-Reader,* copyright © 1971 by Richard Wilbur. "Seventh Grade" from *Baseball in April and Other Stories,* copyright © 1990 by Gary Soto. "Primer Lesson" from *Slabs of the Sunburnt West* by Carl Sandburg, copyright 1922 by Harcourt Brace & Company and renewed 1950 by Carl Sandburg. "Fog" from *Chicago Poems* by Carl Sandburg, copyright 1916 by Holt, Rinehart and Winston and renewed 1944 by Carl Sandburg. "The Algonquin Cinderella" from *World Tales: The Extraordinary Coincidence of Stories Told In All Times, In All Places* by Idries Shah, copyright © 1979 by Technographia, S.A., and Harcourt Brace & Company. "Lonely Particular" from *Revolutionary Petunias & Other Poems,* copyright © 1972 by Alice Walker. Excerpt from *In Search Of Our Mothers' Gardens: Womanist Prose,* copyright © 1983 by Alice Walker, and "Women" from *Revolutionary Petunias & Other Poems,* copyright © 1970 by Alice Walker. "The Enemy" from *Once,* copyright © 1968 by Alice Walker. Reprinted by permission of Harcourt Brace & Company.

HarperCollins Publishers, Inc. Selected excerpts from *An American Childhood* by Annie Dillard. Copyright © 1987 by Annie Dillard. "How the Snake Got Poison" from *Mules and Men* by Zora Neale Hurston. Copyright © 1935 by Zora Neale Hurston. Copyright renewed 1963 by John C. Hurston and Joel Hurston. "Sarah Cynthia Sylvia Stout Would Not Take The Garbage Out" from *Where The Sidewalk Ends* by Shel Silverstein. Copyright © 1974 by Evil Eye Music, Inc. "A Boy and a Man" from *Banner in the Sky* by James Ramsey Ullman. Copyright 1954 by James Ramsey Ullman. Reprinted by permission of HarperCollins Publishers, Inc. "Rikki-tikki-tavi" from *The Jungle Book* by Rudyard Kipling. Excerpt from "King Arthur: The Marvel of the Sword" from *The Book of King Arthur and His Noble Knights* by Mary MacLeod (J. B. Lippincott).

Harvard University Press and the Trustees of Amherst College "I'm Nobody" (poem #288) from *The Poems of Emily Dickinson,* Thomas H. Johnson, editor, Cambridge, Mass.: The Belknap Press of Harvard University Press, Copyright © 1951, 1955, 1979, 1983 by the President and Fellows of Harvard College. Reprinted by permission of the publishers and the Trustees of Amherst College.

John Hawkins & Associates, Inc. "My Furthest-Back Person—The African" by Alex Haley, published July 16, 1972, by *The New York Times Magazine.* Copyright © 1972 by Alex Haley. Reprinted by permission of John Hawkins & Associates, Inc.

Heinemann Educational Publishers, division of Reed Educational & Professional Publishing Ltd. "Tenochtitlan: Inside the Aztec Capital" from *The Aztecs* by Jacqueline Dineen. Copyright © 1992 by Heinemann Educational Publishers. Reprinted by permission of the publisher.

Bill Hilgers, Esq., for the Estate of Barbara Jordan "All Together Now" by Barbara Jordan, orginally published in *Sesame Street Parents,* July/August 1994. Reprinted by permission.

Henry Holt and Company, Inc. "The Pasture," copyright 1939, © 1967, 1969 by Holt, Rinehart and Winston, Inc. "Stopping by Woods on a Snowy Evening," copyright 1923, © 1969 by Holt, Rinehart and Winston, Inc. From *The Poetry of Robert Frost* edited by Edward Connery Lathem. Reprinted by permission of Henry Holt and Company, Inc. From "Birches" by Robert Frost. Copyright © 1969 by Holt, Rinehart and Wilson, Inc.; copyright © 1962 by Robert Frost; copyright © 1975 by Leslie Frost Ballantine.

Edward D. Hoch "Zoo" by Edward D. Hoch, copyright © 1958 by King-Size Publications, Inc.; © renewed 1986 by Edward D. Hoch. Reprinted by permission of the author.

Houghton Mifflin Company From "St. Crispian's Day Speech" from *Henry V* by William Shakespeare, G. Blakemore Evans (Editor), *The Riverside Shakespeare*. Copyright © 1974 by Houghton Mifflin Company. "Phaethon, Son of Apollo," from *Greek Myths*. Copyright 1949, © renewed 1977 by Olivia E. Coolidge. "Icarus and Daedalus" from *Old Greek Folk Stories Told Anew* by Josephine Preston Peabody, The Riverside Press. "The Village Blacksmith" from *The Poetical Works of Longfellow*, Cambridge Edition, 1975. Reprinted by permission of Houghton Mifflin Company. All rights reserved.

Indiana University Press "Heartache" by Anton Chekhov from pp. 328–333 of *From Karamzin to Bunin* edited by Carl Proffer. Published by Indiana University Press. Reprinted by permission of the publisher.

International Paper Company "How to Enjoy Poetry" by James Dickey from the Power of the Printed Word Program. Reprinted by permission of International Paper Company.

Japan Publications, Inc. "On sweet plum blossoms," "Has spring come indeed?" and "Temple bells die out" by Bashō. Reprinted from *One Hundred Famous Haiku* by Daniel C. Buchanan, with permission from Japan Publications, copyright © 1973.

Alfred A. Knopf, Inc. "Mother to Son" from *Collected Poems* by Langston Hughes. Copyright © 1994 by the Estate of Langston Hughes. "The People Could Fly" from *The People Could Fly* by Virginia Hamilton. Text copyright © 1985 by Virginia Hamilton. Illustrations copyright © 1995 by Leo and Diane Dillon. "Annabel Lee" from *The Complete Poems and Stories of Edgar Allan Poe, with Selections from His Writings*, edited by Arthur Hobson Quinn. Reprinted by permission of Alfred A. Knopf, Inc.

Trustees of Leland Stanford Junior University c/o William Saroyan Foundation "The Hummingbird That Lived Through Winter" from *Dear Baby* by William Saroyan. Copyright 1935, 1936, 1939, 1941, 1942, 1943, 1944 by William Saroyan. Reprinted by permission of the Trustees of Leland Stanford Junior University c/o William Saroyan Foundation.

H.N. Levitt "Winslow Homer: America's Greatest Painter" by H. N. Levitt from *Boy's Life*, September 1986. Copyright H. N. Levitt 1986. Reprinted by permission of the author.

Little, Brown and Company From *Let's Steal the Moon* by Blanche Serwer Bernstein. Copyright © 1970, 1987 by Blanche L. Serwer (text). "The Real Story of a Cowboy's Life" from *The West: An Illustrated History* by Geoffrey Ward. Copyright © 1997 by The West Company. "Justin Lebo" from *It's Our World, Too!* by Phillip Hoose. Copyright © 1993 by Phillip Hoose. Used by permission of Little, Brown and Company. "Aunt Leaf" from *Twelve Moons* by Mary Oliver, copyright © 1972, 1973, 1974, 1976, 1977, 1978, 1979 by Mary Oliver. "The Hippopotamus" and "The Caterpillar" from *Verses from 1929 On* by Ogden Nash. Both first appeared in *The Saturday Evening Post*. Copyright 1) 1935 by the Curtis Publishing Company. Copyright 2) 1949 by Ogden Nash; renewed 1976 by Frances Nash, Isabel Nash Eberstadt, and Linell Nash Smith. Used by permission of Little, Brown and Company.

Liveright Publishing Corporation "In Just" by E. E. Cummings, copyright 1923, 1951, © 1991 by the Trustees for the E. E. Cummings Trust. Copyright © 1976 by George James Firmage, from *Complete Poems: 1904–1962* by E.E. Cummings, edited by George J. Firmage. Reprinted by permission of Liveright Publishing Corporation.

Alan Lomax "The Dying Cowboy" from *Cowboy Songs and Other Frontier Ballads* collected by John A. Lomax and Alan Lomax. Copyright © 1910, 1916, 1938 by The Macmillan Company. Copyright © 1938 by John A. Lomax. Used by permission of Alan Lomax.

Louisiana State University Press "Flint" by Christina Rossetti from *The Complete Poems of Christina Rossetti*, edited by R.W. Crump, © 1986, Louisiana State University Press. Reprinted by permission.

Jay Macpherson "Narcissus" by Jay Macpherson from *Four Ages of Man: The Classical Myths*. Copyright © 1962 by Jay Macpherson. Used by permission of the author.

Naomi Long Madgett "Life" from *One and Many* by Naomi Long Madgett. Copyright 1956; from *Remembrances of Spring*, 1993. Reprinted by permission of the author.

The Edna St. Vincent Millay Society c/o Elizabeth Barnett, Literary Executor "The Courage That My Mother Had" by Edna St. Vincent Millay, from *Collected Poems*, HarperCollins. Copyright © 1954 by Norma Millay Ellis. All rights reserved. Used by permission of Elizabeth Barnett, Literary Executor.

William Morrow & Company, Inc. "Winter" from *Cotton Candy On A Rainy Day* by Nikki Giovanni. Copyright © 1978 by Nikki Giovanni. Used by permission of William Morrow & Company, Inc.

John Murray (Publishers) Ltd. "The Dying Detective" from *The Game's Afoot* by Michael and Mollie Hardwick. Copyright © 1969 by Michael & Mollie Hardwick. Reprinted by permission of John Murray (Publishers) Ltd.

New American Library "Miracles" from *Leaves of Grass* by Walt Whitman.

W.W. Norton & Company for the author "The Microscope" by Maxine Kumin. Copyright © 1963 by The Atlantic Monthly Company, Boston, Mass. Reprinted by permission of the author.

Hugh Noyes on behalf of the Trustees of Alfred Noyes Literary Estate. "The Highwayman" from *Collected Poems* by Alfred Noyes (J. B. Lippincott). Reprinted by permission.

NTC Contemporary Books "No Gumption" from *Growing Up* by Russell Baker. Copyright © 1982 by Russell Baker. Reprinted by permission of NTC Contemporary Books.

Naomi Shihab Nye "The Rider" by Naomi Shihab Nye. Copyright © Naomi Shihab. First appeared in *Invisible*, a chapbook from Tribolite Press, Denton, TX. By permission of the author, Naomi Shihab Nye.

Harold Ober Associates Incorporated "Stolen Day" by Sherwood Anderson, originally published in *This Week* Magazine. Copyright 1941 by United Newspapers Magazine Corp. Copyright renewed 1968 by Eleanor Copenhaver Anderson. Reprinted by permission of Harold Ober Associates Incorporated.

Pantheon Books, a division of Random House, Inc. "His Just Reward" from *Swedish Folktales and Legends* by Lone Thygesen Blecher and George Blecher. Copyright © 1993 by G & L Blecher Inc. "Djuha Borrows a Pot" from *Arab Folktales* by Inea Bushnaq. Copyright © 1986 by Inea Bushnaq. Reprinted by permission of Pantheon Books, a division of Random House, Inc.

Raymond R. Patterson "Martin Luther King" by Raymond R. Patterson. Copyright © 1971 by Raymond R. Patterson. Reprinted by permission of the author.

Philomel Books, a division of Penguin Putnam Inc. From *Yeh Shen: A Cinderella Story from China* by Ai-Ling Louie. Copyright © 1982 by Ai-Ling Louie. Used by permission of Philomel Books, a division of Penguin Putnam Inc.

Penguin Putnam, Inc. "Independence Hall" from *On The Road With Charles Kuralt* by Charles Kuralt. Copyright © 1985 by CBS Inc. "Our Finest Hour" from *The Osgood Files* by Charles Osgood. Copyright © 1986, 1987, 1988, 1989, 1990, 1991 by Charles Osgood. Reprinted by permission of Penguin Putnam, Inc. *Ribbons* by Laurence Yep, copyright © 1992 by Laurence Yep from *American Girl Magazine*, Jan/Feb 1992. An expanded version of *Ribbons* by Laurence Yep is available from G.P. Putnam's Sons.

G.P. Putnam's Sons, a division of Penguin Putnam Inc. "Two Kinds" by Amy Tan from *The Joy Luck Club* by Amy Tan. Copyright © 1989 by Amy Tan. From "Was Tarzan a Three-Bandage Man?" from *Childhood* by Bill Cosby. Copyright © 1991 by Bill Cosby. Reprinted by permission of G.P. Putnam's Son, a division of Penguin Putnam, Inc.

The Putnam Publishing Group "Rip Van Winkle" from *A Legend of the Kaatskill Mountains* by Washington Irving. G.P. Putnam & Sons, 1871.

Random House, Inc. "Melting Pot" from *Living Out Loud* by Anna Quindlen. Copyright © 1987 by Anna Quindlen. Reprinted by permission of Random House, Inc. "Father William" from *The Complete Works of Lewis Carroll* by Lewis Carroll.

Regent Music Corporation "Abraham, Martin, and John" by Richard Holler. © 1968, 1970 (Renewed) Regent Music Corporation. All Rights Reserved. Used by permission of Regent Music Corporation. International Copyright Secured.

Marian Reiner "Feelings About Words" from *Words, Words, Words* by Mary O'Neill. Copyright © 1966 by Mary O'Neill. Copyright renewed 1994 by Erin Baroni and Abigail Hagler. "Thumbprint" from *A Sky Full of Poems* by Eve Merriam. Copyright © 1964, 1970, 1973 Eve Merriam. Copyright renewed 1992 Eve Merriam, 1998 Dee Michel and Guy Michel. "Onomatopoeia" from *It Doesn't Always Have To Rhyme* by Eve Merriam. Copyright © 1964, 1992 Eve Merriam. Reprinted by permission of Marian Reiner.

Rock and Roll Hall of Fame and Museum From "Rhythm and Blues: Let the Good Times Roll" and from *Joel Whitburn's Top R&B Singles 1942–1988,* Menomonee Falls, Wis., Record Research, Inc. 1988. Reprinted by kind permission of the Rock and Roll Hall of Fame and Museum, Cleveland, Ohio.

Wendy Rose "Loo-wit" from *The Halfbreed Chronicles and Other Poems* (West End Press) by Wendy Rose. Copyright © 1985 by Wendy Rose. Reprinted by permission of the author.

St. Martin's Press, Incorporated, and Harold Ober Associates Incorporated "Cat on the Go" from *All Things Wise and Wonderful* by James Herriot. Copyright © 1976, 1977 by James Herriot. Reprinted by permission.

Scribner, a division of Simon & Schuster Excerpts from "The Ancient Enmity," retitled "Rattlesnake Hunt," from *Cross Creek* by Marjorie Kinnan Rawlings. Copyright 1942 by Marjorie Kinnan Rawlings; copyright renewed © 1970 by Norton Baskin and Charles Scribner's Sons. "A Day's Wait" from *Winner Take Nothing* by Ernest Hemingway. Copyright 1933 Charles Scribner's Sons. Copyright renewed © 1961 by Mary Hemingway. Reprinted with the permission of Scribner, a division of Simon & Schuster, Inc.

The Rod Serling Trust "The Monsters Are Due On Maple Street" by Rod Serling. Copyright © 1960 Rod Serling; © 1988 by Carolyn Serling, Jodi Serling and Anne Serling. Reprinted by permission of The Rod Serling Trust. All rights reserved.

Estate of Robert Service c/o William Krasilovsky, Esq., Feinman & Krasilovsky "The Cremation of Sam McGee" by Robert Service. 1910 Dodd Mead & Co. Reprinted by permission.

Simon & Schuster Books for Young Readers, an imprint of Simon & Schuster Children's Publishing Division "Papa's Parrot" by Cynthia Rylant from *Every Living Thing* by Cynthia Rylant. Copyright © 1985 Cynthia Rylant. "The Lion and the Statue" and "The Fox and the Crow" from *The Fables of Aesop,* Selected, Told Anew and Their History Traced by Joseph Jacobs. Copyright © 1964 Macmillan Publishing Company. Reprinted with the permission of Simon & Schuster Books for Young Readers, an imprint of Simon & Schuster Children's Publishing Division

Society of Authors as the Literary Representative of the Estate of James Stephens "Washed In Silver" by James Stephens from *Collected Poems.* Copyright © 1943 by James Stephens. Reprinted by permission of the Society of Authors as the Literary Representative of the Estate of James Stephens.

Society of Authors as Representative of The Literary Trustees of Walter de la Mare "Me" by Walter de la Mare from *The Complete Poems of Walter de la Mare.* Copyright © 1969, published by Faber and Faber. Reprinted by permission of The Literary Trustees of Walter de la Mare, and The Society of Authors as their representative.

Gary Soto and Poetry "Oranges" by Gary Soto. First appeared in *Poetry,* copyright © 1983 by The Modern Poetry Association and is reprinted by permission of the author and the Editor of *Poetry.*

Sports Illustrated Magazine Reprinted courtesy of *Sports Illustrated* March 2, 1998. Copyright © 1998, Time Inc. "Golden Girls" by Johnette Howard. All rights reserved.

Stoddart Publishing Co. Limited "I Am a Native of North America" by Chief Dan George, from *My Heart Soars.* Copyright © 1974 by Clarke Irwin. Reprinted by permission of Stoddart Publishing Co., Limited.

Piri Thomas "Amigo Brothers" by Piri Thomas from *El Barrio.* Copyright © 1978 by Piri Thomas. Reprinted by permission of the author, Piri Thomas.

Rosemary A. Thurber "The Night the Bed Fell" by James Thurber. Copyright © 1933, 1961 James Thurber, from *My Life and Hard Times,* published by Harper & Row. Reprinted by permission.

Rosemary A. Thurber and the Barbara Hogensen Agency "The Princess and the Tin Box" from *The Beast in Me and Other Animals* by James Thurber. Copyright © 1948 by James Thurber. Copyright © renewed 1976 by Helen Thurber and Rosemary A. Thurber. Reprinted by arrangement with Rosemary A. Thurber and the Barbara Hogenson Agency.

Time Life Syndication From "Thanksgiving Inventory" by Roger Rosenblatt, published in *Time,* December 1, 1997. Copyright © 1997 Time Inc. Reprinted by permission of Time, Inc.

University of Notre Dame Press From *Barrio Boy* by Ernesto Galarza. Copyright © 1971 by University of Notre Dame Press. Reprinted by permission.

Villard Books, a division of Random House, Inc. From *Into Thin Air* by Jon Krakauer. Copyright © 1997 by Jon Krakauer. Reprinted by permission of Villard Books, a division of Random House, Inc.

Mai Vo-Dinh "The Little Lizard's Sorrow" from *The Toad is the Emperor's Uncle, Animal Folktales from Viet-Nam,* told and illustrated by Mai Vo-Dinh. Copyright © 1970 by Mai Vo-Dinh. Reprinted by permission of the author.

Warner Bros. Publications U.S. Inc. "Bring Back Nelson Mandela" by Hugh Masekela. © 1988 Kalahari Music (BMI). All Rights o/b/o Kalahari Music for the World administered by Warner Chappell Music Ltd. (PRS). All Rights o/b/o Warner Chappell Music Ltd. for the Western Hemisphere administered by Warner-Tamerlane Publishing Corp. (BMI) All Rights Reserved. Used by permission of Warner Bros. Publications U.S. Inc., Miami, Fla. 33014

Rob Weisbach Books, a division of William Morrow & Company "Stepping Out With My Baby" from *Babyhood* by Paul Reiser. Copyright © 1997 by Paul Reiser. Reprinted by permission.

Writers & Artists Agency *A Christmas Carol: Scrooge and Marley* by Israel Horovitz, an adaptation of Charles Dickens's *A Christmas Carol.* Copyright © 1994 by Fountain Pen, Inc. All rights reserved. Reprinted by permission.

Note: Every effort has been made to locate the copyright owner of material reprinted in this book. Omissions brought to our attention will be corrected in subsequent editions.

Art Credits

Cover © Jerry Driendl/FPG International Corp.; **vii t.:** *Portrait,* Pamela Chin Lee, Courtesy of the artist; **vii b.:** *La Grande Famille (The Great Family),* René Magritte, Private Collection/Lauros-Giraudon, Paris, ©2000 C. Herscovici, Brussels/Artists Rights Sociey (ARS), New York; **viii:** Chris Thomaidis/Tony Stone Images; **ix t.:** Corel Professional Photos CD-ROM™; **ix b.:** *La Bonne Aventure (Good Fortune),* 1939, René Magritte, Gouache on paper, 33.5 x 40.7 cm., Museum Boymans-van Beuningen, Rotterdam, ©2000 C. Herscovici, Brussels/Artists Rights Society (ARS), New York; **x t.:** Corel Professional Photos CD-ROM™; **x b.:** Bryce Flynn/Stock, Boston/PNI; **xi t.:** *Happy Cat,* Christian Pierre, Private Collection/SuperStock; **xii t.:** image ©Copyright 1997 PhotoDisc, Inc.; **xii b.:** © 1990 Terry Heffernan; **xiii t.:** *Simultaneous Contrasts: Sun and Moon,* 1913, Robert Delaunay, Oil on canvas, 53" diameter, Collection, The Museum of Modern Art, New York, Mrs. Simon Guggenheim Fund; **xiii b.:** *Nolan Ryan* by LeRoy Neiman, Copyright ©1981 LeRoy Neiman, Inc. All Rights Reserved; **xiv l.:** Ebenezer Scrooge celebrating in the Guthrie Theater's 1994 production of *A Christmas Carol* adapted by Barbara Field. Photo credit: Michal Daniel.; **xiv r.:** *Over view of family walking dog on the street,* William Low, Courtesy of the artist; **xv t.:** image ©Copyright 1997 PhotoDisc, Inc.; **xv b.:** ©The Stock Market/Peter Steiner; **xvi:** *The Chariot of Phaeton racing through the skies.* Copper engraving, 1606, Corbis-Bettmann; **1:** © Stock Illustration Source, Inc.; **2:** Thomas Victor; **3:** The Bettmann Archive; **5:** "Then Came a Dog and Bit the Cat" from Had Gadya (Tale of a Goat), 1919, E. Lissitzky, The Jewish Museum/Art Resource, NY. ©1997 Artists Rights Society (ARS), New York/VG Bild-

Kunst, Bonn.; **6:** *La Cour d'un Ferme,* June 28, 1983, London, Christie's (The Farmyard)/The Bridgeman Art Library, London/New York, ©2000 Artists Rights Society (ARS), New York/ADAGP, Paris; **11:** *Untitled,* Jean-Francois Podevin, © Stock Illustration Source, Inc.; **12:** Robert Foothorap; **13:** *Portrait,* Pamela Chin Lee, Courtesy of the artist; **14:** UPI/Corbis-Bettmann; **17:** *Mandarin Square: Badge with peacock-insignia-3rd civil rank. China,* 17th–20th century, Unknown artist, Yale University Art Gallery; **18–19:** Corbis-Bettmann; **20:** *Chinese Girl under Lanterns,* Winson Trang, Courtesy of the artist; **23:** *Portrait,* Pamela Chin Lee, Courtesy of the artist; **24:** Courtesy of Amy Tan; **28 t.:** Courtesy of the Library of Congress; **28 m.:** The Granger Collection, New York; **28 b.:** © Faber & Faber Ltd; **29:** Corel Professional Photos CD-ROM™; **30–31:** Frank Orel/Tony Stone Images; **32–33:** Michael P. Gadomski/Photo Researchers, Inc.; **36:** AP/Wide World Photos; **37:** © Faith Ringgold, 1986, The Purple Quilt (detail), 91" x 72", acrylic on canvas with pieced fabric borders; **38–39:** Betty Press/Panos Pictures; **41:** © 1998 ABC, Inc. All rights reserved.; **43:** © 1998 ABC, Inc. All rights reserved.; **49:** Culver Pictures, Inc.; **51:** Corel Professional Photos CD-ROM™; **52:** Corbis-Bettmann; **58:** *Drawing from an 1894 edition of Sir Thomas Malory's Le Morte D'arthur,* Aubrey Beardsley, The Granger Collection, New York; **61:** The Print and Picture Collection, Free Library of Philadelphia; **64:** Tracy Frankel/ The Image Bank; **69:** Diana Ong/SuperStock; **70:** Larry Burrows/Life Magazine © Time Warner Inc.; **71:** Oscar Burriel/Photo Researchers, Inc.; **73:** Herve Pelletier/SuperStock; **78 t.:** Corbis-Bettmann; **78 m.:** *Christina Rossetti* (1830–1894), english poet, wood engraving after Dante Gabriel Rossiti, The Granger Collection, New York; **78 b.:** Dianne Trejo; **79:** Corel Professional Photos CD-ROM™; **81:** *La Grande Famille (The Great Family),* René Magritte, Private Collection/Lauros-Giraudon, Paris, ©2000 C. Herscovici, Brussels/SuperStock Artists Rights Society (ARS), New York; **82:** *Three Fruit,* Ashton Hinrichs/SuperStock; **86:** Globe Photos; **87:** The Granger Collection, New York; **89:** Culver Pictures, Inc.; **92:** Courtesy Broadway Books; **93:** © Allsport/Alan Levenson; **95:** © Allsport/Ken Levine; **96:** AP/Wide World Photos; **98:** Paul Berger/Tony Stone Images; **103:** Francisco Cruz/SuperStock; **106:** © David Ridley/Stock Illustration Source, Inc.; **108:** Thomas Victor; **109:** Corel Professional Photos CD-ROM™; **112–113:** Corel Professional Photos CD-ROM™; **114:** Corel Professional Photos CD-ROM™; **119:** Private Collection/Diana Ong/ Superstock; **120 t.:** Courtesy of the Author. Photo by Carolyn Soto.; **120 b.:** John Barrett/Globe Photos; **121:** Vicky Kasala/The Image Bank; **122–123:** D. Young-Wolfe/PhotoEdit; **122:** Mary Kate Denny/PhotoEdit; **123 b.:** Photo Courtesy of Will Faller; **123 inset:** Mary Kate Denny/ PhotoEdit; **124:** Bob Daemmrich/The Image Works; **128 t.:** Corel Professional Photos CD-ROM™; **128 b.:** Corel Professional Photos CD-ROM™; **129 t.:** Corel Professional Photos CD-ROM™; **129 b.:** Corel Professional Photos CD-ROM™; **130:** Corel Professional Photos CD-ROM™; **134 t.:** Courtesy of the Library of Congress; **134 m.:** Photo by Bachrach; **134 b.:** *Rudyard Kipling,* oil on canvas, P. Burne-Jones, Courtesy of the National Portrait Gallery, London; **135:** Corel Professional Photos CD-ROM™; **136:** Photo Researchers, Inc.; **138–139:** Chris Thomaidis/ Tony Stone Images; **142:** *Washington Irving* (detail): Daniel Huntington, National Portrait Gallery, Smithsonian Institution, Washington, D.C./Art Resource, NY; **144:** *Rip in the Mountains,* Albertus Del Orient Brower, Shelburne Museum, Shelburne, Vt.; **146:** *Rip at the Inn,* Albertus Del Orient Brower, Shelburne Museum, Shelburne, Vt., Photograph by Ken Burris; **151:** *Rip Van Winkle Asleep,* Albertus Del Orient Brower, Shelburne Museum, Shelburne, Vt.; **152:** John Quidor, *Return of Rip Van Winkle,* 1849, Andrew W. Mellon Collection, © Board of Trustees, National Gallery of Art, Washington; **160:** Corel Professional Photos CD-ROM™; **163:** MBTA Marketing Communications; **165:** *Untitled (Two Girls Talking),* Pierre-Auguste Renoir/SuperStock; **166 t.:** New York Public Library; **166 m.t.:** Nationwide News Service; **166 m.b.:** Courtesy of the Library of Congress; **166 b.:** Corbis-Bettmann; **167:** *The Banjo Lesson,* c. 1894, pastel, 28" x 22 ½", Virginia Museum of Fine Arts, Richmond, The Adolf D. and Wilkins C. Williams Fund. Photo: Katherine Wetzel. © 2000 Virginia Museum of Fine Arts; **168:** *Organdy Collar,* 1936, Edmund Archer, Collection of Whitney Museum of American Art; **170:** Colonial Williamsburg Foundation; **172–173:** Corel Professional Photos CD-ROM™; **182:** *Farmyard with woman milking cow, from the Da Costa Book of Hours,* Bruges, c. 1515, The Pierpont Morgan Library/Art Resource, NY; **186:** Corel Professional Photos CD-ROM™; **191:** Michael Newman, PhotoEdit; **194–195:** *Couple on the Road,* Diana Ong/SuperStock; **197 t.:** Corel Professional Photos CD-ROM™; **197 b.:** Garden in the interior of a palace: a young lady and her servant, from Recueil de miniatures, Giraudon/Art Resource, NY; **199:** SuperStock; **200–201:** border Hideki Fujii/The Image Bank; **202–204 border:** Hideki Fujii/The Image Bank; **202–203:** Pal Hermansen/Tony Stone Images; **207:** *Untitled,* © Antar Dayal/Stock Illustration Source, Inc.; **208 t.:** AP/Wide World Photos; **208 b.:** Villard Books; **209:** Alex Stewart/The Image Bank; **210–211:** Tony Stone Images; **215:** © Jean-Marc Boivin/Photo Research-ers, Inc.; **218:** Corel Professional Photos CD-ROM™; **225:** Reuters/Gary Caskey/ Archive Photos; **228 t.:** *Alfred Lord Tennyson,* c. 1840, S. Laurence, Courtesy of the National Portrait Gallery, London; **228 m.:** *William Shakespeare,* (detail), Artist unknown, Courtesy of the National Portrait Gallery, London; **228 b.:** Thomas Victor; **229:** Courtesy of the Director, National Army Museum, London; **230:** *Charge of the Light Brigade at the Battle of Balaklava,* 1854, Artist Unknown/SuperStock; **232–233:** © United Artists/Archive Photos; **238:** Corel Professional Photos CD-ROM™; **243:** *The Voice,* 1930, Agnes Pelton, Collection of the Jonson Gallery of the University of New Mexico Art Museum, Albuquerque. Bequest of Raymond Jonson; **244 t.:** The Mark Twain House, Hartford, Conn.; **244 b.:** Thomas Victor; **245:** © The Stock Market/Jeffrey W. Myers; **252–253:** Corel Professional Photos CD-ROM™; **256:** Corel Professional Photos CD-ROM™; **258 t.:** Dimitri Kessel/Life Magazine; **258 m.:** AP/Wide World Photos; **258 b.:** Courtesy of the Library of Congress; **259:** *The White Veil,* 1909, William L. Metcalf, Museum of Art, Rhode Island School of Design, Gift of Mrs. Gustav Radeke; **260:** Philip F. Chaudoir/Tranquality; **263:** *La Bonne Aventure (Good Fortune),* 1939, René Magritte, Gouache on paper, 33.5 x 40.7 cm., Museum Boymans-van Beuningen, Rotterdam, ©2000 C. Herscovici/ARS, New York; **266:** © Phyllis Picard, Stock, Boston/PNI; **271:** Lynn Saville; **274–275:** *The Fight Interrupted,* William Mulready, Victoria & Albert Museum/Art Resource, NY; **276:** Corbis-Bettmann; **277:** "Briggs Suffocating" by James Thurber, Barbara Hogenson Agency, Photo by Eric H. Antoniou; **280:** My Life and Hard Times Copyright ©1933 by James Thurber. Copyright © renewed 1961 by James Thurber. Reprinted by arrangement with Rosemary A. Thurber and The Barbara Hogenson Agency.; **281:** "Briggs and Rex," by James Thurber, Barbara Hogenson Agency, Photo by Eric H. Antoniou; **285:** *View of Toledo,* Domenikos Theotokopoulos, The Metropolitan Museum of Art, H. O. Havemeyer Collection, Bequest of Mrs. H.O. Havemeyer, 1929. (29.100.6).; **286 t.:** Thomas Victor; **286 b.:** *Carl Sandburg,* Miriam Svet, The National Portrait Gallery, Smithsonian Institution, Washington, D.C./Art Resource, NY; **287:** Greg Martin/SuperStock; **288–289:** Dr. E.R. Degginger; **290–291 border:** Dr. E.R. Degginger; **290:** *Untitled,* Rob Wood, Illustration by Wood Ronsaville Harlin, Inc.; **292–293 border:** Dr. E.R. Degginger; **292–293 border:** Dr. E.R. Degginger; **292:** *A New Planet,* K.F. Yuon, Tretiakov Gallery, Moscow, Russia/SuperStock; **294–295 border:** Dr. E.R. Degginger; **294–295 border:** Dr. E.R. Degginger; **294:** *Sunrise IV,* 1937, Arthur Dove, Hirshhorn Museum and Sculpture Garden, Smithsonian Institution; **298 t.:** UPI/ Corbis-Bettmann; **298 b.:** Villard Books, Photo © John Isaac; **299:** image © Copyright 1997 PhotoDisc, Inc.; **306–307:** Image © Copyright 1997 PhotoDisc, Inc.; **308–309 t.:** Kansas State Historical Society, Topeka, Kans.; **308–309 b.:** Courtesy of the Library of Congress; **310–311 border:** Courtesy of the Library of Congress; **315:** Corel Professional Photos CD-ROM™; **316:** Corel Professional Photos CD-ROM™; **320:** PhotoEdit; **325:** *The Cabinetmaker,* Jacob Lawrence, Hirshhorn Museum and Sculpture Garden, Smithsonian Institution, Gift of Joseph H. Hirshhorn, 1966. Photo by Lee Stalsworth; **326 t.:** *Sir Arthur Conan Doyle* (detail), H. L. Gates, The National Portrait Gallery, London; **326 m.:** John Murray Publishers, London; **326 b.:** John Murray Publishers, London; **327:** *Sherlock Holmes,* Frederic Dorr Steele, The Granger Collection, New York; **328 t.:** Culver Pictures, Inc.; **328 b.:** *The Death of Theodore Gericault (1791–1824) with his friends Colonel Bro de Comeres and the painter Pierre-Joseph Dedreux-Dorcy* (1789–1874), 1824 by Ary Scheffer (1795–1858), Louvre, Paris, France/The Bridgeman Art Library International Ltd., London/New York; **331:** Culver Pictures, Inc.; **334:** The Granger Collection, New York; **336:** Culver Pictures, Inc.; **343:** Hawaii Department of Agriculture; **344 t.:** Richard Connelly; **344 m.t.:** Photo by Michael Nye; **344 m.b.:** Arte Publico Press; **344 b.:** *Thomas Hardy* (detail), R.G. Eres, Courtesy of the National Portrait Gallery, London; **345:** Bryce Flynn/Stock, Boston/PNI; **346–347 border:** Bryce Flynn/Stock, Boston/PNI; **347:** Bill Bachmann/New England Stock Photo; **348–349 border:** SuperStock; **349:** *Bicycles,* Robert Vickrey, 32 ½" x 46"

© Robert Vickrey/Licensed by VAGA, New York, NY; **350–351:** Jeff Greenberg/Omni-Photo Communications, Inc.; **352–353:** © David Madison 1997; **356:** © David Madison 1997; **357:** © David Madison 1997; **362:** Michael Newman/PhotoEdit; **367:** Richard Hutchings/PhotoEdit; **370–371:** *Snap the Whip,* Winslow Homer, Butler Institute of American Art, Youngston, Ohio, Bridgeman Art Library, London/SuperStock; **372:** CBS Photo Archive; **373:** CBS Photo Archives; **379:** *Essor,* 1981, Andre Rouillard/SuperStock; **380:** John Wyand; **381:** *Happy Cat,* Private Collection/Christian Pierre/SuperStock; **382:** Gunnar Kullenberg/SuperStock; **386:** Christian Grzimek/OKAPIA/ Photo Researchers, Inc.; **390:** Hans Reinhard/OKAPIA/OKAPIA/Photo Researchers, Inc.; **393:** GARFIELD © Paws, Inc. Dist. by Universal Press Syndicate. Reprinted with permission. All rights reserved.; **396 t.:** Rollie McKenna; **396 m.t.:** New York Public Library Picture Collection; **396 m.m.:** Photo by Victor Kumin; **396 m.b.:** *E. E. Cummings* (detail), 1958, Self Portrait, The National Portrait Gallery, Smithsonian Institution, Washington, D.C./Art Resource, NY; **396 b.:** AP/Wide World Photos; **397:** Charles Gupton/ Tony Stone Images; **398 t.:** John Shaw/Tom Stack & Associates; **398 b.:** Tom & Dee Ann McCarthy/PhotoEdit; **399 border:** John Shaw/Tom Stack & Associates; **400:** *You Are Old, Father William,* 1865, Sir John Tenniel, The Granger Collection, New York; **401:** *You Are Old Father William II,* 1865, Sir John Tenniel, The Granger Collection, New York; **403 t.:** Photo Researchers, Inc.; **403 b.:** Corel Professional Photos CD-ROM™; **404:** John Lei/Stock, Boston; **405:** Illustration from "Where the Sidewalk Ends" ©1974 by Evil Eye Music, Inc. Used by permission of HarperCollins Publishers; **406:** Illustration from "Where the Sidewalk Ends" ©1974 by Evil Eye Music, Inc. Used by permission of HarperCollins Publishers; **410:** AP/Wide World Photos; **415:** *Central Park,* Gustavo Novoa, Wally Findlay Galleries, New York/SuperStock; **416 t.:** Photo by Patricia M. Hoch; **416 m.t.:** UPI/Corbis-Bettmann; **416 b.:** Courtesy of the Estate of Carl Van Vechten, Joseph Solomon, EXECUTOR, The National Portrait Gallery, Smithsonian Institution, Washington, D.C./Art Resource, NY; **417:** Steve Bly/Tony Stone Images; **421:** Corel Professional Photos CD-ROM™; **421:** Charles W. Mann/Photo Researchers, Inc.; **422–423:** E. Hanumantha Rao/Photo Researchers, Inc.; **428 t.:** Corbis-Bettmann; **428 b.:** Jeff Katz/Gamma Liaison; **429:** Courtesy of Doug McCollum; **430:** Art Resource, NY; **436:** *Water Carrier by Moonlight,* Marc Chagall, ©1989 by The Metropolitan Museum of Art, Bequest of Scofield Thayer, 1982 (1984.433.56) ©2000 Artists Rights Society (ARS), New York/ADAGP, Paris; **440:** Myrleen Cates/PhotoEdit; **445:** Lynn Saville; **448–449:** *Youth and Old Age,* Norman Rockwell, Photo Courtesy of The Norman Rockwell Museum at Stockbridge, Reproduced courtesy of the Norman Rockwell Family Trust.; **450:** Corbis-Bettmann; **451:** © Hirz/ Archive Photos; **454–455:** *Nighthawks,* 1942, Edward Hopper, oil on canvas, 84.1 × 152.4 cm., Friends of American Art Collection 1942.51. Photograph ©1998, The Art Institute of Chicago. All Rights Reserved.; **456:** Culver Pictures, Inc.; **457:** Culver Pictures, Inc.; **458:** Culver Pictures, Inc.; **461:** "Through the Looking Glass" by Lewis Carroll, Illustrated by John Tenniel, Fairstreet Archives; **462:** Rudyard Kipling, oil on canvas, P. Burne-Jones, Courtesy of the National Portrait Gallery, London; **463:** John Mitchell/Photo Researchers, Inc.; **464:** Clem Haagner/Photo Researchers, Inc.; **466–467:** E. Hanumantha Rao/Photo Researchers, Inc.; **469:** R. Dev/Photo Researchers, Inc.; **470–471:** Paolo Koch/Photo Researchers, Inc.; **472:** Dinodia/Omni-Photo Communications, Inc.; **478:** UPI/Corbis-Bettmann; **479:** Brian Parker/Tom Stack & Associates; **480:** Corel Professional Photos CD-ROM™; **482:** Image © Copyright 1997 PhotoDisc, Inc.; **485:** *The Pond,* 1985, Adele Alsop, Courtesy of Schmidt Bingham Gallery, NYC.; **493:** *General with Sword,* Francisco Vidal, Courtesy of the artist; **494–495:** *Mexican Market,* Ira Moskowitz, Courtesy of the artist; **498:** David Young-Wolff/PhotoEdit; **500:** Jane Burton/Bruce Coleman, Inc.; **503:** *Looking Along Broadway Towards Grace Church* (detail), 1981, Red Grooms, Agnes Gund Collection, Courtesy Marlborough Gallery, ©2000 Red Grooms/Artists Rights Society (ARS), New York; **504 b.:** Prentice Hall; **504 t.:** Corbis-Bettmann; **505:** Hulton Getty Images/Tony Stone Images; **506–507:** RIA-NOVOSTI/SOVFOTO; **507:** Grant Smith/Corbis; **509:** SOVFOTO/AH; **513 t.r.:** George Kadish, Courtesy of United States Holocaust Memorial Museum Photo Archives; **513 t.l.:** George Kadish, courtesy of United States Holocaust Memorial Museum Photo Archives; **514 t.l.:** Main Commission for the Investigation of Nazi War Crimes, Courtesy of United States Holocaust Memorial Museum Photo Archives; **516 b.l.:** National Archives, courtesy of United States Holocaust Memorial Museum Photo Archives; **516 b.r.:** National Archives, Courtesy of United States Holocaust Memorial Museum Photo Archives; **517 t.r.:** Shraga Wainer, Courtesy of United States Holocaust Memorial Museum Photo Archives; **517 t.l.:** Shraga Wainer, Courtesy of United States Holocaust Memorial Museum Photo Archives; **518:** Hulton Getty Images/Tony Stone Images; **522 t.:** BridgeWater Books; **522 b.:** John Craig Photo; **523:** *Four Piece Orchestra,* 1944, Ben Shahn, © Estate of Ben Shahn/ Licensed by VAGA, New York, N.Y.; **524 t.:** ©1990 Terry Heffernan; **524–525 b.:** Photo by Silver Burdett Ginn; **527 t.:** *Three Studies of a Dancer in Fourth Position,* Charcoal and pastel with stumping, with touches of brush and black wash on greyish-tan laid paper with blue fibers (discolored from pinkish-blue). c. 1879/80, 48 x 61.5 cm. Bequest of Adele R. Levy, 1962.703. Photograph ©1994, The Art Institute of Chicago. All rights reserved.; **526-527 b.:** Photo by Silver Burdett Ginn; **528–529 b.:** Photo by Silver Burdett Ginn; **528 t.:** *Madame X,* 1993, Liu Hung, Courtesy Steinbaum Krauss Gallery, New York, N.Y.; **530:** Photo by Silver Burdett Ginn; **530 t.r.:** Main Commission for the Investigation of Nazi War Crimes, Courtesy of United States Holocaust Memorial Museum Photo Archives; **532–533:** *Morning at the Jackson Ave. Ferry,* Gilbert Fletcher, Courtesy of the artist; **534:** *Four Piece Orchestra,* 1944, Ben Shahn, © Estate of Ben Shahn/Licensed by VAGA, New York, N.Y.; **537:** *Disequilibrium,* 1987, Catherine Redmond, Courtesy of the artist; **543 l.:** Rock and Roll Hall of Fame and Museum, Michael Ochs Archives/Venice, CA; **543 r.:** The Rock and Roll Hall of Fame and Museum; **544:** Tony Freeman/PhotoEdit; **549:** Simon & Schuster; **552–553:** *The Mellow Pad,* 1945–51, Stuart Davis, The Brooklyn Museum; **554:** Thomas Victor; **555:** *The Starry Night,* 1889, Vincent van Gogh, Oil on canvas, 29" x 36 ¼", Collection, The Museum of Modern Art, New York, N.Y. Acquired through the Lillie P. Bliss Bequest; **557:** *Simultaneous Contrasts: Sun and Moon,* 1913, Robert Delaunay, Oil on canvas, 53" diameter, Collection, The Museum of Modern Art, New York, N.Y. Mrs. Simon Guggenheim Fund; **559:** *The Starry Night,* 1889, Vincent van Gogh, Oil on canvas, 29" x 36 ¼", Collection, The Museum of Modern Art, New York, N.Y. Acquired through the Lillie P. Bliss Bequest; **563:** *Self-Portrait,* 1967, Andy Warhol, The Andy Warhol Foundation for the Visual Arts, Inc./ARS, NY/Art Resource, NY; **564 t.:** Corbis-Bettmann; **564 b.:** Thomas Victor; **565:** *The Deadline,* Norman Rockwell, Photo Courtesy of The Norman Rockwell Museum at Stockbridge, Printed by permission of the Norman Rockwell Family Trust Copyright ©1938 the Norman Rockwell Family Trust; **566–567 l.:** Saturday Evening Post Cover, March 28, 1931, © The Curtis Publishing Company, Illustrator: Norman Rockwell, Printed by permission of the Norman Rockwell Family Trust Copyright ©1931 the Norman Rockwell Family Trust; **566 r.:** *Saturday Evening Post* cover, August 10, 1935, Illustrated by G. Brehm, © The Curtis Publishing Company; **567 l.:** *Saturday Evening Post* cover, 1937, Illustrated by Frances Tipton Hunter, ©The Curtis Publishing Company; **567 r.:** *Saturday Evening Post* cover, September 2, 1939, © The Curtis Publishing Company, Illustrator: Norman Rockwell. Printed by permission of the Norman Rockwell Family Trust Copyright ©1939 the Norman Rockwell Family Trust; **568:** Russell Baker; **569:** Russell Baker; **571:** Illustrated by Frances Tipton Hunter, © The Curtis Publishing Company; **572:** Illustrated by G. Brehm, © The Curtis Publishing Company; **576–577:** Yuri Dojc/The Image Bank; **578–579:** Flip Chalfant/The Image Bank; **584 t.:** John Kleihans; **584 b.:** Courtesy, William Lace; **585:** *Nolan Ryan,* by LeRoy Neiman, Copyright © 1981 LeRoy Neiman, Inc. All Rights Reserved.; **586:** *Prisoners from the Front,* 1866, Winslow Homer, The Metropolitan Museum of Art, Gift of Mrs. Frank B. Porter, 1922 (22.207), Copyright ©1980 The Metropolitan Museum of Art; **588:** *The Gulf Stream,* 1899, Winslow Homer, The Metropolitan Museum of Art, Wolfe Fund, 1906, Catharine Lorillard Wolfe Collection, (06.1234), Copyright ©1980 The Metropolitan Museum of Art; **590–591:** AP/Wide World Photos; **592:** ©Allsport/D. Stohmeyer; **596:** Lynn Saville; **601:** Untitled, © Ivan Lee Sanford/Stock Illustration Source, Inc.; **602 t.:** AP/Wide World Photos; **602 m.t.:** AP/Wide World Photos; **602 m.m.:** Mae Galarza; **602 m.b.:** Alan Markfield/Globe Photos; **602 b.:** UPI/Corbis-Bettmann; **603:** *Owh! In San Pao,* 1951, Stuart Davis, Oil on canvas, 52 ¼" x 41 ¾", Collection of Whitney Museum of American Art. Purchase; **604:** *The Declaration of Independence,* John Trumball, Yale University Art Gallery Yale University Art Gallery; **607:** S. Dimmitt/Photo Researchers, Inc.; **608:** S. Dimmitt/ Photo Researchers, Inc.; **609 border:** S. Dimmitt/Photo Researchers, Inc.; **609 b.:** S. Dimmitt/Photo Researchers, Inc.; **610:** S. Dimmitt/Photo Researchers, Inc.; **611:** John